POLITICAL HANDBOOK
OF EUROPE
2007

REGIONAL POLITICAL HANDBOOKS OF THE WORLD

Political Handbook of Europe 2007

Editors: Arthur S. Banks, Thomas C. Muller, William R. Overstreet
Associate Editors: Judith Isacoff, John Riley Jr.
Assistant Editors: Tony Davies, Thomas Lansford
Contributing Editors: Mary H. Cooper, John Greenya, January Layman-Wood, Patrick G. Marshall, Michael D. McDonald, John Morris, John Roy, Brian Sulkis, Steven L. Taylor
Production Assistants: Nathaniel Bouman, Thomas Scalese, Erin Stanley, Kathleen Stanley

CQ Press

Sponsoring Editor: Doug Goldenberg-Hart
Chief, Editorial Acquisitions, Reference Publishing: Andrea Pedolsky
Managing Editor: Stephen D. Pazdan
Production Editor: Joan Gossett
Copy Editors: Kathleen Savory, Anna Socrates
Production and Research: Timothy Arnquist, Kate Ostrander, Ilya Plotkin, Kate Stern
Manager, Electronic Production: Paul P. Pressau
Manager, Print and Art Production: Margot W. Ziperman

Senior Vice President and Publisher: John A. Jenkins
Director, Reference Publishing: Kathryn C. Suárez
Director, Editorial Operations: Ann Davies

President and Publisher, Congressional Quarterly Inc: Robert W. Merry

POLITICAL HANDBOOK OF EUROPE 2007

Introduction by Charles Hauss
George Mason University

CQ PRESS

A DIVISION OF CONGRESSIONAL QUARTERLY INC.

WASHINGTON, D.C.

CQ Press
1255 22nd Street, NW, Suite 400
Washington, DC 20037

Phone: 202-729-1900; toll-free, 1-866-4CQ-PRESS (1-866-427-7737)

Web: www.cqpress.com

Cover design: TGD Communications
Composition: Pooja Naithani and the production staff at TechBooks-Delhi

Maps courtesy of International Mapping Associates

⊗ The paper used in this publication exceeds the requirements of the American National Standard for Information Sciences–Permanence of Paper for Printed Library Materials, ANSI Z39.48-1992.

Printed and bound in the United States of America

10   09   08   07   06   1   2   3   4   5

Library of Congress Cataloging-in-Publication Data

Political handbook of Europe 2007.
    p. cm.
  Includes bibliographical references and index.
  ISBN-13: 978-0-87289-360-3 (alk. paper)
  ISBN-10: 0-87289-360-X (alk. paper)
  1. Europe–Politics and government–20th century–Handbooks, manuals, etc.   2. Europe–Politics and government–21st century–Handbooks, manuals, etc.   3. International agencies–21st century–Handbooks, manuals, etc.   I. Title.
  JN12.P584 2007
  320.9403–dc22   2006037763

CONTENTS

INTERGOVERNMENTAL ORGANIZATION ABBREVIATIONS

Memberships in non-UN intergovernmental organizations are listed at the end of each country's section under Intergovernmental Representation. An asterisk in the list below indicates a nonofficial abbreviation. In the country profiles, associate memberships are in italics.

*AC	Arctic Council	EIB	European Investment Bank
BIS	Bank for International Settlements	ESA	European Space Agency
		EU	European Union
*BLX	Benelux Economic Union	Eurocontrol	European Organization for the Safety of Air Navigation
BSEC	Organization of the Black Sea Economic Cooperation		
		G-7/G-8	Group of Seven/Group of Eight
CBSS	Council of the Baltic Sea States	G-10	Group of Ten
CEI	Central European Initiative	IEA	International Energy Agency
CERN	European Organization for Nuclear Research	NATO	North Atlantic Treaty Organization
*CEUR	Council of Europe	*NC	Nordic Council
CIS	Commonwealth of Independent States	NIB	Nordic Investment Bank
		OECD	Organization for Economic Cooperation and Development
EBRD	European Bank for Reconstruction and Development	OSCE	Organization for Security and Cooperation in Europe
EFTA	European Free Trade Association	WEU	Western European Union

PART ONE

INTRODUCTION

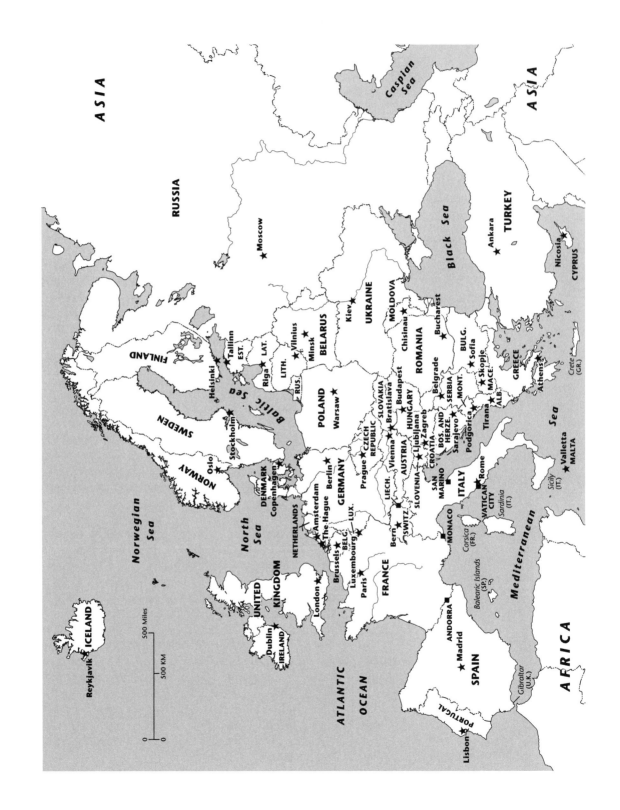

INTRODUCTION TO EUROPE

What Is Europe

At first glance, this does not seem to be a difficult question. Europe is a continent whose boundaries have been recognized for centuries—the Atlantic to the Urals. But the reality is more complicated in two respects.

First, some parts of Europe are not culturally or politically European. Three countries—Armenia, Azerbaijan, and Georgia—that are culturally far more Asian than European are not discussed here. By contrast, Russia and Turkey are included, even though most of the land mass of those countries lies in Asia.

Second, the European countries have never had much in common. Liberal thought, the industrial revolution, and democracy all took root in the West far earlier and far more solidly than in the East. Then, between 1945 and 1991, the cold war made Eastern and Western Europe even more different than alike. Since the collapse of communism, the two parts of Europe have grown closer to some degree. Nonetheless, democracy and capitalism are on a shakier footing to the east of the old iron curtain. Some of those states have disintegrated and seen the first wars in Europe since 1945. Perhaps most importantly of all, their citizens are far poorer than their counterparts in the West.

History I: How Europe Evolved Until 1989

In order to understand how Europe became what it is today, one has to divide its history into two phases. The first phase examines developments in Europe before 1989 and the end of the cold war. The second phase examines where Europe is heading in the 21st century to help explain why Europe is so different today from what it was a decade or a generation ago.

Many people assume that Europe has always had well-defined nation-states with reasonably clear and accepted borders. After all, there was an England, a France, and a Russia in medieval times. But, in reality, their borders kept changing. More importantly, their governments had very little power.

The modern state began to emerge in the 16th century. Some political scientists date the creation of the modern state a century later in 1648 and the signing of the Treaty of Westphalia. The treaty ended nearly a century of religious war and established the principle of national sovereignty by asserting that rulers had the right to govern their own countries without outside interference.

Sovereignty was a reality in name only. To be sure, some states became far more powerful domestically, including England, France, and, to a lesser degree, Spain. But it would be more than two centuries before a unified Germany or Italy emerged. To the east, most of the region was subsumed under one of three multiethnic empires—Austro-Hungarian, Russian, and Ottoman. States there date only from the collapse of these empires during World War I.

The creation of the first modern states following Westphalia also reveals two other important trends in early modern Europe: the rise of national identity and deep divides over religious faith. Eventually, these factors affected every country, and their different impacts go a long way toward explaining why there are still such widespread differences across the continent.

The development of what would eventually become national identity was a gradual process. Over time, people came to think of themselves as English as well as Kentish, French as well as Dauphinois, or Spanish as well as Castilian. However, national identity wasn't as simple as it might seem. Nations and states rarely developed in tandem. Most Germans came to think of themselves as German, but there was no Germany. Even the most advanced states contained minorities whose members were antagonistic toward the national government (and who developed rival national identities), such as the Scots with England or the Bretons with France. Furthermore, most of Eastern Europe was a mélange of ethnic groups living next to each other, with a growing Jewish population scattered almost everywhere. As these people began to develop national identities, their incorporation into the three big empires became increasingly problematic.

Meanwhile, Europe came to be deeply divided by religion. Until Martin Luther posted his 95 theses on a church door in Wittenberg in 1517, almost all of Europe was Roman Catholic—parts of the East belonged to one of the Orthodox churches. Luther's actions helped lead to a split between Catholics and what came to be a number of Protestant sects and sparked the wars of religion mentioned earlier. Religious violence flared from time to time after Westphalia but did not reach the intensity of the earlier war-laden century. Even as the period of religious wars ended, almost every country still had an official religion. And, until near the end of the 20th century, people's religion or degree of religious practice was typically the best predictor of how they voted.

In the century and a half after Westphalia, another important new trend arose in Western (but rarely in Eastern) Europe. The Enlightenment included such developments as liberal thought and the scientific revolution. It was the first serious step toward the most important developments of the 19th century: democracy and capitalism.

The desire for democracy led to the French revolution and those that swept much of Europe in 1848. Those attempts failed. (In the meantime, the British gradually expanded the right to vote and continued transferring real power from the monarch to the Parliament.) At the end of the 19th century, nearly all of Europe was ruled by authoritarian kings and emperors. Even so, these rulers were challenged by people demanding more democracy.

The late 18th and early 19th centuries also saw the rise of market-based capitalism. Capitalist businessmen clamored for more economic freedom from the restrictions and economic practices their countries inherited from feudalism. Many went beyond demands for economic freedom to political liberty as well.

Capitalism also sparked the industrial revolution with its belching factories and overcrowded cities. The industrial revolution brought unprecedented riches to the capitalists but unprecedented misery to the new working class. Many of them turned to the new ideology of socialism, including its revolutionary version, communism, based on the writings of Karl Marx and Friedrich Engels. By the end of the century, some socialists had begun to believe that profound reform could be achieved through democratic institutions rather than the upheaval of socialism. Nonetheless, much of Europe was now divided between capitalists and socialists.

In sum, by 1900, political life in a given country was largely defined by how it had been affected by the development of the nation and state, religious belief, support for and opposition to democracy, and industrialization and the attendant clash between workers and owners. Those issues lingered when, 14 years later, the world was wracked by World War I. The "Great War" intensified these divisions and added some new ones.

Together, the two world wars of the 20th century changed many things in Europe, but not the key divisions growing out of the social, economic, and political transformation of the preceding centuries.

World War I was dubbed the war to end all wars. The unanticipated carnage and its political implications deepened existing divisions along class lines. More importantly, it led to the creation of nine new Eastern European states out of the remnants of the three great empires. One of those was the

Soviet Union (USSR), the first country to adopt Marxism-Leninism as its organizing principle and implement state socialism. The war and its resolution also produced a backlash among nationalists of several countries who were angered by their leaders' failure to achieve war aims. Through a complicated causal path (which also included the depression of the 1930s), racist and fascist governments came to power first in Italy and then, under Hitler, in Germany.

Hitler's seizure of power led to World War II and the Holocaust. Nazi Germany's defeat also led to the division of Europe on the two sides of the iron curtain following the defeat of Germany and its allies.

For the next half century, Europe was divided between east and west. As British Prime Minister Sir Winston Churchill put it shortly after he left office in 1945, "From Stettin in the Baltic to Trieste in the Adriatic an iron curtain has descended across the Continent." The Soviet Union dominated the countries on the east side of the curtain. Those in the West adopted liberal democratic regimes, became American allies, and joined the North Atlantic Treaty Organization (NATO); those in the East became members of the Warsaw Pact.

During the first 20 years of the cold war, the world came close to World War III and nuclear holocaust on several occasions. The most important of these events in Europe was the construction of the Berlin wall in 1961. To keep its citizens from fleeing to the west, the East German authorities with the backing of the USSR constructed a wall around East Berlin. The Berlin wall came to symbolize the conflict between East and West.

The Cuban missile crisis the following year was even more dangerous since it took the world to the brink of global war. After the crisis ended the United States and Soviet Union found ways of not threatening each other in such a direct and dangerous manner, in so-called "proxy wars," including the war in Vietnam.

Most observers assumed that the cold war and the accompanying standoff between the superpowers would last indefinitely. The idea that the cold war was a permanent fact of life became ever

clearer during Ronald Reagan's first term as U.S. president (1981–1984), when his administration faced off against the leadership of an aging Soviet team headed by Leonid Brezhnev.

Then, the impossible happened.

As a result of unexpected and amazing protests from the grassroots level, communist "satellite" regimes in Eastern Europe were toppled in 1988 and 1989. (Moscow acquiesced to the changes because the USSR was suffering from economic crises and reeling from its own internal leadership transitions.) Only in Romania was there any violence, including the public execution of the Ceauşescu family, who had run the country with an iron fist for more than 20 years.

The Soviet Union held on into the 1990s—but just barely.

In the summer of 1991, President Mikhail Gorbachev went on vacation to his family's dacha on the Black Sea in Ukraine. Just before he was due to return to Moscow to sign a Union Treaty that would have given unprecedented powers to the remaining republics, hard-liners staged a coup attempt that might have been one of the most inept in history. Gorbachev and his government seemed to have survived. On returning to Moscow, he claimed that political life would continue as if the coup had not happened.

By the end of the year, the three Baltic republics had declared their independence. Most of the other former Soviet republics followed suit and formed the Commonwealth of Independent States. On December 31, the red flag with the hammer and sickle was taken down from the Kremlin, never to be flown again.

The cold war was over.

History II: Since the End of the Cold War

As the cold war was ending, both President Gorbachev and incoming U.S. President George H.W. Bush spoke about a new world order. Within months, global events suggested a new world *disorder* instead.

Europe itself receded from the world's political center stage as Iraq, terrorism, and other issues grabbed global attention. Nonetheless, European events remained vitally important.

In the short term, most European states joined Operations Desert Shield and Desert Storm in the aftermath of Iraq's occupation of Kuwait in 1991. Their involvement hid two important changes that have roiled the continent ever since.

Transformation in Eastern Europe

The first change concerned the countries of Eastern Europe. The former communist regimes underwent two unprecedented transformations at once. They moved from a communist to a democratic form of government, which meant shifting from one-party rule to multiparty competition. Simultaneously, they made the transition from a centrally controlled socialist economy to one governed largely by a free market. Neither of these transformations was easy.

Three of the countries did not survive. The Soviet Union, of course, disintegrated into its 15 constituent republics, some of which had trouble surviving on their own (which is demonstrated most tragically in Russia's ongoing civil war with separatist rebels in Chechnya). Czechoslovakia peacefully split into two parts, which became the Czech Republic and Slovakia.

To say the least, Yugoslavia did not collapse as easily. That country was never one whose member republics lived in harmony. For reasons that went beyond the collapse of cold war antagonisms, Yugoslavia was being pulled apart long before 1989.

After the Berlin Wall came down, Yugoslavia went through a wrenching period of transition, as economic turmoil and ethnic and religious tensions led to wars between Serbia and Bosnia and Herzegovina and Croatia. More than a quarter of a million people were killed in Bosnia and Herzegovina alone. Ten times that number became either international refugees or displaced persons inside their own borders.

One country became six.

Not all former Soviet satellites were torn asunder. Nonetheless, all went through difficult economic and political transformations in which people's standards of living plummeted. To cite one example, the life expectancy of Russian men dropped by more than ten years at the same time that most people worldwide could expect to live into their 90s. The life expectancy of men was but the most visible sign of a difficult decade for the post-Soviet countries economically and politically.

European Integration

The second change was the creation of the European Union (EU). In 1951 a group of visionaries formed the European Coal and Steel Community, which eliminated internal tariffs on those products for Germany, France, Luxemburg, Belgium, Italy, and the Netherlands. Six years later, those same countries signed the Treaty of Rome, which created the European Economic Community and formed a free-trade zone for all goods in the region.

By the 1990s the EU had established a single, integrated economy throughout Western Europe and included the 15 most powerful countries on the continent as members (Switzerland and Norway refused to join). In 1992 the EU's member states ratified the Treaty of Maastricht, which, in turn, led to the creation of the euro as the continental currency, as well as institutions that were more powerful than any single nation state. As of early 2007 the EU will have 27 members, including 10 of the former communist countries.

Twenty-first Century Issues

Traditional Divisions

Most European countries are divided in ways that reflect the antagonisms discussed above. Although these differences are declining in relative importance, three of them are worth discussing here.

First is the cleavage over religion. Many West European countries have substantial numbers of

Protestants and Catholics. Even those that seem to be homogeneous in this dimension (such as France and Italy) have conflicts over the role of religion in political life. (In these countries, the question is not whether one is Catholic or not, but how devoted people are to their faith.) Since the 1950s public opinion polls have indicated that the more often a respondent went to church, the more likely he or she was to vote for conservative parties and candidates. As the faiths have evolved, especially Catholicism, this trend has become less powerful. Still, 31 percent of practicing Catholics voted for French President Jacques Chirac on the first ballot of the 2002 presidential election, 11 percent more than for the population as a whole. As church attendance continues to decline, the impact of religion will likely do so as well. Nonetheless, given the importance of religion in European political life, faith will remain an important, if diminishing, divide, for years to come.

Second is the persistence of class conflict, whose roots date back at least to the first works written by Marx and Engels during the revolutions that swept Europe in 1848. They had noticed how much the industrial revolution was changing life in Europe and North America. The two argued that the new division between the capitalist owners of the means of production and the working class (which they called the proletariat) would transform political life as well.

As Marx and Engels saw things, the only option the working class had was revolution, since the capitalist bourgeoisie would never give up power voluntarily. By the turn of the 20th century, however, some socialists had become convinced that sweeping reforms could be passed through the legislatures of the newly emerging democracies. Even though the socialist world became deeply divided on the issue of a revolutionary or evolutionary path to socialism, most class conscious workers voted for parties that represented one or the other wing of the working class movement.

During the course of the 20th century, the world continued to change in ways that Marx and Engels had not expected. They had assumed that the working class would grow dramatically and remain at or near the poverty line.

From the 1950s onward, more and more workers moved into the middle class, both in terms of the jobs they held and the lifestyles they enjoyed. Today, far more Europeans work in offices than in factories. Still, in countries like the UK, which does not have a serious religious divide, most workers vote for the left; middle class voters tend to split their votes, but a higher proportion of the middle class votes for the right.

Third, most countries that had important ethnic divisions at the beginning of the 20th century also developed political parties divided along those lines. None was more evident than Belgium whose population is about 60 percent Dutch speaking Flamands and 30 percent French speaking Walloons. No Belgian political party winning more than 5 percent of the vote appeals across linguistic lines. Indeed, as linguistic tensions mounted in the late 1960s, all the major nationwide parties split in two.

Religion, class, and ethnicity still matter. But they do so less and less. As in most industrialized democracies, the number of people practicing their religion has plummeted, which may come as a surprise to American readers. Most people, too, describe themselves as middle class. And, even in a country like Belgium, at least 10 percent of the population describes itself as mixed linguistic or ethnic background.

New Divisions

Europe has changed dramatically since the Berlin wall fell in 1989. The historical disputes still count, but new ones are replacing them.

The most obvious of these new divisions are those growing out of the collapse of communism on the eastern side of the iron curtain. It should be remembered that the Eastern European countries had few, if any, open divisions during the nearly half century of Soviet-style rule. While use of the term totalitarian may be an exaggeration, especially following the upheavals in Hungary in 1956, Czechoslovakia in 1968, and Poland in 1980–1981, there were few opportunities for people who opposed these regimes to press their point of view.

Few people regret the loss of the dictatorial communist regimes. Many, however, object to the loss of state-sponsored housing, health care, and education, which were all provided more or less for free.

In short, one of the key divisions in contemporary Eastern Europe is between the parties on the left that hearken back to the more stable communist past and those that want as rapid a transition to a democratic and capitalist system as possible. In some of the countries, parties on each side of the divide have governed in the nearly 20 years since state socialism collapsed.

None is more interesting than Poland (which, as this was written, was the first country to have twin brothers as president and prime minister). Although the Solidarity movement, which led the overthrow of the communist regime, has disappeared, partisan competition in Poland has been largely between reformed communists and former dissident organizations that grew out of Solidarity.

The few countries in the West that still had a large communist party by the 1980s have seen them all but disappear. In Italy, the party system has collapsed so much that it is hard to tell how many votes orthodox Marxists got in the 2006 victory by the left (how one should categorize a party called Daisy-Democracy is Freedom, which blended its candidates into a broader coalition, is another question). Easier to comprehend is France, where the French Communist Party won under 5 percent of the vote in the 2002 legislative elections and fared even worse in the presidential ballot that same year.

The issues that do seem to matter reflect divisions that have emerged since the late 1960s and have been well documented by political scientist Ronald Inglehart. Although Inglehart's research methods have been criticized, his findings have been consistent during nearly 40 years of polling.

Inglehart and his colleagues have discovered that the old division between working class and middle class is disappearing. Instead, many middle class voters have moved to the left; many workers have become conservatives because of what he calls the split between materialists and postmaterialists.

Materialists have been the losers in what is often called the shift to a postindustrial society. If Inglehart understands the world properly, materialists are worried about their personal security in two ways. First, they are being left behind economically in societies in which knowledge matters more than the ability to work hard on a shop floor. Second, many of them live in ethnically divided neighborhoods, especially in the big European cities that have seen massive waves of nonwhite immigrants since the 1960s.

Materialists, whose parents voted for the left, now tend to vote for conservatives who claim to represent traditional values of both nationality and the working class. In other words, materialists tend to be frightened by the social changes sweeping around them.

Many are offended by the cultural changes that have accompanied the influx of non-Western immigrants, who are often at odds with their new host culture on everything from cuisine to language. In the first years of the 21st century, most Western European countries have experienced protests from the immigrant communities and a concomitant backlash at the polls from the groups who feel most threatened economically and physically by the diversification of their countries.

By contrast, postmaterialists were mostly conservative voters well into the 1960s. But Inglehart argues that as a growing generation of highly educated, middle class people no longer have to worry about their physical security, they can pay more attention to "higher level values." These values range from satisfaction with one's job to a concern with the environment, issues that most materialists do not have the time, money, or energy to concentrate on.

Postmaterialists burst onto the political scene during the 1960s during the protests over the Vietnam war and related issues on both sides of the Atlantic. In Europe this led to a resurgence of interest in Marxism, not from the working poor but from affluent intellectuals.

In the 1990s and 2000s, this split between materialists and postmaterialists is apparent in two overlapping issues.

As noted earlier, the first of these is the way people relate to race. Even such seemingly homogeneous countries as Italy and Ireland have experienced substantial immigration from outside of Western Europe. The Roma in Dublin and the Libyans in Rome have a very visible profile. That has produced significant resentment reflected, for instance, in the support for anti-immigrant and nationalist parties like former Italian prime minister Berlusconi's Forza Italia Party and even more in France's National Front, which now routinely wins more than 15 percent of the vote.

The other issue is European economic and political integration, which is discussed in more detail below. Many materialists feel as threatened by the growing power of European institutions as they do by immigration: to the surprise of many, French voters rejected a referendum to ratify the proposed European Constitution in 2005. The "no" vote in France effectively killed the draft treaty, but it almost certainly would also have lost in a number of other countries, including the UK.

On the other side of the political coin, postmaterialists tend to be strong supporters of both racial and ethnic plurality and European integration. Few have much to fear professionally or personally from immigrants, because most have job security and live in neighborhoods where citizens can safely walk their dogs late in the evening.

Postmaterialists are also most likely to benefit from European integration. Major European cities are now international hubs with tens of thousands of (often) young executives, engineers, and attorneys working for the multinational companies located there. This is not just true of Paris, London, and Rome but also of smaller cities such as Reading in the UK and Sophia Antopolis in France, around which Europe's equivalents of Silicon Valley have sprung up.

How Europeans Cope

People and Politics

People participate (or don't as the case may be) in four main ways.

Acting Individually The first is as individuals. Average citizens may not have a lot of direct influence over political life, but they can write their member of parliament or send a letter to the editor of a newspaper. Both of those options are more effective in the United States than in Europe because members of the House and Senate have more flexibility in how they act than their European counterparts and because the United States has more decentralized media rather than the national press that is common in most European countries.

Interest Groups The second route is to form, join, or advocate through interest groups (which some political scientists call interest articulation). Interest groups focus on a small number of issues of importance to their members. In the last few decades, trade unions and trade associations have been the most influential of them.

People join interest groups because they think those organizations can help them with particular issues. Thus, unions defend the wages, benefits, and other goals of workers; trade associations do the same for businesses.

In some countries, unions and trade associations have had privileged access to government. Thus, in Germany, both the "peak associations" of labor and management were formally included in what were called concerted action discussions at various points from the 1960s onward. Similarly, the British Labour Party has long had a close and formal association with the Trade Unions Congress, while the Conservative Party has had the same kind of link to the Confederation of British Industries.

Over the last 20 years, unions have lost membership everywhere as the work force has increasingly moved into the harder to organize service sector. Big business has also lost some of its clout as small, entrepreneurial firms have come to play a larger role in an economy dominated by innovative, high-tech firms.

Environmental and antiracist interest groups have gained support, especially in countries such as France where racial divisions have been most pronounced. In others, such as the UK, where opposition to immigration and the EU have been most pronounced, interest groups on the other end of the political spectrum have gained prominence.

Political Parties and Elections The third, and main, way Europeans participate is through voting for political parties (a process that some political scientists call interest aggregation). Few interest groups have any serious desire or hope of winning national power (or of even drawing enough concentrated support to win an election). Most political parties would like to do so either on their own or as part of a broadly based coalition that wins a majority of seats in the national parliament (see the next section).

Sometimes, the distinction between parties and interest groups can get confusing, since some parties—the French Greens or National Front, for instance—have no chance of actually winning elections. Nonetheless, that is the goal their leadership sets out, and even some small parties, like the French Greens, have served as minor members of a left-wing coalition that could not come to office without their support.

It is increasingly difficult to put European political parties into a single set of categories. But the following list includes those that can be found in many of the larger countries:

- Greens and others who represent the postmaterialist left. In Germany, France, and elsewhere, they have been part of coalition governments. Nowhere, however, have they consistently won as much as 10 percent of the vote in parliamentary elections.
- Communists and others on the far left. As noted earlier, communist parties have lost most of their support since the end of the cold war. That also holds for Trotskyite and Maoist parties that

actually occasionally outpoll traditional communist parties in Italy and France.
- Social democratic parties are the inheritors of the groups who broke away from the revolutionary Marxist groups in the late 19th or early 20th centuries. Most have dropped any pretensions of still being Marxist or radical in any meaningful sense of the term. Typically, groups like the French *Parti socialiste* or Britain's Labour Party are among the handful of parties that have a realistic chance of winning power.
- Liberals or radicals. Both names are actually misnomers in the early 21st century, especially for an American frame of reference. European liberals tend to be upper middle class business executives who support free-market capitalism and "liberty," hence their name. Radicals were radical only in a 19th-century context, when to be a left-winger meant supporting a free market, democracy, and the separation of church and state. In some countries (e.g., France) the liberals and radicals have all but disappeared. Rarely do they win a lot of the vote. Nonetheless, they hold the balance of power in Germany, where they have served as a junior member of the governing coalition for almost all the time that the Federal Republic has been an independent state—although since the 2005 election, the christian democrats and social democrats run the country through a large or "grand" coalition.
- Christian democrats are pivotal parties in most countries that have large Catholic populations, though they have disappeared in France and Italy. As of 2006 christian democrats were in power in Germany, the Netherlands, and a number of smaller countries.
- One of the most troubling trends in modern European politics has been the rise of a far right that echoes the antidemocratic movements that helped bring the likes of Hitler and Mussolini to power before World War II. Twelve of the 15 members of the EU (before it expanded eastward in 2004) have right-wing parties with little more than thinly veiled racist and ultranationalist appeals. The most prominent has been France's National Front, whose leader, Jean-Marie Le Pen,

routinely wins between 15 and 20 percent of the vote in presidential elections. Although other parties have not done quite as well, the Italian Northern League and the Austrian Freedom Party have been part of governing coalitions.

New Forms of Protest and Terrorism Political scientists are just beginning to pay attention to the often violent European protest movements that began in the 1990s and gained new prominence after 9/11. Almost every country in the West and most in the East now have substantial numbers of nonwhite immigrants, many of whom have had children who automatically become citizens.

The waves of immigration have always been somewhat controversial, starting with the arrival of the first large number of Jamaicans and Indians to the UK in the late 1940s. The numbers of immigrants swelled during the economic boom, which lasted until the Organization of the Petroleum Exporting Countries' oil embargo of 1973–1974.

There was a grudging acceptance of the immigrants because they took jobs that native workers were no longer willing to accept, such as garbage collection, construction, and street sweeping. White Europeans may not have enjoyed having Africans, Arabs, Turks, or Asians in their communities, but they realized that they contributed to the economy.

When the economic downturn began in the mid-1970s, however, resentment began to rise toward the immigrants and their children who were, of course, not immigrants. That is hardly surprising in countries such as France and Germany, where the unemployment rate reached record highs and stayed there for most of a quarter century. In other words, the jobs white Europeans once rejected no longer seemed all that undesirable. Moreover, many working class whites and immigrants lived in the same or adjacent neighborhoods. The fact that many male immigrants came without their families led some white Europeans to worry that they were "paying too much attention" to European women.

Until the late 1990s, the racism growing out of those fears did not have a major political impact other than in the fringe support for the far-right parties mentioned in the previous section. In fact, Britain and France, in particular, maintained policies that made it easy for people to enter the country claiming political asylum.

By the late 1990s, however, opposition to asylum seeking and other forms of immigration grew. Some analysts estimated that as many as 20 million people a year fled their home countries for a variety of reasons. Hundreds of thousands of them tried to get into the EU member countries, as well as Norway and Switzerland, each year. Many were stopped at the borders and forced to live in detention camps. Many more, it seems, illegally entered Western Europe in ways that would remind many American readers of their border with Mexico.

Those tensions took on a new dimension for at least one group of immigrants after 9/11. As the world learned in the days after the terrorist attacks, at least one of the cells of hijackers was a group of Arabs who had lived in Germany for many years.

Since then, Europe has seen two forms of protest from Muslims that are hard to directly tie to either al-Qaida or 9/11, though some links obviously exist.

The first are terrorist attacks themselves, the most important of which occurred in Madrid and London. On March 11, 2004, bombs placed on 13 suburban trains (three did not explode) killed nearly 200 people and wounded at least 2,000 in Madrid. On July 7, 2005, four buses were bombed in London, killing 52 people. Two weeks later a smaller and less devastating attack occurred. A year later, British authorities foiled a planned attack that might have led to the bombing of as many as ten airplanes on transatlantic routes. In short, Europe has become a target of the same loosely organized groups of terrorists who attacked the World Trade Center and the Pentagon in 2001.

In the long run, it may well be that the discontent of young Muslims in general may prove increasingly disruptive for the countries with substantial populations of immigrants and their children. Soccer fans were exposed to the underlying anger of young Muslims when the French star Zinedine Zidane responded to a racist slur by the Italian player (and his former teammate) Marco

Materazzi by head-butting him, thereby costing his team the championship.

But the anger of these marginalized immigrants is far more deeply rooted. France, in particular, has seen extensive civil unrest among young Muslims. Throughout the autumn of 2005, thousands of them took to the streets in protests that started in a Paris suburb (following the death of two youths fleeing the police) and then spread to the rest of the country. The rioters hurled stones at police and set cars on fire. In a few places, they also desecrated Jewish cemeteries and synagogues.

In Sum

The political engagement of Europeans and the organizations they work through has taken two main forms since the individual countries became at least fragile democracies.

The first reflects the divisions dating back to the major upheavals that made contemporary Europe—the nation and state, religion, democracy, and social class. The second involves the disputes that arose only in the 1960s. Then, one might have expected the preeminent groups to come from the political left, whether the protesters of 1968 or the Greens who took the place of these protestors organizationally. In fact, the most important contemporary political splits benefit the right, including opposition to European integration and the growing diversification of European populations, including the rise of militant Islam and the terrorism it may encourage in its wake.

Governing I: The States

As noted previously, modern states spread from the countries who were signatories of the Treaty of Westphalia until they covered almost all the inhabited territory on the planet. In Europe, those state boundaries have changed dramatically over the centuries for various reasons, including, most recently, the collapse of the Soviet Union, Czechoslovakia, and Yugoslavia, and the unification of Germany. Whatever the geopolitical changes that have occurred in Europe, the states

created at least since the end of World War I and the Treaty of Versailles have had enduring boundaries for almost a century.

An important difference, however, exists among European states. Of all the European countries covered in this book, no two have exactly the same constitution or set of state institutions. Nonetheless, they share some common features.

Since the collapse of the central European empires at the end of World War I, all of the European countries have had constitutions. If nothing else, those documents have been the building blocks around which their states were built.

There is one glaring exception. The UK does not have a written constitution. Instead, its regime and rules of the game are determined by a series of laws passed by Parliament and customs that virtually everyone accepts.

Otherwise, the European countries all have written constitutions. In the West, most date from the end of World War II, when their governments were reconstituted after years of occupation. In some countries, including France, Spain, and Portugal, regime changes since the late 1950s led to new constitutions being written and ratified.

On the other side of the former iron curtain, one of the most important misconceptions is that the "satellite" countries did not have constitutions or other similar documents. In fact, they did.

However, those constitutions bore little relation to the way politics there actually played itself out. The state socialist regimes gave the communist party and other institutions not mentioned in most constitutions the lion's share of political power.

Core Principles

At the heart of all European constitutions is a version of the parliamentary system, which was created by the British in the late 19th and early 20th centuries. American readers, familiar with the system of checks and balances (separation of powers) that makes it possible for the U.S. Congress to block legislation proposed by the President and vice versa, often find parliamentary systems odd. The U.S. government acts slowly and normally only after a series of compromises in congressional committees and on the House and Senate floors. This is a deliberate choice reflecting the Founding Fathers' desire to create a system in which no branch could dominate any other.

By contrast, a parliamentary system allows governments to act in a fast and coherent manner to effectuate major policy changes. In Europe, because even the most presidential systems have a parliamentary core, the latter is far more important for anyone trying to understand European politics.

That is the case because a parliamentary system holds a prime minister and his or her cabinet (the government) responsible to parliament. If the government loses a key vote that is taken as a vote of confidence, typically it has to resign. At that point, two things can happen, neither of which are seen as positive outcomes. On the one hand, the prime minister or the head of state can dissolve parliament and call for new elections within a matter of weeks, the exact amount of time depending on the country and its constitution. On the other hand, the current parliament can try to construct a new majority government drawn from members currently in office.

In either case, a lost vote of confidence is seen as a failure on the part of the sitting government. As a result, supporters of the government and the party or parties that support it in parliament almost always vote to support it on key pieces of legislation. It is easiest to see how this works in the UK. There the government sends signals about its intentions not only during an election but in the "Speech from the Throne," or "Queen's Speech," which is read every time the House of Commons returns to session. In fact, the speech is written by the prime minister and reflects what he or she hopes to accomplish during the current session. Should the House of Commons reject anything included in the Queen's speech, that would be taken as a lost vote of confidence and almost certainly lead to the dissolution of parliament and a new election.

The British Model

As noted above, the UK represents the model of what a parliamentary system is like. In prac-
tice, however, not even the governments most based on the British system, such as those in Canada, Australia, and New Zealand, mirror its institutions. Even so, the British, or Westminster, institutions have been a great inspiration to parliaments adopted elsewhere.

Most countries (Sweden is an exception) have a bicameral legislature, which means their parliaments have two houses. Unlike the United States where the House of Representatives and the Senate have relatively equal powers, in most parliamentary systems, the upper house is basically powerless.

The UK is the classic case in which the upper house, the House of Lords, is a relic of the feudal period. Parliament began as an effort to bring the nobility and the commoners together to help chart the country's future. A thousand years ago, the House of Lords was by far the more important branch. By 1900 the House of Commons had taken the ascendant role and had become the source of almost all legislative and governmental power.

When the Liberal government was elected in 1906, it stripped all powers of the House of Lords if it did not agree to endorse all bills passed in the lower house that were part of the government's formal program, today embodied in the Queen's Speech that opens all new sessions of Parliament.

In short, for the last century, the British have only had one house of parliament that "counts," the House of Commons. Its membership varies in size from election to election depending on population shifts. In 2005 members were elected from 646 districts in England, Scotland, Wales, and Northern Ireland.

No one officially runs for an office other than his or her own local district. Thus, Prime Minister Tony Blair ran for reelection from the coal-mining town of Sedgefield near Durham and Newcastle.

In practice, everyone in the country knew that Blair would remain prime minister if Labour kept its majority because, in a parliamentary system, the leader of the majority party becomes the head of government.

Even more importantly, Britain almost always elects a single party with a clear majority in Parliament because of its "first past the post" electoral system (see below). As in the United States, any number of candidates can run in a given district or constituency. Unlike the case in the United States, five to seven candidates normally do so in each one. However, because whoever gets the most votes in a given district wins it (hence, first past the post), only Labour and the Conservatives win a significant number of seats given their support throughout the country. The Liberal Democrats, Scottish, Welsh, and Northern Irish parties do win seats in their regional strongholds (among them, they won 92 of 646 districts in the 2005 election), but only once since the mid-1920s have the minor parties denied either Labour or the Conservatives an outright majority of seats, although neither "major" party has ever won a majority of the national vote.

In short, the majority party forms the cabinet, something Labour has done since its victories at the polls in 1997, 2001, and 2005. At that point, the party leader becomes prime minister and appoints the rest of the cabinet, as well as about 60 other officials who become junior ministers serving under cabinet ministers.

Unlike the United States, all of the prime minister's appointees have to be members of parliament who retain their seat in the legislature while serving in government. Most are members of the House of Commons. (In the summer of 2006, only two appointees belonged to the House of Lords, a number that is likely to decrease further when and if the Labour Party enacts reforms to reduce the already limited powers of the upper house of Parliament.)

Because all recent governments other than the short-lived Labour minority cabinet of 1974 have enjoyed a majority, they have been able to act quickly and decisively to implement the party's program. Debate in the House of Commons is acrimonious. However, the outcome of the votes MPs cast is all but always predictable in advance. There have been times when significant numbers of government "backbenchers" voted against their prime minister's policies, most recently over the war in Iraq. However, Prime Minister Blair never came close to losing a vote of confidence. Indeed, "violating the party whip" on more than an isolated occasion normally leads to the end of a politician's career.

Other Common Denominators All European countries use some form of a parliamentary system. No two are alike, however, and many are very different from the Westminster model.

Sweden, for instance, does not have an upper house. Germany only allows for a vote demonstrating no confidence in the current government if the dissidents are simultaneously prepared to form a new cabinet.

Three overlapping factors account for most of the differences: constitutional structures, electoral laws, and the complexity of the competition among the political parties.

Constitutions. Britain is unique in that it does not have a written constitution. Instead, the constitution consists of laws and traditions that are understood and accepted by virtually everyone in the country.

Some European countries have had many constitutions over the years because they have had a number of unstable regimes. France probably has had the most since it has had five republics, three monarchies, two empires, and a neofascist government that collaborated with the Germans during World War II.

Germany, Italy, Belgium, the Netherlands, and the Scandinavian countries come closest to the British model. All have either a president or monarch as head of state, but, as in the UK, these men and women have little power other than to help end political deadlocks over forming new governments.

The German constitution is unique because after World War II the Allied occupying powers had great influence over its content, including features that made it difficult for a new Nazi or far-left party to come to power. The most important of these is the constructive vote of no confidence mentioned earlier. Because opponents of the government have to have their own alternative administration ready, only two serious attempts at a vote of confidence have occurred in the *Bundestag* (the lower house) in almost 60 years. In 1972 Willy Brandt's socialist-led coalition government came within two votes of losing power. A decade later, his successor, Helmut Schmidt, did lose a vote but actually orchestrated it himself because he knew he no longer had the support of his coalition partners.

The German constitution also gives unusual powers to the upper house, the *Bundesrat*. The *Bundesrat* is composed of members of the 16 German states. The states have representatives in numbers roughly proportional to the size of their populations. The actual people who attend *Bundesrat* meetings is determined by the issues on the agenda. As was the case during most of the 1990s and early 2000s, the opposition parties had more seats than the government; thus, the *Bundesrat* has served its intended role of exerting some kind of check over the *Bundestag*. Generally speaking, the *Bundesrat* must approve any legislation that affects the states, and since the federal constitution gives the states extensive powers, almost all legislation on domestic policy matters must be approved by both houses.

Furthermore, the German constitution provides for the Federal Constitutional Court, which is one of the strongest national supreme courts outside of the United States. Most other countries limit what their highest courts can do; the UK does not have any provisions for judicial review or the power to rule against acts of Parliament and other policies. The German court, by contrast, has ruled on most major issues, including abortion, bans on extremist parties, and German participation in the EU.

France's constitution is the most different from the classical parliamentary model and has now been widely copied in many former communist countries of the old Soviet bloc, including Russia, Poland, and the Czech Republic. Because the average government under the Third (1875–1940) and Fourth (1946–1958) Republics lasted nine months before resigning in anticipation of a lost vote of confidence, Charles de Gaulle and his colleagues who wrote the Fifth Republic's constitution set out to strengthen the executive and weaken Parliament. Among other things, the government can deny members of the National Assembly the right to propose amendments, does not allow it to raise expenditures or lower taxes from the government's proposed budget, removes large areas of domestic and foreign policy from the parliament's purview, and even limits when the assembly and the Senate can meet.

The Fifth Republic also created the first dual executive in which the head of state's power rivals (and often exceeds) that of the prime minister. The president of the republic has been directly elected since 1962. Most of the time, the presidency and the National Assembly have been controlled by the same coalition of parties. Under those circumstances, the president's powers have far outstripped those of the prime minister, who was no more influential than a typical American vice president. For ten years between 1986 and today, the presidency and the Parliament were dominated by different parties, requiring a practice that the French call cohabitation, in which the president and prime minister represent different parties and share power in an equitable manner.

One key feature of French decision making does not appear in the constitution at all. France has a network of elite institutions of higher education that are far more prestigious than the conventional universities. Graduates of such *grandes écoles* as the National School of Administration (ENA) or the Polytechnic School (*Polytechnique*) start their careers in the French civil service. After a decade of service to the state, they can engage in *pantouflage* (literally translated as putting on soft, cushy slippers) and become either politicians or corporate executives. Well over a third of cabinet members and two-thirds of top corporate executives started their careers at ENA or *Polytechnique*. Especially under the Gaullist parties, this "iron triangle" of bureaucrats, politicians, and corporate executives operated behind the scenes to make most important policy decisions and was more responsible than anyone else in France for forging what is now the fourth most dynamic economy in the world.

In Western Europe, most constitutions are at least 30 years old. They are widely accepted as are the democratic practices they call for. Although many people may disagree with their government's policies on social services, Iraq, or European integration, as in the United States, next to no one objects to the constitutional order or the political regimes.

The same certainty does not exist in regard to either democracy or political stability in Central and Eastern European countries that abandoned communism between 1989 and 1991. Some, including Poland, Hungary, the Czech Republic, and Slovakia, seem well on their way to democratic stability by, for instance, having at least two elections in which one party or coalition was defeated and peacefully and gracefully left office in favor of another. That cannot be said for most of the countries of the former Yugoslavia, Ukraine, or Russia, where democracy and the rule of law are tenuously supported, including by many of these countries' leaders.

Electoral Systems. Either the constitution or a regular law lays out how elections are conducted and can have a dramatic impact on how a country is governed. Electoral law can be a political football as governments change the procedures to help promote their own chances or hurt those of their opponents, as has happened in France and Italy three times since the 1980s. President Vladimir Putin's government is doing the same in Russia today, prompting some of the most penetrating criticisms of democracy there.

The first main type of electoral system is the British or American first past the post system mentioned earlier. Under this system, the country is divided into single member districts for electing the lower house. Any number of candidates who meet certain legal criteria (usually a small number of signatures on a nominating petition) can run in a given geographic district. But whoever gets the most votes (a plurality) wins the seat.

This system can distort the popular will as demonstrated at the voting booth. The largest party tends to win far more seats than its share of the national vote would suggest. Thus, in 2005, Britain's Labour Party won 35 percent of the vote and 55 percent of the seats in the House of Commons. By contrast, the Conservatives won almost 32 percent of the vote but barely 30 percent of the seats. The most seriously hurt were the smaller parties, which

won almost a third of the vote but barely 10 percent of the seats, almost all in Scotland, Wales, and Northern Ireland, where minority ethnic groups are concentrated. In short, first past the post systems tend to squeeze small parties and yield clear, even exaggerated, legislative majorities. In fact, in the United States where there are not such concentrations of minority groups, "third" parties have done poorly in congressional elections, although some third party or independent candidates have done reasonably well in recent contests for the White House.

Most European countries use some form of proportional representation, which guarantees parties will have seats in parliament roughly equivalent to their share of the national vote. Proportional systems operate in many ways. Ireland uses a single transferable vote in which voters rank all the candidates running in a given constituency. The candidate who comes in last on the basis of first preferences is eliminated and his or her ballots are reassigned to the remaining candidates on the basis of voters' second choices. That process of dropping the candidate who is now in last place and reallocating ballots continues until one of the remaining ones has a majority of "preferences."

Most proportional systems, however, do not work that way. The majority of countries do not have single member districts but are instead divided into much larger constituencies in which many candidates run. In the Netherlands and elsewhere, there is only one single national constituency. Each party presents a list of candidates, and if it wins 35 percent of the vote, the top 35 percent of the people on the list are elected. There are some variations on the way proportional representation is used. Sweden, Germany, and others set a minimum threshold of 4 or 5 percent of the vote that a party has to reach to win *any* seats. Germany and Russia have combined single member districts with proportional representation in hybrid systems, but in the former, at least, the overall results have all but completely mirrored the proportional result.

Proportional representation tends to have exactly the opposite outcome from first past the post elections. Even in Germany and Sweden, a party does not have to do all that well nationally to gain seats in parliament. Thus, in the 2003 Dutch election, nine parties won seats, including the Political Reformed Party, which won two seats with only 150,000 (1.6 percent) votes. The two largest parties, the Social Democrats and Christian Democrats, won slightly less than 30 percent each.

In effect, with some exceptions, it is usually impossible to form a majority government in proportional representation countries. One of the major parties has to form a coalition with one or more of the smaller ones. In the Netherlands, the Christian Democrats, who won a plurality, were given the first opportunity to form a government, which they did with two of the larger minor parties. So far, that government has worked smoothly and effectively.

But that can only happen if the partners agree to cooperate, especially on issues they do not agree on. In the Netherlands and elsewhere, this has led to periods of consociational democracy, in which historical adversaries agreed to make public policy through consensus formation.

In other countries it has led to gridlock. That was certainly the case in France under the Third and Fourth republics and Italy before the electoral reforms in 1992 and 2006. Perhaps most tragically of all, this kind of fragmentation occurred in the German party system between 1919 and 1933. The inability to form effective governments (and public frustration with the lack of political order) was one of the reasons why Hitler was able to rise to power.

France uses a different system altogether, which has recently been copied by many Eastern European countries, known as single member districts, two ballots. As in the United States and the UK, the country is divided into single member districts for the all important elections to the National Assembly. It is also quite easy for candidates to get on the ballot.

However, candidates only win if they get a majority of the vote in their districts, which happens quite rarely even in a landslide election like the one in 2002 that confirmed the Gaullist coalition in office. If no one gets a majority, a second ballot is held the following week. Any candidate who wins at least 12.5 percent of the vote *may* run in the second round, where the winner is the person who wins the most votes, whether he or she has a majority or not. One of the pressures this system has put on the parties is to force them to make strategic choices about who should run and who should withdraw for the decisive round of voting. For the most part, only a single candidate from the left and Gaullist coalitions runs so that neither of them dilutes its vote by running, say, a socialist and a green. The National Front is not part of this coalition-building process, but with no willing partners and a vote that varies between 10 and 18 percent, it almost never wins any seats. In other words, the system tends to favor the two largest coalitions of parties who also agree to stay together for the five-year life of the assembly. Thus, in 2005 the Gaullist Union for the Presidential Majority and the Socialist-led coalition of the left won *all* of the 577 seats contested in mainland France.

Presidential elections are held under similar rules. Any candidate who gets 500 signatures from members of parliament, regional assemblies, and local governments (of which France has more than 35,000) can get on the ballot for the first round.

Unlike assembly elections, only the top two candidates can run in the second round, which is held two weeks later. Put simply, even more than legislative elections, presidential ones put the emphasis on the strength of candidates who have a chance of winning a majority in the second ballot—despite the fact that 16 (a record) ran on the first ballot in 2002.

The 2002 election put the majoritarian emphasis of the second ballot in sharp relief. As has been the case in every election, no candidate won a majority requiring a second ballot. However, to the surprise of many the racist nationalist Jean-Marie Le Pen nosed out the socialist Lionel Jospin for second place. The left was therefore frozen out of the second ballot for the first time since 1969. Its supporters had to choose between the moderate conservative incumbent, Jacques Chirac, whom most of them despised, and the even more hated Le Pen. Most chose Chirac. Le Pen's vote went up by less than 1 percent between the two rounds. Chirac won more than 80 percent of the vote.

Party Competition. The rules surrounding the conduct of elections obviously explain a lot about the divisions and competition among parties. But rules do not explain everything.

Most European countries are experiencing changes in their party systems that go beyond anything electoral law can account for. In most of the former communist countries, there is not much of a historical legacy for parties to build on. Even in the Czech Republic and a handful of others that at least had somewhat successful experiences with democracy during the interwar period, there was little or nothing people could draw on after roughly a half century of totalitarian rule. Some parties with precommunist histories, such as the Liberals in several countries and the Freeholders in Hungary, were re-created. But, it is important to remember that no one under 70 had ever voted in a free and competitive election in any of those countries.

In some cases, as a result, the number and strength of the parties has fluctuated tremendously in the last decade and a half. There is no more graphic example of that than Russia. There, the leading party has been a so-called "party of power," created by the incumbent president or prime minister to promote his own ambitions. Putin's party, Unified Russia, cruised to victory in the 2005 *Duma* election even though the party was little more than a loose grouping of politicians loyal to the president. As is the case in many of these countries, the former communists came in a distant second, although the Russian communists had reformed less than their former colleagues to the west. Most of the other, smaller parties were new. Perhaps most telling of all, a third of the single member districts were won by independents with no links to any of the parties.

In the West, center-left and center-right parties have dominated the political scene for the better part of a half century. Usually, that pits a social democratic party against either a christian democratic or secular coalition, whose policies have not differed all that much in most countries in recent years.

At least since the 1980s, those parties have seen their share of the vote decline. This reflects not only a larger percentage of the electorate choosing the Greens, the far right, or some other relatively new party, but also a sharp decline in turnout, which reached record lows in the most recent elections in the UK and France.

Governing II: European Integration

The most sweeping changes in contemporary Europe do not involve events in individual countries but instead the trend toward European integration. The *Washington Post*'s T. R. Reid has written a book entitled *The United States of Europe*. His title is an exaggeration, but Europeans are handing more and more of their national sovereignty over to international European institutions, even if their political leaders rarely acknowledge that fact publicly. That process formally started with the creation of the North Atlantic Treaty Organization after World War II. More important, because its responsibilities go far beyond defense and security, is the European Union (EU), which has a profound impact on the way most Europeans live. Moreover, NATO is still largely dominated by the United States while Europeans all but completely control the EU. Other international governmental organizations involving Europe, such as the Western European Union and the Organization for Security and Cooperation in Europe, either have limited powers or are increasingly subordinated to the EU.

Historical Origins

European integration is not a new idea. Leaders from Julius Caesar to Adolph Hitler have dreamed about uniting the continent under their control. Until the last 75 years or so, the assumption was that integration could be achieved only by force. After World War I, a number of young intellectuals began promoting the idea that another, even bloodier, war could only be prevented if Europeans put aside their national differences and created some sort of unified, continent-wide political system. Obviously, they failed, because World War II took more than four times the number of lives than did the first one and shattered political systems throughout the continent, especially after the onset of the cold war split it in two.

In the occupied countries in the West, some of the men and women who resisted the Nazis and their domestic collaborators revived the idea of European integration. Unlike their interwar predecessors, the likes of Jean Monnet in France and Paul-Henri Spaak in Belgium understood that Europe could only be united gradually. Following an academic theory that later came to be known as functionalism, they argued that Europe could only be built one task or function at a time. They hoped that each success would make it possible for proponents of integration to move farther and faster later on. European integration has not proceeded quite that simply or smoothly, but its history since the early 1950s has paralleled the premises of functionalism, albeit with more fits and starts than the likes of Monnet or Spaak would have imagined.

From ECSC to EU

The first steps toward European integration were inspired by national security concerns. Once Europe was divided between East and West by the iron curtain, policy makers on both sides of the Atlantic realized that only a strong Western Europe could resist what was feared as the expansionist impulses of Soviet-led communism. Everyone understood that strength in that sense was both an economic and military concern.

That led the American government to commit the equivalent of $100 billion at today's values to rebuilding Western Europe through the Marshall Plan. Much of northern France and Germany were in ruins, and the German GDP was on the order of $500 per capita, again in today's terms.

The next step was the creation of NATO in 1949, which the Soviets matched by creating the Warsaw Pact. The creation of the Federal Republic of Germany (West Germany) and the German Democratic Republic (East Germany) only intensified the tensions that came close to taking the world to the

brink of World War III, at least until the construction of the Berlin Wall in 1961.

Lost somewhat in the national security concerns at the time was the establishment of the European Coal and Steel Community (ECSC) in 1951. It set in motion a long chain of events that led to the EU of today.

Visionaries like Monnet and Spaak convinced mainstream politicians that the solution to economic recovery lay in rebuilding such key industries as coal and steel. Coal and iron are core ingredients in the production of steel, which was used for making everything from automobiles to railroad track. What's more, most coal and iron deposits were close to the Rhine, the river that also formed borders separating France, Germany, Belgium, the Netherlands, and Luxembourg. Italy was close enough to the Rhine watershed that its coal and iron deposits would be clearly integral to any development strategy. Note, too, that despite the fact that the UK had massive iron and coal reserves, it was not asked to join nor was it interested in joining the ECSC.

The ECSC was a seemingly simple institution. The six member states agreed to eliminate tariffs on coal and steel products that crossed their mutual borders. They also imposed common tariffs on coal and steel products that came from outside the community (including the UK), which would be used to provide the community with income to support its work. They also created a series of institutions on the community and national governmental levels that were later transformed into those of the EU.

The ECSC was a rousing success. Therefore, in 1957, the same alliance of visionaries and conventional politicians agreed to sign the Treaty of Rome. This treaty did two things. First, it eliminated tariff barriers on all goods and services (or so they thought) among the six member countries by creating the European Economic Community (EEC). Second, it created the European Atomic Energy Community (Euratom) to develop peaceful uses of nuclear power. Euratom soon became an afterthought. It is noted here only because it was, in fact, where the Internet was created in the late 1980s. The European Organization for Nuclear

Research, or CERN, its main laboratory, also strad-dles Swiss and French territory.

The EEC experienced difficult times in the 1960s. French President Charles de Gaulle's con-cerns about ceding sovereignty from his own coun-try led him to twice block British applications to join. There were times when it seemed as if the EEC would collapse.

But after de Gaulle's resignation as French pres-ident in 1969, he was replaced by Georges Pompi-dou, who had been one of those interwar visionaries as a young man. Pompidou was, thus, less skepti-cal of the EEC than his predecessor and mentor. Therefore, he made it possible for the UK, Ireland, Denmark, and Norway to join (the Norwegians sub-sequently decided not to do so in a referendum) in 1972–1973. Thus began the process of broadening European institutions by adding new members.

The EEC then renamed itself the European Community (EC) on the assumption that it was going to become more than just a customs union. It also began plans to add more members, including Spain, Greece, and Portugal (which only emerged from military dictatorship in the 1970s).

Many European leaders also realized that the community had to deepen or add more powers if it was to move forward in the ways the function-alists had anticipated. This came to a head in the mid-1980s with the release of a report stating that remaining barriers to trade sapped the EC of what could be several percentage points more of eco-nomic growth per year. That drain on productivity came from rules that limited where people could work and regulations individual countries imposed on truck drivers at their borders to slow down the flow of goods transported by foreigners. In 1985 the influential former French finance minister, Jacques Delors, was named president of the European Com-mission (see below). He seized on a number of legal and political precedents such as the 1979 *cassis de Dijon* case, in which the European Court of Justice ruled that any product that met safety and health standards in one member country met them in all. With all this momentum, he helped push through the Single European Act (SEA) in 1986. Over the next six years, the EC would eliminate the remain-

ing barriers to trade. These improvements would, for instance, allow any citizen, except attorneys, to work in any member country and require mem-ber governments to purchase their own goods and services from vendors throughout the EC.

In 1992 the EC took perhaps its most symboli-cally important step. The member states signed the Treaty of Maastricht, which changed the name to the European Union to reflect the fact that it did far more than economic policy. To that end, it outlined three "pillars" of the EU's activities: the common market, a common foreign and security policy, and a variety of policies concerned with judicial and regulatory matters. The treaty also laid out criteria for creation of a common currency, the euro, which was gradually introduced in the financial markets and went into general circulation a decade later.

During the 1990s the EU also added new mem-bers Finland, Sweden, and Austria, which meant that only Norway (which turned down member-ship again in a referendum) and Switzerland (which never wanted to join) were outside the EU among countries to the west of the former iron curtain. In 2004 the EU added ten more members, including Cyprus, Malta, and the eight most prosperous and democratic countries from the former Soviet bloc.

The EU suffered one of its most serious setbacks in 2005 when voters in a number of countries re-jected a draft constitution, which would have sim-plified some of the most complicated procedures. It is likely that European leaders will make another attempt at drafting a constitution, but that probably will not happen until at least the end of this decade.

Governance in the EU

Like many international government organiza-tions, the EU has four main decision bodies. But unlike those other organizations, the EU has real decision-making power, which can normally be enforced in part because the member states have agreed to share their sovereignty with it and be-cause the EU is not dependent on the member states for much more than 10 percent of its funding.

The Council of the European Union (CEU) has to ratify all major new decisions that would either deepen the powers or broaden the membership of the EU. It meets in two forms, both of which are based on membership drawn from the national governments. Every six months, there is a summit meeting attended by the heads of government of the member states. As needed, the CEU meets to deal with specific issues, with each country sending its relevant cabinet minister(s). When the EEC was first formed, all council votes had to be unanimous, which gave every country what amounted to veto power, something that France used to paralyze the new body in the 1960s. The CEU now votes on the basis of a complicated system of qualified majority voting. Each country gets a certain number of votes based roughly on its population that it casts as a bloc. A bill, or directive, needs to win substantially more than a majority of the votes in a system that guarantees that a combination of some large and some smaller countries will be needed for passage. When and if there is a constitution, this system will change again.

Needless to say, the CEU tends to reflect the priorities and the interests of the national governments. That is less true of the European Commission, which is the day-do-day executive of the EU. As of 2004 each member state names one commissioner, who swears an oath of allegiance to the EU and agrees not to take instruction from his or her home government. That is sometimes honored in the breach since commissioners have had long and distinguished careers in their home countries.

Commissioners serve five-year terms that can be renewed once. Commissioners have substantive responsibilities akin to those of a cabinet member and supervise most of the 15,000 or so civil servants who work for the EU. The commission has the power to directly legislate on minor matters and has been the body that has initiated most of the major deepening and broadening reforms since the early 1960s.

The European Parliament has traditionally been the weakest link in the EU. Until 1979 its members were appointed by national parliaments. That year, they were directly elected for the first time, and the members of the European Parliament, or MEPs, have gradually asserted their influence. Now, the

parliament must approve almost all legislation and approve newly appointed members of the commission, as well as the annual budget. The parliament still has its difficulties. Most elections for it are decided on the basis of national issues rather than European ones. Furthermore, only 732 MEPs represent more than 400,000,000 citizens. That has led some observers to talk about a "democratic deficit" that has contributed to declining popular support for the EU since shortly after the Maastricht Treaty went into effect.

The European Court of Justice (ECJ) has one judge per country. Like the commissioners, the justices take an oath of allegiance to the EU. Early on, the ECJ ruled that because of the nature of the Treaty of Rome in 1957, it could practice judicial review and thus rule on the constitutionality of EU actions. In fact, it has jurisdiction over member states, their citizens, all corporations doing business in Europe, and the EU itself. Some of its seemingly minor rulings have opened the door to major decisions, including passage of the Single European Act. In recent years, it has had the most publicity for its attempts to compel such U.S.-based companies as Microsoft, Apple, and General Electric to meet European as well as U.S. legal standards.

Public Policy

Despite their shared commitment to democracy, most European countries have very different public policies from the United States. Americans typically have a strong preference for limited government. By contrast, Europeans have long embraced what political scientists call an interventionist state that offers extensive social services and has a major role in helping steer what remain predominantly capitalist economies.

Domestic Policy in the West

The first part of this discussion applies primarily to Western Europe, where there is a long tradition of state involvement in social and economic affairs. In the last century or so of its monarchy, France practiced a policy of *dirigisme,* in which the government "directed" much of the economy. That term is still used today. Social service programs date from the late 19th century, when the new German government, led by Otto von Bismarck, introduced health and old age insurance in an attempt to stem the growing support for the socialist party and the trade unions.

Today, most of Western Europe is covered by an extensive network of social programs, some of which provide direct services and some of which provide financial support. Every country has a health program that covers the medical expenses of everyone. In some countries, it is insurance based; in the UK no money changes hands when a patient sees a doctor. The government covers most tuition costs at universities. Each country has an extensive mass transit system that includes train stations in some towns with as few as 2,000 residents.

The government also has played a major role in the economy. After World War II, the government bought or "nationalized" firms representing something on the order of 20 percent of the overall economy. These included public utilities, companies that collaborated with the Germans, most armaments firms, and some businesses that were on the brink of failure but were deemed vital national interests, such as the coal mines in Europe. Most countries, too, had informal networks, such as the iron triangle in France and other groups that made economic policy by consensus among state, business, and labor leaders through what is often called corporatism.

These programs have not been without their critics. The social service benefits are expensive. While Americans pay about a third of their incomes in taxes, Britain has the lowest rates in Western Europe—about 42 percent of total income—and the figure tops 50 percent in Germany and Scandinavia. There is also growing concern about the quality of national health care, where many people now take out supplemental private insurance policies to avoid long waiting lists. Because these programs are so popular, there has been little significant change in the state's role despite efforts to do so by, for instance, conservative leaders such as Britain's Margaret Thatcher.

The interventionist state, where large industrial sectors or firms were publicly owned and operated, has been undercut far more dramatically. First, many of the state-owned industries did not perform well. Second, and more importantly, as globalization spread and companies—public and private—had to compete beyond national borders, it made little sense to keep telecommunications, airlines, or even armaments companies in purely national hands. Last but by no means least, the EU bars most direct state aid or subsidies to business, which had the indirect effect of placing them in reasonably free markets. (Agricultural subsidies are another matter.)

Domestic Policy in the East

Eastern Europe had to make far more profound policy changes after the collapse of communism. Under communist rule, the party and state controlled everything. Virtually all industries were owned by the state and operated in a command economy where state planners determined what they should produce and what they would charge for their goods and services. Citizens received even more extensive social service benefits than their colleagues to the west.

However, there was a glaring problem. Nothing worked well. Comforts and conveniences were in short supply and were thus rationed or shared. Most urban Russians lived in three room *kommunalka aparnments* in which they shared kitchens and bathrooms with dozens of neighbors. Used cars were cheaper than new ones, because they were readily available. The most frequent cause of fires in Moscow was spontaneously exploding televisions. Drivers who had cars took their windshield wipers with them after they parked; otherwise, they would be stolen.

Almost everything the countries made was of such poor quality that it could not be sold on global markets, including most Soviet weapons. This did not pose too much of a problem as long as communist countries only traded with each other.

In short, when communism collapsed, the former Soviet bloc had to make two simultaneous transitions, neither of which had been attempted before.

They had to move both from totalitarian government to democracy and from a centrally planned economy to a capitalist one. To make matters more difficult, none of the countries had significant experience with the subtleties and complexities of either.

As suggested earlier, the transition to democracy has not been an easy one, other than in the countries that entered it with the strongest ties to the West, such as Poland, Hungary, the Czech Republic, Slovakia, and, perhaps, Slovenia. More common are regimes such as Russia's, in which the two postcommunist presidents have increasingly concentrated power in their own hands, helped create a new elite of "oligarchs" who control as much as half of the economy, and all but ignored, if not encouraged, rampant corruption.

The same kind of pattern emerges for the economy. Most leaders were advised by Western experts to engage in shock therapy, through which the economy would be privatized and subjected to global fiscal and budgetary standards as soon as possible. Not every country adopted shock therapy in a wholehearted manner. Nonetheless, as many economists expected, the therapy shocked these countries indeed. But with unintended results.

Few firms could profitably be sold and those that could were normally sold to foreign investors. GDP plummeted as did living conditions. The average life expectancy of a Russian man declined by 10 years between the mid-1980s and 2000. Inflation was rampant; at times cab drivers preferred to be paid in packs of Marlboro cigarettes because their domestic currency kept losing its value.

In this decade, however, many of the economies have finally begun to stabilize. A combination of foreign investment and the emergence of a group of entrepreneurs have sparked a domestic recovery. Russia has benefited from the sale of its oil during a time of rapid energy price increases. Still, these countries are far poorer than their counterparts in the West. Some have a per capita GDP that barely tops $2,000 a year. A few have topped $10,000. Russia's is barely over $4,000. Most Western European states have a per capita GDP of at least $20,000; some are well over $30,000.

In tangible terms, Eastern Europe is developing two very different economies. A small elite is profiting from the reforms and living lives recognizable in the West. Thus, Moscow has one of the highest concentrations of luxury cars in the world. Meanwhile, older, less educated people who live largely on fixed incomes have a standard of living little different from that under communism; in some cases, they are worse off. To make matters even more complicated, most of the guaranteed social services provided under communist regimes have been eliminated. They may have been poorly delivered, but everyone did get at least rudimentary health care and subsidized homes and holidays.

The Eastern European governments still have a lot to do to ensure sustained recoveries and establish some modicum of equality. The private sector may be able to provide the former, but there is little historical evidence that markets alone can help shrink economic inequalities.

Foreign Policy

Political science has traditionally drawn a sharp distinction between comparative politics and international relations, with foreign policy part of the latter. That intellectual division has not made sense for Europe at least since the onset of the cold war, let alone since its disappearance or today's war on terrorism.

For most of the cold war period, Europe was divided into two all but completely unified and almost constantly hostile camps. A few countries remained at least somewhat neutral—Sweden, Finland, Switzerland, and Yugoslavia. Otherwise, they lined up with the American-led NATO in the West or the Soviet-organized Warsaw Pact in the East.

The United States accepted a degree of flexibility among its allies. During the 1970s, West Germany went farther than Washington would have preferred in reestablishing ties with the East. In the 1980s, a number of European governments objected to the deployment of U.S. cruise and Pershing nuclear missiles on European soil. Perhaps most dramatically of all, President de Gaulle took France out of the NATO command and forced its headquarters out of the country in 1966, ushering in a 40-year period when French-American relations were often rather tense.

However, on issues that mattered deeply to the United States, the NATO countries almost always fell into line, including France. Thus, despite massive protests against the war in Vietnam, all NATO members at least officially supported Washington's policies.

The Soviet Union did not tolerate even that level of dissent within its sphere of influence. The regimes in the "satellite" countries were all carbon copies of the party-state in Moscow. Leaders who showed any inclination to follow an independent path were replaced. The only exceptions were Yugoslavia and Albania, where local communist parties had come to power on their own and were not beholden to the USSR.

There were massive upheavals in East Germany, Hungary, the former Czechoslovakia, and Poland between the mid-1950s and the early 1980s. Soviet troops intervened in the first three, deposing reformist leaders, and endorsed the imposition of martial law in Poland in 1981.

When even larger protests broke out again in 1988, the communist regimes could not survive what turned out to be a dual challenge. Their own powers at home were weakened and could not eliminate protest movements that typically had millions of participants. Meanwhile, Mikhail Gorbachev had launched his reform program in Moscow and had decided that supporting aging hard-line leaders in the East was not worth the effort or the money. As noted earlier, all the communist regimes allied to the Soviet Union had collapsed by New Year's Eve when the red flag was lowered from the Kremlin for the last time.

Since then, most Eastern European countries have shifted their foreign policies in ways that support the United States. This is hardly surprising since most Eastern European leaders had been dissidents under communist rule and had long held pro-American views, even if they could not express them in public. Indeed, eight former Soviet-bloc countries that joined the EU, as well as Belarus and Romania, are also members of NATO. Russia and the countries still under its sway, such as Ukraine, remain hostile to any further NATO expansion.

There has been more disunity in this decade than at any point in the postwar period largely because of the war on terrorism, at least using the flexible definition of it used by the Bush administration since the 2003 invasion and occupation of Iraq. After the terrorist attacks of 9/11 almost all European countries rallied to the defense of the United States. Within three weeks, NATO leaders had ruled that the attacks violated Article 5 of the NATO treaty and thus required all member states to come to the aid of the United States. Many sent small contingents of troops to Afghanistan, where the stabilization and reconstruction effort had become officially NATO-led by 2005.

Subsequent foreign policy decisions have not been as unified. While virtually every European leader was convinced that removing Saddam Hussein and his regime from power in Iraq was a desirable goal, not all of them were convinced that the Bush administration's argument for going to war when and how it did was acceptable. France, Germany, and Russia were the most vocal critics. As permanent members of the United Nations Security Council, France and Russia (with China) effectively made the creation of the kind of broad coalition used to fight the 1991 Gulf War impossible. Of the major European powers, only Britain, Italy, and Spain supported the U.S. actions. And with new left of center governments in Rome and Madrid, these two countries have withdrawn their troops as well.

There also has been some criticism of the way the United States is handling the war on terrorism, per se. The attacks in New York and Washington, D.C., were among the most spectacular terrorist incidents in history. But one should not forget that Britain, France, Spain, Germany, and other countries had plenty of experience with terrorism dating back at least to the 1950s. As a result, many Europeans have a more nuanced understanding of terrorism and are more inclined to address its root causes than is the leadership in Washington. This includes Britain and Spain, which have experienced massive attacks of their own since 2001.

Tensions reemerged in 2005 about the best ways to deal with the threats posed by the alleged nuclear weapons programs in North Korea and Iran. The United States emphasized the dangers and the need for firmness, starting with President Bush's remarks about the "axis of evil" in his 2002 State of the Union Address. Most European leaders favor a more diplomatic overture to the two countries, especially those that have strong economic ties with Iran.

Russia is the country least in the European foreign policy mainstream. President Putin has been the one leader most hostile to American foreign policy initiatives. In part, this reflects real policy differences on such issues as Iraq and Iran. In part, it reflects Russian desire to return to the ranks of the world's great powers, which its leadership thinks means retaining a degree of independence from the United States and NATO.

The EU's Impact on Policy

With the launch of the euro and other innovations since Maastricht, the EU probably has more influence than the national governments on economic life. Trade, employment, and taxation policies are increasingly similar from country to country. The new central bank sets a common monetary and fiscal policy for all the member states. European rules about job safety and other microeconomic issues take precedence over domestic ones. And, of course, the euro makes international travel and commerce far easier. Besides, it allows consumers in Ireland to see that they pay a lot more money for everything from automobiles to alcohol than Spaniards or Italians pay. Not everything in the economy is perfect. To cite the most obvious example, Denmark, Sweden, and the UK have not adopted the euro, though the new currency is used in those countries in many urban areas.

The EU's track record has been far more mixed for the other two pillars. The Schengen agreement allows for the free movement of people across the borders of member states. In other words, one goes through passport control when entering one's first EU state but after that, travel within Europe is open. However, the British and Irish never agreed to Schengen, and with growing concern about illegal immigration by asylum seekers and others, pressure is growing to modify the Schengen provisions.

The EU has had a hard time, however, developing a common foreign and security policy. That became clear almost immediately after Maastricht when the Germans, in particular, broke with most of their allies on Yugoslavian policy and when it became clear that the EU did not have the diplomatic clout to stop the fighting. Still, there have been some notable accomplishments. The EU now negotiates for all its member states as a whole in trade negotiations. It is in the process of creating a rapid deployment force that could be sent to places such as Kosovo should fighting break out.

Toward 2010

Looking back over the events and developments across the continent, at least one thing is clear about Europe: political life will continue to change, and much of that change will be impossible to predict even a year in advance.

One can be reasonably certain that the next decade will be different from this one. The three most visible and controversial European leaders will have left the political scene: Blair, Chirac, and Putin (unless the Russian president engineers a constitutional change). The EU is stuck in a period of political lethargy after nearly two decades of broadening and deepening, and many think it will have to move toward a constitution and devise better ways to integrate the new members from Eastern Europe.

The last 60 years have been marked by unprecedented shifts. If one had made predictions about the Europe of today in 1946, 1956, 1966, 1976, or even 1986, they most likely would have been wrong. That is a trend that most certainly will continue.

Charles Hauss teaches political science at George Mason University and is a senior associate at Search for Common Ground.

PART TWO

GOVERNMENTS

ALBANIA

REPUBLIC OF ALBANIA

Republika e Shqipëri

The Country

The Republic of Albania, one of the smallest and least advanced of European nations, is located at the mouth of the Adriatic, where it is flanked by Serbia and Montenegro on the north, Macedonia on the east, and Greece on the southeast. A mountainous topography has served to isolate its people and retard both national unity and development. The two main ethnic-linguistic groups—the Ghegs north of the Shkumbin River and the Tosks south of that river—together embrace 97 percent of the population. Albanian (*shqip*) is an independent member of the Indo-European language group. There are two dialects corresponding to the ethnic division, the Tosk dialect being in official use. A majority of the population has traditionally been Muslim, but in 1967 Albania was proclaimed an atheist state with religious observances proscribed until lifting of the ban by the post-Communist government in April 1991. (Recent estimates describe 70 percent of the population as "nominally" Muslim, 20 percent Orthodox Christian, and 10 percent Roman Catholic.) Because the country has one of Europe's highest population growth rates, some 60 percent of its inhabitants are reported to be under 26 years of age. More than 20 percent of the successful candidates in the 1991 balloting for the People's Assembly were women, but only eight women were elected in 2001 and ten in 2005. There is only one woman in the current cabinet.

Throughout the Communist era, agriculture was dominated by state farms and collectives. In mid-1991, however, the new government adopted a policy of gradually returning the land to peasant ownership or control, yielding a pattern of excessively small holdings with overall productivity one-tenth that of the European Union (EU). Nearly all farmland is now privately owned, and agriculture, primarily at the subsistence level, accounts for more than half of GDP. Chrome, nickel, and copper are mined, although the mining sector remains significantly outdated despite recent interest from foreign investors. Industry accounts for about 12 percent of GDP, while the fledgling fishing sector has been targeted for government support.

With per capita income estimated at no more than $340 in 1993, Albania was classified as Europe's only "least developed" country. The demise

of the socialist system had yielded soaring inflation, paralysis in the industrial sector, massive unemployment, and a huge state budget deficit. Subsequently, however, Albania temporarily became one of Europe's fastest-growing economies, achieving GDP growth of 11 and 8 percent in 1993 and 1994, respectively, albeit from a very low base. Although the discovery in 1995 of new oil reserves offered promise of greater self-sufficiency, the economy was devastated in late 1996 and early 1997 by the collapse of the "pyramid" financial schemes that had attracted heavy investment from much of the population. (It was subsequently estimated that Albanians were bilked of $1.2 billion through the schemes.) Consequently, GDP contracted by 7 percent in 1997 before rebounding to a robust annual average of nearly 8 percent growth in 1998– 2000.

Annual per capita income had reportedly grown to more than $2,000 by 2005, in part due to GDP growth that had averaged 6 percent annually for several years. Moreover, annual inflation was running at only a little over 2 percent, partly in response to the government's tight fiscal policies. Nevertheless, Albania remained one of the poorest countries in Europe, with the informal sector (i.e., the untaxed sector) reportedly outstripping the formal sector. Remittances from workers abroad (an estimated 800,000 from Italy, Greece, and other Western European countries) continued to underpin the Albanian economy. (Ethnic Albanians constitute important segments of the population in several countries in the region, prompting discussion in some quarters of the possible formation of a "Greater Albania.") Most basic goods, including food, are imported. The leading trading partners are Italy and Greece, with whom traditional links were revived in the wake of the Communist collapse.

Despite political discord in Albania in the late 1990s and first half of the 2000s, international lenders such as the International Monetary Fund (IMF) and the World Bank continued to support the government's recovery programs. The IMF praised the government for "steadfast pursuit of sound macroeconomic policies" while urging focus on what was generally conceded to be widespread fraud and corruption, particularly in the customs service and judiciary. Hopes for Albania's eventual EU accession will depend on, among other things, establishment of sufficient border controls to combat trafficking in drugs and arms, successful completion of bank reform currently underway under international supervision, and further privatization of inefficient state-run enterprises. Other current government priorities include modernization of the port at Durrës, additional infrastructure improvements, and development of the energy sector. The government is also attempting to promote the fledgling tourist industry and otherwise attract foreign investment by encouraging "more modern business practices." Meanwhile, heavy migration from the poor mountainous regions to urban areas has compromised basic services and complicated an already unsatisfactory (by Western standards) electoral process.

Government and Politics

Political background

Following almost 450 years of Turkish suzerainty, Albania was declared independent in 1912 but remained in a state of confusion until a monarchy was proclaimed in 1928 by President Ahmad Bey ZOGU, who ruled as King Zog until Albania was invaded and annexed by Italy in 1939. During the later stages of World War II, the Communist-led National Liberation Front under Gen. Enver HOXHA was able to assume control of the country, proclaiming its liberation from the Axis powers on November 29, 1944. Hoxha's provisional government obtained Allied recognition in November 1945 on the condition that free national elections be held. Subsequently, on December 2, 1945, a Communist-controlled assembly was elected, and the new body proclaimed Albania a republic on January 11, 1946. The Albanian Communist Party, founded in 1941, became the only authorized political organization in a system closely patterned on other communist models. Renamed the Albanian Party of Labor (*Partia e Punës e Shqipërisë*—PPS) in 1948, its Politburo and Secretariat continued to wield decisive control.

Political Status: Independent state since 1912; Communist regime established in 1946; interim democratic constitution adopted April 29, 1991; permanent constitution approved by national referendum on November 22, 1998, and signed into law by the president on November 28.

Area: 11,100 sq. mi. (28,748 sq. km.).

Population: 3,069,275 (2001C); 3,189,000 (2005E).

Major Urban Centers (2005E): TIRANË (TIRANA, 387,000), Durrës (107,000), Elbasan (90,000), Shkodër (83,000), Vlorë (80,000), Korçë (53,000).

Official Language: Albanian.

Monetary Unit: Lek (market rate July 1, 2006: 96.56 lekë = $1US).

President: Gen. (Ret.) Alfred MOISIU (formerly Socialist Party of Albania); elected by the People's Assembly on June 24, 2002, and sworn in on July 24 to a five-year term in succession to Rexhep MEJDANI (formerly Socialist Party of Albania). (Upon election the president is constitutionally required to discard formal party affiliation.)

Prime Minister: Sali BERISHA (Democratic Party of Albania); nominated by the president on September 3, 2005 (following the legislative elections of July 3), approved by the People's Assembly on September 10, and inaugurated on September 11 to succeed Fatos Thanos NANO (Socialist Party of Albania).

Despite extensive second-echelon purges from 1972 to 1977, very little turnover in the top political leadership occurred prior to a number of Politburo changes announced on November 7, 1981, at the conclusion of the Eighth PPS Congress. Shortly thereafter, on December 17, Mehmet SHEHU, who had served as chair of the Council of Ministers since 1954, was officially reported to have committed suicide at "a moment of nervous distress." (Three years later, party officials declared that Shehu had been "liquidated" because he had interfered with the "unbreakable unity of the party with the people.") On November 22, 1982, a newly elected People's Assembly named Ramiz ALIA to succeed Haxhi LLESHI as president of its Presidium (head of state), while an ensuing reorganization of the Council of Ministers was widely interpreted as a purge of former Shehu supporters.

On April 11, 1985, after a prolonged illness that had kept him from public view for nearly a year, Hoxha died of a heart condition at Tirana. Two days later, Alia (who had assumed a number of Hoxha's functions during the party leader's illness) became only the second individual to be named PPS first secretary since World War II.

As late as January 1990 President Alia displayed a hard-line posture in regard to the pace of change in Eastern Europe. In April, however, he proclaimed an end to Albania's policy of diplomatic isolation, and in early May the People's Assembly approved a number of major reforms, including an end to the ban on religious activity, liberalization of the penal code, increased autonomy in enterprise decision making, and the right to passports for all Albanians over the age of six. On December 11, following widespread popular demonstrations, liberalization was further advanced by a declaration that other parties would be recognized, with the Democratic Party of Albania (*Partia Demokratike e Shqipërisë*—PDS), the country's first opposition formation in 46 years, being launched the following day.

Student-led demonstrations at the capital on February 20, 1991, prompted Alia to declare presidential rule and, two days later, to appoint a provisional government headed by the politically moderate Fatos Thanos NANO. At multiparty balloting on March 31 and April 17 the Communists secured 168 of 250 legislative seats, largely on the basis of their strength in rural areas, while the opposition PDS won 75. The restructured assembly fell into discord at its opening session because of a PDS boycott prompted by the killing of four party members on April 2. On May 9 the president nonetheless appointed Nano to head a new all-PPS government. A fresh wave of street violence ensued, and on June 5 a respected economist, Ylli BUFI, was named to head an interim coalition government that was installed on June 12, coincident with redesignation of the PPS as the Socialist Party of Albania (*Partia Socialiste e Shqipërisë*—PSS). The new administration contained 12 representatives from the PSS, 7 from the PDS, and 5 from smaller groups that had failed to win assembly seats.

On December 4, 1991, the PDS announced that it was withdrawing from the government coalition because of foot-dragging by the PSS in regard to political reform. Two days later Prime Minister Bufi resigned in favor of Vilson AHMETI, the first non-Marxist government head since World War II. On December 22, ten days after a rally of 20,000 people called for his resignation, President Alia agreed to the scheduling of a new general election.

At two-stage balloting on March 22 and 29, 1992, the PDS won close to a two-thirds majority in a reduced assembly of 140 seats, and on April 3 Alia resigned. Elected by the assembly as Albania's new head of state on April 9, PDS leader Sali BERISHA immediately named Aleksander MEKSI to succeed Ahmeti as prime minister of a tripartite administration that included representatives of the smaller Social Democratic Party of Albania (*Partia Socialdemokrat e Shqipërisë*—PSDS) and Albanian Republican Party (*Partia Republikane Shqiptare*—PRS), in addition to three independents.

In September 1992 former president Alia was placed under house arrest after reportedly being charged with abuse of power and misuse of state funds, while in July 1993 Nano was charged with corruption during his brief premiership. In 1994 both former leaders received substantial prison sentences. (Alia was released in July 1995, although he was rearrested in February 1996 on charges of "genocide" and "crimes against humanity." See PSS in Political Parties, below, for details on the resolution of those charges.) Collaterally, the Albanian authorities also took action against the Democratic Union of the Greek Minority (*Omonia*); although prison terms for five *Omonia* leaders were later rescinded, a further crackdown against Greek separatists was mounted in March 1995.

President Berisha suffered an unexpected rebuff on November 6, 1994, when a referendum on a post-Communist constitution yielded a 53.9 per-

cent majority against the proposed draft (which in October had failed to secure the required two-thirds legislative majority). The president responded by carrying out a major ministerial reshuffle on December 4. Although the PRS and the PSDS announced their withdrawal from the government, the two PSDS cabinet members promptly formed the breakaway Social Democratic Union of Albania (*Bashkimi i Social Demokratiket i Shqipërisë*—BSDS) and remained in their posts. The reshaped administration retained a comfortable parliamentary majority and derived some benefit from an economic upturn in 1994 and 1995.

A controversial Genocide Law enacted in September 1995 authorized the barring from public life until 2002 of Communist-era officials found to have committed crimes against humanity for political, ideological, or religious motives, while associated legislation adopted in November provided for the "screening" of the past records of senior political and other figures. Under these measures, some 70 opposition candidates (notably of the ex-Communist PSS) were barred from standing in the legislative elections held May–June 1996.

The first-round balloting on May 26, 1996, was so riddled with malpractice and fraud (as confirmed by international observers) that the main opposition parties boycotted the second round on June 2, as protest demonstrations in Tirana and elsewhere were broken up with considerable police brutality. The official results of the balloting gave the PDS 122 of the 140 seats, with 10 going to the PSS and the other 8 being shared by three parties. The PDS thus acquired substantially better than the two-thirds majority required for passage of constitutional amendments, one of its campaign pledges having been to draw up a fully democratic post-Communist constitution. The substantially changed government sworn in on July 12, under the continued premiership of Meksi, contained 22 PDS representatives, with two posts going to the reinstated PRS and one to the BSDS.

The collapse in early 1997 of the so-called pyramid financial schemes pushed the country to the brink of anarchy, and pressure mounted on President Berisha to resign and call new elections. On

February 11 the PRS withdrew from the government, and, with dissent growing even within his own PDS, Berisha on March 1 made a concession to his critics and ordered the resignation of the government. However, on March 2 the government declared a state of emergency, and, as "rebels" seized control of about one-third of the nation (primarily in the south), Berisha turned to his security forces and "northern vigilantes" to defend the regime. Berisha was reelected president (unopposed) by the assembly on March 3, and he soon offered amnesty to the southern rebels and began negotiations with the opposition, which included the ad hoc Forum for Democracy, led by a number of former political prisoners. The opposition demanded Berisha's resignation, early elections, and installation of a government of technocrats to deal with economic problems. Berisha, also under pressure from the EU and the Organization for Security and Cooperation in Europe (OSCE), on March 12 announced the formation of an interim "government of reconciliation." The cabinet, led by the PSS's Bashkim FINO as the new prime minister, included all the major parties. However, Berisha refused to resign as president unless he was repudiated in an election, and the southern rebels declined to lay down their arms until he resigned.

In the face of that impasse, the UN Security Council on March 29, 1997, endorsed a proposal by the OSCE that affirmed the right of self-selected nations to accept the Albanian government's call for foreign military intervention. Fearing that refugees, disorder, and a torrent of smuggled weapons would spill into adjoining states unless the Albanian conflict was resolved, eight nations in mid-April sent a total of about 5,900 troops to Albania under "Operation Alba," designed to help provide humanitarian aid and keep the peace pending new elections. Meanwhile, Leka ZOGU, exiled son of King Zog, had returned to Albania on April 13 to campaign for a return of the monarchy. However, in a national referendum on June 29, a monarchy proposal was endorsed by only one-third of the voters.

New legislative elections were conducted on June 29, 1997, after a compromise was reached on enlargement of the assembly to include additional proportional representation. In balloting that was marred by violence but was ultimately deemed "reasonably free and fair" by the OSCE, the PSS overwhelmed the PDS by better than a three-to-one margin (101 seats to 28, including the results of runoff balloting in July). After a period of uncertainty as to his intentions, President Berisha resigned on July 23, and the assembly elected Rexhep MEJDANI of the PSS to succeed him the next day. PSS chair Fatos Nano (freed from jail during the recent domestic unrest and subsequently officially pardoned by Berisha) was again sworn in as prime minister on July 25, heading a coalition government of the PSS, PSDS, the Party of the Democratic Alliance (*Partia e Alenca Demokratike*—PAD), Albanian Agrarian Party (*Partia Agrare e Shqipërisë*—PAS), and the Union for Human Rights Party (*Partia e Bashkimi për te Drejtat e Njeriut*—PBDNj). Former prime minister Fino of the PSS was named deputy prime minister. Meanwhile, Operation Alba was concluded.

Although the southern rebellion subsided following the installation of the PSS-led government, conflict erupted again in August 1998 when six members of the PDS were arrested on charges relating to the repression of the domestic unrest the previous year. In addition, the killing of a prominent PDS activist, Azem HAJDARI, on September 12 outside PDS headquarters prompted thousands of PDS-led protesters to march on government buildings at Tirana the following day. Gunfire was exchanged, and Nano and his cabinet were forced to flee their offices and go into hiding. Demonstrations continued for several days (some 7 people died and nearly 80 were injured) as Berisha called for the resignation of Nano, who in turn accused his PDS adversary of attempting a coup. However, the international community, fearful that Albania was about to repeat the civil strife of 1997, strongly pressured both camps to negotiate a settlement. Order was consequently restored, in part due to Berisha's plea for calm.

Prime Minister Nano resigned on September 28, 1998, and was succeeded by PSS Secretary General Pandeli MAJKO, who was sworn in on

October 2 after receiving the endorsement of the PSS as well as President Mejdani. Majko's cabinet, as approved by the assembly on October 8, comprised the same five parties as the previous government. In keeping with one of Majko's declared priorities, a long-delayed constitutional referendum was held on November 22, the new basic law (see Constitution and government, below) receiving a reported 93.5 percent approval level in a turnout of just above 50 percent of the voters.

The appointment of Majko (at 30 years old, then the youngest prime minister in Europe) was initially perceived as a potentially stabilizing influence, particularly since he had no association with previous Communist governments. However, conflict with the "old guard" quickly surfaced, and Majko stepped down in late October 1999 after losing a PSS leadership battle with Nano. He was succeeded by Deputy Prime Minister Ilir META, whose revamped cabinet easily secured assembly endorsement despite a boycott of the vote by most legislators from the PDS-led Union for Democracy and the United Albanian Right.

The legislative election of June 24 and July 8, 2001, saw the PSS retain a majority, but with fewer seats. Despite PDS complaints of ballot-rigging and other irregularities, international observers regarded the campaign and balloting as fundamentally free and fair. Prime Minister Meta, having renegotiated a coalition agreement with the PSDS, PAD, PAS, and PBDNj, won a parliamentary endorsement for his new cabinet on September 12.

Following sustained friction between him and PSS leader Nano, Prime Minister Meta resigned on January 29, 2002. On February 7 the president invited former prime minister Majko to form a cabinet, which, as endorsed by the assembly on February 22, comprised the same five parties as the outgoing government.

Extensive squabbling over the nomination of the next president of the republic resulted in the selection of a compromise candidate—Gen. (Ret.) Alfred MOISIU—who was endorsed by both the PSS and the PDS. (Moisiu secured 97 of 140 votes in the assembly, comfortably above the required three-fifths [84] majority that was required.) Moisiu took office on July 24, 2002, and the following day Prime Minister Majko retired to make way for Nano, after the PSS had voted to make Nano its parliamentary leader. Nano's new cabinet was sworn in on August 1; it included the PSS, PAS, and PBDNj, but not the PSDS, which objected to losing the post of deputy prime minister.

Former Prime Minister Meta was persuaded to join the July 2002 cabinet as deputy prime minister and foreign affairs minister. However, Meta quit the government a year later, prompting another severe internal PSS dispute that culminated in Meta and a group of PSS legislators forming a new party called the Socialist Movement for Integration (*Lëvizja Socialiste për Integrim*—LSI). Meanwhile, in late December 2003 Nano appointed a new cabinet that included the PSDS and the PBDNj and was also supported by several small parliamentary parties.

The PDS and its allies in the new Alliance for Freedom, Justice, and Welfare (*Aleanca për Liri, Drejtësi, dhe Mirëqenie*—ALDM) secured 74 seats in the July 3, 2005, legislative balloting. Despite initial protests from the PSS over the conduct of the poll, PDS leader Sali Berisha was approved as the new prime minister by an 84–53 vote in the assembly on September 10. Berisha was inaugurated the following day as head of a center-right coalition government that comprised the PDS, Agrarian Environmental Party (*Partia Agrare Ambientaliste*—PAA), PBDNj, and members of two ALDM components (the PRS and the New Democrat Party [*Partia Demokrate e Re*—PDr]).

Constitution and government

A constitution adopted in December 1976 did not significantly alter the system of government introduced three decades earlier. Under its provisions, the former People's Republic of Albania was redesignated as the Socialist People's Republic of Albania and the PPS was identified as "the sole directing political power in state and society." Private property was declared to be abolished, as were the "bases of religious obscurantism"; financial dealings with "capitalist or revisionist monopolies or states" were also outlawed. Under the interim basic law of April 1991, all of these stipulations were abandoned, with the country's name being foreshortened to "Republic of Albania."

The constitution that was approved in a national referendum on November 22, 1998, and signed into law by the president on November 28 codified many of the changes implemented in 1991. The new basic law was described as a "Western-style" document modeled most directly on the German and Italian examples. It describes Albania as a "democratic republic" in which individual human rights (including religious freedom) are guaranteed, as are those of ethnic minorities. Private property rights are also protected, and emphasis is given to a "market-oriented" economy.

The supreme organ of government is the unicameral People's Assembly, none of whose members can be nominated by groups representing ethnic minorities. The assembly, which sits for four years, elects the republic's president, who is precluded from holding party office and is limited to two five-year terms. The powers of the president, particularly those regarding the authority to govern by decree in times of emergency, were substantially diluted in the 1998 constitution. Responsibility for day-to-day governmental administration rests with the Council of Ministers, whose head serves as prime minister. The prime minister is appointed by the president, who, upon the proposal of the prime minister, also nominates the Council of Ministers for approval by the assembly. Should the assembly endorse a nonconfidence motion in the Council of Ministers, the president is directed to appoint a new prime minister in an effort to nominate an acceptable council.

The judiciary includes a Supreme Court and district and local courts. For purposes of local administration, Albania is divided into 36 districts (*rrethët*), the municipality of Tirana, over 200 localities, and 2,500 villages. Local councils, elected by direct suffrage for three-year terms, are the governing bodies in each subdivision.

Foreign relations

Albania's pursuit of an antirevisionist and antiimperialist foreign policy was long conditioned by geography and shifting relationships among external Communist powers. Until 1990 there were four principal phases in dealings with the outside world. The period immediately after World War II was marked by a dependence upon Yugoslavia that lasted until the latter's expulsion from the Cominform in 1948. The second phase was one of accord with the Soviet Union, Albania remaining a close ally of the USSR until the softening of Soviet policy toward Yugoslavia after the death of Stalin. President Hoxha subsequently flouted Soviet leader Nikita Khrushchev in a 1957 speech praising Stalin, thereby opening an ideological cleavage between the two countries. Three years later, Soviet efforts to enlist Albania's support in its dispute with the People's Republic of China were rebuffed, and in 1961 Tirana severed diplomatic relations with Moscow. The third phase was one of dependence on China, as Tirana, which was instrumental in gaining UN membership for China, accepted the latter's view of world affairs until the post-Maoist regime moved toward détente with the West. In mid-1977 Albania severely criticized Chinese foreign policy toward both the United States and the third world, the estrangement culminating in Beijing's suspension in July 1978 of all economic and military assistance. Formal diplomatic relations were retained, however.

In the wake of the dispute with "imperialist-revisionist" China, the Hoxha regime entered the fourth phase of pre-1990 foreign policy by seeking new trade links with a variety of socialist and nonsocialist countries, exclusive of the two superpowers, both of whose policies were consistently branded by Tirana as inimical to Albania's independence and security. Improved relations with Yugoslavia, whose Kosovo province is populated largely by ethnic Albanians, were jolted by a wave of riots involving Serbian security forces March–May 1981, after which the status of Kosovo became a major issue between the two countries.

Negotiations with the Federal Republic of Germany yielded an agreement in September 1987 to establish diplomatic links after Tirana had abandoned its insistence on reparations for World War II damage. During the same month Greece announced the end of a state of war that had technically existed since an Italian invasion from

Albania in October 1940. The action was preceded by a settlement of border issues that effectively voided Athens' long-standing claim to a portion of southern Albania (known to the Greeks as Northern Epirus) populated by a sizable ethnic Greek community.

Albania's transition to multiparty democracy in 1990 and 1991 brought about a transformation in its external relations. On July 30, 1990, it was announced that diplomatic relations were to be reestablished with the Soviet Union after a break of 29 years, and on August 16 Tirana declared that it would become the 141st signatory to the 1969 Nuclear Non-Proliferation Treaty. A week earlier Albania had been granted observer status at the Vienna talks of the Conference on Security and Cooperation in Europe (CSCE, precursor of the OSCE), with full membership following on June 19, 1991. On March 15, 1991, formal relations with the United States, severed since 1939, were restored, paving the way for a visit by U.S. Secretary of State James Baker, who was greeted by some 300,000 cheering residents of Tirana on June 22. Meanwhile, diplomatic relations had been reestablished with Britain on May 29, while links to the Vatican were restored on July 4.

In the wake of perceived Western indifference to the growing threat to ethnic Albanians and other Muslims in former Yugoslavia, particularly in the Yugoslavian province of Kosovo and in Macedonia, Albania was reportedly admitted to the Organization of the Islamic Conference (OIC) in December 1992. The OIC membership subsequently became controversial, however. In mid-1998 Prime Minister Nano argued that appropriate legal steps had not been taken regarding the original application for membership and that Albania's accession had not been official. In part, Nano's position was apparently influenced by his preference for orienting Albania toward Europe rather than the Islamic world. In that context, his government launched, with U.S. assistance, a crackdown on Islamic fundamentalists in 1998. Following Nano's resignation in September, government officials indicated that Albania was prepared to "reactivate" relations with the

OIC, which subsequently offered broad support for Albania's role in housing the primarily Muslim Kosovo refugees in 1999. In May 1993 President Berisha appealed to the United States and the North Atlantic Treaty Organization (NATO) to dispatch forces to Kosovo to prevent "ethnic cleansing" of Albanians.

Relations with Greece worsened in the post-Communist era due to a mass exodus of ethnic Greeks from Albania, attendant border incidents, and renewed Albanian fears of Greek territorial designs. Despite the signature of a series of cooperation agreements by the Albanian and Greek prime ministers in May 1993, tensions flared again in April 1994 as a result of the killing of two Albanian border guards during a raid by activists of the Greek-based Northern Epirus Liberation Front (NELF). Further deterioration, beginning in May, because of an Albanian crackdown on alleged ethnic Greek subversives was partially reversed by a visit to Tirana by the Greek foreign minister in March 1995 and by collateral Greek action against NELF militants. The improvement in bilateral relations yielded a Greek-Albanian friendship treaty in March 1996 that called for cooperation in various fields, as well as mutual respect for the rights of minorities.

Albania became a signatory of NATO's Partnership for Peace in February 1994, while Council of Europe membership was conferred in June 1995. A U.S.-Albanian military cooperation agreement was signed in October 1995, following an official visit to Washington by President Berisha a month earlier, and a U.S. military aid package worth over $100 million was approved in April 1996. Meanwhile, Albania's relations with Italy and other EU countries continued to be complicated by the role of Albanian Adriatic ports as staging areas for illegal immigrants of various origins seeking to reach Western Europe. (In 1995 Italy had deployed additional naval units in the Adriatic to intercept vessels carrying such immigrants and ensure their immediate return to Albania.)

In late 1998 and early 1999 new Prime Minister Majko carefully endorsed Western policy regarding Kosovo, that is, that the province should seek autonomy within Yugoslavia, not independence, despite significant sentiment within the Albanian populace for the latter. Not surprisingly, the government strongly endorsed the military campaign that NATO launched against Serbia in late March 1999, although the initiative produced an influx of some 450,000 refugees from Kosovo. A NATO force of more than 5,000 personnel was stationed in Albania until September 1999 in connection with the anti-Serbian operation, Tirana subsequently expressing the hope that support for NATO in the campaign would facilitate Albania's eventual accession to that alliance. During the ethnic fighting in neighboring Macedonia in 2001, Prime Minister Meta also made his intentions clear: although supporting the cause of ethnic Albanian rights, he condemned violent acts, rejected militant calls for border changes, and disavowed any interest in formation of a "Greater Albania."

Possibly in continued appreciation of NATO's action to protect the ethnic Albanian population in Kosovo, Albania supported the U.S./UK-led invasion of Iraq in 2003 and contributed a small contingent of troops to the NATO mission in Iraq. Collaterally, the Nano government, keenly focused on potential accession to the EU, maintained its distance from the independence movement among ethnic Albanians in Kosovo. In early 2006 new Prime Minister Berisha referred to the "will for independence" among the population in Kosovo, perhaps thereby signaling a shift in attitude from the previous administration regarding that delicate issue.

Current issues

The PSS, PDS, and a number of smaller parties signed a pledge prior to the July 2005 assembly elections to wage a "fair campaign" under new guidelines developed in cooperation with the OSCE and the Council of Europe. The pact was designed to prevent a repeat of the problems that had plagued the national poll in 2001 and the local balloting in 2003. Among other things, the pervasive past irregularities had created the impression that Albania had fallen significantly behind most other "transition" countries in Europe in regard to democratization and adherence to the "rule of law." When initial results in 2005 indicated a victory for the PDS and its allies in the ALDM, Prime Minister Nano, whose PSS had held power since 1997, decried the vote as "unacceptable" and the winners as "illegitimate," thereby raising the specter of yet another sustained political imbroglio. However, in early September Nano formally accepted the results, paving the way for what was considered to be the first "peaceful" transfer of power in Albania since the fall of Communism.

The OSCE reported that the 2005 balloting complied only partially with international standards, citing insufficient voter registration procedures, the declining role of women in the electoral process, the continual "marginalization" of minorities, and the apparent subversion of the "spirit" of the proportional component of the poll by the major parties. Several violent incidents were also reported in connection with the campaign, although observers noted an improvement over previous elections in that regard. It was also noted that the level of "personal attacks" had declined. Overall, the conduct of the election appeared to surpass, if just barely, the minimum requirements for the international community to conclude that sufficient progress had been achieved. For his part, new Prime Minister Berisha, for whom the balloting represented an apparently final victory in his "intense personal rivalry" with Nano, pledged to pursue a broad reform agenda designed to combat corruption, improve the business climate, and reduce poverty. Many of the proposed changes were geared toward facilitating eventual EU and NATO accession for Albania. The EU cautioned that substantial reforms were required before accession talks could begin in earnest, although in June 2006 it signed a stabilization and association agreement with Albania, which had fallen well behind other Balkan countries such as Croatia and Macedonia on that front. Meanwhile, observers noted that severe parliamentary infighting in the first half of 2006 did not bode well for agreement on proposed electoral revisions such as the possible direct election of the president.

Political Parties

Until December 1990, when the first opposition party was recognized, Albania accorded a monopoly position to the Albanian Party of Labor (*Partia e Punës e Shqipërisë*—PPS), which served as the core of the Democratic Front of Albania (*Fronti Demokratik ë Shqipërisë*—FDS), a mass organization to which all adult Albanians theoretically belonged. Although numerous parties were registered in 1991 and the first half of 1992, the People's Assembly in July 1992 banned all parties identifiable as "fascist, antinational, chauvinistic, racist, totalitarian, communist, Marxist-Leninist, Stalinist, or Enverist," the last in reference to former Communist leader Enver Hoxha. However, the 1992 law was revised in 1998 to repeal the ban against communist parties (among other things), although proscription was maintained against "antinational, anti-Albanian, antidemocratic, and totalitarian" groups. There are no current restrictions on parties based on ethnicity, religion, or regional status, as long as such parties do not denigrate other groups.

The Albanian election commission announced that 57 parties registered for the 2005 legislative elections, with 14 of them participating in electoral coalitions for the national proportional balloting.

Government and Government-Supportive Parties:

Democratic Party of Albania (*Partia Demokratike e Shqipërisë*—PDS). The PDS was launched during a rally in Tirana on December 12, 1990, and was legalized a week later. The party sought protection of human rights, a free-market economy, and improved relations with neighboring states. It won 75 of 250 legislative seats at the balloting of March 31 and April 7, 1991, and joined the PSS in a coalition government on June 12.

At the election of March 1992, the PDS, strongest in the north, won 92 of 140 assembly seats, and on April 9 its chair, Sali Berisha, was named president of the republic. The party was awarded all but four portfolios in the Meksi govern-

ment of April 1992. Serious postelection tensions in the PDS were highlighted by the departure of six moderate leftists in July 1992 to form the PAD (below), after which the PDS-led government was accused of authoritarian leanings. The party leadership responded by expelling several rightists, who later formed the ultranationalist PDDS (see PDr).

In March 1995 Eduard SELAMI was dismissed as PDS chair for criticizing President Berisha's effort to secure approval of a new constitution by referendum. His acting successor, Tritan SHEHU, was formally installed in April 1996, as the PDS launched an election campaign advocating lower taxes and more privatization. Later the same month, Selami and seven members of the PDS national council, including Secretary General Tomor DOSTI, were ousted. Although the party's landslide victory in the May–June balloting was tarnished by evidence of widespread voting irregularities, a new PDS-dominated government took office in July. However, the PDS was crushed in the legislative elections of June–July 1997, dropping from 122 to 28 seats. (The PDS participated in the 1997 balloting in a Union for Democracy [*Bashkimi për Demokraci*—BD] coalition that also included the PLL, BSDS, PDKS, PBD, a number of other small parties, and various cultural associations. The BD won only 31 seats, including the 28 PDS seats. Meanwhile, another smaller conservative grouping—the United Albanian Right [*Djatha e Bashkuar e Shqipërisë*—DBS]—won 4 seats. Members of the DBS included the PBK, PRS, PDDS, and LD.)

PSS/PDS friction continued following the 1997 balloting, reportedly fueled by animosity between Berisha and the PSS's Fatos Nano. Consequently, the PDS boycotted most legislative activity. Six high-ranking PDS members were arrested in August 1998 on charges related to suppression of the 1997 domestic unrest, and the tension between the two leading parties almost erupted into civil war in September after Azem Hajdari, a controversial PDS legislator and Berisha protégé, was assassinated outside PDS headquarters in Tirana. Although Hajdari's murder remained unsolved, an extraordinary PDS congress voted in July 1999 to end the party's ten-month assembly boycott. Subsequently, Berisha was able to beat back a challenge from Genc POLLO, leader of the PDS reform wing, for the party's chair at the October 1999 regular congress. In January 2001 Pollo finally broke from the PDS and established the Democrat Party (PD, see below).

Prior to the 2001 legislative balloting, the PDS organized the Union for Victory (Bashkimi për Fitore) coalition with the PLL, BLD, PBK, and PRS. The coalition was largely a successor to the Union for Democracy of 1997. The Union for Victory was a more successful effort than its predecessor in organizing all the leading conservative elements and secured 46 seats. (Berisha claimed that massive irregularities had cost the PDS and its allies many other seats.)

The PDS signed electoral cooperation agreements for the July 2005 legislative balloting with seven small groupings that had coalesced as the ALDM (below). Under the unique arrangements, the PDS presented one candidate in each of the 100 single-member constituencies, although 15 of those candidates reportedly were in fact members of various ALDM components. Collaterally, the PDS urged its supporters to vote for the ALDM in the national proportional balloting.

Leaders: Sali BERISHA (Prime Minister and Chair of the Party), Bamir TOPI (Parliamentary Leader), Jozefina TOPALLI (Chair of the Presidency of the People's Assembly), Ridvan BODE (Secretary General).

Alliance for Freedom, Justice, and Welfare (*Aleanca për Liri, Drejtësi, dhe Mirëqenie—* ALDM). The PDS-supportive ALDM was formed by the groups below prior to the July 2005 legislative poll. A number of members of the ALDM components were included among the formal PDS candidates in single-member districts, while PDS supporters were encouraged to vote for the ALDM in the proportional balloting. (Although the ALDM parties were listed separately on the proportional ballot, a vote for any of the parties was counted as a vote for the ALDM as a whole.) Due to the PDS support, the ALDM secured 33 percent of the proportional vote and was accorded 18 assembly seats (the PRS, 11; PDr, 4; PDKS, 2; and BLD, 1).

Liberal Democratic Union (*Bashkimi Liberal Demokrat—*BLD). The BLD was launched as the Social Democratic Union of Albania (*Bashkimi i Social Demokratikët i Shqipërisë—* BSDS) in January 1995 by Teodor Laço and Vullnet ADEMI, formerly of the PSDS, who had opted to remain in the government in the December 1994 reshuffle, notwithstanding the decision of the parent party to go into opposition. Laço retained his post in the government appointed in July 1996, even though the BSDS had won no seats in the May–June election. His moderating influence was also apparent in late 1998 and early 1999, when he encouraged the Union for Democracy to end its legislative boycott, arguing it could serve more effectively as a genuine opposition party via full parliamentary participation. By then, the party had been transformed into the BLD.

Leaders: Arjan STAROVA (Chair), Teodor LAÇO.

National Front Party (*Partia Balli Kombëtare—* PBK). The PBK is descended from the anticommunist wing of the National Front created in 1942 to oppose Axis occupation. The then PBK leader, Abaz Ermenji, returned to Albania in October 1995 after 49 years in exile. The party won three of the United Albanian Right's four seats to the assembly in the 1997 election. In 2002 Ermenji was defeated in his attempt to retain the PBK leadership.

Reports surrounding the July 2005 legislative poll referenced electoral cooperation between the PBK (under Alimadhi's leadership) and the PDS. However, other reports also referenced PDS cooperation with the **Democratic National Front Party** (*Partia Balli Kombëtar Demokrat—*PBKD), which had reportedly been formed in 1998 by Hysen SELFO, former deputy chair of the PBK who had been expelled from the parent group as a result of conflict with Ermenji. The nature of the relationship of the two parties was unclear.

Leaders: Adriatík ALIMADHI, Abaz ER-MENJI, Shkelqim ROQI.

Albanian Republican Party (*Partia Republikane Shqiptare*—PRS). Third-ranked at the 1991 balloting, the PRS is an urban formation with links to the Italian Republican Party, from which it appears to have drawn financial support. It was awarded the transport and communications portfolio in 1992, despite having won only one assembly seat. The first PRS congress in June 1992 was marred by a major split, resulting in the creation of distinct centrist and right-wing groups.

The PRS withdrew from the ruling coalition in December 1994, criticizing the government's "shortcomings" but pledging itself to "constructive" opposition. It was reinstated with two posts in the government appointed in July 1996, despite winning only three seats in the preceding assembly election. The PRS again exited the government in February 1997 and, amid growing public disorder, called for it to resign. The party secured one of the United Albanian Right's four seats in the 1997 balloting for the assembly.

Early in November 1997, PRS Chair Sabri Godo denounced the PDS at a PRS party congress and said conservatives should rally around the PRS, which could become a "third force" against communism. Saying his legislative duties kept him too busy to lead his party, Godo relinquished the chair to a 32-year-old, Fatmir Mediu. However, Godo continued to serve as chair of the parliamentary constitutional commission that drafted the new basic law implemented in November 1998. Mediu was appointed to the PDS-led cabinet in September 2005, the PRS having secured 11 seats in the July legislative balloting as part of the ALDM.

Leaders: Fatmir MEDIU (Chair), Sabri GODO (former Chair), Çerçiz MINGOMATAJ, Arian MADHI.

Christian Democratic Party of Albania (*Partia Demokristiane e Shqipërisë*—PDKS). A member of the 1977 Union for Democracy coalition, the PDKS drew support mainly from Shkodër and other northern Catholic towns. It won 1 percent of the vote in the 2001 legislative poll. The then chair of the PDKS, Zef BUSHATI, was appointed Albania's ambassador to the Vatican in 2002 and was succeeded as PDKS leader by Nikolle Lesi, a well-known editor. The PDKS secured two seats in the 2005 assembly elections as part of the ALDM.

Leader: Nikolle LESI.

Democratic Union Party (*Partia Bashkimi Demokrat*—PBD). Another member of the 1977 Union for Democracy coalition, the PBD captured 0.6 percent of the vote in the 2001 general election.

Leaders: Remiz NDREU, Ylber VALTERI.

New Democrat Party (*Partia Demokrate e Re*—PDr). Also referenced simply as the Democrat Party (*Partia Demokrate*—PD), the PDr, originating in the reform wing of the PDS, was organized in January 2001 by former PDS leader Genc Pollo, who had already established a six-member reformist group in the People's Assembly. The new formation also incorporated the former Movement for Democracy (*Lëvizja për Demokraci*—LD) and the Democratic Party of the Right of Albania (*Partia Demokratike e Djatha e Shqipërisë*—PDDS), both of which were participants in 1997's United Albanian Right. The LD had been launched by PDS dissidents in April 1997, while the PDDS dated to March 1994. One of the PDDS's founders, Petrit KALAKULA, had served as agriculture minister in 1993 until being dismissed for making allegedly profascist assertions in the People's Assembly. At the 2001 general election the PDr won six legislative seats.

In 2002 former LD leader Dashamir SHEHI (then the PDr secretary general) and several other PDr legislators attempted unsuccessfully to push Pollo out of the PDr leadership. Shehi and the others subsequently formed a new party (see PDRn, under PLL, below).

As part of the ALDM, the PDr secured four seats in the proportional component of the July 2005 assembly balloting, and Pollo was named to the new PDS-led cabinet in September.

Leaders: Genc POLLO, Nard NDOKA.

Human Rights League Party (*Partia Lëvizja për te Drejtat dhe Lirite e Njeriut—PLDLNj*). The PLDLNj is led by Ligoraq Karamelo, a former legislator and former member of the PBDNj. Among other things, Karamelo in early 2006 joined other activists in criticizing the PBDNj and *Omonia* for failing recently to address the concerns of the Greek minority adequately.

Leaders: Ligoraq KARAMELO.

Agrarian Environmental Party (*Partia Agrare Ambientaliste—PAA*). The PAA is a successor rubric for the Albanian Agrarian Party (*Partia Agrare e Shqipërisë—PAS*), which upon its formation in 1991 called for the privatization of all previously collectivized property, credit arrangements for farmers, and job stimulation for those thrown out of work by the collapse of collectivization. The PAS won one seat in the 1997 assembly election and three in 2001. The PAA was given a deputy ministerial post in the December 2003 PSS-led cabinet.

Although the PAA continued to cooperate with the PSS for the July 2005 assembly poll (at which the PAA secured four seats in the proportional balloting [on a vote share of 6.6 percent]), Lufter Xhuveli accepted a post in the new PDS-led government formed in September.

Leader: Lufter XHUVELI (Chair).

Union for Human Rights Party (*Partia e Bashkimi për te Drejtat e Njeriut—PBDNj*). The PBDNj was established in February 1992 following the enactment of legislation banning parties based on "ethnic principles." The new law was aimed in particular at the **Democratic Union of the Greek Minority** (*Bashkimia Demokratik i Minoritet Grek*), referenced as *Omonia*, the transliter-

ation of the Greek word for "harmony." The PBDNj became the electoral successor of *Omonia*, winning two assembly seats in March 1992 as against *Omonia*'s five seats in 1991.

Representing the southern ethnic Greek community, *Omonia* had been formed by clandestine opponents of the former regime in December 1989 and was officially launched a year later under the leadership of Theodori BEZHANI and Sotiris KYRIAZATIS. Presumed to have strong links to several parties in Greece, particularly New Democracy, *Omonia* contended that any territorial change between Albania and Greece should come only from negotiation and agreement, publicly distancing itself from such militant ethnic Greek groups as the **Northern Epirus Liberation Front** (NELF). *Omonia* nevertheless attracted the wrath of Albanian nationalists, and six prominent *Omonia* members were among many ethnic Greeks detained in May 1994 in a government crackdown on suspected subversion. In September five of the six were convicted by a Tirana court of treason and other charges, including "carrying out the orders of a foreign secret service," and were sentenced to prison terms of between six and eight years. However, one of the five received a presidential pardon in December, while the other four were released in February 1995 after the Court of Appeals had identified "procedural violations" in their trial.

The PBDNj was credited with winning three assembly seats in 1996 and four in 1997. It joined the PSS-led coalition in July 1997, a decision reportedly opposed by some members of *Omonia*, which had maintained a separate identity as a cultural organization despite usually close ties with the PBDNj. Vasil MELO, then leader of the PBDNj, defended the 1998 constitution as providing sufficient protection for minorities, although *Omonia* leaders in January 2000 called for greater attention to minority issues, particularly the provision of educational services in Greek where appropriate. *Omonia* was led at the time by Vangjel Dule, elected in 1998 following a leadership crisis that had resulted in the removal of Kyriazatis in 1996.

The PBDNj won three proportional seats, with 2.6 percent of the vote, at the 2001 election. Dule was elected chair of the PBDNj at a party congress in February 2002 that Melo derided as "illegitimate and manipulated." The PBDNj was given one portfolio in the December 2003 cabinet led by the PSS.

It was reported in early 2005 that *Omonia,* under the leadership of Jani JANI, had decided to present its own candidates for the July assembly poll after an absence of 14 years from the electoral process. *Omonia* reportedly agreed to support the PBDNj in the proportional balloting in return for the PBDNj's support for some *Omonia* candidates in the single-member districts. After securing two proportional seats (on a vote share of 4.1 percent), the PBDNj was given the ministry of labor, social affairs, and equal opportunities in the new PDS-led cabinet.

Leader: Vangjel DULE (President).

Opposition Parties

Socialist Party of Albania (*Partia Socialiste e Shqipërisë*—PSS). The PSS is a successor to the Communist Party of Albania (*Partia Komuniste e Shqipërisë*—PKS), which was launched in November 1941 under the supervision of Yugoslav emissaries and became the ruling single party following World War II. The PKS was renamed the Albanian Party of Labor (*Partia e Punës e Shqipërisë*—PPS) in 1948.

In 1990 the PPS Central Committee proposed a number of drastic changes in the country's constitution, including a provision that would prohibit the president of the republic from serving as party first secretary. In accordance with this requirement, President Alia stepped down as first secretary on May 4, 1991. A month earlier, at the conclusion of the country's first multiparty balloting since World War II, the PPS had won a better than two-thirds majority in the new People's Assembly. However, due to subsequent popular unrest, it was forced to participate in a "nonpartisan" governing coalition on June 12, at which time it adopted its current name. In light of these developments, a rump group organized the new Albanian Communist Party (see PKS, below).

At the March 1992 general election the PSS won only 38 of 140 seats with 25 percent of the vote. As a result, Alia resigned as president of the republic, and the party, for the first time, moved into opposition. Alia and his successor as party leader, Fatos Thanos Nano, were both arrested in mid-1993, Nano being convicted in April 1994 of having mishandled $8 million in Italian aid funds during his 1991 incumbency as prime minister. His 12-year prison sentence was upheld by the Supreme Court in August, prior to which Alia and nine former colleagues had also received prison sentences. Alia was released in July 1995, but he was imprisoned (along with several other members of his former administration) in February 1996 on charges of "genocide" and "crimes against humanity" in connection with the alleged killing or internment of Albanians who had attempted to flee the country during his tenure. Nano also remained in prison during the May–June 1996 election, from which many PSS candidates were barred because of their Communist affiliations. Opposition protests over the conduct of the balloting were headed by the PSS, which was officially credited with ten seats despite boycotting the second round.

In a communication from his prison cell in July 1996, Nano proposed that the PSS should become a genuinely reformist party and drop all references to Marxism in its constitution. In the rebellion of early 1997 (see Political background, above), Nano and Alia escaped from prison along with hundreds of others. Nano was subsequently pardoned by President Berisha, who was under pressure to include the PSS in an interim "government of reconciliation." Meanwhile, Alia fled the country, returning in December after having been declared innocent of all outstanding charges by the Albanian courts in October.

In March 1997 Berisha named Bashkim Fino of the PSS as prime minister, and early assembly elections were scheduled for June, with runoffs in July. The PSS, showing its greatest strength in the south, swept to victory, taking 101 seats, which, with 18 seats secured by five allies (the PSDS, PAD, PAS, PBDNj, and PUK [see below]) in an Alliance of State coalition, gave the party a secure margin for amending the constitution. The new assembly elected Rexhep Mejdani, secretary general of the PSS, to be president, and he invited Nano, as prime minister, to form a new government, which was sworn in on July 25. Following severe political turmoil in September 1998, Nano resigned as prime minister and was succeeded by PSS Secretary General Pandeli Majko. Nano also resigned his PSS chair in early 1999. However, although he had announced he would launch a new political movement that, among other things, would be "neither communist nor anticommunist," Nano made a comeback at the October PSS Congress, defeating Majko for the chair by a vote of 291–261. PSS Deputy Chair Ilir Meta was subsequently selected to be the new prime minister by a vote of 68–45 in the PSS steering committee over Makbule ÇEÇO, the governor of Tirana, who was designated to be deputy prime minister.

At the 2001 national election the PSS barely retained its majority, winning 73 seats in a downsized People's Assembly. After receiving the party's endorsement on August 20, Meta again negotiated a coalition government with previous partners the PSDS, PAD, PAS, and PBDNj.

Nano was reelected chair of the PSS at a December 2003 congress that also demanded that PSS legislators toe the party line on major votes or else quit the party. Meta and a number of PSS legislators subsequently left the PSS to form the LSI (below).

The PSS in early 2005 reportedly announced plans to contest the July legislative poll under informal cooperative arrangements with the PSDS, PAS, PBDNj, and a faction of the PAD. As part of that pact, the PSS called upon its supporters to vote for the smaller parties in the nationwide proportional balloting. However, that initiative was undercut by the fact that each party presented a separate nationwide list, thereby precluding the kind of cohesion exhibited by the PDS-aligned ALDM (above). In addition, the PSS presented its own candidate in each single-member constituency, sometimes in direct competition with candidates from its "allies."

Following the defeat of the PSS in the July 2005 balloting, Nano resigned as the PSS chair in September. He was succeeded by Edi Rama (the mayor of Tirana), who defeated former president Mejdani for the post.

Leaders: Edi RAMA (Chair), Fatos Thanos NANO (Former Prime Minister), Gramoz RUÇI (Former Secretary General), Ben BLUSHI (Political Secretary), Pandeli MAJKO (Secretary General and Parliamentary Leader).

Social Democratic Party of Albania (*Partia Socialdemokrat e Shqipërisë*—PSDS). The PSDS was launched in 1991 on a platform of moderate socialism; it finished third at the 1992 poll, winning seven assembly seats, and became a junior partner in the new government headed by the PDS. Following the president's November 1994 referendum defeat, the PSDS officially withdrew from the coalition, although the two cabinet representatives previously associated with the party opted to retain their portfolios as members of the breakaway BSDS.

The PSDS formed an alliance, called the Pole of the Center (*Poli i Quendres*—PQ), with the PAD for the 1996 legislative poll as a centrist alternative to the ruling PDS on the right and the PSS on the left; the PQ secured no seats in that election. However, the PSDS offered some joint candidates with the PSS for the June 1997 balloting, at which nine PSDS members were elected, and the PSDS joined the subsequent coalition government. After winning four seats at the 2001 election, it again joined the government. The PSDS declined to join the July 2002 cabinet because it was not offered the post of deputy prime minister that it had previously held. However, the PSDS returned to the cabinet in December 2003, and, despite his steady criticism of perceived administration failures, PSDS Chair Skënder Gjinushi said the party would support the PSS-led government in the run-up to the July 2005 legislative poll and beyond. The PSDS secured seven seats (on a vote share of 13 percent) in the proportional component of the 2005 balloting.

Leaders: Dr. Skënder GJINUSHI (Chair and Former Deputy Prime Minister), Engjell BEJTJA (General Secretary).

Socialist Movement for Integration (*Lëvizja Socialiste për Integrim*—LSI). A left-of-center splinter from the PSS, the LSI was launched under the leadership of former prime minister Ilir Meta, who had been feuding with PSS leader Nano for several years. (Meta had resigned from the cabinet in 2003 after issuing a "blistering attack" on Nano; he subsequently tried unsuccessfully to force Nano out of the PSS chair.) Nine PSS legislators reportedly joined the LSI, which ran separately from all other parties in the 2005 legislative poll, securing five seats (four on a vote share of 8.4 percent in the proportional balloting).

Leader: Ilir META (Chair and Former Prime Minister), Pellumb XHUFI (Deputy Chair), Ndre LEGISI.

Party of the Democratic Alliance (*Partia e Alenca Demokratike*—PAD). The PAD was launched in October 1992 by a number of parliamentarians, including PDS cofounder Gramoz Pashko, in opposition to what was termed the "autocratic rule" of President Berisha. One of the PAD's activists was killed on January 14, 1994, during a rally that had generated what the government termed "pro-Serbian statements." Several prominent PAD candidates were barred (because of their allegedly Communist past) from the 1996 legislative balloting, which the PAD contested unsuccessfully as part of the PQ alliance with the PSDS. The party won two assembly seats in the 1997 election (having presented its own candidates for that balloting) and joined the new PSS-led government. It remained in the government after the 2001 election, at which it took three seats. However, a split in the party left its status in the government in limbo in 2002. One faction, led by Arben Imani and including at least one legislator, announced in May that it was taking the PAD out of the Alliance of State on the grounds that effective governance was being compromised by PSS infighting. However, another faction, led by Neritan Çeka, reaffirmed its support for the government and named new members to fill the party vacancies created by the "defection" of Imani and his supporters. The factionalization continued into 2005 with Çeka and his supporters cooperating informally with the PSS while Imani's group aligned with the PDS. Competing, at least partially, as an ally of the PSS, the PAD secured three proportional seats (on a vote share of 4.8 percent) in the July 2005 legislative poll.

Leaders: Neritan ÇEKA, Arben IMANI, Gramoz PASHKO.

Social Democracy Party of Albania (*Partia Demokracia Sociale e Shqipërisë*—PDSSh). Formed in April 2003 by several disgruntled members of the PSDS (including Paskal Milo, a former member of the PSDS presidency), the PDSSh described itself as a center and center-left grouping devoted to the concerns of a populace that was "tired of the left's unkept promises." The PDSSh subsequently appeared to move in and out of the PSS-led Coalition for Integration, although it was reportedly supportive of the coalition during the run-up to the July 2005 legislative balloting. The PDSSh secured two proportional seats (on a vote share of 4.3 percent) in the 2005 assembly balloting.

Leader: Paskal MILO (Chair).

Other Parties Participating in the 2005 Assembly Elections

Movement of Legality Party (*Partia Lëvizja e Legalitetit*—PLL). The PLL was founded in 1991 as the political wing of the monarchist movement, which has marginal support in Albania but some following among Albanians living abroad. The movement's 50th anniversary celebrations in Tirana in November 1993 were briefly attended by Leka Zogu, son of the late King Zog (who had fled the country in 1939). Leka Zogu, having returned to Albania to rally support for a referendum on the monarchy (held simultaneously with the June 29, 1997, assembly election), subsequently went back to South Africa and was later threatened with arrest, should he return to Albania, for leading an armed rally in Tirana at which there was a fatal shoot-out. Reporting on the early balloting, Prime Minister Fino had initially estimated that 53 percent favored a monarchy, but official results subsequently put the figure at 33 percent, which the PLL insisted was a fraudulent count. The PLL won three seats in the collateral assembly election.

Leka Zogu and a group of his supporters were arrested in South Africa in early 1999 on charges of illegal possession of a large cache of weapons. Meanwhile, the government alleged that PLL supporters had in effect been involved in a coup attempt. In late 1999 Leka Zogu was sentenced in absentia by a court in Tirana to three years in prison, and the assembly defeated an amnesty motion in his case in mid-2000.

However, Leka Zogu was permitted by invitation of the assembly to return to Albania in mid-2002 as a "common citizen." Although he initially indicated he would not pursue a political career, in mid-2004 he launched a **Movement for National Development** (*Lëvizja për Zhvillim Kombëtar—LZhK*) that comprised the PLL; the **Conservative Party** (*Partia Konservatore—PKons*), led by Armando RUÇO; and the small **Renewal Democratic Party** (*Partia Demokratika e Rinovor—PDRn*), led by Dashamir SHEHI, who had recently split from the PDr. The LZhK's "law and order" platform for the 2005 legislative balloting called for anticorruption measures (including judicial reform) and pursuit of integration with the EU and NATO. Leka Zogu also endorsed independence for Kosovo, although he retreated from previous support for formation of a "Greater Albania."

Leader: Ekrem SPAHIA (Chair).

Albanian Communist Party (*Partia Komuniste e Shqiptare—PKS*). The PKS was organized in 1991 by a rump of the PPS after the parent group adopted the PSS rubric. Although accorded legal recognition in November 1991, the PKS was subsequently outlawed by the mid-1992 ban on "extremist" organizations. When the 1992 law was repealed in April 1998, the PKS was in effect reregistered. It won about 0.9 percent of the vote in 2001.

Leader: Hysni MILLOSHI.

Party of National Unity (*Partia e Unitetit Kombëtar—PUK*). Organized in June 1991 by former Communists, the PUK forged links with Kosovo's Albanian community. Its posture of extreme nationalism is said to be supported, in part, by Albanian "Mafia" groups in Turkey and elsewhere. PUK leader Idajet Beqiri was sentenced to a six-

month prison term in July 1993 for asserting that President Berisha sought to create a fascist dictatorship. In January 1996 Beqiri was again arrested, this time charged with crimes against humanity as a communist-era prosecutor. However, he was subsequently pardoned along with members of the PSS. (Beqiri has subsequently also been referenced as a leader of the underground AKSh, below.)

The PUK earned one seat in the 1997 election as a member of the PSS-led Alliance of State. It won only 0.2 percent of the vote and no seats in 2001.

The PUK participated in the 2005 assembly elections with several other small parties in a coalition called the **Albanian Social Parties + National Unity Party** (*Partite e Spektrit + Partia e Unitetit Kombëtar—PSS + PUK*). Other components of the coalition included the **Environmentalist Party** (*Partia Ambientaliste—PA*), led by Nasi BOZHEKU; the **Albanian Party of Labor** (*Partia Punëtore Shqiptare—PPS*), led by Xhevdet PATAJ; and the **Party for the Defense of Workers' Rights** (*Partia për Mbrojtjen e te Drejtave te Punëtorëve—PMDP*), led by Ymer KURTI and Kadri Mehmat ISUFAG.

Leader: Idajet BEQIRI (Chair).

Albanian Homeland Party (*Partia Shqiptare Atdheu—PShA*). Initially denied legal status in 2004 on the grounds that it was a religion-based (Muslim) grouping, the PShA was subsequently permitted by the Court of Appeals to register for the 2005 assembly balloting. The leader of the PShA, Artan Shaqiri, is a prominent young religious leader who, among other things, has called for the introduction of religious education into the Albanian school system.

Leader: Artan SHAQIRI.

Other parties that competed in 2005 included the **Albanian Business Party** (*Partia e Biznesit Shqiptar—PB*), led by Luan SHAZIVARI; the **Albanian Green Party** (*Partia Te Gjelbërite Shqipërisë—PGjSh*), led by Edlir PETANAJ; the **Albanian Force Party** (*Partia Forca Albania—PFA*), led by Iledin PILLATI; the **Albanian National Security Party** (*Partia e Sigurise Kombëtare Shqiptare—PSKS*), led by Haxhi

BARDHI; the **Albanian Party for Democracy and New Europe** (*Partia Demokracia e Re Europiane Shqiptare*—PDRESh), led by Koçi TAMIRI; the **Albanian Socialist Alliance Party** (*Partia Aleanca Socialiste Shqiptare*—PASS), led by Rasim MULGECI; the **Albanian Workers' Movement Party** (*Partia Lëvizja Punëtore Shqiptare*—PLPS), led by Shefqet MUSARAJ; the **Alliance for Welfare and Solidarity Party** (*Partia Aleanca për Mirëqenie dhe Solidaritet*—AMS), led by Brixhida KOKEDHIMA; the **Democratic Monarchist Movement Party of Albania** (*Partia Lëvizja Monarkiste Demokrate Shqiptare*—PLMDS), led by Guri DUROLLARI; the **Emigration Party of Albania** (*Partia Emigracioni Shqiptar*—PES), led by Kostaq PAPA; the **National League Party of Albania** (*Partia Lidhja Kombëtare Shqiptare*—PLKS), led by Ismet MEHMETI; the **National Reconciliation Party of Albania** (*Partia e Pajtimit Kombëtar Shqiptar*—PPKS), led by Spartak DOBI; the **National Union Party of Albania** (*Partia Bashkesia Kombëtare Shqiptare*—PBKS), led by Henry PEROLLI; the **Popular Alliance Party** (*Partia Aleanca Popullore*—PAP), led by Fatjon SOFTA; the **Reform Democratic Party of Albania** (*Partia e Reformave Demokratike Shqiptare*—PRDS), led by Skënder HALILI; the **Republican Union Party of Albania** (*Partia Bashkimi Republikan Shqiptar*—PBRS), led by Zane LLAZI; and the **Social Christian Party of Albania** (*Partia Socialkristiane e Shqipërisë*—PSKS), led by Fran BRUKA. (The PB, PBRS, PFA, PDRESh, and PRDS attempted to participate in the proportional component of the 2005 legislative balloting in a coalition called the Democratic Movement for Integration [*Lëvizja Demokratike për Integrim*—LDI], but that electoral alliance was invalidated by the electoral commission because of what were deemed to be defects in lists of support signatures.)

Other Party

Macedonian Alliance for European Integration. Launched in mid-2005, this grouping was described as the first "ethnically-based" party to be registered. It pledged to support the interests of the Macedonian minority in Albania.
Leader: Eftim MITREVSKI.

Underground Group

Albanian National Army (*Armata Kombëtare Shqiptare*—AKSh). Described as a "shadowy" grouping, the AKSh promotes establishment of a "Greater Albania" to include the current Albania, Kosovo, and portions of western Macedonia and southern Serbia and Montenegro. It is reportedly a major component of the cross-national Albanian National Unification Front (*Frontit për Bashkimin Kombëtare Shqiptar*—FBKSh). The AKSh has been declared a terrorist organization by the UN Mission in Kosovo and the United States. Macedonia courts have also sentenced several purported AKSh members to prison for alleged participation in bomb attacks in Macedonia in 2003. After being active in Kosovo, Macedonia, and Serbia in the first years of the current decade, the AKSh was reported in 2004 to have gone "completely underground" following the arrest by NATO of several AKSh leaders.

In December 2004 one AKSh leader, Gafur Adili, was placed under house arrest in Tirana for his alleged encouragement of AKSh members to "intervene" in Macedonia. Meanwhile, another reported AKSh leader, Idajet Beqiri, was released from prison in Tirana after the Court of Appeals overturned his conviction for "inciting interethnic hatred." (Beqiri had been arrested in Germany and extradited to Albania.)

In late 2005 Serbian representatives claimed that the FBKSh/AKSh had perpetrated a number of attacks on Serbs in Kosovo. For his part, Adili reportedly said that he believed an ethnic war would be "inevitable" in Kosovo if that province was granted independence.
Leaders: Gafur ADILI, Idajet BEQIRI.

Legislature

The **People's Assembly** (*Kuvënd Popullore*) is currently a unicameral body of 140 deputies, 100 of whom are chosen from single-member

Cabinet

As of August 1, 2006

Prime Minister	Sali Berisha (PDS)
Deputy Prime Minister	Ilir Rusmali (PDS)

Ministers

Agriculture, Food, and Consumer Protection	Jemin Gjana (PDS)
Defense	Fatmir Mediu (PRS)
Economy, Trade, and Energy	Genc Ruli (PDS)
Education and Science	Genc Pollo (PDr)
Environment, Forestry, and Water Administration	Lufter Xhuveli (PAA)
Finance	Ridvan Bode (PDS)
Foreign Affairs	Besnik Mustafaj (PDS)
Health	Maksim Cikuli (PDS)
Integration	Arenca Troshani (PDS) [f]
Interior	Sokol Olldashi (PDS)
Justice	Aldo Bumçi (PDS)
Labor, Social Affairs, and Equal Opportunities	Koço Barka (PBDNj)
Public Affairs, Transport, and Telecommunications	Lulzim Basha (PDS)
Tourism, Culture, Youth, and Sports	Bujar Leskaj (PDS)

[f] = female

constituencies in single-round plurality balloting. (Prior to 2005, successful candidates in the single-member constituencies required a majority vote; runoff balloting was conducted if no candidate secured more than 50 percent of the vote in the first round.) The remaining 40 members are selected by proportional representation from party lists, assuming a minimum vote share of 2.5 percent for individual parties and 4 percent for coalitions. (Voters cast two votes, one for a candidate in their district and one for a party or coalition in the nationwide poll.)

Following the election of July 3, 2005 (and reballoting on August 21, 2005, in three districts for which the initial vote was invalidated by the electoral commission), the seats were distributed as follows: the Democratic Party of Albania (PDS), 56 (all single-member mandates); the Socialist Party of Albania, 42 (all single-member); the PDS-aligned Alliance for Freedom, Justice, and Welfare, 18 (all proportional: the Albanian Republican Party, 11; the New Democrat Party, 4; the Chris-

tian Democratic Party of Albania, 2; and the Liberal Democratic Union, 1); the Social Democratic Party of Albania, 7 (all proportional); the Socialist Movement for Integration, 5 (1 single-member and 4 proportional); the Agrarian Environmental Party, 4 (all proportional); the Party of the Democratic Alliance, 3 (all proportional); the Social Democracy Party of Albania, 2 (both proportional); the Union for Human Rights Party, 2 (both proportional); and independent, 1 (single-member).

Chair of Presidency: Jozefina TOPALLI.

Communications

Press

Albanian newspapers tend to be highly politicized in their reporting, whether they are independent or represent a political party, although a degree of nonpartisan journalism has emerged in connection with the country's recent political liberalization. In addition, the People's Assembly voted on

September 4, 1997, to protect freedom of the press, replacing a 1993 law that restricted access to information and made editors liable for heavy fines if they published "punishable material." International observers described coverage of the 2005 legislative elections as "generally balanced."

The following are published at Tirana: *Koha Jonë* (Our Time, 400,000), leading independent daily; *Zëri i Popullit* (Voice of the People, 105,000), PSS daily; *Rilindja Demokratike* (Democratic Revival, 50,000), PDS daily; *Bashkimi* (Unity, 30,000); *Republika* (Republic), PRS daily; *Progresi Agrar* (Agrarian Progress), twice-weekly PAS organ; *Albanian Daily News*, daily in English; *Gazeta Shqiptare* (Albanian Gazette), independent daily; *Shekulli*, independent daily; *Ekonomia*, daily; *Korrieri,* independent daily; *Tema,* daily; *Panorama,* daily; *Klan*, weekly.

News Agency

The principal source for both domestic and foreign news is the official Albanian Telegraph Agency (*Agjensi Telegrafike Shqiptar*—ATS).

Broadcasting and Computing

Radio and Television of Albania (*Radio Televizioni Shqiptare*), a government facility, dominates broadcasting. Radio Tirana transmits internationally in a number of languages. There is a largely state-financed national television station (TVSH) and several privately owned national television stations, including *TV Arberia* and *TV Klan*. There were approximately 564,000 television receivers and 50,000 personal computers serving 30,000 Internet users in 2003. In May 1997 the assembly passed a law providing for private ownership of radio and television stations, although a government commission controls licensing.

Intergovernmental Representation

Ambassador to the U.S.
Aleksander SALLABANDA

U.S. Ambassador to Albania
Marcie B. RIES

Permanent Representative to the UN
Adrian NERITANI

IGO Memberships (Non-UN)
BSEC, CEI, CEUR, EBRD, Eurocontrol, IDB, Interpol, IOM, OIC, *OIF*, OSCE, WCO, WTO

ANDORRA

PRINCIPALITY OF ANDORRA

Principat d'Andorra (Catalan)
Principalité d'Andorre (French)
Principado de Andorra (Spanish)

The Country

A rough, mountainous country of limited dimensions, Andorra is set in a large drainage area of the Pyrenees between France and Spain. The main stream is the Riu Valira, which has two branches and six open basins. The indigenous residents are of Catalan stock and represent about one-third of the population; foreign residents include Spaniards (about 37 percent of the total population), Portuguese (13 percent), and French (7 percent). Virtually all of the inhabitants are Roman Catholic. The traditional mainstays of the economy were farming and animal husbandry, but tourism, which accounts for 80 percent of GDP, and the transshipment of goods are presently the most important sources of income. Apart from the transmission of power from a hydroelectric plant at Les Escaldes to southern France and the Spanish province of Barcelona, the main exports are machinery and electrical goods, paper, graphic arts products, textiles, foodstuffs, tobacco products, and cattle. The main trading partners are Spain and France, with Andorra having gained a reputation as "the Hong Kong of the Pyrenees" because of money laundering and other services attractive to financiers from nearby countries. Andorra's status as a duty-free principality has also reportedly generated a substantial contraband trade, particularly involving tobacco.

Andorra experienced steady economic growth from the late 1980s into the early 1990s, with negligible unemployment (a steady influx of foreign workers having been required to fill jobs in the booming tourism sector). Growth slowed in the mid-1990s, primarily as a result of the international economic downturn, the related drop in consumer demand in Spain and France, and a decline in tourist arrivals. Although the economy subsequently improved, international attention focused more and more on the perceived negative aspects of the country's "tax haven" status (see Current issues, below).

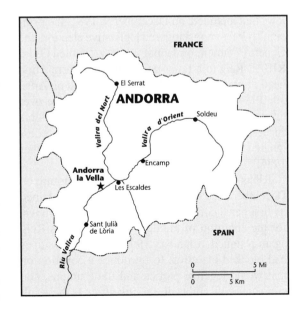

Government and Politics

Political Background

Andorra is the last independent survivor of the *Marca Hispanica* (or March states), a series of several former Spanish countries that served as buffer states and were established by Charlemagne around 800 A.D. to keep the Muslim Moors from advancing into Christian France. Charlemagne, who granted a charter to the Andorran people in return for their fighting the Moors, is credited as the founder of the country. The unique political structure of Andorra dates from 1278, when an agreement on joint suzerainty (a *paréage*) was reached between the French count of Foix, whose right ultimately passed to the president of the French Republic, and the Spanish bishop of the nearby See of Urgel. The first personal meeting between coprinces since 1278 occurred on August 25, 1973, when President Georges Pompidou and Bishop Joan MARTI y Alanís met at Cahors, France, to discuss matters affecting the future of the principality, while on October 19, 1978, President Valéry Giscard d'Estaing and Mgr. Martí y Alanís attended 700th anniversary ceremonies at Andorra la Vella.

Under new constitutional arrangements (see below) that included, on December 9, 1981, the principality's first nonstaggered legislative election, the General Council, on January 8, 1982, named Oscar RIBAS Reig to a four-year term as Andorra's first head of government. Ribas Reig resigned on April 30, 1984, as the result of a lengthy dispute over tax policy, the council on May 21 electing as his successor Josep PINTAT Solans, who was redesignated following a general election in December 1985.

Ribas Reig returned to power after balloting on December 10, 1989, and in 1990 Andorra obtained its first penal code, providing, among other things, for the abolition of the death penalty. Ribas Reig again resigned in January 1992 after conservatives had blocked his effort to introduce a constitution that would legalize parties and trade unions, and guarantee civil rights. Retaining office as the result

of legislative balloting on April 5 and 12, he announced that the new council's principal task would be to draft a basic law for submission to a popular referendum. The process was completed on March 14, 1993, when, in a turnout of 76 percent of the 9,123 eligible voters, 74.2 percent approved what was in effect Andorra's first written constitution. The adoption of the new basic law represented a conscious attempt by progressive elements led by Ribas Reig to bring Andorra into line with other European states in terms of prescribed civil and social rights, although in many respects the principality remained a feudalistic state whose social practices were governed by clerical canons of morality and whose politics were often determined by family loyalties.

In Andorra's first multiparty elections, held on December 12, 1993, Ribas Reig's National Democratic Grouping (*Agrupament Nacional Democràtic*—AND) emerged as the strongest party in the General Council, with Ribas Reig being reelected head of government on January 19, 1994. These victories confirmed the ascendancy of the modernizing political forces led by Ribas Reig, who said that his new government would give priority to fiscal and tax reforms and to the development of tourism. Nevertheless, in the emerging new party structure, conservative elements retained considerable influence in the General Council, and on November 25, following rejection of his 1995 budget, Ribas Reig again resigned and was succeeded on December 21 by Marc FORNÉ Molné of the Liberal Union (*Unió Liberal*—UL), the second-largest party in the General Council. Communal elections in December 1995 were notable for returning two women mayors, who broke the previous male mayoral monopoly.

Following premature dissolution of the General Council on January 1, 1997, new legislative balloting was conducted on February 16, with the UL capturing 16 seats to 6 for the AND and Forné being reelected as head of government by the new council on March 21; the new cabinet took office on April 4. Forné was reelected for another term following new balloting for the General Council

Political Status: Sovereign "Parliamentary
Co-Principality," with the President of the
French Republic and the Spanish Bishop of
Urgel possessing certain powers as joint heads
of state under constitution approved March 14,
1993, with effect from May 4.
Area: 180 sq. mi. (467 sq. km.).
Population: 72,320 (2003C); 75,000 (2005E).
Major Urban Center (2005E): ANDORRA
LA VELLA (22,000).
Official Language: Catalan (French and
Spanish are also used).
Monetary Units: There is no local currency.
The French franc and the Spanish peseta both
circulated until 2002, when Andorra adopted
the euro (market rate July 1, 2006: 1 euro =
$1.28US).
French Co-Prince: Jacques CHIRAC;
became Co-Prince May 17, 1995, upon
inauguration as President of the French
Republic.
Permanent French Delegate: Philippe
MASSONI.
Spanish Episcopal Co-Prince: Mgr. Joan Enric
VIVES Sicilia; became Co-Prince May 12,
2003, upon induction as Bishop of See of
Urgel.
*Permanent Episcopal Delegate: Nemesi
MARQUES Oste.*
Head of Government (*Cap del Govern*):
Albert PINTAT Santolària (Liberal Party of
Andorra); elected to succeed Marc FORNÉ
Molné (Liberal Party of Andorra) for a
four-year term by the General Council on May
27, 2005, following the legislative balloting of
April 24.

on March 4, 2001, at which his Liberal Party of
Andorra (*Partit Liberal d'Andorra*—PLA), as the
UL had been renamed, captured 15 seats, the AND
having splintered into two new parties, which together had gained 11 seats. A new PLA government
was appointed on April 9.

The PLA won 14 seats in the April 24, 2005,
General Council poll under the leadership of Albert
PINTAT Santolària, who was subsequently elected
as head of government with the support of the Andorran Democratic Center (*Centre Demòcrata Andorrà*—CDA).

Constitution and Government

The 1993 document defines Andorra as an independent "parliamentary co-principality" in which
sovereignty is vested in the people (i.e., Andorran citizens), although the Spanish and French co-
princes remain joint heads of state, with defined
and largely symbolic powers. The text provides for
an independent judiciary, civil rights, and elections
by universal suffrage (of citizens) to the legislative
General Council. For the first time, membership in
political parties and trade unions is permitted, and
the government is empowered to raise revenue by
taxation and other means. As joint suzerains, the
French president and the bishop of Urgel are represented respectively by the prefect of the French
department of Pyrenees-Orientales and the vicar
general of the Urgel diocese. Their resident representatives in Andorra bear the titles of *viguier de
France* and *veguer Episcopal.*

Under a Political Reform Law approved after
a stormy legislative debate in November 1981, a
head of government (*cap del govern*) was created
for the first time, while the former first and second syndics were redesignated as syndic general
(chair) and sub-syndic (sub-chair) of the General
Council, with the *syndic général* remaining, by protocol, the higher-ranked official. Legislators were
formerly elected every two years for staggered
four-year terms; under the 1981 reform, the council as a whole sits for four years, designating the
head of government (who appoints a cabinet) for a
like term.

Women were enfranchised in 1970 and in 1973
were permitted to stand for public office. Second-
generation Andorrans were allowed to vote in 1971
and first-generation Andorrans over the age of 28
were accorded a similar right in 1977.

The judicial structure is relatively simple. The
viguiers each appoint two civil judges (*battles*),
while an appeals judge is appointed alternately
by each co-prince. Final appeal is either to the

Supreme Court at Perpignan, France, or to the Ecclesiastical Court of the Bishop of Seo de Urgel,
Spain. Criminal law is administered by the *Tribunal de Corts*, consisting of the *battles*, the appeals judge, the *viguiers*, and two members of the
General Council (*parladors*).

Local government functions at the district level
through parish councils, whose members are selected by universal suffrage. At the lower levels there are *communs* and *corts*. The former are
ten-member bodies elected by universal suffrage;
the latter are submunicipal advisory bodies that
function primarily as administrators of communal
property.

Foreign Relations

Although President Pompidou and Bishop Martí
y Alanís agreed in 1973 that Andorra could send indigenous representatives to international meetings,
the understanding was subsequently repudiated by
President Giscard d'Estaing, and the Principality's
external relations continued to be handled largely
by France. An Andorran delegation did, however,
participate in a conference of French and Spanish Pyrenean regions held at Jaca, Spain, under
the auspices of the Council of Europe June 7–10,
1982.

On January 1, 1986, Spain joined France as a
member of the European Community (EC), subsequently the European Union (EU), but it was
not until September 1989 that an Andorran customs union with the EC was negotiated. Approval of the agreement by the General Council
in March 1990 yielded the country's first international treaty in more than 700 years, the union
coming into effect on July 1, 1991. Substantially
more indicative of emerging international status
was Andorra's admission to the UN on July 28,
1993.

On June 3, 1993, Andorra signed friendship and
cooperation treaties with France and Spain, while
on October 2 President Mitterrand paid an official
visit to the principality. On November 10, 1994,
Andorra became the 33rd full member of the Council of Europe.

Current Issues

Both major political parties pledged during the
1997 campaign to pursue greater foreign investment by, among other things, reducing government regulation of economic activity. The UL's
strong margin in the nationwide balloting (42 percent to the AND's 28 percent) was less important
to its overall comfortable victory than its success
in parish balloting, where its electoral alignment
with leading regional groupings contributed to the
capture of 10 of the 14 parish seats on the council.

In furtherance of the government's desire for
closer integration with Europe, an Andorran law
against the export of contraband went into effect
in May 1998 after the EU, particularly the United
Kingdom, complained that cigarette traffickers, using Andorra as a distribution center, were supply-
ing EU black markets with tobacco. Andorra felt
obliged to crack down on tobacco traffickers, who
have been operating from the principality for generations, because of the government's interest in expanding its limited 1991 customs agreement with
the EU.

In November 1998 EU finance ministers focused
on the formulation of a common method for taxing
nonresident bank accounts, particularly in neighboring non-EU countries such as Andorra where
bank secrecy rules attract foreign money. Andorra
was also subsequently advised to bring its tariffs
and duties into conformance with EU standards,
which could jeopardize its "duty free" allure, a
key factor in the tiny nation's mainstay tourism
industry. The banking sector continued to receive
scrutiny in 1999 and 2000, the Organization for
Economic Cooperation and Development (OECD)
in June 2000 including Andorra in its list of 35 "tax
havens" that could face sanctions unless greater
transparency was provided.

Marc Forné Molné characterized the 2001 legislative success of the PLA (43 percent in the nationwide balloting) as an indication of the electorate's desire for stability. However, the issue
of money-laundering subsequently continued to
haunt Andorra, the OECD in 2002 including the
country on a list of seven "uncooperative" nations

against which sanctions might be levied unless new standards were established regarding transparency in the financial sector and the exchange of information with other countries.

As of mid-2005 Andorra remained on the OECD's "uncooperative" list, although a degree of accommodation appeared imminent with the EU through an agreement that would permit Andorran banks to charge a withholding tax on foreign deposits rather than reveal secret information about the accounts. As part of the new accord, which went into effect July 1, 2005, the EU also pledged to expand its cooperation with Andorra on the environment, transportation, communications, and other issues.

It was unclear if the international financial issues played a significant role in the April 2005 legislative balloting. Although the PLA lost its majority, it was still able to claim the vote represented an endorsement of recent policies, particularly regarding further integration "to some degree" with the EU. For its part, the surging Social Democratic Party (*Partit Socialdemòcrata*—PS) accused the PLA of failing to keep past electoral policies. (Forné, constitutionally prohibited from serving another term as head of government, also lost his legislative seat when the PS won the seats from his parish.)

Political Parties

Although political parties were technically illegal until March 1993, various unofficial groupings had contested elections in the 1970s and 1980s. The December 1993 balloting was the first held under multiparty auspices, with 18 associations of various kinds presenting or endorsing candidates.

Government and Government-Supportive Parties

Liberal Party of Andorra (*Partit Liberal d'Andorra*—PLA). The PLA was initially launched as the Liberal Union (*Unió Liberal*—UL) prior to the December 1993 legislative poll, at which the UL won five seats and 22 percent of the vote. After a year of opposition, the right-of-center formation came to power in December 1994.

Its constituent **Liberal Party** (*Partit Liberal*—PL) joined the Liberal International in 1994.

UL won 16 seats in the February 1997 legislative elections, securing 42 percent of the vote in the balloting for the national seats (good for 6 seats) and 10 parish seats. (The UL parish seats were won by groupings that campaigned under unique local party rubrics.) The working majority for Head of Government Marc Forné Molné was subsequently improved when councillors representing the now-defunct **Union of the People of Ordino** (*Unió del Poble d'Ordino*—UPd'O) joined the UL in forming a parliamentary faction. The UL adopted the PLA rubric prior to the March 2001 legislative balloting. The PLA secured 41.2 percent of the national vote in the 2005 legislative poll, which gained the party 14 seats in the General Council. After ten years in office, Marc Forné Molné was not allowed to seek a new term.

Leaders: Albert PINTAT Santolària (Head of Government and Leader of the Party), Pere CANTURRI Campos (Secretary General).

Andorran Democratic Center (*Centre Demòcrata Andorrà*—CDA). This grouping was launched in 2000 as the Democratic Party (*Partit Demòcrata*—PD), the second party to spin off from fragmentation of the AND (below). The PD won five seats in the 2001 legislative poll, three of them on a 22.4 percent vote share in the national constituency. The CDA secured two seats in the national poll of 2005 on an 11 percent vote share; it participated in that balloting in coalition with a small grouping called **Segle 21.** The CDA subsequently agreed to support the new PLA government in the legislature.

Leader: Enric TARRADO Vives (Parliamentary Leader and 2005 candidate for head of government).

Other Parliamentary Parties

Social Democratic Party (*Partit Socialdemòcrata*—PS). The PS was formed in 2000 when the National Democratic Grouping (*Agrupament Nacional Democràtic*—AND) split into two new parties. Formed in 1979 as the Andorran

Cabinet

As of March 1, 2006

| Head of Government | Albert Pintat Santolària |

Ministers

Agriculture and the Environment	Pere Torres Montellà
Economy	Joel Font Coma
Education and Professional Organizations	Roser Bastida Areny [f]
Finance	Ferran Mirapeix Lucas
Foreign Affairs, Culture, and Cooperation	Juli Minoves Triquell
Health, Social Welfare, and Family	Montserrat Gil Torné [f]
Housing, Youth, Higher Education, and Research	Meritxell Mateu Pi [f]
Justice and Interior	Josep Maria Cabanes Dalmau
Sports and Volunteerism	Carles Font Rossell
Territorial Planning	Manuel Pons Pi Farré
Tourism	Antoni Puigdellívol Riberaygua

[f] = female

Democratic Party, the center-left AND had emerged as the strongest party in the December 1993 elections, winning eight seats and 26.4 percent of the vote on a platform of modernization. Its leader, Oscar Ribas Reig, therefore remained head of government (having first attained the post in 1982) with the support of the ND. However, he was forced to resign in November 1994 when the coalition collapsed. The AND was definitively relegated to second-party status in the February 1997 General Council balloting, when it won four national seats (based on 28 percent of the vote) and the two seats from the parish of Encamp.

The PS also appeared to have subsumed New Democracy (*Nova Democràcia*—ND), which had been founded prior to the 1993 balloting at which it won five seats on a 19.1 percent vote share. The party's strength fell to two seats on a 17 percent share of national balloting in 1997.

The PS won six seats in the March 2001 legislative balloting, four of them on a 28 percent vote share in the national polling. The PS improved significantly to 38.1 percent of the national vote in the 2005 poll, securing a total of 12 seats.

Leader: Jaume BARTUMEU Cassany (Leader of the Party).

Democratic Renovation (*Renovació Democràtica*—RD). The RD won 6.2 percent of the vote (no seats) in the 2005 national balloting. It apparently participated in a joint list with the PS called the PS/RD Alternative (*L'Alternativa PS/RD*) in four parishes in the 2005 poll, and several reports indicated that one of the parish seats nominally won by the PS in fact was won by a member of the RD.

Leaders: Patrick GARCIA Ricart (Leader of the Party), Ricard de HARO Jimenez.

Other Parties and Groups

Greens of Andorra (*Verds D'Andorra*—VA). The recently formed VA secured 3.5 percent of the vote (no seats) in the 2005 legislative poll.

Leader: Isabel LOZANO Muñoz.

Lauredian Union (*Unió Laurediana*). A local party, this grouping won two parish seats in the 2001 legislative balloting but did not compete on a national level. The successful candidates of the Union subsequently joined the PLA parliamentary group in the General Council. There was no reference to the Union in the 2005 legislative poll.

Legislature

The **General Council** (*El Consell General*) is a unicameral body consisting of 28 members. Fourteen councillors are elected from national party lists in proportion to the percent of votes received by the parties participating in nationwide balloting. The remaining 14 councillors are elected in separate parish voting, the party with a plurality in each of the seven parishes winning that parish's two seats. Following the most recent election of April 24, 2005, the distribution of seats was as follows: Liberal Party of Andorra, 14 (6 national seats and 8 parish seats); the Social Democratic Party, 12 (6, 6); and the Andorran Democratic Center, 2 (2, 0).

Syndic General: Joan GABRIEL.

Communications

Press

The domestic press consists of two dailies, *Diari d'Andorra* (Andorran Diary, 3,000) in Andorra la Vella and *El Periòdic d'Andorrá* (Andorran Newspaper) in Escaldes-Engordany, plus the weeklies *Poble Andorra* (Andorran People, 3,000), *Informacions* (News), and *7 Dies* (7 Days), all issued at Andorra la Vella. In addition, French and Spanish newspapers have long circulated in the principality.

Broadcasting and Computing

In 1981 the question of control over Andorran airwaves resulted in the government ordering the principality's two radio stations, the French-owned *Sud-Radio* and the commercial, privately owned Spanish *Radio Andorra*, off the air. The dispute arose over the co-princes' refusal to permit effective nationalization of the broadcast facilities, which had extensive audiences in both France and Spain. Under a compromise approved by the General Council in September, the right of the Andorran people to operate (but not necessarily own) radio stations was acknowledged, and the General Council was granted full sovereignty over any stations broadcasting solely within Andorra. In 1984 *Radio Andorra* returned to the air, with an *Antena 7* television facility initiating programs of Andorran interest from the Spanish side of the border in 1987. In January 1991 a domestic service, *Televisióde Andorra*, initiated four hours of daily programming. *Ràdio i Televisió d'Andorra* (Andorran Radio and Television) has been the public service broadcaster since 2000 and operates *Ràdio Nacional d'Andorra* (RNA) and *Andorra Televisió* (ATV). There were approximately 48,000 television receivers in use in 2003 and 24,500 Internet users in 2001.

Intergovernmental Representation

Andorra's quite limited foreign relations are largely conducted through the French co-prince.

Ambassador to the U.S.
(Vacant)

U.S. Ambassador to Andorra
Eduardo AGUIRRE Jr. (resident in Spain)

Permanent Representative to the UN
Julian VILA COMA

IGO Memberships (Non-UN)
CEUR, Interpol, *OIF,* OSCE, WCO

AUSTRIA

REPUBLIC OF AUSTRIA

Republik Österreich

Note: Final results of the legislative balloting on October 1, 2006, indicated that the opposition Austrian Social Democratic Party won a plurality with 35.3 percent of the vote for the National Council (*Nationalrat*); the Austrian People's Party, 34.3 percent; the Freedom Party of Austria, 11 percent; The Greens, 11 percent; and the Alliance for the Future of Austria, 4.1 percent. The seats will be distributed as follows: Austrian Social Democratic Party, 68; the Austrian People's Party, 66; the Freedom Party of Austria, 21; The Greens, 21; and Alliance for the Future of Austria, 7. President Heinz Fischer subsequently asked Austrian Social Democratic Party leader Alfred Gusenbauer to form a new coalition government.

The Country

Situated at the crossroads of Central Europe, Austria is topographically dominated in the south and west by the Alps, while its eastern provinces lie within the Danube basin. The vast majority of the population is of Germanic stock, but there is an important Slovene minority in the province of Carinthia. Approximately 90 percent of the population is Catholic, although religious freedom is guaranteed. Women made up 41 percent of the official labor force in 1996, concentrated in sales, agriculture, and unskilled manufacturing; women currently hold about 32 percent of Federal Assembly seats.

Austria has a mixed economy; despite recent privatizations, the state still owns or holds major shares in many large industries. Although limited in scope by the mountainous terrain, agriculture continues to provide much of the domestic food requirements, with an emphasis on grains, livestock, and dairy products. Agriculture accounts for about 3 percent of GDP, the industrial sector accounts for 32 percent, and services for more than 65 percent. During the 1970s Austria's economic growth rate, averaging 3.4 percent a year, was one of the highest among industrialized countries. It fell back to

2 percent annually during the 1980s, but Austrian business garnered a larger share of world trade, and by 1986 Austrian investment abroad exceeded capital inflow for the first time. With the collapse of Eastern European Communism in 1989, the country was favorably positioned to regain its historic role as a pivotal economic power in the region.

Political Status: Federal republic established in 1918; reestablished in 1945 under Allied occupation; independence restored under Four-Power Treaty of July 27, 1955.

Area: 32,376 sq. mi. (83,853 sq. km.).

Population: 8,032,926 (2001C); 8,186,000 (2005E). The 2001 figure includes foreign workers.

Major Urban Centers (2005E): VIENNA (1,554,000), Graz (222,000), Linz (178,000), Salzburg (142,000), Innsbruck (112,000).

Official Language: German.

Monetary Unit: Euro (market rate July 1, 2006: 1 euro = $1.28US).

Federal President: Heinz FISCHER (Austrian Social Democratic Party); elected on April 25, 2004, and sworn in for a six-year term on July 9 to succeed Thomas KLESTIL (nonparty), who had been constitutionally precluded from running for a third term and who had died on July 6.

Federal Chancellor: Wolfgang SCHÜSSEL (Austrian People's Party); sworn in on February 4, 2000, to succeed Viktor KLIMA (Austrian Social Democratic Party) following the election of October 3, 1999; formed new government on February 28, 2003, following legislative elections of November 24, 2002.

Thus, exports to Czechoslovakia increased 72 percent during 1990, while Austrian firms were involved in 30 percent of new joint ventures in that country and in 35 percent of those in Hungary.

Real GDP grew by about 2 percent annually from 2004 to 2006, with inflation averaging 2 percent annually during the same period and unemployment measuring 4.5 percent in mid-2005. The current government (installed in 2000) has emphasized conservative economic policies, including deregulation, pension reform, control of budget deficits, and privatization of state-run enterprises. The administration also has approved sharp cuts in corporate taxes, in part to help the economy "compete" effectively following the admis-

sion to the European Union (EU) in May 2004 of four neighboring countries (the Czech Republic, Hungary, Poland, and Slovakia) with historically lower tax rates. EU expansion has been a boon for the Austrian banking sector and has generally presented promising trade opportunities. However, some critics have argued that cheap labor in the acceding countries might undermine the Austrian labor force.

Government and Politics

Political Background

Austria was part of the Habsburg-ruled Austro-Hungarian Empire until the close of World War I, the Austrian republic being established in November 1918. Unstable economic and political conditions led in 1933 to the imposition of a dictatorship under Engelbert DOLLFUSS, while civil war in 1934 resulted in suppression of the Social Democratic Party and Dollfuss's assassination by National Socialists. Hitler invaded Austria in March 1938 and formally incorporated its territory into the German Reich.

With the occupation of Austria by the Allies in 1945, a provisional government was established under the Social Democrat Karl RENNER. Following a general election in November 1945, Leopold FIGL formed a coalition government based on the Austrian People's Party (*Österreichische Volkspartei Partei*—ÖVP) and the Austrian Social Democratic Party (*Sozialdemokratische Partei Österreichs*—SPÖ). The coalition endured under a succession of chancellors until 1966, when the ÖVP won a legislative majority and Josef KLAUS organized a single-party government. In 1970 the Social Democrats came to power as a minority government under Dr. Bruno KREISKY. Subsequent elections in 1971, 1975, and 1979 yielded majority mandates for Chancellor Kreisky.

Following legislative balloting on April 24, 1983, in which the SPÖ failed to retain clear parliamentary control, Kreisky, in accordance with a preelection pledge, resigned in favor of Vice Chancellor Fred SINOWATZ, who formed a coalition government on May 24 that included three members of the third-ranked Freedom Party of Austria (*Freiheitliche Partei Österreichs*—FPÖ).

In a runoff election on June 8, 1986, that attracted world attention because of allegations concerning his service in a German unit guilty of demonstrable atrocities in the Balkans during World War II, former UN secretary general Kurt WALDHEIM, an independent supported by the ÖVP, defeated the SPÖ candidate, Kurt STEYRER, for the Austrian presidency. In protest, Chancellor Sinowatz and three other cabinet members resigned, a new SPÖ-FPÖ government being formed under the former finance minister, Dr. Franz VRANITZKY, on June 16.

The government collapsed in mid-September 1986 after the FPÖ elected Jörg HAIDER, a far-right nationalist, as its chair, thereby rendering it unacceptable as a coalition partner for the Social Democrats. At the ensuing lower house election of November 23, the SPÖ lost ten seats, though retaining a slim plurality, and on January 14 Vranitzky formed a new "grand coalition" with the ÖVP. The coalition continued with a somewhat restructured cabinet following legislative balloting on October 7, 1990, that yielded a substantial gain for the nationalist FPÖ opposition. The FPÖ continued to gain strength in a series of provincial elections in 1991, and its 16.4 percent support in the first round of presidential elections on April 26, 1992, was assumed to have provided the margin that enabled the ÖVP candidate, Thomas KLESTIL, to defeat the Social Democrats' Rudolf STREICHER in a runoff vote on May 24.

Provincial elections in Carinthia, Salzburg, and Tirol in March 1994 yielded significant gains for the FPÖ, mainly at the expense of the ÖVP. In June the government achieved one of its key aims, when a referendum gave a decisive two-to-one verdict in favor of accession to the EU, despite opposition from the FPÖ and The Greens (*Die Grünen*). In October, however, the coalition parties were chastened by federal election results showing postwar percentage lows for both, while the FPÖ made a

further advance. In the absence of any acceptable alternative (and to keep the FPÖ out of office), the SPÖ and the ÖVP agreed to continue their coalition under Vranitzky's chancellorship.

The SPÖ-ÖVP government achieved its central policy objective when Austria became an EU member on January 1, 1995; however, Chancellor Vranitzky's authority was further undermined by the resignation of four disaffected SPÖ ministers in March and by a major dispute between the coalition parties on measures needed to reduce the budget deficit. An accommodation proving unattainable, the government resigned on October 12, with an early election being called for December 17. Contrary to forecasts, the balloting yielded gains for both the SPÖ and the ÖVP, the former appreciably so, while the FPÖ unexpectedly lost ground. After lengthy negotiations, the SPÖ and ÖVP succeeded in resolving their differences, enabling Vranitzky to enter his fifth term as chancellor on March 12, 1996.

In the first direct election for the European Parliament in October 1996, the SPÖ (with 29.1 percent of the vote) finished second to the ÖVP (29.6 percent) while the FPÖ secured a surprisingly high 27.6 percent. The relatively poor showing by the SPÖ was subsequently seen as a factor in Chancellor Vranitzky's resignation on January 18, 1997, in favor of Finance Minister Viktor KLIMA, who made substantial changes in the SPÖ ministerial contingent in the government formed on January 29.

On April 19, 1998, President Klestil, running as an independent with the support of the ÖVP and the FPÖ, was reelected with 63.4 percent of the vote, leaving four other candidates far behind.

The federal election of October 3, 1999, ended the "grand alliance" of the SPÖ and ÖVP when the FPÖ placed second, with 27 percent of the vote, virtually tied with the ÖVP. (At more than 33 percent, the SPÖ secured first place, but it was the party's worst postwar showing.) Among other things, the former coalition partners could not agree on how to deal with a troublesome budget deficit. Consequently, after three months of negotiations, the ÖVP turned to the FPÖ, notwithstanding the threat of sanctions by the EU, which was alarmed by the anti-immigration and anti-EU rhetoric of FPÖ populist Haider, who resigned as party leader amid a storm of international criticism. A center-right/far-right coalition of the ÖVP and FPÖ was subsequently sworn in on February 4, 2000, with the ÖVP's Wolfgang SCHÜSSEL as chancellor.

In early September 2002, Susanne RIESS-PASSER, the vice chancellor and leader of the FPÖ, resigned both posts following a rebellion within the FPÖ led by Haider, who opposed the government's decision to forestall planned tax cuts in the wake of severe flooding in August. Announcing that the ÖVP could no longer work with the FPÖ, Chancellor Schüssel dissolved the National Council, and new elections were held on November 24. The ÖVP won a plurality of 79 seats, and Schüssel intensely pursued a coalition government with either the SPÖ or The Greens. Those efforts ultimately failed, however, and Schüssel was forced to turn again to the FPÖ, a new ÖVP-FPÖ government being installed on February 23, 2003.

In presidential elections on April 25, 2004, Heinz FISCHER of the SPÖ defeated the ÖVP's Benita FERRARO-WALDNER by 52.4 percent to 47.6 percent. Outgoing President Klestil, who was constitutionally precluded from seeking a third term, died on July 6, and Schüssel temporarily assumed the duties of president until Fischer was inaugurated on July 9.

In April 2005 the FPÖ was replaced as the junior coalition partner by the new Alliance for the Future of Austria (*Bündnis Zukunft Österreich*—BZÖ), formed by former FPÖ members, including Haider, who had recently been marginalized in the FPÖ.

Constitution and Government

Austria's constitution, adopted in 1920 and amended in 1929, provides for a federal democratic republic embracing nine provinces (*Länder*), including Vienna, which also serves as the capital of Lower Austria. Although most effective power is at the federal level, the provinces have considerable latitude in local administration. The na-

tional government consists of a president whose functions are largely ceremonial, a cabinet headed by a chancellor, and a bicameral Federal Assembly (*Bundesversammlung*). The chancellor is appointed by the president from the party with the strongest representation in the lower house, the National Council (*Nationalrat*); the upper house, the Federal Council (*Bundesrat*), which represents the provinces, is restricted to a review of legislation passed by the National Council and, for the most part, has only delaying powers, although approval of the assembly in full sitting is required in certain situations.

Each province has an elected legislature (*Landtag*) and an administration headed by a governor (*Landeshauptmann*) designated by the legislature. The judicial system is headed by the Supreme Judicial Court (*Oberster Gerichtshof*) and includes two other high courts, the Constitutional Court (*Verfassungsgerichtshof*) and the Administrative Court (*Verwaltungsgerichtshof*). There are also four higher provincial courts (*Oberlandesgerichte*), 17 provincial and district courts (*Landes-und Kreisgerichte*), and numerous local courts (*Bezirksgerichte*).

Province and Capital	Area (sq. mi.)	Population (2001C)
Burgenland (Eisenstadt)	1,531	277,260
Carinthia (Klagenfurt)	3,681	558,290
Lower Austria (administered from Vienna)	7,402	1,550,940
Salzburg (Salzburg)	2,762	517,510
Styria (Graz)	6,327	1,183,250
Tirol (Innsbruck)	4,883	679,720
Upper Austria (Linz)	4,625	1,381,592
Vorarlberg (Bregenz)	1,004	353,670
Vienna	160	1,550,874

A two-year commission studying constitutional reform known as the "Austria Convention" submitted a report to the National Council in January 2005. Any further action on its recommendations is subject to legislation by the National Council.

In June 2005 the constitution was amended to permit Carinthia to nominate a new candidate to take the province's slot in the rotating presidency of the Federal Council, thus blocking Siegfried KAMPL from ascending to the presidency of the upper house (see BZÖ, under Political Parties, below).

Foreign Relations

The Austrian State Treaty of 1955 ended the four-power occupation of Austria; reestablished the country as an independent, sovereign nation; and forbade any future political or economic union with Germany. In October 1955 the Federal Assembly approved a constitutional amendment by which the nation declared its permanent neutrality, rejected participation in any military alliances, and prohibited the establishment of any foreign military bases on its territory. In November 1990 a number of treaty articles (primarily involving relations with Germany) were declared obsolete by the Austrian government because of the recent political and legal changes in Eastern Europe, although the document's major provisions, including a ban on the acquisition of nuclear, biological, and chemical weapons, were reaffirmed.

The European Community (EC—forerunner to the EU) opened a bilateral mission in Vienna in April 1988, and, despite manifest Soviet displeasure, Austria formally submitted an application to join the EC in July 1989. While EC membership remained the priority, Austria also cultivated relations with post-Communist Central and Eastern Europe, taking a lead in the Central European Initiative (CEI) established in March 1992 on the basis of earlier regional cooperation. Intended to counter the economic power of the reunited Germany, the CEI grouping corresponded in part with the old Habsburg domains and was thus seen by some as the embryo of a resurgent Austrian economic empire.

On the basis of terms agreed upon in March 1994 and strongly recommended by the government, accession to the EU was endorsed by Austrian voters in a referendum on June 12 by a convincing margin of 66.4 to 33.6 percent. On January 1, 1995, Austria (together with Finland and Sweden) ceased to be on the European Free Trade Association (EFTA) side of the European Economic Area (EEA) table, where it had sat for just a year, and instead became a full EU member.

On February 10, 1995, Austria joined NATO's Partnership for Peace. It also obtained observer status at the Western European Union (WEU), while stressing that it would retain its long-standing neutrality. In April 1995 Austria became a signatory of the Schengen Accord, which provided for free movement among a number of EU states, and in November it agreed to contribute 300 soldiers to the NATO-commanded Implementation Force (IFOR) in Bosnia-Herzegovina.

Although the December 1995 election again showed that most Austrians rejected antiforeigner extremism and xenophobia, the immigration issue continued to be highly sensitive. Among other things, an influx of migrants and refugees from Eastern Europe and the former Yugoslavia had prompted the government to tighten restrictions on entry, particularly for immigrants from Bosnia-Herzegovina.

Austria's role in a united Europe took center stage in 1998. In March Austria was 1 of 11 nations recommended for inclusion in the EU's Economic and Monetary Union (EMU), which became effective January 1, 1999. With a budget deficit of 2.7 percent of GDP for 1997, Austria was well within the 3 percent EMU criteria established by the Maastricht Treaty. However, Vienna's role in the "new Europe" did not include participation in an expanding NATO.

The success of the radical FPÖ in 1999 renewed questions about Austria's commitment to European integration and created image problems for Vienna reminiscent of the Kurt Waldheim years. Following the formation of a governing coalition that included the anti-immigrant FPÖ in 2000, the EU imposed diplomatic sanctions against Austria. France and Belgium were among the strongest backers of the sanctions, but by May 2000 at least six EU members reportedly were looking for a face-saving way to end them, especially as Vienna threatened to block EU reforms and EU enlargement. On September 12 the EU lifted the sanctions but pledged to monitor the activities of the FPÖ. Subsequently, the

National Council approved the EU's Treaty of Nice in November 2001. The Austrian legislature in May 2005 ratified the proposed new EU constitution (although a majority of the Austrian public appeared to be against the measure). By 2005 Austria had regained what one journalist described as "surprising international respectability" only five years after falling into the status of "pariah state" because of the FPÖ.

This newfound credibility in European diplomatic circles was shaken somewhat at a October 2–3, 2005, meeting of EU foreign ministers in Luxembourg called to clear remaining hurdles to opening accession talks with Turkey. Austria attempted to put the brakes on full EU membership for Turkey, proposing instead a "privileged partnership" status. Popular support for the EU has been declining in Austria given the rapid expansion of EU membership, popular rejection of the EU constitutional referenda in France and the Netherlands, squabbling between Britain and France over EU budgets, and high unemployment attributed to the influx of foreign workers. The Turkish accession in particular enjoys little popular support in the country, and the radical-right parties have called for a popular referendum on the question. At the Luxembourg meeting, however, Austria withdrew its veto once it secured concessions that Croatia's case for EU membership would be put on a faster track (Croatia is within Austria's cultural and economic sphere of influence in southern Europe). Austria assumed the six-month rotating EU presidency on January 1, 2006.

A recent controversy with the neighboring Czech Republic concerns a nuclear power plant in Temelin, 40 miles from the Austrian border. In protest, demonstrators blocked border crossings in 2000 and Austria at one point threatened to block EU membership for the Czech state if the plant were brought on line. In December 2000 Chancellor Schüssel and Czech Prime Minister Zeman, meeting in Melk, Austria, agreed to arrange consultations regarding safety and inspection issues, but the status of the facility remained controversial. Similar controversy stirred in late 2005 amid reports that neighboring Slovenia was considering building a new nuclear power plant to meet future energy needs.

In 2006 relations with neighboring Italy were strained by a flare-up of old sensitivities over the status of the Italian alpine province Trentino-Alto Adige. Provincial leaders in the German-speaking communities of Alto Adige signed a petition seeking "protection and guardianship" under any new Austrian constitutional arrangements adopted in the future by the National Council, specifically guarantees of the subregion's right to autonomous status and of protection of its German language, culture, and traditions. Soon thereafter Italian President Ciampi canceled a scheduled visit to Vienna in March 2006 citing the proximity of the Italian national elections.

Current Issues

Following Chancellor Schüssel's failure in 2001 and 2002 to shed the FPÖ as the junior partner in his governing coalition, the center-right/radical-right government faced the difficult task of having to reduce one of the highest budget deficits in the EU while satisfying its antitax conservative constituency as well as those voters the coalition had won over with costly populist campaign promises. The administration faced numerous work stoppages in the public sector and the nation's first general strike (in May 2003) in more than 50 years. Nevertheless, the government remained committed to pension reform, privatization measures, and budget restraint. In addition, in October 2003 the government adopted what were widely described as the most restrictive asylum laws in the EU. The government also announced in January 2006 that it would extend until 2009 labor market restrictions on the freedom of movement into Austria for citizens from the new EU member states in response to persistent high domestic unemployment.

In a surprise move in an election year, the government prepared to sell a 49 percent stake in the nationally owned postal service in early 2006, despite the threat of strikes from postal union leaders. Compulsory military service for Austrians was reduced to six months in 2006.

Despite his reported decline in popularity polls, Schüssel in mid-2005 was seen as still firmly in control and expected to run again. The results of the October 2005 provincial elections, however, cast doubt on whether the center-right/radical-right coalition will survive new elections intact. With the ÖVP and SPÖ in a virtual tie in early 2006 opinion polls, speculation centered on a revival of a "grand coalition" (as in the aftermath of the 2005 German election) or an alliance with The Greens following the October 1, 2006 national elections.

Political Parties

Government Coalition

Austrian People's Party (*Österreichische Volkspartei Partei*—ÖVP). Catholic in origin, the ÖVP developed out of the prewar Christian Social Party. Dominated by farmers and businesspeople, it advocated a conservative economic policy and strongly supported EU accession. The dominant government party from 1946 to 1970, the ÖVP was thereafter in opposition for 16 years, with longtime party chair Aloïs Mock standing down in 1980 following provincial election reverses. Damaged by its support of Kurt Waldheim at the 1986 presidential poll, the party lost ground in November legislative balloting and opted to return to a "grand coalition" as junior partner to the SPÖ. The coalition was maintained despite further losses in 1990 and 1994 (the overall decline being only partially disguised by the easy victory of ÖVP nominee Thomas Klestil in the 1992 presidential poll).

The ÖVP's 1994 vote share of 27.7 percent was a postwar low, with the party close to being overtaken on the right by the radical FPÖ (see below). The setback led to the ouster of Vice Chancellor Erhard BUSEK as party chair in April 1995 and the appointment of Wolfgang Schüssel as his successor, although the coalition with the SPÖ was maintained. ÖVP ministers precipitated the collapse of the coalition in October and an early election in December, at which the ÖVP vote unexpectedly improved to 28.3 percent. The "grand coalition" with the SPÖ was resumed in March 1996. However,

the party slipped in the October 1999 parliamentary election to less than 27 percent, tied for second place with the FPÖ at 52 seats each. Schüssel, favoring reforms that a divided SPÖ would not accept, became a reluctant partner with the FPÖ and was sworn in as chancellor on February 4, 2000 (see Political background, above, for subsequent developments).

The ÖVP's results in the provincial elections in October 2005 were mixed. The party increased its share in Vienna to 49 percent but lost control over the provincial assembly and governorship to the SPÖ in Styria. Its national coalition partner, the BZÖ, fared badly, however, undermining confidence that the ÖVP-BZÖ coalition could survive the next parliamentary election. The party's national poll numbers eroded in 2006 because of persistent high unemployment, opposition to its attempts to curtail the pension system, and the negative impact of allegations that work visas were sold at Austrian embassies when Schüssel served as foreign minister in the mid-1990s.

Leaders: Dr. Wolfgang SCHÜSSEL (Federal Chancellor and Chair of the Party), Dr. Aloïs MOCK (Honorary President of the Party), Andreas KHOL (President of the National Council), Reinhold LOPATKA (Secretary General), Wilhelm MOLTERER (Leader of Parliamentary Group).

Alliance for the Future of Austria (*Bündnis Zukunft Österreich*—BZÖ). Disgruntled FPÖ members, including all of the FPÖ cabinet ministers and most of the FPÖ legislators, launched the BZÖ in April 2005. The BZÖ, which elected prominent right-winger Jörg Haider as its chair, therefore became the junior partner in an ÖVP-BZÖ coalition government and avoided a fall of the coalition government that would have triggered early national elections. In the same month Siegfried Kampl, a BZÖ member from Carinthia who was scheduled to assume the rotating presidency of the Federal Council in July 2005, tarred the new party's image by denouncing deserters from the Nazi-era Austrian armed forces. Amid a storm of protest Kampl pledged to resign his seat but reneged on the promise in May 2005, and he subsequently resigned his membership in the BZÖ.

In the October 2005 provincial elections the BZÖ secured less than 2 percent of the vote in Vienna (and thus no representatives), and also failed to win any seats in the Styrian provincial assembly. The poor results immediately cast doubt on the BZÖ's potential fortune in the national polls slated for October 2006, specifically its ability to win the 4 percent needed to retain seats in the parliament, and therefore its ability to remain a viable governing coalition partner for the ÖVP. Following the provincial elections Haider made overtures to reunite with the FPÖ but was rebuffed.

Responding to the success of the populist antiforeigner appeals of the FPÖ, in December 2005 Haider called for expulsion of any foreigners who were unemployed or charged with a crime, stricter enforcement of immigration quotas, government approval of Muslim religious instructors, and greater school emphasis on the integration of foreign-born students.

Leaders: Jörg HAIDER (Chair of the Party and Governor of Carinthia), Hubert GORBACH (Vice Chair), Karin GASTINGER and Heike TRAMMER (Deputy Chairs), Uwe SCHEUCH (Speaker), Ursula HAUBNER.

Opposition Parties

Freedom Party of Austria (*Freiheitliche Partei Österreichs*—FPÖ). Formed in 1956 as successor to the League of Independents, which drew much of its support from former National Socialists, the FPÖ in the early 1970s moderated its extreme right-wing tendencies in favor of an essentially liberal posture. Its coalition with the SPÖ after the 1983 election, the first time that it had participated in a federal administration, collapsed as the result of the election of rightist Jörg Haider as party chair in 1986. Nonetheless, the FPÖ made substantial gains at the expense of both the SPÖ and the ÖVP in the National Council balloting of November 1986 and at provincial elections in March 1989. On the basis of a platform stressing opposition to immigration from Eastern Europe,

it nearly doubled its lower house representation in 1990, almost entirely at the expense of the ÖVP.

In November 1992 the FPÖ launched an "Austria First" campaign for a referendum on the immigration issue, which was rejected in September 1993 by a large majority in the legislature. Three months later, moderate elements broke away to form the Liberal Forum (see below), which subsequently replaced the FPÖ as the Austrian affiliate of the Liberal International. Haider's anti-EU stance failed to prevent a decisive referendum vote in favor of entry in June 1994; in the October federal election, however, the FPÖ advanced further, its 22.5 percent vote share enabling Haider to claim that he was on course to win the chancellorship. In January 1995 the party attempted to broaden its appeal by forming a "citizens' movement," *Die Freiheitlichen* (Freedom Movement), that rejected "old-style party politics."

Although the FPÖ unexpectedly fell back to 21.9 percent in the December 1995 federal balloting and remained in opposition, it rebounded to capture nearly 28 percent of the vote in the October 1996 elections to the European Parliament. In March 1999 the party won the regional election in Carinthia, Haider's home province, with 42 percent of the vote. It was the first time the party had won a provincial election. Haider's victory was capped in April by his election as governor by the Carinthian legislature, which had been dominated by the SPÖ for about 50 years.

The FPÖ tied for second with the ÖVP in the October 1999 parliamentary election, picking up 12 seats to bring its total to 52. The disintegration of the grand coalition allowed the FPÖ to join the government, but only after agreeing with the ÖVP to end its opposition to EU membership and EU enlargement. When this failed to satisfy the FPÖ's critics abroad, Haider resigned as party leader, effective May 1, 2000, in favor of a Haider loyalist. Political analysts viewed this as a purely tactical move.

The party lost significant ground at provincial elections in Styria, Burgenland, and Vienna in late 2000 and early 2001. It also performed poorly in the November 2002 legislative balloting (18 seats on a 10.2 percent vote share), the June 2004 poll for the European Parliament (6.3 percent of the vote), and the March 2005 municipal elections in Lower Austria. As a result, the FPÖ announced that many "far-rightists" were being removed from top party posts. In the ensuing internal struggle, however, Haider and his supporters (who advocated maintaining the coalition government with the ÖVP) lost the battle and immediately quit the FPÖ to form the BZÖ (see above), the FPÖ thereby losing most of its legislative representation and all its cabinet ministries.

Now led by the new party chair Heinz-Christian Strache (elected on April 23, 2005, at the party congress in Salzburg) the FPÖ contested the provincial elections in October 2005 on an anti-immigration and anti-EU platform in a bid to recapture the support of its right-wing populist base. This strategy moved the FPÖ to the right of the BZÖ, which had a more pragmatic approach because of its membership in the government. In the Vienna provincial election the FPÖ won 15 percent of the vote, but in Styria, a traditional FPÖ stronghold, the party failed to win any representation in the provincial assembly. In early 2006 the party launched a national petition for a referendum on the EU-related issues regarding Turkish admission to the EU as well as Austria's continued neutrality and its level of participation in the EU.

Leader: Heinz-Christian STRACHE (Chair of the Party), Martina SCHENK and Hans WEIXELBAUM (Vice Chairs), Herbert KICKL, Harald VILIMSKY, and Karlheinz KLEMENT (General Secretaries).

Austrian Social Democratic Party (*Sozialdemokratische Partei Österreichs*—SPÖ). Formed in 1889 as the Social Democratic Party and subsequently redesignated the Austrian Socialist Party (*Sozialistische Partei Österreichs*) before reassuming its original name in 1991, the SPÖ represents the overwhelming majority of workers and part of the lower middle class; as such, it advocates progressive taxation, high social expenditure, and economic planning. After serving as junior coalition partner to the ÖVP from 1947 to 1966, the SPÖ re-

turned to office as a minority government in 1970 under Bruno Kreisky, who won an absolute majority in 1971 and retained it in the 1975 and 1979 elections. A party congress in 1978 renounced state ownership as a necessary element of a democratic socialist economy. Losing its overall majority in 1983, the SPÖ formed a coalition with the FPÖ, with Kreisky yielding the chancellorship and party leadership to Fred SINOWATZ. Sinowatz resigned in June 1986 over the Waldheim affair and was replaced by Franz Vranitzky.

In September 1986, in light of the FPÖ's sharp swing to the right, the SPÖ terminated the government coalition, but it lost ground in resultant elections, opting in January 1987 to re-form a "grand coalition" with the ÖVP. This provoked the resignation of Kreisky as SPÖ honorary chair, on the grounds that Vranitzky had turned his back on socialism in favor of the "banks and bourgeoisie." Nonetheless, a party congress in October gave qualified support to the government's privatization program.

The "grand coalition" was maintained after the 1990 election, with the SPÖ remaining the largest party; it was also preserved after the October 1994 balloting, when the SPÖ vote slipped to a postwar low of 34.9 percent, and after the December 1995 election, when the SPÖ recovered to 38.1 percent.

Following the SPÖ's relatively poor performance in the October 1996 balloting for the European Parliament, Vranitzky in January 1997 resigned as chancellor and was succeeded by Finance Minister Viktor Klima, who was also elected to replace Vranitzky as SPÖ chair at a special party congress in April.

In the parliamentary elections of October 1999, the SPÖ representation fell from 71 to 65 seats on a vote share of 33 percent, although the SPÖ retained a legislative plurality. After months of negotiations with the ÖVP, the grand coalition collapsed, reportedly over the unwillingness of the labor wing of the SPÖ to agree to budget cuts necessary to keep deficit spending within bounds. In February 2000 Klima resigned as party chair.

The SPÖ improved to 36.5 percent of the vote and 69 seats in the November 2002 elections, although it lost its legislative plurality to the ÖVP. In 2004 Heinz Fischer became the first member of the SPÖ in 30 years to be elected to the nation's largely ceremonial presidency, while the SPÖ's Gabi Burgstaller was elected governor of Salzburg after decades of conservative control of that province. The provincial turnover continued in late 2005 with the election of Franz VOVES as governor of Styria province, leaving the SPÖ with four of the nine provincial governorships, and costing the ÖVP its majority in the Federal Council in 2006.

Following its success in the October 2005 provincial elections the SPÖ enjoyed a slight lead over the ÖVP in national opinion polls, but the surge in popular opinion shrunk to a virtual tie in early 2006 amid a deepening banking fraud scandal associated with a bank owned by the Austrian Trade Union Federation, which has close ties to the SPÖ. A government investigation revealed in March 2006 that the bank had averted failure via a massive loan guarantee from the trade union federation strike fund. A subsequent poll revealed that most Austrians believed that SPÖ Chair Alfred Gusenbauer had knowledge of the events surrounding the bailout.

In response to the 2005 energy price and supply disruptions across Europe, the SPÖ leadership in early 2006 announced a renewable energy initiative as part of the party's platform for the parliamentary elections later in the year.

Leaders: Alfred GUSENBAUER (Chair of the Party), Heinz FISCHER (President of the Republic), Doris BURES and Norbert DARABOS (Federal Executive Directors), Bettina STADLBAUER (General Secretary), Josef CAP.

The Greens (*Die Grünen*). Austria's principal ecology-oriented party, *Die Grünen* was organized as the Green Alternative (*Die Grüne Alternative—* GAL) during a congress in Klagenfurt on February 14 and 15, 1987, of three groups that had jointly contested the 1986 election: the **Austrian Alternative List** (*Alternative Liste Österreichs—*ALÖ), a left-wing formation with links to the West German Greens; the **Citizens' Initiative Parliament** (*Bürgerinitiative Parlament—*BIP); and the VGÖ

(see below). After failing in a bid to retain its organizational identity, the VGÖ withdrew, leaving the GAL, with seven National Council deputies, one seat short of the minimum needed to qualify as a parliamentary group. The party overcame the difficulty in 1990 by winning ten seats, with three more being added in 1994 on a 7 percent vote share before declining to 4.8 percent and nine seats in December 1995. In 1993 it adopted its present name but continued to offer national candidate lists as The Greens–The Green Alternative. A July 2001 party congress passed a new platform based on core principles of ecology, solidarity, autonomy, grassroots democracy, nonviolence, and feminism.

Die Grünen became the fourth-largest parliamentary party following the October 1999 election when it gained 5 additional seats, for a total of 14, with 7.4 percent of the vote. It improved to 9.5 percent of the vote and 17 seats in 2002.

Leaders: Alexander Van der BELLEN (Chair), Michaela SBURNY (Vice Chair), Eva Glawischnig-Pieszcek and Dr. Madeleine PETROVIC (Deputy Chairs), Peter PILZ, Peter SCHIEDER.

Other Parties that Contested the 2002 Election

Liberal Forum (*Liberales Forum—*LiF). The LiF was founded in February 1993 by five FPÖ deputies opposed to the party's nationalist agitation, among them the FPÖ presidential candidate in 1992, Dr. Heide SCHMIDT. In the October 1994 federal balloting, the LiF limited the gain for its parent party by winning 11 seats on a 5.9 percent vote share, although it slipped to 5.5 percent and 10 seats in December 1995. Party Leader Schmidt ran in the presidential election of April 1998 and came in a distant second (with 11.4 percent of the votes) in a field of five. She resigned her leadership position when the party lost all 10 seats in 1999 on a vote share of 3.65 percent, less than the 4 percent threshold required for representation. The LiF managed to secure only 0.1 percent of the vote in 2002.

Leaders: Alexander ZACH (Chair), Roland GATT and Gabriele METZ (Deputy Chairs).

Austrian Communist Party (*Kommunistische Partei Österreichs*—KPÖ). The KPÖ, founded in 1918, supports nationalization, land reform, and a neutralist foreign policy. Its strength lies mainly in the industrial centers and in trade unions, but it has not been represented in the legislature since 1959 and obtained only 0.3 percent of the vote in 1994, 0.5 percent in 1999, and 0.6 percent in 2002. The KPÖ did, however, surpass the BZÖ vote total in the October 2005 provincial election in Vienna, finishing in fifth place to the BZÖ's sixth place, but well short of the 5 percent necessary to win representation in the provincial assembly.

Leader: Walter BAIER (Chair).

Christian Electoral Union (*Christliche Wählergemeinschaft*—CWG). The CWG won 0.2 percent of the vote in the parliamentary election of 1994 and dropped to 0.1 percent in 1999 (when it contested seats in three provinces) and 0.04 percent in 2002.

Leader: Karl ANGERER.

Other parties that contested the 2002 balloting included the **Socialist Left Party** (*Sozialistische Links Partei*—SLP), which received 0.08 percent of the vote after being launched in 2000 by disaffected members of the SPÖ, and **The Democrats** (*Die Demokraten*), which secured 0.05 percent of the vote under the leadership of Andreas KOLAR.

Other Parties

The Independents (*Die Unabhängigen*—DU). Founded by Richard Lugner, the DU is a populist party that opposes the eastward expansion of the EU and the patronage system long dominated by the grand coalition of the ÖVP and SPÖ. Lugner, an entrepreneur often compared to Donald Trump because of their associations with celebrities and high society, drew almost 10 percent of the vote when he entered the 1998 presidential race. The DU won 1 percent of the vote in the 1999 parliamentary election.

Leader: Richard LUGNER.

United Greens of Austria (*Vereinte Grünen Österreichs*—VGÖ). Founded in 1982, the VGÖ is an essentially conservative grouping that is concerned with air pollution and nuclear power safety. It contested the 1986 election in coalition with the ALÖ and the BIP (see above, under The Greens), but withdrew from the coalition after formation of the GAL in 1987. Its one National Council seat was lost in 1990 and not regained in 1994 (when it won only 0.1 percent of the vote). In early 1999 local elections, the VGÖ and the GAL cooperated in some jurisdictions. The VGÖ did not contest the October 1999 national poll.

Leader: Adi PINTER.

Other fringe parties have included the **Austrian Family Party** (*Österreichische Familienpartei*—ÖFP), founded in 1982 by Leopold KENDÖL, president of the Austrian Catholic Family Association; the **Austrian Natural Law Party** (*Österreichische Naturgesetz Partei*—ÖNP); the **Best Party** (*Die Beste Partei*—DBP); the **Civic Greens of Austria** (*Bürgerliche Grüne Österreichs*—BGÖ); the Marxist **League of Democratic Socialists** (*Bund Demokratischer Sozialisten*—BDS); the far-right **People's Extra-Parliamentary Opposition** (*Volks Ausserparlamentarische Opposition*—VAPO); the **People's True Extra-Parliamentary Opposition** (*Volkstreue Ausserparlamentarische Opposition*—VtAPO), a radical antiforeigner movement whose leader, Gottfried KÜSSEL, was given an 11-year jail term in October 1994; and the **Socialist Alternative** (formerly called the Revolutionary Marxist Group [*Gruppe Revolutionärer Marxisten*]), a Trotskyist formation led by Hermann DWORCZAK.

The regionally based **Unity List** (*Enotna Lista*—EL), founded in 1975, is an ethnic party of the Slovene minority in Carinthia led by Vladimir SMRTNIK.

In the 2004 balloting for the European Parliament, two Austrian seats (on a 14 percent vote share) were won by an independent list headed by Hans-Peter MARTIN, a member of the European Parliament since 1999 who had gained significant attention for his campaign against the perceived exorbitant financial allowances accorded some of his peers.

Cabinet

As of May 1, 2006

Chancellor	Dr. Wolfgang Schüssel (ÖVP)
Vice Chancellor	Hubert Gorbach (BZÖ)

Ministers

Agriculture, Forestry, Environment, and Water Management	Josef Pröll (ÖVP)
Defense	Günther Platter (ÖVP)
Economic Affairs and Labor	Martin Bartenstein (ÖVP)
Education, Science, and Culture	Elisabeth Gehrer (ÖVP) [f]
Finance	Karl-Heinz Grasser (ind.)
Foreign Affairs	Ursula Plassnik (ÖVP) [f]
Health and Women's Issues	Maria Rauch-Kallat (ÖVP) [f]
Interior	Liese Prokop (ÖVP) [f]
Justice	Karin Miklautsch (BZÖ) [f]
Transportation, Innovation, and Technology	Hubert Gorbach (BZÖ)
Social Security, Generations, and Consumer Protection	Ursula Haubner (BZÖ) [f]

[f] = female

Legislature

The bicameral **Federal Assembly** (*Bundesversammlung*) consists of a Federal Council (upper house) and a National Council (lower house).

Federal Council (*Bundesrat*). The upper chamber as of 2006 consisted of 62 members representing each of the provinces on the basis of population, but with each province having at least three representatives. Chosen by provincial assemblies in proportion to party representation, members serve for terms ranging from five to six years, depending on the life of the particular assembly. The presidency of the council rotates among the nine provinces for a six-month term. In the council as of January 2006, the Austrian Social Democratic Party held 29 seats; Austrian People's Party, 26; The Greens, 4; and 3 seats were occupied by members with no official party affiliation.

President: Gottfried KNEIFEL (through December 2006).

National Council (*Nationalrat*). The lower chamber consists of 183 members elected by universal suffrage from 25 electoral districts for maximum terms of four years. At the most recent election of November 24, 2002, the Austrian People's Party won 79 seats; the Austrian Social Democratic Party, 69; the Freedom Party of Austria, 18; and The Greens, 17. (*See headnote*).

President: Andreas KHOL.

Communications

All news media operate freely and without government restrictions, though the establishment in 2000 of a media regulatory bureau to monitor the "objectivity" of radio and television journalists alarmed libertarians.

Press

The following are published daily in Vienna, unless otherwise noted: *Kronen Zeitung* (1,080,500 daily, 1,332,400 Sunday), independent; *Der Kurier* (385,000 daily, 607,000 Sunday), independent; *Kleine Zeitung* (Graz and Klagenfurt, 277,000), independent; *Salzburger Nachrichten* (Salzburg, 135,000), independent;

OberÖsterreichische Nachrichten (Linz, 120,000), independent; *Tiroler Tageszeitung* (Innsbruck, 100,000), independent; *Die Presse* (100,000), independent; *Der Standard* (100,000 daily, 152,000 Sunday); *Neue Zeit* (Graz, 71,000), Socialist; *Vorarlberger Nachrichten* (Bregenz, 65,000); *Wiener Zeitung* (40,000), government organ, world's oldest daily (f. 1703); *Kärtner Tageszeitung* (Klagenfurt, 36,000), Socialist.

News Agencies

The domestic agency is *Austria Presse-Agentur* (APA); numerous foreign agencies also maintain bureaus in Vienna.

Broadcasting and Computing

The Austrian Broadcasting Company (*Österreichischer Rundfunk*—ÖRF), which operates television and radio media, is state owned but protected in its operation from political interference under the broadcasting law. In October 1989 the government moved to end the ÖRF's monopoly by licensing private broadcasting. Currently, there is one national commercial television broadcast service, and one national commercial radio network competing with the ÖRF public broadcasting services. There were approximately 7.1 million television receivers and 3.3 million personal computers serving 3.7 million Internet users in 2003.

Intergovernmental Representation

Ambassador to the U.S.
Eva NOWOTNY

U.S. Ambassador to Austria
Susan Rasinski McCAW

Permanent Representative to the UN
Gerhard PFANZELTER

IGO Memberships (Non-UN)
ADB, AfDB, BIS, CEI, CERN, CEUR, EBRD, EIB, ESA, EU, Eurocontrol, IADB, IEA, Interpol, IOM, OECD, OSCE, PCA, WCO, WTO

BELARUS

REPUBLIC OF BELARUS

Respublika Belarus

The Country

Located adjacent to Poland in the western region of the former Soviet Union, Belarus is bordered on the north by Latvia, on the northwest by Lithuania, on the east by the Russian Federation, and on the south by Ukraine. Approximately 78 percent of its population is Belarusan, 13 percent Russian, 4 percent Polish, and 3 percent Ukrainian. The predominant religion is Eastern Orthodox, with another 10 percent of the population professing Roman Catholicism. A 2002 law recognized the leading role of the Russian Orthodox Church and prohibited publication and missionary work by churches that had not been registered for at least 20 years. Women make up about half the labor force. Following the October–November 2004 legislative elections, women held 29 percent of the seats in the lower house and 32 percent in the upper house.

Much of Belarusan territory is low-lying swampland from which substantial quantities of peat are mined, while extensive forests support a major timber industry. The leading crops include grains (rye, oats, wheat), potatoes, and sugar beets. Agriculture, which continues to be dominated by state and collective farms, now accounts for about 10 percent of GDP, overall output having declined steadily since 1993. Industrial output includes machinery, chemicals, processed foods, and wood and paper products, with industry as a whole constituting about 37 percent of GDP in 2003.

Belarus initiated a privatization and price deregulation program in 1994 in consultation with the International Monetary Fund (IMF), but progress was slow amid GDP contraction that averaged nearly 14 percent annually in 1993–1995. Suspended in July 1994 because of rampant corruption, the privatization program was somewhat hesitantly relaunched in March 1995. Belarus is generally considered "the most unreformed" of the former European Soviet republics, and the state continues to control most assets and economic activity. The private-sector share of GDP stands at about 25 percent.

GDP growth in the latter half of the 1990s was sporadic, peaking at 11.4 percent in 1997 but declining to 3.4 percent in 1999 before recovering to 5.8 percent in 2000. Inflation was a major problem, the consumer price index soaring by 182 percent in 1998 and 251 percent in 1999. With Russia as

its leading trading partner, Belarus was hit hard by the 1998 Russian ruble crisis; shortages of food and other essential goods occurred, and the value of the Belarusan ruble plummeted. The subsequent Russian recovery benefited foreign trade, while the value of the Belarusan currency was stabilized in September 2000 by adoption of a unified exchange rate. Inflation for 2000 remained high, at 108 percent, but over the following three years dropped to about 25 percent, according to government sources. GDP growth in 2001–2002 averaged slightly under 5 percent annually but then approached 7 percent in 2003. For 2004, inflation continued its descent and by mid-2005 had reached 11 percent. Growth for 2004 surpassed 10 percent and remained rapid, at 7.1 percent, in 2005, but the IMF projected a slowdown to 4.0 percent for 2006.

Government and Politics

Political Background

Merged with Poland in the 16th century after a lengthy period of Lithuanian rule, Byelorussia became part of the Russian Empire as a result of the Polish partitions of 1772, 1793, and 1795. A major battlefield during World War I, the region was reconquered by Red Army troops following a declaration of independence in 1918 and became a constituent republic of the Union of Soviet Socialist Republics (USSR) in 1922. In 1939 a western area that had been awarded to Poland in 1921 was reclaimed and incorporated into the Byelorussian SSR.

On July 27, 1990, Byelorussia emulated a number of its sister republics by issuing a declaration of sovereignty. On August 25, 1991, following the abortive Moscow coup against USSR President Mikhail Gorbachev, the Byelorussian Communist Party was suspended, and the Supreme Soviet proclaimed the republic's "political and economic independence." On September 18 its name was changed to Belarus, and Stanislau SHUSHKE-VICH was designated chair of the Supreme Soviet, succeeding Nicholai DEMENTEI, who had been obliged to resign after displaying support for the Moscow hard-liners. Belarus hosted the December 8 tripartite meeting with Russia and the Ukraine that proclaimed the demise of the Soviet Union, and its capital, Minsk, was named as the "normal" venue for meetings of the Commonwealth of Independent States (CIS) that was formally launched on December 21.

Belarus became fully independent with virtually all of its Soviet-era power structure and personnel still in place. In 1992 disputes between the government and the non-Communist opposition became more heated, although the ruling establishment successfully resisted a campaign for the calling of new elections. While the Supreme Soviet voted to lift the suspension of the Communist Party, its property remained under state ownership. Strains then intensified between Shushkevich, a free-market nationalist, and the chair of the Council of Ministers, Vyacheslau KEBICH, a veteran Communist who favored state control of the economy and close ties with Moscow. In January 1994 Shushkevich's opponents won legislative approval of a censure motion that accused him of "personal immodesty" (i.e., corruption). Shushkevich resigned and was succeeded on January 28 by Mechyslaw HRYB (Mechislav GRIB), a former Communist apparatchik who shared Kebich's enthusiasm for closer economic and military cooperation with Russia.

In the first round of balloting for the newly created office of president on June 23, 1994, Alyaksandr LUKASHENKA, a pro-Russian anticorruption campaigner, topped a six-man field with 44.8 percent of the vote. Lukashenka, running as an independent, went on to defeat Kebich by a near 6–1 margin in a two-way second-round poll on July 10. Lukashenka's nomination of Mikhail CHYHIR (CHIGIR) as prime minister secured legislative approval on July 21.

Despite opposition calls for an early legislative poll, the preindependence Supreme Council elected in April 1990 concluded its five-year term. Attempted replenishment took place on May 14 and 28, 1995, when only 119 of the 260 legislative seats were filled, well short of the two-thirds constitutionally required for a quorum. In referenda also

Political Status: Formerly the Byelorussian Soviet Socialist Republic, a constituent republic of the Union of Soviet Socialist Republics; declared independence on August 25, 1991; new constitution declared to be in force by the government on November 27, 1996, following approval by national referendum on November 24.

Area: 80,155 sq. mi. (207,600 sq. km.).

Population: 10,045,237 (1999C); 9,799,000 (2005E).

Major Urban Center (2005E): MIENSK (Minsk, 1,775,000).

Official Languages: Belarusan and Russian (the latter being the first language of most inhabitants).

Monetary Unit: Belarusan Ruble (official rate July 1, 2006: 2,143 rubles = $1US).

President: Alyaksandr LUKASHENKA; elected at popular runoff balloting on July 10, 1994, and inaugurated for a five-year term on July 20, succeeding Mechyslaw HRYB (Mechislav GRIB), who, as chair of the Supreme Council, had theretofore served as head of state; term extended to 2001 by constitutional referendum of November 1996; reelected on September 4–9, 2001, and inaugurated on September 20; reelected for a third term on March 19, 2006, and sworn in on April 8.

Prime Minister: Syarhey SIDORSKY (Sergei SIDORSKY); named acting prime minister on July 10, 2003, by the president, who had dismissed Prime Minister Henadz NAVITSKI (Gennady NOVITSKY) on the same day; endorsed as prime minister by the House of Representatives on December 19, 2003, and appointed to that post by the president later that same day; reconfirmed on April 17, 2006.

held on May 14 the government secured large "yes" votes (of between 78 and 83 percent in a turnout of 64.5 percent) on four proposals that, among other things, accorded the Russian language equal status with Belarusan, called for economic integration with the Russian Federation, and granted the president the right of parliamentary dissolution.

The 119 deputies elected in May included contingents of Communists, Agrarians, and conservative independents, almost all supportive of the government's pro-Russian line and unenthusiastic about market reform. Accordingly, the preferred option of President Lukashenka was that the outgoing Soviet-era legislature should reduce the quorum requirement in the new body to two-fifths (i.e., to 104) so that the seated deputies could conduct legislative business. However, two attempts to transfer authority to them failed in June, the majority preference of the old legislators being to maintain the status quo pending new elections for the unfilled seats. Opposition parties, which were barely represented among the candidates elected in May, complained that this course effectively left the country without a legislature, the mandate of the previous body having expired in March. The political impasse was eased somewhat when further elections on November 29 and December 10 increased the number of seats properly filled to 198. The Communists and Agrarians ended up with a substantial majority of party-based seats, although the largest number (95) went to "unaffiliated" candidates, most of whom were thought to support the president.

President Lukashenka subsequently continued to pursue enhancement of his powers, proposing sweeping constitutional revision in mid-1996 in view of an ongoing dispute with the Constitutional Court and his opponents in the Supreme Council over what they charged were his efforts to "rule by decree." Prime Minister Chyhir resigned on November 18 to protest Lukashenka's plans, the president naming Deputy Prime Minister Syarhey LING to serve as acting prime minister.

A highly controversial referendum on November 24, 1996, officially yielded a majority of more than 70 percent in favor of an amended constitution supporting a strengthened presidency and the extension of Lukashenka's current term from five to seven years, until 2001. Competing proposals put forward by the Supreme Council, which sought to curtail presidential powers, were overwhelmingly rejected by voters. Before the balloting, anti-Lukashenka Supreme Council members had initiated impeachment proceedings, and a reported 10,000 demonstrators had protested in Minsk. Nevertheless, the government, rejecting assertions that the referendum results were undemocratic and the official tally padded, declared the amended constitution in force on November 27.

Among other things, the document provided for a new bicameral parliament, although more than 40 members of the Supreme Council refused to recognize the referendum's legitimacy and continued to meet in rump sessions as the former legislature's "13th convocation." Having won support for their stance from the European Union (EU), the United States, and many other countries, on January 1997 the defiant legislators initiated a shadow cabinet, the Public Coalition Government–National Economic Council (subsequently the National Executive Council—NEC), chaired by Genadz KARPENKA. On January 15 President Lukashenka announced a cabinet reshuffle that was formally confirmed on February 19 by the new House of Representatives, which comprised those legislators who had been elected to the Supreme Council in 1995 and who accepted the legitimacy of the new constitution.

On January 10, 1999, 43 members of the rump Supreme Council announced a "presidential" election for May 16, in conformance with the 1994 constitution. Organizations supporting the move included the three largest opposition parties, the Belarusan Popular Front "Revival" (*Narodni Front Belarusi "Adradzhennie"*—NFB-A), the Belarusan Social Democratic Party "People's Assembly" (*Belaruskaya Satsyal-Demakratychnaya Partya "Narodnaya Hramada"*—BSDP-NH), and the United Civic Party of Belarus (*Abyadnanaya Hramadzyanskaya Partya Belarusi*—AHPB). By March the exiled leader of the NFB-A, Zyanon PAZNYAK, and former prime minister Chyhir had been certified as presidential candidates by the opposition's Central Electoral Commission (CEC). Ultimately, however, the CEC was forced to declare the results of the May balloting invalid because of official harassment, resultant organizational difficulties, and Paznyak's decision to withdraw on May 13 over procedural objections. The opposition had been further damaged in April by

Karpenka's death; he was succeeded as leader of the shadow cabinet by former head of state Mechyslaw Hryb. The opposition suffered another setback on July 22 when Semyon SHARETSKY, the speaker of the Supreme Council, fled to Lithuania. A day earlier the rump legislature, noting the July 20 expiration of President Lukashenka's term under the 1994 constitution, had declared Sharetsky to be the legal president of Belarus.

On February 18, 2000, President Lukashenka replaced Prime Minister Ling with Vladimir YERMOSHIN, the chair of the Minsk Executive Committee (mayor), who was confirmed on March 14 by the House of Representatives. Controversial elections to the House took place on October 15, although much of the opposition, linked through a Coordinating Council of Democratic Forces, called for a boycott. Official results showed a turnout of 61 percent, but some opposition leaders and observers charged that vote totals had been inflated to ensure reaching the statutory minimum of 50 percent. Only about 50 of the 562 official candidates for office represented the opposition, many others having been disqualified on technicalities or intimidated into withdrawing. Following a second round on October 29, the election results were declared valid in 97 of 110 constituencies, with the remaining seats being filled in March–April 2001.

Although most of the opposition united behind Uladzimir HANCHARYK (Vladimir GONCHARIK) of the Belarusan Federation of Trade Unions for the presidential election of September 4–9, 2001, President Lukashenka claimed some 76 percent of the disputed vote. Inaugurated on September 20, he nominated a new prime minister, Henadz NAVITSKI (Gennady NOVITSKY), on October 1. Formation of a new Council of Ministers was concluded by mid-December.

On July 10, 2003, President Lukashenka dismissed Prime Minister Navitski and several agricultural officials and named a deputy prime minister, Syarhey SIDORSKY, to head the cabinet in an acting capacity. Sidorsky's elevation to prime minister was completed on December 19, following endorsement by a 111–9 vote of the House of Representatives earlier in the day.

During the second half of 2003 opposition forces began organizing for the 2004 legislative election. The principal alliances to emerge from the process were the Popular Coalition "Five-Plus" and the European Coalition "Free Belarus." The Five-Plus brought together the AHPB and the NFB-A as well as the Party of Communists of Belarus (*Partya Kamunistau Belaruskaya—PKB*) and the Belarusan Social Democratic Assembly (*Belaruskaya Satsyal-Demakratychnaya Hramada—BSDH*), while the Free Belarus grouping included the BSDP-NH.

On September 7, 2004, Lukashenka announced that the October 17 balloting also would include a referendum on ending the two-term limit for presidents. Although the opposition united in an effort to defeat the constitutional change, the referendum easily passed, according to the official results, thereby permitting Lukashenka to seek a third term in 2006. The simultaneous election for the House of Representatives saw the opposition parties shut out: of the 110 contested seats, only 12 were won by party candidates, all of them government supportive.

Although President Lukashenka's term was not due to expire until September 2006, on December 16, 2005, Parliament unanimously endorsed holding the next presidential election six months early. At a National Congress of Democratic Forces, held October 1–2, 2005, the leading opposition parties, including those in the Five-Plus and European Coalition alliances, had selected as their joint candidate Alyaksandr MILINKEVICH, a nonpartisan academic and experienced nongovernmental organization leader. To no one's surprise, Lukashenka emerged the victor at the March 19, 2006, election, winning 82.6 percent of the vote. According to the Central Electoral Commission, Milinkevich finished second, with 6.1 percent of the vote, in the four-way contest, the conduct of which was uniformly condemned by Western monitors.

Constitution and Government

After a two-year gestation period, a new constitution secured legislative approval on March 15, 1994, and entered into force on March 30. It de-

fined Belarus as "a unitary, democratic, socially orientated, law-governed state" that aspired to be nuclear-free and neutral. It provided for an executive president to be directly elected by universal adult suffrage for a once-renewable five-year term. The president served as commander in chief; could declare a state of emergency; and had authority to appoint the prime minister, cabinet, and judges. Under constitutional amendments approved in May 1995, he also could dissolve the legislature "in the event of systematic or gross violation of the constitution." The legislature was the unicameral, 260-member Supreme Council, also directly elected for a five-year term. A Constitutional Court of 11 judges served as the final authority on legislative and executive acts, although its status was brought into question by the creation in April 1996 of a separate Constitutional Council attached to the presidency. An impeachment law adopted on February 1, 1995, specified that the president could be removed from office by a two-thirds majority of the legislature because of criminal activity, infringement of the constitution, or an expression of popular nonconfidence in a national referendum.

Under a simplification of local government structures given legislative approval on October 6, 1994, village and some town councils were abolished, while district and regional councils were made less bureaucratic. By a decree of November 1994, the president assumed the authority to appoint and dismiss senior local government officials in the country's six regions (*voblasti*) and the municipality (*horad*) of Minsk, the aim being to create a "vertical chain of power."

The powers of the presidency were vastly expanded in controversial basic law revisions approved by national referendum on November 24, 1996. The changes extended the current president's term of office and gave him the authority to nullify decisions of local councils, set election dates, and call parliament into session as well as dissolve it. The president also was empowered to appoint half the members of the Constitutional Court, as well as the chief justice, and officials of the Central Electoral Commission. The unicameral legislature was replaced by a two-chamber body consisting of 110 members in a House of Representatives and a

64-member upper house called the Council of the Republic. A referendum on October 17, 2004, eliminated the two-term limitation on the presidency.

Foreign Relations

Although not then an independent country, Byelorussia was accorded founding membership in the United Nations in a move by the Western Allies to reconcile Stalin to the creation of a world organization that would appear to have a built-in anti-Soviet majority. In contrast, it did not join the IMF and World Bank until July 1992. By then, Belarus had been recognized by a wide variety of foreign governments. In January 1992 Council of Ministers Chair Kebich, in a prelude to full diplomatic relations, had become the first leader of a former Soviet republic to visit China.

After protracted diplomatic exchanges, independent Belarus ratified a series of agreements by which it renounced its inherited nuclear weapons. Under one of the accords, signed in Washington on July 22, 1992, the U.S. government pledged $59 million to assist in dismantling about 80 Belarus-based SS-25 missiles. Under a further agreement in December 1993, Russia obtained the right to guide seven CIS members, including Belarus, in defense policy. (The Russians reported that they had removed the last nuclear missiles in November 1996.) Belarus joined NATO's Partnership for Peace program in January 1995, although it proceeded more slowly than many other countries in negotiating the specifics of its participation in the program. In April 1999 Belarus suspended its interactions with NATO to protest the bombing of Yugoslavia, but it resumed its participation in August.

In February 1995 Belarus and Russia signed a friendship and cooperation treaty, significant sentiment having been voiced in both countries for a degree of bilateral reintegration in view of the lack of progress within the CIS. Among other things, the pact provided for joint border protection and the eventual creation of a single administration to run an economic and monetary union. The process culminated in the signature in Moscow on April

2, 1996, of a far-reaching Treaty on the Formation of the Community of Sovereign Republics (CSR), which envisioned military and political cooperation as well as economic union. Russian Prime Minister Viktor Chernomydrin became the first chair of the CSR executive committee upon entry into force of the treaty on August 20. Provision also was made for the eventual establishment of a CSR Supreme Council (comprising governmental and legislative leaders of both nations) to serve as the grouping's ruling body, assisted by a CSR Parliamentary Assembly consisting of an equal number of representatives from the Belarusan and Russian legislatures.

Little progress was made throughout the rest of 1996 and early 1997 in implementation of the CSR pact, and Russian President Boris Yeltsin and Belarusan President Lukashenka attempted to reinvigorate the process on April 2, 1997, by signing a revised treaty and initialing a lengthy "Charter of the Union" that, although watered down somewhat at the last minute, provided specifics regarding the extent and timing of integration. Despite opposition from various constituencies in both countries, the two presidents on May 23 signed the charter, which formally came into effect on June 11 following ratification by the Belarusan and Russian legislatures. All citizens of both nations were declared "citizens of the Community," and other countries were pointedly invited to join. The union remained largely symbolic, however, although the new Parliamentary Assembly in December approved the first CSR budget, with financing for military cooperation and anticrime and customs measures.

On December 8, 1999, Yeltsin and Lukashenka signed yet another agreement, a Treaty on the Creation of a Union State, that was quickly passed by the legislatures of both countries. Although specifying that Russia and Belarus would retain sovereignty and "territorial integrity," the document, like its predecessors, called for establishing joint executive and legislative bodies, a common currency, a joint taxation system, and coordinated defense, foreign, and economic policies. On April 25, 2000, the Council of Ministers of the Union met for the first time. A monetary union was to have been established by January 2005, but adoption of a single currency has been repeatedly postponed, in part because no agreement has been reached on what compensation Belarus will receive to offset the consequent economic damage. In the meantime, work has proceeded on a constitutional draft, but basic issues remain unresolved, including, especially, questions related to sovereignty. (One nonstarter put forward by Russian President Putin in August 2002 called for, in effect, Russia's absorption of Belarus.) In 2003–2004, amid signs of diminished Belarusan enthusiasm for the overall union, the atmosphere was further clouded by differences related to natural gas purchases from Russia and the sale to Russia's Gazprom of a stake in the Belarusan gas distribution network.

At a January 2006 session of the Supreme Council of the Union, which was attended by Presidents Lukashenka and Putin, agreements were signed covering, among other things, freedom of movement and equal rights. The draft "Constitutional Act" remained unfinished, although some officials indicated that a referendum on the draft might be held late in 2006.

Relations with Western European countries and institutions have suffered because of their objections to the Lukashenka regime's political practices. Recent efforts to mediate between Lukashenka and the opposition and to encourage free and fair elections have been unavailing despite initiatives by the "parliamentary troika" of the European Parliament, the Parliamentary Assembly of the Organization for Security and Cooperation in Europe (OSCE), and the Parliamentary Assembly of the Council of Europe (PACE).

Citing erosion of human rights and democracy in Belarus, in November 2002 the EU and the United States imposed a travel ban on President Lukashenka and seven other government officials. A month earlier, the last foreign member of the OSCE Advisory and Monitoring Group in Belarus (AMG) had been obliged to leave the country due to the expiration of her visa. The Lukashenka regime, alleging that the AMG had repeatedly aided the opposition and interfered in the country's internal affairs, refused to accept the credentials of or to renew visas for AMG personnel until the mission's mandate was revised. In late December the OSCE and Belarus agreed to scrap the AMG and establish in its place a new OSCE office in Minsk to assist "in further promoting institution building," to help with economic and environmental activities, and to monitor events. In February 2003 the OSCE Parliamentary Assembly restored Belarus's membership, but in the same month the European Parliament adopted a resolution that criticized the Lukashenka regime for an adverse human rights climate and "indiscriminate attacks" on opponents, journalists, human rights activists, and others. In April the EU and the United States lifted their travel bans, but they continued to criticize the Lukashenka regime's failure to meet democratic standards.

Current Issues

President Lukashenka's regime, described by U.S. Secretary of State Condoleezza Rice in April 2005 as "the last true dictatorship" in Europe, has come under increasing international criticism for its authoritarianism. In March 2005 the European Parliament adopted a resolution that also called the government a dictatorship, while in March the UN Human Rights Commission passed a resolution condemning human rights abuses. As the 2006 presidential election approached, the EU warned that future relations would depend on the fairness and openness of the contest. Not surprisingly, OSCE monitors had concluded that the October 2004 legislative election fell "significantly short" of democratic standards for fairness and transparency.

Despite such external pressure, the Belarusan opposition continued to face official obstructions, a lack of access to the state-run media, and prosecutions that critics of the regime have branded as political reprisals. For example, Mikalay STATKEVICH, head of the BSDP-NH, and youth organizer Pavel SEVYARYNETS were convicted in 2005 of spearheading protests against the conduct of the 2004 parliamentary elections. Other detained oppositionists include two former members of Parliament, Andrey KLIMAU and Syarhey SKREBETS, and Mikhail MARYNICH, the last of whom was convicted in late 2004 of stealing several computers that had been donated by the U.S. embassy for use by the public association he headed. Moreover, as of early 2006 authorities had failed to solve the disappearances in 1999 of former minister of the interior Yuri ZAKHARENKA and deputy speaker of the rump Supreme Council Victar HANCHAR (Victor GONCHAR). Both men are believed to have been murdered, with suspicion falling on a secret police unit.

Although the main opposition parties, despite ideological and policy differences, united in October 2005 behind Alyaksandr Milinkevich for the 2006 presidential contest, not even the candidate himself expressed confidence that Lukashenka could be defeated at the polls. In late January 2006, speaking to a Polish interviewer, Milinkevich asserted that the opposition's goal was not to win the election but to set the stage for further political action. ("Because in fact there are no elections in our country, and as long as this regime exists there will not be.") Lukashenka, meanwhile, repeatedly rejected any suggestion that Belarus might undergo a bloodless revolution similar to those in other former Soviet republics, stating in January 2005, "There will be no rose [Georgian], orange [Ukrainian] or banana revolutions in our country." In late December 2005 he signed into law legislation imposing prison sentences on those convicted of such crimes as organizing antigovernment demonstrations, joining banned organizations, or disseminating false information about the country.

Officially, 92.9 percent of Belarus's voters turned out for the March 2006 presidential contest, the results of which brought some 10,000 anti-Lukashenka demonstrators into Minsk's October Square on election night. For the most part, the police adopted a hands-off approach until March 24–25, when hundreds of protesters were arrested. Although some 500 Russian monitors concluded that the election had evidenced only "technical imperfections," with no significant impact on the results, most international observers rejected the government's conduct as totally unacceptable. The OSCE, in particular, attacked a "climate of intimidation"

imposed by internal security personnel. According to various reports, opposition campaign workers had been arrested, harassed, and assaulted, and state employees had been coerced into voting for the incumbent. Following another opposition rally on April 26, Five-Plus leaders Milinkevich, Alyaksandr BUKHVOSTAW, Syarhey KALYAKIN, and Vintsuk VYACHORKA all received short sentences. Milinkevich vowed to fight on at the head of a "For Freedom" movement.

Political Parties

As in post-Soviet Russia, top Belarusan officials have generally avoided direct involvement in political party activity while in office, despite (or because of) their earlier associations with the Soviet-era Communist Party. Unlike in Russia, however, where party politics has often dominated proceedings in the powerful State Duma, under the disputed 1996 constitution the less powerful Belarusan legislature has been controlled by Lukashenka loyalists rather than by party caucuses.

In Belarus political and personal support for the head of state and prime minister has often coalesced in broad alliances of assorted parties, nongovernmental organizations, and interest groups. The Popular Movement of Belarus (*Narodni Dirzhenie Belarusi*—NDB), organized in 1992, embraced both the hard-line left and the pan-Slavic right on a joint platform advocating maintenance of close relations with Russia and resistance to Western capitalist encroachment. It supported the conservative prime minister, Vyacheslau Kebich, against the reformist head of state, Stanislau Shushkevich, in 1992–1993, as well as Kebich's unsuccessful presidential candidacy in 1994. During the Lukashenka era the NDB gave way to the **Belarusan Popular Patriotic Union—BPPU** (*Belaruski Narodna Patryatychny Sayuz*), which was established in September 1998 by some 20 government-supportive parties and groups, many of them former NDB participants. Founding members of the BPPU included the Communist Party of Belarus (KPB), whose leader, Victar Chykin, was named BPPU executive secretary; the Republican Party of

Labor and Justice (RPPS); the now-defunct Slavic Assembly "White Russia" (*Slavyanski Sabor "Belaya Rus"*); the Movement for Democracy, Social Progress, and Justice; and several military and veterans' organizations. The Liberal Democratic Party of Belarus (LDPB) also was identified as an initial participant; its chair, Syarhey Haydukevich, a former NDB leader, was named BPPU deputy executive secretary, although for a time the LDPB and Haydukevich leaned toward opposition. The BPPU has endorsed unification of Belarus and Russia as well as continued state domination of the economy.

Opposition policy coordination has often been lacking despite unifying efforts spearheaded by the largest parties: the Belarusan Popular Front "Revival" (NFB-A), the United Civic Party of Belarus (AHPB), and the Belarusan Social Democratic Party "People's Assembly" (BSDP-NH). In January 1997, in the wake of the disputed November 1996 constitutional referendum, the NFB-A, the AHPB, the Agrarian Party of Belarus (APB), the Party of Communists of Belarus (PKB), and other anti-Lukashenka organizations established a "shadow" cabinet, the Public Coalition Government-National Economic Council (PCG-NEC), under Genadz Karpenka, that in October 1997 was reorganized as a National Executive Committee (NEC). After Karpenka's death in April 1999, the NEC was led by his former deputy, Mechyslaw Hryb. The legislative branch of the opposition "government" was the rump of the Supreme Council elected in 1995 (the 13th convocation).

In late January 1999 a Congress of Democratic Forces of Belarus met in an attempt to consolidate the opposition. This led in mid-February to the establishment of a Coordinating Council of Democratic Forces (CCDF), which had already existed since at least 1997 on a more informal basis. "Founding" groups were the NFB-A, the AHPB, the BSDP-NH, the Association of Nongovernmental Organizations, the Charter-97 (*Khartiya-97*) human rights group, and the Congress of Democratic Trade Unions; other participants have included the Belarusan Labor Party (BPP), the Belarusan Social Democratic Assembly (BSDH), and the Belarusan

Women's Party "Hope" (BPZ-N). Chaired by the AHPB's Anatol Lyabedzka, the CCDF called for a boycott of the November 2000 legislative election, but the effort was only partially successful.

Under a presidential decree issued in January 1999, all 27 officially registered political parties, all public associations, and all trade unions were required to reregister under stricter standards regarding, for example, national membership. Only 17 parties met the new criteria when the reregistration period expired in August; most of the others had not applied, while the Party of Common Sense (*Partya Zdarovaga Sensu*—PZS) and the Belarusan Christian Democratic Unity (*Belaruskaya Khrystsiyanska Demakratychnaya Zluchnasts*—BKDZ) were denied official recognition for technical reasons. In 1998 half a dozen other small parties had already been disbanded by order of the Supreme Court. In August 2001, with the presidential election approaching, the CCDF suspended its activities, but it was revived in January 2002.

In mid-2003, looking toward the parliamentary balloting scheduled for October 2004, opposition elements began organizing alliances. The largest of these, encompassing the AHPB, the BSDH, the NFB-A, the PKB, and the BPP as well as a number of smaller parties and nongovernmental organizations, adopted the name **Popular Coalition "Five-Plus"** (*"V-Plyus"*) in early November. Despite ideological and other differences, the participating organizations endorsed a uniform "Five Steps to a Better Life" platform that emphasized economic and social dignity for everyone, job creation and worker protection, self-governance and equality before the law, budget transparency and an end to official corruption, and "mutually beneficial friendly relations with all neighboring and EU countries." At the same time, a **European Coalition "Free Belarus"** (*"Svabodnaya Belarus"*) was taking shape under the leadership of the BSDP-NH, the BPZ-N, the Charter-97, a number of youth groups, and assorted public associations. On September 13, 2004, shortly after Lukashenka announced that a referendum on repealing the two-term limit for presidents would be included on the October ballot, the two alliances, the **Young Belarus** (*Maladaya Belarus*) youth coalition, and the **Republic** (*Respublika*) faction of opposition deputies in the House of Representatives announced that they would campaign jointly against the change under the slogan "Say No! to Lukashenka."

The only major party boycotting the October election and referendum was the Conservative-Christian Party of the Belarusan Popular Front (KKhP-NFB), but none of the opposition parties, and none of the few *Respublika* incumbents who were permitted to contest the election, won any seats. Only 12 were won by declared party candidates, all of them government supportive.

In November 2004 most opposition leaders agreed that they would select a single candidate for the 2006 presidential contest. Late in the same month they organized a **Permanent Council of Democratic Forces** that included the original Five-Plus members (technically minus the BPP, which had been deregistered by the government), the Free Belarus parties, the Belarusan Ecological Party of the Greens, the Public Youth Organization "Civil Forum," the Young Front, and various nongovernmental organizations. At a National Congress of Democratic Forces, held October 1–2, 2005, in Minsk, this "unified opposition" endorsed the unaffiliated Alyaksandr Milinkevich as their 2006 presidential candidate by a vote of 399–391 over the AHPB's Lyabedzka. Shortly after the congress the PKB's chair, Syarhey Kalyakin, assumed leadership of the pro-Milinkevich Political Council of Democratic Forces. In addition to President Lukashenka, there were three other party candidates—the LDPB's Haydukevich, the KKhP-NFB's Zyanon Paznyak, and Alyaksandr Kazulin of the newly organized Belarusan Social Democratic Party "Assembly" (BSDP-H)—as well as three independents who subsequently formed initiative groups in preparation for getting on the 2006 ballot. In mid-February 2006 the Central Election Commission officially registered Haydukevich, Kazulin, Lukashenka, and Milinkevich for the ballot.

During 2005 the government had continued to tighten party regulations, in part through a new law that requires parties to have offices in Minsk and at least four regional capitals. In addition, the new law prohibited official party offices from being located in residences or residential complexes, which placed a considerable burden on some of the cash-strapped opposition groups. As of January 2006 there were 17 registered parties in Belarus.

Progovernment Parliamentary Parties

Agrarian Party of Belarus (*Agrarnaya Partya Belarusi*—APB). The APB was founded in 1994 in opposition to the restoration of peasant land ownership in Belarus, as advocated by the Belarusan Peasants' Party (*Belaruskaya Syalarskaya Partya*—BSP), which was deregistered in 1999. The APB returned 33 candidates in the 1995 legislative balloting and later attracted 13 "unaffiliated" deputies to its group in the Supreme Council, of which party chief Semyon Sharetsky was elected chair. The party ruptured in 1996, with Sharetsky and his supporters disavowing the results of the November constitutional referendum. Sharetsky continued as the chair of the opposition's reconstituted Supreme Council but, fearing for his safety, ultimately fled to Lithuania in July 2000. On March 31 a congress of the APB had pledged its loyalty to President Lukashenka.

In 2004 the APB won three House seats.

Leader: Mikhail SHYMANSKI (Chair).

Communist Party of Belarus (*Kommunisticheskaya Partya Belarusi*—KPB). The Soviet-era Communist Party had originated as a regional committee of the Russian Social Democratic Labor Party (formed in 1904). Established as the ruling party of the Soviet Socialist Republic of Byelorussia in 1920, the party suffered heavily during the terror of the 1930s, and thereafter remained wholly subservient to Moscow. However, the conservative Minsk leadership miscalculated when it backed the abortive coup by hard-liners in Moscow in August 1991. In the immediate aftermath, many party officials were ousted, independence from the USSR was declared, and the party itself was suspended, its property being nationalized. The party was subsequently relegalized as the Party of Communists of Belarus (PKB, below) and backed the ouster of reformist head of state Stanislau Shushkevich in January 1994. Embracing the concept of multipartyism, the PKB contested the mid-1994 presidential elections in its own right by supporting Vasil NOVIKAU, who placed last of six in the first round with only 4.6 percent of the vote. Nevertheless, the Communists' strong organization enabled them to win 42 seats in the 1995 Assembly election, a plurality that later rose to 44 because of accessions by independents.

Tensions in the party were revealed in September 1996 when First Secretary Syarhey Kalyakin was publicly criticized by several other party leaders for aligning with opponents of President Lukashenka. The factionalization culminated with a pro-Lukashenka group headed by Victar CHYKIN readopting the KPB designation at a congress in November, while Kalyakin's supporters continued to operate as the PKB. The KPB subsequently endorsed the president's push for reintegration with Russia, and in 1998 Chykin was chosen as leader of the BPPU. Nevertheless, at its August 2000 congress the party paradoxically claimed to be part of the opposition. At the October 2004 general election the KPB won eight seats in the House of Representatives.

Leader: Tatsyana HOLUBEVA (Chair).

Liberal Democratic Party of Belarus (*Liberalna-Demakratychnaya Partya Belarusi*—LDPB). Registered in March 1994 under the leadership of Vasil KRYVENKA, the LDPB views itself as the Belarusan counterpart of Russia's ultranationalist Liberal Democratic Party and therefore advocates close links with Russia. It subsequently allied with pro-Lukashenka forces as a founding member of the BPPU. By March 1999, however, responding in part to what it considered unfair official tactics against its candidates for local soviets, the party was distancing itself from other presidential supporters, claiming that democratic elections were impossible.

The LDPB initially refused to participate in the opposition boycott of the October 2000 House of Representatives election, but it withdrew from the voting before the second round because of alleged electoral violations. It subsequently announced that it would rejoin the opposition Coordinating Council. Reelected chair of the party at a congress in August 2000, Syarhey Haydukevich described himself as Lukashenka's "very decent rival" for the presidency in 2001, and in late November he announced plans to create a center-left electoral bloc, the New Belarus Unity, to support his candidacy. At the September 2001 poll he officially won only 2.5 percent of the vote.

At a September 2003 extraordinary convention, supporters of the party's deputy chair, Aleh MARKEVICH, voted their opposition to Haydukevich's leadership, but the Ministry of Justice subsequently ruled in the chair's favor. At a December 2003 convention the attendees voiced support for Haydukevich, reelected him chair, and expelled Markevich and others. The LDPB won one House seat in October 2004. In 2005 Haydukevich announced that he would seek the presidency again in 2006. At the balloting he finished third, with 3.5 percent of the vote.

Leaders: Syarhey HAYDUKEVICH (Sergei GAIDUKEVICH, Chair), Uladzimir KARUNAS (Deputy Chair).

"Five-Plus" Parties

Belarusan Labor Party (*Belaruskaya Partya Pratsy*—BPP). The BPP was established in 1993. Although the Supreme Court canceled its registration in August 2004 over technical irregularities, party leader Alyaksandr Bukhvostaw remained a principal participant in the Five-Plus coalition and later in the Permanent Council of Democratic Forces. Bukhvostaw, also a leader of the country's independent trade union movement, headed the initiative group in support of the unified opposition's 2006 presidential candidate, Alyaksandr Milinkevich.

Leader: Alyaksandr BUKHVOSTAW.

Belarusan Popular Front "Revival" (*Narodni Front Belarusi "Adradzhennie"*—NFB-A). The NFB-A was launched in June 1989 at a conference in Vilnius, Lithuania, of pro-independence groups. They chose as their leader Zyanon Paznyak, an archaeologist who in 1988 had published evidence of mass graves found at Kurapaty, near Minsk, on the site of a detention/execution camp established on Stalin's orders in 1937. The NFB-A defines itself as a broad popular movement with a "closely integrated" political party, the **Party of the Belarusan Popular Front,** which was established in 1993.

In the April 1990 Supreme Soviet elections in Belarus, the NFB-A won only 34 of 360 seats against an entrenched Communist hierarchy. In August 1991 it welcomed the declaration of independence. Remaining in opposition, the NFB-A attacked the slow pace of political and economic reform and then opposed the presidential constitution introduced in March 1994, on the grounds that a democratic parliament had not yet been elected. It also opposed the treaty on monetary union with Russia and participation in the CIS security pact. In the direct presidential poll of June–July 1994, Paznyak drew only a 13.9 percent vote share and was eliminated in the first round. The Front failed to win parliamentary representation in 1995.

The issuance of a warrant for his arrest after an antigovernment demonstration in April 1996 caused NFB-A Chair Paznyak to flee abroad. Granted asylum by the United States, he was reelected chair in absentia at the party congress in June 1997 and later agreed to serve as the NFB-A standard-bearer in the controversial symbolic presidential election in May 1999.

A major split in the party occurred following a July 31–August 1, 1999, congress, at which neither Paznyak nor his principal challenger, Deputy Chair Vintsuk Vyachorka, received sufficient votes to resolve a leadership dispute occasioned by Paznyak's continuing exile and his alleged authoritarianism. With another leadership vote expected in October, the party ruptured; at a congress on September 26, 1999, the Paznyak supporters "renamed" the party the Conservative-Christian Party of the BNF (KKhP-NFB, below) and continued to claim leadership of the NFB-A. A month later the NFB-A elected Vyachorka as its new chair.

In 2005 Vyachorka was one of the early supporters behind Alyaksandr Milinkevich's quest for the presidency in 2006.

Leaders: Vintsuk VYACHORKA (Chair), Yury KHADYKA (Deputy Chair).

Belarusan Social Democratic Assembly (*Belaruskaya Satsyal-Demakratychnaya Hramada—* BSDH). The BSDH held its founding congress in February 1998 under the leadership of former Supreme Council chair Stanislau Shushkevich, who called for restoration of the 1994 constitution. The new formation attracted many members of the Belarusan National Party (*Belaruskaya Natsyanalnaya Partya—*BNP), including its chair, Anatol Astapenka. (The BNP was not reregistered in 1999.)

In 2003 the United Social Democratic Party (USDP), led by Alyaksey Karol, merged into the BSDH. Karol's party had been denied registration following its August 2002 formation through merger of a faction of the Belarusan Women's Party "Hope" (below) and the unregistered Belarusan Social Democratic Party (*Belaruskaya Satsyal-Demakratychnaya Partya—*BSDP). The BSDP, dating from December 2001, had been formed by Karol and other defectors from the BSDP-NH (below).

In April 2005, over Shushkevich's objection, elements of the BSDH voted to merge with the BSDP-NH. Shushkevich's supporters ultimately retained control of the party, however, and he continued his efforts to seek the presidency in 2006. One of four candidates selected to vie for the endorsement of the unified opposition, Shushkevich withdrew before the secret balloting by the National Congress of Democratic Forces in October 2005.

Leaders: Stanislau SHUSHKEVICH (Chair), Anatol ASTAPENKA and Alyaksey KAROL (Deputy Chairs).

Party of Communists of Belarus (*Partya Kamunistau Belaruskaya—*PKB). The PKB originated as the refashioned Soviet-era Communist Party, but in November 1996 a major split occurred over whether to support President Lukashenka. As a result, the Lukashenka supporters became the Communist Party of Belarus (KPB, above), with the oppositionist faction retaining the PKB designation.

While not opposed to closer ties with Russia, the PKB rejects Soviet-style rule and loss of Belarusan sovereignty. It has called for democratic reforms, including reduction of presidential powers and transfer of authority to soviets. It condemned the 2000 House of Representatives election as a "farce," despite polling better than expected. Party leader Syarhey Kalyakin was initially a presidential candidate in 2001 but withdrew in a show of unity behind Vladimir Goncharik.

Looking toward the 2006 presidential race, Kalyakin was again named as the party's preferred candidate. Following the October 2005 decision of the unified opposition to support Alyaksandr Milinkevich, Kalyakin became a leading figure in the Milinkevich campaign.

Leaders: Syarhey KALYAKIN (Chair), Alena SKRYHAN and Valery UKHNALYOV (Central Committee Secretaries).

United Civic Party of Belarus (*Abyadnanaya Hramadzyanskaya Partya Belarusi*—AHPB). The promarket AHPB was founded in October 1995 as a merger of several groups—most notably the professional/technocratic United Democratic Party of Belarus (*Abyadnanaya Demakratychnaya Partya Belarusi*—ADPB), led by Alyaksandr DABRAVOLSKY—that had contested the first round of that year's legislative balloting in an alliance called the Civic Accord Bloc. The leader of the merged party, Stanislau BAHDANKEVICH, had the previous month been dismissed as president of the National Bank after disagreeing with President Lukashenka's pro-Russian policies. (The ADPB itself had been formed in 1990 as a merger of three prodemocracy groupings, including Communists for Perestroika and the Democratic Party, and had initially been a constituent of the opposition NFB-A.) In the 1995 legislative balloting the AHPB won 9 seats in its own right, forming the Civic Action parliamentary group, which rose to 18 members with the adhesion of "unaffiliated" deputies.

In February 1996 the AHPB entered into an alliance with the small Belarusan Christian Democratic Unity (*Belaruskaya Khrystsiyanska-Demokratychnaya Zluchnasts*—BKDZ), which had been founded in 1991 as successor to the pre-Soviet Christian Democratic Association. On January 8, 1997, the party hosted the first meeting of the opposition "shadow cabinet," the PCG-NEC. It subsequently continued its anti-Lukashenka stance, organizing demonstrations against the government and boycotting the 2000 legislative election.

Anatol Lyabedzka was reelected party chair in May 2004 and was subsequently endorsed as the party's 2006 presidential candidate. At the opposition's National Congress in October 2005, he finished second to Alyaksandr Milinkevich, 391 votes to 399, in balloting to select the unified opposition's candidate.

Leaders: Anatol LYABEDZKA (Anatol LEBEDKO, Chair), Yaraslaw RAMANCHUK (Deputy Chair).

Belarusan Ecological Party of the Greens (BEPG). The BEPG was established in June 1998 by merger of the Belarusan Ecological Party (*Belaruskaya Ekalagichnaya Partya*—BEP) and the Belarusan Green Party (*Belaruskaya Partya Zyalenych*—BPZ). In addition to supporting the rational use of natural resources, it advocates human rights and preferential funding for health, education, and social programs. In 2004 the party supported the Five-Plus alliance.

Leaders: Mikalay KARTASH, Mikhail FRYDLAND.

"Free Belarus" Parties

Belarusan Social Democratic Party "People's Assembly" (*Belaruskaya Satsyal-Demakratychnaya Partya "Narodnaya Hramada"*—BSDP-NH). The BSDP was founded in 1991 as a latter-day revival of the Revolutionary *Hramada* Party (founded in 1902), which spearheaded the early movement for the creation of a Belarusan state but was outlawed following declaration of the Soviet Socialist Republic in January 1919. The revived party participated initially in the opposition NFB-A, supporting the latter's unsuccessful candidate in the 1994 presidential poll. It contested the 1995 legislative election in its own right, winning 2 seats and later increasing its parliamentary group to 15 members. In 1996 it merged with the Party of Popular Accord (PPA), which dated from 1992.

The party organized unsanctioned anti-Lukashenka rallies in 1996–1999, for which party leader Statkevich was jailed repeatedly. Tactical differences with other opposition parties emerged in 2000, with Statkevich opposing the boycott of the October legislative election and advocating nomination of a single opposition candidate—one acceptable to Communists and nationalists alike—to run against Lukashenka in 2001.

In December 2004, seeking to bring together the country's moderately leftist parties, Statkevich led formation of an organizational committee for a "United Social Democratic Party of Belarus." Other participants in the unification effort included the BSDP-NH's principal Free Belarus partner, namely the Belarusan Women's Party "Hope" (below), and the civic organization *Perspectiva*. In the same month, partly as a result of his allegedly autocratic style and his strong support for Belarusan EU membership, dissident elements within the BSDP-NH expelled Statkevich, whose supporters then held a competing conference and expelled several key Statkevich opponents. In January 2005 the Ministry of Justice ruled in favor of the opponents, who then elevated Anatol LYAWKOVICH (LEVKOVICH) to chair. In February 2005, however, Statkevich's supporters reinstated him and endorsed his candidacy for president in 2006.

In April 2005 elements of the BSDP-NH and the BSDH voted to merge as the Belarusan Social Democratic Party "Assembly" (BSDP-H, below), with Alyaksandr Kazulin as chair, but Statkevich retained control of the BSDP-NH majority. In May he was convicted of participating in illegal protests against the conduct of the October 2004 election and was sentenced to three years' detention and community service. He was transferred to house arrest in November 2005, but the conviction meant that he was ineligible to run for president in 2006.

Leaders: Mikalay STATKEVICH (Chair), Alyaksandr ARASTOVICH (First Deputy Chair).

Belarusan Women's Party "Hope" (*Belaruskaya Partya Zhanchyn "Nadzeya"*—BPZ-N). Founded in 1994, the social democratic BPZ-N split in August 2002 over the issue of unification with the unregistered Belarusan Social Democratic Party (BSDP—see the BSDH, above). Competing party congresses resulted, after which supporters of theretofore Women's Party leader Valyantsina PALEVIKOVA followed her into the new United Social Democratic Party (USDP, also under the BSDH). (After the government refused to register the new party, Palevikova ultimately joined the AHPB.)

In September 2002 the Ministry of Justice declared that the Palevikova faction had not had the authority to disband the BPZ-N. The ministry instead granted recognition to the more government-supportive faction, which had the active backing of trade union leader Leanid KOZIK, a former deputy head of the presidential administration. That faction had elected Valyantsina Matusevich as Palevikova's successor. Subsequently, however, the BPZ-N returned to active opposition and helped form the Free Belarus alliance. After the October 2004 election the BPZ-N joined the BSDP-NH in seeking to unify the country's social democratic parties.

Leader: Valyantsina MATUSEVICH (President).

Other Parties

Belarusan Patriotic Party (*Belaruskaya Patryatychny Partya*—BPP). The BPP was launched in November 1994 as the Belarusan Patriotic Movement (*Belaruski Patryatychny Rukh*—BPR) in support of President Lukashenka, who had been elected earlier in the year as an independent advocating anticorruption, economic reform, and an economic and military alliance with Russia. Ideologically close to the radical Russian nationalist Vladimir Zhirinovsky, the BPR was officially credited with winning only 1 seat in the 1995 legislative balloting; however, many of the 95 "unaffiliated" deputies belonged to the presidential tendency and subsequently formed the dominant Accord (*Zgody*) group in the Supreme Council.

The BPR adopted its present name at its fourth congress, in October 1996. It continues to be staunchly pro-Lukashenka and pro-Russian.

Leader: Nikolai ULAKHOVICH (Chair).

Belarusan Social Democratic Party "Assembly" (*Belaruskaya Satsyal-Demokratychnaya Party "Hramada"*—BSDP-H). Formation of the BSDP-H, ostensibly by merger of the BSDH and the BSDP-NH, was announced in April 2005 under the leadership of Alyaksandr Kazulin, a former rector of Belarusan State University who had recently joined the BSDP-NH. The "merger" was opposed by BSDH leader Stanislau Shushkevich as well as by BSDP-NH leader Mikalay Statkevich, who had originally supported the idea but had since found himself fighting a challenge to his leadership. In the end, Statkevich and Shushkevich prevailed, leaving Kazulin's supporters, including former BSDH deputy chair Mechyslaw Hryb, with a considerably diminished organization. In September 2005 the Permanent Council of Democratic Forces, preparing to unite behind a single opposition candidate for president in 2006, rejected Kazulin and his party's participation at the October National Congress of Democratic Forces, the BSDH having accused him of playing a divisive role. Kazulin nonetheless continued his quest for the presidency and was officially registered as a candidate in February 2006. He finished last in the four-way contest, with only 2.2 percent of the vote.

Leaders: Alyaksandr KAZULIN, Mechyslaw HRYB (Mechislav GRIB).

Conservative-Christian Party of the Belarusan Popular Front (*Konservativnaya Khrystsiyanska Partiya–Narodni Front Belarusi*—KKhP-NFB). The strongly nationalist KKhP emerged from a congress held on September 26, 1999, by supporters of Zyanon Paznyak within the NFB-A. It was registered as a party on February 28, 2000. The party staunchly opposes the Lukashenka regime and union with Russia and has attacked OSCE efforts to mediate between the opposition and the government as lending legitimacy to the present regime. The KKhP was a principal organizer of an "All-Belarusan Congress" that met on July 29, 2000, in Minsk and condemned any agreements that would result in a loss of Belarusan independence and sovereignty. Paznyak was reelected party leader in December 2003.

The party boycotted the October 2004 election, the only significant opposition party to do so. As expected, Paznyak later stated that he would run for president in 2006, but in January 2006, from exile in the United States, he endorsed conducting a "people's vote." The plan called for anti-Lukashenka voters to cast fake ballots, leave with the real ballots, and submit the latter to an independent commission as evidence of opposition to the incumbent.

Leaders: Zyanon PAZNYAK (Chair, in exile), Yuryy BELENKI and Syarhey PAPKOW (Deputy Chairs).

Republican Party of Labor and Justice (*Respublikanskaya Partya Pratsy i Spravyadlivasti*—RPPS). Established in 1993, the RPPS won one seat in the 1995 Supreme Council election. In 1998 it participated in formation of the BPPU. At the 2004 election the RPPS lost its only House seat.

Leader: Anatol NETYLKIN.

Social Democratic Party of Popular Accord (*Satsyal Demakratychnaya Partya Narodnay Zgody*—SDPNZ). The SDPNZ was formed in 1997 by Leanid SECHKA and other former members of the Party of Popular Accord who had opposed the latter's 1996 absorption by the BSDP-NH. It rejected participation in the opposition boycott of the October 2000 election and was credited with winning two seats in the House of Representatives after the first round. The party failed to win any seats in 2004.

Leader: Syarhey YARMAK.

Cabinet

As of March 15, 2006

Prime Minister	Syarhey Sidorsky
First Deputy Prime Minister	Uladzimir Syamashka
Deputy Prime Ministers	Ivan Bambiza
	Vasil Dalhalyow
	Vasil Hapeyew
	Andrei Kabyakov
	Alyaksandr Kosinets

Ministers

Agriculture and Food	Leanid Rusak
Architecture and Construction	Genadz Kurachkin
Communications and Information Technology	Uladzimir Hancharenko
Culture	Uladzimir Matvejchuk
Defense	Col. Gen. Leanid Maltsau
Economy	Mikalay Zaychanka
Education	Alyaksandr Radzkow
Emergency Situations	Col. Enver Baryyew
Energy	Alyaksandr Aheyew
Finance	Mikalay Korbut
Foreign Affairs	Syarhey Martynaw
Forestry	Pyotr Syamashka
Health (Acting)	Viktar Rudenka
Housing and Municipal Services	Uladzimir Belakhvostau
Industry	Anatol Rusetski
Information	Uladzimir Rusakevich
Interior	Maj. Gen. Uladzimir Naumau
Justice	Viktar Halavanov
Labor and Social Security	Antanina Morava [f]
Natural Resources and Environmental Protection	Lyavontsy Kharuzhyk
Revenue and Taxes	Hanna Dzyayko
Sport and Tourism	Alyaksandr Grigorov
Statistics and Analysis	Uladzimir Zinowski
Trade	Alyaksandr Ivankow
Transportation and Communications	Uladzimir Sasnowski

[f] = female

In January 2005 Pavel Sevyarynets stepped down as leader of the **Young Front** (*Malady Front*) youth organization in favor of new cochairs, Syarhey BAKHUN and Dzmitryy DASHKE-VICH. Sevyarynets remained involved in the Permanent Council of Democratic Forces while attempting to form a new Christian Democratic party. In May 2005 he was sentenced to three years' detention and community service for organizing illegal demonstrations against the conduct of the October 2004 election.

The government has denied registration to the **Party of Freedom and Progress** (*Partya Svabody i Pragrzsu*—PSP), which held its founding congress in November 2003 under the leadership of Uladzimir NAVASYAD, who at that time was a member of the House of Representatives. In May 2005 the PSP held its third founding congress as part of its effort to meet requirements for registration, but in October the Ministry of Justice again ruled against it. Navasyad also has been associated with the **Public Youth Organization "Civil Forum"** as well as the Free Belarus coalition.

Other recently active parties include the **Belarusan Green Party** (*Belaruskaya Partya Zyaleny*—BPZ), led by Aleh HRAMYKA; the pro-Lukashenka **Belarusan Social-Sporting Party** (*Belaruskaya Satsyalna-Sportyunaya Partya*—BSSP), which won one seat in the House of Representatives in 2000 but none in 2004; and the **Republican Party** (*Respublikanskaya Partya*—RP), founded in 1994 and led by Uladzimir BELOZOR.

Legislature

The controversial amended constitution of November 1996 provided for abolishing the unicameral Supreme Council and establishing a two-chamber **National Assembly** (*Natsionalnoye Sobrani*) consisting of a House of Representatives and a Council of the Republic. Although the referendum approving the constitution was declared "nonbinding" by the Constitutional Court and denounced as illegitimate by some opposition parties, a majority of the Supreme Council members on November 28 voted to abolish the Council and appointed themselves to the new House of Representatives. However, an anti-Lukashenka rump subsequently continued to meet as the Supreme Council, arguing that it remained the legitimate legislature.

Council of the Republic (*Soviet Respubliki*). The upper house has 64 members: 8 elected by local soviets from each of the country's 6 regions and the municipality of Minsk, plus 1 appointed by the president from each division. The most recent elections occurred in August–November 2004, with the first session of the new Council opening on November 15 (although the president had not yet named all of his appointees).

Speaker: Henadz NAVITSKI.

House of Representatives (*Palata Predstaviteley*). The constitutional revisions of November 1996 provided for direct election of a 110-member lower house for a four-year term. More than 100 members of the former Supreme Council met for the first time as the new House shortly after voting to abolish the Supreme Council on November 28, 1996.

The most recent election took place on October 17, 2004, with runoff balloting in one district on October 27 and a repeat election on March 20, 2005, in another district where neither of the candidates in the initial balloting had received 50 percent support. The vast majority of the 109 deputies elected in October were Lukashenka loyalists who had run without party affiliation. The Central Electoral Commission described 12 of the winners as party candidates: Communist Party of Belarus, 8; Agrarian Party of Belarus, 3; Liberal Democratic Party of Belarus, 1.

Speaker: Uladzimir KANAPLYOW.

Communications

Although media independence and the freedom to disseminate information are protected by the constitution and in law, the government continues to control electronic news transmission and newspaper distribution. Independent, opposition publications have been subjected to a variety of threats and pressures, most commonly allegations of libeling or defaming President Lukashenka and other officials. As a consequence, journalists have been jailed and publications fined. On other occasions printing equipment has been confiscated by tax authorities and licenses denied. In the two months preceding the October 2004 legislative election the Ministry of Information temporarily banned a dozen publications, citing technical violations of their registration certificates.

Press

The following are published daily in Minsk in Belarusan, unless otherwise noted: *Sovetskaya Belorussiya* (Soviet Byelorussia, 430,000), government organ, in Russian; *Respublika* (Republic,

120,000), government organ, in Belarusan and Russian; *Narodnaya Hazeta* (People's Newspaper, 90,000), government organ, in Belarusan and Russian; *Vechernii Minsk* (Evening Minsk, 90,000), in Russian; *Zvyazda* (Star, 90,000), government organ; *Dobry Vechar* (Good Evening, 40,000), independent; *Narodnaya Volya* (People's Will, 27,000), independent, in Belarusan and Russian. There also are a number of party organs, including *Naviny BNF* (Belarusan Popular Front News). In addition to *Narodnaya Volya*, which has been repeatedly targeted by the government, leading opposition publications include *Belorusskaya Delovaya Gazeta* (Belarusan Business News), which publishes four times a week.

News Agencies

The domestic facility is the Belarus Information Agency (Belta, originally the Belarus Telegraphy Agency), headquartered in Minsk. The Belarusan Information Company (BelaPAN) also provides news and other services.

Broadcasting and Computing

Broadcasting continues to be dominated by the National State Television and Radio Company. Smaller, private stations broadcast in the larger cities. In 2003, transmission facilities previously used by major Russian TV channels were assigned by the government to regional usage. There were approximately 3.8 million television receivers and 1.4 million Internet users in 2003. The government is the only legal Internet service provider.

Intergovernmental Representation

Ambassador to the U.S.
Mikhail KHVOSTOV

U.S. Ambassador to Belarus
George A. KROL

Permanent Representative to the UN
Andrei DAPKYUNAS

IGO Memberships (Non-UN)
CEI, CIS, Interpol, IOM, NAM, OSCE, PCA, WCO

BELGIUM

KINGDOM OF BELGIUM

Koninkrijk België (Dutch)
Royaume de Belgique (French)
Königreich Belgien (German)

The Country

Wedged between France, Germany, and the Netherlands, densely populated Belgium lies at the crossroads of Western Europe. Its location has contributed to a history of ethnic diversity, as manifested by linguistic and cultural dualism between the Dutch-speaking north (Flanders) and the French-speaking south (Wallonia). The Flemings and Walloons respectively constitute 58 percent and 31 percent of the total population, with 11 percent being effectively bilingual; most of the remainder are a small German-speaking minority located along the eastern border. In contrast to the linguistic division, 75 percent of the population is Roman Catholic, with small minorities of Jews, Protestants, and Muslims.

The economy is largely dominated by the service sector, which provides 74 percent of GDP and employs 73 percent of the nation's labor force. Belgium's industry, responsible for less than 24 percent of GDP, was traditionally concentrated in textiles, steel, and glass, but emphasis has shifted to production of machinery, fabricated metals, food, and chemicals. Agriculture occupies less than 2 percent of the labor force and accounts for only 1.4 percent of GDP, although it supplies three-quarters of food requirements. Unemployment has hovered around 8 percent since 2000, dipping to 7.9 percent in 2004 but projected to rise to 8.2 percent in 2006.

A substantial regional imbalance exists: most modern industries (mainly chemicals) and services (mostly of the high-technology variety) are disproportionately located in Flanders, while older, declining enterprises tend to be concentrated in French-speaking Wallonia. A source of regional and ethnic tension, this disparity was accentuated by the move to a federal governmental structure in the early 1990s, despite government efforts to reduce the imbalance.

Moderate but steady economic growth prevailed during most of the two decades after World War II, but the annual increase in GDP fell to an average of less than 2 percent in the decade following

the OPEC-induced "oil shock" of 1973–1974, one of the lowest rates among industrialized nations. Higher growth in the late 1980s was accompanied by a persistent 10 percent unemployment rate and was followed by recession, with the economy contracting by 1 percent in 1993 and with unemployment rising to 12 percent. Growth of some 2 percent a year resumed in 1994–1995, and expansion continued at a solid rate throughout the rest of the decade.

GDP grew by an average of only 1 percent annually in 2001–2003, before improving by 2.4 percent in 2004. Increases in oil prices and reduced exports caused the country's GDP growth to fall again to an estimated 1.5 percent in 2005. The International Monetary Fund (IMF), however, projects a GDP growth rate of 2.1 percent for 2006. Throughout this period, Belgium has won praise from the IMF for its ability to maintain a balanced federal budget.

Government and Politics

Political Background

After centuries of Spanish and Austrian rule and briefer periods of French administration, Belgium was incorporated into the Kingdom of the Netherlands by the Congress of Vienna in 1815. Independence was proclaimed on October 4, 1830, and Prince LEOPOLD of Saxe-Coburg was elected king in 1831, although Belgian autonomy was not formally recognized by the Netherlands until 1839. In the 20th century, the country was subjected to German invasion and occupation during the two world wars.

Since World War II, Belgium has been governed by a series of administrations based on one or more of its three major political groups: Christian Democratic, Socialist, and Liberal. Beginning in the early 1960s, however, the traditional system was threatened by ethnic and linguistic antagonism between the Dutch- and French-speaking regions. By a series of constitutional amendments in 1970–1971, substantial central government powers were to be devolved to regional councils for Flanders, Wallonia, and Brussels (nominally bilingual but in fact largely French speaking), while German speakers also were recognized as forming a distinct cultural community.

Under the Egmont Pact of 1977, Belgium's major parties agreed, after years of discord, on the establishment of a federal system based on Flanders, Wallonia, and Brussels. However, in August 1978 the Supreme Court ruled that certain aspects of the plan were unconstitutional, and on October 11 the government of Prime Minister Léo TINDEMANS was forced to resign. At the ensuing general election of December 17 the distribution of seats in the House of Representatives remained virtually unchanged, and on April 3, 1979, a new center-left government was formed under Dr. Wilfried MARTENS of the Christian People's Party (*Christelijke Volkspartij*—CVP) that included five of the six participating parties in the outgoing government.

In early January 1980 Prime Minister Martens, bowing to militant Flemish pressure, announced the postponement of self-government for Brussels while committing his government to the establishment of regional bodies for Flanders and Wallonia. In response, representatives of the Democratic Front of French Speakers (*Front Démocratique des Francophones*—FDF) withdrew on January 16, leaving the government without the two-thirds majority needed for constitutional revision and forcing its resignation on April 9. Nonetheless, Martens succeeded in forming a "grand coalition" on May 18 that included representatives of the two Liberal parties—the Flemish Liberals and Democrats (*Vlaamse Liberalen en Demokraten*—VLD) and the Liberal Reformation Party (*Parti Réformateur Libéral*—PRL)—as well as the CVP; the Christian Social Party (*Parti Social Chrétien*—PSC); and two Socialist formations, the *Parti Socialiste* (PS) and the *Socialistische Partij* (SP). Requisite constitutional majorities thus having been restored, the government was able to secure parliamentary approval during July and August 1980 to establish councils for the Dutch- and French-speaking regions.

Alleviation of the constitutional crisis brought to the fore a number of long-simmering differences on

Political Status: Independence proclaimed October 4, 1830; monarchical constitution of 1831 most recently revised in 1970.

Area: 11,781 sq. mi. (30,513 sq. km.).

Population: 10,296,350 (2001C); 10,454,000 (2005E).

Major Urban Centers (2005E): BRUSSELS (urban area, 999,000), Antwerp (urban area, 457,000), Ghent (230,000), Charleroi (200,000), Liége (185,000), Bruges (117,000), Namur (106,000).

Official Languages: Dutch, French, German.

Monetary Unit: Euro (market rate July 1, 2006: 1 euro = $1.28US).

Sovereign: King ALBERT II; ascended the throne on August 9, 1993, following the death of his brother, King BAUDOUIN.

Heir to the Throne: Prince PHILIPPE, son of the king.

Prime Minister: Guy VERHOFSTADT (Flemish Liberals and Democrats), designated to form a new government by the king on June 23, 1999, following the election of June 13; sworn in at the head of a six-party cabinet on July 12, 1999, succeeding Jean-Luc DEHAENE (Christian People's Party), who had tendered his resignation on June 14; sworn in at the head of a new government on July 12, 2003, following the election of May 18.

economic and defense policies. As a result, the government resigned on October 4, 1980, and 12 days later Martens announced the formation of a center-left coalition (CVP, PSC, SP, and PS). On April 8, 1981, Martens stepped down as prime minister in favor of the CVP's Mark EYSKENS, but a general election on November 8 yielded little in the way of party realignment in either legislative house. Eventually, on December 17, Martens secured approval for a center-right administration that included both Liberal parties while excluding the Socialists. Having introduced an economic-austerity program, the coalition marginally increased its majority at parliamentary balloting on October 13, 1985, a new government (Martens's sixth) being sworn in on November 28.

In the late 1980s renewed linguistic controversy erupted over specifics of regionalization. Particularly controversial was the status of a group of villages in southeastern Flanders (Les Fourons/Voeren) whose French-speaking majority doggedly resisted the authority of the surrounding Dutch-speaking region. Amid fierce interparty discord, Martens was again forced to resign on October 15, 1987. At the ensuing election of December 13 the Christian parties lost ground, and the Socialists achieved a plurality for the first time since 1936. A 144-day impasse followed, with Martens responding on May 6, 1988, to the king's request to form a new five-party government that encompassed the Christian parties, the Socialists, and the Flemish nationalist People's Union (Volksunie—VU), while again excluding the Liberals.

In September 1991 the VU ministers withdrew over an arms export controversy. As a result, Prime Minister Martens stepped down for the seventh time, precipitating a general election on November 24, at which all four coalition parties lost seats without collateral gains by the opposition Liberal parties. Against a groundswell of anti-immigration sentiment, the main victor was the militant Flemish Bloc (Vlaams Blok—VB), which overtook the less extreme VU; two Ecologist parties also registered substantial gains. Another lengthy interregnum ensued before the CVP's Jean-Luc DEHAENE succeeded in forming a four-party Christian–Socialist administration (Belgium's 35th since World War II) on March 7, 1992.

Although the Dehaene government lacked the two-thirds parliamentary majority required to enact constitutional amendments, the St. Michael Accords of September 29, 1992, enabled it to win a historic vote on February 6, 1993; by dint of support from the VU and the Ecologists, it mustered the necessary House majority for a constitutional amendment transforming Belgium from a unitary state into a federation of its linguistic communities. The decision was formally confirmed by the House on July 14.

On July 31, 1993, a reign that had spanned more than four decades came to an end with the death of

King Baudouin, whose brother, Prince Albert of Liége, was crowned on August 9.

Belgium was saved from having to find a new prime minister when the Franco-German nomination of Dehaene as European Union (EU) Commission president was vetoed by Britain in June 1994 on the grounds that he was too federalist.

Meanwhile, the ruling coalition had been weakened by the Agusta-Dassault scandal, involving the Socialist parties' alleged receipt of some $3.2 million in kickbacks for expediting the award of military contracts to Italian and French firms in 1988–1989. The allegations later extended to the Flemish Socialists, notably to former prime minister Guy SPITAELS and to Willy CLAES, who had been economics minister in 1988 and who was appointed NATO secretary general in September 1994. Accordingly, the Agusta affair figured prominently in the campaign for early general elections held on May 21, 1995, the first under the new federal constitution. The government parties again secured about 50 percent of the vote among them, and Dehaene was reappointed prime minister on June 23 at the head of the same four-party coalition, although with some personnel changes. The government subsequently faced severe difficulties in attempting to meet the criteria for participation in the EU's Economic and Monetary Union (EMU), and related job and spending cuts precipitated widespread public-sector protest strikes in 1995 and 1996.

In October 1995 the Belgian lower house voted to lift the parliamentary immunity of Claes, so that he could be brought to trial on Agusta-Dassault affair charges. As a consequence, he resigned as NATO secretary general, and in December 1998 he and a dozen other individuals were convicted of corruption, with Claes receiving a suspended three-year sentence.

Not surprisingly, the 1999 national electoral campaign largely focused on high-level corruption and law enforcement concerns as well as on the merits of further devolution to Flanders, Wallonia, and Brussels. In late May, however, attention dramatically shifted with the revelation that for two months the government had delayed notifying the public that a factory had distributed animal feed contaminated by the chemical dioxin, a suspected carcinogen. Amid considerable confusion about the extent of the contamination and what steps were needed to ensure a safe food supply, the Dehaene government was voted out of office at balloting on June 10.

Dehaene's CVP lost 7 of the 29 lower house seats it had won in 1995, permitting the VLD, with 23 seats, to fashion a 94-seat, six-party majority coalition with the PS, SP, PRL, and two environmental parties, the Ecologists (*Ecologistes Confédérés pour l'Organisation de Luttes Originales—* ECOLO) and the Live Differently (*Anders Gaan Leven*—Agalev). The new prime minister, VLD leader Guy VERHOFSTADT, and his cabinet were sworn in on July 12. Following the general elections of May 18, 2003, Verhofstadt remained in office as head of another coalition government that comprised the VLD, PS, Socialist Party-Differently (*Socialistische Partij-Anders*—SP.A), Reformist Movement (*Mouvement Reformateur—* MR), and SPIRIT (*Sociaal, Progressief, International, Regionalistisch, Integraal-democratisch en Toekomstgericht*—SPIRIT).

Constitution and Government

Belgium's constitution of 1831 (as amended) provides for a constitutional monarchy with a parliamentary form of government (voting being compulsory). Executive power is theoretically exercised by the monarch, who is head of state, but actual power rests with the prime minister and his cabinet, both responsible to a bicameral legislature. The judicial system, based on the French model, is headed by the Court of Cassation, which has the power to review any judicial decision; it may not, however, pass on the constitutionality of legislation, for which advisory opinions may be sought from a special legal body, the Council of State. There also are assize courts, courts of appeal, and numerous courts of first instance and justices of the peace.

The ethnic-linguistic reorganization finally enacted in 1993 involved the creation of three self-governing regions, Dutch-speaking Flanders, French-speaking Wallonia, and bilingual Brussels, each with directly elected assemblies of 124 (including 6 from Brussels), 75, and 75 members, respectively. There also are cultural councils for the Dutch-speaking and French-speaking communities (the former being identical with the Flanders assembly and the latter being indirectly constituted by the Wallonia assembly members and 19 members of the Brussels assembly), as well as a 25-member directly elected cultural council for the small German-speaking minority in eastern Belgium. The regional governments of Flanders, Wallonia, and Brussels are responsible to the respective assemblies, exercising broad social and economic powers; only defense, foreign relations, and monetary policy are reserved to the federal government, the size of which has been reduced as responsibilities have been devolved to the regions. Also reduced, as of the 1995 election, was the size of the central legislature (see Legislature, below). Local administration is based on ten regions and nearly 600 communes.

On October 25, 2001, Princess MATHILDE gave birth to a daughter, Princess ELISABETH Thérése Marie Héléne, second in line to the throne after her father, Prince PHILIPPE. Male primogeniture had been eliminated from the law of succession in 1991.

Foreign Relations

Originally one of Europe's neutral powers, Belgium since World War II has been a leader in international cooperation. It was a founding member of the United Nations, NATO, the Benelux Union, and all of the major West European regional organizations. Its only overseas possession, the former Belgian Congo, became independent in 1960, while the Belgian-administered UN Trust Territory of Ruanda-Urundi became independent in 1962 as the two states of Rwanda and Burundi.

Belgium contributed to the U.S.-led multinational coalition that liberated Kuwait in early 1991. In September 1991 Belgian troops were sent to Zaire (now the Democratic Republic of the Congo)

to oversee the evacuation of Belgian nationals from that strife-torn state, the action marking an effective end to Belgium's close relationship with its former colony. Belgian nationals also came under serious threat when Rwanda descended into bloody anarchy in April 1994. After ten Belgian soldiers attached to the UN had been killed at Kigali airport, Belgian paratroopers were sent in to assist with the evacuation of foreign nationals.

The cornerstone of Belgium's external policy remains active participation in the EU. Having initially expressed some misgivings about the rapid reunification of Germany in 1990, Belgian political leaders agreed for the most part that European integration was the best means of preventing any revived threat from the country's powerful eastern neighbor. Belgium was a prime mover of the Schengen accord providing for the abolition of border controls between certain EU members, as inaugurated in March 1995, although in November 2000 the Verhofstadt government, responding to anti-immigrant sentiment and a rising number of asylum cases, announced that it favored tighter restrictions. (In the spring of 2005 the Parliament approved the proposed new EU constitution.)

In late 2001 the Verhofstadt government hailed a 35-country agreement on international diamond certification as a necessary step toward ending the illegal trafficking in so-called conflict or "blood" diamonds. In 2000 a UN report had criticized the Antwerp diamond market, the largest in the world, for "lax controls and regulations" that permitted gem transactions to finance wars in Africa. By the time of the 2001 agreement, Belgium had already signed certification agreements with Angola, Botswana, the Democratic Republic of the Congo, Guinea, and Sierra Leone.

The Verhofstadt administration sided with many other European governments in opposing the U.S./UK-led invasion of Iraq in 2003. However, relations with Washington subsequently improved when Belgium agreed to send fighter planes to Afghanistan to help provide security for elections.

Belgium irritated both the United States and Israel with its laws that allowed individuals to file cases in Belgian courts for crimes against

humanity by individuals outside of Belgian jurisdiction. Palestinians and Lebanese living in Belgium brought a case against Israeli Prime Minister Ariel Sharon in 2001, and cases were brought
against U.S. President George W. Bush and British
Prime Minister Tony Blair in 2003 in connection
to the war in Iraq. The cases were all ultimately
dismissed and the law was amended in 2004 to
make such charges more difficult to bring. Under
the revised law, complainants must show a direct
link between themselves and the alleged crime.
In addition, if the alleged crimes occurred outside
Belgium and the accused are not Belgian, the government can refer the cases to the International
Criminal Court in the Netherlands.

Current Issues

In July 1999 Guy Verhofstadt became Belgium's
first Liberal prime minister in more than a century.
His "blue-red-green" coalition cut broadly across
ideological lines, bringing together the rightist Liberals, the Socialists, and the Greens, while excluding the Christian Democrats from the national government for the first time in 40 years. As part of a
lengthy coalition agreement, the government committed itself to tax cuts, a reduction in the public-
debt burden, a ten-year phase-out of nuclear energy
beginning in 2015, deregulation of the electricity
industry, and improved health care.

Although the new government survived its first
year in office without encountering a new crisis,
the electorate remained fractured along ethnic, linguistic, regional, and ideological lines. At the October 2000 local elections most of the government
parties fared well, but the far-right Flemish Bloc
(VB) captured the headlines by achieving larger
gains, including winning one-third of the votes in
Antwerp, the country's second-largest city. Often
compared ideologically to Austria's Freedom Party,
the VB had campaigned on a separatist and anti-
immigrant platform at a time when Belgians were
increasingly concerned about the steady influx of
aliens.

Prime Minister Verhofstadt's refusal to send
troops to support U.S.-UK actions in Iraq appar-

ently contributed to the success of the VLD and
its coalition partners in the May 2003 general elections. Unemployment, national security, and taxes
also played prominent roles in the campaign, although the leading parties differed only slightly
in their approach to those issues. Not surprisingly,
those parties tended to avoid discussion of immigration and ethnicity. (Immigrants, many of them
Muslims, from Africa and the Middle East were
estimated to comprise about 5 percent of the Belgian population, raising questions regarding criteria for citizenship, possible limitations on immigration, and the need to balance immigration policies
with national security and antiterrorist concerns.)
However, the VB eagerly focused on those issues,
quickly rising from a minor party (with only about
10 percent of the vote in 1999) to being the largest
party in Flanders (with 25 percent of the vote in
2003). (For subsequent developments regarding the
VB, see Flemish Interest, under Political Parties,
below.)

Addressing another dominant concern (the aging workforce and the related issue of rising pension costs), the government in 2005 announced
plans to raise the minimum retirement age from
58 to 60 and also limit certain longstanding retirement benefits. In response, hundreds of thousands of workers in October initiated the first general strike in 12 years. The nation's three largest
unions subsequently threatened additional strikes,
arguing that the government had not done enough
to bring young people into the workforce. Complicating matters for the administration was an IMF
analysis that wages were rising more quickly in Belgium than in neighboring countries, which the IMF
argued might erode Belgium's "competitiveness."

Political Parties

Belgium's leading parties were long divided
into French- and Dutch-speaking sections, which
tended to subscribe to common programs for general elections. Beginning in the late 1960s, the
cleavages became more pronounced, leading eventually to formal separation as the country moved
to a federal structure. Collaterally, the dominance

of the three principal groupings (Christian Democratic, Socialist, and Liberal) has been eroded somewhat by an increase in the strength of numerous smaller ethnic and special-interest groups.

Government Parties

Flemish Liberals and Democrats (*Vlaamse Liberalen en Demokraten*—VLD). In 1961 Belgium's traditional Liberal Party changed its name to the Party for Freedom and Progress (*Partij voor Vrijheid en Vooruitgang*—PVV), its Flemish wing becoming autonomous in 1970. Having participated in various coalitions in the 1970s, both the PVV and its Walloon counterpart were in government with the CVP and PSC in 1981–1988. They were regarded as occupying the coalition's right wing, in part because of their reluctance to accept federalization. In the 1991 Chamber balloting the PVV increased its vote share to 11.9 percent but remained in opposition. In November 1992 it opted for the VLD designation, to which it appended "Citizens' Party" (*Partij van de Burger*).

A smaller-than-anticipated rise to 13.1 percent of the Chamber vote (for 21 seats) in 1995 prompted the resignation of Guy Verhofstadt as party president. However, in June 1997 he was reelected as party president after only one round of voting, and he completed his comeback by being named prime minister after the June 1999 election, at which the VLD led all parties with 14.3 percent of the Chamber vote and 23 seats.

During the 2003 election campaign, the VLD continued to emphasize deregulation and tax reduction, while arguing that new EU legislation should demonstrate it would not diminish the purchasing power of European citizens or have a negative impact on employment.

In 2004 the VLD did poorly in regional elections, falling from second to third place among Flemish political parties.

In a federal cabinet reshuffle in July 2004, VLD Chair Karel DE GUCHT was made minister for foreign affairs, replacing Louis MICHEL. Former Flemish Prime Minister Bart Somers took over as party president.

Leaders: Guy VERHOFSTADT (Prime Minister), Bart SOMERS (President), Fientje MOERMAN (Secretary General).

Socialist Party (*Parti Socialiste*—PS). Until formal separation in October 1978 the PS was the dominant French-speaking wing of the historic Belgian Socialist Party (*Parti Socialiste Belge*—PSB), an evolutionary Marxist grouping organized in 1885 as the *Parti Ouvrier Belge*. Both the PS and the SP (below) have trade-union roots and are essentially pragmatic in outlook, concentrating on social welfare and industrial democracy issues within a free-enterprise context.

Becoming the largest lower-house bloc in the 1987 elections (for the first time since 1936), the two Socialist parties joined a center-left coalition but lost ground in the 1991 balloting, the PS vote slipping to 15.6 percent. It remained in office and also headed the regional governments of Wallonia and Brussels, but from 1993 it was badly compromised by defense-related bribery scandals, which necessitated the resignations of several senior PS figures. It won a lower-house vote share of 11.9 percent (for 21 seats) in 1995. Despite retaining only 19 seats on 10.2 percent of the vote in 1999, it remained in the new VLD-led government. The PS focused on unemployment, industrial policy, and education during the 2003 election campaign, while supporting expansion of the EU.

Leaders: Elio DI RUPO (President), Christie MORREALE (Vice President), Jean-Pol BARAS (General Secretary).

Reformist Movement (*Mouvement Reformateur*—MR). The MR was formed in March 2002 through the merger of the Liberal Reformist Party (*Parti Réformateur Libéral*—PRL), the Democratic Front of French Speakers (*Front Démocratique des Francophones*—FDF), and the Citizens' Movement for Change (*Mouvement des Citoyens pour le Changement*—MCC).

The PRL had been formed in May 1979 under the leadership of Jean GOL by merger of the Party of Walloon Reform and Liberty (*Parti des Réformes et de la Liberté en Wallonie*—PRLW) and the Brussels-based Liberal Party (*Parti Libéral*—

PL). Electorally weaker than its Flemish counterpart, the PRL was in government in 1981–1988 but slipped to a vote share of 8.2 percent in the 1991 Chamber elections. In 1995 it campaigned with the FDF on a joint list that captured 10.3 percent of the Chamber vote and 18 seats. PRL leader Gol (a former deputy premier) died in September 1995 and was succeeded by Louis Michel.

The FDF, a formation of French-speaking Brussels interest groups founded in 1964, seeks to preserve the French character of the Belgian capital. It participated in a center-left coalition in 1977–1980 to help enact the Egmont Pact on devolution, under which Brussels became a separate (bilingual) region, but it made little progress in the 1980s. The FDF won only 1.5 percent in the 1991 balloting.

Disavowing the role of a traditional party, the MCC was organized by Gérard DEPREZ in March 1998, after his January expulsion from the PSC (below). The MCC was formally constituted the following October.

At the 1999 general election the PRL again joined with the FDF as well as with the recently formed MCC. The joint federation list won 18 lower-house seats on a 10.1 percent vote share, and the PRL then elected to join the Verhofstadt government. In December 2000 the PRL president, Daniel DUCARME, announced his intention to start the MR, which in 2002 became the country's second largest Liberal party. However, the MR achieved only moderate gains in the 2003 balloting (24 seats on an 11.4 percent vote share in the Chamber).

Leaders: Didier REYNDERS (President of the Party and Deputy Prime Minister), Louis MICHEL, Jacques SIMONET (Secretary General).

Socialist Party-Differently (*Socialistische Partij-Anders*—SP.A). Originally known as the Socialist Party (*Socialistische Partij*—SP), this grouping was until October 1978 the Dutch-speaking wing of the historic Belgian Socialist Party. It has participated in all coalitions involving its French-speaking counterpart while becoming markedly less supportive of state ownership than the PS. It slipped to a 12 percent vote share

in the 1991 national balloting and won 12.6 percent (for 20 lower-house seats) in May 1995. The SP also was heavily implicated in the Agusta bribery scandal, its former chair, Frank VANDENBROUCKE, becoming the most senior ministerial casualty when he was obliged to resign as deputy prime minister and foreign minister in March 1995. Party Chair Louis TOBBACK, who had been named deputy prime minister and interior minister in April 1998, resigned in September after a Nigerian was killed in custody while resisting forcible deportation.

At the June 1999 balloting the SP won only 14 Chamber seats on 9.6 percent of the vote but was able to negotiate a role in the VLD-led coalition government that was formed in July. On the initiative of its current chair, the SP appended the term *Anders* to its name in August 2001 and then also adopted the additional designation "Social Progressive Alternative" (*Sociaal Progressief Alternatief*).

Positioning itself as a prolabor and environmentally friendly party, the SP.A (which also vigorously opposed the U.S.-led invasion of Iraq) ran in coalition with SPIRIT (below) in the 2003 general election. The SP.A did very well, increasing its share of the national vote from 9 percent to 15 percent. As a result, in part, the SP.A is part of the current federal coalition government.

In 2004 the party did not show as well as expected in regional elections for the Flemish parliament. One result was an eventual leadership change, with Steve STEVAERT being replaced by Caroline Gennez, who in turn was replaced by Johan Vande Lanotte.

Leaders: Johan Vande LANOTTE (President), Caroline GENNEZ (Vice President), Alain André (National Secretary).

SPIRIT (*Sociaal, Progressief, International, Regionalistisch, Integraal-democratisch en Toekomstgericht*—SPIRIT). The "Social, Progressive, International, Regionalist, Integrally Democratic and Forward-Looking" SPIRIT was established in November 2001 following the demise of the People's Union (VU). It represented the merger of the VU's progressive "Group of the Future" (*Toekomstgroep*) with the VU's 1999 electoral partner, the left-leaning Complete Democracy for the 21st Century (*Integrale Democratie voor de 21ste Eeuw*—ID21), which dated from 1998. A number of key members of the VU's "middle group" also joined the SPIRIT, which adopted "Free Flemish, European, Global Democrats" as a descriptive and vowed to reject participation in politically expedient alliances. The new party claimed two senators and four Chamber deputies as members.

Following its successful coalition in the 2003 general elections with the SP.A, the SPIRIT joined the new cabinet at the secretary-of-state level.

Leaders: Geert LAMBERT (Chair), Stefan WALGRAEVE (Vice President), Annelies STORMS (Vice President), Willy WILMS (Party Secretary).

Opposition Parties

Christian Democratic and Flemish (*Christen-Democratisch en Vlaams*—CD&V). The CD&V was called the Christian People's Party (*Christelijke Volkspartij*—CVP) until September 2001. The CVP and the PSC (below) were joint heirs to the former Catholic Party (*Parti Catholique Belge*—PCB), which traced its origins to 1830 and traditionally upheld the position of the Catholic Church in Belgium. It included representatives of commercial and manufacturing interests as well as of the working classes. Following World War II the PCB was reshaped into two wings, the CVP and PSC, which remained closely linked until the 1960s. Both Christian parties are now nondenominational and, with substantial representation from the Catholic Trade Union Federation (the country's largest labor organization), favor a variety of social and economic reforms. Consistently the plurality parliamentary party until 1999, the CVP provided the prime minister in a long series of recent coalitions, with Wilfried Martens serving for 13 years until 1992. Following its 1993 congress, the CVP committed itself to "refocus on renewal." Its

lower-house vote share of 17.2 percent and its 29 seats gave it plurality status in May 1995, but it fell to 22 seats and a 14.1 percent share in June 1999, as a consequence of which Prime Minister Jean-Luc Dehaene resigned. The party's current designation was formally adopted at a party congress on September 29, 2001, soon after which a number of members defected to the NCD (below).

The CD&V defined itself as a moderate alternative to the Verhofstadt government in the 2003 general elections. However, the party's very public stance favoring Turkey's accession to the EU apparently cost it some vote share. In the June 2004 balloting for the European Parliament, the CD&V allied itself with the N-VA (below).

CD&V did very well in the 2004 regional Flemish elections, reestablishing itself as the largest party in Flanders.

Leaders: Jo VANDEURZEN (President), Cathy BERX (Vice President), Wouter BEKE (Vice President).

Flemish Interest (*Vlaams Belane*—VB). This grouping was formally known as the Flemish Bloc (*Vlaams Blok*—VB), which contested the election of December 1978 as an alliance of the National Flemish Party (*Vlaamse Nationale Partij*—VNP) and the Flemish People's Party (*Vlaamse Volkspartij*—VVP). The right-wing Flemish Bloc was formally constituted as a unified party in May 1979. Capitalizing on an upsurge in anti-immigrant sentiment, it increased its lower-house representation sixfold (to 12) in 1991, with a 6.6 percent vote share, ahead of the more moderate People's Union (VU; see N-VA, below). In the 1994 local elections it won a 29 percent plurality in Antwerp but was excluded from the mayoralty by the other parties. Its share of the Chamber vote in 1995 was 7.8 percent, for 11 seats, rising to 9.9 percent and 15 seats in 1999. In the October 2000 local elections the VB made additional gains, prompting the Flemish *De Morgen* paper to comment, "One in three Antwerp citizens believes in fear, intolerance, unadulterated racism, and law and order."

The party became increasingly nationalistic in the 2003 election campaign, decrying the

"Islamization of Europe" and calling for independence for the Flemish part of Belgium. After the Flemish Bloc won 18 seats in the Chamber vote, the Supreme Court upheld a lower court's decision that the Bloc's policies violated antiracist laws. Consequently, the Bloc disbanded in November and reformed as Flemish Interest, which ran a vigorous anti-immigration campaign in the 2004 balloting for the European Parliament.

Leaders: Frank VANHECKE (President), Karel DILLEN (Founder and Honorary President), Filip DEWINTER, Geof ANNEMANS, Roeland RAES, Yves BUYSSE (Political Secretary).

Democratic Humanist Center (*Centre Démocrate Humaniste*—CDH). This party was originally called the Christian Social Party (*Parti Social Chrétien*—PSC), the French-speaking (Walloon) counterpart of the CVP. (The PSC and the CVP established autonomy in the late 1960s and formally separated in 1972.) The substantially smaller PSC was subsequently a junior partner in coalitions headed by the CVP, its vote share falling to 7.8 percent in the 1991 national balloting and 7.7 percent of the Chamber vote (for 12 seats) in 1995. At the 1999 election the PSC saw its vote share drop to 5.9 percent (10 seats) despite efforts to redefine itself as a "party-movement" with a broader focus on mediating between civil society and the state. In May 2002 a PSC congress agreed to adopt the CDH rubric. The name change apparently reflected a desire to emphasize the party's support for social welfare, the CDH's 2003 campaign emphasizing the need for high levels of government intervention in the economy as well as a "Christian ethic" to guide public and private actions.

Leaders: Joëlle MILQUET (President), Andre ANTOINE (First Vice President), Melchior WATHELET (Second Vice President).

National Front (*Front National*—FN). Inspired by the French party of the same name and based in the Walloon community, the right extremist FN was founded in 1983 on a platform of opposition to non-European immigration. It won one Chamber seat in 1991 with 1.1 percent of the vote and took two seats on 2.3 percent of the lower-house vote in 1995. In 1999 it fell back to one seat and 1.5 percent.

Leader: Daniel FERET (President).

New Flemish Alliance (*Nieuw-Vlaamse Alliantie*—N-VA). The N-VA was established in mid-October 2001 by the largest, most conservative faction of the recently defunct People's Union (*Volksunie*—VU).

Also known as the Flemish Free Democrats (*Vlaamse Vrije Democraten*), the nationalist VU had been founded in 1954 and had championed an autonomous Flanders within a federal state. After steady electoral advance on a "socially progressive, tolerant, modern, and forward-looking platform," the VU first entered the government in 1977–1978 in a center-left coalition that enacted key stages of regional devolution under the Egmont Pact. This was regarded as insufficient by its militant wing, which later joined the Flemish Bloc (VB). The VU was again in government in 1988–1991 but was overtaken by the VB in the 1991 elections, when it slipped to 5.9 percent of the lower-house vote. It secured 4.7 percent in 1995 and claimed five seats, but then in 1999 advanced to 5.6 percent and eight seats in coalition with the ID21 (see SPIRIT, above). Intraparty ideological differences led to the VU's demise in the summer of 2001, shortly after it had been embarrassed by the forced resignation of Johan SAUWENS, interior minister of the Flemish regional government, because of his association with a pro-Nazi organization.

The N-VA's principal goal is formation of an independent Flanders republic. Regarded as the heir of the VU (but having rejected *Nieuwe Volksunie* as its name), the NV-A also attracted members of the VU's middle wing, while the more liberal "Future" wing subsequently joined the ID21 in establishing the SPIRIT. Like its predecessor, the N-VA adamantly rejects the far-right posture of Flemish Interest and frames its argument for Flemish independence on the basis of international law and the principle of self-determination.

In the federal elections in 2003 the N-VA won only 5 percent of the vote and a single seat in Parliament. In February 2004 the party formed an alliance with the CD&V and won six seats in the Flemish Parliament.

Leaders: Bart De WEVER (Chair), Frieda BRE-POELS (Vice President), Louis IDE (Vice President), Mark DEMESMAEKER (Secretary).

Ecologists (*Ecologistes Confédérés pour l'Organisation de Luttes Originales*—ECOLO). Formed in 1978, the Walloon-based ECOLO, which takes a libertarian approach to environmentalism, won 5 House seats in 1985, 2 of which were lost in 1987. It recovered strongly in 1991, capturing 10 lower-house seats and a 5.1 percent vote share, which slipped to 4.0 percent and 6 seats in 1995. In June 1999 the party advanced to 7.4 percent and 11 seats, thereafter joining the new VLD-led government. However, it was dropped from the government following its disappointing performance in the 2003 general election.

Leaders: Isabelle DURANT, Jean-Michael JAVAUX and Claude BROUIR (Federal Secretaries).

Other Parties

Green! (*Groen!*). ECOLO's Flemish counterpart, this party was formally known as Live Differently (*Anders Gaan Leven*—Agalev), which obtained four lower-house seats in the 1985 balloting, six in 1987, and seven in 1991, when its vote share was 4.9 percent. Agalev fell back to 4.4 percent of the Chamber vote (for five seats) in 1995. Loosely allied with the VLD and ECOLO, Agalev won 7 percent of the vote in 1999 and then joined the governing coalition. The new party name was adopted in November 2003, Agalev having won no seats in the May general election.

In 2003 the party also gave permission to local divisions to form alliances with other parties. In November 2003 the party replaced Dirk HOLEMANS as party leader with Vera Dua.

Leaders: Vera DUA (President), Lieve HEENE (Party Secretary).

New Christian Democrats (*Nieuwe Christen Democratie*—NCD). The NCD was established by former CVP president Johan Van Hecke in the wake of his October 2001 expulsion from the CD&V (the renamed CVP) for unauthorized contacts with the VLD president, Karel de Gucht. Van Hecke had been associated with the more liberal elements of the CVP. He was joined in the new venture by former agriculture minister Karel Pinxten, who had recently called for formation of a new party uniting progressive Christian Democrats and Flemish Liberal Democrats.

Leaders: Johan VAN HECKE (President), Karel PINXTEN.

Alive (*Vivre Intensement vers l'Avenir de Notre*—VIVANT). Charging that the traditional Belgian parties have not addressed the problems of average workers transitioning from an industry-based to a service-based economy, VIVANT won 2.1 percent of the lower-house vote in 1999 but declined to 1 percent in 2003. The party also did poorly in regional elections in 2004.

Leaders: Roland DUCHATELET (President), Joseph MEYER.

Belgium's smaller political parties include the **Humanist Feminist Party** (*Humanistische Feministische Partij/Parti Féministe Humaniste*—HFP/PFH), founded in 1972 as the Unified Feminist Party (*Vereenigde Feministische Partij/Parti Féministe Unifié*—VFP/PFU) and renamed in 1990; the **Humanist Party of Belgium** (*Parti Humaniste de Belgique*—PHB), which was active in 1984–1989 and then revived in 1994; the nationalist **New Belgian Front** (*Front Nouveau de Belgique/Front Nieuw Belgïe*—FNB), established in 1997 by former FN member Marguerite BASTIEN; and the Flemish **Social-Liberal Democrats** (*Sociaal-Liberale Democraten*—SoLiDe), led by François-Xavier ROBERT.

Among a number of Walloon regionalist parties is the **Rally Wallonia-France** (*Rassemblement Wallonie-France*—RWF), which was founded in November 1999 by merger of three small parties supporting unification with France: the Walloon Rally (*Rassemblement Wallon*—RW), the rump of a party that had been consolidated by merger in the 1960s and had participated in the coalition government of 1974–1977 before disintegrating into assorted factions in the 1980s; the Walloon

Cabinet

As of March 6, 2006

Prime Minister	Guy Verhofstadt (VLD)
Deputy Prime Ministers	Patrick Dewael (VLD)
	Laurette Onkelinx (PS) [f]
	Didier Reynders (MR)
	Freya Van den Bossche (SP.A) [f]

Ministers

Agriculture and the Self-Employed	Sabine Laruelle (MR) [f]
Budget and Public Enterprise	Freya Van den Bossche (SP.A) [f]
Civil Service, Social Integration, Urban Policy, and Equal Opportunities	Christian Dupont (PS)
Development Cooperation	Armand De Decker (VLD)
Defense	André Flahaut (PS)
Economy, Energy, Foreign Trade, and Science Policy	Marc Verwilghen (VLD)
Employment	Peter Vanvelthoven (SP.A)
Environment and Pensions	Bruno Tobback (SP.A)
Finance	Didier Reynders (MR)
Foreign Affairs	Karel De Gucht (VLD)
Interior	Patrick Dawael (VLD)
Justice	Laurette Onkelinx (PS) [f]
Social Affairs and Public Health	Rudy Demotte (PS)
Transport	Renaat Landuyt (SP.A)

Secretaries of State

Administrative Simplification	Vincent Van Quickenborne (VLD)
E-government	Peter Vanvelthoven (SP.A)
European Affairs	Didier Donfut (PS)
Family and Disabled Issues	Gisèle Mandaila Malamba (MR) [f]
Financial Modernization and Combatting Tax Fraud	Hervé Jamar (MR)
Public Enterprise	Bruno Tuybens (SPA)
Sustainable Development and Social Economy	Els Van Weert (SPIRIT) [f]

[f] = female

Democratic Alliance (*Alliance Démocratique Wallonne*—ADW), a 1985 splinter from the RW; and the Walloon Movement for the Return to France (*Mouvement Wallon pour le Retour à la France*—MWRF). The RWF Brussels branch is the *Rassemblement Bruxelles-France* (RBF). The party leadership includes Claude THAYSE (President) and Paul-Henri GENDEBIEN (Founding President). Other small Walloon formations include the **"France" Party** (*Parti "France"*—PF), which advocates unification with France; the leftist **Walloon Party** (*Parti Wallon*—PW), which was founded by merger in 1985 and which won 0.2 percent of the lower-house vote in 1999; and the extreme right-wing **Walloon Bloc** (*Bloc Wallon*—BW), which was established in April 2000 but split into competing factions led by Hubert DEFOURNEY and Georges HUPIN in May 2001.

Parties representing the German-speaking community include the **Christian Social Party** (*Christlich-Soziale Partei*—CSP), which is led by Mathieu GROSCH and which won one European Parliament seat in 1994 and 1999 in alliance with the CVP. The **Party of Belgian German-Speakers** (*Partei der Deutschsprächigen Belgier*—PDB), led by Guido BREUER, was founded in 1971. The **Party for Freedom and Progress** (*Partei für Freiheit und Fortschritt*—PFF), led by Ferdel SCHRÖDER, was associated in 2001 with plans by the PRL's Daniel Ducarme to form a Reformist Movement.

Parties of the left include the Wallonia-based **Communist Party** (*Parti Communiste*—PC), led by Pierre BEAUVOIS, and the Flanders-based **Communist Party** (*Kommunistische Partij Vlaanderen*—KP), led by Jos DE GEYTER. Both trace their origins to the historic Belgian Communist Party (*Parti Communiste de Belgique/Kommunistische Partij van België*—PCB/KPB) founded in 1921. Having evolved from wings of a unitary party in the 1960s to autonomous sections in 1982, in 1989 the PC and KP established a federation—the Belgian Communist Union (*Union des Communistes de Belgique/Unie van Kommunisten van België*—UCB/UKB)—that lasted until 1995, when they completely separated. Neither has held a Chamber seat since 1985. The Maoist **Belgian Party of Labor** (*Partij van de Arbeid van België/Parti du Travail de Belgique*—PvdA/PTB), currently led by Nadine ROSA-ROSSO, was established in 1979 in opposition to the Eurocommunist line of the PCB/KPB. Other small formations include the **Left Socialist Party-Movement for a Socialist Alternative** (*Linkse Socialistische Partij-Mouvement pour une Alternative Socialiste*—LSP-MAS) and the Trotskyite **Socialist Workers' Party** (*Parti Ouvrier Socialiste/Socialistische Arbeiders Partij*—POS/SAP).

Legislature

The bicameral **Parliament** (*Federale Parlament/Parlement Fédérale*) consists of a Senate and a House of Representatives, both elected for four-year terms and endowed with virtually equal powers. The king may dissolve either or both chambers on the advice of the prime minister.

Senate (*Senaat/Sénat*). The upper house consists of 71 members, of which 40 are directly elected (25 from Flanders, 15 from Wallonia), 21 are indirectly elected (10 each by the Flemish Council and the French Council, and 1 by the German Council), and 10 are appointed by the elected senators (6 Flemish and 4 Walloon). At least six of the Walloon senators must be legally resident in Brussels, as must at least one of the Flemish senators. In addition, the reigning monarch's children or Belgian heirs are senators by right from the age of 18, with voting rights from the age of 21. As a result of the election of May 18, 2003, the distribution of seats (with directly elected seats in parentheses) was as follows: Flemish Liberals and Democrats, 12 (7); Socialist Party-Differently/SPIRIT, 11 (7); Socialist Party (Walloon), 11 (6); Reformist Movement, 10 (5); Christian Democratic and Flemish, 9 (6); Flemish Interest, 8 (5); Democratic Humanist Center, 3 (2); Ecologist, 2 (1); National Front, 2 (1); independent Flemish, 2; independent French, 1; vacant, 1.

President: Anne-Marie LIZIN.

House of Representatives (*Kamer van Volksvertegenwoordigers/Chambre des Représentants*). The lower house consists of 150 deputies directly elected by proportional representation and compulsory adult suffrage from multimember electoral districts. Each district's complement of deputies is in proportion to population. The election of May 18, 2003, yielded the following distribution of seats: Flemish Liberals and Democrats, 25; Socialist Party (Walloon), 25; Reformist Movement, 24; Socialist Party-Differently/SPIRIT, 23; Christian Democratic and Flemish, 21; Flemish Interest, 18; Democratic Humanist Center, 8; Ecologists, 4; National Front, 1; New Flemish Alliance, 1.

President: Herman DE CROO.

Communications

Under the basic law of May 18, 1960, information transmission (i.e., news and current affairs) cannot be censored by the government.

Press

The following are published daily at Brussels, unless otherwise noted: *Krantengroep De Standaard* (including *De Gentenaar* of Ghent, *Het Nieuwsblad*, and *De Standaard*, 370,000), in Dutch, independent; *Het Laatste Nieuws* (310,000), in Dutch, independent; *Le Soir* (180,000), in French, independent; *La Meuse* (Liège, including *La Lanterne* of Brussels, 130,000), in French, independent; *Gazet van Antwerpen* (Antwerp, 120,000), in Dutch, Christian Democratic; *Het Volk* (Ghent, 120,000), in Dutch, Christian Democratic; *La Libre Belgique* (including *Gazette de Liège,* 80,000), in French, independent; *La Dernière Heure* (70,000), in French, Liberal.

News Agencies

The official agency is *Agence Télégraphique Belge de Presse/Belgisch Pers-telegraafagentschap* (*Agence Belga/Agentschap Belga*); private facilities include *Centre d'Information de Presse* (Catholic), *Agence Europe*, and *Agence Day*. Numerous foreign agencies also maintain bureaus in Belgium.

Broadcasting and Computing

The French-language *Radio-Télévision Belge de la Communauté Française* (RTBF), the Dutch-language *Vlaamse Radio- en Televisieomroep* (VRT), and the German-language *Belgisches Rundfunk- und Fernsehzentrum* (BRF) are government-owned systems operated by cultural councils, under grants made by Parliament. In 1999, there were approximately 6.4 million television receivers in use, while 2.6 million personal computers served 2.0 million Internet users.

Intergovernmental Representation

Ambassador to the U.S.
Franciskus VAN DAELE

U.S. Ambassador to Belgium
Tom C. KOROLOGOS

Permanent Representative to the UN
Johan C. VERBEKE

IGO Memberships (Non-UN)
ADB, AfDB, BIS, BLX, BOAD, CERN, CEUR, EBRD, EIB, ESA, EU, Eurocontrol, G-10, IADB, IEA, Interpol, IOM, NATO, OECD, OIF, OSCE, PCA, WCO, WEU, WTO

BOSNIA AND HERZEGOVINA

REPUBLIC OF BOSNIA AND HERZEGOVINA

Republika Bosna i Hercegovina

CONSTITUENT "ENTITIES":
FEDERATION OF BOSNIA AND HERZEGOVINA

Federacija Bosne i Hercegovine

SERB REPUBLIC OF BOSNIA AND HERZEGOVINA

Republika Srpska Bosne i Hercegovine

Note: Final results of the presidential elections held October 1, 2006, are as follows: Haris Silajdžić (Party for Bosnia and Herzogovina) won election as the Bosniac Member of the Presidency of the Republic of Bosnia and Herzegovina with 62.8 percent of the vote; Željko Komšić (Social Democratic Party of Bosnia and Herzogovina) won election as the Croat Member of the Presidency of the Republic of Bosnia and Herzegovina with 39.6 percent of the vote; Nebojša Radmanović (Alliance of Independent Social Democrats) won election as the Serb Member of the Presidency of the Republic of Bosnia and Herzegovina with 53.3 percent of the vote. (For additional election results, see note on page 134.)

The Country

A virtually landlocked Balkan country with less than eight miles of Adriatic coastline, Bosnia and Herzegovina is bordered on the west and north by Croatia, and on the east by Serbia and Montenegro. The capital, Sarajevo, is located in the northern Bosnian region, while Mostar is the principal town in the Herzegovinian south. Serbo-Croat is the principal language of an otherwise diverse population encompassing approximately 1.9 million Muslim Slavs (Bosniacs), 1.4 million Eastern Orthodox Serbs, and 820,000 Roman Catholic Croats. Women make up about 17 percent of the national House of Representatives but none hold seats in the upper house.

The agricultural sector accounts for about 17 percent of GDP, compared to 35 percent for

industry and 47 percent for services. Timber is an important product in the north, in addition to maize, wheat, and potatoes, while the largely deforested south yields tobacco and various fruits and vegetables. Natural resources include fairly extensive deposits of lignite, iron ore, bauxite, manganese, and copper, as well as considerable hydroelectric capacity. Industrial output is low, however, and the economy overall compares unfavorably with those of most other regional republics. Leading industrial exports include wood and paper products and iron and steel. Principal trading partners are Croatia, Serbia and Montenegro, Germany, Slovenia, and Italy.

The economy collapsed as a result of the internal conflict of 1991–1995, which destroyed much of the infrastructure and displaced several million people. The GDP contracted by some 80 percent, and per capita GDP fell from $2,450 in 1990 to about $500 in 1995. Following the November 1995 peace accord, GDP grew in real terms by 86 percent in 1996, 37 percent in 1997, and 10 percent in 1998 as the manufacturing sector began its recovery, led by wood products, textiles and clothing, and processed foods and beverages. However, much of the growth was fueled by extensive foreign aid, donors such as the European Union (EU), the United States, the World Bank, and the International Monetary Fund (IMF) having contributed over $5 billion to assist in economic development and, by extension, to help solidify the country's complicated and fragile political structure. The introduction of the convertible mark and the establishment of countrywide customs procedures in 1998 were seen as significant steps in bonding the economies of the two political entities in Bosnia and Herzegovina, although the Serb Republic continued to lag behind the Federation in development, in part because of Western dismay over nationalist political activity. Lenders have encouraged the governments of the state and the entities to privatize government-controlled enterprises in order to attract private external investment, but action has been limited in that regard.

In 1999 growth remained at 10 percent and then fell to 5.5 percent in 2000, in part because of a decline in donor reconstruction aid. In 2001 the GDP grew by about 4.3 percent, followed by 5.3 percent in 2002, 4.0 percent in 2003, and 5.7 percent in 2004. For 2005 the IMF estimated growth at 5.4 percent. Overall output nevertheless remains significantly below its prewar level. Meanwhile, unemployment has been estimated at 25 percent or more.

Government and Politics

Political Background

Settled by Slavs in the 7th century, Bosnia annexed what came to be known as Herzegovina in the mid-15th century, with both subsequently being conquered by the Turks. At the 1878 Congress of Berlin the territories were placed under the administration of Austria-Hungary, which continued to recognize Turkish sovereignty until formal annexation in 1908. The June 1914 assassination of the Austrian imperial heir in Sarajevo by a Serbian nationalist led directly to the outbreak of World War I. In 1918 the country became part of the Kingdom of the Serbs, Croats, and Slovenes, which was officially renamed Yugoslavia in October 1929. In November 1945 Bosnia and Herzegovina became one of the six constituent republics of the Communist-ruled Federal People's Republic of Yugoslavia.

During November–December 1990, in the constituent republic's first multiparty balloting since World War II, the three leading nationalist parties (appealing to Bosniacs, Serbs, and Croats) won an overwhelming collective majority in the restructured 240-member bicameral assembly, limiting the previously dominant League of Communists to only 19 seats. In a separate poll on November 18, the three groups also captured all 7 seats in the republican presidency. A month later the three announced that Alija IZETBEGOVIĆ, a Bosniac, would become president of the state presidency; Jure PELIVAN, a Croat, would become prime minister; and Momčilo KRAJIŠNIK, a Serb, would become president (speaker) of the assembly.

Declarations of independence by Croatia and Slovenia on June 25, 1991, precipitated incursions

Political Status (Republic): Former constituent republic of the Socialist Federal Republic of Yugoslavia; declared independence on March 3, 1992. (The Dayton agreement of November 21, 1995, specified that the institutions of the existing republic government were to function until the holding of countrywide elections, after which a new central government would be formed with joint Federation-Serb participation and retention of purely internal functions by each of the two constituent "entities." The existence of a single state of Bosnia and Herzegovina and other provisions of the Dayton accords were confirmed by an international treaty signed in Paris, France, on December 14. Elections were held on September 14, 1996, and the central and entity governments were subsequently established in stages.)

Political Status (Federation): Federation of the areas of the Republic of Bosnia and Herzegovina containing majority Bosniac (Muslim) and Croat populations authorized by framework agreement of March 18, 1994, which envisaged the Federation as a sovereign nation that would pursue a loose political confederation with Croatia; federation agreement "reinforced" by Dayton accord of November 10, 1995, with permanent territorial boundaries established by Dayton accord of November 21, under which, in revision of the 1994 agreement, it was decided that the Federation would be an entity within the Republic of Bosnia and Herzegovina.

Political Status (Serb Republic): Proclaimed by leaders of Serbian-held areas of the republic on March 27, 1992; established (under revised territorial boundaries) as an entity of the Republic of Bosnia and Herzegovina under the Dayton accord of November 21, 1995.

Area (Republic): 19,741 sq. mi. (51,129 sq. km.). At the launching of the Federation in 1994 the area under its control totaled some 30 percent of the former area of the Republic of Bosnia and Herzegovina, the balance being under Serb control. Under the Dayton accord of November 21, 1995, approximately 51 percent of the country's total area was assigned to the Federation and the remaining 49 percent, to the Serb Republic.

Population (Republic): 4,377,033 (1991C); 4,232,000 (2005E, including nonresidents).

Major Urban Centers (2005E): SARAJEVO (380,000), Banja Luka (165,000).

Official Languages: Serbian, Croat, Bosnian.

Monetary Unit: Convertible Mark (official rate July 1, 2006: 1.53 convertible marka = $1US).

Chair of the Presidency of the Republic of Bosnia and Herzegovina: Sulejman TIHIĆ (Bosnian Member); rotated to chair for an eight-month term on February 28, 2006, succeeding Ivo Miro JOVIĆ (Croatian Member).

Bosniac Member of the Presidency of the Republic of Bosnia and Herzegovina: Sulejman TIHIĆ (Party of Democratic Action); elected for a four-year term on October 5, 2002, and inaugurated on October 28, succeeding Beriz BELKIĆ (Alliance for Change/Party for Bosnia and Herzegovina).

Croat Member of the Presidency of the Republic of Bosnia and Herzegovina: Ivo Miro JOVIĆ (Croatian Democratic Union of Bosnia and Herzegovina); elected on May 4, 2005, by the House of Representatives of the Republic of Bosnia and Herzegovina, confirmed on May 9 by the Croat members of the republic's House of Peoples, and sworn in on May 18 to complete the four-year term of Dragan ČOVIĆ (Coalition/Croatian Democratic Union of Bosnia and Herzegovina), who had been elected on October 5, 2002, but had been dismissed on March 29, 2005, by High Representative Paddy Ashdown because of corruption allegations.

Serb Member of the Presidency of the Republic of Bosnia and Herzegovina: Borislav PARAVAC (Serbian Democratic Party of Bosnia and Herzegovina); elected April 9, 2003, by the House of Representatives of the Republic of Bosnia and Herzegovina and confirmed on April 10 by the Serb members of the republic's House of Peoples, to complete the four-year term of Mirko SAROVIĆ (Serbian Democratic Party of Bosnia and Herzegovina), who had been elected on October 5, 2002, but had resigned on April 2, 2003, after being implicated in spying and armaments scandals.

President of the Federation of Bosnia and Herzegovina: Niko LOZANČIĆ (Croatian Democratic Union); elected for a four-year term by votes of the Federation House of Representatives on January 21 and 24, 2003, and confirmed by the Federation House of Peoples on January 27; sworn in on January 27, succeeding Safet HALILOVIĆ (Alliance for Change/Party for Bosnia and Herzegovina). (On January 22 a joint presidential/vice presidential list had failed to win sufficient Serb votes for confirmation by the House of Peoples. The January 24 repeat vote by the House of Representatives constitutionally prevailed over the lack of Serb backing when the House of Peoples voted for a second time on January 27.)

Vice Presidents of the Federation of Bosnia and Herzegovina: Sahbaz DŽIHANOVIĆ (Party for Bosnia and Herzegovina), a Bosniac, and Desnica RADIVOJEVIĆ (Party of Democratic Action), a Serb; elected by the Federation House of Representatives (on a joint list with the president of the Federation) and confirmed by the Federation House of the Peoples in January 2003; sworn in on January 27, for terms concurrent with that of the president, succeeding Karlo FILIPOVIĆ (Alliance for Change/Social Democratic Party of Bosnia and Herzegovina).

President of the Serb Republic of Bosnia and Herzegovina: Dragan ČAVIĆ (Serbian Democratic Party of Bosnia and Herzegovina); elected for a four-year term on October 5, 2002, and sworn in on November 28, succeeding Mirko SAROVIĆ (Serbian Democratic Party of Bosnia and Herzegovina).

Vice Presidents of the Serb Republic of Bosnia and Herzegovina: Adil OSMANOVIĆ (Party of Democratic Action), a Bosniac, and Ivan TOMLJENOVIĆ (Social Democratic Party of Bosnia and Herzegovina), a Croat; elected on October 5, 2002, and sworn in on November 28, for terms concurrent with that of the president of the Serb Republic, succeeding Dragan ČAVIĆ (Serbian Democratic Party of Bosnia and Herzegovina).

Prime Minister of the Republic of Bosnia and Herzegovina (Chair of the Council of Ministers): Adnan TERZIĆ (Party of Democratic Action); nominated by the presidency of the republic on December 22, 2002, following the general election of October 5, and elected by the republic's House of Representatives on December 23, succeeding Dragan MIKEREVIĆ (Party for Democratic Progress of the Serb Republic).

Prime Minister of the Federation of Bosnia and Herzegovina: Ahmet HADŽIPAŠIĆ (Party of Democratic Action); nomination announced by the president of the Federation on February 13, 2003; confirmed by the Federation House of Representatives on February 14, succeeding Alija BEHMEN (Alliance for Change/Social Democratic Party of Bosnia and Herzegovina).

Prime Minister of the Serb Republic of Bosnia and Herzegovina: Milorad DODIK (Alliance of Independent Social Democrats); nominated by the president of the Serb Republic on February 4, 2006, and confirmed by the National Assembly on February 28, succeeding Pero BUKEJLOVIĆ (Serbian Democratic Party of Bosnia and Herzegovina), whose government had lost a no-confidence vote in the National Assembly on January 26.

by the Serb-dominated Yugoslav army, and by early September fighting had spread to Bosnia and Herzegovina. On September 12 a Serbian "autonomous province" was proclaimed on the border with Montenegro, with a number of interior "autonomous regions" being announced by Serb militants later in the month.

At a referendum on February 29–March 1, 1992, in Bosnia and Herzegovina, 99.4 percent of the participants endorsed secession from Yugoslavia, although most Serbs boycotted the poll; on March 3 President Izetbegović issued a proclamation of independence. Subsequently, on March 18, leaders of the country's three main ethnic groups concluded an agreement in Sarajevo that called for division of Bosnia and Herzegovina into three autonomous units based on the "national absolute or relative majority" in each locality. However, most Serbs continued to insist that Bosnia and Herzegovina be included in Yugoslavia, while many Bosniacs, despite the Sarajevo accord, also called for rejection of the division along ethnic lines.

On March 27, 1992, Bosnian Serbs proclaimed a "Serb Republic of Bosnia and Herzegovina" with Dr. Radovan KARADŽIĆ as its president. As ethnic conflict mounted, the UN Security Council in April authorized the deployment of a sizable UN Protection Force (UNPROFOR), although its mandate was to facilitate the distribution of humanitarian aid rather than to engage in active peacekeeping. Subsequently, the Serbs tightened their grip on eastern Bosnia, while stepping up their attack on Sarajevo. By mid-May the siege of the capital had created severe shortages of food and medical supplies, with Foreign Minister Haris SILAJDŽIĆ appealing to the Security Council for the creation of "security zones" similar to those used to protect Kurds in Iraq after the 1991 Gulf war. Soon thereafter, the UN withdrew its military and civilian personnel from Sarajevo, and it was not until June 26 that the Security Council issued an ultimatum to the Serbs to place their heavy weapons under UN control or face international military action to open Sarajevo's airport to relief supplies.

By late 1992 Serbian nationalists controlled approximately 70 percent of Bosnia and Herzegovina, with Croatian forces holding much of the remainder. In March 1993 agreement appeared to have been reached among President Izetbegović, Bosnian Serb leader Karadžić, and Bosnian Croat leader Mate BOBAN on a peace plan advanced by former U.S. secretary of state Cyrus R. Vance (on behalf of the UN) and Britain's Lord Owen (on behalf of the European Community) to create a new decentralized state divided into ten semiautonomous provinces. The plan was repudiated, however, by the self-styled Bosnian Serb parliament on April 2. On June 7 the Bosnian government felt obliged to cooperate with a UN Security Council resolution that would recognize Bosniac "safe areas" in the six enclaves of Bihać, Goražde, Sarajevo, Srebrenica, Tuzla, and Žepa.

Shortly thereafter, in negotiations chaired by Lord Owen and former Norwegian foreign minister Thorvald Stoltenberg (the new UN mediator), a provisional agreement was reached in Geneva that envisaged the division of Bosnia and Herzegovina into three ethnically based states under a federal or confederal constitution. By November, however, the viability of the Owen-Stoltenberg plan for a "Union of Three Republics" had evaporated, with Bosnia Serb leader Karadžić calling for a currency union between the Bosnian Serb Republic and Serbia proper, Izetbegović insisting that the Croats guarantee Bosniac access to the Adriatic, and intra-Muslim conflict in the northwestern enclave of Bihać yielding the proclamation of an "Autonomous Province of Western Bosnia" under the leadership of dissident Bosnia presidency member Fikret ABDIĆ. In addition, Serbian forces had renewed their bombardment of Sarajevo, while fighting between Croats and Bosniacs continued in Mostar.

On February 8, 1994, hard-line Bosnian Croat leader Boban resigned as president of the separatist "Croatian Republic of Herceg-Bosna," which had been proclaimed in August 1993, and on February 24 Bosnian government and Croat forces agreed to a general cease-fire. Subsequently, at a Washington ceremony hosted by U.S. President Clinton on March 18, Bosnian and Croatian representatives signed a framework agreement for a federation of the Bosnian Muslim and Croat populations, together with a preliminary accord on establishment of a loose confederation involving the proposed federation and Croatia. On March 24 the Assembly of the Bosnian Serb Republic declined to endorse the plan.

On May 30, 1994, Krešimir ZUBAK, a Bosnian Croat, was elected to a six-month term as president of the new Federation of Bosnia and Herzegovina, with Haris Silajdžić, who had been named prime minister of Bosnia and Herzegovina in October 1993, being designated the Federation's prime minister. However, at the expiration of his term on November 30, Zubak refused to step down, arguing that if the presidency passed to the Bosniac vice president, Ejup GANIĆ, no major office would then be held by an ethnic Croat.

Despite the impasse, both Croat and Bosniac leaders reaffirmed their support for the Federation on February 5, 1995.

An international "Contact Group" (France, Germany, Russia, the United Kingdom, and the United States) on July 6, 1994, presented a package of peace proposals that called for awarding 51 percent of Bosnian territory to the Muslim-Croat Federation, with key areas placed under protection of either the UN or the EU. While the plan would have permitted the Serbs to retain a number of "ethnically cleansed" areas, they would have been obliged to cede about a third of their currently held territory to the Federation. Although branded as "seriously flawed," the plan was accepted by the Bosnian government, but, as in the case of the Vance-Owen and Owen-Stoltenberg plans, it was rejected by the Serbs, who continued to insist on Serb access to the Adriatic, control of Sarajevo, and the right to confederate areas under their control with Serbia and Montenegro.

Responding to a continued logjam in the political negotiations, former U.S. president Jimmy Carter undertook a nonofficial mediatory mission to Bosnia and Herzegovina on December 18–20, 1994, establishing the basis for a four-month cease-fire that came formally into effect on December 31. The cease-fire generally held in the Sarajevo area but was regularly punctuated by outbreaks of fighting elsewhere, notably around Bihać, which had fallen to Bosnian government troops in August 1994. Hopes of diplomatic progress quickened on March 21, 1995, when President Slobodan Milošević of Serbia held his first-ever unmediated talks with a Bosnian government envoy, but as the cease-fire neared its April 30 expiry date the contending armies prepared to resume hostilities, having apparently used the lull to rearm and regroup.

New fighting in May 1995 yielded further Bosnian Serb advances and renewed heavy shelling of Sarajevo, to which the external powers responded by calling a UN/NATO air strike on an ammunition dump near Pale (the Bosnian Serb capital) on May 25. The Bosnian Serb military reacted by taking some 400 UN peacekeepers as hostages to deter additional strikes, thereby creating a major international crisis. Britain and France responded by dispatching several thousand additional "rapid reaction" troops (plus heavy weapons) to the area, with the stated aim of "protecting" UN peacekeepers.

Intensive negotiations led to the phased release of all the UN hostages by early July 1995, with UN and Western spokespersons denying persistent reports that the Bosnian Serbs had been promised a cessation of air strikes in return. By then a Bosnian government offensive around Sarajevo had petered out, and Bosnian Serb forces were on the advance in eastern Bosnia, threatening the three Muslim-populated safe areas close to the Serbian border (Srebrenica, Žepa, and Goražde). Srebrenica was overrun by the Bosnian Serbs on July 11, with most of its Muslim population fleeing or disappearing, despite the presence of 200 inadequately armed UNPROFOR troops in the town. (The world subsequently learned that some 7,500 Muslim men and boys had been massacred—the worst such incident in Europe since the end of World War II.) On July 25, with Žepa also having fallen to the Bosnian Serbs, NATO announced detailed plans for the protection of the third and largest eastern safe area at Goražde.

The killing of 37 people in a Sarajevo market on August 28, 1995, provoked NATO to launch "Operation Deliberate Force," involving heavy air strikes against Serb positions. Having finally lost patience with the inability of the European powers and new EU mediator Carl Bildt, a former Swedish prime minister, to end the conflict, the U.S. government took charge of Western diplomacy and secured the signature of a 60-day cease-fire agreement on October 5. This was followed on November 1 by the launching of new talks at a Dayton, Ohio, air base. The negotiations produced several historic accords among Presidents Tudjman of Croatia, Milošević of Serbia, and Izetbegović of the Republic of Bosnia and Herzegovina, the last of which had continued to function in tandem with the Federation's new government. On November 10 Tudjman and Izetbegović agreed to "reinforce" the provisions of the 1994 federation agreement, the resultant government having exercised little real authority. In addition, the Croatian and Bosnian leaders accepted the "reunification" of Mostar to serve as the capital of the Federation. Finally, on November 21 a comprehensive settlement was reached regarding the permanent political status of Bosnia and Herzegovina, and the agreement was formally signed in Paris on December 14.

The Dayton accords specified that Bosnia and Herzegovina would remain a single state under international law but would be partitioned into Bosniac-Croat and Serb "entities" that would enjoy substantial autonomy. The (Bosniac-Croat) Federation of Bosnia and Herzegovina was awarded 51 percent of the country's territory, including all of Sarajevo, while the Serb Republic of Bosnia and Herzegovina obtained 49 percent, including several areas once inhabited by Bosniacs. All the parties undertook to cooperate with the International Criminal Tribunal for the former Yugoslavia (ICTY), which had been established in The Hague by decision of the UN Security Council in 1993. Those indicted by the tribunal were to relinquish public office. Final authority to interpret the nonmilitary terms of the agreement in Bosnia and Herzegovina was granted to the Office of the High Representative of the International Community, whose head would be endorsed by the Security Council after nomination by a Peace Implementation Council of 55 governments and multilateral organizations.

Compliance with the agreement was to be assured by the speedy deployment of a 60,000-strong Implementation Force (IFOR), which would operate under NATO command but would draw contingents from non-NATO countries and be subject to UN authorization. Including some 20,000 U.S. troops (the first American ground involvement in Bosnia and Herzegovina), IFOR began to arrive at the end of 1995, replacing the ill-starred UNPRO-FOR contingent. A quick cessation of open hostilities and the withdrawal of opposing forces to the designated cease-fire lines were achieved by the end of January 1996, although interethnic clashes and altercations with IFOR occurred throughout the year. The tensest situations involved the ethnically mixed cities of Brćko and Mostar, the latter split between Bosniacs and Croats in the Federation.

In late January 1996 Hasan MURATOVIĆ (nonparty) was installed as prime minister of the Republic of Bosnia and Herzegovina in succession to Silajdžić, while Izudin KAPETANOVIĆ became prime minister of the Federation. The previous month Rajko KASAGIĆ had been elected the new prime minister of the Serb Republic of Bosnia and Herzegovina; however, as a moderate favored by Western governments, Kasagić quickly came into conflict with the Bosnian Serb president, Radovan Karadžić, who in May 1996 announced Kasagić's dismissal and replacement by Gojko KLIČKOVIĆ, a hard-liner. This controversial action served to intensify international pressure for the ouster of Karadžić, one of several prominent Bosnian Serbs indicted for alleged war crimes by the ICTY and therefore disqualified from public office under the Dayton agreement. After failed efforts by the first high representative, Carl Bildt, U.S. negotiators stepped in and, with Belgrade's backing, secured the formal resignation of Karadžić from all his offices on July 19, with Vice President Biljana PLAVŠIĆ taking over as acting president of the Serb Republic.

At the same time, evidence began to mount that atrocities had been committed during the recent hostilities. The discoveries served to intensify calls for those responsible to be brought before the UN tribunal, which began its first actual trial of a suspect in May 1996. In addition to Karadžić, the 75 persons indicted by the tribunal by mid-1996 included Gen. Ratko MLADIĆ, the Bosnian Serb military commander; Mico STANŠIĆ, the Serbian secret police chief; and a number of prominent Bosnian Croats.

Karadžić's departure from office (although not from dominant influence in the Serb Republic) unblocked the political obstacles to presidential and legislative elections supervised by the Organization for Security and Cooperation in Europe (OSCE). Within Bosnian Federation territory, former prime minister Silajdžić mounted a challenge to President Izetbegović, seeking to rally moderate nonsectarian opinion to his new Party for Bosnia and Herzegovina (*Stranka za Bosnu i Hercegovinu*—SBiH). In the Serb Republic, the new acting president,

Biljana Plavšić, also succeeded Karadžić as presidential candidate of the Serbian Democratic Party of Bosnia and Herzegovina (*Srpska Demokratska Stranka Bosne i Hercegovine*—SDS).

Despite last-minute controversies and much confusion, the elections went ahead on September 14, 1996, involving what OSCE officials described as the most complex popular consultation in the history of democracy. In addition to separate balloting in the Bosniac, Serb, and Croat communities for a three-member presidency of Bosnia and Herzegovina, there were separate elections in the Federation and in the Serb Republic for the House of Representatives of Bosnia and Herzegovina, as well as separate balloting for the House of Representatives of the Federation and for the National Assembly of the Serb Republic. Last but not least, there was a presidential election in the Serb Republic.

The official results confirmed the dominance of the main nationalist parties of the three ethnic groups, namely the Bosniac Party of Democratic Action (*Stranka Demokratske Akcije*—SDA), the Serb SDS, and the Croatian Democratic Union of Bosnia and Herzegovina (*Hrvatska Demokratska Zajednica Bosne i Hercegovine*—HDZ-BiH). In the contests for the three-member presidency of the state, President Izetbegović of the SDA took 80 percent of the Bosniac vote, Momčilo Krajišnik of the SDS took 67 percent of the vote in the Serb Republic, and Krešimir ZUBAK of the HDZ-BiH took 89 percent of the Croat vote. Of the three, Izetbegović had won the most votes and was therefore, under the Dayton accord, elected chair of the presidency of Bosnia and Herzegovina. In the legislative contests, the SDA achieved a plurality in the House of Representatives of Bosnia and Herzegovina and a majority in the lower house of the Federation, while the SDS won a majority in the Serb Assembly. In the Serb Republic's presidential election, Plavšić was confirmed in office with 59 percent of the vote. Despite substantial accumulated evidence of widespread electoral irregularities and intimidation, the election results were certified by the OSCE on September 29.

The inaugural meeting of the new presidency of Bosnia and Herzegovina took place in Sarajevo on October 5, 1996, but it was not attended by Krajišnik, who claimed that security concerns prevented his leaving Serb-controlled territory. Similar reasons were cited by the Serb members for their absence from the inaugural session of the new House of Representatives of Bosnia and Herzegovina, held the same day. Western mediators induced Krajišnik to attend a session of the presidency on October 22, when he swore an oath of allegiance to the constitution of Bosnia and Herzegovina.

The worst fighting since the signature of the Dayton agreement erupted in mid-November 1996, on the eastern line of separation, as Bosnian Serbs mounted armed resistance to Bosniacs who were attempting to return to their former homes. In early December NATO authorized a new Stabilization Force (SFOR) to take over when the IFOR mandate expired on December 20. The SFOR was given an 18-month mandate, with 17 non-NATO countries also agreeing to contribute to its total of 31,000 personnel. The United States was the leading NATO contributor with 8,500 troops, and the SFOR was placed under the command of a U.S. general.

On December 12, 1996, the collective presidency appointed the SBiH's Silajdžić and Boro BOSIĆ of the SDS to cochair the new six-member Council of Ministers of the Republic of Bosnia and Herzegovina. Five days later the leaders of the previous Bosnian Republic formally transferred authority to the new Federation, while Bosnian Croats collaterally announced that the Croatian Republic of Herceg-Bosna had ceased to exist. On December 18 the House of Representatives of the Federation elected Edhem BIĆAKČIĆ of the SDA as prime minister of the Federation's Council of Ministers; the National Assembly of the Serb Republic also reconfirmed the SDS's Kličković as prime minister of the Serb Republic during December. The central government was formally approved by the House of Representatives of the Republic of Bosnia and Herzegovina on January 3, 1997.

An indirect presidential election in the Federation was held on March 18, 1997, Krešimir Zubak having continued to hold the office until then, despite his elevation to the central presidency the previous fall. Vladimir ŠOLJIĆ of the HDZ-BiH, representing Croats, was elected as the new Federation president, while Ejup Ganić of the Bosniac SDA was elected vice president. Under the power-sharing arrangement in the Federation constitution, the two men would exchange positions on January 1, 1998, with Ganić serving out the remaining year of the presidential term.

Local elections, which had been postponed several times since September 1996, were finally held throughout the country on September 13–14, 1997, under the auspices of the OSCE, with the SFOR providing security at polling stations. Meanwhile, political affairs in the Serb Republic had been complicated by a power struggle between President Plavšić's Banja Luka faction and the Karadžić-led Pale faction of the SDS. In late June Plavšić was detained by police in Belgrade and taken to Pale by alleged Karadžić loyalists, only to be freed by NATO forces and escorted back to Banja Luka. On July 3 she ordered the dissolution of the largely pro-Karadžić National Assembly. The SDS challenged the dissolution, called for Plavšić's resignation, and on July 19 expelled her from the party. On August 15 the Constitutional Court of the Serb Republic ruled against the dissolution of the assembly, but Carlos Westendorp, the new high representative, quickly overruled the court.

Plavšić and Krajišnik signed a peace accord mediated by Serbian President Milošević in Belgrade in September 1997. As part of their agreement, new elections were held for the Serb Republic's National Assembly in late November. The SDS and its coalition allies from the Serb Radical Party of the Serb Republic (*Srpska Radikalna Stranka Republike Srpske*—SRS) fell three seats short of a majority, and initial parliamentary sessions were unable to agree upon a government. When a coalition of all other parties in the assembly finally selected a pro-Western moderate, Milorad DODIK of the small Party of Independent Social Democrats (*Stranka Nezavisnih Socijaldemokrata*—SNSD), as the new prime minister on January 18, 1998, the SDS and SRS deputies temporarily walked out and vowed to ignore all new legislation.

A new cabinet for the Serb Republic was sworn in on January 31, 1998, but there were no Mus-lims among the ministers nor any representatives from Karadžić's stronghold in Pale. The assembly further underscored its majority stance against Karadžić by voting to transfer the Serb Republic's seat of government from Pale to Banja Luka, where Plavšić supporters dominated. In June the assembly also endorsed a no-confidence motion against Assembly Speaker Dragan KALINIĆ and Deputy Speaker Nikola POPLAŠEN, both hard-liners, and elected moderates to replace them.

Another full round of state and entity elections took place on September 12–13, 1998, nationalist candidates performing well in most executive races despite a moderate decline in support for nationalist parties in the three legislatures. Izetbegović easily won reelection to the Bosniac seat on the central presidency as the candidate of the SDA-backed Coalition for a Unified and Democratic Bosnia and Herzegovina (*Koalicija za Cjevolitu Demokratsku Bosnu i Hercegovinu*—KCD), while hard-liner Ante JELAVIĆ of the HDZ-BiH secured the Croat seat. However, in a result that was widely applauded in the West, Momčilo Krajišnik was defeated for the Serb seat by Živko RADIŠIĆ of the new *Sloga* (Accord) coalition, which comprised Plavšić's recently established Serbian People's Alliance (*Srpski Narodni Savez*—SNS), Radišić's Socialist Party of the Serb Republic (*Socijalisticka Partija Republike Srpske*—SPRS), and Dodik's SNSD.

At the same time, Western officials were dismayed by Poplašen's victory over Plavšić in the race for president of the Serb Republic. Following the election, Poplašen nominated Kalinić to replace Dodik, but the assembly rejected that appointment. Poplašen then nominated Brane MILJUŠ of the SNSD for the post, but Miljuš was immediately expelled from his party for agreeing to the appointment; his nomination was also rejected by the assembly. The Poplašen/Dodik standoff continued into March, with moderates in the assembly attempting to limit Poplašen's authority, particularly his control of the military and security forces. The situation was further complicated by impending NATO action against Yugoslavia because of its policies in Kosovo. Poplašen was particularly supportive of Belgrade. On March 5, 1999, High Representative Westendorp announced the "dismissal" of Poplašen as president for "abuse of power" in his attempt to oust Dodik. However, Poplašen refused to accept the directive, his position having been strengthened by Serb anger (even among moderates) over the ruling by an international arbitration panel that the city of Brčko, which had been under de facto Serbian control, should be designated as a "neutral" (multiethnic) city under the central presidency. Meanwhile, events had proceeded more smoothly as far as the government of the Federation was concerned, Prime Minister Bičakčić having been reappointed to head a revamped government on December 12, 1998.

On December 28, 1998, the central presidency named Silajdžić to continue as a cochair of the central Council of Ministers and nominated Svetozar MIHAJLOVIĆ of *Sloga* and the SNS to succeed hard-liner Bosić as the Serb cochair. (Neven TOMIĆ, a Croat, was asked to remain as deputy chair.) However, Mihajlović's appointment was strongly criticized by the SDS and Poplašen, and the central House of Representatives did not confirm the appointments until February 3, 1999, following a series of negotiations that apparently mollified the Serbian hardliners.

In August 1999 Wolfgang Petritsch, the Austrian ambassador to Yugoslavia and EU special envoy for Kosovo, was named to succeed High Representative Westendorp, and in October he prohibited Poplašen and two other SRS officials from competing in local and general elections scheduled for 2000. At the same time, he rejected the application of Serb Vice President Mirko SAROVIĆ of the SDS to become the Serb Republic's president, and the office therefore remained vacant for another 14 months. In the Federation, Vice President Ejup Ganić rotated to the presidency on January 1, 2000, exchanging offices with Ivo ANDRIĆ-LUŽANSKI (HDZ-BiH); the two had been elected to the rotating offices by the Federation Parliament on December 11, 1998.

On April 12–13, 2000, the Republic of Bosnia and Herzegovina's Parliamentary Assembly voted to abandon the practice of having two chairs head the Council of Ministers. Instead, as with the collective presidency, the leadership would rotate among the three ethnic constituencies every eight months. The decision was partly a response to acrimonious differences between Cochairs Mihajlović and Silajdžić, the former having accused the latter of, among other things, "war-mongering" and attempting to undermine ethnic parity. On April 26 the presidency nominated for the post Tihomir GLIGORIĆ of the SPRS, whom Prime Minister Dodik had dismissed as deputy prime minister of the Serb Republic in January, but the nomination failed to muster sufficient support in the central House of Representatives and was withdrawn on May 8. Two weeks later the presidency nominated independent economist Spasoje TUŠEVLJAK, also a Serb, and he was confirmed as prime minister on June 6, succeeding Silajdžić and Mihajlović. On June 22 the House endorsed the Tuševljak cabinet.

Meanwhile, Dodik's differences with the SPRS, including his dismissal of Gligorić, had led the SPRS to announce its withdrawal from the Serb Republic's *Sloga* government in February 2000. Dodik nevertheless retained enough support to continue as prime minister, until losing a September 7 no-confidence vote, 43–1, in the 83-member National Assembly. Declaring the vote unconstitutional, Dodik stated that he would remain in office until the November 11 election, at which he was challenging Sarović for the presidency of the Serb Republic.

On October 14, 2000, Minister of Human Rights and Refugees Martin RAGUŽ of the HDZ-BiH was nominated to succeed national Prime Minister Tuševljak, collateral with Živko Radišić's rotation to the chair of the collective presidency in succession to Alija Izetbegović, who had decided to retire from office. (Tuševljak and Radišić, both Serbs, were prohibited from filling the two positions simultaneously.) The House of Representatives confirmed Raguž on October 18.

The parliamentary elections of November 11, 2000, saw many voters move away from hard-line nationalist parties at the central level and in the Bosniac-Croat Federation, the principal beneficiary being the new multiethnic Social Democratic Party of Bosnia and Herzegovina

(*Socijaldemokratska Partija Bosne i Hercegovine*—SDP), which pulled even with the Bosniac SDA and surpassed both the Serb SDS and the Croat HDZ-BiH. In the Serb Republic, however, the SDS continued its dominance, easily winning a plurality in the legislature and seeing its candidate for president, Vice President Sarović, defeat Prime Minister Dodik two-to-one. Sarović took office on December 16, and a week later he nominated a centrist, Mladen IVANIĆ of the year-old Party for Democratic Progress of the Serb Republic (*Partija Demoktatskog Progresa Republika Srpska*—PDP), as Serb prime minister. Confirmed on January 12, 2001, the multiparty Ivanić government included at least one member of the SDS, Trade Minister Goran POPOVIĆ. Less than a week later, however, in response to wide international criticism and, more specifically, U.S. threats to cut off aid if the SDS remained in the government, Popović resigned. Although refusing to identify his other ministers' party affiliations, Ivanić announced that they would not participate in partisan activity while in office.

With the 42 seats in the central House of Representatives distributed among 13 parties after the November 2000 election, the SDP, with 9 seats, had announced that it was prepared to open negotiations on forming a government with all but the main nationalist parties—the SDA (8 seats), the SDS (6 seats), and the HDZ-BiH (5 seats). Led by the SDP chair, Zlatko LAGUMDŽIJA, an Alliance for Change (*Alijanse za Promene*) was established on January 13, 2001, encompassing the SDP, the SBiH, and eight other parties. Together, they controlled 17 seats in the House, and on February 22, with the support of several moderate Serb parties, the SDP's Božidar MATIĆ won parliamentary approval of a multiparty Council of Ministers. Prime Minister Matić, a Bosniac, had been nominated by a majority of the collective presidency—over the objections of the HDZ-BiH's Ante Jelavić—after the House of Representatives rejected the redesignation of the Croat Raguž on February 7.

On July 1, 2000, a sharply divided central Constitutional Court had ruled that the country's constitution extended the constituent status of all three major ethnic communities throughout the entire country and required that the separate constitutions of the Federation and the Serb Republic be brought into line with the central document. The plurality Bosniac constituency praised the decision, whereas the smaller Serb and Croat constituencies feared a loss of concessions that had been recognized at Dayton. Seeking to protect their standing, some Croat leaders demanded that the Dayton agreement be renegotiated.

Under the leadership of Copresident Jelavić, on October 28, 2000, some nine Croat parties formed an unofficial Croatian National Assembly (*Hrvatskih Narodnog Sabora*—HNS), which on March 3, 2001, declared a boycott of the Federation government as well as establishment of a "Croatian self-administration" for cantons having Croat majorities. Jelavić stated that the HNS would consider revoking the self-administration edict if the government met a list of demands, including rescindment of recent changes that had been made by the OSCE to electoral rules. Those changes allowed all members of the Federation's ten cantonal assemblies, whatever their ethnicity, to elect the Croat members of the central government's upper parliamentary chamber, the House of Peoples, thereby increasing the prospects of multiethnic parties and potentially diminishing the power of the HDZ-BiH. On March 7 High Representative Petritsch removed Jelavić from the central presidency because of his involvement in the autonomy movement, which violated the Dayton agreement.

Confronted by nearly universal condemnation, including that of the government in Zagreb, on March 16, 2001, the HNS announced a two-month postponement in self-rule, and on March 20 the new House of Peoples was constituted as scheduled. A week later the central House of Representatives elected Jozo KRIŽANOVIĆ (SDP) to Jelavić's former seat in the collective presidency, and Beriz BELKIĆ (SBiH) to the Bosniac seat, replacing Halid GENJAC (SDA), who for five months had served as Alija Izetbegović's interim replacement.

Meanwhile, on February 27–28, 2001, the Federation Parliament had elected two members of the Alliance for Change, Karlo FILIPOVIĆ of the SDP and Safet HALILOVIĆ of the SBiH, to the

Federation's rotating presidency/vice presidency. The previously announced departure from office on January 11, 2001, of Prime Minister Bičakčić had also opened the way for the Alliance (with some 70 seats in the 140-seat House of Representatives) to forge the Federation's first nonnationalist government, which won lower-house approval on March 12. Headed by Prime Minister Alija BEHMEN of the SDP, the cabinet was dominated by the SDP and the SBiH but also included several independents.

On June 22, 2001, central Prime Minister Matić resigned following the failure of the Parliamentary Assembly to pass an elections bill designed to address the Constitutional Court's concerns about ethnic constituencies. Passage also would have opened the way for Bosnia and Herzegovina's admission to the Council of Europe. On July 10 the central presidency nominated as his replacement the SDP's Lagumdžija, who had been serving as foreign minister. Legislative confirmation followed on July 18. Lagumdžija was succeeded in the rotating post on March 15, 2002, by Dragan MIKEREVIĆ of the PDP.

On April 19, 2002, a month before being succeeded as high representative by Lord Paddy Ashdown of the United Kingdom, Wolfgang Petritsch promulgated constitutional amendments and electoral law changes for the Federation and the Serb Republic, neither of which, in his assessment, had mustered sufficient legislative support for achieving the ends outlined in the July 2000 Constitutional Court decision. With the overarching goal of instituting political equality among Serbs, Croats, and Bosniacs, Petritsch's revisions mandated significant changes to the structure of the entities' legislatures as well as requirements that all ethnic groups be represented at all levels of government.

On October 5, 2002, voters went to the polls to elect (1) at the national level, the three members of the presidency plus the House of Representatives; (2) in the Federation, the House of Representatives and cantonal assemblies; and (3) in the Serb Republic, a president, two vice presidents, and the National Assembly. Overall, the three principal nationalist parties—the Bosniac SDA, the Serb SDS, and the Croat HDZ-BiH (in coalition with other,

smaller Croat parties)—had the greatest success in the legislative contests in addition to sharing the tripartite presidency. On October 28 Dragan ČOVIĆ (HDZ-BiH), Mirko Sarović (SDS), and Sulejman TIHIĆ (SDA) were inaugurated as the triumvirate, although Sarović's tenure was brief: he resigned on April 2, 2003, after being implicated in the sale of armaments to Iraq, despite a UN embargo, and in efforts by Bosnian military intelligence agents to spy on NATO and EU personnel. Sarović was succeeded a week later by Borislav PARAVAC (SDS).

Dragan ČAVIĆ (SDS) was inaugurated as president of the Serb Republic on November 28, 2002. Niko LOZANČIĆ (HDZ-BiH) was sworn in on January 27, 2003, as president of the Federation, following his election by the new Federation Parliament. Also in January, new national and Serb Republic prime ministers—Adnan TERZIĆ (SDA) and Dragan Mikerević (PDP), respectively—won legislative approval. A new Federation prime minister, Ahmet HADŽIPAŠIĆ (SDA), was confirmed in February.

Objecting to High Representative Ashdown's recent dismissals of Serb officials for noncooperation with the ICTY, Serb Prime Minister Mikerević resigned in December 2004 and was succeeded in February 2005 by Pero BUKEJLOVIĆ (SDS). Less than two months later, on March 29, Ashdown dismissed the Croat member of the national presidency, Dragan Čović, who had refused to step down voluntarily in response to corruption allegations dating back to his 2000–2003 tenure as Federation deputy prime minister. His replacement, Ivo Miro JOVIĆ (HDZ-BiH), was confirmed by the national Parliamentary Assembly in early May.

Led by the SNSD, on January 26, 2006, opposition forces in the Serb National Assembly ousted the Bukejlović government by passing a no-confidence motion 44–29. Crucial support for the motion came from the PDP, which had withdrawn from the SDS-led administration in late November 2005, citing the slow pace of reform. The SDS subsequently indicated that it would join the opposition at both the national and Serb Republic levels. On February 4 Serb President Čavić designated a former prime minister, the SNSD's Milorad Dodik, to form a new government, which was endorsed by the National Assembly on February 28.

Meanwhile, the International Criminal Tribunal in The Hague has continued its work. On April 3, 2000, former member of the presidency Momčilo Krajišnik was arrested by the SFOR and delivered to The Hague, where he pleaded not guilty to charges that included genocide, crimes against humanity, and violations of the Geneva Convention. On January 10, 2001, former Serb president Biljana Plavšić, having confirmed a widespread rumor that she had been secretly indicted, turned herself in and pleaded innocent to similar charges. On October 2, 2002, however, she pleaded guilty to crimes against humanity. All other charges were dropped, and on February 27, 2003, she was sentenced to 11 years in prison. As of August 2006 the two "most wanted" Bosnians, Radovan Karadžić and Ratko Mladić, remained at large, and the Krajišnik trial was continuing in The Hague.

Constitution and Government

The Dayton peace agreement of November 1995 laid down a new constitutional structure under which the Republic of Bosnia and Herzegovina, while having a single sovereignty, was to consist of two "entities," namely the (Bosniac-Croat) Federation of Bosnia and Herzegovina, and the Serb Republic (*Republika Srpska*) of Bosnia and Herzegovina. Responsibilities accorded to the central republican government include foreign relations, trade and customs, monetary policy, international and interentity law enforcement, immigration, international and interentity communications and transportation, interentity policy coordination, and air traffic control. The institutions of the central republic include a three-person presidency (one Bosniac, one Croat, and one Serb), a Council of Ministers, a bicameral legislature, a judicial system, and a central bank. The presidency has exclusive control over foreign affairs and the armed forces, while the chair of the Council of Ministers (prime minister), who is appointed by the presidency and confirmed by the House of Representatives, is the head of government.

The judicial branch is headed by a State Court (with criminal, administrative, and appellate divisions), which began functioning in January 2003. A nine-member Constitutional Court (four judges nominated by the Federation House of Representatives, two by the Serb National Assembly, and three noncitizens nominated by the president of the European Court of Human Rights in consultation with the presidency), like the State Court, functions at the national level, while both entities have their own, separate court systems. A High Judicial Council, with participation by international jurists, screens candidates for judicial and prosecutorial positions.

Government functions not specifically vested in the Republic of Bosnia and Herzegovina are regarded as the responsibility of the entities, although some of these may eventually revert to the central administration by agreement of the parties. The Dayton agreement provides for the protection of human rights and the free movement of people, goods, capital, and services throughout the country. It also commits the entities to accept binding arbitration in the event of their being unable to resolve disputes and to cooperate with the orders of the UN International Criminal Tribunal in The Hague. Any person indicted by the tribunal or the Bosnian justice system may not hold appointed or elected office.

In 2000 the Constitutional Court ruled that all citizens should have equal standing throughout the country, which resulted in an April 2002 decision by the High Representative to amend the Federation and Serb Republic constitutions. As a consequence, proportional ethnic representation was mandated at all levels of government and the judiciary. In addition, with effect from the October 2002 election, the Federation's bicameral parliament was reconfigured, and a new Council of Peoples, with limited powers, was established in the Serb Republic. (See the discussion of the various legislative bodies in the Legislatures section, below.)

The Muslim-Croat federation agreement of March 18, 1994, provided that indirectly elected representatives of the two ethnic communities would serve alternate one-year terms as president and vice president, although no change in the initial appointments of May 1994 were made prior to the September 1996 legislative elections. From 2002, however, the president serves a four-year term, supported by two vice presidents from the other two communities. The president nominates a government headed by a prime minister for legislative endorsement. Ministers must have deputies who are not from their own constituent group. Local government is based on ten cantons, each with its own elected assembly, and municipalities, each with an elected council and mayor. The judiciary includes both Constitutional and Supreme Courts as well as cantonal and municipal courts. There is also provision for a Human Rights Court.

The government of the Serb Republic of Bosnia and Herzegovina, declared in March 1992 and recognized under the 1995 Dayton accord, is headed by a directly elected president. Since 2002 he has been assisted by two vice presidents, instead of one, representing the other ethnic communities. The National Assembly, directly elected by proportional representation, elects the prime minister upon the nomination of the president. The separate Council of Peoples, elected by the ethnic caucuses of the National Assembly, was first constituted in 2003. At the local level administration is based on municipalities, each with an elected assembly and a mayor. The judiciary is headed by a Supreme Court and a Constitutional Court and also includes district and basic courts.

At present, the entire executive, legislative, and judicial structure, at both the central and entity levels, is subject to decisions by the Office of the High Representative of the International Community, a position established to oversee implementation of the Dayton accords. The high representative, who is nominated by an international Peace Implementation Council and confirmed by the UN Security Council, has broad powers to issue decrees, dismiss officials who violate the accords, and establish civilian commissions.

Foreign Relations

On December 24, 1991, prior to its declaration of independence, Bosnia and Herzegovina joined Croatia, Macedonia, and Slovenia in requesting diplomatic recognition from the European Community (EC, later the EU). However, the first foreign power to recognize its sovereignty was Bulgaria on January 16, 1992, with the EC according recognition on April 6 and the United States taking similar action the following day. On May 22 Bosnia and Herzegovina was admitted to the UN, thereby qualifying for immediate membership in the Conference on Security and Cooperation in Europe (CSCE, subsequently the OSCE). Amid escalating interethnic conflict and Serbian advances, the republican presidency formally declared on June 20 that a "state of war" existed with the rump Yugoslav federation (Serbia and Montenegro).

Although Western governments were initially unwilling to provide more than humanitarian assistance to the increasingly besieged Bosnians, in May 1993 the UN Security Council created six "safe areas" (including Sarajevo) for Bosniacs. UNPROFOR attempted to expedite the delivery of aid to isolated Bosnian civilians, while on February 28, 1994, in the first offensive action by NATO in its 44-year history, allied aircraft enforcing a "no-fly zone" over Bosnia and Herzegovina shot down four Serbian attack aircraft. Further UN/NATO air strikes on Bosnian Serb positions followed in April and November, although without noticeably denting Serb military capacity.

Regionally, Bosnia and Herzegovina became a member of the Central European Initiative (CEI), originally formed in 1989 as a "Pentagonal" group of Central European states committed to mutual and bilateral economic cooperation; however, development of relations with the Council of Europe and other bodies was stalled by the unresolved internal conflict. In the wider international arena, the Sarajevo government obtained some diplomatic backing from the Nonaligned Movement, and, as an observer at the Organization of the Islamic Conference (OIC) summit in December 1994, President Izetbegović received numerous pledges of financial and other support from member states.

In accordance with the Dayton peace agreement, the UN Security Council on November 22,

1995, voted to lift the arms embargo on former Yugoslavia (formal implementation following on June 18, 1996), while on December 14 the Bosnian and rump Yugoslav governments accorded one another formal recognition. After protracted negotiations, in June 1996 the three Bosnian governments together with Croatia and Serbia proper signed an OSCE-brokered agreement in Florence, Italy, under which they were to reduce their holdings of five categories of offensive weaponry to specified levels within 16 months.

Both the Serb Republic and the Bosniac-Croat Federation signed "special relations" treaties with their ethnic confreres in Yugoslavia (now called Serbia and Montenegro) and Croatia, respectively, even though such treaties are considered by some to be in conflict with both the Dayton accords and the Bosnian constitution. In addition, an agreement was negotiated between the Republic of Bosnia and Herzegovina and Croatia in 1998 providing each country with trade advantages. The Federation also concluded an agreement (despite some opposition from Bosniac leaders) establishing extensive cooperation with Croatia. Formal diplomatic relations were established with Yugoslavia in December 2000, following the change of government in Belgrade. The first summit of the presidents of Yugoslavia, Croatia, and Bosnia and Herzegovina (including the two entity presidents) convened in Sarajevo on June 15, 2002, although a number of difficult issues, including dual citizenship for ethnic Croats and Serbs, were not addressed. A dual citizenship agreement with Yugoslavia was concluded in October 2002 and one with Croatia in August 2005.

Membership in the Council of Europe was achieved in April 2002. Three months earlier Bosnian security officials had turned over to the United States six Algerians whom Washington suspected of having connections to the al-Qaida terrorist network. They had been held since October 2001, but the Bosnian courts had recently ruled that there were insufficient grounds for their continued detention.

In June 2004 NATO reduced its troop level from 12,000 to 7,000, and six months later, on December 4, the SFOR mission concluded. At that time the EU's newly established EUFOR assumed the peacekeeping mandate, utilizing basically the same troops. The changeover had been authorized by the UN Security Council in November. (Two years earlier an EU Police Mission had replaced the UN Mission in Bosnia and Herzegovina [UNMIBH], which the UN had described as "the most extensive police reform and restructuring mandate ever undertaken by the United Nations.") A total of 22 EU member states and 11 other countries pledged personnel for EUFOR's "Operation Althea." At the same time, the U.S. military presence in Bosnia was reduced from 700 to about 250 personnel. Their responsibilities focused on military training, the search for suspected war criminals, and antiterrorism.

Current Issues

In February 2005 Paddy Ashdown, acknowledging broad domestic dissatisfaction with the extraordinary powers still being wielded by his office, stated that the time was rapidly approaching for ending the foreign oversight, a conclusion seconded by his successor, Christian Schwartz-Schilling, who assumed office on January 31, 2006. Writing in the *International Herald Tribune* of February 2, he said that he would have to "step back" for Bosnia to achieve full sovereignty. He further stated, "It is not possible to decree reconciliation, opportunity and prosperity. Institutions that have been created by imposition will never function effectively unless Bosnians of all ethnicities buy in to them and until Bosnian citizens expect them, and not international organizations, to deliver reform."

Virtually all experts have concluded that Bosnia's viability as a unitary state requires significant changes in its structure, but achieving that goal will not be easy. Copresident Sulejman Tihić, a Bosniac, has called for reshaping Bosnia into a unitary but decentralized country with state, regional, and local governments. The more hard-line Serbian parties oppose any changes that strengthen the central government to the detriment of the Serb entity. The HDZ-BiH has advocated elimination of the entities or creation of a third, Croat entity from Federation communes where Croats predominate.

Meeting in Washington on November 22, 2005, to mark the tenth anniversary of the Dayton accords, leaders from all three ethnic groups, pressured by the EU as well as the United States, agreed that they would take "first steps" toward comprehensive institutional reforms, including the abandonment of the tripartite republican presidency. Signatories to the "Washington declaration" included the three copresidents and leaders from eight parties: the Serbian SDS, SNSD, and PDP; the Bosniac SDA, SBiH, and SDP; and the Croat HDZ-BiH and an ally, the Croatian National Union (*Hrvatska Narodna Zajednica*—HNZ). Nevertheless, the first round of talks on constitutional reform concluded in mid-January 2006 without a comprehensive agreement. The participants agreed to strengthen the role of the state-level prime minister and cabinet as well as the role of the national House of Representatives, but consensus on replacing the copresidency and resolving other issues remained elusive. With an eye toward elections due to be held in October 2006, a target date of March 2006 had been set for completing the reform process, but some party leaders later backed away from that commitment.

Also at the Washington meeting in November 2005, Bosnian Serb leaders pledged to take "all possible measures and actions" in pursuit of Radovan Karadžić and Ratko Mladić if the two fugitives did not voluntarily surrender. Capturing both has long been one of the key prerequisites for Bosnian membership in NATO's Partnership for Peace (PfP) program and for a closer relationship with the EU. In the latter regard, on November 25 formal negotiations opened with the EU on a Stabilization and Association Agreement (SAA), a first step toward joining the EU as well as, more immediately, improving trade relations and accessing development capital. The talks had been delayed until passage of legislation restructuring the country's ethnically divided police force, as insisted upon by the European Commission. The resulting Directorate for Police Restructuring Implementation met for the first time in late January 2006.

It wasn't until November 2004 that the Serb Republic formally apologized for the 1995 Srebrenica massacre. The apology did little to bridge ethnic differences, however, and many Serb nationalists complain that the world has paid too little attention to atrocities committed against the Serb population during the 1992–1995 civil war. In November 2004 the International Committee of the Red Cross reported that more than 16,000 individuals from the conflict remain missing. The Office of the UN High Commissioner for Refugees has estimated that of the 2.2 million who had fled the strife, about 1.0 million have returned and that some 500,000 of those still living abroad may want to repatriate, although the number of registered returns has fallen off dramatically since the 108,000 of 2002: only 3,600 occurred in the first half of 2005. There are no accurate figures indicating how many returnees have sold their homes and moved to communities where they are in the ethnic majority. In addition, some 200,000 individuals remain internally displaced.

In September 2005 the ICTY for the first time transferred a prisoner for trial to a Balkan state. In March the Bosnia and Herzegovina State Court had inaugurated a Department of War Crimes, and by September ICTY prosecutors had requested the ICTY to transfer the cases of 14 suspects to Sarajevo. Initially, international prosecutors and judges will predominate.

Political Parties

For four and a half decades after World War II, the only authorized political party in Yugoslavia was the Communist Party, which was redesignated in 1952 as the League of Communists of Yugoslavia (*Savez Komunista Jugoslavija*—SKJ). In 1989 noncommunist groups began to emerge in the republics, and in early 1990 the SKJ approved the introduction of a multiparty system, thereby effectively triggering its own demise. In Bosnia and Herzegovina the party's local branch was succeeded by the League of Communists of Bosnia and Herzegovina–Party of Democratic Changes (SK BiH-SDP; see SDP, below). Political parties have flourished, despite opposition complaints of alleged "repressive" efforts on the part of the leading nationalist parties, especially during election campaigns.

During the 1990s a number of coalitions emerged to contest elections at the central and entity levels. The most prominent, the Coalition for a Unified and Democratic Bosnia and Herzegovina (*Koalicija za Cjevolitu i Demokratsku Bosnu i Hercegovinu*—KCD), was formed prior to the 1997 balloting for the Serb National Assembly by the Party of Democratic Action (SDA), the Party for Bosnia and Herzegovina (SBiH), the Civic Democratic Party (GDS), and the Liberal Party (LS). It won 16 seats at that poll and then, at the September 1998 elections, emerged as the leading group in both the central House of Representatives and the Federation House of Representatives, while finishing second in the Serb National Assembly. In addition, its candidate for the Bosniac seat on the central presidency, Alija Izetbegović of the SDA, was elected with nearly 87 percent of the vote within the ethnic group and 31 percent of the overall national vote (the most of any candidate). The KCD failed to hold together, however, as the other participants moved further away from the strongly nationalist SDA.

Another coalition, Accord (*Sloga;* also translated as Unity), was established in June 1998 to present joint moderate candidates in the September balloting, at which Živko Radišić of *Sloga*'s Socialist Party of the Serb Republic (SPRS) won the Serb central presidential seat with 51.2 percent of the ethnic vote and 21.8 percent of the national total. However, *Sloga* leader Biljana Plavšić of the Serbian People's Alliance (SNS) was defeated in her attempt at reelection as president of the Serb Republic. Milorad Dodik, the leader of a third *Sloga* party, the Party of Independent Social Democrats (SNSD), served as prime minister of the Serb Republic from January 1998 until after the November 2000 election. By then, *Sloga* had dissolved, with the SPRS having withdrawn from the Serb government the preceding February.

No broad coalitions emerged to fight the November 2000 elections, but as a consequence of subsequent efforts to prevent the strongly nationalist SDA, Croatian Democratic Union (HDZ), and Serbian Democratic Party (SDS) from maintaining their predominance, on January 13, 2001, ten moderate parties signed an agreement to establish the Alliance for Change (*Alijanse za Promene*). Initial participants were the Social Democratic Party of Bosnia and Herzegovina (SDP), the SBiH, the New Croatian Initiative (NIH), the GDS, the Croatian Peasants' Party (HSS), the Bosnian-Herzegovinian Patriotic Party (BPS), the Republican Party (RS), the Liberal Democratic Party (LDS), and two pensioners' parties. With the support of a number of other moderate parties, the Alliance, led by the SDP and the SBiH, won control of the central and Federation parliaments and by late March held the Bosniac and Croat seats in the central presidency, the offices of president and vice president of the Federation, and the premierships of both the state and the Federation. In June 2002 it was announced that the Alliance had disbanded, most of its component parties having decided against a coalition approach to the October elections.

In all, 57 parties, some of them grouped into 9 coalitions, were verified by the national Election Commission to contest the October 2002 balloting. More than 70 parties competed in the October 2004 local elections—the first under Bosnian administration—at which the nationalists SDS, HDZ-BiH, and SDA won control in 99 of 122 municipalities.

Parties Represented in the 2002–2006 Central House of Representatives

Party of Democratic Action (*Stranka Demokratske Akcije*—SDA). Organized in May 1990 by Alija Izetbegović, Fikret Abdić (now of the DNZ, below), and others, the SDA is a nationalist grouping representing Bosnian Muslims (Bosniacs). Favoring both decentralization and a unitary state, it obtained substantial pluralities in the 1990 legislative and presidency elections, thereafter dominating the republican government in coalition with other parties. In April 1996 the SDA was weakened by the formation of the breakaway Party for

Bosnia and Herzegovina (SBiH, below), but it nevertheless remained the leading Bosniac party in the September elections. In addition to competing in the Federation, the SDA was the driving force behind formation of the KCD alliance in the Serb Republic.

With the party having performed poorly at local elections, in April 2000 it registered a vote of no confidence in the leadership of its deputy chairs, Halid GENJAC and Ejup GANIĆ, who were replaced in May by Edhem Bičakčić, the Federation prime minister, and Sulejman Tihić. At virtually the same time the party expelled Ganić for refusing to resign as president of the Federation, a position he had assumed on a rotational basis at the end of 1999 after having served a year as vice president. In October 2000 the SDA's dominant figure, Alija Izetbegović, left the collective presidency, citing age and ill health, with Genjac assuming the Bosniac seat on an interim basis. Izetbegović died in 2003.

At the November 2000 election the SDA remained the strongest party in the Federation, winning 38 seats in the House of Representatives on a 27 percent vote share. In the simultaneous balloting for the central House of Representatives, it finished second, with about 20 percent of the vote and 8 seats, while in the Serb Republic it captured 7 percent of the vote and 6 National Assembly seats. In January 2001 Prime Minister Bičakčić left the office he had held for four years to resume his position as general manager of the state electricity company, but shortly thereafter High Representative Wolfgang Petritsch dismissed him because of corruption allegations.

The SDA emerged from the 2002 elections as the dominant Bosniac party, winning a leading 10 seats in the national House of Representatives, capturing twice as many seats as any other party and 33 percent of the vote in the downsized Federation House of Representatives, and retaining its status as the leading Bosniac party in the Serb Republic, where its candidate for president, Adil OSMANOVIĆ, led all other Bosniac candidates and thus was inaugurated as one of two vice presidents. In addition, Party Chair Tihić won the Bosniac seat in the national presidency, while Desnica RADIVOJEVIĆ

finished fourth among Serb candidates. New national and Federation coalition governments were then formed under the SDA's Adnan Terzić and Ahmet Hadžipašić, respectively.

Leaders: Sulejman TIHIĆ (Copresident of the Republic and Chair of the Party), Bakir IZETBEGOVIĆ (Vice Chair), Adnan TERZIĆ (Prime Minister of the Republic), Ahmet HADŽIPAŠIĆ (Prime Minister of the Federation), Šefik DŽAFEROVIĆ (Speaker of the House of Representatives of the Republic).

Party for Bosnia and Herzegovina (*Stranka za Bosnu i Hercegovinu*—SBiH). The SBiH was launched in April 1996 by Haris Silajdžić, who had resigned as prime minister of the central government in January after disagreeing with fundamentalist elements of the ruling SDA. The new party aimed to appeal to all ethnic communities and had some success in the September 1996 balloting, winning ten seats in the House of Representatives of the Federation and two in the central House of Representatives, while Silajdžić polled 14 percent in the presidential contest. For the 1997 National Assembly election in the Serb Republic, the SBiH joined the SDA in the KCD alliance, where it remained for the September 1998 balloting.

Meanwhile, Silajdžić had returned to the copremiership of the central government in January 1997 and continued in that office until the April 2000 passage of a new Council of Ministers law and the resultant appointment of a single prime minister, Spasoje Tuševljak, two months later. At the November elections, the SBiH, running independently, captured 5 seats in the central House of Representatives (on a 12 percent vote share) and 21 seats in the Federation's lower house (15 percent vote share). It also won 4 seats (on 5 percent of the vote) in the Serb Republic's National Assembly. In January 2001 it joined the SDP as a leading force behind formation of the antinationalist Alliance for Change, and in late February the Federation House of Representatives confirmed the party's secretary general, Safet Halilović, as vice president for a year in the Federation's rotating presidency/vice presidency. Silajdžić announced his retirement from politics in September 2001 but in 2002 ran for the Bosniac seat in the state presidency, finishing a close second with 35 percent support. The SBiH won 6 seats in the national House of Representatives, second to the SDA, and 15 seats in the Federation lower house, while retaining its 4 seats in the Serb National Assembly. Following the elections the SBiH joined in the governing coalitions at the national and entity levels.

Leaders: Safet HALILOVIĆ (Former President of the Federation of Bosnia and Herzegovina and Chair of the Party), Haris SILAJDŽIĆ (Former Chair of the Party and Former Cochair of the Council of Ministers of the Republic of Bosnia and Herzegovina), Sahbaz DŽIHANOVIĆ (Vice President of the Federation).

Serbian Democratic Party of Bosnia and Herzegovina (*Srpska Demokratska Stranka Bosne i Hercegovine*—SDS). Formed in July 1990, the SDS serves as the main political organ of the Serbian population. Almost from the birth of the party, hard-line nationalists began purging more moderate factions. The party was technically banned in 1992, after its electoral victories in 1990, due to the role of party leader Radovan Karadžić in the war. In August 1995 Karadžić was indicted for war crimes and thus became, under the later Dayton accords, ineligible to hold office. Nevertheless, he was reelected as party president in June 1996 and named as its nominee for president of the Serb Republic. However, bowing to joint U.S.-Serbian pressure, he soon stepped down from his party office and relinquished the party's presidential nomination to the new acting Serb Republic president, Biljana Plavšić. Those changes notwithstanding, the SDS remained essentially under the control of Karadžić.

A split subsequently opened up between the more moderate Banja Luka faction of the SDS, led by Plavšić, and the hard-line Pale faction of Karadžić and Momčilo Krajišnik (then a member of the presidency of the Republic of Bosnia and Herzegovina). The fissure caused a constitutional crisis and resulted in the expulsion of Plavšić from the SDS and the formation of her own party, the

Serbian People's Alliance (SNS, below). Once the conflict was resolved, the SDS saw its representation drop precipitously (45 to 24 out of 83) in the November 1997 balloting for the National Assembly of the Serb Republic, allowing the opposition to exclude the SDS from government for the first time.

Dragan Kalinić was named chair of the SDS in June 1998, shortly after his controversial dismissal as speaker of the National Assembly (see Political background, above). Kalinić subsequently accused Plavšić and her supporters of conducting an anti-SDS "witch hunt" in the media, and he threatened a boycott of the September 1998 national and entity balloting. The party ultimately decided to participate in the elections, but its representation fell even further in the National Assembly (to 19). Krajišnik, who also had the support of the Serb Radical Party (SRS, below), was defeated in his campaign for reelection to the central presidency, securing 45 percent of the votes within the Serb population. However, the SDS supported the successful candidate in the race for president of the Serb Republic—Nikola Poplašen of the SRS.

At the November 2000 elections the SDS again easily finished first in Serb National Assembly balloting, capturing 31 seats on a 38 percent vote share, and its candidate for president of the Serb Republic, Serb Vice President Mirko Sarović, also proved successful, winning 50 percent of the vote and narrowly avoiding a runoff. When the new National Assembly convened, Kalinić was again chosen as speaker. At the central level, the SDS won 6 seats in the House of Representatives on a 15 percent vote share.

Although Sarović attempted to distance himself and the party from the extreme nationalism of the past and from Karadžić, many observers remained skeptical of statements from the SDS leadership that Karadžić no longer held sway behind the scenes. On April 3, 2000, former member of the presidency Krajišnik, himself under indictment, was arrested by the SFOR and quickly transported to The Hague, where he pleaded not guilty to charges that included genocide, crimes against humanity, and violations of the Geneva

Convention. (His trial opened in February 2004 and was ongoing two years later.)

At the October 2002 general election the SDS remained the leading Serbian party at the national level, winning five seats in the House of Representatives and the Serb seat in the collective presidency, and retained both the presidency of the Serb Republic and a plurality in the Serb National Assembly. In April 2003, however, Mirko Sarović stepped down from the tripartite national presidency over allegations related to a spying scandal and violations of a UN embargo against arms sales to Iraq. He was arrested in November 2005 on corruption charges.

As of August 2006 Radovan Karadžić and a number of other internationally indicted Bosnian Serbs remained at large, which in the previous two years had prompted High Representative Paddy Ashdown to dismiss dozens of Serb officials, including then party chair Dragan Kalinić, for noncompliance with the ICTY. Dragan Čavić took over the party reins and in March 2005 was formally elected to the chair.

In January 2006, as a consequence of the Serbian National Assembly's vote of no confidence in the Pero Bukejlović government, the SDS moved into the role of what Čavić termed "constructive opposition" at both the national and entity levels.

Leaders: Dragan ČAVIĆ (President of the Serb Republic and Chair of the Party), Mladen BOSIĆ (Deputy Chair), Borislav PARAVAC (National Co-president), Dragan KALINIĆ, Pero BUKEJLOVIĆ (Former Prime Minister of the Serb Republic).

Croatian Democratic Union of Bosnia and Herzegovina (*Hrvatska Demokratska Zajednica Bosne i Hercegovine*—HDZ-BiH). The HDZ-BiH was launched in August 1990, reportedly on the initiative of its counterpart in Croatia. It ran third in the 1990 balloting and joined the postelection government. Serious strains developed when the party spearheaded the declaration of the ethnic Croat Republic of Herceg-Bosna in 1993, headed by HDZ-BiH leader Mate Boban. Under pressure from Zagreb, the party participated in the creation of the (Muslim-Croat) Federation of Bosnia-Herzegovina

in March 1994, following which Boban was replaced as HDZ-BiH leader. In the September 1996 post-Dayton legislative balloting, the HDZ-BiH had no serious challengers where the voters were Croats.

Prior to the September 1998 elections a number of HDZ-BiH candidates were banned from competing by the OSCE for what was perceived as "blatant support" from Croatian television. Nevertheless, the party emerged as the second largest grouping (behind the KCD) in the Houses of Representatives of the state and the Federation, and its chair, Ante Jelavić, a former defense minister of the Federation, was elected to the Croat seat on the central presidency, with nearly 53 percent of the Croat vote.

On March 7, 2001, the Office of the High Representative dismissed Jelavić from the presidency because of the support he had voiced, in violation of the Dayton agreement, for the unofficial Croatian National Assembly's declaration of "Croatian self-administration." He had been reelected party chair at a congress in July 2000, by which time the party had drafted a new statute severing its connection to Croatia's HDZ. (The latter party, following the death of Croatian President Tudjman in December 1999, had already discontinued its ideological and financial support of the HDZ-BiH.) Following the congress, the HDZ-BiH lost one of its senior members, former foreign minister Jadranko Prlić, who had failed to win a leadership post and who denounced the party for rejecting democratic change. Prlić subsequently joined the New Croatian Initiative (NHI, below).

At the November 2000 general election the party remained the leading Croat formation despite winning only 5 seats in the central House of Representatives, with 12 percent of the vote. It fared better in the Federation election, finishing third, with 25 seats in the lower house and 18 percent of the vote, but it was excluded from the new Alliance for Change government. On February 7, 2001, the Alliance and other parties in the state-level House of Representatives also rejected the collective presidency's nomination of the HDZ-BiH's Martin Raguž to be sole prime minister of

Bosnia and Herzegovina. Raguž, who had been serving as prime minister under a rotation system since October 18, 2000, subsequently served as coordinator of the "Croatian self-administration."

At the October 2002 elections the HDZ's Dragan Čović easily won the Croat seat in the collective presidency, capturing 62 percent of the Croat vote as the candidate of the **Coalition** (*Koalicija*) formed by the HDZ and the small **Croatian Demo-Christians** (*Hrvatski Demokršćana*—HD). At the Federation level the *Koalicija* also included the **Croatian National Union** (*Hrvatska Narodna Zajednica*—HNZ, also translated as the Croatian People's Community), led by Mate BANDUR, with a fourth partner, the **Croatian Christian Democratic Union** (*Hrvatska Kršćanska Demokratska Unija*—HKDU), joining in the Serb Republic. The *Koalicija* won 4 seats in the national House of Representatives and finished second, with 16 seats, to the SDA in the Federation House. (Running independently, the right-wing, nationalist HKDU won 1 seat in the Federation lower house, as it had in 2000.) In January 2003 the Federation Parliament elected the HDZ's Niko Lozančić as the Federation president. In 2004 a number of HDZ hard-liners left the party and formed the Croatian Bloc (HB, below), which is closely connected to the HB in Croatia.

In October 2004 Jelavić, former Federation president Ivo Andrić-Lužanski, and five other Croats pleaded not guilty to charges stemming from the 2001 declaration of Croat self-administration. A year later Jelavić fled to Croatia to avoid incarceration for embezzlement of aid funds in the 1990s. Because of his dual citizenship, Croatia would not extradite him.

A party session in June 2005 elected ousted national copresident Dragan Čović party president by a vote of 283–258 over Bozo LJUBIĆ. Čović's predecessor, Bariša ČOLAK, had withdrawn from the contest following criticism of his leadership. Čović's corruption trial opened in late 2005.

Leaders: Ivo Miro JOVIĆ (National Copresident), Dragan ČOVIĆ (Former National Copresident and President of the Party), Niko LOZANČIĆ (President of the Federation and Deputy President

of the Party), Nevenko HERCEG (Secretary General).

Social Democratic Party of Bosnia and Herzegovina (*Socijaldemokratska Partija Bosne i Hercegovine*—SDP, or *Socijaldemokrati*). The multiethnic SDP was formed in February 1999 as a merger of the Democratic Party of Socialists (*Demokratska Stranka Socijalista*—DSS) and the Social Democrats of Bosnia and Herzegovina (*Socijaldemokrati Bosne i Hercegovine*). The two had reportedly been pressured by social democratic parties in Western European countries to coalesce in order to better oppose the nationalist parties dominating affairs in Bosnia and Herzegovina.

Also styled the Socialist Democratic Party (*Socijalistička Demokratska Partija*—SDP), the DSS had been formed in June 1990, initially as the Democratic Socialist League of Bosnia and Herzegovina (*Demokratski Socijalistički Savez Bosne i Hercegovine*—DSS-BiH). As such, it was the successor to the local branch of the former ruling "popular front" grouping, the Socialist League of the Working People of Yugoslavia (*Socijalistički Savez Radnog Narodna Jugoslavija*—SSRNJ). Later, it absorbed the League of Communists of Bosnia and Herzegovina–Party of Democratic Changes (*Savez Komunista Bosne i Hercegovine–Stranka Demokratskih Promjena*—SK BiH-SDP), which had resulted from reorganization of the republican branch of the SKJ after its withdrawal from the federal organization in March 1990. Subsequently, the DSS was a member of the United List (ZL; see HSS, below) but left after the September 1996 elections.

The Social Democrats of Bosnia and Herzegovina was the new name adopted in May 1998 by the former Union of Bosnian Social Democrats (*Zajednica Socijalistička Demokratska Bosna—*ZSDB), led by Selim BESLAGIĆ. The ZSDB was originally established in September 1990 as the Alliance of Reform Forces of Yugoslavia (*Savez Reformskik Snaga Jugoslaviji za Bosnu i Hercegovinu*—SRS-BiH). As such, it was the local affiliate of the postcommunist Alliance of Reform Forces that had been launched by the federal prime minister, Ante Marković, several months earlier. Beslagić, a Muslim, was elected mayor of Tuzla in 1990 and subsequently emerged as one of the country's leading proponents of a multiethnic approach to government and culture.

With firm support from most of the international community, the SDP made major inroads against the nationalists in the local elections of April 2000 and then at the balloting for the central and Federation legislatures in November 2000. Nationally, the SDP won a slim plurality (9 of the 42 lower house seats) in November, while it finished second, with 37 seats, in the Federation's House of Representatives. With the party president, Zlatko Lagumdžija, having spearheaded formation of the Alliance for Change in January 2001, SDP leaders quickly assumed leading positions at both governmental levels. By late March they held the Croat seat in the central presidency, the presidency of the Federation, and both prime ministerships.

By 2002, however, the SDP had lost considerable ground to the more nationalist parties. Following the October 2002 election, the SDP held only 4 seats in the national House of Representatives, 15 seats in the downsized Federation House, and no major executive office (except for Vice President Ivan TOMLJENOVIĆ in the Serb Republic). A former Federation prime minister, Alija Behmen, had finished third among Bosniac candidates for the state presidency, while Mladen GRAHOVAC had finished seventh in the contest for the Serb seat.

Partly as a consequence of the poor showing at the polls, the party split over the issue of whether to join nationalist-led coalition governments. Opponents retained control of the party, which led a dissident group to establish the Social Democratic Union (SDU-BiH, below) in December 2002. At its third congress, held in February 2005, the SDP reelected President Lagumdžija.

Leaders: Zlatko LAGUMDŽIJA (Former Prime Minister of the Republic of Bosnia and Herzegovina and President of the Party); Alija BEHMAN, Željko KOMŠIĆ, and Slobodan POPOVIĆ (Vice Presidents); Svetozar PUDARIĆ (General Secretary).

Alliance of Independent Social Democrats (*Savez Nezavisnih Socijaldemokrata*—SNSD). The SNSD was formally established in 1996 as the Party (*Stranka*) of Independent Social Democrats and adopted its present name in May 2002, upon completion of a merger with the Democratic Socialist Party (*Demokratska Socijalistička Partija*—DSP).

After participating in the NSSM-SMP electoral alliance in 1996 (see SPRS, below), the SNSD ran its own candidates in the November 1997 balloting for the National Assembly of the Serb Republic, winning two seats. The SNSD's leader, Milorad Dodik, was subsequently elected prime minister of the Serb Republic, pledging to conduct governmental affairs on a nonpartisan basis. The SNSD improved to six seats in the 1998 election for the National Assembly of the Serb Republic. In December 1999 the Social Liberal Party (*Socijalno-Liberalna Stranka*—SLS) merged with the SNSD, with its former leader, Rade DUJAKOVIĆ, being named an SNSD deputy chair.

Prime Minister Dodik finished second in the Serb Republic's presidential contest in November 2000, winning about 26 percent of the first-preference vote. At the central level, the SNSD competed in alliance with the DSP, but the coalition managed to win only a single seat in the House of Representatives. In the Serb Republic, running on its own, the SNSD tied for second with the Party for Democratic Progress of the Serb Republic (PDP, below), taking 11 seats in the National Assembly.

The DSP had been formed by dissidents from the Socialist Party of the Serb Republic (SPRS, below) following the latter's decision in February 2000 to withdraw from the Serb Republic's ruling *Sloga* coalition. Opposition to the withdrawal had led to a number of expulsions from the SPRS, including that of former party leader Nebojša Radmanović. In November 2000 the DSP won four seats in the Serb Republic's National Assembly.

In October 2002 the SNSD's Radmanović finished second in the balloting for the Serb seat in the national presidency, winning 20 percent of the vote. The party finished second in the balloting for the

Serb National Assembly, winning 19 seats, while its candidate for president of the Serb Republic, Milan Jelić, likewise came in second. The SNSD also won 3 seats in the national House of Representatives and 1 in the Federation House.

In October 2003 the SNSD, the Democratic People's Alliance (DNS, below), and the SPRS joined in a "Charter for the Future" and called for early general elections in an effort to oust the three leading Serb, Bosniac, and Croat nationalist parties. In January 2006 the SNSD, as the leading opposition party in the Serb National Assembly, introduced a no-confidence motion against the SDS-led government of the Serb Republic. With the support of the PDP (below), which had withdrawn its support from the government in November 2005, the motion passed and the government fell. In early February the SNSD's Dodik was designated prime minister and asked to form a new administration.

Leaders: Milorad DODIK (Prime Minister of the Serb Republic and Chair of the Party); Nebojša RADMANOVIĆ (Executive Board President); Milan JELIĆ, Velimir KUNIĆ, and Krstan SIMIĆ (Vice Chairs); Igor RADOJIČIĆ (General Secretary).

Party for Democratic Progress of the Serb Republic (*Partija Demoktatskog Progresa Republika Srpska*—PDP). The founding congress of the PDP was held on September 26, 1999, under the leadership of prominent economist Mladen Ivanić, a centrist. After having registered a modest success at the April 2000 local elections, the PDP finished in a tie for second in the November balloting for the Serb National Assembly, winning 11 seats on a 13 percent vote share. Its candidate for president of the Serb Republic, Momčilo TEPIĆ, finished third. In the election for the central House of Representatives, the party won 2 seats and 5 percent of the vote. A month later Serb Republic President Mirko Sarović nominated Ivanić as prime minister of the Serb entity. In 2001 the PDP joined the Alliance for Change.

At the October 2002 balloting the PDP won two seats in the national House of Representatives and finished third in the Serb Republic lower house, with 11 percent of the vote and nine seats. Its candidate for president of the Serb Republic, Dragan Mikerević, also finished third, with 8 percent of the vote, but he was subsequently named prime minister of the entity. He resigned in December 2004 to protest recent dismissals by the Office of High Representative and related "threats and ultimatums" by the West. In November 2005 the PDP withdrew its support from the SDS-led Bukejlović government, which fell in January 2006. A month later, the PDP accepted three positions in Milorad Dodik's new multiparty cabinet.

Leaders: Mladen IVANIĆ (Former Prime Minister of the Serb Republic and Chair of the Party), Dragan MIKEREVIĆ (Former Prime Minister of the Serb Republic), Branko DOKIĆ (2002 candidate for the presidency of Bosnia and Herzegovina), Nevenka TRIFKOVIĆ (General Secretary).

Bosnian Party (*Bosanska Stranka*—BOSS). BOSS won one seat in the Federation's House of Representatives in the September 1998 balloting, while its candidates for the Muslim and Croat seats on the central presidency received 1.3 percent and 0.7 percent of the vote, respectively. In 2000 it won two seats in the Federation's lower house and then added one more in 2002, when it also won one seat in the state-level lower house. Its candidate for the state presidency, Faruk BALIJAGIĆ, won only 2 percent of the Bosniac vote.

Leader: Mirnes AJANOVIĆ.

Croat Democratic Union (*Hrvatska Demokratska Unija*—HDU). The HDU was organized in May 2002 by Miro Grabovac Titan and other former members of the HDZ-BiH who sought a less nationalist posture. For the October 2002 elections the HDU joined forces with the small People's Party "Working for Prosperity" (NS-RzB, below) in forming the **Economic Bloc "Croat Democratic Union for Prosperity"** (*Ekonomski Blok HDU–Za Boljitak*). The coalition won one seat in the national legislature (although its successful candidate, Mladen Potočnik of the NS-RzB, subsequently joined the Republican Party—see below) and two in the Federation lower house. In the Serb Republic the Croatian Peasants' Party (HSS, below) also participated in the Economic Bloc.

Leader: Miro GRABOVAC TITAN (President).

Democratic People's Union of Bosnia and Herzegovina (*Demokratska Narodna Zajednica Bosne i Hercegovine—DNZ*). A Muslim party, the DNZ was launched in April 1996 by Fikret Abdić as the successor to his Muslim Democratic Party (*Muslimanska Demokratska Stranka—MDS*), which had been founded in 1993 in the Muslim-populated northern town of Bihać. A former chicken farmer, Abdić had been a member of the state presidency for the ruling SDA but had later cooperated with the Bosnian Serbs in the defense of Bihać, until its capture by government forces in August 1994. Earlier, he had attempted to proclaim an "Autonomous Province of Western Bosnia."

Abdić won 6.2 percent of the vote in the 1998 balloting for the Bosniac seat on the central presidency. The party also captured one seat in the national House of Representatives and three in the Federation House, retaining all four in 2000. In July 2001 Abdić went on trial in Croatia, where he had resided since 1995, charged with war crimes dating back to 1992–1995. Found guilty in July 2002 and sentenced to 20 years in prison, Abdić chose to run for the national presidency from his prison cell while appealing the conviction; he finished fourth, with 4 percent of the Bosniac vote. At the same time the DNZ won one seat in the state House of Representatives and two in the Federation's lower house. Abdić's sentence was reduced to 15 years by the Croatian Supreme Court in March 2005, but with the verdict having been confirmed, he resigned as DNZ president in May.

Leader: Rifet DOLIĆ (President).

Free Democrats (*BH Slobodnik Demokrata—BHSD*). The Free Democrats was established in May 2005 under the leadership of Sead Avdić, a former speaker of the national House of Representatives. After having been reelected to the lower house in October 2002 as a member of the SDP, he left that party in late 2002 and was elected president of the newly formed SDU-BiH (below). Only a year

later, he decided to sit in the House of Representatives as an independent. At the BHSD's founding convention Avdić described the new party as social democratic and committed to human rights and a market economy.

Leaders: Sead AVDIĆ (President); Nikola TOMIĆ, Vedran DODIK, and Amila DIZDAREVIĆ (Vice Presidents).

New Croatian Initiative (*Nova Hrvatska Inicijativa—NHI*). The NHI was founded in June 1998 by Krešimir Zubak, a former Croat member of the central presidency, and a group of supporters who had recently left the HDZ-BiH. Zubak described the NHI as "Christian Democratic" in orientation and committed to peaceful political existence with Muslims and Serbs, in contrast to the HDZ-BiH, which he described as still in pursuit of political separation. Zubak finished third (with 11.4 percent of the vote) in the race for the Croat seat on the central presidency in the September balloting, while the NHI secured representation in all three legislatures.

At the November 2000 elections the NHI held its single seats at the national and Serb Republic levels but fell from four to two seats in the Federation's House of Representatives. The NHI joined the Alliance for Change in early 2001 and accepted ministerial posts in the resultant national and Federation governments.

At the October 2002 election the NHI won one seat in the national House of Representatives, two in the Federation lower house (one representative was dismissed in March 2003 by the Office of the High Representative because of corruption allegations), and one in the Serb National Assembly. Its candidate for the Croat seat in the state presidency, Mijo ATIĆ, finished a distant third, with 9 percent of the vote. In March 2004 Atić and a number of other NHI leaders attempted to remove Zubak from the party leadership, but Zubak was reelected at a party assembly, prevailing 173–31 over Drago VRBIĆ.

In March 2005, looking toward the 2006 elections, the NHI and four other small, moderate opposition parties—the Croat Peasants' Party (HSS), the Liberal Democratic Party (LDS), the Civic Democratic Party (GDS), and the Pensioners' Party (SPU), all below—signed a cooperation statement.

Leader: Krešimir ZUBAK (Chair).

Pensioners' Party of Bosnia and Herzegovina (*Stranka Penzionera/Umirovljenika*—SPU). The SPU won one seat in the national House of Representatives and two seats in the Federation lower house at the October 2002 elections.

Leader: Husein VOJNIKOVIĆ.

People's Party "Working for Prosperity" (*Narodna Stranka "Radon za Boljitak"*—NS-RzB). A Croat party established in mid-2002, the NS-RzB joined with the HDU to form the Economic Bloc "Croat Democratic Union for Prosperity" (see HDU, above) prior to the October elections; the bloc's sole successful candidate was the NS-RzB's Mladen Potočnik, who subsequently became leader of the Republican Party (below). The Economic Bloc's candidate for the Croat seat in the presidency, NS-RzB leader Mladen Ivanković-Lijanović, finished second, with 17 percent support. In March 2005 he was charged in the scandal that led to the dismissal of the Croatian member of the state presidency, Dragan Čović.

Leader: Mladen IVANKOVIĆ-LIJANOVIĆ.

Republican Party (*Republikanska Stranka*—RS). The RS was formed in 1993 by Stjepan KLJUIĆ, who had been elected to Bosnia-Herzegovina's collegial presidency in 1990 as a representative of the HDZ-BiH but had become unhappy at the parent party's identification with ethnic Croat aims. Thus, the present party strongly favors a multiethnic state.

In legislative contests the RS and the Liberal Bosniac Organization (LBO), campaigning as the Center Coalition (*Koalicija Centra*—KC), won one seat in the Federation House of Representatives in 1998. Human rights activist Senka NOŽICA won 3.1 percent of the vote as the RS candidate for the Croat seat on the central presidency.

In August 2000 the RS and the Liberal Social Party (*Liberalno Socijalna Partija*—LSP) agreed to run jointly in the November elections, at which the RS again won one seat in the Federation's lower house. It then joined the Alliance for Change in January 2001. In October 2002 the party failed to hold its Federation seat; Kljuić won 5 percent of the Croat vote for the central presidency. In 2003 he became a foreign policy adviser to the HDZ-BiH's winning candidate, Dragan Čović. The party's current president was elected to the national House of Representatives from the Economic Bloc "Croat Democratic Union for Prosperity."

In January 2006 the Republican Party joined four other small organizations in forming the **Alliance of Parties of the Political Center** (*Savez Stranaka Političkog Centra*—SSPC), which voiced support for a new constitution and rapid integration into NATO and, in the next decade, the EU. Partners in the SSPC include the **Bosnian Podrinje People's Party** (*Bosansko Podrinjska Narodna Stranka*—BPNS), led by Seid KARIĆ, and the **Bosnia-Herzegovina Party of Rights** (*Bošanskohercegovačka Stranka Prava*—BSP), led by Besim ŠARIĆ.

Leaders: Mladen POTOČNIK (President), Fuad SILAJDŽIĆ.

Serb Radical Party of the Serb Republic (*Srpska Radikalna Stranka Republike Srpske*—SRS). Related to the Serbian Radical Party in Serbia, the SRS is widely seen as an extension of the Pale faction of the SDS. It increased its electoral performance in the November 1997 National Assembly election, gaining 8 seats for a total of 15, before declining to 11 in 1998. The SRS supported the SDS's Momčilo Krajišnik in the 1998 campaign for the Serb seat on the central presidency, with the SDS in turn supporting the SRS's Nikola Poplašen in his successful run for president of the Serb Republic.

On March 5, 1999, the Office of the High Representative removed Poplašen from the presidency for abuse of power, which included efforts to dismiss Prime Minister Dodik. Poplašen refused to step down, however, and the office remained vacant until December 2000. Moreover, in November 1999 the High Representative prohibited the SRS from participating in the April 2000 local elections and the November 2000 general election, citing obstruction of the Dayton accords by party leaders. As a consequence, a number of party members ran for office under the banners of other Serb parties.

Reelected president of the party in early May 2002, Poplašen stepped down less than a month later so that the SRS could compete in the October election. (Earlier, the High Representative had announced that parties would be ineligible if their official leadership included individuals who had been banned from holding office.) At the general election the SRS won one seat in the national House of Representatives and four seats in the Serb National Assembly. Ognjen Tadić, the SRS candidate for the Serb seat in the national presidency, finished third, with 9 percent of the vote, while Radislav Kanjerić finished fifth in the election for president of the Serb Republic.

In December 2002 the party split, primarily over the issue of support for inclusion of the Bosniac SDA in the Serb government. The more nationalist group, which included Kanjerić and Tadić, ultimately established the SRS "Dr. Vojislav Šešelj" (SRS-VŠ, below). The other faction, based in Banja Luca, elected a new leadership and retained three of the four SRS deputies in the National Assembly. In February 2006 the party withheld its support from the new Dodik government.

Leader: Milanko MIHAJLICA (President).

Socialist Party of the Serb Republic (*Socijalistička Partija Republike Srpske*—SPRS). Founded in June 1993, the SPRS has been affiliated with Slobodan Milošević of Yugoslavia and his Socialist Party, although one wing of the party was very close to other social democratic parties in Europe. The SPRS was the driving force behind the Peoples' Union for Peace–Union for Peace and Progress (*Narodni Savez za Mir–Savez za Mir i Progres*—NSSM-SMP), an alliance of five parties that competed in the 1996 elections to the central and Serb Republic legislatures, winning two seats in the former and ten in the latter. However, the NSSM-SMP did not compete as an alliance in the September 1997 municipal elections or the November 1997

Serb Republic Assembly poll. Two NSSM-SMP components—the Yugoslav Alliance of the Left and the New Radical Party—competed on their own in the 1997 balloting without success. A third component—the Social Liberal Party, which later merged with the SNSD (above)—competed in the municipal elections in an alliance with the SPRS.

Running on its own, the SPRS secured nine seats in the National Assembly of the Serb Republic in 1997, improving to ten in 1998, at which time its president, Živko Radišić, was elected to the presidency of the Republic of Bosnia and Herzegovina as the *Sloga* candidate.

In February 2000 the party leadership decided to withdraw from the governing coalition in the Serb Republic. Observers attributed the move in part to Prime Minister Dodik's dismissal of his deputy prime minister, Tihomir Gligorić of the SPRS, in January. A number of opponents of the withdrawal were soon expelled from or left the party voluntarily to form the DSP (see SNSD). In late April the country's collective presidency nominated Gligorić for the post of central prime minister, but the nomination was withdrawn in early May without a vote in the House of Representatives, support being insufficient for confirmation. At the November 2000 elections the SPRS won one seat at the central level and four in the Serb Republic's National Assembly.

In February 2002 Živko Radišić was ousted as party president and replaced by Petar Djokić. In May Radišić formally resigned from the SPRS and subsequently joined the newly organized People's Party of Socialists (NPS, below), which prompted the SPRS to request that he step down as the Serb member of the national presidency.

At the October 2002 elections the SPRS won one seat in the national House of Representatives and three in the Serb National Assembly. Its candidate for the national presidency, Dargutin ILIĆ, won under 4 percent of the Serb vote, while Djokić, its candidate for president of the Serb Republic, won 5 percent.

In January 2006, contrary to a directive from the party leadership, National Assembly members Nedjo DJURIĆ and Dragutin ŠKREBIĆ voted against the no-confidence motion that ousted the Bukejlović government in the Serb Republic. The party then expelled them.

Leaders: Petar DJOKIĆ (President), Tihomir GLIGORIĆ (Vice President), Živko MARJANAC (Secretary General).

Other Parties Represented in the Federation's House of Representatives

Bosnian-Herzegovinian Patriotic Party (*Bosanskohercegovačka Patriotska Stranka*—BPS). The BPS won two seats in the Federation's House of Representatives in 1998, while its candidate for the Bosniac seat on the central presidency, Sefer Halilović, a former commander of the Bosnia and Herzegovina army, finished third with 5.7 percent of the vote. At the November 2000 elections the BPS won one seat in the national House of Representatives and two in the Federation's lower house. It subsequently joined the Alliance for Change, and Halilović was named to the Behmen cabinet in the Federation.

In October 2002 the BPS won only one seat in the Federation's lower house. Its candidate for the Bosniac seat in the state presidency, Emir ZLATAR, won less than 2 percent of the vote.

On November 15, 2005, the ICTY acquitted Halilović of charges related to the killing of Croatian civilians by troops under his command. He had surrendered to the ICTY in September 2001.

Leader: Sefer HALILOVIĆ.

Civic Democratic Party (*Gradjanska Demokratska Stranka*—GDS). The centrist GDS participated in the KCD alliance in 1997–1998. In November 2000 it won a single seat in the Federation's House of Representatives, after which it joined in forming the Alliance for Change. It again won one Federation seat in October 2002.

Leader: Ibrahim SPAHIĆ.

Croatian Party of Rights (*Hrvatska Stranka Prava*—HSP). Directly linked to the HSP in Croatia, the nationalist HSP won two seats in both the 1996 and 1998 balloting for the Federation's House of Representatives. In 2000 it dropped to one seat, which it retained in 2002 as part of a coalition with the **United Croatian Party of Rights** (*Ujedinjena Hrvatska Stranka Prava*—UHSP).

Leader: Zdravko HRSTIĆ (Chair).

Croatian Peasants' Party of Bosnia and Herzegovina (*Hrvatska Seljačka Stranka Bosne i Hercegovine*—HSS). Affiliated with a similar party in Croatia, the HSS was formed in the early 1990s by moderate Croat leader Ivo Komsić, who was named to the collective presidency in November 1993. Komsić subsequently played a significant role in negotiations leading up to the 1995 Dayton accords, and in 1996 he was the candidate for the Croat seat on the new central presidency from the United List (*Združema Lista*—ZL), a coalition of five parties devoted to a multiethnic approach to affairs in Bosnia and Herzegovina. (Otherwise, the parties in the ZL—the HSS, the Muslim Bosniac Organization [*Muslimanska Bošnjačka Organizacija*—MBO], the Republican Party [RS, above], and the two predecessors of the SDP, the Democratic Party of Socialists [DSS] and the Union of Bosnian Social Democrats [ZSDB]—spanned the political spectrum in orientation.) Komsić finished second in his race, with 10.1 percent of the vote, while the ZL's candidate for the Bosniac seat on the central presidency, Sead Avdić (later of the SDP, SDU-BiH, and BHSD), finished fourth in his race with only 2.3 percent of the vote. Meanwhile, the ZL secured seats in all three legislatures. Komsić later joined the SDU-BiH.

The HSS won one seat in the Federation's House of Representatives in both 1998 and 2000. In January 2000 it participated in forming the Alliance for Change. In October 2002 it retained its Federation seat. It also has close ties to the NHI.

Leader: Marko TADIĆ (President).

Croatian Right Bloc (*Hrvatski Pravaški Blok*—HPB). Formed in June 2002 in an effort to unite various Croatian "parties of rights" (except the HSP), the HPB unsuccessfully contested the national legislative election in October but won one Federation seat.

Leader: Željko KOROMAN (2002 Croat candidate for the central presidency).

Liberal Democratic Party (*Liberalno Demokratska Stranka*—LDS). Formation of the centrist LDS was announced in May 2000 by the Liberal Party of Bosnia and Herzegovina (*Liberalna Stranka Bosne i Hercegovine*—LS-BiH) and the Liberal Bosniac Organization (*Liberalna Bošnjačka Organizacija*—LBO). A formal unification congress was held a month later. The new party won one seat in the Federation's House of Representatives in November 2000 and subsequently joined in formation of the Alliance for Change. It again won one Federation seat in 2002, while the party's chair took 1 percent of the Bosniac vote for the state presidency.

Leader: Rasim KADIĆ (Chair).

Pro-European People's Party (*Proeuropska Narodna Stranka*—ProENS). The ProENS was established in April 2002 under the leadership of a former foreign minister and NHI member, Jadranko Prlić. The party platform called for ethnic cooperation and the formation of expert-based governments.

The party had little success at the October 2002 polling, winning only one seat in the House of Representatives of the Federation, where it ran in coalition with the **Party of Youth of Bosnia and Herzegovina** (*Stranka Mladih Bosne i Hercegovine*—SMBiH). In April 2004 Prlić surrendered to the ICTY, which had indicted him for persecution of Muslims in the Croat separatist Herceg-Bosna. He was released in September while awaiting the start of his trial; as of February 2006 no date had been set.

Leaders: Jadranko PRLIĆ (Chair), Nermin VILA.

Other Parties Represented in the Serb Republic's National Assembly

Alliance of National Revival (*Savez Narodnog Preporoda*—SNP). Led by a former SDS official, Mirko Banjac of the DNS (below), the SNP was established in March–April 2002 by organizations that included the **Party of Serb Unity** (*Stranka Srpskog Jedinstva*—SSJ), the **People's Party of the Serb Republic** (*Narodna Stranka Republika Srpska*—NS), and the **Serb Patriotic Party** (*Srpska Patriotska Stranka*—SPAS). At the October 2002 election the SNP won one seat in the Serb National Assembly, but differences over whether to support the new multiparty Serb Republic government, plus dissatisfaction with Banjac's leadership style, led the NS and the SPAS as well as many of the SNP's officials to leave the Alliance. Those departing also included the SNP's National Assembly member, Radivoje TRBIĆ of the SPAS, who has become a leader of the assembly's Centrist Caucus.

Leader: Mirko BANJAC.

Democratic People's Alliance of the Serb Republic (*Demokratski Narodni Savez Republike Srpske*—DNS). The DNS (also translated as the Democratic National Alliance) was established on June 16, 2000, by anti-Plavšić members of the SNS (below) following their failed attempt to oust her as party leader. Ideologically moderate, the DNS parted ways with the SNS primarily for reasons of personality. At the November 2000 elections it failed to win a seat in the central House of Representatives but took three in the Serb National Assembly, one more than the SNS.

In 2002 the DNS won three seats in the Serb legislature but none nationally. Its candidate for the Serb seat in the national presidency, Milorad COKIĆ, finished far down the list, with only 3 percent support. The party chair, Dragan KOSTIĆ, was equally unsuccessful in his bid for president of the Serb Republic.

In March 2005 the current party chair, Marko Pavić, was charged with abuse of power during his earlier tenure as a minister in the Serb government.

Leaders: Marko PAVIĆ (Chair), Mirko BANJAC.

Serbian People's Alliance of the Serb Republic (*Srpski Narodni Savez Republike Srpske*—SNS). Formed by Serb Republic President Biljana Plavšić (whose name was often appended to the party title) following her expulsion from the SDS in mid-1997, the SNS is a more moderate nationalist formation than the SDS and has been more willing to accept the Dayton accords than its parent party. Its power base is in Banja Luka, where under Plavšić much more room was allowed for dissent than in Pale. The stated goal of the party was to "be based around the original program of the SDS." It saw immediate success in the 1997 National Assembly elections, winning 15 seats, and in 1998 it won 12. However, Plavšić failed in her bid for another term.

Although Plavšić was reelected president of the party in September 1999, differences over her leadership surfaced in 2000, in part because of the party's lack of success at the April local elections. In May the party failed to support her effort to remove Vice President Jovan MITROVIĆ, whom she accused of fostering hard-line policies, and in early June proceeded to elect Dragan Kostić as her replacement. On June 15, however, a court decision reinstated her on technical grounds, after which Kostić and his supporters withdrew to form the Democratic National Alliance (DNS, above). Plavšić retained the support of her Sloga comrade, Serb Republic Prime Minister Milorad Dodik of the SNSD, despite the opposition of the rest of the cabinet.

On January 10, 2001, Plavšić surrendered to the International Criminal Tribunal for the former Yugoslavia in The Hague, having learned of a sealed indictment against her for genocide and crimes against humanity during the civil war, when she had governed alongside Radovan Karadžić. On October 2, 2002, she pleaded guilty to crimes against humanity—seven other charges were dropped—and on February 27, 2003, was sentenced to 11 years in prison. (She has been serving her sentence in Sweden.)

At the October 2002 election the SNS met with little success, winning only one seat in the Serb National Assembly. Svetozar RADIVOJEVIĆ won only 1 percent of the vote for the Serb seat in the national presidency.

Leader: Branislav LOLIĆ (Chair).

Serb Radical Party "Dr. Vojislav Šešelj" (*Srpska Radikalna Strana "Dr. Vojislav Šešelj"*—SRS-VŠ). The SRS-VŠ resulted from a split in the SRS (above) following the October 2002 elections.

The more nationalist Bijeljina-based SRS faction, led by national presidency candidate Radislav Kanjerić and Serb presidential candidate Ognjen Tadić, opposed inclusion of the Bosniac SDA in the new Serb entity government.

In November 2003 the Kanjerić wing held a founding assembly for the new party. Named in honor of the ultranationalist Serb leader Vojislav Šešelj, who had been indicted as a war criminal by the ICTY, the party was initially known as the Serb Radical Alliance "Dr. Vojislav Šešelj" (*Srpski Radikalni Savez "Dr. Vojislav Šešelj"*). One of the four SRS members elected to the Serb National Assembly in 2002 chose to join the SRS-VŠ.

Leaders: Radislav KANJERIĆ (President), Milan LAZIĆ, Ognjen TADIĆ (General Secretary).

Other parties winning one seat in the Serb National Assembly were the **Democratic Party of the Serb Republic** (*Demokratska Stranka Republike Srpske*—DSRS), currently led by Predrag KOVAČEVIĆ; the **Democratic Patriotic Party** (*Demokratska Patriotska Stranka*—DPS), led by Predrag RADIĆ and Darko JOTANOVIĆ; and the **Pensioners' Party of the Serb Republic** (*Penzionerska Stranka Republike Srpske*—PSRS).

Additional Parties

Croatian Bloc (*Hrvatski Blok*—HB). In mid-2004 a number of former hard-line members of the HDZ left the party to form the HB, which is closely connected to the HB in Croatia. Marko TOKIĆ, a former HDZ secretary general whom the Office of High Representative had banned from politics, was considered a behind-the-scenes actor in forming the group. In October 2004 Tokić was one of six individuals indicted for threatening the territorial integrity of the Federation by attempting to organize Croat self-rule in 2001. In 2005 the HB was one of the strongest supporters of establishing a third, Croat entity.

Leaders: Mario VASILJ (Chair), Ivan MADUNIĆ, Marko KRILIĆ.

People's Party of Socialists (*Narodna Partija Socijalista*—NPS). The NPS (sometimes translated as the National Party of Socialists) was

Cabinet

Republic of Bosnia and Herzegovina

As of August 15, 2006

Prime Minister	Adnan Terzić (SDA)

Ministers

Civil Works	Safet Halilović (SBiH)
Defense	Nikola Radovanović (ind.)
European Integration	Adnan Terzić (SDA)
Finance and Treasury	Ljerka Marić (HDZ) [f]
Foreign Affairs	Mladen Ivanić (PDP)
Foreign Trade and Economic Relations	Dragan Doko (HDZ)
Human Rights and Refugees	Mirsad Kebo (SDA)
Justice	Slobodan Kovač (ind.)
Security	Bariša Čolak (HDZ)
Transport and Communications	Branko Dokić (PDP)

Note: The ministers of defense and justice were endorsed by the SDS.

Federation of Bosnia and Herzegovina

As of August 15, 2006

Prime Minister	Ahmet Hadžipašić (SDP)
Deputy Prime Ministers	Gavrilo Grahovac (SBiH)
	Dragan Vrankić (HDZ)

Ministers

Agriculture, Water Management, and Forestry	Marinko Božić (HDZ)
Culture and Sports	Gavrilo Grahovac (SBiH)
Development and Entrepreneurship	Mladen Čabrilo (SBiH)
Education and Science	Zijad Pašić (SDA)
Energy, Mining, and Industry	Vahid Hećo (SBiH)
Finance	Dragan Vrankić (HDZ)
Health	Vjekoslav Mandić (HDZ)
Interior	Mevludin Halilović (SDA)
Justice	Borjana Krišto (HDZ) [f]
Labor and Social Affairs	Radovan Vignjević (SDA)
Refugees and Displaced Persons	Edin Mušić (SDA)
Tourism and Environment	Katica Čerkez (HDZ) [f]
Trade	Maid Ljubović (SBiH)
Transport and Communications	Nedžad Branković (SDA)
Urban Planning	Ferid Otajagić (SBiH)
Veterans and War Disabled	Zahid Crnkić (SDA)

Serb Republic of Bosnia and Herzegovina

As of August 15, 2006

Prime Minister	Milorad Dodik (SNSD)

Ministers	
Administration and Local Government	Nebojša Radmanović (SNSD)
Agriculture, Water Management, and Forestry	Slaven Pekić (PDP)
Economic Affairs and Coordination	Jasna Brkić (ind.) [f]
Economy, Energy, and Development	Milan Jelić (SNSD)
Education and Culture	Anton Kasipović (ind.)
Finance	Aleksandar Džombić (SNSD)
Health and Social Welfare	Ranko Škrbić (SNSD)
Interior	Stanislav Čadjo (SNSD)
Justice	Omer Višić (SBiH)
Labor and Veterans	Boško Tomić (PDP)
Refugees and Displaced Persons	Omer Branković (SDA)
Science and Technology	Bakir Ajanović (ind.)
Trade and Tourism	Predrag Gluhaković (SPRS)
Transport and Communications	Nedeljko Čubrilović (DNS)
Urbanism, Civil Engineering, and Ecology	Fatima Fetibegović (SBiH) [f]
Without Portfolio	Branislav Borenović (PDP)

[f] = female

organized in April 2002, primarily by former members of the SPRS (above). The party was joined in June by former Serb member of the state presidency Živko Radišić, who had been ousted as SPRS president in February. In July the SPRS defense minister of the Serb Republic, Slobodan Bilić, resigned from the cabinet and also joined the NPS.

At the October 2002 election the new formation fared poorly, winning no legislative seats. Its candidate for the national presidency, Tomislav Taušen, won under 0.4 percent of the vote, while its two candidates for Serb Republic president (a Serb and a Croat) were equally unsuccessful.

Leaders: Tomislav TAUŠEN, Slobodan BILIĆ, Živko RADIŠIĆ, Goran BOBAR (Secretary General).

Social Democratic Union of Bosnia and Herzegovina (*Socijaldemokratska Unije Bosne i Hercegovine*—SDU-BiH). The SDU-BiH was organized in December 2002 by former members of the SDP who, following losses at the polls in October, had failed to change the party's policy of nonparticipation in nationalist-dominated governing coalitions. Among those forming the SDU-BiH was Sead Avdić, who was named the new party's

president but in late 2003 announced his decision to sit in the national House of Representatives as an independent. He subsequently formed the Free Democrats (above). A current vice president, Miro Lazović, sits in the Federation upper house.

Leaders: Sejfudin TOKIĆ (President), Miro LAZOVIĆ and Ivo KOMŠIĆ (Vice Presidents).

Legislatures

The 1995 Dayton accords provided for a bicameral **Parliamentary Assembly** (*Parlamentarna Skupština*) of the Republic of Bosnia and Herzegovina, a bicameral **Federation Parliament** (*Parliamenta Federacije*) of the Federation of Bosnia and Herzegovina, and a unicameral legislature of the Serb Republic of Bosnia and Herzegovina. A second legislative body for the Serb Republic was created by constitutional amendment in 2002.

Prior to the November 2000 elections, the Provisional Election Commission introduced multimember constituencies for the Serb legislature and the lower houses of the national and Federation parliaments. In addition, parties were authorized to submit separate lists of candidates for compensatory seats that would be awarded as needed to ensure proportionality of representation.

Parliamentary Assembly of the Republic of Bosnia and Herzegovina

House of Peoples (*Dom Naroda*). The upper chamber has 15 members: 5 Bosniacs and 5 Croats elected by their respective ethnic caucuses in the House of Peoples of the Federation, and 5 Serbs elected by the National Assembly of the Serb Republic. All members serve four-year terms. The office of speaker rotates every eight months among three members, one from each ethnic community. The upper house was most recently constituted on January 31, 2003, with the following party breakdown:

Bosniacs: Party of Democratic Action, 4 seats; Party for Bosnia and Herzegovina, 1.

Croats: Croatian Democratic Union of Bosnia and Herzegovina, 3; Croatian National Union, 1; Social Democratic Party of Bosnia and Herzegovina, 1.

Serbs: Serbian Democratic Party of Bosnia and Herzegovina, 3; Party for Democratic Progress of the Serb Republic, 2.

Speakers: Velimir JUKIĆ, Goran MILOJEVIĆ, Mustafa PAMUK.

House of Representatives (*Zastupnički Dom/ Predstavnički Dom*). The lower chamber consists of 42 directly elected members (28 from the Federation and 14 from the Serb Republic), who serve four-year terms. The office of speaker rotates every eight months among three members, one from each ethnic community. The balloting of October 5, 2002, yielded the following results: Party of Democratic Action, 10 seats; Party for Bosnia and Herzegovina, 6; Coalition of the Croatian Democratic Union and the Croatian Demo-Christians, 5; Serbian Democratic Party of Bosnia and Herzegovina, 5; Social Democratic Party of Bosnia and Herzegovina, 4; Alliance of Independent Social Democrats, 3; Party for Democratic Progress of the Serb Republic, 2; Bosnian Party, Democratic People's Union of Bosnia and Herzegovina, Eco-

nomic Bloc "Croat Democratic Union for Prosperity," New Croatian Initiative, Pensioners' Party of Bosnia and Herzegovina, Serb Radical Party of the Serb Republic, and Socialist Party of the Serb Republic, 1 each.

Speakers: Šefik DŽAFEROVIĆ, Martin RAGUŽ, Nikola ŠPIRIĆ.

Parliament of the Federation of Bosnia and Herzegovina

House of Peoples of the Federation (*Dom Naroda Federacije*). The upper chamber comprises 58 members (17 Bosniacs, 17 Croats, 17 Serbs, and 7 others) indirectly elected by the entity's 10 cantonal assemblies. The current House first convened on January 16, 2003, but without its full complement of Serb delegates: procedures specified in the newly implemented electoral law proved inadequate for filling all of the seats allotted to the Serb minority, which had won a total of only 9 seats in the cantonal assemblies. The following party breakdown is for the 52 filled seats: Coalition of the Croatian Democratic Union, Croatian Demo-Christians, and Croatian National Union, 12; Party of Democratic Action, 11; Social Democratic Party of Bosnia and Herzegovina, 11; Party for Bosnia and Herzegovina, 10; Alliance of Independent Social Democrats, 3; Democratic People's Union of Bosnia and Herzegovina, 2; Croatian Right Bloc, 1; Pensioners' Party of Bosnia and Herzegovina, 1; and Social Democratic Union (subsequently sitting as an independent), 1. As of mid-2006 the full complement of Serb seats remained unfilled.

Speaker: Slavko MATIĆ.

House of Representatives of the Federation (*Zastupnički Dom Federacije*). The lower chamber has 98 directly elected members. The balloting of October 5, 2002, resulted in the following distribution of seats: Party of Democratic Action, 32; Coalition of the Croatian Democratic Union, Croatian Demo-Christians, and Croatian National Union, 16; Social Democratic Party of Bosnia and Herzegovina, 15; Party for Bosnia and Herzegovina, 15; Bosnian Party, 3; Democratic People's

Union of Bosnia and Herzegovina, 2; Economic Bloc "Croat Democratic Union for Prosperity," 2; New Croatian Initiative, 2; Pensioners' Party of Bosnia and Herzegovina, 2; Alliance of Independent Social Democrats, Bosnian-Herzegovinian Patriotic Party, Civic Democratic Party, Coalition of the Pro-European People's Party and the Party of Youth of Bosnia and Herzegovina, Croatian Christian Democratic Union of Bosnia and Herzegovina, Croatian Party of Rights, Croatian Peasants' Party of Bosnia and Herzegovina, Croatian Right Bloc, and Liberal Democratic Party, 1 each.

Speaker: Muhamed IBRAHIMOVIĆ.

Legislative Bodies of the Serb Republic

Council of Peoples (*Vijeće Naroda*). The Council of Peoples, which was established as part of the constitutional amendments implemented in 2002, has limited powers on "issues of vital national interest," its primary mandate being to ensure that no ethnic group is disadvantaged by legislative acts of the National Assembly. Its 28 members (8 Serbs, 8 Bosniacs, 8 Croatians, and 4 others) are elected by the respective ethnic caucuses in the National Assembly. The first council was constituted on March 20, 2003, after a delay caused by difficulties related to selection of Bosniac delegates. Party representation was as follows: Alliance of Independent Social Democrats, 7; New Croatian Initiative, 4; Party of Democratic Action, 4; Democratic Party of the Republic of Serbia, 3; Party for Bosnia and Herzegovina, 3; Social Democratic Party of Bosnia and Herzegovina, 2; Socialist Party of the Serb Republic, 2; Democratic People's Alliance of the Serb Republic, Party for Democratic Progress of the Serb Republic, and Serb Radical Party of the Serb Republic, 1 each.

Chair: Remzija KADRIĆ.

National Assembly of the Serb Republic (*Narodna Skupština Republike Srpske*). The unicameral body consists of 83 directly elected members. The balloting of October 5, 2002, yielded the following distribution of seats: Serbian Democratic Party of Bosnia and Herzegovina, 26; Al-liance of Independent Social Democrats, 19; Party for Democratic Progress of the Serb Republic, 9; Party of Democratic Action, 6; Party for Bosnia and Herzegovina, 4; Serb Radical Party of the Serb Republic, 4; Social Democratic Party of Bosnia and Herzegovina, 3; Socialist Party of the Serb Republic, 3; Democratic People's Alliance of the Serb Republic, 3; Alliance of National Revival, Democratic Party of the Serb Republic, Democratic Patriotic Party, New Croatian Initiative, Pensioners' Party of the Republic of Serbia, and Serbian People's Alliance of the Serb Republic, 1 each.

Speaker: Igor RADOJIČIĆ.

Communications

Throughout the Bosnian conflict media were dominated by nationalist elements, and incidents of violence or intimidation against journalists by government functionaries, police, and fervent nationalists continued to be reported in subsequent years. In June 2000 a group of editors protested that "every form of pressure" was being brought to bear against freedom of the press. In 2005, however, the French organization Reporters Without Borders ranked Bosnia and Herzegovina among those newly independent countries that are "very observant of press freedom."

Press

The following newspapers are dailies published in Sarajevo, unless otherwise noted: *Dnevni Avaz* (Daily Voice, 40,000), Bosniac; *Slobodna Bosna* (Free Bosnia, 30,000), weekly; *Dani* (Days, 25,000), weekly; *Oslobodjenje* (Liberation, 15,000), Bosniac; *Jutarnje Novine* (Morning News, 10,000), Bosniac; *Glas Srpski* (Serbian Voice, Banja Luca, 7,000), government organ, Serbian; *Nezavisne Novine* (Independent News, Banja Luca, 7,000), Serbian; *Dnevni List* (Daily Paper, Mostar), Croatian.

News Agencies

Based in Sarajevo, the Federal News Agency (*Federalna Novinska Agencija*—Fena) operates at the state level; it was established in 2001 by merger of the Bosniac BH Press and the Mostar-based News Agency of the Croatian People in Bosnia and Herzegovina (HABENA). Other news organizations include the Serbian Press Agency (*Srpska Novinska Agencija*—SRNA) and the private Independent News Agency (ONASA).

Broadcasting and Computing

In 2001 the Office of the High Representative established a Communication Regulatory Agency for broadcasting. The nationwide broadcasting facility is the Public Broadcasting Service of Bosnia and Herzegovina, which operates BH TV1 and BH Radio 1. A 2005 media law specifies that BH TV1 equally serve the three principal ethnic communities from three centers located in Sarajevo, Banja Luca, and Mostar. The Federation and the Serb Republic also support public services. There are, in addition, roughly 200 private radio and television stations, most with limited range; some are controlled by the leading Bosniac, Croatian, and Serb political parties. There were approximately 1.5 million television receivers and 100,000 Internet users in 2003.

Intergovernmental Representation

Ambassador to the U.S.
Bisera TURKOVIĆ

U.S. Ambassador to Bosnia and Herzegovina
Douglas L. McELHANEY

Permanent Representative to the UN
Miloš PRICA

IGO Memberships (Non-UN)
BIS, CEI, CEUR, EBRD, Eurocontrol, Interpol, IOM, OSCE

Note: Legislative balloting on October 1, 2006, yielded the following results for the House of Representatives of the Parliamentary Assembly of the Republic of Bosnia and Herzogovina: the Party of Democratic Action won 9 seats; Party for Bosnia and Herzogovina, 8; Alliance of Independent Social Democrats, 7; Social Democratic Party of Bosnia and Herzegovina, 5; Croatian Democratic Union of Bosnia and Herzegovina/Croatian National Union, 3; Croats Together Coalition, 2; Serbian Democratic Party of Bosnia and Herzegovina, 3; Bosnian-Herzegovinian Patriotic Party, 1; Democratic People's Alliance of the Serb Republic, 1; Democratic People's Union of Bosnia and Herzegovina, 1; Party for Democratic Progress of the Serb Republic, 1; and the People's Party "Working for Prosperity," 1.

Final results for balloting for the Serb Republic's National Assembly, also held on October 1, 2006, are as follows: the Alliance of Independent Social Democrats won 41 seats; the Serbian Democratic Party of Bosnia and Herzegovina, 11; Party of Democratic Progress for the Serb Republic, 8; Democratic People's Alliance of the Serb Republic, 4; Party for Bosnia and Herzegovina, 4; Socialist Party of the Serb Republic, 3; Party of Democratic Action, 3; Serb Radical Party of the Serb Republic, 2; and the Social Democratic Party of Bosnia and Herzegovina, 1.

Final results for the House of Representatives of the Federation elections held on October 1, 2006, are as follows: the Party of Democratic Action won 28 seats; Party for Bosnia and Herzegovina, 24; Social Democratic Party of Bosnia and Herzegovina, 17; Croatian Democratic Union of Bosnia and Herzegovina/Croatian National Union/Croatian Party of Rights, 8; Croats Together Coalition, 7; Bosnian-Herzegovinian Patriotic Party, 4; Patriotic Bloc (Bosnian Party/Social Democratic Union of Bosnia and Herzegovina), 3; People's Party "Working for Prosperity," 3; Democratic People's Union of Bosnia and Herzegovina, 2; Alliance of Independent Social Democrats, 1; and the Croatian Party of Rights/New Croatian Initiative, 1.

BULGARIA

REPUBLIC OF BULGARIA

Republika Balgariya

Note: In the second round of the presidential election held on October 29, 2006, incumbent Georgi Parvanov won reelection with 75.9 percent of the vote, while challenger Volen Siderov (National Union Attack) took 24.1 percent. President Parvanov won 64 percent of the vote in the first-round election held on October 22; however, the Bulgarian constitution requires a second round if voter turnout is below 50 percent. Voter turnout in the second round was 41 percent.

The Country

Extending southward from the Danube and westward from the Black Sea, Bulgaria occupies a key position in the eastern Balkans adjacent to Macedonia, Romania, Serbia and Montenegro, Greece, and Turkey. Like Greece and Macedonia, the country includes portions of historic Macedonia, and tensions with neighboring states long existed because of the Bulgarian tendency to consider all Slavic-speaking Macedonians as ethnic Bulgarians. (More than 83 percent of Bulgaria's population is so classified, while there are sizable minorities of Turks [about 9.4 percent] and Roma [officially 4.7 percent but probably higher].) The predominant language is Bulgarian, a component of the southern Slavic language group. While religious observances were discouraged under the Communist regime, the principal faith remains that of the Bulgarian Orthodox Church; there is also a substantial Muslim minority (estimated at 800,000), in addition to small numbers of Catholics, Protestants, and Jews.

Traditionally an agricultural country, Bulgaria achieved a measure of industrialization after World War II under a series of five-year plans. As a result, machine building, ferrous and nonferrous metallurgy, textile manufacturing, and agricultural processing grew in importance, with agriculture accounting for only 14 percent of GDP by the end of Communist rule in 1990. Subsequently, reforms were introduced that included the removal of price subsidies on many basic commodities, currency flotation, privatization of land and small businesses, and decentralization of state enterprises. The transition proceeded slowly, however, and economic problems were exacerbated by the dismemberment of the Soviet Union, which had long taken about 60 percent of the country's exports. Further difficulties were caused by UN sanctions

against Serbia and Montenegro, primarily in the form of blocked exports to Western Europe, that contributed to a decline in GDP by an estimated 15–20 percent in 1992 and a rise in unemployment to 15 percent. Economic contraction slowed to about 5 percent in 1993, with 1 percent growth reported in 1994 (Bulgaria being among the last former Communist-bloc countries to register such recovery). Inflation worsened to 122 percent and unemployment to 20 percent in 1994. Conditions improved somewhat in 1995, when official figures showed a 3 percent increase in GDP. However, a further deterioration in the first half of 1996, exacerbated by corruption and entrenched resistance to economic change, brought Bulgaria to the brink of financial collapse: the value of the lev plummeted, banks failed, inflation soared, basic commodities were in short supply, and the prospect of debt default loomed. As a consequence, GDP fell by a further 7 percent in 1997, and the consumer price index soared by 550 percent as a new government scurried to implement a "shock" package of economic reforms that included faster privatization. In a remarkably rapid turnaround, aided by assistance from the International Monetary Fund (IMF), the World Bank, and others, growth of 3.5 percent was recorded for 1998, while inflation dropped to under 2 percent. Although annual growth reached 5 percent in 2000, inflation rose to 11.4 percent.

GDP grew by 4.2 percent in 2004 and finally returned to its level of 1989, although unemployment remained high (more than 14 percent) and Bulgarian wages remained among the lowest in Europe. (The average Bulgarian earned about $170 per month.) The IMF and other international institutions praised the center-right governments of 1997–2005 for tight fiscal policies that, among other things, reduced the ratio of public debt to GDP, limited budget deficits, improved the investment climate (in part through privatization of public enterprises), and generally facilitated economic stability. Nevertheless, collateral constriction of labor, health, educational, and other benefits generated unrest within a significant portion of the populace, creating major issues in regards to Bulgaria's planned accession to the European Union (EU) in 2007 (see Current issues). The Socialist-led government installed in 2005 announced plans to loosen fiscal policies, generating concern on the part of the IMF.

Government and Politics

Political Background

Bulgarian kingdoms existed in the Balkan Peninsula during the Middle Ages, but the Ottoman Turks ruled the area for 500 years prior to the Russo-Turkish War of 1877–1878; full independence was not achieved until 1908. Long-standing territorial ambitions led to Bulgarian participation on the losing side in the Second Balkan War (1913) and in both world wars. Talks aimed at the country's withdrawal from World War II were interrupted on September 5, 1944, by a Soviet declaration of war, followed by the establishment four days later of a Communist-inspired "Fatherland Front" government. The monarchy was rejected by a 92 percent majority in a disputed referendum held September 8, 1946, after which King SIMEON II, who had come to the throne at age six in 1943, went into exile, and a "People's Republic" was formally established on December 4, 1947, under the premiership of the "father of Bulgarian Communism," Georgi DIMITROV, who died in 1949. Communist rule was consolidated under the successive regimes of Vulko CHERVENKOV and Anton YUGOV. From 1954 until his ouster in November 1989, Todor ZHIVKOV, occupying various positions within the government and party hierarchies, maintained his status as Bulgaria's leader while continuing the pro-Soviet policies instituted by his predecessors.

The collapse of East European communism did not become a factor in Bulgarian politics until November 3, 1989, when upwards of 9,000 demonstrators marched at Sofia in the first prodemocracy rally in the country's postwar history. One week later a number of key Politburo changes were announced, including the replacement of Zhivkov as party general secretary by the reformist foreign minister, Petur MLADENOV. On November 17 the National Assembly named Mladenov to succeed Zhivkov as head of state, and the following day

Political Status: Communist constitution of May 18, 1971, substantially modified on April 3, 1990; present name adopted November 15, 1990; current democratic constitution adopted July 12, 1991.

Area: 42,823 sq. mi. (110,912 sq. km.).

Population: 7,928,901 (2001C); 7,779,000 (2005E). More than 900,000 Bulgarians have emigrated since 1989.

Major Urban Centers (2005E): SOFIA (1,194,000), Plovdiv (337,000), Varna (323,000), Bourgas (213,000), Rousse (182,000).

Official Language: Bulgarian.

Monetary Unit: Lev (official rate July 1, 2006: 1.53 leva = $1US). (On July 5, 1999, the lev was redenominated at the rate of 1,000 old leva = 1 new leva.)

President: Georgi PARVANOV (Bulgarian Socialist Party, from which he resigned following his election); sworn in for a five-year term on January 19, 2002, and assumed office on January 22, having been popularly elected in the second round of presidential balloting on November 18, 2001, succeeding Petar STOYANOV (originally Union of Democratic Forces, later independent).

Vice President: Angel MARIN (Bulgarian Socialist Party); sworn in January 19, 2002, and assumed office on January 22 for a term concurrent with that of the president, succeeding Todor KAVALDZHIEV (Union of Democratic Forces).

Chair of the Council of Ministers (Prime Minister): Sergei STANISHEV (Bulgarian Socialist Party); nominated by the president following the legislative elections of June 25, 2005, and inaugurated on August 16 in succession to Simeon SAXECOBURG-GOTSKI (Simeon SAXE-COBURG-GOTHA; National Movement Simeon II).

citing ethnic hostility, and abusing his powers of office. (He was convicted of embezzlement and sentenced to seven years imprisonment on September 1, 1992. He died in 1998, having been released from house arrest the previous year.)

In multiparty elections held on June 10 and 17, 1990, the Bulgarian Socialist (formerly Communist) Party (*Balgarska Sotsialisticheska Partiya*—BSP) captured a majority of National Assembly seats, with the recently launched Union of Democratic Forces (*Sayuz na Demokratichni Sili*—SDS) trailing by nearly 100 seats. Nevertheless, President Mladenov was obliged to resign on July 6 in the wake of evidence that he had endorsed the use of tanks to crush an antigovernment demonstration in late 1989. After nearly a month of political stalemate, the assembly elected SDS chair Zhelyu ZHELEV as his successor on August 1. On September 19, after efforts to form a coalition had failed, a new all-Socialist cabinet was announced under the continued premiership of Andrei LUKANOV (first appointed in February 1990). However, Lukanov resigned on November 29 after two weeks of street protests and a four-day general strike. On December 7 a politically independent judge, Dimitur POPOV, was named premier designate, and on December 20 he succeeded in forming a coalition administration that included eight Socialists, four representatives of the SDS, and three Agrarians.

Despite a boycott by many opposition parliamentarians, who demanded a referendum in the matter, a democratic constitution was adopted on July 12, 1991, followed by a new legislative poll on October 13. Emerging with a narrow four-seat plurality, the SDS, with support from the ethnically Turkish Movement for Rights and Freedoms (*Dvizhenie za Prava i Svobodi*—DPS), installed Filip DIMITROV on November 8 as head of the country's first wholly non-Communist government since World War II.

On January 19, 1992, in the second round of Bulgaria's first popular presidential poll, Zhelev was reelected to a five-year term, with his SDS running mate, Blaga DIMITROVA, becoming vice president. However, the balloting was unexpectedly close (53.5 percent for Zhelev, 46.5 percent for his

50,000 persons assembled at the capital to applaud the new government. On December 13 Zhivkov was formally expelled from the party; subsequently, the former leader was indicted on a variety of charges that included misappropriating state property, in-

BSP-backed nonparty opponent, Velko VALKA-NOV), largely because of differences between numerous SDS constituent formations, some of which had chosen to campaign separately. One area of contention stemmed from the union's dependence on parliamentary support from the DPS. Not surprisingly, parliamentary confirmation of the Dimitrov administration was accompanied by reversal of a ban, introduced by the Communists, on optional Turkish-language instruction in the secondary schools.

In March 1992 the National Assembly completed work, initiated a year earlier, on land privatization, providing for all agricultural cooperatives to be phased out and permitting foreign investors to participate, as minority members, in joint land ventures with Bulgarians. However, other promised reforms remained stalled, including a decommunization bill, amid serious labor unrest and a growing conflict between President Zhelev and the Dimitrov government over their respective responsibilities. The SDS tried to respond by organizing pro-Dimitrov rallies, but a DPS decision on September 23 to withdraw its support from the government proved fatal. On October 28 the government was defeated 121–111 on a nonconfidence motion and was obliged to resign. An interregnum ensued, during which the BSP wasted its constitutional opportunity to nominate a successor premier. The initiative passed to the DPS, which nominated the president's economic adviser, Lyuben BEROV, to form a nonparty administration of "national responsibility." Somewhat unexpectedly, with the backing of BSP and SDS dissidents, Berov obtained parliamentary approval on December 30 by 124 votes to 25, with the bulk of the SDS deputies abstaining.

The longevity of the Berov administration was assisted by the increasing disarray of the SDS, growing conflict between Zhelev and the SDS, defections to the government side, and the preference of the BSP for a government that it could influence and control rather than for official power as such. However, Berov was incapacitated by a heart attack on March 8, 1994, and President Zhelev announced on April 2 that he was withdrawing political support from the government because of the slow pace of privatization and a failure to attract foreign investment. The ailing Berov sought to regain the initiative on June 28 by launching a much-delayed mass privatization scheme for some 500 state-owned companies; finance officials also successfully concluded a rescheduling of Bulgaria's $10 billion external debt, enabling IMF and World Bank credit lines to be reactivated. Political pressure nevertheless mounted on the government, which resigned on September 2. Attempts by the president to find an alternative were thwarted by the preference of the BSP and the SDS for early elections, pending which a caretaker cabinet was installed on October 18 under Bulgaria's first woman prime minister, Reneta INDZHOVA.

At the legislative poll of December 18, 1994, Bulgarian voters continued the East European trend of restoring ex-Communist parties to power, according the BSP and two minor party (Agrarian and Ecoglasnost Political Club [*Politicheski klub Ekoglasnost*—PKE]) allies an overall majority of 125 of the 240 seats. By contrast, the SDS obtained only 69, its electoral appeal having been eroded by the decision of several of its factions to stand independently. As a result, 35-year-old BSP leader Zhan VIDENOV was sworn in on January 26, 1995, as prime minister of a government that included two members of the Bulgarian Agrarian National Union–People's Union (*Balgarski Zemedelski Naroden Sayuz–Naroden Sayuz*—BZNS-NS), one PKE member, and several nonparty technocrats reputed to favor market reforms. At that stage less than 40 percent of state-owned land had been restored to private ownership, and only 35 of the country's 3,000 large and medium-sized industrial enterprises had been privatized.

Despite a deteriorating economic situation, the BSP polled strongly in local elections in October–November 1995, winning 41 percent of the vote and 195 of the 255 mayoralties at issue, while the SDS, with 24.7 percent, took Sofia and other major cities.

Party politics in 1996 focused on the presidential election in November, for which incumbent Zhelyu Zhelev declared his candidacy. Because Zhelev had fallen out with the SDS since his 1992 election, the opposition held a primary to find a joint candidate, with Zhelev running as the nominee of the People's Union (*Naroden Sayuz*—NS) coalition and the SDS endorsing Petar STOYANOV, a little-known lawyer. The outcome of the primary balloting on June 1 was a decisive 65.7 percent majority for Stoyanov, who thereupon received Zhelev's endorsement. The ruling coalition parties supported the BSP foreign minister, Georgi PIRINSKI, but his candidacy was effectively blocked by a controversial Constitutional Court ruling on July 23 that, having been born in the United States of Bulgarian émigré parents, he did not meet the constitutional requirement of being Bulgarian by birth. On September 2 the Supreme Court rejected the BSP's appeal, and the BSP culture minister, Ivan MARAZOV, was drafted as a replacement. Stoyanov was subsequently the easy victor, heading the first-round balloting on October 27, 1996, with 44.1 percent of the vote and then obtaining 60 percent in a two-way runoff against Marazov on November 3.

In the wake of Stoyanov's victory, Videnov resigned as prime minister and leader of the BSP on December 21, 1996, the assembly accepting his resignation on December 28. The SDS immediately called for the installation of a caretaker government pending proposed early assembly elections. However, the BSP, ignoring massive public demonstrations in support of the SDS proposal, insisted upon its right (as leading parliamentary party) to name a new prime minister, and on January 7, 1997, it tapped Interior Minister Nikolai DOBREV to succeed Videnov. Public opposition again quickly erupted. Strikes and protests began to paralyze the country, and several hundred demonstrators were injured by police after invading the assembly. On January 11 President Zhelev announced he would not invite Dobrev to form a new government, arguing that such a government would not be viable. Consequently, the government was stalemated when Stoyanov took office on January 22, 1997. After weeks without a prime minister and a siege of the assembly by SDS supporters, the BSP in early February finally agreed to allow Stoyanov to appoint an interim government, which,

as announced on February 12, was led by Stefan SOFIANSKI, the mayor of Sofia. The interim government immediately initiated economic reforms designed to stabilize the currency and control food and fuel shortages while preparing for new assembly elections on April 19. In that balloting, the SDS-led United Democratic Forces (*Obedineni Demokratichni Sili*—ODS) scored a massive victory, securing 137 seats to 58 for the BSP-led Democratic Left (*Demokratichna Levitsa*—DL). ODS leader Ivan KOSTOV, an economist and former finance minister, was named prime minister on May 21, pledging that his new cabinet would steadfastly pursue the reforms launched by Sofianski.

Although the economy experienced a remarkably swift turnaround, the Kostov government's standing in the polls had declined by early 2001, in large part because the economic gains had not produced a notable advance in living standards. By April, with a general election only two months away, the BSP was presenting a serious challenge to Kostov's incumbency. However, on April 6 the political landscape underwent a tectonic shift when the former king, Simeon SAXE-COBURG-GOTHA, after 55 years in exile, announced formation of a National Movement Simeon II (*Natsionalno Dvizhenie Simeon Tvori*—NDST) that would contest the National Assembly election. Although the party was refused registration on technical grounds, two small parties agreed to register for the election as a coalition under the NDST designation, thereby providing visibility to a slate of candidates loyal to Simeon. Immediately, Kostov's ODS and the BSP-led Coalition for Bulgaria (*Koalicija za Balgariya*—KzB) saw their poll standings plummet, and at the June 17 balloting the NDST secured 120 of the assembly's 240 seats. The ODS and the KzB trailed with 51 and 48 seats, respectively. Although Simeon had not run for office himself, on July 12, as expected, he received the coalition's endorsement as prime minister. Picked by President Stoyanov to form a cabinet, the former king, having adopted the common name Simeon SAXECOBURGGOTSKI (see NDST under Political Parties, below, for additional information on this name usage), received legislative endorsement on July 24. He was sworn in as the head of an NDST-dominated Council of Ministers that included two DPS and two BSP members. (Despite the participation of the BSP members in the cabinet, the BSP said it had made no political commitment to the government and would in fact remain in "constructive opposition.")

At presidential balloting on November 11, 2001, President Stoyanov, running as an independent but with NDST support, won only 35 percent of the vote on a low voter turnout of 39 percent. His chief rival, BSP Chair Georgi PARVANOV, took 36 percent and at second-round balloting on November 18 won with 54 percent.

On July 16, 2003, Prime Minister Saxecoburggotski announced a cabinet reshuffle and expansion designed, among other things, to facilitate Bulgaria's planned accession to the EU and the North Atlantic Treaty Organization (NATO). However, in March 2004 the NDST/DPS coalition became a minority government when a group of NDST legislators left that grouping to launch a new party called New Time. Although New Time supported the government in several subsequent no-confidence votes, in early February 2005 it joined the opposition parties in demanding the government's resignation for having failed to achieve its promises of 2001. However, New Time ultimately voted against a no-confidence motion on February 11 (thereby preserving the coalition) as part of an accord whereby New Time joined the cabinet in a February 21 reshuffle.

The BSP-led KzB led all parties by winning 82 seats in the assembly balloting on June 25, 2005. After seven weeks of difficult negotiations, BSP leader Sergei STANISHEV was inaugurated on August 16 as head of a center-left KzB/NDST/DPS coalition government.

Constitution and Government

The constitution of July 1991 describes Bulgaria as a republic with a democratic parliamentary form of government. It guarantees freedom of association, religion, and opinion. It supports an economy based on "market forces" and a respect for private property. It provides for a president and vice president, elected jointly for no more than two five-year terms by majority vote of at least 50 percent of those eligible to cast ballots (a second ballot confined to the top two tickets otherwise being required). The president nominates the chair of the Council of Ministers (prime minister), who must be confirmed (and can ultimately be dismissed) by the National Assembly. The assembly, popularly elected for a four-year term, is a unicameral body of 240 members, who may not concurrently hold ministerial office. The highest judicial organs are a Supreme Court of Cassation, which oversees application of the law by lower courts, and a Supreme Administrative Court, which rules on the legality of acts by government organs. There is also a Constitutional Court that interprets the basic law and rules on the constitutionality of legislation and decrees. At the local level Bulgaria encompasses 28 administrative regions, each headed by a governor appointed by the Council of Ministers. There are nearly 300 elected municipal councils, each of which appoints a mayor as chief administrative officer for the duration of its four-year term.

The National Assembly may amend the constitution by the casting of majorities of 75 percent on three separate days. On September 24, 2003, the assembly passed the first constitutional amendments to the 1991 constitution, giving life tenure to magistrates and granting them immunity against charges except in cases of criminal misconduct or abuse of office. (The changes were part of a broader effort to harmonize the legal system with EU standards.)

Foreign Relations

A longtime Bulgarian alignment with the Soviet Union in foreign policy reflected not only the two countries' economic and ideological ties, but also a traditional friendship stemming from Russian assistance in Bulgarian independence struggles. In January 1977 Bulgaria's network of relations with West European governments was completed by an exchange of ambassadors with post-Franco Spain. Ties between Bulgaria and the Vatican, broken in 1949, were restored in December 1990, despite allegations of involvement by the (then) hard-line Communist regime in an attempt on the pope's life in 1981.

Bulgarian-Turkish relations have fluctuated. Although Bulgaria permitted over 100,000 ethnic Turks to emigrate in 1968–1978, subsequent efforts toward assimilation of those that remained (including the forced adoption of Bulgarian names) generated pronounced tension with Ankara. Sofia emphatically rejected all "Turkish accusations" in the matter, calling the Bulgarian Turks "a fictitious minority" and claiming that the name changes were merely those of Bulgarians voluntarily reversing a process mandated during Ottoman rule.

In May 1989, following a series of clashes between ethnic protestors and security police in the Islamic border region, a large number of Bulgarian Muslims took advantage of newly issued passports to cross into Turkey. However, in August Ankara closed the border to stem an influx that had exceeded 310,000. In late December, following the downfall of the Zhivkov regime, National Assembly Chair Stenko TODOROV told a group of Turkish demonstrators at Sofia that henceforth "everybody in Bulgaria [would] be able to choose his name, religion, and language freely."

In October 1991 the Bulgarian and Greek prime ministers signed a 20-year friendship treaty, with Athens offering support for its neighbor's application to join the European Community (EC, subsequently the EU). However, relations with Greece cooled in January 1992, following the inclusion of Macedonia in the former Yugoslav republics to which Bulgaria accorded recognition. Athens, which had long refused to acknowledge a separate Macedonian nationality (whereas Bulgaria had traditionally contended that all Macedonians were ethnically Bulgarians), responded by appealing to its EC partners to limit or halt aid to Sofia. Earlier, on May 7, Bulgaria was admitted to membership in the Council of Europe.

On March 4, 1992, Prime Minister Dimitrov met with U.S. President Bush in Washington. Six days later, in the first such visit since 1917, Defense Minister Dimitur LUDZHEV traveled to Ankara to sign a technical and defense cooperation agreement with Turkish authorities. Bulgaria also entered into a 10-year friendship and cooperation treaty with the Russian Federation on August 4 during a visit to Sofia by President Yeltsin (who two days later confirmed Moscow's recognition of Macedonia).

In March 1993 Bulgaria completed negotiations on an association agreement with the EU and the same month signed a free trade agreement with the European Free Trade Association (EFTA). The new Bulgarian-Russian treaty was ratified during a visit by Prime Minister Berov to Moscow in April, but Bulgaria remained committed to developing its Western ties. In February 1994 it became a signatory of NATO's Partnership for Peace, and in May it was one of nine East European states to become an "associate partner" of the Western European Union (WEU). An exchange of high-level visits with Russia in September 1995 confirmed the stability of bilateral relations, although a reference by President Yeltsin in March 1996 to the possibility of Bulgaria joining an economic union of the former Soviet bloc sparked a furor in Sofia, with the Videnov government denying allegations by President Zhelev that it had held clandestine talks with Moscow.

In February 1997 the caretaker government of Stefan Sofianski announced its intention to seek full membership for Bulgaria in NATO. That position was reaffirmed by incoming Prime Minister Kostov in April, when he also said Bulgaria would seek EU membership. Although NATO did not include Bulgaria in the "first wave" of new members approved in June, the alliance subsequently indicated that Bulgaria was a "strong contender" for the next round of expansion. Meanwhile, Bulgaria was also left off the EU's "fast track" membership list approved in 1997; however, EU officials said it was only a matter of "when" and not "if" Bulgaria would eventually join, assuming continued economic reform on the part of the government. In January 1999 Bulgaria became a member of the Central European Free Trade Agreement (CEFTA, see Foreign relations in article on Poland).

In February 1999 Bulgaria appeared to have resolved its last major outstanding regional dispute when it reached agreement with Macedonia concerning the language to be used in bilateral accords. A number of agreements had been held up for six years because of Bulgaria's insistence that Macedonian was a dialect of Bulgarian and not a language in its own right. (The issue reflected deeper concerns regarding the status of self-described Macedonians in Bulgaria as well as the two countries' concern over each other's possible territorial claims). In an apparent easing of Bulgaria's stance, the 1999 accord authorized the use of the languages recognized by each country's constitution. Several bilateral accords were subsequently concluded, including one providing for military cooperation. Relations with Ankara were also described in early 1999 as greatly improved, border demarcation issues having been resolved and the Turkish business sector having found significant investment opportunities in the vastly improved Bulgarian economy.

Early in 2000 Bulgaria began formal accession talks with the EU, but it remained a "second tier" prospect. In May the National Assembly approved a resolution, 189–3, to pursue membership in the EU as well as NATO.

At NATO's Prague Summit in November 2002, Bulgaria was one of seven Central and East European states invited to join the Alliance. As part of its preaccession protocols (signed in May 2003), Bulgaria subsequently enacted a series of military reforms. The National Assembly formally endorsed accession by a vote of 226–4 on March 18, 2004, and Bulgaria joined the Alliance on March 29.

Perhaps in consonance with the NATO developments, the Saxecoburggotski government supported the U.S.-led invasion of Iraq in 2003. In return, the U.S. provided guarantees on the repayment of Iraq's foreign debt to Bulgaria (these payments had been suspended since 1990). After the fall of the regime of Saddam Hussein, Bulgaria deployed one of the larger contingents in the U.S.-led coalition (some 500 troops). (The Bulgarian troops were withdrawn from Iraq in December 2005.)

On the other major international front, Bulgaria completed the final "chapters" in negotiations toward EU accession in late 2004, and in April 2005 a treaty was signed whereby it was envisioned that

Bulgaria would become a member of the EU as of January 1, 2007. However, that date was contingent on Bulgaria making promised reforms designed to combat corruption (and collateral organized crime), address lingering human rights concerns (particularly regarding minorities), and continue its progress toward meeting the EU's economic criteria. (See Current issues, below, for subsequent information.)

Allegations arose in 2005 that secret U.S. prisons had operated in Bulgaria and that Bulgaria had permitted use of its airports by U.S. planes transferring prisoners to other undisclosed locations as part of the controversial U.S. "rendition" program. However, Bulgarian officials denied the allegations, and in 2006 Bulgaria announced an agreement under which U.S. forces would be allowed to use several military airfields and bases in Bulgaria for at least the next ten years. It was also reported that NATO bases in Bulgaria had been authorized to be used for any potential NATO operations in the Caucasus region.

Current Issues

Simeon Saxecoburggotski in 2001 became the first former East European monarch to assume a republican office. Although nostalgia for the monarchy had undoubtedly contributed to the NDST's victory, a more significant factor appeared to be voter dissatisfaction with both the center-right Kostov government and with the Socialists. Somewhat paradoxically, Simeon had become the "new face" in Bulgarian politics. However, his lack of governmental experience raised questions as to how well he could govern and whether he could fulfill a campaign commitment to make measurable economic gains within 800 days. Nonetheless, the government subsequently scored significant successes with the country's accession to NATO in 2004 and progress toward EU accession as early as 2007.

The NDST had fallen sharply in public opinion polls leading up to the 2005 assembly elections. Among other things, the NDST-led government was apparently widely perceived as having been ineffective in combating corruption and organized crime. In addition, average Bulgarians reportedly were disappointed that the "prosperity" promised through the implementation of IMF reforms had failed to trickle down to needy segments of the population such as pensioners. Prime Minister Saxecoburggotski's efforts to reform health care and education were also apparently seen as inadequate. Finally, the administration faced the penchant by Bulgarian voters to force change at every election (no government has ever been reelected). Consequently, the assembly campaign was tumultuous, particularly after the emergence of the National Union Attack (*Nacionalno Obedinenie Ataka*), an extreme right-wing grouping with populist overtones. (*Ataka* campaigned on an antiminority/antiimmigrant platform that also proposed severing ties with NATO, the EU, and the IMF.)

Seven coalitions or parties (including *Ataka*) secured seats in the June 2005 assembly poll, making for the "most fragmented" legislature in history. Not surprisingly, it proved difficult for the BSP-led KzB to form a new government. The NDST rejected initial overtures from the KzB, insisting that Saxecoburggotski should remain as prime minister. The KzB subsequently proposed a minority government with the DPS, but the assembly rejected that concept. As international pressure for a resolution grew amid concern that Bulgaria's proposed EU accession was being threatened by the instability, the NDST eventually agreed to join the KzB and DPS in a cabinet led by the BSP's young (38 years old), "reform-minded" leader, Sergei Stanishev. The new administration immediately announced that maintaining the EU accession schedule was its top priority. However, as of early 2006 a "cloud of uncertainty" continued to hang over that issue, most observers agreeing that little progress had been achieved regarding judicial reform, corruption, and organized crime. (Regarding the latter, more than 150 gangland murders [some under very public circumstances] had been reported over the last five years.) In May the EU announced that it was delaying until October a decision on whether to continue with the planned January 1, 2007, date or to postpone Bulgaria's accession for a year. Meanwhile, perhaps with an eye on the presidential

elections scheduled for late 2006, the BSP-led center-left government announced plans to increase government spending to deal with a variety of social issues.

Political Parties

Prior to the political upheaval of late 1989, Bulgaria's only authorized political parties were the Bulgarian Communist Party (*Balgarska Komunisticheska Partiya*—BKP) and the Bulgarian Agrarian National Union (*Balgarski Zemedelski Naroden Sayuz*—BZNS), which formed the core of the Fatherland Front (*Otechestven Front*), a Communist-controlled mass organization that also included the trade unions, the Communist youth movement, and individual citizens. In the wake of the ouster of longtime KPB leader Todor Zhivkov in 1989, a large number of opposition groups surfaced, while the KPB changed its name to the Bulgarian Socialist Party (BSP). Since then, parties and coalitions have proliferated. For the 2001 legislative election the Central Election Commission registered 65 parties; it was subsequently reported that 42 coalitions or parties took part in that balloting. By 2004 there were some 80 registered parties, and a new electoral law was approved prior to the 2005 assembly poll with the intent of reducing the number of small parties. Among other things, parties were required to provide signatures of support from at least 5,000 people. Financial deposits were also required of any party presenting legislative candidates, with the deposits being returned only if the party secured more than 1 percent of the national vote. Consequently, only 22 parties or coalitions contested the 2005 balloting.

Government Parties

Coalition for Bulgaria (*Koalicija za Balgariya*—KzB). Established in preparation for the 2001 legislative election, the KzB was the descendant of the BSP-led but less inclusive Democratic Left (*Demokratichna Levitsa*—DL). The DL had been formed prior to the 1996 presidential election by the BSP, the Ecoglasnost Political Club (PKE, below), and the BZNS-AS (see below), which had contested the 1994 legislative election in alliance and had then formed the subsequent government under the BSP's Videnov. The three-party coalition saw its representation fall from 125 seats in 1994 to 58 in 1998. In May 2000 the PKE left the DL.

In November 2000 the parliamentary delegations of the BSP, the BSDP, the OBT, and the PDSD announced a cooperative agreement that led in January 2001 to formal establishment of a New Left political program. On January 25 the formation was announced of the more encompassing KzB, which won 48 seats in the 2001 assembly balloting. At that time its membership comprised the BSP, at least one faction of the BZNS-AS, the BSDP, PDSD, KPB, the United Labor Bloc (OBT), and the Alliance for Social Liberal Progress (*Alians za Sotsialliberalen Progress*— ASLP). However, the OBT left the KzB for the Coalition of the Rose in early 2005, and there were no reports concerning the ASLP as far as the 2005 KzB structure was concerned. Meanwhile, the ZPB and the DSH reportedly joined the KzB for the 2005 balloting.

The KzB won 82 seats in the 2005 assembly elections on a 31 percent vote share, having campaigned on a platform pledging to, among other things, promote higher wages and additional jobs for Bulgarian workers.

Leader: Sergei STANISHEV (Prime Minister).

Bulgarian Socialist Party (*Balgarska Sotsialisticheska Partiya*—BSP). The BSP resulted from a change of name by the Bulgarian Communist Party (*Balgarska Komunisticheska Partiya*—BKP) on April 3, 1990. The BKP had traced its origins to an ideological split in the old Social Democratic Party, the dissidents withdrawing in 1903 to form the Bulgarian Workers' Social Democratic Party, which became the Communist Party in 1919. Banned in 1934, the party came to power in 1944 in the wake of the Red Army's military success and, in coalition with other "progressive" forces, took full control from 1946. Todor Zhivkov became leader in 1954, maintaining a rigid pro-Soviet orthodoxy almost until his ouster in November 1989. The BKP's "leading role" in state and society was terminated on January 1990, when an extraordinary party congress renounced "democratic centralism," restructured its leadership bodies, and endorsed "human and democratic socialism" in the context of a "socially oriented market economy."

As the BSP, the party retained a legislative majority at multiparty elections in June 1990, but in December it accepted a coalition under the premiership of the opposition SDS (below). At a new poll in October 1991 a BSP-led alliance was narrowly defeated by the SDS, the BSP thus going into opposition for the first time since 1944. In a leadership contest at a BSP congress in December, Zhan Videnov, advocate of a "modern left-socialist party," easily defeated a reformist social democratic opponent. In December 1992 most BSP deputies backed the formation of the nonparty Berov government, under which the party reasserted its influence. In further elections in December 1994 the BSP, joined by the PKE and the BZNS-AS, won an overall assembly majority, with 43.5 percent of the vote.

The major financial crisis of May 1996 accentuated underlying divisions within the coalition, with the two smaller partners threatening to leave the government unless personnel changes where made. Within the BSP a powerful conservative wing attached the blame to the Videnov modernizers and to over-hasty economic liberalization, whereas the Videnov supporters cited entrenched Soviet-era personnel and attitudes. Seeking to occupy the middle ground in the controversy, Videnov also came under attack from the BSP right wing, organized as the Association for Social Democracy.

When Videnov resigned from the premiership in December 1996, he also relinquished his role as party chair, an extraordinary BSP congress subsequently selecting Deputy Chair Georgi Parvanov as his successor. Although new elections were also held for the BSP Supreme Council and its 15-member Executive Board, hard-liners continued to dominate both bodies, and they insisted on trying to exercise the BSP's right to choose a new prime minister, despite massive public demonstrations in support of installation of an interim government pending early elections (see Political background, above). However, the prime minister-designate, Interior Minister Nikolai Dobrev, finally capitulated in early February 1997 to pressure for the BSP to relinquish its mandate, his decision to go against the party hard-liners being widely praised domestically and internationally as preventing further severe political conflict and possibly even civil war.

Following the Democratic Left's poor showing in the April 1998 legislative balloting, the BSP leadership announced it would support the new ODS government's economic reform policies but would oppose the Bulgarian bid for NATO membership. Continued friction was subsequently reported between Parvanov's moderate camp and party hard-liners, the latter enjoying the support of the large number of pensioners and veterans in the BSP. In May 2000 Parvanov, now backing integration into NATO, was easily reelected chair, although the party's electoral defeat in June 2001 led a faction headed by the former parliamentary chair, Krasimir PREMYANOV, to call for Parvanov's resignation. The Saxecoburggotski cabinet of July 2001 included two members of the BSP (later reduced to one), but the party itself remained outside the government, choosing to abstain during the July 24 confirmation vote in the National Assembly.

Designated on September 30, 2001, as the BSP presidential candidate, Parvanov won in second-round balloting in November, after which he resigned from the party in the interest of national unity. He was succeeded as BSP leader by Sergei Stanishev, who was named prime minister following the 2005 assembly poll, the BSP having embraced "Euro-style socialism" and having for the most part removed hard-line communists from influential party positions.

Leaders: Sergei STANISHEV (Chair), Georgi PIRINSKI, Rumen Stoyanov OVCHAROV.

Bulgarian Agrarian National Union "Aleksandur Stamboliyski" (*Balgarski Zemedelski Naroden Sayuz "Aleksandur Stamboliyski"*—BZNS-AS). The BZNS-AS is one of several current groups claiming direct descent from the historic BZNS that had been founded in 1899. The BZNS's most prominent leader, Aleksandur Stamboliyski, was an Agrarian prime minister killed in a right-wing coup in 1923. After World War II a pro-Communist rump BZNS was allowed pro forma assembly and government representation as part of the Fatherland Front, usually holding the agriculture portfolio. Asserting its independence as communism began to crumble, the BZNS replaced longtime leader Petur TANCHEV in November 1989 and refused to join the Lukanov government of February 1990; nevertheless, the anti-Communist BZNS-Nikola Petkov faction broke away to join the opposition SDS. The rump BZNS won 16 assembly seats in June 1990 but lost them all in October 1991. A complex sequence of abortive unity schemes and further splits ensued in Agrarian ranks, one outcome being the creation of the BZNS-AS, which contested the 1994 elections in alliance with the victorious BSP. The BZNS-AS also participated in the DL for the 1996 presidential balloting. It was reported that an "1899" faction of the BZNS-AS, led by Dragmir SHOPOV, had participated in the KzB for the 2001 assembly elections. However, reports about the 2005 assembly balloting indicated no participation by the 1899 faction, with the KzB apparently claiming the support of the BZNS-AS faction led by Svetoslav Stoyanov SHIVAROV.

Bulgarian Social Democratic Party (*Balgarska Sotsialdemokraticheska Partiya*—BSDP). A member of the Socialist International, the BSDP traces its descent from the historic party founded in 1891 and more especially from the secession of its nonrevolutionary wing in 1903. Left-wing Social Democrats participated in the Communist-led Fatherland Front that came to power in 1944, the BSDP being merged with the Communist Party in 1948. Over the next four decades exiles kept the party alive as the Socialist Party, which was reestablished in Bulgaria in 1989 under the leadership of Petar DERTLIEV, a veteran of the pre-1948 era. In March 1990 the party reinstated the BSDP title in view of the imminent decision of the Communist Party to rename itself the BSP. As a component of the SDS, the BSDP took 29 seats in the June 1990 assembly election. The following month Dertliev was the initial SDS candidate for the presidency, but he subsequently withdrew in favor of Zhelyu Zhelev.

The BSDP supported the decision of some SDS elements to enter a BSP-dominated coalition government in December 1990 but thereafter came into conflict with the promarket policies of the SDS leadership, arguing that privatized industries should become cooperatives where possible. In the October 1991 assembly election it headed a separate SDS-Centre list, which failed to surmount the 4 percent barrier. The BSDP backed Zhelev's successful candidacy in the January 1992 direct presidential balloting and thereafter sided with the president against the SDS minority government. Following the appointment of a nonparty government in December 1992, the BSDP warned that it marked a reassertion of communist influence. From March 1993, seeking to establish a credible third force between the BSP and an SDS seen as moving to the right, the BSD launched a series of center-left alliances, culminating in the DAR (below). However, the BSDP joined the SDS-led ODS for the April 1997 legislative balloting, although only 1 of the 137 successful ODS candidates belonged to the BSDP.

Late in 1998 the BSDP split, and Petar Dertliev led a wing of the party into the opposition. That group joined the United Labor Bloc (OBT) in establishing a Social Democratic Union (*Balgarska Sotsialdemokraticheska Sayuz*—BSDS) in preparation for the 1999 local elections. Dertliev died in November 2000.

For the 2001 legislative election the Social Democrats remained fractured. One of the principal branches renegotiated its standing within the ODS, the former Dertliev wing joined the KzB, and another "united group" participated in the coalition led by the BEL (below).

The claim to status as the "legitimate" BSDP remained contentious prior to the 2005 assembly balloting, with a faction led by Petar AGOV running as part of the KzB and a faction led by Yordan NIHRIZOV reportedly participating in the ODS. (Some reports indicated that Nihrizov's supporters had earned the "official" right to the BSDP rubric in 1997, with Agov's supporters subsequently sometimes being referenced as the Party of the Bulgarian Social Democrats.) Both Agov and Nihrizov won seats in the 2005 elections.

Political Movement "Social Democrats" (*Politichesko Dvizhenie "Sotsialdemokrati"*—PDSD). The PDSD was established in 2000 following a split within the Euroleft (below, under BSD) over the parent group's direction and leadership. The new formation pledged to advance social democratic interests as well as openness and accountability in government.

Leader: Nikolay KAMOV (Coordinator).

Communist Party of Bulgaria (*Komunisticheska Partiya na Balgariya*—KPB). The KPB, established in 1997, supports EU accession and a mixed economy.

Leader: Aleksandur PAUNOV (First Secretary).

Green Party in Bulgaria (*Zelena Partiya na Bulgaria*—ZPB). Established in 1989, the environmentalist ZPB participated in the 1990 elections in coalition with the SDS. The ZPB was split in 1991 by the formation of the PKE (below) and subsequently participated in several widely varied electoral alliances.

Leader: Aleksandur KARAKACHANOV.

Movement for Social Humanism (*Dvizhenie za Sotsialen Humanizum*—DSH). The DSH was launched in 1995 by BSDP dissidents.

Leader: Alexander RADOSLAVOV.

Civil Union "Roma" (*Grazhdansko Obedinenie "Roma"*). This grouping was launched in March 2001 by some nine nonparty Roma advocacy groups and three parties.

Leader: Toma TOMOV.

Nonparty KzB participants included the **All People Committee for Protection of National Interests** (*Obshtonaroden Komitet za Zashtita na Natsionalnite Interesi*), led by Dobromir ZADGORSKI; the **Confederation of Romas "Europe"** (*Konfederacija na Romite "Evropa"*), which promotes Roma integration and is led by Petar GEORGIEV; the **Fatherland Union** (*Sayuz na Otechestovo*), chaired by Ginyo GANEV; the **Bulgarian Anti-Fascist Union** (*Balgarski Antifashistki Sayuz*—BAFS), led by Velko VULKANOV; the **National Association "United Bulgarian Citizens"** (*Natsionalno Sdruzhenie "Obedineni Balharski Grazhdani"*), established in 2001 on behalf of a civil society, and chaired by Andrei PANTEV; the **Political Club "Trakya"** (*Politicheski Klub "Trakya"*), a recently organized group supporting the cause of Thracian immigrants, chaired by Todor BOYADJIEV; and the **Women's Democratic Union** (*Demokratichen Sayuz na Zhenite*), founded in 1990 to advance the political, legal, social, and economic standing of women, and led by Emilia MASLAROVA.

National Movement Simeon II (*Natsionalno Dvizhenie Simeon Tvori*—NDST). Formation of the NDST party was announced on April 6, 2001, by the former king, Simeon Saxe-Coburg-Gotha (an English translation of the family's original German name), a month after he had returned from exile in Spain. On April 28, however, the Supreme Court upheld an April 23 ruling by the Sofia City Court denying registration to the NDST party because it failed to meet legal requirements. In order to get on the ballot for the June National Assembly election, the former monarch's supporters quickly negotiated an arrangement with two small, officially sanctioned parties, the **Party of Bulgarian Women** (PBW) and the **Movement for National Revival "Oborishte"** (which refers to the site of a 19th-century uprising against the Ottomans), whereby they agreed to contest the election as the NDST. Thus, the NDST was registered as a coalition by the Central Election Commission on May 2. At the June balloting, the formation won 120 seats and a 42.7 percent vote share, far outdistancing its opponents. Simeon II, who was not himself a parliamentary candidate, subsequently accepted the nomination as prime minister. (It was announced that the former king had adopted the common name Saxecoburggotski for the premiership. However, even government sources continued to refer to him regularly as Prime Minister Saxe-Coburg-Gotha or Prime Minister Saxe-Coburg, usages that also subsequently prevailed in news reports.)

The NDST was formally registered as a political party in April 2002, and the prime minister was elected as party leader after initially indicating he would not pursue that post in the interest of party unity.

Five NDST legislators had left the party in March 2002 to protest their leader's perceived failure to follow up on his campaign promises, while 11 others formed New Time (below) in 2004. The NDST fell to 53 seats (on a vote share of 20 percent) in the 2005 assembly elections.

Leaders: Simeon SAXECOBURGGOTSKI (Simeon SAXE-COBURG-GOTHA; Former Prime Minister of the Republic and President of the Party), Daniel Vassilev VALTCHEV (Deputy Prime Minister), Anelia MINGOVA (Parliamentary Leader).

Movement for Rights and Freedoms (*Dvizhenie za Prava i Svobodi*—DPS). Representing the Turkish minority, the DPS won 23 assembly seats in June 1990; it became the swing party in October 1991 by winning 24 seats and in late 1992 played a crucial role in the ouster of the SDS government and the advent of the nonparty Berov administration. The DPS was weakened in 1993 by defections and splits as well as by the emigration to Turkey of many of its supporters, and its representation fell to 15 seats on a 5.4 percent vote share in December 1994. The DPS polled strongly in ethnic Turkish areas in local elections in October–November 1995, winning 26 mayoralties, and in 1996 participated in the ODS in support of the presidential candidacy of Petar Stoyanov.

A split was reported in the party in early 1997 over the decision by Ahmed Dogan not to remain aligned with the ODS for the April legislative balloting and instead to form a broad Alliance for National Salvation (*Obedinenie za Natsionalno Spasenie*—ONS). As configured for the 1997 legislative balloting, the ONS also included an ideologically incongruous mix of liberal minor centrist, environmental, and monarchist parties. The ONS nevertheless secured 19 seats in the 1997 balloting, as compared to 15 for the DPS in 1994. It broadly supported the ODS government for most of the rest of the year before the DPS in December charged Prime Minister Kostov with pursuing "populist measures, rather than reforms."

In preparation for the 1999 local elections the DPS helped establish the Liberal Democratic Union (LDS; see LS, below). Following the 2001 legislative election a dispute between Dogan and former deputy chair Osman Oktay over party direction threatened a split in the DPS, which had been invited to join the Saxecoburggotski government as a junior partner. In July 2003 several members of the DPS (including Oktay) who were reportedly disillusioned with the party's leadership helped to launch a new party, the Democratic Wing Movement.

For the 2001 assembly elections, the DPS led a coalition that also included the Liberal Union and Euroroma (see below); the coalition won 21 seats. In 2005 the DPS secured 34 seats on a vote share of 13 percent.

Leader: Ahmed DOGAN (President).

Other Parliamentary Parties

National Union Attack (*Nacionalno Obedinenie Ataka*). The "ultra-nationalistic" *Ataka* was formed under the leadership of controversial television journalist Volen Siderov in April 2005 by several movements and parties that opposed NATO, EU, and IMF membership for Bulgaria. *Ataka* also demanded the abolition of the DPS (the leading ethnic Turkish party) for being "unconstitutional," contributing to the broad perception of *Ataka* as a right-wing, antiminority formation. (One of the group's slogans was "Bulgaria for the Bulgarians.") *Ataka* also opposed the participation of Bulgarian troops in the U.S.-led operation in Iraq and demanded that the sale of Bulgarian lands to foreigners be banned. Surprising most observers (many of whom condemned *Ataka*'s leadership for engaging in "hate speech"), *Ataka* finished fourth in the June 2005 assembly poll, securing 21 seats on an 8 percent vote share.

Leader: Volen SIDEROV.

United Democratic Forces (Obedineni Demokratichni Sili—ODS). The "anti-Communist," primarily center-right ODS was launched by a number of groups opposed to the BSP-led government elected in 1994. In an unusual procedure, the coalition conducted a primary in June 1996 to determine its presidential candidate, the two contenders being Petar Stoyanov of the SDS and incumbent President Zhelyu Zhelev, the nominee of the People's Union (Naroden Sayuz—NS), an alliance of the BZNS-NS and the DP. (The NS had secured 18 seats on a vote share of 6.5 percent in the 1994 assembly elections.) Stoyanov easily defeated Zhelev and went on to victory in the November national election. As configured for the presidential balloting, the ODS included not only the SDS and the NS but also the Movement for Rights and Freedom (DPS, above). However, the DPS opted out of the coalition for the April 1997 legislative balloting, at which the ODS won a majority of 137 assembly seats and presented Ivan Kostov of the SDS as the next prime minister. The reconfigured ODS won only 51 seats on an 18.2 percent vote share at the June 2001 election, prompting Kostov's resignation. For the November 2001 presidential election, Stoyanov chose to run as an independent, although he received the ODS's endorsement.

The ODS subsequently suffered severe factionalization, most notably when Kostov and his supporters left the SDS in February 2004 to form the DSB (below). In addition, the NS left the ODS in March 2004 to form its own legislative grouping, claiming 11 seats. The ODS fell to 20 seats on a 7.7 percent vote share in the 2005 assembly poll. It subsequently declined to support the new BSP/NDST/DPS coalition government.

Following the poor performance by the ODS in the 2005 assembly poll, Nadezhda Mikhailova was succeeded as ODS chair by Stoyanov, who immediately called for cooperation among all center-right parties for subsequent elections.

Leader: Petar STOYANOV.

Union of Democratic Forces (*Sayuz na Demokratichnite Sili*—SDS). The SDS was launched in late 1989 as a loose opposition coalition of intellectual, environmental, trade union, and other groups. Chaired by Zhelyu Zhelev (a dissident philosophy professor of the Zhivkov era), the SDS entered into talks with the government and negotiated arrangements for multiparty elections in June 1990, which were won by the BSP. Nevertheless, the new assembly elected Zhelev as president of Bulgaria in August 1990, while SDS opposition forced the resignation of the BSP government in November and its replacement by a coalition that included SDS members.

Dissension between moderate and radical elements resulted in the presentation of three distinct SDS lists in the election of October 1991: the main SDS-Movement, the SDS-Centre, and the SDS-Liberals. The outcome was a narrow plurality for the main SDS, which won 110 of the 240 seats and 34.4 percent of the vote, with neither of the other SDS lists gaining representation. The main SDS proceeded to form Bulgaria's first wholly noncommunist government since World War II, headed by Filip Dimitrov, with the external support of the ethnic Turkish DPS. In direct presidential elections in January 1992, Zhelev secured a popular mandate, winning 53 percent of the second-round vote.

However, serious strains quickly developed between the president and Prime Minister Dimitrov, while the SDS assembly group became racked with dissent. The government fell in October 1992 and was replaced by a nonparty administration under Lyuben Berov, with the support of some 20 SDS dissidents.

Seen as increasingly conservative, the anti-Berov SDS in mid-1993 mounted demonstrations against President Zhelev for his alleged backing of "recommunization," but defections of left-inclined deputies reduced SDS assembly strength to below that of the BSP by early 1994. In June the remaining SDS deputies launched a boycott of the assembly, prompting the resignation of the Berov government in September. However, an assembly poll in December resulted in defeat for the grouping, which moved quickly to install Ivan Kostov (a former finance minister) as its new leader on December 29, 1994. With 69 of the 240 assembly seats, it formed the principal opposition to the BSP-led government.

The SDS led the protests against the BSP in early 1997, finally forcing the calling of early elections. In preparation for the April balloting, an SDS conference in February 1997 approved the reformation of the coalition into a political party. (For a list of the members of the SDS prior to its establishment as a single party, see the 1997 *Handbook*.) Following the electoral loss of June 2001, Ivan Kostov resigned as party chair and was replaced by a former chief secretary, Ekaterina MIKHAILOVA. Although regarded as a "natural partner" by the NDST, the SDS declined to join the Saxecoburggotski government, at least in part because it objected to inclusion of an ethnic formation, the DPS. Nadezhda Mikhailova, the ODS parliamentary leader, was elected chair at the March 2002 SDS congress.

In 2004 the SDS was divided by a leadership struggle between Kostov and Nadezhda Mikhailova. At a January 2004 meeting, Nadezhda Mikhailova was reelected as party leader, prompting Kostov and a group of 26 SDS legislators to leave the SDS on February 23 (see DSB, below). The SDS was therefore left with only 14 legislative seats. In October 2005 Nadezhda Mikhailova was defeated in her bid to retain the SDS leadership by Petar Stoyanov, the former president of Bulgaria.

Leaders: Petar STOYANOV (Chair and Former President of the Republic), Nadezhda MIKHAILOVA (Former Chair).

Democratic Party (*Demokraticheska Partiya* —DP). Descended from the conservative Christian party of the same name founded in 1896, the DP was revived in 1989 and joined the opposition SDS. Following the SDS victory in the October 1991 elections, the DP's president, Stefan SAVOV, was elected president of the National Assembly. However, he resigned in September 1992 after being named in a censure motion that was tabled by the BSP and supported by some SDS deputies. (Savov died in January 2000.) The DP formed the NS with the BZNS-NS in 1994 and participated in that grouping as part of the ODS in the 1997 and 2001 assembly balloting. However, following the apparent collapse of the NS, the DP served as a single component of the ODS for the 2005 poll.

Leader: Aleksander PRAMATARSKI (Party Chair).

Saint George Day Movement (*Dvizhenie Gergyovden*—DG). The recently formed DG participated in the 2001 assembly poll in a coalition with the VMRO (below) that secured 3.6 percent of the vote, reportedly appealing to young liberal voters. The DG joined the ODS for the 2005 poll.

Leader: Lyuben DILOV Jr.

The small **National Democratic Party** (*Natsionalno Demokraticheska Partiya*—NDP) also joined the ODS for the 2001 and 2005 assembly poll.

Democrats for a Strong Bulgaria (DSB). Dissatisfaction with the leadership of the SDS prompted party leader and former prime minister, Ivan Kostov, and SDS Deputy Chair Ekaterina Mikhailova to quit the SDS and form the DSB in

February 2004. Twenty-six deputies left the SDS to help launch the DSB, and they were later joined by two other DSB parliamentarians.

Campaigning on a strongly "anti-Communist" (and thereby anti-BSP) platform, the center-right DSB won 17 seats on a 6.4 percent vote share in the 2005 assembly elections.

Leaders: Ivan KOSTOV (Chair and Former Prime Minister), Ekaterina MIKHAILOVA (Deputy Chair).

Bulgarian People's Union (*Bulgarski Naroden Sayuz*—BNS). The BNS was formed by the following three groups as an electoral coalition prior to the 2005 assembly poll. Described as a "complicated venture," the center-right BNS won 13 seats on a 5.2 percent vote share.

Bulgarian Agrarian National Union–People's Union (*Balgarski Zemedelski Naroden Sayuz–Naroden Sayuz*—BZNS-NS). The BZNS-NS is led by Anastasia Dimitrova-Moser, the daughter of G. M. DIMITROV, a prewar Agrarian leader who had emigrated to the United States after World War II. She had been a key participant in earlier struggles for supremacy among the many factions claiming descent from the historic BZNS, becoming leader of the BZNS-Nikola Petkov (named after an Agrarian leader who was executed in 1947) in February 1992. The Petkov group was then a member of the SDS, but the latter became increasingly divided after it lost power in December 1992, with the result that Dimitrova-Moser led a section of the BZNS-NS into a separate alliance with the DP.

The BZNS-NS launched the NS coalition with the DP in 1994 and participated in the ODS in the 1997 and 2001 assembly poll before serving as the core component of the BNS for the 2005 legislative elections.

Leader: Anastasia DIMITROVA-MOSER, Borislav KITOV.

Internal Macedonian Revolutionary Organization (*Vatreshna Makedonska Revolucionerna Organizacija*—VMRO). The "moderate-nationalist" VMRO participated in an electoral coalition with the DG (above) in the 2001 assembly elections before helping to launch the BNS in 2005

Leader: Krassimir KARAKACHANOV.

Union of Free Democrats (*Sayuz na Svobodnite Demokrati*—SSD). The SSD was formed in 2001 by Stefan Sofianski, the former prime minister and the mayor of Sofia who had recently split from the ODS over the refusal by the ODS to support the new NDST-led government. Sofianski resigned as mayor of Sofia after being elected to the assembly on the BNS ticket in 2005.

Leader: Stefan SOFIANSKI (Former Prime Minister).

Other Parties Participating in the 2005 Legislative Elections

New Time. A center-right group, New Time was launched in March 2004 by 11 legislative deputies from the NDST to protest the perceived slow implementation of reforms and Prime Minister Saxecoburggotski's willingness to compromise with the socialist parties in the assembly. New Time is led by Miroslav Sevlievski, a former member of the NDST's Political Council. New Time failed to reach the 4 percent threshold in the 2005 assembly poll.

Leaders: Miroslav SEVLIEVSKI, Emil KOSHLUKOV, Borislav TSEKOV.

Coalition of the Rose. Formed prior to the 2005 assembly balloting, the Coalition of the Rose was perceived primarily as a left-wing grouping, although it cooperated with a number of "diverse" elements in the elections. Included in the latter were the **National Patriotic Alliance** (led by Georgi GANCHEV, the former leader of the BBB [below]) and the **Democratic Wing Movement** (lead by Turkish leader Osman OKTAY, who had split from the DPS in 2003). The coalition secured 1.3 percent of the vote in 2005.

Leaders: Krustyo PETKOV, Alexander TOMOV.

Bulgarian Social Democracy (*Bulgarska Sotsialdemokratsia*—BSD). The BSD was formed in early 2003 by the BEL, the Bulgarian United Social Democrats, and others. The new formation reportedly did well in the 2003 municipal elections.

Leader: Alexander TOMOV.

Bulgarian Euroleft (*Balgarska Evrolevica*—BEL). The BEL, social-democratic in orientation, was organized as the Euroleft Coalition (*Koalicija Evrolevica*—KEL) prior to the April 1997 legislative balloting under the leadership of former deputy prime minister Alexander Tomov. Tomov, along with a group of supporters, had broken from the BSP in 1994 to compete in elections under the banner of the Civic Union of the Republic, which narrowly missed achieving the 4 percent threshold for representation. The ranks of the KEL were enlarged by more BSP defectors in the wake of the collapse of the Videnov government as well as by recruits from other leftist organizations. The KEL won 14 seats in the 1997 poll, subsequently solidly aligning itself with the ODS in support of economic reform and EU and NATO membership for Bulgaria. It became a formal political party at a congress in March 1998, subsequently operating as the BEL, which in December agreed to participate with the Social Democratic Union (BSDS) in the 1999 local elections.

For the 2001 assembly poll, the BEL served as the core component of a three-party left-wing electoral coalition that also included the **Bulgarian United Social Democrats** (a BSDP splinter led by Vulkana TODOROVA) and a faction of the BZNS led by Georgi PINCHEV. The BEL was subsequently described as the "backbone" of the BSD.

Leader: Alexander TOMOV.

United Labor Bloc (*Obedinen Blok na Truda*—OBT). Formed by trade unionists in May 1997 to represent the interests of "the middle class," the OBT in December 1998 announced an electoral accord with the Dertliev branch of the BSDP for the 1999 local elections. The OBT was a member of the KzB for the 2001 legislative poll, and OBT leader Krustyo Petkov secured one of the KzB seats. However, Petkov (also head of the influential Confederation of Independent Trade Unions) left the KzB in April 2005 in favor of participation in the Coalition of the Rose.

Leaders: Krustyo PETKOV (Chair), Rumen GEORGIEV.

National Movement of Rights and Freedoms (*Natsionalno Dvizhenie za Prava i Svobodi*—NDPS). The NDPS, said to have significant support in northeastern Bulgaria, was formed in 1998 as a breakaway from the DPS under the leadership of Gyuner Tahir. The NDPS was initially slated to participate in the ODS for the 2001 assembly elections, but shortly before the balloting Tahir announced the NDPS was severing its ties to the coalition because the ODS had failed to honor an agreement regarding the status of NDPS candidates.

Leader: Gyuner TAHIR.

Euroroma (*Evroroma*). A "sociopolitical" organization formed to support the interests of the Roma minority throughout the region, Euroroma competed as a political party in the 2005 assembly balloting in Bulgaria, securing slightly more than 1 percent of the vote.

Leader: Vassil BOYANOV.

Other parties and coalitions that competed unsuccessfully in the 2005 assembly elections included the Federation of Free Business, led by banker Emil HURSEV; Movement "Forward Bulgaria" (*Dvizhenie "Napred Balgariya"*), which had participated, under the leadership of Beltcho IVANOV, as a nonparty supporter of the KzB in the 2001 assembly balloting; and the Bulgarian Christian Coalition (*Balgarska Khristiyanska Koalitsiya*), which had contested national legislative elections since 1997.

Other Parties

Liberal Union (*Liberalen Sayuz*—LS). The LS was the latest in a series of liberal democratic organizations associated with Dimitur Ludzhev and former president Zhelyu Zhelev. Predecessors included Ludzhev's New Choice Liberal Union, which began as a grouping of dissident SDS assembly members in 1993 and was then formalized in July 1994. For the 1997 legislative poll the New Choice joined the ONS, and then in December 1998 it united with the DPS, Zhelev's Liberal Democratic Alternative (LDA), and the Free Radical Democratic Party of Kiril BOYADZHIEV in the Liberal Democratic Union, which Zhelev described as a true successor to the "original" SDS. The LS participated in the 2001 assembly balloting in coalition with the DPS, but there were no reports of any LS role in the 2005 poll.

Leaders: Rumen DANOV, Zhelyu ZHELEV (Former President of the Republic).

Bulgarian Business Bloc (*Balgarski Biznes Blok*—BBB). The BBB was founded in November 1990 by leading businessman Valentin MOLLOV as a right-wing, promarket formation advocating the conversion of Bulgaria into a tariff- and tax-free zone. It won 1.3 percent of the vote (and no seats) in the 1991 election but attracted growing support under the new leadership of the charismatic Georgi Ganchev, a former fencing champion. In the December 1994 assembly election the BBB broke through to representation, winning 4.7 percent of the vote and 13 of the 240 seats. Ganchev finished third in the first round of the 1996 presidential poll (with 22 percent of the vote). The BBB captured 12 assembly seats in 1997, although several defections were subsequently reported in the wake of dissent over BBB policy. In effect, the party split, with Ganchev and Hristo Ivanov both claiming to be chair. In early 1999 it was reported that the BBB was no longer formally represented in the assembly, all of its former legislators apparently having either joined other parties or decided to serve as independents. In 2001 Ganchev contested the presidency as the candidate of the Georgi Ganchev Bloc (*Blokat na Zhorzh Ganchev*—BZG), and he led a new grouping (the National Patriotic Association) in the 2005 legislative poll, cooperating with the Coalition of the Rose.

Ecoglasnost Political Club (*Politicheski Klub Ekoglasnost*—PKE). The PKE is one of several factions that emerged from the original prodemocracy Ecoglasnost movement, which dominated the first post-Communist governments headed by the SDS. It participated in the SDS-Center alliance in the 1991 elections but opposed the SDS government's shift to the right in 1992. Further policy tensions developed after the SDS went into opposition in December 1992, with the result that the PKE opted to join an alliance headed by the BSP for the December 1994 assembly election. The PKE was part of the BSP-led Democratic Left until May 2000, when it withdrew from the coalition because of what it termed the BSP's "pro-NATO course."

Leaders: Stefan GAYTANDZHIEV (Chair), Georgi GEORGIEV (Former Minister of the Environment).

Democratic Alternative for the Republic (DAR). The DAR was launched in September 1994, mainly on the initiative of the BSDP, as an autonomous alliance of center-left parties that had formed part of the SDS. Their calculation that a separate identity would be advantageous in the December assembly elections proved to be mistaken: the DAR's yield of 3.8 percent of the popular vote was below the 4 percent minimum requirement for representation.

Other components of the DAR at that time included the **Alternative Social-Liberal Party** (*Alternativna Sotsialliberlna Partiya*—ASP), led by Nicolai VASILEV; the **Alternative Socialist Association** (*Alternativo Sotsialistichesko Obedinenie*—ASO), led by Manol MANOLOV; the **Bulgarian Labor Social Democratic Party** (*Balgarska Rabotnicheska Sotsialdemokraticheska Partiya*—BRSP); and the ZPB (above). Although the BSDP and the ZPB joined other alliances for the 1997 legislative balloting, a rump DAR still presented its own candidates (without success). By 2001 the DAR was moribund. Although its individ-

ual components remained active, only the BSDP remained a significant party nationally.

United Macedonian Organization—Party for Economic Development and Integration. Founded in February 1998 and based in the Pirin region, near the border with Macedonia, this ethnic party is generally referred to as **OMO "Ilinden"-Pirin** (*Obedineti Makedonski Organizacii "Ilinden,"* the fourth word being a reference to a failed 1903 Macedonian uprising begun on the feast day of St. Elijah, August 2). Committed to human rights and European integration, the party won three seats in the 1999 municipal elections before being banned by the Constitutional Court in February 2000.

Leaders: Ivan SINGARIYSKI, Ivan GARGAVELOV (Secretary).

Small groups that unsuccessfully contested the June 2001 legislative elections included the **Coalition Simeon II** (*Koalicija Simeon II*—KSII), which attracted 3.4 percent of the vote, leading most observers to conclude that voter confusion because of its name had cost the NDST an outright majority in the National Assembly. Other groups were the **National Union for Tzar Simeon II** (*Natsionalno Obedinenie za Car Simeon II*—NOCS), which won 1.1 percent of the vote; the **Union Bulgaria** (*Sayuz Balgariya*—SB), 0.7 percent; and the **Coalition "National Union Tzar Kiro"** (*Koalicija "Natsionalno Obedenenie Car Kiro"*), 0.6 percent.

Other recently active formations include the **Bulgarian Communist Party-Marxist** (*Balgarska Koministicheska Partiya-Marksismu*—BKP-M), a group led by Boris PETKOV that considers itself the true successor of the former BKP; the **Bulgarian Communist Party-Revolutionary** (*Balgarska Komunisticheska Partiya-Revoliucionna*—BKP-R), formed in March 1991 and claiming, under the leadership of Angel TSONEV, to be the only truly Marxist-Leninist grouping remaining in Bulgaria; the **Bulgarian National Radical Party** (*Balgarska Natsionalna Radikalna Partiya*—BNRP), led by Ivan GEORGIEV; the **Christian Democratic Union** (*Hristiyan Demokraticheska Sayuz*—

Cabinet

As of September 1, 2006

Prime Minister	Sergei Stanishev (BSP)
Deputy Prime Ministers	Emel Etem (DPS) [f]
	Ivailo Georgiev Kalfin (KzB)
	Daniel Vassilev Valtchev (NDST)

Ministers

Agriculture and Forestry	Nikhat Tahir Kabil (DPS)
Culture	Stefan Lambov Danailov (BSP)
Defense	Dr. Vesselin Bliznakov (NDST)
Disaster Management Policy	Emel Etem (DPS) [f]
Economy and Energy	Rumer Stoyanov Ovcharov (BSP)
Education and Science	Daniel Vassilev Valtchev (NDST)
Environment and Water	Dzhevdet Chakarov (DPS)
European Affairs	Meglena Shtilianova Kuneva [f]
Finance	Plamen Vassilev Oresharski
Foreign Affairs	Ivailo Georgiev Kalfin (KzB)
Health	Dr. Radoslav Nenkov Gaydarski (BSP)
Interior	Rumen Yordanov Petkov (BSP)
Justice	Georgi Petkov Petkanov (NDST)
Labor and Social Affairs	Emilia Maslarova (BSP) [f]
Public Administration and Administrative Reform	Nicolay Vassilev Vassilev (NDST)
Regional Development and Public Works	Assen Dimitrov Gagauzov (BSP)
Transport	Petar Vassilev Mutafchiev (BSP)

[f] = female

HDS); the **Citizen's Party of Bulgaria** (*Grazhdanska Partiya za Balgarija*—GPB), formed in late 1999 and chaired by former interior minister Bogomil BONEV, who finished third in the November 11, 2001, presidential election; the **Conservative Union,** established in 2001 by Hristo BISEROV, formerly a chief secretary of the SDS; the **Democratic Alliance** (*Demokraticen Alians*—DA), led by 2001 presidential contestant and former caretaker prime minister Reneta INDZHOVA; and the **Bulgarian Union** (*Sajuz Balgarija*—SB), led by 2001 presidential candidate Petar BERON.

Legislature

The **National Assembly** (*Narodno Sobranie*) is a unicameral body of 240 members proportionally elected from party lists for four-year terms. Parties or coalitions must secure at least 4 percent of the national vote to receive seats. At the most recent balloting of June 25, 2005, the Coalition for Bulgaria won 82 seats; the National Movement Simeon II, 53; the Movement for Rights and Freedom, 34; the National Union Attack, 21; the United Democratic Forces, 20; the Democrats for a Strong Bulgaria, 17; the Bulgarian People's Union, 13.

Chair: Georgi PIRINSKI.

Communications

Press

In April 2004 Freedom House described the press as only "partially free" in Bulgaria because of government control of state media and reported that Bulgaria was one of the few countries in the world in which press freedom had declined recently.

The following are dailies published at Sofia unless otherwise indicated: *24 Chasa* (24 Hours, 330,000), *Noshten Trud* (Night Labor, 330,000), trade union organ; *Trud* (Labor, 200,000), trade union organ; *Standart* (Standard, 110,000), independent; *Narodno Delo* (People's Cause, Varna, 60,000), independent; *Zemya* (Earth, 50,000), former ministry of agriculture organ, now independent; *Nov Glas* (New Voice, Lovech, 50,000), independent; *Chernomorsky Far* (Black Sea Lighthouse, Bourgas, 37,000); *Vecherni Novini* (Evening News, 35,000), former BKP organ, now independent.

News Agencies

The official facility is the Bulgarian Telegraph Agency (*Bulgarska Telegrafna Agentsiya*—BTA). A number of foreign agencies, including *Agence France-Presse* and Reuters, maintain offices in Sofia.

Broadcasting and Computing

Broadcast media laws were approved in 1997 providing for an independent, seven-member National Council for Radio and Television appointed by the National Assembly and the president. Directors of national radio and television are nominated by nongovernmental journalism organizations and approved by the council. In January 2001 about 200 Bulgarian journalists accused the council of violating procedures and demanded its resignation.

In the dominant public service sector, *Bulgarsko Radio* (BR) operates over four national networks, while *Bulgarska Televiziya* (BTV) transmits over two channels. The most influential nationwide private television stations are bTV and Nova. Radio Darik is an important private radio station. Foreign satellite channels can also be received, including Cable News Network (CNN). In 2003 there were approximately 4.0 million television receivers and 400,000 personal computers serving 650,000 Internet users.

Intergovernmental Representation

Ambassador to the U.S.
Elena POPTODOROVA

U.S. Ambassador to Bulgaria
John Ross BEYRLE

Permanent Representative to the UN
(Vacant)

IGO Memberships (Non-UN)
BIS, BSEC, CEI, CERN, CEUR, EBRD, Eurocontrol, Interpol, IOM, NATO, OIF, OSCE, PCA, WCO, WTO

CROATIA

REPUBLIC OF CROATIA

Republika Hrvatska

The Country

With a long western coastline on the Adriatic Sea, Croatia half-encircles Bosnia and Herzegovina in an arc that extends north and eastward to the province of Vojvodina in Serbia and Montenegro; it also borders Hungary in the northeast and Slovenia in the northwest. At independence, Croats comprised 78 percent of the population, which also included a 12 percent ethnic Serb component, concentrated south of the capital, Zagreb, and along the western Bosnian border; however, an exodus from these areas in the 1995 hostilities reduced the Serb population to an estimated 2–3 percent. Forests covering more than a third of the country have supported a major timber industry, while agricultural activity in the eastern Pannonian plain is devoted to the growing of wheat, maize, and potatoes, in addition to the raising of cattle, sheep, pigs, and poultry. Extensive mineral resources, including hydrocarbons, bauxite, iron ore, and copper, helped make Croatia the most industrialized component of the former Yugoslav federation, with a GDP per capita substantially higher than that of Yugoslavia as a whole. However, the onset of regional conflict in the early 1990s, resulting in the loss of about 30 percent of Croatian territory to the Serbs, inflicted substantial damage on Croatia's economy and decimated the important tourist industry. National output declined by 50 percent in 1992, during which the annual inflation rate peaked at 662 percent. A partial recovery in 1993–1994 was offset by the high cost of supporting hundreds of thousands of refugees from strife-torn areas of former Yugoslavia. Croatia's recovery of most of its territory and the Dayton Accords of late 1995 stimulated the economy, which, despite continued high unemployment, subsequently exhibited relatively strong growth and low inflation. Also supporting that progress were structural reforms pursued by the government beginning in 1993, including the privatization of state-run enterprises, reduction of tariffs, rehabilitation of the banking sector, and revision of the pension system. GDP growth averaged about 6 percent annually from 1995 to 1998, with inflation running just below 4 percent and unemployment at about 17 percent at the end of that period.

Political Status: Former constituent republic of the Socialist Federal Republic of Yugoslavia; constitution proclaiming Croatian sovereignty promulgated December 21, 1990; independence declared June 25, 1991; dissociation from Yugoslavia approved by the Croatian Assembly effective October 8, 1991.

Area: 21,829 sq. mi. (56,538 sq. km.).

Population: 4,437,460 (2001C); 4,440,000 (2005E).

Major Urban Centers (2005E): ZAGREB (687,000), Split (185,000), Rijeka (134,000).

Official Language: Croatian.

Monetary Unit: Kuna (market rate July 1, 2006: 5.66 kune = $1US).

President: Stjepan MESIĆ (Croatian National Party); elected in runoff balloting on February 7, 2000, and inaugurated on February 18 for a five-year term (Vlatko PAVLETIĆ [Croatian Democratic Union—CDU], the chair of the House of Representatives, had been serving as acting president since November 26, 1999, following a ruling by the Constitutional Court that longtime President Franjo TUDJMAN [CDU] had become temporarily incapable of performing his duties due to illness. Tudjman died on December 10, prompting new elections); reelected in runoff balloting on January 16, 2005, and inaugurated for a second five-year term on February 18.

Prime Minister: Ivo SANADER (Croatian Democratic Union); appointed by the president on December 9, 2003, to form a new government, following legislative elections on November 23, 2003, and inaugurated on December 23 in succession to Ivica RAČAN (Social Democratic Party of Croatia).

Real GDP declined by 0.4 percent in 1999, in part because of regional economic disruption arising from the conflict in Kosovo. In addition, by that time it had become apparent that enthusiasm for free-market reform within the administration of longtime President Franjo TUDJMAN had been for the most part rhetorical rather than grounded in deeply held convictions. Critics charged the gov-

ernment with retaining too much control of industry and generally mismanaging an economy noted for widespread corruption, an emphasis on political patronage, and a lack of transparency. The new government installed in early 2000 immediately pledged to promote foreign investment, accelerate privatization, and pursue membership in the European Union (EU) and NATO, which had remained distant from Tudjman. GDP grew by 3.2 percent in 2002 and 4.3 percent in 2001, with inflation declining from 7.4 percent at the end of 2000 to 1.8 percent at the end of 2003. However, unemployment remained high (14.3 percent) in 2003, and repayment on the $9 billion foreign debt continued to hinder government initiatives. In 2005 improvement continued, with GDP reported at a real 4.3%, compared with 3.8% in 2004. However, cause for concern remained, as foreign debt equaled 84% of GDP, an increase of 12% since the end of 2004.

Economic restructuring slowed prior to the 2003 legislative elections, many market reforms having proven unpopular with some citizens. The new government installed in late 2003 pledged to further privatize state-run enterprises (notably in the banking and energy sectors) in pursuit of assistance from the International Monetary Fund (IMF) and membership in the EU by 2007 (see Current issues, below).

Government and Politics

Political Background

The greater part of historic Croatia was joined with Hungary in a personal union under the Hungarian monarch from the early 12th century until after World War I, except for a period of Ottoman Turkish rule from 1526 to the early 18th century. By the 19th century Serbo-Croat had evolved as the common language of Croats and Serbs (the two main South Slav groups), although the Catholic Croats use the Latin alphabet and the Orthodox Serbs use Cyrillic script. In December 1918 the country became part of the Kingdom of the Serbs,

Croats, and Slovenes, which was officially renamed Yugoslavia in October 1929. When the Germans invaded Yugoslavia in April 1941, an "Independent State of Croatia" was proclaimed by the *Ustaše* movement, a fascist grouping whose brutality (including the massacre of tens of thousands of Serbs) induced much of the population to support the Communist-inspired Partisan forces led by Josip Broz TITO. In November 1945 Croatia became one of the six constituent republics of the Federal People's Republic of Yugoslavia under the one-party rule of what became the League of Communists of Yugoslavia.

On April 22 and May 6–7, 1990, in the first multiparty balloting since World War II, the right-wing Croatian Democratic Union (*Hrvatska Demokratska Zajednica*—HDZ) won 208 of 349 seats in the constituent republic's tricameral legislature, which on May 30 named HDZ leader Dr. Franjo Tudjman state president and his associate, Stjepan MESIĆ, president of the Executive Council (prime minister). On July 22 the word "Socialist" was deleted from the constituent republic's official name and the Executive Council was redesignated as the government. Three days later Serb leaders in Croatia issued a statement proclaiming their community's right to sovereignty and autonomy. The action was followed on October 1 by the Serbs' proclamation of three "autonomous regions" encompassing districts within Croatia where they were in a majority. Subsequently, on December 21, the assembly, in an action boycotted by Serb deputies, approved a new constitution that formally asserted the republic's sovereignty, including the right to secede from the federation.

On February 8, 1991, in response to a directive from the collective state Presidency of Yugoslavia that all "unauthorized" military units surrender their arms to federal authorities within ten days, Croatia and Slovenia concluded a mutual defense pact. Three weeks later, Croatia's Serb enclaves announced the formation of a "Serbian Autonomous Region of Krajina," which promptly declared its intention to secede from Croatia and subsequently, on joining with adjacent Serb areas of Bosnia and Herzegovina, assumed the name "Republic of Serbian Krajina" (RSK).

In a May 19, 1991, referendum 83.6 percent of Croatia's registered electorate voted for dissociation from Yugoslavia, and on June 25 the republic joined Slovenia in declaring independence. The Croatian government shortly thereafter accepted a three-month moratorium on the dissociation process, as urged by the European Community (EC, subsequently the European Union—EU) in an effort to prevent a military conflict. (Due to the presence of a significant Serbian population in Croatia, Serbian leaders had indicated a much stronger inclination to resist Croatia's secession, as opposed to Slovenia's.) As part of the EC-brokered negotiations, Mesić was named president of the Yugoslavian Collective State Presidency on July 1, although the appointment ultimately proved to be essentially meaningless. The long-feared civil conflict immediately erupted, with the Serb-dominated Yugoslav National Army (JNA), openly allied with local Serb insurgents, winning control of nearly one-third of Croatia by early September. The Croatian government refused to extend the July dissociation moratorium beyond its three-month deadline and announced formal separation from Yugoslavia effective October 8. (Although Mesić remained in his federal post until he declared that "Yugoslavia no longer exists" and resigned on December 5, the Croatian legislature, upon approving the resignation, backdated it to October 8.) The fierce Serb-Croat conflict subsided following the declaration of a cease-fire on January 3, 1992, and the acceptance by both sides of a UN Security Council resolution of January 8 that provided for the deployment of a peacekeeping force in sensitive areas. Accordingly, advance units of the UN Protection Force (UNPROFOR) arrived on March 9.

On August 2, 1992, Croatia's first elections since independence involved balloting for both the House of Representatives and the presidency. The HDZ maintained its substantial overall majority in the legislative contest, and President Tudjman received a decisive 57 percent popular mandate to serve another term, with Hrvoje ŠARINIĆ taking office as prime minister on September 8.

Subsequently, in polling for the new upper House of Counties in February 1993, the HDZ was again the victor, gaining majorities or pluralities in 20 of the 21 constituencies. The Šarinić government resigned on March 29, 1993, and was succeeded on April 3 by another HDZ-dominated administration, headed by Nikica VALENTIĆ.

In 1993–1994 the opposition parties, as well as some HDZ members, claimed that the government had authoritarian tendencies and that a distinct "cult of personality" was emerging around Tudjman. As a result, the government's parliamentary majority was reduced in April 1994 by the withdrawal of some 18 liberal HDZ deputies to form the Croatian Independent Democrats (*Hrvatski Nezavisni Demokrati*—HND), with the attendant acrimony provoking an opposition boycott of parliament until September.

Zagreb's overriding priority in 1995 remained the recovery of the third of Croatia's territory that had come under Serb control in the 1991–1992 fighting. Croatia launched a major military offensive on April 30, and its forces quickly overran Serb positions in western Slavonia. Serb forces in the RSK retaliated by shelling Zagreb on May 2–3, killing civilians and strengthening Croatia's post-1994 alliance with the Bosnian Muslim-Croat Federation. In a new offensive in late July and early August, Croatian forces overran Serb positions in western Krajina, capturing the capital, Knin, on August 4 and prompting the mass flight of ethnic Serbs from the area. As a result of the Croatian advances, the only part of Croatia still under Serb control in late 1995 was eastern Slavonia, on the border with Serbia proper (see Foreign relations, below, for subsequent developments regarding eastern Slavonia).

Buoyed by military success, the Tudjman government was confirmed in power in lower house elections on October 29, 1995, although the ruling HDZ failed to achieve its target of a two-thirds majority, which is required for constitutional amendments. A new HDZ government appointed on November 7 was headed by Zlatko MATEŠA, a close associate of the president. The HDZ consolidated its strength in the upper house balloting of April 13–15, 1997, securing 40 of 63 elective seats, while Tudjman was reelected to another five-year term by receiving 61 percent of the votes in the presidential election of June 15.

Early in 1998 the nation was rocked by a series of protests over a new 22 percent value-added tax. By the end of the year, the HDZ had been further weakened by a succession struggle between party moderates and hard-liners, with several of President Tudjman's leading advisers quitting the government over allegations that party right-wingers were using the intelligence service to spy on and smear the moderates.

Tudjman's deteriorating health in late 1999 prompted a constitutional crisis because no process had been put in place to deal with such a situation. On November 24 the legislature approved new legislation that permitted the Constitutional Court on November 26 to declare Tudjman "temporarily incapacitated"; presidential authority therefore devolved on an acting basis to Vlatko PAVLETIĆ, the chair of the House of Representatives and a longtime close associate of Tudjman's. Tudjman died on December 10.

A coalition of four parties led by the Social Democratic Party of Croatia (*Socijaldemokratska Partija Hrvatshe*—SDP) and the Croatian Social-Liberal Party (*Hrvatska Socijalno-Liberalna Stranka*—HSLS) surprised most observers by winning a substantial plurality of 71 seats in the balloting for the House of Representatives on January 3, 2000, while the HDZ's representation fell to 46 seats. The SDP's Ivica RAČAN was inaugurated as prime minister on January 27 to lead a reformist government that included the HSLS as well as four smaller parties (the Croatian Peasant Party [*Hrvatska Selijačka Stranka*—HSS], the Croatian National Party [*Hrvatska Narodna Stranka*—HNS], the Istrian Democratic Assembly [*Istarki Demokratski Sabor*—IDS], and the Liberal Party [*Liberalna Stranka*—LS]) that had won 24 house seats as an electoral coalition.

In retrospect, at least, the collapse of the HDZ following the death of President Tudjman in late 1999 should not have been considered a surprise. The economy was in the midst of a recession, unemployment was high, and the administration was perceived as riddled with corruption. In addition, Tudjman's decade of autocratic rule had kept Croatia largely outside the reformist movement so prevalent in many of the other former Communist states. In particular, Western capitals criticized Tudjman's record on minority rights, the slow pace of democratic reform, and his lack of enthusiasm for full implementation of the Dayton Accords provisions, particularly the return of Serbian refugees to Croatia and the extradition of Croatian military leaders as requested by the UN International Criminal Tribunal for the Former Yugoslavia (ICTY).

Although many analysts expected the SDP/HSLS coalition to dominate the first round of presidential balloting on January 24, 2000, its candidate, Dražen BUDIŠA of the HSLS, finished second to Stjepan Mesić, the candidate of the HNS/HSS/IDS/LS coalition. Mesić outdistanced Budiša by 56 percent to 44 percent in the runoff on February 7.

Despite its remarkable achievement in ousting the HDZ from power in 2000, the new coalition government subsequently experienced internal conflict on a regular basis. In June 2001 the IDS left the government because of the refusal by the other coalition members to support its request that Italian be made an official language in Istria, the peninsula near the head of the Adriatic Sea with many ties to Italy. A number of HSLS ministers also quit the cabinet in July to protest the government's decision to extradite several generals to the ICTY for possible prosecution regarding war crimes in the 1991–1995 fighting. The HSLS finally left the coalition completely in early July 2002 because of its opposition to the government's recent agreement with Slovenia over the operation of the Krsko nuclear power plant, located in Slovenia but paid for in part by Croatia during Communist rule. (The HSLS opposed the provision that forced Croatia to handle radioactive waste from the plant.) Račan and his government resigned on July 5, but Račan retained the prime ministership in a new government (comprising the SDP, HSS, HNS, LS, and several HSLS dissidents) that was approved by the House of Representatives on July 30.

The HDZ regained a plurality in the November 2003 balloting for the House of Representatives and managed to form a minority government that included a minister from the Democratic Center and was supported in the legislature by the HSLS, HSS, and several independent deputies. Ivo SANADER of the HDZ was named prime minister.

President Mesić, supported by a number of center-left parties, was reelected for a second five-year term by securing 65.9 percent of the vote in runoff balloting on January 16, 2005.

Constitution and Government

The 1990 constitution defined the Republic of Croatia as a unitary (and indivisible), democratic, and social state, in which power "comes from and belongs to the people as a community of free and equal citizens." The highest values of the republic were stated to be freedom, equal rights, national equality, peace, social justice, respect for human rights, inviolability of ownership, respect for legal order, care for the environment, and a democratic multiparty system of government. Legislative power was vested in a bicameral assembly, both houses of which were directly elected and sat for four-year terms. The "supreme head of the executive power" was the president, who was directly elected for a five-year term and who, subject to parliamentary confirmation, appointed the prime minister and, on the proposal of the latter, other members of the government.

Significant changes to the constitution were approved by the House of Representatives on November 9, 2000, primarily to reduce the power of the president. According to those revisions, the prime minister and the cabinet are now appointed by the legislature, although the president remains commander in chief of the military. Another important change was made in March 2001 when the House of Representatives (by then controlled by reformist parties) voted to abolish the upper house (the House of Counties), which was still dominated by the HDZ.

The ordinary court system is headed by a Supreme Court, whose judges are appointed and relieved of duty by a 15-member Judicial Council of the Republic elected by the House of Representatives. There is also provision for a Constitutional Court, whose members are elected by the House of Representatives at the proposal of the upper house for eight-year terms. The main local self-government units are 21 counties (*Zupanije*) and more than 500 towns and other small municipalities.

On December 12, 1997, the legislature approved a constitutional amendment proposed by President Tudjman forbidding Croatia from joining a union with any Yugoslav or Balkan state.

Foreign Relations

Germany unilaterally recognized Croatia on December 23, 1991, with the EC following with recognition of both Croatia and Slovenia on January 15, 1992. Croatia and Slovenia established diplomatic relations with each other on February 17, 1992. On that same date, Russia accorded diplomatic recognition to Croatia. The United States followed suit on April 7. On May 22 Croatia joined Slovenia and Bosnia and Herzegovina in gaining admission to the UN. The mandate of the UNPROFOR forces deployed in Croatia from March 1992 was regularly renewed thereafter, although with increasing reluctance on Croatia's part.

Admitted to the Conference on (later Organization for) Security and Cooperation in Europe (CSCE/OSCE) in March 1992 and to the IMF in January 1993, Croatia also developed its regional links, becoming a member of the Central European Initiative (CEI), originally formed in 1989. The government declared its aim of accession to the EC/EU and to other Western bodies, while seeking Western support for recognition of Croatia's former borders.

In January 1993 Croatia launched an offensive to recover territory lost in 1991 to what had become the Serb-controlled RSK. However, despite some strategic successes on the part of the Croatian thrust, the RSK remained viable, and sporadic fighting continued, although not on the scale of the escalating conflict in Bosnia and Herzegov-

ina. In May 1993 the Tudjman government signed the Vance-Owen peace plan for Bosnia and Herzegovina, albeit clearly without any expectation that it would be implemented in the form proposed. In June, Tudjman and Serbian President Slobodan Milošević reportedly reaffirmed their aim of bringing about the eventual partition of Bosnia and Herzegovina between Croatia and Serbia on the basis of an "orderly" transfer of population. In 1994, however, advocates of a resumption of the earlier Croat-Muslim alliance gained the ascendancy in Zagreb. The result was the signing on March 18 of a U.S.-brokered agreement between Bosnian Croats and Muslims providing for a federal structure in the neighboring republic (see article on Bosnia and Herzegovina), accompanied by a preliminary accord envisaging the creation of a confederation between the new Bosnian federation and Croatia, with each remaining sovereign entities.

In October 1994 Croatia welcomed the creation of the so-called Zagreb Four (Z-4) mini-contact group (the UN, EU, United States, and Russia), which was charged with resolving the Croat-Serb deadlock. Speedy progress seemed to be made by the Z-4 under a December agreement reestablishing essential services between Croatia and the RSK and reopening major roads; however, the accord was suspended by the RSK in February 1995 after Croatia had given formal notice of terminating the UNPROFOR mandate. In the same month Croatia rejected a Z-4 peace plan as "unacceptable" in its "structure, basic provisions, title, and preamble." On March 6 the military commanders of Croatia, the Bosnian government, and the Bosnian Croats concluded a formal alliance in response to a military pact between Croatian Serb and Bosnian Serb forces announced on February 20. A week later President Tudjman bowed to U.S. and German pressure by agreeing to the renewal of the UNPROFOR mandate from March 31, on condition that most UN forces would be stationed on Croatia's international borders.

In the wake of Croatian military successes in 1995 and the restoration of government control over most of Croatia, President Tudjman was a key participant in the Dayton Accords talks that yielded a Bosnian peace agreement in November and was a signatory of the accord at Paris in December. On November 30 the UN Security Council voted to withdraw UN troops from Croatia by mid-January 1996. In a state of the nation address on January 15, Tudjman reported that, in what he called the "homeland war" of 1991–1995, Croatia proper had suffered 13,583 deaths and nearly 40,000 people injured, as well as material damage estimated at some $27 billion.

Although the status of Serb-held eastern Slavonia did not feature in the accords, Croatia's endorsement of the agreement was predicated on an international understanding that the area would be restored to Croatian rule. An agreement signed by Croatia and local Serb leaders on November 12, 1995, provided for the reintegration of eastern Slavonia into Croatia within two years, during which a UN-sponsored transitional administration would exercise authority. In January 1996 the UN Security Council approved the deployment of a 5,000-strong peacekeeping force (the UN Transitional Administration for Eastern Slavonia, Baranja, and Western Sirmium—UNTAES) to supervise the demilitarization of the area, which began in May as the Serbs of the region elected a new leadership that appeared to be reconciled to the eventual restoration of Croatian rule. (Croatia formally reassumed authority over Slavonia on January 15, 1998, following the expiration of the UNTAES mandate. A small UN support group was collaterally assigned to remain in the region to monitor relations between the Croatian police and returning displaced persons.) The progress made on the Slavonian front in 1996 enabled Zagreb, following talks between Presidents Tudjman and Milošević near Athens on August 7, to sign a formal accord with Belgrade on August 23 providing for the establishment of full diplomatic relations between Croatia and Federal Yugoslavia. Collaterally, Croatia increased pressure on the Bosnian Croats to accept federation with the Bosnian Muslims, to which end Presidents Tudjman and Izetbegović of Bosnia, conferring in Geneva on August 14, reached agreement on detailed steps to inject substance into a federation structure theretofore existing only on paper.

Croatia appeared to have achieved membership in the Council of Europe on April 24, 1996, when the organization's Parliamentary Assembly voted in favor of admission. However, in an unprecedented reversal, the Council's Committee of Ministers decided on May 14 to defer a decision on the recommendation on the ground that Croatia had not acted upon a 21-point program on democracy and human rights previously negotiated with the council. Not until further assurances had been received from Zagreb did the ministers, on October 16, agree to Croatia's admission, which was formally accomplished on November 6.

After years of negotiations, Croatia tentatively accepted two agreements with Bosnia and Herzegovina on November 22, 1998. The Ploce-Neum accord gave Bosnia, which had very limited sea access, the right to use Croatia's large-vessel port of Ploce, while the Croatians gained transit rights through Bosnia's Neum region without border formalities. A second treaty called for a "special relationship" between Croatia and the Muslim-Croat Federation of Bosnia and Herzegovina.

Although Croatia continued to express an interest in joining the EU and the North Atlantic Treaty Organization (NATO) during the latter years of the Tudjman administration, Zagreb satisfied neither group that it was committed to key prerequisites for inclusion, including press freedom, fair elections, civilian control of the military, and full implementation of the Dayton peace agreements (particularly the return of Serb refugees). As a result, NATO took no immediate action on Croatia's application to join the Partnership for Peace program. However, Zagreb voiced support for NATO air strikes against Serbia in March 1999, and Foreign Minister Mate GRANIĆ claimed on April 1 that he had obtained a security guarantee from NATO in the event that the conflict in Kosovo spread.

Following Tudjman's death in late 1999 and the subsequent installation in early 2000 of a reformist government, Croatia's relations with the West improved with remarkable speed. In May membership in NATO's Partnership for Peace program was approved, in December Croatia joined the World Trade Organization, and in October 2001 Zagreb signed an association agreement with the EU.

In April 2002 Croatia negotiated an agreement to delineate the border between Croatia and Montenegro. In 2003 President Mesić and the president of Serbia and Montenegro exchanged mutual apologies for atrocities committed during the civil war.

President Mesić was outspoken in his opposition to the U.S./UK-led invasion of Iraq in early 2003, and Croatia rebuffed a request to contribute troops to that initiative. However, relations with Washington improved following the installation of the HDZ government in late 2003, Croatia subsequently agreeing to permit the United States to use Croatian airspace and waters in future military action. In May 2006, Vice President Dick Cheney made a visit to Croatia, which the *New York Times* called "...a reward for Croatia, which Mr. Cheney said had made substantial progress in recent years. It has shed its nationalist image and helped to bring its last remaining Croatian war crimes suspect, Gen. Ante Gotovina, to the International Criminal Tribunal for the Former Yugoslavia. Croatia is now regarded as the favorite among the former Yugoslav states to be accepted into the European Union and NATO."

Current Issues

In 2000 President Mesić, described, in sharp contrast to longtime president Tudjman, as "unpretentious" and "mild-mannered," immediately reversed his predecessor's positions on many issues that had been perceived as retrograde; he also pledged to eliminate covert support to Croatians in Bosnia and Herzegovina who were opposed to the current political structures in that country. Prime Minister Račan also strongly endorsed the reformist agenda, vowing to pursue Croatia's eventual full membership in the EU and NATO with vigor. The international community responded keenly to the government's new directions. However, some initiatives provoked conflict within the coalition government and certain sectors of the

population. For example, mass protest demonstrations were staged in 2001 in connection with the extradition of several generals to The Hague for prosecution by the ICTY. The return of the HDZ to government control in late 2003 was not seen as a surprise, considering the fragmentation of the SDP-led coalition and its perceived failure to invigorate the economy. New prime minister Sanader promised economic, military, and judicial reforms, primarily aimed at entry into the EU. In 2004 the EU authorized the start of formal accession negotiations, in part because of Croatia's apparent willingness to cooperate more enthusiastically with the ICTY. Croatia indicated it hoped to gain EU membership by 2007, but progress stalled in April 2005 when the UN accused the Croatian government of poor faith in extraditing alleged war criminals to the ICTY. (The government argued that it had been unable to locate Ante GOTOVINA, one of the most prominent suspected war criminals, although the ICTY alleged Gotovina was being shielded by supporters that included Croatian officials.) In the May 2005 local elections, the far-right Croatian Party of Rights (*Hrvatska Stranka Prava*—HSP) saw its representation triple in consonance with growing popular antipathy toward the ICTY. Sanader subsequently strongly criticized the ICTY for expanding the list of Croatians it hoped to bring to trial. On October 3, 2005, ICTY's chief prosecutor issued a positive report on Croatia's cooperation with the tribunal, and as a result accession negotiations recommenced. Croatia's chances for EU membership brightened considerably in December 2005, when Gotovina was arrested by Spanish authorities in the Canary Islands, partially as a result of intelligence information provided by the Croatian government. Since the arrest and transfer of Gotovina to The Hague in late 2005, Croatia has continued to cooperate fully with the ICTY.

Political Parties

For four and a half decades after World War II, the only authorized political party in Yugoslavia was the Communist Party, which was redesignated in 1952 as the League of Communists of Yugoslavia (*Savez Komunista Jugoslavija*—SKJ). In 1989 noncommunist groups began to emerge in the republics, and in early 1990 the SKJ approved the introduction of a multiparty system, thereby effectively triggering its own demise.

Government and Government-Supportive Parties

Croatian Democratic Union (*Hrvatska Demokratska Zajednica*—HDZ). Founded in June 1989, the right-wing HDZ won a decisive majority of seats in the 1990 elections in each of the three assembly chambers in the Croatian constituent republic within Federal Yugoslavia. After leading Croatia to independence in 1991, the HDZ won a further overall parliamentary majority in the 1992 balloting, when the party's leader was popularly returned as head of state with 56.7 percent of the vote. Having previously headed a coalition government, the HDZ was the sole ruling party until, after winning a majority in upper house balloting in February 1993, it accepted the small Croatian Peasant Party (below) as a ministerial partner. In September 1994 ideological conflict flared when extreme rightist Vladimir Šeks resigned as deputy prime minister but was speedily elected chair of the party's parliamentary group. Strengthened by Croatian military advances against the Serbs, the HDZ retained a comfortable lower house majority on a 45.2 percent vote share in October 1995. In the upper house elections of April 1997, the HDZ won 40 of 63 elected seats, while President Tudjman in June won a landslide victory in the presidential balloting. He was also unanimously reelected as party president in February 1998. Tudjman appeared to side with party hard-liners in a succession struggle leading to the resignation of two top presidential advisers in October 1998. The hard-liners, who reportedly shared with Tudjman a desire to carve Croatian territory from Bosnia and Herzegovina, were led by Ivić PAŠALIĆ, the president's special adviser for domestic affairs, who many observers believed was the likely successor to the president.

Following Tudjman's death in late 1999, Pašalić lost the HDZ leadership election to Mate GRANIĆ,

who finished a disappointing third in the first round of the 2000 presidential poll with 22.4 percent of the vote. The party's fortunes also slid significantly in the January 2000 legislative balloting as it secured only 24 percent of the vote and 46 seats. Granić subsequently left the HDZ (along with three other HDZ legislators) to form the Democratic Center. Meanwhile, Ivo Sanader was selected as the new HDZ president in 2000, Pašalić being expelled from the party in July 2002 for characterizing Sanader's reelection as "illegal." (Pašalić subsequently formed the Croatian Bloc–Movement for a Modern Croatia).

The HDZ expelled three legislators from the party in 2005 for advocating greater regional autonomy.

Leaders: Ivo SANADER (Prime Minister and Chair), Jadranka KOSOR (Deputy Prime Minister and Deputy Chair), Vladimir ŠEKS (Speaker of the House of Representatives and Parliamentary Leader), Joso ŠKARA (Secretary General).

Croatian Peasant Party (*Hrvatska Seljačka Stranka*—HSS). Originally founded in 1904 as the Croatian Popular Peasant Party and influential in the interwar period, the HSS was relaunched in November 1989 as a party committed to pacifism, localism, and economic privatization. It won 3 lower house seats in August 1992 and 5 upper house seats in February 1993, thereafter accepting ministerial representation in coalition with the dominant HDZ. It switched to opposition status for the October 1995 election, winning 10 seats as a member of the Joint List Bloc (*Zajednica Lista*—ZL), which also included the HNS, HKDU, IDS, and SBHS. The ZL took second place on an 18.3 percent vote share, which yielded a total of 18 seats (10 for the HSS, 4 for the IDS, 2 for the HNS, and 1 each for the HKDU and SBHS). However, the ZL did not present candidates for the April 1997 House of Counties balloting, its members variously running their own candidates, collaborating with other Bloc components, or even aligning with parties outside the Bloc. The HSS presented a number of joint candidates with the HSLS in that balloting.

CROATIA 1 6 5

The HSS contested the 2000 legislative balloting in coalition with the IDS, HNS, and LS, the coalition securing 16 percent of the vote and 24 seats (16 for the HSS). The so-called Opposition Four also presented the successful 2000 presidential candidate—Stjepan Mesić of the HNS. In the 2003 legislative elections, the HSS ran outside of its previous coalition. The party won 9 seats or just over half of its previous representation. The HSS subsequently supported the HDZ-led government, although it did not receive any cabinet posts. The HSS supported President Mesić in the 2005 presidential election.

Leaders: Josip FRISCIC (Chair of the Party), Josip M. TOBAR (Honorary Chair), Stjepan RADIĆ (Honorary President), Ivan STANČER (Vice President), Stanko GRČIĆ (General Secretary).

Croatian Social-Liberal Party (*Hrvatska Socijalno-Liberalna Stranka*—HSLS). Founded in May 1989, the HSLS was characterized as a traditional European liberal grouping. Having performed modestly in the 1990 election, it became the second-strongest and main opposition party in August 1992, winning 14 lower house seats and, for its leader, a creditable 21.9 percent of the presidential vote. Securing 16 seats in the 1993 upper house balloting, the HSLS took part in an opposition boycott of Parliament in mid-1994. In the 1995 lower house balloting the HSLS took 11.6 percent of the vote, confirming its status as the single strongest opposition party. However, in April 1997 balloting for the House of Counties, the HSLS slipped from 16 to 6 seats of its own, although it had supported successful candidates from the HSS in some districts. In the June presidential race, HSLS candidate Vlado GOTOVAĆ, who was beaten up by an army officer at a rally and couldn't finish the campaign, came in third in the three-man race despite having the backing of a number of other opposition parties. The HSLS's showing in the 1997 elections apparently indicated it was declining in strength relative to the SDP, and divisions within the HSLS came to a head at the party's congress in November when a deadlock between Gotovać and his longtime rival Dražen BUDIŠA prevented the election of a

party president. Aside from the leadership issue, the party was also divided over whether to cooperate with the HDZ. On December 6, following his defeat by Budiša in the party's presidential election, Gotovać and his leading supporters resigned from the party to form a new grouping called the Liberal Party (below).

Budiša, also endorsed by the SDP, finished second in the first round of presidential balloting in 2000 with 27.7 percent of the vote and lost the runoff with 44 percent. Meanwhile, the HSLS, now described as a "mildly nationalistic, socially conservative" party, won 24 seats in the 2000 elections to the House of Representatives as part of a coalition with the SDP, PGS, and SBHS. Although the HSLS joined the government following that balloting, Budiša's relationship with Prime Minister Račan of the SDP proved conflictual, and the HSLS officially left the cabinet in July 2002, although some HSLS members kept their posts and left the party. The HSLS ran with the Democratic Center in an electoral coalition in the 2003 elections.

Leaders: Durda ADLEŠIĆ (President), Zlatko KRAMARIĆ (Deputy President), Želimir JANJIĆ, Hrvoje VOJKOVIĆ, Stanko ZRILIĆ (Vice Presidents).

Democratic Center (*Demokratski Centar*—DC). The DC was founded in March 2000 by former foreign minister Mate Granić (the unsuccessful HDZ presidential candidate in the recent election) and several HDZ legislators. The DC advocated Croatia's accession to the EU and NATO and other efforts to improve "international integration." In the 2003 House of Representatives elections, the DC joined the HSLS in a coalition. The DC subsequently joined the HDZ-led coalition government.

Leader: Vesna ŠKARE-OŽBOLT (Chair).

Other Parliamentary Parties

Social Democratic Party of Croatia (*Socijaldemokratska Partija Hrvatske*—SDP). Founded in 1937 as the Communist Party of Croatia and redesignated in 1952 as the League of Communists of Croatia (*Savez Komunista Hrvatske*—SKH), the SDP was runner-up to the HDZ in the 1990 balloting, winning 75 of 349 legislative seats outright, in addition to 16 captured in joint lists with other parties. Then called the Party of Democratic Changes (*Stranka Demokratskih Promjena*—SDP) to signify its rejection of communism, it slumped to only 11 seats (out of 138) in the 1992 election. The party changed its name again in April 1993 when it became the Social Democratic Party of Croatia, angering another leftist party of the same name (*Socijaldemokratska Stranka Hrvatske*—SDSH), with which it would merge a year later. (The SDSH, launched in December 1989, had won 1 seat in 1990 and was a member of the ruling coalition until August 1992, when its leader, Antun VUJIĆ, finished last of eight presidential candidates.)

The sole successful SDP candidate in the 1993 upper house polling was returned by virtue of an alliance with the HSLS. The united SDP performed better in the October 1995 lower house election, winning 8.9 percent of the vote. In the April 1997 elections to the upper house, the SDP showed further strength (in frequent alliance with the HNS), and in the June presidential campaign SDP candidate Zdravko TOMAC ran second (21 percent) in the three-way race. The SDP's gains in both races indicated to some observers that it had displaced the HSLS as the strongest opposition party.

The SDP participated in an electoral coalition in the 2000 legislative elections with the HSLS, PGS, and SBHS. The coalition secured 47 percent of the vote and 71 seats; SDP leader Ivica Račan subsequently formed a coalition government. However, the joint SDP/HSLS presidential candidate, Dražen Budiša of the HSLS, finished second in the 2000 presidential poll.

In the 2003 legislative elections the SDP formed a new coalition with the LS, IDS, and Libra. The SDP developed a broader coalition in 2005 to support the candidacy of President Mesić.

Leaders: Jerko ZOVAK (President/Party Council), Mirko PAČAREK (Vice President), Jadranka FILIPOVIĆ (Chief Secretary).

Croatian National Party   (*Hrvatska Narodna Stranka*—HNS). Formed in January 1991, the HNS is also very widely known as the Croatian People's Party. The HNS secured lower house representation by the co-option of five deputies elected in 1990 under other party labels. It is an antitraditionalist grouping committed to political pluralism and a free-market economy. The party won six seats in the 1992 legislative election, with its leader securing 6 percent of the presidential vote. It slipped to two seats in 1995 and ran joint candidates with the SDP in the 1997 House of Counties balloting.

The HNS participated in the 2000 legislative elections in a coalition with the HSS, IDS, and LS, gaining 2 of the coalition's 24 seats. Despite its modest status in the realm of Croatian parties, the HNS served as the springboard for the successful presidential campaign in 2000 of Stjepan Mesić, a founding member of the HDZ who had broken from President Tudjman in 1994 and joined the HNS in 1997. Mesić won 41.1 percent of the vote in the first round of the presidential poll and 56.0 percent in the runoff.

In the 2003 elections, the HNS joined a coalition with the SBHS and the PGS. In 2005 Mesić was reelected president with support from an SDP-led coalition.

Leaders: Stjepan MESIĆ (President of the Republic), Vesna PUSIĆ (President), Savka DABČEVIĆ-KUČAR (Honorary President), Andrija DUJIĆ, Jozo RADOŠ, Josip POSAVEC, Morana PALIKOVIĆ-GRUDEN (Vice Presidents).

Liberal Party   (*Liberalna Stranka*—LS). The LS was founded in January 1998 by defectors from the HSLS, including HSLS founders such as Vlado Gotovac, its presidential candidate in 1997, and a number of HSLS legislators. The LS sees itself as a guardian of the democratic principles on which the HSLS was founded, including staunch opposition to the HDZ. The LS was part of the "Opposition Four" coalition with the HSS, HNS, and IDS in the 2000 legislative balloting. Gotovac died in late 2000. In 2003 the LS participated in an electoral alliance with the SDP. The LS supported President Mesić in the 2005 presidential polling.

Leader: Zlatko BENAŠIĆ (President).

Alliance of Croatian Coast and Mountains Department   (a.k.a. Primorian Goranian Union)

(*Primorsko Goranski Savez*—PGS). Initially established in March 1990 as the Rijeka Democratic Alliance (*Riječki Demokratski Savez*), the party changed its name in 1996 to reflect its activities beyond the Rijeka region. Its platform advocates respect for all ethnic groups, a free-market economy, and civil liberties. The PGS ran in coalition with the SDP and the HNS for the House of Counties in 1997; by virtue of the success of SDP candidates in some of those races, the PGS was referenced as a parliamentary party, although no PGS members were legislators in their own right. In the 2000 balloting for the House of Representatives the PGS secured two seats as part of an electoral coalition with the SDP, HSLS, and SBHS. The PGS campaigned in a coalition with the HNS and the SBHS in the 2003 legislative elections. In the 2005 presidential election the PGS joined the pro-Mesić coalition.

Leader: Nikola IVANIŠ (President).

Istrian Democratic Assembly (*Istarki Demokratski Sabor*—IDS). Founded in February 1990, the IDS represents ethnic Italians and other minorities in Istria, advocating the creation of a "trans-border region" encompassing Croatian, Slovenian, and Italian areas. In the 1992 lower house balloting it formed a regional front with **Dalmatian Action** (*Dalmatinska Akcija*—DA), led by Mira LJUBIĆ-LORGER, and the Rijeka Democratic Alliance (see PGS, above), which won six seats, of which the IDS took four. In the 1993 upper house election the IDS took 66 percent of the vote in Istria, winning one elective seat and being allocated two more by presidential prerogative. In 1995 the IDS tally as part of the ZL was four seats. The party won two seats in the April 1997 elections for the House of Counties. In August the IDS called a meeting of several opposition parties to agitate for changes in electoral law that would reduce the power of the presidency and make referendums mandatory for all key issues.

The IDS won four seats in the 2000 balloting for the House of Representatives in coalition with the HSS, HNS, and LS. The IDS joined the January 2000 cabinet formed by the SDP's Ivica Račan but left the government in June 2001. The IDS again campaigned with the SDP coalition in the 2003 House election, and it also joined the SDP-led coalition that supported President Mesić in his 2005 reelection campaign.

Leaders: Ivan JAKOVČIĆ (President), Emil SOLDATIĆ (Secretary General).

Party of Liberal Democrats (*Stranka Liberalnih Demokrata*—Libra). Libra was formed in 2002 by former members of the HSLS when the HSLS left the SDP-led coalition government over the handling of the Krsko nuclear power plant issue with Slovenia. Libra deputies continued to support the government after the departure of the HSLS. Libra sought to appeal to younger, more educated urban voters with a centrist, economically liberal platform. In the 2003 House of Representatives elections, Libra joined the SDP-led electoral coalition and secured three seats. Libra also participated in the SDP-led coalition that supported President Mesić in the 2005 presidential election.

Leader: Jozo RADOS.

Croatian Party of Rights (*Hrvatska Stranka Prava*—HSP). A far-right formation established in 1990, the HSP is descended from a prewar nationalist party of the same name. Discord among party leaders for 1991 led a faction to form the **Croatian Democratic Party of Rights** (*Hrvatska Demokratska Stranka Prava*—HDSP) in June 1992. The HSP went on to win five seats in the August 1992 lower house election, its (then) president, Dobroslav PARAGA, taking 5.4 percent of the vote in the national presidential contest. Thereafter, the party came under pressure from the authorities, which in October asked the Constitutional Court to ban the HSP and instituted legal proceedings against three leading members. The HSP's military wing, called the Croatian Defense Association (*Hrvatska Obrambeni Savez*—HOS), was heavily involved in interethnic conflict; from mid-1993 steps were taken by the authorities to integrate the HOS into the official security forces. Paraga was ousted from the party leadership in September 1993, subsequently forming the breakaway HSP-1861. The HSP narrowly surmounted the 5 percent threshold in the October 1995 legislative balloting, securing four seats.

The HSP contested the 2000 legislative balloting in coalition with the HKDU, securing four of the five seats won by the coalition. Meanwhile, Anto Dapić, president of the HSP, won 1.8 percent of the votes in the first round of the 2000 presidential poll. In the 2003 House of Representatives elections, the HSP formed a coalition with the Democratic Party of Zargorje (ZDS) and the Medimurian Party (MS). Only the HSP secured representation with eight seats. Slaven Letica was the HSP candidate in the 2005 presidential polling. He placed fifth with 7.59 percent of the vote.

Leaders: Anto DAPIĆ (President), Slaven LETICA (2005 presidential candidate).

Independent Democratic Serbian Party (*Samostalna Demokratska Srpska Stranka—* SDSS). Based in Vukovar, a major town in Slavonia, the SDSS was founded as the Independent Serbian Party in October 1995; the party adopted its current name in March 1997 in time for Serbs to contest the local elections in April. It quickly merged with the Party of Serbs (*Stranka Srpski—* SS) led by Milorad Pupovac. (The SS, advocating democratic and liberal principles, had been launched in 1993 and included the *Prosveta* ["Enlightenment"] movement.) The SDSS initially was formed to represent ethnic Serbs in Slavonia, but the merged party aimed to address the concerns of the 120,000 Serbs throughout Croatia. However, in its first outing, the party limited itself to contests for local and county assemblies and did not seek representation in the upper house at Zagreb. Ethnic Croatian parties won 16 of the 27 districts in eastern Slavonia, with 11 going to the SDSS. Following the April elections to the House of Counties, President Tudjman appointed SDSS party leader Vojislav Stanimirović and another ethnic Serbian leader, Jovan BAMBURACA, to the upper house, accounting for two of the five appointments the president made to that body. To the surprise of some analysts, the SDSS was unsuccessful in the 2000 balloting for the House of Representatives. However, in the 2003 legislative election, the SDSS gained the three seats reserved for the Serb minority. In exchange for support on key issues, the HDZ-led government agreed to advocate on behalf of SDSS priorities, including refugee return and increased minority rights.

Leaders: Vojislav STANIMIROVIĆ, Milorad PUPOVAC.

Other minor parties that gained representation in the 2003 elections included the **Croatian Pensioners' Party** (*Hrvatska Stranka Umirovljenika—* HSU), led by Vladimir JORDAN; and the **Croatian Democratic Peasant Party** (*Hrvatska Demokratska Seljačka Stranka—*HDSS), led by Ivan MARTAN.

Other Parties and Groups

Croatian Party of Slavonia and Baranja (a.k.a. Slavonian-Baranian Croatian Party) (*Slavonsko-Baranjska Hrvatska Stranka—*SBHS). Founded in December 1992, the SBHS aimed to represent ethnic Croats in what had been Serb-majority Croatian territory occupied by Serb forces in the 1991–1995 conflict. It won one lower house seat in 1995 as a member of the Joint List Bloc. It retained that seat in the 2000 elections for the House of Representatives in which it participated in a coalition with the SDP, HSLS, and PGS. The SBHS joined the HNS-led coalition, along with the PGS, for the 2003 legislative balloting but failed to gain any seats.

Leaders: Damir JURIĆ (President), Zdenko MARUS (Secretary General).

Croatian Christian Democratic Union (*Hrvatska Kršćanska Demokratska Unija—* HKDU). The HKDU was formed in December 1992 by the **Croatian Christian Democratic Party** (*Hrvatska Kršćanska Demokratska Stranka—*HKDS), led by Ivan CESAR, and a majority faction of the Croatian Democratic Party of Rights (HDSP, above), led by Marko Veselica, both constituents dating from 1989. (Veselica had spent 11 years in jail during Communist rule.) The HKDS had participated in the ruling coalition from 1990 but lost its two lower house seats in August 1992, Cesar placing seventh in the concurrent presidential poll. As part of the ZL, the HKDU won one seat in the 1995 lower house balloting. The HDS and HKDS decided to remain legally independent for a transition period, which apparently included the 1997 House of Counties elections. The HKDU secured one seat in the 2000 balloting for the House of Representatives, which it contested in coalition with the HSP. The HKDU failed to gain representation in the House in the 2003 legislative elections. Anto Kovačević, the party's candidate in the 2005 presidential balloting, received less than 1 percent of the vote.

Leaders: Petar ĆURLIN (President), Marko VESELICA (Honorary President).

Serbian People's Party (*Srpska Narodna Stranka*—SNS). Founded in May 1991, the SNS (also known as the Serbian National Party) is an ethnic party that advocates a market economy, civil rights, and membership in the EU. Although much of Croatia's ethnic Serb population was not under Zagreb's jurisdiction at the time of the August 1992 election, the SNS returned three deputies on a platform of opposition to the Serb separatism represented by the self-proclaimed Republic of Serbian Krajina. Following Zagreb's recovery of Krajina in 1995 and the resultant exodus of many ethnic Serbs, the SNS won only two seats in the October election. Its representation fell to one in the 2000 balloting for the House of Representatives. The SNS did not secure any seats in the 2003 House elections.

Leaders: Ivica GAŽI (President), Josip MANOLIĆ (Honorary President).

Croatian Independent Democrats (*Hrvatski Nezavisni Demokrati*—HND). Led by the (then) presiding officers of Croatia's parliament, the HND was formed on April 30, 1994, by some 18 left-of-center dissident deputies of the ruling HDZ (including former President of the Government Stjepan Mesić), who charged President Tudjman with authoritarianism and an ill-advised policy of waging war with Bosnia's Muslims. Both party leaders were replaced in their parliamentary posts by HDZ regulars. The HND failed to surmount the 5 percent barrier in the October 1995 lower house balloting but won one constituency seat. A dispute divided the party leadership in October 1996, and Mesić subsequently joined the HNS. In 2002 it was reported that one disaffected HDZ legislator had left that party and joined the HND. The HND did not gain any seats in the 2003 House of Representatives elections.

Leaders: Josip MANOLIĆ (President), Marija DUIĆ (Secretary General).

Social Democratic Union of Croatia (*Socijaldemokratska Unija Hrvatske*—SDUH). Founded in May 1992, the SDUH was formed from the Reformists of Croatia and the League of Social Democrats of Croatia. Led by a prominent economist, the SDUH was one of several parties hoping to rally left-wing elements in the postcommunist era. It won 3.2 percent of the vote in 1995, thus failing to achieve representation.

Leaders: Boško VUČINIĆ (President), Branko HORVAT (Former President).

Croatian Democratic Republican Party (*Hrvatska Demokratska Republikanska Stranka*—HDRS). The HDRS was launched in October 2000 via merger of Croatian Spring (*Hrvatska Prolječa*—HP) and two other small opposition parties.

Leader: Josko KOVAĆ.

Other parties include the **Croatian Bloc–Movement for a Modern Croatia** (*Hrvatski Blok–Pokret za Modernu Hrvatsku*), formed in 2002 and led by 2005 presidential candidate Ivić PAŠALIĆ; the **Croatian Liberation Movement** (*Hrvatski Oslobodilaćki Pokret*—HOP), led by Ivan CURIĆ and Slavko GRUBIŠIĆ; the **Croatian Popular Party** (*Hrvatska Pučka Stranka*—HPS), whose leader, Tomislav MERČEP, won 0.9 percent of the vote in the first round of the 2000 presidential election and 0.1 percent in 2005; the **Croatian Pure Party of Rights** (*Hrvatska Čista Stranka Prava*—HCSP), Luka PODRUG (President); the

Croatian Republicans (*Hrvatski Republikanci—HR*), led by Tomislav BOGDANIĆ; the **Croatian Republican Party** (*Hrvatska Republikanska Stranka—HRS*), led by Borko JURIN; the **Croatian Republican Union** (*Hrvatska Republikanska Zajednica—HRZ*), an outgrowth of the HRS, led by Mario M. OSTOJIĆ; the **Democratic Party of Zagorje** (*Zagorska Demokratska Stranka—ZDS*), led by Stanko BELINA; the **Homeland Civic Party** (*Domovinska Gradjanska Stranka—DGS*), which won 0.2 percent of the vote in the 1995 balloting for the House of Representatives under the leadership of Drago MINTAS; the **Medimurian Party** (*Medimurska Stranka—MS*), which campaigned in a coalition with the HSP and ZDS in 2003; the **Movement for Human Rights/Party of Ecologically Conscious Citizens** (*Pokret za Ljudska Prava/Stranka Ekološki Sujesnih Gradana—POL/SESG*), led by Rikard MORITZ; the **New Alternative Party,** led by Aljoša BABIĆ; **New Croatia** (*Nova Hrvatska—NH*), whose candidate, Ante PRKAČIN, won 0.30 percent of the vote in the first round of the 2000 presidential balloting and 0.28 percent in 2005; the **Party of Democratic Action of Croatia** (*Stranka Demokratske Akcije Hrvatske—SDAH*), led by Semso TANKOVIĆ; and the **Socialist Workers Party of Croatia** (*Socijalistička Radnička Partija Hrvatske—SRPH*), a leftist, anti-NATO grouping formed in October 1997 under the leadership of Stipe ŠUVAR.

Other parties that participated in the 1997 county elections and have been referenced recently as still active include the **Croatian Citizen Peasant Party** (*Hrvatska Gradansko Seljačka Stranka—HGSS*), led by Stjepan VUJANIĆ; **Croatian Dalmation Home** (*Hrvatski Dalmatinski Dom—HDD*), formed in May 1996 and led by Goran SLADOLJEV; **Croatian Peasant Labor Party** (*Hrvatska Seljačko Radnička Stranka—HSRS*), led by Josip DENT; the **Gypsy Party of Croatia** (*Stranka Roma Hrvatske—SRH*), led by Stevo DURDEVIĆ; the **Istrian Independent Party** (*Istarska Nezavisna Stranka—INS*), led by Franko ŠTURMAN; and the **Istrian Party** (*Istarska Stranka*), led by Miro BOŽAC.

Other minor parties are the **Albanian Christian Democratic Party of Croatia** (*Albanska Demokršćanska Stranka Hrvatske—ADMSH*), led by Mikel MARKAJ; **Central European Action** (*Srednjoeuropska Akcija—SEA*), led by Damir MILIĆ; the **Christian Social Union** (*Kršćanska Socijalna Unija—KSU*), formed in 1999 under the leadership of Nikša SENTIĆ; the **Citizen Party of Sisak** (*Sisačka Gradanska Stranka—SGS*), led by Božidar PINTARIĆ; the **Croatian Defense Order** (*Hrvatski Obranbeni Red—HOR*), led by Branimir PETENER; the **Croatian Democratic Republican Party** (*Hrvatska Demokratska Republikanska Stranka—HDRS*), founded in 2000 under the leadership of Joško KOVAĆ; the **Croatian Ecological Alliance** (*Hrvatski Ekološki Savez—HES*), led by Zlatko SVIBEN; the **Croatian Homeland Party** (*Hrvatska Domovinska Stranka—HDMS*); **Dalmatian Action** (*Dalmatinska Akcija—DA*), led by Mira LJUBIĆ-LORGER; the **Democratic Party of Pensioners** (*Demokratska Stranka Umirovljenika—DSU*), founded in 2001 under the leadership of Zlatko MAVRLJA; the **Freedom Party of Croatia** (*Slobodarska Stranka Hrvatske*), formed in 2001 under the leadership of Boris BABIĆ; the **Green Left of Croatia** (*Zelena Ijevica Hrvatske—ZEL*), led by Zvjezdana CIKOTA (President); the **Green Party** (*Zelena Stranka—ZS*), led by Zoran PIŠL; the **Island's Democratic Party** (*Otočna Demokratska Stranka—ODS*), led by Tomislav OROVIĆ; the **Italian Democratic Union** (*Talijanska Demokratska Zajednica–Unione Democratica Italiana—TDZ-UDI*), led by Tulio PERSI; the **Party of Croatian State Rights** (*Stranka Hrvatkog Dravnog Prava—SHDP*), led by Nikola BIĆANIĆ; the **Party of Danubian's Serbs** (*Partija Podunavskih Srba—PPS*), led by Radivoj LESKOVAC; the **People's Assembly of Rab** (*Rapski Pučki Sabor—RPS*), led by Milijenko MATIJEVIĆ; the **Serbian Democratic Party of Baranja** (*Srpska Demokratska Baranjska Stranka—SDBS*), led by Ljubomir MIJATOVIĆ; and the **South Croatian Party** (*Južnohrvatska Stranka—JHS*), formed in 2001 under the leadership of Srećko KLJUNAK.

Cabinet

As of April 30, 2006

Prime Minister	Ivo Sanader
Deputy Prime Ministers	Jadranka Kosor [f]
	Damir Polenčec

Ministers

Agriculture, Forestry, and Water Management	Petar Čobanković
Culture	Božo Biškupić
Defense	Berislav Rončević
Economy, Labor, and Enterprise	Branko Vukelić
Environmental Protection, Physical Planning, and Construction	Marina Matulović Dropulić [f]
Family, Veterans' Affairs, and Intergenerational Solidarity	Jadranka Kosar [f]
Finance	Ivan Šuker
Foreign Affairs and European Integration	Kolinda Grabar Kitarović
Health and Social Welfare	Neven Ljubičić
Interior	Ivica Kirin
Justice	Ana Lovrin (HDZ) [f]
Maritime Affairs, Tourism, Transport, and Development	Božidar Kalmeta
Science, Education, and Sports	Dragon Primorac (ind.)

[f] = female

Note: Except where indicated otherwise, all of the above ministers are members of the Croatian National Party.

Legislature

Under the 1990 constitution, the Croatian **Assembly** (*Sabor*) consisted of an upper House of Counties (županijski Dom) and a lower House of Representatives, both popularly elected for four-year terms. The new bicameral structure was implemented by elections to the House of Representatives in August 1992 and, following the passage of legislation establishing the country's 21 counties, to the House of Counties in February 1993. The House of Counties was abolished (effective upon the expiration of its current term in May 2001) by a vote in the House of Representatives in March 2001.

House of Representatives (*Zastupnički Dom*). The present House comprises 140 members elected from ten regular constituencies (14 seats each) under a proportional system that requires a party to receive 5 percent of the vote in any constituency to gain representation from that constituency. An additional 5 members are elected (on a plurality basis) to represent ethnic minorities (1 each for Serbian, Hungarian, and Italian minorities; 1 shared by the Czech and Slovak minorities; and 1 shared by the Austrian, German, Ruthenian, Ukrainian, and Jewish minorities), while up to 15 are elected on a proportional basis by Croatians living abroad. (The number of seats from the diaspora is determined at each election via comparison of voter turnout relative to previous turnouts.)

The most recent balloting, held November 23, 2003, resulted in the election of 152 members (including 7 representing Croatians living abroad). The seat distribution was as follows: the Croatian Democratic Union, 66; the coalition of the

Social Democratic Party of Croatia (SDP), the Istrian Democratic Assembly (IDS), the Liberal Party (LS), and the Party of Liberal Democrats (Libra), 43 (SDP, 34; IDS, 4; Libra, 3; LS, 2); the coalition of the Croatian National Party (HNS), the Primorian-Goranian Union (PGS), and the Slavonian-Baranian Croatian Party (SBHS), 11 (HNS, 10; PGS, 1); the Croatian Peasant Party, 10; the coalition of the Croatian Party of Rights (HSP), the Democratic Party of Zagorje (ZDS), and the Medimurian Party (MS), 8 (HSP, 8); the coalition of the Croatian Social-Liberal Party (HSLS) and the Democratic Center (DC), 3 (HSLS, 2; DC, 1); the Croatian Pensioners' Party, 3; the Independent Democratic Serbian Party, 3; the Croatian Democratic Peasant Party, 1; independents, 4.

Chair: Vladimir ŠEKS.

Communications

Government control of the media was heavy under the Tudjman administration, a situation that was attracting ever-increasing international and domestic criticism prior to Tudjman's death in late 1999. Restrictions were subsequently relieved substantially as part of the new government's efforts to present a reformist image to Western capitals.

Press

The following are dailies published in Serbo-Croat: *Večernji List* (Evening Paper, Zagreb, 300,000); *Slobodna Dalmacija* (Free Dalmatia, Split, 110,000); *Jutarnji List* (Zagreb, 100,000); *Novi List* (New Paper, Rijeka, 60,000); *Vjesnik* (Courier, Zagreb, 50,000), formerly progovernment, now independent; *Novi Vjesnik* (New Courier, Zagreb, 45,000); *Glas Slavonije* (Slavonia News, Osijek, 25,000); *Glas Istre* (Istrian News, Pula, 18,000). Weeklies include *Nacional* (Zagreb, 80,000); *Globus* (Zagreb, 180,000); *Feral Tribune* (Split, 50,000), satirical.

News Agency

The official government body since 1990 has been the HINA News Agency.

Broadcasting and Computing

Croatian Radio-Television (*Hrvatska RadioTelevizija*) broadcasts in Serbo-Croat over three nationwide radio stations and three television channels. Croatian television was controlled by the government until 2000 and was criticized internationally for biased reporting and favoritism in its election coverage. In October 1997, for example, the OSCE called on two stations to broadcast public apologies for having "failed to meet even minimally acceptable standards" of fairness. After a long dispute with the government and a demonstration by 100,000 supporters in November 1996, independent Radio 101 received a five-year license in November 1997. Also in November 1997, Radio Vukovar resumed broadcasting in the eastern Slavonian city for the first time since its fall to a Serbian assault six years earlier. The first license for a nationwide private station (Nova TV) was issued in July 2000. In 2003, there were approximately 1.3 million television receivers and 850,000 personal computers serving 1.0 million Internet users.

Intergovernmental Representation

Ambassador to the U.S.
Nevin JURICA

U.S. Ambassador to Croatia
Ralph FRANK

Permanent Representative to the UN
Mirjana MLADINEO

IGO Memberships (Non-UN)
BIS, CEI, CEUR, EBRD, Eurocontrol, IADB, Interpol, IOM, OSCE, PCA, WCO, WTO

CYPRUS

REPUBLIC OF CYPRUS

Kypriaki Dimokratia (Greek)
Kibris Cumhuriyeti (Turkish)

The Country

Settled by Greeks in antiquity, conquered by the Ottoman Empire in 1571, placed under British administration in 1878, and annexed by Britain in 1914, Cyprus has been independent since 1960 (although effectively partitioned since 1974). The largest island in the eastern Mediterranean, it supports diverse and often antagonistic ethnic groups and traditions. More than 75 percent of the population speaks Greek and belongs to the Orthodox Church, while more than 20 percent is Turkish-speaking Muslim; adherents of other religions account for less than 2 percent.

Although Cyprus was historically an agricultural country, the Greek Cypriot rural sector presently employs only about 13 percent of the total labor force and contributes less than 6 percent of GDP (the corresponding Turkish Cypriot figures being 25 and 12 percent, respectively). Nonetheless, vegetables, fruits, nuts, and wine rank with clothing and footwear as leading exports. Following the de facto partition of the island into Greek and Turkish sectors in 1974, rebuilding in the south emphasized manufacturing of nondurable consumer goods, while the more severely damaged north has relied on its citrus groves, mines, and tourist facilities as well as on direct budgetary assistance from Turkey (estimated at around 20 percent of budgeted expenditure in recent years). Whereas 70 percent of predivision productive resources had been located in the north (including 80 percent of the island's citrus groves and 60 percent of tourist installations), the postdivision southern economy rapidly outdistanced that of the north, achieving consistently high annual growth rates and virtually full employment. In addition to developing tourism and agriculture, Greek Cyprus diversified into financial, shipping, and other services, becoming a major offshore banking center and suffering only a temporary downturn as a result of the 1990–1991 Gulf crisis.

The economy performed well in the first half of the 1990s, growth averaging more than 4 percent annually and unemployment remaining negligible. However, disturbances along the dividing line

between the Greek Cypriot and Turkish Cypriot territories in 1996 led to a decline in tourism, the collateral slowdown in economic growth being exacerbated by the effect of drought in 1996–1997 on agricultural production. Subsequently, the economic focus was on efforts to harmonize policies in areas such as taxation, customs, and government spending with those of the European Union (EU), with which Cyprus began conducting formal accession negotiations in 1998. With one of the strongest economies among the EU candidate states, Cyprus completed 24 out of 29 chapters in the EU accession process by late 2001. However, some economic slowdown was noted, mainly due to the global recession and declining tourism revenues.

GDP grew by 4.1 percent in 2001, 2.1 percent in 2002, and 1.9 percent in 2003. In order to join the EU, the government initiated broad reforms in the banking sector and agreed to raise taxes on its offshore financial companies. Accession to the EU on May 1, 2004, was seen as providing significant opportunities for economic growth, although the unresolved political division of the island continued to be a significant complication. In 2004 GDP grew by 3.5 percent, with inflation (2.5 percent) and unemployment (3.4 percent) remaining well below European averages. In addition, by that time per capita annual income had reportedly reached about 80 percent of EU norms. Current government priorities include deficit reduction (in part through pension reform and wage constraint for public sector workers) and overall labor market reform.

The northern economy (on which reliable figures are scarce) appears to have made only limited progress since 1974, being hard hit by the collapse in 1990 of the Polly Peck International fruit-packaging and tourism conglomerate (which had accounted for a third of the Turkish Republic of Northern Cyprus's [TRNC] GDP and 60 percent of its exports) and by external rulings banning imports from the TRNC as an unrecognized entity. The TRNC announced a five-year plan for economic development in 1997, although progress appeared to continue to depend on a resolution of the political statement on the island. Meanwhile,

aid from Turkey remained the major support for the TRNC, which, by using the Turkish lira as its unit of currency, has been forced to deal with rapid inflation, unlike the Greek Cypriot sector.

The UN-controlled border between the TRNC and the south opened to some trade and travel in 2004, although the TRNC government charged that the Greek Cypriot government was limiting trade from the north through overly officious administrative requirements. The TRNC also objected to decisions by the Greek Cypriot government to block some EU assistance (see article on Cyprus: Turkish Sector). However, in 2005 the TRNC reported that GDP per capita, previously only 20 percent of the Greek Cypriot figure, had risen to $7,000 in 2004, mostly because of a construction boom associated with the tourism sector.

Government and Politics

Political Background

The conflict between Greek and Turkish Cypriot aspirations shaped the political evolution of Cyprus both before and after the achievement of formal independence on August 16, 1960. Many Greek Cypriots had long agitated for *enosis,* or the union of Cyprus with Greece; most Turkish Cypriots, backed by the Turkish government, consistently rejected such demands, opposed the termination of British rule in 1960, and advocated division of the island into Greek- and Turkish-speaking sectors. Increased communal and anti-British violence after 1955 culminated in the Zürich and London compromise agreements of 1959, which provided for an independent Cyprus guaranteed by Greece, Turkey, and Britain, and instituted stringent constitutional safeguards for the protection of the Turkish minority. These agreements expressly prohibited either union with Greece or partition of the island between Greece and Turkey.

The government of Archbishop MAKARIOS proposed numerous constitutional changes in November 1963, including revision of articles considered inviolable by the Turkish Cypriots. The proposals led to a renewal of communal conflict, the

Political Status: Independent republic established August 16, 1960; member of the Commonwealth since March 13, 1961; under ethnic Greek majority regime until coup led by Greek army officers and subsequent Turkish intervention on July 20, 1974; Turkish Federated State proclaimed February 13, 1975, in Turkish-controlled (northern) sector; permanent constitutional status under negotiation (currently suspended) despite proclamation of independent Turkish Republic of Northern Cyprus (TRNC) on November 15, 1983.

Area: 3,572 sq. mi. (9,251 sq. km.), embracing approximately 2,172 sq. mi. (5,625 sq. km.) in Greek-controlled (southern) sector and 1,400 sq. mi. (3,626 sq. km.) in Turkish-controlled (northern) sector.

Population: 913,000 (2001E, including Greek sector census figure of 703,529 and an estimate of 209,000 for the Turkish sector); a comparable overall estimate for 2005 would be 976,000, assuming accuracy of the 2001 TRNC figure, which includes settlers from Turkey (approximately 55 percent).

Major Urban Centers (Urban Areas, 2005E): NICOSIA/LEFKOSÍA (224,000, excluding Turkish sector), Limassol/Lemesós (175,000), Larnaca/Lárnax (77,000), Paphos/Néa Páfos (54,000). In 1995, city names were changed by the government as part of a campaign to standardize them in accordance with their Greek pronunciation; however, both names are accorded official status.

Official Languages: Greek, Turkish.

Monetary Unit: Cyprus Pound (market rate July 1, 2006: 1 pound = $2.22US). (Following its accession to the European Union in May 2004, Cyprus announced plans to adopt the euro "as soon as possible.")

President: Tassos PAPADOPOULOS (Democratic Party); elected in first-round popular balloting on February 16, 2003, and inaugurated for a five-year term on March 1, succeeding Glafcos CLERIDES (Democratic Rally).

Vice President: Vacant. Rauf R. DENKTAŞ, then president of the Turkish Republic of Northern Cyprus (see article on Cyprus: Turkish Sector), was elected vice president by vote of the Turkish Community in February 1973, but there has been no subsequent vice-presidential balloting.

---

withdrawal of Turkish Cypriots from the government, and, in 1964, the establishment of the UN Peacekeeping Force in Cyprus (UNFICYP), whose mandate was thereafter regularly extended for six-month periods by the Security Council (the cumulative cost of the operation being put at over $2 billion by 1996). Further conflict broke out in 1967, nearly precipitating war between Greece and Turkey.

Following the 1967 violence, Turkish Cypriots moved to implement an administration for their segment of the island. This organization, known as the Turkish Cypriot Provisional Administration, constituted a de facto government in the Turkish communities. The Turkish Cypriot withdrawal also meant that from 1967 until the Turkish military intervention in July 1974 the prime conflicts were between the Makarios regime and radicals in the Greek community (led, until his death in January 1974, by Gen. George GRIVAS).

On July 15, 1974, the Greek Cypriot National Guard, commanded by Greek army officers, launched a coup against the Makarios government and installed a Greek Cypriot newspaper publisher and former terrorist, Nikos Giorgiades SAMPSON, as president following the archbishop's flight from the island. Five days later, Turkish troops were dispatched to northern Cyprus, bringing some 1,400 square miles (39 percent of the total area) under their control before agreeing to a cease-fire. On July 23 the Sampson government resigned and the more moderate presiding officer of the Cypriot House of Representatives, Glafcos CLERIDES, was sworn in as acting president. On the same day, the military government of Greece fell, and on July 25 representatives of Britain, Greece, and Turkey met in Geneva in an effort to resolve the Cyprus conflict. An agreement consolidating the cease-fire was concluded on July 30, but the broader issues were unresolved when the talks collapsed on

August 14. Upon his return to Cyprus and resumption of the presidency on December 7, Makarios rejected Turkish demands for geographical partition of the island, although he had earlier indicated a willingness to give the Turks increased administrative responsibilities in their own communities.

On February 13, 1975, Turkish leaders in the occupied northern sector proclaimed a Turkish Federated State of Cyprus (see map) with Rauf DENKTAŞ, the nominal vice president of the republic, as president. Although the action was immediately denounced by both President Makarios and Greek Prime Minister Caramanlis, the formation of a Turkish Cypriot Legislative Assembly was announced on February 24.

Extensive negotiations between Greek and Turkish representatives were held in Vienna in April 1977, following a meeting between Makarios and Denktaş in February. Although it was revealed that the more recent Greek proposals embraced the establishment of a bicommunal federal state, the Makarios government insisted that only 20 percent of the island's area be reserved for Turkish administration, while the Turks countered with demands that would entail judicial parity and a presidency to rotate between Greek and Turkish chief executives.

Archbishop Makarios died on August 3, 1977, and was succeeded, as acting president, by Spyros KYPRIANOU, who was elected on August 31 to fill the remaining six months of the Makarios term. Following the kidnapping of Kyprianou's son on December 14 by right-wing extremists, Clerides withdrew as a contender for the presidency, and Kyprianou became the only candidate at the close of nominations on January 26, 1978. As a result, the election scheduled for February 5 was canceled, Kyprianou being installed for a five-year term on March 1. In April 1982 the two government parties, the Democratic Party (*Demokratiko Komma*—Deko) and the (Communist) Progressive Party of the Working People (*Anorthotiko Komma Ergazomenou Laou*—AKEL) agreed to support Kyprianou for reelection in February 1983.

In a three-way race that involved Clerides and Vassos LYSSARIDES, the leader of the United Democratic Union of Cyprus–Socialist Party (*Ethniki Demokratiki Enosi Kyprou–Sosialistiko Komma*—EDEK-SK), who technically withdrew on January 4, Kyprianou won reelection on February 13, 1983, securing 57 percent of the vote. Nine months later, on November 15, the Turkish Cypriot Legislative Assembly unanimously approved the declaration of an independent TRNC.

President Kyprianou and Turkish Cypriot leader Denktaş met at UN headquarters January 17–20, 1985, for their first direct negotiations in five years. Prior to the meeting, the two had endorsed a draft proposal to establish a federal republic that entailed substantial territorial concessions by the Turkish Cypriots and the removal of foreign troops from the island. Although UN Secretary General Javier Pérez de Cuéllar declared that the gap had "never been so narrow" between the two sides, the talks collapsed after Kyprianou had reportedly characterized the plan as no more than an "agenda." Subsequently, the government's coalition partner, AKEL, joined with the opposition Democratic Rally (*Demokratikos Synagermos*—Desy) in blaming Kyprianou for the breakdown in the talks and calling for his resignation as president.

At the conclusion of a bitter debate on the president's negotiating posture, the House of Representatives voted unanimously on November 1, 1985, to dissolve itself, paving the way for an early legislative election. In the balloting on December 8, Kyprianou's Deko gained marginally (though remaining a minority grouping), while the opposition failed to secure the two-thirds majority necessary to enact a constitutional revision that would require the chief executive to conform to the wishes of the House.

Deprived of the backing of AKEL, Kyprianou placed third in first-round presidential balloting on February 14, 1988. In a runoff election one week later, George VASSILIOU, a millionaire businessman running with AKEL endorsement, defeated Clerides by securing a 51.5 percent majority.

On August 24, 1988, Presidents Vassiliou and Denktaş met in Geneva for the first summit talks between the two communities in over three years, with formal negotiations being resumed in

September. By June 1989 deadlock had again been reached, an acceptance in principle by both sides of the UN-proposed concept of a bicommunal, bizonal federation under one sovereignty being negated by fundamental differences on implementation. More positively, a UNFICYP-supervised "deconfrontation" accord was implemented in May 1989 involving the withdrawal of both sides' forces from 24 military posts along the central Nicosia/Lefkosía sector of the "Attila Line" dividing the island.

A new round of UN-sponsored talks that opened in New York in February 1990 ended prematurely the following month when a demand by Denktaş for a "right of self-determination" was construed by Vassiliou as a demand for separate sovereignty. Relations were further exacerbated by the Greek Cypriot government's application in July for entry into the European Community (EC, subsequently the EU). Benefiting from association with Vassiliou's high negotiating profile, AKEL registered the biggest advance in legislative balloting on May 19, 1991, but Desy retained a narrow plurality as Deko representation plummeted.

U.S. and UN diplomatic initiatives in 1991–1992 yielded further intercommunal talks, with the UN in mid-1992 suggesting a demarcation of Greek and Turkish sectors under a federal structure that would entail the transfer of about 25 percent of TRNC territory to Greek Cypriot administration. The UN plan was described as "totally unacceptable" by Denktaş, who warded off growing criticism from TRNC hard-liners by reiterating his self-determination/sovereignty demand for Turkish Cypriots. Also divided were the Greek Cypriots, with AKEL and Desy broadly supporting Vassiliou's acceptance of the UN plan, whereas Deko and the EDEK-SK complained that the president was accepting effective partition. Because of the continuing deadlock, the UN Security Council in November 1992 proposed that confidence-building measures (CBMs) should be implemented to lay the basis for an overall settlement, including reduction of troop levels, some small transfers of TRNC territory to UN administration, and the reopening of Nicosia international airport (closed since 1974).

However, differences on the CBM proposal proved to be as intractable as those on the fundamental issues.

Veteran Desy leader Clerides emerged as the surprise victor in Greek Cypriot presidential balloting on February 7 and 14, 1993, when Vassiliou (again backed by AKEL) headed the first round with 44.2 percent but was narrowly defeated in the runoff contest (50.3 to 49.7 percent). During the campaign the Desy leader's previous support for the Vassiliou line had mutated into forceful criticism, thus enabling Deko and the EDEK-SK (whose joint candidate was eliminated in the first round) to swing behind Clerides in the second round. A new government appointed by Clerides on February 25 contained six Desy and five Deko ministers.

Hopes that Clerides would break the deadlock in the Cyprus negotiations were quickly disappointed. On the other hand, because of continuing economic progress in Greek Cyprus, the administration went into legislative balloting on May 26, 1996, in a buoyant mood. Desy retained its narrow plurality of 20 seats, Deko lost 1 of its 11, and AKEL managed only a 1-seat advance, to 19; the remaining seats went to the EDEK-SK, 5; and the new Free Democrats Movement (*Kinima ton Eleftheron Demokraton*—KED), 2.

The Desy-Deko coalition headed by President Clerides collapsed when the Deko central committee decided to break from the government on November 4, 1997, after Clerides revealed his intention to seek reelection in the February 1998 elections. The five Deko cabinet members who consequently resigned were replaced by nonparty ministers. There were seven candidates in the February 1998 presidential balloting: President Clerides; George IACOVOU, an independent backed by AKEL and Deko; George Vassiliou, former president and the leader of the KED; Nikos ROLANDIS, leader of the Liberal Party (KP); EDEK-SK President Vassos LYSSARIDES; Nicholaos KOUTSOU of New Horizons (NO); and independent candidate Alexis GALANOS, who had broken from Deko over its endorsement of Iacovou.

Iacovou led Clerides by a very slight margin in the first-round balloting (40.61 to 40.06 percent) on February 8, with Lyssarides finishing third with 10.59 percent. The EDEK-SK took no position regarding the runoff, but the other first-round contenders endorsed Clerides, who secured a 50.8 to 49.2 percent victory in the second round on February 15 at which a 94 percent turnout was reported. On February 28 Clerides announced a new "national unity" government comprising, in addition to Desy, the KP, EDEK-SK, United Democrats, and several Deko "rebels." Among other things, the multiparty cabinet was reportedly designed to present a unified stance regarding EU membership and proposed reunification talks. However, the EDEK-SK resigned from the government in late 1998 as the result of a dispute regarding the proposed deployment of Russian missiles on the island (see Current issues, below).

In legislative balloting on May 27, 2001, AKEL secured a plurality of 20 seats, followed by Desy with 19. In presidential elections on February 16, 2003, Tassos PAPADOPOULOS of Deko, campaigning on a hard-line platform regarding the proposed UN reunification plan, won a first-round election with 51.5 percent of the vote. His new coalition cabinet was sworn in on March 1, 2003.

On July 14, 2003, after the breakdown of negotiations between the Greek and Turkish Cypriots over reunification, the Greek Cypriot House of Representatives unanimously approved EU entry. Greek Cypriots rejected the UN-brokered peace plan on April 24, 2004, thereby ensuring that only the Greek areas of Cyprus joined the EU on May 1, 2004 (see Current issues, below).

The government of Tassos Papadopoulos emerged stronger than ever from parliamentary elections on May 21, 2006. In an election that was considered to be primarily a referendum on the government's position with respect to reunification of the island and relations with Turkey, Greek Cypriot voters strongly endorsed the Papadopoulos government's hard-line policies. Papadopoulos's Deko party attracted 17.9 percent of the vote, up from 14.8 percent in 2001. At the same time, parties that came out in favor of a recent UN plan for power sharing with the Turkish Cypriots all showed an erosion of support at the polls.

Constitution and Government

The constitution of 1960, based on the Zürich and London agreements, provided for a carefully balanced system designed to protect both Greek Cypriot and Turkish Cypriot interests. A Greek president and a Turkish vice president, both elected for five-year terms, were to name a cabinet composed of representatives of both groups in specified proportions. Legislative authority was entrusted to a unicameral House of Representatives, with 35 Greek and 15 Turkish members to be elected by their respective communities. In addition, Greek and Turkish Communal Chambers were established to deal with internal community affairs. Collateral arrangements were made for judicial institutions, the army, and the police. Following the original outbreak of hostilities in 1963 and the consequent withdrawal of the Turkish Cypriots from the government, there were a number of changes, including merger of the police and gendarmerie, establishment of a National Guard, abolition of the Greek Communal Chamber, amendment of the electoral law, and modification of the judicial structure.

Subsequent to withdrawal, the Turkish community practiced a form of self-government under the Turkish Cypriot Provisional Administration, an extraconstitutional entity not recognized by the government. It formed a Turkish Cypriot Provisional Assembly composed of the 15 Turkish members of the national legislature and the 15 representatives to the Turkish Cypriot Communal Chamber. In early 1975 the Provisional Administration was reorganized as a Turkish Federated State in the northern sector of the island, followed by a unilateral declaration of independence in November 1983 (see article on Cyprus: Turkish Sector). From the December 1985 election the national membership of the House of Representatives was increased to 80 seats, although only the 56 Greek Cypriot seats were filled in that and subsequent contests.

Prior to the intervention by mainland Turkish forces, the island was divided into six administrative districts, each headed by an official appointed by the central government. Municipalities were governed by elected mayors.

Foreign Relations

Cyprus is a member of the UN and several other intergovernmental organizations. On a number of occasions Archbishop Makarios made diplomatic overtures toward third world countries, although, even prior to the 1974 conflict, internal problems made it difficult for him to follow up on such initiatives.

As a result of the events of 1974, the domestic situation became in large measure a function of relations with Greece and Turkey, two uneasy NATO partners whose range of disagreement has by no means been confined to Cyprus. Britain, because of its treaty responsibilities in the area, has long played a major role in attempting to mediate the Cyprus dispute, while the United States, prior to the George H. W. Bush presidency, played a less active role. The intercommunal talks, held intermittently since 1975, were initiated at the request of the UN Security Council, which has assumed the principal responsibility for truce supervision through the UNFICYP.

In October 1987 the government concluded an agreement with the EC to establish a full customs union over a 15-year period commencing January 1, 1988; in July 1990 it submitted a formal application for full membership. In October 1993 the Council of Ministers of the EU called on the Brussels Commission to begin "substantive discussions" with Cyprus to prepare for accession negotiations. The result was agreement by the EU's Corfu summit in June 1994 that Cyprus would be included in the next round of enlargement negotiations due to begin in 1996 or 1997. Uncertainties remained, however, as to linkage between EU accession and resolution of the basic Cyprus question, especially in light of vehement opposition by both the TRNC and Turkey to the Greek Cypriots' unilateral pursuit of membership. (Formal negotiations regarding the accession of Cyprus to the EU were launched in March 1998, and substantial progress was reported over the next year in bringing Cyprus's economic policies in line with EU requirements, the eventual membership of Cyprus being widely described as "inevitable." Collaterally, Cyprus has also applied for membership in the Western European Union.)

Turkish Cypriot hostility to Greek Cypriot EU aspirations was compounded when the European Court of Justice ruled on July 5, 1994, that all EU imports from Cyprus would require authorization from the Greek Cypriot government, thus in effect banning direct trade between the EU and the Turkish sector. President Denktaş informed the UN Security Council on July 26 that resumption of the peace talks was contingent on cancellation of the court's ruling, while TRNC Assembly resolutions of late August called for defense and foreign policy coordination with Turkey and rejected a federal Cyprus solution as required by the UN, urging instead "political equality and sovereignty" for the Turkish sector.

Pursuant to an agreement of November 16, 1993, placing Cyprus within "the Greek defense area," joint Greek–Greek Cypriot military exercises were held for the first time in October 1994. Seven months later, President Clerides headed a visit to Athens by the Greek Cypriot National Council (consisting of the main party leaders) for a "unity" meeting with Greek government ministers. Concurrently, closer relations were established between the Greek Cypriot government and Russia, which in March 1995 informed Turkey of its firm commitment to a federal solution to the Cyprus problem in accordance with UN resolutions. Following the November 2002 elections in Turkey, the new government of Recep Tayyip Erdoğan began to increase pressure on the TRNC to accept UN efforts at a peace settlement in order to improve Turkey's chance of EU membership.

Current Issues

Amid persistent deadlock in intercommunal negotiations, the Greek Cypriot side took some comfort from the specific condemnations of Turkish Cypriot intractability that issued regularly from the UN secretary general and Security Council beginning in 1992. President Clerides subsequently adopted a tougher stance by categorically ruling out any formal talks on a "confederation" and insisting that further discussions be based on the UN-endorsed concept of a bicommunal federation preserving a single sovereignty.

While continuing to attach importance to American and British mediation, the Greek Cypriot government gave increasing priority to the "EU route" to a settlement, believing that its application for full EU membership could yield a breakthrough in the intercommunal deadlock. Under this scenario, the Turkish Cypriot side would perceive the potential benefits of EU membership to the beleaguered northern economy, and would accordingly be brought to accept a federal "one sovereignty" settlement as the Greek Cypriot application progressed. However, hopes of a speedy breakthrough were dashed in August 1996 when Greek Cypriot antipartition demonstrators clashed with Turkish soldiers and civilians after penetrating the UN buffer zone. An international mediation effort to ease the tension between the two communities was subsequently launched by France, Germany, and the UK.

The UN negotiator for Cyprus, Diego Cordovez, presented President Clerides and President Denktaş with a draft agreement for the establishment of a federal Cyprus in 1997. However, President Denktaş restated his demand that Cyprus suspend its application for EU membership before talks proceeded. The prospects for any future rapprochement remained slim, as Denktaş met with the Turkish minister of foreign affairs, İsmail Cem, and announced that a joint committee would be formed to implement "partial integration" between TRNC and Turkey.

In December 1997 the EU summit at Luxembourg included Cyprus among the six countries for whom formal membership negotiations would be launched in the spring of 1998 (Turkey being pointedly excluded from the list), and the TRNC subsequently suspended all bicommunal activities.

The Greek Cypriot government invited the TRNC to appoint representatives to the Cypriot team being established to negotiate with the EU; however, the Denktaş administration rejected the overture, reportedly out of concern (in part, at least) that it would be in a "subservient" position under such arrangements.

Tension between the Greek Cypriot government and the TRNC escalated sharply in late December 1998 when Clerides announced the impending deployment of Russian missiles on Greek Cypriot soil. Turkey quickly threatened possible military intervention, and the EU said it would suspend accession talks with Cyprus if the plan was pursued. Consequently, Clerides agreed to have the missiles deployed instead on the Greek island of Crete, with Greece maintaining "operational control" of the weapons. Subsequently, the administration called upon the international community to bring greater pressure on Ankara and the TRNC to return to the bargaining table. However, although both Washington and the UN pledged to intensify their mediation efforts, little hope for compromise had appeared by May 1999, nationalists having achieved significant gains in April 1999 balloting in Turkey and no sentiment for a "unitary state" having surfaced in the TRNC.

In August 2000 Cyprus came under pressure from the Organization for Economic Cooperation and Development (OECD) to change its image as an "international tax haven." The *Financial Times* reported that over 40,000 offshore companies were registered but only about 1,200 had a physical presence on the island.

Apparently in consonance with Greek-Turkish rapprochement (see articles on Turkey and Greece), the tension between Greek and Turkish Cypriots eased considerably after a major earthquake hit western Turkey in mid-August 1999, the Cypriot government sending monetary and humanitarian aid to Turkey. However, the improved relations failed to produce any breakthrough in a series of UN proximity talks conducted through 2000. In what some saw as a compromise step, Denktaş in 2001 backed away from his insistence of Cypriot recognition of the TRNC as a precondition to resuming talks and proposed in December a "partnership republic" instead of confederation.

For most of 2002 the Greek and Turkish sides conducted periodic negotiations that failed to produce tangible results. However, a report published in October by the European Commission announced that Cyprus, among others, had fulfilled the political criteria for admission to the EU and was expected to have fulfilled the economic and other criteria in time to sign an accession treaty in the spring of 2003 in anticipation of membership in 2004. Consequently, international pressure intensified for resolution of the Turkish/Cypriot dispute. (Although the EU made it clear that Cyprus's accession was not contingent on a political settlement and that the EU was prepared, if necessary, to admit only the "Greek" part of Cyprus, it was clear that the preference was strong for the island's entry as a "unified entity.") In an effort to solve the deadlock, UN Secretary General Kofi Annan launched a comprehensive plan in early November in which he proposed a "Swiss-model" for reunification in which the two component states would have equal status and substantial autonomy.

Central to Annan's plan was the return of property from the Turkish Cypriots to the Greek Cypriots and compensation for property losses in both communities. Annan's proposal envisioned a reduction of the TRNC from 36 percent of the island to 28.5 percent. The plan would displace 42,000 Turkish Cypriots and allow 85,000 Greek Cypriots to return to their former homes.

Tensions between the two communities increased with the February 2003 presidential election of Tassos Papadopoulos, who demanded that all Greek refugees have their property restored as part of any reunification. Despite apparent concessions from Denktaş regarding partial reopening of the border and some proposed land return, little progress was achieved in subsequent talks as Papadopoulos retained his hard-line stance.

In early 2004 Papadopoulos agreed to present the revised UN reunification plan to a national referendum, although he campaigned against the plan, demanding more concessions from the TRNC, particularly in regard to property reparations. Conse-

quently, the plan was defeated by Greek Cypriots by a three-to-one margin on April 24, and, as a result, only the Greek Cypriot sector joined the EU on May 1. (Voters in the TRNC handily supported the plan.) Although bitterness continued on both sides, new reunification talks were launched in mid-2005, Papadopoulos arguing that the island was "too small" to remain divided. (See article on Cyprus: Turkish Sector for additional information on the reunification issue.)

In January 2006, Turkey added a new twist to the ongoing political dance by offering to open Turkish ports and airspace to Greek Cypriot carriers in return for an end to bans on direct trade between the northern and southern sectors of Cyprus. Many observers saw the move as a Turkish ploy to attract support for Turkey's bid to join the EU, and one that Turkey did not expect the Greek Cypriot government to respond to in a positive way. Indeed, while the EU commissioner for enlargement, Olli Rehn, described the proposal as worthy of consideration, Greek Cypriot President Papadopoulos dismissed the proposal.

Political Parties

Throughout the 14 years preceding the Turkish intervention, the Cypriot party system was divided along communal lines. As a result of population transfers, the Greek parties now function exclusively in the south, while the Turkish parties function in the north. All are headquartered within the divided city of Nicosia. The Greek parties are listed below (see article on Cyprus: Turkish Sector for Turkish parties).

Government Parties

Democratic Party (*Demokratiko Komma—Deko*). The Democratic Party is a center-right grouping organized in 1976 as the Democratic Front to support President Makarios's policy of "long-term struggle" against the Turkish occupation of northern Cyprus. The leading component of the government alliance in the House of Representatives after the 1976 election, at which it won 21 seats, its representation fell to 8 seats in 1981.

In December 1985 it obtained 16 seats (28 percent) in an enlarged House of 56 members, after its former coalition partner, AKEL (below), had supported a censure motion against (then) President Kyprianou. Deko absorbed the Center Union (*Enosi Kentrou*—EK), a minor formation led by former chief intercommunal negotiator Tassos Papadopoulos, in February 1989. It won 11 legislative seats in 1991 and endorsed Clerides for the presidency in 1993, then slipped to 10 seats (on a 16.5 percent vote share) in May 1996.

The run-up to the February 1998 presidential election produced a serious split in Deko, whose leadership formally endorsed (along with AKEL) the candidacy of independent George Iacovou. Many Deko members reportedly objected to that endorsement, and Deko Vice President Alexis GALANOS presented himself as a candidate, securing 4 percent of the vote in the first round of balloting. Galanos (and, apparently, many of his backers) supported Clerides in the second round, and several Deko "rebels" were appointed as independents to the new coalition government, with Galanos being named a presidential advisor. Galanos, a former president of the House of Representatives, was subsequently identified as the leader of a new **Eurodemocratic Renewal Party**.

Deko's vote share fell to 14.8 in the May 2001 balloting and the party's legislative representation slipped to nine seats.

Kyprianou, former president of the republic and a founder of Deko, stepped down as president of the party in 2000 due to ill health; he died in March 2002.

Kyprianou was replaced by Tassos Papadopoulos, who adroitly gained the support of AKEL and the Social Democrats' Movement (Kisos) in the February 2003 presidential election with a campaign that emphasized the need for more concessions from the TRNC in negotiations for a permanent peace plan. He won the election with 51.5 percent of the vote.

Deko did well in parliamentary balloting in May 2006, with its share of the vote increasing to 17.9 percent.

Leaders: Tassos PAPADOPOULOS (President of the Republic and Party President), Nicos CLEANTHOUSE (Deputy President), Vassilis PALMAS (Secretary General).

Progressive Party of the Working People (*Anorthotiko Komma Ergazomenou Laou*—AKEL). Organized in 1941 as the Communist Party of Cyprus, AKEL dominates the Greek Cypriot labor movement and claims a membership of about 15,000. Its support of President Kyprianou, withdrawn for a period in 1980 because of the latter's handling of "the national issue," was renewed in September when the government agreed to a renewal of intercommunal talks; it was again withdrawn as a result of the breakdown in talks at UN headquarters in January 1985. The party won 12 legislative seats in 1981 and 15 in 1985; it endorsed the candidacy of George Vassiliou in 1988.

In January 1990 a number of dissidents, including 4 of the Politburo's 15 members, were dismissed or resigned in a controversy over democratic reforms that led to the creation of Adesok (see below, under the EDE) by 5 of the party's (then) 15 parliamentarians. None was reelected in May 1991 balloting, in which AKEL representation increased to 18 seats. A further advance, to 19 seats (and 33 percent of the vote), was registered in May 1996. AKEL supported independent George Iacovou in the February 1998 presidential poll. The party got a surprising victory in the May 2001 balloting with 34.7 percent of the vote and became the largest party in the legislature with 20 seats. AKEL supported Deko candidate Papadopoulos in the 2003 presidential elections, and the party received four posts in the new Council of Ministers.

Though still holding the most seats in Parliament, AKEL's share of the vote dropped to 31.1 percent in parliamentary elections in May 2006, resulting in a loss of two seats.

Leaders: Dimitris CHRISTOFIAS (Secretary General and the President of the House of Representatives).

Social Democrats' Movement (*Kinima Sosial-dimokraton*—Kisos). This grouping was formerly known as the Unified Democratic Union of Cyprus–Socialist Party (*Ethniki Demokratiki Enosi Kyprou–Sosialistiko Komma*—EDEK-SK), a moderately left-of-center grouping that supported a unified and independent Cyprus. The EDEK-SK had concluded an electoral alliance with the Democratic Front and AKEL in 1976 but campaigned separately in 1981, its three representatives refusing to support the government after the new House convened. Its chair, Dr. Vassos Lyssarides, campaigned for the presidency in 1983 as leader of a National Salvation Front; although announcing his withdrawal prior to the actual balloting as a means of reducing "polarization" within the Greek Cypriot community, he was nonetheless credited with obtaining a third-place 9.5 percent vote share. The party obtained six legislative seats in 1985. Lyssarides ran fourth in the first round of the 1988 presidential poll, after which EDEK-SK threw its support to George Vassiliou. The party improved to seven seats in the 1991 House election but fell back to five in May 1996 (on a 10 percent vote share). Lyssarides secured 10.6 percent of the votes in the first round of the February 1998 presidential balloting. Although the EDEK-SK did not endorse President Clerides in the second round (encouraging members to vote for the candidate of their choice), the party was given the defense and education portfolios in the subsequent coalition government. However, the EDEK-SK withdrew from the government following Clerides's decision to cancel the proposed deployment of Russian missiles on the island in December.

After adopting its current name in 1999, the party fell to 6.5 percent of the vote in the 2001 legislative balloting. Kisos supported Deko candidate Tassos Papadopoulos in the 2003 presidential elections and received two posts in the new coalition government.

In part as a result of the party's support for Papadopoulos's hard-line position against power sharing with Turkish Cyprus, Kisos performed well in the May 2006 parliamentary elections, earning 8.9 percent of the vote and increasing its share of seats in Parliament to five.

Leaders: Yiannakis OMIROU (President), Kriakos MAVRONICOLAS (Deputy President), Antonis KOUTALIANOS (General Secretary).

Opposition Parties

Democratic Rally (*Demokratikos Synagermos*—Desy). The Democratic Rally was organized in May 1976 by Glafcos Clerides following his resignation as negotiator for the Greek Cypriots in the intercommunal talks at Vienna. The Rally has long favored a strongly pro-Western orientation as a means of maintaining sufficient pressure on the Turks to resolve the communal dispute. It secured 24.1 percent of the vote in 1976 but won no legislative seats. Its fortunes were dramatically reversed in the 1981 balloting, at which it obtained 12 seats, with 7 more being added in 1985. The party absorbed the small New Democratic Alignment (*Nea Demokratiki Parataxi*—Nedipa), led by Alekos MIHAILIDES, prior to the 1988 presidential balloting, at which Clerides was defeated in the second round. The party won a plurality of 19 seats at the legislative election of May 1991, with an additional seat going to its coalition partner, the Liberal Party (*Komma Phileleftheron*—KP). Glafcos Clerides withdrew from the party presidency upon being elected president of the republic in February 1993, following which he appointed a government of Desy and the Democratic Party (above). A Desy-Liberal alliance won 20 seats in the May 1996 election, with a vote share of 34 percent, all seats going to Desy candidates. In February 1998 the KP officially merged with Desy. The KP had been organized in 1986 by Nikos ROLANDIS (formerly a close associate of President Kyprianou), who supported George Vassiliou in 1988. It secured 1 legislative seat as an electoral partner of Desy in 1991 but failed to retain it in 1996. Rolandis won less than 1 percent of the vote in the first round of the 1998 presidential balloting and, after throwing his support behind President Clerides in the second round, was subsequently named to the February 1998 cabinet as minister of commerce, industry, and tourism. In the first round of the February 2003 presidential elections, Clerides received 38.8 percent of the vote.

Desy saw its share of the vote drop nearly 4 percent in parliamentary balloting in May 2006, with the party attracting 30.3 percent of the vote and losing 1 of the 19 seats it had held, a result analysts attribute to the party's support for the UN reunification plan.

Leaders: Nicos ANASTASIADES (President), Averof NEOPHYTOU (Deputy President), Eleni VRAHIMI (Secretary General).

European Party (*Evropaiko Komma—* EVROKO) Founded in July 2005, EVROKO is a center-right party focused on reaching a functional settlement to the division of the island. The party ran in the May 2006 elections on a platform opposing the proposed UN reunification plan and earned 5.8 percent of the vote and three seats in Parliament.

Leader: Dhimitrios SILLOURIS.

United Democrats (*Enomeni Demokrates—* EDE). The leftist EDE was formed in 1996 by members of the Free Democrats Movement (*Kinima ton Eleftheron Demokraton—*KED) and the Democratic Socialist Reform Movement (*Ananeotiko Demokratico Sosialistiko Kinema—* Adesok). The center-left KED had been launched in April 1993 by former president George Vassiliou following his unexpected failure to win a second term in February. He pledged that the new group would "contribute to the . . . struggle of our people in solving our national problem" and "promote the admission of Cyprus into Europe." The party won two seats on a 3.6 percent vote share in the May 1996 election.

The Adesok had been launched in early 1990 by a number of AKEL dissidents (including five House deputies), favoring settlement of the Cyprus issue on the basis of UN resolutions. It failed to retain legislative representation in the 1991 and 1996 elections, securing only 1.45 percent of the vote in the latter.

Vassiliou won 3 percent of the vote in the first round of the February 1998 presidential balloting

and supported President Clerides in the second round. Vassiliou was subsequently named as the government's chief EU negotiator, while the EDE was also given the ministry for agriculture, natural resources, and the environment in Clerides's new coalition government. The EDE won a single seat in May 2001 with 2.5 percent of the vote. The party lost that seat in the May 2006 elections, winning only 1.6 percent of the vote.

Leaders: Mikhalis PAPAPETROU (President), Praxoula Antoniadou KYRIAKOU (First Vice President), Nicolas SHIANIS (Secretary General).

New Horizons (*Neoi Orizontes—*NO). NO was launched in early 1996 as a right-of-center party backed by the Church and advocating that Cyprus should be a unitary rather than a federal state. It failed to win representation in the May 1996 election. Party leader Nicos Koutsou won less than 1 percent of the vote in the first round of the 1998 presidential balloting. The NO was described as supportive of the government sworn in on February 28, 1998, although it apparently did not receive a cabinet post. The party received 3 percent of the vote in the May 2001 balloting and won a single seat. In the 2003 presidential election Koutsou received 2.1 percent of the vote.

Leaders: Nicos KOUTSOU (Chair and 1998 presidential candidate), Stelios AMERIKANOS (Secretary General).

Ecological Environmental Movement– Cyprus Green Party (*Kinima Oikologoi Perivallontistoi*). The Cyprus Green Party was established as a political party in February 1996 but failed to make much impact in the May 1996 election, winning only 1 percent of the vote. The party managed to gain legislative representation for the first time in the May 2001 balloting. It received 1.98 percent of the vote and won a single seat. The party repeated that performance in the May 2006 elections, attracting 2 percent of the vote and retaining its single seat.

Leaders: George PERDIKIS (General Secretary), Savvas PHILIPPOU (Deputy General Secretary).

Cabinet

As of June 1, 2006

President	Tassos Papadopoulos (Deko)
Deputy Minister to the President	Khristodhoulos Pasiardhis (ind.)

Ministers

Agriculture, Natural Resources, and Environment	Timmy A. Efthimiou (ind.)
Commerce, Industry, and Tourism	Yiorgos Lillikas (AKEL)
Communications and Works	Haris Thrasou (AKEL)
Defense	Kyriakos Mavronikolas (Kisos)
Education and Culture	Pefkios Georgiades (Deko)
Finance	Michalis Sarris
Foreign Affairs	George Iacovou (ind.)
Government Spokesman	Kypros Chrysostomides (ind.)
Health	Andreas Gavrielides
Interior	Andreas Christou (AKEL)
Justice and Public Order	Doros Theodorou (Kisos)
Labor and Social Insurance	Christos Taliadoros (Deko)

Fighting Democratic Movement (*Agonistiko Dimokratiko Kinima*—ADIK). The ADIK is a center-right breakaway formation from Deko that was launched in 1999. It won a single seat with 2.16 percent of the vote in the May 2001 balloting.

Leader: Dinos MICHAILADES (President), Yiannis PAPADOPOULIS (Secretary General).

Legislature

The Cypriot **House of Representatives** (*Vouli Antiprosópon/Temsilciler Meclisi*) is a unicameral body formerly encompassing 35 Greek and 15 Turkish members, although Turkish participation ceased in December 1963. By contrast, the balloting of December 8, 1985, was for an enlarged House of 56 Greek members. At the most recent election of May 21, 2006, the Progressive Party of the Working People won 18 seats; the Democratic Rally, 18; the Democratic Party, 11; the Social Democrats' Movement, 5; the European Party, 3; and the Ecological Environmental Movement–

Cyprus Green Party, 1. There are also 24 seats nominally reserved for Turkish Cypriots.

President: Dimitris CHRISTOFIAS (AKEL).

Communications

The material that follows encompasses Greek-sector media only; for Turkish media, see article on Cyprus: Turkish Sector.

Press

The following newspapers are published daily at Nicosia in Greek, unless otherwise noted (circulation figures are daily averages for 2002): *Phileleftheros* (Liberal, 26,000), independent; *Simerini* (Today, 9,000), right-wing; *Apogevmatini* (Afternoon, 8,000), independent; *Haravghi* (Dawn, 9,000), AKEL organ; *Alithia* (Truth, 11,000), right-wing; *Agon* (Struggle, 5,000), right-wing; *Cyprus Mail* (4,000), independent, in English; *Machi* (Battle, 3,000), right-wing.

News Agencies

A Greek-sector Cyprus News Agency (*Kypriakon Praktoreion Eidiseon*—KPE) was established in 1976; numerous foreign bureaus maintain offices in Nicosia.

Broadcasting and Computing

Prior to the 1974 conflict, broadcasting was controlled by the semigovernmental Cyprus Broadcasting Corporation (*Radiofonikon Idryma Kyprou*—RIK) and the government-owned *Radyo Bayrak* (RB) and *Radyo Bayrak Televizyon* (RBT). At present, radio service in the Greek sector is provided by the RIK, in addition to 3 private island-wide and 24 local stations. The RIK maintains television service from its station at Mount Olympus, while the RB and the RBT stations broadcast from the Turkish sector. The Greek channel ET-1 is rebroadcast on Cyprus, while radio service is also provided by the BBC East Mediterranean Relay and by the British Forces Broadcasting Service, Cyprus. There were approximately 363,000 television receivers and 200,000 personal computers serving 779,000 Internet users in the Greek sector in 2003.

Intergovernmental Representation

Ambassador to the U.S.
Euripides L. EVRIVIADES

U.S. Ambassador to Cyprus
Ronald L. SCHLICHER

Permanent Representative to the UN
Andreas D. MAVROYIANNIS

IGO Memberships (Non-UN)
CEUR, CWTH, EIB, EU, Eurocontrol, Interpol, IOM, NAM, OSCE, PCA, WCO, WTO

CYPRUS: TURKISH SECTOR

TURKISH REPUBLIC OF NORTHERN CYPRUS

Kuzey Kıbrıs Türk Cumhuriyeti

Government and Politics

Political Background

The Turkish Cypriots withdrew from participation in the government of the Republic of Cyprus in January 1964 in the wake of communal violence precipitated by Archbishop MAKARIOS's announcement of proposed constitutional changes in November 1963 (see map, page 173). In 1967 a Turkish Cypriot Provisional Administration was established to provide governmental services in the Turkish areas, its representatives subsequently engaging in sporadic constitutional discussions with members of the Greek Cypriot administration. Meanwhile, an uneasy peace between the two communities was maintained by a UN peacekeeping force that had been dispatched in 1964. The constitutional talks, which ran until 1974, failed to bridge the gulf between Greek insistence on a unitary form of government and Turkish demands for a bicommunal federation.

A Turkish Federated State of Cyprus was established on February 13, 1975, following the Greek army coup of July 15, 1974, and the subsequent Turkish occupation of northern Cyprus. Rauf DENKTAŞ, nominal vice president of the Republic of Cyprus and leader of the National Unity Party (*Ulusal Birlik Partisi*—UBP), was designated president of the Federated State, retaining the office as the result of a presidential election on June 20, 1976, in which he defeated the Republican Turkish Party (*Cumhuriyetçi Türk Partisi*—CTP) nominee, Ahmet Mithat BERBEROĞLU, by a majority of nearly four to one. He was reelected for a five-year term in June 1981, remaining in office upon proclamation of the Turkish Republic of Northern Cyprus in November 1983.

Intercommunal discussions prior to the death of Archbishop Makarios on August 3, 1977, yielded apparent Greek abandonment of its long insistence on unitary government but left the two sides far apart on other issues, including Greek efforts to secure a reduction of approximately 50 percent in the size of the Turkish sector and Turkish demands for virtual parity in such federal institutions as the presidency (to be effected on the basis of communal rotation) and the higher judiciary.

Prior to the breakdown in discussions between Denktaş and Greek Cypriot leader Spyros KYPRIANOU at UN headquarters in January 1985, the Turks had made substantial concessions, particularly in regard to power sharing and territorial demarcation of the projected federal units. Specifically, they had abandoned their earlier demand (revived in 1991) for presidential rotation and had agreed on a reduction of the area to be placed under Turkish local administration to approximately 29 percent of the island total. However, the two sides were unable to agree on a specific timetable for Turkish troop withdrawal, the identification of Turkish-held areas to be returned to Greek control, or a mechanism for external guarantees that the pact would be observed. In announcing on January 25 that presidential and legislative elections would be held in June, President Denktaş insisted that neither the balloting nor the adoption of the TRNC constitution should be construed as efforts to "close the door to a federal solution."

The constitution was approved by 70 percent of those participating in a referendum on May 5, 1985, with the leftist CTP actively campaigning for a "no" vote. At the presidential poll on June 9, Denktaş was accorded a like margin, while the UBP fell two seats short of a majority at the legislative balloting of June 23. On July 30 a coalition government involving the UBP and the Communal Liberation Party (*Toplumcu Kurtuluş Partisi*—TKP), with Derviş EROĞLU as prime minister, was confirmed by the assembly.

The Eroğlu government fell on August 11, 1986, after the TKP had refused to endorse a proposal to expand the scope of trade and investment in the sector. However, the prime minister was able to form a new administration on September 2 that included the center-right New Dawn Party (*Yeni Doğus Partisi*—YDP) as the UBP's coalition partner.

President Denktaş drew 67.5 percent of the vote in securing reelection to his fourth five-year term on April 22, 1990. Subsequently, a rift developed between Denktaş and Eroğlu over the conduct of negotiations with the south, the prime minister advocating a harder line on concessions to the Greek Cypriots than did the president. As a result, a group of dissidents withdrew from the UBP in July 1992 to form the Democratic Party (*Demokrat Parti*—DP) to which Denktaş transferred his allegiance in late October, thereby provoking a power struggle with UBP leader Eroğlu, who became highly critical of the president's "unacceptable concessions" in negotiations with the Greek Cypriots.

Denktaş eventually gained the upper hand by calling an early assembly election on December 12, 1993, in which the UBP, although retaining a narrow plurality, lost ground, while the DP and the CTP both registered gains. The outcome was the formation on January 1, 1994, of a center-left DP-CTP coalition headed by DP leader Hakki ATUN, which supported the Denktaş line in the intercommunal talks.

In the run-up to the 1995 presidential balloting, Atun resigned as prime minister on February 24 after the CTP had opposed President Denktaş's preelection offer to distribute to TRNC citizens the title deeds of Greek Cypriot property in the north. In the presidential contest on April 15 and 22, Denktaş for the first time failed to win an outright majority in the first round (taking only 40.4 percent of the vote), although he scored a comfortable 62.5 to 37.5 percent victory over Eroğlu in the second. Protracted interparty negotiations were needed to produce, on June 3, a new DP-CTP administration headed by Atun. The coalition again collapsed in November, following the resignation of the CTP deputy premier, Ösker ÖZGÜR, but it was reestablished the following month with Mehmet Ali TALAT of the CTP as Atun's deputy. The DP-CTP coalition government resigned on July 4, 1996, and the UBP's Eroğlu was again given, on August 1, 1996, the job of forming a new government. A UBP-DP coalition cabinet headed by Eroğlu was approved by the president on August 16, 1996.

In the legislative balloting of December 6, 1998, the UBP improved from 17 to 24 seats. On December 30 President Denktaş approved Eroğlu to head a new UBP-TKP coalition government, the DP having fallen into dispute with the UBP over economic policies and cabinet representation. The legislature approved the new cabinet on January 12, 1999, by a strict party-line vote of 31–18. Denktaş won 43.6 percent of the vote in the first round of presidential balloting on April 15, 2000, while UBP candidate Eroğlu received 30.1 percent; the TKP's Mustafa AKINCI, 11.7 percent; the CTP's Mehmet Ali Talat, 10 percent; and Arif Hasan TAHSIN of the Patriotic Unity Movement (*Yurtsever Birlik Hareketi*—YBH), 2.6 percent. Three other minor candidates each got less than 1 percent of the vote. The second round of balloting, scheduled for April 22, was canceled when Eroğlu withdrew on April 19 after the TKP decided to back neither of the candidates for the second round. Denktaş was sworn in on April 24.

After a series of disagreements between the coalition partners (mainly regarding the direction to be taken in foreign relations), the UBP-TKP government resigned on May 25, 2001. President Denktaş asked Eroğlu to form a new government, and a UBP-DP coalition was appointed on June 7.

Political Status: Autonomous federal state proclaimed February 13, 1975; independent republic (thus far recognized only by Turkey) declared November 15, 1983; TRNC constitution approved by referendum of May 6, 1985.

Area: Approximately 1,400 sq. mi. (3,626 sq. km.).

Population: 200,587 (1996C); 221,000 (2005E), on the basis of Turkish Cypriot claims, which include nonindigenous settlers (more than half of the total). The latter figure has not been adjusted to accord with a March 2006 census report of 264,172. The 2006 result has been challenged by Greek Cypriots, who base their estimates on the known Turkish population in 1974, increased by subsequent rates of increase in the south plus an adjustment for emigration.

Major Urban Centers (2005E): LEFKOŞA (Turkish-occupied portion of Nicosia, 42,200), Gazi Mağusa (Famagusta, 37,100).

Principal Language: Turkish.

Monetary Unit: Turkish New Lira (market rate July 1, 2006: 1.59 liras = $1US). Use of the Cyprus pound as an alternative unit of exchange was terminated on May 16, 1983.

President: Mehmet Ali TALAT (Republican Turkish Party); elected in first round of popular balloting on April 17, 2005, and inaugurated April 24 for a five-year term in succession to Rauf R. DENKTAŞ (nonparty).

Prime Minister: Ferdi Sabit SOYER (Republican Turkish Party); asked on April 25, 2005, to form a government by Mehmet Ali Talat, who had resigned as prime minister on April 20 following his election as president; formed new coalition government on April 28, 2005, following the approval of President Talat and the Assembly of the Republic.

The CTP returned to a plurality (19 seats) in the December 14, 2003, assembly balloting, and Talat formed a CTP-DP coalition government on January 13, 2004. However, only two days after the TRNC population had endorsed a UN plan for reunifica-

tion (see Current issues, below), the coalition became a minority government when two DP legislators quit the party to protest the administration's pro-unification stance. After numerous attempts by Talat and the UBP's Eroğlu to form coalition governments failed, new assembly elections were held on February 20, 2005. The CTP increased its seat total to 24, and Talat was able to form a more secure CTP-DP coalition cabinet on March 16.

Talat secured 55.6 percent of the vote in the first round of presidential balloting on April 17, 2005, with Eroğlu finishing second with 22.7 percent. Talat resigned as prime minister on April 20 and was inaugurated as president on April 24. The following day, Ferdi Sabit SOYER, a close ally of Talat and CTP stalwart, formed another CTP-DP coalition government.

Constitution and Government

The constitution of the TRNC provides for a presidential-parliamentary system headed by a popularly elected chief executive, who cannot lead a party or be subject to its decisions. The president appoints a prime minister, who (unlike other ministers) must be a member of the legislature and whose government is subject to legislative recall. Like the president, the 50-member Assembly of the Republic is elected for a five-year term (subject to dissolution) and its presiding officer, who is chosen at the beginning of the first and fourth year of each term, becomes acting head of state in the event of presidential death, incapacity, or resignation. The members of the Supreme Court, composed of a president and seven additional judges, also form a Constitutional Court (five members) and a Court of Appeal and High Administrative Court (three members each). Lesser courts and local administrative units are established by legislative action.

Current Issues

The European Council meeting held in late 1997 decided that Cyprus would be included in the first group of applicants to join the expanded EU, while determining that "political and economic conditions" required for the membership of Turkey were not satisfied. The EU also expressed a wish "to see activated the Cyprus government's wish to include the Turkish Cypriots in the negotiating delegation." However, President Denktaş of the TRNC indicated his unwillingness to proceed with negotiations unless further international recognition of the TRNC was forthcoming, and new discussions were not launched as expected. In August, Denktaş attempted to counter the UN push for reunification by formally proposing a confederation of "equal states," with the UN continuing to patrol the border. That proposal was quickly rejected by most of the international community, despite Denktaş's assessment that "Turks and Greece on Cyprus are like oil and water. They can no longer be mixed."

Tension between the TRNC government and opposition parties and groups became more severe with Denktaş's decision to withdraw from the talks with the Greek Cypriot side in late 2000. However, observers noted some easing after Denktaş decided to resume dialogue in 2002 after the EU indicated that Cyprus had fulfilled the necessary criteria to begin accession negotiations in 2003 with the goal of membership in 2004, with or without resolution of the dispute with the TRNC. Denktaş reportedly made several unilateral offers regarding land return and the reopening of the border, but talks were described as deadlocked by March 2003. Attention subsequently focused almost exclusively on the plan forwarded by UN Secretary General Kofi Annan under which the island would be reunified in a loose confederation with the Greek Cypriot and Turkish Cypriot sectors retaining broad autonomy in most domestic areas. (For complete details on the Annan plan, see Current issues in article on Cyprus.)

With the encouragement of new Prime Minister Talat of the CTP (which had led all parties in the December 2003 assembly balloting), the voters in the TRNC endorsed the reunification plan by a 65 percent "yes" vote in a national referendum on April 24, 2004. Unfortunately for the TRNC, however, the plan was rejected by a three-to-one margin by the Greek Cypriot community. Consequently, the TRNC was "left out in the cold" when Cyprus acceded to the EU with nine other new members on May 1. (Many Turkish Cypriots reportedly blamed President Denktaş's relatively hard line on the issue for the negativity of the Greek Cypriots.) The EU immediately pledged substantial economic assistance to the TRNC as a reward for the "yes" vote regarding reunification. However, the stark reality of the situation became clear in October when Cyprus vetoed an EU plan to establish trade relations with the TRNC. The government of Cyprus indicated that too much assistance to the TRNC might embolden Turkish Cypriots still hoping for additional recognition for the TRNC.

The early legislative elections of February 2005 in the TRNC were widely viewed as a strong endorsement of reunification, the Turkish Cypriots clearly having suffered political and economic isolation since Cyprus's accession to the EU. Following Talat's election in April to succeed hawkish President Denktaş (who, at 81 years old, had decided to retire), prounification forces again saw reason for hope. Negotiations, again centered on the Annan plan, subsequently resumed in an atmosphere that led one observer to conclude nearly "everyone seems to want reunification." Included on that list were Russia (which had been unconvinced in early 2004), the United States (which sent economic development missions to the TRNC), Greece, and Turkey (for whom the stakes may have been higher than for any of the others). Turkey, hoping to begin its own EU accession process, keenly desired an end to the island's split in view of the fact that either Greece or Cyprus could block its entry. In July, Turkey signed a protocol that would (upon approval by the Turkish legislature) extend its long-term customs union with the EU to the ten new EU members, including Cyprus. However, Turkey, which still maintained some 30,000–40,000 troops in the TRNC, insisted its decision did not constitute recognition of the Greek Cypriot government. (Turkey was the only country to recognize the TRNC government and the only European country yet to recognize the Greek Cypriot government.)

Despite continued heavy international pressure, no substantive negotiations toward reunification were conducted throughout the remainder of 2005. Further exacerbating the situation, Cyprus late in the year forced the EU to withhold $140 million in aid earmarked for the TRNC. On a more positive note, the TRNC assembly in December ratified legislation permitting Greek Cypriots to seek the return of property seized in the north following the 1974 partitioning of the island. (The commission established to adjudicate the property returns [or reparations] was described as fully operational as of May 2006.)

UK Foreign Secretary Jack Straw met with TRNC President Talat in the TRNC in January 2006, prompting strong criticism from Greek Cypriot leaders who accused some EU members of attempting to "legitimize" the northern government. In return, Straw described the current Greek Cypriot stance as "not conducive" to reunification. The complex EU issues subsequently continued to dominate TRNC affairs. Just a day after formally authorizing the start of EU accession talks with Turkey, the EU in February announced it would release $165 million to the TRNC for infrastructure development. However, although Cyprus accepted that decision (reluctantly), it continued to block the proposed easing of the EU trade sanctions against the TRNC. For its part, Turkey pressed for a comprehensive settlement of the island's status, rather than a "piecemeal" approach. As a result, even discussions on minor "technical" issues such as immigration and environmental protection were stalled as of May.

The legislative elections in the south in May 2006 (see article on Cyprus for details) appeared to indicate growing popular support for President Papadopoulos's negative stance toward the UN reunification plan. Collaterally, TRNC President Talat acknowledged that Turkish Cypriots had become "greatly disheartened and pessimistic" over the lack of progress in talks with the Greek Cypriots and the ongoing economic "isolation" of the north. Nevertheless, Talat said his government had not yet reached the point of pursuing additional international recognition of the TRNC as an independent entity, preferring instead to retain its support for the UN plan.

Political Parties

Most of the Turkish Cypriot parties share a common outlook regarding the present division of the island. Differences have surfaced, however, as to the degree of firmness to be displayed in negotiations with the Greek community.

Government Parties

Republican Turkish Party (*Cumhuriyetçi Türk Partisi*—CTP). A Marxist formation at the time, the CTP campaigned against the 1985 constitution because of its alleged repressive and militaristic content. For the 1990 election (at which it lost 5 of 12 seats won in 1985) the CTP joined with the TKP and YDP (see DP, below) in a coalition styled the Democratic Struggle Party (*Demokratik Mücadele Partisi*—DMP). It made a comeback to 13 seats in the 1993 balloting, entering a coalition with the DP that effectively collapsed in February 1995 on the issue of Greek Cypriot property rights but was reconstituted in May. Two further coalition collapses and reconstitutions in 1995 led to the ouster of Ösker ÖZGÜR as CTP leader in January 1996. A DP-CTP coalition government under the leadership of Hakki ATUN resigned on July 4, 1996, and the CTP became the main opposition party. However, it was supplanted in that regard by the DP following the 1998 legislative balloting, at which CTP representation fell from 13 to 6 seats on a vote share of 13.4 percent. In part, the electoral decline was attributed to the CTP's stance that negotiations should be resumed with Greek Cypriot officials regarding a settlement of the political stalemate on the island. Chair Mehmet Ali Talat ran as the party's presidential candidate on April 15, 2000, and received 10 percent of the vote.

The CTP competed in the 2003 assembly elections under the rubric of the CTP–United Forces (*CTP–Birleşik Güçler*—CTP-BG) to reflect its attempt to broaden its base through extended cooperation with nongovernmental organizations and independent voters on an anti-Denktaş, pro-EU platform. The CTP-BG secured a plurality of 19 seats in the 2003 balloting on a vote share of 35 percent.

Talat subsequently formed a coalition government with the DP, which continued in office following the February 2005 assembly balloting in which the CTP-BG's vote share grew to 44 percent (good for 24 seats).

Leaders: Mehmet Ali TALAT (President of the TRNC), Ferdi Sabit SOYER (Prime Minister of the TRNC and Chair of the Party), Omer KALYONCU (Secretary General).

Democratic Party (*Demokrat Parti*—DP). The DP was formed in 1992 by a group of pro-Denktaş UBP dissidents who advocated a more conciliatory posture in the intercommunal talks than did the party mainstream. It was runner-up in the 1993 legislative balloting, thereupon entering into a majority coalition with the CTP (above). In 1993 the DP accepted the **New Dawn Party** (*Yeni Doğuş Partisi*—YDP), led by Ali Özkan ALTINIŞIK, into its ranks. The DP-CTP coalition government ended on July 4, 1996, and the UBP's Derviş Eroğlu formed a new coalition government with the DP as a partner on August 16, 1996. However, the DP moved into opposition status following the December 1998 legislative poll, at which it secured 22.6 percent of the vote. Meanwhile, in September 1998 the DP had reportedly accepted the Free Democratic Party (*Hür Demokrat Parti*—HDP) into its ranks. The HDP, led by İsmet KOTAK and Özel TAHSİN, was one of several parties launched following the 1990 election. Prior to the 1993 election the HDP had joined with two smaller groups, the Homeland Party (*Anavatan Partisi*—AP) and the Nationalist Justice Party (*Milliyetçi Adalet Partisi*—MAP), led by Zorlu TÖRE, in a coalition styled the National Struggle Party (*Milli Mücadele Partisi*—MMP). The DP extended support to Rauf Denktaş in the 2000 presidential election. The DP became the junior partner in the new coalition government announced with the UBP in June 2001. Following the December 2003 balloting, the DP joined an unsteady CTP-led coalition. Two of the seven DP legislators resigned from the party in April 2004 to protest the government's prounification stance, forcing early elections in

February 2005, at which the DP gained six seats on a 13.5 percent vote share. Mustafa Arabacioğlu won 13.2 percent of the vote in the first round of the April 2005 presidential poll.

Leaders: Serdar DENKTAŞ (Chair and Deputy Prime Minister), Mustafa ARABACIOĞLU (2005 presidential candidate).

Opposition Parties

National Unity Party (*Ulusal Birlik Partisi*—UBP). The right-wing UBP was established in 1975 as an outgrowth of the former National Solidarity (*Ulusal Dayanışma*) movement. Originally committed to the establishment of a bicommunal federal state, it captured three-quarters of the seats in the Turkish Cypriot Legislative Assembly at the 1976 election but was reduced to a plurality of 18 seats in 1981 and survived a confidence vote in the assembly on September 11 only because the motion failed to obtain an absolute majority. The UBP's former leader, Rauf Denktaş, was precluded by the constitution from serving as president of the party or from submitting to party discipline while president of the republic; nevertheless, he was instrumental in launching the breakaway DP in 1992 after clashing with party leader Derviş Eroğlu, who moved to an increasingly propartition stance. The UBP retained its plurality in the 1993 balloting but remained in opposition. Eroğlu took Denktaş to the second round in the 1995 presidential election, winning 37.5 percent of the vote. Staying in the opposition until a DP-CTP coalition government came to an end on July 4, 1996, the UBP rose to power as a member of a coalition government with the DP on August 16, 1996. The UBP increased its vote share to over 40 percent in the 1998 legislative balloting, Eroğlu subsequently forming a coalition with the TKP. Eroğlu ran as presidential candidate for the UBP on April 15, 2000, and won 30.1 percent of the vote at the first round. He withdrew from the race on April 19 prior to the scheduled second round between himself and Denktaş. The UBP-TKP coalition broke down in May 2001, and Eroğlu formed a new government with the DP in

June. However, he was obliged to resign the prime ministership following the December 2003 legislative balloting, in which the UBP was outpolled by the CTP 35 percent to 33 percent. The UBP secured 19 seats on a vote share of 31.7 percent in the February 2005 assembly balloting, while Eroğlu finished second in the first round of presidential balloting in April with 22.7 percent of the vote. Citing the need for "fresh blood" in the party's leadership, Eroğlu resigned as UBP chair in late 2005. He was succeeded on a permanent basis in February 2006 by Hüseyin Ozgurgun.

Leaders: Hüseyin OZGURGUN (Chair), Dr. Derviş EROĞLU (Former Prime Minister, Former Chair of the Party, and 2005 presidential candidate), Turgay AVCI (Secretary General).

Peace and Democracy Movement (*Barış ve Demokrasi Hareketi*—BDH). The BDH is a coalition of leftist parties that joined together to improve their electoral opportunities prior to the 2003 legislative elections. The grouping was formed under the leadership of Mustafa Akıncı, formerly the party leader of TKP, which provided the core of the BDH. Other constitutive parties of the BDH included the **Socialist Party of Cypress** (*Kıbrıs Sosyalist Partisi*—KSP) and the **United Cyprus Party** (*Birleşik Kıbrıs Partisi*—BKP). The BDH won six seats in the 2003 assembly balloting but only one in the 2005 poll (on a 5.8 percent vote share). Following the poor electoral showing in 2005, some core components reportedly left the BDH, although the BDH continued its institutional existence under the leadership of Akıncı.

Leader: Mustafa AKINCI (Chair), Mehmet ÇAKICI (Secretary General).

Communal Liberation Party (*Toplumcu Kurtuluş Partisi*—TKP). Also known as the Socialist Salvation Party, the TKP is a left-of-center grouping organized in 1976. The six assembly seats won by the party in 1976 were doubled in 1981, two of which (for an enlarged chamber) were lost in 1985. The TKP joined the Eroğlu government in July 1985 but withdrew in August 1986.

In 1989 the TKP absorbed the Progressive People's Party (*Atılımcı Halk Partisi*—AHP), which itself had resulted from the merger in early 1986 of the Democratic People's Party (*Demokratik Halk Partisi*—DHP) and the Communal Endeavor Party (*Toplumsal Atılım Partisi*—TAP). The DHP, which advocated the establishment of an independent, nonaligned, and biregional Cypriot state, was organized in 1979 by former prime ministers Nejat KONUK and Osman ÖREK, both of whom had left the UBP because of dissension within the party. The TAP was a centrist party formed in 1984.

The TKP's legislative representation fell from ten seats to seven in 1990 and to five in 1993. It rebounded to seven seats (on a vote share of 15.4 percent) in December 1998 and became the junior partner in the subsequent coalition government with the UBP. Chair Mustafa Akıncı ran as the TKP's presidential candidate on April 15, 2000, and received 11.7 percent of the vote. The TKP subsequently decided to encourage its voters to vote for their candidate of choice for the second round, a move that caused the UBP's Eroğlu to withdraw from the race. Following the breakdown of the coalition government with the UBP in May 2001, the TKP joined the opposition. Chair Akıncı subsequently stepped down as the party leader, and the post was assumed by the former secretary general, Hüseyin Angolemli.

Leaders: Hüseyin ANGOLEMLİ (Chair), Güngör GÜNKAN.

Other Parties That Competed in the 2003 Legislative Elections

Nationalist Peace Party (*Milliyetçi Barış Partisi*—MBP). The MBP was formed as the result of a merger between the MAP and the center-right **Renewal Progress Party** (*Yenilikci Atilim Partisi*—YAP). In the 2003 legislative elections, the MBP received 3.23 percent of the vote. Its cochairs are Ali Riza GORGUN and former UBP member and former president of the legislature, Ertuğrul HASIPOĞLU.

Nationalist Justice Party (*Milliyetçi Adalet Partisi*—MAP). The far-right-wing MAP supports unification with Turkey and extension of Turkish citizenship to northern Cypriots. The party gained one seat in the assembly after a former DP parliamentarian, Kenan AKIN, defected to the MAP in December 2000. In 1993 the party had joined with the HDP and AP to form MMP (see above, under DP). The MAP backed President Denktaş in the 2000 presidential election.

Leader: Zorlu TÖRE (Chair).

Solution and EU Party (*Cözüm ye AB Partisi*—ÇABP). Established as a prounification grouping in 2003, the ÇABP secured 2 percent of the vote in the December 2003 legislative poll.

Leader: Ali EREL.

Other Parties

Patriotic Unity Movement (*Yurtsever Birlik Hareketi*—YBH). The left-wing YBH was formed as a result of a merger of the New Cyprus Party (*Yeni Kıbrıs Partisi*—YKP) and some former members of the CTP (above) in 1998. The YKP had been founded in 1989 by Alpay Durduran, the TKP/AHP 1985 presidential candidate. In 1998 Durduran urged Turkish Cypriot leaders to return to the bargaining table with their Greek Cypriot counterparts.

The YBH favors the unification of the island and equal treatment for all Cypriots, including Greek Cypriots. In 2003 the YBH filed suit with the European Court of Human Rights to challenge the electoral process of the TRNC. The party presented Arif Hasan TAHSİN as its candidate in the first round of presidential balloting in 1999.

Leaders: Alpay DURDURAN (Chair).

National Revival Party (*Ulusal Diriliş Partisi*—UDP). The UDP was founded on November 18, 1997, under the leadership of Enver Emin. A precursor of the UDP had been founded in 1994 as the National Birth Party (*Ulusal Doğuş Partisi*).

As of November 1995, it had one seat in the assembly. The National Birth Party then merged with the DP and ceased its legal existence. The UDP secured 4.6 percent of the vote and no seats in the December 1998 legislative balloting. The UDP backed President Denktaş in the presidential election on April 15, 2000.

Leaders: Enver EMİN (Chair), Mustafa ERBİLEN (Secretary General).

Reports on the 1998 legislative balloting indicated that a **National Resistance Party** (*Ulusal Direnis Partisi*—UDİP) had received 4.5 percent of the vote, and the recently formed **Our Party** (*Bizim Parti*—BP), led by Okyay SADIKOĞLU, had received 1.2 percent. The BP, described in 1998 as the first Islamist grouping to participate in a TRNC election, supported President Denktaş in his reelection bid.

On August 25, 2000, Arif Salih KIRDAĞ formed the **Freedom and Justice Party** (*Özgürlük ve Adalet Partisi*—ÖAP) to "safeguard bank victims' rights." In December a new centrist formation, the **New Democracy Party** (*Yeni Demokrasi Partisi*), was founded by Eşref DÜSENKALKAR. In January 2001 the **Liberal Party** (*Liberal Parti*—LP) was launched by Kemal BOLAYIR and Ünal Aki AKİF. In 2004 the **Free Thought Party** was reportedly launched under the leadership of Salih COSAR; the party's initial membership reportedly included two defecting DP legislators, although one subsequently returned to the DP fold.

Legislature

A Turkish Cypriot Legislative Assembly, formerly the Legislative Assembly of the Autonomous Turkish Cypriot Administration, was organized in February 1975. Styled the **Assembly of the Republic** (*Cumhuriyet Meclisi*) under the 1985 constitution, it currently contains 50 members, who are elected for five-year terms on a proportional basis in which parties must surpass a 5 percent threshold to gain representation. Following the election of December 14, 2003, the Republican Turkish Party (CTP) held 19 seats; the National Unity Party

Cabinet

As of June 1, 2006

Prime Minister	Ferdi Sabit Soyer (CTP)
Deputy Prime Minister	Serdar Denktaş (DP)

Ministers

Agriculture and Forestry	Hüseyin Yalçın Öztoprak (DP)
Economy and Tourism	Derviş Kemal Deniz (DP)
Education and Culture	Canan Öztoprak (CTP)
Finance	Ahmet Uzun (CTP)
Foreign Affairs	Serdar Denktaş (DP)
Health and Social Assistance	Esref Vaiz (CTP)
Interior	Özkan Murat (CTP)
Labor and Social Security	Sonay Adem (CTP)
Public Works and Transportation	Salih Usar (CTP)
Youth and Sports	Özkan Yorgancioğlu (CTP)

(UBP), 18; the Democratic Party (DP), 7; and the Peace and Democracy Movement (BDH), 6.

Defections from the DP in late April 2004 cost the CTP-DP coalition government its legislative majority. Consequently, early elections were held on February 20, 2005, with the CTP winning 24 seats; the UBP, 19, the DP, 6; and the BDH, 1.

President: Fatma EKENOĞLU.

Communications

Press

Freedom of the press is guaranteed under the 1985 constitution, save for legislative restrictions intended to safeguard public order, national security, public morals, or the proper functioning of the judiciary. The following are published in Nicosia in Turkish: Kıbrıs (Cyprus), "populist" monthly; *Birlik* (Unity), center-right daily (affiliated with the UBP); *Halkın Sesi* (Voice of the People), daily; *Avrupa* (Europe), independent leftist; *Yeni Düzen* (New Order), CTP organ; *Ortam* (Situation), TKP organ; *Yeni Demokrat* (New Democrat), DP organ; and *Vatan* (Homeland). In addition, a number of mainland Turkish papers circulate, of which the leaders are *Sabah* (Morning), *Milliyet* (Nationality), and *Hürriyet* (Liberty).

News Agency

The Turkish-sector facilities are Turkish Agency Cyprus (*Türk Ajansı Kıbrıs*—TAK) and the Northern Cyprus News Agency (*Kuzey Kıbrıs Haber Ajansı*).

Broadcasting

Broadcasting in the Turkish sector is controlled by *Radyo Bayrak* and *Bayrak Radyo Televizyon* (BRT). There were approximately 306,000 radio and 77,400 television receivers in the sector in 1999. In addition to *Radio Bayrak* and the BRT, there are two private radio stations, *First FM* and *Kıbrıs FM*, and two private TV channels.

Intergovernmental Representation

The Turkish Federated State did not seek general international recognition and maintained no missions abroad, except for a representative in

New York who was recognized by the UN as official spokesperson for the Turkish Cypriot community; it did, however, participate in an Islamic Conference meeting on economic cooperation in Ankara, Turkey, held November 4–6, 1980. The present Turkish Republic of Northern Cyprus has proclaimed itself independent but has been recognized as such only by Turkey, with whom it exchanged ambassadors on April 17, 1985.

IGO Memberships (Non-UN)
ECO, OIC

CZECH REPUBLIC

Česká Republika

Note: The election for the Chamber of Deputies on June 2–3, 2006, produced the following distribution of seats: Civic Democratic Party (ODS), 81 seats; Czech Social Democratic Party, 74; Communist Party of Bohemia and Moravia, 26; Christian and Democratic Union–Czech People's Party (KDU-SL), 13; and the Green Party (SZ), 6. Mirek Topolánek, the leader of the ODS, was sworn in on September 4, 2006 but subsequently failed in his efforts to form a coalition government that would have included the ODS, KDU-SL, and SZ, who controlled 100 of the 200 seats in the Chamber of Deputies. Consequently, on September 4 Topolánek formed a minority government comprising nine members of the ODS and six independents. On October 3, the new government was rejected in a 99–96 vote of no confidence before the Chamber of Deputies; the entire cabinet subsequently resigned on October 11.

The Country

Situated at the geographical heart of Europe, the Czech Republic consists of about 60 percent of the area of the former Czechoslovak federation. It is bounded by Slovakia on the east, Austria on the south, Germany on the west, and Poland on the north. Incorporating the old Czech "crown lands" of Bohemia and Moravia (plus part of Silesia), the country has a population that is 90.4 percent Czech; small ethnic minorities include Slovaks, Poles, Germans, Gypsies, and Hungarians (Magyars). The 2001 census did not list "Moravian" as an ethnic category, although 373,294 respondents identified themselves as such. The inhabitants are to a large extent nominally Roman Catholic but encompass a sizable Protestant minority.

Contending with the upland nature of much of the terrain and moderate soil quality, agriculture nonetheless features an extensive dairy sector, as well as traditional strength in the cultivation of grains, potatoes, and hops. The Czech industrial sector, centered at Ostrava and Prague, includes the Škoda automobile manufacturer (which became part of the German Volkswagen group in 1991) and producers of steel, armaments, heavy machinery, glass, and footwear. Export of electrical and electronic goods has grown significantly in recent years. Tourism is another important source of foreign currency.

In postwar Eastern Europe, Czechoslovakia ranked second only to the German Democratic Republic in per capita income, although Slovakia had long been less affluent than Bohemia and Moravia. From 1990 the post-Communist government's economic reform efforts focused on removal of restrictions on private enterprise, including the sale of

government-owned businesses; modernization of the country's industrial base; and encouragement of foreign investment. These changes accentuated the economic differences between the Czech and Slovak republics, in that progress toward a market economy was much more rapid in the former than in the latter. The economic divergence fueled pressure for political separation, leading to the "velvet divorce" agreements of late 1992 and final separation on January 1, 1993.

After contracting by about 20 percent from 1991 to 1993, the Czech economy grew by 2.6 percent in 1994 and over 4 percent in 1995. By the end of 1995 some 90 percent of state enterprises, with a total capital value of around $35 billion, had been privatized. However, the Czech Republic experienced recession in 1997–1998 that raised questions about the country's ability to meet the economic criteria for proposed accession to the European Union (EU). Prospects improved markedly in 2000, with the government moving forward rapidly on additional reforms, including banking sector privatization.

GDP grew by 3.1 percent in 2003 and (accelerated by the Czech Republic's accession to the EU on May 1, 2004) by 4.7 percent in 2004 and 6.0 percent in 2005. Meanwhile, inflation registered 2.8 percent in 2004 and 1.9 percent in 2005, and unemployment stood at 8.3 and 7.9 percent in 2004 and 2005, respectively. A number of economic reforms were required for EU membership, some of which contributed to political discord (see Current issues). Nevertheless, foreign investors remained keenly interested in the Czech Republic, particularly with an eye on the large market in neighboring Germany.

Government and Politics

Political Background

From its establishment in 1918 until its dismemberment following the Munich agreement of 1938, Czechoslovakia was the most politically mature and democratically governed of the new states of Eastern Europe. Due mainly to the preponderant role of Soviet military forces in the liberation of the country at the close of World War II, the Communists gained a leading position in the postwar cabinet and assumed full control in February 1948.

The trial and execution of such top Communist leaders as Vladimír CLEMENTIS and Rudolf SLÁNSKÝ during the Stalinist purges in the early 1950s exemplified the country's posture as a docile Soviet satellite under the leadership of Antonín NOVOTNÝ, first secretary of the Communist Party and (from 1957) president of the republic. By 1967 growing unrest among intellectuals and students had produced revolutionary ferment, which led in early 1968 to Novotný's ouster and his replacement by Alexander DUBČEK as party first secretary and by Gen. Ludvík SVOBODA as president. Dubček, a prominent Slovak Communist, rapidly emerged as the leader of a popular movement for far-reaching political and economic change.

A reformist cabinet headed by Oldřich ČERNÍK took office in April 1968 with a program that included strict observance of legality, broader political discussion, fewer economic and cultural restrictions, and increased Slovak autonomy under new constitutional arrangements designed in part to provide for redress of economic disadvantages. Widely hailed within Czechoslovakia, the so-called Prague Spring was sharply criticized by the Soviet Union, which, on August 20–21, 1968, invaded and occupied the country in concert with the other Warsaw Pact nations except Romania.

The period after the 1968 invasion was characterized by the progressive entrenchment of more conservative elements within the government and the party and by a series of pacts that specified Czechoslovakia's "international commitments," set limits on internal reforms, and allowed the stationing of Soviet troops on Czech soil. For a time, the pre-August leadership was left in power, but Dubček was replaced by Gustáv HUSÁK as party leader in 1969, removed from his position in the Presidium, and expelled from the party in 1970. Černík retained his post as chair of the government until 1970, when he was also expelled from the party. The actions against the "Prague Spring" leaders were paralleled by widespread purges of other

Political Status: Independent Czechoslovak Republic proclaimed in 1918; People's Republic of Czechoslovakia established June 9, 1948; redesignated Czechoslovak Socialist Republic on July 11, 1960; renamed Czech and Slovak Federative Republic on April 21, 1990; present Czech Republic proclaimed upon separation of the constituent components of the federation on January 1, 1993.

Area: 30,450 sq. mi. (78,864 sq. km.).

Population: 10,230,060 (2001C); 10,196,000 (2005E).

Major Urban Centers (2005E): PRAGUE (1,165,000), Brno (368,000), Ostrava (312,000), Plzeň (163,000).

Official Language: Czech.

Monetary Unit: Koruna (official rate July 1, 2006: 22.31 koruny = $1US). Separate currencies for the Czech Republic and Slovakia, both called the koruna and initially at parity with each other, came into force on February 8, 1993.

President: Václav KLAUS (Civic Democratic Party); elected by the Parliament in the third round of balloting on February 28, 2003, and sworn in for a five-year term on March 7, to replace Václav HAVEL (nominated by ruling coalition headed by the Civic Democratic Party).

Prime Minister: (*See headnote.*) Jiří PAROUBEK (Czech Social Democratic Party); appointed by the president on April 25, 2005, to succeed Stanislav GROSS (Czech Social Democratic Party), who had resigned the same day.

reformers during 1969–1971, some 500,000 party members ultimately being affected. President Svoboda, although reelected by the Federal Assembly to a second five-year term in 1973, was replaced on May 29, 1975, by Husák, who retained his party posts. Husák was unanimously reelected president in 1980 and 1985.

The policies of reconstruction (*perestroika*) advanced in the Soviet Union following Mikhail Gorbachev's assumption of power in 1985 proved par-

ticularly difficult for the Czech leadership to emulate, since it appeared the government was being called upon to implement reforms that it had been charged with eradicating after 1968. Thus, the designation in mid-December 1987 of Miloš JAKEŠ to succeed Husák as party leader seemed to represent a compromise between hard-line conservatives and Gorbachev-oriented liberals. Over the course of 1988, numerous members of Charter 77 (formed by prominent playwright Václav HAVEL and other dissidents to monitor compliance with both domestically and internationally mandated human rights obligations) were arrested, as were hundreds of Roman Catholics. There were notable dissident protests in August 1988 on the 20th anniversary of the Soviet-led invasion and again in October on the 70th anniversary of the country's independence.

As elsewhere in Eastern Europe, the edifice of Communist power crumbled quickly in Czechoslovakia in late 1989. On November 20, one day after formation of the opposition Civic Forum under Havel's leadership, 250,000 antiregime demonstrators marched in Prague, and government leaders held initial discussions with Forum representatives the next day. On November 22 Dubček returned to the limelight with an address before an enthusiastic rally at Bratislava, and on November 24 Karel URBÁNEK was named to succeed Jakeš as party general secretary. In the course of a nationwide strike on November 28 (preceded by a three-day rally of 500,000 in Prague), the government agreed to power sharing, but an offer on December 3 to allocate a minority of portfolios to non-Communist ministers was rejected by opposition leaders. Two days later the regime accepted loss of its monopoly status, and on December 10 President Husák resigned after swearing in the first non-Communist-dominated government in 41 years, under the premiership of Marián ČALFA. On December 29 the assembly unanimously elected Havel as the new head of state.

The Civic Forum and its Slovak counterpart, Public Against Violence, won a substantial majority of federal legislative seats at nationwide balloting on June 8 and 9, 1990, with Čalfa (who had resigned from the Communist Party on January 18) forming a new government on June 27 and Havel being elected to a regular two-year term as president on July 5. However, during 1991 the anti-Communist coalition, its major objective achieved, crumbled into less inclusive party formations. In November negotiations between federal and republican leaders over the country's future political status collapsed, with the Federal Assembly becoming deadlocked over the issue of a referendum on separate Czech and Slovak states. With the legislature's presidium having called an election for June, a contest between Czech Finance Minister Václav KLAUS and former Slovak prime minister Vladimír MEČIAR emerged. Klaus favored a right-of-center liberal economic policy with rapid privatization; Mečiar preferred a slower transition to capitalism for the eastern republic, where unemployment, at 12 percent, was three times that of the Czech lands. The two retained firm control of their respective regions in federal and national balloting on June 5–6, after which Mečiar returned to the post of Slovak prime minister, with Klaus choosing to serve as prime minister of a Czech, rather than a federal, administration.

In postelection constitutional talks, the Czech side argued that there should be either a properly functioning federation with a strong central administration or a speedy separation. When the Slovak side rejected Prague's concept of a continued federation, Klaus moved quickly for a formal dissolution, which was endorsed by the two governments by late August 1992. Since majority public opinion in both republics opposed separation, the left-wing opposition parties mounted determined rearguard resistance to the governmental plan, which on October 1 failed to obtain the required three-fifths majority in the federal parliament. Amid growing constitutional confusion, Klaus and Mečiar on October 6 drew up virtually identical separation blueprints, to come into effect on January 1, 1993. On November 25 the plan secured the backing of 183 of the 300 federal deputies—3 more than the required minimum—during a historic vote in which several opposition members broke party discipline by voting in favor. Concurrently, a proposal by the left-wing parties that the separation issue should be submitted to a popular referendum was rebuffed.

Following the official birth of the new state on January 1, 1993, Klaus remained as the Czech Republic's prime minister, heading an ongoing coalition of his own Civic Democratic Party (*Občanská Demokratická Strana*—ODS), the Civic Democratic Alliance (*Občanská Demokratická Aliance*—ODA), and the Christian and Democratic Union–Czech People's Party (*Křest'anská a Demokratická Unie–Česká Strana Lidová*—KDU-ČSL). On January 26 the Czech Parliament endorsed the government's unopposed nomination of Havel as president for a five-year term. Other constitutional institutions were subsequently put in place, including a Constitutional Court. Legislation adopted in July 1993 declared the former Communist regime to have been illegal and lifted the statute of limitations on politically motivated crimes committed during the Communist era.

In October 1994 the government was shaken by the disclosure of alleged corruption in the much-vaunted privatization program. Klaus strove to calm public fears, but the left-wing opposition parties were boosted in their claim that overly hasty privatization was mainly benefiting profiteers and criminals. Nevertheless, the ODS took some 30 percent of the vote, well ahead of the other parties, in the November local elections.

Relative political stability and economic progress in 1995 appeared to confirm the Czech Republic as being the ex-Communist state closest to achieving Western European standards, although a substantial gap remained to be closed. In the campaign for legislative elections on May 31–June 1, 1996, the ruling coalition parties stressed the need for continuity, while the left-wing parties called for political change amid widespread public disquiet about the negative social consequences of rapid transition to a market economy. The results yielded an unexpected setback for the government, which was reduced to minority status (99 seats) in the new Chamber of Deputies, while the Czech Social Democratic Party (*Česká Strana Sociáln Demokratická*—ČSSD) quadrupled its support; the Communists also gained ground, although the left fell well short of an aggregate majority. The outcome was the formation on July 4 of a minority center-right coalition of the ODS, ODA, and KDU-ČSL under the continued premiership of Klaus, who also received a conditional promise of external support from the ČSSD. The ČSSD continued its electoral advance in November in the nation's first Senate balloting, securing 25 seats to the ODS's 32.

In the wake of an ODS campaign financing scandal and mounting evidence that the Czech economic "miracle" had been somewhat illusory, Klaus, under pressure from Havel, ODS dissidents, and his coalition partners, submitted his resignation on November 30, 1997, although he agreed to stay on in a caretaker capacity. On December 17 Havel invited Josef TOŠOVSKÝ, governor of the central bank, to form a government, which, as approved on January 2, 1998, included anti-Klaus representatives from the ODS, members of the ODA and the KDU-ČSL, and a number of unaffiliated "technocrats." Subsequently, on January 20, Havel was reelected to a second five-year term, albeit by only one vote in the second round of parliamentary balloting. Eight days later the government won a confidence motion by a vote of 123–71, thanks in part to the support of the ČSSD, which had agreed only upon the condition that early elections be held in the summer.

The ČSSD won a plurality of 74 seats in the legislative balloting of June 19–20, 1998, followed by the ODS with 63 seats. However, neither Miloš ZEMAN, the prime minister-designate of the ČSSD, nor the ODS's Klaus was able to form a majority coalition government following the balloting. Zeman was ultimately appointed on July 17 as a result of an "opposition contract" under which the ODS agreed to support the ČSSD in crucial legislative votes, if necessary, while remaining outside the government. On the following day he announced a ČSSD cabinet, in which many ministries went to former members of the Communist Party. President Havel formally appointed the new cabinet on July 22, and it received a 73–39 vote of confidence in the Chamber of Deputies on August 19, the ODS

deputies, as agreed, not participating in the vote. The 24 deputies from the Communist Party of Bohemia and Moravia (*Komunistická Strana Čech a Moravy*—KSČM) also abstained.

The ČSSD won a plurality of 70 seats at the June 14–15, 2002, balloting for the Chamber of Deputies. On July 15 Vladimír ŠPIDLA of the ČSSD was sworn in to head a new cabinet comprising the ČSSD, the KDU-ČSL, and the Freedom Union–Democratic Union (*Unie Svobody Demokratická Unie*—US-DEU).

It took three rounds of contentious balloting to choose a new president in 2003, after incumbent President Václav Havel announced his intention to resign at the end of his term. As a result, following Havel's resignation on February 2, the duties of the president were temporarily divided between the prime minister and the speaker of the Chamber of Deputies. Finally, on February 28, Václav Klaus of the ODS was declared the victor over Jan SOKOL of the ČSSD.

President Klaus remained a vocal opponent of the Czech Republic's accession to the EU, but a national referendum on July 13–14, 2003, endorsed membership by a 77 percent yes vote. Consequently, the Czech Republic joined the EU with nine other new members on May 1, 2004. However, the cutbacks and other reforms required by the EU appeared to erode support for Prime Minister Špidla, who resigned on June 30 in the wake of the fifth-place performance by the ČSSD in the recent balloting for the European Parliament. He was succeeded by former deputy prime minister and interior minister Stanislav GROSS, who also assumed leadership of the ČSSD. Gross's new government (also comprising the ČSSD, KDU-ČSL, and US-DEU) won approval by a vote of 101–98 in the Chamber of Deputies on August 24.

The ODS led all parties in the November 2004 elections to the country's recently established regional councils with a reported 36 percent of the vote. The KSČM finished second with 21 percent of the vote, followed by the ČSSD with 14 percent.

The KDU-ČSL members resigned from the cabinet in late March 2005 as the result of questions raised concerning Prime Minister Gross's financial affairs (see Current issues). Gross resigned on April 25, and he was succeeded by the ČSSD's Jiří PAROUBEK, who immediately announced a cabinet comprising the same three parties and many of the ministers who had belonged to the previous government. Gross resigned as party chair on September 24, 2005.

Constitution and Government

Adopted by the (then) Czech National Council on December 16, 1992, the constitution of the Czech Republic came into effect on January 1, 1993, upon the dissolution of the Czechoslovak federation. It defines the Czech Republic as a unitary state with legislative power vested in a bicameral parliament, in which three-fifths majorities are required for the passage of constitutional amendments. Considerable executive authority is exercised by the president, who is elected for a five-year term by Parliament. The president appoints the prime minister and, in consultation with the prime minister, the Council of Ministers. A new Council of Ministers must pass a vote of confidence in the Chamber of Deputies within one month of the council's appointment.

The National Council decided that much Czechoslovak federal law would continue to apply in the Czech Republic; however, in cases of conflict between Czech and federal law, the former would apply. Following the deletion from the Czechoslovak Constitution in December 1989 of the guarantee of Communist power, a systematic revision of legal codes was initiated to reestablish "fundamental legal norms," including the appointment of judges for life. A revision of the criminal law included abolition of the death penalty and provision of a full guarantee of judicial review, while a law on judicial rehabilitation facilitated the quashing of almost all of the political trials of the Communist era. Commercial and civil law revisions established the supremacy of the courts in making decisions relating to rights. In July 2000 Parliament passed electoral revisions that, for purposes of decentralization, established 14 regional assemblies.

Foreign Relations

The collapse of Communist rule in late 1989 led to a transformation of Czechoslovakia's external relations, establishing new parameters that were subsequently inherited by the independent Czech Republic. On December 14 the newly installed non-Communist foreign minister, Jiří DIENSTBIER, declared that the 1968 agreement under which Soviet troops were stationed in Czechoslovakia was invalid because it had been concluded under duress. Subsequently, during a visit by President Havel to Moscow on February 26–27, 1990, the Soviets agreed to withdraw most of their forces by May, with the remainder to leave by July 1991 (a pledge that was honored, amid considerable Czech fanfare, on June 25, 1991).

In September 1990 the Federative Republic signaled its return to the international financial community by rejoining the International Monetary Fund (IMF) and the World Bank; a founding member of both institutions, it had withdrawn from membership in 1954 after a dispute with the IMF over consultation on exchange restrictions. On January 21, 1991, Czechoslovakia joined with Hungary and Poland in withdrawing from participation in the Warsaw Pact (disbanded soon thereafter), while in June of that year the (Soviet-bloc) Council for Mutual Economic Assistance (Comecon) was formally dissolved after the failure of half-hearted proposals for a successor body. (See *Political Handbook of the World 1991* for articles on both groupings.) Meanwhile, Czechoslovakia had been admitted to the Council of Europe on February 21 and had publicly set membership of the European Community (EC, subsequently the EU) and the North Atlantic Treaty Organization (NATO) as key objectives. On December 16, 1991, an EC-Czechoslovak association agreement was signed.

The goal of eventual EC membership was the joint aim of the "Visegrád" cooperation bloc formed on February 15, 1991, by Czechoslovakia, Hungary, and Poland. Czechoslovakia also participated in the Central European Initiative (CEI) created on January 28, 1992, and on March 18 became the first former Communist state to ratify the European Convention of Human Rights. President Havel signed a ten-year friendship treaty with the Russian Federation in Moscow on April 1, as well as a collateral agreement with the Commonwealth of Independent States (CIS), settling outstanding issues related to the withdrawal of Soviet troops.

On December 21, 1992, the Visegrád countries concluded a Central European Free Trade Agreement (CEFTA), to which the Czech and Slovak republics were deemed to have acceded at their attainment of separate sovereignty on January 1, 1993. (See Poland, Foreign relations, for additional information about CEFTA.) In May 1999 the four Visegrád states held their first summit since 1994 in renewed furtherance of regional cooperation.

On January 19, 1993, the UN General Assembly admitted the Czech and Slovak republics to membership, dividing between them the seats on various subsidiary organs that had been held by Czechoslovakia. The Czech Republic also became a member of the Conference on (later Organization for) Security and Cooperation in Europe (CSCE/OSCE), the European Bank for Reconstruction and Development (EBRD), and the Council of Europe. After some delay, revised association agreements were signed by the EC with the Czech Republic and Slovakia on October 4, 1993. Meanwhile, President Havel had signed a further friendship and cooperation treaty with Russia during a visit by President Yeltsin in August. The treaty was finally ratified by Parliament in September 1995.

A priority for the new Czech Republic was to normalize its relations with Slovakia. A temporary currency union between the two countries quickly broke down, while the notional existence of a customs union did not prevent a dramatic slump in bilateral trade in 1993. Progress was made in 1994 in implementing some 30 bilateral treaties and agreements, covering such matters as the division of federal property, debt settlement, and border arrangements. However, disputes persisted, notably over outstanding Slovak debts and the Czech rejection of a Slovak proposal for joint citizenship for the 300,000 Slovaks in the Czech Republic. At prime ministerial meetings on November 24, 1999, and

May 22, 2000, the two republics resolved their remaining property and debt disputes.

It became clear in 1994 that neither NATO nor the EU envisaged the speedy accession of the former Communist states. In the case of NATO, the Czech government welcomed, though without great enthusiasm, the alternative Partnership for Peace program (becoming a signatory in March), while instituting major army reforms designed to bring about compatibility with NATO norms and to reduce the Czech military complement from 85,000 to 65,000. In July 1997 NATO invited the Czech Republic, Hungary, and Poland (but, notably, not Slovakia) to join the alliance, and formal entry occurred on March 12, 1999.

The Czech Republic joined with the other Visegrád states in a continuing effort to promote NATO expansion to other Central and East European states. The Czech Republic in particular sought the inclusion of Slovakia in NATO as a means to secure the state's eastern borders and to enhance Slovakia's democratic prospects. At NATO's 2002 Prague Summit, seven states from the region, including Slovakia, were invited to join the alliance (formal accession occurred in March 2004).

On January 23, 1996, the Czech Republic formally applied for EU membership despite domestic opposition from the unreconstructed left and the ultra-nationalist right. In December 1997 the EU included the Czech Republic in the so-called first wave of potential new members (see EU article for details), and entry negotiations began in the spring of 1998 in anticipation of accession within five years.

At the EU Copenhagen Summit in December 2002, the Czech Republic was one of ten states invited to join the EU. In a referendum held on June 13–14, 2003, Czechs approved EU entry on a vote of 77.3 percent in favor and 22.7 against. Differences between the government and the president were evident during the referendum's campaign, as Klaus declined to publicly campaign in support of accession. The Czech Republic joined the EU on May 1, 2004. Klaus continued to challenge integration with the EU in February 2005 when he asked the Constitutional Court to rule whether the EU Constitution is in harmony with the Czech Constitution, to which the court responded that the case had no standing since the EU Constitution had not yet been adopted or submitted to Klaus for signing. Throughout 2005 the EU repeatedly warned the Czech Republic that it lagged far behind in adopting directives related to a wide range of economic activity, even initiating proceedings in some cases.

Prague's quest for EU membership had been complicated by the issue of the property of the Sudeten Germans expelled from Czechoslovakia immediately after World War II. German government officials had warned that the Czechs would have to negotiate on this issue, whereas Prague insisted that it would accept liability only for property confiscated after the Communist takeover in 1948. In January 1994 the Czech government adopted a draft law providing for the restitution of certain Jewish properties expropriated after 1938; however, a preamble defined this measure as exceptional and as not providing a precedent for claims in respect to the Sudeten Germans. In March 1995, moreover, the Constitutional Court upheld the legality of the 1945 expulsion of the ethnic Germans and the confiscation of their property. The issue was prominent during the 1996 Czech election campaign, after the German finance minister, Theo Waigel, had on May 25 called on the Prague government to apologize for the postwar treatment of the Sudeten Germans. His remark drew a public rebuke from Prime Minister Klaus and a request from the Czech foreign minister that German politicians stop "lecturing" Czechs about events surrounding World War II. Czech parliamentary debate on the issue was capped on March 5, 1997, when the Senate followed the lower chamber in approving (54 votes to 25) the Czech-German declaration already ratified by Germany. In that document Germany expressed its regret for its occupation of Czech territory, while Prague took a similar stance regarding excessive brutality in expelling ethnic Germans. Both sides agreed not to strain their relationship by pursuing further legal or political claims arising from the war.

A recent regional dispute has involved the start-up in October 2000 of the Temelin nuclear power plant. Austria, in particular, objected to completion of the facility, and in September environmentalists blocked border crossings with Austria and Germany in protest. In December the Austrian and Czech governments reached a measure of accommodation, agreeing to a new EU-supervised environmental impact study. However, tension over the plant resurfaced in 2001, with Austria threatening to block the Czech Republic's proposed accession to the EU unless safety issues were resolved. Late in the year Prime Minister Zeman announced that some $27 million would be spent to alleviate the concerns.

About 500 Czech troops have served in the NATO-led Kosovo Force (KFOR) since that operation began in 1999, and a much smaller contingent has served in Bosnia and Herzegovina. The Špidla administration declined a request to contribute troops to the U.S./UK-led invasion of Iraq in 2003, although the subsequent governments provided a small contingent of support staff to assist coalition efforts in that country, and Czech troops have been participating in the NATO Multinational Force in Afghanistan since March 2004.

Current Issues

Upon his installation as prime minister in 2002, Vladimír Špidla made it clear that EU accession was his top priority. To that end, the government initiated bank reforms, introduced new tax measures, and reduced public spending in order to bring the deficit down to EU standards. However, those initiatives caused a split within the ČSSD (whose left-wingers accused Špidla of caving in to the demands of the rightist elements of the KDU-ČSL and the US-DEU) and discord within sections of the population adversely affected by the cutbacks. Consequently, only a little more than a month after the Czech Republic joined the EU, voters appeared to turn against the ČSSD in the June 2004 elections to the European Parliament, giving the ČSSD only 8.8 percent of the vote, compared to 30 percent for the ODS and 20 percent for the surging

KSČM. New Prime Minister Stanislav Gross soon raised public sector wages, while also indicating his administration would attempt to improve the economic climate for the business community. However, Gross's tenure was cut short after only nine months when questions lingered over financial arrangements involved in his private property dealings. For his part, Jiří Paroubek, Gross's successor in April 2005, pledged to lower income taxes but still attempt to reduce the budget deficit, which to many observers sounded like a standard (but probably unattainable) campaign platform in advance of the "wide-open" legislative elections scheduled for mid-2006. Paroubek also promised to push for Czech ratification of the surprisingly controversial new proposed EU Constitution.

Both houses of the Czech Parliament have debated measures that would allow for the direct election of the president, particularly in view of the difficulties associated with the past two presidential elections. (Opinion polls consistently show that public sentiment is in favor of direct elections.) On June 4, 2003, the government approved legislation for popular presidential elections in which the winning candidate would have to receive a majority of the vote in the first round of balloting or face a runoff election. Since it entails a constitutional change, the legislation must be approved by three-fifths majorities in both houses of Parliament; neither house has yet been able to achieve the needed votes.

On August 30, 2005, the finance ministry announced the delay from 2009 to 2010 for adopting the euro because of the need for much deeper fiscal reforms in order to bring the annual public sector deficit into compliance with the EU's convergence criteria specified in the Maastricht Treaty.

Political Parties and Groups

From 1948 to 1989 Czechoslovakia was under effective one-party rule, although the National Front of the Czechoslovak Socialist Republic (*Národní Fronta*—ČSR), controlled by the Communist Party (*Komunistická Strana Československa*—KSČ), included four minor parties in addition to trade-union, farmer, and other groups. Termed by its most visible leader, Václav Havel, as a "temporary organization" to assist in the transition to democratic rule, the Civic Forum (*Občanské Fórum*—OF) was formally launched by a number of anti-Communist human rights groups on November 19, 1989; nine days later, in conjunction with its Slovak counterpart, it negotiated the settlement under which the KSČ agreed to give up its monopoly of power. Having won the June 1990 general election, the OF in February 1991 split into two wings, a majority of its leadership later voting to establish the Civic Democratic Party (ODS), while others participated in the launching of the Civic Movement (see under ČSNS, below).

During 1992, specifically Czech and Slovak parties became far more influential than those attempting to maintain federal constituencies, thus setting the stage for the breakup of the federal system at the end of 1992. On the establishment of the independent Czech Republic on January 1, 1993, the parties that had claimed a federal identity ceased to do so.

Government Parties

Czech Social Democratic Party (*Česká Strana Sociálně Demokratická*—ČSSD). First organized in 1878, the ČSSD was the plurality party at Czechoslovakia's first parliamentary election in 1920 but went underground in 1939. In 1948 it was forced to merge with the KSČ, resurfacing as a separate party in late 1989. It won no seats at the 1990 federal election, after which its Czech and Slovak wings became, in effect, separate parties. In the June 1992 election the ČSSD won 16 seats in the Czech National Council. It mounted strong opposition to the proposed "velvet divorce" between Czechs and Slovaks, arguing in favor of a "confederal union," but eventually accepted the inevitability of the separation. At its first postindependence congress in February 1993, the party formally renamed itself the "Czech" SSD and said it would seek to provide a left-wing alternative to the neoconservatism of the ruling coalition.

Benefiting from public unease over the social consequences of economic transition, the ČSSD achieved a major advance in the 1996 Chamber election, to 61 seats and 26.4 percent of the vote. It opted to give qualified external support to a further center-right coalition, the immediate reward being the election of the ČSSD Chair Miloš Zeman as president of the new Chamber of Deputies. At its congress of March 1997 the party reelected Zeman as chair and endorsed his call for confrontation with the coalition government. The ČSSD supported the transitional government of Josef Tošovský in the January 1998 parliamentary confidence vote with the provision that early elections would be called. The party won a plurality of 74 seats in the June 1998 legislative balloting (on the strength of 32.3 percent of the vote), leading to the installation of a minority ČSSD government led by Zeman, with external ODS support.

Objecting to the continuing pact with the ODS, Petra BUZKOVÁ resigned as deputy chair in January 2000. A frequent critic of Prime Minister Zeman, she was subsequently reported to be targeted by "Operation Lead" (Pb, her initials, represents lead in the periodic table of elements), apparently an effort by Zeman supporters to discredit her.

The ČSSD fared poorly in 13 regional assembly elections in November 2000, winning control of none and capturing only 15 percent of the vote. At simultaneous balloting for 27 Senate seats, the party won just 1, for a loss of 8, leaving it far behind the Quad Coalition (see below) and the ODS.

In the 2002 Chamber of Deputies elections, the ČSSD won 70 seats, making it the largest party in the lower house. Vladimír Špidla replaced Zeman as prime minister and chair of the party. Špidla formed a coalition government with the KDU-ČSL and US-DEU. In the October 25–26, 2002, Senate elections, the ČSSD won just 7 seats, bringing its representation in the upper house down to 11 from 15 (compared with 26 for the ODS). In 2003 dissidents within the ČSSD refused to support Špidla's presidential candidate, Jan Sokol, which contributed to the victory by Václav Klaus of the ODS. In response, Špidla forced the leader of the dissidents, Trade and Industry Minister Jiří RUSNOK, to resign. In EU elections in June 2004, the ČSSD came in fifth and won only 2 seats. Špidla

resigned on June 26, 2004, and was replaced by Stanislav Gross as prime minister and party leader. Gross was in turn succeeded by Jiří Paroubek in April 2005 (see Political background and Current issues for additional information).

Leaders: Jiří PAROUBEK (Prime Minister and Chair); Stanislav GROSS (Former Prime Minister); Bohuslav SOBOTKA, Martin STAREC, Zdeněk ŠKROMACH, Petr VÍCHA, Jana VAŇHOVÁ (Vice Chairs).

Christian and Democratic Union–Czech People's Party (*Křest'anská a Demokratická Unie– Česká Strana Lidová*—KDU-ČSL). The KDU-ČSL is descended from the Czechoslovak People's Party that had been founded in 1918, banned in 1938, and revived in 1945 as a component of the Communist-dominated National Front. From late 1989 it sought to reestablish its independence, joining the broad-based coalition government appointed in December. In June 1990 Josef BARTONČÍK was removed as party chair amid allegations that he had been a secret police informer. The party contested the election of the same month in an alliance that won 19 seats in the Czech National Council. Included in the postelection Czech coalition government, the alliance suffered defections in late 1991, and in April 1992 it was officially redesignated as the KDU-ČSL, which in the June 1992 election won 15 seats in the Czech National Council. The party became a member of the ODS-led Czech coalition government that took the republic to independence in January 1993, after which it no longer advocated autonomy for Moravia, from which it had long drawn the bulk of its support.

In late 1995 the KDU-ČSL was strengthened by the adhesion of five deputies of the KDS (see below, under Civic Democratic Party), who rejected the latter's decision to merge with the dominant ODS; however, the party fell back to 18 seats in the 1996 Chamber balloting.

The KDU-ČSL increased its representation to 20 (on a vote share of 9 percent) in the 1998 balloting for the Chamber of Deputies. Josef LUX, chair of the party, subsequently resigned his post and withdrew from political life in September due to illness. The party chose Jan Kasal as his successor in May 1999, with Kasal then being succeeded by Cyril Svoboda at a May 2001 party conference. In the elections for the Chamber of Deputies in 2002, the KDU-ČSL won 21 seats.

At a party conference on November 8, 2003, Miroslav Kalousek defeated incumbent party leader Cyril Svoboda by a vote of 164 to 131 to become the chair of the KDU-ČSL.

Leaders: Miroslav KALOUSEK (Chair); Jan KASAL (First Deputy Chair); Milan ŠIMONOVSKÝ (Deputy Chair and Deputy Prime Minister, Minister of Transport and Communications); Cyril SVOBODA (Deputy Chair and Foreign Minister); Roman LÍNEK, Pavol LUKŠA (Deputy Chairs).

Freedom Union–Democratic Union (*Unie Svobody–Demokratická Unie*—US-DEU). As a result of dissension in the ODS over the leadership of Václav Klaus and his handling of a campaign finance scandal, nearly half of the ODS's 69 deputies reportedly left the party to form the Freedom Union (*Unie Svobody*—US) on January 17, 1998. Defections of ODS cabinet members to the US were also subsequently reported. The US won 19 seats on a vote share of 8.6 percent in the June balloting for the Chamber of Deputies.

Party Chair Jan RUML resigned in December 1999, with his successor being elected in February 2000. In late 2001 the US and the Democratic Union (*Demokratická Unie*—DEU) announced that the two groups would be merged, the new party to be known as the US-DEU. A right-wing formation founded in June 1994, the DEU won one Senate seat in 1996 but none in 2000. The merged US-DEU won ten seats in the 2002 balloting for the Chamber of Deputies.

On December 6, 2003, DEU leader Ratibor MAJZLIK led 300 supporters in a mass defection after failing to oust the US-DEU leadership at a party conference. In June 2004 other defectors from the DEU formed a new political party, the **Democratic Union of the Czech Republic,** or DEU-CR. The new party was led by Jan DORANT.

On June 14, 2004, Pavel Němec became party chair when Petr MAREŠ resigned after the US-DEU's poor performance in the European Parliament elections (the party failed to win any seats).

Leaders: Pavel NĚMEC (Chair and Deputy Prime Minister, Minister of Justice); František PELC, Ivo LUDVÍK, Svatopluk KARÁSEK (Vice Chairs).

Opposition Parties

Civic Democratic Party (*Občanská Demokratická Strana*—ODS). The ODS resulted from the inability of the Civic Forum leadership in early 1991 to transform the somewhat diffuse movement into a formal party. Intensely anti-Communist, it quickly built a strong organization and concluded an electoral alliance with the Christian Democratic Party (*Křest'ansko-Demokratická Strana*—KDS), which had originated in the mid-1980s as an unofficial ecumenical Christian group calling for political pluralism. Under the leadership of Václav BENDA, a leading dissident in the Communist era, the KDS was established as a distinct party in December 1989. In the June 1992 election the ODS/KDS became the leading formation both at the federal level and in the Czech National Council, ODS leader Václav Klaus heading the Czech regional administration. Upon formal separation from Slovakia on January 1, 1993, the Czech coalition headed by the ODS became the government of the independent Czech Republic, with Klaus continuing as prime minister.

In November 1995 the ODS formally merged with the KDS under the ODS rubric, although five of the ten KDS deputies preferred to join the Christian and Democratic Union–Czech People's Party (KDU-ČSL, above). The ODS lost ground in the spring 1996 balloting for the Chamber of Deputies, falling to 68 seats, but Klaus was able to form a minority coalition. However, allegations of irregularities regarding campaign finances intensified in 1997, contributing to the collapse of the Klaus government in late November. Klaus was reelected chair at the ODS Congress in December, and he finally decided that the party would not participate in the "transitional" government led by Josef Tošovský. Many party dissidents, reportedly upset with Klaus's autocratic style and the alleged financial improprieties, objected to the chair's directive, and four ODS members accepted positions in the January 1998 government. Anti-Klaus legislators subsequently resigned from the ODS to form the new Freedom Union (see above), and several cabinet members reportedly also left the party. Klaus was unable to forge a coalition government following the June 1998 legislative balloting (at which the ODS secured 63 seats, second to the ČSSD) and subsequently endorsed an "opposition contract" that permitted installation of a ČSSD minority government.

Following the November 2000 partial Senate election, the ODS held 22 seats in the upper house, second to the Quad Coalition. In regional assembly contests, the party won control of six and tied the Quad Coalition in a seventh.

In the June 2002 Chamber of Deputies elections, the ODS won 58 seats and continued as the leading opposition party. Klaus resigned as party leader on November 2, 2002, in order to run for the presidency and was replaced at a party conference by Mirek Topolánek on December 15. After three contentious rounds of balloting in Parliament, Klaus was elected president on February 28, 2003.

The ODS dominated the balloting in 2004 for the country's 13 regional councils (established in 2000) with 36 percent of the vote.

Leaders: Mirek TOPOLÁNEK (Chair of the Party); Václav KLAUS (President of the Republic and Honorary Chair of the Party); Petr NEČAS (First Deputy Chair); Pavel BÉM, Petr BENDL, Ivan LANGER, Miroslava NĚMCOVÁ (Deputy Chairs).

Quad Coalition (*Čtyřkoalice*—4K, or *4Koalice*). The center-right Quad Coalition was formed prior to the November 1998 Senate and municipal elections by the Christian and Democratic Union–Czech People's Party, Freedom Union, Democratic Union, and the Civic Democratic Alliance (discussed below). It won 13 of the 27 contested Senate seats at that election and 17 of 27 in November 2000. Following the latter balloting, the coalition controlled 39 of the 81 Senate seats, more than enough to prevent the ČSSD and ODS from passing constitutional amendments. At simultaneous balloting for 13 newly established regional legislatures, the grouping finished second to the ODS, winning 23 percent of the vote and gaining control of 5 assemblies. Earlier, on September 28, the four constituent parties had agreed to elect a common leader in January 2001, establish a shadow cabinet by March 2001, and offer a joint candidate list for the 2002 parliamentary election. In the most recent elections it has cooperated with two reform-minded civic initiatives, "Impulse '99" and "Thanks, Now Leave," both of which objected to the opposition pact between the ODS and the ČSSD. In early 2002 it was announced that the Quad Coalition would be dissolved in the wake of the financial problems within the ODA that had forced its withdrawal from the grouping. However, the KDU-ČSL and the recently merged US-DEU announced that they would present joint candidates in the June legislative balloting on a "Coalition" list.

Communist Party of Bohemia and Moravia (*Komunistická Strana Čech a Moravy*—KSČM). Established under its present name in March 1990, the KSČM is descended from the Communist Party of Czechoslovakia (KSČ) founded in 1921 by the pro-Bolshevik wing of the ČSSD. The KSČ was the only East European Communist Party to retain legal status in the 1930s, until it was banned in the aftermath of the 1938 Munich agreement. Its leaders returned from Moscow at the end of World War II as the dominant element of a Soviet-sponsored National Front and effectively seized sole power in 1948. In March 1990, as non-Communists took over leading government posts, the Czech component of the KSČ relaunched itself as the KSČM, with a socialist rather than a Marxist-Leninist orientation. At the June 1990 multiparty election, the Communists took second place in the Czech National Council, winning 32 of the 200 seats. They then went into opposition for the first time since 1945, amid a continuing exodus of party members.

In mid-1991 the KSČ was officially dissolved, but both the KSČM and its Slovak counterpart remained "Czechoslovak" in orientation. In the

June 1992 election the KSČM-led Left Bloc won 35 of the 200 Czech National Council seats and subsequently resisted dissolution of the federation. Following the creation of the independent Czech Republic in January 1993, the party experienced much internal strife, including the resignation of Jiří SVOBODA as leader over the rejection of his proposal to drop "Communist" from the party's title. He was replaced in June 1993 by the conservative Miroslav Grebeníček, whose election precipitated the formation of the breakaway SDL (below), followed by the departure in December 1993 of what became the SLB (below). The secessions meant that the KSČM had lost a majority of its ten deputies elected in 1992; however, it recovered strongly in the 1996 balloting, winning 22 seats, whereas the various breakaway groups failed to obtain representation. The KSČM fared even better in the 1998 balloting for the Chamber of Deputies, winning 24 seats on the strength of 11 percent of the vote. Following the November 2000 Senate election, it held 3 seats (a loss of 1) in the upper house.

In balloting for the Chamber of Deputies in June 2002, the KSČM won 41 seats. It joined the conservative ODS as the opposition to the coalition government. In the 2004 elections for the European Parliament, the party exceeded analysts' expectations, apparently because of growing popular discontent with the coalition government. The KSČM received the second-largest number of votes with 20.3 percent of the total vote and won 6 seats. Considered one of the "least reformed" communist parties among the countries recently admitted to the EU, the KSČM in 2005 campaigned against the proposed new EU Constitution. The party took an important modernizing step when on September 20, 2005, hard-line leader Miroslav GREBENÍČEK stepped down as chair.

Leaders: Vojtěch FILIP (Chair); Miroslav GREBENÍČEK, Karel KLIMŠA, Jiří DOLEJŠ, Václav EXNER, František TOMAN (Vice Chairs); Pavel KOVARČÍK.

Civic Democratic Alliance (*Občanská Demokratická Aliance*—ODA). The right-wing ODA was launched in December 1989, and it contested the June 1990 multiparty election as part of the victorious Civic Forum, participating in both the federal and Czech republican governments. It contested the June 1992 election in its own right, winning 14 of the 200 Czech National Council seats on a 5.9 percent vote share. As a member of the subsequent Czech coalition government headed by the ODS, it supported the creation of a separate Czech Republic. Its promarket line is similar to that of the ODS, the main difference being its greater emphasis on regional self-government. The party lost 1 of its 14 Chamber seats in the 1996 election.

Chair Jan KALVODA, the target of reports that he falsely claimed to have a doctorate, resigned from government positions and did not seek reelection at the party congress in March 1997, when the ODA elected Michael ŽANTOVSKÝ to succeed him. However, Žantovský, a spokesperson for President Havel, could not reconcile rival party factions; he stepped down in November and was replaced by Deputy Premier Jiří Skalický. The friction evidently could not be contained, as a number of right-wing members left to form the Conservative Consensus Party (SKS). In mid-February 1998 Skalický resigned as chair of the ODA in a fight involving a campaign finance scandal, and several other prominent ODA members (including cabinet ministers) reportedly also left the party. The ODA chose not to contest the election for the Chamber of Deputies in June 1998, party leaders calling upon ODA supporters to vote for candidates from the ODS or US. The ODA was dropped from the Quad Coalition in early 2002 after it failed to make arrangements to pay off its substantial debt from previous campaigns.

In the 2002 elections for the Chamber of Deputies, the ODA received less than 1 percent of the vote, leaving the party with one seat in the Senate as its sole representation in Parliament.

Leaders: Jiřina NOVÁKOVÁ (Party Chair); Jaromír Mário CÍSAŘ, Petr BAŠÍK (Vice Chairs).

Association of Independent Candidates and European Democrats (*Sdružení Nezávislých a Evropští Demokraté*—SNK-ED). The merger of the SNK and the ED was formalized on December 12, 2005. Formed prior to the 2002 elections and led by former ODS leader Josef Zieleniec and Igor Petrov, the Association of Independents (SNK) was a center-right party that, unlike the ODS, was highly supportive of European integration. The party sought to appeal to young conservatives who were dissatisfied with the more nationalistic ODS. In the 2002 elections for the Chamber of Deputies, the SNK received 2.8 percent of the vote. However, it won two seats in the 2002 Senate elections. The SNK formed a coalition with the European Democrats (ED) in 2004, having substantial success in the June 2004 balloting for the European Parliament (three seats on an 11 percent vote share).

Leaders: Josef ZIELENIEC (Political Leader and Former Foreign Minister); Jan KASL (First Deputy Chair); Igor PETROV, Jaromír GAJDÁČEK (Deputy Chairs).

Other Parties That Contested Recent Elections

Association for the Republic–Czech Republican Party (*Sdružení pro Republiku–Republikánská Strana Česká*—SPR-RSČ). Founded in 1990, the right-wing SPR-RSČ advocated economic protectionism, drastic cuts in the state bureaucracy, military neutrality, nonparticipation in such international organizations as the IMF, measures against "unadaptable" minorities (particularly the Gypsies), and the reintroduction of capital punishment. Obtaining its main support in northern Bohemia, the party won 14 seats in the 200-member Czech National Council in June 1992. In 1993 the party experienced serious dissension within its parliamentary group, the membership of which had fallen to seven deputies by mid-1994. The party was further weakened in August by the defection of members to the new **Patriotic Republican Party** (VRS). Campaigning on an anti-Gypsy and anti-German platform, it advanced to 18 seats (and 8 percent of the vote) in the 1996 Chamber election but failed to win any seats in the November Senate election.

Only hours after Parliament had lifted his immunity, SPR-RSČ Chair Miroslav Sládek was arrested on charges of spreading racial hatred. While in prison, he ran unsuccessfully as the party's presidential candidate against Václav Havel in January 1998. Sládek was subsequently acquitted of the charges against him.

The SPR-RSČ won no seats in the 1998 balloting for the Chamber of Deputies, its vote total falling to 3.9 percent amid accusations of financial impropriety as well as an apparent decline in public support for Sládek's xenophobic views. The party split into several smaller parties in 2002, including the Republicans and the Republicans of Miroslav Sládek (see below).

Communist Party of Czechoslovakia (*Komunistická Strana Československa*—KSČ). Its name indicating a rejection of the dissolution of Czechoslovakia, the KSČ was founded in March 1995 as the Party of Czechoslovak Communists (*Strana Československých Komunistů*—SČK) by Miroslav Štěpán, a former head of the Prague Communist Party who had been expelled from the KSČM. Štpán formed the SČK after his release from a 30-month jail term for having ordered the breakup of prodemocracy demonstrations in the late 1980s. In April 1996 the SČK was barred from the forthcoming legislative balloting on the ground that it had failed to pay the required deposits for its candidates. The SČK was renamed the KSČ at a congress in December 1999, at which time it asserted that the KSČM "abuses" the term "Communist Party." It did not contest the 2002 election to the Chamber of Deputies.

Leader: Miroslav ŠTĚPÁN (General Secretary).

Czech National Social Party (*Česká Strana Národně Sociální*—ČSNS). The ČSNS adopted its current name in September 1997, having previously been called the Free Democrats–Liberal National Social Party (*Svobodní Demokraté–Liberálni Národně Sociální Strana*—SD-LNSS). The centrist SD-LNSS was formed as a merger of the SD and LNSS in late 1995, although most LNSS deputies rejected the union and later launched a separate, short-lived parliamentary group, the Civic National Movement (*Občanské Národní Hnutí*—ONH). The SD component, dating as such from 1993 and led by Jiří DIENST-BIER, grew out of the Civic Movement (OH) wing of the Civic Forum (OF) launched in 1991 but was unrepresented in the 1992–1996 Parliament. The LNSS was descended from the National Socialist Party (founded in 1897), which played a dominant role in the interwar period and was a member of the postwar Communist-led National Front, becoming the Czechoslovak Socialist Party (*Československá Strana Socialistická*—ČSS) in 1948. Unsuccessful in the 1990 election, the ČSS in 1991 merged with the former Agrarian Party (*Zemědělská Strana*—KS) and the Green Party (SZ, below) to form a Liberal Social Union (*Liberálně Sociální Unie*—LSU) that won 16 Czech National Council seats in 1992 but thereafter suffered dissension and broke up. Most of the old ČSS component opted in June 1993 to form the centrist-inclined LNSS.

Dienstbier, a prominent dissident during the Communist era and subsequently Czechoslovakia's foreign minister, later left the SD-LNSS. In November 2000 he competed unsuccessfully as a ČSSD senatorial candidate. A year earlier the ČSNS had indirectly achieved lower house representation when Marie MACHATÁ, who had been elected from the Freedom Union, joined the party. (She technically sits as an independent.) In the 2002 lower house elections, the ČSNS received only 0.81 percent of the vote.

Leaders: Jaroslav ROVNÝ (Chair), Vikto TRKAL (Deputy Chair).

Party of Democratic Socialism (*Strana Demokratického Socialismu*—SDS). The SDS was established in June 1997 by merger of the Democratic Left Party (*Strana Demokratiké Levice*—SDL) and the Left Bloc Party (*Strana Levého Bloku*—SLB). The SDL dated from June 1993, when a reformist faction led by Josef MEČL separated from the KSČM, which had declined to change its name. The SLB dated from December 1993, when another KSČM faction led by former presidential candidate Marie STIBOROVÁ departed because of the Communists' new conservative leadership. At the time, the SLB claimed the support of a majority of the parliamentary deputies

who had been elected in 1992 on the Left Bloc program, but it failed to win representation in the 1996 balloting.

In April 1998 the party's chair, Vasil MOHORITA, resigned to join the ČSSD and called for the SDS to dissolve. Nonetheless, the SDS presented candidates in the 2002 elections, but the party received only 475 votes nationwide for their candidates to the Chamber of Deputies.

Leader: Jiří HUDEČEK.

Green Party (*Strana Zelených*—SZ). Originally founded in 1989 and prominent in the "Velvet Revolution," the SZ failed to win representation in the 1990 election. For the 1992 poll it joined the broader Liberal Social Union but reverted to independent status in November 1993. The party was barred from the 1996 legislative elections for failing to put up the required deposit. The SZ received 2.36 percent of the vote in the 2002 legislative elections for the Chamber of Deputies.

Leaders: Martin BURSÍK (Chair); Dana KUCHTOVÁ (First Deputy Chair); Petr ŠTPÁNEK, Džamila STEHLÍKOVÁ (Deputy Chairs).

The Moravians (*Moravané*). The Moravians formed from the December 17, 2005, merger of the **Moravian Democratic Party** (*Moravská Demokratická Strana*—MDS) and the **Movement for an Independent Moravia and Silesia-Moravian National Union** (*Hnutí Samosprávné Moravy a Slezska-Moravské Národní Sjednocení*—HSMS-MNS). The MDS was formed in April 1997 by merger of the Moravian National Party (*Moravská Národní Strana*—MNS) and the Bohemian-Moravian Center Union (*Českomoravská Unie Středu*—ČMUS). The ČMUS was derived from the Movement for Self-Governing Democracy–Association for Moravia and Silesia (*Hnutí za Samosprávnou Demokracii–Společnost pro Moravu a Slezsko*—HSD-SMS), founded in 1990 in support of a demand that the historic province of Moravia-Silesia should have status equivalent to Bohemia and Slovakia. In the 1990 election the HSD-SMS took third place in the Czech National Council, winning 22 seats, 8 of which were lost in 1992. Thereafter, strains developed between moderates and a radical faction favoring extraparliamentary action. The proparliamentary Bohemian-Moravian Center Party (*Českomoravská Strana Středu*—ČMSS) was announced in January 1994, the new title indicating the party's intention to extend its activities to Bohemia. Later in the year it joined other centrist groups, including the Liberal Social Union (*Liberálně Sociální Unie*—LSU), the Farmers' Party (*Zemědělské Strany*—ZS), and the Christian Social Union (*Křest'ansko Sociální Unie*—KSU), in a loose alliance, the ČMUS. Formal merger occurred in February 1996. For the 1998 election the party cooperated with the HSMS-MNS.

Ivan Dřímal, the former MNS leader, was reelected MDS chair in April 2000. In elections for the Chamber of Deputies in 2002, the MDS received just 0.27 percent of the vote. With the long-term goal of self-rule for Moravia and Silesia, the Moravians hoped for a better showing in the upcoming June 2006 election for the Chamber of Deputies.

Leaders: Pavel DOHNAL (Chair); Pavel HÁLA (First Deputy Chair); Milan TRNKA, Jan SMEJKALl (Deputy Chairs).

Independent Democrats (*Nezávislí Demokraté*—ND, or NEZDEM). The NEZDEM was founded on June 23, 2005, by former ČSSD member of parliament Jana Volfová with the help of Vladimír Železný, leader of the Independents (*Nezávislí*). The Independents (the NEZ) was founded in 1995 by Železný, a former Nova TV general director, as a center-right, euro-skeptic party. In the 2002 senatorial elections, the NEZ won two seats. In the 2004 EU parliamentary elections, the NEZ received 8.2 percent of the vote and gained two seats. Bowing to the fact that Železný's name was better known than that of the ND, the latter was renamed Independent Democrats (Chair V. Železný), with the chair's name becoming a formal component of the party name, on December 4, 2005. The NEZDEM then merged with the Party for a Secure Life (*Strana za Životní Jistoty*—SŽJ), which focused on senior citizens and other eco-

nomically vulnerable groups, under the name Independent Democrats. (See *Political Handbook of the World 2005–2006* for history of the SŽJ.)

Leaders: Vladimír ŽELEZNÝ (Chair); Jana VOLFOVÁ, Martin FRAŠKO, Petr HUDLÍK, Václav MUSÍLEK, Václav RÝZNAR, Bla VÁVROVSKÁ (Deputy Chairs).

Path of Change (*Cesta Změny*). Path of Change is a centrist party founded in 2001 by Jiří Lobkowicz. The party supports continued free-market reforms and is pro-European integration; however, it accuses the established parties of cronyism and corruption. The Path of Change also strongly supports the direct election of the president. Soon after its formation, a leadership struggle led Monika PAJEROVÁ, one of the student leaders of the Velvet Revolution, to leave the group and establish a rival party, Hope. In the 2002 elections for the Chamber of Deputies, the Path of Change received less than 1 percent of the vote. It was able to gain one seat in the October Senate elections.

Leader: Jiří LOBKOWICZ.

Other parties that contested the 2002 or 2006 legislative elections or the 2004 elections for the European Parliament included the **Czech Right** (*Česká Pravice*—CP), which was registered in January 1994 (unless noted, all of the parties in this list received less than 1 percent of the vote in the various elections); the **Liberal Reform Party** (*Liberální Reformní Strana*—LIRA), led by Milan HAMERSKÝ; the **Movement of Independents for a Harmonic Development of Community and Town** (*Hnutí Nezávislých Za Harmonický Rozvoj Obcí a Míst*—HNHROM) which won one seat in the Senate in the October 2002 elections; the **Republicans** (Republikáni), a right-wing, euro-skeptic party founded on March 4, 2002, by former members of the Association for the Republic–Czech Republican Party; the **Republicans of Miroslav Sládek** (*Republikani Miroslava Sládka*—RMS), a far-right party formed in 2002 by Miroslav SLÁDEK and former members of the Association for the Republic–Czech

Cabinet

As of June 1, 2006 (*see headnote*)

Prime Minister	Jiří Paroubek (ČSSD)
Deputy Prime Ministers	Zdeněk Škromach (ČSSD)
	Pavel Němec (US-DEU)
	Milan Šimonovský (KDU-ČSL)
	Bohuslav Sobotka (ČSSD)
	Jiří Havel (ČSSD)

Ministers

Agriculture	Jan Mládek (ČSSD)
Culture	Vítzslav Jandák (ind.)
Defense	Karel Kühnl (US-DGU)
Education, Youth, and Sport	Petra Buzková (ČSSD) [f]
Environment	Libor Ambrozek (KDU-ČSL)
Finance	Bohuslav Sobotka (ČSSD)
Foreign Affairs	Cyril Svoboda (KDU-ČSL)
Health	David Rath (ČSSD)
Industry and Trade	Milan Urban (ČSSD)
Information Technology	Dana Bérová [f]
Interior	František Bublan (ind.)
Justice	Pavel Němec (US-DEU)
Labor and Social Affairs	Zdeněk Škromach (ČSSD)
Regional Development	Radko Martínek (ČSSD)
Transport	Milan Šimonovský (KDU-ČSL)
Without Portfolio	Pavel Zářecký (ind.)

[f] = female

Republican Party; the **Right Bloc** (*Pravý Blok—*PB); and the **Romany Civic Initiative** (*Romská Občanská Iniciativa*—ROI), a party promoting the interests of Gypsies.

In addition, new parties emerged, including the far right **Law and Justice Party** (*Právo a Spravedlnost*—PaS), formed on January 28, 2006, from the merger of National Unification, the Workers' Party, the Democractic Party of Social Justice, and the Agrarian Party; the **Union of the Left** founded in 2005 and currently led by Piotr MUSIAL; and the **Romany Social Democratic Party** (*Romská Demokratická Sociální Strana*—RDSS), established in April 2005 and supporting the integration of Romany minorities into mainstream society.

Legislature

The **Parliament of the Czech Republic** (*Parlament České Republiky*) consists, under the 1992 constitution, of a Senate and a Chamber of Deputies. To achieve the transition to separate statehood on January 1, 1993, the composition of the lower house was decreed to be identical to that of the previous Czech National Council (*Česká Národní Rada*) elected in June 1992. The parliament operated as a single-chamber legislature until an entirely new Senate was elected in 1996.

Senate (*Senát*). Under legislation enacted in September 1995, the 81 members of the upper house are elected on a majoritarian basis for a six-year term from single-member constituencies, with one-third of the seats normally being renewed every two years. All 81 seats were filled in the first election held November 15–16 and November 22–23, 1996.

The most recent balloting for 27 seats was held November 5–6 and November 12–13, 2004. As of June 1, 2006, the seats were distributed as follows: Civic Democratic Party, 35; Christian and Democratic Union–Czech People's Party, 11; Czech Social Democratic Party, 6; Freedom Union–Democratic Union, 3; Communist Party of Bohemia and Moravia, 2; Association of Independents and European Democrats, 2; Civic Democratic Alliance, 1; Movement of Independents for a Harmonic Development of Community and Town, 1; independents, 20.

President: Přemysl SUBOTKA.

Chamber of Deputies (*Sněmovna Poslanců*). The lower house consists of 200 deputies directly elected for a four-year term by universal suffrage of those aged 18 and over. The thresholds for representation are 5 percent of the national vote for single parties, 7 percent for alliances of two or three parties, and 10 percent for alliances of four or more parties. In early 1998 the Chamber of Deputies approved a constitutional amendment cutting its current term in half in order to permit new elections in June. Following balloting held on June 19–20, 1998, the seats were distributed as follows: Czech Social Democratic Party, 74; Civic Democratic Party, 63; Communist Party of Bohemia and Moravia, 24; Christian and Democratic Union–Czech People's Party, 20; Freedom Union, 19.

Under controversial electoral reform legislation passed in July 2000, with effect from 2002 the thresholds for representation were raised to 5 percent for single parties, 10 percent for two-party alliances, 15 percent for three-party alliances, and 20 percent for alliances of four or more parties. The reforms also increased the number of electoral districts from 8 to 35.

As of June 1, 2006, the seats in the Chamber were distributed as follows: the Czech Social Democratic Party, 70; Civic Democratic Party, 57; Communist Party of Bohemia and Moravia, 41;

Christian and Democratic Union–Czech People's Party, 21; Freedom Union–Democratic Union, 10; unclassified, 1. The next election was scheduled for June 2–3, 2006. (*See headnote.*)

President: Lubomír ZAORÁLEK.

Communications

Press

The following dailies are published in Czech at Prague, unless otherwise noted: *Blesk* (Lightning, 420,000), Swiss-owned independent tabloid; *Mladá Fronta Dnes* (Youth Front Today, 350,000), former organ of the Socialist Union of Youth; *Právo* (Justice, 350,000), former KSČM organ (called *Rudé Právo* until September 1995), now independent; *Slovo* (Free Word, 230,000); *Hospodářské Noviny* (Economic News, 130,000), business paper; *Večerník Praha* (Evening Prague, 130,000); *Svoboda* (Freedom, Ostrava, 100,000); *Lidové Noviny* (People's News, 68,320), independent; *Haló Noviny* (Hello News), KSČM organ.

News Agencies

The state-owned domestic service is the Czech News Agency (*Česká Tisková Kancelář*—ČTK, or Četeka). Numerous foreign agencies also maintain bureaus in Prague.

Broadcasting and Computing

The former federal broadcasting structures ended on January 1, 1993, when the state-funded Czech Radio (*Český Rozhlas*) and Czech Television (*Česká Televize*) assumed full responsibility within the Czech Republic. The strict government control of the Communist era had ended in 1991, when the supervision of broadcasting was transferred to independent authorities approved by the respective parliaments. In March 1991 the republics were authorized to license independent radio and television stations, with the first independent TV outlet, Nova Television, being launched in Prague in 1994. There are presently several dozen private radio stations in addition to national networks. There were approximately 5.5 million television receivers and 2.1 million personal computers serving 2.7 million Internet users in 2003.

Intergovernmental Representation

Ambassador to the U.S.
Petr KOLÁŘ

U.S. Ambassador to the Czech Republic
William J. CABANISS

Permanent Representative to the UN
(Vacant)

IGO Memberships (Non-UN)
BIS, CEI, CERN, CEUR, EIB, EU, Eurocontrol, IEA, Interpol, IOM, NATO, OECD, OSCE, PCA, WCO, *WEU*, WTO

DENMARK

KINGDOM OF DENMARK

Kongeriget Danmark

The Country

Encompassing a low-lying peninsula and adjacent islands strategically situated at the mouth of the Baltic, Denmark has a largely homogeneous population, although a degree of controversy has emerged in regard to the entry of increasing numbers of asylum seekers and the families of immigrant workers. A vast majority (95 percent) of the inhabitants belong to the state-supported Evangelical Lutheran Church. Approximately 46 percent of the wage labor force is female, with 40 percent of working women concentrated in "female intensive" service and textile manufacturing jobs; in government, women currently hold about one-half of cabinet posts and one-third of national legislative seats, with significantly less representation at the local level.

About three-quarters of Denmark's terrain is devoted to agriculture, and most of the agricultural output is exported (chiefly meat, dairy products, and eggs). However, industrialization was substantial after World War II, with manufactures (principally machinery and electrical equipment, processed foods and beverages, chemicals and pharmaceuticals, textiles, clothing, and ships) accounting for about 70 percent of total exports by 1990. After a dip early in the decade, economic growth recovered to about 3 percent a year in 1993 and 1994 and 4 percent in 1995, but unemployment remained high at around 10 percent. For 1996–1998, annual GDP growth ranged from 2.4 to 3.0 percent, the government being given high marks by the international financial sector for structural

reforms, including tightened labor benefits, implemented in the mid-1990s. GDP growth declined to about 1.3 percent in 1999 but rose again to 2.9 percent in 2000, although inflation remained higher than in most neighboring countries, at 2.9 percent for the year. Denmark's economy, while generally sound, has slowed in the past few years. While GDP growth had picked up in 2000, it dropped to 1.0 percent in 2001 and 1.6 percent in 2002. Nevertheless, Denmark managed to post a trade surplus of $8.3 billion and a current account balance of $5 billion for 2002.

Although a member of the European Community/European Union (EC/EU) since 1973,

Political Status: Constitutional monarchy since 1849; under unicameral parliamentary system established in 1953.

Area: 16,629 sq. mi. (43,069 sq. km.).

Population: 5,349,212 (2001C); 5,385,000 (2005E). Area and population figures are for mainland Denmark; for Greenland and the Faroe Islands, see Related Territories, below.

Major Urban Center (2005E): COPENHAGEN (502,000; metropolitan area, 2,050,000).

Official Language: Danish.

Monetary Unit: Krone (market rate July 1, 2006: 5.83 kroner = $1US).

Sovereign: Queen MARGRETHE II; proclaimed queen on January 15, 1972, following the death of her father, King FREDERIK IX, on January 14.

Heir to the Throne: Crown Prince FREDERIK, elder son of the queen.

Prime Minister: Anders Fogh RASMUSSEN (Liberal Party); formed coalition government on November 27, 2001, following the election of November 20, succeeding Poul Nyrup RASMUSSEN (Social Democratic Party); returned to office following election of February 8, 2005.

Denmark voted by referendum in September 2000 not to join the EU's Economic and Monetary Union (EMU).

Government and Politics

Political Background

The oldest monarchy in Europe, Denmark has lived under constitutional rule since 1849 and has long served as a model of political democracy. Its multiparty system, reflecting the use of proportional representation, has resulted since World War II in a succession of coalition governments, most of minority status. The Social Democratic Party (*Socialdemokratiet*—SD) maintained its prewar position as the strongest single party, heading coali-

tion governments in 1947–1950, 1953–1968, and 1971–1973, latterly under the premiership of Anker JØRGENSEN. After two years of a nonsocialist minority government under Poul HARTLING of the Liberal Party (*Venstre*), Jørgensen returned following the 1975 election, heading a series of minority coalitions until 1982, when he was succeeded by Poul SCHLÜTER of the Conservative People's Party (*Konservative Folkeparti*—KF) as head of another minority government that included the Liberals, Center Democrats (*Centrum-Demokraterne*—CD), and the Christian People's Party (*Kristeligt Folkeparti*—KrF).

The first Conservative prime minister since 1901, Schlüter faced heavy opposition to his proposed austerity measures. For the first time since 1929, the budget failed, and he was forced to call an early election on January 10, 1984, which yielded a decrease in class-alliance voting, with Danes supporting the traditional Conservative outlook on economic issues, including lowered interest rates. As a result, Schlüter remained in office as head of the existing four-party government.

On April 14, 1988, the opposition SD secured legislative approval of a resolution requiring that vessels from the North Atlantic Treaty Organization (NATO) be formally "reminded" of Denmark's 31-year-old ban on nuclear weapons. Prime Minister Schlüter responded by calling a snap election for May 10, at which the socialist bloc suffered a marginal loss, while the rightist FP, theretofore unacceptable as a government coalition partner, registered a 43 percent gain in representation. Since the anti-NATO forces nonetheless retained a narrow majority, the prime minister submitted his resignation and moved into caretaker status, ultimately forming a minority three-party government encompassing the Conservatives, the Liberals, and the RV on June 3.

In a referendum on June 2, 1992, Danish voters by a 50.7 to 49.3 percent majority rejected the Maastricht Treaty of the previous December that provided for a common European currency and pledged EC members to seek common foreign and security policies. While both EC and Danish leaders were surprised by the outcome, it reflected a widely held view that increased European integration would lead to a loss of Danish national identity. The rejection came despite a number of safeguards that had been built into the treaty, including optional adherence to the common currency.

Unwilling to accept the electorate's decision on the Maastricht Treaty, the government on October 27, 1992, secured a "national compromise" agreement between seven of the eight parliamentary parties (the exception being the FP) setting out terms of joint support for the treaty in a second referendum. Its main stipulations were that Denmark would be able to opt out of the proposed single European currency, defense policy coordination, cooperation on legal and police matters such as immigration control, and EU citizenship arrangements. These requirements were largely accepted by the EC heads of government meeting in Edinburgh (Scotland) on December 11–12.

Having headed five minority center-right governments since 1982, Schlüter resigned in January 1993 after a judicial report had found that he had misled Parliament in 1989 over government policy on the admission of the relatives of Tamil refugees from Sri Lanka already in Denmark (the so-called "Tamilgate" scandal). The SD leader, Poul Nyrup RASMUSSEN, thereupon formed Denmark's first majority government since 1971, securing the agreement of the RV, CD, and KrF for a center-left coalition that commanded a one-seat majority in Parliament. The new administration promptly called a further referendum on the Maastricht Treaty on May 18, 1993. This time the Danish version of the instrument, including the opt-outs agreed upon in Edinburgh, received endorsement by 56.8 percent of those voting.

Despite government efforts to combat unemployment and to reform tax policies, economic progress was slow, and the coalition parties performed poorly in local elections in November 1993. Rasmussen encountered further difficulty in February 1994, when the newly appointed social affairs minister, Bente JUNCKER, was obliged to resign over a leak of controversial and unsubstantiated information about a political opponent.

She subsequently left the Center Democrats to sit as an independent in the *Folketing* (Parliament), where the government was thus reduced to technical minority status with 89 of the 179 seats.

The ruling coalition suffered an overall reversal in the June 1994 European Parliament balloting, at which two specifically anti-European lists obtained over a quarter of the votes cast. The same pattern was apparent in national balloting on September 21, although government losses were less than some had predicted. While the KrF failed to surmount the 2 percent barrier, the SD remained the largest party, with 34.6 percent. The opposition Liberals made significant gains, overtaking the Conservatives as the second leading party, but that advance was partially offset by entry of the Red-Green Unity List into the *Folketing*. The outcome was the appointment on September 26 of a minority center-left coalition, headed by Rasmussen and consisting of his SD, the RV, and the CD. Although the government as formed commanded only 76 seats (including one of the two Greenland deputies) in the 179-member *Folketing*, it could rely on the external support of the Socialist People's Party (*Socialistisk Folkeparti*—SF) and the Red-Green Unity List on most issues. Its position was nevertheless precarious, faced by a center-right opposition with a seat total of 83.

The Rasmussen administration in 1995 set as its main priority the reduction of unemployment, which was still running at around 11 percent in a country that had enjoyed full employment for most of the postwar period. However, the government's scope for concrete policy action continued to be circumscribed by an equal commitment to preserving the parity of the krone within the unofficial narrow band of the EU's exchange rate mechanism. Meanwhile, the center-right opposition contended that the government was shirking necessary pruning of Denmark's generous welfare provision and of the extensive rights and benefits accorded to Danish labor.

The government's position became even more tenuous in mid-December 1996 when the two CD cabinet members resigned their posts after the CD had unsuccessfully opposed the terms on which the 1997 budget secured parliamentary endorsement. Meanwhile, Denmark's relations with its self-governing dependencies, the Faroe Islands and Greenland, remained strained as the result of economic problems in the former and security issues in the latter. (Recent opinion polls had shown significantly increased support for greater autonomy in both territories.)

The SD maintained its front-runner status in the November 1997 municipal elections, although its percent of the vote dropped slightly as the far-right, flatly "anti-immigration" Danish People's Party (*Dansk Folkeparti*—DFp) made a strong electoral debut with nearly 7 percent support. In February 1998 Rasmussen announced that legislative elections would be held on March 11, some six months early, in part at least to prepare for the upcoming national referendum on the EU's recent Amsterdam Treaty (see article on EU for details). Surprising many observers, the SD and its coalition allies once again managed to secure a narrow 90-seat majority in the *Folketing* with the support of two deputies from the Faroes and Greenland. Rasmussen reshuffled his cabinet on March 23, although incumbents were reappointed to most major portfolios. Subsequently, in a referendum on May 28, the Danish voters endorsed the Amsterdam Treaty by a 55–45 percent vote, although on September 28, 2000, in a major reversal for the government, they rejected participation in the EU's euro zone by 53–47 percent.

In what proved to be a disastrous political miscalculation, Prime Minister Nyrup Rasmussen called an early election on October 31, 2001, expecting to ride a recent surge in popularity to another term. Instead, voters on November 20 awarded a plurality of 56 seats to the center-right Liberal Party, and on November 27 Liberal leader Anders Fogh RASMUSSEN announced formation of a minority government in coalition with the KF, which had won 16 seats. Eighteen seats short of a majority in the 179-seat *Folketing*, Fogh Rasmussen was forced to rely on external support from the DFp, which held 22 legislative seats.

In elections held on February 8, 2005, Danish voters sent a mixed message to the government. The ruling center-right Liberal Party won 52 seats in the *Folketing*, a significant drop from the 56 seats it won in 2001. The largest opposition party (the SD) also lost ground, dropping from 52 seats to 47 seats. The parties that made gains were smaller, right-wing parties. Both the DFp and the Conservative People's Party picked up 2 seats, winning 24 and 18 seats, respectively.

While Danish voters seem to be calling for a more conservative approach, especially on economic and immigration issues, they nevertheless ensured that Prime Minister Rasmussen would be the first Liberal leader to win a second consecutive term of office. Despite the strong showing by the DFp, a coalition partner, Rasmussen ruled out a formal role for the party in his government because the DFp did not back Denmark's closer integration into the EU, a major aim of the Liberal Party.

Constitution and Government

The constitution adopted in 1953 abolished the upper house of Parliament while leaving intact the main outlines of the Danish political system. Executive power, nominally vested in the monarch, is actually exercised by a cabinet responsible to the *Folketing*, a legislative body that includes representatives from the Faroe Islands and Greenland. The judicial system is headed by a 15-member Supreme Court and encompasses two high courts, local courts, specialized courts for labor and maritime affairs, and an ombudsman who is appointed by the *Folketing*. Judges are appointed by the Crown on the advice of the minister of justice.

Under a major reform enacted in 1970, the former 25 regional districts were reduced to 14 counties (*amtskommuner*), each governed by an elected council (*amtsiåd*) and mayor (*amtsborgmester*). The counties in turn are divided into 277 local administrative units, each featuring an elected communal council (*kommunalbestyrelse*) and mayor (*borgmester*). The city of Copenhagen is governed by a city council (*borger repræsentation*) and an executive consisting of a head mayor (*over-borgmester*), five deputy mayors (*borgmestie*), and five aldermen (*rådmænd*).

Foreign Relations

Danish foreign policy, independent but thoroughly Western in outlook, emphasizes support for the United Nations, the economic integration of Europe, and regional cooperation through the Nordic Council and other Scandinavian programs. Formerly a member of the European Free Trade Association (EFTA), Denmark was admitted to the EC on January 1, 1973; dissatisfaction with fishing agreements led to the withdrawal of newly autonomous Greenland from the EC in 1982, followed by sporadic conflict with individual community members, particularly the United Kingdom, over North Sea fishing rights. Although committed to collective security, the Danish government long resisted pressure by NATO to increase its defense appropriations in real terms; indeed, responding to widespread popular agitation, the Social Democrats and their allies were able, in May 1984, to force legislation making Denmark the first NATO member to withdraw completely from missile deployment. Danish voters in February 1986 endorsed (by popular referendum) continued participation in the EC; however, leftist opposition parties in the *Folketing* succeeded in enacting measures to further reduce effective involvement in NATO, including, in April 1988, the passage of legislation reiterating a long-standing (but unenforced) ban on visits by nuclear-equipped vessels. While the EC issue dominated Danish foreign (and domestic) policy in 1992–1993, the government continued to attach importance to Nordic and other regional cooperation. In March 1992 it became a founding member of the ten-nation Council of the Baltic Sea States, while in May it was an enthusiastic signatory of the European Economic Area (EEA) treaty between the EC and most EFTA countries.

The 2003 invasion of Iraq was a contentious issue in Denmark as it was in much of Europe. The *Folketing* voted in March 2003 to send troops to Iraq, with 93 of the *Folketing*'s 179 members voting for the measure. Denmark contributed a warship, a submarine, and 160 troops to the 2003 attack on Iraq. After the downfall of the Saddam Hussein regime, a 460-member Danish peacekeeping force

was sent to Iraq and in 2005 Denmark had approximately 500 troops stationed there. Despite deep divisions within parliament and among the public over the decision to join the invasion of Iraq, however, the issue of the subsequent occupation of Iraq was not a particularly contentious one in Denmark.

On August 6, 2004, Denmark and Greenland signed a pact with the United States allowing the latter to upgrade its early warning radar facility at Thule. Helge Sander, science minister, announced in October 2004 that Demark is going to map the seabed north of Greenland to explore a geological case for claiming the North Pole for Denmark.

A referendum on the EU constitution was scheduled for September 27, 2005. The constitution is reportedly supported by more than four-fifths of the Danish parliament.

Denmark's relationship with many Islamic countries was seriously damaged when the *Jullands-Posten*, the country's largest-circulation newspaper, published political cartoons of caricatures of the Prophet Mohammed on Sept. 30, 2005. Many Muslims were upset by publication of the cartoons since depictions of the Prophet Mohammed are forbidden under Islamic religious law. On October 24, Prime Minister Rasmussen declined to meet with ten ambassadors from Islamic countries who were protesting the cartoons, saying that he neither possessed nor wanted the power to limit freedom of the press.

On January 26, 2006, Saudi Arabia withdrew its ambassador from Denmark. Libya followed suit by closing its embassy in Denmark on January 29. On February 5, rioting Muslims in Beirut set the Danish Embassy on fire. A boycott of Danish products quickly spread throughout the Middle East, seriously affecting sales for several Danish companies.

Current Issues

Three issues have dominated Danish politics in the past few years: full Danish participation in the EU, a sluggish domestic economy, and immigration. The prominence of these three issues went a long way toward explaining the results of the general election in February 2005, which returned the

Liberal Party to the head of government. The Liberal Party cautiously favored a tighter integration with the EU, and poll results indicate a majority of Danes agreed with that position. The Liberal Party was also generally pro-business and in favor of holding down taxes, a popular position in view of a limping economy.

However, no issue has dominated Danish attention as much as immigration. With international terrorism on the rise and concern growing that immigrants are a burden on an already generous social services system that Denmark is struggling to sustain in challenging economic times, many Danes have grown increasingly vocal in their opposition to current levels of immigration. In May 2002 the *Folketing* approved a new immigration law restricting the ability of Danes under the age of 25 to bring non-EU citizens into the country by marrying them. Under the new law, immigrants must also pay a deposit of $8,180 to be held against any claims made on the welfare system. Immigrants must also prove a "close attachment" to Denmark. In August 2002 the government followed up the new law with an offer of cash to Afghan asylum seekers who agreed to return home. In February 2004 Prime Minister Rasmussen detailed proposals to amend immigration laws to specifically restrict the entry of Muslim clerics. Imams would be required to prove they were educated, could support themselves, and were "worthy." The tightening of immigration laws and policies has had some effect. The number of asylum seekers entering Denmark was cut in half in 2002, from 12,512 in 2001 to 5,047 in 2002. In 2001, 6,263 noncitizens were granted permission to remain in Denmark, a number that was cut to 4,067 in 2002. Despite criticism of Denmark's changes in its immigration laws by the United Nations High Commissioner for Refugees and by the Council of Europe's human rights commissioner, recent polls continue to show public support for further limits on immigration, and the most recent general election saw an increase in public support for the Danish People's Party, which regularly calls for greater restrictions on immigration.

The international uproar over the publication of cartoons depicting the Prophet Mohammed has, if anything, further heightened public concerns over immigration. Approval ratings for Prime Minister Rasmussen—who has repeatedly declined to apologize for publication of the cartoons and who has argued for tighter restrictions on immigration—have remained above 50 percent, significantly higher than that of any opposition politician. In March 2006 the government indicated it would not press charges against the newspaper that first published the cartoons.

Political Parties

Government Parties

Liberal Party (*Venstre*—V). Founded in 1870 as the Agrarian Party but currently representing some trade and industrial groups as well as farmers, the Liberal Party (commonly referenced in Danish as *Venstre* [Left] rather than *Liberale Parti*) stands for individualism as opposed to socialism in industry and business, reduction of taxation through governmental economy, relaxation of economic restrictions, and adequate defense. Its parliamentary representation rose from 22 in 1988 to 29 in 1990, while the party was the main victor in the September 1994 national election, winning 23.3 percent of the vote and 42 seats, although it remained in opposition.

At the 2001 election the Liberals won 31 percent of the national vote and a plurality of 56 seats, permitting the party chair, Anders Fogh Rasmussen, to forge a center-right minority government on November 27. In the general election in February 2005, the Liberal Party won 29 percent of the vote and 52 seats in parliament, 4 fewer than it had won in the previous election. Nevertheless, the party's showing was strong enough to allow party leader and Prime Minister Rasmussen to win a second term in office at the head of a minority coalition government, with the support of the Conservative People's Party and the Danish People's Party.

Leaders: Anders Fogh RASMUSSEN (Prime Minister and Chair), Lars Løkke Rasmussen (Vice Chair), Jens Skipper RASMUSSEN (Secretary General).

Conservative People's Party (*Konservative Folkeparti*—KF). Founded in 1916 as an outgrowth of an earlier Conservative grouping (*Højre*), the KF mainly represents financial, industrial, and business groups. It supports adequate defense, protection of private property, sound fiscal policy, and lower taxation. Under the leadership of Poul SCHLÜTER, the party recovered from a low of 5.5 percent of the vote in 1975 to 14.5 percent in 1981, enabling Schlüter to form a center-right coalition in 1982, which remained in office for more than a decade. A further surge to 23.4 percent in 1984 was followed by a decline to 16 percent in 1990 and the resignation of Schlüter in January 1993.

The KF has not recovered from its decline in popularity in the early 1990s. In the 1998 general elections, in fact, the party lost 11 seats, winning a total of only 16, a loss attributed in part to support being drawn off by the emergence of the right-wing Danish People's Party. Nevertheless, since 2001 the party has been able to sustain a high profile in government as the junior partner in the coalition government led by the Liberal Party. The Conservative People's Party leader, Bendt Bendtsen, currently serves as Denmark's minister for economic and business affairs. In the 2005 general election, the Conservative Party marginally improved its representation, winning 10.3 percent of the vote and 18 seats in parliament.

Leader: Bendt BENDTSEN (Chair).

Government-Supportive Party

Danish People's Party (*Dansk Folkeparti*—DFp). The DFp was launched in October 1995 by dissident deputies of the right-wing Progress Party (FP), including former FP leader Pia Kjaersgaard. While espousing similar policies, the DFp is regarded as being to the right of the parent party. The nationalistic DFp, openly anti-immigrant, did very well in the November 1997 municipal elections and was one of the biggest winners in the March 1998 national election, more than tripling its parliamentary representation by adding 9 seats to the 4 it won in 1994. Its vote share rose to 12 percent in the November 2001 general election, at which it won 22 seats, making it the third-largest political party in Denmark. The party retained that position in the February 2005 general election, winning 24 seats. While the Danish People's Party disagrees with the ruling Liberal Party over the latter's support for increasing integration with the EU, the DFp has supported the government because of its efforts to restrict immigration.

Leaders: Pia KJAERSGAARD (Chair), Peter SKAARUP, (Deputy Chair).

Other Parliamentary Parties

Social Democratic Party (*Socialdemokratiet*—SD). Founded in 1871, the SD mainly represents industrial labor and advocates economic planning, full employment, extensive social security benefits, and environmental planning. The Social Democratic Party has been the ruling party of Denmark for most of the past 75 years. Most recently, the SD led the ruling government coalition from 1993 until 2001. In the 2005 elections the SD won 47 seats in the *Folketing*, a loss of 5 seats from the previous elections. The party nevertheless has the second-largest number of seats in parliament. On April 12, 2005, Helle Thorning-Schmidt, 38, was elected leader of the SD, becoming the first woman to head the party.

Leaders: Helle THORNING-SCHMIDT (Party Leader), Jens CHRISTIANSEN (Secretary General).

Socialist People's Party (*Socialistisk Folkeparti*—SF). The SF was formed in 1958 by former Communist Party chair Aksel LARSEN, who had disagreed with Moscow over the suppression of the 1956 Hungarian Revolution. Subsequently, the party advocated left-wing socialism independent of the Soviet Union, unilateral disarmament, opposition to NATO and Danish membership in the EC, and Nordic cooperation. It has often acted as an unofficial left wing of the SD, concentrating on influencing the platform and voting patterns of the larger party. Traditionally anti-EU, the party was split at its August 1997 congress when parliamentary leader Steen GADE resigned his post in order to campaign for ratification of the EU's

Amsterdam Treaty. In the February 2005 elections the Social People's Party attracted 6 percent of the vote and won 11 seats in the *Folketing*.

Leaders: Villy Søvndal (Chair), Jakob NØRHØJ (Deputy Chair).

Radical Liberal Party (*Det Radikale Venstre*—RV). Also characterized in English as a "Social Liberal" grouping, the RV was founded in 1905; it represents mainly small landowners and urban intellectual and professional elements. In domestic affairs, the party advocates strengthening of private enterprise in a social-liberal context; in foreign affairs, it is pacifist in outlook and has recently strengthened its formerly lukewarm pro-European stand. With a record of often joining or endorsing SD-led governments, it nevertheless supported the Schlüter KF-led coalition in 1982. Following the September 1987 election, (then) parliamentary leader Niels Helveg PETERSEN rebuffed Anker Jørgensen's appeal to realign with the Social Democratic and Socialist People's parties, thereby precluding the establishment of a new Socialist administration. The RV was awarded five cabinet posts in the 1988 Schlüter government, but withdrew from formal participation in 1990.

The party has attracted liberal voter support in the wake of the victory by the center-right parties in the 2001 elections. Most recently, the RV gained 8 seats in the February 2005 election, bringing its total to 17.

Leaders: Søren BALD (President), Marianne SAXTOFT (Vice President).

Red-Green Unity List (*Enhedslisten-De Rød-Grønne*). The Red-Green formation was launched in 1989 as a coalition of three left-wing/environmentalist groups: the VS and DKP (below) and the Trotskyist **Socialist Workers' Party** (*Socialistisk Arbejderparti*—SAP), the last led by Søren SONDERGAARD. The Maoist **Communist Workers' Party of Denmark** (*Danmarks Kommunistisk Arbejderparti*—DKA) joined the coalition in 1991. Strongly opposed to EU membership and the Maastricht process, the Unity List achieved a breakthrough in the September 1994 general election, winning 3.1 percent of the vote

and six seats. Officially, the party has no chair, but rather is directed by a 21-person collective leadership. The Unity List lost one of its six seats in the March 1998 elections with a vote share of 2.7 percent. It lost another in 2001, when its vote share totaled 2.4 percent. The party did significantly better in the February 2005 election, attracting 3.4 percent of the vote and increasing its seats in parliament to six. The party claims that Unity List members of the *Folketing* tithe a part of their parliamentary salary to the party to ensure that their net income is comparable to that of a skilled worker.

Left Socialist Party (*Venstresocialisterne*—VS). The VS split from the SF in 1967 and achieved representation in the legislature for the first time in 1968–1971. In 1984 the party's "revolutionary" wing, informally known as the "Leninist" faction, broke with the leadership over its unwillingness to organize cadres along traditional communist lines. Two members defected to the SF in July 1986. Subsequently, the party was weakened by growing factionalization, with the "Red Realists" favoring cooperation with the SF and the "Left Oppositionists" following a rigid Marxist-Leninist line. The VS has maintained a distinct identity within the Red-Green Unity List.

Leaders: Karen NYGARD, Henrik FOR-CHAMMER, Albert JENSEN. (There is no titular chair, the principal leadership being regarded as collective.)

Communist Party of Denmark (*Danmarks Kommunistiske Parti*—DKP). The DKP was formed in 1919, achieved parliamentary representation in 1932, and participated in the immediate postwar coalition government. The party was greatly weakened by the 1956 Hungarian revolt and the schism that subsequently led to the formation of the Socialist People's Party. Its representation in the *Folketing* following the 1973 election was its first since 1956. However, it lost all of its seven legislative seats at the 1979 balloting. As a member of the Red-Green Unity List coalition, the DKP remains a loose network of militants rather than a full-fledged party. In 1990 a Marxist-Leninist faction of the group opposed to participation in the Unity List formed the **Communist Forum** (*Kommunistisk Forum*), which became the **Communist Party in Denmark** (*Kommunistisk Parti i Danmark—KPiD*) in November 1993 under the leadership of Betty Frydensbjerg CARLSSON.

Other Parties

Christian Democrats (*Kristelig Demokraterne—KD*). The KD was originally formed as the Christian People's Party (*Kristeligt Folkeparti—KrF*) in 1970 in opposition to abortion and liberalization of pornography regulations. The party achieved representation in the *Folketing* for the first time in 1973 and placed two representatives in the center-left coalition formed in January 1993. The KrF vote slipped to 1.1 percent in the June 1994 European elections (insufficient for representation) and took only 1.8 percent in the September national balloting, thereby exiting from both the *Folketing* and the government. The KrF returned to the *Folketing* following the March 1998 election, in which it won four seats on a vote share of 2.4 percent. It retained all four in 2001.

The KrF changed its name to Christian Democrats in October 2003 in an attempt to enhance its public image, prompting the resignation of party chair Jann SJURSEN. He was replaced by Marianne Karlsmose. The KD won only 1.7 percent of the vote in the 2005 general election, which was not enough to win any seats in parliament.

Leader: Marianne KARLSMOSE (President), Sten F. MORTENSEN (Vice President), Kristian ØHRSTRØM (Vice President).

Center Democrats (*Centrum-Demokraterne—CD*). The CD grouping was formed in November 1973 by the dissident Social Democrat Erhard JAKOBSEN to protest "leftist" tendencies in the government and plans for increased taxation, in the belief that traditional "Left" and "Right" political distinctions were no longer appropriate in contemporary Denmark. The party scored an electoral breakthrough in the 1973 balloting (14 seats) and was involved in the center-right coalition government in 1982–1988. It also joined the SD-led government in 1993 before resigning over policy differences in December 1996. Campaign-ing in the March 1998 election on a platform of protecting welfare programs and accommodating refugees and immigrants, the CD added three seats to the five it had won in 1994. In 2001 it won only 1.8 percent of the votes and no seats. In 2005 the party was only able to attract 1 percent of the vote, and again failed to win a seat in parliament.

Leaders: Bjarne MØGELHØJ (President), Henning BORCHERT-JØGENSEN (Vice President).

Danish political movements that contested the 1994, 1999, and 2004 European Parliament elections included the **June Movement** (*Juni Bevægelsen*), led by Jens-Peter BONDE and named after the month of the 1992 initial rejection of the Maastricht Treaty; it won 15.2 percent of the vote and two seats. The **People's Movement against the European Union** (*Folkesbevægelsen mod EU*) took 10.3 percent of the vote and two seats (against 18.9 percent and four seats in 1989) in the 1994 European Parliament balloting and one seat in 1999 and 2004.

Legislature

The *Folketinget* (also frequently rendered as *Folketing*) is a unicameral legislature whose members are elected every four years (subject to dissolution) by universal suffrage under a modified proportional representation system. Of its present membership of 179, 135 are elected in 17 metropolitan districts, with 40 additional seats being divided among those parties that have secured at least 2 percent of the vote but whose district representation does not accord with their overall strength. In addition, the Faroe Islands and Greenland are allotted two representatives each. In the most recent election of February 8, 2005, the Liberal Party won 52 seats; the Social Democratic Party, 47; the Conservative People's Party, 18; the Social Liberal Party, 17; the Socialist People's Party, 11; and the Red-Green Unity List, 6. The Faroes are represented by members of the islands' People's Party and Republican Party, while Greenland's members belong to the Forward and Eskimo Brotherhood parties (see Related Territories, below).

President: Christian MEJDAHL.

Cabinet

As of May 1, 2005

Prime Minister	Anders Fogh Rasmussen (V)

Ministers

Culture	Brian Mikkelsen (KF)
Defense	Søren Gade (V)
Development Cooperation	Ulla Tørnaes (CV) [f]
Economic Affairs and Business Affairs	Bendt Bendtsen (KF)
Education and Ecclesiastical Affairs	Bertel Haarder (V)
Employment	Claus Hjort Frederiksen (V)
Environment and Nordic Cooperation	Connie Hedegaard (KF)
Family and Consumer Affairs	Lars Barfoed (KF)
Finance	Thor Pedersen (V)
Food, Agriculture, and Fisheries	Hans Christian Schmidt (V)
Foreign Affairs	Per Stig Møller (KF)
Interior and Health	Lars Løkke Rasmussen (V)
Justice	Lene Espersen (KF) [f]
Refugees, Immigration, and Integration Affairs	Rikke Hvilshøj (V) [f]
Science, Technology, and Innovation	Helge Sander (V)
Social Affairs and Gender Equality	Eva Kjer Hansen (V) [f]
Taxation	Kristian Jensen (V)
Transport and Energy	Flemming Hansen (KF)

[f] = female

Communications

Press

Freedom of the press is constitutionally guaranteed, and newspapers and magazines are privately published. Many newspapers reflect political party viewpoints, although most are not directly owned by a party. The following newspapers are published in Copenhagen, unless otherwise noted: *Ekstra Bladet* (159,500 weekdays, 192,900 Sunday), independent Radical Liberal; *BT* (149,910 weekdays, 190,053 Sunday), independent Conservative; *Politiken* (153,000 weekdays, 205,000 Sunday), independent Radical Liberal; *Morgenavisen Jyllands-Posten* (Viby, 172,000 weekdays, 269,000 Sunday), independent; *Berlingske Tidende* (160,000 weekdays, 195,000 Sunday), independent Conservative; *Erhvervs-Bladet* (110,000 daily); *Jydske Vestkysten* (Esbjerg, 94,234 weekdays, 106,157 Sunday); *Ålborg Stiftstidende* (Ålborg, 72,000 weekdays, 92,000 Sunday), independent; *Fyens Stiftsti-dende* (Odense, 66,000 weekdays, 98,000 Sunday), independent; *Århus Stiftstidende* (Århus, 72,743 weekdays, 93,772 Sunday), independent; *Det Fri Aktuelt* (42,262 daily), Social Democratic; *Borsen* (42,700 daily).

News Agencies

The domestic agency, owned by the Danish newspapers, is *Ritzaus Bureau;* numerous foreign bureaus also maintain offices in Copenhagen.

Broadcasting and Computing

Radio and television stations have traditionally been controlled by the government-owned, non-commercial *Danmarks Radio* (now *DR Radio*). The monopoly was terminated by the *Folketing* in 1986, which sanctioned the immediate establishment of independent local radio broadcasting, with a nationwide commercial television channel commencing operation in late 1988, followed by a satellite television station in 1991. There were approximately 5.0 million television receivers and 3.7 million personal computers serving 2.9 million Internet users in 2003.

Intergovernmental Representation

Ambassador to the U.S.
Friis Arne PETERSEN

U.S. Ambassador to Denmark
James P. CAIN

Permanent Representative to the UN
Ellen Margrethe LØJ

IGO Memberships (Non-UN)
AC, ADB, AfDB, BIS, CBSS, CERN, CEUR, EBRD, EIB, ESA, EU, Eurocontrol, IADB, IEA, Interpol, IOM, NATO, NC, NIB, OECD, OSCE, PCA, WCO, WTO

Related Territories

Faroe Islands (Faerøerne, or Føroyar).

The Faroe Islands (numbering 18) in the North Atlantic have been under Danish administration since 1380. Their area is 540 square miles (1,399 sq. km.), the population is 51,000 (2005E), and the capital is Tórshavn (population 16,900 [2001E]). The principal language is Faroese, with most inhabitants also Danish-speaking. Fishing and sheep raising are the most important ingredients of the islands' economy, which in 1992–1993 entered an unprecedented crisis due to the disappearance of fish stocks as well as the collapse of a 1980s investment boom and resultant heavy indebtedness.

The islands, which send two representatives to the *Folketing*, constitute a self-governing territory within the Danish state. A 32-member local legislature (*Løgting*) elects an administrative

body (*Landsstýri*) headed by a chair (*løgmadur*). The Crown is represented by a high commissioner (*ríkisumbodsmadur*). The islands have been represented on the Nordic Council since 1969.

The principal political groups are the **Union Party** (*Sambandsflokkurin*), which urges the retention of close links to metropolitan Denmark; the **Social Democratic Party** (*Javnarflokkurin*); the conservative-liberal **People's Party** (*Fólkaflokkurin*); the left-wing **Republican Party** (*Tjóveldisflokkurin*), which advocates secession from Denmark; the **Home Rule Party** (*Sjálvstýrisflokkurin*); the **Progressive and Fisheries Party** [and] **Christian People's Party** (*Framburs–Fiskivinnuflokkurin Kristeligt Folkeparti*); the **Labor Front** (*Verkmannafylkingin*), founded in 1994 by dissident Social Democrats and trade unionists; and the **Center Party** (*Miflokkurin*).

At elections on July 7, 1994, all of the above parties won representation in the islands' 32-member legislature. The leading formation was the Union Party (eight seats), whose leader was sworn in on September 15 as prime minister of a center-left coalition that also included the Social Democrats, the Labor Front, and the Home Rule Party. The previous coalition had consisted of the Social Democratic, Republican, and Home Rule parties.

At the national election of September 21, 1994, the two Faroe Islands' seats in the Danish *Folketing* were won by candidates of the Union and People's parties. In 1996 the Social Democratic Party was replaced in the government coalition by the People's Party while the Social Democratic Party and the People's Party each secured one seat in the March 1998 Danish *Folketing* balloting.

In the legislative elections of April 30, 1998, the dominant issue was the islanders' growing demand for sovereignty, which was embraced in varying degrees by candidates across the political spectrum. Anti-Copenhagen sentiment was inflamed by continuing controversy over the Faroese government's 1993 purchase of a failing Danish-owned bank, one of only two on the islands, whose condition the Faroese alleged had been misrepresented by the Danes. The Republican Party led the 1998 balloting, winning 8 seats with a vote share of 23.8 percent, followed closely by the Social Democratic Party and the People's Party. Anfinn KALLSBERG, leader of the People's Party, subsequently formed an 18-seat coalition government consisting of his own party, the Republicans, and the Home Rule Party. In August the new government said it would seek independence while remaining under the Danish monarchy and monetary system, hoping to submit independence to a referendum.

Meanwhile, after many years of talks, the failure of island and British negotiators to settle a boundary dispute over a potentially large oil and gas field on the ocean floor, in the so-called White Zone in the North Atlantic, prevented the Faroese from going forward with exploration of the site. The government hopes to end the islands' dependence on the fishing industry, which accounts for about 95 percent of exports, as well as reduce unemployment (12 percent in 1997) and the need for subsidies from Denmark, which provides about one-third of the islands' government budget.

In May 1999 representatives from the Faroe Islands, Denmark, and the United Kingdom reached a settlement of the dispute over the maritime border after 21 years of negotiations. The islands were granted sovereignty over some 40 square miles of the area in question, further fueling the drive for independence in view of the potential new oil wealth. However, the Danish government in March 2000 hardened its stance on the independence question, announcing that Danish subsidies (estimated at $110 million per year) would cease 4 years after independence rather than being phased out over a 15–20 year transition period as proposed by Faroese leaders. In early February 2001 the Faroese government announced May 26 as the date for a referendum on the issue of full sovereignty by 2012, but in March the vote was called off because of declining support in the face of Copenhagen's firm position on the subsidies.

In January 2003 government officials from the Faroe Islands and Denmark began talks aimed at transferring responsibility in several policy areas to the Faroese government. On June 26, 2003, the talks culminated in the signing of an agreement that transferred authority over the Faroese judicial system, police, and civil law. Responsibility for security for the Faroe Islands remains with Denmark. In December 2003 the governing coalition collapsed when the Republican Party withdrew its support as the result of charges of an accounting scandal involving the administration of Prime Minister Anfinn Kallsberg (People's Party). On January 20, 2004, parliamentary elections resulted in the anti-independence Union Party winning 23.7 percent of the vote. While this was the highest percentage won by any party, it was down 2.3 percent from the Union Party's showing in the 2002 elections. On February 3, 2004, the Union Party (SF), the Social Democratic Party (JF), and the People's Party (FF) formed a new coalition government with Social Democrat Joannes Eidesgaard as prime minister. The three parties together hold 21 seats in the 32-member parliament.

High Commissioner: Birgit KLEIS.

Prime Minister: Joannes EIDESGAARD (Social Democratic Party).

Greenland (Grønland, or Kalaallit Nunaat).

Encompassing 840,000 square miles (2,175,600 sq. km.), including an extensive ice cover, Greenland is the second-largest island in the world, after Australia. The population, which is largely Eskimo, totals approximately 59,000 (2005E), with residents of the capital, Nuuk (Godthåb), accounting for some 15,200. The indigenous language is Greenlandic. Fishing, mining, and seal hunting are the major economic activities. A number of oil concessions were awarded to international consortia in 1975, but most were subsequently abandoned.

Although under Danish control since the 14th century, the island was originally colonized by Norsemen and only through an apparent oversight was not detached from Denmark along with Norway at the Congress of Vienna in 1815. It became an integral part of the Danish state in 1953 and was granted internal autonomy, effective May 1, 1979, on the basis of a referendum held January 17. The island continues, however, to elect two representatives to the Danish *Folketing*. After achieving autonomy, the island government sought compensation from the United States for the 1953 relocation of indigenous villagers during the construction of U.S. airbases in the northwest. Also persistently controversial was the crash in 1968 of an American B-52 bomber near the Thule base and the eventual disclosure that it had been carrying nuclear weapons, in breach of the Danish ban on nuclear weapons on its territory.

At a pre-autonomy general election held April 4, 1979, the socialist **Forward** (*Siumut*) party obtained 13 of 21 seats in the new parliament (*Landsting*), and *Siumut* leader Jonathan Motzfeldt subsequently formed a five-member executive (*Landsstyre*). Other participating groups included the **Solidarity** (*Atássut*) party, led by Lars CHEMNITZ, which obtained the remaining 8 seats, and the pro-independence **Eskimo Brotherhood** (*Inuit Ataqatigiit*—IA).

At the balloting of April 1983 for an enlarged *Landsting* of 26 members, the *Siumut* and *Atássut* parties won 12 seats each, Motzfeldt again forming a government with the support of two IA representatives. A further election on June 6, 1984, necessitated by a nonconfidence vote two months earlier, yielded a formal coalition of the *Siumut* and IA parties, which had obtained 11 and 3 seats, respectively. However, a disagreement ensued regarding the prime minister's alleged "passivity" over the projected installation of new radar equipment at the U.S. airbase at Thule, forcing another early election on May 26, 1987, the results of which were *Siumut* and *Atássut*, 11 seats each; *Inuit Ataqatigiit*, 4; and a new political party, *Issittup Partiia* (Polar Party), representing the business community and fishing industry, 1. On June 9 Motzfeldt succeeded in forming a new administration based on the previous coalition.

The "Thule affair" returned to prominence in January 1995, when the metropolitan government announced a parliamentary inquiry into the 1968 crash, amid continuing demands from Greenlanders for compensation for its alleged consequences, including a high local incidence of cancer. Controversy intensified in July when the Danish foreign minister disclosed that as early as 1957 the U.S. government had informed the then prime minister that nuclear weapons were present in Greenland and that he had raised no objection.

In September 1997 former Prime Minister Motzfeldt returned to the premiership, Johansen, a strong proponent of the exploitation of Greenland's mineral and oil wealth, having moved into the business sector. In the Danish *Folketing* balloting of March 11, 1998, *Siumut and Atássut* each won 1 seat, with the *Siumut* deputy becoming allied with the government coalition. In the *Landsting* election of February 16, 1999, *Siumut* won 11 seats, *Atássut,* 8; the IA, 7; and independents, 5. Among the major issues were calls for more autonomy from Denmark, proposed adoption of the euro should Denmark join the EU's Economic and Monetary Union, and oil exploration. Following the election, *Siumut* and the IA formed a new coalition government under the leadership of Motzfeldt, *Atássut* returning to opposition.

In September 1999 Danish Prime Minister Rasmussen formally apologized to Greenland's indigenous population for the forced relocation of villagers in 1953 in connection with the construction of U.S. bases. New controversy developed in 2000 when Russia objected to U.S. plans to build a radar station in Greenland.

While autonomy remained an ongoing issue in the country's politics, domestic issues were highlighted in the December 3, 2002, parliamentary elections. The new Democratic Party (*Demokratüt*), which stressed issues of improving Inuit education and relieving the housing shortage, received 15.6 percent of the vote and won 5 seats in the *Landsting*. The biggest winner of the election—in which fully 75 percent of the country's 38,000 voters cast ballots—was the ruling Forward Party (*Siumut*), which won 10 seats and formed a new coalition government under Prime Minister Hans Enoksen. The left-wing Eskimo Brotherhood Party (*Inuit Ataqatigüt*) won 8 seats and the pro-independence Solidarity Party (*Atussut*) won 7 seats.

In May 2003 Greenland and Denmark signed an agreement stipulating that in exchange for Greenland's support for modernization of the U.S. radar station at Thule, Greenland would be consulted on all foreign affairs matters relating to the island. In September 2003, however, things took a different turn when the Forward Party ended its coalition with the conservative Solidarity Party and formed a new government in coalition with the Eskimo Brotherhood Party. The Eskimo Brotherhood Party is pro-independence and opposes upgrading of the U.S. radar station at Thule.

High Commissioner: Peter LAURITEEN.
Prime Minister: Hans ENOKSEN (Siumit).

ESTONIA

REPUBLIC OF ESTONIA

Eesti Vabariik

Note: Toomas Hendrik Ilves (Social Democratic Party) was elected president on September 23, 2006, defeating incumbent president Arnold Rüütel (People's Union of Estonia) with 174 votes from the 347-member electoral college. The election was decided by the electoral college after three rounds of voting in Parliament failed to give either candidate the two-thirds majority (68 votes) required for election.

The Country

The northernmost of the three former Soviet Baltic republics, Estonia is bordered on the north by the Gulf of Finland, on the east by Russia, and on the south by Latvia. As of January 1, 2005, 68.5 percent of the population was Estonian, 25.7 percent Russian, 2.1 percent Ukrainian, 1.2 percent Belarusan, and 0.8 percent Finnish. During 1979–1989 the number of ethnic Estonians dropped by 3.2 percent, and in June 1990 the government established quotas for the admission of "foreign citizens." (In 1998–1999, largely due to Estonia's efforts to be admitted to the European Union [EU], the citizenship requirements were eased.) The 2000 census showed that only 29.2 percent of the population pertained to a specific religious faith, the vast majority of whom were Christian, either Lutheran (46.4 percent of religious persons) or Orthodox Christian (43.8 percent). More than a third professed having no religious affiliation (34.1 percent), while another 14.6 percent could not define a specific religious affiliation.

The manufacturing sector provides about 16 percent of the country's GDP, with agriculture, forestry, and fishing contributing 3.5 percent and wholesale and retail trade accounting for 11.5 percent of GDP. Tallinn is supplied with gas extracted from extensive deposits of oil shale. Still, Estonia is a net importer of gas from Russia. The country is well endowed with peat, some of which is used for the generation of electricity, and with phosphate, from which superphosphate is refined.

Estonia in June 1992 became the first former Soviet republic to abandon the ruble in favor of its own national currency, the kroon. The immediate impact of the action was to slow the rate of inflation from over 1,000 percent to 90 percent in 1993,

Political Status: Absorption of independent state by the Soviet Union on August 6, 1940, repudiated by Estonian Supreme Council on March 30, 1990; resumption of full sovereignty declared August 20, 1991, and accepted by USSR State Council on September 6; present constitution approved in referendum of June 28, 1992.

Area: 17,462 sq. mi. (45,227 sq. km.).

Population: 1,370,000 (2000C); 1,346,000 (2005E).

Major Urban Centers (2005E): TALLINN (395,000), Tartu (101,000), Narva (68,000).

Official Language: Estonian.

Monetary Unit: Kroon (official rate July 1, 2006: 12.24 krooni = $1US). Pegged at one-eighth of a Deutsche mark, the kroon was introduced on June 20, 1992.

President: (*See headnote.*) Arnold RÜÜTEL (People's Union of Estonia); elected by electoral college vote on September 21, 2001, and sworn in for a five-year term on October 8, succeeding Lennart MERI.

Prime Minister: Andrus ANSIP (Estonian Reform Party); nominated by the president on March 31, 2005, following the resignation of Juhan PARTS (Union for the Republic) on March 24 in response to the adoption by the Estonian Parliament (*Riigikogu*) of a nonconfidence motion against the administration's justice minister; sworn in (along with new government) on April 13.

although real GDP plunged by 26.3 percent during the year (as contrasted with declines of 12.6 percent in 1991 and 3.6 percent in 1990), in part because of a shortfall in oil and other needed supplies from neighboring Russia.

Under the influence of free-market reforms introduced in 1992 as well as the return of most of the "Baltic gold" held by the Bank of England and other Western depositaries since the Soviet takeover in 1940, signs of recovery began to emerge in mid-1993, and Estonia subsequently became one of the best-performing transition economies. Real GDP growth reached 10.4 percent in 1997, but in 1998 growth slowed to 5.0 percent, in part due to the effects of the Russian financial crisis. Foreign investment reached a new high in 1998, and, for the first time since the government adopted policies designed to reorient the economy toward the EU, a majority of exports went to EU countries (led by Sweden and Finland). Meanwhile, exports to Russia declined to 13 percent of the total.

Estonia recorded an economic contraction of 0.7 percent in 1999, the most damaging factor being export shortfalls caused by the regional impact of the Russian crisis. However, the economy subsequently performed extremely well (7.3 percent growth in 2000, 6.5 percent in 2001, and 6.0 percent in 2002), earning the Estonian government high marks from both the EU and the International Monetary Fund (IMF) for its economic policies. On the negative side, unemployment stood at 10.3 percent in 2002 (down from 13.7 percent in 2000). Among the fiscal issues facing the administration were expected increases for defense expenditures necessitated by Estonia's accession to the North Atlantic Treaty Organization (NATO) in April 2004. More recently, the Estonian economy has shown continued improvement, with real annual GDP growth rates of 6.7, 7.8, and 9.8 percent, respectively, from 2003 through 2005. Also, by the fourth quarter of 2006 the unemployment rate had fallen to 7.0 percent, while the inflation rate had risen to 4.2 percent for the 12 months through February 2006. Higher inflation necessitated postponing the planned adoption of the euro (which requires inflation below 3.0 percent) from 2007 to 2008. Nevertheless, on May 9, 2006, the Estonian Parliament (*Riigikogu*) ratified the EU Constitution.

Government and Politics

Political Background

Ruled by the Livonian Knights for the greater part of the 13th to 15th centuries and by Sweden until its defeat by Peter the Great in the Great Northern War of 1700–1721, Estonia was granted local autonomy by Russia in April 1917. A declaration of independence in February 1918 was followed by German occupation, but the country's sovereign status was recognized by the Versailles peace treaty of June 28, 1919, and by the Soviet-Estonian Tartu treaty of February 2, 1920. In September 1921 Estonia was admitted to the League of Nations.

In March 1934, under a new constitution adopted two months earlier, Estonia succumbed to the virtual dictatorship of Konstantin PÄTS. In February 1936 the 1934 instrument was revoked, and Estonia formally returned to a democratic system under a basic law of July 29, 1937, that provided for a presidency (to which Päts was elected in April 1938) and a two-chambered parliament. In October 1939 the country was forced to accept Soviet military bases, and on August 6, 1940, it was incorporated into the USSR under a secret protocol of the German-Soviet nonaggression pact of August 23, 1939. German occupation in 1941–1945 was followed by the restoration of Estonia's status as a Soviet republic.

On November 12, 1989, the Estonian Supreme Soviet unilaterally annulled the 1940 annexation, and in February 1990 it abolished provisions in its constitution that accorded a "leading role" to the Communist Party. On March 30 what had become styled as the Supreme Council called for eventual independence, and on May 8 it repudiated the designation "Estonian Soviet Socialist Republic" in favor of the earlier "Republic of Estonia." In February 1991 ethnic Estonians conducted private balloting for a "Congress of Estonia," and a referendum on March 3 yielded a 77.8 percent vote in favor of independence; a declaration to such effect on August 20 was accepted by the USSR Supreme Soviet on September 6.

At legislative balloting on March 18, 1990, a majority of seats had been won by proindependence groups, notably the Estonian Popular Front (*Eesti Rahvarinne*), whose chair, Edgar SAVISAAR, was named prime minister on April 3. Savisaar's appointment had been preceded on March 29 by the reappointment of Arnold RÜÜTEL as legislative chair (de facto president of the republic).

Savisaar resigned on January 23, 1992, after the government had failed to win enough legislative votes to support a state of emergency for coping with post-Soviet food and energy shortages. On January 30 the Supreme Council approved the formation of a new coalition administration, with Tiit VÄHI as caretaker prime minister. In general elections on September 20, Rüütel won a substantial plurality (42.2 percent) of the votes cast in presidential balloting, although in the legislative returns his Secure Home (*Kindel Kodu*) grouping ran second to the Fatherland ("Pro Patria") National Coalition (*Rahvuslik Koonderakond Ismaa*—RKEI), which supported Lennart MERI. Since neither presidential candidate had secured a majority, the choice was constitutionally assigned to the legislature, where a three-party nationalist alignment on October 5 endorsed Meri by a narrow margin. On October 21 a coalition government of the RKEI, the Moderates, and the Estonian National Independence Party was sworn in under the premiership of the RKEI's Mart LAAR. The goals of the new administration included the reinforcement of Estonian statehood, defense of democracy, economic stabilization, the creation of environmental and social guarantees necessary for the development of a market economy, the restoration of a civil society, and integration into Europe.

Following the appointment of a new economy minister in January 1993, Estonia experienced an economic upturn, during which the government's popularity was also enhanced among ethnic Estonians by the passage in June of nationality legislation effectively defining ethnic Russians as foreigners. President Meri delayed signing the measure to give time for the Council of Europe and the Conference on (later Organization for) Security and Cooperation in Europe (CSCE/OSCE) to examine its content. The law as finally enacted in July incorporated clarifications of the social security rights of ethnic Russians and dropped a requirement that foreigners' residence permits had to be renewed every five years. Local referenda on July 16–17, in which the predominantly ethnic Russian inhabitants of the towns of Narva and Sillamae voted in favor of autonomy, were declared illegal by the Estonian authorities.

On November 15, 1993, the government survived a parliamentary no-confidence motion, but in 1994 pressure mounted on Laar, who admitted to having an abrasive personal style. His fate was sealed when on September 2 the president of the Bank of Estonia, Siim KALLAS, revealed that in 1992 the prime minister had secretly ordered the sale of 2 billion rubles to the breakaway Russian republic of Chechnya, in contravention of an agreement with the IMF that the rubles would be transferred to the Russian central bank. On September 26 a no-confidence motion was carried with the support of 60 deputies, and Laar was replaced on October 20 by Andres TARAND, theretofore nonparty environment minister, who was endorsed by the legislature on October 27 and formed a moderately reshuffled government in early November.

Parliamentary elections on March 5, 1995, gave Estonian voters an opportunity to pass judgment on recent political events. The outcome was a humiliating defeat for the Pro Patria alliance, while the Moderates alliance (endorsed by Prime Minister Tarand) also lost ground. The main victor, with a plurality of 41 seats, was the relatively conservative alliance known as the Coalition Party and Rural Union (*Koonderakonna ja Maarahva Ühendus—* KMÜ), headed by the 1992 caretaker prime minister, Tiit Vähi, who on April 12 formed a new coalition government of the KMÜ and Edgar Savisaar's Estonian Center Party (*Eesti Keskerabond—* K). Prime Minister Vähi took pains to deny that his government was dominated by ex-Communists and asserted that it would continue the promarket reforms of its predecessors. Six months later Savisaar was dismissed as interior minister over allegations that he had authorized secret tape-recordings of the recent coalition negotiations. When the Center Party backed Savisaar, Vähi tendered the resignation of the whole government and proceeded to form a new majority coalition in which the Estonian Reform Party (*Eesti Reformierakond—*RE), led by Kallas, replaced the Center Party.

Allegations that President Meri's sympathies inclined toward Moscow on bilateral issues underscored contentious presidential balloting in the *Ri-*

igikogu in August 1996. Nominated for a second term by a cross-section of deputies, the incumbent was at first opposed, as in 1992, only by Arnold Rüütel of the Estonian Rural People's Party (*Eesti Maarahva Erakond*—EME). Meri led in three successive ballots of the deputies on August 26, 27, and 28, without obtaining the required two-thirds majority of the full complement of 101 members. In accordance with the constitution, the speaker subsequently transferred the contest to an electoral college of 374 members (the 101 parliamentarians plus 273 local council representatives), whereupon two additional candidates were nominated. They were eliminated in the first electoral college ballot on September 20, with Meri prevailing over Rüütel in the second later the same day by 196 votes to 126. The reelected president pledged to use his further term to press for Estonia's full integration into European structures, particularly the EU and the North Atlantic Treaty Organization (NATO).

In November 1996 Vähi renewed the alliance between his Estonian Coalition Party (*Eesti Koonderakond*—KE) and Savisaar's Center Party, which broke the RE's hold on the Tallinn city council. The RE then withdrew from the government and the ruling coalition, leaving six ministerial posts vacant. The Progress Party (*Arengupartei*—AP), recently formed by a group of Center Party dissidents, rejected Vähi's invitation to join the government. As a consequence, Vähi formed an exclusively KMÜ minority government that President Meri approved on December 1.

On February 25, 1997, Vähi resigned, two weeks after narrowly surviving a no-confidence vote. The KE named Mart SIIMANN, its caucus head, as its candidate for prime minister. However, he was unsuccessful in persuading former partners in the Center Party or the RE to join his new government, which, as formed on March 14, included most of the previous KMÜ ministers. The AP was given one portfolio.

The KE secured only 7 seats in the March 7, 1999, election, as did its former KMÜ partner, the EME. Although a resurgent Center Party led all parties with 28 seats, the Fatherland Union (18 seats), RE (18 seats), and Moderates (17 seats) coalesced to form a center-right government, with Mart Laar returning to the prime minister's post.

With President Meri ineligible for a third term, the 2001 presidential election was again decided by electoral college vote after the Parliament proved unable to give any nominee the necessary two-thirds majority. The governing coalition's initial candidate, former prime minister Andres Tarand of the Moderates, narrowly finished second to the Center Party's Peeter KREITZBURG in the first round of parliamentary balloting on August 27 and then stepped aside, to no avail, for Peeter TUL-VISTE of the Fatherland Union for the second and third ballots a day later. As a consequence, a 367-member electoral college convened on September 21 and, on a second ballot, chose Arnold Rüütel, now of the opposition People's Union of Estonia (*Eestimaa Rakvaliit*—ERL), over the RE's Toomas SAVI by a vote of 186–155.

Due to increasing conflict among the government coalition partners (see Current issues in the article on Estonia in the 2000–2002 *Handbook* for details), Prime Minister Laar on December 19, 2001, announced his intention to resign. He was succeeded by Siim Kallas, former finance minister and current chair of the RE, who formed a new Center Party/RE cabinet on January 28.

Municipal elections in October 2002 were most notable for the strong performance by the recently launched Union for the Republic (*Res Publica*—RP). Campaigning on an anticorruption and anticrime platform, they won nearly one-quarter of the votes in the March 2, 2003, legislative balloting, tying the Center Party for the most seats (28). Declining a coalition offer from the Center Party, the RP subsequently agreed to an RP/RE/ERL government that was inaugurated on April 10 under the leadership of the RP's youthful chair, Juhan PARTS.

In April 2005 a new ruling coalition was formed under Prime Minister Andrus Ansip when the Center Party replaced RP in the government, joining existing government coalition members RE and ERL. By November, the coalition had added 5 more seats in the parliament for a total of 58 after three RP defectors joined the RE and three Centrists joined the

ERL. Meanwhile the Center Party lost a net total of one member in the same period. In May 2006 the governing councils of the RP and the Pro Patria Union agreed to a merger, which was to be finalized in June.

Constitution and Government

In September 1991 the Supreme Council appointed a Constitutional Assembly (*Põhiseaduslik Assamblee*), composed of 60 members drawn equally from itself and the Congress of Estonia, a 495-member body elected in March 1990 by citizens of prewar Estonia and their descendants. The new basic law that emerged from the assembly's deliberations provided for a parliamentary system and a presidency with defined powers. Providing no voting rights for Russians residing in Estonia unless they qualified for citizenship, the document was approved by a reported 93 percent majority on June 28, 1992. Independent Estonia's first presidential election in September 1992 was by popular vote, with the 101-member *Riigikogu* then choosing from the two top contenders because neither had won an overall majority of the votes cast. However, subsequent presidential elections were to be by parliamentary ballot, with the successful candidate needing a two-thirds majority of all the deputies (i.e., at least 68 votes). If after three ballots no candidate has succeeded, the decision passes to an electoral college in which the deputies are joined by a larger number of local representatives and in which a simple majority vote suffices. The president serves a five-year term and is limited to two terms. (The 1992 election was for a four-year term on a one-time basis.) The president nominates the prime minister and approves the latter's nominations for the cabinet, all subject to legislative approval. The *Riigikogu* is elected via direct party-list balloting in 11 districts. Most seats are distributed on a proportional basis within each district, although some are allocated as "national compensation mandates" to parties securing at least 5 percent of the nationwide vote.

Administratively, the country is divided into 15 counties (*maakond*), which are subdivided into commenes (*vald*), and 6 major towns (the other urban areas being subordinate to the counties). In February 2003 the *Riigikogu*, in the first amendment to the constitution since its adoption, lengthened the term of office for local councils from three to four years.

Foreign Relations

Soviet recognition of the independence of the Baltic states on September 6, 1991, paved the way for admission of the three to the CSCE on September 10 and admission to the UN on September 17. Prior to the Soviet action, diplomatic recognition had been extended by a number of governments, including, on September 2, the United States, which had never recognized the 1940 annexations. Estonia was admitted to the IMF in 1992 and to the Council of Europe in 1993.

Regionally, Estonia, Latvia, and Lithuania concluded a Baltic Economic Cooperation Agreement in April 1990, which led on September 24, 1991, to a customs union agreement intended to permit free trade and visa-free travel between their respective jurisdictions. Nevertheless, with each state adopting its own currency and establishing customs posts on its borders, the development of trade among them was slow. Estonia was a founding member of the Council of the Baltic Sea States (see separate article) in 1992, which served as a conduit for Swedish and other Scandinavian involvement in Estonia's quest for modernization.

In early 1995 relations between Estonia and Latvia were strained by a series of "fish wars" stemming from competing claims to territorial jurisdiction in the Gulf of Riga. In essence, the dispute turned on Estonian insistence on a prewar equal division of the gulf, while Latvia sought to establish the principle of common use, except for a four-mile coastal zone. Lengthy negotiations yielded an agreement on a compromise line in 1996.

Postindependence Estonia's key objective of securing the withdrawal of Russian troops from its territory was complicated in 1993 by Moscow's intense criticism of alleged discrimination against ethnic Russians under Estonia's new citizenship law. Western pressure persuaded Moscow to adhere to an August 1994 deadline for withdrawal, subject to Russian retention of the Paldiski communications base for an additional year. Prior to the Russian withdrawal, President Yeltsin on June 26 decreed that the Russian-Estonian border should be based on the Soviet-era line, thus effectively rejecting the Estonian contention that the 1920 border should be restored. In November 1995 Estonia bowed to reality by agreeing in principle to the maintenance of the existing border, but relations with its powerful neighbor remained tense. Tallinn sought to gain international support for its contention that Estonia's 500,000-strong ethnic Russian population was the result of Moscow-directed settlement during the half-century of Soviet rule. In an effort to bring closure to its difficult negotiations with Russia over a border treaty, Estonia had dropped its insistence that the treaty include mention of the 1920 Tartu Treaty and had accepted demarcation lines unilaterally set by the Russians. However, in January 1997 the Russians threatened sanctions and said they would not sign the treaty until Estonia stopped alleged human rights violations against its ethnic Russians. (The Council of Europe, which ended its human rights monitoring in Estonia on January 30, praised Tallinn for making rapid progress but noted areas that needed improvement.) In December 1998 Estonia adopted legislation allowing children who had been born in Estonia to ethnic Russians to become Estonian citizens, a measure that was welcomed by the Council of Europe, OSCE, and, to a certain extent, Moscow, although Russia pressed for further liberalization regarding stateless adult ethnic Russians. Subsequently, in March 1999, tentative agreement was reached on demarcation of the Russian-Estonian border that would involve the transfer of only a small amount of territory. As of 2004, however, no formal boundary accord had been signed. Meanwhile, the status of ethnic Russians in Estonia continued to be a contentious issue. Although a significant number of them had achieved Estonian citizenship, it was estimated in 2004 that 120,000 had opted for Russian citizenship because of language and other restrictions, while more than 170,000 remained "stateless." (Noncitizens are ineligible to vote in national elections, although all permanent residents, regardless of citizenship status, can participate in local balloting.) On May 18, 2005, Russia and Estonia signed two territorial treaties, one on the common land border and the other on delimitation of the maritime zones in the Gulf of Finland and Gulf of Narva. However, Russia withdrew from the treaty a month later after the *Riigikogu* made references to the Russian occupation while ratifying the treaty in June.

Estonia became a signatory of NATO's Partnership for Peace in February 1994, subsequently reiterating its desire for full NATO membership and also for eventual accession to the EU. It made significant progress toward the latter goal on June 13, 1995, when it joined the other two Baltic republics in signing an association agreement with the EU that placed them on the same footing as the other East European applicant states. In December 1997 the EU invited Estonia, but not the other Baltic states, to join the first wave of EU expansion, and formal membership negotiations began in March 1998. Among other things, the EU called upon Estonia to make it easier for ethnic Russians to become citizens.

Although it was not among the three states invited by NATO to join the alliance in April 1999, Estonia was among five others designated as prime candidates for the next accession phase. In what some called a consolation prize for not gaining quick admission to NATO, Estonia joined its Baltic sister states in signing the Charter of Partnership with the United States in January 1998. In March 2000 Defense Minister Jüri LUIK presented Estonia's plan for joining NATO, including a proposal to increase defense spending to 2 percent of the GDP by 2002, to conform with NATO standards. A NATO summit in November 2002 formally invited Estonia to accede to the alliance, and Estonia was among seven new members admitted to NATO in April 2004. (The *Riigikogu* had endorsed the NATO initiative in March.)

Estonian forces have been participating in operations in Kosovo and in Bosnia and Herzegovina. In June 2003, upon the request of the Iraqi Interim Government, Estonia deployed a light infantry platoon to operation Iraqi Freedom. The Estonian Parliament extended the Estonian Defence Forces mission in Iraq until December 31, 2006.

Current Issues

The surprising success of the fledgling Union for the Republic (RP) in the October 2002 local elections and the March 2003 *Riigikogu* balloting was seen in large part as a protest vote against the entrenched parties. Young people in particular were reportedly attracted by the RP's anticorruption platform and underlying interest in prying the fingers of the "old guard" off the levers of authority. (At 36, Juhan Parts was the youngest prime minister in Europe, and the ministers in his new cabinet averaged only 44 years of age.) In addition, the RP's "Choose Order!" campaign slogan also appeared to resonate with so-called "enlightened rightists" interested in, among other things, lower tax rates.

Despite its emphasis on "new politics," the new center-right coalition government in 2003 did not deviate from plans laid by previous administrations for Estonia's accession to NATO and the EU. In a decision perceived as a means of bolstering ties with the United States and thereby improving Estonia's NATO "credentials," the Parts administration offered military personnel to support the U.S.-led post–Saddam Hussein coalition in Iraq. (The Kallas government in February 2003 had signed, along with leaders of other former Soviet-bloc European states, an open letter of support for the George W. Bush administration's Iraqi policies.) Although public opinion polls initially showed popular support for EU accession to be weak, the government initiated a broad pro-EU campaign that contributed to a 66.8 percent "yes" vote on the question in a national referendum on September 14. The *Riigikogu* in January 2004 also endorsed EU accession, formally achieved on May 1. In addition, the legislature set a target date of 2007 (later pushed back to 2008 because of high inflation) for adoption of the euro. Despite those developments, voter turnout was low (27 percent) for the June European Parliament balloting, at which the governing

RP won no seats while the Social Democratic Party (as the Moderates had been renamed) secured three of the six seats. These were ominous signs for the RP, and ultimately led to Prime Minister Parts' resignation on March 24, 2005, after the Parliament adopted a no-confidence motion against the administration's justice minister. A new government was appointed on April 13, headed by Andrus Ansip of the Estonian Reform Party, with the Center Party taking the place of the RP in the new ruling coalition.

Political Parties

The first opposition parties since World War II began to emerge in 1988, but their impact was little more than that of political pressure groups until 1990. Largely because of a split within the Estonian Communist Party on the independence issue, the legislative distribution of seats was blurred following Estonia's first contemporary multiparty balloting on March 18, 1990. Thus, the principal adversaries were not parties, per se, but two prosecessionist formations and a movement (supported largely by ethnic Russians) opposed to independence, with Communists distributed across all three slates. Following independence in 1991, the earlier broad movements gradually broke up into a large array of smaller parties and groupings, which formed a variety of electoral alliances in 1992 and 1995. In November 1998 the Parliament banned electoral alliances in future balloting in an apparent attempt to reduce the number of small parties, although the use of joint lists was permitted in the March 1999 legislative poll.

Government Parties

Estonian Reform Party (*Eesti Reformierakond*—RE). The RE was founded in late 1994 by Siim Kallas, who as president of the Bank of Estonia had played a key role in the downfall of the Pro Patria prime minister, Mart Laar, in September, but had then failed to secure legislative endorsement as his successor. Described as "liberal rightist" in orientation, the RE incorporated the Estonian Liberal Democratic Party (*Eesti Liberaaldemokraatlik Partei*—ELDP), which had contested the 1992 election as part of the winning Pro Patria coalition but had withdrawn in June 1994 to protest Prime Minister Maar's leadership style. The RE won 16.2 percent of the vote in the March 1995 legislative poll, after which Kallas resigned from his post at the bank.

Having at first remained in opposition, the RE replaced the Estonian Center Party (below) in the coalition government in October 1995, with Kallas becoming foreign minister. However, the RE withdrew from the government in late 1996, although it subsequently was reported to have agreed not to be "obstructionist." As was the case with the Fatherland Union and the Moderates, the RE was given five cabinet posts in the new coalition government formed after the March 1999 legislative balloting, in which the RE had secured 18 seats on a 15.9 percent vote share. After the collapse of that three-party coalition, the RE in January formed a new government with the Center Party, with Kallas assuming the post of prime minister. The RE secured 19 seats on a 17.7 percent vote share in the March 2003 *Riigikogu* poll and accepted "junior" status in the subsequent RP/RE/ERL government, Kallas declining a ministerial post with an announced preference to concentrate on his role as a legislator. The replacement of the RP by the Center Party in the government coalition in April 2005 allowed the RE to place Andrus Ansip in the post of prime minister.

Leaders: Andrus ANSIP (Party Chair and Prime Minister), Eero TOHVER (Secretary General).

People's Union of Estonia (*Eestimaa Rahvaliit*—ERL). The ERL was established in October 1999 as successor to the Estonian Rural People's Party (*Eesti Maarahva Erakond*—EME). In June 2000 the ERL absorbed the Estonian Rural Union (*Eesti Maaliit*—EM) and the Estonian Pensioners' and Families' Party (*Eesti Pensionäride ja Perede Erakond*—EPPE).

The EME, also often referenced as the Country People's Party, had been founded in September 1994 and helped to rally agrarians to the KMÜ. The

EME leader, Arnold Rüütel, was chair of the Estonian Supreme Soviet in the Soviet era but had supported moves to throw off Moscow rule, becoming independent Estonia's first head of state. He won a plurality in the 1992 presidential elections as the Secure Home candidate but lost to the Pro Patria nominee in the decisive legislative balloting.

Although the EME was a prominent member of the KMÜ-led government, it defected from the KMÜ on key votes in 1998 regarding the budget as well as the ban on electoral alliances. It further distanced itself from the Coalition Party (see KE, below) and the KMÜ in early 1999 when it announced plans to form a postelectoral coalition government with Edgar Savisaar's Center Party. A number of members of the Progress Party, including prominent politician Andra VEIDEMANN, subsequently agreed to run on the EME list, but the party nonetheless managed only seven seats (7.3 percent of the vote).

The EM was founded in March 1991 and took eight of the KMÜ seats in March 1995. The EM reached an agreement in January 1998 with the opposition Center Party to support each other in the Parliament in order to protect Estonian farmers and their markets. The EM then ran on the KE list in the March 1999 legislative balloting, as did the EPPE.

The EPPE descended from the Estonian Democratic Justice Union/Pensioners' League (*Eesti Demokraatlik Õigusliit/Pensionäride Ühendus—* EDÕL/PÜ), which dated from 1991 but was not represented in the Parliament elected in 1992. The EPPE's immediate predecessor, the Estonian Pensioners' and Families' League (*Eesti Pensionäride ja Perede Liit*—EPPL), won six legislative seats in 1995 as part of the KMÜ.

Following the formation of the ERL, the new grouping was reported to have the largest membership among Estonian parties. The ERL announced it would oppose the government's policies, which it described as "hostile to the peasantry." The ERL's Rüütel won the presidency on September 21, 2001, in a second-round electoral college ballot. The ERL secured 13 percent of the vote and 13 seats in the March 2003 legislative balloting, its membership having been bolstered by a proposed merger with

the New Estonia Party (*Erakond Uus Eesti*—UE). (See the 2000–2002 *Handbook* for details on the UE.)

Leaders: Arnold RÜÜTEL (President of the Republic), Villu REILJAN (Chair), Mai TREIAL (Vice Chair).

Estonian Center Party (*Eesti Keskerakond*— EK). Launched in October 1991 as the Estonian People's Center Party (*Eesti Rahva-Keskerakond*— ERKE), the party adopted its current name in April 1993. Founded by Edgar Savisaar, the Center Party is an offshoot of the Estonian Popular Front (*Eesti Rahvarinne*), a broad proindependence movement that coalesced in 1988 but split into various parties after independence. The Center Party used the Front's designation in the 1992 election, winning 15 seats (with 12.2 percent of the vote) and achieving a creditable third place for its presidential candidate, Rein TAAGEPERA. As Front party chair, Savisaar was prime minister from April 1990 to January 1992, having previously been chair of the Soviet-era Estonian Planning Committee.

The Center Party absorbed the Estonian Entrepreneurs' Party (*Eesti Ettevõtjate Erakond*— EEE) prior to the March 1995 balloting, at which it won 14.2 percent of the vote. It took four portfolios in the subsequent coalition, with Savisaar becoming interior minister. In October 1995, however, Savisaar's dismissal over an alleged phone-tapping scandal precipitated his party's exit from the government, with Savisaar himself being replaced as party chair by Andra Veidemann. Having initially declared his retirement from political life, Savisaar made a comeback at the head of anti-Veidemann elements in early 1996, securing reelection as chair in late March. Two months later the Veidemann group launched the Progress Party (see New Estonia Party, above, under ERL), to which the Center Party lost 7 of its 16 deputies. In July the state prosecutor closed the Savisaar case, having found nothing criminal in the former minister's conduct.

In May 1998 the Center Party absorbed the Estonian Greens (*Eesti Rõhelised*), which had been launched in 1991 as a coalition of several organizations and had secured one legislative seat in 1992. Allied with the Estonian Royalist Party (*Eesti*

Rojalistlik Partei—ERP), the Greens contested the 1995 balloting in the unlikely Fourth Force (*Neljas Jõud*—NJ), which failed to win any seats. Among other things, the Green movement drew attention to the huge environmental damage resulting from the Soviet military presence in Estonia, which government experts in 1994 said would cost $4 billion to remedy.

Described as a "canny populist," Savisaar led the Center Party to a first-place finish in the March 1999 balloting (28 seats and 23.4 percent of the vote) on a platform calling for a progressive income tax, continued farm subsidies, and other measures designed to appeal to segments of the populace wary of recent free-market economic reforms. Prior to the balloting, the party announced it hoped to form a new government with the EME (see ERL, above), but between them they secured only 35 seats and could find no other suitable coalition partners. The Center Party then remained in opposition to the three-party coalition government formed in March. After the demise of the government in January 2002, the Center Party was admitted to the new cabinet.

Savisaar was reelected mayor of Tallinn in 2002, and the party retained its popularity at the March 2003 legislative poll, leading all parties with 25.4 percent of the vote. However, it was unable to persuade the RE to pursue a coalition government and subsequently returned to opposition status. When the RP dropped out of the government in March 2006, the EK took its place a month later and formed a new government with the remaining governing parties.

Leaders: Edgar SAVISAAR (Chair and Minister of Economic Affairs and Communications), Enn EESMAA (Vice Chair), Mailis Reps (Vice Chair and Minister of Education and Research).

Opposition Parties

Union for the Republic (*Res Publica*—RP). Formed originally by young anti-Soviet activists (including several prominent academicians) as a political "club" in 1989, the rightist RP became a formal party in December 2001. Apparently appealing to Estonians dissatisfied with Estonia's cen-ter and center-left parties, the RP gained about one-quarter of the vote in the local and regional elections in 2001. Similar results (24.6 percent of the vote nationally) in the 2003 national legislative poll secured 28 seats for the RP, which subsequently formed a coalition government with the RE and ERL under the leadership of the RP's Juhan Parts, who, at age 36, became Europe's youngest prime minister. When the Parliament passed a no-confidence vote against the justice minister, Parts and the rest of the RP withdrew from the government, to be replaced in the ruling coalition by the Center Party.

Leaders: Taavi VESKIMÄGI (Chair), Siim KISLER (Vice Chair), Marko MIHKELSON (Vice Chair), Tõnis PALTS (Vice Chair and Mayor of Tallinn).

Fatherland Union (*Erakond Isamaaliit*—IL). The Fatherland Union (also referenced as the Pro Patria Union) was launched in December 1995 by merger of the Fatherland ("Pro Patria") National Coalition (*Rahvuslik Koonderakond Isamaa*—RKEI) and the Estonian National Independence Party (*Eesti Rahvusliku Sõltumatuse Partei*—ERSP). Having dominated the previous government, the two parties had contested the March 1995 election in alliance as the Pro Patria/ERSP Bloc (*Isamaa ja ERSP Liit*) but had retained only eight seats on a 7.9 percent vote share and had gone into opposition.

The RKEI had been formed in early 1992 as an alliance of four Christian democratic and right-of-center parties seeking to make a complete break with the Communist era. In September 1992 the alliance elected a plurality of 29 deputies (with 22 percent of the vote), who the following month joined with the ERSP contingent and others to elect Lennart Meri as president. RKEI leader Mart Laar then turned the alliance into a unitary formation and was named to head a coalition government. After encountering serious difficulties, due in part to his self-confessed "dictatorial" methods, he was ousted as prime minister in September 1994.

At its founding in August 1988 the ERSP had been the only organized non-Communist party in the USSR. Although centrist in ideology, it was consistently more anticommunist than other proindependence formations, declining to participate in the 1990 Estonian Supreme Soviet elections and instead organizing the alternative "Congress of Estonia." Following independence in 1991, it was the country's strongest party, but it was eclipsed by the RKEI in the September 1992 balloting, ERSP Chair Lagle PAREK taking fourth place in the presidential contest with only 4.3 percent of the vote. Thereafter, the ERSP became a junior coalition partner in the Laar government.

Mart Laar returned to the prime minister's post in March 1999 as head of the new three-party coalition government installed following legislative balloting in which the Fatherland Union had finished second with 18 seats on a 16.1 percent vote share. However, his coalition collapsed in late 2001, and his party moved into opposition following the installation of the new RE/Center Party government.

Laar resigned as chair of the Fatherland Union following the party's poor performance in the October 2002 local elections, in which, among other things, it lost all 13 of its seats on the Tallinn municipal council. Laar was succeeded by Tunne KELAM, deputy speaker of the parliament. The Fatherland Union's electoral slide continued in the March 2003 legislative poll, at which it secured only seven seats on a vote share of 7.3 percent. In the 2004 election to the European Parliament, the first for Estonia, the IL won 10.5 percent of the popular vote and 1 of the six seats from Estonia. In May 2006 the IL agreed to merge with the RP, which had left the ruling coalition in March. The new party, launched in June, is to be called Pro Patria and Res Publica Union.

Leaders: Tõnis LUKAS (Chair), Kaia IVA (Vice Chair and Former Mayor of Türi), Andres HERKEL (Vice Chair), Tarmo LOODUS (Secretary General).

Social Democratic Party (*Sotsiaaldemokraatlik Erakond*—SDE). The SDE is the successor (as of 2003) to the Moderates (*Rahvaerakond Mõõdukad*—M), launched in 1990 as an electoral coalition of the Estonian Social Democratic Party (*Eesti Sotsiaaldemokraatlik Partei*—ESDP)

and the Estonian Rural Center Party (*Eesti Maa-Keskerakond*—EMKE).

The ESDP had descended from the historic party founded in 1905 and maintained in exile during the Soviet era. Relaunched in Estonia in 1990 as a merger of three social democratic and workers' parties, it became part of the independence movement, its strong anticommunism enabling it to participate in right-oriented postindependence governments. Founded in 1990 to represent the interests of Estonia's farming community, the EMKE differed from other agrarian formations in that it gave full backing to promarket policies.

Mõõdukad won 12 legislative seats in the 1992 election, its campaign including charges on behalf of the EMKE that the rural parties in the Coalition Party and Rural Union (KMÜ; see Estonian Coalition Party, below) alliance were dominated by former communists. *Mõõdukad* subsequently joined the new Pro Patria-led government, although the ESDP sought to preserve a social welfare dimension to the promarket reforms favored by the other members of the coalition. *Mõõdukad* lost half of its representation in the 1995 balloting, despite the endorsement of Prime Minister Andres Tarand. The alliance established a more formal structure in April 1996, with Tarand being elected chair.

The Moderates ran on a joint list for the 1999 legislative poll with the newly formed Estonian People's Party (*Eesti Rahvaerakond*—R); the two groupings formally merged after that balloting, resulting in the party's new Estonian name (*Rahvaerakond Mõõdukad*). The People's Party had been launched in March 1998 by the Estonian Farmers' Party (*Eesti Talurahva Erakond*—ETRE) and the Republican and Conservative People's Party (*Vabariiklaste ja Konservatiivide Rahvaerakond "Parempoolsed"*—VKRE). The latter, by its own choice rendered "Right-Wingers" in English, had been established in September 1994 under Chair Karin JAANI, who, along with most of her Republican, Conservative, and Christian democratic colleagues, had left the Pro Patria-led coalition government in June. *Parempoolsed* won five seats in the March 1995 election on a 5 percent vote share.

In early April 1998 the People's Party elected Foreign Affairs Minister Toomas Hendrik Ilves (who had touched off a controversy when he had joined the ETRE in late 1997) as chair and initially agreed to support the KMÜ in the legislature. However, the effort to stabilize the ruling coalition failed, the People's Party subsequently announcing it supported neither the governing coalition nor the opposition. Ilves resigned from his cabinet post in November, under pressure from rural elements in the KMÜ. However, he returned to the post in the coalition government named in March 1999, the *Mõõdukad*/People's Party joint list having won 17 seats on a 15.2 percent vote share. Collaterally, *Mõõdukad* Chair Tarand was elected to head the nine-member council established by the governing parties to coordinate their activities and legislative initiatives.

At a party congress on May 18, 2001, Tarand stepped down as chair in what proved to be an unsuccessful pursuit of the state presidency. He was succeeded as chair by Ilves. Like the Fatherland Union, the Moderates performed poorly in the 2002 local elections, prompting the resignation of Ilves as party chair. The decline continued in the March 2003 legislative balloting (six seats on a 7 percent vote share), and in early 2004 party delegates approved the adoption of the SDE rubric to reflect the party's policies more accurately. Subsequently, the SDE surprised analysts by securing three seats (including one for Ilves) in the June 2004 voting for Estonia's six seats in the European Parliament. In the October 2005 local elections, the SDE won 6.43 percent of all votes cast, an improvement over the 4.39 percent the party won in 2002.

Leaders: Ivari PADAR (Chair); Toomas Hendrik ILVES (Former Chair); Eiki NESTOR, Katrin SAKS (Vice Chairs); Andres TARAND (Former Chair); Randel LÄNTS (Secretary General).

Other Parties Contesting the 2003 Legislative Elections

Estonian United Russian People's Party (*Eestimaa Ühendatud Vene Rahvapartei*—EÜVRP). The EÜVRP is the recently adopted name of the **Estonian United People's Party** (*Eestimaa Ühendatud Rahvapartei*—EÜRP). Then considered the strongest of the numerous ethnic Russian

parties in Estonia, the EÜRP participated in the March 1995 election in the alliance known as Our Home Is Estonia (*Meie Kodu on Eestimaa*), along with the Russian Party of Estonia (see VEE, below) and the Russian People's Party of Estonia (*Eesti Vene Rahvapartei*—EVRP). *Meie Kodu* strongly opposed the 1993 Estonian citizenship law, which, by limiting the franchise to citizens, prevented the alliance from obtaining a higher vote among the estimated 20–30 percent ethnic Russian component of the populace. The grouping secured six seats, the legislators subsequently coalescing as a parliamentary Russian Faction.

The EÜRP contested the March 1999 balloting on a joint list with the ESDTP (below) and the VÜP (see VEE, below); the list secured six seats. In May 2000 Viktor ANDREJEV, a leader of the EÜRP, signed a cooperation agreement with Yevgenii PRIMAKOV, the leader of the Fatherland/All Russia faction of the Russian Duma. The agreement was denounced by main Estonian parties as a "sign of EÜRP's disloyalty to the country." In 2000 EÜRP leader Sergei IVANOV left to form the VBEE (see VEE, below). The EÜRP legislators voted to approve the new coalition government formed in January 2002.

In mid-2002 the EÜRP called for a merger of all the Russian parties in Estonia, but the party ultimately did not participate in the enlargement of the VEE (see below). Instead, the EÜRP adopted the EÜVRP rubric in December. Campaigning in support of the estimated 170,000 Russians who had yet to achieve Estonian citizenship, the EÜVRP secured only 2.24 percent of the vote in the 2003 legislative balloting, meaning that for the first time since independence no Russian party would be represented in the *Riigikogu*. The party's electoral slide continued in the 2005 local elections, in which it won less than 1 percent (0.69) of all votes cast, much lower than the 4.31 percent it won in the 2002 local elections.

Leaders: Yevgeny TOMBERG (Chair), Sergei SERGEYEV, Anatoli YEGEROV (Secretary General).

Russian Party of Estonia (*Vene Erakond Eestis*—VEE). The VEE was formed in 1994 under

Sergei KUZNETSOV, and competed in the *Meie Kodu* coalition of ethnic Russian groupings in 1995. In 1996 the VEE absorbed much of the Russian People's Party of Estonia (EVRP), but VEE membership was undercut in 1997 by the formation of the breakaway Russian Unity Party (*Veni Üntsuspartei*—VÜP), which participated in the EÜRP joint list in the 1999 legislative balloting. Running independently in that poll, the VEE failed to gain representation on a 2.0 percent vote share.

In December 2002 the VÜP announced it was merging back into the VEE, along with two other parties—the Russian Baltic Party in Estonia (*Vene Balti Erakond Eestis*—VBEE) and the Unity of Estonia Party. The VBEE had been established in June 2000 by Sergei Ivanov, a former leader of the EÜRP. The Unity grouping had been launched in October 2001 under the leadership of Igor PISAREV, who objected to the party being labeled as an ethnic Russian formation, stating that the formation was dedicated to establishing a "stable middle class."

Although the enlarged VEE claimed a membership of 4,000 and a bigger constituency than the EÜVRP, it secured only 0.18 percent of the vote in the 2003 legislative elections, and only 0.3 percent of the June 2004 vote for the European Parliament. Subsequently, the VÜP, VBEE, and Unity were occasionally referenced as still maintaining separate identities.

Leaders: Stanislav CHEREPANOV (Chair), Pavel CYRIL (General Secretary).

Estonian Social Democratic Labor Party (*Eesti Sotsiaalde-mokraatlik Demokraatlik Tööpartei*—ESDTP). Undeterred by the ouster from power of the Estonian Communist Party (*Eestimaa Kommunistlik Partei*—EKP) during the transition to independence, elements of the old party adopted the name of Estonian Democratic Labor Party (*Eesti Demokraatlik Tööpartei*—EDTP) in 1992, asserting that the party now had a democratic socialist orientation. It unsuccessfully contested the 1995 election within the Justice (*Õiglus*) alliance, which also included the Party for Legal Justice (*Õigusliku Tasakaalu Erakond*—ÕTE), led

by Peeter TEDRE. The EDTP's subsequent efforts to establish ties with the Estonian Social Democratic Party were rebuffed. The party changed its name to Estonian Social Democratic Labor Party in December 1997. The ESDTP contested the 1999 poll on the joint list of the EÜRP. Running independently in the 2003 balloting, the ESDTP won only 0.42 percent of the vote, and in the 2004 European Parliament balloting only 0.5 percent of the vote.

Leaders: Sirje KINGSEPP (Chair), Malle SALUPERE (Vice Chair).

Estonian Christian People's Party (*Eesti Kristlik Rahvapartei*—EKRP). Established in December 1998, the EKRP earned 2.4 percent of the vote in the 1999 legislative poll and 1.1 percent in 2003.

Leader: Aldo VINKEL (Chair), Paul RÄSTA (Vice Chair).

Estonian Independence Party (*Eesti Iseseivuspartei*—EIP). An opponent of Estonia's accession to the EU, the EIP was founded in November 1999 after its predecessor, the Future's Estonia Party (*Tuleviku Eesti Erakond*—TEE), was denied ballot access for failing to meet registration requirements. The EIP won 0.55 percent of the vote in the 2003 legislative balloting, and in the 2005 local elections it won 0.14 percent of the vote.

Leaders: Vello LEITO, Peeter PAEMURRU (Chairs).

Other Parties

The Democrats-Estonian Democratic Party (*Demokraadid-Eesti Demokraatlik Partei*—EDP). The EDP was formally established in February 2001 as successor to the Estonian Blue Party (*Eesti Sinine Erakond*—ESE). The ESE, dating from late 1994 and chaired by Neeme KUNINGAS, had competed unsuccessfully in the 1995 and 1999 legislative balloting, garnering 1.6 percent of the vote in the more recent election. In late 2000 the EDP was envisaged as a merger of the ESE and the Progress Party, but most members of the latter soon withdrew from the agreement and went on to form the UE. The EDP won 1.2 percent of the vote and no seats in the 2004 European Parliament elections.

Leader: Jaan LAAS (Chair), Endel KALJUS-MAA (Vice Chair), Märt MEESAK (Secretary).

Farmers' Assembly (*Põllumeeste Kogu—* PK). Founded in 1992, the conservative PK contested the 1995 election as part of the KMÜ. Having formed part of the subsequent government majority, the PK withdrew in February 1996, claiming that ministers were disregarding farmers' interests. It contested the 1999 poll on its own, failing to secure representation.

In mid-2002 it was announced that the PK would merge with the Conservative Club to form a new party called the National Conservative Party–Farmer's Assembly, which later attempted, under the leadership of Mart HELME, to coalesce with the EIP (see above) for the 2003 legislative poll. The proposed merger with the EIP fell through, however, and leaders indicated that the earlier merger also remained in question, some members of the Farmer's Assembly apparently preferring to retain an independent identity for their grouping.

Estonian Coalition Party (*Eesti Koonderakond—*KE). The KE was founded in December 1991, its leader, Tiit Vähi, becoming caretaker prime minister in January 1992. At the September 1992 balloting the party was part of the Secure Home coalition, a broadly conservative grouping that contained many former communists and supported the unsuccessful 1992 presidential candidacy of former Soviet-era leader Arnold Rüütel. The Secure Home alliance won 17 legislative seats in the 1992 poll on a 13.6 percent vote share and formed the main parliamentary opposition until 1995.

The KE was the dominant component of the Coalition Party and Rural Union (*Koonderakonna ja Maarahva Ühendus—*KMÜ), which was created for the March 1995 legislative election by the KE, EME, EM, EPPL, and PK. Campaigning on a platform promising agricultural subsidies and increased social expenditures, the KMÜ secured a plurality of 41 seats (18 for the KE) and

32.2 percent of the vote. Consequently, Vähi was named prime minister of a KMÜ coalition government, which also initially included the Center Party. When Vähi resigned in February 1997, he was succeeded by Mart SIIMANN, the head of the KE's parliamentary group. However, the governing coalition continued to decline (see Political background, above), and the KE won only seven seats on a 7.6 percent vote share in the March 1999 poll. (The EM and the EPPE ran on the KE joint list, but the EME ran independently.) The KE reportedly considered participating in the new coalition government established after that poll before deciding to become part of what Siimann pledged would be the "constructive opposition."

In August 2001 the party chair indicated that the KE was not interested in serving as a "niche party" and would in all likelihood be dissolved at a party congress in November. Meanwhile, the KE's sole remaining member of Parliament, former prime minister Siimann, was spearheading formation of a new political association, **With Reason and Heart**. Indeed, in November the party congress decided to disband the KE, while Siimann reportedly postponed his plans to transform With Reason and Heart into a political party. The KE was formally dissolved in November 2002.

Other recently established parties include the **Estonian Freedom Movement** (*Eesti Vabadusliikumine—*EVL), led by Andris TAMMELA; the **Estonian Pensioners' Party** (*Eesti Pensionäride Erakond—*EPE), formed in May 2001 and led by Ants TAMME; the **Republican Party** (*Vabariiklik Partei—*VP), formed in October 1999 and registered under the leadership of Kristjan-Olari LEPING in February 2001; and For Human Rights in a United Latvia, led by Tatyana ZDANOK.

Legislature

The former Supreme Soviet/Council (*Ülemnõukogu*) ceased to exist on September 14, 1992, prior to balloting on September 20 for a new unicameral **Parliament** (*Riigikogu*) of 101 members.

Cabinet

As of May 12, 2006

Prime Minister	Andrus Ansip (RE)

Ministers

Agriculture	Ester Tuiksoo (ERL) [f]
Culture	Raivo Palmaru (EK)
Defense	Jürgen Ligi (RE)
Economic Affairs and Communications	Edgar Savisaar (EK)
Education and Research	Mailis Reps (EK) [f]
Environment	Villu Reiljan (ERL)
Finance	Aivar Sõerd (ERL)
Foreign Affairs	Urmas Paet (RE)
Internal Affairs	Kalle Laanet (EK)
Justice	Rein Lang (RE)
Population Affairs	Paul-Eerik Rummo (RE)
Regional Affairs	Jaan Õunapuu (ERL)
Social Affairs	Jaak Aab (EK)

[f] = female

Note: RE = Estonian Reform Party (*Eesti Reformierakond*), ERL = People's Union of Estonia (*Eestimaa Rahvaliit*), and EK = Estonian Center Party.

At the most recent election of March 2, 2003, the Estonian Center Party and the Union for the Republic each won 28 seats; the Estonian Reform Party, 19; the People's Union of Estonia, 13; the Fatherland Union, 7; and the Moderates (subsequently the Social Democratic Party), 6.

Speaker: Eng ERGMA.

Communications

Press

Due to economic difficulties, press circulation declined sharply after independence, although no major daily had been forced to cease publication as of mid-1994. The following are Estonian-language dailies published at Tallinn unless otherwise noted: *Postimees* (Postman, 59,000), leading Tartu paper; *Rahva Hääl* (Voice of the People, 175,000), government organ; *Eesti Ekspress* (Estonian Express, 40,000), weekly; *Eesti Päevaleht* (Daily, 40,000); *Õhtuleht* (Evening Gazette, 20,000); *Äripäev* (Daily Business, 15,000); *Hommikuleht* (Morning Paper, 14,500); *The Baltic Times* (14,000), English-language weekly; *Estoniya* (Estonia, 11,000), in Russian; *The Baltic Independent* (7,200), English-language weekly.

News Agencies

The Estonian Telegraph Agency (*Eesti Teadate Agentuur*—ETA) coordinates its services with Latvian and Lithuanian agencies. The Baltic News Service (BNS) began operations in 1991.

Broadcasting and Computing

Estonian Radio (*Eesti Raadio*) broadcasts in Estonian, Russian, Swedish, Finnish, English, Esperanto, Ukrainian, and Belarusan; Estonian Television (*Eesti Televisoon*) and two foreign-owned commercial stations transmit in Estonian and Russian. In August 2001 the cabinet approved combining the state radio and TV operations as the Estonian National Broadcasting Company (*Eesti*

Rahvusringhaaling). There were approximately 1.2 million television receivers and 300,000 personal computers serving 500,000 Internet users in 2003.

Intergovernmental Representation

Ambassador to the U.S.
Jüri LUIK

U.S. Ambassador to Estonia
Aldona WOS

Permanent Representative to the UN
Tiina INTELMANN

IGO Memberships (Non-UN)
BIS, CBSS, CEUR, EBRD, EIB, EU, IOM, Interpol, NATO, NIB, OSCE, PCA, WCO, WTO

FINLAND

REPUBLIC OF FINLAND

Suomen Tasavalta (Finnish)
Republiken Finland (Swedish)

The Country

A land of rivers, lakes, and extensive forests, Finland is, except for Norway, the northernmost country of Europe. Over 93 percent of the population is Finnish-speaking and belongs to the Evangelical Lutheran Church. The once-dominant Swedish minority, numbering about 7 percent of the total, has shown occasional discontent but enjoys linguistic equality; there also is a small Lapp minority in the north. Women constitute approximately 48 percent of the labor force, concentrated in textile manufacture, clerical work, human services, and the public sector (with women holding 70 percent of all public sector jobs). Female participation in elective bodies is currently around 37.5 percent.

Finland underwent a tumultuous economic transformation in the 1980s and 1990s that ultimately modernized and diversified what was previously an agriculturally based economy. Once having prided itself on its ability to "live on its forest," Finland now devotes less than 8 percent of its labor force to agriculture and forestry, according to recent estimates. Finland's traditional leading exports of wood, paper, pulp, and other forestry-related products remain important sources of revenue, but during the 1990s they were supplanted as the leading merchandise earners by consumer electronics, especially mobile phones produced by Nokia, the largest private employer in Finland. Ranked the most competitive market by the World Economic Forum 2005–2006, the service sector composed 62 percent of Finnish GDP, and industry and agriculture composed 34 and 4 percent, respectively. In particular, Nokia dominated the global cellular phone market in the 1990s and not only helped lift the country out of a recession in 1993 but sparked six years of unprecedented nationwide growth. Additionally, the erstwhile traditional socialist state is continuing to privatize and centralize the state-owned corporations as it seeks to make these firms more competitive in the global economy.

Finland has enjoyed steady growth since the mid-1990s, with GDP rising on average approximately 4 percent per year. Growth peaked in 2000

Political Status: Independent since December 6, 1917; republic established July 17, 1919, under presidential-parliamentary system.

Area: 130,119 sq. mi. (337,009 sq. km.).

Population: 5,181,115 (2000C); 5,241,000 (2005E).

Major Urban Centers (2005E): HELSINKI (551,000), Espoo (239,000), Tampere (208,000), Turku (178,000).

Official Languages: Finnish, Swedish.

Monetary Unit: Euro (market rate July 1, 2006: 1 euro = $1.28US).

President: Tarja HALONEN (Finnish Social Democratic Party); reelected in second-round balloting on February 29, 2006, and inaugurated for a six-year term on March 1, 2006.

Prime Minister: Matti VANHANEN (Finnish Center); designated by the president on June 24, 2003, following the legislative election earlier that day; sworn in on June 24, 2003, as part of a three-party coalition government replacing Anneli JÄÄTTEENMÄKI (Finnish Center), who had resigned on June 18, 2003.

formal declaration of independence dates from December 6, 1917, and its republican constitution from July 17, 1919, although peace with Soviet Russia was not formally established until October 14, 1920. Soviet territorial claims led to renewed conflict during World War II, when Finnish troops distinguished themselves both in the so-called Winter War of 1939–1940 and again in the "Continuation War" of 1941–1944. Under the peace treaty signed at Paris in 1947, Finland ceded some 12 percent of its territory to the USSR (the Petsamo and Salla areas in the northeast and the Karelian Isthmus in the southeast) and assumed reparations obligations that totaled an estimated $570 million upon their completion in 1952. A Treaty of Friendship, Cooperation, and Mutual Assistance with the Soviet Union, concluded under Soviet pressure in 1948 and renewed in 1955, 1970, and 1983, precluded the adoption of an anti-Soviet foreign policy.

Finnish politics from World War II to the late 1980s was marked by the juxtaposition of a remarkably stable presidency under J. K. PAASIKIVI (1946–1956), Urho K. KEKKONEN (1956–1981), and Mauno KOIVISTO (1981–1994) and a volatile parliamentary system that yielded a sequence of short-lived coalition governments based on shifting alliances. Most were center-left administrations in which the Finnish Social Democratic Party (*Suomen Sosiaalidemokraattinen Puolue*—SSDP) played a pivotal role, especially under the premierships of Kalevi SORSA between 1972 and 1987. A significant change occurred at the election of March 15–16, 1987, in which the conservative National Coalition (*Kansallinen Kokoomus*—Kok) gained nine seats, drawing to within three of the plurality Social Democrats. On April 30, for the first time in 20 years, a Kok leader, Harri HOLKERI, became prime minister, heading a four-party coalition that included the SSDP, the Swedish People's Party (*Ruotsalainen Kansanpuolue/Svenska Folkpartiet*—RKP/SFP), and the Finnish Rural Party (*Suomen Maaseudun Puolue*—SMP), the last eventually withdrawing in August 1990. In second-round electoral college balloting on

at 6 percent, and annual GDP growth remained between 1 and 2 percent during 2001–2004. Despite a labor dispute in the paper industry, overall growth remained strong in 2005 at 3.2 percent, and the GDP is expected to grow at 3.5 percent in 2006. In contrast, unemployment has remained high, hovering between 8 and 9 percent during 2000–2006.

Finland was a founding member of the European Union's (EU) Economic and Monetary Union (EMU) on January 1, 1999.

Government and Politics

Political Background

The achievement of Finnish independence followed some eight centuries of foreign domination, first by Sweden (until 1809) and subsequently by virtue of Finland's status as a Grand Duchy within the prerevolutionary Russian Empire. The nation's

February 15, 1988, President Koivisto (SSDP) easily won election to a second six-year term.

In the face of mounting economic adversity that included surging unemployment, high interest rates, and a drastically weakened GDP, both the Kok and the SSDP fared poorly at the parliamentary poll of March 17, 1991, with the opposition Finnish Center (*Suomen Keskusta–Finlands Centern*—Kesk), led by Esko AHO, emerging as the core of a new center-right coalition that included the Kok, the RKP/SFP, and the Finnish Christian Union (*Suomen Kristillinen Liitto*—SKL). The balloting produced a record number of legislative turnovers, approximately two-thirds of the incumbents being denied reelection.

Following the 1991 election, Prime Minister Aho announced a drastic stabilization program to alleviate the country's worst recession since World War II. In November, with the economy continuing to worsen, the markka was devalued by 12.3 percent, while labor agreed to a wage freeze until 1993. In an effort to avoid further devaluation, the government in April 1992 announced public sector cuts equivalent to approximately 2 percent of GDP. Another devaluation, in the form of a decision to let the markka float vis-à-vis other European currencies, was nonetheless ordered in September.

Unexpectedly selected as the SSDP candidate in preference to former premier Sorsa, career diplomat Martti AHTISAARI was the comfortable victor in presidential elections held in two rounds on January 16 and February 6, 1994. In the runoff balloting, he took 53.9 percent of the vote, against 46.1 percent for Defense Minister Elisabeth REHN of the RKP/SFP.

Having agreed with Brussels in March 1994 on terms for entry into the European Union (EU, formerly the European Community—EC), Finland became the first of the three Scandinavian aspirants to conduct a referendum on the issue. Most of the political establishment favored entry, and Prime Minister Aho had deflected opposition from the farming constituency of his own Kesk party by appointing a vocal EU critic, Heikki HAAVISTO,

as foreign minister in charge of the entry negotiations. The decision of the small anti-EU SKL in June to leave the coalition proved to be only a minor setback. Held on October 16, the referendum yielded a 53 to 47 percent margin in favor of entry, the majority "yes" vote of urban southern areas outweighing the mainly "no" verdict of the rural north.

With EU entry safely accomplished on January 1, 1995, the Aho government faced a general election amid continuing economic adversity, a modest upturn in 1994 not having reduced unemployment appreciably (unemployment peaked at 22 percent). The result of the balloting on March 19 was a swing to the left, the Social Democrats achieving their highest postwar vote share and the Left-Wing Alliance (*Vasemmistoliitto*—Vas) also gaining ground. A month later SSDP leader Paavo LIPPONEN formed an ideologically diverse ("rainbow") coalition government that included the RKP/SFP, Kok, the Vas, and the Green League.

The electoral swing to the left in 1995 was attributed to public disenchantment with the harsh economic consequences of the previous government's free-market, deregulatory policies, which were seen as having accentuated the damaging effects of international economic recession. It also appeared that Finnish voters sought to balance the new international course represented by EU membership with familiar welfare state policies at the domestic level. There was nevertheless consensus within the new coalition that the austerity program instituted by the previous government should be continued, albeit with greater emphasis on job creation.

The SSDP retained its plurality in the legislative balloting of March 21, 1999, although its seat total declined from 63 to 51. The Kok finished second with 48 seats, followed by the Kesk, whose total jumped from 39 in 1995 to 46. After several weeks of negotiations, the five parties of the previous coalition agreed to form a new government, which was installed on April 15 under Lipponen's continued leadership.

Foreign Minister Tarja HALONEN of the SSDP led seven candidates in first-round presidential balloting on January 16, 2000, with 40 percent of the vote. She defeated Aho, 51.6 to 48.4 percent, in the runoff poll on February 6 and was inaugurated as Finland's first female president on March 1.

The recent trend of close elections continued on March 16, 2003, as the Kesk captured 55 seats; the Kesk formed a three-party coalition government on April 15 with the former ruling SSDP (53 seats) and the RKP/SFP (8 seats) headed by the Kesk's Anneli JÄÄTTEENMÄKI. With the appointment of Jäätteenmäki, Finland became the only country in Europe with both a female president and prime minister. However, Jäätteenmäki resigned on June 18 following a major dispute over the possible leaking of secret documents (see Current issues, below). She was succeeded on June 24 by Matti VANHANEN of the Kesk.

President Halonen won reelection in January 2006, narrowly defeating Sauli NIINISTÖ, 51.8 to 48.2 percent, in the second round of the election. The election largely focused on the future direction of Finland's relationship with Europe, the North Atlantic Treaty Organization (NATO), and the effects of globalization (see Foreign relations, below).

Constitution and Government

The constitution of 1919 provided for a parliamentary system in combination with a strong presidency, which in practice has tended to grow even stronger because of the characteristic division of the legislature (*Eduskunta/Riksdagen*) among a large number of competing parties. The president is directly elected (since 1994) for a six-year term in two rounds of voting if no candidate obtains an absolute majority in the first. The head of state is directly responsible for foreign affairs and, until recently, shared domestic responsibilities with the prime minister and the cabinet. The *Eduskunta*, a unicameral body of 200 members, is elected by proportional representation for a four-year term, subject to dissolution by the president. The judicial system includes a Supreme Court, a Supreme

Administrative Court, courts of appeal, and district and municipal courts.

Administratively, Finland is divided into 12 provinces (*läänit*), which are subdivided into municipalities and rural communes. The 11 mainland provinces are headed by presidentially appointed governors, while the Swedish-speaking island province of Åland enjoys domestic autonomy (see Related Territory, below).

After decades of piecemeal reform of constitutional law, the *Eduskunta* on February 12, 1999, endorsed the text of a new constitution and, following the elections of March, the new basic law also was formally approved by the new legislature. The new constitution, which entered into force on March 1, 2000, strengthened the powers of Parliament at the expense of the presidency by, among other things, limiting the president's authority in domestic matters (e.g., future prime minister-designates will be named by the Parliament, not the president).

Foreign Relations

Proximity to the Soviet Union and recognition of that country's security interests were decisive factors in the shaping of post–World War II Finnish foreign policy, although Helsinki followed a course of strict neutrality and abstention from participation in military alliances. The desire "to remain outside the conflicting interests of the Great Powers," formally recorded in the Soviet-Finnish treaty of 1948, did not preclude active and independent participation in such multilateral organizations as the United Nations (UN), the Nordic Council, and eventually the Organization for Economic Cooperation and Development. Finland also was a leading proponent of the Conference on (later Organization for) Security and Cooperation in Europe (CSCE/OSCE), in recognition of which the landmark CSCE Final Act of 1975 was concluded at Helsinki.

Joining the European Free Trade Association (EFTA) at its inception in 1960 as an associate member, Finland, on a similar basis, became in 1973 the first free-market economy to be linked to the Soviet bloc's Council for Mutual Economic Assistance. In 1985 it became a full member of EFTA. Despite continuing ties to its eastern neighbor, trade with the Soviet Union declined sharply after 1988, with the country moving to adopt EC industrial standards to protect its access to the EC's impending unified market. On January 20, 1992, the 1948 treaty was formally superseded by a new Russo-Finnish mutual cooperation pact, and on March 18 Finland applied for EC membership. As a prelude to EC entry, Finland became a signatory on May 2 of the European Economic Area treaty between the EC and EFTA countries. Earlier in March it had become a founding member of the Council of the Baltic Sea States.

Negotiations on EC/EU membership opened formally in February 1993 and were successfully completed in March 1994, entry being duly accomplished January 1, 1995, following final parliamentary approval on November 18. In April 1994 Finland became linked to NATO by joining the alliance's Partnership for Peace program. Approximately one-third of the Finns favor joining NATO, and the issue became central during the 2006 presidential election. President Halonen's reelection, however, is a strong indication that Finland will likely stay outside of NATO and will stay the traditional course of neutrality.

In response to the ongoing crisis in Iraq, Finland has joined the International Reconstruction Fund Facility for Iraq and pledged $6.2 million for reconstruction. Finnish firms also have won reconstruction contracts. However, the government has rejected U.S. requests for Finnish peacekeeping forces to be deployed to Iraq. Meanwhile, on the domestic front, the current government has pledged to address the issue of chronically high unemployment.

A key factor in the Finnish vote to enter the EU was a belief that membership would afford protection against a revival of Russian imperialism. Much discussion had been generated by the strong showing of Vladimir Zhirinovsky's ultra-nationalist Liberal Democrats in the 1993 Russian election and of Zhirinovsky's declared aim of restoring Finland to the Russian empire. The subsequent course of

Moscow's external policy provided little reassurance for the Finns. Indeed, President Boris Yeltsin of Russia reopened old wounds when he was in Helsinki for a summit with President Clinton in March 1997. Yeltsin said Russia was opposed to any attempt by Finland to join NATO. His remark and the summit itself renewed discussion of Finland's balancing act on the political continuum between East and West. Notwithstanding its participation with NATO and the EU, Finland sought to maintain friendly relations with Moscow by signing six economic and military cooperation accords with Russia during a visit to Helsinki by Prime Minister Chernomyrdin in May 1996. Relations with Russia have steadily improved as President Halonen and Russian President Putin reportedly have forged a strong working relationship that has yielded agreements in 2006 on immigration along their common border and a Russian pledge to pay off its outstanding debt originating back to the Soviet Era.

Finland assumed the six-month rotating EU presidency on July 1, 2006.

Current Issues

The 2003 Iraq War played an important role in Finnish domestic and foreign policy. In early 2003 President Halonen and Prime Minister Lipponen called for Iraqi compliance with the UN Security Council resolutions. However, they asserted that UN weapons inspectors had not found any clear evidence justifying an attack against Iraq. As late as March 2003 Finland's foreign minister maintained that, without an additional Security Council mandate, any preemptive war against Iraq would be "illegal and should not be allowed."

During the March 2003 elections, however, Kesk leader Anneli Jäätteenmäki allegedly leaked foreign ministry documents to the news media that seemed to indicate that Prime Minister Lipponen would ultimately support the U.S. coalition against Iraq. The issue resonated with the Finnish electorate who, by a 79 percent majority, did not favor any kind of military action against Iraq, and the Kesk won an exceptionally close legislative election. However, Jäätteenmäki resigned as prime minister after only two months in office when coalition partner SSDP withdrew its support for her because of the leaked documents issue. (Jäätteenmäki apologized for the release of the papers but denied they were secret. In March 2004 she was acquitted on all charges related to the matter.) The scandal reportedly has raised issues about the Finnish public's trust in government—previously ranked by Transparency International as one of the world's least corrupt—as well as the future direction of Finland's foreign policy.

In 2006 Finland began construction of the first nuclear power plant in the Baltic region since the Chernobyl accident in 1986. Currently under construction on Eurajoki, the reactor is scheduled to come online in 2009. With limited domestic energy resources, Finland derives about two-thirds of its energy from foreign sources and nuclear energy offers an avenue to avoid increased levels of dependence on Russian fossil fuels.

Political Parties

Finland's multiparty system, based on proportional representation, prevents any single party from gaining a parliamentary majority. Although still used for assessment of broad electoral trends, the traditional classification of parties into "socialist" and "nonsocialist" became less relevant in the 1980s, as policy differences eroded and coalitions were formed across what remained of the right-left ideological divide.

Government Parties

Finnish Center (*Suomen Keskusta–Finlands Centern*—Kesk). The group that was formed in 1906 as the Agrarian Union (*Maalaisliitto*) and renamed the Center Party (*Keskustapuolue*) in 1965 has traditionally represented rural interests, particularly those of the small farmers. Because of major population shifts within the country, it now draws additional support from urban areas. The party surged from 40 parliamentary seats in 1987 to a plurality of 55 in 1991, with the 37-year-old

Esko Aho becoming the youngest prime minister in Finnish history, but also, amid economic recession, the most unpopular by 1994. The party slumped to 44 seats in the 1995 balloting, after which it went into opposition. It secured 48 seats in 1999.

Aho also served as the Kesk standard-bearer in the 2000 presidential campaign, finishing second with 34.4 percent in the first-round voting and nearly defeating the SSDP's Tarja Halonen in the second round on the strength of a last-minute popularity surge based in part on his opposition to EU sanctions against Austria. The Kesk continued to gain strength and earned 55 seats in the 2003 elections.

Prime Minister Vanhanen opted to run for the January 2006 presidential elections and finished third in the first round of voting with 18.6 percent of the vote. He has continued to aggressively integrate Finland into the European and global economy while adopting a more moderate position on social issues. For instance, Vanhanen met with Muslim leaders and expressed disappointment that cartoons depicting the Prophet Mohammad had been posted on the website of Suomen Sisu, a Finnish right-wing nationalist group.

Leaders: Matti VANHANEN (Prime Minister and Chair), Mauri PEKKARINEN (Minister of Trade and Industry and Leader of the Parliamentary Group), Eero LANKIA (Secretary General), Markus OJAKOSKI, and Mari Johanna KIVINIEMI (Deputy Group Chair).

Finnish Social Democratic Party (*Suomen Sosiaalidemokraattinen Puolue*—SSDP). The SSDP was formed in 1899 as the Finnish Labor Party. It is supported mainly by skilled laborers and lower-class, white-collar workers, with additional support from small farmers and professionals. It has been the largest party in the legislature following virtually every election since 1907, one of the most conspicuous exceptions being in 1991 when, running second to the Center Party, its parliamentary representation dropped from 56 to 48 seats. Having been in office continuously since 1966, the party went into opposition in 1991. Paavo Lipponen led the party to a major victory (in Finnish terms) in the 1995 elections, the SSDP vote share increasing by over six points to 28.3 percent. However, the SSDP declined to 51 seats on a vote share of 22.9 percent in 1999.

After Martti Ahtisaari decided not to run in the May 1999 primary for the party's 2000 presidential nomination, the SSDP elected Foreign Minister Tarja Halonen as its candidate. As is the custom for Finnish presidents, Halonen resigned from the party following her election in order to serve in a nonpartisan capacity.

In the March 2003 parliamentary elections, the SSDP held onto its 53 seats but was unable to maintain its majority position in the coalition government. Lipponen stepped down as prime minister and assumed the role of the speaker of Parliament.

President Halonen stood for reelection in January 2006 and won after the second round of voting in a surprisingly close election against Sauli Niinistö (the Kok party). Reaffirming the party's center-left position, Halonen defended the role of the welfare state in protecting citizens' rights and needs in a globalized world. Support from the labor unions played a critical role in her victory.

Party Chair Paavo Lippon announced in March 2006 that he would resign his position after holding the post for more than 12 years. The SSDP is scheduled to hold party elections in June 2006. Arja Alho, a member of parliament, has announced his intention to run for the party's chief leadership position.

Leaders: Paavo LIPPONEN (Speaker of Parliament and Chair of the Party), Sade TAH-VANAINEN (Vice Chair), Eero HEINALUOMA (Secretary), Tarja FILATOV, Arja ALHO.

Swedish People's Party (*Ruotsalainen Kansanpuolue/Svenska Folkpartiet*—RKP/SFP). Liberal in outlook, the SFP has represented the political and social interests of the Swedish-speaking population since 1906. Consistently taking 5 to 6 percent of the overall vote and with strong indirect support in the predominantly Swedish Åland Islands (see Related Territory), it has participated in a variety of postwar coalitions. In the 1994 presiden-

tial balloting, its candidate, Elisabeth Rehn, was the surprise runner-up in the first round but lost in the runoff to Ahtisaari. The RKP/SFP won 12 seats in the 1995 and 1999 legislative polls, while Rehn declined to 7.9 percent of the vote in the first-round presidential balloting in 2000. The RKP/SFP suffered a serious setback in the March 2003 parliamentary elections by retaining only 7 of its 10 seats.

Leaders: Jan-Erik ENESTAM (Minister of the Environment and Chair), Elisabeth REHN (1999 presidential candidate), Christina GESTRIN (Parliamentary Group Leader), Ulla ACHRÉN (Secretary General).

Other Parliamentary Parties

National Coalition Party (*Kansallinen Kokoomus*—KK or Kok). A conservative party formed in 1918, the Kok is the prime representative for private enterprise and the business community as well as for landowners. At the March 1979 general election, it displaced the SKDL (see Vas, below) as the second-largest parliamentary party. Retaining this position in 1983 and 1987, the Kok's success in the latter election enabled it to return to government (after 21 years in opposition) as head of a coalition government. The party dropped to third place in 1991, when its representation plummeted from 53 to 40 seats and it became a junior coalition partner. It continued in this status following a marginal decline to 17.9 percent in the 1995 balloting. However, in 1999 the Kok made the biggest gain of any of the 13 parties by picking up 7 additional seats. Riitta Uosukainen, speaker of the Parliament, gained 12.8 percent of the vote in the first round of the 2000 presidential balloting.

In the March 2003 parliamentary elections the Kok won 40 seats, a drop from the 45 seats it held after the 1999 election. The Kok has placed Finland's role in the EU as the centerpiece of its platform. It favors enlargement of the EU while simultaneously calling for clarifying and strengthening the rules that govern that institution. Sauli Niinistö continued these themes in his 2006 presidential bid. Embracing globalization and free trade,

Niinistö called for a greater role of Finland in both European and transatlantic affairs.

Leaders: Jyrki KATAINEN (Chair); Harri JASKARI (Secretary General); Marjo Matikainen-Kallström, Jari KOSKINEN, Paula RISIKKO (Vice Chairs); Sauli NIINISTÖ (2006 presidential candidate).

Left-Wing Alliance   (*Vasemmistoliitto*—VL or Vas). Vas was launched in April 1990 during a congress at Helsinki of representatives of the leading Communist and left-socialist groups. Following the congress, the Finnish Communist Party (*Suomen Kommunistinen Puolue*—SKP) and its electoral affiliate, the Finnish People's Democratic League (*Suomen Kansan Demokraattinen Liitto*—SKDL), voted to disband. (The SKP reorganized in 1994; see SKP, below.)

The SKDL front had been created in 1944 by the pro-Soviet SKP (founded in 1918) and had established a sizeable electoral constituency, winning a narrow plurality in 1958 and participating in various center-left coalitions until 1982. Meanwhile, in 1969 the SKP had split into majority "revisionist" and minority "Stalinist" wings, the latter being formally ousted in 1984. In 1986 the SKP launched its own Democratic Alternative front, which achieved little more than to weaken the SKDL. The alliance and adoption of a left socialist and anti-EC/EU platform at the 1990 congress alleviated most of these old rifts, with Vas advancing to 11.2 percent of the vote in 1995 and joining a coalition government headed by the Social Democrats. Vas won 20 seats in the 1999 poll, down 2 from 1995.

Vas gained an additional seat in the 2003 parliamentary elections to reach a total of 19 seats. Reacting against the economic pressures associated with globalization and the free movement of capital, Vas has defined its role as a defender of Finnish labor and agriculture.

In May 2006 Vas elected Martti Korhonen party chair. Korhonen immediately announced his intention to make "progressive tax reform" and the expansion of social welfare programs for the poor as centerpieces of the party's message for the 2007 election. Additionally, he indicated his willingness to join the next governing coalition.

Leaders: Martti KORHONEN (Chair), Esko SEPPÄNEN (Member of European Parliament), Ralf SUND (Secretary and Party Election Coordinator), Pekka RISTELÄ (Secretary for International Affairs).

Green League   (*Vihreä Liitto*—VL or Vihr). The Vihr was launched in 1988 as an unstructured alliance of several mainstream environmentalist organizations, including the **Green Parliamentary Group** (*Vihreä Eduskuntaryhmä*), which had won 2 seats in 1983, 4 in 1987, and 10 in 1991. The Vihr fell back to 9 seats on a 6.5 vote share in 1995 (but nevertheless entered government for the first time) before rebounding to 11 seats in 1999. Heidi HAUTALA, a member of Parliament, served as the Vihr presidential candidate in 2000, collecting 3.3 percent of the first-round votes. Vihr earned its best ever result in the March 2003 parliamentary elections, increasing its number of seats from 11 to 14. The current party leadership was elected at a party conference on May 22, 2005.

Leaders: Tarja CRONBERG (Party Chair); Sulevi RIUKULEHTO; Anni SINNEMÄKI; Ville NIINISTÖ, Janne LÄNSIPURO (Deputy Chairs); Ari Heikkinen (Secretary).

Christian Democrats in Finland   (*Suomen Kristillisdemokraatit*—KD). The KD adopted its present name at a May 2001 party conference, having previously been called the Finnish Christian Union (*Suomen Kristillinen Liitto*—SKL). The SKL was formed in 1958 to advance Christian ideals in public life. It won eight legislative seats in 1991 and joined a Center-headed coalition before withdrawing in 1994 because of its opposition to EU accession. It lost one of its seats on a 3 percent vote share in 1995 and won ten seats in 1999. Emphasizing the need to reform the Finnish economy to be more socially and ecologically responsible, the KD suffered a setback in the March 2003 parliamentary elections, losing three of its seven seats. KD is making increasing employment, guaranteeing the accessibility of basic services, and enhancing family life its central messages for the 2007 parliamentary election.

Leaders: Paivi RÄSÄNEN (Chair), Annika KOKKLO (Secretary General), Sari ESSAYAH (Secretary).

True Finn Party   (*Perussuomalaiset*—PS). Formerly known as the Finnish Rural Party (*Suomen Maaseudun Puolue*—SMP), the PS has roots that extend back to a small Poujadist faction that broke from the Agrarian Union in 1956. As a protest group representing farmers and merchants, the SMP made substantial gains in the 1983 election, winning 17 seats and subsequently joining the government coalition; its representation fell to 9 seats in 1987, and it was awarded only one cabinet post as a member of the Holkeri coalition. It withdrew from the coalition in August 1990, slipped to 7 seats in 1991 and, having opposed EU membership, retained only 1 seat in 1995 (with a 1.3 percent vote share). The renamed grouping won 1 seat in 1999 with a vote share of 1 percent. During the March 2003 election, the PS adopted a platform that mixed socialism with a hard-line, right-wing populist stance that emphasized low taxes, encouraged small businesses, and advocated relief for personal debt. Its resurgence as an alternative party has been in part credited to the charismatic personalities of its new leader, Timo Soini.

Leaders: Timo SOINI (Chair and presidential candidate), Raimo VISTBACKA (Vice Chair), Hannu PURHO (Public Relations Officer), Tony HALME (Member of Parliament).

For Åland in the Diet   (*För Åland I Rikselagen*). This is a regional party whose platform is based upon a conservative ideology that stresses "free-thinking cooperation." Since 1948 the party has won a single seat in every parliamentary election.

Other Parties Contesting the 2003 Legislative Election

Ecological Party   (*Ekologinen Puolue*—EP). The EP is a populist party launched in 1990 as a "non-ideological" alternative to the left-leaning Green Union. Sometimes known as the Eco-Diverse Party, its best showing at the polls was in 1995, when it captured one seat. In 1999 the EP failed to win any seats, and in 2003 it managed only 0.2 percent of the vote and again did not earn any seats.

Leaders: Pertti VIRTANEN (Chair), Jukka WALLENIUS (Party Secretary).

Liberals   (*Liberaalit*). This grouping was launched as the Liberal People's Party (*Liberaalinen Kansanpuole*—LKP) in 1965 as a merger of the former Finnish People's Party and the Liberal Union. Having participated in most governments from 1966, the LKP contested the 1979 election in alliance with the Kesk and in 1982 voted to merge with that party while retaining its own identity. The LKP formally reestablished its independence in 1986, although many of its former supporters remained in the Kesk, and the LKP won no legislative seats in 1987, 1991, or 1995. It participated (unsuccessfully) in an electoral alliance with the NSP in 1999. In 2001 the LKP changed its name to the Liberals.

Leaders: Ilkka INNAMAA (Chair), Toni HEINONEN, Janne VAHALA (Deputy Chair).

Communist Party of Finland   (*Suomen Kommunistinen Puolue*—SKP). A descendant of the original SKP (see Vas, above), the current SKP emerged at a congress in 1994 held by communists wishing to maintain a separate identity outside Vas. The reforged grouping opposed many policies of the subsequent "rainbow" government coalition and formally registered as a party in February 1997. The SKP secured only 0.8 percent of the vote in the 1999 legislative poll and also failed to capture any seats in the March 2003 parliamentary election.

Leaders: Yrgö HAKANEN (Chair), Riita TYNJÄ (Vice Chair), Arto VIITANIEMI (General Secretary).

Communist Workers' Party   (*Kommunistinen Tyoväenpuolue*—KTP). The KTP was launched in May 1988 by a group of former Democratic Alternative Stalinists. The party contested the 1991, 1995, 1999, and 2003 elections

Cabinet

As of May 1, 2006

Prime Minister	Matti Vanhanen (Kesk)
Deputy Prime Minister	Eero HEINÄLUOMA (SSDP)

Ministers

Agriculture and Forestry	Juha Korkäoja (Kesk)
Culture	Tanja Karpela (Kesk) [f]
Defense	Seppo Kääriäinen (Kesk)
Education	Antti Kallomäki (SSDP)
Environment	Jan-Erik Enestam (SFP)
Finance	Eero Heinäluoma (SSDP)
Foreign Affairs	Erkki Tuomioja (SSDP)
Foreign Trade and Development	Mari Kiviniemi (Kesk) [f]
Health and Social Services	Liisa Hyssälä (Kesk) [f]
Interior	Kari Rajamäki (SSDP)
Justice	Leena Luhtanen (SSDP) [f]
Labor	Tarja Filatov (SSDP) [f]
Minister of Finance (Coordinate)	Ulla-Maj Wideroos (RKP/SFP) [f]
Regional and Municipal Affairs	Hannes Manninen (Kesk)
Social Affairs and Health	Tuula Haatainen (SSDP) [f]
Trade and Industry	Mauri Pekkarinen (Kesk)
Transport and Communications	Lenna Luhtanen (SSDP) [f]

[f] = female

under the rubric "For Peace and Socialism," winning less than 0.1 percent of the vote in 2003.

Leaders: Hannu HARJU (Chair), Heikki MÄNNIKKÖ (General Secretary).

Other parties contesting the 2003 election were the **Natural Law Party** (*Luonnonlain Puolue—* LLP) (less than 0.1 percent of the vote); **Pensioners for the People** (*Elakeläiset Kansan Asialla*) (0.2 percent); **Force for Change in Finland** (0.4 percent); and **Finnish People's Blue-Whites** (0.2 percent).

Legislature

The **Parliament** (*Eduskunta/Riksdagen*) is a unicameral body of 200 members elected by universal suffrage on the basis of proportional representation in 15 districts. Its term is four years, although the president may dissolve the legislature and order a new election at any time. Following the election of March 16, 2003, the seat distribution was as follows: Finnish Center, 55; Finnish Social Democratic Party, 53; National Coalition Party, 40; Left-Wing Alliance; 19; Green League, 14; Christian Democrats in Finland, 7; Swedish Peoples Party, 8; True Finn Party, 3; For Åland in the Diet, 1.

Speaker: Paavo LIPPONEN.

Communications

Finland enjoys complete freedom of the press; broadcasting is largely over government-controlled facilities.

Press

Newspapers are privately owned, some by political parties or their affiliates; many others are controlled by or support a particular party. The following are dailies published in Helsinki in Finnish, unless otherwise indicated: *Helsingin Sanomat* (446,380), independent; *Ilta-Sanomat* (218,289), independent; *Aamulehti* (Tampere, 135,478), National Coalition; *Turun Sanomat* (Turku, 115,142), independent; *Iltalehti* (134,777), independent; *Kaleva* (Oulu, 85,151), independent; *Maaseudun Tulevaisuus* (84,000, triweekly); *Kauppalehti* (85,292), independent; *Keskisuomalainen* (Jyväskylä, 77,135), independent; *Savon Sanomat* (Kuopio, 67,219), Center Party; *Hufvudstadsbladet* (52,523 daily, 61,000 Sunday), in Swedish, independent; *Demari* (17,252), organ of the Finnish Social Democratic Party.

News Agencies

The Finnish News Agency (*Oy Suomen Tietotoimisto*—STT/*Finska Notisbyrån Ab*—FNB) is a major independent facility covering the entire country; most leading international bureaus also maintain offices in Helsinki.

Broadcasting and Computing

Broadcasting is largely controlled by the state-owned Finnish Broadcasting Company (*Oy Yleisradio Ab*), which offers radio programming in both Finnish and Swedish and services two television channels; there is one commercial television channel, MTV 3, in addition to the offerings of local TV outlets. There were approximately 4.0 million television receivers and 2.3 million personal computers serving 2.8 million Internet users in 2003.

Intergovernmental Representation

Ambassador to the U.S.
Pekka LINTU

U.S. Ambassador to Finland
Marliyn WARE

Permanent Representative to the UN
Kirsti LINTONEN

IGO Memberships (Non-UN)
AC, ADB, AfDB, BIS, CBSS, CERN, CEUR, EBRD, EIB, ESA, EU, Eurocontrol, IADB, IEA, Interpol, IOM, NC, NIB, OECD, OSCE, PCA, WCO, WTO

Related Territories

Åland Islands (Ahvenanmaa).

Lying in the Gulf of Bothnia between Finland and Sweden, the Ålands encompass more than 6,500 islands, less than 10 percent of which are populated. The total land area is 599 square miles (1,552 sq. km.), inclusive of inland water. The capital is Mariehamn (*Maarianhamina*) on Åland Island. The inhabitants, an overwhelming majority of whom are Swedish-speaking, were estimated to total 26,000 in 2001.

The islands were under Swedish rule until 1809, when Finland was ceded to Russia and they became part of the Finnish Grand Duchy. When Finland declared its independence in 1917, the islanders expressed a desire for reversion to Sweden but were obliged to settle for internal autonomy, a status that was confirmed by a League of Nations decision in 1921.

While constitutionally one of Finland's 12 provinces, the islands were granted expanded autonomy in 1951 and again in 1991 (effective January 1, 1993). Provisions included enhanced legislative and fiscal authority, in addition to a recognition of regional citizenship, the right to tax alcohol sales, and full control of postal services. In 1988 the principle of majoritarian parliamentary government was introduced, supplanting a system whereby any party electing at least 5 deputies to the 30-member legislature (*Lagting*) could secure representation in the Executive Council (*Landskapsstyrelse*). The leading political groups are the **Center Party** (*Åländsk Center*), the **Moderate Party** (*Frisinnad Samverkan*), the **Åland Social**

Democratic Party (*Ålands Socialdemokrater*), the **Liberal Party of Åland** (*Liberalerna på Åland*), and the **Greens of Åland** (*Gröna på Åland*), the first three of which formed a coalition government after the election of October 20, 1991. In the October 1995 election the Social Democrats ran fourth (4 seats) and were not included in the coalition of the Center (9 seats) and Moderate (6 seats) parties, which invited an independent to join with them in forming a new government.

At the election of October 17, 1999, the Center and Liberal parties each won 9 seats, while the Moderates dropped to 4 and the Social Democrats to 3. A **Progress Group** (*Ålands Framstegsgrupp*) won 1, with the remaining seats being taken by the **Independents** (*Obunden Samling*). Once again the Center and Moderate parties, joined by the Independents, formed a governing coalition. The islands' single representative in the Finnish Parliament has consistently been returned by the **Åland Coalition** (*Åländsk Samling*), grouping all the main local parties, and normally joins the parliamentary group of the Swedish People's Party. (The current representative is described as a member of For Åland in the Diet [see above].)

In the October 17, 2003, elections, the Liberal Party of Åland and the Center Party each won 7 seats, followed by the Social Democrats with 6; the **Free-Thinking Cooperation Party**, 4; the **Nonaligned Rally Party**, 3; the **List for Åland's Future**, 2; and the Progress Group, 1.

In a separate referendum on EU accession, held on November 20, 1994, the Åland islanders followed the rest of Finland (and Sweden) by voting in favor, but by the much larger margin of 73.7 to 26.3 percent. Thanks to the islands' special tax-free status, negotiated by Helsinki when Finland joined the EU in 1995, tourism is thriving, and Mariehamn has become a center for Baltic Sea ferry services.

Chair (Lantråd) of the Landskapsstyrelse (Prime Minister): Roger NORDLUND (Center Party).

Speaker (Talman) of the Landsting: Gun CARLSON.

FRANCE

FRENCH REPUBLIC

République Française

The Country

The largest country of Western Europe in area and once the seat of a world empire extending into five continents, France today is largely concentrated within its historic frontiers, maintaining its traditional role as the cultural center of the French-speaking world but retaining only a few vestigial political footholds in the Pacific and Indian Oceans and the Americas. While 94.4 percent of the population of metropolitan France, which includes the island of Corsica, are citizens, immigration has become a major political issue, the principal foreign ethnic groups being of North African (Arab), Portuguese, Turkish, Italian, Spanish, and German origins. French is the near-universal language, although German has co-official status in Alsace schools, and Alemannic, Basque, Breton, Corsican, and other languages and dialects are spoken to some extent in outlying regions. The Roman Catholic Church, officially separated from the state in 1905, is predominant, but there are substantial Protestant and Jewish minorities as well as a growing Islamic population, and freedom of worship is strictly maintained. Women constituted 47 percent of the labor force in 2000, concentrated in clerical, sales, and human services sectors; female representation in the national legislature almost doubled in the 1997 elections to just under 11 percent and rose in 2002 to over 12 percent.

In addition to large domestic reserves of iron ore, bauxite, natural gas, and hydroelectric power, France leads Western European countries in the production and export of agricultural products; it also is an important exporter of chemicals, iron and steel products, automobiles, machinery, precision tools, aircraft, ships, textiles, wines, perfumes, and *haute couture*. The industrial sector contributes about one-fourth of GDP and employs a like share of the workforce, with the service sector accounting for most of the balances. Agriculture now accounts for only 3 percent of GDP and employment.

Post–World War II economic planning, associated particularly with the name of Jean MONNET, contributed to the strengthening and expansion of an economy that had been traditionally characterized by fractionalization of industry and inefficient production techniques. The key turning point was

Political Status: Republic under mixed parliamentary-presidential system established by constitution adopted by referendum of September 28, 1958, and instituted on October 4.

Area: 211,207 sq. mi. (547,026 sq. km.).

Population: 58,518,395 (1999C); 60,737,000 (2005E). Area and population figures are for metropolitan France (including Corsica); for overseas departments and other dependent jurisdictions, see Related Territories, below.

Major Urban Centers (2005E): PARIS (2,147,000); Marseilles (797,000); Lyons (473,000); Toulouse (435,000); Nice (338,000); Nantes (277,000); Strasbourg (275,000); Montpellier (249,000); Bordeaux (233,000); Rennes (210,000); Le Havre (186,000); Saint-Étienne (176,000).

Official Language: French.

Monetary Unit: Euro (market rate July 1, 2006: 1 euro = $1.28US).

President: Jacques CHIRAC (Union for a Popular Movement); elected May 7, 1995, and inaugurated May 17 for a seven-year term, succeeding François MITTERRAND (Socialist Party); reelected for a five-year term in runoff balloting on May 5, 2002, and inaugurated on May 16.

Premier: Dominique de VILLEPIN (Union for a Popular Movement); appointed by the president on May 31, 2005, succeeding Jean-Pierre RAFFARIN (Union for a Popular Movement), who had tendered his resignation earlier that day.

France's participation in the European Community (EC, subsequently the European Union—EU) from the formation of the European Coal and Steel Community in 1951 and the resultant linking of its economy to that of the more dynamic Federal Republic of Germany.

The dirigiste policies of successive governments in the 1970s and 1980s yielded steady growth averaging 2.5 percent a year in 1981–1990. In terms of GDP, France remained far behind Germany but pulled well ahead of the United Kingdom, estab-

lishing itself as the industrialized world's fourth largest economy until overtaken in 1999–2000 by a resurgent United Kingdom.

From a peak of over 12 percent in 1996–1997, unemployment dropped to 8.5 percent in 2001. Meanwhile, real GDP growth of 3.5 percent was achieved in 1998, 3.2 percent in 1999, and 4.2 percent in 2000, before slowing to about 2.1 percent in 2001. Thereafter, unemployment began rising again, climbing to 9.5 percent in 2003, while the GDP showed little growth (1.3 percent in 2002 and 0.9 percent in 2003). For 2004 the rate of economic expansion improved to 2.1 percent, while the government undertook policy initiatives, including health care and pension reforms, that were expected to help ease future fiscal shortfalls, which in 2002–2005 exceeded the permissible limit (3 percent of GDP) set by the EU's Economic and Monetary Union (EMU). For 2005 the annualized unemployment rate once again approached 10 percent, while youth unemployment exceeded 20 percent (see Current issues, below). GDP growth for the year slipped to 1.5 percent.

Government and Politics

Political Background

For most of the century after its Revolution of 1789, France alternated between monarchical and republican forms of government, the last monarch being NAPOLEON III (Louis Napoleon), who was deposed in 1870. Overall, the republican tradition has given rise to five distinct regimes: the First Republic during the French Revolution; the Second Republic after the Revolution of 1848; the Third Republic from 1870 to 1940; the Fourth Republic, proclaimed in October 1946 but destined to founder in the 1950s on dissension occasioned by the revolt in Algeria; and the Fifth Republic, established in 1958 by Gen. Charles DE GAULLE, who had headed the first postwar government.

Reentering public life at a moment of threatened civil war, de Gaulle agreed in May 1958 to accept investiture as premier on the condition that he be granted decree powers for six months and a mandate to draft a new constitution that would be submitted to a national referendum. Following adoption of the constitution and his designation by an electoral college, de Gaulle took office on January 8, 1959, as president of the Fifth Republic, naming as premier Michel DEBRÉ. De Gaulle's initially ambiguous policy for Algeria eventually crystallized into a declaration of support for Algerian self-determination, leading in 1962 to the recognition of Algerian independence in spite of open opposition by French army leaders in Algeria and widespread terrorist activities in Algeria and metropolitan France.

Debré's resignation in April 1962 marked the end of the decolonization phase of the Fifth Republic and was followed by the induction as premier of Georges POMPIDOU, who was confirmed in office by a November 1962 election that gave the Gaullists an absolute majority in the National Assembly. Pompidou's premiership, which continued until mid-1968, was marked by heavy stress on the modernization of French economic and military power as well as by a more independent foreign policy that featured improved relations with the Soviet Union, recognition of Communist China, and opposition to U.S. policy in Vietnam and elsewhere.

Under a 1962 constitutional amendment calling for direct election of the president, de Gaulle won a second term in December 1965 over a variety of opposition candidates. The closeness of the election, which required a runoff between de Gaulle and François MITTERRAND, leader of the newly formed Federation of the Democratic and Socialist Left (*Fédération de la Gauche Démocrate et Socialiste*—FGDS), reflected a marked decline in the president's earlier popularity. The Gaullists were further set back by the parliamentary election of March 1967, in which they lost their majority in the National Assembly and became dependent on the support of the Independent Republicans (*Républicans Indépendants*—RI), led by Valéry GISCARD D'ESTAING.

The Fifth Republic was shaken in May–June 1968 by a period of national crisis that began with student demonstrations and led to a nationwide general strike and an overt bid for power by leftist political leaders. After a period of indecision, de Gaulle dissolved the National Assembly and called for a new election, which yielded an unexpectedly strong Gaullist victory. Maurice COUVE DE MURVILLE, who succeeded Pompidou as premier in July 1968, was entrusted by de Gaulle with responsibility for directing a program of far-reaching internal reconstruction. However, following popular rejection of regional devolution and other constitutional proposals in a referendum held in April 1969, de Gaulle resigned, and the president of the Senate, Alain POHER, succeeded him as interim president of the republic. (De Gaulle died in November 1970.)

Former premier Pompidou, the Gaullist candidate, emerged as front-runner in first-round presidential balloting and defeated Poher (a centrist accorded reluctant support by the left) in a runoff election in June 1969. Inaugurated for a seven-year term five days later, Pompidou appointed Jacques CHABAN-DELMAS, president of the National Assembly, as premier in a cabinet that included former prime minister Debré as minister of defense and Giscard d'Estaing as minister of economy and finance. The revelation that Premier Chaban-Delmas had utilized tax loopholes to personal advantage contributed to circumstances that led to his resignation and replacement in July 1972 by Pierre MESSMER, a committed Gaullist. Despite a loss of some 100 seats, the Gaullists succeeded in retaining an assured majority in the legislative election of March 1973, and Messmer was redesignated as premier.

President Pompidou's death in April 1974 led to what was essentially a three-way presidential race among François Mitterrand, joint candidate of the Socialist Party (*Parti Socialiste*—PS), the French Communist Party (*Parti Communiste Français*—PCF), and other left-wing parties; Giscard d'Estaing for the center-right Independent Republicans; and Chaban-Delmas for the Gaullists. In the first round of the election Giscard d'Estaing outpolled Chaban-Delmas, and he went on to defeat Mitterrand in the May runoff with 50.7 percent of the vote. Although he was the first non-Gaullist president of the Fifth Republic, Giscard d'Estaing bowed to political reality by appointing a vigorous young Gaullist, Jacques CHIRAC, as premier.

By mid-1976 the government faced mounting problems, including renewed demonstrations by students opposing educational reform, substantial gains by the left in recent cantonal elections, one of the most devastating droughts in West European history, a growing export deficit, and spiraling inflation. In August Premier Chirac resigned, charging that the president would not grant him sufficient authority to deal with the nation's problems; he was immediately replaced by the politically independent Raymond BARRE, an economist.

Chirac's departure left France for the first time in over two decades without a Gaullist as either president or premier. Chirac proceeded, in late 1976, to reorganize the Gaullist party into the new Rally for the Republic (*Rassemblement pour la République*—RPR). Legislative balloting in March 1978 saw the "government majority," comprising the RPR and a new Giscardian coalition, the Union for French Democracy (*Union pour la Démocratie Française*—UDF), obtain a substantially larger margin of victory than in 1973.

At the first round of the presidential balloting in April 1981, Giscard d'Estaing narrowly led a field of ten candidates (including Chirac for the RPR), but he was defeated by Mitterrand at the May runoff by a 3.5 percent margin. In National Assembly balloting a month later, the Socialists secured a commanding legislative majority, and Pierre MAUROY, who had succeeded Barre as premier in May, announced a new Socialist-led government that included four Communists and one member of the Left Radical Movement (*Mouvement des Radicaux de Gauche*—MRG). From March 1983 the government also included a representative of the small Unified Socialist Party (*Parti Socialiste Unifié*—PSU).

In the face of increasingly overt criticism by the Communist Party and of substantial left-wing losses in balloting for the European Parliament in June 1984, Premier Mauroy felt obliged to submit his resignation; he was succeeded in July by Laurent FABIUS.

During 1985 the prospect of "cohabitation" between a Socialist president and a rightist government loomed as former premier Chirac forged a conservative alliance between the RPR and the UDF. While the Socialists remained the largest single party in the National Assembly after the election of March 1986, the RPR/UDF grouping drew within a few seats of a majority and, with Chirac's redesignation as premier, *"la république à deux têtes"* became a reality. The delicate balance persisted until the 1988 presidential election, at which Mitterrand was the principal candidate of the left, while the rightist vote was split between Chirac, former premier Barre of the UDF, and Jean-Marie LE PEN of the far-right National Front (*Front National*—FN). Mitterrand obtained a decisive plurality of 34.1 percent in first-round balloting and a 54.3 percent majority in the May runoff against Chirac, becoming the first incumbent in the 30-year history of the Fifth Republic to win reelection by popular vote.

Following Mitterrand's second triumph, the Socialists and their allies registered substantial gains at an early legislative poll in June 1988. Although the left fell short of an overall majority, Michel ROCARD, who had been named to head a minority administration in May, was able to form a new government with the support of a number of centrists and independents.

Faced with dwindling legislative support that had necessitated the withdrawal of a series of government measures, Rocard resigned in May 1991 and was succeeded by the country's first female premier, Edith CRESSON. Cresson's approval rating soon fell, however, and after an unprecedented Socialist drubbing at regional elections in March 1992 she was replaced by her finance minister, Pierre BÉRÉGOVOY.

The Bérégovoy government registered some success in insulating France from the worst effects of a deepening international recession, and in September 1992 it convinced a narrow majority of voters to support the EC's Maastricht Treaty (see Foreign relations, below). Domestically, the Socialists encountered increasing difficulties that were accentuated by the aging Mitterrand's waning reputation and the rivalries of his potential Socialist successors. Also besetting the government were a series of scandals and pervasive public fears over third world immigration—fears that both the FN and the "respectable" conservative parties sought to articulate.

At the legislative election of March 1993 the RPR/UDF achieved greater gains than had been expected. Having won a combined share of 40 percent of the first-round vote, the RPR (247 seats) and UDF (213) emerged from the second round with 80 percent of the 577 assembly seats. The PS and its allies, with 20 percent in the first round, retained only 70 of their 282 seats. Although increasing its first-round vote to 13 percent, the FN secured no representation, whereas the unreconstructed French Communists retained 23 of 26 seats. Bracing himself for a further period of "cohabitation," Mitterrand accepted the RPR's nomination of Edouard BALLADUR, a former finance minister, as the new premier.

The first round of presidential balloting on April 23, 1995, gave the Socialist Lionel JOSPIN a surprise lead with 23.3 percent, but the crucial outcome was Chirac's second-place showing (20.8 percent) over Balladur (18.6 percent). Of the other contenders, Le Pen secured the FN's best-ever vote (15 percent). In the May 7 runoff Chirac took 52.6 percent of the vote against Jospin. After a speedy transfer of power from the terminally ill Mitterrand on May 17, Chirac named Alain JUPPÉ, his campaign manager and the incumbent foreign minister, to head a new RPR/UDF government. At his inauguration Chirac pledged to restore "the social cohesion of France," with the reduction of unemployment as his central priority.

The new government quickly ran into problems, beginning with the disclosure in June 1995 that luxury Paris apartments owned by the city had been allocated to senior Gaullists (including Chirac and Juppé) at strikingly low rents. By-election and Senate election reversals for the center-right parties in September, combined with plummeting opinion poll ratings, impelled Juppé to resign on November 7 so that he could form a slimmer and reshaped government. It was immediately faced with widespread industrial action by public sector workers protesting against government economic policy, particularly a mooted reform of the country's costly social security system.

In a surprising decision, President Chirac in April 1997 announced that parliamentary elections would be held on May 25 and June 1, ten months earlier than required. The first round was a disaster for the government, as the RPR/UDF secured only 30 percent of the vote. Consequently, Prime Minister Juppé, whose popularity had plummeted, announced he would resign no matter what the final results of the balloting were, and President Chirac assumed control of the foundering government campaign. Chirac's personal appeal for support from the electorate had little effect, however, and the PS and its allies emerged from the second-round balloting with 274 seats, while the RPR fell to 134 and the UDF to 108. Intense negotiations with the Communists, who had won 38 seats, finally produced a potential legislative majority in support of the PS, and Jospin was sworn in as prime minister on June 3. In addition to the PCF, the new cabinet appointed on June 5 included the Greens (*Les Verts*); the Radical Socialist Party (*Parti Radicale Socialiste*, previously the MRG and subsequently renamed the *Parti Radicale de Gauche*—PRG); and an anti-Maastricht PS splinter, the Citizens' Movement (*Mouvement des Citoyens*—MdC).

The Socialist surge continued in the March 1998 regional elections, at which the governing coalition won 39.4 percent of the vote, followed by the center-right opposition with 35.6 percent and the FN with 15.5 percent. Although the left took over control in a number of regional councils, several UDF incumbents retained regional presidencies thanks to the controversial support of the FN.

In the first round of presidential voting on April 21, 2002, President Chirac emerged as the front-runner, with a lackluster 19.8 percent of the vote in a field of 16 candidates, but the second-place finish of the FN's Le Pen (16.9 percent) sent shockwaves through the political system and generated considerable international criticism. Undercut by a splintering among left and green parties, which had eight candidates on the ballot, and humiliated by his 16.2 percent showing, Premier Jospin immediately announced that he would retire from politics. Forces of the mainstream left, facing no viable alternative, joined with the center-right in rallying around Chirac, and at the runoff balloting on May 5 the incumbent received 82.2 percent of the vote. Buoyed by his success, Chirac then authorized formation of a new electoral coalition, the Union for the Presidential Majority (*Union pour la Majorité Présidentielle*—UMP), at the opening of the legislative campaign later in May.

With the RPR, much of the UFD, and most of the Liberal Democracy (*Démocratie Libérale—DL*) as its principal components, the UMP swept the National Assembly balloting on June 9 and 16, 2002, claiming 355 seats, to 140 for the PS, 21 for the PCF, and none for the FN. On June 17 President Chirac appointed as premier Liberal Democrat Jean-Pierre RAFFARIN, who had been serving as interim premier since May 6. Premier Raffarin's cabinet encompassed ministers from a number of center-right parties, chiefly the RPR, as well as independents. In November 2002 the UMP was reorganized as a unitary party, the Union for a Popular Movement (*Union pour un Mouvement Populaire*—UMP).

In balloting for regional councils on March 21 and 28, 2004, the UMP was resoundingly defeated by a PS/PCF/Greens coalition, which won 20 of 21 mainland regional councils. In response, Premier Raffarin, who had promoted an unpopular reform agenda aimed at tightening pensions and other social benefits, offered his resignation to President Chirac on March 30. Chirac refused the offer, however, and immediately named Raffarin to head a reshuffled cabinet that was announced on March 31. Less than three months later the government suffered another major defeat, this time in the elections for the European Parliament; whereas the left again made significant advances, the UMP's share of the vote dropped to 16.6 percent, compared to 1999's 25.9 percent for the UMP's predecessor parties.

On February 28, 2005, paving the way for a national referendum on an EU constitution, a joint session of the Senate and National Assembly amended the French constitution to make it compatible with the proposed EU document. Despite Parliament's 730–66 vote (with 96 abstentions) in favor of the changes, nearly 55 percent of the voters rejected the May 29 referendum, dealing another blow to Chirac. Two days later Premier Raffarin tendered his resignation, with Chirac thereupon naming the minister of the interior, Dominique de VILLEPIN, as Raffarin's successor. The streamlined cabinet, announced on June 2, was most notable for the appointment of the UMP's president, Nicolas SARKOZY, as minister of state, a position second to premier.

Constitution and Government

The constitution of the Fifth Republic, accepted by a national referendum on September 28, 1958, retained many traditional features of France's governmental structure while significantly enhancing the powers of the presidency in a mixed presidential-parliamentary system. The president, originally chosen by an electoral college but now directly elected in accordance with a 1962 constitutional amendment, holds powers expanded not only by the terms of the constitution itself but also by President de Gaulle's broad interpretation of executive prerogative. In addition to his power to dissolve the National Assembly with the advice (but not necessarily the concurrence) of the premier, the president may hold national referenda on some issues and is granted full legislative and executive powers in times of emergency. A partial check on his authority is the existence of a Constitutional Council, which supervises elections, passes on the constitutionality of organic laws, and must be consulted on the use of emergency powers. In France's first major constitutional revision in 11 years, a "congress" (joint session) of the Senate and National Assembly voted in October 1974 to extend the right to recommend constitutional review of legislation (theretofore confined to the president of the republic, the prime minister, and the two parliamentary presidents) to groups of 60 senators or 60 deputies.

The broad scope of presidential authority has curtailed the powers of the premier and the Council of Ministers, whose members are named by the president (upon the recommendation of the prime minister) and over whose meetings the president is entitled to preside. The cabinet has, however, been strengthened vis-à-vis the National Assembly, in that there are limits to the conditions under which the government can be defeated. Ministers are forbidden to hold seats in Parliament.

The legislative capacity of the once all-powerful National Assembly is now greatly circumscribed. No longer permitted to set its own agenda, the assembly must give priority to bills presented by the government, which can open debate on a bill and propose amendments. The assembly can pass specific legislation in such fixed areas as civil rights and liberties, liability to taxation, the penal code, amnesty, declarations of war, electoral procedure, and the nationalization of industries; however, it can only determine "general principles" in the areas of national defense, local government, education, property and commercial rights, labor, trade unions, and social security. Unspecified areas remain within the jurisdiction of the executive, and no provision is made for the National Assembly to object to a government decree on the ground that it is within a parliamentary mandate. The assembly has, however, played a more assertive role recently, making greater use of its powers of parliamentary oversight to investigate the conduct of foreign policy and to judge the conduct of government ministers.

The Senate, most of whose members are indirectly elected by an electoral college, was reduced under the Fifth Republic to a distinctly subordinate status, with little power other than to delay the passing of legislation by the National Assembly. The 1958 constitution further provided that if the presidency of the republic becomes vacant, the president of the Senate will become president ad interim, pending a new election. A separate consultative body, the Economic and Social Council, represents the country's major professional interests and advises on proposed economic and social legislation.

The judicial system was reorganized in December 1958. Trial procedure was modified, and the lower courts were redistributed by abolishing the judges of the peace (*juges de paix*) and replacing them with *tribunaux d'instance*. The higher judiciary consists of courts of assize (*cours d'assises*), which handle major criminal cases; courts of appeal (*cours d'appel*), for appeals from lower courts; and the Court of Cassation (*Cour de Cassation*), which judges the interpretation of law and the procedural rules of the other courts.

In accordance with his election campaign pledges, President Chirac secured the adoption on July 31, 1995, of a series of constitutional amendments described as the most significant in over 30 years. Among the changes were conversion of the annual parliamentary sitting from two short terms into a single nine-month session from October to June; an increase in the range of issues that could be put to referendum, to include public service, economic, and social questions; and simplification of the procedure for lifting the immunity of parliamentarians charged with criminal offenses.

In June 1999 both houses of the legislature approved an amendment "favoring equal access to women and men to elected positions," the most direct consequence being a requirement that political parties nominate men and women in equal proportion for public office, effective with the March 2001 local elections (in towns of 3,500 or more). Another 1999 amendment authorized the "transfer of competencies" needed to establish the EU's economic and monetary union and, under the 1997 Treaty of Amsterdam, to establish rules governing immigration, border controls, and free movement of persons. Additionally, a July 1999 amendment recognized, in accordance with a 1998 treaty, the jurisdiction of the UN-sponsored International Criminal Court. In September 2000 French voters approved a referendum reducing the presidential term from seven to five years, effective with the 2002 election.

The territory of metropolitan France (outside Paris) is divided into 22 regions and 96 departments (*départements*), the latter subdivided into some 37,000 communes. In addition, there are

4 overseas departments—French Guiana, Guadeloupe, Martinique, and Réunion—and a number of other overseas jurisdictions. The administrative structure is identical in all regions and departments. Each department is headed by a commissioner of the republic (*commissaire de la république*), the traditional title of prefect (*préfet*) technically being abandoned with the enactment of decentralization legislation in March 1982, although continuing in general use. While the commissioner continues to be appointed by and responsible to the central government, some of the commissioner's traditional administrative and financial functions have been transferred to locally elected departmental assemblies (*conseils généraux*) and regional assemblies (*conseils régionaux*). The smallest political unit, the commune, has a popularly elected municipal council (*conseil municipal*) headed by a mayor.

In December 1999 negotiations had opened between the central government and Corsican representatives on autonomy for Corsica. The resultant Matignon Accords, which were approved in July 2000 by the Corsican Assembly, called for devolving administrative and a degree of legislative authority in such areas as finance, tourism, culture, the environment, and education as well as the teaching of the Corsican language. Most politicians on the right, including Chirac, objected to what they regarded as a weakening of the republic, but on December 18, 2001, a significantly amended autonomy bill won final parliamentary approval. In January 2002, however, the Constitutional Council declared unconstitutional key elements of the plan. In March 2003 the French legislature approved constitutional amendments designed to permit decentralization not only in Corsica but also throughout France's regions and in many of its overseas dependencies. On July 6 Corsican voters narrowly rejected, 51 percent to 49 percent, a referendum on administrative devolution for the island.

Foreign Relations

French foreign policy as developed under President de Gaulle was dominated by the objective of restoring France's former leading role in international affairs and its independence of action on the international scene. This was particularly evident in de Gaulle's strenuous effort to establish an independent nuclear force and his collateral refusal to sign treaties banning nuclear testing and proliferation. Within the Europe of "the Six" (the founding members of the EC: Belgium, France, the Federal Republic of Germany, Italy, Luxembourg, and the Netherlands), France accepted the economic provisions of the Treaty of Rome but consistently resisted all attempts at political integration on a supranational basis, twice vetoing British membership in the EC. Within the Atlantic community, France accepted the provisions of the North Atlantic Treaty but withdrew its own military forces from NATO control in 1966 and refused the use of its territory for Allied military activities. Denouncing the United States for alleged "hegemonic" tendencies in international political, economic, and financial affairs, de Gaulle sought to restrict U.S. capital investment in France, assailed the "privileged" positions of the dollar and pound as international reserve currencies, and reduced French cooperation in international monetary arrangements. In world politics, France under de Gaulle's leadership tended to minimize the significance of the UN and its agencies (although remaining a member of the Security Council) and initiated a variety of foreign policy ventures of a more or less personal character, among them a close alignment with the Federal Republic of Germany in 1962–1963, recognition of Communist China in 1964, intermittent attempts to establish closer relations with the Soviet Union, persistent criticism of U.S. actions in Vietnam, condemnation of Israeli policy during and after the 1967 Arab-Israeli conflict, and cultivation of French-speaking Canadian separatist elements.

The most pronounced foreign policy change under President Pompidou was the adoption, as early as December 1969, of a more flexible attitude toward British admission to the EC. In April 1972 he called for a massive "yes" vote in a national referendum on the issue. While the referendum was not strictly necessary because of the Gaullist legislative majority, 68 percent of the participating voters responded affirmatively, and the EC was enlarged in early 1973.

President Giscard d'Estaing introduced a more positive posture of cooperation with the United States and other Western powers, based in part on a close personal relationship with West German Chancellor Helmut Schmidt. Rapidly emerging as one of the world's most traveled heads of state, Giscard d'Estaing became in 1976 the first French president in 16 years to visit Britain, while a 1979 trip to West Berlin was the first by a postwar French leader.

Although viewed at the outset of his incumbency as a consummate statesman, President Mitterrand attracted opprobrium because of the sinking, by French agents, of the antinuclear Greenpeace vessel *Rainbow Warrior* in Auckland harbor, New Zealand, in July 1985, for which an international arbitration tribunal in October 1987 assessed damages of $8.1 million. Resulting from what was apparently the first arbitration between a sovereign nation and a private organization, the settlement was separate from a UN-negotiated award of $7 million to New Zealand and the payment of unspecified damages to the family of a Greenpeace photographer who had been killed in the incident.

From 1970 the principal vehicle for cooperation with other French-speaking nations was the Agency for Cultural and Technical Cooperation (*Agence de Coopération Culturelle et Technique*—ACCT), which was succeeded in 1998 by the International Organization of the Francophonie (*Organisation Internationale de la Francophonie*—OIF), which in 2006 had 49 full members. The first in an ongoing series of francophone summits convened in Paris in February 1986.

Periodic Franco-African summit conferences also are held. Until about 1990 French governments gave fairly indiscriminate backing to incumbent leaders in French-speaking Africa, often sending troops to maintain them in power at moments of crisis. In accord with global trends, recent French policy has been to make financial and other assistance conditional upon progress toward democracy

and greater economic realism. Accordingly, French forces have been deployed on several occasions to assist with the quashing of army insurrections.

The French foreign policy establishment was ill-prepared for the post-1989 collapse of communism in Eastern Europe and, especially, for the rapid reunification of Germany in 1990. Having been deprived of its self-assumed role as the Soviet bloc's chief "interlocutor" in the West, France moved to solidify its special relationship with Germany, agreeing in May 1992 to form a joint Franco-German army corps as the nucleus of a future European army (see article on the EU). The Socialist-led government also strongly supported the EC's Maastricht Treaty on political and economic union, which the French electorate endorsed by a narrow majority (51.04 percent).

French forces participated in the U.S.-led multinational expedition that liberated Kuwait from Iraqi occupation in 1991 and also contributed significantly to the unsuccessful U.S.-led UN effort in 1992–1993 to prevent Somalia's descent into anarchy. Non-UN French forces were rapidly deployed in June 1994 to contain the carnage in Rwanda but were withdrawn in late August.

France shared responsibility for the failure of the EC and other European structures to make an effective response to the escalating conflict in former Yugoslavia in 1992, later becoming a member of the Contact Group (with Britain, Germany, Russia, and the United States) charged with expediting a Bosnian settlement. French troops continue to be deployed as peacekeepers in the region.

A moratorium on the controversial French nuclear testing program at Mururoa Atoll in the South Pacific, declared in April 1992, was followed by France's signature on August 3, 1992, of the UN Treaty on Non-Proliferation of Nuclear Weapons. As reaffirmed in a February 1994 defense white paper, however, French strategy continued to give primacy to nuclear deterrence while laying stress on more effective conventional forces capable of rapid deployment. Also in 1994, France was fully represented at a September meeting of NATO defense ministers for the first time since 1966.

Newly installed President Chirac generated intense controversy on June 13, 1995, by announcing the resumption of French nuclear testing at Mururoa. Spokespersons explained that a limited testing program would yield the data for future computer simulation of nuclear explosions, thereby permitting France to accede to a test ban treaty. In October France sought to defuse regional criticism by announcing that in 1996 it would join with the United States and Britain in signing the 1985 South Pacific Nuclear Free Zone Treaty. Following the sixth test in the series on January 27, 1996, President Chirac announced that he had decided to end French nuclear tests "permanently," and in September France signed the UN-sponsored Comprehensive Nuclear Test Ban Treaty, which it ratified in April 1998.

Although relations between Paris and London were strengthened during this period, the cornerstone of French external policy remained the alliance with Germany and the determination of the two governments to be the joint driving force of a new phase of EU integration, starting with the move to a single currency by the end of the century. Meanwhile, France quarreled with the United States throughout the rest of 1996 over a number of issues, including NATO reform; policy in the Middle East (Paris called for greater pressure on Israel to further the peace process); and the U.S. Helms-Burton Act, which authorized penalties for trading with Cuba.

The decline of French influence in Africa was highlighted in 1997 by the overthrow of Zairian dictator Mobutu, who had been a longtime client of the French government. The victorious rebels, led by Laurent Kabila, operated from the Zairian border with assistance from Rwanda, whose own francophone Hutu regime had been overthrown by Tutsi rebels in 1994. In addition, French attempts at mediation in the 15-year separatist civil war in the Casamance region of Senegal in 1997 actually seemed to spark fighting there rather than reduce tensions.

Upon taking office in mid-1997, Premier Jospin announced a reevaluation of French policy in Africa to counter what he called the "paternalistic" approach of previous governments. Changes subsequently included a reduction in the number of French troops stationed in Africa, resistance to further military intervention on that continent, and a reallocation of development assistance to increase the influence of humanitarian, as opposed to strategic, considerations. Such decisions by a premier marked a departure from the tradition of presidential control of foreign, particularly African, policy. The monopoly of executive authority over foreign affairs was further eroded in March 1998 when the National Assembly took the unprecedented step of initiating a parliamentary inquiry into French military involvement in and policy toward Rwanda.

French reintegration into NATO's military command structure stalled in 1998 over French demands for the appointment of a European, presumably French, commander of NATO's southern command. Despite this dispute, France actively supported NATO's policy toward Serbia, both by committing ground troops to a peacekeeping force based in Macedonia and by participating in the NATO air strikes against Yugoslavia during the Kosovo crisis in March–June 1999. French President Chirac also was a vocal proponent of the use of NATO ground troops in Yugoslavia, if necessary. At the same time, France supported establishment of a separate European military capability and subsequently committed significant personnel to the new EU-backed rapid reaction force.

Since the September 11, 2001, attacks on the United States, France has been at the forefront of European efforts to halt terrorism and break up underground terrorist cells. Dozens of suspected terrorists, the majority of them North African, have been arrested and put on trial; many radical Muslims clerics have been deported; and new antiterrorism measures have been enacted. Although France has been widely praised by the U.S. Bush administration for its antiterrorism efforts, relations with Washington took a sharp downturn beginning in late 2002, when Paris emerged as perhaps the most vocal critic of U.S. efforts to marshal international support in the UN Security Council for military action against the Saddam Hussein regime in Iraq. France's sharp opposition to the U.S.-led invasion of Iraq in March 2003 provoked a spate of anti-French sentiment in the United States that sometimes descended into the absurd, as when the chair of the Committee on House Administration ordered cafeterias in the U.S. House of Representatives to expunge the name "french fries" from their menus and replace it with "freedom fries." Subsequently, Washington and Paris appeared to be making a concerted effort to repair relations, with Presidents Bush and Chirac meeting in Brussels, Belgium, in early 2005, during a European visit by the American executive.

Current Issues

The May 2005 referendum defeat of the proposed EU constitution was generally interpreted not only as a blow to further European integration but also as a reflection of growing dissatisfaction with the French government's domestic policies. The quick resignation of Premier Raffarin was thus expected. What was more surprising, however, was President Chirac's decision to elevate Interior Minister Dominique de Villepin to the premiership and then to name Nicolas Sarkozy as, in effect, de Villepin's second-in-command.

Sarkozy, the most openly ambitious of France's likely presidential candidates for 2007, had drawn the wrath of some UMP members in April, when he stated in an interview that he was prepared to challenge President Chirac should the incumbent seek a third term. Those leveling criticism at Sarkozy included de Villepin, who apparently harbors his own presidential aspirations even though he has never served in an elective office. Meanwhile, the man whom many once considered Chirac's likely successor, former premier Alain Juppé, had been convicted in January 2004 of misusing public funds while serving as secretary general of the RPR and deputy mayor of Paris under Chirac. Juppé was initially barred from holding public office for ten years, but on appeal the ban was reduced to one year.

Well before his 2002 reelection Chirac himself had been implicated in a series of party fundraising scandals dating back to his long tenure as mayor of Paris. He was further damaged in 2001 by revelations that he had paid for family holidays from secret, but apparently legal, funds collected during his premiership in the 1980s and that he had made extraordinarily large cash payments for household expenses while mayor. On October 10, 2001, he won a final decision from the Court of Cassation that he could not be prosecuted or investigated while president, although the court also made it clear that his years in office would not be counted under the statute of limitations.

France has recently seen a spate of other scandals, including the siphoning of funds from the formerly state-owned Elf Aquitaine oil company to provide some $400 million in illegal payments to political parties, politicians, and foreign officials. As a result of another corruption investigation, 47 party activists and business executives went on trial in March 2005 for allegedly having received $40 million in kickbacks from school building contracts in the 1990s. That trial concluded in October with the conviction of 38 individuals, including 3 former government ministers, who were fined and received suspended sentences.

Meanwhile, the conservative Chirac government has continued to roll back social benefits, which undoubtedly contributed to the weakness of the UMP at the polls in 2004. One of its initiatives softened the 35-hour maximum workweek instituted under Prime Minister Jospin, provoking demonstrations by labor union opponents. In addition, government services were widely blamed when an August 2003 heat wave killed 15,000 people, most of them elderly.

An extended national debate over the wearing of Muslim headscarves by schoolchildren culminated in a December 2003 recommendation by a presidential commission that, in the interest of maintaining the secular state, the wearing of conspicuous religious symbols—not only headscarves, but also Jewish yarmulkes, Sikh turbans, large crucifixes, and the like—should be restricted in state schools and colleges. In the context of an upsurge in the incidence of anti-Muslim and anti-Semitic assaults, opponents attacked the recommendation as justifying discrimination against minorities, especially the Muslim immigrant population. In February–March 2004 both legislative houses approved the recommended ban by wide margins, and it entered into effect in September. Implementation proceeded without major disruptions despite numerous local incidents.

The headscarves issue had the additional consequence of drawing considerable attention to the status of the growing Muslim community in France, which, numbering 5–10 million according to various estimates, has faced major social barriers to integration, including widespread discrimination in housing and employment. On October 28, 2005, in the Paris suburb of Clichy-sous-Bois, young Muslims, mainly of North African and sub-Saharan descent, initiated a wave of violent rioting triggered by the deaths of two youths during a police chase. Over the next several days the disturbances expanded into other Parisian suburbs, long notorious for high unemployment, decrepit "council estate" housing, crime, and conflicts with police. By November 8 the riots had spread to some 300 communities, prompting Prime Minister Villepin to declare a 12-day state of emergency that Parliament later extended for three additional months.

Speaking to the nation on November 14, 2005, President Chirac cited the rioting—the most severe since 1968—as evidence of a "profound malaise" and the "poison" of discrimination. He also announced a public service program targeted at training 50,000 young people by 2007. By mid-November the "popular revolt" (to quote a police intelligence agency report) had significantly diminished in intensity, although the state of emergency was not lifted until January 4, 2006. More than 250 schools and 200 other public buildings had been burned or attacked and 10,000 vehicles destroyed. Arrests totaled 4,800.

Even before the rioting, the government had moved to reduce youth unemployment, which averaged 22 percent nationwide but was understood to exceed 50 percent in some areas, including Muslim communities. In August 2005 the Council of Ministers had adopted and implemented by decree, with effect from September 1, a controversial youth employment plan permitting employers with fewer

than 20 employees to dismiss workers under the age of 26 without explanation during their first two years of employment. Promoted by Prime Minister Villepin as a way to increase workplace flexibility and decrease unemployment at no cost to the government, the measure also exempted young workers from being included in the employers' head counts for tax and other legal purposes.

The New Recruitment Contract (*Contrat Nouvelles Embauches*—CNE) plan was widely condemned by labor unions, students, and many liberal and left-wing politicians, whose objections to the government's underlying assumptions were stiffened by parliamentary passage in early March 2006 of legislation that expanded the scheme to larger employers. Taking to the streets in a series of general strikes, opponents of the so-called First Job Contract (*Contrat Première Embauche*—CPE) law argued that the measure would have the adverse consequence of giving employers an incentive to fire the young before their two-year contracts had expired and then to hire youthful replacements, thus creating a class of temporary workers. Although the legislation received the approval of the Constitutional Court on March 30, President Chirac, addressing the nation on March 31, indicated that he would promulgate the measure but immediately suspend its implementation while changes were considered by Parliament.

By then, CPE opponents had already scheduled a fifth general strike for April 4, the fourth, a week earlier, having drawn into the streets an estimated 1 million people (3 million, according to leading trade unions) and tied up transport and other services in Paris. In the end, on April 10 Chirac announced that the CPE would be scrapped rather than revised. De Villepin was left expressing regret that his intentions in promoting the bill had been misperceived, while Sarkozy may have benefited from his having called for suspension of the law even before President Chirac's March 31 address.

Less than a month later, with de Villepin's critics already having written off his chances of winning the presidency, the prime minister was facing yet another crisis. The "Clearstream Affair," named after a Luxembourg-based bank, Clearstream

International, had begun in 2004 with an anony-mous accusation that various businessmen, intel-ligence agents, and politicians, including Nico-las Sarkozy, owned secret bank accounts as part of a complex web of corruption centering around defense contracts. The corruption allegations had been completely discredited in 2004, but a subse-quent investigation into the attempted smear had recently uncovered the apparent source of the plot, a vice president of the European Aeronautics De-fense and Space Company (the Airbus manufac-turer) who was a former associate of de Villepin. Furthermore, although the prime minister was not implicated in the original bogus accusation, the investigating magistrates had uncovered evidence that together de Villepin and President Chirac, hav-ing heard the allegation about hidden accounts, may have improperly initiated their own inquiry into Sarkozy's finances.

All this had begun leaking to the press in April 2006, causing a public furor. Chirac and de Villepin denied any impropriety, but in mid-May the Social-ists introduced a no-confidence motion against the government. Given the UMP's overwhelming ma-jority in the National Assembly, on May 16 the mo-tion received only 190 of the 289 votes needed for passage. On the following day, de Villepin stated that it would be "irresponsible" were he to resign at a time of such turmoil. Sarkozy, meanwhile, was rumored to be preparing to resign from the cabi-net as a first step toward distancing himself from Chirac and de Villepin and launching his presiden-tial bid.

Political Parties

Although the particulars have changed almost beyond recognition since World War II, the cur-rent French party system nevertheless displays, in its broad structure, many similarities with that pre-vailing more than half a century ago. The left con-tinues to be dominated by the Socialists and Com-munists, save that the former, since a relaunch in the early 1970s, have far outstripped the latter as an electoral force. An array of small formations still compete in the political center, largely grouped from 1978 until 2002 under the umbrella of the Union for French Democracy (UDF). De Gaulle's political heirs, campaigning from 1976 until 2002 as the Rally for the Republic (RPR) and now as the Union for a Popular Movement (UMP), are the main force on the conservative right; however, there remains a substantial populist far-right con-stituency, now represented by the National Front (FN). The only significant new phenomenon of the last half-century has been the "green" movement.

Government Parties

Union for a Popular Movement (*Union pour un Mouvement Populaire*—UMP). The present UMP was established as a unitary party at a congress on November 17, 2002. It had been launched in May 2002 as the Union for the Presidential Majority (*Union pour la Majorité Présidentielle*—UMP), a center-right electoral al-liance that included, principally, the Rally for the Republic and elements of both the Liberal Democ-racy (DL) and the Union for French Democracy (but not the Democratic Force faction of UDF leader François Bayrou). It won a majority of 355 seats at the June 2002 National Assembly election, the expectation then being that before year's end it would organize as a unified political party. Ob-servers also speculated that President Chirac, in naming Jean-Pierre Raffarin of the DL as premier, was attempting to bring the DL majority into the fold despite a lack of enthusiasm on the part of DL leader Alain MADELIN. At the same time, the se-lection of former premier Alain Juppé to head the UMP on an interim basis was seen by many as a first step toward establishing the former premier as Chirac's heir apparent.

The Rally for the Republic (*Rassemblement pour la République*—RPR) had been estab-lished in December 1976 as successor to the Union of Democrats for the Republic (*Union des Démocrates pour la République*—UDR), itself heir to various formations descended from the Union for the New Republic (*Union pour la Nouvelle République*—UNR), launched by de Gaulle in 1947. The RPR was organized as the personal vehicle of Jacques Chirac in his political rivalry with President Giscard d'Estaing, which had resulted in Chirac's resignation as premier in August 1976. At the election of March 1978 the RPR emerged as the largest single party in the National Assembly.

After placing third in first-round presidential balloting in April 1981, Chirac announced that his supporters should vote "according to their conscience" in the runoff, thus denying a critical measure of support to Giscard d'Estaing in his losing contest with François Mitterrand in May. At the legislative election in June the RPR ran second to the Socialists, its representation falling from 153 to 85. In April 1985 the RPR concluded an alliance with the UDF (below) for the 1988 assembly election, after which the two groups' 286-seat plurality enabled Chirac to form a government in "cohabitation" with the Socialist presidency.

Having lost to Mitterrand in the second round of the April–May 1988 presidential race, Chirac was challenged within the RPR after the Socialists regained legislative ascendancy in June. The RPR's capture of an assembly plurality in 1993 provided a springboard for Chirac's third run for the presidency, although the RPR prime minister, Edouard Balladur, also chose to stand. Effective campaigning carried Chirac to a second-round victory in May 1995. In October the postelection premier, Alain Juppé, was installed as RPR president in succession to Chirac.

Splits in the RPR continued through the 1997 legislative elections, one issue being whether to co-opt or to repudiate the anti-immigrant stands of the increasingly popular FN. After the disappointing first round of voting in May 1997, Juppé announced his resignation as premier, and later in the summer he was replaced as party leader by long-time rival Philippe SÉGUIN, described as a "partially recanted" former opponent of greater European integration.

In May 1998 Séguin accepted the RPR's alignment with the UDF and the DL in The Alliance, an unsuccessful effort to provide cohesion for the center-right parties. He argued for a RPR/UDF/DL joint list for the June 1999 elections to the European Parliament, but the UDF opted out. In addition, a segment of the RPR, led by Charles Pasqua, also broke from the party's leadership to join with the MPF (below) to present its own list for the June balloting on a platform opposing further European integration. In April 1999 Séguin stepped down from the RPR presidency, claiming he had been undermined by Chirac and his supporters. Nicolas Sarkozy, theretofore secretary general of the RPR, was subsequently named interim president, but he resigned after the party fell to third place, behind the Socialists and Pasqua's Rally for France and the Independence of Europe list (RPF-IE, below), at the European Parliament elections in June. Meanwhile, President Chirac's standing was being undercut by continuing accusations of illegal fundraising while he was mayor of Paris. Both the electoral setback and the ongoing scandal may have contributed to the rejection of Chirac's candidate, Jean-Paul DELEVOY, at the party presidential contest in December. The winner, Michèle ALLIOT-MARIE, became the first woman to head the RPR.

Following his massive reelection victory against the FN's Jean-Marie Le Pen in May 2002, Chirac used his revived standing to organize the Union for a Presidential Majority and then to lead it to a sweeping victory at the June National Assembly elections. In preparation for conversion of the alliance to the unitary UMP, the RPR voted to dissolve in September 2002. The new formation also incorporated the LD and attracted much of the UDF and many members of Pasqua's RPF-IE. In October 2002 the Radical Party (RRRS, below) voted to associate with the UMP while retaining its separate identity.

The Liberal Democracy (*Démocratie Libérale*—DL), originally the Republican Party (*Parti Républican*—PR), was organized as the PR in May 1977 as a merger of the former National Federation of Independent Republicans (*Fédération Nationale des Républicains Indépendants*—FNIR) and several smaller groups supportive of President Giscard d'Estaing. The FNIR, founded by Giscard d'Estaing in 1966, was made up primarily of independents originally affiliated with the National Center of Independents and Peasants (CNIP, below). Although more conservative than the Gaullists in domestic policy, it was more pro-NATO and "European" in its international outlook. In 1974 Giscard d'Estaing formally severed his affiliation with the FNIR in his search for a new "presidential majority." He became chair of the UDF in June 1988. For the 1993 legislative election the PR served as the organizational core of the UDF.

The PR changed its name to the DL following the 1997 legislative election, at which the center-right parties had lost control of the National Assembly and the national government. In May 1998 DL leader Alain Madelin, described as one of the country's "most vociferous" advocates of a free-market economy, announced that the DL was withdrawing from the UDF but would participate in The Alliance with the UDF and RPR. In the first round of the 2002 presidential election Madelin finished tenth, with 3.9 percent of the vote. Most DL National Assembly candidates agreed to run on the UMP list in June 2002, although two were elected on a separate DL list. Madelin—reluctantly, according to some observers—later led the DL into the unified UMP party.

During its November 2002 founding congress, at which it presented its guiding values as liberty, responsibility, solidarity, the nation, and Europe, the UMP elected Alain Juppé as chair and Philippe DOUSTE-BLAZY as secretary general. Juppé, who was convicted in January 2004 of misusing public funds in 1988–1995 while an aide to Chirac and secretary general of the RPR, received an 18-month suspended sentence and was banned from public office for ten years (reduced to one year, on appeal). In July he resigned as UMP chair, with Nicolas Sarkozy then being elected as his replacement in November.

By then, the UMP had suffered significant losses at the regional elections of March 2004, at which it won only 1 of 22 mainland regional councils, and at the June balloting for the European Parliament, taking only 17 of 77 seats on a 16.6 percent vote share. A spate of government ministers lost in the March balloting, as did Valéry Giscard d'Estaing.

Although President Chirac had yet to make a formal announcement, by early 2006 most observers had concluded that he would not seek a third term as president in 2007. Thus the contest for the party's endorsement was generally viewed as pitting Nicolas Sarkozy against Prime Minister Villepin, whose chances were significantly damaged by the youth labor law controversy in early 2006. Late in 2005 Sarkozy had convinced the PS Political Bureau to hold a primary to select a presidential candidate—a change in party rules that was clearly intended to enhance his prospects.

Leaders: Jacques CHIRAC (President of the Republic), Dominique de VILLEPIN (Premier), Nicolas SARKOZY (President of the Party), Jean-Claude GAUDIN (Presidential Delegate), Bernard ACCOYER (Parliamentary Leader), Pierre MÉHAIGNERIE (Secretary General).

Forum of Social Republicans (*Forum des Républicains Sociaux*—FRS). The FRS was organized by Christine Boutin, a socially conservative UDF dissident who won 1.2 percent of the 2002 presidential vote. In June 2002 she was elected to the National Assembly on the UMP list. The FRS subsequently became an associate party of the UMP.

Leader: Christine BOUTIN (President).

National Center of Independents and Peasants (*Centre National des Indépendants et Paysans*—CNIP). Dating back to the 1940s and a significant force through the 1950s, the CNIP has long supported the free-enterprise system, the North Atlantic alliance, and European integration. Although not directly linked to either the RPR or the UDF, it was allied with the center-right coalition in the 1981 and 1986 legislative elections. Continuance of the relationship in 1993 was precluded by the CNIP's de facto support of the FN's anti-immigrant position, although it retained a presence in Parliament, under the "Various Right" label. At present, the CNIP is an associate party of the UMP; members are permitted to hold joint enrollment.

Leaders: Annick de ROSCOAT (President), Bernard BEAUDET (Secretary General).

Radical Party (*Parti Républicain Radical et Radical-Socialiste*—RRRS). Founded in 1901, the Radical Party was the leading party of the prewar

Third Republic and a participant in many Fourth Republic governments. Technically the Radical and Radical Socialist Republican Party, but also known as the *Parti Valoisien* from a Rue de Valois address in Paris, the Radicals maintained their traditional anticlerical posture but were more conservative than the Socialists in economic and social matters.

The Radical majority's refusal to join the Union of the Left with the Socialists and Communists caused the exit of a left-wing faction in 1972 to form the Left Radical Movement (see Left Radical Party, below). Radicals held ministerial office under the presidency of Giscard d'Estaing (1974–1981), during which the party sought to forge greater center-left unity. In July 1977 the Movement of Social Liberals (*Mouvement des Sociaux Libéraux*—MSL), which had been organized in February 1977 by Olivier STIRN (a former Gaullist secretary of state), announced its incorporation into the Radical Party. (Stirn relaunched the MSL as a separate group in October 1981, but it dissolved in 1984.)

In 1978 the Radicals became founding members of the UDF (below). Almost eliminated from the National Assembly in the 1981 Socialist landslide, the Radicals recovered somewhat in the 1986 elections and held office in the subsequent "cohabitation" government. However, the party fell back to three seats in 1988 and again went into opposition. It returned to office following the center-right assembly landslide of March 1993. In 2002 it aligned with the UMP while maintaining its separate identity.

Leaders: André ROSSINOT (Copresident), Jean-Louis BORLOO (Copresident of the Party and Minister of Employment, Social Cohesion, and Housing), François LOOS (Minister-Delegate for Industry), Aymeri de MONTESQUIOU (First Vice President), Renaud DUTREIL (Secretary General).

Union for French Democracy (*Union pour la Démocratie Française*—UDF). The UDF was founded in February 1978 by a number of right-centrist parties, including the Radical Party (RRRS, above), plus several smaller groups in the governing coalition. It supported Valéry Giscard d'Estaing in the 1981 presidential campaign, albeit unofficially as the incumbent voiced a desire to stand as a "citizen candidate" unidentified with any specific grouping. Collaterally, it became possible for individuals to become "direct affiliates" of the UDF without holding membership in one of its constituent groups. In line with its 1985 accord with the RPR, the UDF was awarded five senior cabinet posts in the government formed after the March 1986 balloting. Having abandoned its pact with the RPR, the UDF became the third-ranked legislative grouping in the immediate wake of the second-round poll of June 1988.

Giscard d'Estaing remained the dominant UDF personality into the 1990s, and during the 1993 legislative campaign he tried, but failed, to establish the UDF as the strongest center-right formation. (For that election the RPR and UDF candidates were grouped in the Union for France [*Union pour la France*—UPF].) In the 1995 presidential race most UDF support went to Edouard Balladur in the first round but swung behind Jacques Chirac in the second. UDF representatives were allocated important posts in the subsequent RPR-led government, while Giscard d'Estaing was invited to give "elder statesman" advice to President Chirac.

Giscard d'Estaing eventually stood down as UDF leader in March 1996 and attempted to confer the succession on Alain Madelin of the Republican Party (*Parti Républicain*—PR), who had been dismissed as economy and finance minister in August 1995. However, delegates at a UDF conference preferred former defense minister and PR President François LÉOTARD.

After dropping from 213 seats in the 1993 legislative poll to 198 in 1997, the UDF also was shaken (as was the RPR) by a poor performance in the March 1998 regional elections. Prompting an immediate crisis within the UDF, five UDF incumbent presidents of regional councils accepted the support of the extreme-right FN to retain their posts. Two resigned shortly thereafter, but the other three were eventually expelled from the UDF, including Charles Millon, who formed his own party, the Lyon-based The Right (*La Droite*), which a year later became the Liberal-Christian Right

(*Droite Libérale-Chrétienne*—DLC; now defunct). Léotard faced criticism from several sides in the dispute. Some prominent UDF members resigned from the party to protest what they had perceived as too hard a line toward UDF/FN regional coop- eration. Others attacked Léotard for reacting too slowly and failing to make a "clean break" with the FN.

The latter camp included François Bayrou of the Democratic Force (*Force Démocrate*—FD), who suggested that the UDF be abolished in favor of a new, single center-right party. For his part, Léotard called for a UDF general congress to determine the union's future and to establish policies on the FN and other issues that were splintering the opposi- tion. In May Léotard endorsed the creation of The Alliance among the UDF, RPR, and DL (see the UMP discussion, above), but shortly thereafter he resigned the UDF presidency because of an offi- cial investigation into alleged financial irregulari- ties during his PR presidency. He was succeeded in September by Bayrou, who continued to lobby for the remaining UDF components to merge. The re- sultant "New" (*Nouvelle*) UDF was established in 1999, although the leading constituent parties re- tained de facto identities. Early in the year the UDF rejected an offer from the RPR and DL to present a joint list at the next European Parliament election.

The Democratic Force had been launched in November 1995 within the UDF as a merger of the Center of Social Democrats (*Centre des Démocrates Sociaux*—CDS) and the Social Demo- cratic Party (*Parti Social-Démocrate*—PSD). The CDS dated from a 1976 merger of the Democratic Center (*Centre Démocrate*—CD) and the Demo- cratic and Progressive Center (*Centre Démocratie et Progrès*—CDP), founded in 1966 and 1969, re- spectively. After the 1988 presidential poll, the CDS established a separate assembly identity as the Union of the Center (*Union du Centre*—UDC) but formally returned to the fold in the 1994 European balloting. The PSD had been adopted as the new name of the former Democratic Socialist Move- ment (*Mouvement des Démocrates Socialistes de France*—MDS) in October 1982. The MDS was a centrist group that participated in the 1973 election

as part of the Reform Movement and was a found- ing member of the UDF in 1978. CDS/FD min- isters featured strongly in the Juppé government appointed after the 1995 presidential election.

Another UDF participant, the Popular Party for French Democracy (*Parti Populaire pour la Démocratie Française*—PPDF), had evolved in July 1995 from the Perspectives and Realities Clubs (*Clubs Perspectives et Réalités*—CPR). Dating from 1965, the CPR had acted as a UDF think tank, providing a political home for centrist intellectuals and obtaining ministerial representation after the center-right election victory in 1993. A prominent member of the PPDF was former PR leader Alain Madelin.

The UDF's Bayrou finished fourth (with 6.8 per- cent of the first-round vote) in the 2002 presiden- tial election. Although some of the UDF joined Chirac's new UMP prior to the June 2002 National Assembly election, Bayrou's supporters, clustered in the FD faction, ran independently under the UDF label, winning 29 seats, for third place.

Leaders: François BAYROU (President), Hervé MORIN (Leader in the National Assembly), Michel MERCIER (Leader in the Senate), François SAUVADET (Spokesperson).

Other Leading Parliamentary Parties:

Socialist Party (*Parti Socialiste*—PS). Orig- inally established in 1905 and known for many years as the French Section of the Workers' Interna- tional (*Section Française de l'Internationale Ou- vrière*—SFIO), the French Socialist Party headed the 1936–1938 Popular Front government of Léon BLUM as well as several postwar coalitions, party leader Guy MOLLET being prime minister of the Fourth Republic's longest-lasting administra- tion in 1956–1957. The advent of the Fifth Re- public in 1958 accelerated the party's electoral de- cline, and in 1965 it joined the broader Federation of the Democratic and Socialist Left (*Fédération de la Gauche Démocrate et Socialiste*—FGDS) chaired by François Mitterrand, leader of the small Convention of Republican Institutions (*Conven- tion des Institutions Républicaines*—CIR). Unlike

Mollet, Mitterrand had opposed de Gaulle's return to power in 1958. Backed by the FGDS and the Communists, Mitterrand secured 44.8 percent of the second-round vote in the 1965 presidential election, while the FGDS made major gains in the 1967 National Assembly balloting. Proposals to convert the FGDS into a unitary party foundered in the wake of the 1968 political crisis, and Mitterrand refused to back the 1969 Socialist presidential candidate, Gaston DEFFERRE, who won only 5 percent of the vote.

After further false starts and bickering between the factions, a "congress of socialist unity" in Épinay in June 1971 elected Mitterrand as leader of the new Socialist Party, which embarked upon a strategy of left-wing union. Major gains in the 1973 legislative election were followed by a narrow second-round defeat for Mitterrand, as candidate of the combined left, in the 1974 presidential balloting, when the margin of Giscard d'Estaing's victory was less than 1 percent. In a 1981 rematch Mitterrand was victorious by more than 3.5 percent, while the PS completed its domination with a National Assembly sweep in June. However, as the result of a Socialist defeat at the assembly election of March 1986, the president was forced to accept the appointment of a rightist administration headed by Jacques Chirac for the remaining two years of his initial term. Mitterrand won a second term by defeating Chirac at second-round presidential balloting on May 8, 1988, while the PS secured a sufficient plurality to regain ministerial control at National Assembly voting in June.

Massively defeated in the March 1993 legislative elections, the PS entered a period of internal turmoil when the former PS prime minister, Michel Rocard, assumed the party leadership with the aim of creating a broader social democratic organization. Rocard was, however, forced to step down as party first secretary when the Socialists fared poorly in the June election for the European Parliament.

Straitened financial circumstances and the implication of various PS officials in corruption cases added to the Socialists' problems in the run-up to the 1995 presidential election. A move to draft the outgoing president of the European Commission, Jacques DELORS, as the Socialist candidate was rebuffed by Delors in December, whereupon a former PS leader and education minister, Lionel JOSPIN, defeated Henri EMMANUELLI for the nomination. Against most expectations, Jospin headed the first-round ballot on April 23 and scored an impressive 47.4 percent in the second on May 7. On June 29 Jospin replaced Emmanuelli as PS first secretary, promising to carry out a thorough reform of party structures and policies. In the 1997 legislative elections, Jospin, criticizing the RPR-led government's austerity plans as detrimental to the French economy, led the PS to a plurality of 241 seats in the National Assembly by promising to lower unemployment.

In the 2002 presidential race a divided left contributed to Jospin's third-place finish, with 16.2 percent of the vote. Humiliated, Jospin announced his retirement from active politics. At the June parliamentary election the PS won only 140 seats, and several months later former first secretary Emmanuelli launched a "New World" caucus within the PS in an effort to redirect the party toward its socialist roots and away from the social liberalism of the party's new first secretary, François Hollande. In May 2003, however, the party reelected Hollande as leader.

At the March 2004 local elections the PS made major gains, heading a coalition with the Communists and Greens that won 20 of 21 mainland regional legislatures, up from 8. The PS also won 28.9 percent of the vote at the June 2004 elections to the European Parliament, capturing 31 of 77 seats, compared to 17 for the UMP. In 2005 the party nevertheless remained divided over the proposed EU constitution: Hollande's majority supported further European integration, but a vocal minority, led by longtime party stalwart Laurent Fabius, objected that it did not meet socialist standards. Following the May 2005 rejection of the proposed constitution by the voters, Fabius and his supporters, who had campaigned for a "no" vote, were ousted from the party leadership.

At a party congress held November 18–20, 2005, at Le Mans, Hollande's "modernizers" and the "traditionalists" attempted to heal the rift that had split the party into half a dozen factions. Among other things, the party agreed to unite behind a platform that called for an increase in the minimum wage, opposition to the controversial new youth labor legislation, and reversal of the government's decision to sell a minority stake in the principal state-owned electrical utility company. In other decisions, Laurent Fabius was restored to the party's executive, and the selection of a 2007 presidential candidate was deferred until November 2006. Leading contenders were expected to be Lionel Jospin, former finance minister Dominique STRAUSS-KAHN, and former family affairs minister Ségolène ROYAL.

Leaders: François HOLLANDE (First Secretary), Jean-Marc AYRAULT (National Assembly Leader), Laurent FABIUS, François REBSAMEN.

French Communist Party (*Parti Communiste Français*—PCF). An offshoot of the SFIO (see the PS, above), the PCF assumed a separate identity in 1920. It was the largest party of the Fourth Republic, but the single-member constituency system introduced by the Fifth Republic limited its parliamentary representation, despite participation in left-wing electoral and policy alliances. The party nonetheless remained a powerful force in local government, dominated the largest French labor organization, the *Confédération Générale du Travail* (CGT), and gathered wide support among the dissatisfied French peasantry. Although opposing NATO and European integration and favoring closer relations with the East, the PCF publicly rejected the Soviet intervention in Czechoslovakia in 1968. In 1976 it formally abandoned the theory of the "dictatorship of the proletariat," although it never embraced revisionist "Eurocommunism" and remained in essence a pro-Soviet party until the demise of the USSR.

Following its formal break with the Socialists in September 1984, the PCF experienced a major rupture between "traditionalists" and "renovators." In 1998 the latter offered their own presidential candidate, who won 2.1 percent of the first-round vote, while the mainstream nominee slumped to a postwar low of 6.8 percent. Expelled from the PCF, the "renovators" formed a New Left (*Nouvelle Gauche*—NG) party, which later became part of the Red and Green Alternatives (see under The Alternatives, below). The PCF leader, Georges MARCHAIS, doggedly resisted internal pressure for a "French perestroika" but conceded in April 1990 that his party had been "duped" by the East European Communists.

In 1993 the PCF retained 23 of 26 legislative seats. In September Marchais declared his intention to resign as PCF general secretary because of ill health, and he formally stepped down after 21 years at the party's 28th congress in January 1994. His successor, Robert Hue, was assigned the title "national secretary" as part of a decision to abandon the traditional commitment to "democratic centralism." Hue took 8.6 percent of the first-round vote in the 1995 presidential balloting, after which the PCF backed Lionel Jospin of the PS in the second round. In the 1997 legislative elections the PCF used its opposition to "Europe at any cost" to increase its legislative presence to 38 seats. Although strongly opposed to French participation in the EMU, the PCF nevertheless joined the new PS-led government, albeit only after several days of what were reported to be intense negotiations.

At the 31st PCF congress, held October 26–28, 2001, Hue was named to the new post of party president and also named as the PCF's 2002 presidential candidate. He finished 11th out of 16, with 3.4 percent of the first-round vote. Earlier, in November 2001, he had been acquitted of charges related to illegal fundraising. At the National Assembly election of June 2002, the PCF won only 21 seats.

In November 2002 Hue announced his intention to step down as president, and he was succeeded in April 2003 by Marie-George Buffet. At the 2004 regional elections the PCF joined the PS and the Greens in a successful electoral coalition.

Leaders: Marie-George BUFFET (National Secretary), Alain BOUQUET (National Assembly Leader).

Left Radical Party (*Parti Radical de Gauche*—PRG). A splinter from the Radical Party, the PRG was organized as the Left Radical Movement (*Mouvement des Radicaux de Gauche—MRG*) prior to participating in the 1973 election as part of the Left Union (*Union de la Gauche—UG*). Its parliamentary strength rose from 10 seats to 14 at the election of June 1981, after it had entered the government in May. It secured only 2 assembly seats in 1986. With an increase to 9 seats in 1988, the party was awarded three cabinet posts in the Rocard government. After essaying a quickly forgotten "second force" within the presidential majority, the MRG shared in the defeat of the left in the March 1993 legislative balloting. It was temporarily strengthened by the adhesion of controversial business tycoon Bernard TAPIE; however, Tapie was later sentenced to prison for bribery and fraud.

The MRG was relaunched under new leadership in January 1996, when it absorbed the small Reunite (*Réunir*) group led by Bernard KOUCHNER (a former Socialist minister). With the aim of sharpening its image, the party also adopted the new single-word name "Radical"—much to the chagrin of the main Radical Party, which in March secured a court ruling that the MRG title should be restored within four months. Reorganized as the Radical Socialist Party (*Parti Radicale Socialiste—PRS*), the party took part in the 1997 elections under a withholding agreement with the PS. The PRS was given one ministerial position and two subministerial positions in the subsequent socialist government. The courts again forced the party to choose another name, resulting in adoption of the present designation at a congress in January 1998.

At the 2002 presidential balloting the PRG's Christiane TAUBIRA, from French Guiana, finished 13th, with 2.3 percent of the vote. At the June 2002 National Assembly election the PRG won seven seats. Jean-Michel Baylet was reelected party president in December 2004.

Leaders: Jean-Michel BAYLET (President), Yvon COLLIN (Delegate General), Bernard CASTAGNEDE (Spokesperson), Elizabeth BOYER (Secretary General).

The Greens (*Les Verts*). The Greens, which organized as a unified ecologist party in 1984, began as an outgrowth of an Ecology Today (*Aujourd'hui l'Écologie*) movement that had presented a total of 82 candidates at first-round National Assembly balloting in June 1981. The Greens declined to present candidates for the 1988 legislative balloting on the ground that only a return to proportional representation would assure them an equitable number of seats. At municipal balloting in March 1989 they ran much more strongly than expected, winning between 8 and 24 percent of the vote in some localities.

Les Verts secured no assembly seats on a minuscule vote share in 1993, despite a noncompetition agreement with the Ecology Generation (below). Partly because of its poor showing, the party, in a decisive move to the left, then elected Dominique VOYNET to succeed 1988 presidential candidate Antoine Waechter, who in 1994 set up the Independent Ecological Movement (below). As the *Les Verts* candidate, Voynet ran eighth of nine contenders in the first round of the 1995 presidential balloting, taking 3.3 percent of the vote. For the 1997 legislative election the Greens cooperated in some districts with the Socialists or the PRS (now the PRG). Having won seven seats, they entered the Socialist Jospin government.

In October 2001 the Greens abandoned their initial 2002 presidential candidate, Alain LIPIETZ, a former Maoist who had previously supported Corsican and Basque separatists. In his place the party nominated Noël MAMÈRE, who ran seventh, with 5.3 percent of the vote, in the first round. *Les Verts* saw its National Assembly representation decline to three seats in June 2002. In January 2003 Voynet was replaced by Gilles LEMAIRE, who was then succeeded by Yann Wehrling two years later.

Leaders: Yann WEHRLING (National Secretary), Mirielle FERRI.

Other Parties of the Right and Center

National Front (*Front National—FN*). The FN, an extreme right-wing formation organized in 1972 on an anti-immigration program, startled observers in June 1984 by winning 10 of the 81 French seats in the European Parliament. It made a scarcely less impressive showing in 1986 by winning 35 assembly seats, while its leader, Jean-Marie Le Pen, secured 14.4 percent of the vote in first-round presidential balloting in 1988. Its loss of all but 1 of its National Assembly seats at the legislative balloting only two months later was attributed to the fact that the June election was conducted under majoritarian rather than proportional representation. Its sole deputy was expelled from the party in October 1988, after which the FN was without lower house representation until a by-election victory in December 1989. That seat was lost in 1993, although the Front increased its first-round vote to 13 percent. In the 1995 presidential poll, Le Pen took a first-round share of 15 percent. In municipal balloting in June the FN tripled its complement of councilors and won control of three large southern towns, where it pledged to give preference to French citizens in the allocation of housing and welfare.

With its policies remaining the focus of countrywide debate, the FN secured nearly 15 percent of the vote in the first round of the 1997 legislative poll. In the second round it chose not to withdraw its third-place candidates, having calculated that this would aid a Socialist victory and thus, in the long term, benefit the FN.

In December 1997, for a second time, Le Pen was convicted under antiracism laws for dismissing Nazi gas chambers as a "detail in history" and was fined some $50,000. In April 1998 Le Pen was found guilty of assaulting a female Socialist candidate during the 1997 legislative election campaign. The sentence included the suspension of civil rights for two years, which was reduced to one year on appeal.

Internal conflicts came to a head in December 1998 when deputy leader Bruno Mégret and several of his supporters were expelled from the FN in a dispute with Le Pen over Mégret's policy of alliances with parties of the moderate right. Mégret and his supporters, including the bulk of party activists, declared their expulsion illegal and organized an extraordinary party congress in January 1999 to elect a new leadership for the party. The schism led to the coexistence of two parties, each

claiming to be "the" FN, but in May the courts ruled that Mégret's group had usurped the FN designation, which led to the new party's selecting "National Republican Movement" (MNR, below) instead.

Although the FN/MNR bifurcation initially appeared to split the far-right vote, as evidenced by the FN's loss of nearly half its 1994 support in the 1999 European Parliament election, Le Pen subsequently took advantage of rising anti-immigrant, anticrime, and "French first" sentiment (as well as a divided left) to pull off a remarkable, unexpected second-place finish in the April 2002 first-round vote for the presidency. By capturing 16.9 percent of the vote, Le Pen brought an end to the political career of Prime Minister Jospin, the leading center-left candidate. However, Le Pen's success had the adverse consequence of drawing all his opponents together in support of President Chirac's reelection, and in the second-round voting in June Le Pen could manage only 17.8 percent of the vote.

At the June 2002 National Assembly election the FN won 11 percent of the vote but no seats. At the March 2004 regional elections the FN won 14.7 percent of the vote in the first round, passing the threshold of 10 percent to contest the second round in most regions. Le Pen, however, was refused a place on the ballot in a southern region because he failed to meet requirements. In September 2005 Le Pen dismissed the mayor of Orange, Jacques BOMPARD, from the party's executive. Bompard responded by calling Le Pen a "Stalinist."

Leaders: Jean-Marie LE PEN (President), Marine LE PEN (Vice President), Bruno GOLLNISCH (Delegate General), Carl LANG (Secretary General).

Rally for France and the Independence of Europe (*Rassemblement pour la France et l'Indépendance de l'Europe*—RPF-IE). Frequently referenced simply as the RPF, the RPF-IE began as an electoral list established by Charles Pasqua's Rally for France and Philippe de Villiers's Movement for France (MPF, below) in preparation for the June 1999 European Parliament balloting, at which the list finished second. The Rally for France had been formed by Pasqua, a former minister of the interior, in June 1998, following his departure from the RPR, which, he claimed, had abandoned the Gaullist ideal of an independent France by submitting to the EU. Although established in November 1999 as a unified party, the RPF-IE broke in two less than a year later when, after a falling out between the two leaders, de Villiers revived the MPF as a separate party.

In 2002 Pasqua intended to run for president of the republic, but he failed to obtain the requisite number of signatures to appear on the ballot. At the June National Assembly election the RPF-IE was credited with winning two seats, although several successful candidates on the UMP list also had RPF-IE affiliations. Pasqua has been investigated for illegal party funding and sale of arms to Angola. He also has been implicated in a kickback scandal involving the Iraqi oil-for-food program in the 1990s—a charge that he has vehemently denied.

Leader: Charles PASQUA (President).

Movement for France (*Mouvement pour la France*—MPF). The MPF was launched in November 1994 as the successor to The Other Europe (*L'Autre Europe*), which had been established before the June 1994 European Parliament election, principally by French-British financier Sir James GOLDSMITH. Opposed to EC/EU economic and monetary integration, the MPF also attacked the 1993 world trade liberalization agreement, which had been negotiated under the auspices of the General Agreement on Tariffs and Trade. In the 1995 presidential balloting, MPF leader Philippe de Villiers (formerly of the UDF) finished seventh out of nine first-round candidates, taking 4.7 percent of the vote.

The MPF formed an alliance with Charles Pasqua's RPR dissidents to contest the June 1999 European Parliament election, and the success of the resultant RPF-IE list led to the establishment of a unified party late in 1999. In less than a year, however, Pasqua and de Villiers parted company, leading de Villiers to revive the MPF. De Villiers, who currently sits in the European Parliament, has recently decried the "Islamicization" of France. In

September 2005 he announced that he intended to seek the presidency in 2007.

Leaders: Philippe DE VILLIERS (President), Guillaume PELTIER (Secretary General).

National Republican Movement (*Mouvement National Républicain*—MNR). The MNR was established in 1999 by Bruno Mégret, a former deputy leader of Le Pen's National Front who had been expelled from the FN in December 1998 because of his support for forming alliances with center-right parties. In January 1999 Mégret's dissident FN faction elected him leader of the "National Front–National Movement," but in May the courts ruled that the party could not use the National Front designation, which led to adoption of the current name. At the first round of the 2002 presidential race Mégret won 2.3 percent of the vote.

In July 2002 the Council of State annulled the results of a March 2001 election in Vitrolles over electoral violations, thereby forcing Mégret's wife, Catherine, to resign as mayor. In revoting in October 2002, the MNR was defeated. In January 2004 Bruno Mégret was convicted of illegal party financing, fined, and given a one-year suspended sentence. In November 2005 the party's National Council decided to begin planning to ensure Mégret a place on the ballot for the 2007 presidential election.

Leaders: Bruno MÉGRET (President), Yves DUPONT (Vice President), Catherine MÉGRET, Annick MARTIN (Secretary General).

Other Parties of the Left

The Alternatives (*Les Alternatifs*). The Alternatives was launched as the Red and Green Alternatives (*L'Alternatives Rouge et Verte*—ARV) in November 1989 by merger of the former Unified Socialist Party (*Parti Socialist Unifié*—PSU) and the New Left (*Nouvelle Gauche*—NG). Initially a self-proclaimed anarcho-syndicalist group, the ARV also described itself as "feminist, ecologist, and internationalist."

Formed in 1960 by a number of Socialist splinter groups, the PSU remained in existence when a minority faction led by Michel Rocard opted to join the Socialist Party in 1975. The rump PSU nevertheless backed Mitterrand in the second-round presidential balloting in 1981 and joined the Mauroy government in March 1983. The NG had been organized by Pierre JUQUIN following his expulsion from the PCF in 1987.

The ARV adopted its current name in 1998, when new statutes described the organization as a political movement dedicated to creating a postcapitalist society based on human liberation, social justice, and harmony with nature. In 2002 it supported President Chirac's reelection in the second round ("for the first and last time") and in June ran unsuccessfully for various National Assembly seats.

Leader: Jean-Jacques BOISLAROUSSIE (Spokesperson).

Ecology Generation (*Génération Écologie—* GE). The GE was formed in 1990 by Brice LALONDE, a former presidential candidate and subsequently an environment minister. "*Les Bleus*" has had no success in national elections, and in 2002 Lalonde failed to obtain the necessary number of signatures to appear on the presidential ballot. The party's current president, France Gamerre, is expected to run in 2007.

Leaders: France GAMERRE (President), Michel VILLENEUVE (Spokesperson), Didier BERNARD (Secretary General).

Republican and Citizen Movement (*Mouvement Républicain et Citoyens—*MRC). The MRC traces its origins to the Citizen's Movement (*Mouvement des Citoyens—*MdC), which was founded in 1993 after the Maastricht referendum, primarily by former PS adherents who were desirous of a "weaker" Europe and who opposed the proposed single EU currency. The MdC had an electoral breakthrough in the 1997 legislative elections, winning seven seats and joining the subsequent PS-led government.

In August 2000 the MdC president, Jean-Pierre Chevènement, resigned as interior minister because of his objections to the proposed Corsican autonomy plan. Running for president in 2002 on a platform that combined leftist economies, law and order, and French independence, he finished sixth,

with 5.3 percent of the first-round vote. At the June National Assembly election, running on a Republican Pole list (*Pôle Républicain—*PR), the party failed to win any seats. It subsequently reorganized as the MRC.

Leaders: Jean-Pierre CHEVÈNEMENT (Honorary President), Georges SARRE (First Secretary).

Workers' Struggle (*Lutte Ouvrière—*LO). The LO is a small Trotskyite party whose leader, Arlette Laguiller, has entered five presidential races since 1974, "not at all to be elected" but to "make heard the workers' voice amid the . . . hypocritical declarations" of the leading candidates, including those of the Socialist and Communist parties. In the 2002 presidential contest Laguiller attracted 5.7 percent of the vote in the first round, her best performance to date. In the 2004 regional elections the LO teamed up with the rival Revolutionary Communist League (LCR, below) in an effort to attract left-wing voters. Laguiller is expected to seek the presidency again in 2007.

Leader: Arlette LAGUILLER.

Minor National Parties

Five additional parties offered presidential candidates in 2002. The Trotskyist **Revolutionary Communist League** (*Ligue Communiste Révolutionnaire—*LCR), which was founded in 1973 by Alain KRIVINE, saw its presidential contender, Olivier BESANCENOT, win 4.3 percent of the national vote, for eighth place. The LCR and the LO (above) joined forces for the March 2004 regional elections. The rural-oriented, anti-EU **Hunting, Fishing, Nature, Traditions** (*Chasse, Pêche, Nature, Traditions—*CPNT) is led by Jean SAINT-JOSSE, who won 4.2 percent of the vote. A former minister of the environment opposed to some of the more leftist policies of the Greens, Corinne LEPAGE of the **Cap 21**—Citizen Action and Participation for the 21st Century (*Citoyenneté Action et Participation pour le 21ème Siècle*)— established the group as a political forum in 1996 and then transformed it into a political movement in 2000; she won 1.9 percent of the 2002 vote. The **Workers' Party** (*Parti des Travailleurs—*PT) was established in 1991 as successor to the Trotskyist Internationalist Communist Party (*Parti Communiste Internationaliste*—PCI); its secretary general, Daniel GLUCKSTEIN, finished last among the 16 presidential candidates in 2002, with only 0.5 percent of the vote. Antoine WAECHTER of the **Independent Ecological Movement** (*Mouvement Écologiste Indépendant*—MEI) failed to obtain sufficient signatures to appear on the presidential ballot; formerly a presidential candidate of the Greens, Waechter left the parent organization and established the MEI in 1993.

Numerous additional minor parties offered candidates for the 2002 National Assembly election, many of them in a small number of departments or districts. Later in 2002 the **Union of Radical Republicans** (*Union des Républicains Radicaux*—U2R) was established by Emmanuel DUPUY (President), Paul BAQUIAST (Secretary General), and other former members of the PRG and the *Pôle Républicain*. Also in 2002, business executive and entrepreneur Christian BLANC, who sits in the National Assembly as a UDF ally, formed the social-liberal **Democratic Energies** (*Energies Démocrates*) movement. Partly in response to recent anti-immigrant sentiment and efforts to ban Islamic headscarves from public schools, the **Party of French Muslims** (*Parti des Musulmans de France*) was established by Mohamed LATRÈCHE.

At present, the most visible French antiglobalization crusader is probably José BOVÉ, a founder of the **Small Farmers' Confederation** (*Confédération Paysanne*) who is regarded as a possible "green" candidate for president in 2007. He first came to widespread attention by wrecking a McDonald's restaurant in Millau in 1997. More recently, he has been arrested on several occasions for destroying fields of genetically modified crops.

Regional Parties and Groups

Parties and groups seeking Corsican autonomy or separation have long been active, but they have drawn increased international attention as proposals for greater Corsican autonomy have made their way through the Parliament. Closest to the political mainstream is the **Corsican Nation** (*Corsica Nazione*) alliance, led by Jean-Guy TALAMONI, which has competed with some success against branches of national parties in regional elections. The largest and most prominent of the militant organizations has been the Corsican National Liberation Front (*Front de Libération Nationale de la Corse/Fronte di Liberazione Naziunale di a Corsica*—FLNC), which was established in 1976 but which in 1990 split into two organizations: the FLNC–Historic Wing (FLNC–*Canal Historique*—FLNC-CH), which is now called the **Corsican National Liberation Front–Union of Combatants** (FLNC–*Union des Combatants*—FLNC-UC), and the FLNC–*Canal Habituel*, the latter of which dissolved in 1997.

The history of the FLNC has been marked by bombings, other terrorist activities, and interfactional feuding, interspersed with periodic cease-fires. An FLNC-CH splinter, the **Armata Corsa**, was established in 1999 by François SANTONI, a former secretary general of *A Cuncolta Indipendentista* (ACI), the legal wing of the banned FLNC-CH; Santoni was murdered in August 2001. In May 2001 the ACI had announced that three additional groups—*Corsica Viva*, *Associu per a Suvranita*, and *U Cullettivu Naziounale*—were joining it in formation of **Independence** (*Indipendenza*). In August 2003 the *Resistenza Corsa*, which had claimed responsibility for a series of bombings earlier in the year, announced that it was merging with the FLNC-UC.

One of the more recent FLNC splinters, the **Corsican National Liberation Front–October 22** (FLNC *du 22 Octobre*) opposed a cease-fire that the FLNC-UC had declared in November 2003 in an effort to establish an alliance to contest the March 2004 regional elections. In February 2004 the *Corsica Nazione*, *Indipendenza*, and other groups organized a National Union List (*Liste d'Unione Naziunale*) led by Jean-Guy Talamoni and another moderate nationalist, Edmond SIMEONI. With the support of the FLNC-UC, the list won 17 percent of the second-round vote at the March balloting. A year later, however, the FNLC-UC ended its cease-fire to protest the trial of 22 nationalists, one of whom, Charles PIERI, was reputedly the

FNLC-UC commander. In May 2005 Pieri was convicted and sentenced to ten years in prison for involvement in illegal fundraising. Nineteen codefendants also were convicted, but two were acquitted, including Talamoni. Since then, the FLNC and the FLNC–October 22 have claimed responsibility for dozens of bombings.

Other recently organized formations include the **Party of the Corsican Nation** (*Partitu di a Nazione Corsa*—PNC), which was established in December 2002 by merger of several groups that rejected the use of violence. In contrast, **Clandestini Corsi** claimed in 2004 to be targeting North African immigrants, whom it accused of involvement in drug trafficking.

There are a number of additional regional organizations of varying degrees of militancy. The **Union of the Alsatian People** (*Union du Peuple Alsacien/Elsass Volksunion*—UPA/EVU) has campaigned for regional autonomy and restoration of links to German-speaking Lorraine. In May 2005 the **Alsatian Corps** (*Elsass Korps*), a neo-Nazi group, was banned. The **Breton Democratic Union** (*Union Démocratique Breton*—UDB), a socialist-oriented group, seeks autonomy for Brittany by nonviolent means. Other regional groups include the federalist **Party for the Organization of a Free Brittany** (*Parti pour l'Organisation d'une Bretagne Libre*—POBL); the separatist **Liberation Front of Brittany–Breton Republican Army** (*Front Libération de la Bretagne–Armée Républicain Breton*—FLB-ARB); and the French Basque **Those of the North** (*Iparretarrak*), which was outlawed in July 1987 following the conviction of its leader, Philippe BIDART, for murder.

Legislature

The bicameral **Parliament** (*Parlement*) consists of an indirectly chosen Senate and a directly elected National Assembly.

Senate (Sénat)

The French Senate, which under the Fifth Republic has been reduced to a limiting and delaying role, currently consists of 331 members. The 304 senators from metropolitan France (including Corsica) are designated by an electoral college that is dominated by municipal council members but also includes National Assembly deputies and regional and departmental council members. Fifteen senators are indirectly elected by the overseas jurisdictions, and 12 are named by the Higher Council of French Abroad (*Conseil Supérieur des Français à l'Étranger*) to represent French nationals overseas.

Under a 2003 reform, the number of senators was increased from 321 at the September 26, 2004, election, with an additional 10 members to be added in 2007 and 5 more in 2010, thus bringing the total membership to 346. In addition, the senatorial term was shortened from nine years (selected by thirds every three years) to six years (selected by halves every three years). The 2004 election for 128 seats produced the following results: Union for a Popular Movement, 57; Socialist Party, 30; Union for French Democracy, 12; French Communist Party, 11; *Divers Droite* (Diverse Right), 7; *Divers Gauche* (Diverse Left), 5; Greens, 3; Left Radical Party, 2; unattached, 1.

As of April 2006 the distribution of seats by senatorial grouping was as follows: Union for a Popular Movement and allies, 155; Socialists and allies, 97; Centrist Union (mainly members of the Union for French Democracy) and allies, 33; Communist, Republican, and Citizen (mainly members of the French Communist Party), 23; Democratic and European Social Rally, 16; unattached, 7.

President: Christian PONCELET.

National Assembly (Assemblée Nationale)

The French Assembly presently consists of 577 deputies elected by two-round, majoritarian voting in single member districts for five-year terms (subject to dissolution). Candidates receiving a majority of the vote in the first round are declared elected; in all other districts, those who receive 12.5 percent of the vote in the first round proceed to the second, in which a plurality is sufficient for election.

At the most recent election of June 9 and 16, 2002, 58 candidates won in the first round, with the final results from both rounds producing the

Cabinet

As of August 15, 2006

Prime Minister	Dominique de Villepin
Minister of State	Nicolas Sarkozy

Ministers

Agriculture and Fisheries	Dominique Bussereau
Civil Service	Christian Jacob
Culture and Communications	Renaud Donnedieu de Vabres
Defense	Michèle Alliot-Marie [f]
Ecology and Sustainable Development	Nelly Olin [f]
Economy, Finance, and Industry	Thierry Breton (ind.)
Employment, Social Cohesion, and Housing	Jean-Louis Borloo (UDF/RRRS)
Foreign Affairs	Philippe Douste-Blazy
Health and Solidarity	Xavier Bertrand
Interior and Regional Development	Nicolas Sarkozy
Justice, Keeper of the Seals	Pascal Clément
National Education, Higher Education, and Research	Gilles de Robien (UDF)
Overseas France	François Baroin
Small and Medium-Sized Enterprises, Trade, Small-Scale Industry, and the Professions	Renaud Dutreil (UDF)
Transportation, Capital Works, Tourism, and Maritime Affairs	Dominique Perben
Youth, Sports, and Associations	Jean-François Lamour (ind.)

[f] = female

Note: Unless otherwise noted, ministers are members of the UMP.

following distribution: Union for the Presidential Majority (subsequently renamed the Union for a Popular Movement, UMP), 355 seats; Socialist Party, 140; Union for French Democracy (UDF), 29; French Communist Party, 21; *Divers Droite* (Diverse Right), 10; Left Radical Party, 7; *Divers Gauche* (Diverse Left), 7; Greens, 3; Liberal Democracy, 2; Rally for France and the Independence of Europe, 2; Movement for France, 1. Note, however, that different news sources, even when relying on postelection data from the Interior Ministry, reported slightly different totals for some parties and groups—typically between 355 and 357 seats for the UMP, for example, and 9 or 10 seats for *Diverse Droite*—in part because a small number of successful candidates carried equivocal or dual affiliations, such as UMP/UDF.

As of April 2006 the National Assembly listed the members as belonging to the following political groups (*groupes politiques*): UMP, 354 plus 10 allies; Socialist, 142 plus 8 allies; UDF, 27 plus 3 allies; Communists and Republicans, 22; unaffiliated, 11.

President: Jean-Louis DEBRÉ.

Communications

France's traditional freedom of the press has been maintained under the Fifth Republic, subject to the restriction that offensive criticism may not be directed against the head of state and that the private lives of politicians may not be reported. This formal freedom has, however, been partially offset by consolidation in ownership of the nation's newspapers, which has contributed to a sharp decline in the number of major Parisian dailies (about 10 at present, contrasted with nearly 30 following World War II and 80 prior to World War I). At the same time, the provincial press has grown in circulation and influence. In all, some 135 dailies are currently published.

Press

The following newspapers are published daily in Paris, unless otherwise noted: *Ouest-France* (Rennes, national circulation, 785,000 daily, 250,000 Sunday); *Le Parisien* (370,000), popular morning independent; *Le Figaro* (365,000), founded 1826, leading morning independent and standard-bearer of the bourgeoisie; *Le Monde* (360,000), independent evening paper with international readership and weekly edition in English, left-of-center; *Sud-Ouest* (Bordeaux, 330,000); *La Voix du Nord* (Lille, 320,000); *Le Journal du Dimanche* (300,000 Sunday); *Le Dauphiné Libéré* (Grenoble, 260,000), leading provincial; *Le Progrès* (Lyon, 260,000); *International Herald Tribune* (245,000), American; *La Nouvelle République du Centre-Ouest* (Tours, 245,000); *La Montagne* (Clermont-Ferrand, 215,000), independent; *La Dépêche du Midi* (Toulouse, 210,000), radical management; *L'Est Républicain* (Nancy, 210,000); *Les Dernières Nouvelles d'Alsace* (Strasbourg, 200,000); *Le Télégramme* (Morlaix, 190,000); *Le Provence* (Marseilles, 170,000), largest southeastern daily, socialist; *Midi-Libre* (Montpellier, 165,000); *Libération* (160,000), left-oriented independent; *Nice-Matin* (Nice, 160,000); *Le Républicain Lorrain* (Metz, 160,000); *Aujourd'hui en France* (150,000 published nationally by *Le Parisien*); *Les Echos* (120,000), financial and economic; *L'Humanité* (120,000), Communist; *L'Union* (Reims, 120,000); *L'Alsace* (Mulhouse, 115,000); *Le Courrier de l'Ouest* (Angers, 100,000), *France-Soir* (90,000), leading evening paper, right-wing orientation; *La Croix* (90,000), Catholic.

News Agencies

The principal French news agency is the semiofficial French Press Agency (*Agence France-Presse*—AFP), founded in 1835, which operates in most countries and many overseas territories in French, English, and Spanish; other agencies include *Agence Parisienne de Presse* (ACP). The leading foreign news agencies also maintain bureaus in France's principal cities.

Broadcasting and Computing

Until 1972 the government-owned French Radio and Television Organization (*Office de Radiodiffusion et Télévision Française*—ORTF) held a monopoly of both domestic and international services. In 1974 legislation was enacted breaking up the ORTF in favor of seven state-financed but independent companies. In 1982 the regulatory function was taken over by a single 9-member committee, which was in turn replaced by a 13-member National Commission of Communication and Franchises (*Commission Nationale de la Communication et des Libertatés*—CNCL) in 1986. In 1989 the Socialist government discarded the CNCL, which many viewed as a vehicle of government control over broadcasting, in favor of a 9-member, independent Higher Audiovisual Council (*Conseil Supérieur de l'Audiovisuel*—CSA). At present there are three "public service" (partially state-administered) television channels (*France 2*, *France 3*, and the partly educational *Arte/La Cinquième*) and three commercial channels (*TF1*, *M6*, and the subscription *Canal Plus*). Cable networks and satellite service also are available. There are several major public radio services (including the all-news *France Info*), plus nearly 3,000 commercial stations, of which only a few transmit nationally. In 2003 there were approximately 38.5 million television receivers in use. Some 21.2 million personal computers served 21.9 million Internet users.

Intergovernmental Representation

Ambassador to the U.S.
Jean-David LEVITTE

U.S. Ambassador to France
Craig Roberts STAPLETON

Permanent Representative to the UN
Jean-Marc DE LA SABLIÈRE

IGO Memberships (Non-UN)
ACS, ADB, AfDB, BDEAC, BIS, BOAD, CERN, CEUR, EBRD, EIB, ESA, EU, Eurocontrol, G-10, G-7/G-8, IADB, IEA, Interpol, IOC, IOM, NATO, OECD, OIF, OSCE, PC, PCA, WCO, WEU, WTO

Related Territories

The former French overseas empire entered a state of constitutional and political transformation after World War II, as a majority of its component territories achieved independence, and most of the others experienced far-reaching modifications in their links to the home country. The initial step in the process of readjustment was the establishment in 1946 of the French Union (*Union Française*) as a single political entity designed to encompass all French-ruled territories. As defined by the constitution of the Fourth Republic, the French Union consisted of two elements: (1) the "French Republic," comprising metropolitan France and the overseas departments and territories and (2) all those "associated territories and states" that chose to join. Vietnam, Laos, and Cambodia became associated states under this provision; Tunisia and Morocco declined to do so. The arrangement proved ineffective, however, in stemming the tide of nationalism, which led within a decade to the independence of the Indochinese states, Tunisia, and Morocco; the onset of the war of independence in Algeria; and growing pressure for independence in other French African territories.

In a further attempt to accommodate these pressures, the constitution of the Fifth Republic as adopted in 1958 established the more flexible framework of the French Community (*Communauté Française*), the primary purpose of which was to satisfy the demand for self-government in the African colonies while stopping short of full independence. Still composed of the "French Republic" on the one hand and a group of "Member States" on the other, the community was headed by the president of the French Republic and endowed with its own Executive Council, Senate, and Court of Arbitration. Initially, 12 French African territories accepted the status of self-governing member states, with only Guinea opting for complete independence. In response to the political evolution of other member states, the French constitution was amended in 1960 to permit continued membership in the community even after independence, but no previously dependent territory elected to participate. The community's Senate was abolished on March 16, 1961, at which time the organization became essentially moribund.

As a consequence of constitutional changes instituted in March 2003, the present French Republic encompasses, in addition to mainland France and Corsica, four overseas departments, one departmental collectivity, two overseas collectivities, two overseas countries, and one extraconstitutional overseas territory. For more on these departments and territories, see *Political Handbook of the World 2007*.

GERMANY

FEDERAL REPUBLIC OF GERMANY

Bundesrepublik Deutschland

The Country

Germany's commanding position in Central Europe and its industrious population have made it a significant factor in modern European and world affairs, despite the political fragmentation that has characterized much of its history. Flat and low-lying in the north and increasingly mountainous to the south, the country combines abundant agricultural land with rich deposits of coal and other minerals and a strategic position astride the main European river systems. A small group of Danish speakers is located in the northwest, and a vaguely Polish group of Sorbian speakers inhabits the southeast of the former German Democratic Republic (GDR, or East Germany); otherwise, the indigenous population is remarkably homogeneous. On the other hand, large numbers of Turkish and other foreign workers who entered the Federal Republic of Germany (FRG, or West Germany) after World War II have more recently been joined by a flood of asylum seekers and other immigrants. (Germany's once substantial Jewish population was virtually destroyed during the Nazi period in 1933–1945 and presently numbers only about 100,000, mostly immigrants from the former Soviet Union.) Protestantism, chiefly Evangelical Lutheranism, is the declared religion of about 38 percent of the population, with Roman Catholics numbering about 34 percent. Women made up 42 percent of the labor force in 2000 but remained severely underrepresented in federal and state governmental and legislative bodies.

Although highly industrialized prior to World War II, the German economy exhibited major regional variations that, coupled with quite dissimilar postwar military occupation policies in the East and the West, yielded divergent patterns of reconstruction and development. West Germany, with a greater resource base, substantial financial assistance from the Western allies, and a strong commitment to free enterprise, recovered rapidly, greatly expanded its industry, and by the 1960s had become the strongest economic power in Western Europe. Communist East Germany recovered more slowly, although experiencing a surge in development that by 1990 placed it among the top dozen nations in industrial output and second only to the Union of Soviet Socialist Republics (USSR) in Eastern Europe.

Political Status: Divided into British, French, Soviet, and U.S. occupation zones in July 1945; Federal Republic of Germany under democratic parliamentary regime established in Western zones on May 23, 1949; German Democratic Republic established under Communist auspices in Soviet zone on October 7, 1949; unified as the Federal Republic of Germany on October 3, 1990.

Area: 137,854 sq. mi. (357,041 sq. km.).

Population: 82,503,000 (2005E). A 1981 census in the GDR yielded a total of 16,705,635, while a 1987 census in the FRG yielded a total of 61,077,042.

Major Urban Centers (2005E): BERLIN (3,507,000), Hamburg (1,743,000), Munich (1,267,000), Cologne (966,000), Frankfurt am Main (649,000), Stuttgart (598,000), Essen (589,000), Dortmund (588,000), Düsseldorf (578,000), Bremen (545,000), Leipzig (531,000), Hannover (514,000), Dresden (500,000), Duisburg (494,000), Bonn (317,000), Chemnitz (253,000). Parliament voted in June 1991 to relocate the capital from Bonn to Berlin, although the actual transfer did not occur until 1999–2000. A 1994 Berlin-Bonn law defined the former capital as a "federal city," and many government and international offices continue to operate or have been established there.

Official Language: German.

Monetary Unit: Euro (market rate July 1, 2006: 1 euro = $1.28US).

Federal President: Horst KÖHLER (Christian Democratic Union); elected by the Federal Convention on the first ballot on May 23, 2004, and inaugurated on July 1 for a five-year term, succeeding Johannes RAU (Social Democratic Party).

Federal Chancellor: Angela MERKEL (Christian Democratic Union); elected by the Federal Assembly and sworn in on November 22, 2005, to succeed Gerhard SCHRÖDER (Social Democratic Party) following legislative elections of September 18.

Political reunification on October 3, 1990, was preceded by the entry into force on July 1 of a State Treaty establishing an economic, monetary, and social union of the two Germanies. The principal objectives of the treaty were to provide for transition from a socialist to a market economy in the East; replacement of the East German currency by the West German deutsche mark; and economic integration, with particular attention to largely obsolete capital stock, severe environmental pollution, and uncertainties about property rights in the former Communist territory. However, the problems, compounded by international recession, proved to be much greater than anticipated. During 1993 united Germany's GDP fell by 2 percent, the most severe decline since 1945, while recovery to 2–3 percent growth in 1994–1995 did not halt a rise in unemployment, which reached 9.5 percent in 1997. GDP growth was steady but gradual during the second half of the decade, averaging 1.5 percent annually from 1996 through 1999 before doubling to 3.0 percent in 2000. At the same time, unemployment gradually fell, descending to 7.9 percent for 2000, while consumer price inflation ranged between 0.6 percent in 1998 and 2.1 percent in 2000. From mid-2000, however, higher oil import prices and a slowdown in the global economy contributed to a falloff in growth.

Germany's economic stagnation continued in the early 2000s, with GDP actually declining in 2003 and unemployment reaching a postwar high of 10.7 percent. The Gerhard SCHRÖDER government attempted to implement a variety of free-market reforms, although it was forced to compromise with leftist elements in the cabinet and legislature. However, economic malaise continued, with GDP growth of only slightly more than 1 percent being achieved in both 2004 and 2005 and unemployment moving to more than 11 percent in early 2006. The "grand coalition" government installed in 2005 pledged to address structural weaknesses in the labor market, to promote job creation, and reduce spending. However, it was clear that Germany in 2006 would violate the European

Union (EU) standard regarding the size of the annual budget deficit (no more than 3 percent of GDP) for the fifth year in a row.

Government and Politics

Political Background

Germany's history as a modern nation dates from the Franco-Prussian War of 1870–1871 and the proclamation in 1871 of the German Empire, the result of efforts by Otto von BISMARCK and others to convert a loose confederation of German-speaking territories into a single political entity led by the Prussian House of Hohenzollern. Defeated by a coalition of powers in World War I, the German Empire disintegrated and was replaced in 1919 by the Weimar Republic, whose chronic economic and political instability paved the way for the rise of the National Socialist (Nazi) Party and the installation of Adolf HITLER as chancellor in 1933. Under a totalitarian ideology stressing nationalism, anti-Communism, anti-Semitism, and removal of the disabilities imposed on Germany after World War I, Hitler converted the Weimar Republic into an authoritarian one-party state (the so-called "Third Reich") and embarked upon a policy of aggressive expansionism that led to the outbreak of World War II in 1939 and, ultimately, to defeat of the Nazi regime by the Allies in 1945.

Following Germany's unconditional surrender on May 8, 1945, the country was divided into zones of military occupation assigned to forces of the United States, Britain, France, and the Soviet Union, whose governments assumed all powers of administration pending the reestablishment of a German governmental authority. Berlin, likewise divided into sectors, was made a separate area under joint quadripartite control with a view to its becoming the seat of the eventual central German government; elsewhere, the territories east of the Oder and Neisse rivers were placed under Polish administration, East Prussia was divided into Soviet and Polish spheres, and the Saar was attached economically to France.

At the Potsdam Conference in July–August 1945, the American, British, and Soviet leaders agreed to treat Germany as a single economic unit and to ensure parallel political development in the four occupation zones, but the emergence of sharp differences between the Soviet Union and its wartime allies soon intervened. Among other things, Soviet occupation policies prevented implementation of the single economic unit plan, forcing the Western powers to adopt joint measures for their zones only. Protesting a proposed currency reform by its Western counterparts, the USSR in June 1948 instituted a blockade of the land and water routes to Berlin that was maintained until May 1949, prompting Britain and the United States, with French ground support, to resort to a large-scale airlift to supply the city's Western sectors.

Having failed to agree with the USSR on measures for the whole of Germany, the three Western powers resolved to merge their zones of occupation as a step toward establishing a democratic state in western Germany. A draft constitution for a West German federal state was approved by a specially elected parliamentary assembly on May 8, 1949, and the Federal Republic of Germany (FRG), with its capital at Bonn, was proclaimed on May 23. The USSR protested these actions and on October 7 announced the establishment in its occupation zone of the German Democratic Republic (GDR), with East Berlin as its capital. An anti-Communist workers' uprising in East Germany in 1953 was ruthlessly suppressed by GDR and Soviet forces.

In West Germany the occupation structure was gradually converted into a contractual relationship based on the equality of the parties involved. Under the London and Paris agreements of 1954, the FRG gained sovereignty on May 5, 1955, when it was admitted to the North Atlantic Treaty Organization (NATO) and the Western European Union (WEU), while on January 1, 1957, the Saar was returned as the result of a plebiscite held in 1955. The Soviet-sponsored GDR had meanwhile also been declared fully sovereign and was accorded formal recognition by Communist, although not by Western, governments. Although Berlin remained technically under four-power control, East Berlin was incorporated into the GDR as its capital, while

West Berlin, without being granted parliamentary voting rights, was accorded a status similar to that of a *land* (state) of the FRG. The FRG-GDR border served as the focal point for much of the Cold War confrontation of the 1950s and 1960s, with intermittent crises triggered by Soviet/East German interruptions or threats of interruption of land access to West Berlin. This tension, accompanied by accelerating immigration from East to West via the open borders inside Berlin, induced the eastern authorities in August 1961 to build the Berlin Wall.

During the eight years following proclamation of the FRG in 1949, the Christian Democratic Union (*Christlich-Demokratische Union*— CDU) under Chancellor Konrad ADENAUER maintained coalition governments with the Free Democratic Party (*Freie Demokratische Partei*— FDP) and other minor groups, thereby excluding the Social Democratic Party (*Sozialdemokratische Partei Deutschlands*—SPD) from power. In 1957 the CDU and its Bavarian affiliate, the Christian Social Union (*Christlich-Soziale Union*—CSU), won a clear majority of legislative seats, but in 1961 and again in 1965 they were forced to renew their pact with the FDP. In 1966 disagreements on financial policy led the FDP to withdraw from the coalition, and Ludwig ERHARD, who had succeeded Adenauer as chancellor three years earlier, was obliged to resign. On December 1 a CDU-CSU/SPD "grand coalition" government was inaugurated, with Kurt-Georg KIESINGER of the CDU as chancellor.

As a result of the election of September 1969, Willy BRANDT, SPD leader as well as vice chancellor and foreign minister of the CDU-CSU/SPD government, became chancellor at the head of an SPD/FDP coalition. Although the coalition was renewed after the November 1972 balloting, widespread labor unrest early in 1974 attested to the increasing inability of the Brandt administration to cope with domestic economic difficulties, including a record postwar inflation of more than 7.5 percent; however, it was the revelation that one of the chancellor's personal political aides was an East German espionage agent that prompted Brandt's resignation on May 6 and his replace-

ment shortly thereafter by former finance minister Helmut SCHMIDT. Former FDP foreign minister Walter SCHEEL, who had served briefly as interim chancellor following Brandt's resignation, was elected federal president on May 15 and was sworn in on July 1, succeeding the SPD's Gustav HEINEMANN.

At a close election on October 3, 1976, the SPD/FDP coalition obtained a substantially reduced majority of 253 out of 496 seats in the *Bundestag* (Federal Assembly), and on December 15 Schmidt was reconfirmed as chancellor. However, growing Christian Democratic strength at the state level gave the CDU-CSU an overall majority in the Federal Convention, which is responsible for electing the president; as a result, *Bundestag* president Karl CARSTENS, the CDU candidate, was elected on May 23, 1979, to succeed President Scheel, who had decided not to seek a second term after being denied all-party support.

Chancellor Schmidt remained in office following the *Bundestag* election of October 5, 1980, at which the SPD gained 4 seats and the FDP gained 14, while the CDU-CSU, led in the campaign by Franz-Josef STRAUSS, minister-president of Bavaria and CSU chair, lost 17.

An extensive reorganization of the Schmidt cabinet in April 1982 pointed up increasing disagreement within the SPD/FDP coalition on matters of defense and economic policy. On September 17 all four FDP ministers resigned, precipitating a "constructive vote of no confidence" on October 1 that resulted in the appointment of Dr. Helmut KOHL as head of a CDU-CSU/FDP government. Subsequently, in mid-December, Kohl called for a nonconstructive confidence vote that was deliberately lost by CDU abstentions, thus permitting the chancellor to call an early election. At the balloting on March 6, 1983, the three-party coalition won 278 of 498 lower house seats, allowing Kohl to form a new government on March 29.

The coalition's mandate was renewed in balloting on January 25, 1987, although the CDU-CSU share of the vote (44.3 percent) was the lowest since the founding of the West German state in 1949. The SPD did marginally better than opinion polls had predicted, drawing 37.0 percent, compared with

38.2 percent in 1983. Gaining strength at the expense of the major parties were the FDP, which was awarded an additional ministry (for a total of four) in the government formed on March 11, and The Greens, whose parliamentary representation increased from 27 to 42.

In October 1989, in response to political upheavals elsewhere in Eastern Europe, antiregime demonstrations erupted in East Berlin and quickly spread to other major cities. In an attempt to quell the growing unrest, East German authorities abolished the restriction on foreign travel for GDR citizens on November 9 and immediately began dismantling sections of the infamous Berlin Wall that had long divided the city. Subsequently, as the Communist regime faced imminent collapse (for details, see the 1990 *Handbook*), appeals for reunification resurfaced, and on February 6, 1990, Kohl announced his readiness "to open immediate negotiations on economic and monetary union." A positive GDR response resulted in agreement on a common monetary system by the German finance ministers in mid-May, effective July 1. On the same day, all border restrictions between East and West Germany were eliminated.

The crucial succeeding stages toward reunification were (1) Chancellor Kohl's agreement with USSR leader Mikhail Gorbachev in Stavropol on July 15–16, 1990, that unified Germany could be a member of NATO; (2) agreement in the "two-plus-four" (the two Germanies plus the four wartime Allies) forum in Paris on July 17 that international legality should be bestowed on Germany by a "treaty of settlement" rather than a peace treaty; (3) the East German Parliament's resolution on August 23 that the five newly restored eastern *länder* (Brandenburg, Mecklenburg-West Pomerania, Saxony, Saxony-Anhalt, and Thuringia) should accede to the Federal Republic; (4) the signature in Berlin on August 31 of a formal unification treaty between East and West Germany; and (5) the signature in Moscow on September 12 by the "two-plus-four" states of a Treaty on the Final Settlement with Respect to Germany, formally terminating the wartime victors' responsibilities for Germany and Berlin.

On October 1, 1990, the four World War II Allies formally suspended their occupation rights, and in a jubilant midnight ceremony in Berlin on October 2–3 the two Germanies were united. On October 4, 144 members of East Germany's disbanded *Volkskammer* joined West German legislators in the inaugural session of an expanded *Bundestag* at Berlin's old *Reichstag* building, while 4 ministers from the East, including its only non-Communist minister-president, Lothar DE MAIZIÈRE, entered the Kohl government as ministers without portfolio. At elections held October 14 in the recreated eastern *länder,* the CDU won control in all but one parliament (Brandenburg, where it ran second to the SPD).

On December 2, 1990, at the first free all-German election in 58 years, Kohl's CDU-CSU/FDP coalition captured 398 of 662 *Bundestag* seats on a 54.8 percent share of the vote, while the opposition SPD secured 239 seats on a vote share of 33.5 percent. On January 17, 1991, Kohl was formally reinvested as chancellor to head a new government containing 11 CDU, 4 CSU, and 5 FDP ministers.

The unexpected pace of German unification virtually transformed the policy agenda of the now-enlarged Federal Republic, including its ongoing commitments to the West and the European Community (EC, subsequently the EU). Among other acute problems, it faced a need for near-total economic conversion in the East, a wave of immigration coupled with mounting antiforeigner feeling, and a variety of political and legal entanglements involving secret police activities in the former GDR and human rights violations committed under the cloak of East German legality.

Because of the involvement of West German expertise and capital, the process of converting the long centrally planned East Germany to a "social market economy" moved forward more quickly and with less short-term difficulty than in neighboring ex-Communist countries. Most leaders conceded, however, that the challenges far exceeded pre-unification expectations. The conversion process was spearheaded by the Trust Agency (*Treuhandanstalt*), responsible for privatizing nearly 8,000 state-owned firms and large agricultural enterprises. After a slow start, the number of sales reached 500 per month by early 1992, although returns were substantially less than anticipated, in part because of the obsolescence of most East German industry, chronic environmental pollution, and the legal uncertainty of deeds subject to claim from pre-Communist owners.

Economic problems resulting from unification heightened popular disquiet over immigration levels, as reflected in substantial electoral gains for the extreme right in successive state and local elections in 1991–1992 and in widening antiforeigner violence. Particular concern arose over open asylum for political refugees, of whom a record number of 438,000 lodged applications in 1992, partly as a result of the exodus from former Yugoslavia. The government responded to the racial violence by banning a number of extremist groups and by decreeing harsher sentences for those convicted of such activity. It also responded to public concern by securing an amendment to the law of asylum (in May 1993) that brought German practice into broader conformity with that of other West European states by empowering the authorities to refuse entry to those deemed to be economic migrants; specifically, asylum would no longer be granted to persons arriving from countries where the rule of law was deemed to be respected, unless direct evidence of political persecution was adduced. However, the government in mid-June indicated that it would ease restrictions on the attainment of citizenship by aliens, while maintaining the "blood principle" of 1913 that conferred the right to nationality on those of ethnic German ancestry irrespective of place of birth or current location. (In January 1999 reform of the citizen law granted automatic citizenship to children born in Germany and allowed immigrants to seek naturalization following eight years of residence.)

Alarmed by the spiraling costs of unification, the Kohl government on January 19, 1993, published proposals for a "solidarity pact" designed to raise necessary revenue. The proposals were initially rejected by the SPD on the grounds that they were socially unjust, but federal/*länder* negotiations re-

sulted in formal signature of the pact on March 13 by government and opposition representatives. The pact provided for increased taxation and expenditure cuts designed to finance the estimated $60 billion annual cost of the subsidies required by the eastern region.

Damaged by economic recession, the coalition's standing also was impaired through 1993 by a series of ministerial resignations for alleged misconduct. In addition, Kohl's credibility suffered when his controversial nominee for the federal presidency was forced to withdraw because of media reaction to his intensely right-wing views. Subsequently, another CDU nominee, Constitutional Court President Roman HERZOG, was elected to the presidency on May 23, 1994, by a slim 53 percent majority of Federal Convention votes.

State and partial local balloting in the early months of the 1994 "year of elections" yielded no clear pattern of voter sympathies, much attention thereby being focused on the all-Germany European Parliament elections on June 12. The results showed that the CDU-CSU had overcome a Europewide swing against incumbent parties by increasing its vote share to 38.8 percent from 37.8 percent in 1989, and its seat total from 32 to 47 in a German contingent that increased from 81 to 99. The European results proved to be a portent, in that the Kohl coalition retained a narrow majority in the federal elections held on October 16, 1994. The CDU-CSU took 41.5 percent of the vote, only 2 points less than in 1990, and won 294 seats in a *Bundestag* enlarged to 672 members, while the SPD managed only a 3-point increase to 36.4 percent and 252 seats. However, the crucial outcome was the FDP's unexpected surmounting of the 5 percent barrier, its 6.9 percent giving it 47 seats, enough to provide a 10-seat majority for a further CDU-CSU/FDP coalition.

The new *Bundestag* duly reelected Kohl as chancellor on November 15, 1994, by 338 votes to 333. Two days later the fifth Kohl government, again a coalition of the CDU-CSU and the FDP, was sworn in, with much the same personnel as its predecessor but with the FDP contingent reduced from five to three ministers. The ruling coalition quickly faced opposition in the *Bundesrat*, where in early 1995 the SPD majority twice rejected the 1995 draft budget approved by the lower house. However, the superior financial authority of the *Bundestag* eventually prevailed in June, by which time internal strife in the SPD had eased the pressure on the government. Mixed state election results in 1995 were followed in March 1996 by contests in Baden-Württemberg, Rhineland-Palatinate, and Schleswig-Holstein that strengthened the coalition parties overall, especially the FDP.

The Kohl forces suffered a string of defeats in the 1998 state elections, which included a surprising 13 percent showing in Saxony-Anhalt by the German People's Union (*Deutsche Volksunion*—DVU), which became the first extreme-right party to win seats in an eastern state legislature. The state elections foreshadowed the results of the September 27 *Bundestag* contest in which the SPD, running its reelected premier of Lower Saxony, Gerhard Schröder, defeated Kohl's CDU-CSU, 40.9 percent to 35.1 percent. Kohl thus became the first incumbent chancellor to be turned out in postwar Germany, and Schröder became the first Social Democratic chancellor in 18 years. Schröder took office on October 27 as the leader of a center-left ("red-green") coalition government with the environmentally oriented Greens (*Die Grünen*), who had won 47 seats with a 6.7 percent vote share.

On May 23, 1999, the SPD's Johannes RAU, former minister-president of North Rhine Westphalia, was elected federal president in a second round of balloting by the Federal Convention. He had narrowly failed to obtain a majority on the first ballot, his principal opponent being the CDU's Dagmar SCHIPANSKI. Sworn in on July 1, Rau became the first president from the SPD since Gustav Heinemann left office in 1974.

Facing polls that showed a severe erosion in support for the administration in advance of the September 23, 2002, balloting for the *Bundestag*, Chancellor Schröder launched a highly vocal campaign against U.S. policy toward Iraq that appeared to resonate with the electorate. Consequently, the

SPD and Alliance '90/The Greens combined for 206 seats, enough for the two parties to maintain their governing coalition. However, by early 2004 public opinion had apparently again turned against the SPD, and Horst KÖHLER of the CDU was elected president of the republic in the first round of balloting in the Federal Convention.

With the SPD's popularity continuing to decline, Chancellor Schröder deliberately lost a no-confidence vote on July 1, 2005, and asked for early elections. President Köhler, after ruminating on the unusual circumstances, finally dissolved the *Bundestag* on July 21. In new balloting on September 18, the SPD led all parties with 222 seats, although the governing SPD/Greens coalition failed to secure a majority. Meanwhile, the CDU-CSU combined for 225 seats, although the conservatives too were unable to put together a working legislative majority with their longtime ally, the FDP. (Both the CDU and the SDP rejected coalition with The Left, a new alliance that had won 54 seats.) Consequently, the CDU-CSU and the SPD reached agreement in mid-November on a "grand coalition," and Angela MERKEL of the CDU was sworn in on November 22 as chancellor and head of a government that included eight ministers form the SPD, six (including Merkel) from the CDU, and two from the CSU.

Constitution and Government

Germany, under the Basic Law (*Grundgesetz*) of May 23, 1949, is a Federal Republic in which areas of authority are both shared and divided between the component states (*länder*) and the federal government (*Bundesregierung*). Responsibility in such areas as economic, social, and health policy is held jointly, with the federal government establishing general guidelines, the states assuming administration, and both typically providing funds. Each state (*land*) has its own parliament elected by universal suffrage, with authority to legislate in all matters—including education, police, and broadcasting—not expressly reserved to the federal government. The latter is responsible for foreign affairs, defense, and such matters as citizenship, migration, customs, posts, and telecommunications.

The major federal components are the head of state, or federal president (*bundespräsident*); a cabinet headed by a chancellor (*bundeskanzler*); and a bicameral Parliament (*Parlament*) consisting of a Federal Council (*Bundesrat*) and a Federal Assembly (*Bundestag*). *Bundesrat* members are appointed and recalled by the state governments; their role is limited to those areas of policy that fall under joint federal-state responsibility, although they have veto powers where specified state interests are involved. The *Bundestag,* elected by universal suffrage under a mixed direct and proportional representation system, is the major legislative organ. It elects the chancellor by an absolute majority but cannot overthrow him except by electing a successor. The president, whose functions are mainly ceremonial, is elected by a special Federal Convention (*Bundesversammlung*) made up of the members of the *Bundestag* and an equal number of members chosen by the state legislatures. Ministers are appointed by the president on the advice of the chancellor.

The judiciary is headed by the Federal Constitutional Court (*Bundesverfassungsgericht*), with the two houses of Parliament each electing half its judges, and also includes a Supreme Federal Court (*Bundesgerichtshof*) as well as Federal Administrative, Financial, Labor, and Social courts. While the constitution guarantees the maintenance of human rights and civil liberties, certain limitations in time of emergency were detailed in a controversial set of amendments adopted in 1968. In addition, the Federal Constitutional Court is authorized to outlaw political parties whose aims or activities are found to endanger "the basic libertarian democratic order" or its institutional structure.

The Federal Republic currently encompasses 16 *länder*, 10 from West Germany and 6 (†; identified in the table below) from the East. (The government proposed reducing the number of states to 8 in the mid-1990s, but that plan ran into difficulty at its first electoral test in May 1996 when Brandenburg voted against merger with Berlin.)

Land and Capital	Area (sq. mi.)	Population (2005E)
Baden-Württemberg (Stuttgart)	13,803	10,765,000
Bavaria (Munich)	27,238	12,505,000
Berlin (Berlin)†	341	3,373,000
Brandenburg (Potsdam)†	15,044	2,581,000
Bremen (Bremen)	156	660,000
Hamburg (Hamburg)	291	1,739,000
Hesse (Wiesbaden)	8,151	6,104,000
Lower Saxony (Hannover)	18,311	8,034,000
Mecklenburg-West Pomerania (Schwerin)†	6,080	1,715,000
North Rhine-Westphalia (Düsseldorf)	13,149	18,115,000
Rhineland-Palatinate (Mainz)	7,658	4,071,000
Saarland (Saarbrücken)	992	1,057,000
Saxony (Dresden)†	6,839	4,276,000
Saxony-Anhalt (Magdeburg)†	7,837	2,484,000
Schleswig-Holstein (Kiel)	6,053	2,842,000
Thuringia (Erfurt)†	5,872	2,348,000

A 32-member commission was appointed in 2003 to propose revision of the constitution to redistribute certain authority from the states to the federal level in order to provide greater efficiency in, among other areas, implementing economic policy and providing social services. Part of the proposal was that the *Bundesrat* (controlled by the states) would accept reduced veto authority over federal legislation. Negotiations in the commission reportedly collapsed in December 2004 over the question of reducing regional control of education. However, it appeared as of early 2006 that general agreement had been reached on legislation regarding "federalism reform," prompted in part by the recent installation of a "grand coalition" government. Under the accord, the number of laws subject to veto by the *Bundesrat* would be reduced from 60 percent of the total to approximately 35 percent. In return for the dilution of power at the national level, the states were to be given greater authority over education, the penal system, and the civil service. The constitutional amendments were slated for formal presentation to the Parliament by the end of the year. (Passage depended on a two-thirds majority in each house.) Supporters hoped the revisions would be implemented in January 2007. Significantly, however, the proposed amendments did not address the contentious issues of revising the formula for distribution of tax revenues between the states and the national government or the proposed merger of small states to make them more "competitive" with the larger states.

Foreign Relations

The post–World War II division of Germany and the anti-Soviet and anti-Communist outlook of most West Germans resulted in very close relations between the Federal Republic and the Western Allies, whose support was long deemed essential both to the survival of the FRG and to the eventual reunification of Germany on a democratic basis. The FRG became a key member of NATO, the EC, and the WEU as well as of the Organization for Economic Cooperation and Development (OECD), the Council of Europe, and other multilateral bodies aimed at closer political and economic cooperation. Participation by the GDR in multilateral organizations was for more than two decades limited primarily to the Soviet-backed Council for Mutual Economic Assistance and the Warsaw Treaty Organization.

The "two Germanies" concept acquired legal standing with the negotiation in November 1972 of a Basic Treaty (*Grundvertrag*) normalizing relations between the FRG and the GDR. While the agreement stopped short of a mutual extension of full diplomatic recognition, it affirmed the "inviolability" of the existing border and provided for the exchange of "permanent representative missions" by the two governments, thus seeming to rule out the possibility of German reunification. On September 5, 1974, following ratification of the Basic Treaty, both Germanies were admitted to the United Nations (UN). Earlier, in August 1970, FRG Chancellor Willy Brandt had signed a nonaggression treaty with the Soviet Union, and the following December he concluded a treaty with Poland by which the Federal Republic gave de facto recognition to Polish acquisition of nearly one-quarter

of Germany's prewar territory. A treaty voiding the 1938 Munich Agreement was negotiated with Czechoslovakia in June 1973 and ratified a year later. The initiation of this program of postwar "reconciliation" earned a Nobel Peace Prize for Brandt in 1971, while its territorial implications were reaffirmed by the Final Act of the 1975 Helsinki Conference on Security and Cooperation in Europe (CSCE) and by a treaty between Poland and newly unified Germany on November 14, 1990.

Formal unification on October 3, 1990, was made possible by a series of "two-plus-four" talks that began on February 13 and concluded on September 12 with the signing of a Treaty on the Final Settlement with Respect to Germany (see Political background, above). The document was, in actuality, a long-delayed World War II peace treaty, under which the wartime Allies terminated "their rights and responsibilities relating to Berlin and to Germany as a whole," with corresponding "quadripartite agreements, decisions, and practices" and "all related Four Power institutions" being dissolved. For their part, the German signatories agreed to assert no territorial claims against other states; to forswear aggressive war; to renounce the manufacture or possession of nuclear, biological, and chemical weapons; to station only non-NATO forces in the East until completion of Soviet troop withdrawal by the end of 1994; and to reduce their overall armed forces from 577,000 (including East German units) to 370,000 by 1995. Collaterally, West Germany on September 13 signed a "Treaty on Good-Neighborliness, Partnership, and Cooperation" with the USSR, which was later accepted by Russia and the other Soviet successor states.

Because of the constitutional ban on deployment of German forces outside the NATO area, Germany did not participate in the 1991 Gulf war, although it sent air force units to Turkey (a NATO member) and made a substantial financial contribution to the U.S.-led effort. In November 1991 Bonn issued a ban on arms shipments to Turkey in the wake of charges that German weapons had been used against minority Kurds. The action generated a series of angry pronouncements from Turkey, with

Turkish President Özal on March 29, 1992, comparing the Kohl regime to Hitler's Germany. A revelation that at least 15 Leopard-1 tanks had been shipped to Turkey despite the ban forced Defense Minister Gerhard STOLTENBERG and a top aide to resign on March 31.

Preunification predictions that the newly enlarged Germany would play a larger and more independent role in world affairs materialized in the early 1990s. Thus, Germany led the world in direct monetary assistance to the Russian Federation, raising anxiety among the less-affluent southern members of the EC as to the loss of investment and aid that would otherwise have stayed within the EC. More controversially, Germany used its new diplomatic leverage to insist on speedy EC recognition of the secessionist Yugoslav republics of Slovenia and Croatia (and later Bosnia and Herzegovina), overriding the more cautious approach of Britain and France. When former Yugoslavia descended into bloody ethnic conflict in 1992, the government authorized a German warship and three reconnaissance aircraft to join a sanctions-monitoring UN/WEU force in the Adriatic, although the German opposition claimed that the deployment was illegal.

Seeking to ground German unification in an EC framework, the Kohl government was firmly committed to the EC's Maastricht Treaty on political and economic union. Ratification of the treaty was completed by the *Bundestag* in December 1992, subject to a Constitutional Court ruling that any future steps toward European union required specific German parliamentary approval. Germany also signed an agreement with France on May 22, 1992, providing for the creation by 1995 of a joint Franco-German army corps, envisaged as the nucleus of a future European military force (see WEU article).

Responding to international criticism of Germany's nonparticipation in the 1991 Gulf war, the government in January 1993 introduced draft constitutional amendments that would enable German troops to be deployed in UN-approved peacekeeping and humanitarian operations. The immediate urgency of the issue lay in whether German air

force personnel could participate in implementing the Security Council's decision of March 31, 1993, to enforce a "no-fly" zone over Bosnia and Herzegovina. In an interim ruling on April 8, the German Constitutional Court upheld a majority cabinet decision that German crews could participate in UN-approved NATO enforcement action, thus rejecting a contention by the FDP, the junior coalition partner, that the cabinet decision had been unconstitutional. On April 21 cabinet approval was given to the dispatch of 1,600 German troops to participate in the UN operation in Somalia. In a definitive ruling on July 12, 1994, the Constitutional Court decreed that German forces could participate in collective defense or security operations outside the NATO area provided *Bundestag* approval was given in each case.

In the wake of visits to Germany by Presidents Yeltsin and Clinton in May and July 1994, respectively, Russian troops completed their withdrawal from Berlin on August 31, with the last allied troops leaving the city on September 8. Finally cleared of Russian troops, Germany stepped up its diplomatic initiatives in Eastern Europe, supporting the quest of its immediate eastern neighbors to join the EU. In the case of the Czech Republic, however, the question of the ethnic Germans expelled from the Sudetenland at the end of World War II remained problematic, despite the signing of a Czech-German "declaration of reconciliation" in 1997. Germany insisted that a resolution of the compensation issue should precede EU admission. (See article on Czech Republic for further information.)

The Franco-German axis subsequently remained strong in the EU, the two countries committing to speedy economic and monetary union in the EU, even if only an "inner core" were ready to participate at the outset. Germany also worked closely with France on evolving plans for a European wing of NATO empowered to act independently of the United States, which contributed to increasing readiness in 1995 to deploy German forces in foreign theaters. Following the allocation of German warplanes and 1,300 troops to the European "rapid reaction force" sent to Bosnia in June, parliamentary approval was given in December for a 4,000-strong German contribution to the Implementation Force (IFOR) set up under the Dayton peace agreement for Bosnia.

Relations with the United Kingdom, already strained by British resistance to Chancellor Kohl's supranational prescriptions for the EU, deteriorated sharply in March 1996 when Germany took the lead in the imposition of a total EU ban on British beef exports because of the prevalence of "mad cow disease" in British herds.

In October 1998 Chancellor-Elect Gerhard Schröder visited Paris to assure the French that Germany remained committed to EU monetary union and strong economic ties to its leading trading partner. Despite preelection promises by Schröder that his government would maintain continuity in foreign policy, the new "red-green" coalition soon raised concern within NATO in November when Bonn tentatively suggested that the alliance renounce its first-strike nuclear policy.

Both the government and the opposition supported EU expansion in 2004, although Germany joined France in backing provisions in the proposed EU constitution that would preserve the influence of the larger states (see article on the EU for additional information). Meanwhile, Germany's relations with the United States were severely compromised by Schröder's strong opposition to Washington's Iraq policies. Among the consequences was an announcement from the United States that 35,000 of the 75,000 U.S. troops in Germany would be deployed to other countries.

In May 2005 both houses of the German legislature approved the proposed new EU constitution. Although some internal party dissension was reported, the leaders of both the SPD and the CDU-CSU called for the ratification process to continue despite the initial rejection of the new EU structure in several countries.

In January 2006 the new chancellor, Angela Merkel, visited Washington and promised a "new chapter" in U.S./Germany relations. She also subsequently endorsed Schröder's concept of a "strategic relationship" with Russia, reportedly concluding that business interests trumped German concerns over the perceived "autocratic drift" in Russia.

Current Issues

In the wake of the terrorist attacks in the United States in September 2001, Germany passed new domestic antiterrorism legislation and quickly launched a crackdown on radical Islamic groups. Germany also authorized troops for the U.S.-led military campaign in Afghanistan against al-Qaida and the Taliban, despite opposition to the deployment from the governing coalition's junior partner (Alliance '90/The Greens) that almost brought about the collapse of the government.

Continued economic doldrums appeared to drain popular support for the administration as elections loomed in September 2002, prompting Schröder to campaign for reelection on a platform that strongly urged the United States not to invade Iraq. Germany also supported France's successful efforts in the UN Security Council to block a resolution that would have authorized force against Iraq. The strategy worked perfectly, as the SPD and the Alliance '90/The Greens were propelled to another coalition government, albeit with a reduced legislative majority.

For his second term, Schröder in late 2002 announced that his administration's priorities would include a number of potentially unpopular fiscal reforms (known as "Agenda 2010"), including new limits on unemployment compensation and pensions, more flexible labor laws, and an increase in the percentage payment required from individuals for health care. The cuts in social spending prompted wide-scale protests in late 2003 and appeared to contribute to a series of disappointing SPD performances in state elections. Moreover, the SPD secured only 21.5 percent of the vote in the June 2004 European Parliament balloting, compared to 44.5 percent for the CDU-CSU.

The SPD decline continued in elections in the long-standing SPD bastion of North Rhine-Westphalia in May 2005, prompting Schröder to suggest that it was time for the national electorate to indicate anew whom it preferred at the helm of government. The presumed alliance of the CDU-CSU and the FDP appeared to enjoy majority support in advance of the September *Bundestag* balloting. However, the lackluster campaign of Angela Merkel, the CDU-CSU standard-bearer, undercut the CDU-CSU momentum, as did the rise of a new electoral alliance called "The Left," which quickly garnered support in the east. Consequently, the elections were considered inconclusive, with neither major party subsequently being able to cobble together a governing coalition. Although Schröder immediately after the election brashly declared the SPD the "victor" and vowed that his party would not participate in any government unless he retained the chancellorship, it became clear after six weeks of "grueling" negotiations that a CDU-CSU/SPD "grand coalition" represented the only hope for even short-term stability. In order to convince the SPD to join the new government, Merkel backtracked on some of the bold proposals for economic liberalization upon which the CDU-CSU campaign had been based. However, the coalition agreement retained support for the 3 percent sales tax proposed by the CDU-CSU, in return for the willingness of the CDU-CSU to accept an increase in the income tax rates for the wealthy.

Merkel, a former physicist, consequently became Germany's first female chancellor, the youngest (51) chancellor since the end of World War II, and the first chancellor to have been born in the former East Germany. Surprising many observers who had criticized her campaign performance, Chancellor Merkel zoomed to a nearly 80 percent approval rating in public opinion polls in the spring of 2006, based in part on the positive reviews of her trips to the United States and Russia. However, by midyear, analysts were suggesting that the "honeymoon" was coming to an end, as conservative leaders from the states started to press for labor law reforms that had been promised to the business sector during the 2005 campaign.

Political Parties

Following unification in 1990, the established West German parties extended their operations into the former GDR, with considerable success, although the Party of Democratic Socialism (PDS)—successor to the former ruling (Communist) Socialist Unity Party of Germany (SED)—retained significant support in the eastern *länder*. The 5 percent vote threshold for both federal and state elections made it difficult for minor parties to achieve legislative representation. Of the 22 parties that contested the October 1994 *Bundestag* election, only 6 were awarded seats, and 1 of those (the PDS) on an ancillary provision.

Under Germany's federal system, power at the state level provides opposition parties with an important counterbalance to the central government. As of July 1, 2006, the SPD and CDU jointly governed Brandenburg, Bremen, Saxony, Saxony-Anhalt, and Schleswig-Holstein. (The SPD had a legislative plurality in Brandenburg and Bremen, while the CDU had a plurality in Saxony, Saxony-Anhalt, and Schleswig-Holstein.) A CDU/FDP coalition governed in Baden-Württemberg, Hesse, Lower Saxony, and North Rhine-Westphalia. (The CDU held a legislative plurality in all of those states, except for Hesse, where it retained its coalition with the FDP despite holding a majority of the legislative seats.) An SPD/PDS coalition governed in Berlin and Mecklenburg-West Pomerania, the SPD holding legislative pluralities in both states. The CSU held a majority of the legislative seats and governed alone in Bavaria, while its partner, the CDU, held legislative majorities and governed alone in Hamburg, Saarland, and Thuringia. The SDP retained a majority of seats in Rhineland-Palatinate in the March 2006 elections and decided to govern alone. (Previously, the SDP has governed in a coalition with the FDP in Rhineland-Palatinate even though the SDP had held a majority of seats.)

Germany has dozens of parties in addition to those discussed below, but none has a national following of electoral significance.

Governing Parties

Christian Democratic Union (*Christlich-Demokratische Union*—CDU). Founded in 1945 as a middle-of-the-road grouping with a generally conservative policy and broad political appeal, the CDU espoused united action by Catholics and Protestants to sustain German life on a Christian basis, while guaranteeing private property and freedom of the individual. Dominated from 1949 to 1963 by Chancellor Konrad Adenauer, the CDU and its Bavarian affiliate, the Christian Social Union (CSU, below), continued as the strongest party alignment within the Federal Republic until 1969, when it was forced into opposition. With a list headed by CSU Chair Franz-Josef Strauss, who had threatened to sever the CDU-CSU bond if denied coalition endorsement in opposing incumbent Chancellor Helmut Schmidt, the CDU suffered a loss of 16 of its 190 *Bundestag* seats at the October 1980 election. However, following a transfer of support by the Free Democratic Party (FDP, below) to the CDU on October 1, 1982, Schmidt was obliged to step down as federal chancellor in favor of the CDU's Dr. Helmut Kohl. Kohl continued as the head of coalition administrations following the *Bundestag* elections of March 6, 1983, and January 25, 1987. After a poor showing at the European Parliament election in June 1989, he regained much of his popularity by waging a vigorous campaign for German unification, which was formally consummated on October 3, 1990.

In the October 1994 federal balloting the CDU won 34.2 percent of the vote and 244 seats, enabling it to continue the government coalition with the CSU and the FDP. In late 1997 the CDU nominated Kohl for the September 1998 elections, but the aging chancellor could not overcome an early lead by his younger and more telegenic opponent, Gerhard Schröder, who capitalized on high unemployment and a desire for change. The CDU-CSU vote share dropped from 41.4 to 35.1 percent (28.4 percent for the CDU), a loss of 49 seats that deposed the ruling coalition. Kohl even failed to win his home seat, returning to the *Bundestag* only because of his position at the top of the party list. The first postwar chancellor to lose as an incumbent, Kohl subsequently resigned as party chair, and in early November Kohl's handpicked successor, Dr. Wolfgang SCHÄUBLE, secured the position of CDU chair.

Both Kohl and Schäuble subsequently fell victim to a major party financing scandal. In late 1999, the Bonn public prosecutor announced a criminal investigation into a decade or more of secret donations and bank accounts controlled by Kohl, who had already admitted receiving millions of undeclared deutsche marks during his tenure as party chair. Schäuble announced his resignation as party chair and parliamentary leader on February 16, 2000, having acknowledged receiving undeclared contributions from an arms dealer in 1994. (On April 10 a party congress elected Angela Merkel chair, making her the first woman and the first East German to head the CDU.) In February 2001 Kohl agreed to pay a fine of over $140,000 in connection with the financing scandal, thereby avoiding probable criminal charges but not a parliamentary inquiry. By that time the party had already been fined approximately $23 million, pending appeal.

In May 2001 three former party and government officials were charged as a result of the ongoing slush fund investigation, while in June the CDU mayor of Berlin was voted out of office on a no-confidence motion as another financial scandal involving senior party members erupted. Shortly afterward, a Swiss investigation into France's Elf Aquitaine oil company reportedly revealed that more than two dozen CDU members might have accepted bribes in connection with the company's purchase of a German refinery in 1992.

Merkel vied for the party's endorsement as candidate for chancellor in the 2002 national elections, but she eventually withdrew from the race when it became clear that support had grown for Edmund Stoiber of the CSU to serve as the joint CDU-CSU candidate.

In 2004, the CDU, CSU, and FDP decided to field a common candidate for the presidency. The coalition candidate, Horst Köhler, was elected president of the republic in May 2004 on the first ballot. In June 2004 the CDU-CSU alliance continued its electoral recovery and won the European Parliament elections with 44.5 percent of the vote and 49 of Germany's 99 seats.

In May 2005 Merkel was nominated without opposition as the CDU-CSU candidate in the upcoming early elections. Although the CDU fell from 190 seats in the 2002 *Bundestag* balloting to 179 in the 2005 poll, it managed to secure a small plurality (in conjunction with the CSU), which subsequently propelled Merkel to the chancellorship.

Leaders: Angela MERKEL (Chancellor and Party Chair), Horst KÖHLER (President of the Republic), Volker KAUDER (Parliamentary Leader), Norbert LAMMERT (President of the *Bundestag*), Ronald POFALLA (General Secretary).

Christian Social Union (*Christlich-Soziale Union—CSU*). The Bavarian affiliate of the CDU, which by mutual agreement is unopposed by the CDU in Bavaria and does not present candidates elsewhere, espouses policies similar to its federal partner but tends to be more conservative. Party chair Franz-Josef Strauss became minister-president of Bavaria following the *land* election of October 15, 1978, and was the unsuccessful CDU-CSU candidate for chancellor at the 1980 national election. Strauss died in 1988.

The CSU's *Bundestag* representation of 53 after the March 1983 election was reduced to 51 by the withdrawal of two deputies to form The Republicans (below) the following November; the party lost 2 additional seats at the balloting of February 1987 but recovered to 51 in December 1990 and retained 50 in 1994 (on a slightly increased national vote share of 7.3 percent). Thereafter, CSU leaders began to distance the party from the CDU's belief in EU economic and monetary union, arguing against a precipitate move to a single currency and in favor of retaining the deutsche mark for the foreseeable future.

The CSU's vote share dropped to 6.7 percent in the September 1998 election, costing the party three seats and helping to turn the losing CDU-CSU coalition out of power. Following the electoral setback, in January 1999 Edmund Stoiber, the minister-president of Bavaria, succeeded Theodor WAIGEL as party head. In January 2002 Stoiber, who had won praise for his handling of economic affairs in Bavaria, was selected as the CDU-CSU candidate for chancellor in the 2002 balloting, and he remained the public leader of the coalition afterward. Stoiber led the CSU to its victory in the September 21, 2003, Bavarian state elections, at which the CSU won 60.7 percent of the vote and 124 of 180 seats. The CSU seat total in the *Bundestag* fell from 58 in 2002 to 46 (on 7.4 percent of the party list votes) in 2005.

Leaders: Edmund STOIBER (Chair of the Party, Minister-President of Bavaria, and 2002 CDU-CSU candidate for chancellor), Markus SÖDER (General Secretary).

Social Democratic Party of Germany (*Sozialdemokratische Partei Deutschlands—SPD*). Founded in the 19th century and reestablished in 1945, the SPD discarded its original Marxist outlook in 1959 and embraced the concept of the "social market." With a powerful base in the larger cities and the more industrialized states, the SPD subsequently stressed a strong central government and social welfare programs and was an early advocate of normalized relations with Eastern Europe. It was the principal opposition party before participating in a coalition with the CDU-CSU from 1966 to 1969. After the election of October 1969 the SPD's Willy Brandt formed a governing coalition with the FDP, Brandt being replaced as chancellor in May 1974 by Helmut Schmidt following an espionage scandal. The coalition continued until October 1982, when the FDP transferred its support to the CDU, thus forcing the SPD into opposition.

Brandt resigned as SPD chair at a stormy leadership meeting in March 1987 after his colleagues had refused to endorse his choice for party spokesperson. Parliamentary leader Hans-Jochen VOGEL was designated as his successor, but the party's relatively poor showing at the 1990 election led Vogel to resign on December 4. He was succeeded by the minister-president of Schleswig-Holstein, Björn ENGHOLM.

Damaged by the revival of an old political scandal, Engholm resigned as chair on May 3, 1993, and he was succeeded on June 13 by Rudolf SCHARPING (then minister-president of Rhineland-Palatinate), who led the SPD to its fourth successive federal election defeat in October

1994. Concurrent SPD advances at the state level gave it a majority in the *Bundesrat*, although in May 1995 the party lost ground in North Rhine-Westphalia and Bremen and in October suffered a major defeat in Berlin (once an SPD stronghold).

Scharping was ousted as SPD chair in November 1995 and was replaced by the more left-wing Oskar LAFONTAINE, the Saarland premier (and 1990 SPD candidate for chancellor). Lafontaine advocated cooperation with The Greens and the (ex-Communist) Party of Democratic Socialism (below) but expressed doubts about the plan for a single European currency and questioned the automatic granting of citizenship to ethnic Germans from Eastern Europe. The first electoral test of such policies, in three state elections in March 1996, yielded a lower SPD vote in each case.

In March 1998 the party selected Gerhard Schröder, the premier of Lower Saxony, to be its 1998 candidate for chancellor on the strength of his reelection victory in the state elections. Claiming to represent the "New Center," Schröder led the SPD to a 40.9 percent vote share at the September *Bundestag* election, moving the party from 252 to 298 seats. Acknowledging its growing support in the East, the party nominated Wolfgang THIERSE to be president of the lower house, making him the first person from the former East Germany to fill that post.

Belying reports that he controlled the party, Lafontaine quit his SPD leadership post in March 1999 after Schröder appeared to wrest control of the party's agenda during a struggle over economic policymaking. In April Schröder formalized his victory, winning the party chair at a special SPD congress.

Although there was growing discontent with the party leadership because of Schröder's reform efforts, the SPD won the 2002 legislative elections, and Schröder formed another coalition government with The Greens. In October 2003 SPD Deputy Chair Rudolf Scharping resigned in protest over Schröder's policies. In February 2004 Schröder announced his resignation as party leader, and Franz Müntefering was elected chair at a party congress in March.

In September 2003 SPD member Johannes Rau announced that he would not seek reelection as president of Germany. The SPD and The Greens choose Gesine SCHWAN, the first female candidate to run for the office. Schwan was defeated by the CDU-CSU/FDP candidate Horst Köhler in May 2004.

Opposition to efforts to move the party to the center, epitomized by Agenda 2010, led a group of SPD members to leave the party and form a new left-wing group (see WASG under The Left, below). In May 2005 former foreign minister Lafontaine resigned from the SPD to become the PDS/WASG standard-bearer, claiming the SPD was pursuing "antisocialist policies."

The SPD fell from 251 seats in the 2002 *Bundestag* balloting to 222 seats in the 2005 poll (at which it secured 34.3 percent of the party list votes). An SPD congress in mid-November elected Matthias PLATZECK, the minister-president of Brandenburg, as the new SPD chair to succeed Müntefering, who had resigned in a dispute with other leaders concerning a new secretary general. However, Platzeck resigned for health reasons in April 2006 and was succeeded by Kurt Beck, the minister-president of Rhineland-Palatinate. By that time concern was reportedly being voiced within the SPD over its declining membership and perceived secondary status in the government coalition.

Leaders: Kurt BECK (Chair of the Party), Franz MÜNTEFERING (Vice Chancellor), Gerhard SCHRÖDER (Former Chancellor), Hubertus HEIL (General Secretary).

Opposition Parties

The Left *(Die Linke)*. This electoral alliance was quickly formed by the two groups below after Chancellor Schröder in May 2005 called for early elections. Showing strength mainly in the ex-Communist eastern states, the alliance secured 54 seats in the September *Bundestag* balloting on a "hard-left" platform with populist undertones. Both the CDU and SPD quickly ruled out coalition talks with PDS and WASG leaders, who in

2006 announced plans for a formal merger by mid-2007.

Leaders: Lothar BISKY (PDS) and Klaus ERNST (WASG) (Chairs), Oskar LAFONTAINE (WASG, 2005 candidate for chancellor).

Party of Democratic Socialism (*Partei der Demokratischen Sozialismus*—PDS). Pressure exerted by Soviet occupation authorities led in April 1946 to formation of the Socialist Unity Party of Germany (*Sozialistische Einheitspartei Deutschlands*—SED) by merger of the preexisting Communist and Social Democratic parties. The SED controlled all East German organizations except the churches for the more than four decades of Communist rule, using the familiar instrument of a National Front organization.

Longtime party leader Erich HONEKER resigned on October 18, 1989, and was replaced as general secretary by Egon KRENZ. On November 11, in the face of rapidly escalating opposition to the dominance of the SED, all of its 22 Politburo incumbents save Krenz quit and were replaced by a substantially smaller body of 11 members. On December 3 Krenz also resigned. Six days later, during an emergency congress, the party abandoned Marxism and renamed itself the Socialist Unity Party of Germany–Party of Democratic Socialism (SED-PDS) under a new chair, Gregor GYSI. It formally dropped the SED component of the name at an election congress in late February 1990. At the all-German balloting of December 1990, the party, campaigning jointly with a **Left List** (*Linke List*), won 17 *Bundestag* seats, with almost all of its combined 2.4 percent vote share coming from the former GDR.

The PDS failed to secure European parliamentary representation in June 1994, but in the October federal election it won 30 *Bundestag* seats. Although taking only 4.4 percent of the national poll (about 18 percent in the eastern states), its return of 3 candidates in the Berlin electoral district qualified it for seats from the proportional pool. In January 1995 a PDS congress endorsed a "left-wing demo-cratic" program and voted down the party's hard-line faction. Financially boosted by a June court ruling that it was entitled to a share of the former SED's assets, the PDS gained ground in the Berlin state election in October, winning 14.6 percent of the vote. The PDS was the only major party to oppose the proposed merger of the states of Berlin and Brandenburg, its advice being heeded by the latter's citizenry in a May 1996 referendum.

In the September 1998 federal elections the PDS won more than 5 percent of the vote nationwide for the first time, although its support continued to come primarily from the East. Its strong showing increased its representation from 30 to 36 seats. In November the PDS formed its first formal governing coalition since reunification when it joined the SPD in a state government in Mecklenburg-Pomerania, with the PDS getting three posts in the eight-member cabinet.

On October 14, 2000, Gabrielle ZIMMER succeeded Lothar Bisky as chair, reflecting an effort by the party's reform wing to move toward the political center. The party subsequently indicated that it would be prepared to enter the federal government in partnership with the SPD after the 2002 election, a possibility that the SPD immediately rejected. Following the elections, party disputes continued over Zimmer's leadership. On June 28, 2003, a special party congress again elected Bisky as chair to succeed Zimmer. In state elections in Brandenburg in September 2004, the PDS had its best electoral success since reunification with 28.3 percent of the vote. The PDS also gained seven seats in the 2004 European Parliament elections.

The PDS had secured only two seats in the 2002 *Bundestag* balloting but was "rejuvenated" by its electoral alliance with the WASG in 2005. (The PDS had apparently adopted the rubric The Left Party/PDS [*Die Linkspartei*/PDS] prior to the 2005 poll.)

Leaders: Lothar BISKY (Chair); Gregor GYSI, Katja KIPPING, Wolfgang METHKING, and Katina SCHUBERT (Deputy Chairs).

Electoral Alternative for Labor and Social Justice (*Wahlalternative Arbeit und Soziale Gerechtigkeit*—WASG). Comprising mostly disaffected members of the SPD and trade unionists led by former foreign minister Oskar Lafontaine, the WASG was launched as a formal party in early 2005. The leaders of the new group accused the SPD leadership, particularly Gerhard Schröder, of having moved to the right in the interest of the business sector.

Leaders: Klaus ERNST, Oskar LAFONTAINE.

Alliance '90/The Greens (*Bündnis '90/Die Grünen*). Constituted as a national "antiparty party" during a congress held January 12–14, 1980, in Karlsrühe, *Die Grünen* was an amalgamation of several ecology-oriented groups formed in the late 1970s. Internal divisiveness contributed to a poor showing at the October 1980 federal election, when the party won only 1.5 percent of the vote. At the 1983 balloting, however, it won 27 *Bundestag* seats on the basis of a 5.6 percent vote share, and by late 1987 it had secured representation in 8 of the 11 Western *länder* parliaments.

In 1985, following serious electoral losses in Saarland and North Rhine-Westphalia, a split emerged between the fundamentalist (*Fundi*) wing of the party, which rejected participation in coalition governments, and the realist (*Realo*) faction composed largely of *Bundestag* members. During what was described as a "chaotic" congress in Nuremberg in September 1986, the *Realos* consolidated their hold over the group, which came close to overtaking the Free Democrats at the federal balloting of January 1987, winning 8.3 percent of the vote and 42 *Bundestag* seats.

In late 1989 a Green Party (*Grüne Partei*) was launched in the East, which joined with the Independent Women's League (*Unabhängige Frauenbund*) in offering a Greens list at the March 1990 *Volkskammer* poll. Not having endorsed unification, the group was unwilling to join forces with its Western counterpart for the all-German balloting in December, entering instead into the anti-unification Alliance '90 coalition, which was able to win eight *Bundestag* seats by meeting the minimum 5 percent vote-share requirement in the former GDR, even though its percentage in the whole of Germany was only 1.2. By contrast, the original Greens, with 3.9 percent share, were unable to secure the necessary 5 percent in the West.

At parallel congresses in Hannover on January 16–17, 1993, the western Greens and Alliance '90 decided to unite under the official name Alliance '90, while styling themselves informally as "The Greens." The merger was formalized during a congress in Leipzig on May 14. At their Mannheim congress in February 1994, The Greens opted in principle for a "red-green" coalition with the SPD after the October federal elections.

The Greens made a further advance in the October 1994 federal balloting, to 7.3 percent and 49 seats. The new parliamentary arithmetic precluded a coalition with the SPD, but The Greens' presence was acknowledged by the election of a party deputy as one of the *Bundestag*'s four vice presidents. A party congress in December 1995 endorsed The Greens' opposition to any external German military role, although 38 percent of the delegates favored participation in UN peacekeeping missions. The Greens subsequently registered gains in state elections, as a result of which "red-green" coalitions governed five states by the end of 1997. At their convention in February 1998, party leaders said their task was to make clear that The Greens' agenda was not limited to environmental policy and that the party was the best hope for comprehensive change.

In the September 1998 federal elections, The Greens dropped from 7.3 to 6.7 percent of the vote, losing 2 of their 49 seats. Nonetheless, they were a viable coalition partner for the SPD, and the inclusion of three Green ministers in the new Schröder regime gave the party its first positions of power in the federal government. While The Greens were generally in agreement with the SPD on economic matters, they took a harder line on environmental issues and succeeded in winning a coalition agreement to oppose NATO's first-strike nuclear policy, complicating Schröder's effort to reassure allies that Bonn remained a reliable partner.

On the heels of a setback at Hesse state elections, The Greens convened a conference in March 1999 that reportedly focused on "philosophical" issues and ended with a pledge to move the group's platform back toward its "roots."

In early 2001 Vice Chancellor Joschka Fischer came under attack for his role as a far-left activist in the 1970s, which included participation in violent street demonstrations and association with various members of such militant organizations as the Baader-Meinhof gang and the Red Army Faction. Despite calls from the CDU and other conservative elements for his resignation, Fischer retained the support of Chancellor Schröder, and in January 2002 he was formally designated as leader of The Greens, a new post in the party, which had previously preferred a collective leadership.

The Greens declined slightly from 55 seats in the 2002 *Bundestag* balloting to 51 in the 2005 poll, at which it received 8.1 percent of the party-list vote. Fischer subsequently stepped down as the party leader after The Greens went into opposition status.

Leaders: Claudia ROTH, Reinhard BÜTI-KOFER (Cochairs); Joschka FISCHER (Former Vice Chancellor and Former Leader of the Party); Renate KÜNASTE, Fritz KUHN (Parliamentary Leaders).

Free Democratic Party (*Freie Demokratische Partei*—FDP). A moderately rightist party that inherited the tradition of economic liberalism, the FDP stands for free enterprise without state interference but advocates a program of social reform. At the 1980 parliamentary election it won 53 seats (14 more than in 1976), in part because of the defection of Christian Democratic voters dissatisfied with candidate Franz-Josef Strauss. Its representation fell to 34 in 1983 but rose to 46 in 1987 and peaked at 79 in 1990, before falling back to 47 in October 1994.

The FDP formed a governing coalition with the SPD following the elections of 1972, 1976, and 1980 but shifted its support to the CDU in October 1982 after a dispute over the size of the 1983 budgetary deficit, thereby causing the fall of the Schmidt government. FDP leader Hans-Dietrich Genscher retained his positions as vice chancellor and foreign minister under the successor government of Helmut Kohl, but he resigned on May 18, 1992.

The failure of the party to win representation in a series of state elections in 1992–1994 generated much criticism of new leader Klaus KINKEL. He obtained a reprieve when the FDP unexpectedly retained a 47-seat *Bundestag* presence in October 1994 (on a 6.9 percent vote share); however, further electoral failures in Bremen and North Rhine-Westphalia in May 1995 obliged Kinkel to vacate the leadership while remaining foreign minister. Named at a special party congress in June, his successor, longtime Hesse leader Dr. Wolfgang GER-HARDT, distanced himself somewhat from Chancellor Kohl by calling for relaxed citizenship laws, termination of the arms embargo against Bosnia's Muslims, and an end to the "solidarity" tax that was financing economic recovery in former East Germany; with an eye to the challenge posed by the rise of The Greens, he also called for a greater focus on environmental issues. In January 1996 the FDP staged a relaunch on a more right-wing economic platform, quickly winning representation in three state elections in March and confirming its new orientation at a party congress in Karlsrühe in June.

In the *Bundestag* elections of September 1998 the FDP lost 4 seats on a vote share of 6.2 percent. In early January 2001 Gerhardt resigned the party chair, with the FDP secretary general, Guido Westerwelle, being formally elected as his successor on May 4 at a party congress. On January 7 Westerwelle had announced that the FDP would compete independently in the scheduled 2002 federal election, thereby severing the party's alliance with the CDU. In May 2002 Westerwelle was named as the FDP's first solo candidate for chancellor. In the 2002 election the FDP won 7.4 percent of the vote and 47 seats. Deputy Chair Jürgen MÖLLEMANN died in a parachute accident on June 5, 2003, a day after the *Bundestag* voted to strip him of immunity over fraud charges.

The FDP in 2005 posted its best results since 1990 when it improved to 61 seats in the 2005

Bundestag poll, at which it secured 9.8 percent of the proportional votes.

Leaders: Guido WESTERWELLE (Chair and 2002 and 2005 candidate for chancellor); Hans-Dietrich GENSCHER, Otto Graf LAMBSDORFF, Walter SCHEEL (Honorary Chairs); Rainer BRÜDERLE, Andreas PINKWART (Deputy Chairs); Cornelia PIEPER; Dirk NIEBEL (Secretary General).

Other Parties Competing in the 2005 Legislative Elections

The Republicans (*Die Republikaner*). The Republicans party was launched in November 1983 by two former Bavarian CSU deputies who objected to Franz-Josef Strauss's "one-man" leadership, particularly in regard to East-West relations. The manifestly ultrarightist group was self-described as a "conservative-liberal people's party" that favored a reunited Germany, environmental protection, and lower business taxes. Although the party claimed a nationwide membership of only 8,500, its West Berlin section obtained 11 legislative seats on the basis of a 7.5 percent vote share in January 1989.

As reunification became a leading German concern, the party's appeal ebbed. It obtained only 2 percent of the vote at state elections in North Rhine-Westphalia and Lower Saxony in early 1990, and in late May its increasingly controversial chair, former Waffen SS officer Franz SCHÖNHUBER, was obliged to resign, although he recovered the post at a party congress in July. The party made a comeback in the Baden-Württemberg state elections in April 1992, winning 11 percent of the vote and 15 seats; in May 1993, moreover, it secured *Bundestag* representation by the defection from the CDU of Rudolf KRAUSE. Prior to the October 1994 *Bundestag* election Schönhuber was again deposed as leader, officially because of an unauthorized meeting with the leader of the DVU (below) but also because of his negative media image. The party received only 1.9 percent of the *Bundestag* proportional vote in 1994, 1.8 percent in 1998, 0.6 percent in 2002, and 0.6 percent in 2005.

Leader: Rolf SCHLIERER (Federal Chair).

National Democratic Party (*Nationaldemokratische Partei Deutschlands*—NPD). Formed in 1964 by a number of right-wing groups, the NPD was subsequently accused of neo-Nazi tendencies but avoided giving clear-cut grounds for legal prohibition. Unrepresented in the *länder* parliaments or in the *Bundestag*, its appeal at the federal level slipped to a record low 0.2 percent of the popular vote in 1980 and recovered only marginally thereafter. In April 1995 NPD leader Günter DECKERT received a prison sentence for incitement to racial hatred and other offenses. On May Day in 1998 the party organized a demonstration in Leipzig by 6,000 neo-Nazis, one of the largest in years, to protest high unemployment and demand the expulsion of immigrants. At the subsequent federal election, the party took 0.3 percent of the vote.

On December 8, 2000, the *Bundestag* approved a government effort to ban the NPD as "anti-Semitic, racist, xenophobic, and violence-supporting." The proposal had already been backed by 14 of 16 *länder* interior ministers and by the *Bundesrat*, although some elements of the CDU as well as the FDP opposed a ban as counterproductive. On March 18, 2003, the Constitutional Court, which had banned only two parties in the previous 50 years, rejected a ban on the party. In 2004 state elections, the NPD gained 9.4 percent of the vote in Saxony—its greatest electoral showing to date.

In February 2005 the NPD held what was called the biggest far-right rally in Germany since World War II. The party reportedly contested the 2005 *Bundestag* elections in alliance with the DVU (below), securing 1.6 percent of the proportional vote. In December 2005 it was reported that 3 of the 12 NPD state legislators in Saxony had resigned from the party to protest the NPD's "Nazi-style" ideology.

Leaders: Udo VOIGT (Chair); Holger APFGL, Peter MARX, Ulrich EIGENFELD (Deputy Chairs).

German People's Union (*Deutsche Volksunion*—DVU). Launched in 1987 by wealthy publisher Gerhard Frey, the DVU was a far-right grouping that, with links to the NPD but claiming not to be neo-Nazi, assumed a strongly anti-immigrant posture, arguing that most Germans wished their country to be "racially pure." It won 6 City Council seats in Bremen in September 1991 and 6 of Schleswig-Holstein's 89 assembly seats on April 5, 1992. The DVU backed The Republicans in the October 1994 federal election in the wake of reports that the two groups might set aside a long-standing rivalry and, in the words of The Republicans' Franz Schönhuber (with apparent reference to the constraints of the 5 percent rule), "build a relationship that will prevent us from blocking our own electoral progress." The DVU's exit from the Bremen legislature in May 1995 (with only 2.5 percent of the vote) was followed by similar failure in Schleswig-Holstein in October (with 4.3 percent). The party shocked the political establishment in the spring 1998 state elections when it received nearly 13 percent of the vote in Saxony-Anhalt, the first time East Germans elected extreme right-wing candidates to a state legislature and one of the strongest showings of a far-right party since the end of World War II. The party spent more than all its opponents combined in a victory viewed by some analysts primarily as a protest vote. In the subsequent federal elections in September, the party received 1.2 percent nationwide. The DUV joined the NPD (above) in an unsuccessful electoral alliance for the 2005 *Bundestag* balloting.

Leader: Gerhard FREY (Chair).

Law-and-Order Offensive Party (*Partei Rechtsstaatlicher Offensive*—PRO). Sometimes translated into English as the Legal Offensive Party, the right-wing PRO was organized in 2000 by jurist Ronald SCHILL, who had earned a reputation as "Judge Merciless" for handing down severe sentences in criminal cases. Schill has argued for voluntary castration of convicted sexual offenders, restoration of the death penalty, removal of the right to asylum from the German constitution, and the imposition of minimum ten-year sentences for serious crimes. The party is based in Hamburg, where it won a surprising 19.4 percent of the vote at the

September 2001 election and was thus largely responsible for the defeat of the SPD-Greens coalition government. The PRO subsequently joined with the CDU and the FDP in forming a new administration in Hamburg. However, in December 2003 the coalition factionalized because of political differences between the PRO and the CDU/FDP. In the 2002 national legislative elections, the PRO received 0.7 percent of the vote. At a party congress on February 23, Mario Mettbach was elected party chair, and PRO founder Schill was expelled from the party. Schill formed an alternative faction, the Pro-Deutsche Mark/Schill Party (Pro-DM/Schill) with the restoration of the deutsche mark as its main priority.

Leader: Mario METTBACH (Party Chair).

The Greys (*Die Grauen*). Formerly a pensioners' group within The Greens, The Greys (also referenced as the Grey Panthers) organized as a separate party in mid-1989 to represent the interests of older citizens. It won 0.8 percent of the federal proportional vote in 1990, 0.5 percent in 1994, 0.3 percent in 1998, 0.2 percent in 2002, and 0.4 percent in 2005.

Leader: Trude UNRUH (Chair).

Other minor parties that obtained at least 0.1 percent of the vote in the September 2005 federal elections were the **Animal Protection Party** (*Tierschutzpartei*—TP); the **Bavaria Party** (*Bayern Party*), which advocates independence for Bavaria; the **Civil Rights Movement Solidarity** (*Bürgerrechtsbewegung Solidarität*—BüSo); the **Ecological Democratic Party** (*Ökologisch-Demokratische Partei*—ÖDP); the **Family Party of Germany** (*Famlienpartei Deutschlands*—FPD); the **Feminist Party** (*Feministische Partie*), which also is identified as **Women** (*Die Frauen*); the **Marxist-Leninist Party of Germany** (*Marxistisch-Leninistische Partei Deutschlands*—MLPD); and the **Party of Bible-Believing Christians** (*Partei der Bibeltreuen Christen*—PBC).

Other Parties

German Communist Party (*Deutsche Kommunistische Partei*—DKP). West Germany's former Communist Party, led by Max REIMANN, was banned as unconstitutional in 1956, although Reimann returned from exile in East Germany in 1969. Meanwhile, plans to establish a new Communist party consistent with the principles of the Basic Law had been announced in September 1968 by a 31-member "federal committee" headed by Kurt BACHMANN. At its inaugural congress in April 1969, the new party claimed 22,000 members, elected Bachmann as chair, and announced its intention to seek a common front with the SPD in the 1969 *Bundestag* election (an offer that was promptly rejected by the SPD). Subsequently, it received financial support from the East German SED, with which it cooperated in a series of "alternative" postwar anniversary celebrations in 1985. The support terminated with the changes in East Germany in late 1989, forcing the DKP to curtail its activities. The party's longtime chair, Herbert MIES, resigned in October 1989 and was replaced by a four-member Council at the tenth congress in March 1990. In the 2002 national legislative elections, the DKP only received 394 votes. A number of DKP members were reportedly included on the candidate lists of The Left (above) in the 2005 *Bundestag* balloting.

Leaders: Heinz STEHR, Nina HAGER.

South Schleswig Voters' Union (*Südschleswigscher Wählerverband*—SSW/*Sydslesvigk Vaelgerforening*—SSV). Founded in 1948 with the approval of the British occupation authorities, the SSW represented the interests of ethnic Danes in northern Schleswig-Holstein. Exempted from the 5 percent threshold rule, it consistently obtained representation in the state legislature, increasing from one to two seats in March 1996 on a 2.5 percent vote share and then to three in 2000 with 4.1 percent of the vote. It fell back to two seats in 2005 with 3.6 percent of the vote.

Leader: Anke SPOORENDONK.

Democratic Party of Germany (*Demokratische Partei Deutschlands*—DPD). The DPD was founded in October 1995 to represent the interests of foreigners in Germany and to oppose racism, being based in the two-million-strong Turkish community. The DPD's prospects for electoral progress are limited by the fact that most non-German immigrants do not have citizenship and are therefore not entitled to vote.

Leader: Sedat SEZGIN (Chair).

Extremist Groups

Although terrorist activity receded in the 1980s, armed groups both of the right and of the left remained active in postunification Germany. Neo-Nazi groups, whose overall membership was estimated in early 1985 at 22,000, were particularly active in the early 1990s, mounting attacks on both foreign residents and Jews. (By the late 1990s the extremists' numbers were reported to have climbed to over 50,000.) They included the **Free Workers' Party** (*Frei Arbeiterspartei*—FAP), reputedly the largest neo-Nazi group at the time of its banning in February 1995; the much smaller, Hamburg-based **National List** (*Nationale Liste*—NL), which also was banned in February 1995; the **German League for People and Homeland** (*Deutsche Liga für Volk und Heimat*—DLVH); the **National Socialist Action Front/National Action** (*Aktionsfront Nationaler Sozialisten/Nationale Aktion*—ANS/NA); various "military sport groups" (*Wehrsportgruppen*), including the *Wehrsportgruppe Hoffman* led by Odfried HEPP and allegedly supported by the Palestine Liberation Organization; and the **Viking Youth** (*Wiking Jugend*—WJ), banned in October 1994. In January 2004 Bavaria banned the far-right Franconian Action Front (*Aktionsfront Fränkische*—FAF). The federal government reportedly banned another neo-Nazi organization, the **Blood and Honor Group**, in 2000.

On the left, the **Red Army Faction** (RAF), an outgrowth of the Baader-Meinhof group of the early 1970s, emerged with an estimated strength of about 500. Following the emplacement of Pershing missiles in 1984, the RAF declared an "anti-imperialist war" and claimed responsibility for over 20 bombings in 1985, mainly at U.S. military and diplomatic installations, which left four dead; the group also claimed credit for the assassination of arms manufacturer Ernst ZIMMERMAN in February 1985. In April 1992 the RAF announced that it would cease its attacks on public officials

Cabinet

As of September 1, 2006

Chancellor	Angela Merkel (CDU)
Vice Chancellor	Franz Müntefering (SPD)
Head, Federal Chancellery	Thomas de Maizière (CDU)

Ministers

Consumer Protection, Food, and Agriculture	Horst Seehofer (CSU)
Defense	Franz Josef Jung (CDU)
Economic Cooperation and Development	Heidemarie Wieczorek-Zeul (SPD) [f]
Economics and Technology	Michale Glos (CSU)
Education and Research	Annette Schavan (CDU) [f]
Environment, Nature Conservation, and Nuclear Safety	Sigmar Gabriel (SPD)
Family, Senior Citizens, Women, and Youth	Ursula von der Leyer (CDU) [f]
Finance	Peer Steinbrük (SPD)
Foreign Affairs	Frank-Walter Steinmeier (SPD)
Health	Ulla Schmidt (SPD) [f]
Interior	Wolfgang Schaüble (CDU)
Justice	Brigitte Zypries (SPD) [f]
Labor and Social Affairs	Franz Müntefering (SPD)
Transportation, Construction, and Urban Affairs	Wolfgang Tiefensee (SPD)

[f] = female

if the government released several of its long-incarcerated members. In apparent response, former RAF activist Günter SONNENBERG was released in mid-May after serving 15 years of a life sentence. In September 1995, however, an RAF member was sentenced to life imprisonment for involvement in terrorist actions in 1977 and 1982. In April 1998 the RAF announced that it had formally disbanded. In May the government pardoned Helmut POHL, an RAF member, who had urged the group to disband in 1996; he had been convicted of a 1981 bombing of a U.S. Air Force base.

In August 1998 the government outlawed the **Revolutionary People's Liberation Party/Front** as well as the **Turkish People's Liberation Party/Front,** splinters of **Dev-Sol** (*Devrimce Sol*), a leftist Turkish group that was founded in Turkey in 1978 on a platform advocating the creation of a "communist society." (Dev-Sol had been originally banned in Germany in 1983.) The government claimed the outlawed groups were extremists who financed their activities through blackmail and violence. In 2003 the government estimated that 30,000 Muslims belonged to radical Islamic groups.

Legislature

The bicameral **Parliament** (*Parlament*) consists of an indirectly chosen upper chamber, the *Bundesrat,* or Federal Council, and an elective lower chamber, the *Bundestag,* or Federal Assembly.

Federal Council (*Bundesrat*). The upper chamber currently consists of 69 members appointed by the *länder* governments, each of whose three to six votes (depending on population) are cast *en bloc*. Lengths of term vary according to state election dates. The presidency rotates annually among heads of the state delegations, usually *länder* minister-presidents. As of July 2006 the seat distribution was as follows: the Christian Democratic Union, 39; the Social Democratic Party of Germany, 17; the Christian Social Union, 6; the Free Democratic Party, 5; and the Party of Democratic Socialism, 2.

President: Peter Harry CARSTENSEN.

Federal Assembly (*Bundestag*). The lower chamber, currently at 614 members, is the world's largest democratically elected legislative body. Deputies are chosen for four-year terms (subject to dissolution by the president) by popular vote under a complicated electoral system combining direct and proportional representation. In balloting on September 18, 2005, for 613 seats (balloting for 1 seat was postponed due to the death of a candidate), the Social Democratic Party of Germany won 222 seats (145 constituency seats and 77 party-list seats); the Christian Democratic Union (CDU), 179 (105, 74); the Left Party, 54 (3, 51); the Alliance '90/The Greens, 51 (1, 50); the Free Democratic Party, 61 (0, 61); and the Christian Social Union, 46 (44, 2). The CDU won the balloting for the outstanding seat on October 2.

President: Norbert LAMMERT.

Communications

Freedom of speech and press is constitutionally guaranteed except to anyone who misuses it in order to destroy the democratic system.

Press

Newspapers are numerous and widely read, and many of the principal dailies have national as well as local readerships. There are some very large publishing concerns, notably the Axel Springer group, which is Europe's largest publishing conglomerate. In the eastern *länder,* most papers were transferred from party to private control in 1990. The circulation figures for the following newspapers are approximate: *Bild-Zeitung* (Hamburg and seven other cities, 5,674,000), sensationalist Springer tabloid; *Westdeutsche Allgemeine Zeitung* (Essen, 1,313,000); *Hannoversche Allgemeine Zeitung* (Hannover, 250,000); *Freie*

Presse (Chemnitz, 502,000), former PDS organ; *Mitteldeutsche Zeitung* (Halle, 414,000), formerly *Freiheit*; *Sächsische Zeitung* (Dresden, 416,000); *Thüringer Allgemeine* (Erfurt, 589,000), formerly *Das Volk*; *Rheinische Post* (Düsseldorf, 443,000); *Süddeutsche Zeitung* (Munich, 400,000), center-left; *Express* (Cologne, 468,000); *Frankfurter Allgemeine Zeitung* (Frankfurt-am-Main, 471,000); *Leipziger Volkszeitung* (Leipzig, 380,000), former PDS organ; *Augsburger Allgemeine* (Augsburg, 375,000); *Südwest Presse* (Ulm, 378,000); *Nürnberger Nachrichten* (Nürnberg, 350,000); *Magdeburger Volksstimme* (Magdeburg, 321,000), former PDS organ; *BZ* (Berlin, 370,000), Springer group; *Hamburger Abendblatt* (Hamburg, 329,000), Springer group; *Neue Osnabrücker Zeitung* (Osnabrück, 322,000); *Kölner Stadt Anzeiger* (Cologne, 305,000); *Hessische/Niedersächsische Allgemeine* (Kassel, 325,000); *Berliner Zeitung* (Berlin, 246,000), independent; *Die Rheinpfalz* (Ludwigshafen, 258,000); *Rhein-Zeitung* (Koblenz, 259,000); *Abendzeitung/8-Uhr-Blatt* (Munich, 256,000); *Ruhr-Nachrichten* (Dortmund, 243,000); *Berliner Morgenpost* (Berlin, 178,000), Springer group.

News Agencies

There are two principal facilities: the German Press Agency (*Deutsche Presse-Agentur*—DPA), which supplies newspapers and broadcasting stations throughout the Federal Republic while also transmitting news overseas in German, English, French, Spanish, and Arabic, and the General German News Service (*Allgemeiner Deutscher Nachrichtendienst*—ADN), which was launched in 1946 as the official East German agency and reorganized in 1990.

Broadcasting and Computing

Terrestrial noncable broadcasting networks are independent, nonprofit, public corporations chartered by the *länder* governments. The coordinating body is the Association of Public Law Broadcasting Organizations of the Federal Republic of Germany (*Arbeitsgemeinschaft der öffentlich-rechtlichen Rundfunkanstalten der*

Bundesrepublik Deutschland—ARD). There are three national terrestrial television channels, the first provided by ARD affiliates, the second by *Zweites Deutsches Fernsehen* (ZDF), and the third (a cultural and educational service) by several of the regional authorities. There also are numerous cable and satellite channels, more than 50 percent of German households (the highest number in Europe) being wired for cable television. In early 1994 a new state-supported cultural service, *Deutschland Radio*, was launched to promote a sense of community between eastern and western Germans. Non-German broadcasters include the American Forces Network, the British Forces Broadcasting Service, Radio Free Europe, Radio Liberty, and the Voice of America, although in July 1994 U.S. President Clinton announced the relocation of Radio Free Europe and Radio Liberty from Munich to the Czech capital, Prague. There were approximately 49.9 million television receivers and 39 million personal computers serving an equal number of Internet users in 2003.

Intergovernmental Representation

Ambassador to the U.S.
Klaus SCHARIOTH

U.S. Ambassador to Germany
William Robert TIMKEN Jr

Permanent Representative to the UN
(Vacant)

IGO Memberships (Non-UN)
ADB, AfDB, BDEAC, BIS, BOAD, CBSS, CERN, CEUR, EBRD, EIB, ESA, EU, Eurocontrol, G-10, G-7/G-8, IADB, IEA, Interpol, IOM, NATO, OECD, OSCE, PCA, WCO, WEU, WTO

GREECE

HELLENIC REPUBLIC

Elleniki Dimokratia

The Country

Occupying the southern tip of the Balkan Peninsula and including some 3,700 islands in the Ionian and Aegean seas, the Hellenic Republic is peopled overwhelmingly by Greeks but also includes minority groups of Turks and others. Some 95 percent of the people speak modern (*dimotiki*) Greek, a more classical form (*katharevoussa*) no longer being employed in either government or university circles. The vast majority of the population belongs to the official Eastern Orthodox Church, which was granted increased autonomy in its internal affairs by a government charter issued in 1969. In 1996 women constituted 37 percent of the paid work force, with three-fifths of those classed as "economically active" in rural areas performing unpaid agricultural family labor; urban women are concentrated in the clerical and service sectors. Female representation in government at all levels is low in comparison to that of most other members of the European Union (EU).

Traditionally based on agriculture, with important contributions from shipping and tourism, the Greek economy since the early 1970s has witnessed substantial increases in the industrial sector, notably in chemical, metallurgical, plastics, and textile production. This expansion has, however, been accompanied by severe inflationary pressures, the consumer price index rising by an average of approximately 20 percent annually (by far the highest within the European Community [EC], subsequently the EU) from 1980 to 1991 before receding to 9 percent in 1995; meanwhile, unemployment remained high at around 10 percent of the labor force.

Greece's budget deficit and public debt in 1997 remained well above the criteria set by the Maastricht Treaty for admission to the EU's proposed Economic and Monetary Union (EMU) and collateral use of the new euro currency; the Greek inflation rate of 5.4 percent was also too high to qualify. Consequently, when the European Commission announced its recommendations in early 1998 on the matter, Greece was the only one of the 12 EU members interested in the EMU not to be invited to participate in its launching in January 1999. However, Greek leaders pledged to pursue further economic improvement to permit EMU membership as soon as possible. In anticipation of that eventuality, the

Political Status: Gained independence from the Ottoman Empire in 1830; military rule imposed following coup of April 1967; civilian control reinstituted July 23, 1974; present republican constitution promulgated June 11, 1975.

Area: 50,944 sq. mi. (131,944 sq. km.).

Population: 10,934,037 (2001C); 11,093,000 (2005E).

Major Urban Centers (2005E): ATHENS (736,000, urban area, 3,254,000), Thessaloniki (Salonika, 356,000, urban area, 822,000), Patras (164,000), Larissa (129,000).

Official Language: Greek.

Monetary Unit: Euro (market rate July 1, 2006: 1 euro = $1.28US).

President: Karolos PAPOULIAS (Panhellenic Socialist Movement); elected by Parliament on February 8, 2005, and sworn in on March 12 for a five-year term succeeding Konstantinos STEPHANOPOULOS (Democratic Renewal), who was constitutionally precluded from a third term.

Prime Minister: Konstantinos (Kostas) KARAMANLIS (New Democracy); nominated on March 8, 2004, and sworn in on March 10 to succeed Konstantinos (Kostas) SIMITIS (Panhellenic Socialist Movement) following elections of March 7.

Greek drachma became part of the EU's Exchange Rate Mechanism in March 1998.

Economic growth (well over 3 percent in both 1997 and 1998) exceeded the EU average, while the budget deficit was trimmed under the strict economic reforms implemented by the SIMITIS administration, which had also spurred stock market optimism. The International Monetary Fund (IMF) and other global financial institutions praised the government extensively for the recent turnaround, although they cautioned that additional measures were necessary, including further privatization of inefficient state-run enterprises and moderation in regard to wage increases in order to reduce inflation, which at about 4.0 percent in 1998 was still outside the Maastricht criteria.

Inflation fell to about 3 percent in 2000, with the budget deficit having declined to only 1.5 percent of GDP, sufficient to permit Greece's formal entry into the EMU and adoption of the euro effective January 1, 2001. At the same time, however, high public debt and unemployment (12 percent) remained problematic, while international financial experts urged the government to work to simplify the tax system, improve public services, and combat corruption within the state sector. Nevertheless, by the end of 2001 the country was enjoying what one journalist called an "unprecedented gloss of prosperity" that had encouraged foreign investors seeking access to emerging markets in nearby countries.

The nation's economic growth subsequently slowed as public spending increased, especially in connection with the government's preparation for the 2004 summer Olympics. The deficit increased to 6 percent of GDP, and Greece's debt-to-GDP ratio expanded to 105 percent, making it one of the highest in the euro zone and creating severe difficulties with the EU. Indeed, in November 2004, Greece's credit rating with Standard & Poor's was lowered to Single A, with the credit agency citing the government's lack of a clear plan to reduce its debt burden.

Greece's budget situation improved markedly in 2005, with the country's finance minister announcing in October that the deficit in 2006 would fall to 2.8 percent, thanks to stronger-than-expected growth and spending curbs.

Government and Politics

Political Background

Conquered by the Ottoman Turks in the later Middle Ages, Greece emerged as an independent kingdom in 1830 after a protracted war of liberation conducted with help from Great Britain, France, and tsarist Russia. Its subsequent history has been marked by championship of Greek nationalist aspirations throughout the Eastern Mediterranean and by recurrent internal upheavals, reflecting, in part, a continuing struggle between royalists and republicans. The monarchy, abolished in 1924, was restored in 1935 and sponsored the dictatorship of Gen. Ioannis (John) METAXAS (1936–1941) before the royal family took refuge abroad upon Greece's occupation by the Axis powers in April 1941. The resumption of the monarchy in 1946 took place in the midst of conflict between Communist and anti-Communist forces that had erupted in 1944 and was finally terminated when the Communists were defeated with British and subsequent U.S. military assistance in 1949. A succession of conservative governments held office until 1964, when the Center Union, a left-center coalition led by Georgios (George) PAPANDREOU, achieved a parliamentary majority. Disagreements with the young King Konstantinos (CONSTANTINE) on military and other issues led to the dismissal of Papandreou in 1965, initiating a series of crises that culminated in a coup d'état and the establishment of a military junta on April 21, 1967. An unsuccessful attempt by the king to mobilize support against the junta the following December yielded the appointment of a regent, the flight of the king to Rome, and a reorganization of the government whereby (then) Col. Giorgios (George) PAPADOPOULOS, a junta member, became prime minister.

In May 1973 elements of the Greek navy attempted a countercoup in order to restore the king, but the plot failed, resulting in formal deposition of the monarch and the proclamation of a republic on June 1. Papadopoulos's formation of a civilian cabinet and the scheduling of an election for early 1974 resulted in his ouster on November 25 by a conservative military group under the leadership of Brig. Gen. Dimitrios IOANNIDES. However, the new regime was forced in July 1974 to call on Konstantinos KARAMANLIS to form a caretaker government preparatory to a return to civilian rule. Karamanlis was confirmed as prime minister following a parliamentary election on November 17, and Michaelis (Michael) STASINOPOULOS was designated provisional president a month later. Stasinopoulos was succeeded as president by Konstantinos TSATSOS on June 19, 1975. On November 28, 1977, eight days after an early elec-

tion in which his New Democracy (ND) party retained control of the legislature by a reduced majority, Karamanlis formed a new government. He resigned as prime minister on May 6, 1980, following his parliamentary designation as president the day before, and he was succeeded on May 9 by Giorgios (George) RALLIS.

At the general election of October 18, 1981, the Panhellenic Socialist Movement (Pasok) swept to victory with a margin of 22 seats on a vote share of 48.1 percent, and Dr. Andreas PAPANDREOU (son of the precoup premier) formed Greece's first socialist administration three days later. Despite ongoing complaints that the Pasok leadership had failed to make good on its election promises, the government was given a vote of confidence at the European Parliament election in June 1984, winning 41.6 percent of the vote and capturing 10 of the 24 available seats.

President Karamanlis resigned on March 10, 1985, after Papandreou had withdrawn an earlier pledge to support his reelection. In a legislative poll on March 29, the Pasok nominee, Christos SARTZETAKIS, was elected to a regular five-year term as head of state. Subsequently, Pasok remained in power, with a reduced legislative margin of 11 seats on a vote share of 45.8 percent, as the result of an early general election on June 2.

Damaged by a series of scandals, Pasok was defeated at legislative balloting on June 18, 1989, by the ND, which, however, fell six seats short of a majority. Two weeks of intense negotiations followed, with the ND and the Communist-led Progressive Left Coalition agreeing on July 1 to form an anti-Pasok administration on condition that its mandate be for only three months and limited to "restoring democratic institutions and cleansing Greek political life." On September 20, Papandreou, his parliamentary immunity having been lifted, was ordered to stand trial on charges of having authorized illegal wiretaps while in office; eight days later the former prime minister and four associates were also indicted for a variety of offenses that included bribery and the receipt of stolen funds.

On October 11, 1989, the president of the Supreme Court, Ioannis (John) GRIVAS, was asked to form an essentially nonpartisan caretaker administration, which was sworn in the following day. At the year's second parliamentary poll on November 5, the ND registered a net gain of only three seats (three short of a majority), with Pasok gaining an equal number. In consequence, the three main parties agreed on November 21 to form a coalition government under a former governor of the Bank of Greece, Xenophon ZOLOTAS.

Despite an announcement on January 26, 1990, that another legislative election would be held on April 8, the all-party Zolotas government collapsed on February 12 because of continuing disagreement among the coalition partners over economic policy, and it was succeeded by a caretaker administration. At the ensuing poll the ND fell one seat short of a majority, but, with the support of the sole Democratic Renewal member, it was able to secure the installation of a government headed by Konstantinos (Constantine) MITSOTAKIS on April 11. Meanwhile, with the ND abstaining, Parliament had been unable to elect a new state president in three rounds of balloting on February 19, February 25, and March 3. The impasse was broken on May 4 by the new Parliament, which returned former president Karamanlis to office.

On January 17, 1992, Pasok leader Papandreou was acquitted of the corruption charges against him. Despite poor health, previous scandals, and a much-publicized divorce from his second wife, he led his party on October 10, 1993, to decisive victory at an early election necessitated by a series of ND parliamentary defections.

In September 1994 the Greek Parliament voted, without the participation of ND deputies, to indict three former ND ministers, including ex–Prime Minister Mitsotakis, on financial corruption charges. However, arguing that a trial would be politically divisive, Papandreou in mid-January 1995 induced Parliament to drop the charges against Mitsotakis.

In parliamentary balloting for a new president, center-right politician Konstantinos (Constantine) STEPHANOPOULOS was elected on the third ballot on March 8, 1995, with 181 votes to 109

for an ND nominee. The votes for the successful candidate, amounting to one more than the required three-fifths majority, came from Pasok and the small Political Spring grouping.

Growing divisions within Pasok were highlighted by the resignation in September 1995 of the commerce, industry, energy, and technology minister, Konstantinos (Kostas) Simitis, because of opposition to his modernization policies in the Pasok executive. When the elderly prime minister fell seriously ill in November, a full-scale succession struggle ensued, with the influence of Papandreou's wife, Dimitra (Mimi) LIANI, proving to be a controversial factor. The recently appointed interior minister, Apostolos-Athanassios (Akis) TSOKHATZOPOULOS, became acting prime minister and appeared to be well-placed in the leadership battle. However, following Papandreou's resignation on January 15, 1996, balloting of Pasok deputies on January 18 resulted in a narrow second-round victory for Simitis, who was sworn in as prime minister four days later.

Arguing that he needed a full-term mandate to deal with the challenges facing the country (and encouraged by high public approval ratings of his initial performance), Simitis called an early general election on September 22, 1996. The outcome was a reduced but still comfortable overall majority of 162 seats (out of 300) for Pasok, with the added bonus that the main opposition ND slipped to 108 seats, while three small left-wing parties polled strongly to win the remaining 30 seats among them. A further Pasok administration sworn in on September 25 contained a number of personnel changes designed to strengthen Simitis's position, although Tsokhatzopoulos, a former general secretary of Pasok and leader of its populist wing, remained in the government, moving to the influential defense portfolio.

The elevation of Konstantinos Simitis to the premiership in January 1996 was seen as marking the end of the Papandreou era of left-leaning populism in the ruling Pasok. A commercial lawyer by profession, Simitis declared a commitment to the modernization of party and government structures, pursuit of a social democratic program, and closer integration within the EU (on which the previous prime minister had always been equivocal).

On the domestic front, the government continued in 1997 and early 1998 to face serious protests over its economic austerity measures. Although the 1997 budget (announced in late 1996) had prompted a large-scale demonstration by farmers and a series of strikes by public- and private-sector workers, Prime Minister Simitis subsequently unveiled yet another tight budget for 1998. Civil servants again went on strike in February 1998 to protest cuts in benefits as well as measures designed to facilitate the privatization of state-run enterprises. Despite continued opposition from workers and other segments of the population supportive of increased spending (such as pensioners and students), the government held fast to its austerity approach in the 1999 budget, Simitis declaring EMU accession on January 1, 2001, to be his top priority.

Pasok infighting and opposition to the government's stringent economic approach contributed to a decline in the ruling party's fortunes in the October 1998 local elections. Consequently, Simitis reshuffled the cabinet in late October, and in November he called for a legislative vote of confidence, which he won by a vote of 163–136, Pasok legislators having been threatened with expulsion from the party if they failed to support the government. The cabinet also took on a new look on February 18, 1999, after the ministers of foreign affairs, the interior, and public order resigned following the politically charged events surrounding the arrest of Kurdish militant Abdullah Öcalan (see Current issues, below).

Simitis called for early elections on April 9, 2000, which produced a surprisingly slim victory of only 1 percent (43.79 percent to 42.73 percent) by Pasok over the ND, which was led by political newcomer Konstantinos (Kostas) KARAMANLIS, the nephew of former prime minister and president Karamanlis. However, due to Greece's complicated proportional representation system (designed to preclude the need for coalition governments), Pasok secured 158 legislative seats, a sufficient majority to permit Simitis to form a new government on April 13.

Meanwhile, the April 2000 elections were described as "bland" and devoid of major policy differences between the two leading parties. Prime Minister Simitis had called the early balloting in the hope of receiving solid endorsement of his economic reforms, which had prepared the country for entry into the EMU. Instead, Pasok eked out its third consecutive term in office (a record for modern Greece) by only 1 percent of the vote, prompting Konstantinos Karamanlis to call the results a "victory" for his ND despite his narrow failure to capture the prime ministership. Among other things, Simitis and Pasok appeared to have suffered some loss of support because of declining social services (necessitated by budget austerity). Therefore, Simitis quickly promised "a new cycle of change" that would return social welfare to the forefront of his government's agenda. At the same time, however, the realities of EMU accession (implemented on January 1, 2001) demanded continued conservative structural reforms, including revision of liberal labor and pension regulations. Vehement opposition to austerity measures continued to plague the administration in 2002, three months of public sector strike action disrupting tourism and hampering government services in the spring in response to the proposed refinancing of the state pension fund.

In the wake of growing discontent over several issues (see Current issues, below), Prime Minister Simitis resigned on February 10, 2004, although he returned to the premiership three days later in a caretaker capacity pending early elections on March 7. After the ND secured a majority of 165 of 300 seats in that balloting, the ND's Karamanlis was named prime minister on March 10.

On February 8, 2005, the Parliament elected Karolos PAPOULIAS, a popular former foreign minister, as the country's next president. Papoulias enjoyed the endorsement of his own party, Pasok, as well as the ND.

Constitution and Government

The possibility of a return to monarchy was decisively rejected at a plebiscite on December 8, 1974, the Greek people, by a two-to-one margin, expressing their preference for an "uncrowned democracy." The republican constitution adopted in June 1975 provided for a parliamentary system with a strong presidency. Under the new basic law (branded as "Gaullist" by political opponents of Prime Minister Karamanlis), the president had the power to name and dismiss cabinet members (including the prime minister), to dissolve Parliament, to veto legislation, to call for referenda, and to proclaim a state of emergency. These powers were lost by a constitutional amendment that secured final parliamentary approval on March 6, 1986. The action restored full executive power to the prime minister, assuming retention of a legislative majority. The unicameral Parliament, whose normal term is four years, elects the president by a complex procedure that requires a two-thirds majority on a first or second ballot, three-fifths on a third or fourth ballot (a legislative dissolution and election being required prior to the fourth), an absolute majority on a fifth ballot, or a relative majority between the two leading contenders on a sixth. A requirement that the head of state be elected by secret ballot was rescinded by a second amendment, also effective in March 1986. The judicial system is headed by the Supreme Court and includes magistrates' courts, courts of the first instance, and justices of the peace.

Traditionally administered on the basis of its historic provinces, Greece is currently divided into 51 prefectures (plus the self-governing monastic community of Mount Athos), with Athens further divided into four subprefectures. Local government encompasses 277 municipalities and 5,757 communities. In January 1987 the government approved a plan to divide the country into 13 new administrative regions to facilitate planning and coordinate regional development.

Foreign Relations

Greece has historically displayed a Western orientation and throughout most of the post–World War II era has been heavily dependent on Western economic and military support. The repressiveness of the 1967–1974 military regime was, however, a matter of concern to many European nations, and their economic and political sanctions were instrumental in Greece's withdrawal from the Council of Europe in 1969. Relations with the United States remained close, primarily because Greece continued to provide a base for the U.S. Sixth Fleet, but the return to democratic rule was accompanied by increased evidence of anti-American feeling.

The most important issue in Greek foreign affairs is its relationship with Turkey, particularly in regard to the Cyprus question, which has been a source of friction since the mid-1950s. The Greek-inspired coup and subsequent Turkish intervention in Cyprus in July 1974 not only exacerbated tension between the two countries, but also served to bring down the military regime of General Ioannides; it also precipitated Greek withdrawal from military participation in NATO. The return of civilian government, on the other hand, brought a renewal of cooperation with Western Europe. Greece announced in September 1974 that it was rejoining the Council of Europe and subsequently applied for full, as distinguished from associate, membership in the EC, with preliminary agreement being reached at Brussels in December 1978 and entry achieved on January 1, 1981.

Greece returned to the NATO military command structure after a six-year lapse, in October 1980. The action was accepted by Turkey's recently installed military regime, although a lengthy dispute between the two countries over continental-shelf rights in (and air channels over) the Aegean Sea remained unresolved.

Prior to the 1981 electoral campaign, Pasok had urged withdrawal from NATO and the EC, in addition to cancellation of the agreement with the United States regarding military bases. During the campaign these positions were modified, Papandreou calling only for "renegotiation" of the terms of membership in the two international groupings.

Although continuing his criticism of the U.S. military presence, the prime minister signed an agreement on September 9, 1983, permitting U.S. military bases to continue operation until the end of 1988. In early 1986 Papandreou again reiterated his intention to "rid the country of foreign bases," and in September he declared, without indicating a timetable, that "our decision to remove . . . nuclear weapons from our country is final and irrevocable." Nonetheless, on May 30, 1990, a new eight-year cooperation agreement was announced that ensured continued operation of two of four U.S. facilities in return for about $350 million a year in military aid. Symptomatically, Parliament approved the agreement in late July by a straight party, one-vote margin.

Meanwhile, controversy with Turkey continued, with tension again escalating as the result of a confrontation between Greek and Turkish fighter planes over the Greek Aegean islands during Turkish military maneuvers in early 1989. The Aegean controversy turns on Turkish refusal to recognize insular sea and airspace limits greater than six miles, on the ground that to do otherwise would convert the area into a "Greek lake."

The territorial waters dispute erupted anew in September 1994, with Greece declaring that it would formally extend its jurisdiction to 12 nautical miles upon entry into force of the UN Convention on the Law of the Sea (UNCLOS) on November 16. Turkey immediately warned that the move would be considered an "act of aggression," and on October 30 Athens announced that it would defer the introduction of what it continued to view as a "sovereign right." It further angered Ankara by reiterating its right to the extension when ratifying the Convention in June 1995, although it made no move to apply it.

In early 1992 there was virtually unanimous Greek opposition to former Yugoslavia's southernmost republic proclaiming its independence as "Macedonia," a name that historically had embraced parts of modern Greece and Bulgaria, as well as of Yugoslavia. As the result of Greek pressure, most Western nations, including the United States, refused for 15 months to recognize the new state, pending resolution of the highly charged dispute. It was not until April 7, 1993, that the two neighbors agreed to open discussion on the issue, with UN membership being granted the following day to "The former Yugoslav Republic of Macedonia" (referenced as FYROM).

In a substantial hardening of Athens's position following the October 1993 election, the incoming Papandreou government closed Macedonia's principal trade route through the port of Salonika on February 17, 1994. The action was taken after six of Greece's EU partners (followed by the United States) had extended diplomatic recognition to the FYROM, thus complicating Greece's assumption of the EU presidency on January 1. In a highly unusual action against one of its members, the EU challenged the Greek embargo in a suit filed with the European Court of Justice (ECJ) on April 13. The Greek government was unabashed, reasserting that it would "never recognize a state bearing the name of Macedonia or one of its derivatives." It accordingly welcomed a decision by the ECJ on June 29 denying the commission's application for an interim injunction ordering the lifting of the blockade. Subsequent UN and U.S. mediation yielded the signature of an "interim accord" in New York on September 13, under which Macedonia agreed to modify its national flag to meet Greek concerns and to affirm that it had no territorial claim on Greece. The thorniest issue, that of the name "Macedonia," was referred to further talks; nevertheless, Greece felt able to lift the trade embargo on October 14.

Greece's relations with its NATO and EU partners went through a serious test over the former's bombing campaign of Yugoslavia that started in late March 1999. With an overwhelming majority of its citizens against the bombing, the Greek government decided not to let its troops join the campaign but still provided logistical support for the NATO force stationed in neighboring Macedonia, a decision highly criticized by the domestic opposition. U.S. President Bill Clinton visited Greece on November 20, 1999, amid fierce protests largely due to widespread anti-West feelings further fueled by the NATO action in Yugoslavia. During the visit, Greece initially withdrew from a proposed antiterrorism pact with the United States; however, the accord eventually went into effect in September 2000 after Greece reversed its position in light of criticism from Washington and several Western European capitals over Greece's "slowness" in fighting the extremist November 17 Revolutionary Organization (see below, under Extremist Groups) that had claimed responsibility for the killing of a British defense attaché on June 19 in Athens.

Greece opposed the U.S.-led invasion of Iraq. Opposition to the war led to widespread antiwar protests during 2003. Nonetheless, the Pasok government granted the United States over-flight and basing privileges during the conflict and did not join fellow NATO members France, Germany, Belgium, and Luxembourg in attempting to block alliance military assistance to Turkey on the eve of the invasion.

Greece's relations with the other members of the EU were strained in 2004 when an EU investigation determined that the country had provided misleading data in joining the euro currency system in 2001. The Greek government had reported deficit spending of 2.5 percent in 1998 and of 1.8 percent in 1999. In fact, the investigation found that the real figures were 4.1 percent for 1998 and 3.4 percent for 1999, both above the 3 percent deficit-spending limit stipulated by the EU. The Karamanlis government blamed the previous Pasok-led government for the false reporting.

In April 2005 Greece became the sixth country to ratify the EU constitutional treaty, with legislators from both the governing New Democracy party and the leading opposition party supporting the treaty.

Current Issues

Prime Minister Simitis in 1996 had declared his desire for better relations with Turkey, but he faced an immediate crisis with Greece's eastern neighbor over an uninhabited islet in the eastern Aegean Sea close to the Turkish coast. Known to the Greeks as Imia and to the Turks as Kardak, the islet was regarded by Greece as part of the Dodecanese chain ceded by Italy after World War II, whereas Ankara claimed that it was among several coastal islets that Italy had ceded to Turkey in 1932. Responding to an apparent assertion of the Turkish claim, Greek forces landed on the islet in late January 1996 to tear down a Turkish flag, as both countries deployed warships in the area. U.S. diplomatic intervention defused the immediate crisis, with the result that both the Greek and the Turkish governments were assailed by right-wing opposition leaders for giving

in to U.S. pressure. In a further escalation in February, Turkey recalled its ambassador from Athens after Greece had blocked an EU aid grant to Turkey, thereby again demonstrating its opposition to the EU-Turkey customs union effective since the beginning of 1996.

Hope for a reduction in Greek/Turkish tension developed in July 1997 when the two countries signed an agreement during the NATO Madrid summit in which they pledged, among other things, not to use force against one another and to respect each other's sovereignty. However, Cyprus conducted war games in mid-October, inviting Greek participation for the first time. Subsequently, Turkish armed forces held military exercises in the self-declared Turkish Republic of Northern Cyprus in early November, further straining relations. Through December each side issued accusations that the other had committed airspace violations over the Aegean Sea. In addition, a Turkish aeronautical exercise in the Aegean Sea in January 1998 sparked furious Greek criticism. Meanwhile, Turkey continued to berate Greece for its perceived role in blocking Turkey's proposed EU membership (see article on the EU) and for allegedly supporting the outlawed Kurdistan Workers Party (PKK, see article on Turkey).

Simitis also continued in the second half of 1998 to foster improved ties with Turkey, as evidenced by his role in convincing the Cyprus government to deploy Russian-made missiles on the Greek island of Crete rather than in Cyprus (see article on Cyprus for details). However, a full-scale diplomatic crisis erupted between Athens and Ankara in February 1999 following the arrest of PKK leader Abdullah Öcalan in Nairobi, Kenya, minutes after he had left the home of the Greek ambassador. It was subsequently revealed that Öcalan had been smuggled into Greece by pro-Kurdish factions, apparently without the knowledge of the government, which nevertheless then had assumed responsibility for Öcalan's protection and transfer to a safe haven; South Africa was reportedly Öcalan's final destination. Öcalan's arrest was a disaster for the Greek government on several fronts. Ankara strongly denounced Athens's actions, suggesting that Greece should be declared an "outlaw state" for "supporting terrorists." At the same time, Greek embassies and foreign missions became targets for militant Kurdish protesters, who accused Greece of having conspired in the arrest. Some domestic critics accused the government of incompetence for being unaware of Öcalan's entry into Greece. (Although pro-Kurdish sentiment is strong in Greece, there would have been little popular or governmental support for harboring Öcalan, according to most analysts, because of how highly provocative such a decision would have been considered by Turkey.) Meanwhile, the government's failure to protect Öcalan once it had accepted that responsibility was perceived as a significant blow to national pride.

Relations between Greece and Turkey improved unexpectedly in the aftermath of an earthquake that hit western Turkey in August 1999. Greece contributed to rescue efforts and extended other aid, gestures that were reciprocated by Turkey when an earthquake struck Athens in September. Underscoring the rapprochement, Greece finally lifted its veto on EU financial aid earmarked for Turkey and, in December, withdrew its opposition to Turkey's eventual EU accession, contingent on resolution of the Cyprus and Aegean questions. Progress toward normalization of relations continued through 2000 as a number of cooperation agreements were signed, although a temporary reversal occurred in October when Greece withdrew its forces from a NATO air exercise in Turkey after Turkey protested the flights of Greek airplanes over sensitive Aegean areas. In November agreement was reached on a procedure for Greece to repatriate illegal Turkish immigrants, estimated to number more than 700,000 in recent years. In March 2002 Greece and Turkey signed an agreement for a 285-kilometer natural gas pipeline through which Turkey would supply Greece with 500,000 cubic meters of gas each day. Finally, it was widely agreed that improved Greek/Turkish relations contributed to the decision in December by Greek and Turkish Cypriots to resume direct talks after a four-year hiatus.

Greek and Turkish Cypriots negotiated throughout 2002 and 2003 to reach an agreement to allow Cyprus to join the EU in May 2004. However, negotiations broke down in 2004, and Greek Cypriots rejected a compromise UN agreement in a referendum on April 24, 2004. Consequently, only Greek Cyprus acceded to the EU in 2004. (See articles on Cyprus and Cyprus: Turkish Sector for additional information.)

Domestically, the Simitis government enjoyed several successes in 2003, particularly in regard to the apprehension of alleged terrorists. However, cost overruns in preparation for the 2004 Olympics constrained the government's ability to provide pay raises for public workers, and widespread protest demonstrations occurred late in the year. Concern also grew that insufficient progress was being made in the construction projects required for the Olympics to be held. The legislative elections were held early (in March) in part to avoid conflict with the summer games. New Prime Minister Karamanlis also assumed the culture portfolio in order to direct Olympic affairs, gaining widespread praise when the games were held in August without major problems. However, the government subsequently faced potential sanctions from the EU for continuing to violate EU rules regarding budget deficits. Karamanlis won a vote of confidence (165–135) in Parliament on June 13, 2005, for his plan to change labor laws and pension benefits in an attempt to rein in deficit spending. The measures, however, did not prevent a series of strikes that plagued the country's economy in 2005 and 2006.

In March 2005 the administration announced broad tax increases in order to enhance revenue, and fiscal improvement was quickly noted. Consequently, the EU told Greece that sanctions could be avoided if the deficit target (3 percent of GDP) could be reached by the end of 2006.

The Karamanlis government faced further erosion of public confidence with the disclosure in February 2006 that the cell phones of several government officials had been bugged by unknown parties for nearly a year. Karamanlis subsequently announced a reshuffling of his cabinet, highlighted by the appointment of the popular mayor of Athens, Dora BAKOYIANNIS, as foreign minister.

An additional looming challenge to Greece's economy emerged on October 17, 2005, when it was announced that bird flu had been detected in a turkey on the island of Oinousa.

Political Parties

Government Party

New Democracy (*Nea Dimokratia*—ND). Formed in 1974 as a vehicle for Konstantinos Karamanlis, New Democracy was, under Karamanlis, a broadly based pragmatic party committed to parliamentary democracy, social justice, an independent foreign policy, and free enterprise. Giorgios (George) Rallis, generally viewed as a moderate centrist, was elected party leader on May 8, 1980, and was designated prime minister the next day, following Karamanlis's election as president of the republic. In the wake of the ND's defeat at the 1981 election, Rallis lost an intraparty vote of confidence, and, in a move interpreted as reflecting the ascendancy of right-wing influence within the parliamentary group, he was succeeded in December by the leader of the party's conservative bloc, Evangelos AVEROFF-TOSSIZZA. The latter resigned as leader of the opposition in August 1984, following the ND's poor showing at the European Parliament balloting in June, the moderates rallying to elect Konstantinos Mitsotakis as his successor over Konstantinos Stephanopoulos. Stephanopoulos, in turn, withdrew with a number of his center-right supporters to form the Democratic Renewal (*Dimokratike Ananeose*—Diana) in September 1985 after Mitsotakis's August redesignation as ND leader, despite the party's legislative loss to Pasok two months earlier. (Diana was dissolved in June 1994, following its inability to win European Parliament representation.)

The party secured a plurality of 145 seats at the legislative balloting of June 18, 1989, following which it agreed to an unlikely (albeit interim) governing alliance with the Progressive Left Coalition (below, under Coalition of the Left, Movements and Ecology) to ensure parliamentary action that would permit the lodging of indictments against former prime minister Papandreou. After the ensuing election of November 5, at which it again fell short of a majority, it joined in a three-way coalition

that included Pasok to govern until new balloting on April 8, 1990, at which it won exactly half of the seats. With Diana's external support, Mitsotakis on April 11 was able to form a new single-party administration, which survived until the early election of October 10, 1993. As a result of the ND defeat, Mitsotakis on October 26 announced his resignation as party leader, and Miltiades EVERT defeated Ioannis VARVITSIOTIS in a race for the succession.

The party was runner-up to Pasok in the June 1994 European Parliament balloting, winning 9 of 25, seats and in a high-profile local victory won the Athens mayoralty in October. In the September 1996 balloting the ND slipped to 38.1 percent of the vote and 108 seats, therefore remaining in opposition. Evert resigned as ND leader in the wake of the poll but later decided to contest the resultant leadership election, thereby aggravating a long-running internal feud that was not resolved by his reelection as leader by the ND caucus in October. Ranged against Evert was former prime minister Mitsotakis, who backed the candidacy of his daughter, former culture minister Dora Bakoyiannis, as well as the candidacies of Stephanos MANOS (former finance minister) and Georgios SOUFLIAS (former education minister). Souflias received the backing of the other two contenders in the unsuccessful bid to prevent Evert from regaining the leadership, following which the party stepped back from the brink of an open split by referring the leadership issue to a full party congress in 1997.

Konstantinos (Kostas) Karamanlis, a nephew of former president Karamanlis (who died in April 1998), was elected as the new president of the party during the fourth congress on March 21, 1997, Evert losing in the first round. Intraparty friction continued in 1998 and 1999, contributing, among other things, to the defection of Manos. However, Manos and the Liberals agreed to support Karamanlis in the April 2000 legislative balloting in which the ND came within one percentage point of assuming governmental control.

In local elections on October 20, 2002, Dora BAKOYIANNIS, a former ND minister of culture and the wife of an assassinated party leader, was elected the first female mayor of Athens with 61 percent of the vote. The ND won other local races as well, demonstrating the growing decline of voter support for Pasok. In the March 7, 2004, elections, the ND won a majority of seats (165) in the Parliament, and Karamanlis was asked to form a government.

Leaders: Konstantinos (Kostas) KARAMANLIS (Prime Minister and President of the Party), Konstantinos MITSOTAKIS (Former Prime Minister and Honorary President of the Party), Vangelis MEIMARAKIS (Party Secretary).

Opposition Parties

Panhellenic Socialist Movement (*Panellenio Sosialistiko Kinema*—Pasok). Founded in 1974 by Andreas Papandreou, Pasok endorsed republicanism and socialization of the economy. In foreign affairs it committed to the dissolution of European military alliances, strict control of U.S. installations in Greece, and renegotiation of Greek membership in the EC. In 1975, in the first of a series of internal crises, the party was weakened by the withdrawal of members who disagreed with Papandreou over a lack of intraparty democratic procedure. However, most of the dissidents rejoined Pasok prior to the 1977 election, at which it won 93 parliamentary seats. The 1981 balloting yielded a Pasok majority, permitting Papandreou to form the country's first socialist government.

On March 9, 1985, Pasok announced that it would not support the reelection of President Karamanlis, offering as its candidate Christos Sartzetakis, who was elected to a five-year term by the legislature in procedurally controversial balloting on March 29. In early parliamentary balloting on June 2 the party secured a somewhat diminished majority that permitted Papandreou to continue as prime minister.

Pasok suffered major reverses at local balloting in October 1986 and was runner-up to the ND at the parliamentary elections of June and November 1989, with its leader not a formal participant in the temporary tripartite alliance formed after the latter poll. The party experienced a further, albeit marginal, decline in April 1990 but rebounded at the municipal balloting in October, both alone and in coalition with the Communists. The depth of continuing fissures within Pasok was illustrated at its second congress held September 20–23, when Akis Tsokhatzopoulos, Papandreou's choice for election to the newly created post of general secretary of the Central Committee, was approved by a bare majority of one vote. By contrast, Papandreou himself was unanimously reelected party leader and eventually returned as prime minister in October 1993. Subsequently, Papandreou was reelected leader by voice vote at the 1994 congress, with Tsokhatzopoulos being reconfirmed by the Central Committee.

Growing divisions within Pasok intensified when Papandreou fell seriously ill in November 1995, the succession struggle being complicated by the political ambitions of his wife, Dimitra LIANI. Following Papandreou's resignation in January 1996, four candidates stood for the Pasok parliamentary leadership (and thus the premiership), the victor in balloting of Pasok deputies being the reformist Konstantinos Simitis, who defeated establishment candidate Tsokhatzopoulos 86 votes to 75 in the second round. Papandreou died on June 23 and was succeeded as Pasok president by Simitis, who on June 30 again defeated Tsokhatzopoulos in balloting at a special party congress, winning 53.5 percent of delegates' votes. He went on to lead Pasok to a further election victory in September, a reduced vote share of 41.2 percent yielding an overall majority of 162 seats.

Simitis was reelected as Pasok leader at a March 1999 congress, although populist influence reportedly grew in the new 180-member Central Committee. Of particular concern to the populist wing were the government's tight economic policies, seen as constituting a threat to organized labor and other traditional Pasok constituencies. After Pasok narrowly won the April 2000 legislative balloting, Simitis was reelected as party leader during an October 2001 congress at which he rebuffed a challenge from the leader of the populist wing, Akis Tsokhatzopoulos, who was subsequently replaced as Greece's minister of national defense.

By 2003 polls showed growing support for Pasok's main political rival, the ND. In response, Simitis resigned as leader of the party and was replaced by Foreign Minister Georgios Papandreou. Papandreou faced voter discontent with the government's management of the economy and the preparations for the 2004 Olympics. In legislative elections in March 2004, Pasok received 40.55 percent of the vote and 117 seats in the Parliament, thereby losing governmental control to the ND.

On January 31, 2006, Papandreou was elected president of the Socialist International, the worldwide organization of socialist parties.

Leader: Georgios PAPANDREOU (Party Leader), Konstantinos SIMITIS (Former Party Leader), Konstantinos (Kostas) SCANDALIDIS (General Secretary).

Coalition of the Left, Movements and Ecology (*Synaspismos tis Aristeras ton Kinimaton Kai tis Oikologias*—SYN). *Synaspismos* was organized as the Progressive Left Coalition (*Synaspismos tis Aristeras kai tis Proodou*) prior to the June 1989 balloting as an alliance of the KKE (below) and the Greek Left (*Elleniki Aristera*—EAR), plus a number of minor leftist formations. The action served to mitigate a deep rupture that had existed in Greek Communist ranks since 1968. While the drive to promote a broad alliance (*symparataxis*) of the "forces of the Left" had been initiated in early 1988 by the KKE's Harilaos Florakis, the Coalition's eventual leaning was closer to that of the EAR. The new formation won 28 parliamentary seats in June 1989, 7 of which were lost the following November. Its representation was unchanged after the April 1990 balloting, two of its deputies having run as Pasok-Coalition candidates. The KKE formally regrouped as a separate party in June 1991, although nearly half of its parliamentary members opted to leave the party and stay within the Coalition.

The Greek Left had been formally launched in 1987 during an April 21–26 constituent congress of the majority faction of the Communist Party of Greece–Interior (*Kommounistiko Komma Elladas–Esoterikou*—KKEs). The action implemented a decision of the KKEs's fourth national conference in May 1986 to reorganize as a more broadly based party of the left, thereby rejecting an appeal by its (then) secretary, Yiannis Banias, that a longstanding specific identification with Marxism-Leninism be retained. The KKEs had been founded in 1968 as the result of a split in the KKE, although the two formations joined with the EDA to contest the 1974 election as members of a United Left coalition. Ultimately emerging as Greece's principal "Eurocommunist" group, the KKEs participated in the 1977 election as a member of the Alliance of Progressive and Left-Wing Forces (*Symmachia Proodeftikon kai Aristeron Dinameon*), winning one of the Alliance's two seats. Unsuccessful in 1981, it regained a single seat in 1985 and subsequently increased its representation under its new name as a member of *Synaspismos*. The EAR dissolved itself in June 1992, being merged into *Synaspismos*, which became a single party.

Following the 1993 election, at which the Coalition fell marginally short of the 3 percent threshold needed for parliamentary representation, Maria DAMANAKI resigned as president, with a party congress electing Nikos Constantopoulos as her successor. Subsequently, the group recovered to win two seats at the June 1994 European Parliament poll and ten seats in the September 1996 general election (on a vote share of 5.1 percent). The Coalition secured only 3.2 percent of the vote (six seats) in the 2000 legislative balloting.

At a party conference in June 2003 *Synaspismos* formally changed its name from the Progressive Left Coalition to the Coalition of the Left, Movements and Ecology in order to appeal to "Green" voters. However, the party continued to use *Synaspismos* as its official designation. In the 2004 elections *Synaspismos* maintained its representation in the Parliament, securing 3.26 percent of the vote and six seats.

Marxist economist Alekos Alavanos was elected president of the party in 2004, replacing Nikos Konstantopoulos, who resigned after a decade in the post.

Leader: Alekos ALAVANOS (President), Nikos HOUNDIS (Secretary).

Communist Party of Greece (*Kommounistiko Komma Elladas*—KKE). Greece's historic communist grouping, from which the more nationalist wing, KKEs (see under Greek Left, above), split in 1968, the KKE became the fourth-largest party in Parliament at the 1977 election but experienced numerous membership defections during 1980 in reaction to leadership support of the Soviet intervention in Afghanistan. It recovered to become the only group other than Pasok and New Democracy to secure parliamentary representation in 1981.

Following the 1984 Europarliamentary election, the KKE distanced itself from Pasok, seeking to attract voters from the latter's left wing and hoping to increase its leverage in the next Parliament should Pasok fail to secure a majority. The KKE's continued unwillingness to support Pasok in second-round balloting contributed to the governing party's poor showing in the 1986 municipal elections.

During the latter half of 1989 the KKE experienced renewed internal dissonance. A dispute with the party's youth organization resulted in the dismissal of the latter's entire Central Committee in late September, while a number of trade-union affiliate members withdrew to form an anti-Coalition "Militant Initiative" in mid-October. Additional defections followed, including the resignation of eight Central Committee members in late November in protest of the formation of an ecumenical administration.

During the party's 13th congress in Athens held February 19–27, 1991, "conservatives" won control of the Central Committee over reformists, 60–51, and proceeded to confound earlier expectations by electing Aleka Papariga, a hard-liner, as general secretary. Although the chances of a realignment within *Synaspismos* appeared to have been improved by the selection of a KKE reformist to succeed Florakis as Coalition president on March 18, Papariga announced in mid-June that she was taking the KKE out of the alliance. Subsequently, seven reformers, including Coalition leader Damanaki, were suspended from the party's Central Committee.

The KKE won 9 parliamentary seats in a vote share of 4.5 percent in October 1993 and 2 European Parliament seats in June 1994. It improved further to 5.6 percent (and 11 seats) in the September 1996 general election. After organizing many of the antigovernment protests and orchestrating anti-West sentiments during and after the NATO bombing of Yugoslavia (see Foreign relations), the KKE won 5.5 percent of the vote at the general election in April 2000, thereby retaining its 11 seats. In the 2004 elections the KKE received 5.9 percent of the vote and 12 seats in the Parliament.

Leaders: Harilaos FLORAKIS (Honorary President), Aleka PAPARIGA (General Secretary).

Other Parties

Democratic Social Movement (*Dimokratiki Kinoniki Kinema*—Dikki). Dikki was formed prior to the September 1996 balloting by a faction of Pasok claiming to be the true representative of the party's socialist heritage. It won a creditable 4.4 percent of the vote in its first electoral contest, yielding nine seats. It lost parliamentary representation, however, after winning only 2.7 percent of the vote at the general election in April 2000. In the April 2004 elections Dikki received 1.79 percent of the vote.

Leader: Dimitris TSOVALOS (President).

Populist Orthodox Rally (*Laikos Orthodoxos Synagermos*—LAOS). The LAOS was formed in 2000 as a far-right, anti-immigrant party that emphasized the "superiority" of the Greek Orthodox religion. The party was created by Georgios Karatzaferis after he was dismissed from the ND. In the 2004 national elections the LAOS received 2.19 percent of the vote and therefore did not gain any representation in the Parliament. The party did, however, attract 4.1 percent of the vote in the 2004 European parliamentary elections and secured one seat.

Leaders: Georgios KARATZAFERIS (President), Othon FLORATOS (Director General).

Other formations and parties that participated unsuccessfully in the 2004 legislative elections included the **Anti-Capitalist Alliance,** the **Centrists' Union,** the **Communist Party of Greece/Marxist-Leninist,** the **Radical Left Front, Christopistia** (loosely "Faith in Christ"), the **Hellenic Front,** the **Liberal Party,** the

Cabinet

As of April 15, 2006

Prime Minister Konstantinos (Kostas) Karamanlis

Ministers

Aegean and Island Policy	Aristotelis Pavlidis
Culture	Georgios Voulgarakis
Development	Dimitris Sioufas
Economy and Finance	Georgios Alogoskoufis
Education and Religious Affairs	Marietta Giannakou [f]
Employment and Social Protection	Savvas Tsitouridis
Environment, Physical Planning, and Public Works	Georgios Souflias
Foreign Affairs	Dora Bakoyiannis
Health and Social Solidarity	Dimitris Avramopoulos
Interior, Public Administration, and Decentralization	Prokopis Pavlopoulos
Justice	Anatasios Papaligouras
Macedonia and Thrace	Giorgios Kalantzis
Mercantile Marine	Manolis Kefalogiannis
National Defense	Evangelos Meimarakis
Public Order	Georgios Voulgarakis
Rural Development and Foods	Evangelos Basiakos
Tourism	Fani Palli-Petralia
Transport and Communications	Mihalis Liapis

[f] = female

Marxist-Leninist Communist Party of Greece Left, the **Militant Socialist Party of Greece,** and the **Organization for the Restructuring of the KKE**.

Although running as independents rather than under party labels, Muslim candidates from two ethnically Turkish districts in Thrace typically outpoll many minor formations with nationwide constituencies.

Extremist Groups

November 17 Revolutionary Organization (*Epanastatiki Organosi 17 Noemvri*—EO17N). The EO17N is a leftist urban guerrilla organization named after the date of the famous Athens Polytechnical High School insurrection, which had been violently crushed by the military junta in 1973. The grouping surfaced in 1975 and subsequently claimed responsibility for numerous assassinations and violent attacks. Among its victims were CIA Station Chief Richard Welch, former police officer Evangelos MALLIOS, and steel magnate Dimitris ANGELOPOULOS. In October 1991 the group claimed responsibility for the murder of a press attaché at the Turkish Embassy in Athens. In July 1992 the EO17N unsuccessfully attempted to assassinate the minister of finance, while in July 1994 it claimed responsibility for the assassination of a Turkish diplomat. In February 1996 an unsuccessful attack on the U.S. Embassy in Athens was believed to have been planned by the EO17N. Subsequently, the EO17N claimed responsibility for the assassination in Athens in June 2000 of a British defense attaché, saying the killing was a response to the NATO air attacks in Yugoslavia in

1999. Greek authorities subsequently came under intensified pressure for the lack of arrests in regard to EO17N activities.

In 2003 Greek authorities made a series of arrests and gained convictions of the top leadership of EO17N. The leader of the organization, Alexandros GIOTOPOULOS, and its alleged main assassin, Dimitris KOUFODINAS, both received multiple life sentences during trials in December 2003. In addition, 12 others were convicted of terrorism charges. The convictions effectively eliminated, even if only temporarily, the operational capabilities of EO17N.

Other terrorist groups include the **May 1st Revolutionary Organization,** the **People's Revolutionary Struggle** (*Epanastatikos Laikos Agonas*— EPA), and the **Revolutionary Nucleus** (*Epanastatikos Pyrenas*—EP), all of which allegedly carried out attacks against "capitalist" and "imperialist" targets throughout the 1980s and 1990s. The People's Revolutionary Struggle split into several factions in 1995. One of these groups, the **Revolutionary Struggle,** exploded three bombs in Athens on May 5, 2004, to protest the Olympics. On May 13 another bomb exploded outside of a bank, while a second device was found and detonated by police. The police also found and destroyed a bomb near an Olympic site on May 19.

A bomb attack at the American College in Athens in October 1998 was attributed to the anarchist **Anti-Power Struggle** grouping, while another anarchist group, **Children of November,** was deemed responsible for the bombing in December of the Athens office of Leon AVRIS, who had been the KKE's candidate for mayor of Athens in 1997. Earlier, in January 1998, Athens police had arrested 15 suspected members of the extreme leftist **Fighting Guerrilla Faction** for alleged complicity in a bombing. In August 2000 a hitherto unknown group, **Anarchic Struggle,** claimed responsibility for attacks on Egyptian, Italian, and Yugoslavian diplomatic cars.

Legislature

The unicameral **Parliament** (*Vouli*) consists of 300 members elected by direct universal suffrage for four-year terms, subject to dissolution. Since 1926 the procedure for allocating seats, usually a form of proportional representation, has tended to vary from one election to another. At the October 1993 balloting simple proportional representation based on the Hagenbach-Bischoff quota was used in the first distribution, with the Hare quota employed in the second for all parties securing a minimum national vote share of 3 percent. Early general elections on March 7, 2004, produced the following results: New Democracy, 165 seats; the Panhellenic Socialist Movement, 117; the Communist Party of Greece, 12; the Coalition of the Left, Movements and Ecology, 6.

Speaker: Anna PSAROUDA-BENAKI.

Communications

The news media operated under severe constraints while the military was in power. Upon the return to civilian rule, censorship was lifted and a number of theretofore banned papers reemerged, although some have since experienced major shifts in circulation. From 1989 to 1992 overall readership dropped by 36 percent, the greatest decline being experienced by Communist and hard-line Pasok organs.

Under the conservative government of Prime Minister Mitsotakis the media were subjected to legislation banning the "unwarranted" publicizing of terrorist activity, including the publication of terrorist manifestos. However, the controversial measure was rescinded in December 1993.

The Karamanlis government enacted legislation in January 2005 banning individuals with large shareholdings in media from owning shares in companies that bid for public contracts. The European Commission has called on Greece to change the law, indicating that it violates EU directives.

Press

The following are dailies published in Athens: *Eleftheros Typos* (Free Press, 167,806), center-right; *Ta Nea* (News, 135,000), center-left; *Eleftherotypia* (Press Freedom, 118,000), center-left; *Ethnos* (Nation, 84,735), center-left; *Apogevmatini* (Afternoon, 72,904), center-right; *Kathimerini*

(Every Day, 34,000), center-right; *Rizospastis* (Radical, 28,740), KKE organ; *Avriani* (Tomorrow, 16,629), center-left; *Star* (16,215), apolitical; *Niki* (Victory, 12,942), center-left; *Eleftheros* (Free, 9,769), center-right; *Mesimvrini* (Midday, 9,089), center-right; *Avgi* (Dawn, 5,400), Eurocommunist; *Estia* (Vesta, 4,759), far-right; *O Logos* (Speech, 2,140), formerly *Democraticos Logos*, center-left; *Eleftheri Ora* (Free Time, 1,026), far-right.

News Agencies

The major domestic service is the Athens News Agency—ANA (*Athinaiko Praktorio Edisseon*—APE). Several foreign bureaus maintain offices in Athens.

Broadcasting and Computing

In 1987 Hellenic Radio-Television (*Elleniki Radiophonia Tileorassi*—ERT) became a joint stock company by merger of ERT-1 (the original ERT, which had been state-controlled since 1939) and ERT-2, the former Information service of the Armed Forces (*Ypiresia Enimeroseos Enoplon Dynameon*—Yened), which had been turned over to civilian operation in 1982. The restructuring yielded two television channels, ET-1 and ET-2 (to which ET-3, broadcasting from Salonika, was subsequently added). In addition, the private Sky (unrelated to the British facility of the same name) is one of a number of commercial channels that were subsequently launched.

Since 1987 for radio and 1989 for television, local non-state-owned stations have been authorized to operate under government licenses issued on advice of the National Radio and Television Council (ESR), a 19-member body representing a variety of political, social, and cultural groups. By early 1993 the ESR had drafted positive recommendations for 1 Greater Athens and 11 national television stations; however, by midyear the government had failed to take action on any private licenses, with the result that approximately 1,500 local radio and some 100 largely local television stations continued to be operated illegally. By 2001 the ESR had begun to issue licenses regularly and to clear the backlog of applications. The ESR also began to fine stations for advertising violations. The two most popular private TV stations are Mega Channel and Antenna, which commenced operations in late 1989 and early 1990, respectively. There were approximately 5.2 million television receivers and 1 million personal computers serving 1.7 million Internet users in 2003.

Intergovernmental Representation

Ambassador to the U.S.
Alexandros P. MALLIAS

U.S. Ambassador to Greece
Charles P. RIES

Permanent Representative to the UN
Adamantios VASSILAKIS

IGO Memberships (Non-UN)
BIS, BSEC, CERN, CEUR, EBRD, EIB, ESA, EU, Eurocontrol, IEA, Interpol, IOM, NATO, OECD, *OIF*, OSCE, PCA, WCO, WEU, WTO

HUNGARY

HUNGARIAN REPUBLIC

Magyar Köztársaság

The Country

Masters for over 1,000 years of the fertile plain extending on either side of the middle Danube, the Hungarians have long regarded their country as the eastern outpost of Western Europe in cultural pattern, religious affiliation, and political structure. More than 90 percent of the present Hungarian population is of Magyar origin; Germans, Gypsies (Roma), Romanians, Slovaks, and Southern Slavs (Croats, Serbs, Slovenes) are the main ethnic minorities. Despite more than four decades of Communist-mandated antireligious policies from the mid-1940s until the late 1980s, about two-thirds of the population is classified as Roman Catholic; there are also Protestant, Eastern Orthodox, and Jewish adherents. In 1998 women accounted for 45 percent of the labor force, concentrated in manufacturing services and the professions.

Although the Hungarian economy was traditionally dependent on the agricultural sector, which was largely collectivized following the Communist assumption of power after World War II, it now accounts for only 5 percent of the GDP. The country remains, however, a net food exporter, with one of the largest agricultural trade surpluses in Eastern Europe. Industry contributed 33 percent of GDP in 1999. In addition to processed foods, leading industrial products, almost all of which require imported raw materials (iron ore, petroleum, copper, crude fibers), are machinery, transportation equipment, electrical and electronic equipment (including computers), chemicals, and textiles. Bauxite, coal, and natural gas are the chief mineral resources.

Largely because of the collapse of trade with other ex-Communist states, Hungary's GDP fell by 20 percent between 1989 and 1993, and both inflation and unemployment registered in double digits. Growth resumed in 1994, at 2.9 percent, but remained slow through the middle of the decade. Steady expansion followed, averaging 4.6 percent annually in 1997–1999 and reaching an estimated 5.5 percent in 2000. Meanwhile, unemployment consistently declined, from 11.5 percent in 1993 to about 6.5 percent more recently (the lowest rate in Eastern Europe), and consumer price inflation, which had averaged over 20 percent in 1993–1997, dropped under 10 percent in 2000. For the 1990s as a whole, Hungary led the region in

Political Status: Independent kingdom created in 1000; republic proclaimed in 1946; Communist People's Republic established August 20, 1949; pre-Communist name revived as one of a number of Western-style constitutional changes approved on October 18, 1989.

Area: 35,919 sq. mi. (93,030 sq. km.).

Population: 10,197,119 (2001C); 10,080,000 (2005E).

Major Urban Centers (2005E): BUDAPEST (1,700,000), Debrecen (209,000), Miskolc (189,000), Pécs (169,000), Szeged (162,000), Györ (131,000).

Official Language: Hungarian.

Monetary Unit: Forint (official rate July 1, 2006: 221.52 forints = $1US).

President: Laszlo SOLYOM; elected (as the candidate of the Federation of Young Democrats–Hungarian Civic Alliance and several other parties) in third-round balloting by the National Assembly on June 7, 2005, and sworn in for a five-year term on August 5, succeeding Ferenc MÁDL.

Prime Minister: Ferenc GYURCSÁNY (Hungarian Socialist Party); formally invited by the president to form a new government on September 26, 2004, following the resignation of Péter MEDGYESSY (Hungarian Socialist Party) on August 27; formed new government on June 9, 2006, following assembly elections on April 9 and 23.

direct foreign investment, and trade burgeoned, especially with the European Union (EU). Led by Germany, EU countries now purchase three-fourths of Hungary's exports and provide two-thirds of its imports.

Hungary was described in a 2000 report from the International Monetary Fund (IMF) as "in the vanguard of the transition economies" seeking EU accession. However, budget deficits began to increase in the early 2000s, prompting the government (under EU pressure) to implement austerity measures. GDP grew by 3.3 percent in 2002 and 2.9 percent in 2003, while inflation, which had been as high as 11.2 percent in 1999, had fallen to 5.7 percent by 2003. Overall, the EU considered the economic progress sufficient to include Hungary among the ten new countries admitted to the EU on May 1, 2004.

The IMF described EU accession as a "tribute" to Hungary's successful transition to a market economy. Solid growth (4 percent) was achieved in both 2004 and 2005 on the strength of increased exports and rising investment. However, the IMF and the EU warned that the budget deficit and public debt remained unacceptably high (see Current issues, below).

Government and Politics

Political Background

Part of the polyglot Austro-Hungarian Empire, the former Kingdom of Hungary lost two-thirds of its territory (including Transylvania) and the bulk of its non-Magyar population at the end of World War I under the 1920 Treaty of Trianon. A brief but bloody Communist dictatorship under Béla KUN in 1919 was followed by 25 years of right-wing authoritarian government under Adm. Miklós HORTHY, who bore the title of regent. Having regained Northern Transylvania from Romania under the 1940 Vienna Award, Hungary joined Germany in the war against the Soviet Union in June 1941 and was occupied by Soviet forces in late 1944. Under a definitive peace treaty with the Allied Powers signed in February 1947, Hungary reverted to its 1920 borders.

Communists obtained only 17 percent of the vote in a free election held in November 1945 but with Soviet backing assumed key posts in the coalition government that proclaimed the Hungarian Republic on February 1, 1946. Seizing de facto control in May–June 1947, the Communists proceeded to liquidate most opposition parties and to establish a dictatorship led by Mátyás RÁKOSI. The remaining parties and mass organizations were grouped in a Communist-controlled "front," while the Hungarian People's Republic was formally established in August 1949.

The initial years of the People's Republic were marked by purges and the systematic elimination of domestic opposition, which included the 1949 treason conviction of the Roman Catholic primate, József Cardinal MINDSZENTY. In the post-Stalin era, however, gradual liberalization led to the outbreak in October 1956 of a popular revolutionary movement, the formation of a coalition government under Imre NAGY, and the announcement on November 1 of Hungary's withdrawal from the Warsaw Pact. Massive Soviet military force was employed to crush the revolt, and a pro-Soviet regime headed by János KÁDÁR was installed on November 4. Nagy was hanged in 1958; Cardinal Mindszenty, who had been freed in the uprising, sought refuge in the U.S. embassy in Budapest, where he remained for 15 years before being allowed to leave the country.

Concerned primarily with consolidating its position, the Kádár government was initially rigid and authoritarian. However, the 1962 congress of the Hungarian Socialist Workers' Party (*Magyar Szocialista Munkáspárt*—MSzMP) marked the beginning of a trend toward pragmatism in domestic policy that was exemplified by the implementation of a program known as the New Economic Mechanism, which allowed for decentralization, more flexible management strategies, incentives for efficiency, and expanded production of consumer goods. At the same time, Hungary strictly adhered to Soviet pronouncements in foreign affairs, as most dramatically demonstrated by the participation of Hungarian troops in the Warsaw Pact invasion of Czechoslovakia in August 1968.

The retreat from Communist domination commenced somewhat earlier in Hungary than elsewhere in Eastern Europe. In May 1988 Kádár was replaced as party general secretary by Károly GRÓSZ, who had been premier since June 1987. Grósz was succeeded as premier by Miklós NÉMETH in November. In early 1989 the National Assembly legalized freedom of assembly and association, and in mid-March 75,000 demonstrators were permitted to assemble in Budapest to demand free elections and the removal of Soviet troops. On May 2, acting on behalf of the Németh government,

security forces began dismantling the barbed-wire fence along the border with Austria, and on May 13, five days after Kádár had been forced into retirement from his ceremonial post as party president, talks began with opposition leaders on transition to a multiparty system. On June 16 the martyred Imre Nagy was formally "rehabilitated" by means of a public reburial attended by some 300,000 persons. On October 7 the MSzMP renounced Marxism and renamed itself the Hungarian Socialist Party (*Magyar Szocialista Párt*—MSzP). On October 23 the non-Communist speaker of the National Assembly, Mátyás SZÜRÖS, became acting president of the republic in the wake of legislative action that abolished the Presidential Council, purged the constitution of its Stalinist elements, and paved the way for the first free elections in more than four decades.

At second-stage legislative balloting on April 8, 1990, the recently formed Hungarian Democratic Forum (*Magyar Demokrata Fórum*—MDF) won a substantial plurality of seats, and on May 3 its chair, József ANTALL, was asked to form a center-right government, consisting of the MDF, the Christian Democratic People's Party (*Kereszténydemokrata Néppárt*—KDNP), and the Independent Smallholders' Party (*Független Kisgazda Párt*—FKgP), that was installed on May 23. Earlier, on May 2, the new parliament had named a noted former dissident, Arpád GÖNCZ, to the post of acting state president. A referendum on direct election of the president (favored by 86 percent of those participating) failed on July 29 because of insufficient turnout, and on August 3 the assembly elected Göncz to a regular five-year term.

In 1991–1992 the Antall government secured the passage of legislation providing compensation for property expropriated during the Fascist and Communist eras, as well as for individuals killed, imprisoned, or deported for political reasons between 1939 and 1989. In addition, an amendment was approved in October 1993 allowing the prosecution of certain crimes committed by state authorities during the 1956 Hungarian uprising.

In February 1992 the FKgP withdrew from the ruling coalition because its blueprints for the restoration of land to pre-Communist owners had not become government policy. However, three-quarters of the 44 FKgP parliamentary deputies continued to support the government, initially as the FKgP "Historical Section" (*Történelmi Tagozat*). Antall carried out a controversial ministerial reshuffle in February 1993, but the government was further weakened at midyear when a right-wing MDF faction led by István CSURKA was expelled from the party and formed the Hungarian Justice and Life Party (*Magyar Igazság és Élat Párt*—MIÉP).

The MDF sought to ensure political continuity despite Antall's early death in December 1993 at the age of 61, his protracted final illness having afforded time for the prime ministerial succession to be formally bestowed on longtime heir-apparent Péter BOROSS, theretofore the interior minister. However, the change of prime minister did nothing to restore the political fortunes of the MDF, which was overwhelmingly defeated in the May 1994 general election by a resurgent MSzP led by Dr. Gyula HORN. Despite his party's commanding majority, Horn sought to dispel overseas concern about the return to power of Hungary's ex-Communists by forming a coalition with the centrist Alliance of Free Democrats (*Szabad Demokraták Szövetsége*—SzDSz), thus generating the two-thirds majority needed for constitutional amendment.

The Horn government declared its commitment to completing its predecessor's successful privatization program, while giving priority to the investigation of alleged corruption in the disposal of state-owned assets. However, in January 1995 the highly respected László BÉKESI resigned as finance minister, claiming that promarket reform was being resisted by other ministers. In February a new finance minister, Lajos BOKROS, and a special privatization minister were appointed amid government admissions that Hungary's economic difficulties were chronic, largely because of spiraling public debt. The announcement of draconian economic austerity measures in March precipitated the resignation of two more MSzP ministers.

The Horn government also faced deep conflict over its effort to draft a new constitution to replace the much-amended Communist-era text. Immediate controversy centered on a proposal by the opposition FKgP for direct election of a president with enhanced powers. The ruling MSzP insisted that such a change would generate political instability; as a result the June 19 presidential balloting again took place in the National Assembly. The outcome was a second five-year term for Arpád Göncz, who easily defeated an independent conservative nominee, Ferenc MÁDL, whose candidacy drew support from several opposition parties.

In late 1995 the failure to produce a new constitution rebounded on the government when the Constitutional Court issued rulings that parts of the March austerity program contravened provisions of the Soviet-era text. The government took steps to bridge the resultant budget shortfall and suffered further ministerial resignations as a consequence. In February 1996 Finance Minister Bokros himself resigned, after his colleagues had declined to endorse the next stage of his deficit-reducing plans.

By early 1998 the MSzP/SzDSz government was being credited with having achieved significant economic progress. Nevertheless, in the May balloting for the National Assembly it appeared to face a backlash by those adversely affected by privatization and austerity measures. The opposition also focused on corruption scandals and rising crime rates. In the first round on May 10, the MSzP secured 32.3 percent of the vote, followed by the center-right Federation of Young Democrats–Hungarian Civic Party (*Fiatal Demokraták Szövetsége–Magyar Polgari Párt*—FiDeSz-MPP) with 28.2 percent. Following the second round on May 24, the FiDeSz-MPP emerged with a plurality of 148 seats, with the MSzP winning 134 and the SzDSz claiming only 24. Consequently, the president asked the 35-year-old FiDeSz-MPP leader, Viktor ORBÁN, to form a new government. After rejecting cooperation with the MSzP and the ultranationalist MIÉP, Orbán reached agreement with the MDF (with which the FiDeSz-MPP had presented joint candidates) and the FKgP. Orbán was sworn in on July 6, and the new cabinet took office on July 8.

On June 6, 2000, the National Assembly elected Ferenc Mádl as President Göncz's successor.

Unopposed, Mádl had received public support from opposition parties as well as the governing coalition, but he nevertheless failed to achieve the required two-thirds majority on the first two ballots. He polled sufficient votes on a third ballot, when only a simple majority was needed for election, and was inaugurated on August 4.

Somewhat earlier than expected, and with preparations for accession to the EU in mind, on December 13, 2001, President Mádl announced a National Assembly election for April 2002. Although opinion polls had forecast a repeat victory for Prime Minister Orbán, whose FiDeSz-MPP had signed an electoral alliance with the MDF in September 2001, the results of the first round of balloting on April 7 gave a slight lead to the opposition Socialists, who won 42.1 percent of the party list vote and 94 total seats, compared to 41.1 percent and 87 seats for the FiDeSz-MPP/MDF. The Socialist candidate for prime minister, former finance minister Péter MEDGYESSY, immediately began discussions with the Free Democrats on formation of a coalition government. At the end of the second round of balloting on April 21, the FiDeSz-MPP/MDF coalition held a plurality of seats (188 to 178 for the Socialists), but Prime Minister Orbán was without a prospective coalition partner, the FKgP having failed to win any seats. Thus a leftist government of the MSzP and the SzDSz took office under Medgyessy on May 27.

In a national referendum on April 12, 2003, voters approved proposed accession to the EU with an 84 percent "yes" vote. (The National Assembly ratified the measure on December 15, and Hungary joined the EU with nine other new members on May 1, 2004.) However, concurrent austerity measures on the part of the government eroded support for Prime Minister Medgyessy, and the government parties fared poorly in the June 2004 European Parliament balloting. Following a dispute between Medgyessy and junior coalition partner SzDSz, Medgyessy announced his resignation on August 25 after apparently having also lost the support of his own party. He was succeeded on September 26 by the MSzP's Ferenc GYURCSÁNY, a wealthy young businessman who had been serving as minister of youth and sports.

On June 7, 2005, Laszlo SOLYOM, who was nominated by the FiDeSz-MPSz (as the FiDeSz-MPP had been renamed [see Political Parties, below]), was elected president in the third round of balloting in the assembly. Solyom was best known for his former post as president of the Constitutional Court.

The governing coalition of the MSzP and SzDSz extended its legislative majority at the assembly balloting of April 9 and 23, 2006. Gyurcsány's government program was approved by a vote of 206–159 in the assembly on June 9, and Gyurcsány on the same day was again sworn in as prime minister to head a reshuffled MSzP/SzDSz cabinet.

Constitution and Government

The constitution of 1949 (as amended in 1972) declared Hungary to be a state in which all power belonged to the working people, the bulk of the means of production was publicly owned, and the (Communist) Hungarian Socialist Workers' Party was the "leading force" in state and society. Under the October 1989 revision, Hungary is described as an "independent democratic state" adhering to "the values of both bourgeois democracy and democratic socialism." In addition, civil and human rights are protected; a multiparty parliamentary system is to be maintained; and executive, legislative, and judicial functions are separated. The former 21-member Presidential Council was replaced by an indirectly elected state president who serves as commander in chief of the armed forces and has the capacity to negotiate international agreements. Subsequently, the unicameral National Assembly approved a law on the activity and financing of political parties, prohibited parties from operating in the workplace (thus invalidating the traditional role of Communist party cells), and approved an electoral law based on a mixed system of proportional and direct representation. The judicial system is jointly administered by the Supreme Court, whose president is named by the legislature, and the ministry of justice. Below the Supreme Court are county, district, and municipal courts. A Constitutional Court was also added in 1989 as successor to a Constitutional Law Council established by the assembly five years before.

The country is administratively divided into 19 counties and 23 cities and towns of county status (including Budapest), about 200 other towns, and nearly 3,000 villages. Council members at the local levels are directly elected, while those at the county level are elected by the members of the lower-level councils. Each council elects an executive committee and a president.

There have been several efforts recently to revamp the national governmental institutions, the most important proposals calling for the introduction of direct elections for president and a reduction in the size of the assembly. Prime Minister Medgyessy attempted to have the reforms presented for a national referendum in June 2004, but the assembly blocked that initiative.

Foreign Relations

Following the failure of the 1956 revolution, Hungary faithfully followed the Soviet lead in international issues, voting with the Soviet bloc in the United Nations (UN), adhering to the Brezhnev Doctrine of the limited sovereignty of Communist states, and serving as a reliable member of the Warsaw Pact, the Council for Mutual Economic Assistance (CMEA), and other multilateral Communist organs. However, relations with its closest Eastern-bloc neighbors were not always smooth. Disputes over the treatment of ethnic Hungarians in Romania caused tension with Bucharest, while Czechoslovak authorities expressed disapproval of Budapest's efforts, launched in the 1960s, to improve relations with the West.

Communist rule having been brought to an end, the new National Assembly voted unanimously on June 26, 1990, to suspend Hungary's participation in the Warsaw Pact and to withdraw from the alliance by late 1991. The departure of Soviet troops was complicated by acrimonious disputes over financial liabilities, which were, however, largely resolved during reciprocal visits by the Russian and Hungarian presidents in November 1992 and June 1993, respectively.

In November 1990 Hungary became the first East European country to be admitted to the Council of Europe, and the following month it became the first from the region to subscribe to the Social Charter of the European Community (EC, subsequently the EU). The goal of eventual EC membership was a joint aim of the "Visegrád" cooperation bloc formed on February 15, 1991, by Hungary, Poland, and Czechoslovakia (subsequently the Czech Republic and Slovakia). Meanwhile, on December 21, 1992, the Visegrád states signed a Central European Free Trade Agreement (CEFTA; see Foreign relations section in article on Poland for additional information). Hungary is also a member of the Central European Initiative (CEI), originally formed in 1989 as a "Pentagonal" group of Central European states committed to mutual and bilateral economic cooperation within the Conference on (later Organization for) Security and Cooperation in Europe (CSCE/OSCE).

Although Hungary repeatedly stated its acceptance of existing borders, its keen interest in the status of the 32 million ethnic Hungarians in neighboring countries caused regional strains in the post-Communist era. Despite Hungarian attempts to curb the inflow, ethnic Hungarians continued to cross the border from Transylvania in substantial numbers, citing rising Romanian nationalism as the reason. The civil war in former Yugoslavia also resulted in an exodus of ethnic Hungarians, in this case from the Serbian-ruled province of Vojvodina, once part of the Austro-Hungarian Empire. Moreover, Slovakia's move to independence on January 1, 1993, increased concern in Hungary over that country's ethnic Hungarian minority.

Taking a less nationalistic line on ethnic Hungarians in neighboring countries, the Horn government elected in May 1994 sought to improve relations with Romania and Slovakia. In February 1995 Hungary signed the Council of Europe's new Convention on the Protection of National Minorities, and the following month it concluded a friendship and cooperation treaty with Slovakia, which guaranteed the existing border and provided formal protection for minority groups (principally ethnic Hungarians in Slovakia).

A long-negotiated treaty dealing with minority rights and other bilateral issues was signed by the Hungarian and Romanian prime ministers on September 16, 1996, in Timişoara in Romanian Transylvania, where 1.6 million ethnic Hungarians form Europe's largest nonimmigrant ethnic minority. The text represented a compromise, but, inevitably, the treaty was fiercely condemned by the nationalist parties of both countries as a capitulation. Both governments considered finalization of the treaty as an important step toward membership in the EU and the North Atlantic Treaty Organization (NATO).

An agreement between Hungary and the European Free Trade Association (EFTA) entered into force on October 1, 1993, while in December Hungary applied for membership in the Organization for Economic Cooperation and Development (OECD). In February 1994 Hungary joined NATO's Partnership for Peace program, and in May it was one of nine such countries offered close nonmembership links with the Western European Union (WEU). However, the priority remained closer relations with the EU, to which Hungary on April 1, 1994, submitted an application for full membership following the entry into force of an association agreement two months earlier. In December 1997 the EU issued a formal invitation to Hungary and five other "first-wave" nations to begin discussions in March 1998 regarding membership protocols.

In August 1995 Hungary joined in signing a CEFTA agreement providing for free trade in most industrial products by 1997, this being undertaken as step toward EU membership for the four CEFTA members. In January 1996 the government committed 400 Hungarian troops to the NATO-commanded International Force (IFOR) charged with implementing the Dayton Accords for Bosnia. Further important integration into Western structures was achieved in March when Hungary enrolled as a full member of the OECD.

In July 1997 NATO invited Hungary, Poland, and the Czech Republic to join the alliance in 1999,

but the extreme extraparliamentary parties in Hungary continued to oppose membership. The seven parliamentary parties reportedly agreed to hold a nonbinding referendum on NATO, but the FiDeSz-MPP later called for a binding vote. The cabinet subsequently reversed its position on the referendum and agreed to be bound by the results. Voters approved NATO accession overwhelmingly (85 percent) on November 16, and Hungary quickly submitted its formal membership application. Accession was achieved on March 12, 1999, at a ceremony in the United States, although the timing was poor for the new NATO members in view of the conflict between the alliance and Yugoslavia. The NATO military action was particularly sensitive for Hungary, since the 340,000 ethnic Hungarians resident in Vojvodina were considered possible targets of Serbian reprisals. Budapest dutifully permitted NATO planes access to Hungarian airspace for attacks on Serbia but otherwise was not involved in the campaign.

A lingering dispute with Slovakia concerns the construction of dams in Gabčkovo, Slovakia, and Nagymaros, Hungary, on the Danube. In September 1997 the International Court of Justice (ICJ) ruled on the long-standing dispute, finding that Hungary had broken a 1977 agreement to collaborate with its neighbor on the project, which was designed to generate electricity, control flooding, and improve navigation. The ICJ also faulted Slovakia for unilaterally proceeding with an alternative plan and directed both sides to negotiate a settlement, which was reached in March 1998. However, the new Hungarian government formed in July annulled the accord, pending further environmental assessment. By early 2001 no definitive solution had been reached, although Slovakia appeared ready to accept that the Nagymaros dam would not be built. However, in April 2004 negotiations were restarted after a two-year hiatus.

Hungary supported U.S. policy toward Iraq in 2003 and deployed 350 troops to support the U.S./UK-led coalition following the fall of Saddam Hussein. However, Hungary's stance strained relations with France and Germany, and, with more than half of the Hungarian population indicating opposition to the war, the Hungarian troops were withdrawn from Iraq by the end of 2004.

In December 2004 Hungary conducted a national referendum on the controversial proposal to offer citizenship to ethnic Hungarians living in other countries. However, the referendum failed because the required 50 percent voter turnout was not achieved.

Current Issues

Upon his installation as prime minister in 2002, Péter Medgyessy announced that EU membership would be his administration's top priority. Consequently, the government enacted a wide range of economic and other reforms, as approved by the assembly in December 2002. However, budget austerity met with discontent in certain sections of the population as well as within the two-party coalition government. Not surprisingly, despite the smooth EU accession in May, the MSzP and SzDSz performed poorly in the June European Parliament balloting, while the FiDeSz-MPSz secured nearly 50 percent of the votes. Tension within the coalition government came to a head in August when Medgyessy attempted to dismiss the SzDSz economy minister. The SzDSz threatened to quit the cabinet over the matter, and a "coup" within the MSzP (see Political Parties) sealed Medgyessy's fate. His successor, Ferenc Gyurcsány, was described as a "modernizing social-democrat" with a probusiness point of view. Some analysts described the shift in the premiership as representing the endgame in the struggle between the "old-guard socialists" and the younger "center-left" generation. However, the "charismatic" Gyurcsány quickly faced severe policy challenges as the EU accused Hungary of having "broken" recent promises regarding the budget deficit and the public debt. In the first half of 2005 Gyurcsány appointed new ministers to complete agricultural reform demanded by the EU and to pursue the fiscal policies necessary to permit Hungary to adopt the euro by 2010. (The assembly in December 2004 had ratified the proposed new EU constitution by a vote of 322–12.)

Gyurcsány resisted pressure from the EU in late 2005 for additional fiscal retrenchment, possibly with an eye on the upcoming 2006 assembly poll. In fact, the prime minister during the campaign promised massive infrastructure spending if reelected. Viktor Orbán of the FiDeSz-MPP, Gyurcsány's main opponent, called for even greater spending initiatives along with tax cuts, although analysts described the platforms of both major parties as unrealistic considering the nation's burgeoning economic crisis. After Gyurcsány's personal popularity helped the MSzP/SzDSz coalition to become the first post-Communist government to be reelected in Hungary, he quickly proposed a dramatic austerity program designed to reduce the budget deficit, which was projected to reach 9.5 percent of GDP in 2006. (EU criteria require a deficit of no more than 3 percent, putting Hungary's goal of adopting the euro by 2010 in peril.) Gyurcsány called for tax increases, restructuring of "bloated" state institutions, reorganization of the "inefficient" education system, consolidation of municipal administrations, and additional promotion of the private sector. However, it remained unclear if the initiatives would receive the necessary approval of the still diverse assembly.

Political Parties

As of late 1988 the sole authorized political party was the Hungarian Socialist Workers' Party (*Magyar Szocialista Munkáspárt*—MSzMP), supported by a Communist-controlled umbrella organization, the Patriotic People's Front (*Hazafias Népfront*), which, prior to the emergence of a number of unofficial formations, embraced virtually all organized groups and associations in the country. In January 1989 the National Assembly legalized freedom of assembly and association, and a month later the MSzMP approved the formation of independent parties, some of which had begun organizing on an informal basis as early as the previous September. In May 1989 talks began on transition to a multiparty system, yielding a historic accord on September 19 that sanctioned broad-ranged participation in national elections.

In 1994 some 40 parties (out of well over 100 officially registered) competed for National Assembly seats, with 8 winning representation. In 1998, 26 offered candidates, 6 successfully; in 2002, 4 of 39 won representation; in 2006, 5 of 48.

Government Parties

Hungarian Socialist Party (*Magyar Szocialista Párt—MSzP*). The origin of the MSzP lies in the June 1948 merger of Hungary's Communist and Social Democratic parties. Known initially as the Hungarian Workers' Party (*Magyar Munkáspárt—MMP*), the merged grouping was reorganized as the Hungarian Socialist Workers' Party (*Magyar Szocialista Munkáspárt—MSzMP*) when János Kádár took over the leadership in the wake of the 1956 revolution. At an extraordinary party congress on October 6–10, 1989, the party renounced Marxism, adopted its current name, and appointed Rezsó NYERS to the newly created post of presidium president. Gyula Horn was, in turn, chosen to succeed Nyers in May 1990 and led the party to a decisive victory in the May 1994 general election with a vote share of 32.6 percent in the first round and 54.2 percent in the second.

A 1996 financial scandal involving the privatization minister, coupled with the unpopularity of austerity measures, pushed the opposition FiDeSz-MPP as well as the FKgP ahead of the MSzP in public opinion surveys. By April 1997 a dissident faction within the MSzP, called the Socialist Democratic Group, was demanding the replacement of Prime Minister Horn as chair of the party. Horn maintained that the government's economic stabilization program and the prospect of NATO and EU memberships would enable the party to repeat its 1994 victory. In December Horn declared that the party was not interested in an electoral agreement with the SzDSz, its coalition partner, for the May 1998 balloting, although it negotiated a cooperative arrangement with the MSzDP. The MSzP won 134 seats in that balloting, down 75 from its 1994 total, and was forced into opposition.

Horn resigned as party leader at the September 1998 MSzP congress and was succeeded by László

KOVÁCS, former foreign minister and leader of the MSzP's parliamentary group. In October 2000, although refusing to accept a new leadership role, Horn asserted that the party under Kovács was "too defensive." Miklós Németh, the last premier of the Communist era, also appeared to be assuming an active role in the party, having recently ended a nine-year appointment with the European Bank for Reconstruction and Development (EBRD).

A party congress in June 2001 chose a former nonparty finance minister, Péter Medgyessy, as the MSzP candidate for prime minister in the next national election. The decision paid off at the polls in April 2002, when the MSzP secured 178 seats, sufficient for it to form a governing coalition with the SzDSz (below).

Voter discontent with economic reforms, electoral losses in the June 2004 EU parliamentary polls, and the dissatisfaction of the Free Democrats all combined to undermine support for Medgyessy. At a MSzP conference in August 2004, party members voted to replace him with Ferenc Gyurcsány, a millionaire businessman who pledged to pursue a "third way" under which socialism would be "tempered" by some free-market policies. Gyurcsány was widely credited with "rescuing" the MSzP from internal strife, and the success of the MSzP/SzDSz coalition in the 2006 assembly poll was attributed to his popularity.

Leaders: Ferenc GYURCSÁNY (Prime Minister), Istvan HILLER (Party Chair), Katalin SZILI (Speaker of the National Assembly), Ildikó LENDAVI (Parliamentary Leader).

Alliance of Free Democrats (*Szabad Demokraták Szövetsége—SzDSz*). Founded in May 1988 as the Network of Free Initiatives (*Szabad Kezdeményezések Hálózata—SzKH*), the SzDSz was reorganized as a political party the following November and held its first general assembly in March 1989. It won 93 legislative seats in 1990, becoming the leading opposition party of the post-Communist era. Factional strife between "pragmatists" and "ideologues" appeared to be healed in November 1992 by the election of Iván PETÓ as party chair.

The party slipped to 69 seats in the May 1994 general election, its first-round voting share being 19.4 percent. Petó could not contain disagreements over whether the SzDSz should stay in the government coalition, a division that was aggravated by the privatization scandal of October 1996, which implicated both coalition partners. Petó offered to resign but was asked to stay on by the party's executive council. The scandal seriously damaged the party in public opinion polls, with the result that in February 1997 Petó was reelected head of the parliamentary caucus by default as more than ten others declined the leadership role. However, in April Petó resigned, despite denying any role in the scandal. He was replaced by Interior Minister Gábor Kuncze, who in November was named the party's candidate for prime minister in 1998. Kuncze resigned as party leader following the May 1998 legislative balloting, at which the SzDSz declined sharply to 24 seats.

A party congress in December 2000 elected the mayor of Budapest, Gábor Demszky, as chair over Gábor FODOR. Demszky stated that his goals included defeating the government in 2002, denying the Socialists a National Assembly majority, and preventing an alliance between the FiDeSz-MPP and the MIÉP. Immediately after the election, the party's parliamentary leader, Gábor Kuncze, resigned his post in view of Demszky's strong criticism of the deputy group. Demszky in turn resigned in June 2001 and was succeeded as chair by Kuncze.

At the 2002 National Assembly election the SzDSz won 20 seats (1 in alliance with the MSzP), all but 3 of them on a proportional basis. A formal coalition agreement with the Socialists was negotiated over the next month, and the government that took office on May 27 included four SzDSz ministers, although cabinet reorganizations later reduced that number to three. The SzDSz was instrumental in forcing the resignation of Prime Minister Medgyessy in 2004 because of fears of potential future electoral losses.

In March 2005 the SzDSz announced that it would henceforth be known as the SzDSz–Hungarian Liberal Party. However, news reports subsequently continued to refer often to the original rubric.

Leaders: Gábor KUNCZE (Chair and Parliamentary Leader), Gábor DEMSZKY (Mayor of Budapest), Bálint MAGYAR (Minister of Education).

Opposition Parties

Federation of Young Democrats–Hungarian Civic Alliance (*Fiatal Demokraták Szövetsége–Magyar Polgari Szövets*ëg—FiDeSz-MPSz). Founded in 1988, the right-wing group then styled simply as the Federation of Young Democrats (FiDeSz) ran fifth in the 1990 parliamentary balloting, winning only 22 of 378 elective seats. Six months later, however, it captured mayoralties in nine of the country's largest cities. Weakened by defections thereafter, its national representation declined further to 20 seats in May 1994. A 35-year age limit on membership was abandoned in April 1993, paving the way for merger with the Hungarian Civic Party (*Magyar Polgari Párt*—MPP) and creation of the FiDeSz-MPP. In September 1997 the parliamentary caucus of the party voted to admit 11 members of the Christian Democratic People's Party parliamentary group (see KDNP, below), which had dissolved, making the FiDeSz-MPP the largest opposition group in the parliament.

The FiDeSz-MPP competed for a number of seats in the May 1998 legislative balloting on a joint list with the Hungarian Democratic Forum (MDF, below). In addition, several FiDeSz-MPP candidates came from the Hungarian Christian Democratic Federation (MKDSz, below), an association recently formed by the former KDNP members. The FiDeSz-MPP emerged from the balloting as the leading party (148 seats) and became the senior member of the coalition cabinet subsequently formed with the MDF and the Independent Smallholders' Party (FKgP, below) under the leadership of the FiDeSz-MPP's young chair, Viktor Orbán. At a party congress in January 2000 the posts of prime minister and party chair were separated.

On September 1, 2001, the party concluded an agreement with the MDF establishing an electoral alliance for the anticipated 2002 National Assembly balloting. In January 2002, 14 Roma parties and groups also agreed to participate in the pact. Although opinion polls had anticipated an Orbán victory, the FiDeSz-MPP/MDF coalition's 188 seats (164 won by the FiDeSz-MPP) were insufficient to organize a new government after the April election.

In May 2003 the FiDeSz-MPP adopted the FiDeSz-MPSz rubric. In July centrists from FiDeSz left the party to form a new political entity, the **New Hungary Party**, which pledged to pursue more moderate policies than the FiDeSz. Meanwhile, Orbán signed an agreement on October 2, 2003, with Florian FARKAS of the Romany Party, *Lungo Drom* (see below). The agreement called for cooperation between the two parties, and FiDeSz pledged to include at least one Romany candidate on its electoral lists. In May 2004 the FiDeSz-MPSz reached an agreement with the Christian Democratic People's Party (KDNP, below) to run joint candidates in the 2004 EU parliamentary elections and the 2006 legislative elections.

The alliance won 164 seats (141 for the FiDeSz-MPSz) in the 2006 assembly balloting, the poll having been widely perceived as a battle for national supremacy between Prime Minister Gyurcsány and Orbán, who campaigned on a populist platform calling for tax cuts and increased government spending. Orbán offered to resign as leader of the FiDeSz-MPSz after the legislative defeat, but a party congress in May reelected him.

Leaders: Viktor ORBÁN (Party President and Former Prime Minister), László KÖVÉR (Chair of the Party), Tibor NAVRACSICS (Parliamentary Leader).

Christian Democratic People's Party (*Kereszténydemokrata Néppárt*—KDNP). A right-of-center grouping, the KDNP claims to be a revival of the Popular Democratic Party, the leading opposition formation in the immediate post–World War II period. The party won 21 assembly seats in 1990 and 22 in May 1994. In 1997 the Christian Democrats signed a cooperation pact with the Smallholders' Party in preparation for the

1998 elections. However, the leadership's alliance-building efforts went too far for the European Union of Christian Democrats, which expelled the KDNP in July for "unacceptable links" to the extremist MIÉP; dissidents within the party also blamed the party leadership for cooperating with extreme nationalists. The divisiveness culminated in the dissolution of the KDNP's parliamentary caucus in mid-1997, with 11 members deciding to work with the FiDeSz-MPP and forming the MKDSz. The fractured KDNP won no seats in the May 1998 legislative poll, having secured only 2.6 percent of the party-list votes in the first round of balloting.

After failing to secure representation in 2002 in the *Centrum* alliance (see below), the KDNP won 23 seats in the 2006 assembly poll in an alliance with the FiDeSz-MPP.

Leader: Tivadar BARTÓK (Chair), Zsolt SEMJÉN (Parliamentary Leader).

Hungarian Democratic Forum (*Magyar Demokrata Fórum*—MDF). The MDF is a right-of-center nationalist group founded in September 1988 with the avowed purpose of "building a bridge between the state and society." The group claimed 15,000 members at the opening of its first national conference at Budapest in March 1989, when it demanded that Hungary again become "an independent democratic country of European culture." It won 165 of 378 elective seats at the April 1990 election. In January 1993 Prime Minister József Antall survived a challenge to his leadership of the MDF from the party's ultranationalist right, led by István Csurka, and in early June Csurka and three parliamentary colleagues were expelled from the party (see MIÉP, below). Antall died on December 12, 1993, and was succeeded, on a temporary basis, by Sándor LEZSÁK, who was named chair of the MDF Executive Committee on February 23, 1994, after yielding the party presidency to Defense Minister Lajos FÜR on February 18. Lezsák withdrew completely from the leadership on June 1, 1994, in view of the MDF's severe decline to 37 legislative seats at the May balloting. On being confirmed as MDF chair in September, Für ruled out a merger with the KDNP "for the time being."

Following Für's decision to stand down, a party congress in March 1996 returned Lezsák to the MDF chair, a decision provoking a centrist faction to form the breakaway Hungarian Democratic People's Party (MDNP, below), leaving the rump MDF with around 20 parliamentary deputies. The MDF contested many seats in the May 1998 legislative balloting jointly with the FiDeSz-MPP, emerging with 17 seats and joining its electoral partner in the coalition government named in July.

At a party congress on January 30, 1999, Justice Minister Ibolya Dávid defeated Lezsák for the party chair. She was overwhelmingly reelected in January 2001 despite criticism from some members and from coalition partners for taking independent initiatives, including "Offer of Peace 2000" ("*Békejobb 2000*"), an effort to strengthen cooperation with the MDNP and other groups accepting "moderate, center-right, Christian Democratic or Christian values."

In April 2002 the MDF won 24 of the National Assembly seats captured by the FiDeSz-MPP/MDF electoral coalition. However, it slipped to 11 seats running on its own in 2006.

Leaders: Ibolya DÁVID (Chair), Károly HERÉNYI (Parliamentary Leader).

Other Parties

Hungarian Christian Democratic Federation (*Magyar Kereszténydemokrata Szövetség—* MKDSz). Established in 1997 by former members of the Christian Democratic People's Party (KDNP, above), the center-right MKDSz is closely allied with the MDF and the FiDeSz-MPP, which included MKDSz members on its candidate list for the 1998 and 2002 elections. It participated in the Orbán coalition government, generally in a junior capacity, although a founding member, Péter Harrach, headed the ministry of family protection and social affairs, and another member, Lászlo NÓGRÁDI, briefly served as minister of transport and water management in 2000.

Leaders: Lászlo SURJÁN, Péter HARRACH, János LATORCAI.

Center Party (*Centrum Párt*). The Center Party was formed in November 2001 as an alliance of the KDNP (above), the two parties listed directly below, and the Third Side for Hungary (*Harmadik Oldal Magyarországért Egyesület*—HOM), a nonpartisan civic forum that had been organized in the preceding February by Mihály Kupa, at that time an independent in the National Assembly, and István GYENESEI, a county official. In founding the *Centrum*—more formally, the Center of Solidarity for Hungary (*Összefogás Magyarországért Centrum*)—the four organizations agreed to contest the 2002 general election jointly, but the alliance won only 3.9 percent of the party-list vote and no seats. The KDNP left *Centrum* to participate in an elecotal coalition with the FiDeSz-MPP in 2006, but the rump *Centrum* also presented its own candidates.

Leader: Mihály KUPA (Chair).

Green Democrats (*Zöld Demokraták—* ZD). The ZD was established as the Green Alternative (*Zöld Alternativa*—ZA) in 1993 by an assortment of ecology-oriented groups, including liberal elements of the increasingly right-wing MZP (below) who had been expelled for their views. The ZA opposed membership in NATO while championing a typical "green" agenda, including environmental protection and opposition to construction of the joint Hungarian-Slovakian dam project on the Danube. The party adopted its present name at a congress in June 2000.

Leader: György DROPPA.

Hungarian Democratic People's Party (*Magyar Demokrata Néppárt*—MDNP). The MDNP was founded in March 1996 by Iván Szabó after he had been defeated in a contest for the presidency of the MDF by Sándor Lezsák. Formerly the MDF parliamentary leader, Szabó attracted 14 other centrist MDF deputies into the new party. By October 1997 Szabó was so frustrated by lack of party discipline that he announced his resignation as chair, but he withdrew it a few days later. He warned the party against being shaped by the expectations of either the government or the opposition, advocating an alternative to both. The MDNP won no seats in the May 1998 legislative poll, having secured only 1.4 percent of the party-list votes in the first round. The party endorsed FiDeSz-MPP/MDF candidates in the second round. Szabó resigned as MDNP leader shortly after the poll, and discussions regarding cooperation and possible reunion were subsequently held by the MDNP and the MDF.

Leaders: Erzsébet PUSZTAI (Chair), Iván SZABÓ (Honorary Life Chair), Péter Ákos BOD.

Independent Smallholders' Party (*Független Kisgazda Párt*—FKgP). Advocating the return of collectivized land to former owners, the FKgP was launched in November 1989 as a revival of the party that dominated Hungary's first postwar election in 1945. The party—formally, the Independent Smallholders', Agrarian Workers' and Civic Party (*Független Kisgazda, Földmunkás és Polgári Párt*)—was subsequently deeply divided over the nature of reparations for property lost during the Communist era. Thus, in December 1989 a number of dissidents led by Imre BOROS withdrew to form the National Smallholders and Bourgeois Party (*Nemzeti Kisgazda és Polgári Párt*—NKgP), most members of which, however, rejoined the parent party in 1991. On February 21, 1992, party leader József Torgyán announced that the party was withdrawing from the government coalition because the MDF had denied it an opportunity to influence policy; the action was accompanied by the expulsion of most of the FKgP's 44 parliamentary deputies, who proceeded to reaffirm their support for the Antall administration. They subsequently announced formation of an FKgP "Historical Section" (*Történelmi Tagozat,* which evolved into the now-defunct United Smallholders' Party [*Egyesült Kisgazda Párt*—EKgP]). In the May 1994 general election the FKgP recovered to win 26 seats.

Following the MDF split in March 1996, the FKgP became the largest opposition party and stepped up its criticism of the Socialist-led government, whose members were described by Torgyán as "disgusting pseudo-liberal worms and vultures." In August Torgyán rejected a proposal by the leader of the nonparliamentary MIÉP (below) for a three-party merger that would have also embraced the KDNP (above). However, in February 1998 the FKgP reached an agreement with the KDNP for an electoral alliance in the second round of the general elections scheduled for May, with weaker candidates yielding to the stronger ones. The FKgP won 48 seats in that balloting, thereby becoming the third leading party. Its subsequent participation in the coalition government led by the FiDeSz-MPP surprised some observers who thought the latter's free-market orientation might conflict with the FKgP's stance in favor of subsidies and other protection for farmers.

In late 2000 a series of scandals allegedly involving Torgyán and other FKgP officials led to a revolt by some senior party members, including Deputy Chair Zsolt LÁNYI and floor leader László CSUCS, who in January 2001 attempted to convene a party session to oust Torgyán. They and three other members of the party's parliamentary delegation announced in January that they would henceforth sit as independents.

On February 8, 2001, Torgyán resigned as minister of agriculture as a result of a financial scandal that also involved his son, and on February 22 his acting replacement, Imre BOROS, ordered an investigation into Torgyán's financial management of the ministry. Party powers responded, unsuccessfully, in March by demanding Boros's dismissal from the government. With the party clearly divided between Torgyán loyalists and reformers, Torgyán was reelected party leader on May 5, but on the same day the FKgP parliamentary faction, meeting separately, elected Lányi as party chair. The latter group attempted to expel Torgyán four days later. A May 17 court decision ordered his reinstatement, but, in a further twist, the National Assembly Procedural Committee on May 28 determined that he should sit as an independent.

In the second half of 2001 the FKgP rupture became a collapse, and at the April 2002 election the party won only 0.8 percent of the party-list vote and no seats.

In July 2001 members of the Lányi group had formed a **Reform Smallholders' Party**

(*Reform Kisgazdapárt*—RKgP), which elected Katalin LIEBMANN as chair in September. Lányi himself established the **Hungarian Smallholders' and Civic Party** (*Magyar Kisgazda és Polgári Párt*—MKgPP) in September. Sándor CSEH and a former FKgP parliamentary leader, Attila BÁNK, led another agrarian grouping, the **Smallholders' Party–Party of the Smallholders' Federation** (*Kisgazdapárt a Kisgazda Svövetség Pártja*), into the 2002 national election. None of the smallholder formations elected any parliamentary candidates.

Leader: József TORGYÁN (Chair).

Hungarian Green Party (*Magyarországi Zóld Párt*—MZP). The MZP was organized in November 1989 and held its founding congress in June 1990. It secured less than 0.5 percent of the vote in 1990, after which its right-wing faction took on an increasingly antifeminist, homophobic, anti-Semitic character. In June 1993 remaining liberal members were expelled. The party has never achieved national representation.

Leader: Zoltán MEDVECZKI (President).

Hungarian Justice and Life Party (*Magyar Igazság és Élet Párt*—MIÉP). The extreme rightwing MIÉP was launched in June 1993 by dissidents of the then-ruling MDF after István Csurka unsuccessfully challenged József Antall for the MDF leadership in January. Conspicuously anti-Semitic, the party stated that Hungary's national revival was being thwarted by a "Jewish-Bolshevik-liberal conspiracy." By late November 1993 the MIÉP boasted 11 assembly deputies, but in the May 1994 balloting it won only 1.6 percent of the first-round vote and no seats. In October 1996 the party attracted tens of thousands of demonstrators to an antigovernment rally in Budapest, while a March 1997 rally against European integration was attended by an estimated 50,000 protesters. The MIÉP's growing influence was also apparent in the May 1998 legislative elections, in which it secured 14 seats—its first ever via the ballot box. The MIÉP was the only parliamentary party in early 1999 to oppose Hungary's accession to NATO.

The party reelected Csurka as chair at a December 2000 conference at which it also encouraged former Hungarian territories toward "a sense of nationhood" and called for formation of a national guard to "expel foreign mafias." Earlier in the year, Csurka had compared Romania's pollution of the Tisza River to genocide.

At the 2002 general election the MIÉP won only 4.4 percent of the list vote, below the threshold for proportional National Assembly seats.

In March 2004 Ernoe ROZGONYI tried to oust Csurka from his leadership position. When this effort failed, Rozgonyi launched a new political party, the **Hungarian National Front** (MNF). The new right-wing party opposed EU membership and Hungarian support for the U.S. intervention in Iraq. The MIÉP contested the 2006 assembly balloting in a **Third Way** coalition with another far-right grouping called the **Movement for a Better Hungary** (*Jobbik Magyarországért Mozgalom*) led by David KOVACS.

Leader: István CSURKA (Chair).

Hungarian Social Democratic Party (*Magyarországi Szociáldemokrata Párt*—MSzDP). Founded in January 1989, the MSzDP was a revival of the party that was forced to merge with Hungary's Communist Party in 1948. During a congress in October 1989, the party split into "historic" and "renewal" wings, but they reunited in October 1993. The MSzDP secured less than 1 percent of the first-round party-list vote in the May 1994 general election. For the 1998 poll it cooperated with the MSzP and, in a few cases, the MP, but it again secured no seats. In 2002 it ran four unsuccessful candidates in conjunction with the MSzP.

Leader: László KAPOLYI (Chair).

New Left Party (*Új Baloldali Párt*). Often referred to simply as the New Left (*Új Baloldal*), the party was formed prior to the 2002 general election as an alliance of eight small parties and other groups. Social democratic in orientation, the alliance had little impact at the polls.

Leaders: László SCHILLER (Chair), Mátyás SZÜROS.

Cabinet

As of September 1, 2006

Prime Minister	Ferenc Gyurcsány (MSzP)

Ministers

Agriculture and Regional Development	József Gráf (MSzP)
Cultural and Education	István Hiller (MSzP)
Defense	Imre Szekeres (MSzP)
Economy and Transport	János Kóka (SzDSz)
Environment and Water Management	Miklós Persányi (SzDSz)
Finance	János Veres (MSzP)
Foreign Affairs	Kinga Gönez (MSzP) [f]
Health	Lajos Molnár (SzDSz)
Justice and Law Enforcement	József Petrétei (MSzP)
Labor and Social Affairs	Péter Kiss (MSzP)
Local Government and Regions	Mónika Lamperth (MSzP) [f]
Prime Minister's Office	György Szilvásy (MSzP)

[f] = female

Workers' Party (*Munkáspárt*—MP). Following the October 1989 party congress of the then-ruling Hungarian Socialist Workers' Party (MSzMP), a group of hard-line Communists who were opposed to formation of the MSzP announced the launching of a János Kádár Society (*Kádár János Baráti Társaság*) as the "only legal heir" to the parent party. Prior to the 1990 balloting the group reappropriated the MSzMP name, but it succeeded in winning only 3.7 percent of the vote. It adopted its present name in 1992.

Improving on its 1994 performance, in the May 1998 poll the MP received 4.1 percent of the first-round party-list votes, but it again failed to win any seats. Gyula Thürmer was reelected chair at the party's 18th congress in February 1999. In April 2002 the party won 2.8 percent of the party-list vote and then threw its support behind the MSzP in the second round.

Leaders: Gyula THÜRMER (Chair); János VAJDA, Éva SZÖLLÓSINÉ FITOS, Attila VAJNAI (Vice Chairs).

Hungarian Welfare Alliance (*Magyar Népjóléti Szövetség*—MNSz). The extreme-right MNSz was formed in 1994 by Albert SZABÓ after a Hungarian court had ordered the dissolution of his previous grouping, the World National Party for People's Power (*Világnemzeti Nepuralmista Párt*—VNP). Szabó, often described as a neo-Nazi, was convicted in 1998 for "inciting hatred against a community" in connection with an anti-Jewish speech in 1996. Despite the opposition of Jewish groups, the MNSz was permitted to present candidates for the 1998 legislative balloting, the party campaigning in opposition to NATO membership and in favor of the "recapture" of former Hungarian territory. Szabó left Hungary in 1999, and the party was dissolved in December 2000.

Roma Organizations

A large number of Roma (Gypsy) parties and civic organizations have been established in the post-Communist era. Few, however, have more than a local or regional following. The larger groups include the **Lungo Drom Alliance**, led by Flórián FARKAS; the **Hungarian Gypsies' Peace Party**, led by Aladar HORVÁTH, who also chairs the Roma Civil Rights Foundation; the **Hungarian Roma Parlament**; and the **Brotherhood Independent Gypsy Organization** (*Phralipe Független Cigány Szervezet*).

On April 9, 1995, the Roma elected a 53-member National Autonomous Authority of the Romany Minority (*Országos Cigány Kisebbségi Önkormányzat*—OCKÖ; also translated as the National Gypsy Minority Self-Government), the first such officially sanctioned advisory body in Eastern Europe. All of the seats were won by the *Lungo Drom*, as they also were at the election held January 23, 1999.

Legislature

The Hungarian **National Assembly** (*Országgyülés*) is a unicameral body consisting of 386 elective deputies (including 8 seats reserved for ethnic minority representation), of whom 210 are returned from regional and national lists on a proportional basis and 176 from single-member constituencies on a majoritarian basis. Following two-stage balloting on April 9 and 23, 2006, the party distribution was as follows: the Hungarian Socialist Party (MSzP), 190 (4 of those seats were won in a coalition with the SzDSz); the electoral alliance of the Federation of Young Democrats–Hungarian Civic Party (FiDeSz-MPP) and the Christian Democratic People's Party (KDNP), 164 (FiDeSz-MPP, 141; KDNP, 23); the Alliance of Free Democrats (SzDSz), 20 (2 of those seats were won in a coalition with the FiDeSz-MPP); the Hungarian Democratic Forum, 11; independent, 1.

Speaker: Katalin SZILI.

Communications

The formerly pervasive censorship was relaxed in 1988, and in June 1992 a 1974 decree authorizing government supervision of radio and television was declared unconstitutional. The Socialist-led government elected in May 1994 pledged itself to "the legal independence of the national public media from the given government, political powers, and power relations." More recently, the Orbán government has been widely criticized by the opposition and various international organizations, including the Office of the UN High Commissioner for Human Rights and the EU, for its apparent efforts to control broadcasting and print media. Its actions have included naming only progovernment nominees to television and radio boards, the ostensible justification being the failure of the opposition parties to agree on their share of nominees. In April 2000 the sale of the country's oldest newspaper, the independent *Magyar Nemzet*, to a progovernment publisher (who proceeded to merge it with the right-wing *Napi Magyarország*) for some $3,700 also raised questions about the government's commitment to press freedom.

Press

The major Budapest papers circulate nationally, but there are also nearly two dozen provincial dailies, all with circulations under 100,000. The following are issued daily at Budapest, unless otherwise noted: *Népszabadság* (People's Freedom, 316,000), former ruling party organ, now German-owned independent; *Metro* (217,000); *Népszava* (Voice of the People, 120,000), organ of the Trades Union Council; *Mai Nap* (Today, 115,000); *Kurír* (Courier, 80,000), founded in 1990; *Magyar Hirlap* (Hungarian Journal, 75,000), British-owned; *Magya Nemzet* (Hungarian Nation, 70,000), progovernment; *Esti Hirlap* (Evening Journal, 70,000), British-owned.

News Agencies

The state-owned Hungarian News Agency (*Magyar Távirati Iroda*—MTI) is the domestic facility; the Associated Press, *Xinhua*, and many of the major European bureaus have offices in Budapest.

Broadcasting and Computing

Domestic service is dominated by *Magyar Rádió*, which also transmits abroad in seven languages, and *Magyar Televízió*, which operates two terrestrial channels. In addition, several commercial television (cable and satellite) channels are operational, together with a number of commercial radio stations. In July 1997 two Western-led consortia received television licenses and ended a 40-year state monopoly when they began broadcasting in October. There were approximately 4.2 million television receivers and 1.1 million personal computers serving 1.6 million Internet users in 2003.

Intergovernmental Representation

Ambassador to the U.S.
Andras SIMONYI

U.S. Ambassador to Hungary
George H. WALKER

Permanent Representative to the UN
Gábor BRÓDI

IGO Memberships (Non-UN)
BIS, CEI, CERN, CEUR, EBRD, EIB, EU, Eurocontrol, IEA, Interpol, IOM, NATO, OECD, OSCE, PCA, *WEU*, WCO, WTO

ICELAND

REPUBLIC OF ICELAND

Lyðveldið Ísland

The Country

The westernmost nation of Europe, Iceland lies in the North Atlantic Ocean just below the Arctic Circle. Although one-eighth of the land surface is glacier, the warm Gulf Stream assures a relatively moderate climate and provides the country's richest resource in the fish that are found in its territorial waters. (It has been estimated that Iceland accounts for 3–5 percent of the world's seafood.) The population is quite homogeneous, the preponderant majority being of Icelandic descent. More than 90 percent of the population adheres to the official Evangelical Lutheran Church, although other faiths are permitted. Approximately 80 percent of adult women work outside the home, mainly in clerical and service sectors. The four-term presidency of Vigdís FINNBOGADÓTTIR (1982–1996) yielded a significant increase in female political representation, with 30 percent of the parliamentary deputies elected in 2003 being women.

Although fishing and fish processing employ only about 9 percent of the labor force, marine products typically account for nearly three-fourths of Iceland's export trade; other leading activities include dairy farming and sheep raising. Recent development efforts have focused on exploiting the country's considerable hydroelectric and geothermal energy supply; thus, aluminum smelting has become an increasingly significant export industry. Foreign investors have been successfully pursued for energy production and smelting, currently estimated to account for about 35 percent of GDP. High-tech industry is also of growing importance.

The European Union (EU), led by the United Kingdom, is the principal export market.

Numerous devaluations of the króna beginning in 1981, chronic inflation that peaked at 86 percent in 1983, a foreign debt amounting to nearly half of the GNP, and decline of the fishing industry due to high costs and depleting stocks contributed to economic adversity through the end of the decade. More efficient exploitation of maritime resources and enhanced domestic industrial capacity yielded some improvements in the early 1990s, with inflation falling to 4 percent in 1993. After stagnating in 1992–1993 and again in 1995 the economy expanded by an annual average of nearly 5 percent in 1996–2000 and by 4 percent in 2000. After a

brief recession in 2002, growth of more than 4 percent was reported in 2003, while unemployment remained at less than 3 percent. Meanwhile, Icelanders continue to enjoy one of the top per capita gross national incomes in the world (estimated at nearly $28,000 in 2002, it had jumped to $38,620 by 2004). In April 2006, some analysts were expressing concern that the boom could be over and a recession was around the corner (see Current issues, below).

Government and Politics

Political Background

Settled by disaffected Norsemen in the last quarter of the ninth century, Iceland flourished as an independent republic and convened its first parliament (Althing) in 930. However, it came under Norwegian rule in 1262 and in 1381 became (along with other Scandinavian countries) a Danish dominion, stagnating for 500 years under neglect, natural calamities, and rigid colonial controls. The island achieved limited home rule in 1874 under the leadership of Jón SIGURDSSON and in 1918 became an internally self-governing state united with Denmark under a common king. Iceland's strategic position in World War II resulted in British occupation after the fall of Denmark in 1940, with military control being transferred to American forces when the United States entered the war in 1941. Full independence was achieved on June 17, 1944.

Coalition government has dominated Icelandic politics, there having been few single-party governments in the nation's history. A significant change in the postwar era was the defeat of a 12-year centrist coalition of the Independence Party and the Social Democratic Party in 1971. The election of June 1974 resulted in a coalition involving the Independence Party (IP) and the Progressive Party (PP), while that of June 1978 yielded a center-left government of the PP, Social Democratic Party (SDP), and the People's Alliance (PA). The latter government fell in October 1979 and, in the wake of an inconclusive legislative election in December, was replaced by a minority SDP administration that was in turn succeeded in February 1980 by a group of IP deputies led by Gunnar THORODDSEN in coalition with the PA and the PP. On June 29 Vigdís Finnbogadóttir, director of the Reykjavík Theatre since 1972, became the world's first popularly elected female head of state when she defeated three other candidates seeking to succeed Kristján ELDJÁRN, who had declined to seek a fourth term.

In March 1983 Prime Minister Thoroddsen requested dissolution of the Althing and announced that he would not be a candidate for reelection. After another inconclusive poll in April, each of the three major party leaders failed in efforts to form a viable coalition. With the president having threatened to name a nonparty administration, Steingrímur HERMANNSSON of the PP finally succeeded, in May, in organizing a cabinet of his own and IP members.

At the election of April 1987, which was marked by an IP loss of five seats and a doubling (to six) of representation by the feminist Women's Alliance (WA), the coalition fell one seat short of a majority, with the prime minister moving into caretaker status until installation in July of the IP's Thorsteinn PÁLSSON as head of an administration that included PP and SDP representatives. Pálsson resigned in September 1988, with Hermannsson returning as head of a new government that included the SDP and the PA; the coalition's marginal legislative strength was significantly enhanced by addition of the recently organized Citizens' Party in September 1989.

Backed by all of the major parties, President Finnbogadóttir was elected to a third four-year term in June 1988. In the first Icelandic challenge to a sitting head of state, Sigrún THORSTEINSDÓTTIR of the small Humanist Party obtained only 5.3 percent of the popular vote.

At the election of April 20, 1991, Independence parliamentary representation rose from 18 to 26, largely at the expense of the Citizens' Party, all of whose seats were lost. On April 30 Davið ODDSSON, who had succeeded Pálsson as IP leader on March 10, was sworn in as head of a bipartisan administration that included the SDP.

Political Status: Independent republic established June 17, 1944; under democratic parliamentary system.

Area: 39,768 sq. mi. (103,000 sq. km.).

Population: 275,264 (1998C); 299,000 (2005E).

Major Urban Center (2005E): REYKJAVÍK (114,000).

Official Language: Icelandic.

Monetary Unit: Króna (official rate July 1, 2006: 76.01 krónur = $1US).

President: Dr. Ólafur Ragnar GRÍMSSON (previously People's Alliance); elected on June 29, 1996, and inaugurated on August 1 for a four-year term, succeeding Vigdís FINNBOGADÓTTIR (nonparty); term extended for an additional four years when no potential opponent met the May 19, 2000, deadline for filing the required number of nominating signatures; reelected on June 26, 2004, and inaugurated for a third four-year term on August 1.

Prime Minister: Geir HAARDE (Independence Party), sworn in on June 15, 2006, to succeed Halldór ÁSGRÍMSSON (Progressive Party), who stepped down after his party's poor showing in the May 27 local elections.

An ongoing austerity program, rising unemployment, and two devaluations of the króna reduced the government's standing in the early 1990s, while the Social Democrats experienced internal divisions that led to a split in September 1994 (see Political Parties, below). A modest economic upturn in 1994 yielded a narrow 32–31 majority for the coalition parties in legislative balloting on April 8, 1995, although the SDP lost many votes to the new Awakening of the Nation list headed by its former deputy chair. Moves to reconstitute the existing coalition proved abortive, the result being a partnership under Oddsson of the IP and PP, which commanded a comfortable majority of 40 seats.

At the opening of the new Althing on October 1, 1995, President Finnbogadóttir announced that she would not seek reelection when her fourth four-year term expired. In popular balloting on June 29, 1996, the former finance minister and former leader of the leftist PA, Ólafur Ragnar GRÍMSSON, defeated four other candidates, winning 40.9 percent of the vote.

In mid-1998 the PA, SDP, and WA agreed to establish an electoral coalition in an effort to unseat Prime Minister Oddsson's government. The resultant Unified Left (The Alliance) failed to make any inroads, however, and Oddsson was returned for a third term at the election of May 8, 1999. A year later, President Grímsson's term was extended for an additional four years when no potential challenger met the nomination deadline. The IP/PP coalition remained in power following the legislative balloting of May 10, 2003, with Oddsson retaining the prime ministership after agreeing to turn the post over to Halldór ÁSGRÍMSSON of the PP partway through his anticipated four-year term. (Ásgrímsson was inaugurated as prime minister on September 15, 2004.) Meanwhile, Grímsson won a third presidential term with 86 percent of the vote on June 26, 2004.

When his party received only 12 percent of the vote in the local elections held on May 27, 2006, Ásgrímsson resigned as prime minister. He was succeeded, on June 15, 2006, by Geir HAARDE, leader of the IP, who immediately announced a cabinet reshuffle.

Constitution and Government

Iceland's constitution, adopted by referendum in 1944, vests power in a president (whose functions are mainly titular), a prime minister, a legislature, and a judiciary. The president is directly elected for a four-year term. The unicameral legislature (Althing) is currently a 63-member body also elected for four years (subject to dissolution by the president) under a proportional system. The prime minister, who performs most executive functions, is appointed by the president but is responsible to the legislature. Eight district courts occupy the lower level of the judicial system, while the Supreme Court sits at the apex. There are also special labor and impeachment courts.

The number of general electoral districts (*Kjöroemi*) has recently been reduced from eight to six, the latter being employed for the first time in the 2003 elections. The number of towns (*Kaupstaðir*) and other municipalities (*sveitarfelög*) was progressively reduced from 204 in 1990 to 104 in 2003, with further consolidation being planned.

Foreign Relations

Nordic links and membership in the North Atlantic Treaty Organization (NATO), together with an economic dependence on fishing, are the principal determinants of Icelandic foreign relations. Attempts to extend its territorial waters from 1952 to 1975 embroiled the country in disputes with a number of maritime competitors. The first "cod war" resulted from the proclamation of a 12-mile limit in 1958 and was terminated by agreements with Britain, Ireland, and West Germany in 1961; a second period of hostilities followed the proclamation of a 50-mile limit in 1973 and was ended by a temporary agreement with Britain the same year. In 1975 a third "cod war" erupted following Iceland's extension of the limit to 200 miles despite an adverse ruling in 1974 by the International Court of Justice on the 50-mile limit. The dispute led Iceland to break relations with the United Kingdom for a period of months in 1976, before reaching a compromise. Less volatile confrontations over economic zones, fishing rights, species depletion, and quotas continued to occur with various countries (Norway, Denmark, Russia) over the ensuing two decades. Subsequently, however, Iceland intensified its efforts to settle remaining fishing disputes. Most prominently, in May 1999 it joined Norway and Russia in signing an agreement regulating catches in the Barents Sea.

Traditionally opposed to maintenance of an indigenous military force, the government in 1973 announced its intention to close the U.S.-maintained NATO base at Keflavík in order "to ensure Iceland's security." The decision was reversed in August 1974 by the conservative administration, although the government requested that Icelanders be employed for nonmilitary work previously done by Americans at the base. Relations with Washington were momentarily strained in March 1985 by press reports that Pentagon contingency plans in-

cluded the movement of nuclear depth charges to the Keflavík base. Shortly thereafter, U.S. officials assured Reykjavík that no such weapons would be deployed without Icelandic approval, while in May the Althing, by unanimous vote, declared the country to be a nuclear-free zone. In January 1994 a new Icelandic-U.S. accord provided for continued U.S. use of the Keflavík base, although with fewer American warplanes stationed there (see Current issues, below, for subsequent developments).

In a move indicative of Scandinavia's historic links to the Baltic states, Iceland on August 26, 1991, became the first country to reestablish diplomatic relations with Estonia, Latvia, and Lithuania. In May 1992 it became a signatory of the European Economic Area (EEA) treaty between the European Free Trade Association (EFTA) and the European Community (EC, later the EU) states, although unlike most other EFTA members it made no effort to join the EC. In November 1992 Iceland became an associate member of the Western European Union (WEU).

The Norwegian electorate's decision in November 1994 not to follow Finland and Sweden into the EU defused the EU debate in Iceland. Those favoring membership had argued that Iceland could not afford to stay out if all four of its Nordic partners were members. However, Norway's negative decision meant that Iceland's chief Nordic competitor in fish exports would have no advantage over Iceland in the vital European market.

An agreement signed in October 1995 provided for Iceland, together with Norway, to accede (as nonvoting members) to the Schengen Accord envisaging the abolition of internal border controls between most EU states. The final details of the arrangement were approved by the EU in November 2000, with effect from March 25, 2001. The agreement enables Denmark, Finland, and Sweden, as EU members, to preserve the 40-year-old Nordic Passport Union with their two non-EU Nordic partners.

In March 1999 whaling reemerged as a foreign policy issue when the Althing voted to rescind a ten-year-old ban. Iceland withdrew from the International Whaling Commission (IWC), in 1992, and it has not signed the UN Convention on

International Trade in Endangered Species. Domestic opinion polls indicate four-to-one approval for a return to whaling, and the government has consistently maintained that limited harvesting of certain species will cause no harm and may even increase fish populations. By a very close vote, the IWC readmitted Iceland in October 2002, despite the fact that Reykjavík refused to accept the moratorium on whaling. In August 2003 Iceland permitted the killing of some 38 minke whales for "scientific purposes," prompting international protest and boycotts of the country's increasingly lucrative ecotourism industry. The following year 39 were killed. In March 2006 Greenpeace, which claims the total has now reached 100, announced it would be sending its ship MV *Arctic Sunrise* to Iceland as a part of its ongoing efforts to convince Iceland to give up whaling.

The Icelandic Crisis Response Unit (ICRU), established in 1997 as a volunteer peacekeeping unit, which successfully managed an airport in Kosovo in 2003, displayed the same ability at the airport in Kabul, Afghanistan in 2004–2005.

Current Issues

Although the IP/PP governing coalition retained a majority in the May 2003 legislative balloting, the IP suffered a significant loss in vote share and seats, prompting the postelection announcement that Prime Minister Oddsson, Europe's senior head of government, would vacate the post early in favor of the PP's Halldór Ásgrímsson. Other factors contributing to the September 2004 "transition" reportedly included Oddsson's compromised health and his indecorous dispute with President Grímsson over a proposed new media law (see Communications, below, for details). Among other things, Grimsson's veto of the bill, reportedly the first use of the office's veto power since independence, suggested to some observers that further exercise of presidential authority, strongly encoded in the constitution but rarely exercised, might be in the offing. Meanwhile, on the government's part, no formal policy changes accompanied the transfer of the prime ministership. However, analysts noted that Ásgrímsson and the PP were noticeably

"more EU-friendly" than Oddsson and the IP, suggesting that eventual EU membership for Iceland might reemerge as a possibility. Also on the international front, Washington in mid-2003 announced plans to withdraw its remaining warplanes from the Keflavík NATO base, declaring their presence in Iceland no longer necessary. However, the Icelandic government and population responded with alarm about being left "without air defenses" and about the possibility the country might eventually need to create its own military forces. Washington subsequently postponed implementation of the decision, in part, apparently, in acknowledgment of the Oddsson government's support for the U.S.-led invasion of Iraq. However, in March 2006 the United States informed Iceland that, in order to redeploy forces to areas of greater need, it had decided to withdraw most of its service members and all of its fighter jets and helicopters from the country by September. Helgi Agustsson, Iceland's ambassador to the United States, said "We are deeply disappointed over this decision."

Haldór Ásgrímsson's resignation as prime minister was seen as an indication of voters' dissatisfaction with his policy of privatization and his support for Iceland's joining the EU. New prime minister Geir Haarde, most recently the foreign minister but also a widely respected former finance minister, quickly addressed concerns that the nation's "overheated" economy was headed for a difficult adjustment. (Analysts predicted that growth might fall from about 4.5 percent in 2006 to 0–1 percent in 2007.) Among other things, Haarde halted government spending on a number of infrastructure projects and negotiated wage concessions with labor unions. He also announced he would lead the negotiations when Iceland and the United States again take up the question of Iceland's defense.

Political Parties

Government Parties

Independence Party—IP (*Sjálfstæðisflokkurinn*). Formed in 1929 by a union of conservative and liberal groups, the IP has traditionally been the strongest party and has participated in most governments since 1944. Although primarily representing commercial and fishing interests, it draws support from all strata of society and is especially strong in the urban areas. It stands for a liberal economic policy, economic stabilization, and the continued presence of NATO forces. A major split occurred in February 1980 when Vice Chair Gunnar THORODDSEN, backed by several Independence MPs, broke with the regular party leadership and formed a coalition government with the Progressive and People's Alliance parties.

The party lost 5 of its 23 seats at the election of April 1987, largely because of the defection of Albert GUMUNDSSON, who had been forced to resign as industry minister in March because of a tax scandal. Party Chair Thorsteinn Pálsson stepped down as prime minister in September 1988 because of a dispute over economic policy. In March 1991 Reykjavík mayor Davíð Oddsson succeeded Pálsson as party chair and formed a government on April 30, following an election at which the party's plurality rose from 18 to 26. The IP lost only 1 seat in the 1995 balloting, winning 37.1 percent of the vote. However, because of losses by its Social Democratic coalition partner it felt obliged to form a new center-right coalition with the PP.

Oddsson was returned to office at the election of May 1999 (the IP having won 26 Althing seats on an improved vote share of 40.7 percent) and at the May 2003 balloting (the IP having secured 22 seats on a vote share of 33.7 percent). On September 27, 2005, Oddsson stepped down from the government and relinquished his post in the party's leadership to become chair of the Board of Governors of the Icelandic Central Bank. He was replaced the next month by Geir Haarde, who in June 2006 became the new prime minister.

Leaders: Geir HAARDE (Chair of the Party and Prime Minister), Kjartan GUNNARSSON (Secretary General).

Progressive Party—PP (*Framsóknarflokkurinn*). Founded in 1916 as a representative of agrarian interests, the Progressive Party has been responsible for many social and economic reforms benefiting agriculture and the fisheries. In the past it expressed qualified support for NATO while advocating the withdrawal of military forces as soon as possible. Although the party placed second in the 1983 balloting, its chair, Steingrímur HERMANNSSON, succeeded in forming a coalition government in which six of the ten cabinet posts were allocated to the Independence Party. The PP did better than anticipated at the 1987 balloting, retaining 13 of its 14 seats, although Hermannsson was unable to form a new government. The party was awarded four ministries in the Pálsson government of July 8, with Hermannsson returning as head of a three-party coalition in September 1988. The PP went into opposition following the election of April 1991, at which its parliamentary representation was unchanged. It returned to government after the 1995 balloting, in which it advanced to 23.3 percent of the vote.

The PP saw its vote share drop to 18.4 percent at the May 1999 election, giving it 12 seats (a loss of 3), but it remained the junior partner in the governing coalition. The PP retained its 12 seats (on a 17.7 percent vote share) in the 2003 balloting. Under an agreement reached following that election, PP leader Halldór Ásgrímsson was sworn in as head of the ongoing PP/IP coalition government in September 2004.

Leaders: Jón SIGURDSSON (Chair), Halldór ÁSGRÍMSSON (Former Prime Minister and Former Chair of the Party), Sigurdor EYTHORSSON (Secretary General).

Opposition Parties

The Alliance (*Samfylkingarinnar*). The Alliance was established as a unified party on May 5, 2000, having originated prior to the May 1999 Althing election as an electoral coalition of three parties: the People's Alliance—PA (*Althýðubandalagið*), the Social Democratic Party—SDP (*Althýðuflokkurinn*), and the Women's Alliance—WA (*Kvennalistinn*). The three were frequently referred to as the Unified Left.

The PA was launched in 1956 as an electoral front of Communists and a smaller group of disaffected Social Democrats. It traditionally advocated a radical socialist domestic program and a neutralist policy in foreign affairs, including Icelandic withdrawal from NATO. Its parliamentary representation rose from eight to nine in 1991 and remained at that level following the 1995 election. Having been the party chair since 1987, Ólafur Ragnar GRÍMSSON stood down in the fall of 1995 in order to contest the June 1996 presidential election, at which he secured a comfortable victory. By then, the PA had moved to an explicitly democratic socialist orientation. Formation of the Unified Left caused a number of PA Althing members to resign from the party, arguing that it had moved too far to the center in accommodating Social Democrats.

The SDP, which dated from 1916, long advocated state ownership of large enterprises; increased social welfare benefits; and continued support for NATO forces, with eventual replacement by Icelanders when conditions permitted. At the 1987 election the party's legislative strength rose from six seats to ten, all of which were retained in 1991, when it joined in coalition with the IP. Unrest over government austerity measures yielded an unsuccessful challenge to the leadership and the formation of the breakaway Awakening of the Nation-People's Movement (*Thjóðvaki-Hreyfing Fólksins*), which was launched for the 1995 election by former SDP deputy chair and social affairs minister Jóhanna Sigurðardóttir. In the 1995 balloting the SDP won only 11.4 percent of the vote and seven seats, while the *Thjóðvaki* won 7.2 percent and four seats. The two groups subsequently reconciled, and Sigurðardóttir became a prominent leader in the Unified Left before the 1999 election.

The WA, which has also been known as the Alliance of the Women's List (*Samtök um Kvennalista*), was organized prior to the 1983 balloting, for which it presented eight candidates, seating three. Said to be the first feminist group in the world to secure such representation, it doubled its seats to six in 1987, one of which was lost in 1991. In 1995 it slipped further to three seats on a 4.9 percent vote share. Its 1996 presidential candidate, Guðrún AGNARSDÓTTIR, finished third, with 26 percent of the vote. Like the PA, the WA lost a number of members who objected to formation of the Unified Left.

In the run-up to the 1999 Althing election The Alliance called for an expansion of social services and family-oriented government policies (such as longer parental leave) while arguing that Iceland should not consider applying for EU membership for at least four years. It also proposed that the U.S. military presence in Iceland should be reduced but did not challenge continued membership in NATO. Effective unity initially proved elusive for the coalition, particularly in regard to bridging the gap between the centrist SDP and its more strongly leftist partners, and it won only 26.8 percent of the vote and 17 seats.

At its May 2000 inaugural session The Alliance announced that a former SDP leader, Össur Skarphéðinsson, had been elected chair by vote of the membership; a former PA leader, Margrét Frímannsdóttir, was named deputy chair. The Alliance increased its vote share to 31 percent and its seat total to 20 in the 2003 legislative election.

Leaders: Össur SKARPHÉÐINSSON (Chair), Margrét FRÍMANNSDÓTTIR (Deputy Chair), Jóhanna SIGURÐARDÓTTIR, Björgrin SIGURDSSON (Secretary General).

Left-Green Alliance (*Vinstrihreyfing-Grænt Frambod*—VGF). Also referenced as the Red-Green Party and the Left-Green Party, the VGF was formed in 1998 by left-leaning Althing members of the People's Alliance and the Women's Alliance who opposed joining the Unified Left. It won 9.1 percent of the vote and six Althing seats in 1999 and 8.8 percent of the vote and five seats in 2003.

Leaders: Steingrímur J. SIGFÚSSON (President), Kristín HALLDÓRSDOTTIR (Vice President).

Liberal Party (*Frjálslyndi Flokkurinn*). The Liberal Party was formed in 1998 by Sverrir Hermannson, former cabinet minister and former director of the national bank of Iceland. It supports decentralization, a free-market system, a social safety net, tax reduction and simplification, separation of church and state, and continued participation in NATO. At the May 1999 Althing election it exceeded most analysts' expectations, winning

Cabinet

As of September 1, 2006

Prime Minister	Geir Hilmar Haarde (IP)

Ministers

Agriculture	Guðni Ágústsson (PP)
Communications	Sturla Böðvarsson (IP)
Education, Science, and Culture	Thorgerður Katrín Gunnarsdóttir (IP) [f]
Environment and Nordic Co-operation	Jónína Bjartmarz (PP) [f]
Finance	Árni M. Mathiesen (IP)
Fisheries	Einer Kristinn Guofinnson (IP)
Foreign Affairs	Valgerður Sverrisdóttir (PP) [f]
Health and Social Security	Siv Friðleifsdóttir (PP) [f]
Industry and Commerce	Jón Sigurðsson (PP)
Justice and Ecclesiastical Affairs	Björn Bjarnason (IP)
Social Affairs	Magnús Stefánsson

[f] = female

two seats on a 4.2 percent vote share. The Liberals continued to improve in the 2003 legislative balloting, securing 7.4 percent of the vote and four seats. (In May 2005 Gunnar Orn Orlygsson left the Liberal Party to join the Conservative Party and support the government. Therefore, since then the Liberal Party has three MPs instead of four.)

Leader: Sverrir HERMANNSON.

Legislature

Iceland's parliament, the **Althing** (*Alingi*), consists of 63 members elected for four-year terms by a proportional system. At the election of May 10, 2003, the Independence Party won 22 seats; The Alliance, 20; the Progressive Party, 12; the Left-Green Alliance, 5; and the Liberal Party, 4.

President: Sólveig PETURSDOTTIR.

Communications

Press

The following are published daily in Reykjavík: *Fréttabladid* (The Newspaper, 80,000), indepen-

dent; *Morgunbladið* (Morning News, 50,000), independent; DV (*Dagblaðið-Visir*, 40,000), independent; and *Dagur-Timinn* (Day-Times, 14,000), Progressive Party organ. Fréttabladid and DV are owned by the Northern Lights groups, which was recently formed by the Baugur Company, a major retailer in Iceland and the United Kingdom. Northern Lights also owns several major radio and television stations. In 2004 the legislature approved a bill sponsored by the Oddsson administration that would have barred companies from simultaneously owning newspapers and broadcasting stations and also severely limited the percentage of a broadcasting company that could be owned by a company enjoying dominance in another economic sector. However, the bill, which would have forced the breakup of Northern Lights (headed by Jon Asgeir JOHANNESSON, a political opponent of Oddsson's), was vetoed by President Grímsson. Subsequently, further consideration of the matter was postponed until after the 2007 legislative balloting.

News Agencies

Agence France-Presse and United Press International have offices in the capital.

Broadcasting and Computing

The Icelandic State Broadcasting Service (*Ríkisútvarpið*) operates numerous radio transmitting and relay stations; national TV service is also provided through its television division (*Ríkisútvarpið-Sjónvarp*). A number of other radio and television broadcasters transmit less widely. In addition, the U.S. Navy broadcasts from the NATO base at Keflavík. There were approximately 110,000 television receivers and 130,000 personal computers serving 195,000 Internet users in 2003.

Intergovernmental Representation

Ambassador to the U.S.
Helgi AGUSTSSON

U.S. Ambassador to Iceland
Carol van VOORST

Permanent Representative to the UN
Hjálmar W. HANNESSON

IGO Memberships (Non-UN)
AC, BIS, CBSS, CEUR, EBRD, EFTA, Interpol, NATO, NC, NIB, OECD, OSCE, PCA, WCO, *WEU*, WTO

IRELAND

REPUBLIC OF IRELAND

Éire

The Country

The present-day Irish Republic, encompassing 26 of Ireland's 32 historic counties, occupies all but the northeastern quarter of the Atlantic island lying 50 to 100 miles west of Great Britain. Animated by a powerful sense of national identity, the population is approximately 95 percent Roman Catholic and retains a strong sense of identification with the Catholic minority in Northern Ireland. However, a constitutional provision according a privileged position to the church was repealed by public referendum in 1972. In 1998 women constituted 34 percent of the paid labor force, concentrated in the clerical and service sectors; female participation in government, traditionally minimal, currently includes the largely ceremonial president, the deputy prime minister, two other cabinet ministers, and about 14 percent of parliamentary representatives.

Historically dependent on farming and animal husbandry, Ireland's economy continues to include a viable agricultural sector, which accounts for 4–5 percent of GNP, 7 percent of exports, and 10 percent of employment. Most farm activity centers on cattle raising and dairying; wheat, barley, sugar beets, and potatoes rank among the leading crops. The industrial sector now contributes about 36 percent of GNP, employs 29 percent of the workforce, and provides roughly 90 percent of export earnings. Exported manufactures include chemicals, computers and electrical machinery, clothing, and textiles as well as beverages and processed foods. Tourism is another significant source of foreign exchange. Leading trading partners include the United Kingdom, the United States, and Germany.

Ireland has been a substantial net financial beneficiary of the European Community (EC, subsequently the European Union—EU) since it became a member in 1973. At the same time, an Industrial Development Authority has had considerable success in attracting foreign investment that helped to generate economic growth averaging 3 percent a year through the 1980s and also in improving the trade balance. During the 1990s Ireland experienced an economic surge, with GDP growth per annum through 1997 averaging 6.5 percent, by far the highest in the EU. In the second half of the decade foreign investment poured into the country, and the high-tech sector, most notably the computer industry, flourished, earning Ireland's

Political Status: Independent state since 1921; under republican constitution effective December 29, 1937.

Area: 27,136 sq. mi. (70,283 sq. km.).

Population: 3,917,203 (2002C); 4,102,000 (2005E).

Major Urban Centers (2005E): DUBLIN (503,000), Cork (121,000), Galway (71,000), Limerick (55,000).

Official Languages: Irish (Gaelic), English.

Monetary Unit: Euro (market rate July 1, 2006: 1 euro = $1.28US).

President (*Uachtarán na hÉireann*): Mary Patricia McALEESE (*Fianna Fáil*); elected on October 30, 1997, and inaugurated for a seven-year term on November 11, succeeding Mary ROBINSON (nonparty); reelected without opposition on October 1, 2004, and sworn in for a second seven-year term on November 11.

Prime Minister (*Taoiseach*): Bartholomew (Bertie) Patrick AHERN (*Fianna Fáil*); nominated by the president, confirmed by the *Dáil*, and sworn in for a five-year term on June 26, 1997, following the election of June 6, succeeding John BRUTON (*Fine Gael*); reappointed for another five-year term on June 6, 2002, following the election of May 17.

economy the label "Celtic Tiger." Reversing a decades-old pattern, immigration began outpacing emigration, with much of the influx being returnees.

GDP growth for 1998 exceeded 8 percent, and Ireland was well positioned to meet the criteria for entry into the European Economic and Monetary Union (EMU) in 1999. In the latter year economic expansion again reached 8 percent. By July 2000, however, some analysts were expressing concern about an annualized inflation rate of 6.2 percent—more than double the average for the 11-country euro zone—which was being fueled by rising wages and consumer demand, labor shortages, low interest rates, a housing boom, and expanding private-sector credit. GDP growth in 2000 remained the EU's highest at about 9 percent, en-

abling the government to propose both substantial spending increases and tax cuts in its 2001 budget. The budget quickly drew a reprimand from the EU, however, because of what were characterized as its inflationary tendencies. For 2000, inflation had again ticked upward, to 7 percent, but it moderated to 4.7 percent in 2002. GDP growth remained strong (6.9 percent) in 2002, although increased government spending produced a deficit after several years of surpluses. One contributor to the additional spending was a major decentralization initiative designed to ease congestion in Dublin by relocating government offices.

The Irish economy continued to demonstrate strength in 2005 and early 2006. Real GDP increased by 4.7 percent in 2005, according to the International Monetary Fund (IMF), with a similar pace projected for 2006. Employment increased by more than 4 percent in 2005, with inward migration playing a significant role. In December 2005, Minister for Finance Brian Cowen introduced a budget for 2006 that promised sustained GDP growth of between 4.5 and 5 percent. The budget also projected revenue of 44.3 billion euros and expenditures of 45.4 billion euros, with the deficit of 1.1 billion euros representing 0.6 percent of GDP. The inflation rate for the year was predicted to run at 2.7 percent. Cowen also revealed plans for reduced taxes on low- and middle-income earners, accompanied by new restrictions on tax loopholes benefiting the wealthy. As of April 2006, IMF assessments of Ireland's economic health praised the country's low unemployment, consistently high growth rate, and fiscal balance.

Government and Politics

Political Background

Ireland's struggle to maintain national identity and independence dates from the beginning of its conquest by England in the early Middle Ages. Ruled as a separate kingdom under the British Crown and, after 1800, as an integral part of the United Kingdom, Ireland gave birth to a powerful revolutionary movement whose adherents first proclaimed the Republic of Ireland during the Easter Week insurrection of 1916 and, despite initial failure, reaffirmed it in 1919. A measure of national independence was accorded by Great Britain through a treaty of December 1921. Under its terms, the 26 counties of Southern Ireland were granted dominion status, the six Protestant-majority counties of Northern Ireland electing to remain within the United Kingdom. The partition was regarded as provisional by the Irish Republic, which until 1998 remained formally committed to incorporation of the northern counties into a unified Irish nation. Under the historic multiparty Good Friday Agreement of April 10, 1998, however, the Irish government acknowledged, as stated in the accompanying British-Irish Agreement, "the legitimacy of whatever choice is freely exercised by a majority of the people of Northern Ireland with regard to its status, whether they prefer to continue to support the Union with Great Britain or a sovereign united Ireland."

Officially known as the Irish Free State from 1922 to 1937, Southern Ireland became the Irish Republic, or simply Ireland (*Éire*), with the entry into force of its present constitution on December 29, 1937. The era's dominant leader was Éamon DE VALÉRA of the Republican (*Fianna Fáil*) party, who served as prime minister for most of the period between 1932 and 1959 and was then president until 1973. Ireland's association with the British Commonwealth was gradually attenuated and finally terminated on April 18, 1949. For most of the next decade governmental responsibility tended to alternate between the *Fianna Fáil* and United Ireland (*Fine Gael*) parties, while from 1957 to 1973 the former ruled under the successive prime ministries of De Valéra (1957–1959), Sean F. LEMASS (1959–1966), and John M. LYNCH (1966–1973).

After calling a surprise election in February 1973, *Fianna Fáil* failed to retain its majority, and a coalition government of the *Fine Gael* and Labour parties was installed under the leadership of Liam COSGRAVE. Lynch returned as prime minister following a *Fianna Fáil* victory in an election held June 16, 1977, but on December 5, 1979, announced his intention to resign and six

days later was succeeded by Charles J. HAUGHEY. Haughey's investiture was widely regarded as the most remarkable comeback in Irish political history: Although ultimately acquitted, he had been dismissed as Lynch's finance minister in 1970 and tried on charges of conspiring to use government funds to smuggle arms to the outlawed Irish Republican Army (IRA).

At the election of June 11, 1981, *Fine Gael* gained 21 lower-house seats over its 1977 total, and on June 30 Dr. Garret FITZGERALD, by a three-vote margin, succeeded in forming a government in coalition with Labour. The new administration quickly increased taxes, announced spending cuts, and permitted higher interest rates, but on January 27, 1982, its first full budget was defeated by a single vote. Following a new election on February 8, the Haughey-led *Fianna Fáil,* backed by three Workers' Party deputies and two independents, returned to office on March 9. Eight months later, unable to reverse economic decline and buffeted by a series of minor scandals within his official family, Haughey lost a no-confidence motion by two votes. The balance of power again shifted at an election on November 24, yielding the installation of another *Fine Gael*-Labour government under FitzGerald on December 14, 1982.

On October 22, 1986, FitzGerald survived a no-confidence motion by one vote, but he lost his parliamentary majority on December 10 with the resignation of a *Fine Gael* conservative. On January 21, 1987, the four-year-old coalition government fell over the issue of budget cuts, which Labour felt would impinge inequitably on welfare programs. At the ensuing general election of February 17 *Fianna Fáil* fell only three seats short of a majority, with a third Haughey administration being approved on March 10 by the barest possible margin on a vote of 83–82, with one abstention. On the basis of public opinion polls that suggested increased support for his administration, Haughey called an early election on June 15, 1989, but *Fianna Fáil*'s net loss of four parliamentary seats obliged him to join with the Progressive Democrats (PD), which had been formed by *Fianna Fáil* dissidents in 1985. On July 12 the *Fianna Fáil*-PD coalition won *Dáil* approval in an 84–79 vote, with Haughey returning as prime minister.

On December 3, 1990, Mary ROBINSON, a left-leaning lawyer who had long campaigned for birth control and legalized divorce, was inaugurated as president, after having defeated *Fianna Fáil* candidate Brian LENIHAN in runoff balloting on November 9. Lenihan, previously an odds-on favorite, had been dismissed from the Haughey administration in late October after confessing that he had lied in denying reports that in 1982 he had urged President Patrick J. HILLERY to act unconstitutionally in appointing a *Fianna Fáil* government without calling for a validating election.

In November 1991 Prime Minister Haughey, besieged by the alleged improprieties of associates, overcame an intraparty vote of no-confidence led by his finance minister, Albert REYNOLDS, who was promptly sacked. However, on January 30, 1992, after being further buffeted by the revival of a 1982 wiretapping scandal, Haughey submitted his resignation, with Reynolds, on February 11, assuming the office that had eluded him three months before. Although *Fianna Fáil* was obliged to retain the PD as its coalition partner, eight former ministers were swept away in an abrupt conclusion to the Haughey era.

On June 18, 1992, a referendum was held on the Maastricht Treaty on more inclusive European union, which voters approved by a 69 percent majority. In the same poll, Irish voters registered two-thirds majorities in favor of guaranteeing the right to travel to other EC states for abortion and the right to obtain information on abortion availability (enacted into law in March 1995). On a third question, however, voters opted by a similar majority against a proposed relaxation of Ireland's strict abortion proscription.

The *Fianna Fáil*-PD coalition collapsed in early November 1992 after Reynolds had accused PD leader Desmond O'MALLEY of giving "dishonest" evidence in an inquiry into fraud in the beef-exporting industry. Defeated by a Labour-proposed no-confidence motion on November 5, Reynolds was forced to call an early election on November 25 and saw his party slump to its worst postwar electoral showing. *Fine Gael* also lost ground sharply, while the Labour Party, under the charismatic leadership of Richard (Dick) SPRING, registered its best-ever result, albeit remaining third-ranked. Having spent the election campaign attacking Reynolds, Labour subsequently found that the new parliamentary arithmetic and the attractions of office dictated the party's first-ever coalition with *Fianna Fáil*. The new government, enjoying an unprecedented 36-seat overall majority, took office on January 12, 1993, with Reynolds continuing as prime minister, Spring becoming deputy prime minister and foreign minister, and Labour nominees being awarded five other posts.

Apparently secure in office, Reynolds was unexpectedly brought down in November 1994 after his nomination of the incumbent attorney general as High Court president drew Labour opposition because the nominee had been reluctant to authorize the extradition to the North of a Catholic priest accused of pedophile offenses. Amid great political drama, featuring accusations that Parliament had been misled, Reynolds resigned on November 17 and was replaced as *Fianna Fáil* leader by his finance minister, Bertie AHERN. However, attempts to reconstitute the previous coalition proved abortive, and on December 15 a three-party minority government was formed under the leadership of John BRUTON (*Fine Gael*) that included Labour and the small Democratic Left. The coalition commanded 82 of the *Dail's* 166 seats but could rely on the support of the Green Party deputy, whereas *Fianna Fáil* and the PD had a combined strength of only 78 seats and so would require the support of all five independents to challenge the government.

In light of the IRA's cease-fire announcement at the end of August 1994 (see Foreign relations, below), the *Dáil* voted on February 1, 1995, to revoke the 1976 Emergency Powers Act, which had enhanced special police powers in force since 1939. The retention of the original 1939 powers, on the grounds that they were needed to combat organized crime, drew strong criticism from civil liberties groups. (The 1976 powers were not reinstated when the IRA called off its cease-fire in February 1996.)

The Bruton government narrowly prevailed when it called on voters to sanction the legalization of divorce in a constitutional referendum on November 25, 1995. With *Fianna Fáil* giving only half-hearted backing to the proposed change, and with the Catholic Church exerting all its influence against, the outcome was a 50.3 percent victory for the affirmative. New statutes facilitating the division of properties in divorce took effect in February 1997.

With a scandal involving alleged payments to political figures reaching longtime *Fianna Fáil* leader Haughey, the government coalition headed by *Fine Gael* decided to call for early *Dáil* elections in 1997. However, the coalition of *Fine Gael,* Labour, and the Democratic Left failed to close a slight gap in opinion polls and lost to *Fianna Fáil* and the allied Progressive Democrats in balloting on June 6. While no party commanded an outright majority, *Fianna Fáil* won 77 seats and the Progressive Democrats 4 seats, enough to secure, with the support of a few independents, a confidence motion and to form a minority coalition government on June 26. Bertie Ahern thus became, at 45, Ireland's youngest prime minister.

On October 30, 1997, the *Fianna Fáil* candidate, Mary McALEESE, won the presidential election to succeed Robinson, who had declined to run for a second term and had stepped down in September to become the United Nations (UN) High Commissioner for Human Rights. Inaugurated on November 11, McAleese, a Catholic from Northern Ireland and professor of law at Queens University at Belfast, had trounced her four opponents with 45 percent of the votes on the first count and then received 59 percent in the runoff against the *Fine Gael* candidate, Mary BANOTTI.

On April 10, 1998, after 22 months of negotiations, the British and Irish governments won agreement on a historic multiparty peace accord for Northern Ireland (see Foreign relations, below, and the United Kingdom: Northern Ireland article). Prime Minister Ahern actively campaigned on behalf of the Belfast (Good Friday) Agreement, which received Parliament's overwhelming assent on April 22 and won the backing of 94.4 percent of republic voters (on a turnout of 55.6 percent) at a referendum on May 22. The approval constituted acceptance of constitutional changes voiding Ireland's claim to sovereignty in the North, although formal enactment of the amendments was delayed until the United Kingdom handed over devolved powers to the Northern Ireland Assembly and executive body on December 2, 1999.

At *Dáil* balloting on May 17, 2002, *Fianna Fáil* won 41.5 percent of the vote and 81 seats, while *Fine Gael* declined to 22.5 percent and 31 seats. Prime Minister Ahern was reappointed on June 6 to head another *Fianna Fáil*-PD government that included many incumbent ministers.

Prior to the 2004 presidential election, a range of parties, including *Fianna Fáil, Fine Gael,* and *Sinn Féin,* supported the incumbent President McAleese. The Green Party tried to present Éamon RYAN for the presidency, but it was unable to garner support for his candidacy. As a result, no other candidate filed to run for the presidency by the October 1 deadline, and McAleese was thus officially declared reelected on October 1.

In January 2005, McAleese, while attending ceremonies marking the 60th anniversary of the liberation of the German concentration camp Auschwitz, caused considerable controversy with the following remark: "They [the Nazis] gave to their children an irrational hatred of Jews in the same way that people in Northern Ireland transmitted to their children an irrational hatred, for example, of Catholics, in the same way that people gave to their children an outrageous and irrational hatred of those who are of different colour and all of those things." Many Protestants took offense at a perceived linking of their attitudes with those of the Nazis; others criticized McAleese for trivializing the Holocaust. McAleese promptly apologized, saying that she was deeply sorry and was devastated by the reaction caused by her comment. She called her choice of words clumsy. "I was trying to make a point about … the things that we have to do to prevent sectarianism and racism in our own time. I said that people in Northern Ireland who taught their children, for example, to hate, for example, Catholics, and I should have gone on to say, and

Protestants, because the truth of the matter is that, of course, sectarianism is a shared problem." Her apology was reported to have been seemingly well received in most quarters, although some Ulster unionists said they believed it would take time for the pain caused by her remarks to diminish.

Constitution and Government

Under Articles 2 and 3 of the Irish constitution as adopted by plebiscite on July 1, 1937, the document applied to "the whole island of Ireland," with Parliament and the government accorded jurisdiction, at least in theory, over the entire "national territory." (As a consequence, residents of Northern Ireland have long been considered citizens of the republic and, accordingly, eligible to hold office in the South.) In the referendum of May 22, 1998, however, Irish voters approved substitute texts for Articles 2 and 3, as specified by the Good Friday Agreement concluded the previous month. The new Article 2 acknowledges "the entitlement and birthright of every person born in the island of Ireland . . . to be part of the Irish nation," but the new Article 3 also recognizes "that a united Ireland shall be brought about only by peaceful means with the consent of a majority of the people, democratically expressed, in both jurisdictions in the island." In addition, Article 3 authorizes creation of shared North-South executive institutions that "may exercise powers and functions in respect of all or any part of the island."

The constitution provides for a president (*Uachtarán na hÉireann*) directly elected for a seven-year term and for a bicameral legislature (*Oireachtas*) consisting of a directly elected lower house (*Dáil*) and an indirectly chosen upper house (*Seanad*) with power to delay, but not to veto, legislation. The *Seanad* may also initiate or amend legislation, but the lower house must approve all such proposals. Presidential and *Dáil* elections are conducted under the single transferable vote system, in which voters indicate their first choices on their ballots and are invited to indicate a preference order for the other candidates. Multiple "counts," in which candidates getting lower "first-choice" vote totals are eliminated and some votes are transferred to second choices, are often required to determine final electoral outcomes. The cabinet, which is responsible to the *Dáil*, is headed by a prime minister (*Taoiseach*), who is the leader of the majority party or coalition and is appointed by the president for a five-year term on recommendation of the *Dáil*. The president has the power to dissolve the *Dáil* on the prime minister's advice. The judicial system is headed by the Supreme Court and includes a Court of Criminal Appeal, a High Court (called the Central Criminal Court for criminal cases), and circuit and district courts. Judges are appointed by the president with the advice of the government and may be removed only by approval of both houses of the legislature.

Local government is based on 4 provinces (Connacht, Leinster, Munster, and part of Ulster), 27 counties (Tipperary counting as two for administrative purposes), and 5 county boroughs (Dublin, Cork, Galway, Limerick, and Waterford), each with elected governing bodies. Eight regional authorities have as part of their mandate coordinating EU matters.

On August 19, 1998, responding to a car-bombing in Omagh, in the North, that claimed 29 lives and injured more than 200 others, Prime Minister Ahern proposed a controversial series of "extremely draconian" antiterrorism measures that included negating the right to silence and adding penalties for withholding information about terrorist crimes. Although opponents argued that the measures would violate human rights conventions, the Parliament passed the legislation in early September. In November 1996, reacting to public fears of organized crime, voters had approved a referendum restricting the right to bail and giving police expanded authority to detain suspects.

Foreign Relations

Independent Ireland has traditionally adhered to an international policy of nonalignment, remaining neutral throughout World War II and subsequently avoiding membership in any regional security structure, in part because of a reluctance to be a military partner of Britain. It has, however, been an active participant in the UN (since 1955), the EC/EU (since 1973), and other multinational organizations. In November 1992 it became an observer member of the Western European Union (WEU), following its endorsement of a defense/security dimension to European integration under the EU's Maastricht Treaty.

Beginning in 1969, Dublin's relations with the United Kingdom were complicated by persistent violence in Ulster and terrorism committed by both the IRA and ultra-unionists. Since the late 1970s the two governments have cooperated in security matters, but aspects of the Northern Ireland problem caused frequent strains. In an effort to improve relations, in 1981 Prime Ministers FitzGerald and Thatcher agreed to establish an Anglo-Irish Inter-Governmental Conference (AIIC) to discuss a range of mutual concerns. The conference convened in January 1982 but subsequently encountered a number of obstacles, including the Haughey government's opposition to UK proposals for devolution of power to the North, its unwillingness to endorse the British position during the UK-Argentinean Falklands conflict, and renewed IRA bombings in London. Further progress was, however, registered in discussions between the two prime ministers in November 1983, leading two years later to an Anglo-Irish Agreement that was subsequently ratified by the Irish and UK parliaments. The pact established a "framework" within which Dublin would have an advisory role in the devolution of power to Northern Ireland but also acknowledged British sovereignty for as long as such status should be desired by a majority of the territory's inhabitants.

Relations between the two governments again worsened in the wake of the *Dáil's* December 1987 ratification of the 1977 European Convention on the Suppression of Terrorism, which sanctioned the extradition of individuals charged with terrorist activity. Irish public opinion had opposed the convention because of British reluctance to modify its Diplock court system, whereby suspected terrorists could be summarily tried without juries in Belfast courts. As a result, "safeguards" were attached by

the *Dáil,* including a stipulation that the Irish attorney general approve all extradition proceedings.

In April 1991 what had become a lengthy, but inconclusive, series of AIIC talks on the future of Northern Ireland were suspended in favor of a new initiative that called for negotiations between political leaders in the North and the Dublin government, followed by a renewal of talks between the British and Irish representatives. After a series of procedural delays, punctuated by a revival of sectarian violence, Irish ministers in June 1992 met with both Catholic and Protestant leaders from Northern Ireland for the first time since 1973. However, the republic's constitutional claim to the North again proved to be a crucial obstacle to progress, the talks being formally terminated in November in favor of a continuation of the AIIC process.

The advent of the *Fianna Fáil*–Labour coalition in January 1993 brought a change of tone in Dublin, which held out the prospect of Irish constitutional changes to accommodate the Northern majority. In May President Robinson became the first Irish head of state to confer with a British monarch by meeting privately with Queen Elizabeth at Buckingham Palace. Familiar strains resurfaced during President Robinson's unofficial visit to Belfast the following month, when she met and shook hands with the *Sinn Féin* leader, Gerry ADAMS. Nevertheless, renewed impetus in UK-Irish consultations culminated in the Downing Street Declaration on Northern Ireland jointly issued by Prime Ministers Major and Reynolds on December 15, 1993.

Representing a new departure in Anglo-Irish relations, the declaration aimed at a cessation of hostilities in Northern Ireland. While assuming that "the people of the island of Ireland" might wish to opt for unification, it reiterated that "it would be wrong to attempt to impose a united Ireland in the absence of the freely given consent of a majority of the people of Northern Ireland." The Irish government then exerted its influence to bring *Sinn Féin* into the negotiating framework, as envisaged in the declaration, provided that *Sinn Féin* renounce violence. The government's efforts were rewarded by an IRA cease-fire announcement on August 31, 1994, after which *Sinn Féin* leader Adams was invited to Dublin, where in October the government launched an all-Ireland Forum for Peace and Reconciliation (FPR). The publication in February 1995 of a UK-Irish "framework document" setting out the parameters for all-party talks on Northern Ireland provided further impetus to the peace process.

A semi-official visit by Britain's Prince Charles on May 31–June 1, 1995, which included meetings with both President Robinson and Prime Minister Bruton, was the first by a member of the royal family since Irish independence in 1922. Nevertheless, Dublin's efforts to expedite formal all-party talks on Northern Ireland became stalled by the UK government's insistence on prior "decommissioning" of terrorist groups' arms. U.S. President Clinton, during a visit in November to London, Northern Ireland, and Dublin, helped the parties work around this impasse with the two governments agreeing to a "twin-track" approach under which decommissioning would be dealt with separately by an international commission chaired by former U.S. senator George J. Mitchell.

Mitchell's report in January 1996 concluded that decommissioning of arms prior to talks was unachievable but called on all groups to renounce violence in favor of democratic means. While both Dublin and London accepted the Mitchell "principles," London's collateral decision to hold elections in the North for a consultative Northern Ireland Forum on Political Dialogue prior to renewed talks was seen in Dublin as responsible for the IRA's decision in February to call off the cease-fire. Nevertheless, the Bruton government supported the British position that *Sinn Féin* could not participate in formal talks without a reinstatement of the cease-fire. The resumption of IRA violence in mainland Britain enabled Dublin to extract from London a firm date of June 10 for the start of talks, in return for accepting that a preceding forum election would be held in Northern Ireland. Following the polling on May 30, Bruton and Prime Minister Major of Britain jointly opened the talks at Belfast's Stormont Castle and by June 12 had persuaded the Unionist representatives to accept former senator Mitchell as plenary chair. Thereafter, the process became bogged down in familiar procedural wrangling.

On June 25, 1997, Prime Minister Bruton and British Prime Minister Tony Blair agreed on a detailed mechanism for arms decommissioning and the need for an IRA cease-fire, which was restored on July 20, 1997, clearing the way for *Sinn Féin* to enter the broad-based peace talks held in Belfast the following September. With progress made on several issues and the cease-fire continuing to hold, newly installed Prime Minister Ahern reaffirmed that the Irish Republic would consider dropping its claim to sovereignty over Northern Ireland, if approved by Irish voters in a constitutional referendum.

In January 1998 Ireland and Britain jointly issued a document entitled "Propositions on Heads of Agreement" that provided the framework for the Good Friday Agreement of April 10. The propositions put forward "balanced constitutional change" by both governments; establishment of a directly elected Northern Ireland Assembly and a North-South ministerial council; formation of British-Irish "intergovernmental machinery"; propositions and adoption of "practical and effective measures" concerning such issues as prisoners, security, and decommissioning of arms. Conclusion of the Good Friday Agreement (for details, see the Northern Ireland article) was accompanied by a new British-Irish Agreement, which replaced the 1985 Anglo-Irish Agreement and committed both governments to carry through on the multiparty peace accord. On November 26 Tony Blair became the first UK prime minister to address the Irish Parliament, using the occasion to lobby for continuation of the peace process and for disarmament to begin.

The arms decommissioning issue remained a sticking point, however, and the Good Friday Agreement was not fully implemented until December 2, 1999. The North-South Ministerial Council held its inaugural meeting on December 13, and four days later representatives of Ireland, the United Kingdom, the Channel Islands, the Isle of Man, and the devolved governments of Northern Ireland, Scotland, and Wales convened in London for the first session of the Council of the Isles.

On the same day Prime Minister Blair hosted the first intergovernmental meeting under the British-Irish Agreement. Throughout 2000 and into 2001 Prime Minister Ahern remained actively involved in holding together the peace process in the face of IRA reluctance to begin active decommissioning. In March 2003 Ahern supported Blair's decision to postpone elections for the Northern Ireland Assembly in response to increasing violence in the North (the elections were held in November 2003). Ahern also participated in talks between the main Northern Irish political parties and the British and Irish governments in December 2003 and January 2004.

Debate on wider aspects of Irish external policy was stimulated by the publication in March 1996 of the first-ever government white paper on the subject, focusing on whether Ireland should abandon its long-standing military neutrality. Speaking in the *Dáil*, Foreign Minister Dick Spring hinted at Irish moves toward NATO and WEU involvement. However, *Fianna Fáil* spokesmen reiterated the party's traditional opposition to participation in any military organization of which Britain was a member, referring with dread to the attendant possibility that British troops would return to Irish Republic soil. Despite a concern by opponents that ratification of the June 1997 Amsterdam Treaty on greater EU integration would ultimately commit Ireland to participation in a unified military force, Irish voters approved the treaty by referendum on May 22, 1998, with 62 percent voting in favor. In 1999 the Ahern government confirmed its interest in joining NATO's Partnership for Peace, which the *Dáil* authorized by a 112–24 vote on November 9, thereby permitting Irish forces to participate in training for multilateral "peace support, search-and-rescue and humanitarian missions." In 2000 Ireland agreed to commit 1,000 troops to a new EU Rapid Reaction Force, although the government secured an agreement that its troops would be deployed only in UN-sanctioned operations.

During the prelude to the 2003 U.S.-led invasion of Iraq, the Irish government permitted U.S. planes to use Shannon airport for stopovers and refuel-

ing. Although that decision prompted several large protests, the *Dáil* in March voted 77–60 to permit continued U.S. access to the airport.

Current Issues

In a June 26, 2000, by-election in Tipperary the *Fianna Fáil* candidate captured only 23 percent of first-preference votes, and the seat was won by an independent. Most analysts interpreted the election as providing additional evidence of public dissatisfaction not only with the governing coalition but also with all the other leading parties following years of revelations about political favors and donations, tax evasion schemes, and gifts to politicians.

The climate of "sleaze" was cited by the Labour Party at the end of June 2000 when it introduced a no-confidence motion against the government. On June 30, countering the no-confidence motion, the government introduced and won a confidence motion by a vote of 84–80 on the strength of independent support. In defending his government's record, Prime Minister Ahern stated that he had no plans to call an early election and intended to serve out his current term, into 2002.

On June 8, 2001, the Ahern administration suffered a serious setback when Irish voters rejected the EU's Treaty of Nice, with 53.9 percent (of a low turnout of 35 percent) opposing further integration as well as institutional revisions needed to accommodate anticipated new members. A major voter concern appeared to be Ireland's potential loss of influence in a significantly expanded union (see the EU article). However, on October 19, 2002, voters approved the Nice treaty in a second referendum, 62.9 percent in favor and 37.1 percent opposed.

On June 11, 2003, a commission found that Ahern and many other members of Parliament had violated limits on campaign spending in the 2002 elections. However, the commission ruled that the violations were not intentional and not criminal. With the commission's report, the government began to dissolve the nine tribunals investigating corruption and set 2006 as the date for final reports.

In January 2003 the Supreme Court ruled that non-Irish parents and relatives of children born in the country did not have an automatic legal right to remain in Ireland. This ruling was followed by a referendum in June in which voters overwhelmingly endorsed a constitutional amendment that prohibited the automatic extension of citizenship to non-EU babies born in Ireland. The court ruling and subsequent constitutional amendment were supported by the government as a means to end the practice of non-EU persons using residence in Ireland as a means to gain legal status within the union.

The June 11, 2004, EU parliamentary elections handed *Fianna Fáil* its worst electoral defeat in history as *Fine Gael* defeated the ruling party for the first time. The election also marked the first time that *Sinn Féin* won a seat in the EU body. Apparently in response to its poor showing, the administration in December announced a significant increase in public spending for retired workers, people with disabilities, and other sectors of the population.

Relations between the Irish government and *Sinn Féin* and IRA deteriorated sharply in late 2004 and early 2005 in the wake of allegations that the IRA was involved in massive money-laundering operations. The government launched raids on a number of alleged IRA locations and confiscated large sums of money, while criticizing *Sinn Féin* leaders for their perceived role (denied by *Sinn Féin*) in directing IRA activity. For his part, Prime Minister Ahern, long a champion of efforts to bring die-hard nationalists "in from the cold," was also reportedly upset by the *Sinn Féin* approach in the talks in December 2004 that failed to resolve the power-sharing dispute in Northern Ireland.

Seemingly significant progress toward the goal of a peaceful Northern Ireland did occur during 2005. In July, the IRA announced that it would agree to permanently dismantle all of its weapons and allow two observers—a Catholic priest and a former president of the Methodist Church in Ireland—to witness the process. In September, the disarmament was reported to have been carried out. However, the IRA's refusal to release details concerning the operation or to allow any visual documentation of the event fed the ongoing skepti-

cism among members of Ian Paisley's Democratic Unionist Party (PUD). With the Democratic Unionists refusing to communicate with *Sinn Féin*, no resumption of negotiations regarding the sharing of power occurred. In April, UK Prime Minister Blair and Ahern gave the two sides until November 24, 2006, to form a government, declaring that if this deadline was not met they would dissolve the Northern Ireland legislature, terminate the salaries of those involved, and select other means for governance of the province.

Political Parties

Government Parties

Fianna Fáil. Founded in 1926 by Éamon de Valéra, *Fianna Fáil* ("Soldiers of Destiny") advocates the peaceful ending of partition, the promotion of social justice, and the pursuit of national self-sufficiency. It held governmental responsibility in 1932–1948, 1951–1954, 1957–1973, 1977–1981, and March–November 1982, and was then in opposition for over four years. During this period Charles Haughey survived a number of challenges to his leadership, most notably from Desmond O'Malley (see PD, below), who withdrew from the party in 1985. O'Malley, sitting as an independent, was joined by one *Fianna Fáil* representative in voting to approve the Anglo-Irish Agreement in November 1985, the remainder of the party voting in opposition. Haughey returned as prime minister after the 1987 election, but the *Fianna Fáil* legislative plurality was reduced from 81 to 77 seats at the June 1989 balloting, creating, for the first time in Irish history, a governmental impasse. Consequently, Haughey turned to the PD and on July 12 formed *Fianna Fáil*'s first coalition government.

Haughey resigned in January 1992 and was succeeded by longtime party rival Albert Reynolds. In November the party suffered its worst electoral showing since World War II, winning only 68 seats, forcing Reynolds to seek support from the Labour Party (below). The coalition collapsed with Reynolds's resignation in November 1994, with *Fianna Fáil* going into opposition while remaining the largest parliamentary party. In the subsequent election of June 1997, however, *Fianna Fáil* increased its strength to 77 seats, enough for party chief Bertie Ahern to form a minority government in coalition with the PD and a few independents. Reynolds campaigned for but lost the party's nomination for the presidency in September 1997 to Mary McAleese, who won the nationwide election the following October.

In merely the latest in a decade-long series of financial scandals, an internal party investigation into illegal political payments led an uncooperative *Fianna Fáil* MP, Liam LAWLOR, to resign his party membership in June 2000. Called before a judicial tribunal on financial corruption, Lawlor remained recalcitrant, drawing a fine of nearly $12,000 and a seven-day jail sentence in January 2001. In the 2002 legislative elections, *Fianna Fáil* won 81 seats in the *Dáil* and 30 seats in the Senate. Ahern formed a new coalition government with the PD on June 6, 2002. McAleese was reelected president, without opposition, in October 2004.

Leaders: Bertie AHERN (Prime Minister and Party Leader), Brian COWEN (Deputy Party Leader), Mary McALEESE (President of the Republic), Martin MACKIN (General Secretary).

Progressive Democrats (*Dan Páirtí Daonlathach*—PD). The PD was organized in December 1985 by former *Fianna Fáil* legislator Desmond O'Malley as an alternative to a "party system ... based on the civil war divisions of 65 years ago." Accused by critics of being a "Thatcherite," O'Malley called for fundamental tax reform, government tax cuts, and support for private enterprise. The party won 14 *Dáil* seats in 1987, 8 of which were lost in the 1989 election, after which it joined with *Fianna Fáil* in a coalition government. It withdrew in 1992, and at the resultant November legislative poll its representation rose from 6 seats to 10. O'Malley resigned as leader in October 1993 and was succeeded by the first female head of a significant Irish party. In the June 1997 elections the PD won 4 seats and joined *Fianna Fáil* in the new government. In the 2002 elections for the *Dáil,* the PD won 8 seats, and it

subsequently formed another coalition government with *Fianna Fáil.*

Leaders: Mary HARNEY (Deputy Prime Minister and Party Leader), Michael McDOWELL (Party President), John HIGGINS (General Secretary).

Opposition Parties

Fine Gael. *Fine Gael* ("Family of the Irish") was formed in September 1933 through the amalgamation of parties that had accepted the 1921 partition, led by *Cumann na nGaedheal* (the ruling party in 1923–1932). It advocates ultimate union with Northern Ireland, financial encouragement of industry, promotion of foreign investment, and full development of agriculture. Its inability to win a majority in the *Dáil* led to the formation of coalition governments with the Labour Party in 1948–1951, 1954–1957, 1973–1977, 1981–1982, and, under the premiership of Garret FitzGerald, 1982–1987. *Fine Gael*'s slump from 70 to 51 seats in the February 1987 election yielded the surprise resignation of FitzGerald, with former justice minister Alan DUKES being named opposition leader.

At the June 1989 election the party increased its parliamentary representation to 55, remaining in opposition. In November 1990 Dukes resigned and was replaced by his more rightist deputy, John Bruton. At the November 1992 balloting *Fine Gael*'s legislative representation fell to 45 seats, its poorest showing since 1948. Nevertheless, the political crisis of late 1994 enabled Bruton to form a three-party coalition government with Labour and the Democratic Left (see under Labour Party, below). In the June 1997 elections *Fine Gael* increased its strength to 54 seats, but the poor showing of Labour forced *Fine Gael* to return to opposition.

In mid-July 2000 Bruton proposed that *Fine Gael* and Labour consider a pre-election pact before the next general election, but a Labour spokesman responded that his party preferred to campaign on its own platform. On January 31, 2001, Bruton lost a confidence vote among the party's MPs, and on February 9 Michael NOONAN, a former minister of justice, succeeded him as leader of the opposition. Noonan in turn resigned after the *Fine Gael*'s poor performance in the 2002 balloting for the House of Representatives (31 seats on a 22.5 percent vote share); he was succeeded by Enda Kenny, a former minister of tourism and trade.

Leaders: Enda KENNY (Leader of the Opposition), John BRUTON (former Prime Minister), Richard BRUTON (Deputy Leader), Tom HAYES (Parliamentary Chair).

Labour Party (*Páirtí Lucht Oibre*). Originating in 1912 as an adjunct of the Trades Union Congress (TUC), the Labour Party became a separate entity in 1930. It has traditionally advocated far-reaching social security and medical services, public ownership of many industries and services, better working conditions and increased participation of workers in management, expanded agricultural production, protection of the home market, and cooperation and ultimate union with Northern Ireland.

In October 1982 its leader in Parliament, Michael O'LEARY, resigned from the party following its rejection of his proposal that Labour commit itself to formation of a coalition government with *Fine Gael* should the Haughey government fall. His successor, Richard (Dick) Spring, promptly negotiated an interparty agreement that permitted a *Fine Gael*–Labour coalition to assume office on December 14. The coalition collapsed because of Labour's objection to budget cuts advanced by Prime Minister FitzGerald in January 1987. In opposition, Labour increased its parliamentary representation from 12 seats to 15 at the June 1989 balloting.

In 1990 Labour joined with the Workers' Party (below) in backing the successful presidential candidacy of Mary Robinson, who had twice been a Labour parliamentary candidate but had left the party in 1985. In November 1992 Labour achieved its best-ever election result, winning 33 seats. In January 1993 the party entered into a majority coalition with *Fianna Fáil* that collapsed in November 1994, largely at Labour's instigation. The party then renewed its alliance with *Fine Gael*,

joining a three-party coalition that also included the Democratic Left. However, in the June 1997 elections Labour's strength was cut to 17 seats, forcing its return to the opposition. The electoral decline precipitated the resignation of Dick Spring as party leader and the announcement by the Labour leadership that henceforth the party was prepared to discuss joining a governing coalition with any party.

Following months of discussions, Labour and the Democratic Left (DL) merged on January 24, 1999, with the former DL president, Proinsias De Rossa, becoming president of the combined grouping. The DL had been launched by a reformist faction of the Workers' Party that withdrew from that party in February 1992. Committed to democratic socialism, rather than Marxism-Leninism, the DL won four legislative seats in November 1992, versus none for the parent party. In December 1994 the DL agreed to join a coalition government with *Fine Gael* and Labour, its leader being given the social welfare portfolio. With the election of June 1997 the DL returned to the opposition, again with four seats in the *Dáil*.

Leaders: Pat RABBITTE (Party Leader), Liz McMANUS (Deputy Leader), Proinsias DE ROSSA (President), Willie PENROSE (Parliamentary Chair), Mike ALLEN (General Secretary).

Sinn Féin. The islandwide *Sinn Féin* ("Ourselves Alone") was formed in 1905 to promote Irish independence and won a majority of the Irish seats in the 1918 UK elections. In conjunction with the Irish Republican Army (IRA), which had been created in 1919 to conduct a guerrilla campaign against British forces, *Sinn Féin* helped lead the revolutionary movement that produced the Irish Free State. Many members left both *Sinn Féin* and the IRA at the formation in 1922 of the *Cumann na nGaedheal* (see *Fine Gael*, above) and in 1926 of *Fianna Fáil*. Its influence substantially reduced, *Sinn Féin* continued its strident opposition to partition while serving as the political wing of the outlawed IRA. A long-standing policy dispute within the IRA eventually led traditional nationalists, committed to continued violence, to form the Provisional IRA in 1969, while the Marxist-oriented rump, primarily devoted to nonviolent political action, continued to represent the "Official" IRA. The rump changed its party name to *Sinn Féin–The Workers' Party* in 1977 to differentiate itself from the Provisional *Sinn Féin* created by the Provisional IRA. In 1982 the Marxists relinquished the *Sinn Féin* identification entirely to the "Provos" and became the Workers' Party (below). (The "Provisional" label is sometimes still used, particularly in reference to the IRA.)

In supporting the IRA's goal of establishing a unified "democratic socialist republic," *Sinn Féin* contested several elections with the proviso that no successful candidate would sit in the *Dáil,* which it did not consider legitimate. At the February 1982 balloting none of *Sinn Féin's* seven candidates was successful, and it did not contest the national election in November. In November 1986, however, a party conference in Dublin voted 429 to 161 in favor of ending the policy against taking up *Dáil* seats. Party President Gerry Adams received support in the action by other leaders, including the Army Council of the IRA, while a splinter group left the conference in protest (see Republican *Sinn Féin,* below). The change in policy won no *Dáil* seats until June 1997, when *Sinn Féin* won one. *Sinn Féin* also scored significant electoral success in Northern Ireland in 1997 (see United Kingdom: Northern Ireland).

At a special party conference held in Dublin on May 10, 1998, *Sinn Féin* overwhelmingly endorsed the April 10 Good Friday Agreement and agreed to take up seats in the proposed Northern Ireland Assembly. Amid speculation that *Sinn Féin* might win sufficient seats at the next general election to warrant its inclusion in a coalition government, in July 2000 the party won the Sligo mayoralty, its first such victory in over three decades. In the 2002 elections *Sinn Féin* won five seats in the *Dáil.* The party also won its first seat in the EU Parliament in the 2004 elections for that body.

Leaders: Gerard (Gerry) ADAMS (President), Mary Lou McDONALD (Chair), Pat DOHERTY (Vice President), Mitchel McLAUGHLIN (General Secretary).

Green Party (*Comhaontás Glas).* Founded in December 1981 as the Ecology Party of Ireland by Christopher FETTES, *Comhaontás Glas* is an Irish expression of the European Green movement. The group adopted the name Green Alliance in 1983 but took its present name in 1987 to clarify its political status. It captured its first legislative seat at the June 1989 balloting, won a different seat in 1992, and has held two of Ireland's 15 European Parliament seats since 1994. The party backed the proposal legalizing divorce that was narrowly approved by referendum in November 1995, although during the campaign it secured a Supreme Court ruling proscribing further government spending in the "yes" cause.

In the June 1997 election the Green Party increased its strength to two seats. With its poll standing on the rise, the party's May 2000 convention featured a contentious debate over possible participation in a coalition government after the next election. The Green Party won six seats in the 2002 elections.

Leaders: Trevor SARGENT (Party Leader), Mary WHITE (Deputy Leader), John GORMLEY (Parliamentary Leader).

Socialist Party (SP). The SP was founded in September 1996 by trade unionists, Dublin community activists, and members of Militant Labour. Advocating public ownership and democratic socialist planning in key sectors of the economy, the islandwide, nonsectarian party won one *Dáil* seat in June 1997. In the parliamentary debate on the Good Friday Agreement of April 10, 1998, SP leader Joe Higgins called for "a democratic and socialist alternative" to the proposed constitutional changes and objected to seeking voter approval of the pact on May 22, arguing against holding simultaneous referenda on the Northern Ireland accord and the EU's Amsterdam Treaty. The SP won one seat in the 2002 elections. The SP has recently been campaigning to abolish the office of the president, and President McAleese's unopposed election in 2004 has provided additional emphasis for the party's efforts.

Leader: Joe HIGGINS.

Other Parties

Workers' Party (*Pairtí na nOibri*). Tracing its origin to the original *Sinn Féin* and known from 1977 until 1982 as *Sinn Féin–*The Workers' Party, the Workers' Party is a product of the independence and unification movements that have spanned most of the 20th century. Marxist in outlook and dedicated to establishment of a united, socialist Ireland, the party captured its first *Dáil* seat in 20 years at the June 1981 election and expanded its representation to three at the February 1982 balloting. After slipping to two seats in November 1993, the party won four seats in 1987 and seven in 1989. In February 1992, however, six of the party's seven MPs, including its leader, Proinsias De Rossa, broke away to form the Democratic Left after their proposal to replace "Leninist revolutionary tactics" with "democratic socialism" was narrowly voted down at a party conference. The rump group failed to secure parliamentary representation in the elections of 1992 and 1997. Its Northern Ireland wing, formerly known as the Workers' Party Ireland Clubs, holds no seats in either the UK House of Commons or the Northern Ireland Assembly.

Leaders: Sean GARLAND (President), John LOWRY (General Secretary), Thomas OWENS (Northern Ireland Regional Secretary).

Republican Sinn Féin. The Republican *Sinn Féin* was formed at the parent party's 1986 conference by some 30 dissidents who were vehemently opposed to participation in a *Dáil* that did not include representatives from Northern Ireland. It is allegedly linked to Northern Ireland's violent Continuity IRA, although party leaders have denied any connection. The party president branded the IRA's May 2000 decision to put its arms dumps under international supervision as "an overt act of treachery."

Leaders: Ruairí Ó BRÁDAIGH (President), Josephine HAYDEN, Des DALTON (Vice Presidents).

Irish Republican Socialist Party (IRSP). Founded in 1974, the IRSP serves as the political wing of a fringe republican paramilitary group, the Irish National Liberation Army (INLA). The IRSP advocates a democratic socialist republic throughout all of Ireland's 32 counties. It opposed the April 1998 Good Friday Agreement as "a betrayal" that "institutionalizes sectarianism, fails to properly address the imperialist role that Britain has played . . . and locks the Irish people into a capitalist alliance." In August 1998, as urged by the party leadership, the INLA announced a cease-fire. In September 1999 the IRSP confirmed that it had drafted a nonaggression pact for presentation to the INLA and loyalist paramilitary groups in Northern Ireland.

Leaders: Willie GALLAGHER, Fra HALLIGAN.

Communist Party of Ireland—CPI (*Páirtí Cummanach na hÉireann*). An islandwide grouping first formed in 1921 and reestablished in 1933, the CPI split into northern and southern factions during World War II and remained separate until 1970. The party continues to advocate a united, socialist Ireland.

Leaders: Eugene McCARTAN (General Secretary).

Other parties include several small religious and profamily parties, many of which were formed in opposition to the legalization of divorce in the constitutional referendum held in November 1995. Perhaps the most widely known is the **National Party,** founded in 1995 under the leadership of Nora BENNIS. Others include the **Christian Solidarity Party,** founded by Gerard CASEY in July 1994 as the Christian Centrist Party and now led by party president Cathal LOFTUS, and the **People of Ireland Party** (*Muintir na nÉireann Paírtí Teoranta*), founded in 1995 and led by Richard GREENE.

An **Independent Fianna Fáil** was established in 1970 by the late Neil BLANEY, a former *Fianna Fáil* minister, and, following his death, was led by his son Harry BLANEY from 1997 until 2002, when he retired and was replaced by his son Niall BLANEY, who sits in the *Dáil* as an independent from Donegal. Other parties with small followings include the **South Kerry Independent Alliance,** the **Natural Law Party,** the far-left

Cabinet

As of May 1, 2006

Prime Minister *(Taoiseach)*	Bertie Ahern (FF)
Deputy Prime Minister *(Tánaiste)*	Mary Harney (PD) [f]

Ministers

Agriculture and Food	Mary Coughlan (FF) [f]
Arts, Sport, and Tourism	John O'Donoghue (FF)
Communications and Marine and Natural Resources	Noel Dempsey (FF)
Community, Rural, and *Gaeltacht* Affairs	Éamon Ó Cuív (FF)
Defense	William O'Dea (FF)
Education and Science	Mary Hanafin (FF) [f]
Enterprise, Trade, and Employment	Michéal Martin (FF)
Environment and Local Government	Dick Roche (FF)
Finance	Brian Cowen (FF)
Foreign Affairs	Dermot Ahern (FF)
Health and Children	Mary Harney (PD) [f]
Justice, Equality, and Law Reform	Michael McDowell (PD)
Social and Family Affairs	Seamus Brennan (FF)
Transport	Martin Cullen (FF)

[f] = female

Socialist Workers' Party, and the anarchist **Workers' Solidarity Movement**.

Legislature

The Irish **Parliament** (*Oireachtas*) is a bicameral body composed of an upper chamber (Senate) and a lower chamber (House of Representatives).

Senate (*Seanad Éireann*). The upper chamber consists of 60 members serving five-year terms. Eleven are nominated by the prime minister and 49 are elected—6 by graduates of the universities and 43 from candidates put forward by five vocational panels: cultural and educational interests, 5 seats; labor, 11; industry and commerce, 9; agriculture, 11; and public administration, 7. The electing body, a college of some 900 members, includes members of the *Oireachtas* as well as county and county borough councilors. The power of the Senate extends primarily to delaying for a period of 90 days a bill passed by the *Dáil*. Technically, the house does not function on the basis of party divisions; however, following the most recent balloting of July 16–17, 2002, its composition was as follows: *Fianna Fáil*, 30 seats; *Fine Gael*, 15; the Labour Party, 5; Progressive Democrats, 4; independents, 6.

Chair (Cathaoirleach): Rory KIELY.

House of Representatives (*Dáil Éireann*). The *Dáil* currently has 166 members (*teachtaí dála*, familiarly called TDs or deputies) elected by direct adult suffrage and proportional representation for five-year terms, assuming no dissolution. At the general election held June 6, 1997, *Fianna Fáil* won 77 seats; *Fine Gael,* 54; the Labour Party, 17; the Progressive Democrats, 4; the Democratic Left, 4; the Green Party, 2; *Sinn Féin*, 1; the Socialist Party, 1; independents, 6. Labour and the Democratic Left merged in January 1999. Following a

June 2000 by-election, *Fianna Fáil* held 75 seats and independents, 8.

At the most recent balloting, held May 17, 2002, *Fianna Fáil* won 81 seats; *Fine Gael,* 31; the Labour Party, 21; the Progressive Democrats, 8; the Green Party, 6; *Sinn Féin,* 5; the Socialist Party, 1; and independents, 13.

Chair (Ceann Comhairle): Rory O'HANLON.

Communications

Although free expression is constitutionally guaranteed, a Censorship of Publications Board under the jurisdiction of the Ministry of Justice is empowered to halt publication of books. Moreover, under the Broadcasting Act 1960, as amended in 1976 and interpreted by the Supreme Court in a July 1982 decision involving a ban against the Provisional *Sinn Féin,* individuals and political parties committed to undermining the state may be denied access to the public broadcasting media.

Press

All newspapers are privately owned and edited, but the Roman Catholic Church exerts considerable restraining influence. The following are English-language dailies published in Dublin, unless otherwise noted: *Sunday Independent* (310,000), pro–*Fine Gael*; *Sunday World* (294,000, including Northern Ireland); *Irish Independent* (170,000), pro–*Fine Gael*; *Evening Herald* (104,000), pro–*Fine Gael*; *The Irish Times* (119,000), independent; *The Star* (107,000), independent; *Sunday Tribune* (90,000), independent; *Cork Examiner* (Cork, 60,000), independent; *Sunday Business Post* (40,000), independent.

News Agencies

There is no domestic facility, although a number of foreign bureaus maintain offices in Dublin.

Broadcasting and Computing

Until mid-1990 *Radio Telefís Éireann* (RTE), an autonomous statutory corporation, operated all radio and television stations, including two television channels (both carrying advertising) and *Radió na Gaeltachta*, which broadcasts to Irish-speaking areas. In 1988 an Independent Radio and Television Commission (IRTC) was established, which in 1989 awarded a franchise for an independent television channel, TV3; at present there are also more than 20 commercial radio stations. In an attempt to preserve and nurture the growth of Ireland's native language, in 1997 the government began subsidizing the nation's first Gaelic-language television channel, *Teilifís na Gaelige*. There were approximately 1.5 million television receivers and 1.8 million personal computers serving 3.9 million Internet users in 2003.

Intergovernmental Representation

Ambassador to the U.S.
Noel FAHEY

U.S. Ambassador to Ireland
James Casey KENNEY

Permanent Representative to the UN
David J. COONEY

IGO Memberships (Non-UN)
BIS, CEUR, EBRD, EIB, ESA, EU, Eurocontrol, IEA, Interpol, IOM, OECD, OSCE, PCA, WCO, WTO

ITALY

ITALIAN REPUBLIC

Repubblica Italiana

The Country

A peninsula rooted in the Alps and jutting into the Mediterranean for a distance of some 725 miles, the Italian Republic includes the large islands of Sicily and Sardinia and other smaller islands in the Tyrrhenian, Adriatic, Ionian, Ligurian, and Sardinian Seas. Rugged terrain limits large-scale agriculture to the Po Valley, the Campagna region around Naples, and the plain of Foggia in the southeast. Among numerous socioeconomic cleavages, there is a vast difference between the industrialized north and the substantially underdeveloped south. Ethnically, however, the Italians form a relatively homogeneous society, the only substantial minority being the approximately 250,000 German-speaking persons in the province of Bolzano (Alto Adige, or South Tyrol), which is part of the region known from 1919 to 1947 as Venezia Tridentina and thereafter as Trentino-Alto Adige and whose more activist leaders have long sought a referendum on return of the province to Austrian sovereignty. Although Italian is the official language, regional variations of the standard Tuscan dialect exist, and in various parts of the country small minorities speak French, German, Ladin (similar to Romansch), Slovene, and Sard (Sardinian). Roman Catholicism is nominally professed by over 90 percent of the population; however, religious freedom is constitutionally guaranteed, and in March 1985 the Chamber of Deputies ratified a revised concordat with the Holy See that terminated Roman Catholicism's status as the state religion. In 1998 women constituted 38 percent of the paid labor force, concentrated mainly in education and the service sector; female participation in political leadership bodies has been estimated at 10 percent.

Despite the fading of an "economic miracle" that characterized a lengthy boom period after World War II, during the 1960s and 1970s Italy's real GDP increased at a yearly average of 4.3 percent and its population at only 0.7 percent, allowing per capita income to double. GDP growth averaged 2.4 percent annually in 1976–1986 but only 1.4 percent over the following decade. At present, the agricultural sector accounts for under 3 percent of GDP, while industry contributes about 28 percent, and services, the balance.

A founding member of the Economic and Monetary Union (EMU) of the European Union (EU), Italy now ranks as one of the world's ten largest economies. Sluggish growth averaging 1.7 percent

Political Status: Unified state proclaimed in
1861; republic established by national
referendum in 1946; under parliamentary
constitution effective January 1, 1948.

Area: 116,303 sq. mi. (301,225 sq. km.).

Population: 56,995,744 (2001C); 58,174,000
(2005E). Figures are de jure. The de facto
figures are 57,110,144 and 58,245,000.

Major Urban Centers (2005E): ROME
(2,539,000), Milan (1,284,000), Naples
(996,000), Turin (870,000), Palermo
(675,000), Genoa (591,000).

Official Language: Italian (German is also
official in Trentino-Alto Adige).

Monetary Unit: Euro (market rate July 1, 2006:
1 euro = $1.28US).

President of the Republic: Giorgio
NAPOLITANO (Democrats of the Left)
elected by the electoral college on May 10,
2006, and inaugurated on May 15 for a
seven-year term, succeeding Carlo Azeglio
CIAMPI (nonparty).

President of the Council of Ministers: (Prime
Minister): Romano PRODI (The Union/Olive
Tree); designated by the president on May 16,
2006, and sworn in on May 17, following the
election of April 9–10, in succession to Silvio
BERLUSCONI (House of Freedoms/*Forza
Italia*), who formally resigned on May 2;
confirmed with his cabinet by vote of the
Senate and Chamber of Deputies on May 19
and 23, respectively.

annually in 1998–1999 was followed by an upsurge
to 3.0 percent in 2000, but the economy then returned to the doldrums, with GDP expansion dropping to 1.8 percent in 2001, 0.4 percent in 2002, and 0.3 percent in 2003. For 2004 the GDP grew at a rate of 1.2 percent, but the growth rate then fell again to a mere 0.1 percent in 2005. In 2001, unemployment, a persistent problem, dropped below 10 percent for the first time since the early 1990s and then fell steadily, reaching 8.1 percent in 2005. In the south, however, the unemployment rate remains double the national rate. Consumer price inflation averaged 2.7 percent a year in 2000–2003 but dropped to 2.3 percent in 2004–2005.

Government and Politics

Political Background

Unified in the 19th century as a parliamentary monarchy under the House of Savoy, Italy fought with the Allies in World War I. Having succumbed in 1922 to the Fascist dictatorship of Benito MUSSOLINI, it entered World War II on the side of Nazi Germany in June 1940 and switched to the Allied side only after Mussolini's removal from office in 1943. Following a period of provisional government, the monarchy was abolished by popular referendum in 1946, and a new, republican constitution went into effect on January 1, 1948. A Communist Party (*Partito Comunista Italiano*—PCI) bid for national power under the leadership of Palmiro TOGLIATTI was defeated in the parliamentary election of April 1948, which established the Christian Democrats (*Partito della Democrazia Cristiana*—DC), then headed by Alcide DE GASPERI, as Italy's strongest political force. Luigi EINAUDI (DC) was elected as the country's first president in May 1948, being succeeded by Giovanni GRONCHI (DC) in 1955 and Antonio SEGNI (DC) in 1962, with the DC leading a succession of concurrent center-right coalition governments. The first important modification in this pattern occurred in 1962 with the formation by the DC's Amintore FANFANI of a center-left coalition that, under a policy of an "opening to the left" (*apertura a sinistra*), sought parliamentary support from the Socialist Party (*Partito Socialista Italiano*—PSI) and from 1964 usually included PSI ministers in the government. As part of the realignment, Giuseppe SARAGAT of the Democratic Socialist Party (*Partito Socialista Democratico Italiano*—PSDI) was elected to replace the ailing Segni as president in December 1964. Saragat was succeeded by Giovanni LEONE (DC) in 1971.

At a bitterly contested election in June 1976, the PCI registered unprecedented gains at the expense of the smaller parties, running a close second to the DC. While another DC-PSI government could technically have been formed, the Socialists had indicated during the campaign that they would no longer participate in a coalition that excluded the PCI. For their part, the Communists agreed to abstain on confirmation of a new cabinet in return for a "government role" at less than the cabinet level. As a result, former prime minister Giulio ANDREOTTI succeeded in organizing an all-DC minority government that survived Chamber and Senate confidence votes in August. Earlier, in July, Pietro INGRAO had become the first Communist in 28 years to be elected president of the lower house.

In January 1978 the Communists, Socialists, and Republicans withdrew their support of the Andreotti government following rejection by the DC of a renewed PCI demand for cabinet-level participation. Negotiations conducted by DC president Aldo MORO resulted, however, in a compromise whereby the Communists settled for official inclusion in the ruling parliamentary majority and a guarantee that they would be consulted in advance on government policy. Andreotti, directed by President Leone to form a new government, organized a cabinet that, with only two changes from the preceding one, took office on March 13. Three days later, five-time prime minister Moro was abducted by the extremist Red Brigades; on May 9 his body was found in Rome after the government, with substantial opposition support, refused to negotiate with the terrorists. Moro had been considered a likely successor to President Leone, who on June 15, six months before the end of his term, resigned in the wake of persistent accusations of tax evasion and other irregularities. Following the interim presidency of Amintore Fanfani, Alessandro PERTINI of the PSI was sworn in as head of state on July 8.

The withdrawal of Communist support led to the collapse of the Andreotti government in January 1979 and, ultimately, to early but inconclusive elections in June, after which Francesco COSSIGA (DC) formed a three-party centrist government that survived a confidence vote in the Chamber only because of abstentions by the Republicans and the PSI. In February 1980 the Socialists withdrew their tacit parliamentary support, forcing the government to resign in March. Within days, however, the PSI agreed to participate in a new DC-led administration, and another three-party cabinet that included the Republicans took office in April. The second Cossiga government survived until September, when it was forced to resign after defeat of an economic reform package.

In October 1980 the PSI and PSDI concluded a "third force" agreement that did not, however, preclude a dialogue to "reconcile Christian and socialist values"; accordingly, the two parties and the Republicans joined a DC-led government under Arnaldo FORLANI that took office in October. Subsequently, it was revealed that a large number of leading officials, including several cabinet members, belonged to a secret Masonic lodge known as "P-2," which had been implicated in a variety of criminal activities. As a result of the scandal, Forlani was forced to submit his government's resignation in May 1981, and in June Giovanni SPADOLINI of the Republican Party (*Partito Repubblicano Italiano*—PRI) became the first non-Christian Democrat since 1945 to be invested as prime minister. The first Spadolini coalition, encompassing the four participants in the previous government plus the Liberals (*Partito Liberale Italiano*—PLI), lasted until August 1982, when the Socialists withdrew. Spadolini was able to form a new government that included the PSI, but differences over economic policy persisted, forcing a second collapse in November.

In December 1982 former prime minister Fanfani returned as head of a four-party coalition that included the DC, PSI, PSDI, and the Liberals. Although Fanfani succeeded in enacting a number of tax reforms, friction arose during the 1983 regional election campaign, and in April PSI leader Bettino CRAXI withdrew his party from the coalition, forcing a new parliamentary dissolution. At the election of June 1983, the Christian Democrats suffered their most severe setback since the party's formation, while the PCI also lost seats. The beneficiaries were the smaller parties, most notably the Republicans. The PSI also gained, and on July 21 Craxi was asked to form Italy's first Socialist-led administration. Rejecting repeated appeals from PCI leader Enrico BERLINGUER to join the Communists in a "democratic alternative" of the left, Craxi assembled a five-party government encompassing the Fanfani coalition plus the Republicans.

In October 1985, amid intense controversy surrounding the hijacking of the Genoa-based cruise ship *Achille Lauro* by Palestinian terrorists, Defense Minister Spadolini led a Republican withdrawal from the cabinet, precipitating Craxi's resignation. However, an accommodation was reached with Spadolini that permitted retroactive rejection of the government's resignation. Craxi again felt obliged to resign in June 1986, after an unexpected defeat on a local finance bill in which numerous coalition deputies played the role of secret-ballot defectors (*franchi tiratori,* or "snipers"), but he was eventually able to form a new government on the basis of the previous five-party alignment.

In February 1987 Craxi announced the "liquidation" of a 1986 pact with the DC that would have permitted them to lead the government for the last year of the parliamentary term; in March, with obvious reluctance, he submitted his resignation. After a series of abortive cabinet-building efforts, former prime minister Fanfani succeeded in organizing a minority administration that lasted only until late April; in a highly unusual move, the Christian Democrats voted to bring down their own government, leading President Cossiga (who had succeeded President Pertini) to call an early general election.

The June 1987 balloting yielded a significant shift of support from the PCI to the PSI, with a marginal gain for the DC and the parliamentary debut of Italy's Greens (*Federazione dei Verdi—* FdV). The Socialists strongly objected to the proposed choice of DC Secretary General Ciriaco DE MITA as prime minister, and President Cossiga somewhat unexpectedly called on the outgoing DC treasury minister, Giovanni GORIA, to head a revived five-party government that took office in July. Goria managed to retain coalition support only until March 1988, when the PSI and PSDI abstained on a controversial nuclear-power vote. Subsequently, after negotiating a record 200-page government program, De Mita, with PSI and Liberal support, returned as head of a new administration. In October De Mita succeeded in ending a 140-year tradition that permitted legislators to vote in secrecy on virtually all important measures. Thenceforth, budgetary matters, particularly, would no longer be subject to "sniper" attack, although secrecy was retained for selected issues, such as civil rights, abortion, and divorce, and for the electoral college selection of a president.

In May 1989 De Mita resigned as prime minister after being attacked by the PSI on a variety of economic and social issues. In July former prime minister Andreotti returned as head of an administration supported by the same five-party coalition as that of his predecessor. The government remained in power until March 1991, when Craxi's PSI withdrew its support, after which Andreotti fashioned a four-party coalition of the DC, PSI, PSDI, and the Liberals. It was Andreotti's seventh government.

The run-up to the general election of April 1992 was preceded by a number of significant changes in the Italian party system. Formation of the Democratic Party of the Left (*Partito Democratico della Sinistra—*PDS) as revisionist heir to the PCI prompted the collateral organization of a hard-line Communist Refoundation Party (*Partito della Rifondazione Comunista—*PRC). In addition, the long-dominant DC was severely challenged in the country's two major regions by the launching of the Northern League (*Lega Nord—*LN), with the Lombard League (*Lega Lombarda—*LL) at its core, and, in the south, by the emergence of an anti-Mafia grouping, The Network (*La Rete*). The new formations were the principal beneficiaries of the April balloting, at which the DC registered its poorest showing since World War II. On April 24 Prime Minister Andreotti announced his resignation, as did President Cossiga the following day, leaving the country without the constitutional capacity to form a new government. A prolonged deadlock over the selection of a new head of state ensued before being effectively broken by the assassination of the country's leading anti-Mafia judge, Giovanni FALCONE, on May 23. On May 25 a shocked electoral college, in its 16th round of voting, named the recently designated Chamber speaker, Oscar Luigi SCALFARO (DC), as Cossiga's successor. Four weeks later, after nearly three months of political paralysis, the PSI's Giuliano AMATO succeeded, on the basis of the same four parties as his predecessor, in forming Italy's 51st postwar administration.

The traditional parties were severely damaged from early 1992 onward by the country's biggest postwar corruption scandal, which started in Milan and centered at first on disclosures that PSI officials had enriched party coffers by systematic abuse of public service contracts. Arrests began in February and continued throughout the year, amid evidence of wrongdoing at all levels of the center-left political establishment. Some 200 Italian parliamentarians were under criminal investigation by early 1993. Although gravely weakened by the widening scandal, the Amato government clung to office through public approval of eight referendums on April 18–19 that called for major political and economic reforms.

On April 22, 1993, Amato announced his resignation, and he was replaced on April 29 by the politically unaffiliated governor of the Bank of Italy, Carlo Azeglio CIAMPI, whose seven-party coalition government included three former Communists (now members of the PDS) and one Green. However, less than 24 hours later the last four resigned because of the chamber's unexpected refusal to lift Craxi's parliamentary immunity to corruption charges. On May 5 a new government was formed, 10 of whose 25 members were unaffiliated.

The "meltdown" of the postwar party structure accelerated in the run-up to a general election on March 26–27, 1994, and included the transformation of the once-dominant DC into the Italian Popular Party (*Partito Popolare Italiano*—PPI). The result was a radically transformed Parliament dominated by the right-wing Freedom Alliance (*Polo della Libertà*—PL), headed by the new *Forza Italia* formation of media tycoon Silvio BERLUSCONI. On May 11 Berlusconi was sworn in as prime minister of a five-party right-wing government that included representatives of the LN and the "postfascist" National Alliance (*Alleaza Nazionale*—AN).

Policy and personal strains quickly paralyzed the new government, however, culminating in the withdrawal of the LN and the resignation of Berlusconi on December 22, 1994. Shortly before his exit the prime minister had been called before Milan magistrates to answer charges of corrupt payments by parts of his business empire. Rebuffing Berlusconi's demand that he should be reappointed or new elections called, President Scalfaro appointed a nonparty banker, Lamberto DINI, as prime minister to head a cabinet of technocrats that took office on January 17, 1995, in the midst of an economic crisis. The discrediting of the old political elite reached new heights in September with the launching of judicial proceedings against Andreotti on charges of association with the Mafia. (He was ultimately acquitted of the final charge in October 1999.)

Having survived a right-wing nonconfidence motion in October 1995 by striking a deal with the PRC, Dini submitted his resignation on December 30 after parliamentary passage of the 1996 budget. An attempt to form a reformist government by former merchant banker Antonio MACCANICO (then nonparty) foundered, whereupon new elections were called three years ahead of schedule. The contest saw the emergence of a broad "Olive Tree" (*L'Ulivo*) alliance of center-left parties that was headed by Romano PRODI (a former left-wing DC minister) and included the PPI, the ex-Communist PDS, and new parties founded by Dini and Maccanico.

The results of the balloting on April 20–21, 1996, gave the Olive Tree parties decisive pluralities in both houses; as a result Prodi on May 17 became prime minister of Italy's 55th postwar government—technically a minority administration, but with promised external support by the PRC. Although the cabinet was predominantly leftist, the government was firmly pro-EU and soon adopted austerity measures to meet the criteria for entry into the proposed EU EMU in 1999. Among other things, the government began to reduce a budget deficit of 6.8 percent of GDP to less than the 3 percent required for participation. In late November the Prodi government claimed an important initial success when the Italian lira was readmitted to the EU exchange rate mechanism after four years of nonparticipation.

The Prodi government survived its first crisis in April 1997 when the PRC refused to endorse military action to restore order in Albania (see Albania article), forcing Prodi to solicit the support of the center-right parties. A more serious challenge arose when Prodi in late September announced his proposed 1998 budget, which called for extensive additional retrenchment, including pension reductions and further welfare cuts. The PRC denounced the budget slashing, forcing Prodi to submit his resignation on October 9. However, public opinion turned on the PRC, which modified its stance sufficiently to permit reinstatement of the government. Subsequently, the Olive Tree alliance scored heavy victories in local elections in November.

Rejecting the proposed 1999 budget, the PRC again withdrew its support, and the government fell on October 9, 1998. Massimo D'ALEMA, leader of the Democrats of the Left (*Democratici di Sinistra*—DS, as the PDS had been renamed), the largest party in the Parliament, was called upon to form a government after Prodi's attempts to regroup proved futile. D'Alema put together a multiparty government that included not only the first Communist cabinet ministers since a unity government in 1947 but also former president Cossiga's recently organized Democratic Union for the Republic (*Unione Democratica per la Repubblica*—UDR), a center-right grouping of moderate democrats and Christian reformers. Sworn in on October 21, D'Alema retained several key ministers, including those who had been the architects of austerity, and pledged to pass the budget that had been Prodi's downfall.

D'Alema submitted his resignation on December 12, 1999, after losing the support of the small, three-party *Trifoglio* ("Clover") parliamentary alliance, which included Cossiga's new Union for the Republic (*Unione per la Repubblica*—UR). Asked to form a new administration by President Carlo Ciampi, who had handily won election as chief of state in May, D'Alema proposed a seven-party government that was largely unchanged except for the addition of the Prodi-sponsored Democrats (*Democratici*). However, D'Alema's second administration proved short-lived: Responding to major gains won by the resurgent center-right in regional elections, the prime minister resigned on April 17, 2000. President Ciampi then turned to former prime minister Amato, D'Alema's minister of treasury and budget, who succeeded in forming an eight-party Olive Tree government that was

sworn in on April 26 and confirmed by the Chamber of Deputies two days later.

With Amato having removed himself from consideration, the Olive Tree endorsed Rome's mayor, Francesco RUTELLI, a Democrat, to lead the alliance into the 2001 general election. On the center-right, Silvio Berlusconi had apparently convinced most of the populace that the string of corruption charges against him were attributable more to overzealous prosecutors than to actual illegalities. Having reconfigured his Freedom Alliance as the House of Freedoms (*Casa delle Libertà*), on May 13 the former prime minister swept back into office with comfortable majorities in both houses of Parliament. The victory had been widely predicted as Italy's complex political dynamics increasingly came to resemble, in effect, a two-party system: the center-right House of Freedoms alliance won 368 seats in the Chamber of Deputies (58.4 percent) and 177 in the Senate (56.2 percent of the elective seats), while the center-left Olive Tree took 247 (39.2 percent) in the lower house and 128 in the upper (40.1 percent). Berlusconi's cabinet, which was sworn in on June 11, included members of his *Forza Italia,* the AN, the LN, and two Christian Democratic parties, plus a handful of independents. Subsequently, the Christian Democrats merged as the Union of Christian and Center Democrats (*Unione dei Democratici Cristiani e di Democratici Centro*—UDC), and the small Italian Republican Party (PRI) decided to join the governing coalition.

Despite his electoral successes, Berlusconi faced charges that he had bribed judges in the mid-1980s to gain control of a food company, an attack that he said was politically motivated. (Prior convictions for bribing tax officials and for making illegal payments to Bettino Craxi's party in 1991 had already been overturned, and other charges had been dismissed.) In an undisguised attempt to undercut the prosecution, Berlusconi's parliamentary majority passed legislation allowing a defendant to request a change of venue if there were "legitimate suspicions" of judicial bias. However, the Supreme Court rejected Berlusconi's bid to move his corruption trial from Milan. Parliament then passed a bill giving immunity from prosecution to the top five office-holders—the president, prime minister, the presidents of the Senate and Chamber, and the head of the Constitutional Court—during their tenure, which meant that the charges against Berlusconi would fall under the statute of limitations by the end of his current term. In January 2004 the Constitutional Court ruled the immunity law unconstitutional, and in April the trial resumed. In the end, Berlusconi was acquitted, although several of his closest colleagues have been convicted of corruption and linked to organized crime.

On April 15, 2005, the UDC leader and deputy prime minister, Marco FOLLINI, withdrew his party from the cabinet, demanding policy and ministerial changes in the wake of major setbacks for the House of Freedoms parties in the local elections of April 3–4. As a consequence, Prime Minister Berlusconi tendered his resignation on April 20 but quickly fashioned a new government. He was sworn in once again on April 23 at the head of a reshuffled Council of Ministers (dubbed "Berlusconi II") that comprised all the House of Freedoms parties, including the UDC.

By the time the 2006 election campaign got under way, polls predicted that a new coalition, the Union (*L'Unione*), headed by Prodi's center-left Olive Tree, was positioned to break Berlusconi's hold on power. Support for Berlusconi had been undermined by growing public discontent over Italy's anemic economy, Berlusconi's grip on the media, persistent charges of corruption against him and other government figures, and the continued presence of some 3,000 Italian troops in Iraq in support of the 2003 U.S. invasion. Nevertheless, Prodi's victory in the April election was by a razor-thin margin in the Chamber (49.8 percent over Berlusconi's 49.6 percent). Ironically, a new electoral law that Berlusconi had shepherded through Parliament in December 2005 ended up giving Prodi's coalition a larger majority of Chamber seats, 348–281, than would otherwise have been the case. The House of Freedoms actually won more votes in the Senate (49.9 percent versus 49.8 percent), but the same electoral change handed Union a 2-seat advantage. On May 16 Italy's newly installed president, Giorgio NAPOLITANO, designated Prodi to be prime minister, and he was sworn in on May 17.

Constitution and Government

The 1948 constitution, which describes Italy as "a democratic republic founded on work," established a parliamentary system with a president, a bicameral legislature, and an independent judiciary. The president, selected for a seven-year term by an electoral college consisting of both houses of Parliament plus delegates named by regional assemblies, appoints the prime minister and, on the latter's recommendation, other members of the Council of Ministers; he may dissolve Parliament at any time prior to the last six months of a full term. The Parliament consists of a Senate and a Chamber of Deputies; the two houses have equal legislative power, and both are subject to dissolution and the holding of new elections. The Council of Ministers is responsible to Parliament and must resign upon passage of a vote of nonconfidence.

Under a modification to electoral arrangements approved by referendum in April 1993, proportional representation was replaced by predominantly "first-past-the-post," constituency-based elections. Subsequent parliamentary implementation of the mandate provided for single-member districts for both the Senate and Chamber, with 75 percent of the contests to be decided by plurality voting (hence no runoffs) and 25 percent by a system of proportional representation that would favor minor parties (subject, in the case of the Chamber of Deputies, to a vote threshold of 4 percent). A referendum held on April 18, 1999, called for abolishing the proportional component of Chamber elections. Although 91 percent of those voting backed the measure, the turnout was 0.4 percent below the 50 percent threshold needed to make the result binding. A repeat referendum on May 21, 2000, attracted only 32 percent of registered voters.

The judiciary is headed by the Constitutional Court (*Corte Costituzionale*) and includes (in descending order of superiority) the Supreme Court of Cassation (*Corte Suprema di Cassazione*), assize courts of appeal (*corti di assize d'appello*), courts of appeal (*corti d'appello*), tribunals (*tribunali*), district courts (*preture*), and justices of the peace (*giudici conciliatori*).

Italy's historically centralized system was substantially modified under the 1948 basic law, which called for the designation of 19 (later 20) administrative regions (*regioni*), 5 of which (Friuli-Venezia Giulia, Sicily, Sardinia, Trentino-Alto Adige, and Val d'Aosta) enjoy special status. Each region has its own administration, including an elected Regional Council (*Consiglio Regionale*). In addition, since April 2000 voters have directly elected presidents in the 15 ordinary regions. (Each special region has its own constitutional provisions.) Subdivisions include 103 provinces and some 8,100 municipalities, all administered by locally elected bodies. In October 2001 a national referendum endorsed a devolution proposal under which the regions would assume greater authority in agriculture, education, health, and other areas. A November 2005 law amending the constitution was rejected by voters in a referendum held on June 25, 2006. The amendments, backed by the Berlusconi government and opposed by Prodi's Union coalition, would have transferred more authority to the regions in the areas of health, education, and law enforcement; increased the powers of the prime minister to include authority to dissolve Parliament and appoint and dismiss ministers; and centralized the tax system. The amendments would have further diminished the powers of the president, already greatly limited under the constitution.

Foreign Relations

Italian rule outside the country's geographical frontiers was terminated by World War II and the Paris Peace Treaty of 1947, by which Italy renounced all claims to its former African possessions and ceded the Dodecanese Islands to Greece, a substantial northeastern region to Yugoslavia, and minor frontier districts to France. A dispute with Yugoslavia over the Free Territory of Trieste was largely resolved in 1954 by a partition agreement whereby Italy took possession of Trieste city and Yugoslavia acquired the surrounding rural area. The essentials of the 1954 agreement were retained in a formal settlement concluded in 1975.

The province of Alto Adige (South Tyrol), acquired from Austria after World War I, was a periodic source of tension between the two countries. In June 1992 they were at last able to notify the United Nations (UN) that outstanding issues related to the South Tyrol question had been resolved. Under the settlement, South Tyrol (Bolzano) was to be given substantial provincial autonomy, including guarantees for use of the German language, within the broader autonomous region of Trentino-Alto Adige.

Internationally, Italy has been a firm supporter of the Atlantic alliance, the UN and its related agencies, and European integration, including EC/EU. Rome has also attempted to forge a "special" relationship with the Arab world. Although affirming a need for action against terrorism, Italian authorities, in the wake of widespread anti-American street demonstrations, reacted coolly to the April 1986 U.S. bombing raid on Libya. By contrast, Italy endorsed a hard-line response to Iraq's seizure of Kuwait in 1990, and Italian forces joined the U.S.-led expedition that liberated Kuwait in early 1991. In early 2003, despite wide public protests, the Berlusconi government backed the U.S.-led ouster of Iraq's Saddam Hussein and later committed some 3,000 troops to the "coalition of the willing."

The post-1989 collapse of communism in Eastern Europe created some regional difficulties for Italy, notably an influx of refugees from Albania and later from former Yugoslavia. Responding to the new political realities, and in part to counter the economic power of reunited Germany, Italy sponsored the *Pentagonale* regional accord with Austria, Hungary, Czechoslovakia, and Yugoslavia; this became the *Esagonale* in 1991 with the accession of Poland, and in 1992, following the breakup of Yugoslavia, was relaunched as the Central European Initiative (CEI). In October 1994 Italy concluded a friendship and cooperation treaty with Russia.

As the former colonial ruler of Somalia, Italy displayed its concern at the descent of the country into anarchy in 1991 and provided 2,600 troops for the U.S.-led peacekeeping force in late 1992. In May 1993 it was one of the first to accord formal recognition to another former territory, the Ethiopian breakaway state of Eritrea. On a state visit to Addis Ababa in November 1997, President

Scalfaro formally apologized for Italy's occupation of Ethiopia in 1936–1941.

The advent of the Berlusconi government in May 1994 yielded strains with Slovenia and Croatia deriving from the Italian right's desire to recover prewar Italian Istria; under Berlusconi, however, Italy confined itself to demanding compensation for Italians dispossessed after World War II, while the successor Dini government dropped Italy's veto on the conclusion of an EU-Slovenia association agreement. The compensation issue was resolved in 1998.

On the Bosnian conflict, Rome's policy of neutrality and negotiation was seen in some quarters as effectively pro-Serb, a charge rejected by the Italian Foreign Ministry. In September 1995 Italy denied permission for U.S. Stealth bombers to use Italian bases for strikes on Bosnian Serb targets, officially in protest against Italy's exclusion from the international Contact Group on Bosnia. In November, however, Italy agreed to assign 2,300 troops to the International Force (IFOR) to be deployed in Bosnia under the Dayton peace agreement. In the wake of an influx of Albanian refugees in early 1997, Italy led a 6,000-strong multinational force which, with UN backing, was credited with helping restore order in Albania (see article on Albania). In 1998, having joined the Contact Group for the former Yugoslavia as its sixth member, Italy backed the sanctions imposed on Belgrade over the Kosovo crisis and in March 1999 joined the air campaign launched by the North Atlantic Treaty Organization (NATO) (see articles on Serbia and Montenegro).

A G-8 summit of leading industrial nations that opened in Genoa on July 20, 2001, was met by an estimated 100,000 antiglobalization demonstrators, including a small minority of violent protesters. Rioting and the resultant police response led to some 300 injuries, the shooting death of a protester by police, nearly 300 arrests, considerable property damage, and an official investigation into possible police misconduct.

In his first foreign-policy address after becoming prime minister, Romano Prodi on May 18, 2006, denounced the war in Iraq as a "grave" mistake, but refrained from stipulating a deadline for the withdrawal of Italian troops. Prodi renewed Italy's commitment to antiterror actions that are sanctioned by the UN. While endorsing Italy's "historic alliance with the United States," he also expressed support for a strong and unified Europe.

Current Issues

The general election of April 9–10, 2006, handed victory to Romano Prodi's nine-party, center-left Union, by a slim margin following a particularly acrimonious, two-month campaign. Voter turnout was high, at 84 percent of the electorate. Ironically, the Union benefited from a Berlusconi-supported change in election law signed on December 21, 2005. The law restored the pre-1993 full proportional representation system for 617 out of 630 seats in 26 constituencies (autonomous Val d'Aosta retained the first-past-the-post system for its single seat, while overseas Italian citizens elected the remaining 12 deputies representing four overseas constituencies). The new law set thresholds for a coalition (10 percent for the Chamber, 20 percent for the Senate) or for a political party (4 percent for the Chamber, 3 percent for the Senate) to win seats. When a coalition or a party with the largest number of votes fails to win 340 Chamber seats, the law stipulates that it will receive enough "bonus" seats to reach the 340-seat level. Berlusconi had argued that the new system would be fairer, while opponents had predicted that it would spur creation of small parties and destabilize government. As it turned out, the bonus arrangement also enabled Prodi's coalition to edge out Berlusconi's coalition by 2 seats in the Senate.

Berlusconi initially refused to accede to Prodi, attributed the result to fraud, and opposed Prodi's choice of Giorgio Napolitano, an 80-year-old former Communist and speaker of Parliament, to succeed outgoing President Carlo Azeglio Ciampi. On May 10 Napolitano won approval by Parliament and regional representatives for a seven–year term and quickly appointed Prodi as prime minister. On May 17 Prodi was sworn in, along with his 25-member cabinet. On May 19 the Senate approved Prodi's coalition by a 165–155 margin, and on May 23 the Chamber, where the Union enjoys a bigger majority, followed suit with a confidence vote of 344–268. Mayoral elections held on May 28–29 in four big cities gave further credence to the general election results. Prodi's Union won in Naples, Rome, and Turin, while Berlusconi's center-right coalition barely held onto power in its stronghold of Milan.

Prodi immediately faced serious challenges to his government's viability, especially Italy's economic problems. Italy's budget deficit was projected to reach at least 4.5 percent of GDP, a full percentage point higher than Berlusconi's government had predicted and well above the 3 percent level required by the EU by 2007. Faced with mounting scrutiny by EU finance ministers and a likely downgrading of Italy's credit rating, Prodi on May 25 pledged to quickly announce a plan to resolve the deficit and the public debt.

Soon after the election Prodi promised to bring about a sharp break with his predecessor's policies on other fronts as well, including constitutional changes enacted by the Berlusconi government, what Prodi called a climate of corruption, and Italy's support for the war in Iraq. While Berlusconi had promised to withdraw Italy's 2,600 troops by the end of the year, Prodi said the time frame would depend on further negotiations.

The Berlusconi government's attempt to present itself as a friend to the Islamic world suffered a blow when Roberto CALDEROLI, a cabinet minister and deputy leader of the anti-immigrant LN, appeared on Italian television in early 2006 wearing a T-shirt depicting caricatures of the Prophet Mohammed. Despite Calderoli's February resignation in the wake of riots in the former Italian colony of Libya and other Muslim cities to protest what they considered an affront to their religion, the affair undermined Italy's long-standing public-relations campaign to the Muslim world.

Political Parties

For more than four decades after World War II, the Italian political scene was dominated by the Christian Democrats (DC) on the center-right and the Italian Communist Party (PCI) on the left. The DC formed the major component of all postwar governments until 1994, while the PCI, although without government representation after 1947, remained the largest Communist formation in Western Europe and by far the largest Italian opposition party. For most of the period, a number of smaller democratic socialist and reformist parties provided the Christian Democrats with sufficient (although varying) political allies to ensure continual center-left government and keep the Communists out of office. On the far right, reorganization of the prewar Fascist Party is constitutionally forbidden, although various postwar parties serving as vehicles for radical right-wing views have come together in what is now the National Alliance.

The established postwar party structure came under increasing challenge in the 1980s, before effectively disintegrating in the early 1990s. On the left, the PCI reacted to the collapse of communism in Eastern Europe by becoming a democratic socialist party. On the right, increasing popular disgust with political corruption in Rome gave rise to various regional movements, especially in the north, seeking the breakup of Italy as a unitary state. On the center-left, the miring of many political leaders in financial and other scandals led to the conversion of the DC into the Italian Popular Party (PPI) but did not prevent a hemorrhage of Christian Democratic support in the 1994 election, which featured a three-way alliance structure of the right, center, and left covering most significant parties. This became a two-way center-left versus center-right contest in the 1996 elections, for which 273 distinct parties and groups registered candidates, and again in 2001. For the 2006 election all the significant parties and many minor ones joined the center-right House of Freedoms alliance or the center-left Union.

Governing Coalition

The Union (*L'Unione*). The Union is the latest iteration of the Olive Tree the center-left coalition that was launched in mid-1995 mainly on the initiative of Romano Prodi, a distinguished economics professor who had held ministerial office as a left-wing Christian Democrat and had joined the successor Italian Popular Party (PPI). By the time of the 1996 elections, the alliance included the centrist parties that had contested the 1994 elections as the Pact for Italy (*Patto per l'Italia*—PI) as well as the left-wing groupings of the 1994 Progressive Alliance (*Alleanza Progressista*—AP), notably the dominant ex-Communist Democratic Party of the Left (DS). It also embraced two parties founded in early 1996, namely Italian Renewal (RI) and the now-defunct Democratic Union (*Unione Democratica*—UD), as well as the regional South Tyrol People's Party (SVP). In the April 1996 balloting the Olive Tree won a decisive plurality in both houses, with the result that the following month Prodi, who had campaigned under the banner of the *Lista Romano Prodi,* became prime minister of a minority center-left government that had assurances of external support from the Communist Refoundation Party (PRC, below).

After the fall of the Prodi government in October 1998 it was unclear if the Olive Tree would remain as a viable coalition inasmuch as the successor regime of Massimo D'Alema collaborated with Francesco Cossiga's more conservative Democratic Union for the Republic (UDR; see UDEUR, below) to form his government. In preparation for the upcoming European Parliament election, Cossiga left the UDR in January 1999 and subsequently established yet another party, the Union for the Republic (*Unione per la Repubblica*—UR), which, as part of the "Clover" (*Trifoglio*) parliamentary alliance with the Italian Democratic Socialists (SDI) and the Italian Republican Party (PRI, below), withdrew its support from the government in December 1999 and forced D'Alema's resignation. With an eye on the 2001 legislative elections, the Clover parties had questioned D'Alema's leadership and a number of proposed administrative changes he had announced, including bringing Romano Prodi's new Democrats (see *La Margherita,* below) into the government. D'Alema quickly formed a second, eight-party government with the addition of the Democrats and the continued participation of the reconfigured rump of the UDR, the UDEUR. Less than four months later, however, D'Alema again resigned following the Olive Tree's

losses to Silvio Berlusconi's forces in regional elections. The subsequent Amato government, with the SDI again participating, remained in office until the Olive Tree alliance, under Francesco Rutelli, suffered a major defeat at the May 2001 election.

After completing a five-year term as head of the European Commission, Prodi returned to active domestic politics. While maintaining the Olive Tree, he set about organizing a broader center-left coalition, initially called the Grand Democratic Alliance (*Grande Alleanza Democratica*—GAD) and then the Union, in preparation for the 2006 election. At the 2006 election, Italian voters residing overseas elected six delegates and four senators running under a single Union ticket.

Leader: Romano PRODI (Prime Minister of the Republic).

Olive Tree (*L'Ulivo*). As the 2006 election approached, the decade-old Olive Tree alliance of Romano Prodi largely remained together, the principal changes being the merger of several constituent parties, including the PPI, into the Democracy Is Freedom–*La Margherita* party and the departure of the Italian Democratic Socialists, which merged with the Italian Radicals and two smaller groups to form the Rose in the Fist alliance (below). In 2004 the coalition adopted the designation United in the Olive Tree (*Uniti nell'Ulivo*)—its logo continues to be used by supportive parties—but then in February 2005 was reconfigured as the **Olive Tree Federation** (*Federazione dell'Ulivo*), which now comprises the three parties listed directly below. Collectively, they won 220 Chamber seats. For the Senate, however, they ran independently, although still under the Union rubric. The Olive Tree won 1 seat in the Senate in Molise, the only jurisdiction where it ran as a single party.

Leader: Romano PRODI, Anna FINOC-CHIARO (Senate Leader).

Democrats of the Left (*Democratici di Sinistra*—DS). Delegates to a March 1990 extraordinary congress of the Italian Communist Party (*Partito Comunista Italiano*—PCI) voted to abandon the traditional name of the organization, which was commonly referenced thereafter as *La Cosa* (The Thing) until announcement in October of a new name, the Democratic Party of the Left (*Partito Democratico della Sinistra*—PDS). Formal adoption of the new name occurred on February 3, 1991, at a final congress of the PCI. The party adopted the current shorter form for its name in February 1998, when it also abandoned the hammer and sickle as its symbol and replaced it with a rose and EU stars.

Formerly a staunch advocate of far-reaching nationalization, land redistribution, and labor and social reforms, the PCI had in recent decades sought to achieve power by parliamentary means and had long been Italy's second-leading party in both voting strength and legislative representation. In foreign policy matters the PCI had maintained an attitude of considerable independence toward the Soviet Union, as championed by Enrico BERLINGUER, an advocate of "Eurocommunism" and the party's secretary general until his death in 1984. Berlinguer's successor, Alessandro NATTA, was in turn succeeded in 1988 by Achille OCCHETTO, who promised a somewhat vaguely defined "new course" of party renewal that in 1990–1991 led to abandonment of much of the traditional party line and the formation of the PDS with a democratic socialist orientation. Having won 16.1 percent of the national vote in 1992, the PDS advanced to 20.4 percent in March 1994, although failing to achieve a breakthrough to political power as a member of the Progressive Alliance (AP). In the June European balloting PDS support slipped, whereupon Occhetto resigned as general secretary.

The PDS made major advances in local and regional elections in late 1994 and April–May 1995, on the latter occasion heading the poll with 24.6 percent of the vote. In July 1995 it took the historic decision to enter a formal center-left coalition, becoming the strongest component of the Olive Tree alliance. Following the latter's victory in the April 1996 legislative elections (in which the

PDS won 21.1 percent of the proportional vote), the party was rewarded with nine posts in the resultant Prodi government, with Walter VELTRONI of the PDS becoming deputy prime minister. Upon succeeding Prodi in October 1998, Massimo D'Alema became the first ex-communist to head a Western European nation. At the April 2006 election the DS again led the Olive Tree alliance. Separately, it won 17.2 percent of the Senate proportional vote and 62 seats.

Leaders: Massimo D'ALEMA (Deputy Prime Minister and President of the Party), Piero FASSINO (National Secretary), Luciano VIOLANTE (Leader in the Chamber of Deputies).

Daisy–Democracy Is Freedom (*Margherita–Democrazia è Libertà*—M-DL). Widely referenced simply as *La Margherita* ("Daisy"), Democracy Is Freedom was formally constituted as a unified party in March 2002. It began in 2001 as the centrist *Margherita* alliance of four parties—The Democrats, the Italian Popular Party (PPI), Italian Renewal (RI), and the Democratic Union for Europe (see UDEUR, below)—intended to counterbalance the leftist DS within the Olive Tree. Under the leadership of Francesco Rutelli the alliance won 14.5 percent of the proportional vote at the May 2001 election. The subsequent formation of the unified party was marred only by the decision of the UDEUR to remain aloof, in part because of objections to Rutelli's continued leadership.

The Democrats (*I Democratici*) dated from a February 1999 announcement by former prime minister Romano Prodi that he planned to form a new party, with the probable name Democrats for the Olive Tree (*Democratici per l'Ulivo*), in an effort to recast *l'Ulivo* and thereby strengthen the center-left prior to the European Parliament elections in June. The new formation's name was soon simplified to the Democrats. Those supporting the new party included Francesco

Rutelli, at that time the mayor of Rome; Antonio MACCANICO, cabinet minister and founder in 1996 of the Democratic Union (UD; see PRI, below); Sen. Antonio Di Pietro, the former Milan magistrate and anticorruption campaigner (see Italy of Values, below); Leoluca ORLANDO, mayor of Palermo and leader of the anti-Mafia Network "Movement for Democracy" (*Rete "Movimento per la Democrazia"*), which had won 2 percent of the national vote as part of the AP in March 1994; and the Hundred Cities for a New Italy (*Centocittà per un'Italia Nuova*) progressive movement. Prodi stepped aside from the leadership in April, having been nominated for the presidency of the European Commission.

The Italian Popular Party (*Partito Popolare Italiano*—PPI), founded by Don Luigi STURZO in the early 20th century, had functioned as Italy's Catholic party until the rise of fascism in 1922. It was revived as the Christian Democratic Party (*Partito della Democrazia Cristiana*—DC) after World War II, balancing clerical influence and ideas of social reform and serving as the mainstay of a succession of governments prior to changing its name in January 1994. By then, the DC had fallen victim to a wave of corruption charges, including assertions that its most prominent member, seventime prime minister Giulio ANDREOTTI, had links to the Mafia. In the March 1994 general election the PPI won only 11.1 percent of the vote as a member of the Pact for Italy (PI).

In opposition, the PPI became deeply divided over whether to form an alliance with Silvio Berlusconi's PL. The controversy yielded an open split in March 1995, when the anti-Berlusconi "Democratic" wing elected Geraldo Bianco as PPI leader in the absence of the previously dominant faction, which disputed the election's legitimacy. In local elections in April–May the two factions competed separately, the "Democrats" winning 6 percent and the pro-Berlusconi faction

3 percent. In July 1995 the pro-Berlusconi faction formally broke away, becoming the United Christian Democrats (see UDC, below), while the rump PPI became a key component of the center-left Olive Tree alliance for the April 1996 legislative elections. In 2001 it won 44 Chamber and 18 Senate seats for the alliance.

The Italian Renewal (*Rinnovamento Italiano*—RI) had been launched in February 1996 by Lamberto Dini, a month after the fall of his year-old government of technocrats. Designated the "Dini RI List" for the April legislative elections, the party won 4.3 percent of the proportional vote. Dini subsequently served as foreign minister under Prime Ministers Prodi, D'Alema, and Amato.

In May 2005 *La Margherita* decided to prepare its own candidate list for the anticipated 2006 general election, although it remained within the Olive Tree and the Union. An element of rivalry between Prodi and Rutelli may have played a part in the decision. *La Margherita* won 10.5 percent of the Senate vote and 39 seats, placing it second to the DS in the Union's Senate standing.

Leaders: Francesco RUTELLI (Deputy Prime Minister and Federal President), Arturo PARISI (President of the Federal Assembly), Anna FINOCCHIARO (Leader in the Senate), Dario FRANCESCHINI (Leader in the Chamber of Deputies and Coordinator of the Federal Executive), Lamberto DINI.

European Republican Movement (*Movimento Repubblicani Europei*—MRE). The MRE was established by left-leaning dissidents within the PRI who objected to Giorgio La Malfa's decision to align with Silvio Berlusconi's House of Freedoms alliance and to support his government following the 2001 election. At a party congress held in May 2006, the MRE called for greater power-sharing with the two larger parties in the Olive Tree alliance.

Leaders: Luciana SBARBATI (Political Secretary), Adriano MUSI (President), Milena MOSCI (Secretary General).

Communist Refoundation Party (*Partito della Rifondazione Comunista*—PRC). In February 1991 a dissident Communist Refoundation Movement (*Movimento di Rifondazione Comunista*) assembled in Rome to revive the old Communist party, following the latter's conversion a week earlier to the PDS (see the DS, above). The new group was formally launched during a conference in Rome in May 1991; a month later the Proletarian Democracy (*Democrazia Proletaria*—DP), a small party with roots in a 1976 leftist electoral alliance, voted to dissolve and join the new group.

Having won 5.6 percent of the vote in the 1992 Chamber of Deputies election, the PRC advanced to 6.0 percent in 1994 as a member of the Progressive Alliance (AP), from which it later distanced itself. In June 1995 the PRC was weakened by the defection of 14 of its 35 lower house deputies in protest at the alleged "isolationism" of the leadership. By mutual agreement, the rump PRC remained outside the center-left Olive Tree alliance in the April 1996 legislative elections, at which it increased its proportional vote to 8.6 percent. It then gave external backing to the minority Olive Tree government formed in May.

For more than two years the PRC was the key player in keeping the Prodi government in power, taking disagreements to the brink on several occasions over economic priorities (a 35-hour week and a plan to stem unemployment in the south) and foreign policy issues (intervention in Albania and expansion of NATO). But the PRC was itself divided in these confrontations, notably when it nearly forced Prodi to resign in October 1997 but backed down when rank-and-file members protested the party's action. A year later, as the PRC withdrew its support of the 1999 budget and Prodi's coalition collapsed, the strains within the PRC split the party. A progov-

ernment faction defected and formed the PdCI (below). At the May 2001 election the PRC won 3 Senate and 11 Chamber seats, all of the latter because of its 5 percent vote share in the proportional balloting. At the 2006 election the party rebounded, winning 41 Chamber and 27 Senate seats.

Leader: Franco GIORDANO (Secretary General), Gennaro MIGLIORE (Leader in the Chamber of Deputies), Giovanni RUSSO SPENA (Senate Leader).

Rose in the Fist (*Rosa nel Pugno*—RnP). The Rose in the Fist was formed in 2005 as an alliance between the Italian Democratic Socialists and Italian Radicals. The alliance was undertaken to strengthen the hand of Italy's historical liberal, socialist, and lay movements in the 2006 general election. The party's platform stresses a range of primarily social-policy goals, including simplified divorce, access to the "day after" contraceptive pill, legalization of civil unions for gay and heterosexual couples, and legalization of doctor-assisted suicide.

The RnP won 18 Chamber but no Senate seats in the 2006 election.

Leaders: Emma BONINO, Enrico BOSELLI.

Italian Democratic Socialists (*Socialisti Democratici Italiani*—SDI). Founded in 1892, the historic Italian Socialist Party (*Partito Socialista Italiano*—PSI) saw the Communists (PCI) break away in 1921 and survived the suppression of the left during the fascist era. In 1947 a major split developed over the question of collaboration with the Communists, a majority faction led by Pietro NENNI aligning itself with the PCI and a minority right-wing group led by Giuseppe SARAGAT forming what became the Italian Social Democratic Party (*Partito Socialista Democratico Italiano*—PSDI) in 1952. In opposition through the 1950s, the PSI participated in the so-called "opening to the left" from 1962, which eventually led to a coalition with the Christian Democrats. The PSI and PSDI merged in 1966 but split again in 1969, with the more conservative elements reforming the PSDI.

Consistently the third-largest party in both houses of Parliament, the PSI was a member of most governments in the 1970s and 1980s, its leader, Bettino Craxi, becoming the first-ever PSI prime minister in 1983 and achieving a postwar record of incumbency before resigning in 1987. Craxi resigned as PSI general secretary in 1993, after 17 years in office, in the face of cautionary warrants indicating that he was under investigation on 50 charges of corruption and illicit party funding. In August Craxi's parliamentary immunity was lifted.

In the wake of charges against numerous other PSI figures, the party slumped to 2.2 percent in the March 1994 parliamentary poll, which some PSI elements contested under the banner of the Democratic Alliance (see under PRI, below), following suit in the European Parliament balloting in June. In July Craxi received a lengthy prison sentence while still facing other charges, along with about 30 other former PSI officials. (By mid-1999 Craxi, a fugitive in Tunisia, faced some 26 years in prison after multiple convictions. He died in January 2000.)

Seeking to recover its former constituency, the PSI transformed itself into the Italian Socialists (*Socialisti Italiani*—SI) in November 1994. For the April 1996 legislative elections the SI cooperated closely with the Italian Renewal (RI) within the broader Olive Tree alliance. In 1998 the PSDI, which had participated in many center-left coalition governments before losing all its lower house seats in 1994, remerged with the SI, with the conjoint grouping adopting the SDI designation. The SDI held one cabinet post in the first D'Alema government but as part of the "Clover" alliance (with the PRI and Francesco Cossiga's Union for the Republic) withdrew its support and forced the prime minister's resignation in December 1999. In February 2000, however, the SDI broke from the "Clover" group when Cossiga's party moved closer to Silvio Berlusconi's Freedom Alliance. Two months later it joined the Amato administration.

Prior to the 2001 national election the SDI joined with the Green Federation (FdV, below) in *Il Girasole* ("Sunflower"), a suballiance within the Olive Tree that went on to win 16 Senate and 18 Chamber seats.

Leaders: Enrico BOSELLI (Secretary), Roberto VILLETTI (Vice Secretary).

Italian Radicals (*Radicali Italiani*). Since 2002 the title of the electoral affiliate of the **Radical Party** (*Partito Radicale*—PR), Italian Radicals is a predominantly libertarian middle-class grouping advocating civil and human rights. The PR more formally identifies itself as a movement associated with the **Transnational Radical Party** (*Partito Radicale Trasnazionale*), which distances itself from national politics.

The PR's membership in the Chamber of Deputies jumped from 4 seats in 1976 to 18 following the June 1979 election—by far the largest gain of any party. In November its secretary general, Jean FABRE, a French citizen, was sentenced by a Paris court to a month in jail for evading conscription. In 1984, after having fled to France, PR deputy Antonio NEGRI was sentenced to 30 years imprisonment for complicity in a variety of terrorist acts, although he and seven others were acquitted in January 1986 of being "moral leaders" of the Red Brigades and other extremist groups.

Gravitating to the right in the 1990s, the PR presented an unsuccessful Pannella List (*Lista Pannella*—LP) at the March 1994 poll as an ally of Berlusconi's Freedom Alliance. For the 1996 election Pannella joined with TV personality and critic Vittorio Sgarbi (now of the Party of Beauty, below) to present a *Lista Pannella-Sgarbi*. At the May 2001 balloting the PR offered a *Lista Pannella-Bonino* that attracted considerable attention in late April and early May when party leader

Emma Bonino staged a hunger strike to protest the media's failure to cover her party's platform. The list failed to win seats in either house, although the *Lista Bonino* won two seats in the European Parliament in 2004.

Leaders: Emma BONINO, Marco PAN-NELLA, Daniele CAPEZZONE (Secretary).

Italy of Values (*Italia dei Valori*—IdV). The Italy of Values movement was established in 1998 as a liberal democratic, law-and-order, reformist organization by Antonio Di Pietro, a former magistrate who had attracted national attention early in the decade for winning convictions against a number of national politicians in the "clean hands" (*Mani Pulite*) anticorruption campaign. Refusing to reestablish ties to the center-left Olive Tree (despite having initially lent support to Romano Prodi's Democrats) but also rejecting participation in the center-right Berlusconi alliance, Di Pietro put forward his organization's own list, the *Lista Di Pietro–Italia dei Valori*, for the May 2001 elections. It failed to win any Chamber seats, narrowly missing the 4 percent threshold for proportional seats, but retained one Senate seat. For the 2004 European Parliament elections the IdV's two successful candidates were Di Pietro and former Communist leader Achille Occhetto. The party won 17 Chamber and 4 Senate seats in the 2006 election.

Leaders: Antonio DI PIETRO (President), Massimo DONADI (Leader in the Chamber of Deputies).

Party of Italian Communists (*Partito dei Comunisti Italiani*—PdCI). Formed shortly after the PRC withdrew support of the Prodi government in October 1998, the PdCI was largely composed of PRC defectors led by Armando Cossutta, formerly the PRC president. However, the 21 deputies who followed Cossutta out of the PRC were insufficient to salvage the Prodi government. Subsequently, the Communists reconciled themselves to being part of a coalition that included former Christian Democrats and received two cabinet posts in the D'Alema government, the first regime in half a century to include communists. The PdCI continued in the subse-quent Amato administration and campaigned as part of the Olive Tree in 2001. At the 2006 election, the party won 16 Chamber seats.

Leaders: Oliviero DILIBERTO (National Secretary), Armando COSSUTTA, Cosimo Giuseppe SGOBIO (Leader in the Chamber of Deputies).

Federation of the Greens (*Federazione dei Verdi*—FdV). The FdV was officially launched in November 1986 as a union of regional Green lists. In its first national election (June 1987) it won 1 Senate and 13 Chamber seats. After merging with the competing Rainbow Greens (*Verdi Arcobaleno*) in December 1990, the FdV in April 1992 improved its standing to 4 Senate and 16 Chamber seats on a national vote share of 2.8 percent. As a member of the Progressive Alliance in March 1994 its share slipped to 2.7 percent. The Greens won a 2.5 percent proportional vote share in the April 1996 legislative elections, following which Edo RONCHI of the FdV was appointed environment minister, a position he retained in the two D'Alema governments. Alfonso Scanio then served as minister of agriculture under Prime Minister Amato. The party won 9 Senate and 8 Chamber seats in May 2001 as part of the "Sunflower" alliance (with the Italian Democratic Socialists) within the Olive Tree. Although the FdV did not join in formation of the Olive Tree Federation in early 2005, it remained closely allied with the Olive Tree parties. The Greens won 15 Chamber seats at the April 2006 election. For the Senate contest, it joined with the PdCI (above) and the small **United Consumers** (*Consumatori Uniti*—CU), led by Bruno DE VITA, in a **Together with the Union** (*Insieme con L'Unione*) list that won 11 seats.

Leaders: Alfonso PECORARO SCANIO (President), Angelo BONELLI (Leader in the Chamber of Deputies).

Popular–UDEUR (*Popolari*—UDEUR). The UDEUR (Democratic Union for Europe/*Unione Democratica per l'Europa*) is the partial successor to the Democratic Union for the Republic (*Unione Democratica per* *la Repubblica*—UDR), which was formed in late 1997 by former president Francesco Cossiga. The UDR quickly attracted deputies and senators from centrist and conservative elements in other parties, including, in February 1998, the CDU and CCD. Intended as Cossiga's vehicle for assembling moderate democrats and Christian reformers into the equivalent of the old Christian Democratic Party (the PPI's predecessor), the UDR played a pivotal role in the October 1998 formation of the D'Alema government, in which it was awarded three portfolios, including defense.

In January 1999 Cossiga announced his resignation as UDR chair, stating that he would be turning his attention to establishing an umbrella group for like-minded parties in preparation for the June 1999 European Parliament elections. Cossiga's resultant Union for the Republic (UR), joined with the SDI and PRI in the "Clover" parliamentary alliance, withdrew its support from the D'Alema government in December 1999, although the rump of the UDR, reorganized in May as the UDEUR, remained in the government. The UDEUR subsequently revised its statute and added *Popolari* to its name. A former president, Irene PIVETTI, who had been expelled from the Northern League in 1996, retired from politics in 2001 to pursue a TV career.

At the 2001 elections the UDEUR participated in the Olive Tree as part of the *Margherita* alliance, but in 2002 it remained aloof when the other *Margherita* parties decided to unify. The UDEUR won 10 Chamber and 3 Senate seats in the 2006 election.

Leaders: Clemente MASTELLA (National Secretary), Mauro FABRIS (Leader in the Chamber of Deputies).

South Tyrolean People's Party (*Südtiroler Volkspartei*—SVP). The SVP is a moderate autonomist grouping representing the German-speaking inhabitants of the South Tyrol (Bolzano/Bozen or Alto Adige). In 1996 the SVP joined the Olive Tree alliance, to which it remained affiliated in May 2001 although offering two candidate lists, the SVP list and the

SVP–Olive Tree list. Together, they won eight Chamber and five Senate seats. In 2004 the SVP ran with the Olive Tree alliance in the balloting for the European Parliament, winning one seat. The SVP won four Chamber and two Senate seats in 2006. A united **Union–South Tyrolean People's Party** ticket won three additional seats in the Senate, bringing the SVP total to five seats in that chamber.

Leaders: Elmar Pichler ROLLE (Leader), Michl EBNER.

Autonomy Liberty Democracy (*Autonomie Liberté Démocratie*). This center-left coalition was created for the 2006 election in the Valle d'Aosta, which is guaranteed one deputy and one senator under the constitution. The coalition included ten parties: *Alé Vallée*, **Alternative Greens** (*Verdi Alternativi*), **Alternative Left** (*Sinistra Alternativa*), **Committee of Valdaostans** (*Comité de Valdôtains*), the DS (*Gauche Valdôtaine*), the IdV, *La Margherita*, the PRC, the RnP, and the **Valle d'Aosta Alive** (*Vallé d'Aoste Vive*).

Consumers' List (*Lista Consumatori*). This small party was founded in 2004 and joined the center-left coalition the following year. It won one seat in the Senate at the 2006 election.

Leaders: David BADINI (National Secretary), Renato CAMPIGLIA (President).

Parliamentary Opposition

House of Freedoms (*Casa delle Libertà*). Organization of the *Casa* was begun in September–October 2000 by Silvio Berlusconi in preparation for the 2001 general election. The new coalition was the successor to his Freedom Alliance (*Polo delle Libertà*—PL), which had been formed prior to the 1994 balloting as a right-wing coalition consisting principally of *Forza Italia* and the Northern League (LN) in the north and a Good Government Alliance (*Polo del Buon Governo*—PBG) of the National Alliance (AN) and the Christian Democratic Center (CCD) in the south. The PL was also supported by the Union of the Democratic Center (*Unione delle Centro Democratico*—UCD), formed by right-wing elements from the

Italian Liberal Party (*Partito Liberale Italiano—* PLI). Having taken power after the March 1994 election, the PL quickly showed strains, yielding the exit of the LN in December and the collapse of the first Berlusconi government.

Minus the LN, the PL structure was retained for the April 1996 elections, although competition between Berlusconi and AN leader Gianfranco Fini damaged its prospects of regaining power. While the PL's aggregate share of the proportional vote, at 44 percent, was above its comparable 1994 tally and ten points higher than that obtained by the center-left Olive Tree alliance, the latter's gains in the constituency balloting and resultant plurality enabled it to form a minority government, to which the PL parties formed the main opposition. At the May 2001 election the House of Freedoms alliance, which had been joined by the New Italian Socialist Party (NPSI), won majorities in both houses of Parliament, permitting Berlusconi to form a new center-right government. As the 2006 general election approached, the alliance remained unchanged from its 2001 configuration, apart from consolidation among Christian Democrats and the addition of the small Italian Republican Party (PRI). At the 2006 election, House of Freedoms won two Senate seats in Trentino-Alto Adige, the only electoral region where it ran as a separate ticket.

Leader: Silvio BERLUSCONI.

Forza Italia (FI). The FI was launched in January 1994, its name being the traditional chant of supporters of the Italian national soccer team (loosely translatable as "Go, Italy!"). Its founder and present leader, Italy's most powerful media tycoon and owner of the leading Milan soccer team, identified the prevention of an electoral victory by the ex-communist Democratic Party of the Left (PDS; see Democrats of the Left, above) as the new group's principal objective. To this end, it organized the right-wing PL.

Although facing corruption charges and other indictments related to his business activities, Berlusconi led the FI in the April 1996 legislative elections, with the FI winning a 21 percent share of the proportional vote and maintaining its status as the strongest PL

component. Despite his continuing legal problems, Berlusconi was elected party president at the FI's national congress in April 1998. He spent much of the next three years successfully fighting a string of indictments and appealing convictions, all while maintaining political opposition to the center-left Olive Tree administrations. At the 2001 election the FI won 29 percent of the proportional vote in the Chamber of Deputies. FI won 79 Senate and 140 Chamber seats in 2006, making it the leading opposition party.

Leaders: Silvio BERLUSCONI (Former Prime Minister of the Republic and President of the Party), Giulio TREMONTI (Vice President), Alfredo BIONDI (President of the National Council), Sandro BONDI (National Coordinator), Elio VITO (Leader in the Chamber of Deputies), Renato Giuseppe SCHIFANI (Senate Leader).

National Alliance (*Alleanza Nazionale—* AN). The AN designation was initially adopted in January 1994 by the nationalist and anticommunist Italian Social Movement-National Right (*Movimiento Sociale Italiano-Destra Nazionale—*MSI-DN) in a move to attract support from former Christian Democrats and other right-wing groups, including Italian monarchists. Generally characterized as neofascist (a label that the party rejected, while revering the memory of Benito Mussolini), the MSI-DN suffered electoral setbacks and splits in the 1970s, although it maintained a substantial parliamentary presence through the 1980s.

In March 1994 the AN won 13.5 percent of the proportional vote as part of the PL, its support being concentrated in southern Italy, where coalition members ran under the label of the Berlusconi-supportive Good Governance Alliance (PBG); six AN ministers were included in the Berlusconi government appointed in May. A Rome congress in January 1995 officially adopted the AN label and deleted most references to fascism in the AN platform, while a hard-line minority opted to form the Social Movement-Tricolor Flame (MS-FT, below).

The regional elections of April–May yielded a modest increase in the AN vote to 14.1 percent, which rose further to 15.7 percent in the April 1996 legislative balloting. In 1998 opinion polls, AN leader Fini was among the most popular politicians in Italy.

Once again allied with the FI, the AN won 12 percent of the 2001 proportional vote and joined the new Berlusconi government, with Fini as deputy prime minister.

AN became the second-largest opposition party in 2006, winning 71 Chamber and 41 Senate seats.

Leaders: Gianfranco FINI (President), Ignazio LA RUSSA (Leader in the Chamber of Deputies), Altero MATTEOLI (Senate Leader).

Union of Christian and Center Democrats

(*Unione dei Democratici Cristiani e di Democratici Centro*—UDC). Frequently referenced simply as the Union of Christian Democrats, the UDC was established in December 2002 by merger of the Christian Democratic Center (*Centro Cristiano Democratico*—CCD), the United Christian Democrats (*Cristiani Democratici Uniti*—CDU), and the European Democracy (*Democrazia Europea*—DE). Prior to the 2001 general election the CCD and CDU had organized the *Biancofiore* ("White Flower") alliance, which won 3.2 percent of the proportional vote as a component of Berlusconi's House of Freedoms.

The CCD had been established by a right-wing faction of the former Christian Democratic Party (see the discussion of the PPI, under *La Margherita*, above). As a member of the victorious Freedom Alliance (PL) coalition in March 1994, it was awarded one portfolio in the first Berlusconi government. In 1996 it and the CDU presented a joint proportional list that won 5.8 percent of the vote. Much of the party, including its leader, Clemente Mastella, joined Francesco Cossiga's UDR (see UDEUR, above) in February 1998. At the 2001 general election the CCD accounted for 24 of the House of Freedoms' lower house seats and 21 seats in the Senate.

The CDU had also been founded, in July 1995, by a minority right-wing faction of the PPI that favored participation in Berlusconi's PL. In February 1998 the CDU broke from the PL, with many of its members joining the new UDR. The CDU supported formation of the D'Alema government in October 1998 but not the Amato administration in April 2000. By then, the linkage to the pro-Berlusconi forces had been reestablished. At the 2001 elections the CDU claimed 17 Chamber and 8 Senate seats.

The DE had been established in November 2000 by Sergio D'ANTONI, a former Christian Democratic trade union leader. Among his supporters was former prime minister Giulio Andreotti. At the May 2001 election the DE party won only 2.4 percent of the proportional vote and therefore failed to win any Chamber seats, but it captured two Senate seats. In April 2004 D'Antoni abandoned the UDC and joined the opposition, and in October 2004 he won a by-election chamber seat as a member of *La Margherita*.

On occasion the UDC has not sided with Prime Minister Berlusconi. In July 2003 it threatened to leave the governing coalition if the government blocked an investigation into possible corruption in his media empire, while in July 2004 it joined the AN in objecting to the proposed 2005 budget. In April 2005 its withdrawal from the government forced the prime minister's resignation, although it then agreed to participate in a reshuffled cabinet.

In September 2004 the nomination of the party president, Rocco Buttiglione, a fervent Catholic, to serve as European Commission vice president and commissioner for Justice, Freedom, and Security was withdrawn because of controversial comments he had made about homosexuality and the role of women in the family.

The UDC won 39 Chamber and 21 Senate seats in 2006.

Leaders: Pier Ferdinando CASINI, Rocco BUTTIGLIONE (President), Lorenzo CESA (Political Secretary), Luca VOLONTÉ (Leader in the Chamber of Deputies), Francesco D'ONFRIO (Senate Leader).

Northern League–Movement for Autonomy (*Lega Nord–Movimento per l'Autonomia*). On February 4, 2006, proponents of greater regional autonomy forged an alliance, called the "Pact for Autonomy," between the Northern League, representing Italy's northern regions, and the Movement for Autonomy, representing Sicily. Supporters of the Northern League had long called for ending the federal government's policy of shunting tax revenues from the industrialized north to the poorer, agricultural south. The alliance marked a departure from prior political trends, which had pitted the wealthier regions of northern Italy against the south. At the 2006 election, the alliance won 26 Chamber and 13 Senate seats.

Northern League (*Lega Nord*—LN). The LN formed in February 1991 as a federation of the Lombard League (*Lega Lombarda*—LL) and sister parties in Emilio Romagna, Liguria, Piedmont, Tuscany, and Veneto. The party's name for the northern regions is "Padania" (the lands of the Po River), a term that the LN's parliamentary groups have included in their names.

Launched in 1979 and named after a 12th-century federation of northern Italian cities, the LL achieved prominence in the 1980s as the most conspicuous of several regional groups to challenge the authority of Rome and, in particular, its use of public revenues to aid the largely impoverished south. It advocated the adoption of a federal system with substantial regional autonomy in most areas save defense and foreign policy. Its xenophobic and scarcely disguised racist outlook included a pronounced anti-immigrant posture.

The LN won 8.7 percent of the national vote in the 1992 general election and 8.4 percent as part of the PL in March 1994. Having joined the Berlusconi government in May, the LN pulled out in December amid much acrimony. In February 1995 it reestablished itself outside the PL and appended "Federal Italy" (*Italia Federale*) to its name, although

a pro-Berlusconi faction that included party leader Umberto Bossi's longtime deputy and Berlusconi's interior minister, Robert Maroni, left the party and reorganized as the Italian Federalist League (*Lega Italia Federale*—LIF). Maroni and Bossi soon reconciled, and the LIF failed to establish itself as an alternative to the LN.

The LN contested the April 1996 legislative elections independently, increasing its support to 10.1 percent of the national proportional vote and winning 59 seats in the lower house and 27 in the Senate, while becoming the strongest party in northern Italy. In opposition to the resultant center-left government, the LN convened a "parliament" in Mantua in late May, at which Bossi, flanked by green-shirted activists, reasserted the league's secessionist aims. When moderates within the party voiced doubts about the secessionist line, Bossi attracted much publicity in August by expelling their leader, former Chamber of Deputies president Irene Pivetti (subsequently of the UDEUR, above). In September Bossi led a three-day LN march and rally, the climax of which was a declaration of independence for the "Republic of Padania" and the formation of a provisional government. However, strong local opposition to the LN's aims, combined with warnings and appeals from senior politicians in Rome, apparently contributed to Bossi's subsequent announcement that he was prepared to negotiate new constitutional arrangements for northern Italy.

In January 1998 Bossi received a one-year suspended sentence for criminal incitement, and in July both he and Maroni received seven-month suspended sentences for resisting authorities and offensive behavior. Having reconciled with the FI, the LN won a surprisingly small 3.9 percent of the proportional vote in 2001 as the FI made significant inroads in the north.

Responding in part to anti-immigrant statements by the party leadership, in 2002 the Council of Europe issued a report describing the LN as "racist and xenophobic." In January 2004 Umberto Bossi resigned from the Council of Ministers because of inadequate progress on regional devolution. The LN nevertheless remained in the government coalition, and in April 2005 the party's 28 deputies and 17 senators helped approve the "Berlusconi II" government. The LN posted slight losses in the April 2006 election, winning 23 Chamber and 13 Senate seats.

Leaders: Umberto BOSSI (Federal Secretary), Roberto CASTELLI (Senate Leader), Roberto MARONI (Leader in the Chamber of Deputies).

Movement for Autonomy (*Movimento per l'Autonomia*—MPA). The MPA was founded on April 30, 2005, by Raffaele Lombardo, formerly president of the UDC in Catania and in the European Parliament, who left the party citing its failure to adequately represent the south's interests at the federal level. His decision to join forces with the Northern League came after Prodi's Union dropped the proposal to build a bridge over the Straits of Messina, joining the mainland and Sicily, from its list of legislative priorities. Lombardo and his supporters had long sought the bridge as a way to end Sicily's economic isolation.

Leader: Raffaele LOMBARDO.

Christian Democracy–New PSI (*DC–Nuovo PSI*). In early 2006, the following two parties agreed to present a unified list in the upcoming national election. The alliance won four seats in the Chamber but none in the Senate.

Leader: Paolo CIRINO POMICINO (Leader in the Chamber of Deputies).

Christian Democracy for the Autonomies (*Democrazia Cristiana per le Autonomie*). The "Nuova DC" aspires to inherit the mantle of the historic Christian Democratic Party (DC) that dominated postwar governments in Italy until its demise amid the embezzlement scandals of the early 1990s. It originated as a splinter group within the UDC led by Gianfranco Rotondi in 2004 and broke off to become a freestanding party that December. The party joined Berlusconi's House of Freedoms coalition in January 2006.

Leaders: Gianfranco ROTONDI (Political Secretary), Publio FIORI (President of the Party, formerly of the AN).

New Italian Socialist Party (*Nuovo Partito Socialista Italiano*—NPSI). The NPSI constitutes an attempt by supporters of the late Socialist leader Bettino Craxi to reestablish the old Italian Socialist Party (PSI; see the SDI, above). The party's first congress convened in January 2001, with Craxi's son Bobo and a former foreign minister in the leadership. Somewhat incongruously, the NPSI found itself allied with the postfascist National Alliance and the other center-right House of Freedoms participants for the May 2001 elections, at which it won only 0.9 percent of the proportional vote in the lower house, where it held two seats. At the 2004 European Parliament elections the NPSI offered some of its candidates on a Socialist Unity (*Unità Socialista*) list. A power struggle between Party President Craxi and Secretary Gianni De Michelis erupted at a party congress in October 2005, when Craxi charged the party was drifting too far to the right. The struggle ended with a January 2006 ruling by the Tribunal of Rome in favor of De Michelis. Craxi subsequently founded a new party, The Socialists (*I Socialisti*, below), which joined Prodi's Union coalition.

Leader: Gianni DE MICHELIS (Secretary).

Italian Republican Party (*Partito Repubblicano Italiano*—PRI). Founded in 1897, the PRI follows Giuseppe Mazzini's moderate leftist principles of social justice in a modern free society. In foreign policy it has long favored a pro-Western stance and continued membership in the Atlantic alliance. From June 1981 to November 1982 the PRI's political secretary, Giovanni Spadolini, served as the first non-DC prime minister in 37 years; thereafter, the party continued its participation in center-left coalitions until going into opposition in April 1991. Having won 4.4 percent of the national vote in 1992, the PRI contested the March 1994 poll as principal member of the Democratic Alliance (*Alleanza Democratica*—AD), which won 1.2 percent of the national vote as part of the more inclusive AP. Having resigned the party leadership in 1988 and been reinstated in January 1994, Giorgio La Malfa again resigned in October 1994 before again being reinstated in March 1995.

In 1996 the Republicans joined with the Democratic Union (*Unione Democratica*—UD) of former PRI leader Antonio Maccanico as a minor element of the successful Olive Tree alliance. In December 1999, however, as part of the three-party "Clover" group, the PRI withdrew its support from Prime Minister D'Alema, which led to his resignation. At the June 1999 election for the European Parliament, it had offered a joint list with the Federation of Liberals (*Federazione dei Liberali*—FdL), which traced its roots to the conservative Italian Liberal Party (*Partito Liberale Italiano*—PLI), a minor participant in many of Italy's post–World War II governments, into the early 1990s. Subsequently, the PRI, under longtime leader Giorgio La Malfa, continued to call for formation of a liberal democratic alliance.

Following the May 2001 election La Malfa led the party into Berlusconi's House of Freedoms alliance, which precipitated a split in the party and formation by dissidents of the Movement of European Republicans (MRE). In April 2005 La Malfa joined the "Berlusconi II" cabinet as minister of EU policy. La Malfa and Party Political Secretary Francesco Nucara won seats in the Chamber in 2006, running on the Forza Italia list. No other PRI members are in Parliament.

Leaders: Giorgio LA MALFA (President), Francesco NUCARA (Political Secretary), Giancarlo CAMERUCCI (Administrator).

One small center-right party founded by Italians living abroad, **For Italy in the World with Tremaglia** (*Partito per Italia nel Mondo con Tremaglia*), won one seat in the Chamber of Deputies as part of the House of Freedoms.

Other Parties

Liberal Reformers (*Riformatori Liberali*). This small libertarian party formed in 2005 in protest against the Italian Radicals' alliance with the Union center-left coalition. In November 2005 the Liberal Reformers joined Berlusconi's center-right House of Freedoms coalition. The party failed to win any seats in the 2006 election.

Leaders: Benedetto DELLA VEDOVA, Marco TARADASH.

The Pact (*Il Patto*). Also identifying itself as the **Party of Liberal Democrats** (*Partito dei Liberaldemocratici*), the Pact is the latest incarnation of Mario Segni's liberal democratic reform movement. In 1994 the *Patto Segni* ran as part of the centrist Pact for Italy (PI), also headed by Segni, who had been a leading anticorruption campaigner within the Christian Democratic Party until breaking away in 1992 to urge reform of the Italian political system. His initial vehicle was the Democratic Alliance, prior to the launching of the PI in January 1994. In the March balloting the Segni Pact won 4.6 percent of the national vote. Although Segni joined in the launching of *L'Ulivo* in 1995, the party renounced its seats in the European Parliament and soon after left the Olive Tree coalition. Segni decided not to compete in the 1996 elections; instead, in July 1996 he formed the Base Committee for the Constituent Assembly (*Comitati di Base per la Costituente*—CoBaC), which called for a popular election of a Constituent Assembly to design a new republic. Segni was reelected to the European Parliament in 1999 but in 2004, running with a former

Senate president, Carlo SCOGNAMIGLIO, Segni failed to hold the seat.

Leader: Mario SEGNI.

Party of Beauty and Reason (*Partito della Bellezza e della Ragione*). Formation of the Party of Beauty was announced in April 2004 by art critic and maverick politician Vittorio Sgarbi, a former undersecretary of culture who had left the Berlusconi government in a dispute over its decision to sell a number of cultural assets. Sgarbi, who received initial support for his efforts from Giorgio La Malfa of the PRI, committed the party to one issue: protecting Italy's cultural heritage. For the 2004 European Parliament elections Sgarbi's party and La Malfa's Republicans offered a joint list. Sgarbi ran under the Consumers' List in 2006 but was unsuccessful.

Leader: Vittorio SGARBI.

Pensioners' Party (*Partito Pensionati*—PP). Dating from 1987, the PP campaigns on behalf of Italy's retirees. In 2004 it became the first such formation to win a seat in the European Parliament. A member of the Union coalition, the PP failed to win seats in the 2006 national election.

Leader: Carlo FATUZZO.

Social Action (*Azione Sociale*—AZ). AZ, originally called Freedom of Action (*Libertà di Azione*), was formed in late 2003 by Alessandra Mussolini, granddaughter of Benito Mussolini. In 1996 she had left the National Alliance following statements in which Gianfranco Fini distanced the AN from historical fascism and her grandfather's legacy. In 2004 Mussolini won a seat in the European Parliament on a **Social Alternative** list (*Alternativa Sociale–Lista Mussolini*). Social Alternative, which comprised AZ and two other parties of the far right—**New Force** (*Forza* Nuova) and the **Social National Front** (*Fronte Sociale Nazionale*)—for the 2006 election, failed to win any seats and dissolved after the election.

Leader: Alessandra MUSSOLINI.

The Socialists (*I Socialisti*). This small party came into being as a result of a schism within the New Italian Socialist Party (NPSI) between followers of NPSI leader Gianni De Michelis, who sup-

ported the party's membership in Berlusconi's governing coalition, and followers of Bobo Craxi, son of former Socialist Prime Minister Bettino Craxi, who challenged the party's drift to the right. Following a court ruling in January 2006 in favor of De Michelis's leadership of the NPSI, Craxi founded The Socialists, which joined Prodi's Union coalition. The Socialists failed to win any seats in the 2006 election.

Leader: Roberto (Bobo) CRAXI.

Social Movement–Tricolor Flame (*Movimento Sociale–Fiamma Tricolore*—MS-FT). Led by Pino RAUTI, the MS-FT emerged from the minority profascism faction of the former MSI-DN, a majority of whose members opted in January 1995 to remain with the AN. Despite having fashioned a limited electoral agreement with the Berlusconi alliance, the party failed to win any Chamber seats in the 2001 election, when it claimed only 0.4 percent of the lower house proportional vote. It failed to hold its one Senate seat in 2006. Rauti himself has withdrawn from active politics.

Leaders: Luca ROMAGNOLI (National Secretary), Roberto BEVILACQUA (Vice National Secretary), Gennaro GARGIULO (Administrative Secretary).

Italy has numerous regional groupings, many of which allied with the Northern League and the Autonomy Movement for the 2006 election. Exceptions included the **League of the Venetian Front** (*Liga Fronte Veneto*) and the **Lombard Alliance League** (*Lega Alleanza Lombarda*), which joined Prodi's Union coalition, and the Veneto-based **Northeast Project** (*Progetto Nordest*), which ran independently for both houses.

Terrorist Groups

In the second half of the 20th century Italy was often buffeted by political terrorism, over 200 names having been used by groups committed to such activity. The most notorious of the left-wing formations, the **Red Brigades** (*Brigate Rosse*), was founded in 1969, reportedly in linkage with the West German Red Army Faction terrorists. The *Brigate Rosse* engaged in numerous killings during the late 1970s, including that of former prime

Cabinet

As of May 17, 2006

Prime Minister	Romano Prodi (ind.)
Deputy Prime Ministers	Massimo D'Alema (DS)
	Francesco Rutelli (M-DL)

Ministers

Agricultural and Forestry	Paolo De Castro (UDEUR)
Communications	Paolo Gentiloni (M-DL)
Culture	Francesco Rutelli (M-DL)
Defense	Arturo Parisi (M-DL)
Economy and Finance	Tommaso Padoa Schioppa (ind.)
Education	Giuseppe Fioroni (M-DL)
Environment	Alfonso Pecoraro Scanio (FdV)
Foreign Affairs	Massimo D'Alema (DS)
Health	Livia Turco (DS) [f]
Higher Education and Scientific Research	Fabio Mussi (DS)
Industry	Pierluigi Bersani (DS)
Infrastructure	Antonio Di Pietro (IdV)
Interior	Giuliano Amato (ind.)
Justice	Clemente Mastella (UDEUR)
Labor	Cesare Damiano (DS)
Social Policy	Paolo Ferrero (PRC)
Transport	Alessandro Bianchi (ind.)

Ministers without Portfolio

Equal Opportunities	Barbara Pollastrini (DS) [f]
European Affairs	Emma Bonino (RnP) [f]
Family	Rosy Bindi (DL) [f]
Fulfillment of Government Programs	Giulio Santagata (M-DL)
Parliamentary Relations and Reform	Vannino Chiti (DS)
Public Administration	Luigi Nicolais (DS)
Regional Affairs	Linda Lanzillotta (M-DL) [f]
Youth and Sports	Giovanna Melandri (DS) [f]

[f] = female

minister Aldo Moro; subsequently, one of its offshoots, the **Union of Fighting Communists** (*Unione dei Comunisti Combattenti*—UCC), claimed responsibility for the 1987 murder of an air force general and the 1988 assassination of Sen. Roberto RUFFILLI, a leading ally of Prime Minister De Mita. In 1998 Renato CURCIO, a cofounder of the Red Brigades and its last leading figure behind bars, was freed from prison after serving 24 years of a 30-year sentence. In May 1999 the Red Brigades apparently resurfaced, claiming responsibility for assassinating Massimo D'ANTONA, an adviser to the minister of labor.

More recently, the Red Brigades have claimed responsibility for several murders, including the assassination in March 2002 of government economic adviser Marco BIAGI. Members continue to be apprehended, including Leonardo

BERTULAZZI, who was arrested in Argentina in November 2002. The reputed head of logistics for the organization, he had been convicted in absentia in 1977 for kidnapping. In May 2004 the EU added the Red Brigades to its list of terrorist organizations.

A militant group calling itself the **Territorial Anti-Imperialist Nuclei** has recently surfaced.

Legislature

The bicameral **Parliament** (*Parlamento*) consists of an upper house, the Senate, and a lower house, the Chamber of Deputies, of roughly equal power.

Senate (*Senato*). The upper house consists of 322 members elected to a five-year term (except for senators for life, currently numbering 7) by universal suffrage under a proportional representation system that was proposed by the Berlusconi government and adopted on December 14, 2005 (recognizing coalitions winning at least 20 percent of the vote and including at least one party winning at least 3 percent of the vote, and parties winning at least 8 percent running independently or in a coalition winning less than 20 percent of the vote). Under a new "majority prize" provision, a coalition winning a majority of votes in a region will automatically be allocated no less than 55 percent of the region's seats, with the rest distributed among other qualifying coalitions and parties. The majority prize applies to all regions but Molise (which elects only 2 senators), Valle d'Aosta (1 senator), and Trentino-Alto Adige (which falls under a separate election law dividing its 6 seats evenly between Italian- and German-speaking senators). Under a law passed in December 2001, Italian citizens residing abroad elect 6 senators representing four districts: Europe; North and Central America; South America; and Africa, Asia, Oceania, and Antarctica.

The April 9–10, 2006, election produced the following results: The Union, 158 seats (Democrats of the Left, 62; Daisy–Democracy Is Freedom, 39; Communist Refoundation Party, 27; Together with the Union, 11; Italy of Values, 4; The Union [present only abroad and in Trentino-Alto Adige], 4; Popular–UDEUR, 3; The Union–South Tyrolese People's Party [present only in Trentino-Alto Adige], 3; South Tyrolese People's Party, 2; Autonomy Liberty Democracy, 1; Consumers List, 1; Olive Tree [present only in Molise], 1); House of Freedoms, 156 (*Forza Italia*, 79; National Alliance, 41; Union of Christian and Center Democrats, 21; Northern League–Movement for Autonomy, 13; House of Freedoms [present only in Trentino-Alto Adige], 2); and Italian Associations in South America, 1.

President: Fausto BERTINOTTI.

Chamber of Deputies (*Camera dei Deputati*). The lower house consists of 630 members elected to a five-year term by universal suffrage, with 617 seats distributed under the new proportional representation system (recognizing coalition lists with a 10 percent threshold that include at least one party receiving at least 2 percent of the vote, separate party lists with a 4 percent threshold, and parties representing linguistic minorities that win at least 20 percent of the vote in their corresponding regions). Valle d'Aosta elects 1 member, and overseas Italian citizens elect the remaining 12 deputies representing the same four districts as in the Senate. Under the new majority prize provision, a coalition that receives a majority of the vote but less than 55 percent of the seats in Italy proper (340 out of 618) automatically is awarded the full 340 seats.

The April 9–10, 2006, election produced the following results: The Union, 348 (Olive Tree, 220; Communist Refoundation Party, 41; Rose in the Fist, 18; Italy of Values, 17; Party of Italian Communists, 16; Federation of the Greens, 15; Popular–UDEUR, 10; The Union [abroad], 6; South Tyrolean People's Party, 4; Autonomy Liberty Democracy, 1); House of Freedoms, 281 (*Forza Italia*, 140; National Alliance, 71; Union of Christian and Center Democrats, 39; Northern League–Movement for Autonomy, 26; Christian Democracy–New PSI, 4; For Italy in the World with Tremaglia [abroad], 1); and Italian Associations in South America, 1.

As of June 2006 the deputies were organized into the following parliamentary groups (deputies may, however, change their affiliation at any time): Olive Tree, 218 members; *Forza Italia*, 134; National Alliance, 72; Communist Refoundation–European Left, 41; Union of Christian and Center Democrats, 39; Northern League, 23; Italy of Values, 20; Rose in the Fist, 18; Greens, 16; Italian Communists, 16; Popular Alliance–Democratic Union for Europe, 14; mixed, 13 (linguistic minorities, 5; autonomy movement, 5; unaffiliated, 3); and Christian Democrats–Socialist Party, 6.

President: Franco MARINI.

Communications

Although freedom of speech and press is constitutionally guaranteed, the collection and release of official news is centered in the Information Service of the Presidency of the Council of Ministers.

Press

Italy's 75 or so daily papers have a relatively low combined circulation. Several of the papers are owned or supported by political parties. Editorial opinion, influenced by the Catholic Church and various economic groups, leans heavily to the right of center. Most of the newspapers are regional, notable exceptions being the nationally circulated *Corriere della Sera*, *La Stampa*, *La Repubblica*, and *Il Giorno*. The following papers are published daily in Rome, unless otherwise noted: *Corriere della Sera* (Milan, 890,000), centrist; *La Repubblica* (750,000), center-left; *La Stampa* (Turin, 540,000; evening edition *Stampa Sera*), center-left; *La Gazzetta dello Sport* (Milan, 530,000), *Il Sole-24 Ore* (Milan, 420,000), business paper; *Il Giornale* (Milan, 350,000), independent center-right; *Il Messaggero* (340,000), center-right; *Il Resto del Carlino* (Bologna, 250,000), independent conservative; *La Nazione* (Florence, 200,000), right-wing; *Il Gazzettino* (Venice, 180,000), independent; *Il Giorno* (Milan, 170,000), independent; *Il Secolo XIX* (Genoa, 160,000), independent; *Il Mattino* (Naples, 140,000), independent; *Avvenire* (Milan, 130,000), Catholic; *Il Tirreno* (Livorno, 110,000), independent; *Giornale di Sicilia* (Palermo, 90,000), independent; *Il Manifesto* (80,000), leftist; *La Gazzetta del Mezzogiorno* (Bari, 80,000); *L'Unione Sarda* (Cagliari, 80,000).

News Agencies

The leading domestic service is the Associated Press National Agency (*Agenzia Nazionale Stampa Associata*—ANSA); there is also a smaller Italian News Agency (*Agenzia Giornalistica Italia*—AGI), plus a number of specialized services. Numerous foreign bureaus maintain offices in the leading Italian cities.

Broadcasting and Computing

Three nationwide radio broadcasting networks and three television channels are operated by *Radiotelevisione Italiana* (RAI), which is responsible to the Ministry of Communications. In 1995 voters approved partial privatization of RAI, although it took nearly a decade to pass implementing legislation. Over 2,000 private radio stations now broadcast locally, as do some 900 private TV stations. The three principal private TV channels are part of Mediaset, Silvio Berlusconi's media empire. There were approximately 26.4 million television receivers and 14.8 million personal computers serving 18.5 million Internet users in 2003.

Intergovernmental Representation

Ambassador to the U.S.
Giovanni CASTELLANETA

U.S. Ambassador to Italy
Ronald P. SPOGLI

Permanent Representative to the UN
Marcello SPATAFORA

IGO Memberships (Non-UN)
ADB, AfDB, BIS, CDB, CEI, CERN, CEUR, EBRD, EIB, ESA, EU, Eurocontrol, G-10, G-7/G-8, IADB, IEA, Interpol, IOM, NATO, OECD, OSCE, PCA, WEU, WCO, WTO

LATVIA

REPUBLIC OF LATVIA

Latvijas Republika

Note: Final results in the legislative elections held on October 8, 2006, are as follows: the People's Party won 23 seats; the Greens' and Farmers' Union, 18; New Era, 18; Harmony Center, 17; Latvia's First Party/Latvia's Way, 10; Fatherland and Freedom/Latvian National Conservative Party, 8; and For Human Rights in United Latvia, 6. On November 1, President Vike-Freiberga asked Aigar Kalvītis to return as prime minister and form a new government. The new government coalition is expected to include ministers from the People's Party, the Greens' and Farmers' Union, and Latvia's First Party/Latvia's Way, and it may also include a fourth party. Without adding a fourth party, the government will have only a one-vote majority in the Parliament.

The Country

The second-largest of the former Soviet Baltic republics, Latvia is bordered on the north by Estonia, on the east by Russia, on the southeast by Belarus, and on the south by Lithuania. In 2005 an estimated 58.8 percent of the population was Latvian, 28.6 percent Russian, 3.8 percent Belarusan, 2.6 percent Ukrainian, 2.5 percent Polish, and 1.4 percent Lithuanian.

Since World War II the country has become largely urbanized, with an industrial capacity that includes steel and rolled ferrous metal products. Cattle and dairy farming are the principal agricultural activities. Natural resources include extensive deposits of peat and gypsum, in addition to forests that have long yielded substantial sawn timber output.

Ramshackle after five decades of Soviet rule, the Latvian economy was severely dislocated by the postindependence transition from command to free-market policies, experiencing sharp declines in industrial and agricultural output, as well as food and energy shortages. Between 1990 and 1993, GDP contracted by an estimated 50 percent, inflation averaged nearly 200 percent a year (peaking at

958 percent in 1992), and unemployment rose to 20 percent. There were signs of recovery in 1994 (with real GDP growth of 2 percent and inflation down to 35 percent), although Latvia lagged behind its two Baltic neighbors in implementing privatization measures. Growth was impeded in 1995 by a series

Political Status: Absorption of independent state by the Soviet Union on August 5, 1940, repudiated by the Latvian Supreme Council on May 4, 1990; resumption of full sovereignty declared August 21, 1991, and accepted by USSR State Council on September 6.

Area: 24,938 sq. mi. (64,589 sq. km.).

Population: 2,377,383 (2000C); 2,331,000 (2005E).

Major Urban Centers (2005E): RIGA (715,000), Daugavpils (110,000), Liepaja (85,000).

Official Language: Latvian.

Monetary Unit: Lats (official rate July 1, 2006: 1 lats = $1.84US). (Following its accession to the European Union in 2004, Latvia announced that it hoped to adopt the euro as its national currency by 2008. Meanwhile, the lats was pegged to the euro in January 2005.)

President: Vaira VIKE-FREIBERGA (nonparty); elected by the *Saeima* on June 17, 1999, and sworn in for a four-year term on July 8, succeeding Guntis ULMANIS (Latvian Farmers' Union); reelected on June 20, 2003, and sworn in for a second four-year term on July 8.

Prime Minister: Aigars KALVĪTIS (People's Party); nominated by the president on November 24, 2004, and confirmed by the *Saeima* on December 2 to succeed Indulis EMSIS (Greens' and Farmers' Union), who had announced his resignation on October 28.

However, international confidence in the economy remained strong, as underscored by Latvia's accession to the World Trade Organization (WTO) in February 1999 and positive comments from the European Union (EU) concerning Latvia's requested membership. Although GDP growth for 1999 was negligible (0.1 percent), it averaged 6 percent annually from 2000 to 2003. Despite that progress, Latvia was the "poorest" of the ten countries that joined the EU in May 2004. By that time, more than 60 percent of Latvia's trade was conducted with EU members.

Growth of 8.5 percent was registered in 2004 and 10.2 percent in 2005, with per capita GNP having risen more than 50 percent since 1995. However, rapidly increasing inflation (6.2 percent in 2004 and 6.9 percent in 2005) was seen as a threat to Latvia's goal of adopting the euro as of 2008.

Government and Politics

Political Background

Conquered by the Livonian branch of the Teutonic Knights in the 13th century, subjected to Polish domination in the 16th, partly ruled by Sweden in the 17th, and absorbed by Russia in the 18th, Latvia came under Bolshevik control in 1917, prior to German occupation in February 1918. Restored to power after German withdrawal in December, the Bolsheviks were defeated by British naval and German army units in March 1919, and a democratic successor regime was recognized by the Soviets in August 1920 under the Treaty of Riga. Admitted to the League of Nations in September 1921, Latvia adopted a new constitution in May 1922, but the country succumbed to a military-backed coup by the prime minister, Karlis ULMANIS, in May 1934. Latvia was obliged to conclude a treaty of mutual assistance with the Soviets in October 1939 and was formally incorporated into the USSR on August 5, 1940.

On January 11, 1990, the Latvian Supreme Soviet voted to abolish constitutional clauses according a "leading role" to the Communist Party, and

of bank failures and collateral difficulties in the broader financial sector, despite real GDP growth of 8.6 percent in 1997 following implementation of a tight monetary policy and other reforms supported by the International Monetary Fund (IMF) and the World Bank. Meanwhile, inflation had declined to 8.4 percent for 1997.

The Russian financial crisis in the second half of 1998 adversely affected the Latvian economy, GDP growth slipping to 3.6 percent for the year and heading into negative figures in early 1999.

on February 15 it condemned the 1940 annexation in favor of a "free and independent State of Latvia" as part of a restructured Soviet Union. The recently formed Latvian Popular Front secured a clear majority in legislative balloting in March and April, and on May 3 the chair of the Supreme Soviet Presidium, Anatolijs V. GORBUNOVS, became head of state by being elected chair of what was redesignated as the Supreme Council; concurrently, the deputy chair of the Popular Front, Ivars GODMANIS, was named prime minister, in succession to Edvzīns BRESIS.

In a March 3, 1991, referendum, 73.68 percent of the participants voted for independence, which was formally declared on August 21 when hardliners attempted a coup in Moscow. After securing the crucial endorsement of Russian president Yeltsin, the independence of all three Baltic republics was, in the wake of the failed coup, accepted by the new USSR State Council on September 6.

In elections to a restored Latvian Parliament (*Saeima*) on June 5–6, 1993, the recently organized Latvian Way (*Latvijas Cexļš*—LC) won nearly a third of the votes and a plurality of 36 of 100 seats. On July 7, in the third round of balloting, the *Saeima* elected Guntis ULMANIS of the Latvian Farmers' Union (*Latvijas Zemnieku Savienība*—LZS) as president of the republic, and on July 20 the *Saeima* confirmed the LC's Valdis BĪRKAVS as head of a governmental coalition that included the LZS.

The Bīrkavs government resigned on July 14, 1994, following the withdrawal of the LZS because a promise to impose protectionist duties on food imports had not been kept. After a government proposed by the right-wing Latvian National Conservative Party (*Latvijas Nacionā Konservatā Partija*—LNNK) had been rejected by the *Saeima* on August 18, a new coalition was approved on September 15 under the premiership of Māris GAILIS of the LC.

Elections to the *Saeima* on September 30 and October 1, 1995, produced a fragmented legislature amid greatly reduced LC support, with nine parties winning representation and the 18-seat tally of the centrist Master Democratic Party (*Demokrātiskā Partija Saimnieks*—DPS, or *Saimnieks*) giving it narrow plurality status. A subsequent attempt to form a conservative coalition was voted down by the *Saeima*, which also rebuffed a government proposed by the *Saimnieks* leader, Ziedonis ČEVERS. President Ulmanis therefore called on a nonparty businessman and former agriculture minister, Andris ŠĶĒLE, who on December 21 obtained parliamentary endorsement (70–24) for a predominantly center-right, eight-party coalition that included the DPS, the LC, and the moderate conservative parties. Least comfortable in the new administration was the Latvian Unity Party (*Latvijas Vienības Partija*—LVP), consisting largely of former Communists, whose conservative orientation quickly brought it into conflict with the more reform-minded parties in the ruling coalition. On the other hand, the prime minister himself enjoyed considerable public support for his aim of achieving financial stability and accelerating the privatization program. Backed by most of the coalition parties, President Ulmanis secured parliamentary election for a second three-year term on June 18, 1996, winning on the first ballot with 53 votes against 25 for Ilga KREITUSE (the *Saeima* speaker and candidate of *Saimnieks*) and a total of 19 for two other candidates.

The increasing assertiveness of the *Saimnieks* as the largest coalition partner subsequently served as a source of instability, as evidenced in late September and early October 1996 by the ouster of Kreituse as *Saeima* speaker (on September 26) and the resignation a week later of her husband, Aivars KREITUSS, as finance minister, amid much internal party acrimony (see Political Parties, below). On October 21, moreover, *Saimnieks* leader Čevers resigned as deputy prime minister, claiming that the prime minister had authoritarian tendencies and that the 1997 draft budget was unfair to "ordinary people," his exit leaving the party with only one cabinet representative.

Turmoil continued into 1997 when Šķéle resigned on January 20 over criticism of his choice of a finance minister by President Ulmanis. The latter, however, renominated Šķéle, and the reinstated prime minister formed another diverse coalition of the LC, LNNK, LZS, DPS, and the Fatherland and Freedom Alliance (*Tēvzemei un Brīvībai*—TB) committed to quickening the pace of economic reform, pursuing foreign investment, and approving the nation's first balanced budget. The new cabinet was installed on February 13. However, Šķéle, increasingly at odds with the parties forming his coalition government (which had lost five ministers by mid-1997 to resignations), resigned again on July 28. The coalition subsequently nominated Economics Minister Guntars KRASTS of the recently merged TB/LNNK to succeed him, the *Saeima* confirming the appointment on July 28.

In April 1998 Krasts dismissed his economics minister, a member of the DPS; the four other DPS ministers immediately quit the coalition, charging the government with responsibility for deteriorating relations with Moscow. At legislative elections on October 3, the newly formed People's Party (*Tautas Partija*—TP), led by popular former prime minister Šķéle, secured a plurality of 24 seats, followed by the LC, 21 seats; the TB/LNNK, 17; and the Popular Harmony Party (*Tautas Saskaņas Partija*—TSP), 16. Meanwhile, in the wake of continued DPS infighting, the former leading legislative party managed only 2 percent of the vote and, consequently, did not win a single seat. Subsequently, nearly two months of negotiations failed to produce an agreement for participation in a new government by the TP, which insisted that Šķéle be named prime minister. Consequently, on November 26 the *Saeima* approved a minority government comprising the LC, TB/LNNK, and the New Party (*Jauna Partija*—JP, which held eight legislative posts) under the leadership of the LC's Vilis KRIŠTOPANS. The coalition as initially constituted appeared extremely fragile, however, and in February 1999 the Latvian Social Democratic Alliance (*Latvijas Sociāldemokratu Apvienāba*—LSDA) was added to the cabinet, its 14 seats giving the government a majority in the *Saeima*.

Seven rounds of voting were required before the *Saeima* was able on June 17, 1999, to agree on Vaira VIKE-FREIBERGA, a well-respected scholar and independent, as the next president. Meanwhile, difficulties continued within the government, and on July 4 Prime Minister Krištopans resigned in response to what he called "an atmosphere of distrust" within the coalition. (Among other things, the TB/LNNK and TP, now in opposition, had recently signed an agreement regarding possible cooperation in a new administration.) On July 16 the *Saeima* approved a new TP, TB/LNNK, and LC government led by the TP's Šķéle. That coalition also proved restless, however, and Šķéle resigned on April 12, 2000. The president on April 25 named the LC's Andris BERZĪNS to head a cabinet that, as constituted on May 5, also included the TB/LNNK, TP, and JP. Although the JP formally withdrew from the government in early 2001, two JP ministers retained their post; they subsequently became members of the new Latvia's First Party (*Latvijas Pirmā Partija*—LPP).

Surprisingly, the LC failed to secure representation in the October 5, 2002, *Saeima* balloting, which was dominated by the recently formed, center-right New Era (*Jaunais Laiks*—JL), the pro-Russian For Human Rights in United Latvia (*Par Cilvē ka Tiesībām Vietnotā Latvijā*—PCTVL), and the TP. The JL leader Einars REPŠE, a former central bank head, was approved on November 7 to head a coalition government comprising the JL, LPP, TB/LNNK, and the new Greens' and Farmers' Union (*Zalo un Zemnieku Savienība*—ZZS). On June 20, 2003, President Vike-Freiberga was reelected by a vote of 88–6, having won the endorsement of nearly all the major parties.

The LPP withdrew from the government in late January 2004 following a dispute between Prime Minister Repše and Deputy Prime Minister Ainārs ŠLESERS of the LPP. Having lost its legislative majority, the government resigned on February 5. Indulis EMSIS of the ZZS was confirmed by the *Saeima* on March 9 to lead a minority government comprising the ZZS, LPP, and TP. It was widely believed that a minority government was approved in order to preclude lengthy negotiations during a time of historic developments for Latvia (NATO and EU accession, see Current issues, below). The Emsis government resigned on October 25, 2004, after, among other things, the

TP voted against the proposed 2005 budget. Aigars KALVĪTIS of the TP (a former economy minister) was approved by the *Saeima* on December 2 to head a majority government comprising the TP, LPP, JL, and ZZS. In April 2006 all JL members of the cabinet resigned after recordings of phone conversations of Transport Minister Ainārs Šlesers were revealed that suggested his possible involvement in a vote-buying scandal in the Jurmala city council elections. Šlesers was forced to resign, but all other members of the LPP retained their cabinet posts. The JL's abandonment of the government coalition was an early move leading up to the October 2006 *Saeima* elections.

Constitution and Government

Partially reactivated in 1990 (prior to formal independence from the Soviet Union), Latvia's 1922 constitution was fully restored in July 1993, confirming the state as a democratic, parliamentary republic with popular sovereignty exercised through a directly elected parliament (*Saeima*). The 100-member body elects the state president by an absolute majority for a four-year term (amended from three years by the *Saeima* on December 4, 1997), which may be followed by one consecutive renewal. The government, headed by a prime minister, serves at the pleasure of Parliament, which also confirms the appointment of judges; however, the latter may be dismissed only by decision of the Supreme Court, as the highest judicial body.

Foreign Relations

Soviet recognition of the independence of the three Baltic states on September 6, 1991, paved the way for their admission to the Conference on (later Organization for) Security and Cooperation in Europe (CSCE/OSCE) on September 10 and admission to the United Nations on September 17. Prior to the Soviet action, diplomatic recognition had been extended by a number of governments, including, on September 2, that of the United States, which had never recognized the 1940 annexations. The path toward foreign recognition was eased on September 4 with the passage of legislation providing for the return of foreign property seized in the wake of the Soviet takeover. Latvia was admitted to the IMF on May 19, 1992, and to the World Bank group on August 9.

Regionally, Latvia concluded a Baltic Economic Cooperation Agreement with Estonia and Lithuania in April 1990. Under the accord, joint ventures were authorized, assuming foreign equity of no more than 50 percent. On September 24, 1991, the three states also reached agreement on a customs union that authorized free trade and visa-free travel among their respective jurisdictions, although implementation of its provisions proceeded very slowly. At the political level, Latvia participated with Estonia and Lithuania to revive cooperation that had existed under the prewar Baltic Council. It was also a founding member of the broader Council of the Baltic Sea States in 1992. In 1997 Latvia moved closer to its stated goal of becoming a member of the Central European Free Trade Agreement (CEFTA) when Warsaw approved a free trade agreement with Riga.

A postindependence objective of securing the withdrawal of Russian troops was complicated by Moscow's intense criticism of alleged discrimination against ethnic Russians in Latvia (see Current issues, below). Western pressure persuaded Moscow to adhere to an August 1994 deadline for withdrawal, subject to Russian retention of the Skrunda communications base for at least four years and with Latvia guaranteeing the social benefits of retired Russian military personnel. Dismantling of the Skrunda base began in late 1998.

In early 1995 relations between Latvia and Estonia were strained by a series of "fish wars" stemming from competing claims to territorial jurisdiction in the Gulf of Riga. At issue was Estonian insistence on a prewar equal division of the Gulf, while Latvia sought to establish the principle of common use, except for a four-mile coastal zone. Following agreement in principle in July that the disputed waters should be divided, a serious confrontation over fishing rights in early 1996 was eased but not resolved by an accord signed by the two prime ministers in April. The previous month Latvia and Lithuania had agreed on the general principles to be applied to the settlement of their maritime boundary dispute.

Latvia became a signatory of NATO's Partnership for Peace in February 1994, subsequently reiterating its desire for full membership and also for accession to the EU. In the latter context, Latvia and the other two Baltic states in July 1995 became the first ex-Soviet republics to sign association agreements with the EU, offering the prospect of eventual full accession. On October 13 Latvia became the first of the three to submit a formal application for EU membership. However, an EU report issued in December 1996 was critical of Latvia in several respects, most notably for what the EU described as extensive corruption at all levels of government.

Latvia joined the two other Baltic nations in rejecting Russia's offer of a unilateral security guarantee in 1997. Collaterally, Prime Minister Krasts pressed for quicker economic reform, which was considered a prerequisite to meeting Latvia's top foreign policy objectives of becoming a member of NATO and the EU. The European Commission asserted that Latvia had met the political criteria for admission but still did not have a sufficiently competitive economy. Consequently, in December 1997 Latvia was not among the six nations formally invited by the EU to begin entry negotiations in the spring of 1998, although it was included among five nations designated as the potential "second wave" of new EU members. Earlier, NATO did not invite Latvia to become a member when it named three candidate nations in July 1997 for the first-round expansion in 1999, but it specifically identified the Baltic states (and two other nations) as strong prospects for membership in the future. On January 16, 1998, the Baltic states and the United States signed a Charter of Partnership, a nonbinding agreement that was seen as supporting the three states' NATO candidacy but hardly guaranteeing it.

Riga's global integrationist desires advanced in October 1998, when the WTO unanimously invited Latvia to become the first Baltic nation to join. Subsequently, the EU indicated it might be willing to begin preaccession talks with Latvia by the end of 1999, provided Riga continued to make progress on economic reforms.

In December the EU formally invited Latvia and nine other countries to join the EU. A national referendum in Latvia on September 21, 2003, endorsed accession with a 67 percent "yes" vote, and Latvia joined the EU on May 1, 2004. Earlier, on March 29, 2004, Latvia had also become a member of NATO after having adopted a number of reforms, including increased spending on the military.

Latvia supported U.S. president George W. Bush in his Iraq policy in 2003, deploying some 130 troops to support the U.S.- and UK-led coalition in Iraq following the fall of Saddam Hussein. In 2004 the *Saeima* approved the continued deployment of the troops until mid-2005 (as of April 2006 Latvian troops remained in Iraq). Apparently in return for Latvia's support on Iraq, the United States subsequently released $20 million in development aid that had been withheld because of Latvia's unwillingness to exempt U.S. soldiers from prosecution in the new International Criminal Court. In April 2006 Latvia cemented closer relations with Japan by opening a new embassy in Tokyo.

Current Issues

One of the most difficult internal issues for Latvia has been that of entitlement to citizenship. In contrast to Estonia and Lithuania, where they are far less numerous, ethnic Russians account for more than a quarter of Latvia's overall population, a considerably reduced figure since independence from Russia in 1991, when more than a third of the population was Russian. Tension between the two groups has long been exacerbated by the inability of most Russians to speak Latvian and the fact that much of the economy has been Russian-controlled. Thus, a major question has been the citizenship status of first-generation residents, many of whom arrived in accordance with a Kremlin-directed effort to weaken Latvia's sense of national identity. The issue featured prominently in the 1995 election, in which parties advocating more restrictive citizenship rules gained ground. On the other hand, in July 1997 President Ulmanis called for granting citizenship to anyone born in the country, regardless of age or ethnicity, and expressed his concern that the split between Latvians and ethnic Russians was growing. The Parliament, however, in February 1998 rejected legislation that would grant automatic citizenship to children born to non-Latvians. The TB/LNNK insisted that all members of the government adhere to an agreement that the citizenship laws would not be changed without unanimous approval of coalition members.

Faced with growing economic pressure from Russia as well as the need to meet European norms on the treatment of minorities, the government began liberalizing the citizenship law with the passage of amendments in April and June 1998. However, the TB/LNNK blocked enactment of the changes pending a popular referendum, which was held simultaneously with the general election in October. Voters approved the liberalization measures by a 52 percent majority, and citizenship was offered to any child born to noncitizen parents in Latvia following independence. The changes also eased the language requirement for adults seeking citizenship, which was expected to permit greater Russian access to such status. The action drew praise from the EU and OSCE and elicited qualified approval from Russia. However, the Latvian-Russian territorial issue, which had appeared headed for resolution in October 1997 after 18 months of discussion had yielded a draft border demarcation agreement, remained unresolved. The agreement was approved by the Latvian cabinet in December 1997, but Moscow failed to endorse the accord in an attempt to delay Latvia's accession to the EU and NATO, which usually requires that all border disputes be settled.

In July 1999 the *Saeima* passed legislation limiting the use of non-Latvian languages in public gatherings, eliciting strong criticism from the EU, OSCE, and Council of Europe. Naturally, Russia also condemned the move, and its Duma voted to prohibit trade with Latvia, although the Russian government declined to implement the retaliatory measure. In view of the intense international pressure, new Latvian president Vaira Vike-Freiberga vetoed the controversial legislation. A revised and more flexible version was passed by the *Saeima* in December, seemingly appeasing Western European critics but not Russia, which still described the law as "discriminatory."

The Council of Europe voted to discontinue its monitoring of Latvian affairs in early 2001, declaring itself satisfied with the observance of human rights and the appropriate integration of previous "noncitizens." Another major milestone was reached in May 2002 when the *Saeima* agreed to permit Russian-speaking candidates in the upcoming legislative elections.

Although the administration of Prime Minister Repše (installed in late 2002) successfully guided Latvia through the final stages of its accession to NATO and the EU, the coalition remained divided on other important issues, and cabinet members reportedly criticized Repše's leadership style. Subsequently, the new minority government of Indulis Emsis was never expected to be in office for long, once the NATO and EU formalities had been completed. That coalition's stature was additionally undercut by the results of the June 2004 European Parliament balloting in which neither the ZZS nor the LPP gained seats. The Kalvītis coalition installed in December was perceived as more stable, albeit only in comparison to the rapid turnover of recent years.

In April 2005 Latvia indicated it had renounced its territorial claims against Russia. However, Moscow declined to sign a formal border treaty unless Riga agreed to stop pursuing possible compensation for "damages" suffered by Latvia under Soviet rule. Latvia's undeniably pro-Western orientation was also evident in the brief visit to Riga by U.S. President Bush on May 7 and the *Saeima*'s approval on June 6 of the proposed new EU constitution.

Latvia's accelerated growth in 2005 and 2006 produced a construction boom in Riga, including a luxury hotel and casino. Nevertheless, the country saw continued emigration, particularly from the smaller villages, as a result of high unemployment. The country's population declined by approximately 75,000 people from 2000 to 2005, and over 190,000 people from 1995 to 2005. The country's continued economic development will likely be a key issue during the campaign for the parliamentary elections on October 7, 2006.

Political Parties

In January 1990 the then Latvian Supreme Soviet revoked the political monopoly of the Latvian Communist Party (*Latvijas Komunistu Partija*—LKP), which was banned on the declaration of independence in August 1991. Having spearheaded the reassertion of national identity, the broadly based Latvian Popular Front spawned a wide array of new and revived parties, with the *Saeima* election of June 1993 being contested by 23 parties or alliances and that of September–October 1995 by 19. The trend continued in the two subsequent elections to the *Saeima*, in 1998 and 2002, in which 21 and 20 parties or alliances, respectively, campaigned. In the most recent election in 2002, only 6 parties met the 5 percent voter support threshold to win seats in the *Saeima*.

Government Parties

People's Party (*Tautas Partija*—TP). Founded in May 1998 by former prime minister Andris Šķéle, the People's Party won a plurality in the October general election, securing 24 seats on a vote share of 21.2 percent. Self-described as center-right, the party's motto and symbol emphasizes "a family of three," parents plus three children, which is the size of the family unit the party says the Latvian economy should be able to sustain. The party, considered pro-business, favors close cooperation with the Baltic states and membership in NATO, the EU, and the WTO. The party's initial success was attributed to the popularity of Šķéle, who was largely credited with Latvia's recent economic recovery. In mid-2002, Raimond Pauls, a well-known composer and political figure, joined the TP. The resignation of the New Era party from the ruling coalition in April 2006, just six months before the 2006 parliamentary elections, posed a significant challenge to the People's Party prospects.

Leaders: Aigars KALVĪTIS (Prime Minister), Andris ŠĶÉLE (Former Prime Minister), Raimond PAULS, Atis SLAKTERIS (Chair).

Latvia's First Party (*Latvijas Pirmā Partija*—LPP). A center-right, Christian grouping known as the "clergyman" party because of the number of pastors among its members, the LPP was founded in May 2002, its leaders including Ēriks Jēkabsons, a Lutheran minister who had returned to Latvia after having fled the USSR for the United States in 1987. Many former members of the New Party (*Jauna Partija*—JP) joined the LPP, including two cabinet members—Ingrida Labucka and Janis Krumins. The JP had been founded in March 1998 by popular composer Raimond Pauls and others and had elected Pauls chair at the party's first congress. With a membership dominated by young professional people, the party won eight seats in the general election of October 1998 on a vote share of 7.3 percent. Its pragmatic, center-left platform included partial privatization of large enterprises (with a controlling share of large monopolies remaining in state hands), liberalization of citizenship laws (conditioned on mastery of Latvian), admission to NATO and the EU, and improved relations with Russia. It received two cabinet posts in the minority government of Prime Minister Krištopans in November. After Krištopans resigned in July 1999, the JP moved into opposition, but it rejoined the government in May 2000.

In January 2001 it was announced that the JP had changed its name to the New Christian Party (*Jauna Kristigo Partija*—JKP), the new rubric representing the grouping's greater religious orientation. Friction with the other members of the coalition government culminated in late January with a group of JP/JKP legislators voting against the administration's position on proposed laws on pensions and real estate taxes. JKP leader Ingrida UDRE announced the party was withdrawing from the government, but Labucka and Krumins chose to retain their posts, the resulting factionalization appearing to precipitate the collapse of the party. Although many members participated in the founding of the pro-EU, pro-NATO LPP, others went in other directions. (Pauls joined the TP, while Udre was on the ZZS ticket for the 2002 balloting.) The LPP suffered a setback when Transport Minister Ainārs Šlesers was forced to step down in March 2006 after recordings of phone conversations were revealed that suggested possible involvement in a vote-buying scheme in Jurmala city council elections. The LPP remained in the ruling coalition despite the demands for removal by the New Era leadership.

Leaders: Juris LUJANS (Chair), Ēriks JĒKABSONS, Ainārs ŠLESERS (Former Deputy Chair of the JP), Oskars KASTENS.

Greens' and Farmers' Union (*Zalo un Zemnieku Savienī*—ZZS). The center-right ZZS, a pro-EU, pro-NATO grouping, was formed by the following two parties to contest the 2002 legislative poll, in which the ZZS won 12 seats. Former prime minister Vilis KRIŠTOPANS was subsequently described as a leader of the ZZS, as was Ingrida UDRE (formerly of the New Party), who was elected speaker of the *Saeima* in November 2002.

Latvian Farmers' Union (*Latvijas Zemnieku Savienība*—LZS). The LZS continues the tradition of a similarly named organization founded in 1917 and prominent in the interwar period until banned in 1934. It resumed activity in July 1990. As suggested by its name, it is primarily devoted to defending rural interests, taking a somewhat conservative position on the nationality issue. Having won 12 seats in the 1993 balloting (with 10.6 percent of the vote), the LZS slipped to 8 seats and 6.3 percent in the 1995 election, which it contested in alliance with the LKDS (below) and the **Democratic Party of Latgale** (*Latgales Demokrātiskā Partija*—LDP), the latter based in the underdeveloped eastern region of Latvia. In 1996 former members of the LVP joined the LZS, giving it 13 seats in the Parliament. However, the party failed to win any seats in the election of October 1998. New party leaders were elected in March 2001, with Guntis Ulmanis, former president of the republic and theretofore honorary chair of the LZS, retiring from the party in the fall.

Leaders: Augusts BRIGMANIS (Chair), Mārtiņš ROZE (Vice Chair), Ingrīda ŪDRE (Vice Chair and Speaker of the 8th Saeima), Jānis LAPÓE (General Secretary).

Latvian Green Party (*Latvijas Zalā Partija*—LZP). Founded in 1990, the LZP endorsed a Green List at the 1993 election, which captured only 1.2 percent of the vote. Despite the party's lack of parliamentary representation, the LZP named a member as the minister of state for environmental protection. The party also obtained representation at the junior level in the center-right government formed in December 1995, having contested the recent election in alliance with the LNNK. The LZP was part of the coalition government formed by Prime Minister Šķéle but was not included initially in the succeeding Krasts coalition of August 1997. Its position in the new government was unclear, though the LZP's Indulis Emsis kept his position as state minister of the environment. For the June 1998 elections the LZP joined an electoral alliance with the LKDS, but the grouping failed to win any seats.

Following the collapse of the Repše government in early 2004, the LZP's Indulis Emsis was named prime minister until December.

Leaders: Indulis EMSIS (Former Prime Minister), Viesturs SILENIEKS (Co-Chair), Raimonds VEJONIS (Co-Chair).

Opposition Parties

New Era (*Jaunais Laiks*—JL). Also referenced as New Time, the JL was launched in February 2002 under the leadership of Einars Repše, who had resigned in November 2001 from his longtime post as president of the central bank, where he had gained popularity for having helped maintain the stability of Latvia's currency during turbulent times. Describing itself as "liberal-right," New Era pledged to combat corruption and drug smuggling, support "honest businessmen," and pursue EU and NATO membership for Latvia.

After the JL secured a plurality of 26 seats in the October 2002 legislative balloting, Repše served as prime minister until early 2004, when his coalition dissolved. New Era joined the ruling coalition led by the People's Party in October 2004, but left the coalition in protest in April 2006 when allegations were made that key members of coalition partner Latvia's First Party were involved in a municipal vote-buying scandal.

Leaders: Einars REPŠE (Chair), Guntis ULMANIS (Former President of the Republic), Edgars Jaunups (General Secretary).

For Human Rights in United Latvia (*Par Cilvēka Tiesībām Vienotā Latvijā*—PCTVL). The PCTVL was first referenced in 1998 when the Popular Harmony Party, Latvian Socialist Party, and Equality, which had no hope as individual parties of meeting the 5 percent threshold for legislative representation, attempted to form an electoral coalition to contest the October balloting under the PCTVL rubric. (A fourth grouping, the Russian Party, subsequently joined the proposed coalition.) However, the government declined to register the PCTVL, citing what it perceived to be a lack of appropriate endorsement by all the governing bodies of the component parties. Consequently, all the candidates envisioned for the PCTVL ticket were instead presented solely under the TSP banner. Of the 16 seats secured, 6 went to TSP members, 5 to Equality members, 4 to LSP members, and 1 to a member of the Russian Party. One of the main campaign issues for the candidates was pursuit of liberalization of the citizenship and language laws so as to better serve the interests of the Russian-speaking population.

The pro-Moscow PCTVL was permitted to run as a coalition in the 2002 legislative balloting, with no reference to the inclusion of the Russian Party, which had reportedly left the grouping in late 2000 in the wake of a dispute with the LSP leadership. The alliance's platform endorsed membership in the EU (despite opposition from Equality) but was perceived as "nebulous" regarding NATO. Although the PCTVL came in second in the legislative poll (25 seats on a 19 percent vote share), its pro-Moscow stance on many issues precluded it from participation in subsequent coalition governments. The PCTVL split in 2003 when first the TSP, and then the LSP, exited over programmatic and apparent personal differences. Members of these breakaway parties who still supported the PCTVL registered a new party, BITE (*Brīvā izvēle tautu Eiropā*, or Free Choice in People's Europe), which subsequently joined the PCTVL coalition. During the European Parliament elections of 2004, the PCTVL won a seat that was filled by Tatjana Ždanoka.

Leaders: Jakovs PLINERS, Tatjana ŽDANOKA (Co-Chairs).

Equality (*Līdztiesība*). Representing the interests of Russian speakers in newly independent Latvia, Equality secured seven seats in the 1993 legislative balloting on a 5.8 percent vote share. The grouping appeared to have been succeeded in 1995 by the LSP, particularly when a joint candidate list was presented under the LSP rubric for the 1995 legislative balloting. However, Equality, also often referenced as the Equal Rights Movement, in fact maintained its separate identity, becoming a core component of the PCTVL in 1998. Some members, including party leader Sergejs DIMANIS, subsequently pushed for a formal merger with the TSP but were rebuffed, prompting Dimanis's resignation as party leader. He was succeeded by Tatjana Ždanoka, noted for her prominent anti-independence stance in the late 1980s and her current intensely anti-EU sentiments. A number of prospective Equality candidates for the 2002 PCTVL electoral list were not permitted to run because of their previous association with the Communist Party.

Leaders: Tatjana ŽDANOKA, Vladimir BUZAYEV (Chair).

Free Choice in People's Europe (*Brīvā Izvēle Tautu Eiropā*—BITE). The BITE was formed under the leadership of Jakovs Pliners by members of the Popular Harmony Party and Latvian Socialist Party after those parties exited from the PCTVL alliance in 2003. The new party promptly joined the PCTVL in 2003. Given that its founding and leadership has been guided by the PCTVL, BITE's platform should be understood as the same as the parent organization, which is to provide equal rights to all residents,

ease naturalization requirements, and allow the Russian language to be used in official spheres.
Leader: Jakovs PLINERS.

Harmony Center (*Saskaņas Centrs*—SC). Formed in July 2005, the SC is an alliance of the Popular Harmony Party, the Latvian Socialist Party, and the newly formed New Center. Its first chair was Riga city councillor and head of New Center Sergejs Dolgopolovs. Dolgopolovs, who was expelled from the National Harmony Party in 2004 after a bitter struggle with longtime leader Jānis Jurkans, handed over leadership of the SC to journalist Nils Ušakovs a few months after the alliance's founding.
Leader: Nils UŠAKOVS.

New Center (*Jaunais Centrs*—JC). The JC was founded by Sergejs Dolgopolovs after he was expelled from the National Harmony Party by former head Jānis Jurkans in 2004. Its program is focused on decreasing social inequality by introducing a progressive income tax, spending more on social programs and less on the military, eliminating ethnic tensions in part by easing the requirements for naturalization, promoting economic growth through improved state support of business, and decentralizing government administration.
Leaders: Sergejs DOLGOPOLOVS (Chair), Leonid KURDJUMOVS (Vice-Chair).

Popular Harmony Party (*Tautas Saskaņas Partija*—TSP). Also rendered as the National Harmony Party, the TSP is the rump of the Harmony for Latvia-Rebirth (*Saskaņa Latvijai-Atdzimšana*) grouping that remained after the formation of the breakaway Political Union of Economists (*Tautsaimnieku Polilitiskā Apvienāba*—TPA). (The TPA was launched in March 1994 by 4 of the 13 *Saeima* delegates elected by Harmony for Latvia-Rebirth. For the fall 1995 balloting the TPA essayed an alliance with the DPS but eventually opted to stand independently, failing to win representation.)
Eschewing ethnic Latvian nationalism, the TSP advocates the coexistence of Latvians and

non-Latvians, with entrenched rights for minority groups. In the 1995 election the TSP won six seats on a 5.6 percent vote share; in July 1996, however, two TSP deputies followed a breakaway group that opted for merger with *Saimnieks*, whereafter the four-strong TSP contingent no longer met the minimum requirement of five seats for recognition as a parliamentary group and so technically became independents. The party regained its standing as a legislative faction when a member of the LSP joined its ranks in September 1997.

After the TSP split from the PCTVL, it tried to become the dominant voice of Latvia's minorities. But in the European Parliament elections in June 2004, the party failed to reach the 5 percent threshold, while former alliance partner PCTVL earned one seat. The TSP also failed to reach the 5 percent threshold for seats in the Riga City Council during the March 2005 election. *Leaders:* Jānis URBANOVIČS (Chair), Aleksandrs BARTAŠEVIČS.

Latvian Socialist Party (*Latvijas Sociālistiska Partija*—LSP). The LSP was launched in 1995 to represent the interests of the non-Latvian population and to urge the adoption of Russian as Latvia's second official language. The LSP's most prominent figure was Alfrēds Rubiks, the former leader of the Latvian Communist Party who had run on the Equality ticket in June 1993 despite the fact that he was in prison awaiting trial for supporting the failed August 1991 coup on the part of hard-liners in Moscow. Rubiks was elected to the *Saeima*, but the new body rejected his credentials. In July Rubiks was sentenced to eight years of imprisonment for conspiracy to overthrow the government in 1991. Nevertheless, he headed the LSP list in the 1995 balloting, in which the party won five seats on a 5.6 percent vote share. Still in prison, Rubiks was also a candidate in the June 1996 presidential contest, receiving five votes in the *Saeima* balloting. He was released from prison in 1997. In 1998 the LSP joined other leftist parties in the For Human Rights in United Latvia

(PCTVL) alliance, which enjoyed solid electoral success through 2002. Along with the TSP, the LSP split from the PCTVL in 2003.

Leader: Alfrēds RUBIKS.

Fatherland and Freedom/Latvian National Conservative Party (*Tēvzemei un Brīvībai/ Latvijas Nacionālā Konservatīvā Partija*—TB/ LNNK). Founded at a joint congress of the Fatherland and Freedom Alliance (*Apvienāba Tēvzemei un Brīvībai*—TB) and the Latvian National Conservative Party (*Latvijas Nacionālā Konservatīvā Partija*—LNNK) on June 21, 1997, the TB/LNNK is a right-wing nationalistic formation favoring repatriation of aliens, stringent laws on citizenship, and protection of the "purity of the Latvian language," although it maintains a pro-EU and pro-NATO posture.

The TB and the LNNK had been members of the National Bloc (*Nacionālā Bloc*), a parliamentary alliance of conservative parties (including the LZP, LZS, LKDS, and LVP) launched in September 1994. Although the National Bloc components for the most part contested the 1995 election independently, all were included in the ensuing center-right coalition government, and all backed the successful reelection bid of President Ulmanis of the LZS in June 1996.

The LNNK had evolved from the Latvian National Independence Movement (*Latvijas Nacionālā Neatkarības Kustība*—LNNK), which was founded in 1988 and adopted the LNNK abbreviation in 1994. (However, recent news reports have often continued to refer to the group using its pre-1997 name.) Ultranationalist and anti-Russian, the LNNK insisted that state benefits should be limited to ethnic Latvians and that no more than 25 percent of non-Latvians should be recognized as citizens. It won 15 seats on a 13.6 percent vote share in 1993 but was somewhat discredited by the far-right agitation of successful LNNK candidate Joahims Zigerists (who later broke away to form the TKL-ZP, below). On the president's invitation, (then) LNNK associate chair Andrejs Krastiņš attempted to form a right-wing government in August 1994 but was rebuffed by the *Saeima*. For the

fall 1995 election the LNNK formed an unlikely alliance with the Latvian Green Party, their joint list winning only 8 seats on a 6.3 percent vote share.

The TB was an alliance of several ultrarightwing groups that was reported to have received support from right-extremists in Germany. It was also viewed as having been the party of the Waffen SS at the time of the German occupation during World War II. The TB won 5.4 percent of the vote and 6 seats in 1993, rising to 11.9 percent and 14 seats in 1995 and thus becoming the strongest National Bloc member. After party leader Māris Grīnblats had tried and failed to form a government, the TB agreed to join a center-right coalition headed by a nonparty prime minister.

The TB/LNNK nominated Guntars Krasts, a pragmatic businessman, for prime minister in July 1997 when the Šķéle coalition government unraveled. In August 1998 the party blocked enactment of amendments that would have liberalized the citizenship law and organized a referendum on a more restrictive policy at the general election of October 1998, which was rejected by voters. Also, the party fared worse in the election (17 seats on a 14.6 percent vote share) than its components did as separate parties in 1995. The TB/LNNK fell to 5.4 percent of the vote and only 7 seats in the 2002 legislative poll.

Leaders: Guntars KRASTS (Former Prime Minister), Jānis STRAUME (Chair), Juris SARATOVS (General Secretary), Māris GRĪNBLATS (Former Deputy Prime Minister and Former TB Chair), Andrejs KRASTIŅŠ (Former LNNK Chair).

Other Parties Contesting the 2002 Legislative Elections

Latvian Way (*Latvijas Ceļš*—LC). The LC was formed as a loose grouping of "personalities" prior to the 1993 election. Displaying a center-right political posture and a liberal-conservative socioeconomic orientation, the group was viewed by many Latvians as a "*nomenklatura*" party because of the former careers of many of its members. Nevertheless, its pivotal parliamentary position enabled it to lead successive coalition governments, its 32.4 percent vote share in 1993 yielding a plurality of 36 seats. Having slumped to 14.6 percent and 17 seats in the 1995 election, the LC became a junior partner in the subsequent broad-based government before assuming a dominant role in the minority government formed in November 1998 following the October balloting in which the LC had picked up 4 additional seats on a reported vote share of 18 percent. The LC, a pro-EU and pro-NATO grouping, did poorly in the 2001 municipal elections, its loss of support being attributed to growing public disenchantment with the national government. Further distress emanated from the 2002 *Saeima* balloting as the LC fell to 4.9 percent of the vote and therefore no seats. Nevertheless LC member Karina PETERSONE serves as the special task minister for society integration affairs in the current government.

Leaders: Andris BERZĪNS (Former Prime Minister), Ivars GODMANIS (Chair), Juris ŠMITS (General Secretary), Valdis BĪRKAVS (Former Chair), Māris GAILIS (Former Deputy Prime Minister).

Latvian Social Democratic Workers' Party (*Latvijas Sociāldemokrātiskā Strādnieku Partija—* LSDSP). Initially formed in 1904 and Latvia's leading party in the 1920s, the LSDSP was relaunched in 1989. However, it secured less than 1 percent of the vote in the 1993 legislative poll. The LSDSP participated in the 1994 municipal elections in various alliances with numerous other small groupings.

In the 1995 national legislative balloting the LSDSP was part of a "Labor and Justice" coalition that also included the Latvian Democratic Labor Party (*Latvijas Demokrātiskā Darba Partija—*LDDP) and others. The LDDP has been formed since April 1990 as a minority breakaway faction of the Latvian Communist Party. In 1995 the LDDP announced (prior to the election) that its name had been changed to the Latvian Social Democratic Party (*Latvijas Sociāldemokrātiskā Partija—*LSDP), although the LDDP rubric was still referenced for the legislative balloting, at which the Labor and Justice coalition failed to gain representation on a

4.6 percent vote share. (The LSDP rubric was used consistently following the election.)

The LSDSP, LSDP, and others formed a **Latvian Social Democratic Alliance** (*Latvijas Sociāldemokrātu Apvienī—*LSDA) for the 1998 legislative elections, surprising observers by securing 12.8 percent of the vote and 14 seats. In May 1999 the LSDSP and LSDP formally merged, with the LSDSP rubric being retained. In public opinion polls of late 2000, the LSDSP was ranked as the most popular party, and it performed well in the March 2001 municipal elections, eventually forming a coalition with the TB/LNNK to govern the Riga City Council. However, the party's fortunes were reversed in late 2001 when a group of its legislators bolted to form the Social Democratic Union (see below) in protest over, among other things, the reported autocratic style of LSDSP Chair Juris Bojārs. Although considered "pro-Moscow," the left-wing LSDSP formally endorsed Latvia's membership in the EU and NATO. The LSDSP lost its legislative representation at the 2002 *Saeima* balloting, securing only 4 percent of the vote.

Leaders: Guntars JIRGENSONS (Chair), Jānis DINEVIČS (Deputy Chair), Ansis DOBELIS (General Secretary).

Social Democratic Union (*Sociāldemokrātu Savienība—*SDS). The SDS was formed in March 2002 by Egils Baldzens and other legislators who quit the LSDSP after Baldzens was defeated in his attempt to wrest the LSDSP chairship from Juris Bojārs. The SDS secured only 1.5 percent of the vote in the 2002 legislative poll.

Leaders: Pēteris SALKAZANOVS (Chair), Marite TEIVANE (Secretary General).

Freedom Party (*Brivibas Partija—*BP). The BP was launched in April 2002 by a group of prominent figures, including Ziedonis Čevers, the former interior minister who had resigned as chair of the DPS following that party's poor performance in the 1998 legislative balloting. The new party espoused "social-liberal" policies and support for EU and NATO membership.

Leader: Ziedonis ČEVERS.

Popular Union "Centrs" (*Politiskā Apvienība "Centrs"*). This electoral alliance was formed for the 2002 legislative balloting by the two groups below, the **Latvian Farmers Party**, and the **Party of Latvia's Freedom** (led by Odisejs KOSTANDA). The alliance won only 0.6 percent of the vote, below the 5 percent requirement for seats in the *Saeima*.

Latvian Democratic Party (*Latvijas Demokrātiskā Partija*—LDP). The LDP is a successor to the Master Democratic Party (*Demokrātiskā Partija Saimnieks*—DPS), itself a descendant of the prewar Democratic Center Party (*Demokrātiskā Centra Partija*—DCP), which was relaunched in 1992 and won 5 seats in the 1993 legislative balloting on a 4.8 percent vote share. The DCP subsequently became simply the Democratic Party before merging with another group in 1994 under the *Saimnieks* rubric (signifying a traditional source of authority, also sometimes rendered in English as "In Charge"). Taking a liberal position on economic issues and exhibiting a moderate national policy orientation, *Saimnieks* won a narrow plurality of 18 seats with 15.1 percent of the vote in the fall 1995 parliamentary election. After its chair, Ziedonis ČEVERS, had failed to form a government, *Saimnieks* opted to join a broadly conservative coalition headed by a nonparty prime minister, although strains with other participants were apparent in 1996. In June 1996 the *Saimnieks* speaker of the *Saeima*, Ilga KREITUSE, was runner-up (with 25 votes) in the parliamentary balloting for the post of state president.

The DPS was strengthened in July 1996 by its absorption of the small Republican Party (unrepresented in the *Saeima*) and by the defection to it of two deputies of the TSP. Internal strains surfaced on September 13, however, when the party council voted to expel the *Saimnieks* finance minister, Aivars Kreituss, for disregarding party policy and for having used his ministerial position to set up a campaign fund for his wife, Ilga, in her recent candidacy for the presidency. Kreituse showed solidarity with her husband by resigning from the party four days later, with the result that on September 26 she was ousted from the *Saeima* speakership, to which another *Saimnieks* nominee was elected. Collaterally, *Saimnieks* became increasingly opposed to the policies of the government to which it belonged, with Čevers resigning as deputy premier in October.

Although the DPS had been the leading party following the 1995 elections, factionalism had weakened it by the time of the general election of October 1998, when it won less than 2 percent of the votes and lost representation in the *Saeima*, prompting party chair Čevers to resign. The grouping adopted the LDP rubric in November 1999.

Leaders: Andris AMERIKS (Chair), Juris CELMIŅŠ (Deputy Chair).

Labor Party (*Darba Partija*—DP). The DP was founded in 1997 by Aivars Kreituss and his wife Ilga Kreituse, after they had been expelled and resigned, respectively, from the DPS. Aivars Kreituss, the DP's founding chair, said the party favored government intervention in the economy to reinvigorate industry and reform agriculture. The party also supports EU integration. The DP joined an electoral alliance with the LKDS and LZP for the June 1998 elections but failed to win representation.

Leaders: Aivars KREITUSS (Chair), Ilga KREITUSE.

Latvia's Revival Party (*Latvijas Atdzimšanas Partija*—LAP). The LAP was founded in 1998 by former legislator Andris Rubins, who had previously helped launch a party known as the People's Union Freedom (*Tautas Kopa Brīvīda*—TKB). Rubins, a right-wing populist, had once served in the *Saeima* as a member of the TKL-ZP. In the 2002 elections for the *Saeima* the LAP won 0.3 percent of the popular vote, which excluded it from winning any seats.

Leader: Andris RUBINS.

Other small parties registered for the 2002 elections included **Latgale Light** (*Latgales Gaisma*,

Cabinet

As of May 1, 2006

Prime Minister	Aigars Kalvītis (TP)

Ministers

Agriculture	Mārtiņš Roze (ZZS)
Children and Family Affairs	Ainars Baštiks (LPP)
Culture	Helēna Demakova (TP) [f]
Defense	Atis Slakteris (TP)
Economy	Aigars Štokenbergs (TP)
Education and Science	Baiba Rivža (LZS) [f]
Environment	Raimonds Vējonis (ZZS)
Finance	Oskars Spurdziņš (TP)
Foreign Affairs	Artis Pabriks (TP)
Health	Gundars Bērziņš (TP)
Interior	Dzintars Jaundžeikars (LPP)
Justice	Guntars Grīnvalds (LPP)
Regional Development and Local Government	Māris Kučinskis (TP)
Special Assignments for Electronic Government Affairs	Ina Gudele (ind.) [f]
Special Assignments for Integration of Society	Karina Pētersone (LC) [f]
Transport	Krišjānis Peters (LPP)
Welfare	Dagnija Staķe (ZZS) [f]

[f] = female

a center-left, pro-Russian regional party led by the mayor of Daugavpils, Richards EIGINS); the right-wing **Latvia's United Republican Party** (*Latvijas Apvienotā Republikānu Partija*—LARP); the **Latvian Party** (*Latviešu Partija*—LP), a far right-wing grouping led by publisher Aivars GARDA; **Māra's Land** (*Maras Zeme*), another right-wing party; **Our Land** (*Mūsu Zeme*), an anti-EU right-wing party; the **Progressive Centrist Party** (*Progresīvā Centriskā Partija*); the **Russian Party** (*Krievu Partija*), a leftist, pro-Russian grouping that opposed NATO and EU membership; and the **Social Democratic Welfare Party** (*Sociāldemokrātiskā Labklājības Partija*—SLP), led by businessman Juris ZURAVLOV.

Additionally, the **Visu Latvijai** (All for Latvia—VL) nationalist youth organization was trans-

formed into a political party in January 2006 under the leadership of Raivis DZINTARS. Its platform includes expelling people who are disloyal to the country and strengthening the role of the Latvian language in society. It was reported that the VL had been seeking an electoral alliance with the more established For Fatherland and Freedom Party, but had been turned down.

Legislature

The Latvian **Parliament** (*Saeima*) is a unicameral body of 100 members with a four-year mandate (extended from three years by a constitutional amendment approved on December 4, 1997) elected by universal suffrage according to proportional representation. (The threshold was increased to 5 percent for individual parties and 7 percent for coalitions in February 1998.) The election of October 5, 2002, resulted in the seats being distributed as follows: New Era, 26; For Human Rights in United Latvia, 25; the People's Party, 20; the Greens' and Farmers' Union, 12; Latvia's First Party, 10; and the Fatherland and Freedom/Latvian National Conservative Party, 7.

Speaker: Ingrida UDRE.

Communications

Press

The first "informal" (i.e., independent) publications began to appear in 1988, of which the most popular (in Latvian, Russian, and English editions) became the Popular Front's *Atmoda* (Awakening). The Communist Party press monopoly was outlawed in 1990, at which time *Diena* (Day) was launched in Latvian and Russian, with a circulation that quickly rose to more than 100,000, but more recently has been about 75,000. Other papers currently published at Riga (Latvian dailies, unless otherwise noted) include *Lauku Avīze* (Country Newspaper, 90,000), weekly; *SM-Segodnya* (SM-Today, 65,000), in Russian; *Neatkarīgā Cīna* (Independent Struggle, 63,000); *Rigas Balss* (Riga Voice, 57,000), in Latvian and Russian; *Vakara Zinas* (Evening News, 53,000); *Labrit* (Good Morning, 36,000), in Latvian and Russian; *The Baltic Times* (12,000); *Biznes i Baltja* (Business and the Baltics, 19,000); *Chas Lilit*, weekly, in Russian; *Sovietskaya Latviya* (Soviet Latvia, 71,300); *Neatkarīga Rita Avīze*; *Dienas Bizness* (Daily Business, 15,000), weekly.

News Agencies

The Latvian Telegraph Agency (*Latvijas Telegrafa Agentura*—LETA) is a Reuters affiliate; it participated in the formation of a regional service, *Baltija*, in 1990.

Broadcasting and Computing

Radio Latvia broadcasts two programs in Latvian and Russian, as well as in Swedish and English; as of 1999, programming was also available from 16 independent stations. Latvian TV cooperates with British (BBC, MTV), German (ZDF), and U.S. (CNN) networks, as well as with individual stations in Poland, France, and Finland. An independent TV station was licensed in 1996. A media law in 1998 required that 51 percent of all radio and television broadcasts be of European origin and that 40 percent be broadcast in Latvian. There were approximately 1.3 million television receivers and 450,000 personal computers serving 936,000 Internet users in 2003.

Intergovernmental Representation

Ambassador to the U.S.
Maris RIEKSTINS

U.S. Ambassador to Latvia
Catherine Todd BAILEY

Permanent Representative to the UN
Solveiga SILKALNA

IGO Memberships (Non-UN)
BIS, CBSS, CEUR, EBRD, EIB, EU, Interpol, IOM, NATO, NIB, OSCE, PCA, WCO, WTO

LIECHTENSTEIN

PRINCIPALITY OF LIECHTENSTEIN .

Fürstentum Liechtenstein

The Country

A miniature principality on the upper Rhine between Austria and Switzerland, Liechtenstein has a predominantly Roman Catholic population whose major language, Alemannic, is a German dialect. Approximately one-third of the current population are resident aliens, most of whom have sought employment in the service sector.

Once dependent on agriculture, which currently employs less than 2 percent of the population despite the continuing importance of dairying and cattle breeding, Liechtenstein underwent considerable industrialization in the post–World War II era, with an emphasis on metallurgy and light industry. Notable products include dental appliances and precision machinery, most of which are exported, principally to Switzerland and the member countries of the European Union (EU). The principality is chiefly known, however, as one of the world's leading "offshore" banking and finance centers, with a history of confidentiality and of low tax rates that have attracted some 80,000 trust and holding companies, virtually all of which maintain no physical presence in the country. At present, the financial industry provides some 40 percent of revenue and has helped Liechtenstein's per capita GNP rank among the world's highest. In recent years external pressure has forced the government to support efforts to end money laundering and the abuse of banking secrecy (see Current issues). Collaterally, the government has attempted to boost tourism and foreign investment in order to improve Liechtenstein's status as a "business center."

Government and Politics

Political Background

The Principality of Liechtenstein, whose origins date back to the 14th century, was established in its present form in 1719. Part of the Holy Roman Empire and after 1815 a member of the German Confederation, it entered into a customs union with Austria in 1852; following the collapse of the confederation in 1866, the principality in 1868 declared permanent neutrality. Formally terminating the association with Austria in 1919, Liechtenstein proceeded to adopt Swiss currency in 1921, and in 1923 entered into a customs union with

Political Status: Independent principality constituted in 1719; current constitution promulgated October 5, 1921; established diplomatic association with Switzerland in 1919 and customs and currency association in 1923.

Area: 61.8 sq. mi. (160 sq. km.).

Population: 34,477 (2004 National Registration); 35,314 (2005E). Both figures include more than 10,000 resident aliens.

Major Urban Centers (2005E): VADUZ (5,010), Schaan (5,700).

Official Language: German (Alemannic).

Monetary Unit: Swiss Franc (market rate July 1, 2006: 1.23 francs = $1US).

Sovereign: Prince HANS-ADAM von und zu Liechtenstein II; assumed the executive authority of the sovereign on August 26, 1984; acceded to the throne at the death of his father, Prince FRANZ JOSEF II, on November 13, 1989. (On August 15, 2004, Prince Hans-Adam turned over most day-to-day governmental responsibility to Crown Prince Alois.)

Heir Apparent: Crown Prince ALOIS von und zu Liechtenstein.

Prime Minister (Chief of Government): Otmar HASLER (Progressive Citizens' Party); confirmed by the *Landtag* on April 5, 2001, following the general election of February 9 and 11, succeeding Mario FRICK (Fatherland Union); reconfirmed by the *Landtag* on April 21, 2005, to head new coalition government following general election on March 11 and 13.

Switzerland, which continues to administer the principality's customs and provides for its defense and diplomatic representation. Liechtenstein's neutrality was respected in both world wars of the 20th century.

From 1938 until April 1997 the government was a coalition of the Progressive Citizens' Party (*Fortschrittliche Bürgerpartei*—FBP) and the Fatherland Union (*Vaterändische Union*—VU). At the legislative election of February 1978 the FBP lost its parliamentary majority (by one seat) for only the second time since 1928, although it received an overall majority of votes cast. The FBP's Walter KIEBER was succeeded as chief of government by the VU's Hans BRUNHART, Kieber staying on as deputy chief until his retirement in 1980 and replacement by Hilmar OSPELT. The legislative strength of the parties remained unchanged at the elections held in 1982 and 1986. Herbert WILLE of the FBP succeeded Ospelt as Brunhart's deputy following the latter election. At an early election in March 1989, occasioned by a walkout of FBP legislative deputies in a dispute over the use of public funds for the construction of an art gallery, the VU retained its one-seat majority in an expanded *Landtag*.

In August 1984, in an unusual action, the aging Prince FRANZ JOSEF had assigned his official responsibilities, without abdication of title, to Prince HANS-ADAM, a business school graduate. When Franz Josef died on November 13, 1989, after a 51-year reign that had made him the world's most durable monarch, he was immediately succeeded by his 44-year-old son.

At the balloting of February 7, 1993, the FBP regained its status as the largest parliamentary party, although limited to a 12-seat plurality in an expanded body of 25 members when the environmentalist Free List (*Freie Liste*—FL) unexpectedly met the 8 percent threshold for representation, winning 2 seats with 10.4 percent of the vote. However, the *Landtag* was dissolved by Prince Hans-Adam on September 15 after Prime Minister Markus BÜCHEL had fallen victim to a nonconfidence motion brought by his own FBP in protest against his leadership methods. At the ensuing election of October 24 the VU secured a majority of 13 seats (with a vote share of 50.1 percent), while the FBP fell back to 11 seats (44.2 percent) and the Free List slipped to 1 seat (8.5 percent). On December 15 the VU's Mario FRICK formed a new coalition administration, with the FBP's Thomas BÜCHEL succeeding him as deputy chief of government. The VU also increased its vote in communal elections in January 1995, winning the mayoralty of Vaduz after nearly 70 years of FBP control of the capital.

Snap *Landtag* elections (nine months early) were held on January 31 and February 2, 1997, with the only change in distribution being the loss of one FBP seat to the FL. Although negotiations were expected to produce another coalition cabinet as a matter of course, the FBP in a surprise move announced on March 10 that it was leaving the government, ostensibly to create an "effective opposition." Consequently, a new all-VU government under Frick's leadership—the first one-party administration since 1938—was nominated by Prince Hans-Adam and installed on April 9 upon approval by the *Landtag*.

At the election of February 9 and 11, 2001, the opposition FBP won 49.9 percent of the vote and gained 3 *Landtag* seats over its previous total, for a majority of 13, guaranteeing the designation of party leader Otmar HASLER as the next chief of government. The previously governing VU took 41.1 percent, for 11 seats, and the Free List captured 8.8 percent and 1 seat. The new legislature confirmed Hasler and an all-FBP cabinet on April 5.

The prince subsequently continued promoting a constitutional reform plan designed to strengthen the monarchy's powers, including giving him the authority to appoint judges with legislative concurrence (rather than the other way around), to dismiss the government or dissolve the *Landtag* without explanation, and to impose emergency rule. Many legislators, in contrast, wanted to limit the monarchy's existing powers, and a minority was known to favor creation of a republic. Hans-Adam repeatedly called for his proposed reforms to be put before the voters, while warning that he would go into exile if a referendum concluded with a negative vote. He even asserted that without the present royal house and its wealth—his personal fortune has been estimated at $4–6 billion—the principality might have little recourse but to seek a union with either Switzerland or Austria to find a successor who would be willing to meet the costs of maintaining the monarchy. In a national referendum on March 14 and 16, 2003, voters approved the prince's demands with a 64 percent "yes" vote. On August 15, 2004, Prince Hans-Adam (following his father's example) transferred most executive power to his son, Crown Prince ALOIS, although Hans-Adam remained monarch and head of state.

The FBP fell to a plurality of 12 seats at the general election of March 11 and 13, 2005, prompting the return of an FBP/VU coalition, headed by Hasler, on April 21.

Constitution and Government

Under the constitution adopted October 5, 1921, the monarchy is hereditary in the male line and the sovereign exercises legislative power jointly with a unicameral Diet (*Landtag*), which is elected every four years by direct suffrage under proportional representation, assuming no dissolution. The chief of government (*regierungschef*) is appointed by the sovereign from the majority party or group in the Diet. The government, which is responsible to both the sovereign and the Diet, also includes a deputy chief (*regierungschef-stellvertreter*) and three additional government councillors (*regierungsräte*) elected by the Diet itself. Elections are held in two constituencies (Oberland and Unterland), while administration is based on 11 communes (*gemeinden*). The judicial system consists of civil, criminal, and administrative divisions: the first two include local, Superior, and Supreme courts, while the third encompasses an Administrative Court of Appeal (for hearing complaints about government officials and actions) and a State Court, both of which consider questions of constitutionality.

The enfranchisement of women at the national level, supported by both major parties and approved unanimously by the legislature, was narrowly endorsed by male voters in July 1984, after having been defeated in referenda held in 1971 and 1973. Approval at the local level was also voted in eight communes, with approval in the remaining three following in April 1986.

Foreign Relations

Liechtenstein maintains an embassy at Bern but is represented elsewhere by Swiss embassies and consulates through an agreement dating from October 27, 1919. Long a participant in a number of United Nations (UN) specialized agencies,

Liechtenstein decided only in December 1989 to seek admission to the UN. The application was approved in 1990. Previously an associate member of the European Free Trade Association (EFTA) because of its customs union with Switzerland, the principality became EFTA's seventh full member on May 22, 1991. The country does not have a standing army but has long been preoccupied with European defense strategy and is an active participant in the Organization for (formerly Conference on) Security and Cooperation in Europe (OSCE/CSCE).

While not making a formal territorial claim, Liechtenstein in 1992 reopened the question of the extensive lands once owned by the grand duke in what was then Czechoslovakia. Ten times the size of Liechtenstein itself, these ducal estates had been confiscated in 1919 by the fledgling Czechoslovak Republic, which in 1938, under Axis pressure, had agreed to return half and to pay compensation for the remainder. The agreement was repudiated by the post–World War II Communist regime and found no more favor with the post-Communist government in Prague. In mid-2001 Liechtenstein submitted its complaint to the International Court of Justice (ICJ). In February 2005 the ICJ refused to rule on the question.

Switzerland's surprise application in May 1992 for membership in the European Community/European Union (EC/EU) caused difficulties for Liechtenstein, which faced the possibility of having to follow suit if it wished to preserve the 1923 customs union between the two states. Of particular concern were proposed labor-mobility rules. Liechtenstein instead favored membership in the proposed European Economic Area (EEA) between the EU and most EFTA countries. The situation subsequently became even more complicated as Swiss voters in early December rejected ratification of the EEA treaty, a development that effectively blocked progress on that nation's EU membership proposal as well (see article on Switzerland). On December 13 the voters in Liechtenstein gave a 55.8 percent endorsement to EEA membership, but EEA participation had to be deferred pending renegotiation of the customs union.

Another national referendum, this time to approve the revised arrangement with Switzerland, was approved by 55.9 percent of those voting on April 9, 1995, with Liechtenstein then acceding to the EEA on May 1.

In 2003 Liechtenstein initially refused to approve expansion of the EEA to include the Czech Republic and Slovakia because of lingering dispute over the post–World War II agreements. Prince Hans-Adam subsequently lifted his veto against the proposed EEA expansion on the condition that negotiations to resolve the dispute would be renewed.

On April 13, 2005, The Independent Historical Commission on Liechtenstein concluded its four-year investigation into allegations that Liechtenstein had robbed Jews during World War II by stating that no assets of Jewish families had been confiscated and that the country had not employed slave laborers.

Current Issues

In May 2000 the Bank for International Settlements (BIS) included the principality on its list of offshore facilities having lax supervision, and a month later the independent Financial Action Task Force (FATF), which had been established with the support of the Organization for Economic Cooperation and Development (OECD), placed Liechtenstein on its list of "noncooperative" jurisdictions in the fight against money laundering. In July the Group of Seven added its criticism of the country's "harmful" tax policies.

Fearing that the repeated attacks would undermine its financial sector, Liechtenstein announced that it would enforce more rigorously those laws already on the books. The government also supplemented its investigative staff, and the *Landtag* passed new legislation to counter money laundering and to aid in identifying account holders who had previously been shielded by intermediaries and foundations. In 2001 the FATF, noting relaxation of banking secrecy, removed the principality from its blacklist, but Liechtenstein remained on the OECD's list of harmful tax havens. Subsequently, in October 2002, the United States sent an undersecretary of the U.S. Treasury to Liecht-enstein with the message that Islamic militants, including financiers with connections to the al-Qaida network, may have been using bank accounts in Liechtenstein to funnel funds to terrorists. Nonetheless, in March 2006, Crown Prince Alois said that he would not do away with bank secrecy, stating that there is no support for such an action among the populace.

With their endorsement in the national referendum of March 2003, the voters effectively turned Prince Hans-Adam into what was described as Europe's sole absolute monarch. The prince's detractors described his vastly enhanced powers as equivalent to "dictatorial" authority, and the Council of Europe threatened to impose sanctions because of the perceived threat to the democratic process. Tension over the matter was only partly defused by the assumption of substantial executive authority by Crown Prince Alois in 2004. Hans-Adam later reportedly indicated that he did not expect to abdicate completely for perhaps 20 more years.

In December 2005, in what it called the first return of an Iraqi aircraft seized under a UN Security Council resolution since the start of the Iraqi War, Liechtenstein handed over to the Iraqi government a business jet reportedly used by Saddam Hussein to transport money and high-ranking government officials.

Political Parties

Government Parties

Progressive Citizens' Party (*Fortschrittliche Bürgerpartei*—FBP). Founded in 1918 as the basically conservative Citizens' Party (*Bürgerpartei*) and sometimes identified as the Bourgeois Party, what subsequently became the FBP held a majority of legislative seats from 1928 to 1970 and from 1974 to 1978. Starting in 1938 it participated with the VU (below) in Europe's longest-serving government coalition. After 15 years as the junior coalition partner, it regained seniority in February 1993 under the premiership of Markus Büchel but lost it in the year's second election in October, when the FBP list was headed by Josef BIEDERMANN.

Following the 1997 election, at which it won a disappointing 10 seats, the FBP withdrew from the coalition government to sit in opposition. Having won 13 seats at the February 2001 election, the FBP formed a one-party administration in early April. However, after slipping to 12 seats (on a 49 percent vote share) in 2005, it reestablished the coalition with the VU.

Leaders: Otmar HASLER (Prime Minister), Matt JOHANNES (Chair).

Fatherland Union (*Vaterländische Union*—VU). Considered the more liberal of the two major parties, the VU (sometimes referred to as the Patriotic Union) was formed with substantial working-class support in 1917 as the People's Party (*Volkspartei*), which controlled the government for the decade 1918–1928. Having adopted its present name in 1936, it served as the junior coalition partner of the FBP (above) from 1938 to 1970, when it won a majority of legislative seats. It lost its coalition seniority in 1974, regained it in 1978, lost it in February 1993, and regained it again the following October. It formed its own government in April 1997 after the FBP voluntarily moved into opposition status. Following the February 2001 election, it declined to reestablish a coalition with the victorious FBP. However, it rejoined the government in April 2005 after securing ten seats (on a 38 percent vote share) in the March general election.

Leaders: Mario FRICK (Former Prime Minister), Klaus Tschütscher (Deputy Prime Minister), Henry FROMMELT (Chair).

Opposition Party

Free List (*Freie Liste*—FL). Less conservative than the traditional parties, the social democratic, environmentalist FL was formed prior to the 1986 election, at which it narrowly failed to secure the 8 percent vote share necessary for parliamentary representation; it again fell short in 1989, in part because 3 percent went to a new Liechtenstein Nonparty List (*Überparteiliche Liste Liechtensteins*—ÜLL). The party finally passed the threshold in the February 1993 balloting, securing 10.4 percent of the vote and two *Landtag* seats. It lost one of those seats the following October, regained it in 1997,

Cabinet

As of June 1, 2006

Prime Minister	Otmar Hasler (FBP)
Deputy Prime Minister	Klaus Tschütscher (VU)

Ministers

Construction and Public Works	Otmar Hasler (FBP)
Cultural Affairs	Rita Kieber-Beck (FBP) [f]
Economic Affairs	Klaus Tschütscher (VU)
Education	Hugo Quaderer (VU)
Environmental Affairs, Land Use Planning, Agriculture, and Forestry	Hugo Quaderer (VU)
Family and Equal Opportunity	Rita Kieber-Beck (FBP) [f]
Finance	Otmar Hasler (FBP)
Foreign Affairs	Rita Kieber-Beck (FBP) [f]
General Government Affairs	Otmar Hasler (FBP)
Home Affairs	Martin Meyer (FBP)
Justice	Klaus Tschütscher (VU)
Public Health	Martin Meyer (FBP)
Social Affairs	Hugo Quaderer (VU)
Sports	Klaus Tschütscher (VU)
Transport and Telecommunications	Martin Meyer (FBP)

[f] = female

and then fell back to a single seat at the February 2001 election before rebounding to three seats (on a 13 percent vote share) in March 2003. By once again winning three seats, in March 2005, the FL Party prevented either of the two larger parties from gaining an absolute majority.

Leaders: Dr. Pepo FRICK, Elisabeth TELLENBACH-FRICK, Adolph RITTER.

Legislature

The **Diet** (*Landtag*) is a unicameral body currently consisting of 25 members directly elected for four-year terms (barring dissolution) on the basis of universal suffrage and proportional representation. At the balloting of March 11 and 13, 2005, the Progressive Citizens' Party won 12 seats; the Fatherland Union, 10; and the Free List, 3.

President: Klaus WANGER.

Communications

Press

The following are published at Vaduz: *Liechtensteiner Woche* (14,000), Sunday; *Liechtensteiner Vaterland* (9,000), daily VU organ; *Liechtensteiner Volksblatt* (9,000), daily FBP organ.

News Agency

The Press and Information Office of the Liechtenstein Government (*Presse und Informationsamt der Fürstlichen Regierung*) issues periodic press bulletins.

Broadcasting

The only transmitter is that of Radio Liechtenstein, which was launched in 1995; reception is otherwise from Swiss facilities. There were approximately 15,600 television receivers in 2003.

Intergovernmental Representation

Ambassador to the U.S.
Claudia FRITSCHE

U.S. Ambassador to Liechtenstein
Peter R. CONEWAY (resident in Switzerland)

Permanent Representative to the UN
Christian WENAWESER

IGO Memberships (Non-UN)
CEUR, EBRD, EFTA, Interpol, OSCE, PCA, WTO

LITHUANIA

REPUBLIC OF LITHUANIA

Lietuvos Respublika

Note: The government of Prime Minister Algirdas Brazauskas resigned on May 31, 2006, in the wake of allegations of financial impropriety surrounding members of the Labor Party (DP), the coalition partner with the largest number of seats in Parliament at that time. President Adamkus designated Lithuanian Social Democratic Party (LSDP) MP Zigmantas Balčytis to form a new government in June, but his nomination was rejected by Parliament. President Adamkus's second nomination, MP Gediminas Kirkilas (LSDP), was approved by parliamentary vote on July 4. A minority government coalition was formed with the Lithuanian Peasant Nationalist Union (LVLS), the Liberal and Center Union (LCS), and former Labor Party members now part of Civil Democracy (CD), and sworn in on July 18; it was formed without participation from the Labor Party, but was supported by the opposition Homeland Union (TS[LK]) party. Labor Party MP defections to the LSDP over the next four months gave the Social Democrats the largest block of votes in Parliament by October.

The Country

The largest of the former Soviet Baltic republics, Lithuania is bordered on the north by Latvia, on the east by Belarus, on the south by Poland, and on the southwest by the detached Russian region of Kaliningrad. At the 2001 census 83.5 percent of the population was Lithuanian, 6.7 percent Polish, 6.3 percent Russian, and 1.2 percent Belarusan. About 79 percent are Roman Catholic, and 4 percent Russian Orthodox, while 16 percent professed no religion.

Following World War II the country passed from a largely agricultural to a substantially industrialized country, with a population that was two-thirds urban in 1986. As of 2004 the industrial sector accounted for about 34 percent of GDP, with paper, plastics, synthetic fibers, and sulfuric acid being leading products. Services accounted for about 60 percent, while agriculture contributed only 6 percent of GDP. Cattle raising and dairy farming, in addition to grain and sugar beet cultivation, are the principal agricultural activities. Natural resources include forest tracts and relatively extensive peat reserves. In 2004 two-thirds of exports went to the European Union (EU), with Germany being the

single largest importer of Lithuanian goods, and Latvia and Russia close behind. Russia remains the leading source of Lithuania's imports, accounting for 23 percent.

Economic disruption consequent upon political change yielded a 50 percent fall in GDP between

1990 and 1993, average annual inflation of some 200 percent, and an estimated unemployment rate of 15 percent by early 1994. Recovery in 1995 yielded economic growth of 3 percent, an inflation rate reduced to 15 percent, and the first trade surplus since independence. GDP growth improved to 4.7 percent in 1996 (despite inflation of 25 percent) and 7.3 percent in 1997 before declining to 5.1 percent in 1998 as the Russian financial crisis started to take a toll on Lithuanian exports. At the same time, inflation declined dramatically, dropping to 8.8 percent in 1997 and to 5.1 percent the following year. The continuing regional impact of the Russian crisis contributed to an economic contraction of 3.9 percent in 1999, but 2000 saw 3.9 percent growth. Inflation remained under control, with consumer prices advancing by only 0.8 percent in 1999 and 1.0 percent the next year, although unemployment rose from 13.3 percent in 1998 to 15.9 percent in 2000. With eventual EU accession as a goal, successive governments accelerated structural reforms, including bank privatization, tax rationalization, and restructuring of the energy sector. In 2002 the administration also announced broad changes in the nation's pension system. GDP grew by 8.9 percent in 2003, while unemployment fell to 12.4 percent. Overall, economic conditions were satisfactory enough to permit EU accession with nine other countries in May 2004. In 2005 GDP grew by 7.5 percent, while unemployment continued to fall to 8.3 percent.

Government and Politics

Political Background

One of the leading states of medieval Europe, with domains extending as far south as the Black Sea, Lithuania was merged with Poland during the 16th century and subsequently absorbed by Russia during the Polish partitions of the 18th. World War I brought with it four years of German occupation. Following the November 1918 armistice, many countries recognized the restoration of Lithuanian independence, which had been declared on February 16 despite the continuing presence of German forces. A democratic government was established in May 1920, but for several more years Lithuania remained beset by Bolshevik, czarist, and Polish interventions, with Vilnius, the capital, being occupied by Poland in 1920 and Kaunas thereupon being declared the provisional capital. A 1926 coup produced the dictatorship of Antanas SMETONA, who remained in power until World War II.

A secret protocol of the German-Soviet "friendship" treaty of September 1939 assigned the greater part of Lithuania to the Soviet sphere of influence; after being compelled to assume the status of a Soviet Socialist Republic in July 1940, the country was formally incorporated into the Soviet Union on August 3, along with Estonia and Latvia. The initial period of Soviet control was marked by executions and the deportation to Siberia of tens of thousands of Lithuanians. German reoccupation quickly followed the onset of German-Soviet hostilities in June 1941, one consequence being the subsequent decimation of Lithuania's Jewish population. Reimposed at the end of World War II, the Soviet annexation was never recognized by Britain and the United States.

In elections to the Lithuanian Supreme Soviet in late February and early March 1990, a majority of seats were won by candidates backed by the Lithuanian Reform Movement (*Sajūdis*), a secessionist formation that cut across ideological lines. On March 11 *Sajūdis* chair Vytautas LANDSBERGIS defeated Algirdas BRAZAUSKAS, the Communist incumbent chair of the Supreme Soviet Presidium, in balloting for the chairship of what was now styled the Supreme Council. Following the election of Landsbergis, the council designated Kazimiera Danutė PRUNSKIENĖ, a *Sajūdis*-endorsed Communist, to succeed Vytautas SAKALAUSKAS as chair of the Council of Ministers (prime minister). Later the same day, Lithuania became the first Soviet republic to declare its independence by repudiating the 1940 annexation and announcing a Provisional Fundamental Law of the Republic of Lithuania, an action that was immediately rejected by Moscow. In April the Soviet Union imposed an economic blockade on the country, and on June 29, following a meeting of Landsbergis and Prunskienė with President Gorbachev in Moscow, the council approved a temporary suspension of

Political Status: Independence from Russia declared February 16, 1918; absorption of independent state by the Soviet Union on August 3, 1940, repudiated on March 11, 1990, by the Lithuanian Supreme Council; independence recognized by the USSR State Council on September 6, 1991; current constitution approved by referendum of October 25, 1992.

Area: 25,174 sq. mi. (65,200 sq. km.).

Population: 3,483,972 (2001C); 3,421,000 (2005E). Substantial emigration occurred in the 1990s, as evidenced by a 1989 census count of 3,674,802.

Major Urban Centers (2005E): VILNIUS (541,000), Kaunas (364,000), Klaipėda (188,000), Šiauliai (130,000), Panevėžys (116,000).

Official Language: Lithuanian.

Monetary Unit: Litas (official rate July 1, 2006: 2.70 litai = $1US). (The litas was pegged to the euro as of February 2, 2002. Lithuania joined the European Union in 2004 and made a formal request on March 16, 2006, to the European Commission and the European Central Bank for an early assessment of its readiness to join the euro zone in January 2007.)

President: Valdas ADAMKUS (nonparty); elected in second-round balloting on June 27, 2004, and inaugurated for a five-year term on July 12 to succeed acting president, Artūras PAULAUSKAS (New Union [Social Liberals]), who had assumed office on April 6 following the removal from office of Rolandas PAKSAS (Liberal Democratic Party) on the same day.

Prime Minister: Algirdas Mykolas BRAZAUSKAS (Lithuanian Social Democratic Party); nominated by the president on June 29, 2001, confirmed by Parliament on July 3, and sworn in at the head of a Social Democratic–New Union (Social Liberal) coalition on July 12, succeeding Rolandas PAKSAS (then a member of the Lithuanian Liberal Union), who had resigned on June 20, and interim incumbent Eugenijus GENTVILAS (Lithuanian Liberal Union); reappointed by the president on March 6, 2003; reappointed by the president and confirmed by the Parliament on November 25, 2004, following legislative elections on October 10 and 24.

its independence declaration. However, subsequent negotiations proved fruitless, and on January 2, 1991, Chair Landsbergis announced an end to the moratorium.

Prime Minister Prunskienė resigned on January 8, 1991, following widespread opposition to price increases that she had authorized. Three days later Soviet army troops moved to occupy key government buildings at Vilnius, precipitating clashes that resulted in the deaths of 14 civilians and injuries to some 700. The Lithuanians responded by refusing to participate in the referendum on the Union Treaty on March 17, mounting instead a February 9 poll on independence that elicited a "yes" vote of 90.47 percent. A number of other incidents involving Soviet troops followed, prior to Moscow's acceptance of independence for all three Baltic republics on September 6 in the wake of the failed August coup by hard-liners in Moscow.

In an effort to overcome legislative paralysis in regard to economic reform, Chair Landsbergis attempted to secure sweeping new executive powers

in a referendum on May 23, 1992. While nearly 70 percent of the votes cast were affirmative, a participation rate of less than half of the electorate doomed the proposal.

Prime Minister Gediminas VAGNORIUS, who had succeeded Prunskienė following the five-day interim incumbency of Albertas ŠIMINAS, resigned, effective May 28, 1992, because of "destructive left-wing forces" that were allegedly inhibiting government efforts "to stabilize the economy, reform the legal system, and manage the country's finances." However, he continued in office on a caretaker basis until the approval of a new government under Aleksandras ABIŠALA on July 23.

In the country's first election since independence, held in two stages on October 25 and November 15, 1992, Lithuanian voters turned away from *Sajūdis* and awarded a parliamentary majority to the Brazauskas-led Lithuanian Democratic Labor Party (*Lietuvos Demokratinė Darbo Partija—* LDDP), which had been formed in 1990 by the secessionist wing of the Lithuanian Communist

Party. In a simultaneous referendum, the electorate gave 78 percent approval to a new constitution. On November 25 Brazauskas was elected chair of Parliament (*Seimas*) and, as such, acting president of the republic. Confirmed in office by direct balloting on February 15, 1993, he named Adolfas ŠLEŽEVIČIUS on March 10 to succeed Abišala as prime minister.

A major political crisis developed in January 1996 over disclosures that the prime minister had withdrawn his personal savings (some $34,000) from a Lithuanian bank two days before its operations had been suspended by the central bank because of financial irregularities. Denying any wrongdoing, Šleževičius rejected opposition calls for his resignation and was backed by the LDDP council. However, eroding support among LDDP deputies culminated on February 8 with the *Seimas* approving, by 94 votes to 24, a presidential decree calling for his resignation, whereupon Laurynas Mindaugas STANKEVIČIUS (minister of administrative reforms and municipal affairs) was named to succeed him. Following the parliamentary endorsement of Stankevičius a week later, a new LDDP government was announced by the president on February 23.

Despite a limited economic upturn in 1996, the LDDP government went down to a comprehensive defeat in legislative elections on October 20 and November 10, retaining only 12 seats out of the 137 filled. The turnout was only 53 percent in the first round and little more than 40 percent in the second. In a decisive swing to the right, the Homeland Union (Lithuanian Conservatives) (*Tėvynės Sajunga* [*Lietuvos Konservatoriai*]—TS[LK]), which had been launched in 1993 as a partial successor to *Sajūdis*, won an overall majority of 70 seats, while other center-right parties also polled strongly. Meanwhile, in four referenda held on October 20, assorted LDDP proposals for constitutional and electoral reform all failed to obtain majority support.

The TS(LK) leader, former chair Landsbergis, was accordingly elected unopposed to the powerful post of chair of the *Seimas* when it reconvened on November 25, 1996, following confirmation that the TS(LK) had opted to govern in alliance with the Lithuanian Christian Democratic Party (*Lietuvos Krikščionių Demokratų Partija*—LKDP) rather than alone. Negotiations between the two parties yielded a formal coalition agreement by early December, and on December 10 a new government received legislative endorsement by 87 votes to 21 and was sworn in. Headed by former prime minister Vagnorius, it included 11 additional TS(LK) ministers and 3 from the LKDP, with two portfolios being allocated to the Lithuanian Center Union (*Lietuvos Centro Sajunga*—LCS).

The TS(LK) continued its steady political progress in the March 1997 local elections, securing 33 percent of the seats, compared to 14 percent for the LDDP. Seven candidates contested the subsequent presidential election, with incumbent Brazauskas having declined to run for reelection. In first-round balloting on December 21, Artūras PAULAUSKAS, a former prosecutor, secured 44.7 percent of the vote, followed by Valdas ADAMKUS with 28 percent and TS(LK) leader Landsbergis with 16 percent. With Landsbergis's support, Adamkus squeaked out a victory in the second round of balloting on January 4, 1998, winning 50.3 percent of the vote. Adamkus, who had worked for Lithuanian independence during four decades in exile in the United States, was inaugurated on February 26. Prime Minister Vagnorius submitted his resignation, but Adamkus subsequently reappointed him to head a somewhat reshuffled cabinet that was confirmed by the *Seimas* on March 10.

Vagnorius's reappointment initially appeared to signal continuity in the government's emphasis on economic reform and anticorruption measures. However, over the next year severe discord developed between Adamkus and Vagnorius on several fronts, most notably the president's contention that his office should be accorded greater responsibility in the interest of the "modernization of the state." Adamkus also urged that greater authority be given to elected local officials, arguing that the TS(LK) administration had adopted a "Soviet-style" approach to government that imposed policies from the top. Consequently, in mid-April Adamkus announced that he had lost confidence in Vagnorius and urged him and his cabinet to resign. Although the prime minister argued that he was being unfairly vilified for having resisted Adamkus's attempts to "usurp" power, he announced his resignation on April 30 and was replaced on an interim basis by Social Welfare and Labor Minister Irena DEGUTIENĖ. Adamkus then tapped the TS(LK) mayor of Vilnius, Rolandas PAKSAS, who was confirmed as prime minister on May 18, and a new cabinet of TS(LK), LKDP, LCS, and independent ministers was sworn in on June 12. The new administration proved short-lived, however, with Paksas resigning on October 27 because of his opposition to sale of a one-third stake in the country's largest enterprise, the Mažeikiai oil refinery, to U.S.-based Williams International. The ministers of economy and finance also resigned, although the majority of the cabinet as well as President Adamkus supported the arrangement. When Paksas's interim replacement, Degutienė, declined the prime ministership, Adamkus instead nominated Andrius KUBILIUS of the TS(LK), who was confirmed by the *Seimas* on November 3. Five days later the LCS announced that it was leaving the government, although its one minister instead quit the party and remained in the cabinet.

Following a poor showing by the TS(LK) at the March 2000 local election, a group of about a dozen deputies led by former prime minister Vagnorius established a Moderate Conservative faction within the *Seimas*, thereby costing the TS(LK) its majority status. Formation of the Moderate Conservative Union (*Nuosaikiųjų Konservatorių Sajunga*—NKS) followed in May. In the same month, President Adamkus announced a legislative election for October 8, and the LDDP, the Lithuanian Social Democratic Party (*Lietuvos Socialdemokratų Partija*—LSDP), and two smaller parties agreed to forge an electoral alliance headed by former president Brazauskas. In the October balloting Prime Minister Kubilius's TS(LK) won only 9 seats (down from 70 in 1996), while the A. Brazauskas Social Democratic Coalition (*A. Brazausko Socialdemokratinė Koalicija*—ABSK) won a plurality of proportional seats. Nevertheless, the ABSK parties' overall total of 51 deputies proved insufficient to form a government. President Adamkus therefore turned to former prime minister Paksas and his four-party "New Policy" (*Naujosios Politikos*) bloc of the Lithuanian Liberal Union (*Lietuvos Liberalų Sajunga*—LLS), the New Union (Social Liberals) (*Naujoji Sajunga [Socialliberalai]*—NS[SL]), the LCS, and the Modern Christian Democratic Union (*Moderniųjų Krikščionių Demokratų Sajunga*—MKDS). Confirmed for the second time as prime minister on October 26, Paksas announced that his new administration's priorities would be education, economic liberalization and tax reform, an improved business climate, government restructuring, and European integration.

Once again, however, issues of economic policy and privatization brought a quick end to Paksas's tenure. On June 18, 2001, the NS(SL) leader and *Seimas* chair, Artūras Paulauskas, called for Paksas to step down; collaterally, the six NS(SL)-selected cabinet ministers resigned. Paksas tendered his own resignation two days later, with the LLS minister of the economy, Eugenijus GENTVILAS, then assuming Paksas's duties on an acting basis. On July 3 the *Seimas* confirmed former president Brazauskas as prime minister at the head of a coalition of the LSDP (with which the LDDP had merged in January) and the NS(SL), the new cabinet being announced on July 5.

The end to Prime Minister Paksas's second brief term in office came about not only because of policy differences between his LLS and Artūras Paulauskas's NS(SL) but also because of the two leaders' political rivalry. Nine days before Paksas's June 2001 resignation, the New Policy parties had attempted to solidify the crumbling foundation of their alliance by forming five working groups that were given the task of reconciling divergent views on tax reform, pension reform, return of nationalized land, the status of the Mažeikiai oil refinery (including contractual arrangements for acquiring Russian crude), and plans for privatizing the national natural gas company.

In first-round presidential balloting on December 22, 2002, President Adamkus led 17 candidates with 35.5 percent of the vote, followed by Paksas (19.7 percent), and Paulauskas (8.3 percent). However, Paksas defeated Adamkus in the runoff election on January 5, 2003, with 54.7 percent of the vote. Prime Minister Brazauskas was reconfirmed on March 6 to head another (only slightly reshuffled) LSDP-NS(SL) coalition government.

In late 2003 President Paksas became embroiled in a controversy concerning his alleged links with a shadowy figure reputed to have ties to organized crime (see Current issues, below). After a special legislative committee alleged that Paksas had, among other things, jeopardized national security, impeachment proceedings were launched in December, resulting in six formal charges against Paksas in February 2004. After Paksas rejected calls for his resignation, the *Seimas* on April 6 found him guilty by large margins of three charges and removed him from office. As mandated by the constitution, Paulauskas (the chair of the *Seimas*) assumed presidential authority on an acting basis.

The first round of a new presidential election was held on June 13, 2004, with Adamkus winning 30.7 percent of the vote, followed by Kazimiera PRUNSKIENĖ of the Union of the Peasants and New Democracy Parties (*Valstiečių ir Naujosios Demokratijos Partiju Sajunga*—VNDPS) with 21.4 percent. (Prunskienė was supported by Paksas after the *Seimas* had ruled that Paksas could not be a candidate.) Adamkus secured the presidency in the second round of balloting on June 27 with 52.6 percent of the vote.

Following Lithuania's accession to the EU on May 1, 2004, the recently formed Labor Party (*Darbo Partija*—DP) burst onto the electoral scene with a strong performance in the June 2004 elections for the European Parliament. It continued its ascendancy in the *Seimas* balloting on October 10 and 24, leading all parties with 39 seats. After lengthy negotiations, Prime Minister Brazauskas was reappointed to head a new coalition government (inaugurated on December 14) comprising the DP, LSDP, NS(SL), and VNDPS.

In April 2006 the ruling coalition barely survived a crisis when the NS(SL) pulled out and removed its members from the cabinet. This ac-

tion was precipitated when coalition partners voted to oust parliamentary chair and NS(SL) member Artūras Paulauskas in a no-confidence vote on April 11. In the ensuing negotiations among the remaining coalition partners, the Labor Party won the vacated cabinet post for Social Security and Labor, while the National Farmers' Union won the prestigious Foreign Ministry.

Constitution and Government

The 1992 constitution accords primacy, as representing the sovereignty of the people, to a Parliament (*Seimas*) elected for a four-year term, although significant powers, particularly in the sphere of foreign policy, are allocated to the president, who is directly elected for a five-year term. The president appoints the prime minister and, on the latter's nomination, other ministers, all subject to the approval of the *Seimas*. The judicial structure is headed by a Constitutional Court and a Supreme Court, whose judges are selected by the *Seimas* from presidential nominations. Members of district and local courts are appointed by the president.

Government at the local level currently encompasses 10 counties (*apskritys*), which are centrally directed and supervised; 44 rural and 12 urban municipalities, which are self-governing; and some 500 neighborhoods. The 56 self-governing units elect local councils, with each council then selecting an executive. The national government proposed in early 1999 that the mayors of larger cities be elected by popular vote, a change that would require a constitutional amendment, and which had yet to be adopted by April 2006.

Foreign Relations

Soviet recognition of the independence of the Baltic states on September 6, 1991, paved the way for admission of the three to the Conference on (later Organization for) Security and Cooperation in Europe (CSCE/OSCE) on September 10 and admission to the United Nations on September 17. More than 30 governments had recognized

Lithuania during late August, though Washington's failure to do so until September 2 visibly annoyed Chair Landsbergis.

Regionally, Lithuania concluded a Baltic Economic Cooperation Agreement with Estonia and Latvia in April 1990. On September 24, 1991, the three states also reached agreement on a customs union that authorized free trade and visa-free travel among their respective jurisdictions, although implementation of its provisions proceeded very slowly. Lithuania was also a founding member of the broader Council of the Baltic Sea States in 1992.

On July 31, 1991, President Landsbergis and Russian President Boris Yeltsin signed an agreement giving Russia rights of transit across Lithuania to its Baltic enclave of Kaliningrad. Subsequently, on February 16, 1992, Landsbergis demanded that former Soviet troops be withdrawn from Kaliningrad on the grounds that their presence had become a "historic anachronism." While firmly rejecting this demand, Russia entered into negotiations on the withdrawal of its troops from Lithuania, where a referendum on June 14 gave 90 percent endorsement to the government's position. Yeltsin responded on September 8 by agreeing to a full withdrawal by August 31, 1993. Despite some last-minute uncertainty, the deadline was met by the Russians, with President Brazauskas having waived a $140 billion compensation claim lodged by his predecessor. Under an economic cooperation agreement concluded on March 6, Russia undertook to supply oil, natural gas, and nuclear energy to Lithuania in exchange for agricultural and manufactured goods. In October 1999 the *Seimas* ratified a border treaty that had been negotiated in 1997, but in June 2000 the legislature also passed a resolution seeking compensation for 50 years of Soviet occupation. (The cost of the occupation was later estimated at $20 billion.) Relations nevertheless remain cordial, with Presidents Adamkus and Putin taking a common tack in March 2001 on the status of Kaliningrad and the free movement of the region's residents through Lithuania.

Independent Lithuania moved quickly to reestablish historically close relations with Poland,

concluding on January 13, 1992, a joint Declaration on Friendly Relations and Cooperation that included a number of economic and ecological provisions and confirmed the existing border between the two countries. In April 1994 President Wałęsa became the first Polish head of state to visit Lithuania in over a century, signing a treaty of friendship and cooperation at Vilnius. In February 1995 President Brazauskas paid a reciprocal visit to Warsaw, which was followed in September by a bilateral accord envisaging that Lithuania would accede to the Central European Free Trade Agreement (CEFTA/Visegrad Group). Lithuania's relations with Moscow-aligned Belarus were more problematical: an economic cooperation agreement concluded on April 2, 1992, included a confirmation of the existing border, but a widely quoted statement by the Belarus defense minister in March had included territorial claims on Lithuania. Relations with Belarus were further complicated when all three Baltic nations condemned the widespread fraud and repression leading up to the March 2006 elections, which resulted in the reelection of President Alyaksandr Lukashenka.

A prime ministerial visit to Israel in October 1994 was intended to consolidate a government apology made the previous month for Lithuania's wartime role in the Nazi genocide of European Jewry. The visit followed heated controversy over the decision of the immediate post-Soviet government to exonerate convicted war criminals on the grounds that Soviet-era trials had been coercive and lacking due process. Under international pressure, incoming President Brazauskas had in March 1993 announced a review of pardons issued by the previous government. Tension between Lithuania and Israel again flared when in March 2006 the Vilnius District Court found Nazi collaborator Algimantas Dailidė guilty of genocide, but failed to impose any punishment due to the defendant's poor health and old age.

Having joined the Council of Europe in May 1993, Lithuania became a signatory of North Atlantic Treaty Organization's (NATO) Partnership for Peace in January 1994, subsequently reiterating its desire for full membership and also for eventual accession to the EU. In the latter context, Lithuania and the other two Baltic states in July 1995 became the first ex-Soviet republics to sign "Europe" (i.e., association) agreements with the EU, offering the prospect of eventual full membership, for which Lithuania submitted a formal application on December 8.

Lithuania was not among the three countries invited in July 1997 by NATO to join the alliance in 1999, strong Russian objections to such expansion contributing significantly to NATO's decision to proceed slowly. However, NATO officials announced that they considered Lithuania and the other two Baltic states to be strong candidates for eventual membership. Lithuanian leaders were also disappointed (albeit not surprised) that Lithuania was not included on the list of countries invited in December by the EU to begin membership negotiations in 1998. However, the EU agreed that talks would continue toward Lithuania's inclusion in the "second wave" of expansion. In October 1999 the EU abandoned the second wave concept and then announced in December that Lithuania could proceed with accession negotiations.

The three Baltic states signed the U.S.-Baltic Charter of Partnership on January 16, 1998, in which Washington affirmed the three nations' sovereignty (without making any military commitments), supported the integration of the trio into Western institutions, and approved three bilateral working groups to advance cooperation. In December the Lithuanian Parliament abolished the death penalty and also began to consider the possible closure of the Ignalina nuclear power plant, which EU members considered obsolete and dangerous; both actions were considered necessary to improve EU membership prospects for Lithuania. In September 1999 Lithuania agreed to decommission one of Ignalina's two reactors by 2005, contingent on receiving sufficient aid toward the $2.5 billion cost.

Lithuania was formally invited in November 2002 to join NATO, while the EU issued a similar invitation in December. On May 10 and 11, 2003, Lithuanian voters approved the EU initiative with a 91 percent "yes" vote in a national referendum. On March 10, 2004, the *Seimas* approved NATO accession by a vote of 100–3, and Lithuania joined NATO on March 29. EU accession followed on May 1, and in November Lithuania became the first EU member to approve (by an 84–4 vote in the *Seimas*) the proposed new EU constitution. On April 26, 2006, the Lithuanian government announced a final effort to win approval to adopt the euro by January 1, 2007.

Lithuania subsequently participated in a number of NATO operations, including missions in the Balkans and Afghanistan. Lithuania also contributed some 330 troops to support the U.S./UK-led coalition in Iraq following the ouster of Saddam Hussein, but by the end of 2005 the country had only approximately 100 troops in Iraq, 50 of whom were under Polish command and would not be replaced after Poland's complete withdrawal in 2006.

Current Issues

Much of the attention of the new administration of Prime Minister Brazauskas in the second half of 2001 was directed toward the goal of receiving invitations to join NATO and the EU. In May, 11 parties had signed an agreement on defense policy, including a commitment to raise defense appropriations to NATO standards. With regard to the EU, considerable work remained to be done on legislation bringing Lithuania into line with European Commission requirements. The 15 months after the October 2000 *Seimas* election were also marked by shifts in political forces, most notably the consolidation of the major leftist parties in the new LSDP. Mergers involving numerous other parliamentary and nonparliamentary formations also occurred (see Political Parties, below).

Lithuania was among seven countries invited by the November 2002 NATO summit to join the alliance; an EU summit in the second week of December also included Lithuania among ten nations approved for eventual EU membership. Although those developments would normally have been expected to bolster the chances for President Adamkus's reelection, observers noted that the president was facing a surge in popular concern over certain negative effects of recent free-market policies, mandated, in part, to meet EU standards.

Consequently, the runoff presidential victory by former prime minister Rolandas Paksas was not considered a surprise. Disenchantment with recent economic policies also apparently contributed to subsequent increased voter interest in new parties such as the DP, which continued to build political strength through 2005.

In October 2003 documents were discovered that allegedly linked President Paksas to Yurii BORISOV, an ethnic Russian alleged to have ties with organized crime. Among other things, it was alleged that Paksas had granted Borisov dual citizenship, despite reported concerns from Lithuanian security services that Borisov might have been involved in smuggling arms. President Paksas's critics charged that Borisov had contributed heavily to Paksas's political finances. In November an emergency session of the *Seimas* established a special committee to investigate the matter, and in December the *Seimas* accepted the committee's report alleging that Paksas had jeopardized national security. After Paksas was removed from office by the *Seimas* in April, the *Seimas* ruled that Paksas could not participate in the upcoming balloting to fill the presidency. (In October 2004 Paksas was acquitted of criminal charges of revealing state secrets, and he vowed to return to politics. However, that goal appeared to be compromised in November when a court in Vilnius found Borisov guilty of blackmailing Paksas while Paksas was president.)

Among the problems faced by the coalition cabinet inaugurated in December 2004 was the need to reduce the budget deficit to meet EU guidelines in advance of adoption of the euro. In May 2005 the finance minister resigned after the coalition partners rejected his proposed 4 percent tax on corporate profits as a means of enhancing the government's revenue. The cabinet lost four additional members over the next year. On June 21, 2005, the leader of the Labor Party, Viktor USPASKICH, was dismissed from the post of economy minister. Then in April 2006, after the parliament ousted NS(SL) leader Artūras Paulauskas from the office of speaker, the speaker's party left the coalition and recalled its two ministers (for foreign affairs and social security and labor) from the government.

Political Parties

The constitutional revision of March 11, 1990, effectively revoked the monopoly of the Lithuanian Communist Party (*Lietuvos Komunistų Partija*—LKP). In August 1991 the party itself was banned and its property confiscated, although its secessionist wing had long since withdrawn to form the Lithuanian Democratic Labor Party (LDDP; see LSDP). Legislation was approved in early 1999 for government funds to be allocated to parties demonstrating backing from at least 3 percent of the voters. More than two dozen parties and coalitions registered to contest the October 2000 parliamentary elections, a number that dropped to 20 for the 2004 parliamentary elections.

Government Parties

Labor Party (*Darbo Partija*—DP). Formed by ethnic Russian businessman Viktor Uspaskich in 2003, the DP is a populist party that supports increased pensions and higher wages for workers. It also presents itself as an alternative to some established parties perceived to be tainted by corruption. Uspaskich was named minister of the economy in the coalition government installed in December 2004, but he resigned that post in June 2005 in the wake of criticism that he may have faced a conflict of interest between his governmental position and his business affairs. Nevertheless, the Labor Party continued as a force in the government, winning the cabinet post for Social Security and Labor in April 2006 when the NS(SL) withdrew from the ruling coalition and recalled its ministers from the cabinet. The party suffered a setback when on May 3, in response to leader Uspaskich's aggressive maneuverings, seven DP members of parliament left the party and together with three deputies from the Liberal Democratic Party formed a new coalition called Civil Democracy.

Leader: Viktor USPASKICH.

Lithuanian Social Democratic Party (*Lietuvos Socialdemokratų Partija*—LSDP). The present LSDP was established by merger in January 2001 of the existing LSDP and the Lithuanian Democratic Labor Party (*Lietuvos Demokratinė Darbo*

Partija—LDDP). Together, they had formed the backbone of the A. Brazauskas Social Democratic Coalition (*A. Brazausko Socialdemokratinė Koalicija*—ABSK), which had been established to present a consolidated list for the proportional component of the October 2000 legislative election. The other ABSK participants were the New Democracy Party (NDP; see LVL, below) and the Lithuanian Russian Union (see LRS, below).

The premerger LSDP was formed in 1896 and reestablished in 1989. It won a 5.9 percent vote share in the 1992 balloting and then improved to 6.7 percent in 1996, when it took 12 parliamentary seats. The LDDP was formed in 1990 by a faction of the former Lithuanian Communist Party (LKP) that initially supported Soviet president Gorbachev's reformist program and subsequently endorsed independence for Lithuania. The LDDP scored a surprising victory at the 1992 parliamentary balloting, winning 42.6 percent of the vote on a platform of gradual transition to a market economy; the party's leader, Algirdas Brazauskas, was subsequently confirmed as president. Considerable party turmoil accompanied the government crisis and ouster of Prime Minister Adolfas ŠLEŽEVIČIUS in early 1996, which contributed to a disastrous showing at the subsequent *Seimas* election: LDDP representation fell to 12 seats.

At the October 2000 election the ABSK won a leading 28 proportional seats, based on a 31 percent vote share, while the LSDP and LDDP won 7 and 14 single-member constituency seats, respectively. The NDP added 2 more constituency seats, but the total of 51 was insufficient for the coalition to establish a government. Following the January 2001 LSDP-LDDP merger, however, Brazauskas was in a position to negotiate formation of a new administration with the New Union (Social Liberals) when the latter party's coalition with the Liberal Union (LLS) dissolved in June.

The LSDP presented joint candidates with the NS(SL) in the 2004 legislative balloting, after which Brazauskas continued as prime minister. The NS(SL) left the coalition in April 2006, but the ruling coalition retained power.

Leaders: Algirdas Mykolas BRAZAUSKAS (Prime Minister and Party Chair), Vytenis Povilas

ANDRIUKAITIS, Česlovas JURŠĖNAS (Deputy Chairs).

Lithuanian Peasant Nationalist Union (*Lietuvos valstiečių liaudininkų sajunga*—LVLS). Until February 2006, the LVL had been known as the Union of the Peasants and New Democracy Parties (*Valstiečių ir Naujosios Demokratijos Partiju Sajunga*—VNDS). The VNDS was formed on December 15, 2001, by merger of the Lithuanian Peasants' Party (*Lietuvos Valstiečių Partija*—LVP) and the New Democracy Party (*Naujosios Demokratijos Partija*—NDP), which had formed a joint faction in the *Seimas* following the October 2000 election. At the last legislative elections in October 2004, the party won 6.6 percent of the popular vote and 10 out of 141 seats. In the 2004 European parliamentary elections VNDS gained 7.4 percent of the vote and returned one member. VNDS candidate Kazimiera Prunskienė won 47.4 percent of the vote in the second round at the presidential elections in June 2004.

The LVP, which traced its origins to 1905, was revived as the Lithuanian Peasants' Union (*Lietuvos Valstiečių Sajunga*—LVS) in 1990 and adopted the LVP designation in 1994. It won one constituency seat in the 1996 parliamentary election and then four in 2000. In March 2001 the party suffered a split when a delegation from Kaunas was not seated at a party congress because two of its leaders had been expelled the previous month for criticizing the leadership of the party chair, Ramūnas Karbauskis. Most of the Kaunas delegation reportedly joined the LSDP in protest. The LVP subsequently helped confirm Prime Minister Brazauskas.

The NDP was launched as the Lithuanian Women's Party (*Lietuvos Moterų Partija*—LMP) in February 1995 under the leadership of Kazimiera Prunskienė, former head of the Soviet-era Association of Women of Lithuania as well as prime minister in 1990 and 1991. In 1992 the Lithuanian Supreme Court ruled that she had been a conscious collaborator with the KGB, which she denied. The LMP won one seat in the 1996 election, after which it adopted the NDP designation. In 2000 the NDP campaigned as part of the ABSK coalition. It won two single-member constituency seats and one proportional seat but left the coalition shortly thereafter.

Leaders: Kazimira Danutė PRUNSKIENĖ (Chair, Parliamentary Leader, and 2004 presidential candidate), Ramūnas KARBAUSKIS (First Deputy Chair).

Other Parliamentary Parties

New Union (Social Liberals) (*Naujoji Sajunga [Socialliberalai]*—NS[SL]). The left-of-center NS(SL) was established in late April 1998 by Artūras Paulauskas, a prosecutor who had easily outdistanced all rivals in the first round of the January 1998 presidential contest but had then finished second in runoff balloting. Prior to the 2000 parliamentary election the NS(SL) joined the Lithuanian Liberal Union (LLS), the Lithuanian Center Union (LCS), and the Modern Christian Democrats (MKDS), all described below, in announcing that after the balloting they would attempt to form a "New Policy" (*Naujosios Politikos*) government. Backed by President Adamkus, the New Policy program advocated liberal democracy, a market economy, and social activism. Following the October balloting, at which the NS(SL) finished third, the New Policy partners came to power under the LLS's Rolandas Paksas. The coalition foundered in June 2001, however, with Paulauskas calling for Paksas to step down and with the six NS(SL)-nominated cabinet ministers resigning. Later in the month Paulauskas negotiated a coalition agreement with the LSDP and joined the new government.

Paulauskas played a leading role in the 2003–2004 impeachment crisis, serving as interim president following the ouster of President Paksas. Paulauskas subsequently chose to return to his duties as chair of the *Seimas* rather than run for a regular presidential term. The NS(SL) presented joint candidates with the LSDP in the 2004 legislative elections and Paulauskas was elected parliamentary chair, a post he would lose in a no-confidence vote on April 11, 2006, in which 94 MPs, including many coalition partners, voted for his removal. In response the NS(SL) withdrew from the ruling coalition.

Leaders: Artūras PAULAUSKAS (Chair of the Party), Vaclovas KARBAUSKIS (Parliamentary Leader), Vaidas PLIUSNIS (General Secretary).

Liberal and Center Union (*Liberalų ir Centro Sajunga*—LCS). Formed in March 2003 via the merger of the three parties below, the LCS gained 18 seats in the October 2004 legislative elections. In addition, LCS leader Artūra Zoukas was reelected as mayor of Vilnius in June 2003.

Leader: Artūra ZOUKAS.

Lithuanian Liberal Union (*Lietuvos Liberalų Sajunga*—LLS). The founding congress of the moderately right-wing LLS took place in November 1990, but the party failed to win any parliamentary seats in 1992. In 1996 it won one. Following a solid performance in the March 1997 local elections, the LLS attempted to position itself as a leader of Lithuanian centrists, broadening its appeal beyond its base in the business community. In December 1999 former prime minister Rolandas Paksas, having resigned from the TS(LK), joined the LLS and quickly ascended to chair.

In the October 2000 election the party made major gains, winning 17.3 percent of the proportional vote and accumulating 34 seats, second only to the ABSK. The LLS then led the New Policy bloc in forming a government under Paksas, but the coalition dissolved in June 2001 when the NS(SL) parted ways with the LLS. In early September, pressured by the party's governing body, Paksas resigned as party chair. At an extraordinary congress held on October 27 Paksas was defeated in his campaign for chair but accepted the post of first deputy chair. In late December 2001 Paksas and ten other deputies announced that they intended to leave the LLS, in part because of a dispute about selecting the party's standard-bearer for the 2002 presidential race. In March the LLS defectors formed the Liberal Democratic Party (below).

Lithuanian Center Union (*Lietuvos Centro Sajunga*—LCS). The LCS originated in 1992 as the Lithuanian Center Movement (*Lietuvos Centro Judėjimas*—LCJ), which contested the

1992 election on a promarket platform and won two *Seimas* seats. Registered as the LCS in 1993, it went on to win 13 seats in 1996 and then joined the center-right TS(LK)-led coalition government in December. In the subsequent presidential election it backed Valdas Adamkus.

In November 1999 LCS Chair Romualdas OZOLAS announced that the LCS was breaking with the government; in response, the LCS minister of justice, Gintaras BALČIŪNAS, left the party and remained in the cabinet. At the October 2000 election the LCS won only two seats, which led to Ozolas's resignation. As part of the New Policy bloc, it joined the second Paksas government.

Modern Christian Democratic Union (*Moderniųjų Krikščionių Demokratų Sajunga*—MKDS). The constituent congress of the MKDS was held in April 2000 following the decision of the "modern" faction of the Lithuanian Christian Democratic Party (LKDP) to part ways with the "conservative" faction. Differences had emerged in fall 1999, but the LKDP held together until after the March 2000 local elections. The MKDS won one parliamentary seat in October 2000.

Homeland Union (Lithuanian Conservatives) (*Tėvynės Sajunga [Lietuvos Konservatoriai]*— TS[LK]). The Homeland Union was launched on May 1, 1993, as a partial successor to the Lithuanian Reform Movement (*Sajūdis*), which had spearheaded the independence campaign. Under the leadership of Vytautas Landsbergis, the broadly based *Sajūdis* was the leading formation at the elections of February and March 1990 but in the face of economic adversity suffered a stinging defeat in 1992, winning only 20.5 percent of the vote. Although the TS(LK) presented itself as a right-of-center party, it indicated that its ranks would be open to former Communists.

Benefiting from the deep unpopularity of the then ruling LDDP, the TS(LK) rose to power in the fall 1996 election with 70 out of 137 seats (although its share of the proportional vote was less than 30 percent). The party was relatively success-

ful in the March 1997 local elections, but Landsbergis finished a disappointing third (with 15.7 percent of the vote) in the first round of the presidential balloting in December. The TS(LK) renewed its 1996 coalition agreement with the Lithuanian Christian Democratic Party (LKDP; see LKD, below) in January 1999; the Lithuanian Center Union (LCS, above) also remained in the government until departing in November 1999, shortly after the TS(LK)'s Andrius Kubilius had been confirmed as prime minister, in succession to Rolandas Paksas.

Following a poor showing in the March 2000 local election, a group of about a dozen deputies loyal to former TS(LK) prime minister Gediminas Vagnorius established a Moderate Conservative faction within the *Seimas*, thereby costing the TS(LK) its majority status. Formation of the NKS splinter (below) followed. In the October 2000 parliamentary election the TS(LK) won only one constituency seat but won eight more on an 8.6 percent proportional vote share.

In November 2003 the TS(LK) absorbed the LDS (below). In February the party dropped the "Lithuanian Conservatives" from its name and became known simply as the TS. In the October 2004 legislative balloting, the TS won 25 seats, thereby becoming the second-largest grouping in the *Seimas*.

Leaders: Vytautas LANDSBERGIS (Former President of the Republic), Andrius KUBILIUS (Chair and 2002 presidential candidate), Rasa JUKNEVIČIENĖ (Deputy Chair), Arvydas VIDŽIŪNAS (General Secretary).

Lithuanian Rightist Union (*Lietuvos Dešiniųjų Sajunga*—LDS). The LDS was formed in October 2001 by merger of four small parties, none represented in the current *Seimas*: the Homeland People's Party (*Tėvynės Liaudies Partija*—TLP), the Independence Party (*Nepriklausombyės Partija*—NP), the Lithuanian Democratic Party (*Lietuvos Demokratų Partija*—LDP), and the Lithuanian Freedom League (*Lietuvos Laisvės Lyga*—LLL).

The TLP had held its founding congress in December 1999 under the leadership of Laima

ANDRIKIENĖ, who had been expelled from the TS(LK) for criticizing the party and government. The NP dated from 1990. In April 1992 its leader, Virgilius ČEPAITIS, was convicted by the Supreme Court of having "deliberately cooperated" with the Soviet KGB. Allied with the Lithuanian National Union (LTS) in the 1992 poll, it took one of the joint list's 4 seats, but in 1996 it won none and in 2000 it chose not to contest the election. Originally founded in 1902, the LDP had been reestablished in 1989. In the 1992 parliamentary poll it ran on a joint list with the LKDP and LPKTS, winning 4 of the coalition's 18 seats. Standing on its own in 1996, it won 2 constituency seats. In 2000 it ran in a loose coalition with the "Young Lithuanians."

Described by one of its founders as a "classical right-wing party," the LDS supports European integration, market economics, and close cooperation with the TS(LK), Christian Democrats, and other like-minded formations. Its chair is a noted film director.

Leaders: Arūnas ŽEBRIŪNAS (Chair), Laima ANDRIKIENĖ, Saulius PEČELIŪNAS (LDP), Valentinas ŠAPALAS (NP), Antanas TERLECKAS (LLL).

For Order and Justice (*Už Tvarka ir Teisinguma*—UTT). The UTT was formed as an electoral coalition of the two groups below in 2004 following the removal from office of President Paksas. The coalition was reportedly designed to minimize voter backlash against Paksas's LDP; there was also concern that the LDP might be prevented from presenting its own candidates. The UTT won 11 seats in the *Seimas* in the October poll on a vote share of 11.4 percent.

Liberal Democratic Party (*Liberalų Demokratų Partija*—LDP). Formed in March 2002 by former prime minister Rolandas Paksas and other LLS defectors, the center-right Liberal Democratic Party pledged to support the business sector and to guarantee "order in the state." Paksas also indicated continued support for Lithuania's eventual inclusion into NATO and the EU, although he vowed

Lithuania would not be "submissive" in dealing with those groupings.

Paksas was elected president of the republic in 2003 but was removed from office in 2004 (see Political background and Current issues for details.) The LDP supported the VNDPS candidate in the 2004 presidential poll after Paksas was ruled ineligible to run.

Leader: Rolandas PAKSAS (Chair, Former Prime Minister, and Former President of the Republic), Valentis MAZURONIS (First Deputy Chair).

Lithuanian People's Union "For Fair Lithuania" (*Lietuvos Liaudies Sajunga "Už Teisingą Lietuvą"*—LLS). The LLS was formed in 2000 by Julius Veselka, who ran successfully as a "self-nominated" candidate in the 2000 legislative elections. The LLS won 11 percent of the vote in the 2002 local elections.

Leader: Julius VESELKA.

Lithuanian Poles' Electoral Action (*Lietuvos Lenkų Rinkimų Akcija*—LLRA). The LLRA began as the Lithuanian Polish Union (*Lietuvos Lenkų Sajunga*—LLS), an ethnic grouping that won four *Seimas* seats in 1992. As the LLRA, it retained only one seat in 1996 but again won two in 2000 and 2004.

Leaders: Valdemar TOMAŠEVSKI and Leokadija POČIKOVSKA (Members of Parliament).

Other Parties

Lithuanian Christian Democrats (*Lietuvos Krišćionys Demokratai*—LKD). The LKD was formed in May 2001 by merger of the Lithuanian Christian Democratic Party (*Lietuvos Krišćionių Demokratų Partija*—LKDP) and the Christian Democratic Union (*Krišćionių Demokratų Sajunga*—KDS).

The LKDP had been organized in 1989 as the revival of a pre-Soviet party originally formed in 1905. It ran third in the 1992 balloting on a joint list with the Lithuanian Democratic Party (LDP; see LDS, above) and the Lithuanian Union of Political Prisoners and Deportees (LPKTS, below).

It won a total of 16 seats, for second place, in 1996 and joined the TS(LK)-led coalition government. In the October 2000 election, however, it secured only 2 seats and 3 percent of the proportional vote. A month later the party chair, Zigmas ZINKEVIČIUS, resigned over what he labeled as secret merger negotiations being conducted by the party's board chair, Algirdas Saudargas, with the KDS.

A smaller formation, the KDS had won a single parliamentary seat in 1992, 1996, and 2000; its deputy, Kazys Bobelis, had also won 4 percent of the vote in the 1997 presidential balloting.

Leaders: Kazys BOBELIS (2002 and 2004 presidential candidate), Valentinas STUNDYS (Chair), Kazimieras KUZMINSKAS (Deputy Chair).

Lithuanian Russian Union (*Lietuvos Rusų Sąjunga*—LRS). An ethnic party representing the Russian minority, the LRS was registered in 1995 but failed to win representation in the 1996 parliamentary election. It won three proportional seats in 2000 as part of the ABSK. It subsequently backed formation of the LSDP-NS(SL) government.

Leaders: Sergejus DMITRIJEVAS, Vladimiras ORECHOVAS, Jurgis UTOVKA.

Lithuanian Freedom Union (*Lietuvos Laisvės Sąjunga*—LLaS). Based in Kaunas and without a significant national following, the LLaS is a right-wing, populist, anti-Semitic formation. Its controversial leader won the party's only seat in the October 2000 parliamentary election; in the proportional component it won 1.3 percent of the national vote. In the 2004 parliamentary election the LLaS won no single-member district seats and just 0.28 percent of the proportional vote.

Leader: Vytautas ŠUSTAUSKAS (Former Mayor of Kaunas).

Moderate Conservative Union (*Nuosaikiųjų Konservatorių Sąjunga*—NKS). The NKS emerged from the Moderate Conservative parliamentary faction that had been formed in late March 2000 by about a dozen Homeland Union *Seimas* deputies loyal to former prime minister Vagnorius. The dissidents were particularly concerned with what they saw as the government's departure from the Conservative economic program, resulting in "public distrust." In May Vagnorius announced formation of the NKS, which was registered in July. In the October *Seimas* election he won the party's only seat. The NKS did not field candidates in the 2004 *Seimas* election.

Leader: Gediminas VAGNORIUS (Chair).

"Young Lithuanians," New Nationalists and Political Prisoners Union (*"Jaunosios Lietuvos," Naujųjų Tautininkų ir Politinių Kalinių Sąjunga*—JLNTPKS). Previously known as the Lithuanian National Party "Young Lithuania" (*Lietuvių Nacionalinė Partija "Jaunoji Lietuva"*), the rightist JLNTPKS retained its one parliamentary seat at the October 2000 election, but won no seats in 2004 despite fielding five candidates for single-member districts.

Leader: Stanislovas BUŠKEVIČIUS (Chair).

Lithuanian National Union (*Lietuvių Tautininkų Sąjunga*—LTS), The LTS is a 1989 revival of a party first formed in 1924. Its 1992 list, which included the Independence Party (NP; see LDS, above), won four parliamentary seats on a 1.9 percent vote share. The LTS slipped to a single seat in 1996.

Party leader Rimantas SMETONA received a minuscule 0.4 percent of the vote in the first round of presidential balloting in December 1997. He subsequently formed the Lithuanian National Democratic Party (LNDP, below), which joined the Lithuanian Freedom League (LLL; see LDS, above) and the LTS in a People's Front (*Tautos Frontas*) coalition for the proportional component of the 2000 parliamentary election. (All of the Front candidates appeared under the LTS designation.) The LTS fielded 31 candidates for both proportional representation and single-member districts in 2004, but won no seats and only 0.21 percent of the proportional vote.

Leader: Gediminas SAKALNIKAS (Chair).

Lithuanian National Democratic Party (*Lietuvos Nacionaldemokratų Partija*—LNDP). The LNDP was formed by former LTS leader Rimantas Smetona in January 1999 on a platform of "moderate nationalism" that included support for

Cabinet

As of August 1, 2006

Prime Minister	Gediminas Kirkilas (LSDP)

Ministers

Agriculture	Kazimira Danutė Prunskienė (LVLS) [f]
Culture	Jonas Jučas (LCS)
Economy	Vytas Navickas (LVLS)
Education and Science	Roma Žakaitiene (LSDP) [f]
Environment	Arūnas Kundrotas (LSDP)
Finance	Zigmantis Balčytis (LSDP)
Foreign Affairs	Petras Vaitiekūnas (LVLS)
Health	Rimvydas Turčinskas (CD)
Interior	Raimondas Šukys (LCS)
Justice	Petras Baguška (CD)
National Defense	Juozas Olekas (LSDP)
Social Security and Labor	Vilija Blinkevičiūtė (LSDP) [f]
Transportation and Communication	Algidas Butkevičius (LSDP)

[f] = female

NATO membership and closer ties to the West, but not for EU membership. At the time, Smetona was widely considered the only "Eurosceptic" deputy in the *Seimas*. The new party failed to win any seats in the 2000 parliamentary election, either in individual constituencies or as part of the People's Front in the proportional component. A party congress in March 2001 elected Kazimieras UOKA as chair, but he ran as a member of the LTS in 2004. The LNDP has been led by neofascist Mindaugas Murza since May 2002. The LNDP did not field candidates for the 2004 parliamentary election.

Leaders: Mindaugas MURZA (Chair), Žilvinas RAZMINAS.

Other parties contesting the 2000 and/or 2004 parliamentary elections included the **Christian Conservative Social Union** (*Krikščionių Konservatorių Socialinė Sajunga*—KKSS), which won 2 percent of the vote in the 2004 national elections; the **Lithuanian Party "Social Democracy 2000"** (*Lietuvos Partija "Socialdemokratija 2000"*), led by Rimantas DAGYS; and the **Lithuanian Union**

of Political Prisoners and Deportees (*Lietuvos Politinių Kalinių ir Tremtinių Sajunga*—LPKTS), which won one parliamentary seat in 1992 and 1996 but was unsuccessful in 2000 and 2004 despite a loose alliance with the TS(LK).

Additional minor parties include the **Lithuanian Economic Party** (*Lietuvos Ūkio Partija*—LŪP); the **Lithuanian Green Party** (*Lietuvos Žalioji Partija*—LŽP), which dates from 1990 and is led by Ruta GAJAUSKAITĖ; the **Lithuanian Humanist Party** (*Lietuvos Humanistų Partija*—LHP), chaired by Leopoldas TARAKEVIČIUS; the **Lithuanian Justice Party** (*Lietuvos Teisingumo Partija*—LTP); the **Lithuanian Party of Christian Democracy**, led by Ignacas UZDAVINYS; the **Lithuanian Reform Party** (*Lietuvos Reformų Partija*—LRP); the **Lithuanian Socialist Party** (*Lietuvos Socialistų Partija*—LSP), led by Albinas VISOCKAS; the **Lithuanian Social Justice Union** (*Lietuvos Socialinio Teisingumo Sajunga*—LSTS); the **National Center Party** (*Nacionalinė Centro Partija*—NCP), led by Romualdas OZOLAS; the **National Progress Party** (*Tautos Pažangos*

Partija—TPP); the **Party of Lithuanian Political Prisoners** (*Lietuvos Politinių Kalinių Partija*—LPKP), led by Zigmas MEDINECKAS; the **Polish People's Party** (*Polska Partija Ludowa*—PPL), formed in 2002 under the leadership of Antonina POLTAWEIC; and the **Republican Party** (*Respublikonų Partija*—RP), led by Kazimieras PETRAITIS. In late 2000 an additional small party, the **Lithuanian Life's Logic Party** (*Lietuvos Gyvenimo Logikos Partija*—LGLP), reportedly saw its ranks swelled by supporters of neofascist leader Mindaugas Murza, whose repeated efforts to register his **Lithuanian National Socialist Party** (*Lietuvių Nacionalsocialinės Partija*—LNP) had been denied on the grounds that it contributed to ethnic hostility. Murza left the LGLP in August 2001 and became chair of the LNDP in May 2002.

Legislature

The former Supreme Council (*Aukščiausioji Taryba*) was redesignated as the **Parliament** (*Seimas*) on July 7, 1992, with a complement of 141 members, of whom 71 are currently elected from single-member constituencies and 70 are elected from party lists by proportional representation subject to a 5 percent threshold. Under changes enacted in June 1996, voters became entitled, with effect from the fall 1996 election, to record a preference for individual candidates on the party lists.

The election of October 10 and 24, 2004, produced the following totals: Labor Party, 39 seats; the coalition of the Lithuanian Social Democratic Party (LSDP) and the New Union (Social Liberals) (NS[SL]), 31 (LSDP, 20; NS[SL], 11); the Homeland Union, 25; the Liberal and Center Union, 18; For Order and Justice, 10; the Union of the Peasants and New Democracy Parties, 10; Electoral Action of Lithuanian Poles, 2; independents, 6.

Speaker: Viktoras MUNTIANAS.

Communications

During the Soviet period all media outlets were required to endorse Communist ideology. Censorship was abolished in 1989.

Press

The following are dailies published at Vilnius in Lithuanian unless otherwise noted: *Lietuvos Rytas* (Lithuania's Morning, 50,000), weekly edition in Russian; *Respublika* (Republic, 50,000); *Kauno Diena* (Kaunas's Day, 50,000); *Kurier Wilenski* (Vilnius Courier, 32,000), in Polish; *Lietuvos Aidas* (Echo of Lithuania); *Echo Litvy* (Echo of Lithuania), in Russian.

News Agency

The Lithuanian Telegraph Agency (ELTA) is state-owned, servicing the local press in Lithuanian and Russian. The only English-language facility is the Baltic News Service (BNS), which operates in all three Baltic countries.

Broadcasting and Computing

Lithuanian Television and Radio Broadcasting (*Lietuvos Radijas ir Televizija*) is the supervising agency. Lithuanian Radio broadcasts in Lithuanian, Russian, Polish, Yiddish, Belarusan, and Ukrainian, while Lithuanian Television offers programs in Lithuanian, Russian, Polish, Belarusan, and Ukrainian. There are also some three dozen independent radio and TV outlets. There were approximately 1.4 million television receivers and 380,000 personal computers serving 696,000 Internet users in 2003.

Intergovernmental Representation

Ambassador to the U.S.
Vygaudus UŠACKAS

U.S. Ambassador to Lithuania
Stephen D. MULL

Permanent Representative to the UN
Dalius ČEKUOLIS

IGO Memberships (Non-UN)
BIS, CBSS, CEUR, EBRD, EIB, EU, Interpol, IOM, NATO, NIB, OSCE, PCA, WCO, WTO

LUXEMBOURG

GRAND DUCHY OF LUXEMBOURG

Grousherzogdem Lëtzebuerg (Letzeburgish)
Grand-Duché de Luxembourg (French)
Grossherzogtum Luxemburg (German)

The Country

Located southeast of Belgium between France and Germany, the small, landlocked Grand Duchy of Luxembourg is a predominantly Roman Catholic country whose native inhabitants exhibit an ethnic and cultural blend of French and German elements. Linguistically, both French and German are widely spoken; the local language, Letzeburgish, is a West Frankish dialect. About one-third of the population now consists of immigrants, while a tight labor market has benefited *fortaliers*, cross-border workers from neighboring countries.

Luxembourg is highly industrialized. Iron and steel products have long been mainstays of the economy and still account for nearly one-third of total exports. A drastic downturn in the industry in the mid-1970s led not only to a major, successful restructuring and modernization plan, but also to economic diversification, focusing on the production of such goods as rubber, synthetic fibers, plastics, chemicals, and small metal products. Luxembourg also became an international financial center, the number of banks rising from 13 in 1955 to more than 210 in 2000. Stock transactions, insurance, and reinsurance have also become of major importance, and Luxembourg currently accommodates more than 12,000 holding companies. Agriculture, which occupies only 2 percent of the labor force, consists primarily of small farms devoted to livestock raising, although viticulture is also of some prominence. Trade is largely oriented toward Lux-embourg's neighbors and fellow participants in the Benelux Economic Union and the European Union (EU, formerly the European Community—EC).

After three decades of burgeoning prosperity, Luxembourg entered an economic deceleration in the early 1990s as recession struck Belgium, France, and Germany, its three most important trading partners. Nevertheless, the principality maintained a positive GDP growth rate and in 1994 resumed solid expansion that soared to 7.5 percent in 2000. In that year a steadily declining unemployment rate fell to 2.6 percent, although consumer price inflation, having registered only 1.0 percent

in the two preceding years, jumped to 3.2 percent. Having entered the EU's Economic and Monetary Union (EMU) in 1999, which is expected to reduce some of the grand duchy's competitive advantages, Luxembourg is actively pursuing financial-sector diversification, particularly in Internet-related services. At present, Luxembourg enjoys the world's highest per capita GNP, which was $42,060 in 2000.

GDP growth averaged only 2.9 percent in 2003 but rebounded in 2004 to 4.5 percent, apparently under the influence of recent reforms initiated by the government (see Current issues, below). Luxembourg also continued to enjoy one of the lowest budget deficits in the EU (1 percent of GDP) as well as one of the lowest unemployment rates (3.9 percent in 2004). In fact, employment opportunities are so good that approximately one-quarter of the workforce is made up of foreign workers. The downside is that the International Monetary Fund (IMF) projects that unemployment will rise to approximately 6 percent by the end of 2006.

Government and Politics

Political Background

For centuries Luxembourg was dominated and occupied by foreign powers, until the Congress of Vienna in 1815 declared it a grand duchy subject to the king of the Netherlands. On Belgium's secession from the Netherlands in 1830, the greater part of Luxembourg went with it (today constituting the Belgian province of the same name); the remainder was recognized as an autonomous neutral state in 1867 and came under the present ruling house of Nassau-Weilbourg in 1890, when the link with the Netherlands was formally severed. An economic union with Belgium was established in 1922, but Luxembourg retains its independent political institutions under a constitution dating from 1868.

Since World War II political power has been exercised by a series of coalition governments in which the Christian Social People's Party (*Chrëschtlech Sozial Vollekspartei*—CSV) has traditionally been the dominant element. For 15 years

beginning in 1959, the government was led by Pierre WERNER, who formed coalitions with both the Socialist Workers' Party of Luxembourg (*Lëtzebuergesch Sozialistesch Arbechterpartei*— LSAP) and the Democratic Party (*Demokratesch Partei*—DP). A month after the election of May 1974, however, the latter two formed a new government under DP leader Gaston THORN. Prior to the election of June 1979 the governing parties agreed to renew their coalition if they succeeded in gaining a parliamentary majority, but a somewhat unexpected shortfall of one seat necessitated a fairly lengthy period of intraparty negotiation that resulted in the formation of a CSV-DP government and the return of Pierre Werner as prime minister.

In the wake of the June 1984 balloting, at which the CSV remained the largest party but the LSAP registered the greatest gain, a new round of negotiations led to a revived center-left CSV-LSAP coalition under former finance minister Jacques SANTER. In the 1989 poll, the three leading parties lost three seats each, with Santer forming a new bipartisan government after the CSV had retained its plurality in a Chamber reduced from 64 to 60 deputies because of a reduction in the size of the electorate.

As in 1989, Luxembourg's 1994 national and European Parliament elections were held on the same day (June 12) to signify the principality's deep commitment to the cause of European unity. Economic policy questions dominated the campaigning for both elections, which produced only marginal shifts in the party balance. Both ruling coalition partners lost 1 seat, while the various opposition parties increased their aggregate representation from 19 to 22 seats.

In July 1994 Prime Minister Santer was unexpectedly named the compromise choice to take over the European Commission presidency in January 1995. His successor in the principality's premiership was another incumbent CSV finance minister, Jean-Claude JUNCKER, who reshuffled the cabinet on January 20, 1995, while reaffirming established policies.

Political Status: Constitutional monarchy, fully independent since 1867; in economic union with Belgium since 1922.

Area: 998 sq. mi. (2,586 sq. km.).

Population: 439,539 (2001C); 456,000 (2005E).

Major Urban Centers (2005E): LUXEMBOURG-VILLE (Lützelburg, 77,000), Esch-sur-Alzette (28,000).

Official Language: Letzeburgish. As a general rule, French is used for administrative purposes, and German for commerce.

Monetary Unit: Euro (market rate July 1, 2006: 1 euro = $1.28US).

Sovereign: Grand Duke HENRI; ascended to the throne October 7, 2000, on the abdication of his father, Grand Duke JEAN.

Heir Apparent: Prince GUILLAUME, son of the grand duke; proclaimed by the grand duke on December 18, 2000.

President of the Government (Prime Minister): Jean-Claude JUNCKER (Christian Social People's Party); sworn in as the head of a Christian Social–Socialist Workers' coalition by the grand duke on January 20, 1995, succeeding Jacques SANTER (Christian Social People's Party), on the latter's appointment as president of the European Commission; sworn in again on August 7, 1999, following election of June 13 and negotiation of a coalition with the Democratic Party; sworn in for a third term on August 2, 2004, after legislative elections on June 13 and the approval of a coalition government with the Socialist Workers' Party of Luxembourg.

In the election of June 13, 1999, both governing parties suffered losses—four seats in the case of the LSAP, enabling the DP to negotiate an agreement with the CSV that brought it into the government for the first time in 15 years. The new Juncker cabinet, sworn in on August 7, included the DP's president, Lydie POLFER, as vice prime minister as well as minister of foreign affairs and external commerce.

On October 7, 2000, Grand Duke JEAN, 79, who had reigned since his mother's abdication in 1964, stepped aside in favor of his son, Grand Duke HENRI. In preparation for his accession, Henri had been designated as his father's "lieutenant-representative" on March 4, 1998. On December 18, 2000, he followed tradition and named his eldest son, Prince GUILLAUME, as heir apparent.

In the June 13, 2004, legislative elections, the CSV increased its number of seats in the Chamber to 24. The LSAP came in second in the election with 14 seats, while the DP lost 5 seats to decline to 10. Juncker announced a new coalition government with the LSAP on July 31, 2004.

Prime Minister Juncker shuffled his cabinet in 2005, reportedly in an effort to deal more effectively with unemployment and budget concerns. The post of defense minister—previously held by Luc FRIEDEN, who had responsibility for the defense as well as for the treasury and budget—was given to Jean-Louis SCHILTZ, who retains his responsibility for communications. At the same time, the culture portfolio was shifted from François BILTGEN to Secretary of State Octavie MODERT.

Constitution and Government

Luxembourg's 1868 constitution has been repeatedly revised to incorporate democratic reforms, to eliminate the former status of "perpetual neutrality," and to permit devolution of sovereignty to international institutions. Executive authority is exercised on behalf of the grand duke by the prime minister and the cabinet, who are appointed by the sovereign but are responsible to the legislature. Legislative authority rests primarily with the elected Chamber of Deputies, but there is also a nonelective Council of State, whose decisions can be reversed by the Chamber. Deputies are elected on a proportional basis from four electoral constituencies (north, center, south, and east). The judicial system is headed by the Superior Court of Justice and includes a Court of Assizes for serious criminal offenses, two district courts, and three justices of the peace. There are also administrative and special social courts and, since 1996, a Constitutional Court. Judges are appointed for life by the grand duke. The country is divided into 3 districts, 12 cantons, and 118 communes. The districts function as links between the central and local governments and are headed by commissioners appointed by the central government.

Foreign Relations

Luxembourg's former neutral status was abandoned after the German occupation of World War II. The country was a founding member of the United Nations (UN) and a leader in the postwar consolidation of the West through its membership in Benelux, the North Atlantic Treaty Organization (NATO), the EC/EU, and other multilateral organizations. Relations with Belgium have long been close.

On July 2, 1992, the Chamber of Deputies overwhelmingly approved the EU's Maastricht Treaty, which provided for unification in economic, political, and defense areas by 1999. In so doing, however, it specified that noncitizens could vote only if they have been in residence for at least ten years and can speak the national language. The stipulation was regarded as crucial in the case of Luxembourg, a third of whose current inhabitants are nonnationals. On May 9, 1994, Luxembourg opted to participate in the "Eurocorps" joint military force, along with Belgium, France, Germany, and Spain.

Luxembourg has continued to support both NATO and the development of an autonomous European security and defense identity. The Juncker government approved NATO expansion at the 2002 Prague Summit. Meanwhile, Luxembourg supported the creation of a European Rapid Reaction Force (ERRF) designed to give the EU the ability to quickly respond to humanitarian and other security crises. Luxembourg contributed 100 troops to the new force. It has also supported increased European cooperation on defense-industrial issues, including the design and production of major arms systems such as aircraft. Such cooperation was seen as a means to protect steel and other manufacturing industries in Luxembourg.

During negotiations of the EU's Treaty of Nice in 2000, Luxembourg joined other small EU states in trying to retain their long-standing level of influence and power in view of planned EU expansion. That effort was generally viewed as successful.

Current Issues

One factor in the weakened support given to both governing parties at the June 1999 election may have been a controversial public sector pension reform plan, which for the first time required employee contributions and which, over the course of four decades, will gradually reduce public sector pensions. Elements within the LSAP itself expressed concern that its long partnership with the CSV had diminished its independence on policy matters, while the decision of party leader and Vice Prime Minister Jacques POOS to retire apparently left the party, in the public's eye, without a strong figure at the helm. As a result, the DP, led by the widely popular mayor of Luxembourg-Ville, Lydie POLFER, gained three seats and replaced the LSAP in Prime Minister Juncker's government. A two-seat gain was also registered by the Action Committee for Democracy and Pension Justice (*Aktiounskomitee fir Demokratie a Rentengerechtegkeet*—ADR), which for more than a decade has lobbied for private sector parity with public pensions.

In addition to pension reform (a growing concern throughout the EU), Luxembourg faced challenges in the early 2000s regarding how its financial sector operated. Within the EU, the United Kingdom and France were particularly vocal in fighting for full information exchange between national tax authorities as the best means of stopping tax evasion on savings income, whereas Luxembourg argued that maintaining its banking secrecy is a necessity if it is to avoid flight of investment accounts to offshore facilities. At the same time, Luxembourg, as well as a number of other countries and offshore dependencies, were pressured by the United States into relaxing bank secrecy rules and cooperating in tax fraud investigations. In January 2001 Luxembourgian banks began withholding taxes on investments from U.S. sources. Nevertheless, in April 2002 Luxembourg remained one of only seven countries listed by the Organization for Economic Cooperation and Development (OECD) as having harmful tax policies.

The pension crisis continued to dominate domestic affairs in 2002, the government reducing some individual and corporate taxes in an effort to encourage additional private pension contributions. The Juncker administration also announced policies designed to attract "high-technology" jobs and otherwise diversify the economy beyond the manufacturing and financial sectors.

In 2003 Luxembourg reached a compromise agreement with the EU under which a 15 percent withholding tax was to be enforced beginning in 2004. (The rate was scheduled to increase gradually to 35 percent by 2010.) In exchange, Luxembourg was permitted to maintain most of its cherished banking secrecy guidelines.

Luxembourg strongly opposed the U.S./UK-led invasion of Iraq in 2003 and subsequently reaffirmed its support for development of an "autonomous" EU defense capability that would not be inordinately subjected to U.S. pressure. Prime Minister Juncker, who assumed the six-month presidency of the EU's European Council in January 2005, also put his political career on the line by campaigning strongly for Luxembourg to approve the proposed new EU constitution. Juncker, reportedly widely respected in EU circles, announced he would resign as prime minister if voters rejected the EU initiative. Consequently, a national referendum on the question on July 10 received a 56.5 percent "yes" vote, making Luxembourg one of the few countries to date in which a direct popular vote approved the suddenly controversial EU initiative.

In early 2006 the Juncker government was preoccupied with the attempted hostile takeover of Arcelor S.A., a Luxembourg-based steel manufacturer, by the Indian-owned Mittal Steel. The proposed takeover has raised concerns over foreign ownership of businesses that are seen as critical to the region. The Indian government has accused European governments opposed to the sale—including Luxembourg, Spain, and France—

of discrimination and has warned that blocking the sale could harm global trade talks. Arcelor is the largest employer in Luxembourg, employing 6,000 workers, and the Luxembourg government is the company's largest shareholder. Despite Juncker's opposition to the takeover, Parliament on March 17 rejected a change in the country's corporate takeover laws that would have made it more difficult for the takeover to succeed.

Political Parties

With a multiparty system based on proportional representation, for decades Luxembourg has been ruled by coalition governments headed by the Christian Social Party or the Democratic Party allied with each other or with the Socialist Workers' Party.

Government Parties

Christian Social People's Party (*Chrëeschtlech Sozial Volekspartei*—CSV/*Parti Chrétien Social*—PCS). Formed in 1914, Luxembourg's strongest single party draws its main support from farmers, Catholic laborers, and moderate conservatives. Often identified as a Christian Democratic grouping, the CSV endorses a centrist position that includes support for the monarchy, progressive labor legislation, assistance to farmers and small businessmen, church-state cooperation, and an internationalist foreign policy. The dominant partner in most postwar coalitions, the CSV's Chamber representation slipped from 22 to 21 seats in 1994 and then to 19 in June 1999. It nevertheless remained the plurality party, and Prime Minister Jean-Claude Juncker continued in office after forging a coalition with the second-ranked Democrats.

In elections on June 13, 2004, the CSV won 36.1 percent of the vote and 24 seats. Juncker formed a new coalition government with the LSAP on July 31, 2004.

Leaders: Jean-Claude JUNCKER (Prime Minister), François BILTGEN (President), Lucien CLEMENT (Vice President), Marie-Josée JACOBS (Vice President), Jean-Louis SCHILTZ (Secretary General).

Socialist Workers' Party of Luxembourg
(*Lëtzebuergesch Sozialistesch Arbechterpartei—*
LSAP/*Parti Ouvrier Socialiste Luxembourgeois—*
POSL). Founded in 1902, the LSAP draws its
major support from urban lower- and lower-middle-
class voters, particularly those affiliated with trade
unions. It advocates extension of the present system of social legislation and social insurance, and
supports European integration, NATO, and the UN.
In 1971 a conservative wing split off to form the
Social Democratic Party, which was dissolved in
1983. In opposition prior to the June 1984 election,
the LSAP subsequently joined the Santer government, winning 18 Chamber seats in 1989 and 17
in 1994. Having fallen to third place, with 13 seats
in 1999, it returned to opposition as Prime Minister Juncker established a center-right government
with the DP. Following the June 13, 2004, elections
(in which it won 23.4 percent of the vote and 14
seats), the LSAP was invited to form a coalition
government with the CSV.

Leaders: Alex BODRY (President), Yves
CRUCHTEN (Vice President), Liane KADUSCH-
ROTH (Vice President), Romain SCHNEIDER
(Secretary General).

Opposition Parties

Democratic Party (*Demokratesch Partei—*
DP/*Parti Démocratique—*PD).The DP includes
both conservatives and moderates and draws support from professional, business, white-collar, and
artisan groups. Also referred to as the "Liberals,"
the party is committed to free enterprise, although
it favors certain forms of progressive social legislation. It is mildly anticlerical and strongly pro-
NATO. It participated in the Werner government
prior to the 1984 election, after which it went into
opposition. It won 11 Chamber seats in 1989 and
12 in 1994. Having moved ahead of the Socialist
Workers' Party in the June 1999 election, winning
15 seats, the DP negotiated a coalition agreement
with the CSV. In the June 13, 2004, elections the
DP received 16.1 percent of the vote and 10 seats.

Leaders: Claude MEISCH (President), Anne
BRASSEUR (First Vice President), Agny DURDU
(Secretary General).

**Action Committee for Democracy and Pen-
sion Justice** (*Aktiounskomitee fir Demokratie
a Rentengerechtegkeet—*ADR/*Comité d'Action
pour la Démocratie et la Justice Sociale—*CADJS).
Organized in 1987 as the Five-Sixths Action Committee (*Aktiounskomitee "5/6-Pensioun fir Jidfer-
een"*), the ADR adopted its present name at a
national congress in November 1992. Initially
championing an across-the-board introduction in
the private sector of pensions worth five-sixths of
final salary (the level then operative for public employees), the party won four Chamber seats in 1989,
five in 1994, seven in 1999, and five in 2004.

Leaders: Roby MEHLEN (President), Gast
GIBERYEN (Parliamentary Group President),
Jean-Pierre KOEPP (Vice President), Fernand
GREISEN (Secretary General).

The Greens (*Déi Gréng/Les Verts*). Organized
at a June 1983 congress as the Green Alternative (*Gréng Alternativ Partei/Parti Vert-Alternatif*),
The Greens won two legislative seats in 1984 but
in 1986 suffered a major split. The party again
won two seats in 1989 and then added three more
in 1994 before reuniting with the Green Ecological Initiative List (*Gréng Lëscht Ekologesch
Initiativ—*GLEI) in 1995. Its current program advocates environmental protection, democracy, social justice, human rights, and similar causes. In the
June 1999 election it won five seats in the Chamber of Deputies. In the June 13, 2004, elections
The Greens won 11.6 percent of the vote and seven
seats in the Chamber.

Leaders: François BAUSCH (Parliamentary
Group President), Abbes JACOBY (Secretary of
the Parliamentary Group).

Other Parties

The Left (*Déi Lénk/La Gauche*). The constituent congress of The Left took place on January
30, 1999, culminating efforts to overcome previous
cleavages and organize political forces to the left
of the social democratic DP and The Greens. Participants included the KPL (below), DP dissidents,
trade unionists, and members of other small left-
wing parties. In the legislative election of June 1999
the new grouping won one seat in the Chamber of

Cabinet

As of April 21, 2006

Prime Minister	Jean-Claude Juncker (CSV)
Vice Prime Minister	Jean Asselborn (LSAP)

Ministers

Agriculture, Viticulture, and Rural Development	Fernand Boden (CSV)
Civil Service and Administrative Reform	Claude Wiseler (CSV)
Cooperation and Humanitarian Affairs	Jean-Louis Schiltz (CSV)
Higher Education and Research	François Biltgen (CSV)
Defense	Jean-Louis Schiltz (CSV)
Economy and Foreign Trade	Jeannot Krecké (LSAP)
Education and Vocational Training	Mady Delvaux-Stehres (LSAP) [f]
Environment	Lucien Lux (LSAP)
Equality of Opportunity	Marie-Josée Jacobs (CSV) [f]
Family and Integration	Marie-Josée Jacobs (CSV) [f]
Finance	Jean-Claude Juncker (CSV)
Foreign Affairs and Immigration	Jean Asselborn (LSAP)
Health and Social Security	Mars Di Bartolomeo (LSAP)
Interior and Territorial Planning	Jean-Marie Halsdorf (CSV)
Justice	Luc Frieden (CSV)
Labor and Employment	François Biltgen (CSV)
Middle Classes, Tourism, and Housing	Fernand Boden (CSV)
National Education and Professional Training	Mady Delvaux-Stehres (LSAP) [f]
Public Works	Claude Wiseler (CSV)
Religious Affairs	François Biltgen (CSV)
Sports	Jeannot Krecké (LSAP)
Transport	Lucien Lux (LSAP)
Treasury and Budget	Luc Frieden (CSV)

Ministers Delegate

Communications	Jean-Louis Schiltz (CSV)
Foreign Affairs and Immigration	Nicolas Schmit (LSAP)

Secretary of State

Agriculture, Viticulture, and Rural Development	Octavie Modert (CSV) [f]
Culture, Higher Education, and Research	Octavie Modert (CSV) [f]
Relations with Parliament	Octavie Modert (CSV) [f]

[f] = female

Deputies. In local balloting in Esch-sur-Alzette in April 2000 The Left finished third, with 12.8 percent of the vote, enabling it to join a majority coalition with the DP and The Greens. The Left's André HOFFMAN resigned his seat in the Chamber of Deputies to join Esch-sur-Alzette's council of aldermen, with the KPL's Aloyse BISDORFF thereupon succeeding him in the national legislature. Bisdorff was subsequently succeeded by Serge UR-BANY. The Left received 1.9 percent of the vote in the June 2004 elections.

The Left has no formal leadership positions; the organization's first ordinary congress in May 2000 elected a 45-member *Nationale Koordination/Coordination Nationale*, which subsequently selected an 11-member *Koordinationsbüro/Bureau de Coordination*.

Communist Party of Luxembourg (*Kommunistesch Partei vu Lëtzebuerg—KPL*/*Parti Communiste Luxembourgeois—PCL*). Established in 1921, the historically pro-Soviet KPL draws its main support from urban and industrial workers and some intellectuals. It advocates full nationalization of the economy and was the only Western European Communist party to approve the Soviet invasion of Czechoslovakia in 1968. The KPL suffered a loss of three of its five parliamentary seats in the 1979 election, retaining the two that remained in 1984. Its longtime leader, René URBANY, died in October 1990, and the party lost its sole remaining Chamber seat in 1994. Many Communist Party officials joined The Left party after the 1994 elections, and the KPL decided not to contest the elections. The KPL received only 0.9 percent of the vote in the 2004 legislative poll.

Leaders: Aloyse BISDORFF, Ali RUCKERT (President).

Green and Liberal Alliance (*Gréng a Liberal Allianz—GaL*). Led by former parliamentary deputy and GLEI member Jup Weber, the new GaL contested the 1999 legislative and European Parliament elections on a more radical eco-leftist platform than that offered by The Greens. The party failed to make an impact, however, and Weber also lost his seat in the European Parliament.

Leader: Jup WEBER.

Two additional parties offered candidate lists in the 1999 parliamentary election: the **Taxpayers' List** (*Lëscht vum Steierzueler*), which competed in the southern constituency; and the **Third Age Party** (*Partei vum 3. Alter*), a pensioners' group that ran in the central constituency. Other recently active small groups include the **Revolutionary Socialist Party** (*Parti Socialiste Révolutionnaire—PSR*) and the **New Left** (*Neue Linke/Nouvelle Gauche—MNG*), both of which participated in formation of *Déi Lénk*. The **Free Party of Luxembourg** (*Fräi Partei Lëtzebuerg—FPL*) received 0.12 percent of the vote in the June 2004 elections.

Legislature

Legislative responsibility is centered in the elected Chamber of Deputies, but the appointive Council of State retains some vestigial legislative functions.

Council of State (*Der Staatsrat/Conseil d'Etat*). The council consists of 21 members appointed for life; 7 are appointed directly by the grand duke, while the others are appointed by him on proposal of the council itself or of the Chamber of Deputies.

President: Marcel SAUBER.

Chamber of Deputies (*Chamber vum Deputéirten/Châmbre des Députés*). The Chamber currently consists of 60 deputies elected for five-year terms (subject to dissolution) by direct universal suffrage on the basis of proportional representation.

In the June 13, 2004, elections the Christian Social People's Party won 24 seats; the Socialist Workers' Party of Luxembourg, 14; the Democratic Party, 10; the Greens, 7; and the Action Committee for Democracy and Pension Justice, 5.

President: Lucien WEILER.

Communications

All news media are privately owned and are free of censorship.

Press

The following newspapers are published daily at the capital, unless otherwise noted: *Luxemburger Wort/La Voix du Luxembourg* (85,000), in German and French, Catholic, CSV organ; *Tageblatt/Zeitung fir Lëtzebuerg* (Esch-sur-Alzette, 30,000), in German and French, LSAP affiliated; *Le Républicain Lorrain* (15,000), in French; *Lëtzebuerger Journal* (10,000), in German, Democratic organ; *Zeitung vum Lëtzeburger Vollek*, KPL organ, in German.

News Agencies

There is no domestic facility; a number of foreign bureaus, including AP, UPI, and *Agence France-Presse*, maintain offices in Luxembourg-Ville.

Broadcasting and Computing

Broadcasting is dominated by CLT-UFA, a privately owned international company formed in 1997, which absorbed the *Compagnie Luxembourgeoise de Télédiffusion*. In addition, there are a number of cultural and satellite outlets. There were approximately 374,000 television receivers and 300,000 personal computers serving 200,000 Internet users in 2003.

Intergovernmental Representation

Ambassador to the U.S.
Joseph WEYLAND

U.S. Ambassador to Luxembourg
Ann Louise WAGNER

Permanent Representative to the UN
Jean-Marc HOSCHEIT

IGO Memberships (Non-UN)
ADB, BLX, CEUR, EBRD, EIB, EU, Eurocontrol, IEA, Interpol, IOM, NATO, OECD, OIF, OSCE, PCA, WCO, WEU, WTO

MACEDONIA

REPUBLIC OF MACEDONIA

Republika Makedonija

Note: The country was admitted to the United Nations in April 1993 as "The former Yugoslav Republic of Macedonia," although international usage of this title (particularly in regard to capitalization) has varied, with the abbreviation FYROM sometimes being invoked. As of 2006, no resolution had been achieved in the dispute with Greece over use of "Macedonia" in the country's official name.

Note: Preliminary results from legislative balloting on July 5, 2006 (with reruns on July 19 in several constituencies) for the Macedonian Assembly (*Sobranje*) indicated the following distribution of seats: the Internal Macedonian Revolutionary Organization–Democratic Party for Macedonian National Unity (VMRO-DPMNE) and coalition allies, 45; the Coalition for Macedonia Together, 32; the Democratic Union for Integration, 18; the Democratic Party of Albanians (DPA/PDSh), 11; the New Social Democratic Party (NSDP), 7; the Internal Macedonian Revolutionary Organization–People's Party, 6; the Democratic Renewal of Macedonia, 1; and the Party for European Future, 1. The leader of the VMRO-DPMNE, Nikola Gruevski, subsequently announced formation of a new government comprising members of the VMRO-DPMNE, DPA/PDSh, NSDP, the Liberal Party of Macedonia, and the Socialist Party of Macedonia. The cabinet was inaugurated on August 26 following approval by the *Sobranje* on the same day.

The Country

The former Yugoslavian component of historical Macedonia is a landlocked country bordered on the east by Bulgaria, on the north by Serbia and Montenegro, on the west by Albania, and on the south by Greece. According to the 2002 census, 64.2 percent of the population is ethnic Macedonian and 25.2 percent ethnic Albanian, with Roma, Serbs, Turks, Vlachs, and others forming smaller groups. Most of the Macedonian majority supports the Macedonian Orthodox (Christian) Church; the Albanians are predominantly Muslim. Women constitute 41 percent of the labor force, compared to 36 percent for men, with the balance of adults engaged in homemaking, unpaid care giving, or the informal economy.

Agriculture has accounted for about 15 percent of GDP and roughly 20 percent of employment in recent years, the principal crops being fruits, vegetables, grains, and tobacco. The industrial sector,

Political Status: Former constituent republic of the Socialist Federal Republic of Yugoslavia; independence proclaimed under constitution of November 17, 1991, on the basis of a referendum conducted September 8.

Area: 9,928 sq. mi. (25,713 sq. km.).

Population: 2,022,547 (2002C); 2,053,000 (2005E). The 2002 census showed that ethnic Macedonians accounted for 64.2 percent and ethnic Albanians for 25.2 percent of the population.

Major Urban Center (2005E): SKOPJE (476,000).

Official Language: Macedonian, in the Cyrillic alphabet, is an official language for the entire country and is the official language for international relations. Albanian, in its own alphabet, is also an official language under recent constitutional revision that authorized any language spoken by at least 20 percent of the population to be used as an official language. Moreover, the languages and alphabets used by at least 20 percent of the citizens in local governmental areas can also be used as official languages. (Local administrations are also permitted to accord official language status to languages spoken by less than 20 percent of their constituents.)

Monetary Unit: New Macedonian Denar (market rate July 1, 2006: 48.83 denars = $1US).

President: Branko CRVENKOVSKI (Social Democratic Union of Macedonia); elected in second-round balloting on April 28, 2004, and sworn in for a five-year term on May 12, succeeding Boris TRAJKOVSKI (Internal Macedonian Revolutionary Organization–Democratic Party for Macedonian National Unity), who was killed in a plane crash on February 26. (Ljubco JORDANOVSKI [Social Democratic Union of Macedonia], the speaker of the assembly, had served as acting president following Trajkovski's death until Crvenkovski's inauguration.)

Chair of the Council of Ministers (Prime Minister): (*See headnote.*) Vlado BUCKOVSKI (Social Democratic Union of Macedonia); approved by a parliamentary vote of confidence on December 17, 2004, succeeding Hari KOSTOV (Social Democratic Union of Macedonia), who had resigned on November 15, 2004.

---

contributing about 32 percent of GDP and 35 percent of employment, principally exports iron and steel, footwear and clothing, nonferrous metals, tobacco products, and beverages (especially wine). Extractable resources include lignite, copper, lead, and zinc. The European Union (EU), led by Germany and Greece, and present-day Serbia and Montenegro are Macedonia's leading trading partners, while the United States is another significant export market.

The poorest of the former Yugoslav republics, Macedonia was economically distressed in the postindependence period by regional conflict and the disruption of established trading links with neighboring countries. Industrial and agricultural production declined sharply, yielding GDP contraction of about one-third in 1990–1993, during which inflation averaged 600 percent per year and unemployment rose to 40 percent. Beginning in 1994 the government initiated a structural reform program suggested by the International Monetary Fund (IMF) and World Bank; initiatives included liberalization of trade regulations, modernization of customs procedures, privatization of state-run enterprises, and reform of the financial sector. In 1998 Macedonia applied for membership in the World Trade Organization (WTO) and the Central European Free Trade Association (CEFTA) and also signaled strong interest in eventual membership in the EU. Severe difficulties remained, however, including a dearth of foreign investment, continued high unemployment (35 percent), and increasing poverty (nearly one-quarter of the population lived below the poverty line). The ethnic Albanian minority appeared hardest hit by the latter two problems, generating additional resentment in a segment of the population already embittered over perceived "second class" treatment by a national government dominated by the Christian majority. Conditions were further complicated by the conflict in Kosovo and the North American Treaty Organization (NATO) campaign against

Yugoslavia in the first half of 1999, which, among other things, triggered a massive influx of ethnic Albanians from Kosovo into Macedonia, blocked the export of Macedonian agricultural products, and raised concern in the minds of potential foreign investors.

GDP plummeted by 4 percent in 2001 and by 2 percent in 2002 before growth of 3.2 percent was achieved in 2003 and 2.5 percent in 2004. The IMF approved a new three-year aid package in September 2005, while the EU formally declared Macedonia as a candidate for EU membership in December (see Current issues, below).

Government and Politics

Political Background

The land from which Alexander the Great launched his empire in the fifth century B.C., but a region of contention thereafter, greater Macedonia was ruled by the Ottoman Turks for five centuries prior to the Second Balkan War and the Treaty of Bucharest of 1913. The 1913 settlement divided most of the territory between Greece and Serbia, the respective portions being known as Aegean (or Greek) Macedonia and Vardar Macedonia (the latter after the region's principal river), while a much smaller portion (Pirin Macedonia) was awarded to Bulgaria. After World War I Vardar Macedonia (South Serbia) became part of the Kingdom of the Serbs, Croats, and Slovenes, which was renamed Yugoslavia in October 1929. After World War II it was accorded the status of a constituent republic of the Communist-ruled federal Yugoslavia.

Following Belgrade's endorsement of a multiparty system in early 1990, Vladimir MITKOV of the newly styled League of Communists of Macedonia–Party of Democratic Change (*Sojus na Komunistite na Makedonija–Partija za Demokratska Preobrazba*—SKM-PDP) was named president of the republican State Presidency, pending a general election. The balloting for a 120-member assembly that was eventually conducted in three stages (on November 11 and 25, and December 9) was marked by ethnic ten-

sion between the Macedonian and Albanian communities and yielded an inconclusive outcome: the opposition Internal Macedonian Revolutionary Organization–Democratic Party for Macedonian National Unity (*Vnatrešna Makedonska Revolucionerna Organizacija–Demokratska Partija za Makedonsko Nacionalno Edinstvo*—VMRO-DPMNE) won a plurality of 37 seats, compared with 31 for the second-place SKM-PDP, and a total of 25 for two Albanian groups. As a result of the stand-off, Kiro GLIGOROV of the SKM-PDP (subsequently the Social Democratic Union of Macedonia [*Socijaldemokratski Sojuz na Makedonija*—SDSM]) was named to succeed Mitkov as president.

On January 25, 1991, the assembly unanimously adopted a declaration of sovereignty that asserted a right of self-determination, including secession from Yugoslavia. On September 8, 75 percent of the republic's registered voters (with most Albanians abstaining) participated in a referendum that endorsed independence by an overwhelming margin. On November 17 the assembly approved a new constitution, and on December 24 Macedonia joined Bosnia and Herzegovina, Croatia, and Slovenia in seeking recognition from the European Community (EC, subsequently the EU). The Albanians reacted on January 11–12, 1992, with a 99.9 percent vote in favor of territorial and political autonomy for their community. While Belgrade tacitly recognized Macedonian autonomy by handing over border posts to Macedonian army units on March 15 and withdrawing its own military forces from the republic 11 days later, most foreign governments withheld recognition because of Greek protests over the country's name (see Foreign relations, below).

A mid-1992 cabinet crisis resulted in the formation of a new coalition headed by Branko CRVENKOVSKI of the SDSM and including the Party for Democratic Prosperity (*Partija za Demokratski Prosperitet*—PDP/*Partisë për Prosperitet Demokratik*—PPD—PDP/PPD), a primarily ethnic Albanian party. The new government introduced short-term emergency economic measures, including devaluations of the denar in

October and December. Meanwhile, in light of an influx of some 60,000 refugees from the war in Bosnia and Herzegovina, the assembly in October approved a 15-year residency as a requirement for Macedonian citizenship.

The prime importance attached by the government to securing full international recognition helped to ensure the survival of the disparate ruling coalition, which had been mandated to cement national unity. Nevertheless, underlying tensions between Macedonians and the ethnic Albanian community surfaced in 1993 amid accusations of Albanian separatism, and in early 1994 the PDP/PPD split into moderate and nationalist factions, the former remaining in the government and the latter joining the opposition.

In presidential balloting on October 16, 1994, Gligorov secured easy reelection as the candidate of an SDSM-led alliance, winning 78.4 percent of the valid votes cast (52.4 percent of the total electorate), against 21.6 percent for the nominee of the VMRO-DPMNE, Ljubčo GEORGIEVSKI. In legislative balloting on October 16 and 30 (with reruns in some constituencies on November 13), the SDSM-led alliance won 95 of the 120 seats, while opting to maintain the coalition with the PDP/PPD under the continued premiership of Crvenkovski. The opposition parties claimed that both the presidential and legislative elections had been riddled with fraud, a view that received some support from international observers.

On October 3, 1995, President Gligorov suffered serious injuries in a bomb attack on his car in Skopje that resulted in two fatalities. Accepting responsibility for failure to protect the president, Dr. Ljubomir FRĚKOVSKI resigned as interior minister, attributing the assassination attempt to an unnamed "multinational financial and economic corporation in a neighboring state," assisted by Macedonian nationals. In accordance with the constitution, the speaker of the assembly, Stojan ANDOV, leader of the Liberal Party of Macedonia (*Liberalna Partija na Makedonija*—LPM; after 1997, known as the LDP), became acting president, serving until Gligorov resumed his duties in January 1996.

In a major cabinet reshuffle in February 1996, Prime Minister Crvenkovski dropped the LPM from the ruling coalition, ignoring specific advice from the president that its previous party composition should be retained. The new lineup, which included Frèkovski as foreign minister, thus featured the dominant SDSM together with lesser participation by the PDP and the Socialist Party of Macedonia (*Socijalistiěeka Partija na Makedonija*—SPM). Andov responded to the ouster of his party by resigning as speaker, being succeeded in March by Tito PETKOVSKI of the SDSM. An LPM attempt in April to force an early election was easily rebuffed, given the government's comfortable parliamentary majority. The SDSM won a plurality of council seats as well as mayoralties in municipal elections in late 1996, the biggest challenge coming from a coalition of right-wing groupings.

In February 1997 an estimated 3,000 Macedonian students protested against a law permitting the Albanian language to be used in teaching at Skopje University's teacher college, reflecting nationalistic sentiment that the government should not yield to perceived separatism on the part of ethnic Albanians. In March the EU formally expressed concern over rising ethnic tensions, and rioting (resulting in 3 deaths, 100 wounded, and 500 arrests) erupted in July in Gostivar over the right to fly the Albanian flag at municipal buildings in ethnic Albanian areas.

Despite ethnic unrest and a financial scandal allegedly implicating government officials, the government survived a confidence vote in March 1997. The financial scandal was caused by the collapse of a pyramid scheme in which 30,000 people may have lost as much as $60 million. The VMRO-DPMNE attempted to exploit the uproar over the alleged swindle by staging an antigovernment rally on May 15 attended by 30,000 protestors. The assembly approved a major cabinet reshuffle on May 29, with Prime Minister Crvenkovski pledging to concentrate on economic reforms and anticorruption measures.

The problems of ethnic Albanians in Kosovo subsequently spilled over into Macedonia, most notably a series of car bomb explosions in January and

February 1998 that were disputably claimed by the Serbian-based Kosovo Liberation Army (KLA). President Gligorov said in early March that the army had prepared a plan for a large-scale movement of Kosovars through Macedonia to Albania in case open war broke out. Meanwhile, the leaders of several ethnic Albanian parties were charged in mid-March with violating (during a pro-Kosovo rally) Macedonian laws limiting the display of Albanian nationalist symbols. In addition, the mayors of Tetevo and Gostivar were imprisoned for flying the Albanian flag over municipal buildings, the government's reaction prompting threats from the PDP and the Democratic Party of Albanians (*Demokratska Partija na Albancite*—DPA/*Partisë Demokratike Shqiptare*—PDSh—DPA/PDSh), under the leadership of longtime Albanian nationalist Arben XHAFERI, to withdraw from governmental institutions in protest.

New legislative balloting was conducted on October 18 and November 1, 1998, resulting in a majority of 62 seats for the VMRO-DPMNE and its electoral partner, the newly formed, probusiness Democratic Alternative (*Demokratska Alternativa*—DA). A governmental crisis was averted after the elections, when prime minister-designate Georgievski negotiated a coalition agreement that included the DPA/PDSh, theretofore perceived as a more militant segment of the Albanian population than the more mainstream PDP/PPD. Georgievski's new VMRO-DPMNE/DA/DPA government, installed on November 30, pledged to further integrate Albanians into Macedonian institutions and society as a whole.

In presidential balloting to replace the retiring Gligorov, the VMRO-DPMNE candidate, Boris TRAJKOVSKI, captured 52.9 percent of the second-round vote on November 14, 1999, outdistancing the SDSM's Tito Petkovski, who had finished first in the initial round on October 31. Trajkovski's victory came with the support of the DA and the DPA/PDSh, both of which had fielded their own candidates in the first round. Official confirmation of Trajkovski's victory was delayed, however, when the Supreme Court ordered that a revote be held on December 5 in selected precincts because of ballot stuffing and other irregularities. The results of the reballoting proved nearly identical to the previous totals, and Trajkovski was inaugurated on December 15.

On November 24, 2000, the DA, citing the slow pace of economic reform, announced its withdrawal from the governing coalition, putting the administration in jeopardy. In August the administration had weathered the defection of six VMRO-DPMNE legislators to the Internal Macedonian Revolutionary Organization–True Macedonian Reform Option (*Vnatrešna Makedonska Revolucionerna Organizacija–Vistinska Makedonska Reformska Opcija*—VMRO-VMRO), but it now needed to negotiate a new coalition agreement in order to survive. With additional support from independent deputies (including four defectors from the DA), a new alliance of the VMRO-DPMNE, the DPA/PDSh, and the LPM received parliamentary assent on November 30.

On February 26, 2001, fighting erupted in Tanuševçi, on the border with Kosovo, precipitated by members of the Albanian National Liberation Army—NLA (*Ushtrisë Çlirimtare Kombëtare*—UÇK) led by Ali AHMETI. By mid-March fighting had spread to the Tetovo area, leading the UN Security Council on March 21 to pass a unanimous resolution condemning "extremist violence" as "a threat to the security and stability of the wider region." In April the DPA and PDP, both having condemned the NLA, began discussions with the government on possible constitutional changes that would address the status of ethnic Albanians. On May 13 the assembly, by a vote of 104–1, approved formation of a national unity government that, in addition to the three parties in the previous Georgievski administration, included the SDSM, the PDP, the VMRO-VMRO, and the Liberal–Democratic Party (*Liberalno–Demokratska Partija*—LDP), which incorporated elements of the LPM. Fighting nevertheless escalated in succeeding weeks, and as of June some 65,000 ethnic Albanians had fled to Kosovo to escape the conflict.

A Western-brokered peace agreement (the Ohrid accords) was achieved on August 13, 2001. Two weeks later NLA members began surrendering their arms to a 3,500-member NATO force, which had entered the country at the request of President Trajkovski. With NATO's "Operation Essential Harvest" having achieved a partial disarmament on schedule, on September 6 the assembly formally approved the peace accords. The pact called in part for constitutional revisions that would excise the privileged status accorded the Macedonian majority and accord the Albanian language official status in areas with an ethnic Albanian population of 20 percent or more. The assembly finally enacted a package of related constitutional amendments on November 16. Five days later, declaring that the national unity government had achieved its aim of restoring domestic stability, the SDSM and LDP resigned from the administration, which was quickly joined by the New Democracy Party (*Nova Demokratija*—ND).

In the parliamentary election of September 15, 2002, former prime minister Branko Crvenkovski's SDSM led a ten-party alliance, the Coalition for Macedonia Together (*Koalitsija Za Makedonija Zaedno—Koalitsija* ZMZ), to a near-majority of 60 seats in the 120-seat *Sobranje*. Prime Minister Georgievski's VMRO-DPMNE and its principal ally, the LPM, managed to win only 33 seats. The Democratic Union for Integration (*Demokratska Unija za Integracija*—DUI/*Bashkimit Demokratik për Integrim*—BDI—DUI/BDI), chaired by former Albanian National Liberation Army leader Ali Ahmeti, won 16 seats and joined a new Crvenkovski coalition government, which was confirmed by the *Sobranje* and took office on November 1.

Macedonia fell into turmoil on February 26, 2004, when President Trajkovski and six of his staff members were killed in a plane crash near Mostar in Bosnia and Herzegovina. Ljubčo JORDANOVSKI served as acting president until elections in April. In the first round of presidential elections on April 14, 2004, Prime Minister Crvenkovski of the SDSM and Sasko KEDEV of the VMRO-DPMNE advanced to a second round, leaving behind two ethnic Albanian candidates. (Former interior minister Ljube BOSKOVSKI was barred from running as an independent because he had not fulfilled a constitutional residency requirement, while Arben Xhaferi, the DPA/PDSh chair, withdrew.) Crvenovski won the April 28 runoff with 62.7 percent of the vote and was sworn in as president on May 12. Interior Minister Hari KOSTOV succeeded him as prime minister and was sworn in on June 2, after a parliamentary vote of confidence. On November 15, however, Kostov resigned, citing corruption and nepotism within the coalition as a reason. He was replaced by Vlado BUCKOVSKI, who also took over as SDSM chair. On December 17 a parliamentary vote of confidence approved Buckovski's coalition government, which included the DUI/BDI.

Constitution and Government

The constitution proclaimed in November 1991 defines Macedonia as a state based on citizenship, not ethnicity, and specifically rules out any territorial claims on neighboring countries. Minority Albanians, however, asserted that the preamble and dozens of provisions of the basic law accorded privileged status to the ethnic and religious Macedonian majority. This perception contributed to the violent events of 2001 and led to enactment of a series of corrective amendments later that year.

The constitution provides for a directly elected president serving a five-year term as head of state and a cabinet, headed by a prime minister, owing responsibility to a unicameral national assembly (*Sobranje*); the assembly is elected for a four-year term by a combination of majority and proportional voting. Ultimate judicial authority is vested in a Supreme Court, with a Constitutional Court adjudicating constitutional issues.

Legislation approved in September 1996 provided for the division of the country's 34 administrative districts into 123 municipalities plus the self-governing capital of Skopje, with areas of ethnic Albanian populations receiving special treatment in the final drawing of boundaries in light of criticism of the initial proposals by ethnic Albanian parties. Municipalities each have an elected mayor and council.

In 2001 the assembly adopted 15 main amendments to the constitution. The principal provisions were a revised preamble referring to nonethnic Macedonian communities as citizens; a "double majority" legislative for the assembly whereby certain legislation would require approval of a minority group; the establishment of Albanian as the second official language in areas where ethnic Albanians constitute 20 percent of the population; and proportional representation of ethnic Albanians in the Constitutional Court, public administration, and security forces. In 2002 the assembly approved new legislation providing for the devolution of greater authority to local government, effectively granting a measure of self-rule to ethnic Albanian regions. In other measures to integrate ethnic Albanians into national life, the assembly passed a controversial law granting the underground Albanian-language university in Tetovo status as a state university. A new citizenship law passed in 2003 enabled foreign nationals to qualify for citizenship after 8 rather than 15 years of legal residence.

In 2004 the assembly passed a redistricting law, known as the Law on Territorial Organization, which will cut the number of administrative districts from 123 to 76 in 2008. The law, which is in accordance with the 2001 Ohrid peace accords, gives local authorities greater powers in regional planning, finance, and health care. The measure was opposed by many ethnic Macedonians who feared that redistricting could lead to partition of the country along ethnic lines. (Albanians will become the majority in 16 of the new municipalities.)

Foreign Relations

Recognition of Macedonia by the EC/EU was stalled by the insistence of Greece, an EC/EU member, that recognition be conditioned on Macedonia's changing its name. Greece based its position on historical considerations, including the fact that its own northernmost province is also named Macedonia. Thus, the EC/EU foreign ministers declared at a meeting in May 1992 that the community was "willing to recognize Macedonia as a sovereign and independent state within its existing borders and under a name that can be accepted by all parties concerned." Outside of the EC/EU, Turkey was unmoved by Greece's concerns, having extended recognition to Macedonia on February 6. On August 6 Russia also recognized the new republic.

On December 11, 1992, the UN Security Council authorized the dispatch of some 700 UN peacekeeping troops and military observers to the Macedonia-Serbia/Kosovo border in an effort to prevent the fighting in Bosnia and Herzegovina from spreading to the south. Subsequently, the Clinton administration in the United States, which had consistently refused to commit ground forces to the Bosnian theater, indicated that it was willing to participate in the Macedonian peacekeeping effort, and on June 18, 1993, the first troops of an eventual 500-strong American contingent arrived to join the UN Preventive Deployment Force (UNPREDEP). The force's mandate was renewed at six-month intervals thereafter, with its size increasing to 1,150 by November 1996.

Disagreements with Greece, including the nomenclature dispute, continued throughout the 1990s. After the Skopje government had formally applied for UN membership on January 7, 1993, a partial Greek concession permitted the new state to join the UN in April as "The former Yugoslav Republic of Macedonia." Under the compromise, a definitive name as well as a related dispute over the use of Alexander the Great's Star of Vergina symbol on the Macedonian flag would have to be negotiated. The new republic was not permitted to fly its flag outside UN buildings until a 1995 U.S.-UN brokered agreement settled on an acceptable flag design.

Strains with Greece were aggravated by the return to power of a socialist government in Athens in October 1993. Greek Prime Minister Andreas Papandreou was incensed by the decision of the leading EU states in December to recognize Macedonia, and on February 16, 1994, after Washington had extended recognition, Athens imposed a controversial partial trade embargo on Macedonia, cutting the landlocked republic off from the northern Greek port of Salonika (Thessaloniki), its main import-export channel, for all goods except food and medicine, and thereby angering other EU members.

UN and U.S. mediation brought Macedonia's dispute with Greece to partial resolution on September 13, 1995, when the respective foreign ministers initialed an agreement in New York covering border definition, revision of the Macedonian constitution to exclude any hint of territorial claims, and the design of the Macedonian flag, which incorporated a sun with rays to replace the disputed star. Following ratification by the Macedonian Assembly, the accord was formally signed in Skopje on October 15, whereupon Greece lifted its trade embargo. In light of the accommodation with Greece, Macedonia was admitted to full membership in the Organization for Security and Cooperation in Europe (OSCE) on October 12, 1995, and to the Council of Europe a week later. Despite the Skopje-Athens 1995 agreement, the Greek government, throughout the rest of the decade and into the next, strongly opposed to the "Republic of Macedonia" name preferred, with equal resolution, by its northern neighbor.

Moves by the Skopje government to counter a developing Belgrade-Athens axis on Balkan matters included the cultivation of relations with Bulgaria, which had recognized Macedonia in January 1992, and with Turkey. However, the Bulgarian policy encountered difficulty in April 1994 when a Bulgarian minister broke off a visit to Macedonia because of Skopje's insistence on the existence of a distinct Macedonian language. Reflecting the traditional Bulgarian view that Macedonians are really Bulgarians (and their language a variant of Bulgarian), the Bulgarian minister's action reminded the international community that Bulgaria had never entirely abandoned its own territorial claim to Macedonia. The two governments appeared to bridge their differences in early 1999, negotiating a compromise on the language question, which had been blocking Bulgaria's ratification of some 20 bilateral agreements. Relations remained cordial in 2000 despite Sofia's banning of an ethnic Macedonian party, which generated outraged protests by nationalistic groups in Macedonia. During a May visit to Skopje, Bulgarian President Petar Stoyanov signed nine bilateral accords and urged continuing friendship and mutual respect.

The Belgrade-Athens axis and Serb claims on Macedonian territory militated against a natural alignment between the Macedonians and their Serb coreligionists, even though Skopje and Belgrade reached a mutual recognition accord in April 1996. The NATO bombing campaign launched against Yugoslavia in March–June 1999 precipitated the temporary flight of more than 250,000 ethnic Albanians into Macedonia from Kosovo. Most non-Albanians, concerned over the broader regional implications of greater autonomy for the Albanian Kosovars, reportedly opposed the NATO action, while ethnic Albanians in Macedonia called upon the government to provide their confreres with massive assistance. In addition, some ethnic Albanians in Macedonia indicated they might join the KLA in combating Serbian forces, raising the specter of a spillover of the conflict into Macedonia, long considered a "firewall" against further spread of the Balkan fighting. However, the DPA/PDSh's Xhaferi successfully appealed for calm among ethnic Albanians in Macedonia, while the government dutifully accepted the temporary deployment of some 12,000 NATO forces in Macedonia as part of the peacekeeping force proposed for Kosovo.

In view of the Kosovo conflict, most UN members had wanted UNPREDEP to continue to function, but China vetoed a further extension of the mission beyond February 28, 1999. The decision appeared directly related, despite Beijing's denials, to Skopje's establishment of relations with Taiwan in January, an action that caused China to sever ties to Macedonia. Some members of the Georgievski government had argued that recognition of Taiwan would produce a much-needed inflow of foreign investment, on top of foreign aid, from the island, but the results did not meet expectations. Skopje renewed diplomatic ties with Beijing on June 18, 2001, as a consequence of which Taiwan immediately broke relations with Macedonia.

In early 2001 Macedonia indicated that it would no longer pursue new diplomatic ties to countries that refused to recognize the country's designation as the "Republic of Macedonia." (The United States officially recognized Macedonia by its constitutional name, the Republic of Macedonia, rather than the UN name of The former Yugoslav Republic of Macedonia in 2004.) Meanwhile, negotiations with Athens over the name issue continued, even while economic ties between the neighbors moved forward. In November 1999, for example, Greece and Macedonia concluded an agreement on construction of a $90 million oil pipeline between Thessaloniki and Skopje, while in April 2000 the National Bank of Greece was one of three foreign investors to purchase Macedonia's largest bank from the government. In May 2002 the Greek and Macedonian defense ministers concluded a military cooperation agreement.

Current Issues

The 1998 legislative election was conducted in a surprisingly calm atmosphere, with international monitors describing the balloting as generally free and fair. Some credit for the success of the VMRO-DPMNE/DA electoral alliance appeared to go to the moderating effect the DA had on the image of VMRO-DPMNE leader Georgievski, whose intense nationalism and virulent anticommunism had theretofore been perceived as presenting a barrier to effective cooperation with the Albanian minority and moderate socialists. The electorate also seemed to endorse the VMRO-DPMNE/DA's anticorruption and probusiness campaign platform, while the SDSM, in power since 1992, appeared to fall victim, to a certain degree, to the "fatigue factor."

The unexpected participation of the DPA/PDSh in the center-right coalition with the VMRO-DPMNE in 1998 represented, in the words of one analyst, an "interesting experiment" in Balkan power-sharing. New Prime Minister Georgievski quickly underscored his integrationist intentions by supporting release of the Albanian officials imprisoned earlier in the year and pledging financial support for the controversial Albanian-language university in Tetovo. The assembly overrode President Gligorov's veto of an amnesty bill in February 1999, after which the mayors of Gostivar and Tetovo, Rufi OSMANI and Aladjan DEMIRI, and some 900 others were freed. Support for the Tetovo university came in July 2000, when the assembly easily passed a higher education law authorizing creation of a private institution structured along lines that had been proposed by OSCE High Commissioner for Minorities Max van der Stoel. The more militant Albanians were not satisfied, however, and continued to call for creation of a public university on par with those in Skopje and Bitola.

The local elections of September 10 and 24, 2000, failed to meet the OSCE's standards for open and fair elections, as had the presidential contest of October–November 1999. In both cases, revotes were required in some districts, amid widespread evidence of voter intimidation, ballot-stuffing, and other irregularities. Particularly in the west, supporters of what were then the two principal ethnic Albanian parties, the DPA/PDSh and the PDP/PPD, clashed during balloting for mayoral and council offices.

Although speculation about a DPA/PDSh-PDP/PPD merger rose in early 2001, the two were unable to reconcile their differences before hostilities between the government and ethnic Albanians erupted in February–March. The prominence of the two parties in the Albanian community was then severely undercut by the formation in June 2002 of the DUI/BID, chaired by former NLA head Ali Ahmeti.

The NLA had officially disbanded in September 2001, but sporadic ethnic clashes continued to occur. With NATO's Operation Essential Harvest having completed its month-long mission, it was succeeded in September by Operation Amber Fox, which had as its principal purpose protecting the international monitors who were assigned to oversee implementation of the provisions of the Ohrid accords. Although initially authorized for three months, Operation Amber Fox was extended several times and ended on December 14, 2004, when it was succeeded by a new operation called Allied Harmony. Unlike Amber Fox, Allied

Harmony was not led by any single country. Meanwhile, the government pushed forward with related legislation, including an amnesty bill that passed in March 2002 and a series of language laws that won approval in June. Another key provision of the Ohrid accords, the formation of ethnically mixed police units, was also being implemented.

Corruption subsequently continued to be a problem. (Transparency International rated Macedonia as among the most corrupt nations in Europe.) Public concern over that issue probably contributed to the ouster of the Georgievski government in the 2002 legislative balloting by the *Koalitsija* ZKM (the new SDSM-led alliance).

Macedonia formally submitted its application for EU membership in 2004, continued adherence by all parties to the Ohrid accords being considered vital to future progress on that front. EU concern was raised when the OSCE criticized the conduct of the March 2005 local elections, but the European Commission deemed Macedonia a "worthy candidate" in November and the EU summit granted official candidate status in December. Substantive EU negotiations were not expected to begin with intensity until after the June assembly balloting, which in the opinion of most observers, needed a "fair and free" stamp of approval from international observers to solidify Macedonia's EU fortunes. Although the assembly in March approved an electoral reform package, a degree of violence and alleged intimidation of voters were reported in the subsequent campaign. Some ethnic Albanians reportedly remained unhappy over what they perceived as slow implementation of policies to protect the rights of minorities. Other campaign nuances included the competition between young, "pro-Western" politicians and long-standing nationalist leaders. (*See headnote.*)

Political Parties

For four and a half decades after World War II, the only authorized political party in Yugoslavia was the Communist Party, which was redesignated in 1952 as the League of Communists of Yugoslavia (*Savez Kumunista Jugoslavija*—SKJ).

In 1989 non-Communist groups began to emerge in the republics, and in early 1990 the SKJ approved the introduction of a multiparty system, thereby triggering its own demise. In Macedonia the party's local branch, the League of Communists of Macedonia (*Sojuz na Komunistite na Makedonija*—SKM), had been succeeded by the SKM-PDP in 1989 (see SDSM, below).

Nearly three dozen parties offered candidates for the 1998 and 2002 elections, on their own, in coalitions, or both.

Government Parties (Prior to the July 2006 Elections)

Social Democratic Union of Macedonia (*Socijaldemokratski Sojuz na Makedonija*—SDSM). The SDSM was the name adopted in 1991 by the League of Communists of Macedonia–Party of Democratic Change (*Sojuz na Komunistite na Makedonija–Partija za Demokratska Preobrazba*—SKM-PDP), which had been launched in 1989 as successor to the SKM. Although the SKM-PDP had run second to the VMRO-DPMNE in the 1990 legislative poll, its nominee, Kiro Gligorov, was subsequently designated president of the republican presidency.

The SDSM was the largest component of the Union of Macedonia (*Sojuz na Makedonija*—SM), an electoral alliance formed for the 1994 presidential and legislative balloting by the SDSM, SPM, and LPM, the three non-Albanian parties of the post-1992 government. The SM supported the SDSM's Gligorov in his successful bid for a second presidential term in 1994, and the SM secured 95 seats (58 for the SDSM) in the controversial concurrent legislative poll, with the SDSM's Branko Crvenkovski remaining as prime minister of the subsequent SM-led government. However, friction developed within the SM, leading to the departure of the LPM from the government in a February 1996 reshuffle. The SM was subsequently described as having collapsed, and minimal cooperation between the SDSM and the SPM was reported in the 1998 legislative elections, from which the SDSM emerged with only 27 seats. (One of the seats credited to the SDSM was won in coalition with the Social Democratic Party of Macedonia [*Socijal-demokratska Partija na Makedonija—*SDPM], which had won a seat in 1994.)

In the 1999 presidential contest, the SDSM candidate, former assembly speaker Tito Petkovski, finished first in the first round, with 32.7 percent of the vote but lost in the November runoff to the governing coalition's candidate. In May 2000 the SDSM and the LDP concluded a cooperation agreement for the upcoming local elections and the next general election. The League for Democracy soon joined the alliance, and all three immediately called for new elections. An SDSM-led rally in Skopje in mid-May attracted 40,000 people, who heard Crvenkovski charge the government with corruption, failure to raise the standard of living, and an inability to fulfill its election promises. However, a year later the SDSM agreed to join a national unity government, although it withdrew in November 2001, noting that the unity government had accomplished its immediate goal of achieving domestic stability.

The SDSM, LDP, and a number of smaller parties formed the **Coalition for Macedonia Together** (*Koalitsija Za Makedonija Zaedno—Koalitsija* ZMZ) to contest the 2002 elections. In 2004 Crvenkovski was elected president of the republic as the candidate of the coalition. The *Koalitsija* ZMZ was renewed by the SDSM, LDP, and other parties (including the **Democratic Party of Serbs in Macedonia**) for the 2006 assembly balloting.

Leaders: Branko CRVENKOVSKI (President), Vlado BUCKOVSKI (Leader), Georgi SPASOV (Secretary).

Liberal-Democratic Party (*Liberalno-Demokratska Partija—LDP).* The centrist LDP was formed in January 1997 by what proved to be a temporary merger of the LPM (below) and the Democratic Party of Macedonia (*Demokratska Partija Makedonija—*DPM). The DPM had been registered in July 1993 under the leadership of a Communist-era prime minister but unexpectedly failed to have much impact in the 1994 balloting. When the DPM and LPM merged as the LDP,

the DPM's Petar Gošev became leader of the new formation.

The LDP won only four seats in the 1998 legislative poll, securing 7.0 percent in the proportional balloting; Gošev resigned as chair in January 1999 in view of that poor electoral performance. In 2000 the LPM was reestablished as a separate party, taking with it three of the four LDP parliamentary deputies. In May 2000 the LDP joined the SDSM in an electoral alliance for the September local elections and the 2002 assembly election. The LDP's participation in the *Koalitsija* ZKM contributed to the coalition's success in the 2004 presidential election.

Leaders: Risto PENOV (President), Petar GOŠEV.

Democratic Union for Integration (*Demokratska Unija za Integracija—*DUI/*Bashkimit Demokratik për Integrim—*BDI—DUI/BDI). The DUI/BDI was formed in June 2002 by Ali Ahmeti, the former head of the Albanian National Liberation Army—NLA (*Ushtrisë Çlirimtare Kombëtare—*UÇK), which had been dissolved in late September 2001 as a consequence of the August peace accord with the government. The principal focus of the DUI/BDI, according to its chair, was the full implementation of the provisions of the Ohrid accords.

In June 2002 the DUI/BDI reportedly entered into merger talks with the **National Democratic Party** (NDP/PDK), another Albanian party led by Kastriot HAXHIREXHA and comprising former members of the NLA. However, the parties ultimately contested the 2002 assembly balloting independently. In 2003 Haxhirexha and Ahmeti announced the merger of the two groups, but other NDP/PDK members disavowed that action, denouncing Haxhirexha, a former critic of the Ohrid accords, for having abandoned the NDP/PDK's pursuit of "federalism." Claiming "no common interest" with the DUI/BDI, the rump NDP/PDK elected new leaders (Basri HALITI [Chair]); Xhegair SHAQIRI, the legislator elected under the NDP/PDK banner in 2002, briefly joined the DUI/BDI but then returned to the NDP/PDK. Meanwhile, some reports in the run-up to the 2006 elections referenced the DUI/BDI-NDP/PDK as presenting candidates, although the NDP/PDK also presented its own candidates, indicating that the split between NDP/PDK factions continued.

Leaders: Ali AHMETI (Chair), Hysni SHAQIRI, Gezim OSTREMI.

Opposition Parties (Prior to the July 2006 Elections)

Internal Macedonian Revolutionary Organization–Democratic Party for Macedonian National Unity (*Vnatrešna Makedonska Revolucionerna Organizacija–Demokratska Partija za Makedonsko Nacionalno Edinstvo*—VMRO-DPMNE). The VMRO was named after a historic group (founded in 1893) that fought for independence from the Turks. The DPMNE, launched by Macedonian migrant workers in Sweden, merged with the VMRO in June 1990.

The VMRO-DPMNE, with significant support within the Slavic population, strongly endorsed a revival of Macedonian cultural identity, its nationalistic stance being broadly perceived as anti-Albanian and right-wing, despite the group's description of itself as representing the "democratic center." The party won a plurality of 39 seats in the 1990 assembly, subsequently serving as the main opposition to the Communist-led government. The VMRO-DPMNE's presidential candidate in 1994, Ljubčo Georgievski, gained 21.6 percent of the vote against the SDSM's Kiro Gligorov. However, the VMRO-DPMNE boycotted the second round of the 1994 legislative balloting, alleging fraud in the first round, in which it had been credited with no seats.

The VMRO-DPMNE competed for many of the single-member district seats in the 1998 legislative balloting in an alliance with the Democratic Alternative (below) called "For Changes." It emerged from that balloting with 49 seats, having led all parties in the proportional contest with 28.1 percent of the vote. By that time, the VMRO-DPMNE appeared to have substantially moderated its platform, presenting itself as dedicated to "reconciliation and progress" and earning description as a "neo-liberal" party. Nevertheless, it was still a sur-prise when Georgievski invited the DPA, a hardline ethnic Albanian grouping, to join his new government. Georgievski was reelected president of the party at a May 1999 congress.

The VMRO-DPMNE presidential candidate, Boris Trajkovski, won the 1999 election over the SDSM candidate, taking 52.9 percent of the vote in second-round balloting on November 14. He had finished second, with 20.6 percent, in the first round two weeks earlier, when the DA and DPA had offered their own candidates. In the September–October 2000 local elections, a VMRO-DPMNE/DA alliance won the majority of mayoralties.

In August 2000, six VMRO-DPMNE deputies defected to the new Internal Macedonian Revolutionary Organization–True Macedonian Reform Option (below). The government's legislative majority was briefly threatened three months later when the DA left the governing coalition, but within days Georgievski had announced the inclusion of the LPM, which, with added independent support, permitted the administration to remain in power.

The VMRO-DPMNE remained in power until the 2004 death of President Trajkovski. In the ensuing presidential election, the VMRO-DPMNE candidate, Sasko Kedev, lost to the *Koalitsija* ZKM candidate, Branko Crvenkovski. Following the VMRO-DPMNE's electoral defeat, Georgievski resigned as president of the party, and Nikola Gruevski was elected to succeed him.

In July 2004 supporters of Georgievski left the VMRO-DPMNE to form the VMRO-NP (below). The VMRO-DPMNE led a coalition with some 13 other (mostly smaller) parties for the 2006 assembly balloting.

Leaders: Nikola GRUEVSKI (President of the Party); Dosta DIMOVSKA, Marjan ǦORČEV (Vice Presidents of the Party); Vojo MIHAJLOVSKI (Secretary).

Democratic Party of Albanians (*Demokratska Partija na Albancite*—DPA/*Partisë Demokratike Shqiptare*—PDSh—DPA/PDSh). The DPA/PDSh was formed in mid-1997 by the merger of the Party for Democratic Prosperity of Albanians in Macedonia (*Partija za Demokratski Prosperitet na Albancite vo Makedonija*—PDPA) and the People's Democratic Party (*Narodna Demokratska Partija*—NDP). The NDP was an ethnic Albanian grouping that resulted from a split between the moderate majority of the ethnic Albanian party (*Partija za Demokratski Prosperitet*—PDP) and an antigovernment minority, led by Ilijaz Halimi, at a congress of the parent party in February 1994. The NDP became the largest nongovernment party after the October–November elections, winning four seats, but lost that status when the LPM joined the opposition in February 1996.

The PDPA had been launched in April 1995 as another breakaway from the PDP by a group opposed to the parent party's participation in the government coalition. Its leader was Arben Xhaferi, a spokesman for the militant Albanian population who had spent many years in the separatist movement in Kosovo before establishing a base in Tetovo in western Macedonia and being elected as an independent to the Macedonian legislature.

The government allegedly refused to recognize the DPA/PDSh after its formation in 1997 on the grounds that the grouping supported unconstitutional demands on behalf of the Albanians. In fact, official government reports on the 1998 legislative election referenced the grouping as the PDPA/NDP, which contested the balloting in partial alliance with the PDP. Following the election, the use of the DPA/PDSh title appeared to gain the government's sanction, particularly after the DPA/PDSh (which had won 11 legislative seats) agreed to join the subsequent VMRO-DPMNE-led coalition government. Xhaferi, described by the *Christian Science Monitor* as the "flint" that could "set Macedonia afire," called his accord with the VMRO-DPMNE's Ljubčo Georgievski "a small miracle." The DPA/PDSh was not officially registered under that name until July 2002.

Following its entrance into the government, the DPA/PDSh appeared to moderate its course, although Deputy Chair Menduh Thaçi remained one of the more hard-line advocates for Albanian rights. In the 1999 presidential election the party's candidate, Muharem NEXIPI, finished fourth, with 14.8 percent of the vote; in the second round,

the DPA/PDSh threw its support to the successful VMRO-DPMNE candidate. The DPA/PDSh won seven seats in the 2002 assembly poll.

Leaders: Arben XHAFERI (Chair), Menduh THAÇI (Deputy Chair), Ilijaz HALIMI.

Party for Democratic Prosperity (*Partija za Demokratski Prosperitet*—PDP/*Partisë për Prosperitet Demokratik*—PPD—PDP/PPD). The PDP/PPD is one of the principal vehicles for supporting ethnic Albanian interests in Macedonia. Launched in May 1990, it operates only in areas with substantial Albanian populations. Subsequent to the 1990 election (in which it won 25 seats), it absorbed a smaller party with the same abbreviation, the Popular Democratic Party (*Partis Demokratis Populare*—PDP), led by Ilijaz HALIMI.

After joining the government in 1992, the PDP/PPD underwent a split at a February 1994 congress between progovernment moderates, led by Dželadin MURATI, and antigovernment nationalists, led by Halimi, who subsequently reorganized as the NDP (see DPA, above). Dubbing itself the "Party of Continuity," the rump PDP/PPD came into sharp conflict with its coalition partners in mid-1994 over the conviction of a group of alleged Albanian separatists, including the honorary president of the PDP/PPD, Mithat EMINI.

Having lost ground in the October–November 1994 assembly balloting, the PDP/PPD continued as a government party, despite participating in a boycott of the assembly by ethnic Albanian deputies from February to July 1995 in protest against a law banning use of Albanian in passports and identity cards. During this period another antigovernment faction broke away as the PDPA (also under the DPA, above), with the rump PDP/PPD remaining in the government coalition.

The PDP/PPD contested the 1998 legislative balloting in partial coalition with the DPA/PDSh (PDPA/NDP), securing 14 seats. However, the PDP/PPD subsequently switched governmental roles with the DPA/PDSh, moving into opposition while the DPA/PDSh joined the new VMRO-DPMNE-led cabinet. Following the poor showing of the party's 1999 presidential candidate, Muhamed HALILI, who finished sixth with

4.2 percent of the vote, the party leadership was replaced virtually en masse in April 2000, President Abdurahman HALITI giving way to Imer IMERI (Ymer YMERI). Although the party competed in the first round of the local elections in 2000, it pulled out of the second round, alleging major irregularities.

With the departure of the DA from the government in November 2000, Imeri apparently agreed to support the opposition in its bid to replace the Georgievski coalition, but he changed his mind when several of the party's assembly members objected. Subsequent talks with the DPA/PDSh's Xhaferi and the VMRO-DPMNE about the PDP/PPD joining the government broke down in late December, in part because a hardline faction demanded that the proposed private Albanian-language university in Tetovo be a state institution and that use of the Albanian language be permitted in the National Assembly—demands that the government was not prepared to accept at that time. Early in 2001 speculation rose that the PDP/PPD and the DPA/PDSh might merge, but that was before the outbreak of hostilities between militant Albanians and the government. International pressure reportedly led the PDP/PPD to join the May 2001 national unity administration.

In May 2002 Haliti returned to the party presidency following Imeri's resignation for health reasons. Secretary General Muhamed Halili was expelled a month later for criticizing Haliti.

The PDP/PPD won two seats in the 2002 assembly poll.

Leaders: Abdylmenaf BEXHETI, Naser ŽIBERI (Parliamentary Leader and Secretary General), Abduljhadi VEJSELI.

Socialist Party of Macedonia (*Socijalistička Partija na Makedonija*—SPM). Formerly styled the Socialist League–Socialist Party of Macedonia (*Socijalistički Sojuz–Socijalistička Partija na Makedonija*—SS-SPM), the SPM is the successor to the local branch of the former "popular front" grouping, the Socialist League of the Working People of Yugoslavia (*Socijalistički Savez Radnog Narodna Jugoslavija*—SSRNJ). For the 1990 elections the SPM formed a partial alliance

with the Party for the Total Emancipation of Roma in Macedonia (*Partija za Celosna Emancipacija na Romite vo Makedonija*—PCERM), led by Faik ABDI, which obtained one seat under the SPM umbrella and retained it in 1994. Meanwhile, the SPM won eight seats as part of the SM alliance with the SDSM. Following the death of Kiro POPOVSKI, Ljubisav Ivanov was elected SPM leader in May 1996.

In the wake of the collapse of the SM in 1996, the SPM contested the proportional seats and some of the single-member district seats in the 1998 assembly balloting in coalition with the PCERM and the Democratic Progressive Party of the Roma in Macedonia (*Demokratska Progresivna Partija na Romite od Makedonija*—DPPRM) as well as some smaller ethnic parties. The coalition was called the Movement for Cultural Tolerance and Civic Cooperation. The movement won only 4.7 percent of the proportional vote and therefore secured no seats, although the SPM won one seat in the contests determined by majority principle. For the 2000 local elections the SPM entered an SDSM-led alliance.

The SPM retained its single seat in the 2002 assembly poll. Subsequently, in December 2003, it announced the formation of a coalition called the **Third Way** that also included the Democratic Alternative (below) and the **Democratic Union** (led by former interior minister Pavle TRAJANOV).

Leaders: Blagoje FILIPOVSKI, Ljubisav IVANOV (President).

Other Parties

Liberal Party of Macedonia (*Liberalna Partija na Makedonija*—LPM*). The LPM was organized initially as the Alliance of Reform Forces of Macedonia (*Sojuz na Reformskite Sili na Makedonija*—SRSM), an affiliate of the federal Alliance of Yugoslav Reform Forces (*Savez Reformskih Snaga Jugoslavije*—SRSJ). In the 1990 balloting it was allied in some areas with the Young Democratic and Progressive Party (*Mlas Demokratska Progresivna Partija*—MDPS), which it later absorbed, adopting the name Reform Forces of Macedonia–Liberal Party (*Reformskite Sili na Makedonija–Liberalna Partija*—RSM-LP) in 1992. Using the shorter LPM rubric, the party won 29 seats in the 1994 election as part of the SM and continued to be a component of the ruling coalition. However, growing friction with the dominant SDSM culminated in ejection of the LPM from the coalition in February 1996, whereupon party leader Stojan Andov resigned as speaker of the legislature and committed the LPM to vigorous opposition.

A 1997 merger with the Democratic Party of Macedonia (DPM) to form the Liberal-Democratic Party (LDP), ended in 2000, when the LPM reemerged as a separate organization. In November 2000 the revived party joined the governing coalition led by the VMRO-DPMNE.

The LPM participated in the coalition led by the VMRO-DPMNE for the 2006 assembly poll.

Leader: Stojan ANDOV.

Democratic Alternative (*Demokratska Alternativa*—DA). Formed in March 1998 by Vasil TUPURKOVSKI, the Macedonian member of the final Yugoslavian State Presidency, the DA presented a strongly "pro-business" platform. It contested many of the single-member district seats in the October legislative election in the "For Changes" alliance with the VMRO-DPMNE, and won 10.1 percent of the vote in the proportional balloting. Having secured 13 legislative seats, the DA was accorded six posts in the subsequent coalition government led by the VMRO-DPMNE.

Tupurkovski finished third in the 1999 presidential race, with 16 percent of the vote. In the 2000 local elections the party again ran in alliance with the VMRO-DPMNE, but on November 24 it left the governing coalition, ostensibly because of the slow pace of economic reform. Personality differences between Tupurkovski and Prime Minister Georgievski may also have contributed to the rupture. As a consequence, four of the party's legislators immediately departed to sit as independents while continuing their support for the government, and three others defected to the VMRO-DPMNE after the new year.

Leaders: Vasil TUPURKOVSKI (Chair), Savo KLIMOVSKI (Former Speaker of the Assembly).

Internal Macedonian Revolutionary Organization–True Macedonian Reform Option (*Vnatrešna Makedonska Revolucionerna Organizacija–Vistinska Makedonska Reformska Opcija*—VMRO-VMRO). Formation of the center-right VMRO-VMRO was undertaken in early 2000 by former finance minister Boris Zmejkovski and other disgruntled VMRO-DPMNE members who objected to Prime Minister Georgievski's alleged authoritarianism and who charged that the promises made by the party in 1998 were not being fulfilled. The party was officially registered on April 5. In late August six assembly deputies announced that they were leaving the VMRO-DPMNE for the VMRO-VMRO, but by the end of the year the 20–25 defections predicted by the new party's leadership had failed to materialize. In a series of charges and countercharges, some of the defectors stated that the parent organization was offering bribes and making threats to retain its members, while the VMRO-DPMNE asserted that Yugoslavia was using the VMRO-VMRO to destabilize Macedonia.

In June 2002, objecting to the increasing political role of former Albanian National Liberation Army members, the VMRO-VMRO withdrew from the government. In June 2005 it was reported that the VMRO-VMRO had merged with the VMRO-DPMNE.

Leader: Boris ZMEJKOVSKI.

Internal Macedonian Revolutionary Organization–Peoples Party (*Vnatrešna Makedonska Revolucionerna Organizacija–Narodna Partija*—VMRO-NP). The VMRO-NP was formed in Skopje in July 2004 by supporters of former VMRO-DPMNE chair and prime minister of the republic Ljubčo Georgievski. The VMRO-NP is a conservative party whose platform closely resembles the VMRO-DPMNE.

Leaders: Vesna JANEVSKA (Chair), Ljubčo GEORGIEVSKI.

New Social Democratic Party (*Nova Socijal Demokratska Partija*—NSDP). The NSDP was formed in November 2005 by former members

Cabinet

As of July 1, 2006 (*see headnote*)

Prime Minister	Vlado Buckovski (SDSM)
Deputy Prime Minister	Musa Xhaferi (DUI/BDI)
Deputy Prime Minister (EU Integration)	Radmila Sekerinska (SDSM) [f]
Deputy Prime Minister (Economic Affairs)	Minco Jordanov
Deputy Prime Minister (Government Affairs)	Jovan Manasievski (LDP)

Ministers

Agriculture, Forestry, and Water Supply	Sadula Duraku (DUI/BDI)
Culture	Blagoja Stefanovski (SDSM)
Defense	Jovan Manasievski (LDP)
Economy	Fatmir Besimi (DUI/BDI)
Education and Science	Aziz Polozani (DUI/BDI)
Environment and Physical Planning	Zoran Shapuric (LDP)
Finance	Nikola Popovski (SDSM)
Foreign Affairs	Ilinka Mitreva (SDSM) [f]
Health	Vladimir Dimov (SDSM)
Internal Affairs	Ljubomir Mihajlovski (SDSM)
Justice	Meri Mladenovska-Gorgievska (SDSM) [f]
Labor and Social Policy	Stevco Jakimovski (LDP)
Local Self-Government	Rizvan Sulejmani (DUI/BDI)
Transport and Communications	Xhemail Mehazi (DUI/BDI)
Without Portfolio	Vlado Popovski (LDP)

[f] = female

of the SDSM who sought a more centrist social-democratic party.

Leader: Tito PETKOVSKI.

Democratic Renewal of Macedonia (*Demokraticka Obnova na Makedonija*—DOM). The DOM was founded in November 2005 by former LDP member Liljana Popovska.

Leader: Liljana POPOVSKA.

Party for European Future (*Partija za Evropska Idnina*—PEI). The PEI is a centrist party that advocates deeper integration with NATO and the EU. The party was formed in March 2006 by Fijat Canoski.

Leader: Fijat CANOSKI.

New Democracy (*Nova Demokratija*—ND). The ND was launched in April 2001 under the leadership of Cedo PETROV, who had previously served as parliamentary leader of the Democratic Alternative. The ND platform advanced respect for human rights, the rule of law, power sharing among the branches of government accession to the EU, and Macedonian independence. It joined the government in November 2001, following the withdrawal of the SDSM and LDP.

In August 2002 the party suffered a serious rupture. One faction sought to expel Foreign Minister Slobodan CASULE and Health Minister Georgi OROVCANEC, who had agreed to run jointly with the VMRO-DPMNE in the September general election, while the other attempted to dismiss Petrov, who had announced that the party would contest the election independently. The status of the party ultimately remained unclear.

Radical Party of Serbs in Macedonia. Established in April 2006, this group was described as a "branch" of the "ultranationalist" Serbian Radical Party.

Leader: Dragisa MILETIC.

Minor ethnic parties that failed to gain representation in the assembly in the 2002 election were the **Union of Romanies of Macedonia** (*Sojuz na Romite na Makedonija*—SRM), led by Amri BAJRAM; the **Democratic Party of Turks in Macedonia** (*Demokratska Partija na Turcite vo Makedonija*—DPTM); the **Democratic Party of Serbs in Macedonia** (*Demokratska Partija na Srbite vo Makedonija*—DPSM); the **Democratic Alliance of Serbs in Macedonia** (DSSM), led by Borivaje RISTIC; the **Democratic Party of Yugoslavs of Macedonia**, led by Zivko LEKOSKI; and the **Union of Ethnic Croats**, led by Marija DAMJANOVSKA.

Other minor parties that participated in the 2006 legislative elections included the **Party for Economic Renewal**, created in April 2006 and led by Belija RAMKOVSKI; the **Communist Party of Macedonia** (*Komunisticka Partija na Makedonija*—KPM), founded in 1992; the **League for Democracy** (*Liga za demokratija*), led by Gjorgji MARJANOVIC; the **Social Democratic Party of Macedonia** (*Socijaldemokratska Partija na Makedonija*—SDPM), established in 1990; and the **Party for Democratic Future**, a recently formed ethnic Albanian party led by Aladjan DEMIRI (the former mayor of Tetevo) and Xhemal ABDIU.

Legislature

The present Macedonian Assembly (*Sobranje*) is a directly elected unicameral body of 120 members, elected for a four-year term through proportional representation from six electoral districts, each with 20 seats. Prior to the 2002 balloting, 85 of the legislators were directly elected in two-round (if necessary) majoritarian balloting in single-member districts; the other 35 were elected on a nationwide proportional basis, with seats distributed to parties winning at least 5 percent of the national vote.

Following the election of September 15, 2002, the seat distribution was as follows: the Coalition for Macedonia Together, 60 (the Social Democratic Union of Macedonia, 43; the Liberal–Democratic Party, 12; others, 5); the Internal Macedonian Revolutionary Organization–Democratic Party for Macedonian National Unity, 33; the Democratic Union for Integration, 16; the Democratic Party of Albanians, 7; the Party for Democratic Prosperity, 2; the National Democratic Party, 1; and the Socialist Party of Macedonia, 1. The next elections were scheduled for July 2006. (*See headnote.*)

Speaker: Ljubco JORDANOVSKI.

Communications

Press

Macedonia appears to have experienced some contraction and conglomeration in print media since 2002. The top three national Macedonian-language dailies—*Dnevnik* (55,000), *Utrinski Vesnik* (30,000), and *Vest* (30,000)—were acquired by a German media conglomerate, Westdeutsche Allgemeine Zeitung (WAZ) at the end of 2002. WAZ became their major stockholder and reportedly planned on amalgamating them into an entity called "Mediapoint Makedonija." The other large Macedonian-language dailies *Večer* and *Nova Makedonija* reportedly were suffering financial difficulties. As of 2003, there were still some smaller papers that published weekly or fortnightly in Macedonian, Albanian, Turkish, and Romani, though these were experiencing financial troubles and were in danger of closing. The government provides annual financial subsidies to all print media.

News Agencies

There are two news agencies: the state-owned Macedonian Information Agency and the privately owned Makfak.

Broadcasting and Computing

Makedonska Radio-Televizja (MRT), formerly Radio-Television Skopje (Radiotelevizija Skopje), broadcasts over six radio and three television programs in Macedonian, Albanian, Turkish, Serb,

Romany, and Vlach. There were approximately 640,000 television receivers and 130,000 Internet users in 2003.

Intergovernmental Representation

Ambassador to the U.S.
(Vacant)

U.S. Ambassador to The former Yugoslav Republic of Macedonia
Gillian MILOVANOVIC

Permanent Representative to the UN
Igor DZUNDEV

IGO Memberships (Non-UN)
BIS, CEI, CEUR, EBRD, Eurocontrol, Interpol, *OIF*, OSCE, PCA, WCO, WTO

MALTA

REPUBLIC OF MALTA

Repubblika ta' Malta

The Country

Strategically located in the central Mediterranean some 60 miles south of Sicily, Malta comprises the two main islands of Malta and Gozo in addition to the small island of Comino. The population is predominantly of Carthaginian and Phoenician descent and of mixed Arab-Italian cultural traditions. The indigenous language, Maltese, is of Semitic origin. Roman Catholicism is the state religion, but other faiths are permitted.

Malta has few natural resources, and its terrain is not well adapted to agriculture. Historically, the country was dependent upon British military installations and expenditures, which were curtailed upon expiry of the 1972 Anglo-Maltese defense agreement in March 1979. The most important industry was ship repair, but the government sought to encourage diversification while at the same time soliciting external budgetary support in lieu of the former British subsidy. These efforts were initially successful, the economy yielding in 1974–1979 double-digit rates of real per capita growth, comfortable current account surpluses, and declining unemployment. Growth slowed thereafter but remained at a healthy annual average of 5.3 percent in the decade 1985–1994 as Malta established itself as a major freight entrepôt, financial center, and tourist destination. However, budget deficits have been significant in recent years, prompting the government installed in October 1996 to restrain spending, accelerate the privatization of several state-run enterprises, and expand economic incentives designed to attract foreign investment and promote industrial development. GDP growth was reported at 4.9 percent in 1997 and 3.4 percent in 1998. Meanwhile, the new government elected in September 1998 pledged to pursue membership in the European Union (EU), its predecessor having preferred negotiations toward a free trade agreement with the EU rather than full-fledged accession. In 1999 the government introduced austerity measures to reduce the 8.6 percent budget deficit as part of efforts to join the EU and adopt the euro as its currency. The budget introduced a 15 percent value-added tax on petroleum, along with other revenue-enhancing measures. Meanwhile, real GDP growth of 4.0 percent and inflation of 2.1 percent were reported for 1999, with unemployment running at about 5.3 percent at the

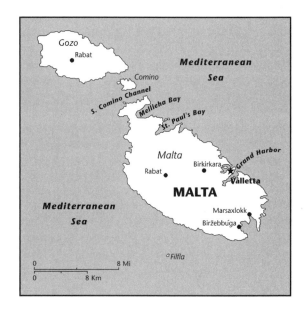

Political Status: Became independent within
the Commonwealth on September 21, 1964;
republic declared by constitutional amendment
on December 13, 1974.

Area: 122 sq. mi. (316 sq. km.).

Population: 397,296 (2002C); 406,000
(2005E).

Major Urban Centers (2005E):
VALLETTA (7,100), Birkirkawa (22,600),
Sliema (12,700).

Official Languages: Maltese, English; Italian is
also widely spoken.

Monetary Unit: Maltese Lira (official rate July
1, 2006: 1 lira = $2.98US). (Following its
entry into the European Union in 2004, Malta
announced plans for adopting the euro as its
official currency by 2008.)

President: Edward (Eddie) FENECH ADAMI
(Nationalist Party); elected on March 29, 2004,
to a five-year term by the House of
Representatives and sworn in on April 4,
succeeding Guido de MARCO (Nationalist
Party).

Prime Minister: Lawrence GONZI (Nationalist
Party); sworn in on March 23, 2004, to replace
Eddie FENECH ADAMI (Nationalist Party),
who resigned the same day in order to run for
the presidency. (Fenech Adami had been sworn
in on April 15, 2003, following legislative
elections on April 12. His original term as
prime minister began on September 6, 1998,
after the election of September 5, when he
succeeded Alfred SANT [Malta Labour
Party].)

end of the year. GDP expansion for 2000 was estimated at 3.8 percent.

Malta's GDP declined by 1.2 percent in 2001 as a
result of the September 11 terrorist attacks and their
subsequent impact on travel and tourism. By 2002
the economy began to grow, and GDP increased by
2.8 percent in 2003 and 1.5 percent (estimated) in
2005. Unemployment remained relatively steady
at slightly more than 5 percent in 2001–2003,
but increased to approximately 7.5 percent in
2005.

Malta's entry into the EU in 2004 was expected
to improve the nation's economy on a variety of
fronts. Already some two-thirds of Malta's trade
was with the EU states, and EU membership was
expected to improve tourism for the islands and increase manufacturing exports (the two main components of the Maltese economy). In addition, the
government pledged to undertake a program of
privatization and enhanced tax administration as
a precondition for membership. In return, Malta
was granted exemptions designed to protect several economic sectors, primarily agriculture and
industry.

Government and Politics

Political Background

Malta has a long history of conquest and rule by
foreign powers. It first came under British control
in 1800, possession being formalized by the Treaty
of Paris in 1814, and its strategic importance being enhanced by the opening of the Suez Canal
in 1869. Ruled by a military governor throughout the 19th century, it experienced an unsuccessful period of internal autonomy immediately following World War I. Autonomy was abolished in
1933, and Malta reverted to its former status as a
Crown Colony. A more successful attempt at internal self-government was initiated in 1947, after Malta had been awarded the George Cross by
Britain for its resistance to Axis air assaults during
World War II. In 1956 the islanders voted three to
one in favor of full integration with Britain, as proposed by the ruling Malta Labour Party (MLP) led
by Dominic (Dom) MINTOFF. However, British
reservations (combined with a change of government in Malta) resulted in 1962 in the submission
of a formal request for independence within the
Commonwealth by Prime Minister Giorgio BORG
OLIVIER of the Nationalist Party (NP), who led
the islands to full sovereignty on September 21,
1964. The first postindependence change of government came in the 1971 election, which returned
the MLP and Mintoff to power. Disenchanted
with the British connection, Mintoff led Malta to

republican status within the Commonwealth in December 1974.

The MLP retained its legislative majority in the elections of September 1976 and December 1981. The results of the 1981 poll were challenged by the opposition NP, which had won a slim majority of the popular vote and, after being rebuffed in an appeal for electoral reform, instituted a boycott of parliamentary proceedings. In a countermove to the boycott, Prime Minister Mintoff declared the 31 Nationalist-held seats vacant on April 26, 1982, with the NP subsequently refusing to make by-election nominations. In March 1983, however, NP leader Edward FENECH ADAMI agreed to resume parliamentary activity on the basis of a commitment from Mintoff to discuss changes in the electoral law.

The interparty talks were suspended in July 1983 in the wake of increasingly violent antigovernment activity and the adoption of a legislative measure that prohibited the charging of fees by private schools and indirectly authorized the confiscation of upwards of 75 percent of the assets of the Maltese Catholic Church. During 1984 the contest erupted into a major conflict between church and state, with the Catholic hierarchy ordering the closure of all schools under its jurisdiction (half the island's total) in September. The schools reopened two months later, with Vatican officials agreeing in April 1985 to the introduction of free education over a three-year period in return for government assurances of noninterference in teaching and participation in a joint commission to discuss remaining church-state issues, including those regarding church property.

Meanwhile, on December 22, 1984, Mintoff had stepped down as prime minister in favor of Karmenu MIFSUD BONNICI, who made no ministerial changes in a government sworn in two days later. The church-state dispute was officially resolved in July 1986, while in January 1987 both the MLP and the NP supported constitutional changes that included modification of the electoral law to ensure that a party winning a majority of the popular vote would have a parliamentary majority.

In a bitterly contested election on May 9, 1987, Labour, as in 1981, won 34 of 65 legislative seats, but, after 16 years in office, lost control of the government because the NP obtained a popular majority and was therefore awarded additional seats. NP leader Fenech Adami was invested as prime minister on May 12. Earlier, at the conclusion of her five-year term on February 15, President Agatha BARBARA had yielded her office, on an acting basis, to the speaker of the House of Representatives, Paul XUEREB. Xuereb retained the position until the House elected the NP's Dr. Vincent TABONE as his successor on April 4, 1989.

In the election of February 22, 1992, the NP won 34 legislative seats with a vote share of 51.8 percent, while the MLP obtained 31 seats with 46.5 percent. Five days later, Fenech Adami formed a new government in which all senior ministers were retained, although in a number of cases with altered portfolios.

On April 4, 1994, former NP leader Ugo MIFSUD BONNICI was sworn in as Malta's fifth president, having been elected by the House of Representatives the same day. Meanwhile, as part of its strategy of preparing for accession to the EU, the government in 1994 enacted legislation that authorized a 15 percent value-added tax (VAT), starting in 1995. This and other government economic policies provoked much labor unrest, including a one-day general strike, backed by the MLP, on October 24, 1994. In March 1995 Fenech Adami carried out a major cabinet reshuffle, bringing in a younger generation of ministers as part of a strategy to retain power in the next general election. However, the prime minister's decision to call an early election on October 26, 1996, proved a miscalculation. Labour confounded the pundits by outpolling the NP 50.7 to 47.8 percent in fiercely contested balloting that drew a record turnout of 97 percent. Although the NP won 34 elective seats to Labour's 31, the 1987 constitutional amendment entitled Labour to 4 additional seats so that it commanded a parliamentary majority. The new Labour government was sworn in on October 28 under the premiership of Alfred SANT, a Harvard-educated former physicist who had headed his party since 1992.

Fulfilling one of its major domestic campaign promises, the Sant government in July 1997 abolished the VAT. Subsequently, the opposition argued that this reversal had contributed to the growing economic problems of budget deficits, rising inflation, and increased unemployment. Meanwhile, in early 1998, union leaders expressed concern over proposed cutbacks in government spending. Subsequently, the government's 1-seat majority evaporated when former prime minister Mintoff, Sant's aging MLP predecessor, deserted the party on two votes relating to a development project in Mintoff's district. Plagued by resignations, bitter attacks from Mintoff, and dissatisfaction within the MLP over Sant's failure to follow traditional patronage policies and his perceived drift to the right, the prime minister called for an election on September 5, 1998, three years early. The NP emerged with 35 seats to the MLP's 30, a result that Sant attributed to his widely unpopular policy of having steeply increased utility rates. The NP's Fenech Adami was once again named prime minister, and he formed a new government on September 8.

On March 29, 1999, voting along straight party lines, the House of Representatives elected the NP's Guido DE MARCO, until then the deputy prime minister and foreign minister, as president.

Membership in the EU became one of the main priorities of Fenech Adami's government. In response to criticism from the MLP, Fenech Adami called a nonbinding referendum on EU membership in 2003. Voting took place on March 8, 2003, with the NP leading the promembership campaign and the MLP vigorously campaigning against accession. Voter turnout was 91 percent with 53.65 percent in favor of EU membership and 46.35 percent against. Sant and other MLP leaders argued that the closeness of the vote, when combined with 9 percent of the eligible voters who did not cast a ballot, meant that the majority of the Maltese did not support membership.

In response, Fenech Adami called for elections on April 12, 2003, just four days before Malta was to sign the accession treaty, to affirm support for membership. In these legislative elections, the turnout was 96.2 percent. The NP received 51.8 percent of the vote and 35 seats; the MLP, 47.5 percent and 30 seats; and the AD, 0.7 percent and no seats. As a result of the loss, Sant did not seek reelection as leader of the MLP. Malta signed

the EU accession treaty on April 16, formally joining on May 1, 2004.

On the eve of presidential elections, Fenech Adami resigned as prime minister on March 23, 2004. He was replaced by Lawrence GONZI (NP), who reshuffled and expanded the cabinet to form a new government that was sworn in on the same day as Fenech Adami's resignation. Fenech Adami was elected president by the House of Representatives on March 29, 2004. He was sworn into office on April 4.

Constitution and Government

The 1964 constitution established Malta as an independent parliamentary monarchy within the Commonwealth, with executive power exercised by a prime minister and cabinet, both appointed by the governor general but chosen from and responsible to Parliament. By constitutional amendment, the country became a republic on December 13, 1974, with an indirectly elected president of Maltese nationality replacing the British monarch as de jure head of state. The president serves a five-year term, as does the prime minister, subject to the retention of a legislative majority. The Parliament consists of a unicameral House of Representatives elected on the basis of proportional representation every five years, assuming no prior dissolution. Under an amendment adopted in February 1987, the party winning a majority of the popular vote is awarded additional House seats, if needed to secure a legislative majority. The judicial system encompasses a Constitutional Court, a Court of Appeal, a Criminal Court of Appeal, and lower courts. Judges for the Constitutional Court and the Court of Appeal are appointed by the president. There is little established local government; however, the island of Gozo is administered by an elected Civic Council in conjunction with a commissioner appointed by the central government.

Foreign Relations

Subsequent to independence, Maltese foreign policy centered primarily on the country's relationship with Great Britain and thus with the North Atlantic Treaty Organization (NATO). A ten-year

Mutual Defense and Assistance Agreement, signed in 1964, was abrogated in 1971 by the Mintoff government. Under a new seven-year agreement, concluded in 1972 after months of negotiation, the rental payments for use of military facilities by Britain were tripled. Early in 1973 Mintoff reopened the issue, asking additional payment to compensate for devaluation of the British pound, but settled for a token adjustment pending British withdrawal from the facilities in March 1979. Rebuffed in an effort to obtain a quadripartite guarantee of Maltese neutrality and a five-year budgetary subsidy from France, Italy, Algeria, and Libya, the Mintoff government turned to Libya. During ceremonies marking the British departure, the Libyan leader, Col. Mu'ammar al-Qadhafi, promised "unlimited" support. In the course of the following year, however, the relationship cooled because of overlapping claims to offshore oil rights, and in September 1980 an agreement was concluded with Italy whereby Rome guaranteed Malta's future neutrality, promising a combination of loans and subsidies totaling $95 million over a five-year period. In 1981 Malta also signed neutrality agreements with Algeria, France, and the Soviet Union, agreeing in March to provide the last with facilities for oil bunkering.

In December 1984 Prime Minister Mintoff announced that the defense and aid agreement with Italy would be permitted to lapse in favor of a new alignment with Libya, which would undertake to train Maltese forces to withstand "threats or acts of aggression" against the island's sovereignty or integrity. Six months later the maritime issue was resolved, the International Court of Justice establishing a boundary 18 nautical miles north of a line equidistant between the two countries.

In March 1986 Prime Minister Mifsud Bonnici met with Colonel Qadhafi in Tripoli, in what was described as an effort to ease the confrontation between Libya and the United States in the Gulf of Sidra. In August the Maltese leader stated that his government had warned Libya of the approach of "unidentified planes" prior to the April attack on Tripoli and Benghazi, although there was no indication that Libyan authorities had acted on the information.

Upon assuming office in May 1987, Prime Minister Fenech Adami indicated that the military clauses of the 1984 agreement with Libya would not be renewed, although all other commitments would be continued. Cooperation between the two countries at the political and economic levels was reaffirmed in 1988, with Libya renewing its $38 million oil supply pact with Malta late in the year.

A member of the United Nations (UN), the Conference on (later Organization for) Security and Cooperation in Europe (CSCE/OSCE), and a number of other international organizations, Malta concluded an association agreement with the European Community (EC) in 1970 and in July 1990 applied for full membership. The government's perseverance in the face of initial reservations in Brussels was rewarded by a decision of the EU summit in Essen in December 1994 that Malta would be included in the next round of enlargement negotiations. While maintaining its neutrality, Malta also joined NATO's Partnership for Peace (PfP) program in April 1995.

Foreign policy issues featured prominently in the October 1996 parliamentary election, which returned the MLP to power, after nearly a decade in opposition. The MLP opposed Maltese accession to the EU in the near future and to membership in NATO's PfP program on the grounds that it violated Malta's 1987 constitutional commitment to neutrality and nonalignment. On taking office, the new Labour prime minister, Alfred Sant, immediately suspended Malta's participation in the PfP, contending that Malta could best promote the stability of the Mediterranean region by a policy of neutrality and stressing that this stance was neither anti-European nor anti-American. He also made it clear, with reference to past Labour governments' close relations with Libya, that Malta would continue to observe UN sanctions imposed on Tripoli over the Lockerbie affair, while expressing the hope that the sanctions would soon be lifted so that Maltese-Libyan commercial relations could be developed.

In regard to the EU, the new government insisted it was "still not time" for Malta to pursue full membership because of the "fragility" of the nation's "economic and industrial structure." However, the administration did not rule out the possibility of joining the EU eventually. Meanwhile, the Sant government and EU officials launched talks toward establishment of a "free trade zone."

Almost immediately following his victory in the snap election of September 1998, Prime Minister Fenech Adami accelerated Malta's pursuit of EU membership, and in February 1999 the European Commission recommended that accession talks with Malta start later in the year. On April 16, 2003, Malta signed the EU accession treaty, along with nine other aspirant countries. However, Fenech Adami did not reverse his predecessor's decision to withdraw from NATO's PfP.

Current Issues

In 1999 Prime Minister Fenech Adami identified EU membership and the problematic condition of government finances as the key issues for his government. Following Malta's reintroduction of the VAT, in February 1999 the European Commission recommended opening talks on EU accession.

The NP government in 2000–2002 continued its efforts to bring the Maltese economy in line with EU standards, sparking further attacks from the MLP, which argued that EU accession in 2004 would freeze crucial foreign investment, decimate Malta's manufacturing and agricultural sectors, and raise administrative costs.

Malta signed the EU accession treaty in April 2003 and the country formally joined the EU on May 1, 2004. European parliamentary elections on June 12, 2004, showed that EU membership remained a contentious issue. Each of the major parties ran a full slate of candidates, and there were a number of fringe and independent candidates as well. The MLP, which ran a euro-skeptic campaign, outpolled the ruling NP, and the AD performed much better than expected. The MLP received 48.4 percent of the vote and three seats, and the NP, 39.8 percent and two seats. The AD gained no seats but had its highest electoral vote in history at 9.3 percent. All new members of the EU are now expected, as a condition of entry, to work toward abandoning their local currencies in favor of the euro. As a step in this direction, it was announced

on April 29, 2005, that the Maltese lira would participate in the European Central Bank's (ECB) Exchange Rate Mechanism II. This move mandated strong fiscal discipline, together with a degree of influence by the ECB in Malta's financial affairs. (As of mid-2006 Malta remained committed to the goal of adopting the euro at the beginning of 2008, although the EU warned that preparations in Malta were not proceeding as quickly as anticipated.)

In March 2006 it was announced that Malta would hold talks with Italy and Libya to discuss joint oil exploration in the Mediterranean. As a result of a previous ruling by the International Court of Justice, Malta had lost claim to some offshore territory to Tunisia. Malta's strategic location has also played an important role in another recently developing issue—the arrival of a wave of illegal immigrants from Africa, many attempting to make their way through Malta to the European mainland. Housing (or sometimes confining) the immigrants has stretched the nation's resources and reportedly generated resentment within the Maltese population.

Political Parties

Government Party

Nationalist Party—NP (*Partit Nazzjonalista*—PN). Advocating the retention of Roman Catholic and European principles, the NP brought Malta to independence. It formerly supported alignment with NATO and membership in the EC, but because of the constitutional pact with Labour in February 1987 adopted a neutral foreign policy. The party obtained 50.9 percent of the vote in the 1981 election without, however, winning control of the legislature. In the 1987 balloting it again obtained only a minority of elective seats, but under the February constitutional amendment was permitted to form a government because of its popular majority. The Nationalists retained power in the 1992 election but were unexpectedly defeated in October 1996, when their share of the popular vote slipped from 51.8 to 47.8 percent. The NP returned to power in the election of September 1998 with a vote share of 51.8 percent. In the April 2003

Cabinet

As of September 1, 2006

Prime Minister	Lawrence Gonzi
Deputy Prime Minister	Tonio Borg

Ministers

Competitiveness and Communications	Censu Galea
Education, Youth, and Employment	Louis Galea
Family and Social Solidarity	Dolores Cristina [f]
Finance	Lawrence Gonzi
Foreign Affairs	Michael Frendo
Gozo (the island of)	Giovanna Debono [f]
Health, the Elderly, and Community Care	Louis Deguara
Investment, Industry, and Information Technology	Austin Gatt
Justice and Home Affairs	Tonio Borg
Resources and Infrastructure	Ninu Zammit
Rural Affairs and the Environment	George Pullicino
Tourism and Culture	Francis Zammit Dimech
Urban Development and Roads	Jesmond Mugliett

[f] = female

Note: All of the above are members of the Nationalist Party.

elections, the NP won 51.8 percent and 35 seats. In March 2004 Fenech Adami was elected president, and NP Vice Chair Lawrence Gonzi became prime minister.

Leaders: Edward FENECH ADAMI (President and Party Chair), Lawrence GONZI (Prime Minister and Vice Chair), Joe SALIBA (General Secretary).

Opposition Parties

Malta Labour Party—MLP (*Partit Laburista*). In power from 1971 to 1987, the MLP advocated a socialist and "progressive" policy, including anticolonialism in international affairs, a neutralist foreign policy, and emphasis on Malta's role as "a bridge of peace between Europe and the Arab world." The party has periodically complained of intrusion by the Catholic Church in political and economic affairs. In the election of December 12, 1981, its share of the popular vote fell to 49.1 percent from 51.2 percent in 1976, but without loss of its three-seat majority in the House of Representatives; its vote share fell further to 48.8 percent in 1987, resulting in a loss of government control because of the constitutional revision. The decline continued to 46.5 percent in the 1992 balloting, after which Karmenu Mifsud Bonnici announced his retirement as party leader. His successor, Alfred Sant, initiated a modernization of the party's organization and policies, while maintaining the MLP's commitment to neutrality and opposition to EU accession. Labour returned to power in the October 1996 election, winning 50.7 percent of the popular vote, but was ousted when it secured only 47 percent in the September 1998 balloting. In the 2003 elections the MLP received 47.5 percent of the vote and 30 seats. As a result of the election, Sant chose not to seek reelection for his leadership post in the MLP.

Leaders: Stefan ZRINZO AZZOPARDI (President), Jason MICALLEF (General Secretary), Alfred SANT (Party Leader), Michael FALZON (Deputy Leader).

Democratic Alternative—DA (*Alternattiva Demokratika*—AD). An ecologically oriented grouping launched in 1989, the AD, also referenced as the Maltese Green Party, ran a distant third in the 1992 balloting, securing no legislative seats on a vote share of 1.7 percent. It was again unsuccessful in 1996, when its vote share slipped to 1.5 percent, and in September 1998, when it won 1.2 percent of the vote. In the 2003 elections the DA received only 0.7 percent of the vote.

Leaders: Harry VASSALLO (Chair), Mario MALLIA (Deputy Chair), Stephen CACHIA (General Secretary).

Legislature

The **House of Representatives** (*Il-Kamra Tad-Deputati*) consists of 65 elective members returned for a five-year term (subject to dissolution) on the basis of proportional representation applied in 13 electoral districts, with additional members being designated if a party obtaining an overall majority of the popular vote fails to win a majority of the elective seats. In the election of September 5, 1998, the Nationalist Party (NP) won 35 seats, and the Malta Labour Party (MLP) won 30. In legislative elections on April 12, 2003, the NP won 35 seats, and the MLP won 30.

Speaker: Anton TABONE.

Communications

Press

The following are Maltese-language dailies published in Valletta, unless otherwise noted: *It-Tóorca* (*The Torch*, 30,000), weekly; *L-Orizzont* (25,000); *Il-Mument* (25,000), weekly; *The Times* (23,000 daily, 35,000 Sunday), in English; *In-Nazzjon Taghna* (20,000); *Lehen Is-Sewwa* (10,000), Catholic weekly; *The Malta Independent* (18,000), in English; and *Alternattiva Zghazagu*, a pro-DA weekly. Business newspapers include *The Malta Business Weekly* and *The Malta Financial and Business Times*.

News Agencies

There is no domestic facility; a number of foreign services, including ANSA, *Agencia EFE*, AP, and Reuters, maintain bureaus in Valletta.

Broadcasting and Computing

In May 1991 a broadcasting bill restructured Xandir Malta, which theretofore provided radio and television services under supervision of the Malta Broadcasting Authority, into an independent corporation; the bill also authorized the launching of ten private commercial radio stations, a number of community radio stations, and a cable television network. Radio broadcasts in several languages are received via Deutsche Welle Relay Malta, while Italian television programs can be received by means of a booster in Sicily. In early 1988 an agreement was concluded with Libya for the launching of a joint regional broadcasting station, the Voice of the Mediterranean. Collapse of the funding agreement caused the station to leave the air at the end of 2004. There were approximately 200,000 television receivers and 110,000 personal computers serving 150,000 Internet users in 2003. By 2005 the number of Internet users had grown to over 300,000 with over 10,000 Internet hosts.

Intergovernmental Representation

Ambassador to the U.S.
John LOWELL

U.S. Ambassador to Malta
Molly BORDONARO

Permanent Representative to the UN
Victor CAMILLERI

IGO Memberships (Non-UN)
CEUR, CWTH, EBRD, EIB, Eurocontrol, EU, Interpol, IOM, NAM, OSCE, PCA, WCO, WTO

MOLDOVA

REPUBLIC OF MOLDOVA

Republicii Moldova

The Country

Located in Eastern Europe, Moldova is bordered on the north, east, and south by Ukraine and on the west by Romania. The breakaway region of Transdnestr lies between the Dnestr (Nistru) River and Ukraine. Approximately 64 percent of the national population is Moldovan, 14 percent Ukrainian, 13 percent Russian, and 4 percent Gagauz (Turkified ethnic Bulgarians of Christian Orthodox faith).

A mild climate and fertile soil permit the cultivation of a wide variety of crops, including grains, sugar beets, fruits, and vegetables, with food processing the leading industry. Metalworking and the manufacture of electrical equipment are also of importance. Excluding Transdnestr, agriculture contributes 25–30 percent of GDP and 40 percent of employment, while industry accounts for 20–25 GDP and under 20 percent of employment. Principal exports are foodstuffs, beverages (notably wine), and tobacco. Russia is the leading trade partner, followed by Romania, Ukraine, and Belarus.

Political and economic transition yielded a slump in GDP of 29 percent in 1992, 9 percent in 1993, and 22 percent in 1994, accompanied by inflation that spiraled to 2,200 percent in 1992 before falling to 840 percent in 1993 and to 115 percent in 1994. Following the financial crisis in Russia in the summer of 1998, Moldova's economy suffered a setback, with GDP falling 6.5 percent after having registered its first growth, 1.6 percent, since independence in 1997. Although consumer price inflation was comparatively tame, at under 8 percent, government debt reached unsustainable heights, exports declined, and, in November, the leu lost almost half its value in one day, creating the most severe currency crisis since independence. In 1999 Moldova suffered another setback, with GDP down by about 4 percent and inflation exceeding 40 percent. The economy recovered in 2000, with growth of 1.9 percent and with inflation halved, and late in the year the International Monetary Fund (IMF) and World Bank agreed to resume lending, conditioned upon Parliament's passing a debt restructuring plan that the government had worked out with the European Bank for Reconstruction and Development (EBRD).

Political Status: Formerly the Moldavian Soviet Socialist Republic, a constituent republic of the Union of Soviet Socialist Republics; declared independence as the Republic of Moldova on August 27, 1991; became sovereign member of the Commonwealth of Independent States on December 21, 1991; new constitution approved on July 28, 1994, and entered into force on August 27.

Area: 13,000 sq. mi. (33,670 sq. km.).

Population: 3,388,071 (2004C); 3,333,000 (2005E).

Major Urban Centers (2005E): CHIȘINĂU (formerly Kishinev, 596,000), Tiraspol (185,000), Tighina (125,00), Bălți (123,000).

Official Language: Moldovan.

Monetary Unit: Moldovan leu (official rate July 1, 2006: 13.34 lei = $1US).

President: Vladimir VORONIN (Party of Communists of the Republic of Moldova); elected by the Parliament on April 4, 2001, and reelected on April 4, 2005, succeeding Petru LUCINSCHI (nonparty).

Prime Minister: Vasile TARLEV (nonparty); nominated by the president on April 11, 2001, and approved by Parliament on April 19, succeeding Dumitru BRAGHIȘ (nonparty).

and sold for scrap, despite the fact that crops have failed for lack of water. Roughly half the people live off subsistence farming, and those who do produce a surplus have difficulty getting it to market, as the country's road network is deficient. With an average wage of only about $70 per month, Moldova reportedly has the lowest standard of living of the former communist states of Europe. One clear result of the economic difficulties is that Moldova has experienced a net loss in population, with an estimated 600,000 Moldovans leaving the country to look for work.

It is, in fact, remittances back home from workers who have left the country that have largely funded the investments that have fueled the country's economic growth.

While the IMF sees encouraging signs in Moldova, the organization remains concerned about the government's lack of progress on structural reforms. "The privatization program has stalled, while corruption remains widespread and government weak," according to a recent Public Information Notice released by the IMF. "Government interference in the private sector—including formal and informal restrictions on exports of certain agricultural goods—casts doubt over the authorities' commitment to market-oriented reforms."

Government and Politics

Political Background

Historic Moldavia lay at the passageway from southern Europe to western Asia and hence was the object of numerous invasions and territorial realignments. Present-day Moldova (the name adopted in June 1990) encompasses the territory of the pre-1940 Moldavian Autonomous Soviet Socialist Republic, which was located within the Ukraine and which was joined to all but the northern and southern portions of Bessarabia upon detachment of the latter from Romania in 1940. With its redrawn borders, the redefined Moldavian SSR became a constituent republic of the USSR.

Since 2000, Moldova's economy has improved steadily. GDP rose 7.8 percent in 2002, although it dropped back to 6.6 percent in 2003 before rebounding to 7.4 percent in 2004. At the same time, inflation had dropped from 15.7 percent in 2003 to 12.6 percent in 2004. The IMF projects further drops in inflation to 10 percent for 2005 and 9 percent for 2006.

The World Bank notes that, between 2000 and 2004, Moldova's GDP had increased by more than 30 percent, and the poverty rate had been cut by more than half.

While Moldova's economy has stabilized somewhat since 2000, it is still in terrible shape. Water pipes that once irrigated fields have been dug up

On July 29, 1989, Mircea SNEGUR was elected chair of the Presidium of the republican Supreme Soviet. Although a member of the Politburo of the Communist Party of Moldova (*Partidul Comunist din Moldova*—PCM), he subsequently endorsed the nationalist demands of the Popular Front of Moldova (*Frontul Popular din Moldova*—FPM), which had been launched earlier in the year.

On August 19, 1990, the Turkic-speaking Gagauz minority in the southern part of the country responded to the prospect of union with Romania by announcing the formation of a "Republic of Gagauzia." On September 2 the Russian majority in the eastern Dnestr valley followed suit, proclaiming a "Dnestr Soviet Republic" (later dropping the "Soviet" descriptor). The Supreme Soviet thereupon went into emergency session, naming Snegur to the new post of executive president on September 3 and empowering him to introduce direct rule "in regions not obeying the constitution." Despite continued unrest, including a pitched battle between police and secessionist militia at a bridge over the Dnestr River on November 2, the situation eased late in the year after the issuance of a threat by Soviet President Mikhail Gorbachev to intervene.

On August 22, 1991, in the wake of the failed Moscow coup against USSR President Gorbachev, PCM First Secretary Grigory YEREMEY resigned from the Politburo of the Communist Party of the Soviet Union (CPSU), and on August 23 President Snegur, who had opposed the Moscow hardliners, effectively banned the PCM. On August 27 Moldova declared its independence and two days later established diplomatic relations with Romania, although those favoring speedy reunification were no longer in ascendancy. In October 1991 the leading pan-Romanian FPM faction came out in opposition to Snegur and called for a boycott of the presidential election set for December 8. Snegur was nevertheless reelected as the sole candidate in a turnout officially given as 82.9 percent, this time drawing his main political support from the pro-independence Agrarian Democratic Party of Moldova (*Partidul Democrat Agrar din Moldova*—PDAM), and on December 21 Moldova became a

sovereign member of the Commonwealth of Independent States (CIS).

In March 1992 ethnic conflict again erupted in the eastern region, with Igor SMIRNOV, the president of the self-proclaimed Dnestr Republic, calling for mobilization of all men between ages 18 and 45. Concurrently, his deputy, Aleksandr KARAMAN, asserted the "very real danger . . . of a Moldovan variant of Yugoslavia" and insisted that the only viable solution would be a confederal republic in which Moldovans, Russians, and Gagauz would have separate autonomous territories. For his part, President Snegur offered special economic status to the Transdnestr region but rejected the concept of a separate republic.

On January 7, 1993, in response to pressure from Romanian officials for reunification, President Snegur called for a referendum on the proposal, which public opinion polls had shown to be supported by no more than 10 percent of the population. A collateral appeal by the president for strengthened Moldovan independence provoked a deep split between pro- and anti-unification deputies, the referendum call ultimately being defeated by one vote. On August 3 Snegur was granted decree powers for the ensuing year to facilitate economic reforms, and in February 1994 his administration indicated that it sought accommodation with Transdnestr on the basis of substantial autonomy for the region, including its own legislative body and the use of distinctive political symbols.

A parliamentary election on February 27, 1994, yielded an overall majority for the PDAM and was followed on March 6 by a referendum in which a reported 95.4 percent of participants voted for maintaining Moldova's separation from both Romania and Russia. A further national unity government under the continued premiership of PDAM's Andrey SANGHELI obtained legislative approval on April 5, its first major act being the introduction of a new devolutionary constitution in August, effectively removing union with Romania as an option, except as a long-term aspiration.

Fortified by an IMF loan, the Moldovan government in March 1995 embarked on a major privatization program intended to dispose of some 1,500 state enterprises in 1995–1996 by a combination of direct sale and issuance of share vouchers to the public. However, resistance to privatization, especially to vouchers, remained prevalent within the state bureaucracy, while opposition parties forecast an outbreak of widespread corruption. Principally because of such opposition within the PDAM, President Snegur in July launched the Party of Rebirth and Conciliation of Moldova (*Partidul Renaşterii şi Concilierii din Moldova*—PRCM).

Although Prime Minister Sangheli was able to announce on August 1, 1995, that the five-year Gagauz conflict was over (see Constitution and government, below), the Transdnestr problem remained more intractable. Seeking a resolution of the latter impasse, President Snegur entered into direct talks with Smirnov, but little progress was made in 1995. On December 24 a territorial referendum yielded an 82.7 percent majority in favor of a draft independence constitution and of separate membership in the CIS. Although the constitution was promulgated in January 1996, the Moldovan government's quest for a political accommodation with the Dnestr Republic leadership was boosted on January 19 when President Snegur secured the signatures of his Russian and Ukrainian counterparts on a joint statement asserting that the Transdnestrian region was part of Moldova but should have special status. Further talks between Snegur and Smirnov culminated in an agreement on June 17 defining the region as "a state-territorial formation in the form of a republic within Moldova's internationally recognized borders." This tortuous wording appeared to satisfy both sides' core demands, although detailed implementation and ratification were expected to be difficult processes. Meanwhile, withdrawal of the Russian 14th Army proceeded slowly, with the Russian military authorities citing various hindrances.

On the domestic political front, President Snegur launched his campaign for reelection in November 1996. A key feature of his platform was that Moldova should move to a more presidential form of government, particularly in respect to authority to appoint and dismiss ministers.

The president also faced obstruction from the opposition-dominated Parliament, which in February voted down a presidential proposal to change "Moldovan" to "Romanian" as the constitutional descriptor of the official language.

Backed by a PRCM-initiated "Civic Movement," Snegur headed the poll in the first round of presidential elections held on November 17, 1996, winning 38.7 percent of the vote against eight other candidates. In second place, with 27.7 percent, came Petru LUCINSCHI, the parliamentary speaker and unofficial PDAM candidate. Lucinschi heavily outpolled the official PDAM nominee, Prime Minister Sangheli, who managed only 9.5 percent and was relegated to fourth place, behind Vladimir VORONIN of the Party of Communists of the Republic of Moldova (*Partidul Comuniştilor din Republica Moldova*—PCRM). Enlivened by a phone-tapping scandal and PDAM allegations that the president's supporters were attempting to rig the outcome, the second round of voting on December 1 featured a runoff between Snegur and Lucinschi, with the latter receiving the formal endorsement not only of the PDAM, but also of the PCRM. The outcome was a decisive victory for Lucinschi, who obtained 54 percent of the vote. Prime Minister Sangheli submitted his resignation on December 3, but the Parliament asked him and his cabinet ministers to continue in office on an acting basis. After Lucinschi was inaugurated on January 15, 1997, he nominated Ion CIUBUC, an economist, to succeed Sangheli. On January 24 the Parliament approved the new government, whose members were selected, according to Ciubuc, not in regard to their political affiliation but rather for their "professional" abilities. The new prime minister pledged that his administration would focus on economic reforms.

Balloting for a new Parliament was held on March 22, 1998, with the PCRM winning a plurality of 40 seats, followed by the pro-Snegur Democratic Convention of Moldova (*Convenţia Democrată din Moldova*—CDM) with 26 seats, the pro-Lucinschi bloc For a Democratic and Prosperous Moldova (*Pentru o Moldovă Democratică şi Prosperă*—PMDP) with 24 seats, and the Party of Democratic Forces (*Partidul Forţelor Democratice*—PFD) with 11 seats. A center-right coalition consisting of the CDM, PMDP, and PFD, called the Alliance for Democracy and Reforms (*Alianţa pentru Democraţie şi Reforme*—ADR), formed a new government on April 21, with Ciubuc as premier. However, unable to stem a growing economic crisis, Ciubuc resigned on February 1, 1999, leaving the ADR deadlocked over his successor. President Lucinschi advanced Serafim URECHEAN for prime minister; however, the prospective premier's effort to form a government of technocrats failed, and he withdrew on February 17. Two days later the president nominated Deputy Prime Minister Ion STURZA for the premiership, and Sturza's cabinet was initially reported to have been approved by 51 legislators in a confidence vote on March 3. However, the Constitutional Court ruled the vote invalid, in that the required majority was 52 votes (50 percent of the 101 legislators, plus 1). Therefore, a new confidence motion was presented on March 12, the government needing an absentee ballot from Ilie ILASCU, a legislator imprisoned in the Dnestr Republic since 1992, to secure a total of 52 votes. (The PCM promised to challenge the absentee ballot, which it alleged to be a forgery.)

The Sturza government fell on November 9, 1999, when the Christian Democrats (*Frontul Popular Creştin Democrat*—FPCD) and a handful of independents (four of whom had left the PMDP a month earlier) joined the Communists in passing a vote of no confidence, citing the government's economic failures. The move followed the defeat several days earlier of a government-sponsored bill to privatize the wine and tobacco industries, rejection of which caused the IMF and the World Bank to suspend release of further loans and credits.

What remained of the former governing alliance, the ADR, broke apart in April 2000 when the principal component of the PMDP, Parliament Speaker Dumitru DIACOV's Movement for a Democratic and Prosperous Moldova (*Mişcarea o Moldovă Democratică şi Prosperă*—MMDP), announced its reconfiguration as the Democratic Party of Moldova (*Partidul Democrat din Moldova*—PDM) and its independence from President Lucinschi and his efforts to strengthen the presidency through constitutional amendment. The struggle over Moldova's system of government took a different direction in July, when Parliament, overriding Lucinschi's vehement veto, overwhelmingly passed constitutional changes that included indirect election of the president by the legislature. A corresponding election law promulgated in October mandated that a presidential candidate would need a three-fifths majority to secure a victory.

In December 2000 neither the PCRM's Voronin nor Pavel BARBALAT, chair of the Constitutional Court, succeeded in marshaling the 61 votes required to win the presidency. Barbalat, who was backed by Diacov's PDM, Snegur's CDM, and the Christian Democrats, repeatedly failed to break 40 votes, while Vladimir Voronin came no closer than 59 (in a third ballot on December 6). A center-right parliamentary boycott prevented a quorum and thus a fourth ballot on December 21, and on December 26 the Constitutional Court ruled that President Lucinschi had the "right and duty" to order new elections. Accordingly, he dissolved Parliament on January 12, 2001, in preparation for a general election. At the balloting of February 25, 2001, the PCRM won a clear majority of 71 seats on a 50.7 percent vote share. The only other formations to win seats were the new Braghiş Alliance (19 seats, 13.3 percent) and the Christian Democrats (11 seats, 8.3 percent). The PCRM landslide ensured the election of Voronin as Moldova's next president and also gave it enough seats to amend the constitution unilaterally.

Since 2002, in part due to pressure from the IMF and the World Bank, the Moldovan government has taken a number of steps to reform the economy and the political system. On June 6, 2002, the Parliament approved a new civil code, which was signed into law on June 11 by President Voronin. The new code was demanded by the IMF to bring the country closer to principles of a market economy. Not coincidentally, the World Bank agreed on June 20 to resume loans to Moldova, which had been suspended in 1999. The bank granted Moldova a $30 million loan for structural adjustments and released the first $10.5 million of a $25 million standby loan. In January 2004 Moldova negotiated an "action plan" with the European Union (EU) and the European Commission (EC) to bring the country closer to EU standards. The action plan involves a wide range of political, economic, and judicial reforms.

In the March 2005 parliamentary elections, the ruling Party of Moldovan Communists (PCRM) failed to win a majority, although the PCRM, with 56 seats, remained the dominant party. The opposition parties, however, threatened a boycott of the presidential vote. Since the PCRM did not win the 61 seats required to elect a president, a boycott would have resulted in new parliamentary elections if two ballots failed to elect a president. Ultimately, however, enough members of the Democratic Moldova Bloc (BMD) voted for Voronin so he was reelected on the second ballot. In the wake of his election victory, Voronin said members of the opposition would be welcome in his new government. He promised the new government would focus on European integration, economic modernization, and the development of democratic values.

Prime Minister Vasile TARLEV promised in April 2005 to form a new government as soon as possible, and he indicated that he would trim the government's staff size by 70 percent.

Despite initial overtures to opposition parties, relations between the PCRM-led government and opposition parties continued to worsen through the latter half of 2005 and into 2006. On October 13, 2005, in a strictly partisan vote, PCRM members of Parliament—which hold a majority—removed the immunity of three opposition members of Parliament prior to charging them with abuse of office.

In response, Our Moldova Alliance, the main opposition party, on November 24 joined the Social Liberal Party in calling for the impeachment of President Voronin. In a statement, the party charged the president with "breaking laws, flouting a ruling of the European Court of Human Rights, offending the Romany ethnic minority with epithets used in relation to the opposition and promoting his own candidate to the post of Chisinau mayor."

Constitution and Government

A new constitution, replacing the 1977 Soviet-era text, secured legislative approval on July 28, 1994, and entered into force on August 27 (the third anniversary of independence). It described Moldova as a "presidential, parliamentary republic" based on political pluralism and "the preservation, development, and expression of ethnic and linguistic identity," defining the state language as "Moldovan" (a close version of Romanian). Executive power continues to be vested in a president, who was directly elected until constitutional changes passed in July 2000 (over President Lucinschi's veto) transformed the country into a "parliamentary republic" and led to passage in September–October of a law establishing procedures for indirect election by the unicameral Parliament. The president names the prime minister, subject to approval by the Parliament, which is elected for a four-year term. Passage of a nonconfidence motion in the Parliament forces the resignation of the Council of Ministers. Other constitutional clauses proclaim Moldova's permanent neutrality and proscribe the stationing of foreign troops on the national territory.

The 1994 constitution authorized "special status" for both the Gagauz region in the south and the Transdnestr region, where separatist activity had broken out in 1990. Statutes providing broad autonomy to Gagauz-Yeri (Gagauzia) went into effect in February 1995, and the following month balloting was conducted to determine which villages wished to be part of the special region. Subsequently, direct elections for a 35-member regional People's Assembly were held in May–June, as was the direct election of a regional executive leader (*bashkan*), who was authorized to carry out quasi-presidential responsibilities.

Meanwhile, the status of Transdnestr remained unresolved. In December 1995 Transdnestrians overwhelmingly endorsed an independence constitution. In May 1997, however, the Moldovan and Transdnestrian leaders, meeting in Moscow, agreed to participate in a single state, although the dynamics of the region's "special status" remained to be defined. At Kyiv, Ukraine, in July 1999 Smirnov and Lucinschi signed a declaration on normalizing relations that committed both sides to a single "economic, judicial, and social sphere within Moldova's existing borders." Nevertheless, subsequent claims by Transdnestr that Chişinău was ignoring its needs and opinions soon led to a renewal of demands for independence. At present, Transdnestr's de facto republican government is led by a strong president who also serves as prime minister; under changes introduced in 2000, a 43-member, unicameral Supreme Soviet was elected on December 10, replacing a bicameral legislature.

In December 2001 Parliament passed a law on local administration that would have replaced Moldova's counties with a district system, but the Constitutional Court declared the measure unconstitutional in March 2002. In January 2003 the government approved new legislation replacing 9 provinces and 2 autonomous regions introduced in 1999 with a structure of 33 districts and 1 municipality.

Foreign Relations

Moldova's first international action following independence in 1991 was to establish diplomatic relations with Romania. On January 16, 1992, Hungary became the first foreign country to exchange ambassadors with the former Soviet republic, although some 70 others, including the United States, had by then recognized Moldovan independence. On March 2 Moldova was admitted to the UN and on April 27 was formally offered membership in the IMF and World Bank. It also joined the Conference on (later Organization for) Security and Cooperation in Europe (CSCE/OSCE).

Possible union with Romania was placed on the agenda by the creation of a parliamentary-level National Council of Reunification in late 1991, while in 1992 government-level meetings were instituted on the basis of a treaty of friendship and cooperation. A growing preference in Moldova for independence meant that by mid-1993 reunification had ceased to be a practical political option. However, spurred by Romania's eagerness to join the North Atlantic Treaty Organization (NATO) and

settle border issues, Moldova and Romania agreed in April 1997 to resume talks on a basic treaty, which was finally initialed on April 28, 2000, by the countries' foreign ministers. As of December 2002 the treaty remained unsigned, in part because Romania has refused to accept references to a separate Moldovan language.

On March 16, 1994, during a visit to Brussels for talks with officials from NATO and the EU, President Snegur signed NATO's Partnership for Peace, while the Moldovan Parliament on April 8 finally ratified membership in the CIS and its economic union. Although Moldovan participation in CIS military or monetary integration was ruled out, the CIS ratification indicated cautious alignment with Moscow, with the aim in particular of securing the long-sought departure of the Russian 14th Army from Transdnestr.

In July 1995 Moldova became the first CIS member to be admitted to the Council of Europe. In December it signed military cooperation agreements with the United States and Ukraine, having concluded a friendship and cooperation treaty with the latter in 1992. A border treaty was concluded with Ukraine in 1999, but objections from factions within the Moldovan Parliament left it unratified at the end of 2000.

In November 1996 Moldova was admitted to membership of the Central European Initiative. In 1997 the government announced its support for negotiations with the EU toward associate membership, perhaps leading eventually to full membership. Regionally, in October 1997 Moldova joined Georgia, Ukraine, and Azerbaijan in forming the GUAM group (currently GUUAM, following the addition of Uzbekistan in 1999).

In recent years, Moldova's foreign relations have directly reflected its internal conflicts to an unusual degree. With large ethnic populations who identify with Romania and Russia, relations with those two countries have been at the forefront of Moldovan foreign relations. Relations with Romania were strained over suggestions by Moldovan President Voronin shortly after he took office that "greater" Moldavia included the Romanian province of Moldavia. Romanian President Ion Iliescu on January 10, 2004, called the idea "a falsification of historical reality and an expression of revisionist inclinations." And while Moldovan Foreign Minister Andrei STRATAN said on February 26, 2004, that Moldova wanted to renew negotiations on a bilateral treaty with Romania, Romania has rejected any treaty talks. Relations with Romania eased somewhat in late 2004. On November 9 Romanian Trade Minister Vasile Radu offered to share Romania's experience in the EU integration process and offered assistance should Moldova encounter an electricity shortage.

Not coincidentally, as Moldova's relations with Romania have improved, its relations with Russia have deteriorated. While President Voronin was considered pro-Russian when he first took office, he has since then gradually adopted more anti-Russian positions, largely as a result of the conflict in Transdnestr. On April 13, 2004, Voronin emphasized that Moldova's relations with Russia were still good, with only the Transdnestr issue being a problem. Voronin said he backs Russia's bid to join the Word Trade Organization (WTO). At the same time, Russia has repeatedly declined to sign a "Declaration on Stability and Security for the Republic of Moldova" sought by Voronin. Russia maintains that such a guarantee of Moldovan sovereignty would be possible only if Moldova guaranteed a peaceful settlement of the Transdnestr issue.

Relations with Russia worsened further in January 2006, when Russia cut off supplies of natural gas to Moldova after the latter declined to accept a 100 percent increase in prices. By mid-January, the two countries agreed on a less dramatic increase in prices. In March, however, the Russian government banned the importing of wine from Moldova and Georgia, purportedly for health reasons. In fact, most analysts characterize Russia's move as retaliation for Moldova's and Georgia's position opposing Russia's entry into the WTO until Russia stops supporting separatists in those two countries and removes troops from their territory.

Moldova has also made efforts to reach beyond purely regional issues. In September 2003, for example, Moldova began participating in postwar security operations in Iraq, at the invitation of the U.S. government. On July 26, 2004, a group of 12 Moldovan demining experts left for Iraq. And on January 21, 2004, Moldova agreed to participate in UN peacekeeping operations. The country pledged to provide up to 73 soldiers for future operations.

Moldova's desire for integration with the EU received a setback on March 10, 2004, when Ivan Borisavijevic, the EC's envoy to Moldova, said that there were serious obstacles on the road to integration, including the Transdnestr conflict, corruption, poverty, and lack of genuine reforms. He estimated it might be 10–15 years before Moldova was ready for integration talks. "The reason rests in a weak economy, an underdeveloped infrastructure, few investments, and much corruption," he said.

Current Issues

The predominant current issue in Moldova remains the status of the Transdnestr region. Chişinău insists that the region remain an integral part of Moldova, while Transdnestrian leaders have fluctuated between demanding outright independence and proposing a confederal system that would feature separate governmental, military, economic, and other institutions. A draft federative plan proposed by former Russian prime minister Yevgeni Primakov in September 2000 was dismissed by Transdnestrian leader Igor Smirnov, who called for the two sides to approach each other as "independent nations." Smirnov may have been jockeying for position, but his quick rejection once again raised the question of where independence advocates were prepared to demonstrate flexibility. They also continued to insist that Russian forces remain in place, whereas in November the OSCE expressed concern that the process of withdrawing Russian troops (numbering about 2,600), as agreed at the 1999 OSCE summit in Istanbul, had yet to begin in earnest. The Russian pullout finally began in late 2001, just a week before Smirnov's December 9 reelection as Transdnestrian president. The Russian withdrawal, however, did not continue.

In 2002 the OSCE issued a draft report calling for a federalized Moldova, with parts of the country having a right to their own legislation and constitution, although the Moldovan constitution and laws would have priority. The OSCE would provide peacekeeping troops. Opposition leader Iurie ROȘCA (PPCD) called the plan "unacceptable" and said that Moldova would "finally and irreversibly disintegrate." The United States announced its support for the plan on August 2, 2002. The OSCE-sponsored talks got under way on August 22, 2002, although no progress resulted.

Russia once again promised the OSCE that it would remove its troops from Transdnestr by the end of 2003. The Moldovan government, however, asked Russia to remain, concerned that unless weapons stocks currently guarded by Russia's remaining 2,000 troops were destroyed or removed they would fall into the hands of separatists. By November 2003, however, President Voronin, a former KGB official, reversed course and refused to sign a Russian-backed plan to extend the stay of the troops. Separatist leader Igor Smirnov promptly threatened to bloc the withdrawal of Russian troops.

In December 2003, Voronin said he supported U.S. Secretary of State Colin Powell's call for an international peacekeeping force. Russia has repeatedly rejected this idea. Dimitrii Rogozin, head of a Russian parliamentary delegation, said on January 30, 2004, that "nobody should influence the Transdnestr peace settlement process." In fact, on May 2, 2004, a Russian defense official said that Russian troops needed to remain in the region to protect Russia's "national-security" interests. On June 1, 2004, Voronin called a new round of negotiations, this time with a different structure. Voronin asked for the United States, Russia, the EU, Romania, and Ukraine to join the talks.

On July 15, 2004, the separatists in Transdnestr raised tensions by shutting down schools in the region that teach Moldovan in Latin script. Transdnestr militia even surrounded a boarding school and refused to allow OSCE staff to deliver food and water, a tactic described by an OSCE official as "simply inhumane." On July 28, 2004, Voronin called Transdnestr leader Smirnov and his colleagues a "group of transnational criminals" and broke off negotiations. On August 2, 2004, separatists blocked rail lines between Transdnestr and Moldova, and on August 5, 2004, the separatists

announced that they were mobilizing reserves for the "Transdnestr Army." Smirnov announced that Transdnestr "is marching on the road to setting up an independent, sovereign state." On October 26, 2004, Russia declared it would not leave Transdnestr until the issue is resolved.

On May 18, 2005, Moldova Deputy Integration Minister Viktor POSTOLAKI told reporters that Moldova's Parliament was developing a draft bill on the status of the separatist Transdnestr region. The legislation reportedly will give the region autonomous status within the Moldovan Republic. Banking and finance, armed forces, customs, and foreign policy would remain under Moldovan authority. Also in early May, the United States backed a Ukrainian proposal for Transdnestr that would involve free elections under the aegis of the EU, the OSCE, the United States, and Russia, as well as replacement of Russian peacekeeping forces with international forces. Separatists in Transdnestr agreed to rejoin talks in mid-May 2005 but declined to allow OSCE inspectors access to the region.

While none of those initiatives have progressed, Moldova has—with support of the United States and the EU—increased pressure on the separatists in Transdnestr by gaining the agreement of Ukraine in March 2006 to refuse exports from the Transdnestr region unless they are approved by Moldovan customs. The separatist government of Transdnestr, which survives primarily thanks to exports through its border with Ukraine, responded by instituting a blockade of train traffic at the border.

The EU also agreed in October 2005 to help Moldova and Ukraine monitor their border to prevent smuggling. The two-year mission will consist primarily of 50 European customs officials and border guards who will train Ukrainian and Moldovan officials.

Political Parties

Moldova's unusually high bar for representation in Parliament—a party must attract 6 percent of the vote, while a two-party bloc need only attract 9 percent and a three-part bloc can earn seats with only 12 percent of the vote—encourages the formation of electoral blocs. Moldovan opposition parties have formed, abandoned, and reformed blocs with great frequency, particularly as parliamentary elections approach. Leading up to the most recent parliamentary elections, on December 2, 2002, the **Social Liberal Party** (SLP) and the **Party of Democratic Forces** (PFD) merged under the name of the **Social Liberal Party**. SLP Chair Oleg Serebrian was elected to lead the new organization. Former PFD chair Valeriu Matei was named deputy chair. On July 19, 2003, a new party, **Our Moldova Alliance** (AMN), was formed by the **Social Democratic Alliance** (ASD), the **Liberal Party** (PL), and the **Alliance of Independents** (AI). And on May 18, 2004, the three primary center-left opposition parties—AMN, the **Democratic Party of Moldova** (PDM), and the **Social Liberal Party** (PSL)—announced the formation of the Democratic Moldova Bloc (BMD). The BMD is led by Serafim Urechean (AMN), the mayor of Chișinău. By January 2005, however, cracks were already showing in the alliance. Three members of the former Braghiș Alliance announced they were running on the Party of Moldovan Communists (PCRM) list. And in October 2005, 30 senior members of the AMN left the party to form a new Party of Social Democracy.

A far-left party, the **Patria-Rodina Political-Civil Union of Citizens**, was created on May 5, 2004, by the **Party of Moldovan Socialists** (PSRM), the **Moldovan Socialist Party** (PSM), the New Komsomol Association, and the Moldovan Communist Party. The group is opposed to integration with the EU and closer relations with the West.

Parties and Blocs Winning Seats in the March 2005 Legislative Elections

Party of Communists of the Republic of Moldova (*Partidul Comuniștilor din Republica Moldova*—PCRM). The PCRM is in part a successor to the Soviet-era Communist Party of Moldova (*Partidul Comunist din Moldova*—PCM). The latter was suspended in August 1991 but achieved legal status in September 1994 as the PCRM even

though many former Communists had by then opted for the Socialist Party (PSM, above) as the successor to the former ruling grouping. The party was not legalized until after the 1994 legislative balloting, but it subsequently attracted defectors from other parties.

In 1996 the PCRM sought to build an alliance of "patriotic popular forces" for the fall presidential election, in which party leader Vladimir Voronin finished third in the first round with 10.3 percent of the vote. The PCRM then backed the successful second-round candidacy of Petru Lucinschi and was awarded two ministries in the new government of Ion Ciubuc. Hard-liners within the PCRM announced in February 1997 they were leaving the party to form a new grouping under the old PCM banner, Voronin dismissing the dissenters as "chameleons."

During the legislative campaign of late 1997 and early 1998 the PCRM called for the "rebirth of a socialist society" in which a "pluralist economy" would be supported by a "strengthened" state sector. Party leaders also expressed support for renewed linkage of the sovereign republics that had emerged following the breakup of the Soviet Union as well as close political and military ties with Russia. The PCRM led all parties in the March 1998 balloting with 30 percent of the vote, which earned it a plurality of 40 seats, including 9 non-PCRM supporters.

For the 1999 local elections it spearheaded formation of a Communist, Agrarian, and Socialist Bloc (*Blocul Comuniștilor, Agrarienilor și Socialiștilor*—BCAS) that also finished first in total district and local council seats. Participants included the PDAM and the PSRM (both below). At the 2001 election the PCRM won 71 seats, enabling it to elect its chair as president.

The PCRM did not fare as well in the 2005 parliamentary elections, winning only 56 seats. Lacking enough votes to ensure the reelection of Voronin as president, and threatened with a boycott of the presidential election by opposition parties, the PCRM reached out to members of the Democratic Moldova Bloc to gain enough votes to ensure Voronin's reelection. Voronin immediately asked

Prime Minister Vasile Tarlev to form a new government.

Leader: Vladimir VORONIN (President of the Republic and Chair of the Party).

Democratic Moldova Bloc (*Blocul Electoral Moldova Democrată*—BMD). The BMD was formed by three center-left parties in May 2004 to compete in the March 2005 parliamentary elections. The bloc won a total of 34 seats in the 2005 elections.

Leader: Serafim URECHEAN.

Our Moldova Alliance (*Alianţă Moldova Noastră*—AMN). The dominant party of the BMD is AMN, a party formed in July 2003 by a joining of three parties: **the Social Democratic Alliance** (ASD), the **Liberal Party** (PL), and the **Alliance of Independents** (AI). The ASD was a successor to the Braghiş Alliance, a group of factions in Parliament supporting then–Prime Minister Dumitru Braghiş who became a co-chair of the AMN, along with Serafim Urechean, who also heads the BMD.

In January 2002 the **Plai Natal** (Motherland) party, which was formed on February 26, 1999, and chaired by Vladimir BABII, joined the AMN. The Liberal Party joined the AMN after itself being created only a year earlier by the merger of the **Party of Rebirth and Reconciliation of Moldova** (*Partidul Renaşterii şi Concilierii din Moldova*—PRCM), the **National Peasant Christian-Democratic Party** (*Partidul Naţional Ţaranesc Creştin Democrat din Moldova*—PNŢCDM), and the **Social Liberal Union** "Force of Moldova." These parties leaned center-right, and their ultimately joining the AMN represents a move to the center-left in the wake of the dramatic victory of the PCRM in the elections in 2001. Among the party leaders are Mircea Snegur, first president of Moldova, and Valeriu MURAVSCHI, former prime minister (1991–1992).

The **Alliance of Independents** was formed in October 2001 and was led by Serafim Urechean, mayor of Chişinău. On October 24, 2005,

the party faced a crisis when 30 members of the national political council, led by former prime minister Dumitru Braghiş, announced they were quitting the alliance over policy changes that moved the alliance further to the right. Braghiş soon announced that he was forming a new party (see Party of Social Democracy, below).

Leader: Serafim URECHEAN (Chair).

Democratic Party of Moldova (*Partidul Democrat din Moldova*—PDM). The second-largest member of the Democratic Moldova Bloc is the PDM, which is chaired by Dumitru Diacov. The PDM was established in April 2000 as successor to the movement "For a Democratic and Prosperous Moldova" (*Miscarea "Pentru o Moldova Democratica si Propera"*—MMDP). The centrist movement had been formed in February 1997 to promote the policies of President Lucinschi. Its leader, Dumitru Diacov, the former deputy speaker of the Parliament, had recently left the Agrarian Democratic Party of Moldova (PDAM) along with a group of other legislators in a policy dispute over support for the government. For the May 1999 local elections the MMDP joined the **Party of Progressive Forces of Moldova** (PFPM), the "New Force" movement, and an unregistered wing of the Social Democratic Party of Moldova under Gheorghe SIMA to form the Centrist Alliance of Moldova, which finished second to the Communist-led BCAS bloc.

In October 1999 the decision of four members of the MMDP's legislative delegation to sit as independents cost the government of Prime Minister Sturza its majority. The formation of the PDM marked Speaker of Parliament Diacov's formal split with President Lucinschi, Diacov having strongly argued against the adoption of a presidential form of government.

Leader: Dumitru DIACOV (Chair), Ion STURZA (Vice Chair).

Social Liberal Party (*Partidul Social Liberal*—PSL). The third founding member of the Democratic Moldova Bloc is the PSL. Formed in May 2001 and chaired by Oleg Sere-brian, the party positions itself as centrist and in favor of domestic political reform and integration with the EU.

In June 2005 three of the party's six deputy chairs—Valeriu MATEI, Alla MINDICANU, and Nicolae DABIJA—quit the party in protest against policies of the party chair that they claimed made the party "an amorphous appendix to the ruling Communist Party."

Leader: Oleg SEREBRIAN (Chair).

Of the 34 seats in Parliament won by the BMD, the AMN won 23 seats, the PDM won 8 seats, and the PSL won 3 seats.

Christian Democratic People's Party (*Partidul Popular Creştin şi Democrat*—PPCD). A pro-Romanian party, the PPCD was known until December 1999 as the Christian Democratic People's Front (*Frontal Popular Creştin Democrat*—FPCD). The FPCD was a February 1992 continuation of the former Popular Front of Moldova (*Frontul Popular din Moldova*—FPM), which was formed in 1989 and became the dominant political group following the eclipse of the Communist Party of Moldova in mid-1991. In May 1993 the party's Executive Committee appointed Iurie Roşca as its chair in place of former prime minister Mircea DRUC, who lived in Romania and had become a Romanian citizen. The FPCD won nine parliamentary seats on a vote share of 7.3 percent at the February 1994 election, subsequently reiterating its commitment to eventual union with Romania. The party backed the unsuccessful reelection bid of President Snegur in the 1996 balloting.

The FPCD broke with the CDM in March 1999 when it boycotted the confidence vote that installed the Sturza government. The FPCD insisted on four portfolios in the government instead of the two it was offered and, as a result, received none. In November it voted with the Communists against the Sturza government, and in December it supported the Braghiş cabinet.

At a December 1999 party congress the renamed PPCD deleted from its manifesto an insistence on Romanian national unity and instead called for Moldovan integration within Europe and "the fulfillment of national unity in full agreement with the will of the people." In June 2000 the party's vice chair, Valentin DOLGANIUC, and a group of supporters resigned, accusing the party chair of creating an "atmosphere of intolerance and dictatorship" and of abandoning the party's principals through an alliance with the PCRM. Roşca subsequently commented that he views eventual unification with Romania as inevitable. The PPCD won 11 parliamentary seats in February 2001.

With the PCRM growing increasingly critical of Russia, the PPCD has continued to move closer to the ruling party, with Roşca even indicating in April 2005 that he would consider joining the cabinet. (No such offer has, however, been forthcoming.)

After the 2005 elections, PPCD seats in Parliament has remained unchanged at 11.

Leaders: Iurie ROŞCA (Chair of Executive Committee).

Other Parties

Patria–Rodina Bloc (*Electoral Bloc Patria–Rodina*—EBPR). The EBPR, was formed in January 2005 by two left-wing parties: the Socialist Party of Moldova (PSM) and the Party of Moldovan Socialists (PSRM). The bloc advocates closer relations with Russia, self-determination for Transdnestr, and elimination of the office of president. The bloc earned only 4.97 percent of the vote in parliamentary elections in 2005, well below the threshold of 9 percent for a two-party bloc to win any seats.

Leader: Boris MURAVSCHI.

Social Democratic Party of Moldova (*Partidul Social Democrat din Moldova*—PSDM). Dating from 1990, the PSDM is but one of many Moldovan parties claiming a social democratic orientation. It contested the 1994 election as the core component of the Social Democratic Electoral Bloc (*Blocul Social-Democrat*—BSD), which secured 3.7 percent of the votes, barely missing the 4 percent threshold for parliamentary representation. In 1997 the party suffered a major split, when a wing supporting President Lucinschi separated and formed the United Social Democratic Party of Moldova (*Partidul Social-Democrat Unit din Moldova*—PSDUM) in conjunction with four other groups: the Republican Party of Moldova (*Partidul Republican din Moldova*—PRM), which had won 0.9 percent of the 1994 vote; the Party of Social Progress (*Partidul Progres Social din Moldova*—PPSM); the Party of Economic Rebirth (*Partidul Renaşterii Economice*—PRE); and the Socialist Action Party (*Partidul Actiunea Socialista*—PAS).

In the 1998 election the PSDM, running on its own, won 1.9 percent of the vote, while the electoral alliance of the PSDUM and the "Hope" Movement received 1.3 percent. The PSDM subsequently reunited; a dissident group led by the PSDUM's former chair, Gheorghe Sima, ran as part of the Centrist Alliance in the 1999 local elections.

Prior to the March 2005 elections, the PSDM accused the ruling PCRM of illegally and unethically controlling the Central Election Commission and the country's media to block access of the opposition parties. The CEC rejected the PSDM charges.

Running without an electoral block in 2005, the PSDM marginally improved its showing, earning 2.92 percent of the vote, a total still well below the threshold required to earn seats in Parliament.

Leaders: Ian MUSUC (Chair).

Party of Socialists of the Republic of Moldova

(*Partidul Socialiştilor din Republica Moldova*—PSRM). The PSRM was organized by the former PSM ideological secretary and Chişinău branch leader, Veronica Abramciuc, following her last-place finish as an independent in the 1996 presidential race. The party won only 0.6 percent of the national vote in the 1998 parliamentary election. For the February 2001 election it joined the new **Republican Party of Moldova** (*Partidul Republican din Moldova*—PRM), which had been established in October 1999 under Valeriu EFREMOV, in forming the **Unity Electoral Bloc** (*Blocul Electoral "Edinstvo"*).

Leaders: Veronica ABRAMCIUC (Co-Chair), Eduard SMIRNOV.

Party of Social and Economic Justice (*Partidul Dreptăţii Social-Economice din Moldova*—PDSEM). Formed in February 1998 in time for the March parliamentary elections, the party was badly embarrassed when 16 of its candidates withdrew from the party and the election in protest against the alleged authoritarian rule of the party leader, who was accused of misappropriating charitable donations for her election campaign. The party received less than 2 percent of the vote in 1998 and was completely marginalized at the 1999 local elections.

With Gen. Nicolae Alexei as its new leader, the PDSEM ran in the 2005 elections on a platform advocating European integration, closer relations with Romania, and popular election of the president. The party, however, did not improve on its previous performance. In 2005 the PDSEM won only 1.66 percent of the vote and failed to win any seats in Parliament.

Leader: Gen. Nicolae ALEXEI.

Party of Social Democracy (*Partidul Social Democrat*—PDS). Founded on April 15, 2006, and led by former prime minister Dumitru Braghiş, the PDS backs a social democratic doctrine and pushes for strong partnerships with the Russian Federation, the United States, and the EU. The party has also taken a position calling for closer relations with Romania and an ultimate withdrawal from the CIS. The party was formed by disgruntled former members of the Our Moldova Alliance.

Leader: Dumitru BRAGHIŞ (Party Leader).

Republican Popular Party (*Partidul Popular Republican*). Founded in 1999 as the **Peasants' Christian Democratic Party** (*Partidul Ţărănesc Creştin Democrat din Moldova*—PTCDM), the party changed its name at a party conference in May 2005 to the Republican Popular Party. The party runs on a platform of improving conditions for the peasants of Moldova. More specifically, it has called for a new Parliament of 51 members, each elected individually. The PTCDM has also called for popular election of the president and a dramatic reduction in the size of government, cutting the current 16 ministries down to at most 6.

Cabinet

As of May 20, 2006

Prime Minister	Vasile Tarlev
Deputy Prime Ministers	Valerian Cristea (without portfolio)
	Zinaida Grecianii (without portfolio) [f]
	Andrei Stratan (Foreign Affairs)

Ministers

Agriculture and Processing Industry	Anatolie Gorodenco
Culture and Tourism	Artur Cozma
Defense	Valeriu Pleşca
Economy and Trade	Valeriu Lazar
Education, Youth, and Sports	Victor Tvircun
Environment and Natural Resources	Constantin Mihailescu
Finance	Mihail Pop
Health and Social Protection	Ion Ababii
Industry and Infrastructure	Vladimir Antosii
Internal Affairs	Gheorghe Papuc
Justice	Victoria Iftodi [f]
Reintegration	Vasile Sova
Transport and Roads	Miron Gagauz

[f] = female

Finally, the party calls for the institution of subsidized loans for peasants.

The PTCDM gathered 1.37 percent of the vote in 2005 and failed to win any seats in Parliament.

Leader: Nicolae ANDRONIC.

Socio-political Republican Movement (*Ravnopravie*—SPRMR). A far-left party, SPRMR advocates closer relations with Russia and Ukraine, seeks introduction of Russian as an official language, and opposes reunification with Romania. The party won 2.83 percent of the vote in the 2005 parliamentary elections, failing to win any seats.

Leader: Valerie KLIMENKO (Chair).

Legislature

In May 1991 the unicameral Supreme Soviet was redesignated as the **Parliament** (*Parlamentul*), which is elected for a four-year term by proportional representation from a single nationwide district subject to a 6 percent threshold rule.

The country's 6 percent threshold for representation in Parliament is the highest in Europe, and it encourages larger parties and blocs. For two-party blocs the threshold is 9 percent, and for three-party blocs it is 12 percent.

Following the March 6, 2005, elections, the 101 seats in Parliament were distributed as follows: Party of Communists of the Republic of Moldova, 56; Democratic Moldova Bloc, 34; Christian Democratic Popular Party, 11.

Speaker: Marian LUPU.

Communications

Press

Moldova's government does not have a good record on press freedom issues. Reports by nongovernment media monitoring groups in Moldova have charged that the government tightly controls the country's electronic media, resulting in coverage biased toward the ruling PCRM party. Indeed, according to a recent statement by the Canada-based International Freedom of Expression Exchange, a nongovernment rights monitoring organization, "Throughout 2003, opposition media outlets that published reports on government corruption or topics deemed troublesome by the Communist administration endured police raids, the confiscation of archival material, detentions, and interrogations, says CPJ. Authorities also employed less-direct forms of intimidation against the opposition press, such as scaring off advertisers and accusing journalists of taking bribes." And a report in 2004 by the Freedom House, a U.S.-based human rights organization, placed Moldova in the category of "unfree states" in its assessment of media independence.

The following are Moldovan dailies published in Chişinău, unless otherwise noted: *Moldova Suverenă* (Sovereign Moldova, 105,000), government organ; *Nezavisimaya Moldova* (Independent Moldova, 60,692), independent, in Russian; *Viaţă Satuli* (Life of the Village, 50,000), triweekly government organ; *Tinerimya Moldovei/Molodezh Moldovy* (Youth of Moldova; 16,486 Romanian, 1,928 Russian); *Ţara* (Homeland, 18,000), PPCD organ; *Trudovoi Tiraspol* (Working Tiraspol, 7,500), antigovernment Russian organ.

News Agency

The domestic facility is the National News Agency "Moldpres" (*Agenţia Naţională de Presă*), headquartered in Chişinău.

Broadcasting and Computing

In March 1994 a presidential decree ordered a consolidation of broadcast activity into a new State Radio and Television Company of Moldova (*Compania de Stat Teleradio-Moldova*). Radio Moldova broadcasts in Moldovan, Russian, Ukrainian, Gagauz, and Yiddish. There were approximately 1.3 million television receivers and 85,000 personal computers serving upward of 270,000 Internet users in 2003.

Intergovernmental Representation

Ambassador to the U.S.
Mihail MANOLI

U.S. Ambassador to Moldova
Heather M. HODGES

Permanent Representative to the UN
(Vacant)

IGO Memberships (Non-UN)
BSEC, CEI, CEUR, CIS, EBRD, Eurocontrol, Interpol, IOM, OIF, OSCE, WCO, WTO

MONACO

PRINCIPALITY OF MONACO

Principauté de Monaco

The Country

A tiny but celebrated enclave on the Mediterranean coast nine miles from Nice, Monaco is surrounded on three sides by France. The principality is divided into four districts: Monaco-Ville (the capital, built on a rocky promontory about 200 feet above sea level), Monte Carlo (the tourist quarter), La Condamine (the business district around the port), and Fontvieille (the industrial district). A majority of the citizenry is of foreign origin, primarily French, but indigenous Monégasques constitute approximately 15 percent of the population and speak their own language, a combination of French and Italian. Roman Catholicism is the state religion, and French is the official language, although other European languages, in addition to Monégasque, are also spoken.

The principality's main sources of income are tourism, import-export trade, its services as a financial center, corporate and indirect taxes, and an expanding industrial base. Shipping is also of growing importance, while gambling, despite the renown of the Monte Carlo Casino and the success of a new American-style casino at Loew's Monte Carlo, has recently accounted for no more than 4 percent of the country's income. Such light industrial products as plastics, processed foods, pharmaceuticals, glass, precision instruments, and cosmetics yield about one-third of the GDP. Customs, postal services, telecommunications, and banking are governed by an economic union with France established in 1956. (Monaco's perceived status as a tax haven has been under substantial scrutiny recently; see Current issues, below.) A Franco-

Monégasque convention of administrative assistance concluded in 1963 brought under French fiscal authority many Monaco-based French companies that the 1956 customs union had virtually freed from taxation.

Concerted land reclamation efforts begun in the 1960s have succeeded in expanding the principality's total area by some 23 percent, with some of the new acreage sold for private development consistent with the government's urban master plan. A new convention center, the Grimaldi Forum, opened in July 2000 as part of a recent effort to attract such business-related activities as conferences and seminars. Development interests also include Internet-based services and expansion of the Port

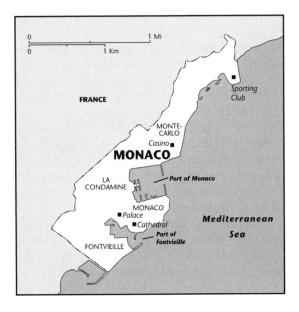

de la Condamine; a floating jetty now under construction is expected to advance Monaco as a base for cruise ships.

In general, the principality's economic health reflects that of France, a period of stagnation in the mid-1990s having been followed since 1997 by a significant recovery. Monaco is also directly dependent on the French labor force: Each business day 30,000 or more French workers cross the border, virtually doubling the population.

Government and Politics

Political Background

Ruled by the Grimaldi family since 1297, the Principality of Monaco has maintained its separate identity in close association with France, under whose protection it was placed in 1861.

A 1918 treaty stipulates that Monégasque policy must be in complete conformity with French political, military, naval, and economic interests; a further treaty of July 17, 1919, provides for Monaco's incorporation into France should the reigning prince die without leaving a male heir.

Monaco's dependence on French-controlled services was emphasized by a dispute that arose in 1962 over the principality's status as a tax refuge under the 1918 treaty. Various pressures, including the setting up of a customs barrier, were invoked by France before a compromise in 1963 paved the way for the signature of new conventions redefining the French-Monégasque relationship. Subsequently, Prince RAINIER III embarked on a three-year struggle with shipping magnate Aristotle S. Onassis for control of the *Société des Bains de Mer* (SBM), a corporation that owns the Monte Carlo Casino, main hotels, clubs, restaurants, and considerable Monégasque real estate. Monaco gained control of the company in 1967 by buying out Onassis's majority shareholdings.

World attention focused briefly on the principality in 1982, following the death of Princess GRACE (the former American actress Grace Kelly) as the result of an automobile accident in the Côte d'Azur region. Subsequently, the passing of the princess was viewed as representing a fiscal as well as personal loss for Monégasques, whose economy, based in large part on tourism, had recently stagnated, with income from both real estate and gambling receding sharply over previous years.

Elections to the National Council in January 1993 appeared to mark a movement toward more competitive politics, although groupings remained electoral lists rather than parties as such. In December 1994 Paul DIJOUD (a former French ambassador to Mexico) was sworn in as Monaco's minister of state (chief minister) in succession to Jacques DUPONT. Dijoud was succeeded on February 3, 1997, by Michel LÉVÊQUE, another long-standing member of the French diplomatic corps who had most recently served as ambassador to Algeria. Elections on February 1 and 8, 1998, resulted in the capture of all council seats by the list of the National and Democratic Union (*Union Nationale et Démocratique*—UND), which had dominated every council election since its formation in 1962.

On January 1, 2000, Patrick LECLERCQ succeeded Michel LÉVÊQUE, who had retired as minister of state. Like his predecessors, Leclercq had a long history of diplomatic service to France, including, most recently, as ambassador to Spain.

The UND's long domination of the National Council came to a surprisingly dramatic end at the balloting of February 6, 2003, when it secured only 3 of the 24 seats in the National Council. The Union for Monaco (*Union pour Monaco*—UPM) secured the other 21 seats.

Prince Rainer died on April 6, 2005, after an extended illness, and he was succeeded immediately by his son, who became Prince ALBERT II. Subsequently, the new sovereign named Jean-Paul PROUST, a former chief of police in Paris, to succeed Leclercq as minister of state.

Constitution and Government

The constitution of December 17, 1962, replacing one of 1911, vests executive power in the hereditary prince, grants universal suffrage, outlaws capital punishment, and guarantees the rights of

Political Status: Independent principality founded in the 13th century; constitutional monarchy since 1911; present constitution promulgated December 17, 1962 (amended in April 2002).

Area: 0.70 sq. mi. (1.81 sq. km.).

Population: 32,020 (2000C); 33,100 (2005E).

Major Urban Center (2005E): MONACO-VILLE (1,000).

Official Language: French.

Monetary Unit: Euro (market rate July 1, 2006: 1 euro = $1.28US). (Although not a member of the European Union [EU], Monaco was authorized by the EU to adopt the euro as its official currency and to mint a limited supply of Monégasque euro coins.)

Sovereign: Prince ALBERT II; acceded to the throne April 6, 2005, following the death of his father, Prince RAINIER III.

Heir Apparent: Princess CAROLINE, sister of the sovereign.

Minister of State: Jean-Paul PROUST; assumed office June 1, 2005, following nomination by the sovereign to succeed Patrick LECLERCQ.

association and trade unionism. The prince rules in conjunction with a minister of state, who is assisted by government councillors and palace personnel, all appointed by the prince. The prince may veto legislation approved by a National Council (*Conseil National*), whose 24 members are elected from single-member districts by universal suffrage for five-year terms. The prince receives advice on constitutional, treaty, and other matters from a 7-member Crown Council, while a 12-member State Council advises in such areas as legislation, regulations, and law and order.

Municipal affairs in the four *quartiers* are conducted by a 15-member elected Communal Council (*Conseil Communal*), with the mayor of Monaco-Ville presiding. The judiciary includes a Supreme Tribunal (*Tribunal Suprême*, president, Roland DRAGO) of 7 members named by the prince on the basis of nominations by the National Council;

courts of cassation, appeal, and first instance; and a justice of the peace.

In January 1992 the National Council approved legislation tightening the principality's citizenship law: Foreign women (but not foreign men) marrying Monégasque citizens would no longer be granted citizenship automatically but would be required to stay with their spouses for at least five years to qualify. In a further decision in December 1992 the council ruled that female citizens should enjoy the existing right of males to pass on their nationality to their children.

Foreign Relations

Monaco's foreign relations are controlled largely by Paris. Although the principality participates indirectly in the European Union (EU) by virtue of its customs union with France, it remains legally outside the EU because of its refusal to sign the Treaty of Rome to protect its status as a tax haven. Prior to joining the United Nations (UN) in May 1993 it maintained a Permanent Observer's office at UN headquarters in New York and had long belonged to a number of UN specialized agencies.

In January 1984 President François Mitterrand became the first French head of state in 23 years to undertake a state visit to the principality. A decade later, in October 1994, Monaco signed an agreement with France providing for coordinated action against money laundering and requiring Monégasque banks and other institutions to report dubious financial transactions to the authorities. However, dissatisfaction with Monaco's progress in this regard surfaced in 1998 when young reformist judges alleged that the "old guard" was being lax in its prosecution. Consequently, overruling Prince Rainier, Paris appointed new prosecutors and chief judges.

Current Issues

Since the late 1990s pressure has mounted for greater transparency in the financial sector to guard against potential money laundering and other corrupt practices. Stung by the criticism (*Le Monde* characterized Monaco as a "refuge for cheats"), the

Cabinet

As of July 1, 2006

Minister of State	Jean-Paul Proust
Ministers	
Finance and Economy	Franck Biancheri
Foreign Affairs	Rainier Imperti
Health and Social Affairs	Denis Ravera
Interior	Philippe Deslandes
Public Works, Environment, and Urban Affairs	Gilles Tonelli

government released a report in January 1999 denying that dubious activity was prevalent in the principality and attacking the "myth" of Monaco as a "superficial playground." In part, the report was seen as a component of the government's unsuccessful campaign to gain membership in the Council of Europe, which reportedly considered Monaco as neither fully sovereign nor sufficiently democratic. French charges of government complicity and deliberate laxness in enforcing financial regulations contributed to Prince Rainier's subsequent angry assertion that it might be time to reexamine the 1918 treaty between France and Monaco. Despite further progress on the financial transparency issue, in 2002 Monaco remained one of only seven jurisdictions cited by the Organization for Economic Cooperation and Development (OECD) as retaining harmful tax policies.

The 2003 National Council election was widely viewed as a generational battle between the "young lion," Stéphane VALERI of the UPM coalition, and the UND's longtime leader, National Council President Jean-Louis CAMPORA, who has served in the council for 30 years. The overwhelming UPM victory was also attributed to the electorate's desire for "modernization," including proposed membership in the Council of Europe.

Prince Rainier's death in 2005 marked the end of a remarkable 55-year reign in which he had shepherded Monaco from a gambling "toytown" into an economically lively and diverse state. Interestingly, Prince Albert, a bachelor, was allowed to succeed his father as the result of constitutional revision in 2002. (The constitution had previously prohibited succession by someone who had no heirs. The changes also provided for Princess CAROLINE, Albert's sister, to become heir apparent.) As expected, Prince Albert pledged to continue his father's policies, although the new government he subsequently appointed included a new department for external affairs, underscoring the need for the principality to keep pace with the fast-changing European landscape. Potentially helpful in that regard was Monaco's acceptance of a proposed EU accord on the tax haven issue under which secret banking centers such as Monaco would withhold taxes on foreign accounts.

Political Parties

In the absence of formal political parties, Monaco's politics were until recently dominated for nearly four decades by the **National and Democratic Union** (*Union Nationale et Démocratique—* UND). Formed in 1962 through the merger of the National Union of Independents (*Union Nationale des Indépendants*) and the National Democratic Entente (*Entente Nationale Démocratique*), the UND won all 18 National Council seats in the elections of 1968, 1978, 1983, and 1988. In addition, the UND list captured 15 seats in the 1993 election, informal reference also being made to it as the Campora List (*Liste Campora*), a reflection of the leadership of Jean-Louis Campora, who was elected president of the new council to succeed long-term UND leader Jean-Charles REY. Two seats were also won in 1993 by the Médecin List (*Liste Médecin*), led by Jean-Louis MEDECIN, the former mayor of Monaco-Ville. The UND list was credited with winning all the seats in the 1998 elections in competition with lists from the **National Union for the Future of Monaco** (*Union Nationale pour l'Avenir de Monaco—UNAM*) and the **Rally for the Monégasque Family** (*Rassemblement de la Famille Monégasque—RFM*). The UNAM and RFM combined forces under an opposition **Union for Monaco** (*Union pour Monaco—UPM*) list led by former UND member Stéphane Valeri for the 2003 balloting, at which the UPM won 21 of 24 seats.

Legislature

The **National Council** (*Conseil National*) is a unicameral body elected via direct universal suffrage for a five-year term. The number of councillors was raised from 18 in 1998 to 24 in 2003. Of the 24 councillors, 16 members are elected by list majority system and 8 members by proportional representation. At the election of February 9, 2003, the Union for Monaco won 21 seats and the National and Democratic Union won 3.

President: Stéphane VALERI.

Communications

Press

The principality publishes an official weekly journal, *Journal de Monaco*, which includes new laws and decrees; other publications include *Monaco Hebdo* and two monthlies, *Gazette Monaco-Côte d'Azur* and *Monaco Actualité*. French newspapers are widely read, and special "Monaco editions" of *Nice-Matin* and *L'Espoir de Nice* are published in Nice.

News Agency

Agence France-Presse is the principal international facility.

Broadcasting

Radio and television broadcasting is government operated, but time is sold to commercial sponsors. *Radio Monte Carlo* (RMC), in which the French government has a controlling financial interest, broadcasts in French, Italian, and various other languages. Trans World Radio, which is maintained by voluntary subscriptions and operates in conjunction with RMC, broadcasts religious programs in many languages. *Télé Monte Carlo* has been broadcasting since 1954. There were approximately 28,000 television receivers in 2003.

Intergovernmental Representation

Monaco maintains consuls general in Washington and New York, while the U.S. consul general in Nice, France, also services American interests in Monaco.

Permanent Representative to the UN
Gilles NOGHES

IGO Memberships (Non-UN)
CEUR, Eurocontrol, Interpol, OIF, OSCE

MONTENEGRO

REPUBLIC OF MONTENEGRO

Republike Crne Gore

Note: At the national election of September 10, 2006, Prime Minister Milo Djukanović's coalition of the Democratic Party of Socialists and Social Democratic Party won a majority of at least 41 seats in the expanded 81-seat Montenegrin legislature. The multiparty Serbian List, headed by the Serbian People's Party, won 12 seats, while the similarly ethnic Serbian coalition of the Socialist People's Party, People's Party, and Democratic Serbian Party won 11. The new Movement for Change also won 11 seats, with most of the balance going to ethnic Albanian groups.

The Country

Montenegro is a Balkan republic, mostly mountainous, with a 180-mile coastline along the Adriatic Sea. The terrain, part of the Karst Plateau, is renowned for its rugged scenery. The country is bordered by Albania to the south, Serbia to the east, and Bosnia and Herzegovina to the north. Pre-1992 Yugoslavia was composed of six constituent republics (Bosnia and Herzegovina, Croatia, Macedonia, Montenegro, Serbia, and Slovenia) that encompassed an area of some 98,800 sq. mi. (255,800 sq. km.) and had nearly 24 million inhabitants. The Federal Republic proclaimed in April 1992, encompassing Serbia and Montenegro, contained approximately 40 percent of its predecessor's area and population. Montenegro is only one-sixth the size of Serbia and has only about one-sixteenth its population.

Montenegrins constitute approximately 43 percent of the population, Serbs approximately 32 percent, Bosniaks about 8 percent, Albanians 5 percent, and various other ethnic groups (e.g., Croats and Roma) the remainder. Eastern Orthodox Christianity predominates, although there is a large Muslim minority, given the long legacy of Ottoman Turkish occupation in the region.

The Montenegrin economy is dependent on export of its industrial and agricultural output. Industrial production, which was badly damaged by the United Nations (UN) economic sanctions imposed against Yugoslavia in the 1990s, is concentrated in hydroelectricity generation (over 2.8 billion kilowatt hours in 2005); metallurgy (aluminum and steel); and the extraction and processing of raw materials, especially bauxite (reserves of bauxite may be surpassed in size only by Russian deposits) and also coal, lumber, and salt. Processing of tobacco

Political Status: Part of the Kingdom of the Serbs, Croats, and Slovenes constituted as an independent monarchy December 1, 1918, and formally renamed Yugoslavia on October 3, 1929; constituent republic of the communist Federal People's Republic of Yugoslavia instituted November 29, 1945, and then of the Socialist Federal Republic of Yugoslavia proclaimed April 7, 1963; constituent republic, along with Serbia, of the Federal Republic of Yugoslavia proclaimed April 27, 1992, and of the "state union" of Serbia and Montenegro established February 4, 2003, under new Constitutional Charter; Republic of Montenegro established June 3, 2006, following a referendum on independence on May 21.

Area: 5,333 sq. mi. (13,812 sq. km.)

Population: 642,000 (2005E).

Major Urban Centers (2005E): PODGORICA (formerly Titograd, 140,000).

Official Languages: The official language is Serbian; however, in areas established by national minorities, their languages are also accorded official status.

Monetary Unit: Euro (market rate July 1, 2006: 1 euro = $1.28 US). The euro has been legal tender in Montenegro since January 1, 2002.

President of Montenegro: Filip VUJANOVIĆ (Democratic Party of Socialists of Montenegro); served as Montenegrin prime minister 1998–2002; elected chair of the Montenegrin Assembly on November 5, 2002, following the legislative election of October 20, and thus became acting president upon the resignation of President Milo DJUKANOVIĆ on November 25; elected president for a five-year term on May 11, 2003, and inaugurated June 13. (The presidential elections of December 22, 2002, and February 9, 2003, had failed to meet the required 50 percent turnout of eligible voters.)

Prime Minister of Montenegro: Milo DJUKANOVIĆ (Democratic Party of Socialists of Montenegro); previously served as prime minister 1991–1998 and as president of Montenegro from 1998 until resigning on November 25, 2002; nominated as prime minister on November 26, 2002, by his predecessor, Acting President Filip VUJANOVIĆ, following the legislative election of October 20; confirmed by the Montenegrin Assembly and sworn in at the head of a new Council of Ministers on January 8, 2003.

and food is also a major manufacturing activity. The industrial sector as a whole employs approximately 30 percent of the total workforce, compared to 68 percent for services. Agriculture and livestock production remain important despite employing only 2 percent of the workforce. Cereals, tobacco, grapes, figs, and olives are the major cash crops; poultry, lamb, goat, and beef are the primary meat products. Agricultural production is situated in the river valleys, mainly along the Zeta River and near Lake Scutari in the southwest. Only about 14 percent of the total area of the country is suitable for cultivation. Another 54 percent is covered with forest or woodlands, much of this in the northeast. Tourism, concentrated along the Adriatic coastline, is a major source of foreign exchange.

Montenegro has moved to privatize ownership of its industrial assets. Montenegrin leaders also hope to generate interest in the Adriatic coastline through expanded tourism and foreign investment in real estate. Challenges include rebuilding neglected infrastructure, curbing public-sector corruption, and suppressing the enormous black-market sector that developed during the period of sanctions. An overarching goal is integration into the European Union (EU).

The per capita annual income is approximately $2,500, with unemployment about 17 percent (although nongovernment sources estimate unemployment as high as 30 percent). More than 12 percent of the population lives below the poverty line. Consumer price inflation was estimated at 3.4 percent in 2004. At independence, Montenegrin leaders claimed that GDP had grown 5 percent in 2005, with inflation at 1.8 percent. The budget deficit was 1.9 percent of GDP.

Government and Politics

Political Background

Following centuries of national struggle against the Turkish and Hapsburg empires, the former Yugoslavia emerged as a unified state with the formation on December 1, 1918, of the Kingdom of the Serbs, Croats, and Slovenes under the Serbian House of Karadjordjević. Uniting the former independent kingdoms of Serbia and Montenegro with the Croatian, Dalmatian, and Bosnian and Herzegovinian territories previously ruled by Austria-Hungary, the new entity (formally styled Yugoslavia on October 3, 1929) was ruled between World Wars I and II as a highly centralized, Serb-dominated state. Following occupation of the country by Nazi Germany and Fascist Italy in April 1941, resistance was led by two rival groups, the proroyalist Chetniks, under Gen. Draža MIHAILOVIĆ, and the Communist-inspired Partisans, led by Marshal Josip Broz TITO, a Croat who sought to enlist all the country's national groups in the liberation struggle. The Partisans' greater effectiveness in opposing the occupation forces and securing Allied aid paved the way for their assumption of power at the end of the war. In March 1945 Tito became prime minister in a "government of national unity"; eight months later, on November 29, the monarchy was abolished and a Federal People's Republic of Yugoslavia, based on the equality of the country's principal national groups, was proclaimed. On January 14, 1953, under a new constitution, Tito was elected president of the republic.

Yugoslavia developed along orthodox Communist lines until 1948, when its refusal to submit to Soviet directives led to its expulsion from the Communist bloc and the imposition of a political and economic blockade by the USSR and its East European allies. Aided by Western arms and economic support, Yugoslavia maintained its autonomy throughout the Stalin era and by the late 1950s had achieved a partial reconciliation with the Warsaw Pact states, although it still insisted on complete independence and the right to find its own "road to socialism." Internally, Yugoslavia had become the first East European country to evolve institutions that moderated the harsher features of communist rule and encouraged the development of a democratic form of communism based on new interpretations of Marxism. A federal constitution promulgated in 1963 consolidated the system of "social self-management" by attempting to draw the people into economic and administrative decision making at all levels; it also expanded the independence of the judiciary, increased the responsibilities of the federal legislature and those of the country's six constituent republics and two autonomous provinces (Kosovo and Vojvodina), and widened freedom of choice in elections.

On May 4, 1980, Marshal Tito, president for life of the republic and of the League of Communists of Yugoslavia (*Savez Komunista Jugoslavija*—SKJ), died at the age of 87, the leadership of state and party thereupon passing to collegial executives—the state presidency and the Presidium of the SKJ Central Committee, respectively. Through the 1980s the federal state presidency and the presidency of the party Presidium rotated on an annual basis among the constituent republics without appreciable dispute.

Economic ills in 1990 set off a series of events that led to the dissolution of greater Yugoslavia into the independent states of Croatia, Slovenia, Bosnia and Herzegovina, and Macedonia, with only Serbia and Montenegro remaining in a diminished federation (see the Bosnia and Herzegovina, Croatia, Macedonia, Slovenia, and Serbia articles). On February 12, 1992, Serbia and Montenegro agreed to join in upholding "the principles of a common state which would be a continuation of Yugoslavia." On April 27 a rump Federal Assembly adopted the constitution of a new Federal Republic of Yugoslavia (FRY), under which elections for a successor assembly were held in Serbia and Montenegro on May 31, 1992.

In 1996 the Democratic Party of Socialists of Montenegro (*Demokratska Partija Socijalista Crne Gore*—DPSCG) achieved a majority in elections for the separate Montenegrin Assembly. On July 15, 1997, Slobodan MILOŠEVIĆ, constitutionally barred from running for a third term as president of Serbia, was elected unopposed as the Yugoslav federal president. However, he continued to face electoral threats to his power.

In Montenegro, a split in the Milošević-allied ruling DPSCG precipitated a 1997 presidential election. On February 21 Montenegrin Prime Minister Milo DJUKANOVIĆ attacked Milošević in a press interview, which, along with his calls for an independent foreign policy and currency for Montenegro, resulted in Djukanović's forced resignation as DPSCG vice president on March 26. The pro-Djukanović faction of the party responded on July 11 by sacking a key Milošević ally, state and DPSCG President Momir BULATOVIĆ, although a month later the pro-Bulatović faction engineered his return as party leader at a DPSCG congress. In the midst of this turmoil Montenegrin Assembly Speaker Svetozar MAROVIĆ announced Montenegrin presidential elections for the fall. Following a ruling by the Constitutional Court, both Djukanović and Bulatović were permitted to run. Although Bulatović, one of eight candidates, claimed a narrow plurality of votes over Djukanović at first-round voting on October 5, his failure to obtain a majority necessitated a second round on October 19, at which Djukanović defeated the two-term incumbent by a mere 5,000 votes.

The new president took office on January 13, 1998, despite violent protests by Bulatović supporters. Through mediation by Yugoslav Prime Minister Radoje KONTIĆ (a Montenegrin), on January 21 the demonstrators agreed to settle for early legislative elections in May 1998. A transitional government under the leadership of the DPSCG's Filip VUJANOVIĆ was appointed on February 4. It included 17 ministers from Djukanović's DPSCG faction, 7 from the opposition, and 4 independents; the Bulatović faction of the DPSCG as well as the proindependence Liberal Alliance of Montenegro (*Liberalni Savez Crne Gore*—LSCG) refused to participate.

Having fallen out of favor with President Milošević, apparently over his stance on the Montenegrin dispute, Prime Minister Kontić lost a confidence vote in the upper chamber of the Yugoslav Federal Assembly on May 18, 1998, and was succeeded the following day by former Montenegrin president Bulatović. On May 31 Montenegrin voters awarded 49.5 percent of the vote and a majority of seats in the Montenegrin Assembly to President Djukanović's For a Better Life electoral coalition, while Bulatović's recently organized Socialist People's Party of Montenegro (*Socialistička Narodna Partija Crne Gore*—SNPCG) claimed 36 percent of the vote and emerged as the leading opposition party. Montenegro's interim prime minister, Vujanović, was reappointed on July 16 to head a government encompassing the three coalition partners: the DPSCG, the People's Party (*Narodna Stranka*—NS), and the Social Democratic Party of Montenegro (*Socialdemokratska Partija Crne Gore*—SDPCG).

In 1999 Montenegrin President Djukanović continued his efforts to distance his administration from federal policies in regard to Kosovo, particularly "ethnic cleansing" of ethnic Albanians, which had precipitated military action by the United States and other North Atlantic Treaty Organization (NATO) countries (see Serbia article for details). Even though Montenegro was not exempt from the NATO air campaign, and despite rumors that the Serbian military was preparing to depose him, on April 21 Djukanović rejected orders that the Montenegrin police were to be placed under the command of the FRY army. Djukanović accused Milošević of using "the pretext of the defense of the country" to displace the civil government. Later, the republican government proposed replacing the federal republic with a looser association in which Montenegro would set its own foreign and military policy and establish independent currency controls.

In a gambit designed to maintain Milošević's hold on power, on July 6, 2000, Milošević's allies pushed through the Federal Assembly constitutional changes authorizing direct election of the president and of the upper legislative house. With most of the opposition continuing its boycott of the federal parliament, the proposals easily received the necessary two-thirds support. The changes, in addition to permitting the incumbent to serve two additional four-year terms, put organization of elections under the FRY instead of the individual republics. On July 8 the Montenegrin Assembly described the changes as "illegal" and "a gross violation of the constitutional rights of the Republic of Montenegro." The Montenegrin legislators nevertheless rejected a proposal for an immediate referendum on Montenegrin independence. On July 27, 2000, Milošević called elections for September, even though his presidential term would not expire until July 2001. The governing coalition in Montenegro quickly announced that it would boycott the balloting, which proved to be a strategic mistake when Milošević was ousted from power.

On December 28, 2000, the NS withdrew from Montenegro's governing coalition in opposition to further movement toward independence. Four months later, President Djukanović entered the Montenegrin Assembly election of April 22, 2001, banking on a strong vote for separation from Serbia, but his DPSCG-SDPCG alliance, styled Victory Is Montenegro (*Pobjeda Je Crne Gore*), failed to achieve more than a slight plurality against the Together for Yugoslavia (*Zajedno za Jugoslaviju*) coalition of the SNPCG, the NS, and the Serbian People's Party (*Srpska Narodna Stranka*—SNS). Three seats short of a majority, Djukanović turned to the Liberal Alliance, which agreed to extend external support to a new Vujanović cabinet, but the government's minority status soon forced the president to backtrack on plans for an immediate independence referendum.

Following the defeat of the Milošević regime and his extradition in 2001 to stand trial for war crimes, on March 14, 2002, the governments of the Federal Republic of Yugoslavia and its two constituent republics announced an "agreement in principle" that would bring the history of Yugoslavia as such to an end, with its replacement by a "state union" to be called Serbia and Montenegro. Over the objections of parties that wanted a separate and independent Serbia, the Serbian legislature ratified the accord 149–79 on April 9. The same day, the Montenegrin legislature voted in favor of the agreement 58–11, despite strong opposition from the SDPCG and the previously government-supportive LSCG, both of which favored Montenegrin independence. Four SDPCG-affiliated ministers quickly resigned from the Montenegrin cabinet, and on April 19, Prime Minister Vujanović submitted his resignation, announcing that his government no longer commanded a legislative majority. At President Djukanović's request, Vujanović attempted to fashion another government, but he was unable to do so, and in July the president called for an early legislative election. Meanwhile, on May 31, both chambers of the Federal Assembly had approved the state union agreement by wide margins.

The Montenegrin Assembly election of October 20, 2002, saw the Democratic List for a European Montenegro (*Demokratska Lista za Evropsku Crnu Goru*), headed by the DPSCG, win 39 of 75 seats, compared to 30 for the opposition Together for Changes (*Zajedno za Promjene*) coalition. Following the election, caretaker Prime Minister Vujanović was elected speaker of the Montenegrin legislature. On November 25 Milo Djukanović resigned as president of Montenegro, and a day later Speaker Vujanović, in his new capacity as acting president, nominated Djukanović for the prime ministership (the office he had previously held from 1991 to 1998). Vujanović then ran in the Montenegrin presidential election of December 22. Although he won an overwhelming majority, a boycott by Together for Changes held the turnout under 50 percent, invalidating the results and forcing a similarly unsuccessful revote on February 9, 2003. In response, the Montenegrin Assembly eliminated the 50 percent requirement, and on May 11 Vujanović was elected president with 63 percent of the vote. On January 8 Djukanović had been confirmed as prime minister.

On January 29, 2003, the Montenegrin Assembly approved the Constitutional Charter for the state union of Serbia and Montenegro. The Federal Assembly concurred on February 4 (by votes of 26–7 in the upper chamber and 84–31 in the lower), thereby excising Yugoslavia from the political map. Under the charter a new state union assembly was elected by and from among the members of the FRY, Serbian, and Montenegrin legislatures, and the new assembly in turn elected the DPSCG's Svetozar Marović, the only candidate, as state union president and chair of the Council of Ministers on March 7.

Under their 2003 EU-backed state union agreement, both Serbia and Montenegro had the right to vote on the question of independence in three years. On May 21, 2006, by a vote of 55.5 percent to 44.5 percent (half a percentage point above the EU threshold for approval), Montenegrins chose independence. Two weeks later, on June 3, the Montenegrin Assembly declared independence. On June 5, although many Serbians were unhappy with what they viewed as an abrupt divorce, the Serbian National Assembly declared Serbia to be the independent successor state to the state union, as had been agreed upon under the charter, and thereby extinguished the last remnants of the former Yugoslavia.

Constitution and Government

Yugoslavia under successive postwar constitutions remained a Communist one-party state until the emergence of a variety of opposition groups at the republican level in early 1990. Political control was long exercised throughout the governmental structure by the Communist Party, known since 1952 as the League of Communists of Yugoslavia (SKJ), and by its "front" organization, the Socialist Alliance of the Working People of Yugoslavia (*Socijalistički Savez Radnog Naroda Jugoslavije*— SSRNJ); by mid-1990, however, the SKJ had collapsed.

The constitution of the Federal Republic of Yugoslavia, adopted on April 27, 1992, provided for a bicameral Federal Assembly, encompassing a Chamber of Republics (with equal representation for Serbia and Montenegro) and a Chamber of Citizens apportioned on the basis of population. The federal president was elected to four-year terms by the assembly until July 2000, when the legislature passed constitutional changes that instituted direct elections for the presidency as well as for the Chamber of Republics. The president was expected to nominate a prime minister from the other constituent republic.

The Constitutional Charter of the state union of Serbia and Montenegro was formally adopted in February 2003 and lasted until both countries chose independence in 2006. It established a presidency with circumscribed powers, although the head of state also served as chair of the Council of Ministers. Elected by and answerable to the unicameral legislature, the Assembly of Serbia and Montenegro, the president served a single four-year term, subject to early dissolution of the legislature. The assembly comprised 91 Serbian deputies and 35 from Montenegro; although initially indirectly elected for two-year terms (subsequently extended), in the future deputies were to be directly elected for four-year terms.

The state union president and the assembly president could not be from the same member state. Shared responsibility also carried through to the defense and foreign affairs portfolios, which had to be held by ministers from different states; each of the two ministers had a deputy from the other state, with the minister and deputy exchanging places halfway through the term of office. Also, the Constitutional Charter established at the apex of the military command structure a Supreme Command Council (SCC), comprising the state union president and the presidents of the two constituent republics. SCC decisions were by consensus.

The Court of Serbia and Montenegro comprised an equal number of judges from each republic. Judges were elected by the state union assembly for a single six-year term. The court was empowered to adjudicate conflicts between the states, disputes between a state and the state union, and issues of compatibility between state union and republican constitutions and laws. It could also hear appeals from citizens regarding rights and freedoms guaranteed by the Constitutional Charter, which called for enforcement of the "provisions of international treaties on human and minority rights and civil freedoms."

Article 60 of the Constitutional Charter specified that after three years a member state could choose to initiate steps toward independence, which had to be approved by referendum in the initiating state. When Montenegro ultimately chose independence, as the charter specified, Serbia became the successor to the state union internationally, thereby inheriting the former federation's membership in the UN and all other international and financial organizations.

Each of the constituent republics had a popularly elected president and unicameral assembly, with a prime minister nominated by the former and confirmed by the latter. The judicial systems included Constitutional and Supreme courts as well as lower-level courts.

Immediately after independence, Montenegrins had yet to craft a process for drafting and approving a new constitution for the republic. The assembly postponed adoption of a new constitution until after new parliamentary elections, but determined that the newly elected deputies will have the power to approve the new charter. As of August 1, 2006, Montenegrins had not determined what system of government will be instituted (presidential, parliamentary, or mixed) nor whether a simple majority or a two-thirds vote of the legislature will be needed to approve a new constitution.

Foreign Relations

In the early 1990s Federal Yugoslavia was ostracized by much of the international community because of military action in support of Serbs in Croatia and in Bosnia and Herzegovina, although Belgrade insisted in early 1992 that all its troops had been withdrawn from both republics. Because of the Bosnian conflict, the UN Security Council on May 30 imposed comprehensive sanctions that included barriers to trade; a freezing of Yugoslavia's foreign assets; severance of air links; a reduction in diplomatic relations; and suspension of sporting, cultural, and technical exchanges. The European Community (EC; predecessor to the EU) ordered a trade embargo, and in November military units from NATO and the Western European Union were detailed to enforce both the UN and EC sanctions. On September 22 the UN General Assembly voted to exclude the FRY from its proceedings and insisted that it apply for UN membership rather than being permitted to succeed to the seat held by its predecessor. In a subsequent "clarification," a Rus-

sian spokesperson insisted that the action referred only to the General Assembly, leaving truncated Yugoslavia the successor state in all other UN bodies. By the end of 1992, however, Yugoslavia had also been suspended from the International Monetary Fund as well as from the Conference on (later Organization for) Security and Cooperation in Europe (CSCE/OSCE) and the Central European Initiative (CEI).

Intensified UN sanctions on the FRY compelled the Belgrade government to take an overtly stronger line with the Bosnian Serbs following the tabling of new peace proposals in early July 1994. Belgrade's reward was UN Security Council approval on September 24, 1994, of a selective suspension of sanctions, including the resumption of international flights to Yugoslavia, the reopening of the Montenegrin port of Bar on the Adriatic, and the restoration of sporting and cultural links. Ultimately, a peace agreement was concluded on November 21, 1995, in Dayton, Ohio (see Bosnia and Herzegovina article), and initialed on behalf of Yugoslavia and the Bosnian Serbs by President Milošević. Suspended the following day, UN sanctions against Belgrade were formally lifted by a unanimous Security Council vote on October 1, 1996 (although FRY assets remained frozen because of disputes and claims from other Yugoslav successor states).

Yugoslavia's standing in the international community improved somewhat in 1997 through Milošević's key role in settling the internal rift in a Bosnian constituent unit, the Serb Republic. Beginning in late February 1998, however, Serbian police and military actions in Kosovo again put Yugoslavia at odds with much of the rest of the world, and on March 31 the UN Security Council imposed an arms embargo on Yugoslavia. A September UN Security Council also called for a cease-fire and condemned the "excessive and indiscriminate use of force" by the Serb military and security units. In November, with an October cease-fire holding, Belgrade barred members of the UN's International Criminal Tribunal for the former Yugoslavia from entering Kosovo to investigate allegations of extrajudicial killings, prompting the U.S. president of the tribunal to brand Yugoslavia as a "rogue state, one that holds the international rule of law in contempt."

Although Yugoslavia stated during the February 1999 peace talks at Rambouillet, France, that it was prepared to consider regional autonomy for Kosovo, it continued to reject a NATO presence on its soil. Immediately following the start of a NATO bombing campaign on March 24, 1999, Belgrade declared a state of war and broke diplomatic relations with France, Germany, the United Kingdom, and the United States. Relations with all four were restored in November 2000 as Yugoslavia, now headed by Vojislav KOŠTUNICA, moved broadly to reestablish its international linkages. The FRY was formally reintegrated into the UN on November 1 and into the OSCE on November 27. In April 2003 it joined the Council of Europe, and two months later it applied for membership in NATO's Partnership for Peace (PfP) program.

At independence in 2006 Montenegro was well positioned to come out from under the international pressure concentrated on Serbia to apprehend and turn over war crimes fugitive Ratko Mladić. "With independence, that hurdle is gone for Montenegro," Prime Minister Djukanović said. "We'll no longer be Serbia's hostage." Within weeks of the independence referendum, and just days after the declaration of independence, President Vujanović sent a letter to the UN seeking membership for Montenegro. The United States, the EU and its member nations, Russia, China, and many other governments quickly recognized Montenegrin independence shortly thereafter. The UN admitted Montenegro as its 192nd member on June 28, 2006, not long after Montenegro became the 56th member of the OSCE.

Current Issues

The declaration of independence adopted by the assembly on June 3, 2006, stated as national priorities joining the UN and other international organizations (such as the World Trade Organization), as well as integration into the EU and NATO. UN membership came early, but EU officials were more cautious, signaling that membership for Montenegro would not be on a fast track. The first step for EU membership will be to legislate domestic reforms to the public sector and the economy in preparation for negotiating an aid and trade pact and a Stabilization and Association Agreement with EU officials later in 2006 (Romania, Bulgaria, and Croatia are ahead of Montenegro in the queue). Montenegro also will seek membership in NATO's PfP program. Under the state union Montenegro shared an army with Serbia (one of the few institutions that was shared, the other being the diplomatic corps); therefore, formation of a professional army will be a priority before joining NATO.

Opposition to independence had come first and foremost from the opposition parties in the assembly, namely the SNPCG, SNS, and NS. Two years earlier, they had been joined by the newly organized Democratic Serbian Party (DSS) in a series of once-a-week protests in the capital, the goal being to force new elections and creation of an interim government. Tensions escalated further when the opposition parties declared a boycott of Parliament after the state-controlled broadcasting service suspended live television broadcasts of the assembly sessions. In the end, however, the opposition could not muster enough votes to proceed with a vote of no confidence.

The removal of the sovereignty issue from the agenda created an issue vacuum for the opposition parties in mid-2006, although they seized on cultural anxieties raised by the slim margin of victory. Petition drives to confer dual citizenship with Serbia sprang up soon after the proindependence votes were counted, and prounion Serb party leaders warned of negative popular reaction to a proposal to make Montenegrin the official language under a new constitution. Meanwhile, the proindependence Bosniak and Albanian leadership was dismayed that the Constitutional Court struck down the Minority Rights Act, which guaranteed seats in the assembly to minority groups based on their proportion in the population (one seat for groups less than 5 percent of the population; three seats for ethnic groups over 5 percent), even if they fell below the usual electoral threshold. The act had been passed just ten days before the referendum, after these leaders had made passage of the bill a condition for their support of independence.

President Vujanović set September 10, 2006, as the date for the next parliamentary election. All parties seemed to be in agreement that the election campaign would be framed by competing visions regarding the legal infrastructure needed to ease integration into the EU and regarding economic reforms, given the poor state of the economy and low standard of living after the removal of sanctions.

Political Parties

For four-and-a-half decades after World War II, Yugoslavia's only authorized political party was the Communist Party, which was redesignated as the League of Communists of Yugoslavia (*Savez Komunista Jugoslavija*—SKJ) in 1952. The collapse of Communist rule in 1989 and 1990 led the formation of a large number of successor and other parties, including several "federal" groupings that sought, without success, to preserve the Yugoslav federation (see the 1994–1995 edition of the *Handbook*, p. 991).

In Montenegro, the Democratic Party of Socialists of Montenegro (DPSCG), successor to the League of Communists of Montenegro, has headed the government since the party's formation in the early 1990s, most recently in alliance with the smaller Social Democratic Party of Montenegro (SDPCG). Joined by the People's Party (NS), they contested the May 1998 Montenegrin election as the For a Better Life (*Da Živimo Bolje*—DŽB) alliance but chose to boycott the federal elections of September 2000, leaving the field to the republic's opposition parties, principally the Socialist People's Party of Montenegro (SNPCG) and the Serbian People's Party (SNS). With the NS having left the government in late December 2000, the DPSCG and the SDPCG formed the Victory Is Montenegro–Milo Djukanović Democratic Coalition (*Pobjeda Je Crne Gore–Demokratska Koalicija Milo Djukanović*) to contest the April 2001 Montenegrin election, at which it won 42 percent of the vote and a plurality of 36 seats. The SNPCG and the SNS were joined by the NS in the opposing, anti-independence Together for Yugoslavia (*Zajedno za Jugoslaviju*) coalition, which finished second, with 41 percent of the vote and 33 seats. In 2002 the DPSCG and the SDPCG formed the Democratic List for European Montenegro–Milo Djukanović (*Demokratska Lista za Evropsku Crnu Goru–Milo Djukanović*), which won 48 percent of the vote. The SNPCG, SNS, and NS ran as the Together for Changes (*Zajedno za Promjene*), which won 38 percent.

In 2006 the assembly opposition parties—the SNPCG, SNS, and NS—which had been joined in 2004 by the newly organized Democratic Serbian Party (DSS), were allied in support of maintaining the state union with Serbia and against the May 21, 2006, independence referendum. Their prounion grouping was defeated by an electoral coalition of pro-independence DPSCG and SDPCG voters, with significant support from the Liberal Party of Montenegro (LPCG) and the ethnic Albanian and Bosniak party leaders and voters.

President Vujanović's decision to set September 10, 2006, as the date for the next parliamentary election fueled a wave of negotiations among the various government and opposition party leaders to forge electoral coalitions and alliances to win a mandate to form the next government.

Government Parties

Democratic Party of Socialists of Montenegro (*Demokratska Partija Socijalista Crne Gore*—DPSCG). The DPSCG is the successor to the League of Communists of Montenegro. It was fourth ranked, with 17 seats, in the federal Chamber of Citizens balloting in December 1992, while retaining a majority in the simultaneous Montenegrin republican Assembly poll with 44 percent of the vote. In the November 1996 elections the party increased its federal representation to 20 seats and maintained its majority at the republican level, winning 45 seats. Historically very close to Slobodan Milošević, the party suffered from intense internal squabbling as increasingly anti-Milošević Prime Minister Milo Djukanović narrowly beat Momir Bulatović in the 1997 Montenegrin presidential election and ousted him from the party leadership. The party split in January 1998, with the Bulatović faction forming the Socialist People's Party of Montenegro (SNPCG, below).

The DPSCG competed in the May 1998 Montenegrin elections as senior partner of the For a Better Life electoral alliance, winning 30 of the coalition's 42 assembly seats. Despite overtures from the anti- Milošević Democratic Opposition of Serbia alliance, the DPSCG chose to boycott the September 2000 federal elections, a major tactical error that left the anti-independence SNPCG in unchallenged control of the Montenegrin delegation to the Chamber of Citizens. At the April 2001 Montenegrin Assembly election the DPSCG-led Victory Is Montenegro coalition finished first but required the external support of the Liberal Alliance (see LPCG below) to organize a government.

At the October 2002 republican election the DPSCG won 30 of the Democratic List's 39 seats. An effort in late 2002 by President Djukanović and Prime Minister Filip Vujanović to, in effect, exchange jobs was finally accomplished in 2003. The DPSCG also held the office of state union president and was the leading Montenegrin party in the state union assembly, although it fully intended to lead Montenegro to independence.

The DPSCG introduced the independence referendum legislation in the assembly and strongly endorsed independence. In July 2006 party leaders engaged in coalition discussions with the SDPCG leadership in anticipation of new elections, despite Djukanović's statements that the party would prefer to contest the elections independently (opinion polls indicated the DPSCG might poll more votes if independent of the SDPCG). After the Constitutional Court ruled the Minority Rights Act unconstitutional, the DPSCG leadership offered guaranteed slots in the assembly to several of the minority parties provided they join the DPSCG in an election coalition, and also promised to pursue legislation or a constitutional provision to undo the court ruling and reinstate the guaranteed legislative seats for ethnic minority parties.

Leaders: Milo DJUKANOVIĆ (Prime Minister of the Republic and President of the Party), Filip VUJANOVIĆ (President of the Republic), Svetozar MAROVIĆ (Former President of the State

Union), Miodrag RADUNOVIĆ (Chair of Executive Committee), Dragan KUJOVIĆ (Vice President), Miodrag VUKOVIĆ (Party Whip).

Social Democratic Party of Montenegro (*Socijaldemokratska Partija Crne Gore*—SDPCG). Dating from the 1992 merger of three parties (two social democratic and one Communist), the SDPCG was strongly pro-independence. It won one federal parliamentary seat in 1996. For the May 1998 Montenegrin Assembly election it participated in the For a Better Life coalition with the DPSCG and the People's Party (below), capturing five seats and joining the government formed in July. It boycotted the 2000 federal election but again ran in coalition with the DPSCG in the April 2001 Montenegrin election. In October Ranko Krivokapić was elected party president, succeeding Žarko RAKČEVIĆ. In October 2002 the SDPCG won nine Montenegrin Assembly seats as part of the Democratic List.

The SDPCG also supported the independence referendum in 2006. In the run-up to the September 2006 elections the leaders of the SDPCG were working to secure a pre-election coalition with the DPSCG and the Croatian and Bosniak party leaders.

Leaders: Ranko KRIVOKAPIĆ (President of the Party and of the Montenegrin Assembly); Ivan BRAJOVIĆ, Miodrag ILIČKOVIĆ, Rifat RASTODER (Vice Presidents).

Civic Party of Montenegro (*Gradjanska Partija Crne Gore*—GPCG). The small GPCG joined the Democratic List for European Montenegro prior to the October 2002 election and was awarded one assembly seat. In 2003 it supported independent presidential candidate Dragab HAJDUKOVIĆ, who won 4 percent of the vote.

Party leader Krsto Pavićević was outspoken in his criticism of the DPSCG leadership following the ruling of the Constitutional Court in July 2006 striking down the Minority Rights Act. He opined that because the court was under the political control of the DPSCG, the court's action could and should be reversed by Prime Minister Djukanović to maintain good faith with the ethnic Bosniak and Albanian parties.

Leaders: Krsto PAVIĆEVIĆ (Chair), Petar BOKAN, Slobodan MEDENICA, Rafet MULIĆ, Ivan VUJOVIĆ, Rade VUJOVIĆ, Neeljko UROVIĆ.

Democratic Union of Albanians (*Demokratska Unija Albanaca—DUA*). In the 2002 legislative election the DUA ran as the **Democratic Coalition "Albanians Together"** (*"Albanci Zajedno"*), which won two seats reserved for the Albanian community. The coalition included two other ethnic Albanian parties: the **Democratic Alliance of Montenegro** (*Demokratski Savez u Crnoj Gori—DSCG*), chaired by Mehmet BARDHI, and the **Party of Democratic Prosperity** (*Partia e Prosperitetit Demokratik—PPD*), led by Osman REXHA. In April 2001 the three had run independently, with the DUA and the DSCG each winning one seat.

Leaders: Ferhat DINOŠA, Gezim HAJDINAGA (Minister for Protection of National and Ethnic Rights).

Other Parliamentary Parties

Socialist People's Party of Montenegro (*Socijalistička Narodna Partija Crne Gore—SNPCG*). The SNPCG was formed in early 1998 by Momir Bulatović following his rupture with the DPSCG. It held its first congress on March 21, 1998, at which 150 members of a governing committee were elected. At the republican election of May 1998 the party came in second, with 29 seats.

Under FRY Prime Minister Bulatović, from May 1998 the party was the junior partner in the FRY government, maintaining strict support for Slobodan Milošević through the September 2000 election. Because the governing Montenegrin coalition boycotted the balloting, the SNPCG virtually swept the Montenegrin polls, winning 19 of the republic's 20 upper house seats and 28 seats in the lower house. With Bulatović having resigned the federal prime ministership following Milošević's concession, the party's vice chair, Zoran ŽIŽIĆ, was selected as his successor by newly installed President Koštunica in late October.

The chair passed from Momir Bulatović to an opponent, Predrag Bulatović (no relation), at a party congress in February 2001, after which the SNPCG formed the Together for Yugoslavia alliance with the SNS and the NS (below) to contest the April Montenegrin legislative election. Following the extradition to The Hague of Slobodan Milošević in late June 2001, Prime Minister Žižić resigned in protest, but he was succeeded in mid-July by another SNPCG member, Dragiša Pešić, who remained in office until the FRY was replaced by the state union. At the 2002 republican election the party won 19 of the 30 seats claimed by the Together for Changes coalition.

The SNPCG joined the other opposition parties (SNS, NS) and the DSS in street protests against the DPSCG-SDPCG government throughout 2004 and the boycott of Parliament in the same year. The SNPCG also spearheaded the prounion coalition in opposition to the 2006 independence referendum. After the vote for independence, Predrag Bulatović steered the party toward a pragmatic "constructive dialogue" on postindependence platform issues, especially the need for a draft constitution, support for more democratic institutions, and engagement with the path toward European integration. Negotiations toward a pre-election coalition with the other opposition parties were complicated by charges by SNPCG leaders of "poaching" tactics by the other opposition parties, especially the SNS, directed at SNPCG voters.

Leaders: Predrag BULATOVIĆ (Chair), Dragiša PEŠIĆ (Former Prime Minister of the FRY), Velizar KALUDJEROVIĆ.

Serbian People's Party (*Srpska Narodna Stranka—SNS*). The SNS was registered as a party in late March 1998 by a dissident faction of the NS. Since then, it has often been in alliance with the SNPCG and the Montenegrin branch of the Serbian Radical Party (SRSCG, below). Although the party continued to support the Milošević regime through the Kosovo crisis, some local party leaders refused to support the federal president's reelection in 2000. At the September balloting the party won two seats in the lower house of the Federal Assembly and one in the upper house. A party congress in February

2001 elected former NS leader Božidar BOJOVIĆ as chair, succeeding Zelidrag NIKČEVIĆ. In October 2002 the SNS won six seats in the Montenegrin Assembly. A year later Bojović was replaced by Andrija Mandić.

The SNS joined the other opposition parties (SNPCG, NS) and the DSS in street protests against the DPSCG-SDPCG government in 2004 and in the subsequent parliamentary boycott. The SNS also enthusiastically joined the prounion coalition in opposition to the 2006 independence referendum. Postreferendum news accounts alleged that SNS party members attributed the success of the referendum vote to the support of ethnic minority voters and therefore demonstrated increased hostility toward ethnic minorities, especially Bosniaks, in Serb-dominated areas.

After independence SNS leaders positioned the party to advocate for policies aimed at protecting the status of Serbs in Montenegro. The SNS launched a petition drive advocating dual Serbian citizenship for Montenegrin Serbs, and party leaders publicly called for measures to preserve cultural autonomy and proportional representation in political institutions for Serbs. SNS leaders also led the drive for a Serbian List of opposition parties in the September 2006 election campaign.

Leaders: Andrija MANDIĆ (President); Bredimir ALEXSIĆ (President of Executive Board); Goran DANILOVIĆ, Novak RADULOVIĆ, Dr. Novica STANIĆ (Vice Presidents).

People's Party (*Narodna Stranka—NS*). Historically an intensely pan-Serbian formation, the NS supported the maintenance of Montenegro's ties with Serbia. It won 14 seats and 13 percent of the vote in the December 1992 Montenegrin election, at which time it also secured 4 federal Chamber seats. In November 1996 an NS coalition with the Liberal Alliance (see LPCG, below) called the People's Accord (*Narodna Sloga*) won 8 federal seats as well as 19 in the Montenegrin Assembly. In March 1997 differences over continuing support for the coalition led supporters of the party's vice chair, Božidar Bojović, to attempt expulsion of the president, Novak KILIBARDA, who was moving closer toward accepting Montenegrin independence. Kilibarda's NS joined the DPSCG in forming the For a Better Life coalition shortly before the May 1998 Montenegrin election, at which it won 7 assembly seats. In the same month the Bojović faction registered a new pro-Belgrade party, the SNS. Kilibarda joined the governing Montenegrin coalition as a deputy prime minister.

In March 2000, rejecting Kilibarda's pro-independence stance, the NS replaced him with Dragan Šoć, the Montenegrin minister of justice. On December 28, objecting to the latest independence moves by President Djukanović, the NS left the governing coalition and subsequently allied itself with the SNPCG for the April 2001 election. In October 2002 it won five assembly seats as part of the Together for Changes coalition.

After independence, the NS leaders, along with the DSS leadership, rebuffed SNS proposals for a Serbian List for the 2006 elections in favor of working to preserve the broader prounion coalition, which had garnered the support of 185000 voters in the May 2006 referendum.

Leaders: Predrag POPOVIĆ (Chair), Dragan ŠOĆ, Budimir DUBAK.

Liberal Party of Montenegro (*Liberalna Partija Crne Gore—LPCG*). The LPCG was established on October 31, 2004, under the leadership of Miodrag Živković, the former chair of the Liberal Alliance of Montenegro (*Liberalni Savez Crne Gore—LSCG*), following his expulsion from the LSCG in September.

Established in 1990 as a strong supporter of independence for Montenegro, the LSCG won 13 seats in the December 1992 republican assembly elections. For the November 1996 polling, the party forged an electoral alliance with the NS, despite their policy differences. Running independently, the LSCG won 5 assembly seats in May 1998. It boycotted the 2000 federal election but won 6 seats at the April 2001 assembly election, after which it supported formation of a minority DPSCG-SDPCG government. Only a year later, however, it withdrew its support over objections to formation of the state union. At the resultant October 2002 Montenegrin Assembly election its representation fell to 4 seats, even though it had made major gains at municipal elections. In the May 2003 three-way republican presidential contest, Živković finished second, with 30 percent of the vote.

In 2004 the party split, largely over the issue of independence, leading to the Liberal Alliance chair's expulsion in September. On March 24, 2005, delegates to an extraordinary conference of the LSCG voted to end the Liberal Alliance party's existence. Longtime party leader Slavko PEROVIĆ condemned Montenegro's intelligentsia and opposition for abandoning their mission, and attacked the Djukanović regime as "mafia-ridden."

With the LSCG now defunct, LPCG leader Živković set his new party in support of independence but continued opposition to the alleged criminality and abuse of power by the Djukanović regime. (In July 2004 he had been found guilty of libeling the prime minister with salacious accusations.)

Leaders: Miodrag ŽIVKOVIĆ (Chair); Bilsen IDRIZOVIĆ, Labud ŠLJUKIĆ, Nikola SAMARDŽIĆ (Vice Chairs).

Other Parties

Democratic Party of Unity. (*Demokratska Stranka Jedinstva*—DSJ). The DSJ is a new party registered in mid-2006 by Zoran Žižić, who was previously vice chair of the SNPCG. Žižić left the SNPCG when that party declined to join the Serbian List coalition in the run-up to the September 10 polls.

Leader: Zoran ŽIŽIĆ (Chair).

Democratic Serbian Party (*Demokratska Srpska Stranka*—DSS). This Montenegrin-based version of the DSS was launched by former SNS party leader Bozidar Bojović in December 2003. The DSS joined the opposition parties' street protests against the DPSCG-SDPCG government throughout 2004. The DSS also joined the prounion coalition in opposition to the 2006 independence referendum. After the referendum DSS leaders rebuffed calls from the SNS for a "Serbian list" to contest the 2006 parliamentary elections, advocating instead for preservation of the larger prounion coalition of parties.

Leaders: Bozidar BOJOVIĆ (Chair), Ranko KADIĆ (Vice Chair), Vukoman FEMIĆ (Vice Chair), Dragica PEJOVIĆ, Miladin JOKSIMOVIĆ.

Group for Change (*Grupa za Promjene*—GZP). Although originally formed as a nongovernmental organization and not a political party, the GZP declared that it would contest the September 2006 legislative elections as the **Movement for Change** (*Pokreta za Promjene*—PzP). The GZP has been a significant participant in public discourse in the past and continued its call for an end to corruption in the public sector. Its principal leaders, Executive Director Nebojša Medojević and Chair Svetozar Jovićević, rank among Montenegro's most respected public figures. Public opinion polls published after the independence referendum show the GZP with stronger support than several of the more established opposition parties.

Leaders: Nebojša MEDOJEVIĆ, Svetozar JOVIĆEVIĆ, Koča PAVLOVIĆ.

People's Accord of Montenegro (*Narodna Sloga Crne Gore*—NSCG). The NSCG (sometimes also referenced as National Unity) was established by former NS leader Novak Kilibarda in February 2001. With fewer than 300 votes, it failed to win any seats at the April Montenegrin Assembly election. In 2002 Kilibarda ran as a member of the DPSCG-led Democratic List for European Montenegro. In 2003 he was named as a member of the new state union assembly.

Leader: Novak KILIBARDA.

People's Socialist Party of Montenegro (*Narodna Socialistička Stranka Crne Gore*—NSSCG). The NSSCG was established in late February 2001 by supporters of former FRY prime minister Momir Bulatović following his ouster from the SNPCG. The party failed to attract significant support at the April 2001 Montenegrin Assembly election, capturing less than 3 percent of the vote and therefore winning no seats. In 2002 it ran as a component of the **Patriotic Coalition for Yugoslavia** (*Patriotska Koalicija za Jugoslavia*—PK), which also included the Serbia-based Yugoslav United Left and Serbian

Cabinet

As of July 1, 2006

Prime Minister	Milo Djukanović (DPSCG)
Deputy Prime Ministers	Dragan Djurović (DPSCG)
	Branimir Gvozdenović (DPSCG)
	Miroslav Ivanišević (DPSCG)
	Jusuf Kalamperović (SDPCG)

Ministers

Agriculture, Forestry, and Water	Milutin Simović (DPSCG)
Culture	Vesna Kilibarda (DPSCG) [f]
Economy	Predrag Bošković (DPSCG)
Education and Science	Slobodan Backović (DPSCG)
Environment and Urban Planning	Boro Vučinić (DPSCG)
Finance	Igor Lukšić (DPSCG)
Foreign Affairs	Miodrag Vlahović (ind.)
Foreign Economic Relations, Trade,	Gordana Djurović (DPSCG) [f]
and European Integration	
Health	Miodrag Pavličić (SDPCG)
Interior	Jusuf Kalamperović (SDPCG)
Justice	Željko Šturanović (DPSCG)
Labor and Social Welfare	Slavoljub Stijepović (DPSCG)
Maritime Trade and Transport	Andrija Lompar (SDPCG)
Protection of National and Ethnic Rights	Gezim Hajdinaga (DUA)
Tourism	Predrag Nenezić (DPSCG)

[f] = female

Radical Party, but again failed to meet the 3 percent threshold.

The NSSCG in 2006 joined the Serbian List coalition in the run-up to the September 10 polls.

Leaders: Momir BULATOVIĆ (Honorary Chair), Novo VUJO-ŠEVIĆ.

Serbian Radical Party in Montenegro (*Srpska Radikalna Stranka Crne Gore*—SRSCG). Founded in Serbia in February 1991, the Serbian Radical Party (SRS) is a quasi-fascist advocate of "Greater Serbia" that emphasizes the importance of its "leader" (*vodj*). The Montenegrin branch of the party, the SRSCG, is closely allied with the Serbian headquarters (see Serbia article). SRSCG joined the Serbian List in the run-up to the 2006 election.

Leaders: Tomislav NIKOLIĆ (Acting Chair), Aleksandar VUČIĆ (General Secretary).

A number of Bosniak parties have also participated in Montenegrin elections. For the 2002 assembly election they were divided into two coalitions: the **Bosniak Democratic Coalition–Harun Hadžić**, which grouped four pro-autonomy Sandžak-based parties (see Serbia article), including the leader's **International Democratic Union** (*Internacionalna Demokratska Unbija*—IDU), and the **Bosniak Coalition** of four parties that supported Montenegrin independence, including the Montenegrin branch of the **Party of Democratic Action** (*Stranka Demokratske Akcije*—SDA). Both Bosniak coalitions fell below 1 percent of the vote.

Legislature

Assembly of the Republic of Montenegro (*Skupština Republike Crne Gore*). The members of the Montenegrin legislature are elected to four-year terms by proportional representation. In general, parties must meet a 3 percent threshold to qualify for seats, although the Albanian minority is guaranteed representation. Results for the election of October 20, 2002, were as follows: Democratic List for European Montenegro, 39 (Democratic Party of Socialists of Montenegro, 30; Social Democratic Party of Montenegro, 7; Citizens' Party, 1; allied independent, 1); Together for Changes, 30 (Socialist People's Party of Montenegro, 19; Serbian People's Party, 6; People's Party, 5); Liberal Alliance of Montenegro, 4; Democratic Coalition "Albanians Together," 2 (Democratic Union of Albanians, 1; Democratic Alliance of Montenegro, 1). The next election, for an expanded, 81-seat house, was scheduled for September 10, 2006. (*See headnote.*)

President: Ranko KRIVOKAPIĆ.

Communications

Press

The following are dailies published in Podgorica in Serbo-Croatian, unless otherwise noted: *Dan*; *Pobjeda*; *Republika*; *Vijesti*; and *Monitor*, weekly.

News Agencies

An independent news agency, MNNews, operates from Montenegro.

Broadcasting and Computing

Montenegro has a state-controlled broadcasting service, *Radio-Televizija Crne Gore,* that operates two radio and two television networks. There are also numerous privately owned stations.

Intergovernmental Representation

Ambassador to the U.S.
(Vacant)

U.S. Ambassador to Montenegro
(Vacant)

Permanent Representative to the UN
Nebojša KALUDJEROVIĆ

IGO Memberships (Non-UN)
OSCE. Following Montenegro's declaration of independence in 2006, Serbia announced that it was assuming all the memberships in intergovernmental organizations formally held by the state union of Serbia and Montenegro. Montenegro was expected to apply for its own membership in those organizations

NETHERLANDS

KINGDOM OF THE NETHERLANDS

Koninkrijk der Nederlanden

Note: The coalition government led by Prime Minister Jan Peter Balkenende resigned on June 29, 2006, when the coalition's smallest member—the D66 party—withdrew its support. D66 departed the coalition after its demands for the resignation of Immigration Minister Rita Verdonk were not heeded. The General Affairs Ministry announced on July 2 that a national election will be held in November. In the meantime, a caretaker government will be formed with the assistance of former prime minister Ruud Lubbers, who will also be responsible for setting a specific date for the national election.

The Country

Facing the North Sea between Belgium and Germany, the Netherlands (often called "Holland," from the name of one of its principal provinces) is noted for the dikes, canals, and reclaimed polder lands providing constant reminder that two-fifths of the country's land area lies below sea level. The largely homogeneous, Germanic population is divided principally between Catholics (31 percent) and Protestants (21 percent), with 40 percent declaring no religious affiliation in 1999. In 2000 women constituted 43 percent of the labor force, concentrated in the services sector; female participation in the central government is approximately 30 percent.

The Netherlands experienced rapid industrialization after World War II, although the industrial sector is now limited to approximately 22 percent of the labor force as compared with 74 percent in the services sector. The traditionally important agricultural sector employs fewer than 4 percent but is characterized by highly efficient methods of production, which are amply rewarded by the common agricultural policy of the European Union (EU, formerly the European Community—EC), of which the Netherlands was a founding member. Leading agricultural products include potatoes, vegetables, sugar beets, wheat, and pork. Since there are few natural resources except large natural gas deposits, most nonagricultural activity involves the processing of imported raw materials. Refined petroleum, chemicals, steel, textiles, and ships constitute the bulk of industrial output. Principal exports include machinery and transport equipment, chemicals and petroleum products, and food. Germany, Belgium, France, and the United Kingdom rank as leading trading partners.

In the early 1980s the economy was stagnating under the influence of persistently high budget

deficits necessitated, in part, by the nation's extensive welfare system, which, among other things, provided disability payments to more than 1 million workers. However, a labor/business pact in 1982 established the basis for significant governmental cost-cutting, private-sector promotion, wage moderation, and more flexible employment regulations. As a result, the economy grew at a real average annual rate of 1.9 percent during 1985–1994. GDP grew by 3.8 percent in 1997 and 4.1 percent in 1998, while inflation remained at about 2 percent annually and unemployment fell to under 5 percent in 1998. The Netherlands easily met the economic criteria required for its participation in the launching of the EU's Economic and Monetary Union (EMU) on January 1, 1999.

GDP growth in 1999 and 2000 held steady at more than 3 percent as inflation remained under control and unemployment continued to decline, reaching 3.6 percent in 2000. However, the economy subsequently deteriorated, with growth of only 1 percent in 2001, 0 percent in 2002, and −1 percent in 2003. Meanwhile, inflation and unemployment climbed to nearly 6 percent in 2002. In addition, the budget surplus of the late 1990s (which had permitted tax reduction) has recently been replaced by a deficit that the Dutch government forecast would reach 3.25 percent of GDP in 2004, thereby creating difficulty for the administration regarding EMU fiscal guidelines. The economy appeared to begin a recovery in 2004 (growth of 1.1 percent), although unemployment continued to rise.

The International Monetary Fund (IMF) cites budgetary restraint and stronger exports as the main factors resulting in further improvement in the country's economy during 2005, when GDP grew another 1.1 percent. What's more, the IMF has forecast a GDP growth rate of 2.6 percent for 2006 and 2.8 percent for 2007.

Government and Politics

Political Background

Having declared independence from Spain in 1581 at the time of the Counter Reformation, the United Provinces of the Netherlands were ruled by hereditary *stadhouders* (governors) of the House of Orange until the present constitutional monarchy was established under the same house at the close of the Napoleonic period. Queen JULIANA, who had succeeded her mother, WILHELMINA, in 1948, abdicated in favor of her daughter BEATRIX in April 1980.

Since World War II the Netherlands has been governed by a succession of coalition governments in which the large Catholic People's Party (*Katholieke Volkspartif*—KVP) typically played a pivotal role prior to its merger into the more inclusive Christian Democratic Appeal (*Christen-Democratisch Appèl*—CDA) in 1980. Coalitions between the KVP and the Labor Party (*Partij van de Arbeid*—PvdA) were the rule until 1958, when the latter went into opposition, the KVP continuing to govern in alliance with smaller parties of generally moderate outlook. A center-right coalition headed by Petrus J. S. DE JONG assumed office in April 1967 and was followed by an expanded center-right government formed under Barend W. BIESHEUVEL in 1971.

The inability of the Biesheuvel government to cope with pressing economic problems led to its early demise in July 1972 and to an election four months later. A 163-day interregnum then ensued before a PvdA-led government organized in May 1973 by Johannes (Joop) M. DEN UYL emerged as the first Dutch administration dominated by the political left. It survived until March 1977, when it collapsed in the wake of a bitter dispute between PvdA and CDA leaders over compensation for expropriated land. After another extended interregnum (the longest in the nation's history), Andreas A. M. VAN AGT succeeded in organizing a government of his CDA and the People's Party for Freedom and Democracy (*Volkspartif voor Vrijheid en Democratie*—VVD) in late December.

At the election of May 1981 the center-right coalition lost its legislative majority and was replaced by a grouping that included the CDA, PvdA, and center-left Democrats 66 (*Democraten 66*—D66), with van Agt continuing as prime minister. The comfortable legislative majority thus achieved

Political Status: Constitutional monarchy established 1814; under multiparty parliamentary system.

Area: 13,103 sq. mi. (33,936 sq. km.).

Population: 15,987,075 (2001C); 16,311,000 (2005E). Since 1971 population records have been maintained by means of a continuous accounting system rather than by total enumerations, the 2001 figure being derived from a January compilation of system components.

Major Urban Centers (2005E): AMSTERDAM (739,000), Rotterdam (596,000), The Hague (seat of government, 468,000), Utrecht (276,000), Eindhoven (209,000).

Official Language: Dutch.

Monetary Unit: Euro (market rate July 1, 2006: 1 euro = $1.28US).

Sovereign: Queen BEATRIX Wilhelmina Armgard; ascended the throne April 30, 1980, upon the abdication of her mother, Queen JULIANA Louise Emma Marie Wilhelmina. *Heir Apparent:* WILLEM-ALEXANDER, Prince of Orange.

Prime Minister: Jan Peter BALKENENDE (Christian Democratic Appeal); sworn in as head of a three-party coalition on July 22, 2002, following general election of May 15, succeeding Willem (Wim) KOK (Labor Party); formed new three-party coalition government on May 27, 2003, following general election of January 22.

Lubbers was forced to resign on May 2, 1989, following coalition disagreement over funding for an ambitious environmental plan, although he remained in office in a caretaker's capacity pending new elections. Because of its perceived antienvironmental posture, the VVD's parliamentary representation dropped from 27 to 22 seats at the balloting on September 6, with the PvdA becoming the CDA's partner in a new center-left administration sworn in on November 7 under Lubbers's leadership. His continuation in office was made possible by a commitment to the PvdA to increase antipollution and social welfare expenditures, financed largely by the imposition of a "carbon dioxide" tax on business firms and a freeze on defense spending in 1991. While the subsequent course of events in Eastern Europe permitted an actual cutback in projected military expenses, the overall economic situation deteriorated.

During the early 1990s traditional Dutch social liberalism led to parliamentary action in several controversial areas. In 1992 the licensing of brothels and sex clubs won parliamentary approval on the ground that it would serve to inhibit the exploitation of prostitutes and facilitate the collection of income tax and state insurance contributions from them. In 1993 the Second Chamber approved legislation under which a doctor would not be prosecuted for administering euthanasia if a 28-point procedure was followed. Also in 1993 the same house approved legislation banning discrimination on grounds of race, nationality, gender, sexual orientation, political views, or religious conviction.

The May 1994 general election marked the withdrawal from Dutch politics of Prime Minister Lubbers, who failed to gain the presidency of the European Commission in June. (The U.S. government vetoed his candidacy for the post of NATO secretary general in 1995, but Lubbers was named to head the United Nations (UN) Office of the High Commissioner for Refugees in 2000.) The CDA campaign in 1994 was headed by Elco BRINKMAN, party leader in the Second Chamber. With Lubbers's departure, the CDA suffered its worst-ever defeat, losing a third of its support. The PvdA also lost ground, but it replaced the CDA

was offset by sharp differences over both defense and economic policy, and the new government collapsed in May 1982. The principal result of balloting in September was a loss of 11 seats by D66 and a gain of 10 by the VVD, Ruud F. M. LUBBERS being installed as head of another center-right government in November following his succession to the CDA leadership in October. Contrary to opinion poll predictions, the CDA won a plurality at the lower house election of May 1986, Lubbers being returned as head of a new center-right government in July.

as the largest parliamentary party, while substantial gains were registered by the VVD and D66. Far-right and far-left parties also gained seats, and two new pensioners' movements made their chamber debuts. The public standing of the outgoing coalition parties was further compromised by the enforced resignations on May 27 of the caretaker ministers of home affairs (PvdA) and justice (CDA) following a Second Chamber vote of no confidence in their handling of measures to combat organized crime. In light of the new parliamentary arithmetic, the outcome of lengthy postelection negotiations was, as expected, the formation in August 1994 of a three-party coalition of the PvdA, VVD, and D66, with Willem (Wim) KOK becoming the first Labor prime minister since 1977.

The new coalition committed itself to a four-year program of retrenchment in social, defense, and other government spending, although deeper welfare cuts were deferred for two years at the PvdA's behest. In addition, the governing parties were broadly united in desiring to meet the "Maastricht criteria" for participation in a single European currency toward the end of the century.

With the government having received wide international praise for the "Dutch model" of sustained economic growth, substantial job creation, and an effective social services sector, the PvdA and the VVD improved their positions in the May 6, 1998, Second Chamber elections, although the D66 slipped significantly. The new government announced by Kok on August 3 comprised six ministers each from the PvdA and the VVD and three from the D66, with the coalition controlling 97 of the 150 seats in the *Tweede Kamer*.

On May 19, 1999, the cabinet resigned following the defeat by one vote in the *Eerste Kamer* of a bill sponsored by the D66 that would have permitted national "corrective referendums" to veto certain economic and social legislative decisions. However, on June 2 the three parties agreed to resume the coalition and to back a revised "consultative referendum" bill under which referendum results would not be binding.

Although the three-party governing coalition flirted with collapse in May 1999, two years of relative stability followed. The biggest controversy to emerge within the government was in fact generated by an unexpected boon, namely budget surpluses for 1999 and 2000, the country's first in a quarter-century. Although the governing partners quickly approved tax cuts and reforms, elements of the left-leaning PvdA also wanted increased expenditures for social programs, while the more conservative VVD pressed for larger tax breaks and reductions in the comparatively high national debt.

At the same time, the Netherlands was also attracting international attention, as it has so frequently in the past, for legalizing controversial social practices. In 2001 it became the world's first country to permit same-sex marriages, and a year later another first-of-a-kind law legalizing euthanasia entered into effect.

Attention in mid-2001 increasingly focused on the upcoming 2002 general election and speculation that Prime Minister Kok might not seek a third term. On August 26 Kok confirmed that he would in fact step down, with the party then turning to its parliamentary leader, Ad MELKERT, to lead it into the balloting. Following local elections in March 2002, however, it appeared that prospects for Labor's continuation in office were declining, given the increasing strength of the CDA and the emergence, farther to the right, of an anti-immigrant populist party, the List Pim Fortuyn (*Lijst Pim Fortuyn*—LPF).

Prime Minister Kok and his cabinet resigned on April 16, 2002, in response to a report that criticized the Dutch military for failing to prevent the July 1995 massacre at the Bosnian "safe haven" of Srebrenica. The government continued to serve in a caretaker capacity until the May 15 general election. Despite the shock of the assassination of LPF leader Pim FORTUYN on May 6 (see Current issues, below), the leaders of the major parties agreed to hold the balloting as scheduled, with the CDA (led by Jan Peter BALKENENDE) securing a plurality of 43 seats in the *Tweede Kamer*, followed by the LPF (26 seats), VVD (24), and PvdA (23).

A CDA/LPF/VVD coalition government was formed on July 22 under Balkenende's leadership. However, it resigned on October 16 as a result of differences over the proposed expansion of the EU, a power struggle within the LPF, and increasing economic difficulties. At early balloting for the *Tweede Kamer* on January 22, 2003, the CDA again achieved a slim plurality (44 seats versus 42 for the PvdA). The CDA initially sought to form a coalition with the PvdA, but negotiations fell apart due primarily to personal animosity between the leaders of the parties. After protracted negotiations, a CDA/VVD/D66 coalition was announced on May 27, with Balkenende retaining the premiership. The coalition proposed a program of reforms to immigration laws, electoral reforms, and changes in the social security program as well as labor laws. The coalition's efforts in these areas have, however, for the most part been frustrated. Indeed, the failure of an electoral reform bill led to the resignation on March 23, 2005, of Deputy Prime Minister and Minister for Government Reform Thom de GRAAF.

On June 29, 2006, the Balkenende government collapsed after several weeks of infighting among the three parties in the coalition government. The smallest of the three parties, D66, withdrew its support for the Balkenende government after calls for the resignaiton of Immigraiton Minister Rita VERDONK were ignored. (See Current issues, below.) Queen Beatrix is expected to call for new elections. Recent opinion polls show the opposition Labor Party with a strong chance of becoming the largest party.

Constitution and Government

Originally adopted in 1814–1815, the Netherlands' constitution has been progressively amended to incorporate the features of a modern democratic welfare state in which the sovereign exercises strictly limited powers. Under a special Statute of December 29, 1954, the Kingdom of the Netherlands was described as including not only the Netherlands proper but also the fully autonomous overseas territories of the Netherlands Antilles and Suriname, the latter ultimately becoming independent in 1975. On January 1, 1986, the island of Aruba formally withdrew

from the Antilles federation, becoming a separate, self-governing member of the kingdom.

Political power centers in the Parliament, or States General (*Staten Generaal*), consisting of an indirectly elected First Chamber and a more powerful, directly elected Second Chamber. Either or both chambers may be dissolved by the sovereign prior to the holding of a new election. Executive authority is vested in a Council of Ministers (*Ministerraad*) appointed by the sovereign but responsible to the States General. An advisory Council of State (*Raad van State*), comprised of the queen and crown prince plus a number of councillors appointed by the queen upon nomination by the Second Chamber, is consulted by the executive on legislative and administrative policy. The judicial system is headed by a Supreme Court and includes five courts of appeal, 19 district courts, and 62 cantonal courts.

For administrative purposes the Netherlands is divided into 12 provinces, the most recent, Flevoland, created on January 1, 1986, from land formed under the more than half-century-old Zuider Zee reclamation project. Each province has its own elected council, which elects an executive, and a sovereign commissioner appointed by the queen. At the local level there are approximately 640 municipalities, each with a council that designates aldermen to share executive responsibilities with a crown-appointed burgomaster.

Foreign Relations

Officially neutral before World War II, the Netherlands reversed its foreign policy as a result of the German occupation of 1940–1945 and became an active participant in the subsequent evolution of the Western community through the Benelux Union, the North Atlantic Treaty Organization (NATO), the Western European Union, the EC/EU, and other West European and Atlantic organizations. A founding member of the UN, the Netherlands also belongs to all of its specialized agencies. The country's principal foreign policy problems in the postwar period stemmed from the 1945–1949 transition to independence of the

Netherlands East Indies (Indonesia); Jakarta's formal annexation in 1969 of West New Guinea (Irian Jaya); and continued pressure, including numerous acts of terrorism, by South Moluccan expatriates seeking Dutch aid in the effort to separate their homeland from Indonesia.

A major foreign affairs issue with profound domestic repercussions turned on the NATO decision in late 1979 to modernize and expand its nuclear arsenal. After intense debate in the Second Chamber, the Dutch acceded to the wishes of their allies but indicated that they would postpone local deployment of 48 cruise missiles in the hope that a meaningful arms control agreement with the Soviet bloc could be negotiated; in the absence of such an agreement, a treaty with the United States authorizing deployment by mid-1989 was finally ratified in February 1986. Preparations for installation of the missiles were, however, suspended prior to the signing of the U.S.-Soviet intermediate-range nuclear force (INF) treaty in December 1987 and were formally terminated upon acceptance of the treaty by the States General in March 1988.

The Netherlands made a naval contribution to the U.S.-led UN coalition in the 1991 Gulf War.

On December 15, 1992, the States General completed its ratification of the EC's Maastricht Treaty on economic and political union. However, the Netherlands' enthusiasm for European integration did not extend to participation in the "Eurocorps" military force inaugurated by France and Germany in 1992, which by mid-1994 also included Belgium, Luxembourg, and Spain. Instead, the Netherlands on March 30, 1994, signed an agreement with Germany providing for the creation of a 30,000-strong Dutch-German joint force that would be fully integrated into NATO and open to other NATO members. The new joint force was formally inaugurated in August 1995, with staff headquarters in Münster, Germany.

Amsterdam took offense in November 1995 when the U.S. government vetoed the candidacy of former prime minister Ruud Lubbers for the post of NATO secretary general, reportedly because of Lubbers's record of concern about German dominance in Europe. (In October 2000 Lubbers

was appointed to head the UN Office of the High Commissioner for Refugees.) Nevertheless, the Netherlands, which had previously committed troops to peacekeeping efforts in Bosnia, assigned 2,100 troops to the NATO-commanded International Force (IFOR) under the Dayton peace accords. The Kok administration was also a solid supporter of NATO action against Yugoslavia in early 1999.

The Hague is home to the International Court of Justice and the UN-sponsored International Criminal Tribunals for the former Yugoslavia and Rwanda (see the discussion under the UN Security Council). A Dutch air base, Kamp Zeist, Utrecht, also served as the trial site for two Libyans accused of the 1988 bombing of Pan Am flight 103 over Lockerbie, Scotland; the Dutch government had permitted the base to be regarded as Scottish territory for the duration of the trial, which concluded with one guilty verdict and one acquittal on January 31, 2001.

The Netherlands' tepid support for the U.S. invasion of Iraq has been a challenge for relations between the two countries. Those relations were further challenged in March 2005 when the Netherlands withdrew its 1,700 troops from Iraq. At the same time, the Netherlands tried to soften the blow by promising to send 25 troops to join a NATO training mission tasked with training Iraqi troops.

Dutch voters also took a step back from European integration when a larger-than-expected 61.5 percent of voters rejected the EU constitution. Prime Minister Balkenende's government had conducted a tepid campaign in favor of the treaty. In June 2006 Balkenende said that any future consideration was to take place in Parliament rather than by referendum.

In February 2006 the Dutch Parliament bowed to entreaties of U.S. and NATO officials and agreed to send up to 1,700 troops to Afghanistan as part of a NATO reconstruction mission.

Current Issues

Events prior to the May 2002 balloting for the *Tweede Kamer* were dominated by the sudden emergence as a major political force of flamboyant Pim Fortuyn, whose promotion of a populist mix of liberal policies (such as the improvement of public services) and rightist positions (such as heavy curbs on immigration and restrictions on rights for ethnic minorities) had struck a chord within a Dutch population increasingly concerned over deteriorating economic conditions and rising crime. Following Fortuyn's assassination on May 6 by an animal rights and environmental activist, consideration was given to postponing the balloting. However, all the major party leaders consented to proceeding as scheduled, with the LPF (the party formed by Fortuyn) winning 26 seats and joining the CDA and VVD in a center-right coalition government. Internal leadership struggles within the LPF quickly compromised the stability of the party and the government, prompting early elections in January 2003. Although the LPF seat total fell to eight in that balloting and the party lost its cabinet status, some of its proposals regarding immigration and crime had become official government policy.

Upon formation of the CDA/VVD/D66 coalition in May, Prime Minister Balkenende promised a crackdown on drug trafficking and other crimes. His administration also tried to combat the burgeoning fiscal crisis through proposed liberalization of labor regulations and reductions in longstanding welfare and pension benefits. However, those measures were met with stiff resistance by trade unions and other elements of society accustomed to the consensus-building approach previously employed in advance of major shifts in economic policies. Despite the government's austerity measures, it was predicted that the budget deficit would exceed 3 percent of GDP and thereby place the Netherlands in violation of the EU's growth and stability pact. (The Dutch government had previously been among the sharpest critics of similar French and German transgressions.) The gathering difficulties culminated in the opposition parties securing a solid majority of the Dutch seats in the June 2004 European Parliament elections. Another factor in the government's poor showing was public opposition to the administration's solid support for U.S. policy in Iraq.

The intertwined issues of immigration and rising anti-Muslim sentiment moved dramatically to the forefront again in November 2004 when Theo van GOGH, a filmmaker who had recently released a movie that focused on Islam's treatment of women, was assassinated, allegedly by an Islamic radical. Numerous anti-Muslim disturbances broke out in the wake of the murder, further threatening the Netherlands' long-time reputation for tolerance. In early 2005 the government announced that stricter qualifications would be imposed on potential immigrants regarding their knowledge of the nation's history and culture. Concurrently, an extensive campaign to combat terrorism was launched, and a number of alleged Islamic militants were either arrested or deported. The immigration and terrorism issues were widely believed to have been major factors in the 61.5 percent "no" vote registered by the Dutch electorate in a national referendum in June on the question of whether the proposed new EU constitution should be approved. (The government and most major parties had called for a "yes" vote.)

In June 2006 the issue of immigration led to the collapse of the Balkenende government. In May, Immigration Minister Rita Verdonk announced that she was considering revoking the citizenship of Ayaan Hirsi Ali, a member of Parliament and an immigrant from Somalia, for having lied on her application for asylum. After public uproar, the government ultimately decided to allow Hirsi Ali to retain her Dutch citizenship, though she had already resigned her seat in Parliament and accepted a job at the American Enterprise Institute, a conservative think tank in the United States. The D66 party, the smallest member of the governing coalition, demanded the resignation of Verdonk in exchange for its continuing support. Verdonk was also under fire from D66 for her proposals to require Dutch to be the only language spoken in the streets of Holland.

On June 29, D66 announced that it was leaving the coalition and Prime Minister Balkenende announced the resignation of his government approximately a year before the next scheduled general election.

Political Parties

The growth of the Dutch multiparty system, which emerged from the tendency of political parties to reflect the interests of particular religious and economic groups, has been reinforced by the use of proportional representation.

Government Parties

Christian Democratic Appeal (*Christen-Democratisch Appèl*—CDA). Party organization in the Netherlands has long embraced a distinction between confessional and secular parties, although the former have experienced a gradual erosion in electoral support. Partly in an effort to counter the anticonfessional trend, the CDA was organized in December 1976 as an unprecedented alliance of the Catholic People's Party (*Katholieke Volkspartij*—KVP) and two Protestant groups, the Anti-Revolutionary Party (*Anti-Revolutionaire Partij*—ARP) and the Christian Historical Union (*Christelijk-Historische Unie*—CHU). The KVP was founded in 1945 as a centrist party supported primarily by Roman Catholic businessmen, farmers, and some workers. It endorsed many social welfare programs while favoring close cooperation between spiritual and secular forces in the community. The ARP, founded in 1879, was the nation's oldest political organization, drawing its principal strength from Calvinist businessmen, white-collar workers, and farmers. The CHU was formed in 1908 by a dissident faction of the ARP. Traditionally more centrist than the parent party, it shared the ARP's Calvinist outlook.

The three constituent parties, which had presented joint lists at the May 1977 parliamentary election, agreed in October 1980 to merge into a unified political grouping. Led by Ruud Lubbers, the CDA obtained a plurality of legislative seats in both 1986 and 1989, aligning itself with the Liberals on the earlier occasion and with Labor on the latter. Under the new leadership of Elco Brinkman for the May 1994 poll, the CDA lost a third of its support (falling from 35.3 to 22.2 percent) and was reduced to the status of second strongest Second

Chamber party. Brinkman resigned as CDA leader in August.

A period of "uncertainty and wrangling" developed within the CDA in the wake of the 1994 electoral decline, the right wing appearing to gain ascendancy in 1997 with selection of Jaap de HOOP SCHEFFER as new party leader. In the May 1998 Second Chamber balloting, the CDA slipped to 29 seats (down from 34) on a vote share of 18.4 percent, although it rebounded strongly to finish first in the March 1999 provincial elections and, thus, in selection of the new First Chamber two months later. De Hoop Scheffer resigned as parliamentary leader in September 2001, citing inadequate support from the party. He was succeeded by Jan Peter Balkenende.

Positioning itself as a "reasoned choice" between the radically conservative LPF (below) and the social-democratic PvdA, the CDA led all parties by securing 43 seats in the May 2002 election to the *Tweede Kamer*. Balkenende subsequently formed a coalition government with the LPF and VVD, but the government collapsed three months later due to divisions within the LPF. Balkenende formed another coalition (this time with the VVD and the D66) following the January 2003 general election, in which the CDA again finished first with 44 seats.

In municipal elections in March 2006, the CDA showed a moderate loss of support, winning 16.9 percent of the vote, a drop of 3.4 percent over the 2002 elections, apparently as a result of an underperforming economy and unpopular pension and health care reforms.

Leaders: Jan Peter BALKENENDE (Prime Minister), M. J. M. VERHAGEN (Chair).

People's Party for Freedom and Democracy (*Volkspartij voor Vrijheid en Democratie*—VVD). The forerunners of the VVD included the prewar Liberal State and Liberal Democratic parties. Organized in 1948, the party drew its major support from upper-class businessmen and middle-class, white-collar workers. Although it accepted social welfare measures, the VVD was conservative in outlook and strongly favored free enterprise and separation of church and state.

The party lost ground in both the 1986 and 1989 elections, on the latter occasion going into the opposition for the first time since 1982. In the May 1994 balloting, however, the VVD advanced from 14.6 to 19.9 percent of the vote and then entered into a coalition with the PvdA and D66 in August. The VVD struck a popular chord with its tough line on immigration and asylum seekers, overtaking the CDA as the strongest party in provincial elections in March 1995. The VVD's Second Chamber seat total rose from 31 to 38 in the May 1998 poll (based on 25 percent of the vote), although it fell to second place behind the CDA in the provincial elections of March 1999. The rise of the LPF (below) cost the VVD in the May 2002 general election, at which VVD representation fell to 23 seats.

Jozias van AARTSEN became party leader when the VVD joined Balkenende's coalition government and former leader Garrit Zalm left the post to become minister of finance. Van Aartsen resigned his position after the party performed poorly in the municipal elections of March 2006. Mark Rutte was elected new party leader on May 31, defeating Immigration Minister Rita Verdonk for the post.

Leaders: Mark RUTTE (Chair), Gerrit ZALM (Deputy Prime Minister).

Democrats 66 (*Democraten 66—D66*). Formed in 1966 as a left-of-center party, the D66 favored the dropping of proportional representation and the direct election of the prime minister. Its stand on other domestic and foreign policy questions was similar to that of the PvdA. It changed its name from Democrats '66 to Democrats 66 in 1986. The party's lower house representation rose from 9 seats in 1986 to 12 in 1989, the latter figure being doubled in 1994 on a vote share of 15.5 percent.

In May 1999 the D66 caused the near-collapse of the government when its proposal for "corrective referendums" (to override certain parliamentary decisions) was defeated by one vote in the

upper house. The matter was resolved in early June when the D66 accepted a compromise that opened the way for nonbinding referendums.

The D66 decline continued in the May 2002 balloting for the *Tweede Kamer*, at which its seat total fell from 14 to 7. After the party secured only 6 seats in the January 2003 election, the D66 became something of a "kingmaker" when it provided the necessary legislative majority for the new coalition government led by the CDA and the VVD.

D66 withdrew its support for the Balkenende coalition government in June 2006, resulting in the collapse of the government. The immediate cause of the party's withdrawal was the failure of Immigration Minister Rita Verdonk to resign, but the party also objected to the Balkenende government's support for sending additional Dutch troops to Afghanistan.

Leaders: Frank DALES (Chair), Thom de GRAAF (Former Deputy Prime Minister), Simone FILIPPINI (Secretary).

Opposition Parties

Labor Party (*Partij van de Arbeid—PvdA*). The Labor Party was formed in 1946 by a union of the former Socialist Democratic Workers' Party with left-wing Liberals and progressive Catholics and Protestants. It favored democratic socialism and was a strong supporter of the UN and European integration. The party program stressed the importance of equality of economic benefits, greater consultation in decision making, and reduced defense spending. In October 1977, against the advice of its leadership, the party's national congress voted in favor of the establishment of a republican form of government for the Netherlands. During the same period, the PvdA strongly opposed both nuclear power generation and the deployment of cruise missiles. Subsequent policy considerations focused on employment; strengthening social security, health care, and education; transport infrastructure; and debt reduction.

At the May 1994 general election the PvdA slipped from 31.9 to 24.0 percent of the vote but overtook the CDA as the largest Second Chamber party with 37 seats. It won 45 seats (on a 29 percent vote share) in May 1998. The PvdA's seat total slipped badly to 23 in the May 2002 balloting for the *Tweede Kamer*, but the party rebounded to 42 seats in January 2003, making it the second largest party in the country.

In municipal elections on March 7, 2006, the PvdA showed a sharp increase in support, raising its share of the vote by 7.6 percent to 23.4 percent from the 2002 elections. Some analysts predict that the PvdA will be the main beneficiary of the resignation in June 2006 of the Balkenende government, since recent opinion polls have projected that the PvdA would win the largest share of parliamentary seats if a snap election were held.

Leaders: Willem (Wim) KOK (Former Prime Minister), Wouter J. BOSS (Chair), Job COHEN (Mayor of Amsterdam).

Socialist Party (*Socialistische Partij*—SP). The left-wing SP increased its vote share from 0.4 percent in 1989 to 1.3 percent in the May 1994 Second Chamber poll, returning two deputies. In preparation for the May 1998 elections, party leaders argued that there was "too much poverty" in the country and criticized a perceived widening of the gap between the rich and poor. It won 3.5 percent of the votes, for five seats. The SP also offered a progressive agenda, in contrast to the LPF, for the 2002 and 2003 elections for the *Tweede Kamer*, securing nine seats both times. In 2005 the SP opposed the proposed new EU constitution.

In municipal elections on March 7, 2006, the SP showed an increase in support, winning 5.7 percent of the vote and more than doubling its number of seats.

Leader: Jan MARIJNISSEN (Chair and Parliamentary Leader).

List Pim Fortuyn (*Lijst Pim Fortuyn*—LPF). The LPF was established as Livable Rotterdam (*Leefbaar Rotterdam*—LR) by political maverick Pim Fortuyn prior to the March 2002 local elections, at which the party succeeded in winning control of the Rotterdam council. The LR platform emphasized an end to immigration and a reversal

of antidiscrimination guarantees for ethnic minorities. (Among other things, Fortuyn described Islam as "backwards.") The party was renamed the LPF in preparation for the general election scheduled for May 15, 2002.

Fortuyn was assassinated on May 6, 2002, nine days before the scheduled balloting, in which the LPF performed remarkably well, winning 26 seats. The LPF subsequently joined the CDA and VVD in a coalition government, but the party soon spun into disarray amid a bitter internal leadership battle and several scandals. Voters in the January 2003 balloting for the *Tweede Kamer* punished the LPF, which won only 8 seats. Underscoring continued party infighting, the eight LPF members of the *Tweede Kamer* announced their "resignation" from the party in August 2004 in a dispute with the party leadership. The LPF subsequently campaigned in 2005 against the proposed new EU constitution.

Leader: G. P. van AS (Chair).

Green Left (*GroenLinks*—GL). The GL was organized as an electoral coalition prior to the 1989 balloting by the Evangelical People's Party (*Evangelische Volkspartij*—EVP), the Radical Political Party (*Politieke Partij Radikalen*—PPR), the Pacifist Socialist Party (*Pacifistisch Socialistische Partij*—PSP), and the Netherlands Communist Party (*Communistische Partij van Nederland*—CPN). It became a permanent party in 1991, when each of its constituent groups voted to disband. The party's vote share declined from 4.1 to 3.5 percent in the May 1994 general election, losing 1 of 6 seats. The GL rebounded strongly in May 1998, when it more than doubled its representation from 5 to 11 seats on a vote share of 7.3 percent. After retaining the 11 seats in the 2002 elections to the *Tweede Kamer*, the GL representation fell to 8 seats in 2003.

Leader: Femke HALSEMA (Chair).

Christian Union (*ChristenUnie*). The Christian Union dates from January 2000, when the Reformational Political Federation (*Reformatorische Politieke Federatie*—RPF) and the Reformed Political Union (*Gereformeerd Politiek Verbond*—GPV) agreed to unify. Appealing to both Calvinists and interdenominational Christians, the RPF had been formed in 1975; it obtained two Second Chamber seats in 1981 and 1982, one in 1986 and 1989, and three in 1994 and 1998. Established in 1948, the more conservative, Calvinist GPV long supported a strong defense policy and the Atlantic alliance but opposed any subordination to a supranational governmental body. It won two Second Chamber seats in each of the last three general elections.

Following the merger, the Christian Union controlled four seats in the First Chamber and five seats in the Second Chamber. The GPV and RPF factions in the Second Chamber formally merged in March 2001. The Christian Union won three seats in the *Tweede Kamer* in 2002 as well as 2003.

Leader: André ROUVOET (Director).

Political Reformed Party (*Staatkundig Gereformeerde Partij*—SGP). Dating from 1918, the SGP is an extreme right-wing Calvinist party that bases its political and social outlook on its own interpretation of the Bible. It advocates strong legal enforcement, including the use of the death penalty, and is against supranational government, which it feels would open society to corrupting influences. Since 1993 women have been banned from active membership.

The SGP retained its existing three Second Chamber seats in the 1989 election but slipped to two in May 1994 before rebounding to three in 1998. It frequently cooperated with the GPV and RPF (see Christian Union), including presentation of joint lists for European Parliament balloting. The SGP won two seats in the *Tweede Kamer* in 2002 and 2003.

Leaders: Bas J. van der VLIES (Chair), C. G. STAAIJ (Secretary).

Other Parties

Center Democrats (*Centrum Democraten*—CD). Despite its name, the CD was actually an extreme right-wing group that urged a total ban on third world immigration. Having in 1989 regained the one lower house seat it had lost in 1986, it advanced to three seats in May 1994, winning 2.5 percent support by capitalizing on popular concern about the changing ethnic composition of Dutch society, particularly the doubling of political asylum admissions from 20,000 in 1992 to 40,000 in 1993. In the May 1998 Second Chamber poll it won only 0.6 percent of the vote and no seats. Party Chair Johannes (Hans) JANMAAT died in 2002, leaving the party's future in doubt.

The Greens (*De Groenen*). Founded in 1983 as a federation of local parties, the conservative Greens won one upper house seat in 1995 on an independent list and retained it in May 1999. Although the party failed to capture any upper or lower house seats in 2003, it remained active at the local level.

Leaders: Jacques de COO (Chair).

Friesian National Party (*Fryske Nasjonale Partij*—FNP). Established in 1962 as a regional party advocating the interest of the people in the province of Friesland, the FNP holds a traditional seat in the *Eerste Kamer*.

The **New Solidarity Union of the Elderly** (*Nieuw Solidair Ouderen Verbond*—NSOV), established in January 1998 by Martin BATENBURG, is one of the more recent in a series of pensioners' parties that have campaigned against attempts to reduce state pension and other benefits for senior citizens. It was preceded by the **General Union of the Elderly** (*Algemeen Ouderen Verbond*—AOV), which in its first year, 1994, won an impressive 3.6 percent of the vote in the general election, entitling it to six seats in the Second Chamber. In 1995 the AOV, also founded by Batenburg, was torn by a bitter internal dispute, as a result of which an effort was made to expel Batenburg and his supporters. In the end, four Second Chamber members left. Other elder parties have included the **55+ Union** (*Unie 55+*), which won one Second Chamber seat in 1994 and presented an unsuccessful joint list with the rump AOV in May 1998. Also running in 1998 was the **Seniors 2000** (*Senioren 2000*), a pensioners' grouping led by former AOV leader Jet NIJPELS; it received less than 0.5 percent of the vote.

Cabinet

As of September 21, 2006

Prime Minister	Jan Peter Balkenende (CDA)
Deputy Prime Ministers	Laurens Jan Brinkhorst (D66)
	Gerrit Zalm (VVD)

Ministers

Agriculture, Nature Management, and Fisheries	Cees Veerman (CDA)
Defense	Henk Kemp (VVD)
Development Cooperation	Agnes van Ardenne (CDA) [f]
Economic Affairs	Laurens Jan Brinkhorst (D66)
Education, Culture, and Science	Maria van der Hoeven (CDA) [f]
Finance	Gerrit Zalm (VVD)
Foreign Affairs	Ben Bot (CDA)
General Affairs	Jan Peter Balkenende (CDA)
Government Reform and Kingdom Relations	Alexander Pechtold (D66)
Health, Welfare, and Sport	Hans Hoogervorst (VVD)
Housing, Physical Planning, and Environment	(Vacant)
Immigration and Integration	Rita Verdonk (VVD) [f]
Interior	Johan Remkes (VVD)
Justice	(Vacant)
Social Affairs and Employment	Aart Jan de Geus (CDA)
Transport, Public Works, and Water Management	Karla Peijs (CDA) [f]

[f] = female

Small parties on the right include the populist **Livable Netherlands** (*Leefbar Nederlands—*LN), which was organized in 2001; the **Netherlands Mobile** (*Nederland Mobiel*), led by W. VAN DER VELDEN; the **New Center Party** (*Nieuwe Midden Partij—*NMP), led by Martin DESSING and previously known as the Dutch Middle Class Party (*Nederlandse Middenstands Partij—*NMP); and the **New National Party** (*Nieuwe Nationale Partij—*NNP), established in 1998 under the leadership of Egbert PERÉE and Henk RUITENBERG. In November 1998 the extremist National People's Party/Center Party '86 (*Nationale Volkspartij/Centrumpartij '86—*NVP/CP '86), led by Stewart MORDAUNT and Martijn FRELING, was banned and ordered dissolved by the courts for inciting racial hatred against asylum seekers.

Other parties include the **Modern Republican Party** (*Republikeinse Moderne Partij—*RMP), which was established in September 2000 under the leadership of H. P. VAN HERWIJNEN to work for adoption of a parliamentary republic and directly elected presidency, and the **Catholic People's Party** (*Katholiek Politieke Partij—*KPP). Minor radical parties on the left include the **New Communist Party of the Netherlands** (*Nieuwe Communistische Partij Nederland—*NCPN), dating from 1992, and the **United Communist Party** (*Verenigde Communistische Partij—*VCP).

In 2004 Paul van BUITENEN (a former member of the European Commission) launched **Transparent Europe**, which secured two seats in the June 2004 balloting for the European Parliament on an antifraud and antiwaste platform. Meanwhile, Geert WILDERS, elected to the *Tweede Kamer* in 2003 as a member of the VVD, resigned from that party in September 2004 and formed a *Groep Wilders* to promote anti-immigration policies and other right-wing causes.

Legislature

The **States General** (*Staten Generaal*) is a bicameral body consisting of an indirectly elected First Chamber and a directly elected Second Chamber.

First Chamber (*Eerste Kamer*). The 75 members of the upper house are indirectly elected by the country's 12 provincial councils for four-year terms. Following the provincial balloting of March 11, 2003, elections to the First Chamber on May 26 gave the Christian Democratic Appeal 23 seats; the Labor Party, 19; the People's Party for Freedom and Democracy, 15; the Green Left, 5; the Socialist Party, 4; the Democrats 66, 3; the Christian Union, 2; the Political Reformed Party, 2; the *Lijst Pim Fortuyn*, 1; and the Friesian National Party, 1.

President: Yvonne TIMMERMAN-BUCK.

Second Chamber (*Tweede Kamer*). The lower house consists of 150 members directly elected (in a single nationwide district under a pure proportional representation system) for four years, subject to dissolution and, under certain circumstances, term extension. Following the election of January 22, 2003, the Christian Democratic Appeal held 44 seats; the Labor Party, 42; the People's Party for Freedom and Democracy, 28; the Socialist Party, 9; the *Lijst Pim Fortuyn*, 8; the Green Left, 8; the Democrats 66, 6; the Christian Union, 3; and the Political Reformed Party, 2.

President: Frans WEISGLAS.

Communications

Press

Newspapers are free from censorship and are published by independent commercial establishments. There is strict separation between managerial and editorial boards. The following are published daily in Amsterdam, unless otherwise noted: *De Telegraaf* (800,000), independent; *Het Algemeen Dagblad* (Rotterdam, 277,000), independent; *De Volkskrant* (288,000), independent Roman Catholic; *Eindhovens Dagblad/Brabants Dagblad* ('s-Hertogenbosch, 300,000); *NRC Handelsblad* (Rotterdam, 237,000), liberal; *Friesch Dagblad* (Leeuwarden, 190,000); *De Gelderlander* (Nijmegen, 190,000), independent Roman Catholic; *Haagsche Courant* (The Hague, 150,000), independent; *De Stem* (Breda, 150,000), Roman Catholic; *Dagblad Tubantia/De Twentsche Courant Tubantia* (Enschede, 150,000); *Noordhollands Dagblad* (Alkmaar, 150,000); *Utrechts Nieuwsblad* (Utrecht, 140,000); *De Limburger* (Maastricht, 140,000), Roman Catholic; *Nieuwsblad van het Noorden* (Groningen, 130,000), independent; *Eindhovens Dagblad* (Eindhoven, 130,000), Roman Catholic; *Trouw* (120,000), Calvinist; *Rotterdams Dagblad* (Rotterdam, 120,000); *Leeuwarder Courant* (Leeuwarden, 110,000), independent progressive; *Het Parool* (89,000), independent.

News Agencies

The Netherlands News Agency (*Algemeen Nederlands Persbureau*—ANP) is an independent agency operated in The Hague and Amsterdam on a cooperative basis by all Dutch newspapers; numerous foreign bureaus maintain offices in The Hague.

Broadcasting and Computing

Public broadcasting by seven associations is coordinated by the Netherlands Broadcasting Corporation (*Nederlandse Omroep Stichting*—NOS) and the Netherlands Programming Corporation (*Nederlandse Programma Stichting*—NPS). The five national public service radio stations are privately owned, as are a dozen regional and several hundred local stations. Public television is available on three channels, and another two are commercial. In addition, cable networks provide foreign commercial and public broadcasts. There were approximately 9.1 million television receivers and 8.2 million personal computers serving 8.5 million Internet users in 2003.

Intergovernmental Representation

Ambassador to the U.S.
Boudewijn Johannes VAN EENENNAAM

U.S. Ambassador to the Netherlands
Roland ARNALL

Permanent Representative to the UN
Franciscus Antonius Maria MAJOOR

IGO Memberships (Non-UN)
ADB, AfDB, BIS, BLX, CERN, CEUR, EBRD, EIB, ESA, EU, Eurocontrol, G10, IADB, IEA, Interpol, IOM, NATO, OECD, OSCE, PCA, WCO, WEU, WTO

Related Territories

The bulk of the Netherlands' overseas empire disappeared with the accession of Indonesia to independence after World War II and the latter's subsequent acquisition of West New Guinea (Irian Jaya). Remaining under the Dutch Crown were the two Western Hemisphere territories of Netherlands Antilles and Suriname, the latter of which became independent on November 25, 1975. As of January 1, 1986, the island of Aruba was politically detached from the Antilles federation, joining it as an internally self-governing territory.

NORWAY

KINGDOM OF NORWAY

Kongeriket Norge

The Country

A land of fjords and rugged mountains bisected by the Arctic Circle, Norway is the fifth-largest country in Western Europe but the second-lowest in population density, after Iceland. In addition to borders with its two Scandinavian neighbors, Sweden and Finland, Norway has also had a common border in the far north with the Soviet Union/Russia since 1944. Three-fourths of the land area is unsuitable for cultivation or habitation, and the population, homogeneous except for asylum-seekers and foreign workers in the south and a small Sámi (Lapp) minority of some 40,000 in the north, is heavily concentrated in the southern sector and along the Atlantic seaboard. For historical reasons the Norwegian language exists in two forms: the Danish-inspired *Bokmål*, and *Nynorsk* (a traditional spoken tongue with a comparatively recent written form); in addition, the Sámi speak their own language, a member of the Finno-Ugrian group. The state-supported Evangelical Lutheran Church commands the allegiance of 88 percent of the population, although a recent survey reportedly concluded that only 10 percent of those members attend church or other Christianity-related activities more than once a month.

Women constitute about 46 percent of the paid labor force, concentrated mainly in clerical, sales, and human service sectors, generally in the lower pay range; about half work part-time. Slightly over one-third of the national legislators elected in 2005 are women, as are 9 of 18 ministers in the current cabinet. (No Norwegian government has been formed since 1986 with less than 40 percent women.) Both the World Economic Forum and the United Nations (UN) Development Program rank Norway second in terms of economic and political gender equality. On January 1, 2006, legislation went into effect requiring publicly owned companies to staff their boards of directors with at least 40 percent women by the next two years.

The Norwegian merchant fleet is one of the world's half-dozen largest and, prior to the discovery of North Sea oil, was the country's leading foreign-exchange earner. Norway continues to export considerable amounts of such traditional commodities as fish and forest products. The development of hydroelectric power in recent decades has made Norway one of the largest exporters of

aluminum and nitrogen products in Western Europe. Since exports and foreign services, including shipping, account for roughly 40 percent of the GNP, the economy is heavily influenced by fluctuations in the world market, although oil and natural gas production have made Norway, on a per capita basis ($42,500 in 2005), one of the most affluent of the world's developed nations. (Norway currently produces more than 3.2 million barrels of oil per day, ranking it among the top ten producers in the world.)

Having recovered from the European currency crisis of September 1992 that led to the floating and devaluation of the krone, Norway has recently enjoyed relatively stable and healthy growth. The GDP, as measured by market value, has nearly doubled since 1980 and the economy has expanded at an average rate of 2.9 percent in 2004 and 3.7 percent in 2005. However, unemployment has remained stubbornly high at 4.5 percent in 2003 and 2004, and 4.2 percent in 2005. Inflation remains in check at 2.5 percent in 2003, and 0.4 percent in 2004 (well below the Norges Bank 2.5 percent target levels for core inflation).

Government and Politics

Political Background

Although independent in its early period, Norway came under Danish rule in 1380. A period of de facto independence, begun in January 1814, ended nine months later, when the *Storting* accepted the Swedish monarch as king of Norway. It remained a territory under the Swedish Crown until 1905, when the union was peacefully dissolved and the Norwegians elected a sovereign from the Danish royal house. Though Norway avoided involvement in World War I, it was occupied from 1940 to 1945 by Nazi Germany, which sponsored the infamous puppet regime of Vidkun QUISLING, while the legitimate government functioned in exile in London.

Norway's first postwar election continued the prewar ascendancy of the Norwegian Labor Party (*Det Norske Arbeiderparti*), and a government was formed in 1945 under Prime Minister Einar GERHARDSEN. Labor continued to rule as a majority party until 1961 and as a minority government until 1965, when a coalition of nonsocialist parties took control under Per BORTEN, leader of the Center Party (*Senterpartiet*—Sp). The Borten government was forced to resign in 1971, following disclosure that the prime minister had deliberately leaked information on negotiations for entering the European Community (EC, later the European Union—EU). A Labor government under Trygve BRATTELI then came to power but was forced from office in September 1972, when EC membership was rejected in a national referendum by 53.5 to 46.5 percent of participants. However, when a coalition government under Lars KORVALD of the Christian People's Party (*Kristelig Folkeparti*—KrF) failed to win the September 1973 general election, Labor returned to power as a minority government. Two years later, Prime Minister Bratteli announced his intention to resign, and on January 9, 1976, Labor's designate, Odvar NORDLI, succeeded him. At the election of September 11–12, 1977, the Labor Party and its ally, the Socialist Left Party (*Sosialistisk Venstreparti*—SV), obtained a combined majority of one seat over four nonsocialist parties, enabling the Nordli minority government to continue in office.

Prime Minister Nordli resigned for health reasons on February 4, 1981, and was succeeded by Gro Harlem BRUNDTLAND, the country's first female chief executive. However, her first minority government fell in the wake of a ten-seat loss by Labor in the election of September 13–14, and on October 14 Kåre WILLOCH formed a minority administration led by the Conservative Party (*Høyre*) with the legislative support of the KrF and the Sp. Partly because of the recessionary effects of Willoch's economic policies, the legislative balloting of September 8–9, 1985, resulted in a near loss of government control. The three ruling parties obtained a total of 78 seats, as opposed to 77 for the Labor and Socialist Left parties, so that the right-wing Progress Party (*Fremskrittspartiet*—Frp), although winning only 2 seats, held the balance of power.

Political Status: Constitutional monarchy established in 1905; under multiparty parliamentary system.

Area: 149,282 sq. mi. (386,641 sq. km.), including Svalbard and Jan Mayen (see Related Territories).

Population: 4,520,947 (2001C); 4,613,000 (2005E).

Major Urban Centers (2005E): OSLO (528,000), Bergen (240,000), Trondheim (156,000), Stavanger (113,000).

Official Language: Norwegian.

Monetary Unit: Krone (official rate July 1, 2006: 6.22 kroner = $1US).

Sovereign: King HARALD V; succeeded to the throne January 17, 1991, upon the death of his father, King OLAV V.

Heir to the Throne: Crown Prince HAAKON Magnus, son of the king.

Prime Minister: Jens STOLTENBERG (Norwegian Labor Party); appointed by the king on October 17, 2005, to succeed Kjell Magne BONDEVIK (Christian People's Party), who had submitted his resignation on October 17, following the election of September 12.

On April 29, 1986, the Willoch government lost a confidence vote on a proposed gas tax increase, the anti-tax Frp voting with the opposition. Ten days later, in the first nonelectoral change in 23 years, Brundtland returned as head of another minority Labor administration. At the parliamentary poll of September 11, 1989, the Labor and Conservative parties both lost ground, with the Conservatives, under Jan P. SYSE, forming a new minority administration in coalition with their former KrF and Sp allies on October 16. However, on October 29, 1990, the Sp deserted the coalition over the issue of foreign financial interests in Norway and agreed to support Labor's return to power under Brundtland on November 3.

The issue that forced the resignation of the Syse government only a year after its installation was the Center Party's objection to the proposed signing of the European Economic Area (EEA) agreement (see article on the European Free Trade Association—EFTA) that would have necessitated revision of Norwegian laws restricting foreign ownership of industrial and financial institutions. Herself dependent on Center Party support, Prime Minister Brundtland declared that her new government would "work for a result that secures national regulation of natural resources and economic activity . . . without locking its position to demands that discriminate [against] citizens of other countries." Thus, Norway joined with other EFTA countries and the 12 EC states in signing the EEA Treaty on May 2, 1992, after securing the addition of clauses designed to meet its concerns.

Controversy over Norway's renewed application for EC/EU membership, approved by the *Storting* in November 1992 and submitted the same month, dominated the general election held on September 13, 1993. The Labor and Conservative parties favored accession (although the former was deeply divided over the issue), whereas the Center, Socialist Left, Christian People's, and Progress parties were opposed. Early predictions of a Labor electoral rout proved wide of the mark: the ruling party gained seats, while the opposition Conservatives lost ground. Other mixed signals on the EU membership question included dramatic Center gains and assorted losses for the Socialist Left, Christian People's, and Progress parties. There being no viable alternative combination, a further Labor minority government was formed by Brundtland on October 7.

Although the Conservatives retained enough seats in 1993 to give Labor a simple parliamentary majority on the EU issue, the anti-EU parties were strong enough collectively to deny the government the three-quarters majority required for approval of formal accession. Thus, there was general agreement that the decisive verdict should be given directly by the electorate in a referendum. The membership terms negotiated by Norway provided ample ammunition for both camps: difficult issues that delayed completion of the negotiations until March 16, 1994, included agriculture and regional policy, the future of Norway's oil and gas reserves, and, above all, fisheries. On the last, a compromise of great complexity was reached that, according to the Norwegian government, enshrined its original refusal to allow a higher EU catch in its waters, whereas the anti-EU camp contended that unacceptable concessions had been made. Similarly, the Center and other anti-EU parties disputed the government's assertion that the terms provided adequate safeguards for Norwegian farmers (among the most heavily subsidized in the world).

The date of the Norwegian referendum was eventually set for November 28, 1994—that is, after those due to take place in the other three applicant countries. With Norwegian opinion much more deeply divided than in Austria, Finland, and Sweden, the government assumed that promembership votes in those countries would be a decisive factor. This proved to be a miscalculation: after intense nationwide debate the Norwegian electorate again rejected EU membership, this time by a margin of 52.2 to 47.8 percent. Having thrown her considerable weight behind the pro-EU campaign, Prime Minister Brundtland acknowledged the outcome as a major defeat. The government's subsequent priority, she said, would be to negotiate appropriate changes to the EEA Treaty that would continue to apply to Norway as a non-EU member, whereas Austria, Finland, and Sweden had all opted to cross to "the EU side of the EEA table."

A desire for continuity was apparent in the resignation of Brundtland as prime minister in October 1996 and the uncontested succession of the Labor chair and parliamentary leader, Thorbjørn JAGLAND. According to Brundtland, the timing of her exit was intended to give Jagland time to establish his authority in advance of the general election due in 1997.

Labor won 65 seats in the September 16, 1997, elections, compared to 25 each for the KrF and the Frp and 23 for the Conservatives. However, Prime Minister Jagland had promised during the campaign to resign if his party polled less than the 36.9 percent of the votes it had received in 1993. Labor having narrowly failed to meet that self-imposed target, Jagland submitted his resignation on October 13. The king invited KrF leader Kjell Magne BONDEVIK to form a new government, which was installed on October 17, despite the fact that the parties in the new coalition (the KrF, Sp, and Liberal Party) controlled only 42 seats in the Storting. Bondevik submitted his resignation on March 10, 2000, with Labor's Jens STOLTENBERG being appointed prime minister on March 17 as head of an all-Labor, minority government.

The election of September 10, 2001, saw Labor narrowly retain its plurality, but with only 43 seats—its worst election returns in nearly a century—and Kjell Bondevik returned to office at the head of a center-right minority coalition of the KrF, the Conservatives, and the Liberals. Controlling only 62 of the Storting's 165 seats, the government required external support from the Frp, which won 26 seats at the election.

In a dramatic reversal, Labor rebounded in the election of September 12, 2005, capturing 61 seats. Stoltenberg was reinstalled as prime minister on October 17 and with the Socialist Left and Center Parties formed a red-green majority in Parliament (collectively they hold 87 of the 169 seats). The 2005 election may prove to be a bellwether of sorts for both the left, as Stoltenberg's government has begun to reverse Bondevik's neoconservative policies, and for the far right with the Progress Party, which won 38 seats and stands as the new principal opposition party (see Current issues, below).

Constitution and Government

The Eidsvold Convention, one of the oldest written constitutions in Europe, was adopted by Norway on May 17, 1814. Executive power is exercised on behalf of the sovereign by a Council of State (Statsråd), which is headed by a prime minister and is responsible to the legislature (Storting). The members of the Storting are elected by universal suffrage and proportional representation for four-year terms. There are no by-elections, and the body is not subject to dissolution. Once constituted, it elects one-fourth of its members to serve as an upper chamber (Lagting), while the remainder serves as a lower chamber (Odelsting). Legislative proposals are considered separately by the two, but most other matters are dealt with by the *Storting* as a whole. Should the cabinet resign on a vote of no confidence, the chair of the party holding the largest number of seats (exclusive of the defeated party) is asked to form a new government. The judicial system consists of district courts (*tingrett*), courts of appeal (*lagmannsrettene*), and a Supreme Court of Justice (*Høyesterett*). Judges are appointed by the king on advice from the Ministry of Justice. In addition to the regular courts, there are three special judicial institutions: a High Court of the Realm (*Riksrett*), consisting of the members of the Supreme Court and the *Lagting*, that adjudicates charges against senior government officials; a Labor Relations Court (*Arbeidsretten*), which handles all matters concerning relations between employer and employee in both private and public sectors; and, in each community, a Conciliation Council (*Forliksråd*), to which most civil disputes are brought prior to formal legal action.

Local government is based on 19 counties (*fylker*); in each county, the central government is represented by an appointed governor (*fylkesmann*). The County Council (*Fylkestinget*), which elects a board and a chair, is the representative institution at the county level. The basic units of local government are urban municipalities and rural communes, each of which is administered by an elected council (*Kommunestyre*), a board, and a mayor.

In 1987, following nearly a decade of agitation by the country's then approximately 20,000 Laplanders, agreement was reached on the establishment of a Sámi assembly of 39 delegates from 13 largely northern constituencies. The new body, constituted at the 1989 general election, has advisory functions in such areas as regional control of natural resources, with decision-making capacity in matters relating to the preservation of Sámi culture.

Foreign Relations

A founding member of the UN and the homeland of its first secretary general, Trygve LIE, Norway was also one of the original members of NATO and has been a leader in Western cooperation through such organizations as the Council of Europe and the Organization for Economic Cooperation and Development. Norway participated in the establishment of EFTA but, in national referendums held in 1972 and 1994, rejected membership in the EC/EU. Regional cooperation, mainly through the Nordic Council, has also been a major element in its foreign policy.

A long-standing concern has been a dispute with what is now the Russian Federation regarding ocean-bed claims in the Barents Sea. At issue is a 60,000-square-mile area of potentially oil-rich continental shelf claimed by Norway on the basis of a median line between each country's territorial coasts and by its neighbor on the basis of a sector line extending northward from a point just east of their mainland border. A collateral disagreement has centered on fishing rights in a southern "grey zone" of the disputed area, where 200-mile limits overlap. In 1977 a provisional agreement was negotiated for joint fishing in an area slightly larger than the "grey zone" proper, which has subsequently been renewed on an annual basis pending resolution of the larger controversy. (Competition over the region—one of the world's richest fishing grounds—culminated in February 2004 in the arrest by the Norwegian Coast Guard of a Russian trawler suspected of concealing 20,000 tons of illegally caught cod.)

The Norwegian government welcomed the transformation of regional power relations following the demise of the Soviet Union in late 1991. Seeking to promote peaceful regional cooperation in the post-Soviet era, Norway became a founding member of the ten-nation Council of the Baltic Sea States in March 1992 and also joined the Barents Euro-Arctic Council set up in January 1993 by the five Nordic countries and Russia. Meanwhile, Norway had not only endorsed the EEA Treaty but had also, in November 1992, accepted associate membership of the Western European Union (WEU), thereby seeking to demonstrate the pro-European axis of its foreign policy. In June 1993 a long-standing dispute with Denmark over the maritime boundary between Greenland and the Norwegian island of Jan Mayen was resolved by an International Court of Justice (ICJ) ruling largely in favor of Norway's claim to a median line delimitation.

In August 1992 Norway attracted international criticism by withdrawing from the International Whaling Commission (IWC) rather than accept an IWC ban on commercial whaling; a month later it joined with Iceland, the Faroe Islands, and Greenland to establish the pro-whaling North Atlantic Marine Mammals Commission. In 1993 foreign disapproval grew when Norwegian vessels resumed commercial whaling despite U.S. threats of trade sanctions and EU warnings that whaling was incompatible with membership.

Norway has demonstrated repeatedly its commitment to NATO by deploying troops in NATO peacekeeping operations in Bosnia, Kosovo, and Afghanistan. As of May 2006 Norway has committed approximately 400 troops and aircraft to the International Security Assistance Force (ISAF) in Afghanistan. Additionally, Norway has signaled its support for Georgia to join the NATO alliance. However, bilateral relations between Norway and the United States have been strained since the U.S. invasion of Iraq in 2003.

Although Norway initially pledged $74 million to aid the reconstruction of Iraq and sent 150 troops to support peacekeeping efforts there, Prime Minister Bondevik described the Iraq war as "regrettable and sad." Rebuffing entreaties from Washington for additional support, the government in 2004 announced that Norway "would give priority to other nations rather than Iraq." Immediately after winning the election of September 12, 2005, Prime Minister Stoltenberg informed President George W. Bush that he would be removing the remaining contingent of Norwegian troops stationed in Iraq. The Norwegian public broadcaster (NPK) reported that in response President Bush declined to meet with Prime Minister Stoltenberg in the White House on May 2, 2006.

On the issue of Nordic cooperation, Norway became enmeshed in an acrimonious fisheries dispute with Iceland in 1994, arising mainly from the latter's determination to fish in the waters around the Norwegian Svalbard islands (see Related Territories, below). In November 1997 Norway concluded an agreement with Iceland and Denmark (on behalf of Greenland) establishing fishing limits in the region.

Current Issues

The Labor Party's promise to increase welfare spending and reverse the tax reforms initiated by former prime minister Bondevik resonated with voters and led to its dramatic victory in the September 2005 election. As expected, Prime Minister Stoltenberg has drawn upon the country's immense oil wealth and has increased spending on education, health, and welfare and in general has swung the domestic policies to the left. This impetus to utilize the profits from oil for social welfare programs has taken on an international side, as the government has initiated an international campaign to work with other petroleum-exporting countries to more effectively use oil revenues for national priorities. Working with such countries as Bolivia, who was in the process of nationalizing its natural gas industry in 2006, Norway has sought to export its domestic model of more equitable distribution of oil wealth.

Despite public opinion polls suggesting that approximately 50 percent of the public favors EU membership, the question appears moot as the Stoltenberg government has announced that it will not apply for EU membership before 2009.

Political Parties

Government Parties

Norwegian Labor Party (*Det Norske Arbeiderparti*—DNA). Organized in 1887, Labor has been the strongest party in Norway since 1927. Its program of democratic socialism resembles those of other Scandinavian Social Democratic parties. The Labor-controlled government supported entrance into the EC in 1972 but was obliged to resign when the proposal was rejected in a national referendum. The party increased its parliamentary representation from 62 seats in

1973 to 76 (2 short of a majority) in September 1977, the Odvar Nordli government continuing in office with the support of the Left Socialists. Gro Harlem Brundtland, who had succeeded Nordli as prime minister on February 4, 1981, was forced to step down following a Labor loss of 10 seats in the September election.

Having declined to enter into a vote-sharing pact with the Left Socialists, Labor nonetheless managed to gain six seats in the September 1985 balloting, placing the two parties' combined strength only one seat short of parity with the nonsocialist alliance. It formed a new minority government supported by the Left Socialists in May 1986 but was forced into opposition after a net loss of eight seats in the September 1989 poll. Brundtland formed her third minority government on November 3, 1990, with the legislative support of the Center Party. In November 1992, following the death of her son, Brundtland resigned as party chair, while continuing as prime minister. An unexpected four-seat Labor gain in the September 1993 elections resulted in a further minority government under Brundtland.

In June 1994 a special Labor conference decided by a 2–1 majority to back EU accession in the November referendum, although substantial rank-and-file Labor opposition to membership contributed to the eventual "no" vote. Brundtland continued as prime minister for two more years, eventually handing over leadership to Thorbjørn Jagland in October 1996. Closely linked to labor unions, the party leadership nevertheless seemed open to finding private sector solutions for the problems of the welfare state, alienating some of its more left-wing supporters. Labor also remained a firm backer of NATO. Although the party won 65 seats in the 1997 election, Jagland resigned as prime minister because the party narrowly missed meeting his self-imposed goal of at least matching the 36.9 percent vote share of 1993. Labor also declined at the municipal balloting (28.2 percent) of September 1999 and in February 2000. After Labor won a dismal 43 *Storting* seats in the September 2001 election, Stoltenberg resigned as prime minister, and he was elected party chair to replace Jagland in November 2002.

Under Stoltenberg's leadership Labor's fortunes turned and led all parties with a reported 27.5 percent of the vote in the September 2003 local elections. Building upon this momentum, Stoltenberg positioned Labor as a true opposition party and moved into an alliance with the Center and Socialist Left Party. This "red-green" alliance proved to be a productive vehicle as Labor won 61 seats and Stoltenberg reclaimed the office of prime minister. As of 2006, it is unclear if this alliance, whose members differ greatly on issues such as trade and NATO membership, will survive. However, indications are that Labor is shifting to a more liberal stance on key domestic issues (e.g., greater use of oil revenues to fund social welfare programs) and international questions (e.g., rejection of calls for a referendum on membership in the EU).

Leaders: Jens STOLTENBERG (Prime Minister and Party Leader), Hill-Marta SOLBERG (Deputy Leader), Thorbjørn JAGLAND (Former Prime Minister), Gro Harlem BRUNDTLAND (Former Prime Minister), Martin KOLBERG (General Secretary), Kathrine RAADIM (International Secretary).

Socialist Left Party (*Sosialistisk Venstreparti—SV*). Organized prior to the 1973 election as the Socialist Electoral Association (*Sosialistisk Valgforbund*), the SV was until late 1975 a coalition of the Norwegian Communist Party (below), the Socialist People's Party (*Sosialistisk Folkeparti—SF*), and the Democratic Socialist/Labor Movement Information Committee against Norwegian Membership in the Common Market (*Demokratiske Sosialister/ Arbeiderbevegelsens Informasjonskomite mot Norsk Medlemskap i EF—DS/AIK*). At a congress held in Trondheim on March 14–16, 1975, the members of the coalition committed themselves to the formation of the new party, although dissolution of the constituent parties was not to be considered mandatory until the end of 1976. In November 1975 the Communist Party decided against dissolution, and in the September 1977 election the SV, damaged in August when two of its deputies leaked a secret parliamentary report on defense negotiations with the United States, retained only 2 of the 16 seats formerly held by the Socialist alliance. The party nonetheless provided the Nordli government with the crucial support needed to maintain a slim parliamentary majority prior to the 1981 balloting, at which it won 2 additional seats. In 1989 the party raised its parliamentary representation from 6 to 17 seats before slipping back to 13 in 1993.

The SV played a prominent role in the successful campaign against EU accession in the November 1994 referendum, thereafter intensifying its opposition to the minority Labor government. In April 1996 SV leader Erik SOLHEIM accused Labor and its Center parliamentary allies of "Americanizing" Norway by a combination of tax cuts for the rich and welfare benefit cuts for the poor. The SV faltered in the 1997 election, dropping from 13 seats to 9. It has toned down its anti-NATO rhetoric in recent years and is now a strong advocate for Norway's "international responsibilities," including foreign aid. The SV more than doubled its representation in the September 2001 election, winning 23 seats.

Looking to build upon its 2001 success, SV continued to move toward more centrist positions and joined Labor and the Center Party to form the red-green alliance in the September 2005 election. As a requirement for joining the alliance, SV agreed to set aside its long-standing demand that Norway withdraw from NATO and muted much of its anti-U.S. rhetoric. However, the Socialist Left Party did more poorly than expected and only retained 15 seats. Some SV members have criticized party leader Halvorsen for moderating the party's critical stance of the United States.

Leaders: Kristin HALVORSEN (Chair and Parliamentary Leader); Øystein DJUPEDAL, Inge RYAN (Deputy Chair); Bård Vegar SOLHJELL (Secretary General); Eugenia TAPIA (International Secretary).

Center Party (*Senterpartiet*—Sp). Formed in 1920 to promote the interests of agriculture and forestry, the Sp was originally known as the Agrarian Party. In the late 1980s it began to take steps to broaden its appeal, changing its name, stressing ecological issues, and advocating reduced workdays for families with small children. Not surprisingly, it also championed the post-1975 government policy of bringing farmers' incomes up to the level of industrial workers, although it remained conservative on some economic, social, and religious matters. The party's parliamentary representation dropped from 12 seats to 11 in 1989. It withdrew from participation in the Syse government in October 1990, causing the collapse of the Conservation coalition; its legislative support of Labor permitted the formation of a new Brundtland administration on November 3. Campaigning on a strongly anti-EU ticket, the Sp made major gains in the September 1993 balloting, increasing its representation from 11 to 32 seats. In the new *Storting* Sp backing was often forthcoming for the minority Labor government, although in June 1996 the party issued a joint statement with Christian People's and Liberal parties envisaging a nonsocialist coalition after the 1997 election. The party suffered a reversal in the September 1997 elections, when EU membership was not an issue, dropping back to its pre-1993 strength of 11 seats, although its vision of a center-liberal coalition government became a reality the following month.

Anne Enger LAHNSTEIN, Sp chair for 16 years, resigned her party post (but not her cabinet position) in March 1999 and was succeeded by Odd Roger ENOKSEN. At the 2001 election the party won ten *Storting* seats, remaining in opposition. Åslaug Haga assumed the party's leadership in 2005 and entered into the red-green alliance with the Labor and Center Parties. By doing so she has further moved the party to a centralist position supporting issues such as oil production in the Barents Sea (under strict environmental standards) and further participation in the global markets. Some members of the party have charged that Haga has abandoned the farmers and the party's traditional agricultural values.

Leaders: Åslaug HAGA (Party Leader), Lars Peder BREKK, Liv Signe NAVARSETE, Magnhild Meltveit KLEPPA (Parliamentary Leader), Dagfinn SUNDSBØ (Secretary General).

Other Parliamentary Parties

Progress Party (*Fremskrittspartiet*—Frp). A libertarian group founded by Anders LANGE in 1974, the anti-EU Progress Party was known until January 1977 as Anders Lange's Party for a Strong Reduction in Taxes, Rates, and Public Intervention (*Anders Langes Parti til Sterk Nedsettelse av Skatter, Avgifter, og Offentlige Inngrep*). Although it lost two of its four seats in the 1985 balloting, the Frp was subsequently invited to join the (then) ruling coalition to offset the Conservatives' losses. Declining to do so, the party held a subsequent balance of power in the *Storting* and provided the crucial votes needed to defeat the Willoch government in April 1986. At the parliamentary poll of September 1989 the Frp emerged as the third-largest party, with 22 *Storting* seats, but in 1993 it suffered a major reverse, winning only 10 seats. In the 1997 elections the Frp regained its strength by winning 25 seats and, with 15.3 percent of the vote, emerged as Norway's second-largest party in the Parliament. The Frp favors dismantling of the welfare state and opposes subsidies of sectors such as fisheries and agriculture. It takes a restrictive stand on immigration issues and favors tough anticrime measures.

Less than a year before the September 2001 election, polls showed the Frp as the country's most popular party, and some analysts began speculating about what direction Norway would take with the Frp's chair, Carl I. HAGEN, as prime minister. The party quickly lost ground, however, most dramatically because of the resignation in February 2001 of its second most influential leader, Terje SÖVIKNES, following a sex scandal in which other party figures were also implicated. Meanwhile, the party was also being torn by sharp differences between its more moderate elements, on the one hand, and its more overtly fascistic and racist wing, on the other. In the end, the party registered a modest loss in vote share, to 14.7 percent, at the 2001 balloting, and won 26 seats. Hagen extended the party's conditional support to the new Bondevik three-party coalition, thereby enabling it to take office in October. The Progress Party secured a re-ported 17.9 percent of the vote in the September 2003 local elections.

By all accounts the September 2005 elections were a tremendous success for the Frp. Positioning themselves as an outside party they campaigned both in defense of a strong welfare state and for radical tax cuts. In particular, Hagen's promise to set gas prices at 12 kroner a liter struck a cord with lower- and middle-class voters. In May 2006 Siv Jensen was elected the party chair and became the first woman leader of the party.

Leaders: Siv JENSEN (Chair), Per SANDDBERG, Per Arne OLSEN (Vice Chairs), Geir MO (Secretary General).

Christian People's Party (*Kristelig Folkeparti*—KrF or KFp). Also known as the Christian Democratic Party, the KrF was created in 1933 with the primary objective of maintaining the principles of Christianity in public life. In addition to support for most Conservative policies, the KrF's agenda subsequently centered on introduction of anti-abortion legislation and increased trade with developing countries. At the 1989 election its legislative strength dropped from 16 to 14 seats, falling further by 1 seat in 1993, when it campaigned against EU membership. The party nearly doubled its representation in September 1997, going up to 25 seats. Joining with the Liberal and Center parties to form a minority coalition government in October, the KrF was permitted to select the new prime minister (former deputy prime minister and foreign affairs minister Kjell Bondevik) because it held the largest bloc of deputies of the three party partners. Bondevik resigned as prime minister in March 2000 following defeat of a government bill in the *Storting*, some observers suggesting he and the KrF may have actually welcomed the opportunity to be in opposition during the run-up to the 2001 elections. Although the party finished with only 22 seats after the September national balloting, Bondevik returned to the prime ministership. Following a poor performance by the KrF in the September 2003 local elections, Valgerd Svarstad HAUGLAND resigned after nearly nine years as KrF chair; she was succeeded in 2004 by Health

Minister Dagfinn Høybråten, considered a strong opponent of proposed EU membership for Norway.

Under Bondevik, Norway enjoyed strong economic growth, with personal incomes rising and the stock market almost tripling. Moreover, inflation remained largely in check while interest rates declined sharply. Despite these gains, Bondevik fell out of favor. His insistence on a conservative fiscal policy and tax cuts seemed out of step with the general public, which favored higher levels of public sector spending. In 2005 the KrF won less than 7 percent of the votes cast and 11 seats. Bondevik announced his retirement from politics shortly after the election.

Leaders: Dagfinn HØYBRÅTEN (Chair), Dagrun ERIKSEN, Knut Arild HAREIDE (Vice Chair), Inger Helene VENÅS (Secretary General), Anita Apelthun SÆLE

Conservative Party (*Høyre*—H). The oldest of the contemporary Norwegian parties (founded in 1884), the *Høyre* (literally "Right") advocates a "modern, progressive conservatism" emphasizing private investment, elimination of government control in the semipublic industries, lower taxes, and a revised tax structure that would benefit business. It has long favored a strong defense policy, not excluding the use of nuclear weapons. Although the party's parliamentary representation declined from 50 seats in 1985 to 37 in 1989, it succeeded in forming a minority coalition administration on October 16, which collapsed a year later upon withdrawal of the Center Party. In the September 1993 balloting, the pro-EU Conservatives slumped from 37 seats to 28. Subsequent moves by some Conservative branches to establish local alliances with the populist Progress Party caused considerable internal dissension, as the national leadership frequently gave parliamentary backing to the minority Labor government, particularly on budgetary matters. In the 1997 elections, the party continued its decline, dropping from 28 to 23 seats. In 2001 the party resurged, winning 38 seats, but its chair yielded to KrF insistence that Kjell Bondevik be prime minister of any KrF-Conservative-Liberal government.

However, the 2005 election proved disappointing as the party captured only 23 seats. Opting to maintain its current leadership, the party reelected Erna Solberg as the chair in 2006. Solberg pledged to refocus the party on the 2007 municipal elections, setting a goal of winning 18 percent of the votes.

Leaders: Erna SOLBERG (Chair), Jan Tore SANNER (Vice Chair), Trond Reidar HOLE (Secretary General), Per-Kristian FOSS.

Liberal Party (*Venstre*—V). Formed in 1884, the Liberal Party, like the Sp, currently stresses ecological issues, while in economic policy it stands between the Conservative and Labor parties. Having suffered defections to splinter groups, the Liberals lost their two remaining parliamentary seats in 1985. In June 1988 the Liberal People's Party (*Det Liberale Folkepartiet*—DLF), which had been formed in 1972 by Liberal dissidents who favored Norway's entrance into the EC and had lost its only parliamentary seat in 1977, rejoined the parent party. After failing to regain *Storting* representation in 1989, the Liberals won one seat in 1993 and took six seats in 1997, joining the subsequent KrF-led coalition government until its dissolution in March 2000. *Venstre* won only two seats in 2001 but again joined Prime Minister Bondevik's governing coalition. In the September 2005 elections the party made its best showing since 1972, wining almost 6 percent of the vote and capturing ten seats.

Leaders: Lars SPONHEIM (Chair), Olaf THOMMESSEN (Vice Chair), Odd Einar DØRUM, Trine Skei GRANDE (Parliamentary Leader), Geir Rune NYHUS (Secretary General).

Coastal Party (*Kystpartiet*). The Coastal Party is the rubric (informal, at least) under which Steinar BASTESEM, a spokesman for whaling interests in the fishing towns of the north, was elected to the *Storting* in September 1997. However, the government subsequently listed him as a member of the Nonpartisan Representatives (*Tverrpolitisk Folkevalgte*—TvF), and in 1999 the party name was given as the Nonpartisan Coastal and Regional

Cabinet

As of May 22, 2006

Prime Minister   Jens Stoltenberg (A)

Ministers

Agriculture	Terje Riis-Johansen (Sp)
Children and Family Affairs	Karita Bekkemellem [f] (A)
Culture and Church Affairs	Trond Giske (Ap)
Defense	Anne-Grete Strom-Erichsen [f] (A)
Education and Research	Oystein Kare Djupedal (SV)
Environment	Helen Oddveig Bjornoy [f] (SV)
Finance	Kristin Halvorsen [f] (SV)
Fisheries	Helga Pedersen [f] (A)
Foreign Affairs	Jonas Gahr Store (A)
Labor and Government Administration	Aslaug Marie Haga [f] (Sp)
Health	Sylvia Kristin Brustad [f] (A)
International Development	Erik Solheim (SV)
Justice and the Police	Knut Storberget (Ap)
Local Government and Regional Development	Aslaug Marie Haga [f] (Sp)
Petroleum and Energy	Odd Roger Enoksen (Sp)
Social Affairs	Bjarne Hakon Hanssen (A)
Trade and Industry	Odd Eriksen (A)
Transport and Communications	Liv Signe Navarsete [f] (Sp)

[f] = female

Party (*Tverrpolitisk Kyst og distriktspartiet*). An internal dispute over party leadership forced Bastesen to step down as chair in 2005.

Leader: Roy WAAGE (Chair).

Other Parties

Red Electoral Alliance (*Rød Valgalianse—RV*). Originally an electoral front for the (Maoist) **Workers' Communist Party** (*Arbeidernes Kommunistparti—AKP*), formed in 1973, the RV subsequently grew to include a substantial number of self-described "independent socialists." Prior to the 1989 elections it joined with the Norwegian Communist Party (NKP, below) to form the Local List for the Environment and Solidarity (*Fylkeslistene for Miljø og Solidaritet—FMS*),

which failed to secure representation. Returning to a separate status, the RV won 1.1 percent of the vote and one *Storting* seat in the 1993 poll, which it lost in 1997. The 2005 election also proved disappointing as RV only earned 1.2 percent of the votes and failed to capture any seats. Torstein Dahle was reelected party president in 2005.

Leaders: Torstein DAHLE (President), Finn Olav ROLIJORDET (Secretary).

Norwegian Communist Party (*Norges Kommunistiske Parti—NKP*). The NKP held 11 *Storting* seats in 1945 but lost all of them by 1961. In March 1975 it participated in the initial formation of the Socialist Left Party, but the following November it voted at an extraordinary congress against its own dissolution. Prior to the 1989 election it joined with the Red Electoral Alliance to form the FMS (under RV, above), which failed to win a seat. The party chose not to contest the 1993 election and obtained only 0.1 percent of the vote in 1997, 2001, and 2005 elections.

Leaders: Kjell UNDERLID, Per Lothar LINDT-NER.

Other recently registered groups include the **Christian Conservative Party** (*Kristent Konservativt Parti*—KKP), the **Generation Party** (*Generasjonspartiet*), the **Green Environmental Party** (*Miljøpartiet De Grønne*), the **Fatherland Party** (*Fedrelandspartiet*—Fp), the **Natural Law Party** (*Naturlovpartiet*), the **New Future Coalition Party** (*Samlingspartiet Ny Fremtid*), the **New Liberal Party** (*Det Liberale Folkepartiet*—DLF), the **Pensioners' Party** (*Pensjonistpartiet*—Pp), the **Society Party** (*Samfunnspartiet*), and the **White Electoral Alliance (Stop Immigration/Repatriate Aliens)** (*Hvit Valgallianse [Stop Innvandringen/Hjelp Fremmede hjem]*).

Legislature

The ***Stortinget*** (also frequently rendered as *Storting*) is a modified unicameral parliament whose members are elected to four-year terms by universal suffrage and proportional representation. Once convened, it divides itself for certain purposes into two chambers by electing one-fourth of its members to an upper chamber (*Lagting*), while the remaining members constitute a lower chamber (*Odelsting*). Each *ting* names its own president; the president of the *Storting* serves for the duration of its term, and the presidents of the two chambers are chosen annually. At the most recent election for 169 seats on September 12, 2005, the Labor Party won 61; the Progress Party, 38; the Conservative Party, 23; the Socialist Left Party, 15; the Christian People's Party, 11; the Center Party, 11; and the Liberal Party, 10.

President of the Storting: Thorbjørn JAGLAND.
President of the Lagting: Inge LØNNING.
President of the Odelsting: Berit BRØBY.

In the 1989 election the Sámi people of northern Norway voted additionally on representatives to a new **Sámi People's Congress** (*Sámediggi*) as replacement for the former Norwegian Sámi Council, which had been viewed as an inadequate defender of Sámi interests. The 39-member Congress has been granted authority in certain areas, such as the future of the Sámi language, the preservation of Sámi culture, and the determination of land use in Sámi-populated areas. Elections are held in tandem with balloting for the Storting, most recently on September 12, 2005.

President: Lars-Anders BAER.

Communications

Freedom of the press is constitutionally guaranteed; radio and television are state monopolies.

Press

Most papers, which tend to be openly partisan, are privately owned by individuals, families, corporations, and political parties. A 1919 ban on Sunday publication was lifted in 1990. The government, which has subsidized the press for decades to promote competition, cut back direct support a total of 30 percent in 1997 and 1998, warning that it would also review whether to continue favorable VAT exemptions. The following are published daily in Oslo unless otherwise noted (circulation figures for 1998): *Verdens Gang* (365,000), independent centrist; *Aftenposten* (288,000), independent conservative; *Dagbladet* (206,000), independent; *Bergens Tidende* (Bergen, 94,000), independent liberal; *Adresseavisen* (Trondheim, 89,000), Conservative; *Stavanger Aftenblad* (Stavanger, 73,000), independent; *Dagens Næringsliu* (69,000); *Fædrelandsvennen* (Kristiansand, 47,000), independent; *Drammens Tidende og Buskeruds Blad* (Drammen, 46,000), independent conservative; *Dagsavisen* (formerly *Arbeiderbladet,* 44,000), formerly a Labor Party organ; *Romerikes Blad* (Lillestrøm, 42,000), pro-Labor; *Haugesunds Avis* (Haugesunds, 39,300), independent;

Sunnmørsposten (Ålesund, 38,000), independent; *Tønsbergs Blad* (Tønsberg, 34,000), independent conservative; *Varden* (Skien, 32,000), independent conservative.

News Agencies

The major domestic facilities are the Norwegian News Agency (*Norsk Telegrambyrå*—NTB), which is jointly owned by the leading newspapers, and the Norwegian Press Service (*Norsk Presse Service*—NPS), which is affiliated with AP; in addition, numerous foreign bureaus maintain offices in Oslo.

Broadcasting and Computing

A state company, *Norsk Rikskringkasting* (NRK), held a monopoly of all broadcasting until 1982, when the first private local radio stations were authorized, while its television dominance ended in 1991 when the *Storting* approved licensing of a new commercial channel (TV2). Three years earlier, the government had granted cable transmission rights to Swedish-based Scansat Broadcasting, whose programs (TV3) are financed by advertising, with six other commercial channels (cable and satellite) being available by late 1994; in addition, British, Danish, Finnish, Swedish, and Russian television is received in some border and coastal areas. There were 4.4 million television receivers and 2.4 million personal computers serving 2.3 million Internet users in 2003.

Intergovernmental Representation

Ambassador to the U.S.
Knut VOLLEBAEK

U.S. Ambassador to Norway
Benson K. WHITNEY

Permanent Representative to the UN
Johan L. LØVALD

IGO Memberships (Non-UN)
AC, ADB, AfDB, BIS, CBSS, CERN, CEUR, EBRD, EFTA, ESA, Eurocontrol, IADB, IEA, Interpol, IOM, NATO, NC, NIB, OECD, OSCE, PCA, WCO, *WEU,* WTO

Related Territories

Norway's principal overseas territories are the islands of the Svalbard group and Jan Mayen, both of which are legally incorporated into the Norwegian state. In addition, Norway has two dependencies in southern waters, Bouvet Island and Peter I Island, and claims a sector of Antarctica.

Svalbard.   Svalbard is the group name given to all the islands in the Arctic Ocean between 10 and 35 degrees East Longitude and 74 and 81 degrees North Latitude, Spitzbergen being the most important island in the group. The islands were placed under Norwegian sovereignty by the 1920 Svalbard Treaty, the 41 signatories of which are entitled to exploit their natural resources, although only Norwegian and Soviet/Russian companies have done so. Coal mining is a major activity in the area, with oil and gas exploration beginning in the late 1980s. Plans have been made to establish an airfield that will be open to international traffic, although protest from local residents has also yielded strict government regulations regarding the allowed number of tourist arrivals. (Russia has also recently expressed concern that the runway could be used for military transport.)

Svalbard has a land area of 23,957 square miles (62,049 sq. km.); its resident population is approximately 2,620 (2005E), of whom some 1,500 are Norwegians, most of the remainder being Russians. In the interests of maintaining the islands' Norwegian status, the Oslo government is committed to large state subsidies for the uneconomic Svalbard coal industry.

In March 1994 the Icelandic government announced its intention to accede to the Svalbard Treaty, its aim being to get access to the rich cod fisheries of the islands' 200-mile zone, where Norway had refused to grant Iceland a catch quota. Penetration of the zone by Icelandic trawlers in 1994 was resisted by Norwegian coastguard vessels, a number of violent incidents occurring. The two sides then drew back from further confrontation, negotiations being assisted by Norway's decision not to join the EU, which meant that the two countries would be equally positioned on access to the EU market for fish products. As the dispute dragged on, the Norwegian Supreme Court in June 1996 upheld a lower court verdict against two Icelandic trawlers apprehended while fishing in the Svalbard protection zone, thus effectively rejecting Iceland's claim to rights in the area. In November 1997, Denmark (on behalf of Greenland), Iceland, and Norway concluded an agreement setting fishing limits in the region.

Governor: Morten RUUD.

Jan Mayen. Jan Mayen is an island of 144 square miles (373 sq. km.) located in the Norwegian Sea, 555 nautical miles from Tromsø. It was incorporated as part of the Kingdom of Norway in 1930. A meteorological station was established on the island during World War II, with navigational and radio facilities added thereafter.

POLAND

POLISH REPUBLIC

Rzeczypospolita Polska

Note: On September 22, 2006, Prime Minister Kaczyński dismissed Deputy Prime Minister Andrzej Lepper of the Self-Defense of the Polish Republic Party from the government after a lengthy dispute over the budget. The resultant coalition crisis was expected to lead to snap elections as early as November if the prime minister proved unable to forge a new parliamentary majority.

The Country

A land of plains, rivers, and forests, Poland has been troubled throughout its history by a lack of firm natural boundaries to demarcate its territory from that of powerful neighbors of both East and West. Its present borders reflect major post–World War II adjustments that involved the loss of some 70,000 square miles of former Polish territory to the former Soviet Union and the acquisition of some 40,000 square miles of previously German territory along the country's northern and western frontiers, the latter accompanied by the expulsion of most ethnic Germans and resettlement of the area by Poles. These changes, following the Nazi liquidation of most of Poland's prewar Jewish population, left the country 96 percent Polish in ethnic composition and 90 percent Roman Catholic in religious faith.

On October 22, 1978, Cardinal Karol WOJTYŁA, archbishop of Kraków, was invested as the 264th pope of the Roman Catholic Church. The first Pole ever selected for the office, Pope JOHN PAUL II was regarded as a politically astute advocate of church independence who had worked successfully within the strictures of a Communist regime. During a June 2–10, 1979, visit by the pope to his homeland, he was greeted by crowds estimated at 6 million. In 1980 the continuing power of the church was perhaps best demon-

strated by the influence exerted by Polish primate Cardinal Stefan WYSZYŃSKI in moderating the policies of the country's newly formed free labor unions while playing a key role in persuading the Communist leadership to grant them official recognition. Cardinal Wyszyński died on May 28, 1981, and he was succeeded as primate on July 7 by Archbishop Józef GLEMP, whose efforts to emulate his predecessor were jolted on December 13 by the imposition of martial law. The result

was a worsening in church-state relations that continued until May 1989, when the Polish *Sejm* voted to extend legal recognition to the church for the first time since 1944. Two months later, Poland and the Holy See established diplomatic relations.

Poland's economy underwent dramatic changes in the years after World War II, including a large-scale shift of the work force into the industrial sector. A resource base that included coal, copper, and natural gas deposits contributed to significant expansion in the fertilizer, petrochemical, machinery, electronic, and shipbuilding industries, placing Poland among the world's dozen leading industrial nations. On the other hand, attempts to collectivize agriculture proved largely unsuccessful, with 80 percent of cultivated land remaining in private hands. Most importantly, the retention of traditional farming methods and the fragility of soil and climatic conditions led to periodic agricultural shortages, which, in turn, contributed to consumer unrest.

In 1987, after the external debt had risen to more than $39 billion, the United States agreed to provide assistance in loan consolidation and rescheduling with the "Paris Club" of Western creditors. The action came after Polish officials had approved limited economic and political liberalization. Far more drastic revision from late 1989 included an end to price controls, the privatization of many state-owned companies, and a variety of other measures intended to introduce a market economy. The immediate consequence was a near 20 percent GDP contraction and annual inflation of 120 percent in 1991–1992, prior to growth of 4 percent a year in 1993–1996, 6.8 percent in 1997, and 4.8 percent in 1998. Growth slowed to 4.1 percent in 1999 and 4.0 percent in 2000 but then dropped to only 1.2 percent in 2001. Inflation remained a problem, averaging 9 percent in 1998–2000 before falling under 4 percent in 2001. Unemployment rose steadily from a low of about 10 percent in 1998 and by 2002 had exceeded 17 percent as a consequence of the economic slowdown.

Poland was the largest of the ten new members to join the European Union (EU) in May 2004, and a year later much of the country was reportedly con-tent with the EU developments to date. Farmers, initially concerned that subsidies in other EU countries would undercut Polish productivity, reported increased exports and welcomed their portion of the significant EU aid provided to Poland. Foreign investment was also continuing at a brisk pace. On the other hand, unemployment remained unacceptably high as did (according to EU standards) the budget deficit.

Poland's economy grew by 5.4 percent in 2005 (up from 3.8 percent in 2004), but its inflation rate rose to 4.4 percent (up from 1.7 percent). Unemployment was down to 19 percent in 2005 from 20 percent in the previous two years.

Government and Politics

Political Background

Tracing its origins as a Christian nation to 966 AD, Poland became an influential kingdom in late medieval and early modern times, functioning as an elective monarchy until its liquidation by Austria, Prussia, and Russia in the successive partitions of 1772, 1793, and 1795. Its reemergence as an independent republic at the close of World War I was followed in 1926 by the establishment of a military dictatorship headed initially by Marshal Józef PIŁSUDSKI. The first direct victim of Nazi aggression in World War II, Poland was jointly occupied by Germany and the USSR, coming under full German control with the outbreak of German-Soviet hostilities in June 1941.

After the end of the war in 1945 a Communist-controlled "Polish Committee of National Liberation," established under Soviet auspices in Lublin in 1944, merged with a splinter group of the anti-Communist Polish government-in-exile in London to form a Provisional Government of National Unity. The new government was headed by Polish Socialist Party (*Polska Partia Socjalistyczna*—PPS) leader Edward OSÓBKA-MORAWSKI, with Władysław GOMUŁKA, head of the (Communist) Polish Workers' Party (*Polska Partia Robotnicza*—PPR), and Stanisław MIKOŁAJCZYK, chair of the Polish Peasant Party

Political Status: Independent state reconstituted 1918; Communist-ruled People's Republic established 1947; constitution of July 22, 1952, substantially revised in accordance with intraparty agreement of April 5, 1989, with further amendments on December 29, including name change to Polish Republic; new interim "small" constitution introduced December 8, 1992; permanent "large" constitution approved by national referendum on May 25, 1997, effective October 17, 1997.

Area: 120,725 sq. mi. (312,677 sq. km.).

Population: 38,230,100 (2002C); 38,148,000 (2005E).

Major Urban Centers (2005E): WARSAW (1,697,000), Łódź (772,000), Kraków (757,000), Wrocław (635,000), Poznań (570,000), Gdańsk (458,000), Szczecin (412,000).

Official Language: Polish.

Monetary Unit: Złoty (market rate July 1, 2006: 3.19 złotys = $1US). (After Poland joined the European Union in May 2004, the Polish government announced that it hoped to adopt the euro as Poland's national currency by 2007. However, that goal proved to be ambitious, and the target date was subsequently pushed back to at least 2009.)

President: Lech KACZYŃSKI (elected as a member of Law and Justice); popularly elected at second-round balloting on October 23, 2005, and inaugurated on December 23 for a five-year term succeeding Aleksander KWAŚNIEWSKI (formerly Democratic Left Alliance). (Presidents are constitutionally required to resign their party affiliations upon inauguration.)

Prime Minister: Jarosław KACZYŃSKI (Law and Justice); designated by the president (upon the recommendation of Law and Justice) on July 10, 2006, and sworn in (along with his new government) on July 14 to succeed Kazimierz MARCINKIEWICZ (Law and Justice), who had announced his resignation on July 10.

(*Partia Stronnictwo Ludowe*—PSL), as vice premiers. Communist tactics in liberated Poland prevented the holding of free elections as envisaged at the Yalta Conference in February 1945, and the election that was ultimately held in 1947 represented the final step in the establishment of control by the PPR, which forced the PPS into a 1948 merger as the Polish United Workers' Party (*Polska Zjednoczona Partia Robotnicza*—PZPR).

Poland's Communist regime was thereafter subjected to periodic crises resulting from far-ranging political and economic problems, accompanied by subservience to Moscow and the use of Stalinist methods to consolidate the regime. In 1948 Gomułka was accused of "rightist and nationalist deviations," which led to his replacement by Bolesław BIERUT and his subsequent imprisonment (1951–1954). By 1956, however, post-Stalin liberalization was generating political turmoil, precipitated by the sudden death of Bierut in Moscow and "bread and freedom" riots at Poznań, and Gomułka returned to the leadership of the PZPR as the symbol of a "Polish path to socialism." The

new regime initially yielded a measure of political stability, but by the mid-1960s Gomułka was confronted with growing dissent among intellectuals in addition to factional rivalry within the party leadership. As a result, Gomułka-inspired anti-Semitic and anti-intellectual campaigns were mounted in 1967–1968, yielding the mass emigration of some 18,000 Polish Jews (out of an estimated 25,000) by 1971. Drastic price increases caused a serious outbreak of workers' riots in December 1970, which, although primarily economic in nature, provoked a political crisis that led to the replacement of Gomułka as PZPR first secretary by Edward GIEREK.

Following a parliamentary election on March 23, 1980, a new austerity program was announced that called for a reduction in imports, improved industrial efficiency, and the gradual withdrawal of food subsidies. Workers responded by demanding wage adjustments and calling strikes, which by August had assumed an overtly political character, with employees demanding that they be allowed to establish "workers' committees" to replace the

PZPR-dominated, government-controlled official trade unions. Among those marshaling support for the strikers was the Committee for Social Self-Defense (*Komitet Samoobrony Społeczej*—KSS), the largest of a number of recently established dissident groups.

On August 14, 1980, the 17,000 workers at the Lenin Shipyard at Gdańsk struck, occupied the grounds, and issued a list of demands that included the right to organize independent unions. Three days later, workers from a score of industries in the area of the Baltic port presented an expanded list of 16 demands that called for recognition of the right of all workers to strike, abolition of censorship, and release of political prisoners. In an emergency session also held on August 17, the PZPR Politburo agreed to open negotiations with the strikers, eventually consenting to meet with delegates of the Gdańsk interfactory committee headed by Lech WAŁĘSA, a former shipyard worker who had helped organize the 1970 demonstrations. On August 30 strike settlements were completed, the 21-point Gdańsk Agreement being approved by the *Sejm* and signed by Wałęsa and the government on August 31. While recognizing the position of the PZPR as the "leading force" in society, the unprecedented document stated, "It has been found necessary to call up new, self-governing trade unions which would become authentic representatives of the working class."

Although most workers along the Baltic coast returned to their jobs on September 1, 1980, strikes continued to break out in other areas, particularly the coal- and copper-mining region of Silesia, and on September 6 First Secretary Gierek resigned in favor of Stanisław KANIA. On September 15 registration procedures to be followed by independent unions were announced, with authority to approve union statutes delegated to the Warsaw provincial court. Three days later, 250 representatives of new labor groups established a "National Committee of Solidarity" (*Solidarność*) at Gdańsk with Wałęsa as chair, and on September 24 the organization applied for registration as the Independent Self-Governing Trade Union Solidarity. The court objected, however, to its proposed governing statutes, particularly the absence of any specific reference to the PZPR as the country's leading political force. Not until November 10—two days before a threatened strike by Solidarity—did the Supreme Court, ruling in the union's favor, remove amendments imposed by the lower court, the union accepting as an annex a statement of the party's role. By December some 40 free trade unions had been registered, while on January 1, 1981, the official Central Council of Trade Unions was dissolved.

The unprecedented events of 1980 yielded sharp cleavages between Wałęsa and radical elements within Solidarity and between moderate and hard-line factions of the PZPR. Fueled by the success of the registration campaign, labor unrest increased further in early 1981, accompanied by appeals from the private agricultural sector for recognition of a "Rural Solidarity." Amid growing indications of concern by other Eastern-bloc states, the minister of defense, Gen. Wojciech JARUZELSKI, was appointed chair of the Council of Ministers on February 11. Initially welcomed in his new role by most Poles, including the moderate Solidarity leadership, Jaruzelski attempted to initiate a dialogue with nonparty groups and introduced a ten-point economic program designed to promote recovery and counter "false anarchistic paths contrary to socialism." The situation again worsened following a resumption of government action against dissident groups, although the Independent Self-Governing Trade Union for Private Farmers–Solidarity (Rural Solidarity), which claimed between 2.5 and 3.5 million members, was officially registered on May 12.

At a delayed extraordinary PZPR congress that convened on July 14, 1981, in Warsaw, more than 93 percent of those attending were new delegates selected in unprecedented secret balloting at the local level. As a consequence, very few renominations were entered for outgoing Central Committee members, while only four former members were reelected to the Politburo. Stanisław Kania was, however, retained as first secretary in the first secret, multicandidate balloting for the office in PZPR history.

Despite evidence of government displeasure at its increasingly political posture, Solidarity held its first national congress in Gdańsk on September 5–10 and September 25–October 7, 1981. After reelecting Wałęsa as its chair, the union approved numerous resolutions, including a call for wide-ranging changes in the structure of trade-union activity. Subsequently, at the conclusion of a plenary session of the PZPR Central Committee held on October 16–18, First Secretary Kania submitted his resignation and was immediately replaced by General Jaruzelski, who, on October 28, made a number of changes in the membership of both the Politburo and Secretariat. Collaterally, Jaruzelski moved to expand the role of the army in maintaining public order.

During the remaining weeks of 1981 relations between the government and Solidarity progressively worsened. On December 11 the union announced that it would conduct a national referendum on January 15, 1982, that was expected to yield an expression of nonconfidence in the Jaruzelski regime. The government responded by arresting most of the Solidarity leadership, including Wałęsa, while the Council of State on December 13 declared martial law under a Military Committee for National Salvation headed by Jaruzelski. Subsequently, a number of stringent decrees were promulgated that effectively banned all organized nongovernmental activity except for religious observances and established summary trial courts for those charged with violation of martial law regulations.

On October 8, 1982, the *Sejm* approved legislation that formally dissolved all existing trade unions and set guidelines for new government-controlled organizations to replace them. The measures were widely condemned by the Catholic Church and other groups, and Solidarity's underground leadership called for a nationwide protest strike on November 10. However, the appeal yielded only limited public support, and Wałęsa was released from detention two days later. On December 18 the *Sejm* approved a suspension (not a lifting) of martial law that voided most of its remaining overt manifestations.

On July 21, 1983, State Council Chair Henryk JABŁOŃSKY announced the formal lifting of mar-

tial law and the dissolution of the Military Committee for National Salvation, the latter body being effectively supplanted four months later by a National Defense Committee, chaired by General Jaruzelski, with overall responsibility for both defense and state security. However, these events were overshadowed by the kidnapping and murder in October 1984 of the outspoken pro-Solidarity cleric, Fr. Jerzy POPIEŁUSZKO of Warsaw, for which four state security officers were ultimately tried and convicted.

Following *Sejm* elections in October 1985, General Jaruzelski succeeded the aging Jabłońsky as head of state, relinquishing the chairship of the Council of Ministers to Zbigniew MESSNER, who entered office as part of a major realignment that substantially increased the government's technocratic thrust. Jaruzelski was reelected PZPR first secretary at the party's tenth congress in mid-1986, during which nearly three-quarters of the Central Committee's incumbents were replaced.

In October 1987 Jaruzelski presented to the PZPR Central Committee a number of proposed economic and political reforms far outstripping Mikhail Gorbachev's "restructuring" agenda for the Soviet Union. Central to their implementation, however, was a strict austerity program, including massive price increases, that was bitterly opposed by the outlawed Solidarity leadership. In the wake of a remarkable referendum on November 29, at which the proposals failed to secure endorsement by a majority of eligible voters, the government indicated that it would proceed with their implementation, albeit at a slower pace than had originally been contemplated.

New work stoppages erupted in Kraków in late April 1988 and quickly spread to other cities, including Gdańsk, before being quelled by security forces. On August 22 emergency measures were formally invoked to put down a further wave of strikes, and six days later the PZPR Central Committee approved a plan for broad-based talks to address the country's economic and social ills. Although the government stated that "illegal organizations" would be excluded from such discussions, a series of meetings were held between

Solidarity leader Wałęsa and Interior Minister Czesław KISZCZAK. On September 19, however, the Messner government resigned after being castigated by both party and official trade union leaders for economic mismanagement. Mieczysław RAKOWSKI, a leading author of the March 1981 economic program, was named prime minister on September 26.

In the wake of further party leadership changes on December 21, 1988, which included the removal of six Politburo hard-liners, a new round of discussions with representatives of the still-outlawed Solidarity was launched on February 6, 1989. The talks resulted in the signing on April 5 of three comprehensive agreements providing for the legalization of Solidarity and its rural counterpart; political reforms that included the right of free speech and association, democratic election to state bodies, and judicial independence; and economic liberalization. The accords paved the way for parliamentary balloting on June 4 and 18, at which Solidarity captured all of the 161 nonreserved seats in the 460-member *Sejm* and 99 of 100 seats in the newly established Senate.

On July 25, 1989, six days after being elected president of the republic by the barest of legislative margins, General Jaruzelski was rebuffed by Solidarity in an effort to secure a PZPR-dominated "grand coalition" government. On August 2 the *Sejm* approved Jaruzelski's choice of General Kiszczak to succeed Rakowski as prime minister; however, opposition agreement on a cabinet proved lacking, and Kiszczak was forced to step down in favor of Solidarity's Tadeusz MAZOWIECKI, who succeeded in forming a four-party administration on September 12 that included only four Communists (although the PZPR was, by prior agreement, awarded both the interior and defense portfolios).

On December 29, 1989, the *Sejm* approved a number of constitutional amendments, including a change in the country name from "People's Republic of Poland" to "Polish Republic," termination of the Communist party's "leading role" in state and society, and deletion of the requirement that Poland must have a "socialist economic system."

Subsequently, on January 29, 1990, formal Communist involvement in Polish politics ended when the PZPR voted to disband in favor of a new entity to be known as Social Democracy of the Republic of Poland (*Socjaldemokracja Rzeczypospolitej Polskiej*—SdRP).

In the face of widespread opposition to his status as a holdover from the Communist era, President Jaruzelski on September 19, 1990, proposed a series of constitutional amendments that would permit him to resign in favor of a popularly elected successor. At first-round balloting on November 25 Wałęsa led a field of six candidates with a 40 percent vote share; in the second round on December 9, he defeated emigré businessman Stanisław TYMIŃSKI by a near three-to-one margin, and he was sworn in for a five-year term on December 22. On January 4, 1991, the president's nominee, Jan Krzysztof BIELECKI, won parliamentary approval as prime minister, with the *Sejm* formally endorsing his ministerial slate on January 12.

In June 1991, amid mounting opposition to government economic policy, President Wałęsa twice vetoed bills calling for a form of proportional representation that he insisted would weaken Parliament by admitting a multiplicity of parties, but he was eventually defeated by legislative override on June 28. As predicted, the ensuing poll of October 27 yielded a severely fragmented lower house, with the Democratic Union (*Unia Demokratyczna*—UD) winning the most seats but no party securing more than 13 percent of the vote. A lengthy period of consultation followed, with an offer by Wałęsa to serve as his own prime minister being met with scant enthusiasm. Unable to secure the reappointment of Bielecki, the president was ultimately obliged to settle on a critic of his free-market strategy, Jan OLSZEWSKI, who narrowly succeeded in forming a government on December 23. Four days earlier Wałęsa had been forced to withdraw a group of proposed constitutional amendments that would have given him authority to appoint and dismiss ministers and to veto parliamentary no-confidence motions, while authorizing a simple rather than a two-thirds *Sejm* majority to enact legislation.

The government was weakened in May 1992 by the successive resignations of the economy and defense ministers, the latter in the wake of allegations he had made concerning the military's involvement in politics. Far more contentious, however, was legislative authorization on May 28 to release secret police files of individuals who had reportedly collaborated with the Communist regime. The action had long been sought by the right-of-center Olszewski government but had been resisted as a violation of human rights by the center-left parties, which insisted that many of the dossiers had been deliberately falsified by departing members of the security forces. Olszewski's subsequent publication of a list of alleged collaborators generated widespread outrage, not least from President Wałęsa, who publicly called for the prime minister's dismissal, and on June 5 the *Sejm* approved a nonconfidence motion by an overwhelming margin.

On June 6, 1992, the *Sejm* endorsed Waldemar PAWLAK, the relatively obscure leader of the PSL, as new prime minister. However, Pawlak was unable, during the ensuing month, to muster sufficient parliamentary support to form a government and was obliged to resign. On July 6 the UD's Hanna SUCHOCKA was confirmed as Poland's first woman prime minister, and five days later she secured *Sejm* approval of a new coalition administration, which included seven parties with ministerial posts and several others pledged to give it parliamentary support. Committed to speedier transition to a market economy, Suchocka's government relaunched the privatization program and secured the reactivation of International Monetary Fund (IMF) credit facilities that had been suspended since 1991. However, Suchocka's austerity policies, including a firm stand against striking coal miners and rail workers, incurred widespread opposition from Solidarity deputies, and on May 28, 1993, her government fell by one vote over a continued tight budget. President Wałęsa responded by refusing to accept the prime minister's resignation, asking Suchocka to remain in office on a caretaker basis pending a new election.

The balloting of September 19, 1993, yielded a pronounced swing to the left, with the SdRP-dominated Democratic Left Alliance (*Sojusz Lewicy Democratycznej*—SLD) winning 37 percent of the legislative seats and the PSL winning 29 percent. Five weeks later, on October 26, the two groups formed a coalition government headed by the PSL's Pawlak.

Conflict between the presidency and the ruling coalition intensified in October 1994, when the government rejected President Wałęsa's dismissal of the defense minister and the legislature voted by a large majority to urge the president to cease interfering in the democratic process. Wałęsa responded by denouncing the Pawlak government and calling for stronger presidential powers, the controversial defense minister being forced out the following month. The crisis deepened in January 1995 amid various policy differences between the president and his government, which yielded the resignation of Pawlak on February 7 after the president had threatened parliamentary dissolution. Collateral strains between the two coalition parties were resolved sufficiently to enable the SLD's Józef OLEKSY, a Communist-era minister, to be sworn in on March 6 as prime minister of a continued SLD-PSL coalition, albeit with half of its members new appointees.

Despite the relative failure of a 1993 effort to form a "presidential" party styled the Nonparty Bloc in Support of Reform (*Bezpartyjny Blok Wspierania Reform*—BBWR), Wałęsa in April 1995 confirmed his candidacy for a second presidential term. His main opponents among 17 other registered candidates were Aleksander KWAŚNIEWSKI of the SLD/SdRP, Jacek KUROŃ of the center-right Freedom Union (*Unia Wolności*—UW), and former prime ministers Olszewski and Pawlak. In the first round of balloting on November 5 Kwaśniewski took a narrow lead, with 35.1 percent against 33.1 percent for Wałęsa. In the runoff contest on November 19 Kwaśniewski won 51.7 percent to 48.3 percent for Wałęsa, despite endorsement of the latter by most of the other first-round candidates and by most center-right parties.

Sworn in on December 22, 1995, Kwaśniewski quickly lost his prime minister, Oleksy, who was obliged to resign on January 24, 1996, over allegations (which he denied) that he had passed information to the Soviet, later Russian, intelligence service. He was replaced on February 8 by Włodzimierz CIMOSZEWICZ of the SLD, heading a further coalition of the SLD and PSL that included six independents.

In preparation for the 1997 legislative elections Solidarity in June 1996 began organizing small center-right parties into the Solidarity Electoral Action (*Akcja Wyborcza Solidarność*—AWS), which ultimately became a coalition of some 36 parties and groups. Despite President Kwaśniewski's popularity and four years of economic growth, the AWS won 201 seats against 164 for the SLD in the balloting on September 21, 1997. The AWS's success was attributed to its alignment with the Catholic Church and its appeal to lingering resentment against the ex-Communists. After protracted negotiations, the AWS signed a coalition agreement with the UW on October 20 and formed a new government on October 31, with Jerzy BUZEK of the leading AWS party, the Social Movement-Solidarity Electoral Action (*Ruch Społeczny-Akija Wyborcza Solidarność*—RS-AWS), as prime minister.

In 1998 and early 1999 Warsaw's imminent entry into the North Atlantic Treaty Organization (NATO) and its preparations for accession to the EU had far-reaching effects on both foreign and domestic policies. With Poland about to become the eastern front line of NATO and the EU, Warsaw was under pressure to tighten its eastern borders, which increased tension with Belarus and raised concerns in Ukraine. Warsaw sought to reassure its former Soviet bloc neighbors and held talks to improve relations with Germany, with whom it hoped to tie up lingering postwar issues, particularly compensation for deported Poles used by the Nazi regime as slave laborers. Poland formally entered NATO on March 12, 1999.

On the domestic front, reforms designed to prepare for EU accession created labor unrest and attendant political fallout. Privatization plans and other reforms, some of which raised the prospects of huge job losses, caused strikes in the coal min-

ing, steel, railway, and defense industries. In trying to curb subsidies and protectionist tariffs, the government alienated farmers, who, under the leadership of radical unionist Andrzej LEPPER of the Self-Defense of the Polish Republic (*Samoobrona Rzeczypospolitej Polskiej*), blocked roads throughout the nation in a series of disruptive protests, the most serious of which began in December 1998 and extended into 1999. At the beginning of 1999 the government was also confronted by opposition to a series of health care reforms, introduction of which led to physician resignations, more strikes, and public confusion. The crisis in health care also contributed to a potential rift in the governing coalition, but the AWS managed to mollify its junior partner, the UW, in late January, in part by dismissing a deputy health minister. The UW nevertheless continued to criticize its senior partner for what it saw as half-hearted pursuit of free-market policies, particularly privatization. Meanwhile, public opinion polls registered increasing dissatisfaction with the AWS and growing support for the leftist SLD.

Policy and leadership differences within the government continued to cause persistent internal friction, and on October 11, 1999, in an effort to stabilize the situation, the AWS and the UW signed a renegotiated coalition agreement. Nevertheless, on June 6, 2000, objecting to Buzek's continuation as prime minister as well as to the inability of the AWS to exert discipline over its disparate components, the UW formally withdrew. The move left the AWS in charge of a minority government, although it continued to receive regular UW support in Parliament and survived until the legislative term ended in 2001.

On October 8, 2000, President Kwaśniewski won reelection with 53.9 percent of the vote despite the presence on the ballot of 11 other active candidates. Second place (17.3 percent) went to an independent, Andrzej OLECHOWSKI, who had previously been associated with the AWS, while Solidarity's Marian KRZAKLEWSKI, despite AWS backing, finished third (15.6 percent). Former president Wałęsa managed only 1 percent of the vote, finishing seventh.

In December 2000 Solidarity announced that it was withdrawing from active politics and turned over to Prime Minister Buzek's RS-AWS its voting rights in the AWS, which was rapidly disintegrating as its various leaders and parties sought to position themselves as the best center-right alternative to the SLD for upcoming parliamentary elections. At the *Sejm* and Senate elections on September 23, 2001, a coalition of the SLD and the much smaller Union of Labor (*Unia Pracy*—UP) claimed a plurality of 216 seats in the lower house and an overwhelming majority in the upper, while Buzek's new coalition, the Solidarity Electoral Action of the Right (*Akcja Wyborcza Solidarność Prawicy*—AWSP), failed to meet the 8 percent threshold for *Sejm* representation. The UW also lost all representation in the *Sejm* as three new formations—the Civic Platform (*Platforma Obywatelska*—PO), with 65 seats; the Law and Justice (*Prawo i Sprawieliwość*—PiS), with 44; and the League of Polish Families (*Liga Polskich Rodzin*—LPR), with 38—split much of the center-right vote. On the far right, Andrzej Lepper's *Samoobrona* entered the *Sejm*, finishing third, with 53 seats.

On October 9, 2001, the SLD/UP completed a coalition agreement with the rural PSL that permitted the SLD's Leszek MILLER, an electrician who had risen through the ranks of the PZPR and the SdRP, to become prime minister of an SLD-dominated cabinet on October 19, concurrent with the opening of the new parliamentary session.

In early March 2003 the PSL left the governing coalition following a disagreement with the SLD over a tax initiative. The government was therefore left with a minority of only 212 seats in the *Sejm*, a situation that was only partially eased by addition of the new Peasant Democratic Party (*Partia Ludowe Democratyczna*—PLD) to the coalition from late March until January 2004. The government remained stressed on several fronts (see Current issues, below), and Miller announced his resignation on May 2, 2004, only one day after Poland had acceded to the EU. President Kwaśniewski immediately designated "technocrat" Marek BELKA of the SLD to succeed Miller, but Belka lost a confirmation vote on May 14 in the *Sejm*, which was then constitutionally permitted to present its own candidate. When the *Sejm* failed to act in that regard, the president reappointed Belka on June 11, and he and his SLD/UP cabinet were confirmed by the *Sejm* on June 24.

Upon his confirmation as prime minister in June 2004, Marek Belka was immediately perceived as at best a caretaker leader of a dying government. That perception was underscored by the poor performance of the SLD and UP in the June European Parliament balloting, at which right-wing and center-right parties rose in prominence.

In the legislative elections on September 25, 2005, the PiS led all parties by securing 155 seats in the *Sejm*, followed by the PO with 133 seats and *Samoobrona* with 56. The SLD was relegated to fourth place with 55 seats. On September 27 the PiS named Kazimierz MARCINKIEWICZ as its choice for prime minister and announced the goal of forming a coalition government with the PO.

The first round of presidential elections was held on October 9, 2005, with a field of 12 candidates. Donald TUSK of the PO won 36.33 percent of the vote, followed by Lech KACZYŃSKI of the PiS with 33.10 percent. On October 23, 2005, Kaczyński bested Tusk 54.04 percent to 45.96 percent to gain the presidency.

President Kwaśniewski on October 24, 2005, formally designated Marcinkiewicz to form a new government. However, the PiS/PO talks collapsed (see Current issues, below, for details), and Marcinkiewicz was sworn in as head of a minority PiS government on October 31. On November 10 the government won a vote of confidence in the 460-seat *Sejm* with 272 votes, thanks to support from *Samoobrona* and the LPR. The PiS ascendancy was completed with Kaczyński's inauguration on December 23. Subsequently, in a May 5, 2006, reshuffle, the LPR and *Samoobrona* formally joined the government, their leaders being named deputy ministers. However, following a series of disputes between Prime Minister Marcinkiewicz and President Kaczyński and his brother Jarosław KACZYŃSKI (the chair of the PiS), Marcinkiewicz resigned on July 10. President Kaczyński immediately named his brother as prime minister-designate, and Jarosław Kaczyński was sworn in as prime minister on July 14 to head an essentially unchanged cabinet. The PiS/LPR/*Samoobrona* government won a vote of confidence in the *Sejm* on July 19 with 240 votes.

Constitution and Government

The constitutional changes of April 1989 provided for a bicameral legislature that incorporated the existing 460-member *Sejm* as its lower chamber and added a 100-member upper chamber (Senate). For the June 1989 balloting it was specified that all of the Senate seats would be free and contested, while 65 percent (299) of the lower house seats would be reserved for the PZPR and its allies (35 on a noncontested "National List" basis). All seats at subsequent elections were to be open and contested. Initially, the combined houses were empowered to elect a state president for a six-year term; however, constitutional changes prior to the December 1990 poll provided for a popularly elected president serving a five-year term. A new "small constitution" became effective on December 8, 1992, having been signed by President Wałęsa on November 17. It redefined the powers of, and relations between, the legislature, presidency, and government. A new "large" constitution, including a charter of liberties and human rights, was approved by a popular referendum on May 25, 1997, by a vote of 56.8 percent.

Parliament sits for a four-year term, save that the *Sejm* may dissolve itself (and by such action end the Senate term) by a two-thirds majority, assuming a quorum of at least 50 percent. The president has widespread authority in foreign and defense matters, with decrees in other areas requiring countersignature by a prime minister who is nominated by the president but must be confirmed by the *Sejm*. The prime minister appoints other ministers, while the president names military leaders and high-level judges. The president may veto legislation but can be overridden by a three-fifths majority of the lower house. There is a Constitutional Tribunal, whose members are appointed by the *Sejm*, while the regular judiciary has three tiers:

regional courts, provincial courts, and a Supreme Court.

As a result of constitutional and administrative reforms in 1975, the number of provinces (voivodships, or *województwa*) was increased from 22 to 49. However, in July 1998, following a contentious debate over boundaries, Parliament reduced the number to 16 (4 more than the government initially proposed). The reduction was part of a package of administrative reforms that also created a "middle tier" of 65 cities and 308 districts (*powiats*) and, in furtherance of decentralization, assigned authority for regional economic development to the voivodships. At the local level, there are nearly 2,500 communes (*gminas*). The prime minister appoints provincial governors (*wojewodowie*); provincial assemblies as well as executives and legislative organs at the lower levels are elected.

Foreign Relations

During most of the postwar era, Polish foreign policy, based primarily on close alliance with the Soviet Union, supported the stationing of Soviet troops in Poland as well as Polish participation in the Warsaw Pact and the Council for Mutual Economic Assistance. The events of the second half of 1980 elicited harsh criticism from the Soviet Union, Czechoslovakia, and East Germany while prompting expressions of concern in the West that the Warsaw Pact might intervene militarily, as it had in Hungary in 1956 and in Czechoslovakia in 1968. Predictably, the Soviet Union and most Eastern-bloc countries endorsed the Polish government's crackdown of December 1981. Western disapproval was alleviated by the lifting of martial law in mid-1983, and Washington withdrew its opposition to Polish membership in the IMF at the end of 1984, facilitating the country's admission to that agency and its sister institution, the World Bank, in June 1986.

In February 1990 Prime Minister Mazowiecki traveled to Moscow for talks with President Gorbachev, reiterating Polish concern that a newly unified Germany might attempt to reclaim land ceded to Poland after World War II. These fears were allayed by the outcome of "two-plus-four" talks between the two Germanies and World War II's victorious powers in July, which yielded a treaty between Bonn and Warsaw on November 14 that confirmed Poland's western border at the Oder and Neisse rivers. Poland's other major foreign policy concern was alleviated when the last Russian military contingent withdrew on September 17, 1993.

On May 21–23, 1992, during President Wałęsa's first visit to Moscow, a friendship and cooperation treaty was concluded that subsequently generated widespread resentment in Poland for its failure to address the issue of Russian responsibility for Stalinist atrocities during World War II. In October this source of strain was reduced when Moscow, bringing to an end over 50 years of false denials, admitted that the former Communist regime had ordered the execution of some 26,000 captured Polish army personnel in Katyn forest in 1940.

On November 2, 1992, Poland's National Defense Committee adopted a new policy based on the assumption that Poland had no natural enemies and no territorial claims on neighboring states. Longer-term security was seen as lying in a Euro-Atlantic system involving Polish membership in NATO. The main thrust of Polish foreign policy, however, was toward membership in the European Community (EC, subsequently the EU). To this end, Poland was a signatory in Kraków on December 21 of the Central European Free Trade Area (CEFTA) treaty with the other "Visegrád" countries of (then) Czechoslovakia and Hungary. Established in 1991 to end trade barriers and establish free trade in Central Europe by 2002, CEFTA was subsequently regarded by some as a form of "training" for EU membership. By mid-1998 CEFTA had grown to include Romania, Bulgaria, and Slovenia, and the former Czechoslovakia was represented by the Czech Republic and Slovakia. Croatia joined CEFTA in January 2003, but five countries (Czech Republic, Hungary, Poland, Slovakia, and Slovenia) left the grouping May 2004 when they joined the EU. Macedonia subsequently announced plans to join Bulgaria, Croatia, and Romania in CEFTA by the end of 2005. Meanwhile, some CEFTA leaders urged expansion of CEFTA to include all the non-EU countries of Southeastern Europe, with an eye on possible creation of a free trade area. Regionally, Poland is also a member of the Central European Initiative (CEI).

Having joined NATO's Partnership for Peace in February 1994, Poland on April 8 followed Hungary's lead in formally applying for admission to the EU. A month later, on May 9, it was one of nine former Communist states to become an "associate partner" of the Western European Union (WEU). Despite the Western thrust, which included a warm reception for U.S. President Clinton during an address to the *Sejm* on July 7, Poland also sought improved relations with Russia and the other members of the Commonwealth of Independent States (CIS). The motivation for the latter was largely economic: Relatively stiff tariffs had generated a deficit in trade with the EU countries, while Poland had previously maintained a trade surplus with the Soviet Union. In December 1997 EU leaders agreed to open entry negotiations with Poland and five other nations, and the first formal talks were held in November 1998. Accession negotiations continued into 2002, with a referendum on admission anticipated for mid-2003.

Under an agreement signed in Paris on July 11, 1996, Poland became the third ex-Communist state (after the Czech Republic and Hungary) to gain full membership in the Organization for Economic Cooperation and Development (OECD). The signing coincided with the end of an official visit to the United States by President Kwaśniewski, during which he received assurances of U.S. support for Poland's accession to NATO. Meanwhile, Poland had assigned 700 troops to the NATO-commanded International Force (IFOR) deployed in Bosnia under the Dayton peace agreements. At the Madrid summit meeting in July 1997, NATO leaders invited Poland and two other former Warsaw Pact nations (the Czech Republic and Hungary) to join the alliance. They became members on March 12, 1999, at ceremonies celebrating NATO's 50th anniversary in Independence, Missouri.

Poland was one of the most supportive countries of the U.S./UK-led invasion of Iraq in 2003, lending some 2,400 troops to the campaign. In a presumably related matter, Prime Minister Miller in April endorsed a plan for Poland to buy 48 American fighter planes for an estimated $3.5 billion as part of a 15-year military upgrade program. (In February 2005 U.S. President George W. Bush pledged $100 million in military aid to Poland.)

On June 7–8, 2003, Polish voters endorsed their country's proposed accession to the EU by a 58.9 percent "yes" vote in a national referendum. Poland joined nine other states as new EU members on May 1.

Tensions rose between Germany and Poland in late 2004 over the issue of reparations from World War II and its aftermath. Representatives of Germans who had been deported from former German territory in 1945–1946 after the territory was incorporated into Poland renewed their campaign for compensation in 2004. In return, Poland threatened to seek reparations from Germany for damage inflicted during the war.

Some European governments had assumed a probusiness, pro-foreign trade bloc (i.e., a PiS-PO government) would emerge from the 2005 elections. However, the PiS minority cabinet and the subsequent PiS-led coalition adopted a nationalistic, euroskeptic approach toward foreign policy. Among other things, other European countries reportedly objected to the new Polish administration's blockage of cross-border takeovers of Polish state-run enterprises slated for privatization. In addition, the EU specifically noted Poland in a resolution condemning perceived growing racism and ultranationalism throughout the continent. Of particular concern to the EU was the inclusion of the LPR in the Polish cabinet in 2006. A further motivation was the assault of the chief rabbi of Poland, Michael SCHUDRICH, in broad daylight in Warsaw in May 2006. The Polish Parliament, in turn, issued a counter-resolution condemning the EU resolution.

Current Issues

While the breakup of the AWS coalition precluded any chance that Prime Minister Buzek would be returned to office at the September 2001 parliamentary election, the extent of the AWSP's loss could fairly be described as ignominious. Because the AWSP participants could not agree to unify as a single party, the coalition was required to obtain 8 percent, rather than 5 percent, of the vote to claim seats in the *Sejm,* and its 5.6 percent return therefore left the AWSP without representation in the lower house. In contrast, the SLD/UP took 41.0 percent of the vote and came within 15 seats of an outright majority. It clearly benefited not only from the popularity of its former leader, President Kwaśniewski, but also from its relative stability when compared to the fractured center-right, which had seen many of its leading figures change affiliation two or more times since the mid-1990s.

The Buzek administration's term in office had been beset by corruption scandals, economic uncertainty, rising unemployment, a looming fiscal crisis, and failure to resolve problems and implement reforms in a range of areas that included health care, pensions, and education. Nor was Buzek able to marshal sufficient support for his government's privatization plan, which the incoming SLD-led administration of Leszek Miller quickly took under review.

Prime Minister Miller's clear priorities were EU accession and the related issue of economic improvement. However, political instability subsequently plagued his SLD/UP government, which avoided a nonconfidence vote primarily because several small parties and a number of independent legislators supported it on key issues to avoid triggering early elections. The June 2003 national referendum clearly provided Miller with a mandate to pursue EU accession despite some antigovernment protests on the part of certain groups who feared possible negative consequences. Ironically, however, Miller resigned on May 2, 2004, only one day after his goal of EU membership for Poland was achieved. It was widely believed that Miller would have faced a nonconfidence vote in the *Sejm* if he had not left office. By that time the SLD had seriously splintered, and the SLD/UP administration had continued its rapid decline in popular esteem due to perceived ongoing corruption and a series of scandals.

Consequently, the dramatic decline of the SLD in the September 2005 legislative balloting was not unexpected, although the plurality achieved by the rightist PiS raised eyebrows domestically as well as throughout the rest of Europe. It was initially widely believed that the PiS would form a center-right government with the PO, but agreement could not be found on the allocation of ministries. (Observers also noted that the pro-EU, probusiness PO had significant policy differences with the nationalist PiS, particularly when successful PiS presidential candidate Lech Kaczyński campaigned on a populist platform that, among other things, promised millions of new homes to underprivileged segments of the population.) As a result, new prime minister Marcinkiewicz had to depend on the support of two diverse "fringe parties"—*Samoobrona* and the LPR—to maintain a legislative majority.

Although the first six months of the Marcinkiewicz government were buffeted by several ministerial resignations and firings, the prime minister himself rose in popularity, appearing to undercut President Kaczyński's political dominance. The president also reportedly considered the prime minister's approach insufficiently aggressive regarding two of Kaczyński's major goals: the cessation of the privatization programs launched by the previous government and a campaign to force former Communists out of government jobs at all levels. The appointment of Jarosław Kaczyński (the president's twin brother) in July 2006 appeared to offer the potential for consolidation of the PiS's nationalistic proclivities, although analysts suggested that EU regulations would restrict dramatic action on the part of the new government. As apparent evidence of the accuracy of that assessment, Jarosław Kaczyński announced shortly after taking office that his government would not permit increased budget deficits, despite calls from the PiS's coalition partners for large welfare increases.

Political Parties and Groups

Prior to 1983 Poland's dominant Communist party, officially known after 1948 as the Polish United Workers' Party (PZPR), exercised its authority through a Front of National Unity (*Front Jednośsci Narodnu*—FJN), which also included two nominally noncommunist groups, the United Peasants' Party (under PSL, below) and the Democratic Party (SD), in addition to various trade union, Catholic, women's, youth, and other mass organizations. In 1983 the Front was superseded by the Patriotic Movement for National Rebirth (*Patriotyczny Ruch Odrodzenia Narodowego*—PRON), but PRON was itself formally dissolved on November 8, 1989, while the PZPR was succeeded by the Social Democracy of the Polish Republic (SdRP) on January 29, 1990. The SdRP served as the core of the subsequent Democratic Left Alliance (SLD) and then dissolved in 1999, when the SLD became a party.

In the early 1980s a number of dissident organizations came into existence, the most important being the Independent Self-Governing Trade Union Solidarity (*Niezależny Samorząd Związków Zawodowych "Solidarność"*—NSZZ Solidarity), in part an outgrowth of the Committee for Social Self-Defense (*Komitet Samoobrony Społeczej*—KSS). (The KSS had been formed in 1977 as successor to the Committee for the Defense of Workers [*Komitet Obrony Robotników*—KOR], which had been organized to provide legal and financial aid to those imprisoned during the 1976 price-hike demonstrations.) Launched during a conference of independent labor groups in Gdańsk on September 17–18, 1980, Solidarity had a membership estimated at 10 million workers, or some 50 percent of the Polish labor force, by mid-1981. It was officially banned upon the imposition of martial law in December 1981, although an underground "Provisional Coordinating Committee" (*Tymczasowej Komisji Koordynacyjnej*—TKK) continued to call for the restoration of independent trade union rights.

In January 1989 the PZPR Central Committee called for gradual relegalization of Solidarity. Roundtable talks between government and union representatives began on February 6 and yielded, two months later, an agreement on political and economic reform, including opposition participation in legislative balloting in June. The Communists were decisively defeated at the June poll.

Lech Wałęsa resigned as Solidarity chair in December 1990, following his election as state president, and was succeeded by Marian Krzaklewski. Since Solidarity was technically not a political party, it participated in the national parliamentary and local elections of 1989 and 1991 through an ad hoc network of civic committees coordinated by a Central Committee appointed by Wałęsa.

Postcommunist Poland's first fully democratic election in October 1991 unleashed a profusion of parties and groupings of all conceivable orientations, several tracing their origins from the Solidarity movement. Of the more than 100 parties active in 1991, no fewer than 29 parties won representation in the 460-seat *Sejm*, none with more than 13 percent of the vote. The scene thereafter was one of constant flux in party allegiance and identity, particularly on the center-right of the political spectrum. Because of a new minimum vote threshold, only seven groups secured parliamentary representation in September 1993. As of mid-1995, however, a total of 275 distinct political parties had achieved official registration.

During the second half of the 1990s the division in Polish politics was most clearly represented by the leftist SLD coalition of President Aleksander Kwaśniewski, who had been elected in 1995, and the center-right Solidarity Electoral Action (*Akcja Wyborcza Solidarność*—AWS) coalition, which was launched in 1996 under the leadership of Solidarity in preparation for the 1997 legislative balloting. Among the other major participants in the AWS were the Conservative Peasant Party (SKL), the Christian National Union (ZChN), the Center Alliance (PC), and the Christian Democratic Party (PChD). In all, more than 30 (mostly small) parties and groups joined the AWS, which won 33.8 percent of the vote at the 1997 legislative elections and secured a plurality of 201 seats in the *Sejm*. Its two most visible figures were Solidarity Chair Krzaklewski and the new prime minister, Jerzy Buzek.

Despite its electoral success, the AWS failed to cohere into a unified party, in part because many of the constituent organizations did not want to merge into a larger grouping that they perceived as dominated by trade unionists. Only about half of the legislators elected under the banner of the AWS

coalition joined a new Solidarity-backed party, the Social Movement-Solidarity Electoral Action (RS-AWS; see Social Movement, below), upon its formation in December 1997.

The third-place finish of Krzaklewski in the 2000 presidential race accelerated the disintegration of the unwieldy AWS, although Prime Minister Buzek managed to remain in office through the full parliamentary term. At the September 2001 legislative election Buzek's new coalition, the Solidarity Electoral Action of the Right (AWSP), failed to meet the threshold for representation in the *Sejm*, and the SLD, in coalition with the Union of Labor (UP), easily outdistanced a handful of recently formed, post-AWS formations—chiefly the Civic Platform (PO), the Law and Justice (PiS), and the League of Polish Families (LPR). Thus, the presidency, the Parliament, and the Council of Ministers are currently dominated by the heirs of Poland's Communist past. The heirs of the Solidarity movement are scattered among a variety of center and right parties.

The 2005 elections brought a substantial change to Polish party politics, with the significant diminution of the electoral strength of the political left and the ascension of the right side of the party system.

Government Parties

Law and Justice (*Prawo i Sprawiedliwość*—PiS). Drawn primarily from conservative elements of the Christian National Union (ZChN, below), the SKL, and the Republican League (*Liga Republikańska*—LR) of Mariusz KAMIŃSKI, the PiS was organized in March 2001 under the leadership of Jarosław Kaczyński, a former editor of *Tygodnik Solidarność* (*Solidarity Weekly*) and a longtime supporter of Lech Wałęsa. In its Christian-democratic orientation the PiS resembled an earlier Kaczyński formation, the now-defunct Center Alliance (*Porozumienie Centrum*—PC; see SKL-RNP), which had been organized in 1991 and had then formed the core of a Center Citizens' Alliance (*Porozumienie Obywatelskie Centrum*—POC) that secured 44 *Sejm* seats the following October. In January 1998 Kaczyński resigned after eight years as PC chair because of the party's decision to remain in the AWS.

Registered as a party in June 2001, the PiS gained additional support through the presence of Kaczyński's twin brother, Lech Kaczyński, who had served in the minority AWS government following the departure of the UW but had been dismissed in July 2001 because of a disagreement with Prime Minister Buzek over the handling of a fraud investigation. The former justice minister, who is regarded as harboring presidential ambitions, brought to the party his reputation as an anticorruption, anticrime campaigner as well as one of Poland's most popular politicians. At the September 2001 elections the PiS won 44 seats in the *Sejm,* based on 9.5 percent of the vote.

In April 2002 the PiS and the Alliance of the Right (*Przymierze Prawicy*—PP) announced their pending merger. The PP (not to be confused with the Polish Agreement [PP], below, under LPR) had been established in March 2001 by Minister of Culture Kazimierz UJAZDOWSKI and former members of the AWS-affiliated SKL and ZChN, including the latter's ex-chair, Marian PIŁKA. Ujazdowski, a close ally of Lech Kaczyński, had headed the Conservative Coalition (*Koalicja Konserwatywna*—KK) before its merger with the SKL in early 1999. In July 2001 he resigned from the Buzek cabinet to protest Kaczyński's sacking.

The PiS consistently opposed the economic policies of the Miller administration, and the Kaczyński brothers regularly accused SLK officials of corruption. That stance appeared to resonate with the public, which accorded the PiS a third-place finish in the June 2004 balloting for the European Parliament.

The 2005 parliamentary elections saw the PiS's share of seats in the *Sejm* increase from 44 in 2001 to 155. The party also won the presidency and a plurality of seats in the Senate.

Leaders: Lech KACZYŃSKI (President), Jarosław KACZYŃSKI (Prime Minister and President of the Party), Kazimierz MARCINKIEWICZ (Former Prime Minister).

Self-Defense of the Polish Republic Party (*Partia Samoobrona Rzeczypospolitej Polskiej—Samoobrona*). The *Samoobrona* Party has its base in the agrarian trade union of the same name. Formed in 1993, the union encompasses about half a million mostly rural members, although the much smaller party has also attracted a high percentage of businessmen disaffected from the rest of the political establishment. Generally regarded as the most militant of Poland's three principal farmers' unions, *Samoobrona* did not become a significant parliamentary force until the 2001 national election, at which the party won 10.2 percent of the vote and 53 seats in the *Sejm*. Following *Samoobrona's* 2001 success at the polls, Andrzej Lepper was named a vice marshal of the lower house, but he was removed from the post in late November, partly as a consequence of provocative statements made against other national figures. Furthermore, on January 25, 2002, the house revoked his parliamentary immunity, and five days later he was fined by an appeals court for defamatory statements made against President Kwaśniewski and others in 1999. In February 2002 Lepper was charged with seven additional counts of slander. However, the charges appeared to enhance Lepper's popularity within the party as well as among segments of the general population, which appeared to be growing increasingly disenchanted with Poland's economic and political (i.e., EU membership) developments.

In 2006 *Sambroona* joined the PiS and the LPR to form a coalition government, with the party's controversial leader, Andrej Lepper, being named deputy prime minister.

Leader: Andrzej LEPPER (Party Leader and Deputy Prime Minister).

League of Polish Families (*Liga Polskich Rodzin*—LPR). Initially formed as a "group of voters," the LPR brought together an assortment of nationalist, predominantly anti-EU, Catholic groups, many of them associated with *Radio Maryja*. Registered as a party on May 30, 2001, the LPR was headed by Antoni MACIEREWICZ, a former interior minister whose efforts to expose former

Communist collaborators contributed to the fall of the Olszewski government in 1992 and who was subsequently expelled from the ZChN. In February 1993 Macierewicz launched the right-wing Christian National Movement–Polish Action (*Ruch Chrześcijańsko–Narodowe-Akcja Polska*—RChN-AP), and in 1995 he participated in the formation of the Movement for the Reconstruction of Poland (ROP, below). He broke from the ROP in late 1997 and established the Catholic National Movement for the Reconstruction of Poland, which in May 1998 shortened its name to the **Catholic National Movement** (*Ruch Katolicko-Narodowy*—RKN) and then joined the AWS. Another LPR founder, Jan ŁOPUSZAŃSKI of the **Polish Agreement** (*Porozumienie Polskie*—PP), had won 0.8 percent of the vote in the 2000 presidential race.

For the 2001 legislative elections the LPR list included not only members of the PP, but also members of the **National Party** (*Stronnictwo Narodowe*—SN) and the ROP. The SN dated from the December 1999 merger of Bogusław KOWALSKI's National Democratic Party (*Stronnictwo Narodowo Demokratyczne*—SND) and an existing SN. In the 2000 presidential election campaign the SN had been a leading supporter of Gen. Tadeusz WILECKI, who won 0.2 percent of the vote.

In September 2001 the LPR won 9 percent of the vote and 38 seats in the *Sejm*. Within six months, however, significant differences had emerged within the parliamentary delegation, pitting Macierewicz supporters against a larger group headed by Roman Giertych. In April 2002 Macierewicz and Jan Łopuszański both reportedly resigned from the party Presidium, and Macierewicz and four other disaffected LPR deputies subsequently resumed coordination under the RKN rubric. Macierewicz served as one of the main opponents to EU membership in the run-up to the 2003 referendum on the issue.

The League became part of the government in May 2006.

Leaders: Marek KOTLINOWSKI, Zygmunt WRZODAK, Roman GIERTYCH (Deputy Prime Minister).

Opposition Parties

Civic Platform (*Platforma Obywatelska—PO*). The PO was organized in January 2001 at the initiative of three prominent politicians: former presidential candidate Andrzej Olechowski, who, running as an independent, had finished second in the 2000 poll with 17 percent of the vote; Donald Tusk, formerly of the Freedom Union (UW, below); and former AWS leader and *Sejm* Speaker Maciej PŁAŻYŃSKI. The new formation's liberal, free-market orientation soon attracted other disparate elements, including much of the previously AWS-supportive Conservative Peasant Party (see SKL-RNP, below) and the right-wing Realpolitik Union (UPR, below). For the 2001 Senate campaign, the PO joined the Solidarity Electoral Action of the Right (AWSP), the UW, and Law and Justice (PiS, above) in a **Senate Bloc 2001** (*Bloc Senat 2001*) in an unsuccessful effort to prevent the SLD from obtaining a majority of seats. In the *Sejm* election the PO finished second, with 12.7 percent of the vote and 65 seats, although a number of deputies elected on its list, including eight from the SKL, chose to sit in the lower house as members of other parliamentary groups.

The PO, which had entered the 2001 elections as a "group of voters," was registered as a political party in March 2002. In April 2003 PO Chair Maciej Płażyński resigned to protest the centrist party's failure to adopt his rightist policies. The PO led all parties in the balloting for the Polish seats in the European Parliament in June 2004.

In the 2005 parliamentary elections the PO won the second largest block of seats with 133, more than doubling the 65 seats that they won in 2001. Initially, they were thought to be in a position to partner with the PiS to form the government, but talks collapsed (see the Current issues, above).

The PO's presidential candidate, Donald Tusk, came in first in the first round of polling in October of 2005 but eventually lost to the PiS candidate in the second round.

Leaders: Grzegorz SCHETYNA (Secretary General), Donald TUSK (Party Chair), Mirosław DRZEWIECKI (Treasurer).

Democratic Left Alliance (*Sojusz Lewicy Democratycznej*—SLD). The SLD was launched prior to the 1991 election as a coalition of the Social Democracy of the Republic of Poland (*Socjaldemokracja Rzeczypospolitej Polskiej*—SdRP) and the previously Communist-dominated All Poland Trade Unions Alliance (*Ogólnopolskie Porozumienie Związków Zawodowych*—OPZZ). The SdRP had been established on January 29, 1990, upon formal dissolution of the Polish United Workers' Party (*Polska Zjednoczona Partia Robotnicza*—PZPR). Formed in 1948 by merger of the (Communist) Polish Workers' Party (*Polska Partia Robotnicza*—PPR) and the Polish Socialist Party (*Polska Partia Socjalistyczna*—PPS), the PZPR claimed approximately 3 million members prior to the events of 1980–1981, as a result of which enrollment declined by nearly 800,000.

At the December 1990 presidential poll the candidate backed by the SdRP, Włodzimierz CIMOSZEWICZ, placed fourth, with 9.2 percent of the vote; by contrast, the SLD was runner-up in the 1991 *Sejm* balloting and then became the largest *Sejm* formation in 1993 by increasing its representation from 60 to 171. Announced in May 1995, the presidential candidacy of SLD/SdRP leader Aleksander Kwaśniewski was subsequently endorsed by some 30 parties and groups, sufficient to yield a comfortable three-point margin of victory for him in the second round of the November balloting. Although the SLD improved its vote share from 1993, increasing from 20.4 to 27.1 percent, it actually won fewer seats (164) in 1997, when it was unable to withstand the pro–Catholic Church, anti-Communist campaign of the AWS. However, following the local elections of October 1998, the SLD controlled 9 of the nation's 16 provinces, having won a vote share of 32 percent.

Upon his election as president in 1995, Kwaśniewski had vacated the SdRP chairship, to which Józef Oleksy was elected in January 1996, three days after his forced resignation as prime minister. After the 1997 election the party chose Leszek Miller to replace Oleksy, who had not run for reelection. Miller's easy victory over Wiesław KACZMAREK, a former economics minister, was considered a blow to reformers who wanted further distance from the party's Communist origins.

Transformation of the SLD into a political party was announced in April 1999, after which the SdRP dissolved, and in July Miller formally took over the leadership of the SLD. Two other coalition partners, the Polish Socialist Party (PPS) and the Movement of Polish Working People (RLP), chose to remain distinct from the new party. All three parties endorsed President Kwaśniewski for reelection in 2000, and on October 8 he claimed a first-round victory against 11 other candidates, winning 53.9 percent of the vote.

In preparation for the September 2001 parliamentary elections the SLD and the Union of Labor (UP, below) forged an electoral coalition (*Koalicja Sojuszu Lewicky Demokratycznej i Unii Pracy*) that captured 41 percent of the national vote and 216 seats, 15 short of a majority. Miller thereupon negotiated a coalition with the Polish Peasants' Party (PSL) and became prime minister. The SLD/UP coalition had even greater success in the majoritarian Senate contest, winning 75 of 100 seats. However, the SLD's popularity subsequently declined amid discontent in some quarters over government austerity measures and disputes among government coalition parties. Miller resigned as SLD president in March 2004, although one of his close allies, Krzysztof JANIK, was elected to succeed him. Miller also resigned as prime minister on May 2, his replacement, Marek Belka, only achieving confirmation as a caretaker prime minister until the 2005 parliamentary balloting after pledging to undo some of the economic measures adopted by the Miller administration. The SLD (weakened by the defection of a group of legislators in March) managed only a fifth-place finish (again in alliance with the UP) in the June 2004 elections to the European Parliament. Janik was defeated in December in his bid for reelection as SLD leader by former prime minister Oleksy, although Oleksy subsequently came under intense scrutiny regarding allegations concerning his activities during Communist rule.

The SLD was repudiated at the ballot box in 2005 when it saw its number of seats in the *Sejm* go from 200 in 2001 to a mere 55.

Leaders: Wojciech OLEJNICZAK (Chair), Grzegorz NAPIERALSKI (General Secretary)

Polish Peasants' Party (*Polskie Stronnictwo Ludowe*—PSL). The original PSL was organized in 1945 by Stanisław Mikołajczyk after the leadership of the traditional Peasant Party (*Stronnictwo Ludowe*—SL), founded in 1895, had opted for close cooperation with the postwar Communist regime. In November 1949, following Mikołajczyk's repudiation by leftist members, the two groups merged as the United Peasant Party (*Zjednoczone Stronnictwo Ludowe*—ZSL), which became part of the Communist-dominated FJN.

In August 1989 a group of rural activists met at Warsaw to revive the PSL on the basis of its 1946 program. In September the ZSL was awarded four portfolios in the Solidarity-led coalition government, and in November the ZSL reorganized into two parties, the Polish Peasant Party-Rebirth (*PSL-Odrodzenie*—PSL-O) and the PSL-*Wilnanóv* (PSL-W). Six months later, the present PSL emerged from a unification congress of the PSL-O, part of the PSL-W, and some members of the PSL-*Solidarność,* which had been formed by former Rural Solidarity members in 1989. The party was nevertheless weakened by continuing controversy between ex-ZSL activists and those who sought to have them purged. The PSL's principal support came from small farmers who opposed the introduction of large-scale agricultural enterprises on the American model.

At the 1991 election the PSL was the core of a Peasant Coalition (*Sojusz Programowy*) that won 48 *Sejm* seats. Running alone, it secured 132 seats in 1993 and formed a governing coalition with the SLD. Amid frequent strains between the coalition parties, the PSL deputy president was dismissed as chair of the *Sejm's* privatization committee in November 1994 on the grounds that he had tried to block or slow down the sell-off of state enterprises.

The PSL lost considerable ground in the 1997 balloting, dropping from 132 seats to 27 on a 7.3 percent vote share. Party leader Jarosław Kalinowski finished fourth, with 6.0 percent of the vote, in the 2000 presidential election. In September 2001 the party won 9.0 percent of the *Sejm* vote, for 42 seats, as a result of which it was positioned to negotiate a governing coalition with the larger SLD/UP alliance. However, Prime Minister Miller of the SLD forced the PSL to leave the government in April 2003 after the PSL voted against its coalition partners on a contentious road tax measure.

Leaders: Waldemar PAWLAK (Chair), Jarosław KALINOWSKI (Former Chair), Zbigniew KUŹMIUK (Parliamentary Leader).

German Minority of Lower Silesia (*Mniejszość Niemiecka Slaska Opolskiego*—MNSO). Representing ethnic Germans in western and northern Poland, the MNSO list won seven seats in the October 1991 balloting, four of which were retained in 1993. It retained two seats in 1997 and 2001 under rules that exempt national minority parties from the 5 percent threshold. Both deputies are from the largest German association, the **German Social and Cultural Society of Opole Silesia** (*Towarzystwo Spoleczno-Kulturalne Niemców na Slasku Opolskim*—TSKN).

Leader: Henryk KROLL (Chair and Parliamentary Leader).

Other Parties

Union of Labor (*Unia Pracy*—UP). Known as Labor Solidarity (*Solidarność Pracy*—SP) in 1991, when it won four *Sejm* seats as a left-wing faction of the original Solidarity movement, the UP captured 41 seats in 1993. With only a 4.7 percent vote share in 1997, the UP failed to meet the 5 percent threshold and therefore retained no seats. Key members, who include representatives of the Belarusan minority, subsequently were reported to have joined the UW early in 1998. The UP was part of the Social Alliance in the October 1998 local elections.

Having lost most of its initial Solidarity members, the UP concluded an electoral coalition with the SLD for the 2001 legislative contests and, following the alliance's success at the polls, joined the new administration under Prime Minister Miller.

Izabela JARUGA-NOWACKA was elected president of the UP at an April 2004 party congress, and she joined the new government formed by the SLD's Marek Belka in May as a deputy prime minister. The UP again presented joint candidates with the SLD in the June 2004 balloting for the European Parliament. In early 2005 it was reported that Jaruga-Nowacka had decided to resign from the UP to participate in the launching of a new left-wing political grouping.

Even running in coalition with the SDPL, the UP was unable to win a single seat in the 2005 elections, after having won 16 in the 2001 contests.

Leaders: Andrzej AUMILLER (Party Leader), Stanislaw CZAJCZYŃSKI (General Secretary).

Polish Social Democracy Party (*Socjaldemokracja Polska*—SDPL). The SDPL was formed in March 2004 by Marek Borowski (a former speaker of the *Sejm*) and some 22 other SLD deputies seeking to distance themselves from the administration of Prime Minister Miller. Although the SDPL declined formal coalition status in the government formed by the SLD's Marek Belka in June 2004, an SDPL member was named minister of health and the SDPL pledged to support the caretaker government in the legislature until the 2005 elections.

In 2005 the SDPL ran in coalition with the UP and failed to gain seats in the legislature.

Leader: Marek BOROWSKI.

Polish Peasants' Bloc (*Polski Blok Ludowy*— PBL). A centrist agrarian party, the PBL was launched by former members of *Samoobrona* in 2002 and subsequently operated in alliance with the PSL.

Leader: Wojciech MOJZESOWICZ.

Peasant Democratic Party (*Partia Ludowe Democratyczna*—PLD). The PLD was founded in February 1998 by Roman Jagieliński, formerly of the PSL. He had been a deputy prime minister and minister of agriculture until he lost support within the PSL and resigned in March 1997. The PLD supported President Kwaśniewski's reelection in 2000 and aligned with the SLD in the 2001 *Sejm* election, a reported six PLD members securing seats

(formally as candidates of the SLD/UP coalition). The PLD agreed to support the revamped Miller government in Parliament in March 2003 but withdrew its support in January 2004, in part apparently as the result of a dispute between Miller and Jagieliński over a possible PLD cabinet post.

Leader: Roman JAGIELIŃSKI.

Movement for the Reconstruction of Poland (*Ruch Odbudowy Polski*—ROP). The radical promarket ROP was formed by former prime minister Olszewski in the wake of his fourth-place showing (with 6.9 percent of the popular vote) in the first round of the November 1995 presidential election. Olszewski had previously been prominent first in the Center Alliance (PC) and then in the Movement for the Republic (RdR), becoming leader of a dissident faction of the latter after his ouster as chair in December 1993. In its first electoral outing in 1997, the ROP was one of only five parties to exceed the 5 percent threshold required to earn parliamentary representation, gaining six seats with a 5.6 percent vote share. The party subsequently remained factionalized, with some of the six legislative winners joining the AWS bloc in Parliament.

In the 2000 presidential contest Olszewski withdrew his candidacy a week before the balloting and urged his supporters to vote for Marian Krzaklewski of Solidarity. In the same contest Darius GRABOWSKI, who had left the ROP in 1999, won 0.5 percent of the vote as an independent. In 2001 the ROP briefly joined Prime Minister Buzek's AWSP coalition but in July opted instead for participation in the League of Polish Families (LPR). Following the September legislative election, however, the ROP broke with the LPR, three deputies in the *Sejm* subsequently identifying themselves as representing the ROP.

Leader: Jan OLSZEWSKI (Chair).

National Pensioners' Party (*Krajowe Przedstawicielstwo Emerytówi Rencistó*—KPEiR). Also referenced in English as the National Party of Retirees and Disability Pensioners, the KPEiR affiliated with the SLD in 1993 but subsequently separated. Many party activists are former members of the PZPR. In addition to advocating small businesses as a vehicle for rural development and job creation, the organization has favored membership in the EU. In 1997 the KPEiR attacked the AWS for "political gangsterism," accusing it of instigating the formation of the KPEiR RP (below), another pensioners' group, to confuse voters and siphon votes. Campaigning under the slogan "Poland First" in 1997, it failed to meet the 5 percent threshold for representation in the *Sejm*. For the local elections of October 1998 it joined a Social Alliance with the PSL and the UP. For the 2001 legislative election it concluded a cooperation agreement with the SLD, and its chair was elected to the *Sejm* on the SLD list. The KPEiR competed (unsuccessfully) in alliance with the PLD in the 2004 elections to the European Parliament.

Leader: Tomasz MAMIŃSKI (Chair).

Social Movement (*Ruch Społeczny*—RS). The RS is the direct heir of the Solidarity movement, with its immediate progenitor being the AWS coalition. Formed by Prime Minister Buzek and his closest supporters as the Social Movement-Solidarity Electoral Action (*Ruch Społeczny-Akcja Wyborcza Solidarność*—RS-AWS) in December 1997, the party shortened its name to the RS at a congress on April 28, 2002.

The initial RS-AWS chair, Marian Krzaklewski of the Solidarity trade union, had stepped down at the group's January 1999 congress in accordance with new guidelines precluding union chairs from holding formal RS-AWS positions. The same congress adopted a platform describing the party as a Christian Democratic grouping devoted to a mixed economy and support for families and social cohesion.

As the AWS coalition disintegrated following Krzaklewski's third-place finish in the October 2000 presidential election (he won only 15.6 percent of the vote), Prime Minister Buzek attempted to shore it up, taking over as leader in January 2001 and heading a newly created National Council. He also urged the remaining AWS parties to reorganize as a unified Solidarity Electoral Action of the Right (*Akcja Wyborcza Solidarność Prawicy*—AWSP), but they insisted on maintaining their independent identities. Thus the AWSP was established on May

23, 2001, not as a party, but as an electoral coalition, by the RS-AWS, the Christian National Union (ZChN), the Polish Party of Christian Democrats (PPChD; see SKL-RNP), and the Movement for the Reconstruction of Poland (ROP). The ROP soon left the coalition, however, and joined the new League of Polish Families (LPR). Moreover, in May the Solidarity Union, having already announced its withdrawal from direct involvement in party politics, withdrew its support for the RS-AWS. All of the remaining AWS parties had already lost key members to other formations, and at the September *Sejm* election the AWSP won only 5.6 percent of the vote, well below the 8 percent threshold needed for a coalition to obtain representation.

Former Prime Minister Buzek stepped down as party chair on October 21, 2001, and was succeeded by Mieczysław JANOWSKI. The latter was in turn succeeded by Sen. Krzysztof Piesiewicz in April 2002, at which time the renamed party attempted to reposition itself at the political center.

Leader: Krzysztof PIESIEWICZ (Chair), Jerzy BUZEK (Former Prime Minister).

Christian National Union (*Zjednoczenie Chrześcijańsko-Narodowe*—ZChN). The ideologically conservative and anti-abortion ZChN was founded in September 1989 from a number of Catholic groups and supported Wałęsa in the 1990 presidential balloting. It contested the 1991 legislative election as the leading element of Catholic Electoral Action (*Wyborcza Akcja Katolicka*—WAK), which won a creditable 49 seats and participated in subsequent center-right administrations. The ZChN was weakened in 1992 when its chair, Wiesław CHRZANOWSKI (then marshal of the *Sejm*), was included on a government list of alleged Communist-era collaborators published by the ZChN interior minister, Antoni Macierewicz, who was expelled from the party and most recently helped form the League of Polish Families (LPR). In the 1993 election the ZChN headed the Homeland (*Ojczyzna*) alliance, which also included the Peasant Alliance (*Porozumienie Ludowe*—PL) and the Conservative Party (PK; see under SKL-RNP, below), but which failed to gain representation.

The ZChN was one of five right-wing groups that formed a "confederation" called the Covenant for Poland (*Przymierze dla Polski*—PdP) in May 1994. None of its members—the Center Alliance (PC) and the Movement for the Republic (RdR) as well as the ZChN, PL, and PK—had crossed the 5 percent vote-share threshold needed to secure *Sejm* representation in 1993. Chrzanowski was succeeded as party leader in March 1995 by Ryszard CZARNECKI, who himself resigned in protest at the party's decision to back Lech Wałęsa in the runoff presidential ballot of November 1995. In May 2000 the party was effectively split when Stanisław ZAJAC narrowly defeated the incumbent, Marian Piłka, for the party chairship. Zajac was in turn succeeded by Jerzy Kropiwnicki in 2002.

Leader: Jerzy KROPIWNICKI (Chair).

Conservative Peasant Party–New Poland Movement (*Stronnictwo Konserwatywno–Ludowe-Ruch Nowej Polski*—SKL-RNP). The SKL-RNP was established in January 2002 by merger of the SKL and the Polish Party of Christian Democrats (*Porozumienie Polskich Chrześcijańskich Demokratów*—PPChD).

Founded in January 1997, the SKL united two small right-wing parties, the Conservative Party (*Partia Konserwatywna*—PK), which had been launched in December 1992 by amalgamation of the Forum of the Democratic Right (*Forum Prawicy Demokratycznej*—FPD) and others, and the Peasant-Christian Alliance (*Stronnictwo Ludowo-Chrześcijańskie*—SLCh). The SKL's founding members included ex-ministers Jan Maria ROKITA and Bronisław KOMOROWSKI, and elements of the Christian Democratic Labor Party (ChDSP, below). At the SKL party congress in late February 1998, two groups joined the SKL: the Party of Republicans (*Partia Republikanów*—PR), led by Jerzy EYSYMONTT, and the Integrative Initiative (*Inicjatywa Integracyjna*—II) faction of the Center Alliance (*Porozumienie Centrum*—PC), led by Wojciech DOBRZYŃSKI. In February 1999 the Conservative Coalition (*Koalicja Konserwatywna*—KK) of Kazimierz Ujazdowski also joined the SKL.

In September 1999 what remained of the Center Alliance, which dated from 1991, and the Christian Democratic Party (*Partia Chrześcijańskich Demokratów*—PChD) announced their merger as the PPChD under Antoni TOKARCZUK, previously the PC chair. Also joining the new formation were former members of an assortment of other small parties that had participated in the AWS. These included the 100 Movement (*Ruch 100*), which had been founded by former foreign minister Andrzej Olechowski, now of the PO; the Polish Peasant Party-Peasant Alliance (*Polskie Stronnictwo Ludowe-Porozumienie Ludowe*—PSL-PL); and the Movement for the Republic (*Ruch dla Rzeczypospolitej*—RdR), which traced its origins to the 1992 formation of the Christian Democratic Forum (*Forum Chrześcijańsko-Demokratyczne*—FChD) by supporters of ousted prime minister Jan Olszewski. In April 2001 the PPChD added to its ranks the Electoral Solidarity (*Solidarni w Wyborach*—SwW) of Jerzy GWIŻDŻ, a longtime ally of former president Lech Wałęsa. Later in the same month the PPChD aligned itself with Prime Minister Buzek's efforts to reshape the AWS. The failure of Buzek's AWSP coalition at the September 2001 poll ultimately led the PPChD to seek a stronger alliance, which led to the 2002 merger with the SKL.

In March 2001 the SKL, theretofore a component of the AWS, had announced that it would leave the government and enter the Civic Platform (PO) in preparation for the September 2001 legislative elections. Following the balloting, however, a number of deputies who had been elected on the PO list established themselves as a separate SKL parliamentary group. In January 2002 the party split over the question of the PO affiliation. One faction, led by Jan Maria Rokita, opted to remain with the PO, and another, led by Artur Balazs, instead approved the merger with the PPChD.

Leaders: Artur BALAZS (President), Janusz STEINHOFF (Vice President), Aleksander HALL, Marek ZAGÓRSKI, Krzysztof TCHÓRZEWSKI (Secretary).

Democratic Party (*Partia Demokratyczna*—PD). A promarket, pro-European grouping hoping to attract centrist support, the PD was launched in the first half of 2005 by Jerzy Hausner (former SLD deputy prime minister) and Władysław Frasyniuk of the UW (below). Hausner had recently quit the SLD after his proposal to cut the federal budget had been rejected. At the launching of the PD, its supporters reportedly indicated that Prime Minister Belka was considering switching his allegiance from the SLD to the PD. (The PD should not be confused with the long-standing party of the same name; see SD, below.)

Leaders: Jerzy HAUSNER, Władysław FRASYNIUK.

Freedom Union (*Unia Wolności*—UW). The UW was organized on April 23–24, 1994, by merger of the Democratic Union (*Unia Demokratyczna*—UD) and the smaller Liberal Democratic Congress (*Kongres Liberalno-Demokratyczny*—KLD). The new formation described itself as a "strong party of the center," committed to market-oriented reforms and a democratic social order, but not insensitive to social justice.

The original UD had been launched by members of the election committees set up by the Solidarity-affiliated Citizens' Movement-Democratic Action (*Ruch Obywatelski Akcja Demokratyczna*—ROAD) to support Prime Minister Mazowiecki's 1990 bid for the presidency. At a congress in May 1991 two additional formations, the left-of-center Social Democratic Movement (*Ruch Demokratyczno Społeczny*—RDS) and the center-right Forum of the Democratic Right (*Forum Prawicy Demokratycznej*—FPD), agreed to merge into the UD. While of somewhat differing outlook, the constituent groups shared a distrust of Wałęsa's "demagogic populism" and strongly favored a slowdown in the imposition of his free-market reform program. The UD led the *Sejm* poll in 1991, securing 62 seats, but it lost its plurality in 1982 when the FPD withdrew before participating in forming the Conservative Party (PK; see SKL-RNP, above). Although improving its representation to 74 in 1993, the UD fell to third place behind the SLD and PSL.

Launched in February 1990, the KLD was the outgrowth of a Gdańsk-based group led by jour-nalist Donald Tusk that had been organized as the Congress of Liberals in 1988. Supported largely by white-collar and private business interests, it favored a free-market economy and the privatization of state enterprises. The KLD won 37 *Sejm* seats in 1991 but failed to reach the 5 percent threshold in 1993.

Having won 60 seats in the 1997 elections, the UW formed a ruling coalition with the AWS after protracted negotiations. UW Chair Leszek BALCEROWICZ, architect of the "shock therapy" economic reforms, was named minister of finance in the new government. At the UW's spring 1998 congress, about 20 activists from the Union of Labor (UP), including prominent Solidarity leader Zbigniew BUJAK, joined the UW.

Differences within the government caused frequent friction between the AWS leadership and the UW, and renegotiation of the coalition agreement in October 1999 only served to delay the UW's departure. On June 6, 2000, the UW formally withdrew, the party's governing council having voted on May 28 to sever its ties because of differences over the leadership of Prime Minister Buzek and the inability of the AWS to exert party discipline over its various components. The move left the AWS as a minority government, although it continued to receive UW support in Parliament.

Following the 2000 presidential election, Chair Balcerowicz was named to head the National Bank, and on December 16 former foreign minister Bronisław GEREMEK was elected to succeed him. Largely excluded from the new leadership, the party's more liberal wing, led by Donald Tusk, thereupon split from the UW and in January 2001 helped form the Civic Platform (PO). At the September 2001 *Sejm* election the UW won only 3.1 percent of the national vote, below the threshold for representation, leading to Geremek's resignation and his replacement by Solidarity stalwart Władysław Frasyniuk. However, the UW recovered somewhat in the June 2004 European Parliament balloting, securing 7.3 percent of the vote and four seats.

Leaders: Władysław FRASYNIUK (Chair), Tadeusz MAZOWIECKI (Former Prime Minister and Former UD and UW Chair), Jacek KUROŃ (1995 presidential candidate).

Christian Democratic Party of the Third Republic (*Chrześcijańska Demokracja III Rzeczypospolitej Polskiej*—ChDRP). The ChDRP was founded on December 1, 1997, by Lech Wałęsa, the former president of Poland and former leader of Solidarity. Wałęsa said the new grouping would not oppose the AWS-UW government but would be available to move toward a position of national influence should that coalition fail. The ChDRP held its first national congress in September 1998.

In July 1998 Wałęsa had announced that a ChDRP deputies team was being established within the AWS *Sejm* floor group. The team's leader, Jerzy Gwiżdż of the Electoral Solidarity (SwW), had formerly been affiliated with the now-defunct Nonparty Bloc in Support of Reform (*Bezpartyjny Blok Wspierania Reform*—BBWR), a formation initially backed by Wałęsa that had won 16 lower house seats in 1993 and then in 1996 joined the "Patriotic Camp" (*Obóz Patriotyczny*—OP) alliance with the Movement for the Republic (RdR), the PSL-PL, and part of the Confederation for an Independent Poland (KPN, below). The effort to advance cooperation between the ChDRP and the AWS was apparently intended, at least in part, to provide a broader base in preparation for Wałęsa's run for the presidency in 2000. After obtaining only 1 percent of the vote, Wałęsa announced his resignation as party leader in October 2000, but he continued to exert a strong influence on the party.

In the years following the 2001 legislative election there were indications that the former president might resume a more active role at the head of a new formation intended to draw together former AWS/Solidarity members who had become disenchanted with current political options. As of 2004 it appeared that the ChDRP had ceased to function, although Wałęsa remained active, serving, among other things, as a mediator in the Ukrainian political crisis late in the year.

Leader: Lech WAŁĘSA.

Confederation for an Independent Poland (*Konfederacja Polski Niepodległej*—KPN). The

KPN is an intensely nationalist group that was formed in September 1979 and then vigorously repressed by the Communist regime. It opposed the Mazowiecki government because of its inclusion of Communists and in 1991 applauded the breakup of the Soviet Union. Having won 46 lower house seats in October 1991, the KPN gave some external support to the Olszewski government that collapsed in June 1992; thereafter it became part of the "hard" opposition to the Suchocka administration. It emerged fifth-ranked, with 22 *Sejm* seats, in 1993.

In the mid-1990s discontent with the leadership of Leszek Moczulski led to a split in the KPN, with the faction led by Adam SŁOMKA calling itself the KPN-OP (below). In July 1997 Moczulski led the parent KPN from the AWS and attempted to establish an alliance of the right. Reelected chair of the KPN in October 2000, Moczulski later indicated a willingness to cooperate with the AWS once again, and in July 2001 the party indicated that it would enter the fall legislative election on Prime Minister Buzek's AWSP list.

Leader: Leszek MOCZULSKI (Chair).

Confederation for an Independent Poland-Patriotic Camp (*Konfederacja Polski Niepodległej-Obóz Patriotyczny*—KPN-OP). The KPN-OP split from the KPN in 1996 under the leadership of Adam Słomka. An AWS deputy chair who had been a persistent critic of the Solidarity coalition for failing to implement its platform and for drifting to the left, Słomka was expelled from the AWS parliamentary caucus in June 1998 after voting against the government's administrative reform plan. Having expressed "deep anxiety" over AWS/SLD cooperation on the measure, Słomka and a handful of other deputies resigned from the AWS caucus, and on July 28 Słomka announced formation of a new electoral bloc, the Homeland Patriotic Movement (*Ruch Patriotyczny "Ojczyzna"*–RPO), that was also joined by an assortment of other right-wing parties and groups, including the ROP, the National Democratic Party (SND; see LPR, above), the Bloc for Poland (BdP, below), and the KPEiR RP (below). In early August the Polish Ecological

Party (PPE "Z"; see Alternative Social Movement, below), theretofore an AWS affiliate, also joined the new group. Presenting candidates as an election committee at the October 1998 local elections, the RPO won under 1 percent of the available seats. The ROP subsequently dropped out of the RPO, while at a congress held in November many delegates showed little enthusiasm when Słomka proposed turning the RPO into a formal political federation.

A KPN-Homeland (KPN-*Ojczyzna*—KPN-O) group within the KPN-OP subsequently caused a split in the party, and in December 2000, under the leadership of Tomasz KARWOWSKI, it voted to expel Słomka. Further to the right than the KPN-OP, the KPN-O signed a controversial cooperation agreement with France's National Front and in 2001 participated in formation of The Alternative. The KPN-OP, meanwhile, put together a Confederation (*Konfederaja*) electoral list for the 2001 *Sejm* election, although Słomka, immediately before the "undemocratic" balloting, called for a boycott.

Leader: Adam SŁOMKA.

Alternative Social Movement (*Alternatywa Ruch Społeczny*). The Alternative was established in March 2001 not as a political party, but as a "social movement." Forty-six mostly populist, anti-EU groups participated in its formation, including the KPN-OP's "Homeland" wing, led by Tomasz Karwowski, and the **Polish Ecological Party** (*Polska Partia Ekologiczna "Zielonych"*—PPE "Z"). At the September 2001 election The Alternative failed to register a significant impact, attracting only 0.4 percent of the vote.

Leaders: Mariusz OLSZEWSKI, Tomasz KARWOWSKI.

Bloc for Poland (*Blok dla Polski*—BdP). The BdP began as a 1997 electoral list organized primarily by the Nonparty Bloc in Support of Reform (BBWR; see ChDRP, above). In the 1998 local elections it participated in the Homeland Patriotic Movement that also included the KPN-OP, among other antiliberal parties. In May 2000 the BdP held its first congress as a party, and in the 2001 legislative election it ran candidates on the list of the PSL.

Leaders: Leszek ZIELIŃSKI (Chair), Andrzej GASIENICA-MAKOWSKI.

Movement of Polish Working People (*Ruch Ludzi Pracy*—RLP). The RLP was established in 1990 by trade unionists and was subsequently associated with the SLD coalition. Upon the conversion of the SLD to a political party in 1999, the leftist RLP chose to retain a separate identity. It remains close to the All Poland Trade Unions Alliance (OPZZ).

Leader: Lech SZYMAŃCZYK.

Polish Socialist Party (*Polska Partia Socjalistyczna*—PPS). Founded in 1892, the PPS went underground during World War II and provided Poland's first postwar prime minister. Although only a small faction was pro-Communist, the party was formally merged with the Communist PPR in 1948 to form the PZPR. The party was revived in 1987 and in March 1990 sponsored a congress of non-Communist leftists. Weakened by internal strife, the PPS failed to secure *Sejm* representation in 1991 or 1993. In February 1996 the two main PPS factions unified under the leadership of 82-year-old Jan MULAK. He was unanimously replaced by Piotr IKONOWICZ at a party congress in April 1998. Although it had been a member of the SLD coalition, in 1999 the PPS did not enter the new SLD party. Ikonowicz won only 0.2 percent of the vote in the 2000 presidential election. In 2003 Ikonowicz formed a new party (see New Left, below), and he was succeeded as PPS chair by Andrzej Ziemski, who pledged to "moderate" the PPS in order to appeal to a broader range of voters.

Leader: Andrzej ZIEMSKI (Chair).

Christian Democratic Labor Party (*Chrześcijańska Demokracja Stronnictwo Pracy*—ChDSP). The ChDSP was organized in early 1989 by a group of Catholic intellectuals as a continuation of the pre-Communist Labor Party (*Stronnictwo Pracy*—SP) that had been suspended in 1946. Standing as the Christian Democrats (*Chrześcijańsko Demokracja*—ChD) in alliance with the PChD (see SKL-RNP, above), the formation won five lower house seats in October 1991. Part of the membership subsequently left to form the SKL in 1997. For the 2001 legislative elections the ChDSP aligned itself with the PiS.

Leader: Andrzej OWSIŃSKI (President).

National Alliance of Pensioners of the Republic of Poland (*Krajowe Przedstawicielstwo Emerytów i Rencistó Rzeczypospolita Polska—* KPEiR RP). Easily confused with the KPEiR, this rightist group of pensioners was formed in July 1997, reportedly at the urging of the AWS, with many former soldiers of the Home Army, the World War II resistance force. Despite attacks from the KPEiR, the KPEiR RP proposed that the two pensioners' groups cooperate. The KPEiR RP, which joined Adam Słomka's RPO in July 1998 and entered the 2001 election on the Confederation list put together by the KPN-OP, favors elimination of income taxes for low-income groups, state land distribution to small farmers, and low-cost sale of government housing to tenants.

Realpolitik Union (*Unia Polityki Realnej—* UPR). The UPR began as an extreme right-wing party of nationalist, anti-Semitic, and Catholic leanings that sponsored a congress with six similarly disposed groups in Warsaw on May 1, 1990. It split into two factions prior to the 1991 election, at which it won three seats. The party joined the "hard" opposition to the Suchocka government of July 1992 but lost its parliamentary representation in September 1993. In January 1996 a faction led by Mariusz DZIERZAWSKI left the UPR and formed the AWS-affiliated Realpolitik Party (*Stronnictwo Polityki Realneij—*SPR). In the 2000 presidential contest (then) UPR Chair Janusz KORWIN-MIKKE won only 1.4 percent of the vote. In early 2001 he voiced support for the new PO, which he compared to the U.S. Republican Party.

Leader: Stanisław WOJTERA (Chair).

Democratic Party (*Stronnictwo Demokraty-czne*—SD). Recruiting its members predominantly from among professional and intellectual ranks, the SD was founded in 1939 as a non-Marxist group and was a Front party during the Communist era. In mid-1989 the party abandoned its alliance with the Communists and in September accepted three portfolios in the Solidarity-led Mazowiecki government. Thereafter, it was seemingly unable to decide what its political profile should be, securing only one *Sejm* seat in the 1991 balloting and none in 1993 or 1997. In 2001 the SD ran in conjunction with the SLD. In June 2002, at the party's 20th congress, delegates replaced Jan KLIMEK as party chair, citing the party's weak performance under his leadership. (The SD should not be confused with the PD [above] that was launched in early 2005.)

Leader: Andrzej ARENDARSKI (Chair).

In preparations for the 2005 general elections, a number of new parties emerged, including the **Center-Left of the Polish Republic** (*Centrolewica Rzeczypospolitej Polskiej*—CRP), founded in support of economic reform in March 2003 under the leadership of Karol KOSTRZERSKI; the **Center Party** (*Centrum*), a pro-EU grouping founded in April 2004 by Dr. Zbigniew RELIGA, an internationally renowned heart surgeon; the **Democratic Left of the Republic of Poland,** launched in April 2005 by, among others, former UP legislator Jerzy MUELLER; the **Greens,** a leftist environmental grouping founded in September 2003 under the leadership of Jacek BOŻEK and Magdalena MOSIEWICZ; the **Initiative for Poland** (*Inicjatywa dla Polski*—IDP), a center-right grouping founded in support of economic reform in June 2003 under the leadership of former treasury minister Aldona KAMELA-SOWINSKA; the **Left-Wing Union of the Third Republic,** launched in March 2005 in support of various social causes; the **New Left** (*Nowa Lewica*—NL), a left-wing "anticapitalist" grouping established in 2003 by former PPS leader Piotr IKONOWICZ; and the **Patriotic Movement,** a right-wing grouping led by Jan OLSZEWSKI and Antoni MACIEREWICZ. (In late 2004 plans were announced for the merger of the Center Party and the IDP.)

Cabinet

As of September 1, 2006 (*see headnote*)

Prime Minister	Jarosław Kaczyński (PiS)
Deputy Prime Ministers	Ludwik Dorn (PiS)
	Roman Giertych (LPR)
	Andrzej Lepper (*Samoobrona*)

Ministers

Agriculture and Rural Development	Andrzej Lepper (*Samoobrona*)
Construction	Antoni Jaszczak (*Samoobrona*)
Culture and National Heritage	Kazimierz Michał Ujazdowski (PiS)
Economy	Piotr Grzegorz Woźniak (PiS)
Environment	Jan Szyszko (PiS)
Finance	Stanisław Kluza (ind.)
Foreign Affairs	Anna Fotyga (PiS) [f]
Health	Zbigniew Religa (ind.)
Interior and Administration	Ludwik Dorn (PiS)
Justice	Zbigniew Ziobro (PiS)
Labor and Social Policy	Anna Kalata (*Samoobrona*) [f]
Marine Economy	Rafał Wiechecki (LPR)
National Defense	Radosław Sikorski (PiS)
National Education	Roman Giertych (LPR)
Regional Development	Grażyna Gęsicka (ind.) [f]
Science and Higher Education	Michał Seweryński (ind.)
Sports	Tomasz Lipiec (ind.)
Transport	Jerzy Polaczek (PiS)
Treasury	Wojciech Jasiński (PiS)
Without Portfolio	Przemysław Gosiewski (PiS)
	Zbigniew Wassermann (PiS)

[f] = female

Legislature

The 1997 constitution provides for a bicameral **National Assembly** (*Zgromadzenie Narodowe*) incorporating as its lower house the existing 460-member *Sejm* and adding a 100-member Senate, each serving four-year terms, subject to dissolution.

Senate (*Senat*). The upper house is elected under a majoritarian system. The Senate cannot initiate legislation but has the power of veto over the *Sejm,* which the latter can overturn only by a two-thirds majority. Following the most recent election of September 25, 2005, the distribution of seats was as follows: Law and Justice, 49; Civic Platform, 34; League of Polish Families, 7; Self-Defense of the Polish Republic, 3; Polish Peasants' Party, 2; unaffiliated, 5.

Marshal: Bogdan Michał BORUSEWICZ.

National Assembly (*Sejm*). Under a proportional system revised in 2001, parties (save for national minority groups) must gain 5 percent of the vote and coalitions need 8 percent to qualify for lower house seats. The distribution following the election of September 25, 2005, was as follows: Law and Justice, 155; Civic Platform, 133; Self-Defense of the Polish Republic, 56; Democratic Left Alliance, 55; League of Polish Families, 34; Polish Peasants' Party, 25; German Minority of Lower Silesia, 2.

Marshal: Marek JUREK.

Communications

Press

Although the leading organs were under government control, the Polish press for most of the Communist era was livelier than in other East European countries, the regime making little effort to halt publication of "uncensored" (*samizdat*) publications, many of which were openly distributed prior to the imposition of martial law in late 1981, when strict censorship was imposed.

Hailed by Lech Wałęsa as the "first independent newspaper from the Elbe to the Pacific," the opposition daily *Gazeta Wyborcza* (Electoral Gazette) commenced publication in Warsaw in May 1989, with a press run that averaged more than 500,000 copies a day. In late 1990 nearly 200 state-controlled newspapers and magazines were privatized, with their number declining sharply thereafter because of increased production costs. There were some 50 dailies in the late 1990s.

The following Polish-language dailies are currently published in Warsaw, unless otherwise noted: *Gazeta Wyborcza* (520,000 daily, 690,000 weekends [*Gazeta Świateczna*]), independent center-left; *Rzecypospolita* (The Republic, 280,000), independent center-right; *Życie Warszawy* (Warsaw Life, 250,000 daily, 460,000 weekends), nonparty; *Trybuna Śląska* (Silesian Tribune, Katowice, 185,000 daily, 800,000 weekends), independent successor to the SdRP's *Trybuna Robotnicza; Czas Krakowski* (Kraków Time, Kraków, 150,000 daily, 260,000 weekends); *Kurier Polski* (Polish Courier, 150,000 daily, 190,000 weekends); *Express Wieczorny* (Evening Express, 140,000 daily,

400,000 weekends), nonparty; *Trybuna* (Tribune, 120,000 daily, 250,000 weekends), launched by the SdRP in late 1989 as successor to *Trybuna Ludu,* the former PZPR Central Committee organ; *Zielony Sztandar* (Green Banner, 100,000), weekly PSL organ; *Gazeta Poznańska* (Poznań Gazette, Poznań, 80,000 daily, 320,000 weekends); *Tygodnik Solidarnoś* (Solidarity Weekly, 65,000), Solidarity union weekly; *Gazeta Krakowska* (Kraków Gazette, Kraków, 60,000 daily, 150,000 weekends). Several papers are also published in the languages of the national minorities (Belarusan, German, Jewish, Russian, Ukrainian).

News Agencies

The Polish Press Agency (*Polska Agencja Prasowa*—PAP), with offices in numerous Polish and foreign cities, transmits information abroad in English. The Polish Information Agency (*Polska Agencja Informacyjna*—PAI), established to assist the PAP, issues foreign-language bulletins and aids foreign journalists. Numerous foreign agencies maintain bureaus in Warsaw.

Broadcasting and Computing

Legislation that came into force on March 1, 1993, introduced new operating rules for public and commercial broadcasting, ending the state monopoly and creating a regulatory Polish National Radio and Television Broadcasting Council. The monolithic *Polskie Radio i Telewizja* was divided into *Polskie Radio* and *Telewizja Polska,* which operate regional as well as national stations. At present, there are both public and private national channels as well as numerous additional radio and television facilities.

In June 1994 Poland's Constitutional Tribunal upheld a broadcast law requirement that radio and TV programming "respect Christian values" by arguing that the admonition fell short of a directive to propagate such values.

There were approximately 17.1 million television receivers and 4.1 million personal computers serving 9.0 million Internet users in 2003.

Intergovernmental Representation

Ambassador to the U.S.
Janusz REITER

U.S. Ambassador to Poland
Victor Henderson ASHE

Permanent Representative to the UN
Andrzej TOWPIK

IGO Memberships (Non-UN)
BIS, CBSS, CEI, CERN, CEUR, EIB, EBRD, EU, Eurocontrol, Interpol, IOM, NATO, OECD, OSCE, PCA, WCO, *WEU,* WTO

PORTUGAL

PORTUGUESE REPUBLIC

República Portuguesa

The Country

Known in antiquity as Lusitania, Portugal overlooks the Atlantic along the western face of the Iberian Peninsula, while including politically the Azores and the Madeira Islands in the Atlantic. Mainland Portugal is divided by the Tagus River into a mountainous northern section and a southern section of rolling plains whose geography and climate are akin to those of northern Africa. The population, a blend of ancient Celtic, Iberian, Latin, Teutonic, and Moorish elements, with a recent admixture of African and other immigrants, is culturally homogeneous and almost wholly affiliated with the Roman Catholic Church, which traditionally exercised commanding social and political influence. Portuguese, the official language, is spoken by virtually all of the population. As of 1998 women comprised 44 percent of the official labor force, concentrated in agriculture and domestic service; female representation in government and politics—despite the participation of a few prominent women, including former prime minister Maria de Lourdes PINTASILGO—averages less than 10 percent. (Although the legislature recently rejected a mandate that women be allotted 25 percent of all posts in the Portuguese Assembly as well as in the Portuguese delegation to the European Parliament, all of the major parties volunteered to observe the proposed quota.)

The economy, one of the least modernized in Europe, retains a somewhat paternalistic structure characterized by limited social services and per capita GNP of only $14,220 in 2004. Although agriculture, forestry, and fishing engage about 24 percent of the population, they contribute only 4 percent of GDP, with half of the country's food needs dependent on imports. Industry, consisting primarily of small manufacturing firms, employs some 35 percent of the labor force and contributes 30 percent of GDP. Exports include textiles, clothing, and electrical machinery as well as such traditional goods as fish products, cork, and olive oil, of which Portugal is one of the world's largest producers. Unemployment, a problem in the late 1970s and early 1980s because of the influx of more than one million persons from former Portuguese colonies, abated substantially upon entry

into the European Community (EC, subsequently the European Union—EU) on January 1, 1986, and remained well below the average for members of the Organization for Economic Cooperation and Development (OECD) in the early 1990s. EC regional development aid helped to sustain a positive annual growth rate prior to a contraction of over 1 percent a year in 1993–1994. Economic growth of 3 percent resumed in 1995–1996 and peaked at 4.2 percent in 1998. By the end of 1997 the unemployment rate had fallen to 6.7 percent and continued to drop thereafter, reaching 4.1 percent in 2000.

In 1998 Portugal was named to be a founding member of the EU's Economic and Monetary Union (EMU) on January 1, 1999, as Lisbon continued to direct an economic recovery program that the International Monetary Fund (IMF) described as being responsible for a "virtuous circle of lower interest rates, vigorous growth, and declining fiscal deficits." However, the economy weakened significantly in 2001, with GDP growth of only about 2.0 percent being achieved. In addition, it was subsequently reported that the government's budget deficit for 2001 was 4.1 percent of GDP, well over the limit (3 percent) set by the EU. Consequently, the new government installed in 2002 initiated a number of measures designed to reduce the deficit, including the cancellation of planned tax cuts and the intensification of the sale of state-owned enterprises to the private sector. However, economic malaise continued, leading to a downturn of 1.2 percent in 2003. Although the economy recovered lost ground in 2004, growth of less than 1 percent occurred in 2005, while unemployment reached 8 percent.

Government and Politics

Political Background

As one of the great European monarchies of late medieval and early modern times, Portugal initiated the age of discovery and colonization and acquired a far-flung colonial empire that was one of the last to be abandoned. Interrupted by a period of Spanish rule from 1580 to 1640, the Portuguese monarchy endured until 1910, when a bloodless revolution initiated a republican era marked by chronic instability and recurrent violence. A military revolt in 1926 prepared the way for the presidency of Marshal António CARMONA (1926–1951) and the assumption of governmental authority by António de Oliveira SALAZAR, an economics professor who became finance minister in 1928 and served as prime minister from 1932 until his replacement because of illness in 1968. Salazar, mistrustful of democratic and socialist ideologies and influenced by Italian Fascism, established economic and political stability, and in 1933 he introduced a "corporative" constitution designed to serve as the basis of a new Portuguese State (*Estado Novo*). With the support of the Catholic Church, the army, and his National Union, the only authorized political movement, Salazar completely dominated Portuguese political life and reduced the presidency to an auxiliary institution.

The later years of Salazar's regime were marked by rising, though largely ineffectual, domestic discontent and growing restiveness in the Overseas Territories. Elections were frequently boycotted by the opposition, and direct presidential elections were eliminated following a vigorous but unsuccessful opposition campaign by Gen. Humberto DELGADO in 1958. Overseas, the provinces of Goa, Damão, and Diu were seized by India in 1961; in the same year, a revolt broke out in Angola, while independence movements became active in Portuguese Guinea in 1962 and in Mozambique in 1964. The attempt to suppress the insurrections resulted in severe economic strain as well as increasing political isolation and repeated condemnation by the United Nations (UN).

The crisis created by Salazar's nearly fatal illness in September 1968 was alleviated by the selection of Marcello CAETANO, a close associate, as the new prime minister. Although he permitted a measure of cautious liberalization, including some relaxation of secret police activity and the return from exile of the Socialist Party leader, Dr. Mário SOARES, Caetano preserved the main outlines of Salazar's policy both in metropolitan Portugal and overseas.

Political Status: Independent republic proclaimed on October 5, 1910; corporative constitution of March 19, 1933, suspended following military coup of April 25, 1974; present constitution promulgated on April 2, 1976, with effect from April 25.

Area: 35,553 sq. mi. (92,082 sq. km.).

Population: 10,355,824 (2001C); 10,547,000 (2005E). Area and population figures include mainland Portugal plus the Azores and the Madeira Islands.

Major Urban Centers (2005E): LISBON (520,000), Porto (Oporto, 248,000).

Official Language: Portuguese.

Monetary Unit: Euro (market rate July 1, 2006: 1 euro = $1.28US).

President: Aníbal CAVACO SILVA (Social Democratic Party); sworn in for a five-year term on March 9, 2006, following election of January 22, succeeding Jorge SAMPAIO (Portuguese Socialist Party), who had served two terms, the maximum allowed under the constitution.

Prime Minister: José SÓCRATES (Portuguese Socialist Party); designated by the president on February 24, 2005, following the legislative election of February 20, and sworn in on March 12 to succeed Pedro SANTANA LOPES (Social Democratic Party).

Prior to the parliamentary election of October 1969, opposition parties were legalized, but they were again outlawed after a campaign in which the official National Union won all 130 seats in the National Assembly. The atmosphere of repression eased again after the adoption in 1971 of constitutional legislation expanding the power of the enlarged National Assembly, granting limited autonomy to the Overseas Territories, abolishing press censorship, and permitting religious freedom. Nevertheless, in the legislative election of October 1973 the ruling Popular National Action (successor to the National Union) won all 150 seats, including 34 representing the Overseas Territories.

In a bloodless coup on April 24, 1974, a group of mainly left-wing military officers calling themselves the Armed Forces Movement (*Movimento das Forças Armadas*—MFA) seized power, ending more than 40 years of civilian dictatorship. The president and prime minister were arrested and flown to Brazil, where they were granted political asylum. The leader of the "Junta of National Salvation," Gen. António Sebastião Ribeiro de SPÍNOLA, assumed the presidency, and on May 15 a center-left cabinet was sworn in with Adelino de PALMA CARLOS as prime minister. After a dispute with the reconstituted Council of State as to the extent of his powers, Palma Carlos resigned on July 9 and was replaced by Gen. Vasco dos Santos GONÇALVES, whose administration recognized the right of the Overseas Territories to "self-determination" with all its consequences, including independence. On September 30 General Spínola also resigned, leaving power in the hands of leftist military officers and civilians. The new president, Gen. Francisco da COSTA GOMES, subsequently reappointed General Gonçalves as prime minister.

In May 1974 Costa Gomes had visited Angola, declaring upon his return that the new government was prepared to offer a cease-fire in Angola, Mozambique, and Portuguese Guinea, with the guerrilla organizations being permitted to organize political parties and to participate in democratic elections. As a result of the initiative, negotiations were undertaken that led to the independence of Guinea-Bissau (formerly Portuguese Guinea) in September, while discussions with insurgent leaders in Mozambique and Sao Tome and Principe resulted in independence for both territories, as well as for Cape Verde, the following year. Although negotiations with Angolan leaders were complicated by the presence of a sizable white minority and by the existence of three major insurgent groups, the formation of a united front by the insurgents opened the way for independence. The front subsequently collapsed, but Portugal withdrew from Angola on the agreed date of November 11, 1975.

On March 11, 1975, right-wing military elements, reportedly acting at the instigation of former president Spínola, had attempted to overthrow the government. Upon failure of the coup, General Spínola flew to Brazil, and the Junta of National

Salvation was dissolved in favor of a Supreme Revolutionary Council (SRC). The latter, sworn in by President Costa Gomes on March 17, was given full executive and legislative powers for the purpose of "directing and executing the revolutionary program in Portugal." Although officers constituted one-third of the cabinet announced on March 25, also included were representatives of the Communist, Socialist, and Popular Democratic parties, as well as of the Portuguese Democratic Movement.

At a Constituent Assembly election on April 25, 1975, the Socialists received 38 percent of the total vote, compared with 26 percent for the Popular Democrats and less than 13 percent for the Communists. The first session of the assembly was convened on June 2, with the Socialists holding 116 of the 250 seats. Despite their commanding legislative strength, the Socialists and Popular Democrats subsequently announced their intention to resign from the government, in part because of a Communist takeover of the Socialist newspaper *República,* and on July 31 a new, essentially nonparty cabinet was formed. However, increasing opposition to Communist influence led, on August 29, to the resignation of Prime Minister Gonçalves and the appointment of Adm. José Baptista Pinheiro de AZEVEDO as head of a new cabinet (the sixth since the 1974 coup) comprising representatives of the three leading parties, as well as of the Armed Forces Movement.

In mid-November 1975 the Communist-led labor unions mounted a general strike in Lisbon, demanding the resignation of the Azevedo government and the formation of an exclusively left-wing "revolutionary government." The strike was followed on November 26 by an uprising of leftist military units that was crushed by loyalist troops responding to government pressure to restore law and order. Although the SRC had previously rebuked Azevedo for his conduct during the strike, the coup's failure was seen as a major defeat for the Communists, and in mid-December, following designation of a new army chief of staff, the council ordered a major reorganization of the armed forces, emphasizing military discipline and the exclusion of the military from party politics.

The new constitution came into effect April 25, 1976, and an election to the Assembly of the Republic was held the same day. The Socialists remained the largest party but again failed to win an absolute majority. On June 27 Gen. António dos Santos Ramalho EANES, a nonparty candidate supported by the Socialists, Popular Democrats, and Social Democrats, was elected to a five-year term as president. The election was a further setback for the Communists, whose candidate, Octávio PATO, finished third, behind far-left candidate Maj. Otelo SARAIVA DE CARVALHO. Three weeks later, on July 16, Dr. Soares was invested as prime minister, heading a Socialist minority government that was, however, endorsed by the other two parties in the presidential election coalition.

Having lost a crucial assembly vote on an economic austerity plan, Soares was forced to resign on December 8, 1977, though he was subsequently able to return as head of a governmental coalition with the conservative Social Democratic Center (*Centro Democrático Social*—CDS) on January 30, 1978. On July 27, however, Soares was dismissed by President Eanes after the CDS ministers had resigned over disagreements on agricultural and health policies, leaving the Socialists without a working legislative majority. His successor, Alfredo NOBRE DA COSTA, was in turn forced to resign on September 14 following legislative rejection of an essentially nonparty program. A new government, also largely composed of independents, was eventually confirmed on November 22 with Dr. Carlos Alberto da MOTA PINTO, a former member of the Social Democratic Party (*Partido Social Democrata*—PSD, the renamed Popular Democratic Party), as prime minister.

Having witnessed assembly rejection of his proposed budget on three occasions since March, Prime Minister Mota Pinto resigned on June 6, 1979. On July 19 Maria de Lourdes Pintasilgo, a member of several previous post-1974 governments, was named to head a caretaker, nonparty government, pending an early legislative election. The balloting of December 2 confirmed Portugal's move toward the extremes of the political spectrum.

Francisco SÁ CARNEIRO, a conservative Social Democrat who in July had formed a Democratic Alliance (*Aliança Democrática*—AD) with the Center Democrats, Monarchists, and disaffected Socialists, led his electoral coalition to a clear majority and was named on December 29 to organize a new government—the 12th since 1974—that was sworn in on January 3, 1980. The Alliance was returned to office with an increased majority at the second legislative election within a year on October 5, 1980.

Prime Minister Sá Carneiro was killed in a plane crash on December 4 and was succeeded as PSD leader and prime minister by Dr. Francisco Pinto BALSEMÃO, who proceeded to organize a new AD cabinet that was sworn in on January 5, 1981. Balsemão continued as head of a reorganized administration on September 1, 1982, prior to resigning on December 19, 1982.

At a general election on April 25, 1983, the Socialists obtained a substantial plurality, enabling Dr. Soares to form a cabinet of nine Socialists, seven Social Democrats, and one independent that assumed office on June 9. However, severe economic difficulties eroded the popularity of the Socialists, while the coalition partners disagreed on the extent of proposed austerity measures. On June 4, 1985, PSD parliamentary leader Aníbal CAVACO SILVA announced his party's withdrawal from the government, although agreeing to a postponement until the signature on June 12 of Portugal's entry accord with the EC. Two days later, Soares was named to head a caretaker administration pending a new election, while declaring himself a candidate for the forthcoming presidential poll.

The October 6, 1985, legislative balloting dealt a serious blow to the Socialists, whose representation was cut nearly in half. The largest vote share, 30 percent, went to the PSD, and Cavaco Silva formed a minority government based on his party's assembly plurality on November 6. The PSD's preferred presidential candidate, the Christian Democrat Diogo FREITAS DO AMARAL, captured nearly half the vote in the initial presidential balloting on January 23, 1986, out of a field of four candidates; however, an unusual coalition of the Socialists, the pro-Eanes Democratic Renewal Party (*Partido Renovador Democrático*—PRD), and the Communist-led United People's Alliance (*Aliança Povo Unido*—APU) succeeded in electing Soares, the remaining center-left candidate, with 51 percent of the vote in the February 16 runoff. Soares, the first civilian head of state in 60 years, was sworn in as Eanes's successor on March 9.

President Soares dissolved the assembly on April 28, 1987, following the April 3 defeat of the Cavaco Silva government on a censure motion that had charged the administration with mismanagement of the economy. At the ensuing poll of July 19, the Social Democrats became the first party in 13 years to win an absolute majority of legislative seats, permitting the incumbent prime minister to return to office on August 17 as head of an all-PSD government. Following his reconfirmation, Cavaco Silva moved to privatize state-owned firms not of "particular importance to the public service" and to reverse a number of post-1974 measures aimed at agricultural collectivization. More importantly, in November 1988 the two leading parties reached agreement on constitutional changes that would strip the basic law of its Marxist elements, reduce the number of legislative deputies, permit the holding of binding national referenda, and accelerate the privatization process.

On January 13, 1991, President Soares gained easy election to a second five-year term on a 70.4 percent vote share that made a runoff unnecessary, while the PSD's retention of its majority in legislative balloting on October 6 permitted Cavaco Silva to retain office at the head of a slightly modified administration on October 28.

With most economic indicators positive or stable, the government took the escudo into the broad band of the EC's exchange rate mechanism (ERM) on April 6, 1992. Five months later it was thrown off course by the European monetary crisis, which led to devaluations of the escudo by 6 percent in November and by 7 percent in May 1993. Deepening economic recession and assorted political problems resulted in a sharp decline in the government's standing, accompanied by an upsurge of "cohabitation" tensions between the president and the prime minister. In December the Socialists outpolled the PSD in local elections, winning their highest-ever share of a nationwide vote.

Continuing economic recession and rising unemployment compounded the government's unpopularity in the later months of 1994, in the face of which Cavaco Silva vacated the PSD leadership in January 1995. He nevertheless remained prime minister in the run-up to the fall general election. At balloting on October 1, the Socialists made substantial gains at the expense of the PSD, although their 112-seat tally left them just short of an overall majority. Of the two smaller parties that won seats, the center-right Popular Party (*Partido Popular*—PP) trebled its representation, while the Communist-dominated Unitary Democratic Coalition (*Coligação Democrática Unitária*—CDU) lost ground. The Socialist leader, António GUTERRES, accordingly formed a minority government at the end of October that was expected to have CDU external support on most issues.

In a presidential election on January 14, 1996, the Socialist candidate and former mayor of Lisbon, Jorge SAMPAIO, scored a comfortable first-round victory, taking 53.8 percent of the vote against 46.2 percent for the PSD's Cavaco Silva. Sampaio was sworn in for a five-year term on March 9. The Socialists extended a string of electoral victories thereafter, unexpectedly adding 3 seats in the assembly election of October 10, 1999 (for a total of 115, exactly half the membership), and retaining the presidency in balloting on January 14, 2001. In the latter contest, President Sampaio won 55.8 percent of the vote, versus 34.5 percent for the PSD's candidate, Joaquim FERREIRA DO AMARAL.

The PSP suffered significant losses in municipal elections on December 16, 2001, and the following day Prime Minister Guterres announced his resignation. On December 28 President Sampaio, following the unanimous advice of the Council of State, dissolved the assembly in preparation for national legislative balloting in March, the Guterres government remaining in place in a caretaker capacity.

At assembly balloting on March 17, 2002, the PSD secured 40.2 percent of the vote and 105 seats, followed by the Socialists (37.9 percent of the vote and 96 seats). On March 28 President Sampaio named José Manuel Durão BARROSO of the PSD to form a new government, and the next day Barroso signed a coalition pact with the PP, which was given three ministerial posts in the new government appointed on April 6.

Prime Minister Barroso resigned on July 5, 2004, to become president of the European Commission. He was succeeded on July 9 by the PSD's Pedro SANTANA LOPES, President Sampaio having rejected calls for early elections. However, in light of the continued decline in popular support for the governing coalition, Sampaio dissolved the assembly on December 10 and directed that new elections be held on February 20, 2005, at which time the PSP gained its first legislative majority (121 seats) since independence. Consequently, the new government installed under the PSP's José SÓCRATES on March 12 included only PSP members and a number of independents.

After months of protests against Sócrates's austerity measures, voters on January 22, 2006, elected former prime minister Cavaco Silva to a five-year term as president. Cavaco Silva, who won 50.6 percent of the vote to defeat five left-wing opponents, is the first center-right president to serve since the restoration of democracy in 1974.

Constitution and Government

The constitution of April 25, 1976, stemmed from a constitutional agreement concluded two months earlier by the leading parties and Costa Gomes in his capacity as chief of state and president of the SRC (subsequently the Council of the Revolution). Under the pact (which superseded an earlier agreement of April 1975), the council, while formally designated as the most important government organ after the presidency, became, in large part, a consultative body with powers of absolute veto only in regard to defense policy. The third most important organ, the Assembly of the Republic, was empowered to override the council (on nonmilitary matters) and the president by a two-thirds majority.

A series of constitutional reforms that came into effect in October 1982 abolished the Council of the Revolution and distributed its powers among a Supreme Council of National Defense, a 13-member Constitutional Tribunal, and an advisory Council of State of 16 members (plus national presidents elected since adoption of the existing basic law): five named by the president, five named by the assembly, and six ex officio (the prime minister; the national ombudsman; and the presidents of the assembly, the Supreme Court, and the regional governments of the Azores and the Madeira Islands).

The president, elected for a five-year term, serves as military chief of staff and as chair of the Council of State, and appoints the prime minister, who is responsible to both the head of state and the assembly. Portugal's judicial system, based on European civil law and heavily influenced by the French model, includes, in addition to the Constitutional Tribunal, a Supreme Court, courts of appeal, and district courts as well as military courts and a Court of Audit.

Administratively, metropolitan Portugal is divided into 18 districts (each headed by a governor appointed by the minister of the interior), which are subdivided into 275 municipalities and more than 4,000 parochial authorities. The Azores and the Madeira Islands are governed separately as Autonomous Regions, each with an elected Regional Assembly and municipal subdivisions (a total of 30). In both regions the central government has been represented since March 2006 by a "representative of the republic" (previously called a minister of the republic), who is appointed by the president.

Foreign Relations

Allied with England since 1373, Portugal nevertheless declared itself neutral in World War II. It currently participates in the North Atlantic Treaty Organization (NATO) and the OECD as well as in the UN and its specialized agencies. It became a member of the Council of Europe in September 1976 and, after years of negotiation, joined Spain in gaining admission to the EC on January 1, 1986.

The country's foreign policy efforts prior to the 1974 coup were directed primarily to retention of its overseas territories at a time when other European powers had largely divested themselves of colonial possessions. This policy yielded isolation in the UN and occasionally strained relations with allied governments. Nevertheless, Portugal remained a valued member of NATO and was honored by a British royal visit in June 1973 to mark the 600th anniversary of the Anglo-Portuguese alliance. Subsequent to the 1974 coup, its African problems were significantly alleviated by the independence of Guinea-Bissau (formerly Portuguese Guinea) in 1974 and of Angola, Cape Verde, Mozambique, and Sao Tome and Principe in 1975.

In late 1975 a dispute arose with Indonesia regarding the status of Portuguese Timor, the country's only remaining Asian possession except for Macao. On December 8 Indonesian Foreign Minister Adam Malik announced that pro-Indonesian parties in the Portuguese (eastern) sector of the island had set up a provisional government and that Indonesian military units had occupied Dili, the capital. Portugal promptly severed diplomatic relations with Indonesia, which had also announced the annexation of Ocussi Ambeno, a small Portuguese enclave on the northern coast of West Timor. On July 17, 1976, Jakarta proclaimed the formal incorporation of the remainder of Timor into Indonesia, although the UN continued to regard Portugal as the territory's legitimate administrative power.

Lisbon's objection to Indonesian control of East Timor was again manifested in the recall of its ambassador to Australia in August 1985, after Australian Prime Minister Bob Hawke had endorsed his predecessor's acceptance of the takeover. Relations with Canberra were further strained in 1989 when Australia concluded a treaty with Indonesia providing for the division of offshore oil resources in the Timor Gap. Claiming that Indonesia's illegal occupation of East Timor rendered the treaty invalid under international law, Portugal in 1991 took the matter to the International Court of Justice (ICJ). In June 1995, however, the ICJ ruled that it had no jurisdiction on the 1989 treaty, as it was precluded from giving a ruling on the legality of Indonesia's annexation of East Timor by Indonesia's nonrecognition of the court's jurisdiction in the matter and because Indonesia was not a party to the case brought by Portugal. UN-prompted "dialogue" between the Portuguese and Indonesian foreign ministers on the East Timor question made no substantive progress in 1995, with Portugal finding little merit in an Indonesian proposal that each side should establish "interest sections" in third-country embassies in Lisbon and Jakarta. Diplomatic relations were not restored with Indonesia until late 1999, following Jakarta's acceptance of an independence referendum in East Timor, which achieved independence as the Democratic Republic of Timor-Leste on May 20, 2002.

In early 1988 Portugal called for a "thorough overhaul" of a mutual defense treaty that permitted the United States to use Lajes air base in the Azores. Although the agreement was not due to expire until 1991, it included a provision for military aid, which the U.S. Congress had sharply reduced in approving the administration's foreign assistance budget for the year. The dispute was eventually settled in January 1989 with Washington pledging to increase levels of both military and economic compensation. An agreement granting a further extension on U.S. use of the Lajes base was signed in Lisbon on June 1, 1995.

In 1989 it was agreed that regular consultative meetings of the foreign ministers of Portugal and the five lusophone African countries would be convened to promote the latter's economic development. In 1991 the six countries plus Brazil agreed upon linguistic standardization, while plans were initiated for a common television satellite channel. Further meetings of the seven Portuguese-speaking states in the early 1990s led to the formal establishment in July 1996 of the Community of Portuguese Speaking Countries (CPLP), with a total population of some 200 million Portuguese speakers (80 percent of them in Brazil). Meanwhile, Portuguese diplomacy had scored a major success in brokering the 1991 Escuril Accord between the warring factions of post-independence Angola.

The 1991 Maastricht Treaty on the economic and political union of what became the EU was ratified by the Portuguese Assembly on December 10, 1992, by a large majority. Two days later the EU's Edinburgh summit agreed to set up a "cohesion fund" for its four poorest members, of which Portugal was one. In March 1995 Portugal participated in the inauguration of the Schengen Accord, under which most EU states undertook to remove internal border controls while strengthening their external barriers to illegal immigrants and criminals.

The Barroso administration vigorously supported the U.S.-led campaign in Iraq in 2003, committing troops to the overthrow of Saddam Hussein and to subsequent security and reconstruction efforts. Responding to increasing public opposition to the war in Iraq and acting on a campaign promise, newly installed Prime Minister Sócrates withdrew Portugal's 120 troops from Iraq in February 2005.

Current Issues

Although European integration has been viewed by many Portuguese as a means of raising the country's economic standing and reducing a traditional reliance on low-wage, unskilled, low-productivity jobs, it has often forced the government to make difficult economic choices. Despite opposition criticism that the previous administration had failed to make significant progress on promised structural reforms in such areas as health care, education, pensions, and social security, the new PSD/PP center-right government installed in April 2002 quickly adopted stringent austerity measures to deal with the rising budget deficit and pledged to reduce defense expenditures. New Prime Minister José Durão Barroso also promised to intensify the government's privatization program and to trim corporate taxes. For its part, the PP, the junior (and more conservative) partner in the coalition government, emphasized the need to tighten immigration regulations.

The EU welcomed the fiscal restraints imposed by the Barroso administration and decided not to impose sanctions on Portugal for violating the EU's stability and growth pact regarding budget deficits.

However, several leading opposition parties called for economic stimulus rather than constraints to deal with rising unemployment (over 7 percent in early 2004) and general stagnation. Strengthened by their victory in the June 2004 European Parliament elections, the PSP and other opposition parties demanded that President Sampaio call for early elections when Barroso resigned in July to become president of the European Commission. Instead, Sampaio opted to pursue "stability" by appointing Pedro Santana Lopes of the PSD to succeed Barroso. The selection of Santana Lopes, who, despite being the mayor of Lisbon, was not well known in the rest of the country and had little experience at the national level, was considered a surprise by many observers. By November it was reported that Santana Lopes was "losing authority" over the cabinet in the wake of a series of "gaffes and mishandled initiatives," prompting Sampaio to accept the need for early assembly elections.

Prior to the February 2005 legislative poll, new PSP leader José Sócrates, described as promarket and pro-European, asked voters to provide him with a PSP majority so that he could administer an "economic shock" designed to reduce unemployment and stimulate growth. Sócrates' wish having been granted, the assembly in March approved his economic package, although observers described the public mood as "somber" in view of the "sacrifice" that would probably be required in regard to higher taxes and cuts in public benefits. The January 22, 2006, election of Cavaco Silva, the sole center-right candidate in the race for president, was seen as a vote of no confidence in the PSP's handling of the economy while prompting hopes that Cavaco Silva would lend weight to the credibility of the government's austerity program. However, Sócrates's May 15 announcement of cuts in pension benefits brought thousands of protesters to the streets.

The government's austerity measures were not enough to improve Portugal's standing in the euro zone. With a projected budget deficit of 5 percent of GDP and a projected public debt of 69 percent of GDP for 2006, Portugal exceeded EU limits on both measures. The EU gave Portugal a deadline of 2008 to meet its budget limit of 3 percent of GDP.

Political Parties

As of November 2005 Portugal had 18 registered parties, although since the 1980s it has progressed toward a largely two-party system dominated by the Portuguese Socialist Party (PSP) and the center-right Social Democratic Party (PSD).

Governing Party

Portuguese Socialist Party (*Partido Socialista Portuguesa*—PSP). Organized in 1973 as heir to the former Portuguese Socialist Action (*Acção Socialista Portuguesa*—ASP), the PSP won a substantial plurality (38 percent) of the vote in the election of April 1975 and 35 percent a year later, remaining in power under Dr. Mário Soares until July 1978. At the December 1979 balloting the PSP lost 33 of the 107 assembly seats it had won in 1976. Its representation returned to a plurality of 101 in 1983, with Dr. Soares being redesignated prime minister on June 9 and continuing in office until forced into caretaker status by withdrawal of the Social Democrats (PSD) from the government coalition in July 1985. The party won only 57 seats at the October election, although Soares succeeded in winning the state presidency in February 1986, at which time he resigned as PSP secretary general.

A party congress in June approved wide-ranging changes aimed at democratizing the party's structure and deleted all references to Marxism in its Declaration of Principles, committing the organization to an "open economy where private, public and social institutions can coexist." Despite the changes, the party's legislative strength gained only marginally (from 57 to 60 seats) at the balloting of July 16, 1987, whereas more appreciable gains (to a total of 72 seats) were recorded at the election of October 6, 1991.

Remaining in opposition, the party elected António Guterres as its leader in February 1992 and registered its best-ever national vote in December 1993 local elections. In the general election of October 1995 the PSP won 112 assembly seats, with Guterres then forming a minority government. In 1996 the PSP's Jorge Sampaio captured the national presidency with a majority in the first round.

In the October 1999 legislative election the PSP fell just short of a legislative majority, winning 115 seats in the 230-seat chamber. President Sampaio continued the party's string of successes in January 2001, easily winning reelection. However, the PSP did poorly in the December 2001 municipal elections, setting the stage for Guterres's resignation as prime minister and the PSP's fall from national power in 2002. Eduardo FERRO RODRIGUES, a former minister in Guterres's 1995 cabinet, was elected in January to succeed Guterres as PSP secretary general and thereby the party's candidate for prime minister. However, Rodrigues resigned the leadership in July 2004 to protest President Sampaio's decision not to call early elections following the resignation of Prime Minister Barroso. Former environment minister José Sócrates was elected as the new PSP leader in late 2004, and, having attempted to move the PSP "to the center," he led the party to a resounding legislative victory in February 2005.

In September 2005 Manuel ALEGRE, a member of the assembly who had lost the race for party leader to Sócrates in 2004, announced that he would seek the presidency in 2006, even though the official Socialist endorsement had gone to 81-year-old former president Soares. At the January 2006 polls Alegre finished second, with 20.7 percent of the vote, while Soares came in third, with 14.3 percent.

Leaders: José SÓCRATES (Prime Minister and Leader of the Party), Jorge SAMPAIO (Former President of the Republic), António GUTERRES (UN High Commissioner for Refugees and Former Prime Minister), Alberto MARTINS (Parliamentary Leader).

Other Parties

Social Democratic Party (*Partido Social Democrata*—PSD). The PSD was founded in 1974 as the Popular Democratic Party (*Partido Popular Democrático*—PPD), under which name it won 26 percent of the vote for the Constituent Assembly on April 25, 1975, and 24 percent in the Assembly of the Republic election a year later. Although it initially advocated a number of left-of-center policies, including the nationalization of key sectors of the economy, a number of leftists withdrew in 1976, and the remainder of the party moved noticeably to the right.

An April 1979 disagreement over leadership opposition to the Socialist government's proposed budget led to a walkout of 40 PSD deputies prior to a final assembly vote. Shortly thereafter, 37 of the 73 PSD deputies withdrew and announced that they would sit in the assembly as the Association of Independent Social Democrats (*Associação dos Sociais Democratas Independentes*—ASDI). The party's losses were more than recouped at the December election, however, when the PSD-led Alliance won a three-seat majority, as a result of which the party president, Francisco Sá Carneiro, was named prime minister. Dr. Francisco Pinto Balsemão was designated party leader in December 1980, following Sá Carneiro's death, and became prime minister in January 1981.

In early 1983 Balsemão announced that he would not stand for another term as party leader, and, following the formal designation of a three-member leadership at a party congress in late February, he was effectively succeeded by Carlos Mota Pinto. The party was runner-up to the PSP at the April election, winning 75 assembly seats. In June 1985 Aníbal Cavaco Silva, who had succeeded Mota Pinto as PSD leader the month before, led a withdrawal from the ruling coalition and formed a minority government after the party had gained a slim plurality at legislative balloting in October. Defeated in a censure vote in April 1987, the PSD became the first party since 1974 to win an absolute majority of seats at the ensuing legislative poll in July. It retained control with a slightly reduced majority of 135 of 230 seats in 1991. A subsequent slide in the PSD's standing, including losses at the 1994 election for the European Parliament, impelled Cavaco Silva to vacate the party leadership in January 1995. At the same time, he hoped to position himself for a presidential challenge.

Under the new leadership of Joaquim Fernando NOGUEIRA, the party went down to an expected defeat in the October 1995 general election, retaining only 88 seats on a 34 percent vote share. In the January 1996 presidential balloting, moreover, Cavaco Silva was defeated by the Socialist candidate in the first round. The party's response at the end of March was to elect as its new leader Marcelo REBELO DE SOUSA, a media personality on the party's liberal wing who had not held ministerial office during the period of PSD rule.

In early 1998 the PSD and PP (below) formed an electoral alliance, styled the Democratic Alternative (*Alternativa Democrática*—AD), with the stated aim of presenting a single list for the upcoming European Parliament and national legislative elections. The AD Pact was formally ratified in February 1999; however, it collapsed the following month, and immediately thereafter Rebelo de Sousa resigned as leader of the PSD. His successor, José Manuel Durão Barroso, a former foreign affairs minister, led the party into the October 1999 election, but the PSD lost 7 of its 88 seats. In 2001 it failed to unseat President Sampaio, with its candidate, Joaquim Martins Ferreira Do Amaral, finishing a distant second (34.5 percent of the vote).

Barroso was named prime minister following the March 2002 legislative balloting, at which the PSD won a plurality of 105 seats. He resigned as prime minister in July 2004 to become president of the European Commission. Pedro Santana Lopes succeeded Barroso as prime minister until the February 2005 legislative poll, at which the PSD fell to 75 seats. Santana Lopes resigned as PSD leader in April. In the 2006 presidential contest former prime minister Cavaco Silva won 50.6 percent of the vote, just enough to avoid a runoff.

Leaders: Luís Marques MENDES (Chair), Aníbal CAVACO SILVA (President of the Republic), Pedro SANTANA LOPES (Former Prime Minister), José Manuel Durão BARROSO (European Commission President and Former Prime Minister).

Unified Democratic Coalition (*Coligação Democrática Unitária*—CDU). Prior to the 1979 election the Portuguese Communist Party (PCP, below) joined with the Popular Democratic Movement (*Movimento Democrático Popular*—MDP)

in an electoral coalition known as the United People's Alliance (*Aliança Povo Unido*—APU). The APU won 47 legislative seats in 1979, 41 in 1980, and 38 in 1985, its constituent formations having campaigned separately in 1983. In the 1986 presidential race, the party formally endorsed the independent Maria de Lourdes Pintasilgo, with some dissidents supporting Francisco Salgado ZENHA of the now-defunct Democratic Renewal Party (*Partido Renovador Democrático*—PRD); following the elimination of both from the runoff, a special Communist Party congress on February 2, 1986, urged Alliance supporters to "hold their nose, ignore the photograph" and vote for Soares.

Apparently disturbed by allegations that it was merely a PCP front, the MDP withdrew from the Alliance in November 1986. The APU was thereupon dissolved in favor of the CDU, which embraced the PCP; a group of MDP dissidents calling themselves the Democratic Intervention (*Intervenção Democrática*—ID), which effectively superseded the MDP; an environmentalist formation, The Greens (*Os Verdes*); and a number of independent leftists. The new group obtained 31 assembly seats in 1987, 7 less than the APU in 1985. In October 1991, having lauded the attempted hardline coup in the Soviet Union two months earlier, the CDU's legislative representation was further reduced to 17. It slipped to 8.6 percent and 15 seats in the October 1995 legislative election but then added 2 more in 1999, when it won 9 percent of the vote.

Portuguese Communist Party (*Partido Comunista Português*—PCP). Founded in 1921 and historically one of the most Stalinist of the West European Communist parties, the PCP was the dominant force within both the military and the government in the year following the 1974 coup. Its influence waned during the latter half of 1975, particularly following the abortive rebellion of November 26, and its legislative strength dropped to fourth place in April 1976, prior to organization of the APU. The party made limited concessions to Soviet-style liberalization at its 12th congress in December 1988 by endorsing freedom of the press and multiparty politics. At a special congress called in May 1990, however, the PCP returned to a basically hard-line posture, although it adopted an initially accommodating attitude to the Socialist minority government that took office in October 1995. It enjoys widespread support in rural and industrial areas.

At the 1999 assembly election the PCP won 15 of the CDU's 17 seats. Its 2001 presidential candidate, António SIMÕES DE ABREU, finished third, with only 5 percent of the vote. In 2005 its assembly representation dropped to 12, and in 2006 its presidential candidate finished fourth, with 8.6 percent of the vote. PCP founder Alvaro Barreirinhas CUNHAL died in June 2005 at the age of 91.

Leaders: Albano NUNES, Jerónimo DE SOUSA (Parliamentary Leader and 2006 presidential candidate), Bernardino SOARES, Carlos CARVALHAS (General Secretary).

Ecologist Party "The Greens" (*Partido Ecologista "Os Verdes"*—PEV). The PEV began in 1982 as the Portuguese Ecologist Movement—"The Greens" Party (*Movimento Ecologista Português—Partido "Os Verdes"*). At the October 1999 election the party won two of the CDU's legislative seats. The PEV subsequently was described as having shifted its emphasis from purely Portuguese environmental issues to broader European concerns. At the 2005 national election the PEV again won two seats.

Leader: Heloísa APOLÓNIA (Parliamentary Leader).

Popular Party (*Partido Popular*—PP). A right-of-center, Christian democratic party founded in 1974 as the Social Democratic Center (*Centro Democrático Social*—CDS), the party is now generally referenced as the PP, although it also uses a combined CDS-PP designation. Strongest in the northern part of the country, a number of its members were named to key government posts following the 1979 and 1980 legislative elections. Despite the party's having lost 8 of 30 assembly

seats at the October 1985 election, its presidential candidate, Diogo FREITAS DO AMARAL, won 46 percent of the vote in first-round presidential balloting in January 1986, but he lost to former prime minister Soares (PSP) in the runoff. Amaral resigned the CDS presidency after the 1991 election, at which the party won only 5 assembly seats. Standing on an anti-EU platform, the PP gained ground in the October 1995 national election, winning 15 seats on a vote share of 9.1 percent.

Despite having repulsed a leadership challenge by Paulo PORTAS, Manuel MONTEIRO resigned as PP president in September 1996 in protest against internal party feuding. He subsequently agreed to return as president, although he announced he would not run again in the party congress scheduled for March 1998. As promised, Monteiro left his party post in March, and at subsequent intraparty balloting Portas finally secured the presidency. A principal architect of the 1998 PSD-PP electoral alliance, Portas nevertheless quickly grew disenchanted with the PSD leadership, and, just prior to the AD's dissolution, the PSD's Rebelo de Sousa accused Portas of publicizing confidential information. Despite a reduced vote share of 8.3 percent, the party retained its 15 assembly seats at the October 1999 election. In 2001 it endorsed President Sampaio for reelection. Portas resigned as the PP leader in April 2005, two months after the party won only 12 assembly seats.

Leaders: José Duarte de Almeida RIBEIRO E CASTRO (Party Leader), Telmo CORREIA, Nuno TEIXEIRA DE MELO (Parliamentary Leader).

Left Bloc (*Bloco do Esquerda*—BE). The BE held its first national convention in February 1999. The alliance included the socialist **Politics XXI** (*Politic XXI*), the Trotskyite Revolutionary Left Front (*Frente da Esquerda Revolucionária*—FER), the Maoist Popular Democratic Union (*União Democrática Popular*—UDP), and the small Trotskyite **Revolutionary Socialist Party** (*Partido Socialista Revolucionário*—PSR). The BE won 2.4 percent of the vote and two seats at the general election of October 1999. Its 2001 presidential contender, Fernando ROSAS, won 3 percent. The BE,

Cabinet

As of July 1, 2006

Prime Minister	José Sócrates

Ministers

Agriculture, Rural Development, and Fisheries	Jaime Silva
Culture	Isabel Pires de Lima [f]
Economy and Innovation	Manuel Pinho
Education	Maria de Lurdes Rodrigues [f]
Environment, Urban Planning, and Regional Development	Francisco Nunes Correia
Finance	Fernando Teixeira dos Santos
Foreign Affairs	Luís Amado
Health	António Correia de Campos
Interior	António Costa
Justice	Alberto Costa
National Defense	Nuno Severiano Teixeira
Parliamentary Affairs	Augusto Santos Silva
Presidency	Pedro Silva Pereira
Public Works, Transport, and Communications	Mário Lino
Science, Technology, and Higher Education	Mariano Gago
Social Security and Work	José António Vieira da Silva

[f] = female

which presents itself as a mainstream, progressive alternative to the PCP, lost two of its constituent parties with the November 2005 dissolution of the UDP and FER.

Leaders: Francisco LOUÇA (Leader of the PSR and 2006 BE presidential candidate), Luís FAZENDA (General Secretary).

Parties that contested the February 2005 assembly balloting unsuccessfully included the **Atlantic Democratic Party** (*Partido Democrático do Atlântico*—PDA), a grouping based in the Azores and the Madeira Islands and led by Carlos da Silva MELO BENTO; the **Humanist Party** (*Partido Humanista*—PH), led by Luís Filipe GUERRA; the **National Renewal Party** (*Partido Nacional Renovador*—PNR), led by José PINTO COELHO; and the **United Socialist Workers' Party** (*Partido Operário de Unidade Socialista*—POUS), formed in 1999 and led by António Aires RODRIGUES.

Legislature

The unicameral **Assembly of the Republic** (*Assembleia da Re-pública*) currently consists of 230 members elected for four-year terms (subject to dissolution) via proportional representation. (Four seats are elected by Portuguese living abroad.) At the most recent balloting on February 20, 2005, the Portuguese Socialist Party won 121 seats; the Social Democratic Party, 75; the Portuguese Communist Party, 12; the Popular Party, 12; the Left Bloc, 8; and the Ecologist Party "The Greens," 2.

President: Jaime GAMA.

Communications

Press

The following newspapers are published daily in Lisbon, unless otherwise noted: *Expresso*

(160,000), influential center-left weekly; *Jornal de Notícias* (Porto, 90,000), centrist; *Correio da Manhã* (85,000), centrist; *O Público* (Lisbon and Porto, 75,000), centrist; *Diário Popular* (70,000); *Jornal de O Dia* (50,000), rightist; *Diário de Notícias* (42,000), centrist; *A Capital* (40,000); *O Primeiro de Janeiro* (Porto, 32,000), centrist; *O Comércio do Porto* (Porto 30,000), rightist.

News Agencies

The leading facility is *Agência Lusa de Informação,* formed in 1987 by merger of *Agência Noticiosa Portuguesa* (Anop) and *Notícias de Portugal* (NP); other domestic services include *Agência Europeia de Imprensa* (AEI) and *Agência de Representações Dias da Silva* (ADS). Numerous foreign agencies also maintain bureaus in Lisbon.

Broadcasting and Computing

In December 1975 the government issued decrees nationalizing television, which had been only partly state owned, in addition to most major radio stations except *Rádio Renascença,* which was owned and operated by the Catholic Church under a 1940 concordat between Portugal and the Vatican. Substantial reprivatization subsequently resulted in a large number of privately owned stations, with remaining state-run radio facilities being controlled by *Radiodifusão Portuguesa* (RDP). Television broadcasting is dominated by the state-owned *Radiotelevisão Portuguesa* (RTP), which has two channels, although by mid-1994 two independent stations (*SIC* and *TVI*) had begun operations. There were approximately 6.5 million television receivers and 1.4 million personal computers serving 2.8 million Internet users in 2003.

Intergovernmental Representation

Ambassador to the U.S.
Pedro CATARINO

U.S. Ambassador to Portugal
Alfred HOFFMAN Jr.

Permanent Representative to the UN
João Manuel Guerra SALGUEIRO

IGO Memberships (Non-UN)
ADB, AfDB, BIS, CERN, CEUR, CPLP, EBRD, EIB, ESA, EU, Eurocontrol, IADB, IEA, Interpol, IOM, NATO, OECD, OSCE, PCA, WCO, WEU, WTO

Related Territories

The Azores and the Madeira Islands have long been construed as insular components of metropolitan Portugal and, as such, were legally distinct from a group of Portuguese possessions whose status was changed in 1951 from that of "Colonies" to "Overseas Territories." Of the latter, the South Asian enclaves of Goa, Damão, and Diu were annexed by India in 1961; Portuguese Guinea became independent as Guinea-Bissau in 1974; and Angola, the Cape Verde Islands, Mozambique, and Sao Tome and Príncipe became independent in 1975. Portuguese Timor (East Timor) was annexed by Indonesia on July 17, 1976, but the action was never recognized by Portugal, and diplomatic relations with Jakarta were not restored until late 1999, after the Indonesian government had accepted the results of the August 1999 independence referendum in East Timor (now Timor-Leste). Macao, which had been defined as a "collective entity" (*pessoa colectiva*) under a governing statute promulgated on February 17, 1976, reverted to Chinese sovereignty in 1999 (see China article). Under the 1976 constitution, the Azores and Madeira are defined as autonomous regions.

Azores (*Açores*). The Azores comprise three distinct groups of islands located in the Atlantic Ocean about 800 miles west of mainland Portugal. The most easterly of the islands are São Miguel and Santa Maria; the most westerly and least densely populated are Corvo and Flores; Fayal, Graciosa, Pico, São Jorge, and Terceira are in the center. There are three political districts, the capitals and chief seaports of which are Ponta Delgada (São Miguel), Horta (Fayal), and Angra do Heroísmo (Terceira). The islands' total area is 890 square miles (2,305 sq. km.), and their resident population (2001C) is 241,800.

Following the 1974 coup, significant separatist sentiment emerged, particularly on Terceira, whose residents feared that the left-wing government at Lisbon might close the U.S. military base at Lajes. In August 1975 a recently organized **Azorean Liberation Front** (*Frente de Libertação dos Açores—* FLA) announced its opposition to continued rule from the mainland. Following the resignation of three appointed governors, the Portuguese government surrendered control of the islands' internal administration to local political leaders and in April 1976 provided for an elected Regional Assembly.

In March 1991 FLA leader José de ALMEIDA was acquitted of treason charges on the ground that there was insufficient evidence of his having incited others to violence. In assembly balloting on October 11, 1992, the Social Democratic Party (PSD) regained its majority, winning 28 of 51 seats. The PSD and the Portuguese Socialist Party (PSP) each won 24 seats in the October 3, 1996, balloting, with the Popular Party (PP) gaining 2 seats and the Portuguese Communist Party (PCP), 1. At the election of October 15, 2000, the PSP claimed a majority of 30 seats, while the PSD dropped to 18. The PP and the Unitary Democratic Coalition (the PCP and The Greens) each won 2 seats. The PSP advanced to 44 of 52 seats in the assembly balloting of October 17, 2004. Three PS and two PSP candidates from the Azores won seats in the National Assembly in the February 2005 Portuguese election.

President of the Regional Government: Carlos Manuel Martins do Vale CESAR (PSP).

Representative of the Republic: José António MESQUITA.

Madeira Islands (*Ilhas da Madeira*). The Madeira Islands consist of Madeira and Porto Santo islands and the uninhabited islets of Desertas and Salvages. Lying west of Casablanca, Morocco, some 500 miles southwest of the Portuguese mainland, they have a total area of 308 square miles (797 sq. km.) and a resident population (2001C) of 245,000. The capital is Funchal, on Madeira Island.

As in the case of the Azores, separatist sentiment exists, the **Madeira Archipelago Liberation Front** (*Frente de Libertação de Arquipélago da Madeira—*FLAM), which advocated independence from Portugal and possible federation with the Azores and the Spanish Canaries, claiming on August 29, 1975, to have established a provisional government. However, both the government that was installed on October 1, 1976, and the elected Regional Assembly that was convened on October 23 were pledged to maintain ties to the mainland.

At balloting on October 15, 2000, the Social Democratic Party (PSD) won its seventh regional election in a row, claiming 41 of the 61 seats in the assembly. The Portuguese Socialist Party (PSP) won only 13 seats and the Popular Party (PP), 3. Alberto João Jardim of the PSD has served as regional president for nearly a quarter of a century. The PSD won 44 of 68 assembly seats in balloting on October 17, 2004. In the February 2005 Portuguese election, three PS and three PSP candidates from the Madeira Islands won seats in the National Assembly.

President of the Regional Government: Alberto João JARDIM (PSD).

Representative of the Republic: Antero Alves MONTEIRO DINIZ.

ROMANIA

România

The Country

Shaped by the geographic influence of the Carpathian Mountains and the Danube River, Romania occupies the northeastern quarter of the Balkan Peninsula. It served historically both as an outpost of Latin civilization and as a natural gateway for Russian expansion into southeastern Europe. Some 88 percent of the population is ethnically Romanian, claiming descent from the Romanized Dacians of ancient times. There are also some 1.8 million Magyars (Hungarians), the largest national minority in Europe, situated mostly in the Transylvanian lands acquired from the Austro-Hungarian Empire after World War I. A sizeable German community that totaled approximately one-half million after World War II has dwindled because of emigration under an agreement concluded in 1977 with West Germany. Traditionally, the Romanian (Greek) Orthodox Church has been the largest religious community. While constituting approximately half of the official labor force, women are concentrated in the agricultural sector because of male urban migration; female participation in political affairs increased significantly under the former Communist regime, but the membership of the current Parliament is only 11.5 percent women in the lower house and 5.8 percent in the upper.

Although one of the world's pioneer oil producers, Romania was long a predominantly agricultural country and continues to be largely self-sufficient in food production. After World War II most acreage was brought under the control of collective and state farms, while the agricultural component of the workforce dropped sharply from 65 percent in 1960 as the result of an emphasis on industrial development—particularly in metals, machinery, chemicals, and construction materials—under a series of five-year plans. Agriculture continues to account for about 15 percent of GDP and to employ about one-third of the labor force. Most farms have now been reprivatized. Leading crops include grains, potatoes, apples, and wine grapes. Industry contributes about one-third of GDP and employs a comparable share of civilian labor. Major exports include clothing, iron and steel, chemicals, and petroleum products (even though Romania is now a net importer of hydrocarbons). By far the leading trading partners are Germany, Italy, and Russia.

Following the overthrow of Nicolae CEAUŞESCU in December 1989 and the new regime's espousal of a free-market orientation,

Political Status: Independence established 1878; People's Republic proclaimed December 30, 1947; designated a Socialist Republic by constitution adopted August 21, 1965; redesignated as Romania in December 1989; presidential multiparty constitution approved in referendum of December 8, 1991.

Area: 91,699 sq. mi. (237,500 sq. km.).

Population: 21,680,974 (2002C); 21,354,000 (2005E).

Major Urban Centers (2005E): BUCHAREST (Bucureşti, 1,886,000), Cluj-Napoca (315,000), Iaşi (314,000), Timişoara (313,000), Craiova (303,000), Constanţa (299,000), Galaţi (291,000), Braşov (274,000).

Official Language: Romanian.

Monetary Unit: New Leu (market rate July 1, 2006: 2.80 new lei = $1US). (The new leu was introduced on July 1, 2005, at the rate of 1 new leu = 10,000 old lei.)

President: Traian BĂSESCU (formerly Democratic Party, currently independent [as constitutionally required]); elected (as the candidate of the Justice and Truth Alliance) in second-round balloting on December 12, 2004, and inaugurated for a five-year term on December 20 in succession to Ion ILIESCU (elected as a member of the Social Democratic Party).

Chair of the Council of Ministers (Prime Minister): Călin POPESCU-TĂRICEANU (National Liberal Party); designated by the president on December 22, 2004, following the legislative elections of November 28 and approved by Parliament on December 28 to succeed Adrian NĂSTASE (Social Democratic Party).

Romania suffered serious economic reversals: a 33 percent contraction of GDP from 1990 to 1993, inflation averaging 140 percent per annum, currency depreciation of 97 percent, and an increase in official unemployment to over 10 percent of the labor force. Limited improvement from 1994 to 1996 included a resumption of growth and a significant reduction in consumer price inflation (to 28 percent in 1995, rising again to 57 percent in 1996), although Romanian living standards remained among the lowest in Europe. The precarious financial situation was highlighted by an enforced 10 percent devaluation of the leu in November 1995 following a sharp fall in its value against hard currencies. In 1997, according to the government, inflation was about 150 percent and GDP declined by about 6 percent. GDP continued to fall during the next two years, dropping by 5.4 percent in 1998 and 3.2 percent in 1999, before recovering in 2000, when growth of 1.6 percent was registered. Inflation remained a problem, however, at more than 40 percent annually in that three-year period, during which disbursements of large loans from the International Monetary Fund (IMF) were often delayed by what the IMF called the country's "stop-and-go" approach to reform and macroeconomic policies. As of late 2000 some 80 percent of the large enterprises that were owned by the state at the end of the Communist era remained under government control, but in February 2001 the government announced a program to privatize 63 large state companies. However, that process was subsequently perceived to be compromised by corruption and other irregularities.

Romania achieved an average annual GDP growth rate of 5.5 percent in 2001–2005, placing it among the fastest growing economies in the region. Unemployment declined to about 5.9 percent in 2005, and inflation fell to about 8.2 percent (down from 9.6 percent in 2004). By that time the IMF reported significant privatization progress, liberalization of the electricity and gas markets, and modernization of the mining sector. Most observers expected economic progress to continue, particular in view of Romania's planned accession to the European Union (EU, see Current issues, below).

Government and Politics

Political Background

Originally consisting of the twin principalities of Walachia and Moldavia, the territory that is now Romania was conquered by the Ottoman Turks in 1504. Recognized as independent at the Berlin Congress in 1878, Romania made large territorial gains as one of the victorious powers in World War I but lost substantial areas to Hungary (Northern Transylvania), to the Soviet Union (Bessarabia and Northern Bukovina), and to Bulgaria (Southern Dobruja) in 1940 under threats from its neighbors and pressure from Nazi Germany. The young King MIHAI (Michael), who took advantage of the entry of Soviet troops in 1944 to dismiss the pro-German regime and switch to the Allied side, was forced in 1945 to accept a Communist-led coalition government under Dr. Petru GROZA. Following rigged elections in 1946, the king abdicated in 1947. The Paris peace treaty in 1947 restored Northern Transylvania to Romania, but not the other territories lost in 1940. Thereafter, the Communists proceeded to eliminate the remnants of the traditional parties, and in 1952, after a series of internal purges, Gheorghe GHEORGHIU-DEJ emerged as the unchallenged party leader.

Following a decade of rigidity, Romania embarked in the early 1960s on a policy of increased independence from the Soviet Union in both military and economic affairs. This policy was continued and intensified under Nicolae Ceauşescu, who succeeded to leadership of the Romanian Communist Party (*Partidul Comunist Român*—PCR) on Gheorghiu-Dej's death in 1965 and became president of the Council of State in 1967. While maintaining relatively strict controls at home, the Ceauşescu regime consistently advocated maximum autonomy in international Communist affairs. These policies were fully endorsed by PCR congresses at five-year intervals from 1969 to 1989, with Ceauşescu being reelected to the top party position on each occasion.

In March 1980 President Ceauşescu was elected to his third term as head of state by the Grand National Assembly. The next day Ilie VERDEŢ, a close associate of the president and an experienced economic planner who had succeeded Manea MĂNESCU as chair of the Council of Ministers in March 1979, presented a new cabinet that included as a first deputy Elena CEAUŞESCU, wife of the president. In the face of increasingly poor economic performance, other significant changes were subsequently made, including the replacement of Verdeţ by the relatively obscure Constantin DĂSCĂLESCU in May 1982.

In November 1989 Romania appeared impervious to the winds of change sweeping over most other East European Communist regimes. Thus, the 14th PCR congress met without incident on November 20–24, and Ceauşescu made a state visit to Iran on December 19–20. During his absence, long-simmering unrest among ethnic Hungarians in the western city of Timişoara led to a bloody confrontation between police and antigovernment demonstrators. The protests quickly spread to other cities, and on December 21 an angry crowd jeered the president during what had been planned as a progovernment rally in Bucharest. By the following day army units had joined in a full-scale revolt, with a group known as the National Salvation Front (*Frontul Salvării Naţionale*—FSN) announcing that it had formed a provisional government. Unlike other East European revolutions, Romania's overthrow of Communist rule involved fierce fighting, in Bucharest and other cities, with many civilian casualties resulting from the government's use of heavy armaments. On December 25 Ceauşescu and his wife Elena, who had been captured after fleeing the capital, were executed following a secret trial that had pronounced them guilty of genocide and the embezzlement of more than $1 billion. On December 26 Ion ILIESCU was sworn in as provisional head of state, with Petre ROMAN, a fellow member of the PCR *nomenklatura*, being named prime minister. The FSN quickly came under attack as a thinly disguised extension of the former regime, and on February 1, 1990, it agreed to share power with 29 other groups in a coalition styled the Provisional Council for National Unity (*Consiliul Provizoriu de Uniune Naţională*—CPUN).

At presidential and legislative elections (the latter involving 6,719 candidates) on May 20, 1990, Iliescu won 85.1 percent of the presidential vote, while the FSN secured 67.0 and 66.3 percent of the votes for the upper and lower houses of Parliament. The balloting went ahead despite demonstrations by opposition parties claiming that they had been accorded insufficient time to organize. The protesters were eventually evicted from Bucharest's University Square in mid-June by thousands of club-wielding coal miners summoned to the capital by the president. On June 20 Iliescu was formally invested for a two-year term as president, with Roman continuing as prime minister.

Following his reappointment, Roman declared that he would pursue an "historic transition from a supercentralized economy to a market economy," adding that the state would "abandon to the greatest possible extent its role as proprietor and manager." Leaders of the small rightist parties responded by articulating a widespread belief that the revolution had been exploited by Communists who were interested only in the overthrow of Ceauşescu. Nevertheless, Roman, who was less identified with the former regime than Iliescu, moved ahead with his reform program, declaring that only "shock therapy" could save the rapidly deteriorating economy from disaster. Thus, prices of essential goods doubled as the result of sharp cuts in state subsidies in April 1991, while a drastic revision of the foreign investment code, urged by the IMF, offered non-Romanian companies full ownership, capital protection, repatriation of profits, and multiyear tax concessions.

Despite rapidly eroding support for the government by mid-1991, the reforms continued unabated, including the enactment of legislation in August that authorized the privatization of all state enterprises except utilities. For their part, the miners responded to soaring inflation by returning to Bucharest in September for three days of violent demonstrations, and on October 1 it was announced that Theodor STOLOJAN, the nonparty finance minister, had been asked to form a new government. By December it was clear that President Iliescu and former prime minister Roman were engaged in a struggle for control of the FSN. Roman had earlier complained of having been driven from office by a "Communist-inspired coup," while the president accused Roman of having flouted an FSN campaign promise of measured conversion to a market economy. Subsequently, Iliescu supporters, formally organized from April 1992 as the Democratic National Salvation Front (*Frontul Democrat al Salvării Naţionale*—FDSN), gained parliamentary support for simultaneous legislative and presidential elections in September, at which Roman's forces were decisively routed.

At his reinvestiture on October 30 President Iliescu endorsed further progress toward pluralism and a market economy, despite having long been accused by opponents of foot-dragging on both counts. Fourteen days later, a deeply divided Parliament ended a five-week impasse by agreeing to the formation of a government led by Nicolae VĂCĂROIU, a relatively unknown tax official then without party affiliation, who proceeded to combine liberal reform with "special care" for its social consequences. In July 1993 the FDSN absorbed three other progovernment parties and adopted a new name, the Social Democracy Party of Romania (*Partidul Democraţiei Sociale din România*—PDSR), which Văcăroiu later joined.

Despite deepening economic misery, the Văcăroiu government endured, with support from the (ex-Communist) Socialist Labor Party (*Partidul Socialist al Muncii*—PSM) and far-right Greater Romania Party (*Partidul România Mare*—PRM). Amid a modest economic upturn in 1994, the government's parliamentary base was strengthened in August by the induction of the rightist Romanian National Unity Party (*Partidul Unităţii Naţionale Române*—PUNR) into coalition status. In the course of 1995, however, the PDSR's relations with all three coalition partners deteriorated sharply, with the result that the PRM and PSM left the government alliance in October, with the exit of the PUNR being finally confirmed in September 1996. Meanwhile, by now reduced to minority status at the national level, the PDSR had been outpolled by the opposition Democratic Convention of Romania (*Convenţia Democrată Română*—CDR) alliance in local elections in June.

In the first round of presidential balloting held on November 3, 1996, incumbent Iliescu (PDSR) headed the poll against 15 other candidates, winning 32.3 percent of the vote. However, he was closely followed by the CDR candidate, Emil CONSTANTINESCU, with 28.2 percent, while Petre

Roman, standing for the Social Democratic Union (*Uniunea Social Democrată*—USD), came in third with 20.5 percent. The USD and most other opposition parties then swung behind the CDR candidate for the runoff polling on November 17. As a result, Constantinescu won a decisive victory over Iliescu by 53.5 percent to 46.5 percent, the incumbent having been weighed down not only by Romania's economic and social deterioration, but also by evidence of abuse of power and pervasive corruption within ruling circles, particularly in connection with the privatization of state assets. In legislative balloting also held on November 3, the CDR won pluralities in both the Senate and the Chamber of Deputies, with the USD also polling strongly as the third grouping, after the PDSR.

Interparty talks following the elections yielded the signature of an agreement on December 6, 1996, providing for Victor CIORBEA, the youthful CDR mayor of Bucharest, to head a majority coalition government with the USD and the Hungarian Democratic Union of Romania (*Uniunea Democrată a Maghiarilor din România*—UDMR), the latter representing Romania's ethnic Hungarian minority. Accorded a 316–152 endorsement by a joint session of the two legislative houses on December 11, the new administration was sworn in the following day. Among other things, the new government reinstated the citizenship of King Mihai, repealing a 1948 decree. He returned to Romania in March 1997 to a warm reception and was later appointed a diplomat at large to help make the case for Romanian membership in the North Atlantic Treaty Organization (NATO). In June the government survived the opposition's first no-confidence motion by a vote of 227 to 158.

Ciorbea's government found it difficult to implement the reforms required to resolve Romania's economic problems, which included GDP contraction, high unemployment, and inflation of about 150 percent. Coalition members, particularly the CDR's Christian and Democratic National Peasants' Party (*Partidul Național Țărănesc Creştin şi Democrat*—PNȚCD) and the USD's Democratic Party (*Partidul Democrat*—PD, an FSN descendant), generally were unable to compromise. In

the wake of persistent feuding and public discord, the cabinet was reshuffled in December, with a number of independents being appointed. On January 14, 1998, the PD withdrew its support from Ciorbea and threatened to quit the government if he did not resign and if no agreement was reached within the coalition on a reform program by March 31. On February 5 the PD's five cabinet ministers resigned, and a new coalition agreement was approved, the open ministerial posts going to the PNȚCD, the National Liberal Party (*Partidul Național Liberal*—PNL), and the Civic Alliance Party (*Partidul Alianța Civică*—PAC). The PD's relationship with the government remained an anomaly: though it considered itself part of the ruling coalition, the party nevertheless set up an opposition-like 17-member committee to monitor the performance of the Ciorbea cabinet. After three months of political instability, Ciorbea resigned on March 30.

On April 2, 1998, President Constantinescu named Radu VASILE, the general secretary of the PNȚCD, to replace Ciorbea; Vasile and his cabinet were sworn in on April 15. The new government included members from the PNȚCD, PD, UDMR, PNL, Romanian Social Democratic Party (*Partidul Social Democrat Român*—PSDR), and Romania's Alternative Party (*Partidul Alternativa României*—PAR). However, in October the PAR quit the coalition government in protest over the slow pace of economic reform.

Himself an economist, Vasile promised to strengthen the market economy by accelerating privatization efforts, and in December 1998 he restructured the government, reducing the number of ministries to quicken the pace of reform. In early 1999, however, his plans were set back by a miners' strike in the Jiu Valley that escalated into Romania's worst civil disorder since 1991. In mid-January the government reached a compromise with the leader of the miners' union, Miron COZMA, agreeing to abandon immediate plans to close unprofitable coal mines. The agreement averted a potential armed conflict between security forces and 20,000 strikers, but in mid-February Cozma and several hundred others were arrested as he led 2,000 miners toward Bucharest in protest against his recent sentencing to 18 years in prison for his role in the September 1991 riots.

With inflation and unemployment at unacceptable levels, and with the leu having fallen by more than one-third of its value between January and mid-March 1999, general dissatisfaction with the state of the economy continued to grow. Squabbling within the governing coalition also persisted, hindering progress on reform measures, and by December Vasile had lost the support of his own PNŢCD, whose ministers, constituting the majority of the cabinet, resigned. On December 13 President Constantinescu dismissed Vasile, naming as interim prime minister the PSDR's Alexandru ATHANASIU, previously minister of labor. Initially, Vasile refused to step down, arguing that the constitution permitted such dismissals only in cases of medical incapacity. Four days later, however, Vasile resigned, thereby defusing a potential constitutional crisis. Constantinescu appointed Mugur ISĂRESCU, the governor of Romania's central bank, as the new prime minister. Isărescu and a largely unchanged Council of Ministers received the legislature's approbation on December 21.

After mid-2000, with presidential and legislative elections approaching, the political alliance behind the governing coalition gradually dissolved. In August 2000 the PNŢCD and several allied parties reconstituted the CDR as the CDR 2000, but minus one of its previous principal components, the PNL. The PD, UDMR, and PNL prepared to contest the elections independently, while in September the PSDR left the government and formed an alliance with the PDSR. The legislative election of November 26 saw the PDSR capture a large plurality in both parliamentary houses, with the xenophobic PRM rising to second place and with the enfeebled CDR 2000 failing to meet the threshold for representation. In the presidential contest, former president Iliescu of the PDSR easily defeated the PRM's Corneliu VADIM TUDOR in a two-way runoff on December 10. Iliescu assumed office on December 21. His choice for prime minister, Adrian NĂSTASE, was confirmed by the Parlia-

ment and sworn in on December 28 at the head of a minority government dominated by the PDSR, with external backing from the PNL and the UDMR. On June 16, 2001, the PDSR and the PSDR completed their merger as the Social Democratic Party (*Partidul Social Democrat*—PSD).

At legislative balloting on November 28, 2004, the PSD, and its ally in the National Union coalition, the Humanist Party of Romania (*Partidul Umanist din România*—PUR), secured a plurality of 132 seats in the Chamber of Deputies. Following closely (with 112 seats) was the Justice and Truth Alliance (*Alianţa Dreptate şi Adevăr*—ADA), which had been formed in 2003 by the PNL and the PD. In concurrent first-round presidential balloting, Prime Minister Năstase led 12 candidates with 41 percent of the vote. The ADA's Traian BĂSESCU finished second with 34 percent of the vote, followed by the PRM's Vadim Tudor with 12.6 percent.

In the presidential runoff on December 12, 2004, Băsescu scored a surprising victory over Năstase, securing 51.2 percent of the vote. On December 28 the Parliament, by a vote of 265–200, approved a cabinet (led by Călin POPESCU-TĂRICEANU of the PNL) comprising the PNL, PD, UDMR, and PUR (which had split from the PSD).

Constitution and Government

Romania's third postwar constitution, adopted in 1965 and amended in 1974, declared the nation to be a "socialist republic," with an economy based on socialist ownership of the means of production. All power was ascribed to the people, but the PCR was singled out as society's leading political force. Supreme state power was nominally vested in a unicameral Grand National Assembly (which was empowered to elect the president of the republic), a Council of State serving as a legislative presidium, a Council of Ministers (cabinet), justices of the Supreme Court, and a chief public prosecutor (procurator general).

Upon assuming power in late 1989, the FSN suspended the basic law, dropped the phrase "Socialist Republic" from the country's official name, and declared its support for a multiparty system and a market economy. The balloting of May 20, 1990, was for a president and a bicameral Parliament, the latter being empowered to draft a new constitution within 18 months, with new elections to follow within 12 months. A revised basic law providing for a strong presidency, political pluralism, human rights guarantees, and a commitment to market freedom was approved by Parliament (sitting as a Constituent Assembly) on November 21, 1991, and ratified by referendum on December 8.

A national referendum held October 18–19, 2003, approved (by a 90 percent "yes" vote) a number of constitutional amendments designed for the most part to facilitate Romania's planned accession to the EU. Among other things, the changes strengthened the protection of human rights (most notably for minority groups) and property rights. In addition, the presidential term was extended from four to five years.

Administratively, Romania is divided into 41 counties plus the city of Bucharest, in addition to a large number of towns and villages. A prefect represents the central government in each county, which elects its own council. Mayors and councils are elected at the lower level.

Foreign Relations

Although historically pro-Western in foreign policy, Romania during its first 15 years as a Communist state cooperated fully with the Soviet Union both in bilateral relations and as a member of the Council for Mutual Economic Assistance, the Warsaw Pact, and the United Nations. However, serious differences with Moscow arose in the early 1960s over the issue of East European economic integration, leading in 1964 to a formal rejection by Romania of all Soviet schemes of supranational planning and interference in the affairs of other Communist countries. Subsequently, Romania followed an independent line in many areas of foreign policy, refusing to participate in the 1968 Warsaw Pact intervention in Czechoslovakia, rejecting efforts to isolate Communist China, and remaining the only Soviet-bloc nation to continue diplomatic

relations with both Egypt and Israel. Prior to the admission of Hungary in 1982, Romania was the only Eastern-bloc state to belong to the World Bank and the IMF.

A constant regional theme of Romania's external relations in the early 1990s was discord with Hungary over the status of Romania's substantial ethnic Hungarian minority population, concentrated in Transylvania. Tension mounted when the ultra-nationalist Gheorghe FUNAR, presidential candidate of the Romanian National Unity Party (*Partidul Unităţii Naţionale Române*—PUNR), was elected mayor of Cluj-Napoca in Transylvania in February 1992, with subsequent restrictions on "anti-Romanian" public meetings. Collaterally, the central government named ethnic Romanians to replace ethnic Hungarian prefects in the two Hungarian-majority counties, the resultant outrage being only partially eased by the appointment of two prefects for each county, one Hungarian and one Romanian.

A second major preoccupation of post-Communist Romania has been the position of Moldova, once the bulk of Romanian-ruled Bessarabia and inhabited predominantly by ethnic Romanians. On September 3, 1991, the Romanian Parliament adopted a resolution endorsing an August 27 declaration of independence by Moldova (the former Soviet Republic of Moldavia), with which Bucharest had established diplomatic relations seven days earlier. On November 2, during a visit to Bucharest, Moldovan Prime Minister Valeriu Muravschi expressed the hope that intergovernmental exchanges could "speed up the process of [his country's] integration with Romania."

Romania's possible interest in uniting with Moldova had contributed to the attempted secession of the latter's Transdnestr (ethnically Russian) and Gagauz (Turkic) majority areas and the onset of armed conflict, in which Bucharest backed the Moldovan authorities, although without intervening militarily. Advancing the concept of "two republics, one nation," the Romanian and Moldovan governments took a gradualist approach to unification and from May 1992 engaged in protracted diplomatic efforts with Russia and Ukraine to bring about a lasting cessation of hostilities between the warring ethnic groups in Moldova. (On the other hand, the Moldovan election of February 1994 yielding a legislative majority for proindependence parties represented a rebuff to the reunification effort.)

Romania was a founding member of the Black Sea Economic Cooperation (BSEC) grouping launched in June 1992, and on February 1, 1993, Romania signed an association agreement with the European Community (EC, subsequently the EU). However, its continuing problems in gaining international acceptance were highlighted by the refusal of the United States to extend most-favored-nation (MFN) trade status until October 1993, although Washington had joined Western European governments in applauding the overthrow of the Ceauşescu regime.

In September 1993 the Parliamentary Assembly of the Council of Europe approved the admission of Romania to the organization. Subsequently, on January 26, 1994, Romania became the first former Communist state to join NATO's Partnership for Peace program, pursuant to its aim of eventual full NATO membership as well as accession to the EU. In the latter context, Romania in mid-1994 secured an EU pledge that it would be treated on a par with the four Visegrád states (Czech Republic, Hungary, Poland, Slovakia) also seeking membership. (On June 22, 1995, Romania became the third ex-Communist state [after Hungary and Poland] to submit a formal application for EU membership, although it was not invited to open accession negotiations until December 1999 [see Current issues, below, for subsequent EU developments].)

The June 1994 advent of a Socialist government in Hungary led to an improvement in Bucharest-Budapest relations, including a visit to Hungary by the Romanian foreign minister in September. Nevertheless, difficulties continued, occasioned by such events as passage in the Romanian Parliament of legislation regulating Hungarian-language education and the display of the flag or the singing of the anthem of another state. Against this background, attempted mediation by the U.S. Carter Center in Atlanta, which Romanian and ethnic Hungarian representatives visited in February 1995, appeared to do little to bridge the ancestral divide.

In a new initiative in September 1995, the Romanian government submitted three draft documents to Hungary covering reconciliation between the two countries, bilateral cooperation, and a code of behavior on treatment of ethnic minorities. Although the response in Budapest was cool, Bucharest persisted, with the result that a 1996 bilateral treaty saw both sides make concessions on the minority question. Hungary renounced any claim to Romanian territory populated by ethnic Hungarians, and Romania undertook to guarantee ethnic minority rights within its borders. Although the treaty commanded majority support in both national legislatures, it attracted fierce criticism from nationalist parties in both Hungary and Romania.

Romanian-Hungarian relations continued to improve after the election of President Constantinescu in November 1996, and in February 1997 the defense ministers of the two countries met and agreed on the formation of a joint peacekeeping force, a move that was seen as enhancing both nations' prospects for gaining entry into NATO. In March, Prime Minister Ciorbea, in the first visit of a Romanian prime minister to Hungary since 1989, signed five agreements. The following month President Arpád Göncz became the first Hungarian head of state to visit Romania, while in June the two nations signed a friendship treaty, confirming existing borders.

Despite support from France, Italy, and Spain, Romania's request to be included in the first-round expansion of NATO was blocked in 1997 by the United States, with U.S. Defense Secretary William Cohen explaining that Washington had said "not yet" rather than simply "no." The rejection was seen as a desire by the United States to placate a nervous Russia and to delay admitting a former Communist state until democracy and free-market reforms had become irreversible. In July U.S. President Clinton, in the first visit to Romania by an American president in more than 20 years, praised the Romanians and encouraged them to stay their course.

Romania became a member of the Central European Free Trade Agreement (CEFTA) on July 1, 1997, expecting to regain access to Eastern and Central European markets as well as to enhance its prospects for NATO membership (see Poland, Foreign relations, for more on CEFTA). A month earlier, the presidents of Ukraine and Romania had signed a friendship treaty, calling existing borders "inviolable" despite earlier friction over the status of Northern Bukovina and Southern Bessarabia, both of which Romania had been compelled to cede to the USSR in June 1940 (see map, p. 1009). Related issues of national identity have delayed conclusion of a basic treaty with Russia, as has Romania's demand that Russia return the state treasury that has been held in Moscow since its delivery there for safekeeping during World War I.

A trip to Romania in May 1999 by John Paul II was the first visit by a Roman Catholic pope to a country with an Orthodox majority since the Great Schism of 1054. Although restricted to Bucharest, the pope was warmly greeted by the patriarch of the Romanian Orthodox Church, TEOCTIST.

A basic treaty between Romania and Moldova was initialed on April 28, 2000, but neither country's legislature ratified the agreement. Subsequently, in November 2002, Romania and Hungary signed an agreement defining the future course of their bilateral partnership and guaranteeing each other support for EU membership.

In 2003 Romania was included in the "second wave" candidates for membership in NATO, to which it formally acceded in March 2004 along with six other countries. Earlier, Romania had contributed a contingent of noncombat troops to the U.S./UK-led operation in Iraq. (As of mid-2006 the government was reportedly considering withdrawing its troops from Iraq.)

In October 2005 Romania and Hungary signed a number of potentially significant agreements providing for cooperation in environmental protection, law enforcement, border security, joint defense programs, and cultural and educational exchanges. The two countries also pledged to pursue common economic policies.

Current Issues

In a nationwide address in July 2000 President Constantinescu, having decided not to seek a second term as president, described Romania's current political parties as conducting "a blind struggle" for power in which "people buy and sell principles, ideologies, seats in the parliament and the cabinet, making use to that end of lies, blackmail, vulgarity, and manipulation." He also noted that his attempts to fight corruption had been held back by the complicity of high-level state institutions.

The final years of the CDR-led government were marked by political infighting and a resultant inability to establish a course that would resolve Romania's economic difficulties. At the same time, the country continued to grapple with the legacy of the Ceauşescu era. The government decided to release files held by the former secret police, the *Securitate*, and supported measures covering restitution for personal property, farmland, and forests seized under the Communists. All of these decisions proved controversial, as did government support for expanding minority-language education (although not for establishing a Hungarian-language university) and for permitting official use of minority languages in local jurisdictions having significant minority communities. Nationalist and conservative opponents vowed to revisit the restitution and minority issues after the November 2000 elections.

The most startling development of the 2000 election season was the increasing support accorded Vadim Tudor's Greater Romania Party (PRM), which saw its share of the legislative vote surge from under 5 percent in 1996 to roughly 20 percent. During the campaign and afterward, the PRM presidential contender showed no inclination to tone down his ultranationalist, anti-Hungarian, anti-Gypsy, anti-Semitic, populist rhetoric, asserting, for example, that Ceauşescu had been "one of the world's great statesmen" and that the IMF and the World Bank were blackmailing Romania, demanding poisonous policy changes in return for vitally needed loans and credits.

An October 2000 evaluation by the European Parliament described Romania's economy as "worrying" and cited numerous other deficiencies, including corruption, the persistent problem of abandoned children, the need for legal reform, and extensive environmental pollution. By that time, the CDR-led government had lost most of its popular support due to continued instability within the coalition (four prime ministers in four years), economic deterioration, and perceived ongoing corruption. In comparison, the PSD-led government installed in late 2000 subsequently enjoyed relative stability and appeared to contribute to a period of economic improvement. Prime Minister Năstase's administration also successfully negotiated accession to NATO and oversaw progress toward EU membership. Consequently, some observers were surprised by Năstase's narrow loss in the late 2004 presidential election to Traian Băsescu of the reform-minded (in rhetorical terms, at least) ADA. Corruption apparently remained on the minds of those who voted for Băsescu, who had earned a reputation for rectitude as mayor of Bucharest. In tandem with the new coalition cabinet formed under the leadership of Călin Popescu-Tăriceanu, Băsescu promised tax reform as well as institutional change that would make Romania "a democracy in real terms." Crucial to the latter goal was judicial reform, some of which was accomplished by legislative action in the first half of 2005.

In April 2005 Romania signed an accession treaty with the EU calling for Romania to become a member in January 2007, although analysts noted that significant reform was still required. Complicating matters at midyear was reported friction between the president and the prime minister on a number of issues.

The dominant issue from mid-2005 to mid-2006 was the fight against corruption, the ADA-led government having pledged to target the major offenders regardless of their political affiliation or status. Anticorruption legislation was presented to the Parliament in late 2005 but met unexpected opposition from within both chambers. Among other things,

the legislators were reportedly concerned that they would lose their own immunity from prosecution in the "clean-up" campaign and would (along with judges) be forced to make their financial assets public. Despite the initial legislative hostility, many of the new laws were ultimately approved, in part due to the efforts of Justice Minister Monica MACOVEI, an independent former human rights activist who gained substantial popular acclaim for her willingness to investigate entrenched interests. The anticorruption campaign produced its first major results in the spring of 2006 when a number of influential politicians (including legislators and cabinet members) were officially placed under investigation.

Supporters of EU integration hoped that the recent corruption investigations would facilitate Romania's EU accession (scheduled for January 2007). However, in April 2006 the EU postponed a decision on the question until October, indicating that Romania "is not there yet." While acknowledging Romania's recent progress, the EU urged further intensification of anticorruption measures as well as agricultural and judicial reform. Despite those concerns, most experts predicted a favorable EU ruling in October regarding Romania's accession.

Political Parties

Until late 1989 Romania's political system was based on the controlling position of the Romanian Communist Party (*Partidul Comunist Român*—PCR). Founded in 1921, the PCR changed its name to Romanian Workers' Party (*Partidul Muncitoresc Român*—PMR) in 1948 after a merger with the left-wing Social Democrats, but the party reassumed its original name at the ninth party congress in 1965. Identified by the constitution as "the leading political force of the whole society," the PCR exercised its authority with the aid of the Front of Socialist Democracy and Unity (*Frontul Democrației și Unității Socialiste*—FDUS), which prepared the approved list of candidates for election to the Grand National Assembly and other bodies.

At the 14th party congress, held in Bucharest November 20–24, 1989, only a month before his overthrow, President Ceauşescu had been unanimously elected to another five-year term as PCR general secretary. Following the rebellion of December 22, the new government of Ion Iliescu declared that the question of banning the PCR would be decided by a popular referendum on January 28, 1990. However, on January 19 the ruling National Salvation Front (*Frontul Salvării Naţionale*—FSN) announced that the decision to schedule the referendum had been "a political mistake," with the result that the party quickly ceased to exist as an organized force.

For the 2004 elections nearly 50 parties and alliances offered candidates.

Government Parties

Justice and Truth Alliance (*Alianţa Dreptate şi Adevăr*—ADA). Launched in November 2003 by the two parties below, the ADA was formed with the goal of presenting a strong opposition front to counterbalance the PSD-led governing coalition. The ADA pledged to combat corruption, restore the independence of the judiciary, protect property rights, pursue EU membership, and adopt promarket economic reforms. ADA candidate Traian Băsescu was elected president in second-round balloting in December 2004, while the ADA (which had finished second in the November legislative balloting to the PSD/PUR alliance) subsequently formed a coalition government with the PUR and the UDMR with PNL leader Călin Popescu-Tăriceanu as prime minister.

The PNL and the PD presented separate candidate lists for the June 2004 local elections (except for Cluj and Bucharest, where joint lists were used). Analysts subsequently described the ADA as "walking a thin line" in representing the sometimes diverse aspirations of the PNL and PD while remaining sufficiently strong as an alliance. Reflecting such concerns, the ADA has two co-presidents (one each from the PNL and PD) and seven members from each party on its 14-member executive

council. There have been talks recently about a formal merger of the two parties, although no official action had been taken by mid-2006.

Leaders: Călin POPESCU-TĂRICEANU (PNL, Prime Minister and Co-President of the Party), Emil BOC (PD, Co-President of the Party).

National Liberal Party (*Partidul Naţional Liberal*—PNL). Founded in the mid-19th century but banned by the Communists in 1947, the PNL was reconstituted in 1990 as a right-of-center party that, in addition to supporting a free-market economy, endorsed resumption of the throne by the exiled King Mihai. (In 1992 the ex-king declined nomination as the PNL presidential candidate.) A founding member of the Democratic Convention (*Convenţia Democrată* Româna—CDR), the PNL withdrew from the alliance in April 1992. Two splinter groups, the party's Youth Wing and the PNL–Democratic Convention (*Partidul Naţional Liberal–Convenţia Democrată*—PNL-CD), the latter led by Nicolae CERVENI, refused to endorse the action and remained affiliated with the CDR. Some of the youth wing members later helped form the Liberal Party 1993 (PL-93), although others, grouped as the New Liberal Party (*Noul Partid Liberal*—NPL), rejoined the PNL at a February 1993 PNL "unification" congress. Ironically, the 1993 congress ultimately led to formation of a third major splinter when the election of Mircea IONESCU-QUINTUS as chair was contested by his predecessor, Radu CÂMPEANU, who went on to form the **PNL–Câmpeanu** (PNL-C).

Having failed to win any chamber seats in September 1992, the PNL later reestablished a presence in the lower house through absorption in May 1995 of the PL-93's Political Liberal Group (*Grupul Politic Liberal*) and the Group for Liberal Unification (*Grupul pentru Unificarea Liberală*) of the Civic Alliance Party (*Partidul Alianţa Civică*—PAC), although chamber rules to inhibit floor crossing meant that the dozen or so PNL representatives were technically classified as independents. The party rejoined the CDR in time for the November 1996 election and won 25 seats in the chamber and 17 in the Senate. The PNL-CD took 5 seats in the lower house and 4 in the upper, but the PL-93, having left the CDR in 1995, won no seats as part of the National Liberal Alliance (*Alianţa Naţională Liberală*—ANL), which it had formed with the PAC.

In February 1997 PNL-CD dissidents, with unofficial support from the CDR, suspended Nicolae Cerveni as chair because of his efforts to join forces with liberals outside the CDR. In June Cerveni loyalists in the PNL-CD united with the PL-93 to form the Liberal Party (*Partidul Liberal*—PL), chaired by Cerveni. In March 1998 the PL and the PNL–Câmpeanu then formed an umbrella group called the Liberal Federation (*Federaţia Liberală*—FL), but differences over the PL's relationship to the PNL and the CDR soon led to a bifurcation of the PL, with Cerveni heading one faction and Dinu PATRICIU, the former PL-93 chair, and his supporters constituting another. In May the Cerveni PL was renamed the Romanian Liberal Democratic Party (*Partidul Liberal Democrat Român*—PLDR), while in July 1999 the Patriciu PL was absorbed by the PNL. At the same time, the PNL-CD and PL-93 ceased to exist. In May 1999 Cerveni agreed to merge his party with the Romanian National Party (PNR; see PD), but differences soon emerged and Cerveni competed for the presidency in November 2000 as the candidate of the PLDR, finishing last among 12 contenders. Like the PLDR, the PNL–Câmpeanu, running independently, failed to win representation in either house in 2000.

In February 1998 the PAC merged with the PNL. The PAC was an outgrowth of the still active **Civic Alliance** (*Alianţa Civică*—AC), which had been organized in November 1990 by a group of trade unionists and intellectuals to provide an extraparliamentary umbrella for post-Communist opposition groups, in partial emulation of East Germany's New Forum and

Czechoslovakia's Civic Forum. At its second congress in July 1991 the AC voted to establish the PAC, under the leadership of literary critic Nicolae MANOLESCU, as its electoral affiliate. At the 1992 general election the PAC won 13 chamber and 7 Senate seats as a component of the CDR.

As the 2000 general election approached, the PNL, increasingly dominated by Deputy Chair Valeriu STOICA, distanced itself from the CDR, and in June 2000 it offered its own candidates at local elections, placing fourth in terms of mayoral victories. When the party formally abandoned the CDR shortly thereafter, Stoica attempted to forge ties to the Alliance for Romania (*Alianţa pentru România*—ApR), but many party members objected, Nicolae Manolescu being the most prominent member to resign as a consequence. In the presidential contest the PNL endorsed former prime minister Theodor Stolojan, but a group headed by Minister of Finance Decebal Traian REMEŞ, accusing the party of a leftward drift, denounced the selection and left to establish a new party that was registered in October as the National Liberal Party–Traditional (*Partidul Naţional Liberal–Tradiţional*—PNL-T). At the November balloting Stolojan finished third, with 11.8 percent of the vote, while the party won 30 seats in the chamber and 13 in the Senate.

A party congress in February 2001 elected Stoica as PNL chair, the octogenarian Ionescu-Quintus having decided to step down. The following November, the ApR signed a merger agreement with the PNL, and the two united under the PNL rubric on January 19, 2002.

The ApR, a center-left party founded in August 1997, had been formed by reformers who had split off from the PDSR. Led by Teodor Meleşcanu, the ApR regarded itself as a "nonconfrontational" opposition party. It claimed 13 deputies in the chamber and 2 senators upon its formation, but at the November 2000 election it failed at the polls, taking only about 4 percent of the vote for each house. Meleşcanu finished seventh in the concurrent presidential balloting, with 1.9 percent of the vote. Prior to the election the ApR had discussed an alliance with the PNL, but the overtures fell through, in part because the PNL refused to accept the ApR leader as its presidential candidate. Because of the ApR's dismal electoral showing, the entire leadership stepped down in early December 2000. At a party conference in March 2001, however, Meleşcanu was returned to office, and the party redefined itself as "social-liberal" (center-right) in orientation. A social democratic (center-left) faction strongly opposed the redefinition. Subsequent efforts by Meleşcanu to negotiate an alliance with the Democratic Party (DP) failed to bear fruit. However, talks with the PNL proved more fruitful, and in 2002 the ApR merged with the PNL, Meleşcanu becoming vice president of the PNL.

With the goal of reuniting all the liberal factions under one banner, in April 2002 the PNL-C absorbed the PNL-T, led by Decebal Traian Remeş. In June the Cerveni wing of the liberal movement (the PLDR) also merged into the PNL-C. At that point, there were only two major liberal groupings—the PNL and the PNL-C. Final consolidation was achieved at the end of 2003 when the PNL-C merged into the PNL. Meanwhile, by that time the Union of Rightist Forces (*Uniunea Forţelor de Dreapta*—UFD) had also merged with the PNL. (See the 2000–2002 *Handbook* for additional information on the UFD.)

Following the launching of the ADA in November 2003, PNL Chair Theodor Stolojan announced plans to seek the ADA's presidential nomination. However, he retired from the race due to health reasons, and the PNL supported the PD's Traian Băsescu. Stolojan also resigned as PNL chair, and he was succeeded by Călin Popescu-Tăriceanu, who became prime minister following the November 2004 legislative elections.

In June 2005 Popescu-Tăriceanu proposed a formal merger of the PNL and the PD, although it was subsequently decided that the current arrangement would continue at least until the 2008 elections.

Leaders: Călin POPESCU-TĂRICEANU (Chair); Gheorghe FLUTUR, Puiu HASOTI, Teodor MELEŞCANU, Dan Rdau RUŞAN (Vice Presidents).

Democratic Party (*Partidul Democrat*—PD). The PD is a direct descendant of the National Salvation Front (FSN), which was described as a "self-appointed" group that assumed governmental power following the overthrow of the Ceauşescu regime. Claiming initially to be a supraparty formation, the Front reorganized as a party in February 1990 and, as such, swept the balloting of May 20. On July 6 it announced that it was further reorganizing under a social-democratic rubric. One day earlier Ion Iliescu had stepped down as FSN president in compliance with a law that prohibited the head of state from serving as the leader of a political party. Subsequently, however, he emerged as de facto leader of the Democratic National Salvation Front (FDSN), which opposed rapid economic reform.

At its first national convention held March 16–17, 1991, the FSN, despite criticism from the Iliescu faction, approved a free-market reform program entitled "A Future for Romania" that was presented by Prime Minister Petre Roman. Although Roman was obliged to step down as chief of government in October 1991, the Front, at its second convention held March 27–29, 1992, reconfirmed him as its president and reiterated its support of the free-market program. With the FDSN faction having separated from the FSN, the FSN ran a distant fourth in the national presidential poll of September 1992, Roman having declined to stand as its candidate; in the legislative balloting the FSN was limited to third place behind the FDSN and CDR, winning 10 percent of the vote.

In May 1993 the FSN reconstituted itself as the Democratic Party–National Salvation Front (*Partidul Democrat–Frontul Salvării Naţionale*—PD-FSN), and in October 1994 it absorbed the Democratic Party of Labor (*Partidul Democrat al Muncii*—PDM). In February 1996 Roman accepted nomination as the PD-FSN candidate in the November presidential election, proclaiming his intention to stand on a social-democratic platform. For the accompanying legislative balloting the PD-FSN not only entered into the Social Democratic Union (USD) with the PSDR, but also sought to rally other proreform groupings under its banner. These efforts yielded third place for Roman in the presidential contest, while the PD-FSN won 43 Chamber and 22 Senate seats in the legislative balloting.

As part of the Ciorbea government the PD, which had dropped the FSN designation, frequently tussled with the PNŢCD (below), particularly over the forced resignation in early 1998 of PD Minister of Transport Traian Băsescu, who had called for more rapid economic reform. The PD briefly withdrew from the cabinet until adoption of a revised coalition protocol, and it remained at the center of governmental turmoil until Ciorbea's resignation in March 1998. The PD subsequently supported both the Vasile and Isărescu administrations, with Petre Roman becoming foreign minister in the latter. Controversy again arose when the PD minister of defense, Victor BABIUC, left the party in March 2000, Roman accusing the National Liberal Party (PLN) of encouraging his departure. Babiuc resigned from the cabinet two days later and in May joined the PNL.

At the November 2000 election the PD finished third, declining to 31 seats in the Chamber of Deputies and 13 in the Senate, and then moved into the opposition when the new Parliament convened. Among the successful senatorial candidates on the PD list was former prime minister Radu Vasile, who, having been expelled from the PNŢCD in early 2000, accepted an invitation to bring his supporters into Cornel BRAHAS's Party of the Romanian Right (*Partidul Dreapta Românesca*—PDR). After overcoming a court challenge from opponents within the PDR, the expanded party then reregistered un-

der Vasile's chairship as the **Romanian People's Party** (*Partidul Popular din România*—PPDR), which espoused authoritarianism, opposed multiculturalism, and described suspicion of foreigners as "a natural instinct." Having had little success at the June local elections, the far-right PPDR chose not to offer its own candidates at the general election in November.

Roman, who had finished the 2000 presidential race in sixth place with 3.0 percent of the vote, subsequently proposed establishing a center-right "Alternative 2004" of the PD, the Alliance for Romania (ApR), and the National Alliance (PUNR-PRN). However, at an extraordinary national convention the following May, he was replaced as chair by Traian Băsescu, recently elected as mayor of Bucharest. (In 2003 Roman formed a new party; see PFDR, below).

Between June and September 2001 the PD absorbed the National Alliance, formation of which had been announced in late July 2000 by the Romanian National Unity Party (PUNR, below) and the Romanian National Party (*Partidul Naţional Român*—PNR). At the November 2000 election the grouping—formally on the ballot as the National Alliance Party (*Partidul Alianţa Naţională* [PUNR-PNR])—won only 1.4 percent of the vote in each house, and in February 2001 the former PUNR leadership indicated their intention to reregister their organization as a separate entity.

The PNR had been founded in March 1998 by the merger of the New Romania Party (*Partidul "Noua Românie"*—PNR) of Ovidiu TRAZNEA and the Agrarian Democratic Party of Romania (*Partidul Democrat Agrar din România*—PDAR) of Mihai BERCA, with the Christian Liberal Party (*Partidul Liberal Creştin*—PLC) joining soon after. The PDAR, an agricultural workers' party launched in 1990 on a nationalist platform, later served as a governing partner of the PDSR, but it withdrew from the alliance in April 1994 in protest over a bill introducing an IMF-mandated land tax. For the 1996 presidential election the PDAR initially nominated Ion COJA, a literature professor and prominent anti-Semite who had temporarily broken with the PUNR. However, the PDAR ultimately joined the Humanist Party (PUR) and the Ecologist Movement (MER) in the unsuccessful National Union of the Center (UNC) alliance, which backed Ion Pop de POPA as its presidential candidate.

In September 1999 Viorel CATARAMĂ resigned as PNR chair, ostensibly to distance the party from a failed company that he had led. His interim replacement, Virgil MĂGUREANU, a former director of the Romanian intelligence service, was elected chair in February 2000. Cataramă ultimately joined the ApR (which merged with the PNL in 2002), while Măgureanu led the PNR into the National Alliance, and then the Alliance, minus the PUNR, into the PD.

Traian Băsescu, then mayor of Bucharest and chair of the PD, became the ADA's successful presidential candidate in 2004. He was succeeded as PD chair by Emil Boc, who in 2005 convinced the delegates at a PD national convention to adopt a platform favoring promarket economic policies, a shift to the center from its former left-leaning doctrine. Boc also launched discussions with other centrist parties regarding possible unification.

Leaders: Emil BOC (Chair), Adrean VIDEANU (Executive Chair), Vasile BLAGA (General Secretary).

Conservative Party (*Partidul Conservator—* PC). The PC is a successor to the Humanist Party of Romania (*Partidul Umanist din România—*PUR), which had been formed in the early 1990s and had subsequently called for adoption of a "third way" that rejected both doctrinaire socialism and "market fundamentalism." The PUR allied with the PSD in 2000 as part of the Social Democratic Pole (see PSD, below, for details). As a result, it subsequently gained legislative seats and representation in the PSD-led cabinet.

For the 2004 legislative elections, the PUR again presented joint lists with the PSD through the Na-

tional Union (*Uniunea Naţională—*UN). However, following that balloting, the PUR deserted the PSD and the UN to join the new government led by the ADA.

In May 2005 the PUR's national convention voted to adopt the PC rubric, although leaders stated that the change did not indicate a revision of what they now declared to be the party's longstanding devotion to conservative doctrine.

Gheorghe COPOS, a state minister (vice prime minister) in the ADA-led coalition government, resigned his cabinet post in June 2006 following his reported indictment on tax evasion charges.

Leaders: Dan VOICULESCU (Chair), Bogdan PASCU (Parliamentary Leader).

Hungarian Democratic Union of Romania (*Uniunea Democrată a Maghiarilor din România—*UDMR/*Româniai Magyar Demokrata Szövetség—*RMDSz). Representing Romania's Hungarian minority, the newly organized UDMR placed second in the legislative poll of May 1990, winning 29 Chamber and 12 Senate seats, despite a mere 7.2 percent vote share; it slipped to fifth in 1992 (with a slightly increased vote share), winning 27 Chamber and 12 Senate seats.

Following the resignation of Géza DOMOKOS as UDMR president, the moderate Béla Marko was elected to the post in January 1993 after protestant bishop Lászlo TÖKÉS, a radical, had withdrawn his candidacy to accept appointment as honorary president. In mid-1995 the UDMR was rebuffed in efforts to establish political cooperation with other opposition parties, who claimed that it had become a party of extreme nationalism, favoring immediate local and regional autonomy for the Hungarian community. However, after the UDMR had won 25 Chamber and 11 Senate seats in November 1996, it was accepted as a member of the CDR-led coalition government.

The UDMR's role in the coalition was frequently strained in subsequent years over Hungarian-language and minority education issues. The organization nevertheless remained part of the successor administrations of Radu Vasile and Mugur

Isărescu. At the election of November 2000 it won 27 seats in the Chamber and 12 in the Senate, while its presidential candidate, György FRUNDA, finished fifth, with 6.2 percent of the national vote. In late December the party extended its external support to the PDSR-led minority government of Prime Minister Năstase, which had indicated it would quickly move forward on legislation designed to permit wider use of ethnic languages in localities and to resolve the status of property confiscated during the Communist era.

In 2003 the UDMR suffered a potential serious setback when several dissident groups announced their "independence" to protest what they considered the "betrayal" of party principles through continued association with the PSD. Among other things, the UDMR rebels accused party leaders of ignoring the grievances of the Hungarian community for the sake of personal gain. Bishop Tökés resigned as the UDMR's honorary president at the 2003 party congress and announced the formation of the Self-Administration of the Hungarian Community from Transylvania (*Autoadminis-trarea Comunităţii Maghiare din Transilvania—*ACMT), to function as an "ad-hoc parliament" within the UDMR. Another formation calling itself the Reformist Bloc (*Blocul Reformist—*BR) also was launched at the congress under the leadership of Timis Toro TIBOR. In addition, following the congress, yet another splinter group (the Hungarian Civic Union [*Uniunea Civică Maghiară—*UCM]) was formed by UDMR members. However, the UCM was not permitted to contest subsequent local elections because the electoral commission ruled it was not an officially recognized party.

The UDMR's decision to join the ADA-led coalition in December 2004 was considered crucial to the establishment of a legislative majority for the cabinet.

Leaders: Béla MARKO (Chair and 2004 presidential candidate), Árpád Francisc MÁRTON (Vice President and Leader in the Chamber of Deputies), Attila VERESTÓY (Vice President and Leader in the Senate).

Opposition Parties

Social Democratic Party (*Partidul Social Democrat—*PSD). The PSD was formally established on June 6, 2001, by merger of the Social Democracy Party of Romania (*Partidul Democraţiei Sociale din România—*PDSR) and the much smaller Romanian Social Democratic Party (*Partidul Social Democrat Român—*PSDR). The two had envisaged their eventual merger in a September 2000 electoral agreement establishing the three-party **Social Democratic Pole of Romania** (*Polul Democrat-Social din România—*PDSR) in partnership with the Humanist Party of Romania (now the PC, see above).

The PDSR had been formed as the "presidential" party on July 10, 1993, by renaming of the Democratic National Salvation Front (FDSN) and its absorption of the Romanian Socialist Democratic Party (*Partidul Socialist Democrat Român—*PSDR), the Cooperative Party (*Partidul Cooperatist—*PC), and the Republican Party (*Partidul Republican—*PR). Less reform-oriented than their colleagues, a number of pro-Iliescu Chamber deputies, styling themselves National Salvation Front–22 December (the date of Ceauşescu's overthrow in 1989), had withdrawn from the parent group in March 1992 and registered as the FDSN in April. The new formation won a plurality of seats in both houses of Parliament in the September 1992 balloting and secured the reelection of Iliescu at the second-round presidential poll of October 11. The Socialist Democrats were a leftist formation that had once been closely allied with the FSN. Their original chair, Marian CÎRCIUMARU, was expelled in August 1990 for a variety of misdeeds. A centrist party favoring free enterprise, the PR was formed in 1991 by merger of an existing Republican Party and the Social Liberal Party–20 May.

Having previously headed a minority government, the PDSR in August 1994 drew the right-wing PUNR (below) into a coalition that continued to attract external support from the Greater Romania Party (PRM) and the Socialist Labor Party (PSM). However, increasing strains resulted in all three withdrawing their support from the government between October 1995 and September 1996, after which the PDSR was technically reduced to minority status in the Chamber of Deputies. Hitherto identified as a nonparty technocrat, Prime Minister Nicolae Văcăroiu announced his adhesion to the PDSR in May 1996. In local elections the following month the PDSR saw its support decline, with former tennis champion Ilie NĂSTASE failing in a bid for the Bucharest mayoralty.

In the November 1996 balloting, Iliescu suffered a second-round defeat in his presidential reelection bid, while the PDSR fell to second place in the legislature (with 21.5 percent of the lower house vote) and went into opposition, whereupon Iliescu assumed the formal party leadership. As the party attempted to regroup in 1997, tensions emerged among the leadership. At the PDSR national conference in June reformers led by former foreign minister Teodor Meleşcanu criticized Iliescu for failing to dissociate the party from corrupt elements. After the conference Meleşcanu and others resigned from the PDSR and formed the Alliance for Romania (ApR; see PNL, above). In June 1999, however, the party agreed to absorb a PUNR splinter, the Alliance for Romanians' Unity Party (PAUR; see PUNR, below).

The left-of-center PSDR descended from the historic party founded in 1893 but was forced to merge with the Communist Party in 1948. Following its reforming in late 1989, several competing groups claimed the inheritance, a court subsequently awarding the PSDR designation to the main faction, which had Socialist International recognition. Standing on the Democratic Convention of Romania (CDR) ticket in the 1992 balloting, the PSDR won 10 Chamber seats and 1 in the Senate. While maintaining its links with some CDR parties for the November 1996 elections, the PSDR established a formal electoral alliance, the Social Democratic Union (*Uniunea Social Democrată—USD*), with the Democratic Party–National Salvation Front (see PD, above), winning 10 of the USD's 53 Chamber seats and 1 of its 23 Senate seats. The USD subsequently agreed to join Victor Ciorbea's CDR-led coalition government.

In July 2000 the PSDR approved a merger with the Socialist Party (*Partidul Socialist—PS*), led by unsuccessful 1996 presidential candidate Tudor MOHORA, while on September 7 it not only agreed to an alliance with the opposition PDSR for the November elections, but to join the PDSR, after the elections, in forming the PSD. Accordingly, on September 8 it formally withdrew from the governing coalition. The agreement with the PDSR prompted longtime party leader Sergiu CUNESCU to resign, asserting that the PSDR had committed "self-enslavery" to an organization that was guilty of "confiscating the revolution" after 1990.

The Social Democratic Pole's 2000 presidential candidate, Ion Iliescu, finished first in the November 26 presidential contest, with 36.5 percent of the vote, and then defeated the Greater Romania Party's Vadim Tudor in the runoff on December 10, taking a 66.8 percent vote share. In the November legislative contests the alliance won 36.6 percent of the vote in the Chamber of Deputies, for a plurality of 155 seats, and 37.0 percent in the Senate, for a plurality of 65 seats. The minority government installed under Adrian Năstase on December 28 included one minister from the PSDR and one from the PUR.

An extraordinary PDSR party conference held in January 2001 unanimously elected Prime Minister Năstase as chair, President Iliescu having resigned in accordance with a constitutional dictate. Upon formation of the PSD, Năstase remained chair.

In November 2001 the Party of Moldovans (*Partidul Moldovenilor—PM*) merged into the PSD. The PM had been organized by the mayor of Iaşi, Constantin SIMIRAD, as a vehicle for forging closer ties between Moldova and Romania. Despite discussions with the PNL in early 2000, the PM had chosen to join the CDR 2000 for the general election in November. In 2003 the PSD absorbed the Socialist Labor Party (*Partidul Socialist al Muncii—PSM*) and the National Revival Socialist Party (*Partidul Socialist al Renaşterii Naţionale—PSRN*).

The PSD participated in the 2004 UN alliance with the PUR, securing a plurality of legislative seats. However, the PSD was forced into opposition when the PUR and the UDMR agreed to join the ADA in a new coalition government. Adrian Năstase was narrowly defeated as the UN candidate in the 2004 presidential poll.

Leaders: Mircea GEOANĂ (Chair), Adrian NĂSTASE (Former Chair and 2004 presidential candidate), Miron MITREA (Vice Chair and General Secretary), Nicolae VĂCĂROIU (Former Prime Minister and Vice Chair), Ion ILIESCU (Former President of Romania and Leader in the Senate), Viorel HREBENCIUC (Leader in the Chamber of Deputies).

Greater Romania Party (*Partidul România Mare*—PRM). The political wing of the extreme nationalist Greater Romania movement, the PRM won a 4 percent vote share in the 1992 legislative balloting. In a speech before a congress that reelected him party chair on March 7, 1993, Corneliu Vadim Tudor praised Nicolae Ceaușescu as a Romanian patriot and portrayed his 1989 overthrow as an "armed attack" by Hungary and the former Soviet Union. From mid-1994 the PRM gave external support to the incumbent government coalition but terminated the arrangement in October 1995 amid much acrimony. Vadim Tudor was subsequently named as the PRM's candidate in the November 1996 presidential election, although by vote of the Senate in April he lost his parliamentary immunity and faced possible legal proceedings on over a dozen assorted accusations. Also in April a PRM congress adopted a "blitz strategy" to be followed if the party came to power, including the banning of the ethnic Hungarian UDMR, strict control of foreign investment, and confiscation of "illegally acquired" property.

In early September 1996 the PRM absorbed the small Romanian Party for a New Society (*Partidul Român pentru Noua Societate*—PRNS), led by Gen. Victor VOICHIȚA. It nevertheless managed only 4.5 percent of the lower house vote in the November election, for 19 Chamber and 8 Senate seats. Vadim Tudor finished fifth in the presidential race, winning 4.7 percent of the vote.

In September 1997 Vadim Tudor canceled plans for an alliance with the PDSR, saying PDSR leader Ion Iliescu's unification effort was designed to return him as head of state. In February 1998 the PRM signed a protocol with Gheorghe Funar's wing of the PUNR, which envisioned the establishment of a Great Alliance for the Resurrection of the Fatherland. The alliance's agenda included a new government and outlawing of the UDMR. Subsequently, however, Funar and his supporters were forced from the PUNR, and he eventually joined the PRM leadership.

In early 1999 Vadim Tudor publicly supported the Jiu Valley miners' strike, but he subsequently expelled the miners' leader, Miron Cozma, from the PRM for bringing the party into "disrepute." Meanwhile, the Senate suspended Vadim Tudor for his having supported the strikers.

The November 2000 elections constituted a major advance for the PRM, which saw its legislative representation jump to 84 seats in the lower house and 37 in the upper, second only to the PDSR; the party's vote share of 19.5 percent in the Chamber and 21.0 percent in the Senate was more than a fourfold increase over its 1996 results. In the presidential race, Vadim Tudor won 28.3 percent of the first-round vote and advanced to a runoff against the PDSR's Iliescu, who, with support from all the other leading parties, prevailed two-to-one over the PRM leader. In the following two years the party lost more than a dozen Chamber deputies as well as other defectors dissatisfied with Vadim Tudor's authoritarian leadership and the party's far-right rhetoric. Principal benefactors were the joint PSD-PUR parliamentary faction (which picked up about a dozen seats), the new Socialist Party of National Revival, and the Romanian Socialist Party.

Prior to the 2004 elections Vadim Tudor expressed remorse for his past actions and recanted previous attacks on various minority groups. He subsequently finished third in the first round of presidential balloting in December, while the PRM secured 48 seats in the Chamber of Deputies.

In March 2005 Vadim Tudor issued a surprise announcement that he was stepping down as PRM leader in favor of Corneliu CIONTU, hitherto deputy chair. It was subsequently reported that the PRM had changed its name to the Popular Greater Romania Party (*Partidul Popular România Mare*—PPRM) and had adopted a more moderate centrist platform. However, the mercurial Vadim Tudor in June returned to the forefront and convinced the party's National Council to rescind the name change and return him to his leadership post. Ciontu was collaterally forced from the party, and he and a group of some 16 PRM deputies announced plans to form a new Popular Party.

Leaders: Corneliu VADIM TUDOR (Chair), Gheorghe FUNAR (Secretary General).

Other Parties Contesting the 2004 Legislative Elections

Romanian Socialist Party (*Partidul Socialist Român*—PSR). Founded in 1992, the small PSR (claiming status as the successor to various socialist parties dating back to 1872) became a parliamentary party in September 2002 with the adherence of two former Greater Romania deputies who had defected to the government earlier in the year. The party thereupon underwent a significant transformation, with one of the deputies, Sever MEŞCA, being elected party chair on October 21. The PSR failed to reach the required threshold for legislative representation in 2004.

Leaders: Ion CIUCA (Chair), Ilie NEACŞU, Vasile OLLEAVU (Executive Chair).

Christian and Democratic National Peasants' Party (*Partidul Naţional Ţărănesc Creştin şi Democrat*—PNŢCD). Founded in the prewar period and banned by the Communists, the National Peasants' Party under its veteran leader, Ion PUIU, refused to cooperate with the FSN because of the large number of former Communist officials within its ranks. Prior to the 1990 election, members of the "historic" PNŢ agreed to merge with a younger group of Christian Democrats as the PNŢCD, with the leadership going to Corneliu COPOSU, another party veteran, who had spent 17 years in jail during the Communist era.

The PNŢCD was one of the core components of the Democratic Convention of Romania (*Convenţia Democrată Română*—CDR), an anti-FSN alliance launched prior to the local elections of February 1992 as a successor to the eight-party Democratic Union (*Uniunea Democrată*—UD) that had been formed in 1990. By then embracing some 18 parties and organizations, the CDR ran second to the FDSN (see PDSR) in the 1992 parliamentary balloting (winning a 20 percent vote share), while its nominee, Emil Constantinescu, was runner-up to Ion Iliescu in the presidential poll. The ethnic Hungarian UDMR was also affiliated, although it presented a separate list in the 1992 election. In June 1995 the CDR rejected the UDMR's overtures for political cooperation between the two groupings, on the grounds that the UDMR had become too nationalistic.

The PNŢCD's Coposu died in November 1995 and was succeeded in January 1996 by Ion DIACONESCU, who defeated Vice President Ion RAŢIU for the post. In the November legislative balloting the promarket PNŢCD was returned as substantially the largest CDR component party, therefore providing the prime minister in the resultant CDR-led coalition government.

Constantinescu again ran for the presidency in 1996, pledging to accelerate the privatization program and encourage domestic and foreign investment in Romania's economy. His candidacy, which had been proposed by the PNŢCD, provoked some opposition within the CDR. Nevertheless, Constantinescu was a strong second in the presidential balloting in November and comfortably defeated President Iliescu in the runoff. In simultaneous legislative elections, the CDR won pluralities in both the Senate (53 seats) and the Chamber (122 seats), with vote shares of 30.7 and 30.2 percent, respectively.

At the time, the center-right CDR included the PNŢCD, the National Liberal Party (PNL), the PNL–Democratic Convention (PNL-CD), Romania's Alternative Party (PAR), the Romanian Ecologist Party (PER), and the Ecological Federation of Romania (FER). In conjunction with the UDMR and the two-party Social Democratic Union (USD), the CDR formed a majority coalition under the PNŢCD's Victor Ciorbea. The CDR remained the core of the government under his successors, Radu Vasile of the PNŢCD and then Mugur Isărescu (nonparty), but by mid-2000 the PNL was preparing to contest the upcoming presidential and legislative elections on its own. The PAR had already withdrawn, in October 1998.

In April 1998 Victor Ciorbea was succeeded as prime minister by the PNŢCD's Radu Vasile, who was in turn replaced in December 1999 by an independent, Mugur Isărescu. The party subsequently decided to support Isărescu's presidential candidacy in 2000, although several members left in August in support of the PNL candidate, former prime minister Theodor Stolojan. Now known as the CDR 2000, the alliance was formally reconstituted on August 31, 2000, under a protocol signed by the PNŢCD, the Union of Rightist Forces (UFD, successor to the PAR), and the FER. Subsequently joining were Ciorbea's new Christian Democratic National Alliance (ANCD; see below), the Traditional National Liberal Party (PNL-T), and the Party of Moldovans (PM). (The PM ultimately merged into the PSD in November 2001.)

At the November 2000 general elections the CDR 2000 was wiped out, winning barely 5 percent of the vote in each house and, as a consequence, no seats. Prime Minister Isărescu, who had received the alliance's endorsement for president, finished fourth in the contest, with 9.5 percent of the vote.

The disastrous showing of the CDR 2000 and the PNŢCD at the November 2000 election led the party's entire leadership to resign, with an interim governing board under Constantin Dudu IONESCU being elected on December 2, pending a party congress in early 2001. At the January session the party elected as chair Andrei MARGA, who defeated Ionescu on a third ballot.

In April 1999 Ciorbea had led a faction out of the PNŢCD and formed the Christian Democratic National Alliance (*Alianţa Naţională Creştin-Democrată*—ANCD). With neither party having won parliamentary seats in November 2000, the ANCD rejoined the parent organization in March 2001. The reunification rapidly led to yet another fissure, however, with Marga resigning as chair and being replaced by Ciorbea in early July. The opposing factions subsequently held competing extraordinary congresses, with Ciorbea being confirmed as chair by the first, on August 14. The forces loyal to Marga held their congress August 17–19 and then, on October 20, established the Popular Christian Party (PPC).

Following a poor showing by the PNŢCD in the mid-2004 local elections, Ciorbea relinquished the party leadership to Gheorghe Ciuhandu, who had just been elected mayor of Timişoara. After another dismal performance in the December 2004 legislative poll (1.85 percent of the vote in the balloting for the Chamber of Deputies), the PNŢCD announced that it would merge with the small Union for Romanian Revival (*Uniunea pentro Renaşterea României*—URR) to form a new **Christian Democrat People's Party** (*Partidul Popular Creştin Democrat*—PPCD) that would espouse a centrist platform. (The URR had been formed in December 2000 following the first round of presidential elections by supporters of Emil Constantinescu.) In 2005 it was reported that the PPCD was soliciting consolidation with other centrist parties.

Leaders: Gheorghe CIUHANDU (Chair), Serban BUBCNEK (First Vice Chair).

Romanian National Unity Party (*Partidul Unităţii Naţionale Române*—PUNR). The PUNR was organized in 1990 as the political arm of the Romanian nationalist Romanian Hearth (*Vatra Românească*). It ran fifth in the 1992 parliamentary balloting on a hard-right ticket, securing 30 Chamber and 14 Senate seats on an 8 percent vote share, and was eventually co-opted into the government coalition in August 1994. Serious coalition tensions developed in mid-1995 when the PUNR demanded to be allocated the foreign affairs portfolio and criticized the government for making too many concessions in seeking better relations with Hungary; after PDSR spokesmen had threatened either to continue as a minority government or to call an early election, the PUNR moderated its position and remained in the coalition. The strains persisted, however, notably over the abrupt dismissal of the PUNR communications minister at the end of January 1996. This led to a major crisis in March, when the PUNR announced its withdrawal from the government, although it was later persuaded to retract. Finally, the prime minister himself initiated the dismissal of the PUNR ministers in early September, after party leader Gheorghe Funar (the mayor of Cluj-Napoca in Transylvania) had delivered a vicious personal attack on the president over what he regarded as unacceptable treaty concessions to Hungary on the minority question. Of the four PUNR ministers, Aurel NOVAC opted to resign from the party and to retain his portfolio as an independent.

Internal PUNR divisions in late 1996 were highlighted by the resignation of Valer SUIAN as secretary general in October. In the following month's elections, Funar made little impact in the presidential contest, while the PUNR's share of the lower house vote slumped to 4.4 percent. In the presidential runoff the PUNR backed Emil Constantinescu of the CDR as the "least bad" candidate. In February 1997 Funar was blamed for the PUNR's poor showing and dismissed as party leader; however, he refused to recognize the legality of his ouster and in the fall claimed the party would join the Alliance for Romania (ApR). After ignoring warnings by the party leadership to drop lawsuits against PUNR members and others, Funar was expelled in November. Subsequently, however, Funar's supporters, including a majority of the party's National Council, restored his party standing, elected him chair, and suspended party chair Valeriu TABĂRĂ. The Tabără faction, which appeared to include most of the party's members of Parliament and 40 of 42 county chairs, said the insurgents' actions were illegal, a position subsequently upheld by a Bucharest municipal court in March 1998. Funar then launched his own party, the Alliance for Romanians' Unity Party (*Partidul Alianţei pentru Unitatea Românilor*—PAUR), which the government refused to register, before joining the PRM. (The PAUR faction ultimately joined the PDSR.)

In October 1999 the PUNR absorbed the Reintegration Party-Dacian-Latin Option (*Partidul Reîntregirii-Opţiunea Daco-Latina*—POD), which had been formed by former Moldovan prime minister Mircea DRUC after his move to Romania.

In July 2000, looking toward the November national elections, the PUNR formed the ultimately unsuccessful National Alliance with the Romanian National Party (PNR; see PD), but in February 2001 its former leaders announced their intention to reregister the PUNR as a separate party. Valeriu Tabără once again assumed the PUNR leadership, but he was succeeded on May 11, 2002, by Gen. (Ret.) Mircea Chelaru, a former chief of the general staff who had resigned under pressure in 2001. The PUNR secured less than 1 percent of the vote in the 2004 balloting for the Senate and Chamber of Deputies.

Leaders: Gen. (Ret.) Mircea CHELARU (Chair).

Ecological Federation of Romania (*Federaţia Ecologistă din România*—FER). The FER was formed prior to the 1996 legislative election, at which it won 1 lower house seat as a component of the CDR. In September 1998 it approved a merger with the Ecologist Movement of Romania (*Mişcarea Ecologistă din România*—MER), which, following the collapse of communism, had been Eastern Europe's largest environmental group, with a reported membership of 60,000. The MER ran fourth in the 1990 legislative election, winning 2.6 percent of the lower house vote and 12 Chamber seats, plus 2.5 percent of the Senate vote and 1 seat. In 1992, however, the MER lost all of its representatives as the ecological movement fractured. In early August 2000 the FER agreed to join the reconstituted CDR 2000. In 2003 it was reported that the FER had participated in the launching of the new Popular Action (see below).

Leader: Ortansa CARTIANU (General Secretary).

Romanian Ecologist Party (*Partidul Ecologist Român*—PER). The PER is an ecological group with a substantially smaller membership than the MER (see FER, above), with which it cooperated in 1992. Standing in its own right as a CDR party in 1996, it won five Chamber seats and one in the Senate.

For the November 2000 parliamentary elections the PER spearheaded formation of an alliance called the **Romanian Ecologist Pole** (*Polul Ecologist din România*) that also included the smaller **Green Alternative Party–Ecologists** (*Partidul Alternativa Verde–Ecologiştii*) and the **Romanian Ecologist Convention Party** (*Partidul Convenţia Ecologistă din România*). The alliance offered a joint candidate list that polled less than 1 percent of the vote in each house. Asked before the election if he would consider an alliance with the larger FER, the PER's Otto WEBER commented that he would not merge with a party of former intelligence service "informers." In early 2003 it was reported that the three ecologist parties had merged under the PER rubric.

Leader: Corneliu PROTOPOPESCU (Chair).

Romanian Workers' Party (*Partidul Muncitoresc Român*—PMR). The PMR was launched in March 1995 by former Communists who claimed that conditions had deteriorated in Romania since the overthrow of Ceauşescu in December 1989. The party subsequently attempted to change its name to the Romanian Communist Party (PCR), but the government refused. It won under 1 percent of the vote at the 2000 general election. In January 2001 the PMR asked that Ceauşescu's remains be exhumed to clarify the circumstances of his death. In mid-2004 it was reported that the PMR had joined with the **United Socialist Party** (*Partidul Socialist Unit*—PSU) to form the **United Left Party**.

Leader: Ilie NEACŞU (Chair), Cristian NICOLAE (Vice Chair).

Roma Party (*Partida Romilor*—PR). Representing Romania's substantial Roma (Gypsy) population, the PR in March 1996 launched an electoral coalition with 11 other Roma groups with the aim of maximizing the impact of the Roma vote in the fall legislative elections. In 2000 the party won only 0.6 percent of the vote for the Chamber of Deputies but claimed one minority seat. The PR reportedly contested the 2004 legislative poll under the rubric of the **Social Democratic Roma Party of Romania** (*Partida Romilor Social Democrată din România*—PRSDR).

Leader: Nicolae PĂUN (Chair), Ivan GHEORGHE.

Popular Action (*Acţiunea Populară*—AP). The AP was formed in mid-2003 by supporters of former president Emil Constantinescu, who was named chair of the new party even though he had announced his retirement from politics following his 2000 presidential defeat. The AP absorbed the Popular Christian Party (*Partidul Popular Creştin*—PPC), which had been formed by the Marga faction of the PNŢCD in 2001. (Andrei Marga, for whom the faction was named, subsequently joined the PNL.)

Leader: Emil CONSTANTINESCU (Chair and Former President of Romania).

Democratic Front of Romania Party (*Partidul Frontul Democrat din România*—PFDR). The PFDR was formed in 2003 by Petre Roman, former prime minister and former chair of the PD. Roman won 1.35 percent of the vote in the first round of the December 2004 presidential balloting.

Leader: Petre ROMAN.

New Generation Party (*Partidul Noua Generaţie*—PNG). The PNG was launched in 2000 under the leadership of Virel LIS, the former mayor of Bucharest. However, Lis subsequently left the party, and the leadership mantle eventually passed to George Becali, the owner of a prominent soccer club. Campaigning on a center-right platform, Becali secured 1.8 percent of the vote in the first round of the December 2004 presidential balloting. In April 2006 it was reported that the party had changed its name to the New Generation Party–Christian Democrat (*PNG–Creştin Democrat*—PNG-CD).

Leader: George BECALI.

Other parties participating in the 2004 legislative balloting included the **Christian Democratic National Party** (*Partidul Naţional Creştin Democrat*—PNCD), the **National Peasant Party** (*Partidul Naţional Ţărănesc*—PNT), the **National Reconciliation Party** (*Partidul Reconcilierii Naţional*—PRN), the **Romanian Party of Pensioners** (*Partidul Pensionarilor din România*—PPR), and the **United Socialist Party** (*Partidul Socialist Unit*).

Cabinet

As of September 1, 2006

Prime Minister	Călin Popescu-Tăriceanu (PNL)

State Ministers

Coordination of Activities Related to Business Environment and Small- to Medium-Sized Companies	Bogdan Pascu (PC)
Coordination of Activities Related to Culture, Education, and European Integration	Béla Markó (UDMR)
Coordination of Economic Activities	(Vacant)

Ministers

Administration and Interior	Vasile Blaga (PD)
Agriculture, Forestry, and Rural Development	Gheorghe Flutur (PNL)
Communications and Information Technology	Zsolt Nagy (UDMR)
Culture and Religious Affairs	Adrian Iorgulescu (PNL)
Economy and Commerce	Ioan-Condruţ Şerbeş (PC)
Education and Research	Michail Hărdău (PD)
European Integration	Anca Daniela Boagice (PD)
Foreign Affairs	Mihai-Răzvan Ungureanu (PNL)
Health	Eugen Nicolăescu (PNL)
Justice	Monica Luisa Macovei (ind.) [f]
Labor, Social Solidarity, and Family	Gheorghe Barbu (PD)
National Defense	Teodor Atanasiu (PNL)
Public Finance	Sebastian Vlădescu (PNL)
Transport, Construction, and Tourism	Radu Mircea Berceanu (PD)
Water and Environmental Protection	Sulfina Barbu (PD) [f]

Ministers Delegate

Commerce	Iuliu Winkler (UDMR)
Control of Internationally Financed Programs	Cristian David (PNL)
Coordination of Cabinet's General Secretariat	Radu Stroe (PNL)
Public Works and Territory Management	Laszlo Borbely (UDMR)
Relations with Parliament	Mihai Alexandru Voicu (PNL)

[f] = female

Legislature

The present Romanian legislature is a bicameral **Parliament** (*Parlament*) consisting of a Senate and a Chamber of Deputies, each with a four-year term. Election is by proportional representation on party lists. Individual parties must meet a 5 percent threshold to claim seats. For two-party alliances the threshold is 8 percent, with 1 percent being added for each additional group, up to a maximum of 10 percent.

Senate (*Senat*). The upper house is currently a 137-member body, distributed after the election of November 28, 2004, as follows: The National Union coalition of the Social Democratic Party (PSD) and the Humanist Party of Romania (PUR), 57 (PSD, 46; PUR, 11); the Justice and Truth Alliance, 49 (National Liberal Party, 28; the Democratic Party, 21); the Greater Romania Party, 21; and the Hungarian Democratic Union of Romania, 10.

Chair: Nicolae VĂCĂROIU.

Chamber of Deputies (*Camera Deputaților*). The lower house currently encompasses 332 seats, 314 filled by election and 18 allocated to minority formations that failed to meet the threshold. Following the general election of November 28, 2004, the elected seats were distributed as follows: the National Union coalition of the Social Democratic Party (PSD) and the Humanist Party of Romania (PUR), 132 (PSD, 113; PUR, 19); the Justice and Truth Alliance, 112 (National Liberal Party, 64; the Democratic Party, 48); the Greater Romania Party, 48; and the Hungarian Democratic Union of Romania, 22. Organizations representing the following ethnic communities also hold individual seats: Albanians, Armenians, Bulgarians, Croats, Czechs and Slovaks, Germans, Greeks, Gypsies (Roma), Italians, Jews, Lipovenian Russians, Poles, Ruthenians, Serbs, Slav Macedonians, Turko-Muslim Tatars, Turks, and Ukrainians.

Chair: Daniel OLTEANU.

Communications

Following the overthrow of Nicolae Ceaușescu in 1989, there was a rapid expansion in the number of mainstream news outlets as well as those devoted to "tabloid" journalism. As a whole, the Romanian media has been criticized for being too heavily influenced by political bias.

Press

In 2002 there were more than 106 dailies and nearly 1,800 periodicals, although some of them have since closed due to a lack of readership and/or advertisers. *Monitorul Oficial* (the Official Monitor) is the government newspaper; it publishes laws and other formal documents that are integral to the legislative process. The leading Romanian-language newspapers published in Bucharest include *Libertatea* (Freedom, 200,000); *Jurnalul Național* (National Journal, 350,000), owned by prominent politician Dan Voiculescu; *Evenimentul Zilei* (Events of the Day, 100,000), a tabloid launched in 1992 that has recently begun in-depth coverage of political news; *Adevărul* (The Truth), which replaced the former Communist Party organ *Scânteia* (The Spark) in 1990; *România Liberă* (The Free Romanian, 70,000); *Curierul Național* (The National Courier); *Cronica Român ă* (The Romanian Chronicles); *Cotidianul* (The Daily); and *Realitatea Românească* (The Romanian Reality). Newspapers published in other cities include *Realitatea* (Reality), published in Timişoara; *Ziarul de Iaşi* (The Iaşi Newspaper), published in Iaşi; *Viața Liberă* (The Free Life), published in Galați; and *Clujeanul*, published in Cluj-Napoca.

News Agencies

The official organ is the Romanian Press Agency (*Agenția de Presă Română*—Rompres). A private news service called Media Fax was launched in 1991 and is currently reportedly used by about 90 percent of the domestic news outlets. ANSA, AP, Reuters, and *Xinhua* are among the numerous foreign agencies that maintain bureaus in Bucharest.

Broadcasting and Computing

Romanian Radio and Television (*Radioteleviziunea Română*) is a state agency controlling most broadcast operations. *Radiodifuziunea Română* transmits domestic programs as well as foreign broadcasts in over a dozen languages, while *Televiziunea Română* and *Televiziunea Națională* offer domestic TV programming. Romania's first independent television station, Soti TV, was forced by financial problems to close in June 1994. Subsequently, a number of private TV stations were established, including the very successful PRO-TV, which features journalists trained in Western news operations. Government interference with Romanian Radio and Television relaxed in 1997, as promised by the Constantinescu government. There were approximately 9.0 million television receivers and 1.8 million personal computers serving 4.0 million Internet users in 2003.

Intergovernmental Representation

Ambassador to the U.S.
Dumitru Sorin DUCARU

U.S. Ambassador to Romania
Nicholas F. TAUBMAN

Permanent Representative to the UN
Mihnea MOTOC

IGO Memberships (Non-UN)
BIS, BSEC, CEI, CEUR, EBRD, Eurocontrol, Interpol, IOM, NATO, OIF, OSCE, PCA, WCO, WTO

RUSSIA

RUSSIAN FEDERATION/RUSSIA

Rossiiskaya Federatsiya/Rossiya

The Country

The world's largest country, with more than three-quarters of the former Soviet Union's land mass (though little more than half of its population), the Russian Federation stretches for more than 5,000 miles from the Baltic Sea in the west to the Pacific Ocean in the east. Its contiguous neighbors lie along an arc that encompasses Norway and Finland in the northwest; Estonia, Latvia, Lithuania, Poland, and Belarus in the west; Ukraine in the southwest; and Georgia, Azerbaijan, Kazakhstan, Mongolia, China, and North Korea in the south. Although there are upward of 100 nationalities, approximately 80 percent of the population is Russian. There are also many millions of ethnic Russians living in the "near abroad" of the other ex-Soviet republics. Women make up about 48 percent of the labor force but remain underrepresented in government. About 10 percent of the current State Duma seats are occupied by women.

Russia possesses a highly diversified and potentially productive economy, including major manufacturing centers in the northwestern, central European, and Ural mountain regions; substantial hydroelectric capacity in the Volga River basin and Siberia; and widespread reserves of oil, natural gas, coal, gold, industrial diamonds, and other minerals. At present, industry contributes about 34 percent of GDP; agriculture, 5 percent; and services, 61 percent.

A commitment to radical economic reform was the centerpiece of Russian government policy following the collapse of the Soviet Union, including price liberalization, currency convertibility, privatization, and encouragement of foreign investment. Despite progress on these fronts, the transition yielded an estimated 25 percent contraction in GDP from 1992 to 1994, with further declines of 6 percent in 1995 and 5 percent in 1996. The inflation rate soared to 1,350 percent in 1992 before being reined back to 131 percent in 1995 and to 22 percent in 1996. The near-collapse of the ruble during a currency crisis in October 1994 left its value at around 4,000 to the U.S. dollar (compared with an official one-to-one rate only five years earlier), with further depreciation taking the rate above 5,500 by late 1996. Currency reform at the end of 1997 restructured the rate to about 6 rubles to the U.S. dollar.

The economy finally saw some recovery in 1997, with GDP rising by a modest 0.4 percent and industrial production by 1.9 percent, while inflation remained manageable at 11 percent. In August 1998, however, the economy went into a tailspin as low world oil prices, a continuing East Asian financial crisis, and Russia's unmanageable debt contributed to a rapid drop in the ruble, which had lost some 70 percent of its value by the first quarter of 1999. For 1998 as a whole, GDP dropped by 4.6 percent and inflation soared to 85 percent. In late April 1999 the International Monetary Fund (IMF), which had suspended loan disbursements to Russia the previous August, agreed to provide an additional $4.5 billion to cover part of Russia's massive debt servicing over the succeeding 18 months, but observers regarded the move as merely a stopgap. For 1999, however, economic growth recovered to 5.4 percent and inflation had dropped at year's end to about 36 percent, a much better performance than initially forecast. A March 2000 report by the Organization for Economic Cooperation and Development (OECD) claimed that the quick turnaround indicated significant progress in Russia's conversion to market economics. For 2000 GDP growth registered 8.3 percent, aided by a boom in world oil prices and the increased competitiveness of the devalued ruble. Growth in 2001 dropped to a still-respectable 5.2 percent, but consumer price inflation remained high, at over 20 percent. Inflation retreated somewhat from 2002 to 2004, with growth moving upward from 4.7 percent in 2002 to 7.3 percent in 2003. In 2001 the government had set a goal of doubling the GDP in a decade—a target still within reach at the end of 2005, growth for the year having been 6.4 percent, following 7.1 percent growth in the previous year.

Government and Politics

Political Background

Russia's early national history was that of a series of small medieval fiefs which gradually united under the leadership of the grand dukes of Moscow in the 15th and 16th centuries, expanding into a vast but unstable empire that collapsed midway through World War I. Military defeat and rising social unrest resulting from that conflict led directly to the "February" Revolution of 1917, which resulted in the abdication of Tsar NICHOLAS II (March 15, 1917, by the Western calendar), and the formation of a Provisional Government whose best-remembered leader was Aleksandr F. KERENSKY. Unable to cope with the country's mounting social, political, economic, and military problems, the Provisional Government was forcibly overthrown in the "October" Revolution of November 7, 1917, by the Bolshevik wing of the Russian Social Democratic Party under Vladimir Ilyich LENIN. The new Soviet regime—so called because it based its power on the support of newly formed workers', peasants', and soldiers' councils, or "soviets"— proceeded under Lenin's guidance to proclaim a dictatorship of the proletariat; to nationalize land, means of production, banks, and railroads; and to establish on July 10, 1918, a socialist state known as the Russian Soviet Federative Socialist Republic (RSFSR). Draconian peace terms imposed by the Central Powers under the Brest-Litovsk Treaty of March 3, 1918, were invalidated by that alliance's eventual defeat in the west, but civil war between the Bolsheviks and the Whites and foreign intervention in Russia lasted until 1922. Other Soviet Republics that had meanwhile been established in the Ukraine, Byelorussia, and Transcaucasia joined with the RSFSR by treaty in 1922 to establish the Union of Soviet Socialist Republics (USSR), whose first constitution was adopted on July 6, 1923. (The Central Asian territories of Turkmenistan and Uzbekistan became constituent republics in 1925, followed by Tajikistan in 1929 and Kazakhstan and Kyrgyzstan in 1936, at which time dissolution of the Transcaucasian SSR yielded separate union status for Armenia, Azerbaijan, and Georgia. The Estonian, Latvian, Lithuanian, and Moldavian SSRs were formally proclaimed in 1940.)

Lenin's death in 1924 was followed by struggles within the leadership of the ruling Communist Party before Joseph Vissarionovich STALIN

Political Status: Formerly the Russian Soviet Federative Socialist Republic (RSFSR), a constituent republic of the Union of Soviet Socialist Republics (USSR); present official designations adopted on April 17, 1992; current constitution approved by referendum of December 12, 1993.

Area: 6,592,800 sq. mi. (17,075,400 sq. km.).

Population: 145,164,000 (2002C); 144,738,000 (2005E).

Major Urban Centers (2005E): MOSCOW (10,150,000), St. Petersburg (formerly Leningrad, 4,105,000), Novosibirsk (1,406,000), Nizhny Novgorod (formerly Gorky, 1,298,000), Yekaterinburg (formerly Sverdlovsk, 1,304,000), Samara (formerly Kuibyshev, 1,152,000), Omsk (1,143,000), Rostov-na-Donu (1,058,000), Volgograd (1,033,000), Vladivostok (587,000).

Official Languages: Russian, in addition to languages recognized by the constituent republics.

Monetary Unit: Ruble (official rate July 1, 2006: 26.85 rubles = $1US).

President: Vladimir PUTIN; nominated as prime minister on August 9, 1999, and confirmed by the State Duma on August 16; became Acting President on December 31, upon the voluntary resignation of President Boris Nikolayevich YELTSIN; inaugurated as president for a four-year term on May 7, 2000, following the March 26 presidential election; reelected on March 14, 2004, and inaugurated for a second term on May 7.

Chair of the Government (Prime Minister): Mikhail FRADKOV; nominated by the president on March 1, 2004, and approved by the Duma on March 5, succeeding Mikhail KASYANOV, who had been dismissed by the president on February 24 and replaced in an acting capacity by Viktor KHRISTENKO; submitted a pro forma resignation following the presidential inauguration of May 7, 2004, but immediately renominated and then reconfirmed on May 12.

emerged in the later 1920s as the unchallenged dictator of the party and country. There followed an era characterized by extremes: forced industrialization that began with the First Five-Year Plan in 1928; all-out collectivization in agriculture commencing 1929–1930; far-reaching political and military purges from 1936 to 1938; the conclusion in August 1939, on the eve of World War II, of a ten-year nonaggression pact with Nazi Germany; the use of Soviet military power during 1939 and 1940 to expand Soviet frontiers at the expense of Poland, Finland, Romania, and the Baltic states of Estonia, Latvia, and Lithuania; and an abrupt end of Nazi-Soviet collaboration when German forces attacked the USSR on June 22, 1941. The subsequent years of heavy fighting, which cost the USSR an estimated 20 million lives and left widespread devastation in European Russia, eliminated the military power of Germany and ultimately enabled the USSR to extend its influence into the heart of Europe.

Stalin's death on March 5, 1953, initiated a new period of political maneuvering among his succes-sors. The post of chair of the Council of Ministers, held successively by Georgy M. MALENKOV (1953–1955) and Nikolai A. BULGANIN (1955–1958), was assumed in March 1958 by Nikita S. KHRUSHCHEV, who had become first secretary of the Soviet Communist Party in September 1953. Khrushchev's denunciation of Stalin's despotism at the 20th Communist Party of the Soviet Union (CPSU) Congress in February 1956 gave impetus to a policy of "de-Stalinization" in the USSR and Eastern Europe, while emphasis in Soviet foreign policy shifted from military confrontation to "competitive coexistence," symbolized by a growing foreign aid program and by such achievements as the launching of the world's first artificial earth satellite, *Sputnik,* in 1957. Khrushchev's policies nevertheless yielded a series of sharp crises within and beyond the Communist world. An incipient liberalization movement in Hungary was crushed by Soviet armed forces in 1956, relations with Communist China deteriorated from year to year, and recurrent challenges to the West culminated in a defeat for Soviet aims in the confrontation with the

United States over Soviet missiles in Cuba in October 1962.

Khrushchev's erratic performance resulted in his dismissal in October 1964 and the substitution of collective rule, under which Leonid I. BREZHNEV became head of the CPSU and Aleksei N. KOSYGIN became chair of the Council of Ministers. In 1965 Nikolai V. PODGORNY succeeded Anastas I. MIKOYAN as chair of the Presidium of the Supreme Soviet and thereby as nominal head of state, while Brezhnev clearly emerged from the 24th Party Congress in 1971 as first among equals. His position as CPSU general secretary was reconfirmed at the 25th and 26th Congresses in 1976 and 1981. In June 1977 the Supreme Soviet designated Secretary Brezhnev to succeed Podgorny as chair of the Presidium.

In October 1980 Kosygin asked to be relieved of his duties as chair of the Council of Ministers because of declining health, and he was replaced by First Deputy Chair Nicolai TIKHONOV. Of more far-reaching consequence was the death of Brezhnev in November 1982 and his replacement as party secretary by Yuri V. ANDROPOV, who had previously served as head of the KGB, the Soviet intelligence and internal security agency. Andropov was named chair of the Presidium in June 1983 but died in February 1984. He was succeeded as CPSU general secretary and, two months later, as head of state by Konstantin Y. CHERNENKO.

Long reputed to be in failing health and widely viewed as having been elevated to the top leadership on a "caretaker" basis, Chernenko died in March 1985. As evidence that the succession had already been agreed upon, the relatively young (54) Mikhail S. GORBACHEV was named general secretary on the following day. The Presidium chairmanship remained temporarily vacant. During the ensuing four years, wide-ranging personnel changes occurred in both the party and the government. In July 1985 the longtime foreign minister, Andrei A. GROMYKO, was named to the Presidium chairmanship, while Nikolai I. RYZHKOV replaced the aging Tikhonov as chair of the Council of Ministers in September. In October 1988 Secretary Gorbachev was elected to the additional post of Presidium chair, with Gromyko moving into retirement. Two months later extensive constitutional revisions introduced a new parliamentary system, competitive elections, heightened judicial independence, and other changes in keeping with Gorbachev's policies of openness (*glasnost*), restructuring (*perestroika*), and greater democracy.

In May 1989 a new, supralegislative Congress of People's Deputies elected Gorbachev to a five-year term as chair of a restructured Supreme Soviet, with Anatoly I. LUKYANOV (vice chair of the Presidium since October) redesignated as Gorbachev's deputy. Following further constitutional amendments in December 1989 and March 1990 that sanctioned a multiparty system, increased the scope of direct elections, and broadened the rights of private property and enterprise, the Congress named Gorbachev in March 1990 to the new post of Union president. Concurrently, it elected Lukyanov chair of the Supreme Soviet.

In June 1990 the Russian Federation issued a declaration asserting the primacy of the RSFSR constitution within its territorial limits. The document also asserted a right to engage in foreign relations and "freely to leave the USSR" in accordance with procedures set forth in Union law. Earlier, on the basis of constitutional reforms approved at the Union level in 1988, the Russian Federation had emulated the central USSR administration by establishing a two-tiered legislative system consisting of a Congress of People's Deputies and a bicameral Supreme Soviet elected by the Congress. On May 29, 1990, the 1,068 Congress deputies, who had been elected in competitive balloting on March 4, elected Boris YELTSIN as chair of the RSFSR Supreme Soviet, and hence, de facto president of the Federation.

On July 20, 1990, Yeltsin announced a "500-day" drive toward a market economy within the Federation, which subsequently became the core of an all-Union plan that secured approval in weakened form three months later. In mid-November, following a meeting with USSR President Gorbachev, Yeltsin called for a central "coalition government of national unity" as a prelude to further Union negotiations.

During the fall and winter of 1990–1991 conservative forces (principally elements of the administrative and Communist Party bureaucracies, the army, the interior police, and the KGB) ranged themselves against Gorbachev's pluralist measures. For a time, the Soviet leader appeared to offer little resistance to the backlash, but a six-month lapse into authoritarianism ended dramatically in April 1991 with a much-heralded "nine-plus-one" conference, at which the participating republics (with Armenia, Georgia, Moldova, and the Baltic states not attending) endorsed a new Union Treaty that called for extensive decentralization in the social, political, and economic spheres. Under the plan, a new constitution would be drafted for a "Union of Soviet Sovereign [rather than Socialist] Republics."

At a nonbinding referendum on the draft of the Union Treaty on March 17, 1991, RSFSR voters had registered 71.3 percent approval, with 69.9 percent also endorsing the creation of a directly elective RSFSR presidency. On April 5 the republican Congress voted to create the office, and on June 12 Yeltsin defeated five other candidates, including former Soviet ministerial chair Nikolai Ryzhkov, for the presidency, with Aleksandr RUTSKOI elected vice president.

During the week of August 19, 1991, a self-proclaimed State Committee for the State of Emergency (SCSE), led by Soviet Vice President Gennadi YANAYEV, responded to Gorbachev's reforms and the new Union proposal by launching an attempted coup. With RSFSR President Yeltsin in the forefront of the opposition, the coup quickly failed and USSR President Gorbachev resumed constitutional authority. By the end of the month, however, most of the republican parties had renounced the authority of the CPSU, Ukraine had declared its independence, and Yeltsin had called upon Gorbachev to recognize the independence of Estonia, Latvia, and Lithuania.

Following Moscow's acceptance on September 6, 1991, of the withdrawal of the Baltic states, the remaining 12 republics, during a meeting at Alma-Ata (Almaty), Kazakhstan, held October 1–2, endorsed a plan for what Gorbachev now characterized as a union of "confederal democratic states." However, in a referendum on December 1 Ukrainians overwhelmingly endorsed complete independence, and one week later at Brest, Belarus, both Russia and Belarus joined Ukraine in proclaiming the demise of the Soviet Union. On December 21 Russia and 10 of its sister republics (with Georgia not participating) proclaimed the formation of the Commonwealth of Independent States (CIS—see under Intergovernmental Organizations), and four days later Gorbachev, the last president of the USSR, resigned.

Meanwhile, in mid-July 1991 the RSFSR Congress of People's Deputies had encountered an impasse over the selection of Yeltsin's successor as chair of the Russian Supreme Soviet. When no candidate managed to muster a majority in six rounds of voting, the former deputy chair, Ruslan KHASBULATOV, who had been accused of an excessively authoritarian leadership style, was named acting chair. Two months later a dispute broke out in the Supreme Soviet over an attempt by the president to augment his executive powers, and on September 27 Ivan SILAYEV resigned as chair of the Council of Ministers. In late October Khasbulatov was confirmed as Supreme Soviet chair and Yeltsin personally took over Silayev's responsibilities, while continuing to press for enhanced capacity to move forward with his economic reforms. On November 1 the added powers were approved, as was authority to suspend actions of the presidents of the autonomous republics within the RSFSR. On November 6 Yeltsin was formally invested as chair of the Council of Ministers. On the same day he issued a decree banning both the Union and the republican Communist parties and nationalizing their assets.

The abolition of most price controls and other "shock therapy" economic measures in 1992 intensified a clash between ministers and legislators, with Khasbulatov warning that the Federation could encounter "a catastrophic decline in living standards, famine [and] social upheaval." The cabinet responded by submitting its resignation on April 12, with members withdrawing en masse from the Congress of People's Deputies. In the end, after defeating a proposal by Khasbulatov that would have stripped the president of most of his powers, the deputies adopted a declaration that permitted a resumption of governmental activity, with an architect of the Yeltsin reform program, Finance Minister Yegor GAIDAR, being named acting chair of the Council of Ministers on June 15. Yeltsin's victory was, however, less than total. He failed in a bid to further augment his executive powers and was precluded from effectively moving on land reform, most notably in regard to privatization.

During the final months of 1992 Yeltsin was forced into an increasingly defensive posture on domestic policy. In October he came under particular attack from an alliance of former Communists and Russian nationalist extremists, whose newly proclaimed National Salvation Front he felt obliged to outlaw after it had indicated a readiness to seize power. Concurrently, he ordered the disbanding of the Directorate for the Supreme Bodies of Power and Government, a 5,000-man armed formation under the personal control of Chair Khasbulatov. Nevertheless, two months later Yeltsin was obliged to abandon Gaidar, his leading reform advocate, and accept as prime minister Viktor S. CHERNOMYRDIN, previously in charge of the state fuel-energy complex.

In early 1993 the contest between Yeltsin and Khasbulatov intensified, with the former campaigning for an April referendum on major provisions of a new constitution and the latter calling for early parliamentary and presidential elections in 1994. In mid-February the two agreed to the convening of an emergency Congress session to address the issue of legislative-executive relations. Although Khasbulatov subsequently abandoned an effort to forge a prior "constitutional agreement" with his rival, Yeltsin indicated that he would proceed with the referendum even, if necessary, without the legally mandated consent of the legislature. The Presidium of the Supreme Soviet responded by approving Khasbulatov's motion to seek a declaration of emergency rule and substantial curtailment of presidential power. On March 5 the Supreme Soviet voted to convene an emergency Eighth Congress, and on March 12–13 the latter

body voted to reject Yeltsin's constitutional proposals and cancel the April referendum. In an address to the Russian people a week later, Yeltsin accused the Congress of having exceeded its authority and announced the signing of a series of presidential decrees introducing a "special regime," which the Constitutional Court on March 23 declared *ultra vires* on the ground that such action could be taken only during a legally declared state of emergency.

On March 28, 1993, during an emergency Ninth Congress, a motion to dismiss Yeltsin secured a substantial majority, but not the two-thirds required for implementation; a similar motion to dismiss Khasbulatov, which required only a simple majority, also failed. The congress then proceeded to authorize an April 25 referendum at which the voters simultaneously voiced support for Yeltsin and his socioeconomic policies as well as for early legislative elections.

Two days before the referendum Yeltsin had unveiled his draft constitution, which called for a strong presidency, a bicameral legislature, and an independent judiciary. Not unexpectedly, the document was rejected on May 7, 1993, by the Supreme Soviet's Constitutional Commission, which preferred a parliament with expanded powers, including the capacity to reject government appointments. Undaunted, the president on June 5 convened a 700-member constitutional conference, which approved his draft on July 12.

Yeltsin's renewed ascendancy was demonstrated on September 16, 1993, by the reappointment of Gaidar as deputy prime minister and economics minister. Moreover, in actions that were immediately repudiated by the Constitutional Court, the president on September 21 issued a decree on constitutional reform, suspended both the Congress of People's Deputies and the Supreme Soviet, called for the election on December 11–12 of a new bicameral legislature, and announced that presidential balloting would take place on June 12, 1994. The congress, assembling in emergency session, responded by voting to impeach the president and named the conservative Rutskoi, whom Yeltsin had suspended as vice president on September 1, as his successor. Yeltsin thereupon mounted a series of measures against his legislative opponents that culminated in the House of Soviets ("White House") being sealed off by some 2,000 troops on September 27. A number of armed clashes followed, with the anti-Yeltsin leaders surrendering on the evening of October 4 after government forces had stormed the building. Overall, the fighting cost some 140 lives, while several hundred people were injured. As the power struggle drew to a close, Yeltsin announced that the December 12 elections would be augmented to include a referendum on the new constitution. However, the proposal for early presidential balloting was abandoned.

In balloting for the State Duma, the lower house of the new Federal Assembly, the proreform Russia's Choice list won a plurality of seats but was strongly challenged by both right- and left-wing opponents. At the same time, 58.4 percent of participating voters approved the new constitution. The most startling success was that of the neofascist Liberal Democratic Party of Russia (*Liberalno-Demokraticheskaya Partiya Rossii*—LDPR), led by Vladimir ZHIRINOVSKY, which secured the largest share (22.8 percent) in the party preference poll and finished second overall in the State Duma race, with 64 of 450 seats.

Events in early 1994 illustrated Yeltsin's increased political vulnerability as a result of the 1993 election. In January both Gaidar and the reformist finance minister, Boris FEDOROV, resigned after failing to secure a number of objectives, including dismissal of the hard-line Central Bank chair, Viktor GERASHCHENKO. A month later the State Duma voted to grant amnesty not only to the leaders of the October 1993 parliamentary maneuverings, but also to those involved in the August 1991 coup attempt. Yeltsin responded on April 28 by concluding a two-year Treaty on Civil Accord with 245 political and social groups. The document specified, inter alia, that controversial constitutional changes would be avoided, that there would be no early elections, that local self-government would be strengthened, and that the rights of ethnic minorities would be supported. Signatories of the document included not only arch-reformer Gaidar but also Zhirinovsky,

whereas some rightists, notably former vice president Rutskoi, denounced it as unconstitutional.

The Treaty on Civil Accord yielded a measure of political stability for the Chernomyrdin government, while steps were taken to reduce the potential for presidential/ministerial tension. At the same time, the slowdown in the pace of economic reform attracted growing criticism from Gaidar, whose party was renamed Russia's Democratic Choice (*Demokraticheskiy Vybor Rossii*—DVR) in June 1994. In October the government was jarred by a major currency crisis that halved the external value of the ruble and led, a month later, to a major reshuffle of economic portfolios.

The Russian government made some progress in 1994 in improving relations with its more fractious constituent republics, concluding accords with Tatarstan in February and with Bashkortostan in August that provided for substantial home rule. However, the self-declared "independent" Republic of Chechnya in the Caucasus proved to be obdurate. In the wake of mounting tensions Russian forces launched a full-scale invasion of the territory on December 11 with the aim of restoring central government authority. Despite fierce Chechen resistance, the Russians finally captured the capital, Grozny, on February 6, 1995, and thereafter extended their control to other population centers.

The invasion of Chechnya dominated Russian politics in the first half of 1995. The action was strongly supported by the nationalist Right but opposed by important elements of the centrist/reformist parties that had usually backed the Yeltsin administration, notably Gaidar's DVR. Ministry of Defense figures in late February 1995 put the number of dead and missing Russian soldiers at about 1,500, but independent observers estimated that some 10,000 Russians might have been killed and that Chechen civilian deaths totaled 25,000 in Grozny alone. International criticism of the action was particularly strong in the Islamic world—the Chechens being predominantly Muslims—and was heightened by Red Cross reports that Russian soldiers had massacred at least 250 civilians during an April assault on the village of Samashki in western Chechnya. Moreover, it appeared that a protracted guerrilla war was a prospect, since the self-styled Chechen "president," Gen. Dzhokhar DUDAYEV, had gone underground with a considerable military entourage. In June 1995 a band of Chechen gunmen seized a hospital in the southern Russian town of Budennovsk, holding over 1,000 people hostage for five days until securing safe passage back to Chechnya in return for the hostages' release. At least 120 people died in the crisis, including about 30 casualties when Russian forces tried unsuccessfully to storm the hospital.

The Chechen attack was perceived as humiliating for Russia and provoked a parliamentary motion of no confidence in the government, directed mainly at the three "power" ministers of defense, interior, and security—all Yeltsin supporters—rather than at Prime Minister Chernomyrdin, who had negotiated the hostages' release. On June 21 the motion was carried by 241 votes to 72, but the result was nonbinding under the constitution unless repeated within three months. With Yeltsin's announcement that several senior ministers and officials would be dismissed, a second motion at the beginning of July failed to obtain the requisite majority. Russian and Chechen negotiators eventually signed a cease-fire agreement on July 30, but general hostilities resumed in October amid continued wrangling over the future political status of Chechnya.

Party political attention from mid-1995 focused on the forthcoming legislative and presidential elections, scheduled for December 1995 and June 1996, respectively. New parties, alliances, and realignments proliferated, including the launching in May of Our Home Is Russia (*Nash Dom–Rossiya—* NDR) by Prime Minister Chernomyrdin, while several prominent figures declared their presidential candidacies, including Zhirinovsky on the far right and Gennadi ZYUGANOV of the Communist Party of the Russian Federation (*Kommunisticheskaya Partiya Rossiiskoi Federatsii—*KPRF). Despite health problems, President Yeltsin subsequently confirmed his candidacy for election to a second term.

The outcome of the State Duma election on December 17, 1995, was a significant victory for the KPRF, which won a plurality of 157 of the 450 seats with 22.3 percent of the party list vote, more than double the tally of the second-place NDR, which managed only 55 seats. In third place came the LDPR with 51 seats, while the reformist Yavlinsky-Boldyrev-Lukin Bloc (*Yabloko*), with 45 seats, was the only other list to achieve the 5 percent threshold for the allocation of proportional seats. In the constituency section, however, a total of 19 other groupings won representation.

President Yeltsin responded to the Communist/conservative electoral advance by making major government changes in January 1996. Several prominent reformers were dropped, including privatization architect Anatoly CHUBAIS as first deputy premier. Andrei KOZYREV was replaced as foreign minister by Yevgeni PRIMAKOV, hitherto chief of foreign intelligence and known to be much less pro-Western than his predecessor. These changes and a collateral slowdown in the privatization program found favor with the dominant KPRF contingent in the State Duma. However, strong condemnation of most aspects of government policy dominated in the subsequent presidential election campaign of KPRF leader Zyuganov, who particularly deplored the decimation of Russia's industrial base that had resulted from espousal of market capitalism.

Held on June 16, 1996, the first round of the presidential balloting found Yeltsin heading the field of ten candidates with 35.3 percent of the vote, but only narrowly ahead of Zyuganov, who obtained 32.0 percent. In third place, with 14.5 percent, came Gen. (Ret.) Aleksandr LEBED, the former Russian military commander in the separatist Moldovan region of Transdnestria, standing as candidate of the nationalist Congress of Russian Communities (*Kongress Russkikh Obshchin—* KRO), while Grigori YAVLINSKY (*Yabloko*) and Zhirinovsky (LDPR) trailed. Within two days of the polling Yeltsin had forged an alliance with Lebed, who was appointed secretary of the National Security Council on June 18. With Lebed's endorsement in the runoff ballot on July 3, Yeltsin won a decisive victory by a margin of 53.7 to 40.3 percent for Zyuganov. Reinaugurated on August 9, President Yeltsin immediately reappointed Chernomyrdin as prime minister, at the head of a reshaped government in which proreform elements regained some of the ground lost in the January reshuffle. In addition, Anatoly Chubais assumed the key post of presidential chief of staff, at a time of mounting concern about the president's health. On securing the Duma's approval of his reappointment, Chernomyrdin stated that the government would press ahead with the main elements of economic reform, including privatization, while giving more attention to ameliorating the negative social aspects of liberalization.

Meanwhile in Chechnya, the collapse of the cease-fire in October 1995 had been followed in January 1996 by major hostage seizures by Chechen rebels. Russian peace overtures were assisted by the death of Chechen leader Dudayev in a Russian rocket attack on April 21, following which his successor, Zelimkhan YANDARBIYEV, concluded a cease-fire agreement with President Yeltsin on May 27. The Chechnya cease-fire again broke down with Yeltsin's reelection, but efforts by the new presidential security adviser, General Lebed, yielded a new agreement on August 31 that provided for the withdrawal of Russian and rebel forces from Grozny. Following Yeltsin's dismissal of Lebed on October 17, on grounds that he had proved to be a disruptive influence, the Russian president concluded yet another peace agreement with the Chechen leadership. The November 23 accord provided for a complete Russian military withdrawal before the holding of presidential and parliamentary elections in Chechnya on January 27, 1997.

The winner in the presidential election was the most moderate of the candidates, Aslan MASKHADOV, who nevertheless continued to favor complete independence. In May Maskhadov and Yeltsin signed a peace treaty that rejected the use of force and postponed final resolution of Chechen-Russian relations to the year 2001. The situation nevertheless remained precarious as Chechen field commanders and extralegal groups continued to engage in abductions, politically motivated murders, and skirmishes with Russian troops along the Chechen frontier.

With President Yeltsin undergoing heart bypass surgery in November 1996 and spending most of the next several months in the hospital, questions about his health dominated the political scene into 1997. Attempts at impeachment by the opposition KPRF and LDPR over the health issue failed to pass constitutional muster, however, and in March Yeltsin significantly restructured the government, bringing in two noted reformers: Anatoly Chubais as a first deputy prime minister (the position from which he had been dismissed in January 1996) and the youthful governor of Nizhny Novgorod, Boris NEMTSOV. In November 1997 Chubais was dismissed as finance minister (but retained as deputy prime minister) following revelations that he had received money for his contribution to a book on privatization in Russia, a scandal widely linked to rivalry between financial conglomerates over the spoils of privatization.

Apparently determined to end infighting within the cabinet and to forge ahead with economic reform despite such adverse signs as a falling stock market and continuing wage arrears, on March 23, 1998, Yeltsin dismissed the government and named Sergei KIRIYENKO, a young reformer, as prime minister. Facing a threat of dissolution by the president after having rejected the nomination twice, the Duma finally approved Kiriyenko on April 24. His tenure proved to be short, however, as Russia's economic plight deepened, precipitated by falling oil prices on world markets and the impact of the recent East Asian financial turmoil. The crisis led on August 17 to a major devaluation of the ruble, the suspension of foreign debt payments, and the rescheduling of domestic short-term debt. Six days later, having dismissed Kiriyenko, Yeltsin nominated a former prime minister, Viktor Chernomyrdin, as his successor. However, the Duma twice rejected the nomination and Chernomyrdin withdrew his candidacy. On September 10 Yeltsin proposed in his stead a political veteran, Foreign Minister Primakov, who, with the support of the KPRF, won easy confirmation the following day.

Primakov's accomplishments included initiating an anticorruption campaign that targeted the "oligarchs," businessmen with powerful political connections who had made fortunes since the breakup of the Soviet Union, largely through the auction of state-owned enterprises in the mid-1990s. A principal target, Boris BEREZOVSKY, had close connections to Yeltsin's entourage ("the family"), and accusations surfaced that the president himself may have been involved, at least indirectly, in illegal business dealings.

On May 12, 1999, Yeltsin dismissed the government of Prime Minister Primakov, who, at the time, had been considered the front-runner to succeed Yeltsin at the expiration of the presidential term in 2000. Primakov's replacement, First Deputy Prime Minister Sergei STEPASHIN, was confirmed by the State Duma on May 19 and thus became Russia's fourth prime minister in 14 months. Among those appointed to the new cabinet over the next month was Finance Minister Mikhail KASYANOV, who had previously served as envoy to the IMF and other multilateral financial institutions.

On August 9, 1999, Yeltsin once again dismissed his prime minister, designating as Stepashin's successor Vladimir PUTIN, theretofore head of the Federal Security Service (successor to the KGB) and secretary of the Security Council. Furthermore, Yeltsin identified Putin as his preferred presidential successor. The State Duma approved Putin's appointment as prime minister on August 16 and a slightly revamped cabinet three days later.

Speaking to the legislature before the confirmation vote, Putin not only outlined his government's economic goals, but also asserted that he would restore order to the North Caucasus and Chechnya. In early February 1999 Chechnya's President Maskhadov, under pressure from opposition field commanders, had issued a decree ordering an immediate transition to Islamic law (Sharia), had curtailed the legislature's powers, and had created a commission to draft an Islamic constitution. On February 9 the field commanders set up a *Shura* (Islamic Council) and subsequently elected Shamil BASAYEV as its leader. On March 19 the instability of the entire North Caucasus region was exacerbated by a devastating bombing in Vladikavkaz, the capital of North Ossetia, which killed at least 50 and injured another 100.

In early August 1999 Chechen rebels commanded by Basayev and Jordanian-born Omar ibn al-KHATTAB invaded Dagestan, capturing several border villages and declaring an independent Islamic state. Federal and Dagestani forces began a counteroffensive and within two weeks had forced the insurgents to withdraw. On August 16 President Maskhadov declared a state of emergency in Chechnya, but the situation continued to deteriorate, culminating in late August and September with several massive bomb blasts in Moscow and elsewhere that destroyed apartment blocks and killed nearly 300. Suspicion immediately fell on Chechen terrorists. Additional incursions into Dagestan prompted tighter security measures and Russian forces renewed the push into Chechnya. By late October nearly 200,000 civilians had fled the fighting, many into neighboring Ingushetia. Emphasizing air power and artillery in an effort to minimize Russian casualties, the strong military response served to strengthen Prime Minister Putin's standing in the polls, leading to speculation that the offensive had been undertaken for political gain. The government, however, asserted that its intention was to convince the entire North Caucasus region—the Republics of Karachayevo-Cherkessia and North Ossetia as well as Chechnya, Dagestan, and Ingushetiathat Moscow would exert its full force to maintain central authority and defeat terrorism.

The December 18, 1999, election to the State Duma saw the KPRF once again claim a plurality (113 seats on a 24 percent vote share), but, more significantly, the combined success of several recently formed, increasingly pro-Putin blocs secured a working majority for the government. Two of the new electoral alliances, Unity (*Edinstvo*) and the Union of Right Forces (*Soyuz Pravyh Sil*—SPS), had been endorsed by Putin. A third, the Fatherland–All Russia bloc (*Otechestvo–Vsya Rossiya*—OVR), led by former prime minister Primakov and Moscow's mayor, Yuri LUZHKOV, found itself undercut by Putin's popularity. Most of the more than 100 representatives elected as independents soon joined progovernment parliamentary factions and deputies' groups.

With Putin's standing secured, President Yeltsin unexpectedly resigned on December 31, 1999, the prime minister thereby becoming acting president pending an election to be held within three months. Putin quickly decreed immunity from prosecution for Yeltsin, although not for "family" members. At the presidential contest of March 26, 2000, Putin garnered 52.9 percent of the vote; of the ten challengers, the KPRF's Zyuganov finished second, with 29.2 percent, and *Yabloko's* Yavlinsky, third (6 percent). Both former Prime Minister Primakov and Mayor Luzhkov of the Fatherland had declined to run in the face of Putin's certain victory. Inaugurated on May 7, Putin nominated Mikhail Kasyanov for the premiership three days later. The State Duma approved the nomination on May 17, and over the next several days approved a revamped cabinet that featured, most notably, major changes in the structure and leadership of economic ministries.

The newly inaugurated Putin wasted no time before initiating steps to consolidate Moscow's authority. On May 13, 2000, he issued a decree establishing seven federal "super-districts" to be funded by Moscow and headed by presidentially appointed envoys empowered to ensure regional compliance with federal law. The move was a clear effort to rein in Russia's 89 territorial units, many of which had exercised considerable autonomy in tax and other areas under Yeltsin. By August Putin had also succeeded in winning reform of the Federation Council, with regional governors and presidents to lose their ex officio seats by 2002, and had secured the authority to dismiss regional leaders for violating federal law (see Constitution and government, below).

Throughout his acting presidency Putin had continued his hard-nosed policies toward the Chechen rebels. Late in December 1999, with Grozny in ruins, federal forces had advanced into the city with the support of pro-Russian Chechen contingents. Heavy street fighting followed the advance, and it

was February 6, 2000, before the government could announce that Grozny had finally been taken. The remaining Chechen rebels retreated, amid heavy casualties, to the southern mountains. At the same time charges of human rights abuses by Russian troops escalated, especially in "filtration camps" established to weed out belligerents, while on April 25 the UN Commission on Human Rights voted to condemn a "disproportionate and indiscriminate use of Russian military forces." By then, pro-Russian Chechen officials were increasingly being targeted for assassination by the rebels, who also continued guerrilla assaults on Russian troops. On June 8 President Putin imposed direct rule on the region, naming Mufti Akhmed KADYROV as governor four days later.

Following the September 11, 2001, terrorist attacks on the United States, public support for Putin's policies in Chechnya appeared to stiffen. On November 18 presidential regional envoy Viktor KAZANTSEV met outside Moscow with Akhmed ZAKAYEV, a representative of President Maskhadov, but the brief talks—the first since the renewed conflict began in 1999—made no progress at resolving the underlying issues or bringing hostilities to a close. In the field, Russian forces continued to take the initiative into 2002 but without obtaining a decisive victory. In April the Chechen rebels confirmed that a leading commander, Khattab, had been killed in action.

In July 2001 Unity, All Russia, and Fatherland organized an alliance that was registered in December as Unity and Fatherland–Unified Russia (*Edinstvo i Otechestvo–Edinaya Rossiya*), and two months later the members of all three voted to dissolve as separate entities. On the right, many of the SPS participants had also merged into a single party, while on the left the continued domination of the KPRF was called into question by factional disputes as the 2003 State Duma election approached. At the December 7 balloting the Putin-supportive Unified Russia captured a majority of seats, while the KPRF lost support to a recently organized Motherland–People's Patriotic Union (*Rodina–Narodno-Patrioticheskii Soyuz*) electoral bloc. In a major setback, neither the SPS nor *Yabloko* met the 5 percent threshold for claiming proportional seats, while the LDPR doubled its representation, to 36 seats. When the State Duma convened, the Unified Russia parliamentary faction surpassed the two-thirds majority needed to approve constitutional changes.

On February 24, 2004, only three weeks before a presidential election, President Putin dismissed the Kasyanov government and on March 1 named Mikhail FRADKOV, Russia's ambassador to the EU, as prime minister. Confirmed by the legislature on March 5, Fradkov completed his streamlined cabinet on March 9. Five days later Putin, running as an independent, easily won reelection, capturing 71.3 percent of the vote against five candidates, the closest of whom, KPRF nominee Nikolai KHARITONOV, managed only 13.7 percent. Required by the constitution to resign following the May 7 presidential inauguration, Fradkov was immediately reappointed by Putin and then reconfirmed on May 12.

With regard to Chechnya, frequent suicide bombings and hostage-taking continued to command international headlines. On October 23, 2002, 41 separatists seized more than 800 hostages at a Moscow theater. An attack by Russian special forces on October 26 killed all the rebels but also resulted in the deaths of some 130 hostages, all but a few of whom fell victim to a paralyzing agent that had been dispersed to disable the Chechens. Two months later suicide bombers attacked the administrative headquarters at Grozny, killing 80 and wounding 150. From May to August 2003 suicide bombers, some of them women (dubbed "black widows" in the Russian media), included in their targets a music festival in Moscow, additional government buildings and a religious festival in Chechnya, and a military hospital in North Ossetia.

On March 23, 2003, a reported 96 percent of Chechen voters endorsed a draft constitution for a self-ruling republic with an elected legislature and president. Akhmed Kadyrov won the Chechen presidential election on October 3 with more than 80 percent of the vote, his principal rivals having withdrawn from the contest, but on May 9, 2004, he was assassinated by a land mine. Prime Minis-

ter Sergei ABRAMOV, who had been in office less than two months, became acting president. On August 29 Maj. Gen. Alu ALKHANOV, theretofore the Chechen interior minister, was elected president with 74 percent of the vote, with his principal rival, Chechen businessman Malik SAIDULLAYEV, having been denied a place on the ballot because of a technicality.

In the most tragic incident of the separatist struggle, on September 1, 2004, some 30 rebels, reportedly including several operatives linked to the al-Qaida network, invaded a school at Beslan, North Ossetia, and took 1,200 teachers, parents, and children hostage under conditions that rapidly deteriorated. Two days later, in a scene fraught with confusion, nearly 340 hostages died during a rescue mission.

Immediately afterward, President Putin moved to consolidate his authority. Legislation passed at his behest during the next six months gave him the power to appoint all of the chief executives of Russia's 89 regions and republics, tightened requirements for registration of political parties, eliminated single-mandate legislative districts beginning with the 2007 State Duma election, and raised to 7 percent the vote threshold needed for parties to claim lower house seats.

The Chechen separatists suffered a significant blow on March 8, 2005, when Aslan Maskhadov died during an operation by the Federal Security Service. Two days later the separatist Chechen State Defense Committee announced that Abdul-Khalim SADULAYEV had succeeded Maskhadov as its chair. Moscow increased its control over the Chechen republic through the parliamentary elections called for November 27, 2005, which were widely criticized for irregularities and low turnout. In those elections the pro-Moscow United Russia party was declared to have won 61 percent of the vote, giving it majorities in both upper and lower chambers. In March 2006 pro-Moscow warlord Ramzan KADYROV, leader of a private army of thousands of irregular troops and son of slain president Akhmed Kadyrov, was approved as prime minister in a unanimous vote of the People's Assembly of Chechnya, succeeding Sergei Abramov, who had resigned in February. Three months later, in mid-June, Abdul-Khalim Sadulayev was killed in a Russian police operation. The separatist foreign minister, Akhmed ZAKAYEV, was named as his replacement. Then, on July 10, Shamil BASAYEV, the Chechen separatist leader who claimed responsibility for spectacular attacks that killed hundreds of Russian civilians over the last decade, including the Beslan school massacre of 2004, died when a nearby truck carrying dynamite blew up.

Constitution and Government

Under the 1993 constitution the Federation president "determine[s] guidelines for the domestic and foreign policy of the state." Directly elected for no more than two consecutive four-year terms, he nominates the chair of government (the prime minister) as well as higher court judges; in addition, he serves as commander in chief of the armed forces, appoints and dismisses the top military commanders, and may issue decrees carrying the force of law. He may reject an initial vote of nonconfidence and upon the repassage of such a measure within three months may call for dissolution of the legislature and new elections. The current basic law makes no provision for a vice president. The president's main advisory body on security issues is the Security Council, whose powers were substantially strengthened by presidential decree in July 1996.

The bicameral Federal Assembly consists of the State Duma and, as an upper house, the Federation Council. The Duma votes on the president's nominee as government chair as well as his choices for other high positions. Legislation must first be approved by majority vote of the entire Duma; rejection by the upper house requires a two-thirds vote of the entire Duma to override. Measures vetoed by the president require approval by two-thirds of both houses. The Federation Council comprises two representatives from each of Russia's 89 territorial components—prior to 2002, the governing executive (governor or, in the case of republics, president) and the leader of the assembly. On August 7, 2000, however, President Putin signed into

law a measure stripping regional officials of their ex officio seats and of their immunity from prosecution. With full effect from January 2002, the regional executives each appoint one member to the council (with legislative concurrence), and each territorial assembly elects a legislative representative. The Federation Council's powers include review of martial law and emergency decrees.

The judicial system includes a Constitutional Court, a Supreme Court, a Supreme Arbitration Court, and lesser federal entities as determined by law. Between 2001 and 2002 Russia introduced codes permitting the sale and private ownership of land, although the sale of agricultural land to foreigners and to companies with majority foreign ownership was prohibited. In July 2002 a new "Western-style" criminal code instituted a jury system nationwide for serious offenses, required police to obtain court warrants for arrests and searches, and set a 48-hour limit on detentions.

Local self-government is conducted through referenda, elections, and other means, with appropriate "consideration for historical and other local traditions." As of mid-2005 the Federation encompassed 21 republics (*respubliki*), 6 territories (*kraia*), 49 regions (*oblasti*), the Jewish autonomous region (*avtonomnaya oblast*) of Birobijan, 10 autonomous areas (*avtonomnie okruga*), and 2 "cities of federal importance" (Moscow and St. Petersburg). By referendum, in December 2003 the Perm region and the Komi-Permyak autonomous area voted to merge, and ultimately united as Perm Krai on December 1, 2005. In April 2005 voters in two additional autonomous areas, Evenki and Taimyr, endorsed their incorporation into Krasnoyarsk Territory, effective in January 2007. Also in 2005, voters in the Kamchatka region and the Koryak autonomous area in the Russian Far Eastern district approved a referendum that will result in their merger on January 1, 2007. Then in a referendum held on April 16, 2006, the people of the Irkutsk region and the Ust-Orda Buryat autonomous area in Siberia voted in favor of merger. This merger activity has been encouraged by the central government as part of a larger plan to consolidate the federal structure to just 28 federal entities, ostensibly to streamline public administration, but apparently also as a way to diminish the political authority of the often restless ethnic areas.

By decree, on May 13, 2000, President Putin established seven overarching federal districts—Central, Far Eastern, North Caucasus (renamed Southern by decree on June 23), Northwest, Siberian, Ural, and Volga—to oversee regional compliance with federal law. Later, in conjunction with the reform of the Federation Council, Putin signed into law two other pieces of legislation intended to restructure the federal relationship, one giving the president authority to dismiss regional heads who violate federal law, and the other permitting regional executives to remove local officials for similar cause. On September 1, again by decree, President Putin established a consultative State Council of the Russian Federation, ostensibly to ensure that executives from all 89 territorial subdivisions have an institutional voice at Moscow. Chaired by the president, the State Council has a seven-member Presidium consisting of a presidentially appointed representative from each of the "super districts." Serving six-month terms, the appointees are chosen by rotation from among the leaders of Russia's constituent republics and regions. Legislation passed in 2004 brought an end to the election of regional governors and republican presidents, who are now appointed by the Federation president with the concurrence of the legislature of the particular jurisdiction.

Foreign Relations

The Russian Federation was generally accepted as successor to the Soviet Union in respect to the latter's international commitments and affiliations, including membership in the United Nations and the Conference on (later Organization for) Security and Cooperation in Europe (CSCE/OSCE). It also assumed the Soviet Union's obligations under international and bilateral treaties, such as those on arms control with the United States. In June 1992 Russia was formally admitted to membership in the International Monetary Fund (IMF) and the World Bank.

In the course of a highly productive summit at Washington held June 16–17, 1992, President Yeltsin was enthusiastically received in an address to a joint session of the U.S. Congress, and Presidents George H. W. Bush and Yeltsin concluded agreements on most-favored-nation trade status and a major extension of the Strategic Arms Reduction Treaty (START) concluded at Moscow in July 1991. Under the START II accord, each nation would be limited to 3,000–3,500 long-range weapons (down from 11,000–12,000 on the eve of START I), while all land-based multiple warhead missiles would be banned. In November 1992 the Supreme Soviet ratified the 1991 START I accord with the United States, although an exchange of ratification documents was deferred until Belarus, Kazakhstan, and Ukraine had signed the 1968 Nuclear Non-Proliferation Treaty (NPT) and agreement had been reached on the disposition of nuclear arms in their possession. (Under a protocol to START I signed at Lisbon in May 1992, the three ex-Soviet republics had agreed that Russia should be the sole nuclear power in the CIS.) By late 1993 Belarus and Kazakhstan had completed these procedures, with Ukraine acceding to the NPT in December 1994. On April 14, 2000, the State Duma, at the urging of President-Elect Vladimir Putin, ratified START II, and on April 22 approved the 1996 Comprehensive Test Ban Treaty (CTBT). On the latter day, however, the legislature also endorsed a revised military doctrine authorizing use of nuclear weapons "if the very existence of the country" were in jeopardy.

With regard to areas of the "near abroad" populated by ethnic Russian minorities, the Yeltsin administration firmly opposed the demands of right-wing nationalists that they be brought under Russian sovereignty. At the same time, it insisted that the rights of Russian minorities must be fully respected by the governments concerned. Thus, in October 1992 Yeltsin suspended the withdrawal of Russian troops from the three Baltic states, citing "profound concern over the numerous infringements of rights of the Russian-speaking population" in Latvia and Estonia, in particular. However, Western pressure and assurances on ethnic Russian rights yielded the withdrawal of Russian forces from Lithuania by August 1993 and from Estonia and Latvia a year later, subject to Russian retention of certain defense facilities for a specified period.

The rapid transformation of Russia's external relations was highlighted in June 1994 when Russia acceded in principle to NATO's Partnership for Peace (PfP) program for former Soviet-bloc and neutral European states, and also signed a new partnership and cooperation agreement with the European Union (EU). The following month President Yeltsin attended part of the G-7 summit at Naples, Italy, with confirmation that Russia would be a full participant in the "political" sessions of future summits. In May 1995 Russia signed two detailed PfP agreements with NATO but repeated its opposition to any eastward expansion of the alliance.

In September 1994 President Jiang Zemin became the first senior Chinese leader to visit Moscow since 1957. Agreements signed on September 3 resolved most bilateral border demarcation disputes and committed each never to use force against the other. Further visits to Moscow by President Jiang in May 1995 and by Premier Li Peng in June continued the rapprochement, which was consolidated by President Yeltsin's April 1996 visit to Beijing. Troop reductions on the Sino-Russian border were agreed to as part of a new "strategic partnership" for the 21st century.

Similar efforts at improving ties with Japan were long stalled due to a dispute over the four southern Kurile Islands seized by the Soviet Union at the end of World War II (see Japan: Foreign relations). In November 1997 President Yeltsin and Japanese Prime Minister Ryutaro Hashimoto pledged to sign a treaty by the year 2000 that would settle the dispute and normalize relations. The two leaders also concluded a fishing agreement covering the Kurile Islands and agreed to further economic cooperation. Following President Putin's inauguration in 2000, however, Russia adopted a less accommodating stance toward formal resolution of the insular question, and several meetings between Putin and successive Japanese prime ministers over the years have concluded without significant progress toward a peace treaty. Russia has announced it would cede two of the four southernmost islands in the extensive archipelago, but Japan insists on all four. As of mid-2006 neither a treaty nor a resolution of the insular dispute appeared likely in the near future.

The dominant foreign policy issue in 1997 was the proposed admission of former Warsaw Pact members Poland, the Czech Republic, and Hungary into an expanded NATO, despite Russian objections and its previous threat to withdraw from the 1990 Conventional Forces in Europe (CFE) treaty. Negotiations held at Moscow in May between NATO Secretary General Javier Solana and Russian Foreign Minister Yevgeni Primakov led to an accord, signed in Paris on May 27, known as the Founding Act. While Russia had sought a treaty, rather than a nonbinding accord, it accepted an agreement to strengthen the OSCE, acquiesced on the need for revisions to the CFE treaty, and received a pledge, but not a guarantee, from NATO that the Western alliance would not place nuclear weapons on the territory of any new member states. While the NATO Founding Act did not give Russia a veto over future NATO decisions, as Yeltsin had desired, a Russian-NATO joint council has afforded Russia a voice in NATO decisions. Russia also received a number of economic concessions, including enhanced status in the G-7, $4 billion in U.S. loan guarantees, and U.S. assistance in joining the Paris Club of official creditors, of which Russia became a member in September. Washington also pledged to support eventual Russian accession to the World Trade Organization (WTO), although in May 2005 the George W. Bush administration stated that it had no timeline for Russian membership.

Russia's objections to the 1990 CFE treaty rested on a desire to limit NATO deployments in the former Warsaw Pact countries. Consequently, on July 23, 1997, at Vienna 16 NATO and 14 former Warsaw Pact states agreed "in principle" on a new draft accord that set national rather than bloc limitations on conventional armed forces.

Also related to the eastward expansion of NATO, Yeltsin advocated closer linkages with CIS member states, in particular regarding economic, political, and military ties between Russia and Belarus. In

1996 the two signed a Treaty on the Formation of the Community of Sovereign Republics (CSR), and in June 1997 the legislatures of both countries ratified a Charter of the Union, which set out a plan for greater integration (see article on Belarus). On December 25, 1998, Yeltsin and Belarusan President Alyaksandr Lukashenka signed several documents on setting up an integrated monetary system and customs policies and on forming a common leadership while retaining national sovereignty. Modeled on the European Union, a formal Union Treaty was signed at Moscow on December 8, 1999, and unanimously ratified on December 22 by the upper houses of both countries. Adoption of a shared currency, the ruble, had been scheduled for 2006, but slow progress in negotiations could push this into 2007. Meanwhile, in September 2003 Kazakhstan and Ukraine joined Russia and Belarus in signing a treaty intended to create a Single Economic Space, which would include a free trade zone and greater coordination of economic policy.

Additional overtures regarding closer ties have been made toward such CIS countries as Armenia, Kazakhstan, and Kyrgyzstan. In contrast, in 2000 Russia announced its withdrawal from the 1992 Bishkek Treaty on visa-free travel among CIS members, citing threats posed by international terrorism, crime, and drug-trafficking, and adding that it preferred to regulate travel bilaterally.

In August 1992 tension between Russia and Ukraine eased in the wake of an agreement to place the former Soviet Black Sea fleet under joint command pending implementation of a June accord to divide the ships equally and jointly finance their bases. At a CIS meeting in April 1994, the two countries agreed that 15–20 percent of the fleet's 800-plus ships (including auxiliary vessels) would be retained by Ukraine, with Russia "purchasing" the remainder of Ukraine's share. Further difficulty then arose over bases for the Russian ships, but the issue was largely resolved in May 1997. Agreements concluded at that time not only permitted Russia to lease half of the Ukrainian naval base at Sevastopol for a period of 20 years, but also signified Russian recognition of Crimea and Sevastopol as Ukrainian territory.

Elsewhere in the region, Russian troops remained deployed in several areas of the "near abroad" following the disintegration of the Soviet Union, but Russian diplomacy rather than military might quickly became central to efforts at resolving various regional conflicts. Hence, Russian negotiators facilitated the cease-fire agreement between Georgia and its breakaway Abkhaz Republic in April 1994, while negotiators in the Moldova/Transdnestria confrontation called for the gradual withdrawal of Russian forces. As of mid-2006, however, definitive resolution of the Transdnestria dispute remained elusive, and Russian troops continued to be stationed there.

Russian contingents have participated in several peacekeeping missions, including a UN-sponsored force in Bosnia and Herzegovina and a CIS contingent in Tajikistan. Russian diplomats also attempted to exert their influence in the inspections dispute between Iraq and the UN and, in 1998 and 1999, in the confrontation between Yugoslavia and NATO over the Kosovo question.

Russian objections to what it considers U.S. military hegemony came to a head on March 23, 1999, when Prime Minister Primakov, who was en route to discussions with the Clinton administration and the IMF, ordered his plane back to Russia upon being informed of NATO's imminent bombing campaign against Yugoslavia. Strong ethnic ties between Russians and Yugoslavia's Serbs contributed to Moscow's pro-Belgrade stance, although former prime minister Viktor Chernomyrdin was a leading mediator during the crisis. Following conclusion in June 1999 of the NATO assault, Russian troops were successfully stationed alongside NATO-led peacekeepers in Kosovo, despite initial disagreements over deployment zones and the chain of command. The mission's success seemed to presage greater Russian cooperation with NATO, and a visit by President Clinton to Russia from June 3 to June 6, 2000, during which he addressed the Federal Assembly, produced a bilateral agreement on disposal of weapons-grade plutonium and on setting up an early-warning center—the first-ever permanent US-Russian military operation—to reduce the risk of accidental nuclear war. In July 2000 the government introduced a new foreign policy doctrine favoring pragmatism, "cooperation with NATO in the interests of security and stability on the Continent," closer ties with such important Asian countries as China and India, and "active dialogue" with the United States. Moscow and Washington continued to differ over the contemplated—but technologically questionable—U.S. limited missile defense plan, with Russian officials charging that the proposed warhead intercept system would violate the 1972 Anti-Ballistic Missile (ABM) Treaty.

The United States formally withdrew from the ABM Treaty in 2002, which provoked the expected outcry from Russia, but intervening events—especially the September 11, 2001, attacks on the United States—had made the development far less significant to U.S.-Russian relations than it might otherwise have been. In the aftermath of the September attacks President Putin was quick to assert that the Chechen rebels had ties to the al-Qaida network of Osama bin Laden, while firm Russian support for U.S. efforts to organize a broad international consensus for its "war on terrorism" apparently served to temper Washington's subsequent criticism of Moscow's Chechnya policy. Putin's intervention on behalf of the United States was also a contributing, if not a decisive, factor in the decision of the Central Asian republics to back the U.S. military campaign against al-Qaida and Afghanistan's Taliban regime.

Meeting in Moscow on May 24, 2002, Presidents Putin and George H. W. Bush signed the Treaty of Moscow (the Strategic Offensive Reductions Treaty—SORT), thereby committing their countries to reduce nuclear stockpiles by two-thirds over the next decade. (The Russian legislature ratified the SORT in May 2003; a vote had been delayed by objections to U.S. policy toward Iraq.) Other summit concerns included improved cooperation in counterterrorism and in trade relations, particularly with regard to the energy sector. On May 28 at Rome, Italy, NATO, and Russia signed the Rome Declaration establishing a NATO-Russia Council for the purpose of discussing such crucial policy matters as nonproliferation, combating terrorism, and peacekeeping. Putin had apparently already signaled that, despite strong objections, Russia would acquiesce in additional NATO expansion into the former Soviet Baltic republics, the trade-off being closer Russian-NATO cooperation in security and political matters. On May 29 a Russian-EU summit at Moscow saw the EU recognize Russia as a market economy, a designation that was echoed by the United States shortly thereafter, thereby advancing Russia's efforts to enter the WTO.

In October 2004 the legislature ratified the Kyoto Protocol on global warming, thereby enabling the protocol to enter into effect. With the United States having refused to consider ratification, a Russian rejection would have doomed the initiative. Although President Putin had earlier expressed reservations as to whether the protocol was in Russia's best interests, ratification had become central to establishing closer relations with the EU.

Current Issues

President Putin's March 2004 reelection largely mirrored his 2000 effort in that the absence of a viable opposition contender permitted him to wage a noncampaign, remaining aloof, refusing to debate other candidates, and relying on the government's overwhelming media advantage to present him in a favorable light. Putin had already demonstrated that he intended to consolidate authority in the president's office, largely at the expense of regional prerogatives, and to significantly reduce the number of competing political parties, and his easy victory cleared the way for him to pursue his agenda. The escalation of attacks against civilians by Chechen separatists—most dramatically in the school seizure at Beslan—further increased public support for Putin and permitted him to act even more quickly and forcefully.

Unified Russia has emerged as the vehicle for what Putin's supporters label "reform" (and his detractors, authoritarianism). Forged from both center-right and center-left parties, Unified Russia espouses "social conservatism"—a blend of market economics, promotion of the middle class, nationalism, and support for social order and stability.

There has, however, been tension between the party's more rightist market forces and those committed to a more "social orientation," some of whom strongly objected to a Putin initiative that replaced guaranteed social service benefits with cash payments. Some within Unified Russia have proposed that their party develop right and left wings, thereby taking advantage of the decline in support for the KPRF, the SPS, and *Yabloko,* but the leadership has rejected any such division.

President Putin's consolidation of power at the center has been interpreted by some observers as marking the ascendancy of the *"siloviki"* (roughly, "the powerful"), individuals with a background in the Soviet KGB or the present Russian security and military services, at the expense of former president Yeltsin's "family"—particularly some of the oligarchs who had amassed fortunes through the sale of state assets in the 1990s. Early targets had been Boris Berezovsky and then Vladimir GUSINSKY, owner of Russia's largest independent media conglomerate, Media-MOST, which had angered the government with its unfavorable coverage of the war in Chechnya. Ultimately, Berezovsky was granted asylum in the United Kingdom and Gusinsky, having been charged with embezzlement and then money-laundering, relocated to Israel, while Media-MOST fell under control of Gazprom, the state-owned natural gas monopoly.

The next high-profile oligarch to come under judicial scrutiny was Mikhail KHODORKOVSKY, the chief executive officer of a leading energy company, Yukos, and reputedly Russia's wealthiest individual—a title once held by Berezovsky. Although the government denied any involvement in the prosecution of Khodorkovsky for tax evasion and fraud, his supporters asserted that he had been targeted as part of a campaign to regain state control of key natural resource industries. (Khodorkovsky was rumored to have discussed the sale of Yukos with U.S.-based Exxon-Mobil.) Moreover, he had contributed funds to the SPS and *Yabloko,* thereby breaking a much-discussed-but-unconfirmed-understanding with the Kremlin that past, questionable dealings would not be prosecuted as long as the oligarchs refrained from direct involvement in opposition politics. Khodorkovsky's trial, which began in June 2004, concluded on May 31, 2005, with a guilty verdict, and he was sentenced to nine years in prison. Meanwhile, Yukos, which allegedly owed tens of billions of dollars in taxes, had seen its production subsidiary auctioned off in December 2004 in what an economic adviser to Putin labeled the "scam of the year." Sold to the only bidder, a previously unknown company, the subsidiary ultimately ended up in the hands of Gazprom. Even though the "Yukos affair" had badly damaged Russia's image among foreign investors, the Russian government seemed determined to break up the company. While the company continued to explore asset sales to pay off the existing tax claims, it was hit again in December 2005 with another $3.5 billion in new tax claims by Russian authorities. By June many experts, and even some company executives, had little hope that the Yukos would survive.

Relations with the U.S. George W. Bush administration remain relatively stable, despite Russia's opposition to the U.S.-led invasion of Iraq in March 2003. Washington, for its part, has criticized the Putin government for growing authoritarianism, but has not been particularly outspoken regarding Chechnya, while the Russian government continues to assert connections between the North Caucasus separatist movements and international terrorism, sometimes justifiably. President Putin received additional support for that view during an October 2004 visit to China, which has sought to establish similar connections to the separatist movement in its Xinjiang Uighur Autonomous Region. Meanwhile, human rights organizations have accused Russia of targeted executions and a panoply of other offenses in Chechnya, leading the Parliamentary Assembly of the Council of Europe (PACE) to threaten Russia with a war crimes tribunal should its human rights record fail to improve. As of mid-2006 the thousands of Russian military and security personnel in Chechnya continued to engage in vigorous offensive operations.

Russia has been near the center of the controversy in 2005 and 2006 over Iran's attempt to develop a nuclear power plant and the capacity to enrich uranium for weapons, in part because Russia supplied the technology to Iran and was directly involved in the construction of the Bushehr plant, and agreed in 2005 to supply nuclear fuel. Washington has repeatedly but unsuccessfully urged Russia to end its involvement. Because of its ties to the project, Russia's cooperation with Western efforts to deter Iran has been critical, and has allowed Russia to steer those efforts toward the development of a package of economic and diplomatic incentives for Iran, which was announced in June 2006, rather than imposing sanctions. As of mid-2006, acceptance of the package was still being negotiated.

In another energy-related controversy, Russia has been accused of using its energy resources to support more aggressive diplomatic relations with its European neighbors. Near the end of 2005 Russia raised the price of gas to its immediate neighbors to more closely approximate the rates paid by EU market countries, roughly doubling the cost. The lone exception, Belarus, was able to enjoy continued below-market prices, but was under pressure to cede a controlling stake of Belarusan pipeline operator Beltransgaz to Russia's state-controlled natural gas monopoly Gazprom. In a separate action in April 2006 Russian leaders threatened to divert energy supplies for Europe to other markets unless Gazprom were allowed direct access to EU markets. The threats were later moderated, but Russia continues to insist on direct access to the EU market.

Political Parties and Groups

The advent of political pluralism in the Soviet Union in 1990 and the suspension of the CPSU in August 1991 stimulated the emergence of over 200 parties, most of which did not survive in the successor Russian Federation. Some three dozen formations were active in the run-up to the December 1993 legislative elections; ten ultimately gained representation in the State Duma. Thereafter, the party scene was characterized by frequent realignments and new formations, particularly among the promarket and centrist groupings broadly supportive of the Yeltsin administration. The launching in

May 1995 of the center-right Our Home Is Russia (NDR) formation as the "government" party and concurrent moves to form a center-left opposition bloc were seen as an attempt by the political establishment to create a two-party system that would exclude from power the ultranationalists on the far right and the revived Communists on the reactionary left. However, both camps retained sizeable popular constituencies in the complex party maneuverings preceding the legislative balloting of December 17, 1995, at which more than 40 parties, movements, and alliances offered candidates.

As of January 1, 1999, the Ministry of Justice reported 141 registered political organizations, over 40 of which had sought official status during December 1998 to meet the eligibility deadline for the December 1999 legislative election. However, electoral laws permitted a political formation registered for less than a full year to contest the election if it constituted an alliance of at least two legally registered parties or movements. In the end, 26 organizations qualified for the election, including several alliances formed in 1999. Of the four most important groups active in September 2000, only the Communist Party of the Russian Federation (KPRF) predated 1998, the other three being the Putin-backed Unity, the left-centrist Fatherland, and the right-centrist Union of Right Forces (SPS).

At the beginning of 2001 there were 56 registered parties and 156 other political groups, but a law passed by both houses of the Federal Assembly in June and subsequently signed by President Putin rewrote registration requirements to the detriment of small parties. The law stipulated that to compete nationally parties must have at least 10,000 members, with no fewer than 100 members registered in each of 45 or more of the country's 89 regions and republics.

The new parties law accelerated a process of political consolidation that had begun in anticipation of its passage. In May 2001, with most of its constituent groups having agreed to a formal merger, the SPS held a congress to authorize its restructuring as a unified party. A second congress in December confirmed the decision, and it was officially registered as such in March 2002. In July 2001 Unity,

All Russia, and Fatherland had formed an alliance that was registered in December as the Unity and Fatherland–Unified Russia; its central component organizations voted to dissolve as separate entities in February 2002, by which time Unified Russia was already being referred to in some circles as the latest "party of power." Consolidations were also taking place among Russia's less significant parties.

For the State Duma election of December 2003 a total of 44 parties were eligible to present candidate lists for the proportional component. (Twenty public associations were also eligible, but only as members of electoral blocs.) In the end, 18 individual parties and 5 electoral blocs competed, with only 3 parties and 1 bloc meeting the 5 percent threshold for proportional seats: Unified Russia; the KPRF; the People's Party of the Russian Federation (NPRF), which had been established in 2001; and the Motherland–People's Patriotic Union bloc, elements of which subsequently united as the Motherland party.

Under legislation passed in December 2004 the minimum registration requirements for parties was raised to 50,000 members, with at least 500 members in each of half the country's regions and 250 in each of the rest. Furthermore, single-mandate districts have been eliminated for future State Duma elections, and the threshold for winning proportional seats was raised to 7 percent of the total national vote. In early 2005 President Putin further proposed that electoral blocs no longer be permitted to compete. Smaller parties uniformly condemned these changes, which were expected to result in no more than a handful of parties winning seats at the 2007 election. Many of the parties that had run in 2003 were already in the process of striking alliances or merging. Additionally, in May 2006 the Duma approved a bill that would strip lawmakers who switched parties of their seats, an action which would effectively eliminate this practice.

Presidential Party

Unity and Fatherland–Unified Russia (*Edinstvo i Otechestvo–Edinaya Rossiya*). In July 2001

Unity (*Edinstvo*), All Russia (*Vsya Rossiya*), and Fatherland (*Otechestvo*) organized an alliance that was registered in December as Unified Russia, with the members of all three then voting in February 2002 to dissolve as separate entities. The Unity bloc, also known as the Inter-Regional Movement "Unity" (*Mezhregionalnoye Dvizhenie "Edinstvo"—Medved* ["Bear"]), had been announced in September 1999 by nearly three dozen leaders of regions and republics (some of whom later withdrew their support) to contest the State Duma elections in December. Backed by President Yeltsin and Prime Minister Putin as a counter to the Fatherland–All Russia bloc, Unity offered no ideological platform and was described by some commentators as a "virtual party." Apparently benefiting from Putin's prosecution of the war in Chechnya and his accompanying rise in popularity, Unity finished second to the KPRF at the December 1999 federal election, winning 23 percent of the vote and 73 seats. In May 2000, with President Putin in attendance, Unity held its founding congress as a political party. On the same day former prime minister Viktor Chernomyrdin's Our Home Is Russia (*Nash Dom–Rossiya*—NDR), having won only 1.2 percent of the party list vote and eight constituency seats at the most recent State Duma election, voted to disband in favor of Unity.

Little more than a year earlier, in April 1999, the organizing committee of All Russia had met in an effort to establish in the Federal Assembly a regionalist power bloc dominated by various regional governors and presidents. Two days later it allied with the Fatherland movement, which had been founded in late 1998 by Yuri Luzhkov, the mayor of Moscow. The resultant Fatherland–All Russia (*Otechestvo–Vsya Rossiya*—OVR) won 13 percent of the party list vote and 66 seats at the December State Duma election.

In April 2001 the Unity faction in the State Duma and the Fatherland–All Russia faction announced that they would work together with the goal of forming a unified party. Within days, two additional parliamentary factions, Russia's Regions and the People's Deputies, had agreed to cooperate with them on selected issues, thereby—at least on paper—creating a 234-seat majority bloc in the State Duma.

At the December 2003 parliamentary election, the unified party, now known as Unified Russia, with President Putin's backing, was the clear victor, winning 36.6 percent of the proportional vote and a slim majority of the filled seats. More importantly, it soon attracted additional support from independents and other parties, enabling its Duma faction to chair all committees and to surpass the two-thirds threshold for making constitutional changes.

In early 2005 some commentators and party members urged that Unified Russia establish left and right wings to better reflect the diversity within the organization and to prepare for the next election cycle. In April the party leadership ruled out any such formal substructure. Party chief Boris Gryzlov noted that the party's main values remained "democracy, civil freedom, sovereignty, and law."

Unified Russia extended its political control by winning regional and local elections held on March 12, 2006. In those elections Unified Russia won 197 out of 359 seats in the eight regional legislative contests, and did well in local elections held in 60 regions across the country.

Leaders: Boris GRYZLOV (Chair of the State Duma), Vladimir PEKHTIN (Deputy Chair of the State Duma), Yuri LUZHKOV (Mayor of Moscow), Oleg MOROZOV, Mintimer SHAIMIYEV (President of Tatarstan), Sergei SHOIGU, Vyacheslav VOLODIN (Secretary of the General Council).

Other Leading Parties in the State Duma

Communist Party of the Russian Federation (*Kommunisticheskaya Partiya Rossiiskoi Federatsii*—KPRF). The KPRF is a late 1992 revival of the former Communist Party of the Soviet Union—CPSU (*Kommunisticheskaya Partiya Sovietskogo Soyuza*—KPSS), which was suspended in August 1991 and banned in November. The KPRF ran third in the legislative poll of December 1993 and thereafter generally opposed the Yeltsin administration, although in January 1995 a Communist was appointed justice minister. At the December State Duma election the KPRF won a plurality of 157 of the 450 seats, including 99 on a 22 percent share of the proportional vote.

KPRF leader Gennadi Zyuganov contested the mid-1996 presidential election on a platform deploring the erosion of Russia's industrial base by IMF-imposed policies and promising to restore economic sovereignty. He finished a close second to President Yeltsin in the first round on June 16, with 32 percent of the vote, but lost to the incumbent in the runoff on July 3, taking 40.3 percent of the vote. The KPRF then sought to consolidate the left-wing and conservative backing obtained by Zyuganov, initiating the formation in August of the opposition People's Patriotic Union of Russia (NPSR—see Patriots of Russia, below).

After having unsuccessfully attempted to forge a "For Victory" (*Za Pobedu*—ZP) electoral coalition of Communists, Agrarians, and others to contest the December 1999 State Duma balloting, the KPRF basically ran independently, with "For Victory" reduced to little more than a slogan. As in 1995, it won a plurality, taking 114 seats and a party list vote share of 24 percent. Three months later Zyuganov again finished second, with 29 percent of the vote, in the presidential contest.

In May 2002 the party's Central Committee expelled three leading members who refused to resign from leadership posts in the State Duma after the ascendant Unified Russia won committee chairs away from the KPRF. The most prominent dissenter was the chair of the Duma, Gennadi SELEZNEV, who subsequently built his patriotic Russia movement (*Rossiya*) into the Party of Russia's Rebirth (below).

At the December 2003 State Duma election the KPRF saw its support halved—to 12.6 percent of the proportional vote and a total of only 52 seats—in part because a significant fraction of the leftist vote was siphoned off by the new Motherland coalition. Sergei GLAZYEV, a former Communist who had sought an electoral alliance with the KPRF before forming the Motherland coalition, was one of several prominent leftists who had grown disenchanted with Zyuganov's continuing leadership, which led, in mid-2004, to further ruptures. In July supporters of Zyuganov and Vladimir TIKHONOV held competing congresses, with the Ministry of Justice ultimately ruling in Zyuganov's favor. Tikhonov went on to form the All-Russian Communist Party of the Future (VKPB, below). Zyuganov also lost the support of Gennadi SEMIGIN, chair of the NPSR, who was expelled from the KPRF and later formed the Patriots of Russia.

The KPRF's 2004 presidential candidate, Nikolai Kharitonov, finished second, with 13.7 percent of the vote. The KPRF has subsequently led opposition to a number of President Putin's initiatives, including changes to social benefits policies. In March 2006 the KPRF came in second in six of eight regions holding legislative elections, improving their representation in five regions. The modest improvement in these regions came in part from the fact that competing leftist party *Rodina* was excluded from the balloting in all but one of the regions. The one region in which it competed, the Altai Republic, *Rodina* came in second.

Leaders: Gennadi ZYUGANOV (KPRF), Nikolai KHARITONOV (2004 presidential candidate), Oleg KULIKOV (Secretary of Central Committee).

Liberal Democratic Party of Russia (*Liberalno-Demokraticheskaya Partiya Rossii*—LDPR). The far-right LDPR was launched at Moscow in March 1990 as an all-Union grouping. Its leader, the xenophobic Vladimir Zhirinovsky, drew over six million votes (7.8 percent) in the 1991 presidential poll. Dubbed "the Russian Mussolini," Zhirinovsky had made a number of extravagant promises, such as providing each Russian with cheap vodka and launching a campaign to reconquer Finland. The party was officially banned in August 1992 on the ground that it had falsified its membership lists; however, it was permitted to contest the 1993 legislative poll, at which it ran second to Russia's Choice overall, while heading the party list returns with 22.8 percent of the national vote.

Although Zhirinovsky signed the April 1994 Treaty on Civil Accord between President Yeltsin and over 200 political groups, his increasingly controversial utterances caused him to be shunned by the political establishment, including his own natural allies. In the December 1995 legislative balloting the LDPR slipped to 11.4 percent of the proportional vote, coming in third place with 51 seats. In the mid-1996 presidential contest, moreover, Zhirinovsky managed only fifth place in the first round, with 5.7 percent of the vote. The LDPR continued to fare poorly in regional elections in 1997.

On October 11, 1999, the Central Electoral Commission disqualified the LDPR party list from the December State Duma election because two of its top three candidates—one of whom was being investigated for money laundering—had not fully declared their assets. With the electoral deadline approaching, Zhirinovsky quickly cobbled together an alternative list, the Zhirinovsky Bloc (*Blok Zhirinovskogo*), based on the small affiliated Spiritual Revival of Russia Party (*Partiya Duhovnogo Vozrozhdeniya Rossii*—PDVR), led by his half-sister Lyubov ZHIRINOVSKAYA and Oleg FINKO, and the Russia Free Youth Union (*Rossiiskii Soyuz Svobodnoi Molodezhi*—RSSM), led by Yegor SOLOMATIN. The bloc won a 6.0 percent party list vote share and 17 seats at the election. In the March 2000 presidential contest Zhirinovsky polled 2.7 percent of the vote, for fifth place.

At the December 2003 State Duma election the LDPR finished with an unexpected 11.5 percent of the proportional vote and a total of 36 seats. This momentum did not last, however. Zhirinovsky, acknowledging President Putin's insurmountable lead going into the 2004 presidential election, chose not to run. The party's candidate, Oleg MALYSHKIN, finished fifth with 2.0 percent of the vote. The LDPR did not reach the threshold for winning seats in two of eight regions holding legislative elections in March 2006, and lost significant ground in the other six.

Leader: Vladimir ZHIRINOVSKY (Deputy Speaker of the State Duma and Chair of the Party).

Motherland (*Rodina*). Motherland began as the Party of Russian Regions (*Partiya Rossiidkikh Regionov*—PRR), which joined the Party of

National Rebirth "People's Will" (below), the Socialist United Party of Russia (Spiritual Heritage) (*Sotsialisticheskaya Edinaya Partiya Rossii [Dukhovnoe Nasledie]*—SEPR), and smaller groups in forming the **Motherland–People's Patriotic Union** (*Rodina–Narodno-Patrioticheskii Soyuz*) electoral bloc in September 2003. Appealing to the patriotic left, the Motherland bloc surprised most observers by drawing support from the Communists and winning 9.0 percent of the proportional vote and a total of 36 State Duma seats in December.

The bloc's principal organizers, Sergei GLAZYEV and Dmitri ROGOZIN, had been associated with a number of political formations since the breakup of the Soviet Union. Glazyev, an economist and coleader of the People's Patriotic Union (NPSR; see under PR, below), a leftist umbrella group, had been named cochair of the small PRR in May 2003. He was also in the leadership of the Congress of Russian Communities (*Kongress Russkikh Obshchin*—KRO), a moderately nationalist movement that dated from 1995 and had previously been led by Yuri SKOKOV and then by Rogozin. Much of the KRO's membership had followed Rogozin into the People's Party (NPRF, below) after its formation in 2001. Glazyev had also recently become the chair of the SEPR, founded in March 2002 by merger of Ivan Rybkin's Socialist Party of Russia (*Sotsialisticheskaya Partiya Rossii*—SPR) and Alexei PODBERYOZKIN's Spiritual Heritage (*Dukhovnoe Nasledie*), which dated from 1996 and 1995, respectively. For the 2003 elections Glazyev had approached the KPRF about an alliance but was turned down, leading to his involvement in forming the *Rodina* alliance with Rogozin.

Rogozin had been expected to bring the KRO into Yuri Luzhkov's Fatherland prior to the 1999 elections, but the two parted company, largely over Luzhkov's alignment with the All Russia movement, which Rogozin saw as a threat to national unity. Instead, the KRO forged an unsuccessful electoral bloc with the Yuri Boldyrev Movement, an eponymous group led by a founder of *Yabloko*. More recently, Rogozin had been serving as pres-

idential envoy for Kaliningrad as well as chair of the State Duma's International Affairs Committee. He left the People's Party in mid-2003 and was expected to join Unified Russia but instead forged the Motherland alliance with Glazyev.

Soon after the bloc's unexpected success in December 2003, their ideological differences and competing political ambitions caused a rupture between Glazyev and Rogozin. In February 2004 Rogozin engineered the renaming of the PRR as the *Rodina* party, after which Glazyev, who had decided to run against President Putin, was removed from the leadership. (Another potential presidential contender from Motherland, former Central Bank chair Viktor Gerashschenko, had not met candidacy requirements.) As an independent, Glazyev finished third, with 4.1 percent of the vote, in the March 2004 balloting. Three months later his new public-political organization, **For a Decent Life** (*Za Dostoinuyu Zhizn*—ZDZ), based on a loyal SEPR faction and various other elements of the Motherland coalition, was denied registration by the Ministry of Justice.

Rodina was barred from all but one of the elections to eight regional legislatures held on March 12, 2006, mostly on relatively minor technical matters, like giving away air fresheners during the campaign. Later in March Rogozin announced his resignation from all senior party posts but remained a member of *Rodina*.

Leaders: Aleksandr BABAKOV (Chair), Yuri JUMPS (Secretary of the Political Council).

People's Party of the Russian Federation (*Narodnaya Partiya Rossiiskoi Federatsii*—NPRF). The NPRF, which was formed from Gennadi RAIKOV's preexisting People's Deputy group in the State Duma, was registered as a party in October 2001. At the December 2003 elections it won only 1.2 percent of the proportional vote and 17 district seats. Its deputies then elected to sit in the Unified Russia parliamentary faction. Citing his duties in the Duma, Raikov stepped down as party chair in April 2004.

At a January 2005 party congress the NPRF adopted a more social-democratic platform and criticized the government's decision to replace guaranteed social service benefits with monetary payments. The party leadership later threatened to pull its deputies from the Unified Russia deputy group, but in May the majority of the NPRF's 17 deputies instead opted to join Unified Russia to ensure their inclusion on the Unified Russia party list for the 2007 Duma election. The maneuvering called into question the continuing viability of the NPRF. Earlier in 2005 a possible merger with the Social Democratic Party of Russia (SDPR, below) had been under discussion, but was not realized.

Leader: Gennadi GUDKOV (Chair).

Yabloko. *Yabloko* ("Apple")—formally, the Russian Democratic Party *"Yabloko"* (*Rossiiskaya Demokraticheskaya Partiya "Yabloko"*)— descends from the Yavlinsky-Boldyrev-Lukin Bloc, an electoral grouping formed in October 1993 by economist Grigori YAVLINSKY, scientist Yuri BOLDYREV, and former ambassador to the United States Vladimir LUKIN, who, while endorsing market reforms, opposed what they viewed as Yeltsin's "shock therapy." Having won 7.8 percent of the party list vote in the December 1993 balloting, *Yabloko* was one of the few Duma factions that refused to sign the April 1994 Civic Accord on the ground that the action was extraconstitutional. Boldyrev left the party in 1994. (In 1999 he formed an electoral bloc with the Congress of Russian Communities [KRO—see the Motherland, above].)

Yabloko finished fourth in the December 1995 legislative balloting, winning 45 seats in total on a share of 6.9 percent of the proportional vote. In the mid-1996 presidential contest Yavlinsky placed fourth in the first round, winning 7.3 percent of the vote and then giving qualified endorsement to Boris Yeltsin in the runoff balloting. Debates over the 1997 and 1998 budgets showed *Yabloko,* rather than the Communists or the nationalists, to be the most uncompromising opponent of the government's spending plans.

In August 1999, barely two weeks after being dismissed as prime minister, Sergei Stepashin joined *Yabloko.* At the 1999 State Duma elections

Yabloko won 21 seats, including 16 on a party list vote share of 5.9 percent; during the campaign it was the only major party to criticize the government's conduct of the war in Chechnya, particularly the bombing of Grozny. Yavlinsky finished third, with 5.8 percent of the vote, at the March 2000 presidential election. In April 2000 Stepashin was elected chief auditor of Russia by the State Duma.

In June 2000 *Yabloko* and the Union of Right Forces (SPS) formed a coordinating council and agreed to merge within two years, Yavlinsky commenting that both regarded the union as a "necessity to consolidate Russia's democratic and liberal forces." The merger failed to materialize, however, and at the 2003 lower house election *Yabloko,* running independently, won only 4.3 percent of the proportional vote and four seats. The poor showing of both *Yabloko* and the SPS rekindled the possibility of a merger, although Yavlinsky has had significant differences with SPS leader Anatoly Chubais. In July 2004 Yavlinsky won reelection as party head over Yuri KUZNETSOV, who had advocated an alliance with the SPS. *Yabloko* and SPS ran on a joint list for election to the Moscow legislature in December 2005, and that same month announced intentions to create a united liberal party. The two parties formed an electoral alliance for the March 2006 elections to eight regional parliaments, but failed to win any seats. In June 2006, the *Yabloko* party congress voted not to pursue the merger with the SPS.

In April 2006, the Russian Ecological Party "The Greens" (*Rossiiskaya Ekologicheskaya Partiya "Zelenye"*—REP "The Greens") agreed to merge with *Yabloko* as a result of its inability to meet more stringent membership requirements for contesting the 2007 parliamentary elections. Originally called the Constructive Ecological Movement of Russia (*Konstruktivno-Ekologicheskoye Dvizheniye Rossii*—KEDR ["Cedar"]) and later the Russian Ecological Party "KEDR," The Greens adopted its last name in February 2002. The KEDR had secured only 0.75 percent of the vote in December 1993, improving to 1.4 percent in December 1995. It joined efforts to forge a broad centrist-socialist bloc before the December 1999 elections but, in attempting to run independently, it was disqualified from the party list on a technicality when one of its top three candidates dropped out. (In April 2000 the Constitutional Court threw out the electoral law provision.) In 2003 The Greens, running independently, won only 0.4 percent of the proportional vote and no State Duma seats.

Leaders: Grigori YAVLINSKY (Chair), Alexei ARBATOV (Deputy Chair).

Party of Russia's Rebirth (*Partiya Vozrozhdeniya Rossii*—PVR). The PVR held its founding congress in September 2002 and was formally registered two months later under the leadership of Gennadi Seleznev, the chair of the State Duma. A longtime Communist, in May 2002 Seleznev had run afoul of Gennadi Zyuganov and been expelled from the KPRF when he refused to resign his chairmanship. While still a member of the KPRF he had started **Russia** (*Rossiya*) as a left-nationalist movement.

For the 2003 State Duma election the PVR forged an electoral bloc with the Russian Party of Life (below). The bloc won only 1.9 percent of the proportional vote but claimed three constituency seats.

Leader: Gennadi SELEZNEV.

Union of Right Forces (*Soyuz Pravyh Sil*—SPS). The SPS emerged as a reform-minded, pro-Western electoral coalition in July and August 1999. Initial participants were former prime minister Sergei Kiriyenko's New Force (*Novaya Zila*—NZ), a market-oriented group that dated from late 1998; Samara Governor Konstantin TITOV's federalist Voice of Russia (*Golos Rossii*—GR), a movement that was envisaged as a bloc of governors rather than as a political party upon its formation in early 1999; and Just Cause (*Pravoye Delo*—PD, also translated as Right Cause), a center-right electoral bloc formed 1998–1999 by Yegor Gaidar, Anatoly Chubais, and a number of other prominent politicians who sought to prevent the Communists from returning to power in the December 1999 election. At a unification conference on August 29 they were formally joined by Irina Khakamada's Common Cause (*Obshchee Delo*—OD), a

liberal, reformist movement that had been established in 1995 with support from a number of women's and youth groups; former deputy prime minister Boris Nemtsov's Young Russia (*Rossiya Molodaya*—RM), which had been formed in late 1998 on a platform that called for market-oriented economic reforms and an end to compulsory military service; and Gaidar's Russia's Democratic Choice (*Demokratichesky Vybor Rossii*—DVR).

The center-right DVR had been organized initially in November 1993 as Russia's Choice (VR), an outgrowth of the Bloc of Reformist Forces: "Choice of Russia" (*Blok Reformistkikh Sil: "Vybor Rossii"*—BRVR), formed five months earlier by a group of radical reformers, most prominently Gaidar and the first deputy chair of the Council of Ministers, Vladimir SHUMEIKO. Although the VR finished first in the lower house election of December 1993, Gaidar and most other radical reformers left the government in January 1994. In June 1994 the VR was formally transformed into a political party, the DVR. In March 1995 the DVR withdrew its support from President Yeltsin in protest against the Russian military action in Chechnya. The DVR, which also objected to the slow pace of economic reform, then helped launch a bloc called the United Democrats (*Obyedinennye Demokraty*—OD), but the DVR/OD won only 3.9 percent of the proportional vote and nine constituency seats at the December 1995 election.

Along with Unity, the SPS received verbal support from Prime Minister Putin going into the December 1999 Duma election, at which it won 29 seats and an 8.5 percent proportional vote share. Although the SPS Coordinating Council announced in February 2000 that it would not endorse any candidate for the upcoming presidential election, various SPS constituent organizations went their own way. Kiriyenko's group supported Acting President Putin, Lev PONOMARYEV's Democratic Russia (*Demokraticheskaya Rosiya*—DR) component of the DVR backed Konstantin Titov, and both Nemtsov and Khakamada campaigned for *Yabloko's* Grigori Yavlinsky.

The SPS established itself as a national organization at a congress on May 20, 2000, at which time it passed a resolution pledging support for "any actions taken by President Putin that do not run counter to the values of liberalism, are in the interests of a free society, and contribute to the country's economic prosperity." A future merger with *Yabloko* was announced in June but was never accomplished.

At a founding congress held May 26–27, 2001, the SPS formally reorganized as a unified party, its (at that time) nine constituent parties having agreed, in the preceding weeks, to dissolve as independent entities. Support within the nine parties was not unanimous, however, and key members of the DVR, in particular, indicated that they would leave the organization. The new party's initial cochairs were Chubais, Gaidar, Khakamada, Kiriyenko, and Nemtsov. In May 2000 Kiriyenko resigned from the party to serve as President Putin's envoy to the Volga federal district.

At the December 2003 State Duma election the SPS suffered a major defeat, winning only 4.0 percent of the proportional vote and three constituency seats. As a consequence, in January 2004 the remaining cochairs resigned, with no replacements being named. In March Khakamada ran for president against Putin without the party's endorsement, finishing fourth, with less than 4 percent of the vote; she subsequently formed Our Choice (below).

At a party congress in May 2005 the SPS chose Nikita Belykh, deputy governor of Perm Oblast, as its new chair, and Leonid Gozman, a colleague of Chubais on the board of the state electricity monopoly, United Energy Systems, as his deputy. Belykh was opposed by Ivan STARIKOV, representing the party faction most opposed to President Putin's policies. The SPS has entertained merging with *Yabloko* in recent years, going so far as supporting a joint list with *Yabloko* for the legislative elections in Moscow in December 2005 and announcing intentions to jointly create a large democratic opposition party that same month. The two parties also formed an electoral alliance for the March 2006 elections to eight regional parliaments, but failed to win any seats. As of mid-2006 a formal merger had not been realized, with the *Yabloko*

party congress in June 2006 voting not to pursue such a merger.

Leaders: Nikita BELYKH (Chair), Leonid GOZMAN (Deputy Chair), Anatoly CHUBAIS, Yegor GAIDAR, Boris NEMTSOV.

Agrarian Party of Russia (*Agrarnaya Partiya Rossii*—APR). The APR represents agro-industrial workers and managers as well as farmers. It was founded in February 1992 as the political arm of several conservative organizations that opposed land privatization, including the Agrarian Union of Russia (*Agrarnyi Soyuz Rossii*—ASR), led by Vasily STARODUBTSEV. In the December 1993 legislative elections the APR ran fourth, winning 7.7 percent of the popular vote, and subsequently aligned itself with the Communist/nationalist opposition in the new State Duma. In June 1995 the APR chair of the State Duma, Ivan RYBKIN, was named head of an electoral bloc embracing assorted regional groups of a rural character; the APR decided to remain outside the new bloc, which was later renamed the Socialist Party of Russia (see under Motherland, above).

Having won only 3.8 percent of the vote in the December 1995 legislative balloting, the APR was allocated no proportional seats but won 20 in the constituency section. The party backed the unsuccessful candidacy of KPRF leader Zyuganov in the mid-1996 presidential contest and also joined the new KPRF-led NPSR alliance in August. Fearing further electoral losses, at the March 1997 party congress the APR moved toward the center by dropping its opposition to the privatization of state-owned land.

In August 1999, 63 of the APR's 79 regional groups voted to join the Fatherland–All Russia electoral alliance for the December legislative election. Starodubtsev (at that time the governor of Tula) and State Duma faction leader Nikolai Kharitonov dissented and remained associated with the KPRF; the latter now heads the Agro-Industrial Union of Russia.

At the December 2003 State Duma election the APR won 3.6 percent of the proportional vote and two district seats. As a consequence the party's chair, Mikhail LAPSHIN, president of the Altai Republic, was unseated at the party's April 2004 congress and replaced by Vladimir Plotnikov, a deputy associated with Unified Russia. The party's 12th Congress, held in October 2004, reaffirmed the party's realignment with the majority party and President Putin's policies.

Leader: Vladimir PLOTNIKOV (Chair).

Other Parties

All-Russian Communist Party of the Future (*Vserossiiskaya Kommunisticheskaya Partiya Budushchego*—VKPB). The VKPB resulted from the July 2004 split within the KPRF over Gennadi Zyuganov's continuing leadership. When competing party congresses led the Ministry of Justice to rule in favor of Zyuganov, the KPRF dissidents formed the VKPB, which was formally registered as a party in December. (The party's initials are identical to those of Lenin's 1917 Bolshevik party.)

Leader: Vladimir TIKHONOV.

Development of Enterprise (*Razvitie Predprinimatelstva*—RP). The business-oriented RP (alternatively translated as Development of Entrepreneurship), which dates from 1998, won one constituency seat in the 2003 State Duma election but took under 0.4 percent of the proportional vote.

Leader: Ivan GRACHEV.

Eurasian Party–Union of Russian Patriots (*Evrazskaya Partiya–Soyuz Patriotov Rossii*—EP-SPR). The EP-SPR, which began as the Eurasian Party of Russia, advocates reintegration of Russia and the other former Soviet republics as a "Eurasian" power. Its leader, Pavel Borodin, has served as state secretary of the Russian-Belarusan Union.

For the 2003 State Duma election the EP-SPR formed an electoral bloc, the **Great Russia-Eurasian Union** (*Velikaya Rossiya-Evraiskii Soyuz*—VR-ES), in partnership with the **Russian Peace Party** (*Rossiiskaya Partiya Mira*—RPM), led by Iosif KOBZON and Vladimir MEDVEDEV, and the **Citizens' Party of Russia** (*Grazhdanskaya Partiya Rossii*—GPR, also translated as the Russian Civic Party), led by D. O. SEREZHETDINOV. The bloc won only 0.3 percent of the proportional vote and one constituency seat.

Leaders: Pavel BORODIN, Abdul-Vakhed NIYAZOV.

Liberal Russia (*Liberalnaya Rossiya*—LR). The LR, which had been formed with the support of the self-exiled oligarch Boris Berezovsky, was registered by the Ministry of Justice in October 2002—not coincidentally, shortly after Berezovsky's expulsion. Since the party's inception, differences had existed between Berezovsky's supporters, who were committed to uniting the anti-Putin opposition, and members committed first and foremost to a liberal ideology. As a consequence, the LR split in two, with both groups claiming the LR name.

A cochair of the anti-Berezovsky LR and vocal critic in the State Duma of the war in Chechnya, Sergei YUSHENKOV, was assassinated in April 2003. Several members of Berezovsky's LR, including cochair Mikhail KODANEV, were convicted in March 2004 of involvement in Yushenkov's murder and received prison sentences of 10–20 years.

In July 2003 Ivan Rybkin, who had previously been a leader of the Agrarian Party and then of the Socialist Party of Russia (SPR; see Motherland, above), was elected cochair of the Berezovsky party, which was not allowed to register prior to the December State Duma election. Berezovsky himself was given asylum in the United Kingdom in September 2003. Meanwhile, the officially registered, anti-Berezovsky LR joined the New Course–Automotive Russia bloc (see the RPR, below) for the election.

The leader of the officially registered LR, Viktor POKHMELKIN, resigned from the party in March 2004 to sit in the State Duma as an independent. At the time, he commented that "the Liberal Russia brand" had been so discredited that "it is indecent for a normal person to admit to having anything to do with it." Shortly before, Ivan Rybkin, alleging that he had been abducted during an otherwise unexplained absence from the campaign, announced his withdrawal from the race for the Federation presidency.

Leader: Alexei YUSHENKOV (Cochair, Official LR).

Our Choice (*Nash Vybor*). Formation of Our Choice was announced in November 2004 by Irina Khakamada, who sought to restore "liberalism with a human face" following the defeat of the SPS and *Yabloko* at the December 2003 State Duma elections. Previously associated with the Party of Economic Freedom (PES, below), the Common Cause movement, and then the SPS, Khakamada had also held various government offices involved in promoting small business and entrepreneurship. In March 2004 she ran for president as an independent, winning 3.8 percent of the vote, for fourth place. In March 2006 the creation of the **People's Democratic Union** (*Narodno-Demokraticheskii Soyuz*), a movement that united left-wing forces and pro-democracy forces beneath a single banner, was announced. It included Khakamada, former prime minister Mikhail Kasyanov, former policy council secretary for the Union of Right Forces Ivan Starikov, former Duma member Nikola Travkin, and other current and former political leaders.

Leader: Irina KHAKAMADA.

Party of Economic Freedom (*Partiya Ekonomicheskoi Svobody*—PES). The PES was organized in June 1992 by Russian entrepreneur Konstantin Borovoi, who joined with the celebrated eye surgeon Svyatoslav Fyodorov (see PST, below) in calling for an even more accelerated pace of economic reform than that advocated by the Gaidar administration. The party was disqualified from the 1993 poll for not following election rules. In the December 1995 legislative balloting, the PES obtained only 0.1 percent of the proportional vote, but its chair won a constituency seat. In December 1998 Borovoi joined in forming an "Anticommunist Front," but he lost his Duma seat in December 1999.

Leader: Konstantin BOROVOI (Chair).

Party of National Rebirth "People's Will" (*Partiya Natsionalnogo Vozrozhdeniya "Narodnaya Volya"*—PNV-NV). People's Will emerged in late 2001 from Sergei Baburin's Russian National Union (*Rossiiskii Obshenarodnyi Soyuz*—ROS). Also translated as the Russian All-People's Union, the ROS had been formed in 1990 and 1991 by fiery populist Baburin to further a nationalist agenda that subsequently called for the restoration of the Soviet Union. The ROS also advocated state ownership of land and major industries as well as strong central economic regulation. Barred from running in 1993, in 1995 it formed the core of the Power to the People (*Naroduvlastiye*) electoral bloc, which also included the Officers' Union (see under Working Russia, below), Elena SHUVALOVA's Movement of Mothers "For Social Justice" (*Dvizhenie Materei "Za Socialnuyu Spravedlivost"*), and other groups, all under the leadership of former Soviet premier Nikolai Ryzhkov. In 1999 the ROS won 0.4 percent of the party list vote and two constituency seats.

Joining the ROS in formation of People's Will were Nina Zhukova's Union of Realists (*Soyuz Realistov*—SR), which had been established in 1995 as an alliance of some 20 centrist groupings, and Russian Revival (*Russkoye Vozrozhdeniye*), a right-wing formation committed to Russian Orthodoxy and traditional culture.

For the 2003 State Duma election People's Will joined the Motherland bloc. It subsequently decided to remain aloof from the unified Motherland party, but late in 2004 a party congress urged continuation of unification discussions, given the tightened requirements for party registration and representation in the State Duma, but by mid-2006 unification had not occurred.

Leaders: Sergei BABURIN (Chair), Alexander KUDIMOV.

Party of Workers' Self-Government (*Partiya Samoypravleniya Trudyashchikhsya*—PST). The PST was formally launched in January 1995 by Svyatoslav FYODOROV, a distinguished ophthalmologist who had previously been a leading member of the Party of Economic Freedom (PES, above) and then of the Russian Movement for Democratic

Reform (*Rossiiskoe Dvizhenie Demokraticheshikh Reform—RDDR*). Aiming to represent the interests of small and medium-sized businesses, it soon joined another new group, the Party of People's Conscience (*Partiya Narodnoi Sovesti—PNS*), led by former prosecutor general Alex KAZANNIK, in an electoral alliance that also included the People's Party of Russia (*Narodnaya Partiya Rossii—NPR*). The PST nevertheless decided to contest the December 1995 legislative election with its own list, which obtained 4.1 percent of the proportional vote and one constituency seat. In the mid-1996 presidential contest, Fyodorov took sixth place in the first round with 0.9 percent of the vote.

In October 1998 the PST joined the center-left coalition led by the UPPL but had scant success at the 1999 State Duma election. Fyodorov died in an air crash in June 2000, his successor as party leader being elected three months later. In January 2003 the PST announced it would be allied with the PVR (above) for the December State Duma election. The party's chair Levon Chakhmakhchyan sits in the Federation Council, but allegations in June 2006 of involvement in a bribery scandal have put his position in jeopardy.

Leader: Levon CHAKHMAKHCHYAN (Chair).

Patriots of Russia (*Patrioty Rossii—PR*). Founder and former Communist Gennadi Semigin announced formation of the PR as a unified political party in April 2005. The previous October Semigin had spearheaded formation of a PR coalition encompassing ten predominantly leftist parties and movements, including his own **People's Patriotic Union of Russia** (*Narodno-Patrioticheskii Soyuz Rossii—NPSR*), which had been organized in 1996 by the KPRF's Gennadi Zyuganov as a means of consolidating left wing, conservative parties and movements. Zyuganov had lost control of the NPSR in mid-2004, however, during the dispute over leadership of the KPRF. Other initial participants in the PR coalition included the All-Russian Communist Party of the Future (VKPB), the Eurasian Party–Union of Russian Patriots (EP-SPR), the National-Patriotic Forces of the Rus-

sian Federation (NPSRF), former Communist Gennadi Seleznev's Party of Russia's Rebirth (PVR), the Party of Workers' Self-Government (PST), the People's Patriotic Party of Russia (NPPR), the Khramov wing of the Russian Labor Party (RPT), the Russian Party of Pensioners (RPP), and the Union of People for Education and Science (SLON). The PR also claimed the support of some 30 public organizations. In early 2005 the coalition concluded cooperation agreements with the People's Party of the Russian Federation, the People's Will, and the Social Democratic Party of Russia.

Since becoming a party in 2005, the PR has achieved significant growth. It took part in five of the eight races to regional legislatures in March 2006, passing the 5 percent threshold to win seats in the parliaments of the Kaliningrad and Orenburg regions, scoring 7.0 and 5.6 percent, respectively. By April 2006 the PR had 75 regional branches.

Leader: Gennadi SEMIGIN (Chair).

People's Republican Party of Russia (*Narodno Respublikanskaya Partiya Rossii—NRPR*). Founded by Gen. Aleksandr Lebed, the NRPR was organized at a founding congress at Moscow in March 1997. The NRPR presented itself as a political alternative to both the regional elite and the KPRF. Running as a candidate of the Congress of Russian Communities (KRO; see Motherland) in the presidential elections in June 1996, Lebed had won 14.5 percent of the first-round vote and subsequently supported Yeltsin against the KPRF in the second round. Lebed was quickly appointed secretary of the National Security Council, a post from which he was dismissed the following October.

The NRPR emphasizes the need for a strong state and greater control over foreign trade and is seen as appealing to the "patriotic" wing of the Russian electorate. Lebed was elected governor of Krasnoyarsk in 1998 and was believed to be positioning himself for the next presidential campaign. Lebed also organized the closely affiliated Honor and Motherland (*Chest i Rodina*) movement, which in February 1999 was split by a dispute over Lebed's alleged "despotism." Among those expelled from the movement was Lebed's longtime associate and head of the Political Council, Yuri SHEVTSOV. In September 1999 Lebed announced that his organization would not present a party list for the December State Duma election, preferring instead to support "mentally sound" candidates for individual seats. Lebed died on April 28, 2002, following a helicopter crash.

At the 2003 legislative election the NRPR won only 0.13 percent of the proportional vote and no seats.

Leader: Nikolai ANDRONIK.

Republican Party of Russia (*Respublikanskaya Partiya Rossii*—RPR). A self-described "left-centrist party of the parliamentary type," the RPR was founded in 1990 by former members of the Democratic Platform within the CPSU. It subsequently helped launch the Democratic Choice bloc. In June 1995 the party announced that former minister Ella PAMFILOVA would head its list in the forthcoming elections. Called the Pamfilova-Gurov-Lysenko Bloc, the list obtained only 1.6 percent of the proportional vote and two constituency seats. Pamfilova subsequently formed the For Civil Dignity movement, while in November 1998 Aleksandr GUROV was named by the Interior Ministry to head an institute charged with fighting organized crime. In 2002 the party was joined by Forward, Russia! (*Vperyod Rossiya!*), led by former finance minister Boris Federov.

In the run-up to the December 2003 State Duma election the RPR joined the anti-Berezovsky wing of the Liberal Russia party (LR, above) and the Motorists' Movement of Russia (*Dvizhenie Avtomobilistov Rossii*—DAR) in forming the **New Course–Automotive Russia** (*Novyi Kurs–Avtomobilnaya Rossiya*—NK-AR) electoral bloc. The bloc won only 0.8 percent of the proportional vote and one constituency seat. In advance of the 2007 parliamentary elections the RPR has engaged in discussions to join forces with the SPS and the Development of Enterprise parties.

Leaders: Vladimir LYSENKO, Boris FEDEROV.

Russian Labor Party (*Rossiiskaya Partiya Truda*—RPT). The RPT was organized in early 2002 under the leadership of Oleg Shein, a deputy in the State Duma, and Sergei Khramov, a union leader. For the 2003 State Duma election the wing of the party led by Shein joined the Motherland coalition, while Khramov supported the Great Russia–Eurasian Union bloc (see the EP-SPR, above). In 2004 Khramov participated in formation of Gennadi Semigin's Patriots of Russia coalition.

Leaders: Oleg SHEIN, Sergei KHRAMOV.

Russian Party of Life (*Rossiiskaya Partiya Zhizni*—RPZh). The RPZh was established in 2002 by Sergei Mironov, chair of the Federation Council. Centrist in nature, the RPZh has focused on quality-of-life issues. It competed in 2003 in partnership with the PVR (above). Mironov won under 1 percent of the vote as a candidate for president in 2004.

Leader: Sergei MIRONOV.

Russian Party of Pensioners (*Rossiiskaya Partiya Pensionerov*—RPP). Dating from 1997, the RPP contested the 2003 State Duma elections in a bloc with the **Party of Social Justice** (*Partiya Sotsialnoi Spravedlivosti*—PSS), led by Vladimir Kishenin, who subsequently united with the Social Democrats (SDPR, below). At the election the bloc won 3.1 percent of the proportional vote but no seats, which contributed to the suspension of the party's chair, Sergei ATROSHENKO, by an extraordinary party congress in January 2004. Valery GARTUNG succeeded him, initially in an acting capacity. In October 2004 the RPP joined in forming the Patriots of Russia coalition.

In February 2005 Gartung broke with Unified Russia, primarily because of his opposition to President Putin's cash-for-benefits reform, which was widely viewed as adversely affecting pensioners. Seemingly as a direct result of this action, it was discovered that Gartung's election as party leader involved irregularities, which ultimately cost him the post that autumn.

Leader: Igor ZOTOV (Chair).

Social Democratic Party of Russia (*Sotsial-Demokraticheskaya Partiya Rossii*—SDPR). The

SDPR was formed in November 2001 by merger of Mikhail Gorbachev's Russian United Social Democratic Party (*Rossiiskaya Obyedinennaya Sotsial Demokraticheskaya Partiya*—ROSDP) and Konstantin Titov's Russian Party of Social Democracy (*Rossiiskaya Partiya Sotsialnoi Demokratii*—RPSD). The ROSDP had been established in March 2000 and registered in May in an attempt to organize a unified social democratic party in opposition to both Communist ideology and unrestrained free-market liberalism. The RPSD dated from February 1995, its first chair, Aleksandr YAKOVLEV, having been a leading adviser to Gorbachev at the end of the Soviet era. Titov, the governor of Samara, became chair in 2000, and for a time the party was closely associated with the SPS.

The SDPR, with Gorbachev as leader and Titov as chair, chose not to contest the 2003 State Duma election, although Titov had sought a cooperative arrangement with Unified Russia. For want of a viable alternative, the party backed Vladimir Putin for reelection in March 2004. Two months later Gorbachev resigned as leader, in part because of disagreements with Titov, who himself subsequently took a less active role in the party. The party's current chair, Vladimir Kishenin, headed the electoral list of the Russian Party of Pensioners–Party of Social Justice (RPP-PSS) bloc for the 2003 State Duma election. In 2005 he brought his PSS into the SDPR.

Leader: Vladimir KISHENIN (Chair).

Union of Communist Parties —**CPSU** (*Soyuz Kommunisticheskikh Partii*—SKP-KPSS). The SKP, which continues to include "Communist Party of the Soviet Union" (CPSU/KPSS) as part of its official name, primarily groups some 20 "old-style" communist groups, although the KPRF also participates. For the December 1995 State Duma election various SKP members joined forces in a list that won 4.6 percent of the proportional vote and one constituency seat. In 1999 the Communists–Workers of Russia–For the Soviet Union bloc (*Kommunisty–Trudyashiesya Rossii–Za Sovetskii Soyuz*) was less successful, winning only 2.2 percent of the party list vote and no seats. Principal participants in the bloc included the Russian Communist Workers' Party (*Rossiiskaya Kommunisticheskaya Rabochaya Partiya*—RKRP), led by Viktor TYULKIN, and the Soviet Homeland movement (*Sovetskaya Rodina*) of Anatoly KRYUCHKOV. Soviet Homeland, established in October 1996, grouped a number of small hard-line ("irreconcilable") parties, including Kryuchkov's **Revolutionary Party of Communists** (*Revoliutsionnaya Partiya Kommunistov*—RPK); Aleksei PRIGARIN's **Russian Communist Party—CPSU** (*Rossiiskaya Kommunisticheskaya Partiya*—RKP-KPSS); the **Russian Workers' Party** (*Rossiiskaya Robochaya Partiya*—RRP), an RKRP offshoot led by Mikhail POPOV; and the **All Union Communist Party of Bolsheviks** (*Vsesoyuznaya Kommunicheskaya Partiya Bolshevikov*—VKPB), led by Nina ANDREYEVA. In July 2000 the SKP chair announced formation of a **Communist Party of the Union of Belarus and Russia.** Earlier, he had characterized the leadership of the KPRF as "social traitors" and "collaborators."

In October 2001 Tyulkin and Kryuchkov were named cochairs of a unified **Russian Communist Workers' Party–Revolutionary Party of Communists (RKRP-RPK).** Since then, a number of the already numerous minor Communist parties have split further.

For the 2003 State Duma election the KPRF included on its list members of the RKRP-RPK and the RKP-KPSS.

Leader: Oleg SHENIN (Chair).

Union of Muslims of Russia (*Soyuz Musulman Rossii*—SMR). Aiming to represent the estimated 20 million Muslims of the Russian Federation, the SMR was founded in early 1995, partly as a response to the Russian military intervention in predominantly Muslim Chechnya.

In May 1998 party leader Nadirshakh KHACHILAYEV was detained in connection with the deaths of three police officers at his home in Dagestan and a brief takeover of government buildings. Subsequently released, Khachilayev went into hiding. The SMR, which supports merger of Dagestan and Chechnya, held an extraordinary congress in

December 1998, in part to permit reregistration following amendments to a law prohibiting formation of religion-based political associations. Khachilayev was captured in October 1999 and sentenced to prison in June 2000; however, he was immediately released under an amnesty program declared by the State Duma. He was assassinated in August 2003 in Dagestan.

Leader: Sheikh Ravil GAINUTDIN.

Women of Russia (*Zhenshchiny Rossii*—ZR). Led by a former Soviet Communist Party official, the ZR is an alliance dedicated to the social and political equality of women. It endorses a "humane" approach to economic reform, the provision of social amenities (including free education and health care), and maintenance of law and order. The ZR won 23 seats in the 1993 State Duma election but in 1995 won only three constituency seats (having secured only 4.6 percent of the proportional vote). The party suffered a significant rupture in 1997 when Yekaterina LAKHOVA left to form the Russian Women's Movement (*Dvizhenie Zhenshin Rossii*—DZR), which allied with Fatherland–All Russia (OVR) for the 1999 elections.

Initially affiliated with the Fatherland–All Russia bloc, the ZR separated from it because of the bloc's "traditionally conservative attitude to the role of women in society." Running independently, the ZR took 2.0 percent of the 1999 party list vote and no seats. In 2003 it supported Unified Russia.

Leader: Galina KARELOVA.

Working Russia (*Rabochaya Rossiya*—RR). A sociopolitical movement, Working Russia (also translated as Labor Russia) is led by Viktor Anpilov, who was expelled from his collateral membership in the RKRP (under SKP, above) in 1996. In 1998 Anpilov undertook to regroup the Stalinists of the Soviet era in a Stalin Bloc–For the Soviet Union (*Stalinsky Blok–Za Sovetsky Soyuz*—SB-ZSS) for the December 1999 legislative elections. Other participants included the **Officers' Union** (*Soyuz Ofitserov*—SO), led by Stanislav TEREKHOV, and Yevgeni DZHUGASHVILI, a grandson of Joseph Stalin. The bloc won 0.6 percent of the party list vote and no seats.

Anpilov has also been associated with other far-left groupings, including a Leninist-Stalinist offshoot of the RKRP. In 2002 he reportedly established the **Communists of Working Russia** (*Kommunisty Trudovoii Rossii*—KTR). In January 2004 the youth wing of Working Russia, the Red Youth Vanguard, unsuccessfully attempted to remove Anpilov from the leadership.

Leader: Viktor ANPILOV.

Other parties and blocs that contested the 2003 State Duma election without success included the nationalist, anti-Western **Conceptual Party "Unity"** (*Kontseptualnaya Partiya "Edinenie"*—KPE), which emerged in 2002 from a quasi-mystical religious movement under the leadership of Konstantin PETROV. The KPE won 1.2 percent of the proportional vote. All of the following parties won less than 0.5 percent: the **Democratic Party of Russia** (*Demokraticheskaya Partiya Rossii*—DPR), which was founded in 1990 (and therefore regards itself as Russia's oldest party) and which was led by Vladimir PODOPRIGORA; the **For Holy Rus** (*Za Svyatuyu Rus*—ZSR), led by Sergei POPOV; the ultra-leftist, pro-Soviet **Peace and Unity** (*Mir i Edinstvo*—ME), led by Sazhi UMALATOVA; the **Russian Constitutional-Democratic Party** (*Rossiiskaya Konstitusionno-demokraticheskaya Partiya*—RKdP, or *Kadets*), led by V. V. VOLKOV; the **True Patriots of Russia** (*Istiinye Patrioty Rossii*—IPR), which was formerly called the Islamic Party of Russia and which was led by Magomed RADZHABOV; the **Union of People for Education and Science** (*Soyuz Liudei za Obrazovanie i Nauku*—SLON), led by Vyacheslav IGRUNOV, one of the original *Yabloko* leaders; and the **United Russian Party "Rus"** (*Obyedinennaya Rossiiskaya Partiya "Rus"*), led by Vladimir SOKOLOV.

Other registered parties include the **Conservative Party of Russia** (*Konservativnaya Partiya Rossii*—KPR), led by Nikolai BOGACHEV following the death of its founder, Lev UBOZHKO, in 2003; **Freedom and People's Power** (*Svoboda i Narodovlastie*—SN), an ally of Motherland that is led by a former

Cabinet

As of July 1, 2006

Prime Minister	Mikhail Fradkov
First Deputy Prime Minister for Economic and Social Affairs	Dmitri Medvedev
Deputy Prime Ministers	Aleksander Zhukov
	Sergei Ivanov

Ministers

Agriculture	Aleksei Gordeyev
Civil Defense, Emergencies, and Natural Disasters	Sergei Shoigu
Culture and Mass Communications	Aleksandr Sokolov
Defense	Sergei Ivanov
Economic Development and Trade	German Gref
Education and Science	Andrei Fursenko
Finance	Aleksei Kudrin
Foreign Affairs	Sergei Lavrov
Health and Social Policy	Mikhail Zurabov
Industry and Energy	Viktor Khristenko
Information Technology and Communications	Leonid Reyman
Interior	Rashid Nurgaliyev
Justice	Vladimir Ustinov
Natural Resources	Yuri Trutnev
Regional Development	Vladimir Yakovlev
Transportation	Igor Levitin
Director, Federal Security Services	Nikolai Patrushev
Director, Foreign Intelligence Service	Sergei Lebedov
Secretary, Security Council	Igor Ivanov
Chief, Government Apparatus	Dmitri Kozak

mayor of Vladivostok, Viktor CHEREPKOV; the **National-Patriotic Forces of the Russian Federation** (*Natsionalno-Patrioticheskie Sil Rossiiskoi Federatsii*—NPSRF), led by Shmidt DZOBLAEV; the anti-liberal, anti-Semitic **People's Patriotic Party of Russia** (*Narodno-Patrioticheskaya Partiya Rossii*—NPPR), led by former defense minister Igor RODIONOV; the **Political Party "Eurasia"** (*Politicheskaya Partiya "Evraziya"*), led by Aleksandr DUGIN; the probusiness **Russian United Industrial Party** (*Rossiiskaya Obyedinennaya Promyshlennaya Partiya*—ROPP); and the small **Union** (*Soyuz*) party, led by A. V.

PRONIN. In December 2004 *Soyuz* agreed to join Gennadi Gudkov's People's Party, as did the RKdP. The radical **National-Bolshevik Party** (*Natsional-Bolshevistskaya Partiya*—NBP), led by writer Eduard LIMONOV, faced liquidation in mid-2005 following unsuccessful efforts to be registered.

In 2005 chess champion Garri KASPAROV, a prospective presidential candidate for 2008, created the centrist **United Civic Front** to unify the opposition to the Putin regime. Earlier, he had helped organize the **Committee 2008** (*Komitet 2008*) movement.

Legislature

The 1993 constitution provides for a **Federal Assembly** (*Federalnoe Sobranie*) consisting of a Federation Council and a State Duma. The normal term for each is four years.

Federation Council (*Sovet Federatsii*). The upper house is a 178-member body to which each of Russia's 89 constitutionally recognized territorial units returns two members, one selected by the unit's executive and one by the unit's legislature. (Prior to January 2002, the chief executive and legislative chair of each unit had served ex officio.) Most members are designated as independents, but a majority now supports Unified Russia.

Chair: Sergei MIRONOV.

State Duma (*Gosudarstvennaya Duma*). The lower house is a 450-member body, half of whose seats are filled by proportional representation from party lists obtaining a minimum of 5 percent of the vote and half from single-member constituencies. The most recent election took place on December 7, 2003, with reballoting on March 14, 2004, in three districts where a plurality of voters rejected all candidates. (A third vote, held on December 5, 2004, was required in one district, while one of the candidates who had won in March was stripped of his seat in June for electoral violations.) The following seat distribution reflects the December 2003 results (party list and single-member constituency seats in parentheses): Unified Russia, 224 (120, 104); Communist Party of the Russian Federation, 52 (40, 12); Liberal Democratic Party of Russia, 36 (36, 0); Motherland–People's Patriotic Union, 36 (29, 7); People's Party of the Russian Federation, 17 (0, 17); *Yabloko,* 4 (0, 4); Party of Russia's Rebirth/Russian Party of Life, 3 (0, 3); Union of Right Forces 3 (0, 3); Agrarian Party of Russia, 2 (0, 2); Great Russia–Eurasian Union, Development of Enterprise, New Course–Automotive Russia, 1 constituency seat each; independents, 67. Note, however, that a number of successful independent candidates were party members who chose to run for district seats without affiliation.

By the opening of the Duma on December 29, 2003, significant realignments had occurred as various parliamentary factions formed. For the 447 filled seats, bloc alignments were reported to be as follows: Unified Russia, 306; Communist Party, 52; Motherland, 38; Liberal Democratic Party, 36; unaffiliated, 15.

Chair: Boris GRYZLOV.

Communications

All mass media are licensed by the government. During the legislative election campaign of December 1999 government opponents, supported by monitors from the OSCE and the European Institute for the Media, frequently charged media bias, while in February 2000 the Union of Journalists asserted that "the threat to the freedom of speech in Russia has for the first time in the last several years transformed into its open and regular suppression," particularly regarding coverage of the war in Chechnya. In June Prime Minister Kasyanov nevertheless identified a free press as "an absolute priority."

The government's direct and indirect control of the media remained undiminished in 2003 and 2004. Immediately before the March 2004 presidential election reports by the OSCE and the Russian Union of Journalists (the latter with funding from the European Commission) concurred that state-controlled television, the public's leading source of news, heavily favored the incumbent, President Putin, in terms of both air time and content. Some state-controlled media outlets gave no coverage at all to the other presidential candidates.

Press

Following the demise of the USSR, many newspapers had to curtail operations because of high printing costs under free market reforms, with average circulation falling by about 60 percent during 1992 alone. The principal government organs of the USSR, *Pravda* and *Izvestiya,* continue to publish as independent newspapers, but with a mere fraction of their Soviet-era circulations. The following are dailies published at Moscow, unless otherwise noted: *Argumenty i Facty* (Arguments and Facts, 2,880,000), independent weekly; *Trud* (Labor, 1,700,000), trade union organ; *Moskovsky Komsomolets* (Moscow Young Communists, 800,000); *Komsomolskaya Pravda* (Young Communist Truth, 790,000), independent; *Novaya Gazeta* (New Gazette, 670,000), weekly; *Rossiiskaya Gazeta* (Russian Gazette, 375,000), Federal Assembly organ; *Moskovskaya Pravda* (Moscow Truth, 320,000), independent; *Sovetskaya Rossiya* (Soviet Russia, 300,000), thrice weekly, independent; *Vechernyaya Moskva* (Moscow Evening, 300,000), independent; *Izvestia* (News, 230,000), independent; *Tribuna* (Tribune, 200,000), industrial; *Moskovskiye Novosti* (Moscow News, 160,000), weekly in Russian and English, independent; *Sankt-Peterburgskiye Vedomosti* (St. Petersburg News, 90,000), organ of St. Petersburg mayoralty; *Pravda* (Truth, 70,000), independent.

News Agencies

In early 1992 the long dominant Telegraphic Agency of the Soviet Union (*Telegrafnoye Agentstvo Sovyetskogo Souza*—TASS) was combined with part of the former Novosti Press Agency (*Agentstvo Pechati Novosti*—APN) to form the Russian Information Telegraph Agency–Telegraphic Agency of the Sovereign Countries (*Informatsionnoye Telegrafnoye Agentstvo Rossii–Telegrafnoye Agentstvo Suverennykh Stran*—ITAR-TASS). Other facilities include a Russian Information Agency–Novosti (*Rossiyskoye Informatsionnoye Agentstvo*–Novosti—RIA-Novosti) as well as several independent agencies, most prominently Postfactum and Interfax. The leading foreign agencies maintain bureaus in Moscow.

Broadcasting and Computing

In early 1991 Russia broke the Soviet government's broadcasting monopoly by establishing its own service, the All-Russian State Television and Radio Broadcasting Company (*Vserossiiskaya Gosudarstvennaya Teleradiokompaniya*—VGTRK), commonly called Russian Television and Radio (*Rossiiskoye Televideniye i Radio*—RTR). The separate Ostankino Russian State Television and Radio Broadcasting Company (*Rossiiskaya Gosudarstvennaya Teleradiokompaniya Ostankino*) was subsequently established. However, the latter was broken up in 1995, its television network becoming Russian Public Television (*Obshestvennoe Rossiiskoye Televideniye*—ORT), which was dominated by Boris Berezovsky's media empire until he sold his stake in 2001. An Independent Television (*Nezavisimoye Televideniye*—NTV) network, owned by Vladimir Gusinsky's Media-MOST, was taken over by the state-run Gazprom in 2001. Subsequently, Gazprom announced that it would sell off its media outlets. In August 2001 a presidential decree established the Russian Television and Radio Broadcasting Network to oversee signal distribution.

In June 2003 the government shut down the independent broadcaster *TVS* and assigned its broadcast frequencies to a sports channel. All of Russia's main terrestrial stations are now at least partially government-owned. There were approximately 96.1 million television receivers and 14 million personal computers serving 6.0 million Internet users in 2003.

Intergovernmental Representation

Ambassador to the U.S.
Yuri V. USHAKOV

U.S. Ambassador to Russia
William J. BURNS

Permanent Representative to the UN
Vitaly I. CHERKIN

IGO Memberships (Non-UN)
AC, APEC, BIS, BSEC, CBSS, CEUR, CIS, EBRD, G-8, Interpol, OSCE, PCA, WCO

SAN MARINO

MOST SERENE REPUBLIC OF SAN MARINO

Serenissima Repubblica di San Marino

The Country

An enclave within the Italian province of Emilia-Romagna, San Marino is the world's oldest and second-smallest republic (after Nauru). Its terrain is mountainous, the highest point being Mount Titano, on the western slope of which is located the city of San Marino. The Sammarinese are ethnically and culturally Italian, but their long history has created a strong sense of identity and independence. The principal economic activities are service-related industries, especially nonresident banking and financial services as well as tourism, and some light manufacturing. Agriculture now employs under 2 percent of the workforce; olives and wine grapes rank with various grains as important crops. Wine, textiles, varnishes, ceramics, woolen goods, furniture, and building stone are chief exports. Traditional sources of income include the sale of coins and postage stamps and an annual budget subsidy from the Italian government. Some 3.3 million tourists visit annually.

By virtue of its economic union with Italy, San Marino became part of the European Economic Community (EEC) in the 1950s. It now has a separate customs union and cooperation agreement with the European Union (EU). The GDP grew steadily throughout the 1990s, averaging 7 percent annually, while the growth of the tourism industry contributed to an influx of cross-border workers (nearly one-fourth of the labor force). The economy slowed to an average growth of 2.8 percent between 2000 and 2002 before stagnating completely in 2003 in the wake of a decline in the manufacturing sector. Growth of 2 percent was estimated for 2004.

Government and Politics

Political Background

Reputedly founded in 301 A.D., San Marino is the sole survivor of the numerous independent states that existed in Italy prior to unification in the 19th century. A treaty of friendship and cooperation concluded with the Kingdom of Italy in 1862 has subsequently been renewed and amended at varying intervals.

Political Status: Independent republic dating from the early Middle Ages; under multiparty parliamentary regime.

Area: 23.6 sq. mi. (61 sq. km.).

Population: 28,753 (2002C); 31,500 (2005E), not including some 13,000 Sammarinese residents abroad.

Major Urban Center (2005E): SAN MARINO (4,800).

Official Language: Italian.

Monetary Unit: Euro (market rate July 1, 2006: 1 euro = $1.28US).

Captains Regent: Antonio CARATTONI (Party of Socialists and Democrats) and Roberto GIORGETTI (Popular Alliance); elected by the Grand and General Council for six-month terms beginning October 1, 2006, in succession to Gian Franco TERENZI (San Marino Christian Democratic Party) and Loris FRANCINI (San Marino Christian Democratic Party).

A coalition of Communists (*Partito Comunista Sammarinese*—PCS) and Socialists (*Partito Socialista Sammarinese*—PSS) controlled the government until 1957, when, because of defections from its ranks, it lost its majority to the opposition Popular Alliance (composed mainly of Christian Democrats and Social Democrats). The San Marino Christian Democratic Party (*Partito Democratico Cristiano Sammarinese*—PDCS) remained the plurality party at the elections of 1959, 1964, and 1969 but required the continuing support of the San Marino Independent Social Democratic Party (*Partito Socialista Democratico Indipendente Sammarinese*—PSDIS) to cement a governing majority. The coalition split over economic policy in January 1973, enabling the Socialists to return to power in alliance with the Christian Democrats. In the September 1974 election (the first in which women were allowed to present themselves as candidates for the Grand and General Council), the Christian Democrats and the Social Democrats each lost two seats, while the Communists and the Socialists experienced small gains.

In November 1977 the Socialists withdrew from the government, accusing the Christian Democrats of being bereft of ideas for resolving the country's economic difficulties. Following a lengthy impasse marked by successive failures of the Christian Democrats, Communists, and Socialists to form a new government, a premature general election was held in May 1978, but the balance of legislative power remained virtually unchanged. Subsequently, the Christian Democrats again failed to secure a mandate, and in July a "Government of Democratic Collaboration" involving the Communists, Socialists, and the Socialist Unity Party (*Partito Socialista Unitario*—PSU, principal successor to the PSDIS) was approved by a bare parliamentary majority of 31 votes. The other PSDIS successor, the San Marino Social Democratic Party (*Partito Socialista Democratico Sammarinese*—PSDS), joined the governing coalition in 1982 but returned to opposition after the May 1983 election, at which the ruling parties gained an additional council seat. The leftist government fell in June 1986, when the Communist and Socialist Unity parties withdrew over foreign policy and other issues. In late July the council, by a 39–13 vote, approved a new program advanced by the Christian Democratic and Communist parties, the first such coalition in the country's history. The coalition was renewed in June 1988, following a general election in May at which the governing parties gained four seats at the expense of a divided Socialist opposition. In 1990 the PCS, responding to recent events in Eastern Europe, recast itself as the San Marino Progressive Democratic Party (*Partito Progressista Democratico Sammarinese*—PPDS).

On February 24, 1992, the Christian Democrats withdrew from their coalition with the PPDS and forged a new ruling alliance with the recently reunified Socialists (see Political Parties, below). The outcome of the May 30, 1993, election was notable for the emergence of three smaller parties, although the ruling center-left coalition of the PDCS and the PSS retained a comfortable majority in the Grand and General Council. The coalition was renewed following the May 1998 legislative elections.

In February 2000 the Socialists withdrew from the government because of policy differences. The Christian Democrats then turned to the PPDS to ensure a new legislative majority, and on March 28 a government of the Christian Democrats, the Progressive Democrats, and the Socialists for Reform (*Socialisti per le Reforme*—SpR) assumed office. In February 2001, with the Christian Democrats having rebuffed efforts to introduce measures aimed at tightening the country's financial and tax regulations, another crisis ensued, leading to premature dissolution of the legislature on March 11.

The legislative election held June 10, 2001, resulted in only minor changes in the makeup of the Grand and General Council. The PDCS remained in the plurality, claiming 25 seats on a vote share of 41.5 percent, while the PSS took 15 seats on 24.2 percent of the vote. Third place (20.8 percent of the vote and 12 seats) went to the newly organized Party of Democrats (*Partito dei Democratici*—PdD), successor to the PPDS, the SpR, and the Movement for Ideas (*Idee in Movimento*—IM). Following the election, the PDCS and PSS established a new coalition, but the PSS again withdrew on June 5, 2002. Subsequently, the PSS, the PdD, and the small San Marino Popular Democratic Alliance (*Alleanza Popolare dei Democratici Sammarinese*—APDS) formed a new government that excluded the Christian Democrats. However, that government collapsed in December and was replaced with a PSS/PDCS coalition; the PdD rejoined the government in December 2003.

Following the election of June 4, 2006, a coalition government was formed by the recently established Party of Socialists and Democrats (*Partito dei Socialisti e dei Democratici*—PSD), which resulted from the merger of the PSS and PdD; the Popular Alliance (*Alleanza Popolare*—AP, the renamed APDS); and the small United Left (*Sinistra Unita*—SU) alliance. The new government presented its program on July 17.

Constitution and Government

Although a document dating from 1600 is sometimes referenced as San Marino's constitution, it is perhaps more accurate to say the republic has no codified, formal constitution but rather a constitutional tradition that is hundreds of years old. Legislative power is vested in the Grand and General Council (*Consiglio Grande e Generale*) of 60 members directly elected for five-year terms, subject to dissolution. A ten-member Congress of State (*Congresso di Stato*), or cabinet, is elected by the council for the duration of its term. Two members of the council are designated for six-month terms as captains regent (*capitani reggenti*). They are the heads of state but under normal circumstances do not set policy; both have equal power. Each is eligible for reelection three years after the expiration of the term. The judicial system encompasses justices of the peace (the only level not entrusted to Italian personnel); a law commissioner and assistant law commissioner, who deal with both civil and criminal cases; a criminal judge of the Primary Court of Claims (involving penalties greater than three years); two Appeals Court judges; and a Council of Twelve (*Consiglio dei XII*), which serves as a final court of appeals in civil cases only.

Administratively, San Marino is divided into nine sectors called castles (*castelli*), each of which is directed by an elected Castle Board led by the captain of the castle, both serving five-year terms (increased from two years in 1994).

Foreign Relations

On March 2, 1992, San Marino was admitted to full United Nations (UN) membership, having previously been accorded observer status with the world body, and on September 23 it became a member of the International Monetary Fund (IMF). The republic is also a member of other international organizations, including the Conference on (later Organization for) Security and Cooperation in Europe (CSCE/OSCE), in whose review sessions it has been an active participant.

The country's relations with Italy (raised to the ambassadorial level in 1979) are governed by a series of treaties and conventions establishing a customs union, regulating public-service facilities, and defining general principles of good neighborly relations. Despite its staunchly reiterated independence, the country's reliance on Italy for a variety of necessities, ranging from daily newspapers to currency, provides little evidence that it will break with a tradition of alignment with Italian social and political processes.

In May 1985 San Marino and China concluded a visa-exemption accord, the first such agreement between Beijing and a West European regime. In February 1997 Secretary of State for Foreign and Political Affairs Gabriele GATTI met with Cuban leader Fidel Castro in Havana, San Marino subsequently continuing to urge the United States to lift its embargo on Cuba.

Current Issues

As in 1998, the 2001 pre-election debate raised questions about the republic's relationship with the EU, which was concerned about San Marino's status as a tax haven. The EU, which in November 2000 proposed an open exchange of information on nonresident investment accounts, maintained that financial secrecy creates an unlevel playing field in the markets, erodes members' tax bases, and facilitates fraud. Indeed, Italian tax officials had launched raids throughout San Marino in July 1998 to snare tax evaders, estimated to cost Rome $600 million annually. The issue appeared resolved, for the most part, by an accord that went into effect in 2005 under which certain tax havens, including San Marino, agreed to withhold taxes on foreign deposits, without disclosing confidential information on those accounts. Meanwhile, in a response to continued economic sluggishness, the government pledged to pursue reform of the pension system and labor regulations, in part to remain "competitive" in view of the more "flexible" labor markets elsewhere in Europe.

The results of the parliamentary election held on June 4, 2006, closely shadowed the April election results in neighboring Italy, where the center-left staged a narrow upset victory over the ruling center-right governing coalition. Although San Marino's Christian Democrats won a one-seat plurality of the seats in the Grand and General Coun-cil, the party passed into the opposition on July 12, when the center-left PSD, AP, and SU formed a governing coalition that excluded it. The Christian Democratic leadership protested that the move violated the will of the electorate, which had given their party the largest share of the votes.

Political Parties

San Marino's older political parties traditionally had close ties with and resembled corresponding parties in Italy, although recent mergers and name changes have led to more distinctive identities.

Governing Coalition

Party of Socialists and Democrats (*Partito dei Socialisti e dei Democratici*—PSD). This party was founded in February 2005 as a merger between the San Marino Socialist Party (*Partito Socialista Sammarinese*—PSS) and the Party of Democrats (*Partito dei Democratici*—PdD), both of which at the time participated in a governing coalition that also included the PDCS.

The leftist PSS and the Communist Party (PCS) ruled jointly during 1945–1957. In 1973 the PSS returned to power upon forming a coalition government with the Christian Democrats that was continued after the 1974 election, at which the party won eight council seats. (It gained an additional representative when the PSDIS, originally a right-wing splinter from the PSS, split in 1975.) In November 1977, however, it withdrew from the coalition, precipitating the fall of the PDCS-led administration. It went on to win eight council seats in 1978 and nine in 1983, entering the government on both occasions. The unprecedented PDCS-PCS coalition formed in July 1986 excluded the PSS.

In 1990 the Socialist Unity Party (*Partito Socialista Unitario*—PSU), the more extreme remnant of the PSDIS, reunited with the PSS, which revived its coalition with the Christian Democrats in February 1992. In the May 1998 balloting the PSS retained its 14 legislative seats, continuing as the junior coalition partner until withdrawing from the government in February 2000. After winning 15 seats in June 2001, the PSS reentered a PDCS-led coalition. A year later it joined the PdD and APDS (both below) in a left-leaning government.

The Party of Democrats (PdD) was established in March 2001 by merger of three groups: the San Marino Progressive Democratic Party (*Partito Progressista Democratico Sammarinese*—PPDS), the Movement for Ideas (*Idee in Movimento*—IM), and a group of reformist Democrats and Socialists ("*I reformisti Democratici e Socialisti*") led by Emma ROSSI.

In the context of the political upheaval of late 1989 in Eastern Europe, the PPDS had been formally launched on April 15, 1990, as heir to the San Marino Communist Party (*Partito Comunista Sammarinese*—PCS), which had won 18 council seats at the May 1988 election. The PCS, a nominally independent offshoot of the Italian Communist Party, had generally followed the line of its Italian parent. The PPDS was forced into opposition following the breakup of its coalition with the Christian Democrats in early 1992, and it fell back to 11 council seats in 1993. For the May 1998 election the PPDS formed a joint list with the IM and a grouping called the Democratic Convention (*Convenzione Democratica*—CD); also included were several independents and two candidates identified with the San Marino Democratic Union (*Unione Sammarinese Democratica*—USD). The combined list won 18.6 percent of the vote, thereby retaining 11 seats, although one representative left the PPDS-IM legislative group in November, initially to sit as an independent. The February 2000 departure of the PSS from the government enabled the PPDS to reestablish a coalition with the Christian Democrats in March, but the resultant government collapsed a year later.

Meanwhile, the leftist IM had been established in 1998 by Alessandro ROSSI as principal successor to the Democratic Movement (*Movimento Democratico*—MD); following the 1998 election, the nascent IM extended its support to the newly formed PDCS-PPDS government. The MD had been formed in 1990 by members of the San Marino Social Democratic Party (*Partito Socialista Democratico Sammarinese*—PSDS), the most moderate of San Marino's several socialist parties and itself a partial successor to the San Marino Independent Social Democratic Party (*Partito Socialista Democratico Indipendente Sammarinese*—PSDIS), which had bifurcated in 1975 (see also PSU, above). At the 1993 general election the MD had won three seats.

Emma Rossi's reformist group was largely a continuation of the Socialists for Reform (*Socialisti per le Reforme*—SpR). The SpR (familiarly, *Reformasi*) had been formed in time for the May 1998 balloting by Rossi, who had earlier resigned from her cabinet post and left the PSS on the ground that the PSS had become too closely aligned with the PDCS. The SpR won two seats in the Grand and General Council, apparently drawing votes from some former MD supporters. In March 2000 Rossi entered the newly formed governing coalition. Formation of the PdD was announced in preparation for the premature election of June 2001. Having won 12 seats at the balloting, the PdD joined in forming the new PSS-PdD-APDS coalition government in mid-2002.

At the 2006 election, the PSD won 31.8 percent of the vote and 20 seats, 7 fewer than the total won in the previous election of 2001 by its constituent parties, the former PSS and PdP, and 1 less than their former coalition partner, the Christian Democrats (PDCS; see below). On July 12 the PSD formed a center-left governing coalition with the Popular Alliance (AP) and United Left (SU).

Leaders: Giuseppe MORGANTI (President), Antonio CARATTONI, Paride ANDREOLI, Mauro CHIARUZZI (Secretary).

Popular Alliance (*Alleanza Popolare*—AP) This centrist, liberal party, formerly known as the San Marino Popular Democratic Alliance for the Republic (*Alleanza Popolare dei Democratici Sammarinesi per la Repubblica*—APDS), was formed prior to the 1993 election under the leadership of former Christian Democrats. The APDS won four Grand and General Council seats in 1993; it secured six seats in 1998 on a 9.8 percent vote share. In 2001 it slipped to five seats and 8.2 percent of the vote. In 2006, the party, now known as the AP, won 12 percent of the vote and seven seats.

Leaders: Roberto GIORGETTI (Coordinator), Tito MASI, Fernando BINDI.

United Left (*Sinistra Unita*—SU). This leftist political alliance was formed in 2005 by the **San Marino Communist Refoundation** (*Rifondazione Comunista Sammarinese*—RCS) and **Zona Franca** (ZF), a PSD splinter. The RCS was founded in 1992 by PCS hard-liners unwilling to accept entry into the PPDS. The new formation won two legislative seats on a 3.4 percent vote share in May 1993 and two seats on a 3.3 percent share in the 1998 legislative contest. It retained both seats in 2001, when it won 3.4 percent of the vote. At the 2006 election the SU won 8.7 percent of the vote and five seats.

Leaders: Ivan FOSCHI (Political Secretary, RCS), Vanessa MURATORI (RCS), Francesca MICHELOTTI (ZF), Alessandro ROSSI (ZF).

Other Parties

San Marino Christian Democratic Party (*Partito Democratico Cristiano Sammarinese*—PDCS). Catholic and conservative in outlook, the PDCS was established in 1948 and first came to power in 1957. In recent years it has been the strongest party in the Grand and General Council, winning at least 21 seats in every election since 1974. It ruled as the senior partner in coalitions with the PSS from 1973 until the latter's withdrawal in December 1977, at which time the PDCS was unable to organize a new government majority and went into opposition. It returned to power in an unprecedented coalition with the Communist Party (subsequently the PPDS) in July 1986, from which it withdrew in February 1992 to revive the alliance with the Socialists. The party again won a plurality in the 1993 balloting, following which its coalition with the Socialists was continued.

The PDCS lost 1 of its 26 seats in the legislative election of May 1998, when it won a 40.9 percent vote share. The February 2000 collapse of the PDCS-PSS coalition led the PDCS to reunite with the PPDS in a tripartite coalition that also included the SPR. Although the PDCS retained its 25 seats at the June 2001 election, a revived PDCS-PSS coalition lasted only one year and the PDCS was forced into opposition. At the June 2006 election the PDCS won 21 seats, more than any other party, but not enough to outweigh the combined strength of 32 seats won by the center-left PSD-AP-SU governing coalition.

Leaders: Pier Marino MENICUCCI (Political Secretary), Gabriele GATTI (Parliamentary Leader), Cesare GASPERONI (Administrative Secretary).

New Socialist Party (*Nuovo Partito Socialista*—NPS). The leftist NPS was founded in November 2005 by defectors from the PSD to restore traditional socialist values for political reform and against corruption the party claimed had infiltrated government.

At the 2006 election the NPS won 5.4 percent of the vote and three seats.

Leaders: Antonio Lazzaro VOLPINARI, Augusto CASALI.

We Sammarinese (*Noi Sammarinesi*—NS). This party, which defends the republic's traditional values, won 2.5 percent of the vote and one seat on the council in 2006.

Leader: Marco ARZILLI.

Sammarinese People (*Popolari Sammarinesi*—Popolari). Founded in 2003, the party won 2.4 percent of the vote and one seat on the council in 2006.

Leader: Romeo MORRI.

San Marino National Alliance (*Alleanza Nazionale Sammarinese*—ANS). The right-wing ANS, linked to the Italian post-fascist National Alliance (*Alleanza Nazionale)* won 1.9 percent of the vote and one seat at the June 2001 council election.

Cabinet

As of October 1, 2006

Captains Regent	Antonio Carattoni (PSD)
	Roberto Giorgetti (AP)

Secretaries of State

Finance and Budget, Postal Service, and State Philatelic Company	Stefano Macina (PSD)
Foreign and Political Affairs, Economic Planning, and Research	Fiorenzo Stolfi (PSD)
Health and Social Welfare, Equal Opportunity, and Social Security	Fabio Berardi (PSD)
Industry, Crafts, Trade, and Relations with the Public Services Company	Tito Masi (AP)
Internal Affairs and Civil Defense	Valeria Ciavatta (AP) [f]
Justice, Government Relations, and Information	Ivan Foschi (SU)
Labor, Cooperation, and Political Youth Movement	Antonello Bacciocchi (PSD)
Public Education, Cultural Institutions, the University, and Social Affairs	Francesca Michelotti (SU) [f]
Territory, Environment Agriculture, and Relations with the State Production Company	Marino Riccardi (PSD)
Tourism, Sports, Telecommunications, and Economic Cooperation	Paride Andreoli (PSD)

[f] = female

In 2006 it won 2.3 percent of the vote and retained its seat on the council.

Leaders: Vittorio Ennio PELLANDRA (President), Glauco SANSOVINI, Lorenz BERTI (Political Secretary).

Sammarinese for Freedom (*Sammarinesi per la Libertà*—SpL). Founded in 2003, the SpL won 1.8 percent of the vote and one council seat in 2006.

Leaders: Guiseppe ROSSI (President), Monica BOLLINI.

Legislature

The **Grand and General Council** (*Consiglio Grande e Generale*) is a unicameral body consisting of 60 members elected on a proportional basis for five-year terms by direct popular vote. The captains regent serve as presiding officers. At the election of June 4, 2006, the San Marino Christian Democratic Party won 21 seats; the Party of Socialists and Democrats, 20; Popular Alliance, 7; United Left, 5; New Socialist Party, 3; Sammarinese for Freedom, 1; Sammarinese People, 1; San Marino National Alliance, 1; We Sammarinese, 1.

*Captains Regent:*Antonio CARATTONI and Roberto GIORGETTI.

Communications

Press

Newspapers and periodicals are published primarily by the government, by some political parties, and by the trade unions. The main publications are *San Marino Oggi* (San Marino Today), daily; *Nuovo Corriere di Informazione Sammarinese* (New Messenger of San Marino Information), daily; *Repubblica Sera* (Evening Republican), daily; *La Tribuna Sammarinese* (San Marino Tribune), daily; *Il Nuovo Titano* (The New Titano), PSS organ; and *San Marino,* PDCS organ.

News Agency

There is no national facility. For foreign news the media rely primarily on the Italian news agency, ANSA.

Broadcasting

The public service San Marino RTV (*Radiotelevisione*) began broadcasting in 1993, while *Radio Televisione Italiano* (RAI) broadcasts a daily information bulletin about the republic under the title *Notizie di San Marino*. There is also one privately owned radio station (*Radio Titano*). Some 23,000 television receivers were in use in 1999.

Intergovernmental Representation

San Marino does not have diplomatic relations with the United States; it does, however, maintain consular offices in Detroit, New York, and Washington, D.C., while U.S. interests in San Marino are represented by the American consulate general in Florence, Italy

Permanent Representative to the UN
Daniele BODINI

IGO Memberships (Non-UN)
CEUR, OSCE

SERBIA

REPUBLIC OF SERBIA

Republike Srbije

The Country

Pre-1992 Yugoslavia was composed of six constituent republics (Bosnia and Herzegovina, Croatia, Macedonia, Montenegro, Serbia, and Slovenia) that encompassed an area of some 98,800 sq. mi. (255,800 sq. km.) with nearly 24 million inhabitants. The Federal Republic of Yugoslavia (FRY), encompassing Serbia and Montenegro, that was proclaimed in April 1992 contained approximately 40 percent of its predecessor's area and population. While Serbia has a Serb ethnic majority somewhat in excess of 60 percent, they are unevenly distributed. There have been particularly destabilizing effects in Serbia's Kosovo and Metohija Province, over 90 percent of whose 1.7 million inhabitants are ethnic Albanians, and in the Sandžak region of western Serbia, where half the population is ethnic Albanian. Serbia's Vojvodina Province, in the north, has a significant ethnic Hungarian minority. Eastern Orthodox Christianity predominates, although Serbia has a large Muslim minority, the largest communities being among ethnic Albanians in Kosovo and in the Sandžak area. Vojvodina has a significant Roman Catholic minority.

Mostly underdeveloped before World War II, the larger Yugoslavia made rapid advances after 1945 under a Communist regime that applied pragmatic and flexible methods of economic management. Initial policies of forced agricultural collectivization were progressively modified following Belgrade's rupture with Moscow in 1948, and private farms subsequently accounted for about two-thirds of agricultural output. In industry, worker participation in the "social self-management" of enterprises was initiated as early as 1950, with later reforms further institutionalizing decentralization while moving the country toward a Western-style market economy. Close trading relations with the West were established during a 1949–1953 economic boycott by the Soviet bloc, and in 1966 Yugoslavia became the first Communist state to conclude a trade agreement with the European Economic Community.

Political transition and the outbreak of regional conflict in mid-1991 caused the economy to deteriorate rapidly, the decline being aggravated by the imposition of economic sanctions by the United Nations (UN) from May 1992 until November

Political Status: Kingdom of the Serbs, Croats, and Slovenes constituted as an independent monarchy December 1, 1918, and formally renamed Yugoslavia on October 3, 1929; constituent republic of the communist Federal People's Republic of Yugoslavia instituted November 29, 1945, and then of the Socialist Federal Republic of Yugoslavia proclaimed April 7, 1963; constituent republic, along with Montenegro, of the Federal Republic of Yugoslavia, proclaimed April 27, 1992, and of the "state union" of Serbia and Montenegro, established February 4, 2003, under new Constitutional Charter; independent Republic of Serbia established June 5, 2006, following Montenegro's declaration of independence on June 3.

Area: 34,116 sq. mi. (88,361 sq. km.). Included in Serbia are the autonomous provinces of Kosovo and Metohija, 4,203 sq. mi. (10,887 sq. km.), and Vojvodina, 8,304 sq. mi. (21,506 sq. km.).

Population: 10,394,026 (from Yugoslavia's 1991 census, excluding Bosnia and Herzegovina, Croatia, Macedonia, and Slovenia); 10,058,000 (2005E), including Kosovo, 2,040,000, and Vojvodina, 2,231,000. A 2002 census figure of 8,134,617 did not include Kosovo.

Major Urban Centers (2005E): BELGRADE (1,117,000), Novi Sad (Vojvodina, 192,000), Priština (Kosovo, 168,000).

Official Languages: The official language is Serbian; however, in areas established by national minorities, their languages are also accorded official status.

Monetary Unit: Dinar (market rate July 1, 2006: 66.70 dinars = $1US) and euro (market rate July 1, 2006: 1 euro = $1.28US). Both the dinar and the euro are legal tender in the United Nations–administered Serbian province of Kosovo.

President: Boris TADIĆ (Democratic Party); elected in second-round balloting on June 27, 2004, and inaugurated for a five-year term on July 11, succeeding Milan MILUTINOVIĆ (Socialist Party of Serbia), whose term had expired on December 29, 2002. In the interim, three chairs of the National Assembly of Serbia—Nataša MIĆIĆ (from December 30, 2002; Civic Alliance of Serbia/Democratic Opposition of Serbia), Dragan MARŠIĆANIN (from February 4, 2004; Democratic Party of Serbia), and Predrag MARKOVIĆ (from March 4, 2004; G17 Plus)—had served as acting presidents, the presidential elections of October 13, 2002, December 8, 2002, and November 16, 2003, having failed to meet the required 50 percent turnout of eligible voters.

Prime Minister: Vojislav KOŠTUNICA (Democratic Party of Serbia); served as president of the Federal Republic of Yugoslavia 2000–2003; named prime minister-designate on February 20, 2004, by acting president Dragan MARŠIĆANIN, following the election of December 28, 2003; confirmed at the head of a minority government by the National Assembly on March 3, 2004, succeeding Zoran ŽIVCOVIĆ (Democratic Party).

1995. Substantial currency devaluations were undertaken in early 1992, with inflation soaring to a historically unprecedented rate of 1 million percent a month by December 1993. The "super dinar" introduced on January 24, 1994, was valued at 13 million old dinars and had the effect of ending hyperinflation. The GDP of Serbia and Montenegro declined by more than 40 percent in the period of 1990–1995. For the rest of the decade, growth averaged only about 2 percent annually.

The agricultural sector accounted for about one-fifth of GDP but employed under 5 percent of the labor force in 2000, the leading crops being maize, wheat, and sugar beets. Industry contributed about two-fifths of GDP and about one-third of employment. Coal, lead, and zinc are mined in significant quantities, particularly in Kosovo. Major exports have included basic manufactures, machinery and transport equipment, and agricultural products.

Beginning in early 1998 escalating violence in Kosovo led to a renewal of international sanctions. The North Atlantic Treaty Organization (NATO) bombing campaign of March–June 1999 severely damaged the country's productive capacity and economic infrastructure, exacting a major toll on bridges, rail lines, roads, power plants, and communications facilities. Following the cessation of hostilities, the Group of Seven (G-7) announced that it would provide only humanitarian aid to Serbia as long as President Slobodan MILOŠEVIĆ remained in power, while a donor conference of over 100 countries and agencies pledged some $2 billion in reconstructive, humanitarian, and administrative assistance for Kosovo. In late September the government claimed that the NATO air war caused $100 billion in damage, compared to the $30–50 billion estimated by international sources. According to FRY government figures, GDP declined by 16 percent in 1999 because of the Kosovo conflict but increased by 5 percent in 2000. Output nevertheless stood at only half of its 1989 level, and 30 percent of the labor force was unemployed.

Real economic growth of 5.5 percent in 2001 was undercut by an inflation rate of more than 90 percent, largely funded by currency depreciation and rising domestic demand for imports. Structural reform and privatization proceeded slowly, contributing to lower GDP growth of 3.8 percent in 2002 for the FRY and 2.7 percent in 2003 for the state union. At the same time, however, inflation fell dramatically, to about 21 percent in 2002 and 11 percent in 2003. For 2004, estimated growth surged to 8 percent, while inflation rose only slightly, to 13 percent. GDP growth in 2005 was estimated at 5.5 percent in the state union as a whole; inflation rose to more than 16 percent.

Government and Politics

Political Background

Following centuries of national struggle against the Turkish and Hapsburg empires, Yugoslavia emerged as a unified state with the formation on December 1, 1918, of the Kingdom of the Serbs, Croats, and Slovenes under the Serbian House of Karadjordjević. Uniting the former independent kingdoms of Serbia and Montenegro with the Croatian, Dalmatian, and Bosnian and Herzegovinian territories previously ruled by Austria-Hungary, the new entity (formally named Yugoslavia on October 3, 1929) was ruled between World Wars I and II as a highly centralized, Serb-dominated state in which the Croats became an increasingly disaffected minority. The Serb-Croat antagonism, which caused many Croats to sympathize with Nazi Germany and Fascist Italy, continued even after the two Axis powers attacked and occupied the country on April 6, 1941, and set up a pro-Axis puppet state of Croatia that included most of Bosnia and Herzegovina. Wartime resistance to the Axis was led by two rival groups, the proroyalist Chetniks, under Gen. Draža MIHAILOVIĆ, and the Communist-inspired Partisans, led by Marshal Josip Broz TITO, a Croat who sought to enlist all the country's national groups in the liberation struggle. The Partisans' greater effectiveness in opposing the occupation forces and securing Allied aid paved the way for their assumption of power at the end of the war. In March 1945 Tito became prime minister in a "government of national unity"; eight months later, on November 29, the monarchy was abolished and a Federal People's Republic of Yugoslavia, based on the equality of the country's principal national groups, was proclaimed. On January 14, 1953, under a new constitution, Tito was elected president of the republic.

Yugoslavia developed along orthodox Communist lines until 1948, when its refusal to submit to Soviet directives led to its expulsion from the Communist bloc and the imposition of a political and economic blockade by the Soviet Union and its East European allies. Aided by Western arms and economic support, Yugoslavia maintained its autonomy throughout the Stalin era and by the late 1950s had achieved a partial reconciliation with the Soviet-led Warsaw Pact states, although it still insisted on complete independence and the right to find its own "road to socialism." Internally, Yugoslavia had become the first East European country to evolve institutions that moderated the harsher features of Communist rule and encouraged the development of a democratic form of communism based on new interpretations of Marxism. A federal constitution promulgated in 1963 consolidated the system of "social self-management" by attempting to draw the people into economic and administrative decision-making at all levels; it also expanded the independence of the judiciary, increased the responsibilities of the federal legislature and those of the country's six constituent republics and two autonomous provinces (Kosovo and Metohija, and Vojvodina), and widened freedom of choice in elections. During the 1970s Yugoslavia rejected the so-called Brezhnev doctrine of "limited sovereignty" among members of the "Socialist commonwealth," reaffirmed its readiness to fight for its independence if necessary, and proceeded with further applications of the "self-management" principle. These efforts culminated in the adoption of a fourth postwar constitution in 1974.

On May 4, 1980, after a four-month illness, Marshal Tito, president for life of the republic and of the League of Communists of Yugoslavia (*Savez Komunista Jugoslavija*—SKJ), died at the age of 87. The leadership of state and party thereupon passed to collegial executives—the state Presidency and the Presidium of the SKJ Central Committee, respectively. The administrative machinery assembled during the 1970s under Tito and his close associate Edvard KARDELJ (who had died in February 1979) continued to run smoothly.

Through the 1980s the federal state Presidency and the presidency of the party Presidium rotated on an annual basis among the constituent republics without appreciable dispute. A significant innovation in 1989 was that Janez DRNOVŠEK (Slovenia) and Borisav JOVIĆ (Serbia) became state president and vice president, respectively, after being elected to five-year terms on the presidential collegium by popular vote of their constituencies, rather than by the earlier procedure of republican or provincial parliamentary selection.

During 1990 both the federal government and the SKJ experienced acute crises as economic ills exacerbated long-standing political animosities. The 14th (extraordinary) SKJ Congress that convened on January 20, 1990, was forced to adjourn three days later because of a split over introduction of a multiparty system and did not reassemble prior to a brief concluding session on May 26. Meanwhile, both Croatia and Slovenia had conducted open elections in which the SKJ's republican counterparts were defeated, the notable exception being in the Croatian presidential race. The situation was further aggravated when the hard-line Jović acceded to the state presidency on May 15.

On July 2, 1990, Slovenia and Macedonia declared their "full sovereignty" within Yugoslavia, while Croatia approved constitutional changes having much the same effect. On the same day a majority of Serbs endorsed a new constitution that, contrary to the federal document, effectively stripped the provinces of Kosovo and Vojvodina of autonomous status. Concurrently, ethnic Albanian delegates to the Kosovo Assembly declared their province independent of Serbia, proclaiming it a constituent republic of the Yugoslav federation. Serbia responded three days later by dissolving the Kosovo legislature.

In a series of multiparty elections during November and December 1990, former Communists won overwhelmingly in Serbia and Montenegro but were decisively defeated in Bosnia and Herzegovina. The balloting occurred at a time of mounting confrontation between the government of Croatia and the Serb-dominated Yugoslav National Army (*Jugoslovenske Narodne Armije*—JNA). On January 20, 1991, Croatia and Slovenia concluded a mutual defense pact. On February 20 the Slovene Assembly voted for phased secession from the federation; eight days later the Serb-populated regions of Croatia opted for effective secession, prior to proclaiming at year's end a self-styled "Republic of Serbian Krajina."

On March 15, 1991, in an apparent effort to trigger military intervention to preserve the federation, Serbian President Slobodan Milošević instigated the resignation of Jović from the federal presidency; the Montenegrin and Vojvodinan representatives promptly followed suit, while the Kosovo representative was summarily dismissed. However, the army refused to move and the Serbs were forced to back down. On March 28 Milošević joined the presidents of the other five constituent republics in a series of summit meetings that yielded agreement on April 11 to hold a referendum on the country's future. On June 6 the presidents were reported to have agreed to a plan whereby the republics would retain sovereignty within Yugoslavia but would not seek international recognition as independent states. However, the relatively prosperous Slovenes subsequently indicated their unwillingness to continue financial support for the less-developed republics, while Croatia feared that its sizable Serbian minority would force geographic dismemberment if it remained in the federation. As a result, the two western republics declared their independence on June 25. Six days later former Croatian prime minister Stjepan MESIĆ was elevated to the now meaningless post of federal president.

That the federation had in fact expired was quickly apparent in the failure of the JNA to mount real opposition to Slovenia's secession, while much more serious JNA engagement in Croatia was mainly directed to backing local Serbs against Croatian government forces. By late August 1991 the latter conflict had yielded a loss by Croatia of nearly one-third of its territory, although some was later retaken. On September 8 Macedonians voted overwhelmingly for a "sovereign and independent" state, while Bosnia and Herzegovina issued a declaration of sovereignty on October 15. On December 5 Mesić resigned as president of the collective presidency, stating "Yugoslavia no longer exists," with the Croatian Assembly backdating the action to October 8, when its declaration of independence had formally come into effect.

On January 15, 1992, one day after the advance contingent of a UN peacekeeping force had arrived in Yugoslavia, the European Community (EC, subsequently the European Union—EU) recognized the independence of Croatia and Slovenia, while on February 12 Serbia and Montenegro agreed to join in upholding "the principles of a common state which would be a continuation of Yugoslavia." Subsequently, in a referendum held February 29–March 1, Bosnia and Herzegovina opted for independence, and on March 26 Macedonia moved in the same direction by securing the withdrawal of JNA forces from its territory.

On April 27, 1992, a rump Federal Assembly adopted the constitution of a new Federal Republic of Yugoslavia (FRY), under which elections for a successor assembly were held in Serbia and Montenegro on May 31. Milošević's Socialist Party of Serbia (*Socijalistička Partija Srbije*—SPS) won a slim majority in the new lower house, the Chamber of Citizens, in part because opposition elements, including the new Democratic Movement of Serbia (*Demokratska Pokret Srbije*—Depos) coalition, boycotted the balloting. On June 15 the assembly elected Dobrica ĆOSIĆ, a well-known writer and political independent, as federal president. Under the new basic law, Ćosić, a Serb, was obligated to name a Montenegrin to the post of prime minister; however, in an unusual move apparently instigated by Milošević in the hope of currying favor in Washington, Ćosić nominated Milan PANIĆ, a U.S. citizen born in Serbia, who was formally confirmed by the assembly on July 14.

Milošević's policies stirred a series of opposition rallies in Belgrade, including a massive turnout on June 28, 1992, that included an appearance by Prince ALEKSANDAR Karadjordjević, the son of Yugoslavia's last king. The Serbian leader soon became increasingly critical of Panić, who, despite serious doubts as to his residential qualifications, ran against Milošević in the Serbian presidential election on December 20 but was soundly defeated. In simultaneous parliamentary balloting Milošević's SPS maintained its dominance of the Serbian National Assembly. Although the SPS lost ground in the FRY's Federal Assembly, the hardliners and anti-Panić forces were sufficiently strong to secure the overwhelming passage of a nonconfidence motion against the prime minister on December 29.

Amid uncertainty stemming from Panić's refusal to resign, his deputy, Radoje KONTIĆ of Montenegro, was named prime minister on February 9, 1993, and on March 2 he formed a new coalition government. Thereafter, as the FRY's international isolation increased because of the worsening conflict in Bosnia and Herzegovina, the ire of the Serbian hard-liners focused on the nonparty federal president, Ćosić, who was considered a moderate in Serbian terms even though he had drafted the intellectual blueprint for a "greater Serbia." The outcome was another success for the hard-liners on May 31 and June 1, when SPS legislators, apparently with the blessing of the Serbian president, joined with those of the ultranationalist Serbian Radical Party (*Srpska Radikalna Stranka*—SRS) to pass motions in both federal chambers asserting that the president had breached the constitution, thus paving the way for his replacement on June 25 by the chair of the Serbian legislature, Zoran LILIĆ.

Thereafter, President Milošević was increasingly aligned with the "greater Serbia" school, although international pressure had obliged him in early May 1993 to accept the Vance-Owen plan for the cantonization of Bosnia and Herzegovina. Milošević was bitterly denounced for his action by the SRS leader, Vojislav ŠEŠELJ, whose call for a nonconfidence vote forced dissolution of the Serbian National Assembly on October 20. In elections on December 19, the SPS increased its strength in the 250-member body from 101 to 123 seats, while SRS representation declined from 73 to 39 in a contest that saw a marked shift to right-wing nationalist attitudes among the opposition parties. Postelection negotiations led to the formation on March 17, 1994, of a Serbian "cabinet of economists" that was headed by Mirko MARJANOVIĆ (SPS) and also included representation for the New Democracy (*Nova Demokratija*—ND) party. At the federal level a new government, reduced in size and restructured to increase its efficiency, was appointed on September 15 under the continued premiership of Kontić.

In 1995 a major offensive by Croatian government forces recovered most of the "Republic of Serbian Krajina" by early August (see Croatia article). This provoked a storm of criticism of Milošević within Yugoslavia, where hard-line leaders accused the president of doing nothing to prevent the greatest military and humanitarian disaster to befall the Serbs since World War II. Political difficulties were compounded by the flight of some 200,000 Serbian refugees from Krajina, most of them into Yugoslavia, where many supported opposition demands for the government's ouster. The muted response of the Serbian president to the Croat successes (and to subsequent advances by allied Muslim and Croat forces in Bosnia) was widely seen as in line with his recent policy of distancing the Belgrade government from the Croatian and Bosnian Serbs, in part to secure a settlement that would fully lift UN sanctions on Yugoslavia (see Foreign relations, below).

Serbian relations with the province of Kosovo remained in a state of crisis in 1995 and 1996 as ethnic Albanians, resisting Serbian attempts to impose political, social, and educational control, established their own underground administration. Elections to the Kosovo Assembly in May 1992, won by the pro-independence Democratic Alliance of Kosovo (*Lidhja Demokratike e Kosovës*—LDK), had been condemned as illegal by Belgrade, which had officially dissolved the body in 1990. Nevertheless, the LDK leader, Ibrahim RUGOVA, was proclaimed president of a self-declared "Republic of Kosovo" (which secured international recognition only from Albania). The leading Muslim parties boycotted the 1993 Serbian National Assembly election, with no more than 10 percent of the Albanians reported to have participated. Secret negotiations between Serbian and Kosovar representatives in mid-1994 made no apparent progress, and the local situation deteriorated in December when Serbian security forces carried out the most sweeping wave of arrests since 1990 in an effort to eliminate the unauthorized police force created by the ethnic Albanians. Tension intensified further in mid-1995 when the Belgrade government announced that Serb refugees from Krajina would be resettled in Kosovo with the aim of redressing the province's ethnic imbalance.

Elections in November 1996 took place amid increasing voter dissatisfaction with government mismanagement, crime, and corruption, as well as with the lack of economic improvement following the suspension a year earlier of UN sanctions. In the balloting for the federal Chamber of Citizens on November 3, 1996, an alliance of Milošević's SPS, the Yugoslav United Left (*Jugoslovenska Levica*—JUL), and the ND won 64 of the 138 seats, while the government-aligned Democratic Party of Socialists of Montenegro (*Demokratska Partija Socijalista Crne Gore*—DPSCG) secured 20 seats.

SRS representation fell to 16, while the Together (*Zajedno*) coalition of moderate opposition parties obtained a disappointing 22 seats in the federal contest. In mid-November, however, following a second round of balloting for local assemblies, the opposition parties claimed victory in most of Serbia's cities, including Belgrade. The SPS-controlled courts and electoral commissions quickly annulled the municipal results, alleging irregularities. In response, the opposition parties, joined by students and later the Serbian Orthodox Church and teachers, staged mass demonstrations of up to 250,000 people in the streets of Belgrade. After 88 days of marches, Milošević, on February 11, 1997, finally felt compelled to have the Serbian National Assembly confirm the opposition electoral victories.

Once in office, the opposition found its hands tied, the pro-Milošević bureaucracy having collaborated with departing SPS politicians in the mass transfer of government property from localities to the SPS-dominated Serbian state. Moreover, cracks began appearing in the facade of the *Zajedno* coalition in the spring of 1997 as its constituent parties were unable to agree on a common candidate for the federal presidency. In the wake of the SPS's nomination of Milošević, the Serbian Renewal Movement (*Srpski Pokret Obnove*—SPO) on June 24 announced withdrawal from (and hence the death of) the coalition, even though two other *Zajedno* parties, the Democratic Party (*Demokratska Stranka*—DS) and the Democratic Party of Serbia (*Demokratska Stranka Srbije*—DSS), continued to cooperate with each other.

On July 15, 1997, Milošević, constitutionally barred from running for a third term as president of Serbia, was elected unopposed as federal president. However, he subsequently continued to face electoral threats to his power as both Serbia (in September) and Montenegro (in October) held presidential and parliamentary elections. Despite boycotts by two of the three main opposition parties and by Albanians in Kosovo, turnout in the first round of Serbian elections on September 21 was reported to have passed the 50 percent threshold needed for them to be valid. In Serbia's parliamentary elec-

tions, Milošević's SPS and allies won a plurality of seats but were faced with having to rely on either the second-place SRS or the third-place opposition SPO for a parliamentary majority. After months of negotiations, on March 24, 1998, the SPS and its ally, the JUL, formed a government with the SRS under the continued leadership of Prime Minister Marjanović.

Meanwhile, in the first round of the Serbian presidential election (also on September 21, 1997), no candidate had won an absolute majority, forcing a runoff between Milošević's hand-picked SPS candidate, Zoran Lilić, and SRS leader Vojislav Šešelj. The results of the October 5 second round favored Šešelj but were annulled by law as turnout had fallen below 50 percent. New first-round elections were held on December 7, with Šešelj facing a new SPS candidate—Foreign Minister Milan MILUTINOVIĆ—and five other candidates. At the December 21 runoff Milutinović handily defeated Šešelj with 59 percent of the vote. The election was subsequently labeled as "fundamentally flawed" by the Conference on (later Organization for) Security and Cooperation in Europe (CSCE/OSCE).

Having fallen out of favor with President Milošević, Prime Minister Kontić lost a confidence vote in the upper chamber of the Federal Assembly on May 18, 1998. He was succeeded the following day by Milošević ally and former Montenegrin president Momir BULATOVIĆ of the recently organized Socialist People's Party of Montenegro (*Socijalistička Narodna Partija Crne Gore*—SNPCG). Bulatović had lost a close bid for reelection in October 1997, largely because of a split between pro- and anti-Milošević forces in his previous party, the DPSCG.

By this point, tensions had worsened in Kosovo, which Serbians considered their historic homeland. Following the murder of four Serbian policemen on February 28, 1998, by members of the separatist Kosovo Liberation Army (KLA), a retaliatory security operation killed 24 ethnic Albanian villagers, many apparently by summary execution. On March 2 some 50,000 protesters demonstrated in Priština, the Kosovar capital, while the United States and the EU, among others, condemned the excessive use of force. Despite a series of diplomatic missions to Belgrade and Priština, the Serbian crackdown continued, provoking additional demonstrations and calls by regional neighbors and the six-member international Contact Group on former Yugoslavia (see Foreign relations, below) for restraint and the opening of talks on Kosovar autonomy. On March 22 ethnic Albanians, in addition to casting ballots for the shadow "Republic of Kosovo" legislature, reelected the LDK's Ibrahim Rugova as shadow president, although some ethnic Albanian parties boycotted the vote, partly in opposition to Rugova's policy of passive resistance in the effort to achieve Kosovar independence.

With daily demonstrations continuing in the province, U.S. diplomats succeeded in convincing President Milošević and Rugova to meet for the first time on May 15, 1998. Although both sides agreed to initiate weekly talks in Priština, the violence in Kosovo continued to escalate as Serbian army and paramilitary security forces, sweeping through Kosovar villages, met strong resistance from the rapidly expanding KLA. In June Milošević rejected diplomatic efforts by U.S. negotiator Richard Holbrooke and Russian President Boris Yeltsin to include the KLA in talks, declare a cease-fire, and withdraw his forces from Kosovo. By then, reports of civilian massacres, torture, and other human rights violations committed by Serbian contingents were regularly surfacing, contributing to the prospect of NATO intervention. On October 12, facing the threat of imminent NATO air strikes, Milošević agreed to begin withdrawing military and security forces from Kosovo and to allow entry of 2,000 international observers supervised by the OSCE. Although violations of the cease-fire occurred on both sides, the first peace monitors were deployed in November. Fighting intensified again in mid-December, but late in the month both sides accepted a local cease-fire brokered by the head of the OSCE mission. In January 1999, however, widespread hostilities resumed despite renewed threats from NATO. On January 15 the worst atrocity of the conflict to date occurred when Serbian forces executed 45 civilians from the village of Račak.

On February 6, 1999, peace talks between Serbian officials and ethnic Albanians—including KLA representatives—opened in Rambouillet, France. Cosponsored by France and the United States, the negotiations were aimed at winning approval of a proposal by the Contact Group that, while acknowledging Serbian sovereignty in Kosovo, envisaged almost complete administrative autonomy for the province, the withdrawal of all but 1,500 Serbian border troops, the rapid disbanding of the KLA, and formation of a new, ethnically balanced police force. The plan would also require Serbia to accept the stationing of NATO troops on its soil, which had become the major sticking point for the Milošević regime. On February 23 both sides accepted the autonomy plan in principle, but despite the urgings of U.S. Secretary of State Madeleine Albright and others, neither signed the accord. Talks resumed in Paris on March 15 and three days later the Kosovar delegation finally signed the pact. However, the talks came to an abrupt halt on March 19 when the Serbian delegation continued to reject the presence of NATO peacekeepers. Holbrooke met with Milošević in Belgrade March 22–23 in a final, futile diplomatic effort to avoid war.

On March 24, 1999, NATO forces from eight countries initiated Operation Allied Force, the most extensive air campaign in Europe since the close of World War II. In the following weeks allied bombing extended throughout Yugoslavia in an effort to force the Milošević regime to accept the Rambouillet agreement. Amid increasing allegations of massacres and other war crimes in Kosovo, Serbian forces stepped up a widespread campaign of "ethnic cleansing" that saw the entire Albanian population forced from some cities and villages, creating an immediate refugee crisis at the borders of Albania and Macedonia. By the end of April the refugee exodus was swelling toward 750,000, with additional hundreds of thousands displaced within the province itself. The main Serbian opposition parties, a number of which had earlier joined various nongovernmental organizations in an umbrella grouping, the Alliance for Change (*Savez za Promene*—SZP), were largely silenced by the country's war footing. The loudest dissenting voice was that of Deputy Prime Minister Vuk DRAŠKOVIĆ of the SPO. Having joined the government on January 18 in a show of national solidarity, he was dismissed on April 28 for having stated two days earlier that the populace should be told, contrary to government contentions, "that NATO is not facing a breakdown, that Russia will not help Yugoslavia militarily, and that world public opinion is against us." In Montenegro, President Milo DJUKANOVIĆ (Bulatović's successor) continued his efforts to distance his administration from federal policies. Even though Montenegro was not exempt from the NATO air campaign, and despite rumors that the Serbian military was preparing to depose him, on April 21 Djukanović rejected orders that the Montenegrin police be placed under the command of the army. Djukanović accused Milošević of using "the pretext of the defense of the country" to displace the civil government.

On May 6, 1999, the G-7 countries plus Russia (G-8) proposed a peace plan providing for "deployment in Kosovo of effective international civil and security presences" and formation of an interim provincial administration under the UN Security Council. On June 3 President Milošević accepted the terms of an amended peace agreement offered by President Martii Ahtisaari of Finland and Russia's Viktor Chernomyrdin, including the deployment in Kosovo (but not the rest of Serbia) of a UN-sponsored, NATO-dominated peacekeeping contingent (Kosovo Force, or KFOR) expected to number some 50,000 troops. The agreement also called for the complete withdrawal of the Serb army, police, and paramilitary forces from Kosovo. On June 10 NATO suspended its bombing campaign and the UN Security Council adopted Resolution 1244, authorizing the international troop deployment and the establishment of an interim civilian administration in Kosovo. The resolution also reaffirmed Yugoslavia's "sovereignty and territorial integrity" but echoed previous calls for "substantial autonomy and meaningful self-administration in Kosovo." The agreement was widely, though often reluctantly, accepted by most

of the opposition, including Serbian nationalists, the principal exception being the SRS, which on June 14 protested by announcing its withdrawal from the coalition government in Serbia. (The withdrawal was technically prohibited by Serbian President Milutinović because of the state of war.) Meanwhile, on May 27 the International Criminal Tribunal for the former Yugoslavia (ICTY) had indicted President Milošević and four others, including the interior minister and army chief of staff, for crimes against humanity related to events in Kosovo.

On June 14, 1999, the UN Security Council received a plan for the civil Kosovo administration: the EU would supervise reconstruction, and the OSCE would oversee institution-building. Humanitarian and administrative matters would primarily fall in the purview of the Office of the UN High Commissioner for Refugees (UNHCR) and a newly established UN Interim Administration in Kosovo (UNMIK), respectively. On June 20, with the Yugoslav army having completely withdrawn from Kosovo, NATO formally concluded its bombing campaign. On the same day NATO and the KLA signed an agreement providing for KLA demilitarization, although Hashim THAÇI, the KLA leader, refused to renounce the eventual goal of Kosovar independence. Most of the 1 million or more Kosovo Albanian refugees and displaced persons were already returning to their homes, contributing to the collateral flight from the province of ethnic Serbs, many of whom feared reprisals.

In July 1999 UNMIK, headed by French Secretary of State for Health Bernard Kouchner, established a consultative, multiethnic Kosovo Transitional Council (KTC), although the LDK's Rugova initially refused to participate because not all the parties in his shadow government were included. In December UNMIK announced formation of an Interim Administrative Council (IAC) of Rugova, Thaçi, and Rexhep QOSJA of the United Democratic Movement (*Lëvizja Bashimit Demokratike*— LBD); a fourth seat on the IAC was reserved for a representative of the Serb community, which refused to participate. By then, forensic specialists from the international war crimes tribunal had already exhumed thousands of Albanian bodies from mass graves in Kosovo. Late in the year, the Albanian death toll was estimated at 4,000–5,000, considerably less than originally projected.

On August 12, 1999, a federal cabinet reshuffle saw the addition of SRS ministers to the Bulatović administration in an effort to shore up support for Milošević. Political opposition to Milošević nevertheless continued to mount, although the SPO's Drašković remained aloof from an SZP campaign launched on September 21 to demand early elections. On January 10, 2000, however, the SPO leader joined his principal opposition rival, Zoran DJINDJIĆ of the DS, in forging a unified strategy that was signed by 16 opposition parties. Earlier, in Montenegro, the republican government had proposed replacing the federal republic with a looser association in which Montenegro would set its own foreign and military policy and establish independent currency controls.

On April 18, 2000, the Eurocorps, with troop contingents from Germany, Spain, France, Belgium, and Luxembourg, took over control of the Kosovo peacekeeping effort from NATO, but KFOR was encountering increasing difficulty in preventing violent clashes between Albanian and Serb communities. The climate of violence was not, however, limited to Kosovo: the Yugoslav defense minister, Pavle BULATOVIĆ, was assassinated in Belgrade on February 7, while the SPO's Drašković was wounded on June 16 in Montenegro.

In a gambit designed to maintain Milošević's hold on power, on July 6, 2000, the SPS pushed through the Federal Assembly constitutional changes authorizing direct election of the president and of the upper legislative house. With most of the opposition continuing its boycott of parliament, the proposals easily received the necessary two-thirds support. The changes, in addition to permitting the incumbent to serve two additional four-year terms, put organization of elections under the FRY instead of the individual republics. On July 8 the Montenegrin assembly described the changes as "illegal" and "a gross violation of the constitutional rights of the Republic of Montenegro." The Montenegrin legislators nevertheless rejected a proposal for an immediate referendum on Montenegrin independence.

On July 27, 2000, Milošević called elections for September, even though his presidential term would not expire until July 2001. The governing coalition in Montenegro quickly announced that it would boycott the balloting. On August 7 the Democratic Opposition of Serbia (*Demokratske Opozicije Srbije*—DOS), ultimately encompassing some 18 parties and a trade union association, nominated Vojislav KOŠTUNICA, leader of the DSS, as their joint presidential candidate. The SPO, running independently, nominated the mayor of Belgrade, Vojislav MIHAJLOVIĆ, raising the prospect of a split in the opposition vote.

Despite allegations of vote-rigging and other irregularities committed by the incumbent's supporters, Koštunica emerged from the September 24 balloting as the likely leader, although the SPS initially claimed otherwise. In the legislative balloting, the DOS won a plurality in the lower house, but the electoral boycott by Montenegro's governing parties left the balance of power in the hands of the pro-Milošević SNPCG. On September 26 the government-controlled election commission admitted that Koštunica held the lead in the presidential tally, but with less than the 50 percent needed to avoid a runoff with Milošević. Rejecting the commission's count, Koštunica refused to participate in a second round scheduled for October 8. In the following days massive street demonstrations called for Milošević to step down, the Serb Orthodox Church began referring to Koštunica as the president, the Yugoslav army made it clear that it would not intervene, and ultranationalist SRS leader Vojislav Šešelj announced that he, too, would support Koštunica's claim to the presidency. On October 4 the Constitutional Court annulled the presidential poll, but two days later, with the country in the grip of a general strike and with pro-DOS demonstrators in Belgrade having burned the Federal Assembly and other buildings, the court reversed itself and declared that Koštunica had won 50.2 percent of the vote (some sources put the total at 55–56 percent). On the same day Milošević conceded, and the new president took office on October 7.

Faced with mounting opposition, the SPS-led government of Serbia resigned on October 21, 2000. The SPS's Milomir MINIĆ assumed office as prime minister on October 24 at the head of a transitional cabinet of the SPS, DOS, and SPO, pending a Serbian National Assembly election set for December 23. On November 4 the Federal Assembly confirmed the nomination of Zoran ŽIŽIĆ of the SNPCG as federal prime minister, Momir Bulatović having resigned on October 9. The Žižić cabinet included an equal number of ministers from the SNPCG and the DOS, plus two reform-oriented, nominally unaffiliated economists with strong ties to the DOS.

Municipal elections in Kosovo were held on October 28, 2000, under UNMIK supervision. Participation by ethnic Serbs was minimal. Rugova's LDK finished first, well ahead of Thaçi's recently formed Democratic Party of Kosovo (*Partia Demokratike e Kosovës*—PDK).

At the Serbian republican election of December 23, 2000, the DOS handily defeated Milošević's SPS, winning 176 of the National Assembly's 250 seats, with 64 percent of the vote. On January 25, 2001, Zoran Djindjić of the DOS-affiliated DS took office at the head of a new DOS-dominated Serbian cabinet that also included members of the DOS-supportive G17 Plus economic think tank and several independents.

On April 1, 2001, after a violent standoff outside the former president's villa, Serbian police arrested Slobodan Milošević on charges of corruption and abuse of power. A debate continued over where he should be tried, as some members of the federal administration called for surrendering him to the ICTY even though President Koštunica opposed any such action in the absence of legislation or a constitutional change authorizing extradition. Within the Federal Assembly efforts to pass extradition legislation were repeatedly stymied by the SNPCG. As a consequence, on June 23 the majority of the federal cabinet—minus the absent Prime Minister Žižić and all but one SNPCG minister—issued a decree on cooperation with the war crimes tribunal. On June 28 the FRY Constitutional Court stayed the decree pending determination of its con-

stitutionality, but Serbian Prime Minister Djindjić and his cabinet, meeting in an emergency session and in near unanimity, discredited the court and refused to accept the stay. Justifying their action under a provision of the Serbian constitution that allows the Serbian government to act unilaterally and temporarily on behalf of the whole country if federal authorities are unable to do so, the Serbian authorities immediately surrendered Milošević to UN representatives, who flew him to the Netherlands. In reaction, FRY Prime Minister Žižić resigned on June 29, although he remained on in a caretaker capacity until the confirmation on July 17 of Dragiša PEŠIĆ, also of the SNPCG.

In the context of a growing rivalry between Federal President Koštunica and Serbian Prime Minister Djindjić, the DSS withdrew from the Serbian coalition government on August 17, 2001, ostensibly over the government's inaction in fighting organized crime. A precipitating factor was the murder earlier in the month of a former secret police agent who had claimed knowledge of connections between government officials and organized crime. In December the DSS's Dragan MARŠIĆANIN resigned under pressure as speaker of the Serbian National Assembly to avert a dismissal motion advanced by Djindjić's allies. The increasing distance between the DSS and the DOS culminated on June 12, 2002, when the DSS withdrew from the Serbian legislature in protest of a government effort to replace 21 DSS deputies for absenteeism and to distribute some of their seats to other parties.

At balloting for a new 120-member Kosovo Assembly on November 17, 2001, Ibrahim Rugova's LDK had won a plurality of 47 seats, while Hashim Thaçi's PDK finished with 26 and the multiparty Serbian Return Coalition (*Koalicija Povratak*—KP) took 22. After opening its first session on December 10 the assembly, which has limited provisional powers, elected a seven-member administrative presidency, but three days later it failed to elect a provincial president; Rugova, the only viable candidate for the office, received 49 votes, well short of the two-thirds needed for election, when rival parties refused to participate. A second attempt on January 10, 2002, again failed, and it wasn't until March 4 that Rugova was finally elected. Under a power-sharing arrangement, Bajram REXHEPI of the PDK was named prime minister of a cabinet that included nine additional members: four from the LDK, two from the PDK, two from the Alliance for the Future of Kosovo (*Aleanca për Ardhmërinë e Kosovës*—AAK), and one from the KP. Meanwhile, on January 21 Michael Steiner of Germany had succeeded Hans Haekkerup of Denmark as head of UNMIK.

On March 14, 2002, the governments of Serbia, Montenegro, and the FRY announced an "agreement in principle" that would bring the history of Yugoslavia as such to an end, with its replacement by a "state union" to be called Serbia and Montenegro. Over the objections of parties that wanted a separate and independent Serbia, the Serbian legislature ratified the accord 149–79 on April 9. The same day, the Montenegrin legislature voted in favor of the agreement 58–11, but dissatisfaction on the part of proindependence parties soon cost the Montenegrin government its majority. On May 31, both chambers of the Federal Assembly approved the state union agreement by wide margins.

In August 2002, with the federal presidency certain to be replaced by a much weaker union presidency, Federal President Koštunica entered the race for the Serbian presidency. At the September 29 election he won a leading 31 percent of the vote. Second place, with 27 percent, went to Miroljub LABUS, the federal deputy prime minister and the hand-picked candidate of Serbian Prime Minister Djindjić. At a runoff election on October 13 Koštunica took about 67 percent of the vote, but the turnout fell under 50 percent, invalidating the results. A repeat election on December 8, which pitted Koštunica against the SRS's Vojislav Šešelj and one other candidate, met the same fate, leaving Serbia without an elected president when Milutinović's term expired near the end of the month.

On January 27 and 29, 2003, the Serbian and then the Montenegrin assemblies approved a Constitutional Charter for the state union of Serbia and Montenegro. The Federal Assembly concurred on February 4 (by votes of 26–7 in the upper chamber and 84–31 in the lower), thereby excising Yugoslavia from the political map. Under the charter a new state union Assembly of Serbia and Montenegro was elected by and from among the members of the FRY, Serbian, and Montenegrin legislatures, and the new assembly in turn elected the DPSCG's Svetozar MAROVIĆ, the only candidate, as state union president and chair of the Council of Ministers on March 7.

Five days later Serbian Prime Minister Zoran Djindjić was assassinated by an organized Belgrade criminal gang, the Zemun Clan, many of whose members had served in Slobodan Milošević's Special Operations Unit (the so-called "Red Berets"). In the following weeks thousands of individuals were questioned in the case, and dozens were ultimately charged with involvement in the crime. Djindjić was succeeded in an acting capacity by Deputy Prime Minister Nebojša ČOVIĆ of the DOS-affiliated Democratic Alternative (*Demokratska Alternativa*—DA), with the Serbian legislature then confirming the DS's Zoran ŽIVKOVIĆ as the new prime minister on March 18, 2003.

Later in the year, the DOS-led government of the Serbian Republic lost its legislative majority, precipitating an early National Assembly election on December 28, 2003. With the DOS alliance having dissolved, the ultranationalist SRS won a plurality of 82 seats but was unable to form a government. Thus, Vojislav Koštunica, who had stepped down as the last president of the FRY on March 3, 2003, was named Serbian prime minister-designate on February 20, 2004, by Dragan Maršićanin—the second of three acting Serbian presidents following the expiration of Milutinović's term in 2002. On March 3, 2004, the newly elected Serbian legislature confirmed Koštunica as the head of a minority government that included his DSS, the allied SPO and New Serbia (*Nova Srbija*—NS), and the G17 Plus. Because of its minority status, the new government depended on parliamentary support from the SPS.

In February 2004, three months after another invalidated Serbian presidential election, the Serbian Assembly eliminated the 50 percent turnout requirement. At a fresh election on June 13 Tomislav NIKOLIĆ of the ultranationalist SRS finished first, with 31 percent of the vote, against a dozen other candidates, including the DS's Boris TADIĆ (28 percent) and independent businessman Bogoljub KARIĆ (18 percent). At runoff balloting on June 27, however, Tadić, having gained the support of most mainstream parties, won 54 percent to Nikolić's 46 percent, and he was inaugurated as Serbian president on July 11.

At the second election for the Kosovo Assembly, held October 23, 2004, President Rugova's LDK again finished first, winning 47 of 120 seats, followed by Thaçi's PDK with 30. For the most part the Serbian community boycotted the balloting, with most of the 10 reserved Serbian seats being awarded to a Serbian List for Kosovo and Metohija (*Srpska Lista za Kosovo i Metohiju*—SLKM) that included members of the KP. On December 3 the newly convened legislature reelected Rugova as president and confirmed a cabinet headed by Ramush HARADINAJ of the AAK, which had finished third, with 9 seats. The minority government also included the LDK and one minister from the Bosniac Coalition "Vakat" (*Koalicija "Vakat"*), plus two (initially unfilled) posts for Serbs. The selection of Haradinaj, a former KLA commander, caused the Serbian government to withdraw from first-ever direct talks with Kosovar officials, which had opened in Vienna, Austria, on October 14, 2003.

Haradinaj's tenure as Kosovo's prime minister proved short, however: on March 8, 2005, he resigned and shortly afterward surrendered to the ICTY to face charges that included crimes against humanity. His successor, the less controversial Bajram KOSUMI, also of the AAK, was confirmed by the legislature on March 23. Less than a year later, on January 21, 2006, President Rugova died of cancer, which began a series of leadership changes. Nexhat DACI, speaker of the Kosovo Assembly, served as acting president until February 10, when Fatmir SEJDIU of the LDK was elected president by the assembly. Prime Minister Kosumi then resigned on March 1, under pressure for stronger leadership during UN-mediated negotiations over Kosovo's future political status. President Sejdiu named Agim CEKU, a former officer in the Croat-

ian Army and more recently a general in the Kosovo Protection Corps, as prime minister on March 10. Ceku left Kosumi's cabinet nearly intact, dismissing only Deputy Prime Minister Adem SALIHAJ of the LDK. Collaterally, Speaker Daci was forced to resign by his party, the LDK, and was replaced by Kole BERISHA, the party's secretary general.

Under their 2003 EU-backed state union agreement, both Serbia and Montenegro had the right to vote on the question of independence in three years. On May 21, 2006, by a half a percentage point above the EU-set threshold of 55 percent for approval, Montenegro's voters chose separation from Serbia, and on June 3 the Montenegrin Assembly passed a declaration of independence. Although many Serbians were unhappy with what they viewed as an abrupt divorce, on June 5 the Serbian National Assembly declared Serbia to be the independent successor state to the state union, as had been agreed upon under the charter, and thereby extinguished the last remnants of the former Yugoslavia. The two countries then began the process of disentangling their institutions.

Constitution and Government

Yugoslavia under successive postwar constitutions remained a Communist one-party state until the emergence of a variety of opposition groups at the republican level in early 1990.

The constitution of the Federal Republic of Yugoslavia, adopted on April 27, 1992, provided for a bicameral Federal Assembly, encompassing a Chamber of Republics (with equal representation for Serbia and Montenegro) and a Chamber of Citizens apportioned on the basis of population. The federal president was elected to a four-year term by the assembly until July 2000, when the legislature passed constitutional changes that instituted direct elections for the presidency as well as for the Chamber of Republics. The president was expected to nominate a prime minister from the other constituent republic.

The Constitutional Charter of the state union of Serbia and Montenegro (including Serbia's Autonomous Province of Vojvodina and Autonomous

Province of Kosovo and Metohija) was formally adopted in February 2003 and lasted until both countries chose independence in 2006. It established a presidency with circumscribed powers, although the head of state also served as chair of the Council of Ministers. The president was elected for a single four-year term by the unicameral legislature, the Assembly of Serbia and Montenegro, which comprised 91 Serbian and 35 Montenegrin deputies; although initially indirectly elected, in the future deputies were to have been directly elected for four-year terms.

The state union president and the assembly president could not be from the same member state. Shared responsibility also carried through to the defense and foreign affairs portfolios, which had to be held by ministers from different states; each of the two ministers had a deputy from the other state, with the minister and deputy to exchange places halfway through the term of office. Also, the Constitutional Charter established at the apex of the military command structure a Supreme Command Council (SCC), comprising the state union president and the presidents of the two constituent republics.

The Court of Serbia and Montenegro, with an equal number of judges from each republic, was empowered to adjudicate conflicts between the states, disputes between a state and the state union, and issues of compatibility between state union and republican constitutions and laws. It could also hear appeals from citizens regarding rights and freedoms guaranteed by the Constitutional Charter, which called for enforcement of the "provisions of international treaties on human and minority rights and civil freedoms."

Each of the constituent republics had a popularly elected president and unicameral assembly, with a prime minister nominated by the former and confirmed by the latter. The judicial systems included Constitutional and Supreme Courts as well as lower-level courts.

Article 60 of the Constitutional Charter specified that after three years a member state could choose to initiate steps toward independence, which had to be approved by referendum in the initiating state. (No such provision was included with regard to Kosovo or Vojvodina.) When Montenegro ultimately chose independence, Serbia became the successor to the state union, thereby inheriting the former federation's membership in the UN and all other international organizations.

The Serbian National Assembly was actively drafting a new constitution in 2005–2006, a matter made more urgent by the end of the state union. The new constitution is slated for completion and ratification by the assembly before the end of 2006. One sticking point for the partners in the Koštunica government was over the method of selecting the president of the republic. The DSS has argued for direct election, while the G17 Plus has advocated selection by the assembly.

Foreign Relations

Following the 1948 break with Moscow, Yugoslavian foreign policy concentrated on maintaining the country's independence from both major power blocs. Though highly critical of U.S. policy in Vietnam and the Middle East, Belgrade was equally critical of the Warsaw Pact intervention in Czechoslovakia in 1968, the Moscow-supported Vietnamese invasion of Kampuchea (Cambodia) in 1978–1979, and the Soviet intervention in Afghanistan in December 1979. The Tito regime consistently advocated peace, disarmament, détente, and aid to anticolonial and developmental struggles of third world countries; along with Egypt's Nasser and India's Nehru, Yugoslavian President Tito was considered a founder of the Nonaligned Movement.

Regionally, relations with Bulgaria were impeded by Sofia's insistence that all Macedonians be recognized as ethnically Bulgarian, while nationalist sentiments among ethnic Albanians, particularly in Kosovo, complicated Yugoslavian-Albanian relations. Long bitterly hostile to the "revisionists" in Belgrade, Tirana did not agree to establish diplomatic relations until 1971, and even then unrest in Kosovo continued to fuel mutual hostility.

Federal Yugoslavia was ostracized by much of the international community because of military action in support of Serbs in Croatia and in Bosnia and Herzegovina, although Belgrade insisted in early 1992 that all its troops had been withdrawn from both republics. Because of the Bosnian conflict, the UN Security Council on May 30 imposed comprehensive sanctions that included barriers to trade, a freezing of Yugoslavia's foreign assets, severance of air links, a reduction in diplomatic relations, and suspension of sporting, cultural, and technical exchanges. The EC ordered a trade embargo, and in November military units from NATO and the Western European Union were detailed to enforce both the UN and EC sanctions. On September 22 the UN General Assembly voted to exclude the FRY from its proceedings and insisted that it apply for UN membership rather than being permitted to succeed to the seat held by its predecessor. In a subsequent "clarification," a Russian spokesman insisted that the action referred only to the General Assembly, leaving truncated Yugoslavia as the successor state in all other UN bodies. By the end of 1992, however, Yugoslavia had also been suspended from the International Monetary Fund (IMF), as well as from the OSCE and the Central European Initiative. Nevertheless, Belgrade was not entirely without external supporters: Greece (an EC/EU member) saw the rump state as a natural ally in its disputes with Macedonia and Albania, while religious and ethnic ties contributed to significant Russian sympathy and diplomatic support for the Serb cause.

Intensified UN sanctions on the FRY compelled the Belgrade government to take an overtly stronger line with the Bosnian Serbs following the tabling of new peace proposals in early July 1994. Drawn up by the five-nation Contact Group (of Britain, France, Germany, Russia, and the United States, together with the UN and EU), the so-called Stoltenberg-Owen plan abandoned the cantonization concept and proposed instead the effective partition of Bosnia and Herzegovina into Muslim/Croat and Serb areas. However, the Bosnian Serbs rejected the plan overwhelmingly, both in their "parliament" and in a referendum held August 27–28. Belgrade's response was to announce the severance of all political and economic ties with

the Bosnian Serbs and to agree on September 14 to the deployment of international observers on the Yugoslav-Bosnian border to monitor compliance with the official blockade.

Belgrade's reward was UN Security Council approval on September 24, 1994, of a selective suspension of sanctions, including the resumption of international flights to Yugoslavia, the reopening of the Montenegrin port of Bar on the Adriatic, and the restoration of sporting and cultural links. Following the intensification of NATO aerial attacks in late August 1995, the Bosnian and Croatian Serb leaders were pressured into accepting the primary role of the Serbian president in peace negotiations with the Contact Group. The Bosnian Serbs could no longer veto settlement proposals deemed acceptable by Belgrade. As a result, after three weeks of intense negotiations between the protagonists conducted under U.S. sponsorship in Dayton, Ohio, a peace agreement was concluded on November 21, 1995 (see Bosnia and Herzegovina article), and initialed on behalf of Yugoslavia and the Bosnian Serbs by President Milošević. Suspended the following day, UN sanctions against Belgrade were formally lifted by a unanimous Security Council vote on October 1, 1996 (although FRY assets remained frozen because of disputes and claims from other Yugoslav successor states).

Yugoslavia's standing in the international community improved somewhat in 1997 through Milošević's key role in settling the internal rift in a Bosnian constituent unit, the Serb Republic. Beginning in late February 1998, however, Serbian police and military actions in Kosovo again put Yugoslavia at odds with much of the rest of the world. On March 10 Bulgaria, Greece, Macedonia, Romania, and Turkey jointly appealed for a dialogue on the Kosovo question, while on March 31 the UN Security Council imposed an arms embargo on Yugoslavia. From April to June the Contact Group, which now included Italy, met several times, with only Russia dissenting from the imposition of various economic sanctions. On June 13 the group called for a cease-fire, the withdrawal of FRY and Serb forces, the stationing of international monitors in Kosovo, and new talks between

Belgrade and ethnic Albanians. A September UN Security Council also called for a cease-fire and condemned the "excessive and indiscriminate use of force" by the Serb military and security units. In November, with the October cease-fire holding, Belgrade barred members of the UN war crimes tribunal from entering Kosovo to investigate allegations of extrajudicial killings, prompting the U.S. president of the tribunal to brand Yugoslavia as a "rogue state, one that holds the international rule of law in contempt."

Although Yugoslavia stated during the February 1999 peace talks in Rambouillet, France, that it was prepared to consider regional autonomy for Kosovo, it continued to reject a NATO presence on its soil. Immediately following the start of the NATO bombing campaign on March 24, 1999, Belgrade declared a state of war and broke diplomatic relations with France, Germany, the United Kingdom, and the United States. Relations with all four were restored in November 2000 as Yugoslavia, now headed by Vojislav Koštunica, moved broadly to reestablish its international linkages. The FRY was formally reintegrated into the UN on November 1 and into the OSCE on November 27. On May 25, 2001, meeting in Vienna, the FRY and the other four Yugoslav successor states reached agreement on the division of assets from the former Yugoslavia. In April 2003 it joined the Council of Europe, and two months later it applied for membership in NATO's Partnership for Peace (PfP) program.

Prior to Montenegro's declaration of independence, the state union's ambitions to join the EU were complicated by the differences between the Serbian and Montenegrin currency, customs, and market regimes. Negotiations with the EU on a Stabilization and Association Agreement (SAA) as a precursor to EU membership primarily stalled, however, because of Serbia's testy relationship with the ICTY and the unresolved status of Kosovo. Although a number of once-prominent Serbian military leaders voluntarily surrendered to the ICTY in 2004 and 2005, the prosecutors in The Hague continued to insist that Belgrade had not rigorously pursued Radovan KARADŽIĆ and Ratko MLADIĆ, the most notorious Bosnian Serb commanders. Some human rights advocates have charged that Serbia has actively protected the two, who are under indictment for genocide and other crimes. The Serbian government has denied the accusations, even though Prime Minister Koštunica has consistently argued that Serbians suspected of criminal acts during the Croatian, Bosnian, and Kosovar conflicts should be tried by a Serbian war crimes court. The matter of cooperation with the ICTY also delayed consideration by NATO of Serbia's participation in its PfP program. Montenegro, after the dissolution of the state union, was free to pursue precursor agreements with the EU and PfP participation independently. Meanwhile, the EU suspended SAA negotiations with Serbia on May 3, 2006, after Belgrade failed once more to apprehend and turn over Mladić.

Current Issues

A 2004 report by the government acknowledged Serbian involvement in the 1995 massacre of some 8,000 Muslim men and boys outside Srebrenica, Bosnia and Herzegovina. In June 2005 a state-run television channel for the first time broadcast videotape showing Serbian paramilitaries executing victims. Although the general public responded with shock and outrage, it remains divided on the overarching issue of societal responsibility. During a visit to Bosnia and Herzegovina in December 2004 President Tadić, a pro-Western moderate and Koštunica's principal political rival since the assassination of Zoran Djindjić, drew considerable international attention by apologizing "to all against whom a crime was committed in the name of the Serbian people." With at least one eye on critics at home, he also insisted that individual criminals, not the Serbian people, should be held accountable and that crimes committed against Serbs during the complex conflicts should not be forgotten. (The first trial of former KLA members concluded in The Hague in November 2005 with one conviction and two acquittals.)

Meanwhile, Slobodan Milošević opened his defense at the end of August 2004, two-and-a-half years after his trial began for alleged offenses in Croatia, Bosnia and Herzegovina, and Kosovo. On March 11, 2006, 444 days into the trial, with only 10 days left, Milošević was found dead of an apparent heart attack in his cell. Carla del Ponte, the ICTY's chief prosecutor, expressed regret, as did numerous international and human rights leaders, that the death of Milošević, the first head of state in history to be tried for war crimes, had prevented "justice from being done." But former U.S. ambassador to the UN Richard E. Holbrooke, the chief architect of the Dayton accords, called this idea "utter nonsense." Holbrooke continued, "After all, the man died in his cell, knowing he would never see freedom again—a fitting end for someone who started four wars (all of which he lost), causing 300,000 deaths, leaving more than 2 million people homeless and wrecking the Balkans." Popular and nationalistic reaction in Serbia to the news of Milošević's death was considerably more sympathetic, giving a boost in support to the ultranationalist SRS and to Milošević's old party, the SPS. The trial of former Serbian president Milan Milutinović began in July 2006, while that of SRS ultranationalist leader Vojislav Šešelj was expected to get under way in October. The two surrendered to the ICTY in January and February 2003, respectively, to defend themselves against charges that include crimes against humanity and violations of the conventions of war. In Serbia, the ongoing trial of several dozen individuals implicated in the Djindjić assassination, including Milorad LUKOVIĆ, the alleged mastermind, was expected to conclude late in 2006.

The tumult created by Milošević's death, the EU rebuke over the failure to deliver Mladić, stalled Kosovo status talks, infighting between the DS and DSS leaders, and Montenegro's independence dealt a blow to the stability of Prime Minister Koštunica's minority government. Following the EU's May 2006 suspension of talks on a preaccession agreement, G17 Plus party leader and Deputy Prime Minister Miroljub Labus resigned from the cabinet. Another G17 Plus leader, Ivana DULIĆ-MARKOVIĆ, an ethnic Croat, was confirmed as deputy prime minister shortly thereafter, despite objections from the SRS. The remaining G17 Plus cabinet ministers have threatened to leave the government if talks with the EU on an SAA have not resumed by October 2006.

In July Belgrade delivered an "action plan" for apprehending Mladić and other fugitives in an attempt to show greater cooperation with the ICTY and restart the SAA negotiations. The plan called for greater cooperation within Serbia's various intelligence and secret service organizations, and greater coordination and communication with the ICTY. International observers and Serbian human rights leaders cast doubt on the feasibility of the proposal, however, given the intense rivalry between these organizations and the pockets of sympathy for the Bosnian Serb fugitives within Serbia's military and secret services. Meanwhile, the SRS has gained public support through its appeals to Serb nationalism, rejection of external pressures, and criticism of the handling of the Montenegro and Kosovo questions. This surge in support for the SRS has raised the stakes over the timing of new elections and also given the SPS more leverage in dealing with the government, which has been dependent on SPS legislative support for passage of its programs. The moderate and centrist parties in government prefer new elections before the question of Kosovo's status has been determined to avoid more backlash or defections to the SRS or SPS from disaffected voters.

With the end of the state union, the foreign and defense ministries were transferred to Serbia, as was the ministry for human rights and minorities; the selection of ministers, however, was complicated by the government's dependence on SPS votes. The SPS assembly delegation bitterly opposed confirming the state union foreign minister, SPO leader Vuk Drašković, long one of Slobodan Milošević's severest critics. Moreover, there is disagreement between President Tadić and Prime Minister Koštunica over who will have the authority to select a new commander for the Serbian armed forces once the state union's military command structure is dissolved.

Kosovo continues to be administered under UN Security Council Resolution 1244. In July 2005 current UNMIK head Søren Jessen-Petersen, a Dane, initiated a handful of pilot decentralization projects to further local government reform and inculcation of democratic standards. Particular attention has been directed toward the status of the minority Serb population. To date, only a small fraction of the estimated 200,000 Serbs who fled the province since 1999 have decided to return. (Ethnic Albanians currently outnumber ethnic Serbs by an estimated 1.8 million to 120,000.) UNMIK is due to report in 2006 to the UN Security Council on the Kosovo government's progress on human rights goals and democratic reforms. Much of this attention is directed toward monitoring the treatment of ethnic Serbs, despite the presence of other ethnic groups in Kosovo, including Romas, Bosniacs, and Turks. Immediate challenges facing the new Kosovo prime minister, Agim Ceku, included satisfying UNMIK and UN demands for protection of minority rights, greater transparency in government, and elimination of corruption. Ceku also is seeking reforms to further European integration for the province.

In February 2006 the UN convened talks in Vienna on the future political status of Kosovo that were also attended by representatives of France, Germany, Italy, Russia, the United Kingdom, and the United States. Serbia's position remained that Kosovo is part of its territory, while Kosovar leaders insisted that the only viable political solution is independence for the province. Progress toward resolution of the political status question was sidetracked immediately by disagreement over more minor issues regarding division of power regionally, and economic, cultural, and religious matters. In June Serbia's government unveiled a proposal dubbed "the platform" that offered Kosovo greater autonomy within Serbia for 20 years while preserving Belgrade's control over foreign affairs, borders and customs, monetary policy, protection of Serb religious and cultural matters, and human rights. Kosovo's ethnic Albanian leaders rejected the proposal outright. The platform also received little support from the parties convened in Vienna. Russia, dealing with its own internal divisions over regional sovereignty, was less inclined to criticize

Serbia for its stance and more inclined to favor initiatives designed to delay a final status decision.

Political Parties

For four-and-a-half decades after World War II, Yugoslavia's only authorized political party was the Communist Party, which was redesignated as the League of Communists of Yugoslavia (*Savez Komunista Jugoslavija*—SKJ) in 1952. Political control was also exercised by its "front" organization, the Socialist Alliance of the Working People of Yugoslavia (*Socijalistički Savez Radnog Naroda Jugoslavije*—SSRNJ). The collapse of Communist rule in 1989–1990 led to the formation of a large number of successor and other parties, including several "federal" groupings that sought, without success, to preserve the Yugoslav federation (see the 1994–1995 edition of the *Handbook*, p. 991).

Until late 2000 the dominant party in Serbia and at the federal level was Slobodan Milošević's Socialist Party of Serbia (SPS). Beginning in 1992 a number of opposition coalitions attempted to dislodge the SPS and its allies. The Democratic Movement of Serbia (*Demokratska Pokret Srbije*—Depos) was formed in May 1992 as an alliance whose principal members were the Serbian Renewal Movement (SPO), New Democracy (ND, subsequently the Serbian Liberals), and, following its separation from the Democratic Party (DS), Vojislav Koštunica's Democratic Party of Serbia (DSS). After having boycotted the May 1992 federal general election, Depos won 20 seats in the lower house of the Federal Assembly and 50 in the Serbian Assembly at the joint December 1992 balloting. Depos quickly fractured, however, although the SPO and the ND, joined by the Civic Alliance of Serbia (GSS), attempted to rejuvenate the alliance (dubbed Depos II) prior to the December 1993 Serbian Assembly election, at which it won 45 seats. In February 1994 the ND decided to support the Serbian government, and that, coupled with a move to the right by the SPO, brought an end to Depos.

In early 1996 the Together (*Zajedno*) coalition was established by the SPO, DS, and GSS, which were later joined by the Democratic Center (DC;

see the DS, below) and, at the federal level, the DSS. The alliance captured a disappointing 22 seats in the federal balloting of November 1996 but was far more successful in municipal elections later in the month, although the federal government did not acknowledge the victories for several months. Thereafter, with Serbian legislative elections approaching, relations between the SPO and its partners turned acrimonious, and in mid-1997 *Zajedno* collapsed.

A more inclusive Alliance for Change (*Savez za Promene*—SZP) originated in a June 1998 agreement by half a dozen parties to adopt a uniform opposition strategy. Among the initial participants were the DS, the GSS, and the Christian Democratic Party of Serbia (DHSS). Organizations joining later included the DC, the Democratic Party of Vojvodina Hungarians (DSVM), the New Serbia (NS), the Association of Free and Independent Trade Unions (*Asocijacija Slobodnih i Nezavisnih Sindikata*—ASNS), some 20 smaller parties, and various civic groups.

A smaller opposition grouping, the Alliance of Democratic Parties (*Savez Demokratskih Partija*—SDP), had been organized in October 1997 by the Alliance of Vojvodina Hungarians (SVM), the League of Vojvodina Social Democrats (LSV), the Reformist Democratic Party of Vojvodina (RDSV, subsequently the RVSP—see the Vojvodina Party, below), the Sandžak Coalition (KS), the Social Democratic Union (SDU), and the Šumadija Coalition (KŠ).

The SZP and SDP, often in conjunction with the SPO, organized or participated in a number of anti-Milošević demonstrations and, beginning in September 1999, a series of opposition roundtables. These led to a January 10, 2000, meeting at which 16 opposition party leaders, spearheaded by the SPO's Vuk Drašković and the DS's Zoran Djindjić, committed their organizations to a joint strategy for forcing early elections. Following the July adoption by the Milošević-controlled Federal Assembly of constitutional changes permitting direct election of the president and the upper house, the opposition prepared for the September 24 federal elections by attempting to forge a comprehen-

sive electoral alliance. Although the SPO and many less-influential parties ultimately chose to remain independent, the unification effort culminated in formation of the Democratic Opposition of Serbia (*Demokratske Opozicije Srbije*—DOS), which on August 7 nominated the DSS's Koštunica for the presidency. By the time of the September balloting the DOS encompassed 18 parties (plus the ASNS), among them the DS, DSS, GSS, NS, and the 6 SDP parties. The DOS followed up its federal victories in September by winning 176 of the 250 seats in the December Serbian National Assembly election.

The cumbersome DOS, which had already suffered defections, dissolved before the December 2003 Serbian legislative election. Although various smaller parties formed coalitions, none was successful. Of the six electoral lists meeting the 5 percent threshold for seats, only one—the SPO-NS—was a formal coalition, although the DS included on its list candidates from several other parties that had recognized their inability to achieve the threshold.

There are, in addition to the parties mentioned above, a plethora of minor formations, many with a predominantly regional or ethnic character in Vojvodina, Kosovo, and Sandžak. As of 2003 there were nearly 275 registered parties in Serbia alone, while over two dozen organizations contested the Kosovo elections of October 2004.

Principal Parties in Serbia

Democratic Party (*Demokratska Stranka*—DS). The descendant of a post–World War I governing democratic party, the DS was revived in December 1989 and held a constituent convention on February 3, 1990, with Dragoljub MIĆUNOVIĆ being elected as the party's first president. A centrist party committed to a democratic multiparty system, human rights, and a free press, the DS boycotted the May 1992 Federal Assembly election. Its reluctance to join the opposition coalition Depos in 1992 resulted in a party split, with the departing faction, the DSS, joining the alliance. Building on its modest success in the December 1992 balloting, the DS won 29 Serbian Assembly seats a year later as the party's turn toward nationalism won it surreptitious support from the Milošević-run media. At the head of the nationalist faction was Zoran Djindjić, who led the electoral campaign and on January 29, 1994, was elected party president in what was essentially a leadership coup against Mićunović, who subsequently formed the Democratic Center (*Demokratska Centar*—DC).

The party returned to active opposition in 1996 by joining *Zajedno*. The SPO's withdrawal in mid-1977 meant the demise of *Zajedno*, and the DS boycotted the 1997 Serbian elections. In 1998 Djindjić joined a number of other opposition politicians in announcing formation of the Alliance for Change (SZP). In 2000 Djindjić was a leading participant in the formation of the DOS as well as coordinator of the SZP. As prime minister of Serbia, he led the more reform-minded majority within the DOS, often in opposition to his chief rival, Vojislav Koštunica of the DSS. Djindjić was assassinated on March 12, 2003. A week later Zoran Živković was confirmed as prime minister.

Following the breakup of the DOS, the DS ran independently in the Serbian legislative election of December 2003, although various candidates from other parties, including the Civic Alliance of Serbia (GSS, below) and the DC, were included on the DS electoral list. The DS's Boris Tadić was elected president of Serbia in June 2004.

In January 2005 the DC merged into the DS. Following its formation in 1995, the DC had participated in both the Depos and the *Zajedno* opposition alliances before forming the DAN Coalition (*Koalicija DAN*) with the ND (now the LS, below) and the Democratic Alternative (DA; see the SDP, below) in December 1999. All three DAN parties then joined the DOS in 2000. Mićunović ran as the DOS candidate in the invalidated Serbian presidential election of November 2003, finishing second. At the 2003 Serbian National Assembly election five DC candidates on the DS electoral list were awarded seats.

Following the separation of Serbia and Montenegro, Tadić backed a call for early elections, before the political status of Kosovo is finalized. He and Prime Minister Koštunica of the DSS, which prefers to schedule elections for early 2007, have been actively discussing the issue with an eye toward the growing popular support for the ultranationalist SRS.

Leaders: Boris TADIĆ (President of the Republic and of the Party), Bojan PAJTIĆ (Vice President), Nenad BOGDANOVIĆ, Slobodan GAVRILOVIĆ, Tamara MILOŠEVIĆ (Secretary).

Democratic Party of Serbia (*Demokratska Stranka Srbije*—DSS). The DSS was established shortly before the December 1992 election by a dissident faction of the Democratic Party that wished to join the Depos opposition bloc in that contest. Under Vojislav Koštunica it later swung further to the right than its parent.

Standing on its own in the December 1993 Serbian Assembly election, the DSS won seven seats. Although a constituent of the *Zajedno* alliance in the November 1996 election, at which it won four seats, the DSS ran separately in some municipalities in the subsequent local balloting. With the DS, it boycotted the 1997 Serbian elections.

In August 2000 Koštunica emerged as the consensus DOS presidential candidate to oppose Slobodan Milošević, and he was declared the winner of the September election in early October. Subsequently, the conservative Koštunica had differences with the DOS majority, not least over the handling of Slobodan Milošević.

In August 2001 the DSS withdrew from the Serbian government, asserting that it was not addressing the problem of organized crime. Relations with the DOS and, more specifically, the DS continued to worsen thereafter, and in December the DSS's Dragan Maršićanin was forced out as speaker of the Serbian National Assembly after being accused of vote rigging. With the rivalry between DS leader Djindjić and Koštunica heating up, the DSS in effect withdrew from the DOS.

Koštunica was denied the Serbian presidency in 2002 when a low voter turnout invalidated elections in October and December. Having led the DSS to a second-place finish, with 17.7 percent of the vote and 53 seats, at the Serbian legislative election of December 2003, he was confirmed as the head of a minority government in March 2004. For the December election the DSS had included on its electoral list a handful of candidates from several small parties, including the People's Democratic Party (*Narodna Demokratska Stranka*—NDS), led by Slobodan VUKSANOVIĆ, which then merged into the DSS in October 2004.

Leaders: Vojislav KOŠTUNICA (Prime Minister of Serbia and President of the Party), Dragan MARŠIĆANIN (Vice President of the Party and 2004 presidential candidate).

G17 Plus. The G17 Plus originated in a think tank of reform-minded, nonparty economists that participated in the FRY and Serbian cabinets following the ouster of Slobodan Milošević. It was established as a political party in December 2002 under the leadership of Miroljub Labus, former FRY deputy prime minister and presidential candidate of the DS. At the December 2003 balloting for the Serbian National Assembly the G17 Plus electoral list finished fourth, with 11.5 percent of the vote and 34 seats, including 3 that went to members of the Social Democratic Party of Serbia (SDP, below). The G17 Plus then joined the minority Koštunica government.

After the EU suspended negotiations with Serbia on a precursor agreement, G17 Plus leader Mladjan Dinkić resigned as deputy prime minister in protest. Other G17 Plus cabinet ministers pledged soon thereafter that they would resign from the government if the EU negotiations had not resumed by October 1, 2006.

Leaders: Čedomir ANTIĆ (President), Ivana DULIĆ-MARKOVIĆ (Deputy Prime Minister), Mladjan DINKIĆ, Miroljub LABUS, Prvoslav DAVINIĆ.

New Serbia (*Nova Srbija*—NS). The NS was organized following the expulsion of Čačak's controversial mayor, Velimir Ilić, from the SPO in 1998 and his subsequent departure from Serbia-Together (*Srbija-Zajedno*), an SPO offshoot. The NS joined the Alliance for Change and then the DOS. In November 2003 Ilić ran third in the invalidated Serbian presidential election. A month later

the NS and the SPO ran as a coalition in balloting for the Serbian legislature, with the NS being awarded nine seats.

Leader: Velimir ILIĆ.

Serbian Democratic Renewal Movement (*Srpski Demokratski Pokret Obnove*—SDPO). The conservative SDPO was formed in May 2005 by nine National Assembly members who left the Serbian Renewal Movement (SPO, below), largely because of differences with the SPO leader, Vuk Drašković. The nine assemblymen then formed a joint legislative caucus with the nine members from the New Serbia party, which had previously been close to the SPO. The SDPO supports the DSS-led government and has called for further European integration.

Leaders: Veroljub STEVANOVIĆ, Vojislav MIHAILOVIĆ.

Serbian Renewal Movement (*Srpski Pokret Obnove*—SPO). The SPO was founded in March 1990 as a merger of four parties, most notably those led by Vojislav Šešelj and Vuk Drašković. However, in less than three months, internal squabbling led to the departure of Šešelj to found a new party, the SRS (below). Without Šešelj the SPO moderated its extreme nationalism and participated in the Depos coalitions in 1992 and 1993. During this time, Drašković spoke out loudly against war crimes and as a result, with his wife Danica, was arrested and allegedly beaten by Serbian police. Following the disappointing showing of *Zajedno* in the 1996 federal election, the SPO was the sole opposition party to contest the 1997 Serbian elections for both parliament and the presidency, finishing third in both contests.

On January 18, 1999, Drašković joined Prime Minister Bulatović's government as a deputy prime minister, but his show of national solidarity ended three months later when comments made contrary to policy led to his dismissal. The other three SPO ministers immediately resigned.

In 2000 the SPO remained aloof from the DOS alliance—a move that Drašković subsequently acknowledged as a mistake. At the September elections the SPO won only one upper house seat, while its presidential candidate, Vojislav Mihajlović, the mayor of Belgrade, took only 3 percent of the vote. At the December balloting for the Serbian assembly, the SPO won under 4 percent of the vote and no seats. Drašković subsequently voiced support for reestablishing Serbia as a constitutional parliamentary monarchy.

For the 2003 Serbian legislative election the SPO joined forces with the New Serbia, winning 13 of the coalition's 22 seats (based on a 7.7 percent vote share). Intraparty differences led in 2005 to formation of the SDPO by nine of the SPO's assemblymen.

Leaders: Vuk DRAŠKOVIĆ (Acting Minister of Foreign Affairs and Chair of the Party), Danica DRAŠKOVIĆ, Vlajko SENIĆ (Deputy Chair).

Serbian Radical Party (*Srpska Radikalna Stranka*—SRS). Founded in February 1991 and runner-up to the SPS at the federal lower house elections of May and December 1992, the SRS is a quasi-fascist advocate of "Greater Serbia" that emphasizes the importance of its "leader" (*vodj*). It withdrew its support of the SPS at both the republican and federal levels in September 1993 and mounted a campaign to undercut the ruling party in the run-up to the 1993 legislative balloting, at which, however, its representation dropped from 73 to 39 seats.

In April 1994 the SRS abolished its paramilitary wing, the Serbian Chetnik Movement (formed in July 1990 as the revival of a World War II army of the same name), following charges that it was guilty of war crimes in Croatia during 1991 and 1992. It was also implicated in the Bosnia and Herzegovina conflict. Party leader Šešelj was given a suspended prison sentence on September 19, 1994, for violence in the assembly but committed the same offense a week later, for which he received an actual four-month sentence. In opposition to his continuing leadership, party dissidents left to form a new party, the Radical Party of the Left Nikola Pašić (*Radikolna Stranka Levice Nikola Pašić*—RSLNP), named after a 19th-century founder of

an SRS precursor. The RSLNP had no success at the polls.

In the November 1996 federal election SRS lower house representation slipped further, to 16 seats. In the first runoff of the 1997 Serbian presidential election, Šešelj appeared to have beaten SPS candidate Zoran Lilić, but due to a low turnout the election was invalidated. Šešelj ultimately lost to new SPS candidate Milan Milutinović in December, though the official count and turnout levels were questionable. In the parliamentary election, the SRS, attacking Milošević as the cause of Serbia's woes, finished a strong second with 82 seats. As a result, the SPS approached the SRS about joining the Serbian government, with Šešelj being named a deputy prime minister in March 1998. The SRS was the only prominent Serb party to reject the June 1999 Kosovo peace plan.

At the federal level, the SRS 2000 presidential candidate, Tomislav Nikolić, finished third, with 6 percent of the vote, while the party captured only 5 seats in the lower house and 2 in the upper. At the December 2000 Serbian National Assembly election the SRS finished third, with 23 seats, a loss of 59. In December 2003, however, with the DOS having dissolved, the SRS won a leading 27.6 percent of the vote and 82 seats, far outdistancing the second-place DSS. Although the victory also gave the SRS a plurality of 30 indirectly elected seats in the new state union assembly, the party was unable to muster enough additional support to form a government in Serbia. Nikolić finished first in the June 2004 balloting for president of Serbia but was defeated in the second round, when he won 46 percent of the vote.

As of August 2006 Vojislav Šešelj was awaiting trial in The Hague on charges that included crimes against humanity from 1991 to 1995. He had surrendered to ICTY authorities in February 2003.

The SRS is likely to emerge from the next legislative election with the largest bloc of seats, but not a majority.

Leaders: Tomislav NIKOLIĆ (Acting Chair), Aleksandar VUČIĆ (General Secretary).

Socialist Party of Serbia (*Socijalistička Partija Srbije*—SPS). The SPS was formed on July 17, 1990, by consolidation of the former League of Communists of Serbia and its associated Socialist Alliance. The party won 194 of 250 seats in the Serbian Assembly at balloting in December 1990, while its leader, Slobodan Milošević, defeated 30 other candidates in retaining the Serbian presidency with a 65 percent vote share. The SPS won a narrow majority (73 of 138 seats) in the federal Chamber of Citizens in May 1992. Following the imposition of UN sanctions on May 30, anti-Milošević social democrats within the party formed several splinter groups; however, Milošević remained firmly in charge and was reelected in December, when the party also retained its pluralities in both the federal and the republican assemblies.

Thereafter, the SPS moved closer to the ultranationalist SRS (above), with which it cooperated to oust President Ćosić from the FRY presidency on June 1, 1993. Four months later the SRS terminated the relationship, prior to the Serbian legislative poll in December, at which the SPS won 123 seats. In late 1995 Milošević dismissed several hard-line nationalists in the SPS leadership who were critical of the Dayton peace accord and supportive of militant factions among the Bosnian Serbs. Subsequently, an SPS-led electoral alliance, the Joint List, which included the JUL and ND (see LS, below), dominated federal parliamentary elections in November 1996 as well as the September 1997 presidential and legislative elections in Serbia.

At the federal presidential election of September 2000 President Milošević finished second, with some 35–37 percent of the vote, although he refused to acknowledge his loss to the DOS's Koštunica until early October. In simultaneous parliamentary elections, the SPS-JUL alliance saw its seat total in the lower house drop to 44, while it won only 7 of Serbia's 20 seats in the newly elective upper house. Although the SPS continued to control the republican government and legislature in Serbia, the success of the DOS precipitated a premature dissolution of the Serbian National Assembly in late October and the swearing in of an

interim coalition government of the SPS, DOS, and SPO, pending an election in late December. In the meantime, a defiant Milošević was reelected party chair at a party congress on November 25.

The erosion of public support for the SPS continued at the December 2000 Serbian Assembly balloting. The SPS won only 37 seats, in contrast to the 86 won in 1997 as part of the Joint List with the JUL and ND. At the December 2003 election it won only 7.7 percent of the votes, good for 22 seats. Milošević, despite being on trial in The Hague, remained the SPS chair until his death in 2006.

Struggles over leadership of the SPS began after Milošević's death. The infighting undermined party unity in the assembly; this threatened the already slim margin of the DS/DSS-led government, which depended on SPS support. On the other hand, the public disaffection with the centrist government coalition has helped improve the SPS's public support, raising the possibility that the SPS could be part of a new government with the SRS after the next legislative ballot.

Leaders: Ivica DAČIĆ (President of Main Board), Zoran ANDJEL-KOVIĆ (Deputy Leader).

Other Serbian Parties

Christian Democratic Party of Serbia (*Demohrišćanska Stranka Srbije*—DHSS). The DHSS dates from 1997, when a dispute with Vojislav Koštunica led a number of DSS members to leave the party under the former DSS vice president, Vladan Batić. He subsequently served as coordinator of the Alliance for Change and as a principal leader of the DOS.

More recently, the DHSS has advocated an independent Serbia. At the December 2003 Serbian legislative election the DHSS headed the **Independent Serbia** (*Samostalna Srbija*) list, which won 1.1 percent of the vote. Other participants were the **Democratic Party "Homeland"** (*Demokratska Stranka "Otadžbina"*), whose Radoslav AVLIJAŠ had attracted little support as a Serbian presidential candidate in November; the **Democratic Movement of Serbia's Roma** (*Demokratska Pokret*

Rumuna Srbije); the **Peasant Party** (*Seljačka Stranka*); and the **Serbian Justice** (*Srpska Pravda*).

Leader: Vladan BATIĆ (President).

Civic Alliance of Serbia (*Gradjanski Savez Srbije*—GSS). The GSS is a radical liberal party founded in November 1992 by internationally known antiwar activist Dr. Vesna PEŠIĆ. A small party whose membership is mainly intellectuals, it fared poorly on its own in the 1992 Serbian elections; however, as part of Depos in the 1993 elections Dr. Pešić won a seat in the Serbian Assembly. The GSS competed as part of *Zajedno* in the 1996 federal and local elections but boycotted the 1997 Serbian elections. It helped establish the Alliance for Change in 1998 and the DOS in 2000.

In December 2003 GSS candidates for the Serbian legislature ran on the DS electoral list, ending up with five seats. In the following year a number of GSS leaders, including the party's president, Goran SVILANOVIĆ, resigned and joined the DS.

Leaders: Nataša MIĆIĆ (President of the Party and Former Speaker of the Serbian National Assembly).

Movement for Democratic Serbia (*Pokret za Democratsku Srbiju*—PDS). The PDS was formed in August 1999 by a former Yugoslav Army chief of staff who had been fired by President Milošević in November 1998 for disagreeing with the government's policies in Kosovo. It joined the DOS in 2000. In March 2002 the party's president was forced to resign as a deputy prime minister in Serbia's cabinet following his detention for allegedly having been a U.S. spy. In March 2005 Perišić turned himself into the ICTY to face charges that included crimes against humanity from 1992 to 1995

Leaders: Momčilo PERIŠIĆ (President), Slobodan VUKSANOVIĆ.

Serbian Liberals (*Liberali Srbije*—LS). The LS adopted its present name in March 2003, having previously been called the New Democracy (*Nova Demokratija*—ND). Founded in July 1990 as the successor to the Serbian Socialist Youth Organization, the ND was an original member of the Depos alliance. It withdrew from the opposition movement in February 1994, announcing that at the republican level it would support the SPS-led administration.

In the November 1996 federal and September 1997 Serbian elections the party, which describes itself as liberal and social democratic, ran on a joint ticket with the SPS and the JUL. In July 1999 the ND was expelled from the electoral alliance, as were its five deputies from the Serbian National Assembly. The move came shortly after the party's president had called for the resignation of both the federal and republican governments.

In December 1999 the ND joined the tripartite DAN Coalition. It also joined the DOS in 2000. At the December 2003 Serbian legislative election the renamed LS won only 0.6 percent of the vote.

Leader: Dušan MIHAJLOVIĆ (President).

Serbian Unity Party (*Stranka Srpskog Jedinstva*—SSJ). The SSJ is an ultranationalist group launched prior to the December 1992 balloting, with the reported support of President Milošević, as a counter to the SRS. Its leader, Željko RAŽNJATOVIĆ ("Arkan"), a commander of the paramilitary Tigers group, had been linked in press reports to a variety of atrocities in Bosnia and Croatia. In the 1992 election the SSJ attracted relatively few votes but nonetheless won five seats, thanks to its geographic concentration in Kosovo. At the December 1993 poll the SRS performed better than expected, denying the SSJ parliamentary representation. The SSJ was completely marginalized in the 1996 federal election, winning less than 5,000 votes.

On March 31, 1999, the ICTY announced that it had sent Belgrade a warrant for Arkan, who had been secretly indicted in September 1997. He was killed by masked gunmen in a Belgrade hotel on January 15, 2000.

The hard-line stance of the SSJ won it 14 seats at the December 2000 Serbian Assembly election. In 2003 it ran under the banner of the **For National Unity–Prof. Borislav Pelević and Marijan Rističević** (*Za Narodno Jedinstvo–Prof. Borislav Pelević i Marijan Rističević*—ZNJ), an electoral list that also included the **National Peasant Party** (*Narodna Seljačka Stranka*—NSS), the National Party (*Narodna Stranka*), the **Serbia Our Home** (*Naš Dom Srbija*—NDS), and the **Serb Party** (*Srpska Stranka*—SS). The ZNJ won only 1.7 percent of the vote. The NSS's Marijan RISTIČEVIĆ finished fourth, with 3 percent of the vote, in the invalidated November 2003 Serbian presidential election.

Leader: Borislav PELEVIĆ (Chair of the Party and 2004 presidential candidate).

Social Democratic Party (*Socijaldemokratska Partija*—SDP). The SDP was established in April 2002 by merger of one wing of the Social Democracy (SD, below) and the Social Democratic Union (SDU, below). (The SD wing loyal to party founder Vuk OBRADOVIĆ ultimately won title to the SD name in the courts.)

The SDU-SD merger proved short-lived: in March 2003 the SDU was reestablished as a separate party.

In October 2003 the SDP withdrew its support for the DOS-led Serbian government, which contributed to the collapse of the government and accelerated the alliance's disintegration. At the December 2003 parliamentary election the SDP candidates joined the G17 Plus electoral list, winning three seats.

In September 2004 Nebojša Čović's Democratic Alternative (*Demokratska Alternativa*—DA) merged into the SDP. The DA, dating from July 1997, met with scant success at the September 1997 polls. It participated in the Alliance for Change but departed and formed the DAN Coalition with the ND (now the LS) and the Democratic Center (see DS, above) in late 1999 before joining the DOS in 2000. At the December 2003 Serbian legislative election the DA won only 2.2 percent of the vote and no seats.

In August 2005 Prime Minister Koštunica asked the SDP to leave the government after two of its three assembly members voted against privatization of the state oil and gas company. Party Chair Čović, who had been serving as head of the Serbia and Montenegro Coordination Center for Kosovo, was then dismissed, and the party formally entered the opposition. Minister of Labor Slobodan LALOVIĆ sided with the government and left the party. In October the SDP concluded a cooperation agreement with former presidential candidate Bogoljub Karić's **"Strength of Serbia" Movement** (*Pokret "Snaga Srbije"*).

Leaders: Nebojša ČOVIĆ (Chair), Slobodan ORLIĆ (Deputy Chair).

Social Democracy (*Socijaldemokratija*—SD). The SD was registered in May 1997, and four months later the party leader, a retired general, ran unsuccessfully in the Serbian presidential election. A founding member of the Alliance for Change, the SD joined the DOS in 2000. The party split in 2002, with one wing then participating in formation of the Serbian SDP (above). Obradović's wing ultimately won title to the SD name and for the 2003 Serbian legislative election formed the **Defense and Justice** (*Odbrana i Pravda*) electoral list with three other small parties: Borivoje BOROVIĆ'S **National Party of Justice** (*Narodna Stranka Pravda*—NSP), the **Party of Workers and Pensioners** (*Stranka Radnika i Penzionera*—SRP), and the **Green Social Democratic Party** (*Socijaldemokratska Partija Zelenih*—SPZ). The list won only 0.5 percent of the vote.

Leader: Vuk OBRADOVIĆ (President).

Social Democratic Union (*Socijaldemokratska Unija*—SDU). The SDU was formed by a University of Belgrade psychologist and former associate of the Civic Alliance, Žarko Korać. He has also been linked to the student-led Resistance (*Otpor*), which repeatedly took to the streets in opposition to the Milošević regime. The SDU participated in the DOS alliance in 2000.

Following an abortive merger with a wing of Social Democracy in 2002, the SDU reemerged as a separate party in March 2003. At the December 2003 Serbian National Assembly election its candidates ran on the DS electoral list, ending up with one seat.

Leader: Žarko KORAĆ (President).

Socialist People's Party (*Socijalistička Narodna Stranka*—SNS). The SNS was established in early 2003 on the basis of the People's Socialists (*Narodni Socijalisti*, sometimes translated as the National Socialists), a floor group in the Serbian National Assembly.

In April 2002 the SPS had expelled party leader Branislav Ivković for undermining party unity, in part by attempting to replace Slobodan Milošević as chair. In June Ivković's faction convened an extraordinary party congress that elected Ivković chair and relegated Milošević to honorary chair for life. Having failed to wrest control of the SPS from Milošević loyalists, in October 2002 Ivković announced his intention to head a splinter party, initially identified as the Party of Socialists, which in November gave rise to the People's Socialists floor group.

The SNS candidate for Serbian president, Dragan Tomić, finished fifth, with 2.2 percent of the vote, at the invalid election of November 2003. For the repeat election of June 2004 Ivković replaced him on the ballot and finished eighth, with under 0.5 percent. At the Serbian National Assembly election of December 2003 the SNS ran as a component of an electoral list called the **Socialist People's Party–People's Bloc–General Nebojša Pavković** (*SNS–Narodni Blok–General Nebojša Pavković*), which won under 1 percent of the vote and thus no seats.

Leaders: Branislav IVKOVIĆ (Chair and 2004 presidential candidate), Dragan TOMIĆ.

Šumadija Coalition (*Koalicija Šumadija—KŠ*). Taking its name from a central Serbian region stretching south from Belgrade, the KŠ was organized in August 1997 in reaction to the disintegration of the opposition alliance *Zajedno*. Its leader later served as coordinator of the Alliance of Democratic Parties. The party joined the DOS in 2000. At the 2003 Serbian elections the KŠ cooperated with the Together for Tolerance coalition (see Sandžak Democratic Party, below), which placed the KŠ leader at the head of its election list.

Leader: Branislav KOVAČEVIĆ (President).

Yugoslav United Left (*Jugoslovenska Levica—JUL*). A successor to the former ruling League of Communists of Yugoslavia, the JUL was launched in mid-1994 by Mirjana Marković, the preferred name of President Milošević's wife, who was reputed to wield considerable government influence and whose fortnightly newspaper column was widely read as a guide to the likely course of political events. An umbrella grouping of some two dozen communist and other leftist organizations, the JUL contested the November 1996 federal elections as well as the September 1997 Serbian elections in alliance with the SPS and ND.

In February 1998 the party's deputy chair, Nenad DJORDJEVIĆ, was arrested for allegedly embezzling some $10 million from the Serbian Health Insurance Fund while serving as its director.

The JUL remained allied to the SPS for the September 2000 election, but in October the SPS announced that it intended to offer a separate candidate list for the December Serbian legislative balloting, at which the JUL failed to obtain any seats. In 2003 the JUL won only 0.1 percent of the vote. In 2005 Marković, who had been in self-imposed exile in Moscow since 2003, was scheduled to stand trial for abuse of power during her husband's period of rule. In July 2006, because of her numerous failures to appear in court, a new warrant for her arrest was issued.

Leader: Mirjana (Mira) MARKOVIĆ.

Other unsuccessful parties/electoral lists contesting the December 2003 Serbian legislative elections were the **Economic Force of Serbia and Diaspora–Branko Dragaš** (*Privredna Snaga Srbije i Dijaspora–Branko Dragaš*); the **Labor Party of Serbia** (*Laburistička Partija Srbije—LPS*), led by Dragan MILOVANOVIĆ; **Resistance** (*Otpor*), which originated in the anti-Milošević, student-led Resistance movement and which became a party in 2003; and the **Union of Serbs of Vojvodina–Dušan Salatić** (*Savez Srba Vojvodine–Dušan Salatić*).

Sandžak Parties

Party of Democratic Action Sandžak (*Stranka Demokratske Akcije Sandžaka—SDA Sandžak*). Linked to the Party of Democratic

Action in Bosnia and Herzegovina, the ethnically Bosniac SDA has distinct organizations based in the Albanian/Muslim communities of the Sandžak region (in southwestern Serbia, adjacent to Montenegro), Montenegro, Preševo, and Kosovo (see under Kosovo Parties, below). A leading advocate of autonomy for Sandžak, the SDA saw 45 of its members convicted of plotting armed insurgency in 1994, although all were pardoned or had their convictions vacated in 1996.

In August 1995 the chair of the SDA Sandžak, Sulejman Ugljanin, came under challenge from party elements who objected to his residence in Turkey and who also wanted to establish closer ties to the Serbian opposition. Led by the party's secretary general, Rasim LJAJIĆ, Ugljanin's opponents held their own party congress and succeeded in reregistering the party under Ljajić. Before long five similarly named Sandžak parties had emerged. Having returned from exile at the end of September 1996, Ugljanin continued at the head of what he deemed the "true" SDA Sandžak and organized a three-party coalition, the **Sandžak List Dr. Sulejman Ugljanin** (*Koalicija "Lista za Sandžak Dr. Sulejman Ugljanin"*—LZS), which won a seat in the November election for the federal legislature and three seats in the Serbian Assembly in 1997.

In August 2000 the Democratic Alliance of Sandžak (*Demokratski Savez Sandžaka*—DSS) joined the Sandžak List. The Democratic Alliance had been formed the preceding January by several parties, including Harun HADŽIĆ's **International Democratic Union** (*Internacionalna Demokratska Unija*—IDU) and the **Bosniac Democratic Party of Sandžak** (*Bošnjačke Demokratske Stranke Sandžaka*—BDSS), led by Esad DŽUDŽEVIĆ. Also in 2000, Ljajić's SDA Sandžak adopted the name Sandžak Democratic Party (SDP, below), which remains the principal regional rival of Ugljanin's SDA.

For the 2003 Serbian election various participants in the Sandžak List, including the BDSS and Bajram OMERAGIĆ's **Social Liberal Party of Sandžak** (*Socijalno-Liberalna Stranka Sandžaka*—SLSS), were included on the DS party list. Ugljanin has also chaired the Bosniac National

Council of Sandžak (*Bošnjačkog Nacionalnog veća Sandžaka*—BNVS), which claims to be the highest representative body of Bosniacs in the region.

Leaders: Sulejman UGLJANIN (President), Nermin BEITOVIĆ (Secretary General).

Sandžak Democratic Party (*Sandžačka Demokratska Partija*—SDP). The SDP (which should not be confused with the Serbian Social Democratic Party—SDP, above) began as the Sandžak SDA faction led by Rasim Ljajić (see SDA Sandžak, above) after the ouster of Sulejman Ugljanin in 1995. Ljajić was also serving as chair of the **Sandžak Coalition** (*Koalicija Sandžak*—KS), which joined the DOS alliance in 2000 despite reservations regarding Vojislav Koštunica's nationalist views. Following the September 2000 election, Ljajić was named to the federal cabinet over the objections of pro-Ugljanin Bosniacs. In October he announced that his SDA would reregister as the SDP, which has remained more willing than the SDA to participate in Serbian politics.

Prior to the December 2003 Serbian legislative election the SDP joined the Alliance of Vojvodina Hungarians (SVM, below) and the League of Vojvodina Social Democrats (LSV) in forming the **Together for Tolerance–Čanak, Kasa, Ljajić** (*Zajedno za Toleranciju*), which drew additional support from several other minority groupings, including Vitomir MIHAJLOVIĆ'S **Democratic Party of Romanies**, the **Democratic Alliance of Bulgarians**, and the **Roma Congress Party** (*Romska Kongresna Partija*—RKP), led by Dragoljub ACKOVIĆ. Together, the coalition parties won 4.2 percent of the vote, short of the 5 percent threshold for seats.

Following the termination of the state union in June 2006, Serbia took over the federal-level Ministry of Human Rights and Minorities, with Ljajić retaining the portfolio on an acting basis.

Leader: Rasim LJAJIĆ (Acting Minister of Human Rights and Minorities, and President of the Party).

Small Bosniac/Sandžak parties include the **Liberal Bosniac Organization** (*Liberalno-Bošnjačka*

Organizacija—LBO); the **Party for Sandžak** (*Stranka za Sandžak*—SzS), headed by Fevzija MURIĆ and Azem HAJDAREVIĆ; the **Sandžak Alternative** (*Sandžačka Alternativa*—SA); the **Sandžak Democratic Union** (*Sandžačka Demokratska Unija*—SDU), led by Rešad HAZIROVIĆ; the **Sandžak Popular Movement** (*Narodni Pokret Sandžaka*—NPS); and the **Social Democratic Party of Sandžak** (*Socijaldemokratska Partija Sandžaka*—SDPS).

Vojvodina Parties

Alliance of Vojvodina Hungarians (*Savez Vojvodjannskih Madjara*—SVM). Founded on June 17, 1994, as an offshoot of the DZVM (below), this minority party won 3 seats in the 1996 federal election and 4 in the 1997 Serbian election. It joined the DOS in 2000 but nevertheless offered a separate candidate list in several constituencies, winning 1 lower house seat at the September federal election and, in conjunction with the DOS, an overwhelming majority of seats in the Vojvodina Assembly election of September–October. In the September–October 2004 election, however, the SVM finished third, with 10 seats, far behind the SRS's 36 and the DS's 34. It suffered similar losses in local council elections but joined in forming a DS-led provincial government.

Leader: Jósef KASZA (Chair).

Democratic Alliance of Croats in Vojvodina (*Demokratski Savez Hrvata u Vojvodini*—DSHV). Founded in 1990, the DSHV represents the small ethnic Croat minority in Vojvodina. For the 2004 Vojvodina election it cooperated with the SVM. In 2005 it welcomed ratification of an Agreement on the Protection of National Minorities between Croatia and Serbia and Montenegro.

Leader: Petar KUNDIĆ (Chair).

Democratic Community of Vojvodina Hungarians (*Demokratska Zajednica Vojvodjannskih Madjara*—DZVM). The DZVM was formed in 1990 to represent the interests of the ethnic Hungarian population of Vojvodina. It obtained three federal and nine republican assembly seats in the December 1992 balloting but lost four of the nine in December 1993. On the latter occasion the DZVM leader, Andraš Agošton, disclosed that proautonomy Hungarian organizations in Vojvodina had been financed from Hungary. The party subsequently became divided between those favoring autonomy for Vojvodina and those advocating cooperation with Belgrade. Agošton was replaced as chair in 1996 and organized the DSVM (below) in 1997. Remaining aloof from the DOS, the party failed to win any seats in the Vojvodina Assembly election in September–October 2000. Still represented on some local councils, it has recently been criticized for cooperating with the SRS in some areas.

Leader: Šandor PAL (Chair).

Democratic Party of Vojvodina Hungarians (*Demokratska Stranka Vojvodjannskih Madjara*—DSVM). The DSVM was formed in February 1997 by Andraš Agošton, former chair of the DZVM. The party did not join the DOS in 2000. It won one Vojvodina Assembly seat in 2004.

Leader: Andraš AGOŠTON.

League of Vojvodina Social Democrats (*Liga Socijaldemokrata Vojvodine*—LSV). The moderate left-wing LSV was a founding member of the Vojvodina Coalition (see the Vojvodina Party, below) and continues to support autonomy for the region. At a party congress in February 2000 its chair launched a campaign for creation of a "Vojvodina Republic" within Yugoslavia. The party competed in the September election as part of the DOS alliance.

In 2004 the LSV led formation of the **Coalition "Together for Vojvodina"** (*Koalicija "Zajedno za Vojvodinu"*), which won seven seats in that year's Vojvodina Assembly election. Other local participants included the **Democratic Vojvodina** (*Demokratska Vojvodina*—DV), the **Union of Vojvodina Socialists** (*Unija Socijalista Vojvodine*—USV), and the **Vojvodina Union–"Vojvodina, My Home"** (*Vojvodjanska Unija–"Vojvodina, Moj Dom"*—VU) as well as the Vojvodina Civic Movement (VGP) and the Vojvodina Movement (VP), both of which later participated in formation of the Vojvodina Party (below). After the election the LSV joined the DS-led provincial government.

Leaders: Nenad ČANAK (Chair), Bojan KOSTREŠ (Speaker of the Vojvodina Assembly).

Vojvodina Party (*Vojvodjanska Partija*). Formation of the Vojvodina Party was accomplished in June 2005 by the merger of half a dozen small parties, including the Reformists of Vojvodina, the Vojvodina Civic Movement (*Vojvodjanski Gradjanski Pokret*—VGP), the Vojvodina Movement (*Vojvodjanski Pokret*—VP), and the Vojvodina Coalition (*Koalicija Vojvodina*—KV). A principal goal of the new formation is full autonomy for the province.

The Reformists of Vojvodina–Social Democratic Party (*Reformisti Vojvodine–Socijaldemokratska Partija*—RVSP) had been called the Reformist Democratic Party of Vojvodina (*Reformska Demokratska Stranka Vojvodine*—RDSV) before adopting the RVSP designation in May 2000. The RDSV won two legislative seats at the December 1992 federal election in a combined list with the DS, and one seat in a combined list with the latter and the Civic Party (*Gradjanska Partija*—GP). It subsequently helped form the KV, which won two lower house seats in the November 1996 federal election, won four in the 1997 Serbian election, and joined the DOS in 2000. For the December 2003 Serbian legislative election the RVSP formed an electoral list called the **Reformists–Social Democratic Parties of Vojvodina-Serbia** (*Reformisti–Socijaldemokratske Partije Vojvodine-Srbije*), which included the DSVM (above). In 2004 the Reformists won two Vojvodina Assembly seats before joining the Vojvodina Party.

Leader: Miroslav ILIĆ.

Kosovo Parties

Democratic Alliance of Kosovo (*Lidhja Demokratike e Kosovës*—LDK). The LDK was founded in 1989 and is the largest Albanian party. Advocating the creation of an independent, demilitarized republic, it won an overwhelming preponderance of seats in a "constituent republican assembly" for the province on May 24, 1992, after which the LDK leader, Ibrahim Rugova, was proclaimed president of a self-declared "Republic of Kosovo." The group boycotted the republican elections of 1993 and 1997 as well as the November 1996 federal balloting.

Rugova, who consistently advocated nonviolence and a negotiated settlement of the Kosovo issue with Belgrade, was reelected president, with over 90 percent of the vote, at the "Republic" elections of March 22, 1998. Collaterally, the LDK again won most of the seats in the shadow legislature. At the November 2001 election the LDK won a leading 47 seats in the Kosovo Assembly, which then elected Rugova president of Kosovo in March 2002. The LDK again won 47 seats in October 2004, after which the new assembly returned Rugova to office for another term. Following Rugova's death on January 21, 2006, Nexhat Daci served as acting president until Fatmir Sejdiu was elected president by the assembly on February 10.

The fallout from Rugova's death led to divisions within the party and the removal of assembly speaker Nexhat Daci and Deputy Prime Minister Adem Salihaj from leadership posts in early 2006. Daci and Salihaj formed a faction after their dismissal.

Leaders: Fatmir SEJDIU (President of Kosovo and Chair of the Party), Eqrem KRYEZIU and Sabri HAMITI (Vice Chairs), Kole BERISHA (Secretary General), Adem SALIHAJ (Former Deputy Prime Minister), Nexhat DACI (Former Speaker of the Kosovo Assembly).

Democratic Party of Kosovo (*Partia Demokratike e Kosovës*—PDK). More radical than the LDK, the PDK was established as the Party of Democratic Progress in Kosovo (*Partia e Progresit Demokratik të Kosovës*—PPDK) in September–October 1999 by Hashim Thaçi, leader of the Kosovo Liberation Army—KLA (*Ushtria Çlirimtare e Kosovës*—UÇK). Although some analysts date the formation of the KLA as far back as 1992, its presence as a loosely linked network of guerrilla bands didn't capture notice until 1996. Its emergence as a major factor in the movement for Kosovar independence occurred in early 1998, during the federal government's crackdown in the province, which was precipitated by the KLA's killing of four Serb policemen. In the following year its greatly expanded forces engaged in numerous clashes with Serb army and paramilitary contingents and at one time claimed to hold 40 percent of the province's territory. Many of its commanders favored not just separation from Yugoslavia, but union in a Greater Albania.

Its lack of a political structure having proved a hindrance, in August 1998 the KLA named the chair of the PPK (see under AAK, below), Adem DEMAÇI, as its political spokesman. Demaçi, who had spent 28 years as a political prisoner, agreed to sever his PPK connections at that time. The KLA's increasing importance to a Kosovo settlement was recognized by its participation in the February–March 1999 Rambouillet-Paris peace talks, although Demaçi, refusing to accept any resolution short of independence, argued against attendance and on March 2 resigned from the KLA leadership. On March 5 a Serbian judge issued an arrest warrant for KLA chief Thaçi, who had been tried in absentia and sentenced to ten years in prison for his activities. Shortly thereafter, the KLA named Thaçi as prime minister of a proposed provisional Kosovar government.

At a PPDK congress in May 2000 the party changed its name to the PDK. In November 2001 it won 26 assembly seats, with Bajram Rexhepi becoming prime minister of Kosovo in March 2002. Following the October 2004 assembly election, at which it again finished second, with 30 seats, the PDK chose to remain outside the governing coalition.

Leaders: Hashim THAÇI (Chair), Vlora CITAKU, Bajram REXHEPI (Former Prime Minister of Kosovo).

Alliance for the Future of Kosovo (*Aleanca për Ardhmërinë e Kosovës*—AAK). The AAK was launched in May 2000 by Ramush Haradinaj, a former KLA commander, as a political alliance that incorporated a number of smaller Kosovar parties, including the Parliamentary Party of Kosovo (*Partija Parlamentare e Kosovës*—PPK). A liberal

party that placed itself ideologically in "the modern European center," in the early 1990s the PPK was a principal rival of Ibrahim Rugova's LDK.

Other parties joining the AAK included the militant **National Movement for the Liberation of Kosovo** (*Lëvizja Kombëtare për Çlirimin e Kosovës*—LKÇK); the **Albanian Party of National Unity** (*Partia e Unitetit Kombëtar Shqiptar*—Unikomb), which later left the AAK and is now led by Muhamet KELMENDI; and the **People's Movement for Kosovo** (*Lëvizjes Popullore e Kosovës*—LPK), which operated predominantly as a KLA-supportive exile group based in Switzerland and Germany.

In November 2001 the AAK won eight assembly seats; on their own, the LKÇK and LPK each won one seat. In 2004 the AAK won nine seats; the LPK, one. Party Chair Haradinaj headed the coalition government formed in December 2004 but resigned in March 2005 to face war crimes charges before the ICTY. He was succeeded by the AAK's Bajram Kosumi, who previously had been a leader of the PPK and the United Democratic Movement (*Lëvizja Bashimit Demokratike*—LBD) of Rexhep Qosja. Kosumi resigned as prime minister on March 1, 2006.

Leaders: Ramush HARADINAJ (Chair), Bajram KOSUMI (Former Prime Minister of Kosovo).

Return Coalition (*Koalicija Povratak*—KP). The Return Coalition was organized by a group of Serbian parties, including the DSS, DA, DS, DHSS, ND, and SD, prior to the 2001 Kosovo Assembly election. Its platform called for an end to Serbian emigration from Kosovo, the return of those Serbs displaced during the Kosovo conflict, an accounting of those missing, a return of Serbian property, and measures to ensure Serb safety and freedom of movement. The only Serbian political group to participate in the November election, it finished third, winning 22 seats.

With the October 2004 Kosovo Assembly election approaching, KP leader Oliver Ivanović led formation of a **Serbian List for Kosovo and Metohija** (*Srpska Lista za Kosovo i Metohiju*—SLKM) that also included the DS and SPO. It won eight seats but refused to join the government.

Leaders: Oliver IVANOVIĆ (Chair), Randjel NOJKIĆ.

ORA ("Hour" or "Time"). ORA was established in 2004 by media entrepreneur Veton Surroi as a reformist initiative with an economic focus. It contested the October 2004 Kosovo Assembly election as the **Citizens' List "ORA"** (*Lista Qytetarë "ORA"*), winning 6 percent of the vote and seven seats, and was organized as a party in December.

Leaders: Veton SURROI (President); Ylber HYSA, Teuta SAHATQIA (Vice Presidents).

Coalition "Vakat" (*Koalicija "Vakat"*). Vakat was established in June 2004 by three parties: the **Democratic Party of Bosniacs** (*Demokratska Stranka Bošnjaka*—DSB/*Partia Demokratike e Boshnjakëve*), the **Democratic Party Vatan** (*Demokratska Stranka Vatan*—DSV/*Partia Demokratike Vatan*), and the **Bosniac Party of Kosovo** (*Bošnjačka Stranka Kosova*—BSK/*Partia Boshnjake e Kosovës*). The DSB was registered in 2001. Both the DSV and the BSK began as local branches of the SDA and became parties earlier in 2004. At the October Kosovo Assembly election Vakat won three seats.

Leaders: Xhezair MURATI (DSB), Sadik IDRIZI (DSV), Husnija BESKOVIĆ (BSK).

Kosovo Democratic Turkish Party (*Kosova Demokratik Türk Partisi*—KDTP). The KDTP was established in 1990 to represent the ethnic Turkish population. In October 2004 it won three Kosovo Assembly seats, as it had in the previous election.

Leader: Mahir YAĞCILAR.

Albanian Christian Democratic Party of Kosovo (*Partia Shqiptare Demokristiane e Kosovës*—PShDK). Dating from 1990, the PShDK mainly represents Catholic ethnic Albanians in Kosovo but includes some Muslims in its ranks. In August 1995 its leader, Mark Krasniqi, rejected autonomy for Kosovo on Belgrade's terms and set international mediation and an end to police repression as conditions for entering into talks. The

party attracted little support at the October 2000 municipal elections in Kosovo, finishing with only a 1.2 percent vote share.

After the 2004 Kosovo Assembly election the PShDK was awarded two seats. Shortly thereafter, a major rift resulted in a disputed February 2005 party convention at which a majority faction replaced Krasniqi with Tadej Rodiqi. The Krasniqi wing subsequently held its own convention.

Leaders: Tadej RODIQI, Zef MORINA, Mark KRASNIQI.

New Democratic Initiative of Kosovo (*Iniciativa e Re Demokratike e Kosovës*—IRDK). At the 2004 Kosovo Assembly election the IRDK contested the seats set aside for the Roma, Ashkali, and Egyptian communities. It won two seats.

Leader: Bislim HOTI.

Serbian Democratic Party of Kosovo and Metohija (*Srpska Demokratska Stranka Kosova i Metohije*—SDSKM). The SDSKM was organized in June 2005 on the basis of the **Citizens' Initiative of Serbia** (*Gradjanska Inicijativa Srbija*—GIS). Despite the objections of the Serbian government, the GIS had contested the Serbian set-aside seats at the 2004 Kosovo Assembly election, winning two of them. In January 2005 party founder Slaviša Petković accepted the post of minister for returns and communities in the Kosovo Council of Ministers.

Leader: Slaviša PETKOVIĆ.

Party of Democratic Action Kosovo (*Stranka Demokratske Akcije Kosovo*—SDA Kosovo/*Partia e Aksionit Demokratik*). Established in 1990, the Kosovo branch of the SDA, like its SDA Sandžak counterpart (above), is based in the Albanian/Muslim community. In 2000 a former party leader, Hilmo KANDIĆ, established a separate **Bosniac Party of Democratic Action of Kosovo** (*Bošnjačka Stranka Demokratske Akcije Kosova*—BSDAK/*Partia e Aksionit Demokratik të Boshnjakëvetë Kosovës*). At the October 2004 Kosovo Assembly election the SDA Kosovo won one seat.

Leader: Numan BALIĆ (Chair).

Cabinet

As of August 1, 2006

Prime Minister	Vojislav Koštunica (DSS)
Deputy Prime Minister	Ivana Dulić-Marković (G17 Plus) [f]

Ministers

Agriculture, Forestry, and Water Management	Goran Živkov (G17 Plus)
Capital Investments	Velimir Ilić (NS)
Culture	Dragan Kojadinović (SPO)
Defense (Acting)	Zoran Stanković
Diaspora	Vojislav Vukčević (SPO)
Foreign Affairs (Acting)	Vuk Drašković (SPO)
Economy	Predrag Bubalo (DSS)
Education and Sport	Slobodan Vuksanović (DSS)
Energy and Mining	Radomir Naumov (DSS)
Finance	Mladjan Dinkić (G17 Plus)
Health	Tomica Milosavljević (G17 Plus)
Human Rights and Minorities (Acting)	Rasim Ljajić (Sandžak SDP)
Interior Affairs	Dragan Jočić (DSS)
International Economic Relations	Milan Parivodić (DSS)
Justice	Zoran Stojković (DSS)
Labor, Employment, and Social Policy	Slobodan Lalović (G17 Plus)
Public Administration and Local Self-Government	Zoran Lončar (DSS)
Religious Affairs	Milan Radulović (DSS)
Science and Environmental Protection	Aleksandar Popović (DSS)
Trade, Tourism, and Services	Bojan Dimitrijević (SPO)

[f] = female

Serbian Resistance Movement (*Srpski Pokret Otpora*—Spot). Originating in the 1980s as an antigovernment movement of ethnic Serbs in Kosovo, the Spot took its present political form in 1995. It opposed independence for Kosovo and what it considered to be the antidemocratic policies of the federal government. In 2004 it formed an electoral alliance with the New Serbia party and businessman Bogoljub Karić's "Strength of Serbia" Movement but, citing security concerns and the request of the Serbian government, later withdrew from the October Kosovo Assembly election.

Leader: Momčilo TRAJKOVIĆ (President).

Nearly 30 parties, "citizens' initiatives," and coalitions contested the 2004 Kosovo Assembly election. Those winning single seats also included the following: the **Citizens' Initiative of Gora** (*Gradjanska Inicijativa Gore*—GIG), representing the Gorani community and led by Rustem IBIŠI; the **Democratic Ashkali Party of Kosovo** (*Partia Demokratike Ashkali e Kosovës*—PDAK), led by Sabit RRAHMONI; the **Justice Party** (*Partia e Drejtësisë*—PD), led by Sylejman ÇERKEZI; the **Liberal Party of Kosovo** (*Partia Liberale e Kosovës*—PLK), led by Gjergj DEDAJ; and the **United Roma Party of Kosovo** (*Partia Rome e*

Bashkuar e Kosovës—PREBK), led by Haxhi Zulfi MERXHA.

Legislature

The **Serbian National Assembly** (*Narodna Skupština Srbije*) comprises 250 members elected to four-year terms by proportional representation. Parties must meet a 5 percent threshold to qualify for seats. At the most recent election of December 28, 2003, the following party lists were successful: Serbian Radical Party, 82 seats; Democratic Party of Serbia, 53; Democratic Party, 37; G17 Plus, 34 (including 3 won by members of the Social Democratic Party); Serbian Renewal Movement–New Serbia, 22; Socialist Party of Serbia, 22.

President: Predrag MARKOVIĆ.

Communications

Historically, news media in Serbia were government-controlled or strictly supervised. A Law on Public Information passed in October 1998 by the Milošević-dominated legislature ostensibly prohibited censorship, although strict penalties could be pronounced for publishing or broadcasting material that the government viewed as undermining the federal republic's or Serbia's territorial integrity. As of February 2000, over 60 cases had been pursued under the 1998 law, the editor of the independent *Danas* describing the heavy fines being levied as "the preplanned wearing down of the targeted media."

In May 1998 the federal government had stepped up its efforts to restrict independent radio and television broadcasts by increasing licensing fees several times over, with only 3 of 38 independents initially being given frequency assignments. The Milošević government generally forbade media dissemination of "propaganda" originating in foreign broadcasts, and efforts were made to restrict access to such sources as the U.S. Radio Free Europe/Radio Liberty. In May 2000 a government campaign against opposition and independent media outlets saw police units raiding the offices of Belgrade's principal TV station, *Studio B*, and two radio outlets in an effort to control their news broadcasts.

Since Milošević's fall from power, greater freedom has prevailed. Plans call for converting state-run broadcasting facilities into public-service companies.

Press

The following are dailies published in Belgrade in Serbo-Croatian, unless otherwise noted: *Blic* (230,000), independent tabloid; *Politika* (130,000), state-run, founded in 1901; *Večernje Novosti* (270,000), evening paper; *Danas,* independent; *Dnevnik* (Novi Sad); *Koha Ditore* (Priština), in Albanian; *Magyar Szó* (Novi Sad), in Hungarian.

News Agencies

The leading domestic facility is the Tanjug News Agency (*Novinska Agencija Tanjug*). In addition, the major foreign agencies have bureaus in Belgrade.

Broadcasting and Computing

Serbia and its autonomous provinces each have a state-controlled broadcasting service: *Radio-Televizija Srbije* in Serbia, *Radio-Televizija Novi Sad* in Vojvodina, and *Radio-Televizija Priština* in Kosovo. Private TV and radio stations have been licensed in increasing numbers. As of 2003 there were approximately 3.2 million television receivers and 1.4 million Internet users in Serbia.

Intergovernmental Representation

Ambassador to the U.S.
Ivan VUJAČIĆ

U.S. Ambassador to Serbia
Michael Christian POLT

Ambassador to the UN
(Vacant)

IGO Memberships (Non-UN)
BIS, BSEC, CEI, CEUR, EBRD, Eurocontrol, Interpol, IOM, OSCE, PCA, WCO

SLOVAKIA

SLOVAK REPUBLIC

Slovenská Republika

The Country

Situated in the geographical center of Europe, Slovakia consists of some 40 percent of the area of the former Czechoslovak federation. It is bounded by the Czech Republic to the west, Poland to the north, the Ukraine to the east, Hungary to the south, and Austria to the southwest. A former province of the Hungarian-ruled part of the Austro-Hungarian Empire, the country has a population that is 86 percent Slovak and 11 percent Hungarian (Magyar), with small minorities of Czechs, Roma (Gypsies), Ruthenes, and Ukrainians. Some 60 percent of the population are Roman Catholics, the other main Christian denominations being Protestant (6 percent) and Orthodox (3 percent).

A substantial proportion of former Czechoslovakia's heavy industry, including armaments and explosives manufacturing, is located in Slovakia, although a considerable agricultural sector, currently contributing about 4 percent of GDP and 6 percent of employment, has been retained. Leading crops are wheat, other grains, and sugar beets. Industry as a whole accounted for 28 percent of GDP and 23 percent of employment in 1999, when the principal manufactures were machinery and vehicles, chemicals and plastics, and processed foods. Leading trade partners are Germany and the Czech Republic.

Long less affluent than Bohemia and Moravia, Slovakia felt that its reform efforts in the immediate post-Communist period accentuated economic differences with the Czech Republic, fueling pressure in Slovakia for the political separation that was eventually implemented on January 1, 1993. State control and central planning were much more entrenched in the Slovak bureaucracy, which continued to be dominated by officials who had prospered under the previous regime. In 1993 Slovakia's estimated per capita GNP was only $1,500, as contrasted with $2,500 in the Czech lands, with Slovak GDP falling by an estimated 5 percent during the year; at the same time, unemployment and inflation in Slovakia rose well above Czech Republic levels, to 15 percent and around 25 percent, respectively. Real GDP growth averaged over 6.6 percent annually in 1995–1997 before dropping to 4.4 percent in 1998 and then to 1.9 percent in 1999, despite rapid export growth. Unemployment, a persistent problem, exceeded 19 percent in December 1999,

while consumer price inflation climbed to 10.7 percent for the year.

The lackluster economic performance was widely attributed to the "authoritarian" policies of the postseparation government, which favored a slow transfer to the free market and retained significant elements of the bloated Communist bureaucracy. Among other things, conditions impeded foreign investment and appeared to threaten the proposed accession of Slovakia to the European Union (EU) and the North Atlantic Treaty Organization (NATO). However, the situation eventually improved in the wake of the installation in 1998 of a center-right administration that implemented numerous belt-tightening measures, including the privatization of state-owned banks and other enterprises. Reform (lower corporate taxes, paring of welfare and pension benefits, and more privatization) intensified even further when the government retained control in the 2002 general election. GDP growth averaged well over 4 percent annually in 2002–2004, with inflation falling to about 7.5 percent by the end of that period. Although unemployment remained high (about 15 percent), Slovakia was otherwise described as one of Central Europe's brightest economic performers upon its accession to the EU in 2004. Despite substantial concern in some quarters over the negative effects of restructuring on the poor, the government in 2004 pledged to restrain spending in order to reduce the budget deficit sufficiently to permit adoption of the euro by 2009. In March 2006 the International Monetary Fund (IMF) estimated real GDP growth of 6.0 percent for Slovakia in 2005 and projected a figure of 6.3 percent for 2006. However, concerns over inflation and unemployment were considered factors in the June 2006 legislative loss by the center-right Dzurinda government (see Political background and Current issues, below).

Government and Politics

Political Background

Founded in 1918, Czechoslovakia was considered to be the most politically mature and democratically governed of the new states of Eastern Europe, but it was dismembered following the 1938 Munich agreement. The preponderant role of Soviet military forces in liberating the country at the close of World War II enabled the Communists to gain a leading position in the postwar cabinet headed by strongly pro-Soviet Premier Zdeněk FIERLINGER, although President Eduard BENEŠ was perceived as nonaligned. Communist control was consolidated in February 1948, and, under Marxist-Leninist precepts, Czech-Slovak differences officially ceased to exist, the two ethnic groups being charged with building socialism in amity and cooperation. (For subsequent political developments during the Communist era, see the article on the Czech Republic.)

As elsewhere in Eastern Europe, the edifice of Communist power in Czechoslovakia crumbled in late 1989. On November 20, one day after formation of the opposition Civic Forum (*Občanské Fórum*—OF), 250,000 antiregime demonstrators marched in Prague, and 24 hours later government leaders held initial discussions with Forum representatives. On November 22 the widely admired Alexander DUBČEK (who had attempted to introduce "socialism with a human face" while serving as leader of the Czechoslovakian Communist Party in the "Prague Spring" of 1968) returned to the limelight with an address before an enthusiastic rally in Bratislava. Following a nationwide strike on November 28 (preceded by a three-day rally of 500,000 in Prague), the regime accepted loss of its monopoly status, and on December 7 Prime Minister Ladislav ADAMEC quit in favor of the little-known Marián ČALFA. On December 10 President Gustáv HUSÁK resigned after swearing in the first non–Communist-dominated government in 41 years, with the Federal Assembly naming Václav HAVEL as his successor on December 29. The Civic Forum and its Slovak counterpart, Public Against Violence (*Verejnost Proti Násili*—VPN), won a majority of federal legislative seats at nationwide balloting on June 8 and 9, 1990, with Čalfa (who had resigned from the Communist Party on January 18) forming a new government on June 27 and Havel being

Political Status: Slovak Republic proclaimed upon separation of the constituent components of the Czech and Slovak Federative Republic (see article on Czech Republic) on January 1, 1993.

Area: 18,933 sq. mi. (49,035 sq. km.).

Population: 5,379,780 (2001C); 5,381,000 (2005E).

Major Urban Centers (2005E): BRATISLAVA (423,000), Košice (234,000), Prešov (92,000).

Official Language: Slovak.

Monetary Unit: Koruna (official rate July 1, 2006: 30.06 koruny = $1US). (Following Slovakia's accession to the European Union in 2004, the Slovakian government announced it hoped that the euro could be adopted as the national currency by 2009.)

President: Ivan GAŠPAROVIČ (People's Union–Movement for Democracy); popularly elected in runoff balloting on April 17, 2004, and inaugurated on June 15 for a five-year term, succeeding Rudolf SCHUSTER (Party of Civic Understanding).

Prime Minister: Robert FICO (Direction–Social Democracy); designated by the president on June 20, 2006, to form a new government following the legislative elections of June 17 and formally appointed by the president on July 4 to head a new coalition government in succession to Mikuláš DZURINDA (Slovak Democratic and Christian Union).

Slovensko—HZDS). In November negotiations between federal and republican leaders over the country's future political status collapsed, with the Federal Assembly becoming deadlocked over the issue of a referendum on separate Czech and Slovak states.

On March 3, 1992, the Federal Assembly presidium scheduled a general election (coinciding with elections to the Czech and Slovak National Councils) for June 5–6, and on April 14 Havel announced that he would seek a further term as president. By then, however, a contest between Czech Finance Minister Václav KLAUS and former Slovak prime minister Vladimír MEČIAR had emerged as the major determinant of federal politics, Klaus favoring a right-of-center liberal economic policy with rapid privatization and Mečiar preferring a slower transition to capitalism for the eastern republic. The two remained in firm control of their respective regions at the election of June 5–6, after which Mečiar returned to the post of Slovak prime minister, from which he had been dismissed in April 1991. Paralleling their differing economic outlooks, the Czech and Slovak leaders entertained divergent views as to the federation's political future. Klaus insisted that Czechoslovakia should remain a state with strong central authority or divide into separate entities, while Mečiar favored a weakened central government with most powers assigned to the individual republics. In the end, the death knell of the combined state was sounded by successful Slovak opposition in the assembly to the reelection of Havel as federal president on July 3. Thereafter, events moved quickly toward formal dissolution, with agreement being reached between the two governments by the end of August and the Slovak National Council adopting an independent constitution on September 1. Ironically, public opinion in both regions opposed separation. Thus, Klaus and Mečiar were obliged to act through the Federal Assembly, 183 of whose deputies (three more than the required minimum) on November 25 endorsed the breakup with effect from January 1, 1993.

The Mečiar government of independent Slovakia quickly came under criticism for its alleged

---

elected to a regular two-year term as president on July 5.

During 1991 the anti-Communist coalition, its major objective achieved, crumbled into less inclusive party formations. The Civic Forum gave rise to two Czech groups in February, while in Slovakia the VPN assumed a new identity, the Civic Democratic Union–Public Against Violence (*Občanská Demokratická Únie–Verejnost Proti Násili*—ODU-VPN), in October after having been substantially weakened by the defection of a Slovak separatist faction, the Movement for a Democratic Slovakia (*Hnutie za Demokratické* dictatorial tendencies and its reluctance to tackle the entrenched position of former Communists in the state bureaucracy. The election of Michal KOVÁČ as president on February 15, 1993, added to the divisions in the ruling HZDS. Although Kováč, a former reform Communist, was then backed by Mečiar, his postelection offer to resign from the HZDS highlighted an internal rift between the prime minister and leading cabinet colleagues. In a cabinet reshuffle in March, Mečiar ejected his main HZDS opponent, Foreign Minister and Deputy Prime Minister Milan KŇAŽKO, who promptly defected from the party to found a new group, the Alliance of Democrats of the Slovak Republic (*Aliancia Demokratov Slovenskej Republiky*—ADSR). Mečiar also insisted on appointing a former Communist military officer, Imrich ANDREJČÁK, as defense minister. The one ministerial representative of the Slovak National Party (*Slovenská Národná Strana*—SNS) thereupon resigned in protest, although the SNS, a strongly nationalistic formation with an anti-Hungarian orientation, announced that it would continue to support the government.

Mečiar governed the country for the next seven months as head of a minority government, failing during this period to entice the (ex-Communist) Party of the Democratic Left (*Strana Demokratickej L'avice*—SDL') to join his administration. In October 1993 the HZDS-SNS coalition was formally revived, this time with the junior partner holding several key portfolios. However, divisions within both ruling parties became uncontainable in early 1994, and damaging defections led to Mečiar's defeat in a parliamentary nonconfidence vote on March 11. Mečiar resigned three days later and was replaced as prime minister on March 16 by Jozef MORAVČÍK, who had resigned as foreign minister the previous month and had set up a new party opposed to the HZDS. He formed a center-left coalition, headed by his own Democratic Union of Slovakia (*Demokratická Únia Slovenska*—DÚS) and including the SDL', which was to hold office pending an early general election.

The ouster of the Mečiar government, described as a "parliamentary putsch" by the former prime minister, served to enflame political antagonisms in the run-up to the election. Particularly venomous were relations between Mečiar and President Kováč, whose open criticism of the HZDS leader had been a major cause of the government's collapse. Nevertheless, in legislative balloting on September 30–October 1, 1994, Mečiar and the HZDS won a plurality, campaigning on a populist platform that appealed to the large rural population. Despite an economic upturn under the Moravčík government, the new DÚS could manage only fifth place, being outpolled by the center-left Common Choice bloc (headed by the SDL'), the Hungarian Coalition (*Mad'arská Koalícia*—MK), and the Christian Democratic Movement (*Křest'ansko-demokratické Hnutie*—KDH). Six weeks later, on December 13, Mečiar embarked upon his third term as prime minister, heading a "red-brown" coalition of the HZDS, the far-right SNS, and the leftist Association of Workers of Slovakia (*Združenie Robotníkov Slovenska*—ZRS) that commanded 83 of the 150 legislative seats.

In March 1995 tensions between Mečiar and President Kováč flared when the latter delayed a bill transferring overall control of the national intelligence agency, the Slovak Information Service (*Slovenská Informačna Služba*—SIS), from the presidency to the government. Although the president signed the bill on April 8, following its readoption by the legislature, the National Council on May 5 passed a motion censuring him for mismanagement of the SIS. The 80-vote tally in favor was below the two-thirds majority required to remove the president; nevertheless, Mečiar backed an HZDS executive call for Kováč's resignation and urged his expulsion from the party. The following month the prime minister called for a national referendum to decide whether Kováč should continue in office, while on June 23 the National Council voted to strip the president of his duties as commander in chief and to transfer them to the government.

On August 31, 1995, the president's 34-year-old son, Michal KOVÁČ Jr., was kidnapped, transported to the Austrian border, and arrested by Austrian police under a 1994 German warrant charging him with fraud (which he denied). Although responsibility for the abduction was unclear, Slovak opposition spokesmen and independent commentators saw a connection between the episode and the continuing constitutional deadlock between the president and prime minister. On September 6 the government majority in the National Council blocked a move to establish an inquiry into the affair.

Early in 1997 the opposition completed a petition drive to hold a referendum on instituting direct presidential elections, but the government suspended the referendum on April 22, claiming that the constitution could only be changed by the Parliament. On May 22 the Constitutional Court ruled that the referendum would be legal, but the government asserted that the result would not be binding and, therefore, should not appear on the same ballot as a separate referendum on whether the Slovak Republic should join NATO. On the eve of the referendum the interior minister, Gustáv KRAJČÍ, ordered new ballots to be printed without the presidential question, creating voter confusion and provoking a boycott. As a result, the turnout was less than 10 percent, invalidating the results.

As was widely expected, in early 1998 the legislature failed to elect a new president, no candidate being able to command the required three-fifths majority. When President Kováč's term expired on March 2, the constitution authorized Prime Minister Mečiar to assume various presidential powers. He quickly dismissed nearly half of the government's overseas ambassadors and canceled further referendums on NATO membership and direct presidential elections. By then, Mečiar had already been attacked for alleged intimidation of the media, abuse of police powers, and the apparent enrichment of cronies through the sale of state-run enterprises. Popular support for his administration continued to decline as the HZDS repeatedly blocked the National Council from selecting a new president and also, in May, changed the electoral law to make it more difficult for small parties to win seats in the legislature (see Constitution and government, below).

At the National Council election of September 25–26, 1998, the HZDS secured only 27 percent of the vote. Although it retained a slim plurality of seats (43, down from 61 in 1994), its only potential coalition partner was the SNS, with 15 seats, the ZRS having failed to achieve representation. Consequently, the newly formed Slovak Democratic Coalition (*Slovenská Demokratická Koalícia*—SDK) allied with the SDL', the Party of the Hungarian Coalition (*Strana Mad'arskej Koalície*—SMK), and the Party of Civic Understanding (*Strana Občianskeho Porozumenia*—SOP) to form a new government on October 30 under the leadership of the SDK's Mikuláš DZURINDA. Dzurinda quickly pledged to repair the nation's international image in order to attract foreign investment and enhance chances for EU and NATO accession. Domestic reform included curtailment of strictures on the media and unions as well as the appointment of an ethnic Hungarian to the newly created post of deputy prime minister for human and minority rights.

In January 1999 the new legislature resolved the presidential impasse by approving the long-delayed constitutional amendment to provide for the direct election of the president. The governing coalition nominated SOP leader Rudolf SCHUSTER, the mayor of Košice (and a former prominent member of the Czechoslovakian Communist Party), as its candidate for the May 15 presidential election. Schuster was initially expected to face the strongest opposition from former president Kováč and actress and former ambassador Magda VÁŠÁRYOVÁ, both of whom ran as nonparty, or "civic," candidates. However, in early April former prime minister Mečiar, who had left the public arena following his regime's 1998 loss, reappeared to announce that he had accepted the nomination of the HZDS for the post, immediately positioning himself as Schuster's primary opponent. On May 15 Schuster garnered 47.4 percent of the vote, shy of the 50 percent needed for an outright victory despite Kováč's late withdrawal in his favor. At runoff balloting on May 29 against Mečiar, who had claimed second place with 37.2 percent support, Schuster won 57.2 percent and was therefore inaugurated on June 15.

The apparent stability of the multiparty Dzurinda government during its first two years in office belied the tensions in the underlying political party structure. In January 2000, acknowledging that the SDK would not outlive the current legislative term, Dzurinda announced that he planned to organize a new party, the Slovak Democratic and Christian Union (*Slovenská Demokratická Krest'anská Únia*—SDKÚ), in preparation for the 2002 election. By the end of the year the Christian Democrats and others had formally withdrawn from the SDK (see discussion in Political Parties, below), although not from the government.

The HZDS led all parties with a plurality of 36 seats in the September 20–21, 2002, legislative balloting followed by the SDKÚ with 28 and the recently formed Direction (*Smĕr*). Despite the HZDS's plurality, Dzurinda was subsequently able to form a new government comprising the SDKÚ, SMK, KDH, and the recently formed New Citizen's Alliance (*Alliancia Nového Občana*—ANO). The coalition fell to minority status in September 2003 when seven SDKÚ legislators left the party.

The first round of new presidential balloting was held on April 3, 2004, with Mečiar leading all candidates with 32.7 percent of the vote, followed by Ivan GAŠPAROVIČ of the new People's Union–Movement for Democracy (*L'udová Únia–Hnutie za Demokraciu*—LU-HZD) with 22.3 percent and the SDKÚ's Eduard KUKAN with 22.1 percent. In the runoff election on April 17, Gašparovič defeated Mečiar with a 59.1 to 40.1 percent vote share.

Dzurinda's minority coalition government collapsed in February 2006, and early legislative elections were called for on June 17, with Direction–Social Democracy (*Smĕr–Sociálna Demokracia—Smĕr*) leading all parties with 50 seats. *Smĕr* leader Robert FICO on July 4 formed a coalition government comprising *Smĕr*, the SNS, and the renamed People's Party–HZDS (*L'udová Strana–HZDS—LS-HZDS*).

Constitution and Government

The constitution of the Slovak Republic came into effect on January 1, 1993, on dissolution of the Czechoslovak federation. It defines Slovakia as a unitary state with a unicameral legislature, the 150-member National Council of the Slovak Republic, which sits for a maximum term of four years. Elections are by proportional representation. Prior to passage of a May 1998 electoral reform, individual parties were required to obtain at least 5 percent of the national vote to claim council seats, while alliances of two or three parties needed at least 7 percent, and alliances of four or more parties, at least 10 percent. Under the amended law, however, all parties, regardless of their participation in coalitions, are required to meet a 5 percent threshold, as a result of which numerous previously allied organizations merged before the September 1998 election (see Political Parties and Groups).

In another major change, a January 1999 constitutional amendment introduced direct presidential elections. Previously, the National Council chose the president by secret ballot, a three-fifths majority being required for election. The president serves a five-year term and performs a largely ceremonial role, although legislation and treaties require his approval and he may dissolve the National Council and declare a state of emergency. In addition, the president appoints the prime minister and, on the latter's recommendation, other government ministers, who are collectively responsible to the legislature.

Under legislation enacted in 1996, Slovakia is divided into eight regions (Bratislava, Trnava, Nitra, Trenčín, Žilina, Banská Bystrica, Prešov, and Košice), which are themselves divided into 79 districts. Regional officials were nominated at the federal level until 2002 (see Current issues, below); district officials are elected.

A feature of the Slovak constitution is its guarantee of the rights of ethnic minorities, including freedom to choose national identity and prohibition of enforced assimilation and discrimination. Under associated legislation, use of minority languages in dealings with public authorities is guaranteed in administrative areas where a minority forms 20 percent or more of the total population.

Earlier, the National Council had decreed that Czechoslovak federal law would continue to apply in Slovakia but that, in cases of conflict between Slovak and federal law, the former would prevail. In addition, following the deletion from the Czechoslovak constitution in December 1989 of the guarantee of Communist power, a systematic revision of legal codes had been initiated to reestablish "fundamental legal norms." A revision of the criminal law included abolition of the death penalty and provision of a full guarantee of judicial review, while a law on judicial rehabilitation facilitated the quashing of nearly all of the political trials of the Communist era. Commercial and civil law revisions established the supremacy of the courts in making decisions relating to rights, and property rights were reinstituted.

Foreign Relations

On December 21, 1992, the "Visegrád" countries (Poland, Hungary, and Czechoslovakia) concluded a Central European Free Trade Agreement (CEFTA), to which the Czech and Slovak republics were deemed to have acceded at their attainment of separate sovereignty on January 1, 1993. (For additional information on CEFTA, see Foreign relations in the article on Poland.) On December 30 the IMF decided to admit both the Czech and Slovak republics as full members, effective January 1. On January 19, 1993, the UN General Assembly admitted the two republics to membership, dividing between them their seats on various subsidiary organs held by the former Czechoslovakia. The two states also became separate members of the Council of Europe, the Conference on (later Organization for) Security and Cooperation in Europe (CSCE/OSCE), and the European Bank for Reconstruction and Development (EBRD), sovereign Slovakia having declared its intention to honor and

fulfill all the international treaties and obligations entered into by the Czechoslovak federation. In October 1993 agreements were signed with the EU transferring the latter's 1991 association agreement with Czechoslovakia to the two successor states in renegotiated form. (For foreign relations of the former federative republic to December 31, 1992, see entry under the Czech Republic article.)

As part of its orientation toward the West, Slovakia in February 1994 joined NATO's Partnership for Peace program for former Communist and neutral states, becoming in addition an associate partner of the Western European Union (WEU) in May. Shortly thereafter, it signed military cooperation agreements with Germany and France, receiving from both countries assurances of support for eventual Slovakian membership in NATO and the EU.

Following the breakup of Czechoslovakia, the Slovak government applied itself to the implementation of some 30 treaties and agreements designed to regulate relations with the Czech Republic, but some aspects of the separation (including the division of federal property, debt settlement, and border arrangements) proved difficult to finalize. A temporary currency union between the two states was terminated on February 8, 1993, accompanied by a dramatic slump in bilateral trade despite the commitment of both sides to a customs union. In 1994 Slovak-Czech trade began to recover, while the Moravčík government upon assuming office in March sought improved relations by moving quickly to conclude an agreement with Prague on police and customs arrangements.

The Czech government's unilateral decision in June 1995 to terminate the payments clearance system operating with Slovakia drew strong condemnation from Bratislava, where Czech charges of Slovak noncompliance with its rules were rejected. The premiers of the two countries met at a CEFTA summit in Brno, Czech Republic, on September 11, when a mutual desire to preserve the Czech-Slovak customs union was expressed. In January 1996 Bratislava and Prague signed a treaty defining the 155-mile Slovak-Czech border and involving land exchanges totaling some 6,000 acres in resolution of outstanding claims. Remaining property and debt disputes were resolved at prime ministerial meetings in November 1999 and May 2000.

Slovakia's relations with neighboring Hungary have long been colored by the presence of a 600,000-strong ethnic Hungarian minority: allegations of official discrimination against it inevitably draw the attention of the Budapest government, which regards itself as the protector of Magyars beyond its borders. Under the 1992–1994 Mečiar government, the influence of the nationalist SNS contributed to a worsening of relations with the ethnic Hungarian community. The 1994 Moravčik government took a more conciliatory line and also sought to improve relations with Budapest. On Mečiar's return to office in December, rapprochement with Hungary continued to be a government aim.

A long-negotiated treaty of friendship and cooperation was signed in Paris on March 19, 1995, by the Slovak and Hungarian prime ministers that recognized the rights of national minorities and enjoined their protection, while declaring the Slovakian-Hungarian border to be "inviolable." The treaty was ratified by the Slovak legislature on March 27, 1996. A remaining disagreement involves the controversial Gabčíkovo-Nagymaros dam being built by Slovakia on the Danube. In early 1999 tentative agreement was reportedly reached for joint operation of the dam and the discontinuation of plans to build another on the Danube, but no final resolution followed. In September 2000 UN Secretary General Kofi Annan apparently offered to mediate the dispute, but Prime Minister Dzurinda rejected the offer as unnecessary.

On June 27, 1995, Slovakia formally submitted an application for full EU membership, and it subsequently expressed its desire to join NATO. However, in July 1997 the Madrid summit of NATO leaders did not include Slovakia among the three former Warsaw Pact nations, including the Czech Republic, invited to join the alliance. Neither was Slovakia numbered in December among the six nations invited to begin formal membership discussions with the EU, though it remained one of five East European countries expected to participate in a "second wave" of expansion. The decisions were

reportedly based on political grounds, including the perceived lack of democratic reforms in Slovakia and its treatment of ethnic Hungarians. The change of government in the fall of 1998 improved Slovakia's prospects for EU and NATO accession, as new Prime Minister Dzurinda indicated his desire to redirect the nation's focus away from Russia and Ukraine (his predecessor's favored direction) and toward the West. Slovakia's standing with regard to NATO admission was also improved by the government's support for the 1999 air campaign against Yugoslavia.

Despite initial objections from the United States, Slovakia was invited on July 28, 2000, to join the Organization for Economic Cooperation and Development (OECD), which the Dzurinda government viewed as further recognition of the country's readiness for full integration with Western institutions. A favorable progress report in November from the European Commission offered additional encouragement that the goal of EU accession by 2004 might be achieved, although the status of Slovakia's large Roma (Gypsy) minority remained a concern.

Slovakia was formally invited in November 2002 to begin membership negotiations with NATO. In what was seen as a related development, Slovakia and a group of other Eastern European countries publicly endorsed the stance of U.S. President George W. Bush regarding Iraq in early 2003. On April 10 the National Council approved NATO accession by a vote of 124–11, and in June Slovakia sent some 100 engineer troops to support the U.S.-led coalition in Iraq (despite the fact that polls indicated that 75 percent of Slovakia's population opposed the war). Slovakia officially joined NATO with six other new members on March 29, 2004. EU accession followed on May 1, a national referendum on May 16–17, 2003, having approved EU membership by a 94 percent "yes" vote, albeit with a modest turnout of only 52 percent. Prime Minister Dzurinda's defeat in the legislative balloting of June 2006 was initially seen as a possible setback in the country's goal of adopting the euro by 2009. However, in July new prime minister Robert Fico announced that he would support the 2009 schedule.

Current Issues

A number of amendments were made to the constitution in early 2001 to permit eventual EU and NATO accession by, among other things, defining the relationship between national and international (i.e., EU) legislation. The basic law revision also cleared the way for the direct election of regional governors and regional legislatures, the first balloting for which was held in December. The HZDS won nearly all the gubernatorial elections and also ran strongly in the legislative polls, propelling former prime minister Mečiar to the forefront of the political scene once again. A negative review from the IMF in March 2002 also created difficulties for the government, although it survived a no-confidence vote forced by the HZDS to protest privatization initiatives. As the campaign for the September legislative balloting commenced, both NATO and the EU warned that a new government led by Mečiar and the HZDS would be unacceptable and would threaten Slovakia's accession plans.

Following the formation of his new coalition government in October 2002, Prime Minister Dzurinda intensified the economic reforms necessary for EU membership and continued to press for NATO accession. However, despite success on both fronts (see Foreign relations, above), the coalition remained divided on many other issues and seemed to lose popularity in the wake of a series of corruption scandals. Consequently, the poor performance of the candidates from the coalition parties in the first round of presidential balloting in April 2004 was not considered a surprise. New President Gašparovič apparently benefited in the second round from concern that a victory by Mečiar might have scuttled the upcoming EU accession and created problems within NATO.

In the second half of 2004 the government imposed additional austerity measures designed to reduce the budget deficit to meet EU standards. Significant public protests greeted those initiatives, particularly on the part of the Roma minority that by nearly all accounts continued to be subjected to ethnic and economic discrimination. However, by mid-2005 it was reported that the population had grown substantially more supportive of the EU in the wake of an economic "boom" fueled in part by an influx of foreign investment and rising demand for Slovakia's exports.

The collapse of the government in February 2006 was caused by the KDH's decision to quit the cabinet in a dispute over abortion policy. (The KDH had unsuccessfully promoted legislation that would have allowed hospital workers to decline to assist in abortions because of their antiabortion religious beliefs.) In the early legislative elections in June, Prime Minister Dzurinda's successful economic record failed to block the advance of *Smĕr*'s Robert Fico, who campaigned on a populist platform that promised reduced taxes, increased social spending, cessation of privatization of state-run enterprises, and the withdrawal of Slovakia's troops from Iraq. Fico, Slovakia's first left-wing prime minister since the fall of communism, also promised that benefits from economic development in the future would be spread across a wider portion of the population. In addition to *Smĕr*'s plurality, the other major development in the legislative poll was the success (20 seats) of the right-wing SNS, a somewhat surprising choice as a junior partner in Fico's new government. Socialists from across Europe criticized the selection of the SNS (and to a lesser degree, the LS-HDZS) to participate in the cabinet. However, Fico, a 41-year-old lawyer, affirmed after the election that his administration would "respect minorities," fulfill Slovakia's NATO commitments, and retain a "pro-EU" posture.

Political Parties and Groups

From 1948 to 1989 Czechoslovakia displayed quite limited elements of a multiparty system through the National Front of the Czechoslovak Socialist Republic (*Národní Fronta—ČSR*), which was controlled by the Communist Party. The Front became moribund in late 1989, as most popular sentiment coalesced behind the recently organized coalition of the Civic Forum (*Občanské Fórum—OF*) in the Czech lands and its Slovak counterpart, the Public Against Violence (*Verejnost Proti*

Násili—VPN), which swept the legislative balloting of June 8–9, 1990. In February 1991 the Slovak prime minister, Vladimír Mečiar, accused the VPN leadership of "not defending the interests of Slovakia" and announced the formation of a minority faction that on June 22 organized separately as the Movement for a Democratic Slovakia (HZDS).

During the first half of 1992 the regional parties became far more influential than those attempting to maintain federal constituencies, thus setting the stage for the breakup of the federation following the June general election, at which the HZDS emerged as the largest party in Slovakia. On the establishment of independent Slovakia on January 1, 1993, those parties that had theretofore claimed a federal identity ceased to do so.

A controversial May 1998 electoral law revision mandated that individual parties, even those in coalitions, would claim National Council seats only if they obtained 5 percent of the national vote. As a direct result, a number of small parties merged with larger formations—principally the HZDS and the Slovak National Party (SNS)—while the principal opposition alliances, the Slovak Democratic Coalition (SDK) and the Hungarian Coalition (MK), technically transformed themselves into unified parties in preparation for the September 1998 election. Both participated in the formation of the multiparty Dzurinda government that took office a month later. In less than a year the diverse SDK began to fracture, leading Prime Minister Dzurinda to announce on January 17, 2000, his intention to organize a Slovak Democratic and Christian Union (SDKÚ), which held a founding congress the following November. By then it had become apparent that the SDK would survive only until the 2002 election campaign, if that long, Dzurinda having announced that he would remain its chair while advancing the SDKÚ as a leading contender for 2002. The SDKÚ congress was soon followed by the withdrawal of the Christian Democratic Movement (KDH) and much of the Democratic Party (DS) from the SDK's parliamentary organization, although both pledged continued support for the government.

Government Parties

Direction–Social Democracy (*Směr–Sociálna Demokracia—Směr*). Formally established at a constituent conference on December 11, 1999, *Směr* quickly emerged as a potentially significant force for the scheduled 2002 general election, on the strength of its leader's popularity. Robert Fico, previously an SDL' deputy chair, had begun organizing the *Směr* early in 1999 as a center-left "third way" party that supports EU accession, political reform, and caution with regard to majority foreign ownership of key industries. In late 2000 opinion polls ranked Fico as the country's most trustworthy and popular politician.

Směr won 13.5 percent of the vote and 25 seats in the September 2002 general election and subsequently served as one of the strongest left-leaning opponents of the Dzurinda government. *Směr* supported Ivan Gašparovič of the HZDS in his successful run for president in 2004.

In early 2005 *Směr* merged with the Social Democratic Party of Slovakia (*Sociálnodemokratická Strana Slovenska—SDSS*) and the Social Democratic Alternative (*Sociálnodemokratická Alternatíva—SDA*), a small party formed by former SDL' ministers that had competed unsuccessfully in the 2002 legislative poll. (For information on the historically significant SDSS, see the 2005–2006 *Handbook*.) The new grouping, which also reportedly attracted former members of the SOP and the SDL', adopted the Direction–Social Democracy rubric, although it continued to be routinely referenced as simply *Směr*. The party secured a plurality of 29.1 percent of the legislative vote in 2006.

Leaders: Robert FICO (Chair and Prime Minister), Pavol PASKA (Deputy Chair), Monika BEŇOVÁ (General Manager).

People's Party–Movement for a Democratic Slovakia (*L'udová Strana–Hnutie za Demokratické Slovensko—LS-HZDS*). The LS-HZDS originated (as the HZDS) in an early 1991 split within the prodemocracy Public Against Violence (VPN) that turned on a dispute between the mainstream leadership and Prime Minister Mečiar, who favored a diluted form of federalism that would offer greater protection for Slovak economic and political interests. Thus, Mečiar issued an essentially nationalist appeal "For a Democratic Slovakia" prior to his dismissal in April 1991 and the formation of the new party in late June. Subsequently, the HZDS became Slovakia's leading party. Returning to power as a result of the HZDS's victory in the June 1992 elections, Mečiar led Slovakia to its separation from the Czech Republic on January 1, 1993, and governed on the basis of an alliance with the right-wing SNS. Thereafter, the party was weakened by breakaways of centrist elements critical of the prime minister's approach, culminating in Mečiar's ouster in March 1994. In opposition, the HZDS remained the country's strongest party. It formed a populist alliance with the smaller RSS (see next paragraph) for the fall national election that headed the returns with 34.9 percent of the vote and thereafter became the dominant party in a "red-brown" coalition with the SNS and the left-wing ZRS.

In July 1998 the HZDS approved the incorporation into its ranks of three groups with which it had previously cooperated: the Party of Entrepreneurs and Tradesmen (*Strana Podnikateľov a Živnostnikov*—SPŽ), led by Ivan SYKORA; the New Agrarian Party (*Nová Agrárná Strana*—NAS), which had been formed in November 1997 by union of the opposition Farmers' Movement of Slovakia (*Hnutie Poľnohospodárov Slovenska*—HPS) and the progovernment Agrarian Party of Slovakia (*Roľnícka Strana Slovenska*—RSS); and the Social Democracy (*Sociálna Demokracia*—SD), a minor party based in Žilina. At the September 1998 national election the HZDS again finished first, but with a bare plurality of 1 over the SDK's 42 seats. In April 1999 Mečiar was reelected party chair and unexpectedly announced his candidacy for president, immediately rising to second place in opinion polls on the strength of his rural base. At runoff balloting on May 29 he lost to the SOP's Rudolf Schuster.

The HZDS held a "transformation" congress in March 2000 in an effort to redefine itself as a center-right "people's party." Mečiar was unanimously reelected chair, and he remained one of the country's most popular public figures. The HZDS led all parties in the 2002 legislative balloting, but 11 of its legislators resigned from the party in May 2003 to launch the People's Union (see LU-HZD, below). Mečiar led all candidates in the first round of the April 2004 presidential poll with 32.7 percent of the vote, but he was defeated in the second round with only 40.1 percent of the vote. Mečiar was reelected chair at a June 2004 HZDS convention, which also adopted the LS-HZDS rubric for the party. The LS-HZDS secured 8.8 percent of the vote in the 2006 legislative poll.

Leaders: Vladimír MEČIAR (Chair and 1999 and 2004 presidential candidate); Anton BLAJSKO, Jan KOVARCIK, Lubos LACKOVIC, Milan URBANI, Viliam VETESKA (Deputy Chairs); František BLANARIK (Secretary).

Slovak National Party (*Slovenská Národná Strana*—SNS). Founded in December 1989, the SNS is an intensely nationalist and anti-Hungarian formation that received 13.9 percent of the vote in the 1990 National Council balloting but only 7.9 percent in June 1992, after which it entered into a coalition with the HZDS. It continued to support the government after the resignation of its sole minister in March 1993 and in October resumed formal coalition status, obtaining several key ministries. Its moderate wing, led by Chair L'udovit Černák, broke away in February 1994 (see NDS-NA, under SDKÚ, below), and the SNS went into opposition after the fall of the Mečiar government in March. In May the SNS Central Council decided that only ethnic Slovaks could be members of the party, which was awarded two portfolios in the coalition formed in December 1994 after winning nine seats in the preceding election. The party advocated a "no" vote on the NATO referendum of May 1997 and joined the ZRS in backing President Mečiar's proposal for a "voluntary exchange of minorities" between Slovakia and Hungary. Its legislative representation rose to 14 in 1998 on a 9 percent vote share.

On June 27, 1998, the Slovak Green Alternative (*Slovenská Zelených Alternatíva*—SZA), led by Zora LAZAROVÁ, merged into the SNS. (For the 1994 election the SZA had participated in a joint list with the HZDS, drawing some environmental support away from the SZS.) On the same day the Christian Social Union (*Křest'anská Sociálná Únia*—KSÚ) ratified a merger agreement signed in May by the SNS's Ján Slota and the KSÚ chair, Viliam OBERHAUSER.

At the 1999 presidential election Slota drew only 2.5 percent of the popular vote, for fifth place, and at a party congress in September he lost his chairmanship. In March 2000 the SNS renewed its alliance with the HZDS, the two parties agreeing to work together in Parliament and in an effort to force an early election. Unlike the HZDS, the SNS opposes NATO membership.

In September 2000 the National Council stripped an SNS MP, Vít'azoslav MORIC, of parliamentary immunity, and in early October he was charged with inciting ethnic and racial hatred for having proposed that "unadaptable Gypsies" be sent to "reservations." The charges were subsequently dropped.

Slota and a number of his supporters were expelled from the SNS in late 2001. They subsequently announced the establishment of a "Real SNS," although the selection of that name was challenged by the SNS proper. The Real SNS was credited with 3.7 percent of the legislative vote in 2002, while the SNS was credited with 3.3 percent. The SNS was surprisingly successful in the 2006 legislative poll, securing 20 seats on a vote share of 11.7 percent.

Leaders: Jan SLOTA (Chair), Jaroslav PAŠKA (First Deputy Chair), Jozef PROKEŠ.

Opposition Parties

Slovak Democratic and Christian Union–Democratic Party (*Slovenská Demokratická Krest'anská Únia–Demokratická Strana*—SDKÚ-DS). Officially registered as a party on February 14, 2000, by Prime Minister Dzurinda (formerly of the KDH), the SDKÚ held its initial congress on November 18–19, 2000. Some 19 deputies and numerous government ministers affiliated with the Slovak Democratic Coalition (*Slovenská Demokratická Koalicia*—SDK) had pledged allegiance to it by the end of the year. The SDK had emerged in 1997 as a loose, philosophically diverse coalition of opposition parties, including the SDSS; SZS; DÚ, which dissolved in favor of the SDKÚ; and the KDH and DS, both of which withdrew in late 2000. In February 1998 the SDK evolved into an electoral alliance, and four months later it officially registered as a unified party in order to ensure that none of its constituent organizations would fail to meet the new 5 percent threshold for claiming National Council seats. As a result, the SDK secured 42 seats in the September 1998 legislative balloting (on 26 percent of the votes) and led the subsequent coalition government. Following the withdrawal of the KDH and DS in late 2000, the SDK deputies numbered 27, including those who had announced support for the new SDKÚ and 2 (including former DÚ deputy chair and "Velvet Revolution" leader Ján BUDAJ) who had formed the new Liberal Democratic Union (see below).

On August 26, 2000, the Democratic Union (*Demokratická Únia*—DÚ), one of the founding members of the SDK, had officially dissolved to join the SDKÚ, as had the minor Slovak Union of Small Tradesmen, Entrepreneurs, and Farmers (*Únie Živnostníkov, Podnikatel'ov a Rolníkov*—ÚŽPR) on June 30. (The ÚŽPR, led by Pavol PROKOPOVIĆ, had cooperated with the SDK at the 1998 election, contributing one seat to the alliance.) The DÚ had been founded at a Bratislava congress on April 23, 1994, as a merger of two components of the coalition government that came to power the previous month: the Democratic Union of Slovakia (DÚS), led by Prime Minister Jozef Moravčík, which had originated in February as a breakaway group of the then-ruling HZDS called the Alternative of Political Realism; and the Alliance of Democrats of the Slovak Republic (*Aliancia Demokratov Slovenské Republiky*—ADSR), another HZDS splinter group formed in June 1993 by Milan Kňažko, who had been ousted as foreign minister three months earlier. Commanding the support of 18 members of the National Council at the time of the merger, the DÚS adopted a centrist orientation and sought to build an alliance of similar formations for the fall 1994 general election. It largely failed to do so, attracting only the National Democratic Party–New Alternative (*Národná Demokratická Strana–Nová Alternatíva*—NDS-NA) onto its list, which polled a poor 8.6 percent vote share and won 15 seats. Founded in March 1994 by a moderate faction of the SNS and led by Ľudovit ČERNÁK, the NDS-NA was formally absorbed by the DÚS in early 1995. In 1998 the DÚS won 12 of the SDK's 42 National Council seats.

The SDK officially dissolved in 2001; some core components formally transferred their allegiance to the SKDÚ, while the DS, SDSS, SZS, and KDH continued as independent parties. Following the 2002 legislative balloting (in which the SDKÚ finished second to the HZDS with 28 seats and 19 percent vote share), Prime Minister Dzurinda was again asked to head a coalition government.

Following his dismissal as defense minister in September 2003, SDKÚ legislator Ivan Šimko launched the Free Forum (below), the defections throwing the SDKÚ coalition into the status of a minority government. Continuing the SDKÚ slide, Eduard Kukan finished third (with 22.1 percent of the vote) as the party's candidate in the first round of presidential balloting in April 2004.

In January 2006 the SDKÚ merged with the Democratic Party (*Demokraticka Strana*—DS), the new grouping adopting the SDKÚ-DS rubric. (For information on the DS, see the 2005–2006 *Handbook*.) In the legislative election of June 2006, Prime Minister Dzurinda and the SDKÚ-DS lost to Robert Fico's *Smĕr,* 29.1 percent to 18.4 percent. Dzurinda said that his reforms "should continue," a rather unlikely prospect as they were one of the main causes of the voters' desire for a change in government.

Leaders: Mikuláš DZURINDA (Former Prime Minister and Chair of the Party), Ivan MIKLOŠ (Former Deputy Prime Minister), Eduard KUKAN (Former Deputy Chair and 2004 presidential candidate), Ivan HARMAN (Former General Secretary).

Christian Democratic Movement (*Křest'ansko-demokratické Hnutie*—KDH). Previously a partner of the Czech Christian Democrats, the KDH presented its own list in Slovakia for the 1990 poll. Its chair, Ján Čarnogurský, served as Slovakian prime minister following Mečiar's dismissal in April 1991. The party went into opposition after the June 1992 election but returned to government in the center-left coalition formed in March 1994. Polling a creditable 10.1 percent and winning 17 seats in the fall election, the KDH again went into opposition and subsequently rejected cooperation overtures from the ruling HZDS. In late 1996 the KDH joined with the DÚS and DS to form the "Blue" opposition alliance, named after the color of the EU flag to demonstrate the participants' pro-Europeanism.

Following the 1998 election, the KDH strongly argued for maintaining its separate identity within the SDK. In response to the formation of the SDKÚ (an obvious rival for Christian Democratic support), the KDH withdrew from the SDK in November 2000, taking with it nine members of the National Council. Late in the month, however, it officially joined the governing coalition. A month earlier Čarnogurský had resigned the party chairship after ten years in office.

The KDH secured 8.3 percent of the votes in the 2002 legislative poll, while its candidate, legislator František Mikloško, won 6.5 percent of the votes in the first round of presidential balloting in April 2004. The KDH won 8.3 percent of the vote in the 2006 legislative poll.

Leaders: Pavol HRUŠOVSKÝ (Chair and Former Speaker of the National Council), František MIKLOŠKO (2004 presidential candidate), Ján ČARNOGURSKÝ (Former Prime Minister), Stanislav VAJCÍK (Secretary General).

Party of the Hungarian Coalition (*Strana Mad'arskej Koalície*—SMK/*Magyar Koalíció Partja*—MKP). The SMK was established in June 1998 as an outgrowth of the Hungarian Coalition (*Mad'arská Koalícia*—MK). Based in Slovakia's

600,000-strong ethnic Hungarian population, the MK had been formed for the 1994 national election by the three parties below, of which the first two had presented a joint list in the 1990 and 1992 elections, winning 7.4 percent of the vote on the latter occasion. In the 1994 balloting the three-party alliance came in third place with 17 seats on a 10.2 percent vote share. The ethnic Hungarian parties were the only groups in favor of across-the-board support of NATO in the 1997 referendum, endorsing membership as well as deployment of nuclear weapons and siting of foreign military bases in Slovakia. In September they called upon Prime Minister Mečiar to resign over his suggestion that Hungary and Slovakia "exchange" minorities, which had reminded them of the postwar deportations 50 years ago. The SMK captured 15 National Council seats in the September 1998 election, at which it won 9.1 percent of the vote.

In August 2000 the party called for establishment of a self-governing region in the south, threatening to withdraw its support for the Dzurinda government. The call came in the context of national plans to establish new local administrative boundaries, creating 12 regions from the current 8. Ethnic Hungarians have objected, in particular, to division of the Komárno region, fearing a dilution of their political power.

The SMK secured 11.7 percent of the vote in the 2006 legislative balloting.

Leaders: Béla BUGÁR (Chair), Pál CSÁKY (Former Deputy Prime Minister), Miklós DURAY (Deputy Chair), Gyula BÁRDOS (Parliamentary Leader).

Other Parties Participating in the 2006 Elections

Free Forum (*Slobodné Fórum*—SF). The SF was formed in November 2003 by seven SDKÚ legislators under the leadership of former defense minister Ivan ŠIMKO. The new grouping subsequently opposed the SDKÚ on most issues, but a March 2004 party conference narrowly elected Zuzana Martináková as chair over Šimko. Re-

ports also surfaced of negotiations for an SF-SDKÚ alliance in future elections. In June 2005 it was reported that Šimko and his supporters had launched a new "neo-conservative, pro-European" party called **New Christian Democracy**.

The SF won 3.5 percent of the legislative vote in 2006.

Leader: Zuzana MARTINÁKOVÁ.

New Citizens' Alliance (*Alliancia Nového Občana*—ANO). Launched in April 2001 by Pavol Rusko, former director of one of the nation's most important private television stations, the ANO described itself as a centrist party. The ANO secured 8 percent of the vote and 15 seats in the 2002 general election, although it was subsequently reported that five legislators had left the party to protest the conservative stance of other parties in the coalition government. Lubo Romo, the ANO candidate in the first round of the April 2004 presidential balloting, received only 0.1 percent of the vote. Several ANO legislators subsequently quit the party. The ANO won 1.4 percent of the legislative vote in 2006.

Leaders: Pavol RUSKO (Chair), Lubo ROMO (Deputy Chair and 2004 presidential candidate).

Communist Party of Slovakia (*Komunistická Strana Slovenska*—KSS). Descended from the original Slovak Communist Party founded in 1939, the present KSS consists of the Marxist-Leninist minority that rejected transformation into the democratic socialist SDL' in 1990. The party won a 2.7 percent vote share in the 1994 legislative balloting and 2.8 percent in 1998. In 1999 its candidate for president attracted only 0.5 percent of the vote. The KSS improved to 6.3 percent of the vote (and 11 seats) in the 2002 legislative poll. However, it failed to secure representation in 2006 on a vote share of 3.9 percent.

Leaders: Josef ŠEVC (Chair), Ladislav JAČA (General Secretary).

People's Union–Movement for Democracy (*Ľudová Únia–Hnutie za Demokraciu*—LU-HZD). The HZD was launched in 2002 by Ivan Gašparovič, a former supporter of HZDS leader and former prime minister Vladimír Mečiar. The defection was attributed to Gašparovič's anger at being left off the HZDS candidate list for the September 2002 National Council balloting. The HZD secured 3.3 percent of the vote in the legislative poll. Subsequently, in May 2003, 11 legislators quit the HZDS to form the People's Union under the leadership of former deputy prime minister Vojtech Tkáč. The LU and the HZD announced a merger in January 2004 and subsequently nominated Gašparovič, a former speaker of the National Council, as the presidential candidate of an LU-HZD-led Confederation of the National Forces of Slovakia that also included the SNS (above) and another small grouping called **Slovak National Unity** (*Slovenská Národná Jednota*—SNJ). Gašparovič surprised most observers by finishing second in the first round of balloting with 22.3 percent of the vote and then handily defeating his former mentor Mečiar in the run-off. Following the election, Gašparovič resigned his post as chair of the LU-HZD so as not to appear beholden to any single party.

Leaders: Josef GRAPA (Acting Chair), Ivan GAŠPAROVIČ (President of the Republic), Vojtech TKÁČ.

Party of the Democratic Left (*Strana Demokratickej L'avice*—SDL'). Following the Communist defeat in late 1989 a Communist Party of Slovakia (*Komunistická Strana Slovenska*—KSS), originally formed in 1939 but subsequently absorbed by the Communist Party of Czechoslovakia, was reestablished. In October 1990 its majority wing renamed itself as the Communist Party of Slovakia–Party of the Democratic Left, which became simply Party of the Democratic Left later in the year.

The SDL' ran third in Slovakian local elections in November 1990 and second in the June 1992 general election. In 1993 it resisted overtures from the then-ruling HZDS to join the government, and in March 1994 it became the strongest component of a new center-left coalition. For the general election in fall 1994, it headed the Common Choice (SV) alliance, which won 18 seats (13 filled by

members of the SDL', which had won 29 seats in 1992). The failure of the SDL' to emulate the recent electoral success of other East European ex-Communist parties was attributed in part to the preference of the old Slovak *nomenklatura* for Mečiar's HZDS.

From 1995 the SDL' experienced internal strife over whether to join the coalition government, as proposed by the HZDS. The election of compromise candidate Jozef Migaš as party leader in April 1996 (in succession to Peter WEISS) failed to end the dissension, which intensified when the SDL' leadership gave qualified external support to the government during a midyear cabinet crisis. Having finished third in the 1998 legislative election with 23 seats, the SDL' signed a coalition agreement under which it accepted six ministerial portfolios, compared with nine for the SDK, three for the SMK, and two for the SOP.

Migaš was reelected chair at a July 2000 party conference despite considerable dissension over antigovernment statements, including his support for a no-confidence motion in April. On December 16, 2000, the SDL' minister of defense, Pavol KANIS, announced that he would shortly leave the cabinet, primarily over allegations concerning the financing of a luxury villa he had built.

Leaders: Lubomir PETRAK (Chair); Jozef MIGAŠ; Lubomír ANDRASSY, Branislav ONDRUŠ (Deputy Chairs).

Association of Workers of Slovakia (*Združenie Robotníkov Slovenska*—ZRS). The ZRS was formed as an independent party in April 1994, having previously been a component of the SDL' (above), on whose list Ján L'upták (a former bricklayer) had won a legislative seat in 1992. Standing on a left-wing platform that urged protection of workers' rights and nonaccession to NATO, it took a 7.3 percent vote share in 1994, won 13 seats, and accepted four portfolios in the new Mečiar coalition government, including that of privatization. In January 1996 the ZRS leadership ordered the closure of the party's Bratislava branch after its members had criticized L'upták for subservience to the prime minister. Although it was a junior partner in the ruling coalition, the ZRS broke with the government in opposition to bank privatization in February 1997. The ZRS also advocated a "no" vote in the referendum on NATO membership. Its fortunes plummeted in the 1998 election, when it lost all its legislative seats upon securing only 1.3 percent of the vote.

Leader: Ján L'UPTÁK (Chair).

Small parties that contested the 2006 legislative poll unsuccessfully included the **Agrarian Party of the Provinces** (*Agrárna Strana Vidieka*—ASV); the **Civic Conservative Party** (*Občianska Konzervatívna Strana*—OKS), led by Peter TATÁR; **Hope** (*Nádej*); the **Left Bloc** (*L'avicový Blok*—L'B); **Mission 21–New Christian Democracy** (*Misia 21–Nová Krest'anská Demokracia*—Misia 21); the **Party of Civil Solidarity** (*Strana Občianskej Solidarity*—S.O.S.); **Slovak Prosperity** (*Prosperita Slovenska*—PS); the **Slovak National Coalition–Slovak Mutuality** (*Slovenská Národná Koalícia–Slovenská Vzájomnost'*—SLNKO); and the **Slovak People's Party** (*Slovenská L'udova Strana*—SL'S).

Other Parties

Party of Civic Understanding (*Strana Občianskeho Porozumenia*—SOP). Founded in February 1998 by former foreign minister Juraj HAMŽÍK and populist Košice Mayor Rudolf Schuster, the SOP supports a "civil society" and an "orientation toward North Atlantic structures." Schuster, a member of the small Carpathian-German minority, served as speaker of the Parliament during and shortly after the Velvet Revolution of 1989. Upon his inauguration as president of Slovakia in June 1999, Schuster resigned as SOP chair; he was succeeded by Pavol HAMŽÍK on June 26.

The SOP apparently did not present candidates in the 2002 legislative elections, and it was reported in 2003 that the party had aligned with *Smĕr*. When Schuster failed to garner *Smĕr*'s support for his presidential reelection campaign, he ran as an independent, securing 7.9 percent of the vote. Schuster subsequently announced his retirement from politics, and the SOP was described as defunct, its members reportedly having been absorbed into *Smĕr*.

Green Party in Slovakia (*Strana Zelených na Slovensku*—SZS). Founded as a party in December 1989, the Greens failed to secure federal parliamentary representation in 1990 but obtained six seats in the Slovak National Council. Having lost all six in the 1992 balloting, it regained two seats in 1994 as part of the Common Choice coalition. In 1998 it won three SDK seats and in late 2000 agreed to work with the newly formed LDÚ on leftist concerns.

Leaders: Ladislav AMBRÓŽ (Chair), Ján RUSNÁK.

Liberal Democratic Union (*Liberálnodemokratická Únia*—LDÚ). Formation of the LDÚ was announced by two DÚS MPs who objected to the latter party's August 2000 decision to dissolve and merge with the SDKÚ. The LDÚ held its founding conference on November 4, electing as its leader a former deputy chair of the defunct DÚ. Philosophically, the new party is closest to coalition partners SZS and SDSS.

Leaders: Ján BUDAJ (Chair), Juraj ŠVEC (Deputy Chair).

Party of Labor and Development (*Strana Práce a Rozvoja*—SPR). The leftist SPR was formed in January 2000 in support of economic and social equality. It opposes NATO membership and the attendant defense upgrades, preferring instead greater investment in such areas as education, health care, and agriculture.

Leader: Ján KALEJA (Chair).

Party of the Democratic Center (*Strana Demokratického Stredu*—SDS). The SDS was formed in October 1999 by Ivan Mjartan as a "modern liberal" party. Mjartan had won 3.6 percent support at the 1999 presidential election. In January 2000 the SDS was joined by the outgoing chair of the Constitutional Court, Milan Čič.

Leaders: Ivan MJARTAN (Chair), Milan ČIČ (Deputy Chair).

Cabinet

As of August 1, 2006

Prime Minister	Robert Fico (*Smer*)
Deputy Prime Ministers	Dušan Čaplovič (*Smĕr*)
	Robert Kaliňák (*Smĕr*)
	Štefan Harabin (LS-HDZS)

Ministers

Agriculture	Miroslav Jureňa (LS-HDZS)
Construction and Regional Development	Marian Janušek (SNS)
Culture	Marek Mad'arič (*Smĕr*)
Defense	František Kašický (*Smĕr*)
Economy	L'ubomír Jahnátek (*Smĕr*)
Education	Ján Mikolaj (SNS)
Environment	Jaroslav Izák (SNS)
European Affairs, Human Rights, and Minorities	Dúsan Čapolovič (*Smĕr*)
Finance	Ján Počiatek (*Smĕr*)
Foreign Affairs	Ján Kubiš (*Smĕr*)
Health	Ivan Valentovič (*Smĕr*)
Interior	Robert Kaliňák (*Smĕr*)
Justice	Štefan Harabin (LS-HDZS)
Labor, Social Affairs, and Family	Viera Tomanová (*Smĕr*) [f]
Transport, Posts, and Telecommunications	Lubomir Vážny (*Smĕr*)

[f] = female

There are 90 or more specifically Romany (Gypsy) parties and nongovernmental organizations in Slovakia. Over the years numerous efforts have been made to form a more unified coalition. In October 2000 14 parties and 29 civic groups announced that they would present a uniform platform to contest the general election scheduled for 2002 and that candidates would run under the banner of the oldest and largest of the Romany parties, the **Romany Civic Initiative** (*Rómska Občanská Iniciatíva*—ROI), founded in 1990 and led by Gejza ADAM. (Adam was dismissed as the ROI chair in March 2001; he was replaced by Milan MIZIC.) On October 23 another leading Romany party, the **Romany Initiative of Slovakia** (*Rómska Iniciatíva Slovenska*—RIS), led by Alexander PATKOLÓ, announced a cooperation agreement with the HZDS, the Romany party having withdrawn in July from a similar agreement with the SDK, which it had accused of failing to keep commitments. Until a February 2000 congress the RIS had been known as the Romany Intelligentsia for Coexistence (*Rómska Inteligencia za Spolunažívanie*—RIZS). A leadership dispute between Patkoló and the party's previous chair, Ladislav FÍZIK, had led to a major rupture in the organization. Adam claimed the support of Fízik for the ROI-led 2002 electoral initiative.

Legislature

The unicameral **National Council of the Slovak Republic** (*Národná Rada Slovenské Republiky*) consists of 150 members directly elected via proportional representation in one countrywide constituency for four-year terms. Parties must secure at least 5 percent of the vote to achieve representation. Following the most recent balloting of June 17, 2006, the seats were distributed as follows: Direction–Social Democracy, 50; the Slovak Democratic and Christian Union–Democratic Party, 31; the Slovak National Party, 20; the Party of the Hungarian Coalition, 20; the People's Party–Movement for a Democratic Slovakia, 15; and the Christian Democratic Movement, 14.

Speaker: Pavol PAŠKA.

Communications

Press

The following dailies are published in Slovak in Bratislava, unless otherwise noted: *Nový Čas* (New Time, 230,000), German-owned independent; *Pravda* (Truth, 170,000), former Communist Party organ, now independent; *Práca* (80,000), organ of Slovak Confederation of Trade Unions; *Slovenská Republika* (80,000), right-wing; *SME* (We Are, 50,000); *Uj Szó* (New Word, 40,000), in Hungarian; *Hospodárske Noviny* (Economic News, 40,000); *Národná Obroda* (National Renewal, 30,000), independent; *Večerník* (Evening Paper, 30,000); *Slovenský Východ* (Slovak East, Košice, 30,000); *Košický Večer* (Košice Evening, 25,000); *Hlas Ľudu* (Voice of the People, 20,000).

News Agencies

Before independence the state-owned Czechoslovak News Agency (*Československá Tisková Kancelář*—ČTK, or *Četeka*) was divided into separate Czech and Slovak concerns, with the latter being renamed the News Agency of the Slovak Republic (*Tlačová Agentúra Slovenskej Republiky*—TASR) in November 1992. A private Slovak News Agency (*Slovenská Tlačová Agentúra*—SITA) has also operated since 1997. A number of foreign agencies also maintain offices in Bratislava.

Broadcasting and Computing

The former federal broadcasting structure ended on January 1, 1993, when the state-funded Slovak Radio (*Slovenský Rozhlas*), with two national networks, and Slovak Television (*Slovenská Televízia*), with two channels, assumed full responsibility in Slovakia. The strict government control of the Communist era had ended in 1991, when the supervision of broadcasting was transferred to authorities approved by the respective parliaments, which subsequently authorized the licensing of independent radio and television stations. There were approximately 2.7 million television receivers and 1.1 million personal computers serving 1.4 million Internet users in 2003.

Intergovernmental Representation

Ambassador to the U.S.
Rastislav KAČER

U.S. Ambassador to the Slovak Republic
Rodolphe M. VALLEE

Permanent Representative to the UN
Peter BURIAN

IGO Memberships (Non-UN)
BIS, CEI, CERN, CEUR, EBRD, EIB, EU, Eurocontrol, Interpol, IOM, NATO, OECD, OSCE, PCA, WCO, WTO

SLOVENIA

REPUBLIC OF SLOVENIA

Republika Slovenija

The Country

Located in the extreme northwest of post-World War II Yugoslavia, with a short Adriatic coastline south of Trieste, Slovenia is bordered on the west by Italy, on the south and east by Croatia, on the northeast by Hungary, and on the north by Austria. The population is predominantly Slovene (90.5 percent), with small Croat, Serb, Magyar (Hungarian), and Italian minorities. About 82 percent of the population is declared Roman Catholic. Women and men are equal participants in the labor force.

While many of its people were engaged in farming and animal husbandry, Slovenia was the most industrialized and economically advanced of the former Yugoslav republics, with substantial output of iron, steel, automotive products, cement, and sulfuric acid. It produced over 20 percent of Yugoslavia's GDP, despite having only 8 percent of the federation's population, and had a per capita GDP double that of Yugoslavia as a whole. Agriculture continues to account for 5 percent of GDP, compared to 39 percent for industry. Leading manufactures include transport equipment, textiles, and chemicals and pharmaceuticals. Tourism is another significant contributor to the economy. The European Union (EU) now accounts for about two-thirds of trade, with Germany and Italy in the lead.

Slovenia's industrial production declined by 21 percent in 1991 (to its 1975 level), while GDP fell by 9 percent and inflation soared to over 200 percent. However, the economy recovered more quickly than was true for the other independent republics of the former Yugoslavia. GDP growth was steady throughout most of the 1990s, averaging close to 4 percent in 1995–1998 and reaching 4.9 percent in 1999. GDP growth was 3.5 percent in 2004. Consumer price inflation has remained under 10 percent annually since 1996, even after the introduction of a value added tax in 1999, while unemployment has declined. In 2003 unemployment was 7.2 percent, while inflation was 3.5 percent. As one of the "fast track" Eastern European candidates for EU membership, Slovenia liberalized foreign investment regulations and privatized state enterprises such as banking, insurance, and telecommunications. In 2002 Slovenia removed all remaining restrictions on foreign investment in Slovenia.

In March 2003 Slovenian voters approved a referendum on EU membership, and the country formally joined the organization on May 1, 2004. In 2005 the government announced new privatization initiatives and further economic reforms to prepare for the expected adoption of the euro as Slovenia's currency in 2007.

Economically, Slovenia is the most prosperous country to emerge from the former Yugoslavia and in general is among the most successful of all former Eastern bloc states. Healthy growth has been forecast by the Slovenian Central Bank into 2008. Additionally, in May 2006 unemployment hit its lowest level since independence.

Government and Politics

Political Background

Previously consisting of a number of Austrian crown lands, modern Slovenia was included in the Kingdom of the Serbs, Croats, and Slovenes, which was officially renamed Yugoslavia in October 1929. During World War II it was divided between Germany, Hungary, and Italy, and in 1945 it became a constituent republic of the Yugoslavian federation.

After 45 years of Communist one-party rule, a six-party Democratic Opposition of Slovenia (*Demokratične Opozicije Slovenije*—Demos) obtained a majority of legislative seats in the tricameral Slovenian Assembly in balloting on April 8 and 22, 1990, with Demos leader Lojze PETERLE being named president of the Executive Council (prime minister) on May 16. However, in the contest for president of the republic the former Communist leader, Milan KUČAN, outpolled three competitors by winning 44.5 percent of the vote in the first round and defeated the runner-up, Demos candidate Jože PUČNIK, with a 58.7 percent vote share in the second. On July 2 the assembly issued a declaration of full sovereignty for the Slovene Republic, and at a referendum on December 23 an overwhelming majority of voters opted for independence.

On February 20, 1991, the assembly approved a resolution announcing the phased "dissociation of Slovenia from Yugoslavia," and on June 25 Slovenia joined neighboring Croatia in issuing a formal declaration of independence. A brief war ensued with federal Yugoslav forces, resulting in the withdrawal of the latter after ten days of relatively minor skirmishing. Having achieved its primary objective, the Demos coalition proved unstable and was formally dissolved in December 1991. This left what became the Party of Democratic Reform (*Stranka Demokratične Prenove*—SDP) and the Liberal Democratic Party (*Liberalna Demokratična Slovenije*—LDS)—with the former having descended from the League of Communists and the latter from the former Communist youth organization—more strongly represented than any other grouping, although Peterle, leader of the conservative Slovenian Christian Democrats (*Slovenski Krščanski Demokrati*—SKD), remained premier.

In early 1992 the government encountered criticism for the slow pace of economic reform, and on April 22 Peterle was obliged to resign upon passage of a parliamentary vote of no confidence. The assembly thereupon named Janez DRNOVŠEK of the LDS to form a new government, which, after being installed on May 14, announced a program that included reducing inflation and unemployment, privatizing the economy, and establishing linkages with international financial institutions.

Despite major problems arising from economic restructuring, the LDS became the strongest parliamentary party in the first post-independence general election, held on December 6, 1992, with the SKD taking second place. In simultaneous presidential balloting, Kučan, abandoning his party affiliation, was returned for a five-year term by 63.8 percent of the vote against seven other candidates. The governmental outcome was the formation of a new center-left coalition under the continued incumbency of Drnovšek, with Peterle as deputy premier and foreign minister.

The new Drnovšek government reaffirmed its commitment to the "Economic Policy Program"

Political Status: Former constituent republic of
the Socialist Federal Republic of Yugoslavia;
independence declared June 25, 1991, on the
basis of a referendum held December 23, 1990;
present constitution adopted December 23,
1991.

Area: 7,818 sq. mi. (20,251 sq. km.).

Population: 1,964,036 (2002C); 1,997,000
(2005E).

Major Urban Centers (2005E): LJUBLJANA
(256,000), Maribor (92,000).

Official Language: Slovene.

Monetary Unit: Tolar (official rate July 1,
2006: 187.42 tolars = $1US) (Slovenia was
slated to adopt the euro as its official currency
on January 1, 2007).

President: Janez DRNOVŠEK (Liberal
Democracy of Slovenia); directly elected in
balloting of November 10 and December 1,
2002, and inaugurated on December 22
succeeding Milan KUČAN (nonparty).

President of the Executive Council (Prime
Minister): Janez JANŠA (Slovenian
Democratic Party) nominated by the president
on November 3, 2004, and confirmed by the
National Assembly on November 9, following
the general election of October 3, to succeed
Anton ROP (Liberal Democracy of Slovenia);
new cabinet confirmed by National Assembly
on December 3, 2004.

aimed at galvanizing the private sector, reforming
fiscal legislation, restructuring the banking system,
and rehabilitating state-owned enterprises. However, in the face of considerable opposition to
any dramatic break with past practices, it took
a cautious line in its economic reform, preferring to adapt existing structures rather than abolish them. Observers noted that the center-left cabinet included former Communists in all the key
economic portfolios. Moreover, President Kučan,
once Slovenia's Communist leader, retained considerable personal influence (and public popularity), even though the 1991 constitution reduced the
presidency to a largely symbolic role.

In June 1993 the president and various ministers became involved in a major arms-trading scandal when some 120 tons of weaponry were discovered at Ljubljana's Maribor airport, apparently
en route from Saudi Arabia to the Bosnian Muslims in contravention of a United Nations (UN)
embargo. Amid conflicting allegations as to who
had instigated the shipment, the affair became a
power struggle between Defense Minister Janez
JANŠA of the Social Democratic Party of Slovenia (*Socialdemokratična Stranka Slovenije*—SDS)
and President Kučan, with the former depicting the
episode as characteristic of the corrupt practices
surrounding the ex-Communist ruling clique. The
confrontation persisted until March 1994, when reported misconduct by military police under the
defense minister's authority prompted the prime
minister to dismiss Janša from the government,
whereupon the SDS joined the opposition.

The transfer to opposition of the SDS was not
seen as affecting survival of the Drnovšek government, which continued to command a parliamentary majority. Indeed, prior to the ouster Drnovšek
had consolidated his assembly support by restructuring the LDS, now called the Liberal Democracy
of Slovenia (*Liberalna Demokracija Slovenije*—
LDS), to include elements of three smaller parties,
two with parliamentary representation.

The SKD's participation in the ruling coalition became strained in 1994, culminating in the
resignation of Peterle from his government posts
in September to protest the selection of an LDS
deputy to be the new president of the National Assembly. Other Christian Democrats continued to
hold important portfolios, however, and the government remained secure in the National Assembly. More ominous for the LDS was the withdrawal of the United List of Social Democrats
(*Združena Lista Socialnih Demokratov*—ZLSD)
from the coalition in January 1996 (in protest
against the prime minister's move to dismiss a
ZLSD minister), while in May a parliamentary nonconfidence vote against the foreign minister, Zoran
THALER, obliged Drnovšek to make a new appointment to the post.

In assembly balloting on November 10, 1996, the LDS remained the largest single party but fell back to 25 seats out of 90, while a center-right Slovenian Spring (*Slovenije Pomladi*—SP) alliance of the Slovenian People's Party (*Slovenska Ljudska Stranka*—SLS), the SDS, and the SKD won a combined total of 45 seats. Drnovšek was asked to remain as head of a caretaker government, and he immediately announced his intention to form a new government comprising the LDS and the other non-SP parties. However, the 45–45 parliamentary split between the SP and the LDS-allied parties delayed not only the quick formation of a new government, but also the election of a permanent prime minister. The latter stalemate was finally broken in early January 1997 when an SKD deputy announced support for Drnovšek, who was reelected on January 9 by a vote of 46–44. Nevertheless, wrangling over the formation of a new cabinet continued for some seven weeks until the SLS broke with the SP to participate with the LDS and the small Slovenian Democratic Party of Pensioners (*Demokratična Stranka Upokojencev Slovenije*—DeSUS) in a government approved on February 27. Subsequently, President Kučan easily won reelection to a second five-year term on November 23, 1997, taking 55 percent of the vote in a field of eight candidates in the first-round balloting, thereby avoiding a runoff.

Drnovšek survived two nonconfidence votes in May and December 1998, both relating to claims by opposition leader Janša that the prime minister knew about a secret 1995 security agreement with Israel and failed in his constitutional duty to make it public. In the December vote, the opposition could muster only 24 votes in the 90-seat National Assembly.

On March 15, 2000, nine SLS ministers announced that they would leave the government on April 15, at which time the SLS and the SKD would merge in preparation for an autumn general election. With the SLS controlling 19 of the government's 49 seats in the National Assembly, Prime Minister Drnovšek faced the imminent demise of his government. On April 3 he proposed adding eight nonparty experts to the cabi-

net, but lack of support forced his resignation on April 8. The unified center-right SLS+SKD Slovenian People's Party (*SLS+SKD Slovenska Ljudska Stranka*—SLS+SKD) put forward Andrej BAJUK as his successor, but Bajuk, an economist with the Inter-American Development Bank who had spent all but a fraction of his life abroad, twice failed to win majority support in the legislature, obtaining 44 votes on April 20—two shy of the required 46—and then 43 on April 26. Following negotiation of a coalition agreement with the SDS, Bajuk won confirmation, 46–44, on May 3, although on May 23 the legislature split evenly on his proposed cabinet, which did not win approval until June 7, also by a 46–44 vote. The new government included eight SLS+SKD ministers, five SDS ministers, and five independents.

The government suffered a serious rupture in late July 2000 when the majority of the SLS+SKD, but not Prime Minister Bajuk, reversed course and joined the LDS in backing retention of proportional representation in the National Assembly. (In a 1996 binding referendum the public had endorsed a majoritarian system, but the legislature had failed to enact the change because of opposition from the left.) As a result, the SDS ended its agreement with the SLS+SKD, and on July 27 President Kučan called an election for October. In the interim, Prime Minister Bajuk left the SLS+SKD and formed the New Slovenia–Christian People's Party (*Nova Slovenija–Krščanska Ljudska Stranka*—NSi), which quickly formed an electoral coalition with the SDS.

At the October 15, 2000, balloting the LDS won a plurality of 34 seats, thereby permitting Prime Minister Drnovšek's return to power in November at the head of a four-party coalition that also included the ZLSD, the SLS+SKD, and the DeSUS. Easily confirmed by the National Assembly on November 17, Drnovšek fashioned a restructured cabinet comprising nine LDS ministers and three each from the ZLSD and the SLS+SKD. In addition, the ZLSD Chair, Borut PAHOR, took over as president of the legislature.

In runoff balloting on December 1, 2002, Prime Minister Janez Drnovšek won the presidency of

Slovenia, capturing about 56.5 percent of the vote against Barbara BREZIGAR, a state prosecutor. Drnovšek resigned as prime minister the next day, and on December 6 President Kučan (who had been barred from seeking a third term) nominated Finance Minister Anton ROP (LDS) as the new prime minister. Confirmed by the National Assembly on December 19, Rop and his cabinet took office on December 20. President Drnovšek was sworn in on December 22 and assumed his duties the following day.

The main priorities of the new president and government were finalizing Slovenia's entry into both the North Atlantic Treaty Organization (NATO) and the EU. In November 2002 Slovenia was invited to join NATO along with six other countries, and in December 2002 Slovenia was one of ten countries that were offered EU membership. At a national referendum on March 23, 2003, voters approved entry into both organizations. EU membership was approved by 89.6 percent of the voters, while NATO membership was supported by 66.1 percent. On March 29, 2004, Slovenia joined NATO and on May 1, it became a member of the EU.

In 2004 the assembly enacted controversial legislation to grant Slovenian citizenship to refugees from the former Yugoslavia (see Current issues, below). Opposition groups argued against the measure, which undermined public support for the LDS-led government and prompted the SLS (the SLS+SKD having returned to the SLS rubric) to withdraw from the government on April 7, 2004. The issue was also prominent in European parliamentary elections on June 13, 2004, in which the opposition NSi received 23.5 percent of the vote and two seats, while an alliance of the LDS and the DeSUS secured 21.9 percent and two seats; the SDS, 17.7 percent and two seats; and the ZLSD, 14.2 percent and one seat. Previously, on February 26, 2004, the National Assembly had approved legislation that required 40 percent of party candidates for the EU seats to be female.

In addition to the unpopular citizenship policy, the ruling coalition faced problems over internal strife surrounding the 2004 legislative elections. On June 24 Rop requested that the assembly approve a no-confidence vote in Foreign Minister Dimitrij RUPEL whom the prime minister accused of cooperating with the opposition. The assembly removed Rupel through a no-confidence vote on July 5 (Rupel subsequently joined the SDS). In the legislative elections on October 3, 2004, the SDS became the largest party in the legislature when it received 29.1 percent of the vote and 29 seats in the assembly, while the LDS only secured 22.8 percent and 23 seats (see Legislature, below). SDS leader Janez Janša was nominated by the president to form a government on November 3. Janša formed a coalition government that included the SDS, NSi, DeSUS, and SLS. The government was approved by the assembly on December 3.

Constitution and Government

The Slovenian elections of April 1990 were the first to be freely contested in former Yugoslavia in 51 years. The current constitution was adopted on December 23, 1991, and has been amended by the Constitutional Act of July 14, 1997, and the Constitutional Act of July 25, 2000.

The head of state is the president, who is directly elected for a five-year term but has a largely ceremonial role (in contrast to the powerful executive presidency of neighboring Croatia). The principal executive officer is the prime minister, who is designated (and may be removed) by the National Assembly.

The 1991 document endorses basic human rights on the European model, one of the aims of the drafters having been to demonstrate Slovenia's suitability for admittance into European democratic organizations. The judiciary includes district and regional courts, with a Supreme Court at the apex. Administratively, Slovenia encompasses 193 municipalities, each consisting of one or more of the country's approximately 2,700 cadastral communities. Municipalities may choose to form larger districts (*upravne enote*), of which there are currently 58.

Foreign Relations

The European Community (EC, later the EU) recognized the independence of both Croatia and Slovenia on January 15, 1992, with the two countries establishing diplomatic relations on February 17. (Relations with Yugoslavia were not normalized until December 8, 2000.) On May 23 Slovenia joined Croatia and Bosnia and Herzegovina in gaining admission to the UN, having two months earlier become a member of the Conference on (later Organization for) Security and Cooperation in Europe (CSCE/OSCE).

In March 1992 Slovenia was admitted to membership of the Central European Initiative (CEI), becoming active in efforts to revive the Slovenian and Italian Adriatic ports as entrepôts for the CEI countries. Slovenian officials recalled that the Trieste-Vienna railway, running through Slovenia, had been one of the first built in continental Europe and saw the CEI as a framework for re-creating the economic links of the imperial era. In the longer term, Slovenia aspired to membership in the EC/EU, as did the other non-EU CEI states. On January 15, 1993, it became a member of the International Monetary Fund (IMF), and in May it was admitted to membership of the Council of Europe. In February 1994 Slovenia joined the Partnership for Peace program launched by NATO the previous month for former Communist and neutral states.

Slovenia contributed troops to the international peacekeeping mission in Bosnia. In addition, Slovenia was instrumental in creating the International Fund for Demining and Mine Victims' Assistance to support demining operations in Bosnia. In March 2004 Slovenia deployed troops and equipment to Afghanistan as part of the UN-led peacekeeping operation. In August, firefighting units were also sent to Kabul, Afghanistan, to train locals.

Unresolved border disputes have strained Slovenia's post-independence relations with Croatia. The issue flared up in October 1994 when the Slovenian Assembly adopted local boundary changes that assigned territory claimed by Croatia to the Slovenian municipality of Piran. Although the Slovenian government quickly called for revision of the measure, Croatia lodged an official protest. Talks at the prime ministerial level in June 1995 were reported to have yielded agreement on "98 percent" of land and maritime border issues. However, relations cooled in December 1997 when Croatia amended its constitution, dropping Slovenes from a list of recognized ethnic minorities and raising suspicions about Zagreb's intentions.

Notwithstanding their bilateral territorial dispute, Slovenia and Croatia remained in agreement on the need to resist any revival of irredentism on the part of Italy, which had long pressed the issue of compensation for Italians whose property in Istria had been appropriated following post-World War II border changes that favored Yugoslavia. The pressure on Slovenia intensified with the advent of the right-wing Berlusconi government in Italy in May 1994, with Rome making it clear that it would block Slovenia's EU membership aspirations until it obtained satisfaction. However, following the fall of Berlusconi in December, the new nonparty Italian government lifted the veto on March 4, 1995, enabling Slovenia to commence associate membership talks with the EU, which were assisted by Spanish mediation on the dispute with Italy. Following the resolution of most outstanding issues, Slovenia signed an association agreement with the EU in June 1996, also lodging an application for full EU membership. In the same month Slovenia became an "associate partner" of the Western European Union (WEU), seeing such status as a necessary precursor to the goal of NATO membership. Subsequently, in February 1998, Slovenia agreed to compensate 21,000 ethnic Italians for property they left behind when they fled to Italy at the end of World War II.

At the NATO Summit Meeting in Prague, on November 21–22, 2002, with formal notification following a few days later, Slovenia was invited to begin accession talks for NATO membership along with six other countries: Bulgaria, Estonia, Latvia, Lithuania, Romania, and Slovakia. On March 29, 2004, Slovenia became a member of NATO, and on May 1, it joined the EU. The assembly approved the proposed EU Constitution on February 2, 2005.

Once in office in December 2004, the Janša government announced its intention to form closer ties to the United States. Tensions between the two countries over the International Criminal Court had strained otherwise very good relations (a bilateral treaty, signed in March 2004, created nonextradition status for U.S. citizens). The United States had already agreed to provide military technical assistance to Slovenia following the 2003 decision to abolish conscription and transition to an all-volunteer military.

Additionally the Janša government has pursued deeper ties with Romania and is actively working to aid Romania's quest to join the EU. Meanwhile, negotiations have continued with Russia over debt repayment. (The Soviet Union owed Slovenia $129 million, which the Slovenian government is seeking to recoup in the form of energy and power plant parts.) Slovenia has also pursued the purchase of 136 tanks from Finland to aid in compatibility with the NATO forces. (The government is looking to increase defense spending to 2 percent of GDP by 2008 [the rate was 1.87 percent in 2006]).

Current Issues

Relations with neighboring Croatia took a step forward after the death of Croatian President Franjo Tudjman in December 1999 and the election of a new president, Stipe Mesič, two months later. Following talks with President Kučan during a March visit to Ljubljana, Mesič described bilateral issues as "solvable with just a little stronger will on both sides." Border concerns, including Slovenian access to Piran Bay, were largely resolved in July 2001, as was a disagreement over management of the jointly owned nuclear power plant at Krško, Slovenia. In September 2004 Slovenian Prime Minister Rop threatened to block Croatia's bid for EU entry over the continuing border issues. Austria has also expressed concern about the safety of the nuclear facility, but a more contentious issue for Vienna and Ljubljana has been Austrian calls, particularly from the right, for Slovenia to renounce the World War II-era decrees under which the Partisan-led Antifascist Council for the National Liberation of Yugoslavia (*Antifašističko Vee Narodnog Oslobodjenja Jugoslavije*—AVNOJ) expelled the German minority from Yugoslavia and confiscated German property. Although former foreign minister Dimitrij Rupel has described the AVNOJ decrees as "a historic fact that cannot be changed," the two governments have been working on an agreement that would clarify the rights of the Slovene minority in Austria as well as those of ethnic Germans in Slovenia.

In 2004 the assembly passed legislation, requested by the Supreme Court, which granted citizenship to residents of Slovenia who had immigrated from other areas of the former Yugoslavia and who had lost their legal status because they failed to apply for citizenship within a six-month grace period following Slovenian independence. (This group became known as the "erased" since they were struck from the census records and therefore were ineligible for government benefits and services.) Conservative and opposition parties forced a national referendum on the issue and on April 4, 2004, voters overwhelmingly rejected the citizenship law with 94 percent voting against amnesty. The government and LDS had urged citizens to boycott the referendum and turnout was low at 31.45 percent. Interior Minister Rado BOHINC vowed to continue registering the erased, and the Supreme Court subsequently ruled that the referendum was illegal.

Ongoing disputes with Croatia over the border continued in 2005–2006, with the most recent issue being that of demarking fishing areas in the Adriatic Sea (the talks over that issue have also included Italy). Energy is a major issue as well, with negotiations ongoing with Russia's Gazprom to construct a natural gas pipeline through Slovenia into Italy. Also, talks are likely to begin soon with the United States concerning the construction of an oil pipeline between the Black Sea and the Adriatic Sea through Slovenia.

Further integration into Europe is a major goal of the current administration, as is general expansion of trade opportunities globally. Among other things, Slovenia is seeking to capitalize upon its location as a natural crossroads between Eastern and Western Europe.

One long-term economic problem that Slovenia shares with other EU members is growing pension and retirement spending. In 2003, 500,000 Slovenians, or one-quarter of the population, were pensioners. In that year pension expenditures accounted for 13 percent of GDP, a figure that is projected to rise to 18 percent by 2020.

Political Parties

For four-and-a-half decades after World War II, the only authorized political party in Yugoslavia was the Communist Party, which was redesignated in 1952 as the League of Communists of Yugoslavia (*Savez Komunista Jugoslavija*—SKJ). In 1989 noncommunist groups began to emerge in the republics, and in early 1990 the SKJ approved the introduction of a multiparty system, thereby effectively triggering its own demise. The most important initial outgrowth of liberalization was the creation of the Democratic Opposition of Slovenia (*Demokratične Opozicije Slovenije*— Demos), an electoral alliance that included the Liberal Democratic Party (LDS), the Slovenian Christian Democrats (SKD, see SLS+SKD), the Slovenian Peasant League (SKZ, forerunner of the Slovenian People's Party—SLS), the Slovenian Democratic League (SDZ; see under DS), the Social Democratic League of Slovenia (SDZS; see SDS), and the Greens of Slovenia (ZS). Demos won 47 of 80 seats in the balloting for the Slovenian Socio-Political Chamber in the spring of 1990, but the coalition collapsed following independence, at the end of 1991. Meanwhile, in Slovenia the SKJ's local branch was succeeded by what became the Party of Democratic Reform (*Stranka Demokratične Prenove*—SDP), whose modest electoral performance in 1992 was partly attributable to the fact that many former Communist leaders had switched to other parties. The SDP joined the new United List (ZL) electoral alliance in November 1992 but declined to join in formation of the United List of Social Democrats (ZLSD) in May 1993. (The SDP is now defunct.)

From the first post-independence general election in December 1992, no single party has been able to command a legislative majority, resulting in coalition governments of shifting membership, all headed by Prime Minister Janez Drnovšek of the LDS except for an interregnum under Andrej Bajuk (initially of the newly merged "SLS–SKD Slovenian People's Party") in April–November 2000. Prior to the November 1996 election, the SLS, SKD, and SDS had formed a center-right electoral alliance, Slovenian Spring (*Slovenije Pomladi*— SP), that won 45 of the National Assembly's 90 seats on a platform that advocated speedier transition to a market economy while, like the LDS, strongly favoring NATO and EU membership. Despite its near-majority, however, the SP was unable to prevent Drnovšek's reconfirmation as prime minister in January 1997, and the coalition was crippled when the SLS agreed to join the new government in late February 1997. Following the October 2000 election Drnovšek succeeded in fashioning a new 58-seat coalition headed by his LDS and also including the ZLSD, the SLS+SKD, and the Slovenian Democratic Party of Pensioners (DeSUS). The 2004 elections saw the end of LDS-dominated governments. Instead, SDS leader Janez Janša created a 49-seat coalition that included the SDS, NSi, DeSUS, and SLS–SKD.

Government Parties

Slovenian Democratic Party (*Slovenska Demokratska Stranka*—SDS). Founded in 1989 as the Social Democratic League of Slovenia (*Socialdemokratska Zevza Slovenije*—SDZS), one of the Demos participants, the SDS has described itself as a "social-democratic party in the traditions of European democracy and the social state." However, the party has adopted center-right policies and aligned itself with Christian Democrat parties and the European People's Party (EPP) in the European Parliament.

Although its presidential candidate in 1992 registered only 0.6 percent of the vote, the party won 3.3 percent and four seats in the legislative election, subsequently participating in the LDS-led coalition government. On the dismissal of party leader Janez Janša as defense minister in March 1994, the SDS joined the parliamentary opposition. In May 1995 it absorbed the National Democrats (*Narodnimi Demokrati*—ND), which had separated from the Slovenian Democratic League (SDZ) in 1991.

As part of the SP in the November 1996 balloting, the party took third place with 16 seats on a 16.1 percent vote share. It remained in opposition until formation of the SLS+SKD-led government of Andrej Bajuk in April 2000. Holding five ministerial portfolios, the SDS remained in the cabinet despite termination of the coalition agreement in July. For the October 2000 election the party concluded a cooperation pact, "Coalition Slovenia" (*Koalicija Slovenija*), with the new NSi (below), and went on to win 15.8 percent of the vote and 14 National Assembly seats.

In September 2003 the party changed its name from the Social Democratic Party of Slovenia (*Socialdemokratična Stranka Slovenije*) to the Slovenian Democratic Party (*Slovenska Demokratska Stranka*), but kept the initials SDS. The change was designed to align the party with center-right groups in the European Parliament, including the EPP. In the European parliamentary elections in June 2004, the SDS secured 17.7 percent of the vote and 2 seats. In legislative elections in October, the SDS became the largest parliamentary group after it won the elections with 29.1 percent of the vote and 29 seats. Party leader Janez Janša was subsequently nominated as prime minister and formed a coalition government on December 3. On May 15, 2005, Janša was reelected as party president at the Eighth SDS Congress.

Leader: Janez JANŠA (Prime Minister and Party President), Jože TANKO (Parliamentary Leader), Dušan STMAD (Secretary-General).

Slovenian People's Party (*Slovenska Ljudska Stranka*—SLS). The SLS is the current rubric of the party that had been named the SLS+SKD Slovenian People's Party (SLS+SKD) in April 2000 upon the merger of the longstanding SLS and the Slovenian Christian Democrats (*Slovenski Krščanski Demokrati*—SKD). The 2000 merger

had occurred following the decision by nine SLS ministers to leave the government.

Claiming descent from a prewar SLS, the People's Party was founded in May 1988 as a nonpolitical Slovenian Peasant League (*Slovenska Kmečka Zveza*—SKZ), which registered as a party in January 1990. It won 11 assembly seats in 1990 as a member of Demos and adopted the SLS designation in 1991. In 1992 it won 10 legislative seats on an 8.7 percent vote share, advancing strongly to 19 seats and 19.4 percent in November 1996 as part of the Slovenian Spring (SP) alliance. The SLS's defection from the alliance in February 1997 was decisive in the formation of a new coalition government led by Prime Minister Drnovšek. SLS President Marjan Podobnik ran a distant second in the November 1997 presidential election with 18.4 percent of the vote.

The SKD was founded in March 1990 by a group of "non-clerical Catholic intellectuals." It was the largest component of Demos, having won 11 assembly seats in the 1990 balloting, after which Lojze Peterle became head of the government that took Slovenia to independence. He remained prime minister following the disintegration of Demos in late 1991, resigning in April 1992 after losing a nonconfidence vote on government economic policy. The SKD became the second strongest parliamentary party in the December 1992 election, winning 15 seats and joining a center-left coalition headed by the LDS, with Peterle as deputy premier. Increasing strains in 1994 yielded Peterle's resignation from the government in September, although other SKD ministers remained in office. In the November 1996 election, as part of the SP, the party slipped to fourth place, winning 10 seats and 9.6 percent of the vote. The defection of SKD deputy Ciril PUCKO broke a deadlock in January 1997, allowing Janez Drnovšek of the LDS to be reelected prime minister. At the 1997 presidential election the party's Jože BERNIK finished third with 9.4 percent of the vote.

At the congress that formally approved the merger into the SLS+SKD in 2000, Franc ZAGOŽEN, the SLS parliamentary leader, was elected party president; his deputies included

Peterle and Andrej Bajuk. The new party immediately claimed a plurality of 28 seats in the 90-seat National Assembly, and on April 28 it renewed its coalition with its former SP partner, the SDS. That agreement produced on May 3 assembly approval of Bajuk as prime minister, although it took until June 7 for the legislature to approve an SLS+SKD-led cabinet. The coalition soon began unraveling, however, over the issue of whether to adopt a majoritarian electoral system. On July 25 most of the SLS—but not Bajuk and Peterle—sided with the LDS and other opposition parties in supporting retention of proportional representation. A day later the SLS+SKD and SDS announced the end of their coalition agreement, although they agreed to remain in a caretaker government pending legislative elections in October. On August 4 Bajuk and Peterle established the New Slovenia–Christian People's Party (NSi, below).

At the October 2000 election the SLS+SKD won only nine seats, on a 9.5 vote share. It subsequently agreed to accept three ministries in a reconstituted LDS-led government. In 2002 the SLS+SKD decided to readopt the SLS rubric. At a party congress in November 2003, Janez Podobnik was elected party president. The SLS withdrew from the LDS-led government in April 2004 over the unpopular citizenship law (see Political background, above). In the October 2004 legislative elections, the SLS received 6.8 percent of the vote and secured seven seats in the assembly. It subsequently joined the SDS-led coalition government.

Leaders: Janez PODOBNIK (President); Nada SKUK, Bojan ŠROT (Vice Presidents); Jakob PRESEČNIK (Parliamentary Leader).

Slovenian Democratic Party of Pensioners (*Demokratična Stranka Upokojencev Slovenije*—DeSUS). Also known as the Grey Panthers, the DeSUS was a component of the leftist ZLSD (below) until opting to contest the November 1996 election in its own right, winning five seats and 4.3 percent of the vote. The party's decision to join the government in February 1997 was crucial in providing the coalition with a slim majority in the

assembly. The DeSUS saw its vote share rise to 5.2 percent in 2000, but it won only four seats. It agreed to accept junior status in the subsequent LDS-led government. DeSUS gained 4.0 percent of the vote and four seats in the 2004 elections. It joined the SDS-led coalition government.

Leaders: Karl ERJAVEC (President), Franc ŽNIDARŠIČ (Parliamentary Leader), Pavel BRGLEZ (General Secretary).

New Slovenia–Christian People's Party (*Nova Slovenija–Krščanska Ljudska Stranka*—NSi). The NSi was established on August 4, 2000, following a split within the SLS+SKD over the issue of adopting a majoritarian electoral system for the National Assembly, as favored by then Prime Minister Bajuk. Like its predecessor, the SKD, the NSi is a conservative, Christian democratic formation supporting deregulation, privatization, a market economy, and membership in both the EU and NATO. For the October 2000 election it concluded a cooperation agreement with the SDS and won eight seats on an 8.8 percent vote share. The NSi received the highest number of votes in the June 2004 European parliamentary elections with 23.5 percent and two seats. The NSi won 9.0 percent of the vote and nine seats in the 2004 National Assembly elections. The party subsequently joined the SDS-led coalition government, and Bajuk was appointed finance minister.

Leaders: Andrej BAJUK (President), Alosz SOK (Parliamentary Leader).

Other Parliamentary Parties

Liberal Democracy of Slovenia (*Liberalna Demokracija Slovenije*—LDS). The LDS was formed in March 1994 as a merger of the main government formation, the Liberal Democratic Party (*Liberalna Demokratična Stranka*—LDS), led by Prime Minister Drnovšek, and three small groupings: a faction of the Democratic Party (see DS, below), including three of its six deputies; all five Green deputies (see ZS, below); and the Socialist Party of Slovenia (*Socialistična Stranka Slovenije*—SSS), led by Viktor ŽAKELJ. In total the new LDS had the support of 30 deputies in the 90-member assembly, with only the SSS (descended from the front organization of the Communist era) being without legislative seats.

Descended from the former Federation of Socialist Youth of Slovenia (*Zveza Socialistična Mladina Slovenije*—ZSMS) and initially styled the ZSMS–*Liberalna Stranka*, the old LDS was formally launched in November 1990. Unlike most Communist youth organizations, the ZSMS had been a substantially independent formation in support of liberal values of individual rights and freedoms since the early 1980s. Having been among the runners-up in the 1990 election, the old LDS became the strongest parliamentary party in the 1992 balloting, with its leader being named prime minister. The new LDS retained this status in November 1996 despite falling to 25 lower house seats on a 27 percent vote share.

Prime Minister Janez Drnovšek was narrowly reelected in January 1997 and subsequently succeeded in establishing a coalition government with the SLS and the DeSUS (both above). However, Bogomir KOVAČ, the LDS candidate for president in November 1997, won only 2.7 percent of the vote, putting him next to last in the eight-man field. The April 2000 departure of the SLS led to Drnovšek's resignation, although he returned to office following the October 2000 election, the LDS having won a plurality of 34 seats with 36.3 percent of the vote.

In balloting on November 10 and December 1, 2002, Drnovšek was elected president of the republic. He nominated Anton Rop as prime minister and Rop was confirmed on December 19. In February 2003 Rop was elected president of the party. The LDS suffered an electoral defeat in the EU elections in which the opposition NSi received 23.5 percent of the vote and 2 seats, while an electoral alliance of the LDS and the DeSUS secured 21.9 percent and 2 seats. The LDS subsequently lost legislative elections in October in which the party received 22.8 percent of the vote and 23 seats, while the SDS received 29.1 percent and 29 seats.

Leaders: Dr. Janez DRNOVŠEK (President of the Republic), Anton ROP (Former Prime Minister,

President of the Party, and Parliamentary Leader), Roman JAKIČ (Secretary General).

United List of Social Democrats (*Združena Lista Socialnih Demokratov*—ZLSD). The ZLSD was originally formed prior to the December 1992 election as a United List (ZL) of groups deriving from the Communist era, winning 14 seats and joining a coalition headed by the LDS. The original components were the SDP, the Social Democratic Union (*Socialdemokratska Unija*—SDU), the Workers' Party of Slovenia (*Delavska Stranka Slovenije*—DSS), and the DeSUS. Of these, the SDR declined to join a formal merger creating the ZLSD in 1993, while the DeSUS reverted to independent status after the ZLSD left the government in January 1996. Advocating neutrality as an alternative to NATO membership (but favoring EU accession), the ZLSD won 9 lower house seats on a 9 percent vote share in the November balloting. At the October 2000 election it won 12 percent of the vote and 11 seats, after which it agreed to join Prime Minister Drnovšek's new government. The ZLSD secured 14.2 percent of the vote and 1 seat in the June 2004 European parliamentary elections. In legislative elections in October 2004, the ZLSD received 10.2 percent of the vote and 10 seats.

Leaders: Borut PAHOR (President), Miran POTRČ (Parliamentary Leader), Uroš JAUŠEVEC (General Secretary).

Slovenian National Party (*Slovenska Narodna Stranka*—SNS). The SNS is an extreme right-wing grouping that stands for a militarily strong and sovereign Slovenia, the family as the basic unit of society, and preservation and restoration of the country's cultural heritage. It won 9.9 percent of the vote and 12 lower house seats in December 1992 but entered a divisive phase in 1993 after party leader Zmago Jelinčič was named as a federal Yugoslav agent. Also contributing to party disunity were disclosures that prominent members were listed in police files as informers in the Communist era. As a result, five of its assemblymen formed an Independent SNS Deputy Group, three others launched a breakaway Slovenian National

Right (*Slovenska Nacionala Desnica*—SND), and one withdrew to sit as an independent.

At the 1996 election the SNS won four seats with 3.2 percent of the vote. It again won four seats in October 2000, on a 4.4 percent vote share. In the 2004 assembly elections, the SNS increased its vote share to 6.3 percent and secured six seats.

Leaders: Zmago JELINČIČ (President and Parliamentary Leader), Sašo PEČE (Vice President).

Other Parties

Youth Party of Slovenia (*Stranka Mladih Slovenije*—SMS). The SMS was organized in July 2000 by former members of youth groups at the universities of Maribor and Ljubljana. Claiming no firm ideology, but emphasizing youth-oriented issues, the party won a surprising four seats in the October 2000 National Assembly election on a vote share of 4.3 percent. It subsequently agreed to support the return of Janez Drnovšek as prime minister. The SMS secured 2.1 percent of the vote in the 2004 National Assembly and therefore did not gain any seats in the legislature.

Leaders: Dominik ČRNJAK (President), Marko DIACI (Parliamentary Leader).

Democratic Party of Slovenia (*Demokratska Stranka Slovenije*—DS). Also calling itself the Slovenian Democrats (*Demokrati Slovenije*), the DS is descended from the Slovenian Democratic League (*Slovenska Demokratična Zveza*—SDZ), which was formed in 1989 and registered as a party in March 1990. One of the strongest supporters of secession, the SDZ participated in the 1990 poll as a member of Demos. In 1991 the SDZ divided, with one faction becoming the Democratic Party (*Demokratska Stranka*—DS) and another becoming the National Democrats (ND; see SDS above). The old DS won six lower house seats in 1992, but in March 1994 three of its deputies, led by Dimitrij Rupel, joined the restructured LDS; of the other three, two opposed dissolution of the DS, which became the current Democratic Party of Slovenia, and one became an independent.

The party won only 2.7 percent of the vote in November 1996 and therefore failed to obtain representation. Party President Tone PERŠAK received 3 percent of the votes in the November 1997 presidential race. At the October 2000 election the DS won under 1 percent, as it did in the 2004 elections.

Leaders: Mihael JURAK (President), Alojz KRAPEŽ (Vice President).

Greens of Slovenia (*Zeleni Slovenije*—ZS). The ZS was formally launched in June 1989, although it had been active as a nonpolitical environmentalist group for a number of years earlier. It was an active participant in Demos and in the 1992 assembly balloting won five seats, with all of the occupants having participated in the postelection coalition. As the ZS-Eco-Social Party, the grouping joined the restructured LDS in 1994. Since then, the parent group has not had parliamentary representation.

For the October 2000 election the ZS joined the **Green Alternative of Slovenia** (*Zelena Alternativa Slovenije*—ZAS), led by Metka FILIPIČ, in a united **Green List** (*Zdreženi Zeleni–Zeleni Slovenije in Zelena Alternativa*) that secured only 0.9 percent of the national vote. In the 2004 assembly elections, the ZS received 0.69 percent of the vote.

Leaders: Vlado ČUŠ (President); Žare LIPUŠČGK, Branimir BAJDE, Andrej ŽELE (Vice Presidents).

Other parties that contested the 2004 assembly elections included (unless indicated, the parties received less than 1 percent of the vote): **Active Slovenia** (*Aktivna Slovenia*—AS), led by Franci KEK, with 2.97 percent of the vote; **Our Slovenia** (*Slovenija je Naša*—SJN), headed by Boris POPOVIČ, 2.6 percent; the **June List** (*Junijska Lista*), with 55 percent female candidates; the **Party of Ecological Movements** (*Stranka Ekoloških Gibanj*—SEG), led by Glorija MARINOVIČ; the **Party of the Slovenian Nation** (*Stranka Slovenskega Naroda*—SSN), led by Borut KORUN; the **Go, Slovenia!** (*Naprez Slovenija*—NPS), headed by Blaž SVETEK; and a coalition of the **Women's Voice Slovenia** (*Glas Žensk Slovenije*—GŽS), led by Monika PIBERL; the

Cabinet

As of July 1, 2006

Prime Minister	Janez Janša (SDS)

Ministers

Agriculture, Forestry, and Food	Marija Lukacic (SDS) [f]
Culture	Vasko Simoniti (SDS) [f]
Defense	Karl Erjavec (DeSUS)
Economic Affairs	Andrej Vizjak (SDS)
Education, Science, and Sports	Milan Zver (SDS)
Environment and Physical Planning	Janez Podobnik (SLS)
Finance	Andrej Bajuk (NSi)
Foreign Affairs	Dimitrij Rupel (SDS)
Health	Dr. Andrej Bručan (SDS)
Higher Education, Science, and Technology	Jure Zupan (NSi)
Interior	Dragutin Mate (SDS)
Justice	Lovro Štrum (NSi)
Labor, Family, and Social Affairs	Janez Drobnič (NSi)
Public Administration	Gregor Virant (SDS)
Transport	Janez Božič (SLS)
Without Portfolio	Ivan Žagar (SLS)

[f] = female

Association for Primorsko (*Zveza Za Primorsko*—ZZP); the **Union of Independents of Slovenia** (*Zveza Neodvisnih Slovenije*—ZNS); and the **New Democracy of Slovenia** (*Nova Demokracija Slovenije*—NDS).

Legislature

Prior to implementation of the 1991 constitution, the Slovene Assembly (*Zbòr*) was a directly elected tricameral body consisting of a Socio-Political Chamber, a Chamber of Associated Labor, and a Chamber of Communes. On December 6, 1992, the first elections were held for a National Assembly and a portion of a National Council.

National Council (*Državni Svet*). The 40 members of the council, who serve five-year terms, are chosen by electoral colleges of local (22 seats) and functional (18 seats) interest groups. The

breakdown is as follows: 4 seats for employer groups; 4 for employee groups; 4 for farmers, trades people, and professions; 6 for noncommercial activities; and 22 for local interests. The council is able to propose new laws, require the holding of referendums relating to legislation, call for a parliamentary inquiry, request the Constitutional Court to review the constitutionality and legality of legislative acts, and direct the National Assembly to reconsider newly passed legislation.

President: Janez SUŠNIK.

National Assembly (*Državni Zbor*). The 90 members of the assembly are elected for four-year terms. Eighty-eight of the members are elected in eight electoral districts by proportional representation. Lists must receive a minimum of 4 percent of the national vote to achieve representation. The remaining 2 seats are reserved for Hungarian and Italian ethnic minorities, with 1 seat going to each group and with each elected in a special nationwide electoral district. The balloting on October 3, 2004, resulted in the following seat distribution: Slovenian Democratic Party, 29; Liberal Democracy of Slovenia, 23; United List of Social Democrats, 10; New Slovenia–Christian People's Party, 9; Slovenian People's Party, 7; Slovenian National Party, 6; Slovenian Democratic Party of Pensioners, 4; minority representatives, 2.

President: France CUKJATI.

Communications

Press

Unless otherwise noted, the following are dailies published in Ljubljana in Slovene: *Delo* (Work, 280,000); *Slovenske Novice* (Slovene News, 360,000); *Večer* (Evening, Maribor, 200,000); *Dnevnik* (Journal, 196,000).

News Agency

The principal facility is the Slovenian Press Agency (*Slovenska Tiskovna Agencija*—STA), headquartered in Ljubljana.

Broadcasting and Computing

Slovenian Radio-Television (*Radiotelevizija Slovenija*) offers national programming in Slovene, Hungarian, and Italian. About 50 radio stations broadcast regionally or locally, and cable television is increasingly common. There were approximately 770,000 television receivers and 650,000 personal computers serving 880,000 Internet users in 2003.

Intergovernmental Representation

Ambassador to the U.S.
Samuel ZBOGAR

U.S. Ambassador to Slovenia
Thomas B. ROBERTSON

Permanent Representative to the UN
Roman KIRN

IGO Memberships (Non-UN)
BIS, CEI, CEUR, EBRD, EIB, EU, Eurocontrol, IADB, Interpol, IOM, NATO, OSCE, PCA, WCO, WTO

SPAIN

KINGDOM OF SPAIN

Reino de España

The Country

Occupying more than four-fifths of the Iberian peninsula (which it shares with Portugal), Spain is separated by the Pyrenees from France and the rest of Europe and includes within its national territory the Balearic Islands in the Mediterranean, the Canary Islands in the Atlantic, and some small North African enclaves, including the *presidios* of Ceuta and Melilla. Continental Spain, a region of varied topography and climate, has been noted more for beauty of landscape than for wealth of resources but possesses valuable deposits of slate, iron, coal, and other minerals, as well as petroleum. The Spanish are a mixture of the original mainly Iberian population with later invading peoples. The population includes several cultural/linguistic groups: Castilians, Galicians, Andalusians, Catalans, and Basques (who claim distinct ethnicity). Regional feelings remain strong, particularly in the Basque and Catalan areas in the north and east, and various local languages and dialects are used in addition to the long-dominant Castilian Spanish. The population is almost entirely Roman Catholic, although religious liberty is formally guaranteed. In 1998 women comprised approximately 37 percent of the labor force, concentrated in domestic and human services and clerical work. Although traditionally minimal, female participation in government is rising. Several parties have adopted quota systems to ensure female access to senior party posts, and the current cabinet is half female.

The Spanish economy was transformed between 1960 and 1972 by mass tourism, the GNP increasing almost fivefold; however, high inflation, un-

employment consistently in excess of 15 percent, and substantial balance-of-payments problems curtailed subsequent growth rates until January 1986, when entry into the European Community (EC, subsequently the European Union—EU) provided a renewed stimulus. Industry currently accounts for about 25 percent of GDP, with the principal industrial exports being automobiles, machinery and electrical equipment, metals and metal products, and processed foods. Textiles and footwear, plastics, ships, petroleum, and chemicals also are of major importance. Agriculture, the traditional mainstay of the Spanish economy, has seen its share of GDP and employment decline to about 3 percent

and 6 percent, respectively. The most important agricultural products continue to be olives and olive oil, cereals, fruits, vegetables, and wines. Fishing also remains significant, with Spain's fleet ranking as one of the world's largest.

Notwithstanding substantial EC/EU funding, the economy experienced severe recession in the early 1990s and an unemployment rate that, at around 25 percent of the labor force in early 1995, was by far the EU's highest. GDP grew by around 3.4 percent in 1997, and unemployment, while still high, fell to about 20 percent as Madrid implemented a strict reform program highlighted by what the International Monetary Fund (IMF) described as "prudent monetary and fiscal policies." Unemployment fell to 18 percent in 1998, and in 1999 Spain was permitted to participate in the launching of the EU's Economic and Monetary Union (EMU), propelled by continued GDP growth (3.8 percent in real terms for 1998) and declining inflation. The economy continued to expand to a rate of 4.2 percent in 1999–2000, above the average for the other states in the Organization for Economic Cooperation and Development (OECD), while unemployment continued its downward trend, falling from 11.5 percent in 2002 to 9.2 percent in 2005. Economic growth dropped to 2.0 percent in 2002 but edged upward thereafter, reaching 2.8 percent in 2004, and 3.4 percent in 2005. By mid-2006 concern had been raised that Spain's economic growth could not be sustained, as it relied primarily on a housing construction boom and other domestic consumption. Spain's trade deficit had grown in 2005 to about 7.3 percent of GDP, the highest in the developed world.

Government and Politics

Political Background

Conquered in the 8th century by North African Moors (Arabs and Berbers), who established a flourishing Islamic civilization in the south of the peninsula, Christian Spain completed its self-liberation in 1492 and went on to found a world empire that reached its apogee in the 16th century and then gradually disintegrated. Monarchical rule under the House of Bourbon continued into the 20th century, surviving the dictatorship of Miguel PRIMO de Rivera in 1923–1930 but giving place in 1931 to a multiparty republic that became increasingly subject to leftist influences, leading to the electoral victory of a Popular Front coalition in 1936. The leftist success provoked a military uprising led by Gen. Francisco FRANCO Bahamonde, precipitating the three-year Civil War in which the republican forces, although assisted by Soviet and other foreign volunteers, were ultimately defeated with aid from Fascist Italy and Nazi Germany. A fascist regime was then established, Franco ruling as leader (*caudillo*) and chief of state with the support of the armed forces; the Catholic Church; and commercial, financial, and landed interests.

Having preserved its neutrality throughout World War II and suffered a period of ostracism thereafter by the United Nations (UN), Spain was gradually readmitted to international society. The political structure was modified in 1947 with the adoption of a Law of Succession, which declared Spain to be a monarchy (although without a monarch), and again in 1967 by an Organic Law confirming Franco's position as chief of state, defining the structure of other government bodies, and providing for strictly limited public participation in elections to the legislature (*Cortes*). Political and administrative controls in effect since the Civil War were considerably relaxed during the early 1960s, but subsequent demands for change generated increasing instability. In December 1973 Prime Minister Luis CARRERO Blanco was assassinated by Basque separatists and succeeded by Carlos ARIAS Navarro.

Franco became terminally ill on October 17, 1975, and on October 30 Prince JUAN CARLOS de Borbón y Borbón, who had previously been designated as heir to the Spanish throne, assumed the powers of provisional chief of state and head of government. Franco died on November 20, and two days later Juan Carlos was sworn in as king, in accordance with the 1947 Law of Succession.

Political Status: Formerly under system of personal rule instituted in 1936; monarchy reestablished November 22, 1975, in accordance with Law of Succession of July 26, 1947, as amended in 1969 and 1971; parliamentary monarchy confirmed by constitution effective December 29, 1978.

Area: 194,896 sq. mi. (504,782 sq. km.).

Population: 40,847,371 (2001C); 43,929,000 (2005E).

Major Urban Areas (2005E): MADRID (3,192,000), Barcelona (1,621,000), Valencia (798,000), Seville (703,000), Zaragoza (648,000), Málaga (543,000), Bilbao (352,000).

Official Languages: Spanish and regional languages (principally Basque, Catalan, Galician, and Valencian).

Monetary Unit: Euro (market rate July 1, 2006: 1 euro = $1.28US).

Monarch: JUAN CARLOS I; invested before the Spanish Legislative Assembly in 1969; sworn in as king on November 22, 1975, following the death of the former chief of state and president of government, Gen. Francisco FRANCO Bahamonde, on November 20.

Heir to the Throne: Prince FELIPE; sworn in as heir apparent on January 30, 1986.

President of Government (Prime Minister): José Luis Rodríguez ZAPATERO (Spanish Socialist Workers' Party); nominated by the king on April 7, 2004, following the parliamentary election of March 14, elected by the Congress of Deputies on April 16, and sworn in on April 18 for a four-year term, succeeding José María AZNAR López (Popular Party).

On July 1, 1976, Arias Navarro resigned as prime minister—reportedly at the king's request—following criticism of his somewhat cautious approach to promised reform of the political system. His successor, Adolfo SUÁREZ González, moved energetically to advance the reform program, securing its approval by the National Council of the National (Francoist) Movement on October 8, by the *Cortes* on November 10, and by the public in a referendum conducted on December 15. The National Movement was abolished by cabinet decree on April 1, 1977, and on June 15 balloting took place for a new, bicameral *Cortes*, with Prime Minister Suárez's Union of the Democratic Center (*Unión de Centro Democrático*—UCD) obtaining a substantial plurality in both houses. A new constitution went into force on December 29, 1978, following overwhelming approval by the *Cortes* on October 31, endorsement in a referendum on December 6, and ratification by King Juan Carlos on December 27. Suárez was formally reappointed on April 2, 1979, a general election on March 1 having yielded no substantial party realignment within the legislature.

During 1979–1980 an increase in terrorist activity, particularly in the Basque region, gave rise to manifest uneasiness within military circles, while the UCD experienced internal dissension following the introduction of a liberal divorce bill that the Catholic Church and most right-wing elements bitterly opposed. On January 29, 1981, Suárez unexpectedly resigned. Before his designated successor had been confirmed, a group of Civil Guards, led by Lt. Col. Antonio TEJERO Molina, seized control of the Congress of Deputies chamber in an attempted coup on February 23. Due largely to the prompt intervention of King Juan Carlos, the rebellion failed, Leopoldo CALVO Sotelo i Bustelo, the UCD secretary general, being sworn in as prime minister on February 26. However, the fissures between moderate and rightist elements within the UCD continued to deepen, with a number of new parties being spawned during late 1981 and the first half of 1982. As a result, lower house UCD representation plummeted to a mere dozen deputies at an election held October 12, when the Spanish Socialist Workers' Party (*Partido Socialista Obrero Español*—PSOE) obtained a comfortable majority (202 to 106 seats) over the Popular Alliance (*Alianza Popular*—AP), an emergent right-wing group that had previously held only a handful of seats. On December 2, PSOE leader Felipe GONZÁLEZ Márquez was inaugurated as the first left-wing head of government since the 1930s. González was sworn in for a second term on July 24, 1986, following an early election on June 22 at which the PSOE, despite marginally declining strength, retained majority control of both houses of the *Cortes*.

At the election of October 29, 1989, the PSOE lost majority control of the Congress of Deputies by one seat. Nonetheless, González continued in office, and on April 5, 1990, he survived a confidence vote because of the absence of four Basque deputies whose attempt to alter the wording of the oath of allegiance had been denied. During 1991 Prime Minister González approached his tenth year in office amid little evidence of declining popularity. With the conservative Popular Party (*Partido Popular*— PP, successor to the AP) engaged in a process of ideological self-examination and with the Communist Party (despite having been an early exponent of "Eurocommunism") reeling from events in Eastern Europe, the Socialists and their leader continued to dominate.

The PSOE government experienced a sharp drop in its popularity in 1992 amid disclosures of financial corruption in ruling party circles. Toward the end of the year the PSOE headquarters in Madrid were raided twice on the orders of a judge investigating illegal sources of finance. Further corruption disclosures in early 1993, combined with continuing economic problems, persuaded González to call a general election four months before constitutionally required. At the balloting of June 6 the PSOE unexpectedly avoided defeat. Although reduced to a plurality of 159 seats in the 350-member Congress of Deputies, the Socialists were able to retain power as a minority government (with a third of the cabinet posts going to independents) by obtaining the parliamentary support of regional parties. In a confidence vote on July 9, the main Catalan (*Convergéncia i Unió*— CiU) and Basque nationalist (*Partido Nacionalista Vasco*—PNV) parties voted with the PSOE, giving the minority government a 181-seat majority. The immediate price of CiU support was a government commitment to transfer 15 percent of taxes raised in Catalonia to the regional Catalan government, with the CiU in February 1994 adding a demand for "real" autonomy for Catalonia.

In April 1994 González secured all-party approval for new anticorruption measures, including the creation of a special prosecutor's office. Although González prevented a new parliamentary committee from investigating past PSOE fund-raising activities, evidence of financial malpractice by the ruling party and the state administration mounted inexorably. The PP leader, José María AZNAR López, obtained considerable political benefit from the scandals, and he led his party to a crushing victory over the PSOE in the European Parliament balloting on June 12. Moreover, in simultaneous regional elections in its stronghold of Andalucía, the PSOE lost its overall majority and had to enlist support from the Communist-led United Left (*Izquierda Unida*—IU) to remain in power.

A further PSOE setback in Basque regional balloting on October 24, 1994, highlighted the government's political and economic difficulties, amid continuing allegations of official wrongdoing and corruption. Two months later, three former senior security officers were arrested in the wake of reports that they had run a secret "death squad" operation against Basque terrorists in the mid-1980s. Centering on the activities of the so-called "Antiterrorist Groups of Liberation" (*Grupos Antiterroristas de Liberación*—GAL), the case took on additional momentum when 14 former political and security officials were indicted in April 1995 on charges ranging from attempted murder to misuse of public funds.

To add to the government's problems, the Basque *Euzkadi ta Azkatasuna* (ETA), which had been engaged in a violent separatist campaign since the 1960s, launched a new wave of terrorist attacks in 1995, including an attempt to assassinate PP leader Aznar in a Madrid car bomb attack on April 19. The episode bolstered Aznar's popular standing, as evidenced by his party's advances in regional elections on May 28.

PSOE hopes of a government revival appeared to be dashed by a sensational press disclosure in mid-June 1995 that a military intelligence unit had intercepted the mobile telephone calls of leading politicians and businessmen, including those of King Juan Carlos. Accepting political responsibility for the operation, Defense Minister Julián GARCÍA Vargas and his immediate predecessor, Narcís SERRA i Serra, resigned from the government. Moreover, the episode brought to a head deepening strains between the PSOE and the Catalan CiU, which on July 17 formally withdrew its parliamentary support for the minority government. Meanwhile, judicial investigations into the GAL affair gathered pace, leading in January 1996 to serious criminal charges against José BARRIONUEVO, who had been interior minister in 1982–1988.

In early parliamentary balloting held on March 3, 1996, the PP won 156 lower house seats, compared to 141 for the PSOE. After protracted negotiations with the main regional parties, PP leader Aznar succeeded in forming a minority government, which secured parliamentary approval on May 4 and was sworn in two days later. The PP's parliamentary margin (186 to 166 seats) relied on external support from Basque (PNV), Catalan (CiU), and Canarian (*Coalición Canaria*—CC) regionalist parties, which won concessions that included a doubling (to 30 percent) of the proportion of income tax revenues accruing to the autonomous regions.

In the succeeding two years public resentment against the ETA grew in response to an increase in civilian deaths. As part of a government crackdown, the entire 23-member national committee of the political wing of the ETA, the *Herri Batasuna* (HB), was placed on trial. All were found guilty and sentenced to a minimum of seven years, although the Constitutional Court ultimately ordered their release in July 1999.

In September 1998 the ETA announced a unilateral cease-fire, and in October an unofficially affiliated political "platform," the "We the Basque Citizens" (*Euskal Herritarrok*—EH), finished third in the regional elections. In December the EH participated in formation of a Basque regional government—a first for an ETA-linked group—with the PNV and the Basque Solidarity (*Eusko Alkartasuna*—EA).

In June 1999 Prime Minister Aznar revealed that government and ETA representatives had initiated direct talks under the 1998 cease-fire, but little was achieved in succeeding months. The ETA continued to insist on the withdrawal of security forces from the Basque region, the release of some 450 jailed comrades (or, at the very least, their transfer to prisons in Basque Country), and an independence referendum. On November 28, citing the lack of progress toward any of its goals, the ETA announced that it would end its cease-fire as of December 3. On January 23, 2000, Prime Minister Aznar, opposition leader Joaquín ALMUNIA Amann of the PSOE, and several former prime ministers led an estimated million people in a Madrid march to protest the resumed campaign of violence. Collaterally, the PNV ended its regional governing alliance with the EH.

At the general election of March 12, 2000, Prime Minister Aznar's PP surpassed expectations, winning an outright majority in both houses of the *Cortes*, including 183 seats in the Congress of Deputies. Reelected prime minister by the lower house on April 26, with external support from the CiU and the CC, Aznar was sworn in for a second term on April 27 at the head of a revamped and expanded cabinet. A ministerial reshuffle announced on July 9, 2002, was highlighted by the selection of Spain's first woman foreign minister, Ana PALACIO Vallelersundi, who was sworn in the following day.

On March 11, 2004, in the worst peacetime attack on Spanish civilians since the Civil War of the 1930s, a series of bombs exploded on four Madrid commuter trains, killing 191 and injuring another 1,400. The bombings had clearly been timed to affect the general election scheduled for March 14. Although the Aznar government immediately focused blame on the ETA, it soon emerged that the coordinated assault had been perpetrated by militants associated with the al-Qaida terrorist network.

A week earlier opinion polls had given the incumbent PP, now led by Aznar's designated successor, Mariano RAJOY Brey, a lead of 5 to 9 percent in the contest for the Chamber of Deputies, but on

March 14 the voters gave the PSOE 42.6 percent of the vote, good for 164 seats, versus 37.6 percent and 148 seats for the PP. The rapid reversal of the PP's fortunes was generally attributed to the bombings, the government's misplaced blame, and underlying public opposition to Spain's military involvement in Iraq following the U.S.-led overthrow of the Saddam Hussein regime. With support from the IU and a handful of regional parties, the PSOE's José Luis Rodríguez ZAPATERO was confirmed as prime minister on April 16 and took office at the head of a 16-member cabinet, half of them women.

Constitution and Government

The 169-article Spanish constitution of 1978, the seventh since 1812, abrogated the "fundamental principles" and organic legislation under which General Franco had ruled as chief of state (*jefe del estado*) until his death in 1975. The document defines the Spanish state as a parliamentary monarchy and guarantees a variety of basic rights, including those of speech and press, association, and collective bargaining. "Bordering provinces" and "island territories and provinces" with common characteristics and/or historic regional status may, under prescribed circumstances, form "autonomous communities," but no federation of such communities is to be permitted. Roman Catholicism was disestablished as the state religion, although authorities were directed to "keep in mind the religious beliefs of Spanish society." Torture was outlawed, the death penalty abolished, and "a more equitable distribution of regional and personal incomes" enjoined.

The powers of the king include nominating a candidate for the post of prime minister, after consulting the parties in the *Cortes*; dissolving the house and calling fresh elections if such approval is not forthcoming; serving as commander in chief of the armed forces, which are specifically recognized as guardians of the constitutional order; and calling referenda. The prime minister, who is empowered to dissolve the *Cortes* and call an election at any time, is assisted by a cabinet that is collectively responsible to the lower house.

Legislative authority is exercised by the bicameral *Cortes*, consisting of a 259-member Senate (208 directly elected territorial representatives plus 51 indirectly chosen by the assemblies of the autonomous regions) and a Congress of Deputies of 300 to 400 (currently 350) members elected on the basis of universal adult suffrage and proportional representation. Both houses serve four-year terms, barring dissolution; each can initiate legislation, although the upper house can only delay measures approved by the lower.

The judicial system is headed by a Supreme Tribunal (*Tribunal Supremo*) and includes territorial courts, provincial courts, regional courts, courts of the first instance, and municipal courts. An independent General Council of Judicial Power (*Consejo General del Poder Judicial*) oversees the judiciary.

The country is divided into 19 regions containing 50 administrative provinces, including the island provinces of Baleares, Las Palmas, and Santa Cruz de Tenerife. Although it was envisaged in 1978 that devolution to the regions would involve only a limited range of powers, such as alteration of municipal boundaries, control of health and tourism, instruction in regional languages, and the establishment of local police agencies, the tendency has been to delegate ever more functions to regional governments.

In October 1979 devolution statutes presented for the Basque and Catalan regions were overwhelmingly approved in regional referenda. In March 1980 elections for regional Legislative Assemblies were held in the Basque provinces of Alava, Guipúzcoa, and Vizcaya, and in the Catalan provinces of Barcelona, Gerona, Lérida, and Tarragona. Similar elections were held in Galicia in October 1981 and in Andalucía in May 1982. By February 1983 autonomy statutes had been approved for the (then) remaining 13 regions, with balloting in each being conducted in May. In 1994 the African enclaves of Ceuta and Melilla were also accorded the status of autonomous regions, bringing the total to 19. The presidents of government of the autonomous regions are elected by the regional legislatures.

Autonomous Region	President of Government [as of July 1, 2006]
Andalucía	Manuel Chaves González (PSOE)
Aragón	Marcelino Iglesias Ricou (PSOE)
Asturias	Vicente Álvarez Areces (PSOE)
Baleares (Balearic Islands)	Jaume Matas Palou (PP)
Canarias (Canary Islands)	Adán Martín Menis (CC)
Cantábria	Miguel Ángel Revilla Roiz (PRC)
Castilla y León	Juan Vicente Herrera Campo (PP)
Castilla–La Mancha	José María Barreda Fontes (PSOE)
Catalunya (Catalonia)	Pasqual Maragall (PSC)
Ceuta	Juan Jesús Vivas Lara (PP)
Euzkadi/País Vasco (Basque Country)	Juan José Ibarretxe Markuartu (PNV)
Extremadura	Juan Carlos Rodríguez Ibarra (PSOE)
Galicia	Emilio Pérez Touriño (PSdeG)
Madrid	Esperanza Aquirre (PP)
Melilla	Juan José Imbroda Ortiz (UPM)
Murcia	Ramón Luis Valcarel Siso (PP)
Navarra	Miguel Sánz Sesma (UPN)
La Rioja	Pedro María Sanz Alonso (PP)
Valencia	Francisco Enrique Camps Ortiz (PP)

Foreign Relations

Neutral in both world wars, Spain sided with the anti-Communist powers after World War II but under Franco was prevented by certain democratic governments from becoming a member of NATO, the EC, and other Western organizations. It was, however, admitted to the UN in 1955 and, in due course, to all of the latter's specialized agencies. The 1970s and early 1980s saw a strengthening of relations with Portugal, France, and West Germany. There also was a reduction of tension with Britain over Gibraltar (see article on United Kingdom: Related Territories), which resulted in reopening of the border in early 1985 and a British commitment to talks from which the sovereignty question was not excluded. Relations with the United States remained cordial following the conclusion in 1970 of an Agreement of Friendship and Cooperation to replace the original U.S.-Spanish defense agreement of 1953. Following the restoration of democracy in 1975–1976, Spain was admitted to the Council of Europe in 1977 and to NATO in 1982, with membership in the EC following on January 1, 1986.

In February 1976 Spain yielded control of its North African territory of Spanish (Western) Sahara to Morocco and Mauritania. The action was taken despite strong protests by Algeria and the passage of a resolution by the UN General Assembly's Committee on Trust and Non-Self-Governing Territories in December 1975 that called for a UN-sponsored plebiscite to permit the Saharans to exercise their right to self-determination. Formerly cordial relations with the Saharan representative group Polisario (see article on Morocco) were broken and its envoys expelled following a late 1985 Polisario attack on two Spanish vessels off the coast near Mauritania.

A major foreign affairs issue in the late 1980s was the U.S. military presence, which, in the course of a NATO referendum campaign in 1986, Prime Minister González promised to reduce. In May voters endorsed NATO membership, but on condition that Spain remain outside the alliance's command structure, ban nuclear weapons from Spanish territory, and reduce the number of U.S. forces in Spain. Subsequent negotiations yielded an agreement in principle on January 15, 1988, whereby the United States would, within three years, withdraw from the Torrejón facility outside Madrid and transfer its 72 F-16 jet fighters to a new base in Italy. The accord, as finalized at UN headquarters in September, contained no provision for continued military or economic assistance to Spain, while permitting U.S. military activity at a number of bases, including naval operations at Rota (near Cadiz); most importantly, it allowed both sides to maintain their positions on nuclear arms, Spain reaffirming its opposition to the presence of such weapons but agreeing not to ask for compliance by inspection of U.S. vessels. In September 1990 González defied Spanish public opinion by contributing three warships to the buildup of allied forces in response to Iraq's August invasion of Kuwait.

In the early 1990s Spain signed a series of agreements placing some of its forces under NATO's "operational control" (the wording being used in deference to the 1986 referendum decision proscribing participation in NATO's command structure). The government sought to deflect criticism of this policy by urging greater defense cooperation between West European states, favoring the Western European Union (WEU) as the appropriate vehicle. A perennial snag for Spain's participation in such moves, however, was its refusal to join in any military activity that appeared to endorse British rule in Gibraltar. The installation of a conservative government in May 1996 was followed by a parliamentary vote in November to permit full participation in NATO (which then had a Spanish secretary general). Meanwhile, control of Gibraltar remained a contentious issue in Spanish-British relations, although a number of administrative accommodations were achieved in 2000.

All-party support for the process of European integration was reflected in the Spanish Parliament's near-unanimous approval of the EC's Maastricht Treaty in October–November 1992. Subsequently, at the EC's Edinburgh summit in December, Spain, together with Portugal, scored a diplomatic success by securing agreement on the creation of a "cohesion fund" for the four poorer members, including itself. Spain was also due to benefit from a similar fund established under the European Economic Area (EEA) agreement signed between the EC and five EFTA countries in March 1993. More recently, in February 2005 Spanish voters overwhelmingly endorsed the proposed EU constitution, which had the support of both the PSOE and the PP.

A frequent source of tension in Spain's external relations continued to be the activities of its 18,000-vessel fishing fleet (the EU's largest), whose crews combined a determination to protect home waters with a desire to exploit distant fishing grounds, often in alleged contravention of conservation and other international agreements. In mid-1994 serious clashes occurred in the Bay of Biscay between Spanish vessels and boats from Britain, France, and Ireland in exercise of their right under EU fisheries policy to catch tuna in Spanish waters. In March 1995 a bitter dispute broke out with Canada over fishing rights and practices in the Northwest Atlantic, which was resolved only after the EU had accepted, with reluctant Spanish concurrence, a sharply reduced catch quota in the area. In the acrimonious exchanges preceding the April settlement, there was widespread outrage in Spain when the UK government, responding to overwhelmingly pro-Canadian public opinion in Britain, vetoed Spanish attempts to invoke EU sanctions against Canada, and in December Spain's endorsement of the admission of three new EU members was forthcoming only after it had secured additional fishing access to Irish and UK waters.

In early 2003, despite wide public opposition, the Aznar government strongly supported the U.S.-led ouster of the Saddam Hussein regime in Iraq and then, in the aftermath, dispatched Spanish forces to aid in peacekeeping and humanitarian efforts. A pledge by PSOE candidate Zapatero to withdraw Spanish troops from Iraq contributed to the March 2004 Socialist victory at the polls. By late May all 1,300 troops had been brought home. An additional source of tension with the United States arose when in November 2005 EADS-CASA, the Spanish subsidiary of the European aerospace consortium, began negotiating the sale of military aircraft to the Venezuelan government of Hugo Chávez, whom the George W. Bush administration has treated with hostility. In June 2006 the United States officially blocked the sale because the planes in question contained U.S. technology.

Current Issues

Prior to the March 2004 terrorist bombings in Madrid, the PP appeared to be on its way to a comfortable victory in the March 14 elections. The Aznar government had weathered a number of difficulties, including a mishandled environmental crisis, caused by the sinking of the Greek oil tanker *Prestige* off the coast of Galicia in November 2002, and labor opposition to reduced unemployment benefits and other economic measures. In June 2002 the unemployment issue had led to the country's first general strike since 1994. The Aznar government had also managed to overcome

80 to 90 percent public disapproval of Spain's military involvement in Iraq. Following the September 2001 al-Qaida attacks on the United States, a majority had backed the U.S.-led "war on terrorism," but many Spaniards questioned why the Aznar government insisted on supporting the Bush administration's position on Iraq. Some analysts suggested that by aligning himself with Washington and its chief ally, London, Aznar hoped to obtain additional support for his tough line toward the ETA. In that regard, however, Spain's most crucial ally remained France, which adamantly opposed the Iraq venture.

Fearing adverse repercussions from the Madrid bombings, the government argued that a defeat at the polls would constitute a victory for the bombers, but it made a crucial miscalculation by placing blame on the ETA, even though initial forensic evidence pointed to Islamic extremists as the likely perpetrators. By election day many Spaniards believed that the government had tried to manipulate the flow of information for political reasons, and voters displayed their anger through the ballot. In succeeding weeks the evidence against Islamic extremists became incontrovertible. By early 2005 some 70 suspects, many of them from Morocco or elsewhere in North Africa, had been arrested, and about 20 remained in custody. On April 11, 2006, 29 suspects were indicted on charges related to the bombings, with the trial expected to begin in 2007. Meanwhile, on September 26, 2005, in Europe's largest trial of Islamic militants, a Spanish court convicted 18 of 24 defendants of belonging to al-Qaida. Among those convicted was Imad Eddin Barakat YARKAS, allegedly the leader of al-Qaida in Spain, who was sentenced to a prison term of 27 years for conspiring in the September 2001 attacks on the United States.

Some dozen seats short of a majority in the Chamber of Deputies, the Zapatero government came into office through the support of a number of small regional parties, including the Catalan Republican Left (*Esquerra Republicana de Catalunya*—ERC), the Canarian Coalition, and the Galician Nationalist Bloc (*Bloque Nacionalista Galego*—BNG). In addition to quickly fulfilling

a campaign pledge to withdraw from Iraq, Prime Minister Zapatero advanced a social agenda that included recognition of gay marriages (approved by both houses of the *Cortes* in 2005) and a more liberal policy toward illegal immigrant workers. In 2002 there were an estimated 200,000 illegal aliens in the Canary Islands alone, while up to a million others entered Spain each year. Zapatero sought to curb the influx by issuing work permits to those who had valid work contracts and could demonstrate that they had been in Spain for at least six months. By May 2005, at the end of the three-month registration period, some 700,000 aliens had taken advantage of the program. Over the course of the next year, immigration from Africa to the Canary Islands had reached crisis proportions, with over 9,000 illegal migrants caught in just the first five months of 2006. In response, the Zapatero government launched a two-prong program to halt would-be migrants on the shores of Senegal and Mauritania using joint Spanish-Mauritanian patrols, and intercept migrants on the high seas with the help of helicopters, planes, and ships from France, Italy, Germany, Britain, Greece, Portugal, and Holland.

Meanwhile, the issue of Basque separatism remained unresolved. Under Prime Minister Aznar, Spain had clamped down on groups associated with the ETA, most significantly the Unity (*Batasuna*) party, successor to the EH. When the Supreme Court outlawed *Batasuna* in March 2003, Basque nationalists began trying to register new formations. The courts ruled against them, however, and as a consequence some 1,500 candidates were disqualified from running in that year's local elections. At the end of 2004 an autonomy plan drawn up by Euzkadi President Juan José IBARRETXE won the approval of the regional legislature, but it was rebuffed by the *Cortes* and the Zapatero government in early 2005. In May the government signaled its willingness to negotiate with the ETA, but only if the separatists renounced terrorism. On March 22, 2006, ETA announce a "permanent ceasefire" to begin on March 24 as a prelude to talks with the government, which began on June 29.

Spain's tendencies toward devolution took another significant step forward in June 2006, when voters in Catalonia overwhelmingly approved a referendum giving their region greater autonomy, including retention of a higher percentage of tax collections and greater authority over judicial appointments, immigration, licensing, and mass transportation. It also recognized Catalan as the "preferential" language over Castilian Spanish, and acknowledged that Catalonia considers itself a distinct nation. Prime Minister Zapatero supported the Catalan referendum and said other regions were free to propose their own such referenda. As of mid-2006 two regions, the Balearic Islands and Andalucía, were already in the process of doing so.

The Catalonia referendum provoked concern in some quarters. In January 2006 the commander of Spain's ground forces, General José MENA Aguado, was sacked for saying in a speech to other officers that the army should intervene if Catalonia's proposed autonomy statutes were approved. The opposition PP also expressed concern that the Catalonia referendum would produce a cascade of similar referenda from the rest of the country's regions, leaving the national government with little authority or financial resources.

Political Parties

The only authorized political formation during most of the Franco era was the Spanish Falange (*Falange Española Tradicionalista y de las Juntas de Ofensiva Nacional-Sindicalista*—FET y JONS), subsequently referred to as "The National Movement." In January 1975, prior to Franco's death, a law permitting the establishment of noncommunist and nonseparatist "political associations" went into effect, and during the next two years a large number of parties, both legal and illegal, proceeded to organize. In March 1976 the Democratic Coordination (*Coordinación Democrática*—CD) was launched as a unified front embracing all strands of the opposition, from Communists to liberal monarchists.

Following a December 1976 referendum on political reform and the subsequent enactment of legislation simplifying the registration of political parties, the CD broke up. Most of its moderate members joined with a number of non-CD parties in establishing UCD, which won the June 1977 election and controlled the government for the ensuing five years. Following a disastrous showing against the PSOE at the October 1982 election, the UCD leadership voted in February 1983 to dissolve the party. By then what was to become the Popular Party had emerged as the main conservative alternative to the PSOE. Although 92.8 percent of the 1996 congressional vote was shared by just five parties (with no other party securing even 1 percent), the development of a straight two-party system was qualified by a diversity of regional parties and continuing support for left-wing groups. There are presently over 2,000 registered national, regional, and local parties.

Government Party

Socialist Workers' Party (*Partido Socialista Obrero Español*—PSOE). Founded in 1879 and a member of the Socialist International, the PSOE, under the young and dynamic Felipe González Márquez, held its first legal congress in 44 years in December 1976, and in 1979 the PSOE became the second-strongest party in the *Cortes*, winning 121 seats in the Congress of Deputies and 68 seats in the Senate at the election of March 1, in conjunction with a regional ally, the Party of Socialists of Catalonia (PSC, below). In April 1978 the Popular Socialist Party (*Partido Socialista Popular*—PSP), which had contested the 1977 election as part of the Socialist Union (*Unidad Socialista*—US), formally merged with the PSOE.

At a centennial congress in May 1979, González unexpectedly stepped down as party leader after a majority of delegates refused to abandon a doctrinal commitment to Marxism. His control was reestablished during a special congress in late September, the hard-liners being defeated by a vote of more than ten to one. At the 1982 election the PSOE/PSC won an absolute majority in both the Congress and Senate, González being invested as prime minister on December 2. In the following year the PSOE absorbed the centrist Democratic Action Party (*Partido de Acción Democrática*—

PAD). Subsequently, the PSOE experienced internal strain as a result of the government's pro-NATO posture, which ran counter to the party's long-standing rejection of participation in any military alliance. The issue was resolved in favor of qualified NATO membership by the March 1986 referendum, held shortly after the PSOE government had taken Spain into the EC.

The PSOE held power with a reduced majority in 1986. Its retention of only 175 lower house seats at the 1989 balloting was blamed, in part, on the emergence in September of a dissident internal faction, Socialist Democracy (*Democracia Socialista*—DS), and the subsequent defection of party members to the IU (below). Thereafter, the PSOE's standing was adversely affected by a series of financial scandals involving prominent party figures, although at an early election in June 1993 the party retained a narrow plurality of 159 seats, sufficient for González to form a minority government with regional party support.

Continuing financial and security scandals led to the defeat of the PSOE in the election of March 1996, which left it with 141 seats in the lower house on a vote share of 35.5 percent. González declined to run for reelection as PSOE general secretary in 1997 and was succeeded by Joaquín Almunia Amann.

In 1999–2000 the PSOE suffered a series of setbacks. On May 14, 1999, Josep BORRELL Fontelles, the party's candidate for prime minister in the next election, withdrew because of a financial scandal involving two former associates. Ten days later the man who had served as the PSOE's president for over 20 years, Ramón RUBIAL Cavia, died. On June 13, at local and regional elections, the PSOE saw its vote share increase, largely at the expense of the IU, but succeeded in gaining control of only one regional government, in Asturias. At the May 2000 national balloting, the party and its affiliates lost ground to the PP, losing 16 of their 141 seats in the lower house and prompting its prime ministerial candidate, Almunia, to immediately resign from the leadership.

Almunia's successor as secretary general, José Luis Rodríguez Zapatero, was elected by a party conference on July 23, 2000, narrowly defeating José BONO Martínez, the heavily favored president of Castilla–La Mancha. Rodríguez Zapatero, whose supporters compared him to the UK's Tony Blair, soon made wholesale changes in the party's hierarchy in the interest of "modernization" and a "New Way" (*Nueva Vía*).

In July 2001 the Democratic Party of the New Left (*Partido Democrático de la Nueva Izquierda*—PDNI), which had been organized in 1996 by former members of the United Left, principally Cristina ALMEIDA and Diego LÓPEZ Garrido, merged with the PSOE. The PDNI had been allied with the PSOE in recent elections.

At the general election of March 2004 the PSOE won an unexpected victory, taking 42.6 percent of the vote and 164 seats (including those won by regional affiliates). With the support of the IU and several small regional parties, Zapatero was confirmed as prime minister in April.

In addition to the PSC, regional parties affiliated with the PSOE include the Basque Socialist Party–Basque Left (PSE-EE, below), the Party of Galician Socialists (PSdeG, below), the **Madrid Socialist Federation** (*Federación Socialista Madrileña*—FSM), the **Socialist Party of Navarra** (*Partido Socialista de Navarra*—PSN), and the **Socialist Party of the Valencian Country** (*Partido Socialista del País Valenciano*—PSPV).

Leaders: José Luis Rodríguez ZAPATERO (Prime Minister and General Secretary of the Party), Manuel CHAVES González (President).

Other National Parties

Popular Party (*Partido Popular*—PP). The PP was known until January 1989 as the Popular Alliance (*Alianza Popular*—AP), which emerged in 1976 as a right-wing challenger to the Union of the Democratic Center (UCD). Following the UCD victory in 1977, most AP deputies in late 1978 joined with representatives of a number of other rightist parties in an alliance that contested the 1979 election as the Democratic Coalition (*Coalición Democrática*—CD), winning nine lower house seats. Despite its Francoist image, the AP opposed the 1981 coup attempt. Prior to the 1982 poll, the UCD national executive, by a narrow margin, rejected a proposal to form an alliance with the AP, although a constituent group, the Popular Democratic Party (*Partido Demócrata Popular*—PDP), formerly the Christian Democracy (*Democracia Cristiana*—DC), elected to do so. At the October voting the AP/PDP coalition, benefiting from the effective demise of the UCD, garnered 106 congressional seats, thus becoming the second-ranked group in the lower house. Although pro-NATO, the AP urged a boycott of the March 1986 referendum on the NATO membership issue in an effort to undermine the González government.

The AP contested the June 1986 election as part of the Popular Coalition (*Coalición Popular*—CP), which included the PDP and secured 105 congressional seats. Describing the outcome as "unsatisfactory," the PDP (with 21 deputies and 11 senators) broke with the Coalition upon convening of the new *Cortes* on July 15, while four members of the AP also defected in opposition to Manuel FRAGA Iribarne's CP/AP leadership. Further disintegration of the CP at the regional level prompted Fraga's resignation as AP president on December 2, 1986. Antonio HERNÁNDEZ Mancha was named AP president (and leader of what remained of the CP) in February 1987.

At a party congress held January 20–22, 1989, the formation undertook a number of moves, including the change of name, to reorient itself toward the center as a moderate conservative alternative to the PSOE. In the same year, it absorbed the Liberal Party (*Partido Liberal*—PL), which nevertheless elected to retain its legal identity. The PP also has, from time to time, had local and regional pacts with a variety of other parties.

The PP retained its second-ranked standing at the October 1989 poll (albeit with a gain of only 1 lower house seat, for a total of 106), and on December 17 won an absolute majority in the Galician Parliament. Recently reinstated party chief Fraga was thereupon installed as regional president, being succeeded as PP leader by José María Aznar. The party was able to mount an impressive opposition threat in the run-up to the June 1993 parliamentary balloting, at which it won 141 congressional and 107 senatorial seats on a vote share of 34.8 percent, less than four points behind the PSOE. Having overtaken the PSOE at the June 1994 European Parliament balloting, the PP solidified its standing as the largest party in the March 1996 national balloting, winning 156 seats and 38.9 percent of the vote, enabling Aznar to form a minority government supported by three regionalist groupings, Catalonia's Convergence and Union (CiU), the Canarian Coalition (CC), and the Basque Nationalist Party (PNV).

At a party congress in January 1999, Aznar's handpicked candidate, Javier ARENAS Bocanegra, was chosen to succeed Francisco ÁLVAREZ Cascos as secretary general. Bocanegra's ascendancy reportedly underlined the prime minister's professed desire to foster the image of a more centrist PP as well as his increasing control over the party.

In March 2000 the PP won 183 seats on an unexpectedly high vote share of 46.6 percent, but the PP's quest for a third term in office failed in March 2004, when its results fell to 37.6 percent and 148 seats. In September 2003 Aznar had confirmed his decision to pass the party reins to his deputy prime minister, Mariano Rajoy.

Leaders: Mariano RAJOY Brey (President), José María AZNAR López (Honorary President), Ángel ACEBES Paniagua (Secretary General).

United Left (*Izquierda Unida*—IU). The IU was formed in April 1986 as an anti-NATO electoral coalition that principally included the Spanish Communists (PCE, below), the **Republican Left** (*Izquierda Republicana*—IR), the **Socialist Action Party** (*Partido de Acción Socialista*—Pasoc), the **Progressive Federation** (*Federación Progresista*—FP), the left-wing liberal **Carlist Party** (*Partido Carlista*—PC), and the libertarian **Humanist Party** (*Partido Humanista*—PH). It won a total of seven congressional seats at the June 1986 election.

The PCE's Julio ANGUITA González resigned as IU general coordinator in November 1991, after opposing suggestions by members of several groups, including the PCE, that the coalition members dissolve as separate entities to form a single party; subsequently, however, he resumed the position. The IU made only marginal headway in the June 1993 election, winning 18 lower house seats with 9.6 percent of the vote. It retained third place in the 1996 national election, winning 21 lower house seats on a 10.6 percent vote share, but thereafter experienced a marked decline. At the June 1999 local elections its vote share fell from 11.7 to 6.5 percent, and at the March 2000 national election it won only 8 congressional seats. In March 2004 the IU won 5.0 percent of the vote and 5 lower house seats.

Other closely linked organizations include the **Ezker Batua** (EB—also translated as **United Left**) in Basque Country and Navarre, the **United Left of the Balearic Islands** (*Esquerra Unida de los Illes Balears*—EU), the **United Left of Valencia** (*Esquerra Unida del País Valenciá*—EUPV), and the Catalan **United and Alternative Left** (*Esquerra Unida i Alternativa*—EUiA). The IU has frequently formed coalitions with other small parties to contest regional elections.

Leaders: Gaspar LLAMAZARES Trigo (General Coordinator), Pedro Antonio RÍOS (Parliamentary Group Coordinator).

Spanish Communist Party (*Partido Comunista de España*—PCE). Founded in 1920 but soon banned, the PCE was legalized in April 1977, following the release from detention in December 1976 of its secretary general, Santiago CARRILLO Solares. On April 19–23, 1977, in Madrid, it held its first legal congress in 45 years, while on May 13 the PCE's most celebrated figure, Dolores IBÁRRURI Gómez ("La Pasionaria"), returned to Spain after 38 years in exile. The PCE and its regional ally, the **Unified Socialist Party of Catalonia** (*Partit Socialista Unificat de Catalunya*—PSUC), secured 20 seats in the Congress of Deputies and 12 seats in the Senate at the June 1977 election. In March 1979, with Ibarruri having declined to seek legislative reelection for reasons of health and age, it placed three additional deputies in the lower house but lost all of its upper house seats. In the context of sharp differences between pro-Soviet and

"Eurocommunist" factions, its congressional representation declined sharply in 1982 to only four members, with the result that Carrillo, the only survivor of the Civil War still to lead a major party, was forced to step down in November. Carrillo's influence was eroded still further by the decision of new party leaders, who favored nonalignment, to adopt internal reforms and work for a "convergence of progressive forces" with other leftist groups, both elective and nonelective; in April 1985 Carrillo and 18 supporters were expelled following an emergency national congress in March, subsequently forming the Spanish Workers' Party–Communist Unity (*Partido de los Trabajadores de España–Unidad Comunista*—PTE-UC), which joined the PSOE in February 1991.

Immediately prior to the 1986 election, a pro-Soviet splinter group, the Spanish Communist Workers' Party (*Partido Comunista Obrero Español*—PCOE), led by Enrique LISTER, voted to disband and rejoin the PCE. Subsequently, in February 1987, a PCE delegation visited Moscow, pledging a strengthening of relations with the Soviet Communists. A second pro-Soviet splinter, the Communist Party of the Peoples of Spain (*Partido Comunista de los Pueblos de España*—PCPE), rejoined the party at a congress of unity in January 1989. The PCPE, led by Ignacio GALLEGO, had broken from the party in 1984 because of the "politico-ideological degeneration . . . which introduced Eurocommunism."

At a party congress in December 1998, the PCE elected Francisco Frutos as its new secretary general.

Leaders: Francisco FRUTOS Gras (Secretary General), Felipe ALCARAZ (Executive President of the Federal Committee).

The Greens (*Los Verdes*). Long a somewhat disparate movement of pacifists, feminists, and ecologists, the Spanish Greens established the Spanish Green Party (*Partido Verde Español*—PVE) in June 1984 and convened their first congress in February 1985. However, a number of the constituent organizations disavowed the action as having been taken without appropriate consultation. At the 1986 election the Green Alternative (*Alternativa Verde*) list fared poorly, and the Greens made little headway thereafter until a congress held at Grenada in 1993 resulted in formation of a Green Confederation. At present, some two dozen regional organizations belong to or have observer status in the Confederation, including the **Basque People's Greens** (*Euskal Herriko Berdeak*—EHB) and the Initiative for Catalonia–Greens (below).

In January 2004 the Greens and the PSOE forged an alliance for the March national election and the June balloting for the European Parliament.

Leaders: Margalida ROSSELLO Pons (President), David HAMMERSTEIN Mintz (Secretary for International Relations).

Spain has a long history of right-wing formations, many of them descendants of the Franco-era **Spanish Falange**. Reduced to little more than a shadow of its former significance, the Falange joined with a number of other neo-fascist groups in forming a National Union (*Unión Nacional*) that secured one legislative seat in 1979. It did not contest the 1982 election to avoid divisiveness within "the forces opposing Marxism." Subsequently, it appeared to have been largely superseded by the formation in October 1984 of a new right-wing grouping, the Spanish Integration Committees (*Juntas Españolas de Integración*), which in 1993 was absorbed by the **National Front** (*Frente Nacional*—FN). Formation of the extreme right-wing FN was announced in October 1986 by Blas PIÑAR López, former secretary general of the New Force (*Fuerza Nueva*), which had been dissolved in 1982. The FN has not contested recent elections, but some of its supporters participated in the **Alliance for National Unity** (*Alianza por la Unidad Nacional*—AUN), with little impact in the 1996 election. With its leader, Ricardo SAENZ de Ynestrillas, in prison for attempted murder, the AUN did not contest the 2000 national election. At the 1996 national election the rump Falange, which had split into "Authentic" and "Independent" wings, secured less than 0.1 percent of the vote. In 2000 a new four-party

far-right electoral alliance, **Spain 2000** (*España 2000*), suffered a similar fate. The four constituent groups in the alliance were the **National Democracy** (*Democracia Nacional*—DN) of Francisco PEREZ Corrales, the **National Workers' Party** (*Partido Nacional de los Trabajadores*—PNT), the **Republican Social Movement** (*Movimiento Social Republicano*—MSR), and the **Spanish Social Apex** (*Vértice Social Español*—VSE). In late 2005 National Democracy, the Falange, and **Spanish Alternative** (*Alternativa Española*) began negotiations to form a new electoral coalition in anticipation of municipal elections in 2007 and general elections in 2008. By May 2006 discussions were said to be well advanced, but with no specific announcement made.

Regional Parties

There are hundreds of regional parties in addition to the local affiliates of the PP, PSOE, and IU/PCE. Grouped by alphabetical order of region, the parties discussed below are represented in the *Cortes* or regional assemblies.

Andalusian Party (*Partido Andalucista*—PA). Known until 1984 as the Andalusian Socialist Party (*Partido Socialista de Andalucía*—PSA), the PA won 1 seat in the Congress of Deputies in 2000 and none in 2004. At the regional level, the PA won 5 of 109 seats in the Andalusian elections in 2000 and 2004.

Leaders: Julián ÁLVAREZ Ortego (Secretary General), Manuel LÓPEZ López (National Secretary for Organization).

Aragonese Party (*Partido Aragonés*—PAR). Called the Aragonese Regionalist Party (*Partido Aragonés Regionalista*—PAR) until February 1990, the PAR is a center-right grouping that retains its predecessors' initials. Although the party did not contest the 1996 national congressional election in its own right, it won three Senate seats on the strength of an alliance with the PP. At the May 2003 regional election it won eight seats and then joined a governing coalition as junior partner to the PSOE, as it had in 1999. At the 2004 national election it failed to win any seats but continued to hold one designated Senate seat.

Leaders: José Ángel BIEL (President), Juan Carlos TRILLO Baigorri (Secretary General).

Aragonese Junta (*Chunta Aragonesista—* ChA). The ChA won five seats in the regional *Cortes* in 1999 and nine at the 2003 election, after which it joined the PSOE in forming a government. Nationally, it won one seat in the 2000 and 2004 congressional polls.

Leaders: Bizén FUSTER (President), José Antonio ACERO (General Secretary).

Majorcan Union (*Unió Mallorquina—*UM). The centrist UM, although previously aligned with the PP, joined the PSOE-led government alliance following the June 1999 regional election, at which it had won three seats. In 2003 it again won three.

Leaders: Maria Antónia MUNAR Riutort (President), Damià Nicolau FERRA (General Secretary).

PSM–Nationalist Union of Majorca (PSM– *Entesa Nacionalista de Mallorca—*PSM-EN). The PSM-EN traces its origins to 1976, when the Socialist Party of the Islands (*Partit Socialist de les Illes—*PSI) was established. In December 1977 the party changed its name to the Socialist Party of Majorca (*Partit Socialista de Malloica—*PSM), to which Nationalist Left (*Esquerra Nacionalista—* EN) was added in 1984. Between then and 1990, when the PSM-EN restyled itself as the PSM– Majorca Nationalists (*PSM–Nacionalistes de Mallorca*), the party contested regional, national, and European elections in a number of alliances with other left-oriented formations. In November 1998 the organization assumed its current name.

Following the June 1999 regional election, the PSOE negotiated an anti-PP governing alliance that was joined by the PSM-EN, which had won 5 of the 59 legislative seats. In May 2003 the PSM-EN retained 4 seats, but the PP returned to power. Nationally, the party contested the March 2004 lower house elections as part of a coalition, the **Balearic Islands Progressives** (*Progressistes per les Illes Balears—*PIB), that also included the IU-affiliated United Left of the Balearic Islands (EU), the regional Greens, and the Catalan Republican Left (ERC, below).

Leaders: Joana Llüisa MASCARÓ Melià (President), Gabriel BARCELÓ Milta (General Secretary).

In addition to the IU-linked EU, other organizations winning seats in the Balearic legislature in May 2003 were the **Progressive Pact** (*Pacte Progressista*), a leftist coalition that claimed five seats, and the **Independent People's Group of Formentera** (*Agrupació Independent Popular de Formentera*), which won one.

Aralar. Named for a Basque mountain range, *Aralar* is a recent nationalist splinter from the now-outlawed *Batasuna* (below). Advocating nonviolence, the party won four seats in the Navarre legislature in May 2003 and one in the Basque regional election in April 2005. For the 2004 national election *Aralar* joined with the Basque Nationalist Party (PNV), the Basque Solidarity (EA), and another nationalist Basque party, **Batzarro**, in the **Navarre Yes** (*Naffaroa Bai—*Na-Bai) coalition, which won one seat in the Chamber of Deputies.

Leaders: Patxi ZABALETA (Coordinator), Uxue BARKOS Berruezo (Na-Bai).

Basque Nationalist Party (*Partido Nacionalista Vasco—*PNV/*Euzko Alderdi Jeltzalea—*EAJ). A moderate party that has campaigned for Basque autonomy since 1895, the PNV obtained a plurality in the 1980 Basque election and formed a regional government headed by Carlos GARAICOETXEA Urizza. After the 1984 regional election a dispute regarding devolution of power to individual Basque provinces led to Garaicoetxea's replacement as premier and party leader by José Antonio ARDANZA in January 1985, with the PNV eventually concluding a legislative pact with the PSOE's local affiliate, the Basque Socialist Party (see PSE-EE, below), while Garaicoetxea joined Basque Solidarity (EA, below).

In 1989 the PNV organized mass demonstrations in Bilbao to pressure separatist militants to end their armed struggle. However, subsequent efforts to form an electoral coalition with the EA and the Basque Left (see PSE-EE, below) failed, and in October 1989 the PNV's representation in the Spanish Congress and Senate fell to five and six seats, respectively. One of the latter was lost in the 1993 balloting, after which the PNV gave intermittent support to the PSOE minority government. In the March 1996 national balloting it retained five lower house seats, whereupon it agreed to support a minority PP government in return for more devolution. However, it later withdrew that support.

At balloting for the Basque regional legislature in October 1998, the PNV led all the parties, but its lack of a majority led it to form a coalition government with "We the Basque Citizens" (EH, the restyled political arm of the ETA) and the EA. In January–February 2000, following a renewal of ETA violence, the PNV ended its alliance with the EH. At the national election in March 2000 the PNV picked up 2 seats in the Congress of Deputies, for a total of 7, while at an early regional election on May 13, 2001, it registered its biggest success in a quarter-century, winning 33 seats (a gain of 6) on a 43 percent vote share.

Having retained seven seats at the March 2004 election, the PNV entered the April 2005 regional election seeking support for the "Plan Ibarretxe," a proposal for increased autonomy that had been put forward by PNV leader and Euzkadi President Juan José Ibarretxe. The plan, which included establishment of a union with French Basque areas as well as Basque representation in the EU, had been described by Prime Minister Zapatero as secessionist and unconstitutional and then rejected by the *Cortes* earlier in the year. At the polls, the PNV lost four seats, and Ibarretxe managed to retain the presidency by only one vote when the regional legislature met in June.

Leaders: Juan José IBARRETXE Markuartu (Basque President), Josu Jon IMAZ (President of the Party), Josune ARIZTONDO Akarregi (Secretary).

Basque Socialist Party–Basque Left (*Partido Socialista de Euzkadi–Euzkadiko Ezkerra—PSE-EE*). The PSE-EE was formed in March 1993 by merger of the PSOE-affiliated Basque Socialist Party, led by Ramón JÁUREGUI, and the smaller, more radical Basque Left, led by Juan María BANDRÉS and Jon LARRINAGA. At the May 2001 regional election the PSE-EE finished third, winning 13 of 75 seats, a relatively weak performance that contributed to the resignation of the party's secretary general, Nicolás REDONDO Terreros, in December. At balloting in April 2005 the party finished second, with 18 seats. Despite the support of the PP, the new PSE-EE leader, Paxti López, lost the contest for regional president to the incumbent, the PNV's Ibarretxe, by one vote.

Leaders: Jesús EGUIGUREN (President), Patxi LÓPEZ (Secretary General).

Basque Solidarity (*Eusko Alkartasuna—EA*). The EA was formed in September 1986 as the Basque Patriots (*Eusko Abertzaleak*) by a group of PNV dissidents, subsequently joined by former Basque premier Carlos Garaicoetxea Urriza. A left-wing nationalist group opposed to political violence, it currently holds one seat in the national Chamber of Deputies. It contested the 1996 election in alliance with the now-defunct Basque Left (*Euskal Ezkerra—EuE*), which had separated from the *Euskadiko Ezkerra* (also translated as Basque Left) in 1993.

In late 1998 the EA agreed to participate in the formation of a Basque regional coalition government with the PNV and EH, and in the May 2001 and April 2005 elections it remained allied with the PNV.

Leaders: Begoña ERRAZTI (President), Unai ZIARRETA (General Secretary).

Communist Party of the Basque Lands (*Partido Comunista de las Tierras Vascas—PCTV/Euskal Herrialdeetako Alderi Komunista—EHAK*). The PCTV/EHAK was established by former members of *Batasuna* after that party was banned in March 2003. At the April 2005 regional election it unexpectedly won nine legislative seats. The subsequent support of two PCTV legislators enabled the PNV's Ibarretxe to retain the regional presidency.

Leaders: Juan Carlos RAMOS Sánchez, Aritz BLAZQUEZ Diz, Javier RAMOS Sánchez, Juan Manuel RODRÍGUEZ Hernández.

Canarian Coalition (*Coalición Canaria—* CC). The CC was formed prior to the 1993 general election as a regional alliance that included the **Canarian Independent Groupings** (*Agrupaciones Independientes de Canarias—*AIC); the socialist **Canarian Initiative** (*Iniciativa Canaria—* ICAN); and the left-wing **Mazorca Assembly** (*Asamblea Majorera—*AM). Also initially part of the alliance were the **Canarian Nationalist Party** (*Partido Nacionalista Canario—*PNC) and the **Canarian Independent Center** (*Centro Canario Independiente—*CCI), predecessor of the current **Canarian Nationalist Center** (*Centro Canario Nacionalista—*CCN). More recently, the CC was joined by the **Lanzarote Nationalist Party** (*Partido Nacionalista de Lanzarote—*PNL).

The AIC, consisting principally of the **Tenerife Independents Group** (*Agrupación Tinerfeña de Independientes—*ATI) and the **Las Palmas Independent Group** (*Agrupación Palmera de Independientes—*API), had captured one congressional seat in the 1989 general election and was subsequently the only non-PSOE party to support Prime Minister González's reelection; in the 1991 regional balloting it took second place behind the PSOE in the Canaries, and the AIC nominee, ATI leader Manuel HERMOSO Rojas, secured the island presidency.

In the 1993 general election the CC returned four deputies and six senators, proceeding thereafter to give qualified support to the minority PSOE government. In September 1994 the CC-led regional government lost its narrow majority when the PNC withdrew from the coalition. The coalition won a plurality of 21 regional assembly seats in 1995, so that Hermoso remained in office. Its four national deputies, reelected in 1996, backed the formation of a PP government in exchange for various concessions. The CC won 25 seats at the June 1999 Canarian election and continued to rule, with PP support. At the May 2000 national balloting the coalition won four Chamber and five Senate seats.

Following the May 2003 regional election, at which the CC won a plurality of 22 seats, the CC and the PP formed a coalition government. Nationally, the CC won three lower house seats in 2004 and then voted to approve the PSOE's Zapatero as prime minister.

Leaders: Paulino RIVERO Baute (President), Adán MARTÍN Menis (Canarian President).

Party of Independents from Lanzarote (*Partido de Independientes de Lanzarote—*PIL). Based on the Canarian island of Lanzarote, the PIL held one seat in the previous Spanish Senate. In March 2001, having been sentenced to a three-year prison term for bribery, Dimas MARTÍN Martín, the PIL president and senator, announced his resignation from both posts. In 2003 the PIL won three seats in the regional legislature as part of the **Canarian Nationalist Federation** (*Federación Nacionalista Canaria—*FNC).

Leader: Celso BETANCOR Delgado (President).

Cantabrian Regionalist Party (*Partido Regionalista Cántabro—*PRC). The PRC is a moderate conservative party that won 6 seats out of 39 in the 1995 and 1999 Cantabrian regional assembly elections.

Following the 2003 election, at which it won eight seats, the PRC held the balance of power and negotiated formation of a governing coalition with the PSOE.

Leader: Miguel Ángel REVILLA Roiz (President of the Cantabria Government).

León People's Union (*Unión del Pueblo Leónes—*UPL). The UPL won three seats in the *Cortes* of Castilla y León in 1999 and 2003.

Leader: Melchor MORENO de la Torre (President).

Catalan Republican Left (*Esquerra Republicana de Catalunya—*ERC). Founded in 1931, the ERC was one of two Catalan republican parties, the other being the Democratic Spanish Republican Action (*Acció Republicana Democrática*

Española—ARDE), granted legal recognition in August 1977. In July 1991 the Catalan radical separatist Free Land (*Terre Lliure*) announced that it was dissolving, with its members being accepted into the ERC. In December 1991 the ERC abandoned its call for federalism, appealing instead for Catalan independence.

The ERC split in late 1996, with its national senator and deputy, together with 4 of its 13 regional deputies, defecting to the Catalan Independence Party (*Partido per la Independencia*—PI), which dissolved in September 1999.

Following the November 2003 regional election, which saw the ERC nearly double its representation, to 23 seats, it joined with the PSOE-affiliated PSC in forming a new regional government. In January 2004, however, party leader Josep Carod-Rovira was forced to resign as head of the government following revelations that he had secretly met with ETA leaders in what he described as an effort to convince them to renounce violence.

At the 2004 national election the ERC won eight seats in the Congress of Deputies, seven more than it had previously held. For the Senate it campaigned as part of the PSC-led Catalan Accord for Progress (ECP; see under the PSC, below).

Leaders: Josep Lluís CAROD-ROVIRA (President), Ernest BENACH i Pascual (President of the Catalan Parliament), Joan PUIGCERCÓS (Secretary General).

Convergence and Union (*Convergéncia i Unió*—CiU). The center-left CiU was formed in November 1978 as a coalition of the **Democratic Convergence of Catalonia** (*Convergéncia Democrática de Catalunya*—CDC) and the **Democratic Union of Catalonia** (*Unió Democrática de Catalunya*—UDC). In its first federal elections (1979) the CiU elected eight deputies and one senator. At the first elections to the Parliament of Catalonia in 1980, the CiU won 43 seats, allowing CDC President Jordi Pujol i Soley to be elected President of Catalonia. The CiU won a majority of seats in the Catalan legislative election of March 1992, and at the national level the CiU secured 17 congressional and 14 senatorial seats in June 1993, after which it gave qualified support to the PSOE minority government. Having initially made greater tax transfers to Catalonia its quid pro quo for supporting the PSOE government, the CiU in February 1994 lodged a demand for full Catalan autonomy and moved into opposition in mid-1995.

The CiU lost seats but retained power in the November 1995 Catalan election, for the first time since 1984 not winning an absolute majority. The 16 lower house seats it secured in the March 1996 national balloting enabled it to extract tax and other concessions in return for backing the new PP government. It retained a slim plurality at the October 1999 Catalan election and at the May 2000 national election won 8 Senate and 15 congressional seats.

In the regional election of November 2003, the CiU won a plurality of seats but surrendered the government to a coalition led by the PSC (below) and ERC. Nationally, the party won four directly elected Senate seats and ten Chamber seats in March 2004. For the European Parliament election of June 2004 the CiU joined the PNV, the BNG (below), and others in the **Galeuca** (for Galician, Euskadi, and Catalonia) coalition.

Leaders: Jordi PUJOL i Soley (Founding President of the CiU and President of the CDC), Artur MAS i Gavarró (President), Josep Antoni DURAN i Lleida (Secretary General), Ramon ESPADALER i Parcerisas (UDC President).

Initiative for Catalonia–Greens (*Iniciativa per Catalunya–Verds*—IC-V). Initially an alliance headed by the PCE-affiliated Unified Socialist Party of Catalonia (PSUC), the IC was established in 1987 and became, in effect, the Catalonian branch of the United Left. Other initial participants in the IC were the Party of Communists of Catalonia (*Partit dels Communistes de Catalunya*—PCC) and the Accord of Left Nationalists (*Entesa Nacionalistas d'Esquerra*—ENE). In 1990 the grouping evolved into a party that then became increasingly close to the Catalan branch of the Greens (*Els Verds*—EV), and together they won 11 seats at the November 1995 regional election. The coalition was formalized as the IC-V in 1998. At the 1999 regional election it won only 3 seats while cooperating with the PSOE-affiliated Party of Socialists of Catalonia (PSC). Nationally, the IC-V won 2 seats in the Congress at the March 2000 election.

In 2003 the IC-V and the allied EUiA (see the IU, above) won nine seats in the regional legislature. At the 2004 national balloting, the IC-V/EUiA won two seats.

Leader: Joan SAURA Laporta (President).

Party of Socialists of Catalonia (*Partit dels Socialistes de Catalunya*—PSC). The regional affiliate of the PSOE, the PSC dates from the late 1970s, when several like-minded leftist parties merged. At the national level, it remains a major contributor to the PSOE's success. In March 2004 it won 18 seats in the lower house. In addition it won 8 in the Senate as part of the **Catalan Accord for Progress** (*Entesa Catalana de Progrés*—ECP), an alliance forged with the ERC, the IC-V, and the United and Alternative Left (EUiA; see under the IU, above).

At the October 1999 Catalan election the PSC, led by Pasqual Maragall, finished a close second to the CiU, winning more votes but ending up with four fewer seats. The PSC had contested the election in alliance with the IC-V. In November 2003 the PSC again finished second in regional balloting but then joined with the ERC to form a government headed by Maragall.

Leaders: Pasqual MARAGALL (President of Catalonia), José MONTILLA (First Secretary).

Galician Nationalist Bloc (*Bloque Nacionalista Galego*—BNG). Founded in 1983, the BNG is a left-wing group that came in third in the 1989 regional election, winning 5 seats out of 75. In the October 1993 balloting in Galicia it more than doubled its vote (to 18.7 percent) and won 13 seats out of 75. In late 1991 it had been joined by the Galician National Party (*Partido Nacionalista Galego*—PNG), which had split from the (now defunct) Galician Coalition (*Coalición Galega*—CG) in 1986. In 2000 the BNG won 3 seats in the national lower house, 1 less than in 2000. At the

regional election of June 19, 2005, it won 13 seats, 4 fewer than in 2001, but sufficient to form a coalition government with the PSOE-affiliated PsdeG (below), thereby ousting the PP from power for the first time in a quarter-century.

Leader: Anxo QUINTANA González.

Party of Galician Socialists (*Partido dos Socialistas de Galicia*—PSdeG). As the regional affiliate of the PSOE, in June 2005 the PSdeG won 25 seats at the Galician election, 8 more than in 2001. It then formed a coalition with the Galician Nationalist Bloc that ousted the PP from power for the first time in a quarter-century.

Leader: Emilio PÉREZ Touriño (President of Galicia and Secretary General of the Party).

Convergence of Navarran Democrats (*Convergencia de Demócratas Navarros*—CDN). The CDN was launched in 1995 by a group that split from the PP-affiliated UPN. It won 10 of 50 regional assembly seats in 1995 but only 3 in 1999 and 4 in 2003.

Leaders: Juan CRUZ Alli (Former President of Navarra and CDN President), José Andrés BURGUETE Torres (Vice President).

Union of the Navarran People (*Unión del Pueblo Navarro*—UPN). A conservative grouping allied with the PP and firmly opposed to the Basque nationalist goal of reincorporating Navarra in Euzkadi, the UPN was formed in 1979 and governed the province from 1991 to 1995, when it went into opposition (although remaining the largest party). At the June 1999 election it won 22 of the 50 legislative seats and recaptured the presidency. It increased its representation by 1 in 2003 and then in 2004 won 2 seats in the national lower house.

Leaders: Miguel SANZ Sesma (President of Navarra and of the UPN), Alberto CATALÁN Higueras (Secretary General).

Rioja Party (*Partido Riojano*—PR). A center-left formation in Spain's main wine-growing area, the PR won one seat in the 1993 general election and two in the 1995 regional contest. Although subsequently unsuccessful at the national level, it retained its regional seats in 1999 and 2003.

Leaders: Miguel GONZÁLEZ de Legarra (President), Javier SAENZ-TORRE Merino (Secretary General).

Valencia Entesa (*Entesa pel País Valenciá*). The leftist *Entesa* ("Accord" or "Agreement") coalition was established in Valencia in June 2002 by the United Left of Valencia (EUPV; see under the IU), the Valencian Greens, and the **Valencian Left** (*Esquerra Valenciana*—EV). The EUPV and the Greens had previously contested local elections together, winning a high of ten seats in the regional assembly in 1995. In the 2003 regional elections *Entesa* won five assembly seats. In March 2004 it won one seat in the national Chamber of Deputies, where its representative sits with the IU group.

Leaders: Isaura NAVARRO (EUPV), Joan RIBÓ i Canut (EUPV).

Illegal Groups

Basque Homeland and Liberty (*Euzkadi ta Azkatasuna*—ETA). Founded in 1959, the ETA has long engaged in a violent separatist campaign directed primarily at police and government targets, although in recent years journalists and anti-ETA civilians have increasingly fallen victim. By 2001 the number of deaths attributed to ETA attacks approached 800.

In 1978 the ETA's political wing was indirectly involved in formation of the United People (HB; see Unity, below) More recently, the HB was the driving force behind the "We the Basque Citizens" (*Euskal Herritarrok*—EH) coalition, which contested the 1998 regional election. The EH participated in the resultant governing alliance until the end of a unilateral ETA cease-fire (September 1998–December 1999) that led to the EH's expulsion. In June 2001 elements of the EH established a unified party, Unity. In its more than three decades of operations the ETA has demonstrated considerable resiliency despite the arrests or deaths of numerous leaders. In September 2000 French authorities captured the reputed ETA chief, Ignacio GRACIA Arregui (also known as Iñaki de

RENTERÍA), for whom a French arrest warrant had been issued in 1987. The French also arrested the suspected ETA military commander, Francisco Xabier GARCÍA Gaztelu, in February 2001 and the alleged head of logistics, Asier OIARZABAL Txapartogi, in September 2001. In September 2002 senior leaders Juan Antonio OLARRA Guridi and Ainhoa MUGIKA Goni were arrested in Bordeaux, France, while in December Ibón FERNÁNDEZ Iradi and half a dozen other ETA leaders were arrested near Bayonne. Fernández Iradi escaped from custody two days later but was recaptured by the French in December 2003. By then, increased French-Spanish cooperation against the ETA was severely hampering the organization's activities, with nearly four dozen suspected operatives having been arrested in October–November 2003 alone. Key suspects arrested in April 2004 included Félix Alberto LÓPEZ de la Calle, a military commander, and Félix Ignacio ESPARZA Luri, a logistics chief; in December alleged political leader Mikel ALBIZU Iriarte and Soledad IPARRAGUIRRE Genetxea, a suspected military commander, were also captured. In response to overtures from the Zapatero government for peace talks, the ETA offered a partial truce in June 2005, involving a commitment not to attack elected officials, an offer that was deemed as insufficient by the government to begin talks. Then on March 22, 2006, the group announced a permanent cease-fire, opening the way for direct negotiations with the government, which began on June 29, 2006.

Unity (*Batasuna*). *Batasuna* descends from the United People (*Herri Batasuna*—HB), which was founded in 1978. Linked with the political wing of the terrorist ETA, the Marxist HB coalition was runner-up in the Basque parliamentary election of March 1980 and obtained 2 lower-house *Cortes* seats in 1982. A decision by the Interior Ministry to withdraw legal recognition from the party was overturned by court action in January 1984. In October 1989 the HB lost 1 congressional seat but surprised observers by announcing that it would occupy its 4 remaining seats, ending a decade-long boycott of elected office above municipal level. However, on November 20, the eve of the *Cortes* opening, HB congressman-elect Josu MUGURUZA was killed and another HB leader, Iñaki ESNAOLA, was wounded in an attack by alleged right-wing terrorists. Subsequently, the remaining HB deputies were expelled for refusing to pledge allegiance to the constitution. The HB won 2 congressional seats and 1 senatorial seat in the 1993 national election; it won 11 regional seats in 1994 but lost its Senate seat in 1996.

Karlos RODRÍGUEZ, an HB leader, compared the party to *Sinn Féin*, the political wing of the Irish Republican Army, in 1997, as ETA supporters staged counter-demonstrations against massive antiviolence protests across Spain. On December 1, 1997, the entire 23-member National Committee was convicted of supporting terrorism, and each member was sentenced to at least seven years in prison. On July 20, 1999, however, the Constitutional Court threw out the convictions.

In September 1998 the HB announced that it would be competing at Basque regional elections the following month as part of a leftist coalition, or "platform," styled We the Basque Citizens (*Euskal Herritarrok*—EH). The EH finished third in the October polling, with 14 seats, and subsequently agreed not only to recognize the legitimacy of the regional legislature, but also to participate in a regional coalition government with the PNV and EA. An ETA decision in November 1999 to end its 14-month cease-fire led directly to the EH's ouster from the PNV-led administration, and at the May 2001 regional election it saw its representation halved and its vote share drop 8 percentage points, to 10 percent. On June 23, 2001, the EH joined in forming the unified *Batasuna* party.

Amid an upsurge in ETA attacks, on April 30, 2002, police detained 11 *Batasuna* members who were suspected of channeling funds to the ETA or laundering "taxes" collected by the ETA. In August a judge suspended the organization's activities for three years and ordered its offices closed, citing its relationship with the ETA. In the same month the national legislature supported a government request that the Supreme Court ban *Batasuna* altogether, and on March 17, 2003, the court concurred.

The ban, which extended to the HB and EH designations, was the first of its kind since the Franco era. Subsequent efforts by *Batasuna* members to register other organizations, most prominently an *Autodeterminaziorako Bilgunea* (AuB) coalition, were rejected.

In May 2003 the United States added *Batasuna* to its list of terrorist organizations, and the United Kingdom followed suit in June. In November 2004 *Batasuna* called for peaceful dialogue among all sides to end the decades of violence. Despite this and other peace initiatives the ban on party activity was extended for two more years by a Spanish court on January 17, 2006, just days before *Batasuna* was to hold a large meeting to outline its political plans. The extension of the ban was supported by the conservative PP but was considered a blow to the Zapatero government, which saw *Batasuna* as an important participant in peace talks.

Leader: Arnaldo OTEGI.

Other leftist groups have included an ETA splinter, the **Autonomous Anticapitalist Commandos** (*Comandos Autónomos Anticapitalistas*—CAA), and the **Antifascist Resistance Groups of October 1** (*Grupos de Resistencia Antifascista del Primero de Octubre*—GRAPO). Spanish and French authorities arrested a dozen alleged GRAPO members, including apparent leader Fernando HIERRO Txomon, in July 2002. A Free Galician Guerrilla People's Army (*Ejército Guerrilleiro de Pobo Gallego Ceibe*—EGPGC) claimed responsibility for a number of attacks throughout Galicia in 1987–1991.

The activities of two Catalan separatist groups, Free Land (see under ERC, above) and the Movement for the Defense of the Land (*Movimiento de Defensa de la Terra*—MDT) prompted the emergence in mid-1986 of a right-wing antiseparatist formation called the Catalan Militia (*Milicia Catalana*). Other right-wing groups have included the National Revolution (*Revolución Nacional*—RN), the Warriors of Christ the King (*Guerrilleros del Cristo Rey*—GCR), the Apostolic Anticommunist Alliance (*Alianza Apostólica Anticomunista*—AAA), and the Antiterrorist Liberation Groups

Cabinet

As of July 1, 2006

Prime Minister	José Luis Rodríguez Zapatero
First Deputy Prime Minister	María Teresa Fernández de la Vega Sanz [f]
Second Deputy Prime Minister	Pedro Solbes Mira

Ministers

Agriculture, Food, and Fisheries	Elena Espinosa Mangana [f]
Culture	Carmen Calvo Poyato [f]
Defense	José Antonio Alonso Suárez
Development	Magdalena Álvarez Arza [f]
Economy and Finance	Pedro Solbes Mira
Education, Science, and Technology	Mercedes Cabrera Calvo-Sotelo [f]
Environment	Cristina Narbona Ruiz [f]
Foreign Affairs	Miguel Ángel Moratinos Cuyaubé
Health	Elena Salgado Méndez [f]
Housing	María Antonia Trujillo Rincón [f]
Industry, Trade, and Tourism	José Montilla Aguilera
Interior	Alfredo Pérez Rubalcaba
Justice	Juan Fernándeo López Aguilar
Labor and Social Affairs	Jesús Caldera Sánchez-Capitán
Public Administration	Jordi Sevilla Segura
Government Spokesperson	María Teresa Fernández de la Vega [f]

[f] = female

(*Grupos Antiterroristas de Liberación*—GAL). The GAL was implicated in nearly two dozen murders in the French Basque region, with investigation of its activities substantiating rumored links with Spanish officials.

Legislature

Traditionally designated as the *Cortes* (Courts), the Spanish legislature was revived by General Franco in 1942 as a unicameral body with strictly limited powers and officially named *Las Cortes Españolas*. Initially, it had no directly elected members, but provision was made in 1967 for the election of 198 "family representatives." The essentially corporate character of the body was retained in 1971, when several new categories of indirectly elected and appointed members were added.

In November 1976 the *Cortes* approved a long-debated Political Reform Bill, which, calling for a largely elected bicameral assembly, secured overwhelming public endorsement in a referendum held on December 15. The new **Cortes Generales**, consisting of a Senate and a Congress of Deputies, held its inaugural session in July 1977. Both houses serve four-year terms, subject to dissolution.

Senate (*Senado*). The upper house currently has 259 members, of whom 208 were directly elected in 2004: 4 from each of the 47 mainland provinces; 6 from Santa Cruz de Tenerife (3 from Tenerife and 1 each from La Gomera, La Palma, and Hierro); 5 from the Balearic Islands (3 from

Mallorca and 1 each from Menorca and Ibiza-Formentera); 5 from Las Palmas (3 from Gran Canaria and 1 each from Fuerteventura and Lanzarote); and 2 each from the North African enclaves of Ceuta and Melilla. The remaining 51 members are designated at varying times (depending on regional elections) by 17 autonomous regional legislatures (Ceuta and Melilla being excluded). Each designates at least 1 senator, with the more popular regions entitled to an additional senator for each million inhabitants. The current distribution is Andalucía, 8; Aragón, 2; Asturias, 2; Balearic Islands, 1; Basque Country, 3; Canary Islands, 2; Cantábria, 1; Castilla y León, 3; Castilla–La Mancha, 2; Catalonia, 7; Extremadura, 2; Galicia, 3; Madrid, 6; Murcia, 2; Navarra, 1; La Rioja, 1; and Valencia, 5.

The overall party distribution after the elections of March 14, 2004, was as follows (directly elected members in parentheses): Popular Party, 126 (102); Spanish Socialist Workers' Party, 96 (81); Catalan Accord for Progress, 16 (12), including 10 (8) for the Party of Socialists of Catalonia, 4 (3) for the Catalan Republican Left, and 2 (1) for the Initiative for Catalonia–Greens; Basque Nationalist Party, 7 (6); Convergence and Union, 6 (4); Canarian Coalition, 4 (3); United Left, 2 (0); Aragonese Party, 1 (0); Galician Nationalist Bloc, 1 (0).

President: Javier ROJO García.

Congress of Deputies (*Congreso de los Diputados*). The lower house currently consists of 350 deputies elected on block lists by proportional representation. Each province is entitled to a minimum of 3 deputies, with 1 deputy each from the African enclaves of Ceuta and Melilla.

The balloting on March 14, 2004, produced the following seat distribution: Spanish Socialist Workers' Party, 164 (including 18 from the Party of Socialists of Catalonia, 10 from the Party of Galician Socialists, and 10 from the Basque Socialist Party–Basque Left); Popular Party, 148 (including 2 on a joint list with the Union of the Navarran People); Convergence and Union, 10; Catalan Republican Left, 9; Basque Nationalist Party, 7; United Left, 5 (including 2 for the Initiative for Catalonia–

Greens–United and Alternative Left coalition and 1 for the Valencia *Entesa*); Canarian Coalition, 3; Galician Nationalist Bloc, 2; Aragonese Junta, 1; Navarre Yes, 1; Basque Solidarity, 1.

President: Manuel MARÍN González.

Communications

Under the 1978 constitution, the right to disseminate true information is guaranteed and prior censorship is outlawed. The most significant restriction is a 1979 law that limits the practice of journalism to those possessing a university degree in the subject.

Press

The following are dailies published in Madrid, unless otherwise noted: *El País* (580,000 daily, 1,040,000 Sunday), progressive; *ABC* (330,000 daily, 760,000 Sunday), monarchist; *El Mundo* (300,000 daily, 360,000 Sunday), center-left; *El Periódico* (Barcelona, 210,000 daily, 380,000 Sunday); *La Vanguardia* (Barcelona, 210,000 daily, 340,000 Sunday), conservative; *El Correo Español y el Pueblo Vasco* (Bilbao, 130,000), independent; *La Voz de Galicia* (La Coruña, 130,000 daily, 160,000 Sunday), Galician regional; *El Diario Vasco* (San Sebastián, 100,000 daily, 120,000 weekend), Basque Country regional; *El País* (Barcelona, 80,000 daily, 140,000 Sunday); *Diario de Navarra* (Pamplona, 60,000), regional; *Heraldo de Aragón* (Zaragoza, 60,000), regional; *Las Provincias* (Valencia, 60,000 daily, 85,000 Sunday), conservative regional; *La Nueva España* (Oviedo, 60,000). In February 2003 the leading Basque-language newspaper, *Euskaldunon Egunkari*, was closed because of alleged links to the ETA.

News Agencies

Domestic agencies include *Agencia EFE*, in which the government is the majority shareholder; *Colpisa*; and *Europa Press*. Numerous foreign agencies maintain bureaus in Madrid.

Broadcasting and Computing

(*Grupo Radio Televisión*) *Española* (RTVE) is the national public broadcasting service. Its radio arm, with five principal domestic networks, is *Radio Nacional de España* (RNE), while *Televisión Española* (TVE) broadcasts internationally as well as domestically. There also are regional public radio and TV services. Private broadcasting was authorized in 1988. The largest private radio service, with over 200 stations, is the *Sociedad Española de Radiodifusión*. There were approximately 35.6 million television receivers and 8.5 million personal computers serving 9.8 million Internet users in 2003.

Intergovernmental Representation

Ambassador to the U.S.
Carlos WESTENDORP

U.S. Ambassador to Spain
Eduardo AGUIRRE Jr

Permanent Representative to the UN
Juan Antonio YÁÑEZ-BARNUEVO

IGO Memberships (Non-UN)
ADB, AfDB, BIS, CERN, CEUR, EBRD, EIB, ESA, EU, Eurocontrol, IADB, IEA, Interpol, IOM, NATO, OECD, OSCE, PCA, WCO, WEU, WTO

Related Territories

Virtually nothing remains of Spain's former colonial empire, the bulk of which was lost with the independence of the American colonies in the early 19th century. Cuba, Puerto Rico, and the Philippines were acquired by the United States in 1898. More recently, the West African territories of Río Muni and Fernando Pó became independent in 1968 as the state of Equatorial Guinea; Ifní was ceded to Morocco in 1969; and the Western (Spanish) Sahara was divided between Morocco and Mauritania in February 1976 (the latter subsequently renouncing its claim on August 5, 1979). Thereafter, the only remaining European possessions in the African continent were the small Spanish enclaves discussed below.

Places of Sovereignty in North Africa (*Plazas de Soberanía del Norte de Africa*). These Spanish outposts on the Mediterranean coast of Morocco, dating from the 15th century, encompass the two enclaves of Ceuta and Melilla, officially referred to as *presidios*, or garrison towns, and three "Minor Places" (*Plazas Menores*): the tiny, volcanic Chafarinas and Alhucemas islands, and Peñón de Vélez de la Gomera, an arid garrison spot on the north Moroccan coast. Ceuta, with an area of 7.4 square miles (19.3 sq. km.) and a population of 74,000 (2005E), and Melilla, with an area of 4.7 square miles (12.3 sq. km.) and a population of 68,000 (2005E), are considered parts of metropolitan Spain, and before being accorded the status of autonomous regions in September 1994, they were organized as municipalities of the provinces of Cádiz and Málaga, respectively. The Minor Places, with military garrisons of about 100 each, are under the jurisdiction of Málaga. In 1985 intense controversy was generated by Madrid's promulgation of a new alien residence law, which required all foreigners living in Spain to reapply for residence or face expulsion; the law, which was directed mainly at fugitives who had entered Spain prior to the conclusion of extradition treaties with a number of European countries, raised serious questions regarding the status of ethnic Moroccan Muslims, who have lived in the enclaves for generations.

In February 1986 government and Muslim representatives agreed to form a commission to conduct a census while examining "ways to integrate Muslims fully into Spanish society." A general strike by Muslims in November, in support of a demand for immediate Spanish nationality, led to violent clashes between Muslims and Europeans. The internal crisis was defused when Prime Minister González announced in February 1987 that citizenship would "normally" be granted to Muslim residents. But Spain continued to oppose the Moroccan claim to the enclaves, resolutely rejecting any parallel with its own claim to British-ruled Gibraltar.

During a state visit to Morocco in July 1991 by King Juan Carlos, the Spanish and Moroccan prime ministers signed a friendship treaty (the first between Spain and an Arab country) providing in particular for the peaceful settlement of disputes between the two countries. Madrid had long felt that any attempt to alter the status of the enclaves would be interpreted by Rabat as an "annexation" of "occupied territory." Thus, it had branded as "unconstitutional" a unilateral pronouncement by Melilla's mayor in early 1993 that the city was an "autonomous community" within Spain. On September 2, 1994, however, the Spanish government approved statutes of autonomy, effective from March 13, 1995, that upgraded the status of the enclaves by authorizing the replacement of their local councils by 25-member assemblies, to which an executive and president would be responsible. The Moroccan government responded by launching a major diplomatic offensive against Spanish possession of the enclaves, contending that the forthcoming reversion of Hong Kong and Macao to China provided an example that Spain should follow. Madrid rejected such arguments, and in 1998 Spanish officials refused a Moroccan invitation to take part in a panel discussion on granting residents of the enclaves dual citizenship.

Tensions flared again in July 2002 when Moroccan police set up camp on the offshore islet of Perejil (also known as Tourah or Leila), five miles west of Ceuta, ostensibly to combat smuggling and drug trafficking. In response, Spain dispatched members of its armed forces to Perejil, which the *New York Times* described as "a barren rock that is home only to a flock of goats." In an effort to mediate the dispute, U.S. Secretary of State Colin Powell proposed that the islet be returned to its pre-July status. Both Spain and Morocco agreed, although Morocco subsequently voiced objection to the presence of a Spanish naval vessel near another islet, Nekor. On July 30 Morocco's King Mohamed VI reasserted his country's claims to Ceuta, Melilla, and the offshore islands and stated that Spain should end its "occupation."

At the elections of June 13, 1999, the recently formed Independent Liberal Group (*Grupo Independiente Liberal*—GIL), led by a mainland mayor, Jesús GIL, won pluralities in the 25-seat assemblies of both Ceuta and Melilla, but in both jurisdictions anti-GIL coalitions prevailed in forming governments. In Ceuta, the GIL won 12 seats but was bested by an alliance of the PP, with 8 seats; the **Democratic and Social Party of Ceuta** (*Partido Democrático y Social de Ceuta*—PDSC), with 3; and the PSOE, with 2. Greater confusion reigned in Melilla, where six parties split the vote: the GIL won 7; the PP, 5; the **Coalition for Melilla** (*Coalición por Melilla*—CpM), 5; the **Independent Party of Melilla** (*Partido Independiente de Melilla*—PIM), 3; the **Union of the Melilla People** (*Unión del Pueblo Melillense*—UPM), 3; and the PSOE, 2. Initially, the CpM leader, Mustafa ABERCHAN Hamed, assumed the presidency, but he soon fell victim to shifts in the governing alliance, losing a censure motion and being replaced in August 1999 by the UPM's Juan José IMBRODA Ortiz.

The balloting on May 25, 2003, was more definitive. In Ceuta the PP won an overwhelming majority, taking 19 seats; the second-place **Cueta Democratic Union** (*Unión Demócrata Ceutí*—UDCE), a Muslim formation led by Muhammad MUHAMMAD Ali, won 3, while the PSOE and PDSC each won 1. In Melilla, Imbroda Ortiz's UPM took 15 seats, followed by the CpM with 7 and the PSOE with 3. In 2004, as in 2000, all six representatives elected to the *Cortes Generales* from the enclaves ran as PP candidates or chose to sit with the PP parliamentary group.

On September 29, 2005, five Africans were shot to death and dozens of others were injured when hundreds of individuals tried to scale the fence separating Morocco from Ceuta. The fatal shots reportedly came from the Morocco side of the border. On the same day Madrid announced that it would deploy some 500 troops to Melilla and Ceuta in an effort to prevent such attempts, which had claimed nine lives in the preceding two months. The incidents led directly to a decision by 60 African and European countries to meet at Rabat, Morocco, in July 2006, in an effort to formulate a strategy that would stem the flow of illegal immigrants into EU countries.

SWEDEN

KINGDOM OF SWEDEN

Konungariket Sverige

Note: At the general election of September 17, 2006, the four-party center-right Alliance for Sweden, led by Fredrik Reinfeldt of the Moderate Coalition Party (MSP), ousted Prime Minister Göran Persson's Social Democratic Labor Party (SdAP) from power. Final election results gave the SdAP 130 seats and 37.2 percent of the vote, well short of the 178 amassed by the MSP (97 seats, 27.8 percent) and its partners, the Center Party (29, 8.3 percent), the Liberal People's Party (28, 8.0 percent), and the Christian Democratic Party (24, 6.9 percent). Also winning legislative seats were the Left Party (22, 6.3 percent) and the Green Ecology Party (19, 5.4 percent). Prime Minister Persson submitted his resignation on September 18, and on the following day Reinfeldt was asked to form a new government.

The Country

Situated on the Baltic side of the Scandinavian Peninsula and projecting north of the Arctic Circle, Sweden is the largest and most populous of the Scandinavian countries. The indigenous population, about 90 percent of which belongs to the Evangelical Lutheran Church, is homogeneous except for Finnish and Sámi (Lapp) minorities in the north. In addition, there are nearly 1 million resident aliens who have arrived since World War II, including some 400,000 Finns and substantial numbers from Mediterranean countries, such as Greece, Turkey, and Yugoslavia. In 2003, 79 percent of women ages 20–64 were in the labor force, compared with 84 percent of men. In 2002 women won 45 percent of the seats in the *Riksdag,* making it one of the most gender-equal parliaments in the world.

Although only 7 percent of the land is cultivated and agriculture, forestry, and fishing contribute only 2 percent of the GDP, Sweden is almost self-sufficient in foodstuffs, while its wealth of resources has enabled it to assume an important position among the world's industrial nations. A major producer and exporter of wood, paper products, and iron ore, Sweden also is a leading vehicle manufacturer and exports a variety of sophisticated capital goods. Despite socialist leadership throughout most of the postwar period, the private sector accounts for more than 90 percent of Sweden's output, although about 30 percent of jobs are in the public sector. Government outlays, primarily in the form of social security and other transfer payments,

Political Status: Constitutional monarchy established on June 6, 1809; under revised constitution effective January 1, 1975.

Area: 173,731 sq. mi. (449,964 sq. km.).

Population: 8,587,353 (1990C); 9,024,000 (2005E).

Major Urban Centers (2005E): STOCKHOLM (767,000), Göteborg (483,000), Malmö (270,000), Uppsala (183,000).

Official Language: Swedish.

Monetary Unit: Krona (official rate July 1, 2006: 7.20 kronor = $1US).

Sovereign: King CARL XVI GUSTAF; succeeded to the throne September 19, 1973, following the death of his grandfather, King GUSTAF VI ADOLF.

Heir Apparent: Princess VICTORIA Ingrid Alice Désirée, daughter of the king.

Prime Minister: (*See headnote.*) Göran PERSSON (Social Democratic Labor Party); took office as head of minority government on March 17, 1996, in succession to Ingvar CARLSSON (Social Democratic Labor Party); remained head of minority government following general election of September 15, 2002.

remained negligible. Further growth of 3.6 percent was recorded in 2000 as unemployment dropped to 4.7 percent.

While Sweden's economy has sustained growth rates in GDP between 1.6 percent and 2.6 percent in recent years, some analysts note that even this moderate level of growth is due primarily to increases in productivity. Unemployment remains a problem. While the official unemployment rate peaked at 6.5 percent in 1999 and dropped to 4.0 percent in 2000 and 2001, it has risen to more than 5 percent in 2004 and 2005. Most recently, Ericsson, the telecom giant, announced that it would eliminate 60,000 jobs over three years.

In June 2005 the Swedish Central Bank surprised markets by cutting the interest rate by half a percentage point in response to data showing the country's economic growth had slowed to 1.4 percent in the first quarter of the year. The Organization for Economic Cooperation and Development (OECD), however, still forecasts a growth rate of 2.8 percent for 2005 and 3.3 percent for 2006. Both projected rates are higher than the OECD average. Nevertheless, the country has been afflicted with unexpected high unemployment, which reached an historical high of 6.9 percent in 2005, with employment in the manufacturing sector suffering the most, with a loss of 10,000 jobs during 2005.

reached nearly 60 percent of net national income in 1990, with total tax revenue equal to 58 percent of GDP (the highest in the developed world).

The worldwide recession in the early 1990s resulted in Sweden's GDP shrinking by 5.2 percent between 1990 and 1993. The government responded with reforms to cut public spending, which were an abnormally high 67.5 percent of the GDP in 1993.

The reforms, combined with an improving world economy, resulted in a resumption of growth in Sweden's economy in 1994, but real unemployment rose to a postwar high of 14 percent by year's end, before falling to around 12 percent by mid-1996. Most aspects of the economy subsequently continued to rebound; GDP grew by 3.6 percent in 1998 and 4.1 percent in 1999, while unemployment declined to less than 6 percent in 1999 and inflation

Government and Politics

Political Background

A major European power in the 17th century, Sweden later declined in relative importance but nevertheless retained an important regional position, including links with Norway in a personal union under the Swedish crown from 1814 to 1905. Neutrality in both world wars enabled Sweden to concentrate on its industrial development and the perfection of a welfare state under the auspices of the Social Democratic Labor Party (*Socialdemokratiska Arbetarepartiet*—SdAP), which was in power almost continuously from 1932 to 1976, either alone or in coalition with other parties.

At the *Riksdag* election of 1968 the Social Democrats under Tage ERLANDER won an absolute majority for the first time in 22 years. Having led the party and the country since 1946, Erlander was succeeded as party chair and prime minister by Olof PALME in October 1969. Although diminished support for the Social Democrats was reflected in the parliamentary elections of 1970 and 1973, the party maintained control until September 1976 when voters, disturbed by a climate of increasing labor unrest and inflation, and declining economic growth, awarded a combined majority of 180 legislative seats to the Center Party (*Centerpartiet*—CP), the Moderate Coalition Party (*Moderata Samlingspartiet*—MSP), and the Liberal People's Party (*Folkpartiet Liberalerna*—FP). On October 8 a coalition government was formed under CP leader Thorbjörn FÄLLDIN. However, policy differences between the antinuclear CP and the pronuclear MSP and FP forced the government to resign in October 1978, providing the opportunity for Ola ULLSTEN to form a minority FP government.

Following the election of September 16, 1979, a center-right CP-MSP-FP coalition with a one-seat majority was formed under former prime minister Fälldin, but on May 4, 1981, the MSP withdrew in a dispute over tax reform. However, the MSP tacitly agreed to support the two-party government to avoid an early election and the likely return of the Social Democrats. Fälldin continued in office until the election of September 19, 1982, at which the Social Democrats obtained a three-seat plurality over nonsocialists, permitting Palme to return as head of an SdAP minority administration supported in Parliament by the Left Party-Communists (*Vänsterpartiet-Kommunisterna*—VpK).

On February 28, 1986, Palme was assassinated in Stockholm by unidentified gunmen, the first postwar West European head of government to be killed while in office. Deputy Prime Minister Ingvar CARLSSON assumed interim control of the government and was confirmed as Palme's successor on March 12. The Social Democrats retained their dominant position at the election of September 18, 1988, with the conservatives losing ground and the Green Ecology Party (*Miljöpartiet de Gröna*—MpG) entering the *Riksdag* for the first time with 20 seats.

Carlsson resigned on February 15, 1990, after losing a key vote on an economic austerity plan that would have placed upper-middle-income taxpayers in a 72 percent bracket while freezing both prices and wages through 1991. He was returned to office 11 days later after accepting a substantially watered-down tax schedule that left most of the country's budgetary problems unresolved. As a result, the Social Democrats experienced their most serious setback since 1928 at triennial legislative balloting on September 15, 1991, falling to 138 seats out of 349; concurrently, the aggregate strength of the four traditional "bourgeois" parties—the CP, MSP, FP, and Christian Democratic Community Party (*Krisdemokratiska Samkällspartiet*—KdS)—rose to 170 seats, due mainly to gains by the MSP and the KdS. While the Left Party (Vp, formerly the VpK) lost ground and the Greens disappeared from the *Riksdag,* the populist New Democracy (NyD) party won a startling 25 seats in its first parliamentary race. The result was the installation of a four-party center-right administration under the MSP's Carl BILDT that was 6 seats short of an assured parliamentary majority and therefore dependent on NyD external support.

Faced with the country's worst postwar economic crisis, Prime Minister Bildt and opposition SdAP leader Carlsson on September 20, 1992, concluded an unprecedented economic pact that called for tax increases and major public spending cuts over five years. However, the new cooperative spirit was badly dented in November, when the SdAP declined to support specific austerity measures, obliging the Swedish authorities to allow the krona to float and thereby to depreciate by 9 percent. Further welfare spending cuts mandated by the 1993–1994 budget ended the already frayed consensus.

Through 1993 the government relied on the NyD in critical parliamentary divisions, but in late March 1994 the NyD withdrew its support following the resignation the previous month of its leader, Count Ian WACHMEISTER. The government also was weakened by the resignation in June of the Center Party environment minister, Olof JOHANSSON, in protest against the granting of final cabinet approval to the construction of the controversial Öresund bridge and tunnel link with Denmark, which environmentalists claimed would gravely damage the Baltic Sea ecosystem. In the campaigning for the fall legislative election the ruling coalition derived some benefit from a modest economic upturn, but the continuing high unemployment and uncertainty about the future of the welfare state gave the opposition Social Democrats powerful ammunition. Overhanging the campaign was the issue of Sweden's projected membership in the European Union (EU, formerly the European Community—EC) from January 1995, on which negotiations had been successfully concluded on March 1.

The outcome of the balloting on September 18, 1994, was a decisive swing to the left, with the Social Democrats and the ex-Communist Vp both gaining ground sharply and the left-oriented Greens reentering the *Riksdag* after a three-year absence. Of the outgoing coalition parties, the MSP held its vote, but the other three all lost seats, while the NyD disappeared from Parliament altogether. Having rejected an FP offer of a majority center-left coalition, the Social Democrats proceeded to form a minority one-party government headed by Carlsson; it enjoyed pledges of external support, albeit qualified, from the Vp and Greens.

Attention then turned to the EU referendum set for November 13, 1994, with the proaccession center-right parties, Social Democratic leadership, and business community ranged against a lively anti-EU coalition of the Vp, Greens, and many rank-and-file Social Democrats. The upshot, in a turnout of 82.4 percent, was a 52.2 to 46.9 percent vote in favor of accession.

On August 18, 1995, Prime Minister Carlsson unexpectedly announced that he would retire in March 1996, more than two years before the expiration of his government's mandate. The early favorite to succeed Carlsson was the deputy premier, Mona SAHLIN; however, press disclosures that she had used an official credit card to pay personal bills forced her exit from politics in November 1995 (although the public prosecutor decided two months later that she had committed no crime). After much initial hesitation, Finance Minister Göran PERSSON was persuaded to become a candidate. Elected chair of the ruling party at an extraordinary congress on March 15, 1996, he was sworn in as prime minister on March 17 at the head of a substantially reshuffled cabinet.

In the general election of September 20, 1998, the SdAP's legislative representation fell to 131 seats (compared to 161 in 1994) on a vote share of 36.6 percent, with the MSP finishing second with 22.9 percent of the vote and 82 seats.

The SdAP's poor performance in the 1998 elections was largely a result of voter dissatisfaction with the government's fiscally conservative policies and its willingness to make cuts in the welfare system. Many voters who had previously voted SdAP reported switching to the Vp, which promised to press the government to increase expenditures on social welfare and employment.

In April 1999 Finance Minister Erik ASBRINK resigned after a disagreement with Persson over the budget. Bosse RINGHOLME replaced him.

In 2002 Prime Minister Persson won his third term in office, thanks to his party's strong showing in the September 15 parliamentary election. The Social Democrats benefited from an economic upturn, with unemployment holding at 4 percent and low inflation, to capture 39.8 percent of the vote, a significant improvement on its 36.4 percent showing in 1998. In addition, just before the elections, Persson had promised to increase spending on welfare.

Persson immediately ruled out a role giving seats in the government to either the Left Party or the Green Party—both coalition partners—because of their opposition to adoption of the euro. The SdAP nevertheless managed to secure parliamentary support from the Vp and MpG to form a minority government. Analysts conjecture that the Vp and MpG agreement was based on an understanding that the government would press for reductions in defense spending and a moratorium on cod fishing in the Baltic Sea.

The biggest loser in the election was the conservative MSP. Running on a platform calling for tax cuts—including abolition of wealth and real estate taxes—a policy many Swedes felt would endanger their system of social benefits, the party managed to win only 15.2 percent of the vote. The Liberal Party was the surprise winner in the election, with its share of the vote nearly tripling to 13.3 percent, a result analysts attributed primarily to the party's call for a language test for citizenship.

Despite Persson's promise to increase welfare spending, in April 2003 the government responded to persistent sluggishness in the economy—marked most notably by an increase in unemployment—by making cuts in welfare benefits amounting to $1.88 billion over two years.

The Swedish political scene was rocked on September 10, 2003, when Foreign Minister Anna LINDH was assassinated in a Stockholm department store. Days later, on September 14, 2003, Swedish voters rejected adoption of the euro by a margin of 56 percent to 42 percent, this despite the measure's strong backing by Prime Minister Persson and the recently murdered foreign minister.

In the wake of voters' decisive rejection of the euro, major Swedish businesses warned that the government needed to institute policies to encourage growth. Michael TRESCHOW, chair of Ericsson, specifically called for reducing taxes on small business and allowing companies to reduce sick benefits.

Prime Minister Persson on October 3, 2003, filled the post of assassinated Foreign Minister Anna Lindh with Laila FREIVALDS, a former justice minister. At the same time, Deputy Prime Minister Margareta WINBERG left the cabinet to take the post of ambassador to Brazil, a move some analysts attributed to her opposition to the euro. Her position was not immediately filled.

On February 11, 2004, a new party was formed to contest elections to the European Parliament in June. The June List (*Juilistan*) was founded by a group of economists and a former head of the Central Bank. Lars WOHLIN, one of the founders, said that, while the party was against joining the Economic and Monetary Union (EMU), it was not against membership in the EU.

The June List surprised analysts by winning 14.4 percent of the vote in the European Parliament elections on June 10, 2004, and securing 3 of Sweden's 19 seats. The ruling SdAP attracted a record-low 24.7 percent of the vote, a result that analysts attribute to Swedish voters' uncertainties about closer integration with the EU. In August the MSP, CP, FP, and Christian Democratic Party (*Kristdemokraterna*—Kd, the renamed KdS) formed the Alliance for Sweden (*Allians för Sverige*) in preparation for the 2006 general election.

Prime Minister Persson announced another broad reshuffling of the cabinet on October 21, 2004. Among the major changes, Mona Sahlin was tapped to head a new Environment and Community Development Ministry. Ibrahim BAYLAN, the first immigrant to become a minister in a Swedish government, was named to head the schools portfolio in a reorganized Education and Culture Ministry. Analysts attributed the changes both as a response to the SdAP's poor performance in the 2004 European Parliament election and as an attempt to reassure voters before the next general election in 2006.

In 2005, for the first time since 1995, the SdAP fell behind the MSP in polls. Most analysts attributed this to a series of scandals—involving housing perks for party members—and continuing high unemployment.

The SdAP suffered another setback in March 2006 when Foreign Minister Laila Freivalds resigned after it was disclosed that her ministry had taken steps to shut down an Internet website with cartoons portraying the Prophet Muhammed. Freivalds had also been criticized for a slow response to the Asian tsunami in 2004 in which more than 500 Swedes died.

Constitution and Government

The present Swedish constitution retains the general form of the old governmental structure, but the king is now only a ceremonial figure (formerly, as nominal head of government, he appointed the prime minister and served as commander in chief of the armed forces). In 1979 the *Riksdag* took final action on making women eligible for succession; thus the present king's daughter, VICTORIA, born in 1977, has become the heir apparent. Any proposed amendment of the constitution must be approved twice by the *Riksdag* in successive legislative terms, that is, a general election must intervene between the first approval and the second.

The chief executive officer, the prime minister, is nominated by the speaker of the *Riksdag* and confirmed by the whole house. The prime minister appoints other members of the cabinet, which functions as a policy-drafting body. Routine administration is carried out largely by independent administrative boards (*centrala ämbetsverk*). Legislative authority is vested in the *Riksdag,* which has been a unicameral body since 1971. The judicial system is headed by the Supreme Court (*Högsta Domstolen*) and includes 6 courts of appeal (*hovrätt*) and 100 district courts (*tingsrätt*). There is a parallel system of administrative courts, while the *Riksdag* appoints four *justitieombudsmen* to maintain general oversight of both legislative and executive actions.

Sweden is administratively divided into 24 counties (including Stockholm) with appointed governors and elected councils and into 289 urban and rural communes with elected councils. The 20,000-strong Sámi (Lapp) community in the north has its own local assembly.

Under legislation approved in 1996, the Evangelical Lutheran Church was effectively disestablished as the Church of Sweden on January 1, 2000, in a termination of church-state legal and fiscal links dating from the 16th century.

Foreign Relations

Sweden has not participated in any war nor joined any military alliance since 1814. Unlike Denmark, Iceland, and Norway, it declined to enter the North Atlantic Treaty Organization (NATO) in 1949, while its determination to safeguard its neutrality is backed by an impressive defense system. A strong supporter of international cooper-

ation, Sweden participates in the United Nations (UN) and all its related agencies; in 1975 it became the first industrial nation to meet a standard set by the OECD, allocating a full 1 percent of its GNP to aid for developing countries (although two decades later the proportion had fallen to 0.8 percent). Sweden also attaches importance to regional cooperation through the Nordic Council, while in 1960 it was a founding member of the European Free Trade Association (EFTA), although its membership in that body ceased upon its accession to the EU in 1995.

Stockholm's traditionally good relations with Moscow were strained during the 1980s and early 1990s by numerous incidents involving Soviet submarines in Swedish waters as well as by intrusions of Russian planes into the country's airspace. However, during an official visit to Moscow by Prime Minister Bildt on February 4–7, 1993, the long-standing controversy appeared to end when the Russians for the first time formally admitted to violations of Swedish territorial waters.

Citing the end of the Cold War and the need to improve its economy by means of increased trade, Sweden applied for membership in the EC on July 1, 1991. To pave the way, it became a signatory of the European Economic Area (EEA) treaty between the EC and certain EFTA countries on May 2, 1992. It also placed emphasis on post-Soviet regional cooperation, becoming a founding member of the ten-nation Council of the Baltic Sea States in March 1992 and of the Barents Euro-Arctic Council (of the five Nordic countries and Russia) in January 1993. Two months later Sweden modified its tradition of neutrality by agreeing to join a NATO military maneuver in August, and in May 1994 it enrolled in NATO's Partnership for Peace program for the neutral and former Communist states of Europe and the ex-USSR. However, governmental and popular sentiment has subsequently remained in favor of continued status outside of full NATO membership.

Relations with Russia were tested once again in November 2002 when Sweden expelled two Russian diplomats. The diplomats were implicated in an investigation of industrial espionage at Ericsson.

Russian officials said they were "bewildered" by the expulsions.

Over the past few years, Sweden has been edging back from its long-standing policy of strict neutrality. While stressing that it was still important for Sweden to remain nonaligned, Prime Minister Persson announced proposals in November 2000 that would more closely involve Sweden in regional security, including a pledge to contribute 1,500 troops to the new European rapid reaction force.

As Sweden's economy has struggled to maintain momentum, and particularly as unemployment has risen in recent years, the country has grown more skeptical about tighter integration among the countries of the EU. In fact, in October 2005, Sweden threatened to withdraw its support for plans to liberalize services within the EU.

Current Issues

Polls, elections, and public commentary all reveal that the priority of Swedish voters and politicians alike continues to be sustaining the country's very generous social welfare system in the face of serious economic challenges. In particular, as the Swedish economy has struggled in recent years, unemployment has become a major issue. As of March 2005 unemployment stood at 5.7 percent, far higher than the 4 percent goal set by the government in 1996. The government reduced its expectations in the 2005 budget by projecting a lowering of the rate to 5.1 percent for that year.

Rising unemployment, and the trimming of welfare benefits, have resulted in an increase in labor conflicts. After secret talks between the government and the Municipal Workers' Union broke down, 47,000 local government employees went on strike on May 12, 2003. Two days later 5,000 electricians joined the strike. The union had called for pay raises and for an increase in the minimum wage. The government reached an agreement with the union on May 28.

At the same time, a rapidly aging work force also has led to greater reliance on immigrant labor in certain sectors. Indeed, about 1 million of Sweden's 9 million people were born outside the country. Rising immigration has, in turn, exacerbated concerns among Swedes over the potential strain on the country's welfare system presented by an additional influx of workers from other EU countries as the EU expands.

While the Swedish government has expressed concerns over immigration, the issue is not as contentious in Sweden as it is in many other EU countries, most notably Denmark and Norway. Nevertheless, in April 2004 the government campaigned for legislation requiring work permits for immigrant workers. Parliament, however, rejected such legislation by a 182–137 vote on April 28.

All of these issues come together in Sweden's consideration of its relationship with the EU and, especially, the EMU. While Swedes have repeatedly shown support for membership in the EU, as long as Swedish sovereignty is protected, they strongly rejected adoption of the euro in 2003. Criticism of the euro is strongest among voters in the 18–30 age bracket. With Sweden's major businesses and its ruling party pushing for the euro, however, the issue promises to be a hot topic leading up to the next general elections in September 2006.

Political Parties

Government Party

Social Democratic Labor Party (*Socialdemokratiska Arbetarepartiet*—SdAP). Formed in the 1880s and long a dominant force in Swedish politics, the SdAP has a "pragmatic" socialist outlook. During more than four decades of virtually uninterrupted power from 1932, it refrained from nationalizing major industries but gradually increased government economic planning and control over the business sector. When its representation in the *Riksdag* dropped to 152 in 1976, the SdAP was forced, despite its sizable plurality, to move into opposition. It regained control of the government in 1982 and, despite a further reduction, maintained control in 1985 and 1988 with the aid of the VpK (see Vp, below). There were few, if any, changes in party ideology and practice following the assassination of Olof Palme and the accession of his deputy, Ingvar Carlsson, to the prime ministership in March 1986. The group was again forced into opposition at the legislative poll of September 1991, when its seat tally fell from 156 to 138. It staged a comeback in 1994, winning 161 seats and 45.3 percent of the vote.

Carlsson's surprise announcement in August 1995 of his impending departure as party leader and prime minister, combined with rapid public disenchantment with the EU, yielded a dramatic slump in SdAP support to only 28.1 percent in the September European Parliament balloting, when three of the seven Social Democrats elected were critical of EU membership. The party was further damaged in November by the enforced exit from politics of Carlsson's deputy and presumed successor, Mona Sahlin, after press disclosures about her financial affairs. The mantle accordingly passed to the finance minister, Göran Persson, who was elected SdAP chair unopposed on March 15, 1996, and appointed prime minister two days later.

Persson led the party to a strong showing in the September 2002 general elections, with the SdAP winning 39.8 percent of the vote.

The party leadership was again thrown into disarray, however, with the assassination of Foreign Minister Anna Lindh, who was considered by many the natural successor to Prime Minister Göran Persson.

The party also has been split over support for the EMU. While the party is officially in favor of the EMU, several party leaders, including Margot WALLSTROM, EU environment commissioner, are against adoption of the euro.

Leaders: Göran PERSSON (Prime Minister and Chair of the Party), Britt Bohlin OLSSON (Parliamentary Leader), Marita ULVSKOG (Secretary General).

Other Parliamentary Parties

Moderate Coalition Party (*Moderata Samlingspartiet*—MSP). Known as the Conservative Party until after the 1968 election and commonly referred to today simply as the Moderate Party, the MSP was organized as a vehicle for the financial and business community and other well-to-do elements. The party advocates tax cuts and reduced governmental interference in the economy. It has long favored a strong defense policy and strongly supported Sweden's accession to the EU. The party joined a center-left coalition government in 1976 but withdrew in 1981 after disagreeing with a tax reform plan. Its *Riksdag* representation dropped from 86 seats in 1982 to 66 in 1988 but rose again to 80 in 1991, when it formed a center-right coalition with the FP, CP, and Christian Democrats (below) under the premiership of Carl Bildt. The Moderates retained 80 seats in the 1994 national balloting (on a slightly higher vote share of 22.4 percent), but an overall swing to the left returned the party to opposition. The MSP was unable to improve its position substantially in the September 1998 *Riksdag* election (82 seats and a 22.9 vote share), thwarting Bildt's determined campaign to return to the prime ministership. Bildt, a prominent EU/UN negotiator in Yugoslavia since 1995, resigned as MSP chair in mid-1999 and was succeeded by Bo LUNDGREN, a former minister of finance.

The party fared even worse in the 2002 general election, with its share of the vote dropping to only 15.2 percent. As a result, party leader Bo Lundgren announced his resignation. Fredrik Reinfeldt replaced him in October 2003 and spearheaded formation of the **Alliance for Sweden** (*Allians för Sverige*) with the FP, CP, and Kd in August 2004.

In a bid to capture the middle ground of Swedish politics prior to the next general election in September 2006, the party dropped its call for radical tax cuts and emphasized instead support for public services.

Leaders: Fredrik REINFELDT (Chair), Mikael ODENBERG (Parliamentary Leader), Sven Otto LITTORIN (Secretary General).

Liberal People's Party (*Folkpartiet Liberalerna*—FP). Originally formed as a parliaentary group in 1895, the first *Folkpartiet* merged with the Liberal Coalition Party in 1900. The two split in 1923 over alcohol issues and reunited in 1934 in today's form as the FP. (The grouping has since often been referred to as the Liberal Party.) The FP draws support from rural free-church movements as well as from professionals and intellectuals. Favoring socially progressive policies based on individual responsibility, the party has sought the cooperation of the Center Party (below) on many issues. It was the only party represented in the minority government of October 1978. The party lost half of its parliamentary representation at the 1982 general election, and in July 1984 former prime minister Ola Ullsten resigned as chair "to make way for more dynamic influences." Benefiting from a marginal loss of support for the governing SdAP and more substantial losses for both of the other major "bourgeois" parties (MCP, CP), the FP gained 30 additional *Riksdag* seats, for a total of 51, at the September 1985 balloting. The party lost 7 of these in 1988, and its parliamentary representation dropped further to 33 in 1991 when it entered a four-party center-right coalition.

After another electoral setback in 1994, to 26 seats on a 7.2 percent vote share, the Liberals reverted to opposition status, with Bengt WESTERBERG standing down as party chair. In June 1996 the FP announced a relaunch as a "bourgeois left" party emphasizing the fight against unemployment and ethnic separation. The party lost 9 of its 26 seats in the September 1998 general election.

The party made dramatic gains in the 2002 general election, winning 13.3 percent of the vote and 48 seats in the *Riksdag*. Analysts attribute the gains to the party's call for a language test for citizenship, a measure aimed at ensuring integration of immigrants rather than curbing immigration.

Leaders: Lars LEIJONBORG (Chair), Anna Grönlund KRANTZ (Parliamentary Leader), Johan JAKOBSSON (Secretary General).

Center Party (*Centerpartiet*—CP). Farmers' representatives first began breaking away from other parties to promote rural rights in 1910, and in 1922 formally launched the Agrarian Party (the precursor to the CP). In return for agricultural subsidies, the party began to support the Social Democrats in the 1930s, occasionally serving as a junior partner in coalition with the SdAP. Since

adopting its present name in 1958, the party has developed nationwide strength, including support from the larger urban centers. It has long campaigned for decentralization of government and industry and for reduced impact of government on the lives of individuals, whereas in the 1970s opposition to nuclear power became its main issue. A major advance to 86 seats in the 1976 election enabled the CP to head a center-right coalition until 1978 under Thorbjörn Fälldin, who returned to the premiership in 1979 despite his party's 22-seat decline in that year's election. In opposition after a further slump of 8 seats in 1982, it continued to lose ground in 1985, 1988, and 1991 (when its tally stood at 31). At a party congress in June 1986, Karin SÖDER was elected to succeed Fälldin, who had resigned six months earlier because of his party's poor showing at the 1985 election. However, Ms. Söder (Sweden's first female party leader) was forced to step down in March 1987 for health reasons. The party's participation in the center-right coalition formed in 1991 was shaken by the resignation in June 1994 of party chair Olof Johansson as environment minister, in opposition to the Öresund bridge project. In the September election the CP was reduced to 27 seats (on a vote share of 7.7 percent) and again went into opposition.

Johansson resigned as party chair in April 1998 and was succeeded in June by Lennart DALÉUS, a staunch opponent of nuclear power who had led the CP's successful 1980 referendum on decommissioning nuclear plants. He promptly announced that the party would no longer cooperate with the SdAP and also voiced reservations about the MSP. He hoped to be part of a centrist government following the September general election, but the CP lost 9 of its 27 seats on a vote share of 5.1 percent.

Daléus was replaced as party leader by Maud Olofsson in 2001. The party fared only slightly better in the 2002 general election, however, winning only 6.2 percent of the vote and 22 seats in Parliament.

Leaders: Maud OLOFSSON (Chair), Åsa TORSTENSSON (Parliamentary Leader), Jöran HÄGGLUND (Secretary General).

Christian Democratic Party (*Kristdemokra-terna*—Kd). Formed in 1964 as the Christian Democratic Coalition (*Kristen Demokratisk Samling*—KDS) to promote Christian values in politics, the KDS adopted the name Christian Democratic Community Party (*Kristdemokratiska Samhällspartiet*—KdS) in 1987 and its current title in 1996. The group claims a membership of more than 25,000 but for two decades was unable to secure *Riksdag* representation, although it did secure a growing number of local and state seats. In September 1984 it entered into an electoral pact with the Center Party, thereby securing its first legislative seat in 1985 despite a marginal 2.6 percent vote share. Excluded completely in 1988, the KdS won 26 legislative seats in 1991 and joined a center-right coalition. Reduced to 15 seats (and 4.1 percent of the vote) in the 1994 balloting, it went into opposition. Opposing adoption of the euro and stressing "cleaner politics," the KdS ran the most successful campaign in its history for the general election of September 1998, winning 42 seats (a gain of 27) on a vote share of 11.8 percent.

Göran Hägglund was elected party leader on April 3, 2004, succeeding Alf SVENSSON, who had been Sweden's longest-serving party leader, with 31 years in the post. The party won 9.1 percent of the vote in 2002 but had seen its poll numbers drop to 3.8 percent by 2004.

Leaders: Göran HÄGGLUND (Chair), Stefan ATTEFALL (Parliamentary Leader), Urban SVENSSON (Secretary General).

Left Party (*Vänsterpartiet*—Vp). Originally formed in 1917 as the Left Social Democratic Party (*Vänster Socialdemokratiska Partiet*—VSdP), renamed the Communist Party (*Kommunistiska Partiet*—KP) in 1921 and the Left Party-Communists (*Vänsterpartiet-Kommunisterna*—VpK) in 1967, the Vp adopted its present name during a congress in Stockholm in May 1990. Long before the decline of communism in Eastern Europe, the party pursued a "revisionist," or "Eurocommunist," policy based on distinctive Swedish conditions. This posture provoked considerable dissent within the VpK before the

withdrawal of a pro-Moscow faction in early 1977. Following the 1982 election, the party agreed to support a new SdAP government; its voting strength became crucial following the SdAP's loss of 7 seats in September 1985 and even more so as the latter's plurality fell by an additional 3 seats in 1988. Having won 16 seats in the 1991 general election, the Vp went into full opposition to the new center-right coalition government. In the 1994 balloting the party achieved its best result since 1948, winning 22 seats on a 6.2 percent vote share.

Having unsuccessfully opposed Sweden's accession to the EU, the Vp made a further strong advance in the September 1995 European balloting, returning three representatives with 12.9 percent of the vote, and nearly doubled its parliamentary representation in the September 1998 elections, winning 43 seats on a vote share of 12.0 percent, its best showing since its formation. Its legislative support subsequently remained crucial in the continuation of the SdAP minority government.

Gudrum SCHYMAN, leader of the party, resigned on January 26, 2003, when discrepancies in her tax returns were made public. Lars Ohly replaced Schyman at a party election on February 20, 2004.

Ohly's appointment highlighted a division between modernist and traditional wings of the party, with Ohly, a former railroad worker, representing the traditionalist wing.

The party—Sweden's fourth largest—faced a possible split in January 2005, largely caused by the party leader's insistence on calling himself a communist. On January 29 more than 150 members met to decide if they should leave the party or work to reform it. Although the party has not broken apart, Ohly still faces a major struggle to keep it together.

Leaders: Lars OHLY (Chair), Lars BÄCKSTRÖM (Parliamentary Leader), Anki AHLSTEN (Secretary).

Green Ecology Party (*Miljöpartiet de Gröna*—MpG). Established in 1981, the Greens benefited at the 1988 election from an upsurge

Cabinet

As of July 13, 2006 (*see headnote*)

Prime Minister	Göran Persson
Deputy Prime Minister	Bosse Ringholm

Ministers

Agriculture, Food, and Consumer Affairs	Ann-Christin Nykvist [f]
Communications and Regional Policy	Ulrica Messing [f]
Defense	Leni Björklund [f]
Education and Culture	Leif Pagrotsky
Employment	Hans Karlsson
Environment	Lena Sommestad [f]
Finance	Pär Nuder
Foreign Affairs	Jan Eliasson
Health and Elderly Care	Ylva Johansson [f]
Industry and Trade	Thomas Östros
Integration, Metropolitan, and Gender Equality Issues	Jens Orback
International Development Cooperation	Carin Jämtin [f]
Justice	Thomas Bodström
Local Government Finances and Financial Market Issues	Sven-Erik Öesterberg
Migration and Asylum Policy	Barbro Holmberg [f]
Preschool Education, Youth Affairs, and Adult Learning	Lena Hallengren
Primary and Secondary Schools	Ibrahim Baylan
Public Health and Social Services	Morgan Johansson
Social Affairs	Berit Andnor [f]
Sustainable Development	Mona Sahlin [f]

[f] = female

Note: All of the above are members of the SdAP.

of popular interest in environmental issues. It has advocated tax reduction for low-income wage earners, increased charges for energy use, and heightened penalties for pollution by commercial establishments and motor vehicle operators. It also has called for the phasing out of nuclear-generated electricity (currently about 45 percent of Sweden's total) and curtailed highway construction. (It is strongly opposed to the Öresund bridge and tunnel project.) The party's parliamentary representation plummeted from 20 seats in 1988 to none in 1991 but recovered to 18 seats (on 5.0 percent of the vote) in 1994.

Prominent on the defeated "no" side in the November 1994 referendum on EU membership, the Greens registered a major advance in the September 1995 European Parliament balloting, winning 4 seats and 17.2 percent of the national vote. The Greens lost 2 seats in the 1998 general election on a vote share of 4.5 percent but agreed to continue to support the SdAP minority government on confidence motions.

The party repeated its showing of 4.5 percent of the vote in the 2002 elections, securing 17 seats in Parliament. The party participated in negotiations with center-right parties after the election before deciding to renew its agreement with the SdAP.

Leaders: Maria WETTERSTRAND, Peter ERIKSSON (Spokespersons); Hådkan WÅHLSTCDT (Secretary General); Mikael JOHANSSON (Parliamentary Leader).

Legislature

The unicameral **Riksdag** consists of 349 members serving four-year terms. (Before the 1994 election the term was three years.) Of the total, 310 are elected by proportional representation in 28 constituencies; the remaining 39 are selected from a national pool designed to give absolute proportionality to all parties receiving at least 4 percent of the vote. Following the election of September 2002, the Social Democratic Labor Party holds 144 seats; the Moderate Unity Party, 55; the Liberal Party, 48; the Christian Democrats, 33; the Left Party, 30; the Center Party, 22; and the Green Ecology Party, 17. The next election was scheduled for September 17, 2006. (*See headnote.*)

Speaker: Böjrn von SYDOW.

Communications

Under Sweden's Mass Media Act, which entered into force in January 1977, principles of noninterference dating back to the mid-1700s and embodied in the Freedom of the Press Act of 1949 were extended to all information media.

Press

Most papers are politically oriented, and many are owned by political parties. The Press Subsidies Bill of 1966 granted state funds to political parties for distribution of their papers in case of financial difficulties. The following are published in Stockholm, unless otherwise noted: *Aftonbladet* (382,000 daily, 486,000 Sunday), Social Democratic; *Expressen* (374,000), liberal; *Dagens Nyheter* (361,000), independent; *Göteborgs Posten* (Göteborg, 265,000), liberal; *Svenska Dagbladet* (188,000), moderate conservative; *Sydsvenska Dagbladet* (Malmö, 115,000), independent liberal; *Dagens Industri* (90,000), business; *Nya Wermlands-Tidningen* (Karlstad, 59,000), moderate conservative; *Arbetet* (Malmö, 55,000), Social Democratic.

News Agencies

The principal domestic facility is the Newspapers' Telegraph Agency (*Tidningarnas Telegrambyrå*—TTB), which is owned by the country's newspapers and other media groups. There are also smaller agencies, such as the Swedish International Press Bureau (*Svensk Internationella Pressbyrån*—SIP), and services run by the leading parties, such as the Swedish Conservative Press Agency (*Svenska Nyhetsbyrån*). In addition, numerous foreign agencies maintain offices in Stockholm.

Broadcasting and Computing

The principal broadcasting services are provided by nonprofit, government-regulated companies: *Sveriges Radio, Sveriges Television,* and *Sveriges Utbildningsradio,* the last of which presents educational programming. Commercial stations also transmit widely. There were approximately 5.7 million television receivers in 2003, with more than two-thirds of all households connected to cable services. Concurrently, some 6.0 million personal computers served 5.6 million Internet users.

Intergovernmental Representation

Ambassador to the U.S.
Gunnar LUND

U.S. Ambassador to Sweden
Michael M. WOOD

Permanent Representative to the UN
Anders LIDEN

IGO Memberships (Non-UN)
AC, ADB, AfDB, BIS, CBSS, CERN, CEUR, EBRD, EIB, ESA, EU, Eurocontrol, G-10, IADB, IEA, Interpol, IOM, NC, NIB, OECD, OSCE, PCA, WCO, WTO

SWITZERLAND

Swiss Confederation

Schweizerische Eidgenossenschaft (German)
Confédération Suisse (French)
Confederazione Svizzera (Italian)

The Country

Situated in the mountainous heart of Western Europe, Switzerland has traditionally set an example of peaceful coexistence among different indigenous ethnic and cultural groups, although a postwar increase in the country's "foreign" population was somewhat less than harmonious. The well-educated, politically sophisticated Swiss generally speak one of four languages: German (63.7 percent), French (20.4 percent), Italian (6.5 percent), and Romansch (0.5 percent). Roman Catholics account for 41.8 percent of the population and Protestants 35.3 percent, while 15.4 percent assume no religious affiliation (as of the year 2000). The previously large influx of foreign workers has ebbed in recent years, although in relation to total population they constitute the highest proportion (20 percent) of any European country except Liechtenstein. Women made up 40 percent of the registered labor force in 1996.

Switzerland's durable goods output is largely based on the production of precision-engineered items and special quality products that are not readily mass produced. Stock raising is the principal agricultural activity, and the chief crops are wheat and potatoes. Tourism, international banking, and insurance are other major contributors to the economy. The country relies heavily on external transactions; foreign exchange earned from exports of goods and services constitutes more than a third of the total national income. Switzerland's GDP of $33,678 per capita makes it one of the world's richest countries.

Switzerland enjoyed a decade of consistent growth following a 1982 recession. However, this period was followed by a new recession that yielded record unemployment (up to 5.1 percent in late 1993) and GDP contraction in 1992–1993. Growth resumed in 1994–1995 (at 2.3 percent a year) and was slow but steady from 1997 to 1999, averaging under 2 percent annually. Recent economic performance has been sluggish, with a growth rate of 0.3

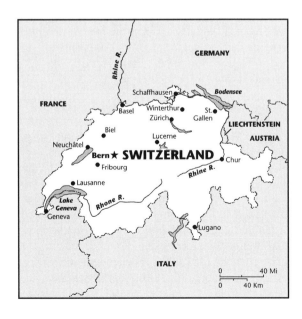

Political Status: Neutral confederation from 1291; equivalent of federal system embodied in constitution of May 29, 1874. A new constitution, which revised and reformed that of 1874, went into effect on January 1, 2000 (as adopted April 18, 1999).

Area: 15,943 sq. mi. (41,293 sq. km.).

Population: 7,204,055 (2000C); 7,434,000 (2005E); figures reference resident population, including noncitizens.

Major Urban Centers (2005E): BERN (118,000), Zürich (327,000), Geneva (177,000), Basel (163,000), Lausanne (109,000).

Official Languages: German, French, Italian. Romansch is recognized as a national language but without full official status.

Monetary Unit: Swiss Franc (market rate July 1, 2006: 1.23 francs = $1US).

President: Moritz LEUENBERGER (Social Democratic Party); elected by the Federal Assembly on December 7, 2005, to succeed Samuel SCHMID (Swiss People's Party) for a one-year term beginning January 1, 2006.

Vice President: Micheline CALMY-REY (Social Democratic Party), elected by the Federal Assembly on December 7, 2005, to succeed Moritz LEUENBERGER (Social Democratic Party) for a term concurrent with that of the president.

percent in 2002 and a contraction of 0.4 in 2003. Matters improved in 2004 with a growth rate of 2.1 percent, which dropped to 1.5 percent in 2005 and picked up again in 2006, when it was projected by the Swiss National Bank to reach at least 2 percent. According to the Organization for Economic Cooperation and Development, unemployment has been on the rise during the early 21st century, going from 2.6 percent in 2001 to 3.2 percent, 4.2 percent, and 4.4 percent in 2002, 2003, and 2004, respectively. Inflation during this period was quite low, with the annual growth rate in consumer prices averaging only 0.9 percent for the period of 1999–2003 and projected to rise marginally, to 1.1 percent, in 2006.

Government and Politics

Political Background

The origins of the Swiss Confederation date back to 1291, when the cantons of Uri, Schwyz, and Unterwalden signed an "eternal alliance" against the Hapsburgs. The league continued to expand until 1648, when it became formally independent of the Holy Roman Empire at the Peace of Westphalia. Following French conquest and reorganization during the Napoleonic era, Switzerland's boundaries were fixed by the Congress of Vienna in 1815, when its perpetual neutrality was guaranteed by the principal European powers. The present constitution, adopted on May 29, 1874, superseded an earlier document of 1848 and increased the powers conferred on the central government by the cantons. The 1874 Constitution was revised by referendum on April 18, 1999, and a new Constitution was put into legal force on January 1, 2000. The changes were primarily aimed at modernizing and updating the 1874 charter, which had been altered 140 times since it was written. The new Constitution was approved by 59 percent of the vote; however, only 35 percent of eligible voters participated in the referendum. In addition to modernizing the document's language, the new Constitution included new provisions pertaining to labor rights and equal opportunity for people with disabilities.

Women have had the right to vote in federal elections since 1971. The Federal Supreme Court ruled in November 1990 that the half-canton of Appenzell-Innerrhoden could no longer serve as Europe's last bastion of all-male suffrage. Despite this, women were denied participation in the Federal Council until quite recently. In February 1984 the Social Democrats nearly withdrew from the government coalition over the issue. The Federal Assembly subsequently reversed itself and approved the Radical Democratic nomination of Elisabeth KOPP, mayor of the Zürich suburb of Zumikon, as a member of the executive body in October of that year. In so doing, the assembly appeared to have ensured that, because of the principle of presidential rotation, the position of nominal head of state would eventually fall to Kopp. However, she was obliged to resign her council post in December 1988 because of advice she improperly gave her husband while a formal money-laundering inquiry was being conducted on a company where he was an officer. On January 1, 1999, Ruth DREIFUSS of the Social Democratic Party became the first woman to hold the presidency of the confederation.

In June 1986 the Federal Assembly approved a series of measures aimed at curbing a refugee influx that included a considerable number of Turks, Sri Lankan Tamils, Ugandans, and Zaireans. In an April 1987 referendum, Swiss voters endorsed proposals restricting immigration and making political asylum more difficult to obtain; additional restrictions (largely procedural in nature) were enacted in October 1988.

In November 1989, Swiss voters rejected a constitutional amendment that would have abolished the country's army by the year 2000, in the highest turnout (69 percent) for a referendum since the women's franchise poll of 1971.

In a September 1990 referendum, voters narrowly rejected a proposal to close the country's five nuclear power stations. However, they did approve a ten-year moratorium on the construction of additional nuclear generation facilities, demonstrating their growing concerns in the wake of the 1986 Chernobyl disaster (although controversial plans to develop deep-buried nuclear waste storage sites were not affected).

In August 1991 the country observed the 700th anniversary of the signing of its initial federal charter (the oldest such document known to exist) with minimal fanfare. Interestingly, immigration was the only issue to have a measurable impact on the 1991 election. The ruling coalition pursued what was described as a "lackluster" campaign that largely avoided the pan-Europe issue, even though the balloting came on the eve of linkage discussions between the European Community (EC, subsequently the European Union—EU) and the much looser European Free Trade Association (EFTA). Four months earlier, in a partial measure of public sentiment, Swiss voters had rejected a package of reforms designed to bring the country's fiscal system into line with those of other European countries. Swiss politics were again dominated by external policy questions in 1992, notably Switzerland's application to join the EC and its signing of the EFTA-EC European Economic Area (EEA) treaty; the Swiss citizenry's rejection of the latter by referendum in December was a serious blow to the government (see Foreign relations, below).

Reeling from the collapse of its European policy, the government stumbled into a political crisis in early 1993 when the Social Democratic Party nominated a woman for federal councilor (i.e., minister). Although the tradition of exclusively male representation had ended in 1984, misogynist tendencies remained strong in the predominantly male Federal Assembly. The first Social Democratic candidate was Christiane BRUNNER, a French-speaking lawyer and trade union official from Geneva whose colorful lifestyle and feminist views caused the assembly to reject her nomination on March 3. The Social Democrats then proceeded to nominate another woman, Ruth Dreifuss, and threatened to leave the government if she were rejected. The assembly elected Dreifuss on March 10 to head the federal interior department.

The issue of Switzerland's military role resurfaced in 1993, following the government's purchase of 34 fighter jets from the United States. This decision prompted the Group for Switzerland Without an Army (GSOA) to launch another popular initiative, not only for the cancellation of the purchase but also for a constitutional amendment to ban all new military aircraft acquisitions until 2000. However, voters rejected both proposals in June 6 referendums by majorities of 57 and 55 percent, respectively. Other referendum outcomes in 1993 demonstrated an unusual degree of popular support for government-proposed economic measures.

Unemployment remained relatively high in 1994 despite an economic upturn, and the government came under strong pressure to adopt tougher policies on immigration and crime. The National Council voted on March 16, 1994, to give the police increased powers to search and detain foreigners who lacked appropriate identification. The following month the government was embarrassed by an Amnesty International report asserting that some Swiss police officers were using unwarranted force against persons in custody, especially foreigners. As a result, government legislation that criminalized racial discrimination and racist propaganda was approved by referendum on September 25 (which enabled Switzerland to ratify the United Nations Convention Against Racial Discrimination). More indicative of the popular mood, however, was another referendum, on December 4, that yielded 73 percent endorsement for tougher action against drug dealers and illegal immigrants.

The issue of accession to the EU dominated a federal lower house election on October 22, 1995, but the result was far from conclusive. The pro-EU Social Democrats achieved their best result ever, winning an extra 12 National Council seats, mainly in the urban areas of Zürich, Basel, and Geneva. However, rural voters favored the strongly anti-EU Swiss People's Party (SVP), which gained four seats. The question of accession was deferred as both parties wished to preserve the four-party coalition that had ruled the country since 1959.

Switzerland has long been considered an ideal example of what political scientist Arend Lijphart calls "consensus democracy" wherein institutional arrangements are such that they maximize the democratic participation of the population. Further, it demonstrates a system wherein a society with significant social cleavages (in this case primarily linguistic but also religious) can establish adequate representation for all groups. It has a multiparty system based on proportional representation (introduced in 1919) and has been governed since 1959 by a coalition of four moderate parties that controls the legislature and determines the composition of the collegial executive body.

Switzerland's ability to ensure sufficient representation is exemplified by its collegial executive, the seven-member Federal Council. The positions of president and vice president rotate among those seven on an annual basis. The seats on the council are allocated among the four largest political parties by what has been dubbed the "Magic Formula." From 1959 to 2003 the Magic Formula granted two

seats apiece to the Christian Democratic People's Party (CVP), the Radical Democratic Party (FDP), and the Social Democratic Party, with the final slot going to the SVP. The substantial electoral success of the SVP in 2003 led to an adjustment of the formula, which resulted in an SVP gain of one seat and the loss of one for the CVP. Indeed, the SVP had threatened to go into outright opposition if they were not awarded the additional seat. This change to the Magic Formula reflects the SVP's growing significance in Swiss politics. The party went from 14.9 percent of the vote for the lower house in 1995 to 22.5 percent in 1999 to almost 27 percent in 2003 (the largest overall share of the votes). The growth in stature of the SVP has come primarily at the expense of the center-right parties (the CVP and the FDP).

Constitution and Government

Under the constitution of 1999, Switzerland is (despite the retention of "confederation" in its official name) a federal republic of 23 cantons, 3 of which are subdivided into half-cantons. The areas of central jurisdiction are largely detailed in the various articles of Title III, Chapter 1 of the 1999 charter. The cantons retain autonomy in a range of local concerns but lack the right to nullify national legislation. Responsibility for the latter is vested in a bicameral parliament, the Federal Assembly, both houses of which have equal authority. The upper house, the 46-member Council of States, is made up of 2 representatives from each undivided canton and 1 from each half-canton; election methods vary from one canton to another. The lower house, the 200-member National Council, is directly elected for a four-year term by universal adult suffrage under a proportional representation system. Legislation passed by the two chambers may not be vetoed by the executive nor reviewed by the judiciary. In addition to normal legislative processes, the Swiss constitution provides for the use of initiatives to amend the constitution and referendums to ratify or reject federal legislation. To go forward, the two require petitions bearing 100,000 and 50,000 signatures, respectively.

Executive authority is exercised on a collegial basis by a Federal Council, whose seven members are elected by the entire Federal Assembly. Each December the assembly elects two of the seven to serve for the following year as president of the confederation (in effect head of state) and vice president of the Federal Council (equivalent to deputy head of state). The president has limited prerogatives and serves as a first among equals. Although the Federal Council is responsible to the legislature, it has increasingly become a nonpolitical body of experts from the leading political parties. Its members are usually reelected as long as they are willing to serve.

The Swiss judicial system functions primarily at the cantonal level; the only regular federal court is the 26-member Federal Supreme Court, which has the authority to review cantonal court decisions involving federal law. Each canton has civil and criminal courts, a Court of Appeal, and a Court of Cassation.

Local government exists on two basic levels: the cantons and the approximately 3,000 communes (municipalities). In some of the larger cantons the communes are grouped into districts, which are headed by commissioners. There are two basic governing organs at the cantonal and communal levels, much like the federal system: a unicameral legislature and a collegial executive. In five cantons and half-cantons (as well as in numerous smaller units) the entire voting population functions as the legislature, while in the others the legislature is elected. As at the federal level, initiatives and referendums may be used to propose, amend, or annul legislation within a canton.

After 30 years of separatist strife in the largely French-speaking, Roman Catholic region of Jura, Swiss voters approved cantonal status for most of the area in September 1978. The creation of the 23rd canton, the first to be formed since 1815, was approved by over 82 percent of those voting in the national referendum. Jura's full membership in the confederation took effect on January 1, 1979. Southern Jura, predominantly Protestant and German-speaking, remained part of Bern. The small German-speaking district of Laufental, having been cut off geographically from Bern by the creation of the Jura canton, voted on September 26, 1993, to be transferred from the Bern canton to the half-canton of Basel-Land.

In a constitutional referendum on March 10, 1996, 76.1 percent of voters supported official recognition of Romansch, the 2,000-year-old language used, in five dialects, by approximately 50,000 inhabitants of the eastern canton of Graübunden (or Grisons). The measure enhanced the "national" status accorded by a 1938 referendum, obliging federal authorities to provide services to Romansch speakers in their own language. However, it did not grant Romansch the same "official" status given to German, French, and Italian; the law requires that all federal documents be issued in those languages.

Canton and Capital	Area (sq. mi.)	Population (2005E)
Aargau/Argovie (Aarau)	542	567,000
Appenzell		
Ausserrhoden (Herisau)	94	53,000
Innerrhoden (Appenzell)	66	15,000
Basel/Bâle		
Basel-Land (Liestal)	165	265,000
Basel-Stadt (Basel)	14	186,000
Bern/Berne (Bern)	2,336	957,000
Fribourg (Fribourg)	645	252,000
Genéve/Geneva (Genève)	109	429,000
Glarus (Glarus)	264	38,000
Graübunden/Grisons (Chur)	2,744	187,000
Jura (Delémont)	323	69,000
Luzern/Lucerne (Luzern)	576	355,000
Neuchâtel (Neuchâtel)	308	168,000
St. Gallen/St. Gall (St. Gallen)	778	458,000
Schaffhausen/Schaffhouse (Schaffhausen)	115	74,000
Schwyz (Schwyz)	351	137,000
Solothurn/Soleure (Solothurn)	305	247,000
Thurgau/Thurgovie (Frauenfeld)	391	233,000
Ticino/Tessin (Bellinzona)	1,085	322,000
Unterwalden		
Nidwalden (Stans)	106	40,000
Obwalden (Sarnen)	189	33,000
Uri (Altdorf)	416	35,000
Valais (Sion)	2,018	290,000
Vaud (Lausanne)	1,243	650,000
Zug/Zoug (Zug)	92	106,000
Zürich (Zürich)	667	1,268,000

Foreign Relations

Swiss foreign policy has historically stressed neutrality and scrupulous avoidance of membership in military alliances. In the interest of maintaining that neutrality, Switzerland chose to remain outside the UN through the Cold War era, although it was accredited as a permanent observer to the organization, was a party to the statute of the International Court of Justice, and belonged to many UN specialized agencies. In 1984 both the National Council and the Council of States approved a government proposal that the country apply for UN membership; however, voters overwhelmingly rejected the action in a referendum on March 16, 1986. Switzerland eventually joined the UN in September 2002 following public endorsement in a March 2002 referendum.

By contrast, the electorate readily approved joining the International Monetary Fund (IMF) and World Bank in a referendum of May 17, 1992. The following day the government announced that it would apply for EC membership, having earlier in the month signed a treaty providing for the creation of the EEA between the EC and EFTA. The EEA treaty generated considerable public debate, culminating in a national referendum on December 6, 1992, at which 50.3 percent of those voting (and 16 of 23 cantons) rejected ratification, despite having been urged to vote in favor by three of the four government parties, the centrist opposition parties, employers, trade unions, and the powerful banking sector. Opposing the measure were the smallest government formation, the Swiss People's Party, and an uneasy coalition of ecologists and rightists. The voter turnout of 78.3 percent was the highest for any referendum since 1947; analysis showed that, whereas the French-speaking Swiss voted overwhelmingly in favor of the EEA, German and Italian speakers were decisively against it.

The Swiss government reiterated its goal of joining the EU in its fall 1993 foreign policy report; however, the December 1992 referendum verdict on the EEA and divisions within the ruling coalition prevented any progress from being made in that direction. There was general agreement that Swiss policy should be concentrated on limiting the negative effects of remaining outside the EU/EEA, to which end negotiations were initiated with the European Commission. The government's strategy received a boost on May 1, 1995, when Liechtenstein acceded to the EEA while retaining its 70-year-old economic and monetary union with Switzerland. This meant that Swiss exporters with outlets in Liechtenstein also could benefit from the tariff concessions available under the EEA accord. The federal government continued its legislative program to bring Swiss law into line with EEA/EU practice, although it was hindered by voters' rejection of attempts to ease existing restrictions on foreign ownership of property in Switzerland in a referendum on June 25, 1995. In late 1998, after four years of negotiations, Switzerland completed a trade agreement with the EU; a national referendum endorsed the measure in May 2000. The government has maintained its stance in favor of eventual accession to the EU, although 76.7 percent of voters rejected a referendum proposal to immediately apply for membership on March 4, 2001. Swiss-EU relations soured somewhat after the EU complained in December 2005 that low corporate tax rates in Switzerland violated the terms of their trade agreement. The Swiss government rebuffed the charge as an unjustified attack on Swiss sovereignty.

There were signs in 1995–1996 of a softening in Switzerland's stance of armed neutrality (usually referenced as dating from 1515 but formalized three centuries later by the Congress of Vienna). On June 3, 1996, Flavio COTTI became the first Swiss foreign minister to address a meeting of the North Atlantic Treaty Organization (NATO); the Swiss government appointed a military attaché to an observer role in NATO soon thereafter. Despite opposition from conservative parties, the government announced on October 30 its plans to enter the NATO Partnership for Peace (PfP) program, while stressing that it had no intention of joining NATO itself. The government also pledged that it would abide by the June 1994 referendum decision precluding any armed participation in PfP peacekeeping exercises, although from December 1995 Switzerland had permitted NATO to fly over its territory and use its railways to supply peacekeeping operations in Bosnia. At a referendum held on June 10, 2001, Swiss voters narrowly approved (by 50.9 percent) permitting armed Swiss troops to participate in international peacekeeping missions. The vote also authorized training with NATO forces, although opponents of the proposal argued that Switzerland's traditional neutrality would be jeopardized.

It was officially confirmed on May 22, 1996, that despite signing the Nuclear Non-Proliferation Treaty (NPT) in 1969, Switzerland had in the same year established a federal commission to develop and maintain a capability to construct nuclear weapons. To that end it had kept a stock of nonenriched uranium (acquired in the 1950s) until 1981; the commission was not disbanded until 1988. In confirming this history, government spokesmen contended that Switzerland was now honoring its commitments under the NPT.

Contemporary Swiss foreign policy has been strongly influenced by the principle of "solidarity," which holds that a neutral state is morally obligated to undertake social, economic, and humanitarian activities contributing to world peace and prosperity. Partly for this reason, Switzerland joined the Inter-American Development Bank in July 1976 as a nonregional member and subsequently agreed to convert assorted debts owed by various developing nations into grants.

The international image of Switzerland as a bastion of banking probity and humanitarian values was damaged in 1995–1997, particularly in the United States and Israel, when new developments emerged in the 50-year-old dispute over the assets of Holocaust victims. In late 1996 releases of archival materials in Switzerland and the former Allied countries stimulated domestic and international criticism of Swiss dealings with Nazi Germany and its victims during World War II. The controversy centered on allegations that Swiss banks had knowingly accepted gold from the Nazis that had either been looted from the central banks of occupied countries or plundered from victims of the Holocaust. (U.S. officials argued that Germany had relied heavily on the sale of the gold to prolong its war effort.) Holocaust survivors and their heirs demanded a new investigation into the thousands of long-dormant Swiss bank accounts that they suspected contained Nazi victims' assets.

The Swiss commercial banks initially assumed an extremely conservative position on the inquiries, concentrating solely on dormant accounts for which complete documentation was available. By late 1997 they had identified some 16,000 such accounts, valued at about $54 million. It was agreed that the unclaimed money would be released through an independent panel; the banks also contributed to a government-sponsored voluntary fund of some $200 million that had been established to assist needy elderly survivors of the Holocaust. However, those measures failed to address the central question of looted gold, and pressure intensified on behalf of the plaintiffs in class-action suits against the banks. Much of the international community criticized the Swiss government for its perceived foot-dragging on the issue.

In early 1998 an independent Swiss commission reported that some $450 million in Nazi gold had been received in Switzerland during the war, about 80 percent having been handled by the Swiss Central Bank and the remainder by private banks. (It was estimated that the gold would be valued at about $4 billion in today's market, without interest.) Another commission concluded shortly thereafter that officials of the Central Bank had been aware that some of the gold had come from the Central Banks of countries overrun by the Germans. Now that a degree of Swiss liability had been conclusively established in their minds, Jewish organizations demanded a settlement, without which a number of U.S. states threatened to discontinue their substantial dealings with Swiss financial institutions.

In April the three major Swiss commercial banks reversed themselves and announced they would pursue a "global settlement" of the claims. Some Jewish leaders described their initial offer in June of $600 million as "humiliating," but a $1.25 billion settlement was eventually reached in August. Most of the money (to be paid out in four installments over three years) was to be used to compensate victims (or their families) of the Holocaust for whom specific claims could not be documented—the so-called "rough justice" approach. The Swiss Central Bank notably refused to participate in the settlement, as the government argued that none of its actions as a neutral state during the war had been improper. That position partly reflected the sentiment of a growing segment of the population, which lashed out against the intense international scrutiny. (In November 1998 a government commission reported that the Holocaust debate had drawn attention to a degree of "latent Swiss anti-Semitism," creating "a political crisis concerning Switzerland's self-image.") In February 2001 the government identified the names on 21,000 accounts considered likely owned by Holocaust victims between 1933 and 1945. Some 100,000 claims were expected to be filed for the dormant accounts.

Swiss banks also face international scrutiny on several other fronts: for their role in providing services for apartheid South Africa during the international embargo; for their reluctance to disclose and freeze the money held by former Zairean president Mobutu Sese Seko; for their alleged involvement in money laundering by organized crime syndicates in Russia; and for "serious shortcomings," according to a September 2000 report by the Federal Banking Commission, in accepting an estimated $500 million in deposits from Nigerian dictator Sani Abacha and his family. An investigation into money laundering via Swiss banks by former Argentine President Carlos Menem began in 2003, but the Swiss suspended the investigation in 2004.

Current Issues

A key development in Swiss politics in recent years has been the increased popularity (and electoral success) of the nationalistic right-wing Swiss People's Party (SVP). The party, including Christopher Blocher, who was elected to the Federal Council in December 2003, proffers a populist, anti-immigration, anti-asylum message. The SVP has long been a central player in national politics, with one seat on the Federal Council. However, its ability to achieve the single highest vote totals in the 2003 election (almost 27 percent) led to the acquisition of a second seat. The popularity of the SVP

in some sectors underscores a profound debate taking place in Switzerland over the country's appropriate role in international politics, specifically in Europe. Concerns about the influx of foreigners into Switzerland (who now constitute roughly 20 percent of the population) have taken on increasing political significance as many Swiss fear the loss of what they view as their unique culture.

While Switzerland did take the historical step of joining the UN on March 2, 2002 (by a vote of 54.1 percent), at the same time it demonstrated linguistic cleavages among the population. The French-speaking areas of the country supported the move, while the German-speaking areas generally disagreed. As such, it is not surprising that the SVP draws a great deal of support from German-speakers. This linguistic division eroded in 2003, when the SVP drew much of its support from French-speaking cantons.

The tensions within the populace over these topics are reflected in many recent votes. In November 2002 voters defeated a measure (offered up by the SVP) to restrict the country's asylum laws by a historically thin margin (4,208 votes, or 0.2 percent). However, on September 26, 2004, provisions that would make it easier for foreigners to become Swiss citizens were defeated. A proposal to ease procedures for citizenship for second-generation immigrants failed 56.8 percent to 43.2 percent, and a provision that would have guaranteed Swiss citizenship for third-generation immigrants at birth failed 51.6 percent to 48.4 percent.

However, in a referendum held on June 5, 2005, 54.6 percent of voters agreed to join the Schengen agreement, which provides for closer security cooperation with the EU and allows persons from other Schengen countries (i.e., most of Europe) to enter Switzerland without passports beginning in 2007. It also will allow for the sharing of information among signatories to the agreement, such as whether an asylum-seeker has sought refuge in more than one country. In a separate referendum, held on September 25, 2005, 56 percent of voters approved a government-sponsored proposal to allow citizens of the ten new EU member states to live and work in Switzerland, provided they had jobs and could support themselves.

Another crucial issue in the past several years has been whether Swiss banks would collect taxes on monies deposited in their banks on behalf of the EU. An agreement, 15 years in the making, was installed starting in July 2005 wherein withholding taxes will be extracted from the accounts in question.

Political Parties

The Swiss political scene is characterized by a multiplicity of political parties but is dominated by a four-party coalition that controls the majority of seats in both houses of the Federal Assembly.

Government Parties

Swiss People's Party (*Schweizerische Volkspartei—SVP/Union Démocratique du Centre—UDC/Unione Democratica di Centro—UDC/Partida Populara Svizra—PPS*). Formed in 1971 by a merger of the former Farmers, Artisans, and Citizens' Party with the Democratic Party, the SVP is a populist, right-wing party with strong agrarian and conservative social tendencies, traditionally based in German-speaking cantons. It advocates a strong national defense as well as the protection of agriculture and small industry. The party appeared to be on the wane around 1990, but its electoral fortunes began to reverse in 1991. The SVP was the only government party to participate in the successful popular opposition to the EEA accord in 1992. In 1995 the SVP increased its electoral support to 14.9 percent, yielding 29 lower house seats—a gain of 4 over 1991—and came within 0.08 percent of the first-place SPS (see below) in 1999. Its ability to capture 26.6 percent of the vote in 2003, largely in French-speaking Switzerland, for a plurality (55) of lower house seats led the Swiss government to alter the formula used to assign seats to the Federal Council. The SVP now has 2 seats on the Council, making it one of the four main governing parties.

Leaders: Ueli MAURER (President), Caspar BAADER (Leader of Parliamentary Group), Gregor A. RUTZ (General Secretary).

Social Democratic Party (*Sozialdemokratische Partei der Schweiz—SPS/Parti Socialiste Suisse—PSS/Partito Socialista Svizzero—PSS/Partida Socialdemocrata da la Svizra—PSS*). Frequently referenced as the Socialist Party, the SPS, which organized in 1888, advocates direct federal taxation and a degree of state intervention in the economy. Although it adopted an essentially reformist social democratic program in 1982, the party also has been influenced by the ecologist and feminist movements. In 1984 it came close to withdrawing from the government after its coalition partners rejected a female SPS nominee for the Federal Council; it secured their acceptance of an alternative female candidate in 1993, after a similar crisis. Since 1992 the former *Partito Socialista Unitario* (PSU), now led by Ilario LODI, has operated as an autonomous section of the national party, the *Partito Socialista, Sezione Ticinese del PSS,* in the Italian-speaking canton of Ticino.

In the 2003 lower house election the SPS won 52 seats on a 23.4 percent vote share, making it the second largest in the chamber behind the SVP. It has 9 seats in the upper house and 2 seats on the Federal Council.

Leaders: Hans-Jürg FEHR (President), Hildegard FÄSSLER (Leader of Parliamentary Group), Thomas CHRISTEN (Secretary General).

Radical Democratic Party (*Freisinnig-Demokratische Partei der Schweiz—FDP/Parti Radical-Démocratique Suisse—PRD/Partito Liberale-Radicale Svizzero—PLR*). Leader of the historic movement that gave rise to the federated state, the FDP is liberal in outlook and stands for strong centralized power within the federal structure. As of 2003 the FDP was the third largest party in the lower house, with 14 seats, and the second largest (14) in the upper house, with 2 seats on the Federal Council.

Leaders: Fulvio PELLI (President), Felix GUTZWILLER (Leader of Parliamentary Group), Guido SCHOMMER (General Secretary).

Christian Democratic People's Party (*Christlichdemokratische Volkspartei der Schweiz—CVP/Parti Démocrate-Chrétien Suisse—PDC/*

Partito Popolare Democratico—PPD/Partida Cristiandemocratica dalla Svizra—PCD). The CVP formed in 1912 as the Swiss Conservative Party by elements long opposed to the centralization of national power; it adopted its present name in 1970. Appealing primarily to Catholics, it traditionally advocated cantonal control over religious education and taxes on alcohol and tobacco while opposing direct taxation by the federal government. Its lower house representation had declined gradually since 1979, falling to 28 seats in 2003 on a vote share of 14.4 percent. As a result, the CVP lost 1 of its 2 seats on the Federal Council to the SVP. However, the CVP still holds the largest number of seats (15 out of 46) in the upper house.

Leaders: Doris LEUTHARD (President), Urs SCHWALLER (Leader of Parliamentary Group), Reto NAUSE (General Secretary).

Other Parliamentary Parties

Green Party of Switzerland–The Greens *(Grüne Partei der Schweiz–Die Grüne/Parti Ecologiste Suisse–Les Verts/Partito Ecologista Svizzero–I Verdi/Partida Ecologica Svizra–La Verda).* The Swiss Federation of Green/Ecology Parties was founded in May 1983 by nine groupings, including two that had gained representation at the cantonal level in Zürich and Luzern the previous month and one that had elected an MP in 1979. The Federation obtained 3 seats in the October 1983 *Nationalrat* election and adopted its present name in 1985. The 9 lower house seats won in 1987 grew to 14 in 1991 but fell back to 9 in 1995 when it received only 5 percent of the vote. The party sustained both its vote share and number of seats in the 1999 lower house elections, in which it worked jointly with the **Green Alliance** *(Grüne Bündnis Alliance Verte)*, an ecologist feminist group, which has since merged with The Greens. The party increased its seat share in the lower house to 13 in 2003.

Leaders: Ruth GENNER (President), Louis SCHELBERT (Leader of Parliamentary Group), Hubert ZURKINDEN (General Secretary).

Liberal Party *(Liberale Partei der Schweiz—LPS/Parti Libéral Suisse—PLS/Partito Liberale Svizzero—PLS).* With a program similar to that of the Christian Democratic People's Party, the LPS (formerly the Liberal Democratic Union) draws support primarily from Protestant circles. It favors a loosely federated structure and opposes centralization and socialism. The ten seats obtained by the party at the 1991 *Nationalrat* balloting represented a single-seat increase over 1987. It slipped to seven seats in 1995, with only 2.7 percent of the vote. It lost one more seat in the 1999 lower house elections when it earned 2.2 percent of the vote. The party continued to decline in 2003, winning only four seats (although it did maintain its 2.2 percent of the vote).

Leaders: Claude RUEY (President), Christophe BERDAT (General Secretary).

Evangelical People's Party *(Evangelische Volkspartei der Schweiz—EVP/Parti Evangélique Suisse—PEV/Partito Evangelico Svizzero—PEV).* Established in 1919, the EVP is committed to a program based largely on conservative Protestant precepts. It retained its three existing lower house seats in 1991 and formed a parliamentary group with the Independents' Alliance. In 1995 it slipped to two seats, with 1.8 percent of the vote, and maintained its parliamentary alliance. It increased its lower house representation to three seats in 1999; it maintained this representation in 2003 elections.

Leaders: Ruedi AESCHBACHER (President), Joel BLUNIER (General Secretary).

Federal Democratic Union *(Eidgenössisch-Demokratische Union—EDU/Union Démocratique Fédérale—UDF/Unione Democratica Federale—UDF).* The EDU/UDF is a Protestant fundamentalist, anti-immigration party. It retained its single seat in the 1995 lower house election and again in 1999, when the party got 1.25 percent of the vote. In 2003 a vote share of 1.3 percent garnered two seats for the party.

Leaders: Hans MOSER (President), Peter BONSACK (Vice President).

Swiss Democrats (*Schweizer Demokraten—*SD/*Démocrates Suisses—*DS/*Democratici Svizzeri—*DS). This party emerged in 1961 as the National Action against Foreign Infiltration of People and Homeland (*National Aktion gegen Überfremdung von Volk und Heimat/Action Nationale contre l'Emprise et la Surpopulation Etrangéres*) and as of 1977 was known as the National Action for People and Homeland (*National Aktion für Volk und Heimat—*NA/*Action National—*AN). The SD adopted its present name prior to the 1991 balloting. It has sought to reduce the number of resident foreign workers as well as the number of naturalizations, although both proposals were overwhelmingly defeated in referendums held in October 1974 and March 1977, respectively. On the other hand, a 1981 law relaxing restrictions on foreign workers, against which the NA had campaigned vigorously, was narrowly overturned by a referendum in June 1982. The party secured three *Nationalrat* seats in 1987 and five in 1991, after which it formed a parliamentary group with the Ticino League (below). In 1995 the party's lower house representation fell to three seats on a vote share of 3.1, then to 1.8 percent and one seat in 1999. In 2003 polling, the party won 1.0 percent of the vote and one seat in the lower house.

Leaders: Bernhard HESS (President), Rudolf KELLER.

Swiss Labor Party (*Parti Suisse du Travail—*PST/*Partei der Arbeit der Schweiz—*PdAdS/*Partito Svizzero del Lavoro—*PSdL). Organized in 1921 as the Swiss Communist Party, outlawed in 1940, and reorganized under its present name in 1944, the PST is primarily urban based and has long maintained a pro-Moscow position. In September 1991 the party removed all references to "communism" and "democratic centralism" from its statutes and the following month increased its *Nationalrat* representation from one to three seats. It retained those seats in the 1995 balloting, after which its deputies affiliated to the Social Democratic parliamentary group. In the 1999 lower house elections, the PST gained 0.9 percent of the vote

and won two seats, which it kept in 2003 with 0.7 percent of the vote. The party's Geneva chapter contested the elections under the title **Alliance of the Left** (*Alliance de Gauche—*AdG) along with a radical socialist grouping called **Solidarities** (*Solidarités*).

Leaders: Alain BRINGOLF (President), Anjuska WEIL, Sonia CRIVELLI.

Alternative List (*Alternative Liste—*AL). Josef Lang, an independent from Zug who aligns with The Greens in Parliament, uses this label, which can also be translated as "Alternative Left." At the 2003 election the party won one seat in the lower house.

Solidarities (*Solidarités*). The Solidarities is a leftist party based in French-speaking portions of Switzerland. Founded in 1992, it first ran as a party in 2003, winning one seat with 0.5 percent of the vote. Some tallies count Christian GROBET as a member of the party when he won his seat in 1999, but at the time he ran as an independent.

Christian Social Party (*Christlichsoziale Partei—*CSP/*Parti Chrétien-Social—*PCS/*Partida Cristian-Sociala—*PCS). A small center-left party, the CSP contested several National Council elections without success until it was able to secure one seat in 1995. The party kept that seat with a vote share of 0.4 percent in 1999 and 2003.

Leaders: Monika BLOCH SÜSS (President), Marlies SCHAFER-JUNGO (General Secretary).

Ticino League (*Lega dei Ticinesi*). The Ticino League is a right-wing formation that advocates greater autonomy for the largely Italian-speaking canton of Ticino. It won two lower house seats in the 1991 balloting, after which it formed a parliamentary group with the Swiss Democrats. It held only one seat in 1995, two seats after the 1999 lower house elections, and back down to one in 2003.

Leader: Giuliano BIGNASCA (President).

Other Parties

Freedom Party of Switzerland (*Freiheitspartei der Schweiz—*FPS). Launched in 1985 as the

Federal Council

As of July 1, 2006

President	Moritz Leuenberger (SPS/PSS)
Vice President	Micheline Calmy-Rey (SPS/PSS) [f]
Federal Chancellor	Annemarie Huber-Hotz (FDP) [f]

Department Heads

Defense, Civil Protection, and Sports	Samuel Schmid (SVP/UDC)
Economic Affairs	Doris Leuthard (CVP/PDC)
Environment, Transportation, Communications, and Energy	Moritz Leuenberger (SPS/PSS)
Finance	Hans-Rudolf Merz (FDP/PRD)
Foreign Affairs	Micheline Calmy-Rey (SPS/PSS) [f]
Interior	Pascal Couchepin (FDP/PRD)
Justice and Police	Christoph Blocher (SVP/UDC)

[f] = female

Swiss Automobile Party (*Schweizer Auto-Partei*), a motorists' pressure group based in German-speaking Switzerland, the Freedom Party is still referred to by that name despite adopting its present rubric in 1994. Having secured two *Nationalrat* seats in 1987, in March 1989 the formation won 12 council seats in the canton of Aargau and a month later won seven seats in Solothurn. Its representation at the federal level rose to eight seats in 1991 after it had added an anti-immigration component to its manifesto. It fell back to seven seats in the 1995 balloting on a 4 percent vote share. The lower house elections in 1999 proved disastrous for the FPS, when its vote share fell under 1 percent and it failed to secure representation. In 2003 the party won 0.2 percent of the vote and no seats.

Leaders: Jürg SCHERRER (President), Walter MÜLLER (Secretary).

Independents' Alliance (*Landesring der Unabhängigen*—LdU/*Alliance des Indépendants*—AdI). Organized in 1936 by progressive, middle-class elements, the LdU represents consumers' interests and advocates liberal and social principles.

In 1991 its lower house representation dropped from eight to six seats, and in 1995 it retained only three seats, its vote share falling to 1.8 percent. It won only one seat in 1999 and did not run in 2003.

Minor far-right formations have included the anti-immigrant, Valais-based **Conservative and Liberal Movement** (*Mouvement Conservateur et Libéral*—MCH), launched in 1986; the **National Socialist Party** (*Nationalsozialistische Partei*—NSP), organized in Zürich by a former National Action vice president in 1986; and the Geneva-based **Vigilance Party** (*Parti Vigilance*—PV). Minor center-left parties include the **Humanist Party** (*Humanistische Partei*—HP), a member of the Humanist International.

Minor left-extremist parties have included the **Socialist Workers' Party** (*Sozialistische Arbeiterpartie*—SAP/*Parti Socialiste Ouvriére*—PSO) established in 1969 as the Marxist Revolutionary League (*Marxistische Revolutionäre Liga/ Ligue Marxiste Révolutionnaire*) by dissident Trotskyite members of the PST, and the

Maoist **Communist Party of Switzerland–Marxist-Leninist** (*Kommunistische Partei der Schweiz–Marxistische-Leninistiche/Parti Communiste Suisse–Marxiste-Léniniste*), founded in 1972.

There are also a number of small interest-group parties, including the **Catholic People's Party of Switzerland** (*Katholische Volkspartei Schweit*—KVP) and the following autonomist groupings in the French-speaking Jura region: the **Jura Alliance** (*Alliance Jurassienne*—AJU) and the **Southern Jura Christian Democratic Party** (*Parti Démocrate-Chrétien du Jura-Sud*—PDCJS).

Legislature

The bicameral **Federal Assembly** (*Bundesversammlung/Assemblée Fédérale/Assemblea Federale*) consists of a Council of States elected by the various cantons and a National Council elected by a uniform procedure throughout the country. As a result of this dual system, the Council of States is more conservative than the National Council, which more closely reflects the relative strength of the political parties within the country.

Council of States (*Ständerat/Conseil des Etats/Consiglio degli Stati*). The upper house consists of 46 members, 2 elected from each of the 20 cantons and 1 from each of the 6 half-cantons. Electoral procedures vary from canton to canton, but the majority of them hold direct elections based on the same franchise as for the National Council. Following the elections of October 19, 2003, the Christian Democratic People's Party held 15 seats; the Radical Democratic Party, 14; the Social Democratic Party, 9; and the Swiss People's Party, 8.

President: Rolf BÜTTIKER.

National Council (*Nationalrat/Conseil National/Consiglio Nazionale*). The lower house consists of 200 members elected for four-year terms by direct popular vote within each canton on a proportional representation basis. The seat distribution resulting from balloting on October 19, 2003, was as follows: Swiss People's Party, 55; Social Democratic Party, 52; Radical Democratic Party, 36; Christian Democratic People's Party, 28; Green Party, 13; Liberal Party, 4; Evangelical People's Party, 3; Federal Democratic Union, 2; Swiss Labor Party, 2; Swiss Democrats, 1; Ticino League, 1; Solidarities, 1; Christian Social Party, 1; and Alternative List, 1.

President: Claude JANIAK.

Communications

Press

The Swiss press is privately owned and free from governmental influence, although editors are accustomed to using discretion in handling national security information. The three most widely read German-language newspapers are *20 Minuten* (782,000), *Blick* (Zürich, 736,000), and *Tages-Anzeige* (Zürich, 573,000). The top three French-language newspapers are *Le Matin* (Lausanne, 331,000), *24 Heures* (Lausanne, 245,000), and *Tribune de Genéve* (Geneva, 187,000). In Italian the three leading newspapers are *Corriere del Ticino* (Lugano, 113,000), *La Rgeione Ticino* (94,000), and *Giornale del Popolo* (Lugano, 63,000).

News Agencies

The domestic facility is the Swiss Telegraph Agency (*Schweizerische Depeschenagentur/Agence Télégraphique Suisse*); in addition, numerous foreign agencies maintain bureaus in Geneva.

Broadcasting and Computing

Broadcasting services are primarily funded by licensing fees, with multilingual programming provided by the Swiss Radio and Television Broadcasting Society (*Schweizerische Radio-und Fernsehgesellschaft/Société Suisse de Radiodiffusion et Télévision*). There are over 115 radio stations and 115 television stations in Switzerland. In 2003 there were approximately 4.7 million television receivers in use, and 6.0 million personal computers served 2.6 million Internet users.

Intergovernmental Representation

Ambassador to the U.S.
Urs ZISWILER

U.S. Ambassador to Switzerland
Peter R. CONEWAY

Permanent Representative to the UN
Peter MAURER

IGO Memberships (Non-UN)
ADB, AfDB, BIS, CERN, CEUR, EBRD, EFTA, ESA, Eurocontrol, G-10, IADB, IEA, Interpol, IOM, OECD, OIF, OSCE, PCA, WCO, WTO

TURKEY

REPUBLIC OF TURKEY

Türkiye Cumhuriyeti

The Country

Guardian of the narrow straits between the Mediterranean and Black seas, present-day Turkey occupies the compact land mass of the Anatolian Peninsula together with the partially European city of İstanbul and its Thracian hinterland. The country, which borders on Greece, Bulgaria, Georgia, Armenia, the Nakhichevan Autonomous Republic of Azerbaijan, Iran, Iraq, and Syria, has a varied topography and is subject to extreme variation in climate. It supports a largely Turkish population (more than 80 percent, in terms of language) but has a substantial Kurdish minority of approximately 12 million, plus such smaller groups as Arabs, Circassians, Greeks, Armenians, Georgians, Lazes, and Jews. Some 98 percent of the populace, including both Turks and Kurds, adheres to the Islamic faith, which maintains a strong position despite the secular emphasis of government policy since the 1920s. Sunni Muslims constitute a substantial majority, but between 10 and 20 percent of the population belong to the Alevi (Alawi) sect of Islam.

Women constitute approximately 36 percent of the official labor force, with large numbers serving as unpaid workers on family farms. While only 10 percent of the urban labor force is female, there is extensive participation by upper-income women in such professions as medicine, law, banking, and education, with the government being headed by a female prime minister during 1993–1995.

Turkey traditionally has been an agricultural country, with about 50 percent of the population still engaged in agricultural pursuits, yet the con-tribution of industry to GDP now exceeds that of agriculture (24.9 and 11.8 percent, respectively, in 2004). Grain (most importantly wheat), tobacco, cotton, nuts, fruits, and olive oil are the chief agricultural products; sheep and cattle are raised on the Anatolian plateau, and the country ranks among the leading producers of mohair. Natural resources include chrome, copper, iron ore, manganese, bauxite, borax, and petroleum. The most important industries are textiles, iron and steel, sugar, food processing, cement, paper, and fertilizer. State economic enterprises (SEEs) account for more than 60 percent of fixed investment, although substantial privatization has recently been decreed.

Political Status: Independent republic established in 1923; parliamentary democracy since 1946, save for military interregna from May 1960 to October 1961 and September 1980 to November 1983; present constitution approved by referendum of November 7, 1982.

Area: 300,948 sq. mi. (779,452 sq. km.).

Population: 67,803,927 (2000C); 72,031,000 (2005E).

Major Urban Centers (2005E): ANKARA (3,587,000), İstanbul (9,770,000), İzmir (2,498,000), Bursa (1,411,000), Adana (1,247,000).

Official Language: Turkish. A 1982 law banning the use of the Kurdish language was rescinded in early 1991.

Monetary Unit: Turkish New Lira (market rate July 1, 2006: 1.59 new liras = $1US).

President of the Republic: Ahmet Necdet SEZER (nonparty); elected by the Grand National Assembly on May 5, 2000, and sworn in for a seven-year term on May 16 to succeed Süleyman DEMİREL (True Path Party).

Prime Minister: Recep Tayyip ERDOGAN (Justice and Development Party—AKP) invited by the president on March 11, 2003, to form a new government, following general elections on November 3, 2002.

Economic growth during the 1960s was substantial but not enough to overcome severe balance-of-payments and inflation problems, which intensified following the oil price increases of 1973–1974. By 1975 the cost of petroleum imports had more than quadrupled and was absorbing nearly two-thirds of export earnings. A major devaluation of the lira in mid-1979 failed to resolve the country's economic difficulties, and in early 1980, with inflation exceeding 100 percent, a $1.16 billion loan package was negotiated with the Organization for Economic Cooperation and Development (OECD), followed in June by $1.65 billion in credits from the International Monetary Fund (IMF). Subsequently, aided by improving export performance and a tight curb on foreign currency transactions, the economy reg-

istered substantial recovery, with inflation being reduced to a still unsatisfactory level of 39 percent in 1987, before returning to 70 percent in 1989. High inflation rates plagued Turkey throughout the 1990s, reaching 99 percent by 1997. An economic stabilization program introduced in 1997 brought the rate down to 55 percent in 1998.

Although annual inflation had been lowered to about 35 percent in 2000 and solid GNP growth (estimated at over 6 percent) had been reestablished, a financial crisis erupted in late February 2001, forcing a currency devaluation and other intervention measures. In April 2001 the government announced it anticipated 3 percent economic contraction for the year. Among other things, resolution of the economic problems was considered a prerequisite to Turkey's long-standing goal of accession to the European Union (EU) (see Foreign relations, below, for details). The IMF approved a $15.7 billion "rescue package" in May 2001 and endorsed up to $10 billion in additional aid in November after the government pledged to intensify its efforts to reorganize the banking sector, improve tax collection, combat corruption, promote foreign investment, and accelerate the privatization program. Consequently, the government narrowly avoided defaulting on its debt repayments, much to the relief of Western capitals for whom Turkey represents a geographic, political, and military linchpin amid the turbulence of the Middle East.

Turkey has weathered the financial crises of 2000–2001 and, thanks in part to conditions imposed by an agreement with the IMF, the economy is stabilizing. Indeed, inflation was down to 12 percent during 2004, and some analysts say the real inflation rate was below 10 percent. The government set a target of 8 percent inflation for 2005. At the same time, the country's real Gross Domestic Product (GDP) grew by 8 percent in 2002 and 6 percent in 2003, and was projected to grow 5 percent in 2004.

Observers give much of the credit for Turkey's improved economic performance to tighter fiscal policies as well as to reform of the financial sector, including especially the creation of an independent

Banking Regulation and Supervision Agency, re-capitalization of the state banks, and tighter auditing procedures. After its 2004 consultations with Turkey, however, the IMF has cautioned that Turkey's economy is still vulnerable. In particular, the IMF has frowned upon recent government-backed increases in wages, which it feared would fuel inflation. And the IMF has called specifically for reform of the social security system, which has large deficits, and called on the government to refrain from large increases in public spending. On April 12, 2005, Turkey and the IMF reached agreement on a $10 billion loan conditioned upon recent and continuing economic reforms.

In April 2006, parliament finally approved a long-sought social-security reform bill that raises the retirement age to 65 and deters abuse of the pension system through "double dipping" by those who retire to qualify for a pension only to then return to work. Despite this important act of belt tightening, and despite the economy being on track for 5 percent growth in 2006, the IMF warned Turkey in May 2006 that the country needed to further rein in government spending.

Government and Politics

Political Background

Present-day Turkey is the surviving core of a vast empire created by Ottoman rule in late medieval and early modern times. After a period of expansion during the 15th and 16th centuries in which Ottoman domination was extended over much of central Europe, the Balkans, the Middle East, and North Africa, the empire underwent a lengthy period of contraction and fragmentation, finally dissolving in the aftermath of a disastrous alliance with Germany in World War I.

A secular nationalist republic was proclaimed in October 1923 by Mustafa Kemal ATATÜRK, who launched a reform program under which Turkey abandoned much of its Ottoman and Islamic heritage. Its major components included secularization (separation of religion and state), establishment of state control of the economy, and

creation of a new Turkish consciousness. Following his death in 1938, Atatürk's Republican People's Party (*Cumhuriyet Halk Partisi*—CHP) continued as the only legally recognized party under his close associate, İsmet İNÖNÜ. One-party domination was not seriously contested until after World War II, when the opposition Democratic Party (*Demokrat Parti*—DP) was established by Celal BAYAR, Adnan MENDERES, and others.

Winning the country's first free election in 1950, the DP ruled Turkey for the next decade, only to be ousted in 1960 by a military coup led by Gen. Cemal GÜRSEL. The coup was a response to alleged corruption within the DP and the growing authoritarian attitudes of its leaders. Many of those so charged, including President Bayar and Prime Minister Menderes, were tried and found guilty of violating the constitution, as a result of which Bayar was imprisoned and Menderes executed.

Civilian government was restored under a new constitution in 1961, with Gürsel remaining as president until his incapacitation and replacement by Gen. Cevdet SUNAY in 1966. The 1961 basic law established a series of checks and balances to offset a concentration of power in the executive and prompted a diffusion of parliamentary seats among several parties. A series of coalition governments, most of them led by İnönü, functioned until 1965, when a partial reincarnation of the DP, Süleyman DEMİREL's Justice Party (*Adalet Partisi*—AP), won a sweeping legislative mandate.

Despite its victory in 1965, the Demirel regime soon became the target of popular discontent and demands for basic reform. Although surviving the election of 1969, it was subsequently caught between left-wing agitation and military insistence on the maintenance of public order, a critical issue because of mounting economic and social unrest and the growth of political terrorism. The crisis came to a head in 1971 with an ultimatum from the military that resulted in Demirel's resignation and the formation of a "nonparty" government by Nihat ERİM, amendment of the 1961 constitution, the declaration of martial law in eleven provinces, the arrest of dissident elements, and the outlawing of the left-wing Turkish Labor Party (*Türkiye İşçi*

Partisi—TİP) and moderate Islamist National Order Party (*Millî Nizam Partisi*—MNP). The period immediately after the fall of the Erim government in 1972 witnessed another "nonparty" administration under Ferit MELEN and the selection of a new president, Adm. (Ret.) Fahri KORUTÜRK. Political instability was heightened further by an inconclusive election in 1973 and by both foreign and domestic policy problems stemming from a rapidly deteriorating economy, substantial urban population growth, and renewed conflict on Cyprus that yielded Turkish intervention in the summer of 1974.

Bülent ECEVİT was appointed prime minister in January 1974, heading a coalition of his own moderately progressive CHP and the smaller, religiously oriented National Salvation Party (*Millî Selâmet Partisi*—MSP). Although securing widespread domestic acclaim for the Cyprus action and for his insistence that the island be formally divided into Greek and Turkish federal regions, Ecevit was opposed by Deputy Prime Minister Necmettin ERBAKAN, who called for outright annexation of the Turkish sector and, along with his MSP colleagues, resigned, precipitating Ecevit's own resignation in September. Both Ecevit and former prime minister Demirel having failed to form new governments, Sadi IRMAK, an independent, was designated prime minister on November 17, heading an essentially nonparliamentary cabinet. Following a defeat in the National Assembly only twelve days later, Irmak also was forced to resign, although he remained in office in a caretaker capacity until Demirel succeeded in forming a Nationalist Front coalition government on April 12, 1975.

At an early general election on June 5, 1977, no party succeeded in gaining a lower house majority, and the Demirel government fell on July 13. Following Ecevit's inability to organize a majority coalition, Demirel returned as head of a tripartite administration that failed to survive a nonconfidence vote on December 31. Ecevit thereupon formed a minority government.

Widespread civil and political unrest throughout 1978 prompted a declaration of martial law in 13 provinces on December 25. The security situation deteriorated further during 1979, and, faced with a number of ministerial defections, Prime Minister Ecevit was on October 16 again obliged to step down, with Demirel returning as head of an AP minority government on November 12.

Divided by rising foreign debt and increasing domestic terrorism, the National Assembly failed in over 100 ballots to elect a successor to Fahri Korutürk as president of the Republic. Senate President İhsan Sabri ÇAĞLAYANGİL assumed the office on an acting basis at the expiration of Korutürk's seven-year term on April 6. On August 29 Gen. Kenan EVREN, chief of the General Staff, publicly criticized the assembly for its failure both to elect a new president and to promulgate more drastic security legislation, and on September 12 he mounted a coup on behalf of a five-man National Security Council (NSC) that suspended the constitution, dissolved the assembly, proclaimed martial law in all of the country's 67 provinces, and on September 21 designated a military-civilian cabinet under Adm. (Ret.) Bülent ULUSU. The junta banned all existing political parties; detained many of their leaders, including Ecevit and Demirel; imposed strict censorship; and arrested upwards of 40,000 persons on political charges.

In a national referendum on November 7, 1982, Turkish voters overwhelmingly approved a new constitution, under which General Evren was formally designated as president of the Republic for a seven-year term. One year later, on November 6, 1983, the recently established Motherland Party (*Anavatan Partisi*—ANAP) of former deputy prime minister Turgut ÖZAL won a majority of seats in a newly constituted, unicameral Grand National Assembly. Following the election, General Evren's four colleagues on the NSC resigned their military commands, continuing as members of a Presidential Council upon dissolution of the NSC on December 6. On December 7 Özal was asked to form a government and assumed office as prime minister on December 13.

Confronted with a governing style that was viewed as increasingly arrogant and ineffective in combating inflation, Turkish voters dealt Prime

Minister Özal a stinging rebuke at local elections on March 26, 1989. ANAP candidates ran a poor third overall, securing only 22 percent of the vote and losing control of the three largest cities. Özal refused, however, to call for new legislative balloting and, despite a plunge in personal popularity to 28 percent, utilized his assembly majority on October 31 to secure the presidency in succession to Evren. Following his inauguration at a parliamentary ceremony on November 9 that was boycotted by opposition members, Özal announced his choice of Assembly Speaker Yıldırım AKBULUT as the new prime minister.

Motherland's standing in the opinion polls slipped to a minuscule 14 percent in the wake of a political crisis that erupted in April 1991 over the somewhat heavy-handed installation of the president's wife, Semra ÖZAL, as chair of the ruling party's İstanbul branch. Both Özals declared their neutrality in a leadership contest at a party congress in mid-June, but they were viewed as the principal architects of an unprecedented rebuke to Prime Minister Akbulut, who was defeated for reelection as chair by former foreign minister Mesut YILMAZ.

Yılmaz called for an early election on October 20, 1991, "to refresh the people's confidence" in his government. The outcome, however, was a defeat for the ruling party, with former prime minister Demirel, now leader of the right-of-center True Path Party (*Doğru Yol Partisi*—DYP), negotiating a coalition with the left-of-center Social Democratic People's Party (*Sosyal Demokrat Halkçı Parti*—SHP) and returning to office for the seventh time on November 21, with the SHP's Erdal İNÖNÜ as his deputy.

Demirel's broad-based administration, which brought together the heirs of Turkey's two oldest and most prominent political traditions (the CHP and the DP), claimed greater popularity—50 percent voter support and more than 60 percent backing in the polls–than any government in recent decades. Thus encouraged, Demirel and İnönü launched an ambitious program to counter the problems of rampant inflation, Kurdish insurgency, and obstacles to full democratization.

On April 17, 1993, President Özal died of a heart attack, and on May 16 the Grand National Assembly elected Prime Minister Demirel head of state. The DYP's search for a new chairperson ended on June 13, when Tansu ÇİLLER, an economics professor, defeated two other candidates at an extraordinary party congress. On July 5 a new DYP-SHP coalition government, committed to a program of further democratization, secularization, and privatization, was accorded a vote of confidence by the assembly, and Çiller became Turkey's first female prime minister.

A major offensive against guerrillas of the Kurdistan Workers' Party (*Partîya Karkerén Kurdistan*—PKK) in northern Iraq was launched on March 20, 1995. Six weeks later the government announced that the operation had been a success and that all of its units had returned to Turkey. The popularity of the action was demonstrated at local elections on June 4, when the ruling DYP took 22 of 36 mayoralties on a 39 percent share of the vote. However, on September 20 a revived CHP, which had become the DYP's junior coalition partner after absorbing the SHP in February, withdrew its support, forcing the resignation of the Çiller government.

On October 2, 1995, Çiller announced the formation of a DYP minority administration that drew unlikely backing from the far-right Nationalist Action Party (*Milliyetçi Hareket Partisi*—MHP) and the center-left Democratic Left Party (*Demokratik Sol Parti*—DSP). However, the prime minister was opposed within the DYP by former National Assembly speaker Hüsamettin CİNDORUK, who resigned on October 1 and was one of ten deputies expelled from the party on October 16, one day after Çiller's defeat on a confidence motion. On October 31 President Demirel appointed Çiller to head a DYP-CHP interim government pending a premature election in December.

At the December 24, 1995, balloting the pro-Islamic Welfare Party (*Refah Partisi*—RP) emerged as the legislative leader, although its 158 seats fell far short of the 276 needed for an overall majority. Eventually, on February 28, 1996, agreement was reached on a center-right coalition that would permit the ANAP's Yılmaz to serve as prime minister until January 1, 1997, with Çiller occupying the post for the ensuing two years and Yılmaz returning for the balance of the parliamentary term, assuming no dissolution.

Formally launched on March 12, 1996, the ANAP-DYP coalition collapsed at the end of May amid renewed personal animosity between Yılmaz and Çiller over the former's unwillingness to back the DYP leader against corruption charges related to her recent premiership. The DYP then opted to become the junior partner in an alternative coalition headed by RP leader Necmettin ERBAKAN, who on June 28 became Turkey's first avowedly Islamist prime minister since the creation of the secular republic in 1923. Under the coalition agreement, Çiller was slated to take over as head of government in January 1998. However, the military reportedly feared that Erbakan's tolerance for rising religious activism would seriously threaten the country's secular tradition, and, after months of pressure from the military, Erbakan resigned on June 18, 1997, with the hope that a new government under the leadership of his coalition partner, Çiller, would bring the paralyzed government back to life. However, on June 20 President Demirel bypassed Çiller, whose DYP had been weakened by steady defections, and selected the ANAP's Yılmaz to return as next prime minister. A new coalition composed of the ANAP, the DSP, and the new center-right Democratic Turkey Party (*Demokrat Türkiye Partisi*—DTP) was approved by Demirel on June 30, and Yılmaz and his cabinet were sworn in the following day.

The new coalition government tried to reverse the Islamic influence of its predecessor and in July 1997 proposed an eight-year compulsory education plan that included the closure of Islamic secondary schools, prompting weeks of right-wing and militant Islamic demonstrations.

The Yılmaz government collapsed on November 25, 1998, when he lost a vote of confidence in the Grand National Assembly following accusations of corruption against members of his cabinet. President Demirel asked Bülent Ecevit to form a new government on December 2, thereby aban-

doning the long-standing tradition of designating the leader of the largest party in the legislature as prime minister. (Such action would have put Recai KUTAN's moderate Islamist Virtue Party [*Fazilet Partisi*—FP] in power, an option opposed by the military.) When Ecevit proved unable to form a government, Demirel turned to an independent, Yalım EREZ, who also failed when former prime minister Çiller rejected his proposal that her DYP be part of a new coalition. After Erez abandoned his initiative on January 6, 1999, President Demirel reinvited Ecevit to form the government. This time Ecevit succeeded in forming a minority cabinet made up of the DSP and independents; the DYP and ANAP agreed to provide external support.

Ecevit's cabinet survived a crisis that erupted in mid-March 1999, when the FP threatened to topple the government and joined forces with disgruntled members of parliament from various political parties who were not nominated for reelection. At balloting on April 18, 1999, Ecevit's DSP received 22 percent of the votes and became the largest party in the assembly with 136 seats. On May 28 Ecevit announced the formation of a coalition cabinet comprising the DSP, MHP, and ANAP. Meanwhile, on May 16 Ahmet Necdet SEZER, chief justice of the Constitutional Court, had been sworn in as the new president following the legislature's rejection of President Demirel's request for constitutional revision that would have permitted him a second term.

In October 2001, the Grand National Assembly approved several constitutional amendments aimed at easing Turkey's path into the EU. The changes provided greater protection for political freedom and civil leaders, including protection for the Kurdish minority. Also, the number of civilians on the National Security Council was increased from five to nine, with the military continuing to hold five seats.

In January 2002, the Constitutional Court banned AKP leader Recep Tayyip ERDOGAN from running for the legislature because of alleged seditious activities. The court also ordered the party to remove Erdogan from party leadership.

In July 2002, Prime Minister Ecevit was forced to call early elections to the Grand National Assembly as a result of resignations causing the DSP-led coalition to lose its majority in the legislature. The general election on November 3, 2002, was a disaster for the ruling DSP. The largest winner was the AKP, which attracted 34.3 percent of the vote and 363 seats in the Grand National Assembly. The only other party to exceed 10 percent of the vote and win seats in the legislature was the CHP, which won 19.4 percent of the vote and 178 seats. The DSP won only 1.2 percent of the vote.

Because Erdogan was prohibited from holding a seat in the Grand National Assembly, AKP deputy leader Abdullah GÜL was appointed prime minister, though Erdogan reportedly acted as de facto prime minister. With its strong numbers in the Grand National Assembly, the AKP was able to enact constitutional reforms allowing Erdogan to become prime minister. Erdogan was elected to the Grand National Assembly on March 9 and was appointed prime minister on March 11. Under AKP leadership, the Grand National Assembly adopted further reforms aimed at eventual accession to the EU, including legislation allowing broadcasting and education in Kurdish. Another piece of legislation would have allowed peaceful advocacy of an independent Kurdish state. This measure was vetoed by President Sezur only to be made law when the Grand National Assembly overrode the veto.

In March 2003, Turkey's Constitutional Court banned the People's Democracy Party (HADEP) from politics as a result of its alleged support for the PKK. In addition, 46 party members were individually banned from politics for five years.

In August 2003, for the first time, a civilian assumed control of the National Security Council. This event followed amendments to the constitution earlier in the year that reduced the number of seats reserved for the military in the council. Another sign of the waning power of the military in Turkey was the fact that, for the first time since the republic was founded in 1923, public spending on education ($6.7 billion) exceeded that spent on defense ($5.6 billion) in 2004.

The AKP further solidified its position with a strong showing in local elections on March 28, 2004, winning 42 percent of the vote. The CHP had the second-best showing, but won only 18 percent of the vote.

Constitution and Government

The 1982 constitution provided for a unicameral, 400-member Grand National Assembly elected for a five-year term, (the membership being increased to 450 in 1987 and 550 in 1995). The president, elected by the assembly for a nonrenewable seven-year term, is empowered to appoint and dismiss the prime minister and other cabinet members; to dissolve the assembly and call for a new election, assuming the concurrence of two-thirds of the deputies or if faced with a government crisis of more than 30 days' duration; to declare a state of emergency, during which the government may rule by decree; and to appoint a variety of leading government officials, including senior judges and the governor of the Central Bank. Political parties may be formed if they are not ethnic- or class-based, linked to trade unions, or committed to communism, fascism, or religious fundamentalism. Strikes that exceed 60 days' duration are subject to compulsory arbitration.

The Turkish judicial system is headed by a Court of Cassation, which is the court of final appeal. Other judicial bodies include an administrative tribunal styled the Council of State, a Constitutional Court, a Court of Accounts, various military courts, and twelve state security courts.

The country is presently divided into 80 provinces, which are further divided into sub-provinces and districts. Mayors and municipal councils have long been popularly elected, save during the period 1980–1984.

Foreign Relations

Neutral until the closing months of World War II, Turkey entered that conflict in time to become a founding member of the United Nations and has since joined all of the latter's affiliated agencies. Concern for the protection of its independence, primarily against possible Soviet threats, made Turkey a firm ally of the Western powers with one of the largest standing armies in the non-Communist world. Largely on US initiative, Turkey was admitted to the North Atlantic Treaty Organization (NATO) in 1952 and in 1955 became a founding member of the Baghdad Treaty Organization, later the Central Treaty Organization (CENTO), which was officially disbanded in September 1979 following Iranian and Pakistani withdrawal.

Relations with a number of Western governments cooled in the 1960s, partly because of a lack of support for Turkey's position on the question of Cyprus. The dispute, with the fate of the Turkish Cypriot community at its center, became critical upon the island's attaining independence in 1960 and nearly led to war with Greece in 1967. The situation assumed major international importance in 1974 following the Greek officers' coup that resulted in the temporary ouster of Cypriot President Makarios, and the subsequent Turkish military intervention on July 20 that yielded Turkish occupation of the northern third of the island (for details see articles on Cyprus and Cyprus: Turkish Sector).

Relations with the United States, severely strained by a congressional ban on military aid following the Cyprus incursion, were strained further by a Turkish decision in July 1975 to repudiate a 1969 defense cooperation agreement and force the closure of 25 US military installations. However, a new accord was concluded in March 1976 that called for reopening of the bases under Turkish rather than dual control, coupled with substantially increased U.S. military assistance. The U.S. arms embargo was finally lifted in September 1978, with the stipulation that Turkey continue to seek a negotiated resolution of the Cyprus issue.

While the Turkish government under Evren and Özal consistently affirmed its support of NATO and its desire to gain full entry to the EC (having been an associate member of the European Economic Community since 1964), relations with Western Europe deteriorated in the wake of the 1980 coup because of alleged human rights violations.

Ankara submitted a formal membership request to the EC, and in December 1989 the EC Commission laid down a number of stringent conditions for admission to the community, including an improved human rights record, progress toward improved relations with Greece, and less dependence on agricultural employment. Because of these concerns, Turkey remained outside the EU upon the latter's inception in November 1993, although, in an action viewed as linked to its EC bid, it had become an associate member of the Western European Union in 1992.

On March 6, 1995, Turkey and the EU agreed to a customs union, which entered into force January 1, 1996. However, in July 1997 the EU Commission included five East European states but excluded Turkey from among those invited to join first-round enlargement negotiations scheduled for early 1998. Moreover, the commission recommended Cyprus for full membership, a decision that was controversial given the lack of a settlement between Turkey and Greece over the Cyprus question. The United States and the EU subsequently assured both sides that Cyprus would not be accepted into the EU until a settlement was reached. In light of improving Turkish/Greek relations, a December 1999 EU summit finally accepted Turkey as an official candidate for membership.

Apart from Cyprus, the principal dispute between Greece and Turkey has centered on territorial rights in the Aegean. In late 1984 Ankara vetoed a proposal by Greek prime minister Papandreou to assign Greek forces on Lemnos to NATO, invoking a long-standing contention that militarization of the island was forbidden under the 1923 Treaty of Lausanne. The controversy revived in early 1989 with Turkey refusing to recognize insular sea and airspace limits greater than six miles on the premise that to do otherwise would convert the area into a "Greek lake." The dispute intensified in September 1994, with Greece declaring that it would formally extend its jurisdiction to 12 nautical miles upon entry into force of the UN Convention on the Law of the Sea on November 16. Turkey immediately warned that the move would be considered an "act of aggression," and on October 30 Athens announced that it would defer the introduction of what it continued to view as a "sovereign right."

In October 1984 an agreement was concluded with Iraq that permitted security forces of each government to pursue "subversive groups" (interpreted primarily as Kurdish rebels) up to a distance of five kilometers on either side of the border and to engage in follow-up operations for five days without prior notification. The hot pursuit agreement notwithstanding, the Turkish government strongly supported UN-endorsed sanctions against Iraq in the wake of its invasion of Kuwait in August 1990. Despite considerable revenue loss, Turkey moved quickly to shut down Iraqi oil pipelines by banning ships from loading crude at offshore terminals. In September, despite opposition criticism, the legislature granted the administration special authority to dispatch troops to the Gulf and to allow foreign forces to be stationed on Turkish soil for non-NATO purposes (most importantly, the stationing of F-111 fighter bombers at İncirlik air base to monitor the UN-sanctioned Iraqi no-fly zone north of the 36th parallel).

In 1994 Ankara angered Moscow by seeking to impose restrictions on shipping through the Bosphorus. The issue was highly charged because of the 1936 Montreaux treaty, which provided complete freedom of transit through both the Bosphorus and Dardanelles during peacetime. Turkey insisted that the new regulations (including the prohibition of automatic pilots for navigation and limitations on dangerous cargo) were prompted only by technical considerations that had not existed at the time of the treaty's adoption.

During 1992 Turkey faced a dilemma in regard to the conflict in Bosnia and Herzegovina. Both the Bosnians and Turkish citizens of Bosnian descent appealed for action to oppose Serbian advances in Muslim areas; however, Atatürk's secularist heirs were reluctant to move in a manner that might be seen as religiously inspired. Deeply opposed to unilateral action, Turkey launched a pro-Bosnian campaign in various international venues, including the UN, the Conference on (subsequently the Organization for) Security and Cooperation in Europe (CSCE/OSCE), NATO, the Council of Europe, and the OIC. Throughout, it urged limited military intervention by the UN and the lifting of the arms embargo for Bosnia should existing sanctions and diplomatic efforts prove ineffective.

The military action launched by Turkey against the Kurds in northern Iraq on March 20, 1995, was condemned by most West European governments. On April 10 the EU foreign ministers, while acknowledging Turkey's "terrorism problems," called on Ankara to withdraw its troops "without delay," and on April 26 the Parliamentary Assembly of the Council of Europe approved a resolution calling for suspension of Turkey's membership if it did not leave Iraq by late June. For its part, the Turkish government reacted angrily to an announcement on April 12 that political exiles had established a Kurdish "parliament in exile" in the Netherlands, and a renewed cross-border offensive was launched by some 30,000 troops on July 5–10. In any event, no action was taken to suspend Turkey's Council of Europe membership, despite further vigorous Turkish action against the Kurdish insurgency. In July 1997 Turkey and the Democratic Party of Kurdistan (DPK) reached a preliminary agreement to boost security in northern Iraq. However, in August Turkish warplanes crossed the Iraqi border to bomb PKK rebel bases, drawing the condemnation of Baghdad.

A major diplomatic dispute erupted in 1998 over Syria's alleged sheltering of PKK rebels, Ankara warning Damascus in October of possible military action unless Syrian policy changed. The crisis was also colored by Syria's concern over the recent rapprochement between Turkey and Israel, which had produced a defense agreement and a recent visit by Prime Minister Yılmaz to Israel. Following intense mediation by several Arab leaders from the region, Syria subsequently agreed that it would not allow the PKK to set up "military, logistical, or financial bases" on Syrian territory. Collaterally, PKK leader Abdullah ÖCALAN was forced to leave Syrian-controlled territory in Lebanon. Öcalan moved to Russia, which, under intense Turkish pressure, also refused him asylum. He then entered Italy, prompting a row between Rome and Ankara. Italy rejected Turkey's extradition request on the grounds that it could not send a detainee to a country that permitted the death penalty. Italy therefore attempted to negotiate Öcalan's transfer to Germany, where he also faced terrorism charges. However, Bonn, apparently fearing violence between its own Turkish and Kurdish minorities, declined to file an extradition request. Consequently, Öcalan was released from detention in Italy in mid-December and reportedly left that country in January 1999 for an unknown destination.

In mid-February 1999 Öcalan was arrested by Turkish security forces shortly after he had left the home of the Greek ambassador in Nairobi, Kenya. The incident proved to be highly embarrassing for the government in Athens. Despite the renewed animosity surrounding Öcalan's arrest, Turkish/Greek relations thawed noticeably in late 1999 when Greece lifted its veto on EU financial aid earmarked to Turkey and accepted a carefully worded agreement that permitted the EU to accept Turkey as a candidate for membership. In early 2000 the two countries agreed to establish a joint commission to "reduce military tensions" in the Aegean and to pursue cooperation in several other areas.

In 2003, Turkey's relationship with the United States faced a major challenge with Turkey's refusal to allow US troops to use Turkish territory as a staging area for the invasion of Iraq in March 2003. Some observers attributed this refusal, which was an embarrassment to the Turkish government and military, to a political power struggle taking place within Turkey. While the governing Justice and Development Party (AKP) was in favor of such cooperation, many nationalistic members of the Grand National Assembly, including some AKP members, were not. Relations with the United States have also been strained over what the Turkish government has seen as a lack of concern with Kurdish terrorist activity in Turkey and northern Iraq. Indeed, in November 2004, Turkish newspapers published unconfirmed reports that the Turkish government had formulated a plan to move 20,000 Turkish troops into northern Iraq to prevent Kurds from taking complete control of Kirkuk. On January 26, 2005, a senior Turkish army general said bluntly that the Turkish military was prepared to intervene if clashes erupted in northern Iraq or if Iraqi Kurds attempted to form an independent state.

Iran and Turkey signed a security agreement on July 30, 2004, to place rebels opposed to either government on each government's list of terrorist organizations.

Relations with Russia have also been further strained by Turkey's ongoing efforts to control the passage of oil tankers through the Bosphorus straits. Turkey says that the increased number of oil tankers represents an environmental threat to Turkey's coastline and waterways. Turkey has imposed tighter regulations on passage, which Russia claims have added greatly to transit time and, accordingly, to costs. In August 2004, Turkey also proposed, and offered to help fund, construction of pipelines to reduce waterborne traffic. Apart from the issue of the Bosphorus strait, however, Turkish relations with Russia have been generally good. Tourism between the two countries has jumped to around $1 billion a year and bilateral commerce has grown to about $6.5 billion.

Iraq resurfaced as a contentious issue between Turkey and the United States in July 2006, when Turkey again called on the United States to crack down on Kurdish rebels based in northern Iraq and made veiled threats to attack rebel bases if steps were not taken against the rebels.

Turkey's relations with the EU also grew more contentious in 2006. When the EU in October 2004 agreed to move forward with negotiations leading to Turkey's accession to the union, it also placed two unusual conditions on the talks. First, the EU Commission stressed that the talks would be open ended and with no guarantee of eventual membership. Secondly, the commission recommended that the negotiations, which could take up to ten years in any case, should be suspended if Turkey is seen to backtrack on reforms. Some observers saw these conditions as providing an opportunity for member countries—some of which are already nervous about Islamic extremism in their own countries—to back out of the arrangement. Nevertheless, on December 17, 2004, Prime Minister Erdogan formally accepted the offer of the EU to proceed with accession talks.

Even as Turkey's bid to join the EU is under consideration, charges that the country is backtracking on its commitment to required social and economic reforms have come to the forefront. On July 14, after the indictment of one author and the confirmation of another's conviction on charges of insulting the government, Olli Rehn, the European official supervising membership talks, warned that the Turkish courts were failing to comply with EU standards. Indeed, according to the Turkish Publishers' Association, 47 writers are being prosecuted on charges that include insulting Atatürk, the founder of modern Turkey, and "inciting racial hatred."

EU representatives have also cited Turkey's failure to open air and sea connections with the Greek sector of Cyprus as a major hurdle to membership. "It is obvious to me Turkey must respect the obligations it has entered into to allow goods coming from Cyprus access to its ports," French president Jacques Chirac told a news conference on July 16. "If it didn't, it would be putting in doubt its capacity" to pursue EU membership. Turkish prime minister Erdogan was apparently unfazed. "So long as the Turkish Cypriots remain isolated, we will not open our ports and airports" to people from Cyprus's Greek zone, Erdogan explained to reporters. "If the negotiations halt, then let them halt," Erdogan said.

On a broader level, the World Bank advised Turkey in March 2006 that it would need to do a better job of getting women into the workforce and children into schools if it wanted to improve its chances of joining the EU.

Current Issues

Three intertwined issues have dominated politics in Turkey over the past several years: accession to the EU, a significant rise in nationalist and Islamist sentiments among the populace, and the continuing Kurdish insurgency in the southeast part of the country.

While the Turkish government, along with the majority of Turks, is in favor of joining the EU, the reforms required before Turkey would be allowed to join are seen by some as interference in Turkish affairs. Nevertheless, since 2001 the Grand National Assembly has enacted a number of reforms aimed at easing the path to joining the EU. In October 2001, the legislature approved constitutional amendments aimed at broadening civil liberties and human rights. In November, legislation granting equal status to women in certain areas was passed. In February 2002, the legislature revoked a law allowing schoolgirls to be forced to undergo "virginity tests." In August 2002, the Grand National Assembly abolished the death penalty in peacetime. And on September 26, 2004, the Turkish parliament approved major revisions to the penal code, specifically aimed at bringing the code in line with those prevalent in the EU. A further reform of the penal code in June 2005 provided greater protections for women and children and imposed harsher penalties for torture and "honor" killings.

In 2005 and 2006, however, European officials have charged Turkey's government with backtracking on some reforms and slowing down implementation of others. European officials, along with some Turks, have also been concerned about the growing tensions between Islamic and secular forces inside Turkey.

While the Erdogan government has been trying to reassure Europe that it is a secular country intent on reform, some domestic moves by the government have generated concern within Turkey—and particularly within the military—that Prime Minister Erdogan, a devout Muslim, is intent on bringing Islamic values into government. The AKP's greatest support is seen by most observers as coming from middle-class, conservative Muslims. Prime Minister Erdogan generated controversy with his proposal in May 2004 to give Islamic schools equal standing with the public schools with respect to gaining admission to secular universities. The proposal—which critics described as a thinly disguised effort to promote religious schools and Islamic law—caused some university rectors to threaten to resign and opposition members of parliament to walk out on hearings in protest.

Most recently, in early March 2006, tensions between Islamic and secular forces were evident in the events surrounding the eventual veto by President

Ahmet Necdet Sezer of the government's nominee for central bank governor. There was speculation that the government of Prime Minister Erdogan nominated Adnan BUYUKDENIZ, an economist and executive at an Islamic-style bank (neither paying nor charging interest), in part because of his religious convictions. In any event, the issue highlighted the distrust between the presidency, judiciary, and the military on the one hand and the government on the other hand.

The rift was also evident in May 2006 following the murder of a senior judge by gunmen who shouted Islamic slogans. Some indications linked the murder to a recent decision upholding a ban on the wearing of traditional Muslim headscarves in public institutions. Prime Minister Erdogan subsequently declined to attend the judge's funeral, which generated further controversy and spurred calls by opposition parties for early elections.

Recent years have also seen a resurgence of domestic unrest. In November 2003 a suicide bombing outside of two of İstanbul's largest synagogues killed 25 people and injured 300 people. Later in the month, suicide bombers attacked the Hong Kong and Shanghai Banking Corporation and the British Embassy, killing 31 people and injuring more than 450. These attacks were attributed to domestic Islamic extremists with possible ties to al-Qaida. Violence from the Kurdish insurgency has also been increasing over the past several years. In September 2003, the Kurdish rebel group PKK announced that it was ending its cease-fire, adopted five years previously, with the Turkish government. In a September 2004 offensive, the largest in five years, government troops killed 11 Kurdish rebels in the southeast province of Hakkari. The government blamed Kurdish rebels for a series of bombings—including two hotel bombings and the bombing of a pop concert—in August and September. The numbers of roadside bombings in the southeastern part of the country have also increased. While the Kurdish population remains generally loyal to the PKK, many Kurds have started to question the rebels' tactics, particularly since government reforms aimed at EU membership have resulted in a steady improvement in rights and protections for Kurds.

As the Erdogan government has shown more reticence in implementing reforms in 2005 and 2006, however, protests in the Kurdish sectors of the southeast have increased. Indeed, widespread protests in April 2006 resulted in the deaths of seven Kurds.

Turkey was also challenged in 2005 with the arrival of bird flu. The government came under criticism for failing to detect the virus in the eastern part of the country for several weeks, allowing it to spread to the point where it may be impossible to contain. By January 2006, at least 15 cases of bird flu had been detected in humans, and the government had destroyed hundreds of thousands of birds in an effort to contain the virus.

Political Parties

Turkey's multiparty system developed gradually out of the monopoly originally exercised by the historic Republican People's Party (*Cumhuriyet Halk Partisi*—CHP), which ruled the country without serious competition until 1950 and which, under Bülent Ecevit, was most recently in power from January 1978 to October 1979. The Democratic Party (*Demokrat Parti*—DP) of Celal Bayar and Adnan Menderes, founded by CHP dissidents in 1946, came to power in 1950, maintained control for the next decade, but was outlawed in consequence of the military coup of 1960, many of its members subsequently entering the conservative Justice Party (*Adalet Partisi*—AP). Other formations included an Islamic group, the National Salvation Party (*Millî Selâmet Partisi*—MSP); the ultra-rightist Nationalist Action Party (*Milliyetçi Hareket Partisi*—MHP); and the leftist Turkish Labor Party (*Türkiye İşçi Partisi*—TİP). All party activity was banned by the National Security Council on September 12, 1980, while the parties themselves were formally dissolved and their assets liquidated on October 16, 1981.

Approval of the 1982 constitution ruled out any immediate likelihood that anything resembling the earlier party system would reappear. In order to qualify for the 1983 parliamentary election, new parties were required to obtain the signatures of at least 30 founding members, subject to veto by the National Security Council (NSC). Most such lists were rejected by the NSC, with only three groups (the Motherland, Populist, and Nationalist Democracy parties) being formally registered for the balloting on November 6 in an apparent effort to promote the emergence of a two-party system. Of the three, only the ruling Motherland Party remained by mid-1986: the Populist Party merged with the Social Democratic Party in November 1985 to form the Social Democratic People's Party (see under CHP, below), while the center-right Nationalist Democracy Party (*Milliyetçi Demokrasi Partisi*—MDP) dissolved itself in May 1986.

In July 1992 the government lifted bans on all of the parties closed during the military interregnum and by mid-1996 their number had risen to over 30, distributed almost equally to the right and left of the political spectrum.

Government Party

Justice and Development Party (*Adalet ve Kalkinma Partisi*—AKP). The AKP was launched in August 2001 by the reformist wing of the FP (see below) as a moderate religious, center-right formation. Out of the former parliamentarians from the FP and other parties, 53 later joined the AKP, making it the second-largest opposition party in the assembly (after the DYP). Some analysts noted that the AKP might prove to be a strong challenger to the coalition parties in the next legislative elections.

In January 2002 the Constitutional Court ruled that AKP president Recep Tayyip Erdogan was ineligible to run for office due to his imprisonment in 1999 on charges of having "incited hatred on religious grounds." In November 2002 elections, the AKP won 34.2 percent of the vote and 363 legislative seats. Abdullah Gül formed his government on November 18, 2002. Erdogan's ineligibility for office was removed when the Turkish Grand National Assembly changed select articles of the Constitution. Erdogan was elected an MP at by-elections on March 9, 2003, and formed his government on March 14, 2003. (AKP's legislative seats went down to 357 by July 2005.)

The party revealed some cracks in its solidarity in February 2005 with the resignation from the government and the party of Erkan MUMCU, the minister for tourism and culture. Mumcu, a liberal and secular member considered a rising star in the party, indicated he was resigning because he felt he could no longer influence government decisions.

Leaders: Recep Tayyip ERDOGAN (President), Idris Naim ŞAHIN (Secretary General).

Opposition Parties

Republican People's Party (*Cumhuriyet Halk Partisi*—CHP). The CHP is a left-of-center party founded in 1923 by Kemal Atatürk. It was dissolved in 1981 and reactivated in 1992 by 21 MPs who resigned from the Social Democratic People's Party (*Sosyal Demokrat Halkçı Parti*—SHP) to reclaim the group's historic legacy. The CHP absorbed the SHP on February 18, 1995.

A member of the Socialist International, the SHP had been formed in November 1985 by merger of the Populist Party (*Halkçı Parti*—HP), a center-left formation that secured 117 seats in the 1983 Grand National Assembly election, and the Social Democratic Party (*Sosyal Demokrat Parti*—SODEP), which was not permitted to offer candidates for the 1983 balloting. A left-of-center grouping that drew much of its support from former members of the CHP, SODEP had participated in the 1984 local elections, winning 10 provincial capitals. The SHP was runner-up to ANAP in November 1987, winning 99 assembly seats despite the defection in December 1986 of 20 of its deputies, most of whom joined the DSP. Its parliamentary representation was reduced to 82 upon formation of the People's Labor Party, whose candidates were, however, entered on SHP lists for the 1991 campaign. Subsequently, 18 of those so elected withdrew from the SHP, reducing its representation to 70.

On September 20, 1995, former CHP chair Deniz Baykal, who had been succeeded by the SHP's Hikmet CETIN at the time of the February merger, was reelected to his earlier post.

Immediately thereafter he withdrew the party from the government coalition, thereby forcing Tansu Çiller's resignation as prime minister. In the resultant December election the CHP fell back to 49 seats on a 10.7 percent vote share. Baykal's CHP gave outside support to the Yilmaz-led ANAP-DSP-DTP coalition government of June 1998. However, amid accusations of corruption against various ministers, the CHP's call for a vote of no confidence against the Yılmaz cabinet brought the coalition down in November 1998. The CHP failed to surpass the 10 percent threshold in the April 18, 1999, elections, securing only 8.5 percent of the vote, and was therefore left out of the assembly. Baykal resigned from his chair's post on April 22. The CHP elected famous journalist and former tourism minister Altan ÖYMEN as its new leader on May 23; however, Baykal regained the post at an extraordinary congress in October 2000, defeating Öymen and two other minor candidates. The CHP's ranks were strengthened in 2002 by defections from the DSP.

In the November 2002 elections the CHP won 19.3 percent of the vote and 178 legislative seats, thus becoming the main opposition party. In October 2004 the New Turkey Party (*Yeni Türkiye Partisi*—YTP) merged with the CHP. YTP had been launched in July 2002 by former DSP cabinet ministers, legislators and members including Ismail Cem, former cabinet minister. TP had scored poorly (1.1 percent) in the November 2002 elections. In January 2005, Baykal's presidency was challenged at a highly explosive CHP Party Congress by Mustafa SARIGÜL, the highly popular mayor of the İstanbul district of Şişli, who eventually lost his bid but vowed to continue his opposition. A few pro-Sarigül legislators left the party following the congress to join the SHP (see below). By mid-2005, CHP was ridden with internal turmoil, with numerous dissidents (including legislators) resigning from the party and charging Baykal with "single-person authoritarian rule." CHP's legislative seats were down to 154 by mid-2005.

Leaders: Deniz BAYKAL (President), Önder SAV (Secretary General).

Motherland Party (*Anavatan Partisi—* ANAP). The right-of-center ANAP supports the growth of private enterprise and closer links to the Islamic world as well as the EU. It won an absolute majority of assembly seats in 1983 and at the local elections of March 1984 obtained control of municipal councils in 55 of the country's 67 provincial capitals. Its ranks having been augmented by most former deputies of the Free Democratic Party (*Hür Demokrat Parti*—HDP), which was formed by a number of independents in May 1986 but dissolved the following December, ANAP won a commanding majority of 292 seats at the election of November 1987. Following the poll, Prime Minister Özal announced that he would seek a merger of ANAP and the DYP to ensure a right-wing majority of sufficient magnitude to secure constitutional amendments without resort to referendums. However, the overture was rebuffed, with DYP leader Demirel describing Özal in September 1988 as an "incompetent man" who represented "a calamity for the nation."

Following Özal's inauguration to the technically nonpartisan post of president of the Republic in November 1989, Yıldırım AKBULUT was named prime minister and party president. Upon his ouster in June 1991 he was succeeded by former foreign minister Mesut Yılmaz. At the early legislative balloting of October 20 ANAP trailed the DYP by only 3 percentage points (24 to 27), but its representation plummeted to 115, leading to the collapse of the Yılmaz administration.

ANAP was runner-up to the RP with a 19.7 vote share at the legislative poll of December 24, 1995, although placing third in representation with a seat total of 132. After considerable delay, it entered into a coalition with the DYP whereby Yılmaz would serve as prime minister for the remainder of 1996, with former prime minister Çiller slated to succeed him for a two-year period on January 1, 1997, Yılmaz had less than three months as head of government, being forced to resign in early June after the DYP had withdrawn from the coalition. ANAP then went into opposition to an RP-DYP coalition, amid much acrimony with its erstwhile government partner. Yılmaz was appointed to form a new cabinet on June 20, 1997, following RP Prime Minister Erbakan's resignation under military pressure two days earlier. Yılmaz's ANAP-DSP-DTP coalition government lasted only five months, however, after which ANAP gave parliamentary support to the Ecevit-led DSP government.

At the elections of April 18, 1999, ANAP fared poorly, securing only 13 percent of the votes and 86 seats. Although the party became a junior partner in the subsequent Ecevit-led government, ANAP's image was subsequently tarnished by press allegations of corruption among some of its members.

ANAP suffered a major electoral defeat in November 2002 and received 5.1 percent of the vote and no legislative seats. Mesut Yılmaz resigned on November 4, 2002, and the party underwent a prolonged and deep crisis. Following the short-lived presidencies of Ali Talip Özdemir and Nesrin Nas, former AKP legislator and minister of Culture and Tourism, Erkan Mumcu became the party's president in April 2005. After being joined by legislators defecting from AKP and CHP, the party had, by mid-2005, 21 legislative seats.

Leaders: Erkan MUMCU (President), Muharrem DOĞAN (Secretary General).

True Path Party (*Doğru Yol Partisi*—DYP). The center-right DYP was organized as a successor to the Grand Turkey Party (*Büyük Türkiye Partisi*—BTP), which was banned shortly after its formation in May 1983 because of links to the former Justice Party of Süleyman Demirel. The new group was permitted to participate in the local elections of March 1984 but won control in none of the provincial capitals. By early 1987, augmented by assemblymen of the recently dissolved Citizen Party (*Vatandaş Partisi*—VP), it had become the third-ranked party in the Grand National Assembly. The DYP remained in third place by winning 59 seats at the November 1987 balloting and became the plurality party, with 178 seats, in October 1991. In November it formed a coalition government under Demirel with the SHP (see under CHP). A second DYP-SHP government was formed by the new DYP leader, Tansu Çiller, following Demirel's assumption of the presidency in May 1993. A new

coalition was formed with the CHP in March 1995, following the latter's absorption of the SHP. However, a CHP leadership change in September led to the party's withdrawal and the collapse of the Çiller government.

The DYP placed second in the December 1995 election (with 19.2 percent of the vote), eventually forming a coalition government with ANAP on March 12, 1996, that featured a "rotating" leadership under which the ANAP's Mesut Yılmaz became prime minister and Çiller was to return to the top post in January 1997. However, animosity between the DYP and ANAP leaders quickly resurfaced, with Çiller calling the prime minister a "sleazeball" (for allegedly expediting press exposés of her questionable use of official funds as prime minister) and withdrawing the DYP's support for the coalition in late May. Overcoming its previous antipathy toward the RP, the DYP the following month entered a new coalition as junior partner of the Islamist party, with Çiller becoming deputy premier and foreign minister, pending a scheduled resumption of the premiership at the beginning of 1998. By mid-January 1997 a parliamentary inquiry had cleared the DYP leader of all corruption charges relating to her tenure as premier. After the DYP-RP coalition collapsed under intense pressure from the military and the secular political establishment in June 1997, the DYP remained in the opposition during the Yılmaz-led ANAP-DSP-DTP coalition. By backing CHP leader Deniz Baykal's proposal for a vote of no-confidence against the Yılmaz government, the DYP facilitated its collapse in November 1998. The DYP then gave outside support to Bülent Ecevit's minority government. The DYP fared badly in the April 1999 elections, securing only 12 percent of the votes and 85 seats.

The DYP experienced a major electoral defeat in November 2002, and received 9.5 percent of the vote and no legislative seats. This defeat prompted Tansu Çiller to resign following the election. Independent legislator and a former hard-line and controversial director of security (national police) Mehmet Ağar was elected president of the party in December 2004. With defections from other parties, the party had, by mid-2005, four legislative seats.

Leaders: Mehmet AĞAR (President), Kamil TURAN (Secretary General).

Social-Democrat People's Party (*Sosyaldemokrat Halk Partisi*—SHP). Launched by former Deputy Prime Minister Murat Karayalçin in hopes of reclaiming the historical legacy of an earlier formation of a similar name, SHP did not contest the November 2002 elections. SHP was later joined by former CHP legislators who had left the party in protest of Deniz Baykal's reelection as the president over challenger Mustafa Sarigül (see above, under CHP). With these additions, by mid-2005, SHP had four legislative seats.

Leaders: Murat KARAYALÇIN (President), Ahmet Güryüz KETENCI (Secretary General).

Party of the People's Rise (*Halkin Yiikselişi Partisi*—HYP). The centrist HYP was established in February 2005 by Yaşar Nuri ÖZTÜRK, a former scholar of Islamic theology who became popular with his "reformist" and modernist interpretations of religion, and a former CHP legislator who had left his party in April 2004 to protest Deniz Baykal's leadership style. Currently Öztürk is the only legislator of the HYP.

Leaders: Yaşar Nuri ÖZTÜRK (President), Yücel AKSOY (Secretary General).

Other Parties

Democratic Left Party (*Demokratik Sol Parti*—DSP). Formation of the DSP, a center-left populist formation, was announced in March 1984 by Rahşan Ecevit, the wife of former prime minister Bülent Ecevit, who was barred from political activity prior to the constitutional referendum of September 1987. At the October 1991 election the party attracted sufficient social democratic support to weaken the SHP (see under CHP, below), although winning only seven seats. It recovered in the December 1995 balloting, winning 76 legislative seats with 14.6 percent of the vote. The DSP became a junior partner in a Mesut Yılmaz-led coalition government that also included the DTP (below), on June 30, 1998. After the Yılmaz-led

coalition government collapsed in November 1998, Ecevit formed a minority government on January 12, 1999, that ruled the country until the early elections of April 18. The DSP became the largest party at that balloting with 22 percent of the votes and 136 seats, and Ecevit subsequently formed a DSP-MHP-ANAP coalition cabinet.

In 2002 the DSP reportedly was riddled with internal dissent, some prominent members resigning to form the TDP in January and the YTP in July. The DSP suffered a major electoral defeat in November 2002, receiving only 1.2 percent of the vote and no legislative seats. Bülent Ecevit resigned leadership of the party and nominated Zeki Sezer, a former cabinet minister, to replace him. Sezer was elected to the position at the party's congress in July 2004.

Leaders: Zeki SEZER (President), Ahmet TAN (Secretary General).

Nationalist Action Party (*Milliyetçi Hareket Partisi*—MHP). Until 1969 the ultranationalist MHP was known as the Republican Peasant Nation Party (*Cumhuriyetçi Köylü Millet Partisi*—CKMP), formed in 1948 by conservative dissidents from the old Democratic Party. Dissolved in 1953, the grouping reformed in 1954, merging with the Turkish Villager Party in 1961 and sustaining the secession of the Nation Party in 1962.

The MHP dissolved following the 1980 military coup; in 1983 its sympathizers regrouped as the Conservative Party (*Muhafazakar Parti*—MP), which then was renamed the Nationalist Labor Party (*Milliyetçi Çalişma Partisi*—MCP) in 1985. (The MHP rubric was reassumed in 1992.) The MHP's extremist youth wing, members of which were known as the Grey Wolves (*Bozkurtlar*), remained proscribed, although similar activities were reportedly carried out under semi-official youth clubs. Holding 17 legislative seats as of September 1995, the MHP's 8.18 percent vote share on December 24 was short of the 10 percent required for continued representation. However, it subsequently acquired two seats from defections.

Historic MHP leader Alparslan TÜRKES died in 1998; following the election of Devlet Bahçeli as the new MHP president, members close to Türkeş's son and wife left the party to form the ATP and UBP.

The MHP won surprising support in the election of April 1999, gathering 18 percent of the votes and gaining 129 assembly seats. Some analysts noted that the party's popular support faded during its years in the coalition government between 1999–2002. Indeed, MHP suffered a major electoral blow in November 2002 when it received only 8.3 percent of the vote and no legislative seats. Although following the election, Devlet Bahçeli initially announced he would step down from his leadership position, he ran for and won the party's presidency again in October 2003.

Leaders: Devlet BAHÇELI (President), M. Cihan PAÇACI (Secretary General).

Felicity Party (*Saadet Partisi*—SP). The SP was formed in July 2001 by the traditionalist core of the Virtue Party (*Fazilet Partisi*—FP), which had been shut down by the constitutional court in June. The Virtue Party had been launched in February 1998 days before a constitutional court decision banned the Islamic-oriented Welfare Party (which was in the coalition government until June 18, 1997) on charges of undermining the secular foundations of the Turkish Republic.

The Welfare Party (*Refah Partisi*—RP) had been organized in 1983 by former members of the Islamic fundamentalist MSP. It participated in the 1984 local elections, winning one provincial capital. It failed to secure assembly representation in 1987.

Having absorbed Aydin MENDERES' faction of the Democrat Party (DP), the RP attained a plurality in the December 1995 election with 21.4 percent of the vote but at that stage was unable to recruit allies for a government. However, the speedy collapse of an alternative administration brought the RP to office for the first time in June 1996, heading a coalition with the DYP. Under intense pressure from the military and secular political establishment, Prime Minister Necmettin ERBAKAN resigned on June 18, 1997, and the RP-DYP coali-

tion failed. On February 22, 1998, the Constitutional Court banned the RP and barred some of its founders, including Erbakan, from political activity for five years.

Some 135 parliamentarians of the proscribed Welfare Party joined the FP, making it the main opposition party in the parliament. Although FP leaders denied their party was a successor to the RP, Turkey's secularists did not find the denial credible. The FP assumed the role of the main opposition party to both the Yılmaz-led ANAP-DSP-DTP coalition government that ended in November 1998 and to the Ecevit-led minority DSP government that was installed in January 1999. Although some analysts initially saw the FP as a likely winner of the general elections in April, the party secured only 15 percent of the votes and 111 seats. Recai Kutan was narrowly reelected as FP chair at the party congress in May 2000, fending off a challenge from a "reformist" wing led by Recep Tayyip ERDOGAN (former mayor of Istanbul) and Abdullah GÜL, which then broke away to launch its own formation, the Justice and Development Party (*Adalet ve Kalkinma Partisi*—AKP) in August 2001 following the banning of the FP in June.

Further weakened by legislative defections and a marked shift of popular support to AKP (see above), FP received an electoral setback in November 2002, winning only 2.5 percent of the vote and no legislative seats.

Leaders: Recai KUTAN (President), Suat PAMUKÇU (Secretary General).

Party of Liberty and Change (*Hürriyet ve Değişim Partisi*—HÜRPARTI). In May 2005, the Democratic Turkey Party (*Demokrat Türkiye Partisi*—DTP) decided to change its name to the Party of Liberty and Change.

The DTP was launched in January 1997 by a group of prominent members of the DYP opposed to the leadership of Tansu Çiller. They included former interior minister İsmet SEZGIN, who had been a close supporter of former DYP leader Suleyman Demirel. The DTP entered the ANAP-led coalition government on June 30, 1998, having secured representation in the assembly in 1997 through defections from the DYP. The DTP assumed an opposition party role after the Yılmaz-led ANAP-DSP-DTP government collapsed in November 1998. The party fared poorly in the April 18, 1999, elections securing less than 1 percent of the votes. In June 2002 a former diplomat, Mehmet Ali BAYAR, was elected to the presidency of the DTP.

In June 2005, Yaşar Okuyan was elected the president of HÜRPARTI.

Leader: Yaşar OKUYAN (President).

Great Unity Party (*Büyük Birlik Partisi—*BP). A nationalist Islamic grouping, the BBP was launched in 1993 by a member of dissident MCP parliamentarians prior to the reactivation of the MHP in 1992. The party, whose members are known as "Turkish-Islamic Idealists" (*Türk-Islam Ülkücüleri*), returned 13 deputies on the ANAP ticket in the 1995 election but subsequently opted for separate parliamentary status. The BBP won only 1.5 percent of the votes in the general election of April 1999. In November 2002, the party received 1.1 percent of the vole and no legislative seats.

Leader: Muhsin YAZICIOĞLU (President).

Democratic Society Party (*Demokratik Toplum Partisi—*DTP). Formerly known as the Democratic People's Party (*Demokratik Halk Partisi—*DEHAP), which was launched in January 1999 by former members of HADEP (People's Democracy Party–*Halkin Demokrasi Partisi*), the Pro-Kurdish DTP was initiated by former legislators Leyla ZANA, Orhan DOĞAN, Hatip DİCLE and Selim SADAK who had joined the Democracy Party (*Demokrasi Partisi—*DEP) in 1994. The Turkish Grand National Assembly had lifted the parliamentary immunity of those four Kurdish politicians and they were arrested and jailed between 1994–2005. Based on concerns that DEHAP would be banned by the Constitutional Court, DTP was launched reportedly as a preemptive "successor" in November 9, 2005. Since its launching, all DEHAP mayors, members and leaders entered the DTP. While DEHAP decided to dissolve itself in December 2005, the Constitutional Court continued with the process of banning the party and started to convene on the case on July 13, 2006.

Leaders: Ahmet TÜRK, Aysel TUĞLUK (Co-presidents).

Party of Nation (*Millet Partisi—*MP). Descended from the original MP, the present party is a more immediate outgrowth of the Reformist Democratic Party (*Islahatçi Demokrasi Partisi—*IDP), a relatively ineffectual right-wing formation that displayed ideological affinities with both the RP and MÇP. Its parliamentary deputies, technically sitting as independents after the 1991 election, readopted the MP name in 1992. It won no seats in 1995 or in 1999. In November 2002, the party won 0.22 percent of the vote and no legislative seats.

Leader: Aykut EDİBALİ (President).

Party of Liberty and Solidarity (*Özgurhik ve Dayantsma Partisi—*ÖDP). Backed by many leftist intellectuals, feminists and human rights activists, the ODP was launched after the December 1995 election as a broad alliance of various socialist factions together with elements of the once powerful Dev-Yol movement (see Extremist Groups, below). Some of the socialist groups, notably the United Socialist Party (*Birleşik Sosyalist Parti—*BSP), had contested the balloting as part of the HADEP bloc. The BSP had been formed as a merger of various socialist factions, including the Socialist Unity Party (*Sosyalist Birlik Partisi—*SBP), itself founded in February 1991 (and represented in the 1991–1995 assembly) as in large part successor to the United Communist Party of Turkey (*Türkiye Birlesik Komünist Partisi—*TBKP), led by Haydar KUTLU and Nihat SARGIN.

The TBKP had been formed in 1988 by merger of the Turkish Communist Party (*Türkiye Komünist Partisi—*TKP) and the Turkish Labor Party (*Türkiye İşçi Partisi—*TİP). Proscribed since 1925, the pro-Soviet TKP had long maintained its headquarters in Eastern Europe, staffed largely by exiles and refugees who left Turkey in the 1930s and 1940s. Although remaining illegal, its activities within Turkey revived in 1983, including the reported convening of its first congress in more than 50 years. The TİP, whose longtime leader, Behice BORAN, died in October 1987, had been formally dissolved in 1971 and again in 1980, but had endorsed the merger at a congress held on the first anniversary of Boran's death. Prior to the November 1987 election the TKP and TİP general secretaries, Kutlu and Sargin, respectively, had returned to Turkey for the prospective merger but had been promptly arrested and imprisoned.

Until early 1990, with the Constitutional Court subsequently confirming a ban on the TBKP. Former TBKP elements were prominent in the new ÖDP. The ÖDP fared poorly in the April 1999 elections, gaining less than 1 percent of the votes. Several constituent groups reportedly left the ÖDP in 2002. In November 2002, the party won 0.34 percent of the vote and no legislative seats.

Leader: Hayri KOZANOGLU (President).

Communist Party of Turkey (*Türkiye Komünist Partisi*—TICP). The TKP was launched in November 2001 as a merger of the Party for Socialist Power (*Sosyalist Iktidar Partisi*—SIP), and the Communist Party (*Komünist Partisi*—KP). The SIP was a continuation of the banned Party of Socialist Turkey (*Sosyalist Türkiye Partisi*—STP). The hard-line Marxist-Leninist SIP contested the 1995 election under the HADEP rubric. It secured less than 1 percent of the vote in 1999. The KP was formed in July 2000 by former SIP members. In November 2002, the party won 0.2 percent of the vote and no legislative seats.

Leaders: Aydemir GÜLER (President), Kemal OKUYAN (Vice President).

Workers' Party (*İşçi Partisi*—IP). The Maoist-inspired IP, founded in 1992, is the successor of the Socialist Party (*Sosyalist Parti*—SP), which was launched in February 1988 as the first overtly socialist formation since the 1980 coup. The party called for Turkey's withdrawal from NATO and nationalization of the economy. The SP was deregistered by order of the Constitutional Court in June 1992, the IP securing less than 0.5 percent of the vote in 1995. Since 2000 the IP, self-described as "national leftist," has garnered public attention due to its staunchly anti-EU stance.

In November 2002, the party received 0.5 percent of the vote and no legislative seats.

Leader: Doğu PERİNÇEK (President).

Other nonparliamentary centrist and rightist groups include the **Liberal Democrat Party** (*Liberal Demokrat Parti*—LDP), a free-market grouping led by Cem TOKER; the **Young Party** (*Genç Parti*—GP), led by controversial media magnate Cem UZAN; the **Party for Independent Turkey** (*Bağımsız Türkiye Partisi*—BTP), led by Haydar BAŞ; and the **Justice Party** (*Adalet Partisi*—AP), which claims to be the legitimate heir of the historic AP. The extreme-right-wing **Party of Luminous Turkey** (*Aydınlık Türkiye Partisi*—ATP), led by Tuğrul TÜRKEŞ, reportedly competes to attract former MHP dissidents. Among other parties are **My Turkey Party** (*Türkiyem Partisi*), led by Durmuş Ali EKER; and the **Party of Land** (*Yurt Partisi*—YP), an ANAP breakaway formation led by former minister Sadettin TANTAN.

The **Revolutionary Socialist Workers' Party** (*Devrimci Sosyalist İşçi Partisi*—DSİP), led by Doğan TARKAN and Ahmet YILDIRIM; the **Turkish Socialist Workers' Party** (*Türkiye Sosyalist İşçi Partisi*—TSİP), led by Mehmet SÜMBÜL; and the **Socialist Democracy Party** (*Sosyalist Demokrasi Partisi*—SDP), a breakaway formation from ÖDP (above), led by Filiz Koçali, are all minor Marxist formations. In late 2001 another pro-Kurdish formation, the **Party of Rights and Liberties** (*Hakve Özgürlükler Partisi*—HAKPAR) was launched by Abdülmerik FIRAT. Other minor center-left formations include the **Equality Party** (*Eşitlik Partisi*); the **Party for Independent Republic** (*Bağımsız Cumhuriyet Partisi*), led by former Foreign Minister Mümtaz SOYSAL; the **Social Democrat Party** (*Sosyal Demokrat Parti*); the **Republican Democracy Party** (*Cumhuriyetçi Demokrasi Partisi*—CDP), led by Yekta Güngör ÖZDEN; and the **Social-Democrat People's Party** (*Sosyaldemokrat Halk Partisi*—SHP), launched by former Deputy Prime

Minister Murat KARAYALÇIN in the hopes of reclaiming the historical legacy of an earlier formation of a similar name (see SHP, above).

Extremist Groups

Pre-1980 extremist and terrorist groups included the leftist **Revolutionary Path** (*Devrimci Yol*—Dev-Yol) and its more radical offshoot, the **Revolutionary Left** (Dev-Sol, below), both derived from the **Revolutionary Youth** (*Dev Genç*), which operated in the late 1960s and early 1970s; some of its members also joined the far leftist **Turkish People's Salvation Army** (*Türkiye Halk Kurtuluş Ordusu*—THKO). The **Turkish People's Liberation Party Front** (*Türkiye Halk Kurtuluş Partisi-Cephesi*—THKP-C), the **Turkish Workers' and Peasants' Liberation Army** (*Türkiye İşçi Köylü Kurtuluş Ordusu*—TİKKO, below), and the **Kurdistan Workers' Party** (PKK, below) all experienced numerous arrests—often leading to executions—of members. In addition, Armenian guerrilla units, composed almost entirely of nonnationals, variously operated as the Secret Army for the Liberation of Armenia (Asala), including a so-called Orly Group; the Justice Commandos for the Armenian Genocide; the Pierre Gulmian Commando; the Levon Ekmekçiyan Suicide Commando; and the Armenian Revolutionary Army. The activities of many of these groups have subsided, notable exceptions being Dev-Sol and the PKK.

Revolutionary Left (*Devrimci Sol*—Dev-Sol). Organized in 1978, Dev-Sol appeared to have retained its organizational vitality after the 1980 crackdown, although many of its subsequent activities took the form of interfactional struggle. Its founder, Dursun KARATAŞ, who had been given a death sentence in absentia that was later commuted to life imprisonment, was arrested by French authorities on September 9, 1994; subsequently, the group claimed responsibility for the murder on September 29 of a hard-line former justice minister, Mehmet TOPAÇ.

In 1993 or earlier Dev-Sol apparently split into two factions, the "Karataş" and the "Yağan"

wings, with the former emerging in March 1994 as the **Revolutionary People's Liberation Party-Front** (*Devrimci Halk Kurtuluş Partisi-Cephesi*—DHKP-C). Violent clashes between the two factions have been reported in a number of European countries, and in August 1998 Germany banned both. DHKP-C militants were active in organizing the hunger strikes and prison riots since December 2000.

Kurdistan Workers' Party (*Partîya Karkerén Kurdistan*—PKK). Founded in 1978, the PKK, under the leadership of Abdullah (Apo) Öcalan, was for a long time based principally in Lebanon's Bekaa Valley and northern Iraq. In southeast Anatolia, where it continues to maintain a presence, the party's 1992 call for a general uprising on March 21, the Kurdish New Year (Nevruz), was generally unheeded. Subsequently, a unilateral cease-fire declared by Öcalan under pressure from northern Iraq Kurdish leaders proved short-lived, and PKK terrorism re-escalated. In late July 1994 Turkish warplanes reportedly completely destroyed a PKK base in northern Iraq, and in mid-August a London court convicted three separatists of a number of attacks on Turkish property in the United Kingdom. Öcalan thereupon reiterated his call for a cease-fire as a prelude to the adoption of constitutional reforms that would acknowledge the "Kurdish identity." The government again failed to respond and in September charged the PKK with responsibility for the killing of a number of Turkish teachers in the southeastern province of Tunceli. Government military offensives against the Kurdish insurgents in 1995–1996 were combined with efforts to eradicate the PKK party organization.

Through 1997 and 1998 extensive Turkish military operations seriously undermined the PKK's ground forces. On April 13, 1998, the PKK's second-highest ranking commander, Şemdin SAKIK, who had left the organization a month earlier, was captured in northern Iraq by Turkish security forces. But the major blow to the organization was without doubt Party Chair Öcalan's arrest by Turkish commandos in Nairobi, Kenya (see under Foreign relations, and Current issues, above), in February 1999. The commander of the PKK's armed wing, People's Liberation Army of Kurdistan (ARGK), Ceril BAYIK, had reportedly threatened Turkish authorities and foreign tourists on March 15, claiming that the whole of Anatolia "is now a battlefield." Some sources also reported a leadership struggle between Bayik and Abdullah Öcalan's brother, Osman ÖCALAN.

From February to July 1999 Kurdish militants engaged in various attacks, including suicide bombings, in response to their leader's arrest. A State Security Court accused Öcalan of being responsible for 30,000 deaths between 1984–1999. He was found guilty of treason and sentenced to death on June 29. During his defense, Öcalan argued that he could "stop the war" if the Turkish state would let him "work for peace" and spare his life. He apologized for the "sufferings PKK's actions may have caused," claiming that the "armed struggle had fulfilled its aims" and that the PKK would now "work for a democratic Turkey, where Kurds will enjoy cultural and linguistic rights." On August 2, Öcalan called on his organization to stop fighting and leave Turkish territory starting September 1. The PKK's "Presidential Council" quickly announced that it would follow their leader's commands, and during the PKK's congress in February 2000, it was announced that the party's political and armed wings would merge into a front organization called the People's Democratic Union of Kurdistan. Some analysts argued that the decision was in line with the PKK's decision to stop its armed struggle and seek Kurdish political and cultural rights within the framework of Turkey's integration with the European Union. In 2001 a small group of renegade PKK members launched the Kurdistan Workers' Party-Revolutionary Line Fighters (*Partîya Karkerén Kurdistan-Devrimci Çizgi Savaşçıları—* PKK-DÇS) with the expressed aim to continue the armed struggle. In April 2002 the PKK decided to dissolve itself (announcing it had fulfilled its "historical mission") to launch a new organization called the Kurdistan Freedom and Democracy Congress (*Kongreya Azadî û Demokrasiya Kurdistan—*KADEK). The KADEK claimed to be

against armed struggle, to have rejected fighting for an independent Kurdish homeland, and to have espoused a "political" line to press for cultural and linguistic rights for Turkey's Kurds as "full and equal members under a democratic and united Turkey." However, in May the EU announced it still considered the PKK a "terrorist organization." The Turkish government continued to claim that the PKK's transformation into KADEK was a "tactical ploy."

In September 2003, KADEK was restyled as the Peoples' Congress of Kurdistan (*Kongra Gelê Kurdistan—*Kongra-Gel). Several high-level defections occurred in the ranks, including that of Osman ÖCALAN, who reportedly joined a splinter group, the Democratic Solution Party of Kurdistan (*Partiya Welatparézén Demokratén Kurdistan—* PWDK) that was established in April 2004. In June 2004, Kongra-Gel announced that the ceasefire declared by Abdullah Öcalan in September 1999 was not respected by the Republic of Turkey and that they would return to "legitimate armed defense" to counter military operations against their "units." In April 2005 it was announced that PKK was reconstituted and the new formation was styled as the PKK–Kongra-Gel. Since the announcements, numerous sporadic clashes have been reported between the Turkish security forces and PKK–Kongra-Gel's armed wing, People's Defense Forces (*Hezen Parastina Gel—*HPG).

Since March 2005, a hitherto unknown group called "Kurdistan Freedom Falcons" (*Teyrêbazên Azadiya Kurdistan —*TAK) has taken responsibility for numerous car bomb explosions and other urban terrorist acts. Although some press reports argued TAK was one among many out-of-control wings of PKK–Kongra-Gel, the organization quickly denounced any links with the group.

Leaders: Abdullah ÖCALAN (Honorary President), Zübeyir AYDAR (President), Murat KARAYILAN (Chair of the Executive Council).

Other extreme left groupings include the **Communist Party of Turkey-Marxist Leninist** (*Türkiye Komünist Partisi-Marksist-Leninist—* TKP-ML) and its armed wing, the **Turkish**

Cabinet

As of August 10, 2006

Prime Minister	Recep Tayyip Erdoğan
Deputy Prime Minister and Minister of Foreign Affairs	Abdullah Gül
Deputy Prime Minister and State Minister	Abrüllatif Şener
Deputy Prime Minister and State Minister	Mehmet Ali Şahin
State Ministers	Beşir Atalay
	Mehmet Aydin
	Ali Babacan
	Kürşad Tüzmen
	Nimet Çubukçu [f]

Ministers

Agriculture and Village Affairs	Mehmet Mehdi Eker
Culture and Tourism	Atilla Koç
Energy and Natural Resources	Mehmet Hilmi Güler
Environment and Forestry	Osman Pepe
Finance	Kemal Unakitan
Health	Recep Akdağ
Industry and Trade	Ali Coşkun
Interior	Abdülkadir Aksu
Justice	Cemil Çiçek
Labor and Social Security	Murat Başesgioğlu
National Defense	Mehmet Vecdi Gönül
National Education	Hüseyin Çelik
Public Works and Housing	Faruk Nafiz Özak
Transport	Binali Yıldırım

Note: All ministers are members of the Justice and Development Party (AKP).

[f] = female

Workers' and Peasants' Liberation Army (*Türkiye İşçi Köylü Kurtuluş Ordusu*—TİKKO), which claimed responsibility for an attack on a police bus in İstanbul in December 2000 in retaliation for government action to break the prison hunger strikes; and the **Communist Labor Party of Turkey-Leninist** (*Türkiye Komünist Emek Partisi-Leninist*—TKEP-L).

On January 17, 2000, Hüseyin VELİOĞLU, reportedly a leader of the **Party of God** (*Hizbullah,* a militant Islamist Sunni group unrelated to the Lebanon-based Shiite *Hezbollah*) was killed and two of his associates were arrested in a shootout with police in İstanbul. The event brought attention to the group, which was believed to have been particularly active in southeast Anatolia in the early 1990s, when *Hizbullah* had reportedly launched a campaign of violence against PKK militants and pro-Kurdish lawyers, intellectuals, and human rights activists. Some unconfirmed press reports claimed that the group members were tolerated if not encouraged by the state security forces, which allegedly explained the fact that none of its members were caught until the shoot-out.

During the months of January and February 2000, police arrested over 400 alleged members of *Hizbullah,* some reportedly civil servants. State security forces also found several safe-houses of the group where they reportedly recovered mutilated bodies of dozens of victims, including famous moderate Islamic feminist Konca KURİŞ, who was kidnapped in July 1998.

On February 10, 2000, the **Great Eastern Islamic Raiders-Front** (*İslami Büyük Doğu Akıncıları-Cephesi*—BDA-C) claimed responsibility for four bomb attacks in İstanbul. The militant Islamist group had previously been accused of masterminding the mob attack on a hotel that left 36 people dead, including many famous leftist and secularist intellectuals and musicians, during a cultural festival in a central Anatolian town, Sivas, on July 2, 1992.

On May 7, 2000, Turkish authorities announced that they had apprehended those responsible for the murder of the former foreign minister and secularist professor, Ahmet Taner Kışlalı, killed on October 21, 1999. Turkish police claimed that those arrested were members of a hitherto unknown militant Islamist group, **Unity** (*Tevhid*), and were also responsible for the murders several years ago of famous leftist newspaper columnist Uğur Mumcu and academician Bahriye Üçok.

Following the arrest of PKK leader Abdullah Öcalan in February 1999, a shadowy far-right group, **Turkish Avenger Brigade** (*Türk İntikam Tugayı*—TİT), issued death threats against pro-Kurdish activists and politicians, and claimed responsibility for attacks on various HADEP buildings. Some unconfirmed reports suggest that the group is merely a facade for occasional "agent-provocateur" activities allegedly linked to factions within the Turkish security forces.

Legislature

The 1982 constitution replaced the former bicameral legislature with a unicameral **Turkish Grand National Assembly** (*Türkiye Büyük Millet Meclisi*) elected for a five-year term on a proportional basis (10 percent threshold).

After the general election of November 2002, the seat distribution was Justice and Development Party, 363; Republican People's Party, 178.

Speaker: Bülent ARINÇ.

Communications

Formal censorship of the media in regard to security matters was imposed in late 1979 and was expanded under the military regime installed in September 1980. A new press law promulgated in November 1982 gave public prosecutors the right to confiscate any publication prior to sale, permitted the government to ban foreign publications deemed to be "a danger to the unity of the country," and made journalists and publishers liable for the issuance of "subversive" material. However, freedom of the press was largely restored in the first half of the 1990s. On July 21, 1997, the Council of Ministers accepted a draft granting amnesty to imprisoned journalists. Under current law, however, journalists still face prosecution and imprisonment for reporting on issues deemed sensitive by the government.

Press

The following are dailies published in İstanbul: *Posta* (680,000), populist; *Hürriyet* (540,000), centrist; *Sabah* (465,000), centrist; *Zaman* (444,000), conservative; *Fanatik* (330,000), sports; *Takvim* (294,000), populist; *Pas Fotomac* (280,000), sports; *Milliyet* (240,000), centrist; *Vatan* (230,000), centrist; *Türkiye* (215,000), conservative; *Akşam* (210,000), conservative; *Güneş* (130,000), populist; *Gözcü* (125,000), sensationalist; *Star* (105,000), populist; *Yeni Şafak* (100,000), moderate religious, pro-AKP; *Dünden Bugüne Tercüman* (98,000), conservative; *Şok* (75,000), sensationalist; *Andolu'da Vakit* (69,000), radical-religious; *Cumhuriyet* (58,000), center left, secularist; *Yeniçağ* (56,000), far-right; *Milli Gazete* (50,000), conservative-religious pro-SP; *Radikal* (41,000), liberal; *Bulvar* (36,000), sensationalist; *Halka ve Olaylara Tercüman* (29,000), conservative Birgün (14,000), left-wing; *Ülkede*

Özgür Gündem (12,000), pro-Kurdish, pro-DEHA; *Ortadoğu* (10,000), far-right, pro-MHP; *Referans* (10,000), finance and economics; *Yeni Asya* (7,500), conservative-religious; *Önce Vatan* (6,500), nationalist; *Günluk Evrensel* (5,500), far-left, pro-EMEP; *Yeni Mesaj* (3,500), far-right, pro-MHP; *Dünya* (2,500), finance and economics; *Hürses* (1,500), finance and economics.

Non-Turkish-language publications include *Jamanak* (daily) and *Nor Marmara* (daily) in Armenian; *Agos* (weekly) in Turkish and Armenian; *Turkish Daily News* (daily) and *The New Anatolian* (daily) in English; *Apoyevmatini* (biweekly) in Greek; *Azadiya Welat* (bimonthly) and *Zend* (monthly) in Kurdish; and *Şalom* (weekly) Sephardic Jewish/ Ladino and Turkish.

News Agencies

The leading news source is the government-owned Anatolian News Agency (*Anadolu Ajansı—AA*). Virtually all of the leading international agencies maintain Ankara bureaus.

Broadcasting and Computing

The state-controlled Turkish Radio Television Corporation (*Türkiye Radyo Televizyon Kurumu—TRT*) currently offers domestic service over several radio networks and television channels. In April 1992 a TRT International Channel (Avrasya) began broadcasting via satellite to an area from Germany to Central Asia, earning third place in international transmission after CNN International and BBC International. In July 1993 a constitutional amendment formally abolished the state broadcast monopoly. In 1994 a Higher Council of Radio and Television (*Radyo Televizyon Üst Kurulu—RTÜK*) was established to oversee all radio and television emissions and programming. The appointed body reports to the prime minister and has the authority to license and shut down radio and television stations for up to a year on the grounds of such offenses as libel and the transmission of "offensive" or "hate-inciting" programs. The council has closed down numerous radio and television stations since its inception and has been widely criticized for using vague criteria that reportedly amount to censorship. There were approximately 26.7 million television receivers and 3.5 million personal computers serving 5.5 million Internet users in 2003.

Intergovernmental Representation

Ambassador to the US
Nabi SENSOY

US Ambassador to Turkey
Ross WILSON

Permanent Representative to the UN
Baki İLKIN

IGO Memberships (Non-UN)
ADB, BIS, BSEC, CEUR, ECO, EBRD, Eurocontrol, IDB, IEA, Interpol, IOM, NATO, OECD, OIC, OSCE, PCA, WCO, *WEU,* WTO

UKRAINE

Ukrayina

The Country

The third largest and second most populous of the former Soviet republics, Ukraine is bordered on the north by Belarus, on the east by Russia, on the south by the Black Sea, and on the west by Moldova, Romania, Hungary, Slovakia, and Poland. Approximately 71 percent of the population is Ukrainian and 22 percent Russian, with no other group greater than 1 percent. The ethnic Russian population is located primarily in eastern Ukraine, where there is significant sentiment in favor of the reestablishment of greater economic, political, and military integration with Russia. The population in western Ukraine is described as strongly anticommunist and supportive of the country's orientation toward Western Europe. Most Ukrainians profess Eastern Orthodoxy, although there is a sizable Roman Catholic community and smaller numbers of Muslims and Jews.

The black-earth steppe of the south, one of the world's most productive farming regions, provided about one-quarter of the former Soviet Union's foodstuffs. Agriculture presently accounts for about 12 percent of GDP and 15 percent of employment. The leading crop is wheat, followed by sugar beets, potatoes, and a wide variety of other vegetables and fruits. Natural resources, including iron, coal, bauxite, zinc, oil, and gas, have long supported a range of manufacturing activity, including metallurgical, machine-building, and chemical production, that accounted for nearly a third of the USSR's industrial output. Industry now contributes about 40 percent of GDP, primarily from mining and metallurgy, and employs some 25 percent of the labor force.

The demise of the Soviet system yielded a 50 percent contraction in economic output in 1990–1994, accompanied by inflation that spiraled to 4,735 percent in 1993 before falling to 890 percent in 1994 and to under 100 percent in 1995. GDP declined by 12.2 percent in 1995, 10.0 percent in 1996, and 3.0 percent in 1997, when inflation fell to 10 percent. A modest recovery appeared possible for 1998 until the economy was rocked by the Russian financial collapse of August, which constrained trade between the two countries and prompted a significant outflow of capital. Consequently, GDP fell by another 1.9 percent for 1998, and inflation increased to 20 percent.

The GDP declined by a modest 0.4 percent in 1999, raising hopes for a turnaround, and in 2000

Political Status: Formerly the Ukrainian Soviet Socialist Republic, a constituent republic of the Union of Soviet Socialist Republics; declared independence on August 24, 1991; new constitution adopted on June 28, 1996.

Area: 233,090 sq. mi. (603,700 sq. km.).

Population: 48,457,000 (2001C); 46,525,000 (2005E).

Major Urban Centers (including suburbs, 2005E): KYÏV (KIEV, 1,771,000), Donèc'k (Donetsk, 4,644,000), Dnipropètrovsk (Dnepropetrovsk, 3,461,000), Charkiv (Kharkov, 2,837,000), L'viv (Lvov, 2,582,000), Odèsa (Odessa, 2,407,000).

Official Language: Ukrainian (replaced Russian in 1990). The Council for Language Policy and the National Orthography Commission are currently working to restore syntax, style, and other aspects of Ukrainian to what they were before the 1930s, when Moscow ordered Ukrainian to be made more uniform with Russian.

Monetary Unit: Hryvna (official rate July 1, 2006: 5.00 hryvnas = $1US).

President: Viktor YUSHCHENKO ("Our Ukraine" Bloc); elected in rerun second-round balloting on December 26, 2004, and sworn in for a five-year term on January 23, 2005, succeeding Leonid Danilovych KUCHMA.

Prime Minister: Viktor YANUKOVYCH (Party of Regions); named by the president on August 3, 2006, after protracted negotiations regarding a coalition government following the legislative elections of March 26 and approved by the Supreme Council on August 4 to succeed Yuriy YEKHANUROV (People's Union "Our Ukraine").

market for Ukraine's exports, led by metals. Inflation, at nearly 26 percent, remained high, but a more fundamental problem was a lack of political consensus on what direction the economy should take. At the end of 2000, virtually all the large Soviet-era state enterprises remained in government hands, while privatization and other market-oriented reforms continued to meet opposition from a Communist-Socialist-Agrarian parliamentary bloc. On the right, politically well-connected entrepreneurs, the so-called oligarchs, also opposed many reform efforts, particularly in the energy sector, where greater transparency and a sharp reduction in barter arrangements among consumers, sellers, and suppliers threatened to undermine a major source of the oligarchs' wealth. The slow pace of reform contributed to delayed disbursements from the IMF and other multilateral lending agencies. In 1999 the IMF also objected to a jump in public spending shortly before the presidential election and to Ukraine's use of accounting practices that inflated foreign currency reserves. The IMF agreed to resume disbursing a $2.6 billion loan in December 2000 after a 14-month interruption.

GDP rose by 9.1 percent in 2001, 4.5 percent in 2002, 9.4 percent in 2003, and 13.5 percent in 2004, led by growth in the industrial sector and strong domestic consumer demand. However, Ukraine remained heavily dependent on imported energy products, particularly from Russia. In addition, the oligarchs retained a near monopoly on the industrial and financial sectors and were perceived as blocking reform of the tax system. The World Bank and IMF pledged additional aid in response to the government's action against money laundering, but the country was still viewed as a high risk by foreign investors.

Upon taking office in early 2005, President Yushchenko pledged to pursue free-market policies and to investigate the some 3,000 nontransparent privatizations that had been completed during the Kuchma administration. Foreign investors initially welcomed the market orientation brought on by the Orange Revolution but were subsequently

the economy expanded for the first time since independence, achieving 6 percent growth. The International Monetary Fund (IMF), which has encouraged stabilization and liberalization measures, attributed the gains to exchange rate depreciation, unexpected resilience in Russia (Ukraine's principal trading partner), and an improved world described as "unnerved" by the political turmoil of late 2005 and the first half of 2006. Meanwhile, the IMF reported that growth had slowed to about 3 percent in 2005, while inflation had risen to an annual rate of nearly 15 percent. On a more positive note for supporters of proposed membership in the European Union (EU) and the World Trade Organization (WTO), the United States in December 2005 formally recognized Ukraine as a market economy, with the EU following suit in February 2006.

Government and Politics

Political Background

Under Polish rule in the 16th century, Ukraine experienced a brief period of independence in the 17th before coming under Russian control in the 18th. Ukraine again proclaimed independence following the overthrow of the tsarist regime in 1917, with the region becoming a battlefield of conflicting forces that eventually yielded a Red Army victory and Ukraine's incorporation into the USSR as one of its constituent republics in 1922. In 1954 the Soviet leadership marked the 200th anniversary of Russia's absorption of Ukraine by transferring the Crimean autonomous republic from Russian to Ukrainian administration, despite its largely ethnic Russian population. Subsequent moves to rehabilitate the original Crimean Tatars, who had been transported to Central Asia during World War II because of alleged collaboration with the Germans, yielded the return of some 250,000 to Crimea by the early 1990s.

On July 16, 1990, the Ukrainian Supreme Soviet, under pressure from nationalist opposition forces, issued a sovereignty declaration that asserted the "indivisibility of the republic's power on its territory," its "independence and equality in external relations," and its right to countermand the utilization of its citizens for military service beyond its boundaries. In a somewhat equivocal vein, however, it failed to claim a right of secession from the Soviet Union and explicitly provided for dual Soviet and Ukrainian citizenship. The less

than clear-cut nature of the declaration prompted widespread nationalist demonstrations, led primarily by student activists. On October 23 the chair of the council of ministers, Vitaliy A. MASOL, responded by submitting his resignation; he was succeeded by Vitold FOKIN.

Ukraine endorsed Soviet President Mikhail Gorbachev's union proposal in April 1991 but, in the wake of the failed hard-line coup against Gorbachev in Moscow, issued a formal declaration of independence on August 24. On August 31 the chair of the Supreme Soviet, Leonid KRAVCHUK, suspended activities of the Communist Party of Ukraine (*Komunistychna Partiya Ukrainy*—KPU), and on September 4 the leader of the KPU legislative bloc announced that the group would disband. On December 1, in a vote held simultaneously with Kravchuk's reconfirmation in direct presidential balloting, Ukrainians overwhelmingly endorsed the August independence declaration. On December 8 the republic joined Belarus and Russia in announcing the demise of the Soviet Union, and on December 21 Ukraine became a founding member of the Commonwealth of Independent States (CIS).

Fokin, who had continued as prime minister upon reorganization of the council of ministers in May 1991, survived a confidence vote on July 1, 1992, following a decision to raise food prices, but he was forced to step down on September 30 amid uncertainty over the direction and pace of the republic's economic reform program. He was succeeded, on an acting basis, by First Deputy Prime Minister Valentin SIMONENKO, who yielded the office on October 27 to Leonid D. KUCHMA, the "technocrat" director of the former Soviet Union's largest arms production complex.

Increasingly battered by conservative parliamentarians opposed to his economic reform efforts, Prime Minister Kuchma submitted his resignation for the fifth time in as many months on September 9, 1993, with the Supreme Council voting acceptance on September 21. Kuchma's deputy, Yukhym ZVYAHILSKIY, was named acting prime minister, although President Kravchuk assumed direct control of the government by decree on

September 27. Three days earlier the Supreme Council had averted a constitutional crisis by agreeing that parliamentary and presidential elections would be held in the first half of 1994.

In apparent reaction to his inability to resolve Ukraine's economic ills, President Kravchuk announced in late February 1994 that he would not seek to remain in office upon expiration of his mandate at midyear. He nonetheless registered as a candidate on April 30, and in first-round presidential balloting on June 26 he won 37.7 percent of the vote, as contrasted with 31.3 percent for former prime minister Kuchma. At the runoff on July 10, Kravchuk lost to his opponent, 45.1 percent to 52.1 percent, critical factors in Kuchma's success being endorsement by the revived KPU and support in the eastern industrialized areas with a heavy ethnic Russian population. At his inauguration on July 19 the new head of state promised gradual electoral reform and closer ties to Russia. Meanwhile, in an apparent overture to his pro-Russian opponents, President Kravchuk had, on June 16, 1994, reappointed Vitaliy Masol as prime minister. Masol eventually resigned in March 1995, reportedly over economic policy differences with President Kuchma, who was seeking more active economic reform. Masol was replaced by Col. Gen. Yevhen MARCHUK, theretofore a deputy premier and state security chair.

The 292–4 parliamentary passage on April 4, 1995, of a motion of nonconfidence backed by both Communist conservatives and reformers precipitated a major political crisis, as President Kuchma reappointed Marchuk on April 8 and tabled proposals to strengthen the powers of the presidency pending the adoption of a new constitution (see Constitution and government, below). The Supreme Council's failure to ratify the changes on May 30 caused the president to threaten a referendum, whereupon the legislature, cognizant of the wide public support for the changes, on June 15 acceded to an interim "constitutional treaty" that granted most of the new powers sought by Kuchma. Conflict over economic reform nevertheless simmered between the legislature and the president, with Kuchma's determined pursuit of a market economy generating strains not only between the president and the KPU-led bloc, but also within the mainly centrist political groups that provided the president's core support.

Prime Minister Marchuk was dismissed by President Kuchma on May 27, 1996, ostensibly for shortcomings in the conduct of economic policy, and was replaced by the first deputy prime minister, Pavlo LAZARENKO. A cabinet reshuffle following the adoption of a new constitution in June 1996 was completed in October. Kuchma also reshuffled his cabinet in February 1997 in an attempt to deal with corruption, stabilize the financial system, and press on with economic reforms. Deputy Prime Minister Viktor PYNZENYK, a leading architect of reform, resigned in April, denouncing the legislature for a lack of commitment to reform. Pynzenyk was replaced by the chair of Ukraine's largest bank, which was reportedly financing businesses closely associated with Kuchma himself. In June, Lazarenko was replaced on an acting basis by First Deputy Prime Minister Vasyl DURDYNETS, ostensibly because of failing health. Lazarenko had faced serious allegations of corruption and blocking reform, and his ouster had reportedly been ordered by Kuchma. In July the legislature approved Kuchma's nomination of Valeriy PUSTOVOYTENKO, minister of cabinet affairs and a member of the People's Democratic Party of Ukraine (*Narodno-Demokratychna Partiya Ukrainy*—NDPU), as the new permanent prime minister.

In late 1997 a new electoral law was adopted to increase the role of political parties in legislative elections by providing for half the legislators to be selected from party lists in nationwide balloting. New Supreme Council balloting was conducted under the revised system for the first time on March 29, 1998. Thanks to a strong performance in the proportional poll, the KDU improved its representation substantially. However, the KDU-led left-wing opposition was still unable to achieve a majority, with many of the independent candidates elected in the single-member districts representing business interests supportive of President Kuchma's economic reform efforts. Consequently,

Prime Minister Pustovoytenko remained in office following the election, although the cabinet was extensively reshuffled in early 1999.

The presidential election of October 31, 1999, saw the incumbent opposed by 12 other candidates, including KPU leader Petro SYMONENKO, Oleksandr MOROZ of the Socialist Party of Ukraine (*Sotsialtstychna Partiya Ukrainy*—SPU), and former prime minister Yevhen Marchuk, who was backed by a number of smaller parties. Meeting in Kaniv in August, Moroz, Marchuk, and two other candidates had agreed that they would unite behind one of their number before the election, but Marchuk's selection on October 25 immediately led Moroz to assert that he would nevertheless remain in the race. A third member of the "Kaniv Four," Oleksandr TKACHENKO, chair of the Supreme Council and leader of the Peasants' Party of Ukraine (*Selyanska Partiya Ukrainy*—SelPU), withdrew in favor of Symonenko, not Marchuk. The first round of presidential balloting ended with Kuchma claiming 36.5 percent of the vote, necessitating a November 14 runoff against the second-place Symonenko, who had won 22.2 percent. With third-place finisher Moroz and the other leftist candidates having thrown their support to the KPU leader for the second round, Kuchma wielded his presidential prerogatives in an effort to secure the victory. On November 3 he dismissed the governors of three regions that had supported either Moroz or Symonenko, and on November 10 he named Marchuk head of the National Security and Defense Council in a transparent bid to gain the 8.1 percent support Marchuk had received as fifth-place finisher in the first round. In the runoff election Kuchma took 57.7 percent of the vote. The Parliamentary Assembly of the Council of Europe and the Organization for Security and Cooperation in Europe (OSCE) were among the observer organizations citing flaws in the conduct of the second round.

Following Kuchma's inauguration for a second term on November 30, 1999, the cabinet resigned, as required by the constitution. The president quickly renominated the incumbent prime minister, but on December 14 the Supreme Coun-

cil rejected Pushtovoytenko by a vote of 206–44. Two days later Kuchma nominated reformist Viktor YUSHCHENKO, the nonparty chair of the National Bank of Ukraine, who was confirmed and sworn in on December 22. The new prime minister came into office pledging a reform program that included "open" privatization, lower inflation, a balanced budget, cuts in the size of the government bureaucracy, payment of remaining wage and pension arrears, and restructuring of the agricultural sector, in which President Kuchma had proposed converting the country's 10,000 collective farms into cooperatives and joint stock companies. Subsequent cabinet changes included the appointment by Kuchma of three new deputy prime ministers, including Yuliya TYMOSHENKO of Fatherland (*Batkivshchnyna*), a former energy industry executive, who assumed responsibility for fuel and energy policy in January.

On January 13, 2000, former president Kravchuk announced formation of a government-supportive parliamentary majority by 11 center-right factions, including his own Social Democratic Party of Ukraine (United) (*Sotsial-Demokratychna Partiya Ukrainy [Obyednana]*—SDPU[O]), and a number of independent deputies. The new Supreme Council majority immediately attempted to remove the SelPU's Tkachenko as parliamentary chair, but obstructionism from the left prevented a vote. Convening in a nearby exhibition hall, the 239-member majority voted Tkachenko out of office on January 21, and on February 1 it elected in his place Ivan PLYUSHCH, who had previously served in the same capacity. The leftist opposition continued to meet in the Supreme Council chamber despite lacking a quorum, but a week later a group of majority deputies forced its way into the building. By February 15 the opposition effort had lost its impetus, and regular parliamentary sessions resumed shortly thereafter.

On November 28, 2000, SPU leader Moroz released to the public audiotapes implicating President Kuchma, Interior Minister Yuriy KRAVCHENKO, and presidential chief of staff Vladimir LYTVYN in a plot to "get rid of" independent journalist and presidential critic Heorhiy

GONGADZE, who had gone missing in mid-September and whose headless body was uncovered near Kyiv in early November. Former presidential bodyguard Mykola MELNYCHENKO had secretly recorded incriminating conversations in the president's office in mid-2000. Kuchma, supported by the prosecutor general's office, insisted that the relevant recordings were fabrications, although participants in other conversations on the tapes attested to their authenticity. In response to the scandal, an anti-Kuchma National Salvation Forum was organized in February 2001, including as a member former deputy prime minister Tymoshenko, who had been dismissed by Kuchma in January after being formally charged with corruption while head of Unified Energy Systems of Ukraine in 1996–1997.

By then, the new center-right parliamentary majority had already dissipated. The country's "oligarchs," seeing their economic fiefdoms threatened by Prime Minister Yushchenko's reform policies, demanded formation of a new government that would better represent their interests. Oligarchs in the forefront of this effort included the SDPU(O)'s Viktor MEDVEDCHUK and Hryhoriy SURKIS; former ministers of the economy Serhiy TYHYPKO, Viktor PYNCHUK, and Andriy DERKACH; all of the recently organized Working Ukraine (*Trudova Ukraina*); and Oleksandr VOLKOV of the even newer parliamentary faction Democratic Union (*Demokratychny Soyuz*). From the opposite side of the political spectrum, the Communists and other leftists joined the oligarchic parties in calling for the market-oriented, centrist Yushchenko to be replaced.

On April 26, 2001, Prime Minister Yushchenko lost a no-confidence vote in the Supreme Council, 263–69, as the Communist and oligarchic parties united against him. He submitted his resignation on April 27, and a day later President Kuchma dismissed the cabinet, which remained in office in a caretaker capacity. On May 29 the Supreme Council confirmed Anatoliy KINAKH, a former first deputy prime minister, as Yushchenko's successor. Kuchma announced the final appointment to a revamped cabinet on July 10.

In the context of ongoing efforts by a frequently fractious opposition to force President Kuchma's resignation or to impeach him (see Current issues, below), Ukrainians elected a new Supreme Council on March 30, 2002. Former prime minister Yushchenko's "Our Ukraine" Bloc (*Blok Viktora Yushchenka "Nasha Ukraina"*—NU) finished with a plurality of 110 seats, followed by the pro-Kuchma "For a United Ukraine!" Electoral Bloc (*Vyborchiy Blok "Za Yedinu Ukrainu!"*—ZYU) with 101, and the KPU with 66. The NU and the KPU were joined by the Yuliya Tymoshenko Bloc (*Blok Yuliyi Tymoshenko*—BYT) and the SPU as the principal opposition formations, which, despite their ideological differences, pledged to renew the effort to force Kuchma from office.

On November 16, 2002, President Kuchma nominated Viktor YANUKOVYCH, the governor of the Donetsk oblast and leader of the recently formed pro-Russian Party of Regions (*Partiya Rehioniv*—PR), to be the new prime minister. The appointment was confirmed with 234 votes in the Supreme Council on November 21.

In the wake of massive protest demonstrations against his administration, Kuchma in early 2004 announced that he would not seek reelection, despite having been authorized to run by the Constitutional Court. The three major presidential contenders thereby became Prime Minister Yanukovych (Kuchma's preference as a successor), former prime minister Yushchenko, and Oleksandr Moroz of the SPU. The first round of balloting on October 31 produced a near dead heat between Yanukovych (40.20 percent of the vote) and Yushchenko (39.01 percent). Election observers reported numerous violations of fair election practices, while opposition parties claimed that the government had been involved in a conspiracy to poison Yushchenko (see Current issues). The government announced that Yanukovych won the November 21 runoff balloting with 49.46 percent of the vote compared to 46.31 percent for Yushchenko, prompting protest demonstrations in major Ukrainian cities as well as an international outcry over perceived fraud on the government's part. The Supreme Council refused to ratify

Yanukovych's victory and ordered a second runoff for December 26, at which Yushchenko, now the leader of an Orange Revolution (so named after his main campaign color) achieved a clear victory with 52 percent of the vote.

Yanukovych initially refused to accept the results, but he eventually resigned as prime minister on December 31, 2005, paving the way for Yushchenko's inauguration on January 23, 2006. The following day Yushchenko named Yuliya Tymoshenko, his main Orange Revolution partner, as prime minister. Her appointment was confirmed on February 4 via 457 votes in the Supreme Council.

Despite the near euphoria that greeted the installation of the new administration in early 2005, infighting soon broke out within the cabinet, and friction over policy differences developed between the president and the prime minister. Consequently, on September 8 Yushchenko dismissed Tymoshenko and her cabinet, Tymoshenko immediately announcing that she and her supporters were crossing over to the opposition. On September 9 Yushchenko nominated Yuriy YEKHANUROV, the governor of the Dnipropėtrovsk region and a member of the NU, to be the next prime minister. The appointment was able to muster only an insufficient 223 votes of support in the Supreme Council on September 20. However, after Yushchenko had reportedly offered significant concessions to Yanukovych, the PR agreed to support Yekhanurov, who was confirmed with 289 votes on September 23. The new cabinet announced on September 27–28 was dominated by the NU, although a number of posts were filled by nonparty technocrats.

Following a controversial gas deal with Russia in early January 2006 (see Current issues), the Supreme Council on January 10 passed a motion of no confidence against the Yekhanurov government. However, the government remained in place pending balloting for a new Supreme Council, which, under recent constitutional revision, would be empowered to appoint most of the new cabinet.

The March 26, 2006, legislative balloting produced a surprising plurality for the PR, with the BYT and NU splitting the Orange Revolution vote (see Legislature, below, for results). Several attempts by the NU and BYT to form a coalition government foundered over the ensuing months, as did the PR's attempts to find sufficient partners to achieve a legislative majority. Consequently, conditions reached a critical point by July, with Yushchenko facing the choice of calling for new elections or accepting an arrangement with his former arch-rival Yanukovych. Finally, on August 3 Yushchenko agreed to nominate Yanukovych to lead a new government dominated by the PR but also including members of the SPU and the NU.

Intertwined with postindependence political developments has been the vexed issue of the status of the Ukrainian autonomous republic of Crimea, where the aspiration of the majority ethnic Russian population for union with Russia generated strains in Moscow-Kyiv relations (see Foreign relations, below), with the added complication of disaffection among the peninsula's original Tatar inhabitants. The election of Yuriy MESHKOV, leader of the secessionist Republican Movement of Crimea (*Republikanskve Dvizheniya Kryma—RDK*), as Crimean president on January 31, 1994, was seen in Kyiv as a threat to the country's territorial integrity. Although he insisted that he was not calling for separation from Ukraine, Meshkov repeated an earlier call for a referendum on the establishment of "an independent Crimea in union with CIS states."

On May 19, 1994, the Crimean legislature voted to restore its proindependence constitution of May 1992, with the Crimean port of Sevastopil declaring in August that it had "Russian legal status." The Ukrainian Supreme Council consequently adopted legislation designed to curb Crimea's autonomy, enacting a measure in November providing for the automatic invalidation of any Crimean legislation in conflict with Ukrainian law. In March 1995, moreover, the Kyiv legislature annulled Crimea's constitution and effectively abolished the presidency, with President Kuchma assuming direct control over the region from April 1. Meshkov denounced these actions as unconstitutional, although plans to hold a referendum on the separatist 1992 basic law were canceled at the end of May. Kuchma rescinded his direct rule decree in August 1995, while asserting that candidates for the Crimea premiership must first be approved by him. In February 1996 the appointment of Arkady DEMYDENKO as Crimean prime minister was so confirmed. On June 3, 1997, Kuchma approved the dismissal of Demydenko after the Crimean parliament had voted three times to sack him. Kuchma agreed to appoint Anatoli FRANCHUK, an ally and former Crimean premier (1994–1995), as prime minister; his cabinet was approved by the Crimean parliament on June 19.

Elections to the Crimean Supreme Council were conducted on March 29, 1998, in conjunction with the balloting for the Ukrainian Supreme Council. Left-wing parties advanced in the Crimean Supreme Council, which elected Leonid HRACH of the Communist Party of Crimea (*Kommunisticheskaya Partiya Kryma*—KPK) as its new speaker. However, in an apparent reflection of the balance of power maintained at the national level, Kuchma named Serhiy KUNITSYN, the leader of the centrist factions in the Crimean Supreme Council, as the new Crimean prime minister on May 19. Subsequently, in January 1999 a new constitution was adopted for Crimea, which, among other things, gave the autonomous republic substantial budgetary authority. Tensions between factions loyal to Hrach and Kunitsyn continued to play out in the following two years, with Hrach repeatedly working through the legislature for Kunitsyn's dismissal. In September 2000 President Kuchma commented that he saw no need to take such an action given the current balance of powers in the province, but on July 18, 2001, the Crimean legislature voted to dismiss Kunitsyn, who ultimately stepped down five days later. Kuchma then named Valeriy HORBATOV as his successor. However, Kunitsyn returned to the prime minister's post in April 2002 following the March legislative elections, which were reportedly marred by numerous irregularities. (Horbatov had been elected to the Ukrainian Supreme Court.)

Tension between Crimea and the national government continued to simmer into 2004, as the Russian nationalists who dominated Crimea pressed for designation of Russia as an official language and for stronger military and political links with Russia. In the wake of the Orange Revolution at the national level in late 2004 and early 2005, Kunitsyn resigned as Crimean prime minister in April 2005, being described as the last major leader of the Kuchma era to leave office. He was succeeded by Anatoliy MATVIYENKO, a close associate of Prime Minister Tymoshenko and a member of the BYT. However, Matviyenko also fell victim to national politics only a few months later when Tymoshenko and President Yushchenko became estranged. Anatoliy BURDYUHOV, a member of the NU, was named in September to replace Matviyenko as head of a Crimean government that included a number of bankers (including Burdyuhov) and increased representation for the Crimean Tatars.

Prior to the March 26, 2006, balloting for the Crimean Supreme Council, the region was described as still polarized along ethnic lines and suffering economic malaise. Not surprisingly, considering the fact that ethnic Russians constitute 60 percent of the Crimean population, the pro-Russian For Yanukovych Bloc won a strong plurality of 44 seats in the new Supreme Council. With President Yushchenko's endorsement, Viktor PLAKYDA was selected in June as the new Crimean prime minister. Plakyda, the former director of the Crimean energy company, announced his intention to focus on economic development. However, political discord continued to dominate regional events as evidenced by major protests against the North Atlantic Treaty Organization (NATO) that forced cancellation of planned Ukraine-U.S. military exercises in June as well as by ongoing calls from members of the Russian Duma for the reannexation of Crimea by Russia.

Constitution and Government

Coincident with his formal reinstallation as Ukrainian head of state on December 5, 1991, Kravchuk's title changed from that of Supreme Soviet chair to president of the republic. Seven months earlier the Council of Ministers had been restructured as a Western-style cabinet headed by a prime minister. The draft of a new constitution published in October 1993 called for retention of most of the existing government structure. It provided for a 450-seat Supreme Council with a four-year mandate and a Council of Ministers guided by a president directly elected for a five-year term.

Under the terms of the June 1995 interim "constitutional treaty," a Constitutional Commission completed work on the draft of a new constitution in March 1996. Despite some opposition to stronger presidential authority at the expense of the legislature, the Supreme Council adopted the new text on June 28. It granted significant new powers to the president, including the right to name the prime minister (with the concurrence of a parliamentary majority) and other officials, and recognized the right to own private property. In addition, it provided for the establishment of a National Security and Defense Council and for the holding of parliamentary and presidential elections in March 1998 and October 1999, respectively. It also specified that parliamentary deputies could not simultaneously hold government appointments. On September 24, 1997, the parliament approved a mixed voting system for the Supreme Council, half of which was therefore directly elected from single-seat constituencies; the remaining 225 seats were apportioned to parties that received at least 4 percent of all ballots cast in separate nationwide balloting.

A number of constitutional revisions were negotiated as part of the resolution of the presidential crisis of late 2004. Under the changes (which went into effect on January 1, 2006), significant authority previously exercised by the president was transferred to the Supreme Council. Although the president retained the formal right to nominate the prime minister, the Supreme Council was empowered to present a candidate for the president's consideration, thereby acquiring de facto control of the post. The Supreme Council was also given control over all cabinet appointments except for the defense and foreign affairs portfolios, which remained under the president's purview. In addition, the Supreme Council was authorized to dismiss the prime minister and cabinet members. The basic law revisions also decree that all 450 members of the Supreme

Council would henceforth be elected by proportional voting.

A Supreme Court was installed in January 1997. There is also a Constitutional Court with members appointed by the president, legislature, and the bar association. In addition, the 2005 Code of Administrative Procedure provided for an additional court system headed by a High Administrative court to deal with a variety of issues, including election-related cases.

Ukraine is divided into 24 provinces (*oblasts*), with Crimea administered as an autonomous republic. The metropolitan areas of Kyiv and Sevastopil (Sevastopol) have special status. Local self-government functions in divisions and subdivisions.

Foreign Relations

Although at the time not an independent country, Ukraine, like Byelorussia (now Belarus), was accorded founding membership in the UN in 1945 as a gesture to the USSR, which feared the world body would have an anti-Soviet bias. Theretofore not a member of the IMF or World Bank, independent Ukraine was admitted to both institutions in September 1992; earlier, it had become a member of the Conference on (subsequently Organization for) Security and Cooperation in Europe (CSCE/OSCE) following the demise of the Soviet Union and the creation of the CIS in December 1991.

Ukrainian leaders insisted following independence that they wished the country to become nuclear free, even though a substantial proportion of the former USSR's nuclear arsenal was located in Ukraine. Although Ukraine was a signatory of the 1992 Lisbon Protocol to the 1991 Strategic Arms Reduction Treaty (START I), designating Russia as the sole nuclear power in the CIS, implementation was delayed by difficulties over the terms demanded by the Ukrainian government and the Ukrainian nationalist opposition. Not until November 1993 did the Supreme Council conditionally ratify START I, while indicating that it was not prepared to endorse the Nuclear

Non-Proliferation Treaty (NPT) without substantial Western security guarantees, financial assistance for weapons dismantling, and compensation for nuclear devices transferred to Russia for destruction. The conditional ratification and statement of terms yielded speedy progress in January 1994 on a tripartite agreement, whereby the United States would provide assistance for the dismantling of nuclear weapons by Ukraine, with warheads being shipped to Russia for destruction. Eventually, Ukraine would receive about $1 billion, via Russia, from the sale of reprocessed uranium from the warheads. In accordance with the agreement, Ukraine began shipping warheads to Russia in early March, and in December Ukraine formally acceded to the NPT, following parliamentary ratification the previous month. On June 1, 1996, President Kuchma announced that Ukraine had completed the process of nuclear disarmament by transferring the last of its warheads to Russia.

Independent Ukraine's relations with Russia were also complicated by the question of the status of Crimea and by a long-running dispute over the ownership of the ex-Soviet Black Sea fleet based in the Crimean port of Sevastopil. In February 1992 Ukraine refused a Russian request for the retrocession of Crimea on the grounds that the CIS agreement included a commitment to accept existing borders, to which the Russian parliament (*Duma*) responded in May by declaring the 1954 transfer to Ukraine unconstitutional and void. The *Duma*'s action was in support of a declaration of independence from Ukraine by the Crimean Supreme Soviet, which the Crimeans repealed after the Ukrainians had voted to annul its content by an overwhelming margin. Subsequently, the Ukrainian foreign ministry issued a statement declaring that "the status of the Crimea is an internal Ukrainian matter which cannot be the subject of negotiation with another state."

In June 1992 an agreement in principle between Presidents Kravchuk of Ukraine and Yeltsin of Russia provided for the Black Sea fleet of more than 800 ships, including auxiliary vessels, to be divided equally between the two countries. Differences nevertheless persisted, accompanied by periodic incidents involving naval personnel in Sevastopil and by nationalist opposition to compromise in both parliaments. In June 1995 Kuchma and Yeltsin reached a further accord, with Russia agreeing to buy part of the Ukrainian half of the fleet, thus increasing its share to 81 percent, and with both sides having naval bases in Sevastopil.

In May 1997 Yeltsin made a state visit to Ukraine to sign a 10-year friendship treaty and to resolve remaining differences over the Black Sea fleet. By virtue of a 20-year lease, the fleet was to be based primarily in Sevastopil. Both the Russian and Ukrainian navies were to use Streletskaya Bay, but the rest of the Black Sea would be used exclusively by Ukraine. Russia also recognized Crimea and the city of Sevastopil as Ukrainian territory. In addition, the agreement settled questions about Ukraine's bilateral debts and its claims on ships the Russians "inherited" upon the dissolution of the Soviet Union. In February 1999 the Russian *Duma* ratified the treaty, which formally recognized, for the first time, Ukraine's sovereignty within its current borders.

Ukraine acceded to NATO's Partnership for Peace program in February 1994, and in June it signed a partnership and cooperation agreement with the EU. An important aspect of the latter accord was the provision of EU aid for closure of the remaining nuclear reactors in Chernobyl, site of the world's worst nuclear accident, in 1986. Having been formally admitted to the Council of Europe in November 1995, Ukraine became a full member of the Central European Initiative (CEI) in May 1996 and was granted observer status within the Nonaligned Movement in September. In September 1997 Ukraine agreed to a plan by which it would join the Central European Free Trade Agreement (CEFTA, see Foreign relations in article on Poland), though no firm timetable was announced. A new EU economic cooperation agreement with Ukraine took effect on March 1, 1998, committing each to increased trade and investment, and Ukraine indicated that it eventually intended to apply for full membership.

As one of the largest recipients of American foreign aid, Ukraine bowed to the United States and

Israel in March 1998 and did not sell turbines for Russian nuclear reactors destined for Iran. The agreement on commercial nuclear technology removed an impediment to improved relations with Washington at a time of sharply increased contacts with NATO officials. Despite the prospect of reprisals by Russia, which asked Kyiv not to cancel the turbine contract, Ukraine tried to maintain the momentum it had gained in July 1997 when it had signed a cooperation charter with NATO. The agreement, reportedly modeled on the Russia-NATO Founding Act of May 1997, established a special relationship (short of membership) that included the exchange of military missions and the establishment of a NATO-Ukraine Commission, through which Ukraine could consult with NATO if it came under an external threat. In March 1998, clarifying its neutrality and its relationship with the Western alliance, Kyiv said it "does not rule out" joining NATO in the future if membership would not jeopardize its relationship with neighbors, particularly Russia. President Kuchma also endorsed the expansion of NATO in March 1999 (again contrary to Moscow's wishes), although he condemned the subsequent NATO military campaign against Yugoslavia.

In June 1997 the presidents of Ukraine and Romania signed a treaty, subsequently approved by their respective parliaments, confirming existing borders and protecting the rights of national minorities. Meanwhile, the informal "Union of Three" alliance of Georgia, Ukraine, and Azerbaijan became identified through the acronym GUAM when Moldova joined the group in October. Earlier, in the fall of 1996, the former Soviet bloc nations had begun to strengthen their economic and political relationships based on a common pro-Western orientation, suspicion of Russia, and the prospects of collaborating on the exploitation of Azerbaijan's Caspian oil. GUAM expanded to the GUUAM upon the accession of Uzbekistan in April 1999. However, in May 2005 Uzbekistan withdrew from the grouping, which in May 2006 changed its name to the GUAM Organization for Democracy and Economic Development.

Having received grant and loan pledges valued in the billions of dollars from the European Bank for Reconstruction and Development (EBRD) and other multilateral agencies as well as individual countries, Ukraine officially shut down the last operating nuclear reactor in Chernobyl on December 15, 2000. The financial and technical assistance was targeted for a range of projects, including construction of a more permanent sarcophagus around the highly radioactive reactor that was destroyed by the 1986 explosion, constructing replacement power facilities, upgrading safety at remaining nuclear plants, and aiding the local population.

A decade after the demise of the Soviet Union, delineation of Ukraine's borders with Moldova and Romania remained somewhat problematic. A treaty concluded with Moldova in 1999 had not been ratified by the Ukrainian Supreme Council as of March 2001. Meanwhile, negotiations with Romania continued over areas encompassing various arms of the Danube, the adjacent delta, the Black Sea continental shelf, and the minuscule Zmiyiny (Serpent) Island in potentially oil-rich waters. Romania has long claimed Northern Bukovina and Southern Bessarabia, which it ceded to the Soviet Union in 1940, and fervent Romanian nationalists remained committed to incorporating the two areas into a Greater Romania.

Ukraine's foreign policy under President Kuchma was driven by two contradictory goals: to maintain friendly relations with Russia on the one hand and to open the door to Europe with a possible view to membership in the EU on the other. In reference to the former, in 2003 Kuchma was elected as chair of the CIS, becoming the first non-Russian to hold the post. In addition, treaties were signed in 2003 delineating the land boundary between Russia and Ukraine as well as resolving the status of the Sea of Azov as joint territorial waters.

At the same time the Kuchma administration sought to counterbalance its close relations with Russia through a policy of engagement with the United States and the EU. In pursuit of this opening to the West, Kuchma sent 1,650 troops to serve in Iraq in 2003, even though the Supreme Council had approved a motion condemning the U.S.-led intervention in Iraq. (The troops were withdrawn in 2005.)

The victory of Viktor Yushchenko in the controversial 2004 presidential race put a strain on Ukraine's relations with Russia, as Putin had openly supported Yushchenko's main opponent, Viktor Yanukovych. However, Yushchenko's first foreign visit after his inauguration was to Moscow, where he pledged continued close relations. On the other hand, Yushchenko intensified Ukraine's efforts to join the EU and endorsed eventual membership in NATO.

In what was seen as at least a significant symbolic initiative, in November 2005 the EU sent 70 police and customs personnel to help combat smuggling along the Ukrainian-Moldovan border. The EU also recognized Ukraine as having a market economy in February 2006, an important step toward further integration.

Current Issues

Independent Ukraine already has a long history of politically tainted charges and countercharges involving corruption and other illegalities, particularly relating to mismanagement of the energy sector. The Gongadze case made Ukraine's political dynamic even more complex. In early 2001 a philosophically incongruous coalition, ranging from Oleksandr Moroz's Socialist Party to the fascist Ukrainian National Assembly (*Ukrainska Natsionalna Asambleya*—UNA), continued to stage a series of militant "Ukraine Without Kuchma" rallies. The National Salvation Forum (NSF), organized by Moroz, Yuliya Tymoshenko, and others, also pressed for President Kuchma's resignation or removal from office, amid indications that the loyalty of Ukraine's oligarchs, who had been among Kuchma's strongest supporters, might be wavering. As a further complication, Kuchma and Prime Minister Yushchenko were not always in agreement, although they jointly condemned the NSF in a February 2001 statement that was also signed by Supreme Council Chair Ivan Plyushch.

According to reports, the president and Yushchenko heatedly disagreed over Kuchma's January 2001 dismissal of Tymoshenko, who quickly donned the mantle of anticorruption, pro-reform martyr. When she was named deputy prime minister for fuel and energy in January 2000, arrears in natural gas payments to Russia were threatening future supplies, and the electricity grid, highly dependent on coal contracts, was in danger of failing. Tymoshenko vowed to fight the sector's oligarchs and to end graft, insisting, for example, that electricity contracts specify transparent cash settlements instead of the barter arrangements that had left the industry open to profiteering and abuse. She asserted later in the year that her reforms had raised cash payments from 10 percent to 60 percent of the total. Her opponents, however, accused her of abusing the emergency powers that she had assumed in March, and in June Minister of Energy and Fuel Serhiy TULUB resigned because of repeated differences with Tymoshenko.

By mid-2000 Tymoshenko was also drawing fire from Kuchma, who was particularly critical of a natural gas deal she had initialed with Turkmenistan to reduce reliance on Russia's Gazprom, to which several of Ukraine's oligarchs had connections. Before entering government, Tymoshenko herself had made a considerable fortune in the energy business, and her standing was further undermined by corruption allegations against her and her husband, who was remanded to custody in August 2000 on charges of embezzlement. In November a report from a special ministerial commission chaired by National Security and Defense Council Chief Yevhen Marchuk created additional controversy by accusing the government of overstating fuel reserves and revenues from the energy sector while understating debt owed by energy companies to the state. Yushchenko condemned the report, and Tymoshenko charged its authors with committing politically motivated inaccuracies. She subsequently characterized her January 2001 removal from office as a reprisal carried out by Kuchma on behalf of "criminal clans of oligarchs." For its part, the prosecutor general's office justified her detention in February–March by citing new evidence that she had paid nearly $80 million in bribes to former prime minister Lazarenko while he was in office.

Lazarenko, his immunity from prosecution having been lifted by the Supreme Council in 1999, continued to face numerous charges in Ukraine, from accepting bribes to ordering contract killings. In June 2000 he pleaded guilty and was convicted in Switzerland of money laundering during his earlier tenure as governor of Dnipropétrovsk. Lazarenko, not to be outdone, charged in 2000 that Kuchma and his aides had themselves embezzled and laundered hundreds of millions of dollars, including proceeds from IMF loans that were used to purchase high-yielding Ukrainian debt.

Another major domestic concern at the beginning of the 2000s was proposed structural changes in governance. In an April 2000 referendum voters overwhelmingly approved four Kuchma proposals that, if enacted, would have cut the number of legislative deputies from 450 to 300, added an appointive upper chamber to represent regional interests, limited legislators' immunity from prosecution, and given the president authority to dismiss the parliament if it went more than a month without a working majority or if it failed to pass the annual budget within three months of submission. Kuchma had lobbied for the measures as a means of furthering "the systematic and efficient work of the legislature," whereas the majority of the Supreme Council saw the referendum as Kuchma's attempt to diminish the council's authority and to install a presidential system of government. In January 2001 the Supreme Council instead passed a bill adopting a strictly proportional party-list system for the next general election, with parties having to achieve 4 percent of the vote to obtain representation. The bill obviously favored the larger parties and factions and could have dramatically altered the balance of power in the Supreme Council. Kuchma promptly vetoed the electoral bill. The debate over such fundamental structural changes continued into 2002 as much of the opposition sought controls on presidential power.

In August 2002 President Kuchma announced formation of a constitutional commission to study reforms in the hope of eliminating the administrative impasses that had characterized governance since independence. Among other things, he called for establishment of a bicameral legislature. However, his lack of a legislative majority precluded progress.

In October 2002 a senior judge opened a criminal investigation in alleged corruption and abuse of power on the part of the Kuchma administration. Although the Supreme Court subsequently ordered the investigation suspended, anti-Kuchma demonstrations were held in major cities in 2003 and 2004, the opposition claiming that inappropriate force was used by security forces to quell the protests.

The dramatic presidential campaign of late 2004 in Ukraine was one the world's most closely watched political developments. One major focus of the global attention was the apparent poisoning of reformist candidate Yushchenko during the campaign. Yushchenko, who nearly died as a consequence of what was initially described as an unknown illness, later claimed that he had been poisoned during a meeting in September with leaders of the Ukrainian security forces. Tests subsequently appeared to verify that Yushchenko was suffering from dioxin poisoning, which, among other things, had left his face severely disfigured. For many observers, the "before and after" photos of Yushchenko seemed to encapsulate the essence of the presidential contest—a corrupt, perhaps criminal, entrenched administration (represented by Kuchma's handpicked candidate as his potential successor, Prime Minister Viktor Yanukovych) versus a rising tide of reformists determined to shake off the last vestiges of a communist past. Of course, such analysis was simplistic, at best, as Yanukovych enjoyed substantial genuine support in industrialized areas of eastern and southern Ukraine, where much of the population spoke Russian and continued to prefer strong ties with Russia. He also appeared generally content with the economic role of the nation's oligarchs.

Meanwhile, Yushchenko campaigned on a generally "pro-Western" platform that called, among other things, for Ukraine's eventual membership in the EU and NATO. Underscoring Ukraine's long-standing geographic schism in that regard, Yushchenko's support was strongest in central and western areas of the country. Russian leader Putin roiled the political waters even further with his blatant endorsement of Yanukovych's candidacy during Putin's state visit to Ukraine in October.

The mass demonstrations in November and December 2004 that prompted the Supreme Court decision to permit new runoff presidential balloting were widely praised by democracy advocates around the world. Most Western capitals appeared to accept the conclusion that the initial poll had been irrevocably fraudulent. At the same time, however, concern arose that the country faced possible fragmentation, perhaps disintegration, if the results of the final runoff were not accepted by both sides. Consequently, Yanukovych's ultimate capitulation, reportedly issued under the duress of intense international pressure, was greeted with great relief. Nevertheless, critics charged the Kuchma/Yanukovych administration with one final example of corrupt government action, achieved through legal maneuvers that delayed Yushchenko's inauguration until late January 2005. Reformists argued that members of the outgoing government used the extra time to enrich themselves and their cohorts in several ways, particularly through additional sales of state-run enterprises at cut-rate prices. Some critics went so far as to allege that systematic "looting" of public resources had taken place.

Yushchenko's appointment of Yuliya Tymoshenko as prime minister in early 2005 was not considered a surprise in view of the electoral pact they had concluded prior to the presidential poll in which Tymoshenko had eschewed presidential ambitions of her own in favor of support for Yushchenko's bid. Tymoshenko's new cabinet contained a number of "Our Ukraine" ministers as well as representatives of the Socialist Party of Ukraine and the Party of Industrialists and Entrepreneurs of Ukraine; the legislators from the Communist Party of Ukraine provided the main opposition to her appointments. The new administration promised immediate reform in many areas, most notably in regard to combating corruption. Consequently, a number of investigations were reportedly launched into the recent spate of privatizations. The government also announced its intention to pursue EU and NATO memberships with vigor. Shortly thereafter, NATO signaled its intention to approve Ukraine's application eventually, provided that the new government enacted the required military reforms. The EU approved a three-year "action plan" designed to facilitate Ukraine's possible membership, although the commitment was reportedly not sufficiently strong for Yushchenko, who was dissatisfied with the EU's failure to set a timetable for formal accession negotiations to begin. In addition to the perceived need for major additional reforms, the EU's caution was also attributed to concern that quicker action might alienate Russia, which for many years had strongly objected to Ukraine's further integration with the West. For his part, U.S. President George W. Bush unequivocally endorsed Ukraine's applications for membership in NATO and the WTO. During Yushchenko's visit to Washington in April, Bush described the Orange Revolution as a prominent example of the "world changing for the better" through democratization, a cornerstone of his stated foreign policy.

In March 2005 the government relaunched the criminal investigation into the Gongadze case, Yushchenko charging that the previous administration had covered up the facts in the matter. However, momentum toward uncovering the details of the previous privatizations was subsequently reported to have slowed. It appeared that enthusiasm for the investigation waned in part due to concern expressed by foreign investors, who reportedly feared that their interests might be compromised by such scrutiny. Consequently, the government announced new guidelines designed to convince investors that "property rights" would henceforth be protected.

Reform efforts also appeared to be compromised by growing friction between President

Yushchenko and Prime Minister Tymoshenko. In April 2005, faced with gasoline prices that had soared by 30 percent, Tymoshenko imposed mandatory price caps. Perhaps in protest, Russian oil suppliers (responsible for 80 percent of Ukraine's oil needs) subsequently cut back on their distribution to Ukraine, causing significant shortages and consumer angst. Consequently, Yushchenko ordered that the price caps be removed, arguing that they ran counter to his administration's commitment to a market economy. Analysts thereafter noted additional problems, including personal rivalries, that were constraining the ability of the disparate elements behind the Orange Revolution to enact change. For example, surprisingly fractious debate was reported in July over legislation geared toward implementing economic reform required for WTO membership. Complaints also greeted Yushchenko's announcement in August concerning plans to revamp the nation's mining sector. Overall, the lack of effective action was seen as eroding the government's credibility both domestically and internationally only six months after the new administration had been installed amid much optimism.

Mutual allegations of corruption from the supporters of Yushchenko and Tymoshenko intensified following Tymoshenko's dismissal in September 2005. Among other things, the president reportedly had to make several compromises, including a pledge not to prosecute the electoral fraud that had surrounded the 2004 elections, to earn the support of the PR for new prime minister Yekhanurov. The new cabinet was described as "pragmatic" and "more cautious" than the Tymoshenko government, which contributed to the apparent growing disillusionment among supporters of the Orange Revolution as the year ended.

In early January 2006 Russia reduced the flow of natural gas to Ukraine in the wake of several months of conflict over prices. An agreement was reached a few days later that permitted a resumption of full deliveries, but opponents of the accord claimed that Ukraine was being forced to double its payments as a "punishment" for the Orange Revolution. Popular discontent also was exacerbated by

the lack of progress in the Gongadze case. (The trial of three police officers charged with involvement in the journalist's death was adjourned indefinitely in February for the judge to assess if state secrets were involved.)

The NU and BYT hoped to form an electoral coalition prior to the March 2006 legislative poll, but continued friction between the leaders of the two groups prevented an agreement. Consequently, the door was opened for a remarkable comeback by former prime minister Yanukovych and his pro-Russian PR. After months of inconclusive coalition negotiations, Yushchenko ultimately "swallowed his pride" and agreed to Yanukovych's return to the premiership in August. (Analysts suggested that Yushchenko's alternative—new elections—would have produced further decline for the NU.) Although the installation of a government resolved the immediate crisis, it was widely believed that the coalition partners would have difficulty finding lasting common ground regarding issues such as economic reform, relations with Russia, the intensity with which to pursue EU membership, and possible accession to NATO. Regarding the latter, Yushchenko, in apparent deference to the anti-NATO SPU, suggested that a national referendum might be held to define Ukraine's final stance.

Political Parties

Leaders of the executive branch (president, prime minister) have tended to distance themselves from direct participation in party politics while in office. Power in the legislative branch is exercised by various shifting Supreme Council factions, most of which have explicit ties to parties.

As of early 2001, there were 110 officially registered parties in Ukraine. In January 2001 a reported 11 parties and 30 civic groups joined the Ukrainian Right-Wing (*Ukrainska Pravytsya*) alliance as a step toward consolidation of anti-Kuchma forces on the right. It was largely superseded, however, by formation in February of a National Salvation Front (NSF), which was organized as a "citizens' initiative," primarily by supporters of Yuliya Tymoshenko. The NSF had as its goals coordinating activities with the "Ukraine Without Kuchma" movement, advancing a center-right legislative agenda, and marshaling diplomatic support for its anti-Kuchma stance. At the same time, other elements on the center-right coalesced around former prime minister Viktor Yushchenko, and in July they announced formation of an electoral bloc, "Our Ukraine" (*Blok Viktora Yushchenka "Nasha Ukraina"*—NU).

A formal accord by the initial participating parties (*Rukh*, KUN, PKNS, RiP, LPU, Solidarity, RKP, and the Youth Party of Ukraine) was signed in early October.

On July 10, 2001, the NSF had formed an electoral committee that, Tymoshenko indicated, was prepared to engage in "peaceful coexistence or cooperation" with Yushchenko, but he ultimately rejected any alliance with Tymoshenko. In early November the NSF was renamed the Yuliya Tymoshenko Bloc (*Blok Yuliyi Tymoshenko*—BYT). Parties in the BYT included Fatherland, USDP, UNP *"Sobor,"* and URP. Also in October, the pro-Kuchma forces established the third principal electoral bloc, **"For a United Ukraine!"** (*Vyborchiy Blok "Za Yedinu Ukrainu!"*—ZYU), which was chaired by Volodymyr LYTVYN, head of presidential administration. The parties in the ZYU included the APU, NDPU, PPPU, PR, and TU. (The ZYU finished second in the 2002 legislative balloting with 102 seats.) Forces on the left continued to be led by the Communist Party of Ukraine (KPU) and the Socialist Party of Ukraine (SPU).

In all, 33 parties and blocs were listed on the ballot for the March 2002 election, which saw "Our Ukraine" win 23.6 percent of the proportional vote and a plurality of 110 seats; "For a United Ukraine!", 11.8 percent and 101 seats; and the Tymoshenko Bloc, 7.3 percent and 22 seats, well behind the KPU (20.0 percent and 66 seats).

Twenty-eight parties competed independently in the March 2006 legislative balloting, while another 50 parties participated in 17 electoral blocs, including a revamped NU and a slightly modified BYT. Under recent changes in the electoral law, parties were required to have been registered for at least one year to participate in the elections.

Government Parties

Party of Regions (*Partiya Rehioniv*—PR). The PR held its initial congress in March 2001 as the culmination of a process that began with the signing of a merger agreement by five centrist parties in July 2000. Connected to Donetsk financial and industrial interests, the nascent PR quickly formed a new parliamentary faction, Regions of Ukraine.

Of the PR's five founding organizations, the Labor Party of Ukraine (*Partiya Pratsi Ukrainy*—PPU) dated from late 1992, when it was organized by elements descended from Soviet-era official unions. Led by Valentyn LANDYK, the PPU participated in the 1998 general elections in the "Together" electoral alliance with the LPU (below). The Party of Regional Revival of Ukraine (*Partiya Rehionalnoho Vidrodzhennya Ukrainy*—PRVU), which won 0.9 percent of the proportional vote in the 1998 legislative election, was led by Donetsk's mayor, Volodymyr RYBAK, and Yukhym ZVYAHILSKIY. The other three founding parties were the recently formed Party "For a Beautiful Ukraine" (*Partiya "Za Krasyvu Ukrainu"*—PZKU), led by Leonid CHERNOVETSKIY; the All-Ukrainian Party of Pensioners (*Vseukrainskoi Partiya Pensioneriv*—VPP), led by Andriy KAPUSTA and Hennadiy SAMOFALOV; and the Party of Solidarity of Ukraine (*Partiya Solidarnosti Ukrainy*—PSU), formed in July 2000 by the Solidarity (*Solidarnist*) parliamentary faction under Petro Poroshenko.

In November 2000 the emerging party had adopted the unwieldy designation Party of Regional Revival "Labor Solidarity of Ukraine" (*Partiya Rehionalnoho Vidrodzhennya "Trudova Solidarnist Ukrainy"*). At the time, it was considered pro-Kuchma while claiming to represent the interests of the regions within a unified state. At the March founding congress, Mykola AZAROV, the controversial chair of the State Tax Administration, was elected chair, although he was quoted as saying he saw the position as temporary. Poroshenko, who had reportedly sought the chairship, continued to lead the separate Solidarity faction in the Supreme Council and ultimately established the Solidarity party (below). With the next legislative election in sight, Azarov resigned as party leader in January 2002 to avoid charges of conflict of interest.

The PR was a principal forum for Viktor Yanukovych in the 2004 presidential elections. The PR was assisted in the 2006 legislative balloting by financial support from billionaire tycoon Rinat AKHMETOV, who was elected on the PR's list, along with a number of his business associates. Western campaign consultants also contributed to the PR's success (a plurality of 186 seats on a vote share of 32.1 percent). The PR advocated "strong ties" to the EU but opposed NATO membership. Yanukovych also pledged to pursue official language status for Russian and improvements in relations with Russia in general.

Leader: Viktor YANUKOVYCH (Prime Minister), Volodymyr SEMYNOZHENKO (Chair).

"Our Ukraine" Bloc (*Bloc "Nasha Ukraina"*—NU). A successor to the NU that participated in the 2002 legislative balloting (at which it led all parties with 111 seats) and presented Viktor Yushchenko as the successful 2004 presidential candidate, the NU comprised the following parties for the 2006 balloting for the Supreme Council. The NU finished third in the election, securing 81 seats on a vote share of 13.95 percent.

Leader: Viktor YUSHCHENKO (President of Ukraine).

People's Union "Our Ukraine" (*Narodni Soyus "Nasha Ukraina"*—NSNU). The pro-presidential, right-of-center NSNU was formed in early 2005 by supporters of President Yushchenko to, among other things, contest the 2006 legislative elections. It was considered to be a successor to "Our Ukraine," the electoral bloc that had supported Viktor Yushchenko's successful presidential campaign. Reports indicated that some 25 component groups of "Our Ukraine" had participated in the launching of the NSNU. Described by some as the next "party of power," the NSNU nevertheless failed to attract a number of major Yushchenko allies.

Meeting in Kyiv on March 5, 2005, some 6,000 delegates to the NSNU's founding congress elected a 120-member Council and an Executive Committee. Deputy Prime Minister Roman Bezmertnyy was elected as head of the Council, while Yuriy Yekhanurov was named head of the Executive Committee. Yushchenko was named as the party's honorary chair. The NSNU's 21-member presidium included five cabinet members.

Like its predecessor, the NSNU advocated market-driven economics and accelerated integration with Europe. It was initially reported that the NSNU planned to contest the 2006 elections in alliance with the BYT and the APU. However, no major mergers had occurred by the time of the organization's July 2005 congress.

Leaders: Viktor YUSHCHENKO (President of Ukraine and Honorary Chair of the Party), Roman BEZMERTNYY (Former Deputy Prime Minister), Yuriy YEKHANUROV (Former Prime Minister and Head of Executive Committee).

Popular Movement of Ukraine (*Narodnyi Rukh Ukrainy—Rukh*, or NRU). *Rukh* was organized in September 1989 as the Popular Movement of the Ukraine for Restructuring (*NRU za Perebudovu*). From the outset it advocated Ukrainian independence, causing its critics among the anti-Communist groups to charge it with being more nationalist than democratic. Its founding chair, the writer Ivan DRACH, appealed to his colleagues to rally behind President Kravchuk after the latter's break with the KPU. Another leader, Vyacheslav CHORNOVIL, who had secured a 25 percent vote share as the party's presidential candidate in 1991, insisted that *Rukh* should continue in opposition. Thereafter, the party remained deeply divided in regard to the president, although agreeing to fill two important positions (first deputy prime minister and economics minister) in the Kuchma administration. It was not formally registered as a party until 1993.

Campaigning on a platform of market reform and opposition to CIS membership, *Rukh* won 20 seats in its own right in the 1994 legislative elections. The party called for Ukraine's integration into NATO and the EU and for other democratic and reformist parties to unite against the left.

Rukh was the second leading party in the 1998 legislative poll, being credited with about 10 percent of the vote in the nationwide proportional balloting. However, it continued to suffer from what one analyst described as a "crisis in direction" occasioned more by personality differences than policy disputes. In January 1999 Chornovil was ousted as chair in favor of Yuriy Kostenko, a former cabinet minister. Chornovil and his supporters subsequently formed a new parliamentary faction called the Popular *Rukh* of Ukraine-1, or *Rukh*-1. Chornovil died in a car accident in March, and Hennadiy UDOVENKO, a former foreign minister, was named acting chair of the new faction.

Kostenko and Udovenko both ran for president in 1999; the former, technically on the ballot as an independent, won 2.2 percent of the vote, and the latter took 1.2 percent. Following a court challenge over the use of the party name, the two factions were registered separately in January 2000, with Udovenko's party assuming the NRU designation and the Kostenko group taking the name **Ukrainian Popular Movement** (*Ukrainskyi Narodnyi Rukh—Rukh*, or UNR).

In November 2000, looking ahead to the next legislative election, Udovenko's NRU announced an electoral alliance with the Congress of Ukrainian Nationalists (KUN) and the Reforms and Order Party (RiP), both discussed below. In early 2001 it appeared that the two *Rukh* parties could well be allies for the next Supreme Council balloting and might even reunite beforehand. However, although both joined the Yushchenko bloc, they failed to resolve their differences before the March 2002 election. Afterward, both branches continued to express an interest in reuniting. In 2004 Udovenko was replaced as head of his faction by Borys Tarasyuk, while Kostenko and his supporters formed the UNP (below).

Leader: Borys TARASYUK.

Party of Industrialists and Entrepreneurs of Ukraine (*Partiya Promislovtsiv i Pidpryyemtsiv Ukrainy—PPPU*). The PPPU was established by Prime Minister Kinakh in late November 2001. Previously the head of the Ukrainian Union of Industrialists and Entrepreneurs, Kinakh was elected to lead the new party at its February 2002 congress. The party's probusiness platform called for such measures as a significant reduction in the value-added tax and the adoption of policies favoring investment and the development of high-tech, export-oriented industry.

Kinakh was named deputy prime minister in the January 2005 cabinet.

Leader: Anatoliy KINAKH (Former Deputy Prime Minister).

Congress of Ukrainian Nationalists (*Konhres Ukrainskykh Natsionalistiv—KUN*). The KUN was founded in October 1992 as an electoral front of the émigré Organization of Ukrainian Nationalists (OUN, below), which had led the struggle against Soviet communism before being finally suppressed internally in the 1950s. Advocating Ukraine's exit from the CIS but divided between pro-capitalists and those favoring a state economic role, the KUN won five seats in the 1994 balloting, although its leader was prevented from standing in a Lviv constituency. The KUN participated in the National Front alliance with the Ukrainian Republican Party and Ukrainian Conservative Republican Party in the 1998 legislative poll.

Leader: Oleksiy IVCHENKO.

Christian Democratic Union (*Khrystiyansko Demokratichnyj Soyuz—KDS*). The KDS was formed in 2003 by the centrist Christian Popular Union Party (*Partiya Khrystiyansko Noradniy Soyuz—PKNS*), the Ukrainian Christian

Democratic Party, and the All Ukrainian Union of Christians. The first two of those groups had participated in the Forward, Ukraine! (*Vpered, Ukraino!*) electoral alliance that had secured 1.7 percent of the national proportional poll in the 1998 legislative balloting. (Forward, Ukraine! subsequently became a party in its own right; see below.)

Leader: Volodymyr STRETOVYCH.

Ukrainian Republican Party "Assembly" (*Ukrainska Respublnkanska Partiya "Sobor"*—URP *"Sobor"*). The center-right URP *"Sobor"* was formed in December 2005 by former UNP *"Sobor"* leader Anatoliy Matviyenko and disaffected members of the Ukrainian Republican Party.

Leader: Anatoliy MATVIYENKO.

Socialist Party of Ukraine (*Sotsialtstychna Partiya Ukrainy*—SPU). Although organized in 1991 by the former leader of the Communist legislative majority, the SPU was described as "not so much a successor to the Communist Party, as a party of economic populism." As such, it urged retention of a major state role in the economy, while favoring priority for workers in privatization. It won 15 parliamentary seats in 1994 and attracted a further 12 independent deputies into its parliamentary group. In early 1996 two SPU deputies, Nataliya Vitrenko and Volodymyr Marchenko, were expelled from the party for criticizing the leadership for deviating from socialist ideals; they subsequently formed the PSP (below).

The SPU and the Peasants' Party of Ukraine (SelPU, below) formed an electoral bloc called "For Truth, for the People, for Ukraine" for the 1998 legislative poll, the alliance being credited with about 8 percent of the national proportional vote. SPU Chair Oleksandr Moroz, a former chair of the Supreme Council, finished third in the 1999 presidential election, taking 11.3 percent of the vote.

In November 2000 Moroz released secret tape recordings implicating President Kuchma in the disappearance of an independent journalist (see Current issues, above) and then helped form the "Ukraine Without Kuchma" movement and the National Salvation Forum. At the March 2002 election the SPU won 22 seats, 20 of them on the basis of a 6.9 percent share of the proportional vote.

The SPU joined the cabinet named in January 2005. It won 33 seats on a vote share of 5.7 percent in the March 2006 legislative poll. The party was initially perceived as a potential partner in a coalition government that would have included the NU and the BYT, but Moroz switched allegiance to the PR, after which Moroz was elected speaker of the Supreme Council.

Leader: Oleksandr MOROZ (Chair and Speaker of the Supreme Council).

Opposition Parties

Yuliya Tymoshenko Bloc (*Bloc Yuliyi Tymoshenko*—BYT). A successor to the BYT formed by supporters of Yuliya Tymoshenko prior to the 2002 legislative balloting (at which it won 22 seats), the BYT comprised the parties listed below for the 2006 elections (at which it secured 129 seats on a vote share of 22.3 percent). The BYT was aided by the inclusion of Levko LUKYANENKO and his supporters from the URP, who had been left without affiliation following a split in the URP. The BYT campaigned on a platform of support for integration with Western Europe and opposition to the recently completed natural gas deal with Russia. Tymoshenko also maintained a populist stance that promised increased welfare spending and wide-ranging corruption investigations.

Leader: Yuliya TYMOSHENKO (Former Prime Minister).

Fatherland (*Batkivshchyna*). Fatherland (also frequently translated as Motherland) was established as a Supreme Council faction in March 1999 by Yuliya Tymoshenko and other members of the All-Ukrainian Association *"Hromada"* (below) who objected to the parent party's support for Pavlo Lazarenko. Ironically, Tymoshenko had once been a close associate of Lazarenko, who had encouraged her to enter politics. Initially numbering about two dozen deputies, the Fatherland faction soon surpassed

"Hromada," which ultimately fell below the 14 adherents needed for official faction status.

In late December 1999 President Kuchma named Tymoshenko to the new Yushchenko cabinet as deputy prime minister for fuel and energy, but by mid-2000 she was already drawing criticism from Kuchma for her handling of the sector. Despite continuing support from the prime minister, she was dismissed from her cabinet post by Kuchma on January 19, 2001, four days after being formally charged with gas smuggling, tax evasion, and document forgery while head of Unified Energy Systems of Ukraine in 1996–1997.

In late 2001 Fatherland absorbed Stepan Khmara's Ukrainian Conservative Republican Party (*Ukrainska Konservatyvna Respublikanska Partiya*—UKRP). Intensely anti-Communist and anti-Russian, the UKRP had been formed in June 1992 by a radical wing of the URP (below) led by Khmara. Then a URP deputy, Khmara had been arrested and put on trial as the result of a scuffle with an undercover KGB agent in November 1990, although the resultant outcry restored his parliamentary immunity in September 1991. Advocating retention of Ukraine's ex-Soviet nuclear arsenal, Khmara won the UKRP's only seat in the 1994 election. The UKRP joined the URP and KUN in the National Front alliance for the proportional component of the 1998 legislative poll. Unlike those parties, however, it did not secure any mandates in the balloting for the seats from the single-member districts. Calling President Kuchma's policies "criminal," Khmara and his party joined the National Salvation Front in early 2001.

Leaders: Yuliya TYMOSHENKO (Former Prime Minister), Oleksandr TURCHYNOV, Stepan KHMARA.

Ukrainian Social Democratic Party (*Ukrainska Sotsial-Demokratychna Partiya*—USDP). The USDP was established in November 1998 by former justice minister Vasyl Onopenko, previously the leader of the Social Democratic Party of Ukraine (United).

In the 1999 presidential election he finished eighth, with 0.5 percent of the vote.

Leader: Vasyl ONOPENKO.

Ukrainian People's Party "Assembly" (*Ukrainskoho Narodnoho Partiya "Sobor"*— UNP *"Sobor"*). Organized in December 1999 by former members of a number of parties, the anti-Kuchma *Sobor* held a February 2001 congress at which it reelected as its leader Anatoliy Matviyenko, a former Kuchma ally and NDPU chair. Matviyenko called for Kuchma's removal from office, blaming him for Ukraine's "slide to authoritarianism."

In October 2005 a *Sobor* congress voted to participate in the BYT in the 2006 legislative elections, thereby splitting the party.

Matviyenko and his supporters left the party to form the URP *"Sobor"* (above) and participate in the NU, while the remaining UNP *"Sobor"* members were reportedly absorbed into other BYT parties.

Communist Party of Ukraine (*Komunistychna Partiya Ukrainy*—KPU). Formerly Ukraine's ruling party, the KPU was banned in August 1991 but was allowed to reregister in October 1993 (without regaining party property of the Soviet era). Petro Symonenko was elected party leader in 1993. Standing on a traditional platform of anticapitalism and antinationalism, the party secured a plurality of seats in the 1994 legislative balloting and subsequently served as the core of the parliamentary opposition to the economic restructuring efforts of President Kuchma.

The KPU's plurality rose in the 1998 legislative poll, the party performing particularly well in the nationwide proportional balloting, winning about 25 percent of the votes. First Secretary Symonenko finished second in the 1999 presidential poll, winning 22.2 percent of the initial vote and 38.8 percent in a runoff against the incumbent. KPU demands of the subsequent Yushchenko government included severance of ties to NATO, designation of Russian as an official language, commitment to a socialist economy, and central planning for state enterprises.

In 2000 it was reported that the KPU had split into two factions. The first was led by Symonenko and remained decidedly antimarket, anti-American, and pro-Russian. The second adopted the name Communist Party of Ukraine-Reformed; its leader was reported to be Mikhail SAVENKO, a "progressive socialist" who was a member of the Working Ukraine faction in the Supreme Council.

At the March 2002 election the KPU took 66 seats, 59 of them on the basis of winning 20.0 percent of the proportional vote. It secured 21 seats in 2006 on a vote share of 3.7 percent.

Leader: Petro SYMONENKO (First Secretary).

Other Parties Participating in the 2006 Legislative Elections

People's Opposition Bloc of Nataliya Vitrenko (*Blok Natalii Vitrenko Narodna Opoziciya*). This extremely pro-Russian and anti-American grouping was formed by the two parties below prior to the 2006 legislative balloting, at which the bloc secured 2.93 percent of the vote, narrowly missing the threshold required for representation. The bloc opposed Ukraine's proposed membership in NATO, the EU, and the WTO, and called for a new union of Belarus, Russia, and Ukraine.

Leader: Nataliya VITRENKO.

Progressive Socialist Party (*Prohresyvna Sotsialistychna Partiya*—PSP). Formed in 1996 by legislators recently expelled from the SPU, the PSP, considered the most radical of the country's leftist groupings, secured 4 percent of the national proportional vote in the 1998 legislative poll. Labeling herself a "true Marxist," the party's 1999 presidential candidate, Nataliya Vitrenko, finished fourth in the balloting, with 11.0 percent of the vote. In early October she and 33 others had been wounded by a grenade attack at a campaign rally.

For the 2002 election Vitrenko organized the **Nataliya Vitrenko Bloc** (*Blok Nataliyi Vitrenko*), which included the PSP and the **Party of Educators of Ukraine** (*Partiya Osvityan*

Ukrainy—POU). The Bloc won 3.2 percent of the proportional vote but no seats.

Leaders: Nataliya VITRENKO (1999 presidential candidate), Volodymyr MARCHENKO.

Rus'-Ukrainian Union Party (*Partiya Rus'ko-Ukrainsky Soyus*—RUS). The RUS was formed in June 2005 by several pro-Russian groupings, including the Russian Bloc, led by Vladimir PASHKOV, and the Russian Movement of Ukraine, led by Oleg LYUTIKOV.

Leader: Ivan SIMONENKO.

Lytvyn Bloc. This electoral bloc was formed prior to the 2006 legislative balloting by the two parties below and the small **Party of All-Ukrainian Union of the Left "Justice"** in support of Supreme Council Speaker Volodymyr Lytvyn. The bloc secured 2.44 percent of the vote.

Leader: Volodymyr LYTVYN (Former Speaker of the Supreme Council).

People's Party (*Narodna Partiya*—NP). The NP is the recently adopted rubric of the former Agrarian Party of Ukraine (*Ahrarna Partiya Ukrainy*—APU), which was established in 1996 to support farmers and which secured 3.7 percent of the proportional vote in the 1998 legislative balloting, just missing the 4 percent threshold necessary to be allocated proportional seats. At the APU's third congress in June 1999, Mykhaylo HLADIY, then deputy prime minister for the agro-industrial complex, was elected leader over the incumbent, parliamentary deputy Kateryna VASHCHUK. The APU supported President Kuchma's reelection in the October–November balloting.

The APU was renamed the People's Agrarian Party of Ukraine in 2004, with Volodymyr Lytvyn becoming its leader. The NP rubric was adopted in 2005.

Leader: Volodymyr LYTVYN.

Ukrainian National Bloc of Kostenko and Plyushch. Comprising center-right parties (including the UNP and the **Party of Free Peasants and Entrepreneurs of Ukraine**), this bloc (formed in advance of the 2006 legislative poll) supported

Yuriy Kostenko (the leader of the UNP) and parliamentarian Ivan Plyushch. The bloc won 1.87 percent of the vote.

Leaders: Yuriy   KOSTENKO,   Ivan PLYUSHCH.

Ukrainian People's Party (*Ukrainska Narodna Partiya*—UNP). The UNP was formed in 2004 by Yuriy Kostenko and other members of the UNR faction of *Rukh*. The UNP reportedly won several mayoral races in the 2006 local elections.

Leader: Yuriy KOSTENKO.

Council (*Viche*). *Viche* is the recently adopted rubric of the Constitutional Democratic Party (*Konstytutsiyno-Demokratychna Partiya*—KDP), a centrist party that participated in the 1998 legislative balloting with the Interregional Reform Bloc (*Mizhrehionalny Blok Reformiv*—MBR) as part of the Social Liberal Association (*Sotsialno Liberalne Obyednannya*—SLOn), which secured 0.9 percent of the proportional vote. For the 2002 legislative poll the KDP joined the Winter Generation Team (*Komanda Ozymoho Pokolinnja*—KOP). Described by the media as appealing to the Ukrainian equivalent of the West's "Generation X," the KOP bloc won 2 percent of the proportional vote at the March 2002 election. It encompassed the KDP, USDP, LDPU, and the **Private Property Party** (*Partiya Privatnoi Vlasnosti*—PPV).

The new name for the KDP was adopted prior to the 2006 legislative balloting, at which *Viche* secured 1.74 percent of the vote.

Leader: Inna BOHOSLOVSKA.

Civil Political Bloc Pora–PRP. Formed in advance of the 2006 legislative poll by the following two groups, this bloc won 1.47 percent of the vote.

Reforms and Order Party (*Reformy i Poryadok Partiya*—RiP). The previously pro-Kuchma RiP secured 3.1 percent of the national proportional vote in the 1998 legislative poll after negotiations for its inclusion in the "Forward, Ukraine!" alliance with the PKNS and UKhDP had fallen through. In December 2000 it joined Udovenko's *Rukh* and the KUN in announcing formation of a center-right electoral bloc. The RiP supported economic reform and greater integration of Ukraine with Western Europe. The RiP participated in the NU for the 2002 legislative poll.

Leader: Victor PYNZENYK (Former Deputy Prime Minister).

It Is Time (*Pora*) The reformist *Pora* was formed in 2005 by members of youth organizations that had supported the Orange Revolution

Leader: Vladyslav KASKIV.

Liberal Party of Ukraine (*Liberalna Partiya Ukrainy*—LPU). Largely based in Donetsk, the LPU was formed in 1991 by Volodymyr Shcherban, who has served as the governor of the Sumy *oblast,* and Yevhen SHCHERBAN, who was assassinated in 1996. The LPU contested the 1998 legislative poll in the "Together" alliance with the Labor Party of Ukraine; the alliance won 1.9 percent of the national proportional vote.

In January 2005 Shcherban left office, and he subsequently reportedly fled Ukraine after an arrest warrant was issued charging him with corruption. (The former governor insisted the charges were politically motivated.) As a result of Shcherban's status, the LPU was not permitted to participate in the NU for the 2006 legislative poll. Running on its own, the LPU won only 0.04 percent of the vote.

Leader: Volodymyr SHCHERBAN.

"Not Right" Bloc (*Blok "Ne Tak"*—Ne Tak). This bloc was formed in December 2005 by parties opposed to the Orange Revolution. It opposed Ukraine's proposed membership in Western organizations such as NATO and the EU. In addition to the SPDU(O), other *Ne Tak* parties included the **All-Ukrainian Political Union "Women for the Future"** (*Vseukrainske Politychne Obyednannya "Zhinky za Majbutnie"*—ZM), which won 2.1 percent of the proportional vote in the 2002 legislative elections under the leadership of Valentyna DOVZHENKO; the small, centrist **Republican Party of Ukraine,** launched in early 2005 by Yuriy BOYKO, a former head of the state gas company; and the **All-Ukrainian Union "Center."** *Ne*

Tak won 1.01 percent of the vote in the 2006 legislative elections.

Social Democratic Party of Ukraine (United) (*Sotsial-Demokratychna Partiya Ukrainy [Obyednana]*—SDPU[O]). Launched in 1990 by the minority leftist faction of the Ukrainian Social Democratic Movement (*Sotsial-Demokratychna Dvizheniya Ukrainy*—SDDU), the SDPU(O) was committed to democratic socialism in the tradition of the Second International, as exemplified by the prewar Ukrainian Social Democratic Workers' Party. The party's failure to win representation in the 1994 legislative poll strengthened those within it favoring reunion with what was now the SDPU.

Although the party included critics and prominent rivals of Kuchma, officials of the Kuchma government were also members. The SDPU(O) attempted a merger with the SDPU (below) late in 1997, but the negotiations failed. However, it displayed surprising strength in the 1998 legislative election, attaining the required threshold of 4 percent to be allocated seats in the nationwide proportional voting.

In December 2001 the Supreme Council ousted the party's chair as first deputy speaker for alleged abuse of authority and related offenses. At the March 2002 election the SPDU(O) won 6.3 percent of the proportional vote and 24 seats.

Leaders: Viktor MEDVEDCHUK (Chair), Leonid KRAVCHUK (Former President), Oleksandr ZINCHENKO (Former Parliamentary Faction Leader).

Working Ukraine (*Trudova Ukraina*—TU). Working Ukraine (frequently translated into English as Labor Ukraine) was organized in March 1999 as a parliamentary faction. A 1998 electoral bloc of the same name, encompassing the Ukrainian Party of Justice (*Ukrainska Partiya Spravedlyvosti*—UPS) and the Civil Congress of Ukraine (*Hromadyanskiy Kongres Ukrainy*—HKU), had won 3 percent of the national propor-

tional vote and one seat, held by the UPS's Andriy DERKACH, who joined the new faction.

Established as a party in June 1999, the TU was initially led by Mykhalyo SYROTA, who was subsequently associated with the Solidarity parliamentary faction. By that time party leadership had passed to former economic minister Serhiy Tyhypko, who was generally regarded as one of Ukraine's most prominent oligarchs. As of February 2001 the party's parliamentary faction comprised 48 deputies, second only to that of the KPU. Having called for formation of a coalition government, the TU subsequently campaigned to unseat Prime Minister Yushchenko.

One of the TU's stalwarts is Viktor PINCHUK, who represents the powerful Dnepropetrovsk clan and is a son-in-law of former president Kuchma. The TU, which had participated in the For a United Ukraine electoral bloc in 2002, secured only 0.09 percent of the vote running on its own in 2006.

Leaders: Serhiy TYHYPKO (Chair), Ihor SHAROV (Former Parliamentary Leader).

Green Party of Ukraine (*Partiya Zelenykh Ukrainy*—PZU). The PZU was formed in 1990 as the political wing of the Green World (*Zeleniy Svit*) movement established in 1987. The party was best known for its campaigning on the Chernobyl issue, but it remained poorly organized as an electoral force. The PZU was credited with only 1.3 percent of the nationwide proportional vote in the 2002 legislative balloting and 0.54 percent in 2006.

Leaders: Vitaliy KONONOV (President), Serhiy KURYKIN (Chair).

Peasants' Party of Ukraine (*Selyanska Partiya Ukrainy*—SelPU). Organized in January 1992 as the rural counterpart of the SPU, the SelPU was committed to land collectivization and opposed to rapid economic reform. By virtue of its strong support in the Soviet-era rural bureaucracy, it won 19 seats in the 1994 legislative balloting and subsequently attracted 31 independent deputies into its parliamentary group. Following the 1998 legislative poll (in which the SeIPU competed in alliance with the SPU), Chair Oleksandr Tkachenko, a strong opponent of IMF-requested economic reform, was elected chair of the Supreme Council. However, in early 2000 he was voted out, in what was dubbed a "velvet revolution," by a pro-Kuchma majority. In 2002 Tkachenko was included on the KPU electoral list. The SeIPU secured 0.31 percent of the vote in the 2006 legislative poll.

Leaders: Oleksandr TKACHENKO (Chair of the Party and Former Chair of the Supreme Council), Serhiy DOVHAN.

Ukrainian National Assembly (*Ukrainska Natsionalna Asambleya*—UNA). The UNA, an essentially fascist grouping, was formed initially as a loose alliance of right-wing parties that from June 1990 to August 1991 styled itself the Ukrainian Interparty Assembly. The UNA compared the situation in Ukraine with that of Germany under the Weimar Republic and in the fall of 1991 organized a paramilitary affiliate, the **Ukrainian National Self-Defense** (*Ukrainska Narodna Sambooborunu*—UNSO), in emulation of the interwar Nazi brown shirts. At least three candidates identified with the UNA were elected in western Ukraine in the 1994 legislative balloting, and the party also polled strongly in Kyiv. It came under legal challenge in 1995 because of its alleged involvement in paramilitary activities at home and abroad and was reportedly banned by order of the Justice Ministry on September 6. However, it was permitted to contest the 1998 legislative balloting, securing 0.4 percent of the national proportional vote. Its registration was subsequently revoked again, but in early 2001 the UNA-UNSO was actively organizing the more militant "Ukraine Without Kuchma" demonstrators. The UNA won less than 0.1 percent of the proportional vote at the 2002 legislative election and 0.06 percent in 2006.

Leaders: Andrij SHKIL (Chair), Oleh VITOVYCH.

Patriots of Ukraine Bloc. Formed in advance of the 2006 legislative balloting, this bloc included the UNKP and the **Patriotic Party of Ukraine** (*Patriotychna Partiya Ukrainy*—PPU), which, under the leadership of Mykola HABER (who had won 0.1 percent of the vote in the 1999 presidential elec-

tion), had organized the **Against All** bloc in the 2002 legislative poll.

Ukrainian National Conservative Party (*Ukrainska Natsionalno-Konservatyvna Partiya*—UNKP). The UNKP was formed in 1992 by merger of the former Ukrainian National Party (*Ukrainska Natsionalna Partiya*—UNP), founded in Lviv under the leadership of Hryhorii PYRKHODKO in October 1989, and the Ukrainian People's Democratic Party (*Ukrainska Narodno-Demokratychna Partiya*—UNDP), a free-market group launched in Kiev in June 1990 under the leadership of Oleksandr BONDARENKO. The UNKP participated in the KNDS coalition in the 1994 legislative balloting.

In 1999 the party dismissed Deputy Chair Viktor RODIONOV for his support of Yevhen Marchuk in the presidential race. The party instead backed President Kuchma and his proreform, pro-European integration policies, although by early 2001 it had joined other rightist groups in criticizing Kuchma for his economic failures, what was perceived as a softened stance toward Russia, and authoritarianism. In late January the UNKP was one of the more than 40 parties and civic organizations forming the Ukrainian Right-Wing alliance.

Leader: Oleh SOSKIN.

Revival Party. This group was founded in 2005 by Heorhiy Kirpa, who was a former minister of transportation. It won 0.96 percent of the vote in the 2006 legislative poll.

Leader: Heorhiy KIRPA.

State Party (*Derzhava Partiya*). Formed by former federal prosecutor Hennadiy Vasylyev, *Derzhava* led a *Derzhava*–Labor Union Bloc that included the **All-Ukrainian Party of Laborers** in the 2006 legislative elections, securing 0.14 percent of the vote.

Leader: Hennadiy VASYLYEV.

Party of National Economic Development (*Partiya Natsionalno Ekonomichnoho Rozvytku Ukrainy*—PNERU). Led by banker Volodymyr

Matviyenko, the PNERU won one seat in the 2002 legislative balloting but fell to a 0.23 percent vote share in the 2006 poll.

Leader: Volodymyr MATVIYENKO.

"For Union" Bloc. This bloc was formed in 2005 by the Union Party, the **Socialist Ukraine Party,** the **Homeland Party,** and the **Slavic Party.** The bloc secured 0.20 percent of the vote in the 2006 legislative poll.

Union Party (*Partiya "Soyuz"*). Essentially a Crimean grouping that advocates creation of a union of Ukraine, Belarus, and Russia, this party secured 0.7 percent of the vote in the 1998 national proportional poll. In 2002 it ran as part of a **Russian Bloc** that also included the **"For a United Russia" Party** and the **Russo-Ukrainian Union Party**.

Leader: Svitlana SAVCHENKO.

Ukrainian Conservative Party. This group is reportedly most well-known for what is perceived to be its anti-Semitic platform. It secured 0.09 percent of the vote in the 2006 legislative elections.

Leader: Heorhiy SHCHYOKIN.

Lazarenko Bloc. Supportive of former Prime Minister Pavlo Lazarenko (as of August 2006 facing a ten-year jail sentence in the United States on money-laundering and other charges), this bloc was formed for the 2006 legislative elections by the two parties below and the **Social Democratic Union** (*Sotsial Demokratychnyy Soyuz*—SDS). (The SDS had been a member of the Unity Bloc [below] for the 2002 poll.) The bloc secured 0.30 percent of the vote in 2006.

Leader: Pavlo LAZARENKO (in custody in the United States).

All-Ukrainian Association "Community" (*Vseukrainske Obyednannya "Hromada"*). Founded in September 1997, *"Hromada"* elected former prime minister Pavlo Lazarenko as its first chair and joined the KPU and other leftist groups in blocking many initiatives proposed by the Kuchma/Pustovoytenko administration. The party's legislative stance appeared less founded in ideology than in Lazarenko's enmity toward Kuchma, who had insisted on Lazarenko's ouster as prime minister in the wake of corruption allegations. *"Hromada"* was credited with about 5 percent of the nationwide proportional vote in the 1998 legislative poll.

In December 1998 Lazarenko was arrested at the border by Swiss authorities on money-laundering charges; he was subsequently released on bail of $2.6 million. Lazarenko left Ukraine for the United States in February 1999, after the Supreme Council had removed his immunity from prosecution and Ukrainian prosecutors had begun preparations to charge him with embezzlement and other malfeasance. The scandal surrounding Lazarenko split *"Hromada,"* with his supporters nominating him as the party's 1999 presidential candidate despite the corruption charges while Lazarenko's opponents coalesced in a breakaway faction called Fatherland (above) under the leadership of Yuliya Tymoshenko.

Lazarenko pleaded guilty to Swiss charges in June 2000. He received an 18-month sentence in absentia, and authorities confiscated $6.6 million from his accounts for return to Ukraine. In October 2002 he remained under custody in the United States, where he faced additional money-laundering charges. Ukraine continued to seek his extradition. In August 2006 Lazarenko was convicted by a U.S. court and sentenced to ten years in prison. His case was immediately appealed.

Leader: Pavlo LAZARENKO (Former Prime Minister).

Social Democratic Party of Ukraine (*Sotsial-Demokratychna Partiya Ukrainy*—SDPU). The SDPU was formed as the SDP by the majority moderate faction of the Ukrainian Social Democratic Movement (SDDU), which split at its inaugural congress in May 1990. Likened to the German SPD, the party urged a complete break with Marxism but attracted only sparse support, winning two seats in 1994.

In February 1995 the SDPU was reregistered following a merger with the Human Rights Party and, according to reports, the Ukrainian Party of Justice (UPS), although the latter contested the 1998 election as part of the Working Ukraine alliance. The SDPU received only 0.3 percent of the proportional vote in the 1998 legislative election. In the 2002 campaign it renewed its claim to being the only truly social democratic party in Ukraine, but it again attracted negligible vote support.

Leader: Yuriy BUZDUHAN.

Bloc of National-Democratic Parties. This bloc was formed for the 2006 legislative balloting by the parties below and others, including the **Christian Liberal Party of Ukraine** and the **Ukrainian Christian Democratic Party**. The bloc secured 0.49 percent of the 2006 vote.

Democratic Party of Ukraine (*Demokratychna Partiya Ukrainy*—DPU). Based in the intelligentsia, the DPU was organized in December 1990 by a number of former members of *Rukh*. It supported strong presidential rule, a social market economy, and withdrawal from the CIS, while placing somewhat greater emphasis on human rights than the URP. Strongly represented in the 1990–1994 legislature, the DPU slumped to two party seats and four associated independents in 1994. It contested the national proportional component of the 1998 legislative poll in an alliance with the PEVK (see Regional Parties, below) called the "Bloc of Democratic Parties—NEP (Power of People, Economy, Order)," which secured 1.2 percent of the vote. In 2002 it joined the liberal **Democratic Union** (*Demokratychnyy Sojuz*—DS) of Volodymyr HORBULIN in a DPU-DS electoral bloc that won four Supreme Council seats.

Leader: Volodymyr YAVORIVSKIY.

People's Democratic Party of Ukraine (*Narodno-Demokratychna Partiya Ukrainy*—NDPU). The NDPU was registered in June 1996 as the result of a merger of centrist politi-

cal forces, including the Party for Democratic Revival of Ukraine (*Partiya Demokratychna Vidrodzhennia Ukrainy*—PDVU), New Wave (*Nova Khvylia*—NK), and the Labor Congress of Ukraine (*Trudova Kogres Ukrainy*—TKU). The PDVU had earlier formed the core of the New Ukraine center-left alliance and had won four seats in the 1994 balloting.

The NK had been launched in 1993 by a number of centrist deputies anxious to provide a promarket alternative to reactionary nationalism. It returned four "independent" deputies from Lviv in the 1994 balloting, partly because of the high profile of Viktor Pynzenyk as the leading reformer in the government. The NDPU was credited with about 5 percent of the nationwide proportional vote in the 1998 legislative balloting.

In June 1999 Anatoliy Matviyenko, the party chair, resigned in opposition to the NDPU's endorsement of President Kuchma for reelection. Matviyenko was particularly critical of Kuchma's economic failures. Prime Minister Pustovoytenko was elected to succeed Matviyenko, who went on to form URP *"Sobor"* (above) later in the year.

Leaders: Valeriy PUSTOVOYTENKO (Chair of the Party and Former Prime Minister), Oleksandr KARPOV.

Forward, Ukraine! (*Vpered, Ukraine!*). Initially formed as an electoral alliance of the PKNS and the Ukrainian Christian Democratic Party for the 1998 legislative poll, Forward, Ukraine! subsequently registered as a party in its own right and participated in the NU in the 2002 legislative poll. Running on its own, Forward, Ukraine! secured 0.02 percent of the legislative vote in 2006.

Popular Movement of Ukraine for Unity (*Narodnyi Rukh Ukrainy za Yednist*). A "third way" *Rukh* splinter that rejected participation in either Yuriy Kostenko's UNR or Hennadiy Udovenko's NRU, this party participated unsuccessfully on its own in the 2002 legislative poll. It secured 0.13 percent of the vote in 2006.

Leader: Bogdan BOIKO.

Other Parties and Groups

Solidarity (*Solidarnist*). Solidarity began as a faction in the Supreme Council. Organized in February 2000, it drew defectors from a number of factions, including Fatherland, the SDPU(O), and the NDPU. In July 2000 the faction leaders established the Party of Solidarity of Ukraine (*Partiya Solidarnosti Ukrainy*—PSU), which subsequently participated in formation of the Party of Regions (PR, above). Differences soon emerged within the latter, however, and the PSU leader, Petro Poroshenko, remained at the head of the separate Solidarity faction in the legislature before organizing the Solidarity party, which participated in the NU for the 2002 legislative balloting.

Leader: Petro POROSHENKO.

Liberal-Democratic Party of Ukraine (*Liberalno-Demokratychna Partiya Ukrainy*—LDPU). The LDPU was founded in Kiev in November 1990 on the premise that "socialism is incompatible with humanism and democracy." Its centrist orientation sharply distinguished it from the right-wing Russian Liberal Democratic Party. In the December 1991 presidential election the LDPU backed the candidacy of Volodymyr HRYNYOV. The LDPU participated in the European Choice electoral alliance with the USDP for the 1998 legislative balloting. The party was refused permission to participate in the 2006 legislative poll for technical reasons.

Leader: Andriy KOVAL.

Ukrainian Republican Party (*Ukrainska Respublikanska Partiya*—URP). The URP was launched during a congress of the Ukrainian Helsinki Union in April 1990, becoming Ukraine's first modern non-Communist party to receive official recognition. Its stated aim was the creation of a "parliamentary republic . . . [with] guaranteed freedom of activity."

In 1992 Mykhaylo HORYN, a cofounder of *Rukh,* joined the URP and was instrumental in organizing the Congress of National Democratic Forces (*Kongres Natsionalno–Demokratychnykh Syl*—KNDS), a coalition of some 20 organizations dedicated to working for national unity under President Kravchuk. In addition to the URP and the Ukrainian Christian Democratic Party, the congress included the DPU and UNKP (both above) and the USDP (below).

The KNDS was credited with winning an aggregate of some 25 seats in the 1994 balloting, although the URP, weakened by the exit of a radical faction that became the Ukrainian Conservative Republican Party (UKRP, see Fatherland, above), won only 11 of those seats, one of its defeated candidates being Horyn. (He subsequently helped form the Republican Christian Party, below). The URP led an unsuccessful effort to impeach President Kuchma in September 1997, accusing him of compromising the nation's sovereignty through the Black Sea treaty with Russia.

The URP contested the 1998 legislative election in a National Front (*Natsionalnyi Front*) alliance with the KUN (above) and the UKRP; however, the front won only 2.7 percent of the national proportional voting and therefore no proportional seats. The URP joined several other right-wing parties in supporting the 1999 presidential candidacy of former Security Service chief and prime minister Yevhen Marchuk, who won 8.1 percent of the vote, for fifth place in the October election.

In late 2001 the URP absorbed Oleksandr SERHIYENKO's Ukrainian Christian Democratic Party (*Ukrainska Khrystiyansko-Demokratychna Partiya*—UKhDP). Based in the Uniate Catholic population of Galicia, the UKhDP had been organized in April 1990 as the outgrowth of a Ukrainian Christian Democratic Front formed in 1989. Its founders hoped to emulate the success of Bavaria's Christian Social Union, before encountering a number of internal controversies that led in 1992 to the withdrawal of a moderate faction to form the Christian Democratic Party of Ukraine (*Khrystiyansko-Demokratychna Partiya Ukrainy*—KhDPU).

At an extraordinary session in October 2005, the URP split into two camps. One faction under the leadership of Levko Lukyanenko retained the

URP rubric, while a larger faction formed the URP *"Sobor"* (above). The rump URP was left without legal standing for the 2006 legislative poll. Consequently, Lukyanenko and several supporters were elected to the Supreme Council as part of the BYT. Following the elections, Lukyanenko said that the URP would be relaunched.

Leaders: Levko LUKYANENKO.

Organization of Ukrainian Nationalists (*Orhanizatsiya Ukrainskykh Natsionalistiv—* OUN). The present OUN was established in Lviv in January 1993 by Ivan KANDYBA and elements of the historic OUN that were critical of the organization's émigré leadership for deciding to set up the Congress of Ukrainian Nationalists (KUN, above) as an electoral arm. Kandyba and his associates instead wanted to reestablish the domestic OUN, which had led opposition to Communist rule until suppressed in the 1950s. To distinguish it from the external group, the new group was initially identified as the "Organization of Ukrainian Nationalists in Ukraine."

Kandyba had previously been chair of the DSU (below) and succeeded in attracting his successor, Volodymyr SHLEMKO, into the OUN in December 1993. Although the OUN and the KUN ran separately in the 1994 legislative election, the OUN was registered not as a party per se, but as a civic association. In 1999 it backed Yevhen Marchuk for the presidency, and in January 2001 it joined in formation of the anti-Kuchma Ukrainian Right-Wing.

Leaders: Mykola PLAVYUK, Orest VASKUL.

Unity Bloc (*Blok "Yednist"*). Led by Kyiv Mayor Oleksandr Omelchenko, the Unity electoral bloc was established prior to the 2002 national election on the basis of his **Ukrainian Party "Unity"** (*Ukrainska Partiya "Yednist"*), which was joined by several other minor formations, including the **Social Democratic Union** (*Sotsial Demokratychnyy Sojuz—*SDS) of Sergei PERESUNKO, the **Young Ukraine** (*Moloda Ukraina—*MU), and the **Ukrainian Justice Party–Union of Veterans, Invalids, and Victims of Chernobyl and the Afghan War** (*Ukrainska Partiya Spravedlivosti–Sojuz Vet-*

*eraniv, Invalidiv, Chornobiltsiv, Afgantsiv—*UPS). The Unity bloc won three Supreme Council seats in 2002.

Leader: Oleksandr OMELCHENKO.

Ukrainian Peasants' Democratic Party (*Ukrainska Selianska Demokratychna Partiya—* USDP). Founded at Lviv in June 1990, the USDP attempted to draw support from rural dwellers committed to individual farming. However, because of the lengthy period of communalization under the Communists, it remained much less influential than the pro-collectivization SelPU (above). The USDP formed an electoral alliance with the LDPU (above) called European Choice of Ukraine (*Yevropeiski Vybir Ukrainy—*YVU) for the 1998 legislative poll. However, the alliance secured only 0.1 percent of the national proportional vote.

Leader: Viktor PRYSYAZHNYUK.

Yabluko. Defining itself as a right-centrist party, *Yabluko* ("Apple") was formed in December 1999 to support Ukraine's capitalists and the middle class. A corresponding faction of about 14 deputies (the minimum required for recognition) formed within the Supreme Council. At the 2002 legislative election, however, it won only 1.2 percent of the proportional vote and no seats.

Leaders: Viktor CHAIKA, Mykhaylo BRODSKIY.

Social-National Party of Ukraine (*Sotsial-Natsionalna Partiya Ukrainy—*SNPU). An extreme nationalist grouping, the SNPU has been described as a "black-shirted," neo-Nazi formation whose emblem is a swastika-like modification of Ukraine's national symbol, the Trident. For the 1998 legislative election it ran with the DSU in a "Less Talk" (*Menche Sliv*) alliance, which secured 0.2 percent of the national proportional vote. In May 2000 the SNPU concluded a cooperation agreement with the like-minded French National Front of Jean-Marie Le Pen, and in January 2001 it signed on as a founding member of the Ukrainian Right-Wing alliance.

Leader: Yaroslav ANDRUSHKIV.

Ukrainian Statehood and Independence (*Derzhavna Samostiynist Ukrainy*—DSU). The DSU was launched in May 1990 by Ivan Kandyba, a former political prisoner, who aspired to recreate the historic Organization of Ukrainian Nationalists (see OUN, above). Pledged to the formation of a "Greater Ukraine," it admitted only Ukrainians with no record of affiliation with the Communists. Volodymyr SHLEMKO replaced Kandyba as DSU leader in December 1992 but came into increasing dispute with deputy leader Roman KOVAL over the latter's calls for Ukraine to be "ethnically cleansed" of Russians and Jews, opting in December 1993 to take his faction into Kandyba's OUN. The rump DSU backed President Kravchuk's unsuccessful re-election bid in 1994, but in legislative balloting it was the most successful of the far-right parties, returning 25 deputies who stood officially as independents. It joined the SNPU in the "Less Talk" electoral alliance in 1998 after the two parties failed to reach agreement on joining the National Front with the Ukrainian Conservative Republican Party (UKRP; see Fatherland, above), the URP, and the KUN.

Other parties in the "Our Ukraine" Bloc in 2002 included the **Republican Christian Party** (*Respublikanska Krystyyanska Partiya*—RKP), which was founded in 1997 by Mykola POROVSKYI, Mykhaylo HORYN, and Mykola HORBAL and which won 0.5 percent of the 1998 proportional vote, and the **Youth Party of Ukraine** (*Molodizna Partiya Ukrainy*—MPU), which is led by Yuriy PAVLENKO and which played a role in the demonstrations that led to the annulment of the first presidential runoff in 2004.

Regional Parties

There are a number of active Crimean parties in addition to branches of many Ukrainian parties. The **Communist Party of Crimea** (*Kommunisticheskaya Partiya Kryma*—KPK), led by Leonid HRACH, was banned in 1991 but permitted to reregister in 1993. The **National Movement of the Crimean Tatars** (*Natsionalyi Dvizheniya Krymskikh Tatar*—NDKT), led by Vashtiy AB-DURAYIMOV, is the oldest of the Crimean Tatar groups, dating from the 1960s and formally established in April 1987. The **National Party** (*Milli Firka*—MF) is a radical Tatar group founded in August 1993 and named after the party that attempted to set up an independent Crimean Tatar republic in 1917–1918. The **Organization of the Crimean Tatar National Movement** (*Organizatsiya Krymskotatarskogo Natsionalnogo Dvizheniya*—OKND), the largest of the Crimean Tatar parties, urges exclusive jurisdiction for the Crimean parliament. The business-oriented **Party for the Economic Revival of Crimea** (*Partiya Ekonomicheskogo Vozrozhdeniya Kryma*—PEVK), which won one seat in the Supreme Council in 1994, has been led by Vladimir SHE-VIOV (Volodymyr SHEVYOV). The secessionist **Republican Movement of Crimea** (*Republikanskoe Dvizheniya Kryma*—RDK) is led by Yuriy MESHKOV, who was elected president of Crimea in January 1994. The **Russian Party of the Crimea** (*Russkoi Partiya Kryma*—RPK) was founded under the leadership of Sergei SHUVAINIKOV in September 1993 as a radical splinter of the RDK. The **For Yanukovych Bloc** was organized in Crimea in 2005 by supporters of former prime minister Viktor Yanukovych, while the **Kunitsyn Bloc** was launched by supporters of former Crimean prime minister Serhiy Kunitsyn. The former won 44 seats on a 33 percent vote share in the March 2006 balloting for the Crimean Supreme Council, while the latter secured 10 seats on a 7.6 percent vote share. The KPK finished fourth in the balloting with 9 seats.

Other regional or ethnically based groups include the **Democratic Movement of the Donbas** (*Demokraticheskoe Dvizheniya Donbassa*—DDD); the **Union for Democratic Reforms** (*Obiednannia Demokratychnykh Peretvoren*—ODP), formed under the leadership of Serhiy USTYCH in December 1993 by former Soviet officials in the Transcarpathia region of western Ukraine; and the **Subcarpathian Republican Party** (SRP), which was established in 1992 to press for Transcarpathian autonomy.

Cabinet

As of September 1, 2006

Prime Minister	Viktor Fedorovych Yanukovych (PR)
First Deputy Prime Minister	Mykola Yanovych Azrov (PR)
Deputy Prime Ministers	Andriy Petrovych Klyuyev (PR)
	Dmytro Volodymyrovych Tabachnyk (PR)
	Volodymyr Rybak Vasylyovych (PR)

Ministers

Agrarian Policy	Yuriy Fedorovych Melnyk
Building, Architecture, Housing, and Communal Services	Volodymyr Rybak Vasylyovych (PR)
Cabinet Affairs	Anatoliy Volodymyrovych Tolstoukhov (PR)
Coal Industry	Serhiy Borysovych Tulub (PR)
Culture and Tourism	Ihor Dmytrovych Likovy (NU)
Defense	Anatoliy Stepanovych Hrytsenko (NU)
Economy	Volodymyr Oleksiyovych Makukha (PR)
Education and Science	Stanislav Mykolayovych Nikolayenko (SPU)
Emergency Situations	Viktor Ivanovych Baloha (NU)
Environmental Protection	Vasyl Heorhiyovych Dzharty (PR)
Family, Youth, and Sports	Yuriy Oleksiyovych Pavlenko (NU)
Finance	Mykola Yanovych Azarov (PR)
Foreign Affairs	Borys Ivanovych Tarasyuk (NU)
Fuel and Energy	Yuriy Anatoliyovych Boyko (PR)
Health	Dr. Yuriy Volodymyrovych Polyachenko (NU)
Industrial Policy	Anatoliy Ivanovych Holovko
Interior	Yuriy Vitaliyovych Lutsenko (SPU)
Justice	Roman Mykhaylovych Zvarych (NU)
Labor and Social Policy	Mykohaylo Mykolayovych Papiyev (PR)
Relations with the Supreme Council	Ivan Ivanovych Tkalenko (PR)
Transport and Communications	Mykola Mykolayovych Rudkovsky (SPU)

Legislature

Supreme Council (*Verkhovna Rada*). Formerly styled the Supreme Soviet, Ukraine's legislature is a unicameral body of 450 members. Under changes to the electoral law effective with the election of March 29, 1998, 225 members were elected directly by a majority voting in single-member districts and 225 were seated via propositional voting from party lists of those parties who met a 4 percent threshold in separate nationwide balloting. The term of office was four years. However under constitutional changes that went into effect in January 2006, all 450 members were designated to be selected via proportional representation from a single nationwide constituency in future elections. In addition, the threshold to secure representation was decreased to 3 percent, while the term of office was increased to five years. The revisions also precluded legislators from changing their allegiances during a legislative term, while no independent candidates were permitted.

Following the balloting of March 26, 2006, the seats were distributed as follows: the Party of Regions (PR), 186 seats (151 PR members and 35 unaffiliated members); the Yuliya Tymoshenko

Bloc, 129 (Fatherland Party, 62; the Ukrainian Social Democratic Party, 8; unaffiliated, 59); the "Our Ukraine" Bloc, 81 (the People's Union "Our Ukraine," 39; the Popular Movement of Ukraine, 10; the Party of Industrialists and Entrepreneurs of Ukraine, 8; the Christian Democratic Union, 3; the Ukrainian Republican Party "Assembly," 3; the Congress of Ukrainian Nationalists, 3; and unaffiliated, 15); the Socialist Party of Ukraine (SPU), 33 (SPU, 29; unaffiliated, 4); and the Communist Party of Ukraine (KPU), 21 (all KPU members).

Speaker: Oleksandr MOROZ.

Communications

Freedom of speech is guaranteed in the Ukrainian constitution, but prior to recent liberalization, opposition publications were frequently subjected to official harassment and libel suits brought by government officials. In January 2001 the chair of the parliamentary committee responsible for freedom of speech and information decried efforts at political censorship, including "selective" financial support offered by the government. Officials were known to limit access to licenses, newsprint, and electricity and to exert pressure on advertisers. Collaterally, domestic and international advocates for freedom of expression criticized the Ukrainian government for inadequately investigating the disappearance and murder of independent journalist Heorhiy Gongadze in 2000. The Parliamentary Assembly of the Council of Europe, for one, cited "intimidation, repeated aggressions, and murders" directed against journalists. At a September 2001 rally marking the anniversary of Gongadze's disappearance, participants unveiled a plaque dedicated to the 18 journalists who had been killed since 1991.

In April 2001 the government's television and radio council appeared ready to hinder domestic transmission of the BBC World Service, the Voice of America, and Deutsche Welle by selling to a new station the frequency on which all three had been transmitted by the independent *Kontinent* radio, with which Gongadze had worked. The government noted that *Kontinent* had failed to meet loan repayments to a state bank, and later in the year it revoked the station's license, ostensibly because of overdue tax payments. The station nevertheless continued to broadcast.

In 2003 Freedom House downgraded its assessment of Ukraine's media status from partially free to not free. Reporters Without Borders reported that more than 50 reporters were arrested in 2003. The government also reportedly continued to use criminal libel cases and civil suits to intimidate the media. In addition, the Kuchma administration passed legislation in 2004 allowing the government to monitor Internet publications and e-mails, an initiative critics claimed was aimed at popular opposition websites. The hard line toward media freedom was perceived as partially responsible for the popular antigovernment sentiment that propelled the Orange Revolution in late December 2004, after which the Yushchenko administration pledged quick liberalization in favor of a Western-style media policy. The OSCE reported that the media coverage of the 2006 legislative elections was significantly improved, with parties and electoral blocs able to communicate their messages to the electorate.

Press

In 1998 *Vseukrainskiye Vedomosti* (All-Ukrainian Gazette) was fined $1.8 million for a mistaken sports report and subsequently ceased publication. *Pravda Ukrainy,* the largest opposition newspaper, was shut down in 1998 on a technicality, although it was permitted to reregister in early 1999. *Kievskie Vedomosti,* the country's oldest independent newspaper, closed down in February 1998 after years of confrontations with national and Kyiv government officials; it resumed publication two months later under changed ownership. At the same time, Kyiv's opposition *Polityka* ceased publication.

The following are dailies published in Kyiv in Ukrainian, unless otherwise noted: *Holos Ukrainy* (Voice of Ukraine, 768,000), Supreme Council organ in Ukrainian and Russian; *Silski Visti* (Rural News, 450,000), former KPU organ;

Demokratychna Ukraina (Democratic Ukraine, 311,300), formerly *Radyanska Ukraina* (Soviet Ukraine), independent; *Uradoviy Kur'er* (Official Courier, 200,000), government organ, now privately owned; *Rabochaya Gazeta/Robitnycha Hazeta* (Workers' Gazette, 176,000), former KPU organ, in Ukrainian and Russian; *Vecherniy Kyiv* (Kiev Evening, 90,000); *Za Vilnu Ukrainu* (Lviv, 50,000), independent; *Pravda Ukainy* (Ukrainian Truth, 358,300), in Russian, independent.

News Agency

The official domestic facility is the Ukrainian National Information Agency (Ukrinform), headquartered in Kyiv; the Ukrainian Independent Information and News Agency (*Ukrayinske Nezalezhne Informatsiyne Agentsvo Novyn*—UNIAN) is a leading independent press source. A number of foreign bureaus, including Reuters, maintain offices in the capital.

Broadcasting and Computing

In February 2000 a unified State Committee for Information Policy, Television, and Radio Broadcasting (*Derzhkominform*) was established, one of its goals being to restrict national broadcasts to the Ukrainian language except in areas with substantial minority communities. The Ukrainian State Television and Radio Company (*Derzhavna Teleradiomovna Kompaniya Ukrainy*) currently broadcasts in Ukrainian and Russian. There were also a limited number of commercial outlets transmitting to approximately 29.6 million television receivers. There were some 1.0 million personal computers serving 950,000 Internet users in 2003.

Intergovernmental Representation

Ambassador to the U.S.
Oleh SHAMSHUR

U.S. Ambassador to Ukraine
John E. HERBST

Permanent Representative to the UN
Valeriy P. KUCHINSKY

IGO Memberships (Non-UN)
BSEC, CEI, CEUR, CIS, EBRD, Eurocontrol, Interpol, IOM, OSCE, PCA, WCO

UNITED KINGDOM

UNITED KINGDOM OF GREAT BRITAIN AND NORTHERN IRELAND

The Country

The United Kingdom of Great Britain and Northern Ireland occupies the major portion of the British Isles, the largest island group off the European coast. The individual identity of its separate regions, each with distinctive ethnic and linguistic characteristics, is reflected in the complex governmental structure of the country as a whole. England, the heart of the nation, accounts for over half the total area and 83 percent of the total population. Wales, conquered in the Middle Ages, has its own capital, Cardiff, and a national language, Welsh, with which some 30 percent of the population have familiarity. Scotland, ruled as a separate kingdom until 1707, has long had its own legal and educational systems; its capital is Edinburgh. Conquered by the English in the Middle Ages, Ireland became part of the UK in 1800 but in 1921 was partitioned into Northern Ireland, whose Protestant majority opted for retention of British status, and the predominantly Catholic Irish Republic. Varieties of the Gaelic language are spoken in both Scotland and Northern Ireland. There are two established churches, the Church of England (Episcopalian or Anglican), with some 1.5 million active members, and the Church of Scotland (Presbyterian), with some 700,000 members. Nonestablished religions include Roman Catholicism, which claims over 4 million adherents; Islam, with 1.5 million; and Methodism, with 400,000. Apart from a legal prohibition on the monarch (who is head of the Church of England) or the heir to the throne becoming a Roman Catholic, religious freedom prevails.

In 2004 women comprised 46 percent of the paid (including part-time) workforce, concentrated in the retail, clerical, and human services sectors. As of July 2006 women held 126 seats in the 646-member House of Commons as well as seven cabinet posts.

Great Britain was the seat of the industrial revolution of the 18th century, and most of its urbanized and highly skilled population is engaged in manufacturing and service industries, mainly transport, commerce, and finance, with agriculture accounting for under 2 percent of GDP and employment. Machinery, basic manufactures, and agricultural products constitute the bulk of British imports. Machinery and transport equipment, basic

Political Status: Constitutional monarchy, under democratic parliamentary regime.

Area: 94,249 sq. mi. (244,104 sq. km.), embracing England and Wales, 58,382 sq. mi. (151,209 sq. km.); Scotland, 30,415 sq. mi. (78,775 sq. km.); Northern Ireland, 5,452 sq. mi. (14,120 sq. km.).

Population: 58,789,194 (2001C), including England, 49,138,831; Scotland, 5,062,011; Wales, 2,903,085; Northern Ireland, 1,685,267; 60,021,000 (2005E).

Major Urban Centers (2005E): *England:* LONDON (urban area, 7,396,000), Birmingham (971,000), Liverpool (464,000), Leeds (451,000), Sheffield (443,000), Bristol (426,000), Manchester (390,000); *Wales:* CARDIFF (300,000); *Scotland:* EDINBURGH (442,000), Glasgow (619,000); *Northern Ireland:* BELFAST (276,000).

Principal Language: English (Scottish and Irish forms of Gaelic are spoken in portions of Scotland and Northern Ireland, respectively, while Welsh is spoken in northern and central Wales).

Monetary Unit: Pound Sterling (market rate July 1, 2006: 1 pound = $1.85US).

Sovereign: Queen ELIZABETH II; proclaimed Queen on February 6, 1952; crowned June 2, 1953.

Heir Apparent: CHARLES Philip Arthur George; invested as Prince of Wales on July 1, 1969.

Prime Minister: Anthony (Tony) BLAIR (Labour Party); invited by the queen on May 2, 1997, to succeed John MAJOR (Conservative Party) following general election of May 1 and formed new government on May 7; continued in office following general elections of June 7, 2001, and May 5, 2005.

manufactures, chemicals, and mineral fuels are the chief exports. Germany, the United States, and Japan rank as the leading trading partners.

The British economy experienced intermittent crises after World War II as the result of factors that included the wartime liquidation of most of the country's overseas assets and a lack of flexi-bility in management and labor practices. Emigration and immigration, featuring the "brain drain" of skilled professional personnel (mainly to the United States) and a concurrent influx of non-white labor from Africa, South Asia, the West Indies, and elsewhere, also produced unsettling economic and social effects, including racial tensions. The oil crisis of 1973–1974 was particularly damaging to the UK economy, but in the late 1970s fiscal constraint and increased exploitation of North Sea oil reserves yielded annual GDP increases of 2–3 percent, despite remaining structural problems. Under the post-1979 Conservative government, policies to increase productivity at first exacerbated the effects of international recession, causing unemployment to rise into the double digits and industrial output to fall. From 1983 the economy experienced something of a boom: Overall economic growth averaged over 3 percent a year from 1983 to 1989, corporate profits rose, productivity was second only to that of Japan, annual inflation fell to around 4 percent, and the government ran a budget surplus.

The "British economic miracle" foundered in the wake of the stock market crash of October 1989. Initially, the government sought recovery by increasing liquidity, but a rapid inflationary surge forced it to apply interest rates at record highs. In October 1990 the pound sterling was placed in the broad band of the European Community (EC) exchange rate mechanism (ERM), which in effect pegged it to the deutsche mark. By then, the economy had entered its deepest and longest recession since the 1930s, aggravated by similar difficulties in other industrial economies. In 1991–1992 overall output dropped by 3.6 percent and unemployment, having fallen to a ten-year low of 5.9 percent in 1989, rose to 10.5 percent by late 1992. In September 1992 massive speculation against the pound sterling forced its withdrawal from the ERM and, in effect, a 20 percent devaluation.

Clear signs of a rebound appeared in 1993, and by April 1994 the GDP had regained its preslump (1990) peak. The recovery continued in 1995–1997, with annual GDP growth averaging about 3 percent. A global slowdown held expansion to

2.2 percent in 1998 and 2.0 percent in 1999, although growth in the last three quarters of the latter year returned to an annualized rate of about 3 percent and helped vault the UK over France and into fourth place among the world's largest economies. Moreover, unemployment stood at only 4 percent, the lowest rate in a quarter of a century, while retail inflation remained below the target of 2.5 percent. Although the Labour administration that took office in 1997 had initially maintained the fiscal restraint imposed during the 18-year reign of the Conservatives, the budget for 2000–2001 proposed significant spending increases, with a focus on improving the national health system and education. According to the International Monetary Fund (IMF), GDP growth for 2000 held at 3.0 percent before dropping to 2.2 percent in 2001 and 2.0 percent in 2002, then rising to 2.5 percent in 2003 and 3.2 percent in 2004.

In its 2005 report, the IMF praised the UK for a "remarkable performance" over the past decade, marked by sustained growth, low inflation, and steadily low unemployment (4.8 percent from 2003–2005). However, GDP growth for 2005 fell to 1.7 percent (the lowest in 13 years), primarily as the result of reduced consumer spending. In addition, unemployment crept up to 5.3 percent in mid-2006. Meanwhile, the UK government rejected a request from the European Union (EU) that it raise taxes or cut spending in order to reduce the "excessive" budget deficit, estimated at 3.4 percent of GDP for the fiscal year 2005–2006. (Although the UK is not a member of the eurozone and therefore is not subject to formal EU sanctions, it has committed itself to the EU's stability and growth pact, which theoretically limits national budget deficits to 3.0 percent of GDP. The UK has missed that target since 2003.)

Government and Politics

Political Background

After reaching its apogee of global influence in the closing decades of the Victorian era, the UK endured the strains of the two world wars with its political institutions unimpaired but with sharp reductions in its relative economic strength and military power. The steady erosion of the British imperial position after World War II was only partially offset by the concurrent development and expansion of the Commonwealth, a grouping that continued to reflect an underlying British philosophy but whose center of gravity shifted to newly developed and developing nations. Despite continuing differences on many issues, the three traditional parties—Conservative, Labour, and Liberal (now the Liberal Democrats)—have in some respects drawn closer together.

The Labour Party, after winning the postwar elections of 1945 and 1950 under the leadership of Clement R. ATTLEE, went into opposition for 13 years while the Conservative Party governed under prime ministers Winston CHURCHILL (1951–1955), Anthony EDEN (1955–1957), Harold MACMILLAN (1957–1963), and Sir Alec DOUGLAS-HOME (1963–1964). A Conservative defeat in the general election of October 1964 returned Labour to power under Harold WILSON. At the election of June 1970 the tide swung back to the Conservatives, who under Edward HEATH obtained a 30-seat majority in the House of Commons. In February 1974 the Conservatives outpolled Labour but fell 3 seats short of a plurality, Wilson returning to head the first minority government since 1929. A second election eight months later gave Labour an overall majority of 3 seats. In April 1976 Wilson unexpectedly resigned and was succeeded as prime minister by Foreign Secretary James CALLAGHAN, who saw Labour's fortunes plummet in the 1978–1979 "winter of discontent" that featured damaging public sector strikes.

In May 1979 the Conservatives obtained 339 seats (a majority of 44) in the House of Commons, enabling Margaret THATCHER to become the first female prime minister in British (and European) history. Benefiting from popular response to her handling of the Falklands war (see Foreign relations, below), the Conservatives surged to a 144-seat majority at the election of June 1983. They retained control of the Commons with a somewhat diminished but still comfortable majority of 102 in June 1987, Thatcher becoming the first prime minister in modern British history to win three consecutive terms.

Following the introduction of a widely disliked community charge ("poll tax") in April 1990, the Conservatives' popularity took a downward turn that was only briefly reversed by public appreciation of Thatcher's firmness in response to the Persian Gulf conflict precipitated by Iraq's invasion of Kuwait in August. Amid a damaging series of by-election defeats for the Conservatives, a sense of crisis was generated by the resignation on November 1 of the deputy prime minister, Sir Geoffrey HOWE, over the prime minister's lack of support for enhanced British participation in the EC. On November 13 the former defense secretary, Michael HESELTINE, reversing an earlier pledge, challenged Thatcher for the party leadership, and at an intraparty poll on November 20 he won sufficient backing to deny the prime minister a first-round victory. Two days later Thatcher announced her intention to resign. In the second-round ballot on November 27 Chancellor of the Exchequer John MAJOR defeated both Heseltine and Foreign Secretary Douglas HURD. Having abandoned the "poll tax" and moderated other aspects of "Thatcherite" policies that had enjoyed his keen support theretofore, Major led the Conservatives to a fourth successive election victory on April 9, 1992, despite economic recession and negative forecasts from opinion pollsters. Although Labour made significant gains, the Conservatives retained a working majority of 336 seats in the 651-member House of Commons.

The Danish referendum vote in June 1992 against the Maastricht Treaty on greater EC economic and political union caused divisions to surface within the Conservative Party between pro- and anti-EC factions, the latter being dubbed "Eurosceptics." Because of the government's modest majority, anti-EC Conservative MPs were able to mount protracted resistance to parliamentary ratification of the Maastricht Treaty until after reversal of the Danish negative vote in May 1993 (see Foreign relations, below).

The opposition Labour Party displayed its own internal fissures over the EC. However, its main task was to revitalize its leadership following the resignation of Neil KINNOCK, who had suffered defeat in two successive general elections. Elected leader in July 1992, John SMITH maintained Kinnock's moderate, pro-EC stance while initiating reviews of Labour's social and constitutional policies.

A rapid Labour rise in the opinion polls in late 1992 was assisted by a series of major government reverses and blunders, amid a European currency crisis that forced the pound sterling out of the EC's ERM.

The withdrawal from the ERM represented a traumatic collapse of government economic policy. In March 1993 Chancellor of the Exchequer Norman LAMONT presented a "budget for jobs" and claimed that the recession was over, but a spiraling budget deficit obliged him to introduce tax increases effective in 1994, some in breach of Conservative election pledges. Major responded on May 27 with a cabinet reshuffle that included the replacement of Lamont by Kenneth CLARKE, hitherto home secretary. Major later sought to recover the initiative by launching a "back to basics" campaign, stressing traditional Conservative values on education, law and order, and other matters.

The issuance of the joint UK-Irish Downing Street Declaration on Northern Ireland in December 1993 yielded some political credit to Major (and led eventually to the historic cease-fire announcement by the Irish Republican Army [IRA] on August 31, 1994—see Northern Ireland article). Conservative fortunes nevertheless continued their decline, and in June 1994 the party lost 16 of its 34 seats in the European Parliament. The clear victor in the balloting was the Labour Party, under the interim leadership of Margaret BECKETT following the sudden death of Smith on May 12. Subsequent Labour leadership elections, for the first time involving all individual party members, resulted in 41-year-old Tony BLAIR emerging an easy winner on July 22, with former union official John PRESCOTT succeeding Beckett as deputy leader. Seeking to appeal to "middle England," Blair accelerated the modernization of Labour policies and structures.

Rocked by scandals, including the press revelation that certain Conservative MPs had accepted "cash for questions" (payment from outside interests for tabling parliamentary questions to ministers), the government continued to face bitter opposition from some of its own backbenchers. On November 28, 1994, eight Conservative "Eurosceptics" rebelled against a financing bill for the EU that the government had made an issue of confidence. The EU issue, the "sleaze factor" resulting from an unremitting flow of sex and financial scandals, and other divisions contributed to all-time low opinion-poll ratings for the Conservatives, who in local elections on May 4, 1995, suffered the party's heaviest postwar defeat.

Amid renewed speculation about his future, Prime Minister Major on June 22, 1995, announced his formal resignation from the party leadership, forcing critics to "put up or shut up" regarding his reelection. All but one cabinet minister declared support for the prime minister, the exception being John REDWOOD, who resigned as secretary for Wales in order to challenge Major on a radical right-wing, strongly Eurosceptic platform. Major emerged the comfortable first-round victor on July 4. The following day the prime minister announced an extensive government reshuffle in which Heseltine was rewarded for his crucial loyalty in the leadership contest by being made first secretary of state and deputy prime minister.

Local elections in May 1996 dropped the Conservatives to third place, behind Labour and the Liberal Democrats, in terms of total local councilors. With allegations of improper financial conduct on the part of Conservative members of Parliament (including junior ministers) being supported by the Nolan Commission on Standards in Public Life, and with time running out on the five-year legislative term, the prime minister on March 17, 1997, asked for a dissolution of Parliament. The election held on May 1 resulted in one of the worst defeats for any governing party in the last century, as the Conservatives won only 165 seats, its losing candidates including 7 cabinet members.

Labour swept to power by securing 418 seats on the strength of 44.4 percent of the vote. In keeping with his "centrist" stance, Blair named a mix of "old hands" and "New Labour modernizers" to the new cabinet appointed on May 7. Following the election, former prime minister Major announced his resignation as Conservative leader, with Eurosceptic William HAGUE defeating the pro-EU Kenneth Clarke in the subsequent contest to lead the party.

Carrying through on one of Labour's most prominent campaign pledges, the Blair administration quickly pursued decisions in Wales and Scotland regarding devolution of regional authority. In a referendum on September 11, 1997, 74 percent of the voters in Scotland approved the proposed creation of a Scottish Parliament, while on September 18 a plan for establishment of a National Assembly was endorsed by 50.3 percent of the voters in Wales. Elections for the two bodies—the first Scottish legislature since 1707 and the first ever in Wales—were held on May 6, 1999, with Labour emerging as the plurality party in both. The Scottish Parliament and Welsh Assembly both held opening ceremonies on July 1, with Queen Elizabeth in attendance in Edinburgh.

The long process of negotiation and accommodation in Northern Ireland, which included the direct involvement of both British and Irish governments, led to the signing on April 10, 1998, of a multiparty peace accord, the Belfast (Good Friday) Agreement, followed on June 25 by the election of a Northern Ireland Assembly. Devolution of powers from London to the assembly and a power-sharing executive occurred on December 2, 1999. Even then, however, a lingering dispute over the disarming of the paramilitary IRA led London to reimpose direct rule on February 11, 2000. On May 30 power was again devolved, the IRA having agreed, earlier in the month, to put its arsenals under international supervision. Little progress was made in the following 16 months, despite repeated negotiating efforts by Prime Minister Blair, Irish Prime Minister Ahern, and others, as paramilitary arms decommissioning, police reform, and withdrawal of British forces continued to be at issue.

On August 10, 2001, and again on September 22 London briefly suspended the assembly as a technical maneuver to avoid calling a new election. The devolved government was given new life by the IRA's October 23 announcement that it had begun decommissioning to "save the peace process," but revelations of IRA spying ultimately led London to reimpose direct rule from October 15, 2002 (see Northern Ireland article for details).

At an early election called by Prime Minister Blair for June 7, 2001, Labour was overwhelmingly returned to office with 412 seats in the House of Commons (6 less than in 1997). A reshuffled cabinet was announced on June 8, and on the same day Conservative leader Hague stepped down despite modest gains by his party in simultaneous local elections.

At the poll of May 5, 2005, Labour, for the first time, registered its third consecutive victory in the House of Commons, albeit with a substantially reduced majority of 355 seats. Prime Minister Blair conducted an only minor cabinet reshuffle on the following day, but his government reorganization was much more extensive on May 5, 2006, following an extremely poor performance by Labour in partial local elections the previous day (see Current issues, below).

Constitution and Government

The UK is a constitutional monarchy that functions without a written constitution on the basis of statutes, common law, and long-standing but flexible traditions and usages, subject since 1973 to EC/EU membership and consequential acceptance of the primacy of EC/EU law. Executive power is wielded on behalf of the sovereign by a cabinet of ministers drawn from the majority party in the House of Commons and, to a lesser degree, from the House of Lords. The prime minister is the leader of the majority party in the House of Commons and depends upon it for support. There is also a historically important Privy Council of government members and some 300 other individuals drawn from public life. Although superseded in importance by the cabinet, it retains an advisory role in

some policy areas and continues to issue "orders in council" under authority of the monarch, who presides over its meetings, or as authorized by Parliament. The Privy Council also reviews legislation passed by the crown dependencies (the Channel Islands and the Isle of Man).

Elected by universal adult suffrage, the House of Commons has become the main repository of legislative and sole repository of financial authority. The House of Lords retains the power to review, amend, or delay for a year legislation other than financial bills and takes a more leisurely overview of legislation, sometimes acting as a brake on the House of Commons. The lower house, which has a maximum term of five years, may be dissolved by the sovereign on recommendation of the prime minister if the latter's policies should encounter severe resistance or if the incumbent feels that new elections would increase the ruling party's majority.

Under legislation approved by the House of Lords 221–81, with Conservatives abstaining, on October 26, 1999, Labour's 1997 campaign pledge to end hereditary membership in the upper house moved forward. The bill, which received royal assent on November 11, authorized formation of an interim upper chamber to include among its members 92 hereditary peers. Meanwhile, the Wakeham Royal Commission appointed in October 1998 continued to draft proposals for a permanently restructured upper body. The final report, issued on January 20, 2000, proposed a chamber of 550 mostly appointed members but with a minority of 65, 87, or 195 to be elected through regional proportional representation. Law lords (Lords of Appeal in Ordinary), lifetime appointees who have traditionally constituted the kingdom's highest court of appeal, would retain their seats. The existing 26 seats held by archbishops and bishops would be supplemented by 5 seats for representatives of non-Christian religions. Other life peers would be gradually phased out and replaced by a combination of appointed and elected members. A Labour white paper published in November 2001 offered an alternative proposal—abolition of all hereditary peers in a 600-member house encompassing 120 directly elected members, 120 appointees, 16 bishops, and most of the balance party nominees in proportion to vote shares in the most recent general election—but the plan was largely abandoned in May 2002, a number of party leaders insisting that a higher proportion of the upper house should be directly elected.

Subsequently, the Blair administration called for abolition of the post of Lord Chancellor, the establishment of a Supreme Court, and, in the wake of devolution, absorption of the offices for Scotland and Wales by a department of constitutional affairs. Thus, in a mid-2003 cabinet reshuffle, the secretaries of state for Scotland and Wales, while retained, were assigned secondary status, with Lord FALCONER of Thoroton named secretary of state for constitutional affairs and invested as Lord Chancellor "for the transitional period."

In March 2004 the House of Lords referred the Constitutional Reform Bill to a special select committee, while the government abandoned plans for a bill to abolish the 92 seats held by remaining hereditary peers.

A year later, on March 25, 2005, royal assent was given to a revised Constitutional Reform Bill that provided for a Supreme Court separate from the House of Lords and, without abandoning the office itself, transferred the judicial function of the Lord Chancellor to a President of the Courts for England and Wales.

Apart from the newly established Supreme Court, the judicial system of England and Wales centers on a High Court of Justice for civil cases, with three divisions (Chancery, Family, and Queen's Bench); a Crown Court for criminal cases; and a Court of Appeal, with civil and criminal divisions. Scotland has its own High Court of Justiciary (criminal) and Court of Session (civil), both including appeal courts, while Northern Ireland has a separate Supreme Court of Judicature, comprising a (civil) High Court of Justice, a (criminal) Crown Court, and a Court of Appeal. In relevant cases, UK citizens and groups have the right of appeal against national legal rulings to the European Court of Human Rights in Strasbourg, France.

Local government in England traditionally encompassed a two-tier structure of county and district (or borough or city) councils, but in recent years dozens of unitary authorities have been established. The traditional structure largely survives in 34 county and more than 200 district councils, although some of the counties have seen unitary authorities established within their geographical boundaries. Under legislation enacted in 1994, Wales and Scotland, formerly with two tiers, moved on April 1, 1996, to a unitary system, with 22 and 32 elected councils, respectively. Northern Ireland has 26 district councils.

Since 1986, when the Greater London Council was abolished, the capital has been governed through 32 boroughs, each with its own elected council, and the Corporation of the City of London, its unique status reflecting its commercial rather than residential character. Additionally, at a referendum held on May 7, 1998, Londoners overwhelmingly approved direct election of a mayor and establishment of a 25-member London Assembly. The first mayoral and assembly elections were held in May 2000, with the new government assuming office on July 3.

Published on July 30, 1998, a government white paper, *Modern Local Government in Touch with the People,* heralded other changes ahead, including greater budgetary freedom for local authorities and separation of executive and legislative responsibilities. In another reform, in December 1998 the government appointed members to eight newly established Regional Development Agencies (RDAs), with a ninth added for London in 2000. Tasks mandated for the RDAs include promoting sustainable economic development, increasing efficiency and competitiveness, and encouraging investment.

The viability of the UK as a political entity has been a matter of major concern for three decades. The most intractable problem has been that of deep-rooted conflict in Northern Ireland between the majority Protestants, most of whom remain committed to the union with Great Britain, and a Catholic minority, substantial elements of which have long sought union with the Republic of Ireland. A multiparty peace accord, the Belfast (Good Friday)

Agreement of April 10, 1998, was approved in Northern Ireland by referendum on May 22, with a new Northern Ireland Assembly being elected on June 25. Devolution of authority from London to the assembly and a Northern Ireland Executive occurred on December 2, 1999, although differences over the decommissioning of weapons held by the IRA resulted in reimposition of direct rule from February 11 to May 30, 2000. Upon devolution, the secretary of state for Northern Ireland retained authority in "excepted and reserved" areas, including law, criminal justice, and foreign affairs. Direct rule was again imposed for 24 hours in August and September 2001, and then for an indefinite period on October 15, 2002, with no recision as of mid-2006 (see article on Northern Ireland).

Although not characterized by the violence endemic in the Irish question, a powerful separatist movement has also developed in Scotland. Alarmed by the growing influence of the Scottish National Party (SNP), which won a third of the Scottish votes in the October 1974 general election, the Labour leadership, in a 1975 government paper, proposed the establishment of elected assemblies for both Scotland and Wales. Despite Conservative criticism that the departure would prove costly and contain "the danger of a break-up of Britain," pertinent legislation was completed in mid-1978. In March 1979, however, referendums yielded rejection of devolution in Wales and approval by an insufficient majority in Scotland. Successive Conservative administrations subsequently ruled out the creation of regional assemblies, although in March 1993 the government, in what was officially described as the first major review of the England-Scotland relationship since 1707, introduced measures to give the 72 Scottish MPs a larger role in decision making.

Immediately after taking power in May 1997, the new Labour government set out plans for new Scottish and Welsh devolution referendums. On September 11 the Scottish electorate voted by a substantial majority for an elected Parliament, and on September 18 Welsh voters approved creation of a National Assembly. Under the Government of Wales Act and the Scotland Act, both passed by the UK Parliament following the referendums, elections for the two new bodies were held on May 6, 1999, with formal transfer of devolved powers occurring on July 1. Although the UK Parliament retains ultimate authority to legislate on all matters, it will not routinely do so in devolved sectors, which include education, health, culture, local government, housing, transportation, and the environment. The Scottish Parliament cannot propose independence from the union, nor can it legislate in reserved areas, which include defense and treaty obligations. Because Wales has a closer legal association with England, the Welsh assembly has a more limited scope than the Scottish Parliament, with no authority to pass primary legislation governing, for example, the legal system or taxation. Both Scotland and Wales, like Northern Ireland, continue to be represented in the UK Parliament and in the Westminster cabinet. With regard to England, the Blair administration has indicated its willingness to go beyond establishing the RDAs and the London Authority (mayor plus assembly) and to devolve powers from the UK government to English regional bodies as the demand arises.

Since 1997 the Labour government has also been examining proportional representation for use in British elections. The 1999 balloting for the new Scottish and Welsh legislatures utilized, for the first time, a combination system in which each voter cast two ballots, one for a constituency representative elected under the traditional "first-past-the-post" basis and the second for a party list from which "top-up" seats were allocated, thereby assuring that the makeup of the legislatures would better reflect each party's overall vote share. A proportional scheme was also introduced for the European Parliament elections held in June 1999. However, many members of the UK House of Commons, including a substantial number of Labour MPs, have not expressed enthusiasm for converting to a basically proportional system for the House, as proposed in the report of the Jenkins Commission on electoral reform in October 1998. In July 2000 Labour confirmed that electoral reform would not have a high priority in the upcoming session of

Parliament and that a referendum on a revised voting system should not be expected in the near future.

In another matter of constitutional significance, the monarchy, with the full support of the Labour government, has recently pledged initiatives to modernize its role in state and society. The decision followed widespread criticism directed at the royal family's allegedly distant demeanor following the death of DIANA, Princess of Wales, the former wife of Prince CHARLES, in an automobile accident in August 1997. In February 1998 Queen ELIZABETH II indicated that she would support abolishing primogeniture with regard to the line of succession, although Parliament has not yet formally considered such a change.

Foreign Relations

Reluctantly abandoning its age-long tradition of "splendid isolation," the UK became a key member of the Allied coalitions in both world wars and has remained a leader in the Western group of nations, as well as one of the world's nuclear-armed powers. Postwar British governments have sought to retain close economic and military ties with the United States while maintaining an independent British position on most international issues. Britain has continued to play an important role in the United Nations (UN) and in collective security arrangements, such as the North Atlantic Treaty Organization (NATO), although after 1957 Britain's withdrawal of most military forces from the Far East and the Persian Gulf substantially diminished its weight in the global balance of power.

The UK's participation in the work of such institutions as the IMF, the General Agreement on Tariffs and Trade/World Trade Organization (GATT/WTO), and the Organization for Economic Cooperation and Development (OECD) reflects its continued central position in international financial and economic affairs as well as its commitment to assist in the growth of less-developed countries. (Similar concerns have also become a focus of the Commonwealth, which was formally established in 1931.) Unwilling to participate in the creation of

the original three EC components (The European Economic Community [EEC], European Coal and Steel Community [ECSC], and European Atomic Energy Community [Euratom]), it took the lead in establishing the European Free Trade Association (EFTA) in 1960. Subsequently, Conservative and moderate Labour leaders began to urge British entry into the EC despite anticipated problems for the UK and other Commonwealth members. France, however, vetoed the British application for admission in 1963 on the ground that the country remained too closely tied to the United States and the Commonwealth to justify close association with the continental nations. With the abandonment of French objections after President de Gaulle's resignation in 1969, a bill sanctioning entry was approved by the House of Commons in October 1971, and Britain was formally admitted to the EC on January 1, 1973. In a referendum held in June 1975, continued membership of the EC was endorsed by a two-thirds majority of participating voters, but enthusiasm for the European venture remained low in Britain over the subsequent two decades.

In late 1979 the Thatcher government won worldwide plaudits for its resolution of the seven-year Rhodesian civil war through a lengthy process of negotiation that culminated in independence under black majority rule in April 1980 (see Zimbabwe article). In September 1981 Belize (formerly British Honduras) secured independence, as did Antigua and Barbuda in November. These were the latest territories to benefit from Britain's post-1957 imperial disengagement, which had seen 18 former possessions, protectorates, and colonies becoming independent during the 1960s, 10 in the 1970s, and 2 (including Zimbabwe) in 1980, to be followed by St. Kitts and Nevis (1983) and Brunei (1984).

The Falkland Islands war that erupted in April 1982 followed nearly two decades of sporadic negotiations between Britain and Argentina in a fruitless effort to resolve a dispute that had commenced in the late 18th century (see Falkland Islands under Related Territories, below). Following the Argentine defeat, the UN General Assembly renewed appeals for a negotiated solution to the sovereignty issue, and since 1984 the UN Committee on Decolonization has routinely passed Argentine-sponsored resolutions asking London to reopen negotiations on the matter. Two days of high-level talks in Madrid, Spain, in February 1990 produced a compromise settlement of conflicting claims to fishing rights and an agreement to restore a seven-year rupture in diplomatic relations, but the sovereignty issue remains unresolved.

In September 1984 Britain and China agreed that the latter would regain possession of Hong Kong in 1997, although the Conservative government continued to rebuff Spanish appeals for the reversion of Gibraltar, given manifest opposition to such a move by its inhabitants (see Special Administrative Region in China article in *Political Handbook 2007* and Gibraltar under Related Territories, below).

While the Thatcher government had reservations about U.S. military intervention in Grenada in 1983, its generally close foreign policy alignment with Washington was demonstrated by endorsement of the U.S. bombing of Libya in 1986, as contrasted with the prevailing view of other EC countries. UK-U.S. cooperation was also a key factor during the Gulf crisis of 1990–1991, with British forces participating in the U.S.-led coalition that expelled Iraq from Kuwait.

In December 1991 the Major government was successful in negotiating various UK opt-outs from the EC's Maastricht Treaty on European union, notably from its commitment to a single European currency and from its jobs-imperiling social policy chapter. However, not until July 23, 1993, did the government obtain final parliamentary authority for its opt-out policy. This followed a stinging attack on the treaty by former prime minister Margaret Thatcher in the House of Lords, who cast her first vote in 34 years against her party's leadership, and came about only after Major had gained the reluctant support of his Conservative opponents in the House of Commons by making the decision a confidence motion. On July 30 a British court rejected the last legal challenge to the treaty, and on August 2 instruments of UK ratification were deposited in Rome.

In October 1997 the new Labour administration signaled a slightly more pro-European position by announcing that Britain would consider joining the EU's Economic and Monetary Union (EMU), but not immediately. Earlier, in May, the incoming foreign secretary had confirmed a Labour commitment to accept the social charter of the EU. In November 1998 the queen gave her assent to legislation that incorporated into British law the 1950 European Convention on Human Rights, with effect from October 2, 2000.

During 1992 UK diplomacy became increasingly preoccupied with the conflict in former Yugoslavia. Although some 3,400 British troops were committed to the UN humanitarian effort by 1994, the government firmly opposed any direct military intervention by external powers and backed both the UN arms embargo and the Vance-Owen diplomatic effort to obtain a negotiated settlement. Following major escalation of the Bosnian crisis in March 1995, London's policy underwent a significant shift. In addition to raising its troop contingent in the former Yugoslavia to 10,000, Britain agreed to contribute an additional 7,000 soldiers to a new NATO-led rapid reaction force charged with providing "enhanced protection" to the UN peacekeeping force. Subsequently, the British government was party to a NATO decision to step up air strikes around the Bosnian capital with the twin aims of relieving pressure on its inhabitants and of forcing Bosnian Serb acceptance of the latest peace plan. Britain gave its full support to the Dayton Accords of December 1995, which brought the conflict to a swift close. British troops remained part of the continuing UN peace force.

Relations with Iran reached a nadir following the late Ayatollah Khomeini's 1989 death sentence against the naturalized British writer Salman RUSHDIE for alleged blasphemy against Islam in his novel *The Satanic Verses*. In September 1998 Iran disassociated itself from the Rushdie *fatwa,* clearing the way for London and Teheran to exchange ambassadors in May 1999.

The Blair administration has been a consistent supporter of the second U.S.-led incursion into Iraq, often at its political peril. A number of the prime minister's key aides resigned over the issue, including parliamentary leader Robin COOK in March 2003 and International Development Secretary Claire SHORT two months later. By far the greatest damage, however, was fallout from the apparent suicide on July 13, 2003, of David KELLY, a ministry of defence weapons expert, who had been the source for alleged reports that Downing Street had "sexed up" a 2002 dossier on Iraqi weapons of mass destruction. (Although Blair, to the apparent detriment of his standing in public opinion polls, continued to support the effort in Iraq through mid-2006, his administration broke with Washington on the issue of the U.S. prison in Guantánamo Bay, arguing that the facility should be closed.)

In April 2004 Blair announced that he would call for a referendum on Britain's commitment to the EU after the next election. However, in June 2005 he said that the government would not proceed with a referendum bill, given the rejection of the EU constitution by the French and Dutch electorates. In mid-2006 the administration indicated that it might approve certain revisions in EU institutions on a "piece-by-piece" basis without a referendum. (Such an approach had been proposed for many countries by EU enthusiasts hoping to "salvage" at least some of the constitutional changes.)

Current Issues

In the first two years after his overwhelming victory at the polls in 1997, Prime Minister Blair moved forward on a broad range of initiatives, including reform of the House of Lords and devolution in Scotland, Wales, and Northern Ireland. Between January 1998 and May 1999, white papers or commission reports addressed the future makeup of local government, various proportional representation schemes, campaign finance reform, freedom of information, and social service reform. At the same time, however, the Blair government downplayed any commitments that might entail substantial increases in spending or taxation, while encroaching even further on traditional Conservative territory by promoting "family values," social responsibility, citizenship, and a hard line on street crime. The "New Labour" program also attacked "something for nothing" welfare policies and proposed pension reform, despite considerable opposition from Labour traditionalists. On April 1, 1999, the first national minimum wage—£3.60 per hour for those 22 and older—was introduced, although trade unionists complained that the rate should have been pegged higher.

One of the most contentious issues during the early years of the Blair administration was if and when to adopt the EU's euro as a replacement for the pound sterling. Although the Blair government consistently supported eventual entry into the EMU, widespread public opposition forced the administration to review its strategy and adjust its timetable. Labour's loss of its majority in the June 1999 elections for the European Parliament not only compelled the party to downplay the euro issue but also helped revivify the predominantly anti-euro Conservative Party.

The Conservatives cited the euro issue as but one example of what they charged was Blair's willingness to set aside principle and change his agenda based on public opinion. Such assertions contributed to a fundamental image problem that was further fueled in July 2000 by a leaked memo in which Blair lamented that he and Labour were perceived as "out of touch with gut British instincts," particularly in such areas as family issues, crime, and immigration. Blair's memo called for "eye-catching initiatives" in the area of family policy and a get-tough approach to crime. In the latter regard, the government was already pursuing policies bound to run up against the European Convention on Human Rights upon its entry into force in October 2000. To the consternation of civil-liberties advocates, Whitehall proposed denying trial by jury in some criminal cases—a proposal that was ultimately abandoned in April 2002—and revoking double jeopardy in murder cases where substantial new evidence has come to light.

The issue of immigration and political asylum also came to the fore in the late 1990s and early 2000s. Some 80,000 aliens applied for political asylum in 2000, up from 5,000 a decade earlier. With the Conservative Party calling for tough measures to discourage "economic migrants" posing as political refugees, Home Secretary Jack STRAW in March 2000 called for a complete reexamination of the 1951 UN Convention on the Status of Refugees. An Immigration and Asylum Bill, passed in November 1999 with effect from April 1, 2000, instituted a voucher system instead of cash payments to asylum seekers and also authorized their dispersal around the country, over the objections of many local authorities.

In the wake of the September 11, 2001, terrorist attacks in the United States, the Blair government stood as the most steadfast supporter of the George W. Bush administration's October decision to launch military attacks against the al-Qaida network and the Taliban regime in Afghanistan. Collaterally, Prime Minister Blair formed a "War Cabinet." Earlier, he had called for tighter domestic security and had initiated steps to freeze assets of suspected terrorist organizations, monitor bank transactions, and introduce fast-track extradition. On December 14 an Anti-Terrorism, Crime, and Security Bill was enacted, although the Conservative majority in the House of Lords had exacted a number of tempering concessions beforehand. In November, anticipating passage of the bill, Secretary BLUNKETT had declared a "public emergency," thereby justifying derogation of a provision in the European Convention on Human Rights that prohibited detention of foreigners without trial.

In April 2004 the House of Commons approved a measure denying UK welfare benefits to asylum seekers unless they registered for work, while efforts continued to stop the flow of illegal immigrants through the Channel tunnel. Four months later, the Home Office published figures showing that applications for political asylum had fallen to a seven-year low and that France had overtaken the UK as the principal destination of EU asylum seekers.

The May 2005 balloting for the House of Commons cut Labour's working majority in half, as both the Conservatives and Liberal Democrats achieved noteworthy gains. The results were similar in the simultaneous partial local elections.

The terrorist threat became a reality on July 7, 2005, with a series of London subway bombings in which 56 persons died, including 4 believed to have been among the perpetrators. Two weeks later, on July 21, the city was subjected to a second, albeit failed, series of attacks in three subway trains and a bus, after which the Blair administration adopted a number of antiterrorist measures, including a catalog of offenses for which foreign militants could be deported. In September the administration introduced new antiterrorism legislation calling, among other things, for an extension of the time a suspect could be held without charges being filed from 14 to 90 days. The following month a number of foreign-based Islamic groups were banned from operating in the UK on the government's assertion that they had ties to al-Qaida. In general, the government's antiterrorism measures appeared to gain acceptance among the population and most political parties. However, the more stringent initiatives fueled a growing debate over the extent to which civil rights should be curtailed in the name of national security.

Attention in early 2006 focused on the ongoing slide of the Labour Party (buffeted by a series of scandals and policy disputes) and the collateral emergence of the new Conservative leader, David CAMERON, as a dynamic actor on the political stage. Both appeared to contribute to the "meltdown" of Labour at the partial local elections in early May, as the government party suffered a third-place finish in vote percentage. Particularly costly (apparently) for Labour was the revelation that several wealthy businessmen who had secretly lent money to the party's 2005 campaign had been nominated by Blair for peerages, status that automatically includes appointment to the House of Lords. Popular discontent was also reported concerning the perceived lax enforcement of deportation laws for foreigners being released from prisons. Although Blair reportedly faced growing criticism from Labour backbenchers, his cabinet reshuffle (the biggest of his tenure) on the day after the elections indicated his intention to pursue additional reform in areas such as education, energy, pensions, and health with vigor. At the same time, Blair pledged that he would resign the premiership in sufficient time to let Gordon BROWN (his apparent successor) establish himself as prime minister prior to the general election due by 2009. (In early September Blair announced that he would hand over the premiership within a year.) Meanwhile, Brown (the chancellor of the exchequer and an architect with Blair of "New Labour") began to speak out on a variety of issues outside the purview of his office, prompting some observers to suggest the Blair/Brown relationship was in effect a "undeclared shared premiership." For his part, Cameron focused on a determined effort to move the Conservatives toward the center on many topics in order to sustain the party's electoral momentum in, among other things, the elections scheduled for the spring of 2007 in Scotland and Wales.

In early August 2006 UK security officials announced that they had uncovered a plot by potential suicide bombers to blow up a number of commercial airliners headed to the United States. More than 25 people were subsequently arrested in connection with the alleged plot.

Political Parties

Government Parties

Labour Party. An evolutionary socialist party in basic doctrine and tradition, the Labour Party (founded in 1900) has moved to the center over the past decade but continues to reflect the often conflicting views of trade unions, doctrinaire socialists, and intellectuals, while seeking to broaden its appeal to the middle classes and white-collar and managerial personnel. The trade unions traditionally constituted the basis of the party's organized political strength and provided the bulk of its income, although their influence over policy formulation and candidate selection has been reduced in recent years.

After periods of prewar minority government and participation in the wartime coalition, Labour won a large parliamentary majority in 1945 under Clement Attlee and between then and 1951 proceeded to create a comprehensive welfare state, while nationalizing some of the "commanding heights" of the economy. Returning to government in 1964 under Harold Wilson, Labour was unexpectedly defeated in 1970. However it returned to power in February 1974 as a minority government, still under Wilson, who in a further election in October 1974 won a narrow victory. In early 1977 resignations and defections deprived the government of its majority, forcing Labour to conclude a parliamentary alliance with the small Liberal Party that lasted until late 1978. Meanwhile, James Callaghan succeeded Wilson as Labour leader and prime minister in April 1976.

Defeated by the Conservatives in the May 1979 balloting, Labour swung to the left and also changed its leadership selection procedure. Designated party leader in November 1980 under the old system of election by Labour MPs, Michael FOOT, a revered representative of Labour's "old left," presided over changes that in 1981 established an electoral college of affiliated trade unions, Labour MPs, and local constituency parties for selection of the party leader and deputy leader. This change, and a mainstream antipathy to the EC, caused a small number of right-wing, pro-EC MPs to break away in March 1981 and form the Social Democratic Party (see under Liberal Democrat Party, below). Foot fought the June 1983 election on a platform of withdrawal from the EC, unilateral nuclear disarmament, and socialist economic policies. Overwhelmingly defeated, he resigned the Labour leadership and was succeeded in October 1983 by Neil Kinnock. A disciple of Foot, Kinnock contested the June 1987 election on broadly the same policies as in 1983 and also suffered defeat. Thereafter, he initiated a radical policy review, which eventually resulted in Labour's dropping its hostility to the EC and to Britain's nuclear deterrent, while supporting market economics (subject to regulation). Kinnock continued Foot's policy of expelling Trotskyites of the "Militant Tendency."

Kinnock suffered a further election defeat in April 1992, although Labour's tally of 271 seats and a 34.4 percent vote share represented a significant gain over the 1987 results. He thereupon resigned and was succeeded by John Smith, a moderate who continued the "modernizing" thrust, notably by forcing through "one member, one vote" arrangements for the selection of Labour candidates and leaders. Smith led Labour to major advances in local balloting in 1993 and 1994 but died on May 12, 1994. He was succeeded in July, under the new voting arrangements, by another "modernizing" lawyer, Tony Blair. In the interim, Labour had won a major victory in the June European Parliament elections, taking 62 of the 87 UK seats with a 42.7 percent vote share, while the "Blair factor" boosted the party's electoral resurgence in subsequent parliamentary by-elections and in local balloting in May 1995. In a symbolic change to Labour's constitution, a special party conference on April 29 agreed to drop its celebrated "clause 4" commitment to "the common ownership of the means of production, distribution and exchange" in favor of a general assertion of democratic socialist aims and values. The trend toward "modernization" of the party continued with efforts to further reduce the role of union block votes. Moreover, Blair moved the party to the center by co-opting Conservative issues—a strategy often compared to that used by Democratic president Bill Clinton against the Republicans in the United States.

Labour's huge victory in the May 1997 balloting for the House of Commons (418 seats) included the election of 101 female Labour MPs, the party having purposefully presented "women only" lists in a number of safe constituencies. Following his accession to the prime ministership, Blair continued to promote "New Labour" in such areas as budget constraint and welfare reform while pressing ahead with promised initiatives on devolution of regional power in Wales and Scotland. Labour's "pro-yes" campaigns on the devolution referenda were conducted in alliance with the Liberal Democrats as well as *Plaid Cymru* in Wales and the Scottish National Party in Scotland.

In May 1998 the party's National Executive Committee (NEC) approved tightened procedures for vetting of parliamentary candidates, the main intention being to weed out those who had voted contrary to party policy or were otherwise deemed unsuitable. Six months later the NEC banned its members from leaking committee discussions and began requiring them to inform the Labour press office before making public comments on NEC matters. The measures offered opponents a further opportunity to label the Blairites as autocratic, as had a decision early in the year to expel two Labour members of the European Parliament, in part for attacking proposed welfare reforms and the leadership's control of the European Parliament candidate list.

Although failing to win a majority in either the new Scottish Parliament or the Welsh National Assembly, Labour emerged from the May 6, 1999, elections as the plurality party in both, taking 56 of 129 seats in Scotland and 28 of 60 in Wales. It entered into a coalition agreement on May 13 with the Scottish Liberal Democrats but in Wales chose to form a minority government under UK Secretary of State for Wales Alun MICHAEL. In a heated battle, Michael, relying on Prime Minister Blair's support, had defeated Rhodri MORGAN for leadership of Welsh Labour three months earlier. A year later, however, on February 9, 2000, Michael resigned as Welsh first minister shortly before the assembly passed a no-confidence motion, 31–27, largely because of his failure to distance himself from London. On February 15 the assembly confirmed Morgan as his successor. (The title of the office was subsequently changed to first secretary.)

At the European Parliament balloting of June 1999 Labour suffered its first major defeat since Blair's assumption of power, taking only 28 percent of the vote and 29 seats, a loss of 33. The defeat was largely explained by voters' opposition to Labour's pro-euro policy.

On February 20, 2000, Blair's preferred candidate for the new London mayoralty, former minister of health Frank DOBSON, won a narrow victory in a party electoral college, defeating leftist MP Ken LIVINGSTONE. The latter won 60 percent support from London party members and 72 percent from labor unions and societies, but Dobson prevailed on the strength of 86 percent support from the third, equally weighted electoral college bloc: Labor MPs, members of the European Parliament, and candidates for the Greater London Authority

(GLA). To the chagrin of the party hierarchy, Livingstone ran as an independent and won the election on May 4. Despite Labour's previous strength in the capital, the party won only 9 seats on the 25-member GLA, equaling the Conservative total. In a further setback on May 4, Labour lost control of 16 of the 73 contested local councils it had previously held.

At the same time, intraparty disputes continued to surface over Prime Minister Blair's "command and control" managerial style (dubbed "control freakery" by opponents), his reliance on a small circle of advisers that critics dubbed "Tony's cronies," and his centrist "New Labour" programs. Peter KILFOYLE, who had resigned as under secretary of state for defense in January 2000, announced in February that he was forming a "heartlands group" of Labour MPs committed to the party's core supporters and traditional, left-of-center policies. Blair nevertheless remained firmly in control of Labour, which handily won the June 2001 House of Commons election, capturing 412 seats on a slightly reduced vote share of 42 percent.

The May 2005 poll was won by Labour with a Commons majority (55 percent) reduced for a number of reasons, including widespread disagreement over constitutional revision, Britain's role in the EU, and Blair's support of the U.S. position in Iraq. The prime minister subsequently reportedly faced growing criticism from left-wing backbenchers opposed to his ongoing reformist agenda. Following Labour's dismal performance in the May 2006 local elections (third place with only 26 percent of the vote), calls intensified for Blair to announce a timetable for his resignation in favor of Gordon Brown (the chancellor of the exchequer), who was widely perceived as Blair's anointed successor. Although the relationship between Blair and Brown had occasionally been cool in the past, Blair indicated in 2006 that he firmly supported Brown as the next Labour leader (see Current issues, above).

Leaders: Anthony (Tony) BLAIR (Prime Minister and Leader of the Party), John PRESCOTT (Deputy Party Leader), Hazel BLEARS (Chair), Gordon BROWN (Chancellor of the Exchequer), Jack STRAW (Leader of the House of Commons), Jack McCONNELL (First Minister of Scotland), Peter WATT (General Secretary).

Co-operative Party. Founded in 1917, the Co-operative Party operates largely through some 200 affiliated cooperative societies throughout Britain. Under a 1927 agreement with the Labour Party, it cosponsors candidates at local, national, and European elections.

Leaders: Gareth THOMAS (Chair), Peter HUNT (General Secretary).

Other UK Parliamentary Parties

Conservative Party. Although in opposition during 1945–1951, 1964–1970, 1974–1979, and since 1997, the Conservative Party (formally the Conservative and Unionist Party, informally the Tory Party) dominated British politics through much of the 20th century, drawing support from business, the middle classes, farmers, and a segment of the working class.

In February 1975 Margaret Thatcher, former secretary of state for education and science, was elected party leader, succeeding Edward Heath, under whom the Conservatives had lost three of the previous four elections. Following the party's return to power in May 1979, a rift developed between moderate members (derogatively styled "wets") and those supporting Thatcher's stringent monetary and economic policies; through the 1980s prominent "wets" were gradually dropped from the government, while others came to terms with "Thatcherism." The party's successful 1983 campaign manifesto called for, among other things, tough laws to curb illegal strikes and privatization of state-owned industry. The emphasis for the June 1987 election was on continued "positive reform" in such areas as fiscal management, control of inflation, greater financial independence for individuals, and improved health care.

Deepening divisions over European policy led in November 1990 to a leadership challenge by former cabinet minister Michael Heseltine, who obtained enough first-round votes to force Thatcher's resignation. But the succession went to the chancellor of the exchequer, John Major, who was regarded as the "Thatcherite" among the three second-round contenders but who quickly jettisoned his predecessor's more controversial policies. The Conservatives fought the April 1992 election on a platform of further privatization (including British Rail and the coal mines), financial accountability in the National Health Service, and freedom of choice in the state education sector. On a vote share of 41.9 percent, the party won its fourth consecutive term, taking 336 (out of 651) seats in the House of Commons, 40 fewer than in 1987.

Postelection difficulties caused a massive slump in the Conservatives' public standing, as evidenced by unprecedented local electoral trouncings in 1993–1994 and the concurrent loss in by-elections of several "safe" Conservative parliamentary seats to the Liberal Democrats. In June 1994 the party also fared badly in European Parliament balloting, falling from 34 to 18 seats (out of 87). Increasing intraparty criticism led Prime Minister Major to place his leadership on the line in June 1995. Reelected the following month with the support of 218 of the 329 Conservative MPs, he proceeded to elevate Heseltine to "number two" status in the Conservative hierarchy.

Additional by-election losses and several defections were followed by another rout in local elections in May 1996, even in the party's southern heartland. By the end of 1996, the government was perilously close to minority status in the House of Commons and reliant on the tactical support of Ulster Unionists to survive until the May 1997 election, at which Conservatives captured only 165 seats. The defeat was so extensive that Major resigned as party leader.

After three rounds of balloting, William Hague, former Welsh secretary, defeated former chancellor of the exchequer and EU advocate Kenneth Clarke to become (at 36) the youngest Conservative leader of the century. The EU issue flared up again later in the year when Clarke, Heseltine, and others objected to the decision by party leaders to maintain opposition to the EU's proposed single currency. Following through on a Hague commitment, in Jan-

uary 1998 the parliamentary delegation approved new procedures for selecting the party leader and challenging the incumbent. Under the new rules all party members, not just MPs, were empowered to vote for the leader.

At the annual party conference in October 1998, Hague reiterated his opposition to a single European currency, citing in support the results of a recently concluded referendum of party members. In February 1999 Heseltine, Clarke, and former prime minister Heath all voiced support for Prime Minister Blair's "national changeover plan" and later joined the cross-party "Britain in Europe" movement.

On December 2, 1998, Hague dismissed the party's leader in the upper house, Viscount CRANBORNE, for failing to consult with him before approving the so-called "Cranborne compromise" with Labour over the hereditary membership of an interim upper house of Parliament (pending full reform of the House of Lords) and over passage of a proportional representation scheme for the European Parliament elections in June 1999. Subsequently, Hague's apparent willingness to accept proportional representation for some elected bodies as well as an end to hereditary voting rights in a new upper chamber drew fire from hard-line Conservatives, as did his initial support for a statement by (then) deputy leader Peter LILLEY in April 1999 that "the free market has only a limited role in improving public services like health, education, and welfare." The right interpreted the statement as further evidence of a retreat from Thatcherism.

As expected, the party fared poorly at the May 6, 1999, elections for the new Scottish Parliament and Welsh National Assembly, although it registered significant gains in simultaneous nationwide local elections. Conservatives took only 18 seats (all of them "top-up") in the 129-member Scottish legislature and 9 (8 "top-up") in the 60-member Welsh Assembly, but, following up on modest gains made locally in 1998, the party displaced the Liberal Democrats as the second largest party at the local level. A month later Conservatives outpolled Labourites at balloting for the European Parliament, winning 36 seats, more than reversing the party's losses in 1994. The trend continued in 2000, when a March by-election victory gave the party its first directly elected seat in the Scottish Parliament, with further gains recorded in May's local council elections.

In October 1999 Hague, in a retreat from an earlier attempt to delineate a "caring" conservatism, had outlined a "common sense revolution" that marked a clear return to Thatcherism. Over the next six months Hague elaborated on his call for tax cuts; repeated his "sterling guarantee" that the party would not adopt the euro during the next Parliament; took a strong Eurosceptic stance, including support for a proposal that the founding Treaty of Rome be renegotiated to permit members to opt out of EU policies unrelated to trade; accused the Labour administration of being soft on criminals, including sexual offenders; and opposed initiatives on homosexual rights. By mid-2000 the party's standing in public opinion polls had risen dramatically. Prior to the turnaround, many observers had expected Hague's leadership to be challenged by Michael PORTILLO, a former defense secretary under John Major who had returned to the House of Commons with a November 1999 by-election win. Hague, showing new confidence, nevertheless awarded Portillo the key role of shadow chancellor of the exchequer in February 2000.

Despite successes in local council elections, the Conservatives failed to make gains against Labour at the election of June 2001, winning 166 seats and 32.7 percent of the vote in England, Scotland, and Wales. As a consequence, Hague resigned on June 8. Although Portillo was initially regarded as his likely successor, the acrimonious leadership contest ultimately narrowed to a choice between Eurosceptic Iain Duncan SMITH and Kenneth Clarke, with Smith winning a clear victory on September 13. However, Smith was forced to resign on October 29, 2003, after losing a vote of confidence among Conservative MPs, and he was succeeded by Michael HOWARD on November 5. Howard himself resigned following the Conservative defeat in May 2005, although the Conservatives had improved their seat total to 197 on a vote share of 32.3 percent.

David Cameron, a youthful (39-year-old) "modernizer," was elected chair of the party in December 2005 by a two-to-one margin of party member votes over David DAVIS. Cameron immediately pledged to move the Conservatives toward the center for upcoming elections, promising a "more compassionate party" that would present a much larger percentage of female candidates (only four of the party's current MPs were women) and minority candidates. The new leader also emphasized environmental issues, called upon businesses to address "social concerns," and announced that it would undermine the party's credibility to pledge tax cuts during the next general election considering the national budget situation. Although the party's right wing reportedly objected to much of Cameron's centrist policies, the immediate results of the shift to the center included resounding success for the Conservatives in the May 2006 local elections (40 percent of the vote) and continued improvement in the party's position in public opinion polls.

Leaders: David CAMERON (Party Leader and Leader of the Opposition); George OSBORNE (Shadow Chancellor of the Exchequer); Andrew MACKAY (Senior Parliamentary Leader and Political Advisor); Francis MAUDE (Chair); Lord ASHCROFT, Bernard JENKIN (Deputy Chairs).

Liberal Democrat Party. A federal organization of largely autonomous English, Welsh, and Scottish parties, the Liberal Democratic Party (routinely referenced as the Liberal Democrats) formed by merger of the Liberal and Social Democratic parties, as approved at conferences of the two groups on January 23 and 31, 1988, respectively. Initially called the Social and Liberal Democratic Party (SLDP), it adopted the shorter name in October 1989.

Reduced to a minority position by the rise of Labour after World War I, the Liberal Party (founded in 1859) continued to uphold the traditional values of European liberalism and sought, without notable success, to attract dissident elements in both of the main parties by its nonsocialist and reformist principles. Despite having won only 13 seats in the election of October 1974, the party played a crucial role in 1977–1978 by entering into a parliamentary accord with Labour, thus, for the first time in nearly 50 years, permitting a major party to continue in office by means of third-party support. In September 1982 the party voted to form an electoral alliance with the Social Democratic Party (SDP), which yielded an aggregate of 23 parliamentary seats in the 1983 election and 27 in 1987.

The SDP had been formally organized on March 26, 1981, by the "gang of four" right-wing Labour dissidents (Roy JENKINS, Dr. David OWEN, William RODGERS, and Shirley WILLIAMS), who strongly objected to the party's swing to unilateralist and anti-European positions. However, after a series of by-election successes in 1981–1982, the SDP lost impetus. Objecting to the proposed merger with the Liberals after the 1987 election, Owen resigned from the SDP leadership in August 1987 and in February 1988 announced the formation of a "new" SDP, which was ultimately dissolved in June 1990. Meanwhile, in July 1988 the merged Liberal Democrats had elected Paddy ASHDOWN as its leader.

At the April 1992 election the Liberal Democrats won 20 seats, which rose to 25 as a result of subsequent by-election victories. The May 1995 and May 1996 local elections saw the Liberal Democrats overtake the Conservatives as the second party (after Labour) in local government, its greatest strength being mainly in the south and west of England. In the May 1997 general election the party increased its representation to 46 seats, adding another with a by-election win in November. Having announced that it would cooperate with the new government, it subsequently agreed to participate in a special cabinet committee established by Prime Minister Blair for regular consultation in areas of "mutual interest."

In May 1999 the party finished fourth in balloting for the new Scottish and Welsh legislatures, but its 17 seats in the Scottish Parliament enabled it to emerge as the junior partner in a coalition administration in Scotland with Labour. As part of the agreement, Sir David STEEL, former leader of the Liberal Democrats, was chosen to be speaker of the Scottish Parliament. In the May local council elections, Conservative gains dropped the Liberal Democrats back to third place in terms of total local seats.

On August 9, 1999, Charles Kennedy was elected party leader, Ashdown having announced in January that he would step down following the June European Parliament (EP) elections. Under a proportional representation system, the Liberal Democrats saw their EP seat total rise to ten, eight more than in 1994, despite a reduced vote share.

In March 2000 the party threatened to stop cooperating with the government if Labour reneged on its campaign pledge to pursue adoption of proportional voting for the House of Commons. The party also remained firmly committed to the EU and adoption of the euro.

In October 2000 the Liberal Democrats joined Labour in forming a coalition government in Wales. At the June 2001 election for the House of Commons, the party gained 6 seats, for a total of 52, although in local elections it lost the two local councils it had controlled. At the 2005 poll, the party gained 10 lower house seats for a total of 62 on a vote share of 22.1 percent.

Kennedy resigned as chair in January 2006 after acknowledging an ongoing struggle with alcoholism. He was succeeded by Menzies Campbell, a former Olympic sprinter and Scottish MP, who was supported by "modernizing rightwingers" in the party. The "modernizers" were described as supportive of "economic liberalism," including the privatization of certain public services. At the same time, the Liberal Democrats remained opposed to British participation to the war in Iraq and expressed concern about the effect on civil rights of recent antiterrorism initiatives. The Liberal Democrats moved into second place (on a 27 percent vote share) behind the Conservatives in the May 2006 local elections.

Leaders: Walter Menzies ("Ming") CAMPBELL (Party Leader), Vincent CABLE (Deputy Leader), Simon HUGHES (President), Paul BURSTOW (Chief Whip), Lord MCNALLY (Leader in the House of Lords).

Scottish National Party (SNP). Founded in 1934, the SNP advocates Scottish independence within the EU. At the 1979 election it lost 9 of its 11 seats in the House of Commons and since then has managed to win no more than 6. The SNP aligned with Labour and the Liberal Democrats in support of a "yes" vote in the September 1997 referendum on creation of a Scottish Parliament.

As the May 6, 1999, elections for the new Parliament approached, Labour pulled away from the SNP in opinion polls, ending speculation that the nationalists could command a parliamentary majority. Although winning only 7 of 73 constituency seats despite a 28.7 percent first-vote share (second to Labour's 38.8 percent), the SNP received an additional 28 "top-up" seats, making it the leading opposition party in the legislature.

At the party's annual conference in September 1999 party leader Alex Salmond predicted that Scotland would be independent by 2007, and in March 2000 the SNP put forward an independence referendum plan that it would pursue if it won the next Scottish election. Four months later Salmond announced that he would resign as SNP leader in September, at which time the party elected John SWINNEY, his deputy, to succeed him. Swinney had been challenged on the left by Alex NEIL.

At the June 2001 UK general election the SNP retained five of the six seats it had previously held. Amid criticism for ineffective election leadership and arguably disappointing results, Swinney resigned in June 2004. Salmond returned as leader following his election on September 3. The SNP returned to a representation of six in the House of Commons in 2005 on a vote share of 17.7 percent of the votes cast in Scotland.

Leaders: Alex SALMOND (Party Leader), Nicola STURGEON (Deputy Leader), Ian HUDGHTON (President), Bruce CRAWFORD (Business Convenor [Party Chair]).

Plaid Cymru (literally, "Party of Wales," usually referred to by its Welsh name, or informally as the Welsh Nationalist Party). Founded in 1925, *Plaid Cymru* sought full self-government for Wales as a democratic socialist republic. In May 1987 it entered into a parliamentary alliance with the SNP to work for constitutional, economic, and social reform in both regions. It elected four MPs in 1992, when it gained 8.9 percent of the Welsh vote (partly through an alliance in six constituencies with the Welsh Green Party). In 1997 the party retained the four seats, and it joined the Labour Party and the Liberal Democrats in urging passage of the September referendum regarding establishment of a Welsh regional assembly.

Plaid Cymru finished second to Labour at balloting for the Welsh National Assembly on May 6, 1999, taking a 28.4 percent first-vote share and winning a total of 17 seats (9 constituency, 8 "top-up"). Labour subsequently backed the party's nominee as speaker of the new legislature, Lord Dafydd ELIS-THOMAS. In June 1999 *Plaid Cymru* won 2 seats in the European Parliament.

In May 2000, citing health reasons, the party's president, Dafydd WIGLEY, resigned. Ieuan Wyn Jones handily won election as his successor on August 3, and at the party's September annual conference he set 2003 as the target date for supplanting Labour as the foremost party in the Welsh National Assembly. At the June 2001 election for the House of Commons, *Plaid Cymru* retained its four seats. Three months later, at its annual conference, the party formally ended its demand for Welsh independence.

At the May 1, 2003, assembly election the *Plaid Cymru* lost 5 of its 17 seats and barely kept its position as the official opposition. Jones resigned as president and assembly leader within a week of the election. Folk singer and politician Dafydd Iwan was subsequently elected party president, with Jones winning reelection as assembly leader. *Plaid Cymru*'s representation in the House of Commons dropped to 3 in 2005 on a vote share of 12.6 percent of the votes in Wales. Jones subsequently warned party members at the *Plaid Cymru* annual conference that internal squabbling was compromising electoral effectiveness.

Leaders: Dafydd IWAN (President), Ieuan Wyn JONES (Assembly Leader), Elfyn LLWYD (Parliamentary Leader).

Respect, the Unity Coalition. Respect was launched in January 2004 by MP George Galloway, who had been expelled from the Labour Party in October 2003 after being found guilty of inciting UK troops in Iraq to disobey orders. Galloway, running technically as an independent, was reelected in 2005 by a constituency heavily populated by immigrants.

Leaders: George GALLOWAY, Linda SMITH.

Green Party of England and Wales. Organized in 1973 as the Ecology Party, the Greens adopted their present name in 1985. (The semiautonomous Welsh branch is the **Welsh Green Party** [*Plaid Werdd Cym*].) The party addresses human rights issues in addition to problems affecting the environment.

The Greens have consistently polled less than 1 percent of the vote for the House of Commons. In June 1999, however, the Greens won two seats in the European Parliament on a 6.3 percent vote share. In November 1999 Lord BEAUMONT of Whitley, a life peer in the House of Lords, resigned from the Liberal Democrats and joined the Greens as their sole member in the UK Parliament. The party secured no lower house seats on a 1.0 percent vote share in 2005.

Leaders: Richard MALLENDER (Chair), Caroline LUCAS (Principal Speaker).

Note: For information on the Democratic Unionist Party, *Sinn Féin*, the Social Democratic and Labour Party, and the Ulster Unionist Party (all represented in the UK House of Commons), see Political Parties and Groups in the article on United Kingdom: Northern Ireland.

Non-Parliamentary Parties

UK Independence Party (UKIP). The UKIP was created in 1993 by Alan SKED and members of the Anti-Federalist League (founded 1991) to oppose what it saw as the surrender of British sovereignty implicit in the terms of the EU's Maastricht Treaty; the party urged withdrawal from the EU. It failed to win any parliamentary seats in 1997 but won 7 percent of the vote and 3 seats in the European Parliament balloting in June 1999. It fared even better in the European poll of June 2004, winning 12 of 75 seats in a third-place showing.

The UKIP's most celebrated MVP, former talk show host Robert KILROY-SILK, resigned from the party in January 2005 to found **Veritas,** a new party dedicated to the restoration of probity in public life.

British National Party (BNP). The BNP was founded in 1982 by a breakaway faction of the fascist National Front (NF). In early 2006 BNP leader Nick Griffin was acquitted of charges of inciting racial hatred related to a speech he gave at a party conference in 2004 in which he reportedly made strongly anti-Muslim remarks. The BNP improved from 7 to 32 seats in the local elections held in May 2006, performing well in the white working-class areas of east London.

Leaders: Nick GRIFFIN (Chair), Roger KNAPMAN.

Recent elections have been contested by some 100 minor formations, none of which secured a significant share of the vote except, in a very few cases, in individual constituencies. Covering the full political spectrum, the small parties highlighted below are among those recently active.

On the left, the **Socialist Labour Party** (SLP) was launched in 1996 by miners' union leader Arthur SCARGILL to protest the perceived rightward drift of the Labour Party. An Independent Labour Network (ILN) was later formed for similar reasons by European Parliament members Ken COATES and Hugh KERR following their expulsion by the Labour leadership for criticizing the party's "Tory policies." In 1999 Coates unsuccessfully sought reelection on an Alternative Labour List, while Kerr joined the Scottish Socialist Party (below). The more militant **Socialist Workers' Party** (SWP), dating from 1950, has recently withdrawn its traditional support for Labour and begun fielding its own candidates; its founder, Tony CLIFF, died in April 2000. A coalition (the London Socialist Alliance) of the SWP and the **Communist Party of Britain** (below) supported Maverick Ken Livingstone's successful campaign for the capital's mayoralty in 2000. In 1997 the

Militant Labour (ML, originally the Militant Tendency within the Labour Party) founded the Trotskyite **Socialist Party** (SP), led by Peter TAAFFE. An ML minority, led by the group's founder, Ted GRANT, remained within Labour as the Socialist Appeal, while the ML's Scottish branch, led by Tommy SHERIDAN, helped form a Scottish Socialist Alliance that, in turn, established the autonomous **Scottish Socialist Party** (SSP) in 1998. In 1999 the SSP took one seat (won by Sheridan) in the new Scottish Parliament, as did the **Scottish Green Party** (SGP), led by Nina BAKER (Governor) and Robin HARPER, the successful candidate. The **Socialist Party of Great Britain** (SPGB), a non-Leninist Marxist group founded in 1904, continues to maintain branches throughout the country.

On the extreme left, the **Communist Party of Britain** (CPB), currently led by Robert GRIFFITHS, split in 1988 from the historical Communist Party of Great Britain (CPGB) to protest the CPGB's conversion to Eurocommunism. The CPGB was founded in 1920, briefly enjoyed parliamentary representation, and was influential in the trade union movement. However, it is now defunct, most of its remaining membership having reorganized in 1992 as the moderate Democratic Left (DL). The DL presented itself as an association rather than a party and so did not contest elections. In 1999, under the leadership of Nina TEMPLE, its membership voted to reorganize as the nondoctrinaire **New Times Network.** Other CPBG remnants include the Marxist-Leninist **New Communist Party** (NCP), formed by dissidents in 1977; the **Communist Party of Great Britain,** which has as its goal reforging the original CPGB; and the **Communist Party of Scotland** (CPS). The **Workers' Revolutionary Party** (WRP) has also undergone extensive splintering; a faction that has retained the WRP name is led by Sheila TORRANCE. WRP offshoots include the Trotskyite **Socialist Equality Party** (SEP, formerly the International Communist Party), the British branch of the International Committee of the Fourth International. Other small groups include the Trotskyite **Alliance for Workers' Liberty** (AWL), led by Sean MATGAMA; the **Revolutionary Communist Group** (RCG); and

the **Revolutionary Communist Party of Great Britain (Marxist-Leninist),** led by Chris COLEMAN.

On the extreme right, the National Front (NF), a fascist grouping founded in 1967, won a number of local council seats in the 1970s but disintegrated thereafter. Most of the NF defected in 1982 to what is now the BNP (above). In 1995 most remaining NF members regrouped under Ian ANDERSON as the **National Democrats** (ND). Founded in 1990, the **Third Way,** despite its roots in the NF, denounced national socialism and instead favored worker participation in industry, adoption of Swiss-style democratic reforms, immigration restrictions, withdrawal from the EU and other multilateral groups, and an ecological agenda. Extremist groups include the violent **Combat 18.**

Other formations include the **Christian People's Alliance** (CPA), launched in May 1999 as a Christian Democratic party and chaired by David CAMPANALE; the anti-abortion **ProLife Alliance; the Liberal Party,** led by Michael MEADOWCROFT, who opposed the conversion of the historic party into what became the Liberal Democrats; **Mebyon Kernow** (literally, "Sons of Cornwall"), a Cornish separatist group formed in 1951 and led by Richard COLE; the **Islamic Party of Britain,** founded in 1989 and led by David Musa PIDCOCK; the **Legalize Cannabis Alliance** (LCA); and the antimonarchist **British Republican Party** (BRP), established in 1998. In addition, the anti-euro **Democracy Movement,** led by Robin BIRLEY, was organized in 1999 as successor to the Referendum Movement, which began in 1994 as the Referendum Party of the late Sir James GOLDSMITH.

Among the numerous British fringe groups are the **Natural Law Party** (NLP), founded in 1992 by practitioners of Transcendental Meditation and led by Dr. Geoffrey CLEMENTS; the **Official Monster Raving Loony Party,** led by Alan (Howling Lord) HOPE since the 1999 suicide of the party's founder, former rock singer (Screaming Lord) David SUTCH; and the individualist **Rainbow Dream Ticket Party,** which advocates abolishing Parliament and instituting government by home-based electronic referenda.

Cabinet

As of September 1, 2006

Prime Minister and First Lord of the Treasury	Tony Blair
Deputy Prime Minister and First Secretary of State	John Prescott

Secretaries of State

Communities and Local Government	Ruth Kelly [f[
Constitutional Affairs	Lord Falconer of Thoroton
Culture, Media, and Sport	Tessa Jowell [f]
Defense	Des Browne
Education and Skills	Alan Johnson
Environment, Food, and Rural Affairs	David Miliband
Foreign and Commonwealth Affairs	Margaret Beckett [f]
Health	Patricia Hewitt [f]
Home Department	John Reid
International Development	Hilary Benn
Northern Ireland	Peter Hain
Scotland	Douglas Alexander
Trade and Industry	Alistair Darling
Transport	Douglas Alexander
Wales	Peter Hain
Work and Pensions	John Hutton
Chancellor of the Duchy of Lancaster	Hilary Armstrong [f]
Chancellor of the Exchequer	Gordon Brown
Chief Secretary to the Treasury	Stephen Timms
Chief Whip (Parliamentary Secretary to the Treasury)	Jacqui Smith [f]
Leader of the House of Commons	Jack Straw
Leader of the House of Lords	Baroness Amos [f]
Lord Chancellor	Lord Falconer of Thoroton
Lord President of the Council	Baroness Amos [f]
Lord Privy Seal	Jack Straw
Minister for the Cabinet Office and for Social Exclusion	Hilary Armstrong [f]
Minister of the Civil Service	Tony Blair
Minister for Women	Ruth Kelly [f]
Minister Without Portfolio	Hazel Blears [f]

[f] = female

Legislature

The **Parliament** serves as legislative authority for the entire UK. Meeting in Westminster (London) with the queen as its titular head, until November 1999 it consisted of a partly hereditary, partly appointed House of Lords and an elected House of Commons, which is the real locus of power. Under the House of Lords Act 1999 the membership of the upper house was restructured (see below).

Following voter approval at separate devolutionary referendums held in Scotland and Wales in 1997, the UK Parliament passed legislation in 1998 that authorized creation of a Scottish Parliament and a Welsh National Assembly. Elections for both legislatures were held for the first time on May 6, 1999. Creation of a New Northern Ireland Assembly was approved by referendum on May 22, 1998, with the initial election occurring a month later, on June 25 (see the Northern Ireland article). All three legislative bodies were elected for four-year terms under a proportional representation system that combined single-member constituencies and "top-up" seats drawn from party lists.

House of Lords. As of October 1999, the House of Lords had 1,330 members, of whom 751 were hereditary peers, either by succession or of first creation. The remaining members included the 2 archbishops and 24 other senior bishops of the Church of England, serving and retired Lords of Appeal in Ordinary (who constituted the nation's highest body of civil and criminal appeal), and other life peers. Only about 200–300 members of the House of Lords attended sessions with any degree of regularity. The House of Lords Act 1999 abolished the hereditary component and replaced it on an interim basis, pending more comprehensive reform, by 92 ex-hereditary members: 75 elected by all the hereditaries according to a predetermined party ratio, 15 house officers elected by the full membership, and 2 appointed royal office holders (the Earl Marshall and the Lord Great Chamberlain). The 75 peers elected on October 29 on a party basis comprised 42 Conservatives, 28 "crossbenchers" (independents), 3 Liberal Democrats, and 2 Labour members. The collateral election of house officers added 9 Conservatives, 2 Labour peers, 2 Liberal Democrats, and 2 crossbenchers.

Initially, the full interim chamber had 670 members, but the subsequent naming of new life peers—most of them Labour supporters, in an effort by the government to achieve political parity—plus the naming in April 2001 of 15 independent "people's peers" by an appointments commission, brought the total to 715 as of July 31, 2001. Following the most recent appointments, as of July 3, 2006, the total was 753: Labour Party, 213; Conservative Party, 210; crossbenchers, 196; Liberal Democrats, 79; Green Party of England and Wales, 1; archbish-

ops and bishops, 26; peers on leave of absence, 12; others, 16.

On June 28, 2006, the House of Lords for the first time elected its own leader as part of broader governmental changes proposed by the prime minister in 2003. The new Lord Speaker, who may serve a maximum of two five-year terms, assumed (effective July 4) the leadership role previously exercised by the Lord Chancellor (the prime minister's appointee and a member of the cabinet). Baroness Hayman of the Labour Party was elected as the first Lord Speaker, and, following the custom of the speaker of the House of Commons, she subsequently withdrew her party affiliation. Meanwhile, legislation proposing a popularly elected component for the House of Lords was expected to be introduced in late 2006 or early 2007.

Lord Speaker: Baroness HAYMAN.

House of Commons. Following the general election of May 5, 2005 (and one subsequent by-election on June 23 in a constituency where initial balloting had been postponed due to the death of a candidate), the House consisted of 646 members directly elected from single-member constituencies for terms of five years, subject to earlier dissolution. The strength of the parties was as follows: Labour Party, 355 seats; Conservative Party, 198; Liberal Democrats, 62; Democratic Unionist Party, 9; Scottish National Party, 6; *Sinn Féin,* 5 (seats not taken); *Plaid Cymru,* 3; Social Democratic and Labour Party, 3; Respect, the Unity, 1; Ulster Unionist Party, 1; independent, 2. (According to long-standing convention, the speaker serves without party affiliation and votes only in case of a tie vote. The current speaker was first elected in 1979 on the Labour Party ticket. Following his designation as speaker in 2000, he withdrew his party affiliation. In the 2001 and 2005 elections he ran as "The Speaker Seeking Reelection.")

Speaker: Michael MARTIN.

Scottish Parliament. Party strength in the 129-member Parliament after the May 1, 2003, election was as follows: Labour Party, 50 seats; Scottish National Party, 27; Conservative Party,

18; Liberal Democrats, 17; Scottish Green Party, 7; Scottish Socialist Party 6; others, 4.

Speaker: George REID.

Welsh National Assembly (*Cynulliad Cenedlaethol Cymru*). Party strength in the 60-member National Assembly after the May 1, 2003, election was as follows: Labour Party, 30 seats; *Plaid Cymru,* 12; Conservative Party, 11; Liberal Democrats, 6; other, 1.

Speaker: Lord Dafydd ELIS-THOMAS.

Communications

Freedom combined with responsibility represents the British ideal in the handling of news and opinion. The press, while privately owned and free from censorship, is subject to strict libel laws and is often made aware of government preferences with regard to the handling of news reports. In late 1989, faced with the prospect of parliamentary action to curb the excesses of the more sensationalist papers, publishers adopted an ethics code that limited intrusion into private lives; offered the objects of press stories reasonable opportunity for reply; provided for appropriately prominent retraction of errors in reporting; precluded payments to known criminals; and barred irrelevant references to race, color, and religion.

A Press Complaints Commission was established by the industry in 1991. Responding to public concerns following the death of Diana, Princess of Wales, in a high-speed motor vehicle accident in August 1997, the commission announced in December 1997 a revised code of conduct that widened the definition of privacy for individuals, prohibited "persistent pursuit" by photojournalists, and offered additional protections for children. In February 1998 Prime Minister Blair offered support for continued self-regulation by the press.

A communications bill, which was first published in May 2002, replaced five current regulatory bodies for the press, television, and radio with a single Office of Communications, the first chair of which was appointed in July. As drafted, the proposal would liberalize ownership restrictions.

Press

Per capita consumption of newspapers in the UK, once the highest in the world, has fallen off substantially in recent years. Major consolidation in ownership has occurred over the past several decades. The best known of the current chains is Rupert Murdoch's News International PLC, which includes among its newspapers the UK's largest daily tabloid, *The Sun;* the largest Sunday tabloid, *The News of the World;* and the influential *Times* and *Sunday Times.* The regional press is also highly concentrated, with 674 titles being owned (in 1996) by 10 corporations. In 2004, there were more than 2,600 regional and local newspapers.

England: The following papers are dailies published in London, unless otherwise indicated: *News of the World* (3,745,000), Sunday, usually pro-Conservative tabloid; *The Sun* (3,301,000), usually pro-Conservative tabloid; *Daily Mail* (2,404,000), pro-Conservative tabloid; *The Mail on Sunday* (2,400,000), pro-Conservative tabloid; *The Mirror* (formerly *Daily Mirror,* 1,777,000); *Sunday Mirror* (1,597,000), pro-Labour tabloid; *The Sunday Times* (1,363,000), pro-Conservative; *Sunday People* (1,275,000), pro-Labour tabloid; *Express on Sunday* (990,000), pro-Conservative tabloid; *The Daily Express* (929,000), pro-Conservative tabloid; *The Daily Telegraph* (907,000), Conservative; *Daily Star* (883,000), pro-Conservative tabloid; *The Sunday Telegraph* (695,000), Conservative; *The Times* (858,000), usually pro-Conservative; *The Observer* (434,000), Sunday, independent; *The Financial Times* (426,000), independent; *Evening Standard* (361,000), moderate Conservative tabloid; *The Guardian* (London and Manchester, 371,000), center-left; *The Independent on Sunday* (212,000), independent; *The Independent* (262,000), independent; *Express & Star* (Wolverhampton, 163,000); *Manchester Evening News* (148,000), independent; *Liverpool Echo* (135,000); *Birmingham Evening Mail* (104,000); *Evening Chronicle* (Newcastle upon Tyne, 92,000); *Leicester Mercury* (90,000); *Shropshire Star* (Telford, 83,000), *Sunday Mercury* (Birmingham, 80,000); *Sunday Sun* (Newcastle upon Tyne,

82,000); *Yorkshire Evening Post* (Leeds, 82,000); *Nottingham Evening Post* (79,000); *Evening Standard* (Stock-on-Trent, 75,000), *The Star* (Sheffield, 75,000); *Evening Post* (Bristol, 61,000); *The News* (Portsmouth, 63,000), *Evening Telegraph* (Coventry, 62,000), *Yorkshire Post* (Leeds, 62,000).

Wales: *South Wales Echo* (Cardiff, 59,000); *South Wales Evening Post* (Swansea, 60,000); *Western Mail* (Cardiff, 44,000).

Scotland: *Sunday Mail* (Glasgow, 585,000), pro-Labour tabloid; *Sunday Post* (Dundee, 514,000), tabloid; *Daily Record* (Glasgow, 479,000), independent tabloid; *Evening Times* (Glasgow, 95,000); *The Press and Journal* (Aberdeen, 89,000); *The Herald* (Glasgow, 79,000), independent, the oldest national newspaper in the English language; *The Courier and Advertiser* (Dundee, 83,000); *Scotland on Sunday* (Edinburgh, 81,000), independent; *The Scotsman* (Edinburgh, 68,000), independent; *Evening News* (Edinburgh, 68,000); *Evening Express* (Aberdeen, 60,000).

Northern Ireland: See next article.

News Agencies

Britain boasts the world's oldest news agency, Reuters, founded by the pioneer German news gatherer Paul von Reuter, who established his headquarters in London in 1851. The company is now a worldwide service controlled by press interests in Britain, Australia, and New Zealand. The other leading agencies included the Associated Press Ltd. (a British subsidiary of the Associated Press of the United States) and the Press Association, founded in 1868.

Broadcasting and Computing

Broadcasting services are provided by the British Broadcasting Corporation (BBC), founded in 1922, and various independent commercial companies. The BBC, which is publicly financed by compulsory license fees, operates two national television services, various satellite channels, five national and four regional radio services, and several dozen local stations. The commercial sector is regulated by the Independent Television Commission (ITC) and the Radio Authority (RA). Funded by paid advertising, the commercial television companies have their own national network, while the fourth national television station (Channel 4) is also financed by advertising but has statutory obligations, including a duty to broadcast a suitable proportion of its transmissions in Wales in the Welsh language. A fifth national television station (Channel 5), also commercially operated, began broadcasting in 1997. There were approximately 50 million television receivers and 24 million personal computers serving 25 million Internet users in 2003.

Intergovernmental Representation

Ambassador to the U.S.
David G. MANNING

U.S. Ambassador to the UK
Robert H. TUTTLE

Permanent Representative to the UN
Sir Emyr JONES PARRY

IGO Memberships (Non-UN)
ADB, AfDB, BIS, CDB, CERN, CEUR, CWTH, EBRD, EIB, ESA, EU, Eurocontrol, G-10, G-7/G-8, IADB, IEA, Interpol, IOM, NATO, OECD, OSCE, PCA, WCO, WEU, WTO

Related Territories

All major, and many minor, territories of the former British Empire achieved full independence in the course of the last century, and most are now members of the Commonwealth, a voluntary association of states held together primarily by a common political and constitutional heritage and, in most cases, use of the English language (see "The Commonwealth" in Intergovernmental Organizations section). In conventional usage, the term Commonwealth also includes the territories and dependencies of the UK and other Commonwealth member countries. As of 2006 the UK retained a measure of responsibility, direct or indirect, for 3 crown dependencies, 11 inhabited territories, 2 essentially uninhabited territories, and the so-called Sovereign Base Areas on Cyprus.

In September 1998, following up on a commitment made at the Dependent Territories Association conference in London the preceding February, the Blair government announced that it intended to introduce legislation that would supersede the 1981 British Nationality Act, which had excluded most colonial residents from British citizenship, and restore their "right of abode" in the UK, which had been revoked in 1962. The dependencies would be restyled British overseas territories. A white paper issued in March 1999 reaffirmed the government's intentions, although the government added that the Caribbean colonies would be required to introduce various criminal justice reforms—for example, abolishing the death penalty and decriminalizing consensual homosexual relations—before attaining the new status. Implementing legislation was passed in 2002, with British citizenship being conferred on citizens of all British overseas territories (except the Sovereign Base Areas) from May 21. Since 2005 many of the territories, with London's cooperation and encouragement, have been studying possible constitutional reforms.

Crown Dependencies

Though closely related to Great Britain both historically and geographically, the Channel Islands and the Isle of Man are distinct from the UK and are under the jurisdiction of the sovereign rather than the state.

Channel Islands. Located in the English Channel off the northwest coast of France, the Channel Islands have been attached to the English Crown since the Norman Conquest in 1066. The nine islands have a total area of 75 square miles (198 sq. km.) and a population (2001C) of 146,993. The two largest and most important are Jersey and Guernsey, each of which has its own parliament (the States) but is linked to the crown through a representative who bears the title lieutenant governor and serves as commander in chief. While the Channel Islands control their own domestic affairs, defense policy and most foreign relations are administered from London. St. Helier on Jersey and St. Peter Port on Guernsey are the principal towns. Because of their mild climate and insular location, the islands are popular tourist resorts, and their low tax rate has attracted many permanent residents from the UK.

The government of Jersey is based in the "Assembly of the States," a 53-member elected body composed of 29 deputies, 12 constables (heads of parishes), and 12 senators, not counting 3 nonvoting ex officio members (attorney general, solicitor general, dean of Jersey) plus the lieutenant governor and a bailiff, who presides over the legislature. Deputies and constables serve three-year terms; senators serve six-year terms, with elections for half their number held triennially. The most recent senatorial election was held October 19, 2005, with the balloting for deputies following on November 23. Candidates ran as independents, although it was reported that 3 of the newly elected deputies were affiliated with the recently formed **Jersey Democratic Alliance** (JDA) and two with the **Center Party.** One senator, Stuart SYVRET, has been associated with the **Jersey Green Party.**

November 2005 marked a major change in Jersey's governmental structure. Under the States of Jersey Law 2005, the previous committee system of governance was replaced by a ten-member cabinet-style system headed by a chief minister. The other nine ministers are nominated by the chief minister from among the membership of Assembly of the States, which then elects each minister individually. The authority of the lieutenant governor to veto resolutions of the States was abolished, and "orders in council," issued by the Privy Council in London, were henceforth to be referred to the States for review. On December 5 Sen. Frank Walker was elected chief minister by a vote of 38–14 over Senator Syvret.

Guernsey is governed through its "States of Deliberation," which comprises 45 people's deputies elected from multi- or single-member districts every four years, 2 representatives from Alderney, 2 ex officio members (attorney general and solicitor general), and a bailiff. Prior to the election of April

21, 2004, the States had included 10 local (parish) representatives, but those seats were eliminated as part of a governmental reform process that also saw, from May 1, 2004, adoption of a ministerial administration. At that time, 43 separate committees were abolished in favor of a Policy Council, comprising a chief minister and 10 other ministers elected from and by the members of the States; 10 departments, each headed by a minister; and 5 "specialist" committees.

The small islands of Alderney, Sark, Herm, Jethou, Brecqhou, and Lihou are usually classified as dependencies of the Bailiwick of Guernsey, although Alderney and Sark have their own legislatures: the States of Alderney, encompassing a president and 10 deputies serving four-year terms (half elected every other year), and the Sark Court of Chief Pleas, comprising 40 hereditary "tenants" (landowners) and 12 deputies elected for three-year terms. In late 2006 an ongoing constitutional reform process is expected to eliminate not only the hereditary seats from the Court of Chief Pleas but also the hereditary feudal post of seigneur of Sark.

Although the Channel Islands are not legally part of the EU, certain EU directives are deemed to apply to them, notably those relating to tariffs and agricultural policy. In February 1995 the Sark Court of Chief Pleas rejected the incorporation of relevant parts of the EU's Maastricht Treaty into Sark law. In November 1999, however, the Court of Chief Pleas voted to rescind a 1611 law that had restricted property inheritance to men. In December the UK Privy Council approved the change, thereby preventing a future challenge in the European Court of Human Rights.

In November 1998 a report presented by the UK Home Office recommended that the Channel Islands and the Isle of Man, which between them have registered some 90,000 offshore businesses, require such operations to provide greater details about their ownership and activities. The report also proposed that the dependencies take additional steps to prevent money laundering and other financial offenses. The June 2000 decision of the OECD to include the Channel Islands and the Isle of Man

among 35 international jurisdictions with harmful tax and investment regimes led the islands' administrations to assert that reform would be pointless unless other, larger jurisdictions, such as Switzerland and Luxembourg, also participated. In early August, however, the islands pledged to cooperate with OECD efforts to eliminate tax crimes perpetrated by offshore corporations, and in February 2002 they were removed from the blacklist.

In a February 2000 ruling with major implications for a number of UK institutions, the European Court of Human Rights determined that a Guernsey flower grower had been denied a fair trial when he appealed a planning decision denying him use of a packing shed as a residence. The original appeal had involved the bailiff of Guernsey, who held executive and legislative as well as judicial responsibilities, thereby calling into question his impartiality, according to the court. The decision increased the likelihood of future challenges against, for example, the UK's lord chancellor, particularly in cases based on policies that the chancellor helps administer.

Lieutenant Governor and Commander in Chief of Jersey: Andrew RIDGWAY.

Bailiff of Jersey and President of the Assembly of the States: Sir Philip M. BAILHACHE.

Chief Minister of Jersey: Frank Harrison WALKER.

Lieutenant Governor and Commander in Chief of the Bailiwick of Guernsey and its Dependencies: Vice Adm. Sir Fabian MALBON.

Bailiff of Guernsey and President of the States of Deliberation: Geoffrey Robert ROLAND.

Chief Minister of Guernsey: Laurence Charles MORGAN.

Isle of Man. Located in the Irish Sea midway between Northern Ireland and northern England, the Isle of Man has been historically connected to Great Britain for over 700 years but remains politically distinct. It has an area of 227 square miles (588 sq. km.) and a population of 76,315 (2001C). The principal town is Douglas, and most income is derived from offshore banking and business services.

The island's self-governing institutions include the High Court of Tynwald (the world's oldest parliament in continuous existence), encompassing a president elected by the Court, the Legislative Council, and the House of Keys. The Legislative Council includes a president, the lord bishop of Sodor and Man, a nonvoting attorney general, and eight others named by the House of Keys, which is a 24-member body popularly elected for a five-year term. The British monarch serves as head of state ("Lord of Man") and is represented by a lieutenant governor, who historically functioned as head of government and presided over an Executive Council. In 1986, however, the office of chief minister was created, and in 1990 a Council of Ministers replaced the Executive Council. Concurrently, the president of the Tynwald assumed many of the responsibilities of the lieutenant governor, who nevertheless still reserves important constitutional powers, including the authority to dissolve the House of Keys. The chief minister, elected by the legislature, nominates the other ministers.

The island levies its own taxes and has a special relationship with the EU, falling within the EU customs territory but remaining fiscally independent of it. In August 2000 the Manx administration joined the Channel Islands in agreeing to work with the OECD on tax harmonization, improved financial transparency, and information exchange.

At the election of November 22, 2001, independents won 19 seats in the House of Keys. The **Alliance for Progressive Government** won 3 seats, and the **Manx Labour Party** won 2. The nationalist **Mec Vannin** (Sons of Mannin), which dates from 1962 and advocates republican independence, boycotts elections.

Following the 2001 polling the incumbent chief minister, Donald Gelling, was unanimously reelected to the post, but he stepped down a year later and was succeeded by Richard CORKHILL. In December 2004 Corkhill resigned because of a financial scandal, and on December 14 Gelling was returned as chief minister.

Lieutenant Governor: Sir Paul HADDACKS.

President of the Tynwald: Noel Quayle CRINGLE.

Speaker of the House of Keys: James Anthony BROWN.

Chief Minister: Donald James GELLING.

Inhabited Overseas Territories

The territory of Gibraltar, described below, remains directly subordinate to the UK, although it enjoys almost complete autonomy in internal affairs. The term "colony" or "crown colony," is often still used in reference to it. For information on other overseas territories of the UK see *Political Handbook of the World 2007.*

Gibraltar. The territory of Gibraltar, a rocky promontory at the western mouth of the Mediterranean, was captured by the British in 1704 and ceded by Spain to the UK by the Treaty of Utrecht in 1713. It has an area of 2.1 square miles (5.5 sq. km.), and its population numbers 29,800 (2005E), of whom about 21,000 are native Gibraltarians. The economy was long dependent on expenditures in support of its air and naval facilities; in recent years, however, tourism and financial services have grown in importance, and special status within the EC/EU has permitted it to transship foreign goods without payment of such duties as value-added taxes. Financial services currently constitute about one-fifth of the economy, significantly more than UK defense expenditures.

British authority is represented by a governor. Substantial self-government was introduced in 1964 and further extended in 1969 by a new constitution that provided for a House of Assembly of 15 elected and 2 ex officio members (the attorney general and the financial and development secretary), plus a speaker appointed by the governor. Of the elected members, no more than eight can represent the same party. The executive Gibraltar Council, chaired by the governor, has four additional ex officio members and five other members, including a chief minister, drawn from the elected members of the House of Assembly. The governor names as chief minister the majority leader in the assembly.

Gibraltar has been the subject of a lengthy dispute between Britain and Spain, which has pressed in the UN and elsewhere for "decolonization" of the territory and has impeded access to it by land and air. A referendum conducted by the British in 1967 showed an overwhelming preference for continuation of British rule, but Spain rejected the results and declared the referendum invalid. Spain's position was subsequently upheld by the UN General Assembly, which called in December 1968 for the ending of British administration by October 1, 1969. A month after promulgation of the 1969 constitution, which guarantees that the Gibraltarians will never have to accept Spanish rule unless the majority so desires, Spain closed its land frontier. In January 1978 Spain agreed to the restoration of telephone links to the city, but the border was not fully reopened until February 1985, following an agreement in November 1984 to provide equality of rights for Spaniards in Gibraltar and Gibraltarians in Spain; in addition, Britain agreed, for the first time, to enter into discussions on the sovereignty issue.

At the election of March 1988 the **Gibraltar Socialist Labour Party** (GSLP) won the permissible maximum of eight legislative seats, its leader, Joe BOSSANO, becoming chief minister. Upon assuming office Bossano declared that most of the residents opposed the 1984 accord with Spain. Earlier, in December 1987, the assembly had rejected a UK-Spanish agreement on cooperative administration of the territory's airport. Quite apart from the impact of exclusive British control on the sovereignty issue, Spain has argued that the isthmus to the mainland, on which the airport is located, was not covered by the 1713 treaty.

The GSLP was again victorious at the election of January 16, 1992, retaining its majority with a vote share of 73 percent; the **Gibraltar Social Democrats** (GSD), led by Peter Caruana, won seven seats and the Gibraltar National Party (GNP), led by Dr. Joseph GARCIA, none. Following the election, Bossano insisted that his party's campaign for greater autonomy from Britain was not anti-Spanish, but "a clear expression of the desire for self-determination." Declining tourism and rising unemployment in 1993 caused further strains with Britain, which Bossano accused of neglecting Gibraltar's interests at the EU level.

The December 1994 round of UK-Spanish foreign ministers' talks on Gibraltar was snagged by heightened Spanish vigilance and consequential delays at the border crossing. Part of the Spanish concern was that Gibraltarians were increasingly supplementing traditional cigarette smuggling operations with drug trafficking and money laundering. In July 1995 UK pressure led the government to table a bill designed to stop money laundering and to bring Gibraltar's offshore banking into line with British and EU standards. Meanwhile, Chief Minister Bossano maintained his refusal to participate in the UK-Spanish talks, calling instead for direct discussions with Madrid on self-determination for Gibraltar.

A more flexible stance by the center-right GSD, which held that negotiations could proceed on any issue other than sovereignty, won the support of 48 percent of voters in a general election on May 16, 1996, with the GSLP slumping to 39 percent. The GSD secured eight assembly seats against seven for the GSLP, with the GNP again failing to win representation despite taking 13 percent of the vote. GSD leader Peter Caruana was sworn in as chief minister, pledging to participate in UK-Spanish talks.

In April 1998, in a shift of strategy, Madrid offered to open bilateral talks with Chief Minister Caruana regarding its recent proposal that Britain and Spain share sovereignty during a transitional period, with Gibraltar ultimately to achieve self-governing status under Spain—a proposal that Caruana and the Blair government dismissed. Later in the year both sides demonstrated a willingness to improve cooperation with regard to overflights of Spanish territory by Royal Air Force and NATO aircraft as well as the use and development of Gibraltar's airport. In 1999, however, a continuing dispute over fishing rights off Gibraltar for Spanish trawlers led Spanish customs officials to enforce strict, time-consuming border controls in retaliation. In October Caruana labeled bilateral talks on sovereignty between London and Madrid as "inappropriate and unacceptable." Instead, he proposed a "two flags, three voices" approach—the third voice being Gibraltar—which Spain has rejected.

In January 2000 Caruana surprised the opposition by calling an election for February 10, three months ahead of schedule. At the balloting his GSD increased its vote share to 58 percent and again claimed eight seats in the House of Assembly. An alliance of Bossano's GSLP and Joseph Garcia's small **Gibraltar Liberal Party** (successor to the GNP) won the other seven elective seats.

Two months later, on April 19, 2000, Spain and Britain announced that they had resolved differences over the territory's administrative status. Madrid's refusal to accept Gibraltar as a "competent authority" had delayed a range of EU business and economic initiatives. Spain agreed to recognize the validity of various documents issued by Gibraltar, including passports and identity cards. Britain agreed to act as a "postal box," relaying communications to and from Spain, which could thereby continue to avoid direct contact with the Gibraltar government. In addition, the agreement cleared the way for Britain to accede to parts of the EU's Schengen agreement on frontier controls, and it opened the way for Gibraltar-based financial corporations to compete throughout the EU. Chief Minister Caruana responded to the announcement of the agreement by saying, "Spain, Britain, and Gibraltar have all preserved their interests; there are no winners and no losers."

For the first time since December 1997, ministerial talks between Spain and the UK resumed on July 26, 2001, and by early 2002 it was clear that the two sides were moving closer toward a joint sovereignty arrangement. However, the prospect of any such arrangement was greeted with scorn by Caruana and generated, over the ensuing months, massive demonstrations by Gibraltarians.

Madrid and London nonetheless pressed ahead and by mid-2002 had reached agreement on joint rule, though differing as to its duration. The UK clearly viewed it as more than "transitional." In addition, Britain insisted that its military bases remain under its control. Caruana, meanwhile, refused to participate in the talks, save as an equal partner. Subsequently, on November 7, Gibraltar mounted a referendum in which 98.9 percent of the participants voted against shared sovereignty. At the most recent general election of November 28, 2003, Caruana's Gibraltar Social Democrats retained its eight seats, while the GSLP-Liberal alliance again won seven.

In October 2004 Spain agreed, for the first time, to give Gibraltar a seat at the negotiating table, which led to the first three-party discussion in December. On February 10, 2005, the first session of a Trilateral Forum, with an open agenda, met in Malaga, Spain. Issues considered by the forum have included the airport and benefits for Spanish workers, but sovereignty has remained off the table.

Governor and Commander in Chief: Sir Francis RICHARDS.

Chief Minister: Peter CARUANA.

UNITED KINGDOM: NORTHERN IRELAND

The Country

Geographically an integral part of Ireland, the six northern Irish counties (collectively known as "Ulster," although excluding three counties of the historic province of that name) are politically included within the UK for reasons rooted in the ethnic and religious divisions introduced into Ireland by English and Scottish settlement in the 17th century. As a result of this colonization effort, the long-established Roman Catholic population of the northern counties came to be heavily outnumbered by Protestants, who assumed a dominant political, social, and economic position and insisted upon continued association of the territory with the UK when the rest of Ireland became independent after World War I. Although a minority, Roman Catholics are strongly represented throughout Northern Ireland and constitute a rising proportion of the total population, currently over 42 percent. Catholic complaints of discrimination, especially in regard to the allocation of housing and jobs and to limitation of the franchise in local elections, were the immediate cause of the serious disturbances that commenced in Northern Ireland during 1968–1969.

Despite recurring political violence, foreign investors have been drawn to Ulster by lucrative financial incentives and its proximity to the European market. After sharing in the UK recession of the early 1990s, Northern Ireland experienced an economic upturn in 1993. The signing of the multiparty Good Friday Agreement in April 1998 served as another spur to growth. A month later London announced a new $500 million economic aid package directed toward encouraging foreign investment, developing small businesses, easing unemployment, and improving labor skills. Tourism, in particular, was targeted for growth, with political stability expected to lead to some 20,000 additional jobs in the industry.

For 1997–1998 Northern Ireland reported record exports, led by expanding sales of transport equipment. Other manufactures include clothing and textiles, food and beverages, and machinery, with the industrial sector accounting for about one-fourth of the GDP. Growth industries include software, telecommunications, and electronics. Agriculture, which dominated the economy until recent years, now accounts for under 5 percent of GDP and employs a similarly small percentage of the workforce; principal crops are barley, wheat, and potatoes. Leading trading partners are the rest of the UK and the United States, although commerce with the Republic of Ireland has been growing. Per capita GNP, which increased to about $16,000 in 1997, continues to lag behind that of the UK as a whole by about 20 percent. However, unemployment is comparable to that in Scotland and Wales and well below the average for Europe.

Government and Politics

Political Background

Governed as an integral part of Ireland, and therefore of the UK, throughout the 19th and early 20th centuries, Northern Ireland acquired autonomous status in 1921 as part of a general readjustment necessitated by the success of the Irish independence movement in the rest of Ireland. The Government of Ireland Act of 1920 provided for a division of Ireland as a whole into separate northern and southern sections, each with its own

Political Status: Autonomous province of the United Kingdom under separate parliamentary regime established in 1921 but suspended March 30, 1972; coalition executive formed January 1, 1974; direct rule reimposed May 28, 1974; consultative Northern Ireland Assembly elected October 20, 1982, but dissolved by United Kingdom June 19, 1986; devolution to (new) Northern Ireland Assembly and multiparty power-sharing Northern Ireland Executive effected December 2, 1999; direct rule reimposed February 11–May 30, 2000, on August 11, 2001, for one day, on September 22, 2001, for one day, and on October 15, 2002.

Area: 5,452 sq. mi. (14,120 sq. km.).

Population: 1,685,267 (2001C); 1,721,000 (2005E).

Major Urban Center (2005E): BELFAST (276,000).

Official Language: English.

Monetary Unit: Pound Sterling (market rate July 1, 2006: 1 pound = $1.85US).

First Minister: Vacant, following resumption of direct rule by the United Kingdom on October 15, 2002.

United Kingdom Secretary of State for Northern Ireland: Peter HAIN; appointed on May 6, 2005, by UK Prime Minister Tony Blair, succeeding Paul MURPHY.

legislature. Enshrined in the December 1921 Anglo-Irish treaty, this arrangement was reluctantly accepted by the Irish nationalist authorities in Dublin but embraced in Northern Ireland as the best available means of continuing as an integral part of the UK. The new government of Northern Ireland was dominated from the beginning by the pro-British, Protestant interests controlling the Ulster Unionist Party (UUP), with militant elements becoming known as "loyalists." Ties with Britain were sedulously maintained, for both religious and historic reasons and because of accompanying economic benefits, including social services and agricultural subsidies. Opposition Catholic sentiment in favor of union with the Irish Republic repre-

sented a continuing but long-subdued source of tension.

Catholic-led "civil rights" demonstrations against political and social discrimination erupted during 1968, evoking counterdemonstrations by Protestant extremists and leading to increasingly serious disorders, particularly in Londonderry (known to Catholics as Derry). In November 1968 the government of Terence O'NEILL proposed a number of reform measures that failed to halt the disturbances and yielded an erosion of support for the prime minister within his own government and party. Parliament was accordingly dissolved, with a new election in February 1969 producing the usual unionist majority but failing to resolve an internal UUP conflict. In April mounting disorder and acts of sabotage led the Northern Ireland government to request that British army units be assigned to guard key installations. Although O'Neill persuaded the UUP to accept the principle of universal adult franchise at the next local government elections, he resigned as party leader on April 28 and as prime minister three days later. His successor in both offices, Maj. James D. CHICHESTER-CLARK, an advocate of moderate reform, was chosen by a 17–16 vote of the UUP over Brian FAULKNER, an opponent of the O'Neill reform program. The government promptly announced an amnesty for all persons involved in the recent disturbances and received a unanimous vote of confidence on May 7.

After renewed rioting in Belfast, Londonderry, and elsewhere during the first half of August 1969, Chichester-Clark agreed on August 19 that all security forces in Northern Ireland would be placed under British command; that Britain would assume ultimate responsibility for public order; and that steps would be taken to ensure equal treatment of all citizens in Northern Ireland in regard to voting rights, housing, and other issues. The subsequent deployment of regular British soldiers in the province was at first welcomed by the Catholic population as affording protection from Protestant incursions into their localities. However, under the influence of the Provisional Irish Republican Army (Provisional IRA or the "Provos"), many Catholics quickly came to see the British troops as an occupying force, and their alienation increased as the result of the internment without trial of several hundred Catholics in August 1971. Growing polarization was highlighted by the formation in 1971 of the ultra-loyalist Democratic Unionist Party (DUP) by a hard-line faction of the UUP led by Dr. Ian PAISLEY.

The situation turned sharply worse on "Bloody Sunday," January 30, 1972, when a prohibited Catholic civil-rights march in Londonderry was infiltrated by hooligan elements, and 14 unarmed civilians died as the result of clashes with British troops. A wave of violence and hysteria followed. Unable to act in agreement with the Belfast regime of Prime Minister Brian Faulkner, who had succeeded Chichester-Clark in March 1971, British Prime Minister Edward Heath announced that he would reimpose direct rule. The Northern Ireland Parliament was prorogued rather than dissolved, and William (subsequently Viscount) WHITELAW was designated to exercise necessary authority through the newly created office of secretary of state for Northern Ireland. With the backing of the three leading British parties, these changes were quickly approved by the British Parliament and became effective, initially for a period of one year, on March 30, 1972. The 1972 death toll from political violence reached 478, the highest annual total during the post-1969 "Troubles."

A plebiscite on the future of Northern Ireland was held on March 8, 1973, but was boycotted by the Catholic parties. An unimpressive 57.4 percent of the electorate voted for Ulster's remaining within the UK, while 0.6 percent voted for union with the Republic of Ireland and the remainder abstained. The British government subsequently organized the election on June 28 of a Northern Ireland Assembly of 80 members to serve a four-year term. This step was formalized on July 18 by passage of a parliamentary bill permitting the devolution of powers to the assembly and an executive, and on November 27 Brian Faulkner was named chief of an executive-designate that included representatives of both Protestant and Catholic factions.

In a meeting in Sunningdale, England, on December 6–9, 1973, that was attended by members of the Irish and UK governments as well as the executive-designate of Northern Ireland, agreement was reached on the establishment of a tripartite Council of Ireland to oversee changes in the relationship between the northern and southern Irish governments. On January 1, 1974, direct rule was terminated. While the (mainly Catholic) Social Democratic and Labour Party (SDLP) endorsed the agreement, the bulk of the Unionist Party rejected it, forcing Faulkner's resignation as party leader on January 7 and as chief executive on May 28, in the wake of which direct rule was again imposed.

In July 1974 the UK Parliament passed the Northern Ireland Act of 1974, which authorized the election of a Constitutional Convention. At balloting on May 1, 1975, the United Ulster Unionist Coalition (UUUC), a grouping of largely "anti-Sunningdale" parties, won 45 of 78 convention seats. On September 8 the UUUC convention members voted 37–1 against the participation of republicans in a future Northern Ireland cabinet, and on November 20 the convention concluded its sitting with a formal report that embraced only UUUC proposals. The convention was reconvened on February 3, 1976, in the hope of reaching agreement with the SDLP and other opposition parties, but it registered no further progress and was dissolved a month later.

The UUUC was itself dissolved on May 4, 1977, following the failure of a general strike called by its more intransigent loyalist components, acting in concert with the Ulster Workers' Council (UWC) and the Ulster Defense Association (UDA), the largest of the Protestant paramilitary groups. With the level of violence having declined, Secretary of State for Northern Ireland Roy MASON proposed in late November that a new attempt be made to restore local rule. The effort was abandoned, however, because of intensified violence in the first quarter of 1978, which prompted the House of Commons in late June to extend the period of direct rule for another year. In the absence of a political settlement, the order was renewed annually thereafter.

Following the failure of another attempt at constitutional talks in early 1980 and a further escalation of violence, seven republican inmates of the Maze prison near Belfast began a hunger strike on October 27 in support of a demand for "political" status. While the strike was called off on December 18 following government promises of improvement in prison conditions, the action was widely publicized and was renewed in March 1981, with ten prisoners ultimately dying, including Bobby SANDS and Kieran DOHERTY, who had won election to, respectively, the UK and Irish parliaments shortly before their deaths. The most significant diplomatic development of the year was a meeting in London on November 6 at which UK Prime Minister Margaret Thatcher and Irish Prime Minister Garret FitzGerald agreed to set up an Anglo-Irish Intergovernmental Council (AIIC) to meet on a periodic basis to discuss matters of common concern.

In early 1982 the Thatcher government secured parliamentary approval for the gradual reintroduction of home rule under a scheme dubbed "rolling devolution." The initiative assumed substantive form with balloting on October 20 for a new 78-member Northern Ireland Assembly. For the first time the Provisional *Sinn Féin* (the political wing of the Provisional IRA) participated in the process, obtaining five seats. The poll was accompanied, however, by an upsurge of terrorist activity, with both the Provisional *Sinn Féin* and the SDLP boycotting the assembly session that convened on November 11 to formulate devolution recommendations.

During a meeting in Hillsborough Castle, Northern Ireland, on November 15, 1985, Prime Ministers Thatcher and FitzGerald concluded an Anglo-Irish Agreement that established an Intergovernmental Conference (IGC) within the context of the AIIC to deal on a regular basis with political and security issues affecting the troubled region. Subsequently, in reaction to unionist maneuvering, the small nonsectarian Alliance Party joined *Sinn Féin* and the SDLP in boycotting the Northern Ireland Assembly, while the 15 unionist MPs resigned their seats in the UK House of Commons to force by-elections as a form of referendum on the Hillsborough accord. (One unionist seat fell

to the SDLP.) On June 19, 1986, the UK government dissolved the assembly, which had become little more than an anti-accord forum for unionists. The dissolution, which signaled the failure of London's seventh major peace initiative in 14 years, did not, however, abolish the body, leaving open the possibility of future electoral replenishment.

In February 1989 agreement was reached on the functions and membership of another joint undertaking provided for in the Anglo-Irish accord: a British-Irish Inter-Parliamentary Body of 25 MPs from each country, including minority party representatives. The first meeting of the new group opened in London on February 26, 1990, but two seats reserved for unionist parliamentarians remained vacant because of their continued opposition to the 1985 accord.

In March 1991 continued tension in the province was momentarily eased by the announcement of agreement on new talks in three "strands": first, discussions between the Northern Ireland "constitutional" parties, focusing on devolution and power sharing, chaired by Secretary of State Peter BROOKE; second, "North-South" talks between the Northern Ireland parties and the UK and Irish governments; and third, "East-West" talks between London and Dublin on replacing the 1985 Anglo-Irish Agreement. Any agreement reached under the talks would be put to referendums in both Northern Ireland and the Republic of Ireland.

Although preliminary first-strand talks opened on schedule on April 30, 1991, the so-called Brooke initiative quickly ran into procedural and political obstacles. Not until June 17 was it possible for full first-strand discussions to begin in Belfast, marking the first formal interparty talks in Northern Ireland in 16 years. However, it became apparent that Brooke had overestimated the willingness of the parties to seek common ground, with the unionist parties remaining resolutely opposed to any formula that appeared to give Dublin a role in Northern Ireland's affairs.

A July 1991 breakdown in the talks was followed by an escalation of sectarian violence, and by January 1992 the number of British troops assigned to the province had risen to 11,500. The conflict nonetheless continued, with the number of killings attributed to Protestant paramilitary groups, principally the Ulster Volunteer Force (UVF) and the Ulster Freedom Fighters (UFF), reportedly approaching those perpetrated by the IRA.

The talks were formally suspended by Brooke on January 27, 1992, pending the outcome of the UK election on April 9. In that contest the 17 Northern Ireland constituencies returned 13 Unionists, while the SDLP increased its representation in the House of Commons to 4 by gaining the West Belfast seat held since 1983 by the *Sinn Féin* president, Gerard (Gerry) ADAMS. In the postelection reshuffle Brooke was replaced as Northern Ireland secretary by Sir Patrick MAYHEW, who on April 17 announced his intention to resume the talks.

On June 30, 1992, representatives of the four leading Ulster formations met in London with an Irish government delegation, the first time since Ireland became independent in 1921 that hard-line unionists had met with Irish officials. On July 1 the participants agreed to undertake sustained negotiations on the North-South relationship, but deadlock soon emerged, in part over the Republic of Ireland's continuing constitutional claim to the whole of Ulster. The talks formally concluded without agreement in early November, whereupon meetings of the IGC resumed. Meanwhile, sectarian violence continued unabated. On August 10, 1992, the UK government announced the banning of the loyalist UDA, bringing the number of proscribed organizations in Northern Ireland to ten.

The advent of a *Fianna Fáil*/Labour coalition government in the Republic of Ireland in January 1993 heralded a more accommodating line by Dublin, and despite continuing IRA bombings in England, the quest for a negotiated settlement appeared to gain momentum. During April and May 1993, SDLP leader John HUME held a series of meetings with *Sinn Féin* leader Adams in what was characterized by Hume as an effort to bring about "a total cessation of all violence." On May 27 Irish President Mary Robinson conferred in London with Queen Elizabeth in the first such meeting between the two countries' heads of state. Most significantly, on December 15, 1993, Prime Minis-

ters John Major and Albert Reynolds issued their Downing Street Declaration. Aiming to bring about the end of hostilities in the province, the declaration acknowledged that "the people of the island of Ireland" might wish to opt for unification but reiterated that "it would be wrong to attempt to impose a united Ireland in the absence of the freely given consent of the majority of the people of Northern Ireland." The declaration thereby raised the possibility that Dublin would take steps to delete its constitutional claim to the North; it also stated that if IRA violence were brought to "a permanent end," *Sinn Féin* could expect to participate in all-party talks. Reaction to the new document was decidedly cool among the unionists, while *Sinn Féin* declined to give an immediate response, preferring instead to call for "clarifications."

The 25-year-old logjam in Northern Ireland appeared to be broken by an IRA announcement on August 31, 1994, that from midnight that day "there will be a complete cessation of military operations" by all IRA units. Noting that "an opportunity to secure a just and lasting settlement has been created," the statement called for "inclusive negotiations." Received with great rejoicing in Northern Ireland, especially among Catholics, the IRA announcement prompted London to take the position that if the cease-fire proved to be a permanent renunciation of violence, *Sinn Féin* would be invited to participate in future negotiations. In Dublin Prime Minister Reynolds took speedier action, receiving Adams on September 5 to discuss the convening of a "forum of peace and reconciliation." Unionist spokesmen, however, described the cease-fire as a public relations ploy and demanded that the IRA surrender its weapons and explosives prior to meaningful talks. On October 13 the three main loyalist paramilitary organizations also declared a cessation of hostilities but made it clear that they would not surrender their weapons until the IRA had done so.

The position of *Sinn Féin,* however, was that arms decommissioning should be dealt with at the talks rather than before and should be part of a complete "demilitarization" of Northern Ireland, including the withdrawal of British troops. This basic impasse persisted, despite the progressive up-grading of the UK government's contacts with *Sinn Féin*. The first public talks between the two sides took place in December 1994 in Belfast, while Adams and Secretary of State Mayhew finally met on May 24, 1995, on the margins of a Washington conference aimed at promoting investment in Northern Ireland.

Meanwhile, the UK and the Irish government, now headed by Prime Minister John Bruton, continued to clarify their positions. A joint "framework document" issued on February 22, 1995, envisaged the creation of a North-South council with "executive, harmonizing or consultative functions" and the restoration of self-government to Northern Ireland under a power-sharing formula. The document also recorded the Irish government's pledge to introduce a constitutional amendment deleting any territorial claim to Northern Ireland, while the UK government would propose constitutional legislation enshrining its commitment to uphold the democratic wish of the Northern majority. Reactions to the document were predictable: conditional approval from Adams, who noted that "its ethos is for one Ireland," but strong condemnation from unionist leaders, with Paisley of the DUP describing it as "Ulster's death warrant."

In early July 1995 violence resurged in conjunction with the annual "marching season," during which Protestant fraternal orders hold upward of 3,000 marches, some through Catholic neighborhoods, chiefly to mark the July 1690 defeat of the Catholic King James II by the Protestant William of Orange at the Battle of the Boyne. Amid fears that the peace process was losing momentum, on July 24 the UK and Irish prime ministers issued a three-part plan under which the disarmament of paramilitary groups would be supervised by an international commission, a target date would be set for the opening of all-party talks, and early release dates would be set for some of the 1,000 republican and loyalist paramilitaries currently serving prison sentences. The timing of decommissioning remained a sticking point, however, with London continuing to insist on paramilitary disarmament as a precondition for all-party discussions. While at-tempting to persuade London to modify its stance, the Dublin government went ahead with its "forum of peace and reconciliation," in which *Sinn Féin,* the SDLP, and a large number of others (but not the main unionist parties) set out their positions on the talks issue and the constitutional future. In September the UUP elected a new leader, David TRIMBLE, who had come to prominence in July by defying a police blockade and leading an Orange Order march through the Catholic neighborhood of Drumcree, near Portadown.

Intensive UK-Irish negotiations in October–November 1995 attempted to confront the decommissioning issue and thereby prepare the way for multiparty negotiations. As a result, on December 15 an international commission headed by former U.S. senator George Mitchell began to address the disarmament question, while a tentative date of February 1996 was set for opening interparty talks. In January 1996 the Mitchell panel proposed that all parties adhere to six principles, including the renunciation of political violence and a commitment to eventual, full decommissioning under international supervision.

Blaming what it labeled British intransigence, the IRA abruptly ended its cease-fire on February 2, when a massive bomb exploded in London, killing two men and causing damage later estimated at up to $300 million. The bombing appeared to catch even *Sinn Féin* off guard, casting doubt on the extent of its influence over the IRA. Security measures in Northern Ireland, which had been relaxed, were rapidly stepped up, and on February 28 both governments demanded an immediate and unequivocal restoration of the cease-fire, pending which *Sinn Féin* would be excluded from talks.

After individual discussions with Northern Ireland parties started in March (the uninvited *Sinn Féin* representatives being turned away), the UK government enacted legislation authorizing election of a consultative Northern Ireland Forum for Political Dialogue. Balloting took place on May 30, returning 90 members from 18 constituencies and a further 20 members from the 10 parties securing the largest shares of the popular vote. Although *Sinn Féin* participated in the election, winning 17 seats on a larger-than-expected vote share, it remained aloof from the Forum. Moreover, the SDLP, with 21 seats, soon withdrew, preferring to concentrate on direct talks. Thus the Forum was left to the two main unionist parties, the UUP (30 seats) and the DUP (24 seats), and to various smaller groupings. The latter included the Ulster Democratic Party (UDP) and the Progressive Unionist Party (PUP), which were described as "close to the thinking of" the leading loyalist paramilitaries, the UDA and the UVF, respectively.

With the Forum effectively sidelined by the absence of the nationalist parties, attention turned to the multiparty negotiations, which opened on June 10, 1996, in Stormont Castle, the seat of the direct-rule administration. Both governments and all of the main parties except *Sinn Féin,* whose leaders were again turned away, took part, although the proceedings were initially stalled by unionist objections to the proposal that former senator Mitchell be the chair. In July the traditional Protestant marches again provoked sectarian altercations, while the IRA and a splinter, the Continuity Army Council, or Continuity IRA, continued their attacks into the autumn and beyond. In October the UUP and the SDLP finally agreed on a full agenda for the Stormont negotiations, while in November the SDLP and *Sinn Féin* requested, among other things, a guarantee that *Sinn Féin* would be admitted to the talks if the IRA declared another cease-fire. Britain and Ireland disagreed, however, on the precise terms for *Sinn Féin*'s participation.

Talks resumed in January 1997 but were suspended in March to await the UK election of May 1, at which the UUP took 10 of Northern Ireland's 18 seats in the House of Commons, followed by the SDLP with 3, and the DUP and *Sinn Féin* with 2 each. Under Prime Minister Tony Blair the new UK Labour government moved swiftly to place Northern Ireland high on the political agenda, with Dr. Marjorie (Mo) MOWLAM assuming office as secretary of state for Northern Ireland. Despite another round of hostilities associated with the Protestant marching season, on July 19 the IRA announced a resumption of the August 1994 cease-fire, opening the way for *Sinn Féin* to join the multiparty

talks when they began again in mid-September. Although *Sinn Féin* had explicitly endorsed the six Mitchell principles, which also included a commitment to abide by the terms of any negotiated peace settlement, the unionists, objecting to *Sinn Féin*'s presence, boycotted the opening session. In late September, however, in a precedent-shattering shift of policy that drew the wrath of hard-line loyalists, the UUP's Trimble agreed to rejoin the talks despite *Sinn Féin*'s presence. Thus, representatives of eight parties—the UUP, SDLP, *Sinn Féin,* UDP, PUP, the Alliance Party of Northern Ireland (APNI), the Northern Ireland Women's Coalition, and the Labour Coalition—gathered in Stormont in October, the principal absentee being Paisley's DUP. In tandem, an Independent International Commission on Decommissioning (IICD), chaired by a retired Canadian general, John de Chastelain, broached the disarmament issue.

In October 1997 Tony Blair met with Gerry Adams, the first such meeting between a UK prime minister and *Sinn Féin* in more than 70 years, while in November the new Irish prime minister, Bertie Ahern, conferred with the UUP's Trimble. Despite such confidence-building steps, little progress was achieved before the Christmas break, during which the leader of the paramilitary Loyalist Volunteer Force (LVF), Billy WRIGHT, was murdered inside the Maze prison by members of the Irish National Liberation Army (INLA). Retaliations ensued, and on January 9, in a spectacular political gambit, Secretary Mowlam met in the Maze with loyalist prisoners and earned their support for continued peace discussions.

Although provocations by paramilitaries on both sides continued, Prime Ministers Blair and Ahern issued a brief framework for peace entitled "Propositions on Heads of Agreement" on January 12, 1998. The outline proposed "balanced" constitutional change by both the UK and Ireland; establishment of a directly elected Northern Ireland legislature and a North-South ministerial body; formation of British-Irish "intergovernmental machinery"; and adoption of "practical and effective measures" concerning such issues as prisoners, security, and decommissioning. The constitutional changes put forward by the prime ministers included excision of the Irish Republic's territorial claim to Northern Ireland, coupled with revision of British constitutional legislation dealing with the UK's authority over affairs in the North. *Sinn Féin* initially evinced little enthusiasm for the proposal, which fell significantly short of the party's longstanding demand for reunification with the South, while unionists expressed concern that creation of a North-South organ would in fact pave the way for reunification.

Early in 1998 the UDP and *Sinn Féin* were separately suspended from the multiparty talks because of cease-fire violations committed by their paramilitary associates, the UFF and the IRA, respectively, but in March both parties were readmitted to Stormont. On March 25 Mitchell set a 15-day deadline for the two governments and the eight participating parties to achieve a final peace plan, which was concluded on April 10 (a day late) following a marathon negotiating session. The Belfast Agreement, which quickly became better known as the Good Friday Agreement, called for the following: (Strand One) creation of a Northern Ireland Assembly with full authority to legislate "in devolved areas," an Executive Committee (Northern Ireland Executive) of ministers drawn from the legislature and headed by a first minister and a deputy first minister, a consultative Civic Forum of community and business leaders, and a continuing role for the secretary of state for Northern Ireland in matters not devolved to the new institutions; (Strand Two) creation of a North-South Ministerial Council; and (Strand Three) establishment of a British-Irish Council with representatives from Ireland and all the British isles, including devolved institutions in Scotland and Wales. In addition to requiring removal from Ireland's constitution of the claim to Northern Ireland from Ireland's constitution, the agreement mandated adherence to human rights and equal opportunity, full decommissioning by May 2000, normalization of security arrangements in Northern Ireland (including the withdrawal of the roughly 17,500 British troops), and formation of an independent commission to review policing procedures. Finally, an assessment of the criminal justice system was to include "an accelerated programme for the release of prisoners" affiliated with those organizations maintaining a "complete and unequivocal" cease-fire. Accompanying the Good Friday Agreement was a new British-Irish Agreement, superseding the 1985 Anglo-Irish Agreement and committing London and Dublin to carry through on the peace arrangements.

With an islandwide referendum—the first such vote since partition—scheduled for May 22, supporters and opponents of the Good Friday Agreement quickly began campaigning. In April David Trimble convinced the UUP as a whole to back the agreement despite vehement opposition from six of his party's ten MPs, the DUP, the small United Kingdom Unionist Party (UKUP), and the fraternal Orange Order. Meeting in Dublin on May 10, a special *Sinn Féin* conference also endorsed the agreement and authorized members to sit in the proposed Northern Ireland Assembly. In the end, the referendum passed with a 71 percent affirmative vote in the North, on a turnout of 81 percent. Balloting for the new 108-member assembly took place on June 25, with 16 parties offering candidates. The UUP obtained a plurality of 28 seats, followed by the SDLP with 24, the DUP with 20, and *Sinn Féin* with 18. In all, opposition unionists claimed 28 seats, just short of the number that would have enabled them to tie up legislation (see Constitution and government, below, for a discussion of rules governing passage of measures requiring "cross-community support").

On July 1, 1998, the new Northern Ireland Assembly elected the UUP's Trimble as first minister and the SDLP's Seamus MALLON as deputy first minister, John Hume having declined the latter nomination. Already, however, a major stumbling block to full formation of the power-sharing Executive Committee, and thus to devolution, had emerged. Whereas Trimble demanded that the IRA begin decommissioning its arms before he would allow *Sinn Féin* to take up any ministerial positions, Gerry Adams argued that the Good Friday Agreement contained no such stipulation.

Once again, the Protestant marching season brought with it a series of violent incidents, including the torching of ten Catholic churches on July 2–3, 1998. Following a ruling by an independent Parades Commission that the traditional Orange Order parade in Drumcree would not be allowed to pass through a Catholic neighborhood, more than 5,000 Orangemen protested at the barricades. A month later, on August 15, in the worst carnage since the "Troubles" began, a car bomb exploded in Omagh, killing 29 and injuring more than 200 others. A recently formed IRA splinter, the "Real IRA," claimed responsibility for the attack, which even the INLA and the Continuity IRA condemned. The bombing provoked Prime Ministers Blair and Ahern to introduce in their respective legislatures antiterrorism measures that Ahern characterized as "extremely draconian." Both parliaments passed similar bills in early September.

On September 10, 1998, for the first time, Trimble and Adams met privately in Stormont, but they made no progress on the decommissioning dispute. Trimble, responding to the announcement on October 16 that he and John Hume had won the Nobel Peace Prize for their efforts, expressed the hope that the decision had not been "premature." On October 31 the negotiators missed the deadline set by the Good Friday Agreement for creation of the "shadow" (predevolution) Executive Committee and the North-South Ministerial Council.

The stalemate appeared broken on December 18 with the announcement in Stormont of a further agreement covering formation of ten government departments and six cross-border bodies, the principal goal being British transfer of authority to the Northern Ireland Assembly and Executive Committee in February 1999. The new agreement provided for the UUP and the SDLP to head three departments each, with *Sinn Féin* and the DUP being responsible for two each. Ministerial nominations would await progress on disarmament. Although the LVF on the same day became the first paramilitary group to turn in some of its weapons, the IRA refused to reciprocate, calling the LVF action a "stunt."

In January 1999 Trimble set February 15 as the date for inaugurating the Executive Committee, while Secretary of State Mowlam established

March 10 as the date for transferring powers to the assembly. However, neither deadline was met. On February 16 the assembly voted 77–26 in favor of the December power-sharing accord and also approved creation of the Civic Forum, the North-South Ministerial Council, the British-Irish Council, and the cross-border bodies. Nevertheless, the decommissioning issue remained unresolved, even after the UUP and *Sinn Féin* held their first party-to-party session the following day. Despite personal efforts by Prime Ministers Blair and Ahern, Secretary of State Mowlam announced on March 9 that she was postponing devolution again, until April 2, Good Friday.

Although all the principal paramilitary groups continued to adhere to cease-fires (despite a notable increase since late 1998 in the number of "punishment beatings" inflicted by gangs against members of their own communities), a prominent nationalist civil rights lawyer, Rosemary NELSON, was killed by a car bomb on March 15, 1999. The apparent perpetrator, the recently organized loyalist Red Hand Defenders (RHD), was quickly added by Secretary of State Mowlam to the list of banned organizations, as was another new loyalist paramilitary group, the Orange Volunteers (OV). At the end of March, Blair and Ahern made another attempt to resolve the decommissioning impasse. They proposed in the Hillsborough Declaration that the UUP, SDLP, *Sinn Féin,* and DUP nominate their members of the Executive Committee and that within one month, in a "collective act of reconciliation," the paramilitaries voluntarily "put beyond use" various arms. Upon IICD certification of the decommissioning, the assembly could confirm the nominees to the Executive Committee. The "changed security situation" would also permit "further moves on normalisation and demilitarisation." On April 13, however, *Sinn Féin* rejected the declaration, reiterating that all parties should adhere to the letter of the Good Friday Agreement, which specified only that decommissioning occur by May 2000. On April 20 Ahern and Blair met in London with UUP, SDLP, and *Sinn Féin* leaders, to no avail. In mid-May London and Dublin set a new deadline of June 30 for formation of the

Executive Committee, but further attempts by Blair and Ahern to broker an agreement proved fruitless. On July 14 Trimble reaffirmed that the UUP would not sit with *Sinn Féin* in a devolved government until decommissioning had begun, prompting Deputy First Minister-elect Mallon to resign on July 15 and Blair to announce that devolution would be further postponed.

Through August 1999, unionists and *Sinn Féin* verbally skirmished over whether the IRA had broken its cease-fire. Meanwhile, former U.S. senator Mitchell had agreed to chair a review of the peace process that opened on September 6 in Belfast and moved on October 12 to London, where the newly appointed secretary of state for Northern Ireland, Peter MANDELSON, insisted that the negotiators had no alternative but to meet the terms of the Good Friday Agreement. "There is no Plan B," he asserted. "It's that or nothing." An effort by both the UUP and *Sinn Féin* to temper their rhetoric prompted Mitchell to extend negotiations beyond an October 23 deadline, and in early November he held meetings with U.S. President Clinton as well as the British and Irish prime ministers. Shortly thereafter, *Sinn Féin* reported that the IRA was prepared to establish contact with General de Chastelain. On November 15–16, in a sequence of carefully worded, coordinated statements, Mitchell, Trimble, and Adams separately endorsed the continuance of devolution and decommissioning. On November 17 the IRA confirmed that, following establishment of the institutions outlined in the Good Friday Agreement, it would name a representative to "enter into discussions" with de Chastelain. In a secret ballot on November 27, 58 percent of the UUP's governing council backed Trimble's cautious acceptance of the IRA initiative. Thus, the UUP gave up its demand that decommissioning had to begin before it would sit with *Sinn Féin* on the power-sharing Northern Ireland Executive.

On November 29, 1999, the Northern Ireland Assembly approved ten nominees to serve in the executive under Trimble and Mallon. The latter had been reaffirmed as deputy first minister by a 71–28 vote of the assembly, thereby negating his July resignation through a legally questionable ma-

neuver that was challenged by the DUP and other hard-liners. (The stratagem circumvented having to jointly reelect Mallon and First Minister Trimble, who probably would not have secured the necessary 30 unionist votes.) On December 1 the UK Parliament authorized devolution, and on December 2 London formally transferred power to the assembly and the executive; however, the cabinet convened minus the two DUP ministers, who refused to sit with the two *Sinn Féin* ministers. On the same day, Dublin formally promulgated the constitutional changes that ended the Irish Republic's claims to the North, and on December 2–3 IRA representatives met for the first time with General de Chastelain. On December 13 the North-South Ministerial Council held its inaugural meeting, and on December 17 representatives of Ireland, the UK, the Channel Islands, the Isle of Man, and the devolved governments of Northern Ireland, Scotland, and Wales gathered in London for the first session of the Council of the Isles.

The IRA's subsequent failure to begin disarming led the UK government to reimpose direct rule on February 11, 2000. In a last-minute effort to salvage the power-sharing government, the IRA had told General de Chastelain that it was prepared to address putting its arms and explosives "beyond use," but the offer came too late to forestall the reimposition. In response, on February 15 the IRA suspended further contacts with de Chastelain.

While attending talks in Washington in mid-March 2000, Trimble indicated that he might consider reinstituting the power-sharing government prior to any actual arms decommissioning by the IRA. The statement catalyzed his opponents within the UUP, and at a March 25 session of the party's governing council he faced a leadership challenge by the Rev. Martin SMYTH. Although Trimble managed to win 57 percent of the council vote, Smyth's supporters, including the influential hard-liner Jeffrey DONALDSON, succeeded in linking restoration of the government to a highly charged symbolic issue: retaining the name of the territory's controversial police agency, the Royal Ulster Constabulary (RUC). On September 9, 1999, Chris Patten, a former UK governor of Hong Kong, had released a report on RUC reform that proposed, among a list of 175 recommendations, changing the force's name to the Police Service of Northern Ireland (PSNI). Unionists had immediately denounced the proposal as well as suggestions that the police oath and insignia be revised to remove all association with the UK. (*Sinn Féin* had responded to the report by repeating its long-held position that the RUC should be abolished.)

Despite a series of diplomatic meetings and public negotiations, little substantive progress on resolving the armaments impasse occurred until May 6, 2000, when the IRA announced that it would accept international inspection of its arms stockpiles and would "completely and verifiably" put its weapons beyond use. As inspectors it nominated Martti Ahtisaari, former president of Finland, and Cyril Ramaphosa, former secretary general of South Africa's ruling party, the African National Congress. London and Dublin quickly proposed that power-sharing be resumed on May 22, but on May 18 Trimble, fearing defeat, postponed a crucial meeting of the UUP governing council. In an effort to defuse the RUC issue, Secretary of State Mandelson agreed to amend pending legislation on RUC reform, adding, for example, mention of the RUC to the legal description of the police service. On May 27, by a vote of 459–403, Trimble again prevailed over the UUP hard-liners, despite the opposition of Deputy Leader John TAYLOR, who viewed Mandelson's concessions as inadequate.

On May 30, 2000, London returned authority to the Northern Ireland Assembly and Executive. In early June Mandelson made additional concessions to garner republican support for the RUC reform legislation, but he left the name-change issue unresolved. At the same time, the new home rule government faced differences over other symbolic issues—principally, the refusal of the *Sinn Féin* ministers to fly the Union Jack over their offices.

On June 25 the IRA stated that it had reopened discussions with de Chastelain's IICD, and on June 26 arms monitors Ahtisaari and Ramaphosa reported that they had conducted their first inspections of IRA stockpiles. In further fulfillment of the Good Friday Agreement, authorities by late July had released more than 425 paramilitary prisoners, loyalist and republican alike, from prison, although Johnny ADAIR, a former leader of the UFF, was returned to prison on August 22 following renewed feuding between loyalist paramilitary groups in July–August. Responding to the outbreak of violence, Secretary of State Mandelson ordered British troops onto the streets of Belfast.

On October 28, 2000, First Minister Trimble overcame another challenge to his leadership when the UUP governing council rejected a hard-line proposal that the party withdraw from the government if the IRA failed to actively begin disarmament by November 30. Trimble instead proposed that he prohibit the executive's two *Sinn Féin* ministers from participating in official North-South meetings until the IRA actively engaged with the IICD. Trimble's decision drew immediate criticism not only from Gerry Adams, but also from Deputy First Minister Mallon. Meanwhile, in the last week of October weapons inspectors Ahtisaari and Ramaphosa conducted their second inspection of IRA stockpiles, as a result of which they described the IRA as "serious about the peace process."

During the first half of 2001 no significant progress was made in resolving three linked issues: IRA decommissioning, as demanded by the unionists; departure of the UK military, as demanded by the republicans; and reform of the RUC, as demanded by both (though with seemingly irreconcilable goals). Renewed negotiating efforts by Prime Ministers Blair and Ahern failed, leading First Minister Trimble to announce in May 2001 that he would resign his office on July 1, in the absence of concrete action by the IRA.

As predicted by Trimble himself, hard-liners made notable gains at the general election of June 7, 2001. Whereas his UUP lost 3 of its 9 seats in the UK House of Commons (having already lost 1 to the DUP at a September 2000 by-election) and 31 of its 185 local council seats, Ian Paisley's DUP gained 2 seats in the House of Commons, for a total of 5, and 40 additional council seats, for a total of 131. The SDLP held steady, retaining its 3 parliamentary seats and losing only 3 of its 120 local council seats, while *Sinn Féin* saw its membership in the House of Commons rise from 2 to 4 and its local council representation increase from 74 to 108.

With a backdrop of renewed sectarian rioting, centered on a Roman Catholic school in a predominantly Protestant area of Belfast, Trimble, as he had threatened, resigned on July 1, 2001. His action automatically vacated the office of deputy first minister. A diplomatic scramble ensued as Ireland and the UK attempted to reinvigorate the peace process before six weeks had passed, after which a new first minister had to be elected, a Northern Ireland Assembly election called, or direct rule reimposed. On August 6 the IICD released a statement confirming that the IRA had accepted a method for putting its weapons "completely and verifiably" beyond use, but in the absence of a timetable and at least a minimal surrender of weapons, the unionists dismissed the agreement as inadequate. Nevertheless, believing that a breakthrough might be near, London decided to exploit a legal loophole and reset the six-week clock by imposing direct rule for a single day beginning at midnight on August 11. The move by Secretary of State for Northern Ireland John REID angered the IRA, however, and it withdrew from its agreement with the IICD. The situation was further complicated by the arrest in Colombia of three alleged IRA members who, according to Colombian authorities, had been assisting the principal leftist guerrilla organization, the Colombia Revolutionary Armed Forces (*Fuerzas Armadas Revolucionarias de Colombia*—FARC). (Gerry Adams subsequently denied accusations that at least one of the men was acting as a *Sinn Féin* representative.) Meanwhile, the sectarian violence in Belfast again worsened, leading Reid to announce on October 12 that the government no longer recognized the cease-fires with the UDA/UFF and the LVF.

Facing increasing international pressure following the September 11, 2001, attacks by Islamic terrorists in the United States, the IRA stated on September 20 that it would renew and accelerate its talks with the IICD. Collaterally, London her-

alded a breakthrough based on the decisions of the SDLP and then the UUP and DUP (but not *Sinn Féin*) to participate in formation of a cross-community Northern Ireland Policing Board as part of a new Police Implementation Plan. (The RUC was formally renamed the PSNI on November 4.) Citing these positive developments, on September 21, with the second six-week period about to expire, London announced another direct-rule interregnum that began at midnight on September 22 and concluded 24 hours later.

On October 18, 2001, the UUP and DUP ministers withdrew from the executive after the assembly had rejected a unionist demand that the two *Sinn Féin* ministers be excluded. Shortly thereafter, Adams and his deputy, Martin McGUINNESS, for the first time explicitly called upon the IRA to begin disarming, and on October 23 both the IRA and the IICD released statements announcing that a quantity of arms had in fact been decommissioned. In response, Trimble announced that the UUP would return to the executive and that he would seek reelection as first minister.

At the assembly's first vote on November 2, two members of the UUP voted against Trimble, leaving him one vote short of the necessary unionist majority, despite unanimous nationalist support. On November 6 he achieved the necessary margin when the assembly allowed three members of the Alliance Party to temporarily redesignate themselves as unionists. However, the DUP was incensed by the maneuver, which led to scuffles outside the assembly.

An additional IRA decommissioning occurred in April 2002, but continuing sectarian violence in Belfast prompted Trimble, in early July, to threaten the withdrawal of the UUP from the assembly if authorities did not take corrective measures. Although he accused the IRA of fomenting the rioting, loyalist paramilitaries appeared to be equally culpable. The annual "marching season" once again led to repeated clashes, and in late July London vowed to stiffen its response to security violations. A week earlier, on July 16, the IRA had issued an unprecedented public apology to the families of its innocent victims.

On October 4, 2002, the *Sinn Féin* offices in Stormont were raided by authorities investigating alleged IRA spying, and two days later Denis DONALDSON, a *Sinn Féin* administrator, was arrested and charged with possessing some 1,200 documents of potential use to paramilitaries. The unionists immediately demanded the resignations or dismissal of the *Sinn Féin* ministers. On October 15, in an effort to forestall the collapse of the peace process, London reimposed direct rule for the fourth time.

Constitution and Government

The Government of Ireland Act of 1920 gave Northern Ireland its own government and a Parliament empowered to act on all matters except those of "imperial concern" (e.g., finance, defense, foreign affairs) or requiring specialized technical input. The royal authority was vested in a governor appointed by the Crown and advised by ministers responsible to Parliament; in practice, the leader of the majority party was invariably designated as prime minister. Parliament consisted of a 52-member House of Commons, directly elected from single-member constituencies, and a Senate, whose 26 members (except for 2 serving ex officio) were elected by the House of Commons under a proportional representation system. Voting for local government bodies was subject to a property qualification that excluded an estimated 200,000 adults, including a disproportionate number of minority Catholics. The effective disenfranchisement of a substantial portion of the Catholic population precipitated the original disturbances in 1968–1969.

Until 1998 British efforts to bring about agreement on a form of coalition government acceptable to both Protestants and Catholics failed to bear fruit. A Northern Ireland Constitution Act of 1973 abolished the office of governor and provided for a regional assembly and executive; however, the executive functioned only in 1974, and the assembly and its successor in 1973–1974 and 1982–1986. A Constitutional Convention in 1975–1976 failed to produce agreement, and the only major constitu-

tional developments for more than a decade thereafter involved the extension of a consultative role to the Irish government by means of various bilateral accords. Accordingly, direct rule, in effect since 1972 (save for January–May 1974), continued through the UK secretary of state for Northern Ireland. Under direct rule local government encompassed 26 elected city, district, and borough councils with very limited responsibilities for refuse collection, street cleaning, recreational facilities, environmental health, and consumer protection.

Following completion of the Belfast Agreement of April 10, 1998 (familiarly called the Good Friday Agreement but also referenced in some official documents as the Multi-Party Agreement), and pending approval of the agreement by referendum on May 22, the British Parliament passed legislation authorizing election of a New Northern Ireland Assembly, the term "New" being dropped upon formal devolution of authority to the body. Elected on June 25, the legislature comprised 108 members from 18 constituencies. Under the terms of the Good Friday Agreement and the Northern Ireland Act of 1998, which Parliament passed in November 1998 and which repealed the Government of Ireland Act of 1920, assembly members individually defined themselves as a "designated unionist," a "designated nationalist," or "other." Decisions requiring "cross-community support"— for example, standing orders, budget allocations, and election of the assembly chair—required either (1) majority approval, including support from a majority of both nationalists and unionists, or (2) assent by a weighted majority of 60 percent, with affirmative votes from at least 40 percent of unionists and 40 percent of nationalists. To further protect the minority, the cross-community provision could be triggered on any other matter if 30 or more assembly members presented a "petition of concern." Assembly members were to be elected for five-year terms, subject to early dissolution by a vote of two-thirds of the entire membership. Devolved legislative authority extended to such areas as agriculture, economic development, tourism, and education, while "excepted and reserved matters" remaining in the hands of the UK Northern

Ireland secretary included international relations, defense, security, criminal justice, taxation, regulation of financial services, national insurance, and regulation of broadcast and telecommunication services. Under devolution, executive authority resided in an Executive Committee of ministers chosen from the leading assembly parties in proportion to their membership in the body. The assembly selected a first minister and a deputy first minister, who stood for election jointly and were required to secure majority support from both nationalists and unionists. In addition to heading the executive, which might have up to ten additional members, the two leaders jointly nominated ministers and junior ministers to two principal intergovernmental bodies, the North-South Ministerial Council and the British-Irish Council (also known as the Council of the Isles), both of which were established under treaties concluded by the UK and Ireland on March 8, 1999. The North-South Ministerial Council had as its mandate bringing together "those with executive responsibilities in Northern Ireland and the Irish Government, to develop consultation, co-operation, and action within the island of Ireland," on both an islandwide and a cross-border basis. Decisions required agreement by both sides. The British-Irish Council, which was to meet at the summit level twice a year and in other formats "on a regular basis," included representatives from Scotland, Wales, the Channel Islands, and the Isle of Man in addition to Great Britain, Northern Ireland, and Ireland, the purpose being "to promote the harmonious and mutually beneficial development of the totality of relationships among the peoples of these islands." Two additional treaties signed on March 8 authorized formation of various implementing bodies and of a British-Irish Intergovernmental Conference, the latter replacing the Anglo-Irish Intergovernmental Council and the Intergovernmental Conference of 1985.

Northern Ireland is represented in the UK House of Commons, currently with 18 seats (increased from 17 in 1997). It also has 3 seats in the European Parliament.

Recent Developments. Despite the continuation of direct rule, elections to the suspended Northern Ireland Assembly were held on November 26, 2003. The results suggested that resumption of the peace process was virtually impossible. For the Protestants, Ian Paisley's DUP, which strongly opposed the 1998 Good Friday Agreement, displaced Trimble's UUP to become the largest party, with 30 seats. For the Catholics, in a similar reversal of the 1998 results, *Sinn Féin* won 24 seats, as opposed to the SDLP's 18.

Despite the 2003 electoral results, multiparty talks were resumed on February 3, 2004, with the DUP and *Sinn Féin* communicating through intermediaries. Subsequently, UK Prime Minister Blair and Irish Prime Minister Ahern held a series of meetings that yielded no consensus on power sharing, while in December Paisley announced a hardening of the DUP position by insisting on photographic evidence of IRA arms decommissioning.

In early 2005 the peace process reached a new point of collapse with the IRA being blamed for an armed attack on Belfast's Northern Bank in December 2004 and thereafter withdrawing its offer to decommission. On April 7 *Sinn Féin* leader Adams drew no response in urging the IRA to abandon its "armed struggle," while an appeal by Blair and Ahern for the IRA to end "all paramilitary and criminal activity" was equally unproductive until late July when, in a potentially historic development, the IRA pledged to lay down its arms and oppose British rule in the future only through peaceful political involvement. Specifically, the IRA announced that it had "formally ordered an end to the armed campaign" and would pursue a "purely political and democratic program through exclusively peaceful means." Promises were also made that the IRA's massive stockpiles of arms (reportedly buried in bunkers throughout Northern Ireland) would be quickly dismantled.

Prime Minister Blair labeled the IRA announcement a step of "unparalleled magnitude," and in August 2005 the UK indicated that it would cut its troop level (then 10,000) in Northern Ireland in half by 2007 in view of the improved security outlook. In addition, in September General de Chastelain said the IICD was satisfied with the decommissioning of the IRA weapons. However, DUP leader Paisley condemned the UK response as "premature," calling for the "dissolution" of the IRA. He and other Protestant leaders also accused the British and Irish governments of "disregarding" loyalist concerns. Consequently, the DUP continued to refuse to meet directly with *Sinn Féin* when Blair and Ahern relaunched negotiations toward another power-sharing government.

In February 2006 the Independent Monitoring Commission (IMC), established by the UK and Ireland in 2004 to monitor armed groups in Northern Ireland, concluded that the IRA was no longer "engaged in terrorism," while Protestant militants had been responsible for more than 20 killings in the fall of 2005. Encouraged by the IRA's "progress," Blair and Ahern subsequently appeared to focus on pressuring the DUP to adopt a more positive negotiating role. In April the two prime ministers declared a deadline of November 24 for the assembly parties to agree on formation of a new executive, without which a "new way to govern" Northern Ireland would be pursued. Analysts suggested that the deadline posed a "veiled threat" to the DUP, as it implied that the alternative to a power-sharing government could be greater control by the Irish Republic. Adams welcomed the announcement, and in May he proposed that Paisley be named as first minister of the proposed new government. However, the offer was emphatically rejected by Paisley (described as *Sinn Féin*'s "most intractable foe"), and little progress was reported through the summer, despite the establishment of a multiparty Preparation for Government Committee and the reconvening of the Northern Ireland Assembly (see Legislature, below). Blair and Ahern consequently scheduled "last-ditch" negotiations for October in Scotland.

Political Parties and Groups

Parties Winning 2003 Assembly Representation

Democratic Unionist Party (DUP). The DUP was founded in 1971 by a hard-line loyalist faction of the UUP, attracting working-class Protestant support for its strongly anti-Catholic, anti-Dublin position. It was consistently the runner-up to the parent party, winning 21 seats in the 1982 assembly election and 3 UK House of Commons seats in June 1983, all of the latter being retained in 1987. The party was represented at the 1988 Duisburg talks by Deputy Leader Peter Robinson, who urged the creation of an alternative to the 1985 Anglo-Irish accord.

A growing schism between the DUP's older and younger members was, in part, responsible for the party leader's decision in May 1990 to agree to political negotiations. The older faction, led by Ian Paisley, had long adhered to a "no negotiation" policy, while the more youthful faction, exemplified by Robinson, advocated the creation of a political and religious dialogue. At the same time, the party mainstream was moving from an "integrationalist" to a "devolutionist" posture that favored a provincial government with relatively strong legislative and executive powers.

The DUP retained its three Westminster seats in the UK balloting of April 1992, after which the failure of yet another round of constitutional talks left the party's internal divisions unresolved. In the Forum elections of May 1996 the party fell into third place, with 19 percent of the vote, and in the May 1997 UK election it lost the constituency of Mid Ulster to *Sinn Féin*.

The DUP strongly opposed *Sinn Féin*'s presence at the Stormont negotiations of 1997–1998 and refused to participate. It campaigned against the Good Friday Agreement and won 20 of the 28 seats captured by unionist oppositionists at the June Northern Ireland Assembly election. Allotted two portfolios in the Northern Ireland Executive, the DUP adopted obstructionist tactics to protest *Sinn Féin*'s presence in the body.

At a September 2000 by-election for a seat in the UK House of Commons, the DUP captured the district from the UUP, prompting Paisley to declare that First Minister Trimble "is finished, absolutely finished." At the UK general election of June 2001 the DUP won 5 seats, a gain of 2 more. In simultaneous local balloting the party added 40 council seats, for a total of 131.

At the Northern Ireland Assembly balloting of November 2003 the party outpolled the UUP for a plurality of 30 seats. At the House of Commons election of May 2005 the DUP increased its representation from 5 to 9, securing 37.7 percent of the vote in Northern Ireland and consolidating its status as the dominant unionist party with a similar advance in the simultaneous local elections. DUP leader Paisley, who had never accepted the provisions of the 1998 Belfast Agreement, subsequently served as the major opponent of talks with *Sinn Féin* toward restoration of a power-sharing government in Northern Ireland (see Current issues, above).

Leaders: Rev. Ian R. K. PAISLEY (Party Leader), Peter ROBINSON (Deputy Leader), James McCLURE (President), Maurice MORROW (Chair), Nigel DODDS (General Secretary).

Ulster Unionist Party (UUP). The UUP, historically Northern Ireland's dominant party, was split by the 1973 Sunningdale Agreement, the anti-Sunningdale majority becoming known as the Official Unionist Party (OUP). The formation of a "joint working party" between the OUP and the DUP (above) was announced in August 1985 to protect "Ulster's interests within the UK." Throughout 1986 the working party attempted to disrupt local government in protest of the Anglo-Irish Agreement of 1985. By contrast, joint OUP-DUP publications in 1987 called for all Northern Ireland parties to negotiate an alternative to the 1985 accord in a spirit of "friendship, cooperation, and consultation." In addition, the OUP, DUP, and the now-defunct Ulster Popular Unionist Party (UPUP) of James KILFEDDER agreed to present only one unionist candidate from each constituency in the 1987 House of Commons elections, at which they retained 13 of 14 seats. The OUP continued to issue conciliatory statements during 1988, but the party's demand that the Anglo-Irish accord be rescinded before any substantive negotiations could take place between unionists and republicans helped derail initiatives advanced at a meeting of the OUP, DUP, Alliance Party, and Social Democratic and Labour Party (SDLP, below) in October in Duisburg, West Germany.

In May 1990 OUP leaders softened their position, reportedly agreeing to tripartite talks between the province's parties and the British and Irish governments in return for "de facto" (temporary) suspension of the bilateral pact. Subsequently, in April 1991, OUP and DUP representatives attended the opening of the Ulster talks as joint unionist negotiators despite the incompatibility of the DUP's "devolutionist" position and the OUP's "integrationalist" call for increased linkage between Ulster and Britain. The Official Unionists won 9 of the 17 Northern Ireland seats in the UK election of April 1992, by which time they had officially adopted the UUP designation to signify continuity with the historic party.

Having held the party leadership since 1979, James MOLYNEAUX stood down in August 1995 and was succeeded by David Trimble, a leading UUP critic of the concessions being made to Dublin in the peace process. Two years later, in a remarkable turnaround, Trimble agreed to sit at the same negotiating table as *Sinn Féin,* and on April 10, 1998, UUP representatives signed the multiparty Good Friday Agreement. Fighting off intraparty opponents, including six of the party's ten members of Parliament, Trimble secured UUP approval of the peace plan, and at the June 25 election the party won a plurality of 28 seats in the 108-seat Northern Ireland Assembly. On July 1 the assembly elected Trimble first minister of the Executive Committee, and in October 1998 he shared the Nobel Peace Prize with the SDLP's John Hume.

On October 9, 1998, a faction within the UUP formed Union First in opposition to the Good Friday Agreement and the presence of *Sinn Féin* in the government. Thereafter, criticism of Trimble continued to grow. Resentment over what hard-line unionists viewed as ill-advised concessions to *Sinn Féin* culminated in a March 25, 2000, challenge to his leadership by the Rev. Martin Smyth. Although the party's governing Ulster Unionist Council (UUC) gave Trimble 57 percent of the vote, Union First's Jeffrey Donaldson and Deputy Leader

John Taylor were both considered to be likely future challengers. On May 27, having threatened to resign in the event of a negative vote, Trimble gained only 53 percent endorsement of the UUC (459–403) to accept the IRA's offer to permit international monitoring of its arms stockpiles.

On October 28, 2000, the UUC reconvened to consider a Donaldson proposal that the UUP withdraw from the government unless the IRA began decommissioning by November 30. Trimble countered by asserting that, as first minister, he would not authorize the government's two IRA ministers to participate in official North-South meetings until the IRA actively engaged with General de Chastelain's IICD. Trimble again won the council's support, 445–374.

Trimble resigned as first minister effective July 1, 2001. A month earlier the UUP had seen its support at the polls decline, costing it 3 of its 9 seats in the UK House of Commons and 31 of its 185 local council seats. Trimble was reelected first minister on November 6, 2001, although he had failed to obtain the needed majority of nationalist votes four days earlier when two UUP members, Peter WEIR and Pauline ARMITAGE, voted against him. Weir was subsequently expelled from the party and joined the DUP in April 2002; Armitage's membership was suspended.

The UUP lost its plurality to the DUP in the Northern Ireland Assembly election of November 26, 2003, and in late December Trimble's most severe intraparty critic, Jeffrey Donaldson, announced that he was quitting the UPP and aligning himself with the DUP. At the UK general election of May 5, 2005, the UUP lost four of its five seats in the House of Commons, including the one held by Trimble, on a share of only 17.8 percent of the votes in Northern Ireland. The UUP also declined in the concurrent local elections, and Trimble, who had apparently suffered from the voters' perception that he and the UUP had been "too soft" regarding *Sinn Féin* and the IRA, promptly resigned as party leader. He was succeeded on June 24 by Sir Reg Empey.

Leaders: Sir Reg EMPEY (Party Leader), David TRIMBLE (Former Party Leader).

Social Democratic and Labour Party— SDLP (*Páirtí Sóisialta Daonlathach an Lucht Oibre*). Founded in 1970 and a member of the Socialist International, the SDLP is a largely Catholic, left-of-center party that has championed the reunification of Ireland by popular consent, with Catholics being accorded full political and social rights in the interim. Its longtime leader, Gerard FITT, participated in the post-Sunningdale Faulkner government and subsequently became the only non-unionist to hold a seat in the UK House of Commons. Fitt resigned as party leader in November 1979 after the SDLP constituency representatives and executive had rejected the government's working paper for the 1980 constitutional conference on devolution. The SDLP won 14 assembly seats in 1982 but joined *Sinn Féin* in boycotting sessions. It won three UK House of Commons seats in 1987 on a platform that attacked the Thatcher government on employment, housing, education, and agricultural policies.

In addition to supporting the 1985 Anglo-Irish Agreement and resultant UK-Irish cooperation on Northern Ireland, the party became an enthusiastic participant in the 1991 Brooke initiative and its successor talks. Seeking a framework for peace, in April and May 1993 SDLP leader John Hume undertook an unprecedented series of meetings with *Sinn Féin* leader Gerry Adams and subsequently helped negotiate the 1994 IRA cease-fire.

The SDLP had mixed results at the polls during the 1990s, picking up one seat in the 1992 UK general election but returning just three MPs in 1997. A year earlier it had won a somewhat disappointing 21 seats in balloting for the Northern Ireland Forum. A strong supporter of the 1998 Good Friday Agreement, the party carried 24 seats, second to the UUP, in the subsequent election for the Northern Ireland Assembly. The party's deputy leader, Seamus Mallon, was elected deputy first minister of the Executive Committee, the position having been turned down by the overtaxed Hume, who served in the European Parliament as well as the UK House of Commons.

Hume received the 1998 Nobel Peace Prize, not only for his contribution to the Good Friday

Agreement, but for having been, over several decades, "the clearest and most consistent of Northern Ireland's political leaders" in the search for peace. In August 2000 Hume announced that he intended to resign his assembly seat but would retain his other positions. On September 17, 2001, however, he indicated that he would step down as party leader, and a day later Mallon made a similar announcement. At a November party conference Mark Durkan was named to replace Hume. Hume retired from public life in February 2004.

At the May 2005 balloting for the UK House of Commons, the SDLP retained (with 17.5 percent of the votes in Northern Ireland) its three seats.

Leaders: Mark DURKAN (Party Leader), Alasdair McDONNELL (Deputy Leader), Patricia LEWSLEY (Chair), Gerry COSGROVE (General Secretary).

Sinn Féin. The islandwide *Sinn Féin* (see also Ireland: Political Parties) serves as the legal political wing of the outlawed Irish Republican Army (see Former and Current Republican Paramilitary Groups, below). In addition to advocating improved living and working conditions for its primarily Catholic, working-class constituency, throughout the 1970s and 1980s it consistently called for the disbanding of British security forces, the withdrawal of Britain from Northern Ireland's government, and negotiation of a political settlement through an all-Ireland constitutional conference.

Its president, Gerard Adams, was *Sinn Féin's* only successful candidate at the 1987 UK general election, but, as in 1983, he refused to occupy his seat in the Commons. In early 1988 the SDLP attempted to forge ties with *Sinn Féin,* but its interest waned in April when *Sinn Féin* refused to "repeal its commitment to limited guerrilla warfare." A second attempt at linkage was broken off in September following the resumption of IRA bombings in downtown Belfast.

Responding to comments made by UK Secretary of State Peter Brooke, in April 1990 Adams said that the IRA might be persuaded to cease terrorist activities if London established a dialogue with *Sinn Féin.* However, *Sinn Féin's* continued re-

fusal to renounce IRA violence led to its exclusion from the April 1991 talks. In April 1992 Adams lost his Westminster parliamentary seat to the SDLP.

The IRA cease-fire declaration of August 31, 1994, yielded enhanced international stature and negotiating prominence for Adams and other *Sinn Féin* leaders. However, the IRA renewed hostilities in February 1996 while continuing to press for unconditional talks. Though successful in both the 1996 Forum elections (winning 15 percent of the vote) and in the May 1997 UK general elections (winning two seats), the party still chose to remain aloof from either political process. Renewal of the IRA cease-fire in July 1997 and *Sinn Féin's* affirmation of its commitment to the six Mitchell principles, including full decommissioning and rejection of political violence, enabled Adams to join the Stormont multiparty peace talks in September. In response, a hard-line faction left the party and formed the 32 County Sovereignty Committee (below).

At a special party session convened in Dublin on May 10, 1998, and attended by a number of furloughed nationalist inmates from prisons in Northern Ireland and Britain, Adams won overwhelming endorsement of the Good Friday peace plan and permission for *Sinn Féin* members to take up seats in the new Northern Ireland Assembly. At balloting for the assembly in June, the party won 18 seats, sufficient for it to claim two positions on the governing Executive Committee upon devolution.

In June 2000 Cathal CRUMLEY became the first member of *Sinn Féin* to be elected mayor of a Northern city, Londonderry, since partition. Earlier in the year the UK government had introduced a bill in the House of Commons that would permit a member of any UK legislature, including the Northern Ireland Assembly, to hold simultaneously a legislative seat in the Republic of Ireland. The Disqualifications Bill, which passed Parliament on November 30, was widely regarded as a "sweetener" for *Sinn Féin* as it permitted the party's assembly members, particularly Gerry Adams, to seek election to the *Dáil.*

At the UK general election of June 2001, *Sinn Féin* doubled its representation in the House of

Commons, to four seats. It also made gains locally, adding 34 council seats to the 74 it had previously held.

On October 4, 2002, the *Sinn Féin* offices in Stormont were raided by authorities investigating IRA spying, and two days later Denis Donaldson, the party's office administrator, was arrested and charged with possessing some 1,200 documents of potential use to paramilitaries. The revelations ultimately contributed to London's reimposition of direct rule on October 15. (The case took a surreal turn in December 2005 when the charges against Donaldson were dropped and Donaldson acknowledged that he had in fact been a British agent for 20 years.)

The party won 24 seats at the Northern Ireland Assembly election of November 2003.

In August 2004 Adams, in an effort to counter the DUP's objection to revival of the peace talks, called publicly for the disbanding of the IRA as a paramilitary force.

Sinn Féin secured five seats (including one by Adams) in the May 2005 UK House of Commons balloting on a share of 24.3 percent of the votes in Northern Ireland. Shortly thereafter, Adams intensified his call for the renunciation of violence, and the IRA subsequently announced its historic pledge to disarm (see Current issues, above). (Adams has never acknowledged having played a leadership role in the IRA, although many observers have ascribed such status to him.) The UK government later in the year agreed to resume normal party funding to *Sinn Féin,* but the United States in 2006 declined to lift its ban on *Sinn Féin* fundraising.

Leaders: Gerard (Gerry) ADAMS (President), Mitchel McLAUGHLIN (Chair), Martin McGUINNESS, Bairbre de BRÚN, Alex MASKEY (Mayor of Belfast), Lucilita BHREATNACH (General Secretary).

Alliance Party of Northern Ireland (APNI). A nonsectarian and nondoctrinaire group founded in 1970 in reaction to growing civil strife, the Alliance Party, like the SDLP, participated in the post-Sunningdale Faulkner government. It won ten assembly seats in 1982 and was the only non-unionist

party to participate in that body's subsequent proceedings. For lack of alternative proposals, the party in 1987 announced continued support of the 1985 Anglo-Irish Agreement, although it called for the additional enactment of a bill of rights for Northern Ireland. It has achieved occasional success in local elections but has never won a seat in the UK House of Commons.

The Alliance was one of the four Ulster parties represented at talks between unionists and republicans in Duisburg, West Germany, in October 1988. Alliance officials attended the opening of the interparty Ulster talks on April 30, 1991, and, although sympathetic to the unionist position, indicated that they would support the SDLP.

Party leader Dr. John ALDERDICE was nominated to the House of Lords in 1996, giving the Alliance representation in the UK Parliament for the first time. It backed the Good Friday Agreement of 1998 but won only six seats at the subsequent assembly election, a performance that led Lord Alderdice to resign the party leadership. UK Secretary of State for Northern Ireland Mo Mowlam immediately named him as initial presiding officer of the assembly.

Party Leader Sean NEESON announced on September 6, 2001, his decision to step down in favor of "a fresh face," with David Ford then being elected in October as his successor. A month later, in a maneuver designed to secure David Trimble's reelection as first minister and thereby avert a collapse of the power-sharing government, three Alliance assembly members temporarily redesignated themselves as unionists. As a result, Trimble was able to secure a bare majority of unionist votes, permitting his return to office.

The party retained its existing six seats at the 2003 assembly election.

Leaders: David FORD (Party Leader), Naomi LONG (Deputy Leader), Geraldine RICE (President), Yvonne BOYLE (Chair), Allan LEONARD (General Secretary).

United Kingdom Unionist Party (UKUP). The UKUP was formed in 1995 to support the successful parliamentary by-election campaign of prominent lawyer Robert McCartney, who opposed the Anglo-Irish Agreement of 1985, the Downing Street Declaration by the British and Irish governments in 1993, and their joint framework document issued in February 1995. McCartney was the only UKUP candidate elected to a constituency seat in the 1996 Forum poll, but the party gained two regional-list seats, providing a place for one of Ireland's most distinguished men of letters, Conor Cruise O'BRIEN. Like the DUP, the UKUP refused to sit at the same table as *Sinn Féin* and therefore boycotted the 1997–1998 Stormont talks. It opposed the resultant Good Friday Agreement but won five unionist seats at the June assembly election.

In October 1998 O'Brien, the party's president, withdrew from membership after he was quoted as suggesting that unionists might better negotiate with constitutional nationalists for a united Ireland instead of facing additional British concessions to extremist republicans. The party suffered another blow in January 1999 when four of its assembly members formed the Northern Ireland Unionist Party (below). At the June 2001 UK election the UKUP lost its only seat in the House of Commons, and in November 2003 it lost four of its five assembly seats.

Leader: Robert McCARTNEY.

Other Parties

Northern Ireland Unionist Party (NIUP). Creation of the NIUP was announced on January 5, 1999, by four of the UKUP's five assembly members. Despite their opposition to formation of a power-sharing government with *Sinn Féin* membership, they had resigned from the UKUP in protest of Robert McCartney's order that the party withdraw from the legislature should *Sinn Féin* be permitted to join the Executive Committee prior to decommissioning. One of the four, Roger HUTCHINSON, was expelled from the party on December 2, 1999, for accepting membership on two assembly committees charged with scrutinizing executive ministries. The NIUP failed to win representation at the 2003 assembly poll.

Leaders: Cedric WILSON (Party Leader), Norman BOYD, Patrick ROCHE.

United Unionist Assembly Party (UUAP). The UUAP was established with effect from September 21, 1998, by three unionists who had been elected to the Northern Ireland Assembly as independents. In April 2000 one of the three, Denis WATSON, a leader of the Orange Order who had been expelled from the UUP for opposing the Good Friday Agreement, was reported to have joined the DUP.

Leaders: Fraser AGNEW, Boyd DOUGLAS.

Progressive Unionist Party (PUP). The PUP emerged out of the loyalist paramilitaries, in this case the Ulster Volunteer Force (UVF). The PUP's leader, David Ervine, served in the UVF and was imprisoned for five years for possession of explosives. The party is distinctive in that, while it is part of the unionist camp, it also champions working-class causes without regard to sect, and the party leader speaks openly of parallels in policy to British Labour. With a definition of unionism based more in the idea of citizenship than in religion, the party has appeared the most flexible of the unionist camp. It signed the 1998 Good Friday Agreement and won two seats in the June Northern Ireland Assembly election, one of which was lost in 2003.

In the wake of the renunciation of violence by the IRA in 2005, Ervine came under increasing pressure to facilitate similar action on the part of the UVF (below). Meanwhile, Ervine in May 2006 formed a controversial alliance with the UUP in the assembly.

Leader: David ERVINE.

Northern Ireland Women's Coalition (NIWC). The NIWC emerged in time for the Forum elections of May 1996, although it won only about 1 percent of the vote. The movement was strongly nonpartisan, with candidates from a range of political persuasions, and nonsectarian. It signed the 1998 Good Friday Agreement and won two assembly seats in 1998, none in 2003.

Leaders: Monica McWILLIAMS (Party Leader), Jane MORRICE, Pearl SAGAR.

Ulster Democratic Party (UDP). The UDP (known in 1981–1989 as the Ulster Loyalist Democratic Party—LDP) was founded in 1978 as the

New Ulster Political Research Group by leaders of the Ulster Defence Association (UDA, below). The UDP had negligible electoral support but served as a channel of communication to the UDA and its supporters. Although a signatory to the 1998 Good Friday Agreement, it has never won assembly representation.

Leaders: Gary McMICHAEL, John WHITE, David ADAMS.

32 County Sovereignty Movement. This *Sinn Féin* splinter was formed in September 1997 as the 32 County Sovereignty Committee by ardent nationalists opposed to Gerry Adams's decision to support the Mitchell principles and join the multiparty negotiations in Stormont. One of its organizers, Bernadette SANDS-McKEVITT, is the sister of Bobby Sands, a leader of the Maze prison hunger strikes who died in 1981. The Movement is believed to be affiliated with the paramilitary Real IRA (below), which claimed responsibility for the August 1998 Omagh bombing. In June 2000 the Movement condemned the IRA's decision to permit international inspections of its arms stockpiles as "the first stop in a decommissioning surrender process."

Other, small parties include the **Northern Ireland Green Party** and **Northern Ireland Labour**. The latter, a predominantly socialist group, was formed following the demise of the Labour Coalition, which had signed the 1998 Good Friday Agreement but won no Northern Ireland Assembly seats. In addition, numerous parties based in the Republic of Ireland have branches in the North. See the Ireland article for discussions of the island-wide **Socialist Party,** the **Workers' Party,** and the **Communist Party of Ireland,** as well as for additional information on *Sinn Féin.*

Former and Current Republican Paramilitary Groups

Irish Republican Army (IRA). In the late 1960s arguments escalated between the dominant socialist faction in the Republican Clubs, as the (illegal) Northern Ireland section of *Sinn Féin*

was then known, and traditional nationalist elements wanting to organize an armed defense of Catholic areas under attack from police and Protestant gangs. The dispute led to the creation in 1969 of a breakaway "Provisional" Army Council that set about rebuilding the IRA, which had withered away since its last terrorist campaign in 1956–1962. The "Provisional" IRA, supported by the "Provisional" *Sinn Féin,* quickly became a large and effective guerrilla organization, defining its aims as British withdrawal from Northern Ireland and the reunification of Ireland as a socialist republic. (Although in frequent use into the 1990s, the term "Provisional" had become redundant in the early 1980s, when the "Official" rump of the *Sinn Féin* became the Workers' Party—see the discussion of *Sinn Féin* in the Republic of Ireland article.)

Especially active in 1971–1976, when it carried out more than 5,000 bombings, a similar number of armed robberies, and more than 15,000 shootings, resulting in many hundreds of security-force and civilian deaths, the IRA was banned under the 1978 Emergency Provisions Act. It continued its activities in Northern Ireland, Britain, and sometimes continental Europe almost without interruption until 1994.

On August 31, 1994, following secret contacts with the British government, the IRA instituted a cease-fire with the aim of making it possible for *Sinn Féin,* which after 1981 had developed a strong electoral following, to take part in negotiations with the British and Irish governments and with regional parties. With *Sinn Féin* remaining marginalized by demands from most parties and the government that the IRA surrender its weapons, the IRA resumed its military activities in February 1996 by exploding a massive bomb in the financial district of London.

The cease-fire was renewed on July 19, 1997, which opened the way for *Sinn Féin* to join the peace negotiations in Stormont two months later. The IRA gave qualified support to the Good Friday Agreement of April 1998 but at the time refused to link decommissioning of its arms to formation of a devolved government for Northern Ireland, as demanded by the plurality UUP. In December 1998 senior IRA leaders elected a seven-member Army Council headed by hard-liner Brian KEENAN, reinforcing the possibility that the cease-fire might be rescinded were *Sinn Féin* to be excluded from the Northern Ireland Executive.

The IRA's continuing refusal to begin disarming before the inauguration of the power-sharing Executive delayed devolution until December 2, 1999, shortly after the IRA had indicated that it was willing to discuss disarmament with Gen. John de Chastelain of the IICD. Nevertheless, no tangible progress was made in the following two months. On February 11, 2000, the IRA offered, in the words of a report from de Chastelain, to "consider how to put arms and explosives beyond use," but the proposal was too late to prevent London's reimposition of direct rule. On May 6, however, the IRA announced that it would accept international monitoring of its arsenals and would "completely and verifiably" put its weapons beyond use. The breakthrough and a subsequent positive UUP response led London, on May 30, to return authority to the Northern Ireland Assembly and Executive. On June 25 the IRA stated that it had reopened discussions with de Chastelain's IICD, and on June 26 arms inspectors reported that they had completed their first visits to IRA caches. Another inspection occurred in May 2001, although the IRA still refused to consider a firm timetable for decommissioning. In early August the IICD announced an agreement on how decommissioning might proceed, but a week later the IRA rescinded its approval because of the August 11 suspension of the power-sharing government. In mid-September it agreed once again to move forward on discussions with the IICD, and on October 23 the IRA announced its first confirmed decommissioning of weapons. An additional, larger decommissioning occurred in April 2002, and on July 16 the IRA issued its first public apology to the families of its innocent victims.

In October 2002 the discovery of alleged IRA spying in official offices in Stormont led to demands from UK Prime Minister Blair, among others, that the IRA reject violence and fully commit itself to peace. The reimposition of direct rule from London on October 15 led the IRA, two weeks later, to discontinue talks with the IICD.

The IRA's alleged involvement in the December 2004 robbery of Belfast's Northern Bank yielded a breakdown in what had appeared to be a promising outcome for the lengthy peace talks. However, momentum returned in mid-2005 when the IRA, following the encouragement of *Sinn Féin* leader Gerry Adams, renounced the use of violence and vowed to disarm (see Current issues, above, for details).

Irish National Liberation Army (INLA). Formed in 1975 by dissident members of the "Official" IRA after that group had adopted a policy of nonviolence, the INLA was banned in 1979 after assassinating a close associate of Margaret Thatcher. A number of INLA members joined the Maze hunger strikes of 1980–1981. Other members of the INLA and its political front, the **Irish Republican Socialist Party** (see Ireland: Political Parties), were killed in internal feuds, in disputes with the IRA, or in attacks allegedly related to the involvement in the drug trade of the INLA itself and a splinter group, the **Irish People's Liberation Organization** (IPLO). The INLA declared a cease-fire on August 22, 1998, in the wake of the Omagh bombing, and reaffirmed it in early August 1999. In March 2000 the INLA stated that it had delivered to the principal loyalist paramilitary groups, the UDA and UVF, a paper on maintaining the cease-fire even in the face of political impasse.

Continuity IRA (CIRA; Continuity Army Council, CAC). Adamantly opposed to the peace process, including the IRA cease-fire announced in 1994, the Continuity IRA broke away from the IRA in 1995 or 1996 and was proscribed in 1997. Some reports characterized it as an armed wing of the Republican *Sinn Féin* (RSF) party (see Ireland: Political Parties), an accusation that the RSF denied. Although itself responsible for a relatively small number of bombings and killings since 1996, the CIRA condemned the August 1998 Omagh bombing as an unjustified "slaughter of the innocents." Believed to number only about 30, the group may have attracted additional members following the cease-fire declared by the Real IRA (below) in September 1998. It remained the only republican group not to have declared a cease-fire and in the first seven months of 2000 claimed responsibility for a number of bombings in Northern Ireland and England. Some antiterrorism agencies suspected, however, that other groups, particularly the Real IRA, may have been using the CIRA as a cover name.

Real IRA. Apparently organized in October 1997 in opposition to the renewed IRA cease-fire and *Sinn Féin*'s participation in the Stormont peace talks, the Real IRA probably numbered no more than 100–150 members. It was believed in some quarters to be serving as the military wing of the 32 County Sovereignty Movement, whose leaders have denied any connection.

In June 1998 reports surfaced that the Real IRA, the Continuity IRA, and the INLA had held a summit in Dundalk, Ireland, and may have agreed to unify their forces. Following the August Omagh bombing, however, the Continuity IRA and the INLA distanced themselves from the attack, for which the Real IRA claimed responsibility. On August 18, three days after the car bombing, the Real IRA announced a "complete cessation of all military activity." On September 8, reportedly after its leaders received personal visits from the IRA, it declared a "permanent" cease-fire, although it was implicated in subsequent bombings, including a number in England. In May 2000 it warned that it was preparing a renewed bombing campaign. Two months later the Real IRA was implicated in a failed effort to smuggle a shipment of explosives and weapons from Croatia, and in September it was branded as the probable perpetrator of two attacks on security bases in the North. In March 2001 authorities implicated the Real IRA in a car-bomb explosion outside the West London offices of the British Broadcasting Corporation. Other bombings in May and August were also attributed to the Real IRA. In May 2002 three Real IRA members pleaded guilty to conspiracy and other charges and received 30-year sentences.

Michael McKevitt, the leader of the Real IRA, was convicted in 2003 of the charge of heading a terrorist organization; he was sentenced to a 20-year prison term. (The verdict was handed down by a nonjury Special Criminal Court authorized to adjudicate terrorism cases following the 1998 Omagh bombing.)

Leader: Michael McKEVITT (in prison).

Former and Current Loyalist Paramilitary Groups

Ulster Defence Association (UDA). Formed in 1971 by the amalgamation of loyalist paramilitary groups, mainly in greater Belfast and Londonderry, the UDA was initially a mass-membership organization involved in street protests and rallies, including the political strike and accompanying intimidation that brought down the power-sharing administration in 1974. It became increasingly involved in sectarian violence, using such cover names as **Ulster Freedom Fighters** (UFF) and "Ulster Young Militants" to claim responsibility for several hundred killings, the vast majority of noncombatant Catholics. From the mid-1970s the UDA also became deeply enmeshed in racketeering in Northern Ireland, while in the late 1980s it obtained significant material support from the apartheid regime in South Africa.

The UFF was banned in 1973, but the UDA remained legal until 1992, when it was proscribed after a British Army intelligence agent operating in the UDA high command was convicted of conspiracy to murder. The case highlighted allegations that the loyalist paramilitaries had benefited extensively from collusion by members of the police, the army, and the intelligence services. In the interim, the UDA had established a political front, the Ulster Democratic Party (UDP), which remained legal.

In 1991 the UDA/UFF joined the Ulster Volunteer Force and the Red Hand Commando (below) in forming a Combined Loyalist Military Command (CLMC) to coordinate paramilitary activities. The CLMC declared a brief cease-fire in 1991 and then an indefinite cease-fire (subsequently violated) in October 1994, four months after the IRA had done so. In October 1997 conflict within the CLMC broke into the open, and the UDA announced its withdrawal, leading to reports that the joint command had disbanded. Within days sporadic intraloyalist violence was reported, without, however, threatening the cease-fire.

Cease-fire violations attributed to the UFF led to suspension of the UDP from the Stormont peace talks in January–March 1998, but on April 25 the UDA announced its support for the Good Friday Agreement. It may now number only several hundred members, although it claimed the support of as many as 40,000 at its peak in the 1970s. In September 1999 UFF leader Johnny Adair was released from prison in accordance with the peace agreement, having served 4 years of his 16-year term for terrorism.

On June 20, 2000, members of the UFF threatened to break its cease-fire, "reserving the right" to defend Protestant homes in the context of "ethnic cleansing" and "intimidation" perpetrated by nationalists. Three days later, however, it retracted its warning. Two months later, Adair's early release was suspended in the context of violent clashes between the UFF/UDA and the UVF/PUP in Belfast. Altercations continued for several more months. On December 15 the UDA, the UVF, and the Red Hand Commando agreed to a truce.

On October 12, 2001, responding to a renewed wave of violence and rioting, Secretary of State for Northern Ireland John Reid declared an end to the government's cease-fire with the UDA/UFF. Adair, having completed his sentence, was released from prison on May 15, 2002.

Ulster Volunteer Force (UVF). The UVF was founded in 1966 and was quickly banned after allegedly killing two Catholics. It was restored to legal status in 1974 to encourage it to become involved in politics through the Volunteer Political Party (later reconstituted as the Progressive Unionist Party—PUP, above). Banned again after several murders in October 1975, the UVF conducted a protracted campaign of sectarian assassinations designed to put pressure on the IRA to halt its

activities, the most active UVF units being based in Belfast, Armagh, and Tyrone.

In general, the UVF held to the CLMC cease-fire of 1994, despite differences with the UDA that reportedly led to the UVF's expulsion from Derry in November 1997. A splinter group, the Loyalist Volunteer Force (below), left the UVF in 1996, and infighting between the two persisted. In January 2000 a UVF commander, Richard JAMESON, was assassinated, with suspicion immediately falling on the LVF. The parent group may now number a few hundred members, compared to 1,500 in the 1970s.

In July and August 2000 a renewed feud with the UFF for control of loyalist territory (and possibly drug trafficking) in Belfast resulted in the redeployment of UK troops in the capital. In December 2000 the UVF joined the UDA and the Red Hand Commando in a truce.

The UK government charged that the UVF was significantly involved with "loyalist riots" that broke out in Belfast in September 2005, and the UVF was also blamed for several murders in connection with its ongoing feud with the LVF. Consequently, the UK signaled that it no longer considered the UVF to be honoring the cease-fire. In mid-2006 the UVF was pressured to disband (as the LVF had), but it refused to "clarify" its stance.

Red Hand Commando (RHC). Formed in 1972 and proscribed since 1973, the small RHC was frequently linked to the UVF, with some reports describing it as nothing more than a cover name for the larger group. The RHC agreed to the December 2000 truce between the UVF and the UDA.

Loyalist Volunteer Force (LVF). Apparently dating from about 1994, the LVF formed within the UVF around the leadership of Billy Wright, who opposed the 1994 cease-fire and any concessions to nationalists. The LVF withdrew from the UVF in 1996 and was banned a year later. On December 27, 1997, Wright was murdered in Maze prison by INLA inmates, after which the LVF was implicated in a number of apparently retaliatory sectarian killings. (Collaterally, unconfirmed reports suggested that the group was permitting UFF paramilitaries to use the LVF name as a cover.)

The LVF declared a unilateral cease-fire on May 15, 1998, but also urged a "no" vote at the May 22 referendum on the Good Friday Agreement. Three months later it called for an "absolute, utter" end to terrorism and made its cease-fire permanent, thereby qualifying its incarcerated members for early release under the peace accord. On December 18, 1998, the LVF became the first paramilitary organization to decommission some of its weapons, a gesture that the IRA labeled a "stunt."

In November 2005 it was reported that the LVF had disbanded after directing its members to discontinue all operations. The decision was described as a "direct response" to the IRA's recent decision to decommission its arms.

Orange Volunteers (OV). Reviving the name of a major loyalist paramilitary group of the 1970s, the Orange Volunteers emerged in 1998 in opposition to the Good Friday Agreement and the cease-fires declared by other loyalist organizations. It subsequently conducted a small number of sectarian attacks. Its membership, apparently numbering no more than a few dozen individuals disaffected from the UDA/UFF and the LVF, may have overlapped that of the Red Hand Defenders (below). In 2000 both groups were added to the U.S. government's annual list of organizations suspected of terrorism.

Red Hand Defenders (RHD). Like the OV, the RHD was formed in 1998 by loyalist rejectionists. In March 1999 it claimed responsibility for the car bombing that killed prominent lawyer Rosemary Nelson. Two days later, Frankie CURRY, a reputed RHD member, was killed in what some officials characterized as an ongoing conflict between loyalist groups engaged in organized crime. The RHD blamed the UVF for Curry's death but denied that he was a member. In January 2002, following the shooting of a postal worker, the RHD indicated that it was disbanding at the request of the UFF, but another shooting in April was attributed to the group. Some analysts argued that the RHD was a cover name for the UDA/UFF.

Legislature

The former bicameral Northern Ireland Parliament was replaced by a unicameral Northern Ireland Assembly under the Northern Ireland Constitution Act of July 1973. The assembly and a Northern Ireland Executive functioned in 1973–1974, while a 1982 act of Parliament led to election of another assembly, initially with consultative powers, in November 1982. With its tasks unfulfilled, the assembly was dissolved in June 1986, although subject to legislative provision that it could be reactivated. On May 30, 1996, provincial elections were held for a 110-member Northern Ireland Forum for Political Dialogue, a nonlegislative body designed to provide a platform for discussion and to assist in choosing delegates to the coming peace talks.

A 108-member body, initially termed the New Northern Ireland Assembly, was elected for a five-year term on June 25, 1998, but was suspended upon the reintroduction of direct rule on October 15, 2002.

At the June 7, 2001, election for the UK House of Commons, the Ulster Unionist Party (UUP) won 6 seats; the Democratic Unionist Party (DUP), 5; *Sinn Féin,* 4; and the Social Democratic and Labour Party (SDLP), 3. At the May 5, 2005, election for the UK House of Commons, the DUP won 9 seats; *Sinn Féin,* 5; the SDLP, 3; and the UUP, 1.

Northern Ireland Assembly. The most recent assembly balloting was conducted on November 25, 2003 (postponed from May 29), although the body remained under suspension, as it had been since the collapse of the power-sharing government in October 2002. The 2003 poll yielded 30 seats for the Democratic Unionist Party, 27 for the Ulster Unionist Party, 24 for *Sinn Féin,* 18 for the Social Democratic and Labour Party, 6 for the Alliance Party of Northern Ireland, 1 for the Progressive Unionist Party, 1 for the United Kingdom Unionist Party, and 1 for an independent. (In June 2006 it was reported that a UUP member of the assembly had defected to the UK Conservative Party.)

The assembly convened "without power" on May 15, 2006, for the first time in three-and-a-half years as part of the revived effort to resolve the governmental impasse, and assembly committees continued to meet throughout the summer.

The next elections were scheduled for May 2007.

Speaker: Eileen BELL.

Cabinet

The Northern Ireland Executive was suspended by the secretary of state for Northern Ireland with effect from October 15, 2002.

Communications

Press, radio, and television are organized along the same lines as in Great Britain.

Press

The following newspapers are published in Belfast: *Belfast Telegraph* (94,600); pro-unionist daily; *Sunday Life* (83,800); *Irish News* (50,000), nationalist daily; *News Letter* (32,000), pro-unionist daily; *Ulster News Letter* (28,800), pro-unionist daily.

VATICAN CITY STATE

Stato della Città del Vaticano

The Country

An enclave surrounding the Basilica of Saint Peter and including 13 other buildings in and around the city of Rome, the Vatican City State, the smallest independent entity in the world, derives its principal importance from its function as the world headquarters of the Roman Catholic Church and official residence of its head, the pope. The central administration of the church is customarily referred to as the Holy See (*Santa Sede*), or more informally as the Vatican. The Vatican City State is the territorial base from which the leadership of the church exercises its religious and ecclesiastical responsibilities for a worldwide Catholic population of more than 1 billion people and over 400,000 Catholic priests. The city state's population, predominantly of Italian and Swiss extraction, is limited mainly to Vatican officials and resident employees and their families. Italian is the language of common use, although Latin is employed in the official acts of the Holy See.

The Vatican's income is based on contributions from Roman Catholic congregations around the world; the sale of postage stamps and souvenirs; and substantial investments in real estate, bonds, and securities. The Administration of the Patrimony of the Apostolic See (*Amministrazione del Patrimonio della Sede Apostolica*) manages its holdings, while the Institute for Religious Works (*Istituto per le Opere di Religione*—IOR) acts as a bank for moneys held by affiliated religious orders. The Vatican's financial status long remained confidential and hence the object of intense speculation. However, an unprecedented announcement in 1979 revealed that the church's operations would be $20 million in deficit for the year. By 1991 a projected deficit of more than $90 million led to a conference at Vatican City on ways to generate more revenue from local dioceses around the world. The resultant

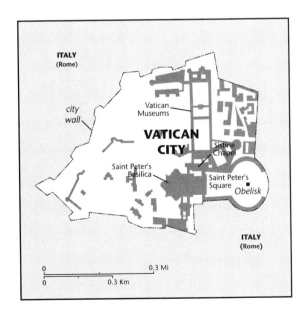

Political Status: Independent sovereign state, under papal temporal government; international status governed by the Lateran Treaty with Italy of February 11, 1929; constitution of June 7, 1929, superseded by a New Fundamental Law signed by the pope on November 26, 2000, with effect from February 22, 2001.

Area: 0.17 sq. mi. (0.44 sq. km.).

Population: 921 (2005E). There are approximately 3,000 lay workers, most of them Italian citizens, who live outside the Vatican.

Official Language: Latin (Italian is the working language).

Monetary Unit: Euro (market rate July 1, 2006: 1 euro = $1.28US). On December 29, 2000, the Vatican and Italy signed an agreement permitting Vatican adoption of the euro, authorization having already been granted in principle by the European Union. Under a 1929 agreement with the Italian government, the Vatican had the right to issue papal coinage in Vatican lire at par with the Italian lira (its total value not to exceed 100 million lire, except in holy years and in the year a council is convened). Since introduction of euro notes and coins in 2002, the Vatican has been permitted to mint its own euro coins, which are issued in small quantities for collectors, as was true of Vatican lire.

Sovereign (Supreme Pontiff): Pope BENEDICT XVI (Josef RATZINGER); elected to a life term by the College of Cardinals on April 19, 2005, succeeding Pope JOHN PAUL II (Karol WOJTYA), who died on April 2, 2005.

Secretary of State of the Roman Curia and Papal Representative in the Civil Government of the Vatican City State: Cardinal Angelo SODANO; appointed by Pope John Paul II on December 2, 1990, while still an archbishop, succeeding Cardinal Agostino CASAROLI, who had resigned on December 1; named a cardinal on May 29, 1991.

Secretary for Relations with States: Archbishop Giovanni LAJOLO; appointed by Pope John Paul II on October 7, 2003, succeeding Archbishop Jean-Louis TAURAN.

President of the Governatorate of Vatican City State: Cardinal Edmund Casimir SZOKA; appointed by Pope John Paul II in 1997. Cardinal Szoka functions as the "mayor" of Vatican City.

remedial action produced a 1993 surplus (the first in more than 20 years) of $1.5 million on income totaling $169 million. Strong investment performance buoyed Vatican finances in the 1990s, but the weakening dollar since 2000 has marked the deficit's return.

Government and Politics

Political Background

Italy's recognition of the Vatican City State in the Lateran Treaty of 1929 terminated a bitter political controversy that had persisted since the unification of Italy in 1860–1870. Before that time the popes had exercised political sovereignty over the city of Rome and substantial portions of the Italian peninsula, where they ruled as territorial sovereigns in addition to performing spiritual and administrative functions as heads of the Catholic Church. The absorption of virtually all territorial holdings by the new Italian state and the failure of Pope PIUS IX to accept the legitimacy of the compensation offered by the Italian Parliament left the Holy See in an anomalous position that was finally regularized after a lapse of two generations. In addition to the Lateran Treaty, by which Italy recognized the independence and sovereignty of the Vatican City State, a concordat was concluded that regulated the position of the church within Italy, while a financial convention compensated the Holy See for its earlier losses. The status of the Vatican City State as established by the Lateran Treaty has since been recognized, formally or tacitly, by a great majority of the world's governments.

Cardinal Josef RATZINGER, who became pope with the title BENEDICT XVI in April 2005, follows one of the longest and most significant papal terms in modern history. Cardinal Karol WOJTYA, archbishop of Kraków, Poland, elected as Pope JOHN PAUL II in 1978, was the most widely traveled pope of any era. He commanded worldwide veneration, even as he moved the church away from the liberal direction of the Second Vatican Council, opened in 1962 during the papacy of Pope JOHN XXIII. Cardinal Ratzinger was a close confidant of John Paul II. From 1981 until John Paul's death, he served as head of the Congregation for the Doctrine of the Faith (once known as the Holy Office of the Inquisition), the Vatican office responsible for maintaining orthodox doctrine throughout the Roman Catholic communion.

Constitution and Government

On November 26, 2000, Pope John Paul II signed a new constitution intended to "harmonize in a legal manner" various governmental changes, such as abolition of the death penalty, which had been introduced since promulgation of the preceding basic law on June 7, 1929. As in the past, the Vatican City State retains the form of an absolute monarchy. Supreme legislative, executive, and judicial power is vested in the pope, who is elected for life and serves concurrently as bishop of Rome, supreme pontiff of the Universal Church, primate of Italy, archbishop and metropolitan of the Province of Rome, and sovereign of the Vatican City State. Assisting the pope in the exercise of his varied responsibilities are the members of two major organs, the College of Cardinals and the Roman Curia (*Curia Romana*).

Members of the college, who numbered 192 as of May 16, 2006, are named by the pope and serve as his chief advisers and coadjutors during his lifetime; upon his death, those under the age of 80 meet to elect his successor. On January 21 and 28, 2001, Pope John Paul named an unexpected total of 44 new cardinals, adding to the dominance of likeminded conservatives in the College of Cardinals. Although the college is still referred to as a conclave, reforms instituted from February 22, 1996, in an "Apostolic Constitution" entitled *Universi Dominici Gregis,* ended the practice of detaining the electors in a locked room until a result emerged, although strict secrecy of the voting process has been maintained. For election, a candidate (usually a cardinal) normally requires a majority of two-

thirds (or two-thirds plus one, depending on the number of electors), but in the event of a protracted deadlock a majority vote may decide to proceed to election by majority. The 1996 change eliminated the options of election by universal acclamation or by delegation to an electoral subcommittee. Also in 1996 the *Domus Sanctae Marthae,* a hospitality residence named after St. Martha, opened within the precincts of Vatican City. This air-conditioned guesthouse is considerably more comfortable than accommodations available to cardinals during previous conclaves, and its existence has been seen as an inducement to older and infirm electors to take more time in coming to a decision. While the papacy is vacant, the full college (meeting in General Congregation) or subcommittees (Particular Congregations) may deal with the ordinary government of the church and of the Vatican City State as well as with any emergency matters arising, with the strict exception of matters that would otherwise be reserved to the authority of the pope.

Apart from conclaves, the full college meets infrequently. A number of cardinals also hold positions on the various bodies that constitute the Curia, which serves as the church's central administrative organ. Political responsibilities have devolved primarily to the Secretariat of State, which in 1988 was divided into two sections, one dealing with general affairs and the other with relations with states. The Secretariat is headed by a secretary of state. The governor of the Vatican works closely with the Secretariat. The governor is currently the same person as the president of the Pontifical Commission for the Vatican City State, a body that seems to have reduced its activity in favor of the Governatorate.

The Vatican City State has its own security force (the Swiss Guard), postal service, coinage, utilities, department store, communication system, and local tribunal with a right of appeal to higher ecclesiastical courts. A papal edict issued in July 1995 set out "rules of conduct" for all Vatican employees, requiring them, on pain of automatic sanctions (including dismissal), to observe Catholic moral doctrines "even in the private sphere" and not to associate with organizations whose "goals are incompatible" with those of the church.

Foreign Relations

The foreign relations of the Holy See are centered primarily on its international status as seat of the church, set in the context of its position as a sovereign entity. Its activities as a sovereign state continue to be governed by the Lateran Treaty and related agreements with the Italian government, which enable it to enter into international agreements and bilateral diplomatic relations in its own right. Worldwide, such diplomatic linkages now total well over 100 (supplemented by unofficial representation in other countries), while the Holy See has permanent observer status at the United Nations (UN), with, as of July 2004, all rights of full membership except that of voting. It is also a full member of certain UN specialized agencies. It participates in the Organization for Security and Cooperation in Europe (OSCE).

The Vatican's close relations with Italy were threatened in the 1980s by the revelation of links between the Institute for Religious Works (IOR), otherwise known as the Vatican bank, and Italy's Banco Ambrosiano, which collapsed in August 1982. The Vatican and the Italian government subsequently appointed a joint commission to investigate the matter, and in May 1984 the IOR agreed "in recognition of moral involvement," but without admission of culpability, to pay 109 creditor banks up to $250 million of a $406 million settlement against Banco Ambrosiano's successor institution.

Earlier, in February 1984, negotiations were concluded on a new Italian-Vatican concordat. Provisions included the abandonment of Roman Catholicism as Italy's state religion and of mandated religious instruction in public schools, although secular authorities would continue to accord automatic recognition to church marriages and full freedom to Catholic schools.

John Paul II exemplified, and Benedict XVI seems to be continuing, a concerted effort to use the papal position to improve relations, not only with non-Catholic Christian entities but also with some non-Christians. The historic breach with Protestant Christendom, dating to the 16th century, was partly overcome in 1982. The Vatican established full diplomatic relations with the United Kingdom and with the Lutheran countries of Denmark, Norway, and Sweden. In contrast, major differences with the Orthodox Christian hierarchy continue to affect the Vatican's relations with a number of countries. In 1992 the Orthodox Church severely criticized Rome for seeking converts in "its" territory, as signified by Pope John Paul's 1991 creation of new dioceses in the former Soviet Union. The ecumenical patriarch, Bartholomew I (representing 15 churches, with 170 million adherents), made a first official visit to the Vatican in June 1995, while a trip by John Paul II to Romania in May 1999 marked the first visit in 1,000 years by a Roman Catholic pope to a country having an orthodox majority. It was followed in May 2001 by a first visit to Greece, where the pope met with Archbishop Christodoulos of the Greek Orthodox Church. At that time John Paul II apologized for the sacking of Constantinople in 1204. The pope subsequently undertook groundbreaking visits to Ukraine (June 2001), Kazakhstan and Armenia (September 2001), and Azerbaijan and Bulgaria (May 2002). The patriarch of Moscow, Aleksei II, remains overtly critical of the Vatican, however, condemning its February 2002 decision to upgrade four previously "temporary" apostolic administrations in Russia to full dioceses.

In January 1984 formal relations at the ambassadorial level were reestablished with the United States after a lapse of 117 years, and a wide range of other linkages followed during the ensuing decade. In the first meeting between a pope and a Soviet head of state, Mikhail Gorbachev was accorded a private audience at the Vatican in December 1989; the meeting served as a prelude to the establishment of official contacts in March 1990. Earlier, in July 1989, relations had been reestablished with Poland after a rupture of more than four decades. Further reflecting the tide of change in Eastern Europe, relations were reestablished with Hungary in February 1990, with Czechoslovakia in April, and with Romania in May. The Vatican established relations with the Russian Federation in December 1991 and with most of the other former Soviet republics during 1992. Speedy recognition was extended to the predominantly Catholic former Yugoslav republics of Croatia and Slovenia in January 1992 and to Muslim-dominated Bosnia and Herzegovina in August.

In addition, relations with Mexico (broken in 1861) were normalized in September 1992, following the deletion of anticlerical clauses from the country's 1917 constitution. As a result of the changes, the church was authorized to own property and operate schools, while priests and nuns were enfranchised and permitted to wear clerical garb in public. On February 1, 1996, President Ernesto Zedillo became the first Mexican head of state to visit the Vatican.

In September 1993 a senior member of the Vatican's Congregation for the Oriental Churches became the highest ranking Catholic official to visit China since the Communist takeover in 1949. Ostensibly responding to an invitation to attend China's National Athletic Games, the emissary reportedly met with "government personalities" amid indications of a possible end to the lengthy estrangement. Further discussions took place between 1996 and 1998, but the Vatican's continuing recognition of the Taiwanese government has prevented normalization with Beijing.

Cordial relations between the Vatican and Israel have gradually evolved during the past quarter-century. Pope John Paul II departed from tradition in strongly endorsing the Egyptian-Israeli peace treaty immediately prior to its signing in Washington in March 1979. In April 1986, in an act without recorded precedent, he was received by the chief rabbi of Rome at the city's central synagogue, where he condemned all forms of anti-Semitism and deplored the genocide inflicted on the Jewish people during World War II. In 1993 a meeting with the chief rabbi of Israel's Ashkenazi Jews—the first such event since the founding of the Jewish State in 1948—paved the way for a December 30 agreement on establishing formal Vatican-Israeli relations, effective June 15, 1994.

The Vatican had long opposed diplomatic ties because of questions regarding Israeli treatment of Palestinians, the status of church property in the Holy Land, and the status of Jerusalem. The first of these concerns had been allayed by a September 1993 agreement between Israel and the Palestine Liberation Organization. A Vatican-Israeli agreement in 1997 covered autonomy for over 1,100 Catholic institutions and holy places while also placing them under state protection. Over the years the church has also shifted its position toward Jerusalem, most recently supporting negotiation of an internationally enforceable statute to protect the city. That stance was included in a February 2000 agreement between the Vatican and the Palestinian National Authority that drew swift Israeli criticism.

In February 2000 John Paul II became the first pope to visit Egypt, and a month later he made the first pilgrimage to the Holy Land by a pope since 1964, visiting Jordan and Israel, including Palestinian-controlled Bethlehem, where he recognized the Palestinians' "natural right to a homeland." Later in the year, responding to the latest wave of Palestinian-Israeli violence, the Pontifical Council for Inter-Religious Dialogue rejected all "exclusive" claims to Jerusalem, noting that the city belongs "to the spiritual patrimony of humanity."

In recent years the Vatican has taken an active interest in global affairs while maintaining its doctrinal opposition to "liberation theology." Pope Benedict, then Cardinal Ratzinger, was considered a leader in that opposition. As head of the Congregation for the Doctrine of the Faith, Ratzinger silenced a number of well-respected liberal Catholic clergy and scholars. In early 1987, in its first attempt to address a global policy issue, the Pontifical Commission for Justice and Peace urged the rescheduling of third world debt, including total remission in "emergency situations." A subsequent wide-ranging papal encyclical deplored the widening gap between rich and poor nations and denounced the ideological rivalry between East and West as having subjected third world countries to imperialistic "structures of sin." In May 1988, during his ninth Latin American tour, John Paul offered his "unconditional support and encouragement to the organizers of labor unions." In a May 1991 encyclical celebrating the 100th anniversary of Pope LEO XII's *Rerum Novarum,* which addressed working-class conditions at the end of the 19th century, John Paul endorsed the free market as "the most efficient instrument for utilizing resources and effectively responding to needs." He added, however, that capitalism should be constrained by legal safeguards rooted in an "ethical and religious" conception of human freedom.

In January 1998 John Paul made a highly publicized trip to Cuba, the only Latin American country that he had not previously visited. In addition to calling upon the government to introduce pluralism, he criticized the long-standing U.S. economic sanctions against Fidel Castro's regime as "unjust and ethically unacceptable." In early 1999, while visiting Mexico, he urged the massive throngs who attended his appearances to use their faith to battle government corruption. He also reemphasized his concern for the "marginalization" of the world's poor by the global effects of unfettered free-market activity.

The Holy See has also participated in a variety of international conferences, including the June 1992 Earth Summit in Rio de Janeiro, where the Vatican managed to keep the issue of population control off the agenda. At the third UN Conference on Population and Development, held in Cairo in September 1994, the Vatican made common cause with traditionalist Muslim governments in opposing any endorsement of abortion and contraception. The September 1995 UN World Conference on Women, in Beijing, concluded with the Vatican endorsing the final declaration but criticizing many liberal elements in the platform for action.

On March 12, 2000, Pope John Paul delivered a far-reaching but nonspecific apology for sins committed by Catholics, the Church's "children," over the two preceding millennia. Without mentioning the Crusades, the Inquisition, or the Holocaust, church leaders cited such offenses as intolerance and discrimination against women, minorities, indigenous peoples, Jews, and the poor. The apology came two years after release of a long-awaited report from the Vatican on the role of the church during the Nazi era. Calling the official document an "act of repentance," the Vatican apologized for the failure of many Roman Catholics to protect Jews during the period. However, it defended the actions of Pope PIUS XII during World War II, claiming his silence regarding Nazi action was necessary to avoid further killings and permit behind-the-scenes assistance to Jews. Some Jewish leaders replied that the statement did not go far enough in addressing the perceived historic role of the church in fostering anti-Semitism.

Current Issues

In his first encyclical, viewed as an inclusive and conciliatory message, issued on January 26, 2006, Pope Benedict XVI affirmed the importance of charity and love, including sexual intimacy, as fundamental expressions of Christian faith. During his first year in office, however, Benedict has mostly lived up to his reputation for conservatism in doctrinal matters, continuing his predecessor's affirmation of traditional teachings on such matters as papal primacy and infallibility, the exclusion of women from the priesthood (while at the same time acknowledging that the church has long marginalized and discriminated against women), and opposition to birth control and gay marriage.

From the first month of his pontificate Pope Benedict spoke out forcefully against a proposed measure to legalize gay marriage in Spain, urging Catholics to work and vote against it. Nonetheless, it passed on July 30, 2005. During a trip to Spain in July 2006, the pope reiterated his stance that the marriage covenant is a "permanent bond" between a man and a woman and "a great good for all humanity."

Since 2001 the Vatican has struggled to deal with the repercussions of a major scandal in the United States and elsewhere involving child sexual abuse by clergy and the institutional church's perceived long-standing indifference to the problem. On November 21, 2001, John Paul voiced an apology to victims, and in January 2002 the Vatican issued new procedures for handling alleged abuse, including trying accused clergy in secret ecclesiastical courts, but without precluding civil and criminal action by secular authorities. In subsequent statements John Paul called pedophilia "grievously evil" and, during a summit of all U.S. cardinals in Rome in April, both a crime and "appalling sin." Such statements did not, however, quell the outcry from much of the laity. Moreover, individual dioceses, which are generally responsible for their own financial affairs, face millions of dollars in settlements to victims, and several have been forced to file for bankruptcy protection. The Vatican's immunity from U.S. prosecution, under the Foreign Sovereign Immunity Act, was challenged in June 2006, when a U.S. district judge ruled that a lawsuit brought against the Vatican for allowing a priest who was a known child molester to be transferred from city to city could proceed. Pope Benedict has shown ambivalence in this matter. One of his earliest acts as pope was to meet with Cardinal Bernard Francis Law, former archbishop of Boston, who had been forced to resign because of his lack of action against pedophile priests. But in May 2006 he asked the Rev. Marcial Maciel Degollado, founder of the conservative Legionaries of Christ and target of multiple molestation charges, to leave the ministry for a life of "prayer and penitence." In November 2005 Benedict officially excluded from the priesthood candidates who support the "gay culture" or have "deep-seated homosexual tendencies," as well as those who are "actively homosexual."

In April 2006 Pope Benedict signaled a possible loosening of the Vatican's ban on all forms of artificial birth control by ordering a study of the use of condoms among people with AIDS and other infectious diseases.

In the arena of relations with the non-Catholic world, Pope Benedict has had a mixed record. He has been largely unsuccessful in improving Jewish-Catholic relations. In May 2005 Benedict met with the Israeli ambassador to the Vatican, promising to visit the main synagogue in Cologne, Germany, during his visit to that city for the August 2005 World Youth Day. He was, however, criticized for failing to mention Israel in a list of countries affected by terrorism. Benedict came under further criticism from Jewish leaders when he failed to explicitly condemn anti-Semitism during a May 2006 visit to the Nazi death camps of Auschwitz and

Birkenau in Poland. He has pressed for freedom of religious expression on behalf of Catholics in India and China and called for negotiations to resolve the U.S.-Iranian standoff surrounding Iran's nuclear program.

Pope Benedict, who initially retained all members of his predecessor's Curia, signaled the official transfer of power in June 2006, when the Vatican announced the retirement, as of September 15, 2006, of Cardinal Angelo SODANO, the Vatican's second most powerful official, and Cardinal Edmund SZOKA, who presides over the Vatican City. Benedict appointed Cardinal Tarcisio BERTONE, archbishop of Genoa, to replace Sodano, and Archbishop Giovanni LAJOLO, currently the Vatican's foreign minister, to replace Szoka, an American who in the 1990s had lifted the veil of secrecy surrounding Vatican finances.

Communications

As the seat of the central organization of the Roman Catholic Church, Vatican City is also the center of a worldwide communications network and of a variety of publicity media directed to both Italian and international audiences. All publications and broadcasting are conducted under church auspices and generally reflect a clerical point of view, though with varying degrees of authority.

Press

L'Osservatore Romano, the semiofficial Vatican daily, and related publications are the principal media for Vatican comment on secular affairs; other publications are primarily concerned with ecclesiastical matters. In addition to *L'Osservatore Romano* (70,000), which also produces weekly editions in English, French, German, Italian, Portuguese, and Spanish, plus a monthly edition in Polish, the leading publications with secular content are the daily *Bollettino Sala Stampa della Santa Sede* (Bulletin of the Holy See Press Office) and the *Annuario Pontificio,* an official annual edited by the Central Statistics Office.

The Roman Curia

As of July 1, 2006

Note: In addition to the bodies noted below, which have political and administrative functions relating to the Vatican as a state, there are numerous other bodies within the Curia with mainly ecclesiastical, theological, ecumenical, disciplinary, cultural, or pastoral functions, including congregations, tribunals, councils, commissions, and committees. The major bodies are referred to as dicasteries of the Roman Curia.

Secretariat of State

Secretary of State	Cardinal Angelo Sodano
Substitute for General Affairs	Archbishop Leandro Sandri
Secretary for Relations with States	Archbishop Giovanni Lajolo

Governatorate of Vatican City State

President	Cardinal Edmund Casimir Szoka
Secretary	Renato Boccardo

News Agencies

The Vatican Information Service (VIS), of the Holy See Press Office, provides daily news in English, French, Italian, and Spanish. *Agenzia Internazionale Fides* (AIF) services news of mission countries throughout the world.

Radio and Television

Radio Vatican (*Radio Vaticana*), located in Vatican City and in Santa Maria di Galeria, outside Rome, broadcasts in about three dozen modern languages and, for liturgical and related purposes, in Latin. A Vatican Television Center (*Centro Televisivo Vaticano*) was established in 1983 to produce and distribute religious programs; it also offers live broadcasts, mainly of events held at the Vatican, that are available to Catholic networks and other satellite links.

Intergovernmental Representation

Apostolic Pro Nuncio to the U.S.
Archbishop Pietro SAMBI

U.S. Ambassador to the Holy See
Francis ROONEY

Permanent Observer to the UN
Archbishop Celestino MIGLIORE

IGO Memberships (Non-UN)
OSCE

PART THREE

INTERGOVERNMENTAL ORGANIZATIONS

ARCTIC COUNCIL

Established: By the Declaration on the Establishment of the Arctic Council, signed September 19, 1996, in Ottawa, Canada.

Purpose: To provide regular intergovernmental consultation on Arctic issues to ensure the well-being of the inhabitants of the Arctic, sustainable development, and the protection of the environment.

Principal Organs: Ministerial Meetings, Senior Arctic Officials Meetings, Secretariat.

Chair: Vitaly Churkin (Russia).

Membership (8): Canada, Denmark, Finland, Iceland, Norway, Russia, Sweden, United States. There are also six "Permanent Participants" representing Arctic indigenous peoples as allowed by the charter: the Aleut International Association, the Arctic Athabaskan Council, the Gwich'in Council International, the Inuit Circumpolar Conference, the Saami Council, and the Russian Association of Indigenous Peoples of the North.

Observers (5): France, Germany, Netherlands, Poland, United Kingdom. Eighteen organizations, including the Association of World Reindeer Herders and the more encompassing United Nations Environment Programme, also have observer status.

Origin and development. Canada first proposed the idea of the Arctic Council in 1989 when concerns about the cultural and environmental degradation associated with modern development arose. In 1994 Canada resurrected the concept of a permanent forum in which diplomats, scientists, and policy analysts could coordinate their efforts toward the protection and management of the fragile Arctic domain. Preliminary discussions were held in June 1995 and August 1996 to draft the council's charter, which was formally signed September 19, 1996, in Ottawa, Canada.

Structure. After initial protest by the United States, it was decided that the Secretariat would not be given a permanent home but would instead rotate every two years, along with the position of chair, among the council members. The charter calls for decisions to be made by consensus at Ministerial Meetings to be held biannually. Meetings of Senior Arctic Officials (SAOs) convene twice a year.

Following the fourth Ministerial Conference on the Arctic Environmental Protection Strategy (AEPS) held June 12–13, 1997, in Alta, Norway, the Arctic Council assumed responsibility for the AEPS and the programs initiated in support of it. Advancing the related overriding goals of environmental protection and sustainable development are five working groups: the Arctic Monitoring and Assessment Program (AMAP); Protection of the Arctic Marine Environment (PAME); Emergency Prevention, Preparedness, and Response (EPPR); Conservation of Arctic Flora and Fauna (CAFF); and the Sustainable Development Working Group (SDWG).

Activities. The Arctic Council has drawn considerable international attention since its formation. Council supporters, describing the Arctic as "an environmental early warning system for our globe," have suggested the group could serve as a model for similar endeavors in other regions. At the same time, the council has steadily expanded its contacts with other intergovernmental forums. For example, the SAO session held November 18–19, 1999, in Washington, D.C., was attended by representatives of the European Union, the Nordic Council of Ministers, the Council of the Baltic Sea States, and the Barents Euro-Arctic Council.

At present, the Arctic Council has three work programs. The Regional Program of Action for the Protection of the Arctic Marine Environment from Land-Based Activities (RPA) was adopted in September 1998 at the first Ministerial Meeting, held in Iqaluit, Canada. The Arctic Climate Impact Assessment (ACIA), with a secretariat based in Fairbanks, Alaska, was formally authorized at the second ministerial session, held October 12–13, 2000, in Barrow, Alaska, as was the Arctic Council Action Plan to Eliminate Pollution of the Arctic (ACAP). The ACIA's principal purpose is "to evaluate and synthesize knowledge on climate variability, climate change and increased ultraviolet radiation and their consequences." The ACAP, which originated in a 1997 report by the AMAP on Arctic pollution, lists reducing the emission of pollutants and forging international cooperative efforts to reduce pollution risks as its primary goals.

Specific Arctic Council projects include assistance to Russia in phasing out polychlorinated biphenyls (PCBs) and managing PCB waste cleanups, as well as assessment of persistent toxic substances (PTS) and radioactive contamination in the region. The SDWG, which held its first session during the May 3–6, 1999, SAO meeting in Anchorage, Alaska, has discussed wide-range projects covering areas such as youth health, telemedicine, regional fisheries, safety in the fishing industry, ecotourism, rural sanitation, and regional transport and transport infrastructure.

Roundtable discussions at the Barrow Ministerial Meeting focused on the ACIA, the future of Arctic cooperation, the effects of contaminants in the region, and the relationship between sustainable development and Arctic communities. At the conclusion of the meeting the position of chair of the Arctic Council passed from the United States to Finland.

The Finnish chair tenure concluded at the third Ministerial Meeting, held October 9–10, 2002, in Inari, Finland, at which time Iceland assumed the council leadership. At the ministerial session, the AMAP presented a report titled "Arctic Pollution 2002," the CAFF outlined recommendations for preservation of regional flora and fauna, and the EPPR presented a "Circumpolar Map of Resources at Risk from Oil Spills in the Arctic."

The fourth Ministerial Meeting, held October 24, 2004, in Reykjavik, Iceland, was dominated by debate over a report from the ACIA on the accelerated pace of climate change related to global warming in the Arctic. The United States reportedly opposed specifying steps to take against climate change, and conference delegates were reported (*Washington Post*, November 25, 2004) as having negotiated forcefully to produce a document that could accommodate the U.S. point of view. At the meeting the ministers also received the Arctic Human Development Report (AHDR) and directed the SDWG to "make full use of the report" to prepare an action plan for sustainable development. The AHDR is an extensive document, the first comprehensive scientific assessment of human well-being to cover the entire Arctic region.

The fifth Ministerial Meeting is to be held October 26, 2006, in Salekhard, Russia. Russia will relinquish the chair at that time.

BANK FOR INTERNATIONAL SETTLEMENTS (BIS/BIZ)

Banque des Réglements Internationaux
Bank für Internationalen Zahlungssausgleich
Banca del Regolamenti Internazionali

Established: By Agreement of Incorporation with the Swiss government dated January 20, 1930, with operations commencing March 17, 1930.

Purpose: "To promote the cooperation of central banks and to provide additional facilities for international financial operations; and to act as trustee or agent in regard to international financial settlements."

Headquarters: Basel, Switzerland. The BIS opened a Representative Office for Asia and the Pacific in Hong Kong in 1998, with a second for the Americas in Mexico City, Mexico, opening in November 2002.

Principal Organs: Board of Directors (16 members), General Meeting, Management.

President and Chair of the Board: Jean-Pierre Roth, Switzerland

Membership (55): Algeria, Argentina, Australia, Austria, Belgium, Bosnia and Herzegovina, Brazil, Bulgaria, Canada, Chile, China, Croatia, Czech Republic, Denmark, Estonia, Finland, France, Germany, Greece, Hong Kong, Hungary, Iceland, India, Indonesia, Ireland, Israel, Italy, Japan, Republic of Korea, Latvia, Lithuania, Macedonia, Malaysia, Mexico, Netherlands, New Zealand, Norway, Philippines, Poland, Portugal, Romania, Russia, Saudi Arabia, Singapore, Slovakia, Slovenia, South Africa, Spain, Sweden, Switzerland, Thailand, Turkey, United Kingdom, United States, and the European Central Bank. As of April 2006 the BIS had not yet resolved the legal consequences of the recent constitutional transformation of a 56th member, the Federal Republic of Yugoslavia, into Serbia and Montenegro.

Official Languages: English, French, German, Italian.

Monetary Unit: Special Drawing Right (SDR) (market rate May 4, 2006, 1.48 SDR = $1US).

Origin and development. The BIS was created to handle post–World War I reparations payments. Though the worldwide economic depression of the 1930s resulted in a moratorium on these payments, the BIS continued to function as the "central bankers' central bank." Its existence was threatened at the end of World War II, when the United States in Bretton Woods proposed its dissolution, but by the 1960s the BIS regained an important role in international monetary affairs. This was a by-product of both the increased importance of monetary policy in international financial relations and the U.S. reliance on "swap arrangements" to finance its balance-of-payments deficit. Furthermore, the role of the BIS was enhanced when the eurocurrency market emerged as an independent force in world politics. Not only was the BIS an active participant in the market, but its annual reports contained valuable data on market size and fluctuations.

While the BIS was traditionally identified as a European bankers' association, the designation became less appropriate as U.S., Canadian, and Japanese banks took an increasingly active role in its policymaking. In 1970 the central bank of Canada became a member, and Japan rejoined after having had its membership lapse from 1952 to 1970 as part of the World War II peace settlement. In June 1992 the status of the central banks of Estonia, Latvia, and Lithuania as BIS members was reactivated after a lapse of more than 50 years. In June 1993 the BIS agreed to divide the capital formerly held by the central bank of Czechoslovakia between the central banks of the Czech Republic and Slovakia.

On June 11, 2001, an Extraordinary General Meeting of the bank canceled the original shares of Yugoslavia (dating to 1931) and the provisional shares issued in June 1997 to the central banks of four of the states that succeeded the Socialist Federal Republic of Yugoslavia. Collaterally, the bank issued new shares to all five successor states— Bosnia and Herzegovina, Croatia, Macedonia, and Slovenia, then joined by the Federal Republic of Yugoslavia—the five having agreed on the division of shares during April–May 2001. Yugoslavia's participation was put in abeyance in 2003 following the country's conversion to the "state union" of Serbia and Montenegro, each component of which has its own central bank. Other recent additions to BIS membership are the central banks of Argentina, Malaysia, and Thailand, as well as the European Central Bank, all of which were invited to join by the BIS Board of Directors in November 1999. In June 2003 similar invitations were extended to the central banks of Algeria, Chile, Indonesia, Israel, New Zealand, and the Philippines.

At an Extraordinary General Meeting on January 8, 2001, the BIS amended its statutes to restrict shares to central banks and require that all privately held shares, about 14 percent of the total, be repurchased (at $9950 per share). A year later, however, representatives of small shareholders sued, claiming undervaluation by the BIS. In November 2002 the Permanent Court of Arbitration ruled in favor of the shareholders, who were to receive approximately 50 percent more per share, but still less than they had sought.

Structure. Administration is vested in three organs: the General Meeting, the Board of Directors, and the Management. The General Meeting is held annually on the second Monday in June. The Board of Directors is responsible for the conduct of the bank's operations at the highest level. The United States, although regularly represented at the bank's meetings, did not occupy the two seats to which it is entitled on the board from World War II until September 1994, at which time the chair of the Board of Governors of the U.S. Federal Reserve System and the president of the Federal Reserve Bank of New York were seated. The Board currently numbers 17: 6 ex officio central bankers from Belgium, France, Germany, Italy, United Kingdom, and United States; 6 named by the ex officio members; and 5 elected. (The BIS statutes provide for up to nine elected governors.)

Working closely with the bank is the privately funded Group of 30, made up of leading central and commercial bankers, who meet periodically to discuss trends within the international banking community.

Activities. Although created to play a role in international settlements, the bank today functions in a variety of capacities. First, it aids member central banks in managing and investing their monetary reserves. Second, it is a major research center, as evidenced by the influence of its annual report in international monetary circles and by its role in collecting and distributing statistical data on international banking and monetary trends. Third, it provides a cooperative forum for central bankers and representatives of international financial institutions. In addition, the BIS acts as or hosts the secretariats of the Markets Committee, formed in 1962 by the Group of 10 (G-10); the Committee on the Global Financial System (CGFS), which was set up in 1971 by the G-10 to track the functioning of financial markets; the Basel Committee on

Banking Supervision (BCBS), established in 1974 by the G-10; the G-10's Committee on Payment and Settlement Systems, dating from 1990; the International Association of Insurance Supervisors (IAIS), founded in 1994, with the Secretariat then being relocated to BIS headquarters in 1998; the Financial Stability Institute (FSI), established by the BCBS and the BIS in late 1998 to advance sound financial standards and practices; the Financial Stability Forum (FSF), formed in 1999; and, since May 2002, the International Association of Deposit Insurers (IADI). Since 1994 the BIS has also served as a "collateral agent," holding and investing collateral for those who purchased bonds issued by Brazil as part of its debt rescheduling. The bank has since taken on a similar role with regard to Peru (1997) and Côte d'Ivoire (1998).

A recent innovation has been bimonthly Global Economic Meetings, which are attended by central bankers from major emerging markets and from the Group of 10. In addition, throughout the year the BIS sponsors meetings that address such matters as financial security, information exchange, and information technology.

The BIS became caught up in 1997 in what a *New York Times* reporter called the "tangled web" of "Nazi gold" which had recently emerged as such a concern in Switzerland and other countries. As a collateral investigation prompted by Washington proceeded independently, BIS officials reported that their own internal review had revealed that a total of 13.5 tons of gold had been transferred to the bank by Nazi Germany, some of which had been re-smelted in an apparent effort to disguise its origin. To help clarify the situation, the BIS agreed to provide information to various investigators and opened its archives for inspection.

Another focus of recent international attention has been the deliberations of the BCBS regarding a New Capital Accord ("Basel II") that would revise risk criteria for determining how much capital banks should hold. A long-awaited draft framework was issued in January 2001, but five months later the BCBS decided to postpone implementation from 2004 until 2005, in part so it would have sufficient time to examine some 250 sets of comments on the proposals. Ultimately, the completed Basel II accord was not released until April 2003, with implementation expected in two phases, one by the end of 2006, and the second by the end of 2007. The measures set forth rigorous criteria for data collection, systems integration, and management that were expected to be expensive and challenging to meet; however, implementation was expected to benefit banks by permitting them to hold less capital to cover operational, credit, and market risks.

The Annual Report issued by the BIS provides an analysis of world economic conditions and problems in addition to summarizing the bank's activities during its fiscal year (April–March).

The 73rd BIS Annual Report (April 2002–March 2003) cited a net profit of 362 million gold francs ($103 million) and total assets of 92.8 billion gold francs ($180 billion, up from $148 billion in 2001) as of March 2003. The report struck a cautious note on the state of the world economy, however, warning of possible deflation if the growth rate did not quicken.

The 74th Annual Report (April 2003–March 2004), while noting a generally improving economic climate, warned against excessive consumer debt, particularly that fueled by cash-out of home equity in the United States and Europe. The report also noted the extent to which the United States' current account deficit was financed by foreigners. For this and subsequent reports the bank switched from reporting in Swiss gold francs to reporting in Special Drawing Rights (SDRs). The SDR is a valuation based on a basket of currencies, and was created by the IMF in 1969 to support the now-defunct Bretton Woods fixed exchange rate system. It has been little used in recent years, but the BIS regards it as an efficient yardstick against which to measure any currency. The 74th report showed assets of SDR million 167,934.80, as against a sum restated in SDRs as 149,619.3 for the previous year. Liabilities were SDR million 158,324.80 as against a restated 140,690.10.

The 75th Annual Report (April 2004–March 2005) noted that the world's major economies were generally growing well, with deflation no longer a concern. Competition for natural resources, however, was beginning to affect the world economy. The report encouraged the United States to get its current account debt more under control. It reported assets of SDR million 180,486.40 and liabilities of SDR million 170,223.10. In September 2005 the bank was instrumental in recovering funds of the former Nigerian dictator Sani Abacha from Swiss banks and returning them to Nigeria.

The bank also issues quarterly reports, and those for December 2005 and March 2006 are somewhat less optimistic about the world monetary outlook. They note a continued rise in asset prices and warn against inflation.

BENELUX ECONOMIC UNION

Union Economique Benelux
Benelux Economische Unie

Established: By Customs Convention signed September 5, 1944, in London, England; entered into force November 16, 1944, becoming fully effective January 1, 1948; present organization created by treaty signed February 3, 1958, in The Hague, Netherlands, effective November 1, 1960.

Purpose: To develop closer economic links among member states; to ensure a coordinated policy in economic, environmental, financial, tourist, transport, and social fields; and to promote a common policy in foreign trade, particularly with regard to the exchange of goods and services with developing countries.

Headquarters: Brussels, Belgium.

Principal Organs: Committee of Ministers, Interparliamentary Consultative Council, Council of the Economic Union, Economic and Social Advisory Council, Benelux Court of Justice, General Secretariat.

Secretary General: Dr. B. M. J. Hennekam (Netherlands).

Membership (3): Belgium, Luxembourg, Netherlands.

Official Languages: French, Dutch.

Origin and development. The origins of the Benelux Economic Union can be traced to 1930 when Belgium, Luxembourg, and the Netherlands concluded a convention with Denmark, Norway, Sweden, and Finland setting forth a joint intention to reduce customs autonomy. In 1932 the Belgium-Luxembourg Economic Union (founded in 1922) and the Netherlands concluded the Convention of Ouchy, by which the three governments agreed not to increase reciprocal customs duties, to reduce import duties, and to eliminate existing commercial restrictions as soon as possible. An impasse of ten years followed, largely because of international tensions and the opposition of several countries to the loss of most-favored-nation status, but in October 1943 in London, England, the three governments in exile concluded an agreement designed to regulate payments and strengthen economic relations after the conclusion of World War II. In September 1944 in London, the same three signed the Dutch-Belgium-Luxembourg Customs Convention, which entered into force November 16, 1944, although economic disparities caused by the war delayed full implementation until January 1948. In June 1953 the governments adopted a protocol embracing social and economic policies, while an additional protocol setting forth a common commercial policy soon followed. Thus the Benelux Treaty of 1958 served primarily to codify agreements that were already concluded.

Structure. The governing body of the union is the Committee of Ministers, which comprises at least three ministers from each member state: the ministers of foreign affairs, economic affairs, and finance. Meeting at least once every quarter, it supervises application of the treaty and is responsible for ensuring that treaty aims are pursued. Decisions are made unanimously.

The Benelux Interparliamentary Consultative Council, established by a convention signed November 5, 1955, predates the establishment of the present organization. The council's 49 members—21 each from Belgium and the Netherlands and 7 from Luxembourg—are chosen from the respective national parliaments. Recommendations by the council to the member states require a two-thirds majority vote; other decisions need only a simple majority.

The Council of the Economic Union, comprising senior officials from the member governments, serves as the principal administrative organ, with responsibility for ensuring implementation of decisions made by the Committee of Ministers and for recommending to the committee any proposals necessary for the functioning of the union. It also coordinates the activities of the union's numerous committees, special committees, and working parties and transmits their proposals, with its own comments, to the Committee of Ministers.

The Economic and Social Advisory Council consists of no more than 27 members (plus an equal number of deputies), one-third from representative social and economic institutions in each country. It may advance proposals on its own initiative to the Committee of Ministers and also renders advisory opinions on matters referred to it by the committee.

The Benelux Court of Justice was established May 11, 1974, in Brussels, Belgium. Comprised of senior judges from the member countries, it interprets common legal rules, either at the request of a national court, in which case the court's decisions are binding, or at the request of a member government, in which case the court serves only in a consultative capacity.

The General Secretariat is headed by a secretary general, always of Dutch nationality, and two deputy secretaries general, one from Belgium and the other from Luxembourg. It includes divisions for General Affairs, Internal Market and Economic Cooperation, Territorial Cross-Border Cooperation, Internal Affairs, and Language.

Activities. Benelux has facilitated the free movement of people, services, goods, and capital between member states by such measures as the abolition of passport controls and labor permits; the elimination of discrimination in regard to working conditions, social benefits, and the right to practice a profession; the removal of import duties and most quotas; and the banning of national discrimination in purchases by public bodies. It also levies uniform customs duties on products imported from non-European Union (EU) countries; acts as a single unit in concluding trade, immigration, and patent agreements with such countries; and operates as a caucus for the member countries, particularly prior to meetings of such intergovernmental economic organizations as the EU and the Organization for Economic Cooperation and Development (OECD). To further disencumber intra-Benelux trade, all internal border formalities have been conducted since 1984 through the use of a shortened form, the so-called Single Administrative Document (SAD), which was subsequently adopted throughout the EU's predecessor, the European Community (EC).

In 1985, Benelux concluded the Schengen Accord with France and West Germany permitting easier border crossing for both individuals and merchandise, while providing for enhanced cooperation in police and security matters. The goal was the elimination of nearly all controls at the internal borders of participating countries by 1990, although delays were encountered in that timetable as other states became signatories (see below). Coordination of the Schengen initiative was entrusted to the Benelux Secretariat.

Internally, Benelux has also focused on environmental concerns, including noise abatement, reduction in water and air pollution, and the creation of union-wide zoning maps. Cross-border cooperation between local authorities in other areas, such as fire, sewer, water, and telecommunication services, was also authorized by a convention that went into effect in 1987.

In May 1988 the Committee of Ministers endorsed a 1988–1992 work program calling for additional Schengen Accord implementation, further steps toward complete realization of the Benelux internal market, and joint action by Benelux members in larger intergovernmental organizations. Throughout 1988 discussion in Benelux organs focused on preparations for the proposed implementation of a single market by the EC on January 1, 1993, with Benelux perceiving itself as a pioneer in such integration and an important potential "motor" for the successful operation of the single market.

Another topic joined EC integration at the top of the Benelux agenda in 1989—the startling pace of political and economic change in Eastern Europe; in particular, the prospect of German unification contributed to a decision in late December to postpone the signing of the Schengen Accord's final convention. However, as the German picture clarified, momentum on the accord was reestablished, and a revised convention was signed June 19, 1990, by the five original signatories. Although border checks were to be lifted to provide free movement of people, the five nations agreed to tighten immigration and police controls and to establish common criteria for granting political asylum.

Italy signed the Schengen convention in November 1990, followed by Portugal and Spain in June 1991 and by Greece in November 1992. Although officials had hoped that, following ratification by the participants, the accord would be implemented on January 1, 1993, various complications arose in 1992 that made this target impossible to achieve. In part, the delay was attributable to the complexities of the ratification process of the EC's 1991 Maastricht Treaty, providing for enhanced political and monetary union of what was styled thereafter the EU. (The Schengen Accord was a collateral part of the Maastricht process, although Schengen cooperation would be "intergovernmental" rather than through established EU channels.) Meanwhile, Benelux pursued economic cooperation with a number of non-EU states, including the recently independent Baltic republics, the increasingly free-market oriented Visegrad group (Czech Republic, Hungary, Poland, and Slovakia), and members of the Association of Southeast Asian Nations (ASEAN).

The Schengen Accord was formally declared ready to enter into force in September 1993, even though ratification was not completed by Italy or Greece. However, the abolition of passport controls within the bloc was subject to a series of postponements because of technical problems with the Schengen Information System (SIS). Located on a police computer at Strasbourg, France, the SIS was intended to help control immigration from non-Schengen countries as well as assist in the fight against drug trafficking and other international crime. Several 1994 target dates proved impossible to meet, and the Schengen Accord eventually entered into force March 26, 1995, for a three-month trial period applicable to seven of the nine signatory states (the Benelux countries, France, Germany, Portugal, and Spain). The nonparticipants were Greece, in which ratification remained outstanding, and Italy, whose domestic ratification in October 1993 was not yet accepted by all other signatories; in both cases, moreover, software incompatibilities obstructed their participation in the SIS.

Austria signed the Schengen Accord on April 28, 1995, while on June 16 a framework agreement was concluded with Denmark, Finland, and Sweden under which they would be able to join the Schengen group without jeopardizing long-established freedom of movement among all five Nordic countries (i.e., including Norway and Iceland, both nonmembers of the EU). Full accession by these four countries would leave Britain and Ireland as the only EU members not to be Schengen signatories, the former out of preference and the latter because of the greater importance of preserving free movement between the republic and the United Kingdom. Difficulties encountered in the April–June 1995 trial period of the Schengen Accord included the refusal of the French authorities to allow cross-border "hot pursuit" of suspected criminals in France, on the grounds that the necessary domestic legislation had not been enacted. After reviewing these and other problems, a meeting of the Schengen executive committee on June 29 rejected a French request for a six-month extension of the trial period, declaring that the accord was "irrevocably in force," whereupon France invoked a clause allowing it to maintain border controls unilaterally for reasons of special national interest.

On January 1, 1997, the Nordic countries (Denmark, Finland, Iceland, Norway, and Sweden) acceded to the Schengen Accord, Iceland and Norway having concluded Cooperation Agreements that allowed them to participate despite their non-EU status. The Greek Parliament ratified the accord the following July, while Austria, Germany, and Italy announced they would implement the Schengen provisions in 1998. Meanwhile, all three Benelux countries received European Commission endorsement for participation in the launching of the EU's Economic and Monetary Union in 1999.

Responsibility for Schengen matters officially passed to the EU under the Schengen Protocol of its 1997 Treaty of Amsterdam, which entered into effect May 1, 1999. Adoption of the treaty necessitated revision of the arrangements permitting Norwegian and Icelandic participation, and on May 18 a replacement "association" agreement was concluded. Full Schengen participation by the Nordic countries was inaugurated March 25, 2001. The United Kingdom and Ireland have been permitted to implement selected Schengen provisions, such as those involving cross-border crime and illegal immigration.

The Benelux countries continue to advocate for even stronger EU institutions and closer cooperation. At the same time, they have focused their attention within Benelux on eliminating remaining obstacles in the "internal market," such as those caused by lack of harmonization in national laws; coordinating Benelux implementation of new EU regulations; and fostering cooperation in such areas as standardization and certification and intellectual property. Cross-border cooperation has also taken on increased importance with regard to town and country planning, the interactions of local authorities, the environment, transport and distribution, and the status and problems of transfrontier workers.

In May 2003, with major expansion of the EU only a year away, Dutch foreign minister Jaap de Hoop Scheffer joined his Czech counterpart Cyril Svoboda in promoting close cooperation between the Benelux and Visegrad Four countries. Their stance reflected concern among many of the smaller current and prospective EU states that their voices would carry less weight under contemplated changes in EU institutions.

April 2004 saw a series of accords designed to improve standardization and harmonize cooperation of police activity in the three countries. The provisions were to be phased in on an ad hoc basis over the next two years, with final implementation due in January 2007.

On November 30, 2005, the Benelux countries renewed an expiring 1999 treaty concerning a common approach to development and the mobility of commerce in the Rhine-Scheldt estuary. This treaty will remain in force until 2011.

CENTRAL EUROPEAN INITIATIVE (CEI)

Established: By agreement signed January 28, 1992, in Vienna, Austria, pursuant to earlier regional cooperation framework inaugurated November 11, 1989, in Budapest, Hungary, and known successively as the "Quadragonale," the "Pentagonale," and the "Hexagonale."

Purpose: To coordinate the implementation of joint projects in fields where advantage can be obtained from the regional harmonization of policies.

Headquarters: Trieste, Italy.

Principal Organs: Meeting of Heads of Government, Conference of Foreign Ministers, Committee of National Coordinators, Executive Secretariat.

Director General: Harold Kreid (Austria).

Membership (17): Albania, Austria, Belarus, Bosnia and Herzegovina, Bulgaria, Croatia, Czech Republic, Hungary, Italy, Macedonia, Moldova, Poland, Romania, Serbia and Montenegro, Slovakia, Slovenia, Ukraine.

Origin and development. On the initiative of the Italian foreign minister, Gianni De Michelis, the "Quadragonale" grouping was created in November 1989 by Austria, Hungary, Italy, and Yugoslavia. This became the "Pentagonale" in May 1990 with the accession of Czechoslovakia, and the "Hexagonale" in July 1991 with the accession of Poland. The initial aim of the grouping was to promote economic and cultural cooperation; however, the dramatic post-1989 political changes in Eastern and Central Europe gave it a new dimension as a vehicle for assisting the revival of democracy in former Communist states. It was also acknowl-

edged, by Italy in particular, that the grouping was intended to be a counterweight to the political and economic power of a united Germany.

In January 1992 the Hexagonale countries (minus Yugoslavia) established the CEI, which was joined later that year by Croatia, Slovenia, and Bosnia and Herzegovina, and by Macedonia in July 1993. Meanwhile, Czechoslovakia's membership had devolved to the Czech Republic and Slovakia on their establishment as separate states in January 1993. On the basis of decisions taken in late 1995, Albania, Belarus, Bulgaria, Romania, and Ukraine became CEI members in May 1996, with Moldova being admitted as the 16th member in November. The October 2000 change of government in the Federal Republic of Yugoslavia (now Serbia and Montenegro) led directly to that country's admission in November 2000.

Structure. The annual heads of government summit and foreign ministers' conferences determine the main areas of cooperation, the chair being held by the member states in turn for a calendar year. The Committee of National Coordinators acts as the link between CEI working groups and the member states. In general, the CEI has refrained from establishing formal institutional structures, and even a 1995 compromise decision to set up a Center for Information and Documentation in Trieste met with some resistance within the membership. The November 28–29, 1997, Meeting of Heads of Government (summit) in Sarajevo authorized conversion of the center into the current Executive Secretariat. Much of the organization's work is conducted through various working groups including agriculture; civil protection; combating organized crime; culture and education; energy;

environment; human dimension; human resource development and training; information and media; interregional and cross-border cooperation; migration; minorities; reconstruction and development; science and technology; small- and medium-size enterprises; tourism; transport; and youth affairs.

Financing for CEI infrastructural and other projects is provided by member states and by international institutions, including the World Bank, the European Bank for Reconstruction and Development (EBRD), the European Investment Bank, and the European Union's PHARE financing program for Eastern and Central European countries. (The acronym derives from the program's initial name, "Poland and Hungary: Action for the Restructuring of the Economy.") A secretariat for CEI projects operates within the EBRD, in London, United Kingdom.

Activities. Yugoslavia organized the Hexagonale summit July 26–27, 1991, in Dubrovnik, but the unfolding Yugoslav crisis resulted in the rump Yugoslav government being excluded when the grouping was reconstituted as the CEI in January 1992. Having unavailingly warned against the dangers of a breakup of the Yugoslav federation, the CEI subsequently admitted four ex-Yugoslav independent states to membership and sought to act as a forum for the resolution of regional conflicts. The July 18, 1992, CEI summit in Vienna appealed for international assistance to cope with the flow of refugees from former Yugoslavia into member states and urged the United Nations to defend the territorial integrity of Bosnia and Herzegovina.

A conference of CEI foreign ministers March 4–5, 1994, in Trieste witnessed clashes between Slovak and Hungarian representatives over the status of the ethnic Hungarian minority in Slovakia. At the fifth CEI summit, held July 15–16 in Trieste, foreign ministers approved a draft declaration on minority rights, intended to be binding on member states and described as going beyond the principles laid down by the Conference on Security and Cooperation in Europe (CSCE, subsequently the Organization for Security and Cooperation in Europe—OSCE) for the treatment of minorities. A CEI ministerial session held April 21–22, 1995, in

Krakow, Poland, condemned recent Serbian attacks on the Muslim-populated UN "safe area" in Biha, Bosnia and Herzegovina, and appealed to all sides of the conflict in that country to honor an extended cease-fire.

A session of CEI premiers and foreign ministers in Warsaw in October 1995 agreed in principle to expand the organization to other regional states, despite some resistance on the ground that the CEI's intended role as a stepping-stone to EU membership would be compromised. The inclusion of five new members (Albania, Belarus, Bulgaria, Romania, and Ukraine) was duly agreed by CEI foreign ministers meeting in late May 1996 in Vienna, in advance of a CEI summit in Rzeszów, Poland, the following month. A further summit in November in Graz, Austria, expanded membership to 16 countries by admitting Moldova; it also agreed to coordinate the fight against drug trafficking and money laundering and to seek cooperation with Russia on questions of an "all-European nature."

A CEI summit November 20–21, 1998, in Zagreb, Croatia, described EU expansion as the most important element in establishing regional stability, particularly in the troubled Balkan region. The CEI leaders also expressed their concern over developments in Kosovo and urged Serbian officials (accused of "ethnic cleansing" by the CEI foreign ministers the previous June) and the leaders of the ethnic Albanians to accept a negotiated settlement.

The November 5–6, 1999, summit in Prague, Czech Republic, was dominated by the situation in Kosovo, with the session's final document extending support to the UN Mission in Kosovo (UNMIK) and the efforts of the associated NATO-led Kosovo Force (KFOR) to maintain peace and security in the troubled province. At the same time, the summit participants expressed interest in the Federal Republic of Yugoslavia (FRY) ultimately joining the CEI. Another major topic of discussion was the recently adopted Stability Pact for South Eastern Europe, sponsored by the EU and grouping some 40 countries interested in helping the regional states "foster peace, democracy, respect for human rights and economic prosperity in order to achieve stability in the whole region."

The November 24–25, 2000, annual summit in Budapest, Hungary, featured the formal admission of the FRY, later known as Serbia and Montenegro, and reemphasized the "fundamental importance" of European integration and EU enlargement. The summit's concluding statement also indicated the CEI's willingness to contribute toward reopening the Danube to free navigation, called for settlement of the Transdnestrian question and the withdrawal of Russian troops from that Moldovan region, supported Ukraine's decision to shut down the final Chernobyl nuclear reactor in December, and encouraged maximum attention to environmental concerns and to enhanced assistance for CEI countries "in special need."

Since then, the CEI has moved forward with many initiatives. For example, meeting in March 2001 in Trieste, the member states' ministers of justice adopted the Trieste Declaration on Judicial Cooperation and Legislative Harmonization as part of their efforts to further cooperation in law enforcement and prosecution. A month later, the ministers of agriculture, meeting in Verona, Italy, focused their attention on food security and related matters. In June 2002 the organization launched a CEI Enterprise Program to support development of small- and medium-size enterprises in the Central and Eastern European states of Bosnia and Herzegovina, Bulgaria, Croatia, Macedonia, Moldova, Slovenia, Ukraine, and Yugoslavia. Other areas receiving attention have included port development, maritime transport in the North Adriatic, development of rail and road links between the eastern member states and western Europe, youth employment and sustainable development, and the role of minority media. In early 2003 preliminary efforts were under way to establish a CEI Parliamentary Assembly comprised of MPs from the member states.

The November 21–23, 2001, CEI summit, held in Trieste under heightened security, was highlighted by discussions related to international terrorism. Meeting in parallel, the associated fourth Summit Economic Forum (SEF), like its three predecessors, brought together business, economic, and political leaders from the member states as well as representatives of such multilateral institutions as the World Bank, the EBRD, and the EU's Stability Pact for a series of meetings that have taken on increasing importance. Discussions have focused on cooperation, exchanges, and investments.

The 2002 CEI summit, which convened November 13–15, in Skopje, Macedonia, emphasized the importance of further EU expansion, even beyond the anticipated May 2004 enlargement. In December 2002 the EU confirmed that Czech Republic, Hungary, Poland, Slovakia, and Slovenia were being offered membership. (Bulgaria and Romania were expected to accede in 2007.) Specific topics discussed at the summit included globalization and efforts to control international terrorism, crime, and illegal migration.

The 2003 summit and SEF, held November 19–21 in Warsaw, Poland, adopted a streamlined Plan of Action for 2004–2006; denounced international terrorism in general and, more specifically, the recent attacks in Istanbul, Turkey; and called for closer cooperation with the EU. The summit's Final Declaration noted that, following the 2004 EU expansion, the CEI would concentrate on helping its non-EU member states join the EU. This message was reinforced at the 2004 summit, held November 25–26 in Portoro, Slovenia, and at the 2005 summit, held November 25 in Piestany, Slovakia.

THE COMMONWEALTH

Established: By evolutionary process and formalized December 31, 1931, in the Statute of Westminster.

Purpose: To give expression to a continuing sense of affinity and to foster cooperation among states presently or formerly owing allegiance to the British Crown.

Commonwealth Center: The Secretariat is located in Marlborough House, London, which also serves as the site of Commonwealth meetings in the United Kingdom.

Principal Organs: Meeting of Heads of Government, Secretariat.

Head of the Commonwealth: Queen Elizabeth II.

Secretary General: Donald McKinnon (New Zealand).

Membership (53, with years of entry): Antigua and Barbuda (1981), Australia (1931), Bahamas (1973), Bangladesh (1972), Barbados (1966), Belize (1981), Botswana (1966), Brunei (1984), Cameroon (1995), Canada (1931), Cyprus (1961), Dominica (1978), Fiji (reentered 1997), Gambia (1965), Ghana (1957), Grenada (1974), Guyana (1966), India (1947), Jamaica (1962), Kenya (1963), Kiribati (1979), Lesotho (1966), Malawi (1964), Malaysia (1957), Maldives (1982), Malta (1964), Mauritius (1968), Mozambique (1995), Namibia (1990), Nauru (1999), New Zealand (1931), Nigeria (1960), Pakistan (reentered 1989, but suspended following military coup of October 1999; readmitted on May 22, 2004), Papua New Guinea (1975), St. Kitts-Nevis (1983), St. Lucia (1979), St. Vincent and the Grenadines (1979), Samoa (1970), Seychelles (1976), Sierra Leone (1961), Singapore (1965), Solomon Islands (1978), South Africa (reentered 1994), Sri Lanka (1948), Swaziland (1968), Tanzania (1961), Tonga (1970), Trinidad and Tobago (1962), Tuvalu (2000), Uganda (1962), United Kingdom (1931), Vanuatu (1980), Zambia (1964). (Zimbabwe, a member since 1980, withdrew in 2003.)

Working Language: English.

Origin and development. A voluntary association that gradually superseded the British Empire, the Commonwealth traces its origins to the mid-1800s, when internal self-government was first introduced in the colonies of Australia, British North America (Canada), New Zealand, and part of what was to become the Union of South Africa. The increasing maturity and independence of these overseas communities, particularly after World War I, eventually created a need to redefine the mutual relationships between the United Kingdom and the self-governing "dominions" that were collectively coming to be known as the "British Commonwealth of Nations." The Statute of Westminster, enacted by the British Parliament in 1931, established the principle that all members of the association were equal in status, in no way subordinate to each other, and united by allegiance to the Crown.

The original members of the Commonwealth, in addition to the United Kingdom, were Australia, Canada, the Irish Free State, Newfoundland, New Zealand, and the Union of South Africa. In 1949 Newfoundland became a province of Canada, and the Irish Republic became an independent state outside the Commonwealth. South Africa ceased to be a member upon becoming a republic in 1961 because of the opposition of the other Commonwealth countries to Pretoria's apartheid policies; however, it was readmitted June 1, 1994, following the installation of a multiracial government. Pakistan withdrew in 1972 but rejoined in 1989, although its membership was suspended in response to the coup of October 1999.

The ethnic, geographic, and economic composition of the Commonwealth has been modified fundamentally by the accession of former colonial territories in Asia, Africa, and the Western Hemisphere. This infusion of racially non-white and economically less developed states had significant political implications, including modification of the Commonwealth's unwritten constitution to accommodate the desire of many new members to renounce allegiance to the British Crown and adopt a republican form of government. In 1949 the pattern was set when Commonwealth prime ministers accepted India's formal declaration that, on becoming a republic, it would accept the Crown as a symbol of the Commonwealth association and recognize the British sovereign as head of the Commonwealth. The movement toward a multicultural identity was solidified by the Declaration of Commonwealth Principles adopted by the heads of government at their 1971 Singapore summit. In addition to acknowledging the organization's diversity, the Singapore Declaration enumerated a set of common principles, including the primacy of international peace and order; individual liberty regardless of racial, ethnic, or religious background; people's "inalienable right to participate by means of free and democratic processes in framing the society in which they live"; opposition to "colonial domination and racial oppression"; and the "progressive removal" of wide disparities in wealth and living standards.

The new thrust was further evidenced by a North-South summit in October 1981, which reflected that most Commonwealth members were developing countries. Subsequently, a 1982 report, *The North-South Dialogue: Making It Work*, proposed many institutional and procedural reforms to facilitate global negotiations on development and related issues, and a 1983 document, *Towards*

a New Bretton Woods, proposed short-, medium-, and long-range changes to enhance the efficiency and equity of the international trading and financial system.

A declaration in October 1987 that Fiji's Commonwealth status had lapsed followed two successive coups, abrogation of the country's constitution, and proclamation of a republic. Readmission required the unanimous consent of the Commonwealth members, and Fiji's application remained blocked until mid-1997 by India on the grounds that appropriate constitutional recognition had yet to be given to the island's Indian population. Fiji was finally readmitted effective October 1, 1997, following the adoption of a new constitution in July, but its membership was suspended in May 2000 following displacement of the elected government. Full participation was restored in late 2001, following democratic elections in August through September.

The October 1991 summit in Harare, Zimbabwe, was noteworthy for the adoption of a declaration redefining the Commonwealth's agenda. The Harare Declaration, drafted under the guidance of a ten-member High Level Appraisal Group, committed all Commonwealth countries, regardless of their political or economic conditions, to promote democracy, human rights, judicial independence, equality for women, educational opportunities, and the principles of "sound economic management."

In a departure from precedent, membership was granted on November 13, 1995, to Mozambique, even though it had never been a British colony and was not at least partly English speaking. A "unique and special" case regarding Mozambique had been presented by its Anglophone neighbors because of regional trade concerns. In 1999 Nauru became the 53rd full member of the Commonwealth after 31 years as a special member, and Tuvalu, also a special member (from 1978), became the 54th full member in 2000. In 2005 Nauru resumed its status as a special member, a category of membership available to very small countries.

In March 2002 Zimbabwe's participation in Commonwealth meetings was suspended as a consequence of a widely condemned presidential election earlier in the month. In response to its continued suspension, Zimbabwe withdrew effective December 7, 2003.

Structure. One of the least institutionalized intergovernmental organizations, the Commonwealth was virtually without permanent machinery until the establishment of its Secretariat in 1965. The symbolic head of the organization is the reigning British monarch, who serves concurrently as constitutional sovereign in those member states that still maintain their traditional allegiance. Since World War II, the heads of government have held biennial meetings, and specialized consultations occur periodically among national ministers responsible for such fields as foreign affairs, defense, finance, education, agriculture, health, trade, legal affairs, science and the environment, and women's and youth affairs. National finance ministers normally convene in the nearest convenient Commonwealth site on the eve of the annual fall meetings of the International Monetary Fund and World Bank to discuss monetary and economic issues.

The Secretariat organizes meetings and conferences, collects and disseminates information on behalf of the membership, and is responsible for implementing collective decisions. The secretary general, who currently serves a four-year term, is assisted by three deputies with responsibilities for political affairs, economic and social development, and development cooperation. Since its reorganization in 2002, the Secretariat has encompassed nine divisions: Communications and Public Affairs, Corporate Services, Economic Affairs, Gender and Human Resources Development, Governance and Institutional Development, Legal and Constitutional Affairs, Political Affairs, Science and Technology, and Special Advisory Services. The organization's technical assistance program is financed primarily through the Commonwealth Fund for Technical Cooperation (CFTC).

The fund is supported by all Commonwealth countries on a voluntary basis, and its governing body includes representatives of all contributors. In addition, a Commonwealth Equity Fund, designed to encourage private sector investment in the emerging stock markets of developing countries, was launched in 1990 and was followed in 1995 by formation of a Commonwealth Private Investment Initiative (CPII). The latter was established to help geographic regions attract capital for small- and medium-sized ventures and for former state enterprises that were being privatized. The first CPII investment fund, for Sub-Saharan Africa, was established in 1996, and others followed. On the political front, a Commonwealth Ministerial Action Group (CMAG) was created in November 1995 to provide guidance toward "good governance" in countries undergoing transition to democracy.

The autonomous Commonwealth Foundation, the formation of which was authorized by the Commonwealth heads of government in 1965, supports nongovernmental organizations, professional associations, and other such bodies. Known informally as the "unofficial Commonwealth," the foundation directs its attention to "inter-country networking, training, capacity-building, and information exchange." The Commonwealth of Learning, likewise authorized by the heads of government and located in Vancouver, Canada, was established in 1987 to promote distance learning and thereby improve access to education and training. Some three dozen additional Commonwealth associations, institutes, councils, and other groups were also established over the years, largely to promote development or disseminate information in such fields as forestry, health, telecommunications, education, journalism, law, and sports. Most are based in London.

Activities. The Secretariat's divisions oversee Commonwealth activities. Among the most prominent, the Political Affairs Division participates in organizing Commonwealth Heads of Government Meetings (CHOGMs), conducts research, aids various committees in their tasks, and monitors political issues and developments of importance to Commonwealth members. Since 1990 its observer missions have also monitored election campaigns, preparations for balloting, and elections in some two dozen Commonwealth countries around the globe, and in 1999 it drafted a "Framework for Principles for Promoting Good Governance and

Combating Corruption." The Economic Affairs Division conducts research and analysis and supports expert groups in such areas as North–South economic relations, protectionist tariffs, reform of the international financial system, debt management, and youth unemployment. Its purview also includes environmental concerns and sustainable development. In the area of technical assistance and development, CFTC provides training, expertise, and advice in the promotion of economic growth, public sector reform, poverty alleviation, infrastructural and institutional development, and capacity building. A Commonwealth Youth Program likewise funded through voluntary contributions, is an effort to encourage youth participation in economic and social development. Among more recent innovations, in 1995 the heads of government endorsed a Commonwealth Plan of Action on Gender and Development.

During the 1980s and early 1990s, the Commonwealth was most prominently identified with its efforts to end apartheid in South Africa, although debate frequently raged within the organization over tactics, especially the imposition of sanctions. Accordingly, the formal readmission of South Africa at midyear was the highlight of 1994, newly elected South African President Nelson Mandela hailing the "sterling contribution" of the grouping to the installation of a nonracial government in Pretoria.

The heads of government meeting held November 8–13, 1995, in Auckland, New Zealand, was dominated by discussion of recent events in Nigeria, which resulted in the suspension of Nigeria's membership and the launching of efforts (ultimately largely unsuccessful) by the Commonwealth to influence the actions of the military regime in Abuja. The governments of Gambia and Sierra Leone were also criticized for their perceived failure to support genuine democratization; the summit established CMAG in part to "guide" developing Commonwealth countries toward abiding by the principles enunciated in the 1991 Harare Declaration.

Nigeria, Gambia, and Sierra Leone were also major topics at the 1997 Commonwealth heads of government meeting held in Edinburgh, Scot-

land. While praising the role Nigeria played in the Liberia conflict, the summit decided to continue the former's suspension because of ongoing human rights abuses and the suppression of democracy by the government. The summit also indicated it might impose sanctions if they would help move Nigeria toward democracy. Sierra Leone was also suspended (until the restoration of President Tejan Kabbah's government in March 1998), and the summit called on Commonwealth members to support the UN and ECOWAS sanctions imposed on that country. In contrast, the government in Gambia was praised for having made progress toward genuine democratization.

Another focus of attention at the summit was the promotion of economic prosperity. The heads of government adopted the Edinburgh Commonwealth Economic Declaration, which called for continued global economic integration with greater attention to the smaller, less developed countries that believed they were being "left behind." To assist the smaller countries, the Commonwealth leaders agreed to support efforts to develop a successor to the Lomé Convention (see European Community section of European Union article), to offer duty-free access to certain markets, and to establish a Trade and Investment Access Facility (TIAF) with initial funding from Australia, Canada, New Zealand, and the United Kingdom. The Commonwealth leaders also endorsed establishing a Commonwealth Business Council, which would meet every two years to ensure that the voice of the "business community" was heard.

In October 1998 CMAG concluded that the Nigerian government had taken enough steps toward democracy to warrant a lifting of sanctions and a resumption of Nigerian participation in some Commonwealth activities. Full participation was restored May 29, 1999, following presidential elections the previous February. In other activities during the year, a Commonwealth ministerial mission lobbied leading providers of aid and loans to developing countries on behalf of small island states, arguing they deserved special consideration because of their extreme exposure to outside political, economic, and environmental forces.

At the November 12–15, 1999, Commonwealth summit in Durban, South Africa, the organization established a ten-member High-Level Review Group (HLRG) comprising the heads of government of Australia, India, Malta, Papua New Guinea, Singapore, South Africa, Tanzania, Trinidad and Tobago, United Kingdom, and Zimbabwe. The HLRG was assigned the task of recommending how the Commonwealth could best meet 21st century challenges. Issues facing the organization included what measures to take in response to corrupt governments and how to reconcile promotion of good governance with the principle of national sovereignty and noninterference in internal affairs. In this context, a number of Commonwealth countries called for expanding CMAG's mandate to allow firmer action where democratic practices were perceived as under threat—for example, in cases of arbitrarily postponed elections, restrictions on freedom of speech and the press, and evidence of persistent human rights violations. To date, such proposals have been met with less than unanimity, however, given that many Commonwealth countries have questionable records with regard to political pluralism and press independence.

Also at the Durban heads of government session, Donald McKinnon, former deputy prime minister and foreign minister of New Zealand, was elected to succeed Chief Eleazar Chukwuemea (Emeka) Anyaoku of Nigeria as secretary general, effective April 2000. McKinnon, who received wise praise for his role in resolving the Bougainville crisis in Papua New Guinea, subsequently indicated that his priorities would include obtaining debt relief for developing countries, promoting democracy, and facilitating technology transfers. The heads of government also confirmed Pakistan's suspension from Commonwealth activities in the wake of the previous month's coup in Islamabad.

Pakistan (like Fiji, Gambia, Sierra Leone, and the Solomon Islands) continued to be one of the countries on the CMAG agenda for 2001. Recent threatening events in Zimbabwe were also discussed at CMAG's March 19–20 session. Collaterally, HLRG established three working groups to consider the Commonwealth's political role, including conflict prevention and the mandate of CMAG; its developmental role, including how to reduce the "digital divide"; and Commonwealth governance and structures.

The CHOGM scheduled for October 2001 was postponed in the wake of the September 11 terrorist attacks in the United States and then rescheduled for March 2–5, 2002, in Coolum, Australia. The meeting's concluding declaration called for a rationalized and streamlined organizational structure, as HLRG's report recommended. Emphasis was also given to "people-centered economic development," good governance and human rights, efforts to bridge the widening gap between rich and poor, and the elimination of terrorism. (Some African participants, however, although condemning the September 11 al-Qaida attacks, expressed concern that the definition of terrorism was too closely tied to U.S. and Western concerns and ignored, for example, that a number of present-day African leaders had themselves been branded as terrorists during the colonial and apartheid eras.) In addition, the assembled heads of government voiced support for the New Partnership for Africa's Development (Nepad), which was launched in 2001 under the auspices of the Organization of African Unity (OAU), and endorsed a new assistance effort for small states. Countries continuing under CMAG scrutiny included Fiji, Pakistan, the Solomon Islands, and Zimbabwe.

In keeping with a summit recommendation that they pursue more active consultations, the Commonwealth foreign ministers convened for the first time in September 2002, during the opening days of the annual UN General Assembly session in New York. At that time the ministers agreed to hold annual meetings.

The next CHOGM, which was held December 5–8, 2003, in Abuja, Nigeria, was dominated by the Zimbabwe issue. Although many African states argued that the Mugabe government could best be engaged by lifting the suspension, opponents prevailed. The Commonwealth proceeded to form a balanced committee of leaders from Australia, Canada, India, Jamaica, Mozambique, and South Africa to pursue "national reconciliation" in Zimbabwe and a rapid return of that country to full participation, but Zimbabwe's governing party quickly voted to terminate membership in the Commonwealth. In acknowledging the withdrawal, Secretary General McKinnon, who was elected to a second term at the CHOGM, expressed his hope that Zimbabwe would rejoin "in due course, as have other members in the past." Also at the CHOGM, membership applications from the Palestinian Authority, Rwanda, and Yemen were rejected.

Four and a half years after the military coup that brought Gen. Pervez Musharraf to power, Commonwealth ministers decided to restore full membership to Pakistan at a May 2004 meeting in London. Ministers insisted that General Musharraf uphold his pledge to step down as chief of the army by the end of the year and expected the country to move forward with democratic reforms. Some African nations, including Nigeria and Tanzania, objected to the readmission of Pakistan because they feared that military rulers, who thought that international sanctions could be reversed, might take power in other countries.

The marriage of Prince Charles, Queen Elizabeth's son and heir to the throne, to Camilla Parker Bowles in April 2005 had implications for the Commonwealth. The British Department of Constitutional Affairs stated on March 21 that Parker Bowles would automatically become queen when Charles became king, despite Charles's declarations to the contrary, unless parliaments of the UK and the Commonwealth countries of which the UK monarch was head of state all agreed to a change in the law. On March 23 the Commonwealth Secretariat announced that Charles would not automatically succeed Queen Elizabeth as head of the Commonwealth when he became king. Instead, the various Commonwealth heads of government would elect the next head of the Commonwealth. Appointing anyone other than the British monarch to this symbolic position would mark a substantial shift away from the organization's British and imperial roots.

The next CHOGM, which was held November 25–27, 2005, in Valletta, Malta, declared that Pakistan could remain a member in full standing as long as General Musharraf resigned from the military within two years. Ugandan President Yoweri Museveni was much criticized for the arrest on treason charges of Uganda's main opposition leader, Col. Kiza Besigye. The European Union received criticism for maintaining agricultural subsidies and for a 36 percent cut in the guaranteed price of sugar—a matter of great concern to Commonwealth Caribbean countries. The summit issued a Statement on Multilateral Trade, calling for agreement on trade subsidies at forthcoming World Trade Organization talks. The 2007 CHOGM meeting will take place in Uganda, unless Commonwealth members continue to question Museveni's policies.

COMMONWEALTH OF INDEPENDENT STATES (CIS)

Sodruzhestvo Nezavisimykh Gosudarstv

Established: During a meeting of 11 of the former constituent states of the Union of Soviet Socialist Republics in Alma-Ata (now Almaty), Kazakhstan, on December 21, 1991.

Purpose: To assist in the orderly transfer of governmental functions and treaty obligations of the former Soviet Union to its independent successor states; to promote coordinated policies in disarmament and national security; and to work toward economic unity among members.

Administrative Center: Minsk, Belarus.

Principal Organs: Council of Heads of State, Council of Heads of Government, Ministerial Councils, Interparliamentary Assembly, Joint Chiefs of Staff, Executive Committee.

Executive Secretary: Vladimir Rushailo (Russia).

Membership (11): Armenia, Azerbaijan, Belarus, Georgia, Kazakhstan, Kyrgyzstan, Moldova, Russia, Tajikistan, Ukraine, Uzbekistan.
    Associate Member (1): Turkmenistan.

Origin and development. Following acceptance on September 6, 1991, of the Baltic states' withdrawal from the Soviet Union, a proposal was advanced for the creation of an economic commonwealth of the remaining Soviet republics. The plan was endorsed by all 12 republics during a meeting on October 1–2 in Alma-Ata, Kazakhstan, although four (Azerbaijan, Georgia, Moldova, and Ukraine) abstained from signing a formal treaty in Moscow on October 18. Less than a month later, on November 14, agreement was reached on the formation of a Union of Sovereign States, which its principal advocate, USSR President Mikhail Gorbachev, characterized as a union of "confederal democratic states." However, the seven republican delegations that attended a subsequent meeting November 25 decided not to initial a draft treaty, returning it to their Supreme Soviets for more consideration. Ukraine's absence from the discussions cast further doubt as to the treaty's viability.

In a referendum December 1, Ukrainians voted overwhelmingly for independence, and one week later, in a highly symbolic meeting in Brest, Belarus, the Russian Federation and Belarus joined Ukraine in proclaiming the demise of the Soviet Union and the establishment of the Commonwealth of Independent States (CIS). On December 13 the five Central Asian republics of Kazakhstan, Kyrgyzstan, Tajikistan, Turkmenistan, and Uzbekistan agreed to join the CIS, which, with the additional endorsement of Armenia, Azerbaijan, and Moldova, was formally launched in Alma-Ata on December 21.

The Azerbaijan legislature voted against ratification of the accord in October 1992. However, following the June 1993 change of government in Baku, the legislature reversed its position, and Azerbaijan's membership was formalized at the

CIS summit in September. Georgia's membership, provisionally endorsed by national leaders in October 1993, was ratified by the Georgian Supreme Council in March 1994. Moldova's parliament ratified CIS membership in April 1994, reversing a negative vote on the question taken the previous August.

After the first six months of its existence, the viability of the CIS appeared in question because little effective action had been taken in economic, political, or military affairs. On the economic front, in seeming contradiction to their stated goal of cooperation, CIS members were preparing to introduce their own national currencies and had instituted numerous cross-border trade restrictions. The Commonwealth had also proved ineffective in resolving the fighting between Armenia and Azerbaijan over Nagorno-Karabakh, ethnic conflict in Moldova, and secularist–Islamic fundamentalist disputes in Central Asian republics.

Meanwhile, tension remained high between Russia and Ukraine, particularly over the status of Crimea and control of the Black Sea fleet. Ukraine was one of five countries (the others being Azerbaijan, Belarus, Kyrgyzstan, and Moldova) that declined to sign a CIS collective security treaty at a May 1992 summit in Tashkent, Uzbekistan. However, a certain CIS momentum appeared to develop following the June agreement between Russia and Ukraine on the Black Sea Fleet dispute (see article on Ukraine).

In March 1992, CIS members (except Azerbaijan, Moldova, and Ukraine) endorsed the creation of a joint CIS military command, which subsequently moved into the former Warsaw Treaty Organization headquarters in Moscow. CIS leaders also backed establishing CIS peacekeeping forces to assist in conflict prevention and resolution within and between member states, and in May most signed a Treaty on Collective Security. However, de facto control of both nuclear and regular forces remained in national hands. In 1993 the participating CIS defense ministers ended the joint military command, preferring less structured and, at least from the Russian perspective, less expensive efforts at military cooperation. In 1999 six

members of the CIS Collective Security Council—Armenia, Belarus, Kazakhstan, Kyrgyzstan, Russia, and Tajikistan, but neither Azerbaijan nor Uzbekistan—renewed their commitment to collective defense for an additional five years. Meeting on April 28, 2003, the six completed arrangements for formation of a separate Collective Security Treaty Organization—CSTO (*Organizacii Dogoora o Kollektivnoi Bezopasnosti*—ODKB). Turkmenistan downgraded its participation to associate status in 2005.

Structure. The Council of Heads of State (the supreme CIS body) and the Council of Heads of Government are required to meet at least every six and three months, respectively, although more frequent meetings were held during the CIS start-up period. In addition, CIS discussions regarding foreign affairs, defense, transportation, energy, the environment, and other areas have been regularly conducted at the ministerial level. Preparation for the various CIS meetings is the responsibility of a permanent administrative staff located in Minsk, Belarus.

An Interparliamentary Assembly was approved by seven CIS states (Armenia, Belarus, Kazakhstan, Kyrgyzstan, Russia, Tajikistan, and Uzbekistan) in April 1992. Subsequently, Azerbaijan, Georgia, Moldova, and Ukraine joined. Although the assembly's first meeting was held in September in Bishkek, Kyrgyzstan, St. Petersburg was subsequently designated its permanent home. The assembly is assisted by its own Secretariat.

In April 1999 the CIS Executive Secretariat was reorganized as the Executive Committee; the executive secretary was given the collateral title of chair of the Executive Committee. Many other organs were subsumed by the new committee, including the Interstate Economic Committee.

Activities. In July 1993 Belarus, Russia, and Ukraine agreed in principle to establish their own "single economic space," reflecting an apparent acknowledgment among the three regional "powerhouses" that effective CIS activity remained a distant prospect. Central Asian states also subsequently voiced concern over the Commonwealth's future, and in 1994 Kazakhstan, Kyrgyzstan, and

Uzbekistan formed a Central Asian Economic Union (CAEU).

Nevertheless, negotiations continued within the CIS, and later in 1994 enthusiasm for economic integration increased substantially. On September 9 the Council of Heads of Government endorsed the creation of an Interstate Economic Committee (IEC), described as the first CIS supranational executive body. Supporters of the proposal anticipated that the IEC would assume control of "transnational systems" (in the energy and communications sectors, for example), with the possible addition of certain industrial and financial corporations jointly owned by member states. They also projected that the new committee would coordinate an integration process that could proceed from a proposed monetary union to a CIS free trade zone and, ultimately, to a full-fledged common market. However, thorny issues remained unresolved, particularly the extent to which members would be willing to turn sovereign powers over to the IEC. (Ultimately, the CIS Executive Committee absorbed the IEC.)

Supporters of genuine economic cooperation were buoyed by the signing of a customs union between Belarus and Russia during the May 1995 CIS summit in Minsk. Meeting in Moscow in November, CIS heads of government signed integration agreements covering gas supplies, external relations, and scientific research, although Russian Prime Minister Viktor Chernomyrdin warned that a solution needed to be found to the problem of nonpayment of CIS members' energy supply debts to Russia. On the eve of the premiers' session, CIS defense ministers formalized their February agreement to create a unified air defense system, which was to be under Russian control and mainly financed by Russia.

Delegates to a CIS summit in Moscow agreed in January 1996 that sanctions should be imposed on the breakaway republic of Abkhazia to compel it to accept Georgian sovereignty; it also extended the mandates of the CIS peacekeeping forces in Abkhazia and Tajikistan. On March 29 the presidents of Russia, Belarus, Kazakhstan, and Kyrgyzstan, meeting in Moscow under CIS auspices, signed a treaty to create "a community of integrated states," i.e., a CIS customs union intended to provide an inner core of CIS members committed to integration.

The CIS enterprise appeared to lose momentum later in 1996 amid mounting criticism that CIS accords were not being implemented. A heads of state summit scheduled for December 1996 to mark the fifth CIS anniversary was postponed into 1997, apparently because of Russian President Boris Yeltsin's health problems, and a session of prime ministers in mid-January 1997 in Moscow was far from united on yet another CIS economic integration plan, which Azerbaijan, Georgia, Ukraine, and Uzbekistan declined to support as drafted. Divisions were also apparent at a meeting of CIS defense ministers later in the month. A majority called for the reinstatement of Gen. Viktor Samsonov as head of the CIS military cooperation staff, thus rejecting the nominee of President Yeltsin, who had removed General Samsonov from the CIS post the previous October upon appointing him chief of the Russian general staff.

Seeking to deflect charges that the CIS was dedicated to "paper creativity," Executive Secretary Ivan Korotchenya claimed in December 1996 that 365 of some 800 treaties and agreements signed within the CIS framework since December 1991 had been implemented, the others having encountered opposition from one or more member states.

The next CIS summit was finally held on March 28, 1997. Once again plans were endorsed by CIS members (with the exception of Georgia) for accelerated integration. The prime ministers of six CIS states also signed an agreement in early October called the "Concept for the Integrated Economic Development of the CIS," but little hope for implementation was provided by the subsequent CIS summit, held October 23 in Chişinău, Moldova. A number of CIS leaders reportedly criticized Russia for failing to provide strong leadership, while Russian leaders warned that excessive concerns with issues of national sovereignty were preventing other members from acting effectively within the CIS. CIS supporters also wondered whether the proliferation of smaller economic groupings among

CIS members was proving counterproductive to the goals of the parent grouping. Blocs included the Belarus-Russia union; the CIS Customs Union of Belarus, Kazakhstan, Kyrgyzstan, and Russia; the Central Asian Economic Community (CAEC, successor to the CAEU) of Kazakhstan, Kyrgyzstan, Tajikistan, and Uzbekistan; and the so-called GUAM grouping of Georgia, Ukraine, Azerbaijan, and Moldova. (Tajikistan joined the CIS Customs Union in February 1999, and the GUAM became the GUUAM after Uzbekistan's admission in April 1999. In February 2002 the participants of the CAEC agreed to reshape it as the Central Asian Cooperation Organization [CACO].)

At the April 1998 summit, entrepreneur Boris Berezovsky, a close political ally of Yeltsin's, was appointed as the Commonwealth's executive secretary. Berezovsky's tenure was short-lived, however, because he soon became a target of an anticorruption investigation in Russia. Yeltsin dismissed him in March 1999 and appointed Yury Yarov his successor a month later.

At the January 20, 2000, Moscow summit, Vladimir Putin, then the acting president of Russia, was elected to chair the Council of Heads of State. The June 20–21 summit in Moscow voiced support for the 1972 Anti-Ballistic Missile Treaty, which CIS saw as threatened by efforts in the United States to implement a national missile defense, and at a meeting on November 30–December 1 in Minsk CIS leaders agreed to move forward with establishment of an antiterrorism center in Moscow. An earlier decision ended the peacekeeping mandate in Tajikistan as of September 16, although the mission in the Georgian region of Abkhazia remained active.

On October 10, 2000, the five constituent states of the CIS Customs Union signed a treaty in Astana, Kazakhstan, authorizing conversion of the organization into the Eurasian Economic Community (EAEC), effective April 2001. EAEC decisions require a two-thirds vote of approval for passage but are then binding on the members. Using a weighted system, Russia was assigned 40 percent of the voting power; Belarus and Kazakhstan, 20 percent each; and Kyrgyzstan and Tajikistan, 10 percent

each. Initial goals of the EAEC, which is modeled on the European Economic Community, were to harmonize tariff and taxation policies, employment regulations, and visa regimes. Armenia, Moldova, and Ukraine have observer status in the EAEC.

Meeting in Yerevan, Armenia, May 25, 2001, the presidents of the six states of the CIS Collective Security Council agreed to move ahead on formation of a 3,000-troop rapid reaction force to be headquartered in the Kyrgyz capital. In recent years the CIS has frequently expressed concern over activities by Islamic extremists in Central Asia. At the Yerevan meeting the heads of state also condemned terrorism, organized crime, and drug trafficking. The session was followed by a full CIS summit on May 31–June 1 in Minsk, where the focus of attention was progress toward establishment of a much-delayed free trade zone.

At an informal summit held on August 1, 2001, in Sochi, Russia, Russian President Putin identified mutual economic concerns as "the sole basis for developing cooperation in all spheres" and described the EAEC, the GUUAM, the CAEC, and similar CIS-related offspring as complementary to the CIS and "a sort of laboratory" where various initiatives could be tested before wider introduction. Putin cautioned, however, that policies adopted by these less-encompassing groups should not interfere with the collective interests of the Commonwealth.

The organization's focus turned once again to terrorism in the wake of the September 11, 2001, al-Qaida attacks against the United States. Particular emphasis was given to closer coordination on counterterrorism and on border security. The most significant shift in policy, however, may have been Russian acquiescence in the positioning of U.S. forces in Central Asia during the U.S.-led "war on terrorism." In connection with the effort to root out terrorist bases in Afghanistan and oust the Taliban regime, Uzbekistan and Kyrgyzstan, in particular, permitted the entry of U.S. contingents. The U.S. military presence was not met with universal acceptance by CIS member states, however, nor was U.S. military assistance in Georgian counterterrorism training. In August 2005 the United States was ordered to vacate its bases in Uzbekistan, and the last U.S. forces were gone by the end of the year.

The tenth anniversary CIS summit in Moscow on November 29–30, 2001, identified stable development and "dignified integration" into the world community as principal Commonwealth goals. President Putin once again lent support to creation of a single economic zone, encouraged respect for minority rights (with an eye toward the millions of Russians living in the former Soviet republics), and defined the regional role of the CIS as that of "unifying, coordinating, and stabilizing."

In April 2002 the six parties to the Collective Security Treaty met in Almaty, Kazakhstan, in furtherance of joint efforts against terrorism, drug smuggling, and illegal immigration. The session concluded with agreement on establishing a more formal security structure and was immediately followed by military exercises involving the Collective Rapid Reaction Forces. Plans for the new security organization were further advanced at the October 6–7, 2002, CIS summit in Chişinău, where the treaty participants signed a charter for the organization. In other business, the summit continued to emphasize efforts against terrorism and the drug trade, discussed measures to boost flagging interstate CIS trade, and reappointed Executive Secretary Yarov for another three-year term.

Meeting on April 28, 2003, in Dushanbe, Tajikistan, the presidents of Armenia, Belarus, Kazakhstan, Kyrgyzstan, Russia, and Tajikistan formally established the Collective Security Treaty Organization and named Nikolai Bordyuzha of Russia as its first secretary general. The CSTO's headquarters in Moscow began functioning at the beginning of 2004. One of the organization's principal assignments was identified as management of the rapid reaction forces.

A CIS summit on September 18–19, 2003, in Yalta, Ukraine, saw the presidents of Belarus, Kazakhstan, Russia, and Ukraine reach agreement on formation of a "Single Economic Space" (SES) that would ultimately harmonize customs, tariff, transport, and related regimes. Although all other CIS members were eligible for membership, some viewed the development with chagrin. Moldovan

President Vladimir Voronin, for one, noted that the agreement once again highlighted a lack of unity within the CIS, and he indicated that as a consequence Moldova "should make the move to more decisive action in the direction of the European Union."

As the SES initiative moved forward in 2004, various disputes arose over the adoption of a single economic agreement for the CIS. Ultimately, the CIS decided to adopt 61 separate agreements to be reviewed at a summit in Yalta in September, when several were signed.

Other fractious issues arose over SES members' move to try to join the World Trade Organization as a single entity. Because of differences that could not be resolved, the members instead decided to approach the WTO separately.

The CIS heads of government met in April 2004 and supported creation of a CIS Reserve Fund, which would help member states in the event of natural disasters. The following month CIS defense ministers met in Armenia and agreed to form a CIS peacekeeping force, and in June they drafted a document that encouraged the CIS and NATO to cooperate in managing a peacekeeping force under UN mandate. Because of increasing concerns about terrorism and border control (and to bolster military cooperation among members), the Secretariat of Defense Ministers was increased from 10 members to 21 in August 2005.

The 38th CIS summit on September 16, 2004, in Astana, Kazakhstan, focused primarily on security and economic issues; the group issued a statement on the fight against international terrorism and vowed to step up the work of the CIS antiterrorist center. A summit on August 16, 2005, in Kazan, Tatarstan, also included adoption of antiterrorism documents but marked the departure of Turkmenistan from full membership. Turkmenistan, which expressed its preference for establishing its international neutrality, remained an associate member. Holding the summit in Kazan was seen as a sign of Tatarstan's increasing independence within the Russian Federation. Meanwhile, internal problems arising from dramatic changes of government in the region—the "rose revolution" in Georgia in 2003, the "orange revolution" in Ukraine in 2004, and the "tulip revolution" in Kyrgyzstan in 2005—did not bode well for the organization's future. President Putin increasingly seemed to see the West as a rival rather than a partner and began to exploit politically Russia's position as a supplier of oil and natural gas. During the winter of 2005–2006 huge increases in the price of natural gas caused outrage and recrimination in such Western-leaning CIS members as

Ukraine and in the EU. There were reports in May 2006 that Georgia and Ukraine were planning to leave CIS, which prompted Russian energy officials to threaten adverse consequences. The EAEC admitted Uzbekistan as a member at a January 2006 summit in St. Petersburg and decided to absorb the CACO to eliminate institutional duplication and more efficiently pursue common objectives and activities related to currency, customs, and a potential free trade area.

COUNCIL OF EUROPE

Conseil de l'Europe

Established: By statute signed May 5, 1949, in London, England, effective August 3, 1949; structure defined by General Agreement signed September 2, 1949.

Purpose: To work for European unity by strengthening pluralist democracy and protecting human rights, seeking solutions to the problems facing European society, and promoting awareness of European cultural identity.

Headquarters: Strasbourg, France.

Principal Organs: Committee of Ministers, Parliamentary Assembly, Secretariat.

Secretary General: Terry Davis (United Kingdom).

Membership (46): Albania, Andorra, Armenia, Austria, Azerbaijan, Belgium, Bosnia and Herzegovina, Bulgaria, Croatia, Cyprus, Czech Republic, Denmark, Estonia, Finland, France, Georgia, Germany, Greece, Hungary, Iceland, Ireland, Italy, Latvia, Liechtenstein, Lithuania, Luxembourg, Macedonia, Malta, Moldova, Monaco, Netherlands, Norway, Poland, Portugal, Romania, Russia, San Marino, Serbia and Montenegro, Slovakia, Slovenia, Spain, Sweden, Switzerland, Turkey, Ukraine, United Kingdom.
    Observers to the Committee of Ministers (5): Canada, Holy See, Japan, Mexico, United States.
    Observers to the Parliamentary Assembly (3): Canada, Israel, Mexico.

Official Languages: English, French. German, Italian, and Russian are also working languages in the Parliamentary Assembly.

Origin and development. In 1946 Winston Churchill put forward his plan for a "United States of Europe," and an implementing program was subsequently drawn up in Hertenstein, Switzerland, by former European resistance fighters. International groups were quickly established, and one of the most important of these, the Union of European Federalists, joined Churchill's United Europe Movement, the Economic League for European Cooperation, and the French Council for United Europe to form an International Committee of Movements for European Unity. Under the leadership of Duncan Sandys of the United Kingdom, the committee organized the first Congress of Europe in The Hague, Netherlands, in May 1948, and called for the establishment of a European Assembly and other measures to unite Western Europe. Meanwhile, the signatories of the five-power Brussels Treaty of March 17, 1948, took up the proposals at the governmental level. These combined efforts came to fruition on May 5, 1949, when the foreign ministers of Belgium, Denmark, France, Ireland, Italy, Luxembourg, Netherlands, Norway, Sweden, and the United Kingdom met in London to sign the Statute of the Council of Europe.

    The organization was conceived as an instrument for promoting increased unity in Western Europe through discussion and, where appropriate, common action in the economic, social, cultural, scientific, legal, and administrative areas, and in the protection of human rights. Matters relating to national defense were specifically excluded from its scope. Greece, admitted in 1949, was obliged to withdraw in 1969 because of alleged violations of human rights by the Papadopoulos military government; it was readmitted in November 1974 after a change of government in July and the holding of parliamentary elections. Turkey's credentials were suspended in May 1981, in response to the military coup the previous September. In September 1983 the assembly also voted to bar members from the new Turkish legislature because of the unrepresentative character of their election. However, the action was rescinded in May 1985, following a report by the council's Political and Legal Affairs Committee that progress had been made over the last year in the restoration of democracy and respect for human rights.

In response to overtures from East European countries, the Parliamentary Assembly in May 1989 created a Special Guest of the Assembly status, which, following the collapse of communism and the breakup of the Soviet Union and Yugoslavia, became an intermediate stage toward full membership for most ex-Communist states, although the admission of some proved contentious because of issues related to human rights and regional conflicts (see Activities, below). Hungary became a full member in 1990, followed by Czechoslovakia and Poland in 1991; Bulgaria in 1992; Romania, Estonia, Lithuania, Slovenia, the Czech Republic, and Slovakia in 1993 (the last two as successors to Czechoslovakia); Latvia, Albania, Moldova, Ukraine, and Macedonia in 1995; the Russian Federation and Croatia in 1996; Georgia in 1999; Armenia and Azerbaijan in 2001; and Serbia and Montenegro in 2003. Meanwhile, Andorra was admitted in 1994 following its promulgation of a democratic constitution and multiparty elections in 1993.

Of the remaining nonmember European states, Belarus has applied for full membership but was suspended from special guest status in January 1997 because of its perceived undemocratic tendencies. A 1998 application for membership by Monaco was not approved because the principality's lack of a parliamentary opposition complicated its ability to guarantee a pluralist delegation. Election law changes followed by elections in February 2003 remedied the situation, and Monaco was admitted as a member on October 5, 2004. The Holy See has observer status.

Structure. The Committee of Ministers, comprised of the foreign ministers of all member states, considers all actions required to further the aims of the council. The decisions of the committee take the form either of recommendations to governments or of conventions and agreements, which bind the states that ratify them. The committee normally meets twice a year in Strasbourg. Most of its ongoing work, however, is performed by deputies who meet collectively almost weekly. Overall policy guidance has recently been provided by meetings of the heads of state and government.

The Parliamentary Assembly, the deliberative organ, can consider any matter within the competence of the council. Its conclusions, if they call for action by governments, take the form of recommendations to the Committee of Ministers. The members of the assembly are drawn from national parliaments and apportioned according to population, the states with the smallest populations having 2 seats and those with the largest, 18. (Countries granted Special Guest of the Assembly status have held seats, although without voting power.) The method of delegate selection is left to the national parliaments. Within the assembly all members participate not as state representatives but as individuals or as representatives of political groups; each delegation includes spokesmen from both the government and the opposition.

Assembly committees cover culture, science, and education; economic affairs and development; environment, agriculture, and local and regional affairs; equal opportunities for women and men; honoring of obligations and commitments by member states (Monitoring Committee); legal affairs and human rights; migration, refugees, and demography; political affairs; rules of procedure and immunities; and social, health, and family affairs. In addition, a joint committee comprises, in equal numbers, members of the assembly and a representative from each member government. A standing committee comprises the chairs of national delegations, the chairs of the general assembly committees, and the Bureau of the Assembly (the assembly president, 18 vice presidents, and leaders of the political groups). The president of the assembly is elected annually for a renewable term; normally he serves a total of three years.

Part of the council's work is carried out by specialized institutions, such as the European Court of Human Rights, the European Youth Foundation, the European Center for Global Interdependence and Solidarity (the North-South Center), the Social Development Fund, and the Congress of Local and Regional Authorities of Europe.

The council's many parliamentary, ministerial, and governmental committees and subsidiary groups are serviced by a Secretariat staff of some 1800 recruited from all member countries. The secretary general is elected by the assembly for renewable, five-year terms from a list of candidates proposed by the Committee of Ministers.

Activities. Except for matters of national and regional defense, the Council of Europe and the Parliamentary Assembly of the Council of Europe (PACE) conduct activities in every conceivable aspect of European political, social, and cultural life. For example, deputies responsible to the Council of Ministers participate in a plethora of rapporteur groups, working parties, and committees concerned with, among other issues, human rights, democratic stability, administrative and budgetary matters, legal cooperation, social and health questions, education and culture, institutional reforms, and relations with the European Union (EU), the Organization for Security and Cooperation in Europe (OSCE), and the Organization for Economic Cooperation and Development (OECD).

Among the most significant achievements of the council are the drafting and implementation of the European Convention for the Protection of Human Rights and Fundamental Freedoms. Signed in November 1950 and entering into force in September 1953, the convention set up the European Commission of Human Rights, comprised of independent lawyers from member states, to examine alleged violations by signatories and to attempt to broker negotiated settlements between the involved parties. A European Court of Human Rights was also established to consider cases in which those negotiations fail. Under the 11th protocol to the human rights convention, on November 1, 1998,

the commission was abolished, with all alleged violations proceeding directly to a new permanent court. The Council of Ministers then approved creation of the new post of Commissioner for Human Rights in May 1999.

In April 1983 a protocol calling for the abolition of capital punishment (except in time of war or threat thereof) was signed by 12 council members; it entered into force in February 1985 and as of January 2003 had been ratified by all member states except Armenia, Russia, and Turkey. An additional protocol, which entered into force in November 1988, seeks to protect the rights of aliens in cases of expulsion, the right of appeal in trial cases, the right of compensation for miscarriage of justice, the right not to be tried twice for the same offense, and the equality of spouses. The most recent additions to the 1950 convention, the 12th and 13th protocols, will enter into effect after ratification by ten members. Protocol No. 12, which was opened for signature November 4, 2000, provides a general protection against discrimination on the basis of sex; race; religion; ethnic, national, or social origin; and political or other opinions. Protocol No. 13, which extends the prohibition against capital punishment to acts committed during war, was opened for signature May 5, 2002, and entered into force on July 1, 2003.

Other landmark conventions include the European Cultural Convention (which entered into force in 1955); the European Convention for the Peaceful Settlement of Disputes (1958); the European Social Charter (1965); the European Convention on the Suppression of Terrorism (1978); the European Convention for the Prevention of Torture and Inhuman or Degrading Treatment or Punishment (1989); the Convention on Laundering, Search, Seizure, and Confiscation of Proceeds from Crime (1993); the Framework Convention for the Protection of National Minorities (1998); the Convention on Human Rights and Biomedicine (1999); and the European Convention on the Exercise of Children's Rights (2000).

Much of the council's attention in recent years has focused on defining its role among the continent's often overlapping organizations, particularly in regard to the "new Europe." It became the official coordinator of human rights issues for the Conference on Security and Cooperation in Europe (CSCE, subsequently the OSCE) following that body's institutionalization in 1990; it also assisted with the establishment of a CSCE Parliamentary Assembly in 1992, in accordance with the council's earlier proposal for an all-European representative forum. In addition, the council's program on democratic institutions has provided assistance to the emerging European democracies in the field of constitutional, legislative, and administrative reform. On the proposal of President Mitterrand of France, made to the Parliamentary Assembly in May 1992, the council held its first summit meeting of heads of state and government October 8–9, 1993 in Vienna, Austria, to consider structural reform of the organization.

Minority and political rights remained prominent council concerns in 1996, particularly in connection with new accessions to full membership. Opposition to Russia's admittance in the Parliamentary Assembly (over the Chechnya military operation and then the Communist victory in the December 1995 State Duma election) was eventually overcome early in 1996 on the strength of various Russian promises. The required two-thirds assembly majority was marshaled in January, with the Committee of Ministers moving swiftly to admit Russia the following month. Even more controversial was Croatia's application, which was approved by the assembly in April but, in an unprecedented move, deferred by the Committee of Ministers in light of concern about the democratic credentials of the Tudjman government and its commitment to the Dayton peace agreement for Bosnia and Herzegovina. On the basis of assurances from Zagreb, Croatia was eventually accorded formal membership in November, its admittance highlighting a recent trend away from insistence on pre-entry observance of council standards toward a policy of monitoring compliance after accession. However, the suspension of the special guest status of Belarus in January 1997 (because the new Belarus constitution adopted in November 1995 was seen as vesting excessive authority in the president)

indicated that basic council standards had not been relaxed.

The second summit of the council's heads of state and government was held October 10–11, 1997, in Strasbourg to pursue the "consolidation of democracy" on the continent and to reconfirm the council's "standard-setting" role in such areas as human rights. The summit's final declaration called on the Committee of Ministers to propose structural reform within the council to promote, among other things, social cohesion, the security of citizens (via programs designed to combat organized crime, government corruption, and terrorism), and cultural diversity within the context of respect for democratic values.

In January 1999, Lord Russell-Johnston, a former leader of the Scottish Liberal Democratic Party, was elected to a three-year term as president of the Parliamentary Assembly. The UK's Terry Davis was also nominated as the council's next secretary general, but in the June election he lost by two votes to Walter Schwimmer of Austria.

During the first half of 2000 renewed fighting in Chechnya generated not only a decision by the Parliamentary Assembly to suspend Russia's voting rights, but also calls for Russia's suspension from the full council. Moscow, in turn, threatened to withdraw from the organization. Admission of special guests Armenia and Azerbaijan proved almost as contentious, although both were formally welcomed in early 2001 on the strength of the argument that simultaneous admission would encourage democratization and resolution of the Nagorno-Karabakh dispute. At the same time, the PACE restored Russia's voting rights, although Moscow has continued to be criticized not only for its actions in Chechnya, but also for an alleged failure to adhere to principles of free speech and press.

On June 21–22, 2001, the council hosted the first world congress on abolition of the death penalty. The council has repeatedly criticized the United States, in particular, for executing convicted criminals and in mid-2001 threatened both the United States and Japan with suspension of their observer status if they did not take steps toward ending capital punishment. On July 1, 2003, Protocol No. 13 to the European human rights convention entered into effect, thereby making prohibition of capital punishment absolute.

The 109th session of the Committee of Ministers convened November 7–8, 2001. Immediately following the September 11 terrorist attacks on the United States, the council had vowed its support for the fight against terrorism and indicated it would consider updating the European Convention on Suppression of Terrorism. The organization also noted it would soon open for signature a Convention on Cyber-Crime and a Second Additional Protocol to the 1959 European Convention on Mutual Assistance in Criminal Matters. On September 25, however, the PACE offered a caution to the United States, describing the attacks as "crimes" rather than acts of war and urging Washington to seek UN Security Council approval before initiating reprisals. The PACE also proposed that the remit of the International Criminal Court (ICC), which the United States has not joined, be expanded to cover international terrorism.

The Convention on Cyber-Crime was opened for signature November 23, 2001, and was to enter into force after ratification by five council members. More than two-dozen member states (plus the United States, Japan, Canada, and South Africa) immediately signed the convention, which entered into force in July 2004.

Five months after the admission of Bosnia and Herzegovina on April 24, 2002, the PACE voted 122–6 in favor of admitting Yugoslavia as soon as its two constituent republics had completed ratification of a new constitution. (The Socialist Federal Republic of Yugoslavia's special guest status was suspended in November 1991; the successor Federal Republic of Yugoslavia was reinstated as a guest in January 2001.) Accordingly, the new "state union" of Serbia and Montenegro was admitted April 3, 2003. (In June 2006, Montenegro declared independence and will therefore have to apply for admission as a separate country.) In contrast, the PACE refused to restore the special guest status of Belarus, let alone approve its admission as a full member, because of lack of democratic progress.

In May 2003, PACE President Peter Schieder voiced concern over ongoing efforts by the United States to convince various countries in Southeast Europe to sign bilateral agreements exempting U.S. officials, military personnel, and nationals from ICC jurisdiction. Moreover, on the agenda for the June 23–27 PACE session was a report on the rights of prisoners held by the United States in Afghanistan or at its Guantanamo Bay, Cuba, base. Other notable reports prepared for the session discussed stem cell research and human organs trafficking. Debate at the summer session focused in part on a Convention on the Future of Europe and the Council of Europe.

Also in May 2003, the anticipated amendment to the suppression of terrorism convention was opened for signature, as was, in May 2005, a new Convention on the Prevention of Terrorism and a Convention on Laundering, Search, Seizure, and Confiscation of the Proceeds from Crime and on the Financing of Terrorism. At the same time the Convention on Action Against Trafficking in Human Beings was also opened.

At its May 16–17, 2005, summit in Warsaw, Poland, the council issued a declaration strengthening its commitment to all aspects of individual freedom and justice. The council established a presence in the fight against human trafficking, corruption, and computer crime. During 2005 and 2006 the council became involved in the controversy over reports that the United States was moving people suspected of terrorism for interrogation in countries in which torture was practiced, and that some Eastern European countries were cooperating with the U.S. Central Intelligence Agency (CIA) by holding such people in secret prisons. The council's special rapporteur, Dick Marty of Switzerland, declared in a June 6, 2006, report that at least 14 European governments were to some degree cooperating with, or at least turning a blind eye to, this program of "extraordinary rendition." His report stated there was clear evidence of aircraft bearing such prisoners flying over and landing in Europe, with Spain, Turkey, Germany, and Cyprus providing "staging posts" for rendition operations, while the UK, Portugal, Ireland, and Greece were "stop-off points." He also stated that Bosnia, Italy, Macedonia, and

Sweden had allowed CIA abductions on their soil. The report also cited evidence for suspicion that Poland and Romania were harboring secret prisons in their territory, a charge that Romania immediately rejected as "speculation," and that the Polish prime minister, Kazimierz Marcinkiewicz, called "libelous."

On May 15, 2006, Russia rotated into the six-month chair of the council's Committee of Ministers. This caused controversy as many believed Russia's record on observing human rights and the rule of law was too weak to justify this position. The Russian response was that compliance was only a matter of time, rather than political will. Russia also complained that the council was trying to impose a pro-Western position on Belarus, where a pro-Russian candidate won a much-disputed presidential election that outside observers from the West declared was tainted by blatant fraud in favor of the incumbent candidate.

COUNCIL OF THE BALTIC SEA STATES (CBSS)

Established: March 5, 1992, by a meeting of foreign ministers of the ten Baltic states in Copenhagen, Denmark.

Purpose: To promote cooperation and coordination among all states bordering on the Baltic Sea or its main links to the open sea; to support new democratic institutions, economic development, humanitarian aid, energy and the environment, culture and education, and transportation and communication.

Headquarters: Stockholm, Sweden.

Principal Organs: Council of Ministers, Committee of Senior Officials, Commissioner of the CBSS on Democratic Development, Secretariat.

Director of Secretariat: Gabriele Kötschau (Germany).

Membership (12): Denmark, Estonia, European Commission, Finland, Germany, Iceland, Latvia, Lithuania, Norway, Poland, Russia, Sweden.

Observers (7): France, Italy, Netherlands, Slovakia, Ukraine, United Kingdom, United States.

Special Participants (6): Baltic Sea Parliamentary Conference, Baltic Sea Seven Islands Cooperation Network, Baltic Sea States' Sub-regional Cooperation, Conference of Peripheral Maritime Regions of Europe-Baltic Sea Commission, Union of the Baltic Cities, Organization for Economic Cooperation and Development.

Origin and development. The idea of an umbrella organization for cooperation among the Baltic Sea states was first raised in the fall of 1991 during a meeting of the Danish and German foreign ministers. Originally, the proposed council was viewed as a vehicle for the Nordic countries and Germany to assist Estonia, Latvia, Lithuania, Poland, and Russia in their transformation into democratic, free-market societies. However, at the March 5–6, 1992, inaugural council meeting, the foreign ministers broadened the scope of proposed cooperation to include other areas, such as the environment, transportation, and education. Military and security matters were specifically excluded from the council's mandate in order not to intrude upon other international organizations.

Structure. The Council of Ministers, comprising the foreign ministers of the member states and a commissioner of the European Commission, meets annually; the chair rotates each year, and the ministerial session takes place in the chair's country. The Council of Ministers provides policy guidance to a Committee of Senior Officials (CSO), which monitors CBSS programs and activities. Since 1996 CBSS has also held informal summit meetings, which are attended by the members' heads of government.

In May 1994 the organization established the autonomous office of Commissioner on Democratic Institutions and Human Rights based in Copenhagen, Denmark. In 2000 the office's mandate was revised, and the title was changed to Commissioner of the Council of the Baltic Sea States on Democratic Development.

A director heads the Secretariat, which was formally inaugurated in October 1998. Its staff includes several senior advisers whose jobs include assisting various CBSS working groups: Assistance to Democratic Institutions, Cooperation on Children at Risk, Economic Cooperation, Nuclear and Radiation Safety, Transportation Issues, and Youth Affairs. In April 2000 the Secretariat launched the Energy Unit, and in January 2001 it started the Baltic 21 Unit to promote sustainable development in accordance with the organization's Agenda 21 action program. The Children's Unit commenced work in June 2002.

In 1994 the CBSS adopted the statutes for the EuroFaculty, which assists in the reform of higher education in business administration, economics, law, and public administration at universities in Estonia, Latvia, and Lithuania. Based originally in Riga, Latvia, the EuroFaculty subsequently initiated an additional project in Kaliningrad, Russia, to integrate the exclave further into regional institutions. A Business Advisory Council was formed in 1996 to assist member countries in privatization and business restructuring and the promotion of small and medium-sized enterprises. Other CBSS bodies include a Task Force on Organized Crime in the Baltic Sea Region and a Task Force on Communicable Disease Control. Members of national and regional legislatures also meet annually at a Baltic Sea Parliamentary Conference.

Activities. Backers of the CBSS expected it to work closely with other European organizations to avoid duplication and the creation of unnecessary bureaucracy. However, because the "new Europe" forced many of the continent's organizations to rethink their missions, the CBSS's purpose was at first unclear. Moreover, political differences within the CBSS (such as the dispute between the Baltic states and Russia over Moscow's reluctance to withdraw forces of the former Soviet military) temporarily hindered institutional progress. Nevertheless, the March 1993 session of the Council of Ministers approved numerous "common guidelines" for future activity; there were approximately 50 proposed CBSS initiatives by that time. Several working groups were also established to report to the CBSS Committee of Senior Officials. Over the next year, the Working Group on Economic Cooperation evaluated ways to expedite customs procedures and border crossings and urged members to support regional transportation and energy projects. Ole Espersen of Denmark became CBSS Commissioner on Democratic Institutions and Human Rights at the Council of Ministers meeting, May 25–26, 1994.

CBSS foreign ministers welcomed the withdrawal of Russian troops from Lithuania and Poland and urged Russia to leave Estonia and Latvia. At the CBSS Council of Ministers session held May 18–19, 1995, in Gdańsk, Poland, Russian officials called upon Commissioner Espersen to address what Moscow perceived to be the "continual infringement" of the civil rights of the Russian-speaking population in Estonia and Latvia. Russia also criticized a "lack of action" by the CBSS in other mandated areas.

Issues addressed by the CBSS in early 1996 included crime and smuggling in the region; some members called for the establishment of uniform CBSS border regulations and controls. At the council's first heads of government summit, held in May in Visby, Sweden, the leaders discussed ways to promote democracy, economic growth, integration, and environmental protection within the region. They also endorsed creation of the Task Force on Organized Crime. The Council of Ministers meeting held in early July in Kalmar, Sweden, focused on strengthening ties with the European Union to which four CBSS members (Denmark, Finland, Germany, and Sweden) already belonged, and four more (Estonia, Latvia, Lithuania, and Poland) were aspiring. The Kalmar meeting also formally endorsed three action programs concerned with participation and stable political development, economic integration and prosperity, and the environment.

In 1997 the Council of Ministers assigned the CSO the task of determining whether or not the CBSS needed a secretariat, and in February 1998 it concluded that a "small and efficient" secretariat should be established in Stockholm, Sweden. The CBSS Secretariat, with Jacek Starosciak of Poland as its director, opened the following October.

At the second meeting of CBSS prime ministers, held January 22–23, 1998, in Riga, Latvia, the heads of government praised past, and supported future, cooperation in the areas of the prevention of organized crime and child molestation, economic integration, civic security, education, environment, and the adaptation and diffusion of information technology. At their seventh annual meeting, held June 22–23 in Nyborg, Denmark, the Council of Ministers adopted Agenda 21 for the Baltic States Region, an action program geared to sustainable development and coordination in agriculture, education, energy, fisheries, forestry, industry, spatial planning, transport, and tourism. Palanga, Lithuania, hosted the June 14–15, 1999, ministerial session.

The third CBSS summit convened April 12–13, 2000, in Kolding, Denmark. The principal topic of discussion was how to restructure the organization to enhance regional integration. At the meeting's conclusion, the heads of government decided that the CBSS should encompass the full range of intergovernmental, multilateral, and cooperative efforts in the region. Two months later, on June 21–22, the Council of Ministers convened in Bergen, Norway, for their ninth session. In addition to naming Helle Degn of Denmark to succeed Commissioner Espersen, the foreign ministers voiced their support of the European Union's "Action Plan for the Northern Dimension"; encouraged continued regional cooperation in energy, the environment, and information technology; and discussed balanced growth.

A notable development at the June 7, 2001, council session in Hamburg, Germany, was adoption of a CSO proposal for a volunteer financing facility, the Fund for Sub-regional Development in the Baltic Sea Region. The ministers also encouraged improved cooperation with regional nongovernmental organizations (NGOs); the first Baltic Sea NGO Forum met on May 28–29 in Lübeck, Germany.

At the fourth CBSS summit, held June 9–10, 2002, in St. Petersburg, Russia, a major topic of discussion was the anticipated impact on Kaliningrad of EU accession by Poland and Lithuania. At the time, residents of the Russian region were accorded visa-free travel across Poland and Lithuania, but adoption of the EU's Schengen rules by the two prospective EU members would bring the practice to an end. Russia, in particular, strongly objected. As in the past, the summit participants voiced their support for the EU's Northern Dimension Action Plan, which focused on the environment, nuclear safety, justice and home affairs, and cross-border projects. The June meeting of government leaders was preceded by a March 5–6 ministerial session in Svetlogorsk, Russia, which marked the tenth anniversary of the CBSS.

The 12th Council of Ministers session, held June 10–11, 2003, in Pori, Finland, continued the emphasis on EU-related matters—particularly the accession of Estonia, Latvia, Lithuania, and Poland to the EU in May 2004—and their broader impact on the non-EU CBSS members. The Russian foreign minister noted that it was CBSS members' "common duty" not to let regional trade ties weaken following EU expansion. The assembled ministers gave their support to the EU "Wider Europe" initiative and the new Northern Dimension plan for 2004–2006. On July 1, 2003, as expected, Poland and Lithuania ended visa-free travel between Kaliningrad and the rest of Russia.

The fifth CBSS summit was held on June 21, 2004, in Laulasmaa, Estonia. It followed closely on the May 1, 2004, expansion of the EU. The final declaration expressed confidence that, with Estonia, Latvia, Lithuania, and Poland now in the EU, European interest in the Baltic region would increase. Noting a recently concluded summit between the EU and Russia the CBSS expressed hope that its mixture of EU and non-EU countries, all of which belonged to the World Trade Organization (WTO), would be good for the political and economic future of the region.

EUROPEAN FREE TRADE ASSOCIATION (EFTA)

Established: By Convention signed January 4, 1960, in Stockholm, Sweden, effective May 3, 1960; updated Convention signed June 21, 2001, in Vaduz, Liechtenstein, with entry into force on June 1, 2002.

Purpose: Initially, to promote economic expansion, full employment, and higher standards of living through elimination of barriers to nonagricultural trade among member states; more recently, to expand trade and other cooperation relations with external countries and to further European integration through a single European Economic Area, extending not only to free trade, but also to deregulation, removal of technical and nontariff barriers to trade, and cooperation with the European Union in the service and agricultural sectors as well as industry.

Headquarters: Geneva, Switzerland.

Principal Organs: Council, EFTA Council Committees, Consultative Committee, EFTA Surveillance Authority, EFTA Court, Secretariat.

Secretary General: William Rossier (Switzerland).

Membership (4): Iceland, Liechtenstein, Norway, Switzerland.

Working Language: English.

   Origin and development. EFTA was established under British leadership in 1959–1960 as the response of Europe's so-called "outer seven" states (Austria, Denmark, Norway, Portugal, Sweden, Switzerland, United Kingdom) to creation of the original six-state European Economic Community (EEC). With the breakdown of negotiations to establish a single, all-European free trade area encompassing both groups, the seven decided to set up a separate organization that would enable the non-EEC states both to maintain a unified position in further bargaining with the "inner six" and to carry out a modest liberalization of trade within their own group. The 1960 EFTA Convention (the Stockholm Convention) resulted. Finland became an associate member of EFTA in 1961; Iceland joined as the eighth full member in 1970. At the start of 1973, however, Denmark and the United Kingdom withdrew upon joining the European Community (EC).

   Unlike the EEC, EFTA was not endowed with supranational features and was not designed to effect a common market or common external tariff, but merely the elimination of internal trade barriers on nonagricultural goods. This objective was met at the end of 1966, three years ahead of schedule. A second goal, a comprehensive agreement permitting limited access to EC markets, led to completion of various trade pacts, the first of which became effective January 1, 1973, concurrent with the initial round of EC expansion.

   Following enlargement of the EC, a further range of activity was unofficially added to the EFTA agenda, and cooperation was extended to more diverse economic matters than the trade concerns specified in the Stockholm Convention. Explicitly recognized by the EFTA Council at its meeting of May 1975, these concerns involved such areas as raw materials, monetary policy, inflation, and unemployment.

   Organized outside EFTA's institutional framework, the first summit in 11 years convened in

May 1977 in Vienna, Austria, and adopted the so-called Vienna Declaration, which prescribed a broad framework for future activities. It included, for example, a resolution calling upon EFTA to become a "forum for joint consideration of wider European and world-wide economic problems in order to make a constructive contribution to economic cooperation in international fora." In pursuit of this goal, a multilateral free trade agreement between the EFTA countries and Spain was signed in 1979 in Madrid, while in 1982 concessions were extended to permit Portugal to expand its industrial base prior to joining the EC. Upon their accession to the larger grouping, it was agreed that Spain and Portugal would conclude special arrangements with EFTA countries.

Cooperation between EFTA and the EC/EU continued to grow, based on general guidelines promulgated in the 1984 Luxembourg Declaration, which endorsed the development of a European Economic Space (EES) including all EFTA and EC countries. The accord called for the reduction of nontariff barriers (the last duties on most industrial trade having recently been removed), more joint research and development projects, and exploratory talks in such areas as transportation, agriculture, fishing, and energy. In an effort to reduce border formalities, EFTA reached agreement with the EC on the use of a simplified customs form, the Single Administrative Document (SAD), to cover trade within and between the two groups. The SAD convention was the first direct agreement between EFTA and the EC, previous pacts having taken the form of similar but separate agreements between each EFTA member and the EC; both the SAD accord and a related convention on common transit procedures became effective on January 1, 1988.

Two years earlier, at the start of 1986, Portugal had left EFTA to join the EC, at which time Finland rose to full EFTA membership. Liechtenstein, which previously participated as a nonvoting associate member by virtue of its customs union with Switzerland, was admitted as a full member in May 1991.

While an EFTA summit in June 1990 again strongly endorsed the EES concept and formal EC-EFTA discussions were immediately begun, the negotiations proved much more difficult than anticipated. The major sticking points were EFTA's request to exempt many of its products from EC guidelines and an inability to agree on a structure through which EFTA could influence EC decision making. Some progress, particularly in regard to the exemptions issue, was reported at a special December session called to "reinvigorate" talks on the European Economic Area (EEA), as the EES had been renamed at the EC's request. In addition, "moment of truth" negotiations in early May 1991 resolved many of the remaining disagreements, with a preliminary accord being signed in October. However, an objection from the European Court of Justice forced the dropping of a proposed EEA legal body from the agreement, and a new pact was signed in May 1992.

The EEA was scheduled to go into effect on January 1, 1993, but its final ratification proved contentious, as was the case with the EC's Maastricht Treaty on political and economic union (see the European Union article). For EFTA the most surprising problem was the rejection of the EEA by a Swiss referendum on December 6, 1992. Despite that jolt, the other EFTA members agreed to pursue the EEA without Switzerland. An adjusting protocol to accommodate the change was signed on March 17, 1993, in Brussels, and by late 1993 all the EC states and the remaining EFTA countries had completed their ratification procedures. (In Liechtenstein, the only other EFTA member to require a popular vote on the question, the EEA was approved by a comfortable margin a week after the Swiss balloting. However, Liechtenstein's customs and monetary union with Switzerland meant that its participation in the EEA had to be deferred.) As finally launched on January 1, 1994, the EEA provided for greatly expanded freedom of movement of goods, services, capital, and labor among the (then) 17 participating nations, home to a population of some 372 million. Having negotiated amendment of the customs and monetary union with Switzerland, Liechtenstein became the 18th EEA member on May 1, 1995.

For four EFTA member states the EEA arrangement was regarded as a stepping-stone to full European Union (EU) membership, Austria having submitted its application as early as July 1989, with Finland, Norway, and Sweden following suit in 1991–1992. Negotiations with all four applicants were completed by early 1994, and referendums later in the year in Austria, Finland, and Sweden approved EU membership. However, Norwegian voters voted "no" on the proposal, as they had once before (in 1972). Consequently, an EFTA ministerial session in December 1994 in Geneva decided that EFTA would continue to function, even though its membership was to fall, as of January 1, 1995, to four countries with a total population of scarcely more than 11 million, nearly two-thirds less than before.

Meeting in June 1999, in Lillehammer, Norway, the EFTA ministers called for the Stockholm Convention to be updated in order to consolidate the EEA regime and a set of agreements between the EU and Switzerland that was about to be concluded. Switzerland had already proposed that the benefits of the new Swiss-EU accords be extended on a reciprocal basis to its EFTA partners. EFTA was also interested in seeing that a revised convention reflect recent developments with regard to its free trade partnerships and multilateral arrangements.

Work on the proposed convention revisions continued through 2000 and into 2001, with the EFTA Council signing the revised EFTA Convention during its ministerial session in Vaduz, Liechtenstein, on June 21–22, 2001. The Vaduz Convention entered into force on June 1, 2002.

Structure. The EFTA Council, the association's principal political organ, consists of one representative from each member state and normally meets two times a year at the ministerial level, twice a month at lower levels. Its responsibilities include supervising the implementation and operation of various free trade agreements and managing relations with the EU. Decisions are generally reached by consensus. Assisting the Council are various standing organs, including the Committee on Customs and Origin Matters, the Consultative Committee (comprising representatives from government and private economic organizations in the member states), the Committee on Technical Barriers to Trade, the Committee of Members of Parliament of EFTA countries, the Committee of Trade

Experts, and the Committee on Third-Country Relations. The last two and the Council are aided by a number of Expert Groups that provide advice on state aid; public procurement; intellectual property; price compensation; trade procedures; legal issues; and services, investment, and establishment. The EFTA Secretariat opened an office in 1988 in Brussels to facilitate cooperation with the EC. In addition, an Office of the EFTA Statistical Adviser is located in Luxembourg.

EFTA also participates in various bodies in connection with the EEA. The EEA Joint Committee, which brings together EFTA, EU, and European Commission representatives, is the main EEA decision making organ, while an EEA Council of EU and EFTA ministers offers overall direction. A Standing Committee of the EFTA States (Switzerland participates as an observer) consolidates the position of EFTA members regarding incorporation of EU laws, regulations, and procedures into the EEA. The Standing Committee is itself assisted by five subcommittees (Free Movement of Goods, Free Movement of Capital and Services, Free Movement of Persons, Flanking and Horizontal Policies, Legal and Institutional Matters) and some 40 working groups. The EEA Joint Parliamentary Committee, which serves as a forum for EEA issues, brings together 12 members from parliaments of the EEA states and 12 members of the European Parliament. In addition, the EEA Consultative Committee focuses on social matters. EFTA has also established its own Brussels-based Surveillance Authority, which monitors implementation of the agreement, and an EFTA Court, sitting in Geneva, as final arbiter of legal disputes.

Activities. In addition to its focus on the EEA, EFTA has devoted considerable energy to expanding other external ties. An EFTA ministerial session in June 1995 saw representatives of the three Baltic republics (Estonia, Latvia, and Lithuania) express interest in negotiating free trade agreements, which formally entered into effect in 1996–1997. EFTA already had similar arrangements with Bulgaria, the Czech Republic, Hungary, Israel, Poland, Romania, Slovakia, Slovenia, and Turkey. Additional free trade agreements were reached with Morocco and the Palestine Liberation Organization ("for the Benefit of the Palestinian Authority") in 1997 and 1998, respectively, and then with Macedonia in June 2000, Mexico in November 2000, both Croatia and Jordan in June 2001, Singapore in June 2002, and Chile in June 2003 (with effect from February 2004).

The agreements with Morocco, the PLO, and Jordan were noteworthy in that they marked a clear decision by the EFTA Council to expand the organization's relationships throughout the Mediterranean region, while the agreement with Mexico marked EFTA's first transatlantic venture, and that with Singapore, the first into the Far East. Other countries and organizations with which EFTA has official relationships include Albania, Algeria, Chile, Colombia, Croatia, Egypt, Jordan, Korea, Lebanon, Macedonia, Mexico, Morocco, Peru, Serbia (as the successor state after the split of Serbia and Montenegro), Tunisia, Turkey, Ukraine, the Gulf Cooperation Council, and the Southern Cone Common Market (Mercosur).

Attention in 2002 and the first half of 2003 largely focused on the planned expansion of the EU to 25 members in May 2004. In the 2002 EFTA annual report the organization's secretary general, William Rossier, had praised the move, noting the "bonding effect of reuniting the European family" and the positive impact on regional stability and security. Under the EEA Agreement, all ten new EU members (Cyprus, Czech Republic, Estonia, Hungary, Latvia, Lithuania, Malta, Poland, Slovakia, and Slovenia) were required to negotiate EEA participation. Two principal stumbling blocks quickly emerged: (1) the EU's request that the three EFTA EEA members increase their contributions toward eliminating economic and social disparities in the poorer EU countries (the ten prospective members plus Portugal, Spain, and Greece), and (2) the need to adjust tariff arrangements affecting Poland's significant fishmeal processing industry. Poland argued that a loss of tariff-free fish imports from Iceland and Norway would devastate its fishmeal industry. The EU, however, insisted that a uniform tariff regime for the entire union had to be maintained.

The EFTA and EEA Councils had hoped to resolve both matters before the ten new EU states signed their accession treaties on April 16, 2003, but they fell short. As a result, the EEA signings were delayed until July 3. The final agreement called for Iceland, Liechtenstein, and Norway to provide some 1.2 billion euros for 2004–2009 for the poorer EU countries, down from the 2.7 billion euros that had initially been requested. On the tariff issue, Poland was forced to give in, and the final agreement authorized a Community-wide duty-free fish import quota significantly smaller than the previous level of Icelandic and Norwegian imports to Poland alone.

The increasingly integrated relationship between EFTA and the EU advanced in other respects recently. For example, the EFTA EEA members have moved forward with plans to join three recently established EU-sponsored organizations—the European Maritime Safety Agency, the European Food Safety Agency, and the European Aviation Safety Agency. At the same time, EFTA ministers also have focused attention on expansion of free trade with non-EU countries. EFTA and the EU have also worked together on a "European Neighborhood Policy," designed to reach out to Eastern European and Mediterranean countries that are currently outside the EEA, and to try to prevent the formation of new barriers.

EUROPEAN ORGANIZATION FOR NUCLEAR RESEARCH (CERN)

Organisation Européenne pour la Recherche Nucléaire

Established: By convention signed July 1, 1953, in Paris, France, effective September 29, 1954.

Purpose: "To provide for collaboration among European States in subnuclear research of a pure scientific and fundamental character, and in research essentially related thereto. The Organization shall have no concern with work for military requirements and the results of its experimental and theoretical work shall be published or otherwise made generally available."

Headquarters: Geneva, Switzerland.

Principal Organs: Council, Committee of Council, Scientific Policy Committee, Finance Committee.

Director General: Robert Aymar (France).

Membership (20): Austria, Belgium, Bulgaria, Czech Republic, Denmark, Finland, France, Germany, Greece, Hungary, Italy, Netherlands, Norway, Poland, Portugal, Slovakia, Spain, Sweden, Switzerland, United Kingdom.

Observers (8): European Commission; India; Israel; Japan; Russia; Turkey; United Nations Educational, Scientific, and Cultural Organization (UNESCO); United States.

Official Languages: English, French.

Origin and development. The European Organization for Nuclear Research was established September 29, 1954, after ratification of a convention drawn up in Paris, France, the preceding July. The convention followed a resolution of the United Nations Educational, Scientific, and Cultural Organization (UNESCO) general conference held in 1950 in Florence, Italy, and an intergovernmental conference convened by UNESCO in December 1951. The organization replaced the *Conseil Européen pour la Recherche Nucléaire* (CERN), which was established February 15, 1952, but retained its predecessor's acronym. One of the original 12 members, Yugoslavia, withdrew in 1961. Austria acceded in 1959 and Spain in 1961; the latter withdrew in 1968 but returned in 1982. CERN was subsequently joined by Portugal (1986), Finland and Poland (1991), Hungary (1992), the Czech Republic and Slovakia (1993), and Bulgaria (1999).

In 2002 India, whose scientists have participated in CERN projects since the 1960s, became the organization's eighth observer. As such, it may participate on a nonvoting basis in all Council sessions.

Structure. The Council of CERN, which normally meets twice a year, is comprised of two representatives—one from government and one from the scientific field—for each member state. The Committee of Council, consisting of the Council president and vice presidents, one or more representatives per member state, plus the chairmen of the Scientific Policy Committee, the Finance Committee, and the European Committee for Future Accelerators, is a less formal forum in which members monitor operations, discuss proposals, and confidentially discuss difficult questions. The Scientific Policy Committee, comprised of some two dozen scientists from member and observer states without regard to geographical distribution, provides the Council with advice on research priorities, resource allocation, management and staffing, and scientific developments and their implications for the organization. The Finance Committee consists of one or more delegates from each member state. The director general, elected by the Council, serves as CERN's head of management, overseeing a directorate and managing various departments focused on research, accelerators and related technology, technical tasks, and administration.

Activities. From a relatively low level in the early years, the use of CERN's experimental facilities has now grown to involve 6,500 visiting scientists from more than 500 universities and research institutes. The CERN staff numbers more than 2,500.

The organization's many accomplishments have included producing in 1981 the first collisions between protons and their antimatter counterparts, antiprotons; verifying the electroweak theory in 1983 that unifies the weak nuclear force and electromagnetic force; announcing in 1984 evidence of the existence of the quark, something previously a matter of theory only; confirming in 1989 that all matter consists of only three families of subatomic particles; and synthesizing in 1995 atoms of antimatter from their antiparticles. In addition, CERN computer scientist Tim Berners-Lee was credited with inventing the World Wide Web in 1990 to provide CERN-affiliated physicists around the world with rapid access to scientific information.

The highlight of 1989 was the inauguration of the Large Electron-Positron Collider (LEP), through which CERN was generally perceived to have outdistanced U.S. rivals, at least temporarily, in the subatomic particle research race. In addition, at its December meeting the Council agreed, in light of the political developments in Eastern Europe,

to provide physicists from that region immediate access to CERN facilities and services pending negotiation of formal arrangements.

In December 1991 the CERN Council unanimously supported a resolution recognizing the Large Hadron Collider (LHC) as the "right machine" for further research in the field of high-energy physics. The LHC, to be built in the same 27-kilometer tunnel housing the LEP collider, would produce head-on proton collisions at much higher energies than previously achieved, causing the protons to be shattered into smaller, very short-lived particles such as quarks.

In 1993 attention focused on negotiations in the United States regarding its Superconducting Supercollider (SSC), for which an 87-kilometer tunnel had been approved in the early 1980s in an effort to propel U.S. scientists to the forefront of high-energy physics. Although construction had begun in Texas in 1992 on the tunnel, the U.S. House of Representatives voted in October 1993 for the "orderly termination" of the project. Consequently, the CERN Council, recognizing the organization's growing status as a "world, rather than a European laboratory," invited nonmembers, especially the United States, to contribute (both scientifically and financially) to the development of the LHC. In addition, in 1993 the CERN Council endorsed a public relations campaign to explain the valuable technical "spin-offs," in areas such as vacuums and cryogenics, from subatomic particle research.

Last-minute budget concerns on behalf of Germany and the United Kingdom delayed a vote on the LHC at the June 1994 Council session, but the project was finally approved at the December meeting after France and Switzerland agreed to provide additional support. However, the threat of German budget cuts on scientific research programs in 1996 again jeopardized the project schedule and contributed to a decision to seek financing from nonmember users, such as Japan, which acquired Council observer status in 1996. Canada, India, and Russia also agreed to contribute funds in 1996. In December 1997 the United States was granted observer status at CERN in return for contributing $531 million in money and material.

(It is estimated that more than 1,000 American scientists could eventually work on the new collider, conducting experiments previously planned for the U.S. collider.)

On November 8, 2000, the LEP was shut down after 11 years in operation to make way for the LHC project, which was targeted to come online in 2005. The 125th Council meeting on June 20, 2003, noted that the LHC project, having overcome several problems in 2001–2002, remained on schedule for a revised 2007 start date. In preparation, an LHC computing grid (LCG) project, involving distributed computing technology, was nearing completion, and discussions were well under way with the European Union on an Enabling Grids for E-science in Europe (EGEE) project that would establish a continent-wide grid infrastructure. The Council session also approved a Medium Term Plan for 2004–2007.

Administrative reorganization at CERN is expected to continue under its new director general, Robert Aymar of France, who succeeded Italy's Luciano Maiani in January 2004. Restructuring plans, based on recommendations of an External Review Committee, include reducing the size of the directorate and reorganizing the more than a dozen divisions into a smaller number of departments. Such functions as public communications, technology transfer, and safety are to be brought into the director general's office. CERN celebrated its 50th anniversary in October 2004.

CERN's international importance only increases as more countries think of developing their own nuclear programs, for peaceful purposes or otherwise. It is noteworthy that in 2005 and 2006 the presidents of both India and Pakistan visited CERN, both signing agreements for improved technical cooperation between CERN and their countries.

EUROPEAN ORGANIZATION FOR THE SAFETY OF AIR NAVIGATION (EUROCONTROL)

Established: By convention signed on December 13, 1960, in Brussels, Belgium, effective March 1, 1963; amended by protocol signed February 12, 1981, effective January 1, 1986. (Convention revisions signed on June 27, 1997, are still undergoing ratification.)

Purpose: To strengthen the cooperation of the contracting parties and to develop their joint activities in the field of air navigation, making due allowance for defense needs and providing maximum freedom for all airspace users consistent with the required level of safety.

Headquarters: Brussels, Belgium.

Principal Organs: Commission, Provisional Council, Agency.

Director General: Víctor M. Aguado (Spain).

Membership (36): Albania, Armenia, Austria, Belgium, Bosnia and Herzegovina, Bulgaria, Croatia, Cyprus, Czech Republic, Denmark, Finland, France, Germany, Greece, Hungary, Ireland, Italy, Luxembourg, Macedonia, Malta, Moldova, Monaco, Netherlands, Norway, Poland, Portugal, Romania, Serbia (as successor state after the split of Serbia and Montenegro), Slovakia, Slovenia, Spain, Sweden, Switzerland, Turkey, Ukraine, United Kingdom.

Official Languages: Dutch, English, French, German, Portuguese.

Origin and development. As early as 1957, governments considered developing an air traffic control procedure that would disregard national frontiers. The growing number of aircraft traveling at ever-higher speed and altitude, the pace at which the aeronautical sciences were advancing, and the greater interdependence of the industrialized states of Western Europe suggested the need for such a joint venture. However, the idea was not officially discussed until January 1958 at the Fourth European Mediterranean Regional Air Navigation Convention of the International Civil Aviation Organization (ICAO) in Geneva, Switzerland. Subsequently, several meetings were held by concerned directors general of civil aviation, and on June 9, 1960, the ministers responsible for civil and military aviation in Belgium, France, the Federal Republic of Germany, Italy, Luxembourg, the Netherlands, and the United Kingdom met in Rome, Italy, to consider a draft convention. Two diplomatic conferences followed (the Italians no longer participating), and the convention was signed at the second of these in December 1960. Ireland acceded to the convention in 1965; Portugal became an associate member in 1976 and a full member in 1986. Greece joined in 1988, Turkey and Malta in 1989, Cyprus in 1991, Hungary and Switzerland in 1992, Austria in 1993, and Denmark and Norway in 1994. In 1995 Slovenia and Sweden joined, followed by the Czech Republic, Italy, and Romania in 1996; Spain, Slovakia, Croatia, Bulgaria, and Monaco in 1997; Macedonia in 1998; Moldova in 2000;

Finland in 2001; Albania in 2002; Ukraine and Poland in 2004; Serbia and Montenegro in 2005; and Armenia in 2006.

Structure. Eurocontrol is currently governed through the Commission, comprised of delegates from each member state (who represent the interests of civil aviation and national defense), and the Provisional Council, comprised of civil aviation officials from the member states. Reporting to the Council are the Performance Review Commission, the Safety Regulation Commission, the Regulatory Committee, the Civil/Military Interface Standing Committee, the Committee of Management, the Enlarged Committee for Route Charges, and the Audit Board. The Eurocontrol Agency, headed by a director general, serves as a secretariat and includes various groups concerned with air traffic management (ATM), training, financial arrangements, and research and development. Upon ratification of Convention revisions signed in 1997, the Commission and the Provisional Council are to become the General Assembly and the Council, respectively; the committee structure will also change, with separate Standing Committees, for example, overseeing the Central European Air Traffic Services (CEATS) and the air traffic control center located in Maastricht, Netherlands.

Eurocontrol's central administration is financed by means of contributions from each member state assessed on the basis of the state's gross national product and the value of the state's route facility cost-base.

Activities. The organization is required to analyze future needs of air traffic and new techniques to meet them; to establish common long-term objectives in the field of air navigation and to establish a common medium-term plan for air traffic services, taking account of the long-term objectives; to coordinate the research and development programs of the member states; and to assist, on request, in the performance of specific air navigation tasks or in the provision and operation of air traffic services.

Specifically, the organization provides air traffic control services, from its Maastricht International Upper Area Control Center, to aircraft operating in the upper airspace of the three Benelux states and the northern part of what was formerly the Federal Republic of Germany on behalf of and at the request of the relevant states. In addition, the CEATS is being developed to serve eight Central European countries (Austria, Bosnia and Herzegovina, Croatia, Czech Republic, Hungary, Italy, Slovakia, and Slovenia).

The organization also prepares and executes studies, tests, and trials at its Research and Development Centre in Brétigny-sur-Orge, near Paris; trains air traffic services personnel at the Institute of Air Navigation Services in Luxembourg; calculates, bills, and collects air navigation route charges at the Central Route Charges Office in Haren, near Brussels; and provides an international air traffic flow management system through its Central Flow Management Unit (CFMU) in Haren.

Despite the wide range of its activity, Eurocontrol falls far short of the common European air control system envisioned at the organization's formation, most members having refused to surrender national prerogatives, such as control of their military airspace and the allocation of lucrative air traffic control equipment contracts. However, in recent years substantial progress has been made in response to growing air traffic congestion in Europe.

In November 1988 the transportation ministers of the (then) 23-member European Civil Aviation Conference (ECAC) called for the development of common air traffic control specifications and operating procedures, asking Eurocontrol to determine the standards. The CFMU evolved as a result of this request. In April 1990 the ECAC approved a comprehensive program, the European Air Traffic Control Harmonization and Integration Program (EATCHIP), to harmonize and integrate air traffic control in Europe and designated Eurocontrol to manage the project. An eight-year period was envisaged for the various national systems involved to adopt common standards and computer software. Other subsequent Eurocontrol activity included an agreement in 1994 to assist NATO's new Partnership for Peace associates from the former Soviet bloc in upgrading surveillance radar facilities.

In April 1995 Eurocontrol's CFMU assumed responsibility for air traffic flow management (not actual air traffic control) in France, and similar measures were subsequently extended within a year to all ECAC members (then numbering 41). In March 1996 Eurocontrol signed a new cooperation agreement with the International Civil Aviation Organization (ICAO) designed, among other things, to eliminate duplication of services.

In December 1996 the Eurocontrol Permanent Commission tentatively approved a far-reaching revision of the Eurocontrol Convention. The changes, which involved a major reorganization (see Structure, above), were expected to streamline operations and facilitate an expansion of services related to aircraft safety; air safety regulations in general; review of airline performance; improved military/civilian cooperation; and implementation of EATCHIP's successor regime, the European Air Traffic Management Program (EATMP). The revised convention was formally signed in June 1997, and some of its provisions were implemented in 1998, prior to formal ratification. (As of mid-2006, the ratification process had not yet been completed.)

During the 1990s Eurocontrol also participated in the Program for Harmonized Air Traffic Management Research (PHARE), and in June 1998 it agreed to participate in development by 2010 of a European Global Navigation Satellite System (GNSS), in cooperation with the European Commission and the European Space Agency (ESA).

It subsequently adopted an ATM 2000+ Strategy, which Eurocontrol described as "a blueprint for developing a seamless, pan-European ATM system." More recently, in furtherance of that goal, Eurocontrol has supported the European Commission's "single sky" initiative with its own "One Sky for Europe" concept, which it has described as a program to treat continental air corridors as a "single, seamless airspace within which traffic can cross national frontiers, supported by a synchronized, integrated system of air traffic management."

The need for the "one sky" approach has become increasingly apparent in recent years because of air corridor congestion. In January 2002 Eurocontrol oversaw what the *Financial Times* described as "the biggest change in the management of European air traffic for 50 years" when a reform halved the vertical separation between aircraft to 1,000 feet in the upper airspace (29,000–41,000 feet). At the same time, Eurocontrol has warned that a lack of airport capacity will become a critical issue by mid-decade.

In October 2002 Eurocontrol became the first international institution to sign an accession protocol with the European Commission; it will become a formal member upon completion of ratification. Additional memberships were expected to follow the expansion of the European Union (EU) to 25 states in 2004. Of the ten new EU members only Poland has joined (November 2003). Ukraine joined Eurocontrol on May 1, 2004, and Armenia on March 1, 2006.

EUROPEAN SPACE AGENCY (ESA)

Established: On a de facto basis by agreement signed at a meeting of the European Space Conference July 31, 1973, in Brussels, Belgium, effective May 1, 1975; de jure establishment achieved after ratification of the ESA Convention on October 30, 1980.

Purpose: To provide for and promote, for exclusively peaceful purposes, cooperation among European states in space research and technology, with a view to their being used for scientific purposes and for operational space applications; to elaborate and implement a long-term European space policy; and progressively to "Europeanize" national space programs.

Headquarters: Paris, France.

Principal Organs: Council (all members), Directorates.

Director General: Jean-Jacques Dordain (France).

Membership (16): Austria, Belgium, Denmark, Finland, France, Germany, Greece, Ireland, Italy, Netherlands, Norway, Portugal, Spain, Sweden, Switzerland, United Kingdom.
  Cooperating States (4): Canada, Czech Republic, Hungary, Romania.

Origin and development. The decision to form the ESA was made at meetings of the European Space Conference in December 1972 and July 1973, culminating 14 years of persistent effort by the Consultative Assembly of the Council of Europe to establish a single European space organization and a common European satellite and launcher program. The long gestation period was in part because of delicate negotiations over which the European Space Research Organization (ESRO) and the European Space Vehicle Launcher Development Organization (ELDO) projects would be continued after their consolidation into the ESA, and in part because of disagreement between France and the Federal Republic of Germany as to the naming of a director general. Austria and Norway, initially observers and subsequently associate members, acceded to full membership January 1, 1987. Finland was an associate member from that date until January 1, 1995, when it became a full member. The 15th member, Portugal, joined in December 1999.

Canada, an ESA observer during the mid-1970s, has been a "cooperating state" since 1979. In April 2003 the ESA and Hungary signed a "European Cooperating State Agreement" that might serve as a model for other countries seeking closer relationship with (and possibly eventual membership in) the ESA. The Czech Republic signed a similar agreement in November 2003, as did Romania in February 2006. In addition, cooperation agreements (as distinguished from cooperating state memberships) have been signed with several other countries.

Structure. The ESA structure was patterned essentially after that of the ESRO, with a Council as its governing body in which each member state has one vote. The management team is headed by a director general, who is elected by the Council. Assisting him are directors who oversee the ESA's programs in such areas as earth observation, industrial matters and technology, launchers, manned spaceflight, and technical and operational support.

The agency also has several national program facilities and four technical establishments: the European Space Research and Technology Center (ESTEC) in Noordwijk, Netherlands; the European Space Operations Centre (ESOC) in Darmstadt, Germany; the European Space Research Institute (ESRIN) in Frascati, Italy; and the European Astronauts Center in Cologne, Germany.

The member states finance the agency, contributing on the basis of a percentage of gross national product to the general and scientific budgets and on an ad hoc basis to other programs. Contributions are also made by nonmember nations that participate in specific programs.

Activities. The ESA has developed or contributed to a variety of satellite programs in many fields, including telecommunications and earth and space observation, while promoting experiments related to the scientific and commercial exploitation of space. Initially a "junior partner" with the United States' National Aeronautics and Space Administration (NASA) on several projects, the agency, through its commercial affiliate Arianespace, now competes directly with NASA in the satellite-launching business. However, ESA-NASA cooperation continues in other areas, such as the Hubble Space Telescope; Spacelab, the self-contained laboratory in which numerous experiments are conducted on U.S. space shuttle flights; and the International Space Station, which also involves Canada, Japan, and Russia.

Central to the overall ESA program is the development of a series of Ariane rockets to propel its own launches from facilities in Kourou, French Guiana. Because the ESA convention prohibits the agency from engaging in profitmaking activities, the launches are conducted by Arianespace, established in 1980 by European aerospace industries and banks in conjunction with the French Space Agency.

Notable ESA achievements include the Giotto probe (launched in 1985) for studying Halley's Comet; the Ulysses solar polar probe (1990); the European Remote Sensing (ERS-1 and ERS-2) satellites for gathering data on the earth's atmosphere, surface, and climate (1990 and 1995); the Infrared Space Observatory (ISO) for studying deep space (1995); the Solar Heliospheric Observatory (SOHO) for expanding knowledge of the sun (1995); the joint NASA-ESA Cassini/Huygens mission to Saturn and its moon Titan (1997), which successfully reached the region of Saturn, transmitting much new information about the planet and its moons, and whose Huygens lander safely reached Titan's surface January 14, 2005; the X-Ray Multi-Mirror (XMM) mission—the first Ariane-5 satellite launch—for studying such phenomena as neutron stars and black holes (1999); the Cluster satellite quartet for examining earth's magnetosphere (2000); and Envisat, ESA's largest and most scientifically advanced earth observation satellite (2001). The Mars Express explorer, which reached Mars orbit in late December 2003, suffered a major failure when its lander was lost during its descent to the Martian surface.

In March 2000 Director General Antonio Rodatà of Italy appointed a committee of three "wise men" (from government, finance, and technology) to examine the ESA's role and to make recommendations for its future. In November the committee proposed, among other things, a closer relationship with the European Union (EU), thereby lending support to the view that, in an era of rapidly increasing European integration, the ESA should effectively become the EU's space agency. A week later the European Union Research Council and the ESA Council adopted a new "European Strategy for Space" to strengthen launch capacities and space technology, to advance scientific knowledge, and to exploit space for the benefit of industry and society. In keeping with these broad goals, the ESA redirected some of its Horizons 2000 Programme toward Small Missions for Advanced Research in Technology (SMART). (SMART-1, the first European spacecraft to orbit the moon, was launched in September 2003.) The ESA has developed closer cooperation with other institutions, including the Russian Aviation and Space Agency and the Chinese National Space Administration. The ESA now has an office in Moscow and is building facilities at its Spaceport in French Guiana to launch Russian Soyuz rockets. Completion is planned in 2007.

The ESA has also entered into a research program, called Double Star, in cooperation with the Chinese National Space Administration. This two-satellite endeavor is expected to continue through December 2006.

One of the projects in which Moscow has expressed an interest is the planned Galileo global positioning system, which appears to have vast commercial possibilities. Galileo, comprising some 30 satellites by 2008, is envisaged as challenging the monopoly of the U.S. military's current navigation and positioning system, even though it is made available without charge for civil uses. The ESA, the European Commission, and the European Organization for the Safety of Air Navigation (Eurocontrol) agreed in 1998 to combine efforts in developing such a Global Navigation Satellite System (GNSS). In March 2002 the EU decided to allocate $3.1 billion for the Galileo project, despite questions from some EU members about its financial feasibility. The U.S. military also expressed concerns about the consequences of deployment, including the danger that NATO transmissions might be compromised, but EU–U.S. differences were resolved in February 2004. The first Galileo satellite was launched December 28, 2005, from Baikonur, Kazakhstan.

In December 2002 an enhanced Ariane-5 launcher with increased load capacity veered off course shortly after launch and blew up, a serious setback that precipitated a review of all Arianespace launch procedures and management. The most immediate consequence of the rocket's failure was a decision to postpone launch of the Rosetta probe, which was scheduled for a 2012 comet interception and was subsequently retargeted (for a 2014 interception) and launched in March 2004.

Five months earlier, in July 2002, the ESA and Eurocontrol signed a five-year renewable agreement on the use of satellite navigation, telecommunications, and other space technology for purposes of civil aviation. In a similar vein, in December 2003 the ESA and the International Mobile Satellite Organization (Inmarsat) signed an agreement on mobile broadband communications that has as its principal goal facilitating broadband capability virtually worldwide, including for ships at sea and aircraft in flight. A low-cost solution allowing fast Internet access for ships at sea became available in April 2006.

In May 2004, the ESA and the EU implemented a framework cooperation agreement that defined two principal goals: establishing "a common basis and appropriate practical arrangements for efficient and mutually beneficial cooperation," and developing an overall European Space Policy designed to link ESA space capabilities and infrastructure with services and applications desired by the EU, and to ensure the EU's unfettered access to the space services it required. The announcement of the agreement coincided with the EU's release of a white paper on space policy that was prepared with ESA assistance.

THE EUROPEAN UNION (EU)

Established: By the Treaty on European Union; initialed by the heads of state and government of the 12 members of the European Communities (EC) on December 11, 1991, in Maastricht, Netherlands; signed by the EC foreign and finance ministers on February 7, 1992; and entered into force November 1, 1993.

Purpose: To strengthen economic and social cohesion; to establish an economic and monetary union, ultimately including a single currency; to implement a common foreign and security policy; to introduce a citizenship of the European Union; to develop close cooperation on justice and home affairs.

Headquarters: Brussels, Belgium. (Some bodies have headquarters elsewhere.)

Principal Organs: European Council (heads of state or government of all members), Council of the European Union (all members), Commission of the European Communities (referred to in all but legal and formal contexts as the European Commission—25 members), European Parliament (732 elected representatives), Court of Justice of the European Communities (informally, the European Court of Justice—25 judges), Court of Auditors (25 members), European Central Bank.

Presidency of the Council of the European Union: Rotates every six months by alphabetical order of member states.

President of the European Commission: José Manuel Durão Barroso (Portugal).

President of the European Parliament: Josep Borrell Fontelles (Spain).

President of the European Court of Justice: Vassilios Skouris (Greece).

President of the Court of Auditors: Hubert Weber (Austria).

President of the European Central Bank: Jean-Claude Trichet (France).

Membership (25): Austria, Belgium, Cyprus, Czech Republic, Denmark, Estonia, Finland, France, Germany, Greece, Hungary, Ireland, Italy, Latvia, Lithuania, Luxembourg, Malta, Netherlands, Poland, Portugal, Slovakia, Slovenia, Spain, Sweden, United Kingdom.

Official Languages: Czech, Danish, Dutch, English, Estonia, Finnish, French, German, Greek, Hungarian, Italian, Latvian, Lithuanian, Maltese, Polish, Portuguese, Slovak, Slovenian, Spanish, Swedish.

Note: The European Union (EU) is the most recent expansion of a process of European integration that was first formalized by the creation of the European Coal and Steel Community (ECSC) in 1952 and then expanded in 1958 by the launching of the European Economic Community (EEC, also known as the Common Market) and the European Atomic Energy Community (Euratom). Especially after entry into force in July 1967 of a merger treaty that established "Common Institutions" for the three European Communities (EC), they had been widely referred to as a singular "European Community" (also EC). On November 1, 2003, the Treaty on European Union (also known as the Maastricht Treaty) added two new "pillars" of cooperation—foreign and security policy, and justice and home affairs—to the original economic pillar created by establishment of the EEC. At that time "EU" became the accepted designation for the collective EC. The Maastricht Treaty also, however, amended the EEC's founding document to replace the term "European Economic Community" with "European Community" (yet again, EC).

The ECSC was terminated when its treaty expired July 23, 2002, but the European Community (i.e., what was originally the EEC) continues to exist, as does Euratom, within the broader framework of the EU; indeed, the EC treaty and the EU treaty merged into one document by the Treaty of Nice, which entered into force February 1, 2003. Although references to EC activity are still correct (and even required) in some legal and other formal situations, common practice has increasingly favored the use of "EU" as an umbrella, particularly given what EU officials themselves have described as "the difficulties of delineating what is strictly EC or EU business."

Origin and development. The formation of the European Communities was one of the most significant expressions of the movement toward European unity that grew out of the moral and material devastation of World War II. For many Europeans, the creation of a United States of Europe seemed to offer the best hope of avoiding a repetition of that catastrophe. Other influences included fear of Soviet aggression and practical experience in economic cooperation gained by administering Marshall Plan aid through the Organization for European Economic Cooperation (OEEC).

These elements converged in a 1950 proposal by French Foreign Minister Robert Schuman envisaging a common market for coal and steel that would, among other things, serve as a lasting guarantee of European peace by forging an organic link between France and Germany. Although the United Kingdom declined to participate in the project, the governments of France, the Federal Republic of Germany, Italy, Belgium, the Netherlands, and Luxembourg agreed to put the "Schuman Plan" into effect through the ECSC treaty, which they signed April 18, 1951, in Paris, France, and that entered into effect July 25, 1952. The original institutional structure of the ECSC, whose headquarters was established in Luxembourg, included a Council of Ministers, an executive High Authority, a parliamentary Assembly, and a Court of Justice.

As the first of the three communities, the ECSC pioneered the concept of a European common market by abolishing price and transport discrimination and eliminating customs duties, quota restrictions, and other trade barriers on coal, steel, iron ore, and scrap. A common market for coal, iron ore, and scrap was established February 1, 1953; for steel May 1, 1953; and for special steels August 1, 1954. Concurrently, steps were taken to harmonize external tariffs on these products. In addition, community-wide industrial policy was facilitated through short- and long-term forecasts of supply and demand, investment guidance and coordination, joint research programs, and regional development assistance. These activities were financed by a direct levy on community coal and steel, the level being fixed by the commission in consultation with the European Parliament.

The next decisive stage in the development of the European Communities was reached with the signature March 25, 1957, in Rome, Italy, of the Treaties of Rome, which established as separate organizations the EEC and Euratom, effective January 1, 1958. (By convention, "Treaty of Rome," in the singular, references just the EEC.) Although Euratom and the EEC from their inception shared the Assembly and Court of Justice already operating under the ECSC, they initially had separate, albeit similar, Councils of Ministers and Commissions. Subsequently, a treaty establishing a single Council of Ministers (formally renamed as the Council of the European Union in 1993) and commission for all three communities was signed by the (then) six-member governments (Belgium, France, Federal Republic of Germany, Italy, Luxembourg, Netherlands) on April 8, 1965, in Brussels, Belgium. However, application of the treaty's provisions was delayed by prolonged disagreement about selecting a president to head the newly merged commission. The choice of Jean Rey of Belgium was ultimately approved, and the new institutions were formally established as of July 1, 1967.

Denmark, Ireland, and the United Kingdom joined the EC on January 1, 1973, followed by Greece on January 1, 1981. Greenland, having become internally independent of Danish rule in 1979, was permitted, on the basis of a 1982 referendum, to terminate its relationship February 1, 1985. Portugal and Spain were admitted to membership January 1, 1986. The former German Democratic Republic became part of the EC as a result of its union with the Federal Republic of Germany in October 1990. (For additional background on pre-EU accessions, see the section on the EC, below.)

As members of the European Free Trade Association (EFTA) participating in the European Economic Area (EEA) with the EU (see separate article on EFTA), Austria, Finland, Norway, and Sweden were formally invited in the spring of 1994 to join the EU on January 1, 1995, assuming ratification of their membership by national referendums. Austria's membership was endorsed by a 66 percent "yes" vote June 12, 1994, while a positive vote also was obtained in the Finnish referendum October 16 and in Swedish balloting November 13. In contrast, Norway voted decisively against EU accession in its referendum November 27–28. Although the Swiss government maintained that Switzerland's membership application remains on file, the rejection of the EEA agreement via a Swiss referendum in December 1992 halted negotiations on EU entry. (More recently, in May 2000 Swiss voters endorsed various economic agreements with the EU, but in March 2001 they decisively rejected applying for admission.)

In late 1985 the European Council approved a number of reforms, most of which were ultimately included in the Single European Act, which amended the Treaty of Rome in ways intended to streamline the decision-making process, open up more areas to EC jurisdiction, and reinvigorate the movement toward European economic and political cooperation. The act, which went into effect July 1, 1987, following ratification by each EC member, called for the establishment of a wholly integrated internal market by the end of 1992, with increased use of majority voting within the Council of Ministers in this and other areas. The powers of the European Parliament also were expanded and, in what many observers considered one of the act's most important provisions, a permanent secretariat, headquartered in Brussels, was established to assist the presidency of the Council of Ministers in

implementing a framework of European political cooperation.

Additional wide-ranging changes to promote political and economic union within the community were included in the Treaty on European Union which, after several years of negotiations (see separate section on the EC, below, for details), was initialed at an EC summit December 9–11, 1991, in Maastricht, Netherlands. The Maastricht Treaty called for establishment of a single currency and regional central bank by 1999 and committed the signatories to the pursuit of "ever closer" political union, including common foreign and security policies.

The plans for economic and monetary union were by far the most specific of the treaty's elements. The EU leaders agreed to launch a European Monetary Institute (EMI) on January 1, 1994, directing that the advisory powers of the EMI would eventually be transformed into the formal authority of a European Central Bank (ECB). It was initially envisaged that both the bank and the proposed single currency might have been operational as early as January 1, 1997, for those countries meeting certain economic criteria and wishing to proceed. However, if that timetable could not be achieved, the single currency was to be established January 1, 1999, and the ECB six months later, although states would still need to "qualify" to participate. A separate "opt-out" protocol gave the United Kingdom the right to make a final decision later on whether to participate in the single currency, while Germany entered a similar stipulation in ratifying the treaty. Denmark's ratification was obtained only after it negotiated an unconditional opt-out from the single currency plan. Sweden, which did not seek a formal opt-out, also chose not to adopt the single currency, at least initially.

Although the 1997 target date was subsequently abandoned (see the Activities section, below), the currencies of the 11 participating countries were permanently linked with the initiation of the Economic and Monetary Union (EMU) on January 1, 1999, at which time the participants also began issuing debt in euros. Two years later, Greece, which had initially failed to qualify on the basis of economic performance, became the 12th EMU member. On January 1, 2002, euro banknotes and coins for public use were introduced in the 12 EMU members (plus Andorra, Monaco, San Marino, and the Vatican); commercial use of old national currencies was discontinued by the end of February 2002. In 2003, Swedish voters rejected adoption of the euro.

The articles on political union in the Maastricht Treaty were more vague, although the treaty introduced the concept of EU "citizenship," designed to confer a variety of rights and responsibilities on all nationals of member states. However, in response to growing European concern about turning too much control over to Brussels, draft references to the union's "federal" nature were dropped from the final text of the treaty, which emphasized instead the notion of "subsidiarity," under which all decisions would be "taken as closely as possible to the citizens." Regarding the proposed common foreign and security policies, the treaty, in one of its most widely discussed provisions, called for the strengthening of the Western European Union (WEU) to "elaborate and implement" defense decisions.

Included in the protocols affiliated with the treaty was a "social policy" charter that requires all EU states (except the United Kingdom) to guarantee a variety of workers' rights. Those provisions were deleted from the treaty proper at the UK's insistence, Prime Minister John Major threatening to repudiate the accord otherwise. Negotiations were also required with Greece, Ireland, Portugal, and Spain to ensure their endorsement of the treaty, the other EC members agreeing to a substantial expansion of development aid to the so-called "poor four."

The EC foreign and finance ministers formally signed the Maastricht Treaty on February 7, 1992, the expectation being that it would proceed smoothly through the required national ratification process in time for its scheduled January 1, 1993, implementation. However, the optimism proved unjustified as Danish voters rejected the treaty, albeit by a very narrow margin, in its first electoral test June 2. Following a strong "yes" majority in the Irish referendum June 18, the treaty was approved without substantial opposition by Greece's and Luxembourg's parliaments in July; however, its future was once again clouded by the September 20 French referendum, which endorsed ratification by only 51 percent. The community was also severely shaken in September by a currency crisis that prompted the United Kingdom and Italy to drop out of the Exchange Rate Mechanism (ERM), set up by the European Monetary System (EMS) in 1979 to limit currency fluctuations.

Facing an apparent "crisis of confidence," the EC leaders convened an emergency summit October 16, 1992, in Birmingham, England, to express their continued support for the Maastricht Treaty while reassuring opponents that some of its more ambitious goals were reduced in scope. Parliamentary approval of the treaty was subsequently achieved by the end of the year in Belgium, Italy, Germany, Netherlands, Portugal, and Spain, although Germany's formal ratification was delayed pending the outcome of a constitutional challenge. In addition, the prospect for a reversal of the Danish position improved when the December 1992 EC summit in Edinburgh, Scotland, agreed to extend Denmark several "opt-out" concessions, most importantly regarding the monetary union plan. Consequently, Danish voters accepted the accord in a second referendum on May 18, 1993. UK ratification, albeit by a very narrow margin, followed in July, and a favorable ruling in the German court case in early October finally cleared the way for implementation of the treaty. The EC heads of state and government held a special summit October 29 in Brussels to celebrate the completion of the ratification process, and the EU was launched when the treaty officially went into force November 1. The Maastricht Treaty and other EU legal texts (the so-called *acquis communautaire*) became immediately applicable to Austria, Finland, and Sweden after their 1995 admission.

A meeting of the European Council on June 16–17, 1997, in Amsterdam, Netherlands, endorsed wide-ranging amendment of the various EC and EU treaties in the interest of broadening the purview of the EU and speeding up the decision-making process. Among other things, the Amsterdam Treaty provided for formal inclusion in the EU treaty structure of (1) the Social Charter (previously relegated to protocol status in 1989); (2) a new employment chapter; (3) the Schengen Accord regarding free movement of people and goods across internal EU borders (see article on Benelux Economic Union for further details); and (4) the so-called "stability and growth pact," designed to enforce "budgetary discipline" on those countries joining the EMU, which was finally launched in 1999. The treaty also removed several policy areas from national control in favor of "common" EU authority, while some additional areas already governed by the EU were moved into the category of requiring only qualified majority approval, rather than unanimous national consent. Agreement also was reached, at least in principle, on giving the European Parliament additional authority and on limiting the size of the commission following the proposed expansion of EU membership. However, many of the provisions were watered down substantially, and several thorny issues were left to further discussion.

As of August 2001 formal membership negotiations were under way with 12 countries. Two had previously concluded Association Agreements with the EC: Malta (signed in September 1963; in force as of December 1964) and Cyprus (December 1972; June 1973). The other ten, all former Soviet Republics or Eastern European entities, had concluded pre-accession "Europe Agreements" (some with the EC prior to inauguration of the EU): Bulgaria (signed March 1993; in force as of February 1995), Czech Republic (October 1993; February 1995), Estonia (June 1995; February 1998), Hungary (December 1991; February 1994), Latvia (June 1995; February 1998), Lithuania (June 1995; February 1998), Poland (December 1991; February 1994), Romania (February 1993; February 1995); Slovakia (October 1993; February 1995); and Slovenia (June 1996; February 1999). In addition, preliminary accession discussions continued with Turkey, which signed an Association Agreement in September 1963, with effect from December 1964.

At a summit held December 12–13, 2002, in Copenhagen, Denmark, the EU formally approved the admission of ten new members: Czech Re-

public, Cyprus (excluding the Turkish Republic of Northern Cyprus), Estonia, Hungary, Latvia, Lithuania, Malta, Poland, Slovakia, and Slovenia. Accession treaties were signed in April 2003, with formal admission, following the necessary ratifications, slated for May 1, 2004. A 2007 target date was set for admission of Bulgaria and Romania, which signed accession treaties April 25, 2005. Croatia was accepted as a candidate country June 18, 2004. Formal membership negotiations with Turkey began in October 2005.

Following the collapse of the Soviet Union, the EC/EU began negotiating cooperative agreements with successor states (plus Mongolia) that, by inclination or geographical location, were not at that time regarded as prospective candidates for admission. As authorized by the Council of Ministers in October 1992, "Partnership and Cooperation Agreements," which require the assent of the European Parliament and ratification by the member states, have been concluded with 12 countries: Armenia (signed April 1996), Azerbaijan (April 1996), Belarus (March 1995), Georgia (April 1996), Kazakhstan (January 1995), Kyrgyzstan (February 1995), Moldova (November 1994), Russia (June 1994), Tajikistan (October 2004), Turkmenistan (May 1998), Ukraine (June 1994), and Uzbekistan (June 1996). A distinctive "Trade and Cooperation Agreement" was concluded with Mongolia in March 1993. Unlike the Europe Agreements, none of these pacts include free trade provisions. As of mid-2006, only the agreements with Belarus and Turkmenistan had not yet entered into force.

The EU also has varying cooperative arrangements with many other countries and regional groups, ranging from Canada and China to EFTA and the Andean Group. (For historical background, see the European Community section, below.) A Euro–Mediterranean Partnership was initiated at a November 1995 conference in Barcelona, Spain, bringing together the EU and 12 (now 10) nonmembers: Algeria, Egypt, Israel, Jordan, Lebanon, Morocco, the Palestinian Authority, Syria, Tunisia, and Turkey as well as Cyprus and Malta.

Structure. The Treaty on European Union authorized the European Council (comprising the heads of state or government of the member states) "to provide the Union with the necessary impetus for its development" and to "define the general political guidelines" for the grouping. The council meets at least twice a year, chaired by the head of state or government of the member state holding the presidency of the EU Council of Ministers. The European Council has convened under its current name since 1974, when it was agreed that European summits, previously called only as deemed necessary, would subsequently be held on a regular basis.

The remaining institutional framework of the EU has the same basic components as those originally allotted to the individual communities: the Council of the European Union (originally the Council of Ministers) to provide overall policy direction, an expert commission charged with the initiation and implementation of EU policies, a European Parliament to represent the public, and a Court of Justice to adjudicate legal issues. A Court of Auditors was added to the communities in 1977.

Depending on the subject under discussion, EU states can be represented on the Council of the European Union by their foreign ministers, as is usually the case for major decisions, or by other ministers. As a result of the Luxembourg compromise in 1966, the principle of unanimity is retained for issues in which a member feels it has a "vital interest." However, changes approved in 1987 reduced the number of areas subject to such veto, the use of qualified majority voting (QMV) in the council being increased to speed up integration efforts. The distribution of votes is as follows: France, Germany, Italy, and the United Kingdom, 29 each; Poland and Spain, 27 each; Netherlands, 13; Belgium, Czech Republic, Greece, Hungary, and Portugal, 12 each; Austria and Sweden, 10 each; Denmark, Finland, Ireland, Lithuania, and Slovakia, 7 each; Cyprus, Estonia, Latvia, Luxembourg, and Slovenia, 4 each; and Malta, 3. Under QMV, passage of a proposal typically requires 232 of the 321 votes (72.3 percent), representing a majority of the member states. If challenged, however, those in the majority must demonstrate that they collectively represent at least 62 percent of the total EU population.

The Maastricht Treaty altered the required makeup of the European Commission and the method of its selection, eliminating country representation, per se, and stipulating only that the commission must include at least one and no more than two individuals from each EU state. However, the 20-member commission that took office in January 1995 preserved the established distribution of two members from each of the "big five" (France, Germany, Italy, Spain, and the United Kingdom) and one each from the smaller states. In November 2004, the commission was expanded to 25 members, one from each state, after a six-month period in which interim commissioners from the ten new states worked alongside those who were serving out their five-year terms. In a complicated selection process, the member states first nominate a commission president and then, in consultation with that person, nominate the full commission. The president and the rest of the commission are subject to confirmation (or possible rejection) by the European Parliament and final appointment "by common accord" of the member states. In general, the commission mediates among the member governments in community matters, exercises a broad range of executive powers, and initiates community action. Its members are completely independent and are forbidden by treaty to accept instructions from any national government. Decisions are made by majority vote, although in practice most are adopted by consensus.

Following were the members of the commission and their principal portfolios as of June 2006:

José Manuel Barroso (Portugal)	President
Jacques Barrot (France)	Vice President; transport
Franco Frattini (Italy)	Vice President; justice, freedom, and security
Siim Kallas (Estonia)	Vice President; administrative affairs, audit, and anti-fraud
Günter Verheugen (Germany)	Vice President; enterprise and industry

Margot Wallström [f] (Sweden)	Vice President; institutional relations and communication strategy
Joaquín Almunia (Spain)	Economic and monetary affairs
Joe Borg (Malta)	Fisheries and maritime affairs
Stavros Dimas (Greece)	Environment
Benita Ferrero-Waldner [f] (Austria)	External relations and European Neighborhood policy
Ján Figel' (Slovakia)	Education, training, culture, and multilingualism
Mariann Fischer Boel [f] (Denmark)	Agriculture and rural development
Dalia Grybauskaité [f] (Lithuania)	Financial programming and budget
Danuta Hübner [f] (Poland)	Regional policy
László Kovács (Hungary)	Taxation and customs
Neelie Kroes [f] (Netherlands)	Competition
Markos Kyprianou (Cyprus)	Health and consumer affairs
Peter Mandelson (United Kingdom)	External trade
Charlie McCreevy (Ireland)	Internal market and services
Louis Michel (Belgium)	Development and humanitarian affairs
Andris Piebalgs (Latvia)	Energy
Janez Potočnik (Slovenia)	Science and research
Viviane Reding [f] (Luxembourg)	Information society and media
Olli Rehn (Finland)	Enlargement of the EU
Vladimir Špidla (Czech Republic)	Employment, social affairs, and equal opportunities

[f] = female

The European Parliament is an outgrowth of the consultative parliamentary assembly established for the ECSC and subsequently mandated to serve in the same capacity for the EEC and Euratom. The parliament's authority, relatively limited at first, has gradually increased over its history. Under a 1975 treaty it was empowered to participate, save for deference to the Council of Ministers in regard to agricultural spending, in formulation of the an-nual EC budget, a draft of which it can reject by a two-thirds vote. The Single European Act and the Treaty on European Union further extended parliament's budgetary powers and ability to affect legislation. In addition, the parliament, previously only authorized to dismiss the entire commission (but not individual members) by a vote of censure, can now reject nominees for individual posts. The parliament, which meets annually (normally in Strasbourg, France) and has a five-year term, must also approve EU treaties as well as the admission of new EU members.

The move to direct elections in all member states in 1979 was followed by the Maastricht Treaty's direction that the Parliament should draw up plans for future elections to take place under uniform voting procedures and constituency arrangements. Some progress was made in this regard for the 1994 elections, notably in that for the first time all EU citizens could vote in their EU country of residence. Following their accession to the EU on January 1, 1995, Austria, Finland, and Sweden initially sent nominated members to the European Parliament, prior to the holding of direct elections in Sweden in September 1995 and in Austria and Finland in October 1996.

The most recent election was held June 10–13, 2004. As a consequence of the previous month's enlargement, the parliament was expanded to 732 seats, allocated as follows: Austria, 18; Belgium, 24; Cyprus, 6; Czech Republic, 24; Denmark, 14; Estonia, 6; Finland, 14; France, 78; Germany, 99; Greece, 24; Hungary, 24; Ireland, 13; Italy, 78; Latvia, 9; Lithuania, 13; Luxembourg, 6; Malta, 5; Netherlands, 27; Poland, 54; Portugal, 24; Slovakia, 14; Slovenia, 7; Spain, 54; Sweden, 19; United Kingdom, 78. Members sit not by nationality, but by political affiliation, as delineated below:

European People's Party/European Democrats (EPP-ED), 268

Austria	Austrian People's Party (ÖVP), 6
Belgium	Christian Democratic and Flemish (CD&V), 4
	Christian Social Party–*Europäische Volkspartei* (CSP-EVP), 1

	Democratic Humanist Center (CDH), 1
Cyprus	Democratic Rally (Desy), 2
	Gia tin Evropi, 1
Czech Republic	Civic Democratic Party (ODS), 9
	Association of Independents and European Democrats (SN/ED), 3
	Christian and Democratic Union–Czech People's Party (KDU-ČSL), 2
Denmark	Conservative People's Party (KF), 1
Estonia	Fatherland Union (IL), 1
Finland	National Coalition Party (Kok), 4
France	Union for a Popular Movement (UMP), 17
Germany	Christian Democratic Union (CDU), 40
	Christian Social Union (CSU), 9
Greece	New Democracy (ND), 11
Hungary	Federation of Young Democrats–Hungarian Civic Party (FiDeSz-MPP), 12
	Hungarian Democratic Forum (MDF), 1
Ireland	*Fine Gael*, 5
Italy	*Forza Italia* (FI), 16
	Union of Christian and Center Democrats (UDC), 5
	Popular Alliance–Democratic Union for Europe (*Popolari*-UDEUR), 1
	South Tyrol People's Party (SVP), 1
	Pensioners' Party (PP), 1
Latvia	New Time (JL), 2
	People's Party (TP), 1
Lithuania	Homeland Union (TS), 2
Luxembourg	Christian Social People's Party (CSV/PCS), 3
Malta	Nationalist Party (PN), 2
Netherlands	Christian Democratic Appeal (CDA), 7
Poland	Civic Platform (PO), 15
	Polish Peasants' Party (PSL), 4
Portugal	Social Democratic Party (PSD), 7
	Popular Party (PP), 2
Slovakia	Slovak Democratic and Christian Union (SDKÚ), 3
	Christian Democratic Movement (KDH), 3
	Party of the Hungarian Coalition (SMK), 2

Slovenia	Slovenian Democratic Party (SDS), 2
	New Slovenia–Christian People's Party (NSi), 2
Spain	Popular Party (PP), 24
Sweden	Moderate Coalition Party (MSP), 4
	Christian Democratic Party (Kd), 1
U. Kingdom	Conservative Party, 25
	Scottish Conservative and Unionist Party, 2
N. Ireland	Ulster Unionist Party (UUP), 1

Party of European Socialists (PES), 200

Austria	Austrian Social Democratic Party (SPÖ), 7
Belgium	Socialist Party (PS), 4
	Socialist Party–Differently (SP.A)/ Spirit Coalition, 3
Czech Republic	Czech Social Democratic Party (ČSSD), 2
Denmark	Social Democratic Party (SD), 5
Estonia	Social Democratic Party (SDE), 3
Finland	Finnish Social Democratic Party (SSDP), 3
France	Socialist Party (PS), 31
Germany	Social Democratic Party of Germany (SPD), 23
Greece	Panhellenic Socialist Movement (Pasok), 8
Hungary	Hungarian Socialist Party (MSzP), 9
Ireland	The Labour Party, 1
Italy	Democrats of the Left (DS), 12
	Italian Democratic Socialists (SDI), 2
	Independents, 2
Lithuania	Lithuanian Social Democratic Party (LSDP), 2
Luxembourg	Socialist Workers' Party of Luxembourg (LSAP), 1
Malta	Malta Labour Party (MLP), 3
Netherlands	Labor Party (PvdA), 7
Poland	Democratic Left Alliance (SLD)/ Union of Labor (UP), 5
	Polish Social Democrats (SDPL), 3
Portugal	Portuguese Socialist Party (PSP), 12
Slovakia	Direction (*Směr*), 2
	Party of the Democratic Left (SDL'), 1
Slovenia	United List of Social Democrats (ZLSD), 1

Spain	Spanish Socialist Workers' Party (PSOE), 24
Sweden	Social Democratic Labor Party (SdAp), 5
U. Kingdom	Labour Party, 19

Alliance of Liberals and Democrats for Europe (ALDE), 88

Austria	Liberals, 1
Belgium	Flemish Liberals and Democrats (VLD), 3
	Reformist Movement (MR), 3
Cyprus	Democratic Party (Deko), 1
Denmark	Liberal Party (V), 3
	Radical Liberal Party (RV), 1
Estonia	Estonian Center Party (K), 1
	Estonian Reform Party (RE), 1
Finland	Finnish Center (Kesk), 4
	Swedish People's Party (RKP/ SFP), 1
France	Union for French Democracy (UDF), 11
Germany	Free Democratic Party (FDP), 7
Hungary	Alliance of Free Democrats (SzDSz), 2
Ireland	Independent, 1
Italy	Democracy Is Freedom–*La Margherita*, 7
	Italy of Values (IdV), 2
	Bonino List, 2
	Movement of European Republicans (MRE), 1
Latvia	Latvian Way (LC), 1
Lithuania	Darbo Party (DP), 5
	Lithuanian Center Union (LCS), 2
Luxembourg	Democratic Party (DP), 1
Netherlands	People's Party for Freedom and Democracy (VVD), 4
	Democrats 66 (D66), 1
Poland	Freedom Union (UW), 4
Slovenia	Liberal Democracy of Slovenia (LDS), 2
Spain	Democratic Convergence of Catalonia (CDC), 1
	Basque Nationalist Party (PNV), 1
Sweden	Liberal People's Party (FP), 2
	Center Party (CP), 1
U. Kingdom	Liberal Democrats (LD), 2

The Greens/European Free Alliance (Greens/EFA), 42

Austria	The Greens, 2
Belgium	Ecologists (ECOLO), 1
	Green!, 1
Denmark	Socialist People's Party (SF), 1
Finland	Green League (Vihr), 1
France	The Greens, 6
Germany	Alliance '90/The Greens, 13
Italy	Green Federation, 2
Latvia	For Human Rights in United Latvia (PCTVL), 1
Luxembourg	The Greens, 1
Netherlands	Green Left (GL), 2
	Transparent Europe, 2
Spain	The Greens, 1 (elected on the PSOE list)
	Initiative for Catalonia–Greens (IC-V), 1
	Catalan Republican Left (ERC), 1
Sweden	Green Ecology Party (MpG), 1
U. Kingdom	Green Party of England and Wales, 2
	Scottish National Party (SNP), 2
	Plaid Cymru, 1

European United Left/Nordic Green Left (EUL/NGL), 41

Cyprus	Progressive Party of the Working People (AKEL), 2
Czech Republic	Communist Party of Bohemia and Moravia (KSČM), 6
Denmark	People's Movement against the European Union, 1
Finland	Left-Wing Alliance (Vas), 1
France	French Communist Party (PCF), 2
	Reunion Communist Party (PCR), 1
Germany	Party of Democratic Socialism (PDS), 7
Greece	Communist Party of Greece (KKE), 3
	Progressive Left Coalition, 1
Ireland	*Sinn Féin*, 1
Italy	Communist Refoundation Party (PRC), 5
	Party of Italian Communists (PdCI), 2
Netherlands	Socialist Party (SP), 2
Portugal	Unified Democratic Coalition (CDU), 2
	Left Block (BE), 1
Spain	United Left (IU), 1
Sweden	Left Party (Vp), 2
U. Kingdom	
N. Ireland	*Sinn Féin*, 1

Independence/Democracy Group (IND/DEM), 37

Czech Republic	Independents (N), 1	
Denmark	June Movement, 1	
France	Movement for France (MPF), 3	
Greece	*Laïkos Orthodoxos Synagermos–G. Karatzaferis* (LA.OS), 1	
Ireland	Independent, 1	
Italy	Northern League (LN), 4	
Netherlands	Christian Union/Political Reformed Party Coalition SGP, 2 (1 each for the Christian Union and the SGP)	
Poland	League of Polish Families (LPR), 10	
Sweden	*Junilistan*, 3	
U. Kingdom	UK Independence Party (UKIP), 11	

Union for Europe of the Nations (UEN), 27

Denmark	Danish People's Party (DFp), 1
Ireland	*Fianna Fáil*, 4
Italy	National Alliance (AN), 9
Latvia	Fatherland and Freedom/Latvian National Conservative Party (TB/LNNK), 4
Lithuania	Union of Peasants and New Democracy Parties (VNDPS), 1
	Liberal Democratic Party (LDP), 1
Poland	Law and Justice (PiS), 7

Unattached, 29

Austria	Martin, 2
	Freedom Party of Austria (FPÖ), 1
Belgium	Flemish Bloc (VB), 3
Czech Republic	Independents (N), 1
France	National Front (FN), 7
Italy	*Alternativa Sociale–Lista Mussolini*, 1
	New Italian Socialist Party (NPSI), 1
	Social Movement–Tricolor Flame (MS-FT), 1
	Socialist Unity, 1
Poland	Self-Defense of the Polish Republic Party (*Samoobrona*), 6
	Movement for a Democratic Slovakia (HZDS), 3
U. Kingdom	UK Independence Party (UKIP), 1
N. Ireland	Democratic Unionist Party (DUP), 1

The Court of Justice of the European Communities (less formally, the European Court of Justice—ECJ), encompassing 25 judges and 8 advocates-general, sits in Luxembourg. In 1989 a Court of First Instance was established to help the ECJ deal with its increasingly large workload. The 25 members of each court are appointed for six years by agreement between the governments of the member states. Both courts can sit in plenary session or in chambers of three or five judges. Since the 2004 EU enlargement, instead of convening in a plenary session, 13 ECJ judges can sit as a "Grand Chamber." The ECJ can sit in plenary session when a member state or an EU/EC institution that is party to the proceedings so requests or in particularly complex or important cases. A European Civil Service Tribunal, comprised of seven judges, is under the Court of First Instance.

The ECJ's principal role is to ensure EU-EC treaties are interpreted and applied properly. Accordingly, it can decide whether acts of the commission, the council, the member governments, and other bodies are compatible with the governing treaties. For example, it ruled in 1986 that the budget approved in December 1985 was invalid because of spending increases voted by the parliament without the concurrence of the Council of Ministers. The ECJ can also rule in cases submitted by national courts regarding interpretation of the treaties and implementing legislation. In a seminal decision, the court ruled in October 1979 that the commission had the authority to represent the EC in global commodity agreement negotiations, with participation by individual member states dependent on such considerations as whether the EC as a whole or the separate states were to be responsible for financial arrangements. The ECJ can also decide if a community institution is in breach of the treaties for failing to act.

In addition, if the court finds that a member state has failed to fulfill an obligation under the treaties, it can impose financial penalties. In December 2001, for example, the ECJ ruled that France's continuing embargo against British beef imports was illegal; France, facing the prospect of heavy fines, finally relented in October 2002. In May 2002 the ECJ announced that henceforth individuals, businesses, and others would be given greater leeway to challenge EU legislation, regulations, and decisions in the ECJ and the Court of First Instance. On September 13, 2005, in what promised to be a landmark case, the ECJ ruled that a 2003 decision allowed the EC, with the support of the European Parliament, to require member states to enforce directives of the EU by means of national criminal law. Ten member states, most notably the UK, had vainly argued against the decision. On November 23 of the same year the EC issued its first list of "EU crimes" that member countries would be required to prosecute. National laws would be used, but penalties would be the same EU-wide. An initial list of EU crimes included environmental crimes and marine pollution, corruption in the private sector, counterfeiting, financial fraud and money-laundering, human trafficking, and improper and destructive use of computers.

The Court of Auditors, first established in 1977, has institutional status on a par with the commission, council, ECJ, and parliament by the Treaty on European Union. The court, whose 25 members are appointed for six-year terms by the council in consultation with the parliament, is responsible for reviewing all EU expenditures and revenues and conducts external audits, sometimes on the spot, of EU as well as national institutions.

The European Monetary Institute (EMI), an interim advisory body that opened January 1, 1994, in Frankfurt, Germany, was transformed into the European Central Bank (ECB) as of June 1, 1998. The ECB's highest decision-making body, the Governing Council, comprises the governors of the central banks of the 12 euro-zone countries plus the 6 members of the ECB Executive Board. The latter is appointed, by consensus, by the euro-zone countries' prime ministers or presidents. Among other things, the Governing Council determines monetary policy for the EMU members and sets ECB interest rates. An additional ECB governing body, the General Council, comprises the ECB president and vice president (who are chosen from among the members of the Executive Board) plus the central bank governors from all the EU countries.

Several other new institutions were approved in connection with the Treaty on European Union,

including a European Environment Agency, located in Copenhagen, and Europol, a new regional police agency. The latter, which opened its headquarters in February 1994 in The Hague, Netherlands, was mandated initially to assist the police forces of member states in collecting and analyzing information regarding drug trafficking and money laundering. However, under the Europol Convention, which was endorsed by the EU heads of state in July 1995 and entered into effect October 1, 1998, Europol can investigate a broader variety of illegalities, including trafficking in nuclear materials, pedophilia, and illegal immigration. Terrorism was added to its mandate in 1998.

Activities. The first of what could appropriately be termed EU summits was held December 11–12, 1993, in Brussels. (For previous EC summits, see section on the EC, below.) With attention focused for two years on the Treaty on European Union ratification process, the EU heads of state and government turned to the region's economic problems, particularly continued high unemployment. The summit adopted an economic recovery plan that appeared to represent a compromise between those advocating activist labor policies and those convinced that government influence was already too great in economic affairs. For the first camp, the summit approved a six-year public works program designed to create jobs in, among other areas, the transportation, energy, environmental, and telecommunications sectors. (Agreement was not reached, however, on the $22 billion annual budget for the initiative that had been proposed by Jacques Delors, president of the commission.) For those looking to the free market to resolve unemployment, the summit called for a reduction in "rigidities" in the European labor market, proposing that minimum wages be lowered and that labor costs that support European social welfare programs be significantly reduced.

In other activity, the European Council endorsed negotiations toward a "stability pact" for Central and Eastern European nations seeking EU membership. The pact would attempt to establish agreement on the protection of minority rights in those countries and create mechanisms for the peaceful resolution of border disputes. Among other things, it was hoped that such an initiative would preclude a repetition of the breakdown that had occurred in the former Yugoslavia, the EU having been criticized for its seeming paralysis in dealing with that situation. The union's potential for effective common foreign policy was also called into question by Greece's unilateral imposition of a partial economic embargo against Macedonia in February 1994 (see article on Macedonia).

The European Council once again tried to emphasize economic affairs during its June 24–25, 1994, summit in Corfu, Greece, one formal highlight of which was the signing of the Partnership and Cooperation Agreement with Russia. Nevertheless, media reports centered on the union's latest political difficulty—the failure of the council to agree on a successor to commission President Delors, who announced his retirement effective January 1, 1995. Although Germany and France reportedly gathered strong support for their preferred candidate, Belgian Prime Minister Jean-Luc Dehaene, UK Prime Minister John Major vetoed Dehaene as too "federalist." Consequently, a special summit was required July 15 in Brussels to approve the selection of a compromise nominee—Jacques Santer, the prime minister of Luxembourg. However, the recently elected European Parliament, some of whose members were upset at not being consulted beforehand, came within 22 votes of rejecting Santer's appointment in late July. Furthermore, nominees to the new commission subsequently faced "grilling" confirmation hearings in the parliament, whose makeup reflected the overall European cleavage between those favoring relatively quick movement toward greater political unity and monetary union and the increasingly vocal "Euro-sceptics," who opposed additional integration.

The focus of the December 9–10, 1994, summit in Essen, Germany, was on EU enlargement, the heads of state of Austria, Finland, and Sweden participating in preparation for the accession of those countries January 1, 1995. The leaders of Bulgaria, Czech Republic, Hungary, Poland, Slovakia, and Romania also attended the summit to discuss in greater detail the criteria for eventual admission. However, despite the obvious "external" fervor for

the EU, enthusiasm within the union subsequently appeared to wane, particularly in regard to the common currency proposal. Turbulence in the financial markets, precipitated in part by the Mexican peso crisis, forced the devaluation of the Spanish peseta and the Portuguese escudo in March, confirming that at least some EU members were retreating from rather than progressing toward the conditions necessary for monetary union. Consequently, the European Council, meeting June 26–27, in Cannes, France, acknowledged that the proposed single currency would not be launched in 1997.

Concern over the monetary issue continued to grow in the second half of 1995 as German officials openly questioned the prospects for some countries, including Belgium and Italy, of qualifying for use of the common currency even by the 1999 final target date. However, the summit held December 15–16, 1995, in Madrid, Spain, reaffirmed the EU's commitment to the 1999 schedule, although it was emphasized that the required economic standards would not be diluted for participation in the monetary union. The EU leaders also agreed that the new currency would be called the "euro."

The December 1995 summit also gave formal approval for creation of an intergovernmental conference (IGC) that was authorized to propose revisions to the EC/EU founding treaties. Issues to be addressed included the possible elimination of the unanimity requirement for major EU decisions, especially with regard to the EU's two new "pillars"—foreign and security policy, and justice and home affairs. Potentially extensive structural changes were also to be considered in the hope that such bodies as the commission and the parliament could become less unwieldy, particularly given the anticipated admission of new members to the union. In addition, ardent integrationists hoped institutional reforms would convince a still largely skeptical European population that the EU was prepared to deal effectively with basic day-to-day concerns, such as unemployment, environmental degradation, and internal security.

Although the IGC was launched in March 1996, little progress was apparent by the time of the June 21–22 summit in Florence, Italy. EU leaders reportedly hoped to provide a boost for the initiative at the summit, but the session was instead dominated by the conflict between the UK and its EU partners over the EU's March ban on exports of UK beef and beef products following the outbreak of bovine spongiform encephalopathy (BSE, the so-called "mad-cow disease") in UK herds. A compromise was quickly reached under which the EU agreed to eliminate the ban gradually (albeit without a specific timetable) in connection with an expanded UK slaughter program. The "mad-cow" issue in and of itself was not widely perceived as representing a long-term threat to the EU; much more problematic, however, was the strong UK response to the ban, the government of John Major having instituted a policy of "noncooperation" in May under which the UK veto was briefly used to block all EU action requiring unanimity. For "Eurosceptics," the beef fracas served as a dramatic reminder of the quagmire the EU could find itself in over many economic issues unless veto powers were substantially reduced. (For subsequent BSE developments and the termination of the beef ban, see the United Kingdom article.)

Continued differences of opinion also were still apparent at the summit regarding the "social dimension" of the EU, as Santer failed to gain approval of his proposed "confidence pact." The pact had called for underspent EU resources to be devoted to some 14 infrastructure projects in connection with an agreement among EU governments, unions, and employers to reduce employee benefits and otherwise make European labor markets more globally competitive.

Attention subsequently focused on negotiations regarding monetary union, German leaders indicating that the entire concept was in jeopardy unless other nations were willing to accept enforceable budgetary discipline as a means of keeping the euro "strong." Bonn's proposed "stability pact" on the matter reportedly met with strong French resistance prior to the EU summit held December 13–14, 1996, in Dublin. However, a compromise favoring the German position was negotiated whereby participants in the monetary union would be subject to mandatory heavy financial penalties

for breaching fiscal guidelines. (One goal of the accord was to preclude countries from attempting to "spend their way out" of future recessions by running up large budget deficits that would weaken the euro.) Agreement also was reached on the creation of a new exchange rate mechanism to determine the relationship of the euro to the currencies of the countries that postponed entry into the monetary union. In addition, the summit endorsed the Dublin Document on Employment, underscoring the continued problem of joblessness, which had somewhat soured the attitude toward further integration on the part of those concerned over how monetary union and devolution of trade authority to Brussels might disrupt local jobs.

Dissension continued within the EU ranks in early 1997 concerning the final IGC proposals on the extent of authority to be turned over by the national governments to EU control. Some members called for the elimination of the national veto completely, endorsing qualified majority voting in all areas and substantial restrictions on "selective cooperation," which permitted frequent "opt-out" decisions by national governments opposed to or uncertain about major EU plans. The Netherlands offered a compromise under which some 25 policy areas would be covered by majority voting, while the national veto would be reserved for "sensitive" issues, such as EU enlargement, direct taxation, and future treaty amendments. However, the UK government labeled the proposal "totally unacceptable." London also opposed the proposed integration of the WEU into the EU.

A special heads of government summit May 23, 1997, in Noordwijk, Netherlands, was buoyed by the presence of the new UK Prime Minister Tony Blair, whose Labour government was decidedly more enthusiastic regarding the EU than its Conservative predecessor. Nevertheless, most of the contentious issues, such as the distribution of voting power between large and small countries on the Council of the European Union, and the size of the commission following expansion, remained unresolved. Consequently, the Amsterdam Treaty signed at the June 16–17 summit contained only vague commitments "in principle" in those areas as well as the extension of majority voting. Although the WEU proposal was formally rejected, integrationists applauded the treaty's inclusion of the Schengen Accord on removal of border controls, the EU Social Charter, and the much-discussed stability pact.

The stability pact was the source of conflict at the summit after new French Prime Minister Lionel Jospin indicated that France was reconsidering its previous commitment to support restrictions on spending because they might interfere with employment programs. The French Socialist government ultimately endorsed the pact, but only after the other EU members agreed to insert an employment chapter into the Amsterdam Treaty and otherwise emphasize the continent's unemployment problem. Consequently, a special summit November 20–21 in Luxembourg was devoted solely to unemployment, the session's joint action plan authorizing a new ECU 10 billion ($11.3 billion) initiative by the European Investment Bank (EIB) to finance small- and medium-sized businesses and to provide comprehensive job training programs for the unemployed.

Despite the perceived weakness of the Amsterdam Treaty, its passage did permit the EU to turn to its two other pressing issues—enlargement and monetary union. Regarding the former, a December 12–13 summit in Luxembourg invited five ex-communist states (Czech Republic, Estonia, Hungary, Poland, and Slovenia) and Cyprus to begin formal membership discussions in March 1998. (The summit followed the recommendations of commission President Santer, although some EU capitals had urged that Bulgaria, Latvia, Lithuania, Romania, and Slovakia be included on the list.) The inclusion of Cyprus among the "first-wave" countries was controversial, particularly because Turkey was pointedly excluded. EU officials said they hoped that both the Cypriot and Turkish communities on Cyprus would participate in the membership negotiations, although the government of the Turkish Republic of Northern Cyprus declined the invitation.

Regarding the "race to the euro," 1997 proved to be a surprisingly successful year for most EU members as self-imposed budgetary constraints and a generally flourishing European economy propelled them toward the criteria established by the Maastricht Treaty. Consequently, in February 1998 the commission recommended that 11 EU states (Austria, Belgium, Finland, France, Germany, Ireland, Italy, Luxembourg, Netherlands, Portugal, and Spain) be invited to participate in the launching of the EMU on January 1, 1999.

On March 26, 1998, Germany officially endorsed the proposed EMU launching, despite that the German Bundesbank questioned the "sustainability" of the financial status of several countries, with Belgium and Italy drawing particular attention because of their high level of official debt. In April the European Parliament called for treaty revisions to ensure the "accountability" of the incoming ECB, suggesting that a monitoring body (including several parliament members) be established to review ECB decisions and activity. An EU summit May 1–3 in Brussels formally agreed that the ECB would open June 1 and would assume responsibility January 1, 1999, for monitoring policy (including setting interest rates) for the countries adopting the euro.

The summit's formal announcement was issued only after protracted negotiations on a president for the ECB. EMI head Wim Duisenberg, the candidate backed by Germany and most other prospective EMU members, finally achieved the nod over Jean-Claude Trichet, whom Paris proposed in what was perceived as an attempt by the French government to convince its citizenry that it would not accept German "domination" in the new European fiscal arrangements. Once again underscoring its expanded assertiveness, the European Parliament criticized the EU leaders for "politicizing" the process. (In November 2003, Trichet succeeded Duisenberg as ECB president.)

Ireland approved the Amsterdam Treaty via national referendum in late May 1998, and Danish voters followed suit shortly thereafter with a 55 percent endorsement. The latter was considered an important test in light of the problems caused in 1993 by the initial Danish rejection of the Maastricht Treaty. Consequently, with final EU-wide ratification of the Amsterdam Treaty seemingly assured, the June 15–16 EU summit in Cardiff, United Kingdom, was relatively quiet, with major decisions being postponed at least until after the German elections scheduled for September.

An informal EU summit October 24–25, 1998 in Pörtschach, Austria, discussed plans for new employment programs and expanded public spending in other areas, illuminating that most EU national governments (including Germany) were now under center-left influence. However, deep divisions remained on the issue of proposed reductions in agricultural subsidies, and the EU summit held December 11–12 in Vienna set March 1999 as a deadline for a settlement. Meanwhile, one of the EU's most serious crises to date had begun to develop over allegations of fraud and corruption in EU budgetary matters. In November the EU Court of Auditors reported uncovering serious "mismanagement," and commission President Santer had already created an internal "anti-fraud" unit.

The EMU was formally launched January 1, 1999, amid great fanfare, with supporters describing it (and the collateral adoption of the euro) as representing the "biggest leap forward" since the Treaty of Rome. However, excitement over that development was quickly dampened in mid-January when the European Parliament appeared poised to approve a censure motion that would have forced the resignation of the commission. The motion was ultimately defeated (293–232), but only after a "peace package" was negotiated under which the commission agreed to the establishment of an independent panel of experts to assess the situation. In March the panel reported that substantial fraud, mismanagement, and nepotism had "gone unnoticed" by the commissioners, many of whom had "lost control" over spending within their areas of responsibility. Consequently, the commission resigned en masse on March 16, and EU leaders convened in a special summit March 24–26 in Berlin to designate Romano Prodi, former prime minister of Italy, as the next president of the commission. Prodi subsequently received the endorsement of the European Parliament; however, the selection of a new commission was delayed until after

the upcoming European Parliament elections. Consequently, Santer and all other commissioners remained in office in a caretaker capacity. The Berlin summit also approved a final 2000–2006 EU budget in which proposed cuts in agricultural subsidies were significantly diluted, mostly at France's insistence. Shortly after the summit, the French legislature ratified the Amsterdam Treaty, paving the way for its entry into force on May 1.

The elections to the European Parliament, held between June 10 and 13 in the differing venues, were notable in that they led to formation of a 233-seat center-right bloc by the European People's Party and the European Democrats (EPP-ED), thereby unseating the Party of European Socialists (180 seats) as the plurality grouping. On September 15 the legislature confirmed Prodi as the head of a new European Commission scheduled to serve out the remainder of its predecessor's term and to start a new five-year term beginning in January 2000. The Prodi commission entered office pledging significant internal reform, although in its first year Prodi himself drew frequently harsh criticism for inefficiency and lack of leadership.

A special two-day heads of government session October 15–16, 1999, in Tampere, Finland, focused on matters related to the EU's third "pillar," justice and home affairs, including immigration, asylum, and organized crime. The summit also marked a change in strategy regarding enlargement, with leaders agreeing that negotiations on accession should be opened with six additional prospective members—Bulgaria, Latvia, Lithuania, Malta, Romania, and Slovakia—early in the new year. (Formal talks began February 15, 2000, in Brussels.) The decision received the assent of the European Council during its summit December 10–11 in Helsinki, putting the six countries on the same footing as the six that were regarded as "fast-track" entries: Cyprus, Czech Republic, Estonia, Hungary, Poland, and Slovenia. The council also formally approved Turkey as a candidate for admission, despite reservations regarding its human rights record. At the same time, the EU recognized the urgency, in advance of enlargement, of preparing institutional reforms and revising current decision-making mechanisms. Accordingly, in February 2000 the EU foreign ministers established an intergovernmental conference directed to present its recommendations for changes to the EU treaties at a year-end summit in Nice, France.

During the same period the EU was moving steadily toward establishing its own military capability. On June 3–4, 1999, a European Council meeting in Cologne, Germany, selected then NATO Secretary General Javier Solana Madariaga of Spain as the first EU high representative for foreign and security policy, a position authorized by the Treaty of Amsterdam. Collaterally, the heads of state and government agreed to begin formalizing a much-debated joint security and defense policy, under which the EU would assume the WEU's defense role and its "Petersberg tasks" (named for the official German guesthouse near Bonn where, in 1992, the WEU defined its future military responsibilities): peacekeeping, humanitarian and rescue missions, and military crisis management. As a further step in the process of taking over the WEU's operational functions, Solana was given the additional role of WEU secretary general in October.

An unprecedented joint meeting of EU foreign and defense ministers November 15, 1999, in Brussels confirmed Solana's WEU appointment and, drawing on the experiences of the conflicts in Bosnia and Kosovo, discussed how to handle future altercations. A central component of the EU strategy was formation of an EU rapid reaction force (RRF) that would be independent of NATO and the United States. A month later, at the Helsinki summit, the European Council authorized formation by 2003 of a 60,000-member RRF that could respond to crises that did not involve NATO as a whole. As the plan continued to evolve over the following year, the EU agreed to work closely with NATO, thereby mitigating U.S. objections. It also agreed to invite the participation in EU-led missions of non-EU states that were NATO members—most particularly, Turkey—as well as non-NATO European countries, such as Russia. Formation of the RRF was given a further go-ahead by the foreign and defense ministers meeting November 20, 2000, in Brussels, although Denmark exercised its right

to opt out. The ministers also agreed to assume the WEU's operational role. Earlier in the year, in April, the WEU/EU Eurocorps, which was inaugurated in November 1993, undertook its most significant mission to date, namely command of the NATO-led Kosovo Force (KFOR) in Yugoslavia.

During 2000 several important developments occurred in the economic sphere. A special heads of government summit March 23–24 in Lisbon introduced a ten-year program, dubbed the "Lisbon Strategy," to develop the EU into "the world's most competitive and dynamic knowledge-driven economy," with attendant goals that included improving the employment rate from 61 percent to 70 percent and achieving an average annual growth rate of 3 percent. (An interim report on this plan's performance, delivered at the March 2006 economic summit in Brussels, indicated that the EU was falling far short of its ambitious goals and economic integration. In particular the Lisbon goal of catching up with the United States by 2010 seemed out of reach.) At the next European Council session, held June 19–20 in Santa Maria da Fiera, Portugal, the EU leaders agreed to institute a system for stopping cross-border tax evasion. Initially, Austria and Luxembourg objected to requirements that they provide information on nonresident banking accounts, but they ultimately acquiesced despite the necessity of revising their bank secrecy laws. The EU scheme called for convincing other international banking and finance centers, including various "off-shore" locations, to agree to exchange information on account holders. If successful, the EU would then introduce a seven-year transitional period during which EU members could choose either to exchange information with other tax authorities or to levy a 20–25 percent withholding tax on the investment earnings of foreign-owned accounts.

The most notable development of 2000 with regard to the EMU concerned efforts to stabilize the sliding euro. On September 22 the ECB and the Group of Seven (G-7) central banks intervened to halt its decline, the value of the currency against the U.S. dollar having dropped by 27 percent since its introduction. The decline nevertheless continued into October, reaching a nadir of $0.82 on October 26 and remaining below $0.90 through the first half of 2001. Meanwhile, in July the EU finance ministers named a committee of "wise men," headed by former EMI president Alexandre Lamfalussy, to examine the operation of EU securities markets and to propose changes in current practices and regulations. In September the Paris, Brussels, and Amsterdam stock exchanges merged as Euronext, the expectation being that bourses in Rome, Madrid, and Luxembourg also might join in the near future. Already second only to London in terms of listings and market capitalization, Euronext anticipated becoming "the first fully integrated cross-border European market for equities, bonds, derivatives, and commodities." As of 2005 it also served stock and derivatives markets in Portugal and derivatives markets in the United Kingdom, and claimed to be Europe's leading stock exchange in terms of trading volume.

In December 2000 the EU's comprehensive review of institutional reform, which included a special summit October 12–15 in Biarritz, France, drew to a close. Meeting on December 7–11, 2000, in Nice, the European Council agreed to significant restructuring of EU institutions, primarily to accommodate 12 new member countries. (The 13th potential member, Turkey, was excluded from the calculations, given that it had not yet begun formal accession negotiations.) Requiring ratification by the European Parliament and all 15 current member countries, the resultant Treaty of Nice bowed to German insistence that the expanded European Parliament and the system of qualified majority voting give greater weight to the populations of the member states.

The Treaty of Nice, which was signed by the members' foreign ministers February 26, 2001, in Brussels, met its first roadblock June 8 when, as if echoing Denmark's 1992 initial rejection of the Maastricht Treaty, some 54 percent of Ireland's voters rebuffed it. EU leaders insisted, however, that expansion plans would proceed and that efforts would be made to address the Irish public's concerns. These included the impact of expansion on Ireland's standing and the status of its military

neutrality in the context of the EU's new military capabilities. Ultimately, the Irish voters were satisfied, and in an October 20, 2002, referendum 62.9 percent endorsed the Treaty of Nice, permitting its entry into force February 1, 2003.

The initial negative Irish vote came in the context of an ongoing debate over the EU's long-term purpose and structure. German leaders, on the one hand, called for even closer integration, including adoption of a federal structure. France, on the other hand, continued to oppose such a model, which it saw as threatening national constituencies. In May, responding to a federalist plan presented by German Chancellor Gerhard Schröder in April, French Prime Minister Lionel Jospin instead proposed a "federation of nation-states." Another area of contention was the Charter of Fundamental Rights, which was drawn up in September 2000 and formally approved by the heads of government at the Nice summit. The charter's firmest opponent, the United Kingdom, argued that its incorporation into the EU treaty was unnecessary because all EU members had already acceded to the European Convention on Human Rights.

During the first half of 2001 the necessity of rethinking the $35 billion annual Common Agricultural Policy (CAP—see the EC discussion for its history) also came to the fore. One crisis alone, the "mad-cow" episode that originated in the United Kingdom, was decimating the CAP budget as the EU covered much of the expense of slaughtering affected herds. The CAP also mandated that the EU buy excess beef, supplies having risen as consumer demand for the commodity dropped and some countries halted imports. On top of that, the first major outbreak of foot and mouth disease in decades, once again primarily in the United Kingdom, further overburdened the CAP budget.

In a significant development for the EU's external relations, the first summit of Balkan states and the EU was held November 24, 2000, in Zagreb, Croatia. The EU pledged more than 4.5 billion euros in aid during 2000–2006 to support "reconstruction, democratization, and stabilization" in Albania, Bosnia and Herzegovina, Croatia,

Macedonia, and Yugoslavia. Most Balkan states had already expressed an interest in eventual EU membership.

During their February 25–26, 2001, meeting in Brussels the EU foreign ministers agreed to abolish virtually all trade barriers for 48 least developed countries, including 39 members of the EC-affiliated African, Caribbean, and Pacific (ACP) group (see the EC discussion). Dubbed the "Everything But Arms" proposal, the initiative made trade in all manufactured and agricultural goods, except armaments, duty- and quota-free, although phase-in periods were established for bananas (to 2006), rice (2009), and sugar (2009)—three commodities that had caused major trade disputes in recent years. Although imports from the affected countries accounted for a minuscule 0.003 percent of all EU imports, the impact on the developing exporters was expected to be considerable: At the time, EU countries absorbed 56 percent of the 48 countries' exports to Europe.

Meeting in mid-June 2001, in Göteborg, Sweden, with U.S. President George W. Bush in attendance, the EU heads of government established 2004 as the firm entry date for the next expansion, although it remained uncertain exactly how many of the eligible countries would be ready for admission at that time. The summit attendees also emphasized the importance of sustainable development in the EU's economic and social strategies, endorsed holding a new round of global trade negotiations, and reaffirmed (in contrast to President Bush) their commitment to meeting the Kyoto Protocol goals on global warming.

With regard to EU-U.S. trade, the summit participants agreed to reduce tensions, which in recent years have been particularly heated over bananas and beef, although the most troublesome issue involved the U.S. Foreign Sales Corporations (FSC) Act. Shortly after the June summit the World Trade Organization (WTO) disputes panel ruled in favor of an EU complaint that the law violates world trade rules by allowing U.S. companies to shelter export income and other foreign sales from tax. The decision was upheld in 2002, thereby requiring a less-than-amiable U.S. Congress to reconsider the FSC

law for the second time, an earlier EU complaint to the WTO having led to a 2000 revision.

In the meantime, on March 23, 2002, responding to a U.S. decision to impose unilateral steel tariffs of between 8 and 30 percent, the EU announced retaliatory tariffs against up to 300 U.S. products. The steel products at issue were manufactured by previously state-owned French, German, Italian, Swedish, Spanish, and UK companies that received subsidies before being privatized. The WTO proceeded to take on the complex issue, while in December the EU and the United States, at a Paris meeting sponsored by the Organization for Economic Cooperation and Development (OECD), agreed to open negotiations on reducing or eliminating steel subsidies.

In the immediate aftermath of the September 11, 2001, terrorist attacks on the United States, the EU heads of government held an emergency meeting September 21 in Brussels, where they extended full support to Washington. An informal summit, which convened October 19 in Ghent, Belgium, focused on the economic and political consequences of the attacks and of the recently launched U.S. "war on terrorism." Subsequent related actions included endorsement of a uniform arrest warrant and a May 2002 decision to freeze the assets of 11 suspected terrorist organizations. Developments at a June 21–22 summit in Seville, Spain, included acceptance of a plan to counter illegal immigration, adopt a common asylum policy, and introduce a common border force. These initiatives are still in development.

Meeting on December 14–15, 2001, in Laeken, Belgium, the heads of government agreed to establish a constitutional convention, to be chaired by former French President Valéry Giscard d'Estaing, to map out a more efficient and democratic structure for the union. On February 28, 2002, the convention began its task, which was expected to extend into 2003. The 105 participants included members of the European Parliament and the European Commission, delegates from each of the 15 member states, and representatives of the 13 prospective member countries. Also in February, the European Parliament approved a program of financial reforms that had been put forward by the Lamfalussy "wise men."

A "skeleton draft" of the proposed constitution for a "union of European states" was published October 28, 2002, but the 46-article document deliberately avoided controversial issues that had yet to be resolved. It did, however, propose reserving powers not specifically conferred by the constitution on EU institutions to the member states. This was seen as an effort to restrain the growth and power of the European Commission in particular.

The January 1, 2002, launch of the euro as legal tender was preceded by the distribution throughout the 12 EMU members of new banknotes and coins worth 660 billion euros ($590 billion). The transition was accomplished without significant disruptions, and at the end of February the French franc, the German deutsch mark, the Italian lira, and the other national currencies were no longer in commercial use. During the next ten months the most significant problem facing a number of euro-zone members was keeping fiscal deficits within targeted limits. In November, France, Germany, and Portugal were all cited for failure to reduce deficits to 3 percent, as required by the EMU's stability and growth pact.

Proposed changes to the CAP and a parallel Common Fisheries Policy (CFP) drew considerable attention in 2002. CAP reform has centered on a shift in emphasis from preventing food shortages to ensuring food safety, environmental standards, and animal welfare. France and Spain, two principal beneficiaries of the existing CAP, voiced objections. Spain also expressed concern over efforts under the CFP to reduce fleet sizes and better manage fish stocks. A December 2002 decision to limit catches of Atlantic cod, haddock, and whiting angered British fishermen in particular.

Problems also persisted with regard to establishing the RRF as part of a comprehensive European Security and Defense Policy (ESDP). The first anticipated RRF mission, to assume control in October 2002 of peacekeepers in Macedonia, required approval of NATO, but Turkey wanted assurances that the RRF would not undertake missions in the Aegean and locations near Turkey. The December 12–13, 2002, Copenhagen summit was highlighted not only by the decision to admit ten new members as of May 2004, but also by completion of a "comprehensive agreement" resolving the dispute with Turkey over the RRF. Under the pact, only EU members and candidates that also are members of NATO or participants in the NATO Partnership for Peace (PfP) program will have access to NATO facilities. Accordingly, Malta and Cyprus are excluded.

Expiration of the ECSC's founding treaty on July 23, 2002, brought the Coal and Steel Community to a close. Perhaps its most significant accomplishment, apart from serving as a model for creation of the EEC, was a decades-long, painful reduction of overcapacity in the community's steel industry. The process included introduction of production quotas, bans on state subsidies, closure of obsolete facilities, modernization of others, restructuring of the market, and expansion of retraining funds and other support for former steelworkers. By 1999 the steel workforce had declined to 280,000 (from 870,000 in 1975), and some 63 million tons of capacity had been eliminated since 1980. In July 2002 all ECSC assets and liabilities were transferred to the EU—technically, after entry into force of the Treaty of Nice, as specified in a treaty protocol. In the interim, ECSC net assets, which were valued at some 1.6 billion euros, were to be managed by the European Commission and then, after completion of the community's liquidation, to be designated as "Assets of the Research Fund for Coal and Steel." Matters related to the coal and steel industries are now addressed within the EU framework.

The European Council met in emergency session February 17, 2003, to discuss the looming crisis in Iraq, but a deep divide separated, on the one hand, France and Germany, which opposed threatened military action, and, on the other hand, the UK, Spain, and Italy, the most vocal supporters of the U.S. President George W. Bush administration's stance against the Saddam Hussein regime. French President Chirac subsequently criticized statements by the eight Eastern European prospective members, plus candidate countries Romania and Bulgaria, for supporting intervention. Iraq policy remained on the agenda at the regular council session March 20–21, which also addressed progress toward achieving the "Lisbon Strategy" goals for economic competitiveness.

On April 16, 2003, at an informal council session, the Czech Republic, Cyprus, Estonia, Hungary, Latvia, Lithuania, Malta, Poland, Slovakia, and Slovenia signed accession treaties. Admission of Bulgaria and Romania was projected for 2007, but Turkey's membership, if approved, was expected a take another decade. A report issued by the commission March 26 had envisaged eventual EU membership for Balkan states Croatia, Albania, Bosnia and Herzegovina, Macedonia, and Serbia and Montenegro (the former Federal Republic of Yugoslavia).

On April 25, 2003, four opponents of the month-old invasion of Iraq met to discuss defense cooperation. At that time Belgium, France, Germany, and Luxembourg decided to establish a headquarters for planning joint military operations, although some critics, especially the UK, viewed the decision as contrary to a prior pledge not to compete with NATO's collective defense mission. A compromise was reached in November, with France and Germany withdrawing their headquarters plan and the UK agreeing to formation of a joint military planning unit independent of NATO. In addition, the EU foreign ministers agreed that common consent would be required to initiate any EU peacekeeping or humanitarian mission and then only if NATO chose not to act. At the December 2003 council summit the defense plan received the approval of the EU leaders, and in January 2004 Nick Witney, an official in the UK Ministry of Defense, was appointed to head the European Defense Agency Establishment Team. A month later France, Germany, and the UK announced their support for forming joint battle groups, each with 1,500 personnel, within the RRF. The first such units (the total number was subsequently set at 13) were to be ready for deployment in 2007. In June 2004 the EU foreign ministers approved establishment of the European Defense Agency (EDA), to be headed by Witney, with responsibilities that in-

cluded improving joint defense capabilities, promoting related research and development, and advancing development of a competitive defense market within the EU. In 2005 the EDA absorbed the functions of the Western European Armaments Group (WEAG), a subsidiary body of the WEU.

Meeting in regular session on June 19–20, 2003, in Salonika, Greece, the council received a draft constitution from the Convention on the Future of Europe and assigned preparation of a final text to an IGC, which was to begin its work in October. In other business, the council indicated its willingness to aid in Iraqi reconstruction and endorsed a statement by the EU foreign ministers on the possible use of military force to prevent the spread of weapons of mass destruction (WMD). Shortly thereafter, council President and Greek Prime Minister Costas Simitis met in Washington with U.S. President Bush, at which time an EU-U.S. extradition treaty was signed. The EU members retained the right to refuse extradition in death penalty cases.

When the IGC on the constitution convened in October 2003, differences over many provisions still required resolution, principal among them the makeup of the European Commission and voting procedures in the proposed Council of Ministers. The draft text called for reducing the commission to 15 members from 2009, but most of the smaller member countries argued that each should continue to be represented by at least one commissioner. With regard to the Council of Ministers, the constitutional text specified a "double majority" system under which passage of a measure would require support from a majority of ministers representing, collectively, at least 60 percent of the total EU population. Spain and Poland, in particular, instead demanded retention of the QMV system specified in the Treaty of Nice. An EU summit December 13 failed to resolve the issues, but the attendees managed to agree on the 2007 admission of Bulgaria and Romania to the union.

In January 2004 the European Commission asked the ECJ to rule on the validity of a November 2003 decision by the EU finance ministers to suspend the stability and growth pact (SGP), thereby avoiding the imposition of penalties against France and Germany for failing to keep their budget deficits in check. In April 2004, with the ECJ not yet having ruled, the commission issued warnings to Greece, Italy, the Netherlands, and Portugal over their deficits. Three months later the ECJ determined that the finance ministers had exceeded their authority in suspending the SGP, but the judges also ruled they could not force the ministers to carry through on the commission's recommendations regarding sanctions. As a consequence, the issue of sanctions was thrown into the political arena, and reform of the SGP became an even more contentious issue.

The March 25–26, 2004, European Council summit was dominated by the March 11 terrorist bombings in Madrid and the subsequent election of a new Spanish government. In addition to appointing a new EU counterterrorism coordinator, the summit participants stated that they intended to act jointly, including with military force, in response to terrorist attacks, and they approved a 50-point plan of action.

In late April 2004 the justice and home affairs ministers sought consensus on another volatile issue, setting minimum standards for treating those seeking political asylum under a proposed Common European Asylum System (CEAS). The CEAS proposal was not, however, universally welcomed, with UN High Commissioner for Refugees Ruud Lubbers describing the plan as intended to reduce standards and "to deter or deny protection to as many people as possible."

As scheduled, the EU's enlargement from 15 to 25 members took place May 1, 2004, with the election of a new European Parliament following on June 10–13. As had been expected following the expansion, the voters returned the center-right European People's Party/European Democrats as the plurality grouping. Somewhat unexpectedly, however, the leading governing parties in 23 of the 25 member states won smaller vote shares than they had in the most recent national elections.

At a June 17–18, 2004, summit of EU leaders a spirit of compromise resolved the remaining disputes over the text of the 350-article EU constitu-

tion. Predictably, the final draft was immediately attacked by the left and the right, by proponents of a unified Europe as well as by opponents fearing the loss of national sovereignty and identity.

If approved by all 25 member countries, the constitution would supersede existing EU treaties. EU law would have primacy over national law in specified areas, when the objectives could best be achieved at the EU level. The European Council would elect an EU president for a once-renewable term of two and a half years and would also choose a minister for foreign affairs. Both positions would be included in the European Commission, which would retain the formula of one member per state for one five-year term, after which the number of commissioners would be reduced to two-thirds the number of member states, filled by rotation. A Council of Ministers would meet in various configurations, depending on the sector involved (e.g., agriculture, transport). The European Parliament, comprising no more than 750 members (a maximum of 96 and a minimum of 6 per country), and the Council of Ministers would jointly "exercise legislative and budgetary functions."

Unless otherwise specified in the constitution, European Council decisions would continue to be by consensus. In the Council of Ministers unanimity would be required in such sensitive areas as foreign policy, defense, and tax law. Otherwise, a "double majority" QMV system would apply, generally requiring support from 55 percent of the member states, representing at least 65 percent of the EU population.

Although the Charter of Fundamental Rights was incorporated into the constitution, its application was to be limited to matters of EU law, with the interpretation of guaranteed rights allowing for national differences based on, for example, tradition. The complete constitution also encompassed 36 protocols, including one amending the Euratom treaty, and 50 "Declarations Concerning Provisions of the Constitution." Meeting October 29 in Rome, the EU heads of government and their foreign ministers signed a constitutional treaty to advance its ratification in all member countries, by referendum or legislative act, by November 2006.

Meanwhile, on July 22, 2004, the new parliament had approved the nomination of Portuguese prime minister José Manuel Barroso to serve as president of the European Commission for 2005–2010. Barroso soon encountered objections to his proposed list of commissioners, however, and on October 27, facing rejection by the parliament, he withdrew the list, even though the new commission was to have been installed November 1. On October 31 the most controversial nominee, Rocco Buttiglione of Italy, a devout Roman Catholic, withdrew his nomination to be commissioner for justice, freedom, and security after having made controversial remarks regarding homosexuality, the role of women in society, and the establishment of North African holding centers for asylum seekers. A controversial Latvian nominee also was dropped, and on November 18 parliament approved the revised commission, which took office four days later.

A November 4–5, 2004, EU summit adopted a new five-year "Hague Program" on freedom, justice, and security that addressed terrorism and organized crime, basic rights and citizenship, and the CEAS. The Hague Program, a follow-up to a plan that was adopted at the 1999 Tampere summit, did not, however, resolve deep divisions over the proposed common asylum plan, especially the use of extraterritorial holding centers. A proposal presented in October suggested establishing pilot centers in Algeria, Libya, Mauritania, Morocco, and Tunisia. While several EU members opposed the centers on humanitarian grounds, France further argued that the centers would attract economic migrants and people traffickers and could destabilize the host governments. There also were fundamental differences over whether asylum seekers who entered the EU would be deported to the centers or whether the centers would be used only to house those who had been intercepted while in transit to EU countries.

The EU summit of December 16–17, 2004, was highlighted by the announcement that accession talks with candidate country Croatia would begin March 17, 2005, provided that the Zagreb government fully cooperated with the International Criminal Tribunal for the former Yugoslavia (ICTY) in The Hague. The summit also confirmed that accession talks with Turkey would begin on October 3, 2005, but several EU members, including France and Italy, had already indicated their likely opposition to admitting the predominantly Asian and Islamic country. Questions also persisted regarding its stance toward Cyprus and its human rights record. Meanwhile, with their accession negotiations having concluded, Bulgaria and Romania were expected to sign accession treaties in April 2005, to be followed by admission January 1, 2007.

In February 2005 President Barroso announced his commission's economic program as well as its social and environmental agenda. The economic program, which acknowledged the EU's lack of progress toward achieving the "Lisbon Strategy" goals, projected 3 percent annual growth and the creation of 6 million new jobs during the 2005–2010 term. To meet these targets, Barroso called for closer cooperation with individual member states, each of which was charged with naming an official to implement and monitor national progress. Policy recommendations included market liberalization, deregulation, and, most controversially, extension of the single market concept to services as well as goods. At a summit March 22–23, 2005, the EU leaders focused on reforming the stability and growth pact, which had largely been disregarded since the 2002 decision of the finance ministers not to impose economic penalties on France and Germany for noncompliance. At the summit the members retained the pact's principal benchmarks—keeping national budget deficits under 3 percent of GDP and public debt under 60 percent of GDP—but basically exempted countries experiencing low or negative growth; excluded from the budget ceiling expenditures for education, defense, foreign aid, and research; and extended the time limits for offending countries to make the necessary adjustments. France, Germany, Italy, and Spain, each of which failed to adhere to the original criteria, were among the countries backing the revisions, which critics described as rendering the pact worthless. The summit also discussed President Barroso's economic agenda for 2005–2010 and requested that the commission reconsider the proposal for liberalizing the service sector.

On January 12, 2005, the European Parliament overwhelmingly endorsed the proposed EU consti-tution, although most UK, Polish, and Czech MEPs voted in opposition. On February 20 Spanish voters became the first to approve the constitution by ref-erendum, but its prospects for unionwide ratifica-tion suffered a major blow May 29 when the French electorate rejected it. Analysts widely interpreted the 54.7 percent "no" vote as, in part, a reflection of dissatisfaction with the current French govern-ment, but on June 1, Dutch voters turned down the constitution by an even larger margin, 61.5 percent to 38.5 percent. The Dutch electorate apparently objected to the rapid pace of enlargement and inte-gration, fearing a loss of national sovereignty and identity as well as an influx of immigrants from the East. Despite the French and Dutch results, many supporters of the constitution urged that the ratifi-cation process continue, although the EU leaders, meeting June 16–17, instead called for a "period of reflection." As of August 2005 the following 15 countries had ratified the proposed constitu-tion: Austria, Belgium, Cyprus, Estonia, Germany, Greece, Hungary, Italy, Latvia, Lithuania, Luxem-bourg, Malta, Slovakia, Slovenia, and Spain. The other eight EU members postponed consideration. If, in the end, five or fewer states failed to ratify the constitution, it could be reconsidered rather than scrapped. In mid-2006, European public opinion seemed to be turning more strongly against the con-stitution, but its supporters inside the EU structure were still enthusiastic about keeping it alive with-out substantial modification.

During the same period a crisis erupted over the 2007–2013 EU budget when the UK refused to accept a reduction in its budget rebate, which was instituted in 1984 when its economic position was much weaker, unless it was accompanied by additional reforms, particularly with regard to the CAP. In June 2003 the EU agricultural ministers approved further "decoupling" of CAP subsidies from productivity and redirected the program to-ward giving farmers flat payments related to rural development and environmental protection. Since

then, the number of excluded or partially affected agricultural products was reduced. Nevertheless, several EU members supported the UK argument that a continuing budgetary emphasis on agricul-ture was misdirected. France, the largest recipient of CAP support and a leading opponent of main-taining the UK budget rebate, disagreed. After pro-tracted negotiations, a compromise was reached in mid-December 2005. The UK agreed to give up ap-proximately 20 percent of its rebate during the com-ing budget period, while the European Commission was asked to hold a "full and wide-ranging" re-view of all EU spending, including the CAP and the UK rebate, and to draw up a report in 2008–2009. On October 27, 2005, British Prime Minis-ter Tony Blair opened a one-day "informal sum-mit" in Hampton Court Palace, near London. The main intention was for EU leaders to discuss eco-nomic trends and globalization as they would affect the EU's future. The meeting, held near the end of Britain's six-month presidency of the EU council, was generally considered not to have accomplished much.

The EU has played a role in lengthy negoti-ations with Iran aimed at forestalling production of weapons-grade uranium. Tehran has repeatedly said its enrichment program is solely for aiding power generation. In early June 2006, Javier Solana delivered to Iran a proposal offering a package of incentives not to produce weapons-grade material. This proposal, whose terms were not immediately made public, was worked out by Germany, France, and Britain on behalf of the EU, and was supported by the United States, Russia, and China.

European Community

(EC)
Communauté Européenne
(CE)

Established: As the European Economic Commu-nity (EEC) by the Treaty of Rome (Italy), signed March 25, 1957, effective January 1, 1958; current name adopted in the Treaty on European Union, effective November 1, 1993.

Purpose: "It shall be the aim of the Community, by establishing a Common Market and progressively approximating the economic policies of Member States, to promote throughout the Community a harmonious development of economic activities, a continuous and balanced expansion, an increased stability, an accelerated raising of the standard of living, and closer relations between its Member States."

Members: (See European Union).

African, Caribbean, and Pacific (ACP) Countries and Territories Affiliated under Cotonou Agreement (78): Angola, Antigua and Barbuda, Bahamas, Barbados, Belize, Benin, Botswana, Burkina Faso, Burundi, Cameroon, Cape Verde Islands, Central African Republic, Chad, Comoro Islands, Democratic Republic of the Congo, Republic of the Congo, Cook Islands, Côte d'Ivoire, Djibouti, Dominica, Dominican Republic, Equatorial Guinea, Eritrea, Ethiopia, Fiji, Gabon, Gambia, Ghana, Grenada, Guinea, Guinea-Bissau, Guyana, Haiti, Jamaica, Kenya, Kiribati, Lesotho, Liberia, Madagascar, Malawi, Mali, Marshall Islands, Mauritania, Mauritius, Micronesia, Mozambique, Namibia, Nauru, Niger, Nigeria, Niue, Palau, Papua New Guinea, Rwanda, St. Kitts and Nevis, St. Lucia, St. Vincent, Samoa, Sao Tome and Principe, Senegal, Seychelles, Sierra Leone, Solomon Islands, Somalia, South Africa, Sudan, Suriname, Swaziland, Tanzania, Timor-Leste, Togo, Tonga, Trinidad and Tobago, Tuvalu, Uganda, Vanuatu, Zambia, Zimbabwe. (Cuba, although regarded as the 79th member by the ACP group, has not approved the Cotonou accord. South Africa is considered a "partial" member, excluded by virtue of its industrialized status from many trade and aid provisions. Its participation is governed by an Agreement on Trade, Development, and Cooperation among the European Community, its Member States, and South Africa, which was signed on October 11, 1999, and by Protocol Three on South Africa of the Cotonou Agreement, signed on June 23, 2000.)

Origin and development. The two treaties establishing the European Economic Community (EEC) and the European Atomic Energy Community (Euratom) were signed in March 1957 in Rome, Italy, and entered into force January 1, 1958. The institutions of the EEC, headquartered in Brussels, Belgium, were broadly fashioned on those of the ECSC, comprising a council of ministers, an executive commission, and the Assembly and Court of Justice already operating under the earlier treaty. Two types of national linkage to the EEC were detailed: full membership, under which an acceding state agreed to the basic principles of the Treaty of Rome, and associate membership, involving the establishment of agreed reciprocal rights and obligations in regard to such matters as commercial policy.

The subsequent central issues of the communities—expansion through admission of additional European states and the sharing of authority by member governments and the communities' main administrative organs—were most acute in the case of the EEC, whose rapid development included a series of crises in which the French government, with its special concern for national sovereignty and its mistrust of supranational endeavors, frequently opposed the other members.

The crucial issue of national sovereignty versus community authority was initially posed in 1965. Ostensibly to protest EEC failure to reach timely agreement on agricultural policy, the French government instituted a boycott of all three communities that was maintained from July 1, 1965, to January 30, 1966, and was ended through an intergovernmental understanding that tended to restrict the independent authority of the Commission to establish and execute community policy.

The membership issue was first brought to the forefront by the decision of the UK, announced in July 1961, to apply for admission to the EEC on condition that arrangements could be made to protect the interests of other Commonwealth states, the other members of the European Free Trade Association (EFTA), and British agriculture. Preliminary discussion of the British bid continued through 1962 but was cut short by France in early

1963 on the general ground that the UK was too close to the United States and not sufficiently European in outlook. A formal UK application for membership in the three communities was submitted in May 1967, with similar bids subsequently being advanced by Ireland, Denmark, and Norway. Action was again blocked by French opposition, despite support for British accession by the Commission and the other five member states. Further negotiations for British, Irish, Danish, and Norwegian membership opened in June 1970, and on January 22, 1972, the treaty of accession and accompanying documents, which provided for expansion to a ten-state organization, were signed in Brussels. Accession was approved by referenda in Ireland (May 11) and Denmark (October 2). However, Norwegian voters, not entirely satisfied with concessions offered for the benefit of their state's agricultural and fishing interests, rejected accession in a national referendum held September 24–25. In the case of the UK, legislation permitting entry was approved by parliament and entered into force October 17, the three accessions becoming effective January 1, 1973. On February 9, 1976, the Council of the European Communities stated that, in principle, it endorsed Greece's request for full membership (an agreement of association was approved in 1962), and a treaty of admission was signed May 28, 1979. Accordingly, Greece became the community's tenth member January 1, 1981.

Negotiations concerning Portuguese and Spanish membership began in October 1978 and February 1979, respectively, but delays resulted from apprehension over the ability of the Iberian states to speed industrial diversification and the projected impact of the two heavily agricultural economies on the EC's Common Agricultural Policy (CAP; see below). Thus, Portugal and Spain were not formally admitted until January 1, 1986.

An association agreement with Turkey was promulgated in 1964 and another with Malta in 1971. In February 1980 community representatives met with the Turkish foreign minister and agreed to strengthen political and commercial ties "with a view to facilitating the accession of Turkey to the Community at a later date." Following the Septem-

ber 1980 military coup in Turkey, the association agreement was suspended briefly, but an expanded set of accords was subsequently negotiated and entered into effect January 1, 1981. Following the declaration of the establishment of the "Turkish Republic of Northern Cyprus," the commission reaffirmed its support for the unity of the Republic of Cyprus and the community's 1973 association agreement with the Greek-dominated government. (Malta as well as Cyprus joined the EU in 2004; Turkey remains a "candidate country.") As of June 2006, Turkey's negotiations for membership were in serious jeopardy over Turkey's refusal to open its ports and airports to Cyprus so long as the Cyprus government refused to open communications with the Turkish-dominated northern half of the island.

Cooperation agreements. Over the years, the EC concluded cooperative agreements with other countries and multilateral groups.

A Convention of Association linking the EEC with 18 African states was signed July 20, 1963, in Yaoundé, Cameroon. A similar agreement was concluded with Kenya, Tanzania, and Uganda on July 26, 1968, in Arusha, Tanzania. Under the UK treaty of accession, all independent Commonwealth states became eligible for association with the community through the Yaoundé Convention, through aid and institutional ties, or through special trade agreements. Both the Yaoundé and Arusha conventions were, however, superseded with the February 28, 1975, signing in Lomé, Togo, of a convention establishing a comprehensive trading and economic cooperation relationship between the EC and 46 (now 78) developing ACP countries and territories. Included in the Lomé Convention's provisions were (1) the granting by the EC of duty-free access on a nonreciprocal basis to all industrial and to 96 percent of agricultural products exported from ACP members; (2) the setting up of a comprehensive export stabilization program (Stabex) guaranteeing income support to the ACP members for their primary products; (3) increased development assistance to the ACP members from EC sources; (4) industrial cooperation between the full members and the associated countries; and (5) the creation of a Council of Ministers, a Committee of Ambassadors, and a Consultative Assembly (superseded in 1985 by the Joint Parliamentary Assembly) to implement the agreement.

A second such convention (Lomé II), which entered into force January 1, 1981, increased community aid from 3.5 billion ECUs to 5.5 billion ECUs ($7.2 billion, at the prevailing rate of exchange) and included a plan to assist ACP producers of copper and tin. In addition, ACP workers in the community were guaranteed the same working conditions, social security benefits, and earning rights as the labor force of EC members. ACP members complained, however, that the new convention was little different from its predecessor, that inflation would consume most of the new aid, and that trade concessions were marginal. Indeed, the conclusion of a September 1980 conference in Luxembourg on the impact of Lomé II was that "trade relations had not dramatically improved and in fact had deteriorated for many ACP members, although those countries as a group had moved back into an overall [trade] surplus with the Community."

Following two years of decline, commodity prices stabilized somewhat during 1982 and 1983. Thus, the negotiations for Lomé III, which opened in October 1983, were less acrimonious than the earlier meetings between the EC and the ACP members. Under the new five-year pact, concluded December 8, 1984, the community agreed to expand the volume of financial resources to 8.5 billion ECUs; however, because of exchange rate slippage the expansion yielded an immediate net dollar value ($6.0 billion) less than that of the Lomé II endowment. The new funds were to be used largely to encourage "self-reliant and self-sustained development," with an emphasis on improving the living standards of the poorest people in the ACP countries and territories.

Negotiations on Lomé IV were launched in October 1988 with ACP leaders hoping to obtain an aid package of at least 15 billion ECUs in view of third world debt problems and difficulties associated with the structural adjustment programs recently implemented in many developing nations. A compromise figure of 12 billion ECUs (about

$14 billion) for five years (1991–1995) was agreed on in December 1989. Most of the other elements of previous conventions were maintained in Lomé IV with additional emphasis being given, among other things, to environmental protection, human rights, and food security. Lomé IV was, however, to cover a ten-year period, twice that of its predecessors; thus, further negotiations were required that yielded another compromise in mid-1995, under which an additional 14.6 billion ECUs (about $19.6 billion) were allocated for the ACP members to the end of the decade.

In April 1997 South Africa became the 71st ACP member to accede to the Lomé Convention. However, under a protocol approved by the commission a month earlier, South Africa was accorded only partial membership because of its comparatively advanced industrial economy. Its current status is governed primarily by a separate Agreement on Trade, Development, and Cooperation among the European Community, its Member States, and South Africa (TDCA), which was signed October 11, 1999, in Pretoria, and excludes South Africa from many of the aid and trade provisions applicable to the other ACP countries.

With Lomé IV due to expire February 28, 2000, negotiations on a successor agreement opened at the end of September 1998 and continued until February 3, 2000, when they were completed in Brussels. Efforts at poverty reduction—the overarching goal of the new 20-year pact—were to be accompanied by political dialog, additional developmental aid, and closer economic and trade cooperation. Formal signing of the "Partnership Agreement to the Lomé Convention" was scheduled for June 8 in Suva, Fiji, but the May coup in that country resulted in the meeting being rescheduled and relocated to Cotonou, Benin, where the signing of the accord, familiarly referred to as the Cotonou Agreement, took place on June 23 before representatives of 92 countries. At the same time, six additional members joined the ACP grouping: Cook Islands, Micronesia, Nauru, Niue, Marshall Islands, and Palau.

In November 1998 Cuba applied for admission, but it put its application on hold in April 2000 because EU members on the United Nations Human Rights Commission voted in favor of a motion condemning the island state's human rights record. The ACP countries later decided to include Cuba in their number, but in May 2003 Havana abandoned its application.

The Cotonou Agreement formally entered into effect April 1, 2003, having been implemented provisionally, pending ratification by the ACP members, all 15 EC/EU members, and the European Parliament. The accord required a waiver from the WTO for the EU to extend trade preferences until 2008, by which time negotiations were to be completed on new economic partnership agreements (EPAs) between the EU and various regional groupings of ACP states. In October 2003 talks opened with the first regional organizations, the Central African Economic and Monetary Community (CEMAC) and the Economic Community of West African States (ECOWAS). The least-developed ACP states, numbering 39 (excluding Cuba), can, however, continue existing preferential arrangements. In the meantime, the ACP members are expected to foster democracy, uphold human rights, and maintain good governance to participate in an aid package amounting to 22.5 billion euros.

After nearly four years of effort by Prime Minister Pierre Trudeau's government to establish a "contractual relationship" between Canada and the EC, a Framework Agreement for Commercial and Economic Cooperation was signed July 6, 1976—the first such accord between the community and an industrialized country. In 1990 the original agreement was superseded by a Declaration of EC–Canada Relations. In the interim, many additional bilateral cooperation agreements were signed, including those with Algeria (1976), Bangladesh (1976), Brazil (1980), China (1978), Egypt (1977), India (1973 and 1981), Israel (1975), Japan (1980), Jordan (1977), Lebanon (1977), Mexico (1975), Morocco (1976), Pakistan (1976), Sri Lanka (1975), Syria (1977), Tunisia (1976), Uruguay (1974), and Yugoslavia (signed in 1980 but suspended following the breakup of Yugoslavia in 1991–1992). A joint cooperation agreement was signed with the five members of the Association of Southeast Asian Nations (ASEAN) in March 1980, with the Andean Group in December 1983, and with the members of the Central American Common Market (CACM) in 1985. In addition, the (then) EFTA members (Austria, Finland, Iceland, Norway, Sweden, and Switzerland), after a longtime reliance on bilateral agreements with the EC, signed a multilateral accord in 1992 to create a European Economic Area (EEA) to promote the freedom of movement of people, goods, services, and capital among the 19 nations involved (see EFTA article).

As a major consequence of the pace of change in Eastern Europe and attendant thaw in East–West relations, the EC in 1989 and 1990 concluded trade and cooperation pacts with Bulgaria, Czechoslovakia, the German Democratic Republic, Hungary, Poland, Romania, and the Soviet Union. Economic links with those nations were previously hindered by the desire of the now-defunct Council for Mutual Economic Assistance (CMEA) to negotiate trade agreements for the group as a whole. Most of these countries soon expressed an interest in full EC membership which, coupled with the subsequent demise of the Soviet Union, necessitated a complete review and significant revision of requirements and procedures for concluding bilateral pacts with post-Communist states. Although several cooperative agreements were concluded between 1991 and October 1993, most were completed following the birth of the EU (see the EU: Origin and development for details).

Activities. Building on the experience of the ECSC, the EC assumed the task of creating a community-wide customs union that would abolish all trade restrictions and establish freedom of movement for all goods, services, labor, and capital. A major part of this task was accomplished by July 1, 1968, a year and a half ahead of the schedule laid down in the Treaty of Rome. All customs duties on community internal trade had been gradually removed, and a common external tariff, likewise arrived at by stages, was ready to be applied. The level of the tariff took into account reductions agreed on in the 1964–1967 "Kennedy Round" negotiations under the General Agreement on Tariffs and Trade (GATT), at which the EC had negotiated as a unit. At the end of the community's "transition period" (December 31, 1969), workers became legally free to seek employment in any member state, although in practice the freedom had already existed.

The Treaty of Rome provided for steps leading toward a full economic union of the member states. To this end, it stipulated that common rules be applied to ensure fair competition and that common policies govern agriculture, transport, and foreign trade. Consequently, the CAP, centrally financed from a conjoint fund, was put into effect July 1, 1968. The product of extremely complex negotiations, it involved common marketing policies with free trade throughout the community, common price levels for major products, a uniform policy for external trade in agricultural products (including export subsidies), and a program to increase the efficiency of community farming. The CAP became, however, a constant source of controversy. ACP members and other major food exporters charged that the CAP, by permitting inefficiency and encouraging production of surpluses, lowered international agricultural prices and led the EC to "dump" such farm commodities as sugar and butter on the world market. The problem was only partially resolved by a commission "green paper," which recommended that a market-oriented pricing policy replace farm subsidies.

Within the community itself, an inequitable burden of CAP financing and the escalating cost of the policy caused dissension and spurred the drafting of a 1981 "agenda for the future" designed to reform the budget by increasing emphasis on social and regional policies and proportionally decreasing agricultural funding. The spiraling cost of CAP subsidies and EC revenue shortfalls forced the community to freeze some CAP payments in October 1983. The problem of finding a compromise package of agricultural and budgetary policy reforms—including budget rebates demanded by the UK—caused the breakup of both the December 1983 Athens and the March 1984 Brussels meetings of the Council of Ministers. The main division between members concerned the extent and speed of reforms of the CAP and the linking of members' contributions to the community budget to their individual wealth and EC benefits.

European leaders meeting in June 1984 in Fontainebleau, France, finally reached accord on budgetary policy. For 1984, Britain was accorded a budget rebate of $800 million and was guaranteed a rebate of two-thirds its net contribution to the community in future years, with EC revenues being enhanced by an increase from 1 percent to 1.4 percent of the value-added tax received from member states. Concessions also were made to limit West Germany's financial burden, with officials expressing hope that progress would thenceforth be made on "relaunching" the community.

Agreement was reached in July 1978 for the establishment of a European currency association to include a joint reserve fund to prevent currency fluctuations between member states and a mechanism by which intracommunity accounts could be settled by use of European Currency Units (ECUs). The resultant European Monetary System (EMS), which included an Exchange Rate Mechanism (ERM) to limit currency fluctuations, came into effect March 13, 1979. In its first decade the ECU became an attractive medium for the issue of bonds by private and public financial institutions, placing the ECU behind only the U.S. dollar and the German deutsch mark in popularity on the international bond market. In May 1983 the community authorized a loan of ECU 4 billion ($3.7 billion) to help France defend its faltering franc until a domestic austerity policy became effective; France threatened to leave the EMS if the loan was not granted.

Beginning in 1985 proponents of unity won a series of endorsements from EC organs and member states for measures designed to create a true internal common market by the end of 1992. New rules were approved to liberalize capital movement across community borders, while other plans included minimizing frontier transport checks and standardizing national tax laws. On January 1, 1988, a lone, shortened customs document, known as the Single Administrative Document, went into effect at all intra-EC borders as well as at those with members of EFTA. Common transit procedures also were implemented to facilitate the movement of goods.

Despite progress toward full integration, EC summits in July and December 1987 broke up without resolution of a spending deficit of about $6 billion over the members' total budgeted contributions of $35 billion. Disagreement continued to center on the controversial CAP subsidies and large-scale storage of surplus food, which accounted for some 70 percent of EC spending despite recent cutbacks in beef and dairy products. In particular, Britain refused to increase its EC contribution until "financial discipline" had been instituted.

In view of the problems involved, an emergency summit in February 1988 in Brussels, Belgium, achieved remarkable results. After marathon negotiations, the participants established a budget ceiling of 1.3 percent of the EC's GNP, set a cap on future growth of agricultural subsidies of no more than three-quarters of increased GNP, approved cuts in the intervention price for surplus farm commodities, and agreed to double aid to the EC's southern members over a five-year period.

With the agricultural and financial crises averted, the EC turned its attention to the single market plan, subsequent rapid progress in that regard generating a surprisingly intense "Euro-enthusiasm." During an uncharacteristically harmonious June summit in Hannover, West Germany, EC leaders described the momentum toward "1992" as "irreversible," particularly in view of an earlier agreement reached by EC finance ministers on a "crucial" plan to end all restrictions on the flow of capital within the community. Governments, financial institutions, and businesses throughout the world also appeared to realize the implications of the EC's progress, their concern about a potential "fortress Europe" prompting reassurances from the EC that the internal market would not "close in on itself" to the detriment of nonmembers.

Additional headway was reported during the next summit, held in December 1988 in Rhodes, Greece, where the informal theme "halfway there, halfway done" reflected that about 50 percent of the legislative program for the internal market was enacted. Nevertheless, the tone of the summit was noticeably more subdued, as it became apparent that several remaining proposals could still prove intractable. In addition, political misgivings again surfaced in some European capitals over the impact on national sovereignty of a fully integrated EC.

The concern was most apparent in London, where the Margaret Thatcher government continued to serve as a brake on EC momentum, particularly in regard to the monetary union plan proposed in April 1989 by a committee headed by European Commission President Jacques Delors of France. The proposal asked EC members to endorse a three-stage program that would include, among other things, the creation of a regional central bank in the second stage and a common currency in the third stage. Despite strong support from most of the other EC countries, UK resistance necessitated a compromise at the summit held in June in Madrid, Spain. Consensus could be reached only on the first stage of the plan, under which EC members agreed to harmonize certain monetary and economic policies beginning in July 1990. Prime Minister Thatcher agreed to allow preparations to proceed for an EC conference on the much more controversial second and third stages of the plan but, on another matter, she opposed as containing unacceptable "socialist" overtones a draft EC charter of fundamental social rights supported by the 11 other national leaders.

In June 1989 the EC was asked to coordinate Western aid to Poland and Hungary from the Organization for Economic Cooperation and Development (OECD), a program (Poland/Hungary Aid for Restructuring of Economies—PHARE) that was later opened to other Eastern European states. In November, emphasizing the community's expanding political role, a special one-day EC summit in Paris expressed its "responsibility" to support the development of democracy throughout Eastern Europe. Some political concerns were also addressed during the regularly scheduled summit in December in Strasbourg, France, notably the growing interest in German unification, which the EC leaders endorsed provided it included recognition of

Europe's postwar borders. In addition, the summit supported the proposed creation of the multibillion dollar European Bank for Reconstruction and Development (see separate EBRD article) to assist economic transformation throughout Eastern Europe. In 1991, as a further measure to promote economic and political reform in the countries that emerged from the Soviet collapse, the EC introduced Technical Assistance to the Commonwealth of Independent States (TACIS), a program that was subsequently expanded to include Mongolia and that has worked closely with the EBRD.

The EC heads of state met for two-day summits in late April and June 1990 in Dublin, Ireland, to further delineate the community's future role in the "new architecture" of Europe. They declared that East Germany would be incorporated into the EC automatically after the creation of a single German state, gave "qualified" support to West German Chancellor Helmut Kohl's call for up to $15 billion in economic assistance to the Soviet Union (seen as a means of reducing Soviet objections to unified Germany's membership in the North Atlantic Treaty Organization), and endorsed a sweeping environmental protection statement.

During their December 1990 summit in Rome, the EC heads of state and government formally opened two parallel conferences: one to consider wide-ranging proposals for EC political union and the other to oversee negotiations on the more fully developed monetary union plan. It was apparent at the Luxembourg summit in June 1991 that the dual conferences had yet to resolve several contentious issues. With several EC leaders facing domestic political problems, no binding decisions were made. However, based on consensus proposals from both conferences, the heads of state and government initialed a Treaty on European Union and numerous related protocols and documents at a pivotal summit on December 9–11 in Maastricht, Netherlands.

In the midst of the individual states' ratification processes, the EC leaders agreed at their December 1992 session to postpone many of the proposals regarding a persistently controversial issue—the free movement of people within the community. Nevertheless, by the target date of January 1, 1993, it was estimated that approximately 80 percent of the previously enacted single market provisions on the free movement of goods, services, and capital was implemented.

With the Maastricht Treaty awaiting only UK ratification, the June 1993 EC summit focused on the community's economic woes, which were contributing as much as any of the other problems to a growing "Euro-pessimism." In particular, the summit proposed measures designed to reduce unemployment, which was above 10 percent in the community. Although French President Mitterrand attempted to portray the session as marking a "psychological recovery" for the EC, the community shortly thereafter experienced another currency crisis less than a year after one led Italy and the UK to abandon the ERM. Faced with a possible total breakdown of the ERM, the EC agreed in early August to let the franc and the six other non-German currencies still in the system float more freely against the mark. However, with UK ratification of the Maastricht Treaty achieved in July, resultant questions about the feasibility of the proposed 1999 single currency soon fell under the purview of the nascent EU.

In a further effort to rationalize the various EC/EU programs and institutions, the 2001 Treaty of Nice amended the existing consolidated versions of the EU and EC founding treaties and merged them into one document.

European Atomic Energy Community

(Euratom)
Communauté Européenne de l'Energie Atomique
(CEEA)

Established: By Treaty of Rome (Italy), signed March 25, 1957, effective January 1, 1958.

Purpose: To develop research, to disseminate information, to enforce uniform safety standards, to facilitate investment, to ensure regular and equitable distribution of supplies of nuclear material, to guarantee that nuclear materials are not diverted from their designated uses, to exercise certain property rights in regard to such materials, to create a common market for the free movement of investment capital and personnel for nuclear industries, and to promote the peaceful uses of atomic energy.

Membership: (See European Union).

Origin and development. Euratom was established in response to the assessment that atomic power on a large scale would be urgently needed to meet the growing energy requirements for economic expansion. The original six ECSC member states also sought to reduce the lead that Britain, the Soviet Union, and the United States had acquired in the field of peaceful uses of nuclear energy. To this end, the members decided to pool their efforts, the area too complex and expensive to be dealt with nationally. Structurally, the Treaty of Rome provided for a council, a commission, and the sharing of the Assembly and Court of Justice already operating under the ECSC.

In December 1969 it was agreed to reshape Euratom so that it could conduct nuclear research under contract for community clients and extend its activities to other scientific research projects, especially those involving noncommunity states. The council also resolved to streamline the community's management, making its operations more flexible and ensuring more effective coordination of its nuclear activities. These reforms took effect in 1971.

Activities. In 1981 an agreement came into force between the community, France, and the International Atomic Energy Agency (IAEA) regarding safeguards on certain nuclear materials, while officials signed long-term agreements establishing conditions for the sale and security within the EC of nuclear materials supplied by Australia and Canada. In November 1995 Euratom and the United States completed negotiations on a controversial new agreement concerning "nuclear cooperation" to replace an accord set to expire at the end of the year. The most contentious element of the pact was a provision giving Euratom members greater latitude in selling plutonium originating from the United States. Previously, Washington had held a veto power over any such transactions; however, the new agreement permitted Euratom members to trade the plutonium within EU borders without U.S. approval. Some U.S. and international groups opposed the measure on the grounds that the plutonium could end up in the control of countries with looser standards, especially given anticipated EU expansion to the east.

Washington also reportedly lodged a protest with Euratom in 1996 concerning a uranium-powered research reactor planned for construction near Munich. The U.S. complaint apparently centered on reported Euratom contacts with Moscow regarding the possible purchase of uranium from Russia for the reactor. For their part, European officials reportedly objected to Washington's presenting itself as the "world policeman" on nuclear issues, noting that the United States had a multibillion-dollar economic stake in the trade of nuclear materials. Despite such strategic differences, in 2000 the United States and Euratom reached a cooperative agreement that covers fusion as well as fission research.

Given that nuclear energy, as of 2004, provided approximately 32 percent of the EU's energy, Euratom continues to be involved in efforts to prevent a disruption of nuclear fuel supplies. For example, since 1960 a Euratom Supply Agency, operating under the commission, has coordinated all of Euratom's contracts for the supply of fissionable material. Inspections of installations that use these supplies are conducted on a regular basis to ensure that nuclear materials are not diverted from peaceful uses and are otherwise maintained under appropriate safeguards.

Because of diminished popular support for nuclear energy, triggered in part by the 1986 Chernobyl disaster in the Soviet Union, the European Commission stopped approving new loans for construction of nuclear power plants within member countries. In June 2004, however, the commission approved a proposal for a Finnish plant, the first in the EU in over a decade and the world's first "third-generation" facility. Given a revived interest in reducing dependence on hydrocarbon sources of energy, the commission also sought a significant increase in Euratom's loan fund. In June 2004 the commission approved a loan of 223.5 million euros for construction of a reactor in candidate country Romania. Bulgaria, which began decommissioning its Soviet-era first-generation nuclear power plants at the urging of the EU, was expected to request similar assistance for new construction. Loans for safety and modernization efforts were also extended to other Eastern European countries, including Russia and Ukraine, where the last Chernobyl reactor was permanently shut down in December 2000. Russia's disruption of natural gas supplies to the EU in the winter of 2005–2006 also led to an increased interest in nuclear power. As of January 2006 the Finnish plant was under construction, France and the Czech Republic announced plans to build more nuclear plants, and Belgium, Italy, Germany, and Sweden had all begun reconsideration of the nuclear power moratorium.

Concurrently, scientists have intensified research on thermonuclear fusion, which many believe could provide power without most of the safety risks and environmental problems associated with fission reactors. The long-term goal of the EU Fusion Programme is "the joint creation of prototype reactors which will lead to electric power plants that meet society's needs: operational safety, respect for the environment, economic viability." Since the first half of the 1980s, fusion research has been conducted at the Joint European Torus (JET), a research and development facility in Culham, United Kingdom. In effect from January 1, 2000, the new European Fusion Development Agreement (EFDA) became operational to govern use of the JET to coordinate fusion technology projects within the EU, and to oversee EU participation in outside endeavors. These endeavors include the international thermonuclear experimental reactor (ITER) project initiated in 1988 by Japan, Russia, and the United States, for which a design was completed in 2001. In addition to the EU, China and South Korea also are participating in the $12 billion project. In June 2005 the partners announced that ITER would be built in Cadarache, France, with a target completion date of 2015.

Much of Euratom's current fusion research looks toward this "Next Step"—that is, construction and operation of an experimental reactor. At the same time, research on the physics of fusion continues, as does longer-range preparatory work for development of a demonstration reactor and, ultimately, a prototype reactor. The full process is expected to take at least another 20 years.

Meanwhile, research in the area of fission also continues, with principal focus on improving operational safety of existing and future reactors as well as the fuel cycle and advancing understanding of radiation protection, including risk assessment, emergency management, severe accident phenomenology, waste management, decommissioning of reactors, and long-term management and restoration of contaminated sites. Past research projects, many stemming from the Chernobyl accident, have involved a wide range of activities, among them treating people exposed to radiation and setting permissible levels of contamination in foodstuffs. Euratom scientists and physicians also have participated in studies examining possible adverse health and environmental consequences associated with the use of depleted-uranium armaments in the Bosnian and Kosovo conflicts during the 1990s.

In December 2002 the European Court of Justice (ECJ), ruling in a dispute brought by the European Commission against the Council of the European Union, stated that Euratom as well as the individual member countries had competence with regard to broader nuclear safety concerns. In a declaration accompanying the Act of Accession to the 1994 global Convention on Nuclear Safety, the council had erred, according to the ECJ, by overly limiting Euratom's role to workplace-related protections and emergency planning, whereas the organization was also competent in safety matters related to siting facilities, design and construction, and operations. The court's decision came at a time when the EU, thanks to enlargement, was about to "inherit" outmoded Soviet-built nuclear plants, further complicating issues of safety and security as well as transport of nuclear materials and disposal of nuclear waste. In May 2005, confirming a 2004 proposal by the commission, the council extended Euratom competence to two international conventions adopted in 1986, the Convention on Early Notification of a Nuclear Accident and the Convention on Assistance in the Case of a Nuclear Accident or Radiological Emergency.

Meanwhile, during the constitutional debates of the Convention on the Future of Europe, the question of Euratom's future role became a significant issue. Some opponents of nuclear power wanted the Euratom treaty to be abolished, which would cut off subsidies to the nuclear power industry, and its safety functions addressed by the proposed European Constitution. Other opponents argued that the Euratom treaty should be "unbundled" from other key EU documents and attached as a protocol to the constitution, thereby making it easier for countries to withdraw from the treaty without affecting their overall standing in the union. In the end, in 2003 the drafting convention left the treaty intact. Later, the European Parliament, which has long sought greater control over Euratom activities, urged the Inter-Governmental Conference (IGC) on the constitution "to convene a Treaty revision conference in order to repeal the obsolete and outdated provisions of that Treaty, especially those relating to the promotion of nuclear energy and the lack of democratic decision-making procedures." The governments of Austria, Germany, Hungary, Ireland, and Sweden also called for convening a special IGC on Euratom and related nuclear matters. In March 2006 the president of the European Commission presented a "green paper" for a common EU energy policy, the core objectives of which were sustainable development, competitiveness, and security of supply.

Euratom research is currently operating in conjunction with the EU's Sixth Framework Program for Research and Technological Development (for 2002–2006) and the associated effort to create a European Research Area (ERA). Because of its status as a separate community, Euratom has its own Framework Program focusing on controlled thermonuclear fusion, management of radioactive waste, and radiation protection. The research budget for the four-year period was set at 1.23 billion euros. In April 2005 the commission proposed a Framework Program for 2007–2011 that, if adopted, would increase Euratom funding to 4.75 billion euros, with the biggest increase slated for fusion research and development.

GROUP OF SEVEN/GROUP OF EIGHT

Established: As the Group of Seven (G-7) during the San Juan, Puerto Rico, summit of leading industrial democracies June 27–28, 1976; first met as the kindred Group of Eight (G-8) after the addition of Russia as a formal participant at the May 15–17, 1998, G-7 summit in Birmingham, United Kingdom.

Purpose: To discuss problems relating to the functioning and structure of the world economy, the international monetary and banking systems, international trade, and other economic and political concerns.

Principal Organs: The G-7/G-8 has no formal organs per se. There are annual summits, twice-a-year (and ad hoc) meetings of finance ministers and central bank governors, and other meetings of government ministers and officials.

G-7 Membership (7): Canada, France, Germany, Italy, Japan, United Kingdom, United States.

G-8 Membership (8): G-7 plus Russia.

Origin and development. The origins of the G-7/G-8 can be traced back to 1962 and the founding of the informal Group of Ten (G-10; see separate article) by Belgium, Canada, France, the Federal Republic of Germany, Italy, Japan, the Netherlands, Sweden, the United Kingdom, and the United States. Also sometimes known as the Group of Eleven since Switzerland joined in 1984, the G-10 encompasses those states that contribute to the General Arrangements to Borrow (GAB), a supplementary loan agreement negotiated to increase the lending resources of the International Monetary Fund (IMF). The GAB was formally launched in October 1962, although prospective members met earlier to examine the international monetary system.

Later in the decade finance ministers and sometimes central bank governors from France, the Federal Republic of Germany, Japan, the United Kingdom, and the United States began to meet as an additional informal caucus that became known as the Group of Five (G-5). As a consequence of discussions at the July 30–August 1, 1975, Helsinki Conference on Security and Cooperation in Europe, the heads of state or government of the G-5 plus Italy convened in November 1975 in Rambouillet, France, to address various economic and financial concerns, including growth, inflation, exchange rates, monetary reform, oil prices, and unemployment. Canada joined as the seventh participant in the San Juan, Puerto Rico, summit in 1976, at which time the assembled leaders agreed on the utility of holding annual sessions. Thus the G-7 was born.

The agendas of the 1976 summit and then the May 7–8, 1977, summit in London, United Kingdom, were broadened to include such concerns as balance-of-payments problems and North-South relations. Also beginning with the 1977 summit, the European Community (subsequently the European Union) was included in discussions, although not as a full participant. At the next summit, held July 16–17, 1978, in Bonn, West Germany, the G-7 issued an unprecedented statement on aircraft hijacking that is widely recognized as the group's first political declaration. Developments at the 1979 summit in Paris included the establishment of the Financial Action Task Force (FATF), which was asked to identify and promote policies that would combat money laundering. (In 2001 the 33-member, independent FATF, which is headquartered at the Paris offices of the Organization for Economic Cooperation and Development, expanded its scope to combat terrorist financing; see the OECD article for additional details.)

Succeeding summits continued to be held by rotation among the member countries, while the agenda expanded to arms control, the environment, political reform, and terrorism. During the second half of the 1980s the G-7 focused its attention on such matters as rectifying trade imbalances, stabilizing exchange rates, combating protectionism, and relaxing debt repayment pressure on the world's poorest countries.

The issue of how best to encourage free-market reform in the Soviet Union and its former satellites in Eastern Europe dominated the G-7 summit July 15–17, 1991, in London, which was attended by Soviet leader Mikhail Gorbachev. Some observers predicted that the meeting might lead to creation of a "Group of Eight," a possibility that U.S. President George H. W. Bush broached at the 1992 summit in Munich, Germany, which Russian President Boris Yeltsin attended. By the 1994 summit in Naples, Italy, Russian participation in most nonfinancial discussions had become the norm, resulting in the designation "Political-8" (P-8). Russia's formal inclusion at the May 15–17, 1998, summit in Birmingham, United Kingdom, marked the birth of the G-8, although the G-7 continues to issue separate statements and communiqués, primarily on financial and economic matters.

Structure. The G-7/G-8 has no permanent secretariat or administrative bodies. Activities coalesce around annual summits of the members' heads of state or government, joined by the president of the European Commission. National delegations also include finance and foreign ministers and a personal representative ("sherpa") of each president, prime minister, or chancellor. Summits typically include a day of private, informal bilateral and multilateral discussions among the leaders. Summits rotate among the G-8 members, with

newest member Russia scheduled to play host for the first time in 2006.

Throughout the year high-level meetings can be held by the members' foreign ministers; by finance ministers and central bank governors; and also by ministers responsible for the environment, justice and interior, labor, development, and other areas. Ad hoc task forces and working groups also have been established.

Activities. In the first half of the 1990s G-7 discussions often centered on how best to support the fledgling free-market systems in the former Communist world. The breakup of Yugoslavia and attendant crises in the Balkans, Russian actions in Chechnya, and the Mexico peso crisis of 1994–1995 also were among the most pressing topics during this period. Terrorism moved to the forefront of the agenda at the June 28–29, 1996, summit in Lyon, France, which took place only a week after the bombing of a U.S. military base in Saudi Arabia. At the urging of U.S. President Bill Clinton, the G-7 leaders approved a 40-point plan to combat crime and terrorism.

With the exception of a brief economic policy discussion, Russia participated fully in the June 20–21, 1997, summit in Denver, Colorado, in the United States. At that session, environmental policies were the focus of considerable debate as the United States and Japan resisted European pressure to set emission targets for greenhouse gases. The 1998 summit in Birmingham, in addition to marking the full inclusion of Russia in most matters, was dominated by the recent dramatic downturn in Asia's economic fortunes and by India's test of a nuclear weapon. In June the G-8 agreed to block all but humanitarian loans from international lenders to both India and Pakistan, which exploded its own nuclear device in response to India's test.

Meeting in February 1999, the G-7 finance ministers and bank governors approved a plan to establish a Financial Stability Forum (FSF), its primary purpose being to prevent economic crises by improving oversight of and information exchange within the world's financial systems. As of early 2004 the forum comprised representatives of the

G-7 countries, the Netherlands, Australia, Hong Kong, Singapore, the European Central Bank, the Bank for International Settlements (BIS), the IMF, the OECD, the World Bank, the Basel Committee on Banking Supervision, the International Accounting Standards Board, the International Organization of Securities Commissions, the International Association of Insurance Supervisors, the Committee on the Global Financial System, and the Committee on Payment and Settlement Systems.

Steps were also taken to include developing countries in discussions related to reform of global financial systems. Largely at the instigation of President Clinton at the November 1997 Asia-Pacific Economic Cooperation (APEC) summit in Vancouver, Canada, a temporary Group of 22 (G-22) took shape. In addition to the G-7 countries, G-22 participants included Argentina, Australia, Brazil, China, Hong Kong, India, Indonesia, South Korea, Malaysia, Mexico, Poland, Russia, Singapore, South Africa, and Thailand. The grouping held its first meeting in April 1998. Less than a year later, on March 11, 1999, a successor Group of 33 (G-33) met for the first time in Bonn, Germany, with a second session convening April 25 in Washington. The 11 additions to the G-22 were Belgium, Chile, Côte d'Ivoire, Egypt, Morocco, Netherlands, Saudi Arabia, Spain, Sweden, Switzerland, and Turkey.

The G-33 was superseded September 26, 1999, by a new Group of 20 (G-20), comprising representatives of the European Union and the IMF/World Bank as well as the G-7 members and the following 11 countries: Argentina, Australia, Brazil, China, India, Republic of Korea, Mexico, Russia, Saudi Arabia, South Africa, and Turkey. Intended to "broaden the dialogue on key economic and financial policy issues . . . and to achieve stable and sustainable world growth that benefits all," the G-20 met for the first time December 15–16 in Berlin, Germany. At its most recent annual meeting, held October 27–29, 2003, in Morelia, Mexico, leading topics included how to avoid the kind of debt payment default that caused a crisis in Argentina late in 2002, how to stop terrorist financing and money laundering, and how to reduce Iraq's overwhelming debt burden.

The June 18–20, 1999, G-7/G-8 summit in Köln, Germany, approved a debt relief package that increased the number of countries eligible for the IMF/World Bank's Heavily Indebted Poor Countries (HIPC) program by 7 to 36. Described as the largest debt-relief program in history, the initiative projected debt relief of up to $90 billion ($70 billion from the G-7 members) over the next several years, in part through IMF reinvestment of proceeds from gold sales. Eligible countries would have to provide assurances that the relief was being channeled into structural reforms and social policy concerns, such as health and education programs. At the summit the G-8 also worked on plans for peacekeeping in Kosovo and, more broadly, reconstruction and development throughout the Balkan states, principally in conjunction with the EU-sponsored Stability Pact for South-Eastern Europe.

At the annual G-7/G-8 summit July 21–23, 2000, in Nago, Okinawa, development funding and debt relief remained a focus of attention, one of the concerns being the slow pace of debt cancellation. Other matters under discussion included achieving gender equality, universal primary education by 2015, and improved health care. On September 22, a day before a scheduled ministerial meeting in Prague, Czech Republic, the G-7 central banks acted to prop up the euro by selling dollars and buying the beleaguered unified currency. That action and rising world oil prices dominated discussions at the ministerial session, which immediately preceded the annual meeting of the IMF and World Bank. At the latter, officials noted that slow progress on debt relief was linked to the failure of the G-7 countries to provide sufficient funding.

The annual G-7/G-8 summit July 20–22, 2001, in Genoa, Italy, took place amid disruptions caused by antiglobalization protests. In addition to the troubled state of the world economy, discussions centered on such topics as cutting emission of greenhouse gases, implementing a development plan for Africa, and overcoming the "digital divide." The session also approved a $1.3 billion fund to help combat AIDS, tuberculosis, and malaria. Meeting in Washington in October 2001, a month after the September terrorist attacks against the United States, the G-7 finance ministers and central bank governors stated their resolve to strengthen the faltering world economy, although they adopted no specific action plan.

Canada hosted the June 26–27, 2002, summit at the resort of Kananaskis, Alberta, sufficiently removed from the nearest large city, Calgary, to ease security concerns not only about terrorism but also about antiglobalization demonstrations. Despite disagreements on particular issues—for example, U.S. tariffs directed against steel and softwood lumber imports and U.S. President George W. Bush's call for Palestinians to replace Yasir Arafat as leader of the Palestinian Authority— several initiatives were approved. The G-8 agreed to a ten-year aid package of $20 billion (half from the United States) to assist Russia and other countries of the former Soviet bloc in securing their remaining nuclear materials. The leaders also agreed to provide additional debt relief under the HIPC initiative, but the $1 billion commitment was far less than some advocates had sought. Similar criticism greeted the G-8 African Action Plan, which confirmed an earlier commitment of $6 billion per year, beginning in 2006, in support of the African Union's New Partnership for Africa's Development (Nepad). UN Secretary General Kofi Annan and the leaders of South Africa, Nigeria, Algeria, and Senegal attended the summit and voiced at least a modicum of support for the program, in return for which potential recipients are expected to introduce wide economic and social reforms.

The June 2–3, 2003, summit in Evian-les-Bains, France, ended with fewer concrete results than its predecessor, in part because of President Bush's planned departure after only 24 hours, but more fundamentally because of lingering ill will attributable to the earlier U.S.-UK decision to invade Iraq and oust the Saddam Hussein regime. Canada, France, Germany, and Russia vocally opposed the March attack and resultant occupation, although the summit participants managed to voice a tepid collective commitment to establishing a sovereign,

stable, and democratic Iraq. Unanimity was evident primarily in a condemnation of nuclear proliferation, the "pre-eminent threat to international security."

Earlier in the year, at a February meeting of G-7 finance ministers and central bankers, some participants had criticized the Bush administration for its large tax cuts and projected fiscal deficits. In February 2004 Japan and the European G-7 members expressed, with greater urgency, their concern about the consequences of a recent steep fall in the value of the U.S. dollar, which the Bush administration, facing a fall election, appeared willing to accept in the expectation that a weak dollar would spur export sales, encourage manufacturing, and create jobs.

Following President Bush's call in April 2004 for more engagement with China in the rich countries' economies, China was invited to participate for the first time in a meeting of the finance ministers and central bank governors at a G-7 meeting on October 1 in Washington. Meanwhile, some of the G-8 countries continued to be at odds with the United States and Britain over financing peacekeeping missions in Iraq, the topic dominating the June 8–10, 2004, summit in Sea Island, Georgia, with Iraqi interim president Sheikh Ghazi Ajil al-Yawar in attendance. In a diplomatic victory for Bush, the UN Security Council on June 9 unanimously adopted a resolution authorizing a multinational force in Iraq, clearly bolstering Bush's position while he met with the world leaders. Bush also pressed for reduction of Iraqi debt and for significantly greater relief for the world's poorest countries. Ultimately, the G-8 failed to agree to a full cancellation of those countries' debt. Instead, they agreed to a two-year extension of their long-running effort to assist in debt reduction.

In 2005, G-7 ministers met often early in the year, struggling to come to terms with debt relief for Africa and many other of the poorest countries. On June 11, in what was described as a "landmark deal" brokered by Britain, the G-7 leaders, meeting in London, agreed to pay to relieve 18 of the poorest countries—most of them in Africa—of some $40 billion in debt. The agreement, the basis of which was hammered out by Blair and Bush a week earlier, would also benefit another nine countries, bringing the total debt reduction tab to some $55 billion. On September 24, 2005, the G-8 pledged to uphold the agreement as well during its summit in Gleneagles, Scotland.

By the end of 2005, the developing world energy shortage was engaging the group's attention, as were ways to combat international terrorism. These concerns were reflected in the report of the December 2–3 meeting of finance ministers and central bank governors in London. The report remained generally positive about global growth, however, despite increased worries over inflation and a warning that the value of a country's currency (China was implied) must reflect economic reality. A similar message about the prospects for economic growth came from the April 21, 2006, meeting of the same group in Washington. The belief was that inflation was being contained, despite the runup in oil prices, and growth in general was good. The group pledged to work for more transparency in oil markets, and it warned against global imbalances and a rise in protectionism.

GROUP OF TEN

Established: As the group of contributing countries to the General Arrangements to Borrow (GAB), negotiated in 1962 in Paris, France, by the Executive Board of the International Monetary Fund.

Purpose: To discuss problems relating to the function and structure of the international monetary system.

Principal Organs: None; communication within the group occurs at regular and ad hoc meetings of ministers, ministerial deputies, and governors or other representatives of the members' central banks.

Membership (11): Belgium, Canada, France, Germany, Italy, Japan, Netherlands, Sweden, Switzerland, United Kingdom, United States.

Nonstate Participants (4): International Monetary Fund (IMF), Organization for Economic Cooperation and Development (OECD), Bank for International Settlements (BIS), European Commission (EC).

Origin and development. The Group of Ten (G-10), also sometimes known as the Group of Eleven since Switzerland's accession to membership in 1984, consists of those states that contribute to the General Arrangements to Borrow (GAB), a supplementary loan agreement negotiated to increase IMF lending resources. The GAB was formally launched in October 1962, although prospective members had met earlier to examine the international monetary system.

Major decisions of the G-10 include a 1966 recommendation that led to the establishment of special drawing rights (SDRs) as a supplementary IMF liquidity resource and support for the IMF's 1983

expansion of the GAB to deal with the potential default of heavily indebted countries. Under the expansion the IMF's lines of GAB credit rose from SDR 6.4 billion to SDR 17 billion (as of early 2004, about 23 billion), plus an additional SDR 1.5 billion made available through an arrangement with Saudi Arabia. The G-10 also backed other changes allowing the use of some GAB resources by non-GAB participants and extended GAB association to certain borrowing arrangements between the IMF and non-GAB participants.

Over the years, G-10 activity became intertwined with, and even supplanted by, several subgroups. In 1967 finance ministers and central bank governors of five G-10 members (France, Federal Republic of, Germany, Japan, United Kingdom, United States) began to meet regularly as an additional informal caucus on international economic monetary developments. They became known as the Group of Five (G-5). In 1975 the G-5 promoted still another forum, comprising the heads of state or government of its members. With the addition of Italy and Canada, the group became known as the Group of Seven (G-7; see preceding article). In general, the G-5 continued to operate in confidence while the G-7 summits generated wide publicity on a broad agenda that grew to include issues well beyond the G-10's purview, such as terrorism and arms control.

Structure. One of the least institutionalized intergovernmental organizations, the G-10 holds meetings at several levels. Ministerial sessions are attended by the finance ministers and central bank governors of member states, the president of the Swiss National Bank, the managing director of the IMF, the secretary general of the OECD, the general manager of the BIS, and the president of the EC Commission. Meetings are held in the spring and fall of each year immediately prior to meetings of the IMF's Interim Committee, with ad hoc sessions called as needed. In addition, the central bank governors typically meet monthly. Members also are represented at as-needed "deputy" meetings attended by high-level civil servants from finance ministries and central banks, joined by senior staff members of the IMF, the OECD Secretariat, the BIS, and the EC. In addition, there are various working and contact groups for particular concerns, such as legal and institutional aspects of the international financial system.

Activities. The G-10 addresses many problems relating to international liquidity, bank lending, monetary policy, trade balances, and other economic issues. Meetings are private, and detailed information on decisions often is not made public. However, broadly worded communiqués are sometimes issued prior to IMF meetings or at times of international economic unrest. The G-10 also produces studies on economic and financial topics and continues to be responsible for approving loan requests under the GAB; such loans are financed only by those states that approve the particular requests, but G-10 members provide "multilateral surveillance" over loan recipients.

At its June 1995 summit in Halifax, Canada, the G-7 urged the G-10 and others to help prevent the kind of financial crisis that beset Mexico the previous winter. In response, the IMF Executive Board established the New Arrangements to Borrow (NAB), effective November 1998, in which 26 states and institutions participate: the 11 G-10 members plus Australia, Austria, Banco Central de Chile (since 2003), Denmark, Finland, Hong Kong Monetary Authority, Republic of Korea, Kuwait, Luxembourg, Malaysia, Norway, Saudi Arabia, Singapore, Spain, and Thailand. In effect, the NAB doubled to SDR 34 billion the resources on which the IMF can draw in the event of a threat to the international monetary system. As of January 2004, the GAB has been activated ten times, most recently in July 1998 to finance an IMF Extended Arrangement for Russia, while the NAB has been activated just once, in December 1998 to provide

a Stand-by Arrangement for Brazil. In line with a G-10 recommendation, the GAB was renewed for the ninth time in November 2002, with effect from December 2003. In November 2003 the NAB also was renewed for a five-year period.

The G-10 met September 27, 2002, in Washington and discussed procedures for resolving debt crises that would benefit both debtors and creditors, including the restructuring of sovereign bonds. The participants also discussed how regulatory, tax, and disclosure policies affect asset markets. A year later, convening September 21 in Dubai, United Arab Emirates, the G-10 noted positive developments in the international economic climate, particularly improvements in the U.S. and Japanese economies and reforms taking place in Europe. The G-10's concluding communiqué also noted, however, that "significant internal and external imbalances" could undermine the ongoing recovery. In addition, the communiqué noted the need to address future fiscal pressures associated with an aging population.

On June 26, 2004, the G-10 central bank governors approved new rules on Banking Capital Adequacy to help stabilize the global financial system by allowing banks to hold more capital to cover risk. The rules were to be implemented in two phases at the ends of 2006 and 2007.

In September 2004, after meeting in Basel, G-10 governors reported an upswing in the global economy, despite high oil prices, and by January 2005 they were predicting nothing short of robust growth. When the per-barrel price of oil topped $60 in June 2005, however, the G-10 governors gave a gloomier assessment, saying that spike would surely dampen economic growth in many areas of the world.

In their latest report, dated September 2005, the group turned to the likely effects of the increasing population reaching retirement age in a period of worldwide deregulation. Its report called for governments to encourage increased transparency and better risk management on the part of private pension schemes and for the promotion of financial literacy among the public in general.

INTERNATIONAL ENERGY AGENCY (IEA)

Established: By the Agreement on an International Energy Program, which was signed by the Council of Ministers of the Organization for Economic Cooperation and Development (OECD) November 15, 1974, in Paris, France.

Purpose: To coordinate the responses of participating states to the world energy crisis and to develop an oil-sharing mechanism for use in times of supply difficulties; to coordinate national energy policies, share relevant information on energy supplies and markets, and establish closer relations between petroleum-producing countries and consumer states.

Headquarters: Paris, France.

Principal Organs: Governing Board, Standing Groups, Committee on Energy Research and Technology, Committee on Non-Member Countries, Secretariat.

Executive Director: Claude Mandil (France).

Membership (26): Australia, Austria, Belgium, Canada, Czech Republic, Denmark, Finland, France, Germany, Greece, Hungary, Ireland, Italy, Japan, Republic of Korea, Luxembourg, Netherlands, New Zealand, Norway, Portugal, Spain, Sweden, Switzerland, Turkey, United Kingdom, United States.

Observers: All other OECD members, as well as the Commission of the European Communities, may participate as observers.

Origin and development. Created as a response by OECD member states to the energy crisis of 1973–1974, the IEA began provisional operation on November 18, 1974, with signatory governments given until May 1, 1975, to deposit instruments of ratification. Norway, one of the original sponsors, did not immediately participate as a full member because of fear that sovereignty over its own vast oil resources might be impaired. Subsequently, Spain, Austria, Sweden, and Switzerland applied for membership, although the last three reserved the right to withdraw if IEA operations interfered with their neutrality. New Zealand was admitted in 1975, and a later agreement with Norway raised it from an associate to a full member. Subsequently, Australia, Greece, and Portugal joined. France and Finland cooperated with the agency until becoming members in 1992. The Czech Republic joined in February 2001, as did South Korea several months later.

Apart from the energy crisis of the 1970s, the most perilous events for the IEA have been the Iran–Iraq war of the 1980s and the Gulf crisis of 1990–1991. In 1984 IEA members discussed plans to be implemented should the Strait of Hormuz be closed because of the Iran-Iraq war. Although one-third of Western Europe's oil was carried through the strait, existing reserves and slackened demand lessened the potential impact of such an eventuality. In addition, members agreed to early use of government-owned or controlled oil supplies to calm the market in cases of disruption.

A week after the Iraqi invasion of Kuwait on August 2, 1990, the IEA Governing Board met in emergency session, urging efforts to avert a possible oil crisis. Another IEA emergency session on January 11, 1991, unanimously approved a contingency plan to ensure "security of supply." Two days after the January 16 launching of Operation Desert Storm against Iraq, the plan was activated and IEA members were directed to make an additional 2.5 million barrels per day of oil available to the market. The IEA reported that 17 countries subsequently released oil from stockpiles during the Gulf war, helping to keep supplies and prices relatively stable.

Structure. The IEA's Governing Board is comprised of ministers of member governments. The board is assisted by three Standing Groups (Emergency Questions, Long-Term Cooperation, and the Oil Market) and two Committees (Energy Research and Technology, and Non-Member Countries). Decisions of the Governing Board are made by a weighted majority except in the case of procedural questions, where a simple majority suffices.

A Coal Industry Advisory Board reports to the Standing Group on Long-Term Cooperation. There also is an Industry Advisory Board on Oil. Working Parties reporting to the Committee on Energy Research and Technology (CERT) focus on Fossil Fuels, Renewable Energy Technologies, and End Use Technologies; a Fusion Power Coordinating Committee also reports to the CERT. The Secretariat includes an Emergency Planning and Preparations Division, which helps carry out the work of the Standing Group on Emergency Questions.

Activities. In the event of an oil shortfall of 7 percent or more the Governing Board can invoke oil-sharing contingency plans and order members to reduce demand and draw down oil reserves. Participating countries agree to maintain oil stocks equal to 90 days' worth of the previous year's net imports. A system of complementary Coordinated Emergency Response Measures (CERM), dating from 1984, may be invoked by the Governing Board under circumstances that do not necessarily constitute a full emergency.

Over the years, the IEA has broadened the scope of its activities to include analyses of various energy sectors as well as "Country Reports" that review energy policies, prices, and developments in key nonmembers as well as in member states. Ties with nonmembers have steadily increased, reflect-

ing their growing energy consumption. The IEA also has confronted nuclear energy issues, particularly as public and governmental support for nuclear power generation declined after the 1986 Chernobyl accident in what is now Ukraine.

Regular publications include the *World Energy Outlook* and annual statistical analyses of the oil, natural gas, electricity, and coal industries. Through "Implementing Agreements" the IEA also helps fund cooperative research efforts involving such areas as alternative energy sources (ocean power, wind, solar, battery, hydro, hydrogen, geothermal, biomass), clean coal technology, hybrid vehicles, energy efficiency, superconductivity, heat pump and heat exchange technology, and nuclear fusion.

The relationship of such environmental issues as rising carbon dioxide emissions, and the consequent "greenhouse effect," to national and international energy goals also has been a major consideration for the IEA. The IEA's 1998 *World Energy Outlook* noted that carbon dioxide emissions were expected to exceed 1990 levels by 70 percent by 2020, with most of this growth occurring in the developing world, especially Asia, and with overall developing world emissions surpassing those of the developed countries by 2010. The 2000 *World Energy Outlook*, anticipating a rise in world energy use of 57 percent between 1997 and 2020, predicted that the emission targets set at the 1997 Kyoto, Japan, session of the Conference of the Parties to the United Nations Framework Convention on Climate Change could not be met.

The *World Energy Outlook* for 2002 predicted that by 2030 fossil fuels would continue to account for 90 percent of energy usage and that over the next three decades consumption of oil would increase at a faster rate than in the preceding 30 years, growing from 75 million barrels per day to 120 million. Consequently, emissions of carbon dioxide are expected to increase by 70 percent. China alone is expected to account for one-fifth of the growth in energy demand.

In 2003 the IEA issued its first *World Energy Investment Outlook*, which concluded that some $16 trillion was needed in energy-related investment by

2030, half of it for transportation and distribution systems. Among those contributing to the report were OPEC, the World Bank, governmental institutions, and various corporations.

The IEA has consistently warned against complacency about energy supplies. Increased energy efficiency on the part of the OECD membership, coupled with constantly improving emergency policies and procedures, has lessened the risk of an "oil shock" similar to that of 1973–1974. Nevertheless, the 1990s saw members' dependency on oil imports approach the level of the 1970s, and as a consequence reserve stocks dropped sharply as a proportion of imports. In addition, given marketplace pressures, oil companies have become less willing to stockpile fuel.

During the biennial International Energy Forum, held in September 2002 in Osaka, Japan, the IEA, OPEC ministers, and other key participants appeared increasingly comfortable about holding discussions in the open rather than behind closed doors. The IEA's contention that suppliers and consumers both benefit from collaborative planning was subsequently reinforced when a confluence of circumstances—the aftermath of a December general strike in Venezuela, Japan's decision to temporarily shut down nuclear plants because of security concerns, unrest in Nigeria, and the March 2003 invasion of Iraq—could have precipitated a major supply crisis. Instead, with the IEA, its members, oil corporations, and OPEC working in concert, no significant supply shortages or price spikes occurred. Meeting on April 28–29, 2003, the IEA Governing Board continued to emphasize the importance of energy security, emergency protection, and economic growth (the "Three E's") and noted "the benefit of reinforced dialogue between producers and consumers of oil, as well as between the IEA and OPEC secretariats."

By the 2005 Governing Board meeting, held on May 3 in Paris, the effect on the oil market of rapid economic growth in China and India became increasingly evident. The final report warned against a business-as-usual approach to energy, stressing the need for more investment and more creative thinking to ensure adequate supplies and reduce the rise in greenhouse gases. The report concludes: "In order to bridge the gap between what is happening and what needs to be done, IEA will help to develop strategies aiming at a clean, clever and competitive energy future. This needs leadership and co-operation."

During 2005 and 2006, gasoline prices rose substantially throughout the developed world, with no promise of a return to previous levels. In addition to increased demand, real or perceived instability in major producer countries, notably in Iran and Nigeria, caused instability in energy markets. In June 2006 the IEA revised upward its estimate of Chinese energy consumption, while noting that higher oil prices appeared to have reduced growth in demand in the United States.

NORDIC COUNCIL

Established: By enabling legislation passed by the parliaments of the founding member states, following agreement at a foreign ministers' meeting on March 16, 1952, in Copenhagen, Denmark, with effect from February 12, 1953.

Purpose: To provide a forum for consultation among the legislatures and governments of the member states on matters of common interest and to promote cooperation on cultural, economic, legal, social, and other matters.

Headquarters: Copenhagen, Denmark.

Principal Organs: Plenary Assembly, Presidium, Secretariat.

Secretary General: Ole Stavad (Denmark).

Membership (5): Denmark (including Faroe Islands and Greenland), Finland (including Åland Islands), Iceland, Norway, Sweden.
Observers: The Sámi (Lapp) local parliaments of Finland, Norway, and Sweden.

Official Languages: Danish, Norwegian, Swedish.

Origin and development. First advocated by Denmark in 1938, the Nordic Council grew out of an unsuccessful attempt in 1948–1949 to negotiate a Scandinavian defense union. A drafting committee set up by the Nordic Interparliamentary Union in 1951 developed the legal basis of the organization, which was established not by treaty but by identical laws adopted by the parliaments of Denmark, Iceland, Norway, and Sweden with effect from February 1953. Finland joined in 1955. A supplementary Treaty of Cooperation (since subject to several amendments) was signed on March 23, 1962, in Helsinki, Finland, to further develop legal, cultural, social, economic, and communications cooperation. In 1970, the Faroe Islands and the Åland Islands were granted separate representation within the Danish and Finnish delegations, respectively. In 1971 a Council of Ministers was created as a separate forum for cooperation among the Nordic governments. In 1984 Greenland was granted separate representation within the Danish delegation.

Structure. The council encompasses 87 members elected by national or territorial parliaments. The Swedish and Norwegian parliaments select 20 representatives each; Iceland's parliament selects 7. Of Denmark's 20 representatives, 16 are selected by the national parliament and 2 each by the parliaments of the Faroe Islands and Greenland. Of Finland's 20 representatives, 18 are selected by the national parliament and 2 by the parliament of the Åland Islands. In principle each delegation reflects the distribution of parties within its parent legislature. Since 1982 there also have been four main political groups (Social Democratic, Conservative, Center, and Socialist) within the council itself.

The elected council members join an unspecified number (usually about 80) of nonvoting government representatives to form the Plenary Assembly, the council's highest decision-making body, which meets once a year for a brief session. The Plenary Assembly's influence emanates primarily from recommendations and statements of opinion addressed to the Nordic Council of Ministers or one or more of the member governments. Under a 2002 restructuring, five committees were created: Business and Industry; Citizens' and Consumer Rights; Culture, Education and Training; Environment and Natural Resources; and Welfare.

A Presidium, consisting of a president and 12 representatives, is appointed each spring by the

Plenary Assembly from among its elected members. It presides over the assembly session and supervises the council's work between meetings, assisted by a Secretariat under the direction of a secretary general. The Secretariat also is responsible for day-to-day contact with the Nordic Council of Ministers and other international organizations.

The **Nordic Council of Ministers,** whose composition varies according to the subject under consideration, is a separate decision-making body, although it works closely with the Nordic Council, and they share various administrative departments. In practice, the Nordic Council of Ministers consists of "specialist ministerial councils" for consumer affairs; construction and housing; culture; drug abuse; education and research; energy; the environment; equality; finance and economics; food, health, and social services; information technology; justice; labor; regional affairs; trade and industry; and transport. (Foreign affairs and defense are outside the organization's purview.) Decisions, which must be unanimous, are binding on the member states save in matters subject to ratification by the national parliaments. The Council of Ministers is assisted by its own Secretariat, located in Copenhagen, Denmark. The current secretary general of that Secretariat is Per Unckel of Sweden. In 1996 the Nordic Council Secretariat was moved from Stockholm, Sweden, to Copenhagen so that it could cooperate more closely with the Secretariat of the Council of Ministers.

Activities. The Nordic Council has provided a forum for consultation among the Scandinavian parliaments on questions of economic, cultural, and legal cooperation. In some areas, the laws of the Nordic countries have been almost completely harmonized, while in others agreement has been reached on common principles or basic legal rules. Particularly impressive results have been obtained in civil and family law. In the commercial field, laws bearing on contracts, installment purchases, instruments of debt, commercial agents, insurance, bills of exchange, and checks are now almost identical, as are those governing copyrights, patents, trademarks, and industrial designs. In 1981 a Nordic Language Convention allowed citizens of one Nordic country to use their native language in court proceedings in another Nordic jurisdiction. An agreement on voting rights was concluded in October 1975, with subsequent revisions allowing all Nordic citizens reciprocal rights of voting and of contesting municipal elections in the country in which they are resident.

Cooperation in social and health policy was formalized in the 1955 Convention on Social Security, augmented in 1975 by an agreement on rights relating to sickness, pregnancy, and birth. A new Convention on Social Security, concluded in 1981, extended additional coverage to individuals temporarily resident in a Nordic country other than their own. In 1973 a Nordic Transport Agreement was enacted to increase efficiency in transportation and communications. Between 1979 and 1983, cooperation in the area of transport increased further with the construction of an interstate highway system, harmonization of road traffic rules, and establishment of a common Scandinavian Airline System. In the economic field, a Nordic Investment Bank (NIB) became operative June 1, 1976 (see section on Regional Development Banks). Additional conventions include a 1974 accord on protection of the environment, a 1981 treaty on Nordic cooperation in development assistance, and a 1982 common labor market agreement that guarantees the right to seek work and residence within all member states.

The 1988 Plenary Assembly endorsed a number of proposals from the Council of Ministers to promote intraregional economic growth as well as heighten extraregional trade. They included the creation of a Nordic Industry Center in Oslo; a program of intensive research and development in biotechnology; extensive cooperation with the European Community (EC) in anticipation of the planned EC single market; expansion of the Nordic Project Fund, set up on a temporary basis in 1982 to help Nordic companies compete for export orders; and establishment of a Nordic Development Fund to provide concessionary loans to projects promoting social and economic development in developing countries. Environmental issues also continued to receive close attention; the assembly met in extraordinary session on November 16 in Helsingör, Denmark, to endorse a wide-ranging antipollution program.

Among the topics discussed at the 1990 Plenary Assembly were the Nordic region's growing contacts with the Soviet Union and other Eastern European nations and the evolving nature of continental relations in the wake of the East-West thaw. At the 1991 Plenary Assembly emphasis was given to cooperation with the Soviet Union's Baltic republics, which were characterized as "natural partners" of the Nordic countries. In its report to the assembly, the Presidium noted that a "comprehensive review" of existing Nordic agreements, treaties, and action programs might be necessary soon to keep pace with the development of "tomorrow's Europe," including cooperation between the EC and the European Free Trade Association (EFTA) in establishing a European Economic Area (see separate article on EFTA).

During the March 1992 Plenary Assembly the Council proposed the short- and long-term reorganization of Nordic agreements and the incorporation of foreign policy and security issues within the cooperation sphere. In other activity, responding to continued economic and political liberalization in the Baltic states, the Council approved funds to aid their private sector industrial development efforts.

In November 1992 a joint statement from the Nordic prime ministers endorsed "a more prominent place" for the council in budgetary affairs, a compromise position that was reluctantly endorsed by the March 1993 Plenary Assembly in Oslo, Norway. Otherwise, attention focused on the complicated negotiations on the European Economic Area (EEA) and on the applications of Finland, Norway, and Sweden to join the EC. The council also welcomed the region's expanding cooperation with Russia.

Relations with the rest of Europe continued to dominate Nordic debate over the next year, particularly as the EC transformed itself into the European Union (EU) with entry into force of the Maastricht Treaty on November 1, 1993. The EU's new "pillar" devoted to a common defense and security policy was of special concern for some Nordic parliamentarians. Apprehension also was expressed during the March 1994 Plenary Assembly that Nordic cooperation would be pushed into the background as Finland, Norway, and Sweden contemplated joining the EU. The council also extended observer status to the Sámi (Lapp) parliaments of Finland, Norway, and Sweden, rejecting, for the time being at least, the request from Sámi representatives that they be accorded full membership privileges.

Attention in 1995 remained focused on interregional issues, such as the future role of the council in view of the admission of Finland and Sweden to the EU. (Norway's voters had rejected EU membership in a November 28, 1994, referendum.) At the Plenary Assembly held February 27–March 2 in Reykjavik, Iceland, the Nordic Council endorsed a recommendation from the Council of Ministers that both councils continue to operate, with priority given to culture, education, and research. In addition, the Nordic prime ministers in August agreed in principle to participate in the proposed Arctic Council, which would provide a forum for consultation among the Nordic countries, Canada, Russia, and the United States on environmental issues (see separate article on the Arctic Council).

As expected, restructuring of the Nordic Council began at the fall Plenary Assembly held in November 1995. In early 1996 many of the organization's institutions were eliminated or consolidated to streamline operations and enhance cooperation. In April, the Nordic Council and the Baltic Assembly, encompassing the parliaments of Estonia, Latvia, and Lithuania, held their first joint conference, in Vilnius, Lithuania.

It was broadly apparent at the 1996 Plenary Assembly in Copenhagen that the Nordic countries still faced significant questions regarding developments in the EU. For instance, parliamentarians from the other council states questioned the wisdom of Finland's announced decision to join the EU's Economic and Monetary Union (EMU) in 1999. The assembly also criticized the EU's Intergovernmental Conference for giving insufficient attention to unemployment policies, long a major priority of Nordic countries.

The growing political dimension of the Nordic Council was evident at the Plenary Assembly of November 10–13, 1997, in Helsinki. After receiving a report from the Nordic defense ministers, the council urged that the definition of security be expanded beyond purely military concerns to include economic, social, and environmental considerations.

International affairs dominated discussions at the November 9–12, 1998, Plenary Assembly— the Nordic Council's 50th such session—held in Oslo. Council members discussed ways of reducing crime in the "Adjacent Areas" (the Baltic states and Russia) and stressed the importance of including some of the Baltic republics in any EU expansion. The environment also was discussed at the assembly, with the Nordic Council receiving a report on pollution caused by nuclear waste and industry on Russia's Kola Peninsula.

In February 1999 a second joint Nordic-Baltic conference convened in Helsinki, the focus of attention being improved cooperation and Russia's economic and security status. In early April the council was joined by representatives of indigenous peoples and of Russia's northwest region in the first Barents parliamentary conference, which focused on welfare, health care, and other social concerns. The November 8–11, 1999, Nordic Council plenary session in Stockholm addressed such issues as the free movement of labor among the member countries and the impact of economic globalization on the Nordic welfare model. Relations with the EU were once again discussed, with Swedish Prime Minister Persson, in particular, opposing formation of a formal Nordic bloc within the EU.

The 52nd Plenary Assembly session on November 6–8, 2000, in Reykjavik, Iceland, called for closer cooperation with Russia on military affairs but still insisted that Russia improve in the areas of human rights, democratization, and free press. Considerable interest greeted publication of a "wise men's" report entitled *Norden 2000—Open to the Winds of the World*, which proposed some 60 specific recommendations for restructuring Nordic cooperation. In addition to calling for a closer relationship between the national parliaments and the

Nordic Council, the report proposed that "Adjacent Areas" be redefined to permit inclusion of Canada and Scotland, for example, in addition to the Baltic region and Russia. The report also identified ten areas in which council members should coordinate their policies: democratic standards, the environment, globalization, technological development, European integration, security, demographics and free migration within the region, culture and education, free trade and economic integration, and welfare and labor policy. Furthermore, the report called for more formal cooperation in matters of developmental assistance, defense, and trade.

Major events during the first half of 2001 included an April 2–3 meeting in Oslo to consider a proposal from the Nordic Council of Ministers on a 20-year strategy for sustainable development. A third joint session of the Baltic Assembly and the Nordic Council opened on May 31, in Riga, Latvia, with the council's president, Sven Erik Hovmand of Denmark, describing Baltic-Nordic cooperation as having achieved an equal partnership of eight countries, replacing a "five plus three" model.

Attention at the 53rd Plenary Assembly, held on October 29–31, 2001, in Copenhagen was dominated by responses to the September terrorist attacks on the United States. Participants also expressed concern about events in the Middle East, called for a strengthened United Nations, and heard a status report on plans to form a joint military brigade capable of peacekeeping and other internationally sponsored missions.

The Plenary Assembly session on October 29–31, 2002, in Helsinki marked a half-century for the Nordic Council. Delegates discussed free movement across open borders and sought greater EU support of the "Northern Dimension" initiative (see the article on the European Union). Immediately before the October 28–30, 2003, Plenary Assembly session in Oslo, the Nordic prime ministers invited prospective EU members Estonia, Latvia, and Lithuania to join the NIB, which had financed projects in developing countries as well as in the Nordic area. (They joined at the beginning of 2005.) Although the new secretary general of the

Nordic Council of Ministers, Per Unckel of Sweden, subsequently stated that he did not anticipate council membership for the three Baltic republics in the near future, he did expect regional cooperation to intensify. In 2003, for the first time, a representative from northwest Russia attended the assembly.

The 2004 session, held on November 1–3 in Stockholm, again focused on cooperation with neighboring countries, including the indigenous peoples of northwest Russia. The assembly dealt with ways to resolve remaining cross-border issues and to ensure cooperation on research projects. The 2005 session, held on October 25–27 in Reykjavik, discussed measures to counter illegal immigration from neighboring countries. Plans for a general reform of the organization's structure were also advanced.

NORTH ATLANTIC TREATY ORGANIZATION (NATO/OTAN)

Organisation du Traité de l'Atlantique Nord

Established: September 17, 1949, by action of the North Atlantic Council pursuant to the North Atlantic Treaty signed on April 4, 1949, in Washington, D.C., and effective August 24, 1949.

Purpose: To provide a system of collective defense in the event of armed attack against any member by means of a policy based on the principles of credible deterrence and genuine détente; to work toward a constructive East–West relationship through dialogue and mutually advantageous cooperation, including efforts to reach agreement on militarily significant, equitable, and verifiable arms reduction; to cooperate within the alliance in economic, scientific, cultural, and other areas; and to promote human rights and international peace and stability.

Headquarters: Brussels, Belgium.

Principal Organs: North Atlantic Council (all members), Defense Planning Committee and Nuclear Planning Group (all members except France), Military Committee (all members).

Chair of the North Atlantic Council and Secretary General: Jaap de Hoop Scheffer (Netherlands).

Membership (26): Belgium, Bulgaria, Canada, Czech Republic, Denmark, Estonia, France, Germany, Greece, Hungary, Iceland, Italy, Latvia, Lithuania, Luxembourg, Netherlands, Norway, Poland, Portugal, Romania, Slovakia, Slovenia, Spain, Turkey, United Kingdom, United States.

Partnership for Peace Participants (20): Albania, Armenia, Austria, Azerbaijan, Belarus, Croatia, Finland, Georgia, Ireland, Kazakhstan, Kyrgyzstan, Macedonia, Moldova, Russia, Sweden, Switzerland, Tajikistan, Turkmenistan, Ukraine, Uzbekistan.

Official Languages: English, French.

Origin and development. The postwar consolidation of Western defenses was undertaken in light of the perceived hostility of the Soviet Union as reflected in such actions as the creation of the Communist Information Bureau (Cominform) in October 1947, the February 1948 coup in Czechoslovakia, and the June 1948 blockade of West Berlin. American willingness to join Western Europe in a common defense system was expressed in the Vandenberg Resolution adopted by the U.S. Senate on June 11, 1948, and subsequent negotiations culminated in the signing of the North Atlantic Treaty on April 4, 1949, by representatives of Belgium, Canada, Denmark, France, Iceland, Italy, Luxembourg, Netherlands, Norway, Portugal, the United Kingdom, and the United States.

The treaty did not prescribe the nature of the organization that was to carry out the obligations of the signatory states, stipulating only that the parties should establish a council that, in turn, would create a defense committee and any necessary subsidiary bodies. The outbreak of the Korean War on

June 25, 1950, accelerated the growth of the alliance and led to the appointment in 1951 of Gen. Dwight D. Eisenhower as the first Supreme Allied Commander in Europe. Emphasis on strengthened military defense of a broad area, reflected in the accession of Greece and Turkey to the treaty in February 1952, reached a climax later that month at a meeting of the North Atlantic Council in Lisbon, Portugal, with the adoption of goals calling for a total of 50 divisions, 4,000 aircraft, and strengthened naval forces. Subsequent plans to strengthen the alliance by rearming the Federal Republic of Germany as part of the European Defense Community collapsed, with the result that the FRG was permitted to establish its own armed forces and, in May 1955, to join NATO.

NATO's gravest problem during the mid-1960s was the estrangement of France over matters of defense. French resistance to military "integration" under NATO reached a climax in 1966 when President de Gaulle announced the removal of French forces from consolidated commands and gave notice that all allied troops not under French command had to be removed from French soil by early 1967. These stipulations necessitated the rerouting of supply lines for NATO forces in Germany; transfer of the alliance's European command from Paris, France, to Casteau, Belgium; and relocation of other allied commands and military facilities. Thereafter, France participated selectively in NATO's operations, although it rejoined the Military Committee in 1996.

During the 1970s NATO suffered from additional internal strains. Early in 1976 Iceland threatened to leave the Organization because of a dispute with Britain over fishing rights off the Icelandic coast. Disputes between Greece and Turkey, initially over Cyprus and subsequently over offshore oil rights in the Aegean Sea, resulted in Greece's withdrawal from NATO's integrated military command and a refusal to participate in NATO military exercises. In October 1980, five months after Greece threatened to close down U.S. bases on its territory, negotiations yielded an agreement on its return as a full participant. However, relations between Greece and Turkey subsequently remained tenuous. (As recently as October 2000 Greece withdrew from a NATO exercise in Turkey when Ankara objected to the flight of Greek aircraft over disputed Aegean islands.)

In June 1980 U.S. President Jimmy Carter reaffirmed his administration's conviction that Spanish membership in NATO would significantly enhance the organization's defensive capability. The Spanish government originally made its application contingent upon Britain's return of Gibraltar and the admission of Spain to the European Community, but Madrid later decided that it could negotiate both issues subsequent to entry. Therefore, following approval in late October by the Spanish *Cortes*, the government formally petitioned for NATO membership, with a protocol providing for Spanish accession being signed by the members in December 1981. A referendum in March 1986 ensured Spain's continued participation with three domestic stipulations: the maintenance of Spanish forces outside NATO's integrated command; a ban on the installation, storage, and introduction of nuclear weapons; and a progressive reduction in the U.S. military presence. In November 1996 the Spanish parliament endorsed Spain's "full participation" in NATO's military structure, which occurred in 1999.

The structure of East-West relations was irrevocably altered by the political whirlwind that swept through Eastern Europe during late 1989 and early 1990, with the demolition of the Berlin Wall (described by one reporter as the "ultimate symbol of NATO's reason for existence") dramatically underscoring the shifting security balance. With communist influence evaporating in many members of the Soviet-led Warsaw Treaty Organization (WTO) and with superpower rapprochement growing steadily, U.S. officials in early 1990 suggested that American and Soviet troop levels could be sharply cut. NATO also endorsed Washington's decision not to modernize the short-range missiles in Europe and agreed to reduce the training and state of readiness of NATO forces.

If any doubt still existed on the issue, a WTO summit in Moscow in early June and a NATO summit in London in early July confirmed the end of

the Cold War. Suggesting that "we are no longer adversaries," Western leaders proposed that a NATO-
WTO nonaggression pact be negotiated. NATO's
"London Declaration" also vowed a shift in military philosophy away from "forward defense," involving heavy troop and weapon deployment at the
East–West frontier, and toward the stationing of
smaller, more mobile forces far away from the former "front lines." The allies agreed that the Conference on (later Organization for) Security and
Cooperation in Europe (CSCE/OSCE) should be
strengthened as a forum for pan-European military and political dialogue and urged rapid conclusion of a conventional arms agreement so that talks
could begin on reducing the continent's reliance on
nuclear weapon systems. They also insisted that
Germany remain a full NATO member upon unification, a condition initially resisted by Moscow but
ultimately accepted as part of the German-Soviet
treaty concluded in mid-July.

As the WTO continued to disintegrate, NATO
pursued its own military retrenchment and reorganization. In May 1991 the NATO defense ministers approved the most drastic overhaul in the
alliance's history, agreeing to reduce total NATO
troop strength over the next several years from 1.5
million to 750,000 (including a cutback of U.S.
troops from the existing 320,000 to 160,000 or
fewer). In addition, it was decided to redeploy most
of the remaining troops into seven defense corps
spread throughout Western and Central Europe.
The new plan also called for the creation of an
Allied Rapid Reaction Corps (ARRC) of 50,000–
70,000 troops to deal quickly with relatively small-
scale crises, such as those that might arise from
the continent's myriad ethnic rivalries. At the same
time, NATO nuclear weapons were retained in Europe as a hedge against a sudden shift in Soviet
policy.

Other issues addressed by NATO in 1991 included a proposed charter change that would permit
"out-of-area" military activity (the alliance's participation in the Gulf war having been constrained
by the restriction against its forces being sent to a
non-NATO country) and the security concerns of
former Soviet satellites in Eastern Europe, several

of which had inquired about admission to NATO.
Although all such overtures were rejected as premature, the ministers called for the development of
a "network of interlocking institutions and relationships" with former communist-bloc nations. The
impulse led to the establishment in December of
the North Atlantic Cooperation Council (NACC)
as a forum for dialogue among the past NATO-
WTO antagonists. Participating in the NACC were
the 16 NATO countries plus Albania, Armenia,
Azerbaijan, Belarus, Bulgaria, Czech Republic,
Estonia, Georgia, Hungary, Kazakhstan, Kyrgyzstan, Latvia, Lithuania, Moldova, Poland, Romania, Russia, Slovakia, Tajikistan, Turkmenistan,
Ukraine, and Uzbekistan. Austria, Finland, Malta,
Slovenia, and Sweden had NACC observer status.

The NACC, which worked in liaison with various NATO bodies and met regularly in conjunction
with the North Atlantic Council, played a growing
role in implementing the "new strategic concept"
endorsed at the November 1991 NATO summit.
While reaffirming the "essential" military dimension of the alliance, the heads of state agreed that a
"political approach to security" would become increasingly important in Europe. Consequently, the
summit called for additional reductions in NATO's
conventional and nuclear forces beyond those proposed in May.

The NATO leaders also endorsed a larger role
for such organizations as the CSCE, the European Community (EC, later the European Union—
EU), and the Western European Union (WEU)
defensive and political alliance in dealing with
the continent's security issues. Significantly, however, the 1991 summit continued to insist that proposed pan-European military forces would "complement" rather than supplant NATO. As further
evidence of the alliance's intention to remain active
in European affairs, the NATO foreign ministers in
May 1992 agreed to make forces available "on a
case-by-case basis" for future peacekeeping missions necessitated by ethnic disputes or interstate
conflict on the continent.

In November 1992 NATO agreed to use its warships, in conjunction with WEU forces, to enforce the UN naval blockade against the truncated

Federal Republic of Yugoslavia. In April 1993 the alliance authorized its jets to monitor the UN ban on flights over Bosnia and Herzegovina. Otherwise, NATO appeared to be locked in a somewhat paralyzing debate on how to deal with the fighting in Bosnia and Herzegovina. In May 1993 U.S. President Bill Clinton suggested that NATO forces be used to create "safe havens" for Bosnian Muslims, but agreement could not be reached within the alliance on the proposal. In midsummer Clinton, who had previously been criticized for not taking a more active role in the Bosnian controversy, suggested that U.S. planes might be used to bomb areas in Bosnia under Serbian control, if requested by the United Nations. Prodded by the new U.S. assertiveness, the NATO defense ministers endorsed the Clinton position and discussed plans for a 50,000-strong NATO peacekeeping force that could be used in the event of a permanent Bosnian cease-fire. Nonetheless, the alliance still appeared to be searching for its proper role in "the confusion of the post–Cold War era."

As proposed by President Clinton, a NATO summit held January 10–11, 1994, in Brussels struck a compromise regarding expansion by launching a highly publicized Partnership for Peace (PfP) program, which extended military cooperation but not full-fledged defense pacts to the non-NATO countries. By mid-1996, 28 nations (including previous WTO members, former Soviet republics, and several longtime "neutral" states) had signed the PfP Framework Document. Among other things, the PfP states pledged to share defense and security information with NATO and to ensure "democratic control" of their armed forces. In return NATO agreed to joint training and planning operations and the possible mingling of troops from PfP states with NATO forces in future UN or OSCE peacekeeping missions.

In other 1994 activity, the alliance continued to draw criticism for its lack of effectiveness in the former Yugoslavia. In what was heralded as a "decisive step," the NATO ambassadors in February agreed to conduct air strikes against certain Serbian targets if requested by the United Nations. Later in the month, in the first such direct military action in the alliance's history, NATO aircraft shot down four Serbian planes that were violating the "no-fly" zone in Bosnia and Herzegovina. In addition, NATO planes bombed several Serbian artillery locations around Sarajevo in April.

Two issues dominated NATO affairs over the next year—the continued conflict in Bosnia and planning for the expected accession of Eastern and Central European countries to the alliance. Regarding the former, NATO responded to growing aggressiveness on the part of Bosnian Serbs by launching a bombing campaign against Serbian positions on August 30, 1995, near Sarajevo. The Serbians subsequently agreed to withdraw their heavy guns from the area as demanded by NATO, the alliance's hard-line approach also apparently contributing to an intensification of peace talks among the combatants in Bosnia. Consequently, NATO tentatively approved the proposed deployment of some 60,000 troops (including 20,000 from the United States) to take over peacekeeping responsibilities from UN forces in Bosnia should a permanent cease-fire go into effect.

By that time a degree of progress had been achieved regarding the alliance's membership plans as well. Among other things, NATO said that applicants would have to display a commitment to democracy and human rights, foster development of a free market economy, establish democratic control of the military, and not become mere "consumers of security." It also was agreed that new members would not have to accept the stationing of NATO forces or nuclear weapons in their territory. NATO members were greatly concerned over a scandal involving Secretary General Willy Claes in the autumn of 1995. Claes, who had succeeded the late Manfred Wörner of Germany in October 1994, was investigated in a corruption case involving a helicopter contract awarded while he was Belgium's economic affairs minister in 1988. As a consequence, he was forced to resign from his NATO post on October 20, 1995.

Further complicating matters for NATO, the subsequent selection process for a new candidate degenerated into a public dispute. The first candidate announced by the European NATO members,

Ruud Lubbers (former prime minister of the Netherlands), was vetoed by the United States, apparently because of a lack of consultation beforehand. France then blocked Uffe Ellemann-Jensen from Denmark, whom the United States supported, reportedly due in part to the candidate's less-than-satisfactory mastery of French. (Many NATO observers also noted that Ellemann-Jensen had recently criticized French nuclear testing.) As a compromise, Javier Solana Madariaga, a prominent member of Spain's Socialist government since 1982, was appointed to the post on December 5. The new secretary general's announced priorities included the expansion of NATO and the promotion of a peace pact in Bosnia. Regarding the latter, the NATO foreign and defense ministers, meeting in joint session on December 5, formally approved the establishment of the peacekeeping force for Bosnia and Herzegovina (called the Implementation Force, or IFOR) to oversee the recently signed Dayton Accord. IFOR began its mission on December 20 (see article on Bosnia and Herzegovina for details).

The other major development at the December 1995 NATO session was an announcement from France that it planned to rejoin the NATO military structure after an absence of nearly three decades. However, it subsequently became apparent that the French decision was contingent on controversial restructuring that would provide greater European control of military affairs on the continent. A degree of progress on that question was perceived at the meeting of NATO foreign ministers on June 2–3, 1996, the United States agreeing that, under some circumstances, the European countries could conduct peacekeeping and/or humanitarian missions on their own under the command of an expanded WEU. However, even though the French defense minister was formally welcomed by his NATO counterparts at their session on June 13, Paris soon after threatened to reverse its recent decision unless Washington agreed to relinquish control of NATO's Southern Command to a European. The United States resisted that demand, primarily because of the prominence of the U.S. Sixth Fleet in the Southern Command.

The U.S.-French debate subsequently deteriorated into a somewhat surprising exchange of "public insults" prior to the meeting of NATO foreign ministers on December 10–11, 1996, at which Paris appeared to back away from its threat to block NATO expansion unless it got its way regarding the Southern Command. Meanwhile, on a more positive note, the NATO ministers endorsed the creation of a new mission for Bosnia and Herzegovina (the 31,000-strong Stabilization Force, or SFOR), scheduled to take over at the end of the month from IFOR. The Bosnian mission had been widely viewed as a major success for NATO, as had the PfP program, many of whose members had lent troops to IFOR. The streamlined SFOR included troops from the United States, Russia, and some 23 other NATO and non-NATO countries including, significantly, Germany, whose commitment of 2,000 soldiers marked the first time that combat-ready German ground troops had been deployed outside NATO borders since World War II.

It also was agreed at the December 1996 session that NATO would make its long-awaited announcement regarding the admission of new members at the summit scheduled for July 8–9, 1997, in Madrid, Spain. Russia immediately denounced any such plans as "completely inappropriate," and the topic dominated NATO affairs in early 1997. While describing expansion as "inevitable," U.S. representatives were reportedly hoping that a special relationship could still be established between the alliance and Russia that would make Moscow less "antagonistic" to the NATO decision. While Russia strongly preferred that Europe abandon NATO and instead focus on strengthening the OSCE, Moscow ultimately accepted NATO enlargement.

Following months of intense negotiations, NATO and Russia signed a Founding Act on Mutual Relations, Cooperation, and Security on May 27, 1997, in Paris, France. Both sides committed to stop viewing each other as "adversaries" and endorsed "a fundamentally new relationship." NATO also stated it had no intention of stationing nuclear weapons or "substantial combat forces" within the borders of new members. In addition, a NATO-Russia Permanent Joint Council (PJC) was established to discuss security issues, which appeared to satisfy Moscow's goal of having a say in NATO decision making, although NATO officials made it clear that Russia would not be able to veto any of the alliance's decisions. Collaterally, Western leaders promised Russia an expanded role in the Group of Seven and other major international forums.

Although Russia remained officially opposed to any expansion of NATO, the new accord permitted NATO to extend membership invitations to the Czech Republic, Hungary, and Poland as of April 1999, assuming ratification by the national legislatures of the NATO members and the three applicants. A number of NATO leaders, led by French President Chirac, had supported the inclusion of Romania and Slovenia in the first round as well but deferred to the U.S./UK position amid reports of complaints over "hegemonic" behavior on the part of the United States. The ruffled feathers were smoothed, however, by the statement from NATO Secretary General Solana that Romania, Slovenia, and the three Baltic states were "strong candidates" for the second round of expansion.

Progress regarding the new members at the Madrid summit served to distract attention from the ongoing conflict between France and the United States. Washington once again refused Paris's demand that a European be put in charge of the Southern Command, and France therefore declined to return to the integrated military command. Meanwhile, at the conclusion of the summit, NATO signed an agreement with Ukraine that established a NATO-Ukraine Commission and provided for cooperation and consultation on a wide range of issues. In other activity in 1997 the alliance replaced the NACC with the Euro-Atlantic Partnership Council (EAPC), which was designed to enhance the PfP program and permit cultivation of broader political relationships among the "partners" and full NATO members. NATO also unveiled a new military command structure, scheduled to be in effect by April 1999. Subsequently, in early 1998, NATO announced it would keep its forces in Bosnia past June, with SFOR's mission now to include civil security. (At the 2004 Istanbul summit, NATO announced it would end the SFOR Mission at the end of 2004.)

Events in 1998 were dominated by NATO's admonitions to Yugoslavia's Serbian leaders regarding their policies in the province of Kosovo, where a crackdown against ethnic Albanian separatists had begun in late February. In June a newly authorized Euro-Atlantic Disaster Response Coordination Center (EDRCC) began operating, its first assignment being to assist Kosovar refugees. In June and August, with the cooperation of PfP members Albania and Macedonia, NATO held military exercises near Yugoslavia's borders, while in October continuing hostilities led NATO to warn Belgrade of imminent air strikes. In response, Yugoslavia agreed to admit OSCE observers and to begin military and security withdrawals from the province. To provide the 2,000-member observer force with air surveillance, NATO placed a coordination unit in Macedonia, where an additional command center was sited in November. Widespread hostilities in Kosovo nevertheless resumed in January 1999. In February peace talks opened in Rambouillet, France, cosponsored by France and the United States, but discussions came to an abrupt halt on March 19 when the Serbian delegation continued to reject one of the proposed peace plan's key provisions, namely the presence of NATO peacekeepers on Serbian soil. On March 24, 1999, NATO forces initiated Operation Allied Force—the first intensive bombing campaign in the Organization's history—which in the following weeks extended throughout Yugoslavia (see article on Serbia and Montenegro for additional details).

Kosovo dampened the alliance's 50th anniversary summit, which was held on April 23–25, 1999, in Washington. Highlights of the summit were the welcoming of the accession of the Czech Republic, Hungary, and Poland (which had been formally admitted at a ceremony at the Truman Library in Missouri on March 12) and the approval of a new Strategic Concept, including a European Security and Defense Identity (ESDI) within the alliance. The summit communiqué acknowledged that the WEU, using "separable but not separate NATO assets and capabilities," could conduct defensive operations without direct U.S. participation. It also noted "the resolve of the European Union to have the capacity for autonomous action" in military matters that did not involve the full alliance. Despite U.S. pressure for NATO to adopt a more global posture, the Strategic Concept continued to limit NATO's purview to the "Euro-Atlantic area," with the communiqué reiterating the primacy of the UN Security Council in international peace and security matters. The summit also saw issuance of a Membership Action Plan (MAP) for future enlargement and the launch of a Defense Capabilities Initiative (DCI), the latter of which emphasized the need for interoperability in command and control and information systems, particularly given the likelihood that future missions will require rapid deployment and sustained operations outside alliance territory. Finally, NATO agreed to build a new headquarters in Belgium, at a cost of about $800 million. (Construction was to begin in 2008, with completion scheduled for 2012.)

On August 5, 1999, NATO approved the appointment (effective the following October) of UK Secretary of State for Defense George Robertson (subsequently Lord Robertson of Port Ellen) as the successor to Secretary General Solana.

Meeting on November 20–22, 2002, in Prague, Czech Republic, the NATO heads of state extended membership invitations to Bulgaria, Estonia, Latvia, Lithuania, Romania, Slovakia, and Slovenia, with formal admission anticipated for 2004. At the same time, the summit approved establishment of a mobile, rapidly deployable NATO Response Force (NRF). Earlier in the year, on May 28, the NATO heads of state had signed the Rome Declaration, which institutionalized a closer working relationship with Moscow through creation of a NATO-Russia Council (NRC) as successor to the NATO-Russia PJC.

The NRF was inaugurated on October 15, 2003. The force numbered 9,000 troops and was placed under the command of British general Sir Jack Deverell. The NRF was scheduled to increase to 25,000 troops by October 2006.

Structure. NATO's complex structure encompasses a civilian component, a military compo-

nent, and a number of partnership organizations. At the apex is the North Atlantic Council (NAC), the principal decision-making and policy organ. It normally meets twice a year at the ministerial level to consider major policy issues, with the participation of the member states' ministers of foreign affairs and/or defense. It also may meet as a summit of heads of state and government. Between ministerial sessions the NAC remains in permanent session at NATO headquarters, where permanent representatives, all of whom hold ambassadorial rank, convene. Decisions at all levels must be unanimous.

The civilian structure includes a Defense Planning Committee (DPC), which dates from 1963; it focuses on a range of matters related to collective defense planning and also offers guidance to military leaders. The DPC typically meets at the permanent representative level but also convenes twice a year as a meeting of defense ministers. The Nuclear Planning Group (NPG) consists of the defense ministers of the countries represented in the DPC. Its purview extends from nuclear safety and deployment to such related matters as proliferation and arms control. Like the NAC, the DPC and NPG may call on a host of committees and other bodies, the most prominent of which are the Senior Political Committee and the Defense Review Committee, to provide expert advice, to assist in preparing meetings, and to follow through on decisions.

The secretary general, who is designated by the NAC, serves as chair of the NAC, the DPC, the NPG, the EAPC, and the Mediterranean Cooperation Group (MCG), as well as joint chair of the NATO-Russia PJC and the NATO-Ukraine Commission. As NATO's chief executive, he has an important political role in achieving consensus among member governments and also can offer his services in seeking solutions to bilateral disputes. At the 2002 Prague summit, the NAC approved a reorganization of NATO's civilian headquarters structure. The new system created a deputy secretary general post and six main divisions, each led by an assistant secretary general. The new divisions are Defense Investment, Defense Policy and Planning, Executive Management, Operations, Political Affairs and Security Policy, and Public

Diplomacy. In addition to the six divisions, plans were made for a newly created NATO Office of Security to be headed by a director. On September 22, 2003, NATO approved the appointment (effective January 5, 2004) of Dutch Foreign Minister Jaap de Hoop Scheffer as successor to Secretary General Lord Robertson. As was the case with many of his predecessors, de Hoop Scheffer's appointment was the result of compromises among the allies. Candidates such as Norway's Defense Minister Kristin Krohn and Portugal's António Vitorino (an EU commissioner) were rejected by France because of their countries' support of the U.S.-led invasion of Iraq, while the U.S. vetoed Canadian Finance Minister John Manley because of his country's opposition to the Iraq war.

The highest military authority is the Military Committee, which operates under the overall authority of the NAC, DPC, and NPG. At its top level the Military Committee is attended by the members' chiefs of defense although, as with the NAC, it is typically in continuous session attended by permanent military representatives from all members. The committee furnishes guidance on military questions, including the use of military force, both to the NAC and to subordinate commands. It also meets with PfP partners on matters of military cooperation. The Military Committee is supported by the International Military Staff (IMS), which includes some 380 military personnel from the member states and 85 civilian personnel. The IMS is led by a three-star officer, currently Vice Admiral Fernado del Pozo of Spain.

Until 1994, the NATO military structure embraced three main regional commands: Allied Command Europe (ACE), Allied Command Atlantic (ACLANT), and Allied Command Channel. However, in 1994 Allied Command Channel was disbanded, and its responsibilities were taken over by ACE. In addition, in 2002 the NAC agreed to dissolve ACLANT as an operational command. It was replaced by Allied Command Transformation (ACT). Each Command is responsible for developing defense plans for its area, for determining force requirements, and for the deployment and exercise of its forces. Except for certain air defense squads

in Europe, however, the forces assigned to the various commands remain under national control in peacetime.

The ACE headquarters, known formally as Supreme Headquarters Allied Powers Europe (SHAPE), is located in Casteau, Belgium. The Supreme Allied Commander Europe (SACEUR) has traditionally been designated by the United States and serves concurrently as Commander-in-Chief of U.S. forces in Europe (CINCEUR). From 1994 ACE had three major subordinate Commands—Northwest (led by a designee of the United Kingdom), Central (led by a designee of Germany), and Southern (led by a designee of the United States). In 1997 NATO defense ministers agreed to reduce the number of command headquarters from 65 to 20 by 1999. The reorganized ACE incorporated two major subordinate commands, Allied Forces North Europe and Allied Forces South Europe, which had a total of seven subregional commands between them as well as separate air and naval component commands. No fewer than nine other commands and staffs fell under the ACE, most of them encompassing rapid reaction forces established in the 1990s. Other major subordinate structures under the ACE are regional headquarters for the West, East, and South Atlantic, plus a Standing Naval Force Atlantic, a Striking Fleet Atlantic, and a Submarine Allied Command Atlantic. There also is a separate Canada–United States Regional Planning Group, originally created in 1940 and incorporated into the NATO command structure in 1949. Its principal task is to recommend plans for the defense of the U.S.-Canada region.

The ACT, with headquarters in Norfolk, Virginia, is headed by the Supreme Allied Commander Transformation (SACT), who is designated by the United States. The current SACT is U.S. Air Force General Lance Smith. The ACT includes the Joint Warfare Center in Stavanger, Norway; the Undersea Research Center in La Spezia, Italy; and the NATO School in Oberammergau, Germany. The ACT's main mission is to transform NATO's military capabilities to respond to new threats and operations.

The NATO Parliamentary Assembly is completely independent of NATO but constitutes an unofficial link between it and parliamentarians of the 26 member countries. In 2004, French Parliamentarian Pierre Lellouche was elected president of the assembly. In addition, PfP partners have associate delegation status in the assembly, which was founded in 1955 as the NATO Parliamentarians' Conference and was subsequently known, until 1998, as the North Atlantic Assembly. By keeping alliance issues under constant review and by disseminating knowledge of NATO policies and activities, the assembly encourages political discussion of NATO matters. During the 1990s its mandate was broadened to include European security as a whole plus economic, environmental, social, and cultural issues relevant to Central and Eastern Europe. The assembly meets twice a year in plenary session, with various committees and study groups convening throughout the year.

Political dialogue also takes place within the 46-member EAPC, which comprises the 26 NATO members plus the 20 PfP partners; the NRC; the NATO-Ukraine Commission; and the MCG. Established in 1997, the MCG grew out of a Mediterranean Dialogue proposed by NATO in 1994 and initiated in 1995, when Egypt, Israel, Jordan, Mauritania, Morocco, and Tunisia agreed to join. Algeria became the seventh non-NATO member in 2000. The MCG is intended to promote mutual understanding and to serve as a forum on security and stability in the Mediterranean region. At the Istanbul summit in June 2004, the NAC decided to enhance the MCG. The seven MCG members were invited to join an enhanced version of the MCG that would be modeled on the PfP through the Istanbul Cooperation Initiative (ICI). The ICI was designed to improve military and intelligence cooperation between NATO and the MCG states and standardize equipment and operational guidelines. In 2006, NATO ministers began searching for a host country in which to establish a joint NATO-MCG training center.

NATO has established more than three dozen subsidiary and related organizations, agencies, and groups that undertake studies, provide advice, formulate policies for referral to the NAC or other NATO decision-making structures, manage specific programs and systems, or provide education and training. Many of these bodies are NATO Production and Logistics Organizations (NPLOs) concerned with technical aspects of design, production, cooperation, and management in communication and information systems, consumer logistics (pipelines, medical services), and production logistics (armaments, helicopters, other aircraft, missiles). Other bodies are concerned with standardization, civil-emergency planning, airborne early warning, air traffic management, electronic warfare, meteorology, and military oceanography.

Recent activities. The dramatic changes in the European political landscape that accompanied the fall of the Berlin Wall and the demise of the Soviet Union substantially altered NATO's perception of its role on the continent. At the same time, the EC was evolving what it initially called a Common Foreign and Security Policy as part of the Maastricht Treaty, which brought the EU into existence in November 1993. In response to these events NATO began developing a framework for Combined Joint Task Forces (CJTFs), which were envisaged as multinational, multiservice contingents that could be quickly deployed for humanitarian, peacekeeping, or defense purposes. In 1996, NATO reached agreement on a European Security and Defense Identity (ESDI), which derived from the EU's interest in being able to take autonomous military action in situations other than those involving NATO in its entirety. Building upon the existing WEU–NATO relationship, the ESDI would be permitted on a case-by-case basis to employ CJTFs, including "separable but not separate NATO assets," for WEU-led missions. Implementation of the CJTF concept began in 1999, and by 2004, three CJTF commands were established, two land-based and one naval. (In November 2000 the WEU's Council transferred its operational role to the EU, in accordance with the EU's 1999 European Security and Defense Policy [ESDP]. Collaterally, the EU, minus Denmark, agreed to establish a Rapid Reaction Force, formation of which was delayed until December 2002, when differences with non-EU member Turkey over access to NATO facilities were resolved.)

During this same period NATO was negotiating cooperative military agreements with Russia, other former Soviet republics, and a number of Eastern and Central European nations under the PfP program. In May 2000 Croatia became a PfP partner and announced that it would ultimately seek full NATO membership. In the same month, the foreign ministers of nine Eastern and Central European PfP countries—Albania, Bulgaria, Estonia, Latvia, Lithuania, Macedonia, Romania, Slovakia, and Slovenia—agreed to apply collectively for NATO membership in 2002. At the same time, many PfP partners were pushing for greater participation in political decisions and military operations, citing the success of their continuing involvement in the SFOR and the Multinational Force in Kosovo (Kosovo Force, or KFOR).

Although NATO was criticized by United Nations Secretary General Kofi Annan, among others, for circumventing the UN in launching the air campaign against Yugoslavia in March 1999, the June 10 Security Council resolution that established the UN Interim Administration Mission in Kosovo (UNMIK) also included provision for the NATO-led KFOR. As of April 2001, KFOR encompassed some 50,000 troops, the bulk of them from NATO and PfP countries, although command had passed a year earlier to the WEU/EU's Eurocorps, consisting of German, French, Spanish, Belgian, and Luxembourgian units. (For additional information on KFOR, see the entries on Serbia and Montenegro and the Security Council.)

The NATO assault on Yugoslavia drew criticism for other reasons, too, and may have led to the early departure of Gen. Wesley Clark of the United States as SACEUR. Clark, who was succeeded by U.S. Gen. Joseph Ralston in April 2000, was believed to have strongly argued for sending ground forces into Kosovo during the conflict, but he had been overruled. The unintentional bombing of the Chinese embassy on May 9, 1999, and the inadvertent bombing of ethnic Albanian refugees pointed out dangers inherent in air warfare, while some human rights organizations charged that NATO had dropped cluster bombs in populated areas, thereby inflicting avoidable civilian injuries. Furthermore, in March 2000 NATO admitted that it had used armor-piercing munitions that incorporated depleted uranium, raising concern in some quarters about environmental pollution. At an NAC meeting in January 2001, Germany, Greece, Italy, and Norway advocated a moratorium on use of depleted uranium shells, pending scientific determination of any increased incidence of cancer, but the United States and United Kingdom objected.

Apart from its peacekeeping missions in the Balkans, NATO is currently engaged in numerous other efforts, including arms control. Having been involved since the height of the Cold War in attempts to reduce conventional as well as nuclear forces, NATO in April 1999 launched an Initiative on Weapons of Mass Destruction (WMD) and authorized creation of a WMD Center within the International Staff in Brussels. In 2001, the George W. Bush administration unilaterally decided to proceed with development of a National Missile Defense (NMD), despite strong objections from most European allies as well as Russia.

Bush's plan was the major topic of discussion at a special one-day NATO summit held on June 13, 2001, in Brussels, the American president declaring that the Anti-Ballistic Missile (ABM) treaty, which currently prohibits the deployment of new missiles as envisioned by the NMD, was a "relic of the past" and needed to be scrapped. The summit, mostly given over to informal discussion among the NATO leaders, was seen as a success for Bush in that many of his European counterparts reportedly agreed to maintain an "open mind" on the NMD, although France and Germany remained explicitly opposed. Some allies also were reportedly reassured by Bush's pledge that Washington would unilaterally reduce the number of U.S. offensive nuclear weapons and would attempt to negotiate a new missile treaty with Russia. Further heartening the European leaders, Bush unequivocally endorsed the ESDP and the "new options" offered by "a capable European force, properly integrated with NATO." In other activity at the summit, the NATO leaders agreed to present a timetable for enlargement at the regular summit scheduled for 2002 in Prague, Czech Republic, and discussed a possible role for NATO in dealing with an intensifying crisis in Macedonia.

On August 22, 2001, responding to a request for assistance from the government of Macedonia, NATO began Operation Essential Harvest, a 30-day mission by some 3,500 troops to help disarm ethnic Albanian groups in that Balkan state. In September NATO authorized Operation Amber Fox, encompassing 700–1,000 personnel, primarily to protect international monitors overseeing implementation of the Macedonian peace plan. On December 16, 2002, Operation Amber Fox was in turn succeeded by a new mission, Operation Allied Harmony, to minimize any further risk of ethnic destabilization. This mission was to be of short duration, with NATO contingents being replaced in 2003 by elements of the EU's newly authorized Rapid Reaction Force.

The day after the September 11, 2001, terrorist attacks on the United States, the NAC invoked the collective self-defense provisions of the founding treaty. The unprecedented decision was followed in October by authorization for specific steps requested by the United States in its efforts to confront international terrorism. These included access to military facilities and intelligence information and the deployment of NATO's airborne early-warning squadron to the United States.

During the rest of 2001 and early 2002 NATO continued to move toward a closer working relationship with Russia. Despite Moscow's assistance in the U.S. "war on terrorism," however, U.S. Secretary of Defense Donald Rumsfeld and others expressed opposition to any arrangement that would significantly increase Russian involvement in military decisions. The negotiating process culminated in the May signing of the Rome Declaration, which not only established the NRC but also authorized the opening of a permanent Russian office at NATO headquarters. Four days earlier presidents Bush and Putin had signed in Moscow a Strategic Offensive Reduction Treaty (SORT) that committed both states to reducing their nuclear stockpiles from 6,000–7,000 warheads to 1,700–2,200 over the next decade.

In line with the 1997 Founding Act, the NRC focused on such areas as control of terrorism, crisis management, nonproliferation, arms control, and theater missile defenses. In addition, the negotiations leading up to the Rome Declaration had a more indirect consequence—namely, an easing of overt Russian opposition to NATO expansion into the Baltic. Meanwhile, Secretary Rumsfeld had begun advocating a redefined international role for NATO forces. Citing the danger that nuclear, biological, or chemical weapons might be obtained by terrorists, at a June 6–7, 2002, meeting of defense ministers in Brussels Rumsfeld called upon NATO to consider preemptive strikes as an option. Lord Robertson, however, responded cautiously; although acknowledging a need for internal reform, he insisted that NATO "will remain a defensive alliance." On July 19 NATO announced that General Ralston would be succeeded as SACEUR by Gen. James Jones, the first U.S. Marine to take command. The announcement was widely interpreted as presaging a strategic shift toward a more flexible military structure, and at an informal meeting of defense ministers on September 24–25 in Warsaw Secretary Rumsfeld called for creation of a mobile strike force.

The November 20–22, 2002, summit in Prague was highlighted by the formal invitation to seven prospective Eastern European members and by an agreement to establish the NRF. In addition, the summit participants pledged their support for deployment of UN disarmament inspectors in Iraq, although some NATO states, particularly France and Germany, remained skeptical of U.S. assertions of Iraqi ties to the al-Qaida terrorist network.

NATO also deployed airborne early-warning planes to help protect the United States and dispatched its Standing Naval Force Mediterranean to the Eastern Mediterranean to support the U.S.-led military operation in Afghanistan and to deter terrorism. In its first major military operation outside of the transatlantic region, in August 2003 NATO assumed command of the International Security

Assistance Force (ISAF) authorized by the UN in Afghanistan. NATO oversaw 5,500 peacekeeping troops in the Kabul region. Efforts to expand the NATO-led mission to more remote regions of the country were constrained by the unwillingness of members and allies to contribute more troops to the ISAF. The inability of the alliance to deploy additional forces demonstrated the growing strain on European member states as the allies tried to maintain operations in areas such as the Balkans, Afghanistan, and Iraq. However, NATO agreed to provide 2,000 additional troops to provide security during the 2004 Afghan elections. In addition, at the 2004 Istanbul summit, NATO leaders agreed to provide troops for at least five provincial reconstruction teams in the Afghan countryside. At the June 2006 Brussels Summit, NATO leaders announced that the alliance would increase its forces in Afganistan to 17,000, allowing the United States to reduce its troop strength from 20,000 to 16,000. NATO also announced at the summit that the United States would succeed British command of the NATO–Afghan mission in 2007.

During the winter of 2002–2003, the United States asked individual NATO states to contribute forces to the anti-Iraq coalition. Belgium, France, Germany, and Luxembourg strongly resisted the U.S. initiative, which was supported by other members such as the United Kingdom, Netherlands, Italy, and Spain. The divide threatened the cohesiveness of the alliance in February 2003 after the antiwar allies blocked a request from Ankara for NATO to provide surveillance aircraft and antimissile batteries to protect Turkey in the event of armed conflict with Iraq. The deadlock was resolved on February 16 by having the Defense Planning Committee (of which France was not a member) resolve the dispute. NATO subsequently authorized the deployment of both early-warning aircraft and antimissile systems.

NATO did not formally participate in the March 2003 invasion of Iraq, but a number of individual NATO members, including the United Kingdom and Poland, contributed troops to the invasion force and to the post–war peacekeeping coalition

that the UN authorized. At the June 2004 summit in Istanbul, interim Iraqi Prime Minister Iyad Allawi requested additional NATO aid. However, the prewar divide continued, and NATO leaders could only reach a compromise whereby alliance forces would train the Iraqi military and police forces. (NATO deployed 300 troops for the training mission, although Belgium, France, Germany, Greece, Luxembourg, and Spain declined to participate.) Nonetheless, the mission marked the second major nontransatlantic security operation by NATO. Also, in its June 28 communique following the summit, the NAC affirmed support for Poland's command of the coalition's multinational division in Iraq.

On January 29, 2003, seven NATO aspirants (Bulgaria, Estonia, Latvia, Lithuania, Romania, Slovakia, and Slovenia) began formal accession negotiations with the alliance. On March 26, 2003, the protocols were signed and the ratification process began. On March 29, 2004, the seven nations became full members of NATO. In June 2006 Putin warned NATO against further expansion to states such as Ukraine; nonetheless, the alliance continued discussions with Ukraine and a range of states including Croatia, Georgia, Armenia, and Azerbaijan. NATO also sought to strengthen ties with nonmembers, and in April 2006 the alliance announced plans for regular security forums with states such as Australia, Finland, Japan, New Zealand, South Korea, and Sweden. Proposals for a global version of PfP were also endorsed.

The seven new members were expected to change the internal dynamics of NATO. All seven supported the U.S.-led invasion of Iraq and favored NATO as the cornerstone of European security, placing them at odds with other NATO members such as France and Germany, which sought a greater security role for the EU.

In line with NATO's broader antiterrorism campaign, the alliance in 2004 sought to bolster its relationship with Mediterranean states, an important topic at the December 2004 meeting of NATO foreign ministers. In June 2005 NATO agreed to provide air and other types of support to the African

Union's proposed peacekeeping mission to the Darfur region of Sudan. NATO eventually provided transport for some 5,000 AU peacekeepers to Darfur and undertook two major humanitarian missions to the region in 2005. NATO provided assistance and support for the United States in the aftermath of Hurricane Katrina and aid for Pakistan following a major earthquake on October 8, 2005.

At the NAC meeting in June 2006 in Brussels, the alliance's defense ministers decided to require all member states to devote 2 percent of their GDP to defense, replacing a longstanding "gentleman's agreement" regarding the 2 percent threshold that only 7 of the 26 NATO members reached in 2005. (The average expenditure per NATO country in 2005 was 1.8 percent.) At the same meeting, the NAC agreed to reorient the alliance so that it could simultaneously conduct six medium-sized operations (of up to 20,000 troops each) and two major missions (of up to 60,000 troops each). The change was designed to better reflect NATO's contemporary range of operations. Finally, the NAC began examining other possible missions for the alliance, including expansion of counter-terrorist and anti-trafficking activities, as well as a greater role in infrastructure security, such as guarding the oil and gas pipelines from Russia to the EU.

ORGANIZATION FOR ECONOMIC COOPERATION AND DEVELOPMENT (OECD/OCDE)

Organisation de Coopération et de Développement Economique

Established: By convention signed December 14, 1960, in Paris, France, effective September 30, 1961.

Purpose: "... to help member countries promote economic growth, employment, and improved standards of living through the coordination of policy [and] ... to help promote the sound and harmonious development of the world economy and improve the lot of the developing countries, particularly the poorest."

Headquarters: Paris, France.

Principal Organs: Council (all full members plus the European Commission), Executive Committee (14 members), Economic Policy Committee, Development Assistance Committee, Secretariat.

Secretary General: Ángel Gurría (Mexico).

Membership (30): Australia, Austria, Belgium, Canada, Czech Republic, Denmark, Finland, France, Germany, Greece, Hungary, Iceland, Ireland, Italy, Japan, Republic of Korea, Luxembourg, Mexico, Netherlands, New Zealand, Norway, Poland, Portugal, Slovakia, Spain, Sweden, Switzerland, Turkey, United Kingdom, United States.
Limited Participant: European Commission.

Official Languages: English, French.

Origin and development. The OECD in the early 1960s replaced the Organization for European Economic Cooperation (OEEC), whose original tasks—the administration of Marshall Plan aid and the cooperative effort for European recovery from World War II—had long been completed, although many of its activities had continued or had been adjusted to meet the needs of economic expansion. By the 1960s the once seemingly permanent post-war shortage of dollar reserves in Western European countries had disappeared, many quantitative restrictions on trade within Europe had been eliminated, and currency convertibility had been largely achieved. This increased economic interdependence suggested the need for an organization in which North American states would participate on an equal footing. Thus, the OEEC, of which Canada and the United States had been only associate members, was transformed into the OECD. The new grouping also was viewed as a means of overseeing foreign aid contributions to less-developed states. It later expanded to include virtually all the economically advanced free-market states. Japan became a full member in 1964, followed by Finland in 1969, Australia in 1971, and New Zealand in 1973. The membership remained static until Mexico's accession in 1994. Subsequently, the Czech Republic (1995), Hungary (1996), Poland (1996), South

Korea (1996), and Slovakia (2000) joined. There also has been discussion of future Russian membership, although there is still widespread disagreement on the matter among long-standing OECD members.

In November 1992 the OECD Council declared the 1961 "limited participation" agreement with the former Yugoslavia void and not in force with any successor states.

Membership is limited to countries with market economies and pluralistic democracies and is granted by invitation only. New countries must be approved by each existing member, giving each country veto power. The 30 member states produce 60 percent of the world's goods and services, leading detractors to label the organization a "rich man's club" in the past. The OECD Center for Cooperation with Non-Members promotes dialogue with 70 nonmember countries, which are invited to subscribe to OECD agreements and treaties and benefit from policy and economic recommendations.

Structure. The Council, the principal political organ, convenes at least once a year at the ministerial level, although regular meetings are held by permanent representatives. Generally, acts of the Council require unanimity, although different voting rules may be adopted in particular circumstances. Supervision of OECD activities is the responsibility of the 14-member Executive Committee, whose members are elected annually by the Council and usually meet once per week. The secretary general, who chairs the regular Council meetings, is responsible for implementing Council and Executive Committee decisions with the assistance of a Secretariat that employs some 2,000 people. The current annual budget is approximately $365 million, 25 percent of which is contributed by the United States. Japan is the next leading contributor.

Probably the best known of the OECD's subsidiary organs is the Development Assistance Committee (DAC), which evolved from the former Development Assistance Group and now includes most of the world's economically advanced states as well as the Commission of the European Communities. The DAC oversees members' official re-

source transfers. The Economic Policy Committee, another major OECD organ, is responsible for reviewing economic activities in all member states. The OECD includes more than 200 committees that produce data, analyses, guidelines, or recommendations affecting policy in every major area of development. The number of committees continues to grow each year. For instance, 11 new committees were created in 2004, and 4 were added by mid-2005 on issues such as combating Internet spam, education, and health. The Committee on International Investment and Multinational Enterprises was responsible for formulating a voluntary code of conduct for multinational corporations, which was adopted by the OECD in 1976. In addition, "high-level groups" have been organized to investigate commodities, positive adjustment policies, employment of women, and many other issues.

To complement the work of the DAC, an OECD Development Center was established in 1962. Its current priorities emphasize the problems of meeting the basic needs of the world's poorest people, with a focus on rural development and appropriate technology in Africa, Asia, and Latin America. Twenty-six members and nonmembers (including Argentina, Brazil, Chile, and India) participate in the center's activities. The Center for Educational Research and Innovation (CERI), established in 1968, works toward similar goals.

The OECD Nuclear Energy Agency (NEA), established in December 1957, supplements national efforts toward peaceful nuclear development. The secretary general participated in the 1974 Washington Energy Conference, and representatives of the United States, Canada, and all of the members of the European Communities except France subsequently agreed to establish a new International Energy Agency (IEA, see separate entry) under OECD auspices. All OECD members except New Zealand and Poland participate in the Nuclear Energy Agency.

Activities. The key to the OECD's major role in international economic cooperation has long been its continuous review of economic policies and trends in member states, each of which submits information annually on its economic status and policies and is required to answer questions prepared by the Secretariat and other members. This "confrontation" review procedure has led to very frank exchanges, often followed by recommendations for policy changes. OECD analyses, generated in part through the use of a highly sophisticated computerized model of the world economy, are widely respected for being free of the political concerns that often skew forecasts issued by individual countries. Furthermore, the OECD has been in the forefront of efforts to combat unstable currencies, massive trade imbalances, third world indebtedness, and high unemployment in industrialized countries.

A degree of controversy developed during the 1989 Council meeting over the recent U.S. citation of Japan, Brazil, and India as "unfair traders" subject to possible penalties. Japan challenged the U.S. decision as a threat to the "open multilateral trading system" and asked for an OECD statement criticizing Washington. Thus, the final communiqué, while not specifically mentioning the United States, condemned any "tendency toward unilateralism." In other activity, the Council strongly urged expanded cooperation for environmental protection and endorsed recent initiatives to reduce third world debt.

On another controversial topic, the OECD, after having completed an extensive review of the cost of farm support, called for the elimination of all agricultural subsidies by wealthier producers. Attempts to overcome substantial differences among members regarding agricultural policy continued at the 1990 Council meeting, the ministers giving the "highest priority" to completing agreements on farm subsidies and other outstanding issues in the Uruguay Round of the General Agreement on Tariffs and Trade (GATT). Other activity during 1990 included the opening of the Center for Cooperation with European Economies in Transition, designed to advise and guide Central and Eastern European countries as they move toward free-market economies.

In mid-1994 the OECD released the results of a two-year study on "structural" causes of unemployment among members. Noting the high rate of unemployment in Europe (about 12 percent) as opposed to the United States (about 6 percent), the report urged European governments to introduce a "new flexibility" in their labor markets. Some recommendations—such as the discouragement of minimum wages, promotion of early retirement, expansion of the part-time work force, and reduction of unemployment benefits—were greeted cautiously by government officials who feared such measures would erode social benefits and the overall standard of living.

Mexico became the first new OECD member in 23 years when, with strong U.S. and Canadian backing, it acceded in May 1994. Argentina and Brazil also were reportedly pressing for inclusion, while the OECD announced it would begin negotiations with the Czech Republic, Hungary, Poland, and Slovakia. Additional Asian representation also became possible, overtures from South Korea reportedly being well received and the OECD announcing its interest in developing closer ties with China, India, and Indonesia. Perhaps most importantly, the OECD signed a cooperation agreement with Russia at the June 1994 ministerial session, pledging to assist Moscow with legal, structural, and statistical reforms to promote Russia's integration into the global economy, an effort that U.S. officials described as the "best investment we can make in our security." In part with a view to the OECD's growing responsibilities, Washington reportedly urged an infusion of "new blood" into the organization's bureaucracy, proposing, among other things, that OECD Secretary General Jean-Claude Paye, whose second five-year term was scheduled to end September 30, be succeeded by a non-European. However, the European nations reportedly insisted that Paye be reappointed, leading to a temporary impasse that necessitated the naming of an interim secretary general, Staffan Sohlman of Sweden, upon the expiration of Paye's term. A compromise was subsequently negotiated November 29, under which Paye was reappointed to the post until June 1, 1996, when he was succeeded by Donald Johnston, a former Canadian minister of economic development. (The OECD decision reportedly was reached following negotiations in a "parallel battle" between Europeans and non-Europeans over the appointment of the first director general of the new World Trade Organization [WTO], Renato Ruggiero of Italy having been tapped for that post.)

At the 1996 ministerial meetings, a preliminary agreement was reached regarding corruption in the developing world. Negotiations subsequently continued on the proposed plan to make the bribing of foreign officials a criminal offense, and in November 1997 the treaty was finalized. (The treaty entered into force on February 15, 1999, following its ratification by 12 signatories.) In other activity, the DAC was directed to use a new formula to monitor the effectiveness of OECD aid on overall development by focusing more on the impact on recipient societies and less on monetary values.

Topics discussed at the 1997 session included unemployment, the aging of OECD members' populations, and regulatory reform. Meanwhile, the OECD established a special liaison committee to assist Russia in developing a market economy and democratic institutions, as well as in qualifying to join the organization.

In January 1998 the OECD established the Center for Cooperation with Non-Members (CCNM) as its "focal point" for discussions on policy and to encourage dialogue with emerging market economies. At the April 1998 Council meeting, negotiations on the multilateral investment agreement, which had been seen as promising, were suspended. The negotiations came to an end later that year following France's withdrawal from them, reportedly because it would lose the ability to protect its domestic movie and television markets under the proposed agreement. Despite this setback, the Council did call for the continued liberalization of world trade and the adherence to WTO rules.

In 1999 the OECD established guidelines for corporate governance, which were considered surprisingly progressive for their time. However, by late 2002 OECD officials urged that the guidelines be toughened in light of the recent years' corporate scandals. Among other things, the OECD argued that independent oversight bodies needed to be established because "self-regulation" had failed,

particularly in the auditing sector. The OECD also called for development of guidelines for pension fund administrators.

Another major focus of OECD attention in recent years has been the harmful effect on international trade and investment of so-called "tax havens" around the globe, which provide foreign depositors with the opportunity to deposit large sums of money with little or no tax consequences. In 2000 the OECD list of countries and territories deemed to be "uncooperative" tax havens comprised Alderney, Andorra, Anguilla, Antigua and Barbuda, Aruba, Bahamas, Bahrain, Barbados, Belize, British Virgin Islands, Cook Islands, Dominica, Gibraltar, Grenada, Guernsey, Isle of Man, Jersey, Liberia, Liechtenstein, Maldives, Marshall Islands, Monaco, Montserrat, Nauru, Netherlands Antilles, Niue, Panama, St. Kitts-Nevis, St. Lucia, St. Vincent and the Grenadines, Samoa, Sark, Seychelles, Tonga, Turks and Caicos Islands, U.S. Virgin Islands, and Vanuatu. Additional momentum in pursuing reform in the havens developed following the terrorist attacks in the United States in September 2001, the George W. Bush administration calling on all banks to help identify and seize accounts that might be linked to terrorist organizations or activity. Many of the small countries on the tax haven "blacklist" initially proposed "solidarity" in resisting reform, arguing that financial services provided much of their income. However, OECD accords with several Caribbean countries in early 2002 appeared to stifle cohesive resistance, and by the end of the year only seven countries (Andorra, Liberia, Liechtenstein, Marshall Islands, Monaco, Nauru, and Vanuatu) were still considered uncooperative on the matter.

The OECD tax haven initiative has been conducted alongside efforts by the Financial Action Task Force (FATF) to combat money laundering through use of another "name-and-shame" blacklist. (The FATF, founded in 1989 by the Group of Seven, is an independent body, but it is housed at OECD headquarters and cooperates extensively with the OECD. Its membership comprises the OECD members [except Czech Republic, Hungary, Republic of Korea, Poland, and Slovakia] plus Argentina, Brazil, European Commission, Gulf Cooperation Council, Hong Kong, and Singapore.) Fifteen countries and territories (Bahamas, Cayman Islands, Cook Islands, Dominica, Israel, Lebanon, Liechtenstein, Marshall Islands, Nauru, Niue, Panama, Philippines, Russia, St. Kitts-Nevis, and St. Vincent and the Grenadines) were included in the FATF's initial blacklist in mid-2000. Bahamas, Cayman Islands, Liechtenstein, and Panama were removed from the list in mid-2001, although Egypt, Grenada, Guatemala, Hungary, Indonesia, Myanmar, Nigeria, and Ukraine were subsequently added to the list. In 2002, reform or promises of reform were sufficient in Dominica, Hungary, Israel, Lebanon, Marshall Islands, Niue, Russia, and St. Kitts and Nevis to persuade the FATF to drop them from the list. By late in the year it had been agreed that the FATF would adopt a less confrontational approach and would rely heavily on "persuasion" by the International Monetary Fund and World Bank to convince recalcitrant countries to intensify their anti–money laundering efforts. In part, the more collegial stance was designed to mollify small or less-developed nations, who argued that stricter guidelines were being imposed on poor countries than those in place in rich nations, much the same as in the case of the OECD tax haven initiative.

By June 2002 Dominica, Grenada, Marshall Islands, Niue, Russia, and St. Vincent and the Grenadines were removed from the blacklist, followed by the Cook Islands, Indonesia, Philippines, and Ukraine by February 2005. The initiative was widely viewed as successful, with most of the 40 countries or territories initially blacklisted cooperating with OECD-imposed guidelines by mid-2003. Myanmar, Nauru, and Nigeria are the remaining three countries on the blacklist. However, a major OECD tax initiative hit a wall in 2003 when some member states were reluctant to join in the establishment of a comprehensive exchange system of banking information to prevent money laundering by terrorist organizations as well as tax evasion by individuals and corporations. In September 2003, Switzerland and Luxembourg balked at the OECD's 2006 deadline for entrance into the system, seeking to preserve their nations' well-established practice of banking secrecy. The two nations blocked an agreement among the member counties, marking the first time member states had used a veto inside the governing Council. The move angered 32 offshore financial centers, including the Cayman Islands, Gibraltar, and Seychelles, which had made commitments to the OECD to exchange banking information on the understanding that there would be a "level playing field." The offshore centers argued they would lose their financial interests to Switzerland, Hong Kong, Singapore, or other countries not included in the initiative. A revolt from the offshore centers was headed off following a meeting with senior OECD officials in October, and it was widely expected that most of the offshore centers would eventually comply with the banking exchange out of fear of being placed on the OECD blacklist. However, international pressure (from the United States, Australia, and other countries) on Switzerland, Austria, Belgium, and Luxembourg to join the banking system have so far been fruitless, making it less likely the initiative will meet its 2006 target. It is estimated that the United States alone loses $70 billion in revenue annually in tax havens. The OECD also is seeking to include Hong Kong and Singapore in the initiative out of fear that tax havens will migrate to Asian markets that do not comply with the banking exchange system.

According to a 2003 OECD report on agricultural reform, efforts to reduce agricultural subsidies had stagnated. The OECD also failed to achieve progress in its efforts to curb steel subsidies as talks with some 38 governments dissolved unceremoniously in 2004. On a more positive note, the organization developed guidelines for private pension fund administrators in the 30 member states.

Pressure was placed on the organization in early 2003 to consider expanding its membership and scope. The OECD created a new working group, headed by the Japanese diplomat Seiichiro Noboru, who was tasked with developing a strategy to dictate the organization's future structure and mission. Noboru recommended that relations be strengthened with the "Big Six" nonmember nations of Brazil, China, India, Indonesia, Russia, and South Africa. The working group was expected to create new criteria for membership, examine the current budgetary system, and assess the geopolitical ramifications of an expanded membership.

OECD Secretary General Johnston announced in January 2005 that he would step down at the conclusion of his second term in May 2006. He recommended that his successor come from an Asian nation, arguing that the "Japanese-Korean-Chinese triangle is going to be the major driving economic force" in the future. In November 2005 the organization elected Ángel Gurría of Mexico, who took office in June 2006. The OECD continues to sponsor conferences and a large number of research papers on topics of interest to its members. Papers particularly focus on the economic circumstances of individual member states. Since 2005, its high-level conferences have dealt with such topics as aging in the developed world, the effect of rising fuel prices and possible shortages, balancing the effects of globalization, and restoring the trust of citizens in their governments.

ORGANIZATION FOR SECURITY AND COOPERATION IN EUROPE (OSCE)

Established: As the Conference on Security and Cooperation in Europe (CSCE) on July 3, 1973, by meeting of heads of states and other representatives of 35 nations in Helsinki, Finland; Helsinki Final Act adopted August 1, 1975; Charter of Paris for a New Europe adopted November 21, 1990; current name adopted at Heads of State or Government Summit on December 5–6, 1994, in Budapest, Hungary.

Purpose: "To consolidate respect for human rights, democracy, and the rule of law, to strengthen peace, and to promote unity in Europe."

Headquarters: Vienna, Austria.

Principal Organs: Heads of State or Government Meeting (Summit), Ministerial Council, Senior Council, Permanent Council, Conflict Prevention Center, Forum for Security Cooperation, Office for Democratic Institutions and Human Rights, High Commissioner on National Minorities, Office of the Representative on Freedom of the Media, Parliamentary Assembly, Secretariats.

Secretary General: Marc Perrin de Brichambaut (France).

Membership (56): Albania, Andorra, Armenia, Austria, Azerbaijan, Belarus, Belgium, Bosnia and Herzegovina, Bulgaria, Canada, Croatia, Cyprus, Czech Republic, Denmark, Estonia, Finland, France, Georgia, Germany, Greece, Hungary, Iceland, Ireland, Italy, Kazakhstan, Kyrgyzstan, Latvia, Liechtenstein, Lithuania, Luxembourg, Macedonia, Malta, Moldova, Monaco, Montenegro, Netherlands, Norway, Poland, Portugal, Romania, Russia, San Marino, Serbia, Slovakia, Slovenia, Spain, Sweden, Switzerland, Tajikistan, Turkey, Turkmenistan, Ukraine, United Kingdom, United States, Uzbekistan, Vatican City State.

Origin and development. The creation of a forum for discussion of East–West security issues was first proposed in the late 1960s. The Soviet Union, in particular, supported the idea as a means of establishing dialogue between the North Atlantic Treaty Organization (NATO) and the Warsaw Treaty Organization (WTO) and formalizing the post–World War II status quo in Europe. Preparatory talks in 1972 led to the establishment of the CSCE on July 3, 1973, in Helsinki, Finland, by the foreign ministers of Canada, the United States, and 33 European countries. After protracted negotiations, their heads of state and government held a summit July 30–August 1, 1975, at the conclusion of which they signed the Helsinki Final Act, which declared the inviolability of national frontiers in Europe and the right of each signatory "to choose and develop" its own "political, social, economic, and cultural systems."

The act called for ongoing discussion of three thematic "baskets"—security, economic cooperation, and human rights—and provided for periodic review of progress toward implementation of its objectives, although no provision was made for a permanent CSCE headquarters or staff. Consequently, the conference operated in relative obscurity and had little impact beyond the establishment of so-called "Helsinki Groups" in the Soviet Union and other Eastern European nations to monitor human rights.

The first two CSCE review conferences, held in Belgrade, Yugoslavia (1977–1978), and Madrid, Spain (1980–1983), produced little of substance, but the third, held in Vienna, Austria (1986–1989), was credited with laying the groundwork for subsequent negotiations that produced the Treaty on Conventional Armed Forces in Europe (CFE), through which NATO and WTO members agreed to substantial arms reductions. The CFE treaty was formally signed at the second CSCE Summit on November 19–21, 1990, in Paris. The NATO and WTO members also signed a joint document declaring they were "no longer adversaries." In addition, the summit adopted the Charter of Paris, which significantly expanded the CSCE mandate and established a permanent institutional framework.

The November 1990 CSCE Summit was viewed by many of the 34 national leaders in attendance as a landmark step toward the establishment of a pan-European security system, a long-standing goal that had seemed unattainable until the dramatic improvement in East–West relations. However, despite the formal opening of the CSCE Secretariat in Prague in February 1991 and a Conflict Prevention Center in Vienna in March, the euphoria over the CSCE's prospects faded somewhat by the time the Council of Foreign Ministers met in June. In light of the perceived potential for instability within the Soviet Union and ongoing ethnic confrontation elsewhere on the continent, Western leaders had recently reaffirmed NATO as the dominant body for addressing their defense and security concerns. In addition, some observers wondered if the CSCE would prove too unwieldy, as its decisions required unanimity and it lacked any enforcement powers.

Albania joined the CSCE in June 1991 and was followed in September by Estonia, Latvia, and Lithuania. Russia subsequently assumed the former USSR seat. The other ten members of the Commonwealth of Independent States (CIS) joined in early 1992, the CSCE having decided to include the five Central Asian republics because of their former inclusion in the Soviet Union. Croatia, Georgia, and Slovenia were admitted in March, followed shortly thereafter by Bosnia and Herzegovina. The Czech Republic and Slovakia were admitted in 1993 following the dissolution of Czechoslovakia, while Macedonia joined the renamed OSCE in October 1995, after Greece lifted its veto. Andorra's accession in 1996 brought the OSCE's active membership up to 54. Yugoslavia (subsequently Serbia and Montenegro) returned to active status in November 2000, Belgrade's membership having been suspended in July 1992. Montenegro joined in June 2006 following its split with Serbia, and the former Serbia and Montenegro membership now officially represents Serbia alone.

The fourth CSCE follow-up session, held from March to July 1992 in Helsinki, focused on reformulating the organization's aims and structures. Its recommendations were adopted as the Helsinki Document by the third CSCE Summit, held in the Finnish capital July 9–10. The text specified that the CSCE's task was now "managing change"; that summit meetings should "set priorities and provide orientation"; that the Council of Foreign Ministers was "the central decision-making and governing body of the CSCE"; and that the Committee of Senior Officials (CSO) was responsible for ongoing "overview, management, and coordination" of CSCE activities. The summit also decided in principle that the CSCE should have its own peacekeeping capability, which should operate in conformity with UN resolutions and in concert with NATO, the CIS, the European Community, and the Western European Union.

Throughout 1994 Russia continued to press for a strengthening of the CSCE, hoping to position it rather than NATO as the preeminent security organization for the "new Europe." Although bluntly dismissive of the notion that it would supplant NATO, Western leaders did agree that the grouping needed, in the words of one participant, "more heft." Thus, the CSCE became the OSCE during the Heads of State or Government Summit on December 5–6 in Budapest, Hungary.

Structure. Prior to the signing of the Charter of Paris in November 1990, the CSCE had little formal structure, operating as what one correspondent described as a "floating set of occasional negotiations." The charter provided for Heads of State or Government Meetings (Summits) and established a Council of Foreign Ministers to meet at least once a year as the "central forum for political consultations within the CSCE process." A Committee of Senior Officials was empowered to carry out the decisions of the council. The charter also authorized the establishment of a Conflict Prevention Center in Vienna, for which a separate secretariat was created, and an Office for Free Elections in Warsaw. The latter body was subsequently renamed the Office for Democratic Institutions and Human Rights (ODIHR).

In 1992 the CSCE also established a Forum for Security Cooperation (for negotiations on further arms control, disarmament, and confidence-building measures) and a High Commissioner on National Minorities. It also adopted a Convention on Conciliation and Arbitration, which led to establishment of a Court of Conciliation and Arbitration to which signatories of the convention could submit disputes. Furthermore, the NATO and former Warsaw Pact members signed an Open Skies Treaty, permitting aerial reconnaissance. (The Treaty entered into effect in January 2002.) In July 1992 the inaugural meeting of the CSCE Parliamentary Assembly took place in Budapest, Hungary.

In addition to adopting the OSCE designation, the December 1994 summit in Budapest enacted several structural changes designed to convey a greater sense of permanency. Thus, the Committee of Senior Officials was renamed the Senior Council and was mandated to meet at least three times a year (once as the Economic Forum). The Ministerial Council (formerly the Council of Foreign Ministers) was mandated to meet in non-summit years. While the Senior Council was given broad responsibility for the implementation of OSCE decisions, day-to-day operational oversight was assigned to

a Permanent Council. OSCE members are generally represented on the Permanent Council by their ambassadors in Vienna, where the main Secretariat offices are located. (The Secretariat also maintains an office in Prague, Czech Republic.)

In 1997 OSCE members approved a plan to create within the Secretariat the post of Coordinator of Economic and Environmental Activities as part of an effort to "strengthen the ability of the Permanent Council and the OSCE institutions to address economic, social and environmental aspects of security." An Office of the Representative on Freedom of the Media was added in 1998. Although the 1994 summit called for upgrading the authority of the OSCE secretary general, the position subsequently remained to a large part subordinate to the organization's chairman-in-office, a post held by a foreign minister of a member country for a one-year term.

Activities. Although most prominently identified since 1990 with its field operations and with election-related activities in the Balkans, the states that succeeded the Soviet Union, and other Eastern European countries, the OSCE has seen its agenda expand to include a wide range of crucial issues facing its membership. Through various seminars, workshops, conferences, conventions, reports, and projects, it continues to address concerns in what it defines as three "dimensions": politico-military, human, and economic. More specifically, the OSCE has been involved in promoting human and minority rights; development of democratic institutions and procedures, including an independent judiciary and a free press; the participation of women in economic and political life; economic and environmental matters; and efforts to halt money laundering, organized crime, the financing of terrorism, and human trafficking, and drugs.

Under the Charter of Paris and, later, the Helsinki Document, the CSCE took on an increasingly prominent role in conflict management, peacekeeping, the promotion of democratic standards, and the monitoring of political, legal, and other developments in Europe and Central Asia. In its first effort at mediation, in July 1991 the

CSCE dispatched a mission to Yugoslavia that had no success in curtailing the violent ethnic conflicts resulting from that country's breakup, despite such subsequent CSCE actions as an arms embargo and the further authorization in August 1992 of the Missions of Long Duration in Kosovo, Sandjak, and Vojvodina. The latter missions, with never more than 20 international personnel, had as their mandate promoting dialogue between the Belgrade government and the ethnic communities in the three regions, but the rump Yugoslavia terminated the missions' memorandum of understanding in 1993. Technically, the regional missions remained in existence until 2001, when Yugoslavia welcomed a new undertaking—the OSCE Mission to Serbia and Montenegro—with a mandate to promote "democratization, tolerance, the rule of law, and conformity with OSCE principles, standards, and commitments." On June 29, 2006, following the separation of Serbia and Montenegro into independent countries, the mission was, in effect, divided into two: the OSCE Mission to Montenegro and the OSCE Mission to Serbia.

In September 1992 the CSCE established the Spillover Monitor Mission to Skopje, which was charged with preventing conflicts elsewhere in the former Yugoslavia from spilling over into newly independent Macedonia. In subsequent years the scope of what is now a joint civilian-military mission was expanded, and in 2001 the number of personnel was increased from under 10 to over 200. As of December 2003 the mission involved some 190 international personnel engaged not only in monitoring but also in police training and development and in implementing the 2001 Ohrid accords, concluded between the minority Albanian population and the Macedonian majority.

A number of other OSCE missions became operational in 1992–1993. Missions to Estonia and Latvia, each comprising under ten representatives, were concerned with institution-building, the inculcation of CSCE principles and, in the case of Estonia, promotion of integration and intercommunal understanding between ethnic Estonians and ethnic Russians; both missions concluded at the end of 2001. In December 1992 a new civilian-military

mission to Georgia was directed to promote negotiations with secessionists in South Ossetia and, secondarily, to assist the UN in its similar efforts with regard to Abkhazia. The Mission in Georgia, which had about 50 personnel in 2003, later took on such additional tasks as building democratic institutions, promoting human rights, and encouraging development of a free press. In addition, a Border Monitoring Operation was directed to watch and report traffic crossing the Georgian border with the troubled Russian republics of Chechnya, Ingushetia, and, from January 2003, Dagestan.

Also in 1992, the "Minsk Process" was fashioned to convene a conference in Minsk, Belarus, that would resolve the Nagorno-Karabakh conflict between Armenia and Azerbaijan. Although the conference has yet to be held, an Initial Operation Planning Group (IOPG), dating from May 1993, was superseded in December 1994 by a High-Level Planning Group (HLPG), which, with nine personnel, continues to meet in Vienna. At the same time, the OSCE agreed to send what would have been its first multinational peacekeeping force to Nagorno-Karabakh if a cease-fire were achieved, but as of June 2006 the deployment had not taken place. In 1995, in a further effort to move toward resolution of the conflict, the OSCE designated a "Personal Representative of the OSCE CiO on the Conflict Dealt with by the OSCE Minsk Conference." The ongoing Minsk Process is co-chaired by France, Russia, and the United States and includes eight other countries in addition to the principals. Separate from the Minsk Process, the OSCE launched a seven-person Office in Yerevan, Armenia, in February 2000 and a six-person Office in Baku, Azerbaijan, in July 2000.

Two other OSCE missions date from 1993. The Mission to Moldova facilitated the formation of a peace plan, which envisaged substantial autonomy for the Transdnestr region; the plan was accepted by the Moldovan government in 1994. The mission currently focuses on providing "advice and expertise" related to such concerns as human and minority rights, democratic transformation, and the return of refugees. Since December 1999 it also has assumed responsibility for "ensuring transparency of the removal and destruction of Russian ammunition and armaments" and coordinating financial and technical assistance for that task. In December 1993 the council also established a Mission to Tajikistan because of the civil war. Deployed in February 1994, the handful of staff members helped secure a peace pact in 1997. In November 2002 the mission was redesignated the Center in Dushanbe (the Tajik capital) with a staff of 16 mandated to "promote the implementation of OSCE principles and commitments" with regard to such concerns as economic and environmental matters; security and stability; and the development of democratic institutions, legal frameworks, and human rights.

In 1995 the OSCE, with the goal of further integrating all five Central Asian members into the organization, established an OSCE Liaison Office in Central Asia in Tashkent, Uzbekistan. In July 1998 the Council decided to open individual offices in Almaty, Kazakhstan; Ashgabat, Turkmenistan; and Bishkek, Kyrgyzstan; in December 2000 the Liaison Office was renamed the Office in Tashkent. As of July 1, 2006, the Office in Tashkent was replaced by the Project Coordinator in Uzbekistan as "a new form of co-operation between the OSCE and the Republic of Uzbekistan, with a view to further develop and consolidate project activities of the OSCE in Uzbekistan." Thus, the OSCE currently has separate offices in each of the Central Asian republics.

In March 1995 the OSCE was authorized by the concluding session of a year-long Conference on Stability in Europe to monitor some 100 "good neighborliness" treaties signed by former Communist countries in Central and Eastern Europe. Thereafter, OSCE envoys were more actively involved in negotiations on various regional conflicts. The OSCE Assistance Group to Chechnya, for instance, helped arrange a series of cease-fires, leading to the conclusion in November 1996 of what appeared to be a definitive accord providing for the withdrawal of Russian forces. The accord failed to hold, however, and in subsequent years the handful of Assistance Group personnel was forced on several occasions to evacuate or otherwise relocate.

Differences with the Russian government led to the closure of the mission in March 2003, although Russia indicated it would continue to work with other OSCE organs, including the ODIHR.

Under the November 1995 Dayton peace agreement for Bosnia and Herzegovina the OSCE was allotted a key role, notably in organizing elections. As of December 2003 the Mission to Bosnia and Herzegovina, numbering some 140 international personnel in more than two dozen field offices, continued to assist with regional stabilization, democracy building, human rights monitoring, and related tasks.

In October 1998 the OSCE, with the approval of the United Nations, undertook its largest mission to date, the Kosovo Verification Mission (KVM). The KVM was authorized for one year and was supposed to verify that all sides of the conflict were in compliance with UN resolutions. It was also directed to monitor elections and help establish a police force and other institutions in Kosovo. Despite the presence of the KVM and several attempts at negotiating an end to the fighting, the violence in Kosovo continued, and the mission had to be withdrawn in March 1999 before NATO initiated its bombing campaign against Yugoslavia. The OSCE returned to Kosovo following the conclusion in June of a comprehensive peace plan that included establishment of a UN Interim Administration Mission for Kosovo (UNMIK), with the OSCE Mission in Kosovo to be responsible for implementing democratic reforms and building governmental institutions. As of June 2005 the mission comprised up to 284 international personnel, plus local staff, with offices in all 30 municipalities.

A number of other field operations continue. The Mission to Croatia, established in 1996, had authorized a maximum of 280 personnel before the termination in 2000 of its Police Monitoring Group; it currently numbers some 51 international personnel engaged in monitoring human rights and treatment of minorities. It also provides advice on democratic institutions and processes. The OSCE Presence in Albania, dating from 1997, includes about 30 personnel based in Tirana and five field offices. The Project Coordinator in Ukraine was introduced in 1999 as the successor to the 1994–1999 OSCE Mission to Ukraine. The Office in Minsk was established in January 2003 as the successor to the Advisory and Monitoring Group in Belarus, which had been established in 1997 but had fallen into disfavor with the government; as of July 2005 there were only five international staff in the office. (Differences between the organization and Belarus arose in part from what were generally described as undemocratic legislative elections in 2001 and the resultant decision of the OSCE Parliamentary Assembly not to seat a Belarusan delegation.)

The Office for Democratic Institutions and Human Rights (ODIHR) has reviewed electoral laws and observed elections in more than two dozen member countries. Frequently, its reports have hightlighted deficiencies in electoral processes, and, on occasion, the OSCE has refused to send monitoring teams. In 1999 it declined to monitor balloting in Kazakhstan because of concerns that the opposition was not being provided adequate opportunity to contest the election. At the end of the year it also declined to monitor upcoming elections in Turkmenistan.

In other field activities, the OSCE has been assisting since 1994 in implementing Russian-Latvian and Russian-Estonian agreements on military pensioners. The OSCE also provided a representative in 1995–1999 to another bilateral agreement between Russia and Latvia regarding the temporary operation and dismantling of the Skrunda Radar Station in Latvia.

The summit of OSCE Heads of State or Government held on December 2–3, 1996, in Lisbon, Portugal, was also attended by representatives of the OSCE's Mediterranean "partners for cooperation" (Algeria, Egypt, Israel, Morocco, and Tunisia), Japan, and South Korea. The summit adopted a lengthy declaration on "a common and comprehensive security model for Europe in the twenty-first century" and resolved in favor of a negotiated revision of the 1990 CFE Treaty, as demanded by Russia in light of its perceived need to deploy additional forces in unstable border regions.

The major event of 1999 was a summit convened on November 18–19 in Istanbul, Turkey. Despite concerns over Russia's renewed offensive in Chechnya, criticism of which led to Russian President Boris Yeltsin's early departure from the meeting, the summit managed to conclude two major agreements. All 54 active member countries signed the new European Security Charter which, in part, reinforced various agreements dealing with security and human rights and called for more rapid response to requests for assistance from member states, particularly with regard to conflict prevention and crisis management. In addition, the 30 states belonging to NATO or the defunct Warsaw Pact signed a revised CFE Treaty, in which all signatories accepted verifiable ceilings for such military equipment as tanks, artillery, and combat aircraft and agreed not to deploy forces outside their borders without approval by the affected country.

A heightened emphasis on opposing terrorism was well in evidence at the December 3–4, 2001, Ministerial Council session in Bucharest, Romania, and at the December 6–7, 2002, session held in Porto, Portugal. In the same vein, the 11th Ministerial Council meeting, held December 1–2, 2003, in Maastricht, Netherlands, voiced support for upgrading passports and other travel documentation to meet minimum security standards, as proposed by the International Civil Aviation Agency (ICAO), and concurred with recommendations by the Forum for Security Cooperation on keeping "manportable air defense systems" from the hands of terrorists. As part of an "OSCE Strategy to Address Threats to Security and Stability in the Twenty-first Century," the session also called for establishment of a Counter-Terrorism Network to coordinate counterterrorism measures, share information, and "strengthen the liaison" among OSCE delegations, government officials, and the new Action against Terrorism Unit (ATU) in the Secretariat.

Taking a broader view, the 2003 Strategy document discussed other sources of instability such as interstate and intrastate conflicts, organized crime, discrimination and intolerance, failure of social integration during a period of mobile migrant populations, environmental degradation, and economic factors (poverty, deepening income disparities, and unemployment). The 2003 ministerial session also endorsed an Action Plan to Combat Trafficking in Human Beings, which called for adding a related special unit in the Secretariat and the appointment by the CiO of a special representative. In addition, the session approved an Action Plan on Improving the Situation of Roma and Sinti (Gypsies) within the OSCE Area.

Extending its range, in 2004 the OSCE held a conference in Berlin on anti-Semitism, agreeing to collect and publish statistics on crimes against Jews in each member country. The conference's final declaration also included measures to fight racism on the Internet and bolster legal systems. Disagreement rather than consensus was widely reported as the outcome of the December 6–8, 2004, OSCE summit in Sofia, Bulgaria. The session ended with no political declaration.

Relations with Russia deteriorated in November 2004 when Moscow claimed the OSCE had taken an "intrusive" interest in the affairs of the former Soviet Union, particularly with regard to the monitoring of elections and borders. It was reported that U.S. and EU diplomats believed the Kremlin was trying to separate Russia from OSCE oversight. Concern over President Vladimir Putin's efforts to consolidate his authority prompted "anxiety" among U.S. officials and contributed to the postponement of a November summit between Russia and the EU. Meanwhile, Russia continued to refuse to uphold its commitment made to the OSCE in 1999 to remove its troops from Georgia and Moldova and prepared to contest the monitoring of the Georgian border. The U.S. ambassador to the OSCE intervened in January 2005 to help resolve the border issue, but nothing was finalized. By March 2005 Russia was criticizing the OSCE

monitoring of legislative elections in Kyrgyzstan. When the disputed elections resulted in the ouster of the Kyrgyz government, the OSCE called for harmony among the country's new leaders and declared that the ousted president, Askar Akayev, should not attempt to return from Russia, whence he had fled. The OSCE's position prevailed, and an election to elect a new president was held in July. Also in 2005, an OSCE conference of justice ministers from Bosnia and Herzegovina, Croatia, and Serbia and Montenegro was held on June 8 in Croatia to discuss cooperation on war crimes trials.

The OSCE, best known for monitoring elections in countries where democracy is relatively new, broke new ground by announcing that it would monitor the 2005 British general election—not with the expectation of finding fraud but as a way to assess the issues around ballot security and postal voting in developed countries. In November 2004 it had conducted a "targeted observation" of legislative and presidential balloting in the United States, and in 2006 it sent teams to both Canada and Italy. During 2005 and the first half of 2006 the OSCE also monitored elections in Albania, Armenia, Azerbaijan, Belarus, Kazakhstan, Kyrgyzstan, Macedonia, Moldova, Tajikistan, and Ukraine as well as the Montenegrin independence referendum of May 2006.

The OSCE was also concerned with the human rights records of Asian and European member countries. It called for an inquiry into the May 2005 shooting of demonstrators in Andijan, Uzbekistan, and warned against erosion of civil liberties in Western countries under pressure to combat terrorism. In June 2006 a Russian diplomat complained that OSCE was applying a double standard in matters of human rights and arms control. (Russia had previously reduced its annual contribution to the organization from approximately $11 million to $8 million, and threatened further reductions.)

ORGANIZATION OF THE BLACK SEA ECONOMIC COOPERATION (BSEC)

Established: As the Black Sea Economic Cooperation by political declaration signed by representatives of 11 states June 24–25, 1992, in Istanbul, Turkey; formalized as the Organization of the Black Sea Economic Cooperation by legally binding charter signed June 5, 1998, in Yalta, Ukraine, effective May 1, 1999, following requisite ratifications.

Purpose: To promote bilateral and multilateral cooperation, particularly in economic matters.

Headquarters: İstanbul, Turkey.

Principal Organs: Council of Foreign Ministers, Committee of Senior Officials, Parliamentary Assembly, Permanent International Secretariat.

Secretary General: Leonidas Chrysanthopoulos (Greece).

Membership (12): Albania, Armenia, Azerbaijan, Bulgaria, Georgia, Greece, Moldova, Romania, Russia, Serbia, Turkey, Ukraine.
  Observer States (13): Austria, Belarus, Croatia, Czech Republic, Egypt, France, Germany, Israel, Italy, Poland, Slovakia, Tunisia, United States.

Origin and development. The formation of an economic grouping of the nations in the Black Sea region was first proposed in the late 1980s by President Turgut Özal of Turkey. After a series of preliminary meetings in 1990 and 1991, the foreign ministers or deputy foreign ministers of Azerbaijan, Armenia, Bulgaria, Georgia, Moldova, Roma-

nia, Russia, Turkey, and Ukraine initialed a declaration outlining the group's objectives in February 1992. The Declaration on Black Sea Economic Cooperation was signed by the heads of state or government of those nine countries plus Greece, which was involved in the earlier negotiations, and Albania during a June 24–25 summit in Istanbul, Turkey.

The Socialist Federal Republic of Yugoslavia also participated in the preliminary talks; however, following the breakup of the SFRY in 1991, its truncated successor, the Federal Republic of Yugoslavia (FRY), was not invited to participate in the BSEC's formal launching because of the other members' concerns over the fighting in Bosnia and Herzegovina. At a Council of Ministers meeting April 18, 2003, Serbia and Montenegro (the reconfigured FRY) and Macedonia were invited to join the BSEC, with Serbia and Montenegro then becoming a member April 16, 2004. After Montenegro and Serbia separated in June 2006, Serbia took the seat of the former union. It was up to Montenegro to apply for membership in its own right, if it chose to do so.

The BSEC Charter, signed at a summit held in Yalta, Ukraine, in June 1998, with effect from May 1, 1999, raised the grouping to an official regional status. Although redesignated as the Organization of the Black Sea Economic Cooperation, the association retained the BSEC acronym.

Structure. The summit of heads of state or government is the highest BSEC policy forum, although the principal decision-making body is the Council of Foreign Ministers, which convenes at least once per year, its chairmanship rotating among members. The council's work is supported by a Committee of Senior Officials and more than a dozen working groups in such areas as agribusiness, combating crime, communications, energy, health care, and transport. There is also an advisory Parliamentary Assembly of the BSEC (PABSEC), which was formed in 1993 and includes a bureau, a standing committee, and three specialized committees: economic, commercial, technological and environmental affairs; legal and political affairs; and cultural, educational, and social affairs. The Permanent International Secretariat, based in Istanbul and headed by a secretary general, began operations in 1994. A Black Sea Trade and Development Bank in Thessaloniki, Greece, opened in 1999 with a primary purpose of funding regional projects. Other organs include a BSEC Coordination Center for economic and statistical information, located in Ankara, Turkey, and an International Center for Black Sea Studies, in Athens, Greece. The BSEC business council serves as a forum for private sector input.

Activities. The framers of the BSEC's founding declaration were careful to stress the new organization's complementarity with the Conference on Security and Cooperation in Europe (CSCE, subsequently the Organization for Security and Cooperation in Europe—OSCE), the European Community (EC, subsequently the European Union—EU), and other regional economic initiatives. Therefore, "institutional flexibility" was endorsed while various working groups assessed the arrangements necessary to promote cooperation in such areas as transportation, communications, energy, tourism, and agriculture without impinging on existing structures.

It was clear, however, that rivalries within the organization (such as those between Greece and Turkey, between Russia and Ukraine, and between Armenia and Azerbaijan) represented significant barriers to effective BSEC activity. Significant intrabloc conflict continued through 1996 as Russia and the Ukraine failed to settle their long-standing dispute over the former Soviet Black Sea fleet and the conflict in Nagorno-Karabakh remained a point

of contention for Armenia and Azerbaijan. Another topic of discussion at the third BSEC summit, held October 25, 1996, in Moscow was the Moldovan demand that all Russian troops be removed from eastern Moldova.

The possibility of creating a free trade zone was the main focus of attention at the February 7, 1997, meeting of foreign ministers held in Istanbul, Turkey, where the then Turkish foreign minister Tansu Çiller expressed her desire for BSEC "integration into Europe." Free trade was also a focus at the June 1998 summit held in Yalta, Ukraine. The Black Sea states expressed their commitment to harmonizing and liberalizing trade regulations in conformance with the World Trade Organization's (WTO) rules and practices. The BSEC also announced its intention to improve its relations with other international organizations, particularly the EU. Some of these ideas were expressed in the BSEC charter, which was signed at the summit. The charter, which incorporated most of the existing structure of the organization, was ratified by all member states effective May 1, 1999.

The 1999 BSEC summit was held November 19 in Istanbul, immediately before an OSCE summit. The BSEC summit declaration noted a desire to move forward from project development to cooperative project implementation. Subsequent initiatives focused on such areas as transport infrastructure and coordination, development of small- and medium-sized enterprises, combating international organized crime, and ecological matters. Meeting April 27, 2001, in Moscow, the Council of Foreign Ministers adopted a "BSEC Economic Agenda for the Future: Toward a More Consolidated, Effective, and Viable BSEC Partnership."

In addition to celebrating the organization's tenth anniversary, the June 25, 2002, summit in Istanbul welcomed adoption of the economic agenda and the concomitant decision to establish a voluntary Project Development Fund. In other business, the participants noted a need for further security and stabilization efforts in the region, condemned all forms of terrorism, and called on all BSEC organs and national authorities to implement a BSEC Agreement on Cooperation in Combating Crime.

The summit also emphasized the importance of establishing with the EU a "tangible relationship" focused on cooperation and coordination.

The eighth meeting of the Council of Foreign Ministers, held April 27, 2001, in Yerevan, Armenia, appointed Secretary General Valeri Chechelashvili to a second three-year term and commented favorably on recent progress toward setting up the Project Development Fund. On July 14–15, three months after receipt of the first contribution—$30,000 from Greece—the fund's steering committee convened for the first time. The subsequent council session, held October 31 in Baku, Azerbaijan, recognized Romania, Russia, Turkey, and the BSEC Business Council for contributions that brought the fund balance to $121,000. In ongoing business, the various BSEC working groups are engaged in tasks that include drafting a protocol on emergency assistance and disaster response, and identifying nontariff trade barriers, preparatory to harmonizing cross-border and customs regulations.

In June 2004 Secretary General Chechelashvili was named Georgia's ambassador to Russia; accordingly, the Council of Foreign Ministers, meeting in October, named Georgia's Tedo Japaridze as his successor. Russia's renewed exertion of its influence, felt also in many other spheres, is demonstrated in increasingly active participation in BSEC. In late 2004 Russia and Greece (a NATO member) agreed to enhance their political dialogue in the context of BSEC and of other organizations of joint interest. At the Council of Foreign Ministers meeting held on April 22–23, 2005, in Komontini, Greece, with the theme "Bringing BSEC closer to the EU," the Russian delegate emphasized the need for all BSEC members (including Russia) to join the WTO. Turkey stayed away from the conference, but Greece pledged to improve relations with its historic adversary.

Since then BSEC has continued to work on several mostly economic and environmental issues. A meeting of the group's environment ministers March 3, 2006, in Bucharest, Romania, produced a declaration calling for increased efforts against pollution and a harmonization of laws to protect marine resources. At the April 26, 2006, meeting of foreign ministers, held in Bucharest, Leonidas Chrysanthopoulos, a Greek career diplomat, was elected secretary general of the organization. One of his first acts in this position was to visit Turkey.

On June 7, 2006, BSEC announced plans to develop "a practical mechanism of cooperation in emergency situations," with Russia hosting the effort.

REGIONAL AND SUBREGIONAL DEVELOPMENT BANKS

Regional development banks are intended to accelerate economic and social development of member states by promoting public and private investment. The banks are not meant, however, to be mere financial institutions in the narrow sense of the term. Required by their charters to take an active interest in improving their members' capacities to make profitable use of local and external capital, they engage in such technical assistance activities as feasibility studies, evaluation and design of projects, and preparation of development programs. The banks also seek to coordinate their activities with the work of other national and international agencies engaged in financing international economic development. Subregional banks have historically concentrated more on integration projects than have regional development banks.

European Bank for Reconstruction and Development (EBRD)

Banque Européenne pour la Reconstruction et la Développement (BERD)

The idea of a multibillion-dollar international lending effort to help revive the economies of East European countries and assist their conversion to free-market activity was endorsed by the heads of the European Community (EC, subsequently the European Union—EU) in December 1989, based on a proposal from French President François Mitterrand. After several months of negotiation in which most other leading Western countries were brought into the project, a treaty to establish the EBRD with initial capitalization of $12.4 billion was signed by 40 nations, the EC, and the European Investment Bank (EIB) on May 29, 1990, in Paris, France. London was chosen as the headquarters for the bank, which proponents described as one of the most important international aid projects since World War II; Mitterrand's special adviser Jacques Attali, who first suggested such an enterprise, was named to direct its operations. The bank officially opened April 15, 1991.

According to the bank's charter, its purpose is to "promote private and entrepreneurial initiative" in East European countries "committed to applying the principles of multiparty democracy, pluralism, and market economics." Although the United Kingdom and the United States originally pressed for lending to be limited entirely to the private sector, a compromise was reached permitting up to 40 percent of the EBRD's resources to be used for public sector projects, such as roads and telecommunications. The bank operated in European Currency Units (ECUs) until January 1, 1999, at which time the ECU was replaced, at par, by the euro.

Although Washington initially opposed its participation, the Soviet Union was permitted to become a member of the EBRD on the condition that it would not borrow more from the bank than it contributed in capital for at least three years, at which point the stipulation would be reviewed. The restriction was imposed because of fears that Soviet needs could draw down most of the EBRD resources and because of U.S. arguments that Moscow had yet to meet the democracy and market orientation criteria. Despite the "net zero" limitation, Moscow was reportedly eager to join the organization because it would be its first capitalist-oriented membership in an international financial institution, and in March 1991 the Supreme Soviet endorsed participation by a vote of 380–1. The net zero condition was eliminated following the breakup of the Soviet Union, with the bank declaring the newly independent former Soviet republics to be eligible for up to 40 percent of total EBRD lending.

The United States is the largest shareholding member, with 12.6 percent of the capital, followed by Germany, France, Japan, Italy, and the United Kingdom, each with 10.7 percent as of December 31, 2001. At the launching of the EBRD the Soviet Union held a 6 percent share, two-thirds of which was subsequently allocated to Russia and the remainder to the other 14 former Soviet republics, all of which (Armenia, Azerbaijan, Belarus, Estonia, Georgia, Kazakhstan, Kyrgyzstan, Latvia, Lithuania, Moldova, Tajikistan, Turkmenistan, Ukraine, and Uzbekistan) joined the bank in 1992. At the end of 2001, Russia held 5 percent of shares, while the EU itself and the European Investment Bank (EIB) each held 3.8 percent. In addition to these 23 members, 39 other states are bank members: Albania, Australia, Austria, Belgium, Bosnia and Herzegovina, Bulgaria, Canada, Croatia, Cyprus, Czech Republic, Denmark, Egypt, Finland, Greece, Hungary, Iceland, Ireland, Israel, Republic of Korea, Liechtenstein, Luxembourg, Macedonia, Malta, Mexico, Mongolia, Morocco, Netherlands, New Zealand, Norway, Poland, Portugal, Romania, Serbia as the successor state after the split of Serbia and Montenegro, Slovakia, Slovenia, Spain, Sweden, Switzerland, and Turkey.

Apart from ordinary resources, at the end of 2001 the EBRD also administered 11 special funds, as follows: the Baltic Investment Special Fund and the Baltic Technical Assistance Special Fund, to aid private sector development of small- and medium-sized enterprises (SMEs) in Estonia, Latvia, and Lithuania; similarly, the Russian Small Business Investment Special Fund and the Russian Small Business Technical Cooperation Special Fund; the Balkan Region Special Fund and the EBRD SME Special Fund, to assist, respectively, in reconstruction and in development of SMEs in Alba-

nia, Bosnia and Herzegovina, Bulgaria, Croatia, Macedonia, Romania, and Yugoslavia; the EBRD Technical Cooperation Fund, to aid in financing technical cooperation projects; the Financial Intermediary Investment Special Fund, to support financial intermediaries in all countries of operation; the Italian Investment Special Fund, to aid modernization, restructuring, expansion, and development of SMEs in selected countries; the Moldova Micro Business Investment Special Fund, to target SME development in Moldova; and the SME Finance Facility Special Fund, to aid SME financing in Bulgaria, Czech Republic, Estonia, Hungary, Latvia, Lithuania, Poland, Romania, Slovakia, and Slovenia. Some 16 countries—including non-EU members Canada, Iceland, Japan, Norway, Switzerland, "Taipei, China," and the United States—have pledged an aggregate of 311 million euros ($278 million) to the 11 funds. At the end of 2001 the eight special investment funds claimed 239 million euros ($213 million) in assets, while the three technical assistance/cooperation funds had a balance of 4.8 million euros ($4.3 million) in remaining available funds.

The first EBRD loans were approved in late 1991. At the first annual meeting of the Board of Governors in April 1992 bank officials reported that 20 loans totaling ECU 621 million (about $770 million) was thus far approved. However, the bank's impact was described as marginal by some East European leaders, and it was widely accepted that lending was restrained by problems in finding reliable borrowers for specific projects. EBRD President Attali reportedly suggested that the bank consider making loans in support of long-term economic restructuring, but the idea was quickly vetoed by the United States as beyond the EBRD mandate and a duplication of World Bank activities.

The second Board of Governors' meeting in April 1993 it was announced that the bank approved 54 investment projects in 1992, involving a total EBRD contribution of ECU 1.2 billion (about $1.5 billion), although actual disbursements for the year totaled only ECU 126 million (about $156 million). The meeting was overshadowed by earlier press disclosures that EBRD disbursement up to the end of 1992 was only half the level of the bank's expenditure on its London offices, staff salaries, travel expenses, and administrative costs. Amid widespread criticism of his style of management, Attali announced his resignation as EBRD president June 25. In August, Jacques de Larosière of France, a former managing director of the International Monetary Fund (IMF), was designated as Attali's successor, and in November the Board of Governors approved internal spending reforms proposed by de Larosière.

At the March 1994 Board of Governors' meeting it was announced that the EBRD earned an approximate $4.5 million profit in 1993, compared to a loss of $7.3 million the previous year. EBRD President de Larosière told the April 1995 annual meeting, however, that he expected the bank's capital base to be exhausted by the end of 1997 under the current rate of lending. Although it was widely conceded that the bank made significant improvement in its "budgetary discipline," Western donors reportedly were awaiting still further reform in bank operations before agreeing to launch replenishment talks.

At the EBRD's annual meeting held in mid-April 1996 in Sofia, Bulgaria, de Larosière called on Eastern European nations to strengthen their banking regulations and supervision. The failure of private banks to follow "basic banking procedures" was contributing to economic difficulties in many Eastern European nations, he said. The shareholders also agreed to double the EBRD's authorized capital from ECU 10 billion to ECU 20 billion (about $25 billion) to accommodate a proposed substantial lending increase. The increase went into effect in April 1997, with 48 of the 60 members depositing their instruments of subscription to the capital increase by the end of the year. President de Larosière said the additional resources would ensure the EBRD would continue to operate "on the cutting edge" of the economic transition in Europe.

With the EBRD emerging in the post-Soviet era as the single largest source of private sector financing in Russia, that country's financial crisis in August 1998 resulted in a loss of 261 million ECUs ($283 million) for the year. At the end of 1998, Russia accounted for about 25 percent of the EBRD's disbursed outstanding loans, but despite the crisis and its "profound impact" throughout the region, only four Russian loans were classified as nonperforming. Overall financing for 1998 totaled 2.37 billion ECUs ($2.57 billion) for 96 projects, down from 108 in 1997. Only a year later, the EBRD had returned to profitability, earning 42.7 billion euros ($43.1 billion) as the region recovered more rapidly than expected.

EBRD President de Larosière announced his retirement in January 1998, and was succeeded in July 1998 by Horst Köhler, president of the German Savings Bank Association. Köhler, who resigned after 20 months in office to become managing director of the IMF, was in turn succeeded in July 2000 by Jean Lemierre, a French financial official.

In recent years the bank has shifted attention from the more developed economies of Central Europe, which absorbed about half of EBRD investments in 1995, toward the east. In its November 2001 Transition Report, the EBRD, looking ahead to the eventual EU accession of ten bank members, urged that all 27 countries of operation continue to receive assistance. Otherwise, a "Brussels lace curtain"—the financial and economic equivalent of the Iron Curtain—might divide the EU from the rest of the continent.

In April 2004 the EBRD announced plans for substantial expansion of lending to its seven poorest members (Armenia, Azerbaijan, Georgia, Kyrgyzstan, Moldova, Tajikistan, and Uzbekistan). In particular, the bank said it would direct support to the private sector in those "early transition" countries.

Lending commitments in 2005 totaled 4.3 billion euros for 151 projects, compared to 4.1 billion euros for 129 projects in 2004, 3.7 billion euros for 119 projects in 2003, and 3.9 billion euros for 102 projects in 2002. Of the 2005 total, 2.5 billion euros went to "early and intermediate transition countries," while 1.1 billion euros went to Russia. The EBRD's 2005 annual report restated the value of its assets on a "fair value" or "mark to market" basis.

European Investment Bank (EIB)

The EIB is the European Union (EU) bank for long-term finance. It was created by the Treaty of Rome, which established the European Economic Community (EEC) on January 1, 1958. The bank, headquartered in Luxembourg, has as its basic function the balanced and steady development of EU member countries, with the greater part of its financing going to projects that favor the development of less-advanced regions and serve the common interests of several members or the whole community. Although industrial modernization remains important, in the context of an expanded community and its transformation into the EU, emphasis has shifted more toward projects involving communications infrastructure, urban development, the environment, energy security, regional development, and crossnational industrial integration. Most recently, "human capital" projects in health and education have taken on greater importance.

The EIB membership is identical to that of the EU (including the ten new members admitted to the EU in May 2004): Austria, Belgium, Cyprus, Czech Republic, Denmark, Estonia, Finland, France, Germany, Greece, Hungary, Ireland, Italy, Latvia, Lithuania, Luxembourg, Malta, Netherlands, Poland, Portugal, Slovakia, Slovenia, Spain, Sweden, and the United Kingdom. Each has subscribed part of the bank's capital of 163.6 billion euros, although most funds required to finance its operations are borrowed by the bank on international and national capital markets. Capital shares range from 0.4 percent of the total for Malta to 16.2 percent each for France, Germany, Italy, and the United Kingdom. Only 5 percent of capital is paid in. Outstanding loans are limited to 2.5 times the subscribed capital.

EIB activities were initially confined to the territory of member states but have gradually been extended to many other countries under terms of association or cooperation agreements. Current participants include 10 countries in the Mediterranean region (Algeria, Egypt, Israel, Jordan, Lebanon, Morocco, Serbia, Syria, Tunisia, and Turkey) and the 77 African, Caribbean, and Pacific (ACP) signatories of the Lomé IV Convention and its successor, the Cotonou Agreement of 2000. Serbia is the successor state after the separation of Serbia and Montenegro, and Montenegro will need to join the EIB as a separate entity should it choose to do so.

The bank is administered by a 25-member Board of Governors (one representative—usually the finance or economy minister—from each EU state) and a 26-member Board of Directors (one from each member state and one representing the European Commission). The president of the bank, appointed by the Board of Governors, chairs the Board of Directors, heads a Management Committee that encompasses eight vice presidents, and oversees the 1,000-plus EIB staff. Other organs include a nine-member Management Committee, a three-member Audit Committee, a General Secretariat, a General Administration Office, and five directorates (Lending Operations in Europe, Lending Operations Outside Europe, Finance, Projects, and Risk Management).

The EIB's lending rose rapidly in the 1990s in response to the "buoyant level of investment" in the member countries, financial requirements arising from the EU single market, and more flexible lending conditions. In addition, the bank began to approve its own loans in Eastern and Central Europe, Latin America, and Asia. Within the community itself, the EIB was directed by the European Council in December 1992 to assist in the development of the economic and monetary union envisioned by the Maastricht Treaty. In addition, in connection with the launching of the EU in November 1993, the EIB was asked to concentrate on trans-European projects (particularly those in the communications, energy, environmental, and transportation sectors) and small- and medium-sized enterprises (SMEs). Some of that activity was directed through a new European Investment Fund (EIF) launched in mid-1994 to provide loan guarantees to projects deemed valuable for "strengthening the internal market." The EIB also participated in the creation of the European Bank for Reconstruction and Development (EBRD, above) to assist in implementing economic reforms and support political democratization throughout Eastern Europe. Other recent initiatives include lending to assist in economic recovery programs in Northern

Ireland and the Gaza Strip/West Bank territory administered by the Palestinian Authority. The EIB also began lending to South Africa, and in 2001 Russia was permitted to begin applying in partial support of environmental projects.

In June 1997 the European Council asked the EIB to increase funding to infrastructure projects and SMEs to promote employment. The EIB, already one of the largest fund sources for such projects, responded by deciding to finance the Amsterdam Special Action Programme (ASAP) for three years. The ASAP channeled funding to the more "labor intensive" areas of health and education and to "innovative, growth oriented" SMEs as well as to infrastructure projects.

In line with a March 2000 decision of the European Council to further increase support for SMEs, the EIB Board of Governors established an "EIB Group" of the EIB and the EIF. The EIB was directed to increase its shares in the latter from the original 40 percent to 60 percent, with the balance held by the European Commission (30 percent) and various European financial institutions (10 percent). The reorganization was intended to improve the group's ability to approve and administer loans, venture capital investments, and SME guarantees. In June 2000 the governors authorized 2 billion euros from EIB profits to be directed toward the EIF's new focus, venture capital, through 2003.

The EIB Group constituted a core component of the EIB's Innovation 2000 Initiative ("i2i"), which earmarked for the following three years 12–15 billion euros for loans involving SMEs and such sectors as health, education, research and development, and information and communications technology. Under its current president, former Belgian finance minister Phillippe Maystadt, the bank has continued to shift its emphasis toward projects involving human resources and advanced technology.

The annual value of signed EIB financing contracts rose incrementally throughout the 1990s, reaching, in the last year of the decade, 31.8 billion euros. The total increased by 13 percent in 2000, to 36.0 billion euros, and to 36.8 billion euros in 2001.

Although the impending expansion of the EU by ten members or more drew considerable attention to the EIB's preaccession assistance, its additional partners around the world also continued to avail themselves of EIB resources. For example, under the 2000 Cotonou pact, total EU aid to the ACP countries for 2002–2006 was set at 15.2 billion euros: 11.3 billion euros as grants from EU members, 2.2 billion euros to be managed by the EIB through an Investment Facility, and some 1.7 billion euros in loans from EIB resources.

In 2001 the EIB agreed to permit lending to Russia for environmental projects in regions that border EIB member states. Subsequently, the bank expanded its authorized capital in 2002–2003 to facilitate the inclusion of ten new members in 2004.

In mid-2004 the EIB became the focus of controversy regarding what critics called an unacceptable lack of transparency in bank dealings. In particular, questions were raised about potential conflicts of interest for directors; consequently, the EIB agreed to publish additional information about its directors and their votes on loan proposals.

In March 2005 the bank announced plans to expand private sector lending in the Southern Mediterranean and to resume lending in Palestinian areas. Lending approvals in 2005 totaled 47.4 billion euros, compared to 43.2 billion euros in 2004, 42.3 billion euros in 2003, and 39.6 billion euros in 2002. Of the 2005 total, 42.3 billion euros went to EU states, and 5.1 billion to other countries. The sectors receiving the most attention were energy, transportation, and the environment. In May 2005 the EIB agreed in principle to make loans to Kosovo, although the region is still formally a part of Serbia.

Nordic Investment Bank (NIB)

A Nordic investment bank was first proposed in June 1957, but its creation was postponed by the founding of the European Free Trade Association. Though further discussed in 1962 and 1964, it was not until June 1, 1976, that an agreement establishing the bank came into force. It is headquartered in Helsinki, Finland.

Prior to 2005, the members of the NIB were the same as those of the Nordic Council: Denmark, Finland, Iceland, Norway, and Sweden. Each country appointed two members to the ten-member Board of Directors, which headed the bank under a rotating chairmanship. In addition, a ten-member Control Committee, on which all five countries are represented, oversaw bank audits and ensured that the bank was managed according to its statutes; the Nordic Council and the Nordic Council of Ministers each appointed five members.

On January 1, 2005, the NIB's membership expanded to include Estonia, Latvia, and Lithuania. In conjunction with the expansion, a new government structure was established for the bank. The most significant change was the creation of an eight-member (one from each member country) Board of Governors as the bank's supreme organ, assuming authority formerly exercised by the Nordic Council of Ministers such as amending bank statutes, deciding on increases in authorized capital stock, and determining membership issues. Decisions by the Board of Governors require unanimity. The Board of Directors, reduced from ten to eight members (again one from each member country) continues to oversee daily bank activity and policies in conjunction with the Control Committee, which now has one member from each member country and two members appointed by the Board of Governors to serve as the committee's chair and deputy chair. The bank is managed by a president (appointed by the Board of Directors for a five-year term) and seven vice presidents.

The main purpose of the bank is to provide financing "on normal banking terms, taking socio-economic considerations into account," for projects that will expand Nordic production and exports and strengthen economic cooperation among member countries. Most NIB loans have gone to projects jointly undertaken by companies or institutions in two or more member countries. Such loans are always issued in conjunction with cofinancing from domestic banks and credit institutions, NIB participation being limited to no more than 50 percent of the total.

In the 1980s the NIB also became an international lender. In 1981 the first loans for joint Nordic projects outside the region were issued after Norway lifted its objection to them. Subsequently, in 1982, the Nordic Council of Ministers established a new Nordic Project Investment Loans (PIL) facility, administered by the NIB, to provide loans for projects "of Nordic interest" in creditworthy developing countries and countries of Central and Eastern Europe. At the direction of the Nordic Council, the bank also helps to administer the Nordic Development Fund, established in 1989 to distribute long-term, interest-free loans to developing countries.

In a major new departure, the Nordic Council of Ministers decided at a March 1990 meeting to establish a Nordic Environmental Finance Company (NEFCO), administered by the NIB, to provide share capital or venture loans for joint projects by Nordic and Central and East European companies in the environmental sector. Formal NEFCO operations were initiated late in the year; in July 1993 NEFCO was reconstituted as a separate organization with its own president, although continued close cooperation with the NIB was expected. Approximately 30 projects were approved by that time, half of them in Poland. NEFCO also continued to participate with the NIB in a supranational task group established to chart the most severe pollution "hot spots" in the Baltic Sea region and facilitate clean-up projects.

In March 1991 the Nordic ministers of finance and economy agreed to provide "know how" and hard currency in support of private sector development in the Baltic states. Through the Baltic Investment Program (BIP), which was launched in 1992, the NIB provided investment and technical assistance, including management and institutional support to the Baltic's national investment banks as well as technical support for the preparation of investment projects and privatization. The BIP concluded its principal activities at the end of 1999, and a two-year phase-out followed.

Jannick Lindbaek, president of the NIB since 1986, left the bank at the end of 1993 to become head of the International Finance Corporation, the World Bank's affiliate for private investment. He was succeeded at the NIB in April by Jón Sigurn, the former governor of the central bank of Iceland. Among the issues facing the new NIB president was the future role of the bank, particularly in light of the accession of two more NIB members (Finland and Sweden) to the European Union (EU) in 1995. Increased cooperation between the NIB and the European Investment Bank (EIB, above) was foreseen as one consequence of the continent's changing political landscape. In addition, the NIB signed an agreement in 1995 with the European Bank for Reconstruction and Development (EBRD, above) to coordinate the activities of the two banks in the Baltic states as well as in Central and Eastern Europe.

In 1996 the Nordic Council of Ministers decided to establish a new environmental loan facility to extend loans to "neighboring areas"—Poland, the Baltic states, and Kalingrad and northwest Russia—for environmental projects. In 2001 the NIB joined with a number of partners—principally the EIB, the EBRD, the World Bank, and the EU Commission—to establish a forum, the Northern Dimension Environmental Partnership (NDEP), for addressing regional environmental problems.

The NIB has also adopted a new definition of what is in the "Nordic interest," expanding its pool of potential clients. A project can now be considered in the Nordic interest "if it has positive effects on employment and business conditions in the Nordic countries, and if it is carried out in one Nordic country by the combined efforts of that country and a non-Nordic one."

As of January 1, 2005, the bank's authorized capital was raised from 4 billion euros to 4.14 billion euros in conjunction with the addition of the three new members. The ordinary lending ceiling rose to 12.67 billion euros. PIL lending authorization, originally set at SDR 350 million, has risen in stages to the current 4.0 billion euros, while the newer environmental loan facility has a ceiling of 300 million euros (raised from 100 million euros in 2003). NIB subscriptions, based on the member countries' GNP, were led at the end of 2004 by Sweden (38 percent), followed by Denmark (22 percent), Norway (20 percent), Finland (19 percent), and Iceland (1 percent). The share amounts in 2005 for the new members were 1.6 percent for Lithuania, 1.1 percent for Latvia, and 0.7 percent for Estonia.

Disbursements in 2005 totaled 2.1 billion euros, compared to 1.3 billion euros in 2004, 1.8 billion euros in 2003, and 1.6 billion euros in 2002. About 1.6 billion euros of the 2005 disbursements remained within the Nordic countries, principally for manufacturing (43 percent), energy (25 percent), and transportation and communication (10 percent). Among non-member countries, loan activity was particularly high in Poland, Brazil, China, and Vietnam.

UNITED NATIONS (UN)

Established: By charter signed June 26, 1945, in San Francisco, United States, effective October 24, 1945.

Purpose: To maintain international peace and security; to develop friendly relations among states based on respect for the principle of equal rights and self-determination of peoples; to achieve international cooperation in solving problems of an economic, social, cultural, or humanitarian character; and to harmonize the actions of states in the attainment of these common ends.

Headquarters: New York, United States.

Principal Organs: General Assembly (all members), Security Council (15 members), Economic and Social Council (54 members), Trusteeship Council (5 members), International Court of Justice (15 judges), Secretariat.

Secretary General: Kofi Annan (Ghana).

Membership (192): See Appendix C.

Official Languages: Arabic, Chinese, English, French, Russian, Spanish. All are also working languages.

Origin and development. The idea of creating a new intergovernmental organization to replace the League of Nations was born early in World War II and first found public expression in an Inter-Allied Declaration signed on June 12, 1941, in London, England, by representatives of five Commonwealth states and eight European governments-in-exile. Formal use of the term United Nations first occurred in the Declaration by United Nations, signed on January 1, 1942, in Washington, D.C., on behalf of 26 states that subscribed to the principles of the Atlantic Charter (August 14, 1941) and pledged their full cooperation for the defeat of the Axis powers. At the Moscow Conference on October 30, 1943, representatives of China, the Union of Soviet Socialist Republics, the United Kingdom, and the United States proclaimed that they "recognized the necessity of establishing at the earliest practicable date a general international organization, based on the principle of the sovereign equality of all peace-loving states, and open to membership by all such states, large and small, for the maintenance of international peace and security." In meetings in Dumbarton Oaks, Washington, D.C., between August 21 and October 7, 1944, the four powers reached agreement on preliminary proposals and determined to prepare more complete suggestions for discussion at a subsequent conference of all the United Nations.

Meeting from April 25 to June 25, 1945, in San Francisco, California, representatives of 50 states participated in drafting the United Nations Charter, which was formally signed June 26. Poland was not represented at the San Francisco Conference but later signed the charter and is counted among the 51 "original" UN members. Following ratification by the five permanent members of the Security Council and most other signatories, the charter entered into force October 24, 1945. The General Assembly, convened in its first regular session January 10, 1946, accepted an invitation to establish the permanent home of the organization in the United States; privileges and immunities of the UN headquarters were defined in a Headquarters Agreement with the U.S. government signed June 26, 1947.

The membership of the UN, which increased from 51 to 60 during the period 1945–1950, remained frozen at that level for the next five years as a result of U.S.-Soviet disagreements over admission. The deadlock was broken in 1955 when the superpowers agreed on a "package" of 16 new members: four Soviet-bloc states, four Western states, and eight "uncommitted" states. Since then, states have normally been admitted with little delay. The exceptions are worth noting. The admission of the two Germanies in 1973 led to proposals for admission of the two Koreas and of the two Vietnams. Neither occurred prior to the formal unification of Vietnam in 1976, while action in regard to the two Koreas was delayed for another 15 years. On November 16, 1976, the United States used its 18th veto in the Security Council to prevent the admission of the Socialist Republic of Vietnam, having earlier in the same session, on June 23, 1976, employed its 15th veto to prevent Angola from joining. Later in the session, however, the United States relented, and Angola gained admission. In July 1977 Washington dropped its objection to Vietnamese membership as well.

With the admission of Brunei, the total membership during the 39th session of the General Assembly in 1984 stood at 159. The figure rose to 160 with the admission of Namibia in April 1990, fell back to 159 after the merger of North and South Yemen in May, advanced again to 160 via the September admission of Liechtenstein, and returned to 159 when East and West Germany merged in October. Seven new members (Estonia, Democratic People's Republic of Korea, Republic of Korea, Latvia, Lithuania, Marshall Islands, and Federated States of Micronesia) were admitted September 17, 1991, at the opening of the 46th General Assembly. Eight of the new states resulting from the collapse of the Soviet Union (Armenia, Azerbaijan, Kazakhstan, Kyrgyzstan, Moldova, Tajikistan, Turkmenistan, and Uzbekistan) were admitted March 2, 1992, along with San Marino. Russia announced the previous December that it was assuming the former USSR seat. Three of the breakaway Yugoslavian republics (Bosnia and Herzegovina, Croatia, and Slovenia) were admitted May 22. Capping an unprecedented period of expansion, Georgia became the 179th member on July 31.

The total dropped back to 178 with the dissolution of Czechoslovakia on January 1, 1993, then moved up to 180 when the Czech Republic and Slovakia joined separately on January 19. On April 8 the General Assembly approved the admission of "The former Yugoslav Republic of Macedonia," the name being carefully fashioned because of the terminological dispute between the new nation and Greece (see Macedonia article). Monaco and newly independent Eritrea were admitted May 28, followed by Andorra on July 28. Palau, which had finally achieved independence following protracted difficulty in concluding its U.S. trusteeship status, became the 185th member December 15, 1994. Kiribati, Nauru, and Tonga were admitted September 14, 1999, and Tuvalu joined September 5, 2000.

A change of government in October 2000 led to the November 1, 2000, admission of the Federal Republic of Yugoslavia (FRY). On September 22, 1992, the General Assembly, acting on the recommendation of the Security Council, decided the FRY could not automatically assume the UN membership of the former Socialist Federal Republic of Yugoslavia. The assembly informed the FRY that it would have to apply on its own for UN membership, and such an application was submitted the following day. However, no action on the request was taken by the assembly because of concern over the Federal Republic's role in the conflict in Bosnia and Herzegovina and, later, its actions regarding the ethnic Albanian population in the Yugoslavian province of Kosovo. As a consequence, the FRY was excluded from participation in the work of the General Assembly and its subsidiary bodies. Throughout this period, however, the UN membership of the Socialist Federal Republic of Yugoslavia technically remained in effect. A certain ambiguity, apparently deliberate, surrounded the issue, permitting the FRY and others to claim that it was still a member, albeit excluded from active participation, while some nations argued that the membership referred only to the antecedent Yugoslavian state. In any event, the flag of the Socialist Federal Republic of Yugoslavia, which was also the flag of the FRY, continued to fly outside UN headquarters with the flags of all other UN members, and the old nameplate remained positioned in front of an empty chair during assembly proceedings. In October 2000 the Security Council, in a resolution recommending admission of the FRY, acknowledged "that the State formerly known as the Socialist Federal Republic of Yugoslavia has ceased to exist." A representative of the FRY took up the empty seat, and a new FRY flag replaced that of the former Yugoslavia.

On September 10, 2002, the UN admitted Switzerland, which had long maintained a permanent observer mission at UN headquarters and had actively participated as a full member of the various UN specialized and related agencies. The Swiss government, having concluded that UN membership in the post–Cold War era would not jeopardize its long-standing international neutrality, sought admission after winning majority support from Swiss voters at a March 2002 referendum. Timor-Leste became the 191st member on September 27.

In 2003 the FRY became the "state union" of Serbia and Montenegro, which dissolved in June 2006, following a successful independence referendum in Montenegro. Accordingly, on June 28 the world's newest independent state, Montenegro, was admitted as the UN's 192nd member. Serbia, as the successor state to the state union, retained the UN seat held to that point by the FRY.

The Holy See (Vatican City State) has formal observer status in the General Assembly and maintains a permanent observer mission at UN headquarters. In July 2004 the UN granted the Holy See the full range of membership privileges, with the exception of voting.

Structure. The UN system can be viewed as comprising (1) the principal organs, (2) subsidiary organs established to deal with particular aspects of the organization's responsibilities, (3) a number of specialized and related agencies, and (4) a series of ad hoc global conferences to examine particularly pressing issues.

The institutional structure of the principal organs resulted from complex negotiations that attempted to balance both the conflicting claims of national sovereignty and international responsibility, and the rights of large and small states. The principle of sovereign equality of all member states is exemplified in the General Assembly; that of the special responsibility of the major powers, in the composition and procedure of the Security Council. The other principal organs included in the charter are the Economic and Social Council (ECOSOC), the Trusteeship Council (whose activity was suspended in 1994), the International Court of Justice (ICJ), and the Secretariat.

UN-related intergovernmental bodies constitute a network of Specialized Agencies established by intergovernmental agreement as legal and autonomous international entities with their own memberships and organs and which, for the purpose of "coordination," are brought "into relationship" with the UN. While sharing many of their characteristics, the International Atomic Energy Agency (IAEA) remains legally distinct from the Specialized Agencies; the World Trade Organization, which emerged from the UN-sponsored General Agreement on Tariff and Trade (GATT), has no formal association with the UN.

The proliferation of subsidiary organs can be attributed to many complex factors, including new demands and needs as more states attained independence; the effects of the Cold War; a subsequent diminution of East-West bipolarity; a greater concern with promoting economic and social development through technical assistance programs (almost entirely financed by voluntary contributions); and a resistance to any radical change in international trade patterns. For many years, the largest and most politically significant of the subordinate organs were the United Nations Conference on Trade and Development (UNCTAD) and the United Nations Industrial Development Organization (UNIDO), which were initial venues for debates, for conducting studies and presenting reports, for convening conferences and specialized meetings, and for mobilizing the opinions of nongovernmental organizations. They also provided a way for less developed states to formulate positions vis-à-vis the industrialized states. During the 1970s both became intimately involved in activities related to program implementation, and on January 1, 1986, UNIDO became the UN's 16th Specialized Agency.

One of the most important developments in the UN system has been the use of ad hoc conferences to deal with major international problems. (For a listing of such conferences and a brief description of their activities, see *Political Handbook of the World 2007*.)

Security Council

Permanent Membership (5): China, France, Russia, United Kingdom, United States. (The other permanent members in late December 1991 accepted Russia's assumption of the seat previously filled by the Union of Soviet Socialist Republics.)

Nonpermanent Membership (10): Terms ending December 31, 2006: Argentina, Denmark, Greece, Japan, Tanzania; terms ending December 31, 2007: Republic of the Congo, Ghana, Qatar, Peru, and Slovakia.

Security Council: Peacekeeping Forces and Missions

In addition to the forces and missions listed below, the United Nations Command in Korea (established on June 25, 1950) remains technically in existence. The only UN member now contributing to the command is the United States, which proposed in June 1975 that it be dissolved. As of mid-2006 no formal action had been taken on the proposal.

United Nations Interim Administration Mission in Kosovo
(UNMIK)

Established: By Security Council resolution of June 10, 1999, which also authorized formation of a Multinational Force in Kosovo (Kosovo Force—KFOR).

Purpose: To promote significant autonomy and self-government in Kosovo; to provide civilian administrative functions, including holding elections; to maintain law and order while promoting human rights and ensuring the safe and voluntary return of Kosovar refugees and displaced persons; to ultimately oversee a transfer of authority to civilian institutions established under a political settlement. KFOR was authorized to establish and maintain a secure environment in Kosovo until such time as the UNMIK Civilian Police could assume this task on a region-by-region basis.

Headquarters: Priština, Kosovo, Serbia.

Head: Joachim Rücker (Germany).

Operational Framework: Four "pillars"—peace and justice; civil administration; democratization and institution-building, under the direction of the Organization for Security and Cooperation in Europe; reconstruction and economic development, under the European Union. KFOR is now under NATO/EU command.

Security Council: International Criminal Tribunals

In the absence of a permanent international court with jurisdiction to prosecute and try cases involving accusations of war crimes, genocide, and crimes against humanity, the Security Council established the International Criminal Tribunal for the former Yugoslavia (ICTY) in 1993 and the International Criminal Tribunal for Rwanda (ICTR) in 1994. Meeting in Rome, Italy, in 1998, a UN conference approved formation of a permanent International Criminal Court (ICC), which by April 2002 had obtained sufficient ratifications for its establishment in July.

As of August 2006 the ICTY had brought public indictments against 161 individuals, including those who had been acquitted and those whose cases had been withdrawn. Twenty-two individuals were serving sentences and 18 had completed their sentences. Fifty-three individuals were detained, nine individuals were on provisional release, and six indicted individuals remained at large.

Biljana Plavšić, former president of the Serb Republic of Bosnia and Herzegovina, was one of the most prominent people to surrender. On November 2, 2002, she pleaded guilty to one count of a crime against humanity for political, racial, and religious persecution, and on February 27, 2003, she was sentenced to 11 years in prison. By far the most prominent figure turned over to the court by national forces was former Yugoslav president Slobodan Milošević, who died on March 11, 2006, during his trial.

As of July 2006 the ICTR had brought public indictments against some 75 individuals and had arrested more than 50 people. Twenty-five cases had reached their conclusion (with 22 convictions), and 25 trials were in progress. The highest-ranking defendant, former Rwandan prime minister Jean Kambanda, pleaded guilty to genocide in 1998 and was sentenced to life in prison.

In August 2000 the Security Council unanimously indicated its support for forming a third war crimes tribunal, for Sierra Leone, that began its proceedings in 2003, although not as a subsidiary body of the Security Council. A similar joint criminal tribunal in Cambodia to prosecute and try former *Khmer Rouges* is expected to begin its proceedings in 2007.

International Criminal Tribunal for the former Yugoslavia
(ICTY)

Formal Name: International Tribunal for the Prosecution of Persons Responsible for Serious Violations of International Humanitarian Law Committed in the Territory of the former Yugoslavia since 1991.

Established: By Security Council resolution of May 25, 1993.

Purpose: To prosecute and try persons who allegedly committed serious violations of international humanitarian law on the territory of the former Yugoslavia since 1991, the subject offenses being genocide, crimes against humanity, and violations of the 1949 Geneva Conventions and the laws or customs of war.

Headquarters: The Hague, Netherlands.

Chief Prosecutor: Carla Del Ponte (Switzerland).

Permanent Judges: Fausto Pocar (Italy, President), Kevin Parker (Australia, Vice President), Carmel A. Agius (Malta), Jean-Claude Antonetti (France), Iain Bonomy (United Kingdom), Liu Daqun (China), Mehmet Güney (Turkey), Theodor Meron (United States), O-gon Kwon (Republic of Korea), Bakone Justice Moloto (South Africa), Alphonsus Martinus Maria Orie (Netherlands), Patrick Lipton Robinson (Jamaica), Mohamed Shahabuddeen (Guyana), Wolfgang Schomburg (Germany), Christine Van Den Wyngaert (Belgium), and Andrésia Vaz (Senegal). There are also 11 *ad litem* judges.

Registrar: Hans Holthuis (Netherlands).

Economic and Social Council: Regional Commissions

The primary aim of the five Regional Commissions, which report annually to ECOSOC, is to assist in raising the level of economic activity in their respective regions and to maintain and strengthen the economic relations of the states in each region, both among themselves and with others. The commissions adopt their own procedural rules, including how they select officers. Each commission is headed by an executive secretary, who holds the rank of under secretary of the UN, while their Secretariats are integral parts of the overall United Nations Secretariat.

The commissions are empowered to make recommendations directly to member governments and to Specialized Agencies of the United Nations, but no action can be taken in respect to any state without the agreement of that state. (For discussion of regional commissions outside of Europe, see *Political Handbook of the World 2007*.)

Economic Commission for Europe
(ECE)

Established: March 28, 1947.

Purpose: To promote economic cooperation, integration, and sustainable development among member countries.

Headquarters: Geneva, Switzerland.

Principal Subsidiary Organs: Committee on Sustainable Energy; Committee on Environmental Policy; Committee on Human Settlements; Committee for Trade, Industry and Enterprise Development; Conference of European Statisticians; Inland Transport Committee; Timber Committee; Secretariat.

Executive Secretary: Marek Belka (Poland).

Membership (56): Albania, Andorra, Armenia, Austria, Azerbaijan, Belarus, Belgium, Bosnia and Herzegovina, Bulgaria, Canada, Croatia, Cyprus, Czech Republic, Denmark, Estonia, Finland, France, Georgia, Germany, Greece, Hungary, Iceland, Ireland, Israel, Italy, Kazakhstan, Kyrgyzstan, Latvia, Liechtenstein, Lithuania, Luxembourg, Macedonia, Malta, Moldova, Monaco, Montenegro, Netherlands, Norway, Poland, Portugal, Romania, Russia, San Marino, Serbia, Slovakia, Slovenia, Spain, Sweden, Switzerland, Tajikistan, Turkey, Turkmenistan, Ukraine, United Kingdom, United States, Uzbekistan. (Israel's long-standing application for membership, based on its "fundamental economic relations" with the European Community and the United States, was approved by ECOSOC in July 1991. The Holy See also participates in the work of the commission in a consultative capacity.)

Recent activities. In 1987 the commission created an ad hoc committee to review ECE structures and functions as part of the UN streamlining campaign. At a special session (the first of its kind), held November 9–10, in Geneva, the commission adopted the committee's recommendations for substantial cuts in the number of ECE subsidiary bodies, reduction in documentation levels, and consolidation or elimination of lower priority programs. The major fields of ECE activity were listed as agriculture and timber, economic projections, energy, environment, human settlements, industry, inland transport, science and technology, statistics, and trade.

In 1988 the ECE resisted further cutbacks as it focused on fast-moving political and economic developments in Europe, including the European Community's drive toward a single internal market and reforms in the centrally planned economies of the Eastern bloc. In fact, describing the commission as uniquely organized to serve as a framework for "all-European integration," ECE officials urged that its role be augmented to take advantage of the continuing reduction in East-West political tensions and economic barriers.

Subsequently, the ECE identified assistance to the Central and Eastern European nations undergoing economic transformation as the commission's top priority, specific areas of concentration including trade facilitation, transport, the environment, statistics, and economic analysis. The commission was also formally delegated by the Conference on Security and Cooperation in Europe (subsequently the Organization for Security and Cooperation in Europe—OSCE) to coordinate economic cooperation agreements emanating from that body. The ECE called on Western donors to increase their aid to the Eastern European countries and the new republics from the former Soviet Union, warning that the "shattered economies" in many might require decades to complete a successful shift to free-market activity.

In 1993 ECOSOC ruled that all the former Soviet republics were eligible to join the ECE, the Asian countries in that group also being entitled to dual membership in the Economic and Social Commission for Asia and the Pacific (ESCAP). Subsequently, Armenia, Azerbaijan, Georgia, Kazakhstan, Kyrgyzstan, Tajikistan, Turkmenistan, and Uzbekistan joined the ECE, bringing total membership, which had been 34 three years before, to 55 by mid-1995. The ECE asked for additional UN resources to deal with the increase, noting that nearly half its members belonged to the "transitional" category and that many of them had experienced a deep economic depression following their reorientation.

ECE attention in 1996 continued to focus on the economies of the Central and Eastern European countries, most of which had become "very open" and heavily influenced by trade with Western European countries. Among other things, the commission offered to help those countries seeking membership in the European Union in developing and implementing a "preaccession strategy." The commission also took part in the inception of the Southeast European Cooperative Initiative (SECI) along with other UN agencies and international organizations. The SECI is designed to help southeastern European countries, from Croatia and Moldova to Turkey, cooperate on economic and environmental matters and become part of "European structures." The initiative's first meeting was held in early December 1996. At the same time, in consonance with overall UN reform efforts, the ECE cut back on the size of its staff, redeployed senior officials "to the field" so they could better understand the needs of the ECE members, and discontinued a number of "obsolete" annual meetings.

The push for reform continued in 1997. At the commission's 50th anniversary session held in late April, the ECE decided to eliminate 60 percent of all programs and 7 of its 14 subsidiary bodies in order to free resources to concentrate on the "core areas" of economic analysis, the environment, human settlements, development of industry and enterprises, population analysis, sustainable energy, agricultural standards, statistics, timber, trade, and transportation. In a continuation of the reform process, the ECE subsequently decided to bolster its cooperation with other UN entities, such as the UN Conference on Trade and Development (UNCTAD).

In March 1998, in conjunction with ESCAP, the ECE inaugurated a Special Program for the Economies of Central Asia (SPECA), specifically the former Soviet republics of Kazakhstan, Kyrgyzstan, Tajikistan, Turkmenistan, and Uzbekistan. The SPECA has focused its attention on such concerns as attracting foreign investment to the region; fostering regional development in transport, including the movement of natural gas and oil; and sustainable use of energy and water.

In May 2000 UN Secretary General Kofi Annan appointed Danuta Hübner of Poland to succeed France's Yves Berthelot as ECE executive secretary, with effect from June. Berthelot was succeeded in 2002 by Brigita Schmögnerová, a former foreign minister and deputy prime minister from Slovakia.

In 2003 the ECE launched a new energy security forum to help prevent insecurity and instability in global energy markets. Other recent activity included expansion of the ECE's convention on environmental matters, considered one of the world's most "far-reaching" treaties in regard to public access to environmental information; establishment of an external commission to evaluate the ECE's future "role, mandate, and functions in light of the changed European institutional landscape"; and agreement to cooperate more closely with the OSCE. In 2005 the ECE, noting that European output and productivity continued to fall behind the levels achieved by the United States, called for intensified regional cooperation to improve the business climate in Europe. At its February 2006 meeting the member states proposed a series of initiatives to increase economic cooperation and integration.

WESTERN EUROPEAN UNION (WEU)

Established: By protocols signed in Paris, France, October 23, 1954, effective May 6, 1955.

Purpose: Collective self-defense and political collaboration in support of European unity.

Headquarters: Brussels, Belgium.

Principal Organs: Council, Inter-Parliamentary European Security and Defense Assembly, Secretariat.

Secretary General: Javier Solana Madariaga (Spain).

Membership (10): Belgium, France, Germany, Greece, Italy, Luxembourg, Netherlands, Portugal, Spain, United Kingdom.
   Associate Members (6): Czech Republic, Hungary, Iceland, Norway, Poland, Turkey.
   Associate Partners (8): Bulgaria, Croatia, Estonia, Latvia, Lithuania, Romania, Slovakia, Slovenia.
   Observers (5): Austria, Denmark, Finland, Ireland, Sweden.

Official Languages: English, French.

Origin and development. The WEU is the direct successor of the five-power Brussels Treaty Organization, which was established by the United Kingdom, France, and the Benelux states through the Treaty of Economic, Social, and Cultural Collaboration and Collective Self-Defense, signed March 17, 1948, in Brussels, Belgium. The Brussels Pact had included provisions for automatic mutual defense assistance and envisioned coordination of military activity. However, de facto responsibilities in those areas were transferred to the 12-power North Atlantic Treaty Organization (NATO) following its creation in 1949. Shortly thereafter, the call for West German rearmament to permit participation in NATO by the Federal Republic of Germany (FRG) led to a revival of interest in a European army. In 1952 the six countries that had recently established the European Coal and Steel Community (ECSC; see the European Union article)—France, West Germany, Italy, and the Benelux countries—signed a treaty to institute a European Defense Community (EDC) that would have placed their military forces under a single authority. Following rejection of the EDC by the French Parliament in 1954, the United Kingdom invited the ECSC countries to revive the 1948 treaty, which was modified and expanded to provide a framework for the rearming of West Germany and its admission to NATO. Under a series of protocols effective May 6, 1955, the Brussels organization was enlarged to include Italy and West Germany and was renamed the WEU.

The protocols redefined the purposes of the organization by including a reference to the unity and progressive integration of Europe; remodeled its institutional structure; established norms for member states' contributions to NATO military forces; provided for limitation of the strength and armaments of forces maintained under national command; took note of the United Kingdom's pledge to maintain forces on the mainland of Europe; acknowledged West Germany's intention to refrain from manufacturing atomic, chemical, biological, and certain other types of weapons; and established an Agency for the Control of Armaments in order to police restrictions on the armaments of all WEU members. The binding defense alliance between WEU members remained in force, but the exercise of military responsibilities remained subordinate to NATO.

The concern over duplication of efforts caused the WEU to transfer many of its social and cultural activities in 1960 to the Council of Europe. However, the union remained active in economic affairs, serving as a link between the European Community (EC) and the United Kingdom after French President Charles de Gaulle's first veto of British entry into the EC in 1963. Activity in that area effectively ceased in the wake of UK admission to the EC in 1973; likewise WEU activity in the political field diminished in proportion to the growth of political consultation within the EC.

Only in 1984, after a lengthy period of relative inactivity, did members call for a "reactivation" and restructuring of the WEU to foster the "harmonization" of views on defense, security, and other military issues precluded from EC debate. At its Council of Ministers meeting held October 26–27 in Rome, Italy, the WEU issued a "Statement of Rome" detailing the tasks of the revived union as assessment of the Soviet threat, increased European arms collaboration, and the formulating of European views on arms control and East-West dialog. The perceived advantages of a revived WEU were the assurance of military aid in case of attack, security cooperation between France and West Germany, and an enhanced capacity to respond to public opinion on European defense issues.

In early 1987 the United Kingdom, which had long relied primarily on security links with the United States, called for strengthening the WEU. In August Britain and France persuaded Belgium, Italy, and the Netherlands to join them in sending naval forces to the Persian Gulf to assist in the U.S.-led escort of oil tankers. Adding to the WEU's heightened visibility, a Council of Ministers meeting held October 1987 at The Hague, Netherlands, approved a strongly worded "Platform on European Security Interests" that stressed the need for the retention of some nuclear forces and an increase in conventional forces in Western Europe to maintain deterrence vis-à-vis the forces of the Soviet-led

Warsaw Treaty Organization (WTO). During 1988 European concern over a possible reduction in the U.S. military commitment on the continent contributed to increased interest in the expansion of WEU membership, with Portugal and Spain signing accession protocols in November.

The post–1989 collapse of European communism and the disintegration of the Soviet Union supplied additional impetus to the WEU regeneration process. Following a November 1991 NATO meeting in Rome that endorsed "specific arrangements for the defense of Europe," the EC's Maastricht summit in December 1991 adopted a Declaration on the Role of the WEU and its Relations with the European Union (EU) and with the Atlantic Alliance, envisaging that the WEU would be responsible for EU defense coordination. Consequently, in the Petersberg (Germany) Declaration of June 1992 the WEU Council of Ministers endorsed the eventual establishment of a permanent WEU military force that could be deployed for peacekeeping, humanitarian and rescue missions, and "crisis management"—collectively, the "Petersberg tasks."

Following Maastricht, the WEU transferred its headquarters from London to Brussels (the seat of the EU) and invited the EC and NATO states that were not already WEU members to become participants. As a result, Greece signed a WEU membership agreement on November 20, 1992; however, that nation's accession was not formally completed until March 5, 1995, following ratification by the individual WEU states. Also in November 1992, EC members Denmark and Ireland became observers, while Iceland, Norway, and Turkey (non-EC NATO members) became WEU associates. New EU members Austria and Sweden were granted observer status on January 1, 1995, followed by Finland on February 3.

In May 1994 the new status of "associate partner" was established for Eastern European states, which were authorized to participate in WEU deliberations as well as future peacekeeping and humanitarian missions. However, the partners were given no vote in any union decisions, nor were they covered by the security guarantee of the 1948

Brussels Treaty. In December 2004 Croatia became the eighth associate partner.

The November 1994 WEU ministerial session adopted "preliminary conclusions" on the formulation of a common European defense policy. Additional progress was reported at the May 1995 meeting of the council, which established a "politico-military support group" to advise on future crises and help formulate possible WEU interventions. The council also approved the creation of a WEU Satellite Center in Torrejón, Spain, to develop satellite-imaging capabilities that would be required in upcoming military operations.

With France spearheading the push for better delineation of an independent European military capability, NATO foreign ministers in June 1996 endorsed a compromise proposal to create a European Security and Defense Identity (ESDI) within the alliance, which, in certain circumstances, could operate under WEU command. The plan centered on the establishment of "combined joint task forces" (CJTFs) for specific peacekeeping and/or humanitarian missions in Europe. It was anticipated that non-NATO countries, such as those involved in NATO's Partnership for Peace (PfP) program, would be invited to participate in the new task forces; the deployment of any NATO forces for such missions would still require unanimous support of the alliance's members.

Although the United States, the United Kingdom, and non-EU member Turkey, in particular, continued to favor leaving military decisions to NATO, the ESDI and subsequent EU decisions were clearly leading toward absorption of the WEU by the EU. In May 1999 the ten full WEU members agreed to a merger in principle with the EU, and the Cologne, Germany, EU summit in June ratified the decision and set the end of 2000 as a target for assumption of what had been the WEU's military role. On November 13, 2000, at a meeting in Marseilles, France, the 28 WEU countries formally decided that the organization's operational capacity for defense and for carrying out the "Petersberg tasks" would be transferred to the EU, which would also take over the WEU Institute for Security Studies at Paris and the Torrejón satellite

facility. At least for the time being, the WEU would maintain a formal existence and some WEU bodies would continue to meet, including the assembly, which had restyled itself as the Inter-Parliamentary European Security and Defense Assembly in June.

Structure. The WEU's decisionmaking body, the Council, traditionally operated through two distinct groupings—the Council of Ministers and the Permanent Council. The Council of Ministers, composed of foreign and defense ministers of WEU countries, normally met twice a year. The Permanent Council was mandated "to discuss in greater detail the views expressed by the Ministers and to follow up their decisions." Comprising ambassadors or other senior officials of member countries, the Permanent Council usually met weekly, its composition alternating between 28 members (all full and associate members, associate partners, and observers) and 21 (all full and associate members and observers).

Although the ministerial-level council continues to exist, it has not met since November 2000; the Permanent Council met most recently in May 2002. Of the WEU's various committees and standing groups, only the Budget and Organization Committee remains active. The EU has assumed the functions of other WEU organs, including the Military Committee, which had been established in 1998 as the WEU's senior military authority.

The WEU's other main organ is the Inter-Parliamentary European Security and Defense Assembly, which is still frequently referenced as the WEU Assembly, as it was originally called. It encompasses the 115 representatives (18 each from France, Germany, Italy, and United Kingdom; 12 from Spain; 7 each from Belgium, Greece, the Netherlands, and Portugal; and 3 from Luxembourg) of the WEU member countries to the Parliamentary Assembly of the Council of Europe. There are also 115 substitutes appointed to the WEU Assembly from members' national parliaments in general proportion to the strength of government and opposition parties. Representatives and substitutes may form political groups within the assembly.

The assembly's regularly scheduled annual meeting, held in Paris, is divided into two sessions, the first in June and the second in December. The assembly, which draws up its own agenda, has functioned as an independent consultative body, making recommendations to the WEU Council and to other intergovernmental organizations, sending resolutions to governments and national parliaments, and rendering its opinion on the annual reports of the council. Its subordinate organs have included a Committee on Defense Questions and Armaments, whose reports have been considered among the most authoritative and incisive published analyses of Western European security needs and developments.

The Western European Armaments Group (WEAG), a subsidiary body of the WEU, originated in NATO's Independent European Program Group (IEPG), which had been formed in 1976 as a forum for improving cooperation in armaments. In December 1992 the IEPG members decided to transfer its functions to the WEU, and in 1993 the group became the WEAG, which had as its principal mission harmonizing and integrating development, production, and procurement of armaments among its members. Meeting at Brussels in November 2004, the defense ministers of the 19 WEAG members (all full WEU states, all associate members except Iceland, and all observers except Ireland) directed their national armaments directors (NADs) to bring the WEAG to a close, given that its functions were to be assumed by the EU's new European Defense Agency (EDA). Thus the WEAG came to an end on May 23, 2005. The related Western European Armaments Organization (WEAO), established in November 1996 as a transitional step toward formation of a long-discussed European Armaments Agency, continues to function in the form of the WEAO Research Cell (WRC), which offers services in defense-related research and technology to members. Provision for establishment of an armaments agency was made in the proposed European Constitution, but in the meantime the WEU continues to provide administrative support for the WRC.

Activities. Throughout most of its history the WEU served as a forum for European security issues, conducting research, issuing reports, and providing advice. Although the WEU helped coordinate the military participation of member states during the 1990–1991 Persian Gulf crisis, the organization did not assume an overt operational role until after the 1992 Maastricht Treaty identified the WEU as the proposed EU's security arm. Collaterally, the WEU Council of Ministers outlined the "Petersberg tasks" of peacekeeping, humanitarian aid and rescue missions, and military crisis management.

Meanwhile, France and Germany had in October 1990 initiated a joint "European Corps" (Eurocorps), consisting initially of a combined brigade of some 4,000 French and German troops. The two governments agreed in May 1992 that the Strasbourg-based force would eventually be enlarged to at least 35,000, while a Franco-German memorandum of November 1992 described the Eurocorps as "forces answerable to the WEU." Seen by its proponents as the embryo of a "European" army in the context of the Maastricht decisions, the Eurocorps concept aroused disquiet, notably on the part of the UK and U.S. governments, that it could undermine NATO cohesiveness in Europe. However, these problems appeared to be resolved by a January 1993 agreement under which the Eurocorps would come under NATO command in an emergency. In October 1993 Belgium agreed to join the Eurocorps, which was formally inaugurated on November 5 under the command of a German general. Spain announced its intended participation the same month and Luxembourg followed suit in May 1994. The Eurocorps was officially declared operational on November 30, 1995, by which time France, Italy, Portugal, and Spain had organized two additional forces, one of ground troops (EUROFOR) and the other with maritime capabilities (EUROMARFOR). These and other multinational contingents were all considered "forces answerable to WEU" (FAWEU).

In July 1992 warships and aircraft of WEU member states, in coordination with NATO, began an operation in the Adriatic code-named "Sharp Guard" to monitor compliance with UN sanctions against rump Yugoslavia (i.e., Serbia and Montenegro). In June 1993 a joint session of the WEU and NATO councils agreed upon a single command and control system for the operation, which continued until June 1996. Beginning in May 1997 the WEU offered Albania assistance through a Multinational Advisory Police Element (MAPE), with a mandate to help in reorganizing and training the Albanian police. In April 1999 the WEU agreed to aid Croatia through a WEU De-mining Assistance Mission (WEUDAM), in support of the Croatia Mine Action Center. Its most significant operational assignment began in April 2000, when the Eurocorps assumed command of the peacekeeping Multinational Force in Kosovo (Kosovo Force, or KFOR).

In October 1999 Javier Solana Madariaga, the departing NATO secretary general, had become secretary general of the Council of the European Union and its first high representative for foreign and security policy. A month later he was also named WEU secretary general in anticipation of the EU's assumption of the WEU's mandate. Thus the November 2000 decision to transfer WEU operational capability to the EU was anticlimactic, leaving as the principal unresolved question the ultimate status of the WEU's assembly and other remaining WEU organs.

An additional issue was the status of the WEU's associate members. In May 1999 the three new NATO members (the Czech Republic, Hungary, and Poland) officially rose from WEU associate partners to associate members. At that time, however, none of the six associate members belonged to the EU, thereby complicating the EU/WEU/NATO relationship. (Turkey was particularly vocal in its objections to the use of its NATO contingents by the EU unless Ankara was given a voice in ESDI decisions.) In June 2001 Secretary General Solana announced that, in view of the WEU's diminished role, no further changes would be made in the status of non-full members.

Since the most recent meeting of the WEU's Permanent Council in May 2002, the WEU has performed "residual functions," chiefly administrative matters, although the Inter-Parliamentary European Security and Defense Assembly continues to meet annually. The 51st meeting was held June 2005 in Paris, at which time it adopted a recommendation on defending against terrorism that called for "a more proactive, not merely reactive, defense strategy, without this signifying a justification for preventive military action." At the 52nd meeting in December 2005, and at the 53rd meeting in June 2006, there were calls for greater public awareness and understanding of the EU's European Security and Defense Policy (ESDP).

PART FOUR

APPENDIXES

APPENDIX A: CHRONOLOGY OF MAJOR EUROPEAN EVENTS, 2006

ALBANIA

June 12. EU and Albania Sign Stabilization and Association Agreement (SAA). The agreement is the first step toward integrating Albania into the EU.

AUSTRIA

January 1. EU Presidency Assumption. Austria assumes the six-month rotating EU presidency.

October 1. Parliamentary Elections. The opposition Social Democratic Party wins a plurality after gaining 35.3 percent of the vote.

BELARUS

March 19. Presidential Elections Dispute. Exit polls show incumbent President Alyaksandr Lukashenka winning a third term in a landslide, amid opposition claims of vote-rigging and violence.

March 20. Western Governments Deem Presidential Election Fraudulent. The United States and EU announce the imposition of sanctions against Belarus following charges of election irregularities.

BELGIUM

September 7. Belgium Foils Terror Plot. Belgian police arrest and charge 17 people with planning a terrorist plot targeting Belgian institutions.

BOSNIA AND HERZEGOVINA

January 26. Directorate for Police Restructuring Implementation Meets for the First Time. As a step toward joining the EU, the country works to restructure its ethnically divided police force through the creation of the Directorate for Police Restructuring Implementation.

January 26. No-Confidence Vote Passes. By a vote of 44–29, Parliament passes a no-confidence vote against the Serb Democratic Party–led government, largely resulting from the ruling government's failure to pass the 2006 budget.

February 28. New Government Assumes Power. Opposition leader Milorad Dodik becomes prime minister. His cabinet excludes members of the nationalist Serb Democratic Party that controlled the government since the 1992–1995 war.

September 27. Court Jails Serb Leader. A tribunal sentences Momčilo Krajišnik to 27 years in prison for war crimes during the Bosnian War; it acquits him on a genocide charge.

October 1. Presidential Elections. In presidential elections, Nebojša Radmanović of the Alliance of Independent Social Democrats wins the Serb seat with 54.8 percent of the vote, Željko Komšić of the Social Democratic Party wins the Croat seat with 40.8 percent of the vote, and Haris Silajdžić of the Party for Bosnia and Herzegovina wins the Muslim seat with 62.1 percent of the vote.

BULGARIA

May 16. Bulgaria Receives a Conditional "Yes" on Joining the EU. The EU Commission confirms that Bulgaria remains on track to enter the EU as planned January 1, 2007; however, fighting organized crime, fraud, and corruption is the priority task before the final decision.

October 17. EU Approves Bulgaria. The EU Enlargement Commission officially approves Bulgaria to join on January 1, 2007.

October 29. Parvanov Reelected. President Georgi Parvanov wins a second five-year term with over 76 percent of the vote in a second round of presidential balloting.

COUNCIL OF EUROPE

June 6. Illegal Detention Report. A report by council Special Rapporteur Dick Marty accuses 14 European nations of illegally cooperating with or ignoring the secret U.S. Central Intelligence Agency program of detention and arrest of terrorist suspects in Europe. The report further charges these nations of maintaining prisons and allowing abductions and secret flights.

CROATIA

September 5. Human Rights Watch Report Denounces Serb Treatment. The report accuses Croatia of neglecting its Serb minority and interfering with the return of refugees of the 1991–1995 civil war to their homes. The report hampers Croatia's EU bid.

October 17. Bush Backs Croatia. U.S. president George W. Bush announces that he will support Croatia's admission to NATO and its bid to enter the EU.

CYPRUS

May 21. Cypriot Parliamentary Elections. President Tassos Papadopoulos's Democratic Party (Deko), with its larger coalition partner the Progressive Party of Working People (AKEL), secures reelection, an indication of support for the government coalition's opposition to the UN-sponsored reunification plan.

July 8. Greek and Turkish Cypriot Leaders Agree to Resume Peace Talks. Cypriot president Tassos

Papadopoulos and Turkish Cypriot leader Mehmet Ali Talat approve a framework for UN-sponsored negotiations, helping to defuse a major crisis in Turkey's EU entry negotiations. These talks are to include issues such as water management and environmental protection.

CZECH REPUBLIC

June 3. Parliamentary Elections Bring New Majority Rule. The center-right, opposition Civic Democratic Party wins plurality; however, incumbent prime minister Jiří Paroubek announces his intention to challenge the result on grounds of unfair opposition campaigning, giving rise to a political stalemate.

August 16. Paroubek Government Resigns. Prime Minister Jiří Paroubek resigns along with his government; Mirek Topolánek is designated to succeed him as prime minister.

September 4. New Government Sworn In. Mirek Topolánek is sworn in as prime minister, as is his newly appointed cabinet.

October 3. Confidence Vote Fails. Prime Minister Mirek Topolánek's government fails to win a confidence vote in the Chamber of Deputies by a 99–96 margin and is forced to resign. A new prime minister will be appointed by President Václav Klaus to attempt a second try.

DENMARK

February 4–6. Cartoon Controversy Results in Deaths. Violent protests ripple across five continents following the republication of Danish cartoons that depicted the Prophet Muhammad, an action forbidden under Islamic law.

June 30. Prime Minister Jan Peter Balkenende Resigns. A dispute with Immigration Minister Rita Verdonk leads to the collapse of the ruling coalition, bringing calls for new, unexpected elections before year's end, likely in November 2006.

ESTONIA

May 6. Parliament Ratifies the EU Constitution. By a vote of 73–1, Estonia becomes the 15th country in the EU to complete the parliamentary stage of ratifying the EU Constitution. All the country's major political parties back ratification.

September 23. Ilves Elected President. Incumbent Arnold Rüütel loses the third round of voting to Toomas Henrik Ilves, who becomes president.

EUROPEAN UNION (EU)

October 14. Condemnation of French Genocide Bill. EU Enlargement Commissioner Olli Rehn criticizes the passing of a French bill criminalizing the denial of an Armenian genocide, suggesting that it will hamper EU enlargement talks with Turkey.

October 17. Europeans Support Iran Sanctions. In light of North Korea's determination to move forward with its nuclear program, the EU decides to back limited UN-imposed sanctions on Iran for refusing to negotiate on its nuclear program.

October 20. Ethiopia Expels Diplomats. Ethiopia allegedly catches two EU diplomats smuggling important Ethiopian criminals out of the country. Ethiopia gives the EU officials 24 hours to leave.

FINLAND

January 29. Incumbent President Tarja Halonen Wins Close Election. A second round of votes results in victory for the incumbent. Despite its narrowness, her victory bolsters indication that Finland will likely stay outside of NATO and pursue neutrality, which emerged as a main issue during the election.

July 1. EU Presidency for Finland. Finland assumes the six-month rotating EU presidency previously held by Austria.

FRANCE

March 18. Labor Protests Plague France. Hundreds of thousands of people march in Paris and other French cities in protest of the First Employment Contract, a proposal giving employers the right to fire workers under the age of 26 in the first two years of their employment. After unrest

spreads to more than 80 cities, the French government withdraws the proposal but protests continue as planned.

May 16. No-Confidence Vote. A vote of no confidence, initiated by Socialists unhappy with President Chirac and Prime Minister de Villepin's investigation of Minister of State Nicolas Sarkozy's role in the "Clearstream Affair," fails by a wide margin.

October 13. Armenian Genocide Legislation Passes. The National Assembly passes legislation making it illegal to deny the Armenian genocide in Turkey as a historical fact. Criticism follows from Turkey, the United States, and the EU.

GERMANY

July 19. The European Commission Suspends Budgetary Disciplinary Proceedings Against Germany. Although having exceeded deficit limitations imposed largely at its own request, Germany receives European Commission approval of its budget plans.

GREECE

May 23. Greek-Turkish Mock Dogfight. A Greek F-16 fighter jet, dispatched to intercept a Turkish jet that had violated Greek airspace, collides with the Turkish jet, resulting in the death of the Greek pilot.

October 15. Local Elections. The ruling New Democracy Party (ND) loses support in local elections, but still is able to take half of the national prefectures. The ND loses the Athens-Piraeus prefecture, the most populous in the nation.

HUNGARY

April 23. Elections Sustain Socialist Coalition. A runoff parliamentary win produces the first administration reelection since the fall of communism in Hungary in 1990. Seizing the victory, Prime Minister Ferenc Gyurcsány proposes an austerity program to reduce the budget deficit, projected to reach 9.5 percent of GDP. Such high levels would nullify the nation's plans to adopt the euro by 2010.

September 18. Protests Erupt Over Prime Minister Scandal. After the public release of a videotape where Prime Minister Gyurcsány admits to lying about the economy in order to secure reelection during the 2006 campaign, protesters take to the streets and demand his resignation.

October 6. No-Confidence Vote. Following weeks of unrest, a no-confidence vote is called on the Gyurcsány government, but the measure fails.

ICELAND

May 27. Prime Minister Resigns. Prime Minister Halldór Ásgrímsson of the Progressive Party resigns when his party receives just 12 percent of the vote in local elections.

June 15. New Prime Minister Takes Power. Geir Haarde of the Independence Party becomes prime minister and reshuffles the cabinet.

IRELAND

September 21. Ahern Payments Scandal Leaks. A report in the *Irish Times* claims that current prime minister Bertie Ahern received payments or loans from a friend and business tycoon while Ahern served as minister of finance in the early 1990s and that he failed to repay or pay taxes on the monies. Under rising scrutiny, Ahern repays the money, along with 5 percent interest, by October 1.

ITALY

April 11. Voters Oust Berlusconi. Italy elects a new prime minister: center-left, former PM Romano Prodi. Incumbent Silvio Berlusconi initially refuses to concede and calls for a recount, but later resigns on May 2.

July 21. Italy Lifts Labor Mobility Restrictions. Italy joins 17 EU states in accepting free movement of labor. The announcement extends worker movement to the 8 newest EU member states.

LATVIA

April 13. New Era Ministers Resign. Following a vote-buying scandal in local elections involving coalition partner Latvia First and its subsequent refusal to leave the coalition, all New Era cabinet ministers resign.

October 8. People's Party Wins Reelection. Led by Prime Minister Aigars Kalvitis, the People's Party secures a plurality in legislative elections, giving it the mandate to form a new coalition government.

LITHUANIA

April 11. New Union (Social Liberal) Party Pulls Out of Coalition. The coalition ousts Artūras Paulauskas, the speaker of the Parliament, prompting a no-confidence vote. As a result, Paulauskas withdraws his New Union (Social Liberal) Party from the coalition.

May 31. Government Collapses. Prime Minister Algirdas Brazauskas resigns along with his entire cabinet, following the departure from the government of the Labor Party, the largest in the coalition.

July 18. New Coalition Government Forms. A four-party, minority coalition government takes office, with former defense minister Gediminas Kirkilas of the Lithuanian Social Democratic Party selected as the prime minister.

October 3. Labor Party Defections. New defections of MPs from the Labor Party give the Lithuanian Social Democratic Party the largest bloc of votes in Parliament.

MACEDONIA

July 5. National Elections Test Aspirations. Prime Minister Vlado Buckovski concedes defeat to the nationalist opposition in elections considered crucial for the country's eventual membership in the EU and NATO.

MOLDOVA

July 7. Transdnestria Bus Bomb. An explosion kills seven people on a bus in Tiraspol, a city in a separatist region, Transdnestria, that is populated mostly by ethnic Russians and Ukrainians.

Moldova downplays the likelihood of terrorist responsibility.

MONTENEGRO

May 21. Montenegrins Vote on Independence. Montenegrins choose independence 55.5 percent to 44.5 percent, breaking the January 2003 EU-devised Constitutional Charter that united Serbia and Montenegro.

June 3. Montenegro Declares Independence. Montenegro secedes from the Serbia and Montenegro state union.

June 28. Admission to the UN. The UN admits Montenegro as a member.

September 10. National Elections. A coalition of the Democratic Party of Socialists and the Social Democratic Party, led by Prime Minister Milo Djukanović, claims victory in the new Montenegrin legislature.

October 3. Djukanović Resigns. Milo Djukanović announces he will not serve as prime minister in the upcoming government, prompting the coalition to nominate Željko Sturanović to form the cabinet.

NETHERLANDS

June 29. Balkenende Government Collapses. After the ruling coalition ignores the Democrats 66 (D66) Party's calls for Immigration Minister Rita Verdonk to resign, the D66 withdraws from the coalition. Subsequently, Prime Minister Jan Peter Balkenende resigns. Balkenende later forms a minority caretaker government to govern until new elections in November.

October 16. Terror Trial Begins. The trial of six Muslims accused of a terrorist plot to attack the Dutch Parliament and murder politicians begins.

NORTH ATLANTIC TREATY ORGANIZATION (NATO)

June 8. North Atlantic Council (NAC) Meeting. A meeting of the NAC, the decision-making body

of NATO, determines that from now on all members will be required to contribute 2 percent of their GDP to defense.

NORWAY

June 12. Government Intervenes in Finance Strike. The Norwegian government, fearing a complete shutdown of the financial sector, forces banks, insurers, and striking workers into arbitration.

POLAND

July 8. Twins Rule. The governing Law and Justice Party votes to name its party leader, Jaroslaw Kaczyński, the country's new prime minister. His twin brother, Lech Kaczyński, is the president of Poland.

September 21. Budget Tussle. Prime Minister Jaroslaw Kaczyński dismisses Self-Defense Party leader Andrzej Lepper over a budget dispute. A crisis results as the coalition looks to secure support or be forced to call for new elections.

October 16. Kaczyński Reinstates Lepper. Self-Defense Party leader Andrzej Lepper returns as deputy prime minister after the ruling Law and Justice Party decides to renew the coalition.

PORTUGAL

January 22. President-Elect Silva. Former prime minister Aníbal Cavaco Silva becomes president.

May 1. Portugal Lifts EU-8 Labor Restrictions. Portugal opens its labor market to citizens of the new EU member states to permit free movement of workers. The nation joins Finland and Spain as adopters of the labor policy.

ROMANIA

May 16. Romania Receives a Conditional "Yes" on Joining the EU. The EU Commission confirms that Romania remains on track to enter the EU as planned on January 1, 2007. Outstanding issues that Romania must further address before a final decision is made include agricultural and tax concerns.

September 27. EU Recommends Admission. A formal EU report recommends that Romania be admitted in 2007 as scheduled.

RUSSIA

January 1. Russia Severs Gas Supply. Russia suspends natural gas flows to Ukraine following a pricing dispute. Countries across Europe report significant reductions in gas supplies, and Russia pledges to restore flows on January 3, after widespread regional disruption.

May 15. Committee of Ministers. Russia rotates to the six-month chair position of the Council of Europe's Committee of Ministers.

October 6. Diplomatic Row with Georgia. Amidst a growing dispute with Georgia stemming from the arrest of Russian officers for espionage, Russia deports at least 130 Georgians, cracks down on immigration, and evacuates its diplomatic staff. Although the officers are released, Russia refuses to back down from its tough policies.

SAN MARINO

June 4. New Coalition Forms. The recently established Party of Socialists and Democrats wins the election, forming a coalition with the Popular Alliance and the United Left.

SERBIA

February 20. Talks Begin on Kosovo. Serbian and Albanian leaders meet for the first time, beginning UN-mediated talks on the future of Kosovo.

March 11. Slobodan Milošević Dies. On trial for war crimes, the former president of Yugoslavia dies in his prison cell of an apparent heart attack.

May 3. EU Suspends Stabilization and Association Agreement (SAA) Negotiations. After Serbia again fails to locate and turn over convicted war criminal Ratko Mladić, the EU suspends SAA talks.

June 5. Independence Declaration. The Serbian National Assembly declares Serbia the legal successor state to the previous union of Serbia and Montenegro.

October 1. G17 Plus Cabinet Ministers Resign. Four G17 Plus cabinet ministers submit their resignations over the lack of cooperation between the government, led by Vojislav Koštunica, and the war crimes tribunal searching for Ratko Mladić.

October 16. Tribunal Report. The Yugoslav war crimes tribunal's chief prosecutor Carla del Ponte accuses Serbia of violating a key precondition of talks for EU membership by not cooperating in the search for Ratko Mladić.

October 16. Talks Remain on Hold. The foreign minister of Finland, Erkki Tuomioja, who holds the current EU presidency, confirms, along with EU Enlargement Commissioner Olli Rehn, that SAA talks with Serbia will remain on hold following the report by UN Chief Prosecutor Carla del Ponte.

SLOVAKIA

February 6. Coalition Government Collapses. The three-party minority ruling coalition government dissolves, bringing new elections.

June 18. Opposition Party Wins Parliamentary Elections. The leftist win results in speculation of whether Slovakia will succeed in adopting the euro in 2009.

SLOVENIA

July 11. Slovenia Receives Approval to Enter the Eurozone. EU finance ministers accept Slovenia's entry into the eurozone, marking the final legal step before Slovenia may adopt the euro in January 2007. This action positions Slovenia to become the first of the May 2004 new EU members to adopt the currency.

SPAIN

March 22. ETA Announces Cease-Fire. The paramilitary Basque Nationalist organization ETA declares a permanent cease-fire as a prelude to talks with the Spanish government.

April 11. Charges for 29 in 2004 Train Bombings. Spanish National Court Judge Juan del Olmo charges 29 suspects for their involvement in the 2004 Madrid train bombings that killed 191 people and wounded more than 1,500.

June 18. Voters Approve Greater Autonomy for Catalonia. Voters approve a referendum expanding the authority of the Catalan government, including greater tax retention and control over immigration and licensing. The results showed 73.9 percent voted for the autonomy plan; turnout was 49 percent.

SWEDEN

March 21. Foreign Minister Laila Freivalds Resigns After Cartoon Fallout. With criticism over her involvement in closing down an Internet site on which the Danish cartoons depicting the Prophet Muhammad had been published, Foreign Minister Freivalds resigns.

September 17. New Coalition Takes Power. Fredrik Reinfeldt becomes prime minister as the Alliance for Sweden defeats the Social Democrats in a surprise victory.

October 14. Trade Minister Quits. Amidst allegations that she did not pay taxes, Trade Minister Maria Borelius resigns after only a week in office. More cabinet members under similar scrutiny are expected to follow her.

SWITZERLAND

October 28–29. Sri Lankan Peace Talks. Switzerland hosts peace talks between the Sri Lankan government and the Tamil Tigers separatist group.

TURKEY

January 23. Accession Talks Set. Turkey and the EU agree on the conditions and purposes of negotiations.

June 12. EU Negotiations Begin. The first of 35 sections of negotiations for admission to the EU opens.

September 22. Merkel Advocates Alternative. German chancellor Angela Merkel, leader of the Christian Democrat Party, promotes a privileged partnership with Turkey, instead of full EU membership.

September 29. Austrian Uneasiness. Alfred Gusenbauer of Austria's Social Democrats Party asserts that Turkey is not ready to enter the EU.

September 30. PKK Declares Ceasefire. The Kurdistan Workers Party (PKK) declares a unilateral cease-fire with the Turkish military.

October 4. Rehn Supports Turkey. EU Enlargement Commissioner Olli Rehn urges European nations to pursue a dialogue with Turkey about EU membership. His support follows attempts by European leaders in Germany, France, and Austria to promote a privileged partnership with Turkey rather than full membership in the EU.

October 7. Austrian Uneasiness Continues. Two Austrian right groups, the Alliance for the Future of Austria and the Freedom Party, assert that Turkey will never be modern enough to enter the EU.

October 13. French Legislation Controversy. Following legislation passed by the French Parliament making it illegal to deny the existence of the early 20th-century Armenian genocide in Turkey, Turkish officials criticize the act. Orhan Pamuk, the 2006 winner of the Nobel Prize in Literature, accuses the French of infringing on freedom of speech.

UKRAINE

January 10. Legislature Passes a Vote of No Confidence. Largely in reaction to the Ukraine-Russian gas deal reached on January 4, Parliament expresses its dissatisfaction with Prime Minister Yuriy Yekhanurov.

March 26. Voters Elect New Parliament. In the first parliamentary elections since the 2004–2005 Orange Revolution that brought opposition leader Viktor Yushchenko to power, the pro-Russian party led by former presidential candidate Viktor

Yanukovych wins the most seats with 32.12 percent of the vote (186 seats). Observers considered the elections a crucial test for democratic transition. Despite the win, the parties of the Orange coalition still hold a majority.

July 18. Demand Made for New Prime Minister. Yanukovych's Party of Regions makes a formal parliamentary coalition proposal to nominate a prime minister, giving President Viktor Yushchenko 15 days to make a decision and augmenting the pro-Western and pro-Russian rivalry growing since the March elections.

August 4. Yanukovych Wins Prime Ministership. Parliament approves Viktor Yanukovych as prime minister, ending a four-month political crisis. Yanukovych received support from former rival Viktor Yushchenko and backing by 271 lawmakers in the 450-member parliament, passing the required majority of 226 votes.

UNITED KINGDOM

January 7. Liberal Democrat Leader Resigns. Charles Kennedy, leader of the third-largest political party in the United Kingdom, announces his resignation after evaporation of support due to revelation of alcohol abuse problems.

August 10. Police Uncover Terrorist Plot. Twenty-four British citizens are arrested in Britain on charges of plotting to detonate liquid explosives on planes flying to the United States.

September 7. Blair Announces Future Resignation. Prime Minister Tony Blair announces that he will step down within one year.

NORTHERN IRELAND

October 13. Northern Ireland Target Date Set. The United Kingdom and Ireland set March 26, 2007, as the target date for a new government to be set up in Northern Ireland that will abide by the peace agreement.

October 17. Northern Ireland Talks Called Off. Historic Northern Ireland talks to be held between Democratic Unionist Party leader Ian Paisley and *Sinn Féin* leader Gerry Adams are called off by Britain.

VATICAN CITY STATE

September 12. Pope Angers Muslims. Pope Benedict XVI's use of an anti-Muslim quote by a Byzantine emperor elicits outrage in the worldwide Muslim community. The pope expresses regret on September 17.

September 25. Pope Meets with Islamic Community. Pope Benedict XVI meets with envoys from the Islamic world to attempt to diffuse tensions rising from his September 12 speech.

APPENDIX B: SERIALS LIST

The Annual Register
The Boston Globe
The Christian Science Monitor
Cyprus Newsletter
The Economist
Editor & Publisher International
The Europa World Year Book
Facts on File
Financial Times
Iceland Reporter
IMF Article IV Reports
IMF Balance of Payments Statistics
IMF Direction of Trade Statistics
IMF Government Finance Statistics
IMF International Financial Statistics
IMF Survey
IMF World Economic Outlook
Keesing's Record of World Events
Le Monde (Paris)

NATO Review
The New York Times
News of Norway
People in Power
Permanent Missions to the United Nations
Radio Free Europe/Radio Liberty
UN Chronicle
UN Handbook
UN Population and Vital Statistics Report
UN Statistical Yearbook
UNESCO Statistician Yearbook
US CIA Heads of State and Cabinet Members
US Department of State, Diplomatic List
The Washington Post
Willings Press Guide
World Bank Atlas
World Bank Country Reports
World Development Report

INDEX

Entries of only a single page number, and the first number in a multiple-page entry, indicate the first or primary reference to that individual. Additional page numbers typically indicate first references in a different section of a profile or in a closely related profile.